TEXAS ALMANAC

2024–2025

Texas State Historical Association

72nd Edition

TEXAS ALMANAC

2024–2025

MANAGING EDITOR
Rosie Hatch

ASSOCIATE EDITOR
Rachel Kaelin

ASSISTANT EDITOR
John Willis

COVER DESIGN
Joel Phillips

ISBN (hardcover) 978-1-62511-074-9
ISBN (flexbound) 978-1-62511-075-6
ISBN (ebook) 978-1-62511-076-3

Library of Congress ISSN: 2378-2188 (Print)
Library of Congress ISSN: 2378-2234 (Digital)

TEXAS STATE HISTORICAL ASSOCIATION

The University of Texas at Austin
3001 Lake Austin Blvd., Suite 3.116, Austin, TX 78703; (512) 471–2600
TSHAonline.org and **LegacyofTexas.com**

Printed in Dallas, Texas, by Taylor Specialty Books
Bound in San Antonio by Universal Bindery
For permission requests, contact **Rosie.Hatch@TSHAonline.org**.

Distributed by Texas A&M University Press and the Texas Book Consortium
4354 TAMU, College Station, Texas, 77843-4354

Order hardcover or flexbound editions at **(800) 826-8911**
or online at **www.tamupress.com**

TexasAlmanac.com

PREFACE

Welcome to the 72nd Edition of the *Texas Almanac*!

This year's feature is "Texas: The Energy State," and it actually contains three stories. The main essay is "Texas Energy: Where We Started and Where We Are Today" on p. 603. From Spindletop to the PEC, from *Dallas* to Houston, read all about how energy shaped our state, how Texas became a leader, and where the journey might take us in the future. The two other essays, "A Brief History of Wind Power" (p. 606) and "How an Invisible Gas Stole the Spotlight" (p. 613), highlight the importance of wind power and natural gas in the state. Nora Ankrum did a phenomenal job writing this feature, and I know you will enjoy reading it.

We also have a new element this year: "Texas Tribune Reports." Each edition of the *Texas Almanac* will always be a reflection of its time, and not everything can be described in a table or a list. That's why we've partnered with The Texas Tribune to include short essays about what is happening today in five important areas: the climate, sports, politics, education, and healthcare. Jump to the beginnings of those chapters to learn more.

Creating this book anew every two years is always a challenge. Obviously, there is a lot of information packed into this 752-page tome. But you'll never truly understand how much information it contains until you go looking up every fact for yourself.

Luckily, I didn't have to do this by myself! I want to thank my fellow editors Rachel Kaelin and John Willis for their dedication to making this book the best it can be. We spent many long days in the office trying hard to get everything exactly right. I also want to thank Joel Phillips, who went through many hardships this year but made time to design another beautiful cover.

Rosie Hatch

Managing Editor, Texas Almanac

"I AM TEXAS" WRITING AND ART CONTEST

I Am Texas is an Annual Competiton that launched after 1,000 kids made history together in 2022 by breaking the Guinness World Record for the Largest Published Book in the World (by kids)! The 2023 *I Am Texas* contest accepted writing and artwork submissions from students in grades 2-12. Elementary students wrote letters to influential Texans both past and present. Middle and high school writers wrote fiction and nonfiction stories inspired by art or artifacts in The Bryan Museum collection. These older writers had the choice to research a specific artifact in the

2022 Winner: Tunkashila "Grandfather" by Sofia Regalado

Museum and write about its history, use an item as a muse for a personal essay, or incorporate an artifact into a creative story.

Students who submitted artwork were asked for their creative interpretation of the "I Am Texas" theme. These young artists used mediums such as oil paint, watercolor, acrylic paint, alcohol marker, and colored pencil and submitted a variety of Texas images including landscapes, bluebonnets, birds, longhorn cattle, and self-portraits.

The 2024 *I Am Texas* writing and art contest has opened for the next group of young writers and artists to show their Texas pride. The Bryan Museum is again accepting submissions through the Submittable platform until April 30, 2024.

Visit iamtx.org to enter!

2023 Winner: The Texas Longhorn by Nathaniel Garza

Texas State Historical Association

An Independent Nonprofit Since 1897

Organized in Austin on March 2, 1897, the Texas State Historical Association is the oldest learned society in the state. Its mission is to "foster the appreciation, understanding, and teaching of the rich and unique history of Texas and, by example and through programs and activities, encourage and promote research, preservation, and publication of historical material affecting the state of Texas." The association's publications include the *Southwestern Historical Quarterly*, more than 150 scholarly books, the Texas Almanac, and the well-known Handbook of Texas Online. The online Handbook, the nation's preeminent state history encyclopedia, attracts 400,000 visitors per month from more than 200 countries and territories around the world. Through its varied education programs, the Association directly serves more than 50,000 elementary through college-aged students each year, while indirectly reaching an additional 86,000 through its teacher training opportunities.

TSHA Board of Directors, 2023–2024

Officers

Hon. Ken Wise
Humble ... President

Gene Preuss
Houston ... Vice President

Andrew J. Torget
Denton ... (2022–2025) Secretary

Ricardo Romo
San Antonio ... Treasurer

Patrick Cox
Wimberley ... Past President

Lance Lolley
Austin ... Past President

Board Members

Carlos R. Hamilton, Jr.
Houston ... (2021–2024)

Stephanie Cole
Arlington ... (2021–2024)

George Diaz
McAllen ... (2021–2022)

Larry Ketchersid
Austin ... (2021–2024)

Bernadette Pruitt
Huntsville ... (2021–2024)

Dolph Briscoe
San Antonio ... (2022–2025)

Sonia Hernandez
Bryan ... (2022–2025)

Kent Hance
Austin ... (2022–2025)

Joy Phillpott
Austin ... (2022–2025)

Lewis F. Fisher
San Antonio ... (2023–2026)

Whit Jones III
Corpus Christi ... (2023–2026)

Joan Marshall
Santa Fe, NM ... (2023–2026)

Mary Jo O'Rear
Corpus Christi ... (2023–2026)

Walter L. Buenger
Bryan ... Chief Historian, Honorary Life Board Member

J. P. Bryan
Houston ... Executive Director, Honorary Life Board Member

John W. Crain
Dallas ... Honorary Life Board Member

Stephen C. Cook
Houston ... Honorary Life Board Member

GREG ABBOTT
Governor of Texas

Greetings,

As the 48th Governor of the great state of Texas, it is my honor to welcome you to the 2024–2025 edition of the *Texas Almanac*, the premier reference for everything Texas.

Texas is the Lone Star State for a reason: We stand apart as a model for the nation. Jobs are growing here, businesses are growing here, and families are growing here. In fact, Texas is growing faster than the nation, and more than eight in 10 who are born here stay here.

Now the 8th-largest economy when compared to the nations of the world, the Texas of today was built on the bold ideas of those who came before us. Men and women who dared to explore the vast new frontier pulled themselves up by their own bootstraps and made a living from the bounty of the land. They innovated, invested, and persevered. And they built an even bigger Texas of tomorrow for the generations yet to come.

I invite you to explore the pages that follow to learn more about the rich and storied history of the Texas and its people, government, economics, natural resources, holidays, diverse cultures, education, recreation, the arts and so much more. Texas is big, and each of our 254 counties has something unique to offer — as do the featured articles in this edition.

If you're not in Texas right now, we invite you to come visit for a while. We're making history every day.

First Lady Cecilia Abbott joins me in thanking the Texas State Historical Association for their dedication to sharing the history and blessings of Texas and for producing this invaluable Almanac preserving the past and present for the future of this great state.

Greg Abbott

Greg Abbott
Governor of Texas

DAN PATRICK
Lt. Governor of Texas

People from all over the world envy Texas; our natural beauty, bustling economy, vibrant culture and rich history are second to none.

The Texas story is one of liberty, perseverance and determination to succeed, and our independence was bought with the blood of our forefathers. Texas history is filled with stories of settlers, immigrants, native peoples, freedmen, outlaws and carpetbaggers, forging their own way forward. Each Texan has contributed to building a better Texas for all of posterity.

Our commitment to God-given freedoms, liberty and the right to self-determination has presented generations of Texans the opportunity to prosper.

The Texas Almanac remains a premier resource to learn about Texas' beautiful history and culture that make our state the light of the United States and the world. Please join me in honoring it as you learn about the greatest state that God ever made: Texas.

Dan Patrick

Dan Patrick
Lt. Governor of Texas

TABLE OF CONTENTS

INDEX OF TABLES

STATE PROFILE

ENVIRONMENT

WEATHER

CALENDAR

RECREATION

SPORTS

COUNTIES

POPULATION

ELECTIONS

GOVERNMENT

LAW ENFORCEMENT

CULTURE & THE ARTS

HEALTH & SCIENCE

EDUCATION

BUSINESS

TRANSPORTATION

AGRICULTURE

Pumpjack in West Texas. Photo by Jonathan Cutrer, jcutrer.com

INDEX OF MAPS

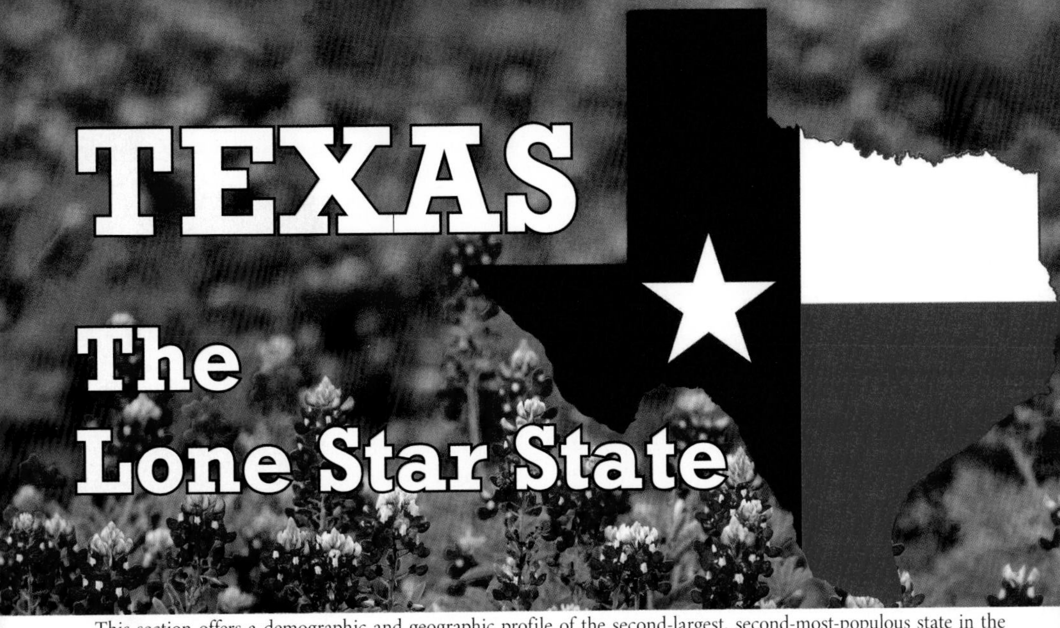

This section offers a demographic and geographic profile of the second-largest, second-most-populous state in the United States. Check the ***Table of Contents*** and the ***Index*** for more-detailed information about each subject.

GOVERNMENT

Capital: Austin
Government: Bicameral Legislature
28th State to enter the Union: Dec. 29, 1845
Present Constitution adopted: 1876
State Senators: 31
State Representatives: 150
Legislative sessions are held for a maximum of 140 days, every 2 years

State motto: Friendship (1930)
Origin of name: Texas, or Tejas, was the Spanish pronunciation of a Caddo Indian word meaning "friends" or "allies."

BUSINESS

Per Capita Personal Income (2021) $59,865
Per Capita Consumption (2021) $45,114
Top spending categories:
Housing and utilities $7,540
Health care $6,593

Non-Farm Employment (2022) 13,199,988
Employment by industry:
Trade, transportation, utilities 2,790,964
Professional and business services 2,075,227
Goods producing 1,963,028
Government .1,911,339
Education and health services 1,751,998
Leisure and hospitality 1,407,325
Manufacturing 924,914
Construction 781,118

(Per capita income/consumption: U.S. Bureau of Economic Analysis. Employment: Texas Workforce Commission.)

POPULATION

Population, 2021 (est.) 29,527,941
Population, 2020 U.S. Census 29,145,505
Population increase, 2020-2021 . . . . 1.3%
Population, 2010 U.S. Census 25,145,561
Population increase, 2010-2021 . . . . 17.4%

Ethnicity, 2020	**Group**	**Percent**
	Anglo	39.7%
	Hispanic	39.3%
	Black	11.8%
	Asian	5.4%
	Other	3.8%

Ten Largest Cities
Houston (Harris Co.) 2,288,250
San Antonio (Bexar Co.) 1,451,853
Dallas (Dallas Co.) 1,288,457
Austin (Travis Co.) 964,177
Fort Worth (Tarrant Co.) 935,508
El Paso (El Paso Co.) .678,415
Arlington (Tarrant Co.) 392,786
Corpus Christi (Nueces Co.) 317,773
Plano (Collin Co.) 288,253
Lubbock (Lubbock Co.) 260,993

Number of counties 254
Largest by pop: Harris Co.. 4,728,030
Smallest by pop: Loving Co. 57

Number of incorporated cities. 1,226
Number of cities of 100,000 pop. or more 40
Number of cities of 50,000 pop. or more 31
Number of cities of 10,000 pop. or more 171

(Population: U.S. Census estimates for 2021. Race: 2020 U.S. Census)

NATURAL ENVIRONMENT

Area (total) .... 268,596 sq. miles
.... (171,901,440 acres)

Land Area .... 261,232 sq. miles
.... (167,188,480 acres)

Water Area .... 7,365 sq. miles
.... (4,713,600 acres)

Geographic Center:
About 15 miles northeast of Brady in northern McCulloch County.

Highest Point:
Guadalupe Peak (8,749 ft.) in Culberson County in far West Texas.

Lowest Point:
Gulf of Mexico (sea level).

Normal Average Annual Precipitation Range:
From 64.4 inches in Jasper County on the Louisiana border to 8.3 inches in Hudspeth County in far West Texas.

Record Highest Temperature:
Seymour, Baylor Co., ... Aug. 12, 1936, 120°F
Monahans, Ward Co., ... June 28, 1994, 120°F
Olney, Young Co., ... June 3, 1998, 120°F
Dryden, Terrell Co., ... June 14, 2008, 120°F

Record Lowest Temperature:
Tulia, Swisher Co., ... Feb. 12, 1899, -23°F
Seminole, Gaines Co.,. .... Feb. 8, 1933, -23°F

ECONOMY

Manufactures: Chemicals and allied products, petroleum and coal products, food and kindred products, transportation equipment.

Farm Products: Cattle, cotton, vegetables, fruits, nursery and greenhouse, dairy products.

Minerals: Petroleum, natural gas, and natural gas liquids.

Top 5 Industries by Contribution to GDP, 2022
Trade, Trans., & Utilities. .... $ 442.8 billion
Financial Activities .... $ 404.9 billion
Professional & Bus. Services .... $ 283.9 billion
Manufacturing .... $ 263.7 billion
Natural Resources & Mining ...... $ 261.6 billion
(2020 Comprehensive Annual Financial Report for the State of Texas)

Top Oil- and Gas-Producing Counties
Oil: Ector County, 3.5 billion bbl (discovery–2023)
Gas: Webb County, 12.1 billion MCF (1993–2022)
(Texas Railroad Commission)

Agriculture (2021):
Total cash receipts. .... $24.8 billion
Animals & products. .... $16.8 billion
All crops .... $8.0 billion
Total exports .... $7.3 billion
Number of farms (estimate) 246,000
Total net farm income .... $8.1 billion
(U.S. Department of Agriculture, National Agricultural Statistics Service Farm Numbers.)

A beautiful sunset near Marfa. Photo by Rosie Hatch

Texas' Rank Among the States

GDP by State, FYE 2022

	State	In Millions
1.	California	$3,598,103
2.	**Texas**	**$2,355,960**
3.	New York	$2,053,180
4.	Florida	$1,389,070
5.	Illinois	$1,033,310
6.	Pennsylvania	$923,089
7.	Ohio	$822,670
8.	Georgia	$755,698
9.	New Jersey	$745,422
10.	North Carolina	$730,072
		United States, $25,462,722

Number of Births, 2022

	State	Total
1.	California	418,523
2.	**Texas**	**389,533**
3.	Florida	224,226
4.	New York	207,484
5.	Pennsylvania	130,003
6.	Illinois	128,315
7.	Ohio	128,221
8.	Georgia	125,827
9.	North Carolina	121,389
10.	New Jersey	102,883
		United States, 3,661,220

Net Electricity Generation, Feb. 2023

	State	Thousand MWh
1.	**Texas**	**38,117**
2.	Pennsylvania	19,678
3.	Florida	17,003
4.	California	15,279
5.	Illinois	14,095
6.	Alaska	10,177
7.	Ohio	9,542
8.	New York	9,310
9.	Michigan	9,165
10.	North Carolina	8,962

Carbon Dioxide Emissions, 2020

	State	Million metric tons
1.	**Texas**	**624.0**
2.	California	303.4
3.	Florida	207.6
4.	Pennsylvania	193.2
5.	Ohio	185.6
6.	Louisiana	183.3
7.	Illinois	169.9
8.	Indiana	154.3
9.	New York	143.4
10.	Michigan	136.8

Number of Farms, 2019

	State	Farms (est.)
1.	**Texas**	**247,000**
2.	Missouri	95,200
3.	Iowa	85,300
4.	Ohio	77,800
5.	Oklahoma	77,300
6.	Kentucky	74,800
7.	Illinois	71,400
8.	California	69,900
9.	Tennessee	69,700
10.	Minnesota	68,000
		United States, 2,023,400

COVID–19 Mortality Rate, 2021

	State	Deaths per 100,000 people
1.	Oklahoma	158.8
2.	Alabama	152.8
3.	**Texas**	**151.4**
4.	West Virginia	146.8
5.	Mississippi	146.3
6.	Wyoming	143.4
7.	Tennessee	142.5
8.	Nevada	141.6
9.	Arizona	139.5
10.	South Carolina	139.2
		United States, 111.4

Sources for these tables are: the Bureau of Economic Analysis, National Center for Health Statistics, U.S. Dept. of Agriculture, and the U.S. Energy Information Administration.

FLAGS OF TEXAS

Texas is called the **Lone Star State** because of its state flag with a single star. The state flag was also the **flag of the Republic of Texas**.

The following information about historic Texas flags, the current flag, and other Texas symbols is from the **Texas State Library & Archives** in Austin. More information is at:

www.tsl.texas.gov/ref/abouttx/index.html#flags

Six Flags of Texas

Six different flags have flown over Texas during eight changes of sovereignty. The accepted sequence of these flags follows:

Spanish: 1519–1821

French: 1685–1690

Mexican: 1821–1836

Republic of Texas: 1836–1845

Confederate States of America: 1861–1865

United States: 1845 to the present

Evolution of the Lone Star Flag

The Convention at Washington-on-the-Brazos in March 1836 allegedly adopted a flag for the Republic that was designed by **Lorenzo de Zavala.** The design of de Zavala's flag is unknown, but the convention journals state that a "Rainbow and star of five points above the western horizon; and a star of six points sinking below" was added to de Zavala's flag.

There was a suggestion the letters "T E X A S" be placed around the star in the flag, but there is no evidence that the Convention ever approved a final flag design. Probably because of the hasty dispersion of the Convention and the loss of part of the Convention notes, nothing further was done with the Convention's proposals for a national flag.

A **so-called "Zavala flag"** is sometimes flown in Texas today that consists of a blue field with a white five-pointed star in the center and the letters "T E X A S" between the star points, but there is no historical evidence to support this flag's design.

The **first official flag of the Republic,** known as the **National Standard of Texas** or **David G. Burnet's**

flag, was adopted by the Texas Congress and approved by President Sam Houston on Dec. 10, 1836. The design "**shall be an azure ground with a large golden star central.**"

The Lone Star Flag

On Jan. 25, 1839, President Mirabeau B. Lamar approved the adoption by Congress of a new national flag. This flag consisted of "a blue perpendicular stripe of the width of one third of the whole length of the flag, with a white star of five points in the centre thereof, and two horizontal stripes of equal breadth, the upper stripe white, the lower red, of the length of two thirds of the length of the whole flag." This is the **Lone Star Flag**, which later became the state flag.

Although Senator William H. Wharton proposed the adoption of the Lone Star Flag in 1838, no one knows who actually designed the flag. The legislature in 1879 inadvertently repealed the law establishing the state flag, but the legislature adopted a new law in 1933 that legally re-established the flag's design.

The red, white, and blue of the state flag stand, respectively, for bravery, purity, and loyalty. The proper **finial** for use with the state flag is either **a star or a spearhead.** Texas is one of only two states that has a flag that formerly served as the flag of an independent nation. The other is Hawaii.

Displaying the State Flag

The Texas Flag Code was first adopted in 1933 and completely revised in 1993. Laws governing display of the state flag are found in sections 3100.002 through 3100.152 of the Texas Government Code:

www.tsl.texas.gov/ref/abouttx/flagcode.html.

Here is a summary of those rules:

★ The Texas flag should be **displayed on state and national holidays** and on special occasions of historical significance, and it should be displayed at every school on regular school days. **When flown out of doors**, the Texas flag should not be flown earlier than sunrise nor later than sunset unless properly illuminated. It should not be left out in inclement weather unless a weather-proof flag is used. It should be flown with the white stripe uppermost **except in case of distress.**

★ **No flag other than the United States flag should be placed above or, if on the same level,** to the state flag's right (observer's left). The state flag should be underneath the national flag when the two are flown from the same halyard. **When flown from adjacent flagpoles**, the national flag and the state flag should be of approximately the same size and on flagpoles of equal height; the national flag should be on the flag's own right (observer's left).

★ **If the state flag is displayed with the flag of another U.S. state, a nation other than the United States, or an international organization**, the state flag should be, from an observer's perspective, to the left of the other flag on a separate flagpole or flagstaff, and the state flag should not be above the other flag on the same flagpole or flagstaff or on a taller flagpole or flagstaff. If the state flag and the U.S. flag are **displayed from crossed flagstaffs,** the state flag should be, from an observer's perspective, to the right of the U.S. flag and the state flag's flagstaff should be behind the U.S. flag's flagstaff.

★ **When the flag is displayed horizontally,** the white stripe should be above the red stripe and, from an observer's perspective, to the right of the blue stripe. **When the flag is displayed vertically,** the blue stripe should be uppermost and the white stripe should be to the state flag's right (observer's left).

★ If the state and national flags are both **carried in a procession,** the national flag should be on the marching right and state flag should be on the national flag's left (observer's right).

★ **On Memorial Day,** the state flag should be displayed at half-staff until noon and then completely raised. **On Peace Officers Memorial Day** (May 15), the state flag should be displayed at half-staff all day, unless that day is also Armed Forces Day.

★ The state flag should not touch anything beneath it or be dipped to any person or thing except the U.S. flag. Advertising should not be fastened to a flagpole, flagstaff, or halyard on which the state flag is displayed.

★ If a state flag is no longer used or useful as an emblem for display, it should be destroyed, preferably by burning. A **flag retirement ceremony** is set out in the Texas Government Code mentioned earlier.

Pledge to the Texas Flag

A pledge to the Texas flag was adopted in 1933 by the 43rd Legislature. It contained a phrase, "Flag of 1836," which inadvertently referred to the **David G. Burnet flag** instead of the Lone Star Flag adopted in 1839. In 2007, the 80th Legislature changed the pledge to its current form:

A person reciting the pledge to the state flag should face the flag, place the right hand over the heart, and remove any easily removable hat.

The pledge to the Texas flag may be recited at all public and private meetings at which the Pledge of Allegiance to the national flag is recited and at state historical events and celebrations.

The pledge to the Texas flag should be recited after the pledge of allegiance to the United States flag, if both are recited.

Honor the Texas flag;
I pledge allegiance
to thee, Texas,
one state under God,
one and indivisible.

TEXAS STATE SYMBOLS

Photo by David Marks/Pexels

State Song

The state song of Texas is "Texas, Our Texas." The music was written by the late William J. Marsh (who died Feb. 1, 1971, in Fort Worth at age 90), and the words by Marsh and Gladys Yoakum Wright, also of Fort Worth. It was the winner of a state song contest sponsored by the 41st Legislature and was adopted in 1929. The wording has been changed once: Shortly after Alaska became a state in January 1959, the word "Largest" in the third line was changed by Mr. Marsh to "Boldest." The text follows:

TEXAS, OUR TEXAS

Texas, our Texas! All hail the mighty State!
Texas, our Texas! So wonderful, so great!
Boldest and grandest, Withstanding ev'ry test;
O Empire wide and glorious, You stand supremely blest.

CHORUS

God bless you Texas!
And keep you brave and strong,
That you may grow in power and worth,
Thro'out the ages long.

REFRAIN

Texas, O Texas! Your freeborn single star,
Sends out its radiance to nations near and far.
Emblem of freedom! It sets our hearts aglow,
With thoughts of San Jacinto and glorious Alamo.
Texas, dear Texas! From tyrant grip now free,
Shines forth in splendor your star of destiny!
Mother of heroes! We come your children true,
Proclaiming our allegiance, our faith, our love for you.

State Motto

The state motto is "Friendship." The word Texas, or Tejas, was the Spanish pronunciation of a Caddo Indian word meaning "friends" or "allies." It was designated by the 41st Legislature in 1930.

State Citizenship Designation

The people of Texas usually call themselves Texans. However, Texian was generally used in the early period of the state's history.

State Seal

The design of the obverse (front) of the State Seal consists of "a star of five points encircled by olive and live oak branches, and the words, 'The State of Texas.' " (State Constitution, Art. IV, Sec. 19.) This design is a slight modification of the Great Seal of the Republic of Texas, adopted by the Congress of the Republic, Dec. 10, 1836, and readopted with modifications in 1839.

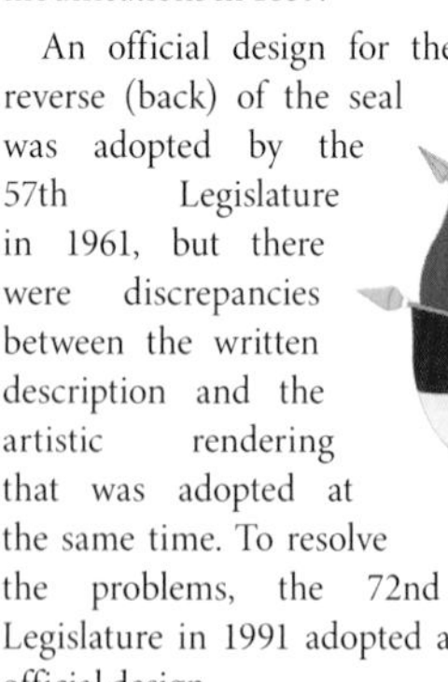

Front of Seal

An official design for the reverse (back) of the seal was adopted by the 57th Legislature in 1961, but there were discrepancies between the written description and the artistic rendering that was adopted at the same time. To resolve the problems, the 72nd Legislature in 1991 adopted an official design.

Back of Seal

The 73rd Legislature in 1993 finally adopted the reverse by law. The current description is in the Texas Government Code, section 3101.001:

"(b) The reverse side of the state seal contains a shield displaying a depiction of:

(1) the Alamo; (2) the cannon of the Battle of Gonzales; and (3) Vince's Bridge.

(c) The shield on the reverse side of the state seal is encircled by:

(1) live oak and olive branches; and (2) the unfurled flags of: (A) the Kingdom of France; (B) the Kingdom of Spain; (C) the United Mexican States; (D) the Republic of Texas; (E) the Confederate States of America; and (F) the United States of America.

(d) Above the shield is emblazoned the motto, 'REMEMBER THE ALAMO,' and beneath are the words, 'TEXAS ONE AND INDIVISIBLE.'

(e) A white five-pointed star hangs over the shield, centered between the flags."

Texas State Symbols

State Bird: The mockingbird (*Mimus polyglottos*) is the state bird of Texas, adopted by the 40th Legislature of 1927 at the request of the Texas Federation of Women's Clubs.

State Flower: The state flower of Texas is the bluebonnet, also called buffalo clover, wolf flower, and el conejo (the rabbit). The bluebonnet was adopted as the state flower, at the request of the Society of Colonial Dames in Texas, by the 27th Legislature in 1901. The original resolution made Lupinus subcarnosus the state flower, but a resolution by the 62nd Legislature in 1971 provided legal status as the state flower of Texas for "Lupinus Texensis and any other variety of bluebonnet."

State Tree: The pecan tree (*Carya illinoinensis*) was adopted as the state tree of Texas by the 36th Legislature in 1919. The sentiment that led to its adoption probably grew out of the request of Gov. James Stephen Hogg that a pecan tree be planted at his grave.

Other State Symbols

In 2001, the Texas Legislature placed restrictions on the adoption of future symbols by requiring that a joint resolution to designate a symbol must specify the item's historical or cultural significance to the state.

State Air Force: The Commemorative Air Force (formerly known as the Confederate Air Force), based in Midland at Midland International Airport, was proclaimed the state air force of Texas by the 71st Legislature in 1989.

State Amphibian: The Texas toad was named the state amphibian by the 81st Legislature in 2009.

State Aquarium: The Texas State Aquarium in Corpus Christi was designated the state aquarium of Texas by the 69th Legislature in 1985.

State Bison Herd: The bison herd at Caprock Canyons State Park was named the official Texas State Bison Herd by the 82nd Legislature in 2011.

State Bluebonnet City: The city of Ennis in Ellis County was designated the state bluebonnet city by the 75th Legislature in 1997.

State Bluebonnet Festival: The Chappell Hill Bluebonnet Festival, held in April, was named state bluebonnet festival by the 75th Legislature in 1997.

State Bluebonnet Trail: The city of Ennis was proclaimed the official state bluebonnet trail by the 75th Legislature in 1997.

State Botanical Garden: The Lady Bird Johnson Wildflower Center, in southwest Austin, was named the State Botanic Garden and Arboretum by the 85th Legislature in 2017. Encompassing 279 acres, it is the largest all-native garden in the state and features more than 800 native plant species.

State Bread: Pan de campo, translated "camp bread" and often called cowboy bread, was named the state bread by the 79th Legislature in 2005. It is a simple baking-powder bread that was a staple of early Texans and often baked in a Dutch oven.

State Cobbler: Peach cobbler was named the state cobbler of Texas by the 83rd Legislature in 2013.

State Cooking Implement: The cast iron Dutch oven was named the cooking implement of Texas by the 79th Legislature in 2005.

State Crustacean: Texas Gulf Shrimp was designated the state crustacean by the 84th Legislature in 2015.

State Dinosaur: *Paluxysaurus jonesi* was proclaimed the state dinosaur by the 81st Legislature in 2009, after it was discovered that the previous state dinosaur, the Brachiosaur Sauropod, Pleurocoelus, (75th Legislature in 1997) had been a misidentification.

State Dish: Chili was proclaimed the Texas state dish by the 65th Legislature in 1977.

State Dog Breed: The Blue Lacy was designated the state dog breed by the 79th Legislature in 2005. The Blue Lacy is a herding and hunting breed descended from greyhound, scent-hound, and coyote stock and developed by the Lacy brothers, who left Kentucky and settled near Marble Falls in 1858.

State Domino Game: 42 was named the state domino game by the 82nd Legislature in 2011.

State Epic Poem: "The Legend of Old Stone Ranch," written by John Worth Cloud, was named the epic poem of Texas by the 61st Legislature in 1969. The work is a 400-page history of the Albany–Fort Griffin area written in verse form.

State Fiber and Fabric: Cotton was designated the state fiber and fabric of Texas by the 75th Legislature in 1997.

State Fish: The Guadalupe bass, a member of the genus *Micropterus* within the sunfish family, was named the state fish of Texas by the 71st Legislature in 1989. It is one of a group of fish collectively known as black bass.

State Flower Song: "Bluebonnets," written by Julia D. Booth and Lora C. Crockett, was named the state flower song by the 43rd Legislature in 1933.

State Folk Dance: The square dance was designated the state folk dance by the 72nd Legislature in 1991.

State Footwear: The cowboy boot was named the state footwear by the 80th Legislature in 2007.

State Fruit: Texas red grapefruit was designated the state fruit by the 73rd Legislature in 1993.

State Gem: Texas blue topaz, the state gem of Texas, is found in the Llano uplift area in Central Texas, especially west to northwest of Mason. It was designated by the 61st Legislature in 1969.

State Gemstone Cut: The Lone Star Cut was named the state gemstone cut by the 65th Legislature in 1977.

State Grass: Sideoats grama (Bouteloua curtipendula), a native grass found on many different Texas soils, was designated the state grass of Texas by the 62nd Legislature in 1971.

State Handgun: The 1847 Colt Walker pistol was named the state handgun by the 87th Legislature in 2021.

State Hashtags: #Texas (state), #TexasToDo (tourism), and #txlege (legislature) were all proclaimed state hashtags by the 84th Legislature in 2015.

State Hat: The cowboy hat was named the state hat of Texas by the 84th Legislature in 2015.

State Health Nut: The pecan was designated the state health nut by the 77th Legislature in 2001.

State Horse: The American Quarter Horse was named state horse by the 81st Legislature in 2009.

State Insect: The Monarch butterfly (*Danaus plexippus*) was designated the state insect by the 74th Legislature in 1995.

State Knife: The 87th Legislature designated the Bowie knife our official state knife in 2021.

State Longhorn Herd: The longhorn herd at Fort Griffin State Historic Site was named the state longhorn herd by the 61st Legislature in 1969.

State Mammals: The state mammals were all designated by the 74th Legislature in 1995:

- **Flying:** Mexican free-tailed bat (*Tadarida brasiliensis*);
- **Large:** Longhorn (*Bos Texanus*);
- **Small:** Armadillo (*Dasypus novemcinctus*).

State Maritime Museum: The Texas Maritime Museum in Rockport was named the state maritime museum by the 70th Legislature in 1987.

State Mushroom: The Texas Star Mushroom (***Chorioactis geaster***) was recognized as the official state mushroom by the 87th Legislature in 2021.

State Music: Western swing was named the state's official music by the 82nd Legislature in 2011.

State Musical Instrument: The guitar was designated the state musical instrument by the 75th Legislature in 1997.

State Native Pepper: The chiltepin (*Capsicum annuum* var. *glabriusculum*) was named the native pepper of Texas by the 75th Legislature in 1997.

State Native Shrub: Texas purple sage (*Leucophyllum frutescens*) was designated the state native shrub by the 79th Legislature in 2005.

State Nickname: "The Lone Star State" was designated the state nickname of Texas by the 84th Legislature in 2015.

State Pastries: Both the sopaipilla and strudel were named the state pastries of Texas by the 78th Legislature in 2003.

State Pepper: The jalapeño pepper (*Capsicum annuum*) was designated the state pepper by the 74th Legislature in 1995.

State Pie: Pecan pie was named the state pie by the 83rd Legislature in 2013.

State Plant: The prickly pear cactus (*Genus Opuntia*) was named the state plant by the 74th Legislature in 1995.

State Plays: There are four official state plays that were designated by the 66th Legislature in 1979:

1. **The Lone Star**
2. **Texas**
3. **Beyond the Sundown**
4. **Fandangle**

A barrel racer competing at Rodeo Austin. Photo by Carol Highsmith, Public Domain

Musician playing the state instrument at Farm Day at San Antonio Missions National Historic Park. Photo by National Park Service, Public Domain

State Pollinator: The Western Honey Bee (*Apis mellifera*) was designated the official pollinator of Texas by the 84th Legislature in 2015.

State Precious Metal: Silver was named the official precious metal by the 80th Legislature in 2007.

State Railroad: The Texas State Railroad was designated the state railroad by the 78th Legislature in 2003. It is a steam-powered tourist excursion train that runs between the towns of Rusk and Palestine.

State Reptile: The Texas horned lizard (*Phrynosoma cornutum*) was named the state reptile by the 73rd Legislature in 1993.

State Rodeo Drill Team: Ghostriders were named the official rodeo drill team of Texas by the 80th Legislature in 2007.

State Saltwater Fish: Red Drum (*Sciaenops ocellatus*) was named the state's saltwater fish by the 82nd Legislature in 2011.

State Sea Turtle: Kemp's Ridley Sea Turtle was named the state sea turtle of Texas by the 83rd Legislature in 2013.

State Seashell: The lightning whelk (*Busycon perversum pulleyi*) was named the state seashell by the 70th Legislature in 1987. One of the few shells that open on the left side, the lightning whelk is named for its colored stripes and is found only on the Gulf Coast.

State Ship: The battleship USS Texas was designated the state ship by the 74th Legislature in 1995. The USS Texas was launched on May 18, 1912, from Newport News, Virginia, and commissioned on March 12, 1914. In 1919, it became the first U.S. battleship to launch an aircraft, and in 1939, it received the first commercial radar in the U.S. Navy. In 1940, the Texas was designated flagship of the U.S. Atlantic Fleet and was the last of the battleships to participate in both World Wars I and II. It was decommissioned on April 21, 1948, and is a State Historic Site, a National Historic Landmark, and a National Mechanical Engineering Landmark. It is docked along the Houston Ship Channel within the San Jacinto Battleground State Historic Site. (Undergoing repairs in drydock in Galveston as of time of publication.)

State Shrub: The crape myrtle (*Lagerstroemia indica*) was designated the official state shrub by the 75th Legislature in 1997.

State Snack: Tortilla chips and salsa was named the state snack by the 78th Legislature in 2003.

State Sport: Rodeo was named the state sport of Texas by the 75th Legislature in 1997.

State Squash: Pumpkin was designated the state squash of Texas by the 83rd Legislature in 2013.

State Stone: Petrified palmwood, found in Texas principally near the Gulf Coast, was designated the state stone by the 61st Legislature in 1969.

State Tall Ship: The Elissa was named the state tall ship by the 79th Legislature in 2005. The 1877 ship makes its home at the Texas Seaport Museum at the port of Galveston.

State Tartan: The Texas Bluebonnet Tartan was named the official state tartan by the 71st Texas Legislature in 1989.

State 10K: The Texas Roundup 10K was named the official state 10K by the 79th Legislature in 2005 to encourage Texans to exercise and incorporate physical activity into their daily lives.

State Tie: The bolo tie was designated the state tie by the 80th Legislature in 2007.

State Vegetable: The Texas sweet onion was designated the state vegetable by the 75th Legislature in 1997.

State Vehicle: The chuck wagon was named the state vehicle by the 79th Legislature in 2005. Texas rancher Charles Goodnight is credited with inventing the chuck wagon to carry food and supplies for the cowboys on trail drives.

State Waterlily: The Nymphaea "Texas Dawn" was named the state waterlily by the 82nd Legislature in 2011. ☆

Explore Texas History

Texas State Historical Association
HANDBOOK OF TEXAS

The *Texas Almanac* has long published feature articles about various aspects of Texas history, all of which are still available on our website, **TexasAlmanac.com**. In recent years, many of those articles were edited and combined to create a single article, "A Brief Sketch of Texas History," which was featured in several editions of the book. That article served its purpose, but a brief look has obvious limitations. After all, the history of Texas is anything but brief.

For this edition we are calling upon our colleagues at the *Handbook of Texas* to present an introductory selection of entries you can read online to learn about the history of Texas. Every entry offers a piece of the fabric of Texas past and present, and just as originally envisioned, the goal of those who write, revise, and edit entries remains ensuring that the *Handbook* is accurate, inclusive, accessible, and reflective of current scholarly standards.

Consider this list a starting point in your further study of Texas history, and explore our chronological overview entries and a few examples of our entries on cities and regions, specific topics, and biographies of deceased individuals. Dig in to these interesting samples of Texas history, and then go on to discover more at the *Handbook of Texas Online,*

https://www.tshaonline.org/handbook

Chronological Overview

Prehistory: *https://www.tshaonline.org/handbook/entries/prehistory*

Spanish Texas: *https://www.tshaonline.org/handbook/entries/spanish-texas*

Texas in the Age of Mexican Independence: *https://www.tshaonline.org/handbook/entries/texas-in-the-age-of-mexican-independence*

Mexican Texas: *https://www.tshaonline.org/handbook/entries/mexican-texas*

Texas Revolution: *https://www.tshaonline.org/handbook/entries/texas-revolution*

Republic of Texas: *https://www.tshaonline.org/handbook/entries/republic-of-texas*

Antebellum Texas: *https://www.tshaonline.org/handbook/entries/antebellum-texas*

Civil War: *https://www.tshaonline.org/handbook/entries/civil-war*

Reconstruction: *https://www.tshaonline.org/handbook/entries/reconstruction*

Late-Nineteenth Century Texas: *https://www.tshaonline.org/handbook/entries/late-nineteenth-century-texas*

Progressive Era: *https://www.tshaonline.org/handbook/entries/progressive-era*

Texas in the 1920s: *https://www.tshaonline.org/handbook/entries/texas-in-the-1920s*

Great Depression: *https://www.tshaonline.org/handbook/entries/great-depression*

World War II: *https://www.tshaonline.org/handbook/entries/world-war-ii*

Texas Post World War II: *https://www.tshaonline.org/handbook/entries/texas-post-world-war-ii*

Texas in the Early Twenty-first Century: *https://www.tshaonline.org/handbook/entries/texas-in-the-early-twenty-first-century*

Biographical

Athanase de Mézières: *https://www.tshaonline.org/handbook/entries/mezieres-athanase-de*

Sam Houston: *https://www.tshaonline.org/handbook/entries/houston-sam*

Stephen F. Austin: *https://www.tshaonline.org/handbook/entries/austin-stephen-fuller*

Mary Eleanor Brackenridge: *https://www.tshaonline.org/handbook/entries/brackenridge-mary-eleanor*

Lyndon B. Johnson: *https://www.tshaonline.org/handbook/entries/johnson-lyndon-baines*

Minnie Fisher Cunningham: *https://www.tshaonline.org/handbook/entries/cunningham-minnie-fisher*

Jesse H. Jones: *https://www.tshaonline.org/handbook/entries/jones-jesse-holman*

Ernie Banks: *https://www.tshaonline.org/handbook/entries/banks-ernest-ernie-mr-cub*

José Francisco Ruiz: *https://www.tshaonline.org/handbook/entries/ruiz-jose-francisco*

Barbara Jordan: *https://www.tshaonline.org/handbook/entries/jordan-barbara-charline*

George T. Ruby: *https://www.tshaonline.org/handbook/entries/ruby-george-thompson*

Jovita Idar: *https://www.tshaonline.org/handbook/entries/idar-jovita*

Lady Bird Johnson: *https://www.tshaonline.org/handbook/entries/johnson-claudia-alta-taylor-lady-bird*

Henry B. González: *https://www.tshaonline.org/handbook/entries/gonzalez-henry-barbosa*

Katherine Stinson: *https://www.tshaonline.org/handbook/entries/stinson-katherine*

Babe Didrikson Zaharias: *https://www.tshaonline.org/handbook/entries/zaharias-mildred-ella-didrikson-babe*

Topical

Spanish Missions: *https://www.tshaonline.org/handbook/entries/spanish-missions*

Slavery: *https://www.tshaonline.org/handbook/entries/slavery*

Battle of the Alamo: *https://www.tshaonline.org/handbook/entries/alamo-battle-of-the*

Civil Rights in Texas: *https://www.tshaonline.org/handbook/entries/civil-rights*

Music: *https://www.tshaonline.org/handbook/entries/music*

Woman Suffrage: *https://www.tshaonline.org/handbook/entries/woman-suffrage*

Germans: *https://www.tshaonline.org/handbook/entries/germans*

African Americans: *https://www.tshaonline.org/handbook/entries/african-americans*

Anglo American Colonization: *https://www.tshaonline.org/handbook/entries/anglo-american-colonization*

LULAC: *https://www.tshaonline.org/handbook/entries/league-of-united-latin-american-citizens*

Kerrville Folk Festival: *https://www.tshaonline.org/handbook/entries/kerrville-folk-festival*

Surface Water: *https://www.tshaonline.org/handbook/entries/surface-water*

Comanche: *https://www.tshaonline.org/handbook/entries/comanche-indians*

People's Party: *https://www.tshaonline.org/handbook/entries/peoples-party*

Houston Astros: *https://www.tshaonline.org/handbook/entries/houston-astros*

San Antonio Spurs: *https://www.tshaonline.org/handbook/entries/san-antonio-spurs*

Witte Museum: *https://www.tshaonline.org/handbook/entries/witte-museum*

Railroads: *https://www.tshaonline.org/handbook/entries/railroads*

Vietnamese: *https://www.tshaonline.org/handbook/entries/vietnamese*

Mexican Americans: *https://www.tshaonline.org/handbook/entries/mexican-americans*

Segregation: *https://www.tshaonline.org/handbook/entries/segregation*

Porvenir Massacre: *https://www.tshaonline.org/handbook/entries/porvenir-massacre*

Armadillo: *https://www.tshaonline.org/handbook/entries/armadillo*

Visual Arts: *https://www.tshaonline.org/handbook/entries/visual-arts*

Cities and Regions

Dallas: *https://www.tshaonline.org/handbook/entries/dallas-tx*

Fort Worth: *https://www.tshaonline.org/handbook/entries/fort-worth-tx*

Houston: *https://www.tshaonline.org/handbook/entries/houston-tx*

Panhandle: *https://www.tshaonline.org/handbook/entries/panhandle*

Trans-Pecos: *https://www.tshaonline.org/handbook/entries/trans-pecos*

Hill Country: *https://www.tshaonline.org/handbook/entries/hill-country*

El Paso: *https://www.tshaonline.org/handbook/entries/el-paso-tx*

Austin: *https://www.tshaonline.org/handbook/entries/austin-tx-travis-county*

San Antonio: *https://www.tshaonline.org/handbook/entries/san-antonio-tx*

Rio Grande Valley: *https://www.tshaonline.org/handbook/entries/rio-grande-valley*

East Texas: *https://www.tshaonline.org/handbook/entries/east-texas*

Permian Basin: *https://www.tshaonline.org/handbook/entries/permian-basin*

The *Handbook of Texas* is a collaborative scholarly project of the Texas State Historical Association (TSHA) that began in 1939 under the direction of Professor Walter Prescott Webb at the University of Texas at Austin to create, "the most useful book that has ever been published in Texas."

- FREE and accessible on computers, phones, and tablets
- More than 27,000 entries by 6,000+ authors
- 7 million page views annually
- 4.2 million visitors annually

A Texas South-Eastern Railroad engine, photographed in 1907. Photo by J.D. Cress, Public Domain

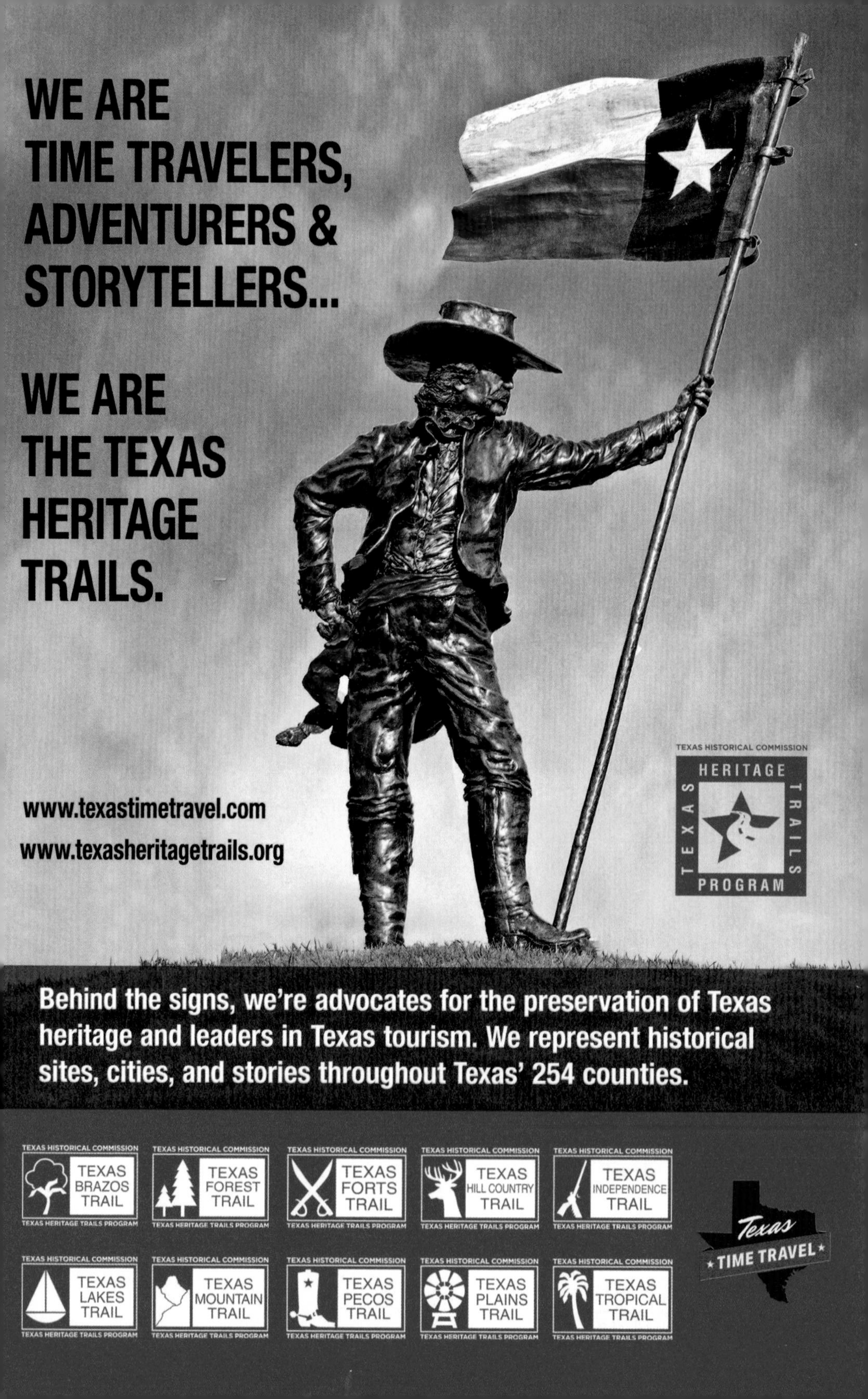
WE ARE
TIME TRAVELERS,
ADVENTURERS &
STORYTELLERS...
WE ARE
THE TEXAS
HERITAGE
TRAILS.
www.texastimetravel.com
www.texasheritagetrails.org
TEXAS HISTORICAL COMMISSION
TEXAS HERITAGE TRAILS PROGRAM
Behind the signs, we're advocates for the preservation of Texas heritage and leaders in Texas tourism. We represent historical sites, cities, and stories throughout Texas' 254 counties.
TEXAS BRAZOS TRAIL
TEXAS FOREST TRAIL
TEXAS FORTS TRAIL
TEXAS HILL COUNTRY TRAIL
TEXAS INDEPENDENCE TRAIL
TEXAS LAKES TRAIL
TEXAS MOUNTAIN TRAIL
TEXAS PECOS TRAIL
TEXAS PLAINS TRAIL
TEXAS TROPICAL TRAIL
Texas TIME TRAVEL

ENVIRONMENT

PHYSICAL REGIONS, GEOLOGY, SOILS

AQUIFERS, RIVERS, LAKES, ESTUARIES & BAYS

PLANT LIFE, FORESTS & GRASSLANDS

WILDLIFE LISTS, THREATENED & ENDANGERED SPECIES

The Physical State of Texas

The Area of Texas

Texas occupies about 7 percent of the total water and land area of the United States. Second in size among the states, Texas has a land and water area of 268,596 square miles, as compared with Alaska's 665,384 square miles, according to the United States Census Bureau. California, the third-largest state, has 163,695 square miles. Texas is as large as all of New England, New York, Delaware, Pennsylvania, Ohio, and Virginia combined.

The state's total area consists of 261,232 square miles of land and 7,365 square miles of water.

Length and Breadth

The longest straight-line distance in a general north-south direction is 801 miles from the northwest corner of the Panhandle to the extreme southern tip of Texas on the Rio Grande southeast of Brownsville. The greatest east-west distance is 773 miles from the extreme eastward bend in the Sabine River in Newton County to the extreme western bulge of the Rio Grande just northwest of El Paso.

Texas' Boundary Lines

The boundary of Texas by segments, including only larger river bends and only the great arc of the coastline, is as follows:

Boundary	Length
Rio Grande	889.0 mi.
Coastline	367.0 mi.
Sabine River, Lake, and Pass	180.0 mi.
Sabine River to Red River	106.5 mi.
Red River	480.0 mi.
East Panhandle line	133.6 mi.
North Panhandle line	167.0 mi.
West Panhandle line	310.2 mi.
Along 32nd parallel	209.0 mi.
TOTAL	**2,842.3 mi.**

Following the smaller meanderings of the rivers and the tidewater coastline, the following are the boundary measurements:

Boundary	Length
Rio Grande	1,254.0 mi.
Coastline (tidewater)	624.0 mi.
Sabine River, Lake, and Pass	292.0 mi.
Sabine River to Red River	106.5 mi.
Red River	726.0 mi.
East Panhandle line	133.6 mi.
North Panhandle line	167.0 mi.
West Panhandle line	310.2 mi.
Along 32nd parallel	209.0 mi.
TOTAL	**3,822.3 mi.**

Latitude and Longitude

The extremes of latitude and longitude in Texas are as follows:

★ From 25° 50' North latitude at the extreme southern turn of the Rio Grande on the south line of Cameron County to 36° 30' North latitude along the north line of the Panhandle, and

★ From 93° 31' West longitude at the extreme eastern point of the Sabine River on the east line of Newton County to 106° 38' West longitude at the extreme westward point of the Rio Grande on the western edge of El Paso.

Named Mountain Peaks in Texas Above 8,000 Feet

The highest point in the state is Guadalupe Peak at 8,749 feet above sea level. Its twin, El Capitan, stands at 8,085 feet and also is located in Culberson County near the New Mexico state line. Both are in Guadalupe Mountains National Park, which includes the scenic McKittrick Canyon.

The elevations used on this page are from various sources, including the U.S. Geological Survey, the National Park Service, and the Texas Department of Transportation. The named peaks above 8,000 feet and the counties in which they are located are listed below.

Name	County	Height
Guadalupe Peak	Culberson	8,749 ft.
Bush Mountain	Culberson	8,631 ft.
Shumard Peak	Culberson	8,615 ft.
Bartlett Peak	Culberson	8,508 ft.
Mount Livermore (Baldy Peak)	Jeff Davis	8,378 ft.
Hunter Peak (Pine Top Mtn.)	Culberson	8,368 ft.
El Capitan	Culberson	8,085 ft.

Elevation Highs and Lows

Highest Town: Fort Davis in Jeff Davis County is the highest town of any size in Texas at 5,050 feet above sea level, and the county has the highest average elevation.

Highest Highway: The highest state highway point also is in Jeff Davis County at McDonald Observatory on Mount Locke, where the road reaches 6,781 feet above sea level, as determined by the Texas Department of Transportation.

Highest Railway: The highest railway point is Paisano Pass, 14 miles east of Marfa in Presidio County, which is 5,074 above sea level.

Lowest Point: Sea level is the lowest elevation determined in Texas, and it can be found in all the coastal counties. No point in the state has been found by the geological survey to be below sea level. ☆

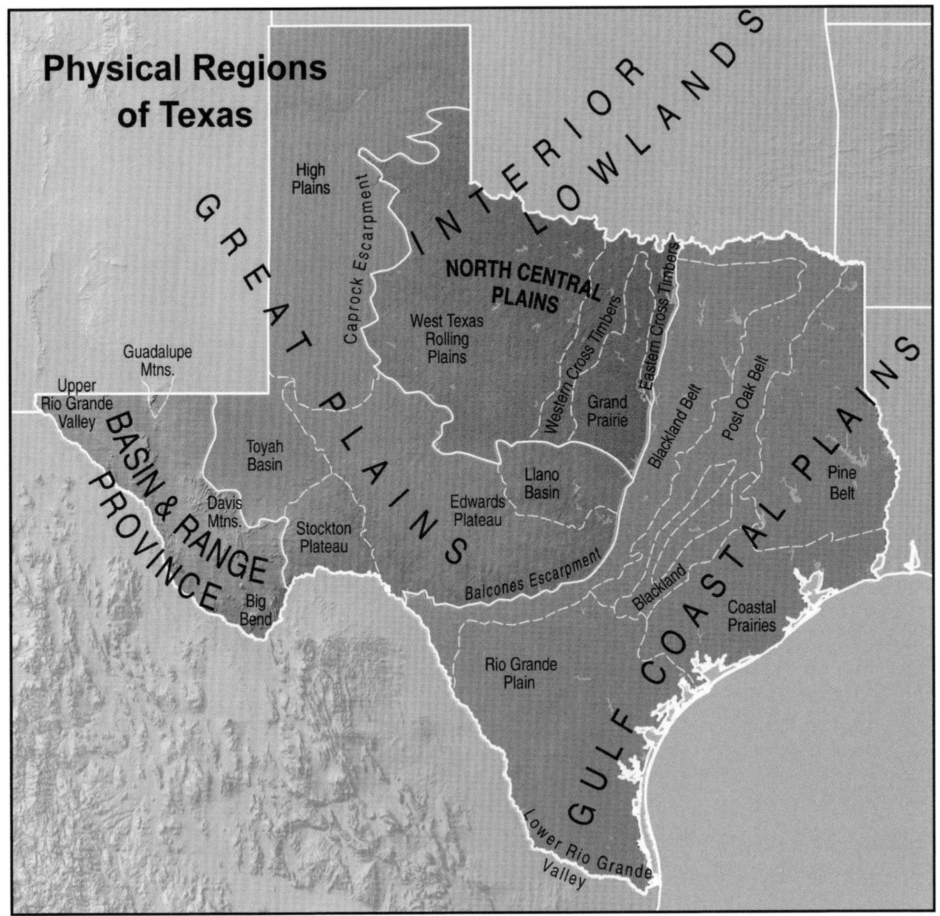

Physical Regions

This section was reviewed by Dr. David R. Butler, Texas State University System Regents' Professor of Geography

The principal physical regions of Texas are usually listed as follows:

I. Gulf Coastal Plains

Texas' Gulf Coastal Plains are the western extension of the coastal plain extending from the Atlantic Ocean to beyond the Rio Grande. Its characteristic rolling to hilly surface covered with a heavy growth of pine and hardwoods extends into East Texas. In the increasingly arid west, however, its forests become secondary in nature, consisting largely of post oaks and, farther west, prairies and brushlands.

The interior limit of the Gulf Coastal Plains in Texas is the line of the Balcones Fault and Escarpment. This geologic fault or shearing of underground strata extends eastward from a point on the Rio Grande near Del Rio. It extends to the northwestern part of Bexar County, where it turns northeastward and extends through Comal, Hays, and Travis counties, intersecting the Colorado River immediately north of Austin. The fault line is a single, definite geologic feature, accompanied by a line of southward- and eastward-facing hills.

The resemblance of the hills to balconies when viewed from the plain below accounts for the Spanish name for this area: balcones.

North of Waco, features of the fault zone are sufficiently inconspicuous that the interior boundary of the Coastal Plain follows the traditional geologic contact between upper and lower Cretaceous rocks. This contact is along the eastern edge of the Eastern Cross Timbers.

This fault line is usually accepted as the boundary between lowland and upland Texas. Below the fault line, the surface is characteristically coastal plains. Above the Balcones Fault, the surface is characteristically interior rolling plains.

A. Pine Belt or "Piney Woods"

The Pine Belt, called the "Piney Woods," extends 75 to 125 miles into Texas from the east. From north to south, it extends from the Red River to within about 25 miles of the Gulf Coast. Interspersed among the pines are hardwood timbers, usually in valleys of rivers and creeks. This area is the source of practically all of Texas' commercial timber production (see Texas Forest Resources, page 73). It was settled early in Texas' history and is one of the oldest farming areas in the state.

This area's soils and climate are adaptable to the production of a variety of fruit and vegetable crops. Cattle raising is widespread, along with the development of pastures planted to improved grasses. Lumber production is the principal industry. There is a large iron-and-steel industry near Daingerfield in Morris County based on nearby iron deposits. Iron deposits are also worked in Rusk and one or two other counties.

A great oil field discovered in Gregg, Rusk, and Smith counties in 1931 has done more than anything else to contribute to the economic growth of the area. This area has a variety of clays, lignite, and other minerals as potentials for development.

B. Post Oak Belt

The main Post Oak Belt of Texas is wedged between the Pine Belt on the east, Blacklands on the west, and the Coastal Prairies on the south, covering a considerable area in East-Central Texas. The principal industry is diversified farming and livestock raising.

It is spotty in character, with some insular areas of blackland soil and some that closely resemble those of the Pine Belt. There is a small, isolated area of loblolly pines in Bastrop, Caldwell, Fayette, and Lee counties known as the "Lost Pines," the westernmost southern pines in the United States. The Post Oak Belt has lignite, commercial clays, and some other minerals.

C. Blackland Belt

The Blackland Belt stretches from the Rio Grande to the Red River, lying just below the line of the Balcones Fault and varying in width from 15 to 70 miles. It is narrowest below the segment of the Balcones Fault from the Rio Grande to Bexar County and gradually widens as it runs northeast to the Red River.

Its rolling prairie, easily turned by the plow, developed rapidly as a farming area until the 1930s and was the principal cotton-producing area of Texas. Now, however, other Texas areas that are irrigated and mechanized lead in farming.

Because of the early growth, the Blackland Belt is still the most thickly populated area in the state and contains within it and along its border more of the state's large and middle-sized cities than any other area. Primarily because of this concentration of population, this belt has the most diversified manufacturing industry of the state.

D. Coastal Prairies

The Texas Coastal Prairies extend westward along the coast from the Sabine River, reaching inland 30 to 60 miles. Between the Sabine and Galveston Bay, the line of demarcation between the prairies and the Pine Belt forests to the north is very distinct. The Coastal Prairies extend along the Gulf of Mexico from the Sabine to the Lower Rio Grande Valley.

The eastern half is covered with a heavy growth of grass; the western half, which is more arid, is covered with short grass and, in some places, with small timber and brush. The soil is heavy clay. Grass supports the densest cattle population in Texas, and cattle ranching is the principal agricultural industry. Rice is a major crop, grown under irrigation from wells and rivers. Cotton, grain sorghum, and truck crops also are grown.

Coastal Prairie areas have seen the greatest industrial development in Texas history since World War II. Chief concentration has been from Orange and Beaumont to Houston, and much of the development has been in petrochemicals and the aerospace industry.

Corpus Christi, in the Coastal Bend, and Brownsville, in the Lower Rio Grande Valley, have seaports and agricultural and industrial sections. Cotton, grain, vegetables, and citrus fruits are the principal crops. Cattle production is significant, with the famed King Ranch and other large ranches located here.

E. Lower Rio Grande Valley

The deep alluvial soils and distinctive economy cause the Lower Rio Grande Valley to be classified as a subregion of the Gulf Coastal Plains. "The Valley," as it is called locally, is Texas' greatest citrus and winter vegetable growing region because of the normal absence of freezing weather and the rich delta soils of the Rio Grande. Despite occasional damaging freezes, the Lower Valley ranks high among the nation's fruit and truck-farming regions. Much of the acreage is irrigated, although dry-land farming also is practiced.

F. Rio Grande Plain

This area may be roughly defined as lying south of San Antonio between the Rio Grande and the Gulf Coast. The Rio Grande Plain shows characteristics of both the Gulf Coastal Plains and the North Mexico Plains because there is similarity of topography, climate, and plant life all the way from the Balcones Escarpment in Texas to the Sierra Madre Oriental in Mexico, which runs past Monterrey about 160 miles south of Laredo.

The Rio Grande Plain is partly prairie, but much of it is covered with a dense growth of prickly pear, mesquite, dwarf oak, catclaw, guajillo, huisache, blackbrush, cenizo, and other cactus and wild shrubs. It is devoted primarily to raising cattle, sheep, and goats. The Texas Angora goat and mohair industry centers in this area and on the Edwards Plateau, which borders it on the north. San Antonio and Laredo are its chief commercial centers, with San Antonio dominating trade.

There is some farming, and the Winter Garden, centering in Dimmit and Zavala counties north of Laredo, is irrigated from wells and streams to produce vegetables in late winter and early spring. Primarily, however, the central and western part of the Rio Grande Plain is devoted to livestock raising.

The rainfall is less than 25 inches annually, and the hot summers cause heavy evaporation, so that cultivation without irrigation is limited.

Over a large area in the central and western parts of the Rio Grande Plain, the growth of small oaks, mesquite, prickly pear (Opuntia) cactus, and a variety of wild shrubs is very dense, and it is often called the Brush Country. It is also referred to as the chaparral and the monte, from a Spanish word that can mean dense brush.)

II. Interior Lowlands

North Central Plains

The North Central Plains of Texas are a southwestern extension into Texas of the interior, or central, lowlands that extend northward to the Canadian border, paralleling the Great Plains to the West. The North Central Plains of Texas extend from the Blackland Belt on the east to the Caprock Escarpment on the west. From north to south, they extend from the Red River to the Colorado River.

A. West Texas Rolling Plains

The West Texas Rolling Plains, approximately the western two-thirds of the North Central Plains in Texas, rise from east to west in altitude from about 750 feet to 2,000 feet at the base of the Caprock Escarpment. Annual rainfall ranges from about 30 inches on the east to 20 inches on the west. In general, as one progresses westward in Texas, the precipitation not only declines but also becomes more variable from year to year. Temperature varies rather widely between summer's heat and winter's cold.

This area still has a large cattle-raising industry with many of the state's largest ranches. However, there is much level, cultivable land.

B. Grand Prairie

Near the eastern edge of the North Central Plains is the Grand Prairie, extending south from the Red River in an irregular band through Cooke, Montague, Wise, Denton, Tarrant, Parker, Hood, Johnson, Bosque, Coryell, and some adjacent counties.

It is a limestone-based area, usually treeless except along the numerous streams, and adapted primarily to raising livestock and growing staple crops. Sometimes called the Fort Worth Prairie, it has an agricultural economy and largely rural population, with no large cities, except Fort Worth on its eastern boundary.

C. Eastern and Western Cross Timbers

Hanging over the top of the Grand Prairie and dropping down on each side are the Eastern and Western Cross Timbers. The two southward-extending bands are connected by a narrow strip along the Red River.

The Eastern Cross Timbers extend southward from the Red River through eastern Denton County and along the boundary between Dallas and Tarrant counties. It then stretches through Johnson County to the Brazos River and into Hill County.

The much larger Western Cross Timbers extend from the Red River south through Clay, Montague, Jack, Wise, Parker, Palo Pinto, Hood, Erath, Eastland, Comanche, Brown, and Mills counties to the Colorado River, where they meet the Llano Basin.

Their soils are adapted to fruit and vegetable crops, which reach considerable commercial production in some areas in Parker, Erath, Eastland, and Comanche counties.

III. Great Plains

A. High Plains

The Great Plains, which lie to the east of the base of the Rocky Mountains, extend into northwestern Texas. This area, commonly known as the High Plains, is a vast, flat, high plain covered with thick layers of alluvial material. It is also known as the Staked Plains or Llano Estacado.

Historians differ as to the origin of this name. Some say it came from the fact that the explorer Coronado's expedition used stakes to mark its route across the trackless sea of grass so that it would be guided on its return trip. Others think that the estacado refers to the palisaded appearance of the

Sunset over the Glass Mountains near Fort Stockton and Alpine. Photo by Jonathan Cutrer, jcutrer.com

Caprock in many places, especially the west-facing escarpment in New Mexico.

The Caprock Escarpment is the dividing line between the High Plains and the lower West Texas Rolling Plains. Like the Balcones Escarpment, the Caprock Escarpment is a striking physical feature, rising abruptly 200 feet, 500 feet, and in some places almost 1,000 feet above the plains. Unlike the Balcones Escarpment, the Caprock was caused by surface erosion.

Where rivers issue from the eastern face of the Caprock, there frequently are notable canyons, such as Palo Duro Canyon on the Prairie Dog Town Fork of the Red River, Blanco Canyon on the White River, as well as the breaks along the Canadian River as it crosses the Panhandle north of Amarillo.

Along the eastern edge of the Panhandle, there is a gradual descent of the land's surface from high to low plains; but at the Red River, the Caprock Escarpment becomes a striking surface feature.

It continues as an east-facing wall south through Briscoe, Floyd, Motley, Dickens, Crosby, Garza, and Borden counties, gradually decreasing in elevation. South of Borden County, the escarpment is less obvious, and the boundary between the High Plains and the Edwards Plateau occurs where the alluvial cover of the High Plains disappears.

Stretching over the largest level plain of its kind in the United States, the High Plains rise gradually from about 2,700 feet on the east to more than 4,000 in spots along the New Mexico border.

Chiefly because of climate and the resultant agriculture, subdivisions are called the North Plains and South Plains. The North Plains, from Hale County north, has primarily wheat and grain sorghum farming, but with significant ranching and petroleum developments. Amarillo is the largest city, with Plainview on the south and Borger on the north as important commercial centers.

The South Plains, also a leading grain sorghum region, leads Texas in cotton production. Lubbock is the principal city, and Lubbock County is one of the state's largest cotton producers. Irrigation from underground reservoirs, centered around Lubbock and Plainview, waters much of the crop acreage.

B. Edwards Plateau

Geographers usually consider that the Great Plains at the foot of the Rocky Mountains actually continue southward from the High Plains of Texas to the Rio Grande and the Balcones Escarpment. This southern and lower extension of the Great Plains in Texas is known as the Edwards Plateau.

It lies between the Rio Grande and the Colorado River. Its southeastern border is the Balcones Escarpment from the Rio Grande at Del Rio eastward to San Antonio and thence to Austin on the Colorado River. Its upper boundary is the Pecos River, though the Stockton Plateau is geologically and topographically classed with the Edwards Plateau.

The Edwards Plateau varies from about 750 feet high at its southern and eastern borders to about 2,700 feet in places. Almost the entire surface is a thin, limestone-based soil covered with a medium to thick growth of cedar, small oak, and mesquite and a varying growth of prickly pear. Grass for cattle, weeds for sheep, and tree foliage for the browsing goats support three industries — cattle, goat, and sheep raising — upon which the area's economy depends. It is the nation's leading Angora goat and mohair producing region and one of the nation's leading sheep and wool areas. A few crops are grown.

Hill Country

The Hill Country is a popular name for the eastern portion of the Edwards Plateau south of the Llano Basin. Its notable large springs include Barton Springs at Austin, San Marcos Springs at San Marcos, Comal Springs at New Braunfels, several springs at San Antonio, and a number of others.

The Hill Country is characterized by rugged hills with relatively steep slopes and thin soils overlying limestone bedrock. High gradient streams combine with these steep hillslopes and occasionally heavy precipitation to produce an area with a significant flash-flood hazard.

C. Toyah Basin

To the northwest of the Edwards and Stockton plateaus is the Toyah Basin, a broad, flat remnant of an old sea floor that occupied the region as recently as Quaternary time.

Located in the Pecos River Valley, this region, in relatively recent time, has become important for many agricultural products as a result of irrigation. Additional economic activity is afforded by local oil fields.

D. Llano Basin

The Llano Basin lies at the junction of the Colorado and Llano rivers in Burnet and Llano counties. Earlier, this was known as the "Central Mineral Region" because of evidence there of a large number of minerals.

On the Colorado River in this area, a succession of dams impounds two large and five small reservoirs. Uppermost is Lake Buchanan, one of the large reservoirs, between Burnet and Llano counties. Below it in the western part of Travis County is Lake Travis.

Between these two large reservoirs are three smaller ones, Inks, Lyndon B. Johnson (formerly Granite Shoals), and Marble Falls reservoirs, used primarily to produce electric power from the overflow from Lake Buchanan. Lake Austin is along the western part of the city of Austin. Still another small lake, Lady Bird Lake (formerly Town Lake), is formed by a low-water dam in Austin.

The recreational area around these lakes has been called the Highland Lakes Country. This is an interesting area with Precambrian and Paleozoic rocks found on the surface. Granitic domes, exemplified by Enchanted Rock north of Fredericksburg, form the core of this area of ancient rocks.

IV. Basin and Range Province

The Basin and Range Province, with its center in Nevada, surrounds the Colorado Plateau on the west and south and enters far West Texas from southern New Mexico on the east. It consists of broad interior drainage basins interspersed with scattered fault-block mountain ranges.

The hiking trails at the Chihuahua Desert Research Center will give you stunning views of the Basin and Range Province of West Texas. Photo by Rosie Hatch

Although this is the only part of Texas regarded as mountainous, these should not be confused with the Rocky Mountains. Of all the independent ranges in West Texas, only the Davis Mountains resemble the Rockies, and there is much debate about this.

Texas west of the Edwards Plateau, bounded on the north by New Mexico and on the south by the Rio Grande, is distinctive in its physical and economic conditions. Traversed from north to south by fault-block mountains, it contains all of Texas' true mountains and also is very interesting geologically.

A. Guadalupe Mountains

Highest of the Trans-Pecos Mountains is the Guadalupe Range, which enters Texas from New Mexico. It abruptly ends about 20 miles south of the boundary line, where Guadalupe Peak, (8,749 feet, highest in Texas) and El Capitan (8,085 feet) are situated. El Capitan, because of perspective, appears to the observer on the plain below to be higher than Guadalupe.

Lying just west of the Guadalupe Range and extending to the Hueco Mountains a short distance east of El Paso is the Diablo Plateau or basin. It has no drainage outlet to the sea. The runoff from the scant rain that falls on its surface drains into a series of salt lakes that lie just west of the Guadalupe Mountains. These lakes are dry during periods of low rainfall, exposing bottoms of solid salt; for years they were a source of commercial salt. West of the Hueco Mountains are the Franklin Mountains in El Paso, with the Hueco Bolson (a down-dropped area approximately 4,000 feet above sea level) separating the two fault-block ranges.

B. Davis Mountains

The Davis Mountains are principally in Jeff Davis County. The highest peak, Mount Livermore (8,378 feet), is one of the highest in Texas; there are several others more than 7,000 feet high. These mountains intercept the moisture-bearing winds and receive more precipitation than elsewhere in the Trans-Pecos, so they have more vegetation than the other Trans-Pecos mountains. Noteworthy are the San Solomon Springs at the northern base of these mountains.

C. Big Bend

South of the Davis Mountains lies the Big Bend country, so called because it is encompassed on three sides by a great southward swing of the Rio Grande. It is a mountainous country of scant rainfall and sparse population. Its principal mountains, the Chisos, rise to 7,825 feet in Mount Emory.

Along the Rio Grande are the Santa Elena, Mariscal, and Boquillas canyons with rim elevations of 3,500 to 3,775 feet. They are among the noteworthy canyons of the North American continent.

Because of its remarkable topography and plant and animal life, the southern part of this region along the Rio Grande is home to Big Bend National Park, with headquarters in the Chisos Basin, a deep valley in the Chisos Mountains. It is a favorite recreation area.

D. Upper Rio Grande Valley

The Upper Rio Grande Valley, or El Paso Valley, is a narrow strip of irrigated land running down the river from El Paso for a distance of 75 miles or more.

In this area are the historic towns and missions of Ysleta, Socorro, and San Elizario, some of the oldest in Texas. Cotton is the chief product of this valley, much of it the long-staple variety. This limited area has a dense urban and rural population, in marked contrast to the territory surrounding it. ☆

Geology of Texas

Source: Bureau of Economic Geology, The University of Texas at Austin; www.beg.utexas.edu

Mountains, seas, coastal plains, rocky plateaus, high plains, forests — all of this physiographic variety in Texas is controlled by the varied rocks and structures that underlie and crop out across the state. The fascinating geologic history of Texas is recorded in the rocks — both those exposed at the surface and those penetrated by holes drilled in search of oil and natural gas.

The rocks reveal a dynamic, ever-changing earth: ancient mountains, seas, volcanoes, earthquake belts, rivers, hurricanes, and winds. Today, the volcanoes and great earthquake belts are no longer active, but rivers and streams, wind and rain, and the slow, inexorable alterations of rocks at or near the surface continue to change the face of Texas.

The geologic history of Texas, as documented by the rocks, began more than a billion years ago. Its legacy is the mineral wealth and varied land forms of modern Texas.

Geologic Time Travel

The story preserved in rocks requires an understanding of the origin of strata and how they have been deformed. **Stratigraphy is the study of the composition, sequence, and origin of rocks**: what rocks are made of, how they were formed, and the order in which the layers were formed.

Structural geology reveals the architecture of rocks: the locations of the mountains, volcanoes, sedimentary basins, and earthquake belts.

The map above shows where rocks of various geologic ages are visible on the surface of Texas today. History concerns events through time, but geologic time is such a grandiose concept, most find it difficult to comprehend. So geologists have **named the various chapters of earth history.**

Precambrian Eon

Precambrian rocks, more than 600 million years old, are exposed at the surface in the Llano Uplift of Central Texas and in scattered outcrops in West Texas, around and north of Van Horn and near El Paso.

These rocks, some more than a billion years old, include complexly deformed rocks that were originally formed by cooling from a liquid state, as well as rocks that were altered from pre-existing rocks.

Precambrian rocks, often called the "basement complex," are thought to form the foundation of continental masses. They underlie all of Texas. The outcrop in Central Texas is only the exposed part of the Texas Craton, which is primarily buried by younger rocks. (A craton is a stable, almost immovable portion of the earth's crust that forms the nuclear mass of a continent.)

Paleozoic Era

During the early part of the Paleozoic Era (approximately 600 million to 350 million years ago), **broad, relatively shallow seas repeatedly inundated the Texas Craton and much of North and West Texas.** The evidence for these events is found exposed around the Llano Uplift and in far West Texas near Van Horn and El Paso, and also in the subsurface throughout most of West and North Texas.

The evidence includes early Paleozoic rocks, sandstones, shales, and limestones, similar to sediments that form in seas today, and the fossils of animals, similar to modern crustaceans: the brachiopods, clams, snails, and related organisms that live in modern marine environments.

By late Paleozoic (approximately 350 million to 240 million years ago), the Texas Craton was bordered on the east and south by a long, deep marine basin called the Ouachita Trough. Sediments slowly accumulated in this trough until late in the Paleozoic Era.

Plate-tectonic theory postulates that the collision of the North American Plate (upon which the Texas Craton is located) with the European and African–South American plates uplifted the thick sediments that had accumulated in the trough **to form the Ouachita Mountains**.

At that time, the Ouachitas extended across Texas. Today, the Texas portion of the old mountain range is mostly buried by younger rocks. Ancient remnants can be seen in the Marathon Basin of West Texas due to uplift and erosion of younger sediments.

The public can see the remains of this once-majestic Ouachita Mountain range at Post Park, just south of Marathon in Brewster County. Other remnants at the surface are exposed in southeastern Oklahoma and southwestern Arkansas.

During the **Pennsylvanian** Period, however, the Ouachita Mountains bordered the eastern margin of shallow inland seas that covered most of West Texas. Rivers flowed westward from the mountains to the seas bringing sediment to form deltas along an ever-changing coastline.

The sediments were then reworked by the waves and currents of the inland sea. Today, these fluvial, delta, and shallow marine deposits compose the late Paleozoic rocks that crop out and underlie the surface of North-Central Texas.

Broad marine shelves divided the West Texas seas into several sub-basins, or deeper areas, that received more sediments than accumulated on the limestone shelves. Limestone reefs rimmed the deeper basins. **Today, these limestone reefs are important oil reservoirs in West Texas.**

These seas gradually withdrew from Texas, and by the late **Permian** Period, all that was left in West Texas were shallow basins and wide tidal flats in which salt, gypsum, and red muds accumulated in a hot, arid land. Strata deposited during the Permian Period are exposed today along the edge of the Panhandle, as far east as Wichita Falls and south to Concho County, and in the Trans-Pecos.

Mesozoic Era

Approximately 240 million years ago, the major geologic events in Texas shifted from West Texas to East and Southeast Texas. The European and African–South American plates, which had collided with the North American plate to form

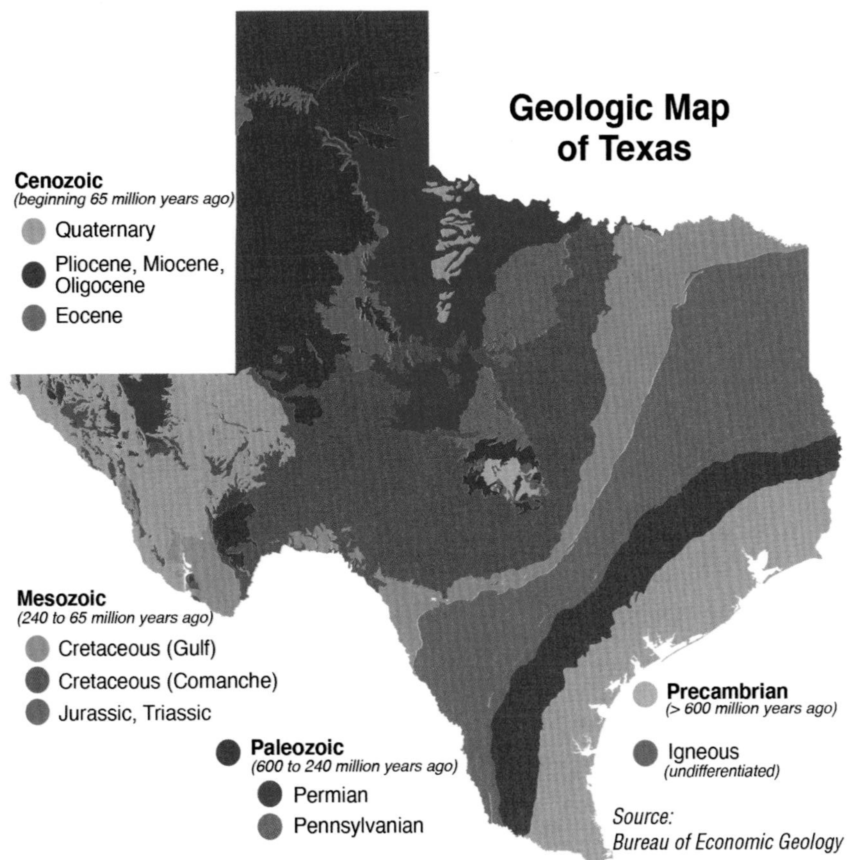

the Ouachita Mountains, began to separate from North America.

A series of faulted basins, or rifts, extending from Mexico to Nova Scotia were formed. These rifted basins received sediments from adjacent uplifts. As Europe and the southern continents continued to drift away from North America, **the Texas basins were eventually buried beneath thick deposits of marine salt within the newly formed East Texas and Gulf Coast basins.**

Jurassic and Cretaceous rocks in East and Southeast Texas document a sequence of broad limestone shelves at the edge of the developing Gulf of Mexico. From time to time, the shelves were buried beneath deltaic sandstones and shales, which built the northwestern margin of the widening Gulf of Mexico to the south and southeast.

As the underlying salt was buried more deeply by dense sediments, the salt became unstable and moved toward areas of least pressure. As the salt moved, it arched or pierced overlying sediments forming, in some cases, columns known as "salt domes." In some cases, these salt domes moved to the surface; others remain beneath a sedimentary overburden. This mobile salt formed numerous structures that would later serve to trap oil and natural gas.

By the early **Cretaceous** (approximately 140 million years ago), the shallow Mesozoic seas covered a large part of Texas, eventually extending west to the Trans-Pecos area and north almost to present-day state boundaries.

Today, the **limestone deposited in those seas is exposed in the walls of the magnificent canyons of the Rio Grande in the Big Bend National Park area** and in the canyons and headwaters of streams that drain the Edwards Plateau, as well as in Central Texas from San Antonio to Dallas.

Animals of many types lived in the shallow Mesozoic seas, tidal pools, and coastal swamps. Today, these lower Cretaceous rocks are some of the most fossiliferous in the state. **Tracks of dinosaurs occur in several places**, and remains of terrestrial, aquatic, and flying reptiles have been collected from Cretaceous rocks in many areas.

During most of the late Cretaceous, much of Texas lay beneath marine waters that were deeper than those of the early Cretaceous seas, except where rivers, deltas, and shallow marine shelves existed.

River delta and strandline sandstones are the reservoir rocks for the most prolific oil field in Texas. When discovered in 1930, this East Texas oil field contained recoverable reserves estimated at 5.6 billion barrels.

The chalky rock that we now call the "Austin Chalk" was deposited when the Texas seas became deeper. Today, the chalk and other Upper Cretaceous rocks crop out in a wide band that extends from near Eagle Pass on the Rio Grande, east to San Antonio, north to Dallas, and east to the Texarkana area. The Austin Chalk and other upper Cretaceous rocks dip southeastward beneath the East Texas and Gulf Coast basins.

The late Cretaceous was the time of the **last major seaway across Texas**, because mountains were forming in the western United States that influenced areas as far away as Texas.

A chain of volcanoes formed beneath the late Cretaceous seas in an area roughly parallel to and south and east of the old, buried Ouachita Mountains. The eruptions of these volcanoes were primarily on the sea floor and great clouds of steam and ash likely accompanied them.

Between eruptions, invertebrate marine animals built reefs on the shallow volcanic cones. Pilot Knob, located southeast of Austin, is one of these old volcanoes that is now exposed at the surface.

Cenozoic Era

At the dawn of the Cenozoic Era, approximately 65 million years ago, deltas fed by rivers were in the northern and northwestern margins of the East Texas Basin. These streams flowed eastward, draining areas to the north and west. Although there were minor incursions of the seas, the Cenozoic rocks principally document extensive seaward building by broad deltas, marshy lagoons, sandy barrier islands, and embayments.

Thick vegetation covered the levees and areas between the streams. Coastal plains were taking shape under the same processes still at work today.

The **Mesozoic marine salt became buried by thick sediments in the coastal plain area**. The salt began to form ridges and domes in the Houston and Rio Grande areas. The heavy load of sand, silt, and mud deposited by the deltas eventually caused some areas of the coast to subside and form large fault systems, essentially parallel to the coast.

Many of these coastal faults moved slowly and probably generated little earthquake activity. However, movement along the Balcones and Luling-Mexia-Talco zones, a complex system of faults along the western and northern edge of the basins, likely generated large earthquakes millions of years ago.

Predecessors of modern animals roamed the Texas Cenozoic coastal plains and woodlands. Bones and teeth of horses, camels, sloths, giant armadillos, mammoths, mastodons, bats, rats, large cats, and other modern or extinct mammals have been excavated from coastal plain deposits.

Vegetation in the area included varieties of plants and trees both similar and dissimilar to modern ones. **Fossil palmwood, the Texas "state stone," is found in sediments of early Cenozoic age.**

The Cenozoic Era in Trans-Pecos Texas was entirely different. There, **extensive volcanic eruptions formed great calderas and produced copious lava flows.** These eruptions ejected great clouds of volcanic ash and rock particles into the air — many times the amount of material ejected by the 1980 eruption of Mount St. Helens.

Ash from the eruptions drifted eastward and is found in many of the sand-and-siltstones of the Gulf Coastal Plains. Lava flowed over older Paleozoic and Mesozoic rocks, and igneous intrusions melted their way upward into crustal rocks. **These volcanic and intrusive igneous rocks are well exposed in arid areas of the Trans-Pecos today.**

In the Texas Panhandle, streams originating in the recently elevated southern Rocky Mountains brought floods of gravel and sand into Texas. As the braided streams crisscrossed the area, they formed great alluvial fans.

These fans, which were deposited on the older Paleozoic and Mesozoic rocks, occur from northwestern Texas into Nebraska. Between 1 million and 2 million years ago, the streams of the Panhandle were isolated from their Rocky Mountain source, and the eastern edge of this sheet of alluvial material began to retreat westward, forming the Caprock of the modern High Plains.

Late in the Cenozoic Era, a great Ice Age descended on the northern North American continent. For more than 2 million years, there were successive advances and retreats of the thick sheets of glacial ice. Four periods of extensive glaciation were separated by warmer interglacial periods. Although the glaciers never reached as far south as Texas, the state's climate and sea level underwent major changes with each period of glacial advance and retreat.

Sea level during times of glacial advance was 300 to 450 feet lower than during the warmer interglacial periods because so much sea water was captured in the ice sheets. The climate was both more humid and cooler than today, and the major Texas rivers carried more water and more sand and gravel to the sea. These deposits underlie the outer 50 miles or more of the Gulf Coastal Plain.

Approximately 3,000 years ago, sea level reached its modern position. The rivers, deltas, lagoons, beaches, and barrier islands that we know as coastal Texas today have formed since that time. ☆

A dissolving salt dome below Daisetta in Liberty County created a large sinkhole in 2008. The sinkhole expanded in 2023. Photo by Roy Luck, CC by 2.0

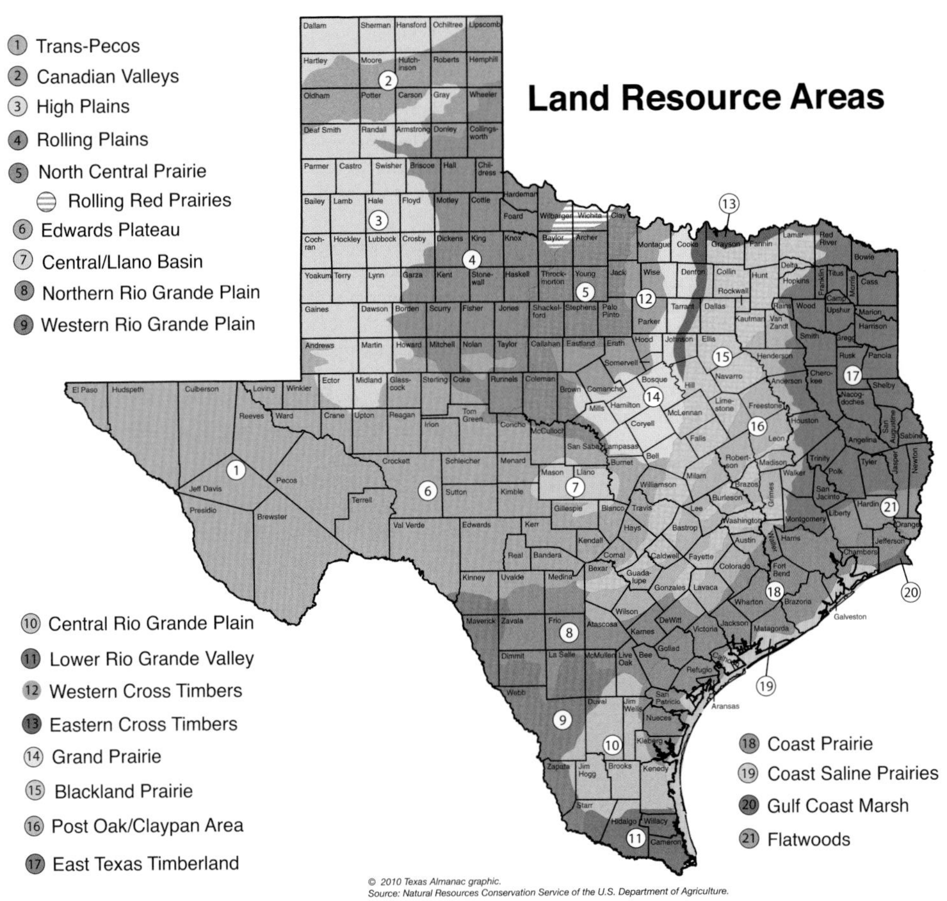

The map above shows the land resource areas of Texas, as defined by the Natural Resources Conservation Service at the U.S. Department of Agriculture. A land resource area is defined as "a geographic area, usually several thousand acres in extent, that is characterized by a particular pattern of soils, climate, water resources, land uses, and type of farming."

Soils of Texas

Source: Natural Resources Conservation Service, U.S. Department of Agriculture, https://www.nrcs.usda.gov/conservation-basics/conservation-by-state/texas

One of Texas' most important natural resources is its soil. Texas soils are complex because of the wide diversity of climate, vegetation, geology, and landscape. More than 1,300 different kinds of soil are recognized in Texas. Each has a specific set of properties that affect its use.

Soils information that was once available only through paper maps or books is now easily accessed online through the Web Soil Survey, found here: https://websoilsurvey.nrcs.usda.gov.

As the state's population continues to move from rural to urban areas, the Web Soil Survey is a tool landowners can use to make land-use and management decisions. This free tool allows landowners to analyze soil data and maps. It is used by farmers and ranchers to find information about soil properties and qualities to optimize agricultural production.

The soil survey is also used by homeowners and commercial builders looking for information on the suitability or the limitations of a building site.

For more information, contact the Natural Resources Conservation Service at 101 S. Main, Temple 76501-7602; (254) 742-9800.

Major Soil Areas

Texas can be divided into **21 Major Land Resource Areas** that have similar or related soils, vegetation, topography, climate, and land uses. Following are brief descriptions of these 21 areas:

Trans-Pecos Soils

The 18.7 million acres of the Trans-Pecos, mostly west of the Pecos River, are diverse plains and valleys intermixed with mountains. Surface drainage is slow to rapid. This arid region is used mainly as rangeland. A small amount of irrigated cropland lies on the more fertile soils along the Rio Grande and the Pecos River. Vineyards are a more recent use of these soils, as is the disposal of large volumes of municipal wastes.

Upland soils are mostly well-drained, light reddish-brown to brown clay loams, clays, and sands. Some have a large amount of gypsum or other salts. Many areas have shallow soils and rock outcrops, and sizable areas have deep sands.

Bottomland soils are deep, well-drained, dark grayish-brown to reddish-brown silt loams, loams, clay loams, and clays. The lack of soil moisture and wind erosion are the major soil-management problems. Only irrigated crops can be grown on these soils, and most areas lack an adequate source of good water.

Upper Pecos, Canadian Valleys and Plains Soils

The Upper Pecos, Canadian Valleys, and Plains area occupies a little over a half-million acres and is in the northwest part of Texas near the Texas–New Mexico border. It is characterized by broad rolling plains and tablelands broken by drainageways and tributaries of the Canadian River. It includes the Canadian Breaks, which are rough, steep lands below the adjacent High Plains. The average annual precipitation is about 15 inches, but it fluctuates widely from year to year. Surface drainage is slow to rapid.

The soils are well drained and alkaline. The mostly reddish-brown clay loams and sandy loams were formed mostly in material weathered from sandstone and shale. Depths range from shallow to very deep.

The area is used mainly as rangeland and wildlife habitat. Native vegetation is mid- to short-grass prairie species, such as hairy grama, sideoats grama, little bluestem, alkali sacaton, vine-mesquite, and galleta in the plains and tablelands. Juniper and mesquite grow on the relatively higher breaks. Soil management problems include low soil moisture and brush control.

High Plains Soils

The High Plains area comprises a vast high plateau of more than 19.4 million acres in northwestern Texas. It lies in the southern part of the Great Plains province that includes large, similar areas in Oklahoma and New Mexico. The flat, nearly level treeless plain has few streams to cause local relief. However, several major rivers originate in the High Plains or cross the area. The largest is the Canadian River, which has cut a deep valley across the Panhandle section.

Playas, small intermittent lakes scattered through the area, lie up to 20 feet below the surrounding plains. A 1965 survey counted more than 19,000 playas in 44 counties occupying some 340,000 acres. Most runoff from rainfall is collected in the playas, but only 10 to 40% of this water percolates back to the Ogallala Aquifer. The aquifer is virtually the exclusive water source in this area.

Upland soils are mostly well-drained, deep, neutral to alkaline clay loams and sandy loams in shades of brown or red. Sandy soils are in the southern part. Many soils have large amounts of lime at various depths and some are shallow over caliche. Soils of bottomlands are minor in extent.

The area is used mostly for cropland, but significant areas of rangeland are in the southwestern and extreme northern parts. Millions of cattle populate the many large feedlots in the area. The soils are moderately productive, and the flat surface encourages irrigation and mechanization. Limited soil moisture, constant danger of wind erosion, and irrigation water management are the major soil-management problems, but the region is Texas' leading producer of three important crops: cotton, grain sorghums, and wheat.

Rolling Plains Soils

The Rolling Plains include 21.7 million acres east of the High Plains in northwestern Texas. The area lies west of the North Central Prairies and extends from the edge of the Edwards Plateau in Tom Green County northward into Oklahoma. The landscape is nearly level to strongly rolling, and surface drainage is moderate to rapid. Outcrops of red beds, geologic materials, and associated reddish soils have led some scientists to use the name "Red Plains." Limestone underlies the soils in the southeastern part. The eastern part contains large areas of badlands (dry terrain with extensive erosion).

Upland soils are mostly deep, pale-brown through reddish-brown to dark grayish-brown, neutral to alkaline sandy loams, clay loams, and clays; some are deep sands.

Many soils have a large amount of lime in the lower part, and a few others are saline; some are shallow and stony. Bottomland soils are mostly reddish-brown and sandy to clayey; some are saline.

This area is used mostly for rangeland, but cotton, grain sorghums, and wheat are important crops. The major soil-management problems are brush control, wind erosion, low fertility, and lack of soil moisture. Salt spots are a concern in some areas.

North Central Prairie Soils

The North Central Prairie occupies about 7 million acres in North Central Texas. Adjacent to this area on the north is the rather small area (less than 1 million acres) called Rolling Red Prairies, which extends into Oklahoma and is included here because the soils and land use are similar.

This area lies between the Western Cross Timbers and the Rolling Plains. It is predominantly grassland intermixed with small wooded areas. The landscape is undulating with slow to rapid surface drainage.

Upland soils are mostly deep, well-drained, brown or reddish-brown, slightly acid loams over neutral to alkaline, clayey subsoils. Some soils are shallow or moderately deep to shale. Bottomland soils are mostly well-drained, dark-brown or gray loams and clays.

This area is used mostly as rangeland, but wheat, grain sorghums, and other crops are grown on the better soils. Brush control, wind and water erosion, and limited soil moisture are the major management concerns.

Edwards Plateau Soils

The 22.7 million acres of the Edwards Plateau are in South Central Texas east of the Trans-Pecos and west of the Blackland Prairie. Uplands are nearly level to undulating except near large stream valleys, where the landscape is hilly with deep canyons and steep slopes. There are many cedar brakes in this area. Surface drainage is rapid.

Upland soils are mostly shallow, stony, or gravelly, dark alkaline clays and clay loams underlain by limestone. Lighter-colored soils are on steep sideslopes and deep, less-stony soils are in the valleys. Bottomland soils are mostly deep, dark-gray or brown, alkaline loams and clays.

Raising beef cattle is the main enterprise in this region, but it is also the center of Texas' and the nation's mohair and wool production. The area is a major deer habitat, and hunting leases produce income. Cropland is mostly in the valleys on the deeper soils and is used mainly for growing forage crops and hay. The major soil-management concerns are brush control, large stones, low fertility, excess lime, and limited soil moisture.

Central or Llano Basin Soils

The Central Basin, also known as the Llano Basin, occupies a relatively small area in Central Texas. It includes parts or all of Llano, Mason, Gillespie, and adjoining counties. The total area is about 1.6 million acres of undulating to hilly landscape.

Upland soils are mostly shallow, reddish-brown to brown, mostly gravelly and stony, neutral to slightly acid sandy loams over granite, limestone, gneiss, and schist bedrock. Large boulders are on the soil surface in some areas. Deeper, less stony sandy-loam soils are in the valleys. Bottomland soils are minor areas of deep, dark-gray or brown loams and clays.

Ranching is the main enterprise, with some farms producing peaches, grain sorghum, and wheat. The area provides excellent deer habitat, and hunting leases are a major source of income. Brush control, large stones, and limited soil moisture are soil-management concerns.

Northern Rio Grande Plain Soils

The Northern Rio Grande Plain comprises about 6.3 million acres in South Texas extending from Uvalde to Beeville. The landscape is nearly level to rolling, mostly brush-covered plains with slow to rapid surface drainage.

The major upland soils are deep, reddish-brown or dark grayish-brown, neutral to alkaline loams and clays. Bottomland soils are mostly dark-colored loams.

The area is mostly rangeland with significant areas of cropland. Grain sorghums, cotton, corn, and small grains are the major crops. Crops are irrigated in the western part, especially in the Winter Garden area, where vegetables such as spinach, carrots, and cabbage are grown. Much of the area is good deer and dove habitat; hunting leases are a major source of income. Brush control, soil fertility, and irrigation-water management are the major soil-management concerns.

Western Rio Grande Plain Soils

The Western Rio Grande Plain comprises about 5.3 million acres in an area of southwestern Texas from Del Rio to Rio Grande City. The landscape is nearly level to undulating except near the Rio Grande where it is hilly. Surface drainage is slow to rapid.

The major soils are mostly deep, brown or gray alkaline clays and loams. Some are saline.

Most of the soils are used for rangeland. Irrigated grain sorghums and vegetables are grown along the Rio Grande. Hunting leases are a major source of income. Brush control and limited soil moisture are the major soil-management problems.

Central Rio Grande Plain Soils

The Central Rio Grande Plain comprises about 5.9 million acres in an area of South Texas from Live Oak County to Hidalgo County. It includes the South Texas Sand Sheet, an area of deep, sandy soils and active sand dunes. The landscape is nearly level to gently undulating. Surface drainage is slow to rapid. Upland soils are mostly deep, light-colored, neutral to alkaline sands and loams. Many are saline or sodic. Bottomland soils are of minor extent.

Most of the area is used for raising beef cattle. A few areas, mostly in the northeast part, are used for growing grain sorghums, cotton, and small grains. Hunting leases are a major source of income. Brush control is the major soil-management problem on rangeland; wind erosion and limited soil moisture are major concerns on cropland.

Lower Rio Grande Valley Soils

The Lower Rio Grande Valley comprises about 2.1 million acres in extreme southern Texas. The landscape is level to gently sloping with slow surface drainage.

Upland soils are mostly deep, grayish-brown, neutral to alkaline loams; coastal areas are mostly gray, silty clay loam and silty clay; some are saline. Bottomland soils are minor in extent.

Most of the soils are used for growing irrigated vegetables and citrus, along with cotton, grain sorghums, and sugar cane. Some areas are used for growing beef cattle. Irrigation water management and wind erosion are the major soil-management problems on cropland; brush control is the major problem on rangeland.

Western Cross Timbers Soils

The Western Cross Timbers area comprises about 2.6 million acres. It includes the wooded section west of the Grand Prairie and extends from the Red River southward to the north edge of Brown County. The landscape is undulating and is dissected by many drainageways including the Brazos and Red rivers. Surface drainage is rapid.

Upland soils are mostly deep, grayish-brown, slightly acid loams with loamy and clayey subsoils. Bottomland soils along the major rivers are deep, reddish-brown, neutral to alkaline silt loams and clays.

The area is used mostly for grazing beef and dairy cattle on native range and improved pastures. Crops are peanuts, grain sorghums, small grains, peaches, pecans, and vegetables. The major soil-management problem on grazing lands is brush control. Waste management on dairy farms is a more recent concern. Wind and water erosion are the major problems on cropland.

Eastern Cross Timbers Soils

The Eastern Cross Timbers area comprises about 1 million acres in a long narrow strip of wooded land that separates the northern parts of the Blackland Prairie and Grand Prairie and extends from the Red River southward to Hill County. The landscape is gently undulating to rolling and is dissected by many streams, including the Red and Trinity rivers. Sandstone-capped hills are prominent in some areas. Surface runoff is moderate to rapid.

The upland soils are mostly deep, light-colored, slightly acid sandy loams and loamy sands with reddish loamy or clayey subsoils. Bottomland soils are reddish-brown to dark gray, slightly acid to alkaline loams or gray clays.

Grassland consisting of native range and improved pastures is the major land use. Peanuts, grain sorghums, small grains, peaches, pecans, and vegetables are grown in some areas. Brush control, water erosion, and low fertility are the major soil concerns in management.

Grand Prairie Soils

The Grand Prairie comprises about 6.3 million acres in North Central Texas. It extends from the Red River to about the Colorado River. It lies between the Eastern and Western Cross Timbers in the northern part and just west of the Blackland Prairie in the southern part. The landscape is undulating to hilly and is dissected by many streams including the Red, Trinity, and Brazos rivers. Surface drainage is rapid.

Upland soils are mostly dark-gray, alkaline clays; some are shallow over limestone and some are stony. Some areas have light-colored loamy soils over chalky limestone. Bottomland soils along the Red and Brazos rivers are reddish silt loams and clays. Other bottomlands have dark-gray loams and clays.

Land use is a mixture of rangeland, pastureland, and cropland. The area is mainly used for growing beef cattle. Some small grain, grain sorghums, corn, and hay are grown. Brush control and water erosion are the major management concerns.

Blackland Prairie Soils

The Blackland Prairies consist of about 12.6 million acres of east-central Texas extending southwesterly from the Red River to Bexar County. There are smaller areas to the southeast. The landscape is undulating with few scattered wooded areas that are mostly in the bottomlands. Surface drainage is moderate to rapid.

Both upland and bottomland soils are deep, dark-gray to black alkaline clays. Some soils in the western part are shallow to moderately deep over chalk. Some soils on the eastern edge are neutral to slightly acid, grayish clays and loams over mottled clay subsoils (sometimes called graylands).

Blackland soils are known as "cracking clays" because of the large, deep cracks that form in dry weather. This high shrink-swell property can cause serious damage to foundations, highways, and other structures and is a safety hazard in pits and trenches.

Land use is divided about equally between cropland and grassland. Cotton, grain sorghums, corn, wheat, oats, and hay are grown. Grassland is mostly improved pastures, with native range on the shallower and steeper soils. Water erosion, cotton root rot, soil tilth, and brush control are the major management problems.

Claypan Area Soils

The Claypan Area consists of about 6.1 million acres in east-central Texas just east of the Blackland Prairie. The landscape is a gently undulating to rolling, moderately dissected woodland also known as the Post Oak Belt or Post Oak Savannah. Surface drainage is moderate.

Gulf Coast marshes are found at Anahuac National Wildlife Refuge, along with a wide variety of wildlife, such as this tri-color heron. Photo by Wally Gobetz, CC by NC-ND 2.0.

Upland soils commonly have a thin, light-colored, acid sandy loam surface layer over dense, mottled red, yellow, and gray claypan subsoils. Some deep, sandy soils with less clayey subsoils exist. Bottomlands are deep, highly fertile, reddish-brown to dark-gray loamy to clayey soils.

Land use is mainly rangeland. Some areas are in improved pastures. Most cropland is in bottomlands that are protected from flooding. Major crops are cotton, grain sorghums, corn, hay, and forage crops, most of which are irrigated. Brush control on rangeland and irrigation water management on cropland are the major soil-management problems. Water erosion is a serious problem on the highly erosive claypan soils, especially where they are overgrazed.

East Texas Timberland Soils

The East Texas Timberlands area comprises about 16.1 million acres of the forested eastern part of the state. The land is gently undulating to hilly and well dissected by many streams. Surface drainage is moderate to rapid.

This area has many kinds of upland soils but most are deep, light-colored, acid sands and loams over loamy and clayey subsoils. Deep sands are in scattered areas, and red clays are in areas of "redlands." Bottomland soils are mostly brown to dark-gray, acid loams and some clays.

The land is used mostly for growing commercial pine timber and for woodland grazing. Improved pastures are scattered throughout and are used for grazing beef and dairy cattle and for hay production. Some commercial hardwoods are in the bottomlands. Woodland management problems include seedling survival, invasion of hardwoods in pine stands, effects of logging on water quality, and control of the southern pine beetle. Lime and fertilizers are necessary for productive cropland and pastures.

Coast Prairie Soils

The Coast Prairie includes about 8.7 million acres near the Gulf Coast. It ranges from 30 miles to 80 miles in width and parallels the coast from the Sabine River in Orange County in Southeast Texas to Baffin Bay in Kleberg County in South Texas. The landscape is level to gently undulating with slow surface drainage.

Upland soils are mostly deep, dark-gray, neutral to slightly acid clay loams and clays. Lighter-colored and more-sandy soils are in a strip on the northwestern edge. Some soils in the southern part are alkaline; some are saline and sodic. Bottomland soils are mostly deep, dark-colored clays and loams along small streams but are greatly varied along the rivers.

Land use is mainly grazing lands and cropland. Some hardwood timber is in the bottomlands. Many areas are also managed for wetland wildlife habitat. The nearly level topography and productive soils encourage farming. Rice, grain sorghums, cotton, corn, and hay are the main crops. Brush management on grasslands and removal of excess water on cropland are the major management concerns.

Coast Saline Prairies Soils

The Coast Saline Prairies area includes about 3.2 million acres along a narrow strip of wet lowlands adjacent to the coast; it includes the barrier islands that extend from Mexico to Louisiana. The surface is at or only a few feet above sea level with many areas of salt-water marsh. Surface drainage is very slow.

The soils are mostly deep, dark-colored clays and loams; many are saline and sodic. Light-colored sandy soils are on the barrier islands. The water table is at or near the surface of most soils.

Cattle grazing is the chief economic use of the various salt-tolerant cordgrasses and sedges. Many areas are managed for wetland wildlife. Recreation is popular on the barrier islands. Providing fresh water and access to grazing areas are the major management concerns.

Gulf Coast Marsh Soils

This 150,000-acre area lies in the extreme southeastern corner of Texas. The area can be subdivided into four parts: freshwater, intermediate, brackish, and saline (saltwater) marsh. The degree of salinity of this system grades landward from saltwater marshes along the coast to freshwater marshes inland. Surface drainage is very slow.

This area contains many lakes, bayous, tidal channels, and man-made canals. About one-half of the marsh is fresh; one-half is salty. Most of it is susceptible to flooding either by fresh water drained from lands adjacent to the marsh or by saltwater from the Gulf of Mexico.

Most of the soils are poorly drained, continuously saturated, soft, and can carry little weight. In general, the organic soils have a thick layer of dark gray, relatively undecomposed organic material over a gray, clayey subsoil. The mineral soils have a surface of dark gray, highly decomposed organic material over a gray, clayey subsoil.

Most of the almost treeless and uninhabited area is in marsh vegetation, such as grasses, sedges, and rushes. It is used mainly for wildlife habitat. Part of the fertile and productive estuarine complex supports marine life of the Gulf of Mexico. It also provides wintering ground for waterfowl and habitat for many fur-bearing animals and alligators. A significant acreage is firm enough to support livestock and is used for winter grazing of cattle. The major management problems are providing fresh water and access to grazing areas.

Flatwoods Soils

The Flatwoods area includes about 2.5 million acres of woodland in humid Southeast Texas just north of the Coast Prairie and extending into Louisiana. The landscape is level to gently undulating. Surface drainage is slow.

Upland soils are mostly deep, light-colored, acid loams with gray, loamy, or clayey subsoils. Bottomland soils are deep, dark-colored, acid clays and loams. The water table is near the surface at least part of the year.

The land is mainly used for forest, although cattle are grazed in some areas. Woodland management problems include seedling survival, invasion of hardwoods in pine stands, effects of logging on water quality, and control of the southern pine beetle. ☆

Lake Nacogdoches during the drought in 2011. Photo by Jeff Attaway, CC by 2.0

Texas Water Resources

Contributed by Dr. Andrew Sansom, leading conservationist and executive director of the Meadows Center for Water and the Environment.

Water shortage is the **most serious** natural resource issue facing Texas today.

Here, as elsewhere in the world, the struggle over the uses to which water should be put — and who has the right to decide on those uses — is **intense and escalating**, particularly as the cyclical occurrence of severe flooding and drought increase. The bottom line is that Texas' population is going to double in the next fifty years and if all the water rights we have issued in our major rivers since Texas was a colony of Spain were fully exercised, many of them would be dry today. Thus, **many of our most iconic rivers**, which are vital to both our economy and the environment, **are at risk**.

Due in part to increasing stress on our rivers and lakes in Texas, we are also increasingly dependent on groundwater from the State's diverse major and minor aquifers. Unfortunately, **we do not recognize in law or policy the hydrologic linkage of our groundwater resources to surface water** — this failure will complicate sound water management of both in the future.

Texas' sensational system of bays and estuaries are arguably the finest such system of any state in the union. These coastal systems provide billions of dollars of economic benefit to the State and constitute some of the most prolific marine ecosystems in the world. What is less understood is that this spectacular natural resource is entirely dependent on continued supplies of freshwater flowing down our rivers and streams to mix with saltwater to **create the unique conditions vital to the existence of so many species of fish and wildlife**. Despite the enormous economic and environmental benefits we receive from these freshwater inflows, we have done a very inadequate job of insuring their continuation.

Historically, we have been reluctant to make difficult choices and decisions relating to water but when faced with crisis we have reacted. Following the drought of the 1950's, which we formally consider the worst on record, we built over 200 major reservoirs for flood control, water supply, and hydropower and they have served us well. However, since the 1970's there has been a dramatic decline in reservoir construction, due to a number of reasons.

More and more communities are creating underground reservoirs in a process called aquifer storage and retrieval, which captures water in times of high flows and stores it to avoid evaporation. We also have millions of acre feet of **brackish groundwater** in Texas **which has been largely untapped** and is less saline than water from the Gulf and closer to the consumer, making it less costly to produce and deliver.

But will that be enough to ensure our future? Despite much progress in water conservation, particularly in cities like San Antonio and El Paso, we still waste far too much water. **It is likely that the key to having a healthy water supply in the future will be increased efficiency.**

Our rivers and streams, our bays, estuaries, and our aquifers not only help define us as a state but are essential components of the one resource that no plant and animal can live without: water. We must do everything we can to make sure it is there for our economy, our environment, and our children. ☆

Major Aquifers of Texas

Sources: Texas Water Development Board, www.twdb.texas.gov

Aquifers are water-bearing rock formations beneath the earth's surface. Texas has a wealth of fresh to slightly saline groundwater in **nine major and 22 minor aquifers** that underlie more than 81% of the state.

Each year, groundwater provides approximately 60% of the water used in the state. Annual water use ranged from 14.2 million acre-feet in 2016 to 18.2 million acre-feet in 2011. In 2020, aquifers provided 55% of the 14.7 million acre-feet of water used by the state.

Approximately 77% of the groundwater produced in 2020 was used for agriculture (mostly for irrigation) and another 18% went to municipal water needs.

For more information about the aquifers of Texas and groundwater management, watch these videos created by the Texas Water Development Board:

www.twdb.texas.gov/groundwater/video/index.asp

Statewide Water Usage, 2020

Source	Volume	Percentage
Groundwater	8.0 million acre-feet	55%
Surface Water	6.2 million acre-feet	42%
Reuse	0.4 million acre-feet	3%

* One acre-foot equals 325,851 gallons of water.

Source: Texas Water Use Summary

Ogallala

The Ogallala Aquifer underlies most of the Texas Panhandle. It is the southernmost extension of the largest aquifer (High Plains Aquifer) in North America. The Ogallala Formation of late Miocene to early Pliocene age consists of heterogeneous sequences of coarse-grained sand and gravel in the lower part, grading upward into clay, silt, and fine sand.

The formation reaches a maximum thickness of 800 feet, and its freshwater saturated thickness averages 95 feet. In Texas, the Panhandle is the most extensive region irrigated with groundwater. About 95% of the water pumped from the Ogallala Aquifer is used for irrigation.

Extensive pumping that exceeds the amount of recharge has resulted in consistently declining water levels throughout much of the aquifer. Water conservation measures promoted by agricultural and municipal users have slowed the rate of decline, and water levels have risen in a few areas. Several agencies are investigating playa recharge and agricultural reuse projects in the aquifer area.

Gulf Coast

The Gulf Coast Aquifer system forms a broad belt parallel to the Texas coastline, extending through 54 counties from the Rio Grande northeastward to the Louisiana border. The aquifer system is composed of Quaternary- and Tertiary-age layers including the Catahoula, Oakville, Fleming, Goliad, Willis, Lissie, Bentley, Montgomery, and Beaumont formations.

The Gulf Coast Aquifer system has been divided into three major water-producing components referred to as the Chicot, Evangeline, and Jasper aquifers. These aquifers are composed of discontinuous layers of sand, silt, clay, and gravel.

The maximum total sand thickness of the Gulf Coast Aquifer system ranges from 700 feet in the south to 1,300 feet in the north. Freshwater saturated thickness averages 1,000 feet. The Gulf Coast Aquifer system is used primarily for municipal, industrial, and agricultural purposes.

Water quality is generally good in the central and northeastern parts of the aquifer but deteriorates to the southwest. Years of heavy pumping have caused significant water-level declines in portions of the aquifer. Some of these declines have resulted in land subsidence, particularly in the Houston-Galveston area.

Edwards Balcones Fault Zone

The Edwards Balcones Fault Zone (BFZ) Aquifer forms a narrow belt extending through the south-central part of the state from a groundwater divide in Kinney County through the San Antonio area northeastward to the Leon River in Bell County. A groundwater divide in Hays County hydrologically separates the aquifer into the San Antonio and Austin regions.

The aquifer is highly permeable, with water occurring in fractures, honeycomb-like zones (or intergranular pores), and solution channels that characterize the Edwards and associated limestone formations of Cretaceous age. Because the aquifer is highly permeable, water levels and spring flows respond quickly to rainfall, drought, and pumping. Aquifer thickness ranges from 200 to 600 feet, and freshwater saturated thickness averages 560 feet in the southern part of the aquifer.

Water from the Edwards BFZ is used primarily for municipal, irrigation, and recreational purposes. The City of San Antonio meets the majority of its water needs with Edwards BFZ water. The aquifer also feeds several well-known recreational springs and underlies some of Texas's most environmentally sensitive areas.

In 1993, the Texas Legislature created the Edwards Aquifer Authority (EAA) to regulate pumping from the aquifer to benefit all users within EAA's jurisdiction. The Barton Springs/Edwards Aquifer Conservation District and the Kinney County Groundwater Conservation District also provide aquifer management in the areas of the aquifer that are not within the EAA boundaries.

The EAA has an active outreach program used to educate the public on water conservation. It also operates several active groundwater recharge sites. The San Antonio River Authority also has a number of flood-control structures that effectively recharge the aquifer.

Carrizo-Wilcox

The Carrizo-Wilcox Aquifer extends from south of the Rio Grande in Mexico through Texas northeastward into Arkansas and Louisiana in a wide band parallel to and northwest of the Gulf Coast Aquifer.

The aquifer consists of the Tertiary-age Wilcox Group and overlying Carrizo Sand Formation of the Claiborne Group. The aquifer is composed of a hydrologically connected system of sand locally interbedded with clay, silt, lignite, and gravel. Although the Carrizo-Wilcox Aquifer reaches 3,000 feet in thickness, the freshwater saturated thickness of the sands averages 670 feet.

Throughout most of its extent in Texas, the aquifer yields fresh to slightly saline water. A little more than half of the water pumped from the aquifer is used for irrigation; the remaining amount pumped is used for municipal, industrial, domestic, and livestock purposes.

Recently, the Carrizo-Wilcox Aquifer has been considered as an alternative water supply for growing central Texas communities that have traditionally used the Edwards BFZ Aquifer to meet municipal needs.

Trinity

The Trinity Aquifer consists of Cretaceous-age Trinity Group formations that extend from the Red River in North Texas southward to the Hill Country of Central Texas. It is composed of several smaller aquifers contained within the Trinity Group. Depending on where they occur in the state, they are referred to as the Antlers, Glen Rose, Paluxy, Twin Mountains, Travis Peak, Hensell, and Hosston aquifers.

These aquifers consist of limestones, sands, clays, gravels, and conglomerates. Their combined freshwater saturated thickness averages about 600 feet in North Texas, and about 1,900 feet in Central Texas. The aquifer discharges to many small springs, with most flowing less than 10 cubic feet per second.

The Trinity Aquifer is primarily used to meet municipal water demands, but also provides water for irrigation, livestock, and other domestic purposes. Extensive development of the Trinity Aquifer in the Dallas–Fort Worth and Waco areas has resulted in water-level declines of 350 feet to more than 1,000 feet, though these declines have slowed with more reliance on surface water and reductions in groundwater pumping.

Edwards-Trinity Plateau

The Edwards-Trinity Plateau Aquifer extends from the Hill Country of Central Texas westward and southwestward to the Trans-Pecos region, covering much of the southwestern part of the state. The aquifer consists of early Cretaceous limestone and dolomites of the Edwards Group and sands

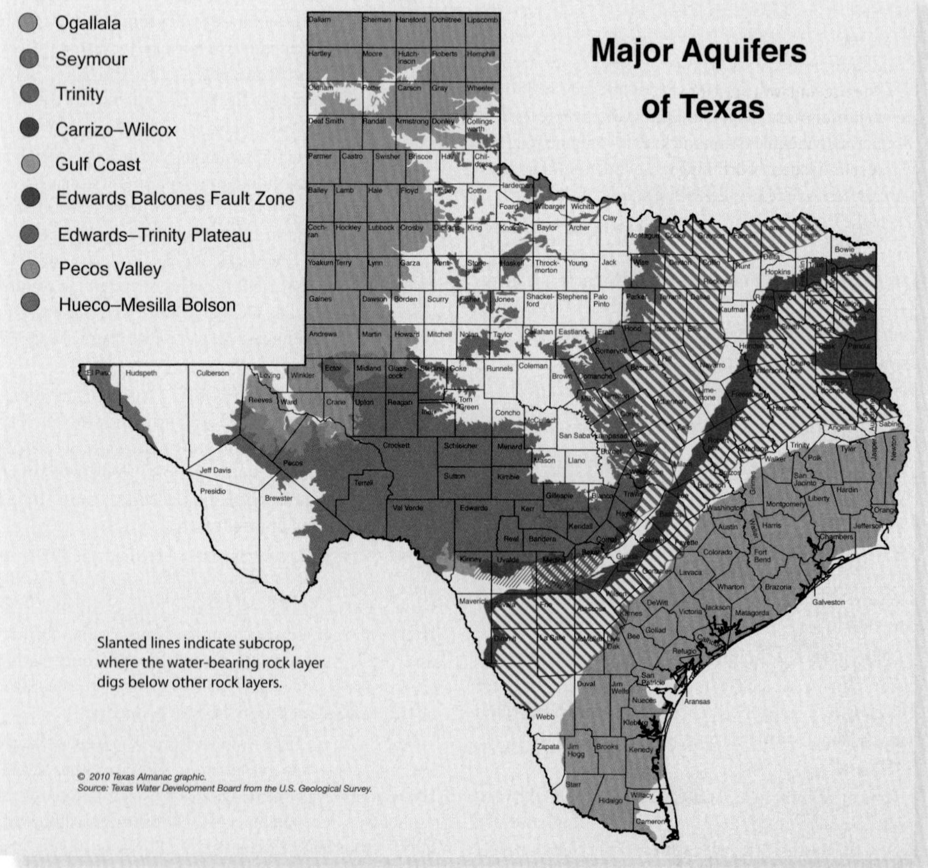

of the Trinity Group. Although the maximum saturated thickness of the aquifer is greater than 800 feet, freshwater saturated thickness averages 433 feet.

The aquifer lies beneath the Edwards Plateau. Near the plateau's edge, along the northern, eastern, and southern margins of the aquifer, groundwater flows towards streams, where water discharges from springs. Irrigation, mainly in the northwestern portion of the region, accounts for more than two-thirds of aquifer use.

Seymour

The Seymour Aquifer extends across north-central Texas. It consists of Quaternary-age, alluvial sediments unconformably overlying Permian-age rocks. Water is contained within isolated patches of discontinuous beds of poorly sorted gravel, conglomerate, sand, and silty clay. These deposits may reach 360 feet in thickness, but most of the Seymour is less than 100 feet thick.

About 90% of the water pumped from the Seymour is used for irrigation. Water quality generally ranges from fresh to slightly saline; however, some areas have moderately to very saline water quality. Nitrate concentrations occur above primary drinking water standards throughout much of the aquifer.

Hueco-Mesilla Bolsons

The Hueco-Mesilla Bolsons Aquifer is located in El Paso and Hudspeth counties in far West Texas. The aquifer consists of Tertiary and Quaternary basin-fill deposits of silt, sand, gravel, and clay that extend northward into New Mexico and westward into Mexico in two basins. The Hueco Bolson, located on the eastern side of the Franklin Mountains, has a maximum thickness of 9,000 feet and is an important source of drinking water for both El Paso and Juárez, Mexico. The Mesilla Bolson, located on the western side of the Franklin Mountains, has a maximum thickness of 2,000 feet.

Historical large-scale groundwater withdrawals, especially for the municipal uses of El Paso and Juárez, have caused major water-level declines. This pumping has also caused a deterioration of the chemical quality of the groundwater in the aquifer, according to El Paso Water Utilities and the United States Geological Survey.

Nearly 90% of the water pumped from the aquifer in the Texas extent of the bolsons is used for public supply. The City of El Paso has reduced its use of groundwater from the Hueco Bolson since 1989, and observation wells indicate that water levels have stabilized from a previously declining trend. El Paso and Fort Bliss also have built the world's largest inland desalination plant in El Paso County, which uses brackish groundwater from the Hueco Bolson.

Pecos Valley

The Pecos Valley Aquifer is located in the upper Pecos River Valley of West Texas. This aquifer, formerly called the Cenozoic Pecos Alluvium, consists of up to 1,500 feet of Tertiary and Quaternary alluvial fill and wind-blown deposits.

The aquifer occupies two hydrologically separate basins: the Pecos Trough in the west and the Monument Draw Trough in the east. The alluvial fill reaches 1,500 feet thick, and freshwater saturated thickness averages about 250 feet. Naturally occurring arsenic and radionuclides occur in excess of primary drinking water standards.

More than 80% of groundwater pumped from the aquifer is used for irrigation, and the remainder is withdrawn for industrial, power supply, and municipal uses. Water-level declines in excess of 200 feet have occurred in Reeves and Pecos counties but have slowed since the mid-1970s as irrigation pumping has decreased. Declines continue in Ward County due to increased municipal and industrial pumping. ☆

Kayakers enjoying a day on the Guadalupe River. Photo by Carolyn Savell, CC by 2.0

Major Rivers of Texas

Sources: Texas Water Development Board, www.twdb.texas.gov; U.S. Geological Survey, https://www.usgs.gov/

Texas contains about 191,000 miles of streams, and the U.S. Geological Survey Geographic Names Information System tracks 11,575 named streams in the state. But amongst all these creeks, brooks, and branches, the 14 major rivers listed here are essential to our everyday lives.

Rio Grande

The Pueblo Indians called this river P'osoge, which means the "river of great water." In 1582, Antonio de Espejo of Nueva Vizcaya, Mexico, followed the course of the Río Conchos to its confluence with a great river, which he named Río del Norte (River of the North). The name Rio Grande was first used, apparently by the explorer Juan de Oñate, who arrived on its banks near present-day El Paso in 1598.

Thereafter the names were often consolidated as Río Grande del Norte. It was shown also on early Spanish maps as Río San Buenaventura and Río Ganapetuán. In its lower course, it early acquired the name Río Bravo, which is its name on most Mexican maps. At times it has also been known as Río Turbio, probably because of its muddy appearance during its frequent rises. Some people erroneously call this watercourse the "Rio Grande River."

This river forms the boundary of Texas and the international U.S.-Mexican border for 889 or 1,254 river miles, depending upon method of measurement. (See Texas Boundary Lines, page 28.)

The U.S. Geological Survey figure for the total length from its headwaters to its mouth on the Gulf of Mexico is 1,900 miles.

According to the USGS, the Rio Grande is tied with the St. Lawrence River (also 1,900 miles) as the fourth-longest North American river, exceeded only by the Missouri-Mississippi, Mackenzie-Peace, and Yukon rivers. Since all of these except the Missouri-Mississippi are partly in Canada, the Rio Grande is the second-longest river entirely within or bordering the United States. It is Texas' longest river.

The snow-fed flow of the Rio Grande is used for irrigation in Colorado below the San Juan Mountains, where the river rises at the Continental Divide. Turning south, it flows through a canyon in northern New Mexico and again irrigates a broad valley of central New Mexico. Southern New Mexico impounds Rio Grande waters in Elephant Butte Reservoir for irrigation of the valley above and below El Paso.

The valley near El Paso is thought to be the oldest irrigated area in Texas because Indians were irrigating crops here when Spanish explorers arrived in the early 1500s.

From source to mouth, the Rio Grande drops 12,000 feet to sea level as a mountain torrent, desert stream, and meandering coastal river. Along its banks and in its valley, Europeans established some of their first North American settlements. Here are situated three of the oldest towns in Texas: Ysleta, Socorro, and San Elizario.

Because of the extensive irrigation, the Rio Grande virtually ends at the lower end of the El Paso valley, except in seasons of above-normal flow.

The river starts again as a perennially flowing stream where the Río Conchos of Mexico flows into it at Presidio-Ojinaga. Through the Big Bend, the Rio Grande flows through three successive canyons, the Santa Elena, the Mariscal, and the Boquillas. The Santa Elena has a river bed elevation of 2,145 feet and a canyon-rim elevation of 3,661. Corresponding figures for Mariscal are 1,925 and 3,625, and for Boquillas, 1,850 and 3,490. The river here flows for about 100 miles around the base of the Chisos Mountains as the southern boundary of Big Bend National Park.

Below the Big Bend, the Rio Grande gradually emerges from mountains onto the Coastal Plains. A 191.2-mile strip on the U.S. side from Big Bend National Park downstream to the Terrell–Val Verde county line has federal designation as the Rio Grande Wild and Scenic River.

At the confluence of the Rio Grande and Devils River, the United States and Mexico have built Amistad Dam, to impound 3,275,532 acre-feet of water, of which Texas' share is 56.2%. Falcon Reservoir, also an international project in Zapata and Starr counties, impounds 2,646,813 acre-feet of water, of which Texas' share in Zapata and Starr counties is 58.6%.

The Rio Grande, where it joins the Gulf of Mexico, has created a fertile delta called the Lower Rio Grande Valley, a major vegetable- and fruit-growing area. The river drains 49,387 square miles of Texas and has an average annual flow of 1,064,613 acre-feet.

Principal tributaries flowing from the Texas side are the Pecos and Devils rivers. On the Mexican side are Río

Average Annual Flow

River	Acre-Feet
Brazos	6,074,000
Sabine	5,864,000
Trinity	5,727,000
Neches	4,323,000
Red	3,464,000
Colorado	1,904,000

Source: Texas Water Development Board

Lengths of Major Rivers

River	Length
Rio Grande	1,900 miles
Red	1,360 miles
Brazos	1,280 miles
Pecos	926 miles
Canadian	906 miles
Colorado	865 miles

Source: Texas Water Development Board

Conchos, Río Salado, and Río San Juan. About three-fourths of the water running into the Rio Grande below El Paso comes from the Mexican side.

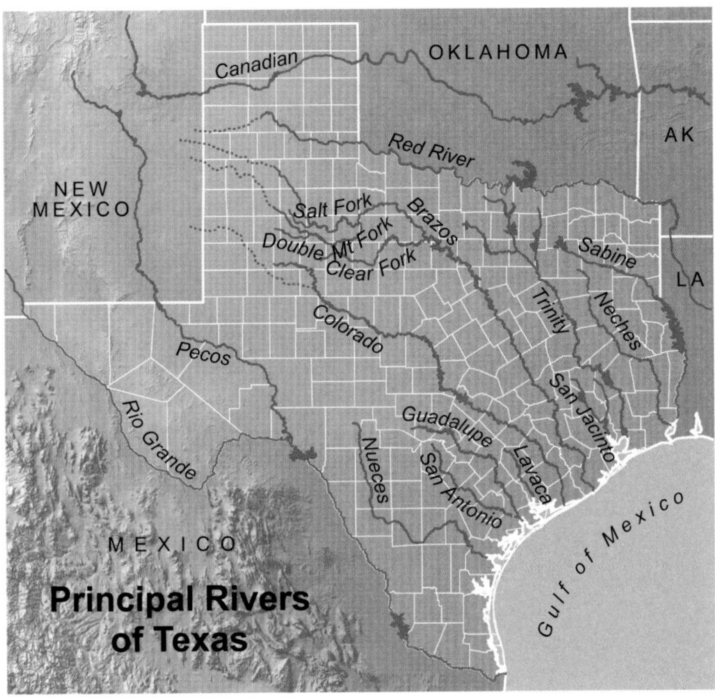

Pecos River

The Pecos, one of the major tributaries of the Rio Grande, rises on the western slope of the Santa Fe Mountains in the Sangre de Cristo Range of northern New Mexico. It enters Texas as the boundary between Loving and Reeves counties and flows 350 miles southeast as the boundary for several other counties, entering Val Verde County at its northwestern corner and angles across that county to its mouth on the Rio Grande, northwest of Del Rio.

According to the Handbook of Texas, the origins of the river's several names began with Antonio de Espejo, who called the river the Río de las Vacas ("river of the cows") because of the number of buffalo in the vicinity. Gaspar Castaño de Sosa, who followed the Pecos northward, called it the Río Salado because of its salty taste, which caused it to be shunned by men and animals alike.

It is believed that the name "Pecos" first appears in Juan de Oñate's reports concerning the Indian pueblo of Cicuye, now known as the Pecos Pueblo in New Mexico, and is of unknown origin.

Through most of its 926-mile-long course from its headwaters, the Pecos River parallels the Rio Grande. The total drainage area of the Pecos in New Mexico and Texas is about 44,000 square miles. Most of its tributaries flow from the west; these include the Delaware River and Toyah Creek.

The topography of the river valley in Texas ranges from semi-arid irrigated farmlands, desert with sparse vegetation, and, in the lowermost reaches of the river, deep canyons.

Nueces River

The Nueces River rises in two forks in Edwards and Real counties and flows 315 miles to Nueces Bay on the Gulf near Corpus Christi. Draining 16,700 square miles, it is a beautiful, spring-fed stream flowing through canyons until it issues from the Balcones Escarpment onto the Coastal Plains in northern Uvalde County.

Alonso de León, in 1689, gave it its name. Nueces, plural of nuez, means nuts in Spanish. (More than a century earlier, Cabeza de Vaca had referred to a Río de las Nueces in this region, but that is now thought to have been the Guadalupe.) The original Indian name for this river seems to have been Chotilapacquen. Crossing Texas in 1691, Terán de los Ríos named the river San Diego.

The Nueces was the boundary line between the Spanish provinces of Texas and Nuevo Santander. After the Texas Revolution of 1836, both Texas and Mexico claimed the territory between the Nueces and the Rio Grande, a dispute that was settled in 1848 by the Treaty of Guadalupe Hidalgo, which fixed the international boundary at the Rio Grande.

Average runoff of the Nueces is about 539,700 acre-feet a year. Principal water supply projects are Lake Corpus Christi and Choke Canyon Reservoir. Principal tributaries of the Nueces are the Frio and the Atascosa rivers. The river terminates in Nueces and Corpus Christi bays along the Coastal Bend.

San Antonio River

The San Antonio River has at its source large springs within and near the city limits of San Antonio. It flows 180 miles across the Coastal Plains to a junction with the Guadalupe River to enter San Antonio Bay along the Gulf Coast. Its channel through San Antonio has been developed into a parkway known as the River Walk.

Its principal tributaries are the Medina River and Cibolo Creek, both spring-fed streams, and this, with its own spring origin, gives it remarkably clear water and makes it one of the steadiest of Texas rivers. Including the Medina River headwaters, it is 238 miles in length.

The river was first named the León by Alonso de León in 1689; the name was not for himself, but he called it "lion" because its channel was filled with a rampaging flood.

Because of its limited and arid drainage area (4,180 square miles) the average runoff of the San Antonio River is relatively small, about 562,700 acre-feet annually.

Guadalupe River

The Guadalupe rises in its North and South forks in western Kerr County. A spring-fed stream, it flows eastward through the Hill Country until it issues from the Balcones Escarpment near New Braunfels. It then crosses the Coastal Plains to San Antonio Bay. Its total length is 409 miles, and its drainage area is 5,953 square miles. Its principal tributaries are the Comal, which joins it at New Braunfels; the San Marcos, another spring-fed stream, which joins it in Gonzales County; and the San Antonio, which joins it just above its mouth on San Antonio Bay.

There has been power development on the Guadalupe near Gonzales and Cuero for many years, and there is also power generation at Canyon Lake. Because of its springs and its considerable drainage area, the Guadalupe has an average annual runoff of more than 1.42 million acre-feet.

The name Guadalupe is derived from Nuestra Señora de Guadalupe, the name given the stream by Alonso de León.

Lavaca River

The Lavaca rises in extreme southwestern Fayette County and flows 117 miles to terminate in Lavaca Bay. Without a spring-fed water source and with only a small watershed, including that of its principal tributary, the Navidad, its flow is intermittent. Runoff averages about 277,000 acre-feet yearly.

The Spanish called it the Lavaca (the cow) because of the numerous bison found near it. It is the principal stream flowing to the Texas Coast between the Guadalupe and the Colorado, and drains 2,309 square miles. The principal lake on the Navidad is Lake Texana.

Colorado River

The Colorado River rises in east-central Dawson County and flows 600 miles to Matagorda Bay. Its drainage area, which extends into New Mexico, is 42,318 square miles. The U.S. Geological Survey puts is total length from source at 865 miles, making it the longest river contained entirely in Texas.

Its average annual runoff reaches a volume of 1.9 million acre-feet near the coast. Its name is a Spanish word meaning "reddish." There is evidence that Spanish explorers originally named the muddy Brazos "Colorado," but Spanish mapmakers later transposed the two names.

The river flows through a rolling, mostly prairie terrain to the vicinity of San Saba County, where it enters the rugged Hill Country and Llano Basin. It passes through a picturesque series of canyons until it issues from the Balcones Escarpment at Austin and flows across the Coastal Plains.

In the Hill Country, a remarkable series of reservoirs has been built to provide hydoelectric power, flood control, and water supply. The largest of these are Lake Buchanan in Burnet and Llano counties and Lake Travis in Travis County. Between the two in Burnet County are three smaller reservoirs: Inks, Lyndon B. Johnson (formerly Granite Shoals), and Marble Falls. Below Lake Travis is the older Lake Austin, largely filled with silt, whose dam is used to produce power from waters flowing down from the lakes above. Lady Bird Lake (formerly Town Lake) is in the city of Austin. This entire area is known as the Highland Lakes Country.

As early as the 1820s, Anglo-Americans settled on the banks of the lower Colorado, and in 1839, the Capital Commission of the Republic of Texas chose the picturesque area where the river flows from the Balcones Escarpment as the site of a new capital of the Republic — now Austin, capital of the state.

The early colonists encouraged navigation along the lower channel with some success. However, a natural log raft that formed 10 miles from the Gulf blocked river traffic after 1839, although shallow-draught vessels occasionally ventured as far upstream as Austin.

Conservation and utilization of the waters of the Colorado are under the jurisdiction of two agencies created by the Legislature — the Lower and Upper Colorado River authorities.

The principal tributaries of the Colorado River are the several prongs of the Concho River on its upper course, Pecan Bayou (farthest west "bayou" in the United States), and the Llano, San Saba, and Pedernales rivers. All except Pecan Bayou flow into the Colorado from the Edwards Plateau and are spring-fed, perennially flowing rivers. In the numerous mussels found along these streams, pearls occasionally have been found. On early Spanish maps, the Middle Concho was called Río de las Perlas.

Brazos River

The Brazos River proper is considered to begin where the Double Mountain and Salt Forks flow together in northeastern Stonewall County; it then flows 840 miles across Texas. The U.S. Geological Survey puts the total length from the New Mexico source of its longest upper prong at 1,280 miles.

With a drainage area of about 42,865 square miles, it is the second-largest river basin in Texas, after the Rio Grande. It flows directly into the Gulf southwest of Freeport in Brazoria County. Its average annual flow approaches 6.1 million acre-feet, the largest volume of any river in the state.

The Brazos' third upper fork is the Clear Fork, which joins the main stream in Young County, just above Possum Kingdom Lake. The Brazos crosses most of the main physiographic regions of Texas: High Plains, West Texas Rolling Plains, Western Cross Timbers, Grand Prairie, and Gulf Coastal Plains.

The original name of this river was Brazos de Dios, meaning "Arms of God." There are several legends as to why. One story is that the Coronado expedition, wandering on the trackless Llano Estacado, exhausted its water and was threatened with death from thirst. Arriving at the bank of the river, they gave it the name "Brazos de Dios" in thankfulness. Another legend is that a ship exhausted its water supply, and its crew was saved when they found the mouth of the Brazos. Still another story is that miners on the San Saba were forced by drought to seek water near present-day Waco and in gratitude called it Brazos de Dios.

Much early Anglo-American colonization of Texas took place in the Brazos Valley. Along its channel were San Felipe de Austin, capital of Austin's colony;

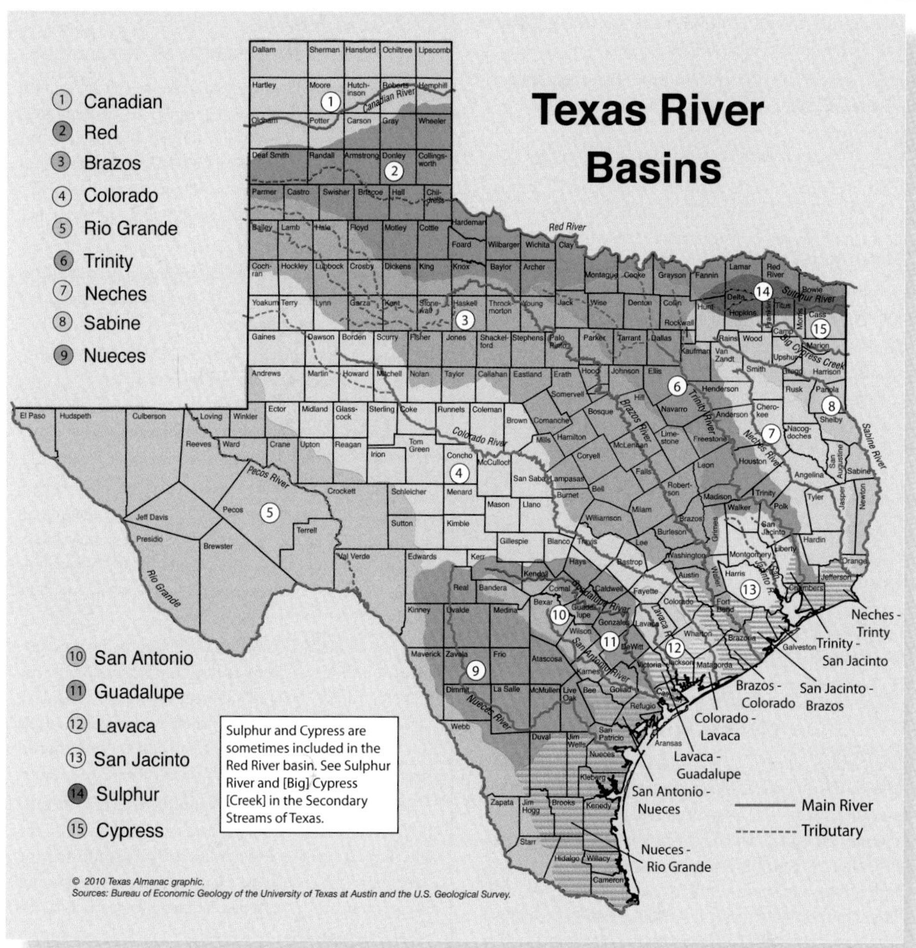

Washington-on-the-Brazos, where Texans declared independence from Mexico; and other historic settlements. There was some navigation of the lower channel of the Brazos in this period. Near its mouth, it intersects the Gulf Intracoastal Waterway, which provides connection with commerce throughout Texas and the Gulf Coast.

Most of the Brazos Valley lies within the boundaries of the Brazos River Authority, which conducts a multipurpose program for development. A large reservoir on the main channel of the Brazos is Lake Whitney (554,203 acre-feet capacity), where it is the boundary line between Hill and Bosque counties. Lake Waco on the Bosque and Belton Lake on the Leon are among the principal reservoirs on its tributaries. In addition to its three upper forks, other chief tributaries are the Paluxy, Little, and Navasota rivers.

San Jacinto River

The San Jacinto is a short river with a drainage basin of 3,936 square miles and an average annual runoff of about 1.36 million acre-feet. It is formed by the junction of its East and West forks in northeastern Harris County and runs to the Gulf through Galveston Bay. Its total length, including the East Fork, is about 85 miles.

Lake Conroe is on the West Fork, and Lake Houston is at the junction of the West Fork and the East Fork. The Houston Ship Channel runs through the lower course of the San Jacinto and its tributary, Buffalo Bayou, connecting the Port of Houston to the Gulf.

There are two stories concerning the origin of its name. One is that when early explorers discovered it, its channel was choked with hyacinth ("jacinto" is the Spanish word for hyacinth). The other is that it was discovered on Aug. 17, St. Hyacinth's Day.

The Battle of San Jacinto was fought on the bank of this river on April 21, 1836, when Texas won its independence from Mexico. San Jacinto Battleground State Historic Site and monument commemorate the battle.

Trinity River

The Trinity rises in its East Fork, Elm Fork, West Fork, and Clear Fork in Grayson, Montague, Archer, and Parker counties, respectively. The main stream begins with the junction of the Elm and West forks at Dallas. Its length is 550 miles, and its drainage area is 17,913 square miles. Because of moderate to heavy rainfall over its drainage area, it has an average annual flow of 5.7 million acre-feet near its mouth on Trinity Bay in the Galveston Bay system.

The Trinity derives its name from the Spanish "Trinidad." Alonso de León named it La Santísima Trinidad (the Most Holy Trinity).

Navigation was developed along its lower course with several riverport towns, such as Sebastopol in Trinity County. For many years, there has been a basin-wide movement for navigation, conservation, and utilization of its water. The Trinity River Authority is a state agency and the Trinity Improvement Association is a publicly supported nonprofit organization that has advocated its development.

The Trinity has in its valley more large cities, greater population, and more industrial development than any other river basin in Texas. On the Coastal Plains, there is large use of its waters for rice irrigation. Large reservoirs on the Elm Fork are Lewisville Lake and Ray Roberts Lake. There are four reservoirs above Fort Worth: Lake Worth, Eagle Mountain Lake, and Lake Bridgeport on the West Fork and Benbrook Lake on the Clear Fork.

Lake Lavon in southeast Collin County and Lake Ray Hubbard in Collin, Dallas, Kaufman, and Rockwall counties are on the East Fork. Lake Livingston is in Polk, San Jacinto, Trinity, and Walker counties.Two other reservoirs in the Trinity basin below the Dallas–Fort Worth area are Cedar Creek Reservoir and Richland-Chambers Reservoir.

Neches River

The Neches rises in Van Zandt County in East Texas and flows 416 miles to Sabine Lake near Port Arthur. It has a drainage area of 9,937 square miles. Abundant rainfall over its entire basin gives it an average annual flow near the Gulf of about 4.3 million acre-feet a year. The river takes its name from the Neches Indians, who the early Spanish explorers found living along its banks. Principal tributary of the Neches, and comparable with the Neches in length and flow above their confluence, is the Angelina River, so named for Angelina (Little Angel), a Hainai Indian girl who converted to Christianity and played an important role in the early development of this region.

Both the Neches and the Angelina run most of their courses in the Piney Woods, and there was much settlement along them as early as the 1820s.

Sam Rayburn Reservoir, near Jasper on the Angelina River, was completed and dedicated in 1965. With a storage capacity of 2.88 million acre-feet, it is the fourth-largest reservoir in Texas. Reservoirs located on the Neches River include Lake Palestine in the upper basin and B. A. Steinhagen Lake located at the junction of the Neches and the Angelina rivers.

Sabine River

The Sabine River is formed by three forks rising in Collin and Hunt counties. From its sources to its mouth on Sabine Lake, it flows approximately 360 miles and drains 7,570 square miles.

Sabine comes from the Spanish word for cypress, as does the name of the Sabinal River, which flows into the Frio River in Southwest Texas. The Sabine has an average annual flow volume of 5.8 million acre-feet.

Water Regulation in Texas

In Texas, water law historically has been different for surface water and groundwater. **Surface water belongs to the state** and, except for limited amounts of water for household and on-farm livestock use, requires a permit for use.

The **Texas Commission on Environmental Quality (TCEQ)** is responsible for permitting and adjudicating surface water rights. The TCEQ is the primary regulator of surface water and polices contamination and pollution of both surface and groundwater.

In general, groundwater is considered the private property of the surface landowner by "rule of capture," meaning the landowner may pump as much water as he wishes from beneath his land for any beneficial use and that does not harm neighboring property.

This right may be limited only by groundwater conservation districts, which are the state's preferred method of groundwater management and provide for the conservation, preservation, protection, recharging, and prevention of waste of groundwater resources within their jurisdictions.

As of August 2021, there are **98 groundwater conservation districts** in Texas, covering nearly 70% of the state. In addition, two subsidence districts cover Harris, Galveston, and Fort Bend counties. Subsidence districts regulate groundwater production to prevent land subsidence: the gradual caving in or sinking of an area of land.

The **Texas Water Development Board (TWDB)** collects data on water quality and availability within the state, plans for future supply and use, and administers the state's funds for grants and loans to finance future water development and supply. See the current members of the TWDB on page 493.

On July 7, 2021, the TWDB voted to adopt the 2022 State Water Plan. It outlines water conservation strategies for meeting projected water supply needs in 2070. The board has also adopted 16 regional water plans focusing on specific parts of the state.

You can see an interactive version of the current state water plan here:

2022.texasstatewaterplan.org/statewide

In addition, Texas has a **Water Conservation Advisory Council**, created in 2007. The council provides reports to the Texas Legislature to make recommendations about funding for water-related programs and suggest legislation to extend the lives of our water resources. Learn more at:

https://savetexaswater.org/

Throughout most of Texas history, the lower Sabine has been the eastern Texas boundary line, although for a while there was doubt as to whether the Sabine or the Arroyo Hondo, east of the Sabine in Louisiana, was the boundary. For a number of years, the outlaw-infested neutral ground lay between them. There was also a boundary dispute in which it was alleged that the Neches River was really the Sabine and, therefore, the boundary.

Travelers over the part of the Camino Real known as the Old San Antonio Road crossed the Sabine at the Gaines Ferry in Sabine County, and there were crossings for the Atascosito Road and other travel and trade routes of that day.

Toledo Bend Reservoir is the largest lake lying wholly or partly in Texas. The reservoir impounds 4.47 million acre-feet of water on the Sabine River in Newton, Panola, Sabine, and Shelby counties. It is the 16th-largest reservoir (in capacity by volume) in the United States. This is a joint project of Texas and Louisiana, through the Sabine River Authority.

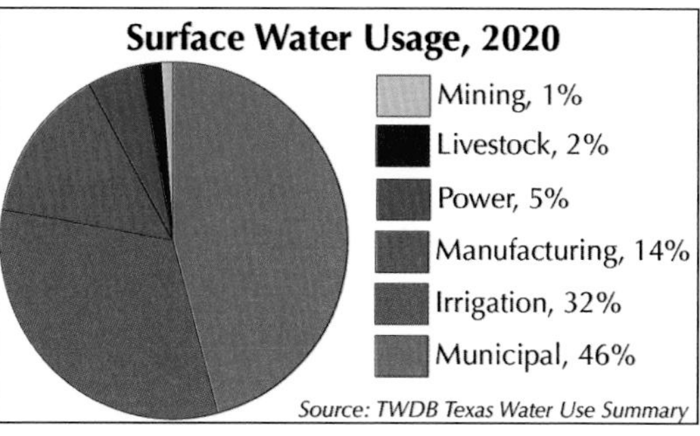

Red River

The Red River, with a length of 1,360 miles from its headwaters, is exceeded in length only by the Rio Grande among rivers associated with Texas. Its original source is water in Curry County, New Mexico, near the Texas boundary, forming a definite channel as it crosses Deaf Smith County, Texas, in tributaries that flow into the Prairie Dog Town Fork of the Red River. These waters carve the spectacular Palo Duro Canyon of the High Plains before the Red River leaves the Caprock Escarpment, flowing eastward.

Where the Red River crosses the 100th meridian at the bottom of the Panhandle, the river becomes the Texas-Oklahoma boundary and is soon joined by Buck Creek to form the main channel, according to the U.S. Geological Survey. Its length in Texas is 695 miles, before it flows into Arkansas, where it swings south to flow through Louisiana.

The Red River, which drains 24,297 square miles in Texas, is a part of the Mississippi drainage basin, and at one time it emptied all of its water into the Mississippi. In recent years, however, part of its water, especially at flood stage, has flowed to the Gulf via the Atchafalaya River in Louisiana.

The Red River takes its name from the red color of the water. This caused every explorer who came to its banks to call it "red" regardless of the language he spoke — Río Rojo or Río Roxo in Spanish, Rivière Rouge in French. At an early date, the river became the axis for French advance from Louisiana northwestward as far as present-day Montague County. There was consistent early navigation of the river from its mouth on the Mississippi to Shreveport, above which navigation was blocked by a natural log raft.

A number of important gateways into Texas from the north were established along the stream, such as Pecan Point and Jonesborough in Red River County, Colbert's Ferry and Preston in Grayson County, and later, Doan's Store Crossing in Wilbarger County. The river was a menace to the early traveler because of both its variable current and its quicksands, which brought disaster to many a trail-herd cow, as well as ox team and covered wagon.

The largest water conservation project on the Red River is Lake Texoma, with a conservation storage capacity of 2.5 million acre-feet.

The Red River's high content of salt and other minerals limits the usefulness of its water along its upper reaches. Ten salt springs and tributaries in Texas and Oklahoma contribute most of these minerals.

The uppermost tributaries of the Red River in Texas are Tierra Blanca Creek, which rises in Curry County, N.M., and flows easterly across Deaf Smith and Randall counties to meet Palo Duro Creek and form the Prairie Dog Town Fork a few miles east of Canyon.

Other principal tributaries in Texas are the Pease and the Wichita in North Central Texas and the Sulphur in Northeast Texas, which flows through Wright Patman Lake, then into the Red River after it has crossed the boundary line into Arkansas.

The last major tributary in Northeast Texas is the Cypress Creek system, which flows into Louisiana before joining with the Red River. Major reservoirs in this basin are Lake O' The Pines and Caddo Lake.

From Oklahoma, the principal tributary is the Washita, which has its headwaters in Roberts County, Texas. The Ouachita, a river with the same pronunciation though spelled differently, is the principal tributary to the Red River's lower course in Arkansas.

The Red River boundary dispute, a long-standing feud between Oklahoma and Texas, was finally settled in 2000 when the boundary was set at the vegetation line on the south bank, except for Lake Texoma, where the boundary was set within the channel of the lake.

Canadian River

The Canadian River heads near Raton Pass in northern New Mexico near the Colorado boundary line and flows into Texas on the west line of Oldham County. It crosses the Texas Panhandle into Oklahoma and there flows into the Arkansas River, a total distance of 906 miles. It drains 12,865 square miles in Texas, and much of its 213-mile course across the Panhandle is in a deep gorge.

A tributary, the North Canadian River, dips briefly into the Texas Panhandle in Sherman County before it joins the main channel in Oklahoma.

One of several theories as to how the Canadian got its name is that some early explorers thought it flowed into Canada. Lake Meredith, formed by Sanford Dam, provides water for several Panhandle cities.

Because of the deep gorge and the quicksand that occurs in many places, the Canadian River has been a particularly difficult stream to bridge. It is known, especially in its lower course in Oklahoma, as outstanding among the streams of the country for the great amount of quicksand in its channel. ☆

Secondary Streams of Texas

In addition to the principal rivers, Texas has many other streams of various size. The following list gives a few of these streams as designated by the U.S. Geological Survey, with additional information from the new Handbook of Texas and previous Texas Almanacs.

Alamito Creek: Formed by confluence of North, South forks 3 mi. N Marfa in Presidio County. Flows SE 82 mi. to Rio Grande 5 mi. S Presidio.

Angelina River: Rises in central Rusk County; flows SE 120 mi. through Cherokee, Nacogdoches, Angelina, San Augustine counties into Sam Rayburn Reservoir, then into Jasper County to the Neches River 12 mi. west of Jasper. A meandering stream through forested country.

Aransas River: Formed 2 mi. N Skidmore in SC Bee County by union of Poesta and Aransas creeks; flows SE 40 mi. forming boundary between San Patricio and Refugio counties; then briefly into Aransas County where it empties into Copano Bay.

Atascosa River: Formed NW Atascosa County by confluence of North, West prongs, flows SE 92 mi. through Atascosa and Live Oak counties into Frio River 2 mi. NW Three Rivers.

Attoyac Bayou: Rises 2.8 mi. NE Mount Enterprise in SE Rusk County; flows SE 67 mi. through Shelby, San Augustine and Nacogdoches counties into Angelina River at Sam Rayburn Reservoir.

Barton Creek: Rises NE of Henly in NW Hays County; flows E 40 mi. through Travis County to Colorado River at Lady Bird Lake in Austin.

Beals Creek: Formed by confluence of Sulphur Springs and Mustang draws 4 mi. W Big Spring SW Howard County; flows E 55 mi. into Mitchell County to mouth on Colorado River.

Big Cypress Creek: Forms in SE Hopkins County E of Pickton; flows SE 60 mi. to mouth on Big Cypress Bayou 3 mi. E Jefferson in Marion County and just before the bayou flows into Caddo Lake. The creek forms the boundary lines between Camp and Titus, Camp and Morris, and Morris and Upshur counties. It passes through Lake Cypress Springs, Lake Bob Sandlin, and Lake O' The Pines, and is part of the Red River drainage basin.

Blackwater Draw: Rises in Curry County, N.M.; flows into Texas in extreme NW Bailey County; flows SE through Lamb, Hale, and Lubbock counties to junction with Yellow House Draw to form North Fork of the Double Mountain Fork Brazos River. Length, 100 mi.

Blanco Creek: Rises near the intersection of Bee, Goliad and Karnes county lines in extreme S Karnes County; flows SE 45 mi. forming boundary of Bee and Goliad counties. Joins Medio Creek in Refugio County to form Mission River.

Blanco Creek: Rises E of Concan in Uvalde County; flows S 44 mi. to Frio River.

Blanco River: Rises W Lindendale in NE Kendall County; flows SE 64 mi. through Blanco and Hays counties; joins San Marcos River, a tributary of the Guadalupe; fed by many springs.

Bosque River: Flows from Lake Waco in McLennan County 5 mi. into Brazos River.

Bosque River, North: Formed at Stephenville by the union of North, South forks in Erath County; flows generally SE 96 mi. through Hamilton, Bosque and McLennan counties into Lake Waco.

Bosque River, South: Rises near Coryell-McLennan county line; flows NE 24 mi. into Lake Waco.

Brady Creek: Rises 14 mi. SW Eden in SW Concho County; flows 90 mi. through McCulloch and San Saba counties into San Saba River 10 mi. SW of Richland Springs.

Brazos River, Clear Fork: Rises 8 mi. E Snyder in Scurry County; flows NE 180 mi. through Fisher, Jones, Haskell, Throckmorton, Shackelford and Stephens counties into Brazos River in S Young County; drainage area 5,728 sq. mi.

Brazos River, Double Mountain Fork: Rises 12 mi. SE Tahoka, Lynn County; flows E 175 mi. through Garza, Kent, Fisher and Haskell counties to confluence with Salt Fork of the Brazos, north of Old Glory in Stonewall County.

Brazos River, North Fork: Formed by union of Yellow House and Blackwater draws in Lubbock; flows SE 75 miles through Crosby, Garza and Kent counties to junction with Double Mountain Fork Brazos River.

Brazos River, Salt Fork: Rises in SE Crosby County; flows 150 mi. through Garza and Kent counties to confluence with Double Mountain Fork in NE Stonewall County to form the main stream of Brazos River.

Buck Creek: Also called Spiller Creek. Rises SE Donley County; flows SE 49 mi. through Collingsworth and Childress counties to Texas-Oklahoma boundary; then 3 mi. through Oklahoma to junction with Prairie Dog Town Fork of Red River NW Hardeman County to form main stream of the Red River.

Buffalo Bayou: Rises in extreme N Fort Bend County; flows E 46 mi. through Houston into San Jacinto River in Harris County. Part of Houston Ship Channel.

California Creek: Rises 10 mi. NE Roby in Fisher County; flows NE 70 mi. through Jones County into Paint Creek in E Haskell County.

Caney Creek: Rises near Wharton in Wharton County; flows 75 mi. through Matagorda County into east end of Matagorda Bay. Centuries ago, the current Caney Creek channel was the channel for the Colorado River.

Capote/Wildhorse Draw: Rises N of Van Horn in Culberson County; runs 86 mi. S through Jeff Davis County to SW of Marfa in Presidio County. One of a number of streams in this area with no outlet to the sea.

Cedar Bayou: Rises 11 mi. NW Liberty in Liberty County; flows 46 mi. S as boundary between Harris County and Liberty and Chambers counties, and into Trinity Bay.

Chambers Creek: Formed SW Waxahachie in Ellis County by union North, South forks; flows SE 45 mi. through Navarro County into Richland Creek at Richland-Chambers Reservoir.

Cibolo Creek: Rises 7 mi. W Boerne in Kendall County; flows SE through Bexar, Comal, Guadalupe and Wilson counties into San Antonio River in Karnes County; 96 mi. in length. Spring-fed, perennially flowing stream.

Coleto Creek: Formed SW of Mission Valley in NW Victoria County by union of Twelve Mile and Fifteen Mile creeks forming boundary between Victoria and Goliad counties. From Coleto Creek Reservoir flows to Guadalupe River in Victoria County.

Comal River: Rises in Comal Springs in City of New Braunfels and flows SE about 2.5 miles to Guadalupe River. Shortest river in Texas by name.

Concho River: Formed at San Angelo by conjunction North, South Concho rivers; flows E 24 mi. through Tom Green County, then 29 mi. through Concho County into Colorado River 12 m. NE Paint Rock. Drainage basin, including North and South Concho, 6,613 sq. mi. A spring-fed stream.

Concho River, Middle: Rises SW Sterling County; flows S, then E 66 mi. through Tom Green panhandle, Irion and Reagan counties into South Concho River at Lake Nasworthy near Tankersley in Tom Green County.

Concho River, North: Rises in S Howard County; flows 137 mi. through Glasscock, Sterling and Coke counties to confluence with South Concho to form Concho River in Tom Green County. Drainage basin, 1,510 sq. mi.

Concho River, South: Rises in C Schleicher County; flows N through Lake Nasworthy to confluence with North Concho River in Tom Green County; length, 41 mi.; drainage basin area 3, 866 sq. mi. Perennial flow from springs.

Cowleech Fork Sabine River: Rises 2 mi. NW Celeste NW Hunt County; flows SE 40 mi. to Lake Tawakoni.

Deep Creek: Rises SE Baird, Callahan County; flows N 55 mi. into Hubbard Creek in Shackelford County near McCatherine Mountain.

Deep Creek: Rises 4 mi. N Fluvanna NW Scurry County; flows SSE 70 mi. to mouth on Colorado River in extreme N Mitchell County.

Delaware River: Rises eastern slope Delaware Mountains in N Culberson County; flows in NE course; crosses Texas-New Mexico state line and enters Pecos River; length, 50 mi.

Devils River: Formed SW Sutton County by union Dry Devils River and Granger Draw; flows SE 95 mi. through Val Verde County into Rio Grande at Amistad Reservoir. Spring-fed, perennially flowing stream throughout most of its course.

Elm Creek: Rises 3 mi. SE Nolan in Nolan County; flows NE 60 mi., passes through Lake Abilene, Buffalo Gap and Abilene in Taylor County and through Lake Fort Phantom Hill into Clear Fork Brazos River near Nugent, SE Jones County.

Frio River: Formed at Leakey in Real County by union of West and East Frio rivers; flows S 190 mi. through Uvalde, Medina, Frio, La Salle, McMullen counties (Choke Canyon Reservoir); joins Nueces River S of Three Rivers in Live Oak County. Drainage area, 7,310 sq. mi. Fed by springs in northern part, where it flows through picturesque canyon.

Greens Bayou: Rises 9 mi. W Aldine, C Harris County; flows ESE into Houston Ship Channel; 42 mi. long.

Hondo Creek: Rises 7.5 mi. NW Tarpley C Bandera County; flows SSE 67 mi. through Medina and Frio counties to Frio River 5 mi. NW Pearsall.

Howard Draw: Rises at Crockett-Reagan county line; flows SSW 45 mi. through Val Verde County to Pecos River near Pandale.

Hubbard Creek: Rises 3 mi. NW Baird N Callahan County; flows NE 62 mi. through Shackelford County; then into Stephens County (Hubbard Creek Reservoir) and joins Clear Fork of the Brazos River 10 mi. NW Breckenridge.

James River: Rises SE Kimble County; flows NE 37 mi. to join Llano River in Mason County.

Jim Ned Creek: Rises 10 mi. NW Tuscola SC Taylor County; flows SE 71 mi. through Callahan and Coleman counties to Brown County to join Pecan Bayou, a tributary of Colorado River.

Johnson Draw: Rises NE Crockett County; runs SSE 66 miles to mouth on Devils River in Val Verde County.

Lampasas River: Rises NW Mills County; flows SE 100 miles through Hamilton, Lampasas, Burnet and Bell counties (Stillhouse Hollow Lake); unites with Leon River to form Little River.

Leon River: Formed by confluence North, Middle and South Forks in NC Eastland County; flows SE 185 mi. through Comanche, Hamilton and Coryell counties to junction with Lampasas River to form Little River in Bell County.

Leona River: Rises N Uvalde in central Uvalde County; flows SE 83 mi. through Zavala County into Frio River in Frio County.

Limpia Creek: Heads in the Davis Mountains on the NE slope of Mount Livermore in Jeff Davis County and flows 52 mi. E, NE and E through Limpia Canyon to disappear at the head of Barrilla Draw in Pecos County. Part of course through Limpia Canyon noted for its scenic beauty.

Little Brazos River: Rises 5 mi. SW Thornton, SW Limestone County; flows 72 mi. SE through Falls and Robertson counties into Brazos River in Brazos County.

Little River: Formed central Bell County by union Leon, Lampasas rivers; flows 75 mi. SE through Milam County into Brazos River.

Devils River is popular for kayaking and tubing. Photo by Patrick Lewis, CC by NC 2.0

Llano River: Formed C Kimble County by union North, South Llano rivers; flows E 100 mi. through Mason, Llano counties to Colorado River. Drainage area, including North, South Llano rivers, 4,460 sq. mi. A spring-fed stream of the Edwards Plateau, known for scenic beauty.

Llano River, North: Rises C Sutton County; flows E 40 mi. to union with South Llano River at Junction in Kimble County.

Llano River, South: Rises in NC Edwards County; flows 55 mi. NE to confluence with North Llano River at Junction in Kimble County.

Los Olmos Creek: Rises central Duval County; flows SE 71 mi. through Jim Wells and Brooks counties; forms boundary between Kenedy and Kleberg counties; into Baffin Bay.

Madera Canyon: Rises N slope Mount Livermore, Jeff Davis County, at altitude of 7,500 ft.; flows 40 mi. NE to join Aguja Creek at Reeves County line to form Toyah Creek, tributary through Pecos River to Rio Grande. Intermittent stream. Noteworthy for its beauty.

Medina River: Rises in North, West prongs in W Bandera County; flows SE 116 mi. through Medina and Bexar counties to San Antonio River. A spring-fed stream. Scenically beautiful along upper course.

Medio Creek: Rises S Karnes County; flows SE 2 mi. through Karnes County, then 7 mi. along boundary Karnes and Bee counties, then SE 37 mi. through Bee County, SE 7 mi. through Refugio County to junction with Blanco Creek to form Mission River.

Mission River: Formed by confluence of Blanco and Medio creeks in C Refugio County; flows SE 24 mi. to mouth on Mission Bay, an inlet of Copano Bay.

Mulberry Creek: Rises NW Armstrong County at Fairview; flows SE 58 mi. through Donley and Briscoe counties into Prairie Dog Town Fork Red River in NW Hall County.

Navasota River: Rises SE Hill County; flows SE 125 mi. through Limestone County and along boundary Leon, Madison, Robertson, Brazos and Grimes counties to Brazos River near Navasota.

Navidad River: Forms at juncture of East and West Navidad rivers in NE Lavaca County; flows 74 mi. through Lavaca and Jackson counties into Lake Texana near Ganado; then joins Lavaca River.

Nolan River: Rises in NW Johnson County; flows S 30 mi. through Lake Pat Cleburne and into Hill County, where it empties into Brazos River at Lake Whitney.

Onion Creek: Rises 1 mi. W of Hays-Blanco county line SE Blanco County; flows SE 37 mi. through N Hays County; then 22 mi. through S Travis County into Colorado River near Garfield.

Paint Creek: Rises in extreme NW Jones County near Tuxedo; flows NE, then SE 53 mi. through SE corner of Stonewall County; then across S Haskell County (Lake Stamford) and into W Throckmorton County to mouth on Clear Fork Brazos River.

Palo Blanco Creek: Rises SE Hebbronville in N Jim Hogg County; flows SE 59 mi. through Duval and Brooks, where it passes through Laguna Salada; then into NW Kenedy County.

Palo Duro Creek: Rises in W Deaf Smith County; flows E 45 mi. into C Randall County to junction with Tierra Blanca Creek near Canyon to form the Prairie Dog Town Fork of the Red River. Lends its name to the notable canyon.

Paluxy River: Formed in E Erath County by convergence of North and South branches at Bluff Dale; flows SE 29 mi. through Hood and Somervell counties to mouth on Brazos River. Dinosaur Valley State Park at a large bend of the river in Somervell County is site of 100-million-year-old dinosaur tracks.

Pease River: Formed by union of North and Middle Pease rivers in NE Cottle County; flows E 100 mi. through Hardeman, Foard and Wilbarger counties into Red River 8 mi. NE of Vernon.

Pease River, Middle: Rises 8 mi. NW Matador in WC Motley County; flows E 63 miles into North Pease River to form the Pease River in NE Cottle County.

Pease River, North: Rises 9 mi. SE Cedar Hill in E Floyd County; flows E 60 mi. through Motley, Hall and Cottle counties. Joins Middle Pease to form Pease River.

Pease River, South: Also called Tongue River. Rises 11 mi. SW Roaring Springs in SW Motley County; flows ENE 40 mi. to mouth on Middle Pease River in W Cottle County.

Pecan Bayou: Formed by union of South, North prongs in SC Callahan County; flows SE 90 mi. through Coleman, Brown (Lake Brownwood) and Mills counties into Colorado River SW Goldthwaite. Westernmost bayou.

Pedernales River: Rises NE corner of Kerr County; flows E 106 mi. through Kimble, Gillespie, Blanco, Hays and Travis counties into Colorado River at Lake Travis. Spring-fed; a beautiful stream.

Pine Island Bayou: Rises near Rye, NE Liberty County; flows 76 mi. SE through Hardin and Jefferson counties into Neches River.

Red River, Prairie Dog Town Fork: Formed by union of Palo Duro and Tierra Blanca creeks in Randall County; flows E 160 mi. through Armstrong, Briscoe, Hall, and Childress counties to junction with Buck Creek to form Red River in NW corner of Hardeman County. Palo Duro Canyon is along course of this stream as it descends from Great Plains.

Red River, North Fork: Rises W Gray County; flows SE 180 mi. through Wheeler County into Oklahoma to junction with the Red River NE Vernon in Wilbarger County.

Red River, Salt Fork: Rises N Armstrong County; flows SE 155 mi. through Donley and Collingsworth counties and into Oklahoma. It joins the Red River opposite the northernmost point of Wilbarger County.

Richland Creek: Rises 3.5 mi. E Itasca N Hill County; flows E 50 mi. through Ellis and Navarro counties, through Navarro Mills Lake and Richland-Chambers Reservoir; then into the Trinity River in Freestone County.

Running Water Draw: Rises 24 mi. WNW Clovis, N.M.; flows ESE into Texas in C Parmer County; then through Castro, Lamb, Hale and Floyd counties to join Callahan Draw 8 mi. W Floydada at head of White River, a tributary of the Brazos River.

Sabana River: Rises at Callahan-Eastland county line; flows SE 50 mi. through Comanche County into Leon River at Proctor Lake.

Sabinal River: Rises 7 mi. N Vanderpool in NW Bandera County; flows S 60 mi. to junction with Frio River in SE Uvalde County. The West Sabinal River, which rises in Real County, joins the main stream at the Bandera-Uvalde county line.

San Bernard River: Rises 1 mi. S New Ulm in W Austin County; flows SE, forming boundary Austin and Colorado counties, 31 mi.; Austin and Wharton counties, 8 mi.; Wharton and Fort Bend counties, 28 mi.; approaches Gulf of Mexico in Brazoria County. Total length, 120 mi. (For more than 100 years locals have reported hearing the wail of a violin from the river. The mystery has never been solved, although some say the musical sounds are caused by escaping gas. The phenomenon has caused the stream to be called the Singing River: Handbook of Texas.)

San Gabriel River: Formed at Georgetown in C Williamson County by union of North and South forks; flows NE 50 mi. into Milam County to join Little River. Originally called San Xavier River.

San Jacinto River, East: Rises E Walker County; flows SE and S 69 mi. through San Jacinto, Liberty, Montgomery and Harris counties into Lake Houston and San Jacinto River.

San Jacinto River, West: Rises E Grimes County NE Shiro; flows SE 90 mi. through Walker County; into Lake Conroe in Montgomery County; then through Montgomery County to Lake Houston in Harris County.

San Marcos River: Formed near N limits City of San Marcos, Hays County, by several large springs, although watershed extends about 10 mi. NE of springs; Blanco River joins the San Marcos River 4 mi. downstream; flows SE 59 mi. as boundary between Guadalupe and Caldwell counties; then through Gonzales County to join Guadalupe River 2 mi. W Gonzales.

Sandy Creek: Rises SW Colorado County; flows SSE 42 mi. through Lavaca, Wharton and Jackson counties into Lake Texana.

San Saba River: Formed W Fort McKavett at Schleicher-Menard county line by union of North Valley and Middle Valley prongs; flows NE 140 mi. through Menard, Mason, McCulloch and San Saba counties into Colorado River 8 mi. NE San Saba. One of the picturesque streams of the Edwards Plateau.

Spring Creek: Rises NE Waller County near Fields Store; flows E 64 mi. forming boundary between Waller and Harris counties, and Montgomery and Harris counties to junction with West Fork San Jacinto River and Lake Houston.

Sulphur River: Formed E Delta County by junction North, South branches; flows E 183 miles forming boundary between Franklin and Red River counties; Titus and Red River counties; Morris and Red River and Bowie counties; then between Bowie and Cass counties, where it flows into Wright Patman Lake; continues on into Red River in S Miller County, Ark.

Sulphur River, North: Rises 1 mi. SW Gober S Fannin County; flows SE, E 54 mi. as boundary between Delta and Lamar counties and to union with South Sulphur River to form Sulphur River.

Sulphur River, South: Rises N Leonard S Fannin County; flows ESE 50 mi. through Hunt County; then as boundary between Hopkins and Delta counties (through Cooper Lake) to union with North Sulphur to form Sulphur River.

Sulphur Springs Draw: Rises in E Lea County, N.M.; enters Texas W Yoakum County at Bronco; flows SE 100 mi. through Terry, Gaines, Dawson, Martin, and Howard counties to confluence with Mustang Creek to form Beals Creek, a tributary of Colorado River.

Sweetwater Creek: Rises 2 mi. W Maryneal, C Nolan County; flows NE 45 mi. through Fisher and Jones counties into Clear Fork Brazos River.

Terlingua Creek: Rises WC Brewster County; flows S 83 mi. into Rio Grande just E Santa Elena Canyon.

Tierra Blanca Creek: Rises N Curry County, N.M.; flows E across Texas state line in SW Deaf Smith County and 75 mi. through Deaf Smith, Parmer and Randall counties to junction with Palo Duro Creek where it forms Prairie Dog Town Fork Red River.

Toyah Creek: Forms near boundary Jeff Davis-Reeves counties; flows NE 50 mi. into Pecos River NC Reeves County.

Trinity River, Clear Fork: Rises NW Poolville in NW Parker County; flows SE 56 mi. through Tarrant County into West Fork Trinity River at Fort Worth.

Trinity River, East Fork: Rises 1.5 mi. NW Dorchester in SC Grayson County; flows S 85 mi. through Collin County (Lake Lavon and Lake Ray Hubbard); then Rockwall and Dallas counties into Trinity River in SE Kaufman County.

Trinity River, Elm Fork: Rises 1 mi. NW Saint Jo in E Montague County; flows 85 mi. SE through Cooke, Denton counties (Ray Roberts Lake and Lewisville Lake) to junction with West Fork to form Trinity River proper at Irving in WC Dallas County.

Trinity River, West Fork: Rises in SC Archer County; flows SE 145 mi. through Jack, Wise (Lake Bridgeport) and Tarrant (Eagle Mountain Lake and Lake Worth) counties to conjunction with Elm Fork to form Trinity River proper in WC Dallas County.

Tule Creek: Formed in Swisher County by union of North, Middle and South Tule draws; flows E 40 mi. through Mackenzie Reservoir and Briscoe County into Prairie Dog Town Fork Red River. Remarkably beautiful Tule Canyon along lower course.

Turkey Creek: Rises near Turkey Mountain EC Kinney County; flows SE 54 mi. through Uvalde, Zavala, Dimmit counties to Nueces River.

Washita River: Rises SE Roberts County; flows E 35 mi. through Hemphill County to Oklahoma state line, then SE to Red River at Lake Texoma. Total length, 295 mi.

West Caney Creek: Rises 1 mi. SW Normangee in SW Leon County; flows SW 11 mi. through NW Madison County to junction with Navasota River on Brazos county line. The historic Old San Antonio Road, a thoroughfare for early Spanish and French explorers, crossed the headwaters of the stream.

White River: Formed 8 mi. W Floydada in WC Floyd County by union of Running Water and Callahan draws; flows SE 62 mi. through Blanco Canyon and White River Lake in Crosby County; then through Garza and Kent counties into Salt Fork Brazos River; principal tributary to Salt Fork.

Wichita River: Formed NE Knox County by union North, South Wichita rivers; flows NE 90 mi. through Baylor (Lake Kemp and Lake Diversion), Archer, Wichita and Clay counties to Red River N Byers.

Wichita River, Little: Formed in C Archer County by union of its North, Middle and South forks; flows NE 62 mi. through Clay County (Lake Arrowhead) into Red River.

Wichita River, North: Rises 6 mi. E East Afton in NE Dickens County; flows E through King, Cottle, Foard counties; then as boundary for Foard and Knox counties; then briefly into Baylor County to junction with South Wichita River to form Wichita River proper NE Vera in Knox County. Length, 100 mi.

Wichita River, South: Rises 10 mi. E Dickens in EC Dickens County; flows E 85 mi. through King and Knox counties to junction with North Wichita to form Wichita River.

Yellow House Draw: Rises in SE Bailey County; flows SE 80 mi. through Cochran, Hockley and Lubbock counties to confluence with Blackwater Draw at Lubbock to form the North Fork of Double Mountain Fork Brazos River. ☆

A group fishing on the Sulphur River near the Wright Patman Dam. Photo by Tony Webster, CC by 2.0

Sunset over the fishing pier on Lake Nasworthy. The largest fish caught in the lake was a 42.5" longnose gar, according to records kept by the TPWD. Photo by John Mueller, CC by NC-ND 2.0

Artificial Lakes and Reservoirs

Sources: U.S. Geological Survey; Texas Water Development Board; New Handbook of Texas; Texas Parks & Wildlife; U.S. Army Corps of Engineers; various river basin authorities; reservoir websites.

The large increase in the number of reservoirs in Texas during the past half-century has greatly improved water conservation and supplies.

As late as 1917, Texas had only four major reservoirs with a total storage capacity of 288,340 acre-feet. (One acre-foot is the amount of water necessary to cover an acre of surface area with water one foot deep, about 325,851 gallons of water.) Most of this capacity was in Medina Lake in southwest Texas, with 254,000 acre-feet capacity, created by a dam completed in May 1913.

By January 2012, Texas had 188 major water supply reservoirs (those with a normal capacity of 5,000 acre-feet or larger) and 21 major non-water supply reservoirs (those that do not have a water supply function). The 188 water supply reservoirs have a total conservation surface area of 1.7 million acres and an original conservation storage capacity of 35 million acre-feet (only Texas' share is counted in border reservoirs). The 21 non-water supply reservoirs have a total normal surface area of 62,079 acres and an original normal storage capacity of 760,000 acre-feet.

According to the U.S. Census Bureau's Master Address File (last updated August 2010), Texas has 5,616 square miles of inland water, ranking it first in the 48 contiguous states, followed by Florida, with 5,027 sq. mi. The only state with more inland water is Alaska, with 19,304 sq. mi.

There are 6,976 reservoirs in Texas with a normal storage capacity of 10 acre-feet or larger.

Natural Lakes in Texas

There are many natural lakes in Texas, though none is of great size. The largest designated natural lake touching the border of Texas is **Sabine Lake**, into which the Sabine and Neches rivers discharge. It is more properly called the **Sabine-Neches Estuary** of the Gulf of Mexico. (Find more information about this estuary on page 66.)

Also near the coast, in Calhoun County, is **Green Lake**, which has about 10,000 acre-feet of storage capacity. It is one of the state's largest natural freshwater lakes.

Caddo Lake, on the Texas-Louisiana border, was a natural lake originally, but its present capacity and surface area are largely due to dams built to raise the surface of the original body of water.

Natural Dam Lake, in Howard County, has a similar history to Caddo Lake.

In East Texas, there are many small natural lakes formed by "horse-shoe" bends that have been eliminated from the main channel of a river. There are also a number of these "horse-shoe" lakes along the Rio Grande in the Lower Valley, where they are called resacas.

On the South Plains and west of San Angelo there are lakes, such as **Big Lake** in Reagan County, that are usually dry.

List of Lakes and Reservoirs

The table that begins below lists the lakes and reservoirs in Texas that have **more than 5,000 acre-feet of storage capacity**. Some industrial cooling reservoirs are not included in this table.

The surface area listed in the table is the **area at conservation elevation** as calculated by the Texas Water Development Board (TWDB). Because sediment deposition constantly changes reservoir volumes over time, storage capacity figures are from the most recent surveys available.

Various methods of computing capacity area are used, and detailed information may be obtained from the TWDB, from the U.S. Army Corps of Engineers, or from local sources. Boundary reservoir capacities include water designated for Texas and non-Texas water. Texas' share will be included in the description.

Information is in the following order: (1) Name of lake or reservoir; (2) year of first impounding of water; (3) county or counties in which it is located; (4) river or creek on which it is located; (5) location with respect to some city or town; (6) purpose of reservoir; (7) owner of reservoir and (8) alternate or previous names. Some of these items, when not listed, are not available. For the larger lakes and reservoirs, the dam impounding water to form the lake bears the same name, unless otherwise indicated. The years in the table refer to first impounding of water. Double years refer to later, larger dams.

The colors shown on the left of the table correspond to the regions on the Texas Lakes map found in the back of this book (hardcover) or the foldout near page 160 (paperback).

Lakes and Reservoirs, Date of Origin	Surface Area (acres)	Storage Capacity (acre-ft.)
Abilene, L.: (1919) Taylor Co.; Elm Cr.; 6 mi. NW of Tuscola; (M-R); City of Abilene	595	7,900
Addicks Reservoir: (1948) Harris Co.; South Mayde Cr.; 1 mi. E of Addicks; (FC-R); USAE; Addicks only has water during times of flood and is dry most of the year	16,780	204,500
Alan Henry, L.: (1993) Garza and Kent counties; Double Mountain Fork, Brazos R; 10 mi. E of Justiceburg; (M-R-Ir.); City of Lubbock	2,800	96,207
Alcoa L.: (1952) Milam Co.; Sandy Cr.; 7 mi. SW of Rockdale; (R-In.); Alcoa Aluminum; also called Sandow L.	914	15,650
Amistad Reservoir, International: (1969) Val Verde Co.; Rio Grande; an international project of the U.S. and Mexico; 12 mi. NW of Del Rio; (C-FC-R-P); International Boundary and Water Commission, U.S. share of conservation capacity is 56.2%; formerly Diablo Reservoir	66,465	3,275,532
Amon G. Carter, L.: (1961) Montague Co.; Big Sandy Cr.; 6 mi. S of Bowie; (M-In.-R); City of Bowie	1,848	27,500
Anahuac, L.: (1936, 1954) Chambers Co.; Turtle Bayou; near Anahuac; (M-Ir.-In.-Mi.); Chambers-Liberty Counties Navigation District; also called Turtle Bayou Reservoir	5,035	33,348
Aquilla L.: (1983) Hill Co.; Aquilla Cr.; 10.2 mi. W of Hillsboro; (FC-R-M); USAE/Brazos R. Auth.	3,084	43,279
Arlington, L.: (1957) Tarrant Co.; Village Cr.; 7 mi. W of Arlington; (M-In.); City of Arlington	1,926	40,188
Arrowhead, L.: (1966) Clay-Archer counties.; Little Wichita R.; 13 mi. SE of Wichita Falls; (M); City of Wichita Falls	14,506	230,359
Athens, L.: (1962) Henderson Co.; 8 mi. E of Athens; (M-FC-R); Athens Municipal Water Auth.; formerly Flat Creek Reservoir	1,799	29,503
Austin, L.: (1893, 1915, 1939) Travis Co.; Colorado R.; in Austin; (M-In.-P); City of Austin, leased to LCRA; Imp. by Tom Miller Dam; 1893 first dam completed in 1893, but failed in 1900. Tom Miller Dam was completed in 1939	1,589	26,644
Ballinger L.: (1947) Runnels Co.; Valley Creek; 5 mi. NW of Ballinger; (M); City of Ballinger; also known as Lake Moonen	500	8,215
Balmorhea L.: (1917) Reeves Co.; Sandia Cr.; 2 mi. SE of Balmorhea; (R-Ir.); Reeves Co. WID No. 1; also known as Lower Parks Reservoir	573	6,350
Bardwell L.: (1965) Ellis Co.; Waxahachie Cr.; 3 mi. SE of Bardwell; (FC-C-R); USAE	3,292	43,917
Barker Reservoir: (1945) Harris-Fort Bend counties; above Buffalo Bayou; (FC only); USAE; Barker only has water during times of flood and is dry most of the year	17,225	270,000
B. A. Steinhagen L.: (1951) Tyler-Jasper counties; Neches R.; 1/2 mi. N of Town Bluff; (C-FC-R-P); USAE; also called Town Bluff Res. and Dam B Res.; Imp. by Town Bluff Dam	10,235	69,259
Bastrop, L.: (1964) Bastrop Co.; Spicer Cr.; 3 mi. NE of Bastrop; (In.-R); LCRA	906	16,590
Baylor L.: (1950) Childress Co.; 10 mi. NW of Childress; (M-R); City of Childress; also called Baylor Creek Reservoir	610	9,220

Abbreviations used in this table: L., lake; R., river; Co., county; Cr., creek; (C) conservation; (FC) flood control; (R) recreation; (P) power; (M) municipal; (D) domestic; (Ir.) irrigation; (In.) industry; (Mi.) mining, including oil production; (FH) fish hatchery; USAE, United States Army Corps of Engineers; WC&ID, Water Control and Improvement District; WID, Water Improvement District; USBR, United States Bureau of Reclamation; Auth., Authority; LCRA, Lower Colorado River Authority; TWDB, Texas Water Development Board; MWD, Municipal Water District; Imp., impounded.

Lakes and Reservoirs, Date of Origin	Surface Area (acres)	Storage Capacity (acre-ft.)
Belton L.: (1954) Bell-Coryell counties; Leon R.; 3 mi. N Belton; (FC-R-M); USAE/Brazos R. Auth.	12,445	432,631
Benbrook L.: (1952) Tarrant Co.; Clear Fk. Trinity R.; 10 mi. SW of Fort Worth; (FC-R); USAE	3,635	85,648
Bivins L.: (1927) Randall Co.; Palo Duro Cr.; 8 mi. NW of Canyon; (M); Amarillo; City of Amarillo; also called Amarillo City Lake	379	5,122
Bob Sandlin, L.: (1977) Titus-Wood-Camp-Franklin counties; Big Cypress Cr.; 5 mi. SW of Mount Pleasant; (In.-M-R); Titus Co. FWSD No. 1; Imp. by Fort Sherman Dam	8,888	203,148
Bonham, L.: (1969) Fannin Co.; Timber Cr.; 5 mi. NE of Bonham; (M); Bonham Municipal Water Auth.	1,056	11,027
Brady Creek Reservoir: (1963) McCulloch Co.; Brady Cr.; 3 mi. W Brady; (M-In.-R); City of Brady	2,020	30,430
Brandy Branch Reservoir: (1983) Harrison Co.; Brandy Br.; 10 mi. SW of Marshall; (In.); AEP-Southwestern Electric Power Co.	1,242	29,513
Brazoria Reservoir: (1954) Brazoria Co.; off-channel reservoir; 1 mi. NE of Brazoria; (In.); Dow Chemical Co.	1,865	21,970
Bridgeport, L.: (1932) Wise-Jack counties; W. Fk. of Trinity R.; 4 mi. W of Bridgeport; (M-FC-R); Tarrant Regional Water District	12,338	372,183
Brownwood, L.: (1933) Brown Co.; Pecan Bayou; 8 mi. N of Brownwood; (M-R); Brown Co. WID No. 1	6,814	131,530
Bryan Utilities L.: (1977) Brazos Co.; unnamed stream; 6 mi. NW of Bryan; (In.); City of Bryan; also called Lake Bryan	818	14,163
Buchanan, L.: (1937) Burnet-Llano-San Saba counties; Colorado R.; 13 mi. W of Burnet; (M-FC-R-P); LCRA	22,452	880,356
Buffalo L.: (1938) Randall Co.; Tierra Blanca Cr.; 2 mi. S. of Umbarger; (C-FC); U.S. Fish and Wildlife Service; Imp. by Umbarger Dam; See Buffalo Lake entry in Wildlife Refuge section for more info. Buffalo Lake is dry most of the year	1,900	18,150
Caddo L.: (1873, 1914, 1971) Harrison-Marion counties, Texas, and Caddo Parish, La.; Cypress Bayou; 29 mi. NE of Marshall; (C-R-M); Northeast Texas MWD; An original natural lake, whose surface and capacity were increased by construction of dams	26,138	129,000
Calaveras L.: (1969) Bexar Co.; Calaveras Cr.; 15 mi. SE of San Antonio; (In.-R); CPS Energy of San Antonio	3,624	63,200
Camp Creek L.: (1949) Robertson Co.; 13 mi. E of Franklin; (R); Camp Creek Water Co.	750	8,550
Canyon L.: (1964) Comal Co.; Guadalupe R.; 12 mi. NW of New Braunfels; (M-R-P-FC); Guadalupe-Blanco R. Auth./USAE	8,308	378,781
Casa Blanca, L.: (1951) Webb Co.; Chacon Cr.; 3 mi. NE of Laredo; (R); Webb Co.; Imp. by Country Club Dam	1,680	20,000
Cedar Creek Reservoir: (1965) Henderson-Kaufman counties; Cedar Cr.; 3 mi. NE of Trinidad; (M-R); Tarrant Regional Water District; also called Lake Joe B. Hogsett	33,099	631,401
Champion Creek Reservoir: (1959) Mitchell Co.; 7 mi. S. of Colorado City; (M-In.); City of Colorado City	1,196	41,580
Cherokee, L.: (1948) Gregg-Rusk counties; Cherokee Bayou; 12 mi. SE of Longview; (M-In.-R); Cherokee Water Co.	3,749	44,475
Choke Canyon Reservoir: (1982) Live Oak-McMullen counties; Frio R.; 4 mi. W of Three Rivers; (M-In.-R-FC); City of Corpus Christi/USBR	25,438	662,821
Cisco, L.: (1923) Eastland Co.; Sandy Cr.; 4 mi. N of Cisco; (M); City of Cisco; Imp. by Williamson Dam	985	29,003
Clyde, L.: (1970) Callahan Co.; N Prong Pecan Bayou; 6 mi. S of Clyde; (M-R); City of Clyde and U. S. Department of Agriculture Soil Conservation Service	449	5,748
Coffee Mill L.: (1939, 1967) Fannin Co.; Coffee Mill Cr.; 12 mi. NW of Honey Grove; (R); U.S. Forest Service	650	8,000
Coleman L.: (1966) Coleman Co.; Jim Ned Cr.; 14 mi. N of Coleman; (M-In.); City of Coleman	1,811	38,076
Coleto Creek Reservoir: (1980) Goliad–Victoria counties; Coleto Cr.; 12 mi. SW of Victoria; (In); Guadalupe-Blanco R. Auth.	3,100	31,040

Abbreviations used in this table: L., lake; R., river; Co., county; Cr., creek; (C) conservation; (FC) flood control; (R) recreation; (P) power; (M) municipal; (D) domestic; (Ir.) irrigation; (In.) industry; (Mi.) mining, including oil production; (FH) fish hatchery; USAE, United States Army Corps of Engineers; WC&ID, Water Control and Improvement District; WID, Water Improvement District; USBR, United States Bureau of Reclamation; Auth., Authority; LCRA, Lower Colorado River Authority; TWDB, Texas Water Development Board; MWD, Municipal Water District; Imp., impounded.

Lakes and Reservoirs, Date of Origin	Surface Area (acres)	Storage Capacity (acre-ft.)
Colorado City, L.: (1949) Mitchell Co.; Morgan Cr.; 4 mi. SW of Colorado City; (M-In.-P); TXU	1,612	30,758
Conroe, L.: (1973) Montgomery-Walker counties; W Fork San Jacinto R.; 7 mi. NW of Conroe; (M-In.); San Jacinto R. Auth., City of Houston/TWDB	19,894	417,605
Corpus Christi, L.: (1930) Live Oak-San Patricio-Jim Wells counties; Nueces R.; 4 mi. SW Mathis; (M-R); City of Corpus Christi; Imp. by Wesley E. Seale Dam	19,748	256,339
Cox Creek Reservoir: Calhoun Co.; Cox Creek; 2 mi. E of Point Comfort; (In); Alcoa Alumninum; also called Raw Water Lake and Recycle Lake	541	5,034
Crook, L.: (1923) Lamar Co.; Pine Cr.; 5 mi. N. of Paris; (M); City of Paris	1,060	9,210
Cypress Springs, L.: (1970) Franklin Co.; Big Cypress Cr.; 8 mi. SE of Mount Vernon; (In-M); Franklin Co. Water Development and TWDB; formerly Franklin Co. L.; Imp. by Franklin Co. Dam	3,252	66,756
Daniel, L.: (1948) Stephens Co.; Gunsolus Cr.; 7 mi. S of Breckenridge; (M-In.); City of Breckenridge; Imp. by Gunsolus Creek Dam	924	9,515
Davis, L.: (1959) Knox Co.; Double Dutchman Cr.; 5 mi. SE of Benjamin; (Ir); League Ranch	585	5,454
Delta Lake Res. Units 1 and 2: (1939) Hidalgo Co.; Rio Grande (off channel); 4 mi. N of Monte Alto; (Ir.); Hidalgo-Willacy counties WC&ID No. 1; formerly Monte Alto Reservoir	2,371	14,000
Diversion, L.: (1924) Archer-Baylor counties; Wichita R.; 14 mi. W of Holliday; (M-In.); City of Wichita Falls and Wichita Co. WID No. 2	3,397	35,324
Dunlap, L.: (1928) Guadalupe Co.; Guadalupe R.; 9 mi. NW of Seguin; (P); Guadalupe-Blanco R. Auth.; (Imp. by TP-1 Dam)	410	5,900
Eagle L.: (1900) Colorado Co.; Colorado R. (off channel); in Eagle Lake; (Ir.); Lakeside Irrigation Co.	1,200	9,600
Eagle Mountain L.: (1934) Tarrant-Wise counties; West Fork Trinity R.; 14 mi. NW of Fort Worth; (M-In.-Ir.); Tarrant Regional Water District	9246	185,087
Eagle Nest L.: (1951) Brazoria Co.; off-channel Brazos R.; 12 mi. WNW of Angleton; (Ir.); T.M. Smith, et al.; also called Manor Lake	N/A	18,000
Eastman Lakes: 8 lakes; Harrison Co.; Sabine R. basin; NW of Longview; Texas Eastman Co.	N/A	8,135
Electra, L.: (1950) Wilbarger Co.; Camp Cr. and Beaver Cr.; 7 mi. SW of Electra; (In.-M); City of Electra	731	5,626
Ellison Creek Reservoir: (1943) Morris Co.; Ellison Cr.; 8 mi. S of Daingerfield; (P-In.); Lone Star Steel	1,516	24,700
E. V. Spence Reservoir: (1969) Coke Co.; Colorado R.; 2 mi. W. of Robert Lee; (M-In.-Mi); Colorado R. MWD; Imp. by Robert Lee Dam	6,372	517,272
Fairfield L.: (1970) Freestone Co.; Big Brown Cr.; 11 mi. NE of Fairfield; (In.); TXU; (formerly Big Brown Creek Reservoir)	2,159	44,169
Falcon International Reservoir: (1954) Starr-Zapata counties; Rio Grande; (International U.S.-Mexico); 3 mi. W of Falcon Heights; (M-In.-Ir.-FC-P-R); International Boundary and Water Commission; Texas' share of total conservation capacity is 58.6%	85,195	2,646,765
Fayette County Reservoir: (1978) Fayette Co.; Cedar Cr.; 8.5 mi. E of La Grange; (P-R); LCRA; also called Cedar Creek Reservoir	2,400	71,400
Forest Grove Reservoir: (1982) Henderson Co.; Caney Cr.; 7 mi. NW of Athens; (In.); TXU	1,502	20,038
Fort Phantom Hill, L.: (1938) Jones Co.; Elm Cr.; 5 mi. S of Nugent; (M-R); City of Abilene	4,213	70,030
Georgetown, L.: (1980) Williamson Co.; N. fork of San Gabriel R.; 3.5 mi. W of Georgetown; (FC-M-In.); USAE	1,307	38,068
Gibbons Creek Reservoir: (1981) Grimes Co.; Gibbons Cr.; 9.5 mi NW of Anderson; (In.); Texas Municipal Power Agency	2,576	27,603
Gilmer Reservoir: (2001) Upshur Co.; Kelsey Creek; 15 mi. N of Longview; 4 mi. W of Gilmer; (M); City of Gilmer	895	12,720
Gonzales, L.: (1931) Gonzales Co.; Guadalupe R.; 4.5 mi. SE of Belmont; (P); Guadalupe-Blanco R. Auth.; also called H-4 Reservoir	696	6,500
Graham, L.: (1929) Young Co.; Flint and Salt creeks; 2 mi. NW of Graham; (M-In.); City of Graham	2,436	45,288

Abbreviations used in this table: L., lake; R., river; Co., county; Cr., creek; (C) conservation; (FC) flood control; (R) recreation; (P) power; (M) municipal; (D) domestic; (Ir.) irrigation; (In.) industry; (Mi.) mining, including oil production; (FH) fish hatchery; USAE, United States Army Corps of Engineers; WC&ID, Water Control and Improvement District; WID, Water Improvement District; USBR, United States Bureau of Reclamation; Auth., Authority; LCRA, Lower Colorado River Authority; TWDB, Texas Water Development Board; MWD, Municipal Water District; Imp., impounded.

Lakes and Reservoirs, Date of Origin	Surface Area (acres)	Storage Capacity (acre-ft.)
Granbury, L.: (1969) Hood Co.; Brazos R.; 8 mi. SE of Granbury; (M-In.-Ir.-P); Brazos R. Auth.; Imp. by DeCordova Bend Dam	8,172	133,858
Granger L.: (1980) Williamson Co.; San Gabriel R.; 10 mi. NE of Taylor; (FC-M-In.); USAE; formerly Laneport L.	4,159	51,822
Grapevine L.: (1952) Tarrant-Denton counties; Denton Cr.; 2 mi. NE of Grapevine; (M-FC-In.-R.); USAE	6,707	163,064
Greenbelt L.: (1967) Donley Co.; Salt Fork of Red R.; 5 mi. N of Clarendon; (M-In.); Greenbelt Municipal and Industrial Water Auth.	668	59,968
Greenville City Lakes: 6 lakes; Hunt Co.; Cowleech Fork, Sabine R.; N of Greenville; (M-R); City of Greenville	N/A	6,864
Halbert, L.: (1921) Navarro Co.; Elm Cr.; 4 mi. SE of Corsicana; (M-In-R); City of Corsicana	549	6,033
Hawkins, L.: (1962) Wood Co.; Little Sandy Cr.; 3 mi. NW of Hawkins; (FC-R); Wood County; (Imp. by Wood Co. Dam No. 3)	776	11,690
Holbrook, L.: (1962) Wood Co.; Keys Cr.; 4 mi. NW of Mineola; (FC-R); Wood County; (Imp. by Wood Co. Dam No. 2)	653	7,790
Hords Creek L.: (1948) Coleman Co.; Hords Cr.; 5 mi. NW of Valera; (M-FC); City of Coleman and USAE	364	8,443
Houston, L.: (1954) Harris Co.; San Jacinto R.; 4 mi. N Sheldon; (M-In.-Ir.-Mi.-R); City of Houston	11,443	136,119
Houston County L.: (1966) Houston Co.; Little Elkhart Cr.; 10 mi. NW of Crockett; (M-In.); Houston Co. WC&ID No. 1	1,330	17,113
Hubbard Creek Reservoir: (1962) Stephens Co.; 6 mi. NW of Breckenridge; (M-In.-Mi.); West Central Texas Municipal Water Auth.	15,687	318,174
Hubert H. Moss L.: (1960) Cooke Co.; Fish Cr.; 10 mi. NW of Gainesville; (M-In.); City of Gainesville	1,121	24,058
Imperial Reservoir: (1912) Reeves-Pecos counties; Pecos R.; 35 mi. N of Fort Stockton; (Ir.); Pecos County WC&ID No. 2	1,530	6,000
Inks L.: (1938) Burnet-Llano counties; Colorado R.; 12 mi. W of Burnet; (M-Ir.-Mi.-P); LCRA	803	14,012
Jacksonville, L.: (1959) Cherokee Co.; Gum Cr.; 5 mi. SW of Jacksonville; (M-R); City of Jacksonville; Imp. by Buckner Dam	1,164	25,732
J. B. Thomas, L.: (1952) Scurry-Borden counties; Colorado R.; 16 mi. SW of Snyder; (M- In.-R); Colorado R. MWD; Imp. by Colorado R. Dam	4,060	199,931
J. D. Murphree Wildlife Management Area Impoundments: Jefferson Co.; off-channel reservoirs between Big Hill and Taylor bayous; at Port Acres; (FH-R); TPWD; formerly Big Hill Reservoir	6,881	32,000
Jim Chapman L.: (1991) Delta-Hopkins counties; Sulphur R.; 3 mi.SE of Cooper; (FC-M-R); USAE; (also called Cooper Lake)	17,958	298,930
Joe Pool L.: (1986) Dallas-Tarrant-Ellis counties; Mountain Cr.; 14 mi. SW of Dallas; (FC-M-R); USAE–Trinity R. Auth. (formerly Lakeview Lake)	7,470	175,358
Johnson Creek Reservoir: (1961) Marion Co.; 13 mi. NW of Jefferson; (In.); AEP-Southwestern Electric Power Co.	650	10,100
Kemp, L.: (1923) Baylor Co.; Wichita R.; 6 mi. N of Mabelle; (M-P-Ir.); City of Wichita Falls and Wichita Co. WID 2	15,357	245,434
Kickapoo, L.: (1945) Archer Co.; N. Fk. Little Wichita R.; 10 mi. NW of Archer City; (M); City of Wichita Falls	5,864	86,345
Kiowa, L.: (1967) Cooke Co.; Indian Cr.; 8 mi. SE of Gainesville; (R); Lake Kiowa, Inc.	560	7,000
Kirby, L.: (1928) Taylor Co.; Cedar Cr.; 5 mi. S. of Abilene; (M); City of Abilene	740	7,620
Kurth, L.: (1950) Angelina Co.; off-channel reservoir; 8 mi. N of Lufkin; (In.); Abitibi Consolidated Industries	726	14,769
Lady Bird L.: (1960) Travis Co.; Colorado R.; in Austin; (R); City of Austin; formerly Town Lake	471	7,338
Lake Creek L.: (1952) McLennan Co.; Manos Cr.; 4 mi. SW of Riesel; (In.); TXU	550	8,400
Lake Fork Reservoir: (1980) Wood-Rains counties; Lake Fork Cr.; 5 mi. W of Quitman; (M-In.); Sabine R. Auth.	26,889	605,061

Abbreviations used in this table: L., lake; R., river; Co., county; Cr., creek; (C) conservation; (FC) flood control; (R) recreation; (P) power; (M) municipal; (D) domestic; (Ir.) irrigation; (In.) industry; (Mi.) mining, including oil production; (FH) fish hatchery; USAE, United States Army Corps of Engineers; WC&ID, Water Control and Improvement District; WID, Water Improvement District; USBR, United States Bureau of Reclamation; Auth., Authority; LCRA, Lower Colorado River Authority; TWDB, Texas Water Development Board; MWD, Municipal Water District; Imp., impounded.

Lakes and Reservoirs, Date of Origin	Surface Area (acres)	Storage Capacity (acre-ft.)
Lake O' the Pines: (1959) Marion-Upshur-Morris counties; Cypress Cr.; 9 mi. W of Jefferson; (FC-C-R-In.-M); USAE; Imp. by Ferrell's Bridge Dam	17,638	241,363
Lavon, L.: (1953) Collin Co.; East Fk. Trinity R.; 2 mi. W of Lavon; (M-FC-In.); USAE	20,595	412,498
Leon, Lake: (1954) Eastland Co.; Leon R.; 7 mi. S of Ranger; (M-In.); Eastland Co. Water Supply District	1,756	28,042
Lewis Creek Reservoir: (1969) Montgomery Co.; Lewis Cr.; 10 mi. NW of Conroe; (In.); Entergy	1,010	16,400
Lewisville L.: (1929, 1954) Denton Co.; Elm Fork of Trinity R.; 2 mi. NE of Lewisville; (M-FC-In.-R); USAE; also called L. Dallas and Garza-Little Elm	27,175	598,902
Limestone, L.: (1978) Leon-Limestone-Robertson counties; Navasota R.; 7 mi. NW of Marquez; (M-In.-Ir.); Brazos R. Auth.	12,486	203,780
Livingston, L.: (1969) Polk-San Jacinto-Trinity-Walker counties; Trinity R.; 6 mi. SW of Livingston; (M-In.-Ir.); City of Houston/Trinity R. Auth.	77,729	1,603,504
Loma Alta Lake: (1963) Cameron Co.; off-channel Rio Grande; 8 mi. NE of Brownsville; (M-In.); Brownsville Navigation District	2,490	26,500
Lost Creek Reservoir: (1990) Jack Co.; Lost Cr.; 4 mi. NE of Jacksboro; (M); City of Jacksboro	413	11,950
Lyndon B. Johnson, L.: (1951) Burnet-Llano counties; Colorado R.; 5 mi. SW of Marble Falls; (P); LCRA; Imp. by Alvin Wirtz Dam; formerly Granite Shoals L.	6,432	131,618
Mackenzie Reservoir: (1974) Briscoe Co.; Tule Cr.; 9 mi. NW of Silverton; (M); Mackenzie Mun. Water Auth.	910	47,151
Marble Falls, L.: (1951) Burnet Co.; Colorado R.; 1.25 mi. SE of Marble Falls; (P); LCRA; Imp. by Max Starcke Dam	613	7,597
Martin Creek L.: (1974) Rusk-Panola counties; Martin Cr.; 17 mi. NE of Henderson; (P); TXU	4,954	75,726
McQueeney, L.: (1928) Guadalupe Co.; Guadalupe R.; 5 mi. NW of Seguin; (P-C-R); Guadalupe-Blanco R. Auth.; Imp. By Abbott Dam	396	5,000
Medina L.: (1913) Medina-Bandera counties; Medina R.; 8 mi. W of Rio Medina; (Ir.); Bexar-Medina-Atascosa Co. WID No. 1	6,059	254,823
Meredith, L.: (1965) Moore-Potter-Hutchinson counties; Canadian R.; 10 mi. NW of Borger; (M-In.-FC-R); cooperative project for municipal water supply by Amarillo, Lubbock and other High Plains cities. Canadian R. Municipal Water Auth./USBR; Imp. by Sanford Dam; Governed by the Canadian R. Compact (1950), Lake Meredith can only hold 500,000 acre-ft. before it must release water to flow to Oklahoma.	7,097	500,000
Millers Creek Reservoir: (1990) Baylor-Throckmorton counties.; Millers Cr.; 9 mi. SE of Goree; (M); North Central Texas Municipal Water Auth. and TWDB	2,212	26,768
Mineral Wells, L.: (1920) Parker Co.; Rock Cr.; 4 mi. E of Mineral Wells; (M); Palo Pinto Co. MWD No. 1	477	5,461
Mitchell County Reservoir: (1993) Mitchell Co.; branch of Beals Creek; (Mi.-In.); Colorado R. MWD	1,463	27,266
Monticello Reservoir: (1972) Titus Co.; Blundell Cr.; 2.5 mi. E. of Monticello; (In.); TXU	1,795	34,740
Mountain Creek L.: (1937) Dallas Co.; Mountain Cr.; 4 mi. SE of Grand Prairie; (In.); TXU.	2,710	22,840
Murvaul, L.: (1958) Panola Co.; Murvaul Bayou; 10 mi. W of Carthage; (M-In.-R); Panola Co. Fresh Water Supply District No. 1	3,507	38,285
Nacogdoches, L.: (1976) Nacogdoches Co.; Bayou Loco Cr.; 10 mi. W of Nacogdoches; (M); City of Nacogdoches	2,180	39,522
Naconiche, L.: (2009) Nacogdoches Co.; Naconishe Cr. and Telesco Cr.; 14 mi. NE of Nacogdoches; (R); Nacogdoches Co.	692	15,031
Nasworthy, L.: (1930) Tom Green Co.; S Concho R.; 6 mi. SW of San Angelo; (R-In.-Ir); City of San Angelo	1,249	9,615
Natural Dam L.: (1957, 1989) Howard Co.; Sulphur Springs Draw; 8 mi. W of Big Spring; An original natural lake, whose surface and capacity were increased by construction of dams; (FC); Wilkinson Ranch/Colorado R. MWD; Natural Dam Lake only has water during times of flood and is dry most of the year	2,272	54,560

Abbreviations used in this table: L., lake; R., river; Co., county; Cr., creek; (C) conservation; (FC) flood control; (R) recreation; (P) power; (M) municipal; (D) domestic; (Ir.) irrigation; (In.) industry; (Mi.) mining, including oil production; (FH) fish hatchery; USAE, United States Army Corps of Engineers; WC&ID, Water Control and Improvement District; WID, Water Improvement District; USBR, United States Bureau of Reclamation; Auth., Authority; LCRA, Lower Colorado River Authority; TWDB, Texas Water Development Board; MWD, Municipal Water District; Imp., impounded.

Lakes and Reservoirs, Date of Origin	Surface Area (acres)	Storage Capacity (acre-ft.)
Navarro Mills L.: (1963) Navarro-Hill counties; Richland Cr.; 16 mi. SW of Corsicana; (M-FC); USAE	4,736	49,827
Nocona, L.: (1960) Montague Co.; 8 mi. NE of Nocona; (M-In.-Mi.); North Montague Co. Water Supply District; also known as Farmers Creek Reservoir	1,362	21,749
North Fork Buffalo Creek Reservoir: (1964) Wichita Co.; 5 mi. NW of Iowa Park; (M); Wichita Co. WC&ID No.3	1,489	15,400
North L.: (1957) Dallas Co.; S. Fork Grapevine Cr.; 2 mi. SE of Coppell; (In.); TXU	800	9,400
Oak Creek Reservoir: (1952) Coke Co.; 5 mi. SE of Blackwell; (M-In.); City of Sweetwater	2,389	39,210
O. C. Fisher L.: (1952) Tom Green Co.; N Concho R.; 3 mi. NW of San Angelo; (M-FC-C- Ir.-R-In.-Mi.); USAE/Upper Colorado R. Auth.; formerly San Angelo L.	1,265	119,445
O. H. Ivie Reservoir: (1990) Coleman-Concho-Runnels counties; 24 mi. SE of Ballinger; (M-In.), Colorado R. MWD; formerly Stacy Reservoir	19,149	554,340
Olmos Reservoir: (1926) Bexar Co.; Olmos Creek, San Antonio R.; 4 mi. N of San Antonio; (FC); San Antonio R. Auth.	889	12,600
Palestine, L.: (1962) Anderson-Cherokee-Henderson-Smith counties; Neches R.; 4 mi. E of Frankston; (M-In.-R); Upper Neches R. Municipal Water Auth.; Imp. by Blackburn Crossing Dam	23,112	367,312
Palo Duro Reservoir: (1991) Hansford Co.; Palo Duro Cr.; 12 mi. N of Spearman; (M-R); Palo Duro R. Auth.	2,407	61,066
Palo Pinto, L.: (1964) Palo Pinto Co.; 15 mi. SW of Mineral Wells; (M-In.); Palo Pinto Co. MWD 1	2,176	27,215
Pat Cleburne, L.: (1964) Johnson Co.; Nolan R.; 4 mi. S. of Cleburne; (M-FC-In.-Ir.); City of Cleburne	1,568	26,008
Pat Mayse L.: (1967) Lamar Co.; Sanders Cr.; 2 mi. SW of Arthur City; (M-In.-FC); USAE	5,638	117,844
Pinkston Reservoir: (1976) Shelby Co.; Sandy Cr.; 12.5 mi. SW of Center; (M); City of Center; formerly Sandy Creek Reservoir	523	7,380
Possum Kingdom L.: (1941) Palo Pinto-Young-Stephens-Jack counties; Brazos R.; 11 mi. SW of Graford; (M-In.-Ir.-Mi.-P-R); Brazos R. Auth.; Imp. by Morris Sheppard Dam	17,914	538,139
Proctor L.: (1963) Comanche Co.; Leon R.; 9 mi. NE of Comanche; (M-In.-Ir.-FC); USAE/Brazos R. Auth.	4,615	54,762
Quitman, L.: (1962) Wood Co.; Dry Cr.; 4 mi. N of Quitman; (FC-R); Wood County; Imp. by Wood Co. Dam No.1	814	7,440
Randell L.: (1909) Grayson Co.; Shawnee Cr.; 4 mi. NW of Denison; (M); City of Denison	311	5,900
Ray Hubbard, L.: (1968) Collin-Dallas-Kaufman-Rockwall counties; E. Fork of Trinity R.; 15 mi. E of Dallas; (M); City of Dallas; formerly Forney Reservoir	20,947	439,559
Ray Roberts, L.: (1987) Denton-Cooke-Grayson counties; Elm Fk., Trinity R.; 11 mi. NE of Denton; (FC-M-D); City of Denton/Dallas/USAE; also known as Aubrey Reservoir	28,646	788,490
Red Bluff Reservoir: (1937) Loving-Reeves counties, Texas; and Eddy Co.; N.M.; Pecos R.; 5 mi. N of Orla; (Ir.-P); Red Bluff Water Power Control District	7,495	151,110
Red Draw Reservoir: (1985) Howard Co.; Red Draw; 5 mi. E of Big Spring; (Mi.-In.); Colorado R. MWD	374	8,538
Richland-Chambers Reservoir: (1987) Freestone-Navarro counties; Richland Cr.; 20 mi. SE of Corsicana; (M); Tarrant Regional Water District.	43,874	1,125,199
Rita Blanca, L.: (1940) Hartley Co.; Rita Blanca Cr.; 2 mi. S of Dalhart; (R) City of Dalhart	524	12,050
River Crest L.: (1953) Red River Co.; off-channel reservoir; 7 mi. SE of Bogata; (In.); TXU	555	7,000
Sam Rayburn Reservoir: (1965) Jasper-Angelina-Sabine-Nacogdoches-San Augustine counties; Angelina R.; (FC-P-M-In.-Ir.-R); USAE; formerly McGee Bend Reservoir	112,590	2,857,077
San Esteban L.: (1911) Presidio Co.; Alamito Cr.; 10 mi. S of Marfa; (Ir.-R); Alpha Twenty One Corp.; Imp. by Alamito Dam	762	18,770
Santa Rosa L.: (1929) Wilbarger Co.; Beaver Cr.; 15 mi. S of Vernon; (Mi.); W. T. Waggoner Estate	1,500	11,570
Smithers L.: (1957) Fort Bend Co.; Dry Creek; 10 mi. SE of Richmond; (In.); Texas Genco	2,480	18,700
Somerville L.: (1967) Burleson-Washington-Lee counties; Yegua Cr.; 2 mi. S of Somerville; (M-In.-Ir.-FC); USAE/Brazos R. Auth.	11,395	150,293

Abbreviations used in this table: L., lake; R., river; Co., county; Cr., creek; (C) conservation; (FC) flood control; (R) recreation; (P) power; (M) municipal; (D) domestic; (Ir.) irrigation; (In.) industry; (Mi.) mining, including oil production; (FH) fish hatchery; USAE, United States Army Corps of Engineers; WC&ID, Water Control and Improvement District; WID, Water Improvement District; USBR, United States Bureau of Reclamation; Auth., Authority; LCRA, Lower Colorado River Authority; TWDB, Texas Water Development Board; MWD, Municipal Water District; Imp., impounded.

Two people from the U.S. Army Corps of Engineers inspecting an inflatable dam near Guthrie for the Red River Chloride Control Project. Many streams that flow through the area pick up salt that was deposited there by ancient sea beds. The salty water is pooled using inflatable dams, then pumped up to 22 miles into Truscott Brine Lake. Photo by USACE Tulsa, CC by 2.0

Lakes and Reservoirs, Date of Origin	Surface Area (acres)	Storage Capacity (acre-ft.)
South Texas Project Reservoir: (1983) Matagorda Co.; off-channel Colorado R.; 16 mi. S of Bay City; (In.); STP Nuclear Operating Co.	7,000	202,600
Squaw Creek Reservoir: (1983) Somervell-Hood counties; Squaw Cr.; 4.5 mi. N of Glen Rose; (In.); TXU	3,169	151,273
Stamford, L.: (1953) Haskell Co.; Paint Cr.; 10 mi. SE of Haskell; (M-In.); City of Stamford	5,316	51,570
Stillhouse Hollow L.: (1968) Bell Co.; Lampasas R.; 5 mi. SW of Belton; (M-In.-Ir.-FC); USAE/Brazos R. Auth.; also called Lampasas Reservoir	6,429	229,881
Striker Creek Reservoir: (1957) Rusk-Cherokee counties; Striker Cr.; 18 mi. SW of Henderson; (M-In.); Angelina-Nacogdoches WC&ID No. 1	1,954	21,799
Sulphur Draw Reservoir: (1992) Martin Co.; Sulphur Springs Draw; 12 mi. NE of Stanton; (FC); Colorado R. MWD	970	7,997
Sulphur Springs, L.: (1950) Hopkins Co.; White Oak Cr.; 2 mi. N of Sulphur Springs; (M); Sulphur Springs Water District; formerly called White Oak Creek Reservoir	1,340	17,747
Sweetwater, L.: (1930) Nolan Co.; Bitter Creek; 6 mi. SE of Sweetwater (M-R); City of Sweetwater	652	12,267
Tawakoni, L.: (1960) Rains-Van Zandt-Hunt counties; Sabine R.; 9 mi. NE of Wills Point; (M-In.-Ir-R); Sabine R. Auth.; Imp. by Iron Bridge Dam	37,325	871,695
Terrell City L.: (1955) Kaufman Co.; Muddy Cedar Cr.; 6 mi. E of Terrell; (M-R); City of Terrell	849	8,594
Texana, L.: (1980) Jackson Co.; Navidad R. and Sandy Cr.; 6.8 mi. SE Edna; (M-Ir); USBR, Lavaca-Navidad R. Auth., Texas Water Dev. Bd.; formerly Palmetto Bend Reservoir	10,312	164,188
Texoma, L.: (1943) Grayson-Cooke counties, Texas; Bryan-Marshall-Love counties, Okla.; (Imp. by Denison Dam) on Red R. below confluence of Red and Washita rivers; (P-FC-C-R); USAE; Texas and Oklahoma each have the right to 50% capacity	71,975	2,516,226
Toledo Bend Reservoir: (1967) Newton-Panola-Sabine-Shelby counties; Sabine R.; 14 mi. NE Burkeville; (M-In.-Ir.-PR); Sabine R. Auth.; Texas and Louisiana each have rights to 50% capacity	178,553	4,472,900
Tradinghouse Creek Reservoir: (1968) McLennan Co.; Tradinghouse Cr.; 9 mi. E Waco; (In.); TXU	2,010	35,124

Abbreviations used in this table: L., lake; R., river; Co., county; Cr., creek; (C) conservation; (FC) flood control; (R) recreation; (P) power; (M) municipal; (D) domestic; (Ir.) irrigation; (In.) industry; (Mi.) mining, including oil production; (FH) fish hatchery; USAE, United States Army Corps of Engineers; WC&ID, Water Control and Improvement District; WID, Water Improvement District; USBR, United States Bureau of Reclamation; Auth., Authority; LCRA, Lower Colorado River Authority; TWDB, Texas Water Development Board; MWD, Municipal Water District; Imp., impounded.

Lakes and Reservoirs, Date of Origin	Surface Area (acres)	Storage Capacity (acre-ft.)
Travis, L.: (1942) Travis-Burnet counties; Colorado R.; 13 mi. NW Austin; (M-In.-Ir.- Mi.-P-FC-R); LCRA; Imp. by Mansfield Dam	19,044	1,115,076
Trinidad L.: (1923) Henderson Co.; off-channel reservoir Trinity R.; 2 mi. S. of Trinidad; (P); TXU	690	6,200
Truscott Brine L.: (1987) Knox Co.; Bluff Cr.; 26 mi. NW of Knox City; (Chlorine Control); Red R. Auth.	3,146	111,147
Twin Buttes Reservoir: (1963) Tom Green Co.; Concho R.; 8 mi. SW of San Angelo; (M-In. -FC-Ir.-R.); City of San Angelo, USBR, Tom Green Co. WC&ID No. 1	6,320	182,454
Twin Oaks Reservoir: (1982) Robertson Co.; Duck Cr.; 12 mi. N. of Franklin; (In); TXU	2,330	30,319
Tyler, L. /Lake Tyler East: (1949/1967) Smith Co.; Prairie and Mud creeks.; 12 mi. SE of Tyler; (M-In); City of Tyler; Imp. by Whitehouse and Mud Creek dams	4,714	77,284
Upper Nueces L.: (1926, 1948) Zavala Co.; Nueces R.; 6 mi. N of Crystal City; (Ir.); Zavala-Dimmit Co. WID No. 1	316	5,200
Valley L.: (1961) Fannin-Grayson counties; 2.5 mi. N of Savoy; (P); TXU; formerly Brushy Creek Reservoir	1,080	16,400
Victor Braunig L.: (1962) Bexar Co.; Arroyo Seco; 15 mi. SE of San Antonio; (In.-R); CPS Energy of San Antonio	1,350	26,500
Waco, L.: (1929) McLennan Co.; Bosque R.; 2 mi. W of Waco; (M-FC-C-R); City of Waco, USAE, Brazos R. Auth.	8,190	189,773
Walter E. Long, L.: (1967) Travis Co.; Decker Cr.; 9 mi. E of Austin; (M-In.-R); City of Austin; formerly Decker L.	1,269	33,940
Waxahachie, L.: (1956) Ellis Co.; S Prong Waxahachie Cr.; 4 mi. SE of Waxahachie; (M-In); Ellis County WC&ID No. 1; Imp. by S. Prong Dam	657	11,642
Weatherford, L.: (1956) Parker Co.; Clear Fork Trinity R.; 7 mi. E of Weatherford; (M-In.); City of Weatherford	1,112	17,812
Welsh Reservoir: (1976) Titus Co.; Swauano Cr.; 11 mi. SE Mount Pleasant; (R-In.); AEP-Southwestern Electric Power Co.; (formerly Swauano Creek Reservoir)	1,269	20,242
White River L.: (1963) Crosby Co.; 16 mi. SE Crosbyton; (M-In.-Mi.); White R. MWD	653	29,880
White Rock L.: (1911) Dallas Co.; White Rock Cr.; within NE Dallas city limits; (R); City of Dallas	995	10,230
Whitney, L.: (1951) Hill-Bosque-Johnson counties; Brazos R.; 5.5 mi. SW Whitney; (FC-P); USAE	23,220	554,203
Wichita, L.: (1901) Wichita Co.; Holliday Cr.; 6 mi. SW Wichita Falls; (M-P-R); City of Wichita Falls	2,200	14,000
William Harris Reservoir: (1947) Brazoria Co.; off-channel between Brazos R. and Oyster Cr.; 8 mi. NW Angleton; (In.); Dow Chemical Co.	1,663	9,200
Winnsboro, L.: (1962) Wood Co.; Big Sandy Cr.; 6 mi. SW Winnsboro; (FC-R); Wood County; (Imp. by Wood Co. Dam No. 4)	806	8,100
Winters, L.: (1983) Runnels Co.; Elm Cr.; 4.5 mi. E Winters; (M); City of Winters (also known as Elm Creek Lake and New Lake Winters)	638	7,779
Worth, L.: (1914) Tarrant Co.; West Fork of Trinity R.; in NW Fort Worth; (M); City of Fort Worth	3,377	33,495
Wright Patman L.: (1957) Bowie-Cass-Morris-Titus-Red River counties; Sulphur R.; 8 mi. SW Texarkana; (FC-M); USAE; (formerly Lake Texarkana)	18,247	97,927

Abbreviations used in this table: L., lake; R., river; Co., county; Cr., creek; (C) conservation; (FC) flood control; (R) recreation; (P) power; (M) municipal; (D) domestic; (Ir.) irrigation; (In.) industry; (Mi.) mining, including oil production; (FH) fish hatchery; USAE, United States Army Corps of Engineers; WC&ID, Water Control and Improvement District; WID, Water Improvement District; USBR, United States Bureau of Reclamation; Auth., Authority; LCRA, Lower Colorado River Authority; TWDB, Texas Water Development Board; MWD, Municipal Water District; Imp., impounded.

Water Conservation Tips

- Check all faucets, pipes, and toilets for leaks.
- Install water-saving showerheads and ultra-low-flush toilets.
- Take shorter showers.
- Never use the toilet as a wastebasket.
- Turn off the water while brushing teeth or shaving.
- Wash full loads of clothes.
- Fully load the dishwasher before starting.
- Rinse dishes and vegetables in a pot of water and not under running water.
- Defrost frozen food in the refrigerator and not under running water.
- Do not over-water landscaping.
- Water the lawn or garden early in the morning or late in evening.

Estuaries and Bays on the Texas Coast

Source: Texas Water Development Board; www.twdb.texas.gov

Texas has 367 miles of coastline along which 11 major river basins and eight coastal basins terminate, bringing fresh water from rivers, streams, and surface runoff to the coast to mix with the Gulf of Mexico seawater. These unique zones, known as estuaries, are a significant feature of the Texas coast.

Texas has seven major estuaries, which are formed by a complex of individual bays separated from the Gulf by barrier islands, and five minor, riverine estuaries, which occur near the mouths of major rivers that flow directly into the Gulf.

Texas estuaries range from the nearly fresh-water Sabine-Neches, which borders Louisiana, to the frequently hypersaline Laguna Madre along the southern coast.

Most Texas bays are shallow, ranging in average depth from two feet to ten feet.

Although each estuary differs in size and hydrological and ecological characteristics, together they support a diverse array of species that serve as the raw materials for a variety of economic activities associated with commercial and recreational fishing, hunting, and birding.

In addition, estuaries provide many other ecological services, such as:

- Water filtration and nutrient regulation through nutrient cycling
- Storm surge protection
- Shoreline stabilization through trapping sediments that support the growth of wetlands

The major estuaries, in order from east to west, include:

Sabine-Neches Estuary (Sabine Lake)

The Sabine-Neches Estuary, commonly known as Sabine Lake, is located along the Texas-Louisiana border and is the smallest of Texas' seven major estuaries with an area of 45,320 acres.

This estuary receives around 14 million acre-feet of fresh water inflow per year from the Sabine and Neches rivers and surrounding coastal watersheds, making it the freshest estuary along the Texas coast. Average bay salinity is eight parts per thousand.

The Sabine-Neches Waterway and Gulf Intracoastal Waterway are important shipping channels in this system.

The estuary is connected to the Gulf by Sabine Pass and lies within Orange and Jefferson counties on the Texas side.

Trinity-San Jacinto Estuary (Galveston Bay)

The Trinity-San Jacinto Estuary, also known as Galveston Bay, is located on the upper Texas coast. It is the largest estuary in Texas, with an area of 345,280 acres, and is the seventh largest in the United States.

Key features include Trinity Bay, Galveston Bay, East Bay, West Bay, and connections with the Gulf at Bolivar Roads, San Luis Pass, and Rollover Pass.

The Houston Ship Channel and the Gulf Intracoastal Waterway are notable man-made features of the system.

This estuary receives on average 11 million acre-feet of fresh water inflow annually from the Trinity and San Jacinto rivers and surrounding coastal watersheds. It is bounded by Bolivar Peninsula and Galveston Island and lies within Chambers, Harris, Galveston, and Brazoria counties.

Colorado-Lavaca Estuary (Matagorda Bay System)

The Colorado-Lavaca Estuary, or Matagorda Bay system, is located along the mid-Texas coast and covers an area of 244,490 acres. The estuary is bounded by Matagorda Island and consists of Matagorda Bay, Lavaca Bay, and several smaller bays, including Carancahua Bay, Tres Palacios Bay, Keller Bay, Cox Bay, and Turtle Bay.

Other key features include Pass Cavallo, the Matagorda Ship Channel, and the Gulf Intracoastal Waterway.

The estuary averages 3.5 million acre-feet of fresh water inflow annually from the Colorado, Lavaca, and Tres Palacios rivers and surrounding coastal watersheds. It is bordered by Matagorda, Jackson, Victoria, and Calhoun counties.

Guadalupe Estuary

The Guadalupe Estuary is located on the mid-Texas coast and covers 148,703 acres. The estuary includes San Antonio Bay, Mission Lake, Hynes Bay, Espiritu Santo Bay, and Mesquite Bay.

This estuary is largely protected from the Gulf by Matagorda Island and typically does not have a direct connection to the Gulf except through Cedar Bayou.

The other closest connection with the Gulf is through Pass Cavallo to the northeast in the Colorado-Lavaca Estuary.

The Guadalupe Estuary typically receives an average of 2.5 million acre-feet of fresh water inflow per year from the Guadalupe and San Antonio rivers and from surrounding coastal watersheds. The estuary lies adjacent to Calhoun, Aransas, and Refugio counties.

Mission-Aransas Estuary

The Mission-Aransas Estuary, located in the Coastal Bend, covers 111,780 acres and consists of Aransas Bay, Copano Bay, and several smaller bays, including Saint Charles Bay, Mission Bay, and Redfish Bay.

The estuary has a direct connection to the Gulf through Aransas Pass but is largely protected by a barrier island, San Jose Island.

Typically, the estuary receives 490,000 acre-feet of freshwater inflow per year from the Aransas and Mission rivers and surrounding coastal basins. The estuary is bordered by Aransas, Refugio, and San Patricio counties.

Nueces Estuary

The Nueces Estuary, located in the Coastal Bend, consists of Nueces Bay, Corpus Christi Bay, and Oso Bay. It spans 106,990 acres and is separated from the Gulf by Mustang Island, except for a direct connection through Aransas Pass.

The Corpus Christi Ship Channel and the Gulf Intracoastal Waterway are notable man-made features of the system.

This estuary typically receives 587,000 acre-feet of fresh water inflow per year from the Nueces River, Oso Creek, and surrounding coastal watersheds. The estuary is bordered by San Patricio and Nueces counties.

Laguna Madre Estuary

The Laguna Madre Estuary is the southernmost major estuary in Texas and extends almost to the Texas-Mexico border.

The Laguna Madre is a unique hypersaline lagoon with an average salinity between 32 and 38 parts per thousand. It is the only hypersaline estuary in the nation and one of only a handful that exist worldwide.

The estuary spans 280,910 acres but is divided by a coastal land mass known as Saltillo Flats, though more commonly referred to as the Landcut, and separated from the Gulf by Padre Island.

The Upper Laguna Madre has one major bay, Baffin Bay, and is hydrologically connected to the Nueces Estuary on its northern end and to the Gulf via the Packery Channel.

San Fernando Creek is the principal source of fresh- water inflow to this arid estuary, where freshwater inflows typically are 326,000 acre-feet per year.

The Lower Laguna Madre has one major bay, South Bay, and is connected to the Gulf via the Port Mansfield Channel and Brazos-Santiago Pass.

The Arroyo Colorado and surrounding coastal watersheds are principal sources of freshwater inflow to the Lower Laguna Madre, providing on average 425,000 acre-feet of inflows per year.

The estuary is bordered by Nueces, Kleberg, Kenedy, Willacy, and Cameron counties.

Minor Estuaries and Bays

Christmas Bay

Southwest of Galveston Bay, this system includes both Bastrop Bay and Drum Bay, and it is protected from the Gulf of Mexico by Follet's Island. It has two connections to the gulf, through Cold Pass and San Luis Pass.

It receives fresh water from runoff and through Bastrop Bayou.

Brazos River Estuary

The Brazos River Estuary, located on the upper Texas coast, is a riverine estuary that flows directly into the Gulf rather than into a system of bays. The estuarine portion of the river occurs near the mouth where tidal water from the Gulf mixes with river water.

Typically, this estuary receives 6.3 million acre-feet of fresh water inflow per year. It is located in Brazoria county.

San Bernard Estuary

The San Bernard Estuary is a minor estuary located along the mid-Texas coast, covering an area of 3,760 acres.

While the San Bernard River flows directly into the Gulf, creating a riverine estuary, neighboring Cowtrap Lake and Cedar Lake are small bays that connect with the Gulf through small tidal inlets.

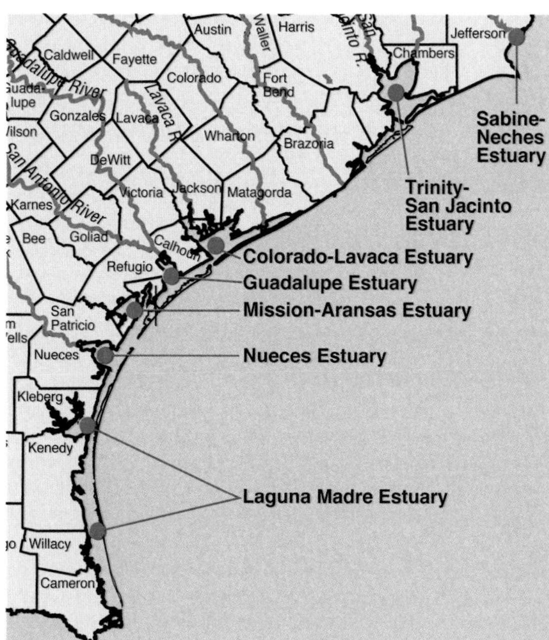

On average, this estuary receives 683,753 acre-feet of fresh water inflow per year from the San Bernard River and surrounding coastal watersheds. It is located in Brazoria and Matagorda counties.

East Matagorda Bay

East Matagorda Bay is a small bay covering an area of 37,810 acres and is separated from the larger estuary by the Colorado River delta. There are no direct sources of river inflow into this bay, which receives an average of 536,165 acre-feet of fresh water per yearfrom runoff of surrounding coastal watersheds.

Rio Grande Estuary

The Rio Grande Estuary forms a natural border between the United States and Mexico and is a riverine estuary, which flows directly into the Gulf with no associated bay system.

The estuarine portion of the river occurs where tides from the Gulf mix with fresh water from the river. Annual average inflow from the Rio Grande is 370,722 acre-feet per year. The estuary is bordered by Cameron County on the north, and Mexico on the south. ☆

Texas Plant Life

Source: This article was updated for the Texas Almanac by Stephan L. Hatch, Director, S.M. Tracy Herbarium and professor, Department of Ecosystem Science and Management, Texas A&M University

The types of plants found in Texas vary widely from one region to the next. This is due to the amount and frequency of rainfall, diversity of soils, and the number of frost-free days. From the forests of East Texas to the deserts of West Texas, from the grassy plains of North Texas to the semi-arid brushlands of South Texas, plant species change continuously.

More than 100 million acres of Texas are devoted to grazing, both for domestic and wild animals. This is the largest single use of land in the state. More than 80 percent of the acreage is devoted to range in the Edwards Plateau, Cross Timbers and Prairies, South Texas Plains, and Trans-Pecos Mountains and Basins.

Sideoats grama, which occurs on more different soils in Texas than any other native grass, was officially designated as the state grass of Texas by the Texas Legislature in 1971.

The 10 principal plant life areas of Texas, starting in the east, are:

1. Piney Woods

Most of this area of some 16 million acres ranges from about 50 to 700 feet above sea level and receives 40 to 56 inches of rain yearly. Many rivers, creeks, and bayous drain the region. Nearly all of Texas' commercial timber comes from this area. There are three native species of pine, the principal timber: longleaf, shortleaf, and loblolly. An introduced species, the slash pine, also is widely grown. Hardwoods include oaks, elm, hickory, magnolia, sweet and black gum, tupelo, and others.

The area is interspersed with native and improved grasslands. Cattle are the primary grazing animals. Deer and quail are abundant in properly managed habitats. Primary forage plants, under proper grazing management, include species of bluestems, rossettegrass, panicums, paspalums, blackseed needlegrass, Canada and Virginia wildryes, purpletop, broadleaf and spike woodoats, switchcane, lovegrasses, indiangrass, and numerous legume species.

Highly disturbed areas have understory and overstory of undesirable woody plants that suppress growth of pine and desirable grasses. The primary forage grasses have been reduced, and the grasslands have been invaded by threeawns, annual grasses, weeds, broomsedge bluestem, red lovegrass, and shrubby woody species.

2. Gulf Prairies and Marshes

The Gulf Prairies and Marshes cover approximately 10 million acres. There are two subunits: (a) the marsh and salt grasses immediately at tidewater, and (b) a little farther inland, a strip of bluestems and tall grasses, with some gramas in the western part. Many of these grasses make excellent grazing.

Oaks, elm, and other hardwoods grow to some extent, especially along streams, and the area has some post oak and brushy extensions along its borders. Much of the Gulf Prairies is fertile farmland, and the area is well suited for cattle.

Principal grasses of the Gulf Prairies are tall bunchgrasses, including big bluestem, little bluestem, seacoast bluestem, indiangrass, eastern gamagrass, Texas wintergrass, switchgrass, and gulf cordgrass. Saltgrass occurs on moist saline sites.

Heavy grazing has changed the native vegetation in many cases so the predominant grasses are the less desirable broomsedge bluestem, smutgrass, threeawns, tumblegrass, and many other less desirable grasses. Other plants that have invaded the productive grasslands include oak underbrush, Macartney rose, huisache, mesquite, prickly pear, ragweed, bitter sneezeweed, broomweed, and others.

Vegetation of the Gulf Marshes consists primarily of sedges, bullrush, flat-sedges, beakrush and other rushes, smooth cordgrass, marshhay cordgrass, marshmillet, and maidencane. The marshes are grazed best during winter.

3. Post Oak Savannah

This secondary forest area, also called the Post Oak Belt, covers some 7 million acres. It is immediately west of the primary forest region, with less annual rainfall and a little higher elevation. Principal trees are post oak, blackjack oak, and elm. Pecans, walnuts, and other kinds of water-demanding trees grow along streams. The southwestern extension of this belt is often poorly defined, with large areas of prairie.

The upland soils are sandy and sandy loam, while the bottomlands are sandy loams and clays.

The original vegetation consisted mainly of little bluestem, big bluestem, indiangrass, switchgrass, purpletop, silver bluestem, Texas wintergrass, woodoats, narrowleaf, post oak, and blackjack oak. The area is still largely native or improved grasslands, with small farms located throughout. Intensive grazing has contributed to dense stands of a woody understory of yaupon, greenbriar, and oak brush.

Mesquite has become a serious problem. Good forage plants have been replaced by such plants as split-beard bluestem, red lovegrass, broomsedge bluestem, broomweed, bullnettle, and western ragweed.

4. Blackland Prairies

This area of about 12 million acres, while called a "prairie," has much timber along the streams, including a variety of oaks, pecan, elm, bois d'arc, and mesquite. In its native state, it was largely a grassy plain — the first native grassland in the westward extension of the Southern Forest Region.

Most of this fertile area has been cultivated, and only small acreages of grassland remain in original vegetation. In heavily grazed pastures, the tall bunchgrass has been replaced by buffalograss, Texas grama, and other less productive grasses. Mesquite, lotebush, and other woody plants have invaded the grasslands.

The original grass vegetation includes big and little bluestem, indiangrass, switchgrass, sideoats grama, hairy grama, tall dropseed, Texas wintergrass, and buffalograss. Non-grass vegetation is largely legumes and composites.

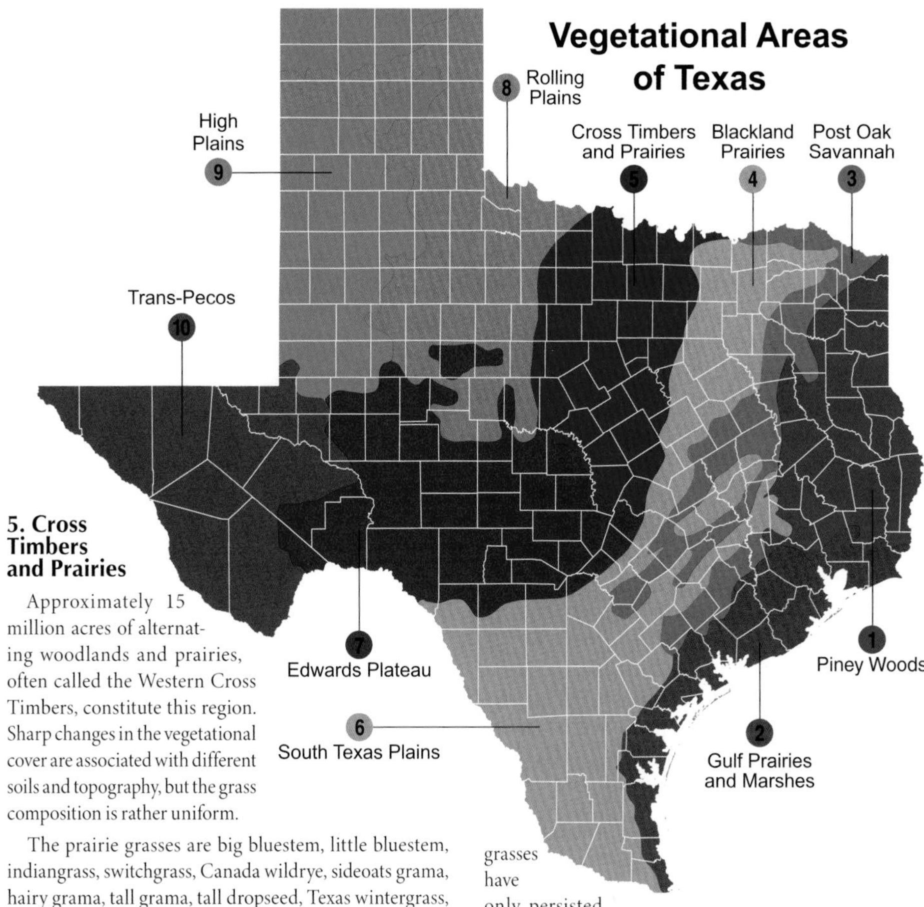

5. Cross Timbers and Prairies

Approximately 15 million acres of alternating woodlands and prairies, often called the Western Cross Timbers, constitute this region. Sharp changes in the vegetational cover are associated with different soils and topography, but the grass composition is rather uniform.

The prairie grasses are big bluestem, little bluestem, indiangrass, switchgrass, Canada wildrye, sideoats grama, hairy grama, tall grama, tall dropseed, Texas wintergrass, blue grama, and buffalograss.

On Cross Timbers soils, the vegetation is composed of big bluestem, little bluestem, hooded windmillgrass, sand lovegrass, indiangrass, switchgrass, and many species of legumes. The woody vegetation includes shinnery, blackjack, post, and live oaks.

The entire area has been invaded heavily by woody brush plants of oaks, mesquite, juniper, and other unpalatable plants that furnish little forage for livestock.

6. South Texas Plains

South of San Antonio, between the coast and the Rio Grande, are some 21 million acres of subtropical dryland vegetation, consisting of small trees, shrubs, cactus, weeds, and grasses. The area is noteworthy for extensive brushlands and is known as the Brush Country, or the Spanish equivalents of chaparral or monte. Principal plants are mesquite, small live oak, post oak, prickly pear (Opuntia) cactus, catclaw, blackbrush, whitebrush, guajillo, huisache, cenizo, and others that often grow very densely.

The original vegetation was mainly perennial warm-season bunchgrasses in savannahs of post oak, live oak, and mesquite. Other brush species form dense thickets on the ridges and along streams. Long-continued grazing has contributed to the dense cover of brush. Most of the desirable grasses have only persisted under the protection of brush and cacti.

There are distinct differences in the original plant communities on various soils. Dominant grasses on the sandy loam soils are seacoast bluestem, bristlegrass, paspalum, windmillgrass, silver bluestem, big sandbur, and tanglehead. Dominant grasses on the clay and clay loams are silver bluestem, Arizona cottontop, buffalograss, common curlymesquite, bristlegrass, pappusgrass, gramas, plains lovegrass, Texas cupgrass, vinemesquite, other panicums, and Texas wintergrass.

Low saline areas are characterized by gulf cordgrass, saltgrass, alkali sacaton, and switchgrass. In the post oak and live oak savannahs, the grasses are mainly seacoast bluestem, indiangrass, switchgrass, crinkleawn, paspalums, and panicums. Today much of the area has been reseeded to buffelgrass.

7. Edwards Plateau

These 25 million acres are rolling to mountainous, with woodlands in the eastern part and grassy prairies in the west. There is a good deal of brushy growth in the central and eastern areas. The combination of grasses, weeds, and small trees is ideal for cattle, sheep, goats, deer, and wild turkey.

This limestone-based area is characterized by the large number of springfed, perennially flowing streams that originate in its interior and flow across the Balcones Escarpment, which bounds it on the south and east. The soils are shallow, ranging from sands to clays, and are calcareous in reaction. This area is predominantly rangeland, with cultivation confined to the deeper soils.

In the east-central portion is the well-marked Central or Llano Basin, centering in Mason, Llano, and Burnet counties, with a mixture of granitic and sandy soils. The western portion of the area comprises the semi-arid Stockton Plateau.

Noteworthy is the growth of cypress along the perennially flowing streams. Separated by many miles from the cypress growth of the moist Southern Forest Belt, they constitute one of Texas' several "islands" of vegetation. These trees, which grow to stately proportions, were commercialized in the past.

The principal grasses of the clay soils are cane bluestem, silver bluestem, little bluestem, sideoats grama, hairy grama, indiangrass, curly-mesquite, buffalograss, fall witchgrass, plains lovegrass, wildryes, and Texas wintergrass.

The rocky areas support tall or mid-grasses with an overstory of live oak, shinnery oak, juniper, and mesquite. The heavy clay soils have a mixture of tobosagrass, buffalograss, sideoats grama, and mesquite.

Throughout the Edwards Plateau, live oak, shinnery oak, mesquite, and juniper dominate the woody vegetation. Woody plants have invaded to the degree that they must be controlled before range forage plants can re-establish.

8. Rolling Plains

This is a region of approximately 24 million acres of alternating woodlands and prairies. The area is half mesquite woodland and half prairie. Mesquite trees have steadily invaded and increased in the grasslands for many years, despite constant control efforts.

Soils range from coarse sands along outwash terraces adjacent to streams to tight or compact clays on redbed clays and shales. Rough broken lands on steep slopes are found in the western portion. About two-thirds of the area is rangeland, but cultivation is important in certain localities.

The original vegetation includes big, little, sand and silver bluestems, Texas wintergrass, indiangrass, switchgrass, sideoats and blue gramas, wildryes, tobosagrass, and buffalograss on the clay soils.

The sandy soils support tall bunchgrasses, mainly sand bluestem. Sand shinnery oak, sand sagebrush, and mesquite are the dominant woody plants.

Continued heavy grazing contributes to the increase in woody plants, low-value grasses such as red grama, red lovegrass, tumblegrass, gummy lovegrass, Texas grama, sand dropseed, and sandbur, with western ragweed, croton, and many other weedy forbs. Yucca is a problem plant on certain rangelands.

9. High Plains

The High Plains, some 19 million treeless acres, are an extension of the Great Plains to the north. Its level nature and porous soils prevent drainage over wide areas.

The relatively light rainfall flows into the numerous shallow "playa" lakes or sinks into the ground to feed the great underground aquifer that is the source of water for the countless wells that irrigate the surface of the plains. A large part of this area is under irrigated farming, but native grassland remains in about one-half of the High Plains.

Blue grama and buffalograss comprise the principal vegetation on the clay and clay loam "hardland" soils. Important grasses on the sandy loam "sandy land" soils are little bluestem, western wheatgrass, indiangrass, switchgrass, and sand reedgrass. Sand shinnery oak, sand sagebrush, mesquite, and yucca are conspicuous invading brushy plants.

10. Trans-Pecos Mountains and Basins

With as little as eight inches of annual rainfall, long hot summers, and usually cloudless skies to encourage evaporation, this 18-million-acre area produces only drought-resistant vegetation without irrigation. Grass is usually short and sparse.

The principal vegetation consists of lechuguilla, ocotillo, yucca, cenizo, prickly pear, and other arid land plants. In the more arid areas, gyp and chino grama, and tobosagrass prevail. There is some mesquite. The vegetation includes creosote-tarbush, desert shrub, grama grassland, yucca and juniper savannahs, pine oak forest, and saline flats.

The mountains are 3,000 to 8,749 feet in elevation and support piñon pine, juniper, and some ponderosa pine and other forest vegetation on a few of the higher slopes. The grass vegetation, especially on the higher mountain slopes, includes many southwestern and Rocky Mountain species not present elsewhere in Texas. On the desert flats, black grama, burrograss, and fluffgrass are frequent.

More productive sites have numerous species of grama, muhly, Arizona cottontop, dropseed, and perennial three-awn grasses. At the higher elevations, plains bristlegrass, little bluestem, Texas bluestem, sideoats grama, chino grama, blue grama, piñon ricegrass, wolftail, and several species of needlegrass are frequent.

The common invaders on all depleted ranges are woody plants, burrograss, fluffgrass, hairy erioneuron, ear muhly, sand muhly, red grama, broom snakeweed, croton, cacti, and several poisonous plants. ☆

Many beautiful flowers can be found on our National Grasslands, like this Lithospermum incisum. Photo by Kerry Woods, CC by NC-ND 2.0

Public Forests and Grasslands in Texas

Sources: U.S. Forest Service, www.fs.usda.gov/texas/ and the Texas A&M Forest Service, tfsweb.tamu.edu

There are **four national forests and five national grasslands in Texas**. These federally owned lands are administered by the U.S. Department of Agriculture Forest Service and by district rangers. The **five state forests** in Texas are managed by the Texas A&M Forest Service.

The national forests are managed to achieve sustainable conditions and provide wildlife habitat, outdoor recreation, water, wood, minerals, and forage for public use while retaining the aesthetic, historic, and spiritual qualities of the land.

In 1960, the Multiple Use–Sustained Yield Act put into law what had been practiced in Texas for almost 30 years: that resources on public lands will be managed so that they are used in ways that best meet the needs of the people, that the benefits obtained will exist indefinitely, and that each natural resource will be managed in balance with other resources.

However, even the most carefully planned system of management cannot foresee factors that can cause drastic changes in a forest. Fire, storms, insects, and disease, for example, can prompt managers to deviate from land management plans and can alter the way a forest is managed.

1. Timber Production

About 486,000 acres of the national forests in Texas are suitable for timber production. Sales of sawtimber, pulpwood, and other forest products are initiated to implement forest plans and objectives. The estimated net growth is more than 200 million board feet per year and is valued at $40 million. A portion of this growth is normally removed by cutting.

2. Cattle Grazing

Permits to graze cattle on national grasslands are granted to the public for an annual fee. About 600 head of cattle are grazed on the Caddo–Lyndon B. Johnson National Grasslands annually. On the Rita Blanca National Grasslands, 5,425 head of cattle are grazed each year, most of them in Texas.

3. Hunting and Fishing

State hunting and fishing laws and regulations apply to all national forest land. Game law enforcement is carried out by the Texas Parks and Wildlife Department.

A wide variety of fishing opportunities are available on the Angelina, Sabine, Neches, and San Jacinto rivers; the Sam Rayburn and Toledo Bend reservoirs; Lake Conroe; and many small streams. Hunting is not permitted on the McClellan Creek National Grassland nor at the Lake Marvin Unit of the Black Kettle National Grassland.

4. Recreational Facilities

An estimated 3 million people visit the recreational areas in the national forests and grasslands in Texas each year, primarily for picnicking, swimming, fishing, camping, boating, and nature enjoyment.

The Sabine and Angelina National Forests are on the shores of Toledo Bend and Sam Rayburn Reservoirs, two large East Texas lakes featuring fishing and other water sports. Lake Conroe and Lake Livingston offer water-related outdoor recreation opportunities on and near the Sam Houston National Forest.

National Forests

National forests in Texas were established by invitation of the Texas Legislature by an Act of 1933, authorizing the purchase of lands in Texas for the establishment of national forests. President Franklin D. Roosevelt proclaimed these purchases on Oct. 15, 1936.

The national forests cover around 640,000 acres in parts of 12 Texas counties.

The four East Texas forests and two North Texas grasslands are under the supervision of the National Forests and Grasslands in Lufkin. The three West Texas grasslands (Black Kettle, McClellan Creek, and Rita Blanca) are administered by the Forest Supervisor in Albuquerque, N.M., as units of the Cibola National Forest.

Each of Texas' National Forests contain wilderness areas, made possible by the Texas Wilderness Act of 1984, introduced by Representative John W. Bryant of Texas' 5th Congressional district, and signed into law by President Ronald Regan. These areas are allowed to return to a completely natural state with limited intervention, and visitors mush follow strict guidelines while within those areas.

(Recreational activities offered in National Forests and Grasslands are listed in the Recreation chapter on page 167.)

Angelina National Forest (154,474 acres) is spread across five East Texas counties: San Augustine, Angelina, Jasper, Nacogdoches and Tyler. The southern portion of the forest is predominantly covered by the longleaf pine. Loblolly and shortleaf pine cover much of the rest of the forest. Angelina NF is home to two wilderness areas: Upland Island (13,331 acres), found south of the Sam Rayburn Reservoir, and Turkey Hill (5,473), north of the reservoir.

Davy Crockett National Forest (161,141 acres) is found in Houston and Trinity counties. This is a diverse forest, with both hardwoods (including white oak, red oak, hickory, chestnut oak, cherry-bark oak, sweetgum, nutall oak, and willow) and pines (loblolly and shortleaf). In the northern part of Davy Crockett NF you'll find the Big Slough Wilderness Area (3,639 acres). The forest also contains the Alabama Creek Wildlife Management Area, 14,500 acres.

Sabine National Forest (160,656 acres) is another wide ranging forest that touches 5 different counties, Sabine, Shelby, San Augustine, Newton, and Jasper, and even forms part of the border between Texas and Louisiana. The forest contains both hardwoods (American beech, southern red oak) and pines (loblolly, shortleaf, and longleaf). The Toledo Bend Reservoir runs along the eastern edge of much of the forest, including the Indian Mounds Wilderness Area (12,369 acres) near the middle.

Sam Houston National Forest (163,037 acres) is about 50 miles north of Houston, with parts found in San Jacinto, Walker, and Montgomery counties. It contains a variety of

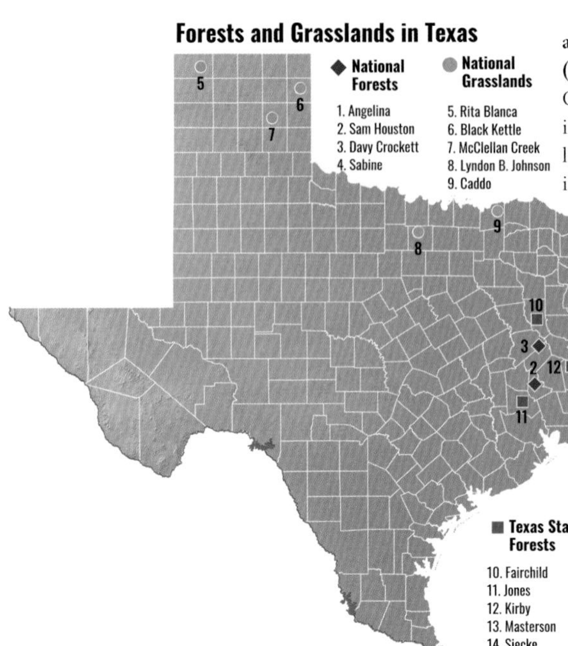

pines and hardwoods, and features redbuds and dogwoods, which are said to create a spectacular show of flowers in mid-February (redbud) and March (dogwood). Part of the forest stretches around the northern end of Lake Conroe, including the Little Lake Creek Wilderness (3,855 acres). Big Creek Scenic Area (1,420 acres) is near the eastern-most part of the forest.

National Grasslands

The national grasslands were originally submarginal Dust Bowl project lands, purchased by the federal government primarily under the Bankhead-Jones Farm Tenant Act (1937). Today they are well covered with grasses and native shrubs.

The national grasslands cover nearly 120,000 acres in six Texas counties. Two of these grasslands extend into Oklahoma, as well.

Lyndon B. Johnson National Grassland (20,250 acres) and **Caddo National Grassland (17,785 acres)** are located northeast and northwest of DFW, with a district ranger office at Decatur. These grasslands provide grazing land for cattle, but also habitat for native wildlife, including white-tailed deer, bobcats, red foxes, and several game birds. Lyndon B. Johnson NG is found mostly in Wise County, with about 60 acres in Montague County. Caddo NG is only in Fannin County. The Bois d'Arc unit of Caddo contains Lake Fannin, Coffee Mill Lake, and Lake Crockett, which are popular for fishing.

Black Kettle National Grassland (31,264 acres) and **McClellan Creek National Grassland (1,449 acres)** are both administered by the Cibola National Forest & National Grasslands in Albuquerque, New Mexico. Black Kettle NG lies mostly in Oklahoma, with a mere 576 acres in Texas' Hemphill County near the town of Canadian; this portion of the grassland is also part of the Lake Marvin Recreation Area. McClellan Creek NG is found near Pampa in Gray County and includes the Lake McClellan Recreation Area. Both grasslands allow livestock grazing, have active oil and gas wells installed, and lie within the Anadarko Basin.

Rita Blanca National Grassland (117,077 acres) is also managed by Cibola National Forest & National Grasslands, in Albuquerque. These grasslands also stretch across the Texas border, from Dallam County (77,366 acres) into Oklahoma (15,653). These grasslands are home to local wildlife and provide food for grazing livestock.

State Forests

Texas has five state forests, all of which are used primarily for demonstration and research. Information about recreation in state forests is provided on page 163.

I.D. Fairchild State Forest: Texas' largest forest is located west of Rusk in Cherokee County. This forest was transferred from the state prison system in 1925. Additional land was obtained in 1963 from the Texas State Hospitals and Special Schools for a total acreage of 2,788.

W. Goodrich Jones State Forest: Located south of Conroe in Montgomery County, it comprises 1,722 acres and is one of the largest working urban forests in the country. It was purchased in 1926 and named for the founder of the Texas Forestry Association.

John Henry Kirby Memorial State Forest: This 630-acre forest in Tyler County was donated by lumberman John Henry Kirby in 1929, as well as later donors. Revenue from this forest is given to the Association of Former Students of Texas A&M University for student-loan purposes.

Paul N. Masterson Memorial Forest: Mrs. Leonora O'Neal Masterson of Beaumont donated these 519 acres in Jasper County in 1984 in honor of her husband, who was a tree farmer and an active member of the Texas Forestry Association.

E.O. Siecke State Forest: The first Texas state forest, it was purchased by the state in 1924. It contains 1,722 acres of pine land in Newton County. An additional 100 acres was obtained by a 99-year lease in 1946. ☆

A family enjoying nature in the pine woods of Bastrop State Park. Photo by Michael Salazar, CC by 2.0

Texas Forest Resources

Source: Texas A&M Forest Service, Texas A&M University System; http://tfsweb.tamu.edu

Forests resources in Texas are abundant and diverse. Forest land covers roughly 38% of the state's land area. According to the Forest Inventory and Analysis (FIA), there are over 63 million acres of forests and woodlands in Texas.

The principal forest region in Texas is called the **East Texas Piney Woods**, due to the abundance of pine-hardwood in the region. The 43-county region forms the western edge of the southern pine region, extending from Bowie and Red River counties in Northeast Texas to Jefferson, Harris, and Waller counties in Southeast Texas. The counties contain 12.0 million acres of forestland and 9.4 million acres of non-forest land.

According to the *East Texas Forestlands, 2020* report, 92% of timberland in East Texas is privately-owned. The largest group of private ownership is family forest landowners (non-industrial, private) with 53% of all timberland. Timber Investment Management Organizations (TIMOs) and Real Estate Investment Trusts (REITs) own 19% of East Texas timberland. Other private owners represent the remaining 20%. State, federal, county, and municipal entities (i.e., public entities) own 8%.

Forest Types

Five major forest types are found in the East Texas Piney Woods. Two are pine-forest types: loblolly-shortleaf and longleaf-slash. These are dominated by the four species of southern yellow pine. In these forests, the various pine trees make up at least 50% of the trees. Loblolly-shortleaf forest is the predominate forest type in the area.

Oak-hickory is the next most common forest type. These are upland hardwood forests in which oaks or hickories make up at least 50% of the trees, and pine species are less than 25%. Oak-pine is a mixed-forest type in which more than 50% of the trees are hardwoods, but pines make up 25%–49% of the trees.

Bottomland hardwood forests can include a variety of trees, including oak, gum, cypress, elm, and ash, and are commonly found along creeks, river bottoms, swamps, and other wet areas.

Other forest types found in East Texas include small acreages of mesquite, exotic hardwoods, red cedar, and unproductive lands that are considered forested but do not meet stocking requirements.

Southern pine plantations, established by tree planting and usually managed intensively to maximize timber production, are an important source of wood fiber. Texas forests include 3.2 million acres of pine plantations, 63% of which are on industrially managed land, 34% on non-industrial private land, and 3% on public land. Genetically superior tree seedlings are usually planted to improve survival and growth.

Growth and Removals

Keeping track of growth and removals on timberland is extremely important as a measure of sustainability. On average, timberland annual net growth in East Texas is about

2020 Forest Inventory Highlights

Resource Attribute	2020	2019	Change
Timberland area (million acres)	11.8	11.8	– 0.2%
Number of trees (billions)	7.1	7.2	– 0.9%
Volume (billion cubic feet)	19.9	19.2	3.7%
Biomass (million tons)	486.1	471.3	3.1%
Net growth (million cubic feet per year)	1,049.0	942.7	11.3%
Removals (million cubic feet per year)	538.8	572.9	– 6.0%
Mortality (million cubic feet per year)	204.5	239.0	– 14.4%

1,049 million cubic feet. Removals of live trees in East Texas timberland is estimated to average 538.9 million cubic feet. Softwood represents 80% of that total. Annual growth exceeds removals by an average of 510.3 million cubic feet.

The 2020 Timber Harvest

Total volume of growing stock removed in 2020 was 538.8 million cubic feet, 6% decrease from the 572.9 million cubic feet removed in 2019.

Texas practices sustainability by keeping annual removals equal to less than the annual net growth observed. In 2020 average annual net growth was estimated to be 1,049 million cubic feet.

Issues Facing Texas Forests

Wildfires

Once a primarily rural concern, wildfires are now a threat statewide. Texas has seen significant fire seasons since 1996, some of which threatened or burned through small towns and cities and destroyed homes. The December 2020 Forest Action Plan, published by Texas A&M Forest Service, cites three factors that are intensifying the threat: population growth, changing land use, and increasing drought frequency.

Information on state wildfire response, wildfire risk assessments, fire department assistance programs, and how homeowners and communities can reduce their wildfire risk is online at: (http://tfsweb.tamu.edu and http://ticc.tamu.edu).

Sustainability

Although East Texas forests have provided jobs and economic growth for more than a century, the resource is coming under increasing pressure with changes in management and use of the piney woods. The forests are being impacted by residential development, ownership changes and parcelization, and population growth.

Urban Forest Sustainability

An estimated 86% of Texans live in urban areas, making urban trees and forests important. Trees reduce urban heat-island effect with shade and evaporative cooling; purify the air by absorbing pollutants, slowing chemical reactions that produce harmful ozone, and filtering dust; reduce storm water runoff and soil erosion; buffer against noise, glare, and strong winds; and provide habitat for urban wildlife.

Texas has seen an increase of 4 million residents since 2010, resulting in rapid urbanization in some areas. That in turn has increased the pressure on the sustainability of trees and forests in urban areas.

Water Resource Protection

Did you know that almost half of Texas' freshwater resources originate on forests? Covering about one-third of the state's land area, those forests and woodlands are integral to keeping a stable supply of clean drinking water for Texans. When those lands are cleared for other uses, our water supply is adversely affected.

Learn more about our state's water resources on page 42. ☆

Beyond the Piney Woods: Texas' Other Tree Regions

In addition to the 12 million acres of timberland in East Texas, there are an additional 51.1 million acres of land in the remainder of Texas that are considered forest-land. These forests consist of mesquite woodlands, oak-hickory forests, juniper woodlands, and other western forest types. These forests do not have the commercial timber value of the East Texas Piney Woods but are environmentally important with benefits of wildlife habitat, improved water quality, recreation, and aesthetics.

- **Post Oak Belt**: The Post Oak Belt forms a band of wooded savannah mixed with pasture and cropland immediately west of the Piney Woods. It extends from Lamar and Red River counties southwest as far as Bee and Atascosa counties. Predominant species include post oak, blackjack oak, and elm. An interesting area called the "Lost Pines" forms an isolated island of southern-pine forest in Bastrop, Caldwell, Fayette, and Lee counties just a few miles southeast of Austin.
- **Eastern and Western Cross Timbers:** The Eastern and Western Cross Timbers cover an area of about 3 million acres in North-Central Texas. The term "cross timbers" originated with the early settlers who, in their travels from east to west, crossed alternating patches of oak forest and prairies and so affixed the name "cross timbers" to these forests.
- **Cedar Brakes:** Farther south in the Edwards Plateau region are the cedar brakes, which extend over 3.7 million acres. Cedar, live oak, and mesquite dominate these steep slopes and rolling hills. Mesquite is harvested for cooking wood, knick-knacks, and woodworking. Live oak in this region is declining because of the oak wilt disease.
- **Mountain Forests:** The mountain forests of the Trans-Pecos region, including Jeff Davis County and the Big Bend, are rugged and picturesque. Several western tree species, including piñon pine, ponderosa pine, southwestern white pine, and even Douglas fir are found there, along with aspen and several species of oak.
- **Coastal Forests:** The coastal forests of the southern Gulf Coast are characterized by a mix of brush and short, scrubby trees. Common species include mesquite, live oak, and acacia. Some of these scrub forests are particularly important as migratory bird habitat.

Do you have forests in your region of Texas? Go explore!

The Blackedge Moray can be found along the Texas coast. Photo by Andrew David, NOAA, Public Domain

Texas Wildlife

Source: This section was written for the Texas Almanac *by Drew R. Davis, Associate Research Scientist, UT Rio Grande Valley, and Travis J. LaDuc, curator of herpetology, Biodiversity Center at UT Austin*

The wide variation in soils, climate, and vegetation in Texas has resulted in a rich diversity of animal life. There are over 1,600 species of vertebrates (animals with backbones) found in Texas, categorized into five groups or classes: fishes, amphibians, reptiles, birds, and mammals. A summary of each class is listed, followed by annotated lists of the species diversity in each of the five groups.

These annotated lists are not intended to be exhaustive, but rather to provide a review of both the common and uncommon species in our state. Those marked by an asterisk (*) are non-native species.

For more information about Texas wildlife, we recommend the following references: The Fishes of Texas database (fishesoftexas.org); the *Texas Natural History Guide* series for reptiles and amphibians (2005–2020, University of Texas Press); *The Texas Ornithological Society Handbook of Texas Birds*, 2nd edition (2014, Texas A&M University Press), *The Mammals of Texas*, 7th edition (2016, University of Texas Press and https://www.depts.ttu.edu/nsrl/mammals-of-texas-online-edition); and David Schmidly's *Texas Natural History: A Century of Change* (2002, Texas Tech University Press).

There are, of course, numerous other regional print and online guides. We encourage you to visit online citizen science platforms such as iNaturalist.org, eBird.org, and HerpMapper.org to learn more about the natural world around you as well and contribute your observations. Go explore!

Fishes

Fishes are a large group of gilled aquatic vertebrates, which include jawless fish, cartilaginous fish, and bony fish. Jawless fish include both hagfish and lampreys, the latter of which only two species are known from Texas. Cartilaginous fish are a class of fish that have skeletons primarily composed of cartilage (rather than bone) and include sharks, skates, and rays.

The final group, the bony fish, is the most diverse and abundant class of fish and is named due to their skeletons being primarily composed of bone (rather than cartilage). More than 34,000 species of bony fish are recognized and include species that range widely in size, shape, and behaviors, making them the most diverse group of vertebrates.

Despite there being more than 560 species of fish from 117 different families in freshwater and marine environments in Texas, fishes are only the second most diverse group of vertebrates in Texas, after birds. In addition to native species, many non-native species of fish have become established in Texas.

Fish are all aquatic, gilled animals that lack limbs with digits. Like amphibians and reptiles, most fish are cold-blooded (or ectothermic), meaning that their body temperatures vary as environmental temperatures change and they cannot self-regulate their temperature. Most fish are covered in scales, which help protect them from predators and pathogens and can help serve as camouflage, but some species like catfish and eels lack scales altogether.

amberjack: see *jack*

American sole: see *flatfish*

anchovy: Three species of anchovy occur in Texas, including the Striped Anchovy (*Anchoa hepsetus*) and Bay Anchovy (*Anchoa mitchilli*). All anchovies occur along the Texas Gulf Coast, inhabiting bays and estuaries and reaching lengths up to 4". These fish are somewhat translucent, with a silver head and broad lateral streak, and a large, rounded head.

barracuda: Three species of barracuda are known from Texas, including the Great Barracuda (*Sphyraena barracuda*), Northern Sennet (*Sphyraena borealis*), and the Guaguanche (*Sphyraena guachancho*). Barracudas are large, predatory fishes that occur in marine waters along the Texas coast, and have large jaws with fang-like teeth, and two dorsal fins that are widely separated.

bass: see *sunfish* or *sea bass*

bowfin: The Bowfin (*Amia calva*) can be found across East Texas. These fish have a long, robust body, a conical head, short barbels, a single long dorsal fin, a large bony gular plate, and are patterned with dark reticulations.

buffalo: see *sucker*

bullhead: see *catfish*

butterfly ray: see *ray*

carp: see *cyprinid*

carpsucker: see *sucker*

catfish: Two families of native catfish are known in Texas. North American catfish consist of at least 11 freshwater species, including the Yellow Bullhead (*Ameiurus natalis*), Channel Catfish (*Ictalurus punctatus*), and Tadpole Madtom (*Noturus gyrinus*). Most species have relatively widespread distributions across the state and vary in their body size and shape, but all species have four pairs of barbels (whiskers). Additionally, three species of blind, aquifer-dwelling species are part of this group: the Toothless Blindcat (*Trogloglanis pattersoni*), Widemouth Blindcat (*Satan eurystomus*), and Mexican Blindcat (*Prietella phreatophila*), which was only discovered in 2016. The second group, sea catfish, is marine, and only two species are known: Hardhead Catfish (*Ariopsis felis*) and Gafftopsail Catfish (*Bagre marinus*). Sea catfish are large fish that lack scales, typically are gray in coloration, and have two or three pairs of barbels. A third, non-native family of catfish called suckermouth armored catfish have been introduced in Texas from Central and South America, and are covered in tough, bony plates, and have a sucker-like mouth.

chub: see *cyprinid*

cichlid: One native species of cichlid, the Rio Grande Cichlid (*Herichthys cyanoguttatus*) can be found in South Texas but has been introduced throughout central Texas. The Rio Grande Cichlid typically has gray background coloration covered in small cream or turquoise-colored spots. Additional species of non-native cichlids also occur in Texas, such as the Blue Tilapia* (*Oreochromis aureus*).

combtooth blenny: Six species of combtooth blennies are known to occur along the Texas coast, including the Molly Miller (*Scartella cristata*) and the Featherduster Blenny (*Hypleurochilus multifilis*). Combtooth blennies have large heads, large eyes, fleshy flaps called cirri between the eyes, compressed and elongated bodies, long and continuous dorsal fins, and rounded caudal fins.

cownose ray: see *ray*

crappie: see *sunfish*

croaker: see *drum*

cusk-eel: see *eel*

cutlassfish: One species, the Atlantic Cutlassfish (*Trichiurus lepturus*) occurs along the Texas coast. These elongated silver fish have a thin, tapering tail, and a large mouth with fang-like teeth.

cyprinid: This group of fishes is the most diverse in Texas, with over 75 recognized species. This group includes species such as the Central Stoneroller (*Campostoma anomalum*), Blacktail Shiner (*Cyprinella venusta*), Common Carp (*Cyprinus carpio*), Shoal Chub (*Macrhybopsis hyostoma*), and Bullhead Minnow (*Pimephales vigilax*). These fish vary greatly in size and specific habitats used, but all occupy freshwater habitats.

damselfish: Four species of damselfish occur in marine habitats off the Texas coast, including the Sergeant Major (*Abudefduf saxatilis*). The Sergeant Major has a deep, laterally compressed body that is silvery-blue and five dark vertical bars.

darter: see *perch*

dolphinfish: The Dolphinfish (*Coryphaena hippurus*) is an elongate, laterally compressed marine fish that has is often metallic blue or green in coloration. Their dorsal fin is long, extending from the head to its deeply forked tail.

drum: Eighteen species of drum occur along the Texas Gulf Coast, many of which are popular sport fish, and include Red Drum (*Sciaenops ocellatus*), Black Drum (*Pogonias cromis*), Freshwater Drum (*Aplodinotus grunniens*), Spotted Seatrout (*Cynoscion nebulosus*), and Atlantic Croaker (*Micropogonias undulatus*). These fish vary greatly in their shape, but all can be relatively large fish, and all have a deep notch separating the dorsal fin into two parts. The Red Drum is the state saltwater fish.

eel: At least six different families of eels are known to occur in marine habitats along the Texas coast. There are seven species of cusk-eel, including the Crested Cusk-eel (*Ophidion josephi*). Cusk-eels have long dorsal and anal fins and their pelvic fins are modified into barbel-like structures occurring below the mouth. There are seven species of snake eels, including the Speckled Worm Eel (*Myrophis punctatus*) and Shrimp Eel (*Ophichthus gomesii*). Snake eels have long, snake-like bodies and often bury among sand or mud substrates. Additional eels, like the Conger Eel (*Conger oceanicus*), Ridged Eel (*Neoconger mucronatus*), Blackedge Moray (*Gymnothorax nigromarginatus*), and

Freckled Pikeconger (*Hoplunnis macrura*) also occur along the Texas coast, but are less abundant. In addition to marine species, one native species of freshwater eel occurs in Texas, the American Eel (*Anguilla rostrata*). This eel has small scales embedded in the skin giving it a smooth appearance, a long snake-like body, and a single continuous dorsal, caudal, and anal fin.

flatfish: Four families of flatfish inhabit coastal waters. Flatfish are flat, laterally compressed fishes, with two eyes on one side of their head, and often bury down into the mud. Flatfish consist of American soles, lefteye flounders, sand flounders, and tonguefish. American soles, including the Lined Sole (*Achirus lineatus*), Fringed Sole (*Gymnachirus texae*), and Hogchoker (*Trinectes maculatus*), have eyes on their right side, fleshy lips, and a distinct caudal fin. Lefteye flounders, including the Twospot Flounder (*Bothus robinsi*), have an oval-shaped, flattened body with eyes on their left side and elongated dorsal and anal fins that are separate from the caudal fin. There are at least 14 different species of sand flounders, including the Southern Flounder (*Paralichthys lethostigma*) and Bay Whiff (*Citharichthys spilopterus*), which are football-shaped, have eyes on the left side of their body, and have both a distinct snout and tail. Tonguefish, such as the Blackcheek Tonguefish (*Symphurus plagiusa*), can be distinguished from other flatfish by having a single continuous dorsal, caudal, and anal fin.

flounder: see *flatfish*

frogfish: Three species of frogfish occur along the Texas coast, including the Sargassumfish (*Histrio histrio*). The Sargassumfish has a short, rounded body with many fleshy extensions, that aid in its camouflage among sargassum (marine algae), and angled limb-like pectoral fins.

gar: Four species of gars are native to Texas, including the Alligator Gar (*Atractosteus spatula*), Spotted Gar (*Lepisosteus oculatus*), Longnose Gar (*Lepisosteus osseus*), and Shortnose Gar (*Lepisosteus platostomus*). All gars have elongated, cylindrical bodies, elongate slender snouts, and bony scales. The Alligator Gar can reach lengths up to 9' and up to 275 pounds.

goby: Fourteen species of gobies are found along the Texas coast, including the Naked Goby (*Gobiosoma bosc*) and Darter Goby (*Ctenogobius boleosoma*). Gobies are small, elongated, bottom-dwelling fishes that have rounded heads with eyes that are positioned close together and on top of the head. Additionally, gobies have pelvic fins that are fused together to form a suctioning disk. Gobies are the most diverse group of marine fishes.

grinnel: see *bowfin*

grouper: see *sea bass*

grunt: Six species of grunts occur in marine habitats along the Texas coast, including the Pigfish (*Orthopristis chrysoptera*), Tomtate (*Haemulon aurolineatum*), and Barred Grunt (*Conodon nobilis*). Grunts are variable in appearance, but all are moderately-sized fishes with mouths that have thick lips. The pharyngeal teeth in these species make a grunting noise when rubbed together, which is how this group was named.

halfbeak: Two species occur along the Texas coast, including the False Silverstripe Halfbeak (*Hyporhamphus meeki*). These unusual-looking fish have round, elongated bodies with a very short upper jaw and an elongated, needle-like lower jaw.

hammerhead shark: see *shark*

herring: Ten species of herrings are found in both marine and freshwater habitats in Texas. Four of the more common species include the Gizzard Shad (*Dorosoma cepedianum*), Threadfin Shad (*Dorosoma petenense*), Gulf Menhaden (*Brevoortia patronus*), and Skipjack Herring (*Alosa chrysochloris*). These silvery fish are important as food for many other fishes and can reach lengths up to 2'. Herrings are variable in their body shape and typically have forked caudal fins.

hind: see *sea bass*

jack: Twenty species of jacks have been recorded along the Texas Gulf Coast, including the Greater Amberjack (*Seriola dumerili*), Crevalle Jack (*Caranx hippos*), and Florida Pompano (*Trachinotus carolinus*). Jacks vary widely in their shape and size but are generally large fish that form schools and are important for commercial fisheries. All jacks have a narrow base of the tail and a deeply forked tail.

killifish: see *topminnow*

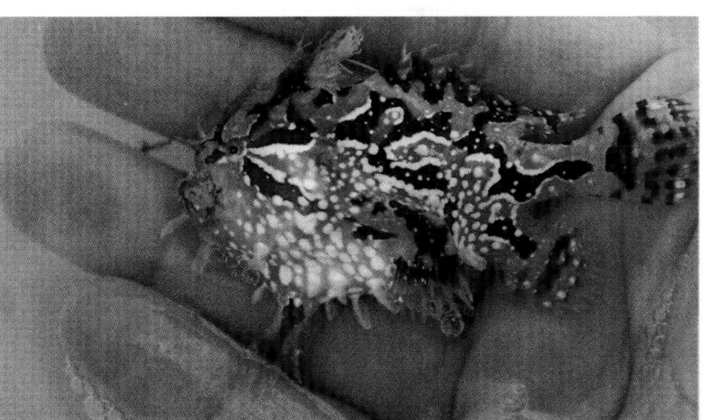

The unusual-looking Sargassumfish blends right in when it hides in its preferred marine algae. Photo by Brandi Noble, NOAA, Public Domain

kingfish: see *drum*

lamprey: Both the Chestnut Lamprey (*Ichthyomyzon castaneus*) and Southern Brook Lamprey (*Ichthyomyzon gagei*) occur in streams and rivers in East Texas. These eel-like fish have a characteristic circular disk-like mouth. The Chestnut Lamprey parasitizes fish as an adult, but adult Southern Brook Lamprey do not feed and rely on previously accumulated energy stores from its filter-feeding larval stage.

lefteye flounder: see *flatfish*

livebearer: There are at least 17 species of livebearers in Texas, including the Western Mosquitofish (*Gambusia affinis*) and Sailfin Molly (*Poecilia latipinna*). These small freshwater fish are widespread across most of Texas and species like the Western Mosquitofish have been widely introduced around the world. As the name suggests, all Texas species are live-bearing, and males have a modified anal fin called a gonopodium.

lizardfish: Three species of marine lizardfish occur along the Texas coast, including the Inshore Lizardfish (*Synodus *foetens*). Lizardfish have elongated cylindrical bodies, large mouths with needle-like teeth, and a large eye.

mackerel: Five species of mackerels are known from the Texas Gulf Coast, with the most abundant being the Spanish Mackerel (*Scomberomorus maculatus*) and King Mackerel (*Scomberomorus cavalla*). Mackerels have elongated, laterally compressed bodies, with a pointed snout. A defining characteristic of these fish is that there is a series of small fins behind both the dorsal and anal fin.

madtom: see *catfish*

menhaden: see *herring*

minnow: see *cyprinid*

mojarra: Nine species of mojarra occur in coastal waters along Texas, including the Spotfin Mojarra (*Eucinostomus argenteus*). Mojarras are silvery fish that are 8–12" in length, with arched backs, deeply forked tails, and a downward-facing mouth to accommodate feeding on bottom-dwelling organisms.

molly: see *livebearer*

mosquitofish: see *livebearer*

mullet: Four species of mullet occur in Texas, including the Striped Mullet (*Mugil cephalus*) and White Mullet (*Mugil curema*). Most mullets are marine, but individuals can also be found in freshwater rivers much further inland. Mullets are silvery in appearance and have an elongated, cylindrical body, a flat head, and a large eye relative to their head size.

needlefish: Four species of needlefish occur along the Texas coast, including the Atlantic Needlefish (*Strongylura marina*), which on occasion move up rivers into freshwater habitats. All needlefish have an elongated, round body with their upper and lower jaws extended into long, narrow beaks that are filled with small teeth.

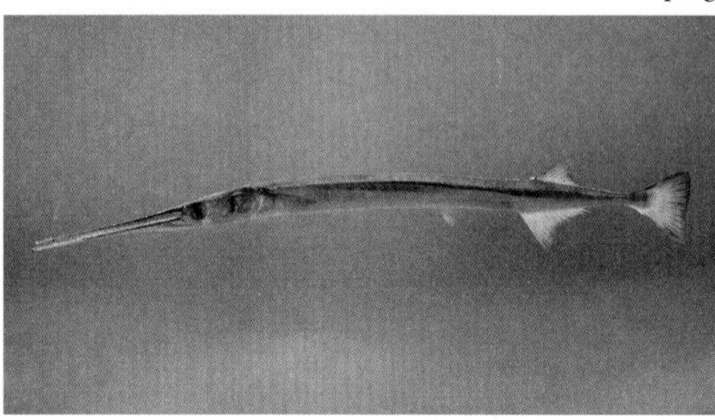

Atlantic needlefish can survive in both sea water and fresh water. Photo by Brandi Noble, NOAA, Public Domain

New World silverside: Five species of New World silversides occur in Texas, including the Brook Silverside (*Labidesthes sicculus*), Rough Silverside (*Membras martinica*), Inland Silverside (*Menidia beryllina*), Texas Silverside (*Menidia clarkhubbsi*), and Tidewater Silverside (*Menidia peninsulae*). Silversides are long slender fish, often with translucent bodies and a silver streak running down the sides of the body. Most species are freshwater, but some also are found in brackish waters.

perch: Over 25 species of perch can be found in freshwater habitats in Texas, including the Plains Orangethroat Darter (*Etheostoma pulchellum*) and the Dusky Darter (*Percina sciera*). These fish are often found in riverine systems and often rest on the substrates or woody debris on the bottom of these habitats. All perch have a dorsal fin that is split into two large lobes or has a narrow connection, and some species have bright colors, especially in breeding males. They get their name due to their darting movements through the water.

pickerel: see *pike*

pike: Two species of pike, the Redfin Pickerel (*Esox americanus*) and Chain Pickerel (*Esox niger*), occur in East Texas. The much more widespread and larger Redfin Pickerel has a long, cylindrical body, with a broad, short, flat snout, and a body coloration that is often green with dark wavy vertical bars and a vertical stripe through the eye. The Chain Pickerel is similar in appearance but is considerably larger than the Redfin Pickerel.

pipefish: This group of seven species includes the Gulf Pipefish (*Syngnathus scovelli*) and the Lined Seahorse (*Hippocampus erectus*). Pipefish have elongate bodies covered in armored plates or spines and tubular snouts, and males possess a brood pouch where they store fertilized eggs from the female until they hatch.

pirate perch: One species of Pirate Perch (*Aphredoderus sayanus*) can be found throughout freshwater habitats in East Texas. Pirate Perch superficially resemble sunfishes but are often quite dark in body coloration with black speckles on a light underside.

pompano: see *jack*

porcupinefish: see *puffer*

porgy: Six species of porgies are known from marine habitats in Texas, including the Pinfish (*Lagodon rhomboides*) and Sheepshead (*Archosargus probatocephalus*). Porgies have laterally compressed, deep bodies and most have teeth that are flattened for grinding.

puffer: Two families of puffers are known from marine habitats along the Texas coastline: puffers and porcupinefish. Puffers, including the Least Putter (*Sphoeroides parvus*), have elongated, globular-shaped bodies covered in small spines (*sometimes unnoticeable*), loose skin on the underside, a beaklike mouth with two teeth in the upper and lower jaw. Porcupinefish, such as the Striped Burrfish (*Chilomycterus schoepfii*), have globular bodies covered in short spines and a beaklike mouth with one upper and lower tooth. Both families can swallow water to expand their bodies when threatened.

pupfish: Six species of pupfish are native to Texas, including the federally endangered Leon Springs Pupfish (*Cyprinodon bovinus*) and Comanche Springs Pupfish (*Cyprinodon elegans*) and the state threatened Conchos Pupfish (*Cyprinodon eximius*), Pecos Pupfish (*Cyprinodon pecosensis*), and Red River Pupfish (*Cyprinodon rubrofluviatilis*). Several of these imperiled species have extremely limited distributions or have suffered widespread declines. Unlike the other species of pupfish, the Sheepshead Minnow (*Cyprinodon variegatus*) remains common and has a widespread distribution across coastal Texas and the Rio Grande drainage, and has been widely introduced into freshwater habitats in Texas.

pygmy sunfish: The Banded Pygmy Sunfish (*Elassoma zonatum*) occurs in freshwater habitats in East Texas. These small (<2" long) fish have a shallow body shape, are laterally compressed, have 9–12 dark bands, and are covered in small dark spots.

ray: Two families of rays occur in shallow estuaries and lagoons along the Texas coast. Butterfly rays, such as the Smooth Butterfly Ray (*Gymnura micrura*), are diamond-shaped and have a short tail with dark lines on it that lacks a dorsal spine. The other family is cownose rays, which is represented by a single species, the Cownose Ray (*Rhinoptera bonasus*). Cownose Rays reach 2–3' in width, are brown on top and white underneath, have a long tail with a venomous barb and get their name from their squared, indented snout and wide-set eyes.

redfish: see *drum*

redhorse: see *sucker*

remora: Four species occur in Texas, including the Remora (*Remora remora*) and the Sharksucker (*Echeneis naucrates*). These marine fish have heavily modified dorsal fins that form an oval-shaped sucker-like organ that allows them to attach to larger marine animals like whales, sea turtles, and sharks.

sand flounder: see *flatfish*

sardine: see *herring*

scorpionfish: Six species of scorpionfish, including the Spotted Scorpionfish (*Scorpaena plumieri*), can be found along the Texas coast. Scorpionfish are large, robust fish with large heads and venomous spines.

sea bass: This group of fish are popular saltwater sport fishes and include hind and grouper. At least 25 species occur along the Texas coast, including the Rock Sea Bass (*Centropristis philadelphica*) and Warsaw Grouper (*Epinephelus nigritus*). Species in this diverse group range in size and shape, but many species are brightly colored, have robust bodies, and large teeth.

seahorse: see *pipefish*

searobin: Nine species of searobins, including the Bighead Searobin (*Prionotus tribulus*), occur along the Gulf Coast of Texas. All searobins have a large, bony head that has numerous spines and ridges and modified pectoral fins that allow the fish to "walk" along the substrate.

seatrout: see *drum*

shad: see *herring*

shark: Sharks include both the requiem and hammerhead sharks, with 13 species found in marine habitats along the Texas coast. Species include the Atlantic Sharpnose Shark (*Rhizoprionodon terraenovae*), which is relatively small, only reaching lengths up to 4', has a pointed snout, and is typically gray in coloration with lighter undersides. The Scalloped Hammerhead (*Sphyrna lewini*) and the Bonnethead (*Sphyrna tiburo*) are easily differentiated from other sharks by their flattened heads that resemble a hammer or shovel and eyes on the outer edges.

shiner: see *cyprinid*

skate: The Roundel Skate (*Raja texana*) occurs along the Texas coastline and can be differentiated from other skates by a dark rounded spot on each pectoral wing. In addition, Roundel Skates have a slightly pointed snout, two dorsal fins at the base of the tail, and lack a serrated spine on their tails.

sleepers: Four species of sleepers can be found in Texas, including the Fat Sleeper (*Dormitator maculatus*), Spinycheek Sleeper (*Eleotris pisonis*), Emerald Sleeper (*Erotelis smaragdus*), and Bigmouth Sleeper (*Gobiomorus dormitor*). All species occur along the Texas Gulf Coast and use both freshwater and brackish habitats. Of these four species, the most abundant appears to be the Fat Sleeper, which has a small, rounded body, two distinct dorsal fins, and black lines along the sides of its face.

snake eel: see *eel*

snapper: Ten species of snappers are known from Texas, including the Red Snapper (*Lutjanus campechanus*) and Gray Snapper (*Lutjanus griseus*), and all are popular sport and commercial fish. Snappers are diverse in their size, pattern, and coloration, but are generally oblong, heavy-bodied, and have pointed snouts with large teeth.

snook: Two species of snook, the Smallscale Fat Snook (*Centropomus parallelus*) and the Common Snook (*Centropomus undecimalis*), occur in coastal waters along South Texas. Snook reach 2–4' in length, have elongate, laterally compressed bodies covered in silvery scales, and a thin dark line running down the length of the body.

stargazer: Stargazers are marine fish that have eyes on the top of their heads and upward-pointing mouths. Species like the Southern Stargazer (*Astroscopus y-graecum*) typically bury in the mud and ambush prey as they pass overhead.

stingray: Four species of whiptail stingrays occur in Texas, and the most common is the Atlantic Stingray (*Dasyatis sabina*). The Atlantic Stingray has a pointed snout and a long, whip-like tail with a serrated spine.

stoneroller: see *cyprinid*

sucker: At least 16 species of suckers can be found across Texas, including the River Carpsucker (*Carpiodes carpio*), Smallmouth Buffalo (*Ictiobus bubalus*), Spotted Sucker (*Minytrema melanops*), and the Gray Redhorse (*Moxostoma congestum*). All suckers have their mouth located on the underside of their head, have thick, fleshy lips, and primarily inhabit freshwater river systems.

suckermouth armored catfish: see *catfish*

sunfish: This group (sometimes also called "perch") includes bass and crappie, all of which are popular freshwater sport fishes. Eighteen species are known from Texas, including the Bluegill (*Lepomis macrochirus*), Green Sunfish (*Lepomis cyanellus*), Longear Sunfish (*Lepomis megalotis*), Largemouth Bass (*Micropterus salmoides*), and White Crappie (*Pomoxis annularis*). Most sunfish species are deep-bodied and laterally compressed, with a series of vertical bars. Crappie are similar in shape to sunfish, but reach larger sizes. Basses are more elongated and with spotting or a large dark stripe down the sides. The Guadalupe Bass (*Micropterus treculii*) is the state fish of Texas.

tarpon: The Tarpon (*Megalops atlanticus*) is a large marine fish that is present along the Gulf Coast of Texas. It can reach lengths of up to 8' in length and weigh more than 350 pounds. The mouth is turned upwards, the last ray of the dorsal fin is elongated, the caudal fin is deeply forked, and it is covered in shiny silver scales.

temperate bass: There are three species of temperate basses in Texas: the native White Bass (*Morone chrysops*) and Yellow Bass (*Morone mississippiensis*) and the non-native Striped Bass* (*Morone saxatilis*). Temperate basses are somewhat deep-bodied, laterally compressed, and have a pointed snout. Species are typically white or silver in appearance with 6–10 dark stripes running the length of the body.

tenpounder: One species, the Ladyfish (*Elops saurus*), occurs along the Texas coastline in bays and estuarine habitats. The Ladyfish has a long, rounded body, silvery scales, a deeply forked caudal fin, and can be up 2–3' in length.

tetra: The Mexican Tetra (*Astyanax mexicanus*) is a small (<4" long) freshwater fish found throughout flowing river systems in south, central and West Texas, and has an oblong, laterally compressed body shape. It is silver in body coloration but has a small black band at the base of the caudal fin. Adult males will have red coloration on the anal fins.

threadfin: The Atlantic Threadfin (*Polydactylus octonemus*) is a marine fish occurring along the Texas coastline and reaches lengths up to 12". These fish have two, widely separated dorsal fins, a deeply forked caudal fin, and 8 soft and flexible pectoral filaments giving it its name.

tilapia: see *cichlid*

toadfish: Two species of toadfish occur in marine habitats along the Texas coast and include the Gulf Toadfish (*Opsanus beta*) and the Atlantic Midshipman (*Porichthys plectrodon*). Both species are ambush predators that wait among muddy substrates. They are scaleless and have numerous barbels or skin flaps that help provide camouflage.

tonguefish: see *flatfish*

topminnow: Thirteen species of freshwater topminnows occur in Texas, including the Blackstripe Topminnow (*Fundulus notatus*) and Plains Killifish (*Fundulus zebrinus*). Topminnows can be found throughout the state, are up to approximately 4" in length, and can be variable in their patterning, with some species having a single horizontal strip down the body, while others have numerous vertical bands.

wahoo: see *mackerel*

Amphibians

Amphibians include frogs, toads, salamanders, newts, and caecilians. Approximately 8,100 amphibian species are found worldwide, and new species are described each year. Texas is home to 70 native species of amphibians, comprising 13 different families and two orders. These species include frogs, toads, salamanders, and newts, but no caecilians. Texas is also home to one introduced species, the Greenhouse Frog.

Amphibians lack claws, although arboreal frogs often have toe pads that assist in climbing and burrowing toads may have spades on the hind feet for digging. Amphibians typically have moist, smooth skin, although species like toads have dry, warty skin. The skin of aquatic frogs is highly permeable to allow gas exchange in aquatic environments. Toads have parotid glands just behind the head. These glands release a toxin to deter predators by irritating their mouths.

All amphibians play important roles in ecosystems. Frogs and toads are primarily herbivorous as larvae and carnivorous as adults, eating insects and other invertebrate pests. Larval salamanders are known to consume mosquito larvae. Further, amphibians are an essential food source for many animals and help to move nutrients from aquatic habitats into upland, terrestrial food webs.

Several of our native amphibians have been accidentally spread and introduced to areas of Texas where they do not naturally occur. For example, the Rio Grande Chirping Frog was widely introduced across the state due to the horticultural trade, and the Green Treefrog became established at Big Bend National Park due to individuals likely hitchhiking on RVs or other camping equipment from areas where this species is native.

amphiuma: There is one species of amphiuma found in Texas, the Three-toed Amphiuma (*Amphiuma tridactylum*). These aquatic salamanders look similar to sirens in that they are elongate and eel-like, but lack external gills, and have four small, frail limbs (sirens have external gills and lack hindlimbs). In aquatic environments, amphiumas can be voracious predators, consuming a wide variety of prey items.

barking frog: The Barking Frog (*Craugastor augusti*) is a secretive species found on the Edwards Plateau in rocky outcrops, though they are also known to inhabit mammal burrows. This species gets its name from the bark-like call it makes. Juveniles have a gray background coloration with numerous black spots covering the body and a light band across the midsection of the body. As adults, this light band darks and becomes less noticeable. Like some other species of frogs, Barking Frogs have skin secretions that can be noxious which serve as an anti-predator defense.

blind salamander: Five species of blind salamanders occur in Texas, all occurring along the Edwards Plateau and Balcones Faultline in central Texas. These five species include the Texas Blind Salamander (*Eurycea rathbuni*), Blanco Blind Salamander (*Eurycea robusta*), Comal Blind Salamander (*Eurycea tridentifera*), Valdina Farms Salamander (*Eurycea troglodytes*), and Austin Blind Salamander (*Eurycea waterlooensis*). Like the closely related spring salamanders, these species are fully aquatic but have reduced or absent vision, as these species occur in aquifers, spring outflows, or within karst habitats where there is little visible light. Several species, such as the Texas Blind Salamander, have lost skin pigmentation and appear white, with elongated limbs.

bullfrog: The American Bullfrog (*Rana catesbeiana*) occurs statewide and is the largest species of frog in North America, having a body length up to 7", and is capable of jumping 3–6'. This large frog lives in large, permanent lakes and wetlands and breeds throughout the summer on warm, humid nights. This species has been widely introduced around the world where it is often farmed for human consumption.

burrowing toad: The Mexican Burrowing Toad (*Rhinophrynus dorsalis*) is an odd-looking, secretive frog that only occurs in extreme South Texas. These frogs are dark gray with small white spots with a red or orange line running down their back. Mexican Burrowing Toads spend the majority of their lives underground and only emerge after heavy rains, often associated with hurricanes or tropical storms. The larval development of Mexican Burrowing Toads is extremely rapid, as the ponds they frequently use dry quickly after filling up after rains.

chirping frog: Texas is home to three species of native chirping frog and one introduced species. The Spotted Chirping Frog (*Eleutherodactylus guttilatus*) can be found in montane regions of West Texas such as Big Bend and the Cliff Chirping Frog (*Eleutherodactylus marnockii*) can be found in the Edwards Plateau. The third native species is the Rio Grande Chirping Frog (*Eleutherodactylus cystignathoides*) which is native to the Rio Grande Valley in South Texas but has great spread throughout much of central and East Texas through the horticultural trade. The non-native Greenhouse Frog* (*Eleutherodactylus planirostris*), originally from the Caribbean Islands, has established populations in Houston, Corpus Christi, and South Padre Island. All chirping frogs are small, mostly leaf-litter-dwelling frogs that get their name from the sound of their call. Additionally, all chirping frogs have direct development, meaning that there is no aquatic swimming tadpole stage and small juvenile frogs hatch from eggs.

chorus frog: Four species of chorus frog occur in Texas. Chorus frogs are closely related to treefrogs and have expanded toe pads on the ends of their digits that allow them to climb up vegetation. The Spotted Chorus Frog (*Pseudacris clarkii*) has a gray background color with irregular green markings and ranges from the panhandle South through central and North Texas into South Texas. Both the Spring Peeper (*Pseudacris crucifer*) and the Cajun Chorus Frog (*Pseudacris fouquettei*) occur in wooded habitats in East Texas. The Strecker's Chorus Frog (*Pseudacris streckeri*) occurs throughout central, east, and North Texas. Most chorus frogs are considerably smaller than treefrogs, except the Strecker's Chorus Frog. Chorus frogs primarily use temporary wetlands that fill up after heavy rains for reproduction. Despite their small size, their call can be surprisingly loud.

congo eel: see *amphiuma*

cricket frog: The Blanchard's Cricket Frog (*Acris blanchardi*) occurs throughout much of Texas except the western panhandle, far West Texas, and South Texas. This small frog is variable in its appearance and can range from grey to green to brown in background coloration with darker markings that can be black, green, or rust-colored. Typically, a dark-colored triangle occurs between the eyes on the top of the head. Blanchard's Cricket Frogs occur along flowing and non-flowing aquatic habitats. Though closely related to treefrogs and chorus frogs, this species has diminished toe pads resulting in more terrestrial behaviors.

dusky salamander: One species of dusky salamander, Spotted Dusky Salamander (*Desmognathus conanti*) has a limited distribution in East Texas. Apparent declines in this species have occurred throughout much of their historic range in the state.

dwarf salamander: One species of dwarf salamander occurs in Texas, the Western Dwarf Salamander (*Eurycea paludicola*). This small, slender species of salamander can be found among leaf litter and logs on forest floors in East Texas. Until recently, this species was part of a single species that ranged from East Texas along the Gulf Coast to North Carolina, that has since been separated into four separate species.

greenhouse frog: see *chirping frog*

Sheep Frogs are typically active after it rains. Photo by Drew R. Davis

leopard frog: Four species of leopard frogs occur in Texas: the Plains Leopard Frog (*Rana blairi*), Rio Grande Leopard Frog (*Rana berlandieri*), Southern Leopard Frog (*Rana sphenocephala*), and Northern Leopard Frog (*Rana pipiens*). All four species look similar to one another and are olive-green to brown in coloration, with dark spots and dorsolateral stripes from the eye to the hindlimb. These large frogs use permanent water bodies and rivers and have powerful hindlimbs that allow them to jump large distances.

mole salamander: Six species of mole salamanders are found in Texas, including the Spotted Salamander (*Ambystoma maculatum*), Eastern Tiger Salamander (*Ambystoma tigrinum*), Western Tiger Salamander (*Ambystoma mavortium*), Marbled Salamander (*Ambystoma opacum*), Small-mouthed Salamander (*Ambystoma texanum*), and Mole Salamander (*Ambystoma talpoideum*). All species are found throughout East Texas, except the Western Tiger Salamander, which occurs in south, west, and North Texas. All species are largely terrestrial and spend much of their time in upland habitats after breeding in wetland habitats. As aquatic larvae, these salamanders are sometimes colloquially called waterdogs or mudpuppies.

mudpuppy: see *waterdog*

narrow-mouthed toad: Two species of narrow-mouthed toads are found in Texas. The Eastern Narrow-mouthed Toad (*Gastrophryne carolinensis*) is restricted to eastern and coastal Texas, the Western Narrow-mouthed Toad (*Gastrophryne olivacea*) occurs throughout much of the state. The Eastern Narrow-mouth Toad is small (>1.5" in length) and is typically brown or gray in coloration with dark flecks and a heavily mottled underside. The Western Narrow-mouthed Toad is similar in size but is typically light gray with small black flecks and an unpatterned underside. Both species spend a large amount of time underground and use ephemeral habitats that fill up after rains for breeding.

The Black-spotted Newt has permeable skin, which makes it highly vulnerable to water pollution. Photo by Drew R. Davis

newt: Two species of newts occur in Texas: the Eastern Newt (*Notophthalmus viridescens*) and the Black-spotted Newt (*Notophthalmus meridionalis*). The Eastern Newt occurs throughout East Texas and parts of coastal Texas while the Black-spotted Newt is restricted to South Texas, where it experienced widespread population declines in recent decades. As a result, the Black-spotted Newt is listed as state-threatened and is a proposed species for federal protection. The Eastern Newt is known to have a terrestrial immature stage called an eft, which is typically bright orange with orange spots outlined in black. As efts mature into adults, they often return to aquatic habitats.

sheep frog: The Sheep Frog (*Hypopachus variolosus*) is closely related to narrow-mouthed toads and is restricted to South Texas. The Sheep Frog is larger than narrow-mouthed toads (2" in length), has a brown background coloration, gray sides with irregular black markings, and a yellow or orange thin stripe down the middle of the back. This species is typically active only after rains where it uses temporary wetlands for reproduction.

siren: Sirens are elongate, slender aquatic salamanders that have external gills behind the head, reduced forelimbs, and no hindlimbs. One species of siren, the Lesser Siren (*Siren intermedia*) is native to Texas and occurs from South Texas up the Gulf Coast and throughout East Texas. These salamanders are sometimes confused as eels due to their body shape and can bury down into the mud at the bottom of wetlands as they dry for prolonged periods and wait for these habitats to fill again after rains.

slimy salamander: The Western Slimy Salamander (*Plethodon albagula*) occurs along the Edwards Plateau and Balcones Faultline in central Texas. These salamanders are black with white speckling along their bodies and can be found under rocks and logs in moist areas in the winter and early spring. As it becomes warm and dry, these salamanders often move deeper underground. Western Slimy Salamanders can secrete a white, sticky substance if disturbed which deters would-be predators.

spadefoot: Spadefoots are toad-like amphibians, which have elliptical (vertical) pupils, smooth skin, and large keratinized spades on their hind feet. Four species occur in Texas: Couch's Spadefoot (*Scaphiopus couchii*), Hurter's Spadefoot (*Scaphiopus hurterii*), Plains Spadefoot (*Spea bombifrons*), and the New Mexico Spadefoot (*Spea multiplicata*). All species spend large amounts of time underground and emerge on warm, wet, rainy nights to forage and reproduce. Like some other species of amphibians, spadefoots are often considered explosive breeders, as reproduction often takes place over a few days following heavy rains when breeding sites (temporary pools) form. Like the Barking Frog and toads, spadefoots can secrete a noxious substance from their skin that is irritating to the eyes and skin of potential predators.

spring peeper: see *chorus frog*

spring salamander: Eight species of spring salamanders occur in central Texas, all occurring in spring outflows and associated stream runs. Most of these species occur in a limited number of localities and have very small ranges. These species include the Salado Salamander (*Eurycea chisholmensis*), Cascade Caverns Salamander (*Eurycea latitans*), San Marcos Salamander (*Eurycea nana*), Georgetown Salamander (*Eurycea naufragia*), Texas Salamander (*Eurycea neotenes*), Fern Bank Salamander (*Eurycea pterophila*), Barton Springs Salamander (*Eurycea sosorum*), and Jollyville Plateau Salamander (*Eurycea *tonkawae*). Most species are federally and state-protected due to their limited occurrence in Texas and the threats these species face.

tiger salamander: see *mole salamander*

treefrog: Six species of treefrogs occur in Texas. The Canyon Treefrog (*Hyla arenicolor*) occurs in rocky, montane habitats in West Texas, and the Squirrel Treefrog (*Hyla squirella*) is restricted to the Texas coast and parts of East Texas. The Green Treefrog (*Hyla cinerea*) occurs throughout East and coastal Texas, West to the Edwards Plateau, and South towards Corpus Christi and an introduced population is present in Big Bend National Park. Two additional species of treefrogs, the Cope's Gray Treefrog (*Hyla chrysoscelis*) and the Gray Treefrog (*Hyla versicolor*) are indistinguishable from one another and only able to be differentiated by the number of chromosomes they have and by their call. Both Cope's Gray Treefrogs and Gray Treefrogs overlap in much of their range throughout east, central, and North Texas. The Mexican Treefrog (*Smilisca baudinii*) is restricted to South Texas and is listed as threatened by TPWD. All treefrogs have expanded toe pads on the tips of their digits which allow them to climb well. Treefrogs are primarily arboreal and can be found near permanent aquatic habitats during the spring breeding season.

true frog: True frogs are a group of large frogs which also include leopard frogs and bullfrogs. Species of true frogs that occur in Texas include the Pickerel Frog (*Rana palustris*) and Green Frog (*Rana clamitans*), which both have relatively large distributions throughout East Texas. The Pickerel Frog looks similar to leopard frogs but has squarish blotches instead of round blotches and yellow or orange coloration on the inside of its hind legs. Despite their name, Green Frogs can also be tan or bronze in coloration and can look similar to American Bullfrogs. These two species can be differentiated by looking at the dorsolateral fold (a fold of skin occurring from behind the eye). In Green Frogs, the dorsolateral fold extends to the hind limb, but in American Bullfrogs, the dorsolateral fold curves around the tympanum (eardrum) and never reaches the hind limb. Both the Pig Frog (*Rana grylio*) and Crawfish Frog (*Rana areolata*) also occur in East Texas but have a much more limited distribution in the state.

true toad: Ten species of toads occur throughout Texas, all varying in size, distribution, and preferred habitats. The largest toad that occurs in Texas is the Mesoamerican Cane Toad (*Rhinella horribilis*) that occurs in extreme South Texas, which can exceed 7" in length. The smallest toad in Texas is the Green Toad (*Anaxyrus debilis*), rarely exceeding 2" in length, which is found across much of the state except East Texas. All other species of toads are similar in size. Likely the rarest toad in Texas is the Houston Toad (*Anaxyrus houstonensis*). The Houston Toad only occurs in a handful of counties in the east-central portion of the state, has suffered widespread population declines, and is both federally- and state-protected. Two of the most widespread and abundant toads in Texas are the Texas Toad (*Anaxyrus speciosus*), which occurs throughout much of Texas except the eastern portion of the state and is also the state amphibian, and the Gulf Coast Toad (*Incilius nebulifer*), which occurs throughout south, central, and East Texas. The American Toad (*Anaxyrus americanus*) occurs in the extreme northeast corner of the state and is similar in appearance to the Fowler's Toad (*Anaxyrus fowleri*), which occupies a larger distribution throughout East Texas. The Great Plains Toad (*Anaxyrus cognatus*) primarily occurs in the Texas panhandle and the Trans-Pecos region. Widespread across west, north, and central Texas, the Red-spotted Toad (*Anaxyrus punctatus*) can be found in rocky, limestone habitats. The Woodhouse's Toad (*Anaxyrus woodhousii*) historically ranged from the Texas panhandle down the Gulf Coast but has experienced declines across much of its range in central Texas. Despite these declines, there remain areas where populations are still robust. Toads typically have dry, warty skin, bony ridges on the top of their head, and large poison glands called parotoid glands behind their eyes. These parotoid glands can secrete noxious compounds which are distasteful and irritating to potential predators.

Squirrel Treefrogs like the one above are often mistaken for Green Treefrogs. As adults they measure about 1.5 inches in length. Photo by Drew R. Davis

waterdog: These salamanders are also occasionally called mudpuppy and one species occurs in Texas: the Gulf Coast Waterdog (*Necturus beyeri*). The Gulf Coast Waterdog occurs in small creek systems in the Big Thicket of East Texas. This species is fully aquatic, has four limbs, and bushy external gills on the sides of its head.

white-lipped frog: The Mexican White-lipped Frog (*Leptodactylus fragilis*) barely makes it into Texas along the Rio Grande in extreme South Texas. In Texas, this species is rare and can only be found after rains, but it is much more common throughout Central America. These frogs appear similar to other true frogs in body shape but have rougher skin, a more pointed snout, and a prominent white stripe along the upper lip. The Mexican White-lipped Frog has a unique nesting habitat unlike other species of frogs in Texas. During reproduction, a foam nest is created from skin secretions and surrounds the eggs. This foam nest helps to prevent the eggs from drying out until the eggs hatch and tadpoles emerge.

Crotalus scutulatus, aka the Mojave rattlesnack or Mojave Green, is one of 11 rattlesnake species found in Texas. Photo by Clinton J. Guadiana

Reptiles

The order Reptilia consists of over 1,200 genera and 11,000 species and includes lizards, snakes, turtles, and crocodilians. Texas is home to 153 native species of reptiles and ten introduced species: Florida Red-bellied Cooter, Bent-toed Gecko, Common House Gecko, Indo-Pacific House Gecko, Tropical House Gecko, Sri Lankan Spotted House Gecko, Mediterranean Gecko, Mexican Spiny-tailed Iguana, Brown Anole, and the Brahminy Blindsnake.

Unlike amphibians, all reptiles have skin that is covered in scales. These scales serve as protection, but also help to prevent water loss, allowing reptiles to tolerate more arid habitats than amphibians.

Most species of reptiles lay eggs, but some species will give birth to live young, such as rattlesnakes. For egg-laying species, young develop in hard or leathery-shelled eggs, which are often laid in a nest and abandoned by the female.

Most reptiles have a well-developed sense of smell and use their tongue to collect chemical compounds from the air and move the compounds to the Jacobson's organ. This chemosensory organ is located on the roof of the mouth and provides sensory feedback for detecting airborne chemicals.

Reptiles also have relatively good vision. Snakes often detect movement with their eyes, and visual cues help them locate prey or attract mates.

Like amphibians, reptiles play an important role in nature as part of the food chain. Within Texas, the highest reptile diversity is located in South and West Texas. The Chihuahuan Desert of West Texas is home to most of the diversity of venomous snakes found in the state, including six species of rattlesnakes. Species like the Pond Slider, Texas Spiny Lizard, and Coachwhip are found across almost the entire state, while species like the Rough-footed Mud Turtle, Reticulate Banded Gecko, and Speckled Racer have extremely limited occurrences in the state.

alligator: The American Alligator (*Alligator mississippiensis*) is the largest reptile in North America and is found across the eastern third of Texas.

alligator lizard: The Texas Alligator Lizard (*Gerrhonotus infernalis*) can be found on rocky hillsides and wooded canyons in central and West Texas. With a long and somewhat prehensile tail, this species can measure over 17" in total length.

anole: The Green Anole (*Anolis carolinensis*) is a frequent visitor seen on fences and trees in the eastern two-thirds of Texas. Sometimes called chameleons because of their ability to change color between brown and green, but they are not related to true chameleons. The Brown Anole* (*Anolis sagrei*) is found along the coast from Brownsville to Galveston and is displacing the native Green Anole in parts of its range.

black-headed snake: Four species of black-headed snakes in Texas reach lengths of 6–8 inches, and a fifth species that lives in West Texas, the Trans-Pecos Black-headed Snake (*Tantilla cucullata*), can grow to 2' in length. The Flat-headed Snake (*Tantilla gracilis*) has a salmon-colored belly and lives in the eastern half of the state. The Plains Black-headed Snake (*Tantilla nigriceps*) is found in West and South Texas as well as the Panhandle.

blindsnake: see *threadsnake*

box turtle: Box turtles have a domed shell with a single hinge on the underside that allows the turtles to completely withdraw their limbs and head into the shell when threatened. These turtles have a generalist diet, consuming worms, insects, and vegetation. The Eastern Box Turtle (*Terrapene carolina*) is primarily found in eastern Texas, while the Ornate Box Turtle (*Terrapene ornata*) is found across most of the remainder of the state.

brownsnake: The Dekay's Brownsnake (*Storeria dekayi*) is one of several small (6–8") snakes found under rocks and logs in both urban backyards and rural settings. Other small snakes that are similar include the Rough Earthsnake (*Haldea striatula*), Smooth Earthsnake (*Virginia valeriae*), Lined Snake (*Tropidoclonion lineatum*), and Western Groundsnake (*Sonora semiannulata*). This group of snakes feeds on a variety of invertebrates, from worms and slugs to centipedes, scorpions, and spiders. Most are brown or tan, though Dekay's Brownsnakes and Lined Snakes are striped, and Western Groundsnakes may be either striped or banded.

bullsnake: see *gophersnake*

chicken snake: see *ratsnake*

chicken turtle: The Chicken Turtle (*Deirochelys reticularia*) is an uncommon species of turtle found in East Texas that looks similar to some sliders in shape and size. This turtle was once widely consumed, and its name refers to the taste of its meat.

coachwhip: see *whipsnake*

collared lizard: The Eastern Collared Lizard (*Crotaphytus collaris*), or Mountain Boomer, is found in rocky areas of central, north, and West Texas. This species has a dark collar around its neck with overall green body color. The Reticulate Collared Lizard (*Crotaphytus reticulatus*) is mostly brown or gray with a network of light lines and dark spots on its back. This species is found in South Texas from Maverick to Hidalgo counties.

cooter: Cooters are large, aquatic turtles that inhabit river systems throughout Texas. Four species of cooters are found in Texas, including one non-native species. The River Cooter (*Pseudemys concinna*) is found throughout East Texas, the Texas Cooter (*Pseudemys texana*) is found throughout central Texas, and the Rio Grande Cooter (*Pseudemys gorzugi*) is found in the Rio Grande and Pecos Rivers of West Texas. The Florida Red-bellied Cooter* (*Pseudemys nelsoni*) is not native to Texas and has been introduced to the headwaters of the San Marcos River and Houston.

copperhead: VENOMOUS. The Copperhead (*Agkistrodon contortrix*) is found in most of the state, except South Texas and the Panhandle. Its copper-colored body with rusty orange or grayish bands help camouflage the snake in leaf litter. They feed on small mammals and insects, particularly, freshly-molted cicadas in the summer.

coralsnake: VENOMOUS. The Texas Coralsnake (*Micrurus tener*) is a common species across south, central, and East Texas. It is infrequently seen because it spends the majority of its life underground, and it feeds almost exclusively on other snakes. Because of variability in color intensity and pattern in Texas Coralsnakes, the commonly used rhyme "red next to yellow, kill a fellow; red next to black, venom lack" is not a reliable method to distinguish venomous coralsnakes from look-a-likes, such as the non-venomous Milksnake (*Lampropeltis triangulum*).

cottonmouth: VENOMOUS. The Cottonmouth (*Agkistrodon piscivorus*), or Water Moccasin, is more commonly encountered in East Texas though populations persist as far west as San Angelo and Junction. Not an aggressive animal; however, it will vigorously defend itself against would-be predators. Defensive behavior includes vibrating its tail and gaping open its mouth, showing off the white lining.

earless lizard: All five species of earless lizards have ears, but they have skin covering the ear opening. The largest species, the Greater Earless Lizard (*Cophosaurus texanus*) is a conspicuous and fast-moving species identified by the black-and-white bands on the bottom of its tail. The Common Lesser Earless Lizard (*Holbrookia maculata*) is found across the west, north, and central portions of Texas. The Keeled Earless Lizard (*Holbrookia propinqua*) is restricted to the sand sheets and dunes of South Texas. The Plateau Earless Lizard (*Holbrookia lacerata*) is found patchily across central Texas, South of the Colorado River and East of the Pecos River. The Tamaulipan Spot-tailed Lizard (*Holbrookia subcaudalis*) is restricted to populations near Del Rio and Kingsville.

earthsnake: see *brownsnake*

gartersnake: Four species occur in the state, primarily feeding on amphibians and fish, but also earthworms. All species have light-colored lines running the length of their dark-colored bodies. The Checkered Gartersnake (*Thamnophis marcianus*) is found everywhere except East Texas. The Black-necked Gartersnake (*Thamnophis cyrtopsis*), found in central and West Texas, is one of the most beautiful snakes in the state with a brilliant orange stripe. Both the Plains Gartersnake (*Thamnophis radix*) and Common Gartersnake (*Thamnophis sirtalis*), though widely found across the north-central and eastern portions of the United States, only have limited ranges in Texas.

gecko: The Texas Banded Gecko (*Coleonyx brevis*) is the smaller of the two native geckos in the state and is found in West and South Texas. The Reticulate Banded Gecko (*Coleonyx reticulatus*) is native to the Big Bend. Six species of geckos have been introduced to Texas. The Mediterranean Gecko* (*Hemidactylus turcicus*) first arrived in Brownsville in the 1950s and is now found as far north as Lubbock and the Red River. Other species like the Tropical House Gecko* (*Hemidactylus mabouia*) and the Sri Lankan Spotted Gecko* (*Hemidactylus parvimaculatus*) are recent arrivals to the state.

glass lizard: The legless Slender Glass Lizard (*Ophisaurus attenuatus*) is restricted to sandy habitats across the eastern half of the state. This species has eyelids and ear openings, distinguishing them from snakes. They can be seen among the coastal dunes on Mustang Island and Padre Island National Seashore where they feed on insects and small vertebrates.

gophersnake: The Gophersnake (*Pituophis catenifer*), sometimes called Bullsnake, can grow to be the longest snake in the U.S., reaching over 9' in length. Found across the western three-quarters of the state, this non-venomous species may hiss and vibrate its tail when threatened. The related

Louisiana Pinesnake (*Pituophis ruthveni*) is a federally-listed species historically found in longleaf pine-oak sandhills habitats in East Texas.

greensnake: The Rough Greensnake (*Opheodrys aestivus*) feeds on spiders and insects, growing to 2' in length in the eastern third of Texas. The Smooth Greensnake (*Opheodrys vernalis*) is thought to be extirpated from the state and is only known from six specimens collected in the 1960s and 1970s.

groundsnake: see *brownsnake*

hog-nosed snake: Hog-nosed snakes are known for their defensive displays towards predators, ending with the snake playing dead. The Eastern Hog-nosed Snake (*Heterodon platirhinos*) prefers to eat toads and is found in the eastern half of the state. The Plains Hog-nosed Snake (*Heterodon nasicus*) is more commonly found in sandy and gravely habitats in West Texas and the Panhandle.

horned lizard: The Texas Horned Lizard (*Phrynosoma cornutum*), or Horny Toad, is the state reptile. Originally found across the majority of the state, it is now restricted to pockets in west, south, and North Texas due to habitat loss and the introduction of invasive grasses and insects. The Greater Short-horned Lizard (*Phrynosoma hernandesi*) is found at higher elevations in the Davis, Guadalupe, and Hueco mountains. The Round-tailed Horned Lizard (*Phrynosoma modestum*) is found mostly in West Texas and the Panhandle and blends into its arid habitats as a rock mimic.

horny toad: see *horned lizard*

iguana: The Mexican Spiny-tailed Iguana* (*Ctenosaura pectinata*) is the only species of iguana found in the state. It was introduced in Brownsville in the 1960s but has not expanded its range outside of Cameron County.

indigo snake: Famed for their ability to eat rattlesnakes, the Central American Indigo Snake (*Drymarchon melanurus*) also eats a variety of mammals, birds, turtles, amphibians, and other snakes. Found in South Texas, this heavy-bodied snake is colored dark black and can grow over 8' long.

The Eastern Musk Turtle is also known as the stinkpot turtle. Photo by Drew R. Davis

kingsnake: The Prairie Kingsnake (*Lampropeltis calligaster*) is found in the grasslands and woodlands of East Texas, with some populations in the Panhandle and South Texas. The Gray-banded Kingsnake (*Lampropeltis alterna*) lives in the drier regions of West Texas and is prized by collectors for its beautiful banding patterns of orange or dark grey. The Common Kingsnake (*Lampropeltis getula*) is found throughout the state, though its pattern is more speckled in East Texas and more dark-blotched in West Texas.

lined snake: see *brownsnake*

loggerhead: see *snapping turtle*

map turtle: Map turtles, sometimes called sawback turtles, are characterized by a keeled ridge down the middle of the shell and numerous yellow lines on their head and limbs and inhabit river systems across the state. The Texas Map Turtle (*Graptemys versa*) is found in the Colorado and Concho rivers and the Cagle's Map Turtle (*Graptemys caglei*) is restricted to the Guadalupe River. Both the False Map Turtle (*Graptemys pseudogeographica*) and the Ouachita Map Turtle (*Graptemys ouachitensis*) are found in river systems in East and North Texas.

milksnake: The Milksnake (*Lampropeltis triangulum*) is a close relative of the kingsnakes. Its bright red, black, and yellow colors help confuse would-be predators that might instead think this snake to be the venomous Texas Coralsnake (*Micrurus tener*). Because of variability in color intensity and pattern in Texas coralsnakes, the commonly used rhyme "red next to yellow, kill a fellow; red next to black, venom lack" is not a reliable method to distinguish coralsnakes from look-a-likes, such as the Milksnake, the Scarletsnake (*Cemophora coccinea*), the Texas Scarletsnake (*Cemophora lineri*), or the Long-nosed Snake (*Rhinocheilus lecontei*).

moccasin: see *cottonmouth*

mountain boomer: see *collared lizard*

mudsnake: The Red-bellied Mudsnake (*Farancia abacura*) is a boldly patterned snake, with dark glossy scales on its back with a bright red belly. It will defend itself when captured by pressing the hard and pointed tip of its tail into the attacker's skin. Occasionally, this species is called a Hoop Snake because of the false myth that it can roll down a hill like a wheel with its tail in its mouth!

mud turtle: Three species of mud turtles are found in Texas, all of which are small (4–6" shell length), secretive species rarely encountered. The Yellow Mud Turtle (*Kinosternon flavescens*) is found throughout most of Texas, except the Piney Woods, and spend a large amount of time in rodent burrows on land, waiting for rains to move into temporary wetlands. The Rough-footed Mud Turtle (*Kinosternon hirtipes*) can only be found in the Alamito Creek drainage of West Texas. The Eastern Mud Turtle (*Kinosternon subrubrum*) occurs across East Texas, often in slow-moving water bodies, including bayous and flooded forests.

musk turtle: These turtles are similar in appearance and ecology to mud turtles, with only two species known in the state. Like mud turtles, musk turtles can discharge a foul-smelling substance from specialized glands on their undersides to deter predators. The Razor-backed Musk Turtle (*Sternotherus carinatus*) gets its name from its shell having small, raised ridges along the midline, and is restricted to aquatic habitats in East Texas. The Eastern

Musk Turtle (*Sternotherus odoratus*) is more widespread across eastern and central Texas and has a smooth top of its shell.

painted turtle: Two species of painted turtles can be found in Texas, both extremely uncommon and limited in their range. The Southern Painted Turtle (*Chrysemys dorsalis*) can be found in extreme northeast Texas and only a few records of the Painted Turtle (*Chrysemys picta*) are known from along the Red River and in far West Texas.

pinesnake: see *gophersnake*

racer: Often a dull green and around 3' in length, the North American Racer (*Coluber constrictor*) is found across the majority of the state, typically in open areas with large amounts of undergrowth. Racers feed on small mammals, birds, reptiles, amphibians, and insects. In East Texas, North American Racers can be brown or tan with some populations being steel-blue or olive intermixed with light white or yellow scales (buttermilk phase).

racerunner: see *whiptail lizard*

ratsnake: Five species of ratsnake occur in Texas. The Western Ratsnake (*Pantherophis obsoletus*), also Chicken Snake, is frequently encountered in the eastern half of the state. It can reach lengths over 5' and spends much of its time in trees, eating squirrels, birds, and bird eggs. The Baird's Ratsnake (*Pantherophis bairdi*) is found only in the Trans-Pecos. This species changes its pattern from blotches (juvenile) to stripes (adult). A mostly gray snake with dark brown blotches, the Great Plains Ratsnake (*Pantherophis emoryi*) is found across most of the state. The Trans-Pecos Ratsnake (*Bogertophis subocularis*) is found in rocky areas of West Texas where it eats mammals, including bats.

rattlesnake: VENOMOUS. Rattlesnakes are seen in every habitat in Texas, with 11 species represented in the state. The largest, the Western Diamond-backed Rattlesnake (*Crotalus atrox*), can reach lengths over 7' and is found everywhere except far East Texas. The Timber Rattlesnake (*Crotalus horridus*) is a heavy-bodied snake found in the hardwood bottomlands of East and North Texas. The Rock Rattlesnake (*Crotalus lepidus*) can reach 2.5' in length and is restricted to the Trans-Pecos. The smallest rattlesnake species in Texas, the Pygmy Rattlesnake (*Sistrurus miliarius*) is found in East Texas, rarely growing longer than 20".

ribbonsnake: The Western Ribbonsnake (*Thamnophis proximus*) is found almost everywhere in the state, except West Texas. It has a series of three stripes down its olive-colored back and is closely related to the gartersnakes.

sea turtle: Five species of sea turtles can be found in saltwater habitats along the Texas coastline. The largest of all sea turtles, the Leatherback Sea Turtle (*Dermochelys coriacea*), has a shell length that exceeds 7' in length and can weigh almost a ton. The Kemp's Ridley Sea Turtle (*Lepidochelys kempii*) is among the rarest and smallest of the sea turtles, which primarily nest along South Padre Island and into coastal Mexico and is designated as the state sea turtle. Other sea turtles include the Green Sea Turtle (*Chelonia mydas*), Hawksbill Sea Turtle (*Eretmochelys imbricata*), and Loggerhead Sea Turtle (*Caretta caretta*). All species of sea turtle are federally- and state-protected and any observed nesting or stranded along the coastline should be reported to appropriate individuals, such as TPWD.

skink: Eight species of skinks in Texas, all with smooth and shiny scales. The smallest species is the Ground Skink (*Scincella lateralis*), often seen scurrying off dirt paths or sidewalks to hide from predators across the eastern three-quarters of Texas. The largest species is the Great Plains Skink (*Plestiodon obsoletus*) and is found in the western half of the state. This species can measure over 1 foot in total length.

The Great Plains Skink can be found as far north as Wyoming. Photo by Drew R. Davis

slider: Two species of sliders are found in Texas. One species, the Pond Slider (*Trachemys scripta*), is among the most common turtle found throughout Texas, occurring in most aquatic habitats. The second species, the Mexican Plateau Slider (*Trachemys gaigeae*) only occurs in the Rio Grande of West Texas.

snapping turtle: Snapping turtles are among the largest freshwater turtles in North America and have a generalist diet, consuming almost anything in the water it encounters, including carrion. Two species of snapping turtles are found in Texas. The Snapping Turtle (*Chelydra serpentina*) is found throughout the central and eastern regions while the Alligator Snapping Turtle (*Macrochelys temminckii*) is restricted to East Texas.

softshell: Softshells get their name from the reduced bony elements in their shell, which gives them a leathery, flexible shell, unlike most other turtles. Having this modified shape gives the turtles the ability to be extremely agile and fast swimmers. These species also have a snorkel-like snout and long necks that allow individuals to raise their heads up and breathe while they are submerged in the sandy bottoms of rivers and streams. Two species of softshells occur in Texas, including the Smooth Softshell (*Apalone mutica*) that is uncommon throughout parts of northern, central, and eastern Texas, and the Spiny Softshell (*Apalone spinifera*) that is much more abundant in suitable habitats across most of Texas.

spiny lizard: Over 10 species of spiny lizards are found in Texas, so-called 'spiny' because of their large, keeled scales that give them a rough appearance. The Crevice Spiny Lizard (*Sceloporus poinsettii*) is unique among Texas spiny lizards as it does not lay eggs but instead gives birth to live young. The Texas Spiny Lizard (*Sceloporus olivaceus*), or Rusty Lizard, prefers to spend their time in trees, often on the opposite side of the trunk from any observers! The

Dunes Sagebrush Lizard (*Sceloporus arenicolus*) is restricted to the shinnery-oak dunes of West Texas near Kermit and Andrews. The Rose-bellied Lizard (*Sceloporus variabilis*) is found in rocky and drier environments in South Texas. The Tree Lizard (*Urosaurus ornatus*) is found on trees and rocks from El Paso to central Texas. The Side-blotched Lizard (*Uta stansburiana*) is found in the western deserts and southern portions of the Panhandle.

terrapin: The Diamond-backed Terrapin (*Malaclemys terrapin*) inhabits brackish waters along the Texas coast from the Louisiana border to Corpus Christi. Throughout the 1800s, this turtle was widely consumed, and population declines were widespread.

threadsnake: The three native species of threadsnakes can initially look like earthworms; however, their tiny tongues and scaled bodies give them away as snakes. Threadsnakes feed on ant and termite larvae. The Texas Threadsnake (*Rena dulcis*) is found in the middle third of Texas; two other species, the New Mexico Threadsnake (*Rena dissecta*) and Western Threadsnake (*Rena humilis*), are found in West Texas. The Brahminy Blindsnake* (*Indotyphlops braminus*) has been introduced to Texas as it hitchhikes around the world, hiding in the soil of plants in the nursery trade.

tortoise: One species of tortoise occurs in Texas, the Berlandier's Tortoise (*Gopherus berlandieri*). This tortoise occurs throughout South Texas and into Mexico and has a domed shell and elephant-like feet. Unlike most other turtles, tortoises spend the majority of their time on land foraging on vegetation.

watersnake: Seven species are known in the state and all are non-venomous. Often, these species are confused with the venomous Cottonmouth (*Agkistrodon piscivorous*). The Diamond-backed Watersnake (*Nerodia rhombifer*) is the largest in the state, often reaching 4', and is found in the eastern two-thirds of Texas. The Plain-bellied Watersnake (*Nerodia erythrogaster*) feeds on amphibians and fish. Both the Brazos River Watersnake (*Nerodia harteri*) and Concho Watersnake (*Nerodia paucimaculata*) are found only in Texas (endemic species).

whipsnake: Whipsnakes are long and slender snakes with large eyes that hunt almost exclusively during the day. The Coachwhip (*Masticophis flagellum*) is found across the entire state and can be found with a variety of body colors: brown, tan, black, and red. Schott's Whipsnake (*Masticophis schotti*) is found in the thornscrub of South Texas and the Striped Whipsnake (*Masticophis taeniatus*) is found in the drier regions of central and West Texas.

whiptail lizard: There are 10 species of whiptail lizards found across the state, with the majority of species found in West Texas. Two species are widely distributed in Texas, except portions of West Texas: the Six-lined Racerunner (*Aspidoscelis sexlineata*), which has six light stripes across its dark back, and the Common Spotted Whiptail (*Aspidoscelis gularis*), which also has light stripes but with additional small light spots between the stripes and across its dark back. The Laredo Striped Whiptail (*Aspidoscelis laredoensis*) is the only species restricted to South Texas, found along the Rio Grande from Val Verde to Cameron counties. The Chihuahuan Spotted Whiptail (*Aspidoscelis exsanguis*) is an all-female species and can reproduce without fertilization from males.

Birds

The order Aves consists of over 2,000 genera and over 10,000 species. Texas is home to 639 species of birds, including purposefully introduced species (e.g., House Sparrow, European Starling) and accidental releases (e.g., Monk Parakeet), as well as recent introductions or range expansions (e.g., Cattle Egret, Red-crowned Parrot). Because many species migrate long distances flying between spring breeding grounds and overwintering sites, some individuals find themselves off-course and are recorded as accidental visitors in our state each year.

Birds are well-known for their vocalizations, which are unique to each species. Calls include courtship songs, alarm calls, and threat displays. Both males and females will vocalize, but the males typically have elaborate songs used to attract mates. Song attractiveness may be enhanced by behavioral displays in some species that include bright colorations and elaborate dances or flight patterns. Some bird species will form single pair bonds (some for life), while other species may breed with more than one partner.

All birds lay eggs; some species may construct elaborate nests from vegetation or build nests in cavities, while some species like Killdeer and nighthawks lay camouflaged eggs directly on the ground. A few species are nest parasites, laying eggs in the nests of other species.

When chicks hatch, they may be altricial (naked, helpless, blind; e.g., songbirds), semi-precocial (downy, dependent, eyes open; e.g., gulls), or precocial (downy, independent, eyes open; e.g., ducklings).

Bird diets vary from scavenging and eating carrion to hunting small and medium-sized vertebrates; other diet items can include invertebrates from grasshoppers to spiders, snails to worms, and many other bird species eat a variety of seeds, fruit, and even nectar. Birds also serve as important diet items for many species.

blackbird: To protect their nests from predators, the Red-winged Blackbird (*Agelaius phoeniceus*) build their nests in dense reeds surrounded by water. A single male will defend a quality patch of nesting area, mating with multiple females that build nests within his territory. Additional species are found in the state, primarily as winter visitors, including the Yellow-headed Blackbird (*Xanthocephalus xanthocephalus*) and the Brewer's Blackbird (*Euphagus cyanocephalus*).

bluebird: Three species. The Eastern Bluebird (*Sialia sialis*) is a welcomed summer resident in the eastern half of the state and a winter resident and migrant across the western half. Bright blue above with a rusty red chest, this species has faced declines across its range, likely due to introduced bird species such as House Sparrow and European Starling.

The male Painted Bunting is often called the most beautiful bird in North America. Photo by Jill D. Miller

bunting: Once seen, a male Painted Bunting (*Passerina ciris*) is a bird not soon forgotten: a deep blue head with a distinct red eye ring, a yellow back, and red breast; almost a 'color-by-numbers' assortment of brilliant colors. A summer resident across much of the state. The male Varied Bunting (*Passerina versicolor*), found along the Rio Grande in West Texas, is equally stunning with its combination of purple, deep blue, and a small amount of red. A male Indigo Bunting (*Passerina cyanea*) is bright blue. Female buntings are inconspicuously colored with a wash of tan or pale yellow covering their body.

caracara: see *falcon*

cardinal: The Northern Cardinal (*Cardinalis cardinalis*) is a frequent and loud visitor to both backyards and mixed forests. A conspicuous bird due to its bright red color (though females are not as bright), this species is monogamous, and the pair remains together throughout the year. Its thick, stout bill is used to feed on seeds.

chachalaca: The Plain Chachalaca (*Ortalis vetula*) is a native species found in the Lower Rio Grande Valley. Also called a Mexican Pheasant, this species can be found on the ground as well as in trees. Eats fruit, leaves, and insects. When multiple animals call at the same time, the loud chorus of 'cha-cha-lac' can be deafening.

chickadee: The Carolina Chickadee (*Poecile carolinensis*) is found across the eastern half of the state. Often seen in a mixed flock with titmice. Feeds on insects as well as seeds and berries. Call is 'chick-a-dee-dee-dee'.

coot: The American Coot, or Mud Hen (*Fulica americana*), is found in ponds and waterways across the state. A dark-gray and black bird with widened toes that aid in swimming. A memorable characteristic of these birds is their ungraceful method of flapping and running across the water's surface to fly.

cormorant: Two species are commonly seen. Great at catching fish, their outer feathers lack waterproofing, an adaptation that enables them to stay underwater rather than float. Often seen along bodies of water as they hold their wings out to dry. The Neotropical Cormorant (*Phalacrocorax brasilianus*) is a common resident across the South and East portions of the state. The Double-crested Cormorant (*Phalacrocorax auritus*) is a winter migrant and visitor.

cowbird: Cowbirds are obligate brood parasites, meaning they do not build their own nests, and instead they lay their eggs in the nests of other species. The baby cowbirds hatch earlier than the other chicks and grow larger, often the only chick to survive and successfully leave the nest. The Brown-headed Cowbird (*Molothrus ater*) and Bronzed Cowbird (*Molothrus aeneus*) are the two most common species in Texas.

crane: Cranes are among the tallest birds in North America, standing over 4' high, but are only winter visitors to Texas. The Sandhill Crane (*Grus canadensis*) is often found in large flocks in open fields where they feed on spent grain. The Whooping Crane (*Grus americana*) is found in coastal marshes where they feed on blue crabs. The Whooping Crane is a critically endangered species with recent surveys estimating the Texas population size to be around 500 individuals.

crow: The American Crow (*Corvus brachyrhynchos*) is a common resident of the Panhandle and eastern half of the state. An omnivorous species with a wide diet, it has been the focus of efforts to control populations because of damage to agricultural areas. The Fish Crow (*Corvus ossifragus*) is found in extreme East Texas; in Texas, the Tamaulipan Crow (*Corvus imparatus*) is known only from a handful of localities in Cameron County.

dove: Many species occur in Texas. Several species are game species, including Mourning Dove (*Zenaida macroura*), White-winged Dove (*Zenaida asiatica*), and White-tipped Dove (*Leptotila verreauxi*). The Rock Dove (*Columba livia*), or Pigeon, can be found in large numbers in urban areas. The

Eurasian Collared-dove* (*Steptopelia decaocto*) first arrived in the state in 1995 and can now be found in every county.

duck: Over 20 species occur in Texas, though most are primarily winter visitors. The Wood Duck (*Aix sponsa*) is an exception, a summer resident across three-quarters of the state. The Northern Shoveler (*Anas clypeata*) uses its remarkably long spatulate bill to filter water, eating plankton and invertebrates. The winter aggregations of Redhead (*Aythya americana*) in the Laguna Madre are the largest in the world. The Muscovy Duck* (*Cairina moschata*) is restricted to counties in the Lower Rio Grande Valley.

Northern Shovelers can also be found in Europe, Asia, and South America. Photo by Rhotodendrites, CC by-SA 4.0

eagle: The Bald Eagle (*Haliaeetus leucocephalus*) is the largest raptor in Texas, feeding on fish and ducks primarily in the eastern third of the state. It can be seen in most of Texas during migration. The Golden Eagle (*Aquila chrysaetos*), with its 7' wingspan, is often associated with mountainous regions where it feeds on mammals, birds, and reptiles.

egret: see *heron*

falcon: Eight species, belonging to two groups, are found in Texas. The larger group possesses long tails and long, narrow wings which enable them to dive at incredible speeds when hunting. Common falcons include the American Kestrel (*Falco sparevius*) and Merlin (*Falco columbarius*), and uncommon falcons include the Peregrine Falcon (*Falco peregrinus*) and the Aplomado Falcon (*Falco femoralis*). Alone in the second group, the Crested Caracara (*Caracara cheriway*) is more like a vulture than a true falcon, with its weak claws but long wings.

finch: Finches are small birds with short, stout bills that primarily feed on seeds and some insects, and often move in flocks. The Lesser Goldfinch (*Spinus psaltria*) is a summer resident of the Trans-Pecos and Lower Rio Grande Valley. The male House Finch (*Haemorhous mexicanus*), with its orange-red head and chest, is found throughout most of the state. The Purple Finch (*Haemorhous purpureus*) is a winter migrant seen in North and East Texas.

flycatcher: Flycatchers have a hunting strategy of catching insects in flight, first spotting them while sitting in the top of a tree or fence post and then flying up to catch the insect and returning to their original spot. With its extremely long tail, the Scissor-tailed Flycatcher (*Tyrannus forficatus*) is a conspicuous resident across much of the state; the Vermillion Flycatcher (*Pyrocephalus rubinus*) is also conspicuous with its brilliantly crimson-colored males. Brown above, yellow below, and with a black mask over its eyes, the Great Kiskadee (*Pitangus sulphuratus*) is well known in South Texas. The Eastern Phoebe (*Sayornis phoebe*) is found in backyards as well as open woodlands. The White-eyed Vireo (*Vireo griseus*) is found across the eastern half of the state, sometimes combining the calls of other species into their own. The Western Kingbird (*Tyrannus verticalis*) is seen in open habitats, often on fence posts or utility lines.

goose: Several species occur as winter migrants, and most can occur in huge populations in the Panhandle and along the coast. Species include the Snow Goose (*Chen caerulescens*), the Ross's Goose (*Chen rossii*), and the Canada Goose (*Branta canadensis*).

grackle: Sociable and eye-catching in many urban areas across the state, these shiny black birds have a showy courtship display and nest in large colonies. Three species occur in Texas: the Common Grackle (*Quiscalus quiscula*) and Great-tailed Grackle (*Quiscalus mexicanus*) are found across much of the state and the Boat-tailed Grackle (*Quiscalus major*) is restricted to a narrow band of habitat close to the ocean along the upper Gulf Coast.

gull: Although gulls are frequently associated with the coast, many species can be found along lakes and marshes far inland from the coast. Gulls rely on their skills as scavengers, grabbing floating items from the water, as well as unattended or abandoned food items from the ground. The Franklin's Gull (*Larus pipixcan*) and the Ring-billed Gull (*Larus delawarensis*) are among the most common gulls seen across the state. With its distinctive "laughing" call, the Laughing Gull (*Leucophaeus atricilla*) is primarily found along the coast.

harrier: see *hawks*

hawk: Hawks are birds of prey in the same family as eagles, kites, and harriers. The Cooper's Hawk (*Accipiter cooperii*) feeds on birds and is often seen in wooded urban backyards. The Northern Harrier (*Circus cyaneus*) can be found gliding low across prairies searching for small vertebrates. The Harris's Hawk (*Parabuteo unicinctus*) is known for cooperatively hunting in social groups. The Red-tailed Hawk (*Buteo jamaicensis*) is found statewide, often seen soaring or perched on telephone poles and fence posts.

heron: Herons and egrets are long-legged and long-billed birds. The Great Blue Heron (*Ardea herodias*) and the Great Egret (*Ardea alba*) are frequently seen around the edges of lakes, marshes, and even in roadside drainage ditches where they feed on fish and other small vertebrates like snakes. The nocturnal Black-crowned Night-heron (*Nycticorax nycticorax*) can be found along urban streams. The Cattle Egret (*Bubulcus ibis*) was unknown in Texas until 1955 as this species spread from Africa to South America in the 1880s (blown across the Atlantic Ocean in giant storms), and then to Florida and Texas in the 1940s and 1950s.

hummingbird: Texas is home to at least 18 species, some species being residents, others only brief migratory visitors. The Ruby-throated Hummingbird (*Archilochus colubris*) is a summer resident in the eastern third of the state; the Black-chinned Hummingbird (*Archilochus alexandri*) is commonly seen in the western two-thirds of the state. The

Lucifer Hummingbird (*Calothorax lucifer*) can be found in the Christmas and Chisos mountains in the Big Bend during the summer; the Green-breasted Mango (*Anthracothorax prevostii*) has been seen sporadically in the Lower Rio Grande Valley, primarily in the fall.

jay: Seven species are recorded from Texas. The Blue Jay (*Cyanocitta cristata*) is the most wide-ranging species, inhabiting rural and urban areas across the state, except West Texas. Eating insects and large amounts of nuts and fruit, this species will also hoard surplus food. The spectacular and distinctive Green Jay (*Cyanocorax yncas*) has slowly been expanding its South Texas range northward towards San Antonio. The Brown Jay (*Psilorhinus morio*) is known only from Starr and Zapata counties.

kestrel: see *falcon*

killdeer: The Killdeer (*Charadrius vociferus*) is a type of plover found throughout Texas, often seen along open fields and grassy lots. They lay their eggs directly on the ground, camouflaged among rocks and pebbles. Well-known for their distraction displays leading predators away from their nests, they will often pretend to have a broken wing.

kingbird: see *flycatcher*

kingfisher: Three resident species in Texas. They hover and dive into the water to catch fish. The Belted Kingfisher (*Megaceryle alcyon*) is found throughout the state. Both the Ringed Kingfisher (*Megaceryle torquata*) and the Green Kingfisher (*Chloroceryle americana*) are restricted to central and South Texas.

kiskadee: see *flycatcher*

kite: Kites are small raptors that feed on insects and small vertebrates, but some species, like the Hook-billed Kite (*Chondrohierax uncinatus*) specialize in snails. Kites can catch and eat insects while in flight or can hover, then swoop down to grab prey off the ground. The Mississippi Kite (*Actiniaa mississippiensis*) can be seen across the state; the White-tailed Kite (*Elanus leucurus*), and the Swallow-tailed Kite (*Elanoides forficatus*) are found in East Texas and along the coast.

meadowlark: Meadowlarks are conspicuous birds found perched on fences along open prairie or grassy habitats. The call of the Western Meadowlark (*Sturnella neglecta*) is a bit more complex than that of the Eastern Meadowlark (*Sternella magna*), but subtle differences in their markings can make the species difficult to tell apart without the aid of their calls.

mockingbird: The Northern Mockingbird (*Mimus polyglottos*) is the state bird of Texas. Known for mimicking songs of other birds to attract mates and intimidate other males; unmated males will sing at night in the spring. Both males and females may vigorously attack would-be predators to defend their eggs and young.

nighthawk: These are nocturnal birds, with large mouths edged with large bristles that act as flytraps, feed at night to catch flying insects. They are also called goatsuckers. They do not build nests, but instead lay camouflaged eggs on bare ground. The Common Nighthawk (*Chordeiles minor*) is seen across the state, whereas the Common Pauraque (*Nyctidromus albicollis*) is restricted to South Texas.

oriole: Orioles are somewhat conspicuous with their bright yellow, orange, or rusty red colors, particularly the males in spring breeding plumage. Nine species reported in the state. The Orchard Oriole (*Icterus spurius*) can be a common resident in East Texas. The Altamira Oriole (*Icterus gularis*) is an orange and black species found only along the Rio Grande in extreme South Texas. The Scott's Oriole (*Icterus parisorum*) is a yellow and black species found across the drier Trans-Pecos region.

osprey: The Osprey (*Pandion haliaetus*) feeds on fish, hovering above the water before plunging in feet first to grab its prey. When flying, they are sometimes confused with gulls, but their sharply hooked beak and dark eye stripe help in their identification.

White-tailed Kites feed primarily on rodents. Photo by Alejandro Bayer Tamayo, CC by SA 2.0

owl: Seventeen species are observed in the state. With large eyes, incredible hearing, and wings adapted to maintain silence in flight, owls are amazing nocturnal predators. More frequently seen owls include the Barn Owl (*Tyto alba*), Great Horned Owl (*Bufo virginianus*), Eastern Screech Owl (*Megascops asio*), Burrowing Owl (*Athene cunicularia*), and Barred Owl (*Strix varia*). In the summer, the small Elf Owl (*Micrathene whitneyi*) can be seen in West Texas.

parakeet: Following several accidental and at least one intentional introduction, the Monk Parakeet* (*Myiopsitta monachus*), or Quaker Parakeet*, is established in several urban areas from Dallas to Austin, San Antonio to Kingsville. The presence of another species found in South Texas along the Rio Grande, the Green Parakeet (*Aratinga holochlora*), may be linked to habitat loss further South in its native range of Mexico.

parrot: A single species, the Red-crowned Parrot (*Amazona viridigenalis*) is found in Texas, common in the metropolitan areas of Cameron, Hidalgo, and Starr counties along the lower Rio Grande border.

Robins are a common sight in backyards across most of the state. Photo by Dori, CC by SA 3.0

pelican: The Brown Pelican (*Pelecanus occidentalis*) is a resident along the Texas coast and may range inland up to 150 miles. The White Pelican (*Pelecanus erythrorhynchos*) is a common winter resident in the eastern half of the state.

phoebe: see *flycatcher*

pigeon: see *dove*

plover: see *shorebird*

prairie chicken: Both the Greater Prairie-chicken (*Tympanuchus cupido*) and the Lesser Prairie-chicken (*Tympanuchus pallidicinctus*) are famed for their elaborate courtship displays: the males gather in tall-grass prairie clearings to dance in a competition for females. The males inflate their large orange neck pouches with air, then force air out with a "boom" that can be heard for over half a mile.

purple martin: see *swallow*

quail: The Northern Bobwhite (*Colinus virginianus*) is the most widespread quail species in Texas, found across all but West Texas. The Gambel's Quail (*Callipepla gambelii*) and the Montezuma Quail (*Cyrtonyx montezumae*) are restricted to the Trans-Pecos; the Scaled Quail (*Callipepla squamata*), or Blue Quail, is found in the Panhandle as well as West and South Texas. All but the Montezuma Quail are legal game species in the state.

rail: Found in both freshwater and brackish marshes, rails are typically heard rather than seen. The Sora (*Porzana carolina*) may be the most conspicuous of the rails, hunting along the open margins in search of seeds and insects. Other species, like the Yellow Rail (*Coturnicops noveboracensis*) and Black Rail (*Laterallus jamaicensis*) are elusive winter migrants to brackish marshes along the coast.

raven: The Common Raven (*Corvus corax*) is a large black bird found in central and West Texas; the Chihuahuan Raven (*Corvus cryptoleucus*) is slightly smaller in size but with a wider distribution in the Panhandle and both West and South Texas. The larger body size, stouter bill, and longer wings distinguish ravens from the crow. Ravens are omnivorous, eating vertebrates, insects, seeds, and fruit.

roadrunner: The Greater Roadrunner (*Geococcyx californicus*) is found across the state, though uncommon in East Texas. They feed on a variety of prey, including insects, spiders, small mammals, small birds, lizards, and snakes, including rattlesnakes, but will also eat fruit and seeds. Other names include Paisano and Chaparral Cock.

robin: The American Robin (*Turdus migratorius*) is known across the state as either a winter visitor (west and South Texas) or as a summer resident (north, central, and East Texas), although its summer range in Texas continues to expand. With its red breast and brown or black back, this species can form large flocks that feed on insects and fruit.

sandpiper: see *shorebird*

shorebird: A large group of wading birds commonly found along the water's edge, whether ocean or freshwater. Shorebirds' long bills are used to probe moist sand and sediment for invertebrates and featherless legs adapted for wading. The Willet (*Tringa semipalmata*) breeds along the Gulf Coast, identified by its black-and-white wing pattern visible during flight. The Spotted Sandpiper (*Actitis macularius*) can be identified by the exaggerated bobbing of its longish tail when walking. The Mountain Plover (*Charadrius montanus*) is a summer resident in open grasslands of the northern Panhandle with some populations wintering in central and South Texas. The secretive and solitary Wilson's Snipe (*Callinago delicata*), the focus of many invented hunts, is an actual game bird found along grassy marshes and meadows.

shrike: The Loggerhead Shrike (*Lanius ludovicianus*), or Butcher Bird, is known for impaling its prey (insects and small vertebrates) on barbed wire fences or sharp-thorned plants. The food items are eaten quickly or saved for future use. Its gray, black, and white body makes this species look similar to a Northern Mockingbird, but its black eye mask and sharp, hooked bill instead help identify it as a shrike.

snipe: see *shorebird*

sparrow: Many of the 30 species of sparrows found in Texas are small brown or gray birds that may be difficult to identify from one another. Identification relies on noting the presence (or absence), number, and color of stripes on their head and bars on their wings. The Chipping Sparrow (*Spizella passerina*) can be found throughout the state, breeding in pockets of the west, central, and East Texas. The Black-throated Sparrow (*Amphispiza bilineata*) is a common species in drier habitats of central, west, and South Texas. The Seaside Sparrow (*Ammodramus maritimus*) is restricted to coastal marshes on the coast. The White-collared Seedeater (*Sporophila torqueola*) is restricted to habitat along the Rio Grande from Val Verde to Starr counties. The ubiquitous House Sparrow* (*Passer domesticus*), distantly related to the New World sparrows, was intentionally released in Galveston in 1867 and spread throughout the state by 1905.

starling: The European Starling* (*Sturnus vulgaris*) was first introduced to North America in New York in 1890. It reached East Texas by 1925 and El Paso in 1939. This aggressive species will often take over cavities and nest boxes, often out-competing native species such as bluebirds and Purple Martins. A visually striking bird in its breeding plumage with a brilliant yellow bill and iridescent black feathers.

swallow: Nine species of small, swift fliers that feed on insects while in flight are found in Texas. The arrival of the first Purple Martin (*Progne subis*) is a harbinger of spring; fall migratory roosts can number in the hundreds of thousands. The Cliff Swallow (*Poetrochelidon pyrrhonota*) has a short, squared tail and builds mud nests in groups on cliffs or bridges. The Barn Swallow (*Hirundo rustica*) has a longer, forked tail and builds small mud nests under the eaves of buildings.

swift: With their long wings and slender bodies, swifts have been called "flying cigars." They are fast fliers, catching and feeding on insects in flight. The Chimney Swift (*Chaetura pelagica*) uses hollow trees and crevices for nesting sites, using saliva to glue together a nest of twigs on the inside of the structure. This species has gained its name because it can utilize man-made structures such as abandoned buildings, silos, and chimneys for nesting sites.

tern: Related to gulls, terns can be found along the coast and inland near lakes and marshes. Terns form large breeding colonies to provide protection in numbers, more experienced adults occupying the center of the colony. The Caspian Tern (*Hydroprogne caspia*) is the largest species in the world. The Royal Tern (*Thalasseus maximus*) and the Sandwich Tern (*Thalasseus sanvicensis*) are restricted to coastal habitats; the Forester's Tern (*Sterna forsteri*) is common along the coast and inland lakes.

thrush: Related to bluebirds and the robin, thrushes are medium-sized birds with melodious calls. Many species are secretive winter migrants, their inconspicuous brown coloration helping hide them in woody brush. The Hermit Thrush (*Catharus guttatus*) is a common winter visitor across the state, with a breeding population in the Davis Mountains. The Wood Thrush (*Hylocichla mustelina*) is a summer resident of East Texas.

titmouse: Titmice in Texas are conspicuous and talkative birds with a noticeable tuft or crest on their head. Often in mixed-species flocks with chickadees and small woodpeckers. The Tufted Titmouse (*Baeolophus bicolor*) is found in the eastern third of the state; the Black-crested Titmouse (*Baeolophus atricristatus*), with a prominent black patch on its crest, is found in the western two-thirds of the state.

turkey: The Wild Turkey (*Maleagris gallopavo*) has a patchwork distribution across Texas, commonly seen in the middle third of state, but in more isolated pockets in West and East Texas. Males use a conspicuous display to attract females: they will strut and gobble, while extending their wings, tail and body feathers. Turkeys often roost in trees at night.

vireo: see *flycatcher*

vulture: With their long wings, both species of vultures are experts at soaring, generally only flapping their wings when they take off from feeding or roosting. Featherless heads and curved bills are adaptations to feeding on carrion. The Black Vulture (*Coragyps atratus*) has a black head and white wingtips when viewed from below; the Turkey Vulture (*Cathartes aura*) has a red head and two-toned (black and white) wings from below: black on the leading edge, gray or white on the trailing edge. Turkey Vultures use both sight and smell to find food, Black Vultures rely more on sight.

warbler: Almost 50 species of warblers, more properly called "wood-warblers," are known from Texas. Many are migrants passing through, while others are breeding summer residents. Many bird watchers anxiously await the last two weeks of April for the peak of spring migration, when birds return from their winter locations in spectacular full breeding plumage. If birds flying from the Yucatan across the Gulf of Mexico encounter strong winds or storms, they will be exhausted from their non-stop flight and "fallout" once they finally reach land. The Golden-cheeked Warbler (*Setophaga chrysoparia*) breeds only in the steep, wooded canyons of central Texas. The population of Colima Warblers (*Oreothlypis crissalis*) found in the Chisos Mountains (Big Bend) is the only U.S. population. The Tropical Parula (*Setophaga pitiayumi*) is a large warbler found in South Texas. The Yellow-rumped Warbler (*Setophaga coronata*) is a common winter visitor to most of Texas.

Caspian Terns are the largest species of tern and can have a wingspan of up to 145 cm (57 in). Photo by Dick Daniels, CC by SA 3.0

waxwing: A conspicuous winter visitor, the Cedar Waxwing (*Bombycilla cedrorum*) moves around in large flocks feeding on berries and fruits. It has a black mask, head crest, and a row of feathers on the wings that are tipped with a bright red waxy substance.

woodpecker: Over a dozen species of woodpeckers occur in Texas, all with sharp, stout bills used to probe wood for insects or used to excavate cavities to nest. At 16" long, the Pileated Woodpecker (*Dryocopus pileatus*) is the largest species in Texas and is found in East Texas; at just under 7", the Downy Woodpecker (*Picoides pubescens*) is one of the smallest and is found across all but West and South Texas. The Acorn Woodpecker (*Melanerpes formicivorus*) is known for storing (and defending) large amounts of acorns wedged into small holes in dead limbs and trees.

wren: Wrens are small brown birds that can be quite vocal when advertising for mates or in defense of their nests. Many species have a white eye-stripe and often hold their tails up at an angle over their backs and are insectivorous. The Carolina Wren (*Thyrothorus ludovicianus*), House Wren (*Troglodytes aedon*), and the Bewick's Wren (*Thryomanes bewickii*) build nests in cavities, often close to human dwellings. The slowly cascading call of the Canyon Wren (*Catherpes mexicanus*) is often heard in rocky areas of West and central Texas.

*The American bison is the largest native land mammal in North America. Photo by **Jack Dykinga**, USDA, Public Domain*

Mammals

Mammals, with a few notable exceptions (the egg-laying monotremes: four species of echidna and the Platypus), are a large group of vertebrates with hair that give birth to live young. There are over 6,400 species worldwide (~1,200 genera), including species-rich groups like rodents, bats, and shrews.

A total of 145 species of native terrestrial mammals occur in Texas, a number exceeded in the United States only by California and New Mexico. Also, 28 species of marine mammals have been reported from the Texas coast or are expected to occur there. A single species of marsupial, the Virginia Opossum, is found in the state.

Mammals are found in every ecoregion across the state, with species diversity highest in the Trans-Pecos. Mammals occupy many different habitats, such as species that live almost entirely underground (moles and gophers), are primarily aquatic (American Beaver, Nutria, River Otter), or can fly (bats) or glide (Flying Squirrel).

Recreational hunting is an important economic activity for the state, with the breeding and hunting of deer impacting the Texas economy by over $1 billion each year. Game animals include White-tailed Deer, Mule Deer, Pronghorn, Javelina, and squirrels. There are also 18 exotics or non-native species that have been introduced by man either accidentally (e.g., Japanese Macaque, House Mouse, Black Rat, Norway Rat) or intentionally (e.g., Nutria, Red Fox, Feral Pig, Axis Deer, Fallow Deer, Sika Deer, Nilgai, Greater Kudu, Eastern Thomson's Gazelle, Sable Antelope, Scimitar-horned Oryx, Common Eland, Aoudad, Blackbuck) and have become established.

armadillo: The Nine-banded Armadillo (*Dasypus novemcinctus*) is one of Texas' most iconic mammals and is the state small mammal. It is found in most of the state except the western Trans-Pecos. It is now common as far north and east as Kansas and Mississippi.

badger: The American Badger (*Taxidea taxus*) is most common in parts of West and South Texas and is occasionally spotted in the eastern part of the state. It is a fierce fighter and is valuable in helping control the rodent population.

bat: Thirty-two species of these winged mammals have been found in Texas, more than in any other state in the United States. Of these, 27 species are known residents, though they are seldom seen by the casual observer. The Mexican Free-tailed Bat (*Tadarida brasiliensis*) and the Cave Myotis (*Myotis velifer*) constitute most of the cave-dwelling bats of central and West Texas. They have some economic value for their deposits of nitrogen-rich guano. Some commercial guano has been produced from Beaver Creek Cavern (Burnet County) and James River Bat Cave (Mason County), and from large deposits in other caves, including Bandera Bat Cave (Bandera County), Blowout Cave (Blanco County), and Devil's Sinkhole (Edwards County). The largest concentration of bats in the world is found at Bracken Cave in Comal County, which is thought to hold between 20 and 40 million bats. The Big Brown Bat (*Eptesicus fuscus*), the Eastern Red Bat (*Lasiurus borealis*), and the Evening Bat (*Nycticeius humeralis*) are found in East and southeast Texas. The Evening Bat and Big Brown Bat are forest and woodland dwelling mammals. The rarer species of Texas bats have been found along the Rio Grande and in the Trans-Pecos. Bats can be observed at dusk near a water source, and many species may also be found foraging on insects attracted to streetlights. Everywhere bats occur, they are the main predators of night-flying insects, including mosquitoes and many crop pests. The state flying mammal of Texas is the Mexican Free-tailed Bat.

bear: The American Black Bear (*Ursus americanus*), formerly common throughout most of the state, is now surviving in remnant populations in mountainous areas of the Trans-Pecos from Big Bend to Del Rio.

beaver: The American Beaver (*Castor canadensis*) is found over most of the state except for the Llano Estacado and parts of the Trans-Pecos.

bighorn: see *sheep*

bison: The largest of native terrestrial wild mammals of North America, the American Bison (*Bos bison*), commonly called buffalo, was formerly found in the western two-thirds of the state. Today, it is extirpated or confined on ranches. Deliberate slaughter of this majestic animal for hides and to eliminate the Plains Indians' main food source reached a peak about 1877–1878, and the American Bison was almost eradicated by 1885. Estimates of the number of buffalo killed vary, but as many as 200,000 hides were sold in Fort Worth at a single two-day sale. Except for the interest of the late Col. Charles Goodnight and a few other foresighted men, the American Bison might be extinct.

buffalo: see *bison*

cat: The Jaguar (*Felis onca*) is probably now extinct in Texas (last recorded in 1948 near Kingsville), along with the Jaguarundi (*Puma yagouaroundi*) and Margay (*Felis wiedii*). The Bobcat (*Lynx rufus*) is found throughout the state in large numbers. The Mountain Lion (*Felis concolor*), also known as the cougar or puma, was once found statewide and is now found in the mountainous areas of the Trans-Pecos and the dense Rio Grande brushland. The Ocelot (*Felis pardalis*) is now restricted to extreme South Texas. The last documented report of a Jaguarundi, was reported from Brownsville in 1986, although unverified reports continue to be described along the length of the Rio Grande. The Margay was last reported before 1852 near Eagle Pass.

chipmunk: The Gray-footed Chipmunk (*Tamias canipes*) is found at high altitudes in the Guadalupe and Sierra Diablo ranges of the Trans-Pecos. See also ground squirrel, with which the chipmunk is often confused in public reference.

coati: The White-nosed Coati (*Nasua narica*), a relative of the raccoon, historically ranged from Brownsville to the Big Bend, but today its distribution is mostly restricted to the Trans-Pecos and it is listed as a threatened species in the state. It inhabits woodland areas and feeds both on the ground and in trees. In Texas, the White-nosed Coati is most commonly seen in Big Bend National Park.

coyote: The Coyote (*Canis latrans*) exists in great numbers in Texas, including in and around urban areas. While a significant predator of Texas livestock, it is also a valuable predator in the balance of nature, providing a layer of protection to crops and rangelands by its control of rodents and rabbits. In terms of economic importance, it is second only to the raccoon in being the most important fur-bearing animal in the state.

deer: The White-tailed Deer (*Odocoileus virginianus*), found throughout the state in brushy or wooded areas, is the most important Texas game animal. Its numbers in Texas are estimated at more than 3 million. The Mule Deer (*Odocoileus heminous*) is found principally in the Trans-Pecos and Panhandle areas and has increased in number in recent years. In Texas, the only native species of Elk (*Cervus canadensis merriami*) was found in the southern Guadalupe Mountains and became extinct about the turn of the 20th century. A separate subspecies of Elk (*Cervus c. canadensis*) was introduced into the same area from South Dakota around 1928. There are currently several herds totaling several thousand individuals. Several exotic deer species have been introduced, mostly for hunting purposes. The Axis Deer* (*Axis axis*) is the most numerous of the exotics. Native to India, it is found mostly in central and South Texas, both free-ranging and confined on ranches. Blackbuck* (*Antilope cervicapra*), also native to India, is the second-most numerous exotic deer in the state and is found on ranches in 86 counties. Fallow Deer* (*Dama dama*), native to the Mediterranean, have been introduced to 93 counties, while the Nilgai* (*Boselaphus tragocamelus*), native of India and Pakistan, is found mostly in Kenedy, Willacy, and Cameron counties. The Sika Deer* (*Cervus nippon*), native of southern Siberia, Japan, and China, has been introduced in 77 counties in central and South Texas.

dolphin: The Atlantic Spotted Dolphin (*Stenella frontalis*) is rather small, long snouted, and spotted; it is purplish gray, appearing blackish at a distance, usually with numerous small white or gray spots on its sides and back. In the Gulf of Mexico, this dolphin is second in abundance only to the Common Bottlenose Dolphin. The Common Bottlenose Dolphin (*Tursiops truncatus*) is stout and short-beaked with sloping forehead, projecting lower jaw, and high dorsal fin. Other species, such as the Clymene Dolphin, Pantropical Spotted Dolphin, Risso's Dolphin, Rough-toothed Dolphin, Spinner Dolphin, and Striped Dolphin are unusual and known in Texas only through strandings along gulf beaches.

ferret: The Black-footed Ferret (*Mustela nigripes*) was formerly found widely ranging through the West Texas country where its main prey, the prairie dog, was formerly plentiful. Related to the mink and weasel, it is now considered extinct in Texas.

fox: The Common Gray Fox (*Urocyon cinereoargenteus*) is found throughout most of the state, primarily in the woods of East Texas, in broken parts of the Edwards Plateau, and in the rough country at the foot of the High Plains. The Swift Fox (*Vulpes velox*) is found in the western third of the state. A second species of Kit Fox (*Vulpes macrotis*) is found in the Trans-Pecos and is fairly numerous in some localities. The Red Fox* (*Vulpes vulpes*), which ranges across central Texas, was introduced for sport.

gopher: Eleven species of pocket gopher occur in Texas. The Botta's Pocket Gopher (*Thomomys bottae*) is found from the Trans-Pecos eastward across the Edwards Plateau. The Plains Pocket Gopher (*Geomys bursarius*) is found from Midland and Tom Green counties east and north to McLennan, Dallas, and Grayson counties. The Desert Pocket Gopher (*Geomys arenarius*) is found only in the Trans-Pecos, while the Yellow-faced Pocket Gopher (*Cratogeomys castanops*) is found in the western third of the state, with occasional sightings along the Rio Grande in Maverick and Cameron counties. The Texas Pocket Gopher (*Geomys personatus*) is found in South Texas from San Patricio County to Val Verde County. Attwater's Pocket Gopher (*Geomys attwateri*) and Baird's Pocket Gopher (*Geomys breviceps*) are both found generally in south-central and coastal Texas from the Brazos River to the San Antonio River and south to Matagorda and San Patricio counties. Jones' Pocket Gopher (*Geomys knoxjonesi*) is found only in far West Texas, while the Llano Pocket Gopher (*Geomys texensis*) is found only in two isolated areas of the Hill Country. Hall's Pocket Gopher (*Geomys jugossicularis*) is restricted to Dallam and Hartley counties in the far northwest Panhandle and Strecker's Pocket Gopher (*Geomys streckeri*) is found only in Dimmit and Zavala counties in South Texas.

ground squirrel: Five species of ground squirrel live in Texas, mostly in the western part of the state. The Rock Squirrel (*Otopermophilus variegatus*) is found throughout the Edwards Plateau and Trans-Pecos. The Rio Grande Ground Squirrel (*Ictidomys parvidens*) occurs throughout much of South Texas, the Trans-Pecos, and almost to the Red River just East of the Panhandle. The Spotted Ground Squirrel (*Xermospermophilus spilosoma*) is found generally in the western half of the state. The Thirteen-lined Ground Squirrel (*Ictidomys tridecemlineatus*) is found in a narrow strip from Dallas and Tarrant counties to the gulf. The Texas Antelope Squirrel (*Ammospermophilus interpres*) is found along the Rio Grande from El Paso to Val Verde County.

Nutria, though not native to Texas, have been increasing their range in the state. Photo by Gzen92, CC by SA 4.0

hog: Feral Hogs (*Sus scrofa*) are found in almost every county in Texas but especially in areas of the Rio Grande and Coastal Plains, as well as in the woods of East Texas. They are descendants of escaped domestic hogs or of European wild hogs that were imported for sport. Their rooting habits can extensively destroy vegetation and soil and their ever-expanding populations threaten many native mammal populations through competition and disease.

javelina: The Javelina or Collared Peccary (*Pecari tajacu*) is found in brushy semidesert areas where Prickly Pear, a favorite food, is found. The Javelina was hunted commercially for its hide until 1939. They are harmless to livestock and to people, though they can defend themselves ferociously when attacked by hunting dogs.

mink: The American Mink (*Vison vison*) is found in the eastern half of the state, always near streams, lakes, or other water sources. Although it is an economically important fur-bearing animal in the eastern United States, it ranked only 13th in both numbers and economic value to trappers in Texas in 2001–2002 trapping season.

mole: The Eastern Mole (*Scalopus aquaticus*) is found in the eastern two-thirds of Texas. Moles cannot see and spend most of their life in underground burrows they excavate for themselves or usurp from other mammals, such as pocket gophers. The burrowing of moles can damage lawns, row crops, and the greens of golf courses. Benefits, however, are aerating soil and eating larval insects that destroy roots of grass and crops.

muskrat: The Common Muskrat (*Ondatra zibethicus*) occurs in aquatic habitats in the northern and southeastern parts of the state as well as along the Pecos River in West Texas. Although the muskrat was once economically valuable for its fur, its numbers have declined, mostly because of the loss of habitat.

nutria: The Nutria* (*Myocastor coypus*) is an introduced species of rodent originally native to South America. It is found primarily in the eastern two-thirds of the state, but they have expanded their range into the Big Bend region. The fur is not highly valued and, because Nutrias are in competition with muskrats, their spread is discouraged. They have been used widely in Texas as a cure-all for ponds choked with vegetation, with spotty results.

opossum: A marsupial, the Virginia Opossum (*Didelphis virginiana*) is found in nearly all parts of the state. The opossum has economic value for its pelt, and its meat is considered a delicacy by some.

otter: Northern River Otters (*Lontra canadensis*) are found in the eastern third of the state. This species has probably been extirpated from the Panhandle and some north-central locations but over the past 20 years, it has been expanding its range back into remaining suitable habitat in East and South Texas.

peccary: see *javelina*

pig: see *hog*

porcupine: The North American Porcupine (*Erethizon dorsatum*) is found from the western half of the state east to Bosque County. It is adapted to a variety of habitats and, in recent years, has expanded into South Texas. Porcupines are expert at climbing trees but are as much at home in rocks as on the ground or in trees. They have a relatively long lifespan; one marked female lived more than 10 years under natural conditions.

prairie dog: Until recent years, probably no sight was so universal in West Texas as the Black-tailed Prairie Dog (*Cynomys ludovicianus*). Naturalists estimated its population in the hundreds of millions, and prairie dog towns often covered many acres with thickly spaced burrows. However, this species has been replaced by livestock and cultivated crops across most of its range, a loss of over 98% of the original population in the state. It is being propagated in several public zoos, notably in the prairie dog town in Mackenzie Park at Lubbock. It has been honored in Texas by the naming of the Prairie Dog Town Fork of the Red River, in one segment of which is located the beautiful Palo Duro Canyon.

pronghorn: The Pronghorn (*Antilocapra americana*) formerly was found in the western two-thirds of the state. It is currently found only in limited areas from the Panhandle to the Trans-Pecos. Despite management efforts, its numbers have been decreasing in recent years.

rabbit: The Black-tailed Jackrabbit (*Lepus californicus*) is found throughout Texas except the Big Thicket area of East Texas. It breeds rapidly, and its long hind legs make it one of the world's faster-running animals. The Eastern Cottontail (*Sylvilagus floridanus*) is found mostly in the eastern three-quarters of the state. The Desert Cottontail (*Sylvilagus audubonii*) is found in the western half of the state, usually on the open range. The Swamp Rabbit (*Sylvilagus aquaticus*) is found in East Texas and the coastal area. The Davis Mountains Cottontail (*Sylvilagus robustus*) is restricted to Jeff Davis County.

raccoon: The Northern Raccoon (*Procyon lotor*) is found throughout Texas, especially in woodlands and near water. It is strictly nocturnal. A raccoon makes its den in a large hollow tree or hollow log, in which it spends the daylight hours sleeping and in which it also rears its young. In western areas, dens usually are in crevices of rocky bluffs.

rats, mice, and voles: There are 40 to 50 species of rats, mice, and voles in Texas of varying characteristics, habitats, and economic destructiveness. The Norway Rat* (*Rattus norvegicus*) and the Roof Rat* (*Rattus rattus*), both non-native species, are probably the most common and most destructive. They also are instrumental in the transmission of several dread diseases, including bubonic plague and typhus. Populations of the Common House Mouse* (*Mus musculus*) are estimated in the hundreds of millions annually. The Mogollon Vole (*Microtus mogolollonensis*) is found only in the higher elevations of Guadalupe Mountains National Park. With its long tail tipped with a white tuft of fur, the state-threatened Texas Kangaroo Rat (*Dipodomys elator*) is restricted to less than a dozen Texas counties near the Red River.

ringtail: The Ringtail (*Bassariscus astutus*) is a cat-sized carnivore resembling a small fox with a long raccoon-like tail. It found statewide but is rare in the extreme South Texas and the Panhandle. Ringtails are nocturnal and live in a variety of habitats, preferring rocky areas, such as rock piles, stone fences, and canyon walls.

sheep: The Mountain or Bighorn Sheep (*Ovis canadensis*), formerly was found in isolated areas of the mountainous Trans-Pecos, but the last native sheep were seen in 1959. Recently, they have been introduced into the same areas with success. The Barbary Sheep* (*Ammotragus lervia*), also called Aoudad, were first introduced to the Palo Duro Canyon area in 1957–1958 and have become firmly established. A multi-partner wildlife restoration project has brought the Bighorn Sheep into the Edwards Plateau, Trans-Pecos, South Texas, Rolling Plains, and Post Oak Savannah regions, including Big Bend Ranch State Park.

shrew: The shrew is one of the smallest mammals. Four species are found in Texas: the Southern Short-tailed Shrew (*Blarina carolinensis*), found in the eastern fourth of the state; the Least Shrew (*Cryptotis parva*), in all but western areas; Elliot's Short-tailed Shrew (*Blarina hylophaga*), known to live in Aransas, Montague, and Bastrop counties; and the Desert Shrew (*Notiosorex crawfordi*), found in the western two-thirds of the state.

A Black-tailed Jackrabbit. Photo by Jim Harper, CC SA 2.5

skunk: There are five species of skunk in Texas. The Eastern Spotted Skunk (*Spilogale putorius*) is found in the eastern half of the state, the Gulf Coast, and across north-central Texas to the Panhandle. A small skunk, it is often erroneously called civet cat. The Western Spotted Skunk (*Spilogale gracilis*) is found in the southwestern part of the state North to Garza and Howard counties and East to Bexar and Duval counties. The Striped Skunk (*Mephitis mephitis*) is found statewide, mostly in brush or wooded areas. The Hooded Skunk (*Mephitis macroura*) was found in limited numbers in the Big Bend and adjacent parts of the Trans-Pecos but may be extirpated from the state. The Hog-nosed Skunk (*Conepatus leuconotus*) is found in across the western, central, and southern portion of the state, as well as the upper Gulf Coast.

squirrel: The Eastern Fox Squirrel (*Sciurus niger*) is found in the eastern two-thirds of the state. The Eastern Gray Squirrel (*Sciurus carolinensis*) is found generally in the eastern third of the state. The Southern Flying Squirrel (*Glaucomys volans*) is found in wooded areas of East Texas. The fox and gray squirrels are important small game animals. See also ground squirrel.

weasel: The Long-tailed Weasel (*Mustela frenata*), akin to the mink, is found statewide but is scarce in West Texas and the far North Panhandle. In general, their predation on mice, ground squirrels, and pocket gophers benefits agricultural interests, though they are known to enter poultry houses and kill chickens.

whale: Some species that are found in the Gulf of Mexico include: Dwarf Sperm Whale (*Kogia sima*); Pygmy Sperm Whale (*Kogia breviceps*), found near the Texas coast where strandings occur relatively frequently; Short-finned Pilot Whale (*Globicephala macrorhynchus*), common in the gulf, where there are numerous strandings and sightings; Sperm Whale (*Physeter macrocephalus*), an endangered species and the most numerous and frequently sighted of the great whales in the gulf. Other species are known in Texas only through strandings on gulf beaches.

wolf: The Red Wolf (*Canis rufus*) was once found throughout the eastern half of the state. It has now been extirpated from the wild, with the only known remnants of the population now in captive propagation. The Gray Wolf (*Canis lupus*) once had a wide range over the western two-thirds of the state. It is now considered extinct in Texas. Both species of wolf are on the federal and state endangered species lists. ☆

Texas' Threatened and Endangered Species

Endangered species are those the TPWD has named as being at risk of statewide extinction. Threatened species are likely to become endangered in the future. The following lists include species that are listed by TPWD as either threatened or endangered as of March 2023 (the most recent list available). The species on these lists vary from those on the federal list of threatened and endangered species managed by the United States Fish and Wildlife Service. Learn more and see the TPWD Conservation Action Plan at: https://tpwd.texas.gov/landwater/land/tcap/.

Threats and Successes

The distribution and abundance of Texas wildlife have changed dramatically over the last 100 years. While a few native species have increased their numbers and expanded their ranges during this period (e.g., White-tailed Deer, Coyote, White-winged Dove), these species are the exceptions. Many species have declined and face continued threats across their shrinking distributions in Texas.

In general, these threats are not focused on individual species, but are widespread risks to ecoregions as a whole, impacting both plant and animal communities. Habitat loss is the primary threat and can include land lost to urbanization and agriculture. The development of land for resource extraction activities contributes to habitat loss and fragmentation. Some technologies, such as wind turbines, have led to the direct mortality of some groups of animals (e.g., birds and bats).

The loss of riparian habitats is often linked to the reallocation or reprioritization of water resources. The suppression of wildfire across many habitats has removed the natural cycle of vegetative change important for maintaining species diversity. Modifications to rainfall patterns and temperatures due to climate change affect the distribution of plant and animal communities as well as the timing of processes and behaviors (e.g., dates for plants to flower and birds to begin migration).

The introduction of invasive grasses (e.g., King Ranch Bluestem, Bufflegrass), aquatic plants (e.g., Hydrilla, Giant Reed), trees (e.g., Chinaberry, Tamarisk), and animals (e.g., Red Imported Fire Ant, Zebra Mussel) has allowed non-native species to outcompete and replace populations of native species across the state. Historical instances of overhunting led to the demise of native Bighorn Sheep, Bison, and Elk; predator control efforts removed the Jaguar and Gray Wolf from the state as well.

All hope is not lost; success stories do exist. Focused conservation efforts have removed species such as the Black-capped Vireo, Concho Watersnake, and American Alligator from the Federal Threatened and Endangered Species List. However, many species still require thoughtful and intensive management plans at local, state, and federal levels to help them remain a part of our state's natural heritage.

To learn more about threats to Texas wildlife and what steps you can do to help conserve native species and their habitats, visit the websites of Texas Parks and Wildlife Department (tpwd.texas.gov), U.S. Fish and Wildlife Service (fws.gov/offices), Natural Resources Conservation Service (nrcs.usda.gov), the Texas Master Naturalist Program (txmn.tamu.edu), private conservation groups like The Nature Conservancy (nature.org/texas), Texas Conservation Alliance (tcatexas.org), and Texas Land Conservancy (texaslandconservancy.org), and species- or location-specific conservation groups, like Audubon Texas (tx.audubon.org) and the Coastal Bend Bays & Estuaries Program (cbbep.org). ☆

Threatened Species

Plants: Cacti: Bunched Cory Cactus, Chisos Mountains Hedgehog Cactus, Lloyd's Mariposa Cactus; **Grasses:** Dune Umbrella-sedge, Small-headed Pipewort; **Trees, Shrubs, Sub-shrubs:** Gypsum Scalebroom, Hinckley's Oak; **Quillworts:** Rock Quillwort; **Wildflowers:** Brush-pea, Earth Fruit, Houston Daisy, Leoncita False Foxglove, Livermore Sweet-cicely, Neches River Rose-mallow, Pecos Sunflower

Invertebrates: Bivalves: Brazos Heelsplitter, False Spike, Guadalupe Fatmucket, Guadalupe Orb, Louisiana Pigtoe, Mexican Fawnsfoot, Salina Mucket, Sandbank Pocketbook, Southern Hickorynut, Texas Fatmucket, Texas Fawnsfoot, Texas Heelsplitter, Texas Pigtoe, Texas Pimpleback, Trinity Pigtoe; **Crustaceans:** Clear Creek Amphipod, Texas Troglobitic Water Slater; **Snails:** Carolinae Tryonia, Caroline's Springs Pyrg, Crowned Cave Snail, Limpia Creek Springsnail, Metcalf's Tryonia, Presidio County Springsnail

Fishes: Catfish: Headwater Catfish, Toothless Blindcat, Widemouth Blindcat; **Coastal Fishes:** Mexican Goby, River Goby; **Large River Fish:** Paddlefish, Shovelnose Sturgeon; **Livebearers:** Blotched Gambusia, Spotfin Gambusia; **Minnows:** Arkansas River Shiner, Bluehead Shiner, Chihuahua Shiner, Chub Shiner, Devils River Minnow, Frio Roundnose Minnow, Medina Roundnose Minnow, Mexican Stoneroller, Nueces Roundnose Minnow, Peppered Chub, Plateau Shiner, Prairie Chub, Proserpine Shiner, Rio Grande Chub, Rio Grande Shiner, Roundnose Minnow, Speckled Chub, Tamaulipas Shiner; **Perches:** Blackside Darter, Guadalupe Darter, Rio Grande Darter; **Pupfish:** Conchos Pupfish, Pecos Pupfish, Red River Pupfish; **Sharks:** Great Hammerhead, Oceanic Whitetip, Shortfin Mako; **Suckers:** Blue Sucker, Western Creek Chubsucker

Amphibians: Black-Spotted Newt, Blanco Blind Salamander, Cascade Caverns Salamander, Georgetown Salamander, Jollyville Plateau Salamander, Mexican Burrowing Toad, Mexican Treefrog, Salado Springs Salamander, San Marcos Salamander, Sheep Frog, South Texas Siren (*Large Form*), Texas Salamander, White-Lipped Frog

Reptiles: Lizards: Mountain Short-Horned Lizard, Texas Horned Lizard; **Snakes:** Black-Striped Snake, Brazos Watersnake, Louisiana Pine Snake, Northern Cat-Eyed Snake, Northern Scarlet Snake, Speckled Racer, Texas Scarlet Snake, Trans-Pecos Black-Headed Snake; **Turtles:** Alligator Snapping Turtle, Cagle's Map Turtle, Chihuahuan Mud Turtle, Green Sea Turtle, Loggerhead Sea Turtle, Texas Tortoise

Birds: Parrots: Red-Crowned Parrot; **Raptors:** American Peregrine Falcon, Cactus Ferruginous Pygmy-Owl, Common Black Hawk, Gray Hawk, Mexican Spotted Owl, Peregrine Falcon, Swallow-Tailed Kite, White-Tailed Hawk, Zone-Tailed Hawk; **Shorebirds:** Black Rail, Piping Plover, Rufa Red Knot, Sooty Tern; **Songbirds:** Arizona Botteri's Sparrow, Bachman's Sparrow, Northern Beardless-Tyrannulet, Rose-Throated Becard, Texas Botteri's Sparrow, Tropical Parula; **Waterbirds:** Reddish Egret, White-Faced Ibis, Wood Stork

Mammals: Bats: Rafinesque's Big-Eared Bat, Spotted Bat; **Carnivores:** American Black Bear, Louisiana Black Bear, White-Nosed Coati; **Marine Mammals:** Atlantic Spotted Dolphin, Dwarf Sperm Whale, False Killer Whale, Gervais' Beaked Whale, Goose-beaked Whale, Killer Whale, Pygmy Killer Whale, Pygmy Sperm Whale, Rough-toothed Dolphin, Short-finned Pilot Whale, West Indian Manatee; **Rodents:** Coues' Rice Rat, Palo Duro Mouse, Tawny-bellied Cotton Rat, Texas Kangaroo Rat

Endangered Species

Plants: Cacti: Black Lace Cactus, Davis' Green Pitaya, Nellie's Cory Cactus, Sneed's Pincushion Cactus, Star Cactus, Tobusch Fishhook Cactus; **Grasses:** Guadalupe Fescue, Little Aguja Pondweed, Texas Wild Rice; **Orchids:** Navasota Ladies'-tresses; **Trees, Shrubs, Sub-shrubs:** Texas Ayenia, Texas Snowbells, Walker's Manioc; **Wildflowers:** Ashy Dogweed, Large-fruited Sand-verbena, Slender Rushpea, South Texas Ambrosia, Terlingua Creek Cat's-eye, Texas Golden Gladecress, Texas Poppy-mallow, Texas Prairie Dawn, Texas Trailing Phlox, White Bladderpod, Zapata Bladderpod

Invertebrates: Beetles: Comal Springs Dryopid Beetle, Comal Springs Riffle Beetle; **Bivalves:** Texas Hornshell; **Crustaceans:** Diminutive Amphipod, Peck's Cave Amphipod, Pecos Amphipod; **Snails:** Diamond Y Springsnail, Gonzales Tryonia, Pecos Assiminea Snail, Phantom Springsnail, Phantom Tryonia

Fishes: Catfish: Mexican Blindcat; **Coastal Fishes:** Smalltooth Sawfish; **Livebearers:** Big Bend Gambusia, Clear Creek Gambusia, Pecos Gambusia, San Marcos Gambusia; **Minnows:** Rio Grande Silvery Minnow, Sharpnose Shiner, Smalleye Shiner; **Perches:** Fountain Darter; **Pupfish:** Comanche Springs Pupfish, Leon Springs Pupfish

Amphibians: Austin Blind Salamander, Barton Springs Salamander, Houston Toad, Texas Blind Salamander

Reptiles: Turtles: Hawksbill Sea Turtle, Kemp's Ridley Sea Turtle, Leatherback Sea Turtle

Birds: Raptors: Northern Aplomado Falcon; **Shorebirds:** Eskimo Curlew; **Songbirds:** Golden-Cheeked Warbler, Southwestern Willow Flycatcher; **Upland Birds:** Attwater's Greater Prairie Chicken; **Waterbirds:** Whooping Crane; **Woodpeckers:** Red-Cockaded Woodpecker

Mammals: Bats: Mexican Long-nosed Bat; **Carnivores:** Jaguar, Jaguarundi, Ocelot, Gray Wolf, Red Wolf; **Marine Mammals:** Blue Whale, Finback Whale, Gulf of Mexico Bryde's Whale, North Atlantic Right Whale, Sei Whale, Sperm Whale ☆

Photos, top to bottom:

Red-Cockaded Woodpecker eating a bug. Photo by U.S. Fish and Wildlife Service Southwest, CC by 2.0

Kemp's Ridley Sea Turtle nesting in the sand. Photo by the National Park Service, Public Domain

Texas Hornshell mussels. Photo by Joel Deluxe, CC by 2.0

Texas Wildlife Management Areas

Source: Texas Parks and Wildlife Department; https://tpwd.texas.gov/huntwild/hunt/wma/

Texas Parks and Wildlife Department is responsible for managing 54 wildlife management areas (WMAs) in the state totaling more than 748,000 acres. Every vegetational area in the state has at least one WMA. (See page 68 for more information about the plant life found in Texas.)

Wildlife management areas are used principally for hunting, but many are also used for research, fishing, wildlife viewing, hiking, camping, bicycling, and horseback riding, when those activities are compatible with the primary goals for which the WMA was established. See the table below for activities available in Texas' WMAs.

Although most WMAs are open year-round, public use access is provided through various permits, depending on the activity. A Limited Public Use Permit ($12) allows access for such activities as birdwatching, hiking, camping, or picnicking.

Call ahead before visiting any WMA to check current conditions, facilities (most do not have public restrooms or drinking water), and possible closures. Learn more about hunting at WMAs on page 176 in the Recreation chapter

For further information, contact the Texas Parks and Wildlife Department, 4200 Smith School Rd., Austin 78744; or call 1-800-792-1112 and choose menu #5, selection #1. ☆

Texas Wildlife Management Areas

Name (Acreage)	County	Hunting	Fishing	Camping	Wildlife Viewing	Hiking	Driving	Bicycling	Equestrian	Comments
Alabama Creek (14,561)	Trinity	★	★	★	★	★	★	★	★	In Davy Crockett NF
Alazan Bayou (2,063)	Nacogdoches	★	★	★	★				★	Near Angelina R
Angelina-Neches/Dam B (12,636)	Jasper/Tyler	★	★	★	★	★		★		Part of B.A. Steinhagen Res.
Atkinson Island (150)	Harris		★		★					Boat access only
Bannister (25,695)	San Augustine	★	★	★	★	★		★	★	In Angelina NF
Big Lake Bottom (3,894)	Anderson	★	★		★					Registration required
Black Gap (103,000)	Brewster	★	★	★	★	★	★	★	★	NW of Big Bend NP
Caddo Lake (8,124)	Marion/Harrison	★	★	★	★				★	Seasonal flooding
Caddo Nat. Grasslands (16,140)	Fannin	★	★	★	★	★		★	★	Separated into two units
Candy Cain Abshier (207)	Chambers				★					Excellent birding spring and fall
Cedar Creek Islands (160)	Henderson		★		★					Wildlife viewing from boat or bank of reservoir only
Chaparral (15,200)	La Salle/Dimmit	★		★	★	★	★	★		Wheelchair accessible trail
Cooper (14,480)	Delta/Hopkins	★	★		★	★		★		Camping: Cooper Lake SP
D.R. Wintermann (246)	Wharton				★					Limited access; bird refuge
East Texas Conservation Center (223)	Jasper									By appointment only
Elephant Mountain (23,147)	Brewster	★		★	★	★	★			Desert bighorn herd
Gene Howe (5,394)	Hemphill	★	★	★	★	★		★	★	Riding March–August only
Gene Howe: W.A. "Pat" Murphy (889)	Hemphill	★	★		★	★				Walk-in access only
Guadalupe Delta (7,411)	Calhoun/Refugio	★	★		★	★		★		Separated into four units
Gus Engeling (10,958)	Anderson	★	★	★	★	★	★	★	★	Drawn hunts in fall and winter
J.D. Murphree (25,852)	Jefferson	★	★		★					Shallow boat recommended
James E. Daughtrey (34,000)	Live Oak/McMullen	★			★					Primitive camping requires special permit
Justin Hurst (15,612)	Brazoria	★	★		★	★		★		On Texas Coastal Birding Trail
Keechi Creek (1,500)	Leon	★								Limited access
Kerr (6,493)	Kerr	★	★		★		★	★		On Guadalupe River
Las Palomas: Anacua (222)	Cameron	★			★					Dove hunting
Las Palomas: Lower Rio Grande Valley (3,311)	Cameron/Hidalgo	★			★	★				Also Presidio County
Lower Neches (7,998)	Orange	★	★		★	★				Coastal marsh
M.O. Neasloney (100)	Gonzales				★	★				Primarily for school groups
Mad Island (7,200)	Matagorda	★			★					Reservations needed for wildlife tours
Mason Mountain (5,300)	Mason	★								Restricted access
Matador (28,183)	Cottle	★	★	★	★	★	★		★	Primitive camping; tours
Matagorda Island (56,688)	Calhoun	★	★	★	★	★		★		1852 lighthouse on N of island
McGillivray & Leona McKie Muse (1,973)	Brown	★								Drawn hunts only
Moore Plantation (26,772)	Sabine/Jasper	★	★	★	★	★		★	★	In Sabine National Forest
Nannie M. Stringfellow (3,666)	Brazoria	★			★					Open for special hunts only
Nature Center (82)	Smith				★	★				Weekday use (8 am–5 pm)

National Wildlife Refuges in Texas

Source: U.S. Fish and Wildlife Service, U.S. Department of the Interior

Texas has more than 470,000 acres in 18 national wildlife refuges that are open to the public. Their descriptions, with date of acquisition in parentheses, follow.

Included in this acreage are two conservation easement refuges, which may be visited at different times of the year for bird watching and wildlife viewing, as well as hunting and fishing. Write or call before visiting to check on facilities and days and hours of operation. On the web: https://www.fws.gov/program/national-wildlife-refuge-system.

Anahuac (1963): The more than 37,000 acres of this refuge are located along the upper Gulf Coast in Chambers County. Fresh and saltwater marshes and miles of beautiful, sweeping coastal prairie provide wintering habitat for large flocks of waterfowl, including geese, 27 species of ducks, and six species of rails. Roseate spoonbills, great and snowy egrets, and white-faced ibis are among the other birds frequenting the refuge. Other species include alligator, muskrat, and bobcat. Fishing, bird watching, auto tours, and hunting are available. Office: Box 278, Anahuac 77514; (409) 267-3337.

Aransas (1937): This refuge complex comprises 115,000 acres including Blackjack Peninsula, Matagorda Island, and three satellite units in Aransas and Refugio counties. Besides providing wintering grounds for the largest wild flock of endangered whooping cranes, the refuge is home to more than 390 species of waterfowl and other migratory birds. Refuge Tour Loop is open daily, sunrise to sunset. Claude F. Lard Visitor Center is open daily, 6:45 a.m. to 7:30 p.m. Other facilities include a 40-foot observation tower and walking trails. Office: Box 100, Austwell 77950; (361) 349-1181.

Attwater Prairie Chicken (1972): Established in Colorado County to preserve habitat for the endangered Attwater's prairie chicken (a ground-dwelling grouse), the refuge comprises 10,528 acres of native tallgrass prairie, sandy knolls, and wooded areas. A 5-mile auto tour loop is available year-round. There are two hiking trails — the Sycamore and the Pipit trails — that traverse the prairie, potholes, and riparian areas. The auto tour loop can also serve as a hiking trail. Refuge open sunrise to sunset. Office: Box 519, Eagle Lake 77434; (979) 234-3021.

Balcones Canyonlands (1992): This 25,000-acre refuge is located in Burnet, Travis, and Williamson counties northwest of Austin. It was established to protect the nesting habitat of two endangered birds: black-capped vireo and golden-cheeked warbler. The Shin Oak Observation Deck is open almost year around (excluding a few weekends in the fall). Hunting available. Open Monday–Friday, 8:00 a.m.–4:30 p.m. Office: 24518 FM-1431, Marble Falls 78654; (512) 339-9432.

Big Boggy (1983): This refuge occupies 5,000 acres of coastal prairie and salt marsh along East Matagorda Bay for the benefit of wintering waterfowl. The refuge is only open to waterfowl hunting in season. Office: 6801 County Road 306, Brazoria, 77422; (979) 964-4011.

Brazoria (1966): The 43,388 acres of this refuge, located along the Gulf Coast in Brazoria County, serve as haven for wintering waterfowl and a wide variety of other migratory birds. The refuge also supports many marsh and water birds, from roseate spoonbills and great blue herons to white-faced ibis and sandhill cranes. Brazoria Refuge is within the Freeport

Texas Wildlife Management Areas

Name (Acreage)	County	Hunting	Fishing	Camping	Wildlife Viewing	Hiking	Driving	Bicycling	Equestrian	Comments
North Toledo Bend (3,650)	Shelby	★	★	★	★	★			★	On Toledo Bend Res.
Old Sabine Bottom (5,158)	Smith	★	★	★	★	★		★	★	Camping at Tyler SP
Pat Mayse (8,925)	Lamar	★	★	★	★	★			★	Remediation ongoing
Playa Lakes: Armstrong (160)	Castro				★					Visitors must stay on the roads
Playa Lakes: Dimmitt (422)	Cottle	★								Limited access
Playa Lakes: Taylor Lakes (530)	Donley	★			★	★				Wheelchair accessible blind
Powderhorn (15,069)	Calhoun	★			★					Birding tours in Spring
Redhead Pond (37)	Nueces				★					Freshwater wetland; part of Great Texas Birding Trail
Richland Creek (13,783)	Freestone/Navarro	★	★	★	★	★		★	★	Call ahead before visiting
Roger R. Fawcett (5,459)	Palo Pinto	★	★							Restricted access
Sam Houston National Forest (161,508)	San Jacinto/Walker	★	★	★	★	★	★	★	★	Also Montgomery County
Sierra Diablo (11,624)	Hudspeth/ Culberson	★								Restricted access
Tawakoni (2,335)	Hunt/Van Zandt	★	★	★	★	★			★	Separated into three units
Tony Houseman/Blue Elbow Swamp (3,985)	Orange	★	★	★	★	★				Canoeing
Welder Flats (1,480)	Calhoun		★		★					Boat access only
White Oak Creek (25,777)	Bowie/Cass/Morris/ Titus	★	★		★	★			★	Camp in Atlanta and Daingerfield SPs
Yoakum Dunes (14,037)	Cochran/Terry/ Yoakum	*In development, not yet open to the public. Commissioned and authorized in 2014, this site will preserve the breeding and nesting habitats of the lesser prairie-chicken, as well as many other native wildlife, including quail, mule deer, and Texas horned lizards.*								

Christmas Bird Count circle, which frequently achieves the highest number of species seen in a 24-hour period. Open daily sunrise to sunset. Hunting and fishing also available. Office: 24907 FM 2004, Angleton, 77515; (979) 922-1037.

Buffalo Lake (1958): Comprising 7,664 acres in the Central Flyway in Randall County in the Panhandle, this refuge contains some of the best remaining shortgrass prairie in the United States. Buffalo Lake is now dry; a marsh area is artificially maintained for the numerous birds, reptiles, and mammals. Available activities include picnicking, auto tour, birding, photography, and hiking. Office: Box 179, Umbarger 79091; (806) 499-3382.

Caddo Lake (2000): Established on portions of the 8,5000-acre Longhorn Army Ammunition Plant in Harrison County, this refuge contains a mature flooded bald cypress forest, with some trees nearly 400 years old. The wetlands support a diverse plant community. The bottomland hardwood forest ecosystem provides essential habitat for migratory and resident wildlife. The wetlands of Caddo Lake are important to migratory birds within the Central Flyway. The area supports one of the highest breeding populations of wood ducks and prothonotary warblers. Bird watching, hunting, equestrian use, auto tour, hiking, and biking are available. Office: (903) 679-9144.

Hagerman (1946): Hagerman National Wildlife Refuge lies on the Big Mineral arm of Lake Texoma in Grayson County. The 4,500 acres of marsh and water and 6,900 acres of upland and farmland provide a feeding and resting place for migrating waterfowl. Bird watching, fishing, and hunting are available. Office: 6465 Refuge Road, Sherman, 75092-5817; (903) 786-2826.

Laguna Atascosa: (1946): This refuge is the southernmost waterfowl refuge in the Central Flyway and contains more than 45,000 acres fronting on the Laguna Madre in the Lower Rio Grande Valley in Cameron and Willacy counties. Open lagoons, coastal prairies, salt flats, and brushlands support a wide diversity of wildlife. The United States' largest concentration of redhead ducks winters here, along with many other species of waterfowl and shorebirds. White-tailed deer, javelina, and armadillo can be found, along with endangered ocelot. Bird watching and nature study are popular; auto-tour roads and nature trails are available. Camping and fishing are permitted within Adolph Thomae Jr. County Park. Hunting also available. Office: 22817 Ocelot Road, Los Fresnos, 78566; (956) 748-3607.

Lower Rio Grande Valley (1979): Part of the 180,000 acre South Texas Refuge Complex, this refuge lies within Cameron, Hidalgo, Starr, and Willacy counties. It comprises more than 100 separate tracts of land, some fallow farm fields connecting healthy habitat that can become travel corridors for wildlife. The refuge includes 11 different habitat types, including sabal palm forest, tidal flats, coastal brushland, mid-delta thorn forest, woodland potholes and basins, upland thorn scrub, flood forest, barretal, riparian woodland, and Chihuahuan thorn forest. Nearly 500 species of birds and over 300 butterfly species have been found there, as well as four of the five cats that occur within the United States: jaguarundi, ocelot, bobcat, and mountain lion. Seasonal hunting and canoe tours are available. Office: 3325 Green Jay Road, Alamo, 78516; (956) 784-7500.

McFaddin (1980): This refuge's 55,000 acres in Jefferson and Chambers counties are of great importance to wintering populations of migratory waterfowl. One of the densest populations of alligators in Texas is found here. Activities on the refuge include wildlife observation, hunting, fishing, and crabbing. Seven boat ramps provide access to inland lakes and waterways; limited roadways. Open daily from sunrise until sunset. Office: Box 358, Sabine Pass, 77655; (409) 971-2909.

Muleshoe (1935): Oldest of the national refuges in Texas, Muleshoe provides winter habitat for waterfowl and the continent's largest wintering population of sandhill cranes. Comprising 5,809 acres in the High Plains of Bailey County, the refuge contains playa lakes, marsh areas, caliche outcroppings, and native grasslands. A nature trail, campground, and picnic area are available. Office: Box 549, Muleshoe 79347; (806) 946-3341.

Neches River (2013): Anderson and Cherokee counties.It was established to protect wintering and nesting habitat for migratory birds of the Central Flyway and the bottomland hardwoods for their diverse biological value. Office: 262 West Highway 79, Jacksonville 75766; (956) 245-9426.

San Bernard (1968): Located in Brazoria and Matagorda counties on the Gulf Coast near Freeport, this refuge's 27,414 acres attract migrating waterfowl, including thousands of white-fronted and Canada geese and several duck species, which spend the winter on the refuge. Habitats, consisting of coastal prairies, salt-mud flats, and saltwater and freshwater ponds and potholes, also attract yellow rails, roseate spoonbills, reddish egrets, and American bitterns. Visitors enjoy auto and hiking trails, photography, bird watching, fishing, and waterfowl hunting in season. Office: 6801 County Road 306, Brazoria, 77422; (979) 964-4011.

Santa Ana (1943): Santa Ana is located on the north bank of the Rio Grande in Hidalgo County. Santa Ana's 2,088 acres of subtropical forest and native brushland are at an ecological crossroads of subtropical, Gulf Coast, Great Plains, and Chihuahuan desert habitats. Santa Ana attracts birders from across the United States who can view many species of Mexican birds as they reach the northern edge of their ranges in South Texas. Also found at Santa Ana are ocelot and jaguarundi, endangered members of the cat family. Visitors enjoy a tram or auto drive, bicycling and hiking trails, and a tower overlook. Office: 3325 Green Jay Road, Alamo, 78516; (956) 784-7500.

Texas Point (1980): Texas Point's 8,900 acres are located in Jefferson County on the upper Gulf Coast, 12 miles east of McFaddin NWR, where they serve a large wintering population of waterfowl and migratory birds. The endangered southern bald eagle and peregrine falcon may occasionally be seen during peak fall and spring migrations. Alligators are commonly observed during the spring, summer, and fall months. Activities include wildlife observation, hunting, fishing, and crabbing. Access to the refuge is by boat and on foot only. Open daily from sunrise until sunset. Office: Box 358, Sabine Pass, 77655; (409) 971-2909.

Trinity River (1994): Established to protect remnant bottomland hardwood forests and associated wetlands, this refuge, located in northern Liberty County off State Highway 787 about 15 miles east of Cleveland, provides habitat for wintering, migrating, and breeding waterfowl and a variety of other wetland-dependent wildlife. A tract south of Liberty includes Champion Lake. Office: Box 10015, Liberty 77575; (936) 336-9786. ☆

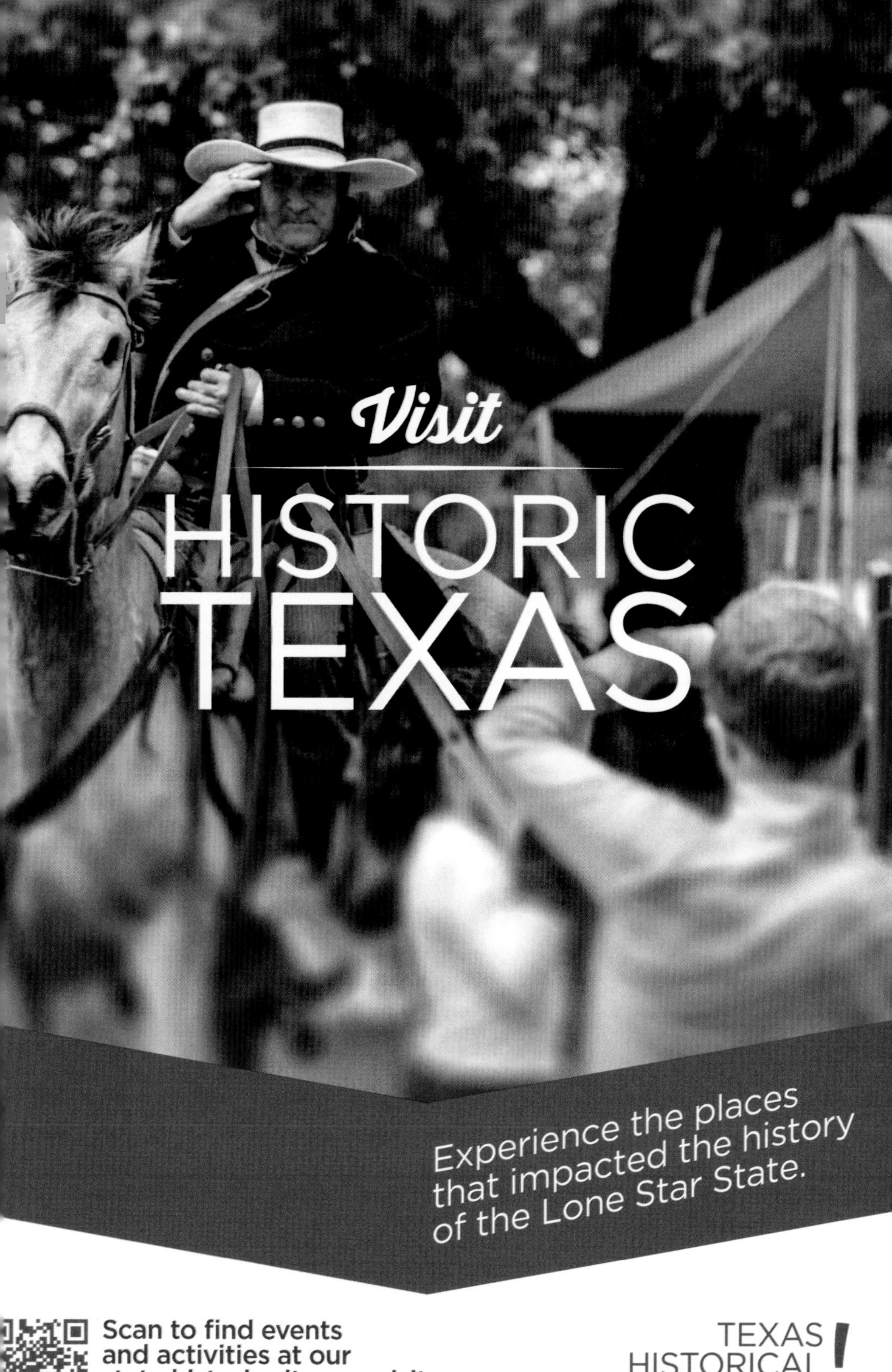
Visit
HISTORIC
TEXAS
Experience the places
that impacted the history
of the Lone Star State.
Scan to find events
and activities at our
state historic sites, or visit
TexasHistoricSites.com
TEXAS
HISTORICAL
COMMISSION
REAL PLACES TELLING REAL STORIES

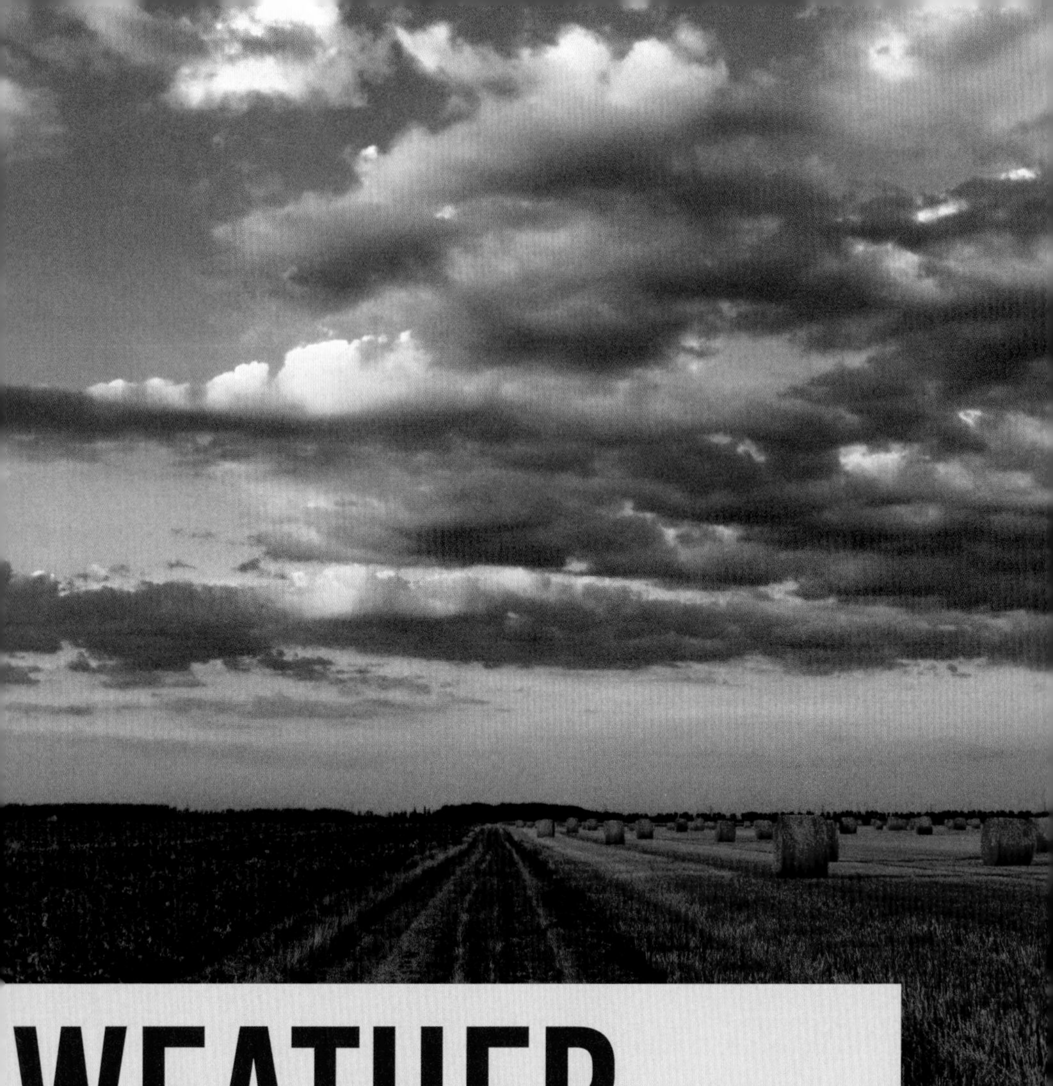

WEATHER

TEXAS TRIBUNE REPORTS: CLIMATE

HIGHLIGHTS & SUMMARIES, 2021 & 2022

TEMPERATURES, PRECIPITATION

TORNADOS, DROUGHTS

DESTRUCTIVE WEATHER

AVERAGES & RECORDS BY COUNTY

TEXAS TRIBUNE REPORTS: CLIMATE

by Erin Douglas, Climate Reporter

THE TEXAS TRIBUNE

As an energy capital and a state frequently impacted by natural disasters and extreme heat, Texas is both a contributor toward and a victim of climate change. Here's a look at how the state is being affected, and how it's responding:

IT'S GETTING HOTTER

The average daily minimum and maximum temperatures in the state both rose by 2.2 degrees Fahrenheit from 1895 to 2020, according to a report from the state's climatologist. The biggest changes in average temperatures were reported in urban areas, where buildings and roads absorb more of the sun's heat, but every Texas county saw an increase.

Even minor shifts in average temperatures require more electricity from the power grid, endanger the health of people who work outdoors, and can alter climate patterns and ecosystems. Heat also increases the prevalence of ground-level ozone pollution, or smog, making it harder for people with asthma and other health concerns to breathe outdoors in major Texas cities.

HURRICANES ARE GETTING MORE POWERFUL

Warming oceans fuel hurricanes, increasing the amount of precipitation, strengthening winds, and resulting in more flooding on land, scientists have found.

Climate change increased the intensity of Hurricane Harvey in 2017, multiple studies found after the storm. Harvey could not have produced so much rain without human-induced climate change, scientists concluded.

Harvey, the costliest U.S. disaster that year, caused $125 billion in damage, and more than 100 people died from direct causes such as flooding and indirect causes such as disruption to medical services, according to a report from the National Hurricane Center.

SEA LEVELS ARE RISING

Sea level rise will also make communities more vulnerable to storm surge during hurricanes, the 2018 National Climate Assessment warned. Already, scientists have observed increases in the number of tidal flood days in areas like Texas' Port Isabel.

Between 2000 and 2019, rising sea levels caused the Texas coastline to retreat, on average, about 1.25 meters, or about 4 feet, per year, according to a 2021 University of Texas Bureau of Economic Geology report for the Texas General Land Office. A 2021 report by the state's climatologist found that a 1-meter relative sea level rise produces a doubling of storm surge risk.

"The places along the Texas coast with the largest rates of sea level rise may have a doubled storm surge risk by 2050 relative to the beginning of the 20th century, purely due to relative sea level rise itself," the report said.

WATER IS BECOMING SCARCE

In the second half of this century, Texas could see "mega-droughts" worse than any previously recorded, according to a 2020 report from Texas A&M and University of Texas at Austin scientists.

The projections are of particular concern for communities like Dallas, which relies entirely on surface water — which is more vulnerable to evaporation — and farmers and ranchers, who rely on rainfall for crops and livestock.

Severe droughts could limit forage growth needed to raise cattle for beef, for example. Droughts, along with disruptions from natural disasters, could strain the state's food supply chains and drive prices up.

RELUCTANCE TO ACT

Many Texas lawmakers have been reluctant to act on climate change, opting instead to fight federal regulations on greenhouse gas emissions, promote the oil and gas industry in the state, and block local governments from passing their own climate initiatives. In the 2023 legislative session, for instance, lawmakers passed a huge economic incentives package to lure companies to Texas, which included the oil and gas industry but excluded wind and solar energy companies. They rejected ideas supported by Democrats to reduce electricity demand — and consequently reduce emissions from electricity production. But they did opt to spend more than $2 billion to boost water supplies and prevent flooding, two of the most destructive climate impacts in Texas as droughts are worsened by higher temperatures and rains and hurricanes get stronger.

Weather

Sources: Unless otherwise noted, this information is provided by Texas State Climatologist John W. Nielsen-Gammon and graduate research assistants Virginia Elliott, Alison Tarter, and William Baule at Texas A&M University. Monthly summaries are supplemented by the National Centers for Environmental Information, Monthly National Climate Report. EF Scale and Saffir-Simpson Hurricane Wind Scale supplied by the National Weather Service.

All temperatures are given in Fahrenheit. C.D.T. stands for "Central Daylight Time." "M.p.h." stands for "miles per hour." "R.A.W.S." stands for "Remote Automatic Weather Station." CoCoRaHS stands for "Community Collaborative Rain, Hail, & Snow Network." Record-setting months are compared against those recorded for the last 128 years, when official sources began recording weather data.

The strengths of tornadoes are expressed using the "Enhanced Fujita Scale," or EF Scale. According to the National Weather Service, the scale refers to a set of wind estimates rather than measurements and is based on damage incurred.

Hurricane categories are recorded according to the Saffir-Simpson Hurricane Wind Scale, which is based on a hurricane's maximum-sustained wind speed. It does not take any other potential hazards into account, such as storm surge or tornadoes.

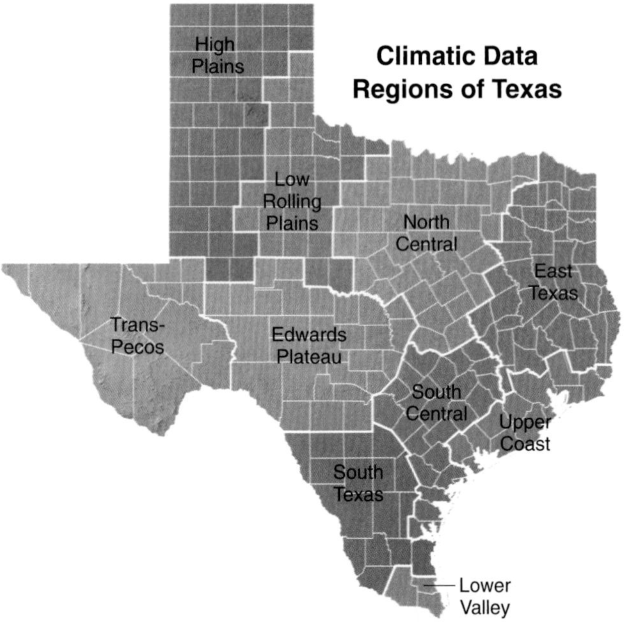

Climatic Data Regions of Texas

Enhanced Fujita Scale: Tornado Strength

EF Rating	3-Second Gust
0	65–85
1	86–110
2	111–135
3	136–165
4	166–200
5	Over 200

Saffir-Simpson Hurricane Wind Scale

Category	Sustained Winds
1	86–110
2	111–135
3 (Major)	136–165
4 (Major)	166–200
5 (Major)	Over 200

Average Temperatures 2021

	High Plains	Low Plains	North Central	East Texas	Trans-Pecos	Edwards Plateau	South Central	Upper Coast	South Texas	Lower Valley
Jan.	38.9	42.7	46.3	48.9	45.0	47.7	54.5	55.2	56.7	61.0
Feb.	34.1	36.8	40.4	44.6	47.4	44.8	50.7	52.3	55.1	59.5
Mar.	51.2	56.4	59.7	60.4	57.4	60.3	64.7	64.5	68.3	70.6
April	56.2	59.8	62.1	63.5	63.3	64.7	69.6	68.7	73.5	76.0
May	66.5	69.1	69.9	71.4	73.5	72.4	75.5	75.7	78.6	79.4
June	77.4	79.0	79.6	80.2	81.3	80.3	82.0	82.4	83.3	83.4
July	77.6	80.7	81.9	81.3	79.7	80.8	82.4	82.9	83.3	83.6
Aug.	78.4	82.0	82.9	82.7	79.1	81.7	84.2	84.6	85.2	86.4
Sep.	75.0	78.5	78.6	77.2	77.0	78.4	80.6	79.4	82.5	83.8
Oct.	63.1	68	69.6	70.5	68.4	70.1	73.9	74.4	77.1	79.1
Nov.	51.3	54.9	56.1	56.1	57.2	58.1	62.0	62.1	65.3	69.0
Dec.	49.2	55.0	59.3	61.2	56.4	60.3	65.8	67.2	67.7	71.1
Ann.	59.9	63.6	65.5	66.5	65.5	66.6	70.5	70.8	73.1	75.2

Precipitation in Inches 2021

	High Plains	Low Plains	North Central	East Texas	Trans-Pecos	Edwards Plateau	South Central	Upper Coast	South Texas	Lower Valley
Jan.	0.66	1.25	2.25	4.72	0.45	1.40	1.61	2.35	0.89	0.97
Feb.	0.24	0.34	1.38	2.76	0.26	0.93	1.22	1.54	0.50	0.41
Mar.	1.24	1.27	2.00	3.22	0.05	0.92	0.98	1.81	0.25	0.46
April	0.55	2.21	3.96	5.22	0.40	1.36	2.10	2.83	0.86	1.07
May	3.94	5.25	7.36	11.18	1.14	4.16	10.06	12.43	5.65	8.00
June	3.60	4.89	3.99	4.85	2.88	2.83	4.96	7.50	3.81	4.15
July	2.95	3.12	3.23	5.52	1.76	3.11	6.66	8.03	5.32	9.70
Aug.	2.04	1.96	3.58	3.21	3.01	2.80	2.79	3.83	2.38	0.97
Sep.	0.65	0.53	0.85	1.60	0.93	1.31	2.75	5.88	1.56	2.36
Oct.	0.90	1.87	3.32	3.12	0.31	2.61	5.37	4.75	1.76	4.15
Nov.	0.05	0.26	1.48	2.64	0.09	0.69	2.29	2.57	1.58	3.69
Dec.	0.01	0.03	0.57	2.44	0.11	0.02	0.93	1.85	0.30	1.33
Ann.	16.83	22.98	33.97	50.48	11.39	22.32	41.72	55.37	24.86	37.26

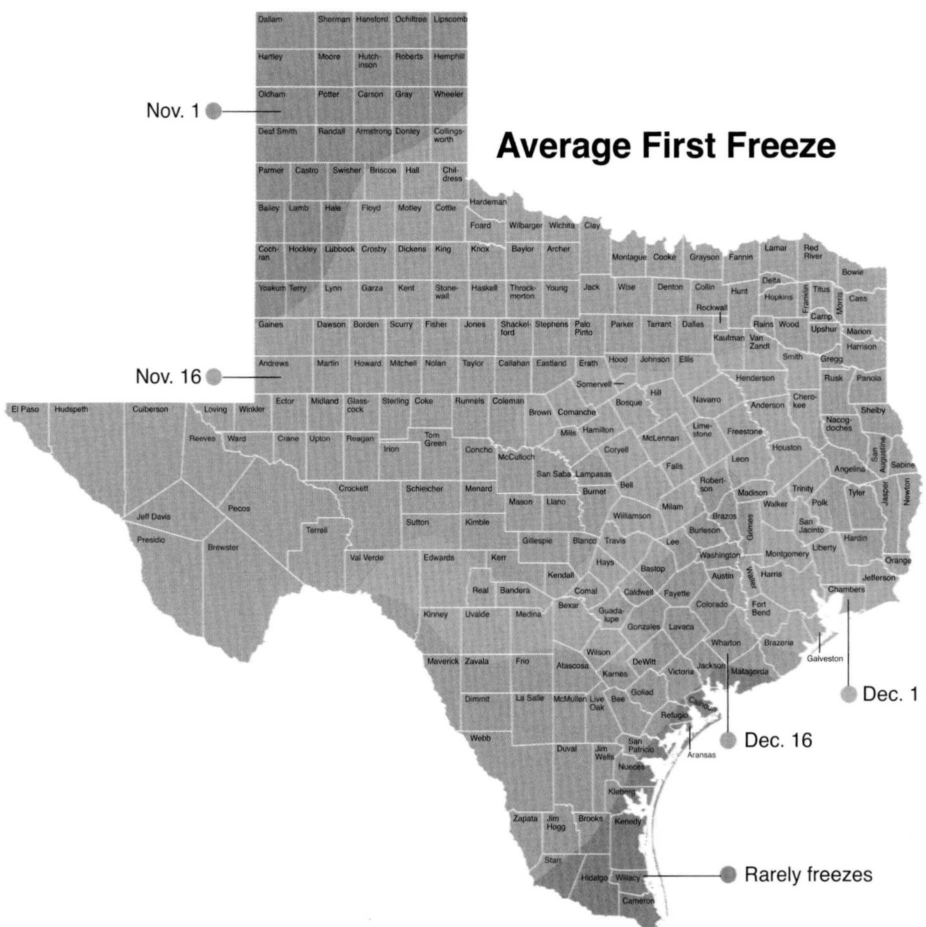

Weather Highlights 2021

January 6, 2021: A squall line ahead of a cold front impacted the Upper Coast region. This line of storms produced strong winds as strong as 50 m.p.h., one-inch hail, and an EF-1 tornado. This tornado occurred near Texas City and caused destruction to a few buildings and an apartment complex.

January 24–25, 2021: A broken line of thunderstorms induced by an upper-level disturbance resulted in high winds up to 75 m.p.h. and severe hail as large as 2.25 inches.

February 11–18, 2021: An Arctic air outbreak resulted in winter weather and extreme cold across the state. Heavy snow and periodic freezing rain occurred, along with bitterly cold temperatures and strong winds. These resulted in extreme wind chill values, power outages due to the extreme demand on the power grid, and loss of water for several days. This entire winter event resulted in 246 deaths. Some were direct deaths from hypothermia and frostbite, and others were indirect deaths from falls, carbon monoxide poisoning, heating-related fires, and car accidents. Cost of damage totaled into the tens of billions of dollars.

2021 Weather Extremes

Lowest Temp.: Lipscomb, Lipscomb Co., February 15	–19°
Highest Temp.: Rio Grande Village, Brewster Co., June 11	117°
24-Hour Precip.: Ganado 1.5 W, Jackson Co., May 17	13.69"
Monthly Precip.: Ganado 1.5 W, Jackson Co., May 17	27.99"
Least Annual Precip.: Castolon, Brewster Co.	6.93"
Greatest Annual Precip.: Ganado 1.5 W, Jackson Co.	75.67"

February 25, 2021: A shallow cold front was responsible for firing scattered thunderstorms across North and Northeast Texas. The main threat was large hail, with the largest falling in Bogata at two inches in size.

March 12–13, 2021: An upper-level disturbance led to a tornado outbreak in the Panhandle: ten EF-Unrated, six EF-0, five EF-1, and two EF-2. These tornadic storms did not cause any fatalities or injuries, but did cause around $1 million worth of damage. Also associated with these storms was severe hail (largest was 2.75 inches) and strong winds (as strong as 70 m.p.h.).

March 16–17, 2021: A dryline-triggered thunderstorms in the Panhandle which dropped large hail (maximum size

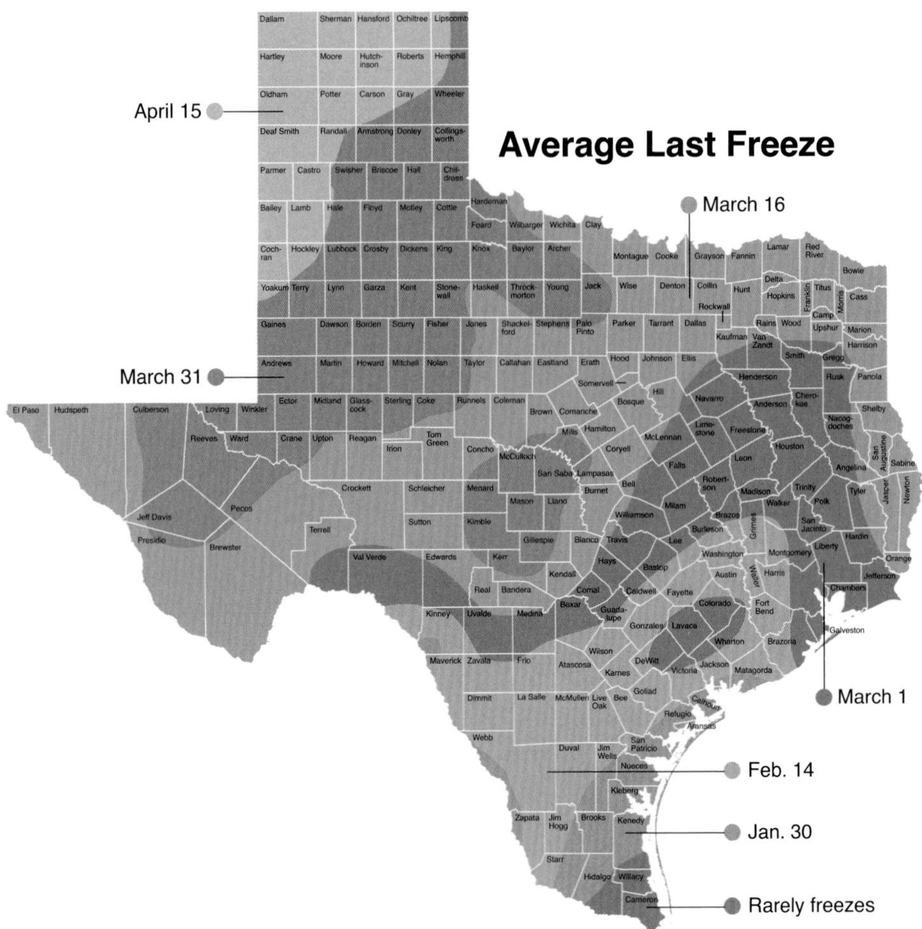

was two inches) and winds as strong as 80 m.p.h. Damages totaled $1 million.

March 22–25, 2021: A low-pressure system was responsible for triggering severe storms across the state. A few tornadoes occurred, including three EF-Unrated and one EF-1. Severe hail up to three inches in size and winds up to 69 m.p.h. were associated with these storms. $460 million in damage resulted.

March 27, 2021: An upper-level disturbance initiated thunderstorm development over East Texas, with one particular supercell being responsible for producing a few tornadoes throughout its lifespan, including two EF-1 and three EF-2. These tornadoes killed one person and injured four. Other threats from these storms included hail up to 1.75 inches and winds up to 61 m.p.h.

April 8–9, 2021: A surface system fired storms across the state that produced severe hail as big as three inches over large swaths of land, as well as winds reaching speeds of 70 m.p.h. Costs totaled up to $21 million.

April 12–15, 2021: A surface system triggered severe storms across the state, bringing with them severe hail. The largest size recorded was a three-inch hailstone. Hail damage totaled $1.3 million.

April 23, 2021: A strong upper-level disturbance led to tornadoes, high winds, and hail across the state. Seven tornadoes in total touched down: five EF-Unrated, one EF-1, and one EF-2. No fatalities or injuries were associated with them. Strong winds up to 61 m.p.h. were observed, along with hail as large as 3.5 inches.

April 27–28, 2021: A slow-moving surface system initiated severe storms across the state. A handful of tornadoes touched down: one EF-Unrated, one EF-0, one EF-1, and one EF-3. No injuries or deaths were related to these. Severe hail also resulted from these storms, with a maximum size of 6.42 inches. This particular hailstone fell in Hondo and was declared the largest hailstone officially recorded in Texas. High winds were the other main threat with these storms, with gusts reaching 96 m.p.h. This storm event resulted in $502 million in damage.

May 3, 2021: A cold front triggered severe thunderstorms that swept across the state, producing tornadoes, hail, and high winds. Six tornadoes touched down: one EF-Unrated, three EF-0, and two EF-2. One of the EF-2 tornadoes occurred in Ellis County and resulted in eight injuries after it struck three semis and one cargo van. Also associated with these storms were strong winds reaching 76 m.p.h. and hail as large as 5.5 inches.

May 7, 2021: An upper level disturbance resulted in severe storms in the Panhandle. An EF-0 tornado touched ground in Gray County, with other locations experiencing high winds up to 63 m.p.h. and one-inch hail.

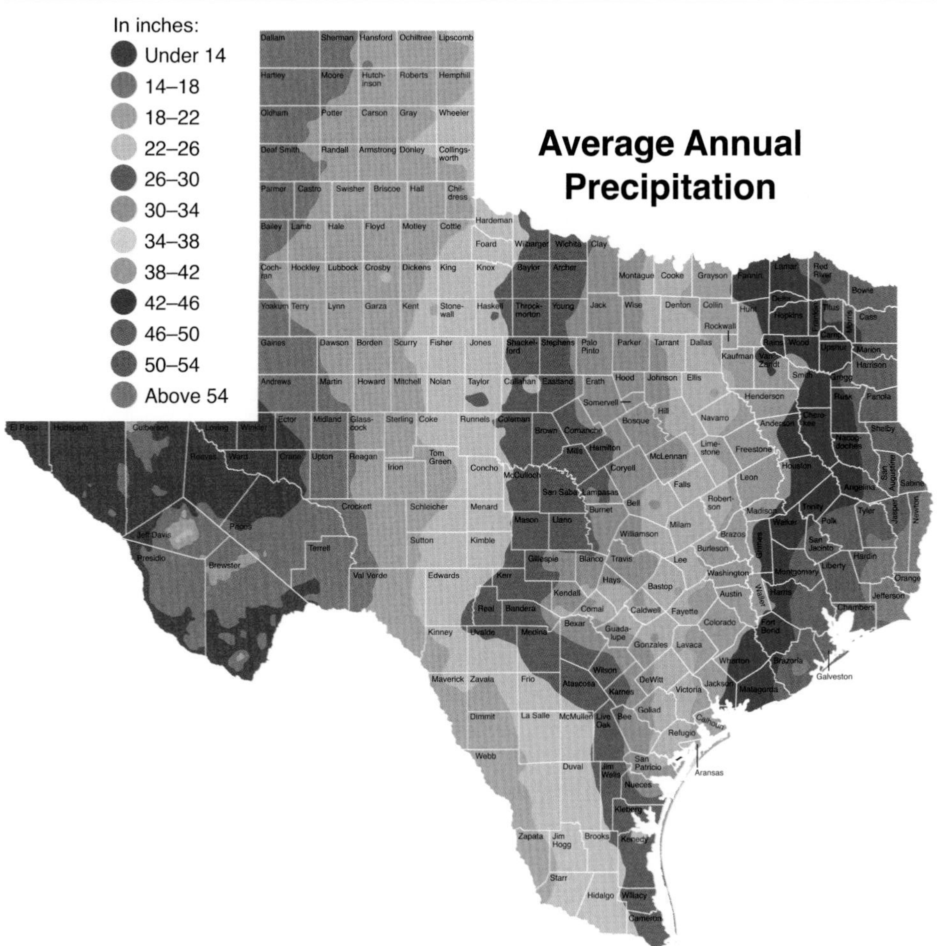

May 9–11, 2021: A strong surface system with a very moist and unstable warm sector initiated severe thunderstorms over a three-day span across the state. Three tornadoes touched down: two EF-0 and one EF-1. Hail as large as four inches fell from these storms, and outflow winds reached speeds of 65 m.p.h.

May 15–20, 2021: A strong, slow-moving upper level disturbance prompted storms over several days throughout Texas. Eighteen tornadoes touched down over the course of this event, including eight EF-Unrated, five EF-0, four EF-1, and one EF-2. Large hail was another significant threat, reaching diameters of 4.25 inches, leading to six injuries. Widespread high winds were also experienced, reaching speeds of 74 m.p.h.

May 25–28, 2021: A surface low-pressure system with an associated dry line and cold front prompted storms across the state over a four day period. Seven tornadoes resulted from these storms: five EF-Unrated and two EF-0. Hail was also abundant with these storms, reaching sizes as large as three inches. Outflow winds were very strong with many of these storms as well, reaching speeds of 78 m.p.h.

May 30–31, 2021: Abundant warm moisture from a southerly low-level jet stream prompted severe storms across the southern portion of Texas. Eight tornadoes resulted from these storms: seven EF-Unrated and one EF-0. Strong winds of 75 m.p.h. and hail as large as 1.75 inches also impacted the area.

June 8, 2021: An upper-level disturbance was responsible for severe thunderstorm development over East Texas. These storms resulted in three EF-0 tornadoes and strong winds from the storm up to 61 m.p.h.

June 24–27, 2021: A surface low-pressure system resulted in severe thunderstorms across the Panhandle. During this time, an EF-Unrated landspout occurred in Hockley County while an EF-1 tornado touched down in Gray County. Strong winds up to 100 m.p.h. and hail as large as two inches also impacted the region.

July 4, 2021: A mid-level, low-pressure center was responsible for severe thunderstorms, which started in the Panhandle and moved south through the state. These storms produced two-inch hail and 74 m.p.h. winds.

July 20, 2021: A stalled surface boundary resulted in storms at the Gulf. A funnel cloud was observed along the Bolivar Peninsula while an EF-0 tornado impacted San Patricio County.

August 2, 2021: A cold front resulted in storms along the coast, causing an EF-0 tornado to impact the Bolivar Peninsula when a waterspout moved onshore.

August 12, 2021: "Popcorn" thunderstorms developed in the southern Panhandle, resulting in high winds up to 58 m.p.h. According to the National Weather Service, popcorn

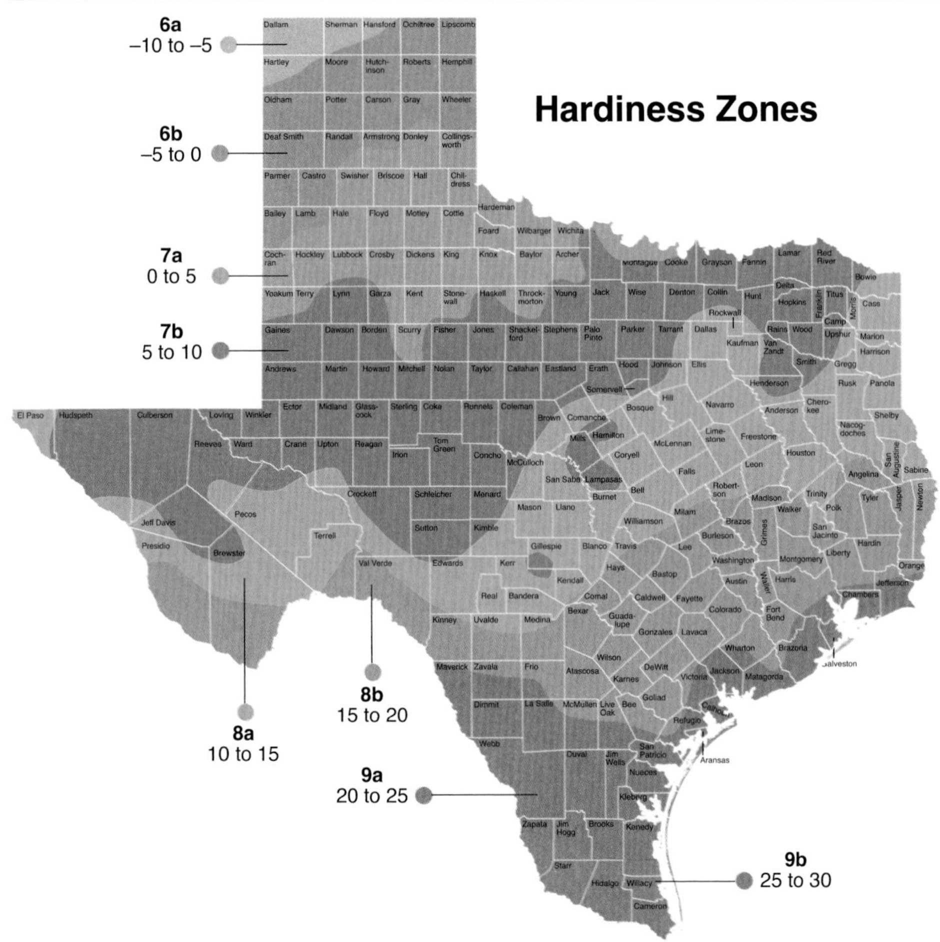

2022 Weather Extremes

Lowest Temp.: Muleshoe No. 1, Bailey Co., February 4	12°
Highest Temp.: Rio Grande Village, Brewster Co., June 8.	117°
24-hour Precip.: Zavalla 2.0 ESE, Angelina Co., August 23	11.68″
Monthly Precip.: Ferris 3.6 E, Ellis Co., August	15.69″
Least Annual Precip.: Rio Grande Village, Brewster Co.	4.65″
Greatest Annual Precip.: Bridge City 1.3 NW, Orange Co.	67.71″

thunderstorms occur most often during the mid- to late summer; they usually have a lifetime of about 30 minutes and don't move much.

September 13–14, 2021: Category 1 Hurricane Nicholas impacted the Gulf Coast over a two-day span. The storm made landfall on the Matagorda Peninsula around midnight on the 14th, moving northeast to Louisiana by day's end. The hurricane caused storm surge near Freeport and Galveston Bay along with heavy rain, resulting in localized flooding.

September 29–30, 2021: An upper-level disturbance prompted severe storms across West Texas. High winds reaching speeds of 62 m.p.h. and severe hail as large as 2.25 inches were produced.

October 26–27, 2021: A strong cold front led to supercells across the southern portion of Texas. There were five tornadoes with these storms: two EF-0 and three EF-2. One of the EF-2 tornadoes led to an injury in Orange County after flipping a mobile home. Although not a huge threat, some of these storms dropped hail as large as 1.5 inches in a few places. Wind was the other primary threat, reaching speeds of 83 m.p.h.

November 10, 2021: A deep upper-level disturbance was conducive for thunderstorm development across Northern Texas. These storms produced two EF-0 tornadoes, hail up to two inches, and 50 m.p.h. winds.

December 10, 2021: A strong cold front prompted storms in northeast Texas, leading to hail as large as two inches and winds up to 52 m.p.h.

December 18, 2021: A cold front moved into an unseasonably warm, moist air mass over South Central Texas, resulting in some severe thunderstorms. Hail up to two inches in size fell while high winds up to 55 m.p.h. also impacted the region. One EF-1 tornado spun up in Montgomery County, but resulted in no fatalities or injuries.

Monthly Summaries 2021

January temperatures varied across the state. Northwestern and western Texas had temperatures 0–2° below normal.

Conversely, northern, eastern, central, and southern Texas were 0–2° above normal, with some parts of eastern and southern Texas being 2–4° above normal. The average temperature for the month was 47.3°, making this month the 43rd-warmest January on record since 1895. Precipitation values for the month also varied.

Western and southeastern Texas received 50% of normal precipitation, with a few parts receiving 25% of normal precipitation. In contrast, eastern, central, and northern Texas received 150% of normal precipitation, with parts of central and eastern Texas receiving 200% of normal. The statewide precipitation average was 1.56 inches, making January 2021 the 54th-wettest January on record.

February temperatures were mostly below-normal. Parts of southeastern, southern, and western Texas experienced temperatures 2–4° above normal with the rest of Texas being below-normal. Western Texas ranged 0–8° below normal, while eastern and central Texas ranged 4–10° below normal. Southern Texas had temperatures 4–6° below normal, and northern Texas was 6–10 degrees below normal with some areas exceeding 10° below. The monthly average temperature was 44.2°, making for the 11th-coldest February on record. Precipitation values varied across the state. Northern, western, central, eastern, and southern Texas received between 25–50% of normal precipitation, with parts of these areas only receiving 5% of normal precipitation. Some areas were on the other side of the spectrum, with parts of central and western Texas receiving between 130–150% normal precipitation amounts. The statewide precipitation average was 0.9 inches, resulting in the 29th-driest February on record.

March experienced above-normal temperatures across Texas. Northern Texas experienced temperatures 0–2° above normal while northeastern Texas had 2–4° above normal temperatures. Western, eastern, and southeastern Texas had temperatures 0–4° above normal, southern Texas had temperatures 0–6° above normal, and central Texas was 2–6° above normal. The monthly average temperature was 59.3°, making March 2021 the 32nd-warmest March on record. This month also saw varying precipitation amounts with most of the state being abnormally dry. Eastern and central Texas saw 50% normal precipitation, while northern Texas received 25–50% of normal. Western and southern Texas saw 5–50% normal precipitation. In contrast, northern Texas received 130–200% normal precipitation. The average precipitation amount across the state was 1.25 inches, making the month the 46th-driest March on record.

April temperatures were below normal for much of the state. Southeastern Texas was 0–2° above normal while southern and far western Texas had temperatures 0–4° above normal. The rest of the state saw temperatures below average; northern, western, central, and eastern Texas were 0–4° below normal. The statewide monthly average was 63.7°, making April 2021 the 34th-coldest April on record. Precipitation varied across the state. Northern, western, and southern Texas ranged from 5–50% of normal precipitation, while southeastern Texas received 50% of normal precipitation. On the other side of the spectrum, North-Central and eastern Texas received 130–150% of normal precipitation, with some parts of North-Central Texas receiving as much as 200% of normal. The average precipitation total for the state was 2.03 inches, making the month the 62nd-driest April on record.

May had temperatures that were below the historical median, with the state experiencing an average of 71.8°. The highest maximum temperature observed over the month was 109° at both Falcon Dam and Castolon. The highest minimum temperature was 79° in many cities along the coast. May 2021 was the fifth-wettest May on record in Texas. The statewide average was 6.04 inches. Nineteen stations with more than 50 years of data set new May records, including Victoria at 20.28 inches and Kingsville with its wettest month ever at 20.94 inches.

June temperatures were ranked above the historical median. June 2021 was the 42nd warmest on record for Texas with an average temperature of 80.5°. The highest maximum temperature of the month was 117° at Rio Grande Village and the highest minimum was 85° at Galveston and Rockport. June was also wetter than the historical median. Texas had its 38th-wettest June on record with a monthly average of 3.47 inches of precipitation.

July was cooler than the state's long-term median, partly because of unusually heavy rainfall. The month's average temperature was an average of 80.6°, making it the 25th-coolest July on record.

Over a hundred daily records were set for lowest maximum temperature. Madisonville, which has 73 years of data, recorded its lowest-ever maximum temperature in July with 76° on July 13. The new record lasted for two days; it was replaced on July 15 by a lowest maximum of 75°. Waco Dam had its lowest July temperature ever, reaching 55° on July 19.

Texas saw particularly large amounts of rain during July 2021, with 4.9 inches ranking the month as 12th historically. A handful of long-term stations across the state had their wettest July on record, highlighted by Rockport at 21.09 inches.

August was the hottest month of the year while being mild historically at 81.9°. A few stations in Texas managed to tie their all-time records for highest August daily minimum temperature. The highest temperature in the region was 109° at Rio Grande Village on August 9. Rainfall was above the historical median, ranking the month as the 38th-wettest August at an average of 2.79 inches.

September temperatures remained warm for the state with an average temperature of 78.3°, making the month the 14th-warmest September of all time. Although warm, no record-high monthly temperatures were set. The hottest temperature seen in the state was 109° at Rio Grande Village on September 21. Conditions were very dry over the course of the month, averaging 1.24 inches of rain and ranking 11th driest historically. Fifteen stations reported zero precipitation and another 16 reported just a trace.

October was very warm for the state with an average of 69.8°; the month ranked 6th-warmest historically. One record-high monthly temperature was set at a long-term station: 104° at Cotulla on October 10, breaking a record set precisely one year earlier. The highest temperature of the month was 106°, which was observed in Rio Grande Village on October 11. The lowest temperatures were observed in Muleshoe on October 16 and Cope Ranch on October 30 at 25°. Precipitation varied throughout the state but averaged close to normal at 2.42 inches. However, about a dozen stations in western Texas failed to record measurable precipitation throughout the month.

November was warmer than normal, averaging 57.3° and ranking as the 31st-warmest November on record. One monthly maximum temperature record was set at Panther Junction in Big Bend National Park, where the temperature reached 92° on November 1. The highest temperature overall was 95° at Rio Grande Village, also in Big Bend National Park. By the end of the month, most of Texas had not yet experienced any temperatures below freezing. Throughout the month, conditions were on the drier side, averaging 1.16 inches of rainfall across the state and ranking the month as the 38th-driest November on record. The largest reported rainfall total was at a station 17 miles northeast of Edinburg with 8.9 inches. Nearby, Falcon Dam set a new record for the month of November with 3.8 inches. Meanwhile, no measurable rainfall was recorded across a broad swath of the Texas Panhandle, with occasional reports of zero rainfall extending southward to the Rio Grande. For some stations near and west of Midland, no measurable rainfall had been recorded since the first week of October.

December had unseasonably warm temperatures. At an average of 59.1° across the state (12.2° warmer than normal), December 2021 was the warmest December on record. 97% of individual stations with sufficient data had their warmest December on record. The highest temperature in the state was 96° in Stamford on December 27, while the lowest temperature was 4° in Lipscomb on December 18. The high temperatures were accompanied by below-normal precipitation. The month ranked the tenth driest on record at 0.62 inches. Substantial portions of western Texas recorded zero measurable precipitation for the month, and for many of those areas, particularly near Amarillo and Midland, this was the second consecutive month without measurable precipitation.

Weather Highlights 2022

January 8–9, 2022: Severe nighttime storms brought tornadoes, strong wind, and hail to southeast Texas, primarily near the Houston metroplex. On the 8th, four EF-0 tornadoes were confirmed in Harris, Liberty, and Montgomery counties on the 8th. These tornadoes were responsible for some minor damage to a few structures, including a hotel, and blew over some trees and open-framed houses. On the 9th, two EF-1 tornadoes touched down in Harris County which destroyed a three-story building's brick facade and uprooted large trees. These storms also brought strong winds, with Sabine County reporting winds up to 70 m.p.h., and ping-pong-ball-size hail was reported in Nacogdoches County. No injuries or deaths were reported with these storms.

January 19–20, 2022: Two thunderstorms produced considerable hail in East Texas, one near Longview and Marshall and the other near Lufkin and Nacogdoches. The maximum hail size reported was 2.5 inches in diameter near Marshall.

February 2–3, 2022: A convective system swept across the state, causing ice storms and severe thunderstorms. Ice and snow shut down nearly all travel from west-Central Texas to North Texas. One death was reported as a result of the extreme cold in Hutchinson County. Severe thunderstorms resulted in large hail up to 2 inches in diameter and strong wind up to 67 m.p.h.

March 14–15, 2022: Two tornadoes were reported along with 23 reports of hail, some as large as golf balls. An EF-1 tornado occurred in Fannin County on the 14th, causing damage to trees and a metal barn. On the 15th, a very brief EF-0 tornado occurred in Galveston County, snapping a large oak tree and damaging roofs.

March 21–22, 2022: A tornado outbreak occurred across the state, dropping 47 reported tornadoes. Five of these had damage tracks of 25 miles or longer. The strongest tornado was an EF-3 which struck Jacksboro, northwest of Fort Worth, injuring nine people. Fifteen tornadoes were rated EF-2, which caused two deaths and 31 injuries, and 15 EF-1 tornadoes resulted in three injuries. Sixteen EF-0 tornadoes also occurred, causing four injuries. Along with these tornadoes were several strong wind and severe hail reports, with hail up to two inches being recorded.

March 30–April 1, 2022: A line of severe storms resulted in tornadoes, strong wind, and severe hail in the eastern portion of Texas. Four EF-1 tornadoes occurred in Rockwall, Red River, Sabine, and Newton counties on the 30th, but resulted in no reported deaths or injuries. Damage included roof destruction and uprooted trees. Half-dollar-size hail and high winds up to 69 m.p.h. were reported in conjunction with these storms.

April 4–5, 2022: Severe thunderstorms struck the northern part of Texas, resulting in six reported tornadoes, hail, and strong wind. Four EF-0 tornadoes occurred in Ellis and Johnson counties and an EF-1 struck Collin County. An EF-2 tornado struck Johnson County, resulting in one injury. Severe hail up to golfball size was observed, and straight-line winds as strong as 75-85 m.p.h. were reported.

April 11–13, 2022: A slow-moving line of storms brought with them four tornadoes, severe hail, and high winds. An EF-Unrated tornado was reported in Coryell County, an EF-0 was reported in Bell County, and an EF-1 was reported in Williamson County. The strongest tornado was an EF-3 in Bell County, which resulted in 23 injuries. High winds of 70 m.p.h. from the squall line caused some power outages, roof damage, and downed trees in North-Central and East Texas.

	Average Temperatures 2022										Precipitation in Inches 2022									
	High Plains	Low Plains	North Central	East Texas	Trans-Pecos	Edwards Plateau	South Central	Upper Coast	South Texas	Lower Valley	High Plains	Low Plains	North Central	East Texas	Trans-Pecos	Edwards Plateau	South Central	Upper Coast	South Texas	Lower Valley
Jan.	37.8	41.7	44.3	46.9	45.2	46.5	51.4	53.4	54.2	58.2	0.17	0.23	0.33	2.04	0.10	0.33	1.28	2.39	0.57	2.00
Feb.	37.4	41.5	44.5	47.2	46.2	46.3	50.9	52.4	54.6	57.4	0.16	0.77	1.71	3.04	0.19	0.52	1.46	1.82	0.34	1.24
Mar.	49.5	54.4	56.9	57.1	56.2	58.5	61.5	61.9	64.8	67.2	0.42	0.35	1.68	4.99	0.01	0.18	1.31	2.65	0.18	0.15
April	61.4	66.3	67.7	67.3	69.0	70.7	73.8	72.9	77.1	79.0	0.16	0.57	2.72	3.59	0.05	0.63	1.08	1.14	1.40	1.73
May	71.8	77.2	76.9	76.5	78.0	80.6	81.9	80.4	84.1	83.4	1.80	2.29	3.44	4.36	0.31	1.61	1.68	2.71	2.65	4.47
June	79.4	83.3	84.3	83.6	83.0	85.0	86.2	85.0	87.4	85.7	1.79	2.45	1.62	1.09	1.65	1.02	1.21	1.44	0.22	0.12
July	84.7	88.8	89.5	87.0	84.6	87.3	88.1	86.3	89.2	88.2	1.90	0.74	0.46	1.51	1.12	0.64	0.53	2.58	0.28	0.48
Aug.	79.3	84.0	85.2	83.8	80.1	83.8	86.0	84.4	86.5	86.8	2.59	3.31	4.05	6.00	4.25	3.34	4.86	7.64	6.11	3.55
Sep.	74.5	78.1	78.8	77.7	74.4	77.8	81.2	80.5	81.4	82.6	0.77	0.80	1.18	1.43	1.58	1.59	1.55	2.10	2.25	3.20
Oct.	60.3	64.8	66.7	66.3	63.7	67.5	71.4	70.5	73.2	76.0	1.75	2.77	3.57	2.99	2.44	1.98	1.59	2.38	1.30	0.65
Nov.	45.4	50.5	53.7	55.8	51.2	54.6	60.3	61.2	62.0	66.4	0.60	1.46	3.76	5.32	0.54	2.37	3.92	7.07	2.79	3.29
Dec.	40.8	45.1	48.9	51.4	49.4	50.9	56.4	57.7	58.5	63.4	0.22	0.80	1.48	5.09	0.28	0.38	1.54	3.35	0.37	0.56
Ann.	60.2	64.6	66.5	66.7	65.1	67.5	70.8	70.6	72.8	74.5	12.33	16.54	26.00	41.45	12.52	14.59	22.01	37.27	18.46	21.44

Severe hail also plagued the area, including a hailstone which fell near Salado on the 13th with a diameter of 5.6 inches.

April 17–19, 2022: Severe storms brought large hail and strong winds in the Edwards Plateau region. The largest hail recorded was 3 inches in Medina County, and wind speeds reached 70 m.p.h., leading to downed limbs and scattered debris.

April 22–23, 2022: A slow-moving line of storms brought large hail and high winds across the state, but primarily to the Panhandle. The 23rd saw the largest hail sizes—two inches in several Panhandle counties—as well as the strongest wind speed, which was 76 m.p.h. in Sherman County.

May 1–5, 2022: A slow-moving system traveled through the state, producing quite a few tornadoes along its way. On the 1st, three EF-Unrated tornadoes occurred in Pecos County and an EF-2 hit Scurry County. On the 4th and 5th, a tornado outbreak occurred, with some tornadoes being tracked for several miles. Five EF-Unrated, three EF-1, one EF-2, and one EF-3 tornado were a result of this outbreak; the EF-2 resulted in one injury. During this period, 428 reports of hail were made, with sizes as large as 3 inches. Additionally, 579 reports of damaging winds were made, with some locations experiencing speeds up to 86 m.p.h.

May 10–17, 2022: A slow-moving and sometimes back-tracking dryline served as the trigger mechanism for several convective cells, which developed in the Panhandle. The primary threat was high winds and severe hail; the strongest winds were 87 m.p.h. in Lamb County and hail was up to 2.75 inches in Stephens County.

May 21–25, 2022: A cold front extending from a lingering low-pressure system brought severe weather over the course of five days across the state. Several tornadoes touched ground: seven EF-Unrated, one EF-0, two EF-1, and four EF-2. No injuries or deaths occurred from these tornadoes. High winds reached speeds of 80 m.p.h. and caused one injury when a vehicle collided with a tree downed by strong winds in Rusk County. Hail up to 3.5 inches caused great damage to cars and structures.

May 31–June 2, 2022: A low-pressure system brought severe thunderstorms to much of the state. These thunderstorms caused two EF-0 tornadoes in Collingsworth County, severe hail up to 3.5 inches, and strong winds up to 81 m.p.h.

June 8, 2022: A cold front was responsible for high winds and hail across the Panhandle. Hail reached up to four inches in size, along with wind gusts as strong as 82 m.p.h. Damage included downed power lines, gas-station canopy destruction, and roof damage.

July 12–14, 2022: A cold front brought high winds and large hail to many parts of the state. Winds reached speeds of 70 m.p.h., causing widespread damage and two injuries when a large tree fell through a mobile home. Half-dollar-size hail was another consequence of these thunderstorms.

July 20–22, 2022: Severe storms initiated across Texas as a result of a weak low-pressure system traveling across the country over this three-day span. The main threat with these storms was strong winds; the maximum recorded was 71 m.p.h. In Port Arthur on the 22nd, a land spout rated as an EF-0 occurred, causing no injuries or damage.

August 5, 2022: Damaging winds of up to 63 m.p.h. from a late evening downburst resulted in an injury in Longview. A tree was blown over, falling onto a vehicle with a person inside.

August 8–10, 2022: A slow-moving cold front resulted in some convective cell development in the Panhandle. One of these cells was responsible for an EF-0 tornado in Dumas which damaged a carport and roof and moved a couple of tractor-trailer rigs 30-40 feet. These storms also produced strong winds up to 65 m.p.h., snapping trees and damaging some metal buildings.

August 14–16, 2022: A low pressure system moving over the southern portion of Texas brought flooding, hail, and a tornado to the region. Intense rainfall brought flash flooding to many counties throughout south Texas over the three-day period as well as severe hail up to 1.75 inches. In Frio County, an EF-0 tornado touched down on the 15th, causing minimal damage. No deaths or injuries were reported with these events.

August 20–25, 2022: A slow-moving low-pressure system was responsible for major flooding and a few tornadoes across the state. Intense rainfall caused notable flooding in the Dallas-Fort Worth area, where thousands of cars were damaged and over a thousand homes were flooded. On the 22nd, this flooding led to a death in Dallas County. An EF-1 tornado occurred in Smith County on the 22nd, while two EF-Unrated tornadoes touched down in Nueces and San Patricio counties on the 23rd and 25th, respectively. These tornadoes caused no deaths or injuries, and damage was minimal.

October 13, 2022: A cold front produced a landspout in Nueces County; it was recorded as an EF-Unrated tornado. No deaths, injuries, or damage was recorded.

October 24, 2022: A dying cold front prompted some severe storms throughout North Central and East Texas. This storm system was responsible for high winds up to 80 m.p.h. and golf-ball-size hail. Most notably, these storms produced an EF-1 tornado in Jarrell, resulting in one injury.

November 4–5, 2022: A cold front pushed across the state, initiating a tornado outbreak. Eleven tornadoes touched down: three EF-1, three EF-2, three EF-3, and two EF-4. One of the EF-3 tornadoes occurred in Morris County, causing one death and eight injuries. One EF-4 tornado caused 13 injuries in Red River County, and the other caused ten injuries in Lamar County. Other threats from these storms included severe hail up to 2.75 inches in size, as well as strong winds as fast as 80 m.p.h.

November 11, 2022: A dryline moving across Central Texas initiated storms that dropped severe hail up to 2 inches in size, leading to widespread damage, including cracked windshields. These storms also brought 60 m.p.h. winds to the region.

December 13–14, 2022: A strong low-pressure system led to a powerful cold front, which caused a tornado outbreak in North Central Texas. Twenty tornadoes touched down: five EF-0, eight EF-1, and seven EF-2. These led to some injuries, including two from an EF-2 tornado in Wise County, five from an EF-1 in Tarrant County, and two from an EF-2 in Collin County. Some of these storms produced hail as large as 2.5 inches and winds up to 90 m.p.h.

December 22–23, 2022: A strong cold front brought high winds up to 80 m.p.h. and extreme cold across Texas, causing large power outages and the widespread freezing of pipes. In Houston, 1,600 bats fell from their roosts due to cold temperatures.

December 29–30, 2022: A dryline caused severe storm development in the eastern portion of the state, resulting in strong winds up to 60 m.p.h. These storms produced an EF-1 tornado in Tyler County that damaged mobile homes and threw a pontoon boat 25 yards into a tree.

Monthly Summaries 2022

January started out very warm for Texas, but quickly turned cool for much of the month. Stations in deep South Texas recorded all-time record-high temperatures for January during the very beginning of the month. The warmest temperature was recorded at Falcon Lake on January 1 with a reading of 99°. By the end of the month, almost the entire state, with the exception of parts of the Lower Rio Grande Valley and the Texas coast, had experienced below-freezing temperatures. In terms of precipitation, conditions were on the dry side. Texas had an average of 0.51 inches, ranking January 2022 as the 14th-driest January on record. Texas reported snow accumulations, with the largest monthly total being 5.6 inches at Texline.

February was a moderately cold month across Texas. The state averaged 45.8°, making the month the 22nd-coldest February on record. The month featured fairly large temperature swings, with two particularly cold episodes in early and late February. The coldest temperature was observed in Muleshoe at -12° on the 4th, while the warmest temperature was observed in Laredo and Alice at 97° on the 22nd. Port Arthur set maximum temperature records for February on February 2nd when it reached 88°. There were no February minimum temperature records set. Precipitation was widely variable across the state. Texas had the 30th-driest February on record at 0.98 inches. Wink and Lipscomb both reported no measurable precipitation throughout the entire month. There was reported measurable snow accumulation, but very little.

March temperatures were generally warmer than the long-term average, but cooler than the most recent three-decade period, 1991–2020. The first triple-digit days occurred along the Rio Grande, with the highest value being 103° at Rio Grande Village on March 30. The temperature stayed above freezing for the entire month in extreme southern Texas and parts of coastal southeast Texas. Three March maximum temperature records were tied at long-term stations on March 28 and March 30. In terms of precipitation, the state was relatively dry. Texas saw its 42nd-driest March on record at 1.2 inches, with 52 stations seeing no measurable precipitation for the entirety of the month. March 22 saw the largest snowfall total for the month at 9.5 inches just south of Amarillo.

April saw very warm temperatures throughout the state. Texas recorded its 14th-warmest April on record, averaging 68.4°, or 2.9° warmer than normal. The hottest temperature of the month was 111° at a R.A.W.S. station in the Santa Ana National Wildlife Refuge in South Texas on April 6. The same day, another R.A.W.S. at Falcon Lake in South Texas reached 110°. These tie for the earliest readings of 110° or greater in the United States, equaling April 6, 1989, when a few stations in Southern California reached or exceeded the 110° mark. Conditions were also very dry in the state. April ranked as Texas' 21st driest on record with slightly more than half of its normal rainfall. Forty-six Texas stations recorded zero precipitation and 16 more recorded trace amounts. Only four out of 27 stations in the Trans-Pecos climate division reported measurable precipitation. The largest single-day rainfall total was 4.87 inches in Sherman.

May saw temperatures well above normal. Texas had its second-warmest May ever at 78°, 4.4° above normal; May 1996 had previously held the record. The hottest temperature was 113° recorded at Rio Grande Village in Big Bend National Park on May 30. About half of the state reached triple digits at least once during the month. One station dropped below freezing: Bravo, in the Panhandle, recorded a minimum temperature of 31° on May 3. In Central Texas, Junction and Goldthwaite set all-time May maximum temperature records, at 106° for Junction and 104° for Goldthwaite; both cities have at least 60 years of weather records. The May average temperature was the hottest on record across a large swath of Texas, from Abilene and San Angelo to Victoria and Galveston and including the major cities of Austin and San Antonio. No stations in Texas set records for coldest temperature recorded in May. Conditions were very dry across the state, making May 2022 the 25th driest on record at an average of 2.25 inches. Colmesneil saw the largest single-day precipitation total at 6.65 inches on May 22, with Rio Grande City reporting 6.5 inches the previous day.

June was particularly warm across the state, extending a pattern established in May. Texas had its fifth-warmest June overall at 83.8°. Many locations across central and southeast Texas recorded their warmest June on record. The hottest temperature recorded during the month was 117° at Rio Grande Village in Big Bend National Park on June 8. That mark was only 3° shy of the all-time temperature record for the state of Texas. Two stations set records for hottest temperature observed during June, including Cotulla (111°) and Fort Worth Naval Air Station (111°). No stations set records for coldest temperature recorded in June. Precipitation was on the dry side, with Texas experiencing its 15th-driest June on record at 1.27 inches. At least 40 stations in Texas reported zero measurable rain. Only three locations reported single-day totals in excess of five inches: Richland Hills, 6.12 inches on June 4; Mansfield, 5.31 inches on June 4; and Quanah, 5.03 inches on June 1.

July was the hottest one Texas ever recorded, averaging 87.3°. The hottest temperature recorded was 115° in Wichita Falls and a few surrounding stations from July 19–20. Several stations set maximum temperature records for July, including Follett. No stations set records for lowest temperature recorded in July. The month was also very dry for Texas, with July 2022 being the fifth driest on record at 0.95 inches. The highest total seen for the state was in Port Arthur at 13.29 inches. Conversely, 176 stations in Texas reported no measurable precipitation for the month.

August was the 22nd hottest out of 128 years for Texas, averaging 83.4°. However, there were no all-time records for highest or lowest temperature. The hottest temperature, 113°, was at Rio Grande Village in Big Bend National Park on August 3. The coldest lowland temperature was 51° at Lipscomb. Although the heat was similar to that of preceding months, August brought much more rain, making for the tenth-wettest August. Four stations in North-Central and East Texas recorded more than 10 inches in a single day: Zavalla (11.68), Blue Mound (11.30), Mesquite (10.88), and Dallas (10.80). Peak monthly totals were 17.99 inches at Zavalla. Seventy-seven stations in Texas recorded over ten inches of rain for the month.

September was warm across Texas, ranking as the 18th warmest at 2.1 degrees above the 20th-century average. No all-time maximum or minimum temperature records were set for the month even though the state still saw triple-digit temperatures on September 21. The month was on the dry side. Seven stations failed to receive measurable precipitation during the entire month. However, the highest total for the state was 9.97 inches at Port Aransas, including 5.86 inches on September 4.

October was near-normal in terms of temperature. The state was close to its historical median value, running slightly cooler than normal for the most part. Five stations topped out at exactly 100°: Waco on October 12, Santa Ana National Wildlife Refuge on October 13, Falcon Dam and Falcon Lake on October 14, and Rio Grande Village on October 23. Precipitation was below normal for the state. Six stations reported no measurable precipitation for the month, but there were a few stations that recording notable accumulations, including one airport (Paris, at 7.64 inches) and five CoCoRaHS stations: Ravenna (8.72 inches), Van Alstyne (8.22), Paris (8.20), Powderly (7.83), and Dodd City (7.77). The largest single-day total was 4.92 inches near Port Arthur on October 29.

In **November,** Texas was near historical median values. Twelve stations reached temperatures of 95° or greater, with the warmest being Falcon Lake reaching 99° on November 4th. The lowest temperature recorded was 8° at Dalhart Airport on November 30th. Jefferson set a monthly record for daily maximum temperature at 89° on November 5th. Precipitation was above normal for the state, making November 2022 the 26th wettest on record. The wettest stations were in Texas City (12.97 inches), Hitchcock (12.72), and Dickinson (11.98). The driest stations included Persimmon Gap and Bravo, each reporting a total of 0.01 inches of precipitation in November.

December was mostly warmer than normal, with the month ranking as the 20th-warmest December on record. An Arctic outbreak in late December led to several stations reporting daily low temperatures below 0°. The warmest temperature recorded was 92° at Santa Ana National Wildlife Refuge near McAllen on December 13th. One long-term station in the state set a monthly record for daily maximum temperature: Beaumont-Port Arthur Airport with 85° on December 3rd. Four long-term stations in the region set monthly records for daily minimum temperature: Eden with 7° on December 23rd, El Campo with 15° on December 23rd, Galveston Scholes Field with 21° on December 23rd, and Harlingen Airport with 27° on December 23rd. Texas experienced its 50th-driest December on record. The wettest stations included Town Bluff Dam (14.18 inches) and Colmesneil, Texas (14.1 inches). Two stations exceeded 7-inch single-day accumulations: near Adkins, Texas (8.02, December 11th) and near Livingston, Texas (7.95, December 11th). Two long-term stations set daily December accumulation records: McCook (2.28) on December 4th and Wingate (2.32) on December 11th. The driest stations in the state reported no accumulated precipitation in December and were located at Ft. Stockton, Crane, Gruver, and Adrian. ☆

Meteorological Data

Source: National Climatic Data Center. Additional data for these locations are listed by county in the table of Texas Climatological Normals for 1981–2010 and Extreme Weather Records by County, beginning on page 126.

City	Temperature		Precipitation					Relative Humidity		Wind			Sun
	No. Days Max. 100° and Above	No. Days Min. 32° and Below	Maximum in 24 Hours	Month & Year	Snowfall (Mean Annual)	Max. Snowfall in 24 Hours	Month & Year	6:00 a.m., CT	Noon, CT	Speed, MPH (Mean Annual)	Highest MPH	Month & Year	Percent Possible Sunshine
Abilene	90	48	6.70	9/1961	3.7	9.3	4/1996	75	50	10.9	55	4/1998	70
Amarillo	61	108	7.25	7/2010	17.2	20.6	3/1934	75	46	12.8	68	6/2008	74
Austin	111	12	15.00	9/1931	1.0	9.7	11/1937	84	57	7.0	52	5/1997	60
Brownsville	123	1	12.19	9/1967	0.0	**	3/1993	90	61	10.4	51	7/2008	59
Corpus Christi	106	4	11.52	6/2006	0.2	2.3	12/2004	90	62	11.7	56	5/1999	60
Dallas-Fort Worth	95	29	5.91	10/1959	1.2	12.1	1/1964	82	56	10.5	73	8/1959	61
Del Rio	131	15	17.03	8/1998	0.9	8.6	1/1985	73	65	8.8	60	8/1970	84
El Paso	99	44	6.50	7/1881	6.9	16.8	12/1987	58	35	8.1	64	1/1996	84
Galveston	30	5	13.91	10/1901	0.2	15.4	2/1895	91	64	11.0	*100	9/1900	62
Houston †	102	10	11.02	6/2001	0.1	2.0	1/1973	90	60	7.5	51	8/1983	59
Lubbock	78	84	7.80	9/2008	8.2	16.3	1/1983	75	46	12.0	70	3/1952	72
Midland-Odessa	101	58	5.99	7/1961	5.1	10.6	1/2012	74	43	10.9	67	2/1960	74
Port Arthur-Beaumont	80	9	17.16	9/1980	0.0	4.4	2/1960	91	64	8.6	105	8/2005	58
San Angelo	102	46	6.25	9/1980	2.4	7.4	1/1978	80	49	9.7	75	4/1969	70
San Antonio	111	15	13.35	10/1998	0.7	13.2	1/1985	84	56	8.2	51	6/2010	60
Victoria	107	11	9.87	4/1991	0.1	2.1	1/1985	91	60	9.5	99	7/1963	49
Waco	104	31	7.98	12/1997	1.2	7.0	1/1949	86	57	10.1	69	6/1961	59
Wichita Falls	98	59	6.22	9/1980	4.2	9.7	3/1989	82	52	11.2	69	6/2002	60
Shreveport, LA §	88	32	10.76	5/2008	1.0	5.6	1/1982	89	59	7.3	63	5/2000	64

*100 mph recorded at 6:15 p.m., Sept. 8, 1900, just before the anemometer blew away. Maximum velocity was estimated to be 120 mph from the northeast between 7:30 p.m. and 8:30 p.m.

†The official Houston station was moved from near downtown to Intercontinental Airport, 12 miles north of the old station.

§Shreveport is included because it is near the boundary line and its data can be considered representative of Texas' east border.

**Trace is an amount too small to measure.

Texas Droughts

Source: Texas State Climatologist and the New Mexico Drought Planning Team.

Drought is difficult to define, and there is no universally accepted definition. The most commonly used drought definitions are based on meteorological, agricultural, hydrological, and socioeconomic effects.

Meteorological drought is often defined as a period when precipitation is diminished in duration and/or intensity. The commonly used definition of meteorological drought is an interval of time, generally on the order of months or years, during which the moisture supply at a given place consistently falls below the climatically appropriate moisture supply.

Agricultural drought occurs when there is inadequate soil moisture to meet the needs of a particular crop at a particular time. Agricultural drought usually occurs after or during meteorological drought but before hydrological drought and can also affect livestock and other dryland agricultural operations.

Hydrological drought refers to deficiencies in surface and subsurface water supplies. It is measured as streamflow and as lake, reservoir, and groundwater levels. There is usually a delay between lack of rain and less measurable water in streams, lakes, and reservoirs. Therefore, hydrological measurements tend to lag other drought indicators.

Socioeconomic drought occurs when physical water shortages start to affect the health, well-being, and quality of life of the people, or when the drought starts to affect the supply and demand of an economic product.

Palmer Drought Severity Index

	High Plains	Low Rolling Plains	North Central	East Texas	Trans–Pecos	Edwards Plateau	South Central	Upper Coast	South Texas	Lower Valley
Frequency	**27**	**28**	**27**	**25**	**28**	**28**	**26**	**26**	**25**	**25**
1901	-2.01	-2.55	-4.58	-2.39	-2.28	-3.14	-3.84	-2.78	-3.21	-5.05
1910	-3.47	-3.89	-5.04	-3.99	-4.21	-4.48	-3.63	-2.51	-3.26	-3.43
1911	-3.69	-4.10	-5.97	-5.02	-4.02	-4.03	-4.21	-4.31	-4.39	-3.03
1917	-3.90	-4.66	-4.53	-4.90	-4.58	-4.88	-6.00	-6.03	-4.56	-3.91
1918	-3.88	-5.97	-6.11	-6.42	-3.75	-5.61	-6.13	-7.00	-4.50	-4.09
1925	-2.96	-3.26	-6.41	-6.20	-3.09	-3.95	-6.09	-5.20	-3.79	-2.51
1934	-4.66	-4.42	-4.84	-3.55	-4.88	-4.51	-2.82	-2.27	-1.54	-1.33
1935	-4.57	-3.83	-0.58	0.19	-4.68	-3.99	0.66	-0.39	0.10	-1.76
1951	-1.65	-3.36	-4.26	-3.84	-4.15	-4.66	-4.64	-4.37	-3.91	-4.10
1952	-4.23	-5.38	-5.53	-3.72	-4.28	-5.10	-4.53	-4.47	-4.45	-3.71
1953	-5.33	-5.41	-3.12	-1.27	-5.67	-4.64	-2.58	-2.21	-5.26	-4.45
1954	-4.46	-4.24	-4.29	-4.27	-4.59	-5.09	-4.87	-3.89	-3.59	-3.38
1955	-4.13	-3.76	-3.81	-3.18	-3.35	-4.78	-4.95	-3.75	-4.59	-3.60
1956	-5.62	-6.25	-6.82	-5.09	-5.47	-6.16	-6.68	-5.72	-4.77	-3.81
1957	-4.94	-5.02	-5.08	-4.92	-4.85	-5.10	-5.82	-5.64	-4.29	-4.12
1963	-2.38	-2.91	-3.95	-3.77	-2.07	-4.29	-4.80	-4.15	-3.71	-3.57
1967	-3.31	-3.42	-4.61	-3.34	-2.55	-4.12	-4.73	-2.99	-3.62	-2.44
1971	-3.33	-4.18	-4.41	-3.11	-2.80	-3.46	-5.01	-3.28	-3.68	-2.70
1974	-4.43	-4.20	-2.44	1.60	-3.44	-3.09	1.26	1.95	-1.29	-1.97
1996	-3.83	-3.57	-4.28	-3.63	-3.76	-3.88	-4.51	-2.59	-3.64	-3.04
2000	-3.88	-3.97	-3.76	-4.34	-4.93	-4.78	-4.39	-5.17	-4.12	-3.73
2006	-4.58	-4.80	-4.93	-4.16	-3.72	-4.14	-5.23	-4.32	-4.73	-4.77
2009	-2.24	-2.97	-3.88	-2.43	-2.35	-3.82	-6.36	-4.23	-5.19	-4.09
2010	-1.13	-1.20	-1.27	-3.67	-2.08	-2.02	-1.49	-1.19	-1.59	-1.68
2011	-6.98	-6.99	-5.99	-6.86	-6.52	-6.39	-6.21	-5.70	-5.45	-4.87
2012	-5.12	-4.75	-3.70	-4.36	-4.93	-3.75	-4.37	-4.72	-4.17	-4.69
2013	-4.16	-4.26	-3.43	-2.94	-3.02	-3.40	-4.47	-3.47	-4.33	-4.94
2014	-3.45	-3.29	-2.56	-1.34	-2.85	-2.93	-3.29	-2.49	-2.72	-1.23
2015	0.69	0.39	0.38	0.84	1.74	0.33	0.41	-0.59	-1.14	-0.56
2016	1.30	2.57	2.85	-2.04	-1.15	1.98	-0.47	-1.63	-1.50	-2.86
2017	-1.15	-1.43	-1.31	-2.40	-1.82	-1.47	-1.72	0.59	-1.97	-3.72
2018	-3.84	-4.35	-3.30	-2.16	-3.18	-3.67	-2.31	0.79	-2.72	-4.09
2020	-3.57	-0.58	1.41	1.63	-4.94	-3.17	-3.74	-0.40	-3.05	-3.22
2021	-3.44	-2.54	-2.16	-2.04	-4.05	-2.64	-3.95	-1.10	-3.50	-2.70
2022	-5.26	-5.53	-6.00	-3.75	-4.63	-5.93	-4.68	-3.69	-4.39	-2.01
PDSI Table Indicators	Moderate drought, PDSI between –2 and –4			Severe drought, PDSI between –4 and –6			Extreme drought, PDSI below –6			

The table on this page uses the **Palmer drought severity index (PDSI)**, the index preferred by the Texas State Climatologist's Office, the National Weather Service, and NOAA. It was developed by meteorologist Wayne Palmer, who first published this method in 1965.

The PDSI is based on a **supply-and-demand model of soil moisture** that factors in temperature, the amount of moisture in the soil, evapotranspiration, and recharge rates. It is most effective in determining long-term drought. Years were included in the table if at least one climate division had a PDSI of -4 or below, as well as the past 10 years, even when no periods of drought occurred. ☆

Normal Annual Rainfall in Inches by Texas Climatic Region

Listed below is the normal annual rainfall in inches for three 30-year periods in each geographical region (see map, p. 106).

Region	HP	LRP	NC	ET	TP	EP	SC	UC	ST	LV
1961–1990	18.88	23.77	33.99	45.67	13.01	24.00	34.49	47.63	23.47	25.31
1971–2000	19.64	24.51	35.23	48.08	13.19	24.73	36.21	50.31	24.08	25.43
1981–2010	20.02	24.85	36.17	48.21	13.16	24.86	35.54	51.14	24.17	24.67

Texas Is Tornado Capital

Source: The Office of the State Climatologist.

An average of 130 tornadoes touch Texas soil each year. The annual total varies considerably, and certain areas are struck more often than others. Tornadoes occur with greatest frequency in the Red River Valley.

Tornadoes may occur in any month and at any hour of the day, but they occur with greatest frequency during the late spring and early summer months, and between the hours of 4:00 p.m. and 8:00 p.m. In the period 1951–2022, 42% of all Texas tornadoes occurred within the three-month period of April, May, and June, with 27% of total tornadoes occurring in May.

More tornadoes have been recorded in Texas than in any other state, which is partly due to the state's size. Between 1951–2022, 9,357 funnel clouds are known to have reached the ground, thus becoming tornadoes. Texas ranks first among the 50 states in the density of tornadoes, experiencing an annual average of 5.25 tornadoes per 10,000 square miles.

The greatest outbreak of tornadoes on record in Texas was associated with Hurricane Beulah in September 1967. Within a five-day period (Sept. 19–23) 115 known tornadoes, all in Texas, were spawned by this great hurricane. Sixty-seven occurred on Sept. 20, a Texas record for a single day.

In May 2015, there were 130 tornadoes, which is a Texas record for a single month. The greatest number of tornadoes in Texas in a single year was 248, which was also in 2015. The second-highest number in a single year was in 1967, when 232 tornadoes occurred in Texas.

On average, May has the highest number of tornadoes with 40. January, February, and December have the lowest average number of tornadoes with 3 each.

The accompanying table, compiled by the National Climatic Data Center, Environmental Data Service, and the National Oceanic and Atmospheric Administration, lists tornado occurrences in Texas, by months, for the period 1951–2022. Additional years are available at texasalmanac.org. ☆

Tornadoes by Year and Month

Year	Jan.	Feb.	March	April	May	June	July	Aug.	Sept.	Oct.	Nov.	Dec.	TOTAL
2022	6	0	53	10	32	0	1	5	0	2	11	21	**141**
2021	1	0	32	11	43	5	1	2	0	5	2	1	**103**
2020	14	0	18	17	24	3	8	2	1	0	2	0	**89**
2019	0	0	12	39	104	13	1	0	2	13	0	0	**184**
2018	5	0	9	4	6	3	3	2	1	22	1	2	**58**
2017	22	17	36	29	43	3	3	25	1	1	0	3	**183**
2016	0	1	14	33	43	4	1	1	5	0	0	0	**102**
2015	0	0	0	48	130	3	0	0	2	20	23	22	**248**
2014	0	0	0	6	15	15	5	0	0	2	0	3	**46**
2013	1	16	0	8	41	3	0	6	0	6	0	3	**84**
2012	22	3	9	36	31	3	0	1	2	3	0	5	**115**
2011	1	1	3	57	20	6	1	4	1	2	8	0	**104**
2010	10	0	0	19	34	23	3	1	12	10	0	0	**112**
2009	0	5	4	48	18	32	2	4	1	4	1	12	**131**
2008	0	3	15	48	33	9	5	1	2	3	1	3	**123**
2007	2	1	56	61	43	21	8	4	14	2	1	3	**216**
2006	0	1	4	20	43	7	3	3	0	9	0	27	**117**
2005	0	0	6	7	27	46	15	4	2	0	0	2	**109**
2004	1	1	27	25	29	34	1	5	0	4	55	2	**184**
2003	0	0	4	31	50	29	6	1	4	12	29	0	**166**
2002	0	0	44	25	61	5	1	4	13	8	0	22	**183**
2001	0	0	4	12	36	12	0	7	15	24	27	5	**142**
2000	0	7	49	33	23	8	3	0	0	10	20	1	**154**
1999	22	0	22	23	70	26	3	8	0	0	0	4	**178**
1998	24	15	4	9	11	6	3	5	3	28	1	0	**109**
1997	0	6	7	31	59	50	2	2	1	16	3	0	**177**
1996	7	1	2	21	33	9	3	8	33	8	4	1	**130**
1995	6	0	13	36	66	75	11	3	2	1	0	10	**223**
1994	0	1	1	48	88	2	1	4	3	9	8	0	**165**
1993	1	4	5	17	39	4	4	0	12	23	8	0	**117**
1992	0	5	13	22	43	66	4	4	4	7	21	0	**189**
1991	20	5	2	39	72	36	1	2	3	8	4	0	**192**
1990	3	3	4	56	62	20	5	2	3	0	0	0	**158**
1989	3	0	5	3	70	63	0	6	3	6	1	0	**160**
1988	0	0	0	11	7	7	6	2	42	4	10	0	**89**
1987	1	1	7	0	54	19	11	3	8	0	16	4	**124**
1986	0	12	4	21	50	24	3	5	4	7	1	0	**131**
1985	0	0	5	41	28	5	3	1	1	3	1	2	**90**
1984	0	13	9	18	19	19	0	4	1	5	2	5	**95**
1983	5	7	24	1	62	35	4	22	5	0	7	14	**186**
1982	0	0	6	27	123	36	4	0	3	0	3	1	**203**
1981	0	7	7	9	71	26	5	20	5	23	3	0	**176**
1980	0	2	7	26	44	21	2	34	10	5	0	2	**153**
1979	1	2	24	33	39	14	12	10	4	15	3	0	**157**
1978	0	0	0	34	65	10	13	6	6	1	2	0	**137**
1977	0	0	3	34	50	4	5	5	12	0	6	4	**123**
1976	1	1	8	53	63	11	16	6	13	4	0	0	**176**
1975	5	2	9	12	50	18	10	3	3	3	1	1	**117**
1974	2	1	8	19	18	26	3	9	6	22	2	0	**116**
1973	14	1	29	25	21	24	4	8	5	3	9	4	**147**
1972	1	0	19	13	43	12	19	13	8	9	7	0	**144**
1971	0	20	10	24	27	33	7	20	7	16	4	23	**191**
1970	1	3	5	23	23	9	5	20	9	20	0	3	**121**
1969	0	1	1	16	65	16	6	7	6	8	1	0	**127**
1968	2	1	3	13	47	21	4	8	5	8	11	16	**139**
1967	0	2	11	17	34	22	10	5	124	2	0	5	**232**
1966	0	4	1	21	22	15	3	8	3	0	0	0	**77**
1965	2	5	3	7	43	24	2	9	4	6	0	3	**108**
1964	0	1	6	22	15	11	9	7	3	1	3	0	**78**
1951-63	6	16	91	175	270	217	68	54	41	44	38	8	**1,028**
Total	200	178	632	1,468	2,519	1,113	276	335	437	416	316	204	**9,357**
Average	3	3	11	23	40	18	5	6	7	7	5	3	**130**
Max	24	20	56	69	130	75	19	34	124	28	55	27	**248**

Extreme Weather Records in Texas

Sources: Office of the State Climatologist and the National Weather Service, Dallas–Fort Worth.

Temperature			
Lowest	-23°F	Tulia	Feb. 12, 1899
	-23°F	Seminole	Feb. 8, 1933
Highest	120°F	Seymour	Aug. 12, 1936
	120°F	Monahans	June 28, 1994
Coldest Winter	41.3°F average		1898–1899
Hottest Summer	86.8°F average		2011

Wind Velocity		
Highest Sustained Wind		
145 mph SE	Matagorda	Sept. 11, 1961
145 mph NE	Port Lavaca	Sept. 11, 1961
Highest Peak Gust		
180 mph SW	Aransas Pass	Aug. 3, 1970
180 mph WSW	Robstown	Aug. 3, 1970

These winds occurred during Hurricane Carla in 1961 and Hurricane Celia in 1970.

Tornadoes		
Waco	McLennan County	May 11, 1953
Wichita Falls	Wichita County	April 3, 1964
Lubbock	Lubbock County	May 11, 1970
Valley Mills	McLennan County	May 6, 1973
Brownwood	Brown County	April 19, 1976
Jarrell	Williamson County	May 27, 1997

Since 1950, there have been six tornadoes of the F-5 category, that is, with winds between 261–318 mph.

Rainfall			
Wettest Year Statewide		2015	41.23 in.
Driest Year Statewide		1917	14.06 in.
Most Annual	Bridge City	2017	109.42 in.
Least Annual	Terlingua	2011	1.30 in.
Most in 24 Hours†	Alvin	July 25–26, 1979	43.00 in.
Most in 18 Hours	Thrall	Sept. 9, 1921	36.40 in.

†Unofficial estimate of rainfall during Tropical Storm Claudette. Greatest 24-hour rainfall at an official site occurred at Albany, Shackelford County, on Aug. 4, 1978: 29.05 inches.

Hail		
Hailstones six inches or greater, since 1950		
7.50 in.	Young County	April 14, 1965
7.05 in.	Burleson County	Dec. 17, 1995
7.00 in.	Winkler County	May 31, 1960
6.42 in.*	Medina County	April 28, 2021
6.00 in.	Ward County	May 10, 1991
6.00 in.	Moore County	June 12, 2010

*Largest documented official hailstone.

Snowfall			
Season	65.0 in.	Romero*	1923–1924
Month	61.0 in.	Vega	Feb. 1956
Single storm	61.0 in.	Vega	Feb. 1–8, 1956
24 hours	26.0 in.	Cleburne	Dec. 21–22, 1929
Annual avg.	24.2 in	Vega, Oldham County	

*Romero was in southwestern Hartley County.

Significant and Destructive Weather

This list of significant weather events in Texas since 1766 was compiled from ESSA–Weather Bureau information, previous Texas Almanacs, the Handbook of Texas, *The Dallas Morning News*, and the Office of the State Climatologist. For historical significant weather dating back to 1766, see texasalmanac.com!

2022

March 21-22, 2022: Tornadoes; North Central and East. A tornado outbreak occurred across the state as a result of a strong dry line, dropping down 47 reported tornadoes. Five of these had damage tracks of 25 miles or longer. The strongest tornado was an EF-3 which struck Jacksboro, injuring nine people. Fifteen tornadoes were rated EF-2, which caused two deaths and 31 injuries, and 15 EF-1 tornadoes resulted in three injuries. Sixteen EF-0 tornadoes also occurred, causing four injuries. These tornadoes resulted in $11.68 million of damage overall.

April 11-13, 2022: Tornado and Hail; North Central and South Central. A slow-moving line of storms brought severe hail and four tornadoes, one significant. An EF-3 tornado occurred in Bell County, reaching wind speeds of 150 to 165 m.p.h. and causing 23 injuries. Severe hail also plagued the area, including a hailstone with a diameter of 5.6 inches that fell near Salado on the 13th. Resulting damage from these storms totaled $2.2 million.

May 1-5, 2022: Tornadoes; Statewide. A slow-moving system traveled through the state, producing quite a few tornadoes along its way. On the 1st, three EF-Unknown tornadoes occurred in Pecos County and an EF-2 hit Scurry County. On the 4th and 5th, a tornado outbreak occurred, with some tornadoes being long-tracked extending several miles. Five EF-Unknown, three EF-1, one EF-2 (resulting in one injury), and one EF-3 tornado were a result of this outbreak. Overall damage from these tornadoes cost $1.03 million.

May 21-25, 2022: Tornadoes; Statewide. A cold front extending from a lingering low-pressure system brought severe weather over the course of four days across the state. Several tornadoes touched ground: seven EF-Unknown, one EF-0, two EF-1, and four EF-2. No injuries or deaths occurred from these tornadoes. Resulting damage from these storms totaled $5.19 million.

November 4-5, 2022: Tornadoes; East. A cold front pushed across the state, initiating a tornado outbreak. Eleven tornadoes touched down: three EF-1, three EF-2, three EF-3, and two EF-4. One of the EF-3 tornadoes occurred in Morris County, causing one death and eight injuries. One EF-4 tornado was in Red River County, causing 13 injuries, and the other was in Lamar County, resulting in ten injuries. These tornadoes were responsible for $25.02 million worth of damage.

December 13-14, 2022: Tornadoes; North Central. A strong low-pressure system led to a powerful cold front which caused a tornado outbreak in the North Central Texas area. Twenty tornadoes touched down: five EF-0, eight EF-1, and seven EF-2. These led to some injuries, including two from an EF-2 tornado in Wise County, five from an EF-1 in Tarrant County, and two from an EF-2 in Collin County. Resulting damage totaled $167,000.

2021

February 11-18, 2021: Snowstorm; Statewide. An Arctic-air outbreak resulted in winter weather and extreme cold across the state. Heavy snow and periodic freezing rain occurred, along with bitterly cold temperatures and strong winds. These resulted in extreme wind chill values, power outages due to the extreme demand on the power grid, and losses of water for several days. This entire winter event resulted in 246 deaths statewide according to official totals. Damages nationally were estimated at $25.9 billion by NOAA, making it the most costly winter storm ever, and the total economic impact in Texas alone may have been as much as $100 billion.

March 12-13, 2021: Tornadoes; Panhandle. An upper level disturbance led to a tornado outbreak in the Panhandle: ten EF-Unrated, six EF-0, five EF-1, and two EF-2. These tornadic storms did not cause any fatalities or injuries, but did cause around $1 million of damage.

April 27-28, 2021: Tornadoes and Hail; Statewide. A slow-moving surface system was responsible for initiating severe storms across the state. A handful of tornadoes touched down: one EF-Unrated, one EF-0, one EF-1, and one EF-3. No injuries or deaths were related to these. Severe hail also resulted from these storms, with a maximum size of 6.42 inches. This particular hailstone fell in Hondo and was declared the largest hailstone officially recorded in Texas. This storm event resulted in $502 million in damage.

May 3, 2021: Tornadoes and Hail; Statewide. A cold front triggered severe thunderstorms that swept across the state, producing tornadoes, hail, and high winds. Six tornadoes touched down: one EF-Unrated, three EF-0, and two EF-2. One of the EF-2 tornadoes occurred in Ellis County and resulted in eight injuries after it struck three semis and one cargo van. Also associated with these storms was hail as large as 5.5 inches. This storm event totaled $4.2 million in damage.

May 15-20, 2021: Tornadoes and Hail; Statewide. A strong, slow-moving upper-level disturbance prompted storms over several days throughout Texas. Eighteen tornadoes touched down over the course of this event, including eight EF-Unrated, five EF-0, four EF-1, and one EF-2. Large hail was another significant threat, reaching diameters of 4.25 inches and leading to six injuries. Storm damages cost $7.5 million.

September 13-14, 2021: Hurricane; Upper Coast. Category 1 Hurricane Nicholas impacted the Gulf Coast over a two-day span. The storm made landfall on the Matagorda Peninsula around midnight on the 14th, moving northeast to Louisiana by day's end. The hurricane caused storm surge near Freeport and Galveston Bay along with heavy rain resulting in localized flooding. $125,000 resulted from the water damage inflicted by the storm.

2020

March 18, 2020: Tornadoes; North Central and High Plains. Severe storms rolled through North Texas and brought a couple of significant tornadoes. Eight were confirmed, with two as strong as EF-2. An EF-1 tornado was confirmed in Graham, and there was widespread damage throughout the area, including damaged buildings, downed power lines, and uprooted trees. Two EF-2 tornadoes, with winds estimated up to 135 m.p.h., were confirmed near Abilene, where several wind turbines were damaged, a small home was destroyed, and at least 75 vehicles were tossed around the area. Hail as large as 2.25 inches was also reported. There were no injuries.

April 22, 2020: Tornado; Upper Coast. A line of severe storms moved through southeastern Texas, bringing an EF-3 tornado in Onalaska and hail up to two inches in diameter. The tornado had peak winds of 140 m.p.h. and was on the ground for 32 miles. Many homes were destroyed and trees were uprooted. Thirty-three people were injured and three were killed.

May 22, 2020: Hail; North Central. Strong instability and moisture brought severe storms through far northern Texas, producing significant hail in Burkburnett. The largest hail reported had a diameter of 5.33 inches. Widespread damage in the area was also reported.

July 25–27, 2020: Hurricane; Lower Valley. Hurricane Hanna, the 2020 Atlantic season's first hurricane, made landfall near Padre Island on July 25th. Winds at this time were around 90 m.p.h. with gusts over 100 m.p.h. Eight to 15 inches of rain fell throughout the Valley, 250,000 people lost power, hundreds of homes were damaged, tens of thousands of tree limbs were blown down, hundreds of trees were uprooted, and there was an estimated $366 million in damage.

September 21–23, 2020: Tropical Storm; South Central. Tropical Storm Beta formed on the 18th in the Gulf of Mexico, slowed considerably, and moved towards the Texas coast. Beta made landfall at Matagorda Bay on the 21st and weakened significantly shortly after. Torrential rainfall caused major flooding in streets, highways, and interstates in Houston, as rainfall surpassed nine inches, forcing road closures. There was one death. Total damage from Beta was estimated at $225 million.

November 24, 2020: Tornado; North Central. Severe storms moved through North Texas, bringing heavy rain and an EF-2 tornado to Arlington. The tornado had wind speeds estimated at 115 m.p.h., stayed on the ground for 5.04 miles, and had a width of 150 yards. Buildings were destroyed, power lines were downed, roads were impassable because of debris, and five people were injured.

2019

April 13, 2019: Tornadoes; East Texas. A large, upper-level storm system moved across the southern Plains states. Severe thunderstorms impacted southeast Texas, producing two EF-3 tornadoes. One of the EF-3 tornadoes hit Franklin with peak winds estimated at 140 m.p.h., injuring 14 people and damaging upwards of 20 buildings. Mobile homes were damaged, cars were overturned, and power lines were downed; about 4,000 people lost power. The other EF-3 tornado touched down near Weches, killing the occupant of a double-wide trailer.

May 20, 2019: Tornadoes and Hail; High Plains. All the ingredients were present for a severe weather outbreak. NWS offices called for a strong chance of long-track, destructive tornadoes, and schools and businesses closed in preparation. Although the outbreak wasn't as significant as expected, tornadoes and hail pummeled northwest Texas. There were seven tornado reports that day, with the strongest being an EF-3 near West Odessa. Hail 5.5 inches in diameter was reported near Wellington, and now holds a record for one of the largest hailstones to fall in the state.

June 9, 2019: Strong Winds; North-Central. Severe thunderstorms moved through northern Texas, bringing heavy rain and strong winds to the Dallas area. Wind damage to power lines caused 350,000 to lose power and collapsed a large construction crane on an apartment building in downtown Dallas. The wind was measured around 70 m.p.h. at Love Field. The crane collapse killed one person and injured five others.

June 24, 2019: Flooding; Lower Valley. The Rio Grande Valley experienced the "Great June Flood II" on this day. Over a foot of rain fell in 6 hours, reaching 15 inches near Santa Rosa. Streets all over the area were flooded, 1,188 homes were destroyed or incurred major damage, more than 100 people had to be evacuated, 45,000 people lost power, 75 m.p.h. winds damaged five mobile homes beyond repair, and many rainfall records were broken.

September 17–19, 2019: Tropical Storm; East Texas and Upper Coast. A tropical disturbance formed near Florida on September 14 and reached the Texas coast on the 17th, becoming Tropical Storm Imelda at 12:45 P.M. C.D.T. The tropical storm made landfall near Freeport at 1:30 P.M. C.D.T. with maximum sustained winds of 40 m.p.h. and weakened to a tropical depression by 7 P.M. that evening. Imelda stalled between Houston and Lufkin from the 17th to the 19th. There was significant flooding in Galveston, Houston, Fannett, Beaumont, Vidor, and Orange, accumulating 30 to 44 inches of rainfall. Vehicles were flooded or stuck on I-10 for 2½ days. Rainfall was measured at 44.29 inches near Fannett, making Imelda the seventh-wettest tropical cyclone to impact the United States, the fifth-wettest in the contiguous United States, and the fourth-wettest in Texas. The flooding killed two people and inundated about 10,000 homes.

October 20, 2019: Tornado; North Central. An upper-level disturbance combining with an unstable atmosphere across northeastern Texas brought severe thunderstorms to the Dallas area. These storms produced golf ball-size hail, strong winds, and seven confirmed tornadoes. The strongest of these was an EF-3, which hit northern Dallas. The tornado was on the ground for 15.8 miles, had maximum winds of 140 m.p.h., remained on the ground for 32 minutes, and caused $1.55 billion in damage, becoming the costliest tornado event in Texas history. In addition to this EF-3, there were two EF-2, two EF-1, and two EF-0 tornadoes in northern Texas.

October 24, 2019: Winter Weather; High Plains. A strong, closed low moved across the Panhandle while a cold front provided significantly colder air across the area. Heavy bands of snow and thundersnow occurred from 9 A.M. C.D.T. on the 24th to 2 A.M. C.D.T. the next day. As much as 11 inches of snow fell in Booker and Miami.

2018

Jan. 16–17, 2018: Winter Weather; North Central Texas. North Texas citizens experienced a frigid Martin Luther King Jr. Day as a strong Arctic cold front pushed through the region. The air mass brought freezing temperatures, snow, sleet, and freezing rain. Two homeless citizens in Dallas lost their lives from the extreme cold conditions.

Jan. 21, 2018: Tornado; East Texas. Unstable atmospheric conditions produced supercell thunderstorms in the Ark-La-Tex midwinter season. Moderate-sized hail and strong winds were products of the intense storms. Reports of an EF-2 tornado on the ground for 7 miles in Bowie County reached an estimated maximum wind speed of 125 m.p.h. Many homes were damaged, as well as injuries sustained by local residents and farm animals with an estimated loss of $2.5 million.

April 3, 2018: Strong Winds; Upper Coast. Strong storms along the Texas coast produced damaging winds and gusts in Harris County. The most damaging winds were short-lived as a phenomenon known as a "microburst", a powerful downward rush of air from a thunderstorm. Sustained winds from this event reached an estimated maximum of 80 m.p.h., causing $2 million in damages to a hangar at Houston Hobby Airport.

May 19–20, 2018: Hail; High Plains. Slow-moving supercell thunderstorms caused a great deal of damage to residents of West Texas during the evening hours and into the night. The storms produced heavy rainfall that led to flash flooding and large hail. The magnitude of hail produced had the greatest toll on residents. Several observations of tennis- to baseball-sized hail were reported during the event which caused an estimated $30 million in damages to property.

June 7, 2018: Severe Weather; High Plains and Low Rolling Plains. A late-spring storm produced heavy rains and destructive winds in West Texas. Estimated winds during this event reached hurricane force, peaking near 115 m.p.h. One family in Scurry County reported an overturned manufactured home that resulted in one injury. Total damages by flash flooding and strong winds were estimated at over $600,000.

June 19–22, 2018: Flooding/Tropical Weather; Lower Valley and South Texas. A low-pressure system originating from the Caribbean made landfall in South Texas in the early days of summer. The system interacted with other atmospheric features to create strong, heavy rain-producing storms. For nearly four days, the region was drenched with continual precipitation that caused widespread flooding. Locally flooded areas saw water depths of 2 to 4 feet. Disaster responders in the region reported more than 2,000 rescues during the event. With at least 20,000 residents and businesses considered affected by the storms, a preliminary estimate of $115 million in property damage was reported.

Oct. 16–17, 2018: Flooding; Central Texas. Strong thunderstorms slowly rolled through Central Texas during the early morning hours bringing torrential downpours to the region. Flash flooding was extensive in the western areas of the region where rainfall totals between 6 to 9 inches caused overfilling of the Llano River, Lake LBJ, Lake Marble Falls, and Lake Travis. One loss of life was reported in Llano County. The combined property damage in Llano, Burnet, and Travis counties exceeded $100 million.

2017

Jan. 14–15, 2017: Ice Storm; High Plains. A strong winter storm made its way from the western US into the Texas Panhandle in the second weekend of January, bringing frigid temperatures, strong winds, ice, and snow. Ice and snow accumulations were measured to be 1-3 inches across the region. Many residents lost power during this event, along with damages to some infrastructure and economic losses to businesses. Total damages were estimated to be nearly $50 million for both Texas and Oklahoma Panhandles.

Jan. 21, 2017: Tornadoes; East Texas. An advancing cold front from the Southern High Plains made its way into East Texas where it interacted with unstable and unseasonably warm air developing into strong thunderstorms and supercells. Twelve tornadoes touched down across the Ark-La-Tex region, with two destructive EF-2s pushing through East Texas. The severe storms were responsible for over $4 million in damages to vehicles, local infrastructure, and resident homes.

March 7, 2017: Fire Weather; High Plains. Hot, dry, and windy conditions led to the ignition of a wildfire in the Texas Panhandle along with other fires within the Great Plains. The Gray County fire took the lives of three who were attempting to save livestock. After more than 521,000 acres of land burned, damages and losses of land, livestock, and infrastructure were estimated to be over $25.1 million.

April 14, 2017: Tornado; High Plains. Strong thunderstorms firing in the Texas Panhandle produced a significant tornadic supercell in the southern High Plains. A post-storm survey conducted by the National Weather Service (NWS) determined that the tornado that tore through Castro County during the early evening hours was an EF-3 with a massive diameter of 1.1 miles. Reports by the NWS affirm no deaths or injuries, though damages were estimated to be nearly $2 million.

April 29, 2017: Tornadoes; East Texas. Four deaths and over 50 injuries were the result of a devastating tornado outbreak in East Texas. There was a total of 7 confirmed tornadoes passing through Henderson, Hopkins, Rains and Van Zandt counties. Post-storm surveys confirmed the strongest storm was an EF-4 that had estimated wind speeds near 180 m.p.h. in Van Zandt County.

June 4, 2017: Hail; West Texas. The development of a strong line of thunderstorms produced strong winds and large hail in Odessa. Five-inch hail and 100 m.p.h. winds were recorded when the storm was at its peak. These conditions significantly damaged vehicles and infrastructure, uprooted trees, and caused power outages across the area. $208 million in damages was sustained from these storms.

August 25–29, 2017: Hurricane; Southeast. Hurricane Harvey made landfall in Southeast Texas, the first Category 4 landfall in the state since 1961. Strong winds and torrential downpours were the most destructive impacts to the region; maximum wind speeds reached 130 m.p.h. and the largest observed rainfall total was 60 inches. There were 68 deaths directly related to the storm and an estimate of $125 billion in damage.

2016

March 9–10, 2016: Flood; East Texas. Multiple days of heavy rain fell across the Sabine River Valley causing massive flooding in the basin. More than 1,500 homes received flood damage, and damage in Texas and Louisiana was estimated at $2.4 billion.

March 17, 2016: Hail; North Central. Intense, warm advection led to thunderstorm development over the western counties of North Texas. Damage from hail as large as tennis balls was estimated at $600 million.

March 23, 2016: Hail; North Central. Severe thunderstorms developed along a dry line as it surged east to the Interstate 35 corridor. Damaging winds, hail, and one tornado caused $2.3 billion in damage.

April 11–12, 2016: Hail; South Central. Severe thunderstorms produced 4.25-inch hail that damaged an estimated 136,000 vehicles and 125,000 homes. Combined damage of $3.5 billion made this the costliest hail storm ever in Texas.

April 17, 2016: Flood; Southeast. Ten to 15 inches of rain in less than 12 hours produced devastating flooding in west Houston in an event called the "Tax Day Flood." There were eight deaths and $2.7 billion in property damage.

May 21–26, 2016: Widespread Severe Weather. Five-inch hail and tornadoes were reported in the Panhandle. Rainfall totals of 6 to 10 inches occurred there and in Southeast Texas. The storms caused four deaths and a combined $1.2 billion in damage.

2015

May 4, 2015: Flood; Lubbock. Dozens of motorists from Lubbock to Tahoka needed to be rescued from their vehicles after driving into deep floodwaters. Combined damage to vehicles, homes, and thousands of acres of wheat crops exceeded $300 million.

May 8, 2015: Hail; Lubbock. Widespread hail damage to homes, businesses, vehicles, and wheat crops. Nearly $500 million of combined property damage and $100 million in crop damage.

May 23–30, 2015: Flash Flood; Central Texas. More than 25 deaths from flash floods and tornadoes from North-Central to South-Central Texas. Flood waters inundated at least 2,585 homes and 73 commercial buildings. Property damage exceeded $1 billion.

October 23–24, 2015: Flash Flood; North Central. Heavy rain led to flash flooding across portions of North-Central Texas. Rainfall totals in flood-damaged areas ranged from 5 inches to 21-plus inches within a 36-hour period. Property damage estimated at $1 billion.

December 26–27, 2015: Tornado; North. A potent storm system brought blizzard conditions to Lubbock and 12 deadly tornadoes to North Texas, followed by significant flooding across parts of North and Central Texas. In total, 15 people died, more than 600 were injured, and tens of thousands of dairy cows in West Texas were killed.

2014

April 3, 2014: Hailstorm; Denton. A severe thunderstorm moving through the Denton area dropped hail as big as softballs, which caused more than $500 million in damages to homes, businesses, and vehicles.

May 11, 2014: Wildfire; Hutchinson County. A wildfire in Hutchinson County destroyed about 100 homes and caused the evacuation of more than 700 residents. The fire burned more than 1,000 acres and caused at least $10 million in damages.

June 12, 2014: Hailstorm; Abilene. A severe hailstorm moving through Abilene dropped hail up to 4.5 inches in diameter across the city. There were 12 injuries and $400 million in property damage.

2013

May 15, 2013: Tornado Outbreak; North Texas. A deadly tornado outbreak in North Texas claimed the lives of six people and injured more than 100 others. $250 million in damages were a result of an EF4 tornado in Mambrino and an EF3 tornado in Cleburne.

May 28, 2013: Hailstorm; Amarillo. A massive hailstorm moving through the Amarillo area dropped hail as big as baseballs and caused $200 million in damages. An estimated 35,000 vehicles and thousands of homes in Amarillo were damaged.

June 5, 2013: Hailstorm; Lubbock. Baseball-sized hail along with winds in excess of 90 m.p.h. caused more than $400 million in property damage in Lubbock. There were numerous reports of damage to homes, vehicles, as well as downed trees and power lines.

October 30–31, 2013: Flash Flooding; Travis County. Six to ten inches of rain fell in Travis County and more than a foot of rain fell near Wimberley and Driftwood. Near Oak Hill, four people died and the flooding caused $100 million in property damage.

2012

Jan. 9, 2012: Supercells; South Texas. Squall-line thunderstorms, hail, and an EF-1 tornado hit southeast of Alice International Airport and parts of Robstown, causing an estimated $5 million in damage. Other straight-line winds and hail caused total damage of $8.66 million.

March 29, 2012: Hail; McAllen. Strong thunderstorms, with wind gusts over 70 m.p.h. at Edinburg Airport, and severe hail up to 2.75 inches caused $50 million in property damage to homes and $1 million to crops. Rainfall between 4–6 inches fell in less than two hours, causing $5 million in flood damage.

April 16, 2012: Tornadoes, Flash Floods; Gregory. Thunderstorms along the Coastal Bend caused four tornadoes, including an EF-1 in Portland, two EF-0 tornadoes in Gregory, and another in Kleberg County. The Portland tornado caused $2 million in damage to homes and property. Around 80 percent of all homes in Gregory were flooded when storms dumped 2–6 inches of rain; some locations received up to 15 inches over several hours. Total damages topped $8.3 million.

April 29, 2012: Hail; Doud. Several severe storms blew up in West Texas near Lubbock with damaging hail and winds. Hailstones up to 4.5 inches fell in Whitharral, and wind gusts up to 95 m.p.h. near Wolfforth tore apart homes and cars. Damage estimates were $20 million from hail in Doud and more than $5 million from wind.

Nov. 22, 2012: Fog; Winnie, Chambers County. Dense fog early Thanksgiving morning caused a massive 150-car pileup on both sides of Interstate-10, causing two deaths and 80 injuries, 12 serious. Vehicular damage was $6 million.

Dec. 19, 2012: Dust Storm; Lubbock. A strong Pacific front kicked up winds up to 70 m.p.h., reducing visibility below 1/2 mile for more than 5 hours, the longest such event since 1977; property damage, $1 million.

Dec. 25, 2012: Heavy Snow; Plano. A moderate cold front and minor storms in North Texas produced wrap-around snow between 3–6 inches that caused 89 traffic accidents and cost $1.2 million.

2011

Jan. 8, 2011: Heavy Snow; Sherman. Between 3–7 inches of snow fell across Northeast Texas, causing hundreds of vehicle accidents, including more than 40 in Sherman and one fatality. Total damage, $1 million.

Feb. 27, 2011: Wildfire; West Texas. High winds and temperatures produced a series of wildfire complexes. The costliest was in Tanglewood, burning 1,659 acres and destroying 26 homes at a cost of $25 million. The biggest was in Willow Creek, burning 24,310 acres and 29 homes at a cost of $10 million. A combination of fires near Lubbock, Matador, Post, and Levelland burned 60,500 acres and several urban dwellings, costing $3.45 million.

March 11, 2011: Wildfire; Aransas. High heat, dry air, and high winds produced several fires in North-Central Texas. More than 10,000 acres burned, including fields of hay bales in Aransas worth $4 million. Three injuries were reported; other property losses were around $1 million.

April 6, 2011: Wildfire; Swenson. A wildfire near Swenson was spawned during critical fire conditions due to a cutting torch. The fire burned for 15 days, burning 122,500 acres of grass and ranchland; damage, $2.54 million.

April 9, 2011: Wildfire; West Texas. Dry conditions near the Pecos River spawned two fires near Midland and Marfa. The former burned 16,500 acres and 34 homes, causing 500 evacuations; the latter was caused by an electrical problem and burned 314,444 acres, 41 homes, and hundreds of cattle and utility poles. Total property damage was estimated at $7.7 million.

April 9–13, 2011: Wildfire; Possum Kingdom Lake. Drought and high winds helped spark a massive fire complex that burned for 16 days, destroying 167 homes, 126 other buildings, and 90% of Possum Kingdom State Park—126,734 acres total. Damage was $120 million, not including the estimated $11 million needed to combat the fire, nor the loss of cattle.

April 15, 2011: Wildfire; Cisco. Dry conditions caused several wildfires in North Texas. The largest was near Cisco, burning around 2,000 acres and destroying five homes. The fires burned 18,000 acres, costing $1.01 million.

April 17, 2011: Wildfire; Oak Hill. Dry conditions and human negligence combined to cause a wildfire in Travis County. Although it covered only 100 acres, it destroyed 11 homes and damage estimates reached $2 million.

April 19, 2011: Hail; North Texas. A series of supercells brought widespread hail ranging from 0.75 inches to 3.5 inches over the course of the 5-hour storm. Damage was around $1 million.

April 25–26, 2011: Supercells; East Texas. An upper level trough brought severe storms to East Texas for two days. On the 25th, three tornadoes touched down in Cherokee and Angelina counties, including two EF-1s; moderate hail was seen and downburst winds of 90-plus m.p.h. were reported. The next day, 10 tornadoes were reported, two of which were EF-1s near Ben Wheeler and Groesbeck, causing injuries. Total damage, $2.72 million.

May 1, 2011: Thunderstorm, Wind; Clyde. Isolated thunderstorms popped up in the Big Country, bringing hail and strong winds. In Clyde, straight-line winds were reported in excess of 100 m.p.h.; damage, $2 million.

May 11, 2011: Thunderstorm, Wind; Scattered Locations. Scattered thunderstorms from Killeen to Burns caused strong winds, hail, flash flooding, and an EF-0 tornado near Lake Kiowa; damage, $1 million.

June 18, 2011: Thunderstorm, Wind; Muenster. Thunderstorms followed by a strong microburst in the early evening and straight-line winds greater than 80 m.p.h. caused widespread damage in excess of $1.36 million.

June 20–21, 2011: Thunderstorm, Wind; East Texas. Severe thunderstorms culminated in strong downburst winds, hail, and an EF-0 tornado. Winds greater than 80 m.p.h. occurred in Nacogdoches and San Augustine, a tornado in Shelby County, and moderate hail; damage, $1.04 million.

June 28, 2011: Thunderstorm Wind, Titus County. Thunderstorms with 65 m.p.h. winds caused widespread damage at a cost of $1.6 million.

Aug. 11, 2011: Flash Flood, Lubbock. Scattered thunderstorms brought heavy rain, wind, and hail to the Lubbock area. Some area received 1–4 inches of rain in an hour, causing high-water damage to homes and vehicles. Farm and weather equipment in Dimmit were damaged by 90 m.p.h. winds. Total damage, $1.18 million.

September–October 2011: Wildfires; Bastrop County. Three separate fires that began Sept. 4 merged into a single blaze east of the city of Bastrop and became known as the Bastrop County Complex fire. The fire destroyed 1,691 homes and much of Bastrop State Park was burned. Declared the most destructive wildfire in Texas history, it was finally extinguished on Oct. 29.

Oct. 9, 2011: Tornado; San Antonio. An EF-1 tornado with winds up to 90–100 m.p.h. tore apart roofs, utility poles, and vehicles; damage, $1 million.

2010

June 9, 2010: Flash Flood; New Braunfels. Storms produced rains in excess of 11 inches, which caused the Guadalupe River to rise over 20 feet in just two hours. Campers, vehicles, boats, homes, and businesses suffered extensive damages along the riverbanks. The flash flood resulted in one death; damage, more than $10 million.

July 2, 2010: Tornado; Hebbronville. An EF-1 tornado that developed following Hurricane Alex caused considerable damage in Hebbronville. Over half of the town's population lost power, and the tornado was reported to be as wide as a football field. Estimated damage, $1.5 million.

July 4, 2010: Flood; Terry, Lubbock, Garza, and Lynn Counties. A series of thunderstorms erupted in the early morning of the Fourth of July over the west South Texas Plains. Local flooding caused roadway closures and damage to more 100 vehicles. More than 300 homes and businesses were affected; economic losses were around $16.5 million.

July 8, 2010: Flood; Starr County. Another storm that formed in the aftermath of Hurricane Alex, dumped an estimated 50 inches or more of rain on the lower Rio Grande Valley over 10 days leading up to the 8th. Falcon Reservoir rose during days of rain and finally spilled over on the 8th. The Rio Grande was nearly 2 miles wide at some points. Estimated damage was around $37 million.

Oct. 24, 2010: Tornado; Rice, Navarro County. An intense EF-2 tornado struck with maximum winds of 135 m.p.h. Vehicles were overturned on Interstate 45 and 11 train cars were derailed when the tornado hit the tracks. The football, baseball, and softball fields of the local high school were damaged; the intermediate school lost the gymnasium roof and suffered a caved-in wall; damage was $1 million.

2009

Jan. 19, 2009: Wildfire; Hidalgo County. Aided by strong gusts, low humidity, lack of rain, and warm temperatures, a wildfire spread across 2,560 acres in Hidalgo County and consumed four buildings at Moore Air Force Base. Damage at the base was $10 million.

March 30, 2009: Hail; Northeast Tarrant County. A strong line of severe storms dumped ping-pong- to baseball-sized hail on numerous cities in northeast Tarrant County. Much of the damage was to automobiles; overall damage was $95 million.

April 11, 2009: Hail; Midland. Up to golf-ball-sized hail caused tremendous damage to homes and vehicles during a severe storm, with an estimated $160 million in roof damage. A woman was pelted in the stomach by a hailstone that broke through the window in her dining room.

May 2, 2009: Thunderstorm, Wind; Irving. The National Weather Service determined that a microburst caused the Dallas Cowboys' bubble practice facility to collapse from winds estimated at 70 m.p.h. Twelve people were injured, including one coach who was paralyzed from the waist down. The damage was estimated at $5 million.

June 11, 2009: Thunderstorm; Wind; Burnet. A peak wind of 67 m.p.h. was measured at the Burnet Airport and numerous planes were flipped or blown across the tarmac. Damage in the city was $5 million.

Sept. 16, 2009: Hail; El Paso. A series of supercell storms produced golf-ball- to tennis-ball-sized hail and the most costly hailstorm in recorded history for the El Paso area. Estimated damage was $150 million.

Dec. 23, 2009: Tornado; Lufkin. An EF-3 tornado touched down in Lufkin, damaging structures, homes, and vehicles. The twister and heavy rains caused damage estimated at $10 million.

2008

March 31, 2008: Hail; Northeast Texas. Severe thunderstorms developed across the Red River valley, many producing large hail that damaged car windows, skylights, and roofs in Texarkana and elsewhere in Bowie County. Damage was estimated at $120 million.

April 10, 2008: Tornadoes; Johnson County. A lone supercell thunderstorm evolved in the afternoon of the 9th, producing tornadoes and large hail. A tornado touched down near Happy Hill and traveled northeast 3 miles to Pleasant Point, where it dissipated. The F-1 tornado, with maximum wind speeds of 90–95 m.p.h., destroyed three homes and damaged more than 30 homes and other buildings. Damage was $25 million.

May 14, 2008: Hail; Austin. A severe thunderstorm southwest of Austin moved northeast across downtown, causing extensive damage from winds and large hail. Large trees and branches were knocked down, and baseball-sized hail and 70–80 m.p.h. winds blew out windows in apartments and office buildings, including the State Capitol. Total damage was estimated at $50 million.

August 18, 2008: Floods; Wichita Falls. An unseasonably strong upper-level storm system moved over North Texas, and several waves of heavy thunderstorms caused heavy rain and widespread flooding in the Iowa Park, Burkburnett, and Wichita Falls areas. In Wichita Falls, at least 118 homes were flooded, 19 of which were destroyed, and residents were evacuated by boat. Burkburnett and Iowa Park were isolated for a few hours because of street flooding. Damage was estimated at $25 million, and Gov. Rick Perry declared Wichita County a disaster area.

Sept. 12, 2008: Hurricane Ike; Galveston. The eye of the hurricane moved ashore near Galveston with central pressure of 951.6 millibars and maximum sustained winds around 110 m.p.h., which made Hurricane Ike a strong category-2 storm. There were 12 deaths directly related to Ike (11 occurring in Galveston County from drowning due to storm surge) and at least another 25 fatalities either due to carbon monoxide poisoning from generators, accidents while clearing debris, or house fires from candles. Storm tide and storm surge caused the majority of property damage at the coast. Damage in Harris, Chambers, Galveston, Liberty, Polk, Matagorda, Brazoria, Fort Bend, San Jacinto, and Montgomery counties totaled $14 billion.

2007

March 29, 2007: Floods; Corsicana. Flash flooding along Interstate 45 submerged two cars in Navarro County, north of Corsicana, and 2 feet of water was reported on I-45 and Texas 31, east of town; damage to businesses, roads, and bridges, $19 million.

April 13, 2007: Hail; Colleyville. Teacup-size hail was reported as strong storms developed in Tarrant County. Hail damage to 5,500 cars and 3,500 homes and businesses was estimated at $10 million.

April 24, 2007: Tornado; Eagle Pass. A large tornado crossed the Rio Grande from Mexico around 6 p.m., striking Rosita Valley, near Eagle Pass. Ten deaths were reported, including a family of five in a mobile home. Golf-ball-sized hail and the tornado struck Rosita Valley Elementary School, leaving only the interior walls standing. Damage indicated wind speeds near 140 m.p.h. and an F-3 level, with a path 1/4-mile wide and 4 miles long. The tornado also destroyed 59 manufactured homes and 57 houses. Total damage was estimated at $80 million.

June 17–18, 2007: Floods; North Texas. Torrential rain fell as an upper-level low lingered for several days. In Tarrant County, one person drowned after her rescue boat capsized. Hundreds of people were rescued from high water. In Grayson County, a woman died in floodwaters as she drove under an overpass, and another death occurred in a flooded truck. Three people in Cooke County died when a mobile home was carried away by floodwaters. Damage was estimated at $30 million in Tarrant County, $20 million in Grayson County, and $28 million in Cooke County.

June 27, 2007: Floods; Marble Falls. Two lines of thunderstorms produced 10–19 inches of rain in southern Burnet County. Hardest hit was Marble Falls, where two young men died in the early morning when their jeep was swept into high water east of town. Damage to more than 315 homes and businesses was $130 million.

Sept. 13, 2007: Hurricane Humberto; Jefferson County. The hurricane made landfall around 1 A.M. in rural southwestern Jefferson County near McFaddin National Wildlife Refuge. Minimum pressure was around 985 millibars, with maximum winds at 90 m.p.h. Flash flooding occurred in urban areas between Beaumont and Orange, as 11 inches of rain fell. Coastal storm tides were 3–5 feet, with the highest storm surge occurring at Texas Point. Humberto caused one death, 12 injuries, and $25 million in damage.

2006

Jan. 1, 2006: Wildfires; North Texas. Several wildfires exploded across North Texas due to low humidity, strong winds, and the ongoing drought. Fires were reported in Montague, Eastland, and Palo Pinto counties. Five injuries were reported, as well as $10.8 million in property damage.

March 12–18, 2006: Wildfires; Borger. A wildfire now known as the Borger wildfire started four miles southwest of Borger, Hutchinson County. It killed seven people and burned 479,500 acres and 28 structures; total property damage, $49.9 million; crop damage, $45.4 million. A second wildfire known as the Interstate-40 wildfire burned 427,696 acres. The Texas Forest Service named the two wildfires the East Amarillo Complex. In all, 12 people were killed; total property damage, $49.9 million; crop damage, $45.4 million.

March 19, 2006: Tornado; Uvalde. An F-2 tornado moved through the Uvalde area causing $1.5 million in property damage. It was the strongest tornado in South- Central Texas since Oct. 12, 2001.

April 11–13, 2006: Wildfire; Canadian. A wildfire 10 miles north of Canadian, Hemphill County, injured two; burned 18,000 acres; and destroyed $90 million of crops.

April 18, 2006: Hail; Gillespie County. Hailstones as large as 2.5 inches in diameter destroyed windows in homes and car windshields between Harper and Doss in Gillespie County. The hail also damaged 70 percent of the area's peach crop, an estimated loss of $5 million.

April 20, 2006: Hail; San Marcos. Hailstones as large as 4.25 inches in diameter (grapefruit-size) were reported south of San Marcos, damaging 10,000 vehicles on the road and another 7,000 vehicles at homes; total damage was estimated at $100 million.

May 4, 2006: Hail; Snyder. Lime-to-baseball-size hail fell across Snyder in Scurry County for at least 15 minutes. The hail was blown sideways at times by 60-to-70-m.p.h. winds. Total damage was estimated at $15 million.

May 5, 2006: Tornado; Waco. A tornado with peak intensity estimated at low F-2 caused damage of $3 million.

May 9, 2006: Tornado; Childress. An F-2 tornado caused significant damage along a 1-1/2-mile path through the north side of Childress in the evening. An instrument at Childress High School measured a wind gust of 109 m.p.h. Property damage was estimated at $5.7 million.

Aug. 1, 2006: Thunderstorms; El Paso. Storms in a saturated atmosphere repeatedly developed and moved over the northwest third of El Paso County, concentrating near the Franklin Mountains. Rainfall reports varied from 4–6 inches within 15 hours, with an isolated report of about 8 inches on the western slope of the mountain range. Four days of heavy rains, combined with the mountains' terrain, led to excessive runoff and flooding not seen on such a large scale in the El Paso area in more than 100 years. Property damage was estimated at $180 million.

2005

March 25, 2005: Hail; Austin. In the evening, the most destructive hailstorm in 10 years struck the greater Austin area. The storm knocked out power to 5,000 homes in northwest Austin. Hail 2 inches in diameter was reported near the Travis County Exposition Center. Total damage was estimated at $100 million.

May 2005–December 2006: Drought; North-Central Texas. In May, portions of the area were upgraded from moderate to severe drought. By month's end, the drought had made significant agricultural and hydrological impacts on the region. In November, many Central Texas counties were added to the drought. The Texas Cooperative Extension estimated statewide drought losses at $4.1 billion, $1.9 billion in North Texas alone.

June 9, 2005: Tornado; Petersburg. An F-3 tornado affected an area from Petersburg in southeast Hale County to portions of southwest and south-central Floyd County. Total damage was estimated at $70 million.

Sept. 23, 2005: Hurricane Rita; Southeast Texas. The eye of Hurricane Rita moved ashore in extreme southwest Louisiana between Sabine Pass and Johnson's Bayou in Cameron Parish with maximum sustained winds of 120 m.p.h., category-3 strength. On the 22nd, Rita had strengthened to a peak intensity of 175 m.p.h. winds. In Southeast Texas, Rita caused 3 fatalities, 3 injuries, and $159.5 million in property and crop damage. Total property damage, $2.1 billion.

Dec. 27, 2005: Wildfire; Cross Plains, Callahan County. The fire started just west of Cross Plains and, fanned by winds gusting near 40 m.p.h., quickly moved east into town. Two elderly people were unable to escape the flames; 16 firefighters were also injured; property damage, $11 million.

2004

June 1–9, 2004: Floods; North-Central Texas. Flash flooding due to an upper air disturbance and a cold front caused damage to more than 1,000 homes. This was the first of many days in which heavy rains fell throughout the state. Estimated damage was more than $7.5 million.

June 21, 2004: Tornadoes; Panhandle. Severe weather kicked up just ahead of a frontal boundary causing damage to Amarillo and the surrounding area. Eight tornadoes were reported around the Panhandle, and there were many reports of hail, topping out at 4.25 inches in diameter in Potter County. Thousands of homes were damaged, and the total damage was estimated at more than $150 million.

July 28–29, 2004: Rainstorm; North-Central Texas. A stationary front led to torrential rainfall in Dallas and Waco. Hundreds of homes were damaged by flash flooding, as 24-hour rainfall totals for the two cities approached 5 inches. Outlying areas of the cities reported as much as 7 inches of rain in a 12-hour period on the 29th. Damage estimates topped $20 million.

Sept. 14, 2004: Storm; Grapeland. A lightning strike during football practice at Grapeland High School, Houston County, caused one death and injuries to 40 players and coaches.

Dec. 24–26, 2004: Snow; Coastal Texas. Large portions of Southeast and South Texas saw their first white Christmas in recorded history. A cold front passed over the state a few days prior to Christmas Eve dropping temperatures below freezing. Another cold front brought snow, which accumulated Christmas Eve night and into Christmas day. Galveston and Houston recorded 4 inches of snow, while areas further south, such as Victoria, had 12 inches. Brownsville recorded 1.5 inches of snow.

2003

Feb. 24–26, 2003: Snow and Ice; North-Central. A severe cold front brought freezing rain, sleet, and snow to the region. Snow accumulations were as high as five inches, resulting in $15 million in damages. Most schools and businesses were closed for this period.

April 8, 2003: Rainstorm; Brownsville. A severe thunderstorm caused one of the most destructive hail events in the history of Brownsville. Hail exceeded 2.75 inches in diameter and caused $50 million in damage to the city. At least five injuries were reported.

July 14–16, 2003: Hurricane Claudette; Port O'Connor. The hurricane made landfall near Port O'Connor in the late morning hours of the 14th. At landfall, wind speeds were more than 90 m.p.h. The system then moved westward toward Big Bend and northern Mexico; one death; two injuries; damage, more than $100 million.

September 2003: Floods and Upper Coast; South Texas. Persistent flooding caused more than $2 million in damage. The remnants of Tropical Storm Grace caused flash flooding along the Upper Coast region near Galveston early in September, with rainfall estimates in Matagorda County ranging from 6–12 inches. During the second half of the month, South Texas was hit with a deluge of rain caused by a tropical wave combined with cold fronts. Monthly rainfall totals ranged from 7–15 inches in the deep south.

2002

March 2002: Storms; Central Texas. Several violent storms occurred, which produced hail, tornadoes, and strong winds. Hail 1-3/4 inches in diameter caused $16 million in damage to San Angelo on the 19th, while 30 people where injured on the same day by an EF-2 tornado in Somerset, Bexar County, that caused $2 million in damage. For the month: 3 fatalities; 64 injuries; damage, $37.5 million.

June 30–July 7, 2002: Rainstorm; Central Texas. Excessive rainfall occurred in the South-Central and Edwards Plateau regions, with some areas reporting more than 30 inches of rain. Damage in the South-Central region alone was nearly $250 million. In Central Texas, 29 counties were devastated by flooding and declared federal disaster areas by President George W. Bush. Total event damage, $2 billion.

Sept. 5–7, 2002: Tropical Storm Fay; Coastal Plains. The storm made landfall along the coast on the 6th. This system produced extremely heavy rainfall, strong damaging wind gusts, and tornadoes. Ten to 20 inches of rain fell in eastern Wharton County. Brazoria County was hit the hardest with about 1,500 homes flooded. The storm produced five tornadoes, flooded many areas, and caused significant wind damage; total damage, $4.5 million.

Oct. 24, 2002: Rainstorms; South Texas. Severe thunderstorms in South Texas produced heavy rain, causing flooding and two tornadoes in Corpus Christi. The most extensive damage occurred across Del Mar College. The storm caused one death and 26 injuries; total damages, more than $85 million.

2001

Jan. 1–31, 2001: Drought; South Texas. The USDA's Farm Service Agency received a Presidential Disaster Declaration in December 2000 because of persistent drought conditions in South Texas; $125 million in damage was reported in the region.

May 2001: Storms; San Antonio and High Plains. Numerous storms caused excessive damage. Four-inch hail caused nearly $150 million in damage in San Antonio on the 6th. On the 30th, supercell thunderstorms in the High Plains produced winds over 100 m.p.h., and golf-ball-sized hail caused more than $186 million in damage. In all, 36 injuried; property and agriculture damage, $358 million.

June–December 2001: Drought. Significant drought-like conditions occurred in Texas from early summer through December. After the yearly drought report was filed, it was determined that total crop damage across the South Plains was about $420 million. Losses occurred to crops such as cotton, wheat, grain sorghum, and corn.

June 5–10, 2001: Tropical Storm Allison; Houston area. The storm dumped large amounts of rain on the city and made landfall on the western end of Galveston Island. Over the next five days, it produced record rainfall, which led to devastating flooding across southeastern Texas. Some weather stations in the Houston area reported more than 40 inches of rain total and more than 18 inches in a 24-hour period. Twenty-two deaths; damage, $5.2 billion.

July–August 2001: Heat. Excessive heat plagued Texas, resulting in 17 deaths in the Houston area.

Oct. 12, 2001: Tornado; Hondo. An F-2 tornado caused $20 million in damage. The tornado injured 25 people and damaged the National Guard Armory, a large hangar at the Hondo Airport, and nearly two dozen aircraft. Also damaged, were some 150 homes in Hondo, 50 on its outskirts, and nearly 100 mobile homes.

Nov. 15, 2001: Rainstorms; Central Texas. Storms caused flash flooding and weak tornadoes in the Edwards Plateau, South-Central, and southern portions of North-Central Texas. Flash flooding caused 8 deaths and 198 injuries.

2000

January–October 2000: Drought. A severe drought plagued most of Texas. Some regions experienced little to no rain for several months during the summer. Abilene saw no rain for 72 consecutive days, while Dallas had no rain for 84 consecutive days during the summer. During July, aquifers hit all-time lows, and lakes and streams fell to critical levels. Most regions had to cut back or stop agricultural activities, which resulted in $515 million in agricultural loss, according to USDA figures.

March 28, 2000: Tornado; Fort Worth. A supercell over Fort Worth produced an F-3 tornado, which injured 80 people and caused significant damage. Flooding killed two people.

May 20, 2000: Rainstorm; Southeast Texas. A flash flood in the Liberty and Dayton area was caused by 18.3 inches of rain falling in five hours. Up to 80 people were rescued from flood waters; property damage, $10 million.

July 2000: Heat; Dallas–Fort Worth. Excessive heat resulted from a high-pressure ridge, particularly from the 12th–21st. DFW Airport reported a 10-day average of 103.3 degrees. College Station had 12 consecutive days of 100 degrees or greater. The heat caused 34 deaths in North and Southeast Texas, primarily among the elderly.

Aug. 2, 2000: Storm; Houston. Lightning struck a tree at Astroworld in Houston injuring 17 teens.

Sept. 5, 2000: Heat. Excessive heat resulted in at least eight all-time high temperature records around the state, one of which was Possum Kingdom Lake, which reached 114 degrees. This day is regarded as the hottest day ever in Texas, considering the state as a whole.

Dec. 13 and 24–25, 2000: Ice and Snow; Northeast Texas. Two major winter storms blanketed the area with up to 6 inches of ice from each storm. Eight inches of snow fell in the Panhandle, while areas in North Texas received 12 inches. Thousands of motorists were stranded on Interstate 20 and had to be rescued by the National Guard; 235,000 people lost electric service from the first storm alone. Roads were treacherous, driving was halted in several counties; total cost of damages from both storms, more than $156 million.

1999

Jan. 22, 1999: Hail; Brazos County. Golf ball- and softball-sized hail fell in the Bryan–College Station area; damage, $10 million to cars, homes, and offices.

May 1999: Storms and Tornadoes; East, Central, West Texas. Numerous severe weather outbreaks caused damaging winds, large hail, dangerous lightning, and numerous tornadoes. An F-3 tornado moved through downtown area and high school of De Kalb, Bowie County, on the 4th, injuring 22 people and causing $125 million in damage to the community. On the same day, two F-2 tornadoes roared through Kilgore simultaneously. On the 11th, an F-4 tornado moved through parts of Loyal Valley, Mason County, and Castell, Llano County, killing one and injuring six. The 25th saw storms produce 2.5-inch hail in Levelland and Amarillo. Total damages, more than $157 million.

August 1999: Heat; Dallas–Fort Worth. Excessive heat throughout the month resulted in 16 fatalities. The airport reported 26 consecutive days of 100 degrees or greater.

1998

March–May, 1998: Drought. According to the Climate Prediction Center, this three-month period ranks as the seventh driest for a region including Texas, Oklahoma, Arkansas, Louisiana, and Mississippi. May 1998 has been ranked as both the warmest and the driest May in this region.

Aug. 22–25, 1998: Tropical Storm Charley; Hill Country. The storm dumped torrential rains in the area that caused flash floods; 13 killed; more than 200 were injured.

Oct. 17–19, 1998: Rainstorm; Hill Country. A massive, devastating flood set all-time records for rainfall and river levels; 25 killed; more than 2,000 injured; damage, more than $500 million from the Hill Country to counties south and east of San Antonio.

1997

May 27, 1997: Tornado; Jarrell. A half-mile-wide F-5 tornado struck Jarrell, Williamson County, leveling the Double Creek subdisivion, claiming 27 lives, injuring 12 others, and causing more than $40 million in damage.

1996

Feb. 21, 1996: Heat. Anomalously high temperatures were reported over the entire state, breaking records in nearly every region. Temperatures near 100 degrees shattered previous records by as many as 10 degrees, and Texans experienced heat more characteristic of mid-summer than winter.

May 10, 1996: Hail; Howard County. Hail up to 5 inches in diameter fell; 48 injuries; property damage, $30 million.

1995

May 5, 1995: Thunderstorm and Hail; Dallas–Fort Worth. A thunderstorm moved across the area with 70 m.p.h. wind gusts and rainfall rates of almost 3 inches in 30 minutes (5 inches in one hour); 20 people killed; 109 injured by large hail, many at Fort Worth's outdoor Mayfest near the Trinity River. With more than $2 billion in damage, NOAA dubbed it the "costliest thunderstorm event in history."

May 28, 1995: Supercell Thunderstorm; San Angelo. The storm produced extreme winds and giant hail, injuring at least 80 people and causing about $120 million in damage. Sixty-one homes were destroyed; more than 9,000 were slightly damaged. In some areas, hail was 6 inches deep, with drifts to 2 feet.

1994

Oct. 15–19, 1994: Rain; Southeast Texas. Extreme amounts of rainfall, up to 28.90 inches over a 4-day period, fell throughout southeastern Texas; 17 killed, mostly in flash flooding. Many rivers reached record flood levels. Houston was cut off as numerous roads, including Interstate 10, were under water. Damage was estimated at $700 million; 26 counties were declared disaster areas.

1983

Aug. 15–21, 1983: Hurricane Alicia. This was the first hurricane to make landfall in the continental U.S. in three years (Aug. 18) and one of the costliest in Texas history ($3 billion). Alicia caused widespread damage to a large section of Southeast Texas, including coastal areas near Galveston and the entire Houston area. Alicia spawned 22 tornadoes; highest winds were estimated near 130 m.p.h. In all, 18 people were killed and 1,800 injured.

Jan. 12–13, 1985: Snowstorm; West and South-Central Texas. A record-breaking snowstorm struck with up to 15 inches falling at many locations between San Antonio and the Rio Grande. San Antonio recorded 13.2 inches of snow on Jan. 12 (the greatest in a day) and 13.5 inches for the two-day total. Eagle Pass reported 14.5 inches of snow.

1982

April 2, 1982: Tornadoes; Northeast Texas. A tornado outbreak with the most severe striking Paris; 10 people killed; 170 injured; 1,000 left homeless; damage, $50 million. In all, seven tornadoes that day left 11 dead and 174 injured.

May 1982: Tornadoes. Texas recorded 123 tornadoes, the most ever in May and one less than the most recorded in any single month in the state; 1 death; 23 injuries.

Dec. 1982: Heavy Snow; El Paso. Snowfall recorded at 18.2 inches was the most to fall there in any month.

1981

May 24–25, 1981: Severe Flooding; Austin. Thirteen killed; 100 injured; damage, $40 million. Up to 5.5 inches of rain fell in one hour west of the city.

Oct. 11–14, 1981: Rain; North-Central Texas. Record rain caused by the remains of Pacific Hurricane Norma reached more than 20 inches in some locations May 24–25, 1981: Severe Flooding. Austin. Thirteen killed; 100 injured; damage, $40 million. Up to 5.5 inches of rain fell in one hour west of the city.

1980

Aug. 9–11, 1980: Hurricane Allen; South Texas. Three persons killed; property and crop damage, $650 million to $750 million; more than 250,000 coastal residents evacuated. The worst damage was along Padre Island and in Corpus Christi; 20 inches of rain fell on extreme South Texas; 29 tornadoes, one of the worst hurricane-related outbreaks.

Summer 1980: Heat. One of the hottest summers in the history of the Lone Star State.

Sept. 5–8, 1980: Hurricane Danielle. The storm brought rain and flooding to southeast and Central Texas; 17 inches of rain fell at Port Arthur; 25 inches near Junction. ☆

Texas Climatological Normals for 1991–2020 and Extreme Weather Records by County through 2022

Sources: Unless otherwise noted, this information is provided by Texas State Climatologist John W. Nielsen-Gammon and graduate research assistants Virginia Elliott, Alison Tarter, and William Baule at Texas A&M University.

Explanations and Sources

The Climatological Normals include Mean Maximum July Temperature, Mean Minimum January Temperature, Average Freeze Dates, Growing Season, and Mean Precipitation. They are calculated every 10 years and are based on the previous 30-year period, which is 1991–2020.

Data for counties where a weather station has not been maintained long enough to establish a reliable mean are interpolated from isoline charts prepared from mean values from stations with long-established records.

Mean Maximum for July is computed from the sum of the daily maxima. Mean Minimum for January is computed from the sum of the daily minima.

Extreme Weather Records include Record High Temperature, Record Low Temperature, and Record Rainfall; they are compiled yearly and are current through 2022.

The far left column lists Texas' 254 counties and identifies the town or landmark nearest to the National Weather Service station used to calculate Climatological Normals. If that weather station is outside the county, the town or landmark is in italics. Extreme Weather Records may have occurred at any weather station in that county and are identified only for Record Rainfall.

An asterisk (*) preceding an Extreme Weather Record means it also occurred on a previous date.

County, Town or Landmark Closest to Station for Normals	Temperature								Average Freeze Dates			
	Mean Max. July	No. at or Above 100°	Mean Min. January	No. at or Below 32°	Record Highest	Record High Date	Record Lowest	Record Low Date	Last in Spring		First in Fall	
	F.	Days	F.	Days	F.	M-D-Y	F.	M-D-Y	Mo.	Day	Mo.	Day
Anderson, Palestine	92.8	8	36.9	38	114	7-26-1954	–6	2-12-1899	Mar.	23	Nov.	9
Andrews, Andrews	95.2	20	33.0	59	113	6-27-1994	–1	2-2-1985	Mar.	18	Nov.	14
Angelina, County Airport	92.4	9	39.4	28	*110	8-19-1909	–2	2-2-1951	Mar.	11	Nov.	15
Aransas, Rockport	91.6	1	48.3	4	107	9-5-2000	9	12-23-1989	Jan.	31	Dec.	25
Archer, Archer City	95.5	29	32.6	57	114	6-28-1980	*–10	12-23-1989	Mar.	25	Nov.	10
Armstrong, Claude	91.2	9	26.0	108	*108	6-28-1980	–16	2-13-1905	Apr.	13	Oct.	27
Atascosa, Pleasanton	96.0	38	42.1	19	*113	8-22-1917	–1	1-31-1949	Feb.	27	Nov.	28
Austin, Sealy	93.4	11	42.9	14	*111	9-4-2000	0	12-23-1989	Feb.	28	Dec.	2
Bailey, Muleshoe NWR	91.6	12	22.1	123	*112	6-28-1994	–21	2-8-1933	Apr.	25	Oct.	19
Bandera, Medina	93.9	13	37.0	44	*110	7-9-1939	*–5	2-2-1951	Mar.	16	Nov.	15
Bastrop, Elgin	94.3	17	41.0	18	*111	9-5-2000	–3	12-23-1989	Mar.	4	Nov.	24
Baylor, Seymour	95.5	31	29.7	69	120	8-12-1936	–14	1-4-1947	Mar.	30	Nov.	6
Bee, Beeville	93.8	14	45.5	9	114	6-22-1990	5	2-12-1899	Feb.	17	Dec.	8
Bell, Stillhouse Hollow Dam	94.1	20	37.7	33	*112	8-11-1947	–5	12-23-1989	Mar.	14	Nov.	20
Bexar, San Antonio Intl. Airport	94.4	18	42.8	14	*113	8-28-2011	*0	1-31-1949	Feb.	26	Nov.	28
Blanco, Blanco	92.4	9	37.2	44	110	9-6-2000	*–6	1-31-1949	Mar.	20	Nov.	10
Borden, Gail	92.6	22	33.7	56	116	6-27-1994	–1	12-23-1989	Mar.	27	Nov.	8
Bosque, Lake Whitney Dam	94.1	28	36.3	43	113	9-5-2000	*–3	12-23-1989	Mar.	15	Nov.	14
Bowie, Texarkana	92.0	10	35.2	46	*112	8-5-2011	–9	2-12-1899	Mar.	15	Nov.	17
Brazoria, Angleton	91.1	0	48.3	4	109	9-4-2000	6	2-12-1899	Jan.	27	Jan	1
Brazos, College Station	94.7	18	43.1	16	112	9-4-2000	–3	1-31-1949	Feb.	27	Nov.	30
Brewster, Alpine	90.9	8	32.5	56	*117	6-17-1992	*–6	1-12-1962	Apr.	2	Nov.	3
Briscoe, Silverton	90.6	9	25.2	111	112	07-15-2020	–10	12-25-2004	Apr.	13	Oct.	28
Brooks, Falfurrias	97.2	41	45.3	10	116	7-13-2016	9	1-12-1962	Feb.	25	Dec.	1
Brown, Brownwood	95.4	30	33.9	55	113	7-19-1925	–6	12-23-1989	Mar.	22	Nov.	10
Burleson, Somerville Dam	95.9	27	36.8	37	114	9-5-2000	3	12-23-1989	Mar.	18	Nov.	9
Burnet, Burnet Muni. Airport	94.1	12	39.7	26	*114	7-11-1917	*–4	12-23-1989	Mar.	6	Nov.	23
Caldwell, Luling	96.2	24	41.2	29	111	8-28-2011	–3	1-31-1949	Mar.	5	Nov.	23
Calhoun, Port O'Connor	91.1	0	47.2	5	*109	8-29-2011	9	12-23-1989	Jan.	30	Dec.	27
Callahan, Putnam	94.0	23	33.6	53	*110	5-28-2011	–8	12-23-1989	Mar.	27	Nov.	7
Cameron, Brownsville	95.1	2	54.9	1	108	8-18-1915	12	2-13-1899	Jan.	6	Jan	2
Camp, *Daingerfield*	91.4	14	36.8	34	111	8-3-2011	*10	12-9-2005	Mar.	8	Nov.	22
Carson, Panhandle	91.3	14	25.2	122	112	6-27-2011	*–10	1-12-1963	Apr.	15	Oct.	29
Cass, Wright Patman Dam	90.9	6	37.1	44	*111	8-5-2011	*–4	02-17-2021	Mar.	4	Nov.	21

Table Highlights

Record Lows in 2021

Twenty-eight new record lows were set in 2021 during Winter Storm Uri, which dumped record amounts of snow on Texas. All 254 counties were affected by Uri; the only parts of Texas that did not record new lows lay in the far West and Panhandle regions.

Rain Records in 2018

Eight rain records were set in 2018. Six of those occurred in the months of September (the third-wettest month in Texas history) and October (the second-wettest month in Texas history). Combined, September–October 2018 are the wettest consecutive months ever.

Rain Records in 2017

Twenty-one rainfall records were set in 2017, 17 of which occurred between August 26 and August 30, during Hurricane Harvey. Six counties recorded more than 20 inches of rain: Galveston, Harris, Jefferson, Lavaca, Liberty, and Orange. The highest rainfall total, 26.03 inches, fell on Port Arthur in Jefferson County.

Rain Records in 2015

Eleven rainfall records were set in 2015, including six records during Oct. 24–25. Most records were set in Central and East Texas and ranged from 9.5 inches in Mineola in Wood County to 18.95 inches in Corsicana in Navarro County.

Record Highs in 2011

Thirty-five new record highs were set in 2011 from the Gulf Coast to West Texas and the Panhandle. The highest records were 118 degrees set in Knox County on June 20 and in Cottle County on June 27. That year began a severe drought that lasted through part of 2015. This period is now considered a "drought of record" by some water suppliers. ☆

Growing Season	Mean Precipitation													Record Rainfall Highest Daily Total		
	January	February	March	April	May	June	July	August	September	October	November	December	Annual			
Days	In.	In.	In.	In.	In.	In.	In.	In.	In.	In.	In.	In.	In.	Location	In.	M-D-Y
234	4.05	3.87	4.11	4.13	4.32	4.50	2.57	3.66	3.31	4.23	3.85	4.20	46.80	Palestine	9.10	8-14-1991
240	0.63	0.62	0.72	0.56	1.32	2.38	1.71	1.55	1.93	1.31	0.55	0.69	13.97	Andrews	7.60	7-2-1914
247	4.66	3.88	4.21	3.69	4.64	4.22	3.34	3.75	3.94	4.73	4.53	4.68	50.27	Zavalla	11.68	08-23-2022
328	2.58	2.01	2.77	2.11	3.40	3.66	3.00	2.37	5.65	3.96	3.01	1.89	36.41	Aransas NWR	14.25	11-1-1974
231	1.68	2.02	2.01	2.43	4.75	3.39	2.51	2.90	2.77	3.77	2.03	2.20	32.46	Olney	8.45	5-15-1989
195	0.71	0.53	1.27	1.45	2.27	2.85	2.82	2.86	1.69	1.75	0.75	0.71	19.66	Claude	6.42	5-16-1951
274	1.98	1.76	2.26	2.36	3.89	3.79	2.63	2.46	3.58	2.72	2.19	1.91	31.53	Rossville	9.09	9-15-1919
279	3.35	2.69	3.36	3.47	5.21	4.20	2.37	3.65	3.93	4.30	3.92	3.45	43.90	San Felipe	12.25	4-18-2016
177	0.51	0.46	0.92	0.73	2.28	2.34	2.31	2.75	2.56	1.68	0.73	0.61	17.88	Muleshoe	5.25	5-16-1951
244	2.23	1.84	3.00	2.54	5.53	3.89	2.51	2.26	4.48	3.29	2.34	2.36	36.27	Vanderpool	11.53	8-1-1978
264	2.96	2.06	3.15	2.73	4.86	2.98	1.97	2.32	2.97	4.02	3.07	3.00	36.09	Smithville	16.05	6-30-1940
222	1.17	1.50	1.93	1.78	3.81	3.84	2.88	2.94	3.23	2.80	1.87	1.24	28.99	Lake Kemp	6.25	9-1-1986
299	1.77	1.56	2.47	2.34	3.08	3.49	3.16	2.82	4.10	2.89	2.47	1.80	31.95	Chase Field	11.55	7-16-1990
251	2.55	2.29	3.26	3.10	4.85	3.43	1.85	2.46	3.74	4.00	2.64	2.80	36.97	Killeen	11.43	9-8-2010
277	1.96	1.74	2.31	2.42	4.40	3.28	2.41	2.15	3.88	3.75	2.08	2.00	32.38	San Antonio	14.33	10-18-1998
236	2.32	1.93	2.86	2.77	4.95	3.21	1.84	2.12	3.72	3.96	2.90	2.23	34.81	Hye	20.70	9-11-1952
226	0.55	0.69	1.08	1.36	2.52	2.39	2.00	2.69	2.54	1.78	1.26	0.59	19.45	Gail	10.79	9-20-2014
243	2.51	2.42	3.49	3.55	4.60	3.85	1.68	2.03	3.83	4.37	2.56	2.69	37.58	Kopperl	11.87	6-23-2014
249	4.26	4.58	4.70	4.88	5.25	4.39	3.40	2.77	3.89	4.78	4.33	5.18	52.41	New Boston	8.15	5-10-2009
338	4.02	2.44	2.91	2.87	3.87	4.74	4.18	4.98	7.06	4.37	4.69	3.80	49.93	Alvin	25.75	7-26-1979
278	3.43	2.90	3.41	2.87	4.60	4.01	1.98	3.10	3.50	4.93	3.31	3.71	41.75	College Station	13.39	10-16-1994
216	0.49	0.42	0.40	0.51	1.01	2.31	2.95	3.04	2.43	1.32	0.58	0.59	16.05	O2 Ranch	7.80	8-6-1920
197	0.69	0.76	1.26	1.64	2.87	3.65	2.42	2.64	2.31	1.82	0.85	0.78	21.69	Quitaque	8.58	6-1-1957
285	1.10	0.92	1.31	1.74	4.42	2.81	2.82	2.24	4.36	3.00	1.42	1.25	27.39	Falfurrias	10.00	9-20-1967
233	1.60	2.20	2.39	2.38	4.25	3.75	2.04	2.63	2.88	3.43	1.72	1.37	30.64	Winchell	8.20	9-23-1955
238	3.17	2.92	3.22	3.33	4.73	3.94	1.88	2.81	3.41	4.34	3.55	3.65	40.95	Somerville Dam	15.25	10-17-1994
262	1.65	1.63	2.66	2.12	3.67	2.85	1.79	1.76	2.89	3.18	2.25	1.93	28.38	Marble Falls	11.00	9-10-1921
263	2.40	2.16	2.74	2.94	4.20	3.55	1.85	2.60	3.42	4.20	2.57	2.76	35.39	Lockhart	13.38	10-18-1998
333	2.84	1.89	2.96	2.41	5.05	4.15	3.80	3.77	4.73	3.84	3.89	2.56	41.89	Point Comfort	14.65	6-26-1960
225	1.20	1.77	2.23	2.08	3.89	3.66	2.36	2.42	2.92	2.87	2.15	1.43	28.98	Baird	10.29	8-3-1978
365	1.08	1.03	1.45	1.47	2.22	2.86	1.98	2.16	5.73	3.83	1.76	1.21	26.78	San Benito	12.67	9-5-1933
259	3.46	4.05	4.62	4.16	4.74	3.85	3.07	2.72	3.66	4.25	3.82	4.68	47.08	Pittsburg	8.11	4-27-1958
196	0.53	0.50	1.24	1.60	2.74	3.22	2.57	3.07	1.91	1.97	0.80	0.91	21.06	Panhandle	8.05	5-16-1951
261	4.10	4.46	4.61	4.24	5.24	4.38	3.64	3.20	3.29	4.28	4.39	4.78	50.61	Linden	8.45	3-28-1989

County, Town or Landmark Closest to Station for Normals	Temperature								Average Freeze Dates			
	Mean Max. July	No. at or Above 100°	Mean Min. January	No. at or Below 32°	Record Highest	Record High Date	Record Lowest	Record Low Date	Last in Spring		First in Fall	
	F.	Days	F.	Days	F.	M-D-Y	F.	M-D-Y	Mo.	Day	Mo.	Day
Castro, Dimmitt	90.6	8	23.5	131	111	7-4-1983	*–12	02-16-2021	Apr.	22	Oct.	23
Chambers, Anahuac	90.3	1	44.8	11	106	7-9-1939	8	12-23-1989	Feb.	12	Dec.	6
Cherokee, Rusk	89.8	6	39.2	27	*111	8-20-1925	–6	02-17-2021	Mar.	7	Nov.	25
Childress, Childress	94.3	30	28.8	76	*117	6-26-2011	–13	1-17-1930	Apr.	3	Nov.	5
Clay, Henrietta	94.7	22	30.8	70	*116	8-7-1951	*–8	12-24-1989	Apr.	1	Nov.	8
Cochran, Morton	92.2	11	25.8	102	111	6-26-2011	–12	1-13-1963	Apr.	11	Oct.	31
Coke, Robert Lee	94.4	25	31.9	63	114	5-25-2000	–9	02-15-2021	Mar.	26	Nov.	7
Coleman, Coleman	95.4	23	36.4	42	114	8-3-1943	–9	12-23-1989	Mar.	14	Nov.	20
Collin, McKinney	91.3	15	36.1	44	115	8-4-2001	–11	12-23-1989	Mar.	10	Nov.	19
Collingsworth, Wellington	96.9	37	29.7	79	117	6-26-2011	–6	12-23-1989	Apr.	1	Nov.	4
Colorado, Columbus	95.7	26	40.7	30	116	9-4-2000	*4	12-24-1989	Mar.	9	Nov.	20
Comal, Canyon Dam	93.6	13	41.6	18	*112	8-4-2011	*2	12-23-1989	Mar.	1	Dec.	1
Comanche, Proctor Reservoir	95.1	23	36.2	56	113	8-3-2000	–8	12-23-1989	Mar.	12	Nov.	18
Concho, Paint Rock	95.1	29	32.1	61	*111	5-29-2011	–8	2-2-1985	Mar.	30	Nov.	5
Cooke, Gainesville	92.1	18	33.8	50	114	8-10-1936	–12	2-12-1899	Mar.	19	Nov.	14
Coryell, Gatesville	94.1	22	37.1	43	*112	9-5-2000	–8	02-16-2021	Mar.	19	Nov.	9
Cottle, Paducah	95.5	39	29.0	71	*118	6-27-2011	*–7	12-24-1989	Mar.	30	Nov.	7
Crane, Crane	95.1	26	33.6	49	115	6-27-1994	–6	2-2-1985	Mar.	16	Nov.	16
Crockett, Ozona	93.7	12	31.9	67	113	8-3-2015	–8	2-2-1951	Mar.	21	Nov.	6
Crosby, Crosbyton	91.5	13	27.6	89	113	6-28-1994	–14	2-12-1899	Apr.	5	Nov.	5
Culberson, Van Horn	93.1	12	31.6	70	112	6-25-1969	–14	2-3-2011	Mar.	21	Nov.	11
Dallam, Dalhart *(6 mi. SW)*	91.6	11	22.4	131	110	6-26-2011	–21	1-4-1959	Apr.	21	Oct.	20
Dallas, Dallas Love Field	95.5	22	39.9	23	115	8-18-1909	–10	2-12-1899	Mar.	2	Nov.	29
Dawson, Lamesa	93.3	17	27.6	93	114	6-28-1994	–12	2-8-1933	Apr.	4	Nov.	4
Deaf Smith, Hereford	91.1	9	23.9	118	111	6-8-1910	–17	2-1-1951	Apr.	17	Oct.	25
Delta, Cooper Dam	92.5	14	36.1	45	110		–1		Mar.	18	Nov.	13
Denton, Denton	94.3	19	35.9	38	*113	7-25-1954	–6	02-16-2021	Mar.	13	Nov.	20
DeWitt, Cuero	96.4	28	43.7	21	114	8-29-2011	2	1-31-1949	Mar.	2	Nov.	27
Dickens, Spur	93.5	23	28.0	89	117	6-28-1994	*–17	2-8-1933	Apr.	6	Nov.	4
Dimmit, Carrizo Springs	98.9	54	39.4	25	*114	6-11-1942	8	12-24-1989	Mar.	5	Nov.	22
Donley, Clarendon	92.8	22	25.3	105	117	8-12-1936	*–13	1-19-1984	Apr.	14	Oct.	26
Duval, Freer	96.8	48	45.5	9	116	6-15-1998	*12	1-24-1963	Feb.	10	Dec.	7
Eastland, Eastland	94.4	17	31.6	68	*115	8-11-1936	–8	12-24-1989	Mar.	30	Nov.	4
Ector, Penwell	93.6	18	33.9	44	116	6-28-1994	–12	2-2-1985	Mar.	15	Nov.	16
Edwards, Rocksprings	90.1	3	38.8	31	110	6-9-1988	0	12-22-1929	Mar.	8	Nov.	25
Ellis, Waxahachie	93.5	15	35.8	33	*115	8-18-2002	*–13	2-5-2011	Mar.	16	Nov.	16
El Paso, El Paso Intl. Airport	92.5	7	33.3	59	115	8-18-1909	–9	2-12-1899	Mar.	24	Nov.	11
Erath, Stephenville	96.0	19	32.9	54	114	8-11-1936	–9	2-12-1899	Mar.	29	Nov.	8
Falls, Marlin	93.6	17	35.3	38	*112	8-11-1969	*–7	1-31-1949	Mar.	21	Nov.	9
Fannin, Bonham	92.1	11	34.5	55	115	8-10-1936	–7	02-16-2021	Mar.	16	Nov.	13
Fayette, La Grange	95.4	29	41.8	19	111	8-23-1917	3	12-23-1989	Mar.	4	Nov.	25
Fisher, Rotan	94.4	27	35.4	55	116	6-27-1994	–12	2-12-1899	Mar.	17	Nov.	15
Floyd, Floydada	91.0	8	26.8	97	111	6-28-1994	–9	1-13-1963	Apr.	7	Nov.	3
Foard, *Truscott*	95.6	38	31.0	66	114		–7		Mar.	28	Nov.	9
Fort Bend, Sugar Land	93.4	8	45.3	7	*108	8-27-2011	8	12-23-1989	Feb.	9	Dec.	13
Franklin, Mount Vernon	93.0	14	36.0	41	112	8-3-2011	*–5	12-23-1989	Mar.	15	Nov.	16
Freestone, Fairfield	92.5	10	37.9	32	*110	9-4-2000	–2	12-23-1989	Mar.	16	Nov.	14
Frio, Dilley	96.7	29	43.4	10	113	9-6-2000	7	12-23-1989	Feb.	16	Dec.	6
Gaines, Seminole	93.4	16	29.1	82	114	6-28-1994	*–23	2-8-1933	Apr.	2	Nov.	6
Galveston, Galveston	90.9	0	50.9	2	106	9-4-2000	7	2-12-1899	Jan.	18	Jan	7
Garza, Lake Alan Henry	93.6	23	31.6	65	116	6-28-1994	–5	02-15-2021	Mar.	29	Nov.	10
Gillespie, Fredericksburg	92.6	10	36.2	42	*109	9-5-2000	–5	1-31-1949	Mar.	18	Nov.	10
Glasscock, Garden City	92.5	17	31.5	72	114	6-27-1994	*–3	12-22-1989	Mar.	31	Nov.	6
Goliad, Goliad	94.1	20	45.0	13	*112	6-14-1998	7	1-12-1962	Feb.	25	Dec.	1
Gonzales, Gonzales	93.9	14	41.8	19	*114	08-10-1962	1	1-31-1949	Feb.	26	Nov.	28

Growing Season	Mean Precipitation													Record Rainfall Highest Daily Total		
	January	February	March	April	May	June	July	August	September	October	November	December	Annual			
Days	In.	In.	In.	In.	In.	In.	In.	In.	In.	In.	In.	In.	In.	Location	In.	M-D-Y
182	0.57	0.54	1.03	1.25	2.64	3.59	2.35	3.10	2.41	2.10	0.70	0.72	21.00	Hart	5.17	6-11-1965
302	4.59	3.07	3.63	4.41	5.39	5.84	5.68	7.02	7.02	4.75	3.85	4.47	59.72	Anahuac	15.87	8-28-1945
263	4.36	4.26	4.46	4.04	4.58	4.51	3.38	3.35	3.67	4.65	3.98	4.88	50.12	Jacksonville	11.00	11-22-1940
217	0.84	1.03	1.52	2.72	3.91	4.04	2.32	2.92	2.49	1.93	1.40	0.98	26.10	Childress Airport	5.32	10-20-1983
221	1.69	1.84	2.59	2.71	4.69	3.59	1.80	3.07	2.59	3.55	2.24	1.67	32.03	Henrietta	6.07	6-23-1959
199	0.62	0.61	1.11	0.87	1.94	2.27	2.36	2.53	2.32	1.48	0.85	0.63	17.59	Morton	4.69	7-7-1960
226	1.06	1.11	1.30	1.65	2.60	2.60	1.54	2.63	2.65	2.11	1.23	0.95	21.43	Robert Lee	8.40	10-13-1957
249	1.31	1.87	2.17	1.96	3.68	3.65	2.09	2.53	2.46	2.69	2.09	1.38	27.88	Burkett	9.47	7-5-2002
254	2.58	2.71	3.54	3.68	4.74	4.13	1.87	2.15	3.10	4.42	3.42	3.45	39.79	Gunter	11.03	5-13-1982
215	0.73	0.86	1.34	1.86	3.24	3.32	2.15	1.92	2.35	2.25	1.19	0.87	22.08	Wellington	9.50	10-3-1986
255	3.67	2.81	3.32	3.77	4.78	5.11	2.93	3.30	3.26	4.69	4.02	3.38	45.04	New Ulm	12.13	4-18-2016
276	2.44	1.98	2.78	2.87	4.46	4.08	2.70	2.43	3.88	4.91	2.88	2.43	37.84	New Braunfels	18.35	10-18-1998
249	1.72	2.08	2.54	2.45	4.43	3.98	1.78	2.32	3.03	3.58	2.09	1.78	31.78	Comanche	8.86	8-19-2004
222	1.06	1.57	1.78	1.51	3.04	3.50	2.05	2.39	2.33	2.36	1.81	1.17	24.57	Paint Rock	8.25	9-9-1980
242	2.21	2.56	3.65	3.92	5.64	4.64	2.91	2.83	3.90	4.36	3.02	3.11	42.75	Gainesville	10.07	7-2-1903
236	2.32	2.54	3.22	3.19	4.14	3.39	2.97	2.97	2.94	4.18	2.63	2.53	37.02	Gatesville	8.67	9-8-2010
223	0.84	0.88	1.62	2.36	3.32	3.54	1.89	2.20	2.93	1.91	1.35	1.04	23.88	Paducah	7.00	6-2-1991
243	0.74	0.53	0.54	0.69	1.32	1.20	0.96	1.39	1.74	1.55	0.84	0.63	12.13	Crane	5.55	8-11-1986
227	0.96	0.88	1.96	1.78	2.81	1.95	1.25	1.81	2.14	2.24	1.26	0.80	19.84	Ozona (22 mi. SE)	8.02	8-18-2007
213	0.79	0.86	1.40	1.82	2.88	2.98	2.40	2.01	2.73	1.73	1.12	0.98	21.70	Crosbyton	5.78	6-30-1913
234	0.47	0.44	0.25	0.22	0.49	1.10	2.05	1.95	1.50	0.94	0.42	0.49	10.32	Pine Springs	9.42	9-12-2014
181	0.47	0.35	0.93	1.25	1.69	2.24	2.51	2.16	1.29	1.64	0.53	0.54	15.60	Bunker Hill	5.25	7-11-1959
272	2.59	2.78	3.45	3.15	4.57	3.83	1.71	2.19	3.10	4.79	2.93	3.23	38.32	Joe Pool Lake	12.05	7-29-2004
212	0.60	0.71	1.01	0.88	2.09	2.36	1.45	1.60	2.89	1.41	1.04	0.80	16.84	Lamesa	6.24	10-10-1985
189	0.64	0.45	1.22	1.09	2.09	3.34	2.34	3.04	1.86	1.85	0.69	0.72	19.33	Hereford	*5.30	8-3-1976
241	3.32	3.45	4.31	4.16	4.91	4.17	3.42	3.04	3.25	5.75	5.01	4.46	49.25	Cooper	8.46	5-13-1982
251	2.20	2.83	3.36	3.67	4.86	3.58	2.29	2.44	2.96	4.64	2.94	2.67	38.44	Isle Du Bois SP	13.00	5-13-1982
270	2.33	1.54	2.76	2.77	4.41	3.92	2.44	2.59	3.57	3.27	2.35	2.27	34.22	Cuero	12.40	6-30-1940
209	0.74	0.84	1.31	1.93	2.77	3.31	2.36	2.39	2.46	2.10	1.21	1.07	22.49	Pitchfork Ranch	7.60	9-18-1996
265	0.98	0.76	1.33	1.15	2.92	1.83	1.74	1.41	3.28	2.05	1.15	0.97	19.57	Carrizo Springs	11.48	10-14-2013
194	0.79	0.66	1.35	2.11	3.45	3.03	2.05	2.90	2.42	2.14	0.92	0.84	22.66	Clarendon	9.25	5-4-2001
304	1.25	1.31	1.92	2.08	2.80	3.07	2.44	2.45	3.35	1.82	1.42	1.24	25.15	Benavides	9.60	9-12-1971
222	1.24	2.01	2.42	1.83	3.76	3.38	1.95	3.12	2.78	3.00	1.92	1.76	29.17	Eastland	7.00	10-13-1957
243	0.68	0.54	0.67	0.70	1.62	1.00	1.47	1.61	1.53	1.27	0.61	0.58	12.28	Pleasant Farms	4.57	8-01-2017
258	1.03	0.93	1.81	1.66	3.35	2.50	1.95	3.10	3.38	3.05	1.66	1.62	26.04	Carta Valley	10.75	8-24-1998
230	0.40	0.48	0.32	0.25	0.30	0.78	1.80	1.76	1.57	1.06	0.51	0.79	10.02	Waxahachie	10.80	9-19-1958
245	2.61	2.72	3.99	3.48	4.31	4.22	2.48	2.91	3.27	4.73	2.93	3.15	40.80	El Paso	6.50	7-9-1881
226	1.84	2.16	2.82	2.91	4.97	3.33	1.99	2.96	3.32	3.32	2.33	2.18	34.13	Huckabay	10.21	4-26-1990
234	3.32	2.87	3.74	3.35	4.97	3.01	1.84	2.23	3.05	4.34	2.94	3.44	39.10	Marlin	11.90	7-31-1903
242	2.81	3.10	4.30	4.01	4.94	4.46	3.21	2.89	4.07	4.58	3.48	3.66	45.51	Bonham	13.30	7-3-1903
267	3.22	2.66	3.23	2.95	4.41	3.61	2.06	2.55	3.61	4.27	3.67	3.39	39.63	La Grange	14.69	8-27-2017
243	0.95	1.33	1.68	1.77	3.15	2.94	1.96	2.18	2.72	2.27	1.53	1.06	23.54	Rotan	6.85	8-13-1972
208	0.71	0.69	1.33	1.47	3.11	3.41	1.82	1.98	2.62	1.45	0.75	0.85	20.19	Floydada	7.75	9-12-2008
227	1.09	1.45	1.71	2.18	3.48	3.43	2.07	2.05	2.89	2.41	1.54	1.13	25.43	Crowell	8.25	9-19-1965
305	3.94	3.03	3.64	3.62	4.30	5.67	3.76	4.95	5.30	5.21	4.42	3.27	51.11	Katy	16.43	8-28-2017
245	3.41	3.73	4.52	4.13	5.07	4.17	3.18	3.10	3.58	4.74	3.86	4.70	48.19	Winfield	10.44	9-15-1913
243	3.65	3.46	3.81	3.29	4.70	4.50	1.77	2.88	3.18	4.23	3.91	4.11	43.49	Oakfield	9.08	06-01-2021
296	1.15	1.24	1.98	1.47	4.02	2.46	2.22	1.96	3.70	2.16	1.42	1.23	25.01	Derby	12.80	5-16-1980
219	0.69	0.72	1.01	1.05	2.23	1.92	2.05	1.78	2.75	1.33	1.00	0.68	17.21	Loop	6.35	10-19-1983
365	4.30	2.14	3.02	2.06	3.04	4.23	3.41	4.71	6.65	5.15	4.28	4.23	47.22	Bacliff	21.62	8-27-2017
225	0.81	0.86	1.37	1.66	2.52	2.99	2.04	1.93	2.13	1.85	1.26	0.80	20.22	Polar	9.00	9-25-1955
235	1.56	1.84	2.50	2.55	4.26	2.98	1.88	2.42	3.25	3.10	2.18	2.04	30.56	Gold	13.80	9-10-1952
219	0.95	0.97	1.27	1.32	2.75	2.06	1.68	2.42	2.45	2.46	1.20	0.87	20.40	Garden City	8.75	7-7-1945
280	2.71	1.73	2.74	2.67	4.54	3.90	2.95	3.41	4.69	3.41	2.33	2.13	37.21	Goliad	12.15	7-16-1990
272	2.37	2.07	2.80	2.82	4.68	3.41	1.95	2.92	3.58	3.94	2.73	2.66	35.93	Gonzales	16.31	8-31-1981

County, Town or Landmark Closest to Station for Normals	Temperature								Average Freeze Dates			
	Mean Max. July (F.)	No. at or Above 100° (Days)	Mean Min. January (F.)	No. at or Below 32° (Days)	Record Highest (F.)	Record High Date (M-D-Y)	Record Lowest (F.)	Record Low Date (M-D-Y)	Last in Spring (Mo.)	Last in Spring (Day)	First in Fall (Mo.)	First in Fall (Day)
Gray, Pampa	90.8	10	24.5	110	113	06-27-2011	–12	1-11-1962	Apr.	14	Oct.	28
Grayson, Sherman	91.1	6	35.7	43	113	08-10-1936	–4	2-16-2021	Mar.	14	Nov.	19
Gregg, Longview	92.7	10	36.1	44	113	08-10-1936	–7	2-12-1899	Mar.	16	Nov.	14
Grimes, *Washington St. Park*	94.1	23	40.3	31	108	08-11-1969	14	1-7-1970	Mar.	7	Nov.	19
Guadalupe, *New Braunfels*	92.8	11	39.1	32	112	09-05-2000	0	1-30-1949	Mar.	8	Nov.	18
Hale, Plainview	91.2	9	27.5	92	112	06-27-2011	–8	2-8-1933	Apr.	6	Nov.	2
Hall, Memphis	94.3	29	27.0	89	*117	08-03-1944	–11	1-18-1930	Apr.	1	Nov.	3
Hamilton, Hico	93.6	11	33.2	54	113	08-11-1936	–11	1-31-1949	Mar.	24	Nov.	7
Hansford, Spearman	91.0	12	21.5	131	111	08-13-1936	–22	1-4-1959	Apr.	21	Oct.	23
Hardeman, Quanah	94.9	23	28.3	78	*119	06-27-1994	–15	12-23-1989	Apr.	4	Nov.	1
Hardin, Evadale	92.1	6	41.3	24	110	09-01-2000	12	2-16-2021	Feb.	25	Nov.	30
Harris, Houston Hobby Airport	92.5	3	48.1	4	111	09-04-2000	5	1-18-1930	Jan.	30	Dec.	28
Harrison, Marshall	92.8	9	34.9	39	*112	08-18-1909	–13	2-16-2021	Mar.	20	Nov.	11
Hartley, Channing	89.4	5	21.9	135	110	9-7-1907	*–20	2-8-1933	Apr.	22	Oct.	24
Haskell, Haskell	93.8	28	30.8	63	115	6-27-1994	*–6	12-23-1989	Mar.	28	Nov.	7
Hays, Dripping Springs	93.5	16	40.8	29	111	9-5-2000	–2	1-31-1949	Mar.	17	Nov.	13
Hemphill, Canadian	92.3	20	19.1	136	*112	6-26-1994	–14	1-5-1942	Apr.	27	Oct.	15
Henderson, Athens	93.1	9	36.5	41	*109	9-5-2000	–6	2-2-1985	Mar.	18	Nov.	12
Hidalgo, McAllen Intl. Airport	98.5	40	54.6	1	113	6-16-1998	10	1-12-1962	Jan.	9	Jan	3
Hill, Hillsboro	94.9	18	35.9	37	113	7-10-1917	–6	12-23-1989	Mar.	21	Nov.	10
Hockley, Levelland	91.4	13	26.7	98	115	6-28-1994	–16	1-13-1963	Apr.	9	Nov.	1
Hood, Cresson	94.7	25	33.1	58	114	8-5-2022	–8	2-16-2021	Mar.	24	Nov.	9
Hopkins, Sulphur Springs	93.0	14	36.0	49	*115	8-10-1969	–10	2-12-1899	Mar.	15	Nov.	14
Houston, Crockett	93.6	19	38.0	31	114	8-18-1909	0	2-1-1951	Mar.	13	Nov.	17
Howard, Big Spring	94.8	25	32.9	54	114	6-28-1994	–7	1-11-1962	Mar.	20	Nov.	13
Hudspeth, Sierra Blanca	96.3	33	28.7	93	115	6-28-1994	–10	2-2-1985	Mar.	29	Nov.	6
Hunt, Greenville	96.0	21	35.3	50	116	8-10-1936	*–4	1-18-1930	Mar.	18	Nov.	16
Hutchinson, Borger	93.7	14	27.6	93	116	7-11-2020	–19	1-8-1912	Apr.	12	Oct.	28
Irion, Cope Ranch	95.3	29	29.8	79	*108	6-9-1985	*–4	2-16-2021	Apr.	9	Oct.	31
Jack, Jacksboro	94.2	20	31.8	56	*113	8-29-2011	–11	2-16-2021	Mar.	28	Nov.	7
Jackson, *Point Comfort*	91.0	1	47.7	5	107	7-27-1954	8	1-31-1949	Feb.	1	Dec.	21
Jasper, Sam Rayburn Dam	93.2	6	42.9	30	109	9-5-2000	*2	2-2-1951	Feb.	24	Dec.	1
Jeff Davis, Fort Davis	90.2	4	32.4	72	*108	6-27-1994	*–10	1-11-1962	Apr.	5	Nov.	1
Jefferson, Port Arthur / Airport	92.2	1	45.8	8	*108	8-31-2000	4	2-12-1899	Feb.	14	Dec.	7
Jim Hogg, Hebbronville	98.5	35	47.9	8	118	7-9-2009	12	12-23-1989	Feb.	4	Dec.	12
Jim Wells, Alice	96.7	23	49.5	4	*114	7-6-1997	11	12-25-1989	Jan.	29	Dec.	29
Johnson, Cleburne	93.5	20	35.3	41	114	9-2-1939	–6	12-23-1989	Mar.	17	Nov.	12
Jones, Anson	94.5	27	31.2	56	118	6-28-1994	*–12	12-23-1989	Mar.	31	Nov.	6
Karnes, Karnes City	95.7	24	40.9	27	112	7-27-1954	6	2-12-1899	Mar.	6	Nov.	20
Kaufman, Kaufman	93.1	17	37.7	39	113	8-10-1936	–7	2-16-2021	Mar.	8	Nov.	21
Kendall, Boerne	92.1	5	38.4	40	112	8-23-1925	–4	1-31-1949	Mar.	15	Nov.	13
Kenedy, *Port Mansfield*	93.8	11	47.1	12	110	6-16-1963	14	1-13-1975	Feb.	17	Dec.	8
Kent, Jayton	95.1	26	29.4	82	116	6-28-1994	–6	2-3-1985	Apr.	1	Nov.	5
Kerr, Kerrville	91.0	9	35.8	46	110	7-27-1954	–7	1-31-1949	Mar.	27	Nov.	7
Kimble, Junction / Co. Airport	94.5	22	35.5	52	112	8-2-2011	–11	12-22-1929	Mar.	25	Nov.	7
King, Guthrie	96.2	33	28.8	87	119	6-28-1994	–10	12-23-1989	Apr.	4	Nov.	3
Kinney, Brackettville	93.2	19	37.9	31	111	6-10-1988	4	1-12-1962	Mar.	11	Nov.	21
Kleberg, Kingsville Air Station	95.7	19	48.4	5	115	6-15-1998	10	12-24-1989	Feb.	3	Dec.	14
Knox, Munday	95.8	31	33.1	56	*118	6-20-2011	–11	1-4-1947	Mar.	26	Nov.	11
Lamar, Paris	94.4	21	35.4	46	112	6-28-1994	*–14	1-13-1963	Mar.	14	Nov.	16
Lamb, Littlefield	91.4	12	24.3	109	*112	7-11-1917	–12	1-31-1949	Apr.	14	Oct.	26
Lampasas, Lampasas	94.9	16	35.5	55	*116	9-8-1893	9	1-12-1962	Mar.	22	Nov.	12
La Salle, Fowlerton	98.3	44	41.1	25	115	8-10-1936	–13	2-12-1899	Mar.	3	Nov.	25
Lavaca, Hallettsville	95.7	13	46.4	13	112	8-29-2011	5	12-23-1989	Feb.	17	Dec.	4
Lee, Lexington	94.2	15	40.5	27	111	9-6-2000	*2	12-23-1989	Mar.	5	Nov.	21

Growing Season	Mean Precipitation													Record Rainfall Highest Daily Total		
	January	February	March	April	May	June	July	August	September	October	November	December	Annual			
Days	In.	In.	In.	In.	In.	In.	In.	In.	In.	In.	In.	In.	In.	Location	In.	M-D-Y
194	0.79	0.63	1.46	2.21	2.84	3.19	2.50	3.09	1.93	2.22	0.98	0.95	22.79	McLean	7.60	4-3-1997
250	2.52	2.76	3.96	3.87	5.54	4.54	2.90	2.88	3.43	4.77	3.50	3.62	44.29	Van Alstyne	9.30	9-22-2018
244	4.27	4.07	4.68	4.34	4.92	4.33	2.50	2.84	3.48	4.33	3.78	4.64	48.18	Longview	12.03	3-9-2016
259	3.53	3.00	3.31	3.35	4.70	4.59	2.23	3.31	3.82	4.69	3.98	3.64	44.15	Richards	11.98	10-16-1994
253	2.31	1.89	2.74	2.46	3.63	3.56	2.98	2.37	3.53	3.16	2.38	2.56	33.57	Kingsbury	9.25	10-9-2002
209	0.68	0.60	1.25	1.52	2.86	2.74	2.38	2.12	1.99	1.63	0.83	0.73	19.33	Plainview	7.00	7-8-1960
215	0.78	0.84	1.38	2.00	3.49	2.92	2.35	2.46	2.44	1.78	1.01	0.83	22.28	Memphis	8.80	6-7-1960
229	2.40	2.81	3.02	3.12	4.39	4.77	2.06	2.73	2.72	3.81	2.20	2.14	36.17	Hamilton	8.20	10-4-1959
182	0.61	0.46	1.25	1.80	2.50	3.32	2.67	2.67	1.71	1.84	0.81	0.97	20.61	Gruver	9.72	6-13-2010
210	0.88	1.19	1.66	1.98	3.52	3.46	2.15	3.03	2.90	2.04	1.58	1.19	25.58	Quanah	8.03	8-2-1995
281	5.23	4.05	3.67	4.49	5.03	6.92	5.23	6.01	5.57	6.05	5.39	5.59	63.23	Kountze	15.50	8-30-2017
330	4.09	2.85	3.28	4.08	5.42	6.09	4.59	5.44	5.76	5.78	3.90	4.34	55.62	Houston-South	20.84	8-27-2017
233	4.20	3.98	5.07	4.78	4.62	4.66	3.65	3.05	3.50	4.67	4.25	4.91	51.34	Harleton	10.50	3-29-1989
183	0.54	0.43	1.12	1.38	1.77	2.64	2.56	2.40	1.55	1.94	0.48	0.88	17.69	Romero	8.27	5-17-1914
225	1.19	1.49	1.98	2.07	3.35	3.78	1.80	2.52	3.25	2.53	1.74	1.25	26.95	Haskell	14.29	8-4-1978
242	2.65	2.10	2.86	2.61	4.29	3.68	2.10	2.11	3.65	3.97	2.94	2.74	35.70	San Marcos	15.78	10-17-1998
170	0.62	0.61	1.41	1.89	3.07	3.46	2.40	2.92	1.78	2.30	0.94	1.16	22.56	Canadian	7.00	6-8-2008
242	3.54	3.88	4.08	3.82	4.30	4.09	2.53	2.64	2.97	5.09	3.49	4.32	44.75	Payne Springs	11.28	10-25-2015
365	0.77	0.72	1.38	1.43	2.03	3.05	2.03	1.81	4.61	2.10	1.17	1.06	22.16	Santa Rosa	15.49	7-28-2020
235	2.74	2.77	3.57	3.68	4.51	3.61	1.65	2.18	3.15	5.05	2.73	3.10	38.74	Aquilla	11.49	10-24-2015
205	0.66	0.60	1.12	1.00	2.40	2.67	2.06	2.29	2.29	1.53	0.87	0.78	18.27	Ropesville	5.06	9-12-2008
228	2.25	2.38	3.28	3.03	4.23	3.82	1.91	2.59	3.01	3.82	2.61	2.29	35.22	Cresson	11.08	6-4-2000
245	3.30	3.63	4.43	4.31	4.30	4.27	3.03	2.92	2.96	4.90	3.98	4.47	46.50	Cumby	8.64	4-11-2017
251	4.13	3.80	3.44	3.68	4.79	5.05	2.53	3.44	3.64	4.45	3.81	4.56	47.32	Crockett	9.11	6-8-2001
239	0.73	0.80	1.15	1.55	2.54	2.49	1.58	2.40	2.39	1.84	1.35	0.78	19.60	Ackerly	6.40	6-9-1993
221	0.57	0.33	0.20	0.21	0.38	0.68	1.58	1.36	1.18	0.87	0.38	0.58	8.32	Dell City	7.10	9-12-2013
244	3.16	3.46	4.42	4.12	5.79	4.16	3.15	2.39	3.84	4.96	3.58	3.98	47.01	Commerce	12.00	8-13-2017
198	0.73	0.57	1.33	2.01	2.71	2.84	2.98	3.73	1.78	1.99	0.93	0.86	22.46	Borger	6.27	9-22-2004
202	0.91	0.90	1.07	1.24	1.81	2.65	1.61	2.60	2.31	1.96	1.10	0.89	19.05	Mertzon	8.35	8-12-1971
225	1.49	2.26	2.95	2.84	4.29	4.01	1.85	2.18	3.14	3.85	1.86	1.94	32.66	Antelope	11.18	5-16-1989
321	3.11	1.84	3.20	2.61	4.25	4.85	3.15	3.42	4.82	3.65	3.57	2.92	41.39	Maurbro	14.80	6-26-1960
280	5.59	4.76	5.44	4.63	4.53	5.54	3.52	4.98	4.44	5.22	5.29	6.09	60.03	Evadale	14.52	9-18-1963
209	0.53	0.41	0.40	0.54	1.19	2.28	2.99	2.65	2.08	1.28	0.57	0.59	15.51	Jasper	8.05	3-29-2018
301	5.32	3.09	3.63	3.92	4.70	6.70	6.85	6.89	6.69	5.47	3.89	4.98	62.13	Port Arthur Reg AP	26.03	8-29-2017
320	1.24	1.17	1.28	1.18	2.42	2.36	2.37	1.45	4.05	2.43	1.27	1.49	22.71	Kaffie Ranch	21.02	9-12-1971
337	1.27	1.35	1.69	0.98	3.49	2.32	2.48	2.62	5.26	2.72	1.58	1.30	27.06	Alice Intl. Airport	13.21	9-13-1951
240	2.61	2.52	3.47	3.08	4.27	3.90	2.11	2.83	3.02	4.43	2.92	2.53	37.69	Lillian	9.30	5-17-1989
221	1.03	1.41	1.53	1.95	3.32	3.56	2.46	2.58	2.26	2.50	1.46	1.37	25.43	Stamford	8.22	8-4-1978
261	1.64	1.61	2.28	2.41	4.38	2.95	2.32	2.66	4.06	3.16	2.32	1.84	31.63	Cibolo Creek	13.75	9-21-1967
256	2.91	3.03	3.48	3.68	4.36	3.57	1.86	2.75	3.41	4.66	3.06	3.40	40.17	Crandall	10.22	4-19-1976
243	2.28	2.22	2.79	2.52	5.28	3.78	2.83	2.80	3.90	3.88	2.92	2.32	37.52	Kendalia	12.32	5-24-2015
300	1.26	1.44	1.93	1.48	3.05	3.22	2.41	2.72	6.16	3.27	1.81	1.58	30.33	Sarita	9.30	10-12-1973
220	0.87	1.12	1.38	1.77	3.12	3.28	2.46	2.13	2.63	2.12	1.42	0.98	23.28	Jayton	*6.50	7-29-2004
226	1.66	1.63	2.35	2.27	4.29	3.31	2.09	1.93	3.73	3.20	2.16	1.94	30.56	Lynxhaven Ranch	15.20	8-2-1978
229	0.89	1.12	2.02	1.82	3.16	2.83	1.48	2.03	2.41	2.15	1.52	1.03	22.46	Junction	8.56	10-08-2018
213	0.95	1.19	1.48	2.04	3.18	3.28	2.05	2.83	2.46	2.00	1.38	0.97	23.81	Guthrie	8.85	7-4-1986
255	0.90	0.95	1.81	1.38	3.27	2.51	1.86	2.61	3.71	2.61	1.35	1.09	24.05	Fort Clark	18.00	6-15-1899
314	1.16	1.17	1.77	1.78	3.50	3.18	1.37	2.30	4.75	2.91	1.43	1.69	27.01	Ricardo	11.30	6-21-1924
232	1.31	1.41	1.87	1.77	3.94	3.61	2.88	2.55	2.12	1.85	1.16	1.23	25.70	Munday	8.00	6-14-1930
266	1.47	1.08	2.11	1.82	3.43	2.65	2.80	1.97	3.86	2.30	1.32	1.45	26.26	Arthur City	10.50	5-12-1920
247	3.08	3.34	4.35	4.70	5.63	4.26	3.51	2.95	3.95	4.62	4.21	4.28	48.88	Olton	6.30	6-4-1985
192	0.65	0.61	1.15	1.05	2.01	2.87	2.22	2.35	2.28	1.31	0.74	0.77	18.01	Lometa	9.50	10-4-1959
238	2.24	2.19	2.96	2.53	4.58	3.53	1.88	2.34	2.45	3.02	2.25	2.20	32.17	Fowlerton	12.80	9-9-2002
297	3.06	2.30	2.99	3.51	4.40	4.54	2.50	3.18	3.67	4.28	3.25	2.74	40.42	Halletsville	20.60	8-27-2017
262	3.08	2.24	2.94	2.61	4.68	3.21	2.11	2.62	3.07	4.59	3.34	3.23	37.72	Fedor	13.00	10-17-1994

County, Town or Landmark Closest to Station for Normals	Temperature								Average Freeze Dates			
	Mean Max. July	No. at or Above 100°	Mean Min. January	No. at or Below 32°	Record Highest	Record High Date	Record Lowest	Record Low Date	Last in Spring		First in Fall	
	F.	Days	F.	Days	F.	M-D-Y	F.	M-D-Y	Mo.	Day	Mo.	Day
Leon, Centerville	93.1	10	36.9	46	113	8-18-1909	–1	12-24-2022	Mar.	20	Nov.	12
Liberty, Liberty	92.9	3	43.0	14	112	8-9-1962	5	12-24-1989	Feb.	21	Dec.	1
Limestone, Mexia	92.5	10	37.9	32	112	8-18-1909	–5	12-23-1989	Mar.	16	Nov.	14
Lipscomb, Lipscomb	92.3	20	19.1	136	*114	6-27-2011	–19	1-19-1984	Apr.	27	Oct.	15
Live Oak, Choke Canyon Dam	95.0	33	44.7	9	112	9-6-2000	11	12-26-1983	Feb.	8	Dec.	6
Llano, Llano	95.3	27	35.9	50	115	7-14-1933	–7	12-22-1929	Mar.	20	Nov.	10
Loving, *Red Bluff Dam*	97.7	50	31.5	69	*112	7-30-1944	0	1-5-1947	Mar.	18	Nov.	10
Lubbock, Lubbock	92.4	13	28.7	84	114	6-27-1994	–17	2-8-1933	Apr.	4	Nov.	2
Lynn, Tahoka	92.2	11	29.8	80	111	6-28-1994	–15	2-8-1933	Apr.	2	Nov.	8
Madison, Madisonville	94.1	13	38.4	35	112	9-5-2000	*–2	1-31-1949	Mar.	16	Nov.	11
Marion, Jefferson	93.0	12	35.5	55	*112	8-5-2011	*–5	12-23-1989	Mar.	18	Nov.	8
Martin, Lenorah	94.8	28	32.7	54	109		*–8		Mar.	26	Nov.	9
Mason, Mason	94.6	19	35.6	51	111	7-12-2022	*3	2-2-1985	Mar.	18	Nov.	13
Matagorda, Bay City	90.2	2	45.0	7	109	9-4-2000	7	12-23-1989	Feb.	20	Dec.	3
Maverick, Eagle Pass	97.4	53	41.0	13	*115	7-25-1944	7	2-12-1899	Feb.	19	Dec.	1
McCulloch, Brady	92.3	15	37.0	43	110	6-29-1980	*–2	1-18-1930	Mar.	14	Nov.	15
McLennan, Waco Reg. Airport	95.5	24	37.9	34	*114	7-23-2018	*–7	1-31-1949	Mar.	15	Nov.	15
McMullen, Tilden	97.2	42	45.3	12	119	7-2-1910	5	12-22-1989	Feb.	13	Dec.	3
Medina, Hondo Muni. Airport	96.1	25	40.7	25	*112	9-5-2000	4	2-1-1949	Mar.	6	Nov.	20
Menard, Menard	93.8	17	31.2	64	114	5-29-1927	–6	1-9-1879	Apr.	7	Oct.	30
Midland, Midland	95.2	24	34.3	58	*116	6-27-1994	*–12	1-11-1962	Mar.	18	Nov.	14
Milam, Cameron	93.1	9	41.0	28	114	7-10-1917	–7	1-17-1930	Mar.	6	Nov.	23
Mills, Goldthwaite	91.8	8	35.3	37	110	8-6-1964	–7	12-23-1989	Mar.	23	Nov.	11
Mitchell, Lake Colorado City	95.1	23	29.5	76	115	6-30-1907	*–7	1-4-1947	Apr.	4	Nov.	5
Montague, Bowie	92.0	13	32.0	64	115	6-28-1980	–12	2-12-1899	Mar.	27	Nov.	9
Montgomery, Conroe	94.4	9	43.8	17	113	9-4-2000	1	2-16-2021	Feb.	24	Dec.	2
Moore, Dumas	90.5	9	23.1	124	*109	6-28-1980	–18	1-5-1959	Apr.	21	Oct.	24
Morris, Daingerfield	91.4	14	36.8	34	112	8-4-1998	–5	2-16-2021	Mar.	8	Nov.	22
Motley, Matador	91.9	18	29.6	72	116	6-28-1994	–6	2-15-2021	Apr.	5	Nov.	4
Nacogdoches, Nacogdoches	91.7	13	37.9	41	*113	9-3-2000	–4	1-18-1930	Mar.	13	Nov.	17
Navarro, Corsicana	93.5	17	36.8	38	*113	7-26-1954	–7	2-12-1899	Mar.	14	Nov.	16
Newton, Toledo Bend Dam	92.9	8	39.0	39	110	6-5-2011	4	1-19-1930	Mar.	9	Nov.	18
Nolan, Roscoe	93.1	18	32.7	57	113	6-27-1994	–11	1-5-1947	Mar.	30	Nov.	8
Nueces, Corpus Christi	93.4	4	49.9	4	113	8-31-1983	*7	2-12-1899	Jan.	28	Dec.	21
Ochiltree, Perryton	93.2	14	24.9	131	*113	6-10-1981	–17	1-7-1988	Apr.	14	Oct.	30
Oldham, Vega	91.5	12	22.7	122	110	7-27-1982	*–17	2-1-1951	Apr.	19	Oct.	23
Orange, Orange	89.4	1	42.1	19	107	9-1-2000	10	12-25-1989	Feb.	28	Nov.	23
Palo Pinto, Mineral Wells	94.6	26	34.8	48	115	8-14-1999	–8	12-23-1989	Mar.	24	Nov.	10
Panola, Carthage	91.6	9	37.9	39	109	9-5-2000	1	12-24-1989	Mar.	8	Nov.	19
Parker, Weatherford	93.1	13	33.7	61	119	6-26-1980	*–11	2-12-1899	Mar.	25	Nov.	8
Parmer, Friona	90.2	6	23.7	118	109	6-19-2017	–15	1-13-1963	Apr.	22	Oct.	23
Pecos, Fort Stockton	94.4	24	37.3	40	117	6-29-1994	–7	1-3-1911	Mar.	8	Nov.	20
Polk, Livingston	93.9	11	41.7	36	116	8-3-2016	*3	12-24-1989	Mar.	1	Nov.	24
Potter, Amarillo	91.2	9	26.0	108	111	6-26-2011	–16	2-12-1899	Apr.	13	Oct.	27
Presidio, Presidio	101.4	96	36.4	25	*117	6-18-1960	–2	1-5-1972	Feb.	23	Nov.	26
Rains, Emory	90.6	10	34.4	54	112	9-5-2000	–5	12-25-1989	Mar.	20	Nov.	12
Randall, Canyon	91.4	10	23.7	107	*109	6-27-2011	–14	2-1-1951	Apr.	15	Oct.	25
Reagan, Big Lake	94.0	14	35.1	56	115	6-28-1994	–9	2-2-1985	Mar.	20	Nov.	14
Real, Camp Wood	93.3	10	36.7	48	*109	9-6-2000	0	11-29-1976	Mar.	12	Nov.	14
Red River, *DeKalb*	92.1	13	33.3	49	115	8-10-1936	*–7	1-18-1930	Mar.	26	Nov.	6
Reeves, Balmorhea	93.8	21	32.1	65	118	6-29-1968	–14	1-11-1962	Mar.	29	Nov.	9
Refugio, Refugio	93.3	6	46.2	11	112	9-5-2000	8	1-12-1962	Feb.	27	Dec.	2
Roberts, Miami	90.5	9	23.3	116	114	6-11-1917	–15	1-5-1942	Apr.	16	Oct.	26
Robertson, Franklin	94.3	16	41.3	24	112	9-4-2000	–1	12-23-1989	Feb.	28	Nov.	28
Rockwall, *Lavon Dam*	91.3	15	36.1	44	*109	7-25-1954	–1	2-16-2021	Mar.	10	Nov.	19

Growing Season	Mean Precipitation													Record Rainfall Highest Daily Total		
	January	February	March	April	May	June	July	August	September	October	November	December	Annual			
Days	In.	In.	In.	In.	In.	In.	In.	In.	In.	In.	In.	In.	In.	Location	In.	M-D-Y
239	3.47	3.22	3.90	3.11	4.65	4.00	2.47	2.71	3.22	4.22	3.63	3.81	42.41	Buffalo	9.19	10-14-1957
286	5.12	3.90	3.98	4.60	5.54	6.05	5.02	5.52	6.85	6.34	4.72	5.18	62.82	Dayton	25.00	8-27-2017
243	3.65	3.46	3.81	3.29	4.70	4.50	1.77	2.88	3.18	4.23	3.91	4.11	43.49	Mexia	8.63	2-4-1986
170	0.62	0.61	1.41	1.89	3.07	3.46	2.40	2.92	1.78	2.30	0.94	1.16	22.56	Booker	7.76	6-9-1997
302	1.51	1.41	2.38	2.01	2.98	2.68	2.76	1.69	3.62	2.33	1.49	1.65	26.51	Whitsett	15.69	9-22-1967
235	1.50	1.67	2.43	2.14	3.86	3.27	1.82	1.59	2.34	3.00	2.07	1.88	27.57	Moss Ranch	13.53	9-11-1952
239	0.80	0.33	0.48	0.22	1.01	0.93	1.48	1.05	1.94	0.97	0.52	0.35	10.08	Mentone	3.79	9-24-1955
210	0.65	0.65	1.10	1.33	2.69	2.58	1.96	1.74	2.55	1.53	0.80	0.75	18.33	Lubbock	7.81	9-12-2008
220	0.76	0.74	1.07	1.34	2.93	2.83	2.29	2.23	2.93	1.66	1.12	0.78	20.68	Tahoka	9.10	5-5-2015
240	4.36	3.35	3.38	3.40	4.86	3.76	2.91	3.42	3.87	4.72	4.34	4.40	46.77	Madisonville	8.89	10-16-2018
236	4.08	4.23	4.83	4.74	5.11	5.10	2.96	2.42	3.77	4.47	3.61	4.42	49.74	Jefferson	9.10	4-26-1921
226	0.77	0.54	0.75	0.85	1.70	1.55	1.45	1.58	1.87	1.18	0.86	0.45	13.55	Tarzan	6.54	9-20-2014
241	1.32	1.88	2.15	2.30	4.21	3.80	2.30	2.01	3.03	2.58	1.94	1.38	28.90	Mason	7.80	10-16-2018
290	3.76	2.53	3.03	3.24	4.44	5.69	4.51	4.27	5.79	4.24	4.00	3.56	49.06	Matagorda	12.20	5-7-1951
287	0.74	0.74	1.18	2.02	2.80	2.20	2.10	1.68	3.29	2.14	1.13	0.81	20.83	Eagle Pass	15.60	6-29-1936
244	1.33	1.71	2.33	2.05	3.79	2.88	2.11	2.21	2.76	2.71	1.87	1.63	27.38	Brady	9.13	7-8-2015
245	2.59	2.68	3.31	3.30	4.44	3.35	1.82	2.05	2.87	4.41	2.71	2.87	36.40	McGregor	13.08	6-16-1964
299	1.09	1.09	2.25	2.12	3.17	2.46	2.87	2.06	3.57	1.92	1.46	1.54	25.60	Calliham	12.00	4-17-2010
263	1.21	1.27	1.88	2.10	3.43	2.94	2.06	1.93	2.76	2.59	1.56	1.18	24.91	Natalia	11.47	9-27-1973
204	1.11	1.35	2.10	2.00	3.40	3.07	1.58	2.00	2.20	2.50	1.80	1.21	24.32	Callan	7.67	10-10-1961
239	0.66	0.58	0.68	0.70	1.57	1.80	1.62	1.72	1.66	1.21	0.72	0.59	13.51	Midland	7.20	5-9-1968
261	2.60	2.35	2.90	2.32	5.28	3.61	2.61	2.51	3.89	4.29	3.11	3.13	38.60	Cameron	12.45	9-10-1921
234	1.70	2.23	2.42	2.23	4.21	4.16	1.82	2.01	2.51	3.49	2.06	1.60	30.44	Goldthwaite	7.20	10-5-1969
216	0.90	1.32	1.68	1.54	2.15	3.05	1.96	2.96	1.90	2.31	1.19	1.04	22.00	Colorado City	8.65	4-6-1900
228	1.64	2.29	3.00	3.04	5.22	4.00	2.63	2.47	3.23	3.62	2.10	2.08	35.32	Bonita	12.47	4-30-2009
285	4.38	3.32	3.46	3.39	5.46	5.21	3.32	4.53	3.69	5.39	4.77	4.10	51.02	Roman Forest	18.88	2019-9-19
183	0.39	0.40	0.98	1.38	1.91	2.27	2.72	2.99	1.66	1.80	0.52	0.68	17.70	Sunray	4.49	10-16-1968
259	3.46	4.05	4.62	4.16	4.74	3.85	3.07	2.72	3.66	4.25	3.82	4.68	47.08	Daingerfield	7.50	7-28-2009
213	0.81	0.89	1.45	1.96	2.77	3.44	2.03	2.68	2.99	1.89	1.08	0.99	22.98	Flomot	7.08	7-9-1994
248	4.46	4.21	4.47	4.01	4.53	4.09	2.88	3.66	4.07	4.34	4.44	4.78	49.94	Nacogdoches	14.22	6-28-1902
246	3.14	3.27	4.01	3.99	4.28	3.77	2.11	2.48	3.28	5.02	3.16	3.61	42.12	Corsicana	18.95	10-24-2015
253	5.30	4.50	5.12	4.68	4.30	4.94	4.66	3.43	3.95	4.23	4.78	5.77	55.66	Deweyville	20.60	9-18-1963
223	0.98	0.99	1.39	1.49	2.79	3.12	1.77	2.20	2.13	2.22	1.15	0.98	21.21	Roscoe	8.28	9-9-1980
331	1.39	1.29	2.28	2.04	3.38	3.56	2.54	2.75	5.42	3.13	2.03	1.93	31.74	Port Aransas	13.89	8-22-1999
197	0.69	0.58	1.51	1.90	2.80	3.20	3.48	2.96	1.86	2.04	0.83	0.97	22.82	Perryton	7.11	5-17-1989
183	0.56	0.40	1.09	1.28	1.83	2.66	2.72	3.26	1.57	2.09	0.64	0.72	18.82	Vega	6.07	5-16-1951
273	5.65	4.18	3.52	4.18	5.14	6.84	5.82	6.71	6.44	5.96	4.71	5.26	64.41	Bridge City	23.82	8-30-2017
231	1.59	2.19	2.98	2.63	4.00	3.55	2.13	2.49	2.66	3.28	2.41	1.89	31.80	Gordon	8.20	5-8-1997
255	4.66	4.23	4.92	4.72	4.35	4.04	3.64	3.44	3.67	4.54	4.44	5.63	52.28	Carthage	9.25	4-14-1991
230	1.96	2.55	3.03	2.69	4.42	3.93	1.86	2.59	3.19	3.76	2.95	2.25	35.18	Weatherford	8.57	8-20-2016
182	0.70	0.48	1.15	1.00	2.14	2.49	2.64	3.13	2.03	1.98	0.75	0.80	19.29	Bovina	4.73	7-21-1918
254	0.65	0.46	0.58	0.79	1.41	1.85	1.79	1.76	1.97	1.29	0.62	0.49	13.66	Bakersfield	7.10	4-30-2007
269	4.53	3.75	3.67	4.33	4.47	5.07	3.22	3.41	4.42	4.56	4.54	5.01	50.98	Corrigan	14.69	10-17-1994
195	0.71	0.53	1.27	1.45	2.27	2.85	2.82	2.86	1.69	1.75	0.75	0.71	19.66	Amarillo	5.89	10-08-2018
275	0.48	0.43	0.52	0.17	0.41	1.04	1.84	1.42	0.95	0.70	0.48	0.48	8.92	Bunton Rch	5.50	8-23-1944
238	3.10	3.46	4.56	4.11	4.64	4.05	3.05	2.77	3.28	4.84	3.37	4.21	45.44	Lake Tawakoni	10.05	10-25-2015
192	0.59	0.40	1.06	0.99	2.25	2.68	2.26	3.03	1.90	1.98	0.68	0.63	18.45	Canyon	7.87	8-29-1968
238	1.03	0.79	0.97	1.47	1.84	2.05	2.10	1.77	2.34	1.60	1.35	0.87	18.18	Big Lake	5.87	8-15-2005
248	1.14	0.99	2.01	1.93	3.46	3.00	2.18	2.94	3.94	2.68	2.10	1.31	27.68	Leakey	11.95	9-26-2016
225	4.13	4.20	4.91	5.40	4.91	4.01	3.25	3.03	4.14	5.32	4.54	4.98	52.82	Avery	9.29	12-28-2015
228	0.66	0.41	0.38	0.50	1.05	1.13	1.82	1.87	2.02	1.09	0.60	0.57	12.10	Red Bluff Dam	7.24	6-19-1984
283	2.25	2.02	3.19	2.25	3.47	3.25	2.11	3.61	3.84	4.04	2.55	2.20	34.78	Austwell	15.96	8-26-2017
192	0.87	0.59	1.35	2.17	3.49	2.91	2.58	3.18	2.08	2.92	0.88	1.13	24.15	Miami	5.58	10-10-1985
277	3.50	2.84	3.75	2.68	4.71	3.68	1.63	3.04	3.03	4.68	3.29	3.78	40.61	Bremond	8.49	8-19-2008
254	2.58	2.71	3.54	3.68	4.74	4.13	1.87	2.15	3.10	4.42	3.42	3.45	39.79	Rockwall	7.08	9-22-2018

County, Town or Landmark Closest to Station for Normals	Temperature								Average Freeze Dates			
	Mean Max. July	No. at or Above 100°	Mean Min. January	No. at or Below 32°	Record Highest	Record High Date	Record Lowest	Record Low Date	Last in Spring		First in Fall	
	F.	Days	F.	Days	F.	M-D-Y	F.	M-D-Y	Mo.	Day	Mo.	Day
Runnels, Ballinger	94.2	26	33.1	52	116	6-30-1907	–6	1-31-1949	Mar.	22	Nov.	10
Rusk, Henderson	93.0	11	37.3	41	*111	9-2-2000	–7	2-16-2021	Mar.	15	Nov.	16
Sabine, *Toledo Bend Dam*	92.9	8	39.0	39	114	8-9-1947	6	2-2-1951	Mar.	9	Nov.	18
San Augustine, Broaddus	92.7	8	37.0	37	112	8-18-1909	1	2-16-2021	Mar.	18	Nov.	13
San Jacinto, Coldspring	94.4	9	43.8	17	110	8-2-1998	3	12-24-1989	Feb.	24	Dec.	2
San Patricio, Sinton	92.8	3	46.9	7	111	9-6-2000	2	2-14-2021	Feb.	1	Dec.	17
San Saba, San Saba	94.1	23	34.8	51	113	8-30-2020	–1	12-23-1989	Mar.	16	Nov.	13
Schleicher, *Fort McKavett*	92.1	8	34.0	56	*107	6-26-1972	–7	2-2-1985	Mar.	22	Nov.	10
Scurry, Snyder	94.1	19	30.5	71	115	8-12-1936	–11	2-2-1985	Mar.	27	Nov.	10
Shackelford, Albany	93.4	23	33.3	57	115	6-27-1972	–13	2-16-2021	Mar.	30	Nov.	8
Shelby, Center	92.9	11	37.3	42	112	9-2-2000	0	2-2-1951	Mar.	13	Nov.	15
Sherman, Stratford	91.3	9	22.0	137	108	6-24-1953	–20	2-9-1933	Apr.	21	Oct.	21
Smith, Tyler	92.2	9	40.3	29	*110	8-3-2011	–8	2-12-1899	Mar.	7	Nov.	21
Somervell, Glen Rose	94.7	25	33.4	63	115	8-19-1984	–15	12-23-1989	Mar.	28	Nov.	7
Starr, Rio Grande City	98.9	63	47.2	6	*116	6-14-1998	7	2-13-1899	Jan.	31	Dec.	17
Stephens, Breckenridge	94.5	25	30.4	70	114	8-12-1936	–8	2-16-2021	Apr.	4	Nov.	3
Sterling, Sterling City	92.5	17	31.5	72	112	6-27-1994	–13	2-2-1985	Mar.	31	Nov.	6
Stonewall, Aspermont	95.2	34	31.0	73	117	6-28-1994	–10	12-23-1989	Mar.	29	Nov.	7
Sutton, Sonora	95.0	16	32.6	70	109	6-28-1980	–8	2-2-1951	Apr.	1	Nov.	6
Swisher, Tulia	89.7	9	24.2	119	111	6-27-2011	*–23	2-12-1899	Apr.	18	Oct.	26
Tarrant, Benbrook Dam	95.8	22	35.4	43	115	8-18-1909	*–12	2-12-1899	Mar.	14	Nov.	16
Taylor, Abilene Reg. Airport	95.1	19	35.5	48	*111	8-3-1943	–9	1-4-1947	Mar.	20	Nov.	10
Terrell, Sanderson	94.2	11	34.1	49	120	6-14-2008	1	12-22-1989	Mar.	11	Nov.	11
Terry, Brownfield	92.8	14	28.1	89	111	6-28-1994	–8	1-14-1963	Apr.	3	Nov.	4
Throckmorton, Throckmorton	95.2	32	31.4	71	119	8-30-1947	–11	12-23-1989	Mar.	29	Nov.	7
Titus, Mount Pleasant	92.3	16	33.9	61	112	7-21-2022	–12	2-2-1951	Mar.	24	Nov.	7
Tom Green, San Angelo	96.1	30	35.4	49	113	6-30-1907	–6	1-18-1930	Mar.	20	Nov.	10
Travis, Austin-Camp Mabry	95.9	29	43.7	12	112	9-5-2000	*–5	1-31-1949	Feb.	20	Dec.	3
Trinity, Groveton	91.3	6	41.0	17	111	9-4-2000	1	12-23-1989	Mar.	1	Nov.	28
Tyler, Town Bluff Dam	90.6	4	39.9	28	*111	9-4-2000	*2	1-31-1949	Mar.	9	Nov.	22
Upshur, Gilmer	91.1	12	34.0	54	114	8-10-1936	–5	2-16-2021	Mar.	26	Nov.	8
Upton, McCamey	95.9	31	34.7	46	*113	6-27-1994	*–2	1-11-1962	Mar.	12	Nov.	16
Uvalde, Uvalde	96.1	25	40.7	25	114	6-9-1910	*6	2-3-1951	Mar.	6	Nov.	20
Val Verde, Del Rio Intl. Airport	97.9	41	42.6	12	*114	7-30-1995	*2	2-3-1985	Feb.	16	Dec.	3
Van Zandt, Wills Point	93.2	13	36.7	41	115	8-18-1909	*–3	2-17-2021	Mar.	11	Nov.	21
Victoria, Victoria Reg. Airport	94.1	10	45.5	9	*111	9-5-2000	*9	1-18-1930	Feb.	18	Dec.	4
Walker, Huntsville	91.3	6	41.0	17	111	7-10-2022	*–2	2-12-1899	Mar.	1	Nov.	28
Waller, *Sealy*	93.4	11	42.9	14	107	8-12-1969	13	1-30-1966	Feb.	28	Dec.	2
Ward, Monahans	97.3	51	28.8	74	120	6-28-1994	–9	1-11-1962	Apr.	3	Nov.	6
Washington, Brenham	93.2	13	41.3	18	113	9-5-2000	–2	1-19-1930	Mar.	2	Nov.	30
Webb, Laredo	100.1	74	48.8	5	116	6-17-1998	5	2-12-1899	Jan.	25	Dec.	17
Wharton, Pierce	94.5	13	44.5	11	112	9-5-2000	3	2-12-1899	Feb.	23	Dec.	5
Wheeler, Shamrock	91.9	16	25.3	97	117	7-12-2011	*–13	1-19-1984	Apr.	9	Oct.	30
Wichita, Wichita Falls Airport	95.3	30	31.8	59	117	6-28-1980	–15	1-4-1947	Mar.	26	Nov.	9
Wilbarger, *Lake Kemp*	95.4	28	30.2	71	119	8-3-1943	–9	12-23-1989	Mar.	27	Nov.	9
Willacy, Raymondville	96.8	21	49.9	3	109	6-6-1916	14	1-13-1962	Jan.	21	Dec.	26
Williamson, Taylor	94.9	21	38.1	28	113	7-11-1917	*–5	1-31-1949	Mar.	6	Nov.	24
Wilson, Floresville	95.7	24	40.9	27	*114	7-6-1984	5	1-21-1985	Mar.	6	Nov.	20
Winkler, County Airport	97.1	51	31.5	65	117	6-27-1994	*–14	1-11-1962	Mar.	26	Nov.	6
Wise, Bridgeport	94.1	23	32.8	61	*115	6-29-1980	*–8	12-23-1989	Mar.	29	Nov.	7
Wood, Mineola	91.9	16	35.3	52	114	6-18-1996	–8	2-16-2021	Mar.	20	Nov.	11
Yoakum, Plains	91.9	13	26.2	99	113	6-27-1994	–12	2-1-1951	Apr.	11	Nov.	1
Young, Olney	95.4	33	31.8	56	*120	6-3-1998	–8	12-23-1989	Mar.	31	Nov.	8
Zapata, Zapata	98.5	59	48.6	4	116	6-16-1998	13	1-4-1911	Jan.	19	Dec.	22
Zavala, Crystal City	97.6	43	45.9	8	115	9-5-2000	6	1-12-1962	Feb.	10	Dec.	10

Growing Season	Mean Precipitation													Record Rainfall Highest Daily Total		
	January	February	March	April	May	June	July	August	September	October	November	December	Annual			
Days	In.	In.	In.	In.	In.	In.	In.	In.	In.	In.	In.	In.	In.	Location	In.	M-D-Y
233	1.01	1.52	1.79	1.56	3.08	3.07	1.67	2.41	2.57	2.20	1.45	1.04	23.37	Wingate	7.68	6-19-1982
247	4.11	4.10	4.63	4.40	4.67	4.76	3.39	3.62	3.82	4.22	4.06	4.63	50.41	Henderson	11.05	3-29-1989
253	5.30	4.50	5.12	4.68	4.30	4.94	4.66	3.43	3.95	4.23	4.78	5.77	55.66	Hemphill	11.70	3-10-2018
240	4.95	5.11	5.22	4.65	4.30	4.80	3.22	4.28	4.18	4.75	4.70	5.40	55.56	San Augustine	10.60	8-18-1915
285	4.38	3.32	3.46	3.39	5.46	5.21	3.32	4.53	3.69	5.39	4.77	4.10	51.02	Oakhurst	16.50	8-28-2017
324	1.65	1.85	2.44	1.83	3.26	3.41	2.80	2.47	5.28	3.86	2.41	1.70	32.96	Welder Wildlife	14.40	9-13-1974
239	1.68	1.98	2.58	1.87	3.93	3.48	2.02	2.02	2.53	3.08	1.80	1.59	28.56	San Saba	11.20	10-5-1969
234	0.84	1.14	1.43	1.49	2.89	2.15	1.74	2.56	2.56	2.76	1.23	1.11	21.90	D. Wilson Ranch	9.51	7-16-1990
227	0.77	1.05	1.56	1.40	2.68	3.14	1.91	2.09	2.75	2.17	1.19	1.06	21.77	Knapp	5.93	5-15-1980
225	1.22	1.73	2.36	2.81	3.39	3.87	2.27	2.11	2.97	2.72	1.93	1.54	28.92	Albany	29.05	8-4-1978
248	5.18	4.81	5.26	4.96	4.46	4.96	3.65	4.18	3.57	4.95	4.89	5.62	56.49	Neuville	10.20	10-30-1941
181	0.51	0.36	1.08	1.41	2.07	2.48	2.53	2.73	1.02	1.70	0.60	0.58	17.07	Stratford	5.60	8-17-1992
257	3.95	4.26	4.25	3.99	4.32	4.78	2.72	2.92	3.23	4.72	3.84	4.68	47.66	Eads	8.24	6-7-1943
225	2.13	2.34	3.00	3.02	4.21	3.78	1.79	2.73	3.01	3.77	2.24	2.23	34.25	Glen Rose	10.73	6-22-2014
321	0.78	0.95	1.25	1.02	2.85	2.76	2.04	1.34	5.12	2.46	1.10	0.80	22.47	Rio Grande City	12.51	9-22-1967
213	1.57	1.89	2.35	2.33	3.92	3.68	2.25	2.53	2.64	2.88	1.88	1.78	29.70	Breckenridge	15.70	10-13-1981
219	0.95	0.97	1.27	1.32	2.75	2.06	1.68	2.42	2.45	2.46	1.20	0.87	20.40	Case Ranch	6.79	9-21-1972
223	0.98	1.22	1.65	1.70	3.07	3.39	2.06	2.71	2.48	1.89	1.33	1.12	23.60	Aspermont	6.92	4-28-1930
221	1.01	1.24	1.55	1.69	2.37	2.62	2.28	2.60	3.21	2.15	1.20	0.74	22.66	Humble Pump Stn	8.60	7-11-1988
189	0.70	0.69	1.36	1.46	2.70	2.94	2.41	2.65	1.99	1.91	0.96	0.77	20.54	Tulia	6.01	10-21-1918
245	2.15	2.38	3.20	3.23	4.54	3.52	1.87	2.45	3.40	4.27	2.71	2.43	36.15	Blue Mound	11.30	8-22-2022
236	1.10	1.29	1.73	1.86	3.21	3.44	1.92	2.53	2.67	2.83	1.40	1.26	25.24	Lawn	9.19	8-4-1978
243	0.56	0.52	0.78	0.62	1.68	2.30	2.02	1.61	1.84	1.15	0.52	0.68	14.28	Dryden	6.30	9-23-1990
215	0.69	0.62	1.07	1.31	2.20	2.67	1.94	1.80	2.56	1.57	0.88	0.74	18.05	Brownfield	7.85	9-21-1936
223	1.24	1.67	2.08	2.16	4.37	3.99	2.37	2.26	3.00	3.06	1.75	1.55	29.50	Throckmorton	6.53	8-4-1978
230	3.56	4.18	4.36	4.55	5.24	4.32	2.90	2.66	3.62	4.61	3.78	4.79	48.57	Mount Pleasant	8.06	11-5-1994
232	0.92	1.20	1.48	1.47	3.05	2.31	1.10	2.42	2.51	2.42	1.16	0.89	20.93	Mathis Field	11.75	9-15-1936
291	2.64	1.89	2.88	2.42	5.04	3.68	1.96	2.74	3.45	3.91	2.92	2.72	36.25	Hill's Ranch	16.02	9-10-1921
272	4.57	3.38	3.85	3.89	4.47	5.45	3.06	4.14	4.47	4.63	4.68	4.73	51.32	Groveton	12.10	10-17-1994
258	4.98	4.85	4.62	4.45	4.68	5.15	4.17	5.03	5.26	4.99	5.12	5.80	59.10	Spurger	11.50	8-30-2017
229	3.76	4.09	4.22	4.66	4.49	4.07	3.05	3.01	3.68	4.57	3.81	4.51	47.92	Gilmer	7.88	4-23-1966
247	0.69	0.55	0.86	1.08	1.26	2.11	1.69	1.88	1.81	1.42	0.82	0.65	14.82	McCamey	9.13	10-4-1986
263	1.21	1.27	1.88	2.10	3.43	2.94	2.06	1.93	2.76	2.59	1.56	1.18	24.91	Montell	20.05	6-29-1913
293	0.61	0.63	1.18	1.50	3.06	2.32	1.50	2.69	2.63	2.08	0.91	0.71	19.82	Del Rio Intl. AP	17.03	8-23-1998
252	3.40	3.59	4.24	3.67	4.85	3.88	2.25	2.64	3.29	4.79	3.94	4.09	44.63	S. County Line	11.55	10-24-2015
291	2.67	1.96	2.99	3.01	5.23	4.21	3.46	3.11	4.53	3.97	2.93	2.34	40.41	Victoria	10.96	5-19-2021
272	4.57	3.38	3.85	3.89	4.47	5.45	3.06	4.14	4.47	4.63	4.68	4.73	51.32	Huntsville	14.75	8-28-2017
279	3.35	2.69	3.36	3.47	5.21	4.20	2.37	3.65	3.93	4.30	3.92	3.45	43.90	Brookshire	16.75	8-28-2017
216	0.67	0.45	0.63	0.44	1.30	1.63	1.87	1.85	2.19	1.52	0.49	0.77	13.81	Grandfalls	5.87	9-4-1986
273	3.66	3.36	3.63	3.56	5.39	4.46	2.58	3.83	4.59	5.07	4.21	3.69	48.03	Brenham	21.46	5-27-2016
329	0.77	0.65	1.34	1.30	2.82	1.81	1.86	1.58	3.87	1.66	0.97	1.05	19.68	Laredo	9.90	8-16-2022
287	3.13	1.95	2.81	3.09	4.79	4.89	4.30	3.92	5.71	5.59	5.69	3.73	49.60	New Gulf	14.00	6-26-1960
202	0.84	0.90	1.70	2.50	3.36	3.73	2.41	2.80	2.42	2.31	1.29	1.03	25.29	Shamrock	8.24	6-4-1995
228	1.20	1.40	2.02	2.50	3.81	3.35	2.02	2.53	2.99	2.88	1.63	1.56	27.89	Wichita V. Farm	8.00	8-15-1971
225	1.15	1.18	2.09	2.57	3.67	4.10	2.37	2.80	3.04	2.53	1.60	1.26	28.36	Vernon	14.82	8-2-1995
340	1.01	1.02	1.40	1.35	3.03	2.58	2.47	2.09	5.56	2.97	0.87	1.12	25.47	Port Mansfield	14.50	7-26-2020
259	2.50	2.24	3.09	3.02	4.25	3.97	2.19	2.64	3.96	3.92	2.71	2.59	37.08	Taylor	16.11	9-10-1921
261	1.64	1.61	2.28	2.41	4.38	2.95	2.32	2.66	4.06	3.16	2.32	1.84	31.63	Falls City	8.83	9-15-1968
222	0.49	0.40	0.72	0.47	1.40	1.27	1.53	1.38	1.55	1.18	0.49	0.50	11.38	NE of Kermit	3.80	9-20-2014
222	1.67	2.21	2.84	3.04	4.55	3.73	2.07	2.18	3.04	3.91	2.19	1.91	33.34	Boyd	9.15	10-31-1981
235	3.67	4.01	4.15	3.80	4.68	3.53	2.67	2.71	3.73	4.99	3.47	5.06	46.47	Mineola	9.50	10-24-2015
200	0.52	0.59	1.04	0.91	1.56	1.99	2.10	2.10	2.48	1.43	0.70	0.77	16.19	Plains	6.11	7-5-1960
222	1.41	1.49	2.58	2.03	3.92	3.41	2.34	2.20	2.53	3.86	1.89	1.59	29.25	Olney	8.74	7-28-2004
341	0.81	0.45	0.66	1.23	2.64	2.61	2.83	1.52	4.37	1.38	1.23	0.67	20.40	Zapata	6.10	4-14-1966
307	1.04	0.85	1.70	1.31	2.23	2.07	2.07	1.92	2.43	2.00	1.00	0.84	19.46	Crystal City	13.88	10-14-2013

ASTRONOMICAL CALENDAR

SEASONS, CHRONOLOGICAL ERAS & CYCLES

MORNING & EVENING STARS, ECLIPSES

AN EXPLANATION OF TEXAS TIME

CALENDARS FOR 2024 & 2025

Astronomical Calendars for 2024 & 2025

Sources: McDonald Observatory; U.S. Naval Observatory's Astronomical Phenomena For The Year 2024; *astropixels.com; and https://in-the-sky.org*

The Year 2024

The year 2024 CE comprises the latter part of the 247th and the beginning of the 248th year of the independence of the United States of America. All dates in this book are given in terms of the Gregorian calendar.

The Seasons

Spring begins on Tuesday, March 19, at 10:06 p.m. (CDT)

Summer begins on Thursday, June 20, at 3:15 p.m. (CDT)

Autumn begins on Sunday, Sept. 22, at 7:44 a.m. (CDT)

Winter begins on Saturday, Dec. 21, at 3:21 a.m. (CST)

Eclipses 2024

Mar. 26: Lunar, penumbral. Visible in parts of Antarctica, W. half of Africa, W. Europe, Americas, Japan, E. half of Australia.

April 8: Solar, total. Visible in Polynesia, N. America (except Alaska), C. America, Greenland, Iceland, Azores.

Sept. 18: Lunar, partial. Visible in parts of Antarctica, Middle East, Africa, Europe, Americas (except W. Alaska), E. part of Polynesia.

Oct. 2: Solar, annular. Visible in Polynesia, part of W. Mexico, Galapagos Islands, S. half of South America, parts of Antarctica, S. Georgia.

The Year 2025

The year 2025 CE comprises the latter part of the 248th and the beginning of the 249th year of the independence of the United States of America.

The Seasons

Spring begins on Thursday, March 20, at 4:02 a.m. (CDT)

Summer begins on Friday, June 20, at 9:42 p.m. (CDT)

Autumn begins on Monday, Sept. 22, at 1:20 p.m. (CDT)

Winter begins on Sunday, Dec. 21, at 9:03 a.m. (CST)

Eclipses 2025

Mar. 14: Lunar, total. Visible in the Americas, Antarctica, and N.E. Russia and W. Africa.

May 5: Solar, partial. Visible in N. E. part of N. America, Greenland, Iceland, parts of W. Europe, part of N.W. Africa, N. part of Russia.

Chronological Eras, 2024

Era	Year	Begins
Julian	6737	Jan. 14
Byzantine	7533	Sept. 14
Jewish (A.M.)*	5785	Oct. 2
Chinese (rén yín)	—	Feb. 10
Roman (A.U.C.)	2777	Jan. 14
Nabonassar	2773	April 17
Japanese	2684	Jan. 1
Seleucidæ (Grecian)	2336	Sept. 14 or Oct. 14
Saka (Indian)	1946	March 21
Diocletian (Coptic)	1741	Sept. 11
Islamic (Hegira)*	1446	July 7

**Year begins at sunset.*

Chronological Eras, 2025

Era	Year	Begins
Julian	6738	Jan. 14
Byzantine	7534	Sept. 14
Jewish (A.M.)*	5786	Sept. 23
Chinese (gui mao)	—	Jan. 29
Roman (A.U.C.)	2778	Jan. 14
Nabonassar	2774	April 17
Japanese	2685	Jan. 1
Seleucidæ (Grecian)	2337	Sept. 14 or Oct. 14
Saka (Indian)	1947	March 20
Diocletian (Coptic)	1742	Sept. 11
Islamic (Hegira)*	1447	June 26

**Year begins at sunset.*

Chronological Cycles, 2024

Dominical Letter	GF	Golden Number (Lunar Cycle)	XI
Epact	19		
Roman Indiction	2	Solar Cycle	17

Chronological Cycles, 2025

Dominical Letter	E	Golden Number (Lunar Cycle)	XII
Epact	0		
Roman Indiction	3	Solar Cycle	18

Morning & Evening Stars, 2024

Morning Stars	
Venus ♀	January 1 through April 28
Mars ♂	January 10 through December 31
Jupiter ♃	June 2 through December 7
Saturn ♄	March 17 through September 8
Evening Stars	
Venus ♀	July 11 through December 31
Jupiter ♃	Jan. 1–May 5; Dec. 7–Dec. 31
Saturn ♄	Jan. 1–Feb. 12; Sept. 8–Dec. 31

Morning & Evening Stars, 2025

Morning Stars	
Venus ♀	April 20 through October 7
Mars ♂	January 1 through September
Jupiter ♃	August through December 31
Saturn ♄	May through August
Evening Stars	
Venus ♀	January 1 through March 17
Jupiter ♃	January 1 through April
Saturn ♄	January 1 through February

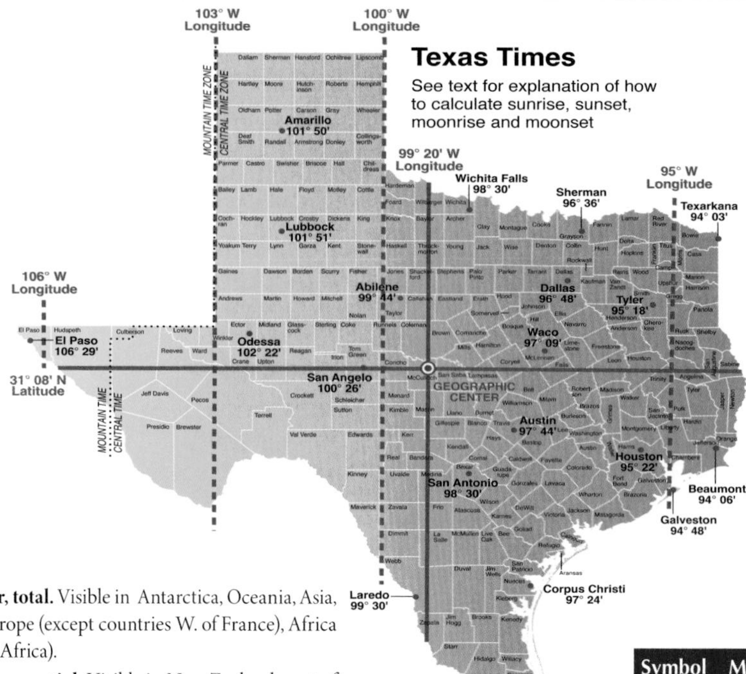

Sept. 7: Lunar, total. Visible in Antarctica, Oceania, Asia, Russia, Europe (except countries W. of France), Africa (except W. Africa).

Sept. 21: Solar, partial. Visible in New Zealand, part of Antarctica.

An Explanation of Texas Time

Times listed here are **Central Standard Time**, except for the period from 2:00 a.m. on the second Sunday in March until 2:00 a.m. on the first Sunday in November, when **Daylight Saving Time**, which is one hour later than Central Standard Time, is in effect.

All of Texas is in the Central Time Zone, except El Paso and Hudspeth counties and the northwest corner of Culberson County, which observe **Mountain Time**. Mountain Time is one hour earlier than Central Time.

All times are calculated for the intersection of 99° 20' west longitude and 31° 08' north latitude, which is **closest to the town of Mercury and** about 15 miles northeast of Brady, McCulloch County. This point is the **approximate geographical center of the state.**

How to Adjust Rise & Set Times

To adjust the time of sunrise or sunset, moonrise or moonset for any point in Texas, apply the following rules:

- For each degree of longitude that the place lies **west** of the 99th meridian, **add four minutes** to the times given in the calendar.
- For each degree of longitude the place lies **east** of the 99th meridian, **subtract four minutes**.

At times there will be considerable variation for distances north and south of the line of 31° 08' north latitude, but this formula will give sufficiently close results.

The map above shows the intersection for which all times given in this chapter are calculated, with some major cities and longitudes to aid in calculating times.

Astronomical Calendars

The calendars on the following pages feature phenomena and planetary configurations of the heavens for 2024 and 2025 in the center columns. The table to the right is a key to those symbols. You'll find find additional keys below the calendars.

Symbol	Meaning
☉	The Sun
☿	Mercury
♀	Venus
●	The Earth
☽	The Moon
♂	Mars
♃	Jupiter
♄	Saturn
♅	Uranus
♆	Neptune
☌	conjunction
☍	opposition

Aspects: Conjunction & Opposition

☌ This symbol, appearing between symbols for heavenly bodies, means they are "in conjunction," that is, having the same longitude in the sky and appearing near each other. For example, ♀ ☌ ☽ means Venus is north or south of the moon by a few degrees. Conjunctions listed in this calendar are separated by 10 degrees or less. Inferior and superior conjuctions mean an inner planet, Venus or Mercury, is in line with the Sun, either between the Earth and the Sun (inferior) or on the opposite side of the Sun (superior).

☍ This symbol means that the heavenly body listed is in "opposition" to the Sun, or that they differ by 180 degrees of longitude.

Common Astronomical Terms

Aphelion: Point at which a planet's orbit is farthest from the sun.

Perihelion: Point at which a planet's orbit is nearest the sun.

Apogee: Point of the moon's orbit farthest from the earth.

Perigee: Point of the moon's orbit nearest the earth.

2024

Times are **Central Standard Time (CST)**, except from **Sunday, March 10 to Sunday, Nov. 3**, during which **Daylight Saving Time (CDT)** is observed. **Boldface times for moonrise and moonset indicate p.m.** Times are figured for the point **31° 08' N 99° 20' W**, the approximate geographical center of the state. See page 138 for explanation of how to get the approximate time at any other Texas point.

1st Month — January 2024 — 31 Days

Day of Year	Day of Month	Day of Week	Planetary Configurations and Phenomena	Sunrise	Sunset	Moon-rise	Moon-set
1	1	Mon	☽ at apogee; ☿ stationary	7:35	5:45	**11:05**	11:22
2	2	Tue	● at perihelion (6 pm)	7:35	5:46	**11:59**	11:48
3	3	Wed	Last qtr. ☽	7:36	5:47		**12:12**
4	4	Thu		7:36	5:48	12:53	**12:38**
5	5	Fri		7:36	5:48	1:48	**1:06**
6	6	Sat	♀ ☌ Antares (1 am)	7:36	5:49	2:47	**1:38**
7	7	Sun		7:36	5:50	3:49	**2:15**
8	8	Mon	♀ ☌ ☽ (1 pm)	7:36	5:51	4:55	**3:01**
9	9	Tue	☿ ☌ ☽ (12 pm)	7:36	5:52	6:01	**3:56**
10	10	Wed	♂ ☌ ☽ (2 am)	7:36	5:52	7:06	**5:00**
11	11	Thu	New ☽	7:36	5:53	8:05	**6:11**
12	12	Fri	☿ gr. elongation W (8 am)	7:36	5:54	8:55	**7:25**
13	13	Sat	☽ at perigee (4 am)	7:36	5:55	9:38	**8:38**
14	14	Sun	♄ ☌ ☽ (3 am)	7:36	5:56	10:15	**9:48**
15	15	Mon	♆ ☌ ☽ (1 pm)	7:36	5:57	10:48	**10:55**
16	16	Tue		7:36	5:58	11:19	
17	17	Wed	First qtr. ☽	7:35	5:58	11:50	12:00
18	18	Thu	♃ ☌ ☽ (2 pm)	7:35	5:59	**12:22**	1:05
19	19	Fri	♅ ☌ ☽ (1 pm)	7:35	6:00	**12:57**	2:10
20	20	Sat	Pluto ☌ ☉ (7 am)	7:35	6:01	**1:37**	3:15
21	21	Sun		7:34	6:02	**2:22**	4:19
22	22	Mon		7:34	6:03	**3:14**	5:20
23	23	Tue		7:34	6:04	**4:10**	6:17
24	24	Wed		7:33	6:05	**5:09**	7:06
25	25	Thu	Full ☽	7:33	6:06	**6:08**	7:48
26	26	Fri		7:32	6:07	**7:07**	8:25
27	27	Sat	☿ ☌ ♂ (9 am)	7:32	6:07	**8:03**	8:56
28	28	Sun		7:31	6:08	**8:58**	9:24
29	29	Mon	☽ at apogee (1 am)	7:31	6:09	**9:51**	9:50
30	30	Tue		7:30	6:10	**10:44**	10:14
31	31	Wed		7:30	6:11	**11:38**	10:39

2nd Month — February 2024 — 29 Days

Day of Year	Day of Month	Day of Week	Planetary Configurations and Phenomena	Sunrise	Sunset	Moon-rise	Moon-set
32	1	Thu		7:29	6:12		11:06
33	2	Fri	Last qtr. ☽	7:29	6:13	12:35	11:35
34	3	Sat		7:28	6:14	1:34	**12:09**
35	4	Sun	Antares ☌ ☽ (6 pm)	7:27	6:15	2:36	**12:49**
36	5	Mon		7:26	6:15	3:41	**1:38**
37	6	Tue		7:26	6:16	4:45	**2:37**
38	7	Wed	♀ ☌ ☽ (12 pm)	7:25	6:17	5:47	**3:44**
39	8	Thu	♂ ☌ ☽ (12 am)	7:24	6:18	6:41	**4:58**
40	9	Fri	New ☽	7:23	6:19	7:28	**6:12**
41	10	Sat	♄ ☌ ☽ at perigee	7:23	6:20	8:09	**7:26**
42	11	Sun		7:22	6:21	8:44	**8:37**
43	12	Mon	♆ ☌ ☽ (12 am)	7:21	6:21	9:17	**9:46**
44	13	Tue		7:20	6:22	9:49	**10:53**
45	14	Wed		7:19	6:23	10:22	
46	15	Thu	♃ ♅ ☌ ☽	7:18	6:24	10:57	12:00
47	16	Fri	First qtr. ☽	7:17	6:25	11:36	1:07
48	17	Sat		7:16	6:26	**12:20**	2:13
49	18	Sun		7:15	6:26	**1:09**	3:15
50	19	Mon		7:14	6:27	**2:04**	4:13
51	20	Tue		7:14	6:28	**3:02**	5:04
52	21	Wed		7:12	6:29	**4:01**	5:48
53	22	Thu	♀ ☌ ♂ (9 am)	7:11	6:30	**5:00**	6:26
54	23	Fri		7:10	6:30	**5:56**	6:58
55	24	Sat	Full **B**	7:09	6:31	**6:51**	7:27
56	25	Sun	☽ at apogee (8 am)	7:08	6:32	**7:45**	7:53
57	26	Mon		7:07	6:33	**8:39**	8:18
58	27	Tue		7:06	6:33	**9:32**	8:43
59	28	Wed	☿ in superior ☌; ♄ ☌ ☉	7:05	6:34	**10:28**	9:08
60	29	Thu		7:04	6:35	**11:25**	9:36

3rd Month — March 2024 — 31 Days

Day of Year	Day of Month	Day of Week	Planetary Configurations and Phenomena	Sunrise	Sunset	Moon-rise	Moon-set
61	1	Fri		7:03	6:36		10:07
62	2	Sat		7:02	6:36	12:25	10:44
63	3	Sun	Antares ☌ last qtr. ☽	7:00	6:37	1:27	11:28
64	4	Mon		6:59	6:38	2:30	**12:20**
65	5	Tue		6:58	6:39	3:31	**1:22**
66	6	Wed		6:57	6:39	4:27	**2:31**
67	7	Thu	♂ ☌ ☽ (10 pm)	6:56	6:40	5:16	**3:44**
68	8	Fri	♀ ☌ ☽ (10 am)	6:55	6:41	5:59	**4:58**
69	9	Sat		6:53	6:41	6:37	**6:10**
70	10	Sun	DST begins (2 am); new ☽	7:52	7:42	8:11	**8:21**
71	11	Mon		7:51	7:43	8:44	**9:32**
72	12	Tue		7:50	7:43	9:17	**10:41**
73	13	Wed	♃ ☌ ☽ (7 pm)	7:49	7:44	9:52	**11:51**
74	14	Thu	♅ ☌ ☽ (6 am)	7:47	7:45	10:31	
75	15	Fri		7:46	7:45	11:14	1:00
76	16	Sat	First qtr. ☽	7:45	7:46	**12:03**	2:06
77	17	Sun	♆ ☌ ☉ (5 am)	7:44	7:47	**12:58**	3:07
78	18	Mon		7:42	7:47	**1:55**	4:01
79	19	Tue	Equinox (10:06 pm)	7:41	7:48	**2:55**	4:48
80	20	Wed		7:40	7:49	**3:53**	5:27
81	21	Thu	♀ ☌ ♄ (8 pm)	7:39	7:49	**4:51**	6:01
82	22	Fri		7:37	7:50	**5:46**	6:31
83	23	Sat	☽ at apogee (10 am)	7:36	7:51	**6:40**	6:57
84	24	Sun	☿ gr. elongation E (5 pm)	7:35	7:51	**7:34**	7:22
85	25	Mon	Full ☽; eclipse (2 am)	7:34	7:52	**8:27**	7:47
86	26	Tue		7:32	7:53	**9:22**	8:12
87	27	Wed		7:31	7:53	**10:19**	8:39
88	28	Thu		7:30	7:54	**11:18**	9:09
89	29	Fri		7:29	7:55		9:44
90	30	Sat	Antares ☌ ☽ (9 am)	7:27	7:55	12:20	10:25
91	31	Sun		7:26	7:56	1:22	11:13

Astronomical Calendar for 2024

4th Month — April 2024 — 30 Days

Day of Year	Day of Month	Day of Week	Planetary Configurations and Phenomena	Sunrise	Sunset	Moon-rise	Moon-set
92	1	Mon	Last qtr. ☽	7:25	7:57	2:22	**12:10**
93	2	Tue		7:24	7:57	3:18	**1:14**
94	3	Wed		7:22	7:58	4:08	**2:23**
95	4	Thu		7:21	7:58	4:52	**3:34**
96	5	Fri	♂ ☌ ☽ (10 pm)	7:20	7:59	5:31	**4:45**
97	6	Sat	♄ ☌ ☽ (3 am)	7:19	8:00	6:06	**5:56**
98	7	Sun	♆ ♀ ☌ ☽ at perigee	7:18	8:00	6:38	**7:05**
99	8	Mon	New ☽; ☉ eclipse (1 pm)	7:16	8:01	7:11	**8:16**
100	9	Tue		7:15	8:02	7:45	**9:27**
101	10	Wed	♃ ♅ ☌ ☽; ♂ ☌ ♄	7:14	8:02	8:23	**10:38**
102	11	Thu	C in inferior m (5 pm)	7:13	8:03	9:05	**11:48**
103	12	Fri		7:12	8:04	9:53	
104	13	Sat		7:10	8:04	10:47	12:54
105	14	Sun		7:09	8:05	11:45	1:53
106	15	Mon	First qtr. B	7:08	8:06	**12:45**	2:44
107	16	Tue		7:07	8:06	**1:45**	3:27
108	17	Wed		7:06	8:07	**2:43**	4:02
109	18	Thu	☿ ☌ ♀ (5 pm)	7:05	8:08	**3:40**	4:33
110	19	Fri	☽ at apogee (8 pm)	7:04	8:08	**4:34**	5:01
111	20	Sat	♃ ☌ ♅ (2 am)	7:03	8:09	**5:28**	5:26
112	21	Sun		7:02	8:10	**6:21**	5:51
113	22	Mon		7:01	8:10	**7:16**	6:16
114	23	Tue	Full ☽	7:00	8:11	**8:12**	6:42
115	24	Wed	☿ stationary (2 am)	6:58	8:12	**9:11**	7:11
116	25	Thu		6:57	8:12	**10:13**	7:45
117	26	Fri	Antares ☌ ☽ (3 pm)	6:56	8:13	**11:15**	8:24
118	27	Sat		6:55	8:14		9:10
119	28	Sun	♂ ☌ ♆ (10 pm)	6:55	8:14	12:16	10:05
120	29	Mon		6:54	8:15	1:14	11:06
121	30	Tue		6:53	8:16	2:05	**12:13**

5th Month — May 2024 — 31 Days

Day of Year	Day of Month	Day of Week	Planetary Configurations and Phenomena	Sunrise	Sunset	Moon-rise	Moon-set
122	1	Wed	Last qtr. ☽	6:52	8:16	2:50	**1:21**
123	2	Thu		6:51	8:17	3:29	**2:30**
124	3	Fri	♄ ☌ ☽ (5 pm)	6:50	8:18	4:04	**3:38**
125	4	Sat	♆ ♂ ☌ ☽	6:49	8:18	4:36	**4:45**
126	5	Sun	☽ at perigee (4 pm)	6:48	8:19	5:07	**5:53**
127	6	Mon	☿ ☌ ☽ (2 am)	6:47	8:20	5:40	**7:03**
128	7	Tue	New ☽	6:47	8:21	6:15	**8:14**
129	8	Wed		6:46	8:21	6:55	**9:25**
130	9	Thu	☿ gr. elongation W (4 pm)	6:45	8:22	7:40	**10:34**
131	10	Fri		6:44	8:23	8:32	**11:38**
132	11	Sat		6:44	8:23	9:30	
133	12	Sun		6:43	8:24	10:31	12:34
134	13	Mon	♅ ☌ ☉ (3 am)	6:42	8:25	11:33	1:21
135	14	Tue		6:42	8:25	**12:33**	2:01
136	15	Wed	First qtr. ☽	6:41	8:26	**1:31**	2:34
137	16	Thu	Juno ☌ ☽ (7 am)	6:40	8:27	**2:26**	3:03
138	17	Fri	☽ at apogee (1 pm)	6:40	8:27	**3:20**	3:29
139	18	Sat	♃ ☌ ☉	6:39	8:28	**4:13**	3:54
140	19	Sun		6:39	8:29	**5:07**	4:18
141	20	Mon		6:38	8:29	**6:03**	4:44
142	21	Tue		6:37	8:30	**7:02**	5:12
143	22	Wed		6:37	8:30	**8:03**	5:44
144	23	Thu	Antares ☌ full ☽	6:37	8:31	**9:06**	6:22
145	24	Fri		6:36	8:32	**10:09**	7:06
146	25	Sat		6:36	8:32	**11:08**	7:59
147	26	Sun	Ceres ☌ ☽ (11 pm)	6:35	8:33		8:59
148	27	Mon		6:35	8:34	12:02	10:05
149	28	Tue		6:35	8:34	12:49	11:14
150	29	Wed		6:34	8:35	1:29	**12:22**
151	30	Thu	Last qtr. ☽	6:34	8:35	2:05	**1:28**
152	31	Fri	♄ ♆ ☌ ☽	6:34	8:36	2:37	**2:34**

6th Month — June 2024 — 30 Days

Day of Year	Day of Month	Day of Week	Planetary Configurations and Phenomena	Sunrise	Sunset	Moon-rise	Moon-set
153	1	Sat		6:33	8:36	3:08	**3:40**
154	2	Sun	♂ ☌ ☽ at perigee	6:33	8:37	3:39	**4:47**
155	3	Mon		6:33	8:37	4:12	**5:55**
156	4	Tue	☿ ☌ ♃; ♀ in superior ☌	6:33	8:38	4:48	**7:05**
157	5	Wed	♃ ☌ ☽ (8 am)	6:33	8:38	5:30	**8:14**
158	6	Thu	New ☽	6:33	8:39	6:19	**9:21**
159	7	Fri		6:33	8:39	7:15	**10:21**
160	8	Sat		6:32	8:40	8:15	**11:12**
161	9	Sun		6:32	8:40	9:18	**11:56**
162	10	Mon		6:32	8:41	10:20	
163	11	Tue		6:32	8:41	11:19	12:32
164	12	Wed		6:32	8:41	**12:16**	1:03
165	13	Thu	Juno ☌ first qtr. ☽	6:32	8:42	**1:11**	1:30
166	14	Fri	☿ in superior ☌ (11 am)	6:33	8:42	**2:04**	1:55
167	15	Sat		6:33	8:42	**2:58**	2:20
168	16	Sun	Spica ☌ ☽ (12 pm)	6:33	8:43	**3:53**	2:45
169	17	Mon		6:33	8:43	**4:50**	3:12
170	18	Tue		6:33	8:43	**5:49**	3:42
171	19	Wed		6:33	8:44	**6:52**	4:17
172	20	Thu	Solstice (3:51 pm)	6:33	8:44	**7:56**	4:59
173	21	Fri	Full ☽	6:34	8:44	**8:58**	5:49
174	22	Sat	Ceres ☌ ☽ (11 pm)	6:34	8:44	**9:55**	6:48
175	23	Sun		6:34	8:44	**10:46**	7:54
176	24	Mon		6:34	8:44	**11:29**	9:03
177	25	Tue		6:35	8:45		10:13
178	26	Wed		6:35	8:45	12:06	11:21
179	27	Thu	♄ ☌ ☽ at perigee	6:35	8:45	12:39	**12:28**
180	28	Fri	♆ ☌ last qtr. ☽	6:36	8:45	1:10	**1:33**
181	29	Sat	☿ ☌ Pollux (4 am)	6:36	8:45	1:41	**2:38**
182	30	Sun	♄ stationary (3 pm)	6:36	8:45	2:12	**3:45**

☉ The Sun ● The Earth ☽ The Moon ☿ Mercury ♀ Venus ♂ Mars ♃ Jupiter ♄ Saturn ♆ Neptune ♅ Uranus ☌= in conjunction ☍= opposition to the ☉

Astronomical Calendar for 2024

7th Month — July 2024 — 31 Days

Day of Year	Day of Month	Day of Week	Planetary Configurations and Phenomena	Sunrise	Sunset	Moonrise	Moonset
183	1	Mon	♂ ☌ ☽ (12 pm)	6:37	8:45	2:47	**4:52**
184	2	Tue	♅ ☌ ☽; ♆ stationary	6:37	8:45	3:26	**6:01**
185	3	Wed	♃ ☌ ☽ (2 am)	6:38	8:45	4:11	**7:07**
186	4	Thu	● at aphelion (11 pm)	6:38	8:44	5:03	**8:09**
187	5	Fri	New ☽	6:39	8:44	6:02	**9:03**
188	6	Sat		6:39	8:44	7:04	**9:50**
189	7	Sun	♀ ☌ ☽ (1 pm)	6:40	8:44	8:06	**10:29**
190	8	Mon		6:40	8:44	9:07	**11:02**
191	9	Tue		6:41	8:44	10:05	**11:30**
192	10	Wed		6:41	8:43	11:01	**11:56**
193	11	Thu		6:42	8:43	11:55	
194	12	Fri	☽ at apogee (2 am)	6:42	8:43	**12:48**	12:21
195	13	Sat	Spica ☌ first qtr. ☽	6:43	8:42	**1:42**	12:46
196	14	Sun		6:43	8:42	**2:38**	1:12
197	15	Mon	♂ ☌ ♅ (3 am)	6:44	8:42	**3:36**	1:40
198	16	Tue		6:44	8:41	**4:36**	2:12
199	17	Wed	Antares ☌ ☽ (2 pm)	6:45	8:41	**5:39**	2:51
200	18	Thu		6:46	8:40	**6:42**	3:37
201	19	Fri		6:46	8:40	**7:42**	4:32
202	20	Sat		6:47	8:39	**8:37**	5:36
203	21	Sun	Full ☽	6:47	8:39	**9:24**	6:46
204	22	Mon	☿ gr. elongation E (1 am)	6:48	8:38	**10:04**	7:57
205	23	Tue	Pluto ☍ (12 am)	6:49	8:38	**10:39**	9:08
206	24	Wed	♄ ☌ ☽ at perigee	6:49	8:37	**11:12**	10:17
207	25	Thu	♆ ☌ ☽ (9 am)	6:50	8:37	**11:43**	11:24
208	26	Fri		6:50	8:36		**12:31**
209	27	Sat	☿ ☌ Regulus; last qtr. ☽	6:51	8:35	12:14	**1:37**
210	28	Sun		6:52	8:35	12:48	**2:45**
211	29	Mon	♅ ☌ ☽ (12 pm)	6:52	8:34	1:25	**3:53**
212	30	Tue	♂ ♃ ☌ ☽	6:53	8:33	2:08	**4:59**
213	31	Wed		6:54	8:32	2:57	**6:02**

8th Month — August 2024 — 31 Days

Day of Year	Day of Month	Day of Week	Planetary Configurations and Phenomena	Sunrise	Sunset	Moonrise	Moonset
214	1	Thu		6:54	8:32	3:53	**6:58**
215	2	Fri		6:55	8:31	4:53	**7:46**
216	3	Sat		6:56	8:30	5:55	**8:27**
217	4	Sun	☿ stationary; new ☽	6:56	8:29	6:56	**9:01**
218	5	Mon	♀ ☿ ☌ ☽	6:57	8:28	7:56	**9:31**
219	6	Tue	☿ ☌ ♀ (9 am)	6:57	8:27	8:52	**9:58**
220	7	Wed		6:58	8:27	9:47	**10:23**
221	8	Thu	☽ at apogee (8 pm)	6:59	8:26	10:40	**10:48**
222	9	Fri		6:59	8:25	11:34	**11:13**
223	10	Sat	Spica ☌ ☽ (4 am)	7:00	8:24	**12:28**	**11:40**
224	11	Sun	☿ ☌ Regulus (4 pm)	7:01	8:23	**1:24**	
225	12	Mon	First qtr. B	7:01	8:22	**2:23**	12:10
226	13	Tue	Antares ☌ ☽ (11 pm)	7:02	8:21	**3:24**	12:45
227	14	Wed	♂ ☌ ♃ (11 am)	7:02	8:20	**4:26**	1:27
228	15	Thu		7:03	8:19	**5:27**	2:17
229	16	Fri		7:04	8:18	**6:23**	3:16
230	17	Sat		7:04	8:17	**7:13**	4:23
231	18	Sun	☿ in inferior ☌ (8 pm)	7:05	8:16	**7:57**	5:34
232	19	Mon	Full ☽	7:06	8:15	**8:35**	6:46
233	20	Tue	♄ ☌ ☽ at perigee	7:06	8:13	**9:10**	7:58
234	21	Wed		7:07	8:12	**9:42**	9:08
235	22	Thu	♆ ☌ ☽ (4 pm)	7:07	8:11	**10:14**	10:17
236	23	Fri		7:08	8:10	**10:48**	11:26
237	24	Sat		7:09	8:09	**11:24**	**12:35**
238	25	Sun	♅ ☌ ☽ (6 pm)	7:09	8:08		**1:44**
239	26	Mon	Last qtr. ☽	7:10	8:07	12:06	**2:52**
240	27	Tue	♃ ♂ ☌ ☽; ☿ stationary	7:10	8:05	12:54	**3:56**
241	28	Wed		7:11	8:04	1:48	**4:54**
242	29	Thu		7:12	8:03	2:46	**5:45**
243	30	Fri		7:12	8:02	3:48	**6:27**
244	31	Sat		7:13	8:01	4:49	**7:03**

9th Month — September 2024 — 30 Days

Day of Year	Day of Month	Day of Week	Planetary Configurations and Phenomena	Sunrise	Sunset	Moonrise	Moonset
245	1	Sun	☿ ☌ ☽; ♅ stationary	7:13	7:59	5:48	**7:34**
246	2	Mon	New ☽	7:14	7:58	6:45	**8:02**
247	3	Tue		7:14	7:57	7:40	**8:27**
248	4	Wed	☿ gr. elongation W (9 pm)	7:15	7:56	8:34	**8:51**
249	5	Thu	♀ ☌ ☽ at apogee	7:16	7:54	9:27	**9:16**
250	6	Fri	Spica ☌ ☽ (11 am)	7:16	7:53	10:21	**9:42**
251	7	Sat	♄ ☍ (11 pm)	7:17	7:52	11:16	**10:10**
252	8	Sun		7:17	7:51	**12:14**	**10:43**
253	9	Mon	☿ ☌ Regulus (1 am)	7:18	7:49	**1:13**	**11:21**
254	10	Tue	Antares ☌ ☽ (7 am)	7:19	7:48	**2:13**	
255	11	Wed	First qtr. ☽	7:19	7:47	**3:13**	12:07
256	12	Thu		7:20	7:46	**4:10**	1:00
257	13	Fri		7:20	7:44	**5:02**	2:02
258	14	Sat		7:21	7:43	**5:48**	3:10
259	15	Sun		7:21	7:42	**6:28**	4:21
260	16	Mon		7:22	7:40	**7:04**	5:32
261	17	Tue	♄ ☌ full ☽ (5 am)	7:23	7:39	**7:37**	6:44
262	18	Wed	♆ ☌ ☽ at perigee	7:23	7:38	**8:10**	7:54
263	19	Thu		7:24	7:36	**8:44**	9:05
264	20	Fri	♆ ☍ (6 pm)	7:24	7:35	**9:20**	10:17
265	21	Sat		7:25	7:34	**10:01**	11:29
266	22	Sun	♅ ☌ ☽; equinox(7:44 am)	7:25	7:33	**10:48**	**12:40**
267	23	Mon	♃ ☌ ☽ (5 pm)	7:26	7:31	**11:41**	**1:48**
268	24	Tue	Last qtr. ☽	7:27	7:30		**2:49**
269	25	Wed	♂ ☌ ☽ (6 am)	7:27	7:29	12:40	**3:43**
270	26	Thu		7:28	7:27	1:41	**4:28**
271	27	Fri		7:28	7:26	2:42	**5:05**
272	28	Sat		7:29	7:25	3:42	**5:37**
273	29	Sun		7:30	7:24	4:40	**6:06**
274	30	Mon	☿ in superior ☌ (3 pm)	7:30	7:22	5:35	**6:31**

Bright stars: Aldebaran, Antares, Spica, Pollux, Regulus. **Minor planets or asteroids:** Pluto, Ceres, Pallas, Juno, Vesta ☌ = in conjunction by 10° or < ☍ = opposition to the ⊙

Astronomical Calendar for 2024

10th Month — October 2024 — 31 Days

Day of Year	Day of Month	Day of Week	Planetary Configurations and Phenomena	Sunrise	Sunset	Moon-rise	Moon-set
275	1	Tue		7:31	7:21	6:29	**6:56**
276	2	Wed	New ☽ at apogee	7:32	7:20	7:22	**7:20**
277	3	Thu		7:32	7:19	8:16	**7:46**
278	4	Fri		7:33	7:17	9:11	**8:13**
279	5	Sat	♀ ☌ ☽ (2 pm)	7:33	7:16	10:07	**8:44**
280	6	Sun		7:34	7:15	11:06	**9:20**
281	7	Mon	Antares ☌ ☽ (1 pm)	7:35	7:14	**12:05**	**10:03**
282	8	Tue		7:35	7:13	**1:05**	**10:52**
283	9	Wed	♃ stationary (1 am)	7:36	7:11	**2:02**	**11:50**
284	10	Thu	First qtr. ☽	7:37	7:10	**2:54**	
285	11	Fri	Pluto stationary (8 pm)	7:37	7:09	**3:40**	12:53
286	12	Sat		7:38	7:08	**4:21**	2:00
287	13	Sun		7:39	7:07	**4:58**	3:09
288	14	Mon	♄ ☌ ☽ (12 pm)	7:39	7:06	**5:31**	4:19
289	15	Tue	♆ ☌ ☽ (12 pm)	7:40	7:04	**6:04**	5:28
290	16	Wed	☽ at perigee (7 pm)	7:41	7:03	**6:37**	6:38
291	17	Thu	Full ☽	7:41	7:02	**7:12**	7:50
292	18	Fri		7:42	7:01	**7:52**	9:03
293	19	Sat	♅ ☌ ☽ (10 am)	7:43	7:00	**8:37**	10:17
294	20	Sun		7:44	6:59	**9:30**	11:30
295	21	Mon	♂ ☌ Pollux; ♃ ☌ ☽	7:44	6:58	**10:28**	**12:37**
296	22	Tue		7:45	6:57	**11:31**	**1:35**
297	23	Wed	♂ ☌ ☽ (2 pm)	7:46	6:56		**2:25**
298	24	Thu	Last qtr. ☽	7:47	6:55	12:34	**3:05**
299	25	Fri	♀ ☌ Antares (1 pm)	7:47	6:54	1:35	**3:40**
300	26	Sat		7:48	6:53	2:34	**4:09**
301	27	Sun		7:49	6:52	3:30	**4:35**
302	28	Mon		7:50	6:51	4:24	**5:00**
303	29	Tue	☽ at apogee (5 pm)	7:50	6:50	5:17	**5:25**
304	30	Wed		7:51	6:49	6:11	**5:50**
305	31	Thu		7:52	6:48	7:05	**6:16**

11th Month — November 2024 — 30 Days

Day of Year	Day of Month	Day of Week	Planetary Configurations and Phenomena	Sunrise	Sunset	Moon-rise	Moon-set
306	1	Fri	New ☽	7:53	6:48	8:01	**6:46**
307	2	Sat		7:54	6:47	8:59	**7:21**
308	3	Sun	DST ends (2 am); ☿ ☌ ☽	6:54	5:46	8:59	**7:02**
309	4	Mon	♀ ☌ ☽ (5 pm)	6:55	5:45	9:59	**7:49**
310	5	Tue		6:56	5:45	10:57	**8:44**
311	6	Wed		6:57	5:44	11:50	**9:45**
312	7	Thu		6:58	5:43	**12:37**	**10:49**
313	8	Fri	First qtr. ☽	6:59	5:42	**1:19**	**11:56**
314	9	Sat	☿ ☌ Antares (2 am)	6:59	5:42	**1:55**	
315	10	Sun	♄ ☌ ☽ (7 pm)	7:00	5:41	**2:29**	1:02
316	11	Mon	♆ ☌ ☽ (7 pm)	7:01	5:40	**3:00**	2:09
317	12	Tue		7:02	5:40	**3:32**	3:16
318	13	Wed		7:03	5:39	**4:05**	4:24
319	14	Thu	☽ at perigee (4 am)	7:04	5:39	**4:42**	5:36
320	15	Fri	♅ ☌ full ☽; ♄ stationary	7:04	5:38	**5:24**	6:49
321	16	Sat	☿ gr. elongation E (1 am)	7:05	5:38	**6:14**	8:03
322	17	Sun	♃ ☌ ☽ (8 am)	7:06	5:37	**7:11**	9:15
323	18	Mon		7:07	5:37	**8:13**	10:20
324	19	Tue		7:08	5:37	**9:19**	11:15
325	20	Wed	♂ ☌ ☽ (2 pm)	7:09	5:36	**10:23**	**12:01**
326	21	Thu		7:10	5:36	**11:24**	**12:38**
327	22	Fri	Last qtr. ☽	7:10	5:36		**1:10**
328	23	Sat		7:11	5:35	12:22	**1:38**
329	24	Sun		7:12	5:35	1:17	**2:03**
330	25	Mon	☿ stationary (9 pm)	7:13	5:35	2:11	**2:28**
331	26	Tue	☽ at apogee (5 am)	7:14	5:35	3:04	**2:52**
332	27	Wed	Spica ☌ ☽ (5 am)	7:15	5:34	3:58	**3:19**
333	28	Thu		7:16	5:34	4:53	**3:48**
334	29	Fri		7:16	5:34	5:51	**4:21**
335	30	Sat		7:17	5:34	6:51	**5:00**

12th Month — December 2024 — 31 Days

Day of Year	Day of Month	Day of Week	Planetary Configurations and Phenomena	Sunrise	Sunset	Moon-rise	Moon-set
336	1	Sun	New ☽	7:18	5:34	7:51	**5:46**
337	2	Mon		7:19	5:34	8:51	**6:39**
338	3	Tue		7:20	5:34	9:46	**7:39**
339	4	Wed	♀ ☌ ☽ (4 pm)	7:20	5:34	10:35	**8:43**
340	5	Thu	☿ in inferior ☌ (7 pm)	7:21	5:34	11:19	**9:49**
341	6	Fri		7:22	5:34	11:56	**10:54**
342	7	Sat	♃ ☍; ♂ stationary (2 pm)	7:23	5:34	12:30	**11:59**
343	8	Sun	♄ ☌ first qtr. ☽	7:23	5:35	**1:01**	
344	9	Mon	♆ ☌ ☽ (2 am)	7:24	5:35	**1:31**	1:04
345	10	Tue	☿ ☌ Antares (4 am)	7:25	5:35	**2:02**	2:09
346	11	Wed		7:26	5:35	**2:36**	3:16
347	12	Thu	☽ at perigee (6 am)	7:26	5:35	**3:14**	4:26
348	13	Fri	♅ ☌ ☽ (3 am)	7:27	5:36	**3:59**	5:39
349	14	Sat	♃ ☌ ☽ (1 pm)	7:28	5:36	**4:52**	6:51
350	15	Sun	Full ☽; ☿ stationary	7:28	5:36	**5:53**	7:59
351	16	Mon		7:29	5:37	**6:58**	8:59
352	17	Tue		7:29	5:37	**8:05**	9:50
353	18	Wed	♂ ☌ ☽ (2 am)	7:30	5:38	**9:09**	10:32
354	19	Thu		7:30	5:38	**10:09**	11:07
355	20	Fri		7:31	5:39	**11:07**	11:37
356	21	Sat	Solstice (3:21 am)	7:31	5:39		**12:04**
357	22	Sun	Last qtr. ☽	7:32	5:40	12:02	**12:29**
358	23	Mon		7:32	5:40	12:55	**12:54**
359	24	Tue	☿ gr. elongation W (8 pm)	7:33	5:41	1:49	**1:19**
360	25	Wed		7:33	5:41	2:43	**1:47**
361	26	Thu		7:34	5:42	3:40	**2:18**
362	27	Fri		7:34	5:43	4:39	**2:55**
363	28	Sat	☿ ☌ ☽ (9 pm)	7:34	5:43	5:40	**3:38**
364	29	Sun		7:35	5:44	6:40	**4:30**
365	30	Mon	New ☽	7:35	5:45	7:38	**5:28**
366	31	Tue		7:35	5:45	8:30	**6:33**

⊙ The Sun ● The Earth ☽ The Moon ☿ Mercury ♀ Venus ♂ Mars ♃ Jupiter ♄ Saturn ♆ Neptune ♅ Uranus ☌= in conjunction ☍= opposition to the ⊙

2025

Times are **Central Standard Time (CST)**, except from **Sunday, March 9 to Sunday, Nov. 2**, during which **Daylight Saving Time (CDT)** is observed. **Boldface times for moonrise and moonset indicate p.m.** Times are figured for the point **31° 08' N 99° 20' W**, the approximate geographical center of the state. See page **138** for explanation of how to get the approximate time at any other Texas point.

1st Month — January 2025 — 31 Days

Day of Year	Day of Month	Day of Week	Planetary Configurations and Phenomena	Sunrise	Sunset	Moonrise	Moonset
1	1	Wed		7:35	5:46	9:16	**7:40**
2	2	Thu		7:36	5:47	9:56	**8:47**
3	3	Fri	♀ ☌ ☽ (9 am)	7:36	5:47	10:31	**9:53**
4	4	Sat	● at perihelion; ♄ ☌ ☽	7:36	5:48	11:03	**10:58**
5	5	Sun		7:36	5:49	11:33	
6	6	Mon	First qtr. ☽	7:36	5:50	**12:04**	12:02
7	7	Tue	☽ at perigee (5 pm)	7:36	5:51	**12:36**	1:07
8	8	Wed		7:36	5:51	**1:11**	2:15
9	9	Thu	♀ gr. elongation E (10 pm)	7:36	5:52	**1:52**	3:24
10	10	Fri		7:36	5:53	**2:41**	4:34
11	11	Sat		7:36	5:54	**3:37**	5:42
12	12	Sun		7:36	5:55	**4:40**	6:45
13	13	Mon	♂ ☌ full ☽ (9 pm)	7:36	5:56	**5:45**	7:39
14	14	Tue		7:36	5:56	**6:51**	8:25
15	15	Wed	♂ ☍ (7 pm)	7:36	5:57	**7:54**	9:03
16	16	Thu	Regulus ☌ ☽ (9 am)	7:36	5:58	**8:53**	9:35
17	17	Fri		7:35	5:59	**9:50**	10:04
18	18	Sat	♀ ☌ ♄ (10 am)	7:35	6:00	**10:45**	10:30
19	19	Sun	☿ at aphelion (8 am)	7:35	6:01	**11:39**	10:55
20	20	Mon	Spica ☌ ☽ at apogee	7:34	6:02		11:20
21	21	Tue	Last qtr. ☽	7:34	6:03	12:33	11:46
22	22	Wed		7:34	6:04	1:28	**12:16**
23	23	Thu	♂ ☌ Pollux (11 am)	7:33	6:04	2:26	**12:50**
24	24	Fri	Antares ☌ ☽ (5 pm)	7:33	6:05	3:25	**1:30**
25	25	Sat		7:32	6:06	4:26	**2:17**
26	26	Sun		7:32	6:07	5:25	**3:13**
27	27	Mon		7:32	6:08	6:20	**4:15**
28	28	Tue		7:31	6:09	7:09	**5:22**
29	29	Wed	New ☽	7:30	6:10	7:52	**6:31**
30	30	Thu		7:30	6:11	8:30	**7:40**
31	31	Fri	♄ ☌ ☽ (10 pm)	7:29	6:12	9:04	**8:47**

2nd Month — February 2025 — 28 Days

Day of Year	Day of Month	Day of Week	Planetary Configurations and Phenomena	Sunrise	Sunset	Moonrise	Moonset
32	1	Sat	♀ ☌ ☽ at perigee	7:29	6:13	9:35	**9:53**
33	2	Sun		7:28	6:13	10:06	**11:00**
34	3	Mon		7:27	6:14	10:37	
35	4	Tue		7:27	6:15	11:12	12:07
36	5	Wed	First qtr. ☽	7:26	6:16	11:51	1:16
37	6	Thu		7:25	6:17	**12:36**	2:25
38	7	Fri		7:24	6:18	**1:29**	3:33
39	8	Sat		7:24	6:19	**2:28**	4:37
40	9	Sun	♂ ☌ ☽ (1 pm)	7:23	6:20	**3:32**	5:33
41	10	Mon		7:22	6:20	**4:37**	6:21
42	11	Tue		7:21	6:21	**5:40**	7:01
43	12	Wed	Regulus ☌ full ☽	7:20	6:22	**6:41**	7:34
44	13	Thu		7:19	6:23	**7:39**	8:04
45	14	Fri		7:19	6:24	**8:34**	8:31
46	15	Sat		7:18	6:25	**9:29**	8:56
47	16	Sun		7:17	6:25	**10:23**	9:21
48	17	Mon	Spica ☌ ☽ at apogee	7:16	6:26	**11:18**	9:47
49	18	Tue		7:15	6:27		10:15
50	19	Wed	♀ at perihelion (12 pm)	7:14	6:28	12:14	10:46
51	20	Thu	Last qtr. ☽	7:13	6:29	1:13	11:23
52	21	Fri	Antares ☌ ☽ (2 am)	7:12	6:29	2:12	**12:06**
53	22	Sat		7:11	6:30	3:10	**12:57**
54	23	Sun		7:10	6:31	4:06	**1:56**
55	24	Mon		7:09	6:32	4:58	**3:01**
56	25	Tue		7:07	6:32	5:44	**4:09**
57	26	Wed		7:06	6:33	6:24	**5:18**
58	27	Thu	New ☽	7:05	6:34	7:00	**6:27**
59	28	Fri	☿ ☌ ☽ (10 pm)	7:04	6:35	7:33	**7:36**

3rd Month — March 2025 — 31 Days

Day of Year	Day of Month	Day of Week	Planetary Configurations and Phenomena	Sunrise	Sunset	Moonrise	Moonset
60	1	Sat	☽ at perigee (3 pm)	7:03	6:35	8:04	**8:45**
61	2	Sun		7:02	6:36	8:37	**9:54**
62	3	Mon		7:01	6:37	9:11	**11:05**
63	4	Tue	☿ at perihelion (8 am)	7:00	6:38	9:49	
64	5	Wed		6:58	6:38	10:34	12:16
65	6	Thu	First qtr. ☽	6:57	6:39	11:25	1:26
66	7	Fri		6:56	6:40	**12:22**	2:31
67	8	Sat	☿ gr. elongation E;♂ ☌ ☽	6:55	6:40	**1:25**	3:30
68	9	Sun	DST begins (2 am)	7:54	7:41	**3:29**	5:19
69	10	Mon		7:52	7:42	**4:32**	6:01
70	11	Tue		7:51	7:43	**5:32**	6:36
71	12	Wed	♄ ☌ ☉ (5 am)	7:50	7:43	**6:30**	7:06
72	13	Thu		7:49	7:44	**7:26**	7:33
73	14	Fri	Full ☽; eclipse (2 am)	7:48	7:45	**8:21**	7:59
74	15	Sat		7:46	7:45	**9:15**	8:24
75	16	Sun	Spica ☌ ☽ (2 pm)	7:45	7:46	**10:10**	8:49
76	17	Mon	☽ at apogee (11 am)	7:44	7:47	**11:06**	9:16
77	18	Tue		7:43	7:47		9:46
78	19	Wed	♆ ☌ ☉ (5 pm)	7:41	7:48	12:03	10:21
79	20	Thu	Equinox (4:02 am)	7:40	7:49	1:01	11:01
80	21	Fri		7:39	7:49	1:59	11:48
81	22	Sat	Last qtr. ☽; ♀ in inferior ☌	7:38	7:50	2:56	**12:42**
82	23	Sun		7:36	7:51	3:48	**1:42**
83	24	Mon	☿ in inferior ☌ (3 pm)	7:35	7:51	4:35	**2:47**
84	25	Tue		7:34	7:52	5:16	**3:55**
85	26	Wed		7:33	7:52	5:53	**5:03**
86	27	Thu		7:31	7:53	6:27	**6:11**
87	28	Fri		7:30	7:54	6:59	**7:21**
88	29	Sat	New ☽; ☉ eclipse (6 am)	7:29	7:54	7:32	**8:31**
89	30	Sun	☽ at perigee (12 am)	7:28	7:55	8:06	**9:43**
90	31	Mon		7:26	7:56	8:44	**10:57**

Astronomical Calendar for 2025

4th Month — April 2025 — 30 Days

Day of Year	Day of Month	Day of Week	Planetary Configurations and Phenomena	Sunrise	Sunset	Moon-rise	Moon-set
91	1	Tue		7:25	7:56	9:27	
92	2	Wed		7:24	7:57	10:17	12:11
93	3	Thu		7:23	7:58	11:14	1:21
94	4	Fri	First qtr. ☽	7:21	7:58	**12:17**	2:24
95	5	Sat	♂ ☌ ☽ (2 pm)	7:20	7:59	**1:21**	3:17
96	6	Sun		7:19	8:00	**2:25**	4:01
97	7	Mon		7:18	8:00	**3:26**	4:38
98	8	Tue	Regulus ☌ ☽ (7 am)	7:17	8:01	**4:25**	5:10
99	9	Wed		7:15	8:02	**5:21**	5:38
100	10	Thu	☿ ☌ ♄ (7 am)	7:14	8:02	**6:15**	6:03
101	11	Fri		7:13	8:03	**7:09**	6:28
102	12	Sat	Spica ☌ full ☽ (8 pm)	7:12	8:03	**8:03**	6:53
103	13	Sun	☽ at apogee (6 pm)	7:11	8:04	**8:59**	7:19
104	14	Mon		7:10	8:05	**9:56**	7:48
105	15	Tue		7:08	8:05	**10:54**	8:21
106	16	Wed	♂ at aphelion (5 pm)	7:07	8:06	**11:52**	8:59
107	17	Thu		7:06	8:07		9:43
108	18	Fri		7:05	8:07	12:48	10:34
109	19	Sat		7:04	8:08	1:41	11:32
110	20	Sun	Last qtr. ☽	7:03	8:09	2:29	**12:33**
111	21	Mon	☿ gr. elongation W (2 pm)	7:02	8:09	3:11	**1:38**
112	22	Tue		7:01	8:10	3:49	**2:43**
113	23	Wed		7:00	8:11	4:23	**3:50**
114	24	Thu	♀ ♄ ☌ ☽	6:59	8:11	4:55	**4:56**
115	25	Fri	☿ ☌ ☽ (8 pm)	6:58	8:12	5:26	**6:05**
116	26	Sat		6:57	8:13	5:59	**7:16**
117	27	Sun	New ☽ at perigee (11 am)	6:56	8:13	6:35	**8:30**
118	28	Mon	♀ ☌ ♄ (2 pm)	6:55	8:14	7:16	**9:46**
119	29	Tue		6:54	8:15	8:04	**11:01**
120	30	Wed		6:53	8:16	9:00	

5th Month — May 2025 — 31 Days

Day of Year	Day of Month	Day of Week	Planetary Configurations and Phenomena	Sunrise	Sunset	Moon-rise	Moon-set
121	1	Thu		6:52	8:16	10:03	12:09
122	2	Fri	Pollux ☌ ☽ (7 pm)	6:51	8:17	11:09	1:09
123	3	Sat	♂ ☌ ☽ (6 pm)	6:50	8:18	**12:15**	1:58
124	4	Sun	First qtr. ☽	6:49	8:18	**1:19**	2:38
125	5	Mon	Regulus ☌ ☽ (1 pm)	6:48	8:19	**2:19**	3:12
126	6	Tue		6:48	8:20	**3:16**	3:41
127	7	Wed		6:47	8:20	**4:11**	4:07
128	8	Thu		6:46	8:21	**5:04**	4:32
129	9	Fri		6:45	8:22	**5:58**	4:57
130	10	Sat	Spica ☌ ☽ at apogee	6:44	8:22	**6:53**	5:23
131	11	Sun		6:44	8:23	**7:49**	5:51
132	12	Mon	Full ☽	6:43	8:24	**8:47**	6:23
133	13	Tue	Antares ☌ ☽ (11 pm)	6:42	8:24	**9:46**	6:59
134	14	Wed		6:42	8:25	**10:43**	7:42
135	15	Thu		6:41	8:26	**11:37**	8:31
136	16	Fri		6:40	8:26		9:26
137	17	Sat	♅ ☌ ☉ (8 pm)	6:40	8:27	12:26	10:26
138	18	Sun		6:39	8:28	1:10	11:29
139	19	Mon		6:39	8:28	1:48	**12:32**
140	20	Tue	Last qtr. ☽	6:38	8:29	2:22	**1:36**
141	21	Wed		6:38	8:30	2:53	**2:40**
142	22	Thu	♄ ☌ ☽ (1 pm)	6:37	8:30	3:24	**3:46**
143	23	Fri	♀ ☌ ☽ (7 pm)	6:37	8:31	3:55	**4:53**
144	24	Sat		6:36	8:32	4:28	**6:04**
145	25	Sun	☽ at perigee (8 pm)	6:36	8:32	5:05	**7:18**
146	26	Mon	New ☽	6:35	8:33	5:49	**8:34**
147	27	Tue		6:35	8:33	6:42	**9:47**
148	28	Wed		6:35	8:34	7:43	**10:52**
149	29	Thu	☿ in superior ☌ (11 pm)	6:34	8:35	8:50	**11:48**
150	30	Fri	Pollux ☌ ☽ (4 am)	6:34	8:35	9:59	
151	31	Sat	♀ gr. elongation W (9 pm)	6:34	8:36	11:05	12:33

6th Month — June 2025 — 30 Days

Day of Year	Day of Month	Day of Week	Planetary Configurations and Phenomena	Sunrise	Sunset	Moon-rise	Moon-set
152	1	Sun	♂ ☌ ☽ (5 am)	6:34	8:36	**12:09**	1:10
153	2	Mon	First qtr. ☽	6:33	8:37	**1:08**	1:42
154	3	Tue		6:33	8:37	**2:04**	2:10
155	4	Wed		6:33	8:38	**2:58**	2:35
156	5	Thu		6:33	8:38	**3:52**	3:00
157	6	Fri	Spica ☌ ☽ (9 am)	6:33	8:39	**4:47**	3:26
158	7	Sat	☽ at apogee (6 am)	6:33	8:39	**5:43**	3:53
159	8	Sun		6:33	8:40	**6:40**	4:23
160	9	Mon		6:32	8:40	**7:39**	4:58
161	10	Tue	Antares ☌ ☽ (5 am)	6:32	8:41	**8:37**	5:39
162	11	Wed	Full ☽; ♀ at aphelion	6:32	8:41	**9:32**	6:27
163	12	Thu		6:32	8:41	**10:23**	7:21
164	13	Fri		6:32	8:42	**11:09**	8:20
165	14	Sat		6:33	8:42	**11:49**	9:23
166	15	Sun		6:33	8:42		10:26
167	16	Mon	♂ ☌ Regulus (9 pm)	6:33	8:43	12:24	11:29
168	17	Tue		6:33	8:43	12:55	**12:32**
169	18	Wed	♄ ☌ last qtr. ☽	6:33	8:43	1:25	**1:35**
170	19	Thu		6:33	8:43	1:55	**2:40**
171	20	Fri	Solstice (9:42 pm)	6:33	8:44	2:26	**3:47**
172	21	Sat	☿ ☌ Pollux (3 pm)	6:34	8:44	3:00	**4:57**
173	22	Sun	☽ at perigee (11 pm)	6:34	8:44	3:40	**6:10**
174	23	Mon		6:34	8:44	4:27	**7:23**
175	24	Tue	♃ ☌ ☉ (10 am)	6:34	8:44	5:24	**8:32**
176	25	Wed	New ☽	6:35	8:45	6:28	**9:33**
177	26	Thu	Pollux ☌ ☽ (2 pm)	6:35	8:45	7:37	**10:23**
178	27	Fri	☿ ☌ ☽ (1 am)	6:35	8:45	8:46	**11:05**
179	28	Sat		6:36	8:45	9:52	**11:40**
180	29	Sun	♂ ☌ ☽ (8 pm)	6:36	8:45	10:55	
181	30	Mon		6:36	8:45	11:53	12:09

☉ The Sun ● The Earth ☽ The Moon ☿ Mercury ♀ Venus ♂ Mars ♃ Jupiter ♄ Saturn ♆ Neptune ♅ Uranus ☌= in conjunction ☍= opposition to the ☉

Astronomical Calendar for 2025

7th Month — July 2025 — 31 Days

Day of Year	Day of Month	Day of Week	Planetary Configurations and Phenomena	Sunrise	Sunset	Moon-rise	Moon-set
182	1	Tue		6:37	8:45	**12:49**	12:36
183	2	Wed	First qtr. ☽ (2 pm)	6:37	8:45	**1:44**	1:02
184	3	Thu	● at aphelion (4 pm)	6:38	8:45	**2:39**	1:27
185	4	Fri	☽ at apogee (9 pm)	6:38	8:45	**3:34**	1:54
186	5	Sat		6:39	8:44	**4:31**	2:23
187	6	Sun		6:39	8:44	**5:29**	2:56
188	7	Mon	Antares ☌ ☽ (12 pm)	6:39	8:44	**6:28**	3:35
189	8	Tue		6:40	8:44	**7:25**	4:20
190	9	Wed		6:40	8:44	**8:18**	5:13
191	10	Thu	Full ☽	6:41	8:43	**9:06**	6:11
192	11	Fri		6:42	8:43	**9:48**	7:14
193	12	Sat		6:42	8:43	**10:25**	8:18
194	13	Sun	♀ ☌ Aldebaran (3 am)	6:43	8:43	**10:58**	9:22
195	14	Mon	☿ at aphelion (8 am)	6:43	8:42	**11:28**	10:26
196	15	Tue		6:44	8:42	**11:57**	11:29
197	16	Wed	♄ ☌ ☽ (5 am)	6:44	8:41		**12:33**
198	17	Thu	Last qtr. ☽	6:45	8:41	12:28	**1:38**
199	18	Fri		6:45	8:41	1:00	**2:46**
200	19	Sat		6:46	8:40	1:37	**3:56**
201	20	Sun	☽ at perigee (9 am)	6:47	8:40	2:20	**5:07**
202	21	Mon		6:47	8:39	3:11	**6:16**
203	22	Tue	♃ ☌ ☽ (11 pm)	6:48	8:39	4:11	**7:19**
204	23	Wed		6:48	8:38	5:17	**8:13**
205	24	Thu	New ☽	6:49	8:37	6:26	**8:58**
206	25	Fri		6:50	8:37	7:34	**9:36**
207	26	Sat	Regulus ☌ ☽ (3 pm)	6:50	8:36	8:39	**10:08**
208	27	Sun		6:51	8:35	9:40	**10:36**
209	28	Mon	♃ ☌ ☽ (3 pm)	6:52	8:35	10:38	**11:02**
210	29	Tue		6:52	8:34	11:34	**11:28**
211	30	Wed		6:53	8:33	**12:29**	**11:54**
212	31	Thu	☿ in inferior ☌ (7 pm)	6:53	8:33	**1:24**	

8th Month — August 2025 — 31 Days

Day of Year	Day of Month	Day of Week	Planetary Configurations and Phenomena	Sunrise	Sunset	Moon-rise	Moon-set
213	1	Fri	First qtr. ☽ at apogee	6:54	8:32	**2:21**	12:23
214	2	Sat		6:55	8:31	**3:18**	12:54
215	3	Sun	Antares ☌ ☽ (9pm)	6:55	8:30	**4:17**	1:30
216	4	Mon		6:56	8:29	**5:14**	2:13
217	5	Tue		6:57	8:29	**6:09**	3:02
218	6	Wed		6:57	8:28	**6:59**	3:58
219	7	Thu		6:58	8:27	**7:44**	5:00
220	8	Fri		6:59	8:26	**8:23**	6:04
221	9	Sat	Full ☽	6:59	8:25	**8:58**	7:10
222	10	Sun		7:00	8:24	**9:30**	8:15
223	11	Mon		7:00	8:23	**10:00**	9:20
224	12	Tue	♀ ♄ ☌ ☽	7:01	8:22	**10:30**	10:25
225	13	Wed		7:02	8:21	**11:02**	11:31
226	14	Thu	☽ at perigee (1 pm)	7:02	8:20	**11:37**	**12:38**
227	15	Fri		7:03	8:19		**1:47**
228	16	Sat	Last qtr. ☽	7:04	8:18	12:18	**2:58**
229	17	Sun		7:04	8:17	1:06	**4:07**
230	18	Mon		7:05	8:16	2:02	**5:11**
231	19	Tue	☿ gr. elongation W (5 am)	7:05	8:15	3:05	**6:07**
232	20	Wed	Pollux ☌ ☽ (7 am)	7:06	8:14	4:12	**6:54**
233	21	Thu	☿ ☌ ☽ (11 am)	7:07	8:13	5:19	**7:33**
234	22	Fri		7:07	8:12	6:24	**8:07**
235	23	Sat	New ☽	7:08	8:10	7:26	**8:36**
236	24	Sun		7:08	8:09	8:25	**9:03**
237	25	Mon		7:09	8:08	9:22	**9:29**
238	26	Tue	♂ ☌ ☽ (12 pm)	7:10	8:07	10:18	**9:55**
239	27	Wed	☿ at perihelion (7 am)	7:10	8:06	11:14	**10:22**
240	28	Thu		7:11	8:05	**12:10**	**10:53**
241	29	Fri	☽ at apogee (10 am)	7:11	8:03	**1:07**	**11:27**
242	30	Sat		7:12	8:02	**2:05**	
243	31	Sun	Antares ☌ first qtr. ☽	7:13	8:01	**3:03**	12:06

9th Month — September 2025 — 30 Days

Day of Year	Day of Month	Day of Week	Planetary Configurations and Phenomena	Sunrise	Sunset	Moon-rise	Moon-set
244	1	Mon		7:13	8:00	**3:58**	12:52
245	2	Tue		7:14	7:58	**4:50**	1:45
246	3	Wed		7:14	7:57	**5:37**	2:43
247	4	Thu		7:15	7:56	**6:18**	3:46
248	5	Fri		7:16	7:55	**6:55**	4:52
249	6	Sat		7:16	7:53	**7:28**	5:58
250	7	Sun	Full ☽; eclipse (1 pm)	7:17	7:52	**7:59**	7:04
251	8	Mon	♄ ☌ ☽ (3 pm)	7:17	7:51	**8:30**	8:10
252	9	Tue		7:18	7:50	**9:02**	9:17
253	10	Wed	B at perigee (7 am)	7:18	7:48	**9:37**	10:26
254	11	Thu		7:19	7:47	**10:17**	11:37
255	12	Fri	♂ ☌ Spica (10 pm)	7:20	7:46	**11:03**	**12:49**
256	13	Sat	☿ in superior ☌ (6 am)	7:20	7:45	**11:57**	**1:59**
257	14	Sun	Last qtr. ☽	7:21	7:43		**3:05**
258	15	Mon		7:21	7:42	12:58	**4:03**
259	16	Tue	♃ ☌ ☽ (6 am)	7:22	7:41	2:03	**4:52**
260	17	Wed		7:22	7:39	3:09	**5:33**
261	18	Thu		7:23	7:38	4:14	**6:08**
262	19	Fri	♀ ☌ ☽ (7 am)	7:24	7:37	5:16	**6:38**
263	20	Sat	♄ ☍ (11 pm)	7:24	7:36	6:16	**7:05**
264	21	Sun	New ☽; ☉ eclipse (3 pm)	7:25	7:34	7:13	**7:31**
265	22	Mon	Equinox (1:20 pm)	7:25	7:33	8:09	**7:57**
266	23	Tue	♆ ☍ (6 am); Spica ☌ ☽	7:26	7:32	9:04	**8:24**
267	24	Wed	♂ ☌ ☽ (10 am)	7:27	7:30	10:00	**8:53**
268	25	Thu		7:27	7:29	10:57	**9:25**
269	26	Fri	☽ at apogee (5 am)	7:28	7:28	11:55	**10:02**
270	27	Sat	Antares ☌ ☽ (12 pm)	7:28	7:27	**12:52**	**10:45**
271	28	Sun		7:29	7:25	**1:48**	**11:34**
272	29	Mon	First qtr. ☽	7:30	7:24	**2:41**	
273	30	Tue		7:30	7:23	**3:29**	12:30

Bright stars: Aldebaran, Antares, Spica, Pollux, Regulus. **Minor planets or asteroids:** Pluto, Ceres, Pallas, Juno, Vesta ☌ = in conjunction by 10° or < ☍ = opposition to the ☉

Astronomical Calendar for 2025

10th Month — October 2025 — 31 Days

Day of Year	Day of Month	Day of Week	Planetary Configurations and Phenomena	Sunrise	Sunset	Moon-rise	Moon-set
274	1	Wed		7:31	7:21	**4:11**	1:30
275	2	Thu	♀ at perihelion (6 am)	7:31	7:20	**4:49**	2:33
276	3	Fri		7:32	7:19	**5:23**	3:37
277	4	Sat		7:33	7:18	**5:55**	4:42
278	5	Sun	♄ ☌ ☽ (10 pm)	7:33	7:16	**6:26**	5:48
279	6	Mon	Full ☽	7:34	7:15	**6:58**	6:56
280	7	Tue		7:35	7:14	**7:32**	8:05
281	8	Wed	☽ at perigee (7 am)	7:35	7:13	**8:11**	9:17
282	9	Thu		7:36	7:12	**8:56**	10:31
283	10	Fri		7:37	7:10	**9:49**	11:45
284	11	Sat		7:37	7:09	**10:50**	**12:56**
285	12	Sun		7:38	7:08	**11:55**	**1:58**
286	13	Mon	♃ ☌ last qtr. ☽ (5 pm)	7:39	7:07		**2:50**
287	14	Tue		7:39	7:06	1:02	**3:34**
288	15	Wed		7:40	7:05	2:08	**4:10**
289	16	Thu	Regulus ☌ ☽ (12 pm)	7:41	7:04	3:10	**4:41**
290	17	Fri		7:41	7:02	4:09	**5:09**
291	18	Sat		7:42	7:01	5:06	**5:35**
292	19	Sun	☿ ☌ ♂; ♀ ☌ ☽	7:43	7:00	6:02	**6:01**
293	20	Mon		7:43	6:59	6:57	**6:27**
294	21	Tue	New ☽	7:44	6:58	7:53	**6:55**
295	22	Wed		7:45	6:57	8:49	**7:26**
296	23	Thu	☿ ☌ ☽ at apogee	7:46	6:56	9:47	**8:01**
297	24	Fri	Antares ☌ ☽ (7 pm)	7:46	6:55	10:44	**8:42**
298	25	Sat		7:47	6:54	11:41	**9:29**
299	26	Sun		7:48	6:53	**12:34**	**10:21**
300	27	Mon		7:49	6:52	**1:23**	**11:19**
301	28	Tue		7:49	6:51	**2:06**	
302	29	Wed	First qtr. ☽; ☿ gr. elong. E	7:50	6:50	**2:45**	12:19
303	30	Thu		7:51	6:50	**3:19**	1:21
304	31	Fri		7:52	6:49	**3:51**	2:24

11th Month — November 2025 — 30 Days

Day of Year	Day of Month	Day of Week	Planetary Configurations and Phenomena	Sunrise	Sunset	Moon-rise	Moon-set
305	1	Sat	♀ ☌ Spica (8 pm)	7:53	6:48	**4:22**	3:27
306	2	Sun	DST ends (2 am); ♄ ☌ ☽	6:53	5:47	**3:52**	3:32
307	3	Mon		6:54	5:46	**4:25**	4:39
308	4	Tue		6:55	5:45	**5:02**	5:50
309	5	Wed	Full ☽ at perigee (4 pm)	6:56	5:45	**5:44**	7:04
310	6	Thu		6:57	5:44	**6:35**	8:20
311	7	Fri		6:57	5:43	**7:34**	9:35
312	8	Sat	☿ ☌ Antares (9 pm)	6:58	5:43	**8:41**	10:44
313	9	Sun		6:59	5:42	**9:50**	11:43
314	10	Mon	♃ ☌ ☽ (2 am)	7:00	5:41	**10:58**	**12:31**
315	11	Tue	Last qtr. ☽	7:01	5:41		**1:11**
316	12	Wed	Regulus ☌ ☽; ☿ ☌ ♂	7:02	5:40	12:03	**1:44**
317	13	Thu		7:03	5:39	1:04	**2:13**
318	14	Fri		7:03	5:39	2:02	**2:39**
319	15	Sat		7:04	5:38	2:57	**3:05**
320	16	Sun		7:05	5:38	3:52	**3:30**
321	17	Mon	Spica ☌ ☽ (4 am)	7:06	5:38	4:47	**3:58**
322	18	Tue		7:07	5:37	5:43	**4:28**
323	19	Wed	☽ at apogee (9 pm)	7:08	5:37	6:40	**5:02**
324	20	Thu	New ☽; ☿ in inferior ☌	7:09	5:36	7:38	**5:41**
325	21	Fri	♅ ☍ (7 am)	7:09	5:36	8:35	**6:26**
326	22	Sat		7:10	5:36	9:29	**7:17**
327	23	Sun	☿ at perihelion (5 am)	7:11	5:35	10:19	**8:13**
328	24	Mon		7:12	5:35	11:04	**9:12**
329	25	Tue		7:13	5:35	11:44	**10:12**
330	26	Wed		7:14	5:35	**12:19**	**11:13**
331	27	Thu		7:15	5:34	**12:50**	
332	28	Fri	First qtr. ☽	7:15	5:34	**1:20**	12:14
333	29	Sat	♄ ☌ ☽ (1 pm)	7:16	5:34	**1:49**	1:15
334	30	Sun		7:17	5:34	**2:20**	2:19

12th Month — December 2025 — 31 Days

Day of Year	Day of Month	Day of Week	Planetary Configurations and Phenomena	Sunrise	Sunset	Moon-rise	Moon-set
335	1	Mon		7:18	5:34	**2:53**	3:25
336	2	Tue		7:19	5:34	**3:32**	4:35
337	3	Wed		7:19	5:34	**4:17**	5:50
338	4	Thu	Full ☽ at perigee (5 am)	7:20	5:34	**5:13**	7:06
339	5	Fri		7:21	5:34	**6:17**	8:20
340	6	Sat		7:22	5:34	**7:28**	9:25
341	7	Sun	♃ ☌ ☽; ☿ gr. elong. W	7:23	5:34	**8:40**	10:20
342	8	Mon		7:23	5:35	**9:49**	11:05
343	9	Tue		7:24	5:35	**10:53**	11:42
344	10	Wed	Regulus ☌ ☽ (12 am)	7:25	5:35	**11:54**	**12:13**
345	11	Thu	Last qtr. ☽	7:25	5:35		**12:41**
346	12	Fri		7:26	5:35	12:51	**1:08**
347	13	Sat		7:27	5:36	1:47	**1:33**
348	14	Sun	Spica ☌ ☽ (10 am)	7:27	5:36	2:42	**2:00**
349	15	Mon		7:28	5:36	3:37	**2:30**
350	16	Tue		7:29	5:37	4:34	**3:02**
351	17	Wed	☽ at apogee (12 am)	7:29	5:37	5:31	**3:40**
352	18	Thu	Antares ☌ ☽ (6 am)	7:30	5:38	6:28	**4:23**
353	19	Fri	New ☽	7:30	5:38	7:24	**5:13**
354	20	Sat		7:31	5:38	8:16	**6:07**
355	21	Sun	Solstice (9:03 am)	7:31	5:39	9:03	**7:06**
356	22	Mon		7:32	5:39	9:44	**8:07**
357	23	Tue		7:32	5:40	10:20	**9:07**
358	24	Wed		7:33	5:41	10:52	**10:07**
359	25	Thu		7:33	5:41	11:22	**11:08**
360	26	Fri	♄ ☌ ☽ (9 pm)	7:34	5:42	11:50	
361	27	Sat	First qtr. ☽	7:34	5:42	**12:19**	12:08
362	28	Sun		7:34	5:43	**12:50**	1:11
363	29	Mon		7:35	5:44	**1:25**	2:17
364	30	Tue		7:35	5:44	**2:05**	3:27
365	31	Wed		7:35	5:45	**2:54**	4:40

⊙ The Sun ● The Earth ☽ The Moon ☿ Mercury ♀ Venus ♂ Mars ♃ Jupiter ♄ Saturn ♆ Neptune ♅ Uranus ☌= in conjunction ☍= opposition to the ⊙

RECREATION

STATE PARKS, NATURAL AREAS & HISTORIC SITES

STATE FORESTS & ARBORETUMS

NATIONAL PARKS, HISTORIC SITES & RECREATION AREAS

NATIONAL FORESTS & GRASSLANDS

BIRDING IN TEXAS

FAIRS, FESTIVALS, SPECIAL EVENTS & MORE...

SPECIAL THANKS TO THE GAGE HOTEL IN MARATHON
AND HOTEL ST. GEORGE IN MARFA
FOR SPONSORING THIS CHAPTER OF THE TEXAS ALMANAC

PHOTO OF SAN JACINTO MONUMENT BY THE TEXAS HISTORICAL COMMISSION

ESTD 1927
Experience Texas History
at one of Texas' Top 10 Resorts
GAGE HOTEL
THIS PROPERTY HAS BEEN PLACED ON THE NATIONAL REGISTER OF HISTORIC PLACES BY THE UNITED STATES DEPARTMENT OF THE INTERIOR
MARATHON, TEXAS | 1.800.884.GAGE | GAGEHOTEL.COM
marfasaintgeorge.com
432.729.3700

Fall foliage at Cooper Lake State Park, South Sulphur unit. Photo by Texas Parks & Wildlife

Texas State Parks and Natural Areas

Sources: Texas Parks and Wildlife, tpwd.texas.gov; and Port Arthur, visitportarthurtx.com/things-to-do/attraction/walter-umphrey-state-park/

Texas' diverse system of state parks and natural areas offers contrasting attractions: mountains and canyons, arid deserts and lush forests, spring-fed streams, sandy dunes, and saltwater surf.

The **Texas Parks and Wildlife Department (TPW)** operates the state parks, state natural areas, and state historic sites listed in this section unless otherwise noted. TPW is dedicated to managing and conserving the state's natural resources and provide recreation opportunities so we can all enjoy the outdoors. The department celebrated its 100th anniversary in 2023.

The following information is a brief glimpse of each park and historic site. Refer to the chart on pages 153–154 for a more complete list of available activities and facilities. Entrance fees range from free to $8 per person unless otherwise stated. There are also fees for guided tours and some activities. Nearby attractions in **green bold** have a separate listing in this chapter.

For the Kids

Our state parks love it when kids get out in nature, and they encourage this with their **Junior Ranger** program. Next time you visit a state park with a little one, pick up a Junior Ranger Journal, loaded with suggested activities, and a Junior Ranger Explorer Pack, containing binoculars, a magnifying glass, and guides to the local flora and fauna. Completing a certain number of activities will earn a badge for that park.

List of State Parks and Natural Areas

Abilene State Park, 16 miles southwest of Abilene on FM 89 and PR 32 in Taylor County, consists of 529 acres that were deeded by the City of Abilene in 1933. Large groves of pecan trees that once shaded bands of Comanches now shade visitors at picnic tables. Nearby is Buffalo Gap, the original Taylor County seat (1878) and one of the early frontier settlements. Buffalo Gap was on the Western, or Goodnight-Loving Trail, over which pioneer Texas cattlemen drove herds to railheads in Kansas.

Atlanta State Park is 1,475 acres located 11 miles northwest of Atlanta on FM 1154 in Cass County; adjacent to Wright Patman Dam and Reservoir. Land acquired from the U.S. Army in 1954 by license to 2004 with option to renew to 2054. Nearby are the historic town of Jefferson and the **Caddo Lake SP** and **Daingerfield SP**.

Balmorhea State Park is 46 acres, four miles southwest of Balmorhea on TX 17 between Balmorhea and Toyahvale in Reeves County. Deeded in 1934–1935 by private owners and Reeves Co. Water Imp. Dist. No. 1 and built by the Civilian Conservation Corps (CCC). Swimming pool (1–3/4 acres) fed by artesian San Solomon Springs; also provides water to aquatic refuge in park. Activities include scuba and skin diving. Motel rooms available at San Solomon Springs Courts. Nearby are city of Pecos, **Fort Davis National Historic Site**, **Davis Mountains SP** and McDonald Observatory.

Bastrop State Park is 6,600 acres, found one mile east of Bastrop on TX 21 or from TX 71. The park was acquired by deeds from the City of Bastrop and private owners in 1933–1935. Site of famous "Lost Pines," an isolated region of loblolly pines and hardwoods. Swimming pool, cabins and lodge are among facilities. A golf course lies adjacent to the park. The state capitol at Austin is 32 miles away; a 13-mile drive through forest leads to **Buescher SP**.

Bentsen–Rio Grande Valley State Park, a scenic park, is along the Rio Grande five miles southwest of Mission off FM 2062 in Hidalgo County. Originally acquired from private owners in 1944, the park's subtropical resaca woodlands and brushlands has grown to 797 acres. Hiking trails provide chance to study unique plants and animals of park. Many birds unique to southern United States found here, including pauraque, groove-billed ani, green kingfisher, rose-throated becard, and tropical parula. Birdwatching tours guided by park naturalists offered daily December–March. The park is one of last natural refuges in Texas for ocelot and jaguarundi. Trees include cedar elm, anaqua, ebony, and Mexican ash. Nearby are Santa Ana National Wildlife Refuge, **Falcon SP**, and Sabal Palm Sanctuary.

Big Bend Ranch State Park, more than 300,000 acres of Chihuahuan Desert wilderness in Brewster and Presidio counties along the Rio Grande, was purchased from private owners in 1988. The purchase more than doubled the size of the state park system, which comprised at that time 220,000 acres. Eastern entrance at Barton Warnock Visitor Center one mile east of Lajitas on FM 170; western entrance is at **Fort Leaton SHS**, four miles east of Presidio on FM 170. The area includes extinct volcanoes, several waterfalls, two mountain ranges, at least 11 rare species of plants and animals, and 90 major archaeological sites. There is little development. Vehicular access is limited. There are longhorns in the park, although they are not part of the official state longhorn herd. Nearby is **Big Bend National Park**.

Big Spring State Park is 382 acres located on FM 700 within the city limits of Big Spring in Howard County. Both city and park were named for a natural spring that was replaced by an artificial one. The park was deeded by the City of Big Spring in 1934 and 1935. The top of Scenic Mountain offers a panoramic view of the surrounding country and a group picnicking pavilion. The "big spring," nearby in a city park, provided watering place for herds of bison, antelope, and wild horses. Used extensively also as campsite for early natives, explorers, and settlers.

Blanco State Park is 105 acres along the Blanco River four blocks south of Blanco's town square in Blanco County. The land was deeded by private owners in 1933. Park area was used as campsite by early explorers and settlers. Red-eared sliders, cricket frogs, Gulf Coast toads, and great blue herons are commonly spotted. **LBJ SP and SHS** and **LBJ National Historic Park** are nearby.

Ready to Plan Your Trip?

The **Texas Department of Transportation** publishes the **Texas State Travel Guide**, a full-color publication with information about attractions, activities, history and historic sites, and the official **Texas Official Travel Map**. You can get both sent to you for free or download a free digital version at the site:

https://www.traveltexas.com/

For up-to-date information about your chosen park or to make camping or tour reservations, visit the TPWD website or call the Central Reservation Center during business hours.

TPWD: **(512) 389-8900**

Toll free: **(800) 792-1112**

TDD **(512) 389-8915**

Find discount passes for youth groups, qualifying seniors, veterans and disabled persons, and families here:

https://tpwd.texas.gov/state-parks/park-information/passes/park-passes

TPWD also operates a free State Park mobile app, available for both iPhone and Android.

Bonham State Park is a 261-acre park located two miles southeast of Bonham on TX 78, then two miles southeast on FM 271 in Fannin County. It includes a 65-acre lake, rolling prairies and woodlands. The land was acquired in 1933 from the City of Bonham. **Sam Rayburn House SHS**, and **Eisenhower Birthplace SHS** are nearby.

Brazos Bend State Park is in Fort Bend County, eight miles east of Damon off FM 1462 on FM 762, approximately 28 miles southwest of Houston. The 4,897-acre park was purchased from private owners in 1976–1977. George Observatory, part of the Houston Museum of Natural Science, is open Saturdays (tickets sold online). The observation deck and tower are ideal spots for viewing and photographing the 270 species of birds, 23 species of mammals, and 21 species of reptiles and amphibians, including American alligator, that frequent the park. Interpretive and educational programs every weekend. Nearby attractions: **Varner-Hogg Plantation SHS** and **Sea Center Texas**.

Buescher State Park is a scenic 1,017 acres, found two miles northwest of Smithville off TX 71 to FM 153 in Bastrop County. Acquired between 1933 and 1936, about one-third deeded by private owner; heirs donated a third; balance from City of Smithville. El Camino Real once ran near park, connecting San Antonio de Béxar with Spanish missions in East Texas. Park land was part of Stephen F. Austin's colonial grant. Some 250 species of birds can be seen. Scenic park road connects with **Bastrop SP** through Lost Pines area.

Caddo Lake State Park, north of Karnack one mile off TX 43 to FM 2198 in Harrison County, consists of 484 acres along Cypress Bayou, which runs into Caddo Lake. A scenic area, it was acquired from private owners in 1933. Caddo legend attributes formation of Caddo Lake to a huge flood.

Today the lake is host to cypress trees, American lotus and lily pads, as well as 71 species of fish. Nutria, beaver, mink, squirrel, armadillo, alligator, and turtle abound. Nearby: **Starr Family Home SHS**, Marshall, and Karnack (birthplace of Lady Bird Johnson).

Caprock Canyons State Park and Trailway, 100 miles southeast of Amarillo and 3.5 miles north of Quitaque off FM 1065 and TX 86 in Briscoe, Floyd, and Hall counties, has 15,313 acres. Purchased in 1975. These canyons provided camping areas for natives of Folsom culture more than 10,000 years ago. Mesquite and cacti in the badlands give way to tall grasses, cottonwood and plum thickets in the bottomlands. Wildlife includes aoudad sheep, coyote, bobcat, porcupine, and fox. A 64-mile trailway (hike, bike, and equestrian trail) extends from South Plains to Estelline.

Cedar Hill State Park, an urban park on 1,826 acres ten miles southwest of Dallas via US 67 and FM 1382 on Joe Pool Lake, was acquired by long-term lease from the Army Corps of Engineers in 1982. Camping mostly in wooded areas. Fishing from two lighted jetties and a perch pond for children. Vegetation includes several sections of tall-grass prairie. Penn Farm Agricultural History Center includes reconstructed buildings of the 19th-century Penn Farm and exhibits; self-guided tours.

Choke Canyon State Park consists of two units, South Shore and Calliham, located on 26,000-acre Choke Canyon Reservoir. Park acquired in 1981 in a 50-year agreement among Bureau of Reclamation, City of Corpus Christi and Nueces River Authority. Thickets of mesquite and blackbrush acacia predominate, supporting populations of javelina, coyote, skunk and alligator, as well as the crested caracara. The 385-acre South Shore Unit is located 3.5 miles west of Three Rivers on TX 72 in Live Oak County and is day-use only, offering birding, fishing, and boating. The 1,100-acre Calliham Unit is located 12 miles west of Three Rivers on TX 72 in McMullen County. The Calliham Unit is a full-service park and offers a variety of camping and sporting facilities. Nearby is James E. Daughtrey Wildlife Management Area.

Cleburne State Park is a 528-acre park located ten miles southwest of Cleburne via US 67 and PR 21 in Johnson County with 116-acre spring-fed lake; acquired from the City of Cleburne and private owners in 1935 and 1936. Oak, elm, mesquite, cedar, and redbud cover white rocky hills. Bluebonnets in spring. Nearby are Fossil Rim Wildlife Center and dinosaur tracks in the Paluxy River at **Dinosaur Valley SP**.

Colorado Bend State Park, encompassing 5,328 acres, is 28 miles west of Lampasas in Lampasas and San Saba counties. Access is from Lampasas to Bend on FM 580 west, then follow signs (access road subject to flooding). Park site was purchased partly in 1984, with balance acquired in 1987. Guided tours to Gorman Falls; crawling cave tours require reservations. Rare and endangered species here include golden-cheeked warbler, black-capped vireo, and bald eagle.

Cooper Lake State Park comprises 3,026 acres just three miles southeast of the town of Cooper in Delta and Hopkins counties. The park was acquired in 1991 from the Army Corps of Engineers. Two units, Doctors Creek and South Sulphur, adjoin 19,300-acre Cooper Lake. South Sulphur offers equestrian camping and horseback riding trails, as well as basketball and volleyball courts. Cooper Wildlife Management Area is nearby.

Copper Breaks State Park, 12 miles south of Quanah on TX 6 in Hardeman County, was acquired by purchase from private owner in 1970. Park features rugged scenic beauty on 1,899 acres, two lakes, grass-covered mesas and juniper breaks. Nearby medicine mounds were important ceremonial sites of Comanches. Nearby Pease River was site of 1860 battle in which Cynthia Ann Parker was recovered from Comanches. Part of state longhorn herd lives at park. Abundant wildlife.

Daingerfield State Park, off TX 49 and PR 17 southeast of Daingerfield in Morris County, is a 551-acre recreational area that includes an 80-acre lake; deeded in 1935 by private owners. This area is the center of the iron industry in Texas; nearby is Lone Star Steel Co. In spring, dogwood, redbuds, and wisteria bloom; in fall, brilliant foliage of sweetgum, oaks, and maples contrast with dark green pines.

Davis Mountains State Park is 2,709 acres in Jeff Davis County, four miles northwest of Fort Davis via TX 118 and PR 3. The scenic area was deeded in 1933–1937 by private owners. First European, Antonio de Espejo, came to area in 1583. Extremes of altitude produce both plains grasslands and piñon-juniper-oak woodlands. Montezuma quail, rare in Texas, visit park. Indian Lodge, built by the Civilian Conservation Corps during the early 1930s, has 39 rooms, a restaurant and a swimming pool. Four-mile hiking trail leads to **Fort Davis National Historic Site**. Other nearby points of interest include the McDonald Observatory and a 74-mile scenic loop through Davis Mountains.

Devils River State Natural Area comprises 37,000 acres in Val Verde County, 22 miles off US 277, about 65 miles north of Del Rio on graded road. It is an ecological and archaeological crossroads. Ecologically, it is in a transitional area between the Edwards Plateau, the Trans-Pecos desert and the South Texas brush country. Archaeological studies suggest occupation and use by cultures from both east and west. Pictograph tours are dependent on staff availability. Reservations are highly recommended.

Devil's Sinkhole State Natural Area, comprising 1,860 acres about six miles northeast of Rocksprings on US 377 in Edwards County, is a vertical cavern. The sinkhole, discovered by Anglo settlers in 1867, was purchased in 1985 from private owners. The cavern opening is about 40 feet by 60 feet, with a vertical drop of about 140 feet. Mexican free-tailed bats live in the sinkhole from late spring to early fall. Access to the park is restricted to guided tours: nature walks, bird tours, and evening bat tours. Call the Devil's Sinkhole Society (830–683–BATS) for availability and to make a reservation. **Kickapoo Cavern SP** is nearby.

Dinosaur Valley State Park, located off US 67 four miles west of Glen Rose in Somervell County, is a 1,525-acre scenic park. Land was acquired from private owners in 1968. Features dinosaur tracks in bed of Paluxy River and two full-scale dinosaur models, originally created for New York World's Fair in 1964–1965, on display. The riverbed featuring the dinosaur tracks was designated a national landmark in 1968. **Cleburne SP** is nearby.

Eisenhower State Park, 423 acres five miles northwest of Denison via US 75 to TX 91N to FM 1310 on the shores of

Lake Texoma in Grayson County, was acquired by an Army lease in 1954. Named for the 34th U.S. president, Dwight D. Eisenhower, who was born nearby at the **Eisenhower Birthplace SHS**. First Anglo settlers came to area in 1835; Fort Johnson was established in area in 1840; Colbert's Ferry established on Red River in 1853 and operated until 1931. Areas of tall-grass prairie and wildflowers. ATV trails available with OHV permit.

Enchanted Rock State Natural Area is 1,644 acres on Big Sandy Creek 18 miles north of Fredericksburg on FM 965 on the line between Gillespie and Llano counties. Acquired in 1978 by The Nature Conservancy of Texas; acquired by the state in 1984. Enchanted Rock is huge pink granite boulder rising 425 feet above ground and covering 640 acres. It is second-largest batholith (underground rock formation uncovered by erosion) in the United States. Natives believed ghost fires flickered at top and were awed by weird creaking and groaning, which geologists say resulted from rock's heating and expanding by day, cooling and contracting at night.

Estero Llano Grande State Park, part of the World Birding Center network, is a 176-acre wetlands refuge 3.2 miles southeast of Weslaco off FM 1015. Birds seen here include waders, shorebirds and migrating waterfowl, as well as coastal species such as Roseate spoonbill and Ibis. Rare spottings include red-crowned parrots and green parakeets. Open daily. Guided tours offered. All-terrain wheelchair available by reservation.

Fairfield Lake State Park is 1,460 acres adjacent to Lake Fairfield, six miles northeast of the city of Fairfield off FM 2570 and FM 3285 in Freestone County. The land had been leased to TPW by Texas Utilities, but the company sold it in 2023. The park closed in June 2023, but the state continues to pursue a deal to save it.

Falcon State Park is 573 acres located 15 miles north of Roma off US 83 and FM 2098 at southern end of Falcon Reservoir in Starr and Zapata counties. Park leased from International Boundary and Water Commission since 1949. Gently rolling hills covered by mesquite, huisache, wild olive, ebony, cactus. Excellent birding and fishing. Nearby are Mexico, Fort Ringgold in Rio Grande City, and historic city of Roma.

Fort Boggy State Park is 1,847 acres of wooded, rolling hills in Leon County near Boggy Creek, about four miles south of Centerville on TX 75. Land donated to TPW in 1985 by Eileen Crain Sullivan. Area once home to Keechi and Kickapoo tribes. Log fort was built by settlers in 1840s; first settlement north of the Old San Antonio Road and between the Navasota and Trinity rivers. Fifteen-acre lake open to small craft. Nearby attractions include **Fort Parker SP** and the Texas State Railroad.

Fort Parker State Park, composed of 759 acres of land and a 700-acre lake, between Mexia and Groesbeck off TX 14 in Limestone County. Named for the former private fort built near present park in 1836, the site was acquired from private owners and the City of Mexia 1935–1937. Nearby is Old Fort Parker Historic Site, which is operated by the City of Groesbeck.

Fort Richardson State Park, Historic Site, and Lost Creek Reservoir State Trailway, located one-half mile south of Jacksboro off US 281 in Jack County, contains 454 acres. Acquired in 1968 from City of Jacksboro. Fort founded in 1867, northernmost of line of federal forts established after Civil War for protection from natives; originally named Fort Jacksboro. In April 1867, fort was moved to its present location from 20 miles farther south; on Nov. 19, 1867, made permanent post at Jacksboro and named for Israel Richardson, who was fatally wounded at Battle of Antietam. Expeditions sent from Fort Richardson arrested natives responsible for Warren Wagon Train Massacre in 1871 and fought Comanches in Palo Duro Canyon. Fort abandoned in May 1878. Park contains seven restored buildings and two replicas. Trailway is nine miles long and ten feet wide, with a smooth improved surface running between the historic site and the north park unit.

Franklin Mountains State Park, created by an act of the legislature in 1979 to protect the mountain range as a wilderness preserve and acquired by TPW in 1981, comprises 24,248 acres, all within El Paso city limits. Largest urban park in the nation. It includes virtually an entire Chihuahuan Desert mountain range, with an elevation of 7,192 feet at the summit. The park is habitat for many Chihuahuan Desert plants including sotol, lechuguilla, ocotillo, cholla, and barrel cactus, and such animals as mule deer, fox, and an occasional cougar. Camping, mountain biking, nature study, hiking, picnicking, rock-climbing. Wyler Aerial Tramway, an aerial cable-car tramway on 195 acres of rugged mountain on east side of Franklin Mountains, is currently closed due to safety concerns. Other area attractions include **Hueco Tanks SP** and **Magoffin Home SHS**.

Galveston Island State Park, on the west end of Galveston Island on FM 3005, is a 2,013-acre site acquired in 1969 from private owners. Study nature amid sand dunes and grassland or enjoy the beach. Four miles of trails throughout the park feature observation platforms and photo blinds. Beach chairs, umbrellas, cabanas, paddleboards, bikes, and e-bikes available for rental; beach wheelchairs free to borrow. Musical productions in amphitheater during summer.

Garner State Park is 1,420 acres of recreational facilities on US 83 on the Frio River in Uvalde County nine miles south of Leakey. Named for John Nance Garner, U.S. Vice President, 1933–1941, the park was deeded in 1934–1936 by private owners. Mini golf, grocery, and laundry facilities on site. Nearby is John Nance "Cactus Jack" Garner Museum in Uvalde. Nearby also are ruins of historic Mission Nuestra Señora de la Candelaria del Cañón, founded in 1749; Camp Sabinal (a U.S. Cavalry post and later Texas Ranger camp) established 1856; Fort Inge, established 1849.

Goliad State Park and Mission Espíritu Santo Historic Site are on 188 acres one-fourth mile south of Goliad on US 183 and 77A, along the San Antonio River in Goliad County. The land was deeded to the state in 1931 by the City and County of Goliad; transferred to TPW 1949. On site is the restored Mission Nuestra Señora del Espíritu Santo de Zúñiga and the El Camino Real de los Tejas Visitors Center. Just 0.6 miles south of the park entrance visitors can tour the **Presidio La Bahía SHS**. An 11-mile drive east on US 59 will take you to the **Fannin Battleground SHS**.

Goose Island State Park, 321 acres ten miles northeast of Rockport on TX 35 and PR 13 on St. Charles and Aransas bays in Aransas County, was deeded by private owners in

Texas State Parks & State Natural Areas

Park	(Special Features)	NEAREST TOWN	Day Use Only	Historic Site/ Museum	Exhibit/Interpretive Cntr	Restrooms	Showers	Trailer Dump Station	Camping	Screened Shelters	Cabins	Group Facilities	Nature Trail	Hiking Trail	Picnicking	Boat Ramp	Fishing	Swimming	Canoe Rentals	Activities/Amenities
Abilene SP		BUFFALO GAP				★	★	★	★	★	★	BG	★	★	★	★	☆	★	★	E, H
Atlanta SP		ATLANTA				★	★	★	★			DG	★	★	★	★	★	★	★	B1
Balmorhea SP	(San Solomon Springs)	BALMORHEA			★	★	★	★	★		★	DG	★		★			★		H, L
Bastrop SP		BASTROP				★	★	★	★		★	BG		★	★		★	★	★	H
Bentsen–Rio Grande Valley SP		MISSION			★	★	★		★			BG	★	★	★					H
Big Bend Ranch SP	(Barton Warnock Center)	LAJITAS		★	★	★			★				★	★	★		☆	☆		B1, E, L
Big Spring SP		BIG SPRING	★			★						DG	★	★	★					B1/2, H
Blanco SP		BLANCO				★	★	★	★	★		DG	★	★	★		★	★	★	H
Bonham SP		BONHAM				★	★	★	★		★	BG		★	★	★	★	☆	★	B1
Brazos Bend SP	(George Observatory)	RICHMOND			★	★	★	★	★	★	★	BG	★	★	★		★			B1/2,E,H
Buescher SP		SMITHVILLE				★	★	★	★	★	★	BG		★	★		★		★	B1/2
Caddo Lake SP		KARNACK			★	★	★	★	★	★	★	BG	★	★	★	★	★		★	
Caprock Canyons SP & TW	(State Bison herd)	QUITAQUE			★	★	★	★	★			BG	★	★	★	★	☆	☆		B1, E, L
Cedar Hill SP		CEDAR HILL		★		★	★	★	★			DG	★	★	★	★	☆	☆	★	B1, H
Choke Canyon SP, Calliham Unit		THREE RIVERS				★	★	★	★		★	BG	★	★	★	★	☆	☆		H
South Shore Unit		THREE RIVERS	★			★						DG			★	★	★			H
Cleburne SP		CLEBURNE				★	★	★	★	★	★	BG	★	★	★	★	★	☆	★	B1, H
Colorado Bend SP	(Cave Tours)	BEND				★	★		★			NG		★	★	★	☆	☆	★	B1
Cooper Lake SP, Doctors Creek Unit		COOPER				★	★	★	★	★	★	BG	★	★	★	★	★	★	★	B1, H
South Sulphur Unit		SULPHUR SPRINGS				★	★	★	★	★	★	DG		★	★	★	★	★	★	B1, E, H
Copper Breaks SP	(State Longhorn herd)	QUANAH			★	★	★	★	★			BG	★	★	★	★	★	☆		B1, E, H
Daingerfield SP		DAINGERFIELD			★	★	★	★	★		★	BG		★	★	★	★	☆	★	
Davis Mountains SP	(Indian Lodge)	FORT DAVIS			★	★	★	★	★			DG		★	★					B1, L, E
Devils River SNA	(Reservations Required)	DEL RIO							★			BG					☆	★		B1
Devil's Sinkhole SNA		ROCKSPRINGS	No access to cavern. Tours of SNA by special request only.																	
Dinosaur Valley SP	(Dinosaur Footprints)	GLEN ROSE			★	★	★	★	★			BG	★	★	★		☆	☆		B1, E
Eisenhower SP	(Marina)	DENISON				★	★	★	★	★	★	DG	★	★	★	★	★	☆		B1, H
Enchanted Rock SNA		FREDERICKSBURG			★	★	★		★			BG	★	★	★					R
Estero Llano Grande SP	(Birding)	WESLACO				★						BG	★	★						B2, H
Fairfield Lake SP		FAIRFIELD	Closed as o August 2023																	
Falcon SP		ZAPATA	★			★	★	★	★	★	★	DG	★	★	★	★	★	☆		
Fort Boggy SP		CENTERVILLE				★	★		★		★	DG		★	★	★	★	☆		B1, H
Fort Parker SP		MEXIA				★	★	★	★	★	★	BG		★	★	★	★	☆	★	B1
Fort Richardson SP, HS & Lost Creek Res. TW		JACKSBORO		★	★	★	★	★	★		★	DG	★	★	★		★	★		B1/2, E
Franklin Mountains SP	(Wyler Aerial Tramway)	EL PASO	★		★	★			★			BG		★	★					B1, R
Galveston Island SP	(Summer Theater)	GALVESTON			★	★	★	★	★		★	DG	★	★	★		☆	☆	★	B1, H
Garner SP		CONCAN				★	★	★	★	★	★	BG		★	★		☆	☆	★	B1
Goliad SP & Mission Espíritu Santo HS		GOLIAD		★	★	★	★	★	★	★		DG	★	★	★		☆	☆		
Goose Island SP		ROCKPORT				★	★	★	★			BG		★	★	★	★			
Government Canyon SNA		SAN ANTONIO				★	★		★			BG	★	★	★					B1
Guadalupe River SP & Honey Creek SNA		BOERNE			★	★	★	★	★			DG		★	★		☆	☆		B1, E
Hill Country SNA		BANDERA				★			★			NG		★						B1, E
Hueco Tanks SP & HS	(Indian Pictographs)	EL PASO		★	★	★	★	★	★			NG	★	★	★					R
Huntsville SP		HUNTSVILLE			★	★	★	★	★	★	★	DG	★	★	★	★	★	☆	★	
Inks Lake SP		BURNET				★	★	★	★		★	DG		★	★	★	★	☆	★	
Kickapoo Cavern SP	(Cave tours, bat colony)	BRACKETTVILLE				★	★	★	★			NG	★	★	★					B1
Lake Arrowhead SP		WICHITA FALLS				★	★	★	★			DG	★	★	★	★	★	☆		B1, E
Lake Bob Sandlin SP		MOUNT PLEASANT				★	★	★	★	★	★	DG		★	★	★	★	☆	★	B1
Lake Brownwood SP		BROWNWOOD				★	★	★	★	★	★	BG	★	★	★	★	★	☆		B1
Lake Casa Blanca International SP		LAREDO			★	★	★	★	★			DG		★	★	★	★	☆		B1
Lake Colorado City SP		COLORADO CITY				★	★	★	★		★	DG	★	★	★	★	★	☆	★	
Lake Corpus Christi SP		MATHIS				★	★	★	★	★	★	DG			★	★	★	☆	★	H
Lake Livingston SP		LIVINGSTON			★	★	★	★	★	★		DG	★	★	★	★	★	☆	★	B1
Lake Mineral Wells SP & TW		MINERAL WELLS				★	★	★	★	★		DG		★	★	★	★	☆	★	B1, E, R
Lake Somerville SP & TW, Birch Creek Unit		SOMERVILLE				★	★	★	★			BG		★	★	★	★	☆	★	B1, E
Nails Creek Unit		LEDBETTER				★	★	★	★			DG		★	★	★	☆	☆	★	B1, E
Lake Tawakoni SP		WILLS POINT				★	★	★	★			BG		★	★	★	★	☆	★	B1
Lake Whitney SP		WHITNEY				★	★	★	★	★	★	BG	★	★	★	★	★	☆		B1

ACTIVITIES/AMENITIES CODES

B1	Mountain biking	**E**	Equestrian facilities and/or trails	**DG**	Day-use group facilities
B2	Surfaced bike trail	**L**	Hotel-type facilities	**NG**	Overnight group facilities
H	Some handicap accessible facilities	**R**	Rock climbing	**BG**	Both day and night group facilities

FACILITIES CODES	★	Facilities or services available for activity	☆	Permitted, but facilities not provided

1931–1935 plus an additional seven acres donated in the early 1990s by Sun Oil Co. Located here is "Big Tree" estimated to be a 1,000-year-old live oak. Excellent birding: rare and endangered whooping cranes can be viewed during winter. Group camp site only for nonprofit youth groups. Nearby: Aransas National Wildlife Refuge.

Government Canyon State Natural Area is an 8,622-acre area in Bexar County, northwest of San Antonio, 3.5 miles northwest of Loop 1604 and FM 471, then 1.6 miles north on Galm Road. Forty miles of trails through native trees such as mountain laurel, Ashe juniper, Mexican buckeye, and Escarpment black cherry. The trail to Zizelmann House (built 1880s) passes dinosaur tracks. Open Friday through Monday. San Antonio and **Landmark Inn SHS** are nearby.

Guadalupe River State Park and Honey Creek State Natural Area comprise 4,232 acres on cypress-shaded Guadalupe River in Kendall and Comal counties, 13 miles east of Boerne on TX 46. The 1,939 acres of parkland was acquired by deed from private owners in 1974 and has four miles of river frontage with several white-water rapids located in a stretch of Guadalupe River noted for canoeing, tubing, and nature study. The Bauer unit provides a primitive experience and is day-use only. Trees include sycamore, elm, basswood, pecan, walnut, persimmon, willow, and hackberry. Honey Creek is only accessible via guided tours, typically offered on weekends.

Hill Country State Natural Area in Bandera and Medina counties, nine miles west of Bandera on FM 1077. The 5,370-acre site was acquired by gift and purchase in 1976. The park is located in typical Texas Hill Country on West Verde Creek and contains several spring-fed streams. It features primitive, hike-in, and equestrian camping and vault toilets.

Hueco Tanks State Park and Historic Site, located 32 miles northeast of El Paso in El Paso County on FM 2775 just north of US 62-180, was obtained from the county in 1969, with additional 121 acres purchased in 1970. The 860-acre park is known for the large natural rock basins that provided water for archaic native hunter-gatherers, Butterfield Overland Mail coach horses and passengers, and other travelers in this arid region. The park features pictographs, an old ranch house and the relocated ruins of a stage station. Wildlife includes gray fox, bobcat, prairie falcons, golden eagles. Guided pictograph tours must be booked at least a week in advance.

Texas State Parks & State Natural Areas

Park	(Special Features)	NEAREST TOWN	Day Use Only	Historic Site/ Museum	Exhibit/Interpretive Cntr	Restrooms	Showers	Trailer Dump Station	Camping	Screened Shelters	Cabins	Group Facilities	Nature Trail	Hiking Trail	Picnicking	Boat Ramp	Fishing	Swimming	Canoe Rentals	Activities/Amenities
Lockhart SP	(Golf course)	LOCKHART				★	★	★	★			DG		★	★		☆	★		B1
Longhorn Cavern SP	(Cavern Tours)	BURNET	★	★	★	★							★	★	★					
Lost Maples SNA		VANDERPOOL			★	★	★	★	★				★	★	★		☆	☆		
Lyndon B. Johnson SP & HS	(State Longhorn herd)	STONEWALL	★	★	★	★						DG	★		★			★		
Martin Creek Lake SP		TATUM				★	★	★	★	★	★	DG		★	★	★	★	☆		B1
Martin Dies Jr. SP		JASPER			★	★	★	★	★	★	★	DG		★	★	★	☆	☆	★	B1
McKinney Falls SP		AUSTIN		★	★	★	★	★	★		★	DG	★	★	★		☆	☆		B1/2,H,R
Meridian SP		MERIDIAN				★	★	★	★	★		BG	★	★	★	★	★	☆	★	H
Mission Tejas SP		WECHES		★		★	★	★	★			BG		★	★		★			
Monahans Sandhills SP		MONAHANS			★	★	★	★	★			DG	★		★					E
Mother Neff SP		MOODY			★	★	★		★			BG		★	★		☆			
Mustang Island SP		PORT ARANSAS				★	★	★	★						★		☆	☆		H
Old Tunnel SP	(Bat viewing, May – Oct.)	FREDERICKSBURG	★			★							★							H
Palmetto SP		LULING				★	★	★	★		★	BC	★	★	★		★	☆	★	
Palo Duro Canyon SP	(Summer Drama: "Texas")	CANYON		★	★	★	★	★	★		★	BG		★	★					B1,E
Pedernales Falls SP		JOHNSON CITY				★	★	★	★				★	★	★		☆	☆		B1, E
Possum Kingdom SP		CADDO				★	★	★	★		★			★	★	★	★	☆	★	H
Purtis Creek SP		EUSTACE				★	★	★	★			DG	★	★	★	★	★	☆	★	B1
Ray Roberts Lake SP, Isle du Bois Unit		PILOT POINT			★	★	★	★	★			BG		★	★	★	★	☆		B1/2, E, H
Johnson Branch Unit		VALLEY VIEW			★	★	★	★	★			DG		★	★	★	★	☆		B1/2, H
Resaca de la Palma SP		BROWNSVILLE	★			★						DG		★						B1, H
San Angelo SP	(State Longhorn herd)	SAN ANGELO				★	★	★	★		★	BG	★	★	★	★	★	☆		B1, E
Sea Rim SP		PORT ARTHUR				★	★	★	★		★		★		★	★	★	☆	★	E
Seminole Canyon SP & HS	(Indian Pictographs)	COMSTOCK		★	★	★	★	★	★				★	★	★					B1
Sheldon Lake SP	(Environmental Learning Center)	HOUSTON	★		★	★								★	☆	★	☆			H
South Llano River SP		JUNCTION		★		★	★	★	★				★	★	★		★	☆		B1
Stephen F. Austin SP		SAN FELIPE			★	★	★	★	★	★	★	BG	★	★	★					
Tyler SP		TYLER				★	★	★	★	★	★	BG	★	★	★	★	★	☆	★	B1
Village Creek SP		LUMBERTON			★	★	★	★	★		★	BG	★	★	★		☆	☆		B1
Walter Umphrey SP		PORT ARTHUR				★		★	★						★	★	★			

ACTIVITIES/AMENITIES CODES

B1	Mountain biking	**E**	Equestrian facilities and/or trails	**DG**	Day-use group facilities
B2	Surfaced bike trail	**L**	Hotel-type facilities	**NG**	Overnight group facilities
H	Some handicap accessible facilities	**R**	Rock climbing	**BG**	Both day and night group facilities

FACILITIES CODES	★	Facilities or services available for activity	☆	Permitted, but facilities not provided

Huntsville State Park is a 2,083-acre recreational area off IH 45 and PR 40 six miles south of Huntsville in Walker County, acquired by deeds from private owners in 1937. Heavily wooded park adjoins Sam Houston National Forest and encloses Lake Raven. At nearby Huntsville are Sam Houston's old homestead (Steamboat House), containing some of his personal effects, and his grave. Approximately 50 miles away is Alabama–Coushatta Reservation in Polk County.

Inks Lake State Park is 1,201 acres of recreational facilities along Inks Lake, nine miles west of Burnet on the Colorado River off TX 29 on PR 4 in Burnet County. Acquired by deeds from the Lower Colorado River Authority and private owners in 1940. Group campsite for nonprofit youth groups. Deer, turkey, and other wildlife abundant. Nearby are **Longhorn Cavern SP** and **Enchanted Rock SNA**. Buchanan Dam, considered the largest multi-arch dam in the nation, located four miles from park.

Kickapoo Cavern State Park is located about 22 miles north of Brackettville on RM 674 on the Kinney/Edwards county line in the southern Edwards Plateau. The park (6,368 acres) contains 20 known caves, two of which are large enough to be significant: Kickapoo Cavern, about 1,400 feet in length, has impressive formations, and Stuart Bat Cave, slightly shorter, supports a large colony of Mexican freetail bats in summer. Public observations of bat flights are available with an entrance permit. Birds include rare species such as black-capped vireo, varied bunting, and Montezuma quail. Open Friday through Monday. Cavern tours on Saturdays by reservation.

Lake Arrowhead State Park consists of 524 acres in Clay County, about 14 miles south of Wichita Falls on US 281 to FM 1954, then eight miles to the park. Acquired in 1970 from the City of Wichita Falls. Lake Arrowhead is a reservoir on the Little Wichita River with 106 miles of shoreline. The land surrounding the lake is generally semiarid, gently rolling prairie, much of which has been invaded by mesquite in recent decades. Park features nine boat ramps and a disc golf course and hosts annual events, including fishing contests and Christmas in the Park.

Lake Bob Sandlin State Park, on the wooded shoreline of 9,400-acre Lake Bob Sandlin, is located 12 miles southwest of Mount Pleasant off FM 21 in Titus County. Trees in the 640-acre park include oak, hickory, dogwood, redbud, maple and pine. Eagles can sometimes be spotted in winter months. Park also features a historical cemetery and bird viewing areas.

Lake Brownwood State Park in Brown County is 538 acres acquired from Brown County Water Improvement District No. 1 in 1934. The park can be reached from TX 279 to PR 15, 16 miles northwest of Brownwood on 7,300-acre Lake Brownwood (near geographical center of Texas). During WW II, the park was a popular rest site for soldiers stationed at nearby Camp Bowie. Nature in the area is diverse, because the park sits where three ecoregions meet: Edwards Plateau, Western Cross-Timbers, and Rolling Plains. (See page 29 for more about the regions of Texas.)

Lake Casa Blanca International State Park, located one mile east of Laredo off US 59 on Loop 20, was formerly operated by the City of Laredo and Webb County and was acquired by TPW in 1990. Park includes 371 acres on Lake Casa Blanca. Features an amphitheater, volleyball, tennis, and basketball courts. Fossils found on site by Lamar University students are exhibited at park headquarters. County-operated golf course nearby.

Lake Colorado City State Park, 500 acres leased from a utility company. It is located in Mitchell County 11 miles southwest of Colorado City off IH 20 on FM 2836. The region features drought-tolerant mesquite trees and abundant wildflowers in spring and summer. More than 300 bird species have been spotted in the park.

A group gathers for the first hike of the year at Hueco Tanks SP. Photo by Texas Parks and Wildlife

Lake Corpus Christi State Park, a 14,112-acre park in San Patricio, Jim Wells, and Live Oak counties. Located 35 miles northwest of Corpus Christi and four miles southwest of Mathis off TX 359 and Park Road 25. Was leased from City of Corps Christi in 1934. Features a wheelchair-accessible 400-foot-long fishing pier and the historic CCC Castle, built by the Civilian Conservation Corps in 1934–1935. Nearby are **Mustang Island SP**, **Choke Canyon SP**, and **Fulton Mansion SHS**.

Lake Livingston State Park, in Polk County, about one mile southwest of Livingston on FM 3126 and PR 65, contains 636 acres along Lake Livingston. Acquired by deed from private landowners in 1971. Near ghost town of Swartwout, a steamboat landing on Trinity River in 1830s and 1850s, as well as **Big Thicket National Preserve** and **Sam Houston National Forest**.

Lake Mineral Wells State Park and Trailway, located four miles east of Mineral Wells on US 180 in Parker County, consists of 3,283 acres encompassing Lake Mineral Wells. In 1975, the City of Mineral Wells donated 1,095 land acres and the lake to TPW; the federal government transferred additional land from Fort Wolters army post. Popular for rock-climbing and rappelling. The 20-mile Lake Mineral Wells State Trailway available for hiking, bicycling, and equestrian use.

Lake Somerville State Park and Trailway, northwest of Brenham in Lee and Burleson counties, was leased from the federal government in 1969. Birch Creek Unit (2,365 acres, reached from TX 60 and PR 57) and Nails Creek Unit (3,155 acres, reached from US 290 and FM 180) are connected by a 13-mile trailway, with equestrian and primitive camp sites, rest benches, shelters, and drinking water. Somerville Wildlife Management Area and **San Felipe SHS** are nearby.

Lake Tawakoni State Park is a 376-acre park in Hunt County along the shore of its namesake reservoir. It was acquired in 1984 through a lease agreement with the Sabine River Authority and opened in 2001. Lake Tawakoni is known for its blue-fin catfish and is host to several fishing tournaments. The park is reached from IH 20 on TX 47 north to FM 2475 about 20 miles past Wills Point.

Lake Whitney State Park is 1,281 acres along the east shore of Lake Whitney west of Hillsboro via TX 22 and FM 1244 in Hill County. Acquired in 1954 by a Department of the Army lease. Located near ruins of Towash, early Texas settlement inundated by the lake. Towash Village named for chief of the Hainai. Park noted for bluebonnets in spring. Hosts an annual youth fishing tournament on the first Saturday in June.

Lockhart State Park is 264 acres, found four miles south of Lockhart via US 183, FM 20 and PR 10 in Caldwell County. The land was deeded by private owners between 1934 and 1937. After Comanche raid at Linnville, the Battle of Plum Creek (1840) was fought in area. The park features a 9-hole golf course and a swimming pool.

Longhorn Cavern State Park, off US 281 and PR 4 about six miles west and six miles south of Burnet in Burnet County, is 646 acres dedicated as a natural landmark in 1971. It was acquired in 1932–1937 from private owners. The cave has been used as a shelter since prehistoric times. Among legends about the cave is that the outlaw Sam Bass hid stolen money there. Confederates made gunpowder in the cave during the Civil War. Cavern operated by concession agreement. Reservations for cave tours are highly recommended. Day-use only. Visitors can camp at nearby **Inks Lake SP**.

Lost Maples State Natural Area consists of 2,174 scenic acres on the Sabinal River in Bandera and Real counties, five miles north of Vanderpool on FM 187. Acquired by purchase from private owners in 1973–1974. Outstanding example of Edwards Plateau flora and fauna, features isolated stand of uncommon Uvalde bigtooth maple. Rare golden-cheeked warbler, black-capped vireo, and green kingfisher nest and feed in park. Fall foliage can be spectacular.

Lyndon B. Johnson State Park and Historic Site, off US 290 in Gillespie County 14 miles west of Johnson City near Stonewall, contains 718 acres. Acquired in 1965 with private donations. Home of Lyndon B. Johnson located north bank of Pedernales River across Ranch Road 1 from park; portion of official Texas longhorn herd maintained at park. Wildlife exhibit includes turkey, deer, and bison. Living-history demonstrations at restored Sauer-Beckmann house. Reconstruction of Johnson birthplace is open to public. Historic structures, swimming pool, tennis courts, baseball field, picnicking. Day use only. Nearby is family cemetery where former president and relatives are buried. In Johnson City is the **Lyndon B. Johnson National Historic Park**, the boyhood home of President Johnson.

Martin Creek Lake State Park, 287 acres, is located four miles south of Tatum off TX 43 and CR 2183 in Rusk County. It was deeded to the TPW by Texas Utilities in 1976. Roadbed of Trammel's Trace, old native trail that became major route for settlers moving to Texas from Arkansas, can be seen. Hardwood and pine forest shelters abundant wildlife including swamp rabbits, gophers, nutria, and numerous species of land birds and waterfowl. Annual perch fishing contest for children ages 4–12 the first Saturday in September.

Martin Dies Jr. State Park is 705 acres in Jasper and Tyler counties on the B. A. Steinhagen Reservoir between Woodville and Jasper via US 190. Land leased from Corps of Engineers since 1964. Named after the decorated WW II veteran, who later served as a state senator and secretary of state. Located at the edge of **Big Thicket National Preserve** and near **Angelina National Forest**. Plant and animal life varied and abundant. Winter bald eagle census conducted at nearby Sam Rayburn Reservoir. Wildscape herb garden. Park is about 30 miles from Alabama and Coushatta Reservation.

McKinney Falls State Park is 744 acres, located about 13 miles southeast of the state Capitol in Austin, off US 183. Acquired in 1970 by gift from private owners. Named for Thomas F. McKinney, one of Stephen F. Austin's first 300 colonists, who built his home here in the mid-1800s on Onion Creek. Ruins of his homestead can be viewed. All-terrain wheelchair available; email the park to reserve. Group camp available only for nonprofit youth groups.

Meridian State Park in Bosque County is a 505-acre park. The heavily wooded land on TX 22 three miles southwest of Meridian was acquired from private owners in 1933–1935. Texas-Santa Fe expedition of 1841 passed through Bosque County near present site of park on Bee

Creek. Endangered golden-cheeked warbler nests here. The fishing pier is ADA accessible.

Mission Tejas State Park is a 364-acre park in Houston County, at the north end of **Davy Crockett National Forest**. Situated 12 miles west of Alto via TX 21 and PR 44, the park was acquired from the Texas Forest Service in 1957. In the park is a representation of Mission San Francisco de los Tejas, the first mission in East Texas (1690). It was abandoned, then re-established 1716; abandoned again 1719; re-established again 1721; abandoned for last time in 1730 when the mission was moved to San Antonio. Also in park is restored Rice Family Log Home, built about 1828.

Monahans Sandhills State Park consists of 3,840 acres of sand dunes, some up to 70 feet high, in Ward and Winkler counties five miles northeast of Monahans on IH 20 to PR 41. Land is leased by state from private foundation until 2056. The dunes were used as meeting place by raiding natives. Rent or purchase a colorful sand disk and try sand-surfing; sand wheelchair available by reservation. Odessa meteor crater is nearby, as is **Balmorhea SP**.

Mother Neff State Park was the first official state park in Texas. It originated with six acres donated by Mrs. I. E. Neff, mother of Pat M. Neff, governor of Texas from 1921 to 1925. Gov. Neff and Frank Smith donated remainder in 1934. The park, located eight miles west of Moody on FM 107 and TX 236, now contains 259 acres along the Leon River in Coryell County. Heavily wooded. Interactive displays in the visitor center.

Mustang Island State Park, 3,954 acres on the Gulf of Mexico in Nueces County, 14 miles south of Port Aransas on TX 361, was acquired from private owners in 1972. Mustang Island is a barrier island with a complicated ecosystem, dependent upon sand dunes. The foundation plants of the dunes are sea oats, beach panic grass and soilbind morning glory. Excellent birding. Explore 20 miles of paddling trails (boat rentals available in Port Aransas). Beach wheelchairs available. **Padre Island National Seashore** 14 miles south. Also nearby: the **Texas State Aquarium** and the USS Lexington Museum.

Old Tunnel State Park sits on 16 acres of land, making it the smallest state park in Texas. Located at 10619 Old San Antonio Road, 14 miles south of Fredericksburg, the park is great for wildlife-viewing opportunities. The abandoned railroad tunnel provides a home to over three million Mexican free-tailed bats and 3,000 cave myotises (mouse-eared bats) from May to October. Reservations to view the bats must be made in advance; tickets can be purchased online or by calling the central reservation center. The park also has a half-mile trail open year-round for birdwatching or for a short hike; there is no fee to access the park before 5 p.m.

Palmetto State Park, a scenic park of 270 acres, is eight miles southeast of Luling on US 183 and PR 11 along the San Marcos River in Gonzales County. Land deeded in 1934–1936 by private owners and City of Gonzales. Named for the tropical dwarf palmetto found there. Diverse plant and animal life; excellent birding. Nearby Gonzales and Ottine important in early Texas history. Gonzales settled 1825 as center of Green DeWitt's colonies.

Palo Duro Canyon State Park consists of 16,402 acres found 12 miles east of Canyon on TX 217 in Armstrong and Randall counties. The land was deeded by private owners in 1933 and is the scene of the annual summer production of the musical drama "Texas." Spectacular one-million-year-old scenic canyon exposes rocks spanning about 200 million years of geological time. Coronado may have visited canyon in 1541. Canyon officially discovered by Capt. R. B. Marcy in 1852. Scene of decisive battle in 1874 between Comanche and Kiowa natives and U.S. Army troops under Gen. Ranald Mackenzie. Also scene of ranching enterprise started by Charles Goodnight in 1876. Part of state longhorn herd is kept here.

Palo Pinto Mountains State Park is currently under development. Comprising 4,871 acres of former ranchland, the new park will have trails for hikers, bikers, and horses, and overnight spaces for RVs and tents. Tucker Lake will be available for fishing, swimming, and boating (no motors). No opening date has been announced as of September 2023. Follow news of the park's development here: https://tpwd.texas.gov/state-parks/palo-pinto-mountains.

Pedernales Falls State Park, 5,212 acres in Blanco County about nine miles east of Johnson City on FM 2766 along the Pedernales River, was acquired from private owners in 1970. Typical Edwards Plateau terrain, with live oaks, deer, turkey and stone hills. The falls, where the river elevation drops by 50 feet across 3,000 feet of rocky limestone riverbed, are the main scenic attraction. Bird blind is wheelchair accessible. Johnson City and **LBJ SP** are nearby.

Possum Kingdom State Park, west of Mineral Wells via US 180 and PR 33 in Palo Pinto County, is 1,529 acres adjacent to Possum Kingdom Lake (20,000 acres) in the Palo Pinto Mountains and Brazos River Valley. Rugged canyons are home to deer, other wildlife, and the lake features many scenic coves along its 300 miles of shoreline. Acquired from the Brazos River Authority in 1940. Museums, restaurants, and entertainment in nearby Mineral Wells, Graham, and Breckenridge.

Purtis Creek State Park is 1,582 acres in Henderson and Van Zandt counties 3.5 miles north of Eustace on FM 316. Acquired in 1977 from private owners. The 355-acre Purtis Creek State Park Lake was designed specifically for fishing and contains largemouth bass (catch-and-release only), and catfish and crappie. Nearby: Texas Freshwater Fisheries Center and Cedar Creek Reservoir.

Ray Roberts Lake State Park is comprised of nine units, but only three of these offer overnight facilities and recreation. The Isle du Bois Unit consists of 1,397 acres on the south side of Ray Roberts Lake on FM 455 in Denton County. Johnson Branch Unit contains 1,514 acres on north side of the lake in Denton and Cooke counties, seven miles east of IH 30 on FM 3002. The Jordan Unit (477 acres on the east side of the lake) features the Lone Star Lodge & Marina. The Greenbelt Unit is a 20-mile multi-use trail between Ray Roberts Dam and Lake Louisville.

Resaca de la Palma State Park, part of the World Birding Center network, is 1,700 semi-tropical acres off US 281, four miles west of Brownsville in Cameron County. Park grounds are open seven days a week year-round from sunrise to sunset. Birding and natural history tours offered. Bike and binocular rentals at the park store. Colorful neo-tropical and Neartic migrant birds have been seen.

Learn about life on a farm in 1850 when you visit the Barrington Plantation in Washington County. Photo by Texas Historical Commission

San Angelo State Park, on O.C. Fisher Reservoir adjacent to the city of San Angelo in Tom Green County, contains 7,677 acres of land, most of which will remain undeveloped. Leased from U.S. Corps of Engineers in 1995. Access is from US 87 or US 67, then FM 2288. Highly diversified plant and animal life. Part of the state longhorn herd is in the park. Nearby is Lake Nasworthy and Fort Concho National Historic Landmark.

Sea Rim State Park in Jefferson County, 20 miles south of Port Arthur, off TX 87, contains 4,141 acres of marshland and 5.2 miles of Gulf beach shoreline, acquired from private owners in 1972. It is prime wintering area for waterfowl. Wetlands also shelter such wildlife as river otter, nutria, alligator, mink, and muskrat. Near McFaddin National Wildlife Refuge.

Seminole Canyon State Park and Historic Site in Val Verde County, nine miles west of Comstock off US 90, contains 2,173 acres; acquired by purchase from private owners 1973–1977. Fate Bell Shelter in canyon contains several important prehistoric native pictographs. Historic interpretive center. Visitors must purchase tickets for tours of rock-art sites online. Nearby are **Amistad National Recreation Area** and the Judge Roy Bean Visitor Center (in Landry).

Sheldon Lake State Park and Environmental Learning Center sit on 2,800 acres in Harris County on Garrett Road two miles east of Beltway 8. Acquired by purchase in 1952 from the City of Houston. Freshwater marsh habitat. Take in panoramic views from the two observation decks on John Jacob Observation Tower. Activities include nature study, birding, and fishing. Wildscape gardens of native plants.

South Llano River State Park, five miles south of Junction in Kimble County off US 377, is a 524-acre site donated to the TPW by a private owner in 1977. Wooded bottomland along the winding South Llano River is the largest and oldest winter roosting site for the Rio Grande turkey in Central Texas. Limited access to roosting area for visitors October through March. Other animals include wood ducks, javelina, fox, beaver, bobcat, and armadillo. Borrow tubes to float down the river or bring your own kayak.

Stephen F. Austin State Park is 663 acres along the Brazos River in San Felipe, Austin County, named for the "Father of Texas." The area was deeded by the San Felipe de Austin Corporation and the San Felipe Park Association in 1940. Site of township of San Felipe was seat of government where conventions of 1832 and 1833 and Consultation of 1835 were held. These led to Texas Declaration of Independence. San Felipe was home of Stephen F. Austin and other famous early Texans; home of Texas' first Anglo newspaper (the Texas Gazette) founded in 1829; postal system of Texas originated here. Area called "Cradle of Texas Liberty." Museum in the park; golf course nearby.

Tyler State Park is 986 acres found two miles north of IH 20 on FM 14 north of Tyler in Smith County. Includes 64-acre lake. The land was deeded by private owners in 1934–1935. Heavily wooded, with 13 miles of trails. Park uses controlled burns to manage the forest. Nearby Tyler is called the Rose Capital of the Nation, with Tyler Rose Garden and annual Tyler Rose Festival. Also in Tyler are Caldwell Children's Zoo and Goodman Museum.

Village Creek State Park, comprising 1,004 heavily forested acres, is located in Lumberton, Hardin County, ten miles north of Beaumont off US 69 and FM 3513. Purchased in 1979 from private owner, the park contains abundant flora and fauna typical of the Big Thicket area. The 200 species of birds native to the area include wood ducks, egrets, and herons. Nature center. Nearby is the **Big Thicket National Preserve**.

Walter Umphrey State Park is operated by Jefferson County on the south end of Pleasure Island off TX 82. Watch ships travelling the Sabine Channel and enjoy nature. Lighted pier for night fishing. For RV site reservations, contact SGS Causeway Bait & Tackle, (409) 985–4811. McFadden National Wildlife Refuge is nearby. ☆

Texas State Historic Sites

Sources: Texas Historical Commission, www.thc.texas.gov; City of Seguin, www.seguintexas.gov/Facilities/Facility/Details/Sebastopol-House-Historic-Site-30; National Museum of the Pacific War, www.pacificwarmuseum.org/; and Texas Parks and Wildlife, tpwd.texas.gov

The **Texas Historical Commission** (THC) is the state agency dedicated to identifying and preserving historic sites. The THC also owns and operates the facilities listed here, unless otherwise noted. Learn more about the agency on page 477 in the Government chapter.

Many sites host events throughout the year. Check the Event Calendar on the THC website to plan your trip:

www.thc.texas.gov/news-events/calendar

Entrance fees range from free to $10 per person unless otherwise stated. There are also fees for guided tours and some activities. Attractions in **purple bold** have a separate listing in this chapter.

List of State Historic Sites

Acton State Historic Site is a 0.006-acre cemetery plot in Hood County where Davy Crockett's second wife, Elizabeth, was buried in 1860. It is 4.5 miles east of Granbury on US 377 to FM 167 south, then 2.4 miles south to Acton. There are no facilities at this site. Nearby attractions include **Dinosaur Valley SP** and **Lake Whitney SP**.

Barrington Plantation State Historic Site, seven miles southwest of Navasota in Washington County on TX 105 and FM 1155, marks the final home of Dr. Anson Jones, the fifth and final president of the Republic of Texas. Visitors can do a self-guided tour of the plantation and Independence

Texas State Historic Sites

Park	(Special Features)	NEAREST TOWN	Day Use Only	Historic Site/ Museum	Exhibit/Interpretive Cntr	Restrooms	Showers	Trailer Dump Station	Camping	Cabins	Group Facilities	Nature Trail	Hiking Trail	Picnicking	Boat Ramp	Fishing	Canoe Rentals	Activities/Amenities
Acton SHS	(Grave of Davy Crockett's Wife)	ACTON	★	★														
Barrington Plantation SHS		WASHINGTON	★	★	★	★					DG			★				
Battleship Texas SHS	(Dry Dock Tours)	GALVESTON	★	★	★													
Bush Family Home SHS		MIDLAND	★	★		★												H
Caddo Mounds SHS		ALTO	★	★	★	★						★		★				H
Casa Navarro SHS		SAN ANTONIO	★	★		★												
Confederate Reunion Grounds SHS		MEXIA	★	★	★	★							★	★		☆		H
Eisenhower Birthplace SHS		DENISON	★	★	★	★					DG							
Fannin Battleground SHS		GOLIAD	★	★	★	★					DG			★				
Fanthorp Inn SHS		ANDERSON	★	★	★	★												
Fort Griffin SHS	(State Longhorn herd)	ALBANY		★	★	★	★	★	★	★		★	★	★		☆	★	
Fort Lancaster SHS		OZONA	★	★	★	★								☆				
Fort Leaton SHS	(Big Bend State Park)	PRESIDIO	★	★	★	★						★		★				
Fort McKavett SHS		FORT McKAVETT	★	★	★	★						★		★				
French Legation SHS		AUSTIN	★	★		★					DG							H
Fulton Mansion SHS		FULTON	★	★	★	★								★				H
Goodnight Ranch SHS	(Goodnight bison herd)	GOODNIGHT	★	★	★	★												
Landmark Inn SHS	(Hotel Rooms)	CASTROVILLE		★	★	★					DG	★		★				L
Levi Jordan Plantation SHS		BRAZORIA	★	★	★	★						★						
Lipantitlán SHS		SAN PATRICIO	★															
Magoffin Home SHS		EL PASO	★	★	★	★								★				H
Mission Dolores SHS	(El Camino Real Trail)	SAN AUGUSTINE		★	★	★	★		★				★	★				H
Monument Hill & Kreische Brewery SHS		LA GRANGE	★	★	★	★					DG	★		★				
National Museum of Pacific War & Adm. Nimitz SHS		FREDERICKSBURG	★	★	★	★					BG	★						H
Port Isabel Lighthouse SHS		PORT ISABEL	★	★		★					DG			★				
Presidio la Bahía SHS	("The Quarters")	GOLIAD		★	★	★				★		★						
Sabine Pass Battleground SHS		SABINE PASS	★	★	★	★								★	★	☆		
Sam Bell Maxey House SHS		PARIS	★	★	★	★												H
Sam Rayburn House SHS		BONHAM	★	★	★	★								★				
San Felipe de Austin SHS		SAN FELIPE	★	★		★												
San Jacinto Battleground SHS		HOUSTON	★	★	★	★					DG	★	★	★		☆		
Sebastopol House SHS		SEGUIN	★	★	★									★				
Starr Family Home SHS		MARSHALL	★	★	★	★					DG							
Varner-Hogg Plantation SHS		WEST COLUMBIA	★	★	★	★				★	DG	★		★		☆		
Washington-on-the-Brazos SHS		WASHINGTON	★	★	★	★					DG			★				

ACTIVITIES/AMENITIES CODES

B1	Mountain biking	**E**	Equestrian facilities and/or trails	**DG**	Day-use group facilities
B2	Surfaced bike trail	**L**	Hotel-type facilities	**NG**	Overnight group facilities
H	Some handicap accessible facilities	**R**	Rock climbing	**BG**	Both day and night group facilities

FACILITIES CODES	★	Facilities or services available for activity	☆	Permitted, but facilities not provided

Hall, and visit the Star of the Republic Museum, containing exhibits about the economic, political, and social history of Texas. Open Wednesday through Sunday. (Located on same site as **Washington-on-the-Brazos SHS**.)

Battleship Texas State Historic Site usually sits within the **San Jacinto Battleground SHS** in LaPorte in east Harris County. Battleship Texas once took part in naval battles during both world wars and was acquired by the state of Texas in 1948. Today the ship serves as a memorial to the servicemen who fought both world wars and as an engineering landmark. **Ship is in dry dock in Galveston undergoing repairs as of September 2023.** Dry dock tours can be booked at https://battleshiptexas.org/drydock/.

Bush Family Home State Historic Site, found at 1412 West Ohio Ave., Midland in Midland County, became the 36th designated historic site in Texas in 2022. The 1,400-sq.-ft. house was built in 1940 and acquired by the Bush family in 1951. First opened to the public as a museum in 2006, the home has been restored to the 1950s and features exhibits about the town and the Bush family. Tours offered Thursday–Sunday, or Tuesday and Wednesday by appointment.

Caddo Mounds State Historic Site in Cherokee County six miles southwest of Alto on TX 21 sits on about 94 acres acquired in 1975. Open for day visits only, park offers exhibits and interpretive trails through reconstructed Caddo dwellings and ceremonial areas, including two temple mounds, a burial mound and a village area typical of people who lived in region for 500 years beginning about 800 CE. Open Tuesday through Sunday. Nearby are Jim Hogg Park, **Mission Tejas SP**, and the Texas State Railroad.

Casa Navarro State Historic Site, on 0.7 acres in downtown San Antonio, was acquired by donation from San Antonio Conservation Society Foundation in 1975. The furnished Navarro House three-building complex, built about 1848, was home of statesman, rancher and Texas patriot José Antonio Navarro. Open Tuesday–Sunday.

Confederate Reunion Grounds State Historic Site, located in Limestone County on the Navasota River, comprises 77 acres. Acquired 1983 by deed from Joseph E. Johnston Camp No. 94 CSA. Entrance is six miles south of Mexia on TX 14, then 2.5 miles west on FM 2705. Historic buildings, two scenic footbridges span the creek; hiking trail to Navasota River for fishing and canoeing. Nearby are **Fort Parker SP** and **Fort Boggy SP**.

Eisenhower Birthplace State Historic Site is six acres off US 75 at 609 S. Lamar, Denison, Grayson County. The property was acquired in 1958 from the Eisenhower Birthplace Foundation. Restoration of home of President Dwight Eisenhower includes furnishings of period and some personal effects of Gen. Eisenhower. Guided tours available; call for schedule. Open Tuesday–Sunday. Town of Denison was established on the Butterfield Overland Mail Route in 1858. Hagerman National Wildlife Refuge and **Eisenhower SP** are nearby.

Fannin Battleground State Historic Site, nine miles east of Goliad in Goliad County off US 59 to PR 27. The 14-acre site was acquired by the state in 1914; transferred to TPW by legislative enactment in 1965. At this site on March 20, 1836, Col. James Fannin surrendered to Mexican Gen. José Urrea after Battle of Coleto; 342 massacred and 28 escaped. The Fannin Memorial Monument and burial site is south of Goliad, near **Presidio la Bahía SHS** and **Goliad SP**.

Fanthorp Inn State Historic Site includes a historic double-pen cedar-log dogtrot house on 1.4 acres in Anderson, county seat of Grimes County, south of TX 90. It was purchased in 1977 from a Fanthorp descendant and opened to the public in 1987. Inn records report visits from many prominent civic and military leaders, including Sam Houston, Anson Jones, and generals Ulysses S. Grant, Robert E. Lee, and Stonewall Jackson. Originally built in 1834, it has been restored to its 1850 use as a family home and travelers' hotel. Open Friday through Sunday.

Fort Griffin State Historic Site is 506 acres 15 miles north of Albany off US 283 in Shackelford County. The state was deeded the land by the county in 1935. Portion of state longhorn herd resides in park. On bluff overlooking townsite of Fort Griffin and Clear Fork of Brazos River valley are partially restored ruins of Old Fort Griffin, restored bakery, replicas of enlisted men's huts. Fort constructed in 1867, deactivated 1881. Nearby are Albany, Abilene, and **Possum Kingdom SP**. Albany annually holds "Fandangle" musical show in commemoration of frontier times.

Fort Lancaster State Historic Site sits on 82 acres located about eight miles east of Sheffield on TX 290 in Crockett County. Acquired in 1968 by deed from Crockett County; Henry Meadows donated 41 acres in 1975. Fort Lancaster established 1855, to guard San Antonio–El Paso Road and protect movement of supplies and immigrants from native hostilities. Site of part of the Camel Corps experiment. Fort abandoned 1861, after Texas seceded from Union. Exhibits on history, natural history, and archaeology. Open Tuesday through Saturday.

Fort Leaton State Historic Site, four miles southeast of Presidio in Presidio County on FM 170, was acquired in 1967 from private owners. In 1848, Ben Leaton built the fortified adobe trading post known as Fort Leaton near present Presidio. Ben Leaton died in 1851. Guided tours available; exhibits trace history, natural history, and archaeological history of area. Operated by TPW and serves as the western entrance to **Big Bend Ranch SP**. Day use only, however camping is available in the state park.

Fort McKavett State Historic Site, 80 acres acquired from 1967 through the mid-1970s from Fort McKavett Restoration, Inc., Menard County and private individuals, is located 23 miles west of Menard off US 190 and FM 864. Originally called Camp San Saba, the fort was built by the War Department in 1852 to protect frontier settlers and travelers on Upper El Paso Road from natives. Camp later renamed for Capt. Henry McKavett, killed at Battle of Monterrey, 1846. Fort abandoned in 1859; reoccupied 1868. Abandoned again 1883. Gen. Wm. T. Sherman once called it "the prettiest post in Texas." More than 25 restored buildings, ruins of many others. Interpretive exhibits.

French Legation State Historic Site, located near downtown Austin, was built in 1841 as a private home for Alphones Dubois, French chargé d'affaires to the Republic of Texas. In 1848 it was purchased by Dr. Joseph W. Robertson, who lived there with his large family and nine enslaved workers. Daughter Lillie Robertson lived in the house her entire life. The state acquired the house after her death and appointed the Daughters of the Republic as custodian. In 2017, HB 3810 transferred the French Legation to the THC. Open Tuesday through Saturday.

Fulton Mansion State Historic Site in Fulton is 3.5 miles north of Rockport off TX Business 35 on South Fulton Beach Rd. in Aransas County. The 2.3-acre property was acquired by purchase from private owner in 1976. A three-story wooden structure built in 1874–1877, it was the home of George W. Fulton, prominent in South Texas for economic and commercial influence; mansion derives significance from its innovative construction and Victorian design. View exhibits at the Fulton Mansion Education and History Center, behind the house. Open Tuesday through Sunday.

Goodnight Ranch State Historic Site, south of the town of Goodnight off US 287 in Armstrong County, is the home of Charles and Mary Ann Goodnight. On the site is J. Evetts Haley Visitor and Education Center where visitors can learn about the area, the Goodnights, and bison. Guided tours of the restored Victorian-style house on the property take about one hour. Open Tuesday through Saturday. **Caprock Canyons SP** is nearby.

Landmark Inn State Historic Site, 5 acres in Castroville, Medina County, about 15 miles west of San Antonio, was acquired through donation by Miss Ruth Lawler in 1974. Castroville, settled in the 1840s by Alsatian farmers, is called Little Alsace of Texas. Landmark Inn built about 1844 as a residence and store for Cesar Monod, mayor of Castroville 1851–1864. Special workshops, tours and events held at the inn; grounds may be rented for receptions, family reunions and weddings. Overnight lodging: all rooms air-conditioned and nonsmoking.

Levi Jordan Plantation State Historic Site, four miles southwest of Brazoria on FM 521 in Brazoria County, was a sugar and cotton plantation established in the 1850s. Owned by descendants until 2001, acquired by the Houston Endowment and donated to TPW in 2022. Today the 90-acre plantation is both an attraction and an active archeological site. View exhibits about the people who lived and worked on the land in the 19th century and watch technicians and historians clean and study artifacts. Open Wednesday through Sunday.

Lipantitlán State Historic Site is five acres, found nine miles east of Orange Grove in Nueces County off Texas 359, FM 624 and FM 70. The property was deeded by private owners in 1937. A fort constructed here in 1833 by Mexican government fell to Texas forces in 1835. Only facilities are picnic tables. **Lake Corpus Christi SP** is nearby.

Magoffin Home State Historic Site, in El Paso, is a 19-room territorial-style adobe on a 1.5-acre site. Purchased by the state and City of El Paso in 1976. Home was built in 1875 by El Pasoan Joseph Magoffin. Furnished with original family artifacts. Parking and information available at the visitor's center, across the street. The site is open Tuesday through Sunday.

Mission Dolores State Historic Site at 701 S. Broadway St. in San Augustine, memorializes the location of a Spanish mission built in 1721 in what is now San Augustine County just 20 miles west of the Texas–Louisiana border. There are no longer any above-ground remains of the mission. Visitors can camp, view interpretive displays at the on-site museum and play frisbee golf. Museum open Tuesday through Saturday.

Monument Hill State Historic Site and Kreische Brewery State Historic Site are operated as one park unit. Monument Hill consists of 40 acres one mile south of La Grange on US 77 to Spur Road 92 in Fayette County. Monument and tomb area acquired by state in 1907; additional acreage acquired from the Archdiocese of San Antonio in 1956. Monument is dedicated to Capt. Nicholas Dawson and his men, who fought at Salado Creek in 1842, in Mexican Gen. Adrián Woll's invasion of Texas, and to the men of the "black bean lottery" (1843) of the Mier Expedition. Remains were brought to Monument Hill for reburial in 1848. The Kreische Complex, on 36 acres, is linked to Monument Hill through interpretive trail. The site includes the brewery and stone-and-wood house built between 1850–1855. One of first commercial breweries in state, it closed in 1884. Smokehouse and barn also in complex. Open daily; guided tours available weekends.

National Museum of the Pacific War and Admiral Nimitz State Historic Site is on seven acres in downtown Fredericksburg, Gillespie County. First established as a state agency in 1969 by Texas Legislature; overseen by the THC and operated by the Admiral Nimitz Foundation. Named for Adm. Chester W. Nimitz of World War II fame, it includes the Pacific War Museum in the Nimitz Steamboat Hotel; the Japanese Garden of Peace, donated by the people of Japan; the History Walk of the Pacific War, featuring planes, boats, and other equipment from World War II; and other special exhibits. Closed Tuesdays. General admission tickets $24; discounts available for veterans, seniors, active military, students, and teachers.

Port Isabel Lighthouse State Historic Site consists of 0.9 acres in Port Isabel, Cameron County. Acquired by purchase from private owners in 1950, the lighthouse was constructed in 1852; visitors over age 5 can climb to top to see the reproduction 3rd Order Fresnel Lens, installed in 2022. Operated by City of Port Isabel.

Presidio la Bahía State Historic Site comprises 45 acres one mile south of Goliad on US 183 and 77A. Established at this site in 1749, the fort took part in six revolutions, making it the most fought-over fort in Texas. Today the site is operated by the Catholic Diocese of Victoria. "Our Lady of Loreto" chapel is the oldest building on the site, and it housed Fannin's troops for a time after they were captured. Re-enactors on the site help visitors understand what life was like when the Presidio was an active fort. Small apartment, "The Quarters," available for overnight stays. Zaragoza Birthplace SHS, Zaragoza plaza and ampitheater, the Fannin Memorial Monument and burial site, and the Angel of Goliad nature trail and plaza are all within walking distance. **Goliad SP** is a half mile north on US 183. An 11-mile drive east on US 59 will take you to the **Fannin Battleground SHS**.

Sabine Pass Battleground State Historic Site in Jefferson County 1.5 miles south of Sabine Pass on Dick Dowling Road, contains 58 acres acquired from Kountze and Couch Trust in 1972. Lt. Richard W. Dowling, with small Confederate force, repelled an attempted 1863 invasion of Texas by Union gunboats. Monument, World War II ammunition bunkers.

Sam Bell Maxey House State Historic Site, at the corner of South Church and Washington streets in Paris, Lamar County, was donated by the City of Paris in 1976. Consists of 0.4 acres with 1868 Victorian Italianate-style frame house, plus outbuildings. Most of furnishings accumulated by Maxey family. Maxey served in Mexican and Civil wars and was two-term U.S. Senator. Open for tours Tuesday through Saturday.

Sam Rayburn House State Historic Site in Bonham, Fannin County, preserves personal belongings, original furniture, and photos just as they were when Sam Rayburn lived here. Visitors can explore the home and grounds to the once powerful and influential Texas politician. Open Tuesday through Saturday.

San Felipe de Austin State Historic Site, located at 220 2nd St. in San Felipe, Austin County, marks the headquarters for Stephen F. Austin's colony in Mexican Texas. Visitors are able to walk the grounds of the former political and economic center of American immigration to Texas before its fall in the war of Texas independence. The site encourages visits from school groups, homeschoolers, and youth groups. Open Wednesday through Sunday. Visitors can camp at the **Stephen F. Austin SP**, one mile away.

San Jacinto Battleground State Historic Site is located 20 miles east of downtown Houston off TX 225 east to TX 134 to PR 1836 in east Harris County. The park is 1,200 acres with a 570-foot-tall monument erected in 1936–1939 in honor of Texans who defeated Mexican Gen. Antonio López de Santa Anna on April 21, 1836, to win Texas' independence from Mexico. The park was purchased by the state in a series of acquisitions between 1899 and the 1930s. Park transferred to TPW in 1965. Elevator ride to observation tower near top of monument; museum. Monument known as tallest free-standing concrete structure in the world at the time it was erected. Interpretive trail around battleground.

Sebastopol House State Historic Site at 704 Zorn Street in Seguin, Guadalupe County, was acquired by purchase in 1976 from Seguin Conservation Society. Today it is owned and operated by the City of Seguin. Built about 1856 by Col. Joshua W. Young of limecrete (concrete made from local gravel and lime), the Greek Revival-style house has been restored to its 1880 appearance. Open Thursday through Sunday. Call the Seguin Parks and Recreation Department, 830-379-4833 for more information. Also of interest in the area is historic Seguin, founded 1838.

Starr Family Home State Historic Site, 3 acres at 407 W. Travis in Marshall, Harrison County. Called Maplecroft mansion, the Greek Revival-style house was home to four generations of the Starr family, powerful and economically influential Texans. Two other family homes also in park. Acquired by gift in 1976; additional land donated in 1982. Open Tuesday through Saturday. Special events during year. **Caddo Lake SP** is nearby.

Varner–Hogg Plantation State Historic Site is 66 acres in Brazoria County, two miles north of West Columbia on FM 2852. Land originally owned by Martin Varner, a member of Stephen F. Austin's "Old Three Hundred" colony; later was home of Texas governor James Stephen Hogg. Property was deeded to the state in 1957 by Miss Ima Hogg, Gov. Hogg's daughter. First rum distillery in Texas established in 1829 by Varner. Open Wednesday through Sunday.

Washington-on-the-Brazos State Historic Site consists of 293 acres found seven miles southwest of Navasota in Washington County on TX 105 and FM 1155. Land acquired by deed from private owners in 1916, 1976 and 1996. Park includes the site of the signing of the Texas Declaration of Independence from Mexico (see the full text on page 446), as well as the site of the later signing of the Constitution of the Republic of Texas. In 1842 and 1845, the land included the capitol of the Republic. Star of the Republic Museum and **Barrington Plantation SHS** are on the same property. ☆

Texas Lakes

Many lakes in Texas have privately owned recreational facilities. The ones in the table below are all managed by the Army Corps of Engineers. See the full list of lakes that have more than 5,000 acre-feet of storage capacity on page 58.

Recreational Facilities, Corps of Engineers Lakes, 2023

Reservoir	Swim Beaches	Boat Ramps	Picnic Sites	Camp Sites	Group Camping	Rental Cabins
Aquilla		★				
Bardwell	★	★	★	★	★	
Belton	★	★	★	★	★	★
Benbrook	★	★	★	★	★	★
Buffalo Bayou	★		★	★		★
Canyon	★	★	★	★	★	★
Cooper	★	★	★	★	★	★
Georgetown	★	★	★	★	★	
Granger	★	★	★	★	★	
Grapevine	★	★	★	★	★	★
Hords Creek	★	★	★	★	★	
Joe Pool	★	★	★	★		★
Lake O' the Pines	★	★	★	★	★	
Lavon	★	★	★	★	★	
Lewisville	★	★	★	★		★
Navarro Mills	★	★	★	★		
O.C. Fisher		★	★	★		
Pat Mayse		★	★	★		★
Proctor	★	★	★	★	★	
Ray Roberts	★	★	★	★	★	
Sam Rayburn	★	★	★	★	★	★
Somerville	★	★	★	★	★	★
Stillhouse Hollow	★	★	★	★		
Texoma	★	★	★	★	★	★
Town Bluff	★	★	★	★		
Waco	★	★	★	★	★	★
Wallisville		★	★			
Whitney	★	★	★	★	★	★
Wright Patman	★	★	★	★	★	

Source: U.S. Army Corps of Engineers

Recreation in State Forests and Arboretums

Source: Texas A&M Forest Service, tfsweb.tamu.edu/

Owned and operated by the Texas A&M Forest Service, our state forests are all working demonstration forests, offering resource education tours by appointment. All Texas State Forests are game sanctuaries with no firearms or hunting allowed, except for those organized by Texas Parks and Wildlife. For general information about the Texas State Forests, see page 71 in the Environment chapter.

The district offices listed below are all open weekdays, 8 am to 5 pm.

E.O. Siecke State Forest: Open year–round during daylight hours. Limited access by vehicle. Forest management demonstration sites throughout. Information, maps, and restrooms are available at the Kirbyville District Office, located at the state forest on FM 82, 4.5 miles southeast of Kirbyville. Phone: (409) 423–2890.

I.D. Fairchild State Forest: Open year–round during daylight hours. Located on US 84, four miles west of Maydelle and 13 miles west of Rusk. Forest management demonstration sites throughout. There are no restroom facilities in this forest. Information and maps at the Jacksonville District Office: 1015 SE Loop 456 in Jacksonville. Phone: (903) 586–7545.

John Henry Kirby Memorial State Forest: Open by reservation only. Located near CR 1550 off Hwy. 69, 15 miles south of Woodville and 16 miles north of Kountze. There are no restroom facilities in this forest. Reservations and maps at the Olive District Office at 3882 Hwy. 69, just north of Kountze. Phone: (409) 246–2484.

Masterson State Forest: Open by reservation only. Located three miles south of Buna and nine miles south of Kirbyville, off TX 62. Reservations and maps can be obtained at the Kirbyville District Office, FM 82, 4.5 miles southeast of Kirbyville. Phone: (409) 423–2890.

W. Goodrich Jones State Forest: Open year–round during daylight hours. Forest management demonstration sites throughout. Three public parking lots on FM 1488. Information, maps, and restrooms are available at the Conroe District Office, located at the state forest on FM 1488, 1.5 miles west of I–45 and five miles south of Conroe. Phone: (936) 273–2261.

Ruth Bowling Nichols Arboretum: Open weekdays, 9 am to 3 pm. Located behind the Jacksonville District Office at 1015 S.E. Loop 456 in Jacksonville. No restroom facilities available. For guided tours, contact the Cherokee County Extension Agent (903) 683-5416.

Olive Scott Petty Arboretum: Open year-round during daylight hours. Limited parking available. Still under development. Located at the Olive District Office at 3882 Hwy. 69, just north of Kountze. Phone: (409) 246–2484.

Kirby Memorial State Forest features a pitcher plant bog. These pitcher plants were photographed in Tyler County. Photo by William L. Farr, CC by SA 4.0

Texas State Forests and Arboretums

Forests	NEAREST TOWN	Reservations Required	Hiking	Biking	Horseback Riding	Wildlife Viewing	Bird Watching	Picnicking	Special Attractions
E.O. Siecke State Forest	Kirbyville		★	★	★	★	★	★	Historical fire tower, the oldest slash pine stand in Texas, Trout Creek
I.D. Fairchild State Forest	Rusk		★	★	★	★	★	★	Red-cockaded woodpecker management area, pond with picnic area
John Henry Kirby Memorial State Forest	Woodville	★	★			★	★		Pitcher plant bog, historical fire tower, John Henry Kirby Historical Marker
Masterson State Forest	Kirbyville	★	★		★		★		Educational loop, pond and picnic area, longleaf seed orchard
W. Goodrich Jones State Forest	Conroe		★	★	★	★	★	★	Red-cockaded woodpecker management area, orienteering course, Sweetleaf nature and fitness trail, two small lakes with limited picknicking and fishing, environmental educator trainings
Arboretums									
Olive Scott Petty Arboretum	Jacksonville		★			★	★		Hazel Tilton outdoor classroom, demonstration gardens, historic trees
Ruth Bowling Nichols Arboretum	Kountze						★	★	Jimmy Hull memorial, ponds, tree identification

Big Thicket National Preserve is a popular place to watch birds and other wildlife. Photo by Matthew Dillon, Flickr, CC by 2.0

National Parks, Historic Sites, Recreation Areas

Source: U.S. Dept of Interior, www.nps.gov/state/tx/index.htm

Below is a list of facilities and activities that can be enjoyed at Texas' two national parks, a national seashore, a biological preserve, a marine sanctuary, and several historic sites, memorials, and recreation areas in Texas. Most are under supervision of the **U.S. Department of Interior**. Recreational opportunities in the state and national forests and national grasslands in Texas are under the jurisdiction of the **U.S. Department of Agriculture**.

Alibates Flint Quarries National Monument consists of 1,371 acres in Potter County. For more than 10,000 years, pre-Columbian Indians dug agatized limestone from the quarries to make projectile points, knives, scrapers, and other tools. The area is presently undeveloped. You may visit the flint quarries on guided walking tours with a park ranger. Tours are at 10:00 a.m. and 2:00 p.m. by appointment from April through October. Off-season tours can also be arranged in March and November, 37084 Alibates Rd., Fritch 79036; (806) 857–6680.

Amistad National Recreation Area is located in Val Verde County on the U.S. side of Amistad Reservoir, an international reservoir on the Texas–Mexico border. The 57,292-acre park's attractions include boating, water skiing, swimming, fishing, camping, and archaeological sites. If lake level is normal, visitors can see 4,000-year-old prehistoric pictographs in Panther and Parida caves, which are accessible only by boat. Check with park before visiting. The area is one of the densest concentrations of Archaic rock art in North America — more than 300 sites. Commercial campgrounds, motels, and restaurants nearby. Marinas located at Diablo East and Rough Canyon. Open year round. 10477 Hwy. 90 W, Del Rio 78840; (830) 775–7491.

Big Bend National Park, established in 1944, has spectacular mountain and desert scenery and a variety of unusual geological structures. It is the nation's largest protected area of Chihuahuan desert. Located in Brewster County in the great bend of the Rio Grande, the 801,000-acre park, which is part of the international boundary between the United States and Mexico, was designated a U.S. Biosphere Reserve in 1976. Hiking, birding, and float trips are popular. Numerous campsites are located in park, and the Chisos Mountains Lodge has 72 non-smoking rooms. Write for reservations to 1 Basin Rural Station, Big Bend National Park, Texas 79834; (855) 765–1324; www.chisosmountainslodge.com. Park open year round; facilities most crowded during spring break. 1 Panther Junction, Big Bend National Park 79834; (915) 477–2251.

Big Thicket National Preserve, established in 1974, consists of 15 separate units totaling 97,000 acres of diverse flora and fauna, often nicknamed the "biological crossroads of North America." The preserve, which includes parts of seven East Texas counties, has been designated an "International Biosphere Reserve" by the United Nations Educational, Scientific and Cultural Organization (UNESCO). The preserve includes four different ecological systems: Southeastern swamps, Eastern forests, Central Plains and Southwestern deserts. The visitor information station is located on FM 420, eight miles north of Kountze. Open daily from 9 a.m. to 5 p.m. Naturalist activities are available by reservation only; reservations are made through the station. Nine trails, ranging in length from one-quarter mile to 18 miles, visit a variety of forest communities. The two shortest trails are handicapped accessible. Trails are open year round, but flooding may occur after heavy rains. Horses permitted on the Big Sandy Horse Trail only. Boating and canoeing are popular on preserve corridor units. Park headquarters are at 6102 FM 420, Kountze 77625; (409) 951–6700.

Blackwell School National Historic Site in Marfa, listed on the National Register of Historic Sites in 2019, is in the works to join the National Park Service as authorized by The Blackwell School National Historic Site Act signed in 2022. The site in Presidio County will open under the National Park System after sufficient land has been acquired and certain required agreements have been completed. Blackwell School, originally known as the Ward or Mexican School, operated as the city's segregated school for Hispanic students starting in 1909. It was closed when the Marfa Independent School District was integrated in 1965. Located at 501 S. Abbott St. in Marfa, the site is currently managed by the Blackwell School Alliance. Open weekends from noon to 4 p.m. and evenings by appointment.

Chamizal National Memorial, established in 1963 and opened to the public in 1973, stands as a monument to Mexican-American friendship and goodwill. The memorial, on 52 acres in El Paso, commemorates the peaceful settlement on Aug. 29, 1963, of a 99-year-old boundary dispute between the United States and Mexico. Chamizal uses the visual and performing arts as a medium of interchange, helping people better understand not only other cultures but their own as well. It hosts a variety of programs throughout the year, including: the fall Chamizal Festival musical event, the Siglo de Oro drama festival (early March), the Oñate Historical Festival celebrating the First Thanksgiving (April), and Music Under the Stars (Sundays, June-August). The park has a 1.8-mile walking trail and picnic areas. 800 S. San Marcial St., El Paso; (915) 532–7273.

El Camino Real de los Tejas was designated a National Historic Trail in 2004. It traces the "royal road" from Mexico to the Red River Valley, established when the area was under Spanish rule. The full route stretched over 2,500 miles, down to Mexico City, and connected to Spanish missions and posts along the way to Los Adaes, the first capital of the Texas province. Today's trail travels many roads, the longest straight route being TX 21 to Hwy. 6 in Louisiana, connecting parks, historic sites, and museums along the way. The National Parks website has tools to help you plan your trip, and photos and videos to learn more about travelers in the past.

El Camino Real de Tierra Adentro became a National Historic Trail in 2000. This royal road brought travelers from Mexico City through what is now El Paso and north into New Mexico, ending near Santa Fe, which was one of the capitals of New Mexico under Spanish rule. This path takes travelers to historic sites and museums along Interstate 25.

Flower Garden Banks National Marine Sanctuary was named after the brightly colored sponges, plants, and other marine life found in the area. The reefs were discovered by snapper and grouper fishermen in the early 1900s. Situated 70–115 miles offshore, the sanctuary is only accessible by boat, so divers interested in visiting can book dive charters that depart from numerous Texas ports, including: Galveston, Freeport, Sabine Pass, and Surfside. The sanctuary protects three separate areas: East Flower Garden Bank and West Flower Garden Bank were designed as a sanctuary under the National Marine Sanctuary Act in 1992, and the algal-sponge communities of Stetson Bank were added to the sanctuary in 1996. Exceptional underwater visibility allows divers to experience spectacular sights, such as giant coral heads, schools of fish, eagle and manta rays, and even majestic whale sharks during summer visits to the area. The banks of the sanctuary include more than a dozen moored dive sites, with typical dive profiles of 70–130 feet. Several ports that offer dive trips are also home to commercial fishing charters for anglers wanting to fish the Flower Garden and Stetson banks. Snappers, jacks, barracuda, and wahoo are just a few of the fish commonly caught by sportfishing enthusiasts. On the web: flower garden.noaa.gov

Fort Davis National Historic Site in Jeff Davis County was a key post in the West Texas defense system, guarding immigrants and tradesmen on the San Antonio-El Paso road from 1854 to 1891. At one time, Fort Davis was manned by black troops, called "Buffalo Soldiers" (because of their curly hair) who fought with great distinction in the Indian Wars. Henry O. Flipper, the first Black graduate of West Point, served at Fort Davis in the early 1880s. The 474-acre historic site is located on the north edge of the town of Fort Davis in the Davis Mountains, the second-highest mountain range in the state. The site includes a museum, an auditorium with daily audio-visual programs, restored and refurnished buildings, a picnic area, and hiking trails. Open year round except Christmas Day. 101 Lt. Flipper Dr., Fort Davis 79734; (432) 426–3224.

Guadalupe Mountains National Park, established in 1972, includes 86,416 acres in Hudspeth and Culberson counties. The park contains one of the most extensive fossil reefs on record. Deep canyons cut through this reef and provide a rare opportunity for geological study. Special points of interest are McKittrick Canyon, a fragile riparian environment, and Guadalupe Peak, the highest in Texas. Camping, hiking on 80 miles of trails, Frijole Ranch Museum, summer amphitheater programs. Orientation, free information, and natural history exhibits available at visitor center. Open year round. Lodging at Van Horn, Texas, and White's City or Carlsbad, NM. 400 Pine Canyon, Salt Flat 79847; (915) 828–3251.

Lake Meredith National Recreation Area, 30 miles northeast of Amarillo, centers on a reservoir on the Canadian River, in Moore, Hutchinson and Potter counties. The 50,000-acre recreational area is popular for water-based activities. Boat ramps, picnic areas, unimproved campsites. Commercial lodging and trailer hookups available in nearby towns. Open year round. 419 E. Broadway, Fritch 79036; (806) 857–3151.

Lyndon B. Johnson National Historical Park includes two separate districts 14 miles apart. The Johnson City District comprises the boyhood home of the 36th president of the United States and the Johnson Settlement, where his grandparents resided during the late 1800s. The LBJ Ranch District can be visited only by taking the National Park Service bus tour starting at the LBJ State Historic Site. The tour includes the reconstructed LBJ Birthplace, old school, family cemetery, show barn, and a view of the Texas White House. Site in Blanco and Gillespie counties was established in 1969 and contains 1,570 acres, 674 of which are federal. Open year round except Thanksgiving, Christmas Day, and New Year's Day. No camping on site; commercial campgrounds, motels in area. 100 Ladybird Ln., Johnson City 78636; (830) 868–7128.

Padre Island National Seashore consists of a 68-mile stretch of a barrier island along the Gulf Coast; noted for white-sand beaches, excellent fishing, and abundant bird and marine life. Contains 133,000 acres in Kleberg, Kenedy, and Willacy counties. Open year round. One paved campground (fee charged) located north of Malaquite Beach; unpaved (primitive) campground area south on beach. Five miles of beach are accessible by regular vehicles; 55 miles are accessible only by 4x4 vehicles. Off-road vehicles prohibited. Camping permitted in two designated areas. Commercial lodging available on the island outside the National Seashore boundaries. 20420 Park Rd. 22, Corpus Christi 78418; (361) 949–8068.

Palo Alto Battlefield National Historical Park preserves the site of the first major battle in the Mexican-American War. Fought on May 8, 1846, near Brownsville, it is recognized for the innovative use of light or "flying" artillery. Participating in the battle were three future presidents: General Zachary Taylor and Ulysses S. Grant on the U.S. side, and Gen. Mariano Arista on the Mexican. The 3,400-acre site in Cameron County is located at the junction of Farm-to-Market roads 1847 and 511. Exhibits at the visitor center interpret the battle as well as the causes and consequences of the war. Phone (956) 541–2785.

Rio Grande Wild & Scenic River is a 196-mile strip on the U.S. shore of the Rio Grande in the Chihuahuan Desert, beginning in Big Bend National Park and continuing downstream to the Terrell-Val Verde County line. There are federal facilities in Big Bend National Park only. Contact Big Bend National Park for more information.

San Antonio Missions National Historical Park preserves four Spanish colonial missions — Concepción, San José, San Juan, and Espada — as well as the Espada dam and aqueduct, which are two of the best-preserved remains in the United States of the Spanish Colonial irrigation system, and Rancho de las Cabras, the colonial ranch of Mission Espada. All were crucial elements to Spanish settlement on the Texas frontier. When Franciscan attempts to establish a chain of missions in East Texas in the late 1600s failed, the Spanish Crown ordered three missions transferred to the San Antonio River valley in 1731. The missions are located within the city limits of San Antonio, while Rancho de las Cabras is located 25 miles south in Wilson County near Floresville. The four missions, which are still in use as active parishes, are open to the public from 9 a.m. to 5 p.m. daily except Thanksgiving, Christmas and New Year's. Public roadways connect the sites, as well as a hike-bike trail. The visitor center for the mission complex is at San José. For more information, write to 2202 Roosevelt Ave., San Antonio 78210; (210) 932–1001.

Waco Mammoth National Monument was designated in 2015 and one of the most recent Texas units of the National Park System. This paleontological site represents the nation's only recorded discovery of a nursery herd of Columbian mammoths. Visitors can view "in situ" fossils including female mammoths, a bull mammoth, and a camel that lived approximately 67,000 years ago.The park is managed in partnership by the National Park Service, the City of Waco, and Baylor University. Welcome Center located at 6220 Steinbeck Bend Dr. It is open every day, except Thanksgiving, Christmas, and New Year's Day. Phone (254) 750–7946. ☆

Sandhill Cranes are known to spend the winter at the Padre Island National Seashore. Photo by USFWS, Flickr, CC by 2.0

National Forests and National Grasslands

U.S. Forest Service, www.fs.usda.gov/texas

For general information about the National Forests and National Grasslands, see page 71 in the Environment chapter. These areas are managed by the U.S. Forest Service, so make sure to visit the link above while planning your trip to learn of any temporary closures or alerts.

An estimated three million people visit the National Forests in Texas for recreation annually. These visitors use established recreation areas primarily for hiking, picnicking, swimming, fishing, camping, boating and nature enjoyment. In the following list of some of these areas, Forest Service Road is abbreviated FSR.

Angelina National Forest

Boykin Springs Recreation Area, 14 miles southeast of Zavalla, has a 6-acre lake and facilities for hiking, swimming, picnicking, fishing, and camping. **Bouton Lake**, 14 miles southeast of Zavalla off TX 63 and FSR 303, has a nine-acre natural lake with primitive facilities for camping, picnicking, and fishing.

Caney Creek on Sam Rayburn Reservoir, ten miles southeast of Zavalla off FM 2743, offers fishing, boating, and camping.

The **Sawmill Hiking Trail** is 2.5 miles long and winds from the Boykin Springs Recreation Area to the Aldridge Sawmill Historic Site, where hikers can explore the remains of the small lumber operation that existed there between 1905 and 1927.

Davy Crockett National Forest

Ratcliff Lake Recreation Area, 25 miles west of Lufkin on TX 7, is a 45-acre lake with facilities for picnicking, hiking, swimming, boating, fishing, and camping. There is also an amphitheater.

The 20-mile-long **4C National Recreation Trail** connects Ratcliff Recreation Area to the Neches Bluff overlook. The **Piney Creek Horse Trail** is 54 miles long and can be entered approximately 5.5 miles south of Kennard off CR 4625. There are two horse camps along this trail system.

Sabine National Forest

Indian Mounds Recreation Area, located 11.5 miles southeast of Hemphill off FM 3382, has camping facilities and a boat ramp. **Lakeview**, on Toledo Bend Reservoir, 21 miles from Pineland, offers camping, hiking, and fishing and can be reached via TX 87, FM 2928, and FSR 120.

Ragtown, 26 miles southeast of Center and accessible by TX 87, is also on Toledo Bend and has facilities for hiking, camping, and boating. **Red Hill Lake**, three miles north of Milam on TX 87, has facilities for fishing, swimming, camping, and picnicking.

Willow Oak Recreation Area on Toledo Bend, 13 miles south of Hemphill off TX 87, offers fishing, picnicking, camping, and boating.

Sam Houston National Forest

Cagle Recreation Area is located on the shores of Lake Conroe, 50 miles north of Houston and five miles west of I-45 at FM 1375. Cagle offers camping, fishing, hiking, birding, and other recreational opportunities in a forested lakeside setting.

Double Lake, three miles south of Coldspring on FM 2025, has facilities for picnicking, hiking, camping, swimming, and fishing. Visitors can also rent canoes and paddleboats. **Stubblefield Lake**, 15 miles west-northwest of New Waverly off TX 1375 on the shores of Lake Conroe, has facilities for camping, hiking, picnicking, and fishing.

The **Lone Star Hiking Trail**, approximately 128 miles long, may be hiked year-round and runs through the Little Lake Creek Wilderness Area and the Big Creek Scenic Area. **Richards–Raven Equestrian Trail** is 19.5 miles with parking for trailers at the trailhead at the intersection of FSR 209 and FM 1791.

Caddo/Lyndon B. Johnson National Grasslands

West Lake Crockett Recreation Area, 12 miles north of Honey Grove (Fannin County) on FM 409, just off FM 100, has a boat-launch ramp and camping sites on a 388-acre lake.

Coffee Mill Lake Recreation Area has camping and picnicking facilities on a 650-acre lake. This area is four miles west of West Lake Crockett Recreation Area.

Black Creek Lake Recreation Area is eight miles north of Decatur (Wise County) and has camping, picnic facilities, a fishing bridge, and a boat-launch ramp on a 30-acre lake.

The **LBJ Multiuse Trail System** comprises nearly 75 miles of biking, hiking, and horseback riding trails that run in the Cottonwood Lake vicinity, north of Decatur. The **TADRA Point** trailhead has facilities for camping, horse camping, restrooms, and and parking.

Black Kettle National Grassland

The Texas portion of this grassland is also known as the **Lake Marvin Recreation Area**, which is open year-round. It provides restrooms and potable water and sites for tent or RV camping and picnicking.

Additional Black Kettle recreational areas are in Oklahoma.

McClellan Creek National Grassland

Lake McClellan Recreation Area provides camping, picnicking, fishing, birdwatching, hiking, and boating. ATV and UTV riders can enjoy a 10-mile designated trail.

Rita Blanca National Grassland

The only developed recreation facility within this grassland in Texas is the **Thompson Grove Picnic Area**, located 14 miles northeast of Texline in Dallam County. ☆

A Northern Crested Caracara spotted in the Attwater Prairie Chicken Preserve. Photo by William L. Farr, CC by SA 4.0

National Natural Landmarks in Texas

Source: National Natural Landmarks Directory, www.nps.gov/subjects/nnlandmarks/nation.htm

Twenty Texas natural areas have been listed on the **National Registry of Natural Landmarks**.

The registry was established by the Secretary of the Interior in 1962 to identify and encourage the preservation of geological and ecological features that represent nationally significant examples of the nation's natural heritage.

The registry currently lists 602 national natural landmarks. Below is the list of those landmarks found in Texas, as of August 2023, and their characteristics (year of listing in parentheses).

Attwater Prairie Chicken Preserve: Colorado County, 55 miles west of Houston in the national wildlife refuge, is rejuvenated Gulf Coastal Prairie, which is habitat for Attwater's prairie chickens. (1968)

Bayside Resaca Area: Cameron County, Laguna Atascosa National Wildlife Refuge, 28 miles north of Brownsville. Excellent example of a resaca, supporting coastal salt-marsh vegetation and rare birds. (1980)

Catfish Creek: Anderson County, 20 miles northwest of Palestine, is undisturbed riparian habitat. (1983)

Caverns of Sonora: Sutton County, 16 miles southwest of Sonora, has unusual geological formations. (1965)

Cave Without a Name: Kendall County, 12 miles northeast of Boerne, is a cave of several rooms that are filled with spectacular formations. (2009)

Devil's Sink Hole: Edwards County, 9 miles northeast of Rocksprings, is a deep, bell-shaped, collapsed limestone sink with cave passages extending below the regional water table. (1972)

Dinosaur Valley: Somervell County, in Dinosaur Valley State Park, four miles west of Glen Rose, contains fossil footprints exposed in bed of Paluxy River. (1968)

Enchanted Rock: Gillespie and Llano counties, 12 miles southwest of Oxford, is a classic batholith, composed of coarse-grained pink granite. (1971)

Ezell's Cave: Hays County, within the city limits of San Marcos, houses at least 36 species of cave creatures. (1971)

Fort Worth Nature Center and Refuge: Tarrant County, within the Fort Worth city limits. Contains remnants of the Grand Prairie and a portion of the Cross Timbers, with limestone ledges and marshes. Refuge for migratory birds and other wildlife, and home to 11 buffalo raised by the center's staff. Educational programs offered for youth and adults. Self-guided hiking. (1980)

Greenwood Canyon: Montague County, along a tributary of Braden Branch, is a rich source of Cretaceous fossils. (1975)

High Plains Natural Area: Randall County, Buffalo Lake National Wildlife Refuge, 26 miles southwest of Amarillo, is a grama-buffalo shortgrass area. (1980)

Little Blanco River Bluff: Blanco County, comprises an Edwards Plateau limestone-bluff plant community. (1982)

Longhorn Cavern, Burnet County: 11 miles southwest of Burnet. Formed at least 450 million years ago, cave contains several unusual geologic features. (1971)

Lost Maples State Natural Area: Bandera and Real counties, 61 miles northwest of San Antonio, contains Edwards Plateau fauna and flora, including unusual bigtooth maple. Largest known nesting population of golden-cheeked warbler. (1980)

Muleshoe National Wildlife Refuge: Bailey County, 59 miles northwest of Lubbock, contains playa lakes and typical High Plains shortgrass grama grasslands. (1980)

Natural Bridge Caverns: Comal County, 16 miles west of New Braunfels, is a multilevel cavern system, with beautiful and unusual geological formations. (1971)

Odessa Meteor Crater: Ector County, 10 miles southwest of Odessa, is one of only two known meteor sites in the country. (1965)

Palo Duro Canyon State Park: Armstrong and Randall counties, 22 miles south-southwest of Amarillo. Cut by waters of the Red River, it contains cross-sectional views of sedimentary rocks representing four geological periods. (1976)

Santa Ana National Wildlife Refuge: Hidalgo County, 7 miles south of Alamo, is a lowland forested area with jungle-like vegetation. It is habitat for more than 300 species of birds and some rare mammals. (1966) ☆

A Hooded Oriole, photographed at the South Padre Island Birding and Nature Center. Photo by lwolfartist, CC by 2.0

Birding in Texas

World Birding Center

The World Birding Center comprises nine birding education centers and observation sites in the Lower Rio Grande Valley designed to protect wildlife habitat and offer visitors a view of more than 500 species of birds. The center has partnered with the Texas Parks and Wildlife Department, the U.S. Fish and Wildlife Service and nine communities to turn 10,000 acres back into natural areas for birds, butterflies and other wildlife.

This area in Cameron, Hidalgo and Starr counties is a natural migratory path for millions of birds that move between the Americas. The nine WBC sites listed here are situated along the border with Mexico. Learn more at **www.theworldbirdingcenter.com/**.

Bentsen–Rio Grande Valley State Park

This is the World Birding Center Headquarters and comprises the 797-acre Bentsen-RGV State Park and 1,700 acres of adjoining federal refuge land near Mission.

The site offers: daily tram service; four nature trails ranging in length from one-quarter mile to two miles; 2-story high Hawk Observation Tower with a 210-foot-long handicapped access ramp; 2 observation decks; 2 accessible bird blinds; primitive camping sites (by reservation); rest areas; picnic sites with tables; exhibit hall; park store; coffee bar; meeting room (available for rental); catering kitchen; bike rentals (1 and 2 seat bikes). Access within the park is by foot, bike and tram only; (956) 585-2858.

Hours: 7 a.m. to 10 p.m., seven days a week.

Edinburg Scenic Wetlands

This 40-acre wetlands in Edinburg is an oasis for water-loving birds, butterflies and other wildlife. The site is currently offering: walking trails, nature tours and classes; (956) 381-9922.

Hours: 8 a.m.–5 p.m., Monday through Thursday; 8 a.m.–6 p.m., Friday and Saturday. Closed Sunday.

Estero Llano Grande State Park

This 230-acre refuge in Weslaco attracts a wide array of South Texas wildlife with its varied landscape of shallow lake, woodlands and thorn forest; (956) 565-3919.

Hours: 8 a.m.–5 p.m., seven days a week.

Harlingen Arroyo Colorado

This site in Harlingen is connected by an arroyo waterway, as well as hike-and-bike trails meandering through the city, Hugh Ramsey Nature Park to the east and the Harlingen Thicket to the west; (956) 427-8873.

Hours: Office, 8 a.m.–5 p.m., Monday through Friday. Nature trails are open seven days a week, sunrise to sunset.

Old Hidalgo Pumphouse

Visitors to this museum in Hidalgo on the Rio Grande can learn about the steam-driven irrigation pumps that transformed Hidalgo County into a year-round farming area. The museum's grounds feature hummingbird gardens, walking trails and historic tours; (956) 843-8686.

Hours: 8 a.m.–6 p.m., Monday through Friday; 9 a.m.–6 p.m., Saturday and Sunday.

Quinta Mazatlan

This 1930s country estate in McAllen is a historic Spanish Revival adobe hacienda surrounded by lush tropical landscaping and native woodland. It is also an urban oasis, where quiet trails wind through more than 15 acres of birding habitat; (956) 688-3370.

Hours: 8 a.m.–5 p.m., Tuesday through Saturday. Open until sunset on Thursdays. Closed Sundays, Mondays, and holidays.

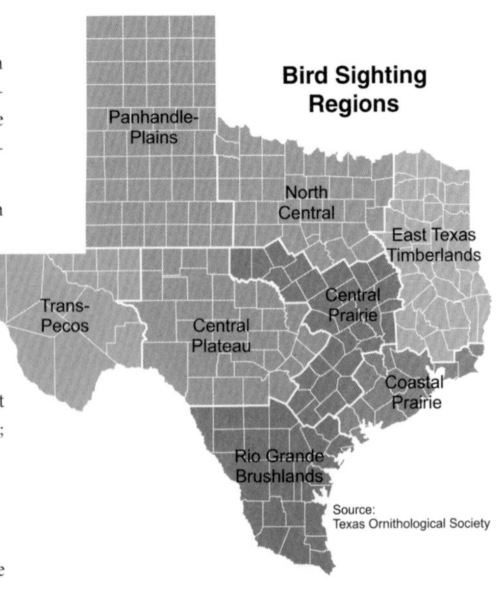

Resaca de la Palma State Park

More than 1,200 acres of wilderness near Brownsville in Cameron County, this site comprises the largest tract of native habitat in the World Birding Center network. Eight miles of trails, bicycles and binoculars available for rent; (956) 350-2920.

Hours: 6 a.m.–10 p.m., seven days a week.

Roma Bluffs

History and nature meet on scenic bluffs above the Rio Grande, where the World Birding Center in Roma is located on the old plaza of a once-thriving steamboat port. Part of a national historic district, the WBC Roma Bluffs includes a riverside nature area of three acres in Starr County. The site offers: walking trails, canoe trips, birding tours, natural history tours and classes; (956) 849-4930.

Hours: 8 a.m.–4 p.m. Tuesday through Saturday, although trails are open seven days a week and are free to the public.

South Padre Island Birding and Nature Center

At the southern tip of the world's longest barrier island, South Padre Island Birding and Nature Center is a slender thread of land between the shallow Laguna Madre and the Gulf of Mexico. This site offers: a nature trail boardwalk and birding tours; 1-800-SOPADRE.

Hours: 9 a.m.–5 p.m., seven days a week.

Great Texas Coastal Birding Trail

This trail winds its way through 43 Texas counties along the entire Texas coastal region. The trail was completed in April 2000 and is divided into upper, central, and lower coastal regions. It includes 308 wildlife-viewing sites and such amenities as boardwalks, parking pullouts, kiosks, observation platforms, and landscaping to attract native wildlife.

Color-coded maps are available, and signs mark each site. Trail maps contain information about the birds and habitats likely to be found at each site, the best season to visit, and food and lodging.

For information, contact: Nature Tourism Coordinator, Texas Parks and Wildlife Department, 4200 Smith School Road, Austin, 78744; (512) 389-4396. On the web: **tpwd.texas.gov/huntwild/wildlife/wildlife-trails/coastal.**

A Vermillion Flycatcher, photographed at the Amistad National Recreation Area in Val Verde County. Photo by Clinton & Charles Robertson, Flickr, CC by SA 2.0

I-20 Wildlife Preserve and Jenna Welch Nature Study Center

The 1-20 Wildlife Preserve is an 87-acre urban playa lake in its natural state in southwest Midland that opened in 2013. It was maintained for many years by the Midland Naturalists and other volunteers, including Jenna Welch, a birding enthusiast and a member of the group. It comprises 3.4 miles of hiking trails, including 1.5 miles of ADA-accessible trails, seven bird observation blinds, four teaching platforms, the 24-foot-tall Hawk Observation Platform, and the Merritt Pavilion.

Jenna Welch Nature Study Center operates an educational outreach program to local schools and area colleges and universities. Land was acquired to build a facility to house the nature study center.

The preserve, at 2201 S. Midland Dr., Midland, 79701, is open to the public daily from dawn until dusk. For more information, call (432) 853-9453. On the web: **www.i20wildlifepreserve.org.** ☆

Texas State Aquarium

Sources: New Handbook of Texas Online; Texas State Aquarium, www.texasstateaquarium.org/

The Texas State Aquarium, 7.3 acres on the southernmost tip of Corpus Christi Beach in Corpus Christi, is operated by the Texas State Aquarium Association, a nonprofit, self-supporting organization established in 1978. Efforts to fund a public aquarium in South Texas began in 1952, and several nonprofit organizations founded over the years eventually grew into the Texas State Aquarium Association.

Since 1978, the association has raised more than $28 million in private and public funding to build and operate the aquarium. Corpus Christi provided $14.5 million, including $4 million from a bond issue.

In 1985, the 69th Texas Legislature declared the project the "Official Aquarium of the State of Texas."

The Jesse H. and Mary Gibbs Jones Gulf of Mexico Exhibit Building was completed in July 1990. In 2003, Dolphin Bay opened for Atlantic bottlenose dolphins and the Environmental Discovery Center opened, featuring a library, a Family Learning Center, and the Flint Hills Resources Distance Learning Studio.

The aquarium's exhibits and research focus on the plants and animals of the Gulf of Mexico and the Caribbean. It is the first U.S. facility to do so.

The Port of Corpus Christi Wildlife Rescue, opened in 2023, is the largest coastal wildlife rescue facility in the state. Visitors can see rescued birds, marine mammals, and sea turtles receive treatment and rehabilitation.

The aquarium is open daily 10 a.m. to 5 p.m. There are admission and parking fees.

For more information, call 1-800-477-GULF. ☆

Sea Center Texas

Source: Texas Parks and Wildlife Department, tpwd.texas.gov/fishing/sea-center-texas/

The Texas Parks and Wildlife Department operates Sea Center Texas: a marine aquarium, fish hatchery, and nature center that educates and entertains visitors. It is located in Lake Jackson, 50 miles south of Houston, off of Texas 288.

The visitor center opened in 1996 and has interpretive displays, a "touch tank," and native Texas habitat exhibits depicting a salt marsh, bay, jetty, reef, and open Gulf waters. The Gulf aquarium features "Cooper," a 50-pound grouper; a green moray eel; a nurse shark; and other offshore species.

Sea Center is one of three marine hatcheries on the Texas coast that produce juvenile red drum, spotted seatrout, and southern flounder for enhancing natural populations in Texas bays. The hatchery can produce 25 million juvenile fish yearly and is a testing ground for production of other marine species. Hatchery tours and educational programs are available by reservation.

A half-acre youth fishing pond introduces youngsters to saltwater fishing through scheduled activities. The pond is handicap accessible and stocked with a variety of marine fish. Sea Center also provides educational activities for children on Fridays from June through August.

The center's wetland area is part of the Great Texas Coastal Birding Trail, where more than 150 species of birds have been identified. They include one acre of salt marsh and three acres of freshwater marsh. Damselflies, dragonflies, butterflies, turtles, and frogs can be sighted off the boardwalk, and an outdoor pavilion is adjacent to butterfly and hummingbird gardens.

Sea Center Texas is operated in partnership with The Dow Chemical Company and the Coastal Conservation Association. Admission and parking are free, though donations are appreciated. Hours are 9 a.m. to 4 p.m. Tuesday through Saturday, and 1 p.m. to 4 p.m. Sunday, except some holidays. Reservations are required for group tours, nature tours, and hatchery tours. For more information, call (979) 292-0100 or email: Seacenter@tpwd.texas.gov. ☆

A cub scout enjoying the touch tank at Texas State Aquarium. Photo by Roy Niswanger, CC 2.0

Fairs, Festivals, and Special Events

Fairs, festivals, and other special events provide year-round recreation in Texas. Some are of national interest, while many attract visitors from across the state. Each county profile in the Counties section also lists events in the Recreation paragraph and following town names. Information here was furnished by event coordinators.

To have your town's event included here, submit your information in the form at:

www.TexasAlmanac.com/submit-event

Abilene: West Texas Fair & Rodeo; September. Founded 1897. www.westtexasfairrodeo.com **Contact:** 1700 Hwy. 36, 79602 rjohnson@expoctc.com (325) 677–4376

Albany: Fort Griffin Fandangle; June. Founded 1938. www.fortgriffinfandangle.org **Contact:** PO Box 2017, 76430 info@fandangle.org (325) 762–3838

Alvarado: Johnson County Pioneers & Old Settlers Reunion; September. Founded 1893. www.alvaradoheritage.com/johnson-county-pioneers-and-old-settlers-reunion.html **Contact:** PO Box 217, 76009 (682) 202–2031

Amarillo: Tri-State Fair & Rodeo; September. Founded 1903. www.tristatefair.com **Contact:** 3301 SE 10th Ave.,79104 (806) 376–7767

Anderson: Grimes County Fair; June. Founded 1952. www.grimescountyfair.com **Contact:** PO Box 630, 77830 (936) 873–4452

Angleton: Brazoria County Fair; October. Founded 1910. www.bcfa.org **Contact:** 901 S. Downing Rd., 77515 contactus@bcfa.org (979) 849–6416

Aransas Pass: Shrimporee; May. Founded 1949. www.aransaspass.org/shrimporee **Contact:** 200 E. Johnson Ave., 78336 (361) 758–2750

Athens: Athens Old Fiddlers Contest & Reunion; May. Founded 1932. athensoldfiddlers.business.site **Contact:** 101 E. Tyler St., 75751 (903) 681–5185

Austin: Rodeo Austin; March. Founded 1938. www.rodeoaustin.com **Contact:** 9100 Decker Lake Rd., 78724 Info@rodeoaustin.com (512) 919–3000

Austin: South By Southwest; March. Founded 1987. www.sxsw.com **Contact:** PO Box 685289, 78768 (512) 467–7979

Austin: Eeyore's Birthday Party; April. Founded 1966. eeyores.org **Contact:** PO Box 12902, 78711 (512) 766–4424

Austin: Austin City Limits Music Festival; October. Founded 2002. www.aclfestival.com **Contact:** info@aclfestival.com

Bay City: Matagorda County Fair & Livestock Show; February-March. Founded 1944. www.matagordacountyfair.com **Contact:** PO Box 1803, 77404 mcfa@matagordacountyfair.com (979) 245–2454

Bay City: Bay City Rice Festival; October. Founded 1945. www.baycitylionsclub.com/rice-festival **Contact:** PO Box 867, 77404 info@baycitylions.com

Beaumont: South Texas State Fair; March. Founded 1907. www.ymbl.org/events **Contact:** 7250 Wespark, 77705 info@ymbl.org (409) 832–9991

Bellville: Austin County Fair & Rodeo; October. Founded 1927. www.austincountyfair.com **Contact:** PO Box 141, 77418 ACFair@austincountyfair.com (979) 865–5995

Belton: Belton 4th of July Celebration & PRCA Rodeo; July. Founded 1919. www.rodeobelton.com **Contact:** PO Box 659, 76513 info@beltonchamber.com (254) 939–3551

Belton: Central Texas State Fair; August-September. www.centraltexasstatefair.com **Contact:** PO Box 206, 76513 info@centraltexasstatefair.com (254) 933–5353

Big Spring: Howard County Fair; September. Founded 1973. www.hcfairtx.org **Contact:** PO Box 2356, 79721 howardcountyfairtx@gmail.com

Boerne: Kendall County Fair; September. Founded 1905. www.kcfa.org **Contact:** 1307 River Rd., 78006 info@kfca.org (830) 249–2839

Brenham: Washington County Fair; September. Founded 1870. www.washingtoncofair.com **Contact:** 1305 E. Blue Bell Rd., 77833 dean@washingtoncofair.com (979) 836–4112

Brownsville: Charro Days Fiesta; February-March. Founded 1938. www.charrodaysfiesta.com **Contact:** 455 E. Elizabeth St., 78520 (956) 542–4245

Burnet: Bluebonnet Festival; April. Founded 1986. bluebonnetfestival.org **Contact:** 101 N. Pierce St., 78611 (512) 756–4297

Burton: Burton Cotton Gin Festival; April. Founded 1990. www.cottonginmuseum.org **Contact:** PO Box 98, 77835 director@texascottonginmuseum.org (979) 289–3378

Caldwell: Kolache Festival; September. Founded 1986. www.burlesoncountytx.com **Contact:** 301 N. Main St., 77836 contact@burlesoncountytx.com (979) 567–0000

Caldwell: Burleson County Fair; September. www.burlesoncountyfair.com **Contact:** PO Box 634, 77836 burlesoncountyfairassoc@gmail.com (979) 567–3938

Canyon: TEXAS Outdoor Musical; June-August. Founded 1967. www.texas-show.com **Contact:** 1514 5th Ave., 79015 info@texas-show.com (806) 651–2181

Chappell Hill: Chappell Hill Bluebonnet Festival; April. chappellhillhistoricalsociety.com **Contact:** 9220 Poplar St., 77426 chappellhillfestivals@gmail.com (979) 203–1242

Clifton: Norse Smorgasbord; November. Founded 1955. visitclifton.org/special-events/norse-smorgasbord **Contact:** 115 N. Ave. D, 76634 oslcnorse1869@gmail.com (254) 675–3962

Clute: Great Texas Mosquito Festival; July. Founded 1981. www.mosquitofestival.com **Contact:** 100 Parkview Dr., 77531 wblackstock@clutetexas.gov (979) 265–8392

Columbus: Colorado County Fair & Rodeo; September. Founded 1978. www.coloradocountyfair.org **Contact:** PO Box 506, 78934 info@coloradocountyfair.org (979) 732–9266

Conroe: Montgomery County Fair & Rodeo; March. Founded 1957. www.mcfa.org **Contact:** 9201 Airport Rd., 77303 info@mcfa.org (936) 760–3631

Corpus Christi: Birdiest Festival in America; April. www.birdiestfestival.org **Contact:** 8545 S. Staples St., 78413 (361) 563–5968

Corpus Christi: Buc Days; May. Founded 1938. www.bucdays.com **Contact:** PO Box 30404, 78463 info@bucdays.com (361) 882–3242

The Houston Livestock Show & Rodeo is the largest event of its kind in the world. Photo by Katie Haugland Bowen, CC 2.0

Corpus Christi: Corpus Christi Beer Festival; June. corpuschristibeerfest.com **Contact:** 100 N. Shoreline Blvd., 78401

Corpus Christi: Dia de los Muertos Festival; October. Founded 2008. www.diadelosmuertoscc.com **Contact:** 623 N. Chaparral St., 78401 (361) 887–6834

Corsicana: Derrick Days; April. Founded 1976. www.derrickdays.com **Contact:** 301 S. Beaton St., 75110 derrickdayscorsicana@gmail.com (903) 654–4850

Dalhart: XIT Rodeo & Reunion; August. Founded 1937. xitrodeoreunion.com **Contact:** president@xitrodeoreunion.com

Dallas: State Fair of Texas; September-October. Founded 1886. www.bigtex.com **Contact:** PO Box 150009, 75315 info@bigtex.com (214) 565–9931

Decatur: Wise County Old Settlers Reunion; July. Founded 1881. www.visitdecaturtx.com **Contact:** 3101 FM 51, 76234 wisecountyreunion@gmail.com (940) 393–0350

De Leon: De Leon Peach and Melon Festival; August. Founded 1917. **Contact:** 5401 Hwy. 6, 76444 pmdeleon@cctc.net (254) 893–6600

Denton: North Texas Fair & Rodeo; August. Founded 1929. www.ntfair.com **Contact:** 2217 N. Carroll Blvd., 76201 info@ntfair.com (940) 387–2632

Edna: Jackson County Youth Fair; October. Founded 1949. www.jcyf.org **Contact:** 284 Brackenridge Pkwy., 77957

Ennis: National Polka Festival; May. Founded 1967. www.nationalpolkafestival.com **Contact:** PO Box 1177, 75120 jennifer@ennis-chamber.com (972) 878–4748

Fairfield: Freestone County Fair; June. Founded 1915. www.fcfar.org **Contact:** PO Box 592, 75840

Flatonia: Czhilispiel; October. Founded 1973. www.czhilispiel.com **Contact:** PO Box 610, 78941 flatoniatxchamber@gmail.com (361) 865–3920

Fort Worth: Fort Worth Stock Show & Rodeo; January-February. Founded 1896. www.fwssr.com **Contact:** PO Box 150, 76101 contact@fwssr.com (817) 877–2400

Fredericksburg: Night in Old Fredericksburg; July. Founded 1963. https://gillespiefair.com/nightinold-fredericksburg **Contact:** 302 E. Austin, 78624 info@gillespiefair.com (830) 997–2359

Fredericksburg: Fredericksburg Food & Wine Fest; October. Founded 1991. www.fbgfoodandwinefest.com **Contact:** 703 N. Llano St., 78624 creativemarketing1975@gmail.com (830) 997–8515

Fredericksburg: Oktoberfest; October. Founded 1981. www.oktoberfestinfbg.com **Contact:** PO Box 222, 78624 creativemarketing1975@gmail.com (830) 997–4810

Freer: Freer Rattlesnake Roundup; April. Founded 1966. **Contact:** PO Box 717, 78357 freercofc@yahoo.com (361) 394–6891

Galveston: Galveston Historic Homes Tour; May. Founded 1974. www.galvestonhistory.org **Contact:** 2002 Strand, 77550 foundation@galvestonhistory.org (409) 765–7834

Galveston: Dickens on The Strand; December. Founded 1974. www.dickensonthestrand.org **Contact:** 2002 Strand, 77550 foundation@galvestonhistory.org (409) 765–7834

Gilmer: East Texas Yamboree; October. Founded 1938. www.yamboree.com **Contact:** PO Box 1378, 75644 office@yamboree.com (903) 843–3759

Glen Flora: Wharton County Youth Fair; April. Founded 1976. www.whartoncountyyouthfair.org **Contact:** PO Box 167, 77443 wcyf@whartoncountyyouthfair.org (979) 677–3350

Graham: Food Truck Championship of Texas; June. foodtruckchampionshipoftexas.com **Contact:** 608 Elm St., 76450 cvb@grahamtexas.org (940) 549–0401

Granbury: Hometown 4th of July Festival; July. Founded 1975. www.granburychamber.com **Contact:** 3408 E. Hwy. 377, 76048 info@granburychamber.com (817) 573–1622

Granbury: Harvest Moon Festival of the Arts; October. Founded 1979. www.granburysquare.com **Contact:** 201 E. Pearl St., 76048 granburyhgma@gmail.com (682) 936–4550

Grand Prairie: Main Street Festival; April. Founded 2014. mainstreetfest.com **Contact:** 200 W. Main St., 75050 (972) 237–8100

Grapevine: GrapeFest; September. Founded 1986. www.grapevinetexasusa.com/grapefest **Contact:** 636 S. Main St., 76051 VisitorInfo@grapevinetexasusa.com (817) 410–3185

Greenville: Hunt County Fair & Livestock Show; April. Founded 1967. www.huntcountyfair.net **Contact:** PO Box 1403, 75403 fairmanager@huntcountyfair.net (903) 454–1503

Groesbeck: Limestone County Fair; March. limestonefair.org **Contact:** PO Box 965, 76642

Hallettsville: Kolache Fest; September. Founded 1996. hallettsville.com/view-event/393/event-info **Contact:** PO Box 313, 77964 visit@hallettsville.com (361) 798–2662

Helotes: Helotes Cornyval; May. Founded 1966. cornyval.org **Contact:** 12210 Leslie Rd., 78023 info@cornyval.org (210) 695–2103

Hempstead: Waller County Fair & Rodeo; September-October. Founded 1946. wallercountyfair.org **Contact:** 21988 FM 359, 77445 office@wallercountyfair.org (979) 826–2825

Hico: Hico Old Settler's Reunion; July. Founded 1883. www.hicotxchamber.org/events **Contact:** PO Box 93, 76457

Hidalgo: Borderfest; March-April. Founded 1976. www.hidalgoborderfest.com **Contact:** PO Box 722, 78557 eventinfo@cityofhidalgo.net

Hitchcock: Galveston County Fair & Rodeo; April. Founded 1938. www.galvestoncountyfair.com **Contact:** PO Box 889, Santa Fe 77510 (409) 986–6010

Hondo: Medina County Fair; September. Founded 1980. **Contact:** PO Box 4, 78861 havefun@medinacountyfair.net (830) 426–5406

Houston: Houston Livestock Show and Rodeo; February-March. Founded 1932. www.rodeohouston.com **Contact:** 3 NRG Park, 77054 questions@rodeohouston.com (832) 667–1000

Hughes Springs: Wildflower Trails of Texas; April. Founded 1971. www.hughesspringstxusa.com **Contact:** PO Box 805, 75656 wft@hughesspringstxusa.com (903) 639–7519

Huntsville: Prison City Film Festival; February. Founded 2018. prisoncityfilmfestival.com **Contact:** 1023 12th St., 77340

Huntsville: Walker County Fair & Rodeo; March-April. Founded 1979. walkercountyfair.com **Contact:** PO Box 1817, 77342 wcfa@walkercountyfair.com (936) 291–8763

Huntsville: Christmas Lighting Fundraiser Festival; November. Founded 2022. www.huntsvilledba.com/christmas-lighting-festival **Contact:** PO Box 6421, 77340 huntsvilledba@outlook.com

Ingram: Texas Arts and Crafts Fair; September. Founded 1973. txartsandcraftsfair.com **Contact:** PO Box 1169, 78025 specialevents@hcaf.com (830) 367–5121

Jefferson: Jefferson Historical Pilgrimage; May. Founded 1948. www.jeffersonpilgrimage.com **Contact:** PO Box 301, 75657 jeffersonpilgrimage@gmail.com (903) 452–3836

Johnson City: Blanco County Fair & Rodeo; August. Founded 1932. www.bcfra.org **Contact:** PO Box 261, 78636 bcfra.info@gmail.com

Kenedy: Bluebonnet Days; April. Founded 1980. kenedychamber.org **Contact:** 205 S. 2nd St., 78119 (830) 583–3223

Kerrville: Kerrville Folk Festival; May-June. Founded 1972. www.kerrvillefolkfestival.com **Contact:** 3876 Medina Hwy., 78028 info@kerrvillefolkfestival.org (830) 257–3600

Kerrville: Kerr County Fair; October. Founded 1980. www.kerrcountyfair.com **Contact:** PO Box 290842, 78029 kcfa@kerrcountyfair.com (830) 257–6833

La Grange: Fayette County Fair; September. Founded 1927. www.fayettecountyfair.org **Contact:** 400 Fair Grounds, 78945 info@fayettecountyfair.org (979) 968–3911

Laredo: Washington's Birthday Celebration; January-February. Founded 1898. www.wbcalaredo.com **Contact:** 1819 E. Hillside Rd., 78041 wbca@wbcalaredo.org (956) 722–0589

Laredo: Laredo International Fair and Exposition; February-March. Founded 1963. www.laredofair.com **Contact:** PO Box 1770, 78045 laredofairexpo@gmail.com (956) 722–9948

Longview: Gregg County Fair; September. Founded 1949. www.greggcountyfair.com **Contact:** 1511 Judson Rd., 75601 ayohe3184@gmail.com (903) 753–4478

Lubbock: 4th on Broadway Festival; July. Founded 1991. www.broadwayfestivals.com **Contact:** PO Box 1643, 79408 (806) 749–2929

Lubbock: Panhandle-South Plains Fair; September. Founded 1914. www.southplainsfair.com **Contact:** PO Box 208, 79408 info@southplainsfair.com (806) 763–2833

Lufkin: Texas State Forest Festival; September. Founded 1938. www.texasforestfestival.com **Contact:** 1200 Ellen Trout Dr., 75904 (936) 634–6644

Luling: Luling Watermelon Thump; June. Founded 1954. www.watermelonthump.com **Contact:** PO Box 188, 78648 admin@watermelonthump.com

Marshall: FireAnt Festival; October. Founded 1983. marshalltexas.com **Contact:** 110 S. Bolivar St., 75670 info@marshalltexas.com (903) 935–7868

Marshall: Wonderland of Lights; November-December. Founded 1984. www.marshalltxchamber.com **Contact:** PO Box 520, 75671

McKinney: Texas Scottish Festival & Highland Games; May. Founded 1986. www.texasscots.com **Contact:** 1705 W. University Dr., 75069 txsf18@texasscots.com (469) 424–1930

Mercedes: Rio Grande Valley Livestock Show; March. Founded 1940. www.rgvls.com **Contact:** 1000 N. Texas, 78570 info@rgvls.com (956) 565–2456

Mesquite: Mesquite Championship Rodeo; June-August. Founded 1957. www.mesquiterodeo.com **Contact:** 1818 Rodeo Dr., 75149 info@mesquiterodeo.com (972) 285–8777

Monahans: Butterfield Festival; July. Founded 1994. www.monahans.org **Contact:** 1525 E. Monahans Pkwy., 79756 chamber@monahans.org (432) 943–2187

Mount Pleasant: Titus County Fair; September. Founded 1975. www.tituscountyfair.com **Contact:** PO Box 1232, 75456 info@tituscountyfair.com

Nacogdoches: Piney Woods Fair; October. Founded 1978. www.nacexpo.net **Contact:** 3805 NW Stallings Dr., 75964 nacexpo@co.nacogdoches.tx.us (936) 564–0849

Nederland: Nederland Heritage Festival; March. Founded 1973. www.nederlandhf.org **Contact:** 1523 Boston Ave., 77627 nhfestival1973@gmail.com (409) 724–2269

New Braunfels: Comal County Fair & Rodeo; September. Founded 1894. www.comalcountyfair.org **Contact:** 701 E. Common St., 78130 info@comalcountyfair.com (830) 625–1505

New Braunfels: Wurstfest; November. Founded 1961. www.wurstfest.com **Contact:** PO Box 310309, 78131 info@wurstfest.com (830) 625–9167

Odessa: Permian Basin Fair & Expo; September. Founded 1975. www.pbfair.com **Contact:** 218 W. 46th St., 79764 pbfair@pbfair.com (432) 550–3232

Palestine: Texas Dogwood Trails Celebration; March-April. Founded 1938. www.visitpalestine.com **Contact:** 825 W. Spring St., 75801 visitorcenter@palestine-tx.org (903) 723–3014

Paris: Red River Valley Fair; September-October. Founded 1911. www.paristx-rrvfair.com **Contact:** 570 Rita Haynes Blvd., 75460 rrvfair@suddenlinkmail.com (903) 785–7971

Pasadena: Pasadena Livestock Show & Rodeo; September. Founded 1949. www.pasadenarodeo.com **Contact:** 7601 Red Bluff Rd., 77507 contactus@pasadenarodeo.com (281) 487–0240

Port Aransas: Whooping Crane Festival; February. Founded 1996. www.whoopingcranefestival.org **Contact:** 403 W. Cotter, 78373 (361) 749–5919

Port Arthur: cavOILcade; October. Founded 1952. cavoilcade.com **Contact:** PO Box 2336, 77643 cavoilcade@portarthur.com (409) 983–1009

Port Lavaca: Calhoun County Fair; October. Founded 1935. www.calcofair.com **Contact:** PO Box 42, 77979 info@calhouncountyfair.com (361) 202–0900

Poteet: Poteet Strawberry Festival; April. Founded 1948. www.strawberryfestival.com **Contact:** PO Box 227, 78065 info@strawberryfestival.com (830) 742–8144

Refugio: Refugio County Fair; March. Founded 1961. www.refugiocountyfair.com **Contact:** 246 Fairgrounds Rd., 78377

Rio Grande City: Starr County Fair; March. Founded 1965. www.starrcountyfair.com **Contact:** PO Box 841, 78582 starrcountyfair@aol.com (956) 488–0122

Rosenberg: Fort Bend County Fair & Rodeo; September-October. Founded 1937. www.fortbendcountyfair.com **Contact:** PO Box 428, 77471 mack@fbcfa.org (281) 342–6171

Salado: Scottish Gathering and Highland Games; November. www.saladomuseum.org **Contact:** 423 S. Main St., 76571 office@saladomuseum.org (254) 947–5232

San Angelo: San Angelo Stock Show & Rodeo; February. Founded 1932. www.sanangelorodeo.com **Contact:** 200 W 43rd St., 76903 (325) 653–7785

San Antonio: CarFest; April. Founded 2016. www.carfestsa.org **Contact:** info@carfestsa.org (210) 890–1909

San Antonio: Fiesta San Antonio; April. Founded 1891. fiestasanantonio.org **Contact:** 110 Broadway, 78205 info@fiestasanantonio.org (210) 227–5191

San Antonio: Texas Folklife Festival; June. Founded 1972. www.texasfolklifefestival.org **Contact:** 801 E. Cesar Chavez Blvd., 78205 texasfolklifefestival@utsa.edu (210) 458–2300

Sanderson: Pachanga; April. Founded 2001. **Contact:** PO Box 734, 79848 sandersonchamberofcommerce@gmail.com (432) 345–2324

Sanderson: Cinco de Mayo Celebration; May. **Contact:** PO Box 734, 79848 sandersonchamberofcommerce@gmail.com (432) 345–2324

Sanderson: 4th of July Celebration; July. Founded 1908. **Contact:** PO Box 734, 79848 sandersonchamberofcommerce@gmail.com (432) 345–2324

Schulenburg: Schulenburg Festival; August. Founded 1976. www.schulenburgfestival.org **Contact:** PO Box 115, 78956

Shamrock: St. Patrick's Day Celebration; March. Founded 1938. www.shamrockstpatricks.com **Contact:** 207 N. Main St., 79079 info@shamrockstpatricks.com (806) 256–2501

Stamford: Texas Cowboy Reunion; June. Founded 1930. www.texascowboyreunion.com **Contact:** 620 N. Swenson, 79553 texascowboyreunion@yahoo.com (325) 514–4132

Sulphur Springs: Hopkins County Fall Festival; October. www.sulphurspringstx.org **Contact:** 125 S. Davis St., 75482 (903) 885–7541

Sweetwater: Rattlesnake Roundup; March. Founded 1958. www.rattlesnakeroundup.net **Contact:** PO Box 416, 79556

Terlingua: Terlingua International Chili Championship; November. Founded 1967. www.casichili.net **Contact:** PO Box 39, 79852 casied@casichili.net

Texarkana: Four States Fair & Rodeo; September. Founded 1940. www.fourstatesfair.com **Contact:** 3700 E. 50th St., Texarkana, AR 71854 office@fourstatesfair.com (870) 773–2941

Todd Mission: Texas Renaissance Festival; October-November. Founded 1974. www.texrenfest.com **Contact:** 21778 FM 1774, 77363 info@texasrenfest.com (800) 458–3435

Tyler: East Texas State Fair; September. Founded 1914. www.etstatefair.com **Contact:** 2112 W. Front St., 75702 info@etstatefair.com (903) 597–2501

Tyler: Texas Rose Festival; October. Founded 1933. www.texasrosefestival.com **Contact:** PO Box 8224, 75711 liz@texasrosefestival.net (903) 597–3130

Waco: Heart O' Texas Fair & Rodeo; October. Founded 1954. www.hotfair.com **Contact:** 4601 Bosque Blvd., 76701 info@HOTFair.com (254) 776–1660

Waxahachie: Scarborough Renaissance Festival; April-May. Founded 1980. www.srfestival.com **Contact:** PO Box 538, 75168 (972) 938–3247

Waxahachie: Gingerbread Trail Tour of Homes; June. Founded 1969. elliscountymuseum.org/gingerbreadtrail **Contact:** 201 S. College St., 75165 admin@elliscountymuseum.org (972) 937–0681

Weatherford: Parker County Peach Festival; July. Founded 1985. www.parkercountypeachfestival.org **Contact:** PO Box 310, 76086 info@weatherford-chamber.com (817) 596–3801

Weatherford: Christmas on the Square; December. Founded 1988. www.weatherford-chamber.com **Contact:** PO Box 310, 76086 info@weatherford-chamber.com (817) 596–3801

West: Westfest; September. Founded 1976. www.westfest.com **Contact:** PO Box 65, 76691 (254) 826–5058

Winnsboro: Autumn Trails Festival; October. Founded 1959. www.winnsboroautumntrails.com **Contact:** PO Box 464, 75494 winnsboroautumntrails@gmail.com (903) 342–1958

Woodville: Tyler County Dogwood Festival; March-April. Founded 1940. www.tylercountydogwoodfestival.org **Contact:** PO Box 2151, 75979 dogwoodfestivaltyco@gmail.com (409) 283–2234

Yorktown: Yorktown Western Days; October. Founded 1959. www.yorktowntx.com **Contact:** PO Box 508, 78164 westerndays@yorktowntx.com (361) 564–2611 ☆

A father and his two sons fishing on Lake Bastrop. Photo by Texas Parks and Wildlife

Hunting and Fishing

Source: Texas Parks and Wildlife Department; http://tpwd.texas.gov

The popularity of hunting and fishing in Texas cannot be denied. Just ask the Texas Parks and Wildlife Department — which should probably be the place you start, because that's where you can find all of the current hunting and fishing regulations for the state.

According to the 2022 State of Texas Annual Cash Report, public hunting, fishing and other participation fees (including sales of hunting and fishing licenses) brought in revenues of $2.5 million in 2021 and $2.7 million in 2022.

Hunting Licenses

A **hunting license** is required of Texas residents and non-residents who hunt any legal bird or animal. Hunting licenses and endorsements are valid during the period Sept. 1 through the following Aug. 31 of each year, except licenses issued for a specific number of days or time periods.

A hunting license (except the non-resident special hunting license and non-resident 5-day special hunting license) is valid for taking all legal species of wildlife in Texas including deer, turkey, javelina, antelope, aoudad (sheep), alligator, and all small game and migratory game birds. Endorsement and tag requirements apply.

A trapper's license is required for all persons to hunt, shoot, or take for sale those species classified as fur-bearing animals or their pelts.

In addition to a valid hunting license:

- An **Archery Endorsement** is required to hunt deer or turkey during Archery-Only open season.
- An **Upland Game Bird Endorsement** is required to hunt turkey, pheasant, quail, or chachalaca. Non-residents who purchase the non-resident spring turkey license are exempt from this endorsement requirement.
- A **Migratory Game Bird Endorsement** and **HIP (Harvest Information Program) Certification** is required to hunt any migratory game birds, including waterfowl, coot, rail, gallinule, snipe, dove, sandhill crane, and woodcock.
- A valid **Federal Duck Stamp** is required of waterfowl hunters age 16 or older.

On the web, information from TPWD on hunting can be found at:**tpwd.texas.gov/huntwild/hunt/**

Hunting and Fishing Licenses Sold

2021	**Volume**
Hunting Licenses	474,854
Fishing Licenses	1,460,842
Combined Licenses	671,013
TOTALS	**2,606,709**
2022*	**Volume**
Hunting Licenses	472,954
Fishing Licenses	1,436,007
Combined Licenses	666,315
TOTALS	**2,575,276**

* Volumes for 2022 are estimated.

Source: 2024–25 Legislative Appropriation Request, TPWD

Texas Lakes

Bodies of water with a normal capacity of 5,000 acre-feet or larger. *Italicized* reservoirs are usually dry.

PANHANDLE PLAINS

1. Palo Duro Reservoir
2. Lake Rita Blanca
3. Lake Meredith
4. Bivins Lake
5. *Buffalo Lake*
6. Mackenzie Reservoir
7. Greenbelt Lake
8. Baylor Lake
9. White River Lake
10. Lake Alan Henry
11. Lake J.B. Thomas
12. Sulphur Springs Draw Reservoir
13. *Natural Dam Lake*
14. Red Draw Reservoir
15. Lake Colorado City
16. Champion Creek Reservoir
17. Mitchell County Reservoir
18. Lake Sweetwater
19. E.V. Spence Reservoir
20. Oak Creek Reservoir
21. O.C. Fisher Lake
22. Twin Buttes Reservoir
23. Lake Nasworthy
24. Ballinger Lake
25. O.H. Ivie Reservoir
26. Hords Creek Lake
27. Lake Winters
28. Lake Abilene
29. Lake Coleman
30. Lake Brownwood
31. Lake Clyde
32. Lake Kirby
33. Lake Fort Phantom Hill
34. Lake Stamford
35. Lake Davis
36. Truscott Brine Lake
37. Santa Rosa Lake
38. Lake Electra
39. Lake Kemp
40. Lake Diversion
41. Lake Kickapoo
42. North Fork Buffalo Creek Reservoir
43. Lake Wichita
44. Lake Arrowhead
45. Millers Creek Reservoir
46. Lake Cooper/Olney
47. Lake Graham
48. Lost Creek Reservoir
49. Possum Kingdom Lake
50. Hubbard Creek Reservoir
51. Lake Daniel
52. Lake Cisco
53. Lake Palo Pinto
54. Lake Leon
55. Proctor Lake

BIG BEND

56. Red Bluff Reservoir
57. Balmorhea Lake
58. Imperial Reservoir
59. San Esteban Lake
60. Amistad International Reservoir

HILL COUNTRY

61. Brady Creek Reservoir
62. Lake Buchanan
63. Inks Lake
64. Lake Lyndon B. Johnson
65. Lake Marble Falls
66. Lake Travis
67. Lake Austin
68. Lady Bird Lake
69. Lake Walter E. Long
70. Lake Georgetown
71. Granger Lake
72. Canyon Lake
73. Medina Lake

PRAIRIES AND LAKES

74. Lake Nocona
75. Hubert H. Moss Lake
76. Lake Texoma
77. Randell Lake
78. Valley Lake
79. Lake Bonham
80. Coffee Mill Lake
81. Pat Mayse Lake
82. Lake Crook
83. River Crest Lake
84. Cooper Lake
85. Lake Sulphur Springs
86. Lake Cypress Springs
87. Greenville City Lakes
88. Lake Tawakoni
89. Terrell City Lake
90. Lake Lavon
91. Lake Ray Hubbard
92. Lake Kiowa
93. Lake Ray Roberts
94. Lewisville Lake
95. Grapevine Lake
96. North Lake
97. White Rock Lake
98. Mountain Creek Lake
99. Joe Pool Lake
100. Lake Arlington
101. Lake Worth
102. Eagle Mountain Lake
103. Lake Weatherford
104. Lake Amon G. Carter
105. Lake Bridgeport
106. Lake Mineral Wells
107. Benbrook Lake
108. Lake Granbury
109. Squaw Creek Reservoir
110. Lake Pat Cleburne
111. Lake Waxahachie
112. Bardwell Lake
113. Cedar Creek Reservoir
114. Forest Grove Reservoir
115. Lake Athens
116. Trinidad Lake
117. Lake Halbert
118. Richland-Chambers Reservoir
119. Fairfield Lake
120. Navarro Mills Lake
121. Aquilla Lake
122. Lake Whitney
123. Lake Waco
124. Tradinghouse Creek Reservoir
125. Lake Creek Lake
126. Belton Lake
127. Stillhouse Hollow Lake
128. Alcoa Lake
129. Lake Limestone
130. Twin Oaks Reservoir
131. Camp Creek Lake
132. Lake Bryan
133. Gibbons Creek Reservoir
134. Somerville Lake
135. Lake Bastrop
136. Fayette County Reservoir
137. Lake Dunlap
138. Lake McQueeney
139. Lake Gonzales
140. Eagle Lake

PINEYWOODS

141. Wright Patman Lake
142. Monticello Reservoir
143. Lake Winnsboro
144. Lake Bob Sandlin
145. Welsh Reservoir
146. Ellison Creek Reservoir
147. Lake O' the Pines
148. Johnson Creek Reservoir
149. Caddo Lake
150. Lake Fork Reservoir
151. Lake Quitman
152. Lake Holbrook
153. Lake Hawkins
154. Gilmer Reservoir
155. Lake Gladewater
156. Eastman Lakes
157. Brandy Branch Reservoir
158. Lake Cherokee
159. Martin Creek Lake
160. Murvaul Lake

GULF COAST
176. Lake Houston
177. *Addicks Reservoir*
178. Sheldon Reservoir
179. *Barker Reservoir*
180. Lake Anahuac
181. J.D. Murphree Wildlife Management Area Impoundments
182. Smithers Lake
183. William Harris Reservoir
184. Eagle Nest Lake
185. Brazoria Reservoir
186. Lake Texana
187. South Texas Project Reservoir
188. Cox Creek Reservoir
189. Coleto Creek Reservoir
161. Lake Tyler/ Lake Tyler East
162. Lake Palestine
163. Lake Jacksonville
164. Striker Creek Reservoir
165. Pinkston Reservoir
166. Lake Naconiche
167. Lake Nacogdoches
168. Lake Kurth
169. Houston County Lake
170. Toledo Bend Reservoir
171. Sam Rayburn Reservoir
172. B.A. Steinhagen Lake
173. Lake Livingston
174. Lake Conroe
175. Lewis Creek Reservoir
SOUTH TEXAS PLAINS
190. *Olmos Reservoir*
191. Calaveras Lake
192. Victor Braunig Lake
193. Upper Nueces Lake
194. Choke Canyon Reservoir
195. Lake Corpus Christi
196. Casa Blanca Lake
197. Falcon International Reservoir
198. Delta Lake Reservoir Units 1 and 2
199. Loma Alta Lake
Hansford
Ochiltree
Lipscomb
Hutchinson
Roberts
Hemphill
Carson
Gray
Wheeler
Armstrong
Donley
Collingsworth
Briscoe
Hall
Childress
Floyd
Motley
Cottle
Hardeman
Wilbarger
Foard
Wichita
Clay
Crosby
Dickens
King
Knox
Baylor
Archer
Montague
Cooke
Grayson
Fannin
Lamar
Red River
Bowie
Garza
Kent
Stonewall
Haskell
Throckmorton
Young
Jack
Wise
Denton
Collin
Hunt
Delta
Franklin
Titus
Morris
Cass
Hopkins
Rockwall
Rains
Wood
Camp
Upshur
Marion
Harrison
Borden
Scurry
Fisher
Jones
Shackelford
Stephens
Palo Pinto
Parker
Tarrant
Dallas
Kaufman
Van Zandt
Smith
Gregg
Howard
Mitchell
Nolan
Taylor
Callahan
Eastland
Erath
Hood
Johnson
Ellis
Henderson
Rusk
Panola
Somervell
Navarro
Hill
Glasscock
Sterling
Coke
Runnels
Coleman
Brown
Comanche
Bosque
McLennan
Limestone
Freestone
Anderson
Cherokee
Shelby
Nacogdoches
San Augustine
Sabine
Reagan
Irion
Tom Green
Concho
McCulloch
Mills
Hamilton
Coryell
Falls
Leon
Houston
Angelina
Crockett
Schleicher
Menard
San Saba
Lampasas
Bell
Robertson
Madison
Trinity
Polk
Tyler
Jasper
Newton
Mason
Llano
Burnet
Milam
Walker
San Jacinto
Sutton
Kimble
Williamson
Brazos
Grimes
Gillespie
Blanco
Travis
Lee
Burleson
Hardin
Val Verde
Edwards
Kerr
Hays
Bastrop
Washington
Montgomery
Liberty
Orange
Kendall
Austin
Waller
Harris
Jefferson
Real
Bandera
Comal
Caldwell
Fayette
Colorado
Fort Bend
Chambers
Bexar
Kinney
Uvalde
Medina
Guadalupe
Gonzales
Lavaca
Wharton
Galveston
Maverick
Zavala
Frio
Atascosa
Wilson
Karnes
DeWitt
Victoria
Jackson
Matagorda
Brazoria
Dimmit
La Salle
McMullen
Live Oak
Bee
Goliad
Refugio
Calhoun
Webb
Duval
Jim Wells
San Patricio
Aransas
Nueces
Kleberg
Zapata
Jim Hogg
Brooks
Kenedy
Starr
Hidalgo
Willacy
Cameron

Game Harvest Estimates

The TPWD conducts random surveys of hunters every year to create estimates of hunter and harvest trends in two categories: small game (23 species total, birds and small mammals) and big game (white-tailed deer, mule deer, and javelina). They collect data not just on what animals were hunted, but also where, and how. You can learn about the methodology and see the full results of these surveys on the web at: **tpwd.texas.gov/publications/huntwild/hunt**

Fishing Licenses

All fishing licenses and endorsements are valid only from Sept. 1 through the following Aug. 31, except licenses issued for a specific number of days or time periods. If you own any valid freshwater fishing package, you will be able to purchase a saltwater stamp and also fish saltwater.

If you own any valid saltwater fishing package, you will be able to purchase a freshwater stamp and also fish freshwater. An all-water fishing package is available that enables anglers to fish both fresh- and saltwater.

Detailed information concerning licenses, endorsements, seasons, and regulations can be obtained from Texas Parks and Wildlife Department, 4200 Smith School Road, Austin 78744, (800) 792-1112 or (512) 389-4820; or on the web at: **tpwd.texas.gov/business/licenses**

Freshwater Fishing

Freshwater fishing in Texas is an activity enjoyed by an estimated 1.21 million recreational anglers. In 2015, these anglers contributed an economic output of approximately $96 million to the Texas economy.

Among the 268 species of freshwater fish in Texas, the most popular fish for recreational fishing are: **largemouth bass, catfish, crappie, and striped, white, and hybrid striped bass**.

Texas anglers can fish in approximately 1,100 public reservoirs and about 191,000 miles of rivers and streams, together totaling 1.7 million acres.

The Texas Parks and Wildlife Department operates field stations, fish hatcheries, and research facilities to support the conservation and management of fishery resources. The hatcheries operated by TPWD raise largemouth and smallmouth bass, as well as catfish, striped and hybrid striped bass, and sunfish.

TPWD has continued its programs of stocking fish in public waters to increase angling opportunities. Many conservation-minded anglers who desire continued quality fishing practice catch-and-release fishing.

Texas Freshwater Fisheries Center

The Texas Freshwater Fisheries Center in Athens, about 75 miles southeast of Dallas, is an $18-million hatchery and educational center, where visitors can learn about underwater life.

The interactive Visitors Center includes aquarium displays of fish in their natural environment. Visitors get an "eye-to-eye" view of three authentically designed Texas freshwater habitats: a Hill Country stream, an East Texas pond, and a reservoir. A marsh exhibit features live American alligators.

2021–2022 Wildlife Game Harvest

Game	Hunters	Harvest Estimates
Dove, combined*	269,954	5,144,658
Duck	87,685	908,185
Gallinule	575	2300
Goose	22,137	93,722
Pheasant	4,600	13,800
Quail, combined**	41,687	420,600
Rabbit	22,712	111,834
Rail	287	n/a
Snipe	2,012	8,625
Squirrel	56,923	408,813
Teal	23,574	253,567
Turkey (fall and spring)	95,763	31,670
Woodcock	2,300	8,625
White-tailed Deer	756,172	827,928
Mule Deer	29,673	9,658
Javalina	36,691	28,192

*Dove, combined includes the following species: Eurasian, mourning, white-tipped, and white-winged.
**Quail, combined includes the following species: bobwhite and scaled.

Source: TPWD Game Harvest Surveys

A casting pond stocked with rainbow trout in the winter and catfish year-round provides a place for visitors to learn how to bait a hook, cast a line, and land a fish. The center has conference facilities and hosts groups by appointment.

The Texas Freshwater Fisheries Center is open Tuesday through Saturday, 9 a.m. to 4 p.m., and Sunday, 1 p.m. to 4 p.m. It is closed on Monday. Admission is charged. The center is located 4.5 miles east of Athens on FM 2495 at Lake Athens. Address: 5550 FM 2495, Athens 75752, or call (903) 676-2277. For more information, visit: **tpwd.texas.gov/spdest/visitorcenters/tffc/**.

Saltwater Fishing

According to the most recent report available, Texas has about 672,000 saltwater anglers (16 years old and older) who spend an estimated $1.1 billion annually on fishing-related expenditures. In 2013, anglers harvested 1.74 million fish from both Texas bays and the Gulf of Mexico off Texas.

The most popular saltwater sport fish in Texas bays are **spotted seatrout, sand seatrout, Atlantic croaker, red drum, southern flounder, black drum, sheepshead, and gafftopsail catfish**.

Offshore, some of the fish that anglers target are **red snapper, king mackerel, Spanish mackerel, dolphinfish, cobia, tarpon, and yellowfin tuna.** ☆

For information about commercial fishing, see page 641 in the Business chapter.

SPORTS

SPECIAL THANKS TO HERITAGE AUCTIONS
FOR SPONSORING THIS CHAPTER OF THE TEXAS ALMANAC

TEXAS TRIBUNE REPORTS: SPORTS

by Ayan Mittra, Senior Managing Editor

THE TEXAS TRIBUNE

The Houston Astros won their second Major League Baseball World Series title in 2022, defeating the Philadelphia Phillies in six games. Before defeating the Phillies, the Astros scored series victories over the Seattle Mariners and the New York Yankees in claiming the American League title. Rookie shortstop Jeremy Peña was the World Series MVP, becoming the first rookie position player to win such an honor. The Astros previously won the World Series in 2017, a championship that has been overshadowed by MLB determining that the Astros illegally used technology to steal signs from their opponents. Texas' other MLB team, the Texas Rangers, who play in the same division as the Astros — the AL West — finished fourth in the division in 2022 with a 68-94 record.

In other sports:

NFL

The Dallas Cowboys finished second in the NFC East, good enough to advance to the playoffs. After winning their Wild Card game against the Tampa Bay Buccaneers, the Cowboys fell to the San Francisco 49ers in the NFC divisional round, 19-12. The Houston Texans finished 3-13-1, a record that netted them the second pick of the 2023 NFL Draft, which they used to pick quarterback CJ Stroud of Ohio State.

NBA

After reaching the Western Conference Finals in 2022, the Dallas Mavericks suffered a setback in the 2022-23 season, falling to a 38-44 record and failing to make the playoffs. The other two Texas NBA teams, the San Antonio Spurs and the Houston Rockets, finished with identical 22-60 records, falling well short of the playoffs. But their consolation: high picks in the 2023 NBA Draft. The Spurs drafted highly touted prospect Victor Wembanyama with the top pick, while the Rockets drafted Amen Thompson with the 4th pick.

COLLEGE FOOTBALL

A Texas team made it to the national championship game as TCU shattered expectations before falling to NCAA champion Georgia, 65-7. TCU defeated Michigan, 51-45, in the Fiesta Bowl to reach the title game after completing an undefeated regular season and only losing to Kansas State in the Big 12 championship game. The University of Texas at Austin tallied an 8-4 regular season record before losing in the Alamo Bowl to Washington. Texas Tech beat Mississippi, 41-25, to win the Texas Bowl and finish with an 8-5 record. The University of Houston also finished with an 8-5 record, while Baylor and Texas A&M finished under .500.

In 2023, UT-Austin will complete its last season as a member of the Big 12 before joining Texas A&M in the Southeastern Conference for the 2024 season. The teams are slated to renew their rivalry in late 2024 at Kyle Field in College Station.

COLLEGE BASKETBALL

Six Texas teams made it to the NCAA's 2023 Division 1 Men's Basketball tournament, with the University of Texas at Austin making it to the Elite Eight. UT-Austin defeated Colgate, Penn State, and Xavier before falling to the University of Miami, which had defeated the University of Houston in its previous game. TCU and Baylor both lost in the second round, with the Horned Frogs losing to Gonzaga and the Bears falling to Creighton. Texas A&M lost in the first round to Penn State, while Texas A&M-Corpus Christi lost in the first round to Alabama.

GOLF

Scottie Scheffler, a Dallas native and a former University of Texas at Austin student, won the 2022 Masters and finished as the top-ranked PGA golfer for the 2021–22 season. Fellow Longhorn Jordan Spieth finished in the top 15 of the rankings.

SOCCER

In only its second season, Austin FC made it to the Western Conference Finals, losing to eventual MLS Cup champion Los Angeles FC, 3-0. Austin FC finished its regular season with 16 wins, 10 losses, and 8 draws. Before losing to LAFC, Austin FC posted a 2-1 over in-state rivals FC Dallas, who finished the regular season with 14 wins, 9 losses, and 11 draws. Texas' other MLS team, the Houston Dynamo, failed to reach the playoffs after finishing with 10 wins, 18 losses, and 6 draws.

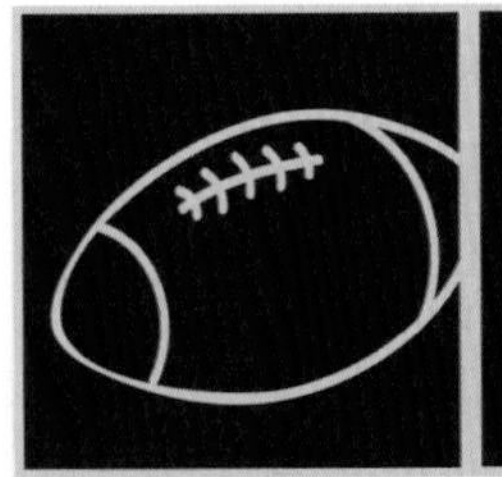

STATE: High School Championships

Sources: The University Interscholastic League at uil.utexas.edu; the Texas Association of Private and Parochial Schools; the Southwest Preparatory Conference; and the Dallas Morning News.

The University Interscholastic League (UIL), which governs literary and athletic competition among public schools in Texas, was organized in 1910 as a division of the University of Texas extension service. Initially, it sponsored forensic competition. By 1920, the UIL organized the structure of the high school football game in response to the growing popularity of the sport in Texas.

The Texas Association of Private and Parochial Schools (TAPPS) is the largest group of private schools in the state with more than 225 member institutions. The interscholastic competition began in 1978 and was significantly expanded when the Texas Christian Interscholastic League ceased to exist in 2000 and many of those schools moved into TAPPS.

The Southwest Preparatory Conference (SPC), established in 1952, is an athletic conference of certain private schools in Oklahoma and Texas.

Not represented are the TAIAO (Texas Association of Independent Athletic Organizations), TCAL (Texas Christian Athletic League), or TCSAAL (Texas Charter School Academic & Athletic League).

Listed are state champions and the game scores. ☆

Football

Year	Conference	Division	Champion	Runner Up
2022-2023	UIL	1A Division I	Westbrook 69	Abbott 24
		1A Division II	Benjamin 68	Loraine 20
		2A Division I	Hawley 54	Refugio 28
		2A Division II	Albany 41	Mart 21
		3A Division I	Franklin 17	Brock 14
		3A Division II	Gunter 42	Poth 7
		4A Division I	China Spring 24	Boerne 21
		4A Division II	Carthage 42	Wimberley 0
		5A Division I	Aledo 52	College Station 14
		5A Division II	South Oak Cliff 34	Port Neches-Groves 24
		6A Division I	Duncanville 28	North Shore 21
		6A Division II	DeSoto 42	Vandegrift 17
	TAPPS	Division I	Logos Preparatory (Sugar Land) 54	Hill Country Christian (Austin) 52
		Division II	Covenant Classical (Fort Worth) 68	First Baptist Christian (Pasadena) 30
		Division III	Christian Heritage Classical (Longview) 36	Bracken Christian (Bulverde) 20
	SPC	3A Division	John Cooper (The Woodlands) 63	Trinity Valley (Fort Worth) 31
		4A Division	Kinkaid (Houston) 17	Houston Episcopal 6
2021-2022	UIL	1A Division I	Westbrook 72	May 66
		1A Division II	Strawn 73	Motley County (Matador) 28
		2A Division I	Shiner 47	Hawley 12
		2A Division II	Stratford 39	Falls City 27
		3A Division I	Lorena 35	Brock 18
		3A Division II	Franklin 49	Gunter 35
		4A Division I	Stephenville 38	LBJ Early College (Austin) 21
		4A Division II	China Spring 31	Gilmer 7
		5A Division I	Katy Paetow 27 (OT)	College Station 24
		5A Division II	South Oak Cliff (Dallas) 23	Liberty Hill 14
		6A Division I	Galena Park North Shore 17	Duncanville 10
		6A Division II	Austin Westlake 40	Denton Guyer 21
	TAPPS	**6-Man Football**		
		Division I	The Emery/Weiner School 69	San Marcos Academy 24
		Division II	Live Oak Classical 46	Faith Academy of Marble Falls 41
		Division III	Covenant Classical (Fort Worth) 68	Bracken Christian 66
		11-Man Football		
		Division I	Parish Episcopal 56	Midland Christian 17
		Division II	Dallas Christian 33	Second Baptist (Houston) 14
		Division III	Cypress Christian (Houston) 16	Trinity Christian (Lubbock) 7
		Division IV	St. Paul Catholic (Shiner) 36	Sacred Heart Catholic (Muenster) 8
	SPC	3A Division	John Cooper (The Woodlands) 49	Cistercian (Irving) 28
		4A Division	Kinkaid (Houston) 42	Episcopal School of Dallas 17

Volleyball

Year	Conference	Division	Champion	Runner Up
2022-2023	UIL	1A	Blum 3	D'Hanis 0
		2A	Windthorst 3	Lindsay 2
		3A	Gunter 3	Bushland 0
		4A	Canyon Randall 3	Aubrey 0
		5A	Colleyville Heritage 3	Frisco Reedy 1
		6A	Dripping Springs 3	Katy Tompkins 0
	TAPPS	1A	Christ Academy (Wichita Falls) 3	Prestonwood Christian North (Prosper) 0
		2A	Ovilla Christian School (Red Oak) 3	Nazarene Christian Academy (Crowley) 0
		3A	Dallas Lutheran School 3	Lubbock Christian School 1
		4A	Grace Prep Academy (Arlington) 3	Prince of Peace Christian (Carrollton) 1
		5A	Liberty Christian School (Argyle) 3	St. Michael's Catholic Academy (Austin) 0
		6A	Prestonwood Christian Academy (Plano) 3	Parish Episcopal School (Dallas) 0
	SPC	3A	Trinity Valley (Fort Worth) 3	Oakridge (Arlington) 1
		4A	Episcopal (Houston) 3	The Hockaday School (Dallas) 0
2021-2022	UIL	1A	Fayetteville 3	Blum 0
		2A	Beckville 3	Thrall 0
		3A	Bushland 3	Gunter 1
		4A	Decatur 3	Celina 0
		5A	Lovejoy (Lucas) 3	Grapevine 0
		6A	Northside Brandeis 3	Keller 2
	TAPPS	1A	Christ Academy (Wichita Falls) 3	Cornerstone Christian (San Angelo) 0
		2A	All Saints Episcopal (Lubbock) 3	St. Joseph (Bryan) 0
		3A	Round Rock Christian 3	Midland Classical 1
		4A	John Paul II (Schertz) 3	Pantego Christian 2
		5A	Fort Bend Christian 3	Prince of Peace Christian (Carrollton) 0
		6A	St. Agnes Academy (Houston) 3	Prestonwood Christian 1
	SPC	N/A	The Hockaday School (Dallas) 3	The Oakridge School (Arlington) 0
2020-2021	UIL	1A	Neches 3	Blum 0
		2A	Iola 3	Crawford 1
		3A	Bushland 3	Goliad 0
		4A	Decatur 3	Wimberley 0
		5A	Lucas Lovejoy 3	Lamar Fulshear 0
		6A	Katy Seven Lakes 3	Klein 1
	TAPPS	1A	Wichita Falls Christ Academy 3	San Antonio The Atonement 0
		2A	Red Oak Ovilla Christian 3	Bulverde Bracken Christian 0
		3A	New Braunfels Christian 3	Midland Classical 0
		4A	Houston Northland Christian 3	Fort Worth Lake Country Christian 1
		5A	Victoria St. Joseph 3	Carrollton Prince of Peace 0
		6A	Argyle Liberty Christian 3	Houston St. Agnes 2

Boys Basketball

Year	Conference	Division	Champion	Runner Up
2022-2023	UIL	1A	Graford 49 (OT)	Jayton 44
		2A	Lipan 50	La Rue La Poynor 46
		3A	Hitchcock 68	Childress 45
		4A	Faith Family Academy (Oak Cliff) 70	Washington (Houston) 56
		5A	Kimball (Dallas) 69	Ellison (Killeen) 48
		6A	Lake Highlands (Richardson) 55	Beaumont United 44
	TAPPS	1A	Kingdom Collegiate (DeSoto) 64	Covenant Academy (Cypress) 37
		2A	Grace Christian Academy (Houston) 64	Bethesda Christian School (Fort Worth) 52
		3A	Lubbock Christian School 55	St. Francis Episcopal School (Houston) 51
		4A	Trinity Christian School (Lubbock) 69	St. Thomas's Episcopal School (Houston)
		5A	TMI Episcopal (San Antonio) 54	St. Michael's Catholic (Austin) 46
		6A	Prestonwood Christian (Plano) 71	John Paul II (Plano) 63
	SPC	3A	Casady (Oklahoma City, OK) 74	The Oakridge School (Arlington) 60
		4A	Houston Christian 81	Episcopal (Bellaire) 78
2021-2022	UIL	1A	Graford 42	Texline 39
		2A	Clarendon 65	Lipan 51
		3A	Madison (Dallas) 53	Cole (San Antonio) 51
		4A	Faith Family (Oak Cliff) 76	Wichita Falls Hirschi 50
		5A	Beaumont United 62	Timberview (Mansfield) 57
		6A	Duncanville 69	McKinney 49
	TAPPS	1A	Christ Academy (Wichita Falls) 67	Robert M. Beren (Houston) 45
		2A	Grace Christian (Houston) 89	Fort Worth Covenant Classical 35
		3A	Hill Country Christian (Austin) 47	Akiba Yavneh Academy of Dallas 40
		4A	Grace Prep (Arlington) 58	John Paul II Catholic (Schertz) 47
		5A	McKinney Christian 56	TMI Episcopal (San Antonio) 51
		6A	John Paul II (Plano) 66	Tomball Concordia Lutheran 56
	SPC	N/A	Houston Episcopal 56	Addison Greenhill 55
2020-2021	UIL	Canceled due to COVID-19 pandemic.		
	TAPPS	1A	Longview Trinity School of Texas 50	Houston Robert M. Beren 33
		2A	Huntsville Alpha Omega 43	Lubbock All Saints Episcopal 38
		3A	Dallas Yavneh 50	Tomball Rosehill Christian 35
		4A	The Woodlands Christian 68	Colleyville Covenant Christian 50
		5A	Frisco Legacy Christian 62	Houston Westbury Christian 59
		6A	Plano John Paul II 51	San Antonio Antonian College Prep 48

Girls Basketball

Year	Conference	Division	Champion	Runner Up
2022-2023	UIL	1A	Nazareth 30	Huckabay 20
		2A	Lipan 53	Gruver 48
		3A	Holliday 58	Fairfield 47
		4A	Waco La Vega 46	Sunnyvale 38
		5A	Frisco Liberty 57	Lubbock Cooper 52
		6A	Northside Clark 42	DeSoto 37
	TAPPS	1A	Harvest Christian Academy (Edinburg) 81	Prestonwood Christian North (Prosper) 25
		2A	Sacred Heart Catholic (Hallettsville) 59	All Saints Episcopal School (Lubbock) 37
		3A	Lubbock Christian School 57	Rosehill Christian School (Tomball) 52
		4A	Dallas Christian School (Mesquite) 41	Geneva School of Boerne 27
		5A	Liberty Christian School (Argyle) 46	Second Baptist School (Houston) 34
		6A	John Paul II (Plano) 65	Bishop Lynch HS (Dallas) 48
	SPC	3A	St. Andrew's (Austin) 55	Trinity Valley (Fort Worth) 34
		4A	Houston Christian 71	Episcopal (Bellaire) 60
2021-2022	UIL	1A	Ackerly Sands 60	Robert Lee 33
		2A	Gruver 50	Stamford 38
		3A	Fairfield 60	Winnsboro 52
		4A	Brownsboro 50	Hardin-Jefferson 49
		5A	Cedar Park 45 (2OT)	Frisco Memorial (40)
		6A	DeSoto 40	South Grand Prairie 23
	TAPPS	1A	Christ Academy (Wichita Falls) 31	Cornerstone (San Angelo) 25
		2A	St. Paul Catholic (Shiner) 31	Bethesda Christian (Fort Worth) 26
		3A	Lutheran High North (Houston) 63	North Dallas Adventist Academy 37
		4A	Lubbock Christian 74	Legacy Prep Christian (The Woodlands) 49
		5A	Dallas Christian 47	Second Baptist (Houston) 41
		6A	John Paul II (Plano) 68	Antonian College Prep (San Antonio) 57
	SPC	N/A	Houston Christian 87	Houston Episcopal High School 43

Boys Soccer

Year	Conference	Division	Champion	Runner Up
2022-2023	UIL	4A	Early College (Hidalgo) 3	Palestine 0
		5A	Lone Star (Frisco) 4	Bel Air (El Paso) 1
		6A	Seven Lakes (Katy) 2	Dripping Springs 1
	TAPPS	Fall 2022	Alcuin School (Dallas) 2	Chinquapin Highlands 0
		Division I	Prestonwood Christian Academy (Plano) 2	Antonian College Prep (San Antonio) 0
		Division II	Legacy Christian Academy (Frisco) 2	St. Joseph Academy (Brownsville) 0
		Division III	Prince of Peace Christian (Carrollton) 3	The Covenant School (Dallas) 1
	SPC	Division II	Cistercian (Irving) 2 (OT)	Casady (Oklahoma City, OK) 1
		Division III	Episcopal (Bellaire) 1	Kincaid (Houston) 0

Year	Conference	Division	Champion	Runner Up
2021-2022	UIL	4A	Boerne 2 (OT)	Celina 1
		5A	Frisco Wakeland 3	Dripping Springs 0
		6A	Austin Lake Travis 1 (4-3 SO)	Plano 0
	TAPPS	Fall 2021	Dallas International 3	Dallas Yavneh 1
		Division I	The Village (Houston) 2	Fort Worth Nolan 0
		Division II	Prince of Peace (Carrollton) 1	Spring Frassati 0
		Division III	Covenant Christian (Colleyville) 5	Houston Cypress 3
	SPC	N/A	Houston The Kinkaid School 1	Oklahoma City, OK Casady School 0

Girls Soccer

Year	Conference	Division	Champion	Runner Up
2022-2023	UIL	4A	Celina 8	Stephenville 1
		5A	Grapevine 1	Frisco 0
		6A	Marcus (Lewisville) 2	Ridge Point (Missouri City) 0
	TAPPS	Division I	Ursuline Academy (Dallas) 5	John Paul II (Plano) 1
		Division II	Faith Christian (Grapevine) 2	St. John XXIII College Prep (Katy) 1
		Division III	The Covenant School (Dallas) 4	John Paul II Catholic (Schertz) 1
	SPC	3A	Trinity Valley (Fort Worth) 1	Country Day (Fort Worth) 0
		4A	Hockaday (Dallas) 2	St. John's (Houston) 1
2021-2022	UIL	4A	Celina 5 (5-3 SO)	Midlothian Heritage 4
		5A	Wakeland (Frisco) 3 (OT)	Grapevine 2
		6A	Southlake Carroll 4	Rockwall 0
	TAPPS	Division I	John Paul II (Plano) 2	St. Pius X (Houston) 0
		Division II	Grapevine Faith 2 (OT)	St. Michael's (Austin) 1
		Division III	John Paul II (Schertz) 2	The Covenant School (Dallas) 0
	SPC	N/A	The Hockaday School (Dallas) 2	St. John's School (Houston) 1

Baseball

Year	Conference	Division	Champion	Runner Up
2022-2023	UIL	1A	Abbott 6	Fayetteville 5
		2A	Harleton 10	Shiner 5 (5 innings)
		3A	Boyd 6	Wall 4
		4A	China Spring 3	Texarkana Liberty-Eylau 2 (12 innings)
		5A	Magnolia West 3	Argyle 2
		6A	Flower Mound (Lewisville) 6	Pearland 4 (6 innings)
	TAPPS	Division I	Trinity Christian (Addison) 7	St. Thomas (Houston) 6
		Division II	Monsignor Kelly Catholic (Beaumont) 4	Midland Christian 2
		Division III	Cypress Christian (Houston) 10	McKinney Christian 7
		Division IV	Temple Christian (Fort Worth) 6	Northland Christian (Houston) 5
		Division V	Ovilla Christian (Red Oak) 11	Sacred Heart Catholic (Hallettsville) 6
	SPC	N/A	Trinity Valley School (Fort Worth) 10	The Oakridge School (Arlington) 1

For track, tennis, and other high school sports champions, see **page 589** in the Education section.

Year	Conference	Division	Champion	Runner Up
2021-2022	UIL	1A	D'Hanis 4	Nazareth 0
		2A	Valley Mills 4	Shiner 2
		3A	London (Corpus Christi) 16	Brock 13
		4A	Sinton 9	Argyle 0
		5A	Georgetown 2	Friendswood 2
		6A	Carroll (Southlake) 8	Reagan (San Antonio) 5
	TAPPS	Division I	Prestonwood Christian Academy (Plano) 5	Central Catholic (San Antonio) 0
		Division II	Second Baptist (Houston) 11	The Brook Hill School (Bullard) 5
		Division III	Bay Area Christian (League City) 5	Lake Country Christian (Fort Worth) 2
		Division IV	Midland Classical Academy 13	Central Texas Christian School (Temple) 6
		Division V	Weatherford Christian 3	St. Paul Catholic School (Shiner) 2
	SPC	N/A	The Kinkaid School (Houston) 5	Episcopal High School (Houston) 3

Softball

Year	Conference	Division	Champion	Runner Up
2022-2023	UIL	1A	Hermleigh 9	D'Hanis 0
		2A	Weimar 4	Como-Pickton 3
		3A	Coahoma 4	Santa Gertrudis Academy 2
		4A	Calallen (Corpus Christi) 9	Liberty 7
		5A	Lake Creek (Montgomery) 8	Canyon (Comal) 0
		6A	Pearland 4	Guyer (Denton) 2
	TAPPS	Division I	John Paul II (Plano) 11	Antonian College Prep (San Antonio) 10
		Division II	Legacy Christian (Frisco) 9	Hyde Park (Austin) 6
		Division III	Cypress Christian (Houston) 5	The Brook Hill School (Bullard) 1
		Division IV	St. Paul Catholic (Shiner) 12	Lubbock Christian (2)
	SPC	3A	Fort Worth Country Day 11	John Cooper (The Woodlands) 1 (5 innings)
		4A	Episcopal High School (Houston) 13	St. John's School (Houston) 0
2021-2022	UIL	1A	D'Hanis 6	Hermleigh 2
		2A	Crawford 3	Lovelady 0
		3A	Hallettsville 6	Coahoma 5
		4A	Liberty 5	Sweeny 0
		5A	Lake Creek 7	Georgetown 0
		6A	Northside O'Connor 7	Lake Ridge 6
	TAPPS	Division I	Antonian College Prep (San Antonio) 18	Bishop Lynch (Dallas) 3
		Division II	Legacy Christian Academy (Frisco) 3	Fort Bend Christian (Sugar Land) 1
		Division III	Holy Cross of San Antonio 4	Lubbock Trinity Christian 0
		Division IV	St. Paul Catholic (Shiner) 17	Ovilla Christian 4
	SPC	N/A	Episcopal (Houston) 7	St. John's School (Houston) 3

Texas College Sports NCAA Champions

Source: National Collegiate Athletic Association, College Football Playoff (collegefootballplayoff.com), and ESPN.

The National Collegiate Athletic Association is a member-led organization dedicated to college athletes and is considered the premier organization for college sports. There are three divisions in the NCAA, only two of which are represented by Texas colleges: Division I and Division II.

Displayed are season champions, conference tournament champions, and the entrants in national championships.

NCAA Division I

Big 12 Conference Champions

The Texas schools in the Big 12 are the University of Texas at Austin (UT, Texas), Texas Tech University (TTU, Texas Tech), Texas Christian University (TCU, Texas Christian), University of Houston (UH, Houston), and Baylor University (BU, Baylor). The University of Houston joined in 2023.

Other schools in the Big 12 are Brigham Young University (BYU), the University of Central Florida (UCF), University of Cincinnati (UC, Cincinnati), University of Kansas (KU, Kansas), Kansas State University (Kansas State, K-State), the University of Oklahoma (OU, Oklahoma), Oklahoma State University (OSU, Oklahoma State), Iowa State University (ISU, Iowa State), and West Virginia University (WVU, West Virginia).

Football

Year	Season	Championship	College Football Playoff
2022	Texas Christian	Texas Christian	Texas Christian lost to the University of Georgia in the CFP playoff game 65-7.
2021	Baylor	Baylor	No Big 12 Texas teams advanced to the College Football Playoff.

Men's Basketball

Year	Season	Tournament	NCAA Division II Men's Basketball Championship
2022	Kansas, Baylor	Kansas	Texas Tech lost to Duke University 78-73 in Sweet Sixteen of national championship.
			TCU lost to University of Arizona 85-80 in second round of national championship.
			Texas lost to Purdue University 81-71 in second round of national championship.
2021	Baylor	University of Texas	Baylor beat Gonzaga 86-70 to win national championship.
			Texas Tech lost to University of Arkansas 68-66 in second round of national championship.
			University of Texas lost to Abilene Christian 53-52 in first round of national championship.

Women's Basketball

Year	Season	Tournament	NCAA Division II Women's Basketball Championship
2022	Baylor	Texas	Texas lost to Stanford 59-50 in Elite Eight of national championship.
			Baylor lost to South Dakota 61-47 in round two of national championship.
2021	Baylor	Baylor	Baylor lost to University of Connecticut 69-67 in Elite Eight of national championship.
			University of Texas lost to South Carolina 62-34 in Elite Eight of national championship.

Baseball

Year	Season	Tournament	Postseason
2023	Texas, Oklahoma State, West Virginia	Texas Christian	Texas Christian University lost to Florida in Men's College World Series.
			Texas lost to Stanford in Super Regionals of national championship.
			Texas Tech lost to Florida in regional finals of national championship.
2022	Texas Christian	Oklahoma	Texas lost to Texas A&M in first game of elimination bracket in Men's College World Series.
			TCU lost to Texas A&M in regional finals of national championship.
			Texas Tech lost to Notre Dame in regional finals of national championship.

Softball

Year	Season	Tournament	Postseason
2023	University of Oklahoma	University of Oklahoma	Texas lost to Tennessee in Knoxville Super Regional 2-0 of national championship.
			Baylor lost to Ole Miss in Salt Lake City Regional elimination bracket of national championship.
2022	University of Oklahoma	Oklahoma State	Texas lost to Oklahoma 2-0 in the finals of the Women's College World Series.

Southeastern Conference Champions

Texas A&M University joined the Southeastern Conference in 2012 and competes in the West Division against Louisiana State University (LSU), the University of Arkansas (U of A, Arkansas), the University of Mississippi (Ole Miss), Mississippi State University (MSU, Mississippi State), the University of Alabama (UA, Bama), and Auburn University (AU, Auburn).

Schools in the East Division are the University of Missouri, the University of Kentucky (UK, Kentucky), Vanderbilt University (Vandy, Vanderbilt), the University of Tennessee (UT, Tennessee), the University of Georgia (UGA, Georgia), the University of South Carolina (USC, South Carolina), the University of Missouri (MU, Mizzou, Missouri) and the University of Florida (UF, Florida).

Football

Year	Division	Season	Championship	College Football Playoff
2022	East	Georgia	Georgia	Texas A&M did not advance to postseason.
	West	Louisiana State		
2021	East	Georgia	Alabama	Texas A&M did not advance to postseason.
	West	Alabama		

Men's Basketball

Year	Season	Tournament	Postseason
2022	Auburn	Tennessee	Texas A&M lost to Pennsylvania State 76-59 in first round of national championship.
2021	Alabama	Alabama	Texas A&M did not advance to postseason.

Women's Basketball

Year	Season	Tournament	Postseason
2022	South Carolina	Kentucky	Texas A&M did not advance to postseason.
2021	Texas A&M	South Carolina	Texas A&M lost to Arizona 74-59 in Sweet Sixteen of national championship.

Baseball

Year	Division	Season	Tournament	Postseason
2023	East	Florida	Tennessee	Texas A&M lost to Stanford in Stanford Regional finals.
	West	Arkansas		
2022	East	Tennessee	Tennessee	Texas A&M lost to Oklahoma in winners' bracket of the Men's College World Series.
	West	Texas A&M		

Softball

Year	Season	Tournament	NCAA Division I Softball Championship
2023	Tennessee	Tennessee	Texas A&M lost to University of Texas in Austin Regional finals.
2022	Arkansas	Arkansas	Texas A&M lost to Oklahoma in Regional.

How National Championships Work

Teams progress differently through NCAA national championships depending on the conference, division, and sport.

Entering Tournaments

Most conferences stage tournaments for their teams at the end of a season. Winning teams get an automatic entry into the NCAA tournament.

Teams can also qualify by being selected for national tournaments by a panel of NCAA judges.

Eliminating Teams

In football and basketball, teams use a single-elimination bracket—one loss, and the team is out.

Baseball and softball use best-of-three games and double-elimination brackets. Double-elimination brackets consist of a winner's bracket, an elimination bracket, and the finals; two losses, and the team is out.

Football Championships

When it comes to football, each conference tackles the national championship in a different way. Schools in the American Athletic, Big 12, Conference-USA, Southeastern, and Sun Belt conferences play in the NCAA Division I Football Bowl Division. A 13-member committee votes on which four teams enter the College Football Playoff semifinals, which rotate annually between the six most important bowl games: the Cotton, Fiesta, Orange, Peach, Rose, and Sugar bowls.

The Southland and Western Athletic Conferences play in the NCAA Division I Football Championship

American Athletic Conference Champions

The 2013-14 season was the first for the AAC after the breakup of the Big East Conference. Texas schools in the AAC are:

- Southern Methodist University
- University of Houston

The University of Houston left the AAC for the Big 12 in the summer of 2023.

Other schools in the conference are the University of Memphis, University of Cincinnati, University of Central Florida, East Carolina University, Temple University, University of South Florida, Tulane University, University of Tulsa, the University of Connecticut, and Wichita State University.

Football

Year	Season	Championship	College Football Playoff
2022	Tulane	Tulane	Neither AAC Texas team entered the College Football Playoff.
2021	Cincinnati, Houston	Cincinnati	Neither AAC Texas team entered the College Football Playoff.

Men's Basketball

Year	Season	Tournament	Postseason
2022	Houston	Houston	Houston lost to Villanova 50-44 in Elite Eight of national championship. Southern Methodist lost to Washington State 75-63 in second round of National Invitation Tournament.
2021	Wichita State	Houston	Houston lost to Baylor 78-59 in Elite Eight.

Women's Basketball

Year	Season	Tournament	Postseason
2022	University of Central Florida	University of Central Florida	Houston lost to Alabama 79-64 in third round of Women's National Invitation Tournament.
2021	South Florida	South Florida	Houston beat Arizona State 50-48 in the Women's National Invitation Tournament Fort Worth Region Consolation Final.

Baseball

Year	Season	Tournament	Postseason
2022	East Carolina	East Carolina	Neither AAC Texas team advanced to the NCAA Division I Baseball Tournament.
2021	East Carolina	South Florida	Neither AAC Texas team advanced to the NCAA Division I Baseball Tournament.

Softball

Year	Season	Tournament	NCAA Division I Softball Championship
2023	East Carolina	Tulane	Neither AAC Texas team advanced to the NCAA Division I Softball Tournament.
2022	East Carolina	East Carolina	Neither AAC Texas team advanced to the NCAA Division I Softball Tournament.

Subdivision, a single-elimination bracket tournament. However, they have no championship games for their football programs, and so rely on being voted in.

Southwestern Athletic Conference schools are eligible for the Football Championship Subdivision championship playoffs, but opt out in favor of the Celebration Bowl.

Baseball and Softball Championships

In baseball and softball, teams progress through the NCAA Divisions I, II, and III Baseball and Softball Championships, referred to here as "national championship." The baseball and softball tournaments are separated into Regionals (double-elimination, with a Winner's Bracket and an elimination bracket, followed by the regional finals), Super Regionals (best of three), and Finals (double elimination in bracket play, then best-of-three for championship title). Division I Regionals and Super Regionals are appended with the locations where the games are played, but omitted here for space.

If Division I baseball and softball teams win the Super Regionals finals, they can progress to the Men's College World Series and Women's College World Series, respectively.

Basketball Championships

In basketball, the terms used for the national championship are, in order of accession: the First Four, first round, second round or "Round of 32," Sweet Sixteen, Elite Eight, and Final Four. Note that the First Four are not part of the first round. To differentiate the NCAA Division I Basketball Championship from the National Invitational Tournaments, which are considered exhibition games and of secondary importance, it is referred to here as "national championship." ☆

C-USA Champions

Texas schools in the West Division of Conference USA in 2023 were:

- Sam Houston State University (SHSU)
- University of Texas at El Paso (UTEP)

Rice University, the University of North Texas (UNT), and the University of Texas at San Antonio (UTSA) left in 2023.

Affiliated Texas universities include Dallas Baptist University (DBU) for baseball; Tarleton State University (TSU) and Texas Christian University (TCU) for beach volleyball; and Stephen F. Austin University (SFA) for bowling.

Other teams in Conference USA are Florida International University (FIU), Jacksonville State University (JSU, Alabama), Liberty University (LU, Virginia), Louisiana Tech University (LA Tech), Middle Tennessee State University (MT), New Mexico State University (NM State), Western Kentucky University (WKU). Kennesaw State University (KSU, Georgia) will join in 2024.

Affiliated non-Texas teams include Tulane University (Louisiana) for beach volleyball and bowling; Florida Atlantic University (FAU), University of Alabama-Birmingham (UAB), and Missouri State (MoState) for beach volleyball; and Arkansas State University (AState), Valparaiso University (Valpo), Vanderbilt (Tennessee), and Youngstown State (Ohio) for bowling.

Football

Year	Division	Season	Championship	College Football Playoff
2022	—	University of Texas at San Antonio	University of Texas at San Antonio	No C-USA Texas teams advanced to the College Football Playoff.
2021	East	Western Kentucky	University of Texas at San Antonio	No C-USA Texas teams advanced to the College Football Playoff.
	West	University of Texas at San Antonio		

Men's Basketball

Year	Division	Season	Tournament	Postseason
2022	East	Middle Tennessee	University of Ala-bama-Birmingham	North Texas lost to Virginia 71-69 OT in second round of National Invitation Tournament.
	West	University of North Texas		
2021	East	Western Kentucky	North Texas	North Texas lost to Villanova 84-61 in second round of national championship.
	West	Louisiana Tech		

Women's Basketball

Year	Division	Season	Tournament	Postseason
2022	East	Charlotte	Charlotte	North Texas lost to Tulsa 75-62 in first round of Women's National Invitation Tournament.
	West	Louisiana Tech		
2021	East	Middle Tennessee	Middle Tennessee	Rice beat University of Mississippi 71-58 in Women's National Invitation Tournament championship game.
	West	Rice		

Baseball

Year	Division	Season	Tournament	Postseason
2022	—	Dallas Baptist	Charlotte	DBU lost to Oral Roberts in Stillwater Regional finals of national championship.
2022		Southern Miss	Louisiana Tech	Dallas Baptist lost to Air Force in Austin Regional elimination bracket of national championship.
2021	East	Charlotte	Old Dominion	No C-USA Texas teams advanced to the postseason.
	West	LA Tech		

Softball

Year	Division	Season	Tournament	NCAA Division I Softball Championship
2023	—	Charlotte	Middle Tennessee	No C-USA Texas teams advanced to the postseason.
2022	East	West Kentucky University	University of North Texas	The University of North Texas lost to Oklahoma State 2-0 in final game of Stillwater Regional.
	West	Louisiana Tech		

Southwestern Athletic Conference Champions

Texas schools in the Western Division of the Southwestern Athletic Conference in 2021 were:

- Prairie View A&M University
- Texas Southern University

The Prairie View A&M Panthers have been in the conference since its founding in 1920 and the Texas Southern Tigers joined the conference in 1954. Other teams in the SWAC Western Division are Grambling State University (Louisiana), Southern University (Louisiana), and University of Arkansas at Pine Bluff.

Schools in the Eastern Division are Jackson State University (in Mississippi), Mississippi Valley State University, Alcorn State University (in Mississippi), Alabama State University, and Alabama A&M University.

SWAC schools opt to play the Celebration Bowl as opposed to the NCAA Division I Football Championships.

Football

Year	Division	Season	Championship	Celebration Bowl
2022	East	Jackson State	Jackson State	North Carolina Central 41, Jackson State 34
	West	Texas Southern		
2021	East	Jackson State	Jackson State	South Carolina State 31, Jackson State 10
	West	Prairie View A&M		
Spring 2021	East	Alabama A&M	Alabama A&M	Alabama A&M 40, University of Arkansas-Pine Bluff 33
	West	University of Arkansas-Pine Bluff		

Men's Basketball

Year	Season	Tournament	Postseason
2022	Alcorn State	Texas Southern	Texas Southern lost to Kansas 83-56 in first round of national championship.
2021	Prairie View A&M, Jackson State	Texas Southern	Texas Southern lost to Michigan 82-66 in first round of national championship.
2020	Prairie View A&M	Canceled	Canceled due to COVID-19 pandemic.

Women's Basketball

Year	Season	Tournament	Postseason
2022	Jackson State	Jackson State	No SWAC Texas teams advanced to the postseason.
2021	Jackson State	Jackson State	No SWAC Texas teams advanced to the postseason.
2020	Jackson State	Canceled	Canceled due to COVID-19 pandemic.

Baseball

Year	Division	Season	Tournament	Postseason
2023	East	Alabama State	Florida A&M	No SWAC Texas teams advanced to the postseason.
	West	Grambling State		
2022	East	Alabama State	Alabama State	No SWAC Texas teams advanced to the postseason.
	West	Southern (Louisiana)		
2021	East	Jackson State	Texas Southern	Texas Southern lost to Fairfield 6-2 in Austin Regional of the NCAA Division I Baseball Tournament.
	West	Prairie View		

Softball

Year	Division	Season	Tournament	NCAA Division I Softball Championship
2023	East	Alabama State	Prairie View A&M	Prairie View A&M lost to Omaha in elimination bracket of Baton Rouge Regional.
	West	Prairie View A&M		
2022	East	Bethune-Cookman	Prairie View A&M	Prairie View A&M lost to Minnesota 13-1 in the elimination round of the NCAA Division I Norman Regionals (5 innings).
	West	Texas Southern		
2021	East	Jackson State	Alabama State	No SWAC Texas team advanced to the postseason.
	West	Texas Southern		

Sun Belt Conference Champions

In 2013, Texas State University (TXST) and the University of Texas at Arlington (UTA) joined the Sun Belt Conference. UTA left in 2022.

Other schools in the conference are the Appalachian State University (App State, North Carolina), Arkansas State University (AState), Coastal Carolina University (CCU, South Carolina), Georgia Southern University (GS), Georgia State University (GSU), James Madison University (JMU), Marshall University (MU, West Virginia), Old Dominion University (ODU, Virginia), University of Louisiana at Lafayette (UL), University of Louisiana Monroe (ULM), University of South Alabama (USA), University of Southern Mississippi (Southern Miss), and Troy University (Alabama).

Football

Year	Division	Season	Championship	College Football Playoff
2022	East	Coastal Carolina	Troy	No SBC teams advanced to the College Football Playoff.
	West	Troy		
2021	East	App State	Louisiana	No SBC teams advanced to the College Football Playoff.
	West	Louisiana		

Men's Basketball

Year	Division	Season	Tournament	Postseason
2022	—	Texas State	Georgia State	TXST lost to UNT 67-63 (OT) in the National Invitation Tournament.
2021	East	Georgia State	Appalachian State	No SBC Texas teams advanced to the postseason.
	West	Texas State		

Women's Basketball

Year	Division	Season	Tournament	NCAA Division I Women's Basketball Championship
2022	—	Troy	University of Texas at Arlington	University of Texas at Arlington lost to Iowa State 78-71 in first round of national championship.
2021	East	Troy	Troy	No SBC Texas teams advanced to the postseason.
	West	Louisiana-Lafayette		

Baseball

Year	Season	Tournament	NCAA Division I Baseball Championship
2023	Coastal Carolina	Southern Miss	No SBC Texas teams advanced to the postseason.
2022	Texas State	Louisiana	Texas State lost to Stanford in the Stanford Regional finals.

Softball

Year	Season	Tournament	NCAA Division I Softball Championship
2022	Louisiana	Louisiana	Texas State lost to Texas A&M in the elimination bracket of the Austin Regional.
2022	Louisiana	Louisiana	No SBC Texas teams advanced to the postseason.

Other Post-Season Tournaments

More than one team from a conference can advance to the NCAA national championships.

If a team does not advance, there are other post-season tournaments they can attend.

NCAA Tournaments

Sometimes, if a team misses an NCAA playoff berth, it might be chosen for the NCAA's invitational tournaments.

In basketball, these are the National Invitational Tournament (NIT, for men's teams), and the Women's National Invitational Tournament (WNIT).

Non-NCAA Tournaments

In basketball, there are four non-NCAA post-season championships for teams that do not make either the national tournament or the invitational tournament: the College Basketball Invitational and the Women's College Basketball Invitational, both hosted by The Gazelle Group, and the Basketball Classic and the Women's Basketball Classic, which are hosted by Eracism and the National Association of Basketball Coaches.

Softball teams can be invited to National Invitational Softball Championship, a tournament sponsored by Triple Crown Sports and the National Fastpitch Coaches Association. ☆

Southland Conference Champions

Texas schools in the Southland Conference in 2023:

- Houston Baptist University
- Texas A&M University–Corpus Christi
- University of the Incarnate Word

Abilene Christian, Lamar, Sam Houston State, and Stephen F. Austin left the Southland Conference in 2021.

Other schools are Central Arkansas University, McNeese State University, the University of New Orleans, Nicholls State University, Northwestern State University, and Southeastern Louisiana University. McNeese, Nicholls, and Northwestern are all in Louisiana

Football

Year	Season	NCAA Division I Football Championship
2022	Southeastern Louisiana, University of the Incarnate Word	University of the Incarnate Word lost to North Dakota State 35-32 in NCAA Division I Football Championship semifinals.
2021	University of the Incarnate Word	University of the Incarnate Word lost to Sam Houston 49-42 in second round of NCAA Division I Football Championship.
2020	Sam Houston	Sam Houston beat South Dakota State 23-21 to win Football Championship.

Men's Basketball

Year	Season	Tournament	NCAA Division I Men's Basketball Championship
2022	Nicholls	University of the Incarnate Word	Texas A&M-Corpus Christi lost to Texas Southern University 76-67 in the First Four.
2021	Nicholls	Abilene Christian	Abilene Christian lost to UCLA 67-47 in second round.
2020	Stephen F. Austin	Canceled	Canceled due to COVID-19 pandemic.

Women's Basketball

Year	Season	Tournament	Postseason
2022	Houston Baptist University	University of the Incarnate Word	University of the Incarnate Word lost to Howard University 55-51 in the First Four of the Women's Basketball Championship.
2021	Stephen F. Austin	Stephen F. Austin	Stephen F. Austin lost to Georgia Tech 54-52 in first round of the Women's Basketball Championship.
2020	Texas A&M-Corpus Christi	Canceled	Canceled due to COVID-19 pandemic.
2019	Lamar	Abilene Christian	Abilene Christian lost to Baylor 95-38 in Basketball Championship first round.
			Stephen F. Austin lost to University of Texas-Arlington 60-54 in Women's National Invitation Tournament first round.
			Lamar lost to South Alabama 73-71 in Women's National Invitation Tournament first round.

Baseball

Year	Season	Tournament	NCAA Division I Baseball Tournament
2023	Nicholls	Nicholls	No SLC Texas teams advanced to the postseason.
2022	McNeese	Southeastern	No SLC Texas teams advanced to the postseason.
2021	Abilene Christian	McNeese	No SLC Texas teams advanced to the postseason.
2020	Canceled	Canceled	Canceled due to COVID-19 pandemic.

Softball

Year	Season	Tournament	NCAA Division I Softball Championship
2023	McNeese	McNeese	No SLC Texas teams advanced to the postseason.
2022	McNeese	McNeese	McNeese lost to Northwestern 10-2 in the Evanston Regional finals of the NCAA Division I Softball Championship.
2021	Stephen F. Austin	McNeese	McNeese lost to LSU 10-2 in Baton Rouge Regional.
2020	Canceled	Canceled	Canceled due to COVID-19 pandemic.

Western Athletic Conference Champions

The Western Athletic Conference was founded in 1962. The University of Texas-Rio Grande Valley (Edinburg) joined in 2013; Tarleton State University (Stephenville) joined in 2020; Abilene Christian University, Lamar University (Beaumont), Sam Houston State University (Huntsville), and Stephen F. Austin State University (Nacogdoches) joined in 2021; the University of Texas at Arlington joined in 2022.

Other schools in the conference are Austin Peay State University (Tennessee), Bellarmine University (Kentucky), California Baptist University, University of Central Arkansas, Eastern Kentucky University, Florida Gulf Coast University, Grand Canyon University (Arizona), Jacksonville University, Lipscomb University (Tennessee), Kennesaw State (Georgia), New Mexico State University, University of North Alabama, University of North Florida, Seattle University (Washington), Southern Utah University, Stetson University (Florida), Queens University Charlotte (North Carolina), Utah Tech, and Utah Valley University.

In 2023, the Western Athletic Conference joined with the ASUN Conference to form the United Athletic Conference.

Football

Year	Season	NCAA Division I Football Championship
2022	Abilene Christian, Stephen F. Austin	No WAC Texas teams advanced to the postseason.
2021	Sam Houston	Sam Houston lost to Montana State 42-19 in quarterfinals.
		Stephen F. Austin lost to University of the Incarnate Word 35-28 in first round.
The WAC did not have a football program between the years of 2013 and 2020.		

Men's Basketball

Year	Season	Tournament	NCAA National Invitational Tournament
2023	Utah Valley	Grand Canyon	Sam Houston lost to North Texas 75-55 in second round of National Invitational Tournament.
2022	NM State, Seattle U, Stephen F. Austin	New Mexico State	No WAC Texas teams advanced to the postseason.
2021	Grand Canyon	Grand Canyon	No WAC Texas teams advanced to the postseason.

Women's Basketball

Year	Season	Tournament	Postseason
2023	Southern Utah	Southern Utah	Stephen F. Austin lost to Arkansas 60-37 in second round of Women's National Invitational Tournament.
2022	Stephen F. Austin	Stephen F. Austin	Stephen F. Austin lost to North Carolina 79-66 in the first round of the NCAA Division I Women's Basketball Championship.
2021	California Baptist	California Baptist	No WAC Texas teams advanced to the postseason.

Baseball

Year	Division	Season	Tournament	NCAA Division I Baseball Tournament
2023	—	Sam Houston	Sam Houston	Sam Houston lost to Oregon St. 3-1 in regional elimination bracket.
2022	West	Grand Canyon	NM State	No WAC Texas teams advanced to the postseason.
	Southwest	Sam Houston		
2021	—	California Baptist, Grand Canyon	Grand Canyon	No WAC Texas teams advanced to the postseason.
2020	—	New Mexico St.	Canceled	Canceled due to COVID-19 pandemic.

Softball

Year	Division	Season	Tournament	NCAA Division I Softball Championship
2023	—	Utah Tech	Grand Canyon	No WAC Texas teams advanced to the postseason.
2022	West	Grand Canyon	Grand Canyon	No WAC Texas teams advanced to the postseason.
	Southwest	Stephen F. Austin		
2021	—	New Mexico St.	Seattle U.	No WAC Texas teams advanced to the postseason.
2020	—	New Mexico St.	Canceled	Canceled due to COVID-19 pandemic.

NCAA Division II

Lone Star Conference Champions

The Lone Star Conference, founded in 1931, has long been the athletic conference for Texas schools in the NCAA second tier of schools, Division II. Texas schools in the conference in 2021 were:

- Angelo State University
- Dallas Baptist University
- Lubbock Christian University
- Midwestern State University
- St. Edward's University
- St. Mary's University
- Texas A&M International University
- Texas A&M University—Commerce
- Texas A&M University—Kingsville
- Texas Woman's University
- University of Texas at Tyler
- University of Texas of the Permian Basin
- West Texas A&M University

Other teams in the conference are Cameron University (Oklahoma), Eastern New Mexico State University, Oklahoma Christian University, Rogers State University (in Oklahoma), University of Arkansas-Fort Smith, and Western New Mexico University. ☆

Football

Year	Season	Title	NCAA Division II Football Championship
2022	Angelo State	Angelo State	Angelo State lost to Colorado School of Mines 42-24 in quarterfinals.
2021	Midwestern State	Midwestern State	Angelo State lost to Colorado School of Mines 34-26 in the quarterfinals.

Men's Basketball

Year	Season	Tournament	NCAA Division II Basketball Championship
2022	Lubbock Christian	West Texas A&M	Lubbock Christian lost to Colorado Mesa 63-62 in the second round.
			Angelo State lost to West Texas A&M 84-76 in the first round.
			Dallas Baptist University lost to Black Hills St. 76-68 in the first round.
			Texas A&M-Commerce lost to Lubbock Christian 80-63 in the first round.
			Texas A&M-Kingsville lost to Colorado Mesa 69-55 in the first round.
			West Texas A&M lost to Black Hills St. 91-77 in the second round.
2021	Lubbock Christian	West Texas A&M	West Texas A&M lost to Northwest Missouri 80-54 in national championship game.
			Lubbock Christian lost to West Texas A&M 101-92 in third round.
			Dallas Baptist lost to West Texas A&M 82-65 in second round.

Women's Basketball

Year	Season	Tournament	NCAA Division II Basketball Championship
2022	West Texas A&M	West Texas A&M	West Texas A&M lost to Glenville St. 103-56 in the Elite Eight.
			Lubbock Christian lost to West Texas A&M 59-54 in the third round.
			Texas Woman's University lost to West Texas A&M 78-73 and Texas A&M-Commerce lost to Lubbock Christian 69-67 in the second round.
2021	Lubbock Christian	Lubbock Christian	Lubbock Christian beat Drury 69-59 to win national championship.
			Texas A&M-Commerce lost to Southwestern Oklahoma 97-79 in regional.

Baseball

Year	Season	Tournament	NCAA Division II Baseball Tournament
2023	Angelo State	Angelo State	Angelo State defeated Rollins 6-5, **winning national championship.**
			UT Tyler lost to Angelo State, St. Edward's lost to Colorado Mesa, and Lubbock Christian lost to St. Edward's in regionals.
2022	Angelo State	Angelo State	Angelo State lost to UT Tyler and West Texas A&M lost to Colorado Mesa in regional elimination brackets.
			Texas A&M-Kingsville lost to Angelo State and St. Edward's lost to Colorado Mesa in regional finals.

Softball

Year	Season	Tournament	NCAA Division II Softball Tournament
2023	Angelo State	UT Tyler	UT Tyler lost to Grand Valley State 2-0 in championship finals.
			West Texas A&M lost to UT Tyler 2-0 in Super Regionals.
2022	UT Tyler	Texas A&M-Commerce	UT Tyler lost to Rogers State 9-3 in finals.
			Texas A&M-Kingsville lost to UT Tyler 6-4 in Super Regionals.
			Texas A&M-Commerce lost to Texas A&M-Kingsville, Lubbock Christian lost to UT Tyler, Angelo State lost to UT Tyler, and St. Mary's lost to Texas A&M Kingsville in regionals.

Football Bowl Games

Sources: ESPN, CBS.

Following are the college football bowl games involving Texas schools, as well as bowl and national championship games held in the state.

2022-2023

Bowl	Winner	Opponent	Date	Place	Stadium
LendingTree Bowl	Southern Miss 38	Rice 24	Dec. 17	Mobile, AL	Hancock Whitney Stadium
New Mexico Bowl	Brigham Young University 24	Southern Methodist University 23	Dec. 17	Albuquerque, NM	University Stadium
Frisco Bowl	Boise State 35	University of North Texas 32	Dec. 17	Frisco	Toyota Stadium
Lockheed Martin Armed Forces Bowl	Air Force 30	Baylor 15	Dec. 22	Fort Worth	Amon G. Carter Stadium
Radiance Technologies Independence Bowl	Houston 23	Louisiana 16	Dec. 23	Shreveport, LA	Independence Stadium
SERVPRO First Responder Bowl	Memphis 38	Utah State 10	Dec. 27	Dallas	Gerald J. Ford Stadium
TaxAct Texas Bowl	Texas Tech 42	Ole Miss 25	Dec. 28	Houston	NRG Stadium
Valero Alamo Bowl	Washington 27	Texas 20	Dec. 29	San Antonio	Alamodome
Tony the Tiger Sun Bowl	Pittsburgh 37	University of California, Los Angeles 35	Dec. 30	El Paso	Sun Bowl Stadium
Fiesta Bowl (Semifinal)	Texas Christian University 51	Michigan 45	Dec. 31	Glendale, AZ	State Farm Stadium
Goodyear Cotton Bowl Classic	Tulane 46	University of Southern California 45	Jan. 2	Arlington	AT&T Stadium
College Football Playoff National Championship	Georgia 65	Texas Christian University 7	Jan. 9	Inglewood, CA	SoFi Stadium

2021-2022

Bowl	Winner	Opponent	Date	Place	Stadium
PUBG Mobile New Mexico Bowl	Fresno State 31	University of Texas at El Paso 24	Dec. 18	Albuquerque, NM	University Stadium
Tropical Smoothie Cafe Frisco Bowl	San Diego State 38	University of Texas at San Antonio 24	Dec. 21	Frisco	Toyota Stadium
Lockheed Martin Armed Forces Bowl	Army 24	Missouri 22	Dec. 22	Fort Worth	Amon G. Carter Stadium
Frisco Football Classic	Miami (OH) 27	University of North Texas 14	Dec. 23	Frisco	Toyota Stadium
SERVPRO First Responder Bowl	Air Force 31	Louisville 28	Dec. 28	Dallas	Gerald J. Ford Stadium
Autozone Liberty Bowl	Texas Tech 34	Mississippi State 7	Dec. 28	Memphis, TN	Liberty Bowl Memorial Stadium
Valero Alamo Bowl	Oklahoma 47	Oregon 32	Dec. 29	San Antonio	Alamodome
Tony the Tiger Sun Bowl	Central Michigan 24	Washington State 21	Dec. 31	El Paso	Sun Bowl Stadium
Goodyear Cotton Bowl Classic (CFP Semifinal)	Alabama 27	Cincinnati 6	Dec. 31	Arlington	AT&T Stadium
Allstate Sugar Bowl	Baylor 21	Ole Miss 7	Jan. 1	New Orleans, LA	Caesars Superdome
TaxAct Texas Bowl	Kansas State 42	Louisiana State University 20	Jan. 4	Houston	NRG Stadium

Major Professional Sports

Sources: ESPN, CBS, team and conference websites.

Major League Baseball

Houston Astros (American League West)

Year	Win	Loss	%	Finish
2022	106	56	0.654	1st in division; **won World Series** against Philadelphia Phillies 4-1 in Game 6.
2021	95	67	0.586	1st in division; lost to Atlanta Braves 4-2 in the World Series.
*2020	29	31	0.483	2nd in division.
*COVID-19 pandemic-shortened season				

Texas Rangers (American League West)

Year	Win	Loss	%	Finish
2022	68	94	0.420	4th in division.
2021	60	102	0.370	5th in division.
2020	22	38	0.414	5th in division.

National Football League (NFL)

Houston Texans (AFC South)

Year	Win	Loss	Tie	%	Finish
2022	3	13	1	0.176	4th in division.
2021	4	13	0	0.235	3rd in division.
2020	4	12	0	0.250	3rd in division.

Dallas Cowboys (NFC East)

Year	Win	Loss	%	Finish
2022	12	5	0.706	1st in division; lost to San Francisco 49ers 19-12 in divisional playoff game.
2021	12	5	0.706	1st in division; lost 23-17 to San Francisco 49ers in wild card round.
2020	6	10	0.375	3rd in division.

National Basketball Association (NBA)

San Antonio Spurs (Southwest)

Year	Win	Loss	%	Finish
2023	22	60	0.268	15th in division; did not advance to playoffs.
2022	34	48	0.415	Lost to New Orleans Pelicans 113-103 in play-in game.
2021	42	30	0.583	Clinched division; lost to LA Clippers 4-3.

Houston Rockets (Southwest)

Year	Win	Loss	%	Finish
2023	22	60	0.268	14th in division; did not advance to playoffs.
2022	20	62	0.244	Did not advance to playoffs.
2021	17	55	0.236	Did not advance to playoffs.

Dallas Mavericks (Southwest)

Year	Win	Loss	%	Finish
2023	38	44	0.463	11th in division; did not advance to playoffs.
2022	52	30	0.634	Lost to Golden State Warriors 4-1 in Western Conference finals.

Women's National Basketball Association (WNBA)

Dallas Wings (Western Conference)

The franchise was founded in 1998 as the Detroit Shock, where it played until 2010. In 2015, it moved to Dallas-Fort Worth from Tulsa. The Wings play in College Park Center at the University of Texas at Arlington.

The WNBA has 12 teams, and its season is played from May to September. The other WNBA team in Texas was the Houston Comets, who were an original franchise when the league was formed in 1997.

The team folded in 2008 when no new owners could be found. ☆

Year	Win	Loss	%	Finish
2021	42	30	0.583	Clinched division; lost to LA Clippers 4-3.

Year	Win	Loss	%	Finish
2022	18	18	0.500	Lost to Connecticut Sun 73-58 in Game 3 of first-round playoff series.
2021	14	18	0.438	Lost to Chicago Sky 81-64 in first round.
2020	8	14	0.364	Did not advance to playoffs.
2019	10	24	0.294	Did not advance to playoffs.

National Hockey League (NHL)

Dallas Stars (Central Division)

Year	Win	Loss	OT* Loss	Finish
2023	47	21	14	8th in league; lost to Vegas Golden Knights 4-2 in conference finals.
2022	46	30	6	5th in league; lost to Calgary Flames 3-2 in first round of playoffs.
2021	23	19	14	Did not advance to playoffs.
2020	37	24	8	Lost to Tampa Bay Lightning 4-2 in Stanley Cup Finals.

*Overtime.

Major League Soccer (MLS)

Austin FC (Western Conference)

Year	Win	Loss	Draw	Finish
2022	16	10	8	2nd in conference; lost to Los Angeles Football Club 3-0 in conference finals.
2021	9	21	4	12th in conference.

FC Dallas (Western Conference)

Year	Win	Loss	Draw	Finish
2022	14	9	11	3rd in conference; lost conference semifinals to Austin FC 2-1.
2021	7	15	12	11th in conference.
2020	9	6	7	6th in conference; lost semifinals to Seattle Sounders 1-0.

Houston Dynamo (Western Conference)

Year	Win	Loss	Draw	Finish
2022	10	18	6	13th in conference
2021	6	16	12	13th in conference
2020	23	4	10	12th in conference

National Women's Soccer League (NWSL)

Houston Dash

Year	Win	Loss	Draw	Finish
2022	10	6	6	4th in league; lost to Kansas City Current 2-1 in NWSL Playoffs quarterfinals.
2021	9	10	5	7th in league.
2020	3	1	0	Season canceled due to COVID-19 pandemic.
2019	7	12	5	7th in league.

Texas Sports Hall of Fame

The Texas Sports Hall of Fame was organized in 1951 by the Texas Sports Writers Association. Each year the honorees are inducted into the Hall of Fame at a gala dinner.

The second such fete in 1952 was headlined by, "That filmland athlete, Ronald Reagan, and his actress wife, Nancy Davis," according to *The Dallas Morning News* on June 9, 1952.

The hall was originally in Grand Prairie in the Dallas-Fort Worth area. The Hall of Fame was closed in 1986 for financial reasons, but in 1991 it was reopened in Waco. In addition to memorabilia, the new location also houses archives.

Under the current selection process, dues-paying members of the Texas Sports Hall of Fame can nominate any number of individuals. (Anyone can become a member.)

The selection committee, chaired by Dave Campbell, founder of *Texas Football Magazine*, reviews all nominees and creates the "Official Voting Membership" ballot. Ballots are then mailed to the voting membership, former Texas Sports Hall of Fame inductees, and the media selection committee.

The results of the balloting are announced in the autumn with the induction banquet following in the winter.

The hall of fame website is at tshof.org. ☆

Year	Inductee	Sport	Texas Connection, Career
2023	Robert Brazile	Football	Houston Oilers; 2-time All-Pro, 7-time Pro Bowl, 1970s All-Decade Team.
	Jose "Cheo" Cruz	Baseball	Houston Astros; led Astros to first-ever division title and postseason appearance; 3rd in National League MVP voting, 1980; led National League in hits.
	Scott Drew	Basketball	Coach; led Baylor men's basketball program to 10 NCAA Tournament appearances, 5 NCAA Tournament Sweet Sixteen appearances, and 2 Big 12 Regular Season Championships.
	Carlette Guidry	Track & Field	Houston native; University of Texas; 23-time All-American, 12-time NCAA National Champion, 17-time SWC Champion, and established 4 school records; Olympian.
	Priest Holmes	Football	San Antonio John Marshall high-school running back; University of Texas; Super Bowl XXXV Champion, 3-time All-Pro, 3-time Pro Bowler, 2002 NFL Defensive Player of the Year.
	Adrian Peterson	Football	Palestine HS; All-American; in NFL, AP NFL MVP Trophy, 2012; 7-time Pro Bowler, 7-time All-Pro, 3-time NFL rushing champion, 2010s All-Decade Team.
	Cynthia Potter	Diving	Houston native; Lamar HS; Olympian (1972, 1976, 1980), winning bronze in 1976; won a total of 28 swimming titles, a record that still stands today; Diver of the Year 3 times.
	Michael Strahan	Football	Texas Southern; 7-time Pro Bowler, led NFL in sacks 2 seasons; NFL Defensive Player of the Year (2001); Super Bowl championship (2008); All-Decade Team (2000s) and Pro Football HOF Class of 2014.
2022	Bob Beamon	Track & Field	University of Texas at El Paso; AAU Indoor Title and Pan-American Games in long-jump (1967); Olympic gold medalist (1968); National Track and Field HOF (1977) and United States Olympic HOF (1983).
	Chris Bosh	Basketball	Lincoln HS, Dallas; 11-time NBA All-Star (2005-2016), 2-time NBA Champion (2012, 2013), Olympic gold medalist (2008). All-Rookie Team 2003-04, All-NBA team in 2006-07. Naismith Memorial Basketball HOF.
	Carly Patterson Caldwell	Gymnastics	American Cup gold medal (all-around, balance beam); Olympics, 2nd American woman to win all-around gold medal since 1984; 27 medals by retirement in 2006; inducted into USA Gymnastics HOF in 2009
	Suzie Snider Eppers	Basketball	Robinson HS first state championship (1970); Baylor All-American
	Manu Ginóbili	Basketball	One of only two players to win an NBA Championship, a Euroleague title, and an Olympic gold medal. Played with the Spurs, claiming four NBA Championships (2003, 2005, 2007, 2014), two NBA All-Star appearances.
	Robert Griffin III	Football	Copperas HS; Baylor quarterback; Big 12 Conference Offensive Freshman of the Year and Big 12 Freshman of the Year; Heisman Trophy; AP College Football Player of the Year; Davey O'Brien Award; Manning Award Washington Redskins (Offensive Rookie of the Year, Pro Bowl in first season).
	Tony Parker	Basketball	San Antonio Spurs, winning four titles (2003, 2005, 2007, 2014); 6-time NBA All-Star, named to 4 All-NBA teams, NBA Finals MVP in 2007
	Mike Renfro	Football	Arlington Heights HS; Texas Christian, All-SWC 3 times, 2nd-team All-American; Houston Oilers; Dallas Cowboys MVP (1985)
	Michael Strahan	Football	Seven-time pro-bowler; led NFL in sacks (2001, 2003); set single-season sack record in 2001; Super Bowl victory (2008).
	Stacy Sykora	Volleyball	Texas A&M; 2-time All American, 3-time Olympian (silver medalist)

Year	Inductee	Sport	Texas Connection, Career
2021	Leroy Burrell	Track & Field	Broke Houston freshman long-jump record (1985-86); Olympic team gold (1992); head track and field coach at University of Houston, 21 seasons; C-USA Coach of the Year 23 times; American Athletic Conference Coaching Staff of the Year 12 years.
	Derrick Johnson	Football	Waco HS, All-State honors as linebacker; 2-time Parade All-American; Texas Football Super Team; US Army All-American Bowl (2001); University of Texas (2001-2004), 2-time consensus All-American, 4-time all-Big 12, Defensive Player of the Year, recipient of Dick Butkus and Bronco Nagurski Awards. 2011-2013 Pro Bowler.
	DeMarcus Ware	Football	12 years as NFL outside linebacker; 2nd Cowboy to ever record 14 sacks in a season; 2016 Super Bowl Champion; 9 Pro Bowler; 4-time First-team All-Pro member, 3-time Second-team All-Pro member, 2-time NFL sacks, NFL 2000s All-Decade Team.
	Charlie Waters	Football	All-ACC quarterback and wide receiver at Clemson; Dallas Cowboys as defensive back (1970), first-team NFL All-Rookie team, 5 Super Bowls, winning 2; 3-time Pro Bowler; Second-Team All-Pro twice.
	Sophia Young-Malcolm	Basketball	2-time Kodak All-American, 1st NCAA title in 2005, Final Four's Most Outstanding Player, consensus first-team All-American, Big 12 Player of the Year, member of Big 12 10th Anniversary Team; All-Big 12 first team for three consecutive years and ended college career as Big 12's all-time leader in points, rebounds, double-doubles. Entered WNBA with San Antonio Silver Stars, 3-time WNBA All-Star, 4-time All-WNBA Team player.
2020	Adrian Beltre	Baseball	Texas Ranger third baseman; 4-time All-Star, 5-time Golden Glove.
	Paul Cass	Tennis	Developed State Team Tournament; coached winning teams.
	Michelle Carter	Track & Field	Red Oak HS (4 shot put state championships); University of Texas, 7-time All American, 5 Big 12 titles, 2006 NCAA Indoor Champion; Rio de Janeiro Olympics gold medalist (2016).
	Clint Dempsey	Soccer	Scored in 3 World Cups; 5th-fastest score in Cup history.
	Shane Lechler	Football	Texas A&M 2-time All-American punter, 1997 All-Big 12 Team; Houston Texans (2013-2017); NFL all-time record holder for career punting average and NFL's 2000's Team of the Decade Punter, 6-time 1st team All-Pro, 7-time Pro Bowler.
	Chuck Sanchelli	Tennis	Founder, volunteer, and member of multiple tennis programs.
	Francie Larrieu Smith	Track & Field	1500-meter title (1970), established 36 US records and 12 world bests in distances from 1,000 to 10,000 meters; just 3rd female American athlete to make 5 Olympic teams; head men's and women's cross country/track and field coach at Southwestern University 1999-2018.
	Kathy Vick	Tennis	Ranked first in Texas in singles, doubles consistently, ages 40-60.
	Teresa Weatherspoon	Basketball	Pineland, TX; 1988 NCAA women's basketball title; WNBA 1997 New York Liberty, retired as franchise's all-time leader in assists and steals; 1988 Olympics (gold), 1992 Olympics (bronze).
	Carol Weyman	Tennis	Founded circuit for junior players, "Road to Little Mo Nationals".
2019	Maureen Connolly Brinker	Tennis	Dallas, 9 Grand Slam singles titles 1950s.
	Tony Franklin	Football	Big Spring, FW Arlington Heights, A&M, NFL kicker 1979–88.
	Andre Johnson	Football	Wide receiver 14 years mostly with Houston Texans.
	Nancy Lieberman	Basketball	First woman coach of men's professionals, for Texas Legends.
	Loyd Phillips	Football	Longview, 1967–69 Chicago Bears, Outland Trophy.
	Greg Swindell	Baseball	Houston Sharpstown High, UT, MLB pitcher 1986–2002.
	Jason Witten	Football	All-Pro tight end, Dallas Cowboys 2003–17.

Go to **texasalmanac.com/topics/sports/texas-sports-hall-fame** for a complete list of inductees beginning with 1951.

Texas Olympic Medalists

Source: United States Olympic Committee.

This is a list of athletes with Texas connections who have won medals in the Olympics including the 2020 games in Tokyo. This list includes those born here or have lived in Texas, as well as U.S. team members who spent their collegiate careers at Texas universities.

Information included is: the athlete's name, the sport and the year, as well as the types of medals (G-Gold, S-Silver, B-Bronze). If the athlete won more than one of the same kind of medal in any one year, the number is noted before the letter code; e.g., 2G indicates that the athlete won two gold medals in the games that year.

The asterisk (*) signifies COVID-19 suspended the 2020 Olympics, which were held from July 23–August 8, 2021.

The symbol (†) following the medal code indicates that the athlete participated in preliminary contests only; the medal was awarded because of membership on a winning team. Years in which the athlete participated but did not win a medal are not included. Track indicates all track and field events except those noted separately.

More results can be seen at texasalmanac.com. ☆

Olympian	Sport	Year	Medal
Abbott, Monica	Softball	2020*	S
Abdallah, Nia Nicole	Taekwondo	2004	S
Adams, Rachel	Volleyball	2016	B
Allen, Chad	Baseball	1996	B
Allman, Valarie	Track	2020*	G
Atkins, Ariel	Basketball	2020*	G
Armstrong, Lance	Cycling	2000	B*
Arnette, Jay Hoyland	Basketball	1960	G
Austin, Charles	Track	1996	G
Baker, Walter Thane	Track	1956	G,S,B
		1952	S
Baptiste, Kirk	Track	1984	S
Barr, Beth	Swimming	1988	S
Bassham, Lanny Robert	Shooting	1976	G
		1972	S
Bates, Michael D.	Track	1992	B
Baz, Shane	Baseball	2020*	S
Beamon, Bob	Track	1968	G
Beck, Robert Lee	Pentathlon	1960	2B
Beckie, Janine	Soccer	2016	B
Bedforth, B.J.	Swimming	2000	G
Berens, Ricky	Swimming	2012	G,S
		2008	G
Berube, Ryan Thomas	Swimming	1996	G
Biles, Simone	Gymnastics	2020*	S, B
		2016	4G,B
Bosh, Chris	Basketball	2008	G
Boudia, David	Diving	2016	S, B
		2012	G,B
Brew, Derrick K.	Track	2004	G,B
Bridgewater, Brad	Swimming	1996	G
Brown, Earlene Dennis	Track	1960	B
Browning, David (Skippy)	Diving	1952	G
Buckner, William Quinn	Basketball	1976	G
Buford-Bailey, Tonja	Track	1996	B
Burrell, Leroy Russel	Track	1992	G
Burrows, Brian	Shooting	2020*	B
Butler, Jimmy	Basketball	2016	G
Campbell, Jane	Soccer	2020*	B
Carey, Rick	Swimming	1984	3G
Carlisle, Daniel T.	Shooting	1984	B

* In January 2013, the International Olympic Committee disqualified Lance Armstrong from the 2000 events he competed in after he was found to have used drugs to enhance his performance.

Olympian	Sport	Year	Medal
Carter, Michael D.	Shotput	1984	S
Carter, Michelle	Shotput	2016	G
Cassell, Ollan	Track	1964	G
Catchings, Tamika	Basketball	2016	G
		2012	G
Chiles, Jordan	Gymnastics	2020*	S
Clay, Bryan E.	Decathlon	2008	G
		2004	S
Clement, Kerron	Track	2016	G
Clemons, Kyle	Track	2016	G
Cline, Nancy Lieberman	Basketball	1976	S
Cohen, Tiffany	Swimming	1984	G
Conger, Jack	Swimming	2016	G
Corbelli, Laurie Flachmeier	Volleyball	1984	S
Cotton, John	Baseball	2000	G
Crocker, Ian	Swimming	2008	G
		2004	G,S,B
		2000	G
Cross-Battle, Tara	Volleyball	1992	B
Crouser, Ryan	Shotput	2020*	G
		2016	G
Daniels, Teahna	Track	2020*	S
Davis, Clarissa G.	Basketball	1992	B
Davis, Jack Wells	Track	1956	S
		1952	S
Davis, Josh C.	Swimming	2000	2S
		1996	3G
Davis, W.F. (Buddy)	High Jump	1952	G
Deadmon, Bryce	Track	2020*	G,B
DeLoach, Joseph N. Jr.	Track	1988	G
Dersch, Hans	Swimming	1992	G
Didrikson, Mildred (Babe)	Track	1932	2G,S
Donie, Scott R.	Diving	1992	S
Drexler, Clyde	Basketball	1992	G
Dumais, Troy	Diving	2012	B
Durant, Kevin	Basketball	2020*	G
		2016	G
		2012	G
Dusing, Nate	Swimming	2004	B
		2000	S

Olympian	Sport	Year	Medal
Eller, Glenn	Shooting	2008	G
Eriksson, Agneta	Swimming	1980	S
Ethridge, Mary (Kamie)	Basketball	1988	G
Farmer-Patrick, Sandra	Track	1992	S
Feigen, Jimmy	Swimming	2016	G
		2012	S†
Fields, Connor	Cycling	2016	G
Finn-Burrell, Michelle Bonae	Track	1992	G
Foerster, Paul	Sailing	1992	S
		2000	S
		2004	G
Forbes, James Ricardo	Basketball	1972	S
Ford, Gilbert (Gib)	Basketball	1956	G
Foreman, George	Boxing	1968	G
Fortenberry, Joe Cephis	Basketball	1936	G
Francis, Phyllis	Track	2016	G
Galloway, Jackie	Taekwondo	2016	B
Garrison, Zina	Tennis	1988	G,B
George, Chris	Baseball	2000	G
Manu Ginóbili	Basketball	2004	G
		2008	B
Gjertson, Doug	Swimming	1992	G,B
		1988	G
Glenesk, Dean William	Pentathlon	1984	S
Goldblatt, Scott	Swimming	2004	G
		2000	S
Gonzáles, Paul G. Jr.	Boxing	1984	G
Gordon, Chris-Ann	Track	2016	S
Gray, Allisha	Basketball	2020*	G
Green, Josh	Basketball	2020*	B
Griner, Brittney	Basketball	2020*	G
		2016	G
Grosso, Julia	Soccer	2020*	G
Guidry, Carlette D.	Track	1996	G†
		1992	G
Haas, Townley	Swimming	2016	G
Hall, Gary Jr.	Swimming	2004	G,B
		2000	2G,S,B
		1996	2G,2S
Hamm, Mia	Soccer	2004	G
		2000	S
		1996	G
Hancock-Benbrook, Vincent	Skeet Shooting	2020*	G
		2012	G
		2008	G
Hannan, Tommy	Swimming	2000	G
Hansen, Brendan	Swimming	2012	G,B
		2008	G
		2004	G,S,B
Hansen, Fred Morgan	Track	1964	G
Hardee, Trey	Track	2012	S
Harkrider, Kiplan P.	Baseball	1996	B
Harrison, Kendra	Track	2020*	S
Hartwell, Erin Wesley	Cycling	1996	S
		1992	B

Olympian	Sport	Year	Medal
Hays, Todd	Bobsled	2002	S
Heath, Michael Steward	Swimming	1984	2G,S
Hedgepeth, Whitney L.	Swimming	1996	G,2S
Hedrick, Chad	Speed Skating	2010	S,B
		2006	G,S,B
Heidenreich, Jerry	Swimming	1972	2G,S,B
Henry, James Edward	Diving	1968	B
Hill, Denean E.	Track	1992	S
		1988	S
		1984	G
Hill, Grant Henry	Basketball	1996	G
Hinds, Natalie	Swimming	2020*	B
Hoffman, Sylvia	Bobsleigh	2022	B
Homfeld, Conrad E.	Equestrian	1984	G,S
Hooker, Destinee	Volleyball	2012	S
Hooper, Darrow	Shotput	1952	S
Horton, Jonathan	Gymnastics	2008	S
Howard, Sherri Francis	Track	1988	S
		1984	G
Hurley, Kelley	Epee Fencing	2012	B
Hurley, Courtney	Epee Fencing	2012	B
Ilyina, Vera	Diving	2004	S
		2000	G
Jackson, Lucious Brown	Basketball	1964	G
Jacobs, Chris	Swimming	1988	2G,S
Jacobs, Lamont	Track	2020*	2G
Jacoby, Lydia	Swimming	2020*	G,S
Johnson, Keldon	Basketball	2020*	G
Johnson, Michael	Track	2000	2G
		1996	2G
		1992	G
Johnson, Rafer L.	Decathlon	1960	G
		1956	S
Jones, John Wesley (Lam)	Track	1976	G
Jordan, DeAndre	Basketball	2016	G
Jordan, Shaun	Swimming	1992	G
		1988	G
Juarez, Ricardo Rocky	Boxing	2000	S
Julich, Robert William	Cycling	2004	B
Kazmir, Scott	Baseball	2020*	S
Keeler, Kathryn Elliott	Rowing	1984	G
Kerley, Fred	Track	2020*	S
Kern, Douglas James	Sailing	1992	S
Kiefer, Adolph	Swimming	1936	G
Kimmons, Trell	Track	2012	S
King, Judith Brown	Track	1984	S
Kleine, Megan	Swimming	1992	G†
Knight, Bianca	Track	2012	G
Kocian, Madison	Gymnastics	2016	G,S
Kolius, John Waldrip	Sailing	1976	S
Lanne, Colleen	Swimming	2004	S
Langkop, Dorothy Franey	Speed Skating	1932	B
Leetch, Brian Joseph	Ice Hockey	2002	S
Lewis, F. (Carl) Carlton	Track	1996	G
		1992	2G
		1988	2G,S
		1984	4G
Lienhard, William Barner	Basketball	1952	G

Olympian	Sport	Year	Medal
Lipinski, Tara K.	Figure Skating	1998	G
Liukin, Nastia	Gymnastics	2008	G,3S,B
Lloyd, Andrea	Basketball	1988	G
Losey, Robert G. (Greg)	Pentathlon	1984	S
Lopez, Diana	Taekwondo	2008	B
Lopez, Mark	Taekwondo	2008	S
Lopez, Steven	Taekwondo	2008	B
		2004	G
		2000	G
Lowe, Sara Elizabeth	Swimming	2004	B
Magers, Rose Mary	Volleyball	1984	S
Malone, Jordan	Speed Skating	2014	S
		2010	B
Manuel, Simone	Swimming	2020*	B
		2016	2G, 2S
Manzano, Leo	Track	2012	S
Marsh, Michael L.	Track	1996	S
		1992	2G
Marshall, Christine	Swimming	2008	B
Matson, James Randel (Randy)	Shotput	1968	G
		1964	G
Matson, Ollie G.	Track	1952	S, B
McFalls, Jennifer Yvonne	Softball	2000	G
McFarlane, Tracey	Swimming	1988	S
McKenzie, Kim	Track	1984	B
McNeir, Forest	Shooting	1920	G
Meadows, Earle	Track	1936	G
Meili, Katie	Swimming	2016	G, B
Mensah-Stock, Tamyra	Wrestling	2020*	G
Mewis, Kristie	Soccer	2020*	B
Middleton, Khris	Basketball	2020*	G
Mills, Ronald P.	Swimming	1968	B
Mitchell, Betsy	Swimming	1988	S
		1984	G, S
Moceanu, Dominique	Gymnastics	1996	G
Montgomery, James P.	Swimming	1976	3G, B
Moore, James Warren	Pentathlon	1964	S
Morrow, Bobby Joe	Track	1956	3G
Mu, Athing	Track	2020*	2G
Munoz, Felipe	Swimming	1968	G
Neilson-Bell, Sandy	Swimming	1972	3G
Nelson, Lianne Bennion	Rowing	2004	S
Newhouse, Frederick V.	Track	1976	G, S
Nott/Cunningham, Tara Lee	Weightlifting	2004	G
Ogbogu, Chiaka	Volleyball	2020*	G
Okafor, Emeka	Basketball	2004	B
Okolo, Courtney	Track	2016	G
Olajuwon, Hakeem	Basketball	1996	G
Olsen, Justin	Bobsled	2010	G
Osterman, Catherine (Cat)	Softball	2020*	S
		2008	S
		2004	G
Paddock, Charles W.	Track	1924	S
		1920	2G, S

Olympian	Sport	Year	Medal
Patterson, Carly	Gymnastics	2004	G, 2S
Patton, Darvis	Track	2004	S
Peirsol, Aaron	Swimming	2008	2G, S
		2004	3G
		2000	S
Perry, Nanceen L.	Track	2000	B
Pesthy, Paul Karoly	Fencing	1964	S
Phenix, Erin	Swimming	2000	G
Pickrem, Sydney	Swimming	2020*	B
Pinder, Demetrius	Track	2016	B
		2012	G
Postma, Joan Spillane	Swimming	1960	G
Potter, Cynthia Ann	Diving	1976	B
Rogers, Raevyn	Track and Field	2020*	S
Rambo, John Barnett	Track	1964	B
Rauch, Jamie	Swimming	2000	S
Retton, Mary Lou	Gymnastics	1984	G,2S,2B
Richards, Robert E.	Track	1956	G
		1952	G
		1948	B
Richards-Ross, Sanya	Track	2012	2G
		2008	G, B
		2004	G
Ritter, Louise	Track	1988	G
Roberts, Dave	Track	1976	B
Roberts, Gil	Track	2016	G
Robertson, Alvin Cyrrale	Basketball	1984	G
Robinson, David M.	Basketball	1996	G
		1992	G
		1988	B
Robinson, Moushaumi	Track	2004	G
Robinson, Robert J.	Basketball	1948	G
Robinzine, Kevin B.	Track	1988	G
Robles, Sarah	Weightlifting	2020*	B
		2016	B
Roe, Frederick	Polo	1924	S
Rogers, Raevyn	Track and Field	2020*	S
Russell, Douglas Albert	Swimming	1968	2G
Russell, John William	Equestrian	1952	B
Salmon, Riley	Volleyball	2008	G
Schneider, Marcus B.	Rowing	1996	B
Schooling, Joseph	Swimming	2016	G
Slay, Brandon Douglas	Wrestling	2000	G
Smith, Clark	Swimming	2016	G
Smith, Dean	Track	1952	G
Smith, Lamont	Track	1996	G
Smith, Owen Guinn	Track	1948	G
Smith, Tommie C.	Track	1968	G
Southern, S. Edward	Track	1956	S
Spencer, Ashley	Track	2016	B
Steinseifer, Carrie	Swimming	1984	2G
Sterkle, Jill Ann	Swimming	1988	2B
		1984	G
		1976	G
Stevenson, Toby	Pole Vault	2004	S
Stulce, Michael S.	Shotput	1992	G
Sullivan, Erica	Swimming	2020*	S
Swoopes, Sheryl Denise	Basketball	2004	G
		2000	G
		1996	G

Olympian	Sport	Year	Medal
Sykora, Stacy	Volleyball	2008	S
Tarmoh, Jeneba	Track	2012	G
Taylor, Robert	Track	1972	G, S
Teagarden, Taylor	Baseball	2008	B
Thomas, Gabby	Track and Field	2020*	S, B
Tinsley, Michael	Track	2012	S
Tisdale, Wayman L.	Basketball	1984	G
Valdez, Jesse	Boxing	1972	B
Van, Allen	Ice Hockey	1952	S
Vollmer, Dana	Swimming	2016	G, S, B
		2012	3G
		2004	G
Walker, Laura Anne	Swimming	1988	B
Walker, Neil	Swimming	2004	G, B
		2000	G, S
Walters, Dave	Swimming	2008	G
Wariner, Jeremy	Track	2008	G, S
		2004	2G
Weatherspoon, Teresa G.	Basketball	1992	B
		1988	G

Olympian	Sport	Year	Medal
Weber-Gale, Garrett	Swimming	2008	2G
Wells, Rhoshii S.	Boxing	1996	B
Wells, Wayne A.	Wrestling	1972	G
Whitfield, Malvin G.	Track	1952	G, S
		1948	G, S
Wilkinson, Laura A.	Diving	2000	G
Williams, Christa L.	Softball	2000	G
		1996	G
Williams, Stacey Ann	Track	2020*	B
Williamson, Darold	Track	2004	G
Wilson, Craig Martin	Water Polo	1988	S
		1984	S
Wolfe, Rowland (Flip)	Gymnastics	1932	G
Woods-Richardson, Simeon	Baseball	2020*	S
Wrightson, Bernard C.	Diving	1968	G
Wylie, Paul Stanton	Figure Skating	1992	S
Young, Earl Verdelle	Track	1960	2G
Zmeskal, Kim	Gymnastics	1992	B

Sha'Carri Richardson after winning the 100-meter world championship title. Photo by Erik van Leeuwen on the third day of the 2023 World Athletics Championships in Budapest, Hungary on August 21, 2023 (Public Domain).

The Fastest Woman in the World

Sha'Carri Richardson, a Dallas native, is a track and field sprinter competing in the 100- and 200-meters. In 2021, she won the women's 100-meter race at the U.S. track and field trials, qualifying for the Olympics. Her win was invalidated when she tested positive for marijuana.

On August 21, 2023, Richardson won the 100-meter world championship title with a personal best of 10.65 seconds at the World Athletics Championships at the National Athletics Centre in Budapest, Hungary.

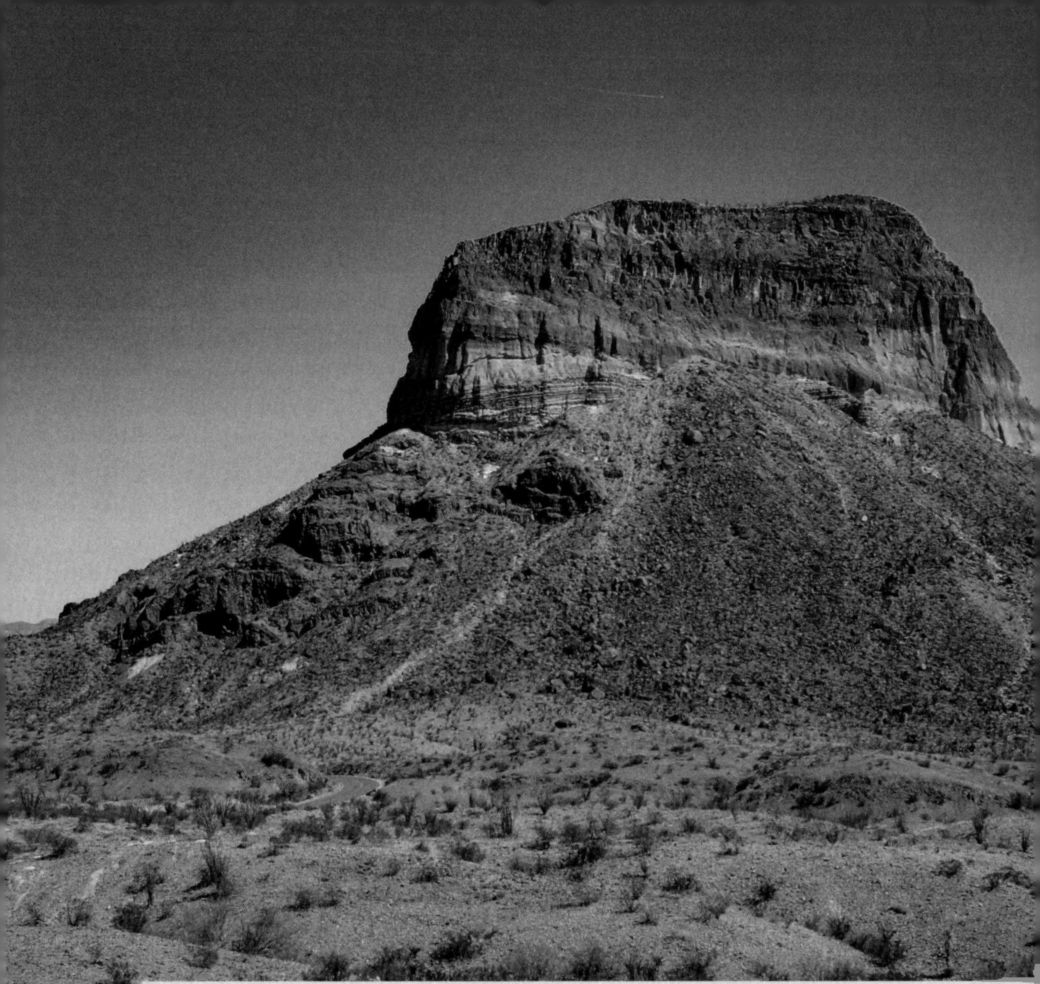

COUNTIES

PHYSICAL FEATURES, ECONOMY, HISTORY, RECREATION

MINERALS, AGRICULTURE, RACE/ETHNICITY, VITAL STATISTICS

TOWNS & POPULATIONS, CLIMATE

MAPS

Counties of Texas

These pages describe Texas' 254 counties and hundreds of towns. Descriptions are based on reports from chambers of commerce, the Texas AgriLife Extension agents, federal and state agencies, the Handbook of Texas, and other sources. Consult the index for other county information.

County maps are based on those of the Texas Department of Transportation and are copyrighted, 2023, as are the entire contents.

Physical Features: Descriptions are from U.S. Geological Survey and local sources.

Economy: From information provided by county judges and county extension agents.

History: From Texas statutes, Fulmore's History and Geography of Texas as Told in County Names, WPA Historical Records Survey, Texas Centennial Commission Report, and the Handbook of Texas.

Race/Ethnicity: Percentage estimates from the official 2020 Census by the U.S. Bureau of the Census. "Anglo" refers to non-Hispanic whites; "Black" refers to non-Hispanic Blacks; "Asian" refers to persons having origins in the Far East, Southeast Asia, or the Indian subcontinent. "Other" includes those of American Indian origin, Pacific Islanders, and those who identify with two or more races. People who identify their origin as Hispanic may be of any race. State of Texas, Race/Ethnicity: Anglo, 39.7%; Hispanic, 39.3%; Black, 11.8%; Asian, 5.4%; Other, 3.8%.

Vital Statistics: Births and Deaths from the Texas Department of State Health Services, Texas Health Data, 2020. Marriage (2019) and Divorce (2017) from the Texas Department of State Marriage/Divorce Indexes. (Divorce data showed 501 divorces with the county specified as "Unknown;" 25 counties were unlisted.)

Recreation: From information provided by county judges and county extension agents. Attempts were made to note activities unique to the area or that point to ethnic or cultural heritage.

Minerals: From county extension agents.

Agriculture: From information provided by county judges and county extension agents. Market value (total cash receipts) of agricultural products sold is from the Census of Agriculture of the U.S. Department of Agriculture that was conducted in 2017, the most recent report available.

Cities: Towns listed include the county seat, incorporated cities, and towns with post offices, as well as certain census designated places (CDP). Population figures for incorporated towns and CDPs are estimates for 2021 from the U.S. Census Bureau. Population estimates for other towns are from local officials received through a Texas Almanac survey. When figures for small portions of major cities are given, they are in brackets, such as **part [52,246] of Dallas** in Collin County.

Sources Of Data Lists

Population (of county): The county population estimates for 2021, U.S. Census Bureau. The line following gives the percentage of increase or decrease from the 2010 U.S. census count.

Area: Total area in square miles, including water surfaces, as determined in the 2010 U.S. census.

Land Area: The land area in square miles as determined by the U.S. Census Bureau in 2010.

Altitude (ft.): Principally from U.S. Geological Survey topographic maps, including revisions available in 2008. Not all of the surface of Texas has been precisely surveyed for elevation; in some cases data are from the Texas Railroad Commission or the Texas Department of Transportation.

Climate: Provided by the National Oceanic and Atmospheric Administration state climatologist, College Station. Data are revised at 10-year intervals to cover the previous three decades. Listed are the latest compilations, as of June 1, 2023, and pertain to a particular site within the county (usually the county seat). The data include: Rainfall (annual mean in inches); Temperature (in degrees Fahrenheit); January mean minimum and July mean maximum. Additional data can be seen in the Weather chapter on pages 126–135.

Workforce/Wages: Prepared by the Texas Workforce Commission, Austin, in cooperation with the Bureau of Labor Statistics of the U.S. Department of Labor. The data are computed from reports by all establishments subject to the Texas Unemployment Compensation Act.

(Agricultural employers are subject to the act if they employ as many as three workers for 20 weeks or pay cash wages of $6,250 in a quarter. Employers who pay $1,000 in wages in a quarter for domestic services are subject also. Still not mandatorily covered are self-employed, unpaid family workers, and those employed by churches and some small nonprofit organizations.)

The work/wage data include (state total, lowest county and highest county included here):

Civ. Labor: Annual civilian labor force for 2022. Texas, 14,662,558; Kenedy County, 147; Harris County, 2,339,651.

Unemployed: The unemployment rate (percentage of workforce) for 2022. Texas, 3.9; Loving County, 0.6; Starr County, 11.0.

Wages: Total wages paid in the fourth quarter of 2022. Texas, $241,863,623,339; King County, $3,218,399; Harris County, $49,707,617,091.

Per Capita Income: Per capita personal income for 2021, as reported by the U.S. Bureau of Economic Analysis. Texas, $59,865; Zapata County, $33,288; Midland County, $126,738.

Property Values: Appraised gross market value of real and personal property from the Comptroller's Property Tax Assistance Division 2022 report.

Retail Sales: Gross retail sales for 2021 as reported by the state Comptroller of Public Accounts.

County Facts Elsewhere In Volume

Anderson County

Physical Features: Forested, hilly East Texas county, slopes to Trinity and Neches rivers; Lake Palestine; sandy, clay, black soils; pines, hardwoods.

Economy: Manufacturing, distribution, agribusiness; poultry farms, hatchery, and processing plant; tourism; hunting and fishing leases; prison units.

History: Comanche, Waco, other tribes. Anglo-American settlers arrived in the 1830s. Antebellum slaveholding area. County created and organized from Houston County in 1846; named for K.L. Anderson, last vice president of the Republic of Texas.

Recreation: Fishing and hunting, streams, lakes; dogwood trails; national wildlife refuge; historic sites; Texas State Railroad depot, park; museums.

Minerals: Oil and gas.

Agriculture: Beef cattle, poultry, hay, truck vegetables, melons, pecans, peaches, wheat, corn, cotton, blueberries. Market value $92.9 million. Timber sold.

Vital Statistics, annual: Births, 543; deaths, 735; marriages, 294; divorces, 39.

Race/Ethnicity: Anglo, 57.1%; Hispanic, 19.2%; Black, 19.7%; Asian, 0.7%; Other, 3.3%.

PALESTINE (18,756) county seat; medical services, education, transportation; clothing, metal, wood products; scientific balloon station; historic bakery; library; vocational-technical facilities; hospital; UT-Tyler extension, community college; Museum of East Texas Culture; hot pepper festival in October.

Other towns include: **Cayuga** (137); **Elkhart** (1,277); **Frankston** (1,114), tourism, packaging industry, oil and gas, commuters to Tyler; depot museum, Square Fair in October; **Montalba** (110); **Neches** (190); and **Tennessee Colony** (300) site of state prisons.

Population	58,402
Change from 2010	–0.1%
Area (sq. mi.)	1,078.0
Land Area (sq. mi.)	1,062.6
Altitude (ft.)	174–773
Rainfall (in.)	46.8
Jan. mean min (°F)	36.9
July mean max (°F)	92.8
Civ. Labor	23,086
Unemployed	3.4%
Wages	$299,523,075
Per Capita Income	$42,444
Property Value	$5,943,553,721
Retail Sales	$634,074,236

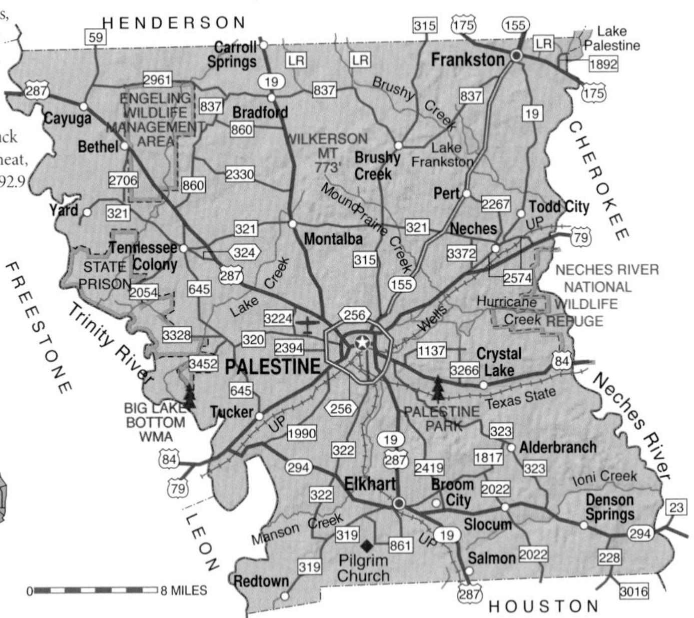

Railroad Abbreviations

AAT . . . . Austin Area Terminal Railroad
AGC . . . . Alamo Gulf Coast Railway
ATK . . . . AMTRAK
ANR . . . . Angelina & Neches River Railroad
ATCX . . . . Austin & Texas Central Railroad
BLR . . . . Blacklands Railroad
BNSF . . . . BNSF Railroad
BOP . . . . Border Pacific Railroad
BRG . . . . Brownsville & Rio Grande Int'l Railroad
CMC . . . . CMC Railroad
DART . . . . Dallas Area Rapid Transit
DGNO . . . . Dallas, Garland & Northeastern Railroad
FWWR . . . . Fort Worth & Western Railroad/Tarantula
GCSR . . . . Gulf, Colorado & San Saba RailwayCorp.
GRR . . . . Georgetown Railroad
GVSR . . . . Galveston Railroad
KCS . . . . Kansas City Southern Railway
KRR . . . . Kiamichi Railroad Company
MCSA . . . . Moscow, Camden & San Augustine RR
PCN . . . . Point Comfort & Northern Railway
PNR . . . . Panhandle Northern Railroad Company
PTRA . . . . Port Terminal Railroad Association
PVS . . . . Pecos Valley Southern Railway
RC . . . . Rusk County Rural Rail Transportation District
RSS . . . . Rockdale, Sandow & Southern Railroad
RVSC . . . . Rio Valley Switching
SAW . . . . South Plains Switching LTD
SRN . . . . Sabine River & Northern Railroad Company
SSC . . . . Southern Switching (Lone Star Railroad)
SW . . . . Southwestern Shortline Railroad
TCT . . . . Texas City Terminal Railway
TIBR . . . . Timber Rock Railroad
TM . . . . The Texas Mexican Railway Company
TN . . . . Texas & Northern Railway
TNER . . . . Texas Northeastern Railroad
TNMR . . . . Texas & New Mexico Railroad
TNW . . . . Texas North Western Railway
TP . . . . Texas Pacifico Transportation
TSE . . . . Texas South-Eastern Railroad Company
TXGN . . . . Texas, Gonzales & Northern Railway
TXR . . . . Texas Rock Crusher Railway
TSSR . . . . Texas State Railroad
UP . . . . Union Pacific Railroad Company
WTJR . . . . Wichita, Tillman & Jackson Railway
WTLR . . . . West Texas & Lubbock Railroad

Andrews County

Physical Features: South Plains, drain to playas; grass, mesquite, shin oak; red clay, sandy soils.

Economy: Natural resources/mining; manufacturing; construction; government/services; agribusiness.

History: Apache, Comanche area until U.S. Army campaigns of 1875. Ranching developed around 1900. Oil boom in 1940s. County created 1876 from Bexar Territory; organized 1910; named for Texas Revolutionary soldier Richard Andrews.

Recreation: Wetlands, bird viewing; museum; camper facilities.

Minerals: Oil and gas.

Agriculture: Beef, cotton, sorghums, grains, hay; pecan orchards; significant irrigation. Market value $10.6 million.

Vital Statistics, annual: Births, 287; deaths, 153; marriages, 93; divorces, 87.

Race/Ethnicity: Anglo, 39.8%; Hispanic, 55.9%; Black, 1%; Asian, 0.5%; Other, 2.7%.

ANDREWS (13,370) county seat; trade center, amphitheatre, hospital.

Other towns include **McKinney Acres** (842).

Population	18,440
Change from 2010	24.7%
Area (sq. mi.)	1,501.1
Land Area (sq. mi.)	1,500.7

Altitude (ft.)	2,862–3,570
Rainfall (in.)	14.0
Jan. mean min (°F)	33.0
July mean max (°F)	95.2
Civ. Labor	9,455
Unemployed	3.2
Wages	$154,136,267
Per Capita Income	$52,943
Property Value	$9,028,141,066
Retail Sales	$254,671,936

Angelina County

Physical Features: Rolling, hilly East Texas county; black, red, gray soils; Angelina National Forest.

Economy: Timber; manufacturers of iron and steel castings, truck trailers, mobile homes; government/services; wood and paper products.

History: Caddoan area. First land deed to Vicente Micheli 1801. Anglo-American setters arrived in 1820s. County created and organized in 1846 from Nacogdoches County; named for legendary Indian maiden Angelina.

Recreation: Sam Rayburn Reservoir; Ellen Trout Zoo, national, state forests, parks; four museums: timber, local history, natural history and art; Forest Festival, Spring Rodeo, Angelina County Fair, spring canoeing Neche River Rendezvous

Minerals: Some natural gas and oil.

Agriculture: Poultry, beef, horticulture, limited Blueberries, Mayhaws and some vegetables. Market value $61.4 million. A leading timber-producing county.

Vital Statistics, annual: Births, 1,167; deaths, 1,155; marriages, 549; divorces, 250.

Race/Ethnicity: Anglo, 57.8%; Hispanic, 22.8%; Black, 14.9%; Asian, 1%; Other, 3.4%.

LUFKIN (34,074) county seat; manufacturing; Angelina College; hospitals; U.S., Texas Forest centers; zoo; Expo Center and Texas Forestry Museum.

Other towns include: **Burke** (692); **Diboll** (4,449); **Hudson** (4,986); **Huntington** (2,019); **Redland** (1,319); **Zavalla** (607).

Population	86,506
Change from 2010	–0.3%
Area (sq. mi.)	864.7

Land Area (sq. mi.)	797.8
Altitude (ft.)	102–460
Rainfall (in.)	50.3
Jan. mean min (°F)	39.4
July mean max (°F)	92.4
Civ. Labor	35,480
Unemployed	4.6%
Wages	$446,265,050
Per Capita Income	$46,170
Property Value	$8,792,025,738
Retail Sales	$1,533,786,068

Aranssas County

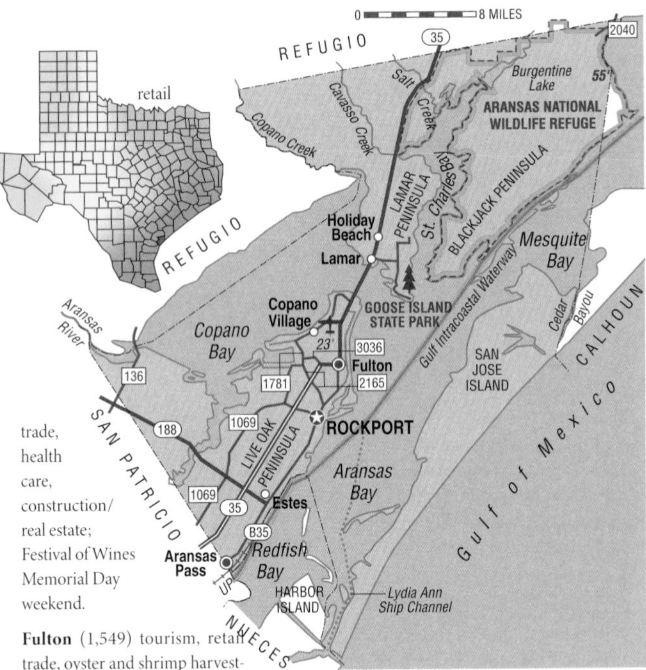

Physical Features: Coastal plains; sandy loam, coastal clays; bays, inlets; mesquites, oaks.

Economy: Tourism, recreational fishing, commercial shrimping, hunting.

History: Karankawa, Coahuiltecan area. Settlement by Irish and Mexicans began in 1829. County created and organized in 1871 from Refugio County; named for Rio Nuestra Señora de Aranzazu, derived from a Spanish palace.

Recreation: Sport fishing, waterfowl hunting; Fulton Mansion; state marine lab; Goose Island State Park; Texas Maritime Museum; bird sanctuaries (a nationally known birding hotspot); Rockport art center; Hummer Bird festival in September.

Minerals: Oil and gas, also oystershell and sand.

Agriculture: Cotton, hay, cow-calf operations. Market value $1.9 million. Fishing, hunting; redfish hatchery.

Vital Statistics, annual: Births, 171; deaths, 435; marriages, 136; divorces, 95.

Race/Ethnicity: Anglo, 66.4%; Hispanic, 25.8%; Black, 1%; Asian, 2%; Other, 4.8%.

ROCKPORT (10,436) county seat; tourism, retail trade, health care, construction/ real estate; Festival of Wines Memorial Day weekend.

Fulton (1,549) tourism, retail trade, oyster and shrimp harvesting, museums, Oysterfest in March; **Holiday Beach** (353); and **Lamar** (1,328).

Also, part [681] of **Aransas Pass**.

For explanation of sources, symbols, and abbreviations, see p. 207 and foldout map.

Population	24,510
Change from 2010	5.8%
Area (sq. mi.)	528.0
Land Area (sq. mi.)	252.1
Altitude (ft.)	sea level–55

Rainfall (in.)	36.4
Jan. mean min (°F)	48.3
July mean max (°F)	91.6
Civ. Labor	9,294
Unemployed	5.3%

Wages	$73,582,292
Per Capita Income	$59,878
Property Value	$5,402,309,260
Retail Sales	$161,323,028

The City Hall in Archer City is in the historic part of town. Photo by Rene Gomez, CC by SA 4.0

Archer County

Physical Features: Northwestern county, rolling to hilly, drained by Wichita, Trinity River forks; Lake Kickapoo, Lake Diversion, Lake Wichita, Lake Arrowhead, Lake Cooper and Lake Olney; black, red loams, sandy soils; mesquites, post oaks.

Economy: Cattle, milk production, oil, hunting leases. Part of Wichita Falls metropolitan area.

History: Caddo, Comanche, Kiowas and other tribes in the area until 1875; Anglo-American settlement developed soon afterward. County created from Fannin Land District in 1858; organized in 1880. Named for Dr. B.T. Archer, Republic commissioner to United States.

Recreation: Hunting of deer, turkey, dove, feral hog, coyote; fishing in area lakes, rodeo in June.

Minerals: Oil and natural gas.

Agriculture: Cow/calf, stocker cattle, dairy, wheat, hay, silage and horses. Market value $72.4 million.

Vital Statistics, annual: Births, 69; deaths, 87; marriages, 15; divorces, 28.

Race/Ethnicity: Anglo, 85.9%; Hispanic, 8.7%; Black, 0.4%; Asian, 0.2%; Other, 4.8%.

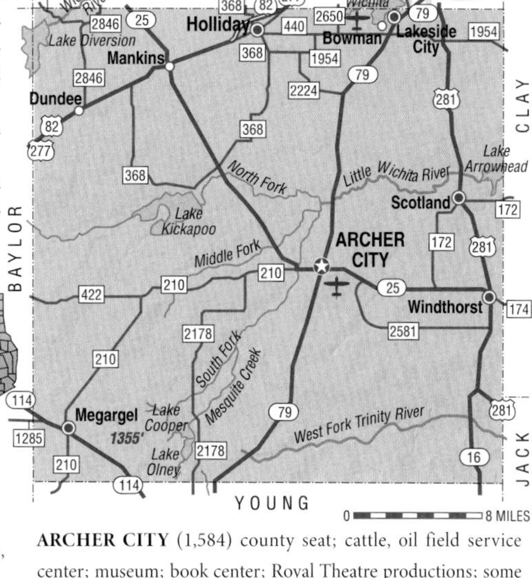

ARCHER CITY (1,584) county seat; cattle, oil field service center; museum; book center; Royal Theatre productions; some manufacturing.

Other towns include: **Holliday** (1,570) Mayfest in spring; **Lakeside City** (1,150); **Megargel** (177); **Scotland** (419); **Windthorst** (344), biannual German sausage festival (also in Scotland).

Population	8,681
Change from 2010	–4.1%
Area (sq. mi.)	925.4
Land Area (sq. mi.)	903.1
Altitude (ft.)	900–1,355
Rainfall (in.)	32.5
Jan. mean min (°F)	32.6

July mean max (°F)	95.5
Civ. Labor	4,013
Unemployed	3.4
Wages	$21,710,223
Per Capita Income	$60,101
Property Value	$2,354,154,920
Retail Sales	$66,349,295

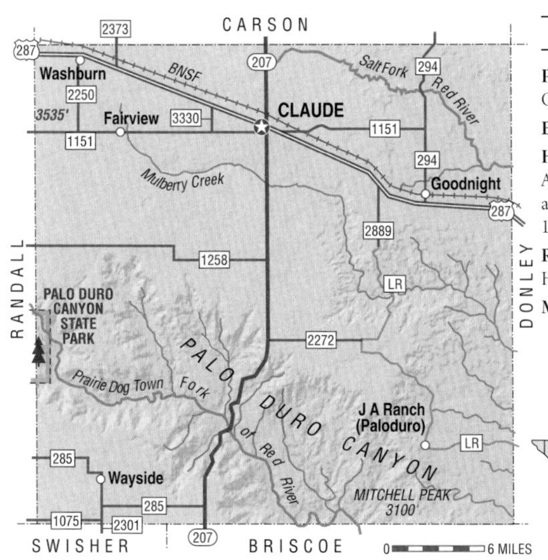

Armstrong County

Physical Features: Partly on High Plains, broken by Palo Duro Canyon. Chocolate loam, gray soils.

Economy: Agribusiness, tourism, commuting to Amarillo.

History: Apache tribal area, then Comanche territory until U.S. Army campaigns of 1874-75. Anglo-Americans began ranching soon afterward. County created from Bexar District, 1876; organized in 1890; name honors pioneer Texas family.

Recreation: Palo Duro Canyon State Park; Goodnight Ranch Home.

Minerals: Sand, gravel.

Agriculture: Stocker cattle, cow-calf operations; wheat, sorghum, cotton and hay; some irrigation. Market value $49.3 million.

Vital Statistics, annual: Births, 22; deaths, 38; marriages, 9; divorces, 11.

Race/Ethnicity: Anglo, 86.2%; Hispanic, 7.8%; Black, 0.3%; Asian, 0.5%; Other, 5.1%.

CLAUDE (1,184) county seat; farm, ranch supplies; glass company; medical center; Caprock Roundup in July.

Washburn (227).

Population	1,839
Change from 2010	–3.3%
Area (sq. mi.)	913.8
Land Area (sq. mi.)	909.1
Altitude (ft.)	2,300–3,535
Rainfall (in.)	19.7

Jan. mean min (°F)	26.0
July mean max (°F)	91.2
Civ. Labor	939
Unemployed	2.8%
Wages	$6,775,792
Per Capita Income	$61,382

Property Value	$854,242,081
Retail Sales	$22,296,181

Atascosa County

Physical Features: On grassy prairie south of San Antonio, drained by Atascosa River, tributaries; mesquites, other brush.

Economy: Coal plant, oil, commuters to San Antonio.

History: Coahuiltecan tribal area; later Apaches and Comanches. Families from Mexico established ranches in mid-1700s. Anglo-Americans arrived in 1840s. County created from Bexar District in 1856 and organized the same year. Atascosa means boggy in Spanish.

Recreation: Quail, deer hunting; museums; river park; theater group, photography.

Minerals: Lignite, oil, gas.

Agriculture: Beef cattle, peanuts, vegetable farming, forage/hay production, turf grass. Some 25,000 acres irrigated. Market value $74.3 million.

Vital Statistics, annual: Births, 678; deaths, 572; marriages, 188; divorces, 107.

Race/Ethnicity: Anglo, 32.8%; Hispanic, 63.7%; Black, 0.7%; Asian, 0.3%; Other, 2.5%.

Population	49,939
Change from 2010	11.2%

For explanation of sources, symbols, and abbreviations, see p. 207 and foldout map.

JOURDANTON (4,127) county seat; coal mining; hospital; park, walking trail; chili cookoff in May, Czech Day in July.

PLEASANTON (10,780) farming, oil-field drilling, health services; cowboy homecoming in August, Longhorn museum; hospital.

Other towns include: **Campbellton** (350); **Charlotte** (1,554); **Christine** (344); **Leming** (549); **Lytle** (2,965) greenhouse, peanuts processed; **Peggy** (22); **Poteet** (2,880) government/services, library, strawberry festival in April.

Area (sq. mi.)	1,221.5
Land Area (sq. mi.)	1,219.5
Altitude (ft.)	180–784
Rainfall (in.)	31.5
Jan. mean min (°F)	42.1
July mean max (°F)	96.0
Civ. Labor	22,510
Unemployed	4.0%
Wages	$216,743,422
Per Capita Income	$46,737
Property Value	$8,205,145,615
Retail Sales	$750,829,511

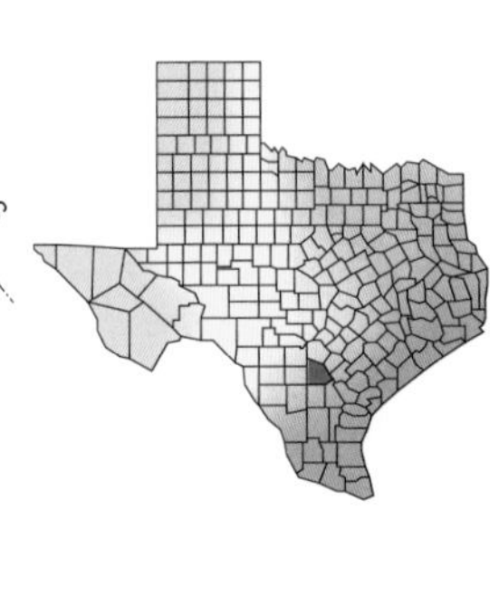

Austin County

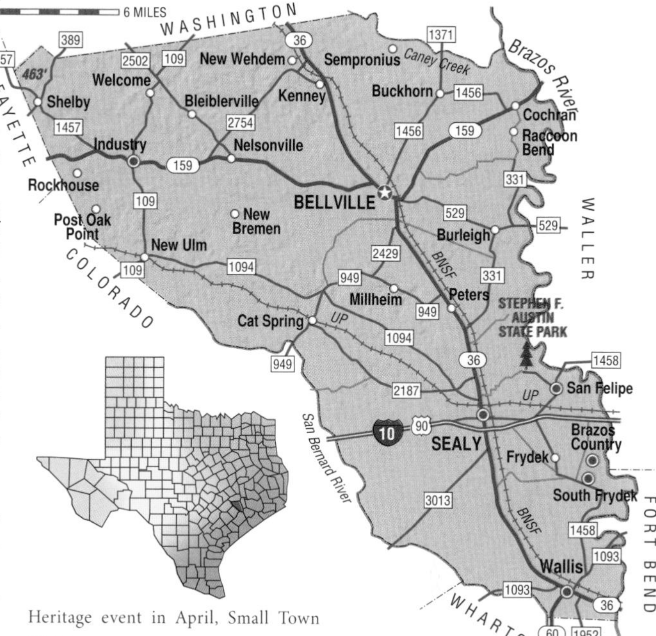

Physical Features: Level to hilly, drained by San Bernard, Brazos rivers; black prairie to sandy upland soils.

Economy: Agribusiness; tourism, government/services; metal, other manufacturing; commuting to Houston.

History: Tonkawa Indian tribal area; reduced by diseases. Birthplace of Anglo-American colonization, 1821, and German mother colony at Industry, 1831. County created and organized in 1837; named for Stephen F. Austin, father of Texas.

Recreation: Fishing, hunting; state park, Pioneer Trail, San Felipe de Austin State Historic Site and Museum, Texas Select Custom Cutlery event (April) and County Fair (Oct), market days and Volunteer Fire Department fundraisers.

Minerals: Oil and natural gas.

Agriculture: Beef production and hay. Also rice, corn, sorghum, nursery crops, grapes, pecans. Market value $33.1 million.

Vital Statistics, annual: Births, 338; deaths, 323; marriages, 113; divorces, 99.

Race/Ethnicity: Anglo, 61.3%; Hispanic, 26.7%; Black, 7.8%; Asian, 0.7%; Other, 3.6%.

BELLVILLE (4,108) county seat; varied manufacturing; hospital; oil. Historic town square shopping, Classic Car Stampede in March, Fruehling Sangerfest German Heritage event in April, Small Town Christmas.

SEALY (6,775) oil-field/military vehicle manufacturing; Blinn College branch; motorsports performance facilities, Fantasy of Lights Christmas in December.

Other towns include: **Bleiblerville** (125); **Brazos Country** (510); **Cat Spring** (200); **Industry** (273); **Kenney** (957); **New Ulm** (391) retail, art festival in April; **San Felipe** (688) colonial capital of Texas; **South Frydek** (210); **Wallis** (1,296) autofest in October.

Population	30,380
Change from 2010 (%)	6.9%
Area (sq. mi.)	656.4
Land Area (sq. mi.)	646.5
Altitude (ft.)	70–463

Rainfall (in.)	43.9
Jan. mean min (°F)	42.9
July mean max (°F)	93.4
Civ. Labor	14,123
Unemployed (%)	3.9

Wages	$223,581,564
Per Capita Income	$58,284
Property Value	$7,766,753,383
Retail Sales	$428,800,977

The town of Kenney has had a post office since 1884. Photo by Djmaschek, CC by SA 3.0

Bailey County

Physical Features: High Plains county, sandy loam soils; mesquite brush; drains to draws forming upper watershed of Brazos River, playas.

Economy: Farm supply manufacturing; electric generating plant; food-processing plants.

History: Settlement began after 1900. County created from Bexar District 1876, organized 1917. Named for Alamo hero Peter J. Bailey.

Recreation: Muleshoe National Wildlife Refuge; "Old Pete," the national mule memorial; historical building park; museum; motorcycle rally; mule deer, sandhill crane, pheasant hunting.

Minerals: Insignificant.

Agriculture: Feedlot, dairy cattle; cotton, wheat, sorghum, corn, vegetables; some 50,000 acres irrigated. Market value $357.0 million.

Vital Statistics, annual: Births, 114; deaths, 70; marriages, 20; divorces, 14.

Race/Ethnicity: Anglo, 31.7%; Hispanic, 65.8%; Black, 0.7%; Asian, 0.1%; Other, 1.7%.

MULESHOE (5,090) county seat; agribusiness center; feed-corn milling; hospital; livestock show.

Other towns include: **Enochs** (80); **Maple** (40).

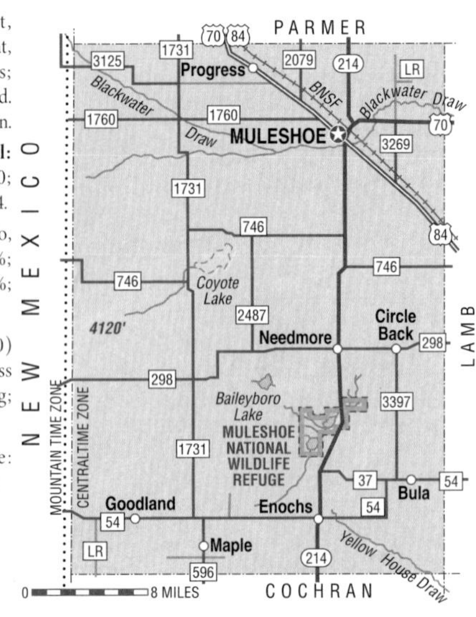

For explanation of sources, symbols, and abbreviations, see p. 207 and foldout map.

Population	6,835
Change from 2010 (%)	–4.6%
Area (sq. mi.)	827.5
Land Area (sq. mi.)	826.8
Altitude (ft.)	3,660–4,120
Rainfall (in.)	17.9
Jan. mean min (°F)	22.1
July mean max (°F)	91.6
Civ. Labor	2,414
Unemployed (%)	4.2
Wages	$31,073,194
Per Capita Income	$51,709
Property Value	$693,114,442
Retail Sales	$66,313,299

Bandera County

Population	21,565
Change from 2010 (%)	5.3%
Area (sq. mi.)	797.6
Land Area (sq. mi.)	791.0
Altitude (ft.)	1,064–2,340
Rainfall (in.)	36.3
Jan. mean min (°F)	37.0
July mean max (°F)	93.9
Civ. Labor	10,624
Unemployed (%)	3.7
Wages	$42,914,259
Per Capita Income	$58,706
Property Value	$5,986,167,626
Retail Sales	$184,897,058

Physical Features: Scenic southwestern county of cedar-covered hills on the Edwards Plateau; Medina, Sabinal Rivers; limestone, sandy soils; species of oaks, walnuts, native cherry and Uvalde maple.

Economy: Tourism, hunting, fishing, ranching supplies, forest products.

History: Apache tribal area, then Comanche territory. White settlement began in the early 1850s, including Mormons and Poles. County created, organized from Bexar, Uvalde counties in 1856; named for Bandera (flag) Mountains.

Recreation: RV parks, resort ranches; Lost Maples and Hill Country State Natural Areas; rodeo, parade on Memorial Day weekend; Medina Lake.

Minerals: Not significant.

Agriculture: Beef cattle, sheep, goats, horses, deer (first in numbers in captivity), small fruit orchards, pumpkins. Market value $6.9 million. Hunting and nature tourism important.

Vital Statistics, annual: Births, 164; deaths, 312; marriages, 115; divorces, 68.

Race/Ethnicity: Anglo, 74.8%; Hispanic, 19.2%; Black, 0.5%; Asian, 0.5%; Other, 5%.

BANDERA (839) county seat; tourism, ranching, service industries; historic sites, Frontier Times Museum.

Other towns include: **Medina** (850) pumpkin patch; **Pipe Creek** (130); **Tarpley** (30); **Vanderpool** (20). Also, the community of **Lakehills** (5,499) on Medina Lake, Cajun Fest (Sept), and **Lake Medina Shores** (696).

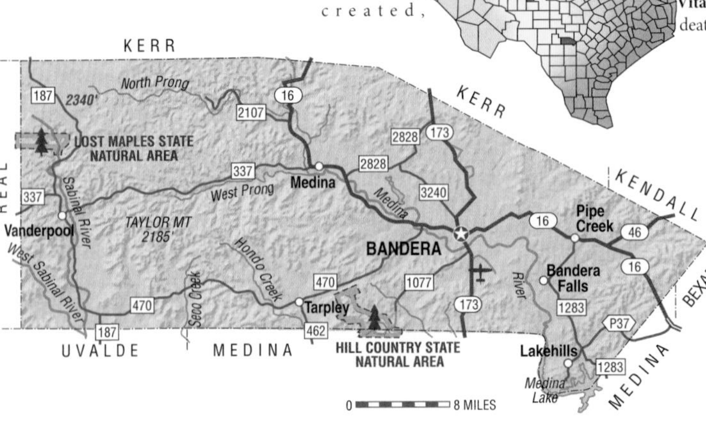

Horses and mules grazing in a pasture near Seymour in Baylor County. Photo by USDA NRCS Texas, Public Domain

Bastrop County

Physical Features: Rolling; alluvial, sandy, loam soils; varied timber, Lost Pines; bisected by Colorado River; Lake Bastrop.

Economy: Government/services; tourism; agribusiness; bio-technology research; computer-related industries; commuters to Austin.

History: Tonkawa Indian area; Comanches also present. Spanish fort established in 1804. County created in 1836, organized in 1837; named for Baron de Bastrop, who aided Moses and Stephen F. Austin in establishing the colony in the 1820s.

Recreation: Fishing, hunting; state parks; Lake Bastrop; historic sites; museum; railroad park; natural science center; nature trails.

Minerals: Lignite and clay.

Population	102,058
Change from 2010 (%)	37.6%
Area (sq. mi.)	895.6
Land Area (sq. mi.)	888.2
Altitude (ft.)	300–729
Rainfall (in.)	36.1
Jan. mean min (°F)	41.0
July mean max (°F)	94.3
Civ. Labor	48,156
Unemployed (%)	3.3
Wages	$275,511,387
Per Capita Income	$44,230
Property Value	$22,506,735,781
Retail Sales	$1,685,118,172

Agriculture: Beef cattle, hay, pecans, turfgrass, feed corn, sorghum. Market value $44.7 million. Pine for lumber, oak for firewood.

Vital Statistics, annual: Births, 1,143; deaths, 824; marriages, 370; divorces, 182.

Race/Ethnicity: Anglo, 47.1%; Hispanic, 42.7%; Black, 5.6%; Asian, 0.7%; Other, 3.9%.

BASTROP (10,434) county seat; government/services, tourism, hospitals, University of Texas cancer research center, federal prison; riverwalk; Yesterfest in April.

ELGIN (10,549) bricks, sausage manufacturing; horse, cattle breeding; medical research; depot museum; Western Days in June, Hogeye festival in October.

Smithville (4,047) government/services, hospital, railroad; parks, hike & bike trails, museums; jamboree on weekend after Easter, Reel Film Expo in May.

Other towns: **Cedar Creek** (4,076); **Circle D-KC Estates** (2,450); **McDade** (1,376) watermelon festival in July; **Paige** (142); **Red Rock** (397); **Rosanky** (1,488) automotive museum; **Wyldwood** (3,718). Also, **Camp Swift** (6,901).

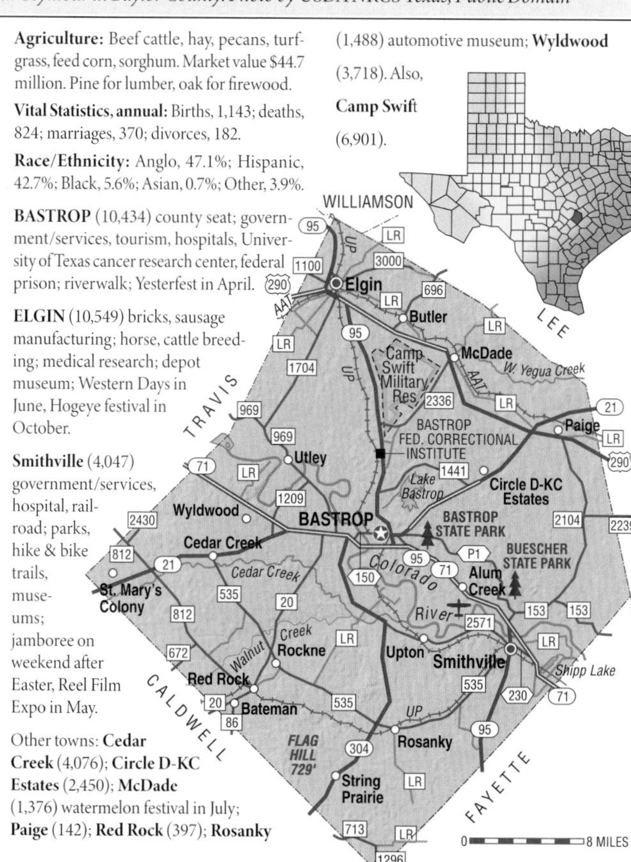

Baylor County

Physical Features: Northwest county; level to hilly; drains to Brazos, Wichita rivers; Lake Kemp, Lake Diversion, Millers Creek Reservoir; sandy, loam, red soils; grassy, mesquites, cedars.

Economy: Agribusiness; retail/service; health services.

History: Comanches, with Wichitas and other tribes also in the area; U.S. Army removed tribes in 1874-75. Anglo-Americans settled in the 1870s. County created from Fannin County in 1858; organized in 1879. Named for H.W. Baylor, Texas Ranger surgeon.

Recreation: Lakes; hunting; settlers reunion, rodeo, go-cart races in July.

Minerals: Oil, gas produced.

Agriculture: Wheat, cattle, cow-calf operations, grain sorghum, cotton, hay. Market value $53.7 million.

Vital Statistics, annual: Births, 45; deaths, 69; marriages, 13; divorces, 3.

Race/Ethnicity: Anglo, 80.7%; Hispanic, 12.7%; Black, 1.5%; Asian, 0.3%; Other, 4.8%.

SEYMOUR (2,584) county seat; agribusiness; hospital; dove hunters' breakfast in September.

Population	3,477
Change from 2010 (%)	–6.7%
Area (sq. mi.)	901.1
Land Area (sq. mi.)	867.5
Altitude (ft.)	1,053–1,537
Rainfall (in.)	29.0
Jan. mean min (°F)	29.7

July mean max (°F)	95.5
Civ. Labor	1,925
Unemployed (%)	2.7
Wages	$18,425,113
Per Capita Income	$58,779
Property Value	$1,284,354,603
Retail Sales	$37,083,381

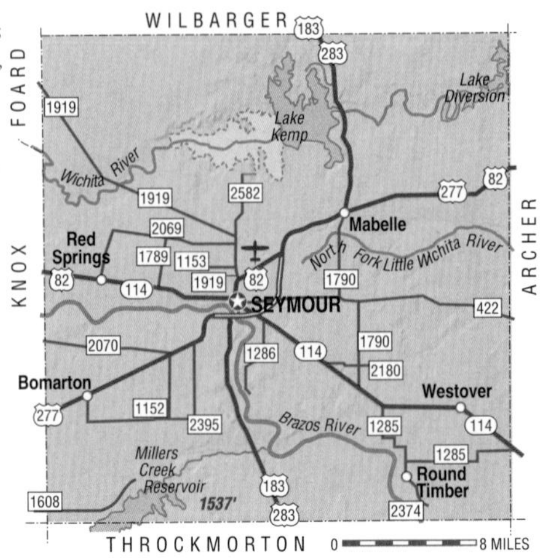

Bee County

Physical Features: South Coastal Plain, level to rolling; black clay, sandy, loam soils; brushy.

Economy: Agriculture, government/services; hunting leases; oil and gas business.

History: Karankawa, Apache, Pawnee territory. First Spanish land grant, 1789. Irish settlers arrived 1826-29. County created from Karnes, Live Oak, Goliad, Refugio, San Patricio, 1857; organized 1858; named for Barnard Bee Sr., secretary of state and diplomat for the Republic.

Recreation: Hunting, birding, camping; historical sites, antiques; rodeo/roping events.

Minerals: Oil, gas produced.

Agriculture: Beef cattle, corn, cotton and grain sorghum. Market value $37.7 million. Hunting leases.

Vital Statistics, annual: Births, 347; deaths, 321; marriages, 110; divorces, 58.

Race/Ethnicity: Anglo, 27.7%; Hispanic, 62.5%; Black, 7.5%; Asian, 0.7%; Other, 1.7%.

BEEVILLE (13,641) county seat; aircraft maintenance, waste-bind manufacturing, retail center; Coastal Bend College; hospital; art museum; Diez y Seis festival in September.

Other towns and places include: **Blueberry Hill** (688); **Mineral** (65); **Normanna** (80); **Pawnee** (85); **Pettus** (640); **Skidmore** (1,265); **Tuleta** (289); **Tynan** (268).

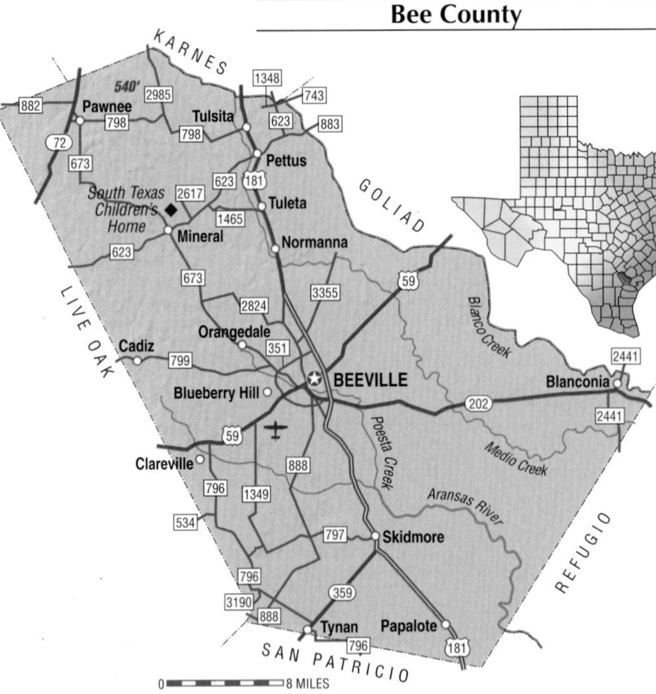

Population	30,924
Change from 2010 (%)	–2.9%
Area (sq. mi.)	880.3
Land Area (sq. mi.)	880.2
Altitude (ft.)	39–540
Rainfall (in.)	32.0
Jan. mean min (°F)	45.5

July mean max (°F)	93.8
Civ. Labor	9,159
Unemployed (%)	5.8
Wages	$91,647,133
Per Capita Income	$34,738
Property Value	$4,283,469,270
Retail Sales	$372,918,453

Bell County

Physical Features: Central Texas Blackland, level to hilly; black to light soils in west; mixed timber; Belton Lake, Stillhouse Hollow Lake.

Economy: Fort Cavazos; manufacturing includes computers, plastic goods, furniture, clothing; agribusiness; distribution center; tourism.

History: Tonkawas, Lipan Apaches; reduced by disease and advancing frontier by 1840s. Comanches raided into 1870s. Settled in 1830s as part of Robertson's colony. A few slaveholders in 1850s. County created from Milam County in 1850; named for Gov. P.H. Bell.

Recreation: Fishing, hunting; lakes; historic sites; exposition center; Salado gathering of Scottish clans in November.

Minerals: Gravel.

Agriculture: Beef, corn, sorghum, wheat, cotton. Market value $77.0 million.

Vital Statistics, annual: Births, 6,102; deaths, 2,818; marriages, 3,541; divorces, 2,035.

Race/Ethnicity: Anglo, 42.3%; Hispanic, 25.2%; Black, 21.8%; Asian, 2.9%; Other, 7.8%.

BELTON (23,845) county seat; University of Mary Hardin-Baylor; government/services; manufacturing; museum, nature center.

KILLEEN (156,261) Fort Cavazos; Texas A&M University–Central Texas and Central Texas College; regional airport; retail center, varied manufacturing; hospital; museums, planetarium; Four Winds Powwow in September.

TEMPLE (85,416) Major medical center with two hospitals and VA hospital; diversified industries; rail and wholesale distribution center; retail center; Temple College, Texas A&M College of Medicine; Azalee Marshall Cultural Activities Center; Czech museum; early-day tractor, engine show in October.

Other towns include: **Harker Heights** (33,560) Founder's Day in October; **Heidenheimer** (224); **Holland** (1,086) corn festival in June; **Little River-Academy** (1,989).

Also, **Morgan's Point Resort** (4,713); **Nolanville** (6,249); **Pendleton** (791); **Rogers** (1,104); **Salado** (2,391) tourism, civic center, amphitheatre, art fair in August; **Troy** (2,468).

Also, part [694] of **Bartlett**.

Fort Cavazos has a population of 24,781.

Population	379,617
Change from 2010 (%)	22.4%
Area (sq. mi.)	1,087.8
Land Area (sq. mi.)	1,051.0

Altitude (ft.)	390–1,227
Rainfall (in.)	37.0
Jan. mean min (°F)	37.7
July mean max (°F)	94.1
Civ. Labor	149,332

Unemployed (%)	4.4
Wages	$1,827,973,091
Per Capita Income	$49,405
Property Value	$42,382,261,852
Retail Sales	$7,326,102,429

For explanation of sources, symbols, and abbreviations, see p. 207 and foldout map.

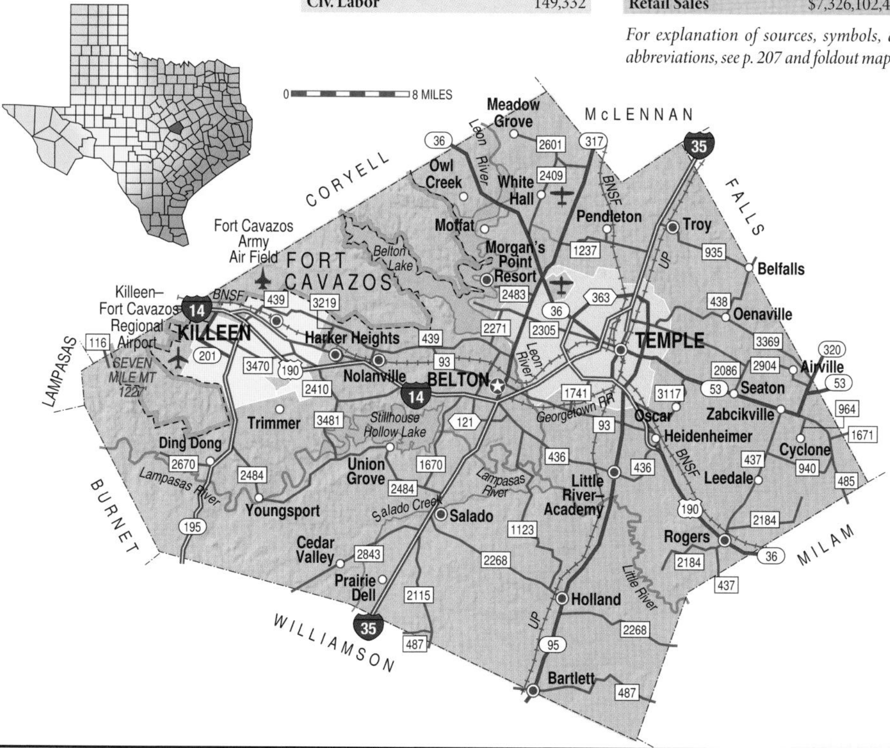

0 8 MILES
McLENNAN
FALLS
MILAM
WILLIAMSON
BURNET
LAMPASAS
CORYELL
FORT CAVAZOS
Fort Cavazos Army Air Field
Killeen–Fort Cavazos Regional Airport
KILLEEN
Harker Heights
Nolanville
BELTON
TEMPLE
Meadow Grove
Owl Creek
White Hall
Moffat
Morgan's Point Resort
Pendleton
Troy
Belfalls
Oenaville
Airville
Seaton
Zabcikville
Oscar
Heidenheimer
Cyclone
Leedale
Little River-Academy
Rogers
Holland
Bartlett
Salado
Prairie Dell
Cedar Valley
Youngsport
Union Grove
Trimmer
Ding Dong
SEVEN MILE MT 1227'
Belton Lake
Stillhouse Hollow Lake
Leon River
Lampasas River
Salado Creek
Little River
Georgetown RR

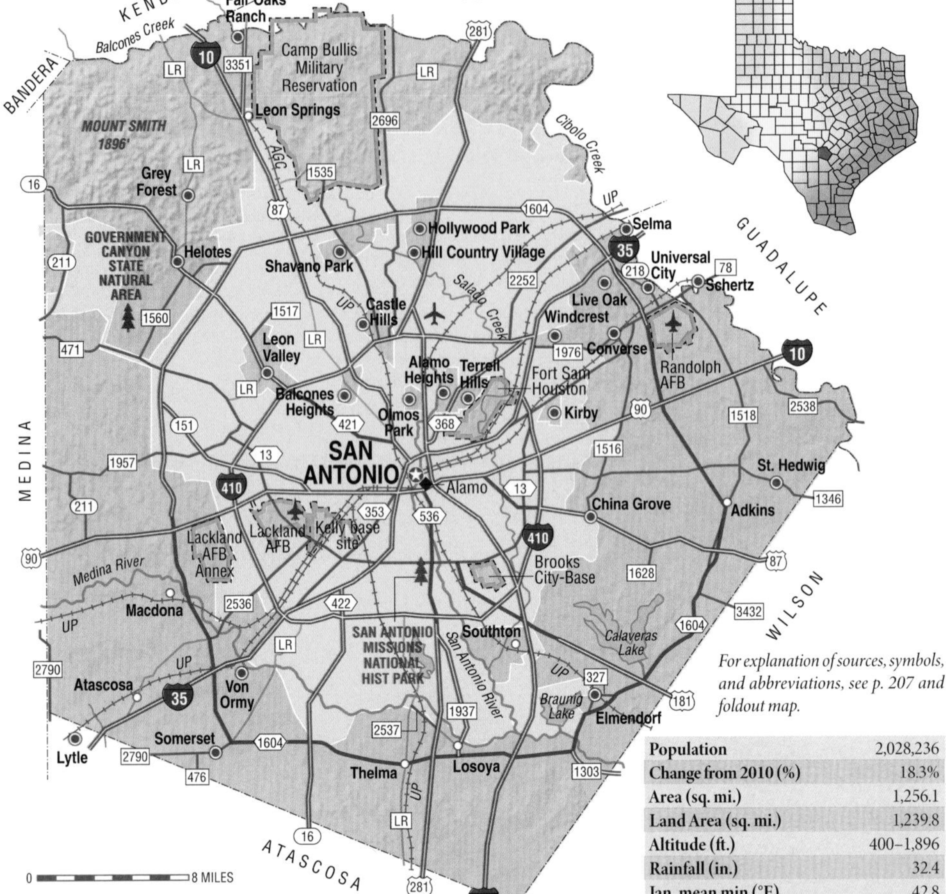

For explanation of sources, symbols, and abbreviations, see p. 207 and foldout map.

Population	2,028,236
Change from 2010 (%)	18.3%
Area (sq. mi.)	1,256.1
Land Area (sq. mi.)	1,239.8
Altitude (ft.)	400–1,896
Rainfall (in.)	32.4
Jan. mean min (°F)	42.8
July mean max (°F)	94.4
Civ. Labor	978,125
Unemployed (%)	3.7
Wages	$14,313,836,178
Per Capita Income	$51,780
Property Value	$271,862,361,111
Retail Sales	$40,554,741,561

Bexar County

Physical Features: On edge of Balcones Escarpment, Coastal Plain; heavy black to thin limestone soils; spring-fed streams; underground water; mesquite, other brush; Braunig Lake, Calaveras Lake.

Economy: Medical/biomedical research and services; government center with large federal payroll, military bases; tourism; education center.

History: Coahuiltecan Indian area; also Lipan Apache and Tonkawa tribes present. Mission San Antonio de Valero (Alamo) founded in 1718. Canary Islanders arrived in 1731. Anglo-American settlers began arriving in the late 1820s. County created and organized in 1836 from Spanish municipality named to honor the duke of Bexar; a colonial capital of Texas.

Recreation: Historic sites include the Alamo, other missions, Casa Navarro, La Villita; River Walk, El Mercado (market), Tower of the Americas, Brackenridge Park, zoo, SeaWorld, HemisFair Park, Institute of Texan Cultures; museums, symphony orchestra; hunting, fishing; NBA Spurs; Fiesta in April, Folklife Festival in June.

Minerals: Gravel, sand, limestone.

Agriculture: Nursery crops, beef cattle, grain sorghum, hay, corn. Market value $67.9 million.

Vital Statistics, annual: Births, 25,247; deaths, 16,664; marriages, 9,120; divorces, 2,693.

Race/Ethnicity: Anglo, 26.7%; Hispanic, 59.3%; Black, 7.4%; Asian, 3.2%; Other, 3.5%.

SAN ANTONIO (1,451,853) county seat; Texas' second-largest city; healthcare/biosciences, government/services, manufacturing, tourism, information technology, aerospace, education, energy; Alamodome. Leon Springs is now part of San Antonio.

Other towns include: **Alamo Heights** (7,392); **Balcones Heights** (2,725); **Castle Hills** (3,947); **China Grove** (1,133); **Converse** (28,643); **Elmendorf** (2,029); **Fair Oaks Ranch** (10,505); **Grey Forest** (489); **Helotes** (9,178) government/services, retail trade, Cornyval Festival in May, Highland games in April, John T. Floore Country Store, Gugger Homestead; **Hill Country Village** (940); **Hollywood Park** (3,106).

Also, **Kirby** (8,100); **Leon Valley** (11,463); **Live Oak** (15,840); **Macdona** (466); **Olmos Park** (2,162); **St. Hedwig** (2,258); **Selma** (11,619, parts in Guadalupe and Comal counties); **Shavano Park** (3,569); **Somerset** (1,765); **Terrell Hills** (5,037); **Universal City** (19,808); **Von Ormy** (1,177); **Windcrest** (5,828).

Part [5,873] of **Schertz**.

Lackland Air Force Base (7,417); **Randolph Air Force Base** (1,842).

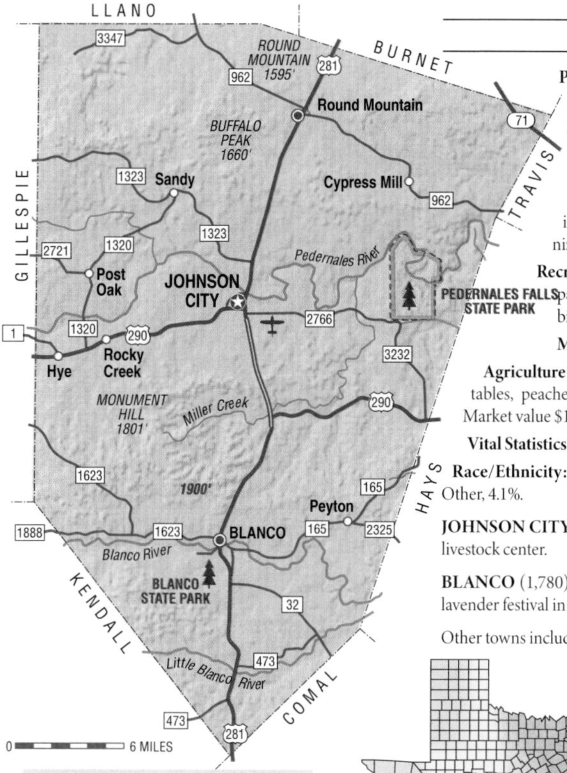

Blanco County

Physical Features: Hill Country county; Blanco, Pedernales rivers; cedars, pecans, live oaks, other trees.

Economy: Tourism, agribusiness/wholesale nursery, ranch supplies, hunting/fishing.

History: Lipan Apache area. Comanches were present when Anglo-Americans settled in the 1850s. County created in 1858 from Burnet, Comal, Gillespie, Hays counties, organized the same year; named for the Blanco (white) River.

Recreation: President Lyndon B. Johnson's boyhood home, state parks, Saur-Beckmann living history farm; hunting, fishing; bike ride in March; scenic drives, wineries/vineyards.

Minerals: Insignificant.

Agriculture: Cow-calf operation, stocker cattle; sheep, goats; hay, vegetables, peaches, grapes, pecans, greenhouse nurseries; limited irrigation. Market value $17.0 million.

Vital Statistics, annual: Births, 82; deaths, 133; marriages, 31; divorces, 51.

Race/Ethnicity: Anglo, 76.6%; Hispanic, 18.4%; Black, 0.6%; Asian, 0.3%; Other, 4.1%.

JOHNSON CITY (1,717) county seat; tourism, electric co-op; art galleries, livestock center.

BLANCO (1,780) tourism, old courthouse, Pioneer museum, nature trail; lavender festival in June.

Other towns include: **Hye** (72) and **Round Mountain** (104).

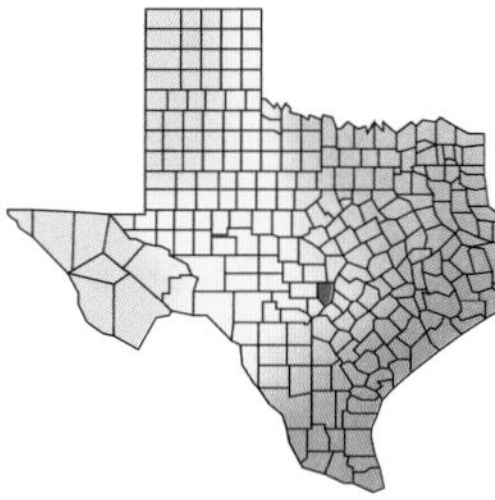

Population	11,886
Change from 2010	13.2%
Area (sq. mi.)	713.4
Land Area (sq. mi.)	709.3
Altitude (ft.)	741–1,900

Rainfall (in.)	34.8
Jan. mean min (°F)	37.2
July mean max (°F)	92.4
Civ. Labor	7,133
Unemployed	2.8%
Wages	$60,203,325
Per Capita Income	$66,088
Property Value	$9,615,911,669
Retail Sales	$104,883,923

Borden County

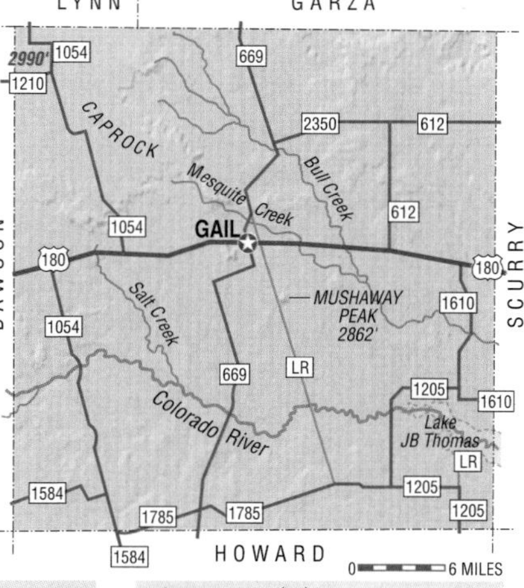

Physical Features: Rolling surface, broken by Caprock Escarpment; drains to Colorado River; sandy loam, clay soils.

Economy: Agriculture and hunting leases; oil; wind turbines and solar farms.

History: Comanche area. Anglo-Americans settled in the 1870s. County created in 1876 from Bexar District, organized in 1891; named for Gail Borden, patriot, inventor, editor.

Recreation: Fishing; quail and deer hunting; Lake J.B. Thomas; museum; junior livestock show in January; Coyote Country Store outdoor music venue.

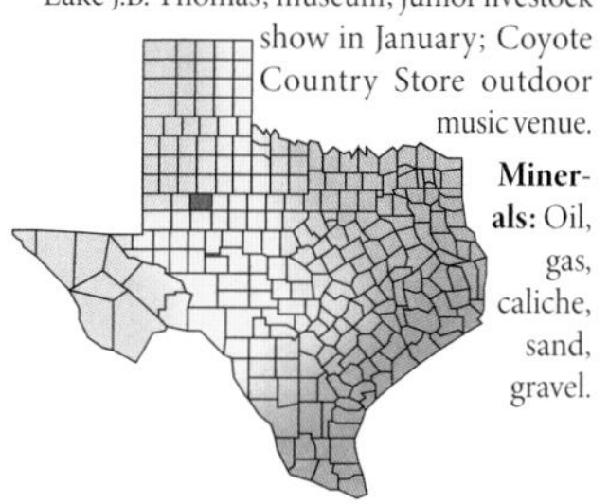

Minerals: Oil, gas, caliche, sand, gravel.

Agriculture: Beef cattle, cotton, wheat, hay, pecans, oats; some irrigation. Market value $28.8 million.

Vital Statistics, annual: Births, 0; deaths, 0; marriages, 4; divorces, NA.

Race/Ethnicity: Anglo, 83.7%; Hispanic, 13.6%; Black, 0.2%; Asian, 0%; Other, 2.5%.

GAIL (173) county seat; museum, antique shop, ambulance service; "star" construction atop Gail Mountain.

Population	617
Change from 2010	-3.7%
Area (sq. mi.)	906.1
Land Area (sq. mi.)	897.4
Altitude (ft.)	2,258–2,990
Rainfall (in.)	19.5
Jan. mean min (°F)	33.7

July mean max (°F)	92.6
Civ. Labor	701
Unemployed	1.9%
Wages	$7,557,804
Per Capita Income	$101,470
Property Value	$1,562,899,234
Retail Sales	$16,558

The Dahl Farmhouse in Bosque County is on the National Register of Historic Places. Photo by Renelibrary, CC by SA 3.0

Bosque County

Physical Features: Hilly, broken by Brazos, Bosque rivers; limestone to alluvial soils; cedars, oaks, mesquites.

Economy: Agribusiness, government/services, small industries, tourism, solar farms.

History: Tonkawa, Waco, and Tawakoni Indian tribes. Settlers from England and Norway arrived in the 1850s. County created and organized in 1854 from the Milam District and McLennan County; named for Bosque (woods) River.

Recreation: Lake Whitney, Meridian State Park, museum at Clifton, fine art conservatory; fishing, hunting; scenic routes, Norwegian smorgasbord at Norse in November.

Minerals: Limestone, gas & oil.

Agriculture: Beef cattle, forages, small grains, and vineyards. Market value $45.1 million. Hunting leases.

Vital Statistics, annual: Births, 181; deaths, 332; marriages, 81; divorces, 38.

Race/Ethnicity: Anglo, 74.7%; Hispanic, 18.2%; Black, 1.3%; Asian, 0.4%; Other, 5.3%.

MERIDIAN (1,407) county seat; food processing, government/services, tourism; retirement home, community college; national championship barbecue cookoff in October.

CLIFTON (3,488) retirement/health care; hospital, nursing school; library; Norwegian historic district; Norwegian Country Christmas.

Other towns include: **Cranfills Gap** (282) Lutefisk dinner in December, Old Rock Church; **Iredell** (310); **Kopperl** (121); **Laguna Park** (1,520); **Morgan** (457); **Valley Mills** (1,243); **Walnut Springs** (815).

Population	18,503
Change from 2010	1.6%
Area (sq. mi.)	1,002.5
Land Area (sq. mi.)	983.0
Altitude (ft.)	410–1,284
Rainfall (in.)	37.6
Jan. mean min (°F)	36.3
July mean max (°F)	94.1
Civ. Labor	8,704
Unemployed	3.7%
Wages	$49,930,452
Per Capita Income	$50,943
Property Value	$7,269,932,028
Retail Sales	$118,258,787

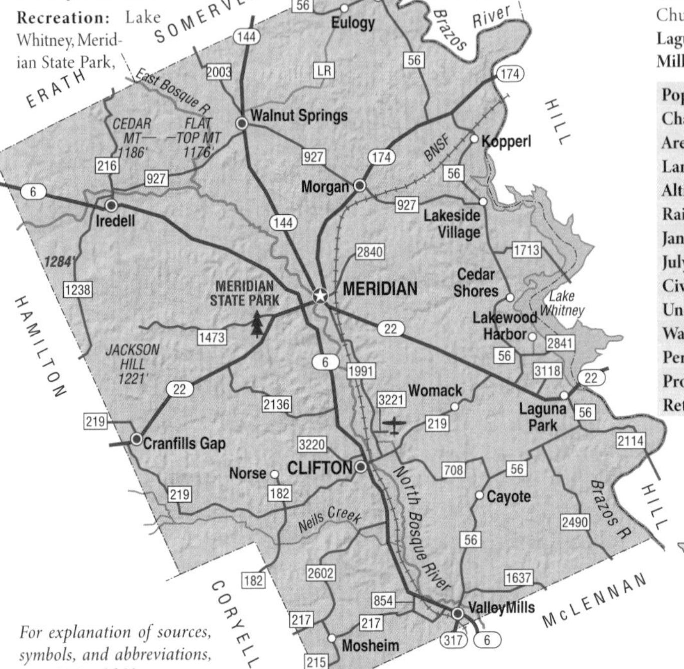

For explanation of sources, symbols, and abbreviations, see p. 207 and foldout map.

Bowie County

Physical Features: Forested hills at northeast corner of the state; clay, sandy, alluvial soils; drained by Red and Sulphur rivers; Wright Patman Lake.

Economy: Government/services, lumber, manufacturing, agribusiness.

History: Caddo tribal area, abandoned in the 1790s after trouble with the Osage tribe. Anglo-Americans began arriving 1815-20. County created and organized in 1840 from Red River County; named for the Alamo hero James Bowie.

Recreation: Lake activities, Crystal Springs beach; hunting, fishing; historic sites; Four-States Fair in September, Octoberfest.

Minerals: Oil, gas, sand, gravel.

Agriculture: Beef cattle, pecans, hay, corn, poultry, soybeans, dairy, nurseries, wheat, rice, horses, milo. Market value $60.1 million. Pine timber, hardwoods, pulpwood harvested.

Vital Statistics, annual: Births, 1,088; deaths, 1,228; marriages, 357; divorces, 435.

Race/Ethnicity: Anglo, 60.1%; Hispanic, 8.2%; Black, 24.9%; Asian, 1.2%; Other, 5.7%.

NEW BOSTON (4,579) site of county courthouse; army depot, lumber mill, steel manufacture, agribusiness, state prison; Pioneer Days in August. The area of Boston, officially designated as the county seat, has been annexed by New Boston.

TEXARKANA (36,017 in Texas, 29,387 in Arkansas) rubber company, paper manufacturing, distribution; hospitals; tourism; colleges; federal prison; Perot Theatre; Quadrangle Festival in September.

Other towns include: **De Kalb** (1,511) agriculture, government/services, commuting to Texarkana, Oktoberfest; **Hooks** (2,514); **Leary** (439); **Maud** (975); **Nash** (3,831); **Red Lick** (937); **Redwater** (851); **Simms** (300); **Wake Village** (5,897).

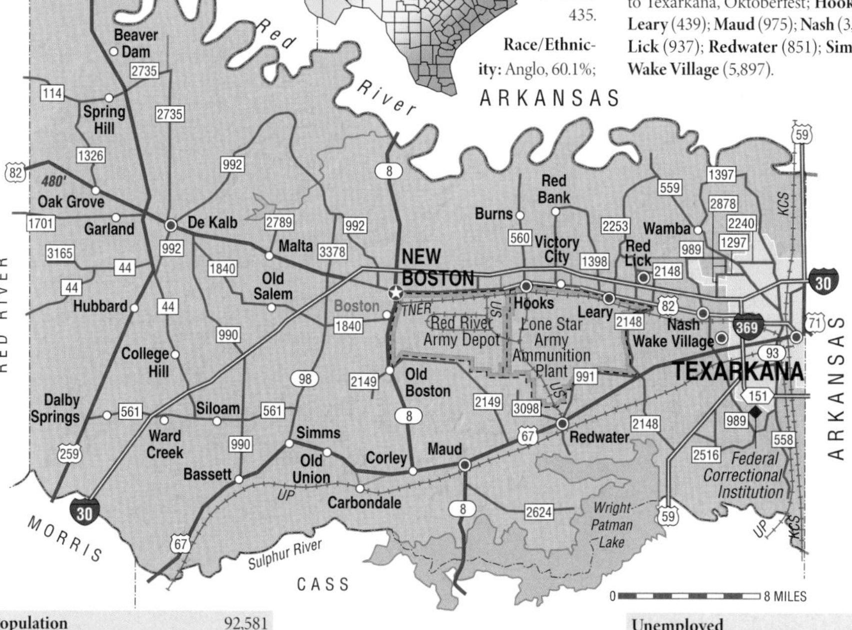

Population	92,581
Change from 2010	0.0%
Area (sq. mi.)	923.0
Land Area (sq. mi.)	885.0
Altitude (ft.)	200–480

Rainfall (in.)	52.4
Jan. mean min (°F)	35.2
July mean max (°F)	92.0
Civ. Labor	38,577

Unemployed	4.6%
Wages	$523,452,469
Per Capita Income	$47,792
Property Value	$10,688,486,811
Retail Sales	$2,102,187,405

A close-up of the architectural details on the federal building in Texarkana. Photo by Carol M. Highsmith, Public Domain

Brazoria County

Physical Features: Flat Coastal Plain, coastal soils, drained by Brazos and San Bernard rivers; Brazoria Reservoir, Eagle Nest Lake, Harris Reservoir, Mustang Lake East/West, San Bernard Reservoirs.

Economy: Petroleum and chemical industry, fishing, tourism, agribusiness. Part of Houston metropolitan area.

History: Karankawa area. Part of Austin's "Old Three Hundred" colony of families arriving in early 1820s. County created 1836 from Municipality of Brazoria, organized in 1837; name derived from Brazos River.

Recreation: Beaches, water sports; fishing, hunting; wildlife refuges, historic sites, plantations; state and county parks; replica of the first capitol of the Republic of Texas at West Columbia.

Minerals: Oil, gas, sand, gravel.

Agriculture: Cattle, hay, rice, soybeans, sorghum, nurseries, corn, cotton, aquaculture, bees. Some 20,000 acres of rice irrigated. Market value $79.5 million.

Vital Statistics, annual: Births, 4,495; deaths, 2,868; marriages, 1,786; divorces, 1,211.

Race/Ethnicity: Anglo, 43.5%; Hispanic, 31%; Black, 14.4%; Asian, 7.1%; Other, 4.1%.

ANGLETON (19,401) county seat; banking and distribution center for oil, chemical, agricultural area; fish-processing plant; hospital.

BRAZOSPORT (60,138) is a community of eight cities; chemical complex, deepwater seaport, commercial fishing, tourism; college; hospital; Brazosport cities include: **Clute** (10,593) mosquito festival in July; **Freeport** (10,594) museum, Riverfest in late April; **Jones Creek** (1,959); **Lake Jackson** (27,879) research & development, museum, sea center, Gulf Coast Bird Observatory; **Oyster Creek** (1,186); **Quintana** (25) Neotropical Bird Sanctuary; **Richwood** (4,761); **Surfside Beach** (656) tourism, St. Patrick's Day parade.

PEARLAND (125,990, parts in Harris, Fort Bend counties) trucking, metal fabrication, oilfield, chemical production; commuting to Houston, NASA; community college; Hindu temple; Winter Fest in January.

Other towns include: **Alvin** (27,576) petrochemical processing, agribusiness, rail, trucking; junior college; hospital; Crawfest and Shrimp Boil in April. **Bailey's Prairie** (781); **Bonney** (183); **Brazoria** (2,845) government/services, retail, manufacturing; library; No-Name Festival in June, Santa Anna Ball in July; **Brookside Village** (1,552).

Also, **Damon** (154); **Danbury** (1,655); **Danciger** (90); **Hillcrest Village** (693); **Holiday Lakes** (1,022); **Iowa Colony** (10,883); **Liverpool** (494); **Manvel** (12,355); **Old Ocean** (150); **Rosharon** (1,721); **Sandy Point** (212); **Sweeny** (3,591) petrochemicals, government/services, hospital, library, Pride Day in May, Levi Jordan Plantation SHS; **West Columbia** (3,611) chemical industry, retail, cattle, rice farming, museum, historic sites, plantation, San Jacinto Festival in April, Stephen F. Austin funeral procession re-enactment in October.

Population	379,689
Change from 2010	21.2%
Area (sq. mi.)	1,608.6
Land Area (sq. mi.)	1,357.7
Altitude (ft.)	sealevel–146
Rainfall (in.)	49.9
Jan. mean min (°F)	48.3
July mean max (°F)	91.1
Civ. Labor	184,468
Unemployed	4.5%
Wages	$1,994,464,752
Per Capita Income	$56,360
Property Value	$74,652,505,595
Retail Sales	$5,323,387,745

For explanation of sources, symbols, and abbreviations, see p. 207 and foldout map.

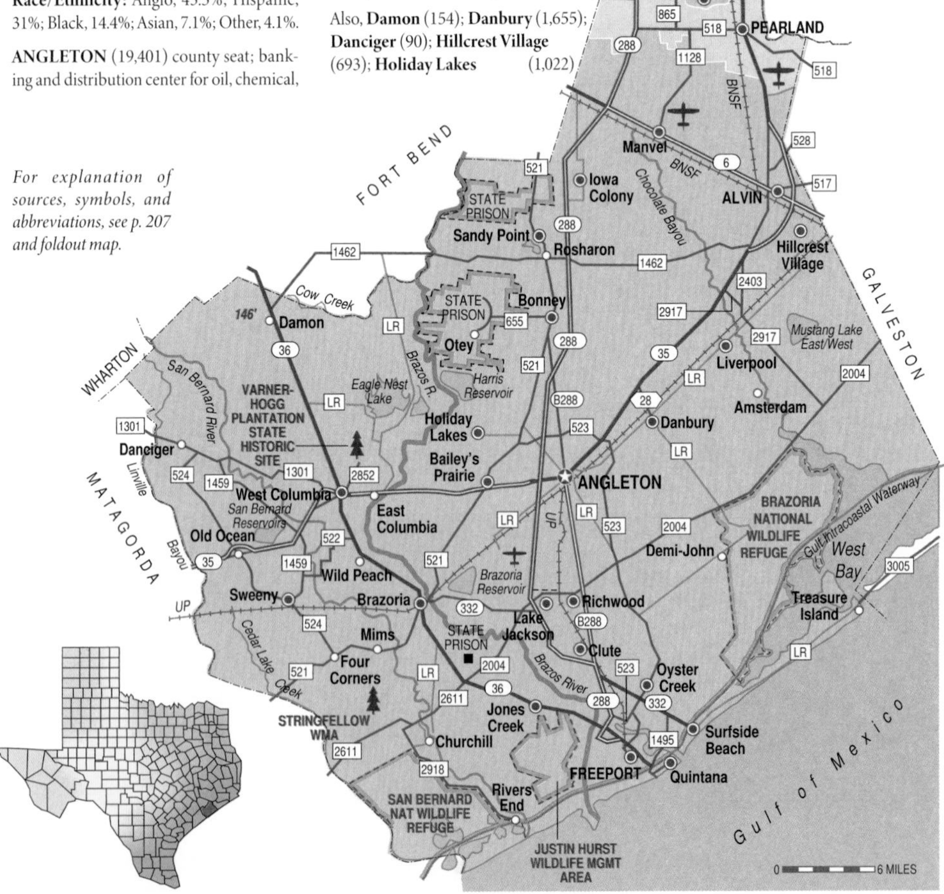

An old municipal building in Bryan has been converted into The Children's Museum. Photo by Larry D. Moore, CC by 4.0

Brazos County

Physical Features: South central county between Brazos, Navasota rivers; Bryan Lake; rich bottom soils, sandy, clays on rolling uplands; oak trees.

Economy: Texas A&M University; market and medical center; agribusiness; computers, research and development; government/ services; winery; industrial parks; tourism.

History: Bidais and Tonkawas; Comanches hunted in the area. Part of Stephen F. Austin's second colony of the late 1820s. County created in 1841 from Robertson, Washington counties and named Navasota; renamed for Brazos River in 1842, organized in 1843.

Recreation: Fishing, hunting; raceway; many events related to Texas A&M activities; George Bush Presidential Library and Museum; winery harvest weekends in August.

Minerals: Sand and gravel, lignite, gas, oil.

Agriculture: Cattle, poultry and eggs, cotton, hay, pecans, turf grass production, grain sorghum, corn, and horses. Market value $91.6 million.

Vital Statistics, annual: Births, 2,636; deaths, 1,341; marriages, 1,159; divorces, 161.

Race/Ethnicity: Anglo, 52.6%; Hispanic, 27%; Black, 10.1%; Asian, 6.3%; Other, 4.1%.

BRYAN (86,866) county seat; defense electronics, other varied manufacturing, agribusiness center; hospitals, psychiatric facilities; Blinn College extension; Brazos Valley African American Museum; steak & grape festival in June, Fiestas Patrias in September.

COLLEGE STATION (120,019) home of Texas A&M University, varied high-tech manufacturing, research; hospital.

Other towns include: **Kurten** (406); **Lake Bryan** (1,555); **Millican** (240); **Wellborn** (400); **Wixon Valley** (232).

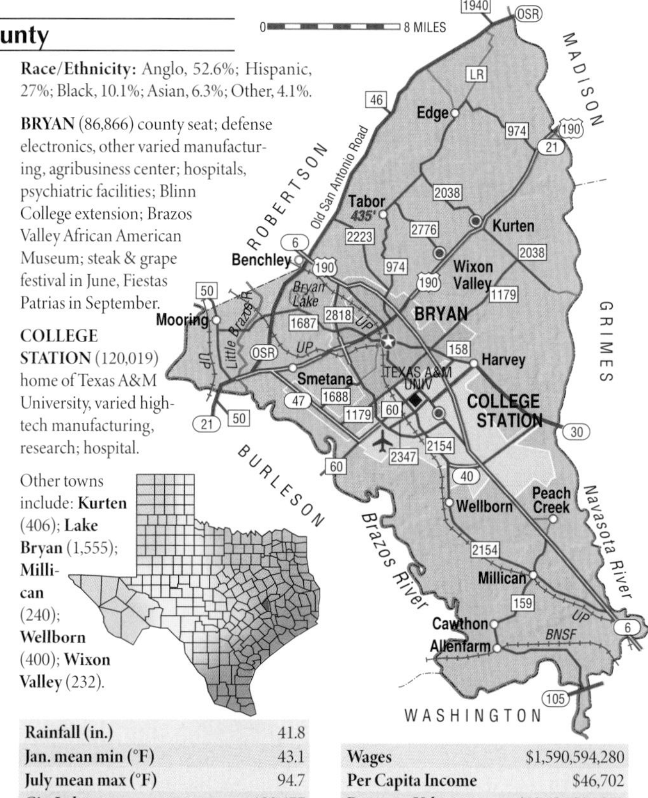

Population	237,032
Change from 2010	21.6%
Area (sq. mi.)	591.2
Land Area (sq. mi.)	585.5
Altitude (ft.)	157–435

Rainfall (in.)	41.8
Jan. mean min (°F)	43.1
July mean max (°F)	94.7
Civ. Labor	128,477
Unemployed	3.1%

Wages	$1,590,594,280
Per Capita Income	$46,702
Property Value	$32,624,384,892
Retail Sales	$4,170,917,277

Brewster County

Physical Features: Largest county, with area slightly less than that of Connecticut plus Rhode Island; mountains, canyons, distinctive geology, plant life, animals.

Economy: Tourism, government services, Sul Ross State University, ranching.

History: Pueblo culture had begun when Spanish explored in the 1500s. Mescalero Apaches in Chisos Mountains; Comanches raided in area. Ranching developed in northern part in the 1880s, with Mexican agricultural communities along river. County created, organized, 1887 from Presidio County; named for Henry P. Brewster, Republic secretary of war.

Recreation: Big Bend National Park, Big Bend Ranch State Park, Rio Grande Wild and Scenic River; ghost towns, scenic drives; hunting; museum; rockhound areas; cavalry post. Also, Barton Warnock Environmental Education Center at Lajitas; cowboy poetry and Western art show in February; Terlingua chili cookoff in November; Artwalk in November, Viva Big Bend Music Festival in July, Big Bend Ranch Rodeo in August.

Minerals: Bentonite.

Agriculture: Beef cattle, meat goats, horses. Market value $16.3 million. Hunting leases important.

Vital Statistics, annual: Births, 75; deaths, 103; marriages, 49; divorces, NA.

Race/Ethnicity: Anglo, 51.8%; Hispanic, 41.5%; Black, 1.7%; Asian, 1%; Other, 4%.

ALPINE (5,815) county seat; ranch trade center, tourism, varied manufacturing; Sul Ross State University; hospital; Art Walk Festival, Spirits of the West Festival, Sul Ross Rodeo.

For explanation of sources, symbols, and abbreviations, see p. 207 and foldout map.

Marathon (427) tourism, ranching center, Gage Hotel, Marathon Basin quilt show in October.

Also, **Basin** (30); **Study Butte** (172), and **Terlingua** (127), Chili Cook-off Championship.

Population	9,450
Change from 2010	2.4%
Area (sq. mi.)	6,192.3
Land Area (sq. mi.)	6,183.7
Altitude (ft.)	1,400–7,825
Rainfall (in.)	16.1
Jan. mean min (°F)	32.5
July mean max (°F)	90.9
Civ. Labor	4,233
Unemployed	3.4%
Wages	$52,637,696
Per Capita Income	$53,014
Property Value	$2,108,590,166
Retail Sales	$120,877,931

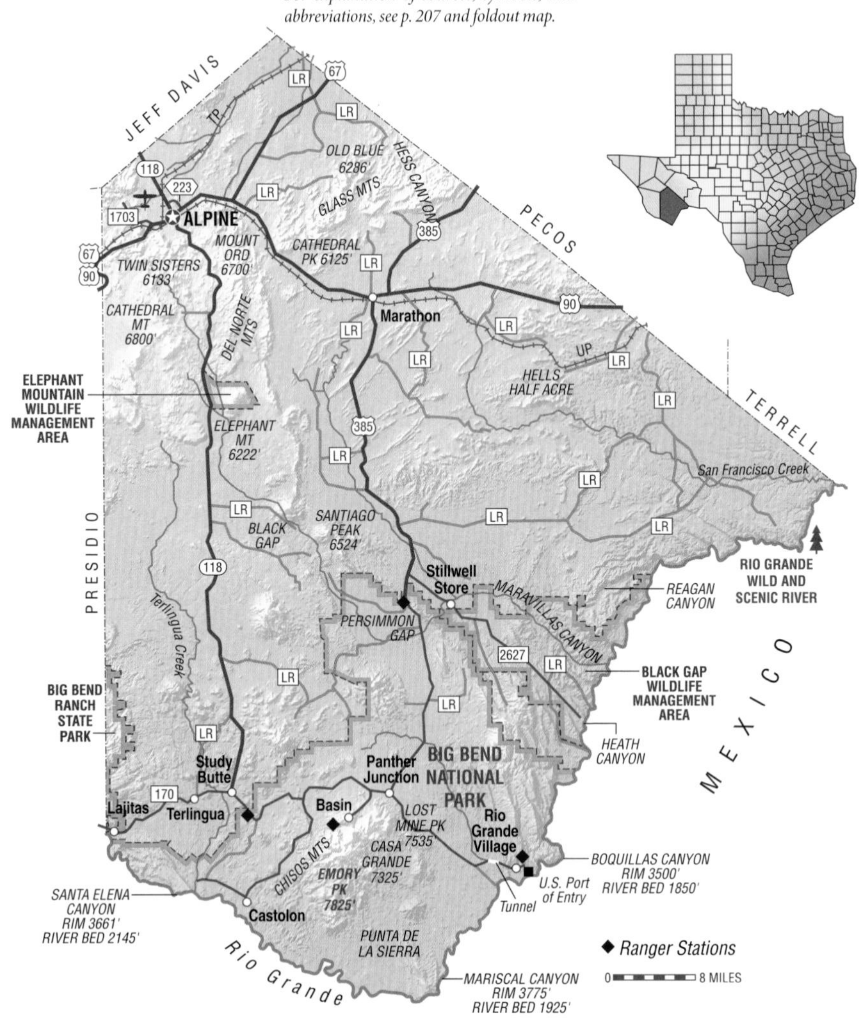

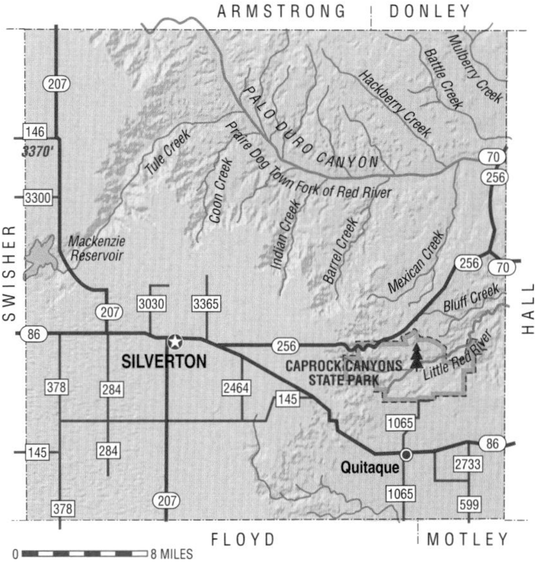

Briscoe County

Physical Features: Partly on High Plains, broken by Caprock Escarpment, fork of Red River; sandy, loam soils.

Economy: Agriculture, government/services.

History: Apaches in area, displaced by Comanches around 1700. Ranchers settled in the 1880s. County created from the Bexar District in 1876 and organized in 1892; named for Andrew Briscoe, Republic of Texas soldier.

Recreation: Hunting, fishing; scenic drives; museum at Quitaque; Caprock Canyons State Park, trailway, bison herd, Clarity tunnel with bats, Mackenzie Reservoir; Briscoe County Celebration in August, Bison Music Festival in September.

Minerals: Insignificant.

Agriculture: Cotton, beef, grain sorghum, wheat, hay. Some 23,000 acres irrigated. Market value $36.6 million.

Vital Statistics, annual: Births, 12; deaths, 28; marriages, 9; divorces, 1.

Race/Ethnicity: Anglo, 70.2%; Hispanic, 25.6%; Black, 1.2%; Asian, 0%; Other, 2.9%.

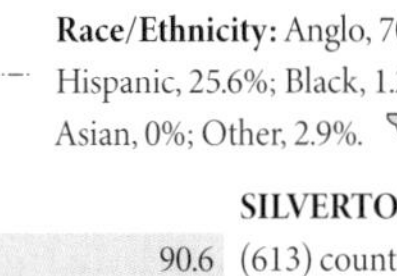

SILVERTON (613) county seat; agribusiness center, irrigation supplies manufactured; clinics.

Quitaque (334) agribusiness, nature tourism, government/services

Population	1,403
Change from 2010	-14.3%
Area (sq. mi.)	901.6
Land Area (sq. mi.)	900.0
Altitude (ft.)	2,064–3,370
Rainfall (in.)	21.7
Jan. mean min (°F)	25.2
July mean max (°F)	90.6
Civ. Labor	603
Unemployed	3.5
Wages	$4,125,633
Per Capita Income	$58,862
Property Value	$761,042,108
Retail Sales	$8,623,812

Brooks County

Physical Features: On Rio Grande plain; level to rolling; brushy; light to dark sandy loam soils.

Economy: Oil, gas, hunting leases, cattle, watermelons and hay.

History: Coahuiltecan Indians. Spanish land grants date to around 1800. County created from Hidalgo, Starr, Zapata counties, 1911; organized in 1912. Named for J.A. Brooks, Texas Ranger and legislator.

Recreation: Hunting, fishing; Heritage Museum, Don Pedrito shrine; Fiesta del Campo in October.

Minerals: Oil, gas production; uranium.

Agriculture: Beef cow-calf operations, stocker; crops include hay, squash, watermelons, habanero peppers. Market value $26.2 million.

Vital Statistics, annual: Births, 95; deaths, 117; marriages, 30; divorces, 4.

Race/Ethnicity: Anglo, 10.2%; Hispanic, 88.2%; Black, 0.1%; Asian, 0.4%; Other, 1%.

FALFURRIAS (4,787) county seat; oil and gas, agricultural, government/services.

Other towns include: **Encino** (71).

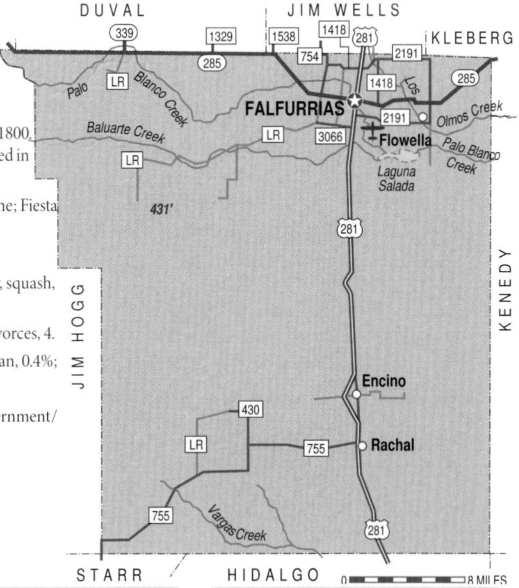

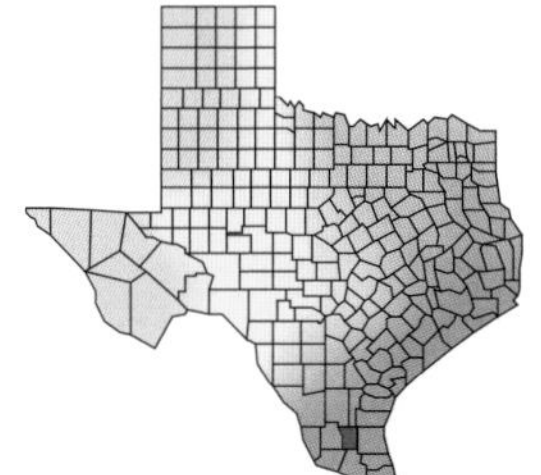

Population	6,994
Change from 2010	–3.2%
Area (sq. mi.)	943.7
Land Area (sq. mi.)	943.4
Altitude (ft.)	46–431
Rainfall (in.)	27.4
Jan. mean min (°F)	45.3
July mean max (°F)	97.2
Civ. Labor	2,381
Unemployed	6.0%
Wages	$32,857,901
Per Capita Income	$43,437
Property Value	$1,369,063,028
Retail Sales	$121,112,262

The Reeves-Womack House in Caldwell is on the National Register of Historic Places. Photo by Renelibrary, CC by SA 4.0

Brown County

Physical Features: Rolling, hilly; drains to Colorado River; Lake Brownwood; varied soils, timber.

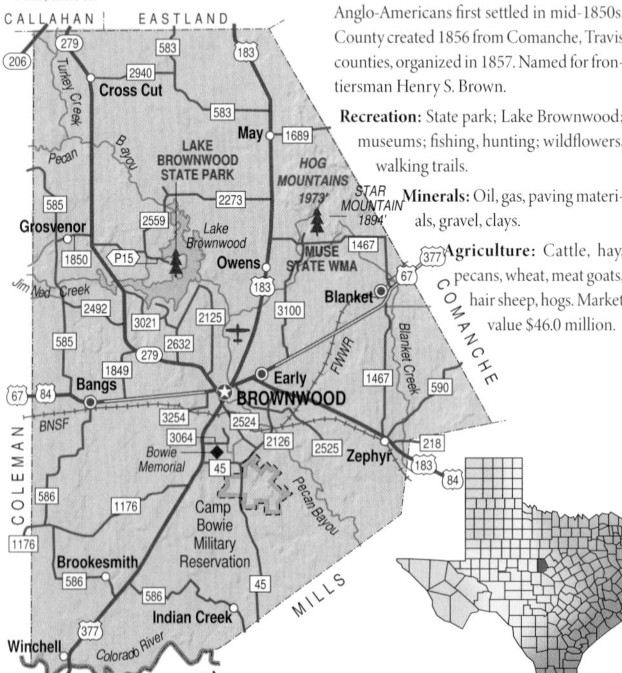

Economy: Manufacturing plants, distribution centers, government/services, agribusiness, medical, education.

History: Apaches; displaced by Comanches who were removed by U.S. Army in 1874-75. Anglo-Americans first settled in mid-1850s. County created 1856 from Comanche, Travis counties, organized in 1857. Named for frontiersman Henry S. Brown.

Recreation: State park; Lake Brownwood; museums; fishing, hunting; wildflowers, walking trails.

Minerals: Oil, gas, paving materials, gravel, clays.

Agriculture: Cattle, hay, pecans, wheat, meat goats, hair sheep, hogs. Market value $46.0 million.

Vital Statistics, annual: Births, 384; deaths, 671; marriages, 227; divorces, 55.

Race/Ethnicity: Anglo, 70%; Hispanic, 21.6%; Black, 3.6%; Asian, 0.7%; Other, 4.2%.

BROWNWOOD (18,770) county seat; rejuvinated downtown with microbreweries and restaurants, manufacturing, retail trade, distribution center; Howard Payne University, MacArthur Academy of Freedom; state substance abuse treatment center; state 4-H Club center; hospital; train museum, aquatic park; Reunion Celebration in September.

Early (3,145) retail, light manufacturing, government/services, agribusiness; motorcycle rally in October.

Other towns include: **Bangs** (1,542); **Blanket** (369); **Brookesmith** (61); **May** (226); **Zephyr** (198). **Lake Brownwood** area (1,595).

Population	38,192
Change from 2010	0.2%
Area (sq. mi.)	957.0
Land Area (sq. mi.)	944.4
Altitude (ft.)	1,230–1,973
Rainfall (in.)	30.6
Jan. mean min (°F)	33.9
July mean max (°F)	95.4
Civ. Labor	15,271
Unemployed	4.3%
Wages	$173,662,495
Per Capita Income	$46,028
Property Value	$7,398,890,312
Retail Sales	$605,995,725

Burleson County

Physical Features: Rolling to hilly; drains to Brazos, Yegua Creek, Somerville Lake; loam and heavy bottom soils; oaks, other trees.

Economy: Oil and gas, tourism, commuters to Texas A&M University, agribusiness.

History: Tonkawa and Caddo tribes roamed the area. Mexicans and Anglo-Americans settled around Fort Tenoxtitlan in 1830. Black freedmen migration increased until 1910. Germans, Czechs, Italians migrated in the 1870s-80s. County created and organized in 1846 from Milam, Washington counties; named for Edward Burleson, a hero of the Texas Revolution.

Recreation: Fishing, hunting; lake recreation; historic sites; Czech heritage museum.

Minerals: Oil, gas, sand, gravel, and water.

Agriculture: Cattle, cotton, corn, hay, sorghum, broiler production, soybeans; Crops are irrigated and dryland; wheat; sunflowers; watermelon; deer & exotic ranches; turfgrass

Vital Statistics, annual: Births, 205; deaths, 255; marriages, 49; divorces, 21.

Race/Ethnicity: Anglo, 63.8%; Hispanic, 21%; Black, 10.5%; Asian, 0.4%; Other, 4.3%.

CALDWELL (4,109) county seat; agribusiness, oil and gas, manufacturing, distribution center, tourism; hospital; civic center, museum; Kolache Festival in September.

Somerville (1,329) tourism, railroad center, some manufacturing; museum; Country Cajun festival in March.

Other towns include: **Chriesman** (30); **Lyons** (505); **Snook** (519) Snookfest in June.

For explanation of sources, symbols, and abbreviations, see p. 207 and foldout map.

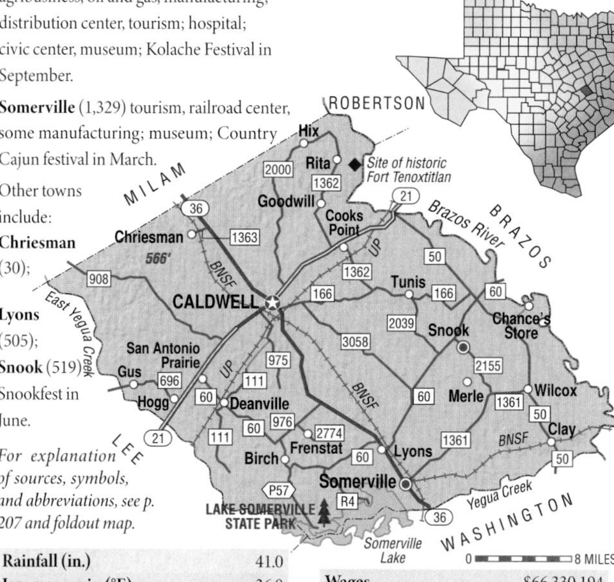

Population	18,051
Change from 2010	5.0%
Area (sq. mi.)	676.8
Land Area (sq. mi.)	659.0
Altitude (ft.)	177–566
Rainfall (in.)	41.0
Jan. mean min (°F)	36.8
July mean max (°F)	95.9
Civ. Labor	8,857
Unemployed	3.6%
Wages	$66,330,194
Per Capita Income	$57,482
Property Value	$5,946,606,241
Retail Sales	$231,591,455

Burnet County

Physical Features: Scenic Hill Country county with Lake Buchanan, Inks Lake, Lake Lyndon B. Johnson, Lake Travis, Lake Marble Falls; caves; sandy, red, black waxy soils; cedars, other trees.

Economy: Tourism, stone processing, hunting leases.

History: Tonkawas, Lipan Apaches. Comanches raided in area. Frontier settlers arrived in the late 1840s. County created from Bell, Travis, Williamson counties, 1852; organized 1854; named for David G. Burnet, provisional president of the Republic.

Recreation: Water sports on lakes; sites of historic forts; hunting; state parks, wildlife refuge; wildflowers; birding, scenic train ride.

Minerals: Granite, limestone.

Agriculture: Cattle, goats, grapes, hay. Market value $14.1 million. Deer, wild hog, and turkey hunting leases.

Vital Statistics, annual: Births, 499; deaths, 591; marriages, 254; divorces, 172.

Race/Ethnicity: Anglo, 70.9%; Hispanic, 22.8%; Black, 1.2%; Asian, 0.9%; Other, 4.3%.

BURNET (6,676) county seat; tourism, government/services, varied industries, ranching; hospital; museums; vineyards; bluebonnet festival in April.

MARBLE FALLS (7,227) tourism, retail, manufacturing; granite, limestone quarries.

Other towns: **Bertram** (1,764); **Cottonwood Shores** (1,512); **Granite Shoals** (5,222); **Highland Haven** (418); **Meadowlakes** (1,922). Also, part of **Horseshoe Bay** [865].

Population	50,954
Change from 2010	19.2%
Area (sq. mi.)	1,021.3
Land Area (sq. mi.)	944.3
Altitude (ft.)	682–1,608
Rainfall (in.)	28.4
Jan. mean min (°F)	39.7
July mean max (°F)	94.1
Civ. Labor	25,614
Unemployed	3.0%
Wages	$235,430,165
Per Capita Income	$59,381
Property Value	$17,624,677,441
Retail Sales	$1,023,046,158

Caldwell County

Physical Features: Varied soils ranging from black clay to waxy; level, draining to San Marcos River.

Economy: Petroleum, varied manufacturing, government/services; part of Austin metro area, also near San Antonio.

History: Tonkawa area. Part of the DeWitt colony, Anglo-Americans settled in the 1830s. Mexican migration increased after 1890. County created from Bastrop and Gonzales counties and organized in 1848; named for frontiersman Mathew Caldwell.

Recreation: Fishing, state park, nature trails, museums, barbecue havens; Luling Watermelon Thump and Lockhart Chisholm Trail roundup in June.

Population	46,791
Change from 2010	22.9%
Area (sq. mi.)	547.2
Land Area (sq. mi.)	545.3
Altitude (ft.)	315–736
Rainfall (in.)	35.4
Jan. mean min (°F)	41.2
July mean max (°F)	96.2
Civ. Labor	21,275
Unemployed	3.5%
Wages	$117,669,491
Per Capita Income	$41,642
Property Value	$7,852,634,252
Retail Sales	$475,276,784

Minerals: Oil, gas, sand, gravel.

Agriculture: Eggs, beef cattle, hay, broilers. Market value $53.6 million.

Vital Statistics, annual: Births, 629; deaths, 482; marriages, 165; divorces, 104.

Race/Ethnicity: Anglo, 36.1%; Hispanic, 55.5%; Black, 4.8%; Asian, 0.5%; Other, 3.1%.

LOCKHART (14,844) county seat; agribusiness center, government/services, tourism, light manufacturing, prison; renowned barbecue at Kreuz, Smitty's, Black's.

Luling (5,518) oil, tourism, agriculture; oil museum; hospital, barbecue cook-off in April.

Other towns include: **Dale** (300); **Fentress** (380); **Martindale** (1,209); **Maxwell** (500); and **Prairie Lea** (320).

For explanation of sources, symbols, and abbreviations, see p. 207 and foldout map.

Calhoun County

Physical Features: Sandy, broken by bays; Green Lake, Powderhorn Lake, Cox Creek Reservoir; partly on Matagorda Island.

Economy: Plastics plants; marine construction; agribusinesses; petroleum; tourism; fish processing, for hire recreational fishing and commercial waterfowl hunting.

History: Karankawa tribal area. Empresario Martín De León brought 41 families in 1825. County created from Jackson, Matagorda, and Victoria counties in 1846; organized the same year. Named for John C. Calhoun, U.S. statesman.

Recreation: Beaches, fishing, water sports, duck, goose hunting; historic sites, county park; La Salle Days in April.

Minerals: Oil, gas.

Agriculture: Cotton, cattle, corn, grain sorghum. Market value $32.1 million. Commercial fishing.

Vital Statistics, annual: Births, 261; deaths, 252; marriages, 110; divorces, 12.

Race/Ethnicity: Anglo, 41.6%; Hispanic, 49%; Black, 1.8%; Asian, 5.5%; Other, 2%.

PORT LAVACA (11,259) county seat; commercial seafood operations, offshore drilling, tourist center; manufacturing; convention center; hospital.

Point Comfort (583) aluminum, plastic plants, deepwater port; **Port O'Connor** (1,084) tourist center, seafood processing, lighted boat parade in December; **Seadrift** (999) commercial fishing, Bayfront Park, Shrimpfest in June.

Population	19,727
Change from 2010	–7.7%
Area (sq. mi.)	1,032.7
Land Area (sq. mi.)	506.8
Altitude (ft.)	sea level–56
Rainfall (in.)	41.9
Jan. mean min (°F)	47.2
July mean max (°F)	91.1
Civ. Labor	12,272
Unemployed	3.7%
Wages	$263,976,333
Per Capita Income	$60,589
Property Value	$7,180,080,301
Retail Sales	$272,835,807

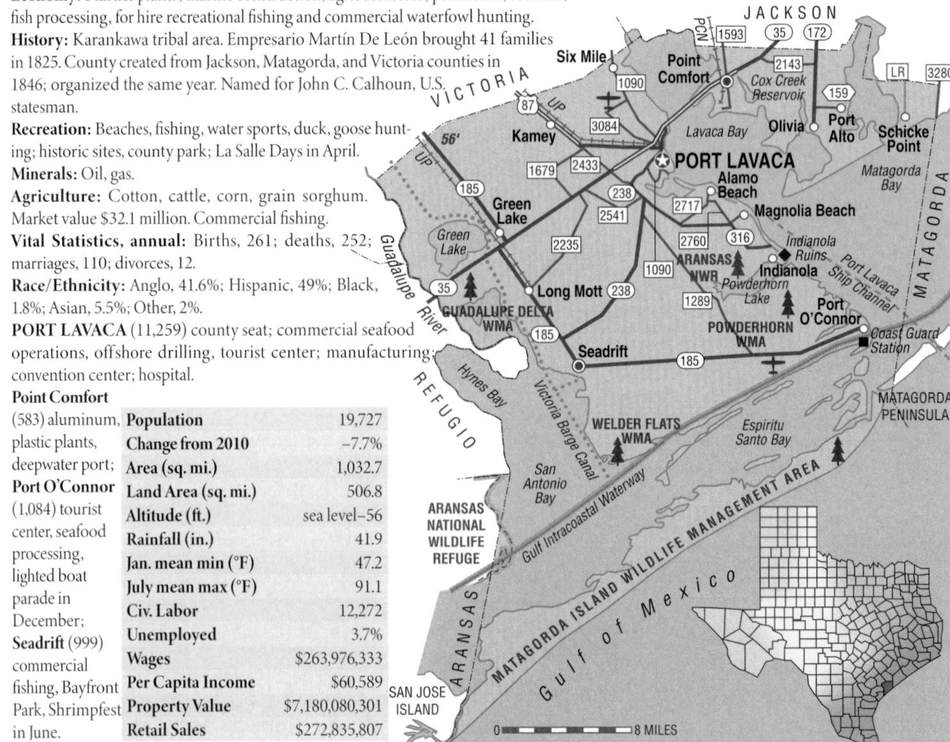

The Rene Robert Cavelier Sieur de La Salle Monument in Indianola was commissioned for the Texas Centennial in 1936. Photo by Larry D. Moore, CC by SA 4.0

Callahan County

Physical Features: On divide between Brazos, Colorado rivers; Lake Clyde, Lake Baird; level to rolling.

Economy: Ranching; feed and fertilizer business; many residents commute to Abilene; 200,000 acres in hunting leases; wind and solar energy, manufacturing.

History: Comanche territory until the 1870s. Anglo-American settlement began around 1860. County created in 1858 from Bexar, Bosque, and Travis counties; organized in 1877. Named for Texas Ranger J.H. Callahan.

Recreation: Hunting, lakes; museums; Baird & Cross Plains Hunters' Feed at deer season.

Minerals: Oil and gas.

Agriculture: Cattle, wheat, sorghum, oats. Market value $31.2 million. Hunting leases important.

Vital Statistics, annual: Births, 123; deaths, 232; marriages, 45; divorces, 14.

Race/Ethnicity: Anglo, 84.3%; Hispanic, 9.5%; Black, 0.9%; Asian, 0.4%; Other, 4.9%.

BAIRD (1,498) county seat; ranching/agricultural trade center, some manufacturing, shipping; historic sites; Railhead Day in May, museum.

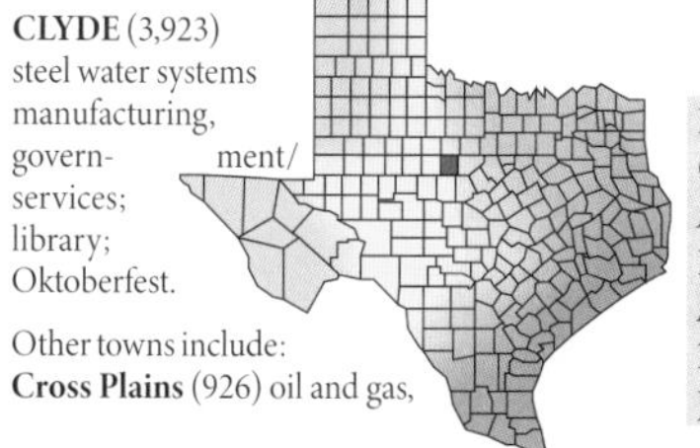

CLYDE (3,923) steel water systems manufacturing, government/services; library; Oktoberfest.

Other towns include: **Cross Plains** (926) oil and gas, agriculture, government/services, home of creator of Conan the Barbarian, museum, Barbarian Festival in April; **Putnam** (65).

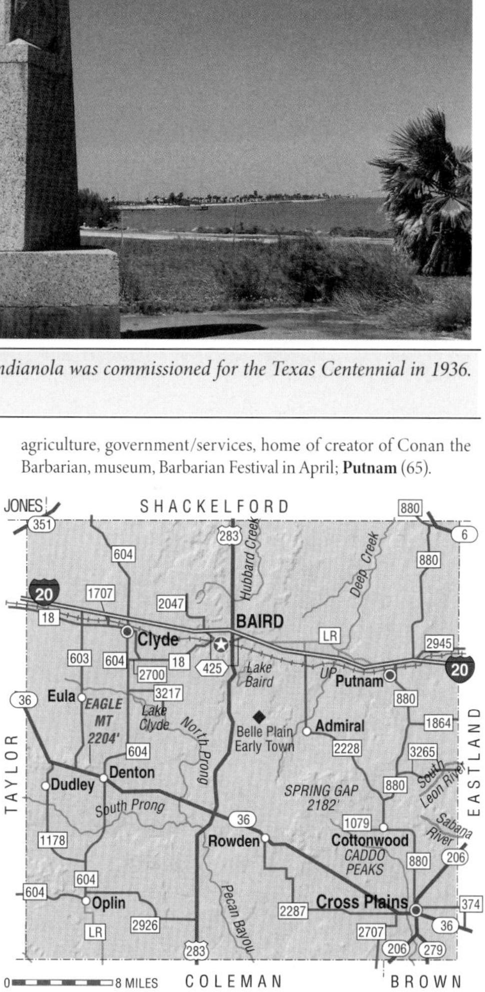

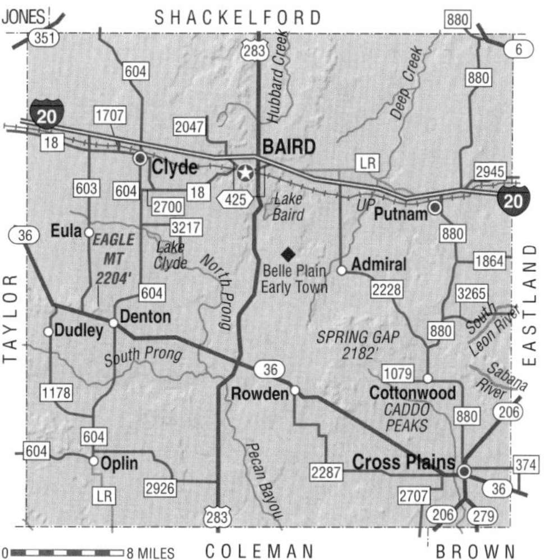

Population	14,115	July mean max (°F)	94.0
Change from 2010	4.2%	Civ. Labor	6,279
Area (sq. mi.)	901.3	Unemployed	3.6%
Land Area (sq. mi.)	899.4	Wages	$42,019,833
Altitude (ft.)	1,350–2,204	Per Capita Income	$50,963
Rainfall (in.)	29.0	Property Value	$2,704,778,997
Jan. mean min (°F)	33.6	Retail Sales	$214,298,216

Cameron County

Physical Features: Southernmost county in rich Rio Grande Valley soils; flat landscape; semitropical climate; Loma Alta Lake.

Economy: Agribusiness, tourism, seafood processing, shipping, manufacturing, government/services.

History: Coahuiltecan tribal area. Spanish land grants date to 1781. County created from Nueces County, 1848; named for Capt. Ewen Cameron of Mier Expedition.

Recreation: South Padre Island: year-round resort; fishing, hunting, water sports; historical sites, Palo Alto visitors center; gateway to Mexico, state parks; wildlife refuge; recreational vehicle center.

Minerals: Natural gas, oil.

Agriculture: Cotton, grain sorghums, vegetables, corn, citrus. Ranked second in sugar cane acreage. Wholesale nursery plants raised. Small feedlot and cow-calf operations. Some 112,000 acres irrigated, mostly cotton and grain sorghums. Market value $122.6 million. Ranked third in value of aquaculture.

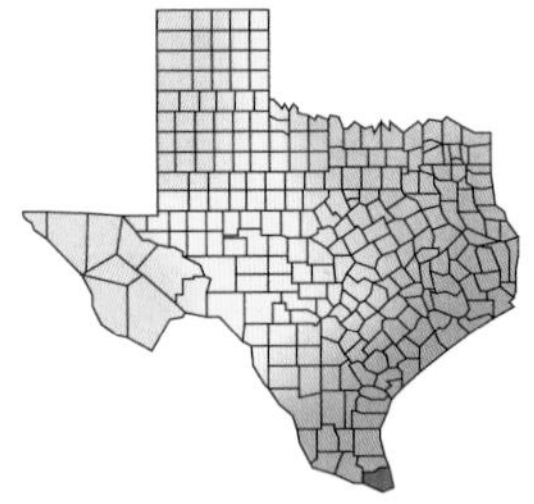

Vital Statistics, annual: Births, 6,019; deaths, 4,220; marriages, 1,701; divorces, 403.

Race/Ethnicity: Anglo, 8.8%; Hispanic, 89.5%; Black, 0.3%; Asian, 0.6%; Other, 0.8%.

BROWNSVILLE (187,831) county seat; international trade, varied industries, shipping, tourism; college, hospitals, crippled children health center; Gladys Porter Zoo, historic Fort Brown; University of Texas–Rio Grande Valley, Texas Southmost College.

Population	423,029
Change from 2010	4.1%
Area (sq. mi.)	1,276.5
Land Area (sq. mi.)	890.9
Altitude (ft.)	sea level–67
Rainfall (in.)	26.8
Jan. mean min (°F)	54.9
July mean max (°F)	95.1
Civ. Labor	177,545
Unemployed	5.7%
Wages	$1,669,119,095
Per Capita Income	$37,861
Property Value	$29,309,024,887
Retail Sales	$6,127,637,448

HARLINGEN (71,925) health care, government/services, tourism; hospitals; college extension campuses; nature center; birding festival in November.

SAN BENITO (24,780) retail center, tourism, agriculture; hospital; museums, arts center, historic buildings; recreation facilities, including walking/jogging trail; ResacaFest on July 4.

SOUTH PADRE ISLAND (2,061) beaches, tourism/convention center, real estate and construction; birding/nature center, Sandcastle Days in October, Spring Break in March.

Other towns include: **Bayview** (501); **Bluetown** (458); **Cameron Park** (5,464); **Combes** (3,040); **Encantada-Ranchito El Calaboz** (1,362); **Indian Lake** (851); **La Feria** (6,814)

Laguna Heights (1,521); **Laguna Vista** (3,605); **Laureles** (3,691); **Los Fresnos** (8,152) Little Graceland Museum, Butterfly Farm, library; **Los Indios** (1,012); **Olmito** (901); **Palm Valley** (1,398).

Also, **Port Isabel** (5,094) tourist center, fishing, museums, old lighthouse, Shrimp Cook-Off in November; **Primera** (5,303); **Rancho Viejo** (2,856); **Rangerville** (197); **Rio Hondo** (2,018); **Santa Maria** (618); **Santa Rosa** (2,423).

For explanation of sources, symbols, and abbreviations, see p. 207 and foldout map.

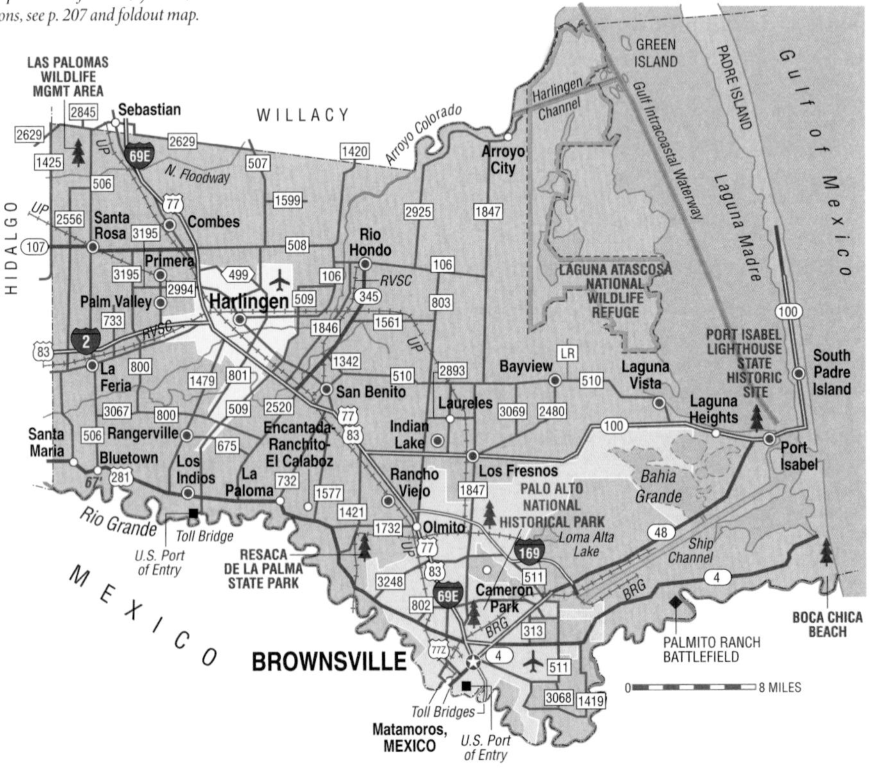

Camp County

Physical Features: East Texas county with forested hills; drains to Big Cypress Creek on the north; Lake Bob Sandlin; third smallest county in Texas.

Economy: Agribusiness, chicken processing and feedmill, timber industries, light manufacturing, retirement center, steel manufacturing, dog food plant.

History: Caddo area. Anglo-American settlers arrived in late 1830s. Antebellum slaveholding area. County created, organized from Upshur County 1874; named for jurist J.L. Camp.

Recreation: Water sports, fishing on lakes; farmstead and airship museum; Pittsburg hot links; Hot Link Festival in April, Pioneer Days in September.

Minerals: Oil, gas, clays, coal.

Agriculture: Poultry and products important; beef, dairy cattle, horses; peaches, hay, blueberries, vegetables. Market value $114.2 million. Forestry.

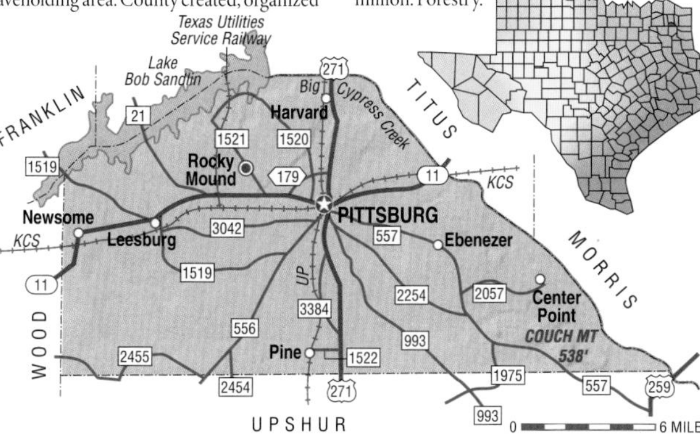

Vital Statistics, annual: Births, 162; deaths, 199; marriages, 67; divorces, 3.

Race/Ethnicity: Anglo, 54%; Hispanic, 25.9%; Black, 15.1%; Asian, 0.8%; Other, 4.2%.

PITTSBURG (4,374) county seat; agribusiness, timber, tourism, food processing, light manufacturing, commuting to Longview, Tyler; hospital; community college; Prayer Tower.

Other towns include: **Leesburg** (128) and **Rocky Mound** (83).

Population	12,616
Change from 2010	1.7%
Area (sq. mi.)	203.2
Land Area (sq. mi.)	195.8
Altitude (ft.)	236–538
Rainfall (in.)	47.1
Jan. mean min (°F)	36.8
July mean max (°F)	91.4
Civ. Labor	5,137
Unemployed	4.5%
Wages	$50,236,928
Per Capita Income	$46,705
Property Value	$2,015,428,924
Retail Sales	$117,377,212

Carson County

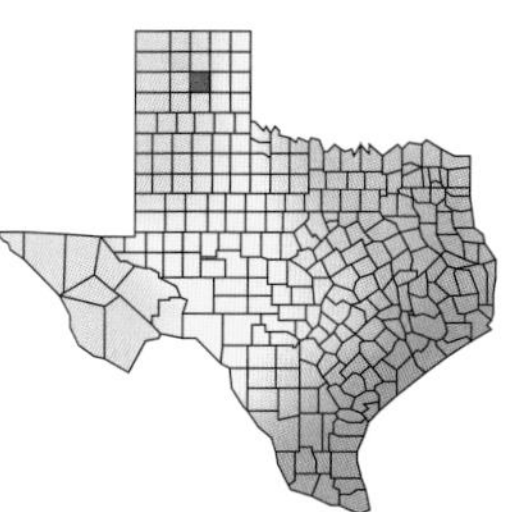

Physical Features: In center of Panhandle on level, some broken land; loam soils.

Economy: Pantex nuclear weapons assembly/disassembly facility (U.S. Department of Energy), commuting to Amarillo, petrochemical plants, agribusiness.

History: Apaches, displaced by Comanches. Anglo-American ranchers settled in the 1880s. German, Polish farmers arrived around 1910. County created from Bexar District, 1876; organized 1888. Named for Republic secretary of state S.P. Carson.

Recreation: Museum, The Cross at Groom; Square House Barbecue in fall.

Minerals: Oil, gas production.

Agriculture: Cattle, cotton, wheat, sorghum, corn, hay, soybeans. Market value $91.8 million.

Vital Statistics, annual: Births, 38; deaths, 97; marriages, 24; divorces, 8.

Race/Ethnicity: Anglo, 83.9%; Hispanic, 9.6%; Black, 0.3%; Asian, 0.3%; Other, 5.8%.

PANHANDLE (2,337) county seat; government/services, agribusiness, petroleum center, commuters to Amarillo; Veterans Day celebration, car show in June.

Other towns: **Groom** (547) farming center, government/services, Groom Day festival in August; **Skellytown** (394); **White Deer** (904) Polish sausage festival in November.

Population	5,746
Change from 2010	–7.1%
Area (sq. mi.)	924.1
Land Area (sq. mi.)	920.2
Altitude (ft.)	2,926–3,595
Rainfall (in.)	21.1
Jan. mean min (°F)	25.2
July mean max (°F)	91.3
Civ. Labor	3,016
Unemployed	3.1%
Wages	$145,325,555
Per Capita Income	$56,357
Property Value	$2,021,470,591
Retail Sales	$170,711,710

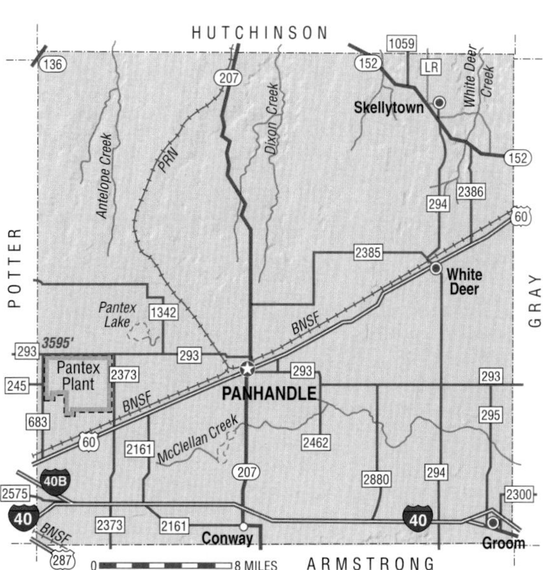

Cass County

Physical Features: Forested Northeast county rolling to hilly; drained by Cypress Bayou, Sulphur River; Wright Patman Lake.

Economy: Timber and paper industries, government/services.

History: Caddoes, who were displaced by other tribes in the 1790s. Anglo-Americans arrived in the 1830s. Antebellum slaveholding area. County created and organized in 1846 from Bowie County; named for U.S. Sen. Lewis Cass.

Recreation: Fishing, hunting, water sports; state park, county park; lake, wildflower trails.

Minerals: Oil, iron ore.

Agriculture: Cattle, poultry. Market value $53.4 million. Timber important.

Vital Statistics, annual: Births, 317; deaths, 528; marriages, 129; divorces, 117.

Race/Ethnicity: Anglo, 73.9%; Hispanic, 4.7%; Black, 15.9%; Asian, 0.4%; Other, 5.1%.

LINDEN (1,786) county seat, timber, agribusiness, tourism; oldest courthouse still in use as courthouse, hospital; Rock and Roll Hall of Fame.

ATLANTA (5,409) Paper and timber industries, government/services, varied manufacturing, hospital, library; Forest Festival in August.

Other towns include: **Avinger** (373) timber, paper industry, steel plant, early cemetery, Glory Days celebration in October; **Bivins** (154); **Bloomburg** (324); **Domino** (74); **Douglassville** (213)

Hughes Springs (1,543) varied manufacturing, warehousing, trucking school, Pumpkin Glow in October; **Kildare** (104); **Marietta** (113); **McLeod** (305); **Queen City** (1,409) paper industry, commuters to Texarkana, government/services, historic sites.

For explanation of sources, symbols, and abbreviations, see p. 207 and foldout map.

Population	28,560
Change from 2010	–6.3%
Area (sq. mi.)	960.3
Land Area (sq. mi.)	937.0
Altitude (ft.)	167–627
Rainfall (in.)	50.6
Jan. mean min (°F)	37.1
July mean max (°F)	90.9
Civ. Labor	12,022
Unemployed	4.7%
Wages	$84,369,558
Per Capita Income	$46,101
Property Value	$4,116,843,543
Retail Sales	$304,269,226

Castro County

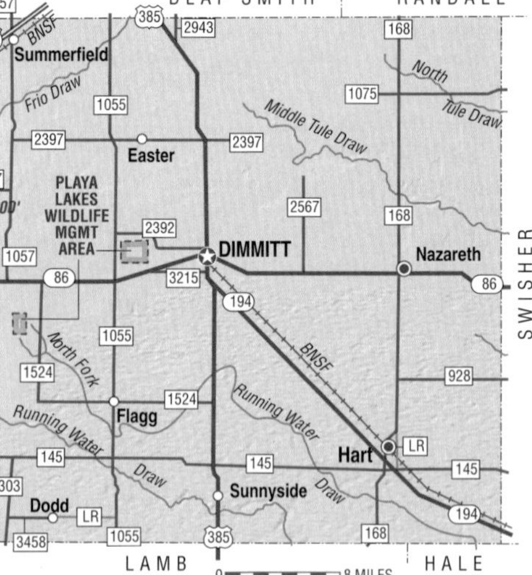

Physical Features: Flat Panhandle county, drains to creeks, draws and playas; underground water.

Economy: Agribusiness.

History: Apaches, displaced by Comanches in the 1720s. Anglo-American ranchers began settling in the 1880s. Germans settled after 1900. Mexican migration increased after 1950. County created, 1876 from Bexar District, organized 1891. Named for Henri Castro, Texas colonizer.

Recreation: Pheasant hunting; Italian POW camp site; Dimmitt Harvest Days celebrated in August.

Minerals: Insignificant.

Agriculture: Beef cattle, dairies (first in number of milk cows), corn, cotton, wheat, sheep. Market value $1.1 billion; third in state.

Vital Statistics, annual: Births, 112; deaths, 87; marriages, 36; divorces, 8.

Race/Ethnicity: Anglo, 31.6%; Hispanic, 64.9%; Black, 1.3%; Asian, 0.3%; Other, 1.9%.

DIMMITT (4,167) county seat; agribusiness center; library, hospital; quilt festival in April.

Other towns include: **Hart** (882) and **Nazareth** (312) German festival/Suds & Sounds in July.

Population	7,374
Change from 2010	–8.5%
Area (sq. mi.)	899.3
Land Area (sq. mi.)	894.4

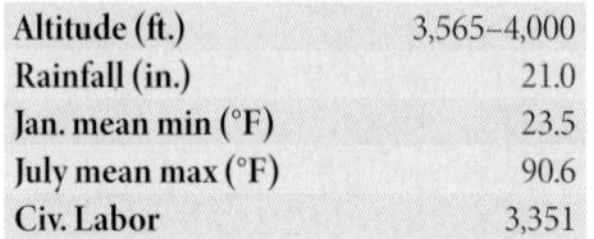

Altitude (ft.)	3,565–4,000
Rainfall (in.)	21.0
Jan. mean min (°F)	23.5
July mean max (°F)	90.6
Civ. Labor	3,351

Unemployed	3.1%
Wages	$31,654,498
Per Capita Income	$81,900
Property Value	$1,845,297,777
Retail Sales	$70,802,290

The Chambers County Courthouse in Anahuac. Photo by Adavyd, CC by SA 4.0

Chambers County

Physical Features: Gulf coastal plain, coastal soils; Lake Anahuac; some forests.

Economy: Water suppliers, banking, chemical distribution facilities, air services, carbon dioxide disposal, retail/shopping.

History: Karankawa and other coastal tribes. Nuestra Señora de la Luz Mission established near present Wallisville in 1756. County created and organized in 1858 from Liberty, Jefferson counties. Named for Gen. T. J. Chambers, surveyor.

Population	48,865
Change from 2010	39.2%
Area (sq. mi.)	871.2
Land Area (sq. mi.)	597.1
Altitude (ft.)	sea level–82
Rainfall (in.)	59.7
Jan. mean min (°F)	44.8
July mean max (°F)	90.3
Civ. Labor	21,015
Unemployed	5.3%
Wages	$360,164,454
Per Capita Income	$60,591
Property Value	$25,732,317,357
Retail Sales	$587,414,295

Recreation: Fishing, hunting; water sports; camping; county parks; wildlife refuge; historic sites; Wallisville Heritage Museum, Chambers County Children's Museum; Texas Gatorfest at Anahuac in September; Texas Rice Festival in October.

Minerals: Oil, gas.

Agriculture: Beef cattle, rice, hay, aquaculture. Market value $19.3 million. Hunting, fishing important.

Vital Statistics, annual: Births, 552; deaths, 385; marriages, 220; divorces, 135.

Race/Ethnicity: Anglo, 64.1%; Hispanic, 23.5%; Black, 6.8%; Asian, 1.3%; Other, 4.3%.

ANAHUAC (1,962) county seat; canal connects with Houston Ship Channel; agribusiness; hospital, library.

WINNIE (2,366) ecotourism; commuting to Beaumont, Houston; rice farming; antiques market; hospital; library, museum; Texas Rice Festival in early October.

Other towns include: **Beach City** (3,208), **Cove** (559), **Hankamer** (226), **Mont Belvieu** (8,337), **Old River-Winfree** (1,310), **Stowell** (2,085), and **Wallisville** (300).Part [4,834] of **Baytown**.

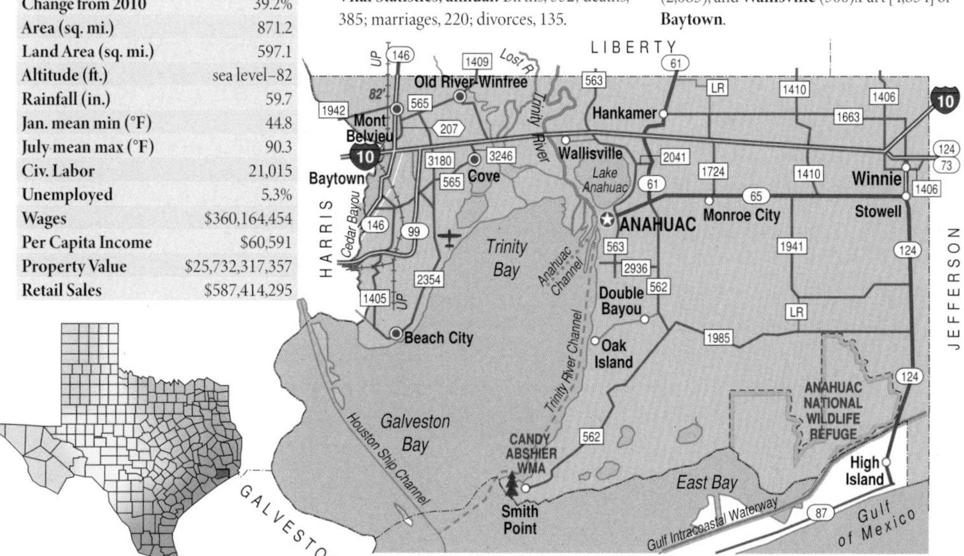

Cherokee County

Physical Features: East Texas county; hilly, partly forested; drains to Angelina, Neches rivers; many streams; Lake Palestine, Lake Striker, Lake Jacksonville; sandy, clay soils.

Economy: Government/services, varied manufacturing, agribusiness.

History: Caddo tribes attracted Spanish missionaries around 1720. Cherokees began settling area around 1820, and soon afterward Anglo-Americans began to arrive. Cherokees forced to Indian Territory 1839. Named for Indian tribe; created 1846 from Nacogdoches County.

Recreation: Water sports; fishing, hunting; historic sites and parks, national wildlife refuge; Texas State Railroad; nature trails through forests; lakes.

Minerals: Gas, oil.

Agriculture: Nurseries (second in the state in value of sales), hay, beef cattle, dairies, poultry. Market value $115.7 million. Timber, hunting income significant.

Vital Statistics, annual: Births, 739; deaths, 684; marriages, 247; divorces, 92.

Race/Ethnicity: Anglo, 59.7%; Hispanic, 23.4%; Black, 12.6%; Asian, 0.5%; Other, 3.8%.

RUSK (5,537) county seat; agribusiness, tourism, state mental hospital, prison unit; historic footbridge, heritage festival in October.

JACKSONVILLE (14,074) varied manufacturing, plastics, agribusiness, tourism, retail center; hospitals, junior colleges; Love's Lookout; Tomato Fest in June.

Other towns include: **Alto** (1,033) farming, timber, light manufacturing, pecan festival in November; **Cuney** (113); **Gallatin** (326); **Maydelle** (250); **New Summerfield** (859).

Reklaw (333, partly in Rusk County); **Shadybrook** (2,191);)**Wells** (867). Part [49] of **Bullard** and part [52] of **Troup**.

For explanation of sources, symbols, and abbreviations, see p. 207 and foldout map.

Population	51,097
Change from 2010	0.5%
Area (sq. mi.)	1,062.2
Land Area (sq. mi.)	1,052.9
Altitude (ft.)	187–775
Rainfall (in.)	50.1
Jan. mean min (°F)	39.2
July mean max (°F)	89.8
Civ. Labor	20,574
Unemployed	4.4%
Wages	$171,772,898
Per Capita Income	$43,376
Property Value	$6,940,282,794
Retail Sales	$544,816,898

This old school building in Newport was built in 1939 by the WPA. Photo by Larry D. Moore, CC by SA 4.0

Childress County

Physical Features: Rolling prairie, at corner of Panhandle, draining to fork of Red River; Baylor Creek Lake, Lake Childress; mixed soils.

Economy: Government/services, retail trade, tourism, agriculture, and healthcare.

History: Apache tribal area, displaced by Comanches. Ranchers arrived around 1880. County created in 1876 from Bexar, Young districts; organized in 1887; named for writer of Texas Declaration of Independence, George C. Childress.

Recreation: Recreation on lakes and creeks, fishing; hunting of deer, turkey, wild hog, quail, dove; parks; county museum.

Minerals: Insignificant.

Agriculture: Cotton, beef cattle, wheat, hay, sorghum, peanuts, vineyards and winery; some 9,000 acres irrigated. Market value $27.2 million. Hunting leases.

Vital Statistics, annual: Births, 58; deaths, 86; marriages, 34; divorces, 10.

Race/Ethnicity: Anglo, 57.8%; Hispanic, 29.1%; Black, 8.6%; Asian, 0.8%; Other, 3.7%.

CHILDRESS (5,844) county seat; agribusiness, hospital, prison unit; settlers reunion and rodeo in July.

Other towns include: **Tell** (20).

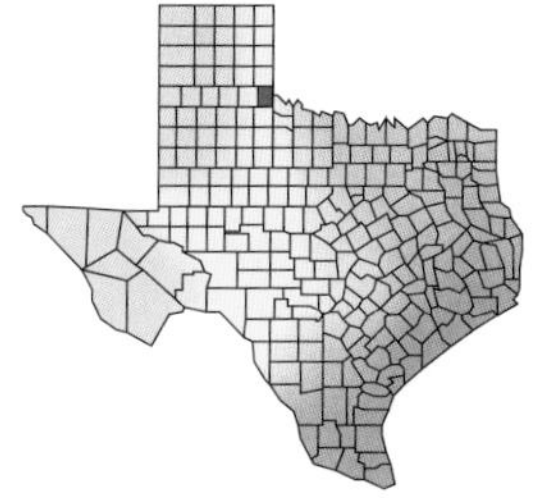

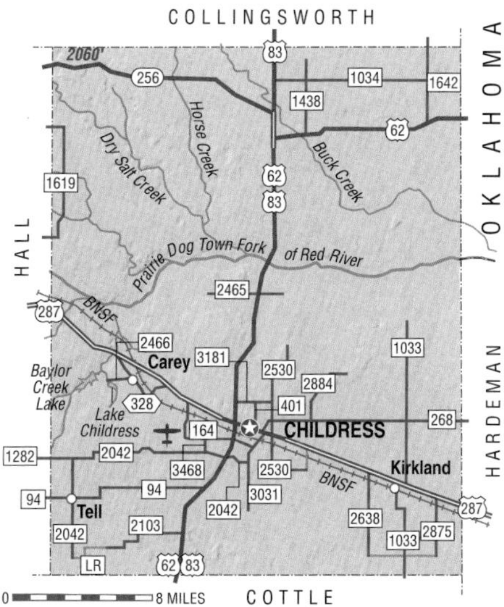

Population	6,736
Change from 2010	–4.3%
Area (sq. mi.)	713.7
Land Area (sq. mi.)	696.4
Altitude (ft.)	1,560–2,060
Rainfall (in.)	26.1
Jan. mean min (°F)	28.8
July mean max (°F)	94.3
Civ. Labor	3,189
Unemployed	2.8%
Wages	$45,100,024
Per Capita Income	$39,953
Property Value	$1,145,740,364
Retail Sales	$139,927,031

Clay County

Physical Features: Hilly, rolling; Northwest county drains to Red, Trinity rivers; Lake Arrowhead; sandy loam, chocolate soils; mesquites, post oaks.

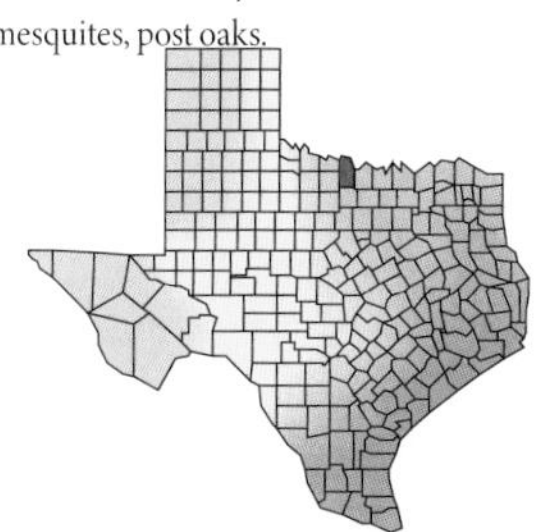

Economy: Oil, agribusiness, commuting.

Population	10,263
Change from 2010	–4.5%
Area (sq. mi.)	1,116.8
Land Area (sq. mi.)	1,088.7
Altitude (ft.)	791–1,200
Rainfall (in.)	32.0
Jan. mean min (°F)	30.8
July mean max (°F)	94.7
Civ. Labor	4,867
Unemployed	3.8%
Wages	$20,308,305
Per Capita Income	$51,938
Property Value	$2,490,116,591
Retail Sales	$228,482,821

History: Wichitas arrived from north-central plains in mid-1700s, followed by Apaches and Comanches. Ranching attempts began in 1850s. County created from Cooke County, 1857; Indians forced disorganization, 1862; reorganized, 1873; named for Henry Clay, U.S. statesman.

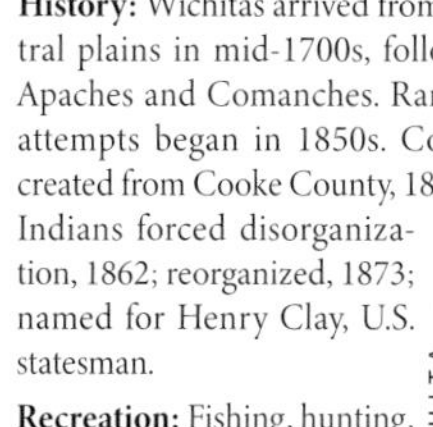

Recreation: Fishing, hunting, horses, water sports; state park; pioneer reunion in September.

Minerals: Oil and gas, stone.

Agriculture: Beef cattle, wheat, pecans, peaches, dairy cattle. Market value $55.7 million. Oaks, cedar, elms sold to nurseries, mesquite cut for firewood.

Vital Statistics, annual: Births, 92; deaths, 147; marriages, 25; divorces, 16.

Race/Ethnicity: Anglo, 87.5%; Hispanic, 6.3%; Black, 0.3%; Asian, 0.5%; Other, 5.4%.

HENRIETTA (3,102) county seat; agribusiness, government/services, manufacturing; hospital; museum; Turkey Fest in April.

Other towns include: **Bellevue** (289), **Bluegrove** (135), **Byers** (453), **Dean** (493), **Jolly** (173), **Petrolia** (516).

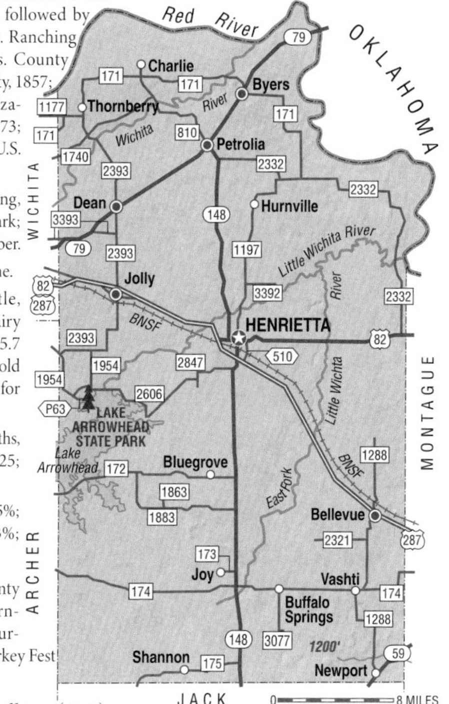

A very old stone gas station in Robert Lee. Photo by Carol M. Highsmith, Public Domain

Cochran County

Physical Features: South Plains bordering New Mexico with small lakes (playas); underground water; loam, sandy loam soils.

Economy: Farming, government/services, retail.

History: Hunting area for various Indian tribes. Ranches operated in the 1880s but population in 1900 was still only 25. Farming began in the 1920s. County created from Bexar and Young districts in 1876; organized in 1924; named for Robert Cochran, who died at the Alamo.

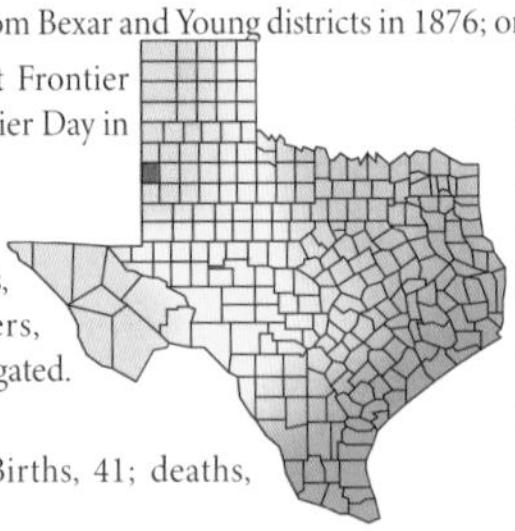

Recreation: Museum; Last Frontier Trail Drive and Buffalo Soldier Day in June.

Minerals: Insignificant.

Agriculture: Cotton, peanuts, sorghum, peas, sunflowers, wheat. Crops 60 percent irrigated. Market value $87.6 million.

Vital Statistics, annual: Births, 41; deaths, 37; marriages, 17; divorces, 5.

Race/Ethnicity: Anglo, 35.8%; Hispanic, 60.0%; Black, 2.4%; Asian, 0%; Other, 1.8%.

MORTON (1,668) county seat; oil, farm center, meat packing, light manufacture; hospital.

Other towns include: **Bledsoe** (132), **Whiteface** (371).

Population	2,516
Change from 2010	−19.5%
Area (sq. mi.)	775.2
Land Area (sq. mi.)	775.2
Altitude (ft.)	3,565–4,000
Rainfall (in.)	17.6
Jan. mean min (°F)	25.8
July mean max (°F)	92.2
Civ. Labor	1,137
Unemployed	4.8%
Wages	$11,167,618
Per Capita Income	$62,305
Property Value	$796,932,646
Retail Sales	$26,128,426

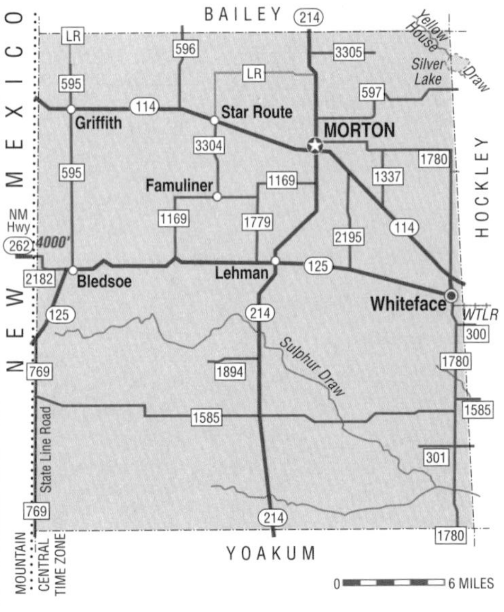

Coke County

Physical Features: West Texas prairie, hills, Colorado River valley; sandy loam, red soils; E.V. Spence Reservoir, Oak Creek Reservoir.

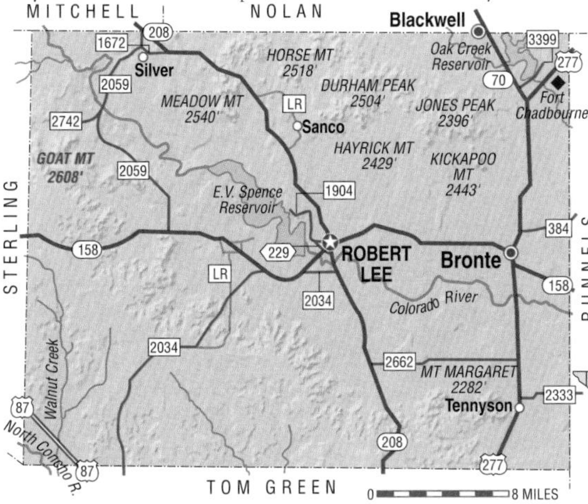

Economy: Oil and gas, government/services, agriculture.

History: From around 1700 to 1870s, Comanche bands roamed through the area. Ranches began operating after the Civil War. County was created and organized in 1889 from Tom Green County; named for Gov. Richard Coke.

Recreation: Hunting, fishing, Caliche Loop birdwatching trail; lakes; Sumac hiking trail; historic sites, Fort Chadbourne, county museum, Fort Chadbourne Days in May; amphitheater.

Minerals: Oil, gas.

Agriculture: Beef cattle, small grains, sheep and goats, hay. Market value $7.8 million.

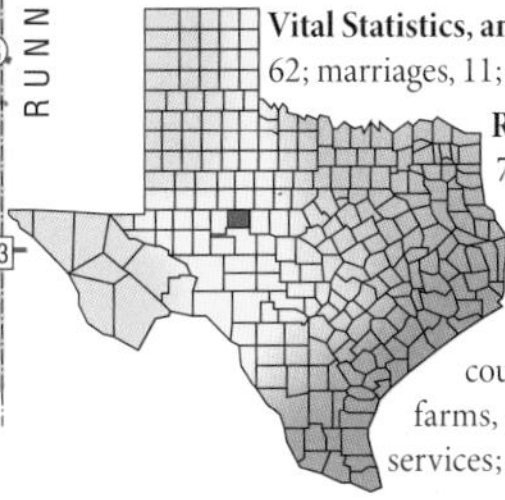

Vital Statistics, annual: Births, 37; deaths, 62; marriages, 11; divorces, 9.

Race/Ethnicity: Anglo, 75.3%; Hispanic, 20.1%; Black, 0.2%; Asian, 0%; Other, 4.4%.

ROBERT LEE (1,022) county seat; oil and gas, wind farms, ranching, government/services; old jail museum.

BRONTE (945) ranching, oil.

Other towns include: **Silver** (34) and **Tennyson** (46). Also, a small part of **Blackwell** (254).

Population	3,321
Change from 2010	0.0%
Area (sq. mi.)	928.0
Land Area (sq. mi.)	911.5
Altitude (ft.)	1,700–2,608
Rainfall (in.)	21.4
Jan. mean min (°F)	31.9
July mean max (°F)	94.4
Civ. Labor	1,535
Unemployed	3.5%
Wages	$12,936,277
Per Capita Income	$48,804
Property Value	$1,815,010,739
Retail Sales	$25,743,129

Coleman County

Physical Features: Hilly, rolling; drains to Colorado River, Pecan Bayou; O.H. Ivie Reservoir, Hords Creek Lake, Lake Coleman; mesquite, oaks.

Economy: Agribusiness, petroleum, ecotourism, varied manufacturing.

History: Presence of Apaches and Comanches brought military outpost, Camp Colorado, before the Civil War. Settlers arrived after organization. County created in 1858 from Brown, Travis counties; organized in 1864; named for Houston's aide, R.M. Coleman.

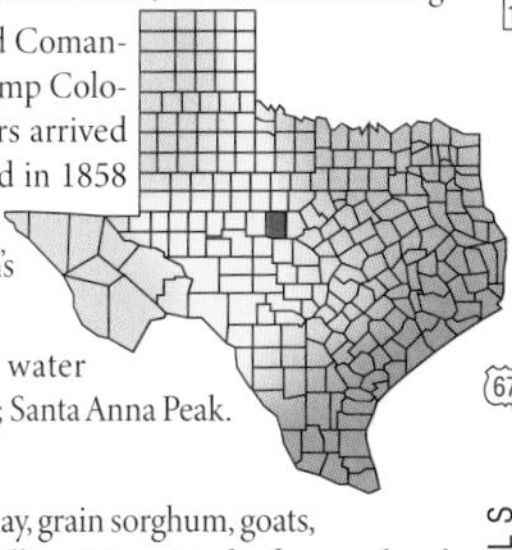

Recreation: Fishing, hunting; water sports; city park, historic sites; lakes; Santa Anna Peak.

Minerals: Oil, gas, stone, clays.

Agriculture: Cattle, wheat, sheep, hay, grain sorghum, goats, oats, cotton. Market value $41.2 million. Mesquite for firewood and furniture.

Vital Statistics, annual: Births, 74; deaths, 152; marriages, 54; divorces, 25.

Race/Ethnicity: Anglo, 78.3%; Hispanic, 15.5%; Black, 1.8%; Asian, 0.4%; Other, 4.0%.

COLEMAN (3,917) county seat; varied manufacturing; hospital, library, museums: Fiesta de la Paloma in October.

SANTA ANNA (1,022) agribusiness, oil, tourism; museum; Funtier days and bison cook-off in May.

Other towns include: **Burkett** (90), **Gouldbusk** (70), **Novice** (121), **Talpa** (127), and **Valera** (18).

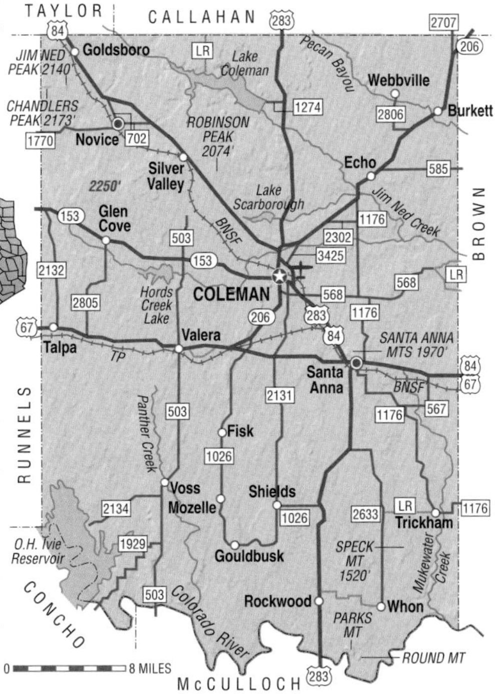

Population	7,735
Change from 2010	–13.0%
Area (sq. mi.)	1,281.4
Land Area (sq. mi.)	1,262.0
Altitude (ft.)	1,289–2,250
Rainfall (in.)	27.9
Jan. mean min (°F)	36.4
July mean max (°F)	95.4
Civ. Labor	3,046
Unemployed	4.3%
Wages	$24,341,641
Per Capita Income	$54,822
Property Value	$2,550,980,996
Retail Sales	$82,239,775

Collin County

Physical Features: Heavy, black clay soil; level to rolling; drains to Trinity; Lake Lavon, Lake Ray Hubbard.

Economy: Government & education services, healthcare, manufacturing plants, retail and wholesale center, Professional, scientific, and administrative and waste management services industries.

History: Caddo tribal area until 1850s. Settlers of Peters colony arrived in the early 1840s. County created, organized, from Fannin County in 1846. Named for pioneer settler Collin McKinney.

Recreation: Fishing, water sports; historic sites; old homes restoration, tours; natural science museum; professional sports teams, soccer (FC Dallas), minor league baseball (Frisco Rough Riders), minor league hockey (Allen Americans), D-league basketball (Texas Legends).

Minerals: Insignificant.

Agriculture: Landscape nurseries, corn, wheat, cattle, hay, grain sorghum, vegetable/specialty crops. Market value $66.8 million.

Vital Statistics, annual: Births, 11,422; deaths, 5,692; marriages, 4,456; divorces, 1,886.

Race/Ethnicity: Anglo, 51.0%; Hispanic, 15.9%; Black, 10.2%; Asian, 17.7%; Other, 5.3%.

McKINNEY (202,690) county seat; agribusiness, trade center, varied industry; hospital, community college; museums.

PLANO (288,253) professional services, banking, finance, insurance, health care/hospitals; community college, university extensions; museums, fine arts organizations, nature preserves, hiking trails; balloon festival in September, AsiaFest in April.

FRISCO (210,719) technical, aerospace industry, hospital, community college.

Other towns include: **Allen** (106,874) retail, manufacturing, wholesale trade, hospital, community college, nature conservatory, natatorium, historic stone dam, Stampede rodeo in October; **Anna** (20,243); **Blue Ridge** (1,187); **Celina** (23,811) museum, historic town square, Fun Day in September.

Also, **Copeville** (243); **Fairview** (10,683) government/services, retail center, commuters, museum, old mill site, wildlife sanctuary, veterans celebration in November; **Farmersville** (3,808) agriculture, light industries, Audie Murphy Day in June.

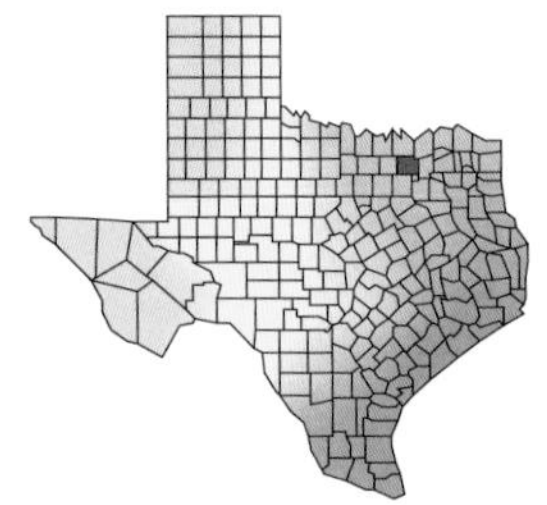

Also, **Josephine** (4,565); **Lavon** (5,342); **Lowry Crossing** (1,695); **Lucas** (8,029); **Melissa** (16,983) industrial plants, library, old town; **Murphy** (21,219); **Nevada** (1,331); **New Hope** (664); **Parker** (5,833); **Princeton** (20,046) manufacturing, commuters, Spring Onion festival in April.

Also, **Prosper** (34,136); **St. Paul** (994); **Westminster** (1,006); **Weston** (299); **Wylie** (59,394) manufacturing, retail, hospital, historic sites, big cat sanctuary, July Jubilee.

Also, part [52,246] of **Dallas**, part [39,134] of **Richardson** and part [10,755] of **Sachse**.

Population	1,109,462
Change from 2010	41.8%
Area (sq. mi.)	886.1
Land Area (sq. mi.)	841.2
Altitude (ft.)	434–810

Rainfall (in.)	39.8
Jan. mean min (°F)	36.1
July mean max (°F)	91.3
Civ. Labor	625,323
Unemployed	3.2%

Wages	$10,698,396,352
Per Capita Income	$77,006
Property Value	$251,288,318,756
Retail Sales	$28,179,587,081

For explanation of sources, symbols, and abbreviations, see p. 207 and foldout map.

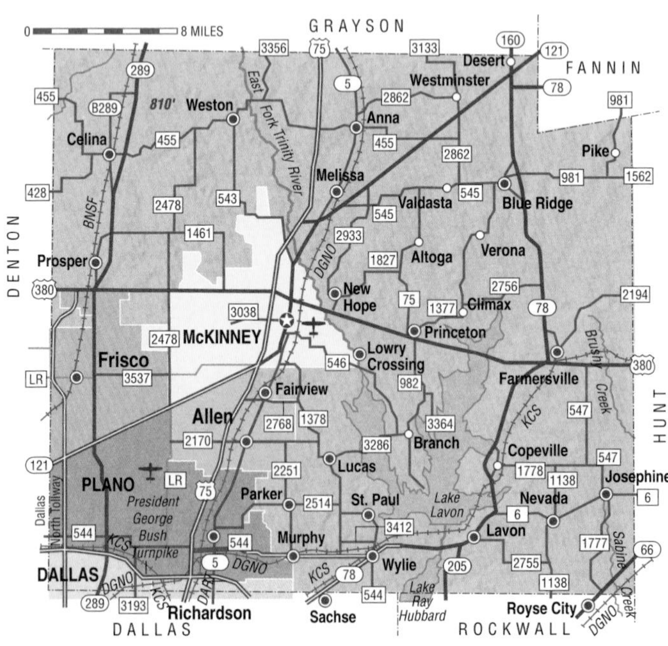

Collingsworth County

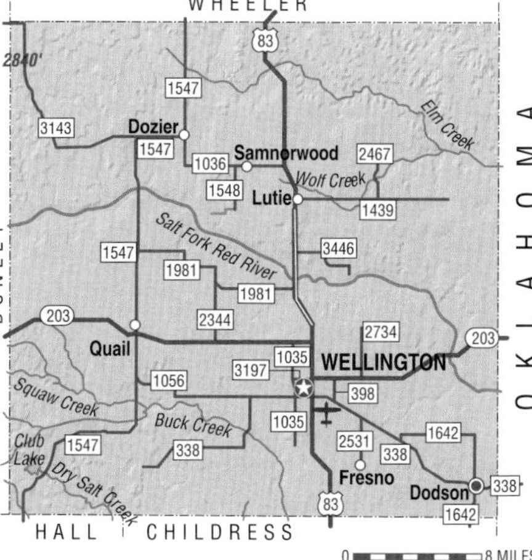

Physical Features: Panhandle county of rolling, broken terrain, draining to Red River forks; sandy and loam soils.

Economy: Agribusiness.

History: Apaches, displaced by Comanches. Ranchers from England arrived in the late 1870s. County created in 1876, from Bexar and Young districts, organized in 1890. Named for Republic of Texas' first chief justice, James Collinsworth (name misspelled in law).

Recreation: Deer, quail hunting; children's camp, county museum, pioneer park; county fair/parade in September.

Minerals: Gas, oil production.

Agriculture: Cotton, peanuts, cow-calf operations, wheat, stocker cattle; 22,000 acres irrigated. Market value $39.7 million.

Vital Statistics, annual: Births, 23; deaths, 48; marriages, 8; divorces, 1.

Race/Ethnicity: Anglo, 61.0%; Hispanic, 31.4%; Black, 4.1%; Asian, 0.3%; Other, 3.3%.

WELLINGTON (1,867) county seat; peanut-processing plants, varied manufacturing, agriculture; hospital, library; restored Ritz Theatre.

Other towns include: **Dodson** (91), **Quail** (25), **Samnorwood** (31).

Population	2,615
Change from 2010	–14.5%
Area (sq. mi.)	919.3
Land Area (sq. mi.)	918.4
Altitude (ft.)	1,750–2,840
Rainfall (in.)	22.1

Jan. mean min (°F)	29.7
July mean max (°F)	96.9
Civ. Labor	1,091
Unemployed	3.5%
Wages	$10,677,548
Per Capita Income	$54,140
Property Value	$774,948,200
Retail Sales	$15,711,301

Colorado County

Physical Features: Located in three soil areas; level to rolling; bisected by Colorado River; Eagle Lake; oaks.

Economy: Agribusiness, oil and gas services, gravel mining.

History: Karankawa and other tribes. Anglo settlers among Stephen F. Austin's Old Three Hundred families. First German settlers arrived around 1840. Antebellum slaveholding area. County created 1836, organized 1837; named for river.

Recreation: Hunting of duck, geese, deer, exotics; canoeing, bicycling; historic sites; prairie chicken refuge; opera house in Columbus, water park in Sheridan.

Minerals: Gas, oil, gravel.

Agriculture: Rice (third in state in acres), cattle, corn, cotton, soybeans, sesame, hay, pecans, nurseries; significant irrigation for rice. Market value $71.0 million.

Vital Statistics, annual: Births, 221; deaths, 305; marriages, 86; divorces, 53.

Race/Ethnicity: Anglo, 57.2%; Hispanic, 29.1%; Black, 10.8%; Asian, 0.4%; Other, 2.5%.

COLUMBUS (3,587) county seat; agriculture, quarrying, manufacturing; hospital; historical sites, homes, museums, walking tour; Magnolia Days festival in May.

Eagle Lake (3,484) rice drying center; hospital; goose hunting; Prairie Edge museum.

Weimar (2,074) agriculture, light industry, meat processing, retail; hospital, library; "Gedenke" (remember) celebration on Mother's Day weekend.

Other towns include: **Altair** (30), **Garwood** (408), **Glidden** (650), **Lone Oak** (50), **Nada** (262), **Oakland** (80), **Rock Island** (447), **Sheridan** (398).

Population	20,630
Change from 2010	–1.2%
Area (sq. mi.)	973.7
Land Area (sq. mi.)	960.3

Altitude (ft.)	125–450
Rainfall (in.)	45.0
Jan. mean min (°F)	40.7
July mean max (°F)	95.7
Civ. Labor	10,213

Unemployed	3.5%
Wages	$99,999,721
Per Capita Income	$59,219
Property Value	$6,942,294,959
Retail Sales	$508,984,312

Comal County

Physical Features: Scenic Hill Country county. Eighty percent above Balcones Escarpment. Spring-fed streams; 2.5-mile-long Comal River, Guadalupe River; Canyon Lake.

Economy: Varied manufacturing, tourism, government/services, agriculture; county in San Antonio metropolitan area.

History: Tonkawa, Waco Indians. A pioneer German settlement 1845. Mexican migration peaked during Mexican Revolution. County created from Bexar, Gonzales, Travis counties and organized in 1846; named for river, a name for Spanish earthenware or metal pan used for cooking tortillas.

Recreation: Fishing, hunting; historic sites; scenic drives, Devil's Backbone; lake facilities; Prince Solms Park, other county parks; Landa Park with 76 species of trees; Gruene historic area; caverns; river resorts; river tubing; Schlitterbahn water park; Wurstfest in November, Wasselfest in December.

Minerals: Stone, lime, sand and gravel.

Agriculture: Cattle, goats, sheep, hogs, horses; nursery, hay, corn, sorghum, wheat. Market value $9.6 million.

Vital Statistics, annual: Births, 1,662; deaths, 1,611; marriages, 982; divorces, 192.

Race/Ethnicity: Anglo, 65.2%; Hispanic, 27.0%; Black, 2.2%; Asian, 1.1%; Other, 4.5%.

NEW BRAUNFELS (98,857) county seat; manufacturing, retail, distribution center; picturesque city, making it a tourist center; Conservation Plaza; rose garden; hospital; library; mental health and retardation center. Gruene is now part of New Braunfels.

Canyon Lake (30,641), which includes Startzville, Sattler, Smithson Valley, Canyon City, Fischer, Hancock, and Spring Branch, retirement and recreation area, tourism, barbecue cook-off in April.

Other towns include: **Bulverde** (5,996) retail center; **Garden Ridge** (4,335);

Also in the county, parts of **Fair Oaks Ranch** [1,418], **Schertz** [1,716] and **Selma** [319].

Population	174,986
Change from 2010	61.3%
Area (sq. mi.)	574.9
Land Area (sq. mi.)	559.5
Altitude (ft.)	560–1,529
Rainfall (in.)	37.8
Jan. mean min (°F)	41.6
July mean max (°F)	93.6
Civ. Labor	82,222
Unemployed	3.5%
Wages	$979,789,102
Per Capita Income	$67,063
Property Value	$48,013,506,193
Retail Sales	$2,979,630,826

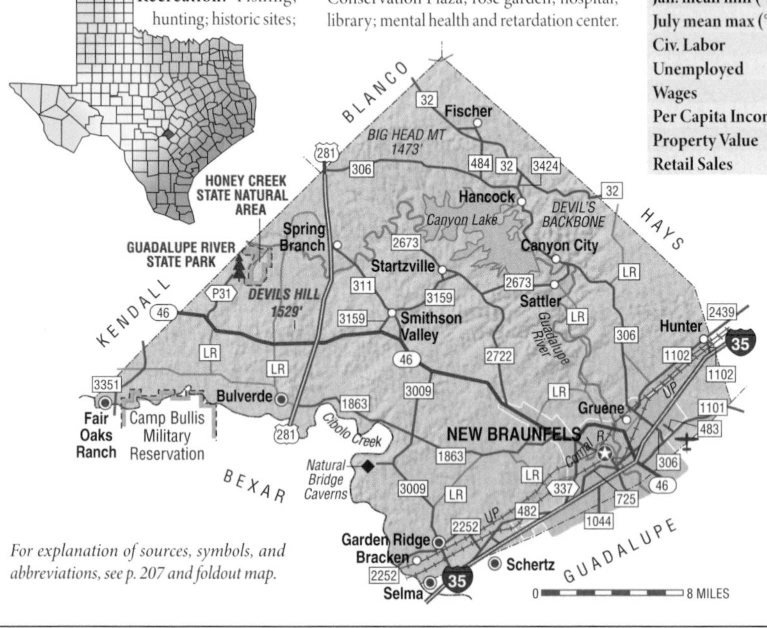

For explanation of sources, symbols, and abbreviations, see p. 207 and foldout map.

The view from a hilltop in Concho County. Photo by USDA NRCS Texas, Public Domain

Comanche County

Physical Features: Rolling, hilly terrain; sandy, loam, waxy soils; drains to Leon River, Proctor Lake; pecans, oaks, mesquites, cedars.

Economy: Agriculture, manufacturing, wind turbines.

History: Comanche area. Anglo-American settlers arrived in 1854 on land granted earlier to Stephen F. Austin and Samuel May Williams. County created and organized in 1856 from Bosque and Coryell counties; named for the Indian tribe.

Recreation: Hunting, fishing, water sports, nature tourism; parks, community center, museums; Comanche Pow-Wow in September, rodeo in July.

Minerals: Limited gas, oil, stone, clay.

Agriculture: Dairies, beef cattle, pecans (first in state in acreage), cotton, hay, wildlife, melons. Market value $173.3 million.

Vital Statistics, annual: Births, 143; deaths, 238; marriages, 56; divorces, 50.

Race/Ethnicity: Anglo, 67.7%; Hispanic, 28.4%; Black, 0.3%; Asian, 0.3%; Other, 3.3%.

COMANCHE (4,235) county seat; plants process feed, food; varied manufacturing; agribusiness; winery; hospital; Ranger College branch; library; state's oldest courthouse, "Old Cora," on display on town square.

De Leon (2,282) pecans, light manufacturing; hospital; car museum, Peach and Melon Festival in August.

Other towns include: **Energy** (70), **Gustine** (402), **Proctor** (57), and **Sidney** (148).

Population	13,775
Change from 2010	–1.4%
Area (sq. mi.)	947.7
Land Area (sq. mi.)	937.8
Altitude (ft.)	1,020–1,847
Rainfall (in.)	31.8
Jan. mean min (°F)	36.2
July mean max (°F)	95.1

Civ. Labor	6,323
Unemployed	3.5%
Wages	$50,892,635
Per Capita Income	$50,112
Property Value	$4,099,185,002
Retail Sales	$179,839,708

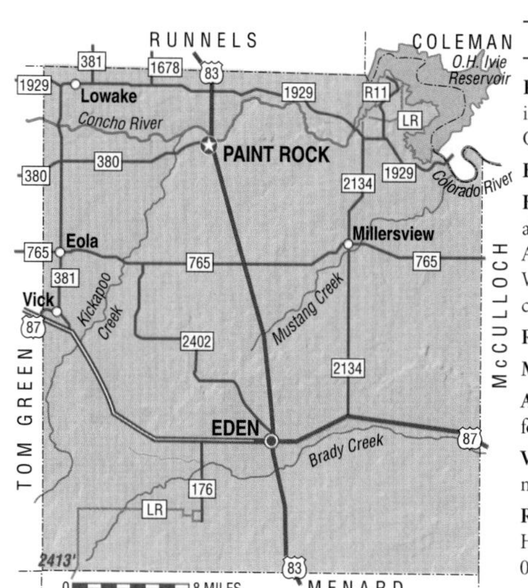

Concho County

Physical Features: On Edwards Plateau; rough, broken to south; level in north; sandy, loam and dark soils; drains to creeks and Colorado and Concho rivers.

Economy: Agribusiness, manufacturing.

History: Athabascan-speaking Plains Indians, then Jumanos in the 1600s, absorbed by Lipan Apaches in the 1700s. Comanches raided after 1800. Anglo-Americans began ranching around 1850; farming began after the Civil War. Mexican-Americans employed on sheep ranches in 1920s-30s. County created from Bexar District in 1858, organized in 1879; named for the river.

Recreation: Famed for 1,500 Indian pictographs; O.H. Ivie Reservoir.

Minerals: Oil, gas, stone.

Agriculture: Sheep, cattle, goats; wheat, feed grains; 2,000 acres irrigated for cotton. Market value $28.1 million.

Vital Statistics, annual: Births, 23; deaths, 34; marriages, 3; divorces, 2.

Race/Ethnicity: Anglo, 63.5%; Hispanic, 31.3%; Black, 2.1%; Asian, 0.6%; Other, 2.6%.

PAINT ROCK (350) county seat; named for Indian pictographs nearby; farming, ranching center.

EDEN (1,543) steel fabrication; hospital; fall fest.

Other towns include: **Eola** (215), **Lowake** (40), and **Millersview** (80).

Population	3,341
Change from 2010	–18.3%
Area (sq. mi.)	993.7
Land Area (sq. mi.)	983.8
Altitude (ft.)	1,421–2,413
Rainfall (in.)	24.6
Jan. mean min (°F)	32.1

July mean max (°F)	95.1
Civ. Labor	1,334
Unemployed	3.1%
Wages	$11,127,169
Per Capita Income	$38,635
Property Value	$2,327,386,068
Retail Sales	$17,428,614

These large fossil ammonites were found in Cooke County. Photo by James St. John, CC by 2.0

Cooke County

Physical Features: North Texas county; drains to Red, Trinity rivers; Ray Roberts Lake, Lake Texoma, Lake Kiowa, Hubert H. Moss Lake; sandy, red, loam soils.

Economy: Oil and gas, varied manufacturing, commuting to Dallas and Fort Worth.

History: Frontier between Caddoes and Comanches. Anglo-Americans arrived in the late 1840s. Germans settled western part around 1890. County created and organized in 1848 from Fannin County; named for Capt. W.G. Cooke of the Texas Revolution.

Recreation: Water sports; hunting, fishing; zoo; museum; park, Gainesville Depot Day/car show in October.

Minerals: Oil, natural gas, sand, gravel.

Agriculture: Beef cattle, horses, forages, wheat, oats, sorghum. Market value $53.8 million. Hunting leases important.

Vital Statistics, annual: Births, 485; deaths, 485; marriages, 306; divorces, 107.

Race/Ethnicity: Anglo, 70.6%; Hispanic, 20.4%; Black, 2.8%; Asian, 0.7%; Other, 5.4%.

GAINESVILLE (17,576) county seat; aerospace, plastics, energy; Victorian homes, walking tours; hospital; community college, juvenile correction unit; Camp Sweeney for diabetic children; World War II Camp Howze site.

Muenster (1,580) varied manufacturing, food processing, water utilities; hospital, museum, Germanfest late April, Oktoberfest.

Other towns include: **Callisburg** (320), **Era** (150), **Lindsay** (1,069) 1919 Romanesque-style church, **Myra** (382), **Oak Ridge** (253), **Rosston** (75), **Valley View** (759), and the residential community around **Lake Kiowa** (2,409).

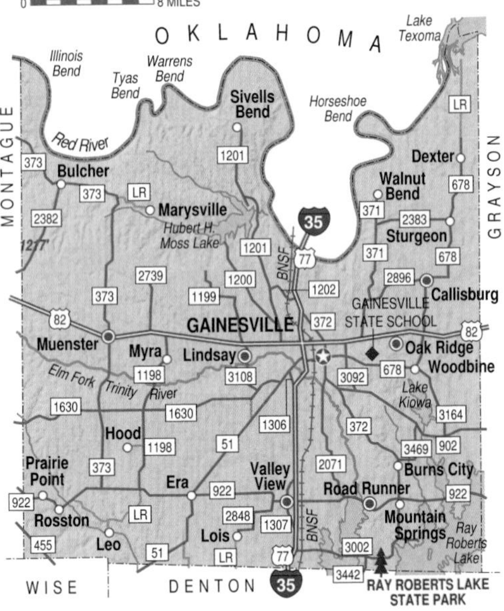

For explanation of sources, symbols, and abbreviations, see p. 207 and foldout map.

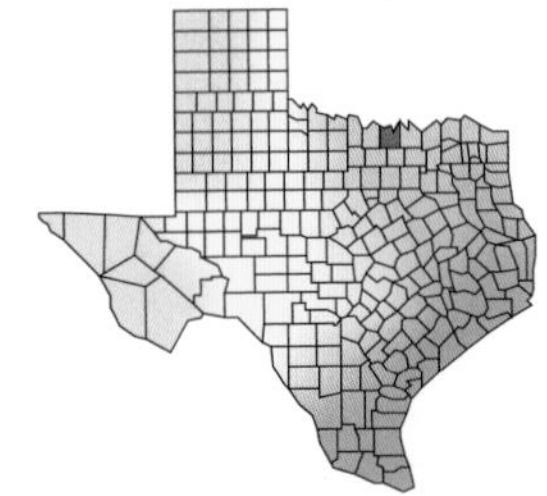

Population	42,244
Change from 2010	9.9%
Area (sq. mi.)	898.4
Land Area (sq. mi.)	874.8
Altitude (ft.)	617–1,217
Rainfall (in.)	42.8
Jan. mean min (°F)	33.8

July mean max (°F)	92.1
Civ. Labor	20,022
Unemployed	3.4%
Wages	$215,590,676
Per Capita Income	$59,800
Property Value	$11,953,609,614
Retail Sales	$817,237,256

Coryell County

Physical Features: Leon Valley in center, remainder rolling, hilly; Belton Lake.

Economy: Fort Cavazos, prisons, agribusiness, manufacturing.

History: Tonkawa area, later various other tribes. Anglo-Americans settled around Fort Gates in late 1840s. Permanent establishment of Fort Hood (now Fort Cavazos) in 1950 changed cultural geography. County created from Bell County, organized 1854; named for local pioneer James Coryell.

Recreation: State park; deer hunting; fishing; lake, Leon River; bluebonnet area; historic homes; log jail; Shivaree in June.

Minerals: Oil and gas.

Agriculture: Beef, forages, oats, wildlife, row crops. Market value $36.3 million. Hunting leases, timber.

Vital Statistics, annual: Births, 913; deaths, 611; marriages, 323; divorces, 271.

Race/Ethnicity: Anglo, 55.6%; Hispanic, 19.8%; Black, 14.2%; Asian, 2.2%; Other, 8.2%.

GATESVILLE (16,854) county seat; prisons, varied manufacturing; hospital; refurbished courthouse; museum; branch Central Texas College; Spurfest in September.

COPPERAS COVE (37,041) business center for Fort Cavazos; industrial filters, other manufacturing; hospital, library; Central Texas College; Rabbit Fest in May.

Other towns include: **Evant** (454, partly in Hamilton County), **Flat** (610), **Jonesboro** (125), **Mound** (214), **Oglesby** (434), **Purmela** (50), **South Mountain** (402). Part [14,415] of **Fort Cavazos**.

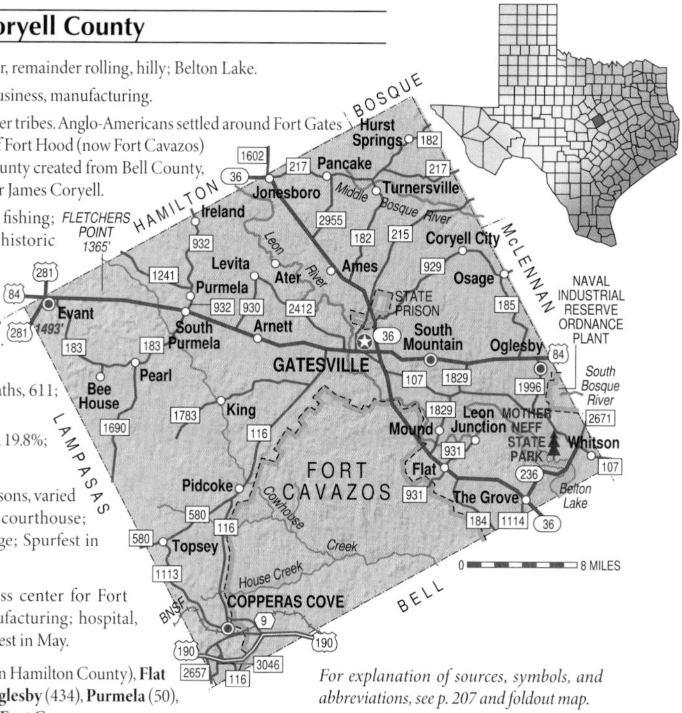

For explanation of sources, symbols, and abbreviations, see p. 207 and foldout map.

Population	84,232
Change from 2010	11.7%
Area (sq. mi.)	1,056.8
Land Area (sq. mi.)	1,052.1
Altitude (ft.)	600–1,493

Rainfall (in.)	37.0
Jan. mean min (°F)	37.1
July mean max (°F)	94.1
Civ. Labor	24,681
Unemployed	4.5%

Wages	$202,174,669
Per Capita Income	$37,476
Property Value	$6,930,910,181
Retail Sales	$662,010,587

A church near Cee Vee in Cottle County. Photo by Leaflet, Public Domain

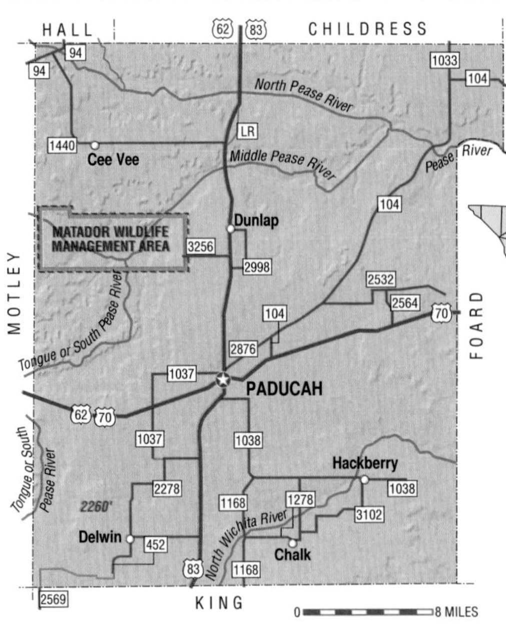

Cottle County

Physical Features: Northwest county below Caprock, rough in west, level in east; gray, black, sandy and loam soils; drains to Pease River.

Economy: Agribusiness, government/services.

History: Around 1700, Apaches were displaced by Comanches, who in turn were driven out by the U.S. Army in the 1870s. Anglo-American settlers arrived in the 1880s. County created in 1876 from Fannin County; organized in 1892; named for George W. Cottle, Alamo hero.

Recreation: Hunting of quail, dove, wild hogs, deer; wildlife management area; City-County Heritage museum, Fiestas Patrias in September, youth horse show in April, Cottle King Old Settlers Reunion & Rodeo in April, Paducah Pickins in March and October.

Minerals: Oil, natural gas.

Agriculture: Beef cattle, sheep, cotton, peanuts, wheat. 3,000 acres irrigated. Market value $27.7 million.

Vital Statistics, annual: Births, 0; deaths, 35; marriages, 3; divorces, NA.

Race/Ethnicity: Anglo, 65.4%; Hispanic, 23.7%; Black, 7.0%; Asian, 0.0%; Other, 4.0%.

Population	1,381
Change from 2010	–8.2%
Area (sq. mi.)	901.6
Land Area (sq. mi.)	900.6
Altitude (ft.)	1,470–2,260
Rainfall (in.)	23.9
Jan. mean min (°F)	29.0
July mean max (°F)	95.5
Civ. Labor	862
Unemployed	2.7%
Wages	$13,064,523
Per Capita Income	$73,613

PADUCAH (1,060) county seat; government/services, library.

Other towns include: **Hackberry** (30).

Property Value	$704,209,695
Retail Sales	$5,671,548

Crane County

Physical Features: Rolling prairie, Pecos Valley, some hills; sandy, loam soils; Juan Cordona Lake (intermittent).

Economy: Oil and gas; agriculture; government/services.

History: Lipan Apache area. Ranching developed in the 1890s. Oil discovered in 1926. County created from Tom Green County in 1887, organized in 1927; named for Baylor University president W. C. Crane.

Recreation: Museum of the Desert Southwest; sites of pioneer trails and historic Horsehead Crossing on Pecos River; hunting of mule deer, quail; camping park; rodeo in May.

Minerals: Oil, gas production.

Agriculture: Beef cattle, goats. Market value $1.9 million.

Vital Statistics, annual: Births, 59; deaths, 48; marriages, 18; divorces, 6.

Race/Ethnicity: Anglo, 28.7%; Hispanic, 67.6%; Black, 1.5%; Asian, 0.5%; Other, 1.8%.

CRANE (3,484) county seat; oil-well servicing and production, foundry, steel, surfboard manufacturing; hospital.

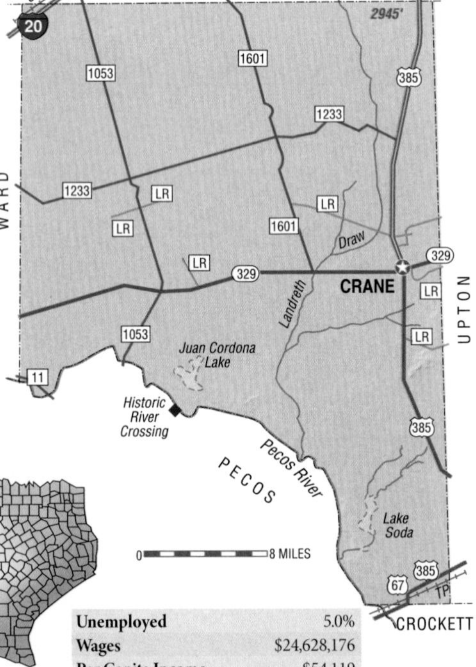

Population	4,680
Change from 2010	7.0%
Area (sq. mi.)	785.7
Land Area (sq. mi.)	785.1
Altitude (ft.)	2,290–2,945
Rainfall (in.)	12.1
Jan. mean min (°F)	33.6
July mean max (°F)	95.1
Civ. Labor	1,627
Unemployed	5.0%
Wages	$24,628,176
Per Capita Income	$54,119
Property Value	$2,279,665,901
Retail Sales	$50,601,921

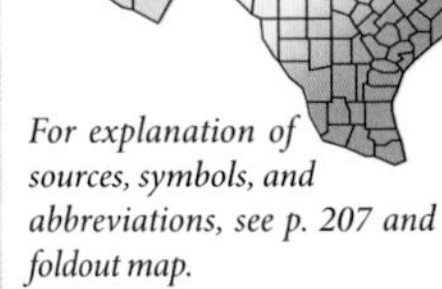

For explanation of sources, symbols, and abbreviations, see p. 207 and foldout map.

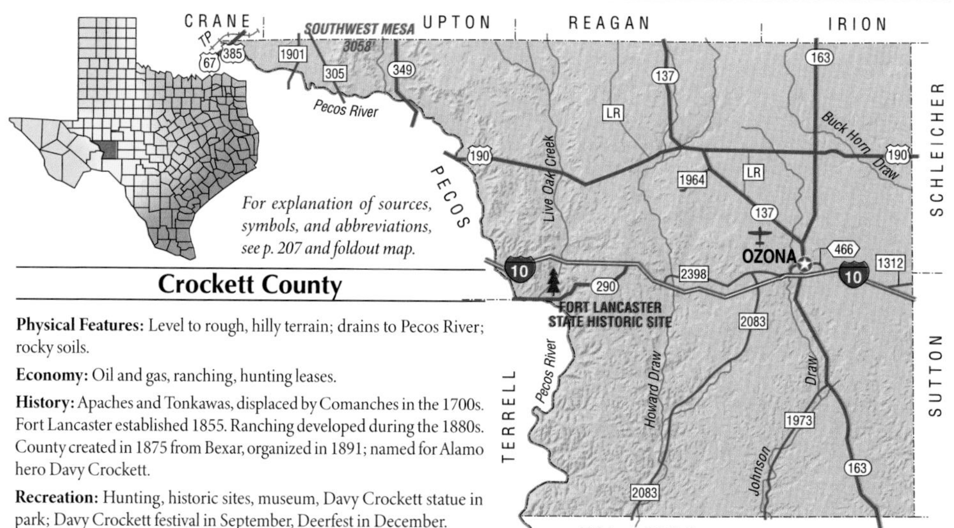

For explanation of sources, symbols, and abbreviations, see p. 207 and foldout map.

Crockett County

Physical Features: Level to rough, hilly terrain; drains to Pecos River; rocky soils.

Economy: Oil and gas, ranching, hunting leases.

History: Apaches and Tonkawas, displaced by Comanches in the 1700s. Fort Lancaster established 1855. Ranching developed during the 1880s. County created in 1875 from Bexar, organized in 1891; named for Alamo hero Davy Crockett.

Recreation: Hunting, historic sites, museum, Davy Crockett statue in park; Davy Crockett festival in September, Deerfest in December.

Minerals: Oil, gas production.

Agriculture: Sheep (first in numbers), goats; beef cattle. Market value $15.4 million.

Vital Statistics, annual: Births, 36; deaths, 61; marriages, 23; divorces, 5.

Race/Ethnicity: Anglo, 34.9%; Hispanic, 62%; Black, 0.6%; Asian, 0.3%; Other, 2.3%.

OZONA (2,343) county seat; ranching, oil & gas, hunting, tourism; health care clinics.

Population	3,068
Change from 2010	−17.5%
Area (sq. mi.)	2,807.4
Land Area (sq. mi.)	2,807.3
Altitude (ft.)	1,720–3,058
Rainfall (in.)	19.8
Jan. mean min (°F)	31.9
July mean max (°F)	93.7
Civ. Labor	1,434
Unemployed	4.0%
Wages	$15,596,708
Per Capita Income	$57,013
Property Value	$3,646,092,458
Retail Sales	$37,637,077

Crosby County

Physical Features: Flat, rich soil above Caprock, broken below; drains into Brazos River forks and playas.

Economy: Agribusiness, tourism, commuters to Lubbock.

History: Comanches, driven out by U.S. Army in 1870s; ranching developed soon afterward. Quaker colony founded in 1879. County created from Bexar District 1876, organized 1886; named for Texas Land Commissioner Stephen Crosby.

Recreation: White River Lake; Silver Falls Park; hunting.

Minerals: Sand, gravel, oil, gas.

Agriculture: Cotton, beef cattle, sorghum; about 112,000 acres irrigated. Market value $86.9 million.

Vital Statistics, annual: Births, 78; deaths, 97; marriages, 17; divorces, 8.

Race/Ethnicity: Anglo, 40.4%; Hispanic, 55.1%; Black, 2.3%; Asian, 0.2%; Other, 1.9%.

CROSBYTON (1,488) county seat; agribusiness center; hospital, Pioneer Museum, Prairie Ladies Multi-Cultural Center, library; Cowboy Gathering in October.

Other towns include: **Lorenzo** (964); **Ralls** (1,639) government/services, agribusiness, museums, Cotton Boll Fest in September.

Population	5,106
Change from 2010	−15.7%
Area (sq. mi.)	901.7
Land Area (sq. mi.)	900.2
Altitude (ft.)	2,250–3,235
Rainfall (in.)	21.7
Jan. mean min (°F)	27.6
July mean max (°F)	91.5
Civ. Labor	2,424
Unemployed	4.1%
Wages	$14,279,863
Per Capita Income	$52,897
Property Value	$1,156,422,804
Retail Sales	$39,739,996

Culberson County

Physical Features: Contains Texas' highest mountain; slopes toward Pecos Valley on east, Diablo Bolson on west; salt lakes; unique vegetation in canyons.

Economy: Tourism, government/services, talc mining and processing, agribusiness, sulfur mining.

History: Apaches arrived about 600 years ago. U.S. military frontier after Civil War. Ranching developed after 1880. Mexican migration increased after 1920. County created from El Paso County 1911, organized 1912; named for D.B. Culberson, Texas congressman.

Recreation: National park; Guadalupe and El Capitan, twin peaks; scenic canyons and mountains; classic car museum, antique saloon bar; frontier days in June, big buck tournament.

Minerals: Sulfur, talc, marble, oil.

Agriculture: Beef cattle; crops include cotton, vegetables, melons, pecans; 6,000 acres in irrigation. Market value $15.9 million.

Vital Statistics, annual: Births, 30; deaths, 36; marriages, 0; divorces, NA.

Race/Ethnicity: Anglo, 20.3%; Hispanic, 75.2%; Black, 0.9%; Asian, 1.3%; Other, 2.3%.

VAN HORN (1,946) county seat; agribusiness, tourism, rock crushing, government/services; hospital.

Other towns include: **Kent** (30).

Population	2,193
Change from 2010	–8.5%
Area (sq. mi.)	3,813.0
Land Area (sq. mi.)	3,812.8
Altitude (ft.)	2,900–8,749
Rainfall (in.)	10.3
Jan. mean min (°F)	31.6
July mean max (°F)	93.1
Civ. Labor	1,153
Unemployed	2.9%
Wages	$29,976,097
Per Capita Income	$71,297
Property Value	$7,829,892,117
Retail Sales	$130,110,839

For explanation of sources, symbols, and abbreviations, see p. 207 and foldout map.

The Empty Saddle Monument in Dalhart. Photo by Billy Hathorn, CC by SA 3.0

Dallam County

Physical Features: Prairie, broken by creeks; playas; sandy, loam soils; Rita Blanca National Grassland.

Economy: Agribusiness, dairies, cheese manufacturing, tourism.

History: Earliest Plains Apaches; displaced by Comanches and Kiowas. Ranching developed in late 19th century. Farming began after 1900. County created from Bexar District, 1876, organized 1891. Named for lawyer-editor James W. Dallam.

Recreation: XIT museum, XIT rodeo in August, pheasant hunting, wildlife, grasslands.

Minerals: none.

Agriculture: A leader in production of grain (corn, wheat, sorghum). Cattle, hogs, dairies, potatoes, sunflowers, beans; substantial irrigation. Market value $634.9 million.

Vital Statistics, annual: Births, 186; deaths, 79; marriages, 39; divorces, 28.

Race/Ethnicity: Anglo, 43.8%; Hispanic, 52.1%; Black, 1.0%; Asian, 0.1%; Other, 2.9%.

DALHART (8,347, partly in Hartley County) county seat; government/services; agribusiness center for parts of Texas, New Mexico, Oklahoma; railroad; cheese plant; grain operations; junior college branch; hospital; prison.

Other towns include: **Kerrick** (35) and **Texline** (460).

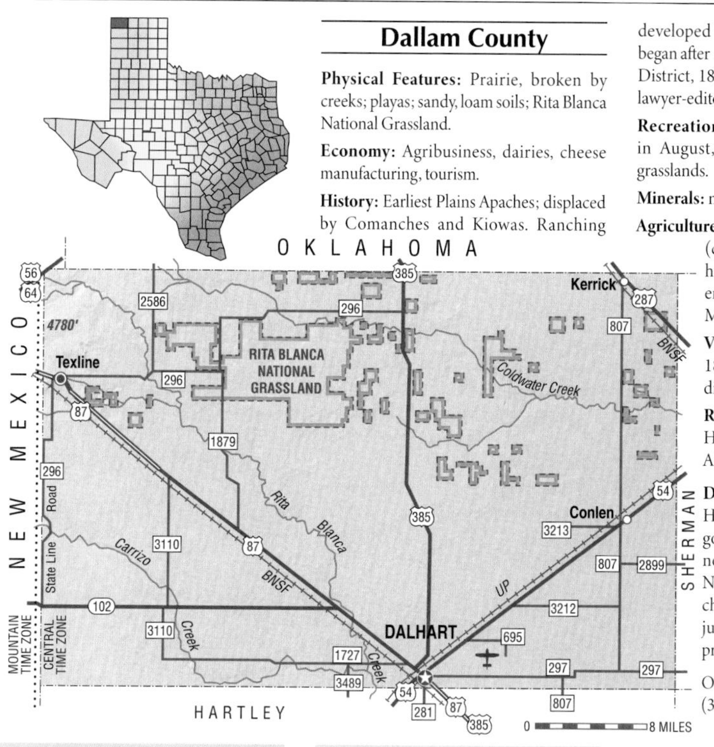

Population	7,172
Change from 2010	7.0%
Area (sq. mi.)	1,505.3
Land Area (sq. mi.)	1,503.3
Altitude (ft.)	3,655–4,780

Rainfall (in.)	15.6
Jan. mean min (°F)	22.4
July mean max (°F)	91.6
Civ. Labor	3,869
Unemployed	2.4%

Wages	$71,714,338
Per Capita Income	$70,511
Property Value	$2,032,102,112
Retail Sales	$116,561,924

Dallas County

Physical Features: Mostly flat, heavy blackland soils, sandy clays in west; drains to Trinity River; Joe Pool Lake, White Rock Lake, Mountain Creek Lake, Lake Ray Hubbard, North Lake.

Economy: A national center for telecommunications, transportation, electronics manufacturing, data processing, conventions and trade shows; foreign-trade zone located at D/FW International Airport, U.S. Customs port of entry; government/services.

History: Caddoan area. Anglo-Americans began arriving in 1840. Antebellum slaveholding area. County created and organized in 1846 from Nacogdoches, Robertson counties; named for U.S. Vice President George Mifflin Dallas.

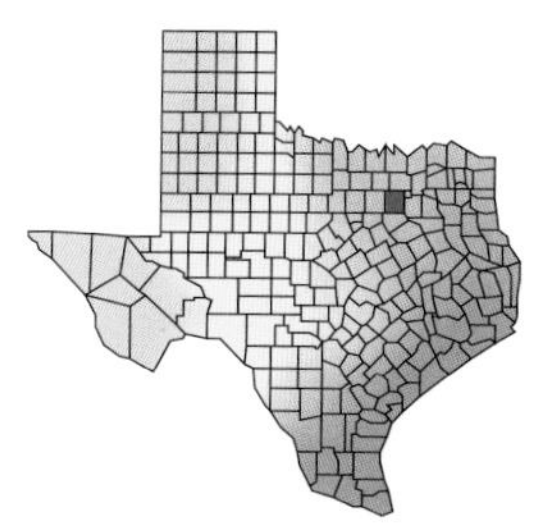

Recreation: One of the state's top tourist destinations and one of the nation's most popular convention centers; State Fair, museums, zoo, West End shopping and tourist district, historical sites, including Sixth Floor museum in the old Texas School Book Depository, site of the assassination of President Kennedy. Also, the Morton H. Meyerson Symphony Center; performing arts; professional sports; Texas broadcast museum; lakes, state park, Audubon center; theme and amusement parks.

Minerals: Sand, gravel, oil and gas.

Agriculture: Horticultural crops, wheat, hay, corn, soybeans, horses. Market value $29.8 million.

Vital Statistics, annual: Births, 36,101; deaths, 19,989; marriages, 8,723; divorces, 7,966.

Race/Ethnicity: Anglo, 27.7%; Hispanic, 40.5%; Black, 21.6%; Asian, 6.9%; Other, 3.2%.

DALLAS (1,288,457) county seat; center of state's largest consolidated metropolitan area and third-largest city in Texas; D/FW International Airport is one of the world's busiest; headquarters for the U.S. Army and Air Force Exchange Service; Federal Reserve Bank; a leader in fashions and in computer operations; hospitals; many hotels in downtown area offer adequate accommodations for most conventions.

GARLAND (242,035) varied manufacturing, community college branch, hospitals, performing arts center.

IRVING (254,198) finance, technology, tourism, distribution center; Boy Scout headquarters and museum; North Lake College; hospitals; parks; Dragon Boat Festival in May.

Other cities include: **Addison** (17,012) general aviation airport, theater center; **Balch Springs** (27,160); part [50,688] of Carrollton (133,251) residential community, distribution center, hospital; **Cedar Hill** (48,557) residential, light manufacturing, retail, distribution center, Northwood University, community college, state park, Penn Farm, Country Day on the Hill in October; **Cockrell Hill** (3,719); **Coppell** (42,221)

Dallas County continued...

distribution, varied manufacturing, office center, hike and bike trails; **DeSoto** (55,729) residential community, light industry and distribution, hospitals; Toad Holler Creekfest in June.

Also: **Duncanville** (39,797) construction, health care, manufacturing; library, museums; Juneteenth celebration; **Farmers Branch** (36,442) distribution center, varied manufacturing, Brookhaven College, hospital; **Glenn Heights** (17,127, partly in Ellis County); most [125,377] of **Grand Prairie** (197,347) wholesale trade, aerospace, entertainment, hospital, library, Joe Pool Reservoir, Indian pow-wow in September, Lone Star horse-racing track; **Highland Park** (8,747); **Hutchins** (5,566) varied manufacturing; **Lancaster** (40,728) residential, industrial, distribution center, Cedar Valley College, Commemorative Air Force museum, Cold War air museum, Bear Creek nature preserve, depot, historic town square, Oktoberfest.

Also: **Mesquite** (147,691) shipping, rail port hub, retail, hospitals, arts center, championship rodeo July – September, rodeo parade in spring, Summer Sizzle festival in June, community college, historical parks; most [77,248] of **Richardson** (116,382) telecommunications, software development, financial services, hospital, library, Wildflower Music Festival in May; **Rowlett** (63,371) residential, manufacturing, government/services, hospital, library, park, hike and bike trails; part [18,287] of **Sachse** (29,042, rest in Collin County) commuting to Dallas, government/services, Fallfest in October; **Seagoville** (18,180507) rural/suburban setting, federal prison, Seagofest in October; **Sunnyvale** (8,062) tile manufacturing, hospital, Samuell Farm, Sunnyfest on July 4; **University Park** (24,849); **Wilmer** (5,332).

Part of **Combine** [870], part of **Ovilla**[291], and part of **Wylie** [1,465].

Population	2,586,050
Change from 2010	9.2%
Area (sq. mi.)	908.6
Land Area (sq. mi.)	871.3
Altitude (ft.)	350–870

Rainfall (in.)	38.3
Jan. mean min (°F)	39.9
July mean max (°F)	95.5
Civ. Labor	1,420,674
Unemployed	3.7%

Wages	$39,072,071,207
Per Capita Income	$72,218
Property Value	$459,594,343,560
Retail Sales	$55,652,716,675

For explanation of sources, symbols, and abbreviations, see p. 207 and foldout map.

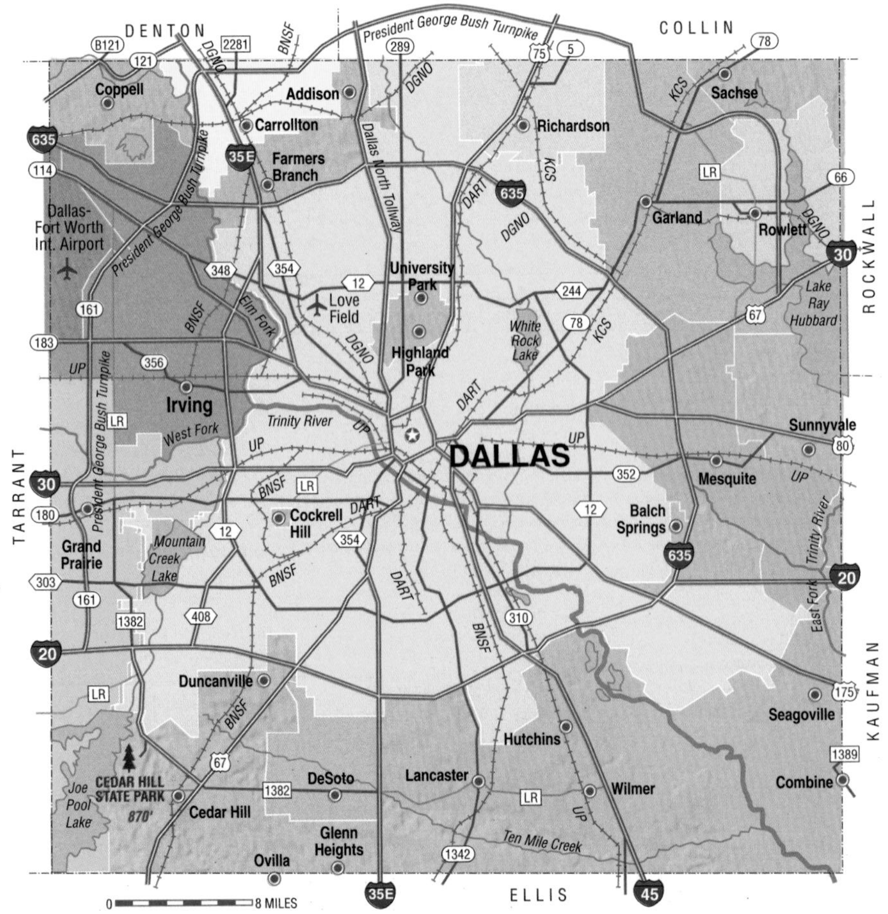

The Dallas Holocaust and Human Rights Museum opened its new location in 2019. Photo by MacTheWikiman, CC by SA 4.0

Dawson County

Physical Features: South Plains county, broken on the east; loam and sandy soils.

Economy: Agriculture, farm and gin equipment manufacturing, peanut plant, government/services.

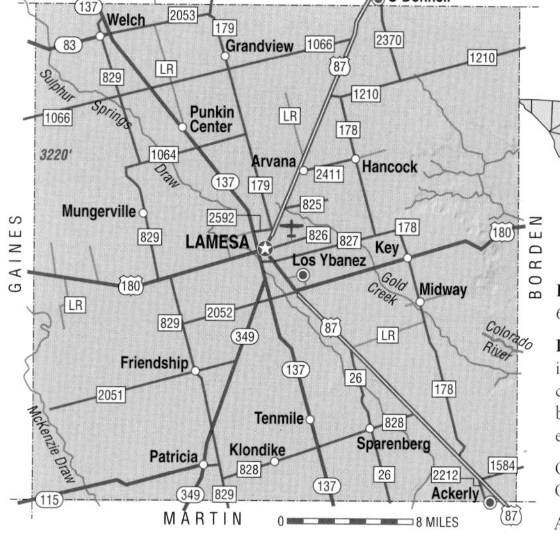

History: Comanche, Kiowa area. Ranching developed in 1880s. Farming began after 1900. Hispanic population increased after 1940. County created from Bexar District, 1876, organized 1905; named for Nicholas M. Dawson, San Jacinto veteran.

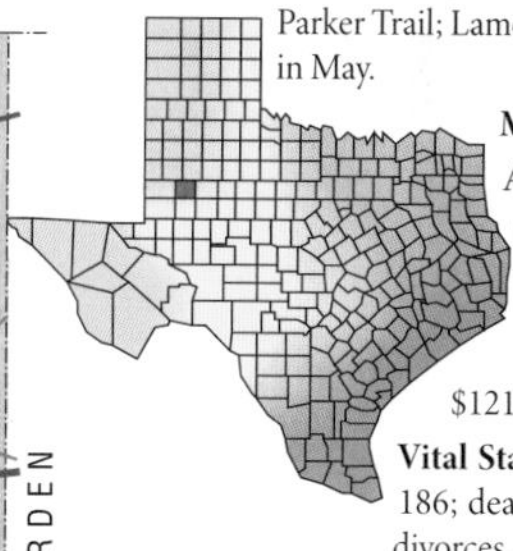

Recreation: Parks, museum, campground, part of Quanah Parker Trail; Lamesa poetry and music fest in May.

Minerals: Oil, natural gas.

Agriculture: Cotton, peanuts, sorghums, watermelons, alfalfa, grapes. 60,000 acres irrigated. Market value $121.3 million.

Vital Statistics, annual: Births, 186; deaths, 192; marriages, 46; divorces, 36.

Race/Ethnicity: Anglo, 36.8%; Hispanic, 54.3%; Black, 6.8%; Asian, 0.4%; Other, 1.6%.

LAMESA (8,751) county seat; agribusiness, food processing, oil-field services, some manufacturing, computerized cotton-classing office; hospital, library; Howard College branch; prison unit; chicken-fried steak festival last weekend in April.

Other towns include: **Ackerly** (265, partly in Martin County), **Los Ybanez** (22) and **Welch** (210).

Also, **O'Donnell** (726, mostly in Lynn County) bust of Dan Blocker.

Population	12,413
Change from 2010	–10.3%
Area (sq. mi.)	902.1
Land Area (sq. mi.)	900.3
Altitude (ft.)	2,580–3,220

Rainfall (in.)	16.8
Jan. mean min (°F)	27.6
July mean max (°F)	93.3
Civ. Labor	4,538
Unemployed	4.4%

Wages	$54,550,858
Per Capita Income	$46,139
Property Value	$1,355,642,730
Retail Sales	$351,392,028

Deaf Smith County

Physical Features: High Plains county, partly broken; chocolate and sandy loam soils; drains to Palo Duro and Tierra Blanca creeks.

Economy: Agriculture, varied industries, meat packing, pet food plant.

History: Apache Indians, were displaced by Comanches and Kiowas. Ranching developed after the U.S. Army drove out the Indian tribes 1874-1875. Farming began after 1900. Hispanic settlement increased after 1950. County created in 1876 from the Bexar District; organized in 1890. Named for famed scout in Texas Revolution, Erastus "Deaf" Smith.

Recreation: Museum, tours, POW camp chapel; Cinco de Mayo, Pioneer Days in May.

Minerals: Insignificant.

Agriculture: Leading agricultural county, dairies, feedlot operations, cotton, wheat, sorghum, corn; 50% irrigated. Market value $1.6 billion, first in state.

For explanation of sources, symbols, and abbreviations, see p. 207 and foldout map.

Vital Statistics, annual: Births, 323; deaths, 200; marriages, 92; divorces, 13.

Race/Ethnicity: Anglo, 22.8%; Hispanic, 74.9%; Black, 0.6%; Asian, 0.2%; Other, 1.5%.

HEREFORD (14,779) county seat; cattle feeding, agriculture, trucking; hospital; Amarillo College branch; aquatic center.

Other towns include: **Dawn** (52).

Population	18,329
Change from 2010	–5.4%
Area (sq. mi.)	1,498.4
Land Area (sq. mi.)	1,496.9
Altitude (ft.)	3,650–4,460

Rainfall (in.)	19.3
Jan. mean min (°F)	23.9
July mean max (°F)	91.1
Civ. Labor	9,015

Unemployed	3.0%
Wages	$117,211,847
Per Capita Income	$60,615
Property Value	$3,552,187,627
Retail Sales	$466,420,277

Delta County

Physical Features: Northeastern county between two forks of Sulphur River; Cooper Lake (also designated Jim Chapman Lake); black, sandy loam soils.

Economy: Agriculture, government/services, retirement location.

History: Caddo area, but disease, other tribes caused displacement around 1790. Anglo-Americans arrived in 1820s. County created from Lamar, Hopkins counties 1870. Greek letter delta origin of name, because of shape of the county.

Recreation: Fishing, hunting; lake, state park; Cooper Cotton Harvest Festival in October.

Minerals: Insignificant.

Agriculture: Beef, hay, soybeans, wheat, corn, sorghum, cotton. Market value $36.3 million.

Vital Statistics, annual: Births, 66; deaths, 90; marriages, 14; divorces, 22.

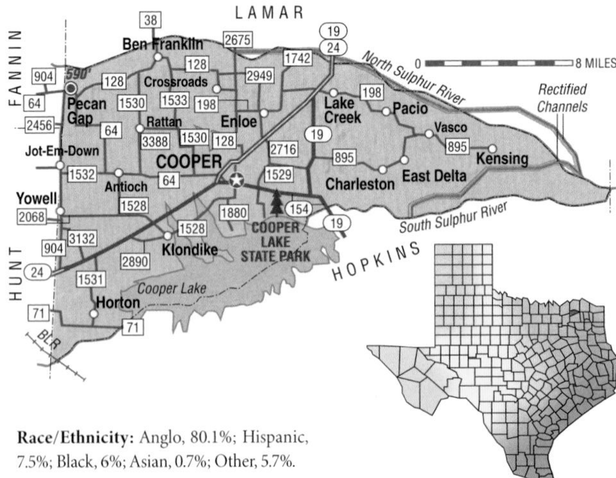

Race/Ethnicity: Anglo, 80.1%; Hispanic, 7.5%; Black, 6%; Asian, 0.7%; Other, 5.7%.

COOPER (1,951) county seat; commuters, industrial park, some manufacturing, agribusiness; museum, library; post office mural.

Other towns include: **Ben Franklin** (60), **Enloe** (90), **Klondike** (175), **Lake Creek** (55), and **Pecan Gap** (181).

Population	5,392
Change from 2010	3.1%
Area (sq. mi.)	277.9
Land Area (sq. mi.)	256.8
Altitude (ft.)	322–590

Rainfall (in.)	49.3
Jan. mean min (°F)	36.1
July mean max (°F)	92.5
Civ. Labor	2,515
Unemployed	4.0%

Wages	$9,623,704
Per Capita Income	$47,471
Property Value	$1,190,014,090
Retail Sales	$86,595,728

Denton County

Physical Features: North Texas county; partly hilly, draining to Elm Fork of Trinity River, Lewisville Lake, Ray Roberts Lake, Grapevine Lake; Blackland and Grand Prairie soils and terrain.

Economy: Varied industries, colleges, horse industry, tourism, government/services; part of Dallas-Fort Worth metropolitan area.

History: Land grant from Texas Congress 1841 for Peters colony. County created, organized, out of Fannin County in 1846; named for John B. Denton, pioneer Methodist minister.

Recreation: Lake activities, parks; universities' cultural, athletic activities, including "Texas Women; A Celebration of History"; "First Ladies of Texas" collection of memorabilia; Little Chapel in the Woods; Texas Motor Speedway; Denton Jazz Festival in April.

Population	941,647
Change from 2010	42.1%
Area (sq. mi.)	953.0
Land Area (sq. mi.)	878.4
Altitude (ft.)	433–980
Rainfall (in.)	38.4
Jan. mean min (°F)	35.9
July mean max (°F)	94.3
Civ. Labor	551,484
Unemployed	3.2%
Wages	$4,658,725,861
Per Capita Income	$68,773
Property Value	$183,197,343,234
Retail Sales	$14,460,443,493

Minerals: Natural gas.

Agriculture: Second in number of horses. Eggs, nurseries, turf, cattle; also, hay, sorghum, wheat, peanuts grown. Market value $123.2 million.

Vital Statistics, annual: Births, 9,965; deaths, 4,822; marriages, 4,295; divorces, 2,779.

Race/Ethnicity: Anglo, 53.6%; Hispanic, 20.2%; Black, 10.5%; Asian, 10.2%; Other, 5.5%.

DENTON (148,146) county seat; universities, manufacturers of trucks (Peterbilt), medical, aviation; hospitals; historic courthouse square; storytelling festival in March.

LEWISVILLE (112,944) commuting to Dallas-Fort Worth, retail center, electronics and varied industries; hospital, library; Celtic Feis & Scottish Highland Games in March.

Flower Mound (77,243) residential community, library, mound of native grasses, bike classic in spring.

Carrollton (133,251, also in Dallas County), hospital.

Other towns include: **Argyle** (4,707) horse farms/training, bluegrass festival in March; **Aubrey** (6,490) horse farms/training, cabinet construction, museum, peanut festival early October; **Bartonville** (1,771); **Copper Canyon** (1,759); **Corinth** (22,690); **Corral City** (36); **Cross Roads** (1,817); **Dish** (437); **Double Oak** (3,054); **Hackberry** (2,961); **Hebron** (803); **Hickory Creek** (5,244); **Highland Village** (15,952); **Justin** (5,031); **Krugerville** (1,920); **Krum** (5,823) commuters, old grain mill, heritage museum, North Pole Days in December; **Lake Dallas** (7,722) light manufacturing, marina, historic downtown, Mardi Gras.

Also: **Lakewood Village** (660); **Lantana** (11,559); **Little Elm** (53,126) real estate, retail, lake activities/beach area, summer concert series; **Northlake** (6,829); **Oak Point** (5,557); **Pilot Point** (4,651) light manufacturing, horse ranches, Fireman's Fest in April; **Ponder** (2,429); **Providence Village** (7,812); **Roanoke** (9,878); **Sanger** (9,380) distribution center, commuters, government/services, lakes, Sellabration in September; **Shady Shores** (2,849); **The Colony** (45,000) retail, business offices, industrial firms; parks, nature trails, salute to veterans on Veterans Day; and **Trophy Club** (13,745) commuters, retail.

Part [28,660] of **Dallas**, part [17,514] **Fort Worth**, part [85,415] **Frisco**, part [5,580] **Plano**, and small parts of **Coppell**, **Celina**, **Prosper**, **Southlake**, **Westlake**.

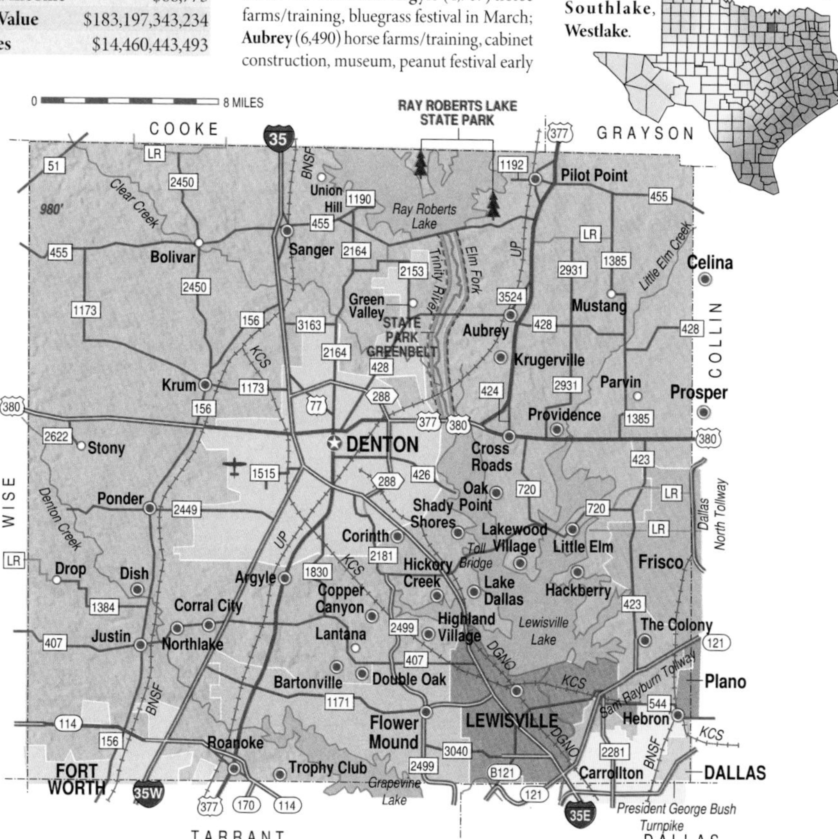

DeWitt County

Physical Features: Gulf Coastal Plain county drained by Guadalupe and tributaries; rolling to level; waxy, loam, sandy soils.

Economy: Oil, tourism.

History: Coahuiltecan area, then Karankawas and other tribes, finally the Comanches. Mexican and Anglo-American settlers arrived in the 1820s. County created, organized, in 1846 from Gonzales, Goliad, and Victoria counties; named for Green DeWitt, colonizer.

Recreation: Hunting, fishing, historic homes, museums, wildflowers, German dance halls.

Minerals: Oil and natural gas, gravel.

Agriculture: Cattle, pecans, row crops. Market value $38.7 million.

Vital Statistics, annual: Births, 246; deaths, 304; marriages, 71; divorces, NA.

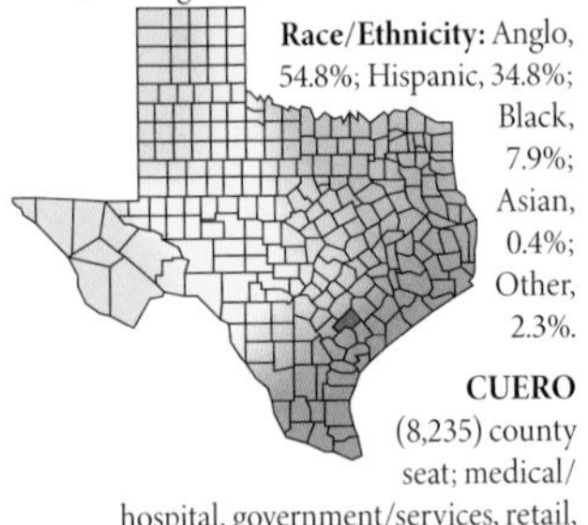

Race/Ethnicity: Anglo, 54.8%; Hispanic, 34.8%; Black, 7.9%; Asian, 0.4%; Other, 2.3%.

CUERO (8,235) county seat; medical/hospital, government/services, retail, ranching, oil and gas; Turkeyfest in October.

Yorktown (1,811) oil and gas, agriculture; library, museum, park, hike/bike trail; Western Days in October.

Other towns include: **Hochheim** (70), **Meyersville** (110), **Nordheim** (330), **Thomaston** (45), **Westhoff** (410).

Part [2,058] of **Yoakum** (5,923 total) cattle, leather, meat processing, hospital, museum, Tom Tom festival in June.

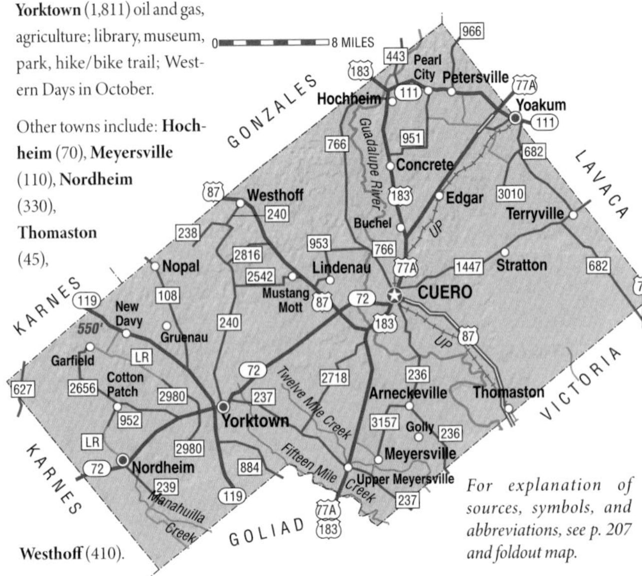

For explanation of sources, symbols, and abbreviations, see p. 207 and foldout map.

Population	19,918
Change from 2010	–0.9%
Area (sq. mi.)	910.5
Land Area (sq. mi.)	909.0
Altitude (ft.)	100–550

Rainfall (in.)	34.2
Jan. mean min (°F)	43.7
July mean max (°F)	96.4
Civ. Labor	9,113
Unemployed	3.4%
Wages	$105,269,703
Per Capita Income	$66,916
Property Value	$9,806,533,078
Retail Sales	$243,158,335

An old gin near Afton in Dickens County. Photo by Aualliso, CC by SA 4.0

Dickens County

Physical Features: West Texas county; broken land, Caprock in northwest; sandy, chocolate, red soils; drains to Croton, Duck creeks.

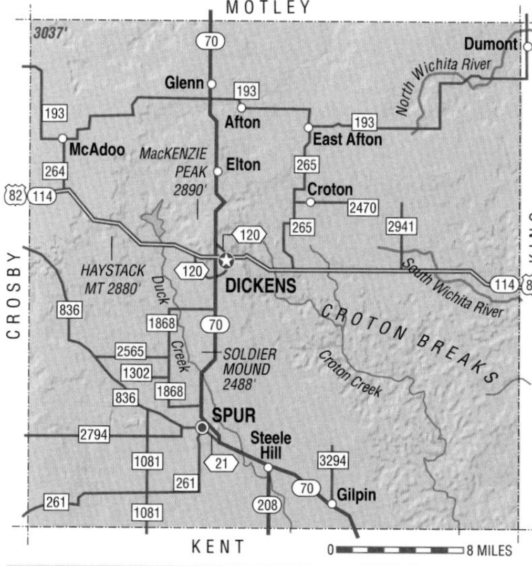

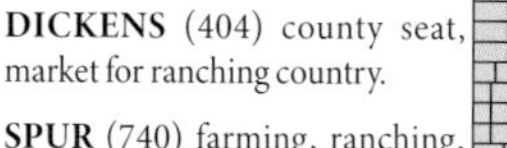

Economy: Agriculture, government services/prison unit, hunting leases, wind farms.

History: Comanches driven out by U.S. Army 1874-75. Ranching and some farming began in late 1880s. County created 1876, from Bexar District; organized 1891; named for Alamo hero who is variously listed as James R. Demkins or Dimpkins and J. Dickens.

Recreation: Hunting, fishing; Soldiers Mound site, Dickens Springs; downtown Spur.

Minerals: Oil, gas.

Agriculture: Cattle, horses, cotton, hay, small grains. Some irrigation. Market value $26.9 million. Hunting leases important.

Vital Statistics, annual: Births, 12; deaths, 41; marriages, 5; divorces, 7.

Race/Ethnicity: Anglo, 66.6%; Hispanic, 28.9%; Black, 1%; Asian, 0.1%; Other, 3.4%.

DICKENS (404) county seat, market for ranching country.

SPUR (740) farming, ranching, hunting, government/services; museum; homecoming in October.

Other towns include: **Afton** (15) and **McAdoo** (75).

Population	1,740
Change from 2010	–28.8%
Area (sq. mi.)	905.2
Land Area (sq. mi.)	901.7
Altitude (ft.)	1,800–3,037
Rainfall (in.)	22.5
Jan. mean min (°F)	28.0
July mean max (°F)	93.5
Civ. Labor	694
Unemployed	4.8%
Wages	$4,484,369
Per Capita Income	$50,869
Property Value	$813,821,946
Retail Sales	$34,013,732

Dimmit County

Physical Features: Southwest county; level to rolling; much brush; sandy, loam, red soils; drained by Nueces River.

Economy: Government/services, agribusiness, petroleum products, tourism.

History: Coahuiltecan area, later Comanches. John Townsend, a Black man from Nacogdoches, led the first attempt at settlement before the Civil War. Texas Rangers forced out the Comanches in 1877. Mexican migration increased after 1910. County created 1858 from Bexar, Maverick, Uvalde, Webb counties; organized 1880. Named for Philip Dimmitt of the Texas Revolution; law misspelled name.

Recreation: Hunting, fishing, campsites, wildlife area; winter haven for tourists; old jailhouse museum.

Minerals: Oil, natural gas.

Agriculture: Onions, pecans, cantaloupes, olives, tomatoes, tangerines, cattle, goats, horses, hay. Market value $28.5 million.

Vital Statistics, annual: Births, 155; deaths, 106; marriages, 27; divorces, NA.

Race/Ethnicity: Anglo, 10.4%; Hispanic, 86.9%; Black, 0.8%; Asian, 0.8%; Other, 1%.

CARRIZO SPRINGS (4,833) county seat; agribusiness center, feedlot, food processing, oil, gas processing, hunting center; hospital; historic Baptist church; Mt. Hope cemetery with 17 Texas Rangers buried; bull riding event in April.

Other towns include: **Asherton** (718), **Big Wells** (487) Cinco de Mayo, **Carrizo Hill** (1,076), and **Catarina** (84) Camino Real festival in April.

Population	8,473
Change from 2010	–15.2%
Area (sq. mi.)	1,334.5
Land Area (sq. mi.)	1,328.9
Altitude (ft.)	410–871
Rainfall (in.)	19.6
Jan. mean min (°F)	39.4
July mean max (°F)	98.9
Civ. Labor	6,154
Unemployed	3.8%
Wages	$98,243,034
Per Capita Income	$55,771
Property Value	$9,439,311,670
Retail Sales	$161,599,822

Kean House in the Cisco Historic District is listed as a Texas Historic Landmark. Photo by Renelibrary, CC by SA 4.0

Donley County

Physical Features: Panhandle county bisected by Red River Salt Fork; Greenbelt Lake, Lelia Lake; rolling to level; clay, loam, sandy soils.

Economy: Agribusiness, government/services, tourism.

History: Apaches displaced by Kiowas and Comanches, who were driven out in 1874-75 by U.S. Army. Methodist colony from New York settled in 1878. County created in 1876, organized 1882, out of Bexar District; named for Texas Supreme Court Justice S.P. Donley.

Recreation: Lake, hunting, fishing, camping, water sports; Col. Goodnight Chuckwagon cook-off in September.

Minerals: Small amount of natural gas.

Agriculture: Cattle top revenue source; cotton, peanuts, alfalfa, wheat, hay, melons; 15,000 acres irrigated. Market value $94.2 million.

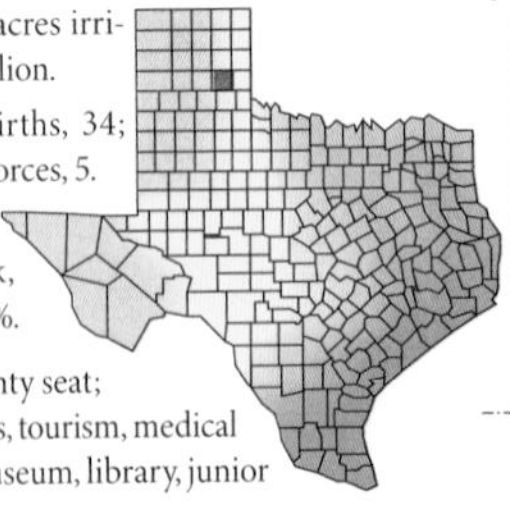

Vital Statistics, annual: Births, 34; deaths, 55; marriages, 20; divorces, 5.

Race/Ethnicity: Anglo, 77.9%; Hispanic, 10.9%; Black, 5.1%; Asian, 0.3%; Other, 5.8%.

CLARENDON (1,867) county seat; higher education, agribusiness, tourism, medical center clinic; Saints Roost museum, library, junior college; restored historic buildings.

Other towns include: **Hedley** (278) cotton festival in October, **Howardwick** (371), and **Lelia Lake** (55).

Population	3,268
Change from 2010	–11.1%
Area (sq. mi.)	933.1
Land Area (sq. mi.)	929.9
Altitude (ft.)	2,080–3,268

Rainfall (in.)	22.7
Jan. mean min (°F)	25.3
July mean max (°F)	92.8
Civ. Labor	1,492
Unemployed	3.6%

Wages	$9,489,625
Per Capita Income	$50,574
Property Value	$909,444,448
Retail Sales	$46,985,123

Duval County

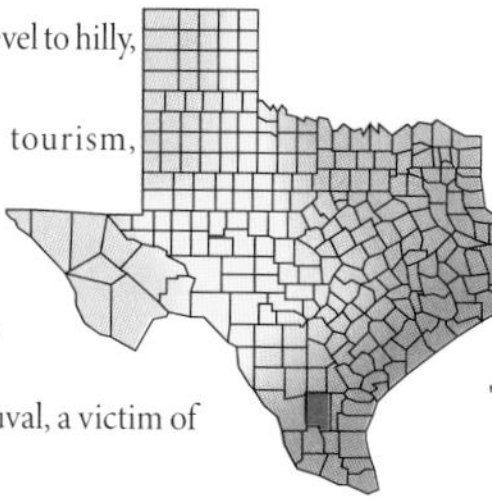

Physical Features: South Texas county; level to hilly, brushy in most areas; varied soils.

Economy: Ranching, petroleum, tourism, government/services.

History: Coahuiltecans, displaced by Comanche bands. Mexican settlement began in 1812. County created from Live Oak, Nueces, and Starr counties in 1858, organized in 1876; named for Burr H. Duval, a victim of Goliad massacre.

Recreation: Hunting, tourist crossroads.

Minerals: Oil, gas, salt, sand, gravel, uranium.

Agriculture: Most income from beef cattle; grains, cotton, vegetables, fruit, hay. Market value $11.0 million.

Vital Statistics, annual: Births, 114; deaths, 137; marriages, 33; divorces, 16.

Race/Ethnicity: Anglo, 9.5%; Hispanic, 81%; Black, 1.5%; Asian, 0.5%; Other, 7.5%.

SAN DIEGO (3,755, part in Jim Wells County) county seat; ranching, oil field, tourist center; hospital.

Freer (2,472) oil and gas, construction, ranching and hunting; rattlesnake roundup in May.

Benavides (1,195) serves truck-farming area.

Other towns include: **Concepcion** (19) and **Realitos** (84).

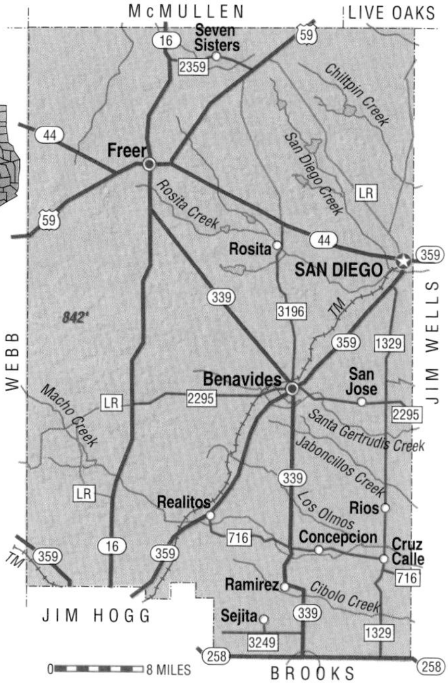

Population	9,756
Change from 2010	–17.2%
Area (sq. mi.)	1,795.6
Land Area (sq. mi.)	1,793.5
Altitude (ft.)	180–842
Rainfall (in.)	25.2

Jan. mean min (°F)	45.5
July mean max (°F)	96.8
Civ. Labor	5,051
Unemployed	4.5%

Wages	$40,475,256
Per Capita Income	$51,887
Property Value	$3,062,601,148
Retail Sales	$51,674,664

Eastland County

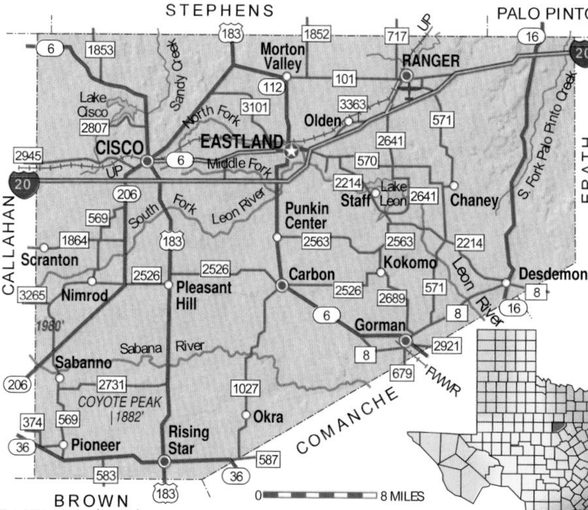

Physical Features: Hilly, rolling; sandy, loam soils; drains to Leon River forks; Lake Cisco, Lake Leon.

Economy: Agribusiness, education, petroleum industries.

History: Plains Indian area. Frank Sánchez among first settlers in 1850s. County created from Bosque, Coryell, Travis counties, 1858, organized 1873; named for W.M. Eastland, Mier Expedition casualty.

Recreation: Hunting, water sports; museums; historic sites and displays.

Minerals: Oil, natural gas.

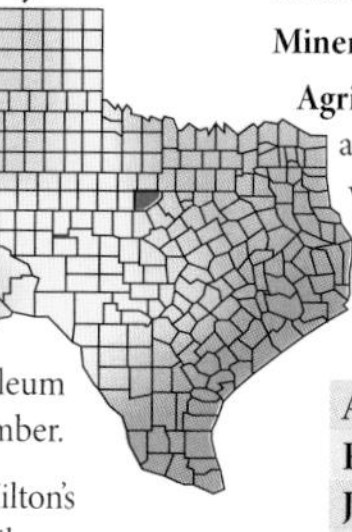

Agriculture: Beef cattle, hay, cotton. Some 9,000 acres irrigated. Market value $23.5 million.

Vital Statistics, annual: Births, 207; deaths, 279; marriages, 104; divorces, 22.

Race/Ethnicity: Anglo, 77%; Hispanic, 16.6%; Black, 1.9%; Asian, 0.5%; Other, 4%.

EASTLAND (3,621) county seat; tourism, government/services, petroleum industries, varied manufacturing; hospital, library; Old Ripfest in September.

CISCO (3,883) manufacturing, distribution, oilfield services; Conrad Hilton's first hotel restored, museums; community college; folklife festival in April.

Ranger (2,276) oil center, varied manufacturing, junior college.

Other towns: **Carbon** (286); **Desdemona** (180); **Gorman** (990) peanut processing, agribusiness, hospital; **Olden** (113), and **Rising Star** (766) cap manufacturing, plant nursery; Octoberfest.

Population	17,864
Change from 2010	–3.9%
Area (sq. mi.)	931.9
Land Area (sq. mi.)	926.5

Altitude (ft.)	960–1,980
Rainfall (in.)	29.2
Jan. mean min (°F)	31.6
July mean max (°F)	94.4
Civ. Labor	6,694
Unemployed	4.6%
Wages	$78,229,205
Per Capita Income	$66,400
Property Value	$4,579,159,872
Retail Sales	$398,381,507

Ector County

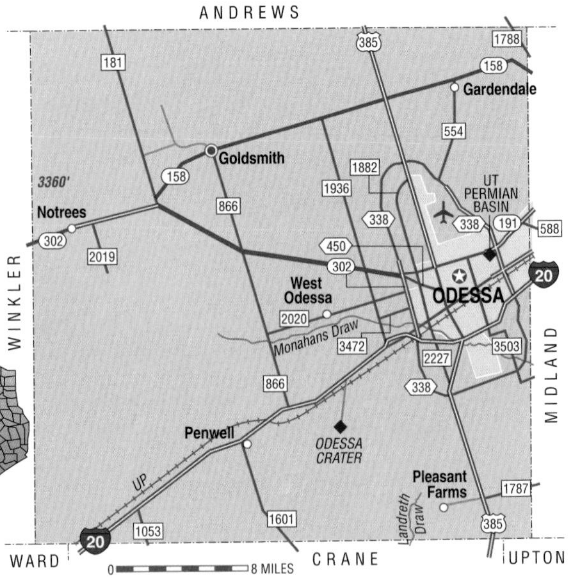

Physical Features: West Texas county; level to rolling, some sand dunes; meteor crater; desert vegetation.

Economy: Center for Permian Basin oil field operations, plastics, electric generation plants.

History: First settlers in late 1880s. Oil boom in 1926. County created from Tom Green County, 1887; organized 1891; named for jurist M.D. Ector.

Recreation: Globe Theatre replica; presidential museum and Bush childhood home; ranching museum, art institute; second-largest U.S. meteor crater, museum; Stonehenge replica.

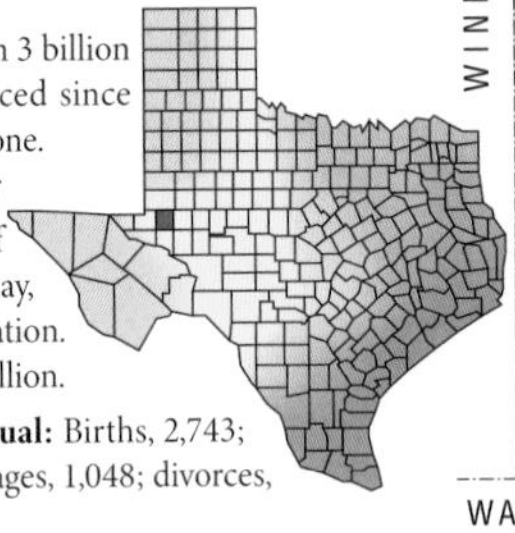

Minerals: More than 3 billion barrels of oil produced since 1926; gas, cement, stone.

Agriculture: Beef cattle, horses are chief producers; pecans, hay, poultry; minor irrigation. Market value $3.4 million.

Vital Statistics, annual: Births, 2,743; deaths, 1,623; marriages, 1,048; divorces, 787.

Race/Ethnicity: Anglo, 30.9%; Hispanic, 60.6%; Black, 4.5%; Asian, 1.4%; Other, 2.7%.

ODESSA (112,483, part in Midland County) county seat; oil and gas, manufacturing, ranching; hospitals; cultural center; Permian Basin Fair and Expo in September.

Other towns include: **Gardendale** (1,268), **Goldsmith** (228), **Notrees** (20), **Penwell** (41), and **West Odessa** (31,927).

Population	161,091
Change from 2010	17.5%
Area (sq. mi.)	901.8
Land Area (sq. mi.)	897.7
Altitude (ft.)	2,780–3,360
Rainfall (in.)	12.3
Jan. mean min (°F)	33.9
July mean max (°F)	93.6
Civ. Labor	83,462
Unemployed	3.9%
Wages	$1,389,178,037
Per Capita Income	$53,610
Property Value	$21,093,027,745
Retail Sales	$4,060,368,616

Edwards County

Physical Features: Rolling, hilly, with caves and spring-fed streams; rocky, thin soils; drained by Llano, Nueces rivers; varied timber.

Economy: Hunting leases, tourism, oil, gas production, ranching.

History: Apache area. First land sold in 1876. County created from Bexar District, 1858; organized 1883; named for Nacogdoches empresario Hayden Edwards.

Recreation: Hunting, fishing; scenic drives; Devil's Sinkhole, Kickapoo Cavern state parks; 4th of July Celebration, PBR Bull Riding, and fish fry and rodeo (Sept).

Minerals: Gas.

Agriculture: Second in number of goats. Mohair-wool production, Angora goats (first in numbers), sheep, cattle, some pecans. Market value $10.9 million. Cedar for fiber.

Vital Statistics, annual: Births, 18; deaths, 34; marriages, 6; divorces, NA.

Population	1,438
Change from 2010	–28.2%
Area (sq. mi.)	2,119.9
Land Area (sq. mi.)	2,117.9
Altitude (ft.)	1,480–2,415
Rainfall (in.)	26.0
Jan. mean min (°F)	38.8
July mean max (°F)	90.1
Civ. Labor	1,201
Unemployed	2.8 %
Wages	$5,833,485
Per Capita Income	$73,981
Property Value	$2,764,517,646
Retail Sales	$23,521,794

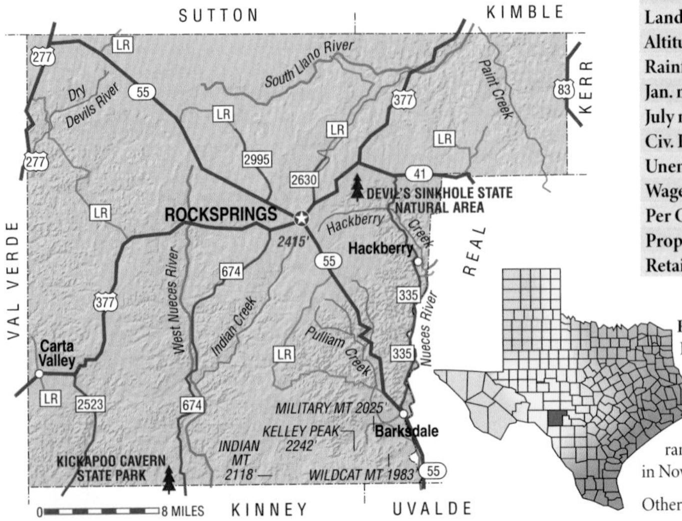

Race/Ethnicity: Anglo, 45.8%; Hispanic, 50.5%; Black, 0.1%; Asian, 0.8%; Other, 2.8%.

ROCKSPRINGS (874) county seat; government/services, hunting, ranching, oil and gas, hunters' barbecue in November.

Other towns include: **Barksdale** (24).

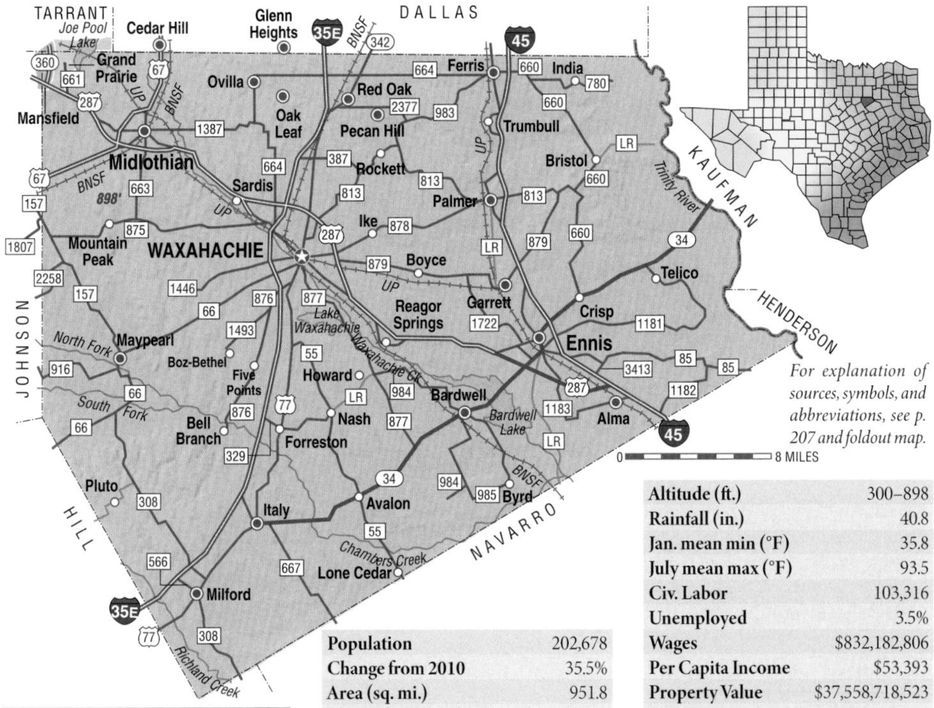

For explanation of sources, symbols, and abbreviations, see p. 207 and foldout map.

Ellis County

Population	202,678
Change from 2010	35.5%
Area (sq. mi.)	951.8
Land Area (sq. mi.)	935.5

Altitude (ft.)	300–898
Rainfall (in.)	40.8
Jan. mean min (°F)	35.8
July mean max (°F)	93.5
Civ. Labor	103,316
Unemployed	3.5%
Wages	$832,182,806
Per Capita Income	$53,393
Property Value	$37,558,718,523
Retail Sales	$2,927,069,674

Physical Features: Blackland soils; level to rolling; Chambers Creek, Trinity River; Bardwell Lake, Lake Waxahachie.

Economy: Cement, steel production, warehousing and distribution, government/services; many residents work in Dallas.

History: Tonkawa area. Part of Peters colony settled in 1843. County created 1849, organized 1850, from Navarro County. Named for Richard Ellis, president of convention that declared Texas' independence.

Recreation: Lakes, fishing, hunting; bluebonnet trails, historic homes, courthouse; Medieval-theme Scarborough Faire in spring.

Minerals: Cement, gas, sand, gravel.

Agriculture: Cattle, cotton, corn, hay, nurseries. Market value $73.1 million.

Vital Statistics, annual: Births, 11,097; deaths, 8,393; marriages, 910; divorces, 330.

Race/Ethnicity: Anglo, 55.3%; Hispanic, 27.0%; Black, 12.3%; Asian, 0.8%; Other, 4.5%.

WAXAHACHIE (43,368) county seat; manufacturing, steel, aluminum, tourism; hospital; colleges, museums; hike/bike trail; Crape Myrtle festival in July.

Ennis (21,210) manufacturing, distribution, agribusiness, tourism; Czech museum and library; hospital; bluebonnet trails, National Polka Festival in May.

Midlothian (37,053) cement plants, steel plant, distribution center, manufacturing; heritage park, cabin; spring fling in April.

Other towns include: **Alma** (392); **Avalon** (400); **Bardwell** (637); **Bristol** (504); **Ferris** (2,857); **Forreston** (400); **Garrett** (854); **Howard** (60); **Italy** (1,981); **Maypearl** (944); **Milford** (730); **Oak Leaf** (1,616); **Ovilla** (4,349); **Palmer** (2,461); **Pecan Hill** (740); and **Red Oak** (15,364) manufacturing, Founders Day in September.

Also, part of **Glenn Heights** [5,063] (mostly in Dallas County). Part of **Grand Prairie** and **Mansfield**.

"Starship Pegasus" was a futuristic restaurant and gift shop in Italy. Photo by Carol M. Highsmith, Public Domain

El Paso County

Physical Features: Westernmost county, in fertile Rio Grande Valley; 7,000-foot mountains; desert vegetation except where irrigated.

Economy: Government, military are major economic factors; wholesale and retail distribution center, education, tourism, maquiladora plants, varied manufacturing, oil refining, cotton, food processing.

History: Various Indian tribes inhabited the valley before Spanish civilization arrived in the late 1650s. Agriculture in area dates to at least 100 A.D. Spanish along with Tigua and Piro tribes fleeing Santa Fe uprising of 1680 sought refuge in the area. County created from the Bexar District in 1849; organized in 1850; named for historic pass (Paso del Norte), lowest all-weather pass through the southern Rocky Mountains.

Recreation: Gateway to Mexico; Chamizal Museum; major tourist center; El Paso Chihuahuas baseball; December Sun Carnival with football game; state parks, mountain tramway, missions and other historic sites.

Minerals: Production of cement, stone, sand and gravel.

Agriculture: Cattle, cotton, pecans (first in state), onions, forage, peppers, some goats and sheep. Third in colonies of bees. 25,000 acres irrigated, mostly cotton. Market value $46.7 million.

Vital Statistics, annual: Births, 2,381; deaths, 1,668; marriages, 6,128; divorces, 21.

Race/Ethnicity: Anglo, 11.3%; Hispanic, 82.6%; Black, 2.8%; Asian, 1.2%; Other, 2.0%.

EL PASO (678,415) county seat; Texas' sixth-largest city and metro area, largest U.S. city on Mexican border. A center for government operations. Federal installations include Fort Bliss, home of the U.S. Army 1st Armored Division, William Beaumont General Hospital, and La Tuna federal prison.

Manufactured products include clothing, electronics, auto equipment, plastics; trade and distribution; refining. Hospitals; museums; convention center; theater, symphony orchestra.

Other towns include: **Anthony** (3,665 in Texas, 8,748 in New Mexico); **Canutillo** (6,393); **Clint** (930); **Fabens** (5,460); **Homestead Meadows North** (6,521); **Homestead Meadows South** (7,981); **Horizon City** (23,162); **Prado Verde** (438); **San Elizario** (10,093), red & green chile war festival in September; **Socorro** (36,236) settled in 1680; **Sparks** (5,169); **Tornillo** (1,360); **Vinton** (2,769); **Westway** (3,726), and **Ysleta** (now within El Paso) settled in 1680, called the oldest town in Texas.

And, **Fort Bliss** (14,226).

Population	867,947
Change from 2010	8.4%
Area (sq. mi.)	1,015.0
Land Area (sq. mi.)	1,012.7
Altitude (ft.)	3,520–7,192

Rainfall (in.)	10.0
Jan. mean min (°F)	33.3
July mean max (°F)	92.5
Civ. Labor	370,586
Unemployed	4.3%

Wages	$3,919,840,863
Per Capita Income	$44,064
Property Value	$73,570,709,437
Retail Sales	$15,541,090,337

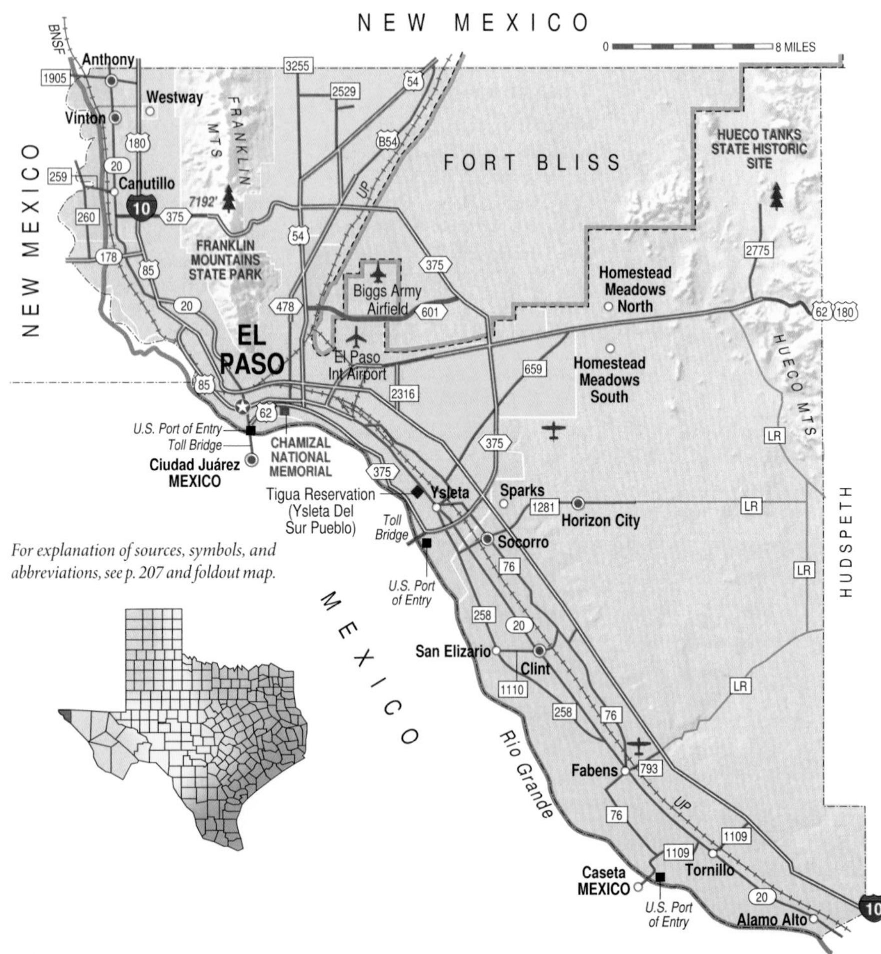

For explanation of sources, symbols, and abbreviations, see p. 207 and foldout map.

Erath County

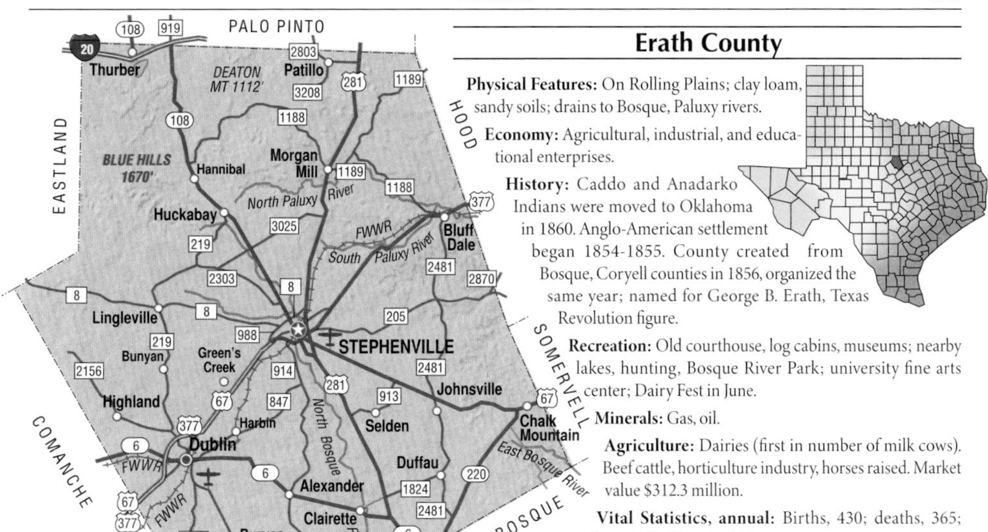

Physical Features: On Rolling Plains; clay loam, sandy soils; drains to Bosque, Paluxy rivers.

Economy: Agricultural, industrial, and educational enterprises.

History: Caddo and Anadarko Indians were moved to Oklahoma in 1860. Anglo-American settlement began 1854-1855. County created from Bosque, Coryell counties in 1856, organized the same year; named for George B. Erath, Texas Revolution figure.

Recreation: Old courthouse, log cabins, museums; nearby lakes, hunting, Bosque River Park; university fine arts center; Dairy Fest in June.

Minerals: Gas, oil.

Agriculture: Dairies (first in number of milk cows). Beef cattle, horticulture industry, horses raised. Market value $312.3 million.

Vital Statistics, annual: Births, 430; deaths, 365; marriages, 249; divorces, 136.

Race/Ethnicity: Anglo, 70.5%; Hispanic, 21.8%; Black, 2.8%; Asian, 0.8%; Other, 4.1%.

Population	43,378
Change from 2010	14.5%
Area (sq. mi.)	1,089.8
Land Area (sq. mi.)	1,083.1
Altitude (ft.)	820–1,670
Rainfall (in.)	34.1
Jan. mean min (°F)	32.9
July mean max (°F)	96.0
Civ. Labor	21,159
Unemployed	3.5%
Wages	$213,088,766
Per Capita Income	$46,906
Property Value	$9,512,992,790
Retail Sales	$731,471,675

STEPHENVILLE (21,199) county seat; Tarleton State University, varied manufacturing; hospital; Texas A&M research and extension center.

Dublin (3,433) dairies, food processing, varied manufacturing, tourism; library; old Dr Pepper plant; grist mill; St. Patrick's Day celebration.

Other towns include: **Bluff Dale** (82); **Lingleville** (269); **Morgan Mill** (206); **Thurber** (48) former coal-mining town; Gordon Center for Industrial History of Texas.

Falls County

Physical Features: On rolling prairie; bisected by Brazos; blackland, red, sandy loam soils; mineral springs.

Economy: Government/services, agribusiness, varied manufacturing, solar farms.

History: Wacos, Tawokanis, Anadarkos in conflict with Comanches. Cherokees alone in area 1830 until 1835 when Anglo-American settlement began. Antebellum slave-holding area. County created, organized, 1850 from Limestone, Milam counties; named for Brazos River falls.

Recreation: Fishing, hunting, camping; Highland Mansion and Falls on the Brazos.

Minerals: Gravel, sand, oil.

Agriculture: Stocker cattle, cow-calf operations, corn, grain sorghum, soybeans, cotton, wheat, oats and pecans, goats, sheep, horses. Some cotton irrigated. Market value $157.9 million.

Vital Statistics, annual: Births, 178; deaths, 199; marriages, 47; divorces, 7.

Race/Ethnicity: Anglo, 51.3%; Hispanic, 23.4%; Black, 21.9%; Asian, 0.3%; Other, 3.2%.

MARLIN (5,543) county seat; agriculture, prison; hospital; museum.

Other towns include: **Chilton** (988); **Golinda** (667); **Lott** (668); **Reagan** (300); **Rosebud** (1,345) feed, fertilizer processing, clothing manufactured; **Satin** (86).

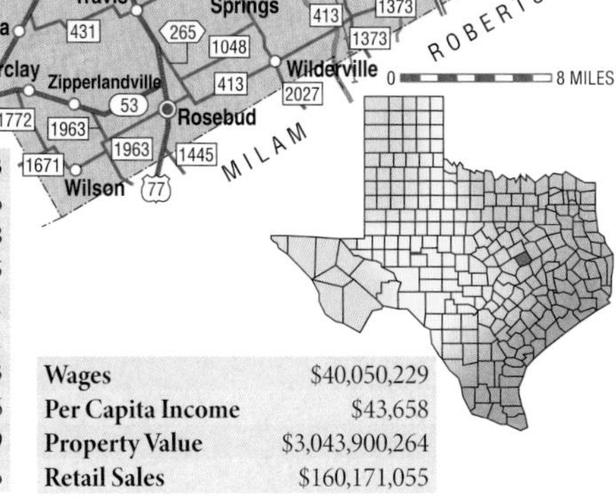

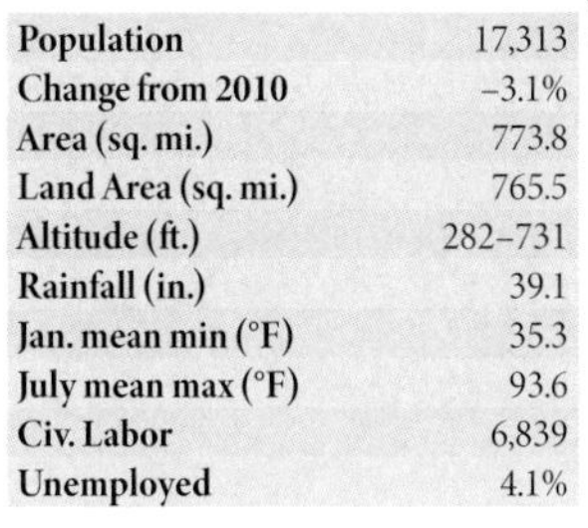

Population	17,313
Change from 2010	–3.1%
Area (sq. mi.)	773.8
Land Area (sq. mi.)	765.5
Altitude (ft.)	282–731
Rainfall (in.)	39.1
Jan. mean min (°F)	35.3
July mean max (°F)	93.6
Civ. Labor	6,839
Unemployed	4.1%
Wages	$40,050,229
Per Capita Income	$43,658
Property Value	$3,043,900,264
Retail Sales	$160,171,055

The Bonham State Park headquarters building was built by the Civilian Conservation Corps. Photo by Larry D. Moore, CC by SA 4.0

Fannin County

Population	36,569
Change from 2010	7.8%
Area (sq. mi.)	898.9
Land Area (sq. mi.)	890.8

Altitude (ft.)	450–800
Rainfall (in.)	45.5
Jan. mean min (°F)	34.5
July mean max (°F)	92.1
Civ. Labor	17,379

Unemployed	3.5%
Wages	$104,106,926
Per Capita Income	$46,449
Property Value	$8,743,441,916
Retail Sales	$426,530,855

Physical Features: North Texas county of rolling prairie, drained by Red River, Bois d'Arc Creek; Coffee Mill Lake, Lake Bonham, Valley Lake; mostly blackland soils; national grasslands.

Economy: Commuting to DFW metroplex, agribusiness.

History: Caddoes who later joined with Cherokees. Anglo-American settlement began in 1836. County created from Red River County in 1837 and organized in 1838; named for James W. Fannin, a victim of the Goliad massacre.

Recreation: Water activities on lakes; hunting; state park, fossil beds; winery; Sam Rayburn home, library; Bois D'Arc festival in May.

Minerals: Sand.

Agriculture: Beef cattle, wheat, corn. Market value $86.3 million. Hunting leases important.

Vital Statistics, annual: Births, 403; deaths, 493; marriages, 151; divorces, 83.

Race/Ethnicity: Anglo, 75.8%; Hispanic, 11.8%; Black, 6.2%; Asian, 0.4%; Other, 5.8%.

BONHAM (10,559) county seat; varied manufacturing, veterans hospital/private hospital, state jail; Sam Rayburn birthday celebration in January.

Other towns include: **Bailey** (231); **Dodd City** (380); **Ector** (497); **Gober** (146); **Honey Grove** (1,753) agribusiness center, varied manufacturing, tourism, historic buildings, library, Davy Crockett Festival in October; **Ivanhoe** (110).

Also: **Ladonia** (612) restored historical downtown, tourism, varied manufacturing, commuters, rodeo; **Leonard** (2,039) government/services, power plant, retail, light industry, museums, community picnic in July; **Randolph** (600); **Ravenna** (183); **Savoy** (732); **Telephone** (210); **Trenton** (773); Windom (196).

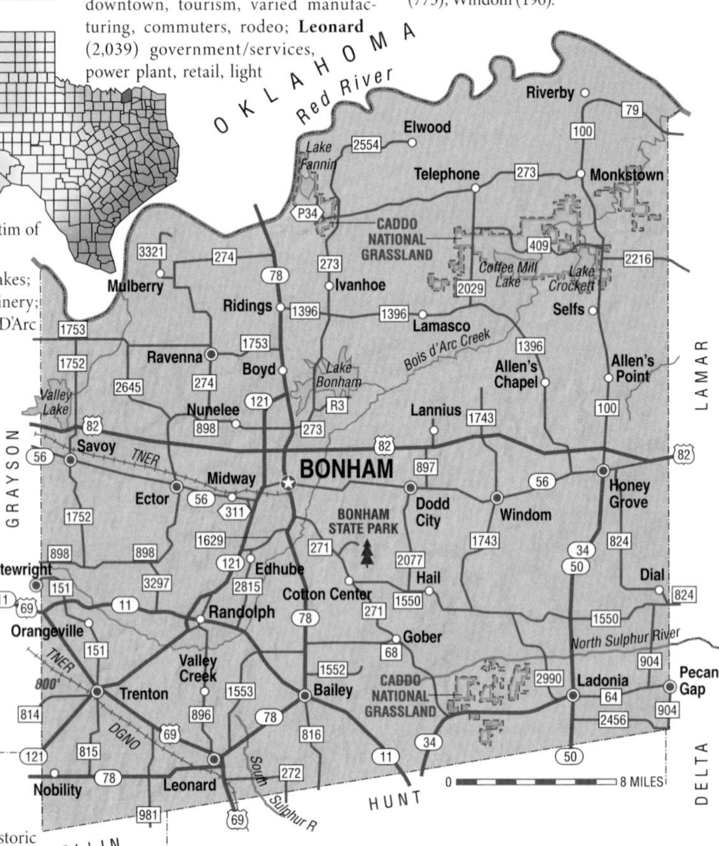

Fayette County

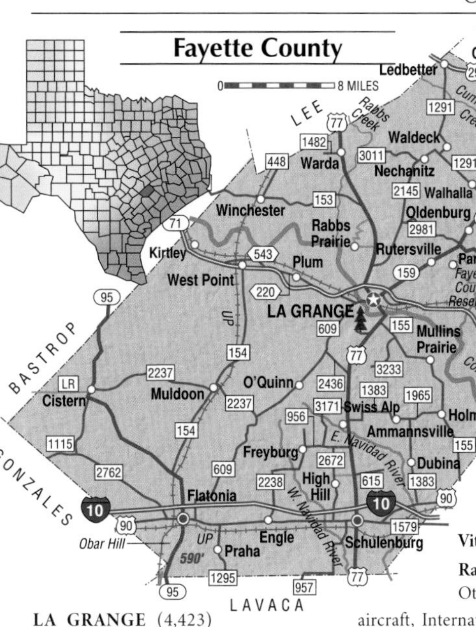

Physical Features: South central county bisected by Colorado River; Fayette County Reservoir; rolling to level; sandy loam, black waxy soils.

Economy: Agribusiness, production of electricity, mineral production, government/services, small manufacturing, tourism.

History: Lipan Apaches and Tonkawas. Austin's colonists arrived in 1822. Germans and Czechs began arriving in 1840s. County created from Bastrop, Colorado counties in 1837; organized in 1838; named for hero of American Revolution, Marquis de Lafayette.

Recreation: Monument Hill, Kreische brewery, Faison Home Museum, other historic sites including "Painted Churches"; hunting, fishing, lake; German and Czech ethnic foods; Prazska Pout in August, Octoberfests.

Minerals: Oil, gas, sand, gravel, bentonite clay.

Agriculture: Beef cattle, corn, hay, sorghum, pecans, dairies. Market value $47.4 million. Firewood sold.

Vital Statistics, annual: Births, 230; deaths, 378; marriages, 83; divorces, 62.

Race/Ethnicity: Anglo, 69.7%; Hispanic, 21.3%; Black, 5.7%; Asian, 0.3%; Other, 3.0%.

LA GRANGE (4,423) county seat; electricity generation, manufacturing, food processing, retail trade, tourism; hospital, library, quilt museum, polka museum, archives; Czech heritage center; Best Little Cowboy Gathering in March.

Schulenburg (2,669) varied manufacturing, food processing; Blinn College extension; aircraft, International Festival Institute, July-August; polka music museums; sausagefest in April.

Round Top (93) music center, tourism; old Lutheran church, heritage museum; antiques shows, April/October; Shakespeare festival in April, Schuetzenfest in September, and **Winedale** (67), historic restorations including Winedale Inn.

Other towns include: **Carmine** (244); **Ellinger** (286) Tomato Festival in May; **Fayetteville** (246) tourism, antiques, old precinct courthouse, Lickskillet festival in October; **Flatonia** (1,336) food production, manufacturing, rail history museum, parks, Czhilispiel in October; **Plum** (582); **Warda** (121); **Warrenton** (186) antique Cadillac museum..

Population	24,687
Change from 2010	0.5%
Area (sq. mi.)	959.8
Land Area (sq. mi.)	950.0
Altitude (ft.)	200–590
Rainfall (in.)	39.6
Jan. mean min (°F)	41.8
July mean max (°F)	95.4
Civ. Labor	11,952
Unemployed	3.5%
Wages	$123,919,611
Per Capita Income	$65,339
Property Value	$10,297,379,816
Retail Sales	$572,236,709

Fisher County

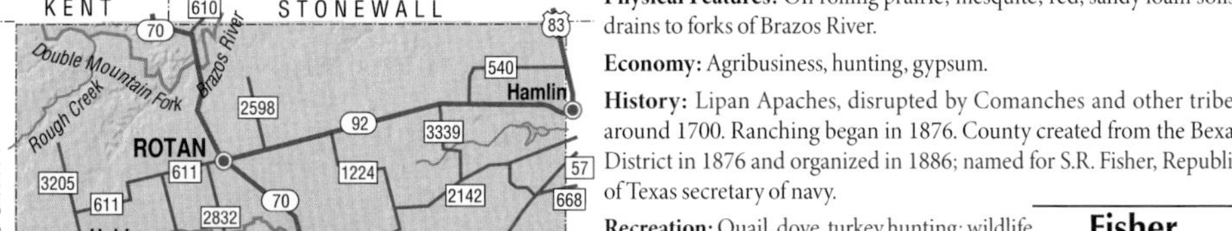

Physical Features: On rolling prairie; mesquite; red, sandy loam soils; drains to forks of Brazos River.

Economy: Agribusiness, hunting, gypsum.

History: Lipan Apaches, disrupted by Comanches and other tribes around 1700. Ranching began in 1876. County created from the Bexar District in 1876 and organized in 1886; named for S.R. Fisher, Republic of Texas secretary of navy.

Recreation: Quail, dove, turkey hunting; wildlife viewing; county fair, rodeo in August in Roby.

Minerals: Gypsum, oil.

Agriculture: Cattle, cotton, hay, wheat, sorghum, horses, sheep, goats. Irrigation for cotton and alfalfa. Market value $35.7 million.

Vital Statistics, annual: Births, 38; deaths, 70; marriages, 8; divorces, 6.

Race/Ethnicity: Anglo, 68.0%; Hispanic, 26.5%; Black, 2.5%; Asian, 0.4%; Other, 2.7%.

ROBY (594) county seat; agribusiness, cotton gin.

ROTAN (1,349) gypsum plant, oil mill, agribusiness. Other towns include: **McCaulley** (36) and **Sylvester** (40). .

Population	3,706
Change from 2010	–6.7%
Area (sq. mi.)	901.8
Land Area (sq. mi.)	898.9
Altitude (ft.)	1,720–2,405
Rainfall (in.)	23.5
Jan. mean min (°F)	35.4
July mean max (°F)	94.4
Civ. Labor	1,641
Unemployed	3.5%
Wages	$11,379,804
Per Capita Income	$57,245
Property Value	$1,666,268,605
Retail Sales	$15,704,168

Floyd County

Physical Features: Flat High Plains, broken by Caprock on east, by White River on south; many playas; red, black loam soils.

Economy: Cotton, wind farm, varied manufacturing, government/services.

History: Plains Apaches in area, and later Comanches. First white settlers arrived in 1884. County created from the Bexar District in 1876 and organized in 1890. Named for Dolphin Ward Floyd, who died at the Alamo.

Recreation: Hunting of pheasant, deer, quail; fishing; Blanco Canyon; Floydada Punkin Day in October; museum.

Minerals: Not significant.

Agriculture: Cotton, wheat, sorghum, corn; pumpkins. Some 260,000 acres irrigated. Market value $196.0 million.

Vital Statistics, annual: Births, 68; deaths, 109; marriages, 26; divorces, 11.

Race/Ethnicity: Anglo, 38.5%; Hispanic, 56.8%; Black, 2.3%; Asian, 0.2%; Other, 2.2%.

FLOYDADA (2,562) county seat; trucking, agriculture, retail, medical clinic, museum.

Lockney (1,637) agriculture center; manufacturing; hospital.

Other towns include: **Aiken** (52), **Dougherty** (91), and **South Plains** (67).

Population	5,350
Change from 2010	–17.0%
Area (sq. mi.)	992.5
Land Area (sq. mi.)	992.1
Altitude (ft.)	2,440–3,345
Rainfall (in.)	20.2
Jan. mean min (°F)	26.8
July mean max (°F)	91.0
Civ. Labor	2,457
Unemployed	4.1%
Wages	$18,727,475
Per Capita Income	$53,292
Property Value	$1,321,949,362
Retail Sales	$47,158,224

Foard County

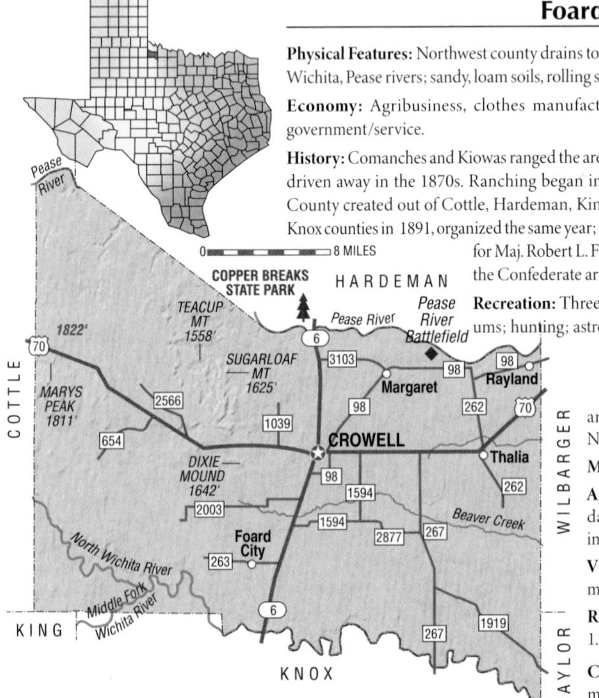

Physical Features: Northwest county drains to North Wichita, Pease rivers; sandy, loam soils, rolling surface.

Economy: Agribusiness, clothes manufacturing, government/service.

History: Comanches and Kiowas ranged the area until driven away in the 1870s. Ranching began in 1880. County created out of Cottle, Hardeman, King, and Knox counties in 1891, organized the same year; named for Maj. Robert L. Foard of the Confederate army.

Recreation: Three museums; hunting; astronomy and ecotourism foundation; wild hog cook-off in November.

Minerals: Natural gas, some oil.

Agriculture: Wheat, cattle, alfalfa, cotton, sorghum, dairies. Market value $14.9 million. Hunting leases important.

Vital Statistics, annual: Births, 12; deaths, 31; marriages, 6; divorces, 4.

Race/Ethnicity: Anglo, 77.2%; Hispanic, 18%; Black, 1.7%; Asian, 0.3%; Other, 2.8%.

CROWELL (749) county seat; retail center, clothing manufacturing; library, Fire Hall museum.

Population	1,080
Change from 2010	–19.2%
Area (sq. mi.)	707.7
Land Area (sq. mi.)	704.4
Altitude (ft.)	1,210–1,822
Rainfall (in.)	25.4
Jan. mean min (°F)	31.0
July mean max (°F)	95.6
Civ. Labor	562
Unemployed	3.2%
Wages	$3,766,591
Per Capita Income	$61,279
Property Value	$969,400,252
Retail Sales	$8,684,757

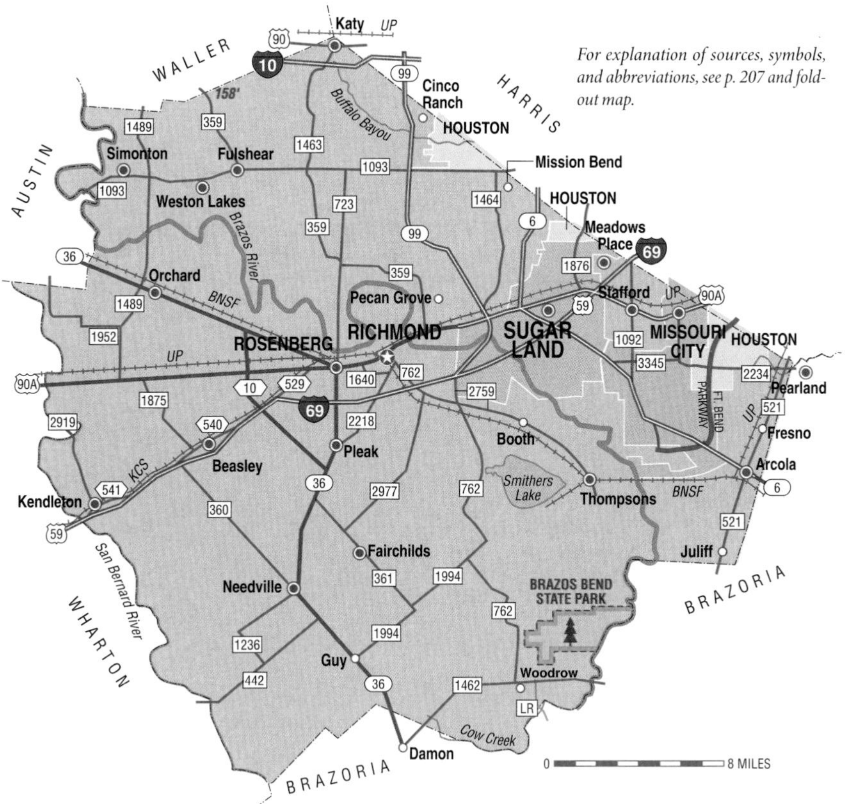

For explanation of sources, symbols, and abbreviations, see p. 207 and fold-out map.

Fort Bend County

Physical Features: On Gulf Coastal Plain; drained by Brazos, San Bernard rivers; Smithers Lake; level to rolling; rich alluvial soils.

Economy: Agribusiness, petrochemicals, technology, government/services; many residents work in Houston.

History: Karankawa groups in area, who retreated to Mexico by the 1850s. Named for river bend where some of Austin's colonists settled in 1824 and built a blockhouse for protection against the Indians. Antebellum plantations made it one of six Texas counties with Black majority in 1850. County created in 1837 from Austin County and organized in 1838.

Recreation: Many historic sites, museums, memorials, parks; George Ranch historical park; Brazos Bend State Park with George Observatory; fishing, waterfowl hunting.

Minerals: Oil, gas, sulfur, salt, clays, sand and gravel.

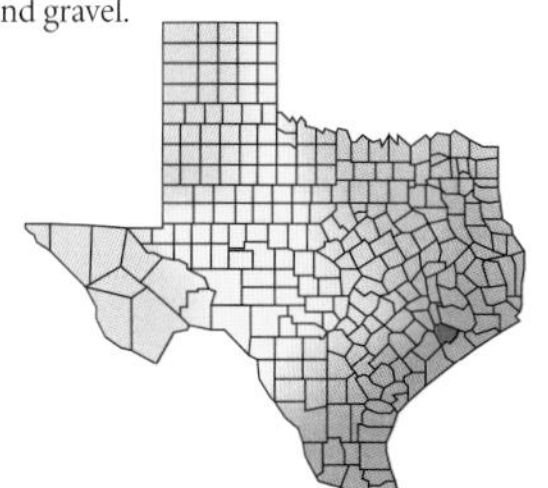

Agriculture: Nursery crops, cotton, sorghum, corn, hay, cattle, horses; irrigation for rice. Market value $85.0 million.

Vital Statistics, annual: Births, 8,816; deaths, 4,545; marriages, 2,880; divorces, 1,883.

Race/Ethnicity: Anglo, 29.6%; Hispanic, 24.1%; Black, 20.4%; Asian, 22.1%; Other, 3.8%.

Population	858,527
Change from 2010	46.7%
Area (sq. mi.)	885.3
Land Area (sq. mi.)	861.5
Altitude (ft.)	46–158
Rainfall (in.)	51.1
Jan. mean min (°F)	45.3

July mean max (°F)	93.4
Civ. Labor	418,649
Unemployed	3.9%
Wages	$3,550,849,054
Per Capita Income	$65,797
Property Value	$139,254,692,176
Retail Sales	$12,188,322,369

RICHMOND (12,233) county seat; foundry; University of Houston branch, Wharton County Junior College branch; Richmond state supported-living center, hospital.

SUGAR LAND (109,373) government/services, prisons, commuting to Houston; hospitals; University of Houston branch; Museum of Southern History. New Territory and Greatwood are now part of Sugar Land.

MISSOURI CITY (74,850, part [5,744] in Harris County) hospital.

ROSENBERG (39,468) varied industry, railroad museum.

Other towns include: **Arcola** (2,156); **Beasley** (599); **Cinco Ranch** (18,399); **Fairchilds** (921); **Fresno** (23,921); **Fulshear** (25,169); **Guy** (239); **Kendleton** (342); **Meadows Place** (4,671); **Mission Bend** (38,772).

Also: **Needville** (3,062) agriculture, commuting, historic Schendel house, historic cemetery, Czech soup supper in January; **Orchard** (315); **Pecan Grove** (19,944); **Pleak** (1,031); **Simonton** (642); **Stafford** (17,364, partly in Harris County); **Thompsons** (163); **Weston Lakes** (4,061).

Also, part [42,352] of **Houston**, part of **Katy** [6,130], hospital, and part of Pearland [5,892].

Franklin County

Physical Features: Small Northeast county with many wooded hills; drained by numerous streams; alluvial to sandy clay soils; Lake Bob Sandlin, Lake Cypress Springs.

Economy: Agribusiness, government/services, retirement area, distribution.

History: Caddoes abandoned the area in the 1790s because of disease and other tribes. First white settlers arrived around 1818. County created in 1875 from Titus County, organized the same year; named for jurist B.C. Franklin.

Recreation: Fishing, water sports; historic homes; wild hog hunting, horse stables; stew cook-off in October.

Minerals: Lignite coal, oil and gas.

Agriculture: Beef cattle, milk production, poultry, hay. Market value $134.1 million. Timber marketed.

Vital Statistics, annual: Births, 122; deaths, 159; marriages, 27; divorces, 33.

Race/Ethnicity: Anglo, 76%; Hispanic, 14%; Black, 3.8%; Asian, 0.7%; Other, 5.5%.

MOUNT VERNON (2,477) county seat; distribution center, manufacturing, tourism, antiques; hospital; nature preserves, museum with Don Meredith exhibit; wine festivals in May and October.

Other towns include: **Scroggins** (150), and part of **Winnsboro** [790, mostly in Wood County], commercial center, Autumn Trails.

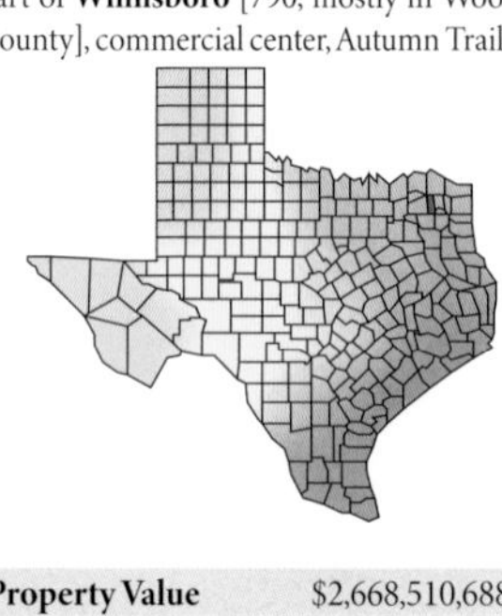

Population	10,464
Change from 2010	–1.3%
Area (sq. mi.)	294.8
Land Area (sq. mi.)	284.4
Altitude (ft.)	300–600
Rainfall (in.)	48.2
Jan. mean min (°F)	36.0
July mean max (°F)	93.0
Civ. Labor	5,361
Unemployed	3.2%
Wages	$43,838,691
Per Capita Income	$51,926
Property Value	$2,668,510,688
Retail Sales	$139,166,647

Freestone County

Physical Features: East central county bounded by the Trinity River; Richland-Chambers Reservoir, Fairfield Lake; rolling Blackland, sandy, loam soils.

Economy: Natural gas, agriculture.

History: Caddo and Tawakoni area. David G. Burnet received land grant in 1825. Seven Mexican citizens received grants in 1833. In 1860, more than half the population was Black. County created in 1850 from Limestone County; organized in 1851. Named for the indigenous stone.

Recreation: Fishing, hunting; lakes; historic sites; state park; Teague amateur rodeo in July.

Minerals: Natural gas, oil.

Agriculture: Beef cattle, peaches (second in acreage), hay, blueberries, horticulture. Market value $68.1 million. Hunting leases.

Vital Statistics, annual: Births, 166; deaths, 281; marriages, 90; divorces, 31.

Race/Ethnicity: Anglo, 65.9%; Hispanic, 16.2%; Black, 14.1%; Asian, 0.3%; Other, 3.4%.

FAIRFIELD (2,896) county seat; government/services, trade center; hospital, museum; wild game supper in July.

TEAGUE (3,447) railroad terminal, oil and gas, government/services, agriculture; library, museum; Parkfest in October.

Other towns include: **Donie** (250), **Streetman** (255), **Wortham** (1,002) agribusiness, blues festivals in September, Blind Lemon Jefferson gravesite.

Population	19,774
Change from 2010	–0.2%
Area (sq. mi.)	892.0
Land Area (sq. mi.)	877.7
Altitude (ft.)	200–608
Rainfall (in.)	43.5
Jan. mean min (°F)	37.9
July mean max (°F)	92.5
Civ. Labor	6,329
Unemployed	5.3%
Wages	$58,271,526
Per Capita Income	$44,014
Property Value	$5,412,075,324
Retail Sales	$228,858,551

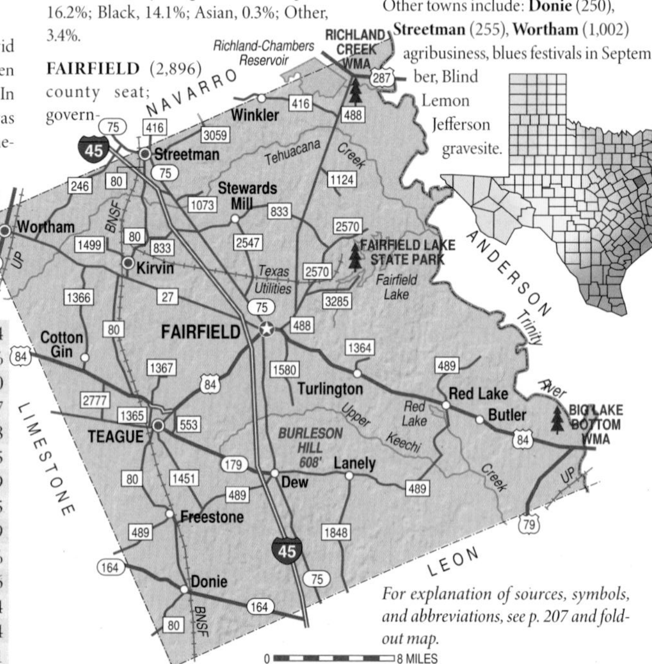

For explanation of sources, symbols, and abbreviations, see p. 207 and fold-out map.

Frio County

Population	18,436
Change from 2010	7.1%
Area (sq. mi.)	1,134.4
Land Area (sq. mi.)	1,133.5
Altitude (ft.)	400–763
Rainfall (in.)	25.0
Jan. mean min (°F)	43.4
July mean max (°F)	96.7
Civ. Labor	9,418
Unemployed	3.4%

Physical Features: South Texas county of rolling terrain with much brush; bisected by Frio River; sandy, red sandy loam soils.

Economy: Agribusiness, oil-field services, hunting leases.

Wages	$102,364,775
Per Capita Income	$39,898
Property Value	$4,212,099,133
Retail Sales	$197,410,064

History: Coahuiltecans; many taken into San Antonio missions. Comanches kept settlers out until after Civil War. Mexican citizens recruited for labor after 1900. County created in 1858 from Atascosa, Bexar, Uvalde counties, organized in 1871; named for the Frio (cold) River.

Recreation: Hunting, Big Foot Wallace Museum, Winter Garden area, splash pad/skate parks.

Minerals: Oil, natural gas, stone.

Agriculture: Peanuts, potatoes, sorghum, cotton, corn, spinach, cucumbers, watermelons, bees (second in number of colonies). Second in vegetables harvested. Market value $124.4 million. Hunting leases.

Vital Statistics, annual: Births, 225; deaths, 190; marriages, 69; divorces, 26.

Race/Ethnicity: Anglo, 16.6%; Hispanic, 77.1%; Black, 3.8%; Asian, 1.1%; Other, 1.4%.

PEARSALL (7,637) county seat; agriculture center, oil and gas, food processing, shipping, government/services; old jail museum; hospital, junior college extension; Cinco de Mayo celebration.

Dilley (3,310) shipping center for melons and peanuts; hospital.

Other towns include: **Bigfoot** (1,390), **Hilltop** (209); **Moore** (122), and **North Pearsall** (1,022).

Gaines County

Physical Features: On South Plains, drains to draws; playas; underground water.

Economy: Oil, gas, cotton, peanuts.

History: Comanche country until the U.S. Army campaigns of 1875. Ranchers arrived in the 1880s; farming began around 1900. County created from Bexar District in 1876; organized in 1905; named for James Gaines, signer of the Texas Declaration of Independence.

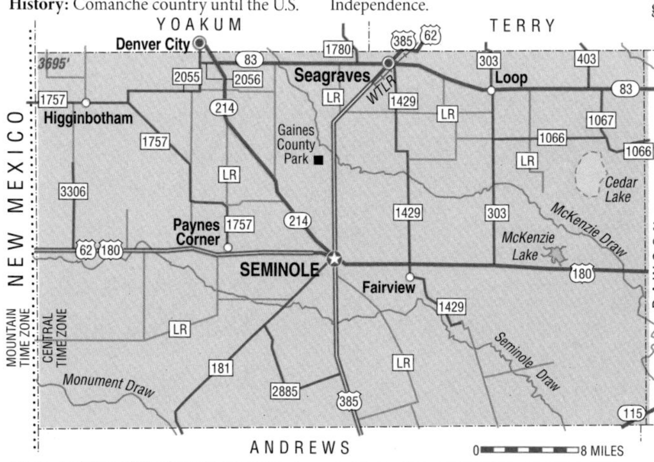

Recreation: Cedar Lake one of largest alkali lakes on Texas plains.

Minerals: Oil, gas.

Agriculture: Cotton (first in bales produced), peanuts (first in acreage), small grains, pecans, paprika, rosemary; cattle, sheep, hogs; substantial irrigation. Market value $188.8 million.

Vital Statistics, annual: Births, 470; deaths, 167; marriages, 165; divorces, 32.

Race/Ethnicity: Anglo, 58.1%; Hispanic, 38.9%; Black, 1.1%; Asian, 0.3%; Other, 1.5%.

SEMINOLE (7,026) county seat; manufacturing, oil and gas, agriculture; hospital, library, museum; Ag & Oil Day celebration in September.

Seagraves (2,185) market for three-county area; cotton, peanut farming; library, museum; Celebrate Seagraves in July.

Other towns include: **Loop** (190). Also, part of **Denver City** (mostly in Yoakum County)..

Population	21,895
Change from 2010	24.9%
Area (sq. mi.)	1,502.9
Land Area (sq. mi.)	1,502.4
Altitude (ft.)	2,935–3,695

Rainfall (in.)	17.2
Jan. mean min (°F)	29.1
July mean max (°F)	93.4
Civ. Labor	10,148
Unemployed	3.0%

Wages	$106,354,343
Per Capita Income	$50,616
Property Value	$5,707,956,648
Retail Sales	$368,809,137

Galveston County

Physical Features: Partly island, partly coastal; flat, artificial drainage; sandy, loam, clay soils; broken by bays.

Economy: Port activities dominate economy; insurance and finance center, petrochemical plants, varied manufacturing, tourism, medical education, oceanographic research, ship building, commercial fishing.

History: Karankawa and other tribes roamed the area until 1850. French, Spanish, and American settlement began in 1815 and reached 1,000 by 1817. County created from Brazoria County in 1838; organized in 1839; named for the Spanish governor of Louisiana Count Bernardo de Gálvez.

Recreation: One of Texas' most historic cities; popular tourist and convention center; fishing, surfing, boating, sailing and other water sports; state park; historic homes tour in spring, Moody Gardens. Also, Mardi Gras celebration; Rosenberg Library; museums; restored sailing ship, "Elissa," railroad museum; Dickens on the Strand in early December.

Minerals: Oil, gas, clays, sand and gravel.

Agriculture: Cattle, aquaculture, nursery crops, rice, hay, horses, soybeans, grain sorghum. Market value $9.2 million.

Vital Statistics, annual: Births, 3,888; deaths, 3,338; marriages, 1,128; divorces, 1,180.

Race/Ethnicity: Anglo, 54.6%; Hispanic, 25.3%; Black, 12.3%; Asian, 3.5%; Other, 4.4%.

GALVESTON (53,219) county seat; tourist center, shipyard, other industries, insurance, port container facility; University of Texas Medical Branch; National Maritime Research Center; Texas A&M University at Galveston; Galveston College; hospitals.

LEAGUE CITY (115,595, part [2,522] in Harris County) residential community, commuters to Houston, hospital.

TEXAS CITY (54,247) refining, petrochemical plants, port, rail shipping; College of the Mainland; hospital, library; dike; Cinco de Mayo, Shrimp Boil in August.

Bolivar Peninsula (2,829) includes: **Port Bolivar** lighthouse, free ferry; **Crystal Beach** seafood industry, sport fishing, tourism, Fort Travis Seashore Park, shorebird sanctuary, Crab Festival in May; **Gilchrist**, and **High Island**.

Other towns include: **Bacliff** (10,567); **Bayou Vista** (1,755); **Clear Lake Shores** (1,263).

Also: **Dickinson** (21,697) manufacturing, commuters, strawberry festival in May; **Friendswood** (41,004, part [10,558] in Harris County); **Hitchcock** (7,408) residential community, tourism, fishing and shrimping, Good Ole Days in August, WWII blimp base, museum.

Also: **Jamaica Beach** (1,072); **Kemah** (1,803) tourism, boating, commuters, museum, Blessing of Fleet in August; **La Marque** (18,697) refining, greyhound racing, farming, hospital, library, Gulf Coast Grill-off in October; **San Leon** (5,144); **Santa Fe** (12,783); **Tiki Island** (1,103).

Population	355,062
Change from 2010	21.9%
Area (sq. mi.)	873.8
Land Area (sq. mi.)	378.4
Altitude (ft.)	sea level–40
Rainfall (in.)	47.2
Jan. mean min (°F)	50.9
July mean max (°F)	90.9
Civ. Labor	169,058
Unemployed	4.4%
Wages	$1,784,675,715
Per Capita Income	$60,071
Property Value	$62,092,272,921
Retail Sales	$5,625,606,722

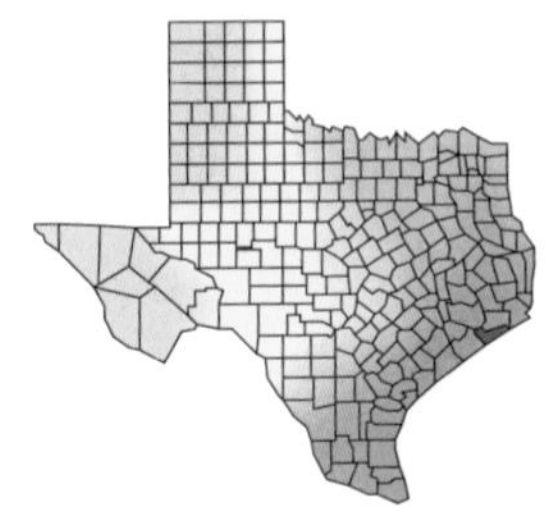

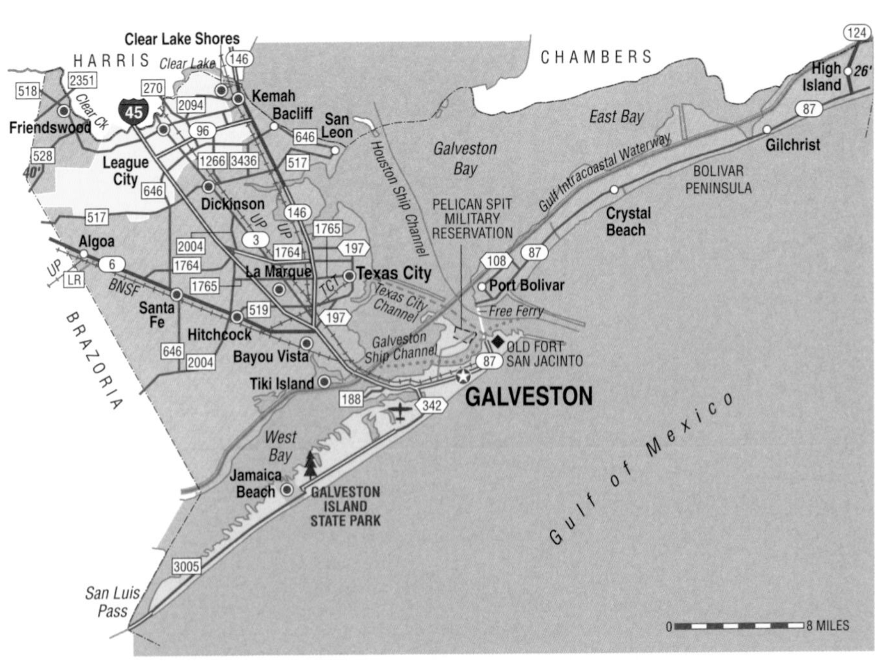

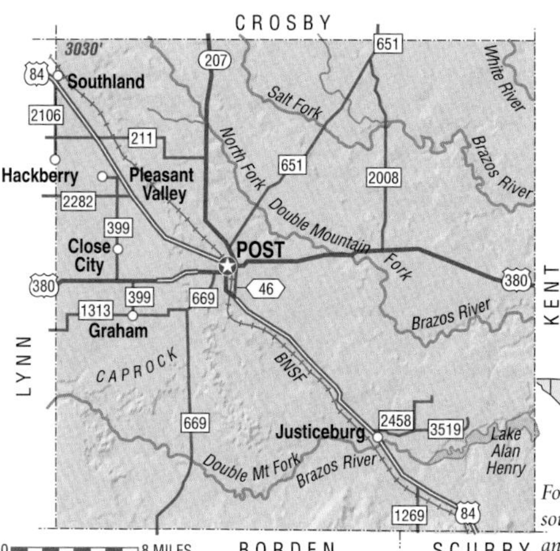

Garza County

Physical Features: On edge of Caprock; rough, broken land, with playas, gullies, canyons, Brazos River forks, Lake Alan Henry; sandy, loam, clay soils.

Economy: Agriculture, oil and gas, trade, government/services, hunting leases.

History: Kiowas and Comanches yielded to U.S. Army in 1875. Ranching began in the 1870s, farming in the 1890s. C.W. Post, the cereal millionaire, established enterprises here in 1906. County created from Bexar District 1876; organized 1907; named for a pioneer Bexar County family.

Recreation: Scenic areas, lake activities, Post-Garza Museum, McCrary Museum, downtown farmers market.

Minerals: Oil, gas, sand, gravel.

Agriculture: Cotton, beef cattle, hay. Some 8,000 acres irrigated. Market value $22.1 million. Hunting leases.

For explanation of sources, symbols, and abbreviations, see p. 207 and foldout map.

Population	5,863
Change from 2010	–9.3%
Area (sq. mi.)	896.2
Land Area (sq. mi.)	893.4
Altitude (ft.)	2,140–3,030
Rainfall (in.)	20.2
Jan. mean min (°F)	31.6
July mean max (°F)	93.6
Civ. Labor	1,964
Unemployed	4.1%
Wages	$20,695,334
Per Capita Income	$36,426
Property Value	$1,162,031,102
Retail Sales	$32,513,212

Vital Statistics, annual: Births, 48; deaths, 67; marriages, 28; divorces, 11.

Race/Ethnicity: Anglo, 37.2%; Hispanic, 56.3%; Black, 4%; Asian, 0.4%; Other, 2.2%.

POST (4,791) county seat; founded by C.W. Post; agriculture, tourism, government/services, prisons; museums, theater.

Gillespie County

Population	27,297
Change from 2010	9.9%
Area (sq. mi.)	1,061.7
Land Area (sq. mi.)	1,058.2
Altitude (ft.)	1,040–2,244
Rainfall (in.)	30.6
Jan. mean min (°F)	36.2
July mean max (°F)	92.6
Civ. Labor	14,654
Unemployed	2.6%
Wages	$151,867,900
Per Capita Income	$78,039
Property Value	$14,243,367,633
Retail Sales	$700,928,036

Physical Features: Picturesque Edwards Plateau area with hills, broken by spring-fed streams.

Economy: Tourism, government/services, agriculture, wine and specialty foods, hunting leases.

History: German settlement founded in 1846 in heart of Comanche country. County created in 1848 from Bexar and Travis counties, organized the same year; named for Texas Ranger Capt. R.A. Gillespie. The birthplace of President Lyndon B. Johnson and Fleet Admiral Chester W. Nimitz.

Recreation: Among leading deer-hunting areas; numerous historic sites and tourist attractions include LBJ Ranch, Nimitz Hotel and Pacific war museum; Pioneer Museum Complex, Enchanted Rock, wineries, produce stands.

Minerals: Sand, gravel.

Agriculture: Beef cattle, wine, hay, peaches (first in acreage). Market value $31.2 million. Hunting leases important.

Vital Statistics, annual: Births, 263; deaths, 389; marriages, 157; divorces, 73.

Race/Ethnicity: Anglo, 74.4%; Hispanic, 21.6%; Black, 0.3%; Asian, 0.5%; Other, 3.2%.

FREDERICKSBURG (11,072) county seat; agribusiness, tourism, wineries, food processing; museum; tourist attractions; hospital; Easter Fires, Oktoberfest.

Other towns include: **Doss** (100); **Harper** (1,203) ranching, deer hunting, Dachshund Hounds Downs race and Trades Day in October; **Luckenbach** (25) saloon, general store and dance hall

Stonewall (512) agribusiness, wineries, tourism, hunting, Peach Jamboree in June, and **Willow City** (22) scenic drive.

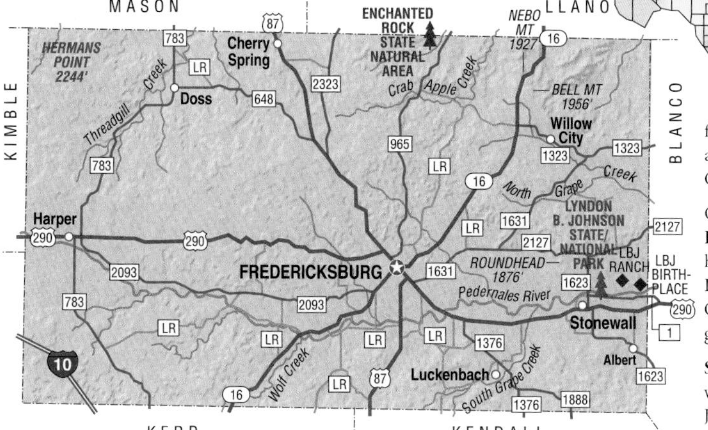

Glasscock County

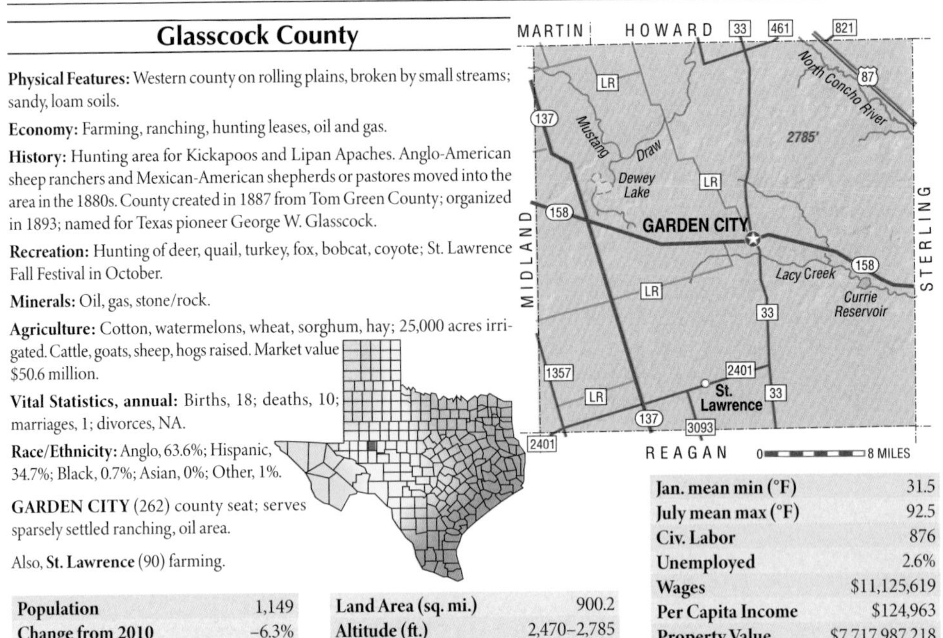

Physical Features: Western county on rolling plains, broken by small streams; sandy, loam soils.

Economy: Farming, ranching, hunting leases, oil and gas.

History: Hunting area for Kickapoos and Lipan Apaches. Anglo-American sheep ranchers and Mexican-American shepherds or pastores moved into the area in the 1880s. County created in 1887 from Tom Green County; organized in 1893; named for Texas pioneer George W. Glasscock.

Recreation: Hunting of deer, quail, turkey, fox, bobcat, coyote; St. Lawrence Fall Festival in October.

Minerals: Oil, gas, stone/rock.

Agriculture: Cotton, watermelons, wheat, sorghum, hay; 25,000 acres irrigated. Cattle, goats, sheep, hogs raised. Market value $50.6 million.

Vital Statistics, annual: Births, 18; deaths, 10; marriages, 1; divorces, NA.

Race/Ethnicity: Anglo, 63.6%; Hispanic, 34.7%; Black, 0.7%; Asian, 0%; Other, 1%.

GARDEN CITY (262) county seat; serves sparsely settled ranching, oil area.

Also, **St. Lawrence** (90) farming.

Population	1,149
Change from 2010	–6.3%
Area (sq. mi.)	901.1
Land Area (sq. mi.)	900.2
Altitude (ft.)	2,470–2,785
Rainfall (in.)	20.4
Jan. mean min (°F)	31.5
July mean max (°F)	92.5
Civ. Labor	876
Unemployed	2.6%
Wages	$11,125,619
Per Capita Income	$124,963
Property Value	$7,717,987,218
Retail Sales	$28,947,409

Goliad County

Physical Features: Coastal Plain county; rolling, brushy; bisected by San Antonio River; Coleto Creek Reservoir; sandy, loam, alluvial soils.

Economy: Government/services, oil/gas, agriculture, electricity-generating plant, tourism.

History: Karankawas, Comanches, other tribes in area in historic period. La Bahía presidio/mission established, 1749. County created, 1836, from Spanish municipality; organized, 1837; name is anagram of (H)idalgo. Birthplace of Gen. Ignacio Zaragoza, hero of Battle of Puebla.

Recreation: Missions, restored Presidio La Bahía, Fannin Battleground; Old Market House museum; lake, fishing, hunting (deer, quail, dove, hogs), camping, canoeing, birding.

Minerals: Production of oil, gas.

Agriculture: Beef cattle, stocker operations and fed cattle are top revenue producers; corn, grain sorghum, cotton, hay; minor irrigation for pasture. Market value $17.7 million. Hunting leases.

Vital Statistics, annual: Births, 52; deaths, 75; marriages, 19; divorces, 5.

Race/Ethnicity: Anglo, 60.6%; Hispanic, 32.6%; Black, 3.4%; Asian, 0.3%; Other, 3.1%.

GOLIAD (1,624) county seat; one of state's oldest towns; power plant; tourism; library; Zaragoza Birthplace State Historic Site, statue; Goliad Massacre re-enactment in March, Diez y Seis celebration in September.

Other towns include: **Berclair** (253), **Fannin** (359), and **Weesatche** (411).

Population	7,163
Change from 2010	–0.7%
Area (sq. mi.)	859.4
Land Area (sq. mi.)	852.0
Altitude (ft.)	50–420
Rainfall (in.)	37.2
Jan. mean min (°F)	45.0
July mean max (°F)	94.1
Civ. Labor	3,198
Unemployed	4.4 %
Wages	$16,383,861
Per Capita Income	$55,947
Property Value	$3,324,536,725
Retail Sales	$46,243,319

For explanation of sources, symbols, and abbreviations, see p. 207 and foldout map.

This Boy Scout building in Garden City was built in 1938. Photo by Larry D. Moore, CC by SA 4.0

Gonzales County

Physical Features: South central county; rolling, rich bottom soils along Guadalupe River and its tributaries; Lake Gonzales; some sandy areas; many oaks, pecans.

Economy: Agribusiness, hunting leases.

History: Coahuiltecan tribal area. Among the first Anglo-American settlements was the DeWitt colony in the late 1820s. County created in 1836; organized in 1837; named for Coahuila y Texas Gov. Rafael Gonzales.

Recreation: Historic sites, homes, Pioneer Village Living History Center, Palmetto State Park, museums, Independence Park.

Minerals: Gas, oil, clay, gravel.

Agriculture: Second in poultry and egg production, cattle; hay, corn, sorghum, pecans, mushrooms. Market value $560.8 million.

Vital Statistics, annual: Births, 290; deaths, 258; marriages, 75; divorces, 58.

Population	19,641
Change from 2010	–0.8%
Area (sq. mi.)	1,069.9
Land Area (sq. mi.)	1,066.7
Altitude (ft.)	200–562
Rainfall (in.)	35.9
Jan. mean min (°F)	41.8
July mean max (°F)	93.9
Civ. Labor	9,527
Unemployed	3.2%
Wages	$98,686,364

Race/Ethnicity: Anglo, 41.5%; Hispanic, 50.4%; Black, 5.5%; Asian, 0.3%; Other, 2.3%.

GONZALES (7,576) county seat; first shot in Texas Revolution fired here; cattle ranching, chicken farming; hospital, college extensions; pioneer village; "Come and Take It" festival in October.

Other towns include: **Belmont** (55); **Cost** (84) First Shot monument; **Harwood** (36); **Leesville** (152); **Nixon** (2,355) poultry-processing plant, Feather Fest in September; **Ottine** (80); **Smiley** (480); **Waelder** (941) Guacamole Fest in September.

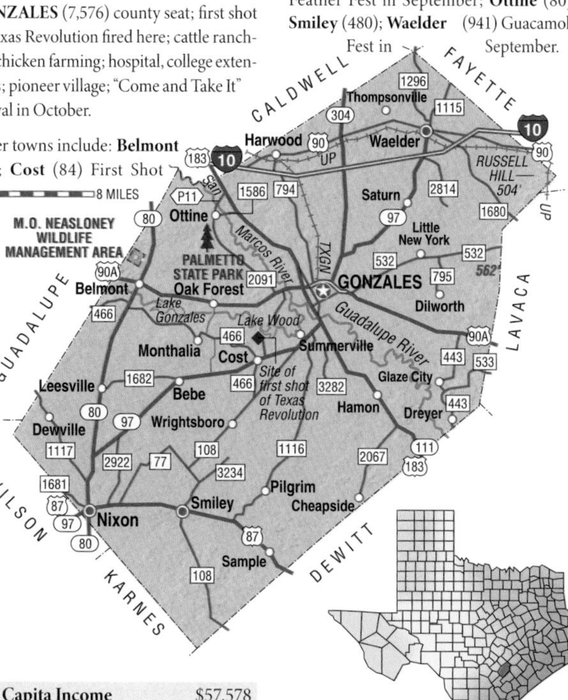

Per Capita Income	$57,578
Property Value	$8,398,890,368
Retail Sales	$320,160,135

Gray County

Population	21,030
Change from 2010	–6.7%
Area (sq. mi.)	929.3
Land Area (sq. mi.)	926.0
Altitude (ft.)	2,450–3,320
Rainfall (in.)	22.8

Jan. mean min (°F)	24.5
July mean max (°F)	90.8
Civ. Labor	7,686
Unemployed	4.5%
Wages	$109,626,451
Per Capita Income	$49,815
Property Value	$2,435,735,786
Retail Sales	$453,588,387

Physical Features: High Plains, broken by Red River forks, tributaries; sandy loam, waxy soils.

Economy: Petroleum, agriculture, government/services.

History: Apaches, displaced by Comanches and Kiowas. Ranching began in the late 1870s. Farmers arrived around 1900. Oil discovered in 1926. County created in 1876 from Bexar District; organized in 1902; named for Peter W. Gray, member of first Legislature.

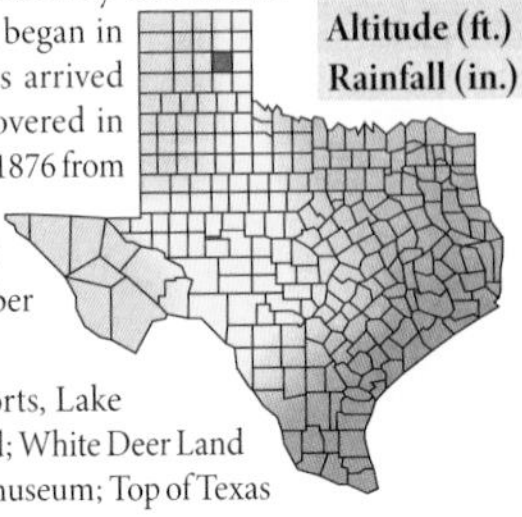

Recreation: Water sports, Lake McClellan and grassland; White Deer Land Museum, barbed-wire museum; Top of Texas livestock show in January.

Minerals: Natural gas, oil.

Agriculture: Cattle, hogs, wheat, cotton, corn, sorghum, hay, milk. Market value $154.6 million.

Vital Statistics, annual: Births, 268; deaths, 294; marriages, 111; divorces, 97.

Race/Ethnicity: Anglo, 61.4%; Hispanic, 29.9%; Black, 3.9%; Asian, 0.6%; Other, 4.2%.

PAMPA (16,474) county seat; petroleum, agriculture; hospital; college; prison; Woody Guthrie museum; Burning the Bricks car show in June.

Other towns include: **Alanreed** (50); **Lefors** (412); **McLean** (654) commercial center for southern part of county.

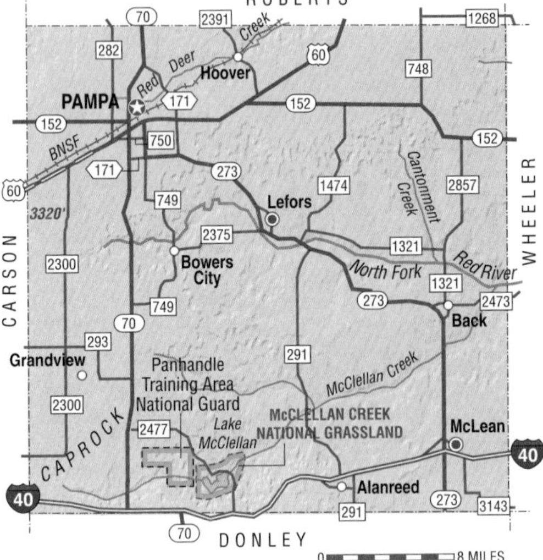

A row of shops in Van Alstyne, Grayson County. Photo by Renelibrary, CC by SA 3.0

Grayson County

Physical Features: North Texas county; level, some low hills; sandy loam, blackland soils; drains to Red River and tributaries of Trinity River; Lake Texoma, Ray Roberts Lake, Valley Lake, Randell Lake.

Economy: A manufacturing, distribution and trade center for northern Texas and southern Oklahoma; nature tourism, mineral production.

History: Caddo and Tonkawa area. Preston Bend trading post established 1836-1837. Peters colony settlers arrived in the 1840s. County created in 1846 from Fannin County, organized the same year; named for Republic Attorney General Peter W. Grayson.

Recreation: Lakes, fishing, hunting, water sports, state park, cultural activities, Hagerman National Wildlife Refuge, Pioneer Village, railroad museum.

Minerals: Oil, gas, gravel, sand.

Agriculture: Wheat, corn, hay, beef cattle, horses. Market value $66.2 million.

Vital Statistics, annual: Births, 1,586; deaths, 1,787; marriages, 767; divorces, 176.

Race/Ethnicity: Anglo, 70.2%; Hispanic, 15.4%; Black, 5.5%; Asian, 1.4%; Other, 7.4%.

SHERMAN (44,873) county seat; varied manufacturing, processors and distributors for major companies; Austin College; hospital.

Denison (25,179) health care, manufacturing, retail center; hospital; Eisenhower birthplace, air force base museum; Main Street Fall festival in October.

Other towns include: **Bells** (1,540); **Collinsville** (1,931); **Dorchester** (69); **Gordonville** (165); **Gunter** (2,255); **Howe** (3,615) manufacturing, agriculture, trucking services, library, Founders' Day in May; **Knollwood** (776); **Pottsboro** (2,613) lake activities, marinas, education, Frontier Days in September; **Preston** (2,217); and **Sadler** (337).

Also: **Southmayd** (1,013); **Tioga** (1,192) Gene Autry museum, festival in September; **Tom Bean** (933); **Van Alstyne** (5,165) retail center, manufacturing, government/services, museum, Grayson County College-South Campus, Fall Der All in October; **Whitesboro** (4,217) agribusiness, tourism, manufacturing, library, Peanut Festival in October; **Whitewright** (1,753) government/services, retail, manufacturing, museum, truck & tractor pull in June.

Population	139,336
Change from 2010	15.3%
Area (sq. mi.)	979.2
Land Area (sq. mi.)	932.8
Altitude (ft.)	500–930

Rainfall (in.)	44.3
Jan. mean min (°F)	35.7
July mean max (°F)	91.1
Civ. Labor	65,789
Unemployed	3.7%

Wages	$682,298,668
Per Capita Income	$52,055
Property Value	$27,991,258,749
Retail Sales	$2,589,111,646

For explanation of sources, symbols, and abbreviations, see p. 207 and foldout map.

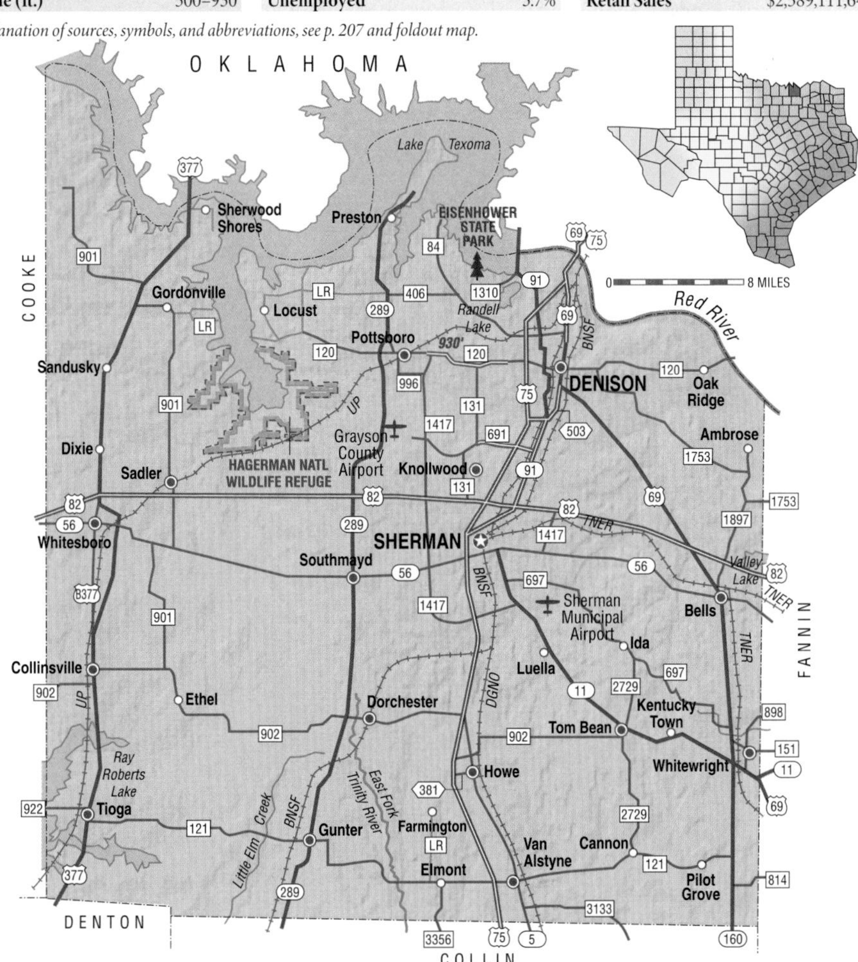

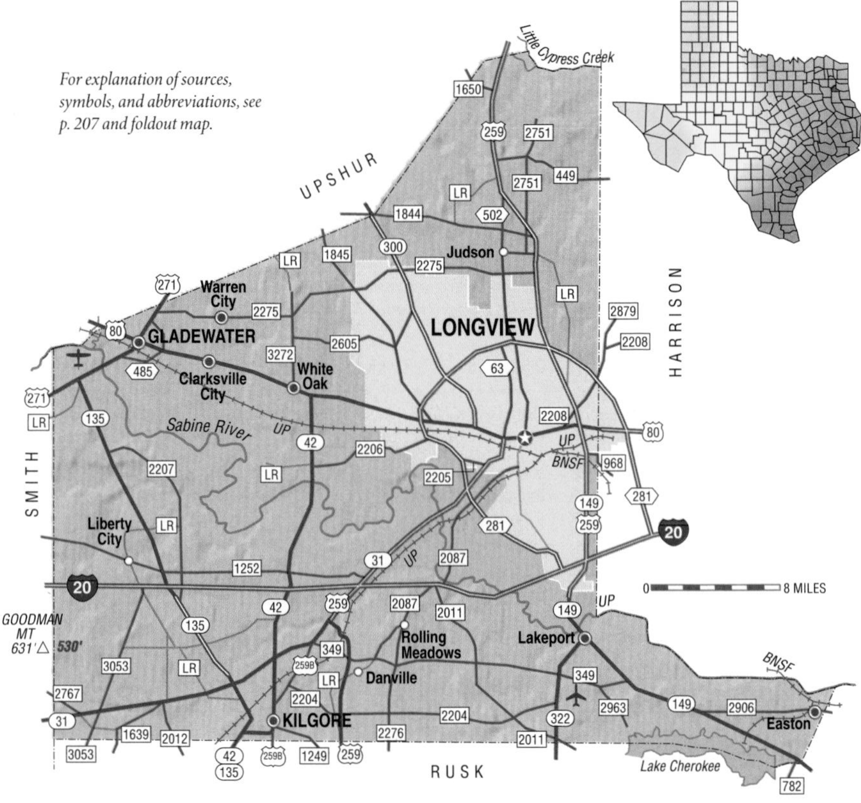

For explanation of sources, symbols, and abbreviations, see p. 207 and foldout map.

Gregg County

Physical Features: A populous, leading petroleum county, heart of the famed East Texas oil field; bisected by the Sabine River; hilly, timbered; with sandy, clay, alluvial soils.

Economy: Oil but with significant other manufacturing; tourism, conventions, agribusiness, and lignite coal production.

History: Caddoes; later Cherokees, who were driven out in 1838 by President Lamar. First land grants issued in 1835 by Republic of Mexico. County created and organized in 1873 from Rusk, Upshur counties; named for Confederate Gen. John Gregg. In U.S. censuses 1880-1910, Blacks were more numerous than whites. Oil discovered in 1931.

Recreation: Water activities on Lake Cherokee, hunting, varied cultural events, East Texas Oil Museum in Kilgore.

Minerals: Leading oil-producing county with more than 3 billion barrels produced since 1931; also, sand, gravel and natural gas.

Agriculture: Cattle, horses, hay, nursery crops. Market value $4.1 million. Timber sales.

Vital Statistics, annual: Births, 1,574; deaths, 1,630; marriages, 922; divorces, 528.

Race/Ethnicity: Anglo, 54.8%; Hispanic, 19.3%; Black, 20.1%; Asian, 1.3%; Other, 4.5%.

LONGVIEW (81,762, small part [2,409] in Harrison County) county seat; chemical manufacturing, oil industry, distribution and retail center; hospitals; LeTourneau University, University of Texas-Tyler Longview center; convention center; balloon race in July.

Kilgore (13,383, part [3,268] in Rusk County), oil, distribution center; Kilgore College, Rangerette museum; Shakespeare festival in summer.

Gladewater (6,137, part [2,369] in Upshur County) oil, manufacturing, tourism, antiques; library, airport, skydiving; Gusher Days in April; daffodils in February-March.

Other towns include: **Clarksville City** (780); **Easton** (763, partly in Rusk County); **Judson** (1,057); **Lakeport** (972); **Liberty City** (2,160) oil, tourism, government/services, Honor America Night in November.

Also: **Warren City** (321); **White Oak** (6,169) oil and gas, commuting to Longview, Tyler; park, Roughneck Days in spring every three years.

Population	124,201
Change from 2010	2.0%
Area (sq. mi.)	275.8
Land Area (sq. mi.)	273.3
Altitude (ft.)	240–530

Rainfall (in.)	48.2
Jan. mean min (°F)	36.1
July mean max (°F)	92.7
Civ. Labor	56,931
Unemployed	4.2%

Wages	$1,078,965,795
Per Capita Income	$52,958
Property Value	$13,906,958,736
Retail Sales	$3,873,124,463

Grimes County

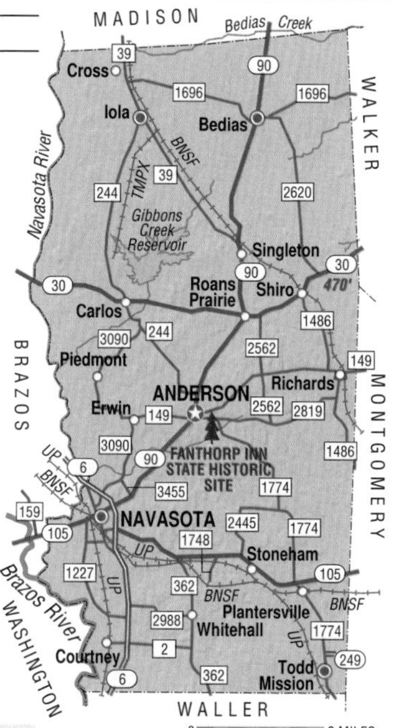

Physical Features: Rich bottom soils along Brazos, Navasota rivers; remainder hilly, partly forested; Gibbons Creek Reservoir.

Economy: Varied manufacturing, agribusiness, tourism, wineries, and wedding venues.

History: Bidais (customs similar to the Caddoes) lived peacefully with Anglo-American settlers who arrived in 1820s, but tribe was removed to Indian Territory. Planter agriculture reflected in 1860 census, which listed 77 persons owning 20 or more slaves. County created from Montgomery County in 1846, organized the same year; named for Jesse Grimes, who signed Texas Declaration of Independence.

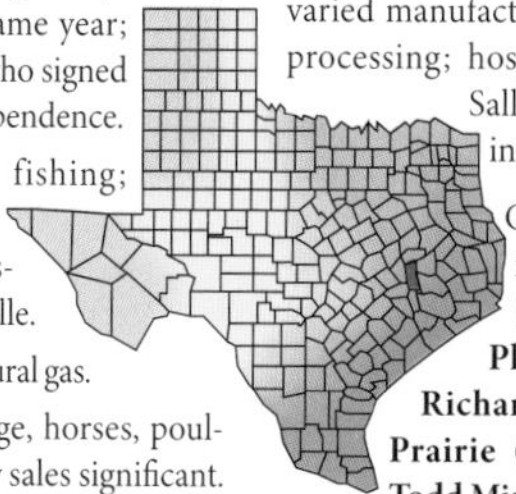

Recreation: Hunting, fishing; Gibbons Creek Reservoir; historic sites; fall Renaissance Festival at Plantersville.

Minerals: Lignite coal, natural gas.

Agriculture: Cattle, forage, horses, poultry; berries, pecans, honey sales significant. Market value $47.5million. Some timber sold, Christmas tree farms.

Vital Statistics, annual: Births, 347; deaths, 355; marriages, 105; divorces, 73.

Race/Ethnicity: Anglo, 57.8%; Hispanic, 25.2%; Black, 13.1%; Asian, 0.3%; Other, 3.7%.

ANDERSON (195) county seat; rural center; Fanthorp Inn historic site; Go-Texan weekend in February.

NAVASOTA (8,068) agribusiness center for parts of three counties; varied manufacturing; food, wood processing; hospital; prisons; La Salle statue; Blues Fest in August.

Other towns include: **Bedias** (370); **Iola** (322); **Plantersville** (473); **Richards** (136); **Roans Prairie** (64); **Shiro** (75); **Todd Mission** (124).

Population	30,287
Change from 2010	13.8%
Area (sq. mi.)	801.6
Land Area (sq. mi.)	787.5
Altitude (ft.)	150–470

Rainfall (in.)	44.2
Jan. mean min (°F)	40.3
July mean max (°F)	94.1
Civ. Labor	11,460
Unemployed	4.5%

Wages	$115,365,433
Per Capita Income	$41,914
Property Value	$8,969,484,280
Retail Sales	$353,063,676

The Whaley House in Longview, Gregg County, is on the National Register of Historic Buildings and is currently home to a law firm. Photo by Tom Reedy, CC by SA 3.0

The Texas Centennial marker for Battleground Prairie is a few miles east of Seguin. Photo by Larry D. Moore, CC by 4.0

Guadalupe County

Physical Features: South central county bisected by Guadalupe River, Lake Dunlap, Lake McQueeney; level to rolling surface; sandy, loam, blackland soils.

Economy: Varied manufacturing, commuting to San Antonio, agribusiness.

History: Karankawas, Comanches, and other tribes until the 1850s. The first Spanish land grant was in 1806 to José de la Baume. DeWitt colonists arrived in 1827. County created, organized, in 1846 from Bexar, Gonzales counties; named for the river.

Recreation: Fishing, hunting, river floating; Sebastopol House, other historic sites; river drive; Fiestas Juan Seguin in June, Diez y Seis in September in Seguin.

Minerals: Oil, gas, gravel, clays.

Agriculture: Cattle, corn, milo, wheat, cotton, hay, nursery crops, pecans. Market value $73.6 million.

Vital Statistics, annual: Births, 1,905; deaths, 1,377; marriages, 536; divorces, 525.

Race/Ethnicity: Anglo, 48.7%; Hispanic, 37.8%; Black, 6.9%; Asian, 1.8%; Other, 4.9%.

SEGUIN (30,902) county seat; varied manufacturing/logistics, health care, government/services; hospital, museums, heritage village; Texas Lutheran University; Pecan Fest in late October.

SCHERTZ (42,622, parts in Bexar and Comal counties) Crescent Bent Nature Park; Bussey's Flea Market weekends.

CIBOLO (33,475) near Randolph AFB; Cibolofest in October.

Other towns include: **Geronimo** (984), **Kingsbury** (134), **Lake Dunlap** (1,412), **Marion** (1,044), **McQueeney** (2,536), **New Berlin** (679), **Redwood** (3,353), **Santa Clara** (771), **Staples** (188).

Also, part [22,602] of **New Braunfels**, part [3,702] of **Selma**, and a small part of **San Marcos**.

Population	177,036
Change from 2010	34.6%
Area (sq. mi.)	714.8
Land Area (sq. mi.)	711.3
Altitude (ft.)	350–952
Rainfall (in.)	33.6
Jan. mean min (°F)	39.1
July mean max (°F)	92.8
Civ. Labor	85,585
Unemployed	3.4%
Wages	$668,455,965
Per Capita Income	$52,190
Property Value	$30,241,090,723
Retail Sales	$2,339,355,623

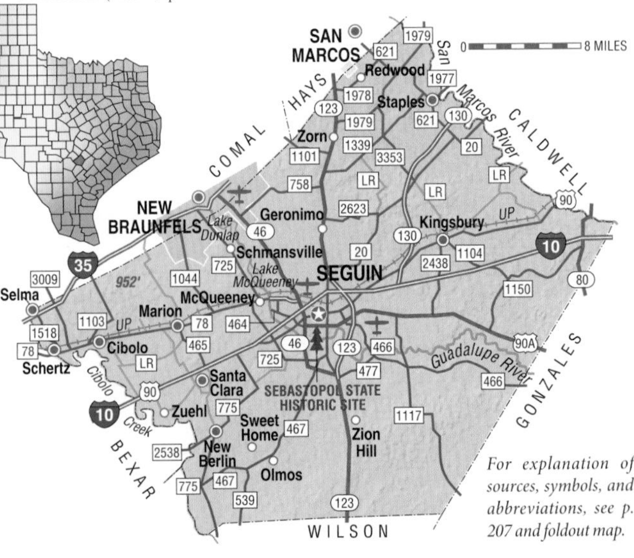

For explanation of sources, symbols, and abbreviations, see p. 207 and foldout map.

Hale County

Physical Features: High Plains; fertile sandy, loam soils; playas; large underground water supply.

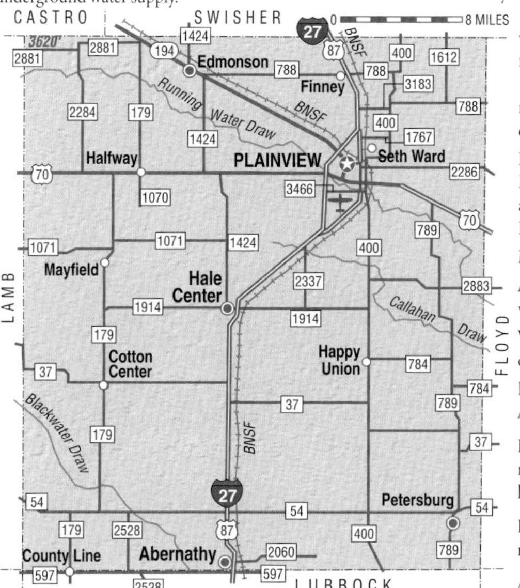

Economy: Agribusiness, food processing/distribution, manufacturing, government/services.

History: Comanche hunters driven out by U.S. Army in 1875. Ranching began in 1880s. First motor-driven irrigation well drilled in 1911. County created from Bexar District in 1876; organized in 1888; named for Lt. J.C. Hale, who died at San Jacinto.

Recreation: Llano Estacado Museum; art gallery, antiques stores; pheasant hunting; Cowboy Days in September at Plainview.

Minerals: Some oil.

Agriculture: Cotton, fed beef, sorghum, dairies, corn, vegetables, wheat. Market value $411.7 million. Irrigation of 200,000 acres.

Vital Statistics, annual: Births, 432; deaths, 454; marriages, 153; divorces, 33.

Race/Ethnicity: Anglo, 32.9%; Hispanic, 59.9%; Black, 4.2%; Asian, 0.5%; Other, 2.5%.

PLAINVIEW (19,739) county seat; agriculture, distribution, corn milling; Wayland Baptist University, South Plains College branch; hospital, library, mental health center; prisons.

Hale Center (2,015) trade center; farm museum, library, parks, murals, cacti gardens.

Abernathy (2,804, part [689] in Lubbock County) government/services, farm supplies, textile plant, gins.

Other towns include: **Cotton Center** (300), **Edmonson** (86), **Petersburg** (982), **Seth Ward** (1,849).

Population	32,220
Change from 2010	−11.2%
Area (sq. mi.)	1,004.8
Land Area (sq. mi.)	1,004.7
Altitude (ft.)	3,180–3,620
Rainfall (in.)	19.3

Jan. mean min (°F)	27.5
July mean max (°F)	91.2
Civ. Labor	11,674
Unemployed	4.9%
Wages	$127,532,854
Per Capita Income	$43,543

Property Value	$3,749,795,731
Retail Sales	$416,574,426

This is a gaging station, used to record the streamflow of Running Water Draw under a bridge in Plainview. Photo by Leaflet, CC by SA 4.0

Hall County

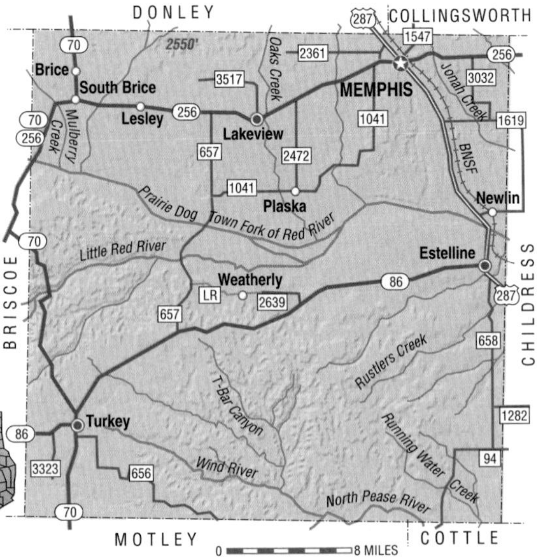

Physical Features: Rolling to hilly, broken by Red River forks, tributaries; red and black sandy loam.

Economy: Agriculture, farm/ranch supplies.

History: Apaches displaced by Comanches, who were removed to Indian Territory in 1875. Ranching began in the 1880s. Farming expanded after 1910. County created in 1876 from Bexar, Young districts; organized in 1890; named for Republic of Texas secretary of war W.D.C. Hall.

Recreation: Hunting of deer, wild hog, dove; Rails to Trails system; Bob Wills museum; Hall County Picnic festival in Memphis in September.

Minerals: None.

Agriculture: Cotton (lint and seed), beef cattle, hay, alfalfa, peanuts. Market value $56.4 million. Hunting leases important.

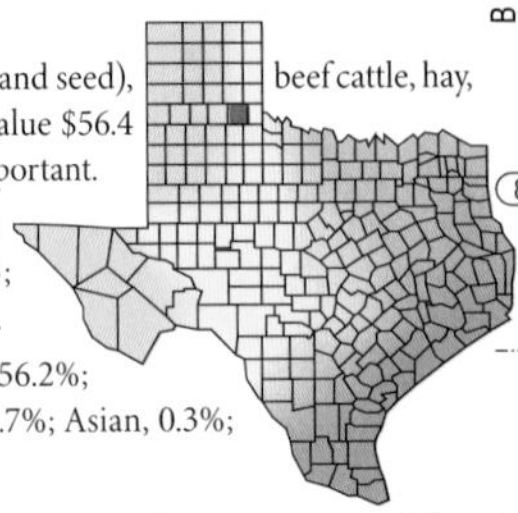

Vital Statistics, annual: Births, 24; deaths, 53; marriages, 5; divorces, NA.

Race/Ethnicity: Anglo, 56.2%; Hispanic, 33.6%; Black, 6.7%; Asian, 0.3%; Other, 3.1%.

MEMPHIS (2,055) county seat; agriculture, foundry, trucking; historic buildings including Presbyterian church (1911); amphitheater built by WPA.

Other towns include: **Estelline** (124), motorcycle rally/chili cookoff in August, **Lakeview** (60), **Turkey** (326) Bob Wills Day in April.

Population	2,845
Change from 2010	–15.2%
Area (sq. mi.)	904.1

Land Area (sq. mi.)	883.5
Altitude (ft.)	1,750–2,550
Rainfall (in.)	22.3

Jan. mean min (°F)	27.0
July mean max (°F)	94.3
Civ. Labor	1,093
Unemployed	4.2%
Wages	$7,874,496
Per Capita Income	$48,706
Property Value	$759,603,236
Retail Sales	$46,467,249

Hamilton County

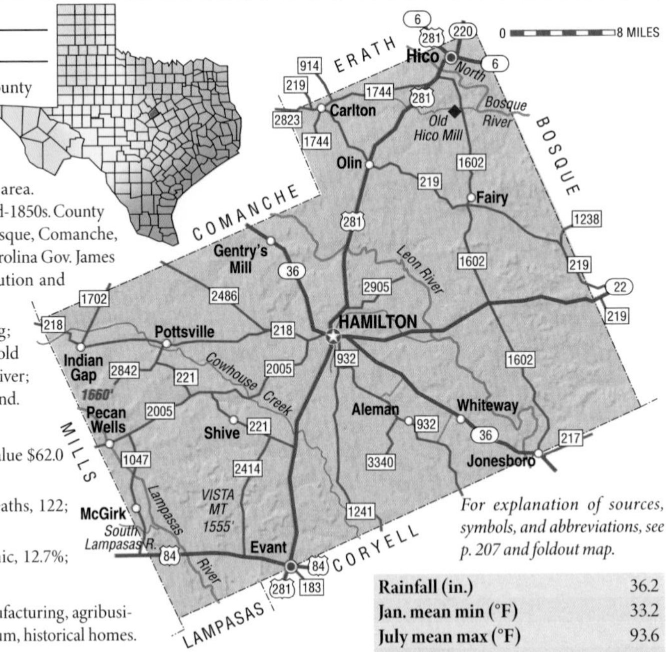

Physical Features: Hilly north central county broken by scenic valleys; loam soils.

Economy: Varied manufacturing, agribusiness, hunting leases, tourism.

History: Waco and Tawakoni Indian area. Anglo-American settlers arrived in the mid-1850s. County created and organized in 1858, from Bosque, Comanche, Lampasas counties; named for South Carolina Gov. James Hamilton, who aided the Texas Revolution and Republic.

Recreation: Deer, quail, dove hunting; Linear Pecan Creek park in Hamilton; old Bulman (bowstring) bridge over Leon River; Hamilton dove festival Labor Day weekend.

Minerals: Natural gas.

Agriculture: Beef, milk, hay. Market value $62.0 million. Hunting leases important.

Vital Statistics, annual: Births, 72; deaths, 122; marriages, 42; divorces, 35.

Race/Ethnicity: Anglo, 82.8%; Hispanic, 12.7%; Black, 0.4%; Asian, 0.4%; Other, 3.7%.

For explanation of sources, symbols, and abbreviations, see p. 207 and foldout map.

HAMILTON (2,871) county seat; manufacturing, agribusiness; hospital and medical clinics; museum, historical homes.

Hico (1,343) tourism, agriculture, varied manufacturing; antiques shops, Billy the Kid museum; steak cookoff in May.

Other towns include: **Carlton** (12), **Evant** (454, partly in Coryell County), **Jonesboro** (125, partly in Coryell County); **Pottsville** (105).

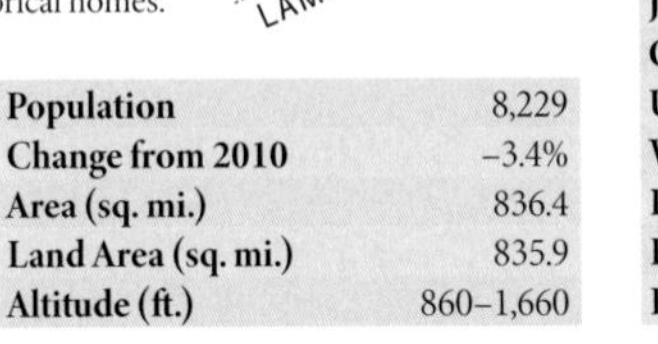

Population	8,229
Change from 2010	–3.4%
Area (sq. mi.)	836.4
Land Area (sq. mi.)	835.9
Altitude (ft.)	860–1,660

Rainfall (in.)	36.2
Jan. mean min (°F)	33.2
July mean max (°F)	93.6
Civ. Labor	3,889
Unemployed	3.4%
Wages	$34,191,030
Per Capita Income	$77,672
Property Value	$4,656,713,685
Retail Sales	$107,802,757

Hansford County

Physical Features: High Plains, many playas, creeks, draws; sandy, loam, black soils; underground water; Palo Duro Reservoir.

Economy: Agribusinesses; oil, gas operations; wind energy.

History: Apaches in area, later pushed out by Comanches around 1700. The U.S. Army removed the Comanches to the Indian Territory in 1874-1875, and ranching began soon afterward. Farmers, including Norwegians, moved in around 1900. County created in 1876, from the Bexar, Young districts and organized in 1889; named for jurist J.M. Hansford.

Recreation: Stationmasters House Museum, hunting, lake activities, ecotourism, Lindbergh landing site.

Minerals: Production of gas, oil.

Agriculture: Large cattle-feeding operations; corn, wheat (first in acreage), sorghum; hogs. Substantial irrigation. Market value $737.4 million.

Vital Statistics, annual: Births, 73; deaths, 54; marriages, 24; divorces, 11.

Race/Ethnicity: Anglo, 48.3%; Hispanic, 49.5%; Black, 0.2%; Asian, 0.2%; Other, 1.8%.

Population	5,159
Change from 2010	–8.1%
Area (sq. mi.)	920.4
Land Area (sq. mi.)	919.8
Altitude (ft.)	2,750–3,378
Rainfall (in.)	20.6
Jan. mean min (°F)	21.5
July mean max (°F)	91.0
Civ. Labor	2,878
Unemployed	2.4%
Wages	$39,276,284
Per Capita Income	$77,093
Property Value	$1,386,306,982
Retail Sales	$69,648,621

SPEARMAN (3,087) county seat; farming, cattle production, oil and gas, wind energy, biofuels; hospital, library, windmill collection; Heritage Days in May with rib cookoff.

Other towns include: **Gruver** (1,108) farm-ranch market, natural gas production, Fourth of July barbecue; **Morse** (251).

Hardeman County

For explanation of sources, symbols, and abbreviations, see p. 207 and fold-out map.

Physical Features: Rolling, broken area on divide between the Pease and Red rivers; Lake Pauline; sandy, loam soils.

Economy: Agriculture, gypsum production, oil and natural gas.

History: Apaches, later the semi-sedentary Wichitas and Comanche hunters. Ranching began in the late 1870s. Farming expanded after 1900. County created in 1858 from Fannin County; re-created in 1876, organized in 1884; named for pioneer brothers Bailey and T.J. Hardeman.

Recreation: State park; lake activities; Medicine Mound aborigine gathering site; Quanah Parker monument; hunting of deer, quail, wild hogs.

Minerals: Oil, natural gas, gypsum.

Agriculture: Wheat, cattle, cotton. Market value $18.0 million. Hunting leases.

Vital Statistics, annual: Births, 42; deaths, 75; marriages, 15; divorces, 14.

Race/Ethnicity: Anglo, 68.8%; Hispanic, 23%; Black, 3.7%; Asian, 0.5%; Other, 4%.

QUANAH (2,272) county seat; manufacturing, farming, ranching, oil and gas; state hospital, general hospital; historical sites; Fall Festival in September.

Other towns include: **Chillicothe** (554) farm market center, hospital.

Population	3,552
Change from 2010	–14.2%
Area (sq. mi.)	696.9
Land Area (sq. mi.)	695.1
Altitude (ft.)	1,250–1,850
Rainfall (in.)	25.6
Jan. mean min (°F)	28.3
July mean max (°F)	94.9
Civ. Labor	1,792
Unemployed	3.5%
Wages	$18,872,714
Per Capita Income	$54,847
Property Value	$1,089,719,340
Retail Sales	$67,527,851

Ghost Road Scenic Drive runs north-south from FM 1293 to FM 787 in Hardin County. Photo by Junglecat, CC by SA 4.0

Hardin County

Physical Features: Southeast county; timbered; many streams; sandy, loam soils; Big Thicket covers much of area.

Economy: Paper manufacturing, wood processing, minerals, food processing, oil and gas; county in Beaumont-Port Arthur-Orange metropolitan area.

History: Lorenzo de Zavala received first land grant in 1829. Anglo-American settlers arrived in 1830. County created and organized in 1858 from Jefferson, Liberty counties. Named for Texas Revolutionary leader William Hardin.

Recreation: Big Thicket with rare plant, animal life; national preserve; Red Cloud Water Park in Silsbee; hunting, fishing; state park; Hogs and Strings Music Festival in October in Kountze.

Minerals: Oil, gas, sand, gravel.

Agriculture: Beef cattle, hay, blueberries, bees and rice. Market value 4.7 million. Timber provides most income; more than 85 percent of county forested. Hunting leases.

Vital Statistics, annual: Births, 698; deaths, 666; marriages, 282; divorces, 279.

Race/Ethnicity: Anglo, 83.5%; Hispanic, 6.1%; Black, 5.4%; Asian, 0.7%; Other, 4.3%.

KOUNTZE (2,163) county seat; government/services, retail center, commuting to Beaumont; library, museum.

SILSBEE (6,851) forest products, rail center, oil, gas; library, Ice House museum.

LUMBERTON (13,802) construction, government/services, tourism; library; Village Creek Festival in October.

Other towns and places include: **Batson** (140); **Pinewood Estates** (1,407); **Rose Hill Acres** (328); **Saratoga** (1,000) Big Thicket Museum; **Sour Lake** (1,792) oil, lumbering; Old Timers' Day in September; **Thicket** (306); **Village Mills** (200); **Votaw** (160), and **Wildwood** (732).

Population	56,973
Change from 2010	4.3%
Area (sq. mi.)	897.6
Land Area (sq. mi.)	890.6
Altitude (ft.)	7–170
Rainfall (in.)	63.2
Jan. mean min (°F)	41.3
July mean max (°F)	92.1
Civ. Labor	24,912
Unemployed	5.2%
Wages	$157,497,982
Per Capita Income	$52,544
Property Value	$6,365,805,952
Retail Sales	$896,964,097

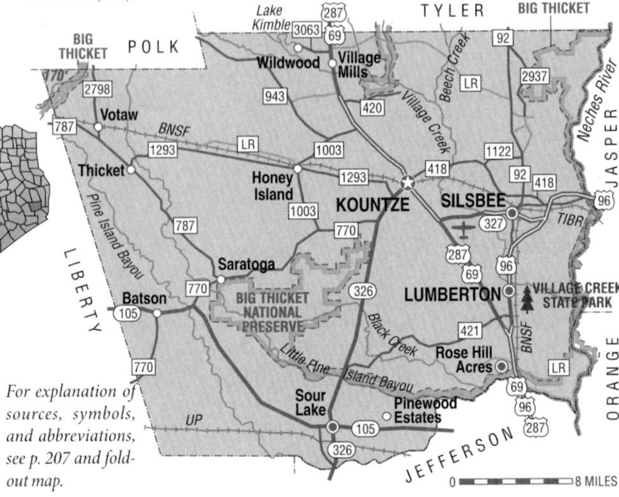

For explanation of sources, symbols, and abbreviations, see p. 207 and fold-out map.

Harris County

Physical Features: Largest county in eastern half of state; level; typically coastal surface and soils; many bayous, canals for artificial drainage; Lake Houston, Sheldon Reservoir; partly forested.

Economy: Highly industrialized county with largest population; more than 92 foreign governments maintain offices in Houston; corporate management center; nation's largest concentration of petrochemical plants; largest U.S. wheat-exporting port, among top U.S. ports in the value of foreign trade and total tonnage. Petroleum refining, chemicals, food, fabricated metal products, non-electrical machinery, primary metals, scientific instruments; paper and allied products, printing and publishing; center for energy, space and medical research; center of international business.

History: Orcoquiza villages were visited by Spanish authorities in 1746. Pioneer settlers arrived by boat from Louisiana in 1822. Antebellum planters brought Black slaves. Mexican migration increased after the Mexican Revolution. County created in 1836 and organized in 1837; named for John R. Harris, founder of Harrisburg (now part of Houston).

Recreation: Professional baseball, basketball, football, soccer; rodeo and livestock show; Jones Hall for the Performing Arts; Nina Vance Alley Theatre; Convention Center; Toyota Center, a 19,000-seat sports and entertainment center; Reliant Stadium and downtown ballpark. Sam Houston Park, with restored early Houston homes, church, stores; Museum of Fine Arts, Contemporary Arts Museum, Rice Museum; Wortham Theater; Hobby Center for Performing Arts; museum of natural science, planetarium, zoo in Hermann Park. San Jacinto Battleground, Johnson Space Center. Fishing, boating, other freshwater and saltwater activities.

Minerals: Among leading oil, gas, petrochemical areas; production of petroleum, cement, natural gas, salt, lime, sulfur, sand and gravel, clays, stone.

Agriculture: Nursery crops, grass (third in acreage of sod), cattle, hay, horses, vegetables, Christmas trees (first in acreage), goats, rice, corn. Market value $50.6 million. Substantial income from forest products.

Vital Statistics, annual: Births, 63,815; deaths, 32,812; marriages, 19,587; divorces, 10,247.

Race/Ethnicity: Anglo, 27.7%; Hispanic, 43%; Black, 18.7%; Asian, 7.3%; Other, 3.3%.

Population	4,728,030
Change from 2010	15.5%
Area (sq. mi.)	1,777.5
Land Area (sq. mi.)	1,703.5
Altitude (ft.)	sea level–310
Rainfall (in.)	55.6
Jan. mean min (°F)	48.1

July mean max (°F)	92.5
Civ. Labor	2,339,651
Unemployed	4.2%
Wages	$49,707,617,091
Per Capita Income	$65,869
Property Value	$850,716,196,280
Retail Sales	$121,558,725,807

HOUSTON (2,288,250, small parts in Fort Bend and Montgomery counties) county seat; largest Texas city; fourth-largest in nation.

A leading center for manufacture of petroleum equipment, agricultural chemicals, fertilizers, pesticides, oil and gas pipeline transmission; a leading scientific center; manufacture of machinery, fabricated metals; a major distribution, shipping center; engineering and research center; food processing; 85 hospitals.

Manufacturing centers make apparel, lumber and wood products; furniture, paper, chemical, petroleum and coal products; publishing center; one of the nation's largest public school systems; prominent corporate center; Go Texan Day (rodeo) in February/March, international festival in March/April.

PASADENA (148,626) residential city with large industrial area manufacturing petrochemicals and other petroleum-related products; civic center; San Jacinto College, Texas Chiropractic College; hospitals; historical museum; Strawberry Festival in May.

BAYTOWN (82,480, part [4,834] in Chambers County) refining, petrochemical center; commuters to Houston; Lee College; hospital, museum, library; historical homes; Chili When It's Chilly cookoff and the Great Bull Run in January.

The Clear Lake Area: which includes **El Lago** (3,006); **Nassau Bay** (5,213); **Seabrook** (13,560); **Taylor Lake Village** (3,617); **Webster** (12,193) tourism, Johnson Space Center, University of Houston-Clear Lake, commuting to Houston; Bayport Industrial Complex includes Port of Bayport; 12 major marinas; hospitals; Christmas lighted boat parade.

Other towns include: **Aldine** (15,887); **Atascocita** (84,222); **Barrett** (3,668); **Bellaire** (16,983) residential city with several major office buildings; **Bunker Hill Village** (3,761); Cloverleaf (25,576); **Channelview** (42,394) hospital; **Crosby** (1,823) government/services, chemical plant, Czech Fest in October; **Cypress** (120,000); **Deer Park** (33,676) ship-channel industries, Totally Texas celebration in April.

Also: **Galena Park** (10,461); **Hedwig Village** (2,328); **Highlands** (7,714) commuters, heritage museum, Jamboree in October; **Hilshire Village** (806); **Hockley** (400); **Huffman** (15,000); **Humble** (16,396) oil-field equipment manufactured, retail center, hospital; **Hunters Creek Village** (4,314); **Jacinto City** (9,378); **Jersey Village** (7,731).

Also: **Katy** (24,005, partly in Fort Bend and Waller counties) corporate headquarters, distribution center, hospitals; museums, park; Rice Harvest festival in October; **La Porte** (35,964) petrochemical industry; depot museum; Sylvan Beach Festival in April; **Mission Bend** (38,772); **Morgan's Point** (271); **Piney Point Village** (3,072); **Sheldon** (2,176); **Shoreacres** (1,530); **South Houston** (15,878).

Also: **Southside Place** (1,826); **Spring** (62,569); **Spring Valley** (4,217); **Tomball** (12,810) health care, oil and gas, retail, hospital, museum, junior college, parks and nature preserve, German festival in March; **West University Place** (14,724).

Small parts of **Cinco Ranch**, **Missouri City**, and **Stafford** (all are mostly in Fort Bend County).

Parts of **Friendswood** [10,558] and **League City** [2,522] (both mostly in Guadalupe County).

Part [8,049] **of Pearland**, (mostly in Brazoria County, also part in Fort Bend County) and part of **Waller** [858] (mostly in Waller County).

Addicks, **Alief**, and **Kingwood** are now within the city limits of Houston.

Harris County

For explanation of sources, symbols, and abbreviations, see p. 207 and foldout map.

A farmer cutting his field in Harrison County. Photo by Carol M. Highsmith, Public Domain

Harrison County

Physical Features: East Texas county; hilly, rolling; over half forested; Sabine River; Caddo Lake, Brandy Branch Reservoir.

Economy: Oil, gas processing, lumbering, pottery, other varied manufacturing.

History: Area was populated by agriculturist Caddo Indians whose numbers were reduced by disease. Anglo-Americans arrived in the 1830s. In 1850, the county had more slaves than any other in the state. County created in 1839 from Shelby County; organized in 1842. Named for eloquent advocate of the Texas Revolution, Jonas Harrison.

Recreation: Fishing, other water activities on Caddo and other lakes; hunting; plantation homes, historic sites; Stagecoach Days in May; Old Courthouse Museum; Old World Store; state park, performing arts; Fire Ant festival in October.

Minerals: Oil, gas, lignite coal, clays, sand and gravel.

Agriculture: Cattle, hay. Also, poultry, nursery plants, horses, vegetables, watermelons. Market value $15.8 million. Hunting leases important. Substantial timber industry.

Vital Statistics, annual: Births, 765; deaths, 769; marriages, 350; divorces, 99.

Race/Ethnicity: Anglo, 61.1%; Hispanic, 14.3%; Black, 19.5%; Asian, 0.7%; Other, 4.4%.

MARSHALL (22,662) county seat; petroleum and lumber processing, varied manufacturing; civic center; historic sites, including Starr Family State Historic Site; hospital; Wiley College, East Texas Baptist University; Wonderland of Lights in December.

Other towns include: **Elysian Fields** (500); **Hallsville** (4,528) government/services, utilities, Western Days in October, museum; **Harleton** (390); **Jonesville** (70); **Karnack** (350); **Nesbitt** (179); **Scottsville** (338); **Uncertain** (88) tourism, fishing, hunting; **Waskom** (1,946) oil, gas, ranching, Howdeo Festival in October; **Woodlawn** (550).

Also, small part [2,409] of **Longview** (mostly in Gregg County).

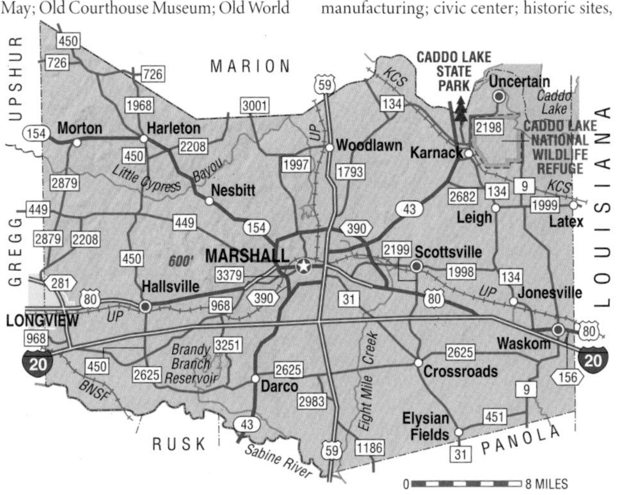

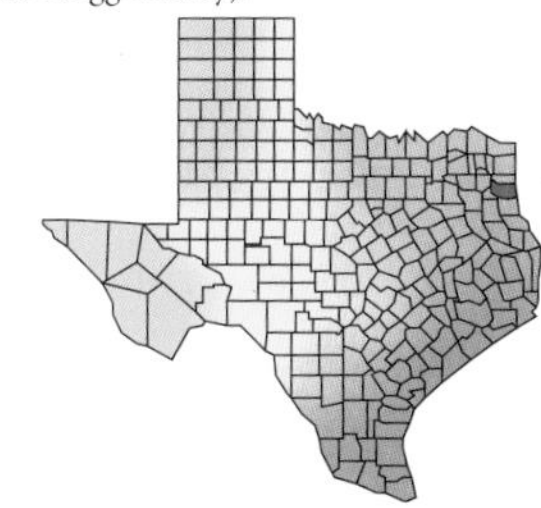

Population	69,150
Change from 2010	5.4%
Area (sq. mi.)	915.8
Land Area (sq. mi.)	900.0
Altitude (ft.)	168–600
Rainfall (in.)	51.3
Jan. mean min (°F)	34.9
July mean max (°F)	92.8
Civ. Labor	28,968
Unemployed	4.5%
Wages	$347,004,450
Per Capita Income	$47,928
Property Value	$11,014,281,487
Retail Sales	$840,963,636

Hartley County

Physical Features: Panhandle High Plains; drains to Canadian River tributaries, playas; sandy, loam, chocolate soils; lake.

Economy: Agriculture, dairies, gas production.

History: Apaches in area, pushed out by Comanches around 1700. The U.S. Army removed the Indians in 1875. Pastores (sheepmen) were in area until the 1880s when cattle ranching began. Farming expanded after 1900. County created in 1876 from the Bexar, Young districts; organized in 1891; named for Texas pioneers O.C. and R.K. Hartley.

Recreation: Lake Rita Blanca activities; ranch museum; XIT Rodeo and Reunion at Dalhart in August.

Minerals: Sand, gravel, oil, natural gas.

Agriculture: Cattle, corn (second in acreage), wheat, hay, dairy cows, vegetables. 155,000 acres irrigated. Market value $1.2 billion. Hunting leases.

Vital Statistics, annual: Births, 56; deaths, 53; marriages, 1; divorces, 14.

Race/Ethnicity: Anglo, 63.2%; Hispanic, 30.3%; Black, 3.5%; Asian, 0.4%; Other, 2.5%.

CHANNING (266) county seat, old XIT Ranch headquarters, Roundup in July.

DALHART (8,347, mostly [5,521] in Dallam County), government/services; agribusiness center for parts of Texas, New Mexico, Oklahoma; railroad; cheese plant; grain operations; junior college branch; hospital; prison.

Also, **Hartley** (368).

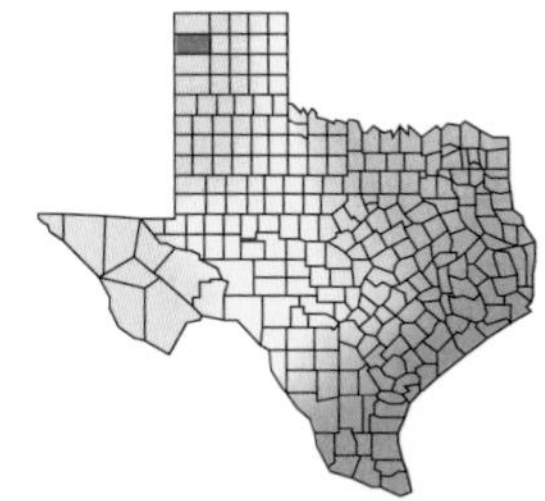

Population	5,397
Change from 2010	–11.0%
Area (sq. mi.)	1,463.2
Land Area (sq. mi.)	1,462.0
Altitude (ft.)	3,340–4,465
Rainfall (in.)	17.7
Jan. mean min (°F)	21.9
July mean max (°F)	89.4
Civ. Labor	2,618
Unemployed	2.0%
Wages	$33,442,675
Per Capita Income	$75,790
Property Value	$1,628,748,438
Retail Sales	$59,785,528

Haskell County

Physical Features: Northwest county; rolling; broken areas; drained by Brazos tributaries; lake; sandy loam, gray, black soils.

Economy: Agribusiness, oil-field operations.

History: Apaches until 1700, then a Comanche area. Ranching began in the late 1870s after the Indians were removed. Farming expanded after 1900. County created in 1858, from Milam and Fannin counties; re-created in 1876 and organized in 1885; named for Goliad victim C.R. Haskell.

Recreation: Lake Stamford activities, fishing tournaments; Haskell arts & crafts show in November; hunting of deer, geese, wild hogs.

Minerals: Oil and gas.

Agriculture: Wheat, cotton, peanuts; 28,000 acres irrigated. Beef cattle raised. Market value $54.3 million.

Vital Statistics, annual: Births, 47; deaths, 84; marriages, 16; divorces, 13.

Race/Ethnicity: Anglo, 67%; Hispanic, 25.4%; Black, 3.3%; Asian, 0.4%; Other, 3.8%.

HASKELL (3,046) county seat; farming center; hospital; city park; Wild Horse Prairie Days in June.

Other towns include: **O'Brien** (92), **Rochester** (248), **Rule** (568) farming, cotton gins/warehouses, oil, mural, park; **Weinert** (175).

Population	5,411
Change from 2010	-8.3%
Area (sq. mi.)	910.3
Land Area (sq. mi.)	903.1
Altitude (ft.)	1,340–1,795
Rainfall (in.)	27.0
Jan. mean min (°F)	30.8
July mean max (°F)	93.8
Civ. Labor	2,771
Unemployed	3.0%
Wages	$23,466,396
Per Capita Income	$54,321
Property Value	$2,030,911,517
Retail Sales	$131,273,990

Hays County

Physical Features: Hilly in west, blackland in east; bisected by Blanco River; on edge of Balcones Escarpment.

Economy: Education, tourism, retirement area, some manufacturing; part of Austin metropolitan area.

History: Tonkawa area, also some Apache and Comanche presence. Spanish authorities attempted the first permanent settlement in 1807. Mexican land grants in early 1830s to Juan Martín Veramendi, Juan Vicente Campos and Thomas Jefferson Chambers. County created in 1843 from Travis County, organized the same year; named for Capt. Jack Hays, a famous Texas Ranger.

Recreation: Fishing, hunting; college cultural, athletic events; African-American museum, LBJ museum; Cypress Creek and Blanco River resorts, guest ranches, Wonder World park.

Minerals: Sand, gravel, cement produced.

Agriculture: Beef cattle, goats, exotic wildlife; greenhouse nurseries; hay, corn, sorghum, wheat and cotton. Market value $21.8 million.

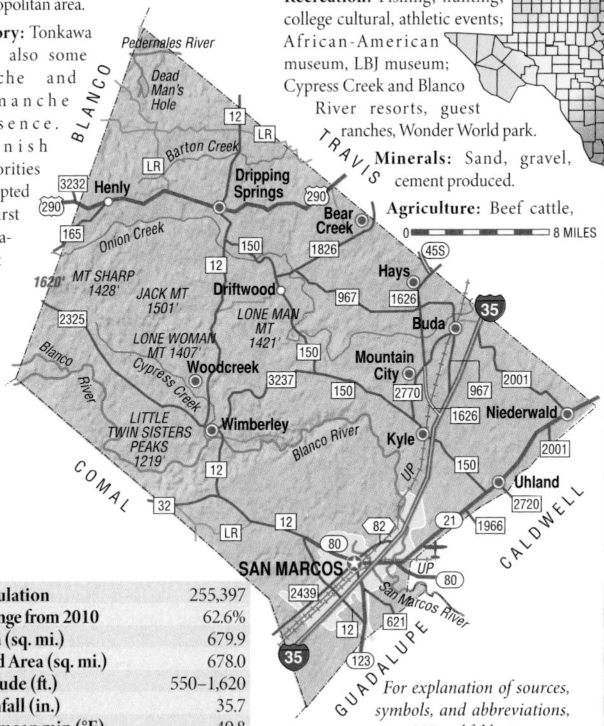

Vital Statistics, annual: Births, 2,802; deaths, 1,340; marriages, 861; divorces, 601.

Race/Ethnicity: Anglo, 50.4%; Hispanic, 38.5%; Black, 3.7%; Asian, 2%; Other, 5.3%.

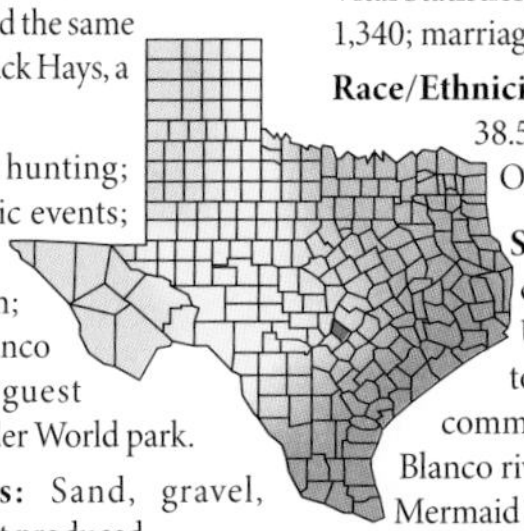

SAN MARCOS (68,580) county seat; Texas State University, outlet center, tourism, distribution center, commuting; hospital; San Marcos, Blanco rivers; jazz festival in February, Mermaid Fest in September.

Kyle (51,789) medical, education, retail center, Claiborne Kyle Log House, Katherine Anne Porter House, 5k Kyle-O-Meter in October.

Other towns include: **Bear Creek** (418); **Buda** (15,643) construction, manufacturing, retail, government/services, Stagecoach park, Weiner Dog races in April; **Driftwood** (87); **Dripping Springs** (5,787); **Hays** (240); **Mountain City** (656); **Niederwald** (671, partly in Caldwell County); **Uhland** (1,667, partly in Caldwell County); **Wimberley** (2,877) tourism, retirement community, artists, historic homes, museum, Blue Hole park/swimming, Jacob's Well spring/natural area, art festival in April; **Woodcreek** (1,804).

Population	255,397
Change from 2010	62.6%
Area (sq. mi.)	679.9
Land Area (sq. mi.)	678.0
Altitude (ft.)	550–1,620
Rainfall (in.)	35.7
Jan. mean min (°F)	40.8

For explanation of sources, symbols, and abbreviations, see p. 207 and foldout map.

July mean max (°F)	93.5
Civ. Labor	138,543
Unemployed	3.0%
Wages	$1,179,098,181
Per Capita Income	$56,097
Property Value	$56,606,376,690
Retail Sales	$4,227,016,987

Hemphill County

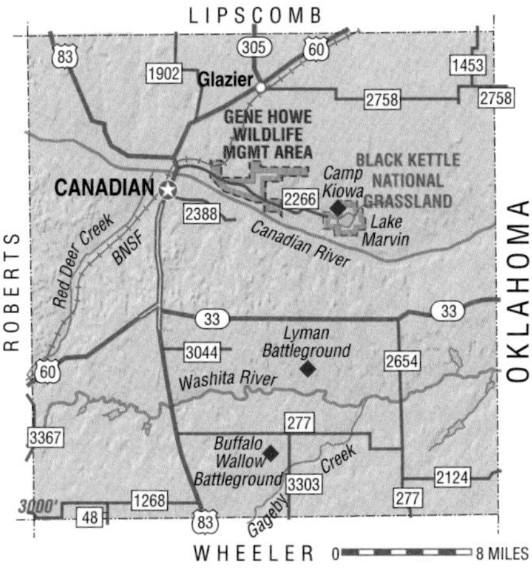

Physical Features: Sloping surface, broken by Canadian, Washita rivers; sandy, red, dark soils.

Economy: Oil, gas, agriculture, tourism, hunting, government/services.

History: Apaches who were in the area were later pushed out by Comanches and Kiowas. The tribes were removed to the Indian Territory in 1875. Ranching began in the late 1870s. Farmers began to arrive after 1900. County created from the Bexar and Young districts in 1876 and organized in 1887; named for Republic of Texas Justice John Hemphill.

Recreation: Lake Marvin; fall foliage tour; hunting, fishing; Indian Battleground, wildlife management area; museum; 4th of July rodeo; prairie chicken viewing in April.

Minerals: Oil, natural gas, caliche.

Agriculture: Cattle, wheat, horses, hay, alfalfa; some irrigation. Market value $138.9 million. Hunting, nature tourism.

Vital Statistics, annual: Births, 30; deaths, 24; marriages, 18; divorces, 8.

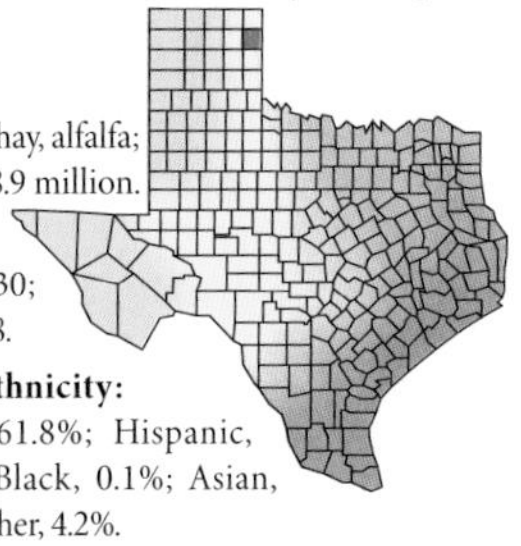

Race/Ethnicity: Anglo, 61.8%; Hispanic, 33.6%; Black, 0.1%; Asian, 0.3%; Other, 4.2%.

CANADIAN (2,248) county seat; oil, gas production; hospital; art foundation.

Population	3,271
Change from 2010	−14.1%
Area (sq. mi.)	912.2
Land Area (sq. mi.)	906.3
Altitude (ft.)	2,170–3,000
Rainfall (in.)	22.6
Jan. mean min (°F)	19.1

July mean max (°F)	92.3
Civ. Labor	1,633
Unemployed	3.3%
Wages	$24,622,358
Per Capita Income	$75,731
Property Value	$1,748,799,081
Retail Sales	$31,723,871

The front entrance to the old elementary school in Malakoff. Photo by Larry D. Moore, CC by SA 4.0

Henderson County

Physical Features: East Texas county bounded by Neches and Trinity rivers; hilly, rolling; one-third forested; sandy, loam, clay soils; timber; Cedar Creek Reservoir, Lake Palestine, Lake Athens, Forest Grove Reservoir; Trinidad Lake.

Economy: Agribusiness, retail trade, varied manufacturing, minerals, recreation, tourism.

History: Caddo tribal area. Cherokees and other tribes migrated into the area in 1819-1820 ahead of white settlement. Cherokees were forced into Indian Territory in 1839. Anglo-American settlers arrived in the 1840s. County created in 1846 from Nacogdoches and Houston counties; organized the same year. County named for Gov. J. Pinckney Henderson.

Population	83,667
Change from 2010	6.5%
Area (sq. mi.)	949.3
Land Area (sq. mi.)	873.8
Altitude (ft.)	256–763

Recreation: Cedar Creek Reservoir, Lake Palestine, other lakes; Purtis Creek State Park; hunting, fishing, bird-watching; ziplining at New York; East Texas Arboretum.

Minerals: Oil, gas, clays, lignite, sulfur, sand and gravel.

Agriculture: Beef cattle, forages, nurseries/horticulture, rodeo stock. Market value $40.2 million. Hunting leases and fishing. Timber important.

Vital Statistics, annual: Births, 955; deaths, 1,320; marriages, 470; divorces, 53.

Race/Ethnicity: Anglo, 75.3%; Hispanic, 13.7%; Black, 5.7%; Asian, 0.6%; Other, 4.7%.

ATHENS (12,890) county seat; agribusiness center, varied manufacturing, tourism, state fish hatchery and museum, hospital, mental health center; Trinity Valley Community College; Old Fiddlers' Reunion in May.

Rainfall (in.)	44.8
Jan. mean min (°F)	36.5
July mean max (°F)	93.1
Civ. Labor	39,001
Unemployed	3.8%

Gun Barrel City (6,378) recreation, retirement, retail center.

Malakoff (2,219) brick factory, varied industry, tourism, library, Cornbread Festival in April.

Other towns include: **Berryville** (852); **Brownsboro** (1,229); **Caney City** (188); **Chandler** (3,400) commuting to Tyler, retail trade, tourism, Pow Wow Festival in October; **Coffee City** (244); **Enchanted Oaks** (354); **Eustace** (1,153); **Larue** (250); **Log Cabin** (749); **Moore Station** (159); **Murchison** (523); **Payne Springs** (750); **Poynor** (288); **Seven Points** (1,402) agribusiness, retail trade, recreation; **Star Harbor** (501); **Tool** (2,212), and **Trinidad** (861).

Also, part of **Mabank** [1,334] (4,562, mostly in Kaufman County).

Wages	$215,253,778
Per Capita Income	$48,594
Property Value	$15,274,511,202
Retail Sales	$1,115,152,108

Hidalgo County

Physical Features: Rich alluvial soils along Rio Grande; sandy, loam soils in north; semitropical vegetation; Anzalduas Channel Dam, Delta Lake, Valley Acres Reservoir.

Economy: Food processing and shipping, other agribusinesses, tourism, mineral operations; Texas' fifth-largest metro area.

History: Coahuiltecan and Karankawa area. Comanches forced Apaches southward into valley in the 1700s; Comanches arrived in valley in the 1800s. Spanish settlement occurred 1750-1800. County created in 1852 from Cameron and Starr counties, organized the same year; named for leader of Mexico's independence movement of 1810, Father Miguel Hidalgo y Costillo.

Recreation: Winter resort, retirement area; fishing, hunting; gateway to Mexico; historical sites; Bentsen-Rio Grande Valley State Park; museums; All-Valley Winter Vegetable Show at Pharr.

Minerals: Oil, gas, stone, sand and gravel.

Agriculture: Ninety percent of farm cash receipts from crops (ranked first in state), principally from sugar cane (first in acreage), grain sorghum (first in acreage), vegetables (first in acreage), citrus, cotton; livestock includes cattle; 184,000 acres irrigated. Market value $311.0 million.

Vital Statistics, annual: Births, 13,383; deaths, 7,239; marriages, 3,992; divorces, 3.

Race/Ethnicity: Anglo, 6.1%; Hispanic, 91.9%; Black, 0.4%; Asian, 1.0%; Other, 0.6%.

EDINBURG (100,483) county seat; vegetable processing and packing, petroleum operations, tourism, clothing; planetarium; the University of Texas-Rio Grande Valley; hospitals; behavioral, health center; museum; Texas Cook'em High Steaks July 4 weekend, Fiesta Edinburg in February.

For explanation of sources, symbols, and abbreviations, see p. 207 and foldout map.

McALLEN (143,920) retail center, medical care/hospitals, government/services; community college; birding center, Mxlan arts/music celebration of Mexican culture in late July.

Mission (86,223) citrus groves, agricultural processing/distribution; hospital; community college; international butterfly park; Citrus Fiesta in January.

Pharr (79,697) agriculture, trading center; trucking; tourism; old clock, juke box museums; folklife festival in February.

Other towns include: **Abram** (1,671); **Alamo** (20,017) live steam museum; **Alton** (18,860); **Doffing** (5,396); **Donna** (16,821) citrus center, varied manufacturing; **Edcouch** (2,720); **Elsa** (5,680); **Granjeno** (287); **Hargill** (1,094); **Hidalgo** (14,239) trade zone, shipping, winter resort, agribusiness, historical sites, library, Borderfest in March; **La Blanca** (3,304); **La Homa** (11,924); **La Joya** (4,587); **La Villa** (2,712); **Linn** (613); **Los Ebanos** (42).

Population	880,356
Change from 2010	13.6%
Area (sq. mi.)	1,582.9
Land Area (sq. mi.)	1,570.9
Altitude (ft.)	28–376
Rainfall (in.)	22.2
Jan. mean min (°F)	54.6
July mean max (°F)	98.5
Civ. Labor	371,985
Unemployed	6.5%
Wages	$3,074,701,037
Per Capita Income	$34,503
Property Value	$62,682,230,460
Retail Sales	$13,605,987,702

Also: **Mercedes** (16,312) "boot capital," citrus, and vegetable center, food processing, tourism, recreation vehicle show in January; **Mila Doce** (7,047); **Monte Alto** (2,136); **Murillo** (8,989); **North Alamo** (4,080); **Palmhurst** (2,602); **Palmview** (15,884); **Palmview South** (2,486); **Peñitas** (6,399); **Perezville** (2,577); **Progreso** (4,904); **Progreso Lakes** (259); **San Carlos** (4,177); **San Juan** (35,577) retirement area, trucking, Shrine of Our Lady of San Juan, Spring Fiesta in February; **South Alamo** (3,228); **Sullivan City** (3,905); **Weslaco** (41,024) agriculture, nature tourism, South Texas College, hospital, Dragonfly Days in May.

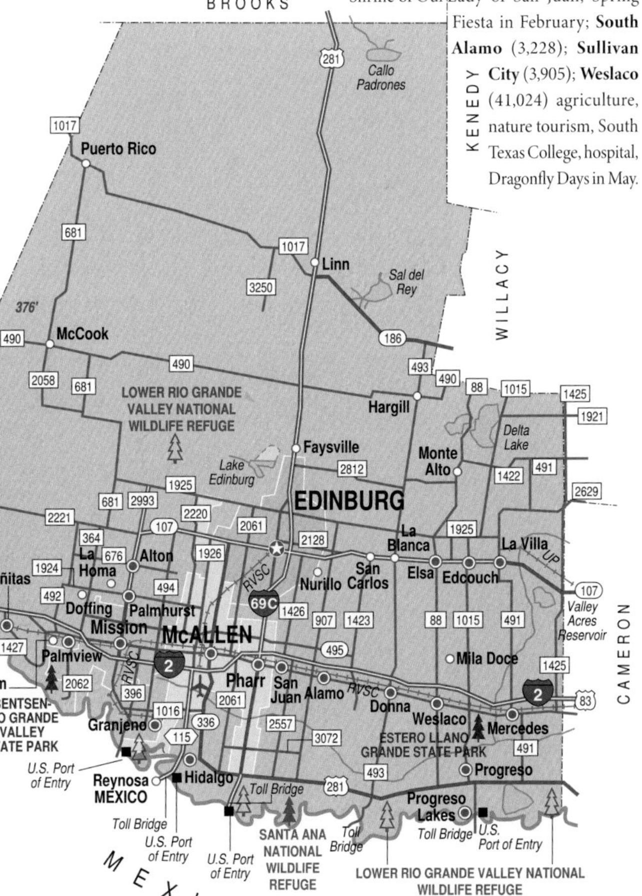

Hill County

Physical Features: North central county; level to rolling; blackland soils, some sandy loams; drains to Brazos; Lake Whitney, Aquilla Lake.

Economy: Agribusiness, tourism, varied manufacturing.

History: Waco and Tawakoni area, later Comanches. Believed to be Indian "council spot," a place of safe passage without evidence of raids. Anglo-Americans of the Robertson colony arrived in the early 1830s. Fort Graham established in 1849. County created from Navarro County in 1853, organized the same year; named for G.W. Hill, Republic of Texas official.

Recreation: Lake activities; excursion boat; Texas Heritage Museum including Confederate and Audie Murphy exhibits, historic structures, rebuilt frontier fort barracks; motorcycle track.

Minerals: Gas, limestone.

Agriculture: Corn, cattle, sorghum, wheat, cotton, dairies, turkeys. Market value $114.0 million. Some firewood marketed.

Vital Statistics, annual: Births, 387; deaths, 526; marriages, 166; divorces, 136.

Race/Ethnicity: Anglo, 67.2%; Hispanic, 22.0%; Black, 5.7%; Asian, 0.5%; Other, 4.5%.

HILLSBORO (8,305) county seat; agribusiness, varied manufacturing, retail, outlet center, tourism, antiques malls; Hill College; hospital; Cell Block museum, restored courthouse; Cotton Pickin' Fair in September.

WHITNEY (2,033) manufacturing, stone works, government/services; hospital; museum; Pioneer Days in October.

Other towns include: **Abbott** (357); **Aquilla** (104); **Blum** (388); **Brandon** (75); **Bynum** (172); **Carl's Corner** (209); **Covington** (270); **Hubbard** (1,405) agriculture, machine shop, antiques, museum, library, Magnolias & Mistletoe Victorian Christmas celebration; **Irene** (170); **Itasca** (1,625); **Malone** (240); **Mertens** (149); **Mount Calm** (290); **Penelope** (182).

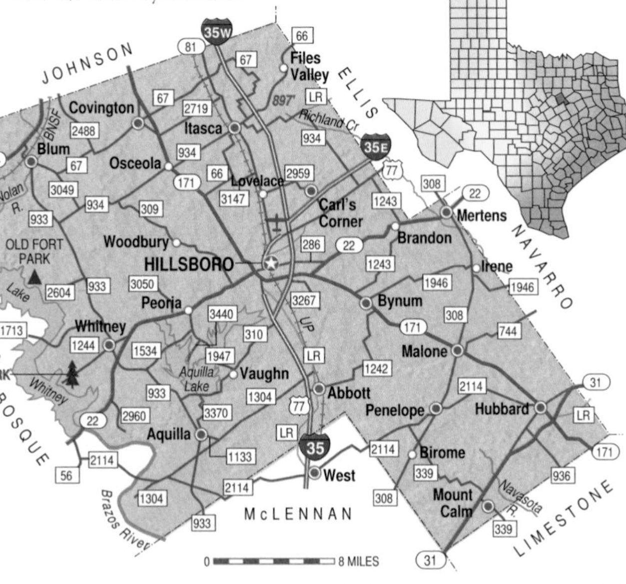

Population	36,471
Change from 2010	3.9%
Area (sq. mi.)	985.7
Land Area (sq. mi.)	958.9
Altitude (ft.)	417–897
Rainfall (in.)	38.7
Jan. mean min (°F)	35.9
July mean max (°F)	94.9

Civ. Labor	17,859
Unemployed	3.9%
Wages	$155,868,817

Per Capita Income	$49,968
Property Value	$7,083,156,356
Retail Sales	$530,077,121

The Lake Whitney Dam on the Brazos River. Photo by the U.S. Army Corps of Engineers, Public Domain

Hockley County

Physical Features: South Plains, numerous playas, drains to Yellow House Draw; loam, sandy loam soils.

Economy: Extensive oil, gas production and services; manufacturing; varied agribusiness.

History: Comanches displaced Apaches in the early 1700s. Large ranches of 1880s brought few residents. Homesteaders arrived after 1900. County created in 1876 from Bexar, Young districts; organized in 1921. Named for the Republic of Texas secretary of war Gen. G.W. Hockley.

Recreation: Sip & Swirl in June; Festival of Lights on the Square; Clovis Horse Sales.

Minerals: Oil, gas, stone; one of leading oil counties with more than 1 billion barrels produced.

Agriculture: Cotton, grain sorghum; cattle, hogs raised; substantial irrigation. Market value $92.0 million.

Vital Statistics, annual: Births, 283; deaths, 324; marriages, 98; divorces, 45.

Race/Ethnicity: Anglo, 45.3%; Hispanic, 49.3%; Black, 2.6%; Asian, 0.2%; Other, 2.5%.

LEVELLAND (12,665) county seat; oil, cotton, cattle center; government/services; hospital; South Plains College; South Plains Bluegrass Music Festival in July.

Other towns include: **Anton** (883); **Opdyke West** (217); **Pep** (30); **Ropesville** (418); **Smyer** (433); **Sundown** (1,265); **Whitharral** (73).

Population	21,363
Change from 2010	–6.9%
Area (sq. mi.)	908.6
Land Area (sq. mi.)	908.4
Altitude (ft.)	3,300–3,730
Rainfall (in.)	18.3
Jan. mean min (°F)	26.7
July mean max (°F)	91.4
Civ. Labor	10,781
Unemployed	3.7%
Wages	$152,092,258
Per Capita Income	$52,586
Property Value	$3,931,290,925
Retail Sales	$298,837,962

Hood County

Physical Features: Hilly; broken by Paluxy, Brazos rivers; sandy loam soils; Lake Granbury, Squaw Creek Reservoir.

Economy: Tourism, commuting to Fort Worth and Dallas, nuclear power plant, agriculture.

History: Lipan Apache and Comanche area. Anglo-American settlers arrived in the late 1840s. County created in 1866 from Johnson and Erath counties, organized the same year; named for Confederate Gen. John B. Hood.

Recreation: Lakes, fishing, scenic areas; summer theater; Gen. Granbury's Bean & Rib cookoff in March; Acton historic site; hike & bike trail.

Minerals: Oil, gas, stone.

Agriculture: Hay, turfgrass, beef cattle, nursery crops, pecans, peaches; some irrigation. Market value $18.9 million.

Vital Statistics, annual: Births, 591; deaths, 900; marriages, 301; divorces, 190.

Race/Ethnicity: Anglo, 80.9%; Hispanic, 12.9%; Black, 0.8%; Asian, 0.8%; Other, 4.6%.

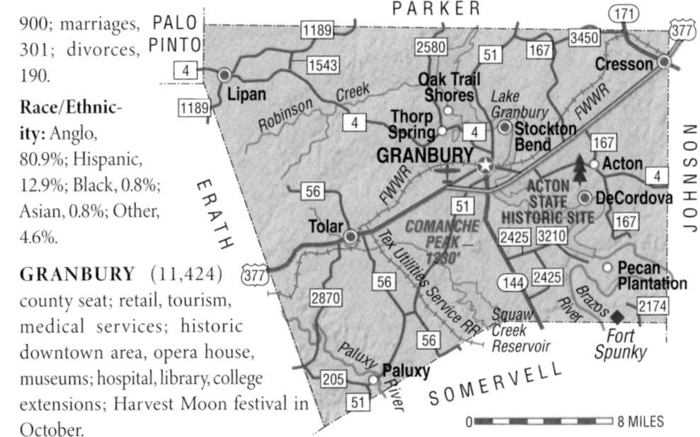

GRANBURY (11,424) county seat; retail, tourism, medical services; historic downtown area, opera house, museums; hospital, library, college extensions; Harvest Moon festival in October.

Other towns include: **Acton** (1,129) grave of Elizabeth Crockett, wife of Davy; **Cresson** (1,849); **DeCordova** (3,104); **Lipan** (520); **Oak Trail Shores** (2,778); **Pecan Plantation** (6,607); **Stockton Bend** (397); **Tolar** (989).

Population	64,222
Change from 2010	25.5%
Area (sq. mi.)	436.8
Land Area (sq. mi.)	420.6
Altitude (ft.)	600–1,230
Rainfall (in.)	35.2
Jan. mean min (°F)	33.1
July mean max (°F)	94.7
Civ. Labor	29,922
Unemployed	3.7%
Wages	$230,448,516
Per Capita Income	$60,912
Property Value	$13,595,564,961
Retail Sales	$1,381,121,710

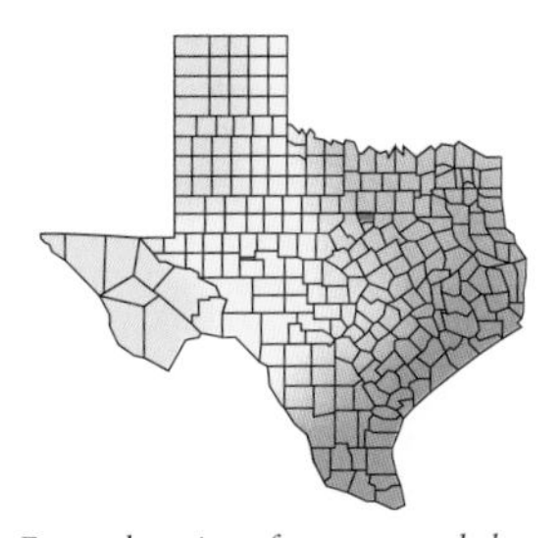

For explanation of sources, symbols, and abbreviations, see p. 207 and foldout map.

The Southwest Dairy Museum in Sulphur Springs. Photo by Michael Barera, CC by SA 4.0

Hopkins County

Physical Features: Varied timber, including pines; drains north to South Sulphur River; Cooper Lake (also known as Jim Chapman Lake), Sulphur Springs Lake; light, sandy to heavier black soils.

Economy: Agribusiness, feed mills; varied manufacturing.

History: Caddo area, displaced by Cherokees, who in turn were forced out by President Lamar in 1839. First Anglo-American settlement in 1837. County created in 1846 from Lamar and Nacogdoches counties, organized the same year; named for pioneer Hopkins family.

Recreation: Fishing, hunting; state park, lake activities; dairy museum; dairy festival in June; stew contest in September.

Minerals: Lignite coal.

Agriculture: Dairies, beef cattle, hay (first in acreage). Market value $253.7 million. Firewood and hardwood lumber marketed.

Vital Statistics, annual: Births, 445; deaths, 523; marriages, 255; divorces, 121.

Race/Ethnicity: Anglo, 70.6%; Hispanic, 17.6%; Black, 6.5%; Asian, 0.8%; Other, 4.6%.

SULPHUR SPRINGS (15,995) county seat; dairy farming, equine center, food processing and distribution, varied manufacturing, tourism; hospital; dairy museum, library, heritage park, music box gallery, civic center.

Other towns include: **Brashear** (280), **Como** (732), **Cumby** (695), **Dike** (170), **Pickton** (300), **Saltillo** (200), **Sulphur Bluff** (280), **Tira** (327).

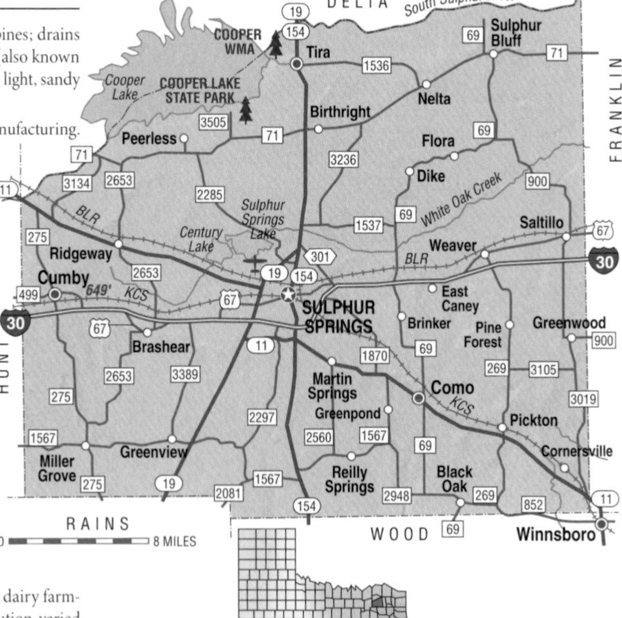

For explanation of sources, symbols, and abbreviations, see p. 207 and foldout map.

Population	37,211
Change from 2010	5.8%
Area (sq. mi.)	792.8
Land Area (sq. mi.)	767.2
Altitude (ft.)	340–649

Rainfall (in.)	46.5
Jan. mean min (°F)	36.0
July mean max (°F)	93.0
Civ. Labor	18,388
Unemployed	3.5%

Wages	$172,075,943
Per Capita Income	$50,272
Property Value	$5,057,474,554
Retail Sales	$859,640,544

Houston County

Physical Features: East Texas county over half forested; rolling terrain, draining to Neches, Trinity rivers; timber production.

Economy: Livestock, timber, government/services, manufacturing, tourism.

History: Caddo group attracted mission San Francisco de los Tejas in 1690. Spanish town of Bucareli established in 1774. Both lasted only a few years. Anglo-American settlers arrived in the 1820s. County created in 1837 from Nacogdoches County by Republic, organized the same year; named for Sam Houston. Cotton plantations before the Civil War had many slaves.

Recreation: Fishing, hunting; national forest; Mission Tejas State Park; 75 historical markers; Houston County Lake.

Minerals: Oil, gas, gravel.

Agriculture: Cattle, hay, watermelons, some cotton and corn. Market value $64.5 million. Hunting leases. Timber principal income source.

Vital Statistics, annual: Births, 187; deaths, 355; marriages, 96; divorces, 21.

Race/Ethnicity: Anglo, 58.7%; Hispanic, 13.9%; Black, 23.4%; Asian, 0.6%; Other, 3.3%.

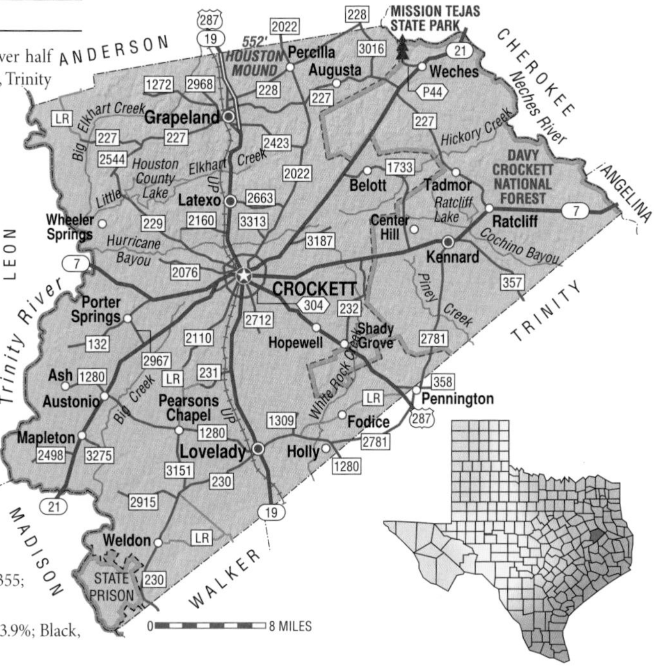

CROCKETT (6,406) county seat; timber, steel and plastic products, clothing manufacturing, hospital; historic sites; Black Expo in February; fiddlers festival in June.

Other towns include: **Grapeland** (1,493) steel, agribusiness, oil and gas, Peanut Festival in October; **Kennard** (280); **Latexo** (242); **Lovelady** (587) Lovefest in February; **Ratcliff** (106).

Population	22,241
Change from 2010	–6.3%
Area (sq. mi.)	1,236.6
Land Area (sq. mi.)	1,230.9
Altitude (ft.)	150–552
Rainfall (in.)	47.3
Jan. mean min (°F)	38.0

July mean max (°F)	93.6
Civ. Labor	10,548
Unemployed	3.6%
Wages	$117,748,504
Per Capita Income	$48,835
Property Value	$4,606,652,030
Retail Sales	$193,316,595

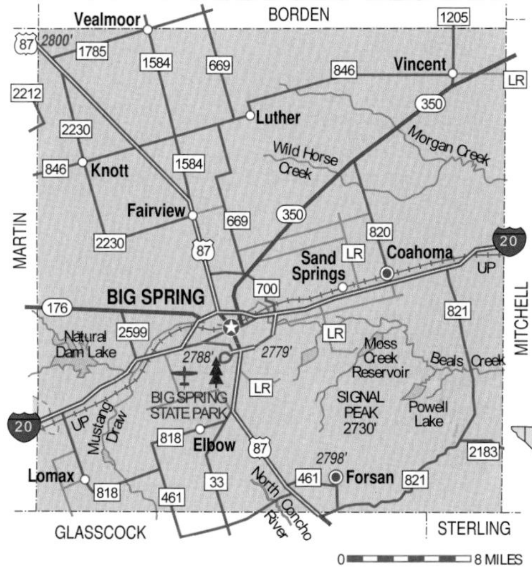

Howard County

Physical Features: On edge of Llano Estacado; sandy loam soils; Natural Dam Lake.

Economy: Agriculture, petrochemicals, government/services.

History: Pawnee and Comanche area. Anglo-American settlement began in 1870. Oil boom in the mid-1920s. County named for V.E. Howard, legislator; created in 1876 from Bexar, Young districts; organized in 1882.

Recreation: Lakes, state park; campground in Comanche Trail Park, Native Plant Trail, museum, historical sites, Pops in the Park in July.

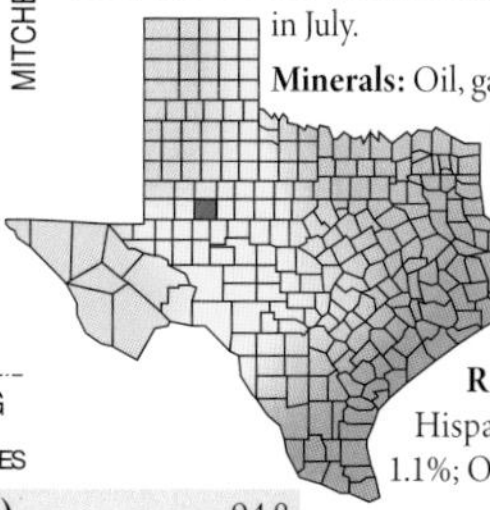

Minerals: Oil, gas, sand, gravel, and stone.

Agriculture: Cotton, beef, hay. Market value $26.9 million.

Vital Statistics, annual: Births, 427; deaths, 466; marriages, 177; divorces, 87.

Race/Ethnicity: Anglo, 45.0%; Hispanic, 46.4%; Black, 4.4%; Asian, 1.1%; Other, 3.2%.

BIG SPRING (25,735) county seat; agriculture, petrochemicals, varied manufacturing; hospitals including a state institution and Veterans Administration hospital; federal prison; Howard College; railroad plaza.

Other towns include: **Coahoma** (914), **Forsan** (219), **Knott** (200), and **Sand Springs** (953).

Population	34,128
Change from 2010	–2.5%
Area (sq. mi.)	904.2
Land Area (sq. mi.)	900.8
Altitude (ft.)	2,180–2,800
Rainfall (in.)	19.6
Jan. mean min (°F)	32.9

July mean max (°F)	94.8
Civ. Labor	13,114
Unemployed	5.1%
Wages	$192,886,415
Per Capita Income	$51,007
Property Value	$10,091,841,192
Retail Sales	$577,371,483

A sign for the Comanche Trail Park in Howard County. Photo by Billy Hathorn, CC by SA 3.0

Hudspeth County

Physical Features: Plateau, basin terrain, draining to salt lakes; Rio Grande; mostly rocky, alkaline, clay soils and sandy loam soils, except alluvial along Rio Grande; desert, mountain vegetation. Fertile agricultural valley.

Economy: Agribusiness, mining, tourism, hunting leases.

History: Mescalero Apache area. Fort Quitman established in 1858 to protect routes to west. Railroad in 1881 brought Anglo-American settlers. Political turmoil in Mexico (1912–1929) brought more settlers from Mexico. County named for Texas political leader Claude B. Hudspeth; created in 1917 from El Paso County, organized the same year.

Recreation: Scenic drives; fort sites; hot springs; salt basin; white sands; hunting; birding; part of Guadalupe Mountains National Park, containing unique plant life, canyons.

Minerals: Talc, stone, gypsum, rare earth minerals.

Agriculture: Most income from cotton, vegetables, hay, alfalfa; beef cattle raised; 18,000 acres irrigated. Market value $17.4 million.

Vital Statistics, annual: Births, 43; deaths, 39; marriages, 0; divorces, NA.

Race/Ethnicity: Anglo, 34.2%; Hispanic, 63.6%; Black, 0.2%; Asian, 0.3%; Other, 1.7%.

Population	3,287
Change from 2010	–5.4%
Area (sq. mi.)	4,571.8
Land Area (sq. mi.)	4,571.0
Altitude (ft.)	3,117–7,484
Rainfall (in.)	8.3
Jan. mean min (°F)	28.7
July mean max (°F)	96.3
Civ. Labor	1,889
Unemployed	4.0%
Wages	$24,092,029
Per Capita Income	$42,500
Property Value	$965,850,888
Retail Sales	$25,483,831

SIERRA BLANCA (676) county seat; ranching center, tourist stop on interstate highway; adobe courthouse; 4th of July fair, livestock show in January.

Other towns include: **Acala** (36); **Dell City** (367) agriculture, government/services, telephone co-op; some of largest water wells in state, Dell Valley Hudspeth fair in September, and **Fort Hancock** (990).

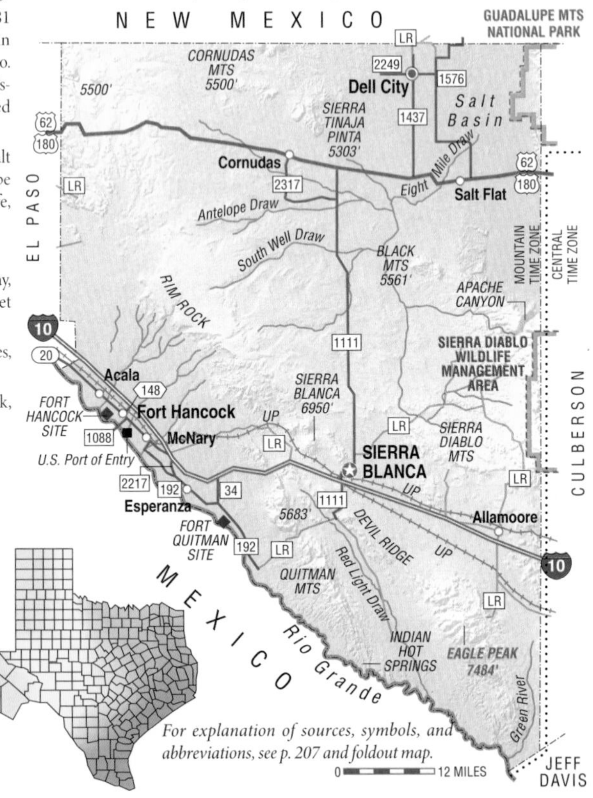

For explanation of sources, symbols, and abbreviations, see p. 207 and foldout map.

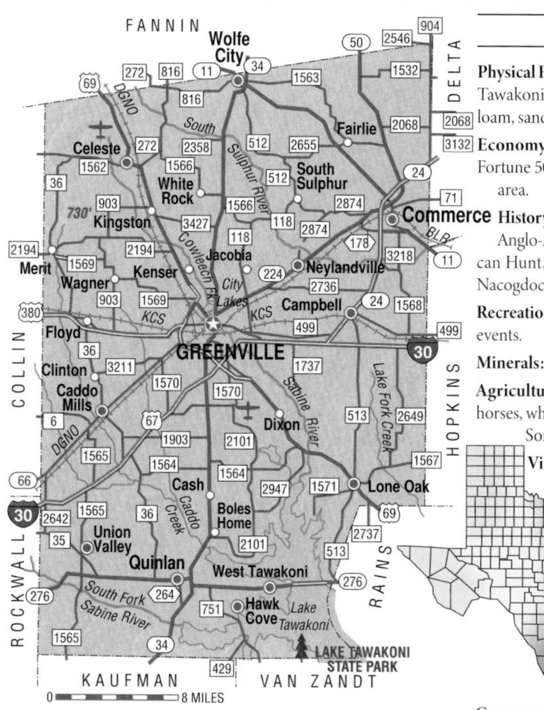

Hunt County

Physical Features: Level to rolling surface; Sabine, Sulphur rivers; Lake Tawakoni, Greenville City Lakes; mostly heavy Blackland soil, some loam, sandy loams.

Economy: Education, varied manufacturing, agribusiness; several Fortune 500 companies in county; many residents employed in Dallas area.

History: Caddo Indians gone by 1790s. Kiowa bands in the area when Anglo-American settlers arrived in 1839. County named for Memucan Hunt, Republic secretary of navy; created in 1846 from Fannin, Nacogdoches counties, organized the same year.

Recreation: Lake Tawakoni sports; Texas A&M University–Commerce events.

Minerals: Sand and white rock, gas, oil.

Agriculture: Cattle, forage, greenhouse crops, top revenue sources; horses, wheat, oats, cotton, grain sorghum. Market value $55.3 million. Some firewood sold.

Vital Statistics, annual: Births, 1,211; deaths, 1,163; marriages, 473; divorces, 201.

Race/Ethnicity: Anglo, 65.6%; Hispanic, 19.7%; Black, 7.8%; Asian, 1.0%; Other, 5.9%.

GREENVILLE (29,578) county seat; varied manufacturing, retail trade, health and government services, commuters to Dallas; hospital; branch of Paris Junior College; cotton museum, Audie Murphy exhibit; fiddle festival in October.

Commerce (8,828) Texas A&M University–Commerce, government/services, varied manufacturing; emergency medical center; planetarium, children's museum; Bois d'Arc Bash in September.

Other towns include: **Caddo Mills** (2,321); **Campbell** (554); **Celeste** (822); **Hawk Cove** (462); **Lone Oak** (725); **Merit** (225); **Neylandville** (68); **Quinlan** (1,455); **Union Valley** (398); **West Tawakoni** (1,932) tourist center, light industry, Lakefest in October; **Wolfe City** (1,406) manufacturing, antiques shops, commuters to Dallas, museum, library, car and truck show in October.

Population	103,394
Change from 2010	20.0%
Area (sq. mi.)	882.0
Land Area (sq. mi.)	840.3
Altitude (ft.)	437–730
Rainfall (in.)	47.0
Jan. mean min (°F)	35.3
July mean max (°F)	96.0
Civ. Labor	46,815

For explanation of sources, symbols, and abbreviations, see p. 207 and foldout map.

Unemployed	3.9%
Wages	$424,649,589
Per Capita Income	$46,801
Property Value	$18,357,493,925
Retail Sales	$1,779,671,143

Clymer Meadow Preserve in Hunt County is a prime example of Texas Blackland Prairie. Photo by Wilafa, CC by SA 4.0

Hutchinson County

Physical Features: High Plains, broken by Canadian River and tributaries, Lake Meredith; fertile valleys along streams.

Economy: Oil and gas, petrochemicals, carbon black plants.

History: Antelope Creek Indian area. Later, Comanches were driven out in U.S. cavalry campaigns of 1874-75. Adobe Walls site of two Indian attacks, in 1864 and 1874. Ranching began in the late 1870s. Oil boom in the early 1920s. County created in 1876 from Bexar Territory; organized in 1901; named for pioneer jurist Anderson Hutchinson.

Recreation: Lake Meredith activities, fishing, camping; Adobe Walls, historic Indian battle site; Alibates Flint Quarries.

Minerals: Oil and gas.

Agriculture: Beef cattle, corn, wheat; about 35,000 acres irrigated. Market value $44.9 million. Hunting important.

Vital Statistics, annual: Births, 231; deaths, 315; marriages, 90; divorces, 70.

Race/Ethnicity: Anglo, 66.9%; Hispanic, 24.1%; Black, 2.0%; Asian, 0.5%; Other, 6.6%.

STINNETT (1,638) county seat; petroleum refining, farm center.

BORGER (12,419) petroleum refining, petrochemicals, nitrogen plant, carbon-black production, oil-field servicing, retail center; Frank Phillips College; museum; hospital; Downtown Merchants Beach Bash in June.

Other cities include: **Fritch** (1,851), **Sanford** (134).

For explanation of sources, symbols, and abbreviations, see p. 207 and foldout map.

Population	20,495
Change from 2010	–7.5%
Area (sq. mi.)	895.0
Land Area (sq. mi.)	887.4
Altitude (ft.)	2,600–3,380
Rainfall (in.)	22.5
Jan. mean min (°F)	27.6
July mean max (°F)	93.7
Civ. Labor	8,487
Unemployed	4.5%
Wages	$133,587,855
Per Capita Income	$50,130
Property Value	$4,245,729,405
Retail Sales	$263,311,135

Irion County

Physical Features: West Texas county with hilly surface, broken by Middle Concho River, tributaries; clay, sandy soils.

Economy: Ranching, oil, gas production, wildlife recreation.

History: Tonkawa Indian area. Anglo-American settlement began in the late 1870s. County named for Republic leader R.A. Irion; created in 1889 from Tom Green County, organized the same year.

Recreation: Hunting; historic sites, including Dove Creek battlefield and stagecoach stops, old Sherwood courthouse built 1900; hunters appreciation dinner in November.

Minerals: Oil, gas.

Agriculture: Beef cattle, sheep, goats; hay, wheat. Market value $9.3 million.

Vital Statistics, annual: Births, 12; deaths, 19; marriages, 8; divorces, 3.

Race/Ethnicity: Anglo, 73.5%; Hispanic, 23.1%; Black, 0.4%; Asian, 0.0%; Other, 3.0%.

MERTZON (771) county seat; farm center, wool warehousing.

Other towns include: **Barnhart** (110).

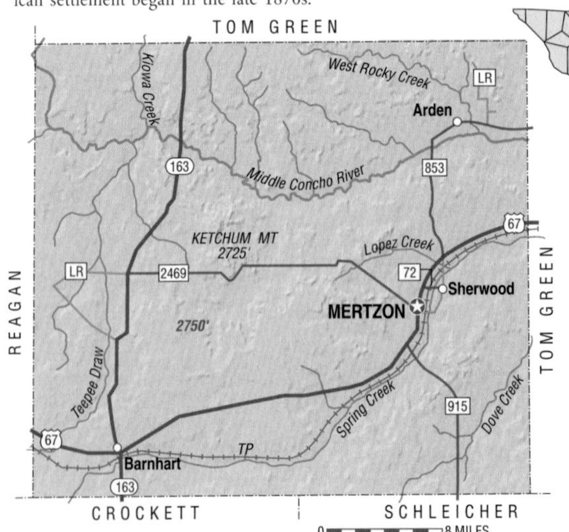

Population	1,552
Change from 2010	–2.9%
Area (sq. mi.)	1,051.6
Land Area (sq. mi.)	1,051.6
Altitude (ft.)	2,000–2,750
Rainfall (in.)	19.1
Jan. mean min (°F)	29.8
July mean max (°F)	95.3
Civ. Labor	790
Unemployed	3.0%
Wages	$16,273,425
Per Capita Income	$78,988
Property Value	$3,409,819,526
Retail Sales	$4,030,272

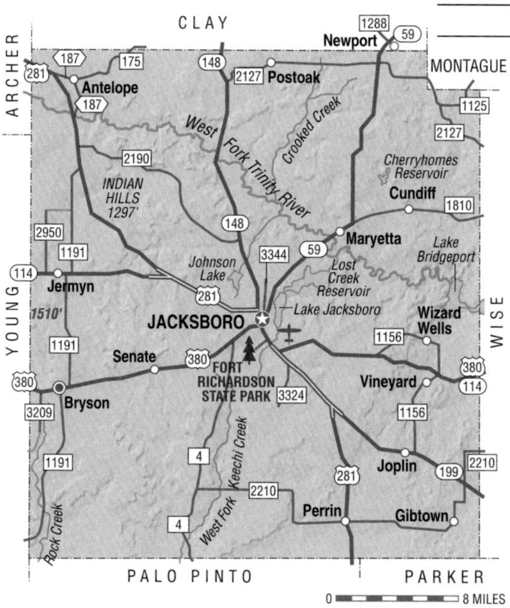

Jack County

Physical Features: Rolling Cross Timbers, broken by West Fork of the Trinity, other streams; sandy, dark brown, loam soils; Lake Bridgeport, Lake Jacksboro, Lost Creek Reservoir.

Economy: Petroleum production, oil-field services, livestock, manufacturing, tourism.

History: A Caddo and Comanche borderland. The first Anglo-American settlers arrived in 1855 as part of the Peters Colony. County named for brothers P.C. and W.H. Jack, who were leaders in Texas' independence effort; created in 1856 from Cooke County; organized in 1857 with Mesquiteville (original name of Jacksboro) as the county seat.

Recreation: Hunting, wildlife leases; fishing; lake activities; Fort Richardson, Texas 4-H Museum (county is birthplace of 4-H clubs in Texas), other historic sites; Lost Creek Reservoir State Trailway.

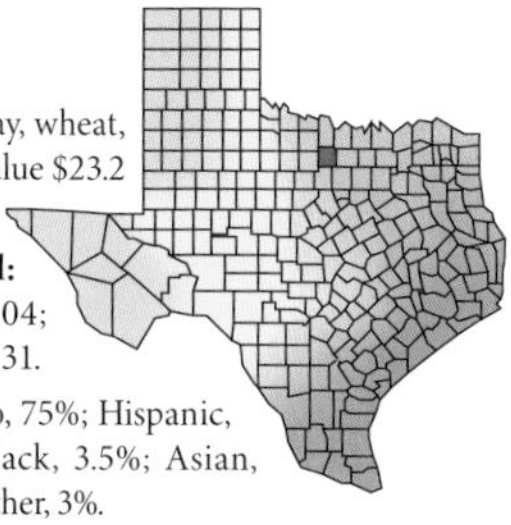

Minerals: Oil, gas.

Agriculture: Cattle, hay, wheat, goats, sheep. Market value $23.2 million. Firewood sold.

Vital Statistics, annual: Births, 80; deaths, 104; marriages, 46; divorces, 31.

Race/Ethnicity: Anglo, 75%; Hispanic, 18%; Black, 3.5%; Asian, 0.5%; Other, 3%.

Population	8,712
Change from 2010	-3.7%
Area (sq. mi.)	920.1
Land Area (sq. mi.)	910.7
Altitude (ft.)	836–1,510
Rainfall (in.)	32.7
Jan. mean min (°F)	31.8

July mean max (°F)	94.2
Civ. Labor	3,443
Unemployed	3.8%
Wages	$38,871,596
Per Capita Income	$45,263
Property Value	$3,196,941,225
Retail Sales	$75,611,661

JACKSBORO (4,209) county seat; agribusiness, petroleum production and services, tourism; hospital; library; Fort Richardson Living History Days in April.

Other towns include: **Bryson** (447), **Jermyn** (75), **Perrin** (54).

The Hutchinson County Veterans Memorial in Borger. Photo by Billy Hathorn, CC by SA 3.0

Jackson County

Physical Features: South coastal county of prairie and motts of trees; loam, clay, black soils; drains to creeks, rivers, bays.

Economy: Plastics manufacturing, agribusinesses.

History: Karankawa area. Lipan Apaches and Tonkawas arrived later. Six of Austin's Old Three Hundred families settled in the 1820s. Mexican municipality, created in 1835, became an original county the following year; named for U.S. President Andrew Jackson. Oil discovered in 1934.

Recreation: Hunting, fishing, birding (southern bald eagle in area); historic sites; Texana Museum; Lake Texana, Brackenridge Plantation campground, state park; Chili Spill in November in Edna, county fair, rodeo in October.

Minerals: Oil and natural gas.

Agriculture: Cotton, cattle, corn, rice; 13,000 acres of rice irrigated. Market value $85.0 million.

Vital Statistics, annual: Births, 201; deaths, 183; marriages, 52; divorces, 42.

Race/Ethnicity: Anglo, 56.8%; Hispanic, 32.2%; Black, 6.3%; Asian, 1.1%; Other, 3.7%.

EDNA (5,944) county seat; oil and gas, chemical plants, agriculture; hospital, library, museums.

Other towns include: **Francitas** (125); **Ganado** (1,982) oil and gas, agriculture, historic movie theater, Crawfish Festival in May; **LaSalle** (110); **La Ward** (189); **Lolita** (715); **Vanderbilt** (492).

Population	15,121
Change from 2010	7.4%
Area (sq. mi.)	856.9
Land Area (sq. mi.)	829.4
Altitude (ft.)	sea level–155
Rainfall (in.)	41.4
Jan. mean min (°F)	47.7
July mean max (°F)	91.0
Civ. Labor	7,127
Unemployed	3.5%
Wages	$75,256,768
Per Capita Income	$51,971
Property Value	$5,032,822,066
Retail Sales	$173,257,921

Jasper County

Physical Features: East Texas county; hilly to level; national forest; Sam Rayburn Reservoir, B.A. Steinhagen Lake; Neches River.

Economy: Timber industries; nature tourism, government/services.

History: Caddo and Atakapa Indian area. Land grants to John R. Bevil and Lorenzo de Zavala in 1829. County created in 1836, organized in 1837, from Mexican municipality; named for Sgt. William Jasper of American Revolution.

Recreation: Lake activities; hunting, fishing; state park, Big Thicket; Butterfly Festival in October at Jasper.

Minerals: Oil, gas produced.

Agriculture: Cattle, plant nurseries, fruits, vegetables. Market value $9.1 million. Timber is major income producer. Hunting leases and fishing tournaments are major income producers.

Vital Statistics, annual: Births, 352; deaths, 531; marriages, 195; divorces, 77.

Race/Ethnicity: Anglo, 72.1%; Hispanic, 6.7%; Black, 16.9%; Asian, 0.3%; Other, 3.9%.

JASPER (7,285) county seat; tourism, government/services, timber; hospital; Angelina College extension; museum; Azalea Festival in March.

Other towns include: **Browndell** (157); **Buna** (1,689) timber, oil, polka dot house, redbud festival in March; **Evadale** (1,168); **Kirbyville** (2,003) electric co-op, government/services, retail, commuters, Calaboose museum, library, Magnolia Festival in April; **Sam Rayburn** (1,100).

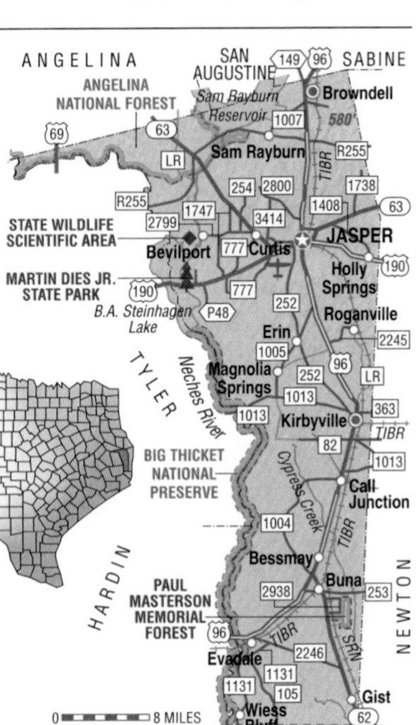

Population	32,975
Change from 2010	-7.7%
Area (sq. mi.)	969.7
Land Area (sq. mi.)	938.9
Altitude (ft.)	10–580
Rainfall (in.)	60.0
Jan. mean min (°F)	42.9
July mean max (°F)	93.2
Civ. Labor	12,645
Unemployed	6.4%
Wages	$117,363,731
Per Capita Income	$49,475
Property Value	$5,746,260,193
Retail Sales	$494,450,379

Boykin Creek in the Angelina National Forest, Jasper County. Photo by William L. Farr, CC by SA 4.0

Jeff Davis County

Physical Features: Highest average elevation in Texas; peaks (Mt. Livermore, 8,378 ft.), canyons, plateaus; intermountain wash, clay, loam soils; cedars, oaks in highlands.

Economy: Tourism, agriculture, McDonald Observatory.

History: Mescalero Apaches in area when Antonio de Espejo explored in 1583. U.S. Army established Fort Davis in 1854 to protect routes to west. Civilian settlers followed, including Manuel Músquiz, a political refugee from Mexico. County named for Jefferson Davis, U.S. Secretary of War, Confederate president; created 1887 from Presidio County, organized the same year.

Recreation: Scenic drives including loop along Limpia Creek, Mt. Livermore, Blue Mountain; hunting; Fort Davis National Historic Site; state park; McDonald Observatory on Mt. Locke; Davis Mountain Preserve; Chihuahuan Desert Research Institute; hummingbird celebration in August.

Minerals: Not significant.

Agriculture: Greenhouse tomatoes, beef cattle, horses, meat goats, vitaculture. Market value $29.3 million. Hunting leases important.

Vital Statistics, annual: Births, 17; deaths, 29; marriages, 12; divorces, NA.

Race/Ethnicity: Anglo, 64.2%; Hispanic, 30.7%; Black, 0.0%; Asian, 0.7%; Other, 4.4%.

FORT DAVIS (1,012), county seat; tourism, government/services, retail; library, Overland and Old Spanish trail museums; "Coolest July 4th in Texas" celebration.

Other town: **Valentine** (108).

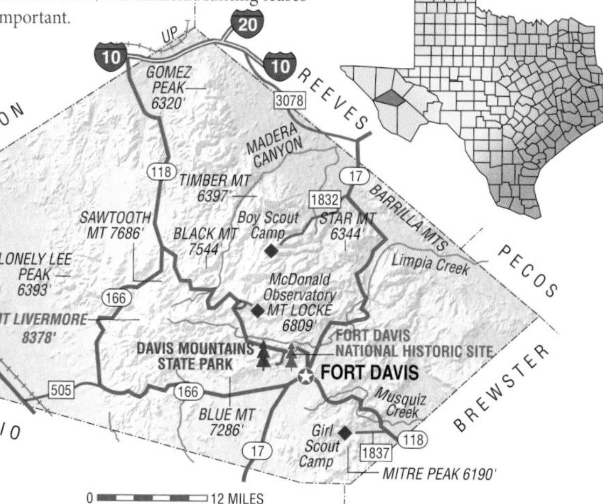

For explanation of sources, symbols, and abbreviations, see p. 207 and foldout map.

Population	1,949
Change from 2010	–16.8%
Area (sq. mi.)	2,264.6
Land Area (sq. mi.)	2,264.6
Altitude (ft.)	3,162–8,378

Rainfall (in.)	15.5
Jan. mean min (°F)	32.4
July mean max (°F)	90.2
Civ. Labor	1,016
Unemployed	3.4%

Wages	$8,916,683
Per Capita Income	$59,302
Property Value	$738,559,488
Retail Sales	$10,068,135

Jefferson County

Physical Features: Gulf Coast grassy plain, with timber in northwest; beach sands, sandy loams, black clay soils; drains to Neches River, Gulf of Mexico.

Economy: Government/services, petrochemical and other chemical plants, shipbuilding, steel mill, port activity, oil-field supplies.

History: Atakapas and Orcoquizas, whose numbers were reduced by epidemics or migration before Anglo-American settlers arrived in the 1820s. Cajuns arrived in the 1840s; Europeans in the 1850s. Antebellum slaveholding area. County created in 1836 from Mexican municipality; organized in 1837; named for U.S. President Thomas Jefferson.

Recreation: Beaches, fresh and saltwater fishing; duck, goose hunting; water activities; Dick Dowling Monument and Park; Spindletop site, energy, fire museums; saltwater lake; J.D. Murphree WMA, McFaddin wildlife refuge, Texas Point wildlife refuge; Lamar University events; historic sites; South Texas Fair in March-April.

Minerals: Large producer of oil, gas, sulfur, salt, sand and gravel.

Agriculture: Rice, hay, beef cattle, crawfish; considerable rice irrigated. Market value $32.3 million. Timber sales significant.

Vital Statistics, annual: Births, 3,192; deaths, 2,958; marriages, 1,450; divorces, 410.

Race/Ethnicity: Anglo, 37.4%; Hispanic, 23%; Black, 32.7%; Asian, 3.9%; Other, 3%.

BEAUMONT (112,556) county seat; oil and gas production, government/services, engineering and industrial services, port; Lamar University, Institute of Technology; hospitals; entertainment district; Neches River Festival in April.

Port Arthur (55,724) oil, chemical activities, shrimping and crawfishing, shipping, offshore marine, tourism; hospitals; museum; prison; Asian New Year Tet, Janis Joplin Birthday Bash in January. Sabine Pass and Port Acres are now within the city limits of Port Arthur.

Other towns include: **Beauxart Gardens** (864); **Bevil Oaks** (1,058); **Central Gardens** (3,377); **China** (1,240); **Fannett** (2,290); **Groves** (16,915) retail center, some manufacturing, government/services, tourism; hospital, pecan festival in October; **Hamshire** (1,420).

Also, **Nederland** (18,331) petrochemical refining, retail center, education; Windmill and French/Acadian museums; extended-care hospital; Tex Ritter memorial and park; heritage festival in March (city founded by Dutch immigrants in 1898).

Also, **Nome** (453); **Port Neches** (13,416) chemical and synthetic rubber industry, manufacturing, library, riverfront park with La Maison Beausoleil, RiverFest in May; **Taylor Landing** (278).

Population	253,704
Change from 2010	0.6%
Area (sq. mi.)	1,112.7
Land Area (sq. mi.)	876.3
Altitude (ft.)	sea level–49
Rainfall (in.)	62.1
Jan. mean min (°F)	45.8

July mean max (°F)	92.2
Civ. Labor	101,171
Unemployed	6.2%
Wages	$1,994,799,086
Per Capita Income	$48,243
Property Value	$39,701,879,150
Retail Sales	$4,718,249,859

For explanation of sources, symbols, and abbreviations, see p. 207 and foldout map.

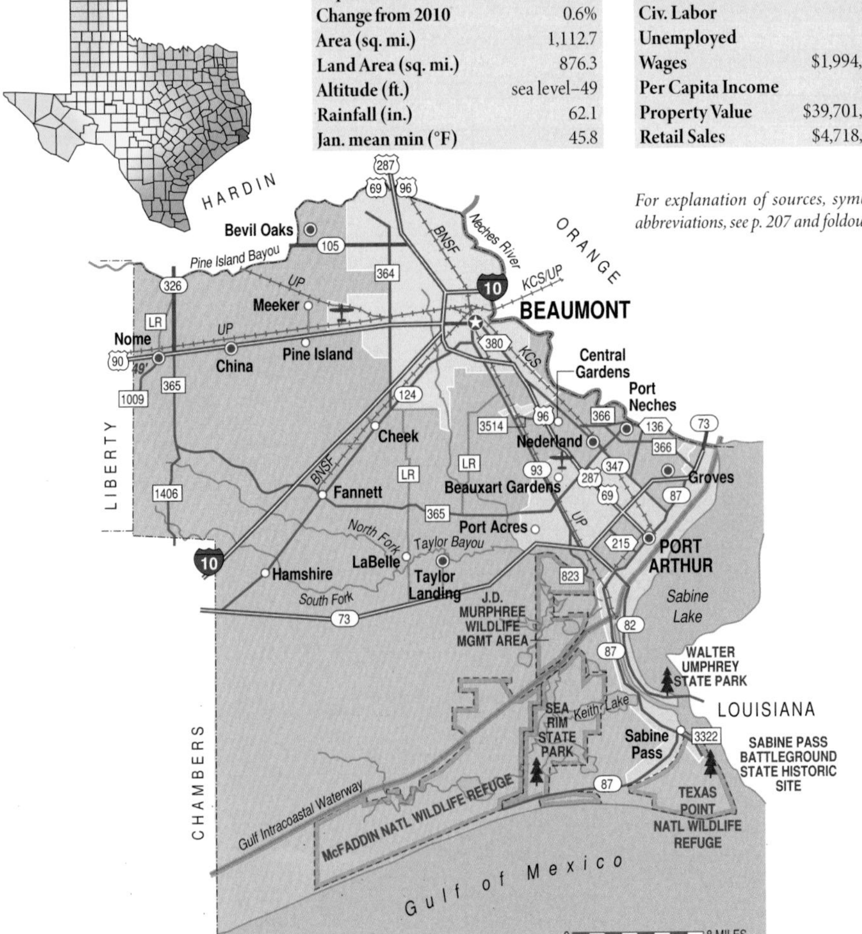

Jim Hogg County

Physical Features: South Texas county on rolling plain, with heavy brush cover; white blow sand and sandy loam; hilly, broken.

Economy: Oil, cattle operations.

History: Coahuiltecan area, then Lipan Apache. Spanish land grant in 1805 to Xavier Vela. County named for Gov. James Stephen Hogg; created and organized in 1913 from Brooks and Duval counties.

Recreation: White-tailed deer and bobwhite hunting.

Minerals: Oil and gas.

Agriculture: Cattle, hay, milk goats; some irrigation. Market value $10.4 million.

Vital Statistics, annual: Births, 56; deaths, 60; marriages, 19; divorces, 1.

Race/Ethnicity: Anglo, 8.6%; Hispanic, 88.5%; Black, 0.1%; Asian, 0.5%; Other, 2.3%.

HEBBRONVILLE (4,283) county seat; ranching, oil-field center.

Other towns include: **Las Lomitas** (90), **South Fork Estates** (38), and **Thompsonville** (216).

Population	4,801	**Rainfall (in.)**	22.7		
Change from 2010	–9.4%	**Jan. mean min (°F)**	47.9	**Wages**	$20,423,089
Area (sq. mi.)	1,136.2	**July mean max (°F)**	98.5	**Per Capita Income**	$43,336
Land Area (sq. mi.)	1,136.1	**Civ. Labor**	1,802	**Property Value**	$1,003,753,796
Altitude (ft.)	230–878	**Unemployed**	5.4%	**Retail Sales**	$41,835,906

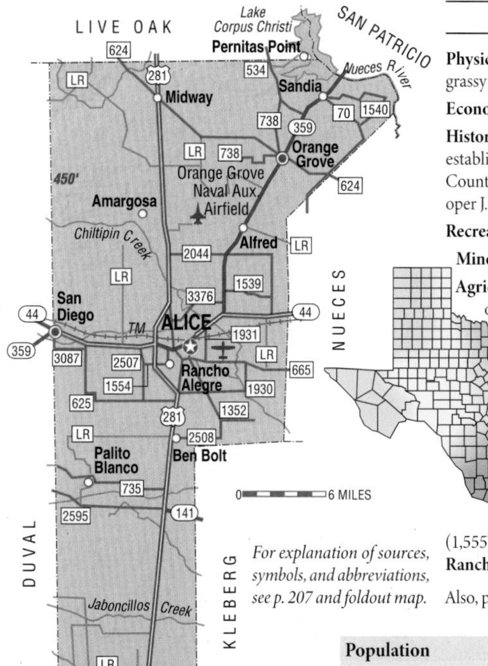

Jim Wells County

Physical Features: South Coastal Plains; level to rolling; sandy to dark soils; grassy with mesquite brush; Lake Corpus Christi.

Economy: Oil and gas production, agriculture, nature tourism.

History: Coahuiltecans, driven out by Lipan Apaches in 1775. Tomás Sánchez established settlement in 1754. Anglo-American settlement began in 1878. County created 1911 from Nueces County; organized 1912; named for developer J.B. Wells Jr.

Recreation: Hunting; fiestas; Tejano Roots hall of fame; South Texas museum.

Minerals: Oil, gas, caliche.

Agriculture: Cattle, sorghum, corn, cotton, dairies, goats, wheat, watermelons, sunflowers, peas, hay. Market value $121.6 million.

Vital Statistics, annual: Births, 540; deaths, 494; marriages, 140; divorces, 132.

Race/Ethnicity: Anglo, 17.9%; Hispanic, 79.3%; Black, 0.5%; Asian, 0.4%; Other, 2.0%.

ALICE (17,761) county seat; oil-field service center, agribusiness, government/services; hospital; Coastal Bend College campus; Fiesta Bandana (from original name of city) in May.

Other towns include: **Alfred** (274); **Amargosa** (125); **Ben Bolt** (1,555); **Orange Grove** (1,183); **Premont** (2,441) wildflower tour in spring; **Rancho Alegre** (1,561); **Sandia** (382).

Also, part [753] of **San Diego** (3,755, mostly in Duval County).

For explanation of sources, symbols, and abbreviations, see p. 207 and foldout map.

Population	38,847	**July mean max (°F)**	96.7
Change from 2010	–4.9%	**Civ. Labor**	15,401
Area (sq. mi.)	868.3	**Unemployed**	5.7%
Land Area (sq. mi.)	865.0	**Wages**	$179,296,295
Altitude (ft.)	50–450	**Per Capita Income**	$50,892
Rainfall (in.)	27.1	**Property Value**	$3,017,515,881
Jan. mean min (°F)	49.5	**Retail Sales**	$541,940,457

Johnson County

Physical Features: North central county drained by tributaries of Trinity, Brazos rivers; lakes; hilly, rolling, many soil types.

Economy: Agribusiness, railroad shops; manufacturing, distribution, lake activities, many residents employed in Fort Worth and Dallas; part of Fort Worth-Arlington metropolitan area.

History: No permanent Indian villages existed in the area. Anglo-American settlers arrived in the 1840s. County named for Col. M.T. Johnson of the Mexican War and Confederacy; created and organized in 1854. Formed from McLennan, Hill, and Navarro counties.

Recreation: Bird, deer hunting; water activities on Lake Pat Cleburne, Lake Whitney; state park; sports complex; museum; Chisholm Trail; Goatneck bike ride in July.

Minerals: Limestone, sand and gravel.

Agriculture: Cattle, hay, horses, dairies, cotton, sorghum, wheat, oats, hogs. Market value $57.9 million.

Vital Statistics, annual: Births, 2,123; deaths, 1,830; marriages, 926; divorces, 460.

Race/Ethnicity: Anglo, 66.3%; Hispanic, 23.7%; Black, 3.6%; Asian, 1.0%; Other, 5.5%.

CLEBURNE (31,999) county seat; manufacturing, oil and gas; hospital, library, museum; Hill College campus; Whistle Stop Christmas.

BURLESON (51,618, part in Tarrant County) agriculture, retail center; hospital.

Other towns include: **Alvarado** (5,111) County Pioneer Days; **Briaroaks** (508); **Coyote Flats** (349); **Cross Timber** (319); **Godley** (1,858); **Grandview** (1,889); **Joshua** (8,098) many residents work in Fort Worth; **Keene** (6,346) Southwestern Adventist University; **Lillian** (1,160); **Rio Vista** (1,078), and **Venus** (5,727).

Also, part [152] of **Cresson** (1,849, mostly in Hood County), and part [4,938] of **Mansfield** (74,368, mostly in Tarrant County).

Population	187,280
Change from 2010	24.1%
Area (sq. mi.)	734.5
Land Area (sq. mi.)	724.7
Altitude (ft.)	500–1,065

Rainfall (in.)	37.7
Jan. mean min (°F)	35.3
July mean max (°F)	93.5
Civ. Labor	89,046
Unemployed	3.5%

Wages	$757,772,490
Per Capita Income	$51,619
Property Value	$25,964,482,879
Retail Sales	$2,882,268,974

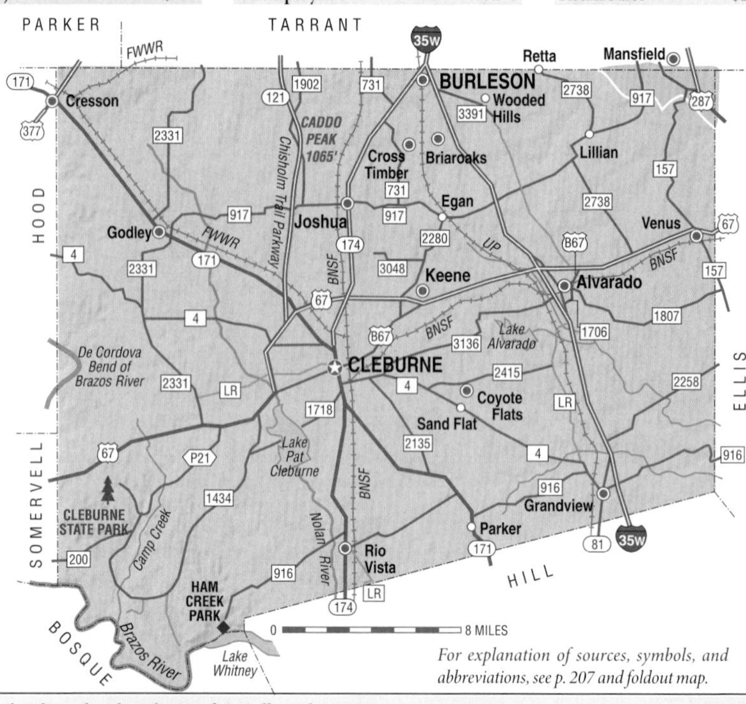

For explanation of sources, symbols, and abbreviations, see p. 207 and foldout map.

Sunset on Lake Alvarado. Photo by HeafMcCall, CC by SA 4.0

Jones County

Physical Features: West Texas Rolling Plains; drained by Brazos River fork, tributaries; Lake Fort Phantom Hill.

Economy: Agribusiness; government/services; varied manufacturing.

History: Comanches and other tribes hunted in the area. U.S. military presence began in 1851. Ranching established in the 1870s. County named for the last president of the Republic, Anson Jones; created in 1858 from Bexar and Bosque counties; re-created in 1876; organized in 1881.

Recreation: Lake activities, hunting, Fort Phantom Hill, Cowboy Reunion July 4 in Stamford.

Minerals: Oil, gas, sand and gravel, stone.

Agriculture: Cotton, wheat, sesame and peanuts; cattle. Some 3,500 acres irrigated for peanuts and hay. Market value $41.5 million.

Vital Statistics, annual: Births, 147; deaths, 262; marriages, 54; divorces, 41.

Race/Ethnicity: Anglo, 58.4%; Hispanic, 28%; Black, 10.1%; Asian, 0.6%; Other, 3%.

ANSON (2,347) county seat; farming center, government/services; hospital; old courthouse, opera house, museums; Cowboys Christmas Ball in December.

STAMFORD (2,977) trade center for three counties, hospital, historic homes, cowboy museum.

HAMLIN (1,879) farm and ranching, oil and gas, electricity/steam plant using mesquite trees, hunting; hospital; museums.

Other towns include: **Hawley** (566), **Lueders** (261) limestone quarries. Small part [5,307] of **Abilene**.

Population	19,873
Change from 2010	−1.6%
Area (sq. mi.)	937.1
Land Area (sq. mi.)	928.6
Altitude (ft.)	1,480–1,970
Rainfall (in.)	25.4
Jan. mean min (°F)	31.2

July mean max (°F)	94.5
Civ. Labor	5,826
Unemployed	4.3%
Wages	$39,464,460
Per Capita Income	$38,914
Property Value	$2,155,544,640
Retail Sales	$234,359,197

Karnes County

Physical Features: Sandy loam, dark clay, alluvial soils in rolling terrain; traversed by San Antonio River; mesquite, oak trees.

Economy: Oil and gas, agribusiness.

History: Coahuiltecan area. Spanish ranching began around 1750. Anglo-Americans arrived in 1840s; Polish in the 1850s. County created in 1854 from Bexar, Goliad, and San Patricio counties, organized the same year; named for Texas Revolutionary figure Henry W. Karnes.

Recreation: Old Helena restored courthouse, hunting, nature tourism, guest ranches.

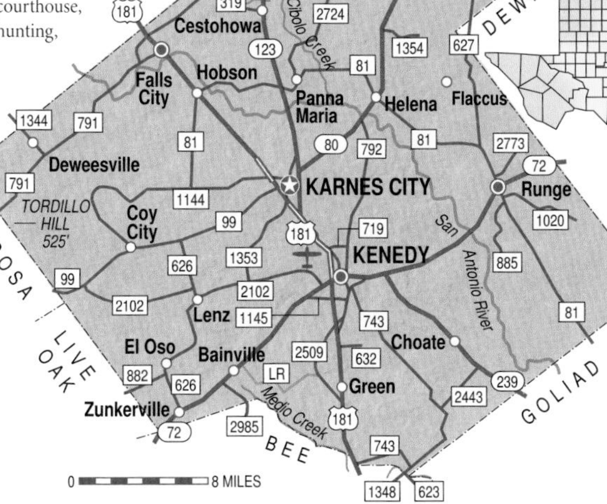

Minerals: Oil, gas, uranium.

Agriculture: Beef cattle, grain, cotton, hay. Market value $29.4 million.

Vital Statistics, annual: Births, 175; deaths, 189; marriages, 18; divorces, 33.

Race/Ethnicity: Anglo, 36.6%; Hispanic, 52.6%; Black, 7.6%; Asian, 1%; Other, 2.2%.

KARNES CITY (3,270) county seat; oil and gas, agribusiness, tourism, processing center, oil-field servicing, manufacturing; library; Lonesome Dove Fest in September.

KENEDY (3,626) farm and oil center, library, dove/quail hunting, prison, hospital; Bluebonnet Days in April.

Other towns include: **Falls City** (544) **Runge** (963) oil and gas services, farming, museum, library.

Population	14,754
Change from 2010	−0.5%
Area (sq. mi.)	753.6
Land Area (sq. mi.)	747.6
Altitude (ft.)	180–580
Rainfall (in.)	31.6
Jan. mean min (°F)	40.9
July mean max (°F)	95.7
Civ. Labor	6,647
Unemployed	3.3%
Wages	$100,566,853
Per Capita Income	$73,144
Property Value	$10,426,984,631
Retail Sales	$190,950,022

Kaufman County

Physical Features: North Blackland prairie, draining to Trinity River; Cedar Creek Reservoir, Lake Ray Hubbard and Terrell City Lake.

Economy: Agriculture, commuting to Dallas, government/services.

History: Caddo and later Cherokee Indians in the area; removed by 1840 when Anglo-American settlement began. County created from Henderson County and organized in 1848; named for member of Texas and U.S. congresses D.S. Kaufman.

Recreation: Lake activities; Porter Farm near Terrell is site of origin of U.S.-Texas Agricultural Extension program; antique centers near Forney; historic homes at Terrell.

Minerals: Gravel, sand, oil, gas.

Agriculture: Beef cattle, horticulture, hay/forage, row crops, horses. Market value $57.1 million.

Vital Statistics, annual: Births, 2,028; deaths, 1,274; marriages, 628; divorces, 433.

Race/Ethnicity: Anglo, 54.1%; Hispanic, 24.9%; Black, 14.8%; Asian, 1.5%; Other, 4.7%.

KAUFMAN (7,379) county seat; government/services, manufacturing and distribution, commuters to Dallas; hospital; Octoberfest.

TERRELL (18,567) agribusiness, varied manufacturing, large outlet center; private hospital, state hospital; community college, Southwestern Christian College; British flying school museum, Jubilee in April.

FORNEY (27,256) important antiques center, light industrial, commuters to Dallas, historic homes, barbecue cook-off in June.

Other towns include: **Combine** (2,358, partly in Dallas County); **Cottonwood** (194); **Crandall** (4,278) Cotton Festival in October; **Elmo** (1,065); **Grays Prairie** (347); **Kemp** (1,178); **Mabank** (4,562, partly in Henderson County) varied manufacturing, tourism, retail trade, Western Week in June; **Oak Grove** (670); **Oak Ridge** (887); **Post Oak Bend** (762); **Rosser** (322); **Scurry** (732); **Talty** (2,710).

Population	157,768
Change from 2010	52.7%
Area (sq. mi.)	807.7
Land Area (sq. mi.)	780.7
Altitude (ft.)	300–611

Rainfall (in.)	40.2
Jan. mean min (°F)	37.7
July mean max (°F)	93.1
Civ. Labor	75,098
Unemployed	3.7%

Wages	$559,389,618
Per Capita Income	$49,494
Property Value	$26,763,189,141
Retail Sales	$2,212,633,410

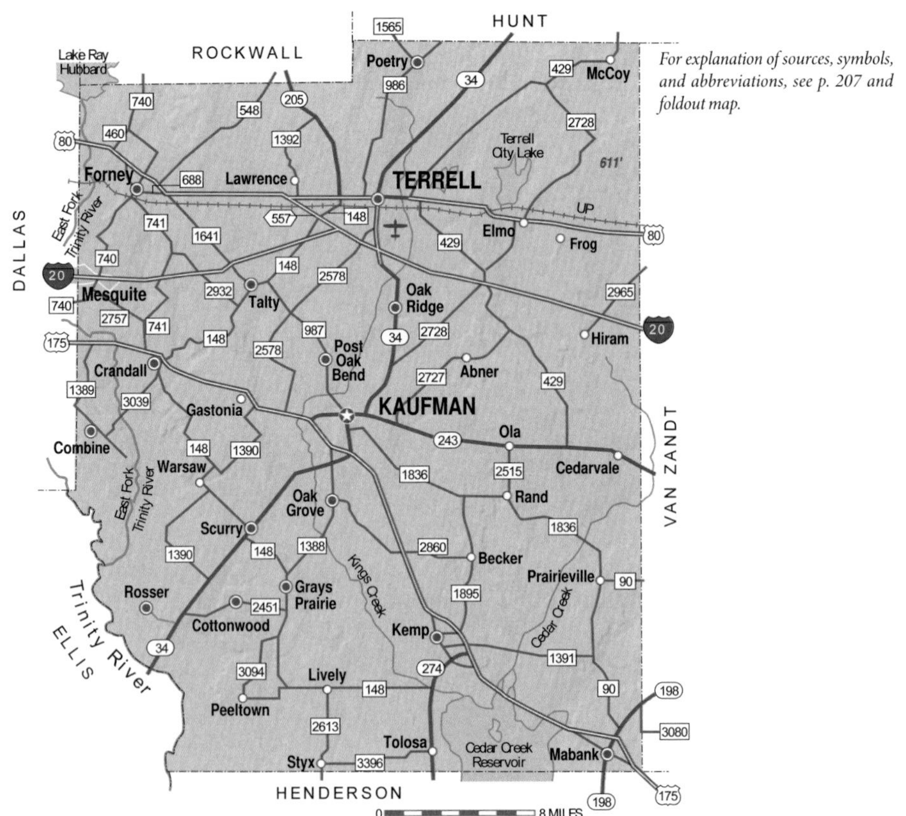

For explanation of sources, symbols, and abbreviations, see p. 207 and foldout map.

Boerne Plaza Park. Photo by Jonmallard, CC by SA 4.0

Kendall County

Physical Features: Hill Country, plateau, with spring-fed streams; caves; scenic drives.

Economy: Government/services, agribusiness, commuters to San Antonio, tourism, retirement area, some manufacturing.

History: Lipan Apaches, Kiowas and Comanches in area when German settlers arrived in 1840s. County created, organized, from Blanco, Kerr counties 1862; named for pioneer journalist-sheepman and early contributor to Texas Almanac, George W. Kendall.

Recreation: Hunting, fishing, exotic wildlife, state parks; Cascade Cavern, Cave Without a Name, Old Tunnel; historic sites; Christmas in Comfort on Saturday after Thanksgiving.

Minerals: Limestone rock, caliche.

Agriculture: Cattle, goats, sheep, hay. Market value $12.4 million. Cedar posts, firewood sold.

Vital Statistics, annual: Births, 385; deaths, 455; marriages, 355; divorces, 65.

Race/Ethnicity: Anglo, 71.7%; Hispanic, 22.6%; Black, 0.7%; Asian, 0.8%; Other, 4.1%.

BOERNE (19,109) county seat; tourism, antiques, some manufacturing, ranching, commuting to San Antonio; library.

Other towns include: **Comfort** (1,955) tourism, farming and ranching, manufacturing, Civil War monument honoring Unionists, library, museum, mountain bike trail; **Kendalia** (149); **Sisterdale** (110); **Waring** (73).

Part [2,355] of **Fair Oaks Ranch** (10,505).

Population	46,788
Change from 2010	40.0%
Area (sq. mi.)	663.0
Land Area (sq. mi.)	662.5
Altitude (ft.)	1,000–2,080
Rainfall (in.)	37.5
Jan. mean min (°F)	38.4
July mean max (°F)	92.1
Civ. Labor	23,745
Unemployed	3.1%
Wages	$296,040,818
Per Capita Income	$96,628
Property Value	$15,563,991,312
Retail Sales	$1,705,701,384

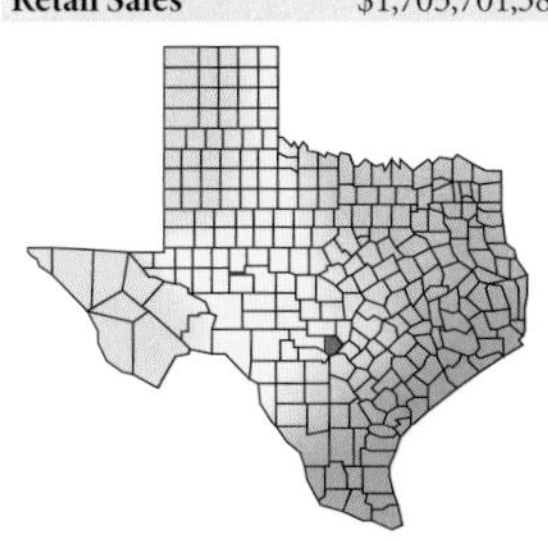

Kenedy County

Physical Features: Gulf coastal county; flat, sandy terrain, some loam soils; motts of live oaks.

Economy: Oil, ranching, nature tourism, hunting leases, wind farm.

History: Coahuiltecan Indians who assimilated or were driven out by the Lipan Apaches. Spanish ranching began in the 1790s. Anglo-Americans arrived after the Mexican War. Among last counties created, organized, 1921 from Cameron, Hidalgo, and Willacy counties; named for pioneer steamboat operator and cattleman, Capt. Mifflin Kenedy.

Recreation: Hunting, fishing, nature tourism.

Minerals: Oil, gas.

Agriculture: Beef cattle, horses. Market value $19.7 million. Hunting leases, nature tourism important.

Vital Statistics, annual: Births, 0; deaths, 0; marriages, 0; divorces, NA.

Race/Ethnicity: Anglo, 20.9%; Hispanic, 74.6%; Black, 0.0%; Asian, 0.0%; Other, 4.6%.

SARITA (164) county seat; cattle-shipping point, ranch headquarters, gas processing; one of the state's least populous counties.

Other towns include: **Armstrong** (6).

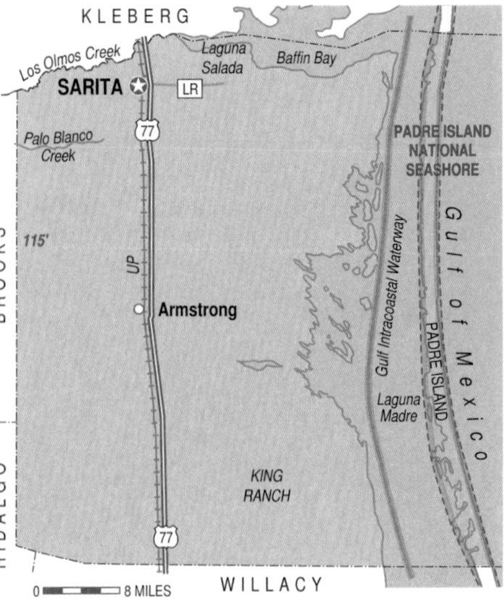

For explanation of sources, symbols, and abbreviations, see p. 207 and foldout map.

Population	340
Change from 2010	–18.3%
Area (sq. mi.)	1,945.8
Land Area (sq. mi.)	1,458.3
Altitude (ft.)	sea level–115

Rainfall (in.)	30.3
Jan. mean min (°F)	47.1
July mean max (°F)	93.8
Civ. Labor	147
Unemployed	6.1

Wages	$3,218,399
Per Capita Income	$47,141
Property Value	$2,354,530,777
Retail Sales	NA

Kent County

Physical Features: Rolling, broken terrain; lake; drains to Salt and Double Mountain forks of Brazos River; sandy, loam soils.

Economy: Agribusiness, oil and gas operations, government/services, hunting leases.

History: Comanches driven out by the U.S. Army in the 1870s. Ranching developed in the 1880s. County created in 1876 from Bexar and Young territories; organized in 1892. Name honors Andrew Kent, one of 32 volunteers from Gonzales who died at the Alamo.

Recreation: Hunting, fishing; scenic croton breaks and salt flat; Winterfest in December.

Minerals: Oil, gas.

Agriculture: Cattle, cotton, wheat, sorghum. Market value $9.9 million.

Vital Statistics, annual: Births, 0; deaths, 17; marriages, 0; divorces, 1.

Race/Ethnicity: Anglo, 87.3%; Hispanic, 10.8%; Black, 0.3%; Asian, 0.0%; Other, 1.7%.

JAYTON (503) county seat; oil-field services, farming center; Summerfest in August.

Other towns include: **Girard** (20).

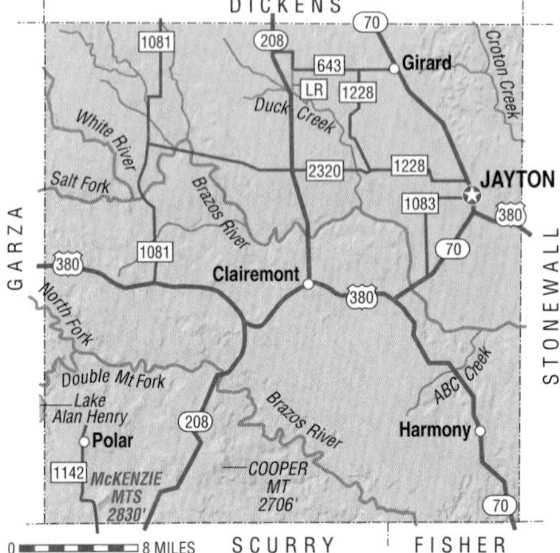

Population	749
Change from 2010	–7.3%
Area (sq. mi.)	902.9
Land Area (sq. mi.)	902.5
Altitude (ft.)	1,740–2,830
Rainfall (in.)	23.3
Jan. mean min (°F)	29.4

July mean max (°F)	95.1
Civ. Labor	627
Unemployed	2.1
Wages	$5,934,905
Per Capita Income	$55,725
Property Value	$969,954,703
Retail Sales	$1,800,063

Kerr County

Physical Features: Picturesque hills, spring-fed streams; dams, lakes on Guadalupe River.

Economy: Tourism, medical services, agribusiness, hunting leases.

History: Lipan Apaches, Kiowas and Comanches in area. Anglo-American settlers arrived in the late 1840s. County created in 1856 from Bexar County; organized the same year; named for a member of Austin's Colony, James Kerr.

Recreation: Youth camps, dude ranches, park, Cailloux and Point theaters, wildlife management area, Cowboy Artists Museum, Kerrville Folk Festival in May/June.

Minerals: none.

Agriculture: Cattle, hay, goats and horses; deer (second in numbers as livestock). Market value $9.3 million. Hunting leases important.

Vital Statistics, annual: Births, 485; deaths, 830; marriages, 274; divorces, 157.

Race/Ethnicity: Anglo, 68%; Hispanic, 25.9%; Black, 1.3%; Asian, 1.1%; Other, 3.7%.

KERRVILLE (24,477) county seat; tourist center, youth camps, agribusiness, aircraft and parts, varied manufacturing; Schreiner University; state hospital, veterans hospital, private hospital; retirement center; retail trade; state arts, crafts show in May.

Other towns include: **Camp Verde** (41); **Center Point** (1,759); **Hunt** (708) youth camps, hospital; **Ingram** (1,813) camps, cabins; **Mountain Home** (96).

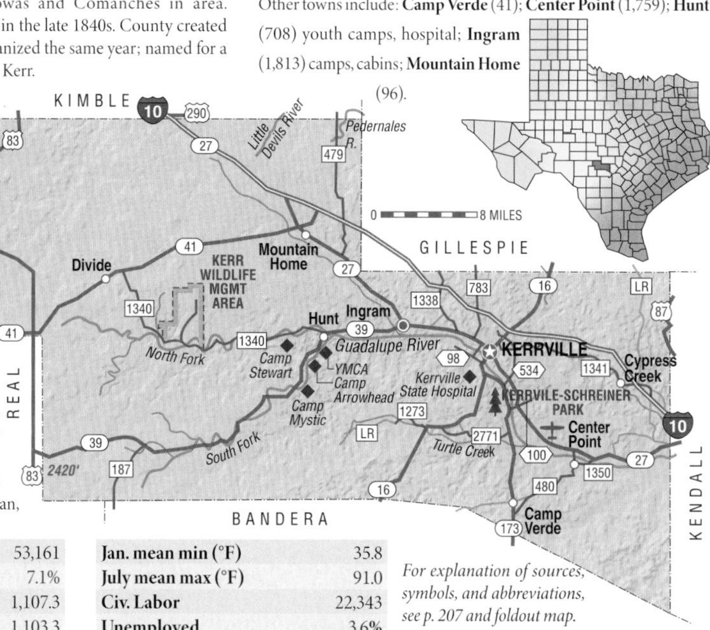

For explanation of sources, symbols, and abbreviations, *see p. 207 and foldout map.*

Population	53,161
Change from 2010	7.1%
Area (sq. mi.)	1,107.3
Land Area (sq. mi.)	1,103.3
Altitude (ft.)	1,404–2,420
Rainfall (in.)	30.6

Jan. mean min (°F)	35.8
July mean max (°F)	91.0
Civ. Labor	22,343
Unemployed	3.6%
Wages	$257,697,180
Per Capita Income	$61,401

Property Value	$10,441,440,483
Retail Sales	$1,336,827,811

Black-bellied Whistling Duck on the Padre Island National Seashore in Kenedy County. Photo by CaptainTom, CC by 2.0

Kimble County

Physical Features: Picturesque Edwards Plateau; rugged, broken by numerous streams; drains to Llano River; sandy, gray, chocolate loam soils.

Economy: Livestock production and market, tourism, cedar oil and wood products, metal building materials.

History: Apache, Kiowa and Comanche area until the 1870s. U.S. military outposts protected the first Anglo-American settlers in the 1850s. County created from Bexar County in 1858 and organized in 1876. Named for George C. Kimble, a Gonzales volunteer who died at the Alamo.

Recreation: Hunting, fishing in spring-fed streams, nature tourism; among leading deer counties; state park; Kimble Kounty Kow Kick on Labor Day, Wild Game dinner on Thanksgiving Saturday.

Minerals: gravel.

Agriculture: Cattle, meat goats, sheep, Angora goats, pecans. Market value $10.9 million.Hunting leases important. Firewood, cedar sold.

Vital Statistics, annual: Births, 54; deaths, 65; marriages, 13; divorces, 10.

Race/Ethnicity: Anglo, 73.2%; Hispanic, 23.0%; Black, 0.2%; Asian, 0.8%; Other, 2.9%.

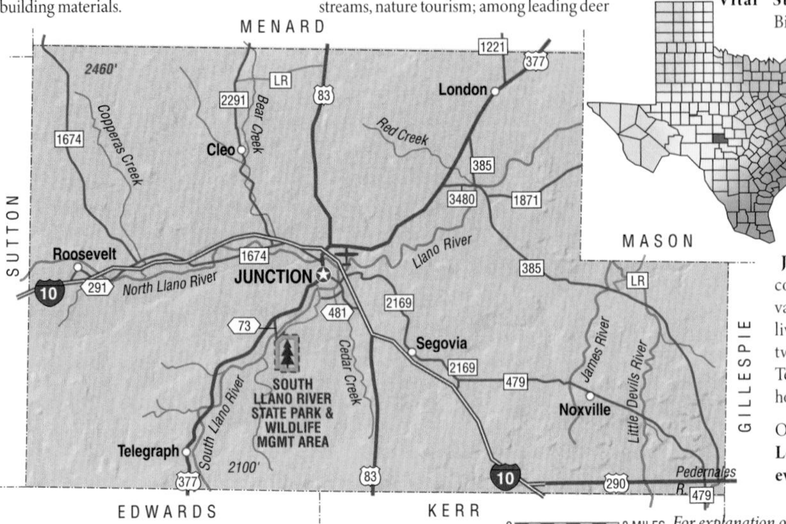

JUNCTION (2,494) county seat; tourism, varied manufacturing, livestock production; two museums; Texas Tech University center; hospital; library, airport.

Other towns include: **London** (180); **Roosevelt** (14).

For explanation of sources, symbols, and abbreviations, see *p. 207 and foldout map.*

Population	4,365
Change from 2010	–5.3%
Area (sq. mi.)	1,251.2
Land Area (sq. mi.)	1,251.0
Altitude (ft.)	1,476–2,460

Rainfall (in.)	22.5
Jan. mean min (°F)	35.5
July mean max (°F)	94.5
Civ. Labor	1,836
Unemployed	3.4

Wages	$14,457,346
Per Capita Income	$54,345
Property Value	$3,501,358,388
Retail Sales	$107,164,960

King County

Physical Features: Hilly, broken by Wichita, Brazos tributaries; extensive grassland; dark loam to red soils.

Economy: Oil and gas, ranching, government/services, horse sales, hunting leases.

History: Apache area until Comanches moved in about 1700. Comanches were removed by U.S. Army in 1874-75 after which ranching began. County created in 1876 from Bexar District; organized in 1891; named for William P. King, a volunteer from Gonzales who died at the Alamo.

Recreation: 6666 Ranch visits, hunting, roping and ranch horse competitions.

Minerals: Oil, gas.

Agriculture: Cattle, horses, wheat, hay, cotton. Market value $13.8 million. Hunting leases important.

Vital Statistics, annual: Births, 0; deaths, 0; marriages, 0; divorces, NA.

Race/Ethnicity: Anglo, 86.8%; Hispanic, 9.4%; Black, 0.0%; Asian, 0.0%; Other, 3.8%.

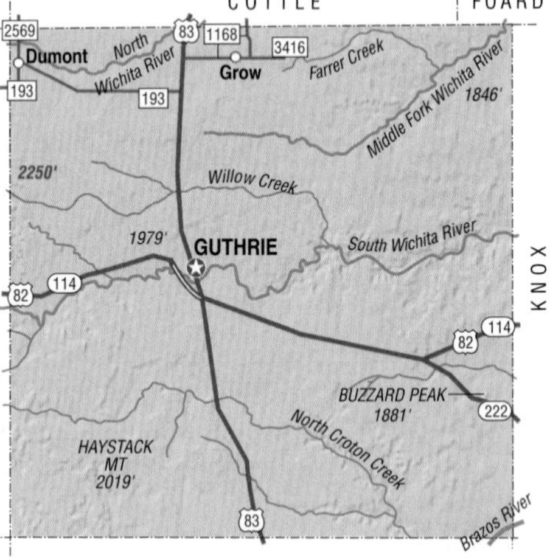

GUTHRIE (164) county seat; ranch-supply center, government/services; community center complex, library; Thanksgiving community supper.

Population	258
Change from 20100	–9.8%
Area (sq. mi.)	913.3
Land Area (sq. mi.)	910.9
Altitude (ft.)	1,450–2,250

Rainfall (in.)	23.8
Jan. mean min (°F)	28.8
July mean max (°F)	96.2
Civ. Labor	582
Unemployed	0.9%

Wages	$6,790,418
Per Capita Income	$91,930
Property Value	$681,475,656
Retail Sales	NA

Kinney County

Physical Features: Hilly, broken by Rio Grande tributaries; Anacacho Mountains; Nueces Canyon.

Economy: Agribusiness, government/services, hunting leases, wind farm, gas pipelines.

History: Coahuiltecans in the area, later Apaches and Comanches arrived. Spanish Franciscans established settlement in the late 1700s. English empresarios John Beales and James Grant established English-speaking colony in 1834. Black Seminoles served as army scouts in the 1870s. County created from Bexar County in 1850; organized in 1874; named for H.L. Kinney, founder of Corpus Christi.

Recreation: Hunting, birding; Fort Clark Springs; Kickapoo Cavern State Park; Seminole Indian cemetery; Juneteenth celebration.

Minerals: Not significant.

Agriculture: Cattle, sheep, goats, hay, sorghum, cotton, corn, oats, wheat, pecans. Market value $5.0 million. Hunting important.

Vital Statistics, annual: Births, 25; deaths, 47; marriages, 15; divorces, 4.

Race/Ethnicity: Anglo, 47.6%; Hispanic, 47.0%; Black, 1.2%; Asian, 0.3%; Other, 4.0%.

BRACKETTVILLE (1,400) county seat; agriculture, tourism; museum, Fort Clark Days in March.

Other towns include: **Fort Clark Springs** (1,338); **Spofford** (47).

Population	3,130
Change from 2010	–13.0%
Area (sq. mi.)	1,365.1
Land Area (sq. mi.)	1,363.1

Altitude (ft.)	790–2,080
Rainfall (in.)	24.1
Jan. mean min (°F)	37.9
July mean max (°F)	93.2
Civ. Labor	1,267

Unemployed	4.7%
Wages	$12,372,774
Per Capita Income	$42,929
Property Value	$2,002,355,653
Retail Sales	$13,263,834

Kleberg County

Physical Features: Coastal plain, broken by bays; sandy, loam, clay soils; tree motts.

Economy: Oil and gas, Naval air station, chemicals and plastics, Texas A&M University – Kingsville, agriculture.

History: Coahuiltecan and Karankawa area. Spanish land grants date to 1750s. In 1853 Richard King purchased Santa Gertrudis land grant. County created 1913 from Nueces County, organized the same year; named for San Jacinto veteran and rancher Robert Kleberg.

Recreation: Fishing, hunting, water sports, park at Baffin Bay; wildlife sanctuary; winter bird watching; university events, museum; King Ranch headquarters, tours; La Posada celebration in November.

Minerals: Oil, gas.

Agriculture: Cattle, grain sorghum, cotton. Market value $52.8 million. Hunting leases and ecotourism important.

Vital Statistics, annual: Births, 376; deaths, 347; marriages, 166; divorces, 79.

Race/Ethnicity: Anglo, 21.7%; Hispanic, 70.6%; Black, 3.2%; Asian, 2.5%; Other, 2.0%.

Population	30,635
Change from 2010	–4.4%
Area (sq. mi.)	1,090.2
Land Area (sq. mi.)	881.3
Altitude (ft.)	sea level–165
Rainfall (in.)	27.0
Jan. mean min (°F)	48.4
July mean max (°F)	95.7
Civ. Labor	13,092
Unemployed	4.8%
Wages	$140,741,432
Per Capita Income	$45,818
Property Value	$3,217,139,712
Retail Sales	$571,759,129

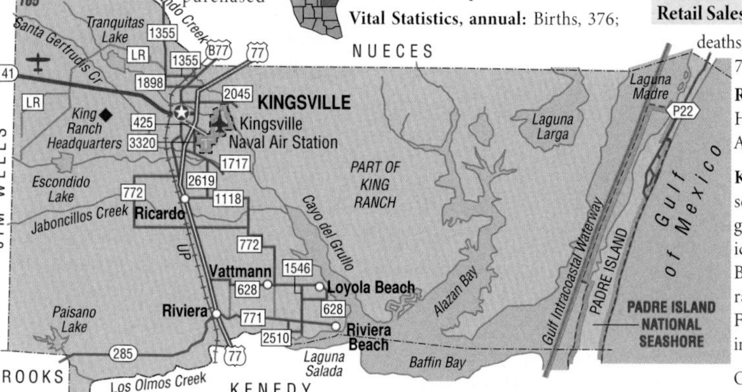

KINGSVILLE (25,069) county seat; government/services, oil, gas, agribusiness, tourism, chemical plant, university, Coastal Bend College branch; hospital; ranching heritage festival in February, King Ranch Breakfast in November.

Other towns: **Ricardo** (1,041), **Riviera** (675).

Knox County

Physical Features: Eroded breaks on West Texas Rolling Plains; Brazos, Wichita rivers; sandy, loam soils; Lake Davis, Lake Catherine, and Truscott Brine Lake.

Economy: Oil, agriculture, government/services.

History: Indian conscripts were used as labor during the Spanish period to mine copper deposits along the Brazos River. Ranching and farming developed in the 1880s. German colony settled in 1895. County created from the Bexar, Young territories in 1858; re-created in 1876; organized in 1886; named for U.S. Secretary of War Henry Knox.

Recreation: Lake activities, fishing, hunting; Knox City seedless watermelon festival in July.

Minerals: Oil, gas.

Agriculture: Wheat, cattle, cotton. Some cotton irrigated. Market value $60.5 million.

Vital Statistics, annual: Births, 43; deaths, 75; marriages, 8; divorces, 17.

Race/Ethnicity: Anglo, 57.7%; Hispanic, 33.7%; Black, 4.4%; Asian, 0.7%; Other, 3.5%.

BENJAMIN (200) county seat; ranching, farm center; veterans memorial.

MUNDAY (1,240) portable buildings, other manufacturing; A&M vegetable research station.

KNOX CITY (1,052) agribusiness, petroleum center; USDA plant materials research center; hospital.

Other towns include: **Goree** (162); **Rhineland** (120) old church established by German immigrants.

Population	3,351
Change from 2010	–9.9%
Area (sq. mi.)	855.5
Land Area (sq. mi.)	850.6
Altitude (ft.)	1,200–1,794

Rainfall (in.)	25.7
Jan. mean min (°F)	33.1
July mean max (°F)	95.8
Civ. Labor	1,484
Unemployed	3.9%

Wages	$12,931,489
Per Capita Income	$50,320
Property Value	$1,631,171,675
Retail Sales	$23,321,343

Lamar County

Physical Features: North Texas county on divide between Red, Sulphur rivers; soils chiefly blackland, except along Red; pines, hardwoods; Pat Mayse Lake and Lake Crook.

Economy: Varied manufacturing, agribusiness, medical, government/services.

History: Caddo Indian area. First Anglo-American settlers arrived about 1815. County created in 1840 from Red River County; organized in 1841; named for second president of Republic, Mirabeau B. Lamar.

Recreation: Lake activities; Gambill goose refuge; hunting, fishing; state park; Trail de Paris rail-to-trail; Sam Bell Maxey Home; State Sen. A.M. Aikin Archives, other museums.

Minerals: Negligible.

Agriculture: Beef, hay, dairy, soybeans (first in acreage), wheat, corn, sorghum, cotton. Market value $73.4 million.

Vital Statistics, annual: Births, 632; deaths, 786; marriages, 317; divorces, 237.

Race/Ethnicity: Anglo, 22%; Hispanic, 73.6%; Black, 3.3%; Asian, 0.1%; Other, 1.0%.

PARIS (24,407) county seat; varied manufacturing, food processing, government/services; hospitals; junior college; museums; Tour de Paris bicycle rally in July.

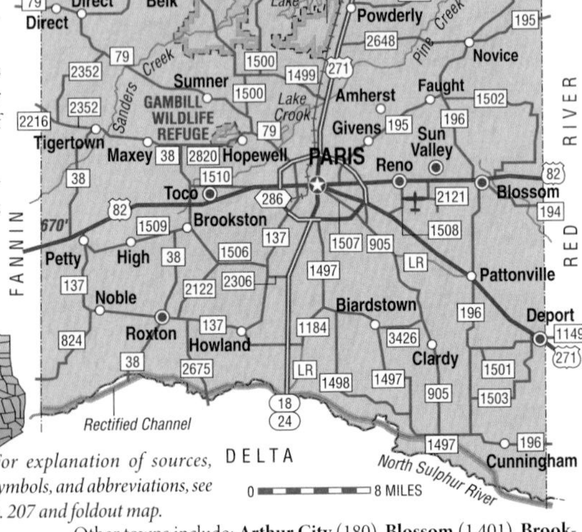

For explanation of sources, symbols, and abbreviations, see p. 207 and foldout map.

Other towns include: **Arthur City** (180), **Blossom** (1,401), **Brookston** (45), **Chicota** (150), **Deport** (551, partly in Red River County), **Pattonville** (180), **Petty** (160), **Powderly** (1,247), **Reno** (3,460), **Roxton** (546), **Sun Valley** (71), **Toco** (91).

Population	50,098
Change from 2010	0.6%
Area (sq. mi.)	933.1
Land Area (sq. mi.)	907.2
Altitude (ft.)	335–970

Rainfall (in.)	48.9
Jan. mean min (°F)	35.4
July mean max (°F)	94.4
Civ. Labor	24,512
Unemployed	4.3%

Wages	$290,953,991
Per Capita Income	$50,699
Property Value	$7,784,367,464
Retail Sales	$965,663,039

Grain elevators near Amherst in Lamb County. Photo by Leaflet, CC by SA 3.0

Lamb County

Physical Features: Rich, red, brown soils on the High Plains; some hills; drains to upper Brazos River tributaries; numerous playas.

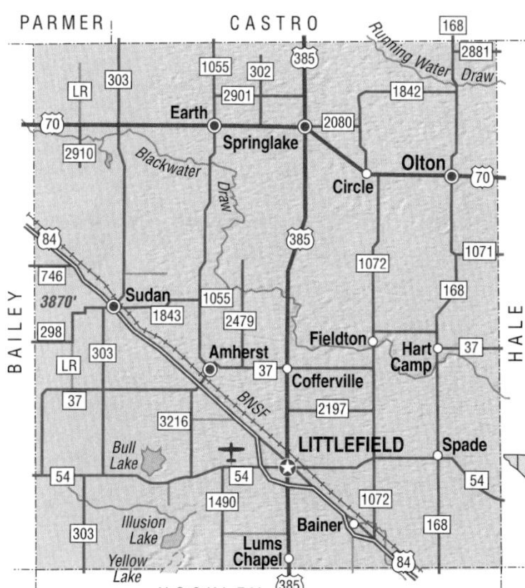

Population	12,898
Change from 2010	-7.7%
Area (sq. mi.)	1,017.7
Land Area (sq. mi.)	1,016.2
Altitude (ft.)	3,390–3,870

Rainfall (in.)	18.0
Jan. mean min (°F)	24.3
July mean max (°F)	91.4
Civ. Labor	5,290
Unemployed	4.0%

Economy: Agribusiness; distribution center; denim textiles.

History: Apache tribes, who were displaced by Comanches around 1700. The U.S. Army pushed the Comanches into the Indian Territory in 1875. Ranching began in the 1880s; farming started after 1900. County created in 1876 from the Bexar District and organized in 1908; named for Lt. G.A. Lamb, who died in battle of San Jacinto.

Recreation: Museums, libraries, Earth Day in April.

Minerals: Oil, stone, gas.

Agriculture: Fed cattle; cotton, corn, wheat, grain sorghum, vegetables, soybeans, hay; sheep. 179,500 acres irrigated. Market value $575.3 million.

Vital Statistics, annual: Births, 181; deaths, 224; marriages, 48; divorces, 15.

Race/Ethnicity: Anglo, 70.6%; Hispanic, 8.8%; Black, 12.7%; Asian, 0.9%; Other, 6.9%.

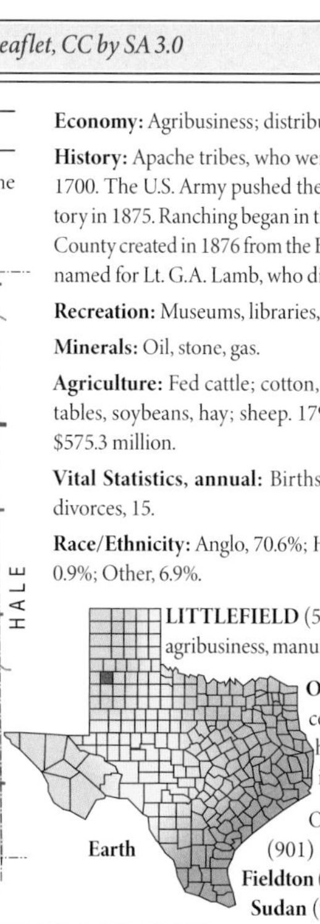

LITTLEFIELD (5,871) county seat; milk processing, agribusiness, manufacturing; hospital, prison, museum.

Olton (1,967) agribusiness, retail center; Sandcrawl museum; pheasant hunt in winter; Sandhills Celebration in August.

Other towns include: **Amherst** (664); **Earth** (901) farming center, dairies, feed lot; **Fieldton** (20); **Spade** (55); **Springlake** (140); **Sudan** (939) farming center, government/services, Homecoming Day in fall.

Wages	$51,117,165
Per Capita Income	$54,689
Property Value	$1,754,868,231
Retail Sales	$112,075,805

The entrance to Horseshoe Falls, a hunting ranch (formerly Lampasas State Park). Photo by Larry D. Moore, CC by SA 4.0

Lampasas County

Physical Features: Central Texas on edge of Hill Country; Colorado, Lampasas rivers; cedars, oaks, pecans.

Economy: Many employed at Fort Cavazos, several industrial plants, agribusinesses, tourism.

History: Mineral springs attracted first Anglo-Americans in 1853. Frontier confrontations between settlers, Comanches continued into 1870s. County created, organized, in 1856 from Bell, Travis counties. Named for river. Some have speculated that an early expedition named river for city of Lampazos in Mexico.

Recreation: Scenic drives; state park; deer hunting, fishing in streams; Hancock Springs free-flow swim area at Lampasas.

Minerals: Sand and gravel, building stone.

Agriculture: Beef cattle, hay, goats, sheep, exotic animals. Market value $18.4 million. Hunting leases, ecotourism.

Vital Statistics, annual: Births, 203; deaths, 285; marriages, 103; divorces, 64.

Race/Ethnicity: Anglo, 38.2%; Hispanic, 57.1%; Black, 3.0%; Asian, 0.0%; Other, 1.7%.

LAMPASAS (7,517) county seat; manufacturing, health care, retail; historic downtown; hospital, college extensions; museum; Spring Ho in July.

Other towns include: **Izoro** (17); **Kempner** (1,182); **Lometa** (766) market and shipping point; Diamondback Jubilee in March.

Population	22,252
Change from 2010	13.1%
Area (sq. mi.)	713.9
Land Area (sq. mi.)	712.8
Altitude (ft.)	800–1,669
Rainfall (in.)	32.2
Jan. mean min (°F)	35.5
July mean max (°F)	94.9
Civ. Labor	9,428
Unemployed	3.7%
Wages	$58,947,288
Per Capita Income	$58,507
Property Value	$4,340,055,511
Retail Sales	$288,165,480

For explanation of sources, symbols, and abbreviations, see p. 207 and foldout map.

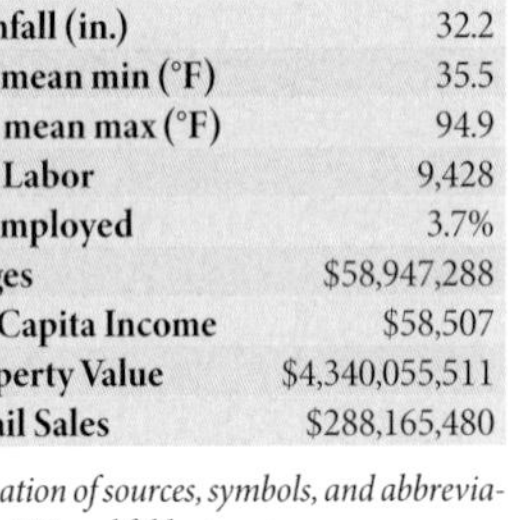

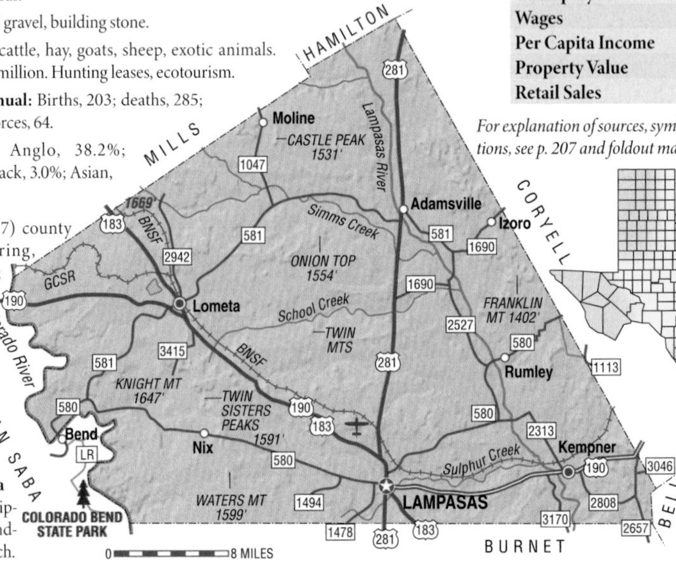

La Salle County

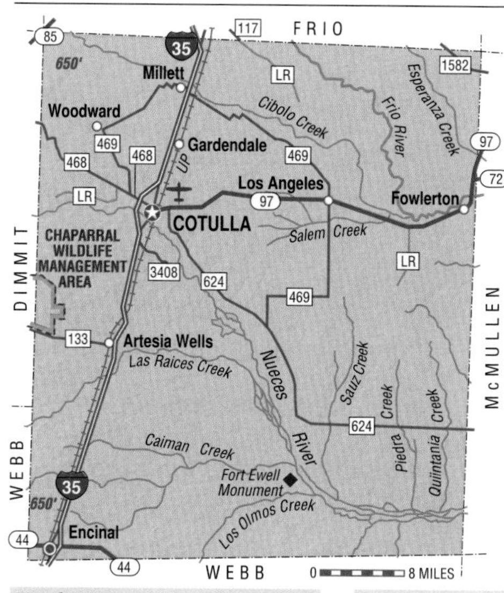

Physical Features: Brushy plain, broken by Nueces, Frio rivers and their tributaries; chocolate, dark gray, sandy loam soils.

Economy: Agribusiness, hunting leases, tourism, government services.

History: Coahuiltecans, squeezed out by migrating Apaches. U.S. military outpost in the 1850s, settlers of Mexican descent established nearby village. Anglo-American ranching developed in the 1870s. County created from Bexar District in 1858; organized in 1880; named for Robert Cavelier Sieur de La Salle, French explorer who died in Texas.

Recreation: Nature trails; school where Lyndon B. Johnson taught; wildlife management area; deer, bird, javelina hunting, fishing; wild hog cookoff in March.

Minerals: Oil, gas.

Agriculture: Beef cattle, peanuts, watermelons, grain sorghum. Market value $6.3 million.

Vital Statistics, annual: Births, 79; deaths, 78; marriages, 34; divorces, NA.

Race/Ethnicity: Anglo, 70.0%; Hispanic, 19.3%; Black, 3.2%; Asian, 1.1%; Other, 6.4%.

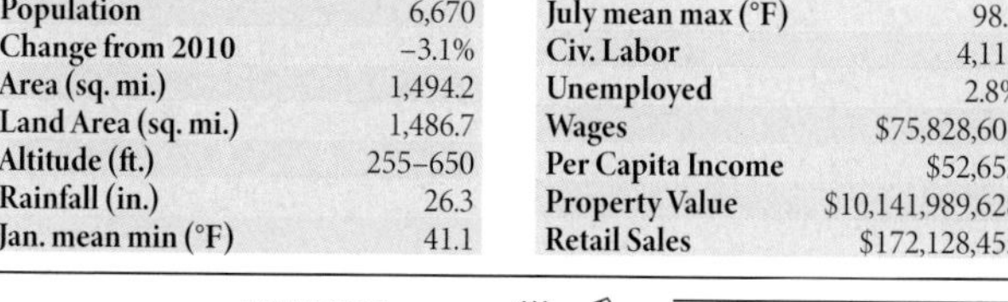

Population	6,670
Change from 2010	–3.1%
Area (sq. mi.)	1,494.2
Land Area (sq. mi.)	1,486.7
Altitude (ft.)	255–650
Rainfall (in.)	26.3
Jan. mean min (°F)	41.1
July mean max (°F)	98.3
Civ. Labor	4,113
Unemployed	2.8%
Wages	$75,828,603
Per Capita Income	$52,652
Property Value	$10,141,989,628
Retail Sales	$172,128,455

COTULLA (3,725) county seat; oil and lodging, state prison; hunting center; Brush Country museum.

Other towns include: **Encinal** (539), **Fowlerton** (66).

Lavaca County

Physical Features: Coastal Plains county; north rolling; sandy loam, black waxy soils; drains to Lavaca, Navidad rivers.

Economy: Varied manufacturing, oil and gas production, agribusinesses, tourism.

History: Coahuiltecan area; later a Comanche area until 1850s. Anglo-Americans first settled in 1831. Germans and Czechs arrived 1880–1900. County created, organized, in 1846 from Colorado, Jackson, Gonzales, Victoria counties. Name is Spanish for cow, la vaca, from name of river.

Recreation: Deer, other hunting, fishing; wildflower trails, historic sites, churches; Fiddlers Frolics in Hallettsville in April.

Minerals: Some oil, gas.

Agriculture: Cattle, forage, poultry, rice, corn, sorghum. Market value $50.5 million. Hunting leases.

Vital Statistics, annual: Births, 227; deaths, 319; marriages, 77; divorces, 48.

Race/Ethnicity: Anglo, 71.6%; Hispanic, 19.4%; Black, 5.8%; Asian, 0.4%; Other, 2.9%.

HALLETTSVILLE (2,742) county seat; retail center; varied manufacturing; agribusiness; museum, library, hospital; domino, "42" tournaments; Kolache Fest in September.

YOAKUM (5,923, partly in DeWitt County); cattle, leather, meat processing; hospital; museum; Tom Tom festival in June.

Shiner (2,154) Spoetzl brewery, varied manufacturing; museum; clinic; Half Moon Holidays in July.

Other towns include: **Moulton** (861) agribusiness, Town & Country Jamboree in July; **Sublime** (75); **Sweet Home** (360).

Population	20,544
Change from 2010	6.7%
Area (sq. mi.)	970.4
Land Area (sq. mi.)	969.7
Altitude (ft.)	85–503
Rainfall (in.)	40.4
Jan. mean min (°F)	46.4
July mean max (°F)	95.7
Civ. Labor	9,159
Unemployed	3.3%
Wages	$71,764,328
Per Capita Income	$62,375
Property Value	$7,273,050,498
Retail Sales	$235,524,084

Lee County

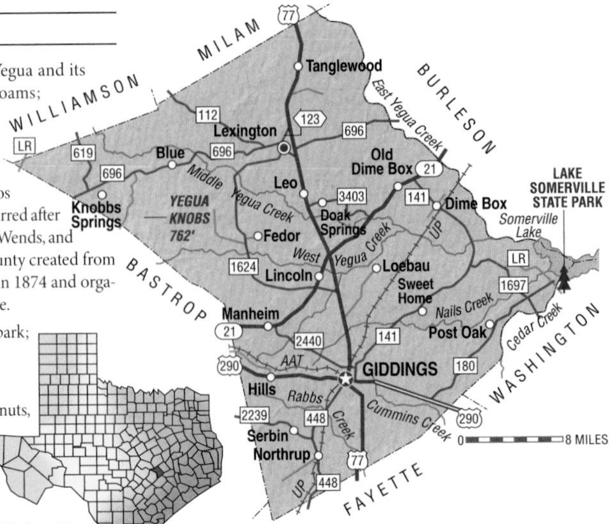

Physical Features: Rolling terrain, broken by Yegua and its tributaries; red to black soils, sandy to heavy loams; Somerville Lake.

Economy: Varied manufacturing, agribusiness, lignite coal operations, government/services.

History: Tonkawas; removed in 1855 to the Brazos Reservation. Most Anglo-American settlement occurred after the Texas Revolution. Slaveholding area. Germans, Wends, and other Europeans began arriving in the 1850s. County created from Bastrop, Burleson, Fayette, Washington counties in 1874 and organized the same year; named for Gen. Robert E. Lee.

Recreation: Fishing, hunting; lake activities, state park; pioneer village; historic sites.

Minerals: Lignite coal, iron ore, gravel.

Agriculture: Beef cattle, hay, nurseries, poultry, peanuts, goats, horses, aquaculture, corn; some irrigation. Market value $56.9 million. Firewood.

Vital Statistics, annual: Births, 209; deaths, 226; marriages, 73; divorces, 65.

Race/Ethnicity: Anglo, 60.7%; Hispanic, 25.6%; Black, 9.3%; Asian, 0.3%; Other, 4%.

GIDDINGS (5,067) county seat; oil/gas, manufacturing, agriculture; museum, old Presbyterian church (1886); rodeo in April.

Other towns include: **Dime Box** (236); **Lexington** (1,231) utility plant, livestock-marketing center, small businesses, log cabins heritage center, homecoming rodeo and barbecue cookoff in May; **Lincoln** (336); **Serbin** (109) Wendish museum.

Population	17,706
Change from 2010	6.6%
Area (sq. mi.)	631.1
Land Area (sq. mi.)	629.0
Altitude (ft.)	238–762
Rainfall (in.)	37.7
Jan. mean min (°F)	40.5
July mean max (°F)	94.2
Civ. Labor	8,734
Unemployed	3.5%
Wages	$86,423,526
Per Capita Income	$56,674
Property Value	$4,943,999,698
Retail Sales	$678,571,304

Leon County

Physical Features: Hilly, rolling, almost half covered by timber; drains to Navasota, Trinity rivers and tributaries; Lake Limestone; sandy, dark, alluvial soils.

Economy: Poultry farming, cattle ranching, hay.

History: Bidais, absorbed into the Kickapoos and other groups. Permanent settlement by Anglo-Americans occurred after the Texas Revolution; Germans arrived in the 1870s. County created and organized in 1846 from Robertson County; named for founder of Victoria, Martín de León.

Recreation: Hilltop Lakes resort area; sites of Camino Real, Fort Boggy State Park; deer hunting.

Minerals: Oil, natural gas.

Agriculture: Poultry, cow-calf production, hay, small grains. Market value $169.4 million. Hardwoods, pine marketed.

Vital Statistics, annual: Births, 199; deaths, 251; marriages, 62; divorces, 52.

Race/Ethnicity: Anglo, 74.2%; Hispanic, 15.6%; Black, 5.9%; Asian, 0.7%; Other, 3.7%.

CENTERVILLE (921) county seat; agriculture, government/services; Christmas on the Square in December.

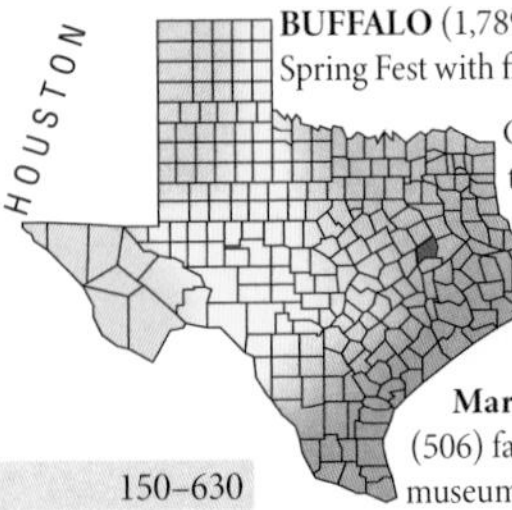

BUFFALO (1,789) oil and gas; library; May Spring Fest with fiddlers' contest.

Other towns include: **Hilltop Lakes** (713) resort and retirement center; **Jewett** (797) steel mill, civic center, museum, library; **Leona** (157) candle factory; **Marquez** (182); **Normangee** (506) farming and tourism; library, museum, city park; **Oakwood** (394).

Population	15,959
Change from 2010	–5.0%
Area (sq. mi.)	1,080.6
Land Area (sq. mi.)	1,073.2
Altitude (ft.)	150–630
Rainfall (in.)	42.4
Jan. mean min (°F)	36.9
July mean max (°F)	93.1
Civ. Labor	6,057
Unemployed	5.2%
Wages	$78,169,647
Per Capita Income	$53,179
Property Value	$5,657,025,887
Retail Sales	$215,824,219

The Dime Box Heritage Society Museum in Lee County. Photo by Larry D. Moore, CC by SA 4.0

Liberty County

Physical Features: Coastal Plain county east of Houston; 60 percent in pine, hardwood timber; bisected by Trinity River; sandy, loam, black soils; Big Thicket.

Economy: Agribusiness; chemical plants; varied manufacturing; tourism; forest industries; prisons; many residents work in Houston; part of Houston metropolitan area.

History: Karankawa tribal area until the 1740s. Spanish established Atascosito settlement in 1756. Settlers from Louisiana began arriving in the 1810s. County named for Spanish municipality, Libertad; created in 1836, organized in 1837.

Recreation: Big Thicket; hunting, fishing; national wildlife refuge; historic sites; Trinity Valley exposition.

Minerals: Oil, gas.

Agriculture: Beef cattle; rice is principal crop. Also nursery crops, corn, hay, sorghum, bees (first in number of colonies). Market value $29.9 million. Some lumbering.

Vital Statistics, annual: Births, 1,259; deaths, 885; marriages, 437; divorces, 300.

Race/Ethnicity: Anglo, 54.6%; Hispanic, 33.6%; Black, 7.7%; Asian, 0.5%; Other, 3.6%.

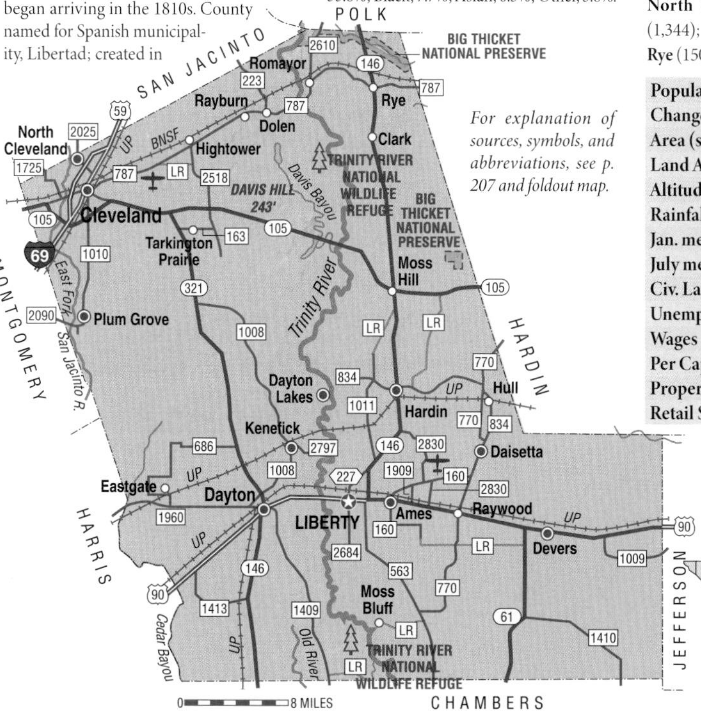

For explanation of sources, symbols, and abbreviations, see p. 207 and foldout map.

LIBERTY (8,539) county seat; petroleum-related industry, agribusiness; library, museum, regional historical resource depository; Liberty Bell, Price Daniel House; hospital; Jubilee in March.

DAYTON (9,134) rice, oil center.

Cleveland (7,999) forest products processed, shipped; tourism; library; museum; hospital.

Other towns include: **Ames** (1,009); **Daisetta** (992); **Dayton Lakes** (50); **Devers** (389); **Hardin** (811); **Hull** (475); **Kenefick** (668); **North Cleveland** (246); **Plum Grove** (1,344); **Raywood** (231); **Romayor** (135); **Rye** (150).

Population	97,621
Change from 2010	29.1%
Area (sq. mi.)	1,176.3
Land Area (sq. mi.)	1,158.4
Altitude (ft.)	3–243
Rainfall (in.)	62.8
Jan. mean min (°F)	43.0
July mean max (°F)	92.9
Civ. Labor	35,293
Unemployed	5.8%
Wages	$264,886,067
Per Capita Income	$42,813
Property Value	$14,859,340,955
Retail Sales	$1,092,956,831

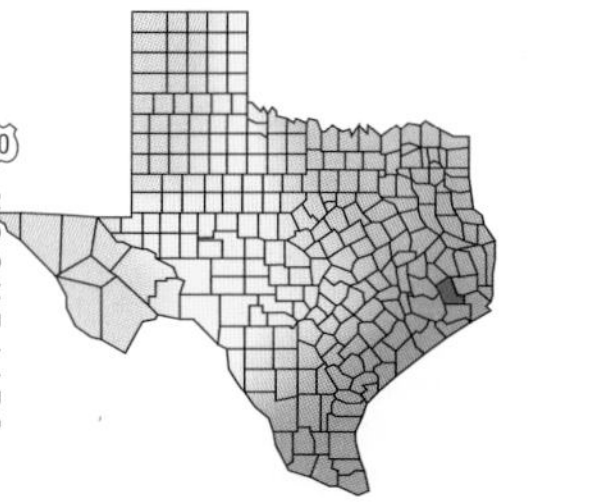

Limestone County

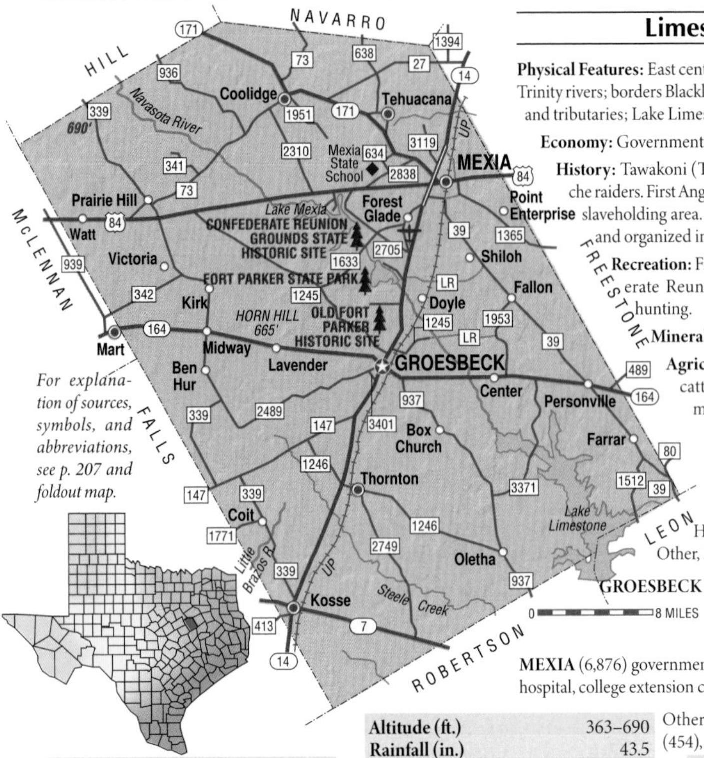

For explanation of sources, symbols, and abbreviations, see p. 207 and foldout map.

Physical Features: East central county on divide between Brazos and Trinity rivers; borders Blacklands, level to rolling; drained by Navasota and tributaries; Lake Limestone.

Economy: Government/services, electricity-generating plant.

History: Tawakoni (Tehuacana) and Waco area, later Comanche raiders. First Anglo-Americans arrived in 1833. Antebellum slaveholding area. County created from Robertson County and organized in 1846; named for indigenous rock.

Recreation: Fishing, lake activities; Fort Parker; Confederate Reunion Grounds; historic sites; museum; hunting.

Minerals: Natural gas, lignite coal.

Agriculture: Hay, corn, wheat, sorghum; beef cattle, horses, poultry. Market value $66.3 million.

Vital Statistics, annual: Births, 273; deaths, 338; marriages, 106; divorces, 72.

Race/Ethnicity: Anglo, 56.6%; Hispanic, 22.6%; Black, 16.4%; Asian, 0.7%; Other, 3.6%.

GROESBECK (3,645) county seat, oil & gas, agriculture, manufacturing, hunting, mining, prison, power generating, hospital, museum.

MEXIA (6,876) government/services [state school], manufacturing; hospital, college extension campus; Boomtown History Day in April.

Other towns include: **Coolidge** (777), **Kosse** (454), **Prairie Hill** (150), **Tehuacana** (224).

Population	22,119
Change from 2010	–5.4%
Area (sq. mi.)	933.2
Land Area (sq. mi.)	905.3

Altitude (ft.)	363–690
Rainfall (in.)	43.5
Jan. mean min (°F)	37.9
July mean max (°F)	92.5
Civ. Labor	8,399
Unemployed	4.6%

Wages	$108,903,754
Per Capita Income	$47,439
Property Value	$4,592,683,144
Retail Sales	$264,717,918

Lipscomb County

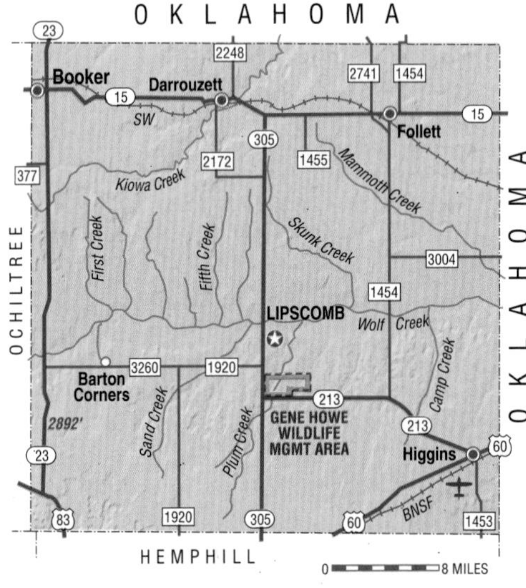

Physical Features: High Plains, broken in east; drains to tributaries of Canadian, Wolf Creek; sandy loam, black soils.

Economy: Oil and gas, agribusinesses, government/services.

History: Apaches, later Kiowas and Comanches who were driven into Indian Territory in 1875. Ranching began in late 1870s. County created in 1876 from Bexar District; organized in 1887; named for A.S. Lipscomb, Republic of Texas leader.

Recreation: Hunting; Wolf Creek museum, prairie chicken booming grounds.

Minerals: Oil, natural gas.

Agriculture: Cattle, corn, wheat, grain sorghum, hay, sunflowers. Some 23,000 acres irrigated. Market value $79.3 million.

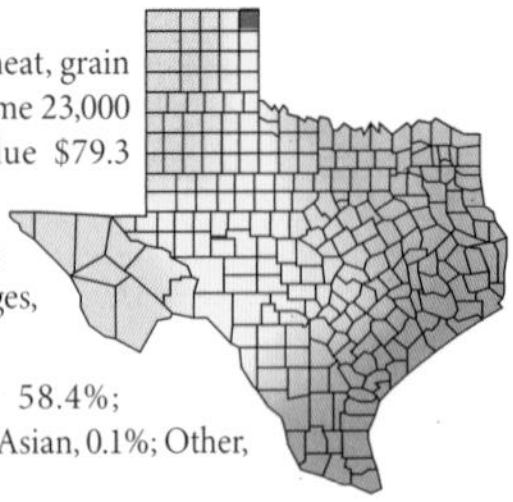

Vital Statistics, annual: Births, 27; deaths, 33; marriages, 8; divorces, 14.

Race/Ethnicity: Anglo, 58.4%; Hispanic, 36.7%; Black, 0.1%; Asian, 0.1%; Other, 4.7%.

LIPSCOMB (34), county seat; livestock center.

BOOKER (1,365, partly in Ochiltree County) trade center, library.

Other towns include: **Darrouzett** (302); **Follett** (362); **Higgins** (345) library, Will Rogers Day in August.

Population	2,931
Change from 2010	–11.2%
Area (sq. mi.)	932.3
Land Area (sq. mi.)	932.2
Altitude (ft.)	2,220–2,892
Rainfall (in.)	22.6
Jan. mean min (°F)	19.1

July mean max (°F)	92.3
Civ. Labor	1,464
Unemployed	3.1 %
Wages	$19,490,765
Per Capita Income	$102,569
Property Value	$704,062,294
Retail Sales	$18,202,510

Historic downtown buildings in Kosse, Limestone County. Photo by Renelibrary, CC by SA 4.0

Live Oak County

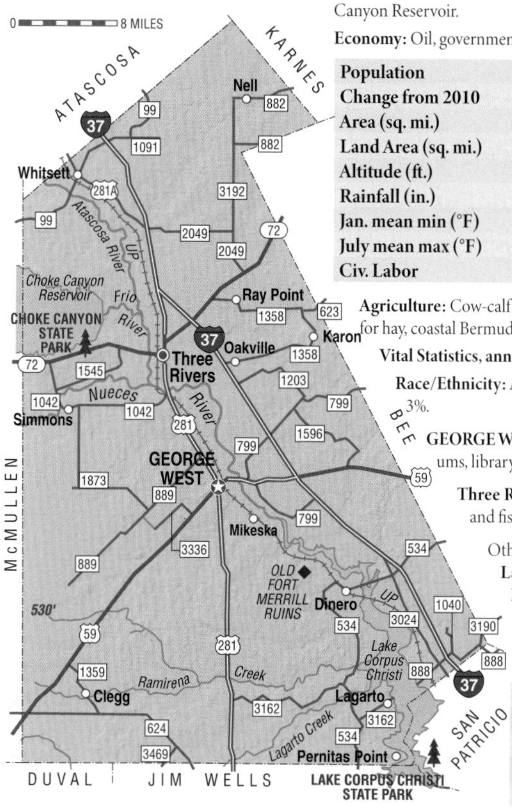

Physical Features: Brushy plains between San Antonio and Corpus Christi, partly broken by Nueces and tributaries; black waxy, gray sandy, other soils; Lake Corpus Christi, Choke Canyon Reservoir.

Economy: Oil, government/services, tourism, agribusinesses.

Population	11,377
Change from 2010	–1.3%
Area (sq. mi.)	1,078.9
Land Area (sq. mi.)	1,039.7
Altitude (ft.)	94–530
Rainfall (in.)	26.5
Jan. mean min (°F)	44.7
July mean max (°F)	95.0
Civ. Labor	4,869

History: Coahuiltecans squeezed out by Lipan Apaches and Spanish. Spanish ranching started in the 1810s. Settlers from Ireland arrived in 1835. County named for predominant tree; created and organized in 1856 from Nueces and San Patricio counties.

Recreation: Lakes; water activities; state park; hunting; historic sites including Fort Merrill (1850s).

Minerals: Oil, gas, sand, gravel.

Agriculture: Cow-calf operations; hogs; corn, grain sorghum, cotton; some irrigation for hay, coastal Bermuda pastures. Market value $19.5 million.

Vital Statistics, annual: Births, 122; deaths, 156; marriages, 50; divorces, 39.

Race/Ethnicity: Anglo, 52.7%; Hispanic, 42.3%; Black, 1.8%; Asian, 0.3%; Other, 3%.

GEORGE WEST (2,192) county seat, ranching, oil and gas operations, museums, library, Dobie Dichos in November.

Three Rivers (1,562) oil and gas, hunting and fishing, agriculture, federal prison.

Other towns include: **Dinero** (344); **Lagarto** (735), **Pernitas Point** (274, partly in Jim Wells County), **Whitsett** (200).

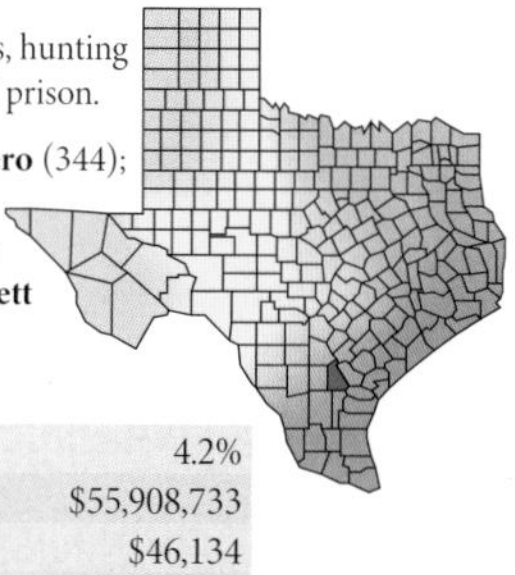

Unemployed	4.2%
Wages	$55,908,733
Per Capita Income	$46,134
Property Value	$6,031,653,693
Retail Sales	$228,697,554

Llano County

Physical Features: Central county drains to Colorado, Llano rivers; rolling to hilly; Lake Buchanan, Inks Lake, Lake Lyndon B. Johnson.

Economy: Tourism, retirement, ranch trading center, vineyards.

History: Tonkawas, later Comanches. Anglo-American and German settlers arrived in the 1840s. County name is Spanish for plains; created and organized in 1856 from Bexar District and Gillespie County.

Recreation: Leading deer-hunting county; fishing, lake activities, major tourist area, Enchanted Rock, eagles' nest on Highway 29, Hill Country Wine Trail in spring.

Minerals: Granite, vermiculite, llanite.

Agriculture: Beef cattle, sheep, goats. Market value $15.7 million. Deer-hunting, wildlife leases.

Vital Statistics, annual: Births, 174; deaths, 377; marriages, 77; divorces, 62.

Race/Ethnicity: Anglo, 82.5%; Hispanic, 11.8%; Black, 0.5%; Asian, 0.6%; Other, 4.6%.

LLANO (3,347) county seat; agriculture, hunting, tourism; hospital; historic district; museum.

KINGSLAND (6,917) tourism, retirement community, recreation, vineyards; library; archaeological center; AquaBoom on July 4.

Other towns include: **Bluffton** (75); **Buchanan Dam** (1,344) hydroelectric industry, tourism, fishing, water sports; **Buchanan Lake Village** (654); **Horseshoe Bay** (4,490, partly in Burnet County); **Sunrise Beach Village** (766); **Tow** (162).

Population	21,978
Change from 2010	13.9%
Area (sq. mi.)	965.9
Land Area (sq. mi.)	934.0
Altitude (ft.)	825–2,000
Rainfall (in.)	27.6
Jan. mean min (°F)	35.9
July mean max (°F)	95.3
Civ. Labor	9,354
Unemployed	3.8%
Wages	$63,757,255
Per Capita Income	$59,689
Property Value	$10,518,374,543
Retail Sales	$208,811,956

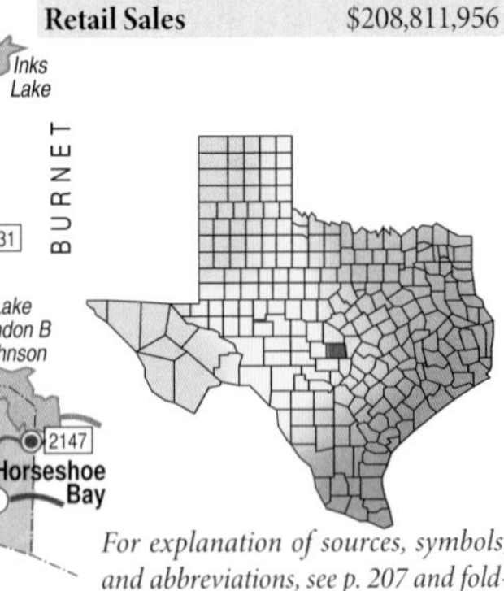

For explanation of sources, symbols, and abbreviations, see p. 207 and fold-out map.

Loving County

Physical Features: Flat desert terrain with a few low-rolling hills; slopes to Pecos River; Red Bluff Reservoir; sandy, loam, clay soils.

Economy: Oil and gas operations; cattle.

History: Land developers began operations in late 19th century. Oil discovered 1925. County created 1887 from Tom Green County; organized 1893, deorganized 1897, again organized 1931, the last organized. Named for Oliver Loving, trail driver. Loving County is our state's (and the country's) least populous.

Recreation: Pecos River, Red Bluff Lake.

Minerals: Oil, gas.

Agriculture: Cattle ranching. Market value $912,000.

Vital Statistics, annual: Births, 0; deaths, 0; marriages, 0; divorces, NA.

Race/Ethnicity: Anglo, 87.5%; Hispanic, 1.6%; Black, 0%; Asian, 0%; Other, 10.9%.

MENTONE (8) county seat, oil-field supply center; the only town.

Population	57
Change from 2010	–30.5%
Area (sq. mi.)	676.7
Land Area (sq. mi.)	668.9
Altitude (ft.)	2,660–3,374
Rainfall (in.)	10.1
Jan. mean min (°F)	31.5
July mean max (°F)	97.7
Civ. Labor	874
Unemployed	0.6%
Wages	$13,933,031
Per Capita Income	$115,158
Property Value	$18,202,084,048
Retail Sales	$16,032,636

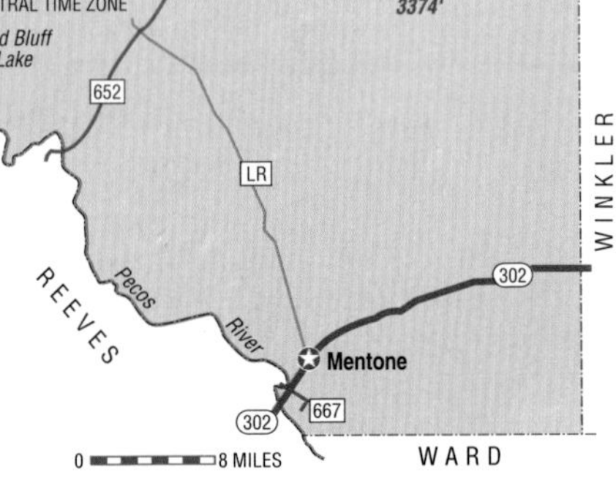

Lubbock County

Physical Features: South Plains, broken by 1,500 playas, upper Brazos River tributaries; rich soils with underground water.

Economy: Among world's largest cottonseed processing centers, a leading agribusiness center, cattle feedlots, varied manufacturing, higher education center, medical center, government/services.

History: Evidence of human habitation for 12,000 years. In historic period, Apache Indians, followed by Comanche hunters. Sheep raisers from Midwest arrived in the late 1870s. Cotton farms brought in Mexican laborers in the 1940s-1960s. County named for Col. Tom S. Lubbock, an organizer of the Confederate Terry's Rangers; county created in 1876 from Bexar District; organized in 1891.

Recreation: Lubbock Lake archaeological site; Texas Tech events; civic center; Buddy Holly statue, Walk of Fame, Lubbock Music Fest in fall; planetarium; Ranching Heritage Center; Panhandle-South Plains Fair, National Cowboy symposium in September; wine festivals; Buffalo Springs Lake.

Minerals: Oil, gas, stone, sand and gravel.

Agriculture: Second in bales of cotton produced. Fed beef, cow-calf operations; poultry, eggs; hogs. Other crops, nursery, grain sorghum, wheat, sunflowers, soybeans, hay, vegetables; more than 155,000 acres irrigated, mostly cotton. Market value $219.5 million.

Vital Statistics, annual: Births, 3,980; deaths, 3,470; marriages, 1,734; divorces, 747.

Race/Ethnicity: Anglo, 49.9%; Hispanic, 35.1%; Black, 8.3%; Asian, 3.1%; Other, 3.6%.

LUBBOCK (260,993) county seat; center for large agricultural area; manufacturing includes electronics, earth-moving equipment, food containers, fire-protection equipment, clothing, other products; distribution center for South Plains; feedlots; museum; government/services; hospitals, psychiatric hospital; wind power center.

Other towns include: **Buffalo Springs** (459); **Idalou** (2,152); **New Deal** (729); **Ransom Canyon** (1,170); **Shallowater** (2,940); **Slaton** (5,811) agriculture, government/services, Harvey House hotel, museums, sausagefest in October; **Wolfforth** (6,008) retail, government/services.

Also, part [689] of **Abernathy** (2,804).

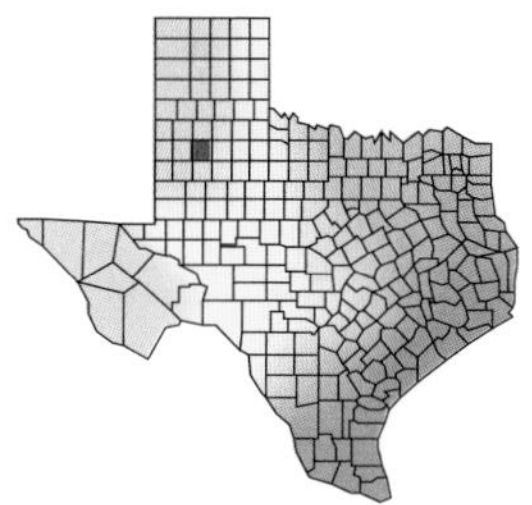

Population	314,451
Change from 2010	12.8%
Area (sq. mi.)	900.7
Land Area (sq. mi.)	895.6
Altitude (ft.)	2,821–3,402
Rainfall (in.)	18.3
Jan. mean min (°F)	28.7

July mean max (°F)	92.4
Civ. Labor	163,740
Unemployed	3.4 %
Wages	$1,968,821,923
Per Capita Income	$50,881
Property Value	$32,907,440,828
Retail Sales	$7,994,332,069

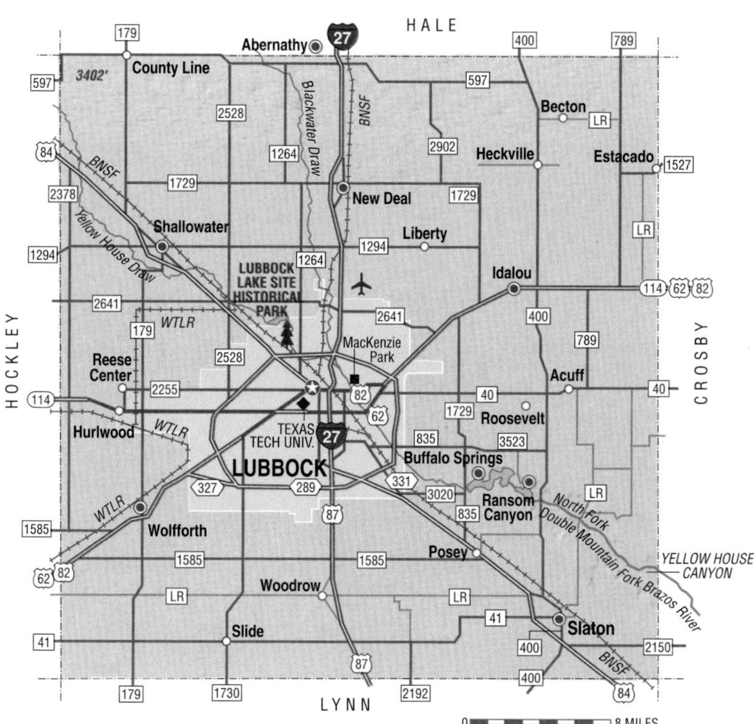

For explanation of sources, symbols, and abbreviations, see p. 207 and foldout map.

Lynn County

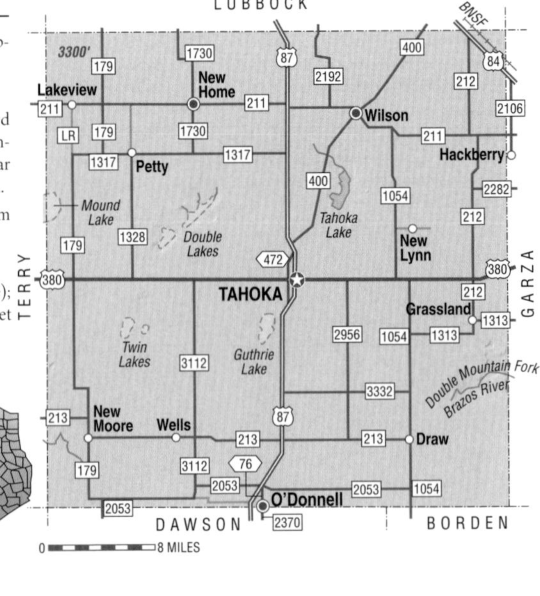

Physical Features: South Plains, broken by Caprock Escarpment, playas, draws; sandy loam, black, gray soils.

Economy: Agribusiness.

History: Apaches, ousted by Comanches who were removed to Indian Territory in 1875. Ranching began in 1880s. Farming developed after 1900. County created in 1876 from Bexar District; organized in 1903; named for Alamo victim W. Lynn.

Recreation: Pioneer museum in Tahoka; Dan Blocker museum in O'Donnell; sandhill crane migration in winter.

Minerals: Oil, natural gas.

Agriculture: Cotton produces largest income (first in acreage); 72,000 acres irrigated. Also, ranching, grain sorghum. Market value $111.4 million.

Vital Statistics, annual: Births, 68; deaths, 93; marriages, 14; divorces, 9.

Race/Ethnicity: Anglo, 52.9%; Hispanic, 42%; Black, 1.9%; Asian, 0.2%; Other, 3%.

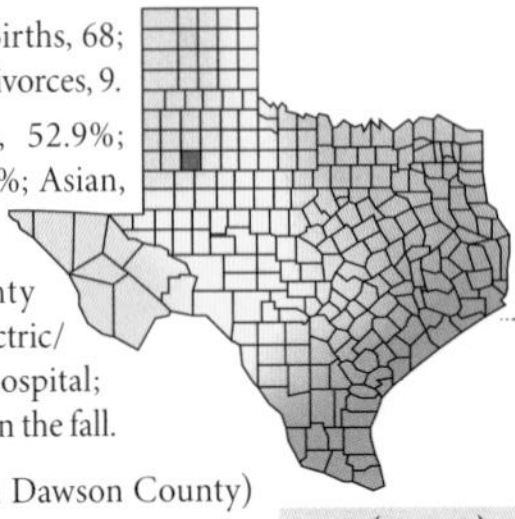

TAHOKA (2,390) county seat; agricultural center, electric/telephone cooperatives; hospital; museum; Harvest Festival in the fall.

O'Donnell (729, partly in Dawson County) commercial center.

Other towns include: **New Home** (335); **Wilson** (444).

Population	5,688
Change from 2010	−3.8%

Area (sq. mi.)	893.5
Land Area (sq. mi.)	891.9
Altitude (ft.)	2,660–3,300
Rainfall (in.)	20.7
Jan. mean min (°F)	29.8
July mean max (°F)	92.2

Civ. Labor	2,876
Unemployed	3.5%
Wages	$28,870,602
Per Capita Income	$58,496
Property Value	$1,631,326,520
Retail Sales	$33,385,440

Wilson City Hall is in the Green Building (the tall brick building on the corner). Photo by Leaflet, CC by SA 3.0

Madison County

Physical Features: Hilly, draining to Trinity, Navasota rivers, Bedias Creek; one-fifth of area timbered; alluvial, loam, sandy soils.

Economy: Prison, government/services, varied manufacturing, agribusiness, oil production.

History: Caddo, Bidai Indian area; Kickapoos migrated from the east. Spanish settlements established in 1774 and 1805. Anglo-Americans arrived in 1829. Census of 1860 showed 30% of population was Black. County named for U.S. President James Madison; created from Grimes, Leon, and Walker counties 1853; organized 1854.

Recreation: Fishing, hunting; Spanish Bluff where survivors of the Gutiérrez-Magee expedition were executed in 1813; other historic sites.

Minerals: sand, oil.

Agriculture: Nursery crops, cattle, horses, poultry raised; forage for livestock. Market value $124.1 million.

Vital Statistics, annual: Births, 176; deaths, 168; marriages, 77; divorces, 13.

Race/Ethnicity: Anglo, 51.9%; Hispanic, 25.4%; Black, 19.2%; Asian, 0.8%; Other, 2.7%.

MADISONVILLE (4,565) county seat; farm-trade center, varied manufacturing; hospital, library; Mudbug & Music in April.

Other towns, **Midway** (184); **Normangee** (506, mostly in Leon County).

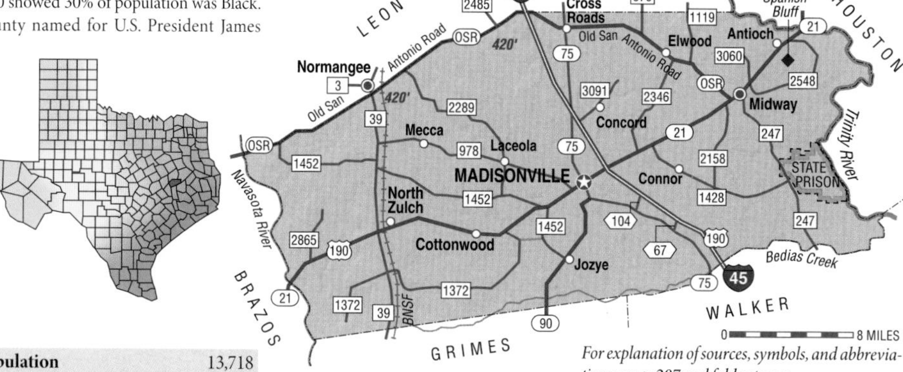

For explanation of sources, symbols, and abbreviations, see p. 207 and foldout map.

Population	13,718
Change from 2010	0.4%
Area (sq. mi.)	472.4
Land Area (sq. mi.)	466.1
Altitude (ft.)	131–420
Rainfall (in.)	46.8

Jan. mean min (°F)	38.4
July mean max (°F)	94.1
Civ. Labor	4,741
Unemployed	4.3%

Wages	$53,967,118
Per Capita Income	$40,859
Property Value	$3,373,473,108
Retail Sales	$349,750,410

Marion County

Physical Features: Northeastern county; hilly, three-quarters forested with pines, hardwoods; drains to Caddo Lake, Lake O' the Pines, Big Cypress Bayou; Johnson Creek Reservoir.

Economy: Agriculture, tourism, forestry, food processing.

History: Caddoes forced out in 1790s. Kickapoo in area when settlers arrived from Deep South around 1840. Antebellum slaveholding area. County created 1860 from Cass County, organized the same year; named for Gen. Francis Marion of American Revolution.

Recreation: Lake activities, hunting, Excelsior Hotel, 84 medallions on historic sites including Jay Gould railroad car, museum, historical homes tour in May, Spring Festival.

Minerals: Iron ore, natural gas, oil.

Agriculture: Beef cattle, hay. Market value $5.9 million. Forestry is most important industry.

Vital Statistics, annual: Births, 91; deaths, 182; marriages, 50; divorces, 40.

Race/Ethnicity: Anglo, 70.6%; Hispanic, 4%; Black, 19%; Asian, 0.5%; Other, 5.9%.

JEFFERSON (1,849) county seat; tourism, syrup works, forestry; museum, library; historical sites.

Other towns include: **Lodi** (175); **Pine Harbor** (809).

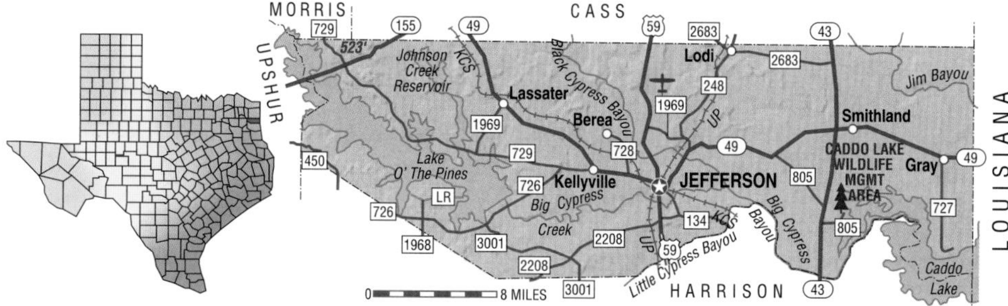

Population	9,645
Change from 2010	–8.5%
Area (sq. mi.)	420.3
Land Area (sq. mi.)	380.9
Altitude (ft.)	168–523

Rainfall (in.)	49.7
Jan. mean min (°F)	35.5
July mean max (°F)	93.0
Civ. Labor	4,208
Unemployed	5.0%

Wages	$20,829,065
Per Capita Income	$47,582
Property Value	$1,494,136,480
Retail Sales	$69,950,309

Martin County

Physical Features: South Plains; sandy, loam soils, broken by playas, creeks; Sulphur Springs Draw Reservoir.

Economy: Oil and gas production, agribusiness.

History: Apaches, ousted by Comanches who in turn were forced out by the U.S. Army in 1875. Farming began in 1881. County created from Bexar District in 1876; organized in 1884; named for Wylie Martin, senator of Republic of Texas.

Recreation: Museum, settlers reunion in July at Stanton.

Minerals: Oil, gas.

Agriculture: Cotton, beef cattle, milo, wheat, horses, meat goats. Market value $54.3 million.

Vital Statistics, annual: Births, 86; deaths, 66; marriages, 20; divorces, 11.

Race/Ethnicity: Anglo, 53.1%; Hispanic, 43.1%; Black, 1.5%; Asian, 0.2%; Other, 2.1%.

STANTON (2,649) county seat; oil and gas production, agribusiness; commuting to Midland, Big Spring; hospital; museum, historic monastery, other historic buildings; Old Sorehead trade days April and October.

Other towns include: **Ackerly** (265, partly in Dawson County); **Lenorah** (83); **Tarzan** (30).

Population	5,211
Change from 2010	8.6%
Area (sq. mi.)	915.7
Land Area (sq. mi.)	914.9
Altitude (ft.)	2,470–2,976
Rainfall (in.)	13.6
Jan. mean min (°F)	32.7
July mean max (°F)	94.8
Civ. Labor	2,798
Unemployed	3.1%
Wages	$42,064,354
Per Capita Income	$84,121
Property Value	$20,409,399,590
Retail Sales	$150,671,987

Mason County

Physical Features: Central county; hilly, draining to Llano and San Saba rivers and their tributaries; limestone, red soils; varied timber.

Economy: Sand plants, agriculture, tourism, hunting.

History: Lipan Apaches in area, driven south by Comanches around 1790. German settlers arrived in the mid-1840s, followed by Anglo-Americans. Mexican immigration increased after 1930. County created from Bexar and Gillespie counties in 1858, organized the same year; named for Mexican War victim U.S. Army Lt. G.T. Mason.

Recreation: Hunting, fishing; kayaking, rock crawling, camping, golf, wine tasting rooms, topaz hunting; historic homes of stone; prehistoric Indian artifacts exhibit; Fort Mason, where Robert E. Lee served; bat cave; wildflower drives in spring, Roundup rodeo in July.

Minerals: Sand, topaz, granite.

Agriculture: Beef cattle, hay, meat goats, viticulture. Market value $21.7 million. Hunting leases important.

Vital Statistics, annual: Births, 33; deaths, 48; marriages, 14; divorces, 5.

Race/Ethnicity: Anglo, 74.6%; Hispanic, 22.3%; Black, 0.1%; Asian, 0.1%; Other, 2.9%.

MASON (2,119) county seat; agriculture, hunting, nature tourism; museums, historical district, homes, rock fences built by German settlers; wild game dinner in November.

Other towns include: **Art** (14), **Fredonia** (55), **Pontotoc** (125).

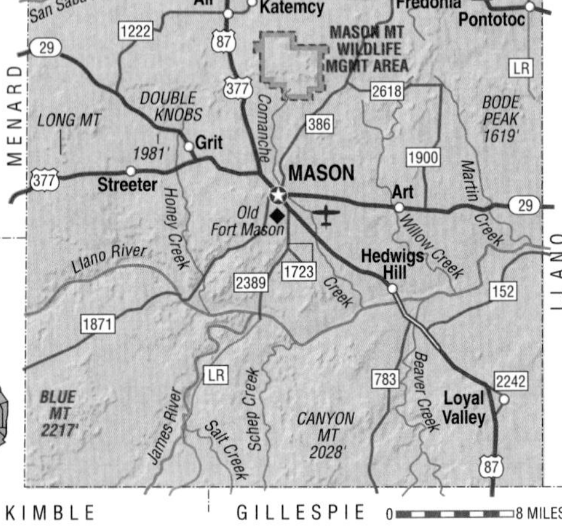

Population	3,943
Change from 2010	–1.7%
Area (sq. mi.)	932.2
Land Area (sq. mi.)	928.8
Altitude (ft.)	1,180–2,217
Rainfall (in.)	28.9
Jan. mean min (°F)	35.6
July mean max (°F)	94.6
Civ. Labor	1,827
Unemployed	3.3%
Wages	$12,180,914
Per Capita Income	$57,094
Property Value	$3,043,957,714
Retail Sales	$27,240,688

The Bay City Regional Airport is east of the town, on FM 2540. Photo by Djmaschek, CC by SA 4.0

Matagorda County

Physical Features: Gulf Coastal Plain; flat, broken by bays; many different soils; drains to Colorado River, creeks, coast; South Texas Project Reservoir.

Economy: Agribusiness, oil and gas fields, refinery.

History: Karankawa tribal area, Tonkawas in the area later. Anglo-Americans arrived in 1822. Mexican immigration increased after 1920. An original county, created in 1836 from a Spanish municipality, named for canebrake; organized in 1837; settled by Austin colonists.

Recreation: Wildlife hunting and viewing, fishing (fresh and salt water), beaches, sailing, historic sites, museums; Bay City rice festival in October.

Minerals: Oil and gas.

Agriculture: Cotton, rice, soybeans, corn, grain sorghum; some 33,000 acres of crops irrigated; cattle, turf, aquaculture (first in value). Market value $124.2 million.

Vital Statistics, annual: Births, 495; deaths, 467; marriages, 178; divorces, 66.

Race/Ethnicity: Anglo, 42.4%; Hispanic, 42.6%; Black, 10.3%; Asian, 1.9%; Other, 2.8%.

BAY CITY (17,882) county seat; government/services, education, nuclear power plant; petrochemicals; agribusiness; hospital, junior college branch.

PALACIOS (4,418) tourism, seafood industry; hospital; Marine Education Center; public fishing piers; Bay Festival on Labor Day.

Other towns include: **Blessing** (249) historic sites; **Cedar Lane** (300); **Collegeport** (80); **Elmaton** (160); **Markham** (983); **Matagorda** (431); **Midfield** (58); **Pledger** (265); **Sargent** (1,319) retirement community, fishing, birding, commercial fishing, barbecue cookoff in April; **Van Vleck** (1,054); **Wadsworth** (507).

Population	36,344
Change from 2010	-1.0%
Area (sq. mi.)	1,612.5
Land Area (sq. mi.)	1,100.3
Altitude (ft.)	sea level–70
Rainfall (in.)	49.1
Jan. mean min (°F)	45.0
July mean max (°F)	90.2
Civ. Labor	17,150
Unemployed	5.9%
Wages	$184,754,887
Per Capita Income	$50,775
Property Value	$10,217,155,750
Retail Sales	$467,279,108

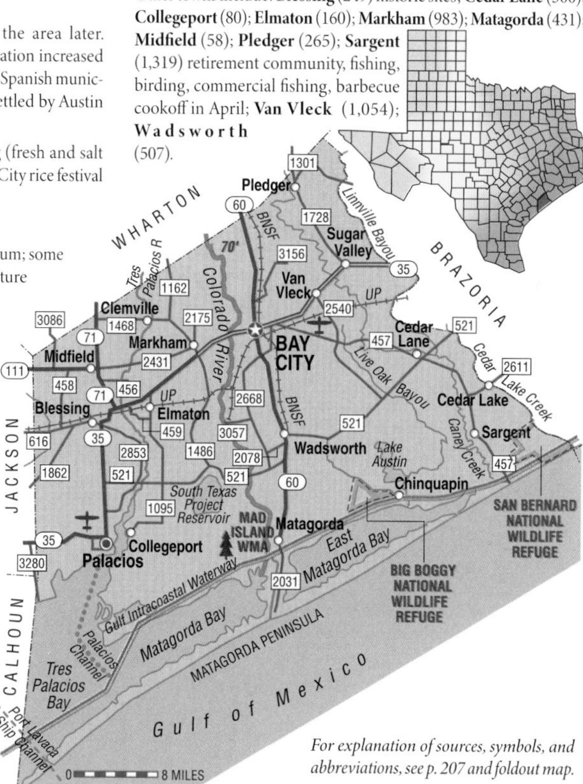

For explanation of sources, symbols, and abbreviations, see p. 207 and foldout map.

Maverick County

Physical Features: Southwestern county on the Rio Grande; broken, rolling surface, with dense brush; clay, sandy, alluvial soils.

Economy: Oil, government/services, agribusiness, tourism.

History: Coahuiltecan area; later Comanches arrived. Spanish ranching began in the 1760s. Anglo-Americans arrived in 1834. County named for Sam A. Maverick, whose name is now a synonym for unbranded cattle; created in 1856 from Kinney County; organized in 1871.

Recreation: Tourist gateway to Mexico; white-tailed deer, bird hunting; fishing; historic sites, Fort Duncan museum.

Minerals: Oil, gas, sand, gravel.

Agriculture: Cattle feedlots; pecans, vegetables, sorghum, wheat; goats, sheep. Some irrigation from Rio Grande. Market value $43.0 million.

Vital Statistics, annual: Births, 1,026; deaths, 688; marriages, 385; divorces, NA.

Race/Ethnicity: Anglo, 2.7%; Hispanic, 94.9%; Black, 0.2%; Asian, 0.3%; Other, 1.8%.

EAGLE PASS (28,596) county seat; government/services, retail center, tourism; hospital; junior college, Sul Ross college branch; entry point to Piedras Negras, Mex., Nacho Festival in Piedras Negras in October.

Other communities include: **Chula Vista** (212), **Eidson Road** (9,743), **Las Quintas Fronterizas** (1,061), and **Rosita** (3,799), all immediately south of Eagle Pass.

Also, **Elm Creek** (3,902); **Fabrica** (1,147); **Seco Mines** (1,064); **Siesta Acres** (1,687); and **Quemado** (112).

Population	58,056
Change from 2010	7.0%
Area (sq. mi.)	1,291.8
Land Area (sq. mi.)	1,279.3
Altitude (ft.)	550–975
Rainfall (in.)	20.8
Jan. mean min (°F)	41.0
July mean max (°F)	97.4
Civ. Labor	23,405

Unemployed	7.9%
Wages	$198,144,469
Per Capita Income	$38,448
Property Value	$5,408,821,331
Retail Sales	$805,888,394

McCulloch County

Physical Features: Hilly and rolling; drains to Colorado River, Brady Creek and Brady Creek Reservoir, San Saba River; black loams to sandy soils.

Economy: Agribusiness, industrial sand production, hunting leases.

History: Apache area. First Anglo-American settlers arrived in the late 1850s, but Comanche raids delayed further settlement until the 1870s. County created from Bexar District in 1856; organized in 1876; named for San Jacinto veteran Gen. Ben McCulloch.

Recreation: Hunting, lake activities, museums, goat cookoff on Labor Day, golf tournaments.

Minerals: Sand, oil, and gas.

Agriculture: Beef cattle and sheep; also small grains, goats, hay, cotton. Market value $22.5 million. Hunting leases.

Vital Statistics, annual: Births, 76; deaths, 124; marriages, 61; divorces, 28.

Race/Ethnicity: Anglo, 64.3%; Hispanic, 31%; Black, 1.2%; Asian, 0.5%; Other, 3%.

BRADY (5,032) county seat; silica sand, oil-field equipment, ranching, tourism, other manufacturing; hospital; Heart of Texas car show in April.

Other towns: **Doole** (74), **Lohn** (149), **Melvin** (124), **Mercury** (166), **Rochelle** (214), and **Voca** (56).

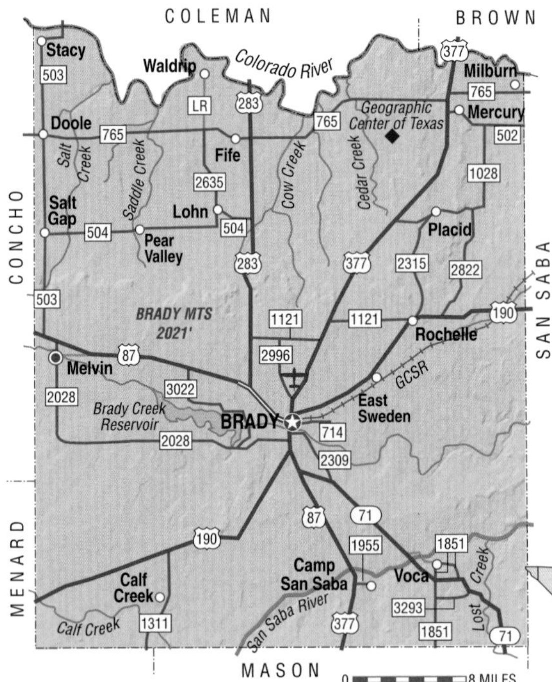

Population	7,533
Change from 2010	–9.1%
Area (sq. mi.)	1,073.4
Land Area (sq. mi.)	165.6
Altitude (ft.)	1,280–2,021

Rainfall (in.)	27.4
Jan. mean min (°F)	37.0
July mean max (°F)	92.3
Civ. Labor	3,151
Unemployed	4.2%

Wages	$29,599,859
Per Capita Income	$45,744
Property Value	$2,778,104,004
Retail Sales	$103,126,218

McLennan County

Physical Features: Central Texas county of mostly Blackland prairie, but rolling hills in west; drains to Bosque, Brazos rivers and Lake Waco, Tradinghouse Creek Reservoir, Lake Creek Lake; heavy, loam, sandy soils.

Economy: Agribusiness, education, health services.

History: Tonkawas, Wichitas and Wacos in area. Anglo-American settlers arrived in the 1840s. Indians removed to Brazos reservations in 1854. County created from Milam County in 1850, organized the same year; named for settler, Neil McLennan Sr.

Recreation: Texas Ranger Hall of Fame, museum; Texas Sports Hall of Fame; Dr Pepper Museum; Cameron Park; drag boat races April and May; zoo; historic sites, homes; museums; libraries, art center; symphony; civic theater; Baylor University events; Heart o' Texas Fair in October.

Minerals: Sand, gravel, limestone.

Agriculture: Corn, silage, wheat, beef cattle, dairies. Market value $179.7 million.

Vital Statistics, annual: Births, 3,199; deaths, 2,742; marriages, 1,376; divorces, 778.

Race/Ethnicity: Anglo, 53.6%; Hispanic, 26.3%; Black, 13.9%; Asian, 1.9%; Other, 4.3%.

WACO (139,594) county seat; manufacturing, higher education, medical services/hospital, government/services, finance; riverside park, historic suspension bridge, zoo; Magnolia Silos market; Waco Mammoth National Monument; wine festival in April.

Hewitt (16,131) medical services/hospital, construction, retail; car show and concert in April.

West (2,557) known for Czech foods; varied manufacturing; Westfest Labor Day weekend.

Other towns include: **Axtell** (300); **Bellmead** (10,575); **Beverly Hills** (1,876); **Bruceville-Eddy** (1,426, partly in Falls County); **China Spring** (1,342); **Crawford** (903); **Elm Mott** (300); **Gholson** (1,262); **Hallsburg** (433); **Lacy-Lakeview** (7,090); **Leroy** (354); **Lorena** (1,791); **Mart** (1,791) agricultural center, some manufacturing, museum, juvenile correction facility.

Also: **McGregor** (5,522) agriculture, manufacturing, distribution; private telephone museum; Frontier Founders Day in September; **Moody** (1,411) agriculture, commuting to Waco, Temple; library; Cotton Harvest fest in September; **Riesel** (1,071); **Robinson** (12,755); **Ross** (251); **Woodway** (9,474).

Part of **Golinda** (667, mostly in Falls County) and part of **Valley Mills** (1,243, mostly in Bosque County).

For explanation of sources, symbols, and abbreviations, see p. 207 and foldout map.

Population	263,115
Change from 2010	12.0%
Area (sq. mi.)	1,060.2
Land Area (sq. mi.)	1,037.1
Altitude (ft.)	350–960
Rainfall (in.)	36.4
Jan. mean min (°F)	37.9
July mean max (°F)	95.5
Civ. Labor	127,001
Unemployed	3.6%
Wages	$1,745,707,728
Per Capita Income	$49,512
Property Value	$37,097,632,938
Retail Sales	$5,163,254,150

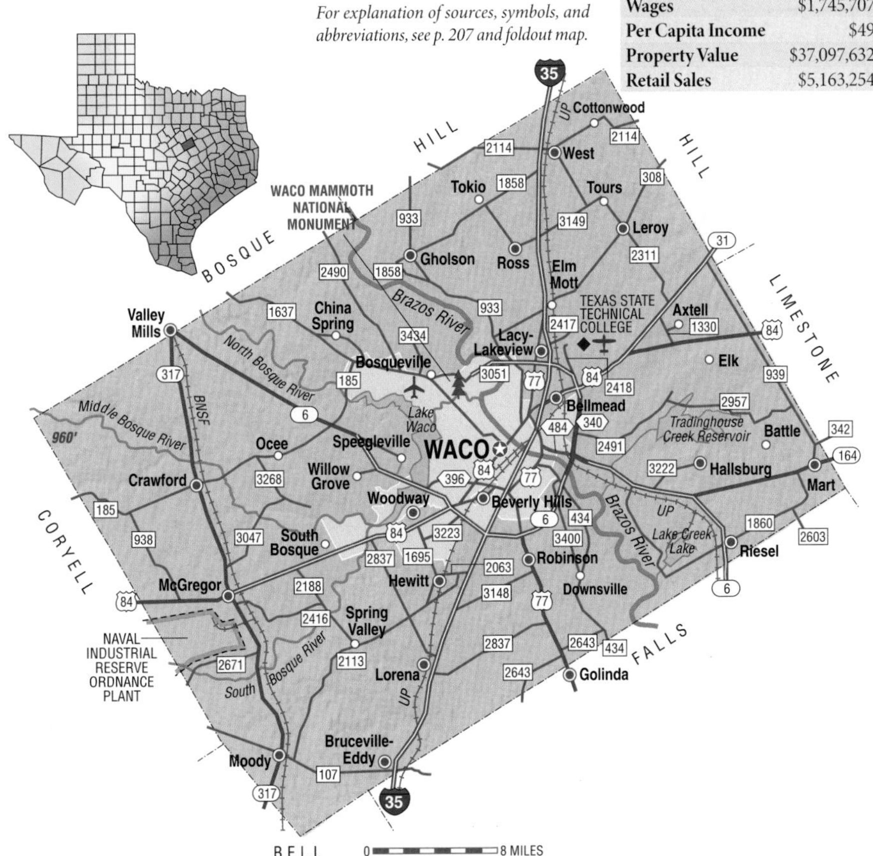

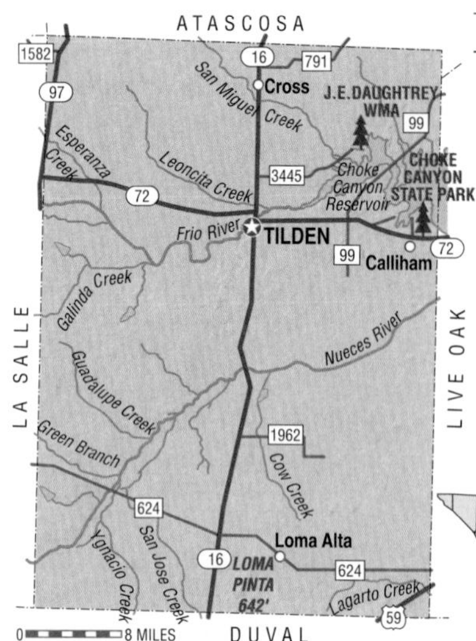

McMullen County

Physical Features: Southern county of brushy plain, sloping to Frio, Nueces rivers and tributaries, Choke Canyon Reservoir; saline clay soils.

Economy: Government/services, retail, agriculture, oil and gas services.

History: Coahuiltecans, squeezed out by Lipan Apaches and other tribes. Anglo-American settlers arrived in 1858. Sheep ranching of 1870s attracted Mexican laborers. County created from Atascosa, Bexar, Live Oak counties 1858; organized 1862, reorganized 1877; named for Nueces River pioneer-empresario John McMullen.

Recreation: Hunting, wildlife viewing; lake activities, state park, wildlife management area; Labor Day rodeo.

Minerals: Gas, oil, lignite coal, caliche, kaolinite.

Agriculture: Beef cattle. Market value $8.3 million. Wildlife enterprises important.

Vital Statistics, annual: Births, 12; deaths, 18; marriages, 3; divorces, NA.

Race/Ethnicity: Anglo, 58.8%; Hispanic, 37.3%; Black, 0.2%; Asian, 0.5%; Other, 3.2%.

TILDEN (301) county seat; oil, gas, lignite mining, ranch center, government/services.

Other towns include: **Calliham** (100).

Population	608
Change from 2010	–14.0%
Area (sq. mi.)	1,156.8
Land Area (sq. mi.)	1,139.4
Altitude (ft.)	150–642

Rainfall (in.)	25.6
Jan. mean min (°F)	45.3
July mean max (°F)	97.2
Civ. Labor	902
Unemployed	1.8%

Wages	$11,290,830
Per Capita Income	$110,273
Property Value	$4,731,909,415
Retail Sales	$20,429,387

Medina County

Physical Features: Southwestern county with scenic hills in north; south has fertile valleys, rolling surface; Medina River, Medina Lake.

Economy: Agribusiness, tourism, commuters to San Antonio.

History: Lipan Apaches and Comanches in area. Settled by Alsatians led by Henri Castro in 1844. Mexican immigration increased after 1900. County created and organized in 1848 from Bexar; named for river, probably for Spanish engineer Pedro Medina.

Recreation: A leading deer area; scenic drives, camping, fishing, historic buildings, museum, market trail days most months.

Minerals: Oil and natural gas.

Agriculture: Cattle, corn, grains, cotton, hay, vegetables, aquaculture; 50,000 acres irrigated. Market value $93.9 million.

Vital Statistics, annual: Births, 597; deaths, 521; marriages, 209; divorces, 142.

Race/Ethnicity: Anglo, 44.0%; Hispanic, 50.2%; Black, 2.5%; Asian, 0.4%; Other, 3.0%.

HONDO (8,387) county seat; flight training center, aerospace industry, agribusiness, varied manufacturing, hunting leases; hospital; prisons; wild game festival in January.

Castroville (3,005) farming; tourism; commuting to San Antonio; Landmark Inn, museum; St. Louis Day celebration in August.

Devine (4,410) commuters, shipping for truck crop-livestock; fall festival in October.

Other towns: **D'Hanis** (615), **La Coste** (1,107), **Natalia** (1,271), **Riomedina** (60), **Yancey** (384). Also, part [817] of **Lytle**.

Population	51,981
Change from 2010	13.0%
Area (sq. mi.)	1,334.4
Land Area (sq. mi.)	1,325.4

Altitude (ft.)	570–1,995
Rainfall (in.)	24.9
Jan. mean min (°F)	40.7
July mean max (°F)	96.1
Civ. Labor	22,681

Unemployed	3.8%
Wages	$128,977,722
Per Capita Income	$50,076
Property Value	$9,672,795,657
Retail Sales	$905,540,865

Menard County

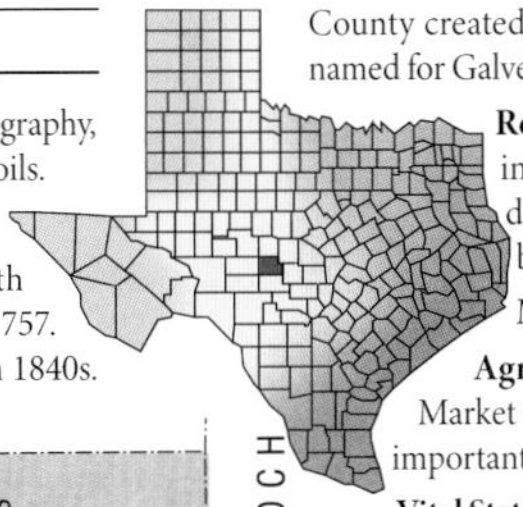

County created from Bexar County 1858, organized 1871; named for Galveston's founder, Michel B. Menard.

Physical Features: West central county of rolling topography, draining to San Saba River and tributaries; limestone soils.

Economy: Agriculture, tourism, oil, gas production.

History: Apaches, followed by Comanches in 18th century. Mission Santa Cruz de San Sabá established in 1757. A few Anglo-American and German settlers arrived in 1840s.

Recreation: Hunting, fishing; historic sites, including Spanish presidio, mission, irrigation ditches; U.S. fort; railroad museum; Jim Bowie barbecue cook-off in May.

Minerals: Oil, gas.

Agriculture: Cattle, sheep, goats, pecans, hay. Market value $9.1 million. Hunting leases, ecotourism important.

Vital Statistics, annual: Births, 14; deaths, 41; marriages, 1; divorces, 4.

Race/Ethnicity: Anglo, 62.7%; Hispanic, 33.7%; Black, 0.6%; Asian, 0.3%; Other, 2.7%.

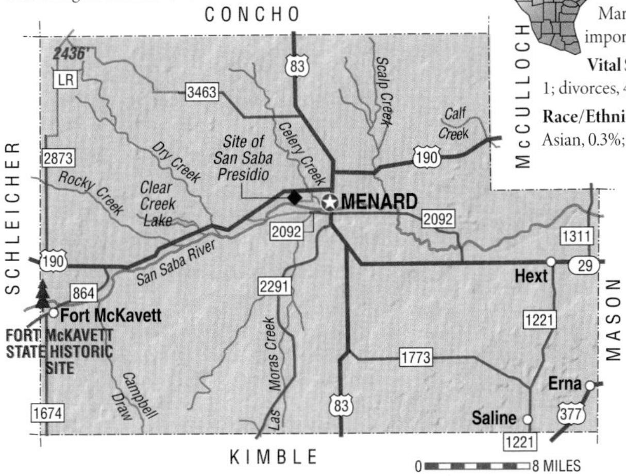

MENARD (1,355) county seat; agribusiness, government/services; Hunters Blowout Ball in early November.

Other towns include: **Fort McKavett** (50); **Hext** (75).

Population	1,982
Change from 2010	−11.6%
Area (sq. mi.)	902.3
Land Area (sq. mi.)	902.0
Altitude (ft.)	1,690–2,436
Rainfall (in.)	24.3
Jan. mean min (°F)	31.2
July mean max (°F)	93.8
Civ. Labor	851
Unemployed	3.8%
Wages	$3,545,496
Per Capita Income	$47,390
Property Value	$1,522,177,180
Retail Sales	$27,396,959

Midland County

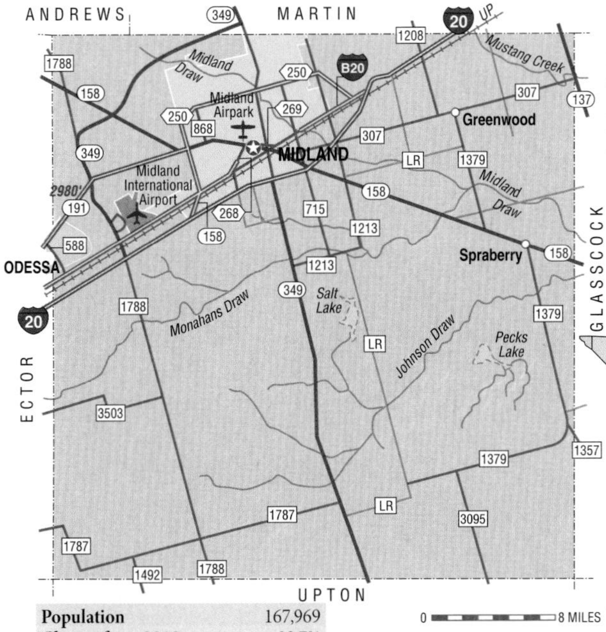

Physical Features: Flat western county, broken by draws; sandy, loam soils with native grasses.

Economy: Among leading petroleum-producing counties; distribution, administrative center for oil industry; varied manufacturing; government/services.

History: Comanches in area in 19th century. Sheep ranching developed in the 1880s. Permian Basin oil boom began in the 1920s. County created from Tom Green County in 1885 and organized the same year; name came from midway location on the railroad between El Paso and Fort Worth. The Chihuahua Trail and Emigrant Road were pioneer trails that crossed the county.

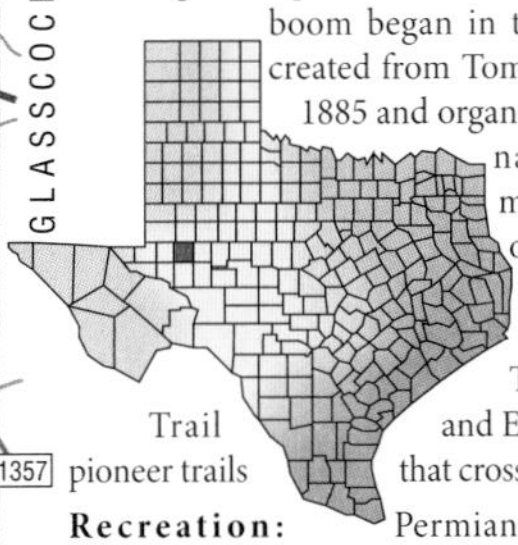

Recreation: Permian Basin Petroleum Museum, Library, Hall of Fame; Museum of Southwest; Commemorative Air Force and Museum; community theater; metropolitan events; Bush Family Home SHS.

Minerals: Oil, natural gas.

Agriculture: Beef cattle, horses, sheep and goats; cotton, hay, pecans; some 11,000 acres irrigated. Market value $16.3 million.

Vital Statistics, annual: Births, 2,919; deaths, 1,312; marriages, 1,228; divorces, 719.

Race/Ethnicity: Anglo, 45%; Hispanic, 43.1%; Black, 6.2%; Asian, 2.3%; Other, 3.4%.

MIDLAND (131,325) county seat; petroleum, petrochemical center; varied manufacturing; livestock sale center; hospitals; cultural activities; community college; polo club, Texas League baseball; Celebration of the Arts in May.

Part [3,803] of **Odessa** (112,483, mostly in Ector County).

Population	167,969
Change from 2010	22.7%
Area (sq. mi.)	902.1
Land Area (sq. mi.)	900.3
Altitude (ft.)	2,550–2,980
Rainfall (in.)	13.5
Jan. mean min (°F)	34.3
July mean max (°F)	95.2
Civ. Labor	105,948
Unemployed	2.9%
Wages	$2,541,031,733
Per Capita Income	$126,738
Property Value	$56,848,651,573
Retail Sales	$4,406,324,173

Milam County

Physical Features: East central county of partly level Blackland; southeast rolling to Post Oak Belt; Brazos, Little rivers; Alcoa Lake.

Economy: Government, construction, retail trade, healthcare, agriculture, accommodation and food services, manufacturing, information, wholesale trade.

History: Lipan Apaches, Tonkawas and Comanches in area. Mission San Francisco Xavier established 1745–1748. Anglo-American settlers arrived in 1834 and a private fort was established in 1840 at Bryant Station to help protect the settlers from Indian raids. County created in 1836 from municipality named for Ben Milam, a leader who died at the battle for San Antonio in December 1835; organized in 1837.

Recreation: Fishing, hunting; historic sites include Fort Sullivan, Indian battlegrounds, mission sites; museum in old jail at Cameron, El Camino Real.

Minerals: Barite, limited oil and gas production.

Agriculture: Cattle, hay, feed corn, cotton. Market value $129.5 million.

Vital Statistics, annual: Births, 295; deaths, 307; marriages, 90; divorces, 52.

Race/Ethnicity: Anglo, 62.1%; Hispanic, 25.3%; Black, 8.5%; Asian, 0.4%; Other, 3.7%.

CAMERON (5,352) county seat; government/services, manufacturing; library; salsa competition in June.

ROCKDALE (5,398) government/services; hospital, juvenile detention center.

Other towns include: **Buckholts** (372); **Davilla** (191); **Gause** (234); **Milano** (398); **Thorndale** (1,287) agribusiness, farming, ranching, antiques, barbecue cook-off in June.

Population	25,106
Change from 2010	1.4%

Area (sq. mi.)	1,021.8
Land Area (sq. mi.)	1,016.9
Altitude (ft.)	250–648
Rainfall (in.)	38.6
Jan. mean min (°F)	41.0
July mean max (°F)	93.1
Civ. Labor	10,297
Unemployed	4.3%
Wages	$73,051,157
Per Capita Income	$45,286
Property Value	$5,682,053,252
Retail Sales	$305,238,904

The Baptist Church in Davilla is on land purchased by the congregation in 1870. Photo by Darryl Pearson, CC by SA 4.0

Mills County

Physical Features: West central county of hills, plateau draining to the Colorado River; sandy, loam soils.

Economy: Agribusiness, hunting leases.

History: Apache-Comanche area of conflict. Anglo-Americans and a few Germans settled in the 1850s. County created and organized in 1887 from Brown, Comanche, Hamilton, Lampasas counties; named for pioneer jurist John T. Mills.

Recreation: Fishing; deer, dove and turkey hunting; Regency suspension bridge; rangeland recreation.

Minerals: Not significant.

Agriculture: Cattle, dairies, sheep (first in numbers), goats, hay. Market value $30.9 million.

Vital Statistics, annual: Births, 28; deaths, 78; marriages, 18; divorces, 17.

Race/Ethnicity: Anglo, 78.5%; Hispanic, 16.3%; Black, 0.6%; Asian, 0.1%; Other, 4.5%.

GOLDTHWAITE (1,715) county seat; agribusiness, hunting; museum; barbecue & goat cook-off in April.

Other towns include: **Mullin** (131); **Priddy** (160); **Star** (97).

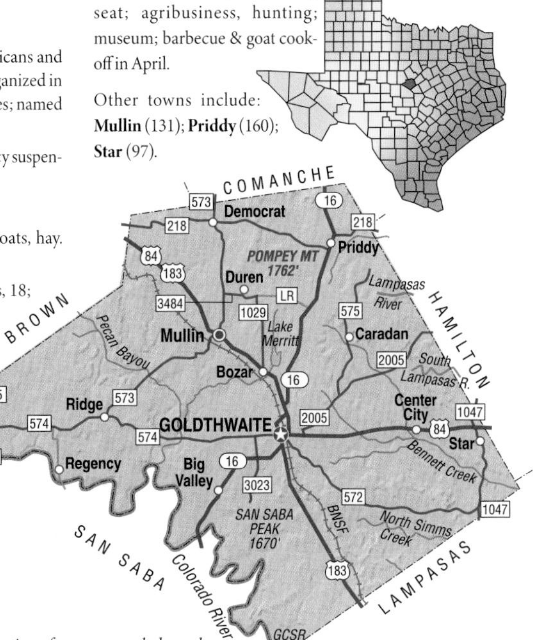

For explanation of sources, symbols, and abbreviations, see p. 207 and foldout map.

Population	4,480
Change from 2010	–9.2%
Area (sq. mi.)	749.8
Land Area (sq. mi.)	748.3
Altitude (ft.)	1,112–1,762
Rainfall (in.)	30.4
Jan. mean min (°F)	35.3
July mean max (°F)	91.8
Civ. Labor	1,910
Unemployed	4.2%
Wages	$13,487,467
Per Capita Income	$51,712
Property Value	$2,868,780,765
Retail Sales	$108,526,885

Mitchell County

Physical Features: Rolling, draining to Colorado and tributaries; sandy, red, dark soils; Lake Colorado City, Mitchell County Reservoir, and Champion Creek Reservoir.

Economy: Government/services, agribusiness, oil, some manufacturing.

History: Jumano Indians in area; Comanches arrived about 1780. Anglo-American settlers arrived in the late 1870s after Comanches were forced into Indian Territory. County created in 1876 from Bexar District and organized in 1881; named for pioneer brothers Asa and Eli Mitchell.

Recreation: Lake activities, state park, museums, hunting.

Minerals: Oil.

Agriculture: Cotton principal crop, grains also produced. Cattle, sheep, goats, hogs raised. Market value $21.7 million.

Vital Statistics, annual: Births, 72; deaths, 92; marriages, 33; divorces, 28.

Race/Ethnicity: Anglo, 48.1%; Hispanic, 38.4%; Black, 10.3%; Asian, 0.6%; Other, 2.5%.

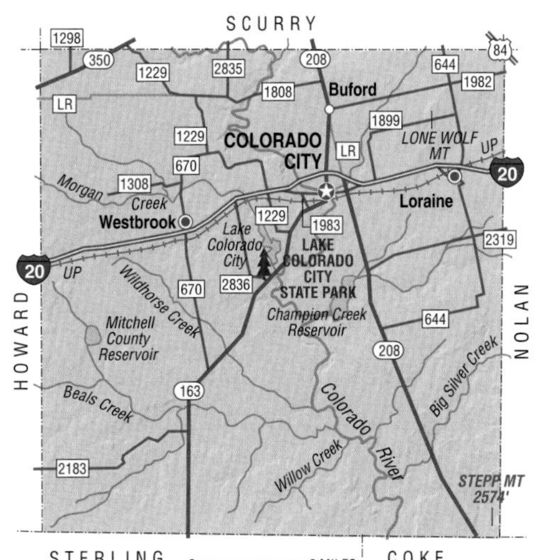

Population	9,070	**July mean max (°F)**	95.1
Change from 2010	–3.5%	**Civ. Labor**	2,309
Area (sq. mi.)	915.9	**Unemployed**	4.4%
Land Area (sq. mi.)	911.1	**Wages**	$27,249,719
Altitude (ft.)	1,930–2,574	**Per Capita Income**	$35,417
Rainfall (in.)	22.0	**Property Value**	$1,725,937,594
Jan. mean min (°F)	29.5	**Retail Sales**	$43,470,437

COLORADO CITY (4,391) county seat; cotton, cattle, oil; hospital/medical services; poppy-mallow blooms at sports complex; goat cook-off in October.

Other towns include: **Loraine** (550) and **Westbrook** (224), trade centers. The community around **Lake Colorado City** (752).

The lighthouse on Lake Conroe in Montgomery County. Photo by Epicanis, CC by SA 3.0

Montague County

Physical Features: Rolling, draining to tributaries of Trinity, Red rivers; sandy loams, red, black soils; Lake Nocona, Lake Amon G. Carter.

Economy: Agribusiness, oil, varied manufacturing, government/services.

History: Kiowas and Wichitas who allied with Comanches. Anglo-American settlements developed in the 1850s. County created from Cooke County in 1857, organized in 1858; named for pioneer Daniel Montague.

Recreation: Lake activities; quail, turkey, deer hunting; scenic drives; museums; historical sites, motorcycle dirt track.

Minerals: Oil, gas, rock.

Agriculture: Beef, hay, pecans, melons, peaches. Market value $33.4 million.

For explanation of sources, symbols, and abbreviations, see p. 207 and foldout map.

Vital Statistics, annual: Births, 210; deaths, 373; marriages, 88; divorces, 42.

Race/Ethnicity: Anglo, 81.9%; Hispanic, 11.8%; Black, 0.4%; Asian, 0.4%; Other, 5.5%.

MONTAGUE (248) county seat.

BOWIE (5,534) varied manufacturing, oil and gas operations; hospital, library; Jim Bowie Days in June.

NOCONA (3,059) athletic goods, boot manufacturing; hospital; art galleries, museums; Wheels & Grills barbecue cook-off and car show in September.

Other towns include: **Ringgold** (100); **Saint Jo** (901) wineries, retail center, art galleries, museums, rodeo in August; **Sunset** (520).

Population	20,409
Change from 2010	3.5%
Area (sq. mi.)	938.3
Land Area (sq. mi.)	930.9
Altitude (ft.)	715–1,318
Rainfall (in.)	35.3
Jan. mean min (°F)	32.0

July mean max (°F)	92.0
Civ. Labor	9,242
Unemployed	3.6%
Wages	$59,129,196
Per Capita Income	$45,716
Property Value	$5,449,744,141
Retail Sales	$216,090,265

Montgomery County

Physical Features: Rolling, half timbered; Sam Houston National Forest; loam, sandy, alluvial soils; Lake Conroe and Lewis Creek Reservoir.

Economy: Varied manufacturing, oil production, medical research, government/services, many residents work in Houston.

History: Orcoquisac and Bidais tribes, removed from the area by the 1850s. Anglo-Americans arrived in the 1820s as part of Austin's colony. County created and organized in 1837 from Washington County; named for Richard Montgomery, American Revolution general.

Recreation: Hunting, fishing; Lake Conroe activities; national and state forests; hiking, boating, horseback riding; historic sites; Texas Renaissance Festival (largest in state) in fall.

Minerals: Natural gas.

Agriculture: Greenhouse crops, hay, beef cattle, horses. Market value $25.8 million. Timber important.

Vital Statistics, annual: Births, 7,433; deaths, 4,672; marriages, 2,825; divorces, 2,041.

Race/Ethnicity: Anglo, 59.9%; Hispanic, 26.4%; Black, 5.5%; Asian, 3.5%; Other, 4.7%.

CONROE (94,400) county seat; government/services, hospital/medical services, commuters to Houston; new Sam Houston State University medical school; community college, museum; Cajun catfish festival in October.

THE WOODLANDS (115,716) commuters to Houston, energy, tourism; college branches, hospitals, museums, parks, concerts, festivals at Mitchell Pavilion.

Other towns include: **Cut and Shoot** (1,139); **Dobbin** (310); **Grangerland** (850); **Magnolia** (2,635) government/services, drilling technology, construction, depot museum; **Montgomery** (2,321) commuters to Houston and Conroe, antiques stores, pioneer museum, street dancing in February; **Oak Ridge North** (3,032); **Panorama Village** (2,547); **Patton Village** (1,730).

Also: **Pinehurst** (4,727); **Porter Heights** (1,167); **Roman Forest** (2,874); **Shenandoah** (3,593); **Splendora** (1,780); **Stagecoach** (588); **Willis** (6,710) commuters to Conroe and Houston; **Woodbranch** (1,412); **Woodloch** (184).

Also, part [6,830] of **Houston** [Kingwood], hospital.

Population	648,886
Change from 2010	42.4%
Area (sq. mi.)	1,076.9
Land Area (sq. mi.)	1,041.9
Altitude (ft.)	50–430

Rainfall (in.)	51.0
Jan. mean min (°F)	43.8
July mean max (°F)	94.4
Civ. Labor	301,853
Unemployed	3.9%

Wages	$3,659,482,204
Per Capita Income	$68,974
Property Value	$114,981,775,004
Retail Sales	$13,615,509,303

For explanation of sources, symbols, and abbreviations, see p. 207 and foldout map.

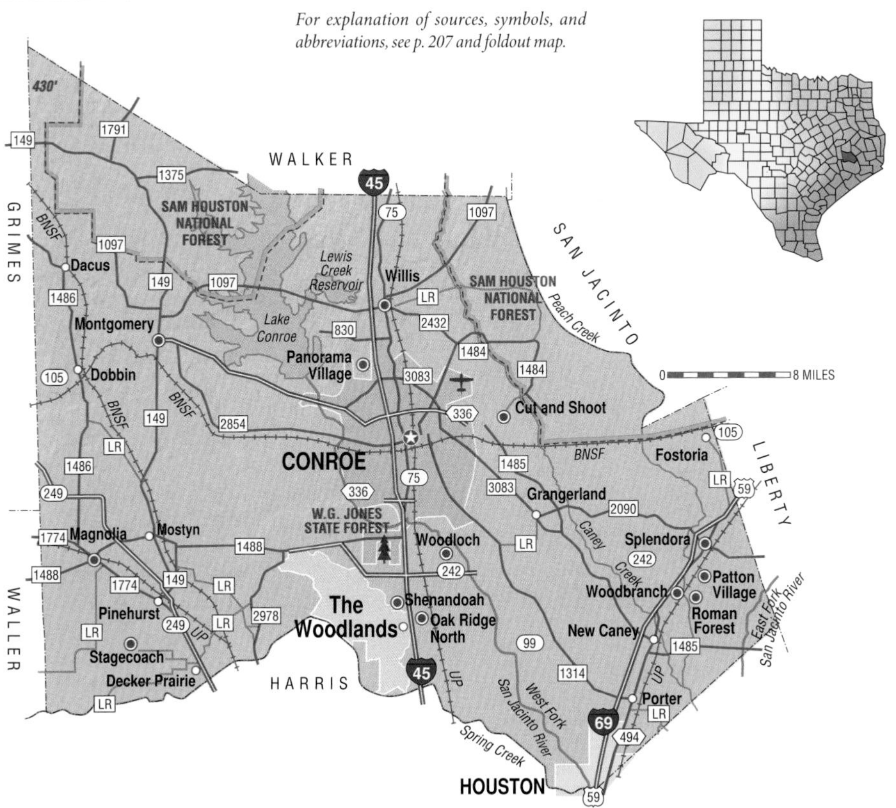

Moore County

Physical Features: Flat to rolling, broken by creeks; sandy loams; Lake Meredith.

Economy: Varied agribusiness, petroleum, natural gas.

History: Comanches, removed to Indian Territory in 1874–1875; ranching began soon afterward. Farming developed after 1910. Oil boom in the 1920s. County created in 1876 from Bexar District; organized in 1892; named for Republic of Texas navy commander E.W. Moore.

Recreation: Lake Meredith activities; pheasant, deer, quail hunting; historical museum; arts center; free overnight RV park; Dogie Days in June.

Minerals: Oil and gas.

Agriculture: Fed beef, corn, wheat, stocker cattle, sorghum, cotton, soybeans, sunflowers. Market value $478.1 million. Irrigation of 122,000 acres.

Vital Statistics, annual: Births, 368; deaths, 192; marriages, 113; divorces, 87.

Race/Ethnicity: Anglo, 30.4%; Hispanic, 59.2%; Black, 3.1%; Asian, 4.6%; Other, 2.7%.

DUMAS (14,290) county seat; tourism, retail trade, varied agribusiness; hospital, hospice, retirement complex.

Other towns include: **Cactus** (3,050); **Sunray** (1,702).

Population	21,118
Change from 2010	–3.6%
Area (sq. mi.)	909.6
Land Area (sq. mi.)	899.7
Altitude (ft.)	2,915–3,825
Rainfall (in.)	17.7
Jan. mean min (°F)	23.1
July mean max (°F)	90.5
Civ. Labor	11,322
Unemployed	2.6%
Wages	$171,096,821
Per Capita Income	$56,634
Property Value	$3,285,792,280
Retail Sales	$381,190,528

Morris County

Physical Features: East Texas county of forested hills; drains to streams, Lake O' the Pines, Ellison Creek Reservoir, Barnes Creek Reservoir.

Economy: Steel manufacturing, agriculture, timber, government/services.

History: Caddo Indians until the 1790s. Kickapoo and other tribes in area 1820s-30s. Anglo-American settlement began in mid-1830s. Antebellum slaveholding area. County named for legislator-jurist W.W. Morris; created from Titus County and organized in 1875.

Recreation: Activities on Lake O' the Pines, small lakes; fishing, hunting; state park.

Minerals: Iron ore.

Agriculture: Beef cattle, broiler production, hay. Market value $44.2 million. Timber industry significant.

Vital Statistics, annual: Births, 135; deaths, 194; marriages, 53; divorces, 7.

Race/Ethnicity: Anglo, 64.4%; Hispanic, 9.9%; Black, 20.4%; Asian, 0.3%; Other, 4.9%.

DAINGERFIELD (2,510) county seat; varied manufacturing, government/services; library, museum, city park, historic theater; Daingerfield Days in October.

Other towns include: **Cason** (173); **Lone Star** (1,407) oil-field equipment manufactured, catfish farming; **Naples** (1,391) trailer manufacturing, livestock, watermelon festival in July; **Omaha** (936), retail center, government/services, commuters.

For explanation of sources, symbols, and abbreviations, see p. 207 and foldout map.

Population	12,030
Change from 2010	–7.0%
Area (sq. mi.)	258.7
Land Area (sq. mi.)	252.0
Altitude (ft.)	228–614
Rainfall (in.)	47.1
Jan. mean min (°F)	36.8
July mean max (°F)	91.4
Civ. Labor	4,473
Unemployed	6.3%
Wages	$46,418,661
Per Capita Income	$47,226
Property Value	$1,352,944,363
Retail Sales	$108,160,058

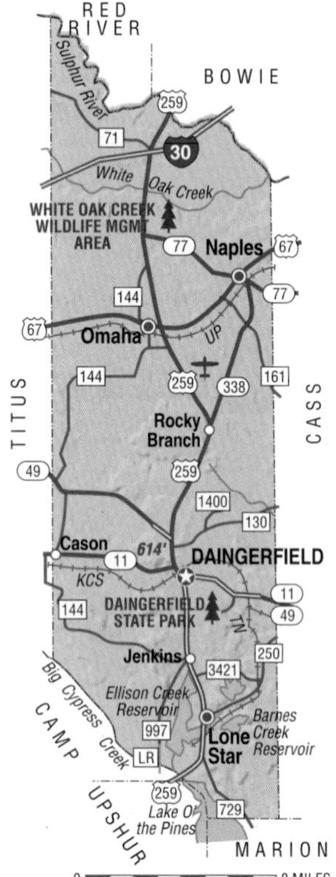

Motley County Museum and Chamber of Commerce. Photo by Barbara Brannon, CC 2.0

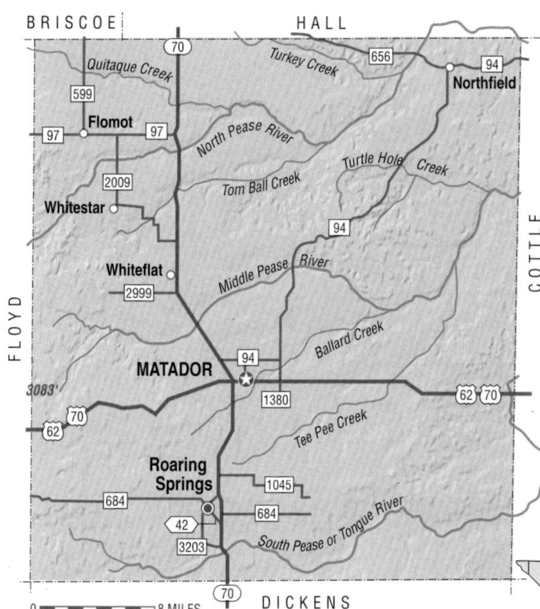

Motley County

Physical Features: Western county just below Caprock; rough terrain, broken by Pease tributaries; sandy to red clay soils.

Economy: Agriculture, government/services, light manufacturing.

History: Comanche tribes in the area, removed to the Indian Territory by the U.S. Army in 1874–1875. Cattle ranching began in the late 1870s. County was created out of the Bexar District in 1876 and organized in 1891; named for Dr. J.W. Mottley, a signer of Texas Declaration of Independence (however, name was misspelled in legislative statute).

Recreation: Quail, dove, turkey, deer, feral hog hunting; Matador Ranch headquarters; spring-fed pool at Roaring Springs; Motley-Dickens settlers reunion in August at Roaring Springs.

Minerals: Minimal.

Agriculture: Beef cattle, cotton, peanuts, hay, wheat. Some irrigation. Market value $15.2 million. Hunting leases important.

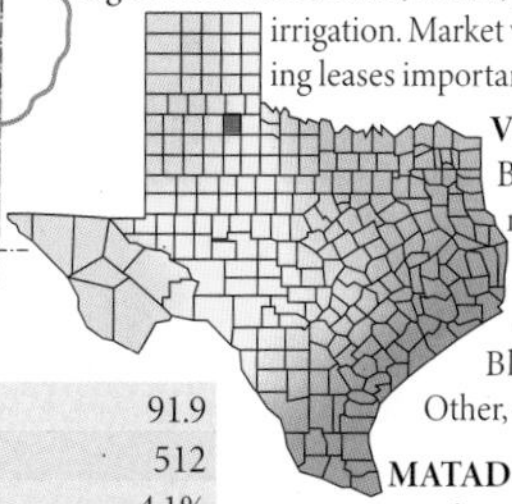

Vital Statistics, annual: Births, 12; deaths, 23; marriages, 5; divorces, 2.

Race/Ethnicity: Anglo, 80.7%; Hispanic, 14.4%; Black, 0.7%; Asian, 0%; Other, 4.2%.

MATADOR (571) county seat; ranching, farming, government/services; museum, historic oil-derrick gas station.

Other towns include: **Flomot** (181) and **Roaring Springs** (214).

Population	1,067
Change from 2010	−11.8%
Area (sq. mi.)	989.8
Land Area (sq. mi.)	989.6
Altitude (ft.)	1,800–3,083
Rainfall (in.)	23.0
Jan. mean min (°F)	29.6

July mean max (°F)	91.9
Civ. Labor	512
Unemployed	4.1%
Wages	$3,273,962
Per Capita Income	$41,754
Property Value	$364,536,815
Retail Sales	$8,266,238

Nacogdoches County

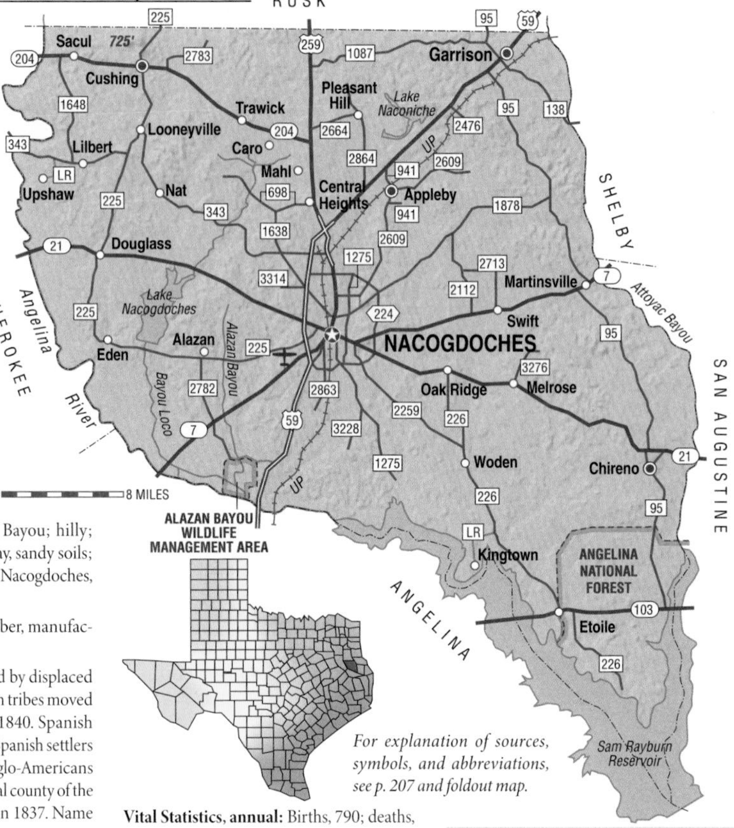

For explanation of sources, symbols, and abbreviations, *see p. 207 and foldout map.*

Physical Features: East Texas county on divide between the Angelina River and Attoyac Bayou; hilly; two-thirds is forested; red, gray, sandy soils; Sam Rayburn Reservoir, Lake Nacogdoches, Lake Naconiche.

Economy: Agribusiness, timber, manufacturing, education, tourism.

History: Caddo tribes, joined by displaced Cherokees in the 1820s. Indian tribes moved west of the Brazos River by 1840. Spanish missions established in 1716. Spanish settlers arrived in the mid-1700s. Anglo-Americans arrived in the 1820s. An original county of the Republic in 1836, organized in 1837. Name comes from Caddo tribe in the area.

Recreation: Lake and river activities; Stephen F. Austin State University events; Angelina National Forest; historic site. Tourist attractions include the Old Stone Fort, pioneer homes, museums, Millard's Crossing Historic Village, Piney Woods Native Plant Center; Azalea Trail in March, Blueberry Festival in June.

Minerals: First Texas oil discovered here, 1866; gas, oil, clay, and stone.

Agriculture: A leading poultry-producing county (third in number of broilers); beef cattle raised. Market value $370.7 million. Substantial timber sold.

Vital Statistics, annual: Births, 790; deaths, 758; marriages, 323; divorces, 155.

Race/Ethnicity: Anglo, 57.5%; Hispanic, 21%; Black, 16.3%; Asian, 1.2%; Other, 4%.

NACOGDOCHES (32,118) county seat; varied manufacturing, lumber mills, wood products, trade center; hospitals; Stephen F. Austin State University; Nine Flags Festival in November/December.

Other towns include: **Appleby** (548), **Chireno** (369), **Cushing** (558), **Douglass** (380), **Etoile** (700), **Garrison** (793), **Martinsville** (350), **Redfield** (117), **Woden** (400).

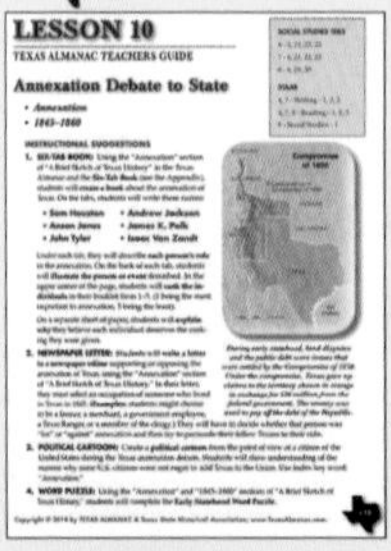

Population	64,668
Change from 2010	0.2%
Area (sq. mi.)	981.2
Land Area (sq. mi.)	946.5
Altitude (ft.)	164–725
Rainfall (in.)	49.9
Jan. mean min (°F)	37.9
July mean max (°F)	91.7
Civ. Labor	28,000
Unemployed	4.3%
Wages	$281,558,422
Per Capita Income	$46,246
Property Value	$8,492,064,044
Retail Sales	$1,066,349,932

The George Taylor Jester House in Corsicana is a Texas Historic Landmark. Photo by Renelibrary, CC by SA 4.0

Navarro County

Physical Features: Level Blackland, some rolling; drains to creeks, Trinity River; Navarro Mills Lake, Richland-Chambers Reservoir, Lake Halbert.

Economy: Diversified manufacturing, agribusinesses, oil-field operations, distribution.

History: Kickapoo and Comanche area. Anglo-Americans settled in the late 1830s. Antebellum slaveholding area. County created in 1846 from Robertson County, organized the same year; named for Republic of Texas leader José Antonio Navarro.

Recreation: Lake activities; Pioneer Village; historic buildings; youth exposition, Derrick Days in April.

Minerals: Longest continuous Texas oil flow; more than 200 million barrels produced since 1895; natural gas, sand and gravel also produced.

Agriculture: Beef cattle, cotton, sorghum, corn, wheat, sunflowers, herbs, horses, dairies. Market value $73.3 million.

Vital Statistics, annual: Births, 645; deaths, 634; marriages, 220; divorces, 77.

Race/Ethnicity: Anglo, 51.3%; Hispanic, 30.5%; Black, 11.9%; Asian, 0.7%; Other, 5.5%.

CORSICANA (25,203) county seat; major distribution center, pecans, candy, fruitcakes; varied manufacturing; agribusiness; hospital; Navarro College; Texas Youth Commission facility.

Other towns include: **Angus** (457); **Barry** (223); **Blooming Grove** (878); **Dawson** (835); **Emhouse** (192); **Eureka** (321); **Frost** (636); **Goodlow** (180).

Also: **Kerens** (1,505) commuting, nature tourism, Cotton Harvest Festival in October; **Mildred** (413); **Navarro** (235); **Oak Valley** (418); **Powell** (101); **Purdon** (133); **Retreat** (432); **Rice** (1,236); **Richland** (265).

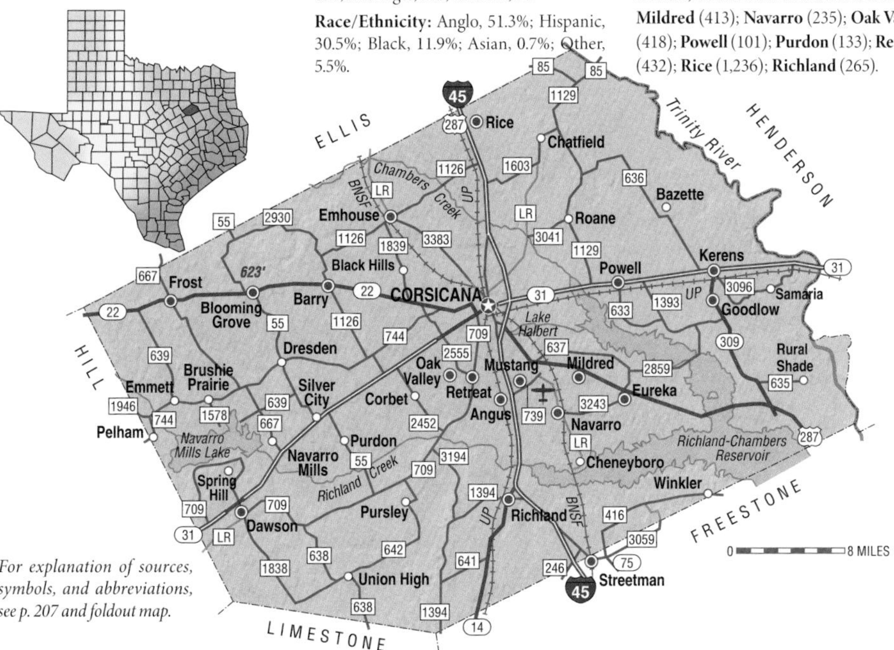

For explanation of sources, symbols, and abbreviations, see p. 207 and foldout map.

Population	53,591
Change from 2010	12.3%
Area (sq. mi.)	1,085.9
Land Area (sq. mi.)	1,009.6
Altitude (ft.)	250–623

Rainfall (in.)	42.1
Jan. mean min (°F)	36.8
July mean max (°F)	93.5
Civ. Labor	23,597
Unemployed	3.9%

Wages	$209,618,769
Per Capita Income	$45,616
Property Value	$8,745,914,006
Retail Sales	$853,748,071

Newton County

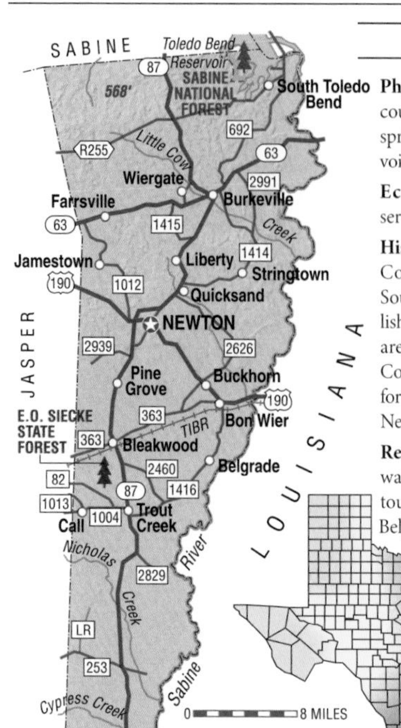

Physical Features: Easternmost Texas county of densely forested hills, valleys; spring-fed streams; Toledo Bend Reservoir; Sabine River; mostly sandy soils.

Economy: Forestry, government/services, tourism.

History: Caddo Indian area. Displaced Coushattas moved across area from South. Anglo-American settlement established in 1830s. Antebellum slaveholding area. County created 1846 from Jasper County, organized the same year; named for American Revolutionary soldier John Newton.

Recreation: Toledo Bend Reservoir, water sports, fishing, hunting, birding, tourism, state forest, Azalea Canyons; Belgrade, site of early town.

Minerals: Oil, gas.

Agriculture: Cattle, hay, nursery crops, vegetables, goats, hogs. Market value $1.6 million. Hunting leases. Major forestry area.

Vital Statistics, annual: Births, 127; deaths, 213; marriages, 38; divorces, 32.

Race/Ethnicity: Anglo, 75.7%; Hispanic, 2.8%; Black, 17%; Asian, 0.2%; Other, 4.3%.

NEWTON (1,991) county seat; lumber manufacturing, plywood mill, private prison unit, tourist center; genealogical library, museum; Wild Azalea festival in March.

Deweyville (519) power plant, commercial center for forestry, farming area.

Other towns include: **Bon Wier** (375); **Burkeville** (603); **Call** (493); **South Toledo Bend** (337); **Wiergate** (350).

For explanation of sources, symbols, and abbreviations, see p. 207 and foldout map.

Population	12,241
Change from 2010	–15.3%
Area (sq. mi.)	939.7
Land Area (sq. mi.)	933.7
Altitude (ft.)	10–568
Rainfall (in.)	55.7
Jan. mean min (°F)	39.0
July mean max (°F)	92.9
Civ. Labor	4,883
Unemployed	6.8%
Wages	$13,485,061
Per Capita Income	$43,123
Property Value	$2,847,471,554
Retail Sales	$41,128,493

Nolan County

Physical Features: On divide between Brazos, Colorado watersheds; mostly red sandy loams, some waxy, sandy soils; Lake Sweetwater, Lake Trammell.

Economy: Farms/ranches, oil/gas, wind energy, government/services.

History: Anglo-American settlement began in the late 1870s. County created from the Bexar, Young districts in 1876; organized in 1881; named for adventurer Philip Nolan, who was killed near Waco.

Recreation: Lakes, hunting, pioneer museum; rattlesnake roundup in March.

Minerals: Oil, gas.

Agriculture: Beef cattle, cotton, sorghum. Market value $36.6 million. Some 3,300 acres irrigated.

Vital Statistics, annual: Births, 202; deaths, 229; marriages, 80; divorces, 9.

Race/Ethnicity: Anglo, 55.2%; Hispanic, 36.3%; Black, 4.2%; Asian, 0.7%; Other, 3.5%.

SWEETWATER (10,513) county seat; wind energy, varied manufacturing, gypsum; hospital; Texas State Technical College; WWII museum.

Other towns include: **Blackwell** (254, partly in Coke County), Oak Creek Reservoir to south; **Maryneal** (50); **Nolan** (60); **Roscoe** (1,244).

Population	14,597
Change from 2010	–4.1%
Area (sq. mi.)	914.0
Land Area (sq. mi.)	912.0
Altitude (ft.)	1,896–2,603
Rainfall (in.)	21.2
Jan. mean min (°F)	32.7
July mean max (°F)	93.1
Civ. Labor	6,782
Unemployed	3.7%
Wages	$82,902,155
Per Capita Income	$52,629
Property Value	$3,923,953,507
Retail Sales	$343,291,932

Nueces County

Physical Features: Southern Gulf Coast county; flat, rich soils, broken by bays, Nueces River, Petronila Creek; includes Mustang Island, north tip of Padre Island.

Economy: Petroleum processing, deepwater port facility, agriculture, tourism.

History: Coahuiltecan, Karankawa and other tribes who succumbed to disease or fled by 1840s. Spanish settlers arrived in the 1760s. Settlers from Ireland arrived around 1830. County name is Spanish for nuts; county named for river; created and organized in 1846 out of San Patricio County.

Population	353,079
Change from 2010	3.8%
Area (sq. mi.)	1,656.0
Land Area (sq. mi.)	835.5
Altitude (ft.)	sea level–150
Rainfall (in.)	31.7
Jan. mean min (°F)	49.9
July mean max (°F)	93.4
Civ. Labor	164,095
Unemployed	4.7%
Wages	$2,231,722,514
Per Capita Income	$52,852
Property Value	$53,876,871,830
Retail Sales	$6,696,390,794

Recreation: Major resort area; beaches, fishing, water sports, birding; Padre Island National Seashore, Mustang Island State Park, Lipantitlan State Historic Site; Art Museum of South Texas, Corpus Christi Museum of Science and History; Texas State Aquarium; Museum of Asian Cultures; professional baseball, hockey; greyhound race track.

Minerals: Oil, gas, sand, gravel.

Agriculture: Grain sorghum (second in acreage), cotton, cattle, wheat, hay, nurseries/turfgrass. Market value $161.0 million.

Vital Statistics, annual: Births, 4,391; deaths, 3,787; marriages, 1,670; divorces, 382.

Race/Ethnicity: Anglo, 30.1%; Hispanic, 61.5%; Black, 3.6%; Asian, 2.2%; Other, 2.7%.

CORPUS CHRISTI (317,773) county seat; seaport, naval bases, varied manufacturing, petroleum processing, tourism; hospitals; museums; Army depot; Texas A&M University-Corpus Christi, Del Mar College; USS Lexington museum, Harbor Lights; Buccaneer Days in late April.

Port Aransas (3,105) deepwater port, tourism, marine research, Coast Guard base, fishing industry; University of Texas Marine Science Institute; museum, beach; Whooping Crane Festival in February; Texas Sand Fest in April.

Robstown (10,157) agriculture, transportation, tourism, petroleum processing; regional fairgrounds; Cottonfest in October.

Other towns include: **Agua Dulce** (688); **Banquete** (425); **Bishop** (3,155) petrochemicals, agriculture, pharmaceuticals, plastics, nature trail; **Chapman Ranch** (200); **Driscoll** (673); **La Paloma-Lost Creek** (670); **North San Pedro** (752); **Petronila** (87); **Rancho Banquete** (517); **Sandy Hollow-Escondidas** (571); **Spring Gardens** (489); **Tierra Grande** (185), and **Tierra Verde** (232).

Annaville, Calallen, and Flour Bluff are now part of Corpus Christi.

A Great Kiskadee spotted at Blucher Park in Corpus Christi. Photo by Liam Wolff, CC by SA 4.0

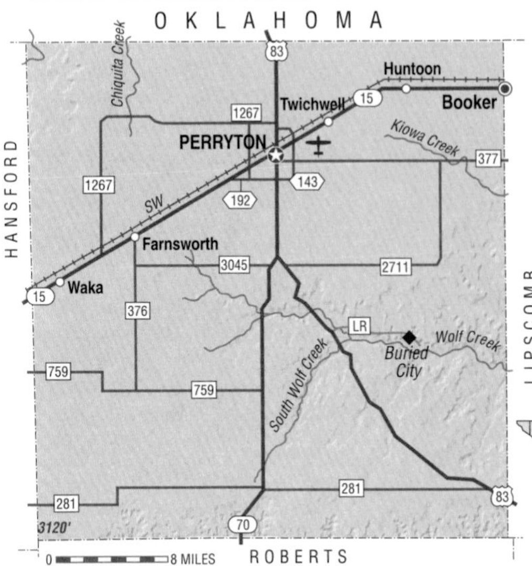

Ochiltree County

Physical Features: Panhandle county bordering Oklahoma; level, broken by creeks; deep loam, clay soils.

Economy: Agribusiness, oil/gas, government/services.

History: Apache groups, who were pushed out by Comanches in late 1700s. The Comanches were removed to the Indian Territory in 1874–1875 by U.S. Army. Ranching developed in 1880s; farming began after 1900. Created from the Bexar District in 1876, organized in 1889; named for Republic of Texas leader W.B. Ochiltree.

Recreation: Wolf Creek park; Museum of the Plains; Prehistoric settlement site of "Buried City"; pheasant hunting, also deer and dove; Wheatheart of the Nation celebration in August.

Minerals: Oil, natural gas, caliche.

Agriculture: Cattle, swine, corn, cotton, wheat (second in acreage), sorghum, hay and forages; some 50,000 acres irrigated. Market value $349.1 million.

Vital Statistics, annual: Births, 125; deaths, 102; marriages, 49; divorces, 32.

Race/Ethnicity: Anglo, 42.4%; Hispanic, 54.6%; Black, 0.1%; Asian, 0.3%; Other, 2.6%.

PERRYTON (8,289) county seat; oil/gas, cattle feeding, grain center; hospital; college.

Other towns include: **Farnsworth** (25); **Waka** (114).

Population	9,782
Change from 2010	–4.3%
Area (sq. mi.)	918.1
Land Area (sq. mi.)	917.6
Altitude (ft.)	2,550–3,120
Rainfall (in.)	22.8
Jan. mean min (°F)	24.9
July mean max (°F)	93.2
Civ. Labor	3,944
Unemployed	3.4%
Wages	$59,752,743
Per Capita Income	$64,247
Property Value	$1,924,512,941
Retail Sales	$84,145,863

Oldham County

Physical Features: Northwestern Panhandle county; level, broken by Canadian River and tributaries.

Economy: Agriculture, wind energy, sand and gravel.

History: Apaches; followed later by Comanches, Kiowas. U.S. Army removed the Indians in 1875. Anglo ranchers and Spanish pastores (sheep men) from New Mexico were in the area in the 1870s. County created in 1876 from Bexar District; organized in 1880; named for editor-Confederate senator W.S. Oldham.

Recreation: Old Tascosa, Cal Farley's Boys Ranch, Boot Hill Cemetery, museums; midway point on old Route 66; County Roundup in August, Boys Ranch rodeo Labor Day weekend.

Minerals: Sand and gravel, oil, natural gas, stone.

Agriculture: Beef cattle; crops include wheat, grain sorghum. Market value $156.0 million.

Vital Statistics, annual: Births, 26; deaths, 20; marriages, 3; divorces, 2.

Race/Ethnicity: Anglo, 75.4%; Hispanic, 17.8%; Black, 1.9%; Asian, 0.6%; Other, 4.4%.

VEGA (869) county seat; farm and ranch trade center; transportation; museums.

Other towns include: **Adrian** (129); **Wildorado** (150). Also, **Cal Farley's Boys Ranch** (150).

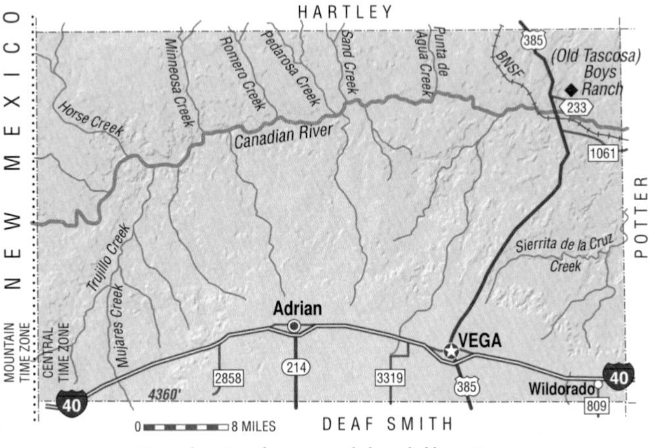

For explanation of sources, symbols, and abbreviations, see p. 207 and foldout map.

Population	1,717
Change from 2010	–16.3%
Area (sq. mi.)	1,501.4
Land Area (sq. mi.)	1,500.5
Altitude (ft.)	3,140–4,360
Rainfall (in.)	18.8
Jan. mean min (°F)	22.7
July mean max (°F)	91.5
Civ. Labor	939
Unemployed	3.0%
Wages	$10,273,969
Per Capita Income	$72,126
Property Value	$1,665,275,092
Retail Sales	$73,974,996

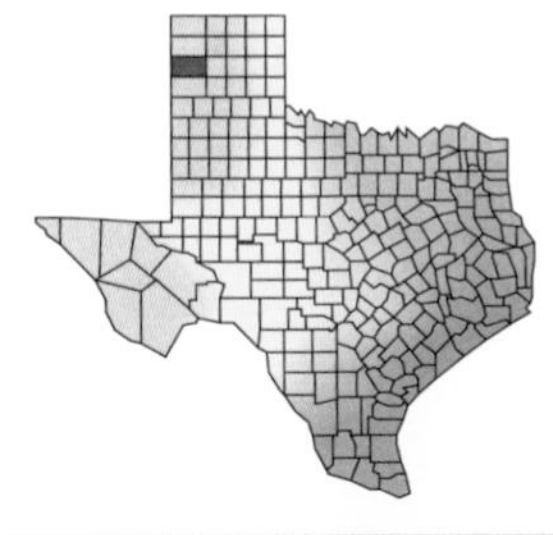

Orange County

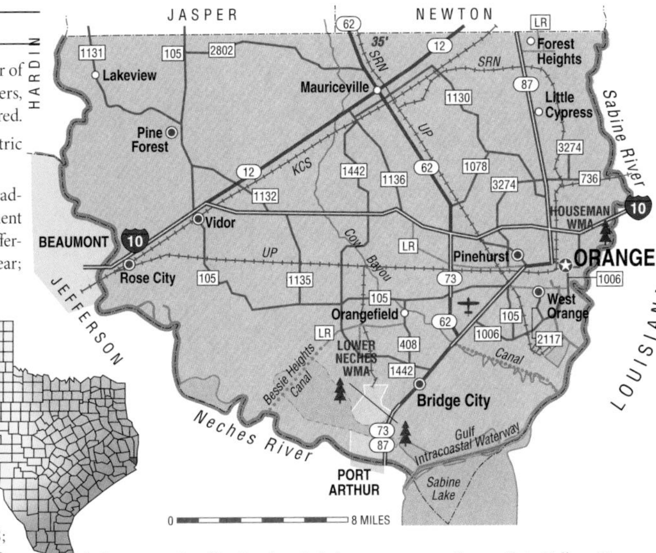

Physical Features: In southeastern corner of the state; bounded by Sabine, Neches rivers, Sabine Lake; coastal soils; two-thirds timbered.

Economy: Oil and gas production, electric power plants, commercial fishing.

History: Atakapan Indian area. French traders in area by 1720. Anglo-American settlement began in the 1820s. County created from Jefferson County in 1852, organized the same year; named for early orange grove.

Recreation: Fishing, hunting, water sports, birding, county park, museums; historical homes, crawfish festival in spring.

Minerals: Oil and gas.

Agriculture: Beef cattle, forages, citrus, bees. Market value $5.0 million. Hunting leases. Timber important.

Vital Statistics, annual: Births, 1,038; deaths, 1,151; marriages, 382; divorces, 259.

Race/Ethnicity: Anglo, 76.6%; Hispanic, 8.6%; Black, 9.4%; Asian, 1.3%; Other, 4.1%.

ORANGE (19,169) county seat; seaport, petrochemical plants, varied manufacturing, food and timber processing shipping; hospital, theater, museums; Lamar State College-Orange; Mardi Gras in February.

Bridge City (9,519) varied manufacturing, ship repair yard, steel fabrication, fish farming, government/services; library; tall bridge and newer suspension bridge over Neches; stop for Monarch butterfly in fall during its migration to Mexico.

Vidor (9,712) steel processing, railroad-car refinishing; library; barbecue festival in April.

Other towns include: **Forest Heights** (1,600); **Little Cypress** (2,173) **Mauriceville** (2,597); **Orangefield** (725); **Pine Forest** (503); **Pinehurst** (2,216); **Rose City** (330); **West Orange** (3,433).

Population	84,742
Change from 2010	3.5%
Area (sq. mi.)	379.5
Land Area (sq. mi.)	333.7
Altitude (ft.)	sea level–35
Rainfall (in.)	64.4
Jan. mean min (°F)	42.1

July mean max (°F)	89.4
Civ. Labor	34,871
Unemployed	5.7%

Wages	$353,741,369
Per Capita Income	$48,912
Property Value	$9,756,164,355
Retail Sales	$1,139,727,627

Veterans Memorial Bridge, also called Rainbow Bridge, crosses over the Neches River and connects Bridge City to Port Arthur. Photo by Aren Cambre, CC by SA 2.5

Palo Pinto County

Physical Features: North central county; broken, hilly, wooded in parts; Possum Kingdom Lake, Lake Palo Pinto; sandy, gray, black soils.

Economy: Varied manufacturing, tourism, petroleum, agribusiness.

History: Anglo-American ranchers arrived in the 1850s. Conflicts between settlers and numerous Indian tribes who had sought refuge on the Brazos River resulted in Texas Rangers removing the Indians in 1856. County created in 1856 from Bosque and Navarro counties; organized in 1857; named for creek (in Spanish name means painted stick).

Recreation: Lake activities, hunting, fishing, state parks, Rails to Trails hiking, biking, fossil park.

Minerals: Oil, gas, clays.

Agriculture: Cattle, dairy products, nursery crops, hay, wheat. Market value $43.2 million. Cedar posts marketed.

Vital Statistics, annual: Births, 344; deaths, 456; marriages, 131; divorces, 142.

Race/Ethnicity: Anglo, 73.1%; Hispanic, 19.8%; Black, 1.9%; Asian, 0.7%; Other, 4.4%.

PALO PINTO (173) county seat; government center.

MINERAL WELLS (14,902) oil and gas, manufacturing, tourism; hospital, Weatherford College branch; art center.

Other towns include: **Gordon** (474); **Graford** (685) retirement/recreation area;**Mingus** (230); **Santo** (308), and **Strawn** (549).

Population	28,686
Change from 2010	2.0%
Area (sq. mi.)	985.5
Land Area (sq. mi.)	951.8
Altitude (ft.)	782–1,530
Rainfall (in.)	31.8
Jan. mean min (°F)	34.8

July mean max (°F)	94.6
Civ. Labor	13,135
Unemployed	3.8%
Wages	$110,115,336
Per Capita Income	$52,042
Property Value	$8,636,781,935
Retail Sales	$456,991,490

Panola County

Physical Features: East Texas county; 60% forested, rolling plain; broken by Sabine, Murvaul Creek; Toledo Bend Reservoir, Lake Murvaul, Martin Creek Lake.

Economy: Gas, oil-field operations, food processing, agribusiness.

History: A Caddo tribal area. Anglo-American settlement established in 1833. Antebellum slaveholding area. County name is Indian word for cotton; created from Harrison, Shelby counties in 1846; organized the same year.

Recreation: Fishing, water activities, hunting; Jim Reeves memorial, Tex Ritter museum and Texas Country Music Hall of Fame; last remaining International Boundary Marker at Louisiana border.

Minerals: Oil, gas, coal.

Agriculture: Broilers, cattle, forages. Market value $100.7 million. Timber sales significant.

Vital Statistics, annual: Births, 264; deaths, 378; marriages, 114; divorces, 82.

Race/Ethnicity: Anglo, 71.6%; Hispanic, 9.7%; Black, 14.4%; Asian, 0.4%; Other, 3.8%.

CARTHAGE (6,533) county seat; petroleum processing, poultry, sawmills; hospital, junior college; Oil & Gas Blast in October.

Other towns include: **Beckville** (736), **Clayton** (125), **DeBerry** (200), **Gary** (338), **Long Branch** (150), **Panola** (305).

Population	22,675
Change from 2010	–4.7%
Area (sq. mi.)	821.3
Land Area (sq. mi.)	801.8

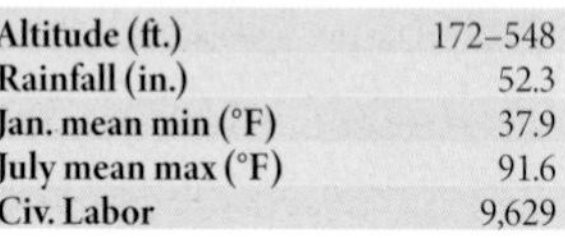

Altitude (ft.)	172–548
Rainfall (in.)	52.3
Jan. mean min (°F)	37.9
July mean max (°F)	91.6
Civ. Labor	9,629

Unemployed	4.6%
Wages	$117,608,805
Per Capita Income	$53,292
Property Value	$7,154,344,400
Retail Sales	$294,485,829

Counties of Texas

A detailed county map accompanies each of 254 county articles on pages 191–369.
Below is the legend to the symbols used on those maps:

Legend to counties

- Principal road
- Secondary road
- Local road
- Divided highway
- 10 Interstate highway
- 377 U.S. highway
- 81 State highway
- 308 Farm-to-market road
- LR Local roads
- 28 Loop
- Railway
- BNSF Railway name
- River or creek
- Lake
- Intermittent water source
- Intracoastal Waterway
- County seat
- Incorporated town
- Unincorporated town
- County boundary
- PECOS Name of neighboring county
- 400' Elevation
- 880' Highest point in county
- Major airport with scheduled jet service
- Municipal airport
- Military airport
- National park or wildlife management area
- Federal land
- State park or wildlife management area
- State land
- Ranger station
- Time zone line
- Boundary of prison or military installation

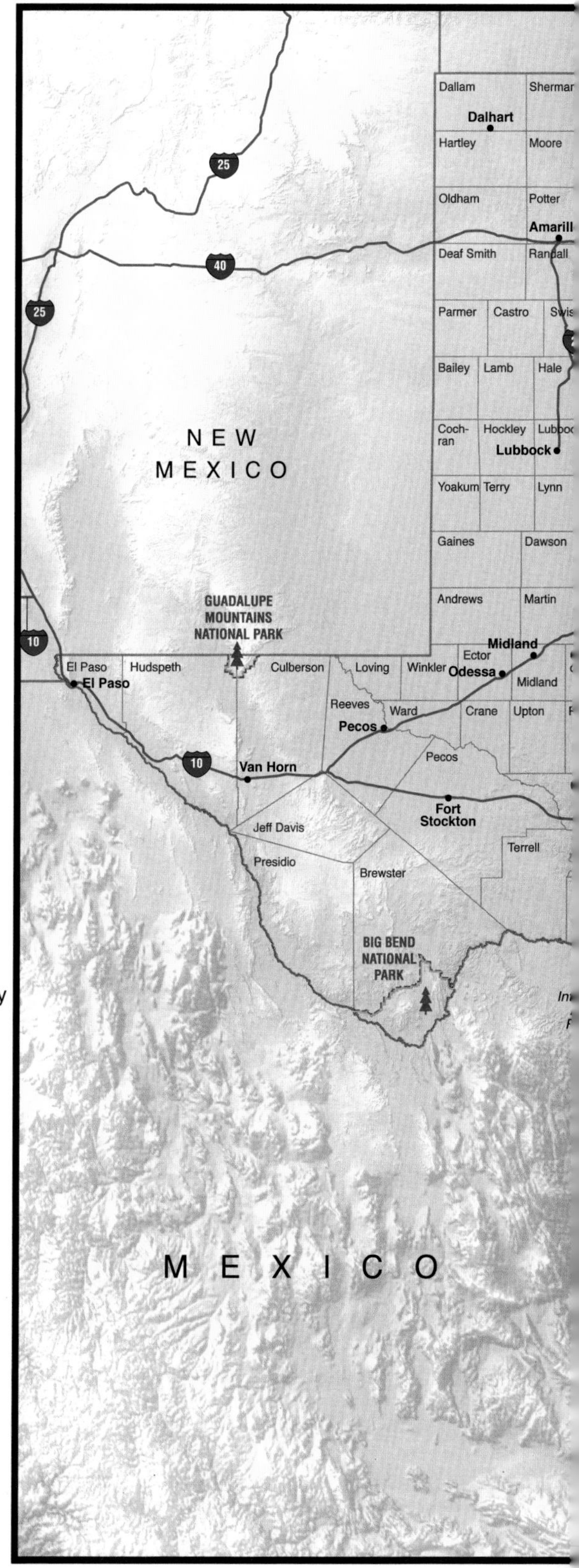

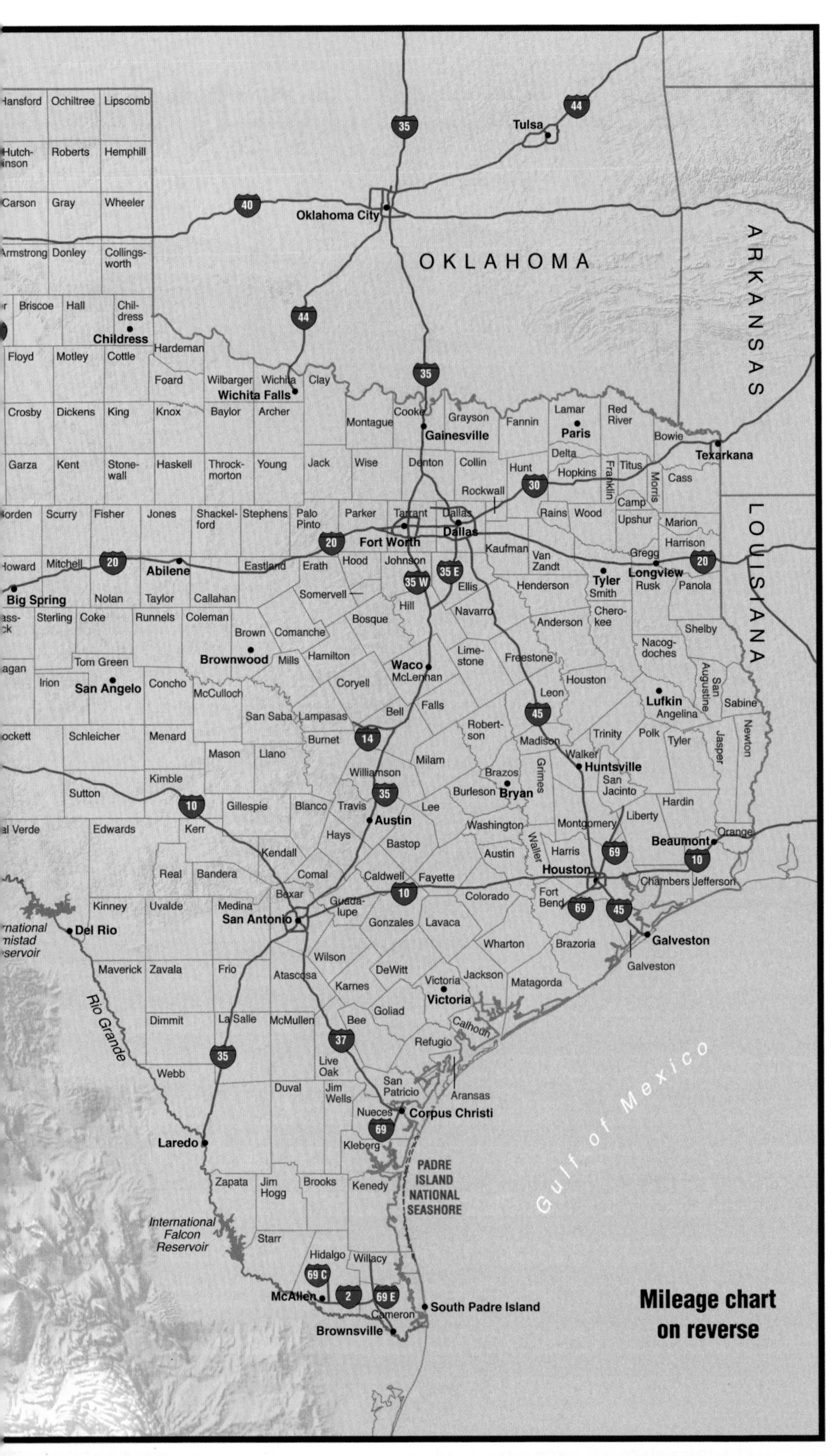

OKLAHOMA
ARKANSAS
LOUISIANA
Gulf of Mexico
Tulsa
Oklahoma City
Ochiltree
Lipscomb
Roberts
Hemphill
Carson
Gray
Wheeler
Donley
Collings-
worth
Briscoe
Hall
Chil-
dress
Childress
Hardeman
Floyd
Motley
Cottle
Foard
Wilbarger
Wichita
Wichita Falls
Clay
Crosby
Dickens
King
Knox
Baylor
Archer
Montague
Cooke
Grayson
Fannin
Lamar
Paris
Red
River
Bowie
Texarkana
Gainesville
Garza
Kent
Stone-
wall
Haskell
Throck-
morton
Young
Jack
Wise
Denton
Collin
Hunt
Delta
Hopkins
Franklin
Titus
Morris
Cass
Rockwall
Camp
Scurry
Fisher
Jones
Shackel-
ford
Stephens
Palo
Pinto
Parker
Tarrant
Dallas
Rains
Wood
Upshur
Marion
Harrison
Fort Worth
Kaufman
Van
Zandt
Gregg
Longview
Mitchell
Abilene
Eastland
Erath
Hood
Johnson
Ellis
Tyler
Smith
Rusk
Panola
Big Spring
Nolan
Taylor
Callahan
Somervell
Henderson
Sterling
Coke
Runnels
Coleman
Hill
Bosque
Navarro
Chero-
kee
Anderson
Shelby
Brown
Comanche
Lime-
stone
Nacog-
doches
Tom Green
Brownwood
Mills
Hamilton
Waco
McLennan
Freestone
Irion
San Angelo
Concho
McCulloch
Coryell
Houston
San
Augustine
Sabine
Leon
Lufkin
Angelina
San Saba
Lampasas
Bell
Falls
Robert-
son
Schleicher
Menard
Burnet
Madison
Trinity
Polk
Tyler
Jasper
Newton
Mason
Llano
Milam
Walker
Williamson
Huntsville
Brazos
Grimes
San
Jacinto
Kimble
Sutton
Burleson
Bryan
Gillespie
Blanco
Travis
Lee
Hardin
Austin
Liberty
Edwards
Kerr
Hays
Washington
Montgomery
Orange
Bastrop
Austin
Waller
Harris
Beaumont
Kendall
Real
Bandera
Comal
Caldwell
Fayette
Houston
Chambers
Jefferson
Bexar
Fort
Bend
Kinney
Uvalde
Medina
Guada-
lupe
Colorado
San Antonio
Del Rio
Gonzales
Lavaca
Galveston
Wharton
Brazoria
Wilson
Galveston
Maverick
Zavala
Frio
Atascosa
DeWitt
Jackson
Victoria
Karnes
Matagorda
Victoria
Goliad
Rio Grande
Dimmit
La Salle
McMullen
Bee
Calhoun
Refugio
Webb
Live
Oak
Duval
Jim
Wells
San
Patricio
Aransas
Nueces
Corpus Christi
Laredo
Kleberg
PADRE
ISLAND
NATIONAL
SEASHORE
Zapata
Jim
Hogg
Brooks
Kenedy
International
Falcon
Reservoir
Starr
Hidalgo
Willacy
McAllen
Cameron
South Padre Island
Brownsville
35
44
40
44
35
30
20
20
20
35 E
35 W
45
14
35
10
69
10
10
69
45
37
35
69
69 C
2
69 E
Mileage chart
on reverse

Parker County

Physical Features: Hilly, broken by Brazos, Trinity tributaries, Lake Mineral Wells, Lake Weatherford; varied soils.

Economy: Agriculture, varied manufacturing, retail sales, government/services, commuting to Fort Worth; part of Dallas-Fort Worth metropolitan area.

History: Comanche and Kiowa area in the late 1840s when Anglo-American settlers arrived. County named for pioneer legislator Isaac Parker; created in 1855 from Bosque, Navarro counties, organized the same year.

Recreation: Water sports; state park and trailway; nature trails; hunting; Peach Festival in July and rodeo days in June; first Monday trade days monthly.

Minerals: Natural gas, oil, stone, sand and gravel, clays.

Agriculture: Beef cattle, greenhouses, hay, horses (first in number), peaches, sheep and goats, vegetables, pecans, aquaculture. Market value $65.0 million.

Vital Statistics, annual: Births, 1,636; deaths, 1,418; marriages, 686; divorces, 437.

Race/Ethnicity: Anglo, 79.4%; Hispanic, 13.4%; Black, 1.1%; Asian, 0.7%; Other, 5.4%.

WEATHERFORD (33,710) county seat; retail center, manufacturing, warehousing, tourism, commuting to Fort Worth, equine industry; hospital, Weatherford College; museums, public gardens, historic buildings.

Other towns include: **Aledo** (5,380); **Annetta** (3,153), **Annetta North** (572), and **Annetta South** (637); **Briar** (5,635); **Dennis** (727); **Hudson Oaks** (2,478); **Peaster** (642); **Reno** (3,100); **Springtown** (3,355); **Willow Park** (5,194).

Population	156,764
Change from 2010	34.1%
Area (sq. mi.)	910.1
Land Area (sq. mi.)	903.5
Altitude (ft.)	700–1,362
Rainfall (in.)	35.2
Jan. mean min (°F)	33.7
July mean max (°F)	93.1
Civ. Labor	74,625
Unemployed	3.3%
Wages	$578,453,615
Per Capita Income	$65,358
Property Value	$27,248,641,449
Retail Sales	$3,348,615,443

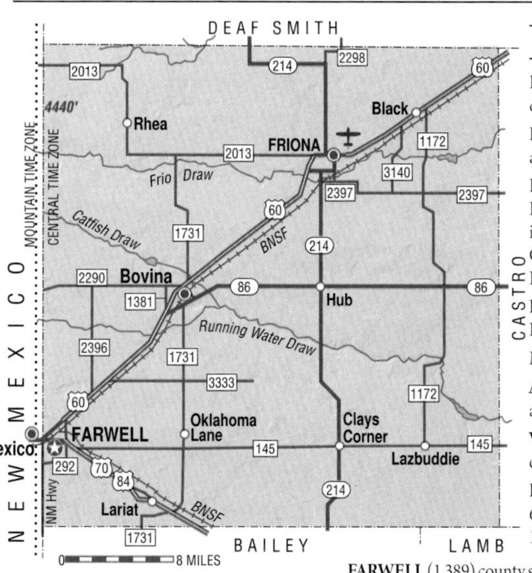

Parmer County

Physical Features: High Plains, broken by draws, playas; sandy, clay, loam soils.

Economy: Cattle feeding, grain elevators, meatpacking plant, other agribusiness.

History: Apaches, pushed out in late 1700s by Comanches and Kiowas. U.S. Army removed Indians in 1874–1875. Anglo-Americans arrived in 1880s. Mexican migration increased after 1950. County named for Republic figure Martin Parmer; created from Bexar District in 1876, organized in 1907.

Recreation: Hunting, playa lake, Border Town Days in July at Farwell.

Minerals: Not significant.

Agriculture: Cattle, dairies; wheat, corn, cotton, sorghum, alfalfa; apples, potatoes. Market value $893.3 million.

Vital Statistics, annual: Births, 169; deaths, 114; marriages, 7; divorces, 24.

Race/Ethnicity: Anglo, 32.3%; Hispanic, 65.9%; Black, 0.5%; Asian, 0.1%; Other, 1.1%.

FARWELL (1,389) county seat; agribusiness, grain storage, farm equipment plants.

FRIONA (4,144) farming, feed lots, feed mill; hospital; museum; Cheeseburger Festival in July.

Other towns include: **Bovina** (1,703) farm trade center; **Lazbuddie** (248).

Population	9,813
Change from 2010	–4.4%
Area (sq. mi.)	885.2
Land Area (sq. mi.)	880.8
Altitude (ft.)	3,785–4,440
Rainfall (in.)	19.3
Jan. mean min (°F)	23.7
July mean max (°F)	90.2
Civ. Labor	5,134
Unemployed	2.4%
Wages	$88,654,252
Per Capita Income	$63,512
Property Value	$1,880,451,455
Retail Sales	$129,759,210

The Pecos County Courthouse in Fort Stockton. Photo by Talshiarr, CC by SA 2.5

Pecos County

For explanation of sources, symbols, and abbreviations, see p. 207 and foldout map.

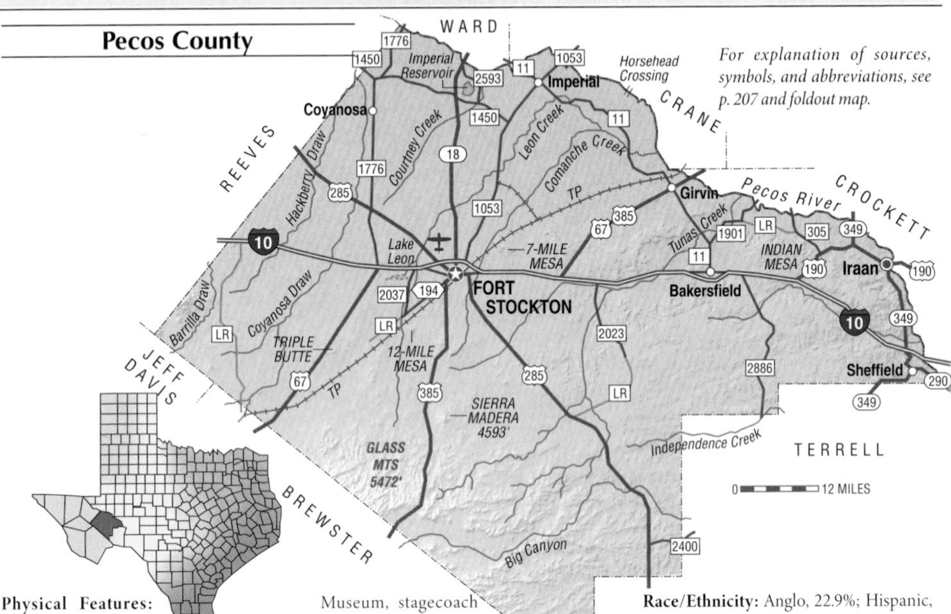

Physical Features: Second largest county; high, broken plateau in West Texas; draining to Pecos and tributaries; Imperial Reservoir, Lake Leon; sandy, clay, loam soils.

Economy: Oil, gas, agriculture, government/services, wind turbines.

History: Comanches in area when military outpost established in 1859. Settlement began after the Civil War. Created from Presidio County in 1871; organized in 1872; named for Pecos River, name origin uncertain.

Recreation: Old Fort Stockton, Annie Riggs Museum, stagecoach stop, scenic drives, Dinosaur Track Roadside Park, cattle-trail sites, archaeological museum with oil and ranch-heritage collections; Fort Stockton Water Carnival in summer.

Minerals: Natural gas, oil, gravel, caliche.

Agriculture: Cattle, alfalfa, pecans, sheep, goats, onions, peppers, melons. Market value $46.2 million. Aquaculture firm producing shrimp. Hunting leases.

Vital Statistics, annual: Births, 217; deaths, 193; marriages, 70; divorces, 13.

Race/Ethnicity: Anglo, 22.9%; Hispanic, 71.4%; Black, 3.3%; Asian, 0.9%; Other, 1.5%.

FORT STOCKTON (8,423) county seat, distribution center for petroleum industry, government/services, agriculture, tourism, varied manufacturing, winery, prison units, spaceport launching small satellites; hospital; historical tours.

IRAAN (1,037) oil and gas center, ranching, farming; hospital, museum; Alley Oop park, county park.

Other towns include: **Coyanosa** (165); **Imperial** (245) center for irrigated farming; **Sheffield** (40) oil, gas center.

Population	15,118
Change from 2010	–2.5%
Area (sq. mi.)	4,764.8
Land Area (sq. mi.)	4,763.9
Altitude (ft.)	2,040–5,472

Rainfall (in.)	13.7
Jan. mean min (°F)	37.3
July mean max (°F)	94.4
Civ. Labor	6,322
Unemployed	4.0%

Wages	$83,555,318
Per Capita Income	$43,661
Property Value	$7,818,545,432
Retail Sales	$456,172,729

Polk County

Physical Features: Rolling; densely forested, with Big Thicket, unique plant, animal life; Neches, Trinity rivers, tributaries; lake.

Economy: Timber, lumber production, tourism, manufacturing.

History: Caddo area; Alabama and Coushatta Indians arrived from Louisiana in the late 1700s. Anglo-American and Hispanic families received land grants in the early 1830s. County named for U.S. President James K. Polk; created from Liberty County and organized 1846.

Recreation: Lake and state park, water activities, fishing, hunting, Alabama-Coushatta Reservation, museum, Big Thicket, woodland trails, champion trees, historic homes.

Minerals: Oil, gas, sand, gravel.

Agriculture: cattle and hay; vegetables raised; income also from blueberries, Christmas trees, honey, horses, and nurseries. Timber and hardwood.

Vital Statistics, annual: Births, 497; deaths, 822; marriages, 273; divorces, NA.

Race/Ethnicity: Anglo, 69.4%; Hispanic, 14.7%; Black, 9.7%; Asian, 0.7%; Other, 5.5%.

LIVINGSTON (5,829) county seat; lumber, tourism, oil; museum, hospital.

West Livingston (7,295) includes Blanchard, East Tempe, Moore Hill, and Polunsky prison unit.

Other towns include: **Camden** (1,200); **Corrigan** (1,480) plywood plant; **Dallardsville** (350); **Goodrich** (258); **Onalaska** (3,143); **Pleasant Hill** (1,060); **Seven Oaks** (69).

Population	51,899
Change from 2010	14.3%
Area (sq. mi.)	1,109.7
Land Area (sq. mi.)	1,057.1
Altitude (ft.)	68–484
Rainfall (in.)	51.0
Jan. mean min (°F)	41.7
July mean max (°F)	93.9
Civ. Labor	18,708
Unemployed	5.5%
Wages	$160,046,818
Per Capita Income	$47,994
Property Value	$7,835,613,067
Retail Sales	$666,285,816

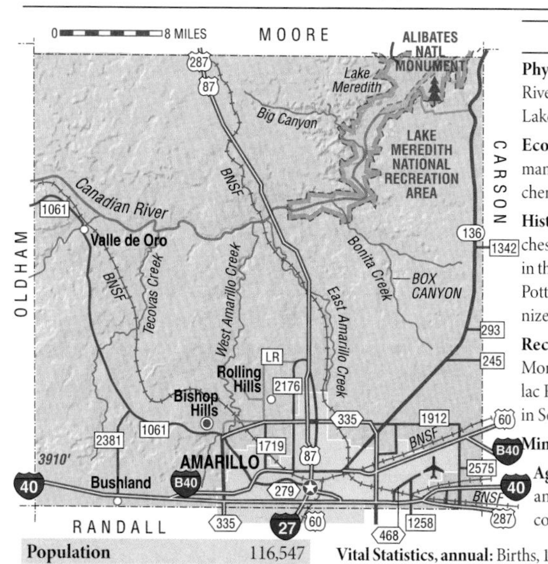

Potter County

Physical Features: Mostly level, part rolling; broken by Canadian River and tributaries; sandy, sandy loam, chocolate loam, clay soils; Lake Meredith.

Economy: Transportation and distribution hub for large area, manufacturing, agribusiness, tourism, government/services, petrochemicals, gas processing.

History: Apaches, pushed out by Comanches in the 1700s. Comanches removed to Indian Territory in 1874–1875. Ranching began in the late 1870s. Oil boom in the 1920s. County named for Robert Potter, Republic leader; created in 1876 from Bexar District; organized in 1887.

Recreation: Lake activities, Alibates Flint Quarries National Monument, hunting, fishing, Wildcat Bluff nature center, Cadillac Ranch car sculpture, professional sports events, Tri-State Fair in September.

Minerals: Natural gas, oil, helium.

Agriculture: Beef cattle production and processing; wheat, sorghum, cotton. Market value $24.8 million.

Vital Statistics, annual: Births, 1,582; deaths, 1,638; marriages, 955; divorces, 235.

Race/Ethnicity: Anglo, 42.3%; Hispanic, 38.1%; Black, 10.1%; Asian, 5.1%; Other, 4.3%.

AMARILLO (201,234) county seat; hub for northern Panhandle oil, ranching, distribution/marketing center, tourism, manufacturing, food processing, prison; hospitals; Amarillo College, Texas Tech University medical, engineering, pharmacy schools; Quarter Horse Hall of Fame, museum.

Other towns include: **Bishop Hills** (207) and **Bushland** (2,581).

Population	116,547
Change from 2010	-3.7%
Area (sq. mi.)	922.0
Land Area (sq. mi.)	908.4
Altitude (ft.)	2,915–3,910
Rainfall (in.)	19.7
Jan. mean min (°F)	26.0
July mean max (°F)	91.2
Civ. Labor	55,077
Unemployed	3.2%
Wages	$1,141,626,948
Per Capita Income	$55,764
Property Value	$12,651,094,895
Retail Sales	$3,101,572,140

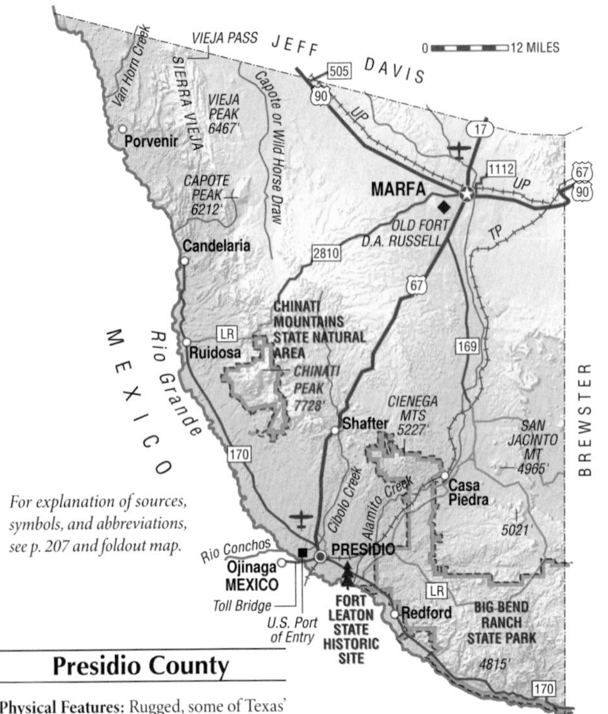

For explanation of sources, symbols, and abbreviations, see p. 207 and foldout map.

Presidio County

Physical Features: Rugged, some of Texas' tallest mountains; clays, loams, sandy loams on uplands; intermountain wash; timber sparse; Capote Falls, state's highest.

Economy: Government/services, ranching, hunting leases, tourism.

History: Presidio area has been cultivated farmland since at least 1200 A.D. Spanish explorers of the 1500s encountered permanent villages along Rio Grande. Jumanos, Apaches, and Comanches in the area when Spanish missions began in 1680s. Anglo-Americans arrived in the 1840s. County created in 1850 from Bexar District; organized in 1875; named for Spanish Presidio del Norte (fort of the north).

Recreation: Hunting; scenic drives along Rio Grande, in mountains; ghost towns, mysterious Marfa Lights; Fort D.A. Russell; Big Bend Ranch State Park; hot springs; Cibolo Creek Ranch Resort; Chinati Foundation art festival in fall. (Chinati Mountains State Natural Area not yet open to public.)

Minerals: Sand, gravel, silver, zeolite.

Agriculture: Cattle, tomatoes, hay, onions, melons. Some irrigation near Rio Grande. Market value $48 million.

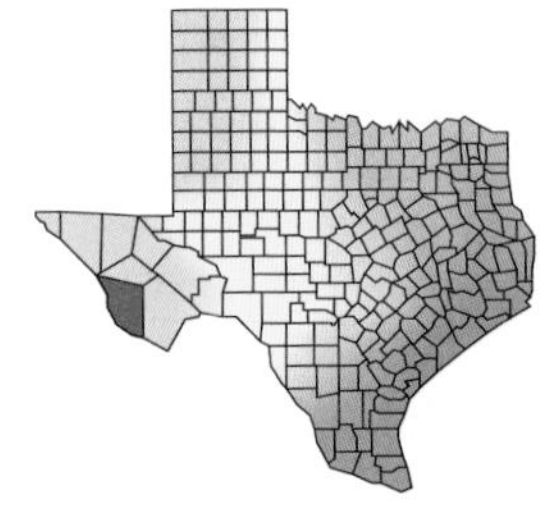

Population	6,140
Change from 2010	–21.5%
Area (sq. mi.)	3,855.9
Land Area (sq. mi.)	3,855.2
Altitude (ft.)	2,400–7,728
Rainfall (in.)	8.9
Jan. mean min (°F)	36.4
July mean max (°F)	101.4
Civ. Labor	3,096
Unemployed	6.2%
Wages	$28,673,932
Per Capita Income	$61,776
Property Value	$16,961,780,215
Retail Sales	$2,430,253,578

Vital Statistics, annual: Births, 74; deaths, 64; marriages, 22; divorces, NA.

Race/Ethnicity: Anglo, 15.7%; Hispanic, 81.4%; Black, 0.4%; Asian, 1.4%; Other, 1.1%.

MARFA (1,750) county seat; ranching supply, Border Patrol headquarters, tourism, art center, gateway to mountainous area; Hotel Paisano, headquarters for movie *Giant*; Agave Festival in June.

PRESIDIO (3,301) international bridge to Ojinaga, Mex., gateway to Mexico's West Coast by rail; Fort Leaton historic site; Dark Skies Music Fest in August.

Other towns include: **Redford** (43); **Shafter** (57) old mining town.

The welcome sign outside Presidio. Photo by Yuan Yufei, CC by SA 3.0

Rains County

Physical Features: Northeastern county; rolling; partly Blackland, sandy loams, sandy soils; Sabine River, Lake Tawakoni, Lake Fork Reservoir.

Economy: Agribusiness, some manufacturing.

History: Caddo area. In the 1700s, Tawakoni Indians entered the area. Anglo-Americans arrived in the 1840s. County, county seat named for Emory Rains, Republic leader; created in 1870 from Hopkins, Hunt, and Wood counties, organized the same year; birthplace of National Farmers Union, 1902.

Recreation: Lake Tawakoni and Lake Fork Reservoir activities; birding, Wild Market Days in fall.

Minerals: Gas, oil.

Agriculture: Beef, forages, dairies, vegetables (second in sweet potato acreage), fruits, nurseries. Market value $22.8 million.

Vital Statistics, annual: Births, 117; deaths, 193; marriages, 81; divorces, 48.

Race/Ethnicity: Anglo, 83.3%; Hispanic, 9.1%; Black, 2.2%; Asian, 0.5%; Other, 5%.

EMORY (1,291) county seat; local trade, tourism, government/ services, commuting to Greenville and Dallas.

Other towns include: **East Tawakoni** (850) and **Point** (765), manufacturing, tourism, tamale fest in September.

Population	12,509
Change from 2010	14.6%
Area (sq. mi.)	258.8
Land Area (sq. mi.)	229.5
Altitude (ft.)	340–570
Rainfall (in.)	45.4
Jan. mean min (°F)	34.4
July mean max (°F)	90.6

Civ. Labor	6,519
Unemployed	3.4%
Wages	$23,475,211
Per Capita Income	$41,563
Property Value	$1,592,721,035
Retail Sales	$68,306,553

Randall County

Physical Features: Panhandle county; level, but broken by scenic Palo Duro Canyon, Buffalo Lake; Bivins Lake; silty clay, loam soils.

Economy: Agribusiness, education, tourism, part of Amarillo metropolitan area.

History: Comanche Indians removed in the mid-1870s; ranching began soon afterward. County created in 1876 from the Bexar District; organized in 1889; named for Confederate Gen. Horace Randal (name misspelled in statute).

Recreation: State park, with Texas outdoor musical drama each summer; Panhandle-Plains Historical Museum; West Texas A&M University events; aoudad sheep, migratory waterfowl hunting in season; Buffalo Lake National Wildlife Refuge; cowboy breakfasts at ranches.

Minerals: Not significant.

Agriculture: Grain sorghum, beef cattle, wheat, silage, cotton, dairies, hay. Market value $479.5 million.

Vital Statistics, annual: Births, 1,602; deaths, 1,403; marriages, 521; divorces, 410.

Race/Ethnicity: Anglo, 67.8%; Hispanic, 22.4%; Black, 3.2%; Asian, 1.9%; Other, 4.6%.

CANYON (15,221) county seat; West Texas A&M University, tourism, commuting to Amarillo, ranching, farm center, light manufacturing, gateway to state park.

AMARILLO (201,234 total, part [100,202] in Potter County) hub for northern Panhandle oil and ranching, distribution and marketing center, manufacturing.

Other towns include: **Lake Tanglewood** (706); **Palisades** (275); **Rockwell Place** (1,445) **Timbercreek Canyon** (445); **Umbarger** (72) German sausage festival in November.

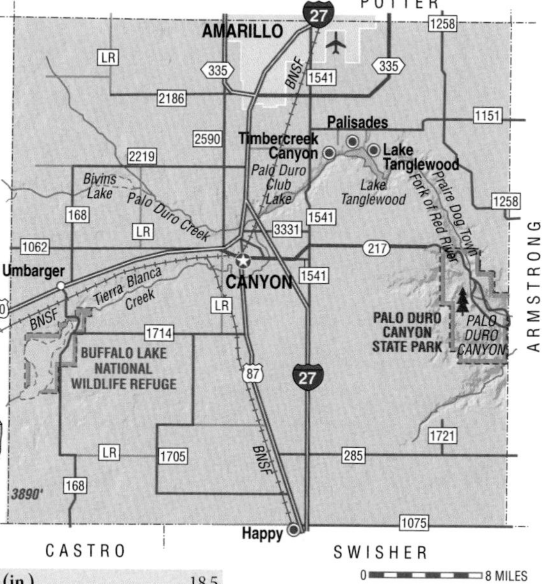

Population	143,854
Change from 2010	19.2%
Area (sq. mi.)	922.4
Land Area (sq. mi.)	911.5
Altitude (ft.)	27,003,890.00

Rainfall (in.)	18.5
Jan. mean min (°F)	23.7
July mean max (°F)	91.4
Civ. Labor	76,100
Unemployed	2.8%

Wages	$480,174,738
Per Capita Income	$56,381
Property Value	$1,912,820,619
Retail Sales	$127,711,720

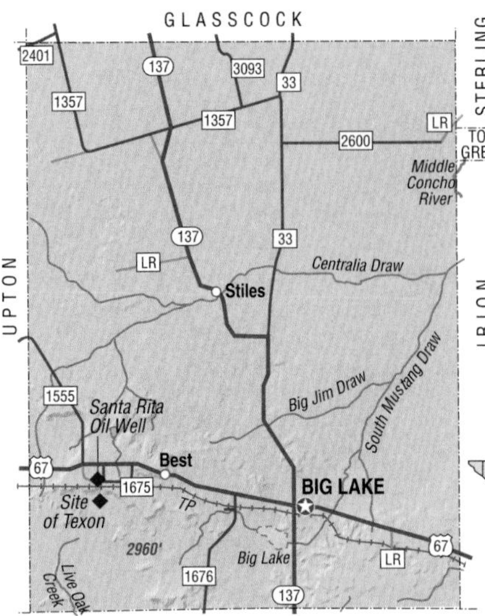

Reagan County

Physical Features: Western county; level to hilly, broken by draws, Big Lake (intermittent); sandy, loam, clay soils.

Economy: Oil and gas production, hunting, ranching.

History: Comanches in the area until the mid-1870s. Ranching began in the 1880s. Hispanic migration increased after 1950. County named for Texas' U.S. Sen. John H. Reagan, first chairman of the Texas Railroad Commission; county created and organized in 1903 from Tom Green County.

Recreation: Site of 1923 discovery well Santa Rita No. 1 on University of Texas land.

Minerals: Gas, oil.

Agriculture: Cotton, cattle, sheep, goats. Market value $18.2 million. Hunting leases important.

Vital Statistics, annual: Births, 56; deaths, 34; marriages, 14; divorces, 15.

Race/Ethnicity: Anglo, 28.6%; Hispanic, 67.4%; Black, 1%; Asian, 0.6%; Other, 2.4%.

BIG LAKE (2,850) county seat; center for oil activities, agriculture, government/services; hospital; Santa Rita festival in summer.

Population	3,253
Change from 2010	−3.4%
Area (sq. mi.)	1,176.0
Land Area (sq. mi.)	1,175.3
Altitude (ft.)	2,370–2,960

Rainfall (in.)	18.2
Jan. mean min (°F)	35.1
July mean max (°F)	94.0
Civ. Labor	1,634
Unemployed	3.5%

Wages	$30,841,451
Per Capita Income	$61,077
Property Value	$8,791,857,016
Retail Sales	$35,970,988

Real County

For explanation of sources, symbols, and abbreviations, see p. 207 and foldout map.

Physical Features: Hill Country, spring-fed streams, scenic canyons; Frio, Nueces rivers; cedars, pecans, walnuts, many live oaks.

Economy: Ranching, tourism, government/services, cedar cutting.

History: Tonkawa area; Lipan Apaches arrived in early 1700s; later, Comanche hunters arrived in the area. Spanish mission established in 1762. Anglo-Americans arrived in 1850s. County created, organized in 1913 from Bandera, Edwards, and Kerr counties; named for legislator-ranchman Julius Real.

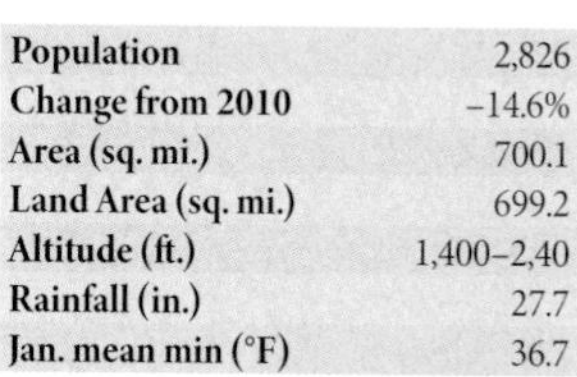

Recreation: Tourist and hunting center, birding, fishing, camping, scenic drives, state natural area.

Minerals: Not significant.

Agriculture: Goats, sheep, beef cattle produce most income. Market value $1.3 million. Cedar posts processed.

Vital Statistics, annual: Births, 27; deaths, 73; marriages, 1; divorces, NA.

Race/Ethnicity: Anglo, 70.3%; Hispanic, 25.1%; Black, 0.8%; Asian, 0.4%; Other, 3.3%.

LEAKEY (333) county seat; tourism, ranching; museums; July Jubilee.

CAMP WOOD (508) tourism, hunting, ranching; medical clinic; San Lorenzo de la Santa Cruz mission site; museum; Lindbergh Park, settlers reunion in August.

Other towns include: **Rio Frio** (50).

Population	2,826
Change from 2010	−14.6%
Area (sq. mi.)	700.1
Land Area (sq. mi.)	699.2
Altitude (ft.)	1,400–2,40
Rainfall (in.)	27.7
Jan. mean min (°F)	36.7
July mean max (°F)	93.3
Civ. Labor	1,143
Unemployed	4.6%
Wages	$8,145,650
Per Capita Income	$55,449
Property Value	$1,992,602,805
Retail Sales	$33,827,431

Red River County

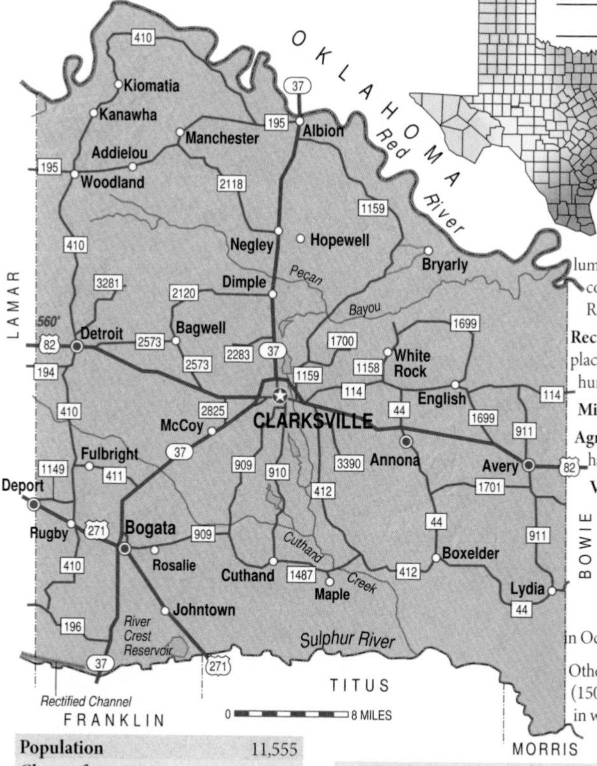

Physical Features: On Red-Sulphur rivers' divide; 39 different soil types; half timbered; River Crest Reservoir.

Economy: Manufacturing, government/services, agriculture.

History: Caddo Indians abandoned the area in the 1790s. One of the oldest counties; settlers were moving in from the United States in the 1810s. Kickapoo and other tribes arrived in the 1820s. Antebellum slaveholding area. County created in 1836 as original county of the Republic; organized in 1837; named for Red River, its northern boundary.

Recreation: Historical sites include pioneer homes, birthplace of John Nance Garner; fall foliage; water activities; hunting of deer, turkey, duck, small game.

Minerals: Small oil flow.

Agriculture: Beef cattle, corn, soybeans, wheat, sorghum, hay. Market value $94.0 million. Timber sales substantial.

Vital Statistics, annual: Births, 110; deaths, 256; marriages, 32; divorces, 42.

Race/Ethnicity: Anglo, 73.3%; Hispanic, 6.6%; Black, 15%; Asian, 0.4%; Other, 4.6%.

CLARKSVILLE (2,790) county seat; varied manufacturing; hospital, library; Historical Society bazaar in October.

Other towns include: **Annona** (183); **Avery** (426); **Bagwell** (150); **Bogata** (1,089); **Detroit** (707) commercial center in west.

Population	11,555
Change from 2010	−10.1%
Area (sq. mi.)	1,056.7
Land Area (sq. mi.)	1,036.6
Altitude (ft.)	260–560
Rainfall (in.)	52.8
Jan. mean min (°F)	33.3
July mean max (°F)	92.1
Civ. Labor	5,144
Unemployed	5.1%
Wages	$32,591,063
Per Capita Income	$53,818
Property Value	$3,274,801,802
Retail Sales	$59,445,509

Reeves County

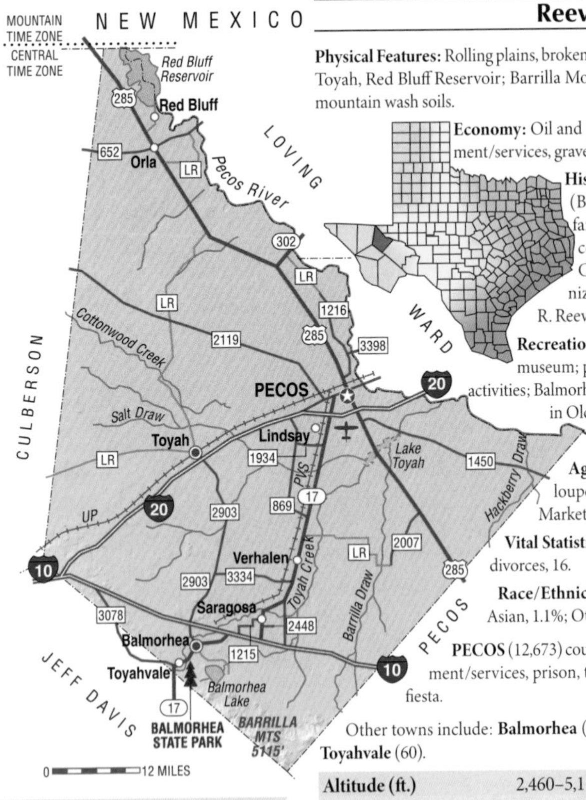

Physical Features: Rolling plains, broken by many draws, Pecos River, Balmorhea Lake, Lake Toyah, Red Bluff Reservoir; Barrilla Mountains on the south; chocolate loam, clay, sandy, mountain wash soils.

Economy: Oil and gas, agriculture, tourism, food processing, government/services, gravel.

History: Jumanos were irrigating crops from springs (Balmorhea) when Spanish explored in 1583. Mexican farmers supplied nearby Fort Davis in the mid-19th century. Anglo-Americans arrived in the 1870s. County created in 1883 from Pecos County; organized in 1884; named for Confederate Col. George R. Reeves.

Recreation: Replica of Judge Roy Bean store, West of Pecos museum; park with javelina, prairie dogs; scenic drives; water activities; Balmorhea State Park with San Solomon Springs pool; Night in Old Pecos, cantaloupe festival in July.

Minerals: Oil, gas, gravel.

Agriculture: Ranching, dairies, hay, cotton, cantaloupes, pecans, pistachios. Some 11,000 acres irrigated. Market value $10.9 million.

Vital Statistics, annual: Births, 214; deaths, 151; marriages, 70; divorces, 16.

Race/Ethnicity: Anglo, 11.5%; Hispanic, 84.8%; Black, 1.5%; Asian, 1.1%; Other, 1%.

PECOS (12,673) county seat; food processing, produce shipping, government/services, prison, tourism, agribusiness; hospital; 16th of September fiesta.

Other towns include: **Balmorhea** (398), **Lindsay** (905), **Saragosa** (185), **Toyah** (61), **Toyahvale** (60).

Population	14,487
Change from 2010	5.1%
Area (sq. mi.)	2,642.1
Land Area (sq. mi.)	2,635.4

Altitude (ft.)	2,460–5,115
Rainfall (in.)	12.1
Jan. mean min (°F)	32.1
July mean max (°F)	93.8
Civ. Labor	8,525

Unemployed	3.4%
Wages	$129,672,903
Per Capita Income	$52,811
Property Value	$33,383,188,638
Retail Sales	$406,967,446

A community park in Balmorhea. Photo by Fortguy, CC by SA 3.0

Refugio County

Physical Features: Coastal plain, broken by streams, bays; sandy, loam, black soils; mesquite, oak, huisache motts.

Economy: Petroleum, petrochemical production, agribusinesses, tourism, commuting to Corpus Christi, Victoria.

History: Karankawa area. Spanish mission, for which the county is named, Our Lady of Refuge, established in 1793. Colonists from Ireland and the United States arrived in the 1830s. Original county of the Republic created in 1836, organized in 1837.

Recreation: Water activities, hunting, fishing, historic sites, wildlife refuge, home of the whooping crane; county fair in March

Minerals: Oil, natural gas.

Agriculture: Cotton, beef cattle, sorghum, corn, soybeans, horses. Market value $35.9 million. Hunting leases.

Vital Statistics, annual: Births, 58; deaths, 110; marriages, 19; divorces, 17.

Race/Ethnicity: Anglo, 42.5%; Hispanic, 49%; Black, 5.9%; Asian, 0.4%; Other, 2.1%.

REFUGIO (2,790) county seat; petroleum, agribusiness center; hospital; museum, historic homes.

Other towns include: **Austwell** (118); **Bayside** (275) resorts; **Tivoli** (645); **Woodsboro** (1,299) commercial center.

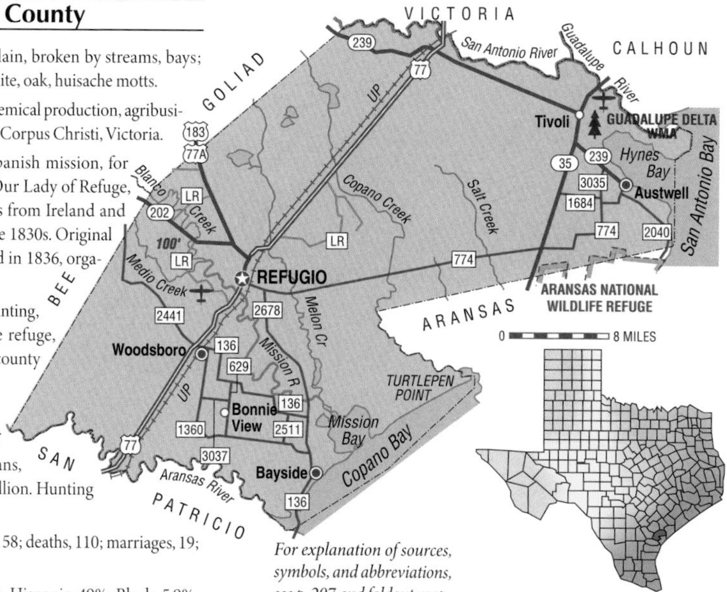

For explanation of sources, symbols, and abbreviations, see p. 207 and foldout map.

Population	6,756
Change from 2010	–8.5%
Area (sq. mi.)	818.2
Land Area (sq. mi.)	77.4
Altitude (ft.)	sea level–100
Rainfall (in.)	34.8
Jan. mean min (°F)	46.2
July mean max (°F)	93.3
Civ. Labor	2,968
Unemployed	4.7%
Wages	$29,188,001
Per Capita Income	$54,475
Property Value	$2,017,194,474
Retail Sales	$94,433,959

Roberts County

Physical Features: Rolling, broken by Canadian River and tributaries; Red Deer Creek; black, sandy loam, alluvial soils.

Economy: Oil-field operations, agribusiness.

History: Apaches; pushed out by Comanches who were removed in 1874–1875 by the U.S. Army. Ranching began in the late 1870s. County created in 1876 from Bexar District; organized in 1889; named for Texas leaders John S. Roberts and Gov. O.M. Roberts.

Recreation: Scenic drives, hunting, museum; national cow-calling contest in June.

Minerals: Production of gas, oil.

Agriculture: Beef cattle; wheat, sorghum, corn, soybeans, hay; 6,300 acres irrigated. Market value $18.3million.

Vital Statistics, annual: Births, 0; deaths, 12; marriages, 5; divorces, 5.

Race/Ethnicity: Anglo, 86.7%; Hispanic, 6%; Black, 0.2%; Asian, 0%; Other, 7%.

MIAMI (521) county seat; ranching, oil center, some manufacturing.

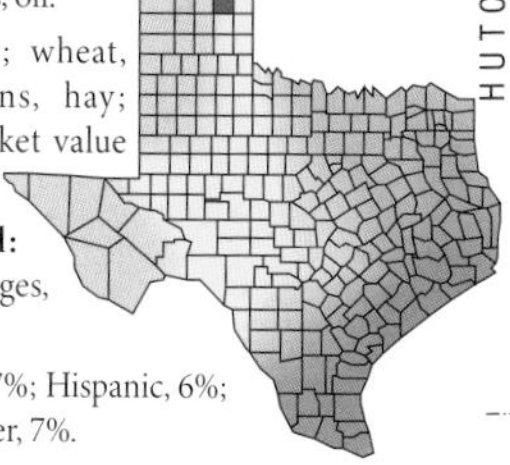

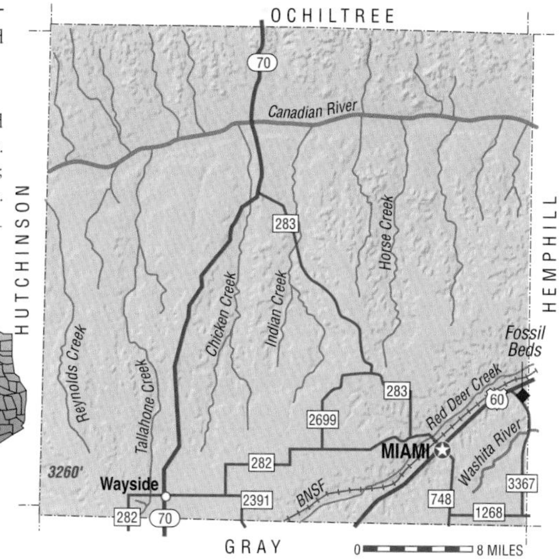

Population	797
Change from 2010	–14.2%
Area (sq. mi.)	924.2
Land Area (sq. mi.)	924.1
Altitude (ft.)	2,380–3,260
Rainfall (in.)	24.2
Jan. mean min (°F)	23.3
July mean max (°F)	90.5
Civ. Labor	399
Unemployed	3.8%
Wages	$5,575,025
Per Capita Income	$56,868
Property Value	$565,684,875
Retail Sales	$1,501,458

The First Methodist Church of Rockwall is on the National Register of Historic Places. Photo by John Hopper, CC by SA 3.0

Robertson County

Physical Features: Rolling in north and east, draining to bottoms along Brazos, Navasota rivers; sandy soils, heavy in bottoms; Lake Limestone, Twin Oaks Reservoir, Camp Creek Reservoir.

Economy: Agribusiness, government/services, oil and gas.

History: Tawakoni, Waco, Comanche, and other tribes. Anglo-Americans arrived in the 1820s. Antebellum slaveholding area. County created in 1837, organized in 1838, subdivided into many others later; named for pioneer Sterling Clack Robertson.

Recreation: Hunting, fishing; historic sites; dogwood trails, wildlife preserves.

Minerals: Gas, oil, lignite coal.

Agriculture: Poultry, beef cattle, cotton, hay, corn; 20,000 acres of cropland irrigated. Market value $158.1 million.

Vital Statistics, annual: Births, 220; deaths, 235; marriages, 51; divorces, 35.

Race/Ethnicity: Anglo, 56.7%; Hispanic, 21.1%; Black, 18.5%; Asian, 0.6%; Other, 3.1%.

FRANKLIN (1,670) county seat; oil and gas, power plants, agriculture; Carnegie library.

HEARNE (4,531) railroad center; depot museum, historic homes, World War II POW camp; Bags & Boards cornhole tournament in September.

Other towns include: **Bremond** (854) mining, agriculture, power utilities, library, museum, Polish Days in late June; **Calvert** (962) agriculture, tourism, antiques, street dance in May, tour of homes; **Mumford** (170); **New Baden** (150); **Wheelock** (225).

For explanation of sources, symbols, and abbreviations, see p. 207 and foldout map.

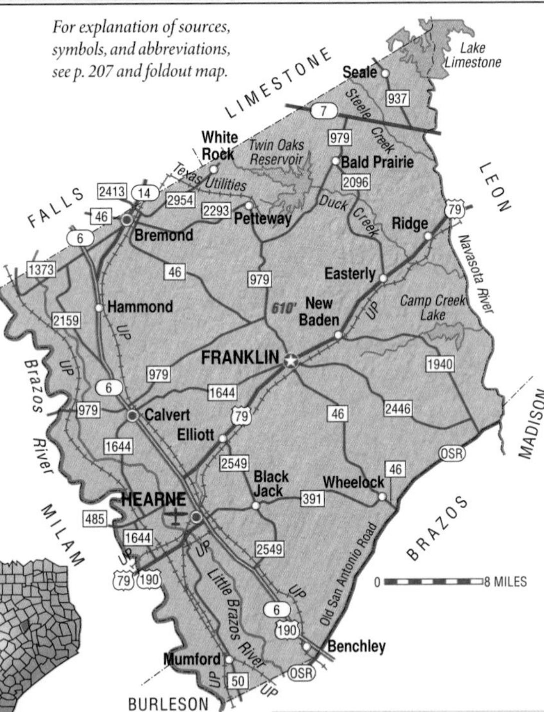

Population	16,958
Change from 2010	2.0%
Area (sq. mi.)	865.4
Land Area (sq. mi.)	855.7
Altitude (ft.)	230–610
Rainfall (in.)	40.6

Jan. mean min (°F)	41.3
July mean max (°F)	94.3
Civ. Labor	7,971
Unemployed	3.8%
Wages	$83,462,437
Per Capita Income	$52,894
Property Value	$6,451,940,472
Retail Sales	$142,552,785

Population	116,381
Change from 2010	48.6%
Area (sq. mi.)	148.7
Land Area (sq. mi.)	127.0
Altitude (ft.)	431–624
Rainfall (in.)	39.8
Jan. mean min (°F)	36.1
July mean max (°F)	91.3
Civ. Labor	59,221
Unemployed	3.3%
Wages	$540,486,375

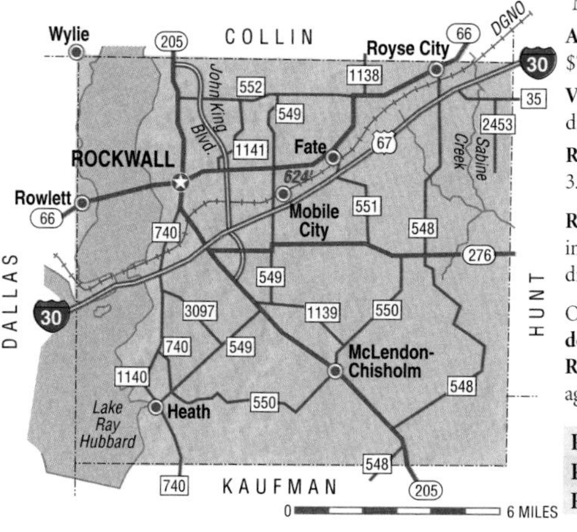

Rockwall County

Physical Features: Rolling prairie, mostly Blackland soil; Lake Ray Hubbard. Texas' smallest county.

Economy: Industrial employment in local plants and in Dallas; in Dallas metropolitan area; residential development around Lake Ray Hubbard.

History: Caddo area. Cherokees arrived in the 1820s. Anglo-American settlers arrived in the 1840s. County created in 1873 from Kaufman, organized the same year; named for wall-like rock formation.

Recreation: Lake activities; proximity to Dallas; unusual rock outcrop.

Minerals: Not significant.

Agriculture: Small grains, cattle, horticulture, horses. Market value $7.8 million.

Vital Statistics, annual: Births, 1,134; deaths, 751; marriages, 1,152; divorces, 321.

Race/Ethnicity: Anglo, 65.1%; Hispanic, 19.1%; Black, 7.6%; Asian, 3.1%; Other, 5.2%.

ROCKWALL (49,669) county seat; commuters, varied manufacturing, government/services; hospital; harbor retail and entertainment district; Founders Day in May.

Other towns include: **Fate** (21,013); **Heath** (10,266); **McLendon-Chisholm** (4,206) Heroes' Day in October; **Mobile City** (145); **Royse City** (15,978) government/services, varied manufacturing, agribusiness, museum, library, Funfest in October.

Per Capita Income	$70,833
Property Value	$22,870,815,545
Retail Sales	$2,599,527,113

Part [7,768] of **Rowlett**, hospital, and a small part of **Wylie**.

Runnels County

Physical Features: Level to rolling; bisected by Colorado and tributaries; sandy loam, black waxy soils; O.H. Ivie Reservoir, Lake Ballinger.

Economy: Agribusiness, oil, government/services, manufacturing.

History: Spanish explorers found Jumanos in area in the 1650s; later, Apaches and Comanches driven out in the 1870s by U.S. military. First Anglo-Americans arrived in the 1850s; Germans, Czechs around 1900. County named for planter-legislator H.G. Runnels; created in 1858 from Bexar and Travis counties; organized in 1880.

Recreation: Deer, dove and turkey hunting; lakes; fishing; antique car museum; historical markers in county.

Minerals: Oil, gas, sand.

Agriculture: Cattle, cotton, wheat, sorghum, dairies, sheep and goats. Market value $53.4 million.

Vital Statistics, annual: Births, 101; deaths, 163; marriages, 53; divorces, 24.

Race/Ethnicity: Anglo, 61.2%; Hispanic, 33.9%; Black, 1.3%; Asian, 0.2%; Other, 3.3%.

BALLINGER (3,580) county seat; varied manufacturing, meat processing; Carnegie Library, hospital, Western Texas College extension; the Cross, 100-ft. tall atop hill; city park; Festival of Ethnic Cultures in April.

Other towns include: **Miles** (907); **Rowena** (197); **Wingate** (113); **Winters** (2,365) manufacturing, museum, hospital.

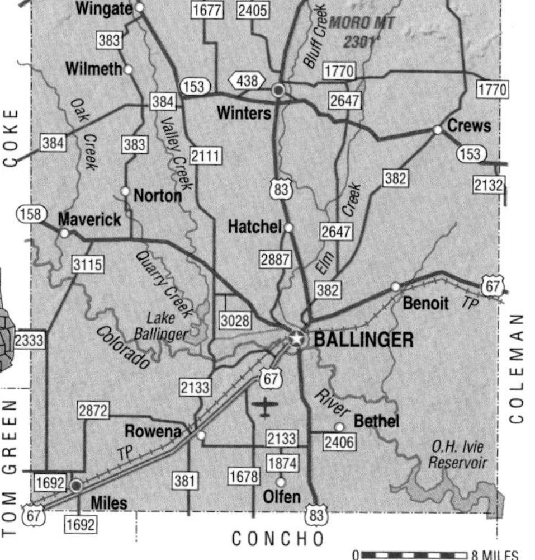

For explanation of sources, symbols, and abbreviations, see p. 207 and foldout map.

Population	9,943
Change from 2010	–5.3%
Area (sq. mi.)	1,057.1
Land Area (sq. mi.)	1,050.9
Altitude (ft.)	1,915–2,301

Rainfall (in.)	23.4
Jan. mean min (°F)	33.1
July mean max (°F)	94.2
Civ. Labor	4,694
Unemployed	3.3%

Wages	$33,728,061
Per Capita Income	$51,307
Property Value	$1,993,032,953
Retail Sales	$122,889,848

Rusk County

Physical Features: East Texas county on Sabine-Angelina divide; varied deep, sandy soils; over half in pines, hardwoods; Martin Creek Lake, Lake Cherokee, Lake Striker.

Economy: Oil and gas, lignite mining, electricity generation, agriculture.

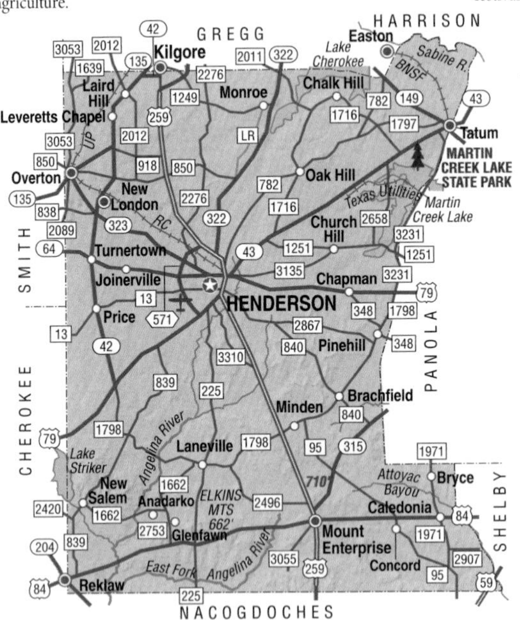

History: Caddo area. Cherokees settled in the 1820s; removed in 1839. First Anglo-Americans arrived in 1829. Antebellum slaveholding area. County named for Republic, state leader Thomas J. Rusk; created and organized from Nacogdoches County in 1843.

Recreation: Water sports, state park, historic homes and sites, scenic drives, site of East Texas Field discovery oil well; Henderson syrup festival in November.

Minerals: Oil, natural gas, lignite.

Agriculture: Beef cattle, forage, poultry, nursery plants. Market value $100.2 million. Timber income substantial.

Vital Statistics, annual: Births, 618; deaths, 682; marriages, 235; divorces, 178.

Race/Ethnicity: Anglo, 61.3%; Hispanic, 18.3%; Black, 15.8%; Asian, 0.4%; Other, 4.1%.

HENDERSON (13,502) county seat; power plant, mining, lumber, state jails; hospital, museum.

Other towns include: **Laird Hill** (300); **Lake Cherokee** (3,336); **Laneville** (169); **Minden** (150); **Mount Enterprise** (504); **New London** (958) site of 1937 school explosion that killed 293 students and faculty; **Overton** (2,274, partly in Smith County) oil, lumbering center, petroleum processing, prison, A&M research center; **Price** (275); **Tatum** (1,340, partly in Panola County); **Turnertown-Selman City** (271).

Also: part [153] of **Reklaw** (333, rest in Cherokee County), and part [3,268] of **Kilgore** (13,383 total, rest in Gregg County).

Population	52,743
Change from 2010	–1.1%
Area (sq. mi.)	938.4
Land Area (sq. mi.)	924.0

Altitude (ft.)	250–710
Rainfall (in.)	50.4
Jan. mean min (°F)	37.3
July mean max (°F)	93.0

Civ. Labor	22,417
Unemployed	4.2%
Wages	$172,554,838
Per Capita Income	$44,874
Property Value	$6,969,219,088
Retail Sales	$471,687,868

The Elias Fleming and Mattie Spharler Crim House in Henderson. Photo by Michael Barera, CC by SA 4.0

Buildings in Downtown Hemphill. Photo by Renelibrary, CC by SA 4.0

Sabine County

Physical Features: Eighty percent forested; 114,498 acres in national forest; Sabine River, Toledo Bend Reservoir on east; Sam Rayburn Reservoir on southwest.

Economy: Timber, government/services, tourism.

History: Caddo area. Spanish land grants in the 1790s brought first Spanish and Anglo settlers. An original county, created in 1836; organized in 1837. Name derived from the Spanish word for "cypress" (sabina).

Recreation: Lake activities, hunting, campsites, hiking trails, marinas, historic homes; McMahan's Chapel, pioneer Protestant church; Sabine National Forest; Lobanillo Swales historic trail.

Minerals: Glauconite, oil.

Agriculture: Beef cattle; forage, fruit raised. Market value $17.7 million. Significant timber industry.

Vital Statistics, annual: Births, 113; deaths, 190; marriages, 56; divorces, 10.

Race/Ethnicity: Anglo, 84%; Hispanic, 4%; Black, 7.4%; Asian, 0.5%; Other, 4.1%.

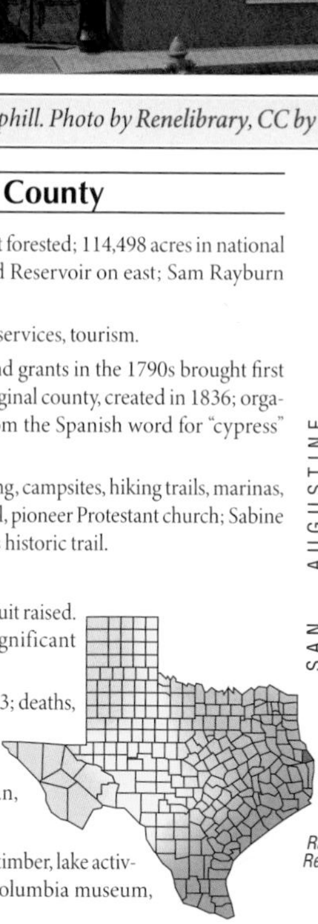

HEMPHILL (1,008) county seat; timber, lake activities, tourism; hospital; NASA Columbia museum, library.

Other towns include: **Bronson** (377); **Brookeland** (300); **Geneva** (200); **Milam** (1,697); **Pineland** (899) timber processing.

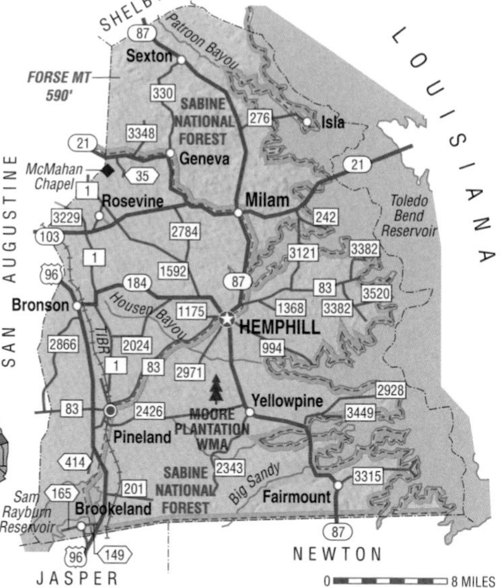

For explanation of sources, symbols, and abbreviations, see p. 207 and foldout map.

Population	10,039
Change from 2010	–7.3%
Area (sq. mi.)	592.3
Land Area (sq. mi.)	530.7
Altitude (ft.)	164–590

Rainfall (in.)	55.7
Jan. mean min (°F)	39.0
July mean max (°F)	92.9
Civ. Labor	3,960
Unemployed	7.0%

Wages	$29,503,403
Per Capita Income	$44,900
Property Value	$1,645,704,713
Retail Sales	$86,113,338

San Augustine County

Physical Features: Hilly East Texas county, 80% forested with 66,799 acres in Angelina National Forest, 4,317 in Sabine National Forest; Sam Rayburn Reservoir; varied soils, sandy to black alluvial.

Economy: Timber, poultry, tourism.

History: Presence of Ais Indians attracted Spanish mission in 1717. First Anglos and Indians from U.S. southern states arrived around 1800. Antebellum slaveholding area. County created and named for Mexican municipality in 1836; an original county; organized in 1837.

Recreation: Lake activities, historic homes, tourist facilities in national forests; sassafras festival in October.

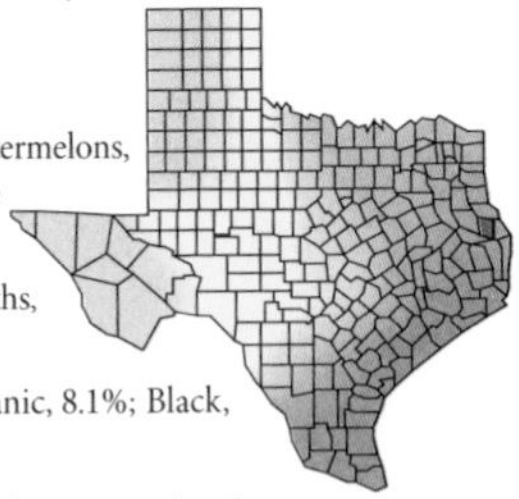

Minerals: Small amount of oil.

Agriculture: Poultry, cattle, horses; watermelons, peas, corn, truck crops. Market value $56.7 million. Timber sales significant.

Vital Statistics, annual: Births, 86; deaths, 173; marriages, 37; divorces, 1.

Race/Ethnicity: Anglo, 66.6%; Hispanic, 8.1%; Black, 22.3%; Asian, 0.5%; Other, 2.6%.

SAN AUGUSTINE (1,854) county seat; logging, poultry farms, tourism; hospital; Mission Dolores museum.

Other towns include: **Broaddus** (186).

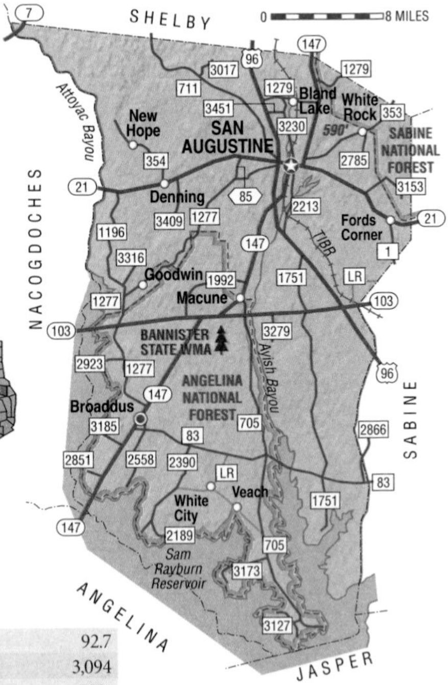

Population	7,922
Change from 2010	–10.6%
Area (sq. mi.)	592.3
Land Area (sq. mi.)	530.7
Altitude (ft.)	164–590
Rainfall (in.)	55.6
Jan. mean min (°F)	37.0
July mean max (°F)	92.7
Civ. Labor	3,094
Unemployed	5.8%
Wages	$31,583,789
Per Capita Income	$50,573
Property Value	$2,085,886,809
Retail Sales	$65,914,232

For explanation of sources, symbols, and abbreviations, see p. 207 and foldout map.

San Jacinto County

Physical Features: East Texas county north of Houston; rolling hills; 80% of area is forested; Sam Houston National Forest; Trinity and East Fork of San Jacinto rivers; Lake Livingston.

Economy: Timber and oil.

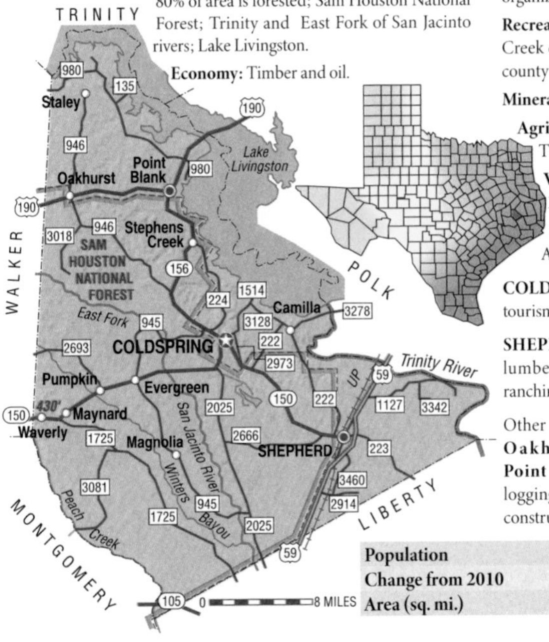

History: Atakapa Indian area. Anglo-Americans arrived in the 1820s. Land grants issued to Mexican families in the early 1830s. County created from Liberty, Montgomery, Polk, and Walker counties in 1869; organized in 1870; named for the battle.

Recreation: Lake activities, hunting, old courthouse and jail; Wolf Creek car show in Coldspring in October. Approximately 60% of county in national forest.

Minerals: Oil, rock, gravel and iron ore.

Agriculture: Beef cattle and forages. Market value $7.2 million. Timber is a principal product.

Vital Statistics, annual: Births, 289; deaths, 379; marriages, 106; divorces, 108.

Race/Ethnicity: Anglo, 70%; Hispanic, 17.6%; Black, 7.6%; Asian, 0.3%; Other, 4.5%.

COLDSPRING (777) county seat; lumbering, oil, farming center, tourism; historic sites.

SHEPHERD (2,045) lumbering, tourism, ranching.

Other towns include: **Oakhurst** (21); **Point Blank** (663) logging, agribusiness, construction.

Population	27,878
Change from 2010	5.7%
Area (sq. mi.)	627.9
Land Area (sq. mi.)	569.2
Altitude (ft.)	62–430
Rainfall (in.)	51.0
Jan. mean min (°F)	43.8
July mean max (°F)	94.4
Civ. Labor	12,048
Unemployed	4.8%
Wages	$25,144,015
Per Capita Income	$46,477
Property Value	$4,684,995,450
Retail Sales	$72,537,352

San Patricio County

Physical Features: Grassy, coastal prairie draining to Aransas, Nueces rivers and to bays; sandy loam, clay, black loam soils; Lake Corpus Christi.

Economy: Oil, petrochemicals, agribusiness, manufacturing, tourism, in Corpus Christi metropolitan area.

History: Karankawa area. Mexican sheep herders in the area before colonization. Settled by Irish families in 1830 (name is Spanish for St. Patrick). Created, named for municipality in 1836; organized in 1837, reorganized in 1847.

Recreation: Water activities, hunting, Corpus Christi Bay, state park, Welder Wildlife Foundation and Park, birdwatching.

Minerals: Oil, gas, gravel, caliche.

Agriculture: Cotton, grain sorghum, beef cattle, corn. Market value $131.3 million. Fisheries income significant.

Vital Statistics, annual: Births, 896; deaths, 770; marriages, 248; divorces, 191.

Race/Ethnicity: Anglo, 38.7%; Hispanic, 55.6%; Black, 1.4%; Asian, 1.2%; Other, 3%.

SINTON (5,562) county seat; oil, agribusiness, tourism; Fiddler's Fest in September.

ARANSAS PASS (8,011, part [681] in Aransas County) deepwater port, shrimping, tourism, offshore oil-well servicing, aluminum and chemical plants; hospital; Shrimporee in May.

PORTLAND (20,536) retail center, petrochemicals, commuters to Corpus Christi; Indian Point pier; Windfest in April.

Other towns include: **Edroy** (285); **Gregory** (1,740); **Ingleside** (9,898) offshore well servicing, chemical and manufacturing plants, commuters, birding, Round Up Days in March; **Ingleside-on-the-Bay** (608); **Lake City** (458); **Lakeside** (3147); **Mathis** (4,354); **Odem** (2,265); **St. Paul** (1,318); **San Patricio** (393); **Taft** (2,818) agriculture, drug rehabilitation center, commuters, wind farm, blackland museum; **Taft Southwest** (1,537).

For explanation of sources, symbols, and abbreviations, see p. 207 and foldout map.

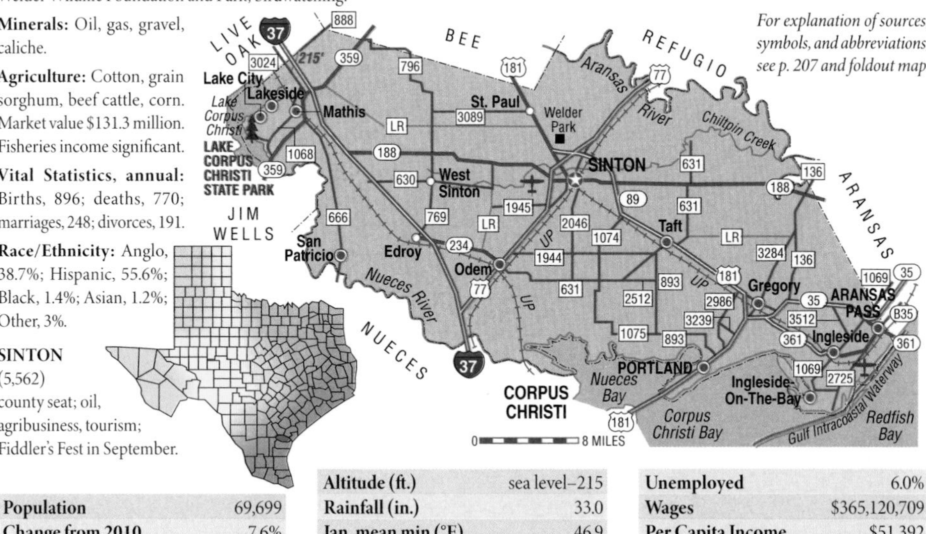

Population	69,699
Change from 2010	7.6%
Area (sq. mi.)	707.8
Land Area (sq. mi.)	693.5

Altitude (ft.)	sea level–215
Rainfall (in.)	33.0
Jan. mean min (°F)	46.9
July mean max (°F)	92.8
Civ. Labor	29,297

Unemployed	6.0%
Wages	$365,120,709
Per Capita Income	$51,392
Property Value	$30,259,685,504
Retail Sales	$1,047,235,703

*The WWI monument in Sinton stands in front of the county courthouse. Photo by **Larry D. Moore, CC by SA 4.0***

San Saba County

Physical Features: West central county; hilly, rolling; bisected by San Saba River; Colorado River on east; black, gray sandy loam, alluvial soils; northern tip of Lake Buchanan.

Economy: Pecan processing plants, tourism, hunting leases.

History: Apaches and Comanches in the area when Spanish explored. Anglo-American settlers arrived in 1850s. County created from Bexar District in 1856, organized the same year; named for river.

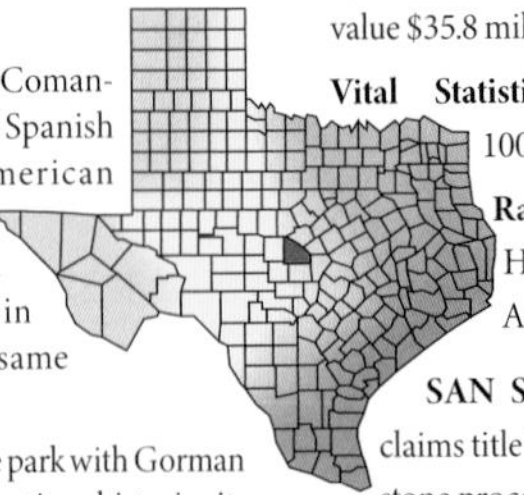

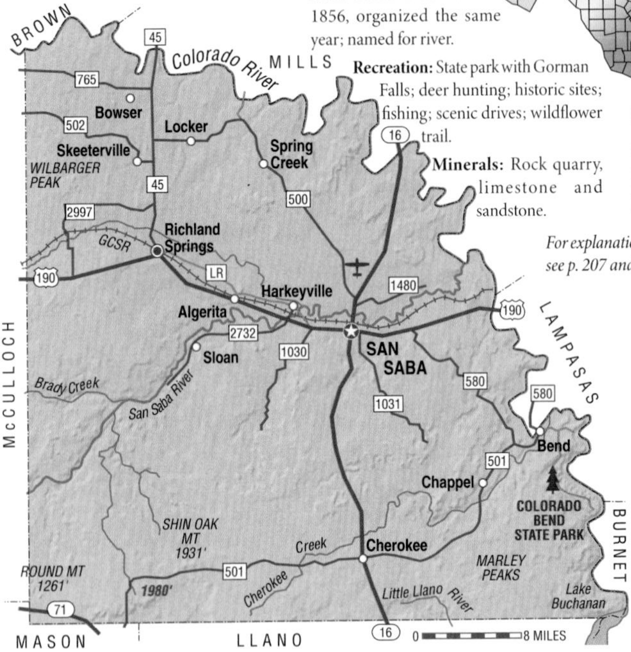

Recreation: State park with Gorman Falls; deer hunting; historic sites; fishing; scenic drives; wildflower trail.

Minerals: Rock quarry, limestone and sandstone.

Agriculture: Cattle, pecans (second in acreage), wheat, hay, some sheep/goats. Market value $35.8 million. Hunting, wildlife leases.

Vital Statistics, annual: Births, 40; deaths, 100; marriages, 17; divorces, 2.

Race/Ethnicity: Anglo, 64.4%; Hispanic, 30.5%; Black, 1.8%; Asian, 0.3%; Other, 2.9%.

SAN SABA (3,151) county seat; claims title "Pecan Capital of the World"; stone processing, varied manufacturing, prison; Cow Camp cookoff in June.

Other towns include: **Bend** (115, partly in Lampasas County); **Cherokee** (175); **Richland Springs** (249).

For explanation of sources, symbols, and abbreviations, see p. 207 and foldout map.

Population	5,827
Change from 2010	–5.0%
Area (sq. mi.)	1,138.4
Land Area (sq. mi.)	1,135.3
Altitude (ft.)	1020–1980
Rainfall (in.)	28.6
Jan. mean min (°F)	34.8
July mean max (°F)	94.1
Civ. Labor	2,237
Unemployed	3.5%
Wages	$17,034,121
Per Capita Income	$43,735
Property Value	$3,178,079,691
Retail Sales	$44,064,990

Schleicher County

Physical Features: West central county on edge of Edwards Plateau, broken by Devils, Concho, San Saba tributaries; part hilly; black soils.

Economy: Oil, ranching, hunting.

History: Jumanos in the area in the 1630s. Later, Apaches and Comanches; removed in the 1870s. Ranching began in the 1870s. Census of 1890 showed third of population from Mexico. County named for Gustav Schleicher, founder of German colony; county created from Crockett County in 1887, organized in 1901.

Recreation: Hunting, livestock show in January, youth and open rodeos, mountain bike events.

Minerals: Oil, natural gas.

Agriculture: Beef cattle, sheep, goats, and cotton, hay. Market value $17.8 million. Hunting leases important.

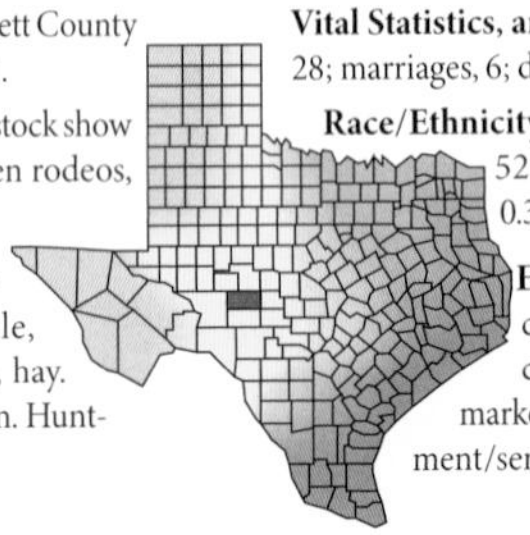

Vital Statistics, annual: Births, 23; deaths, 28; marriages, 6; divorces, 7.

Race/Ethnicity: Anglo, 45%; Hispanic, 52%; Black, 0.6%; Asian, 0.3%; Other, 2.1%.

ELDORADO (1,585) county seat; oil activities, center for livestock, mohair marketing, woolen mill, government/services; hospital.

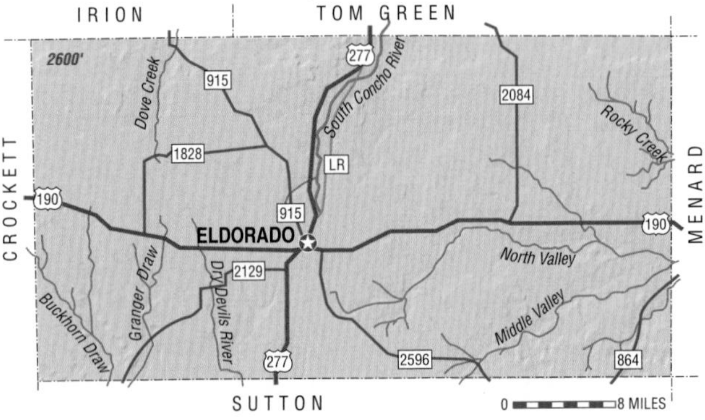

Population	2,429
Change from 2010	–29.8%
Area (sq. mi.)	1,310.7
Land Area (sq. mi.)	1,310.6
Altitude (ft.)	2,070–2,600
Rainfall (in.)	21.9
Jan. mean min (°F)	34.0
July mean max (°F)	92.1
Civ. Labor	1,244
Unemployed	3.5%
Wages	$9,280,246
Per Capita Income	$51,775
Property Value	$1,491,228,712
Retail Sales	$8,451,219

One of the buildings at Western Texas College in Snyder. Photo by Lnichols1971, CC by SA 4.0

Scurry County

Physical Features: Plains county below Caprock, some hills; drained by Colorado, Brazos tributaries; Lake J.B. Thomas; sandy, loam soils.

Economy: Oil, government/services, agribusiness, manufacturing.

History: Apaches; displaced later by Comanches who were relocated to Indian Territory in 1875. Ranching began in the late 1870s. County created from Bexar District in 1876; organized in 1884; named for Confederate Gen. W.R. Scurry.

Recreation: Lake J.B. Thomas water recreation; Towle Memorial Park; museums, community theater, White Buffalo Days and Bikefest in October.

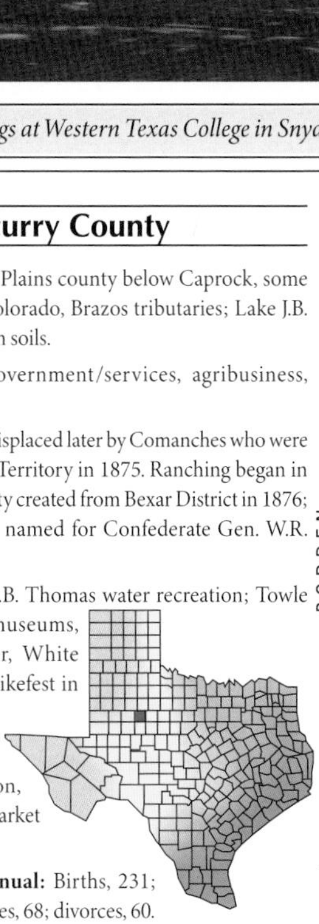

Minerals: Oil, gas.

Agriculture: Cotton, wheat, cattle, hay. Market value $45.2 million.

Vital Statistics, annual: Births, 231; deaths, 223; marriages, 68; divorces, 60.

Race/Ethnicity: Anglo, 51%; Hispanic, 42.2%; Black, 3.5%; Asian, 0.5%; Other, 2.8%.

SNYDER (11,264) county seat; oil, wind energy, agriculture; Western Texas College, hospital, museum; Western Swing fest in June.

Other towns include: **Dunn** (75); **Fluvanna** (84); **Hermleigh** (428); **Ira** (250).

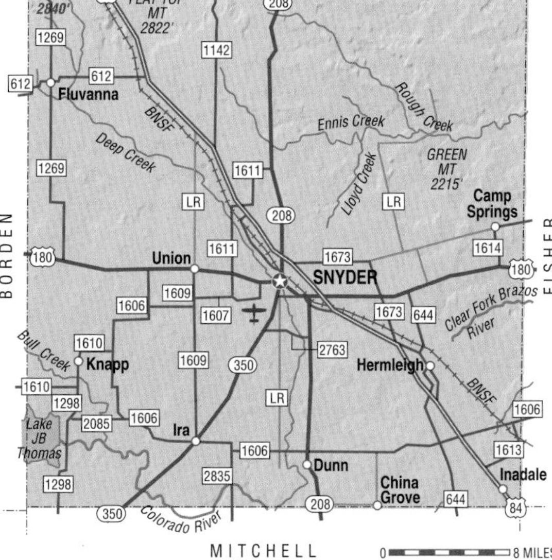

Population	16,824
Change from 2010	-0.6%
Area (sq. mi.)	907.5
Land Area (sq. mi.)	905.4
Altitude (ft.)	1,800–2,840
Rainfall (in.)	21.8
Jan. mean min (°F)	30.5

July mean max (°F)	94.1
Civ. Labor	6,283
Unemployed	4.1%
Wages	$94,780,210
Per Capita Income	$47,138
Property Value	$4,587,440,225
Retail Sales	$300,254,231

A restored Gulf gas station in Albany. Photo by Carol M. Highsmith, Public Domain

Shackelford County

Physical Features: Rolling, hilly, drained by tributaries of Brazos; sandy and chocolate loam soils; lake.

Economy: Oil and ranching, some manufacturing, hunting leases.

History: Apaches; driven out by Comanches. First Anglo-American settlers arrived soon after establishment of military outpost in the 1850s. County created from Bosque County in 1858; organized in 1874; named for Dr. Jack Shackelford (sometimes referred to as John), Texas Revolution hero.

Recreation: Fort Griffin historic site, courthouse historical district, hunting, lake, outdoor activities, June Fandangle musical about area history.

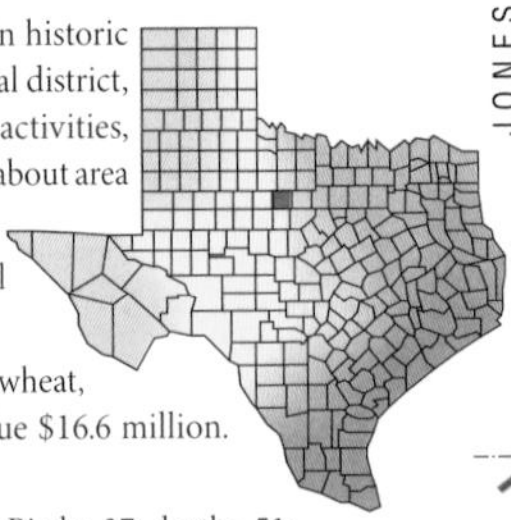

Minerals: Oil, natural gas.

Agriculture: Beef cattle, wheat, hay, cotton. Market value $16.6 million. Hunting leases.

Vital Statistics, annual: Births, 37; deaths, 51; marriages, 11; divorces, 8.

Race/Ethnicity: Anglo, 84.1%; Hispanic, 11.7%; Black, 0.6%; Asian, 0.5%; Other, 3.1%.

ALBANY (1,927) county seat; oil, ranching, hunting; medical clinics; historical district, Old Jail art center, car museum.

Other town: **Moran** (236).

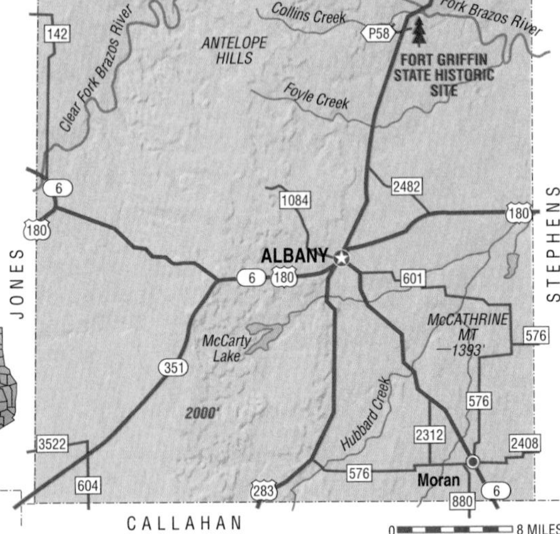

Population	3,212
Change from 2010	–4.9%
Area (sq. mi.)	915.6
Land Area (sq. mi.)	914.3
Altitude (ft.)	1,150–2,000
Rainfall (in.)	28.9
Jan. mean min (°F)	33.3

July mean max (°F)	93.4
Civ. Labor	1,830
Unemployed	2.7%
Wages	$25,723,730
Per Capita Income	$93,075
Property Value	$1,751,973,418
Retail Sales	$21,000,235

Shelby County

Physical Features: East Texas county; partly hills, much bottomland; well-timbered, 67,762 acres in national forest; Attoyac Bayou, other streams; Toledo Bend Reservoir, Pinkston Reservoir; sandy, clay, alluvial soils.

Economy: Poultry, timber, cattle, tourism.

History: Caddo Indian area. First Anglo-Americans settled in the 1810s. Antebellum slaveholding area. Original county of the Republic, created in 1836; organized in 1837; named for Isaac Shelby of the American Revolution.

Recreation: Toledo Bend Reservoir activities; Sabine National Forest; hunting, fishing, camping; historic sites, restored 1885 courthouse.

Minerals: Natural gas, oil.

Agriculture: First in poultry and egg production. Beef cattle and hay. Market value $467.6 million. Timber sales significant.

Vital Statistics, annual: Births, 295; deaths, 330; marriages, 128; divorces, 72.

Race/Ethnicity: Anglo, 60%; Hispanic, 19.5%; Black, 15.8%; Asian, 1.5%; Other, 3.1%.

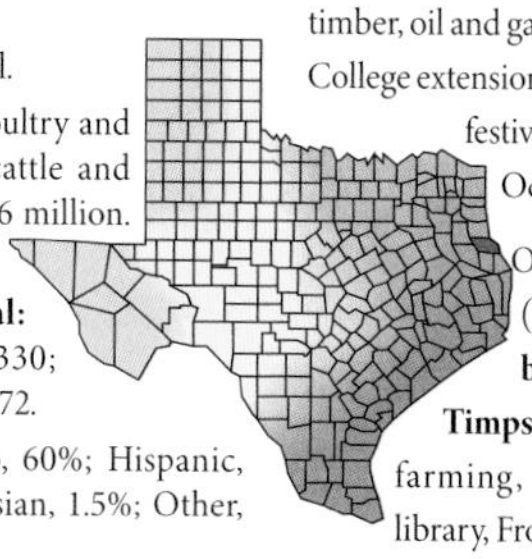

CENTER (5,133) county seat; poultry, timber, oil and gas, tourism; hospital, Panola College extension, museum; What-A-Melon festival in July, poultry festival in October.

Other towns include: **Huxley** (359); **Joaquin** (728); **Shelbyville** (199); **Tenaha** (991); **Timpson** (991) livestock, timber, farming, commuters, genealogy library, Frontier Days in July.

Population	23,939
Change from 2010	–5.9%
Area (sq. mi.)	834.6
Land Area (sq. mi.)	795.6
Altitude (ft.)	174–630
Rainfall (in.)	56.5
Jan. mean min (°F)	37.3
July mean max (°F)	92.9
Civ. Labor	11,029
Unemployed	4.2%
Wages	$108,237,668
Per Capita Income	$54,640
Property Value	$3,137,254,392
Retail Sales	$354,031,725

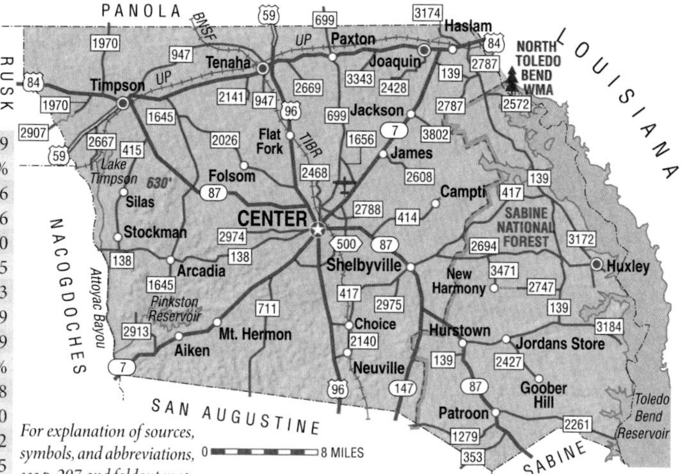

For explanation of sources, symbols, and abbreviations, see p. 207 and foldout map.

Sherman County

Physical Features: A northern Panhandle county; level, broken by creeks, playas; sandy to dark loam soils; underground water.

Economy: Agribusiness, tourism.

History: Apaches; pushed out by Comanches in the 1700s. Comanches removed to Indian Territory in 1875. Ranching began around 1880; farming after 1900. County named for Republic of Texas Gen. Sidney Sherman; created from Bexar District in 1876; organized in 1889.

Recreation: Depot museum; pheasant, pronghorn hunting, jamboree and rodeo in July.

Minerals: Natural gas, oil.

Agriculture: Beef and stocker cattle, wheat, corn, milo, cotton; 127,000 acres irrigated. Market value $838.1 million.

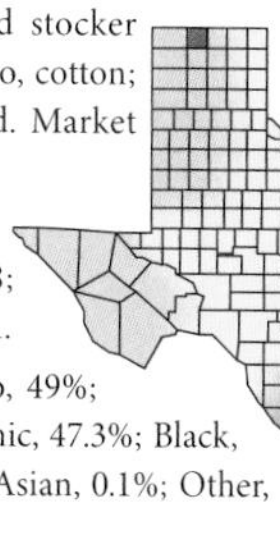

Vital Statistics, annual: Births, 54; deaths, 28; marriages, 10; divorces, 1.

Race/Ethnicity: Anglo, 49%; Hispanic, 47.3%; Black, 0.4%; Asian, 0.1%; Other, 3.3%.

STRATFORD (1,953) county seat; agribusiness, petroleum, tourism, birdseed packaging.

Texhoma (1,115 [with 259 in Texas]) other principal town.

Population	2,798
Change from 2010	–7.8%
Area (sq. mi.)	923.2
Land Area (sq. mi.)	923.0
Altitude (ft.)	3,200–3,805
Rainfall (in.)	17.1
Jan. mean min (°F)	22.0
July mean max (°F)	91.3
Civ. Labor	1,377
Unemployed	2.8%
Wages	$15,615,742
Per Capita Income	$122,945
Property Value	$1,385,554,190
Retail Sales	$74,061,967

Smith County

Population	237,186
Change from 2010	13.1%
Area (sq. mi.)	949.7
Land Area (sq. mi.)	921.5
Altitude (ft.)	275–671
Rainfall (in.)	47.7
Jan. mean min (°F)	40.3
July mean max (°F)	92.2
Civ. Labor	112,049
Unemployed	3.7%
Wages	$1,578,583,512
Per Capita Income	$60,284
Property Value	$30,644,784,848
Retail Sales	$6,104,061,425

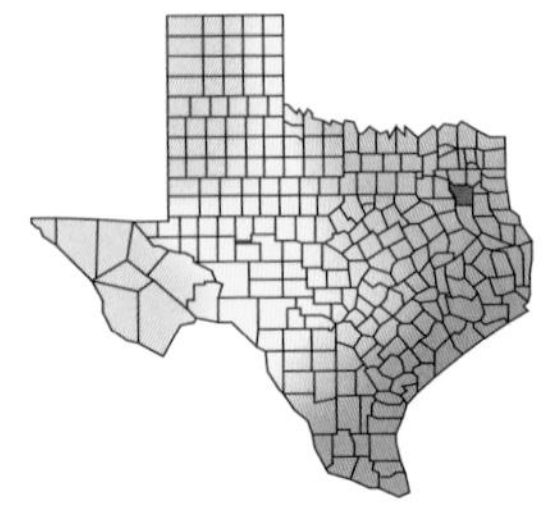

Physical Features: Populous East Texas county of rolling hills, many timbered; Sabine, Neches rivers, other streams; Lake Palestine, Lake Tyler, Lake Tyler East; alluvial, gray, sandy loam, clay soils.

Economy: Medical facilities, education, government/services, agribusiness, petroleum production, manufacturing, distribution center, tourism.

History: Caddoes of area reduced by disease and other tribes in the 1790s. Cherokees settled in the 1820s; removed in 1839. In the late 1820s, first Anglo-American settlers arrived. Antebellum slaveholding area. County named for Texas Revolution Gen. James Smith; county created and organized in 1846 from Nacogdoches County.

Recreation: Activities on Palestine, Tyler lakes; Tyler Botanical Garden, rose garden; state park; Goodman Museum; Caldwell Zoo; collegiate events; Juneteenth celebration, Rose Festival in October, Azalea Trail, East Texas Fair in September/October.

Minerals: Oil, gas.

Agriculture: Horticultural crops and nurseries, beef cattle, forages, fruits and vegetables, horses, Christmas trees. Market value $53.6 million. Timber sales substantial.

Vital Statistics, annual: Births, 2,894; deaths, 2,726; marriages, 1,395; divorces, 782.

Race/Ethnicity: Anglo, 57.6%; Hispanic, 20.3%; Black, 16.3%; Asian, 1.8%; Other, 4.1%.

TYLER (107,192) county seat; health services, education, retail center, varied manufacturing; University of Texas at Tyler, Tyler Junior College, Texas College, University of Texas Health Science Center; hospitals, nursing school; museums, Camp Ford historic park; styles itself, "City of Roses".

Other towns include: **Arp** (926) Strawberry Festival in April; **Bullard** (3,706, part in Cherokee County); **Emerald Bay** (1,292); **Hideaway** (3,251); **Lindale** (6,313) distribution center, foundry, varied manufacturing, CountryFest in October; **New Chapel Hill** (626); **Noonday** (616); **Troup** (2,039, part in Cherokee County) plastic manufacturing, motorcyle customization; **Whitehouse** (8,734) commuters to Tyler, government/services, Christmas on Main in December; and **Winona** (643).

Part [161] of **Overton** (2,274 total, mostly in Rusk County).

For explanation of sources, symbols, and abbreviations, see p. 207 and foldout map.

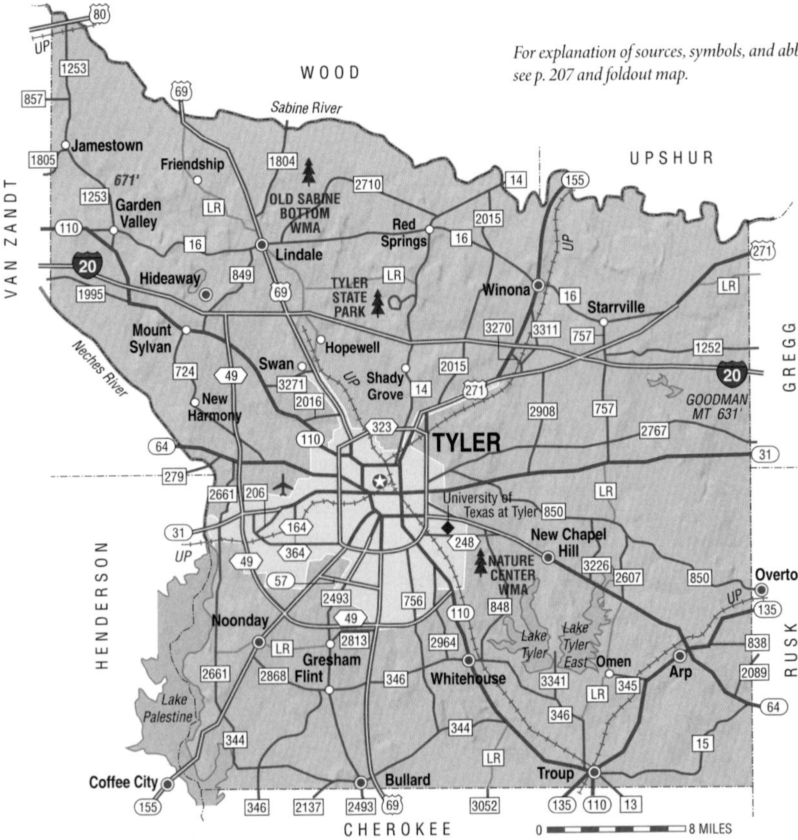

Somervell County

Physical Features: Hilly terrain southwest of Fort Worth; Brazos, Paluxy rivers; Squaw Creek Reservoir; gray, dark, alluvial soils; second-smallest county.

Economy: Nuclear power plant, tourism.

History: Wichita, Tonkawa area; Comanches arrived later. Anglo-Americans arrived in the 1850s. County created in 1875 as Somerville County from Hood County, organized the same year. Spelling was changed in 1876; named for Republic of Texas Gen. Alexander Somervell.

Recreation: Fishing, hunting; unique geological formations; dinosaur tracks in state park; Glen Rose Big Rocks Park; Fossil Rim Wildlife Center; nature trails, museums; exposition center; Paluxy Pedal bicycle ride in October.

Minerals: Sand, gravel, silica, natural gas.

Agriculture: Cattle, hay. Market value $4.1 million. Hunting leases important.

Vital Statistics, annual: Births, 65; deaths, 113; marriages, 48; divorces, 21.

Race/Ethnicity: Anglo, 76.2%; Hispanic, 18.3%; Black, 0.4%; Asian, 0.6%; Other, 4.5%.

GLEN ROSE (2,848) county seat; nuclear power plant, tourism, farm trade center; hospital; Hill College branch.

Other towns include: **Nemo** (56); **Rainbow** (121).

Population	9,469
Change from 2010	11.5%
Area (sq. mi.)	192.0
Land Area (sq. mi.)	186.5
Altitude (ft.)	550–1310
Rainfall (in.)	34.3
Jan. mean min (°F)	33.4
July mean max (°F)	94.7
Civ. Labor	4,573
Unemployed	3.8%
Wages	$63,074,262
Per Capita Income	$54,826
Property Value	$4,231,825,546
Retail Sales	$67,397,184

Starr County

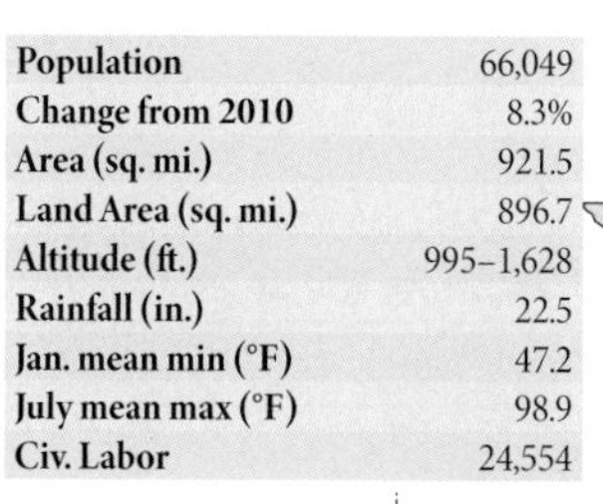

Population	66,049
Change from 2010	8.3%
Area (sq. mi.)	921.5
Land Area (sq. mi.)	896.7
Altitude (ft.)	995–1,628
Rainfall (in.)	22.5
Jan. mean min (°F)	47.2
July mean max (°F)	98.9
Civ. Labor	24,554
Unemployed	11.0%
Wages	$153,284,018
Per Capita Income	$34,933
Property Value	$3,898,602,868
Retail Sales	$660,425,377

Physical Features: Rolling, some hills; dense brush; clay, loam, sandy soils, alluvial on Rio Grande; Falcon Reservoir.

Economy: Vegetable packing, other agribusiness, oil processing, tourism, government/services.

History: Coahuiltecan Indian area. Settlers from Spanish villages that were established in 1749 on south bank began to move across river soon afterward. Fort Ringgold established in 1848. County named for Dr. J.H. Starr, secretary of treasury of the Republic; county created from Nueces County and organized in 1848.

Recreation: Falcon Reservoir activities; deer, white-wing dove hunting; access to Mexico; historic houses, Lee House at Fort Ringgold; grotto at Rio Grande City; Roma Fest in November.

Minerals: Oil, gas, sand, gravel.

Agriculture: Beef and fed cattle; vegetables, cotton, sorghum; 8,500 acres irrigated for vegetables. Market value $47.2 million.

Vital Statistics, annual: Births, 1,115; deaths, 717; marriages, 306; divorces, NA.

Race/Ethnicity: Anglo, 1.8%; Hispanic, 97.7%; Black, 0%; Asian, 0.2%; Other, 0.3%.

RIO GRANDE CITY (15,670) county seat; government/services, tourism, agriculture; hospital, college branches; trolley tours; Vaquero Days in February.

Roma-Los Saenz (11,505) agriculture center; La Purísima Concepción Visita.

Other towns include: **Delmita** (132); **El Cenizo** (328); **Escobares** (2,569); **Fronton** (249); **Garceño** (340); **Garciasville** (60); **La Grulla** (1,207); **La Puerta** (669); **La Rosita** (100); **Las Lomas** (1,882); **La Victoria** (188); **Los Alvarez** (190); Mikes (1,394); **North Escobares** (174); **Salineño** (71); **San Isidro** (182); **Valle Vista** (699).

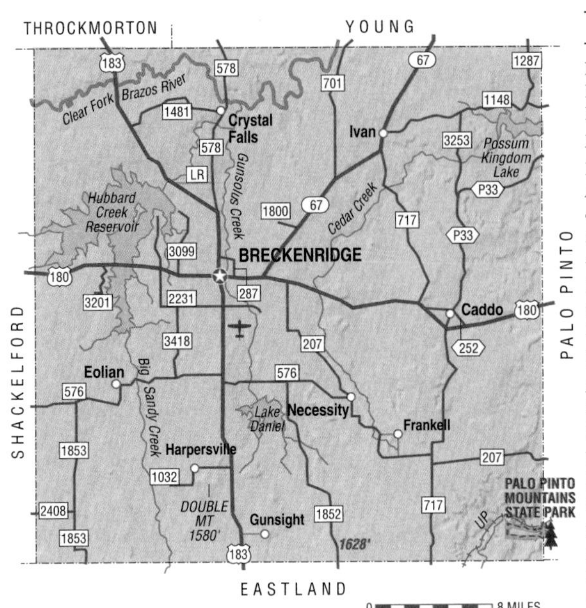

Stephens County

Physical Features: West central county; broken, hilly; Hubbard Creek Reservoir, Possum Kingdom Lake, Lake Daniel; Brazos River; loam, sandy soils.

Economy: Oil, agribusiness, manufacturing, recreation.

History: Comanches, Tonkawas in the area when Anglo-American settlement began in the 1850s. County created as Buchanan in 1858 from Bosque County; renamed in 1861 for Confederate Vice President Alexander H. Stephens; organized in 1876.

Recreation: Lake activities, state park, hunting, campsites, historical points, Swenson Museum, Sandefer Oil Museum, aviation museum, Frontier Days in May.

Minerals: Oil, natural gas, stone.

Agriculture: Beef cattle, hogs, goats, sheep; wheat, oats, hay, peanuts, grain sorghum, cotton, pecans. Market value $10.6 million.

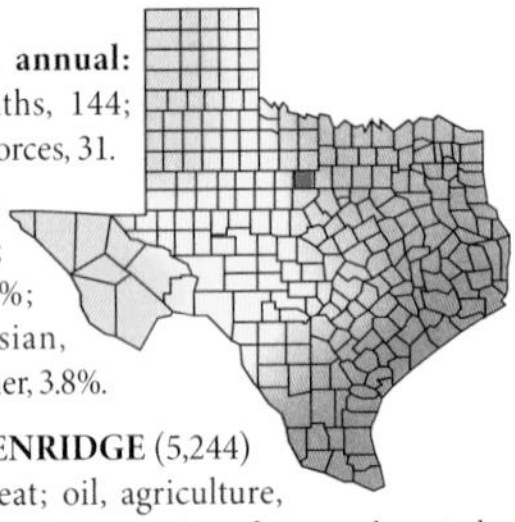

Vital Statistics, annual: Births, 111; deaths, 144; marriages, 35; divorces, 31.

Race/Ethnicity: Anglo, 68.7%; Hispanic, 24.2%; Black, 2.6%; Asian, 0.7%; Other, 3.8%.

BRECKENRIDGE (5,244) county seat; oil, agriculture, oil-field equipment, aircraft parts; hospital, prison, Texas State Technical College branch, library.

Other towns include: **Caddo** (70) gateway to Possum Kingdom State Park.

Population	9,173
Change from 2010	-4.7%
Area (sq. mi.)	1,229.1
Land Area (sq. mi.)	1,223.2
Altitude (ft.)	125–580
Rainfall (in.)	29.7
Jan. mean min (°F)	30.4

July mean max (°F)	94.5
Civ. Labor	4,073
Unemployed	3.7%
Wages	$45,819,685
Per Capita Income	$48,498
Property Value	$2,102,932,358
Retail Sales	$101,108,770

A rest stop and historical marker at the site where Rath City once stood in Stonewall County. Photo by Leaflet, CC by SA 3.0

Sterling County

Physical Features: Central prairie, surrounded by hills, broken by Concho River and tributaries; sandy to black soils.

Economy: Ranching, oil and gas, government/services.

History: Ranching began in the late 1870s after the Comanches, Kickapoos, and other tribes were removed by the U.S. Army. County named for buffalo hunter W.S. Sterling; created in 1891 from Tom Green County, organized the same year.

Recreation: Hunting of deer, quail, turkey, dove; hunters appreciation dinner in November; cowboy festival in June.

Minerals: Oil, natural gas.

Agriculture: Cattle, sheep/goats, horses, wheat, hay; about 600 acres irrigated. Market value $7.7 million. Hunting leases important.

Vital Statistics, annual: Births, 18; deaths, 14; marriages, 0; divorces, NA.

Race/Ethnicity: Anglo, 63.2%; Hispanic, 32.7%; Black, 0.2%; Asian, 0.1%; Other, 3.8%.

STERLING CITY (1,122) county seat; farm, ranch trade center, oil-field services.

For explanation of sources, symbols, and abbreviations, see p. 207 and foldout map.

Population	1,381
Change from 2010	20.8%
Area (sq. mi.)	923.5
Land Area (sq. mi.)	923.5
Altitude (ft.)	2,000–2,760

Rainfall (in.)	20.4
Jan. mean min (°F)	31.5
July mean max (°F)	92.5
Civ. Labor	525
Unemployed	4.0%

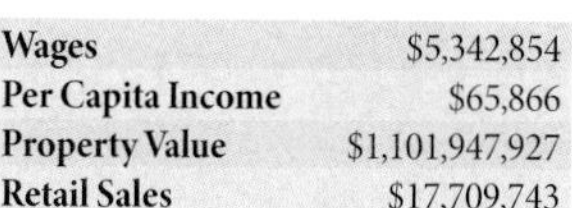

Wages	$5,342,854
Per Capita Income	$65,866
Property Value	$1,101,947,927
Retail Sales	$17,709,743

Stonewall County

Physical Features: Western county on Rolling Plains below Caprock, bisected by Brazos forks; sandy loam, sandy, other soils; some hills.

Economy: Agribusiness, light fabrication, government/services.

History: Anglo-American ranchers arrived in the 1870s after Comanches and other tribes were removed by U.S. Army. German farmers settled after 1900. County named for Confederate Gen. T.J. (Stonewall) Jackson; created from Bexar District in 1876, organized in 1888.

Recreation: Deer, quail, feral hog, turkey hunting.

Minerals: Gypsum, gravel, oil.

Agriculture: Beef cattle, wheat, cotton, peanuts, hay. Also, grain sorghum, meat goats and swine. Market value $15.5 million.

Vital Statistics, annual: Births, 0; deaths, 28; marriages, 4; divorces, 2.

Race/Ethnicity: Anglo, 76.9%; Hispanic, 18.2%; Black, 1.4%; Asian, 0.4%; Other, 3.1%.

ASPERMONT (759) county seat; oil field and ranching center, light fabrication; hospital; livestock show in February.

Other towns include: **Old Glory** (100) farming center.

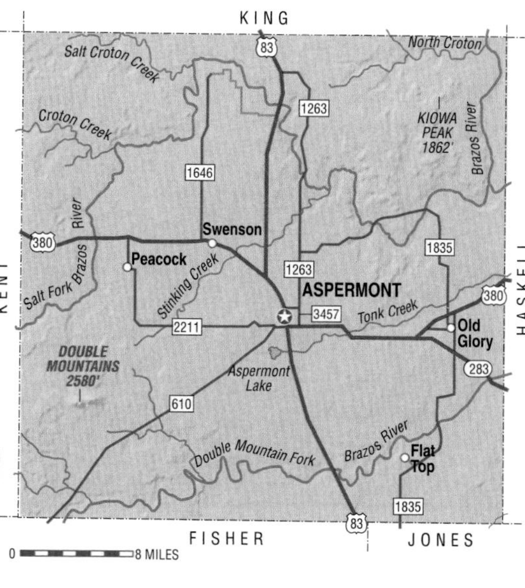

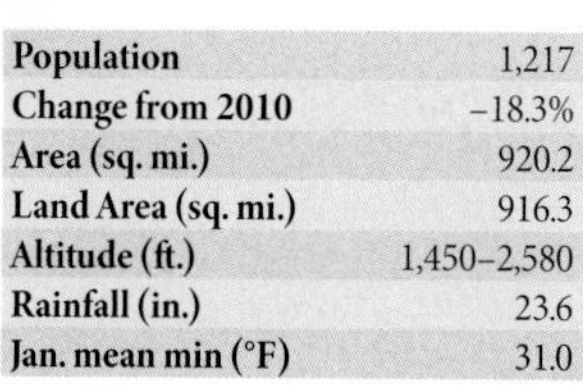

Population	1,217
Change from 2010	−18.3%
Area (sq. mi.)	920.2
Land Area (sq. mi.)	916.3
Altitude (ft.)	1,450–2,580
Rainfall (in.)	23.6
Jan. mean min (°F)	31.0

July mean max (°F)	95.2
Civ. Labor	695
Unemployed	3.0%
Wages	$11,545,728
Per Capita Income	$73,182
Property Value	$877,733,480
Retail Sales	$26,268,472

Sutton County

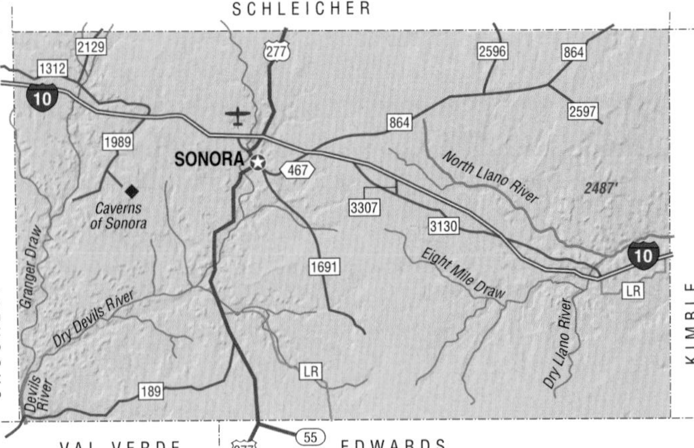

Physical Features: Southwestern county; level in west, rugged terrain in east, broken by tributaries of Devils, Llano rivers; black, red loam soils.

Economy: Natural gas, ranching, hunting.

History: Lipan Apaches drove out Tonkawas in 1600s. Comanches, military outpost, and disease forced Apaches south. Anglo-Americans settled in 1870s. Mexican immigration increased after 1890. County created from Crockett in 1887; organized in 1890; named for Confederate Col. John S. Sutton.

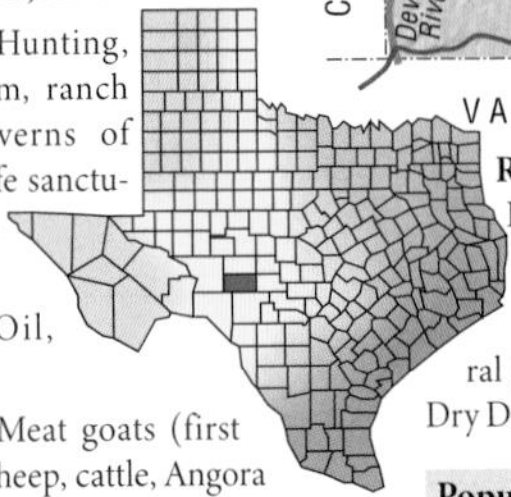

Recreation: Hunting, Miers Museum, ranch museum, Caverns of Sonora, wildlife sanctuary, Cinco de Mayo.

Minerals: Oil, natural gas.

Agriculture: Meat goats (first in numbers), sheep, cattle, Angora goats (second in numbers). Exotic wildlife. Wheat and oats raised for grazing, hay; minor irrigation. Market value $10.4 million. Hunting leases important.

Vital Statistics, annual: Births, 35; deaths, 49; marriages, 14; divorces, 6.

Race/Ethnicity: Anglo, 35.6%; Hispanic, 62.1%; Black, 0.2%; Asian, 0.2%; Other, 2%.

SONORA (2,462) county seat; natural gas production, ranching, tourism; Dry Devils River Music Flood in October.

Population	3,319
Change from 2010	−19.6%
Area (sq. mi.)	1,454.4
Land Area (sq. mi.)	1,453.9
Altitude (ft.)	1,840–2,487
Rainfall (in.)	22.7

For explanation of sources, symbols, and abbreviations, see p. 207 and foldout map.

Jan. mean min (°F)	32.6
July mean max (°F)	95.0
Civ. Labor	1,034
Unemployed	5.7%
Wages	$19,229,675
Per Capita Income	$68,431
Property Value	$1,770,638,232
Retail Sales	$81,199,490

This mercantile building in Sonora was built in 1903, listed on the National Register of Historic Places in 1978, and became a Recorded Texas Historic Landmark in 1982 Photo by Larry D. Moore, CC by 4.0

An old train depot and historic building in Tulia. Photo by Renelibrary, CC by SA 4.0

Swisher County

Physical Features: High Plains; level, broken by Tule Canyon and Creek; playas; large underground water supply; rich soils.

Economy: Cotton processing, manufacturing.

History: Apaches; displaced by Comanches around 1700. U.S. Army removed Comanches in 1874. Ranching began in the late 1870s. Farming developed after 1900. County named for J.G. Swisher of Texas Revolution; county created from Bexar, Young territories in 1876; organized in 1890.

Recreation: Mackenzie battle site, Picnic celebration in July at Tulia.

Minerals: Not significant.

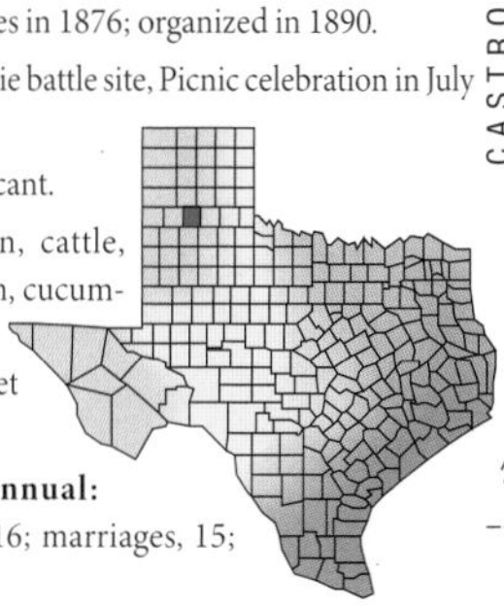

Agriculture: Cotton, cattle, wheat, corn, sorghum, cucumbers. Some 65,000 acres irrigated. Market value $623.9 million.

Vital Statistics, annual: Births, 78; deaths, 116; marriages, 15; divorces, NA.

Race/Ethnicity: Anglo, 46.2%; Hispanic, 45.1%; Black, 5.8%; Asian, 0.1%; Other, 2.7%.

TULIA (4,474) county seat; agriculture, government/services, manufacturing; hospital, library, museum.

Other towns include: **Happy** (613, partly in Randall County); **Kress** (608); **Vigo Park** (36).

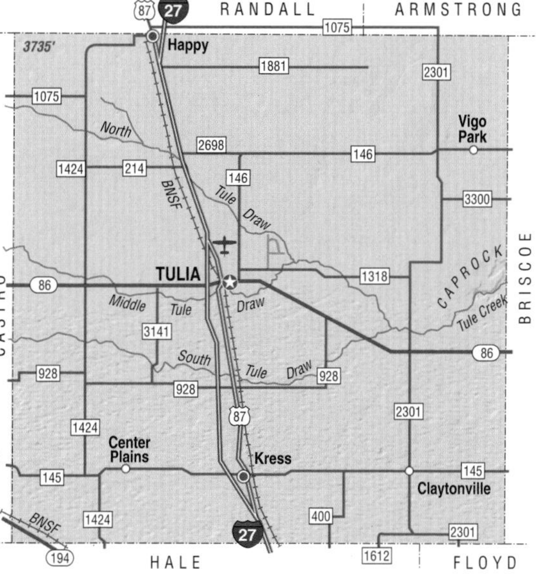

Population	7,008
Change from 2010	−10.8%
Area (sq. mi.)	900.7
Land Area (sq. mi.)	890.2
Altitude (ft.)	3,160–3,735
Rainfall (in.)	20.5
Jan. mean min (°F)	24.2

July mean max (°F)	89.7
Civ. Labor	2,583
Unemployed	4.0%
Wages	$20,959,015
Per Capita Income	$72,623
Property Value	$943,986,533
Retail Sales	$56,941,069

Tarrant County

Physical Features: Part Blackland, level to rolling; drains to Trinity; Lake Worth, Grapevine Lake, Eagle Mountain Lake, Benbrook Lake, Joe Pool Lake, Lake Arlington.

Economy: Tourism, planes, helicopters, foods, mobile homes, electronic equipment, chemicals, plastics among products of more than 1,000 factories, large federal expenditure, D/FW International Airport, economy closely associated with Dallas urban area.

Population	2,126,477
Change from 2010	17.5%
Area (sq. mi.)	902.3
Land Area (sq. mi.)	863.6
Altitude (ft.)	420–960
Rainfall (in.)	36.2
Jan. mean min (°F)	35.4
July mean max (°F)	95.8
Civ. Labor	1,140,773
Unemployed	3.6%
Wages	$17,062,513,179
Per Capita Income	$58,940
Property Value	$325,684,497,038
Retail Sales	$44,849,478,338

History: Caddoes in area. Comanches, other tribes arrived about 1700. Anglo-Americans settled in the 1840s. Named for Republic of Texas Gen. Edward H. Tarrant, who helped drive Indian tribes from area. County created in 1849 from Navarro County; organized in 1850.

Recreation: Scott Theatre; Amon G. Carter Museum; Kimbell Art Museum; Modern Art Museum; Museum of Science and History; Casa Mañana; Botanic Gardens; Fort Worth Zoo; Log Cabin Village, all in Fort Worth. Also, Six Flags Over Texas at Arlington; Southwestern Exposition, Stock Show; Convention Center; Stockyards Historical District; Texas Rangers and Dallas Cowboys at Arlington, other athletic events.

Minerals: Production of cement, sand, gravel, stone, gas.

Education: Texas Christian University, Texas Wesleyan University, The University of Texas at Arlington, Arlington Baptist University, and Tarrant County College

Agriculture: Hay, beef cattle, wheat, horses, horticulture. Market value $29.4 million. Firewood marketed.

Vital Statistics, annual: Births, 26,640; deaths, 16,364; marriages, 10,991; divorces, 7,553.

Race/Ethnicity: Anglo, 42.9%; Hispanic, 29.4%; Black, 17%; Asian, 6.1%; Other, 4.7%.

FORT WORTH (935,508, small parts in Denton, Parker and Wise counties) county seat; a major mercantile, commercial and financial center; airplane, helicopter and other manufacturing plants; hospitals/health care; distribution center; oil and gas; stock show and rodeo January/February.

A cultural center with renowned art museums, Bass Performance Hall; many conventions held in downtown center; agribusiness center for wide area with grain-storage and feed-mill operations; adjacent to D/FW International Airport.

ARLINGTON (392,786) General Motors plant, tourism, the Texas Rangers baseball team, AT&T Stadium, retail, hospitals, bowling museum, art museum; Scottish festival in June.

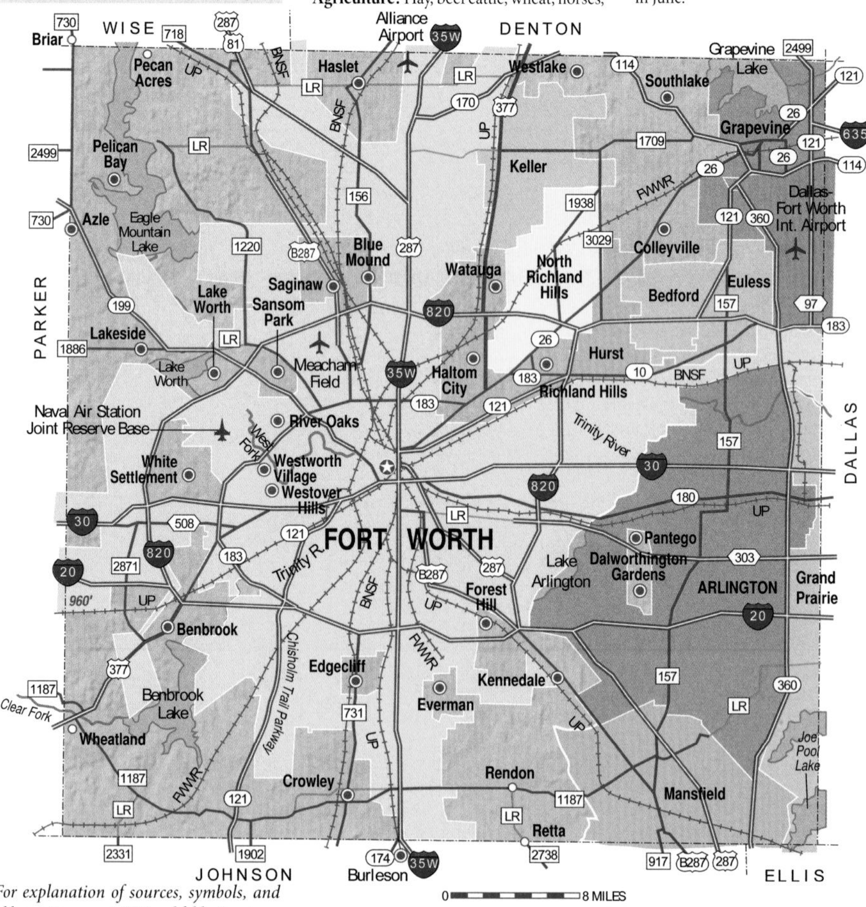

For explanation of sources, symbols, and abbreviations, see p. 207 and foldout map.

Tarrant County continued...

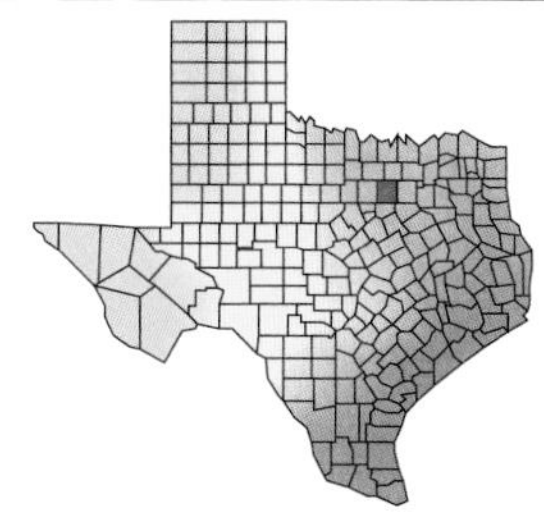

Other towns include: **Hurst** (40,055); **Euless** (60,500); **Bedford** (49,187) helicopter plant, hospital, Celtic festival in fall (these three contiguous cities are sometimes referred to as H.E.B.).

Azle (13,518, partly in Parker County) government/services, retail, medical care/hospital, commuters to Fort Worth, museum, Sting Fling festival in September; **Benbrook** (24,605) varied manufacturing, hospitals; **Blue Mound** (2,359); **Briar** (5,635, parts in Wise and Parker counties).

Also, **Colleyville** (25,986) medical services, commuters, government/services, steak cookoff in October; **Crowley** (19,333) varied manufacturing, government/services, hospital; **Dalworthington Gardens** (2,273); **Edgecliff Village** (3,761); **Everman** (6,067); **Forest Hill** (13,818).

Also, **Grapevine** (50,872) tourist center, distribution, near the D/FW International Airport, hospitals, museums, art galleries, Grapefest in September; **Haltom City** (45,746) light manufacturing, food processing, medical center, library; **Haslet** (2,371) commuters, government/services, Memorial Day celebration; **Keller** (45,397) Bear Creek Park.

Also, **Kennedale** (8,463) commuters, printing, manufacturing, library, drag strip; **Lakeside** (1,624); **Lake Worth** (4,674) retail, tourism, museum, nature center; **Mansfield** (74,368, partly in Johnson, Ellis counties) varied manufacturing, retail, government/services, commuters, hospital, community college, library, museum, parks, Mansfield Rocks in July; **North Richland Hills** (70,209) hospital; **Pantego** (2,528); **Pelican Bay** (2,236); **Rendon** (14,597); **Richland Hills** (8,484).

Also, **River Oaks** (7,524); **Saginaw** (24,011) manufacturing, distribution/trucking, food processing/flour mill, Train & Grain festival in October; **Sansom Park** (5,388); **Southlake** (31,105) technology, financial, retail center, hospital, parks, Oktoberfest; **Watauga** (23,313); **Westlake** (1,683); **Westover Hills** (641); **Westworth Village** (2,602).

Also, **White Settlement** (18,084) aircraft manufacturing, drilling equipment, technological services, museums including Civil War museum, parks, historic sites; industrial park; settlers day festival in fall.

Also, part [9,815] of **Burleson** (51,618, rest in Johnson County) and part [71,948] of **Grand Prairie** (197,347 total, mostly in Dallas County).

2022–2023 Media Market Rankings

Rank	TV Homes	Share
1. New York	7.7 million	6.2%
2. Los Angeles	5.8 million	4.7%
3. Chicago	3.6 million	2.9%
4. Philadelphia	3.1 million	2.5%
5. Dallas/Fort Worth	**3.0 million**	**2.5%**
6. Atlanta	2.7 million	2.2%
7. Houston	**2.7 million**	**2.2%**
8. Washington D. C.	2.6 million	2.1%
9. Boston	2.6 million	2.1%
10. San Francisco	2.6 million	2.1%

Source: Nielsen Media Research

The photo below won an Honorable Mention in the second round of the TPW photo contest. Photo by Jordyn Fischer

Taylor County

Physical Features: Prairies, with Callahan Divide, draining to Colorado River tributaries, Brazos River forks; Lake Abilene, Lake Kirby; mostly loam soils.

Economy: Agribusiness, oil and gas production, education, Dyess Air Force Base.

History: Comanches in the area about 1700. Anglo-American settlers arrived in the 1870s. Named for Alamo heroes Edward, James, and George Taylor, brothers; county created from Bexar, Travis counties in 1858 and organized in 1878.

Recreation: Abilene State Park, lake activities, Nelson Park Zoo, college events, Western Heritage ranch rodeo in May, as well as the West Texas Fair in September at Abilene. Taylor County Expo Events-Western Heritage in May and West Texas Fair & Rodeo in September, Horse Events, Stock-shows, and Concerts, Frontier Texas Museum, The Grace Museum, downtown SODA District, and a new downtown Conference Center Hotel & Convention Center, and Dyess Air Force Base Air-show in the Spring

Minerals: Oil, natural gas.

Agriculture: Beef cattle, small grains, cotton, milo. Market value $31.5 million.

Vital Statistics, annual: Births, 1,933; deaths, 1,631; marriages, 1,010; divorces, 163.

Race/Ethnicity: Anglo, 61%; Hispanic, 24.3%; Black, 7.7%; Asian, 2%; Other, 5.1%.

ABILENE (125,070, a small part in Jones County) county seat; retail center, oil and gas, military, colleges; hospitals, Abilene State School; Fort Phantom Hill (in Jones County). Wylie is now part of Abilene.

Other communities include: **Buffalo Gap** (569) historic sites; **Impact** (20); **Lawn** (312); **Merkel** (2,457) oil and wind energy, ranching, hunting, commuting, museum, health clinic, part of Bankhead Highway (early 1900s transcontinental route); classic car show in March; **Ovalo** (225); **Potosi** (4,720); **Trent** (293); **Tuscola** (847); **Tye** (1,192).

Population	143,326
Change from 2010	9.0%
Area (sq. mi.)	919.3
Land Area (sq. mi.)	915.6
Altitude (ft.)	1,640–2,490

Rainfall (in.)	25.2
Jan. mean min (°F)	35.5
July mean max (°F)	95.1
Civ. Labor	68,871
Unemployed	3.3%

Wages	$900,583,418
Per Capita Income	$58,316
Property Value	$17,083,743,262
Retail Sales	$2,804,700,358

For explanation of sources, symbols, and abbreviations, see p. 207 and foldout map.

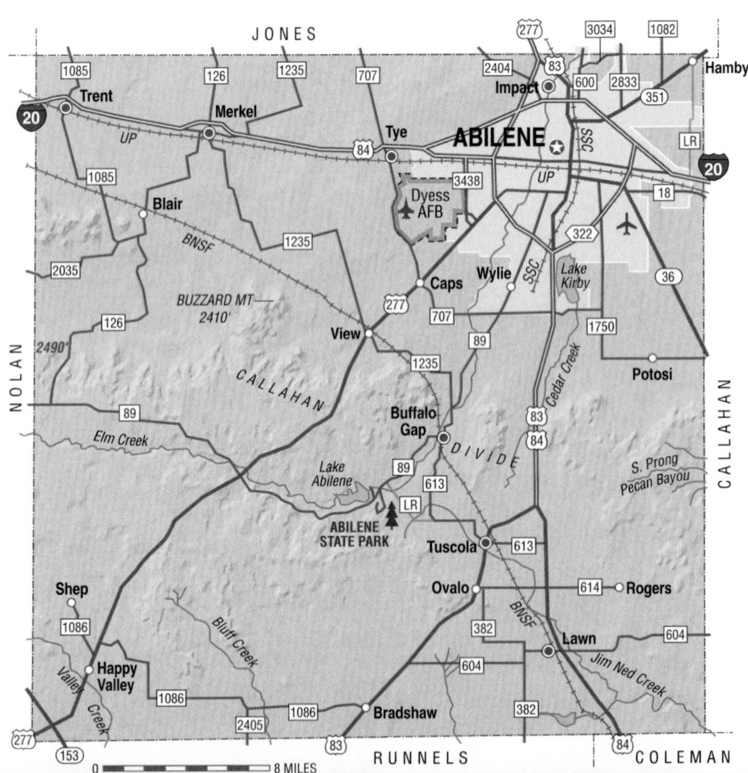

Your Texas. Your History.

Become a member of the TSHA. Learn more at join.tshaonline.org

Terrell County

Physical Features: Trans-Pecos southwestern county; semi-mountainous, many canyons; rocky, limestone soils.

Economy: Ranching, hunting leases, oil/gas exploration, tourism.

History: Coahuiltecans, Jumanos, and other tribes left many pictographs in area caves. Sheep ranching began in the 1880s. Named for Confederate Gen. A.W. Terrell; county created in 1905 from Pecos County, organized the same year.

Recreation: Nature tourism, hunting, especially white-tailed and mule deer, Rio Grande Wild and Scenic River, varied wildlife, hiking trail; Snake Days in June, Prickly Pear Pachanga in October.

Minerals: Gas, oil, limestone.

Agriculture: Goats (meat, Angora); sheep (meat, wool); some beef cattle. Market value $4.2 million. Wildlife leases important.

Vital Statistics, annual: Births, 0; deaths, 14; marriages, 2; divorces, NA.

Race/Ethnicity: Anglo, 46.3%; Hispanic, 48.7%; Black, 1.1%; Asian, 0.7%; Other, 3.3%.

SANDERSON (664) county seat; ranching, hunting, tourism, government/services; museum.

Other town: **Dryden** (13).

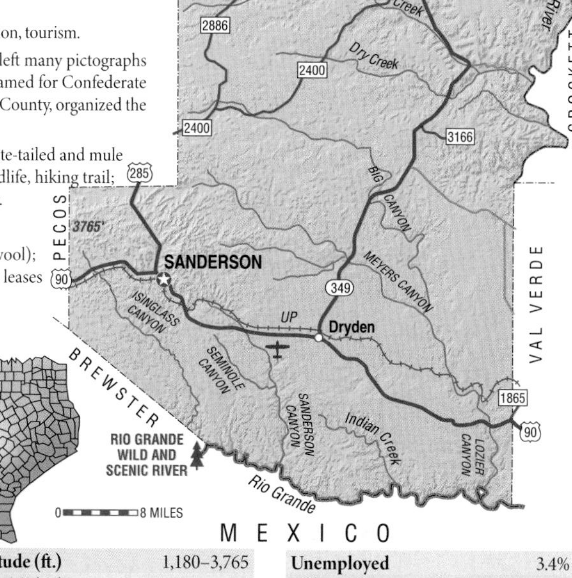

Population	724
Change from 2010	−26.4%
Area (sq. mi.)	2,358.1
Land Area (sq. mi.)	2,358.0

Altitude (ft.)	1,180–3,765
Rainfall (in.)	14.3
Jan. mean min (°F)	34.1
July mean max (°F)	94.2
Civ. Labor	410

Unemployed	3.4%
Wages	$3,979,728
Per Capita Income	$63,481
Property Value	$711,446,089
Retail Sales	$2,834,440

Terry County

Physical Features: South Plains, broken by draws, playas; sandy, sandy loam, loam soils.

Economy: Oil-field services, agribusiness, peanut processing.

History: Comanches removed in the 1870s by U.S. Army. Ranching developed in the 1890s; farming after 1900. Oil discovered in 1940. County named for Confederate Col. B.F. Terry, head of the Eighth Texas Cavalry (Terry's Texas Rangers). Created from the Bexar District in 1876; organized in 1904.

Recreation: Museum, aquatic center, vineyard festival in July, harvest festival in October.

Minerals: Oil, gas, salt mining.

Agriculture: Cotton is principal crop; peanuts (third in acreage), grain sorghum, guar, wheat, melons, cattle, grapes. 98,000 acres irrigated. Market value $136.9 million.

Vital Statistics, annual: Births, 165; deaths, 175; marriages, 63; divorces, 24.

Race/Ethnicity: Anglo, 38.9%; Hispanic, 55.5%; Black, 3.3%; Asian, 0.3%; Other, 2%.

BROWNFIELD (8,916) county seat; oil-field services, government/services, vineyards, peanut processing; hospital; Gobble Wobble Wine Run in November.

Other towns include: **Meadow** (592); **Wellman** (224).

Population	11,754
Change from 2010	−7.1%
Area (sq. mi.)	890.9
Land Area (sq. mi.)	888.8
Altitude (ft.)	3080–3600
Rainfall (in.)	18.1
Jan. mean min (°F)	28.1

July mean max (°F)	92.8
Civ. Labor	4,653
Unemployed	4.1%
Wages	$36,878,773
Per Capita Income	$45,353
Property Value	$1,297,652,107
Retail Sales	$221,440,812

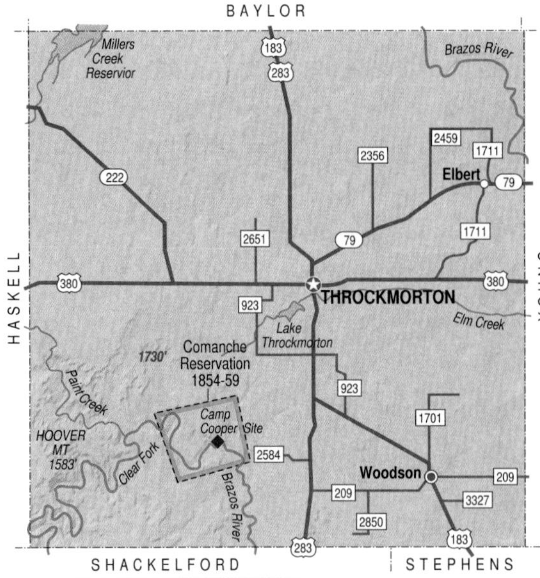

Throckmorton County

Physical Features: Northwest county southwest of Wichita Falls; rolling, between Brazos forks; red to black soils.

Economy: Oil, agribusiness, hunting.

History: Site of Comanche Indian Reservation 1854-59. Ranching developed after Civil War. County named for Dr. W.E. Throckmorton, father of Gov. J.W. Throckmorton; county created from Fannin in 1858; organized in 1879.

Recreation: Hunting, fishing; historic sites include Camp Cooper, site of former Comanche reservation, restored ranch home; Millers Creek Reservoir; Pioneer Day in June.

Minerals: Natural gas, oil.

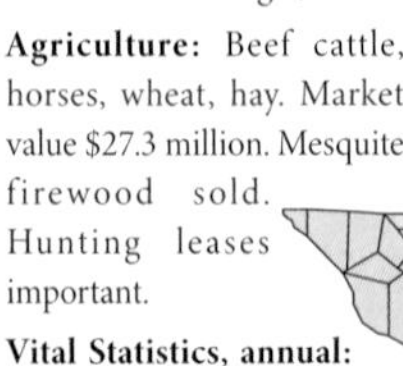

Agriculture: Beef cattle, horses, wheat, hay. Market value $27.3 million. Mesquite firewood sold. Hunting leases important.

Vital Statistics, annual: Births, 18; deaths, 17; marriages, 5; divorces, 1.

Race/Ethnicity: Anglo, 86.7%; Hispanic, 10.1%; Black, 0.1%; Asian, 0.2%; Other, 3%.

THROCKMORTON (749) county seat; varied manufacturing, oil-field services; hospital; Old Jail museum.

Other towns include: **Elbert** (8); **Woodson** (229).

Population	1,495
Change from 2010	–8.9%
Area (sq. mi.)	915.5
Land Area (sq. mi.)	912.6
Altitude (ft.)	1,100–1,730
Rainfall (in.)	29.5
Jan. mean min (°F)	31.4
July mean max (°F)	95.2

Civ. Labor	738
Unemployed	3.1%
Wages	$4,724,874
Per Capita Income	$69,390
Property Value	$1,778,167,093
Retail Sales	$9,488,565

Titus County

Physical Features: Northeast Texas county; hilly, timbered; drains to Big Cypress Creek, Sulphur River; Lake Bob Sandlin, Welsh Reservoir, Monticello Reservoir.

Economy: Agribusiness, varied manufacturing, electric power generation.

History: Caddo area. Cherokees and other tribes settled in the 1820s. Anglo-American settlers arrived in the 1840s. Named for pioneer settler A.J. Titus; county created from Bowie and Red River counties in 1846, organized the same year.

Recreation: Fishing, hunting, lake activities, state park, rodeo, railroad museum, flower gardens.

Minerals: Lignite coal, oil, gas.

Agriculture: Poultry, beef cattle, hay, horticulture, horses. Market value $149.3 million. Timber sales significant.

Vital Statistics, annual: Births, 426; deaths, 341; marriages, 178; divorces, 50.

Race/Ethnicity: Anglo, 42.9%; Hispanic, 43.8%; Black, 9.2%; Asian, 0.8%; Other, 3.2%.

MOUNT PLEASANT (16,079) county seat; tourism, varied manufacturing, food-processing plants; hospital; Northeast Texas Community College; PineFest in April, Juneteenth.

Other towns include: **Cookville** (105); **Millers Cove** (72); **Talco** (488); **Winfield** (422).

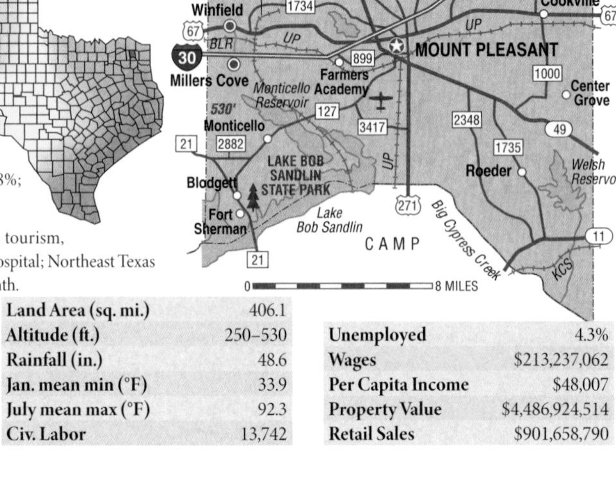

Population	31,183
Change from 2010	–3.6%
Area (sq. mi.)	425.6

Land Area (sq. mi.)	406.1
Altitude (ft.)	250–530
Rainfall (in.)	48.6
Jan. mean min (°F)	33.9
July mean max (°F)	92.3
Civ. Labor	13,742

Unemployed	4.3%
Wages	$213,237,062
Per Capita Income	$48,007
Property Value	$4,486,924,514
Retail Sales	$901,658,790

The Concho River flows through San Angelo. Photo by Michael Barera, CC by SA 4.0

Tom Green County

Physical Features: Plains, rolling hills, broken by Concho forks; loams in basin, stony hillsides; Lake Nasworthy, Twin Buttes Reservoir, O.C. Fisher Lake.

Economy: Agribusiness, trade center for area, education, medical center, government/services.

History: Jumano Indians attracted Spanish missionaries around 1630. Comanches controlled the area when the U.S. military established the first outpost in the 1850s. Anglo-American settlement occurred after the Civil War. County created from the Bexar District in 1874 and named for Gen. Tom Green of the Texas Revolution; organized in 1875; twelve other counties were created from the original area.

Recreation: Water sports, hunting, Fort Concho museum, symphony, Christmas at Old Fort Concho, February rodeo.

Minerals: Oil, natural gas.

Agriculture: Cotton, beef cattle, goats, sheep (third in number), small grains, milo. About 30,000 acres irrigated. Market value $100.0 million.

Vital Statistics, annual: Births, 1,481; deaths, 1,430; marriages, 827; divorces, 345.

Race/Ethnicity: Anglo, 52%; Hispanic, 39.2%; Black, 3.3%; Asian, 1.4%; Other, 4%.

SAN ANGELO (99,667) county seat; government/services, retail, transportation, education; hospitals, Angelo State University, Howard Junior College branch; riverwalk; Museum of Fine Arts, drag boat races in June.

Other towns include: **Carlsbad** (613); **Christoval** (299); **Grape Creek** (4,024); **Knickerbocker** (94); **Mereta** (131); **Vancourt** (131); **Veribest** (115); **Wall** (329); **Water Valley** (203).

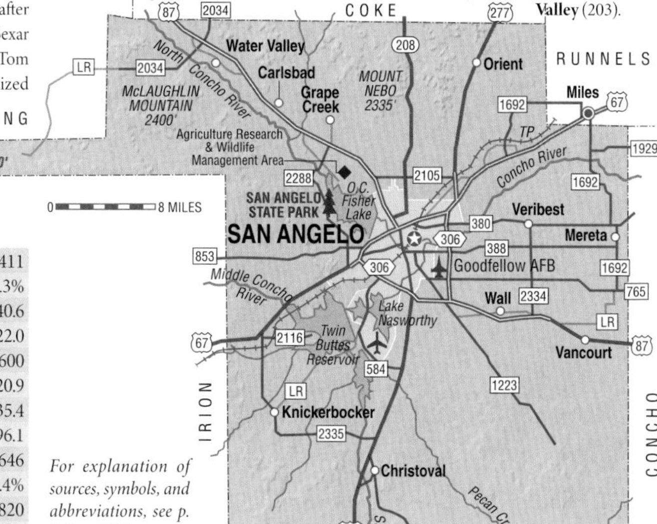

For explanation of sources, symbols, and abbreviations, see p. 207 and foldout map.

Population	119,411
Change from 2010	8.3%
Area (sq. mi.)	1,540.6
Land Area (sq. mi.)	1,522.0
Altitude (ft.)	1,675–2,600
Rainfall (in.)	20.9
Jan. mean min (°F)	35.4
July mean max (°F)	96.1
Civ. Labor	55,646
Unemployed	3.4%
Wages	$656,126,820
Per Capita Income	$59,877
Property Value	$13,009,843,221
Retail Sales	$2,521,044,194

Travis County

Physical Features: Central county of scenic hills, broken by Colorado River; Lake Travis, Lake Austin, Lady Bird Lake, Walter E. Long Lake; cedars, pecans, other trees; diverse soils, mineral deposits.

Economy: Government/services, education, technology, research, and industry.

History: Tonkawa and Lipan Apache area; Comanches, Kiowas arrived about 1700. Spanish missions from East Texas temporarily relocated near Barton Springs in 1730 before removing to San Antonio. Anglo-Americans arrived in the early 1830s.

Population	1,305,154
Change from 2010	27.4%
Area (sq. mi.)	1,023.0
Land Area (sq. mi.)	990.2
Altitude (ft.)	400–1,421
Rainfall (in.)	36.3
Jan. mean min (°F)	43.7
July mean max (°F)	95.9
Civ. Labor	822,494
Unemployed	2.8%
Wages	$20,500,181,275
Per Capita Income	$81,708
Property Value	$428,706,910,568
Retail Sales	$25,667,333,002

County created in 1840, when Austin became Republic's capital, from Bastrop County; organized in 1843; named for Alamo commander Col. William B. Travis; many other counties created from its original area.

Recreation: Colorado River lakes, hunting, fishing; McKinney Falls State Park; LBJ Presidential Library, Lady Bird Johnson Wildflower Center; collegiate, metropolitan, governmental events; official buildings and historic sites; museums, including Bullock state history museum; Sixth St. restoration area; scenic drives; many city parks; South by Southwest film, music festival in March.

Minerals: Production of lime, stone, sand, gravel, oil and gas.

Agriculture: Cattle, nursery crops, hogs; sorghum, corn, cotton, small grains, pecans. Market value $28.1 million.

Vital Statistics, annual: Births, 15,161; deaths, 6,967; marriages, 7,382; divorces, 3,494.

Race/Ethnicity: Anglo, 47.5%; Hispanic, 32.6%; Black, 7.5%; Asian, 7.7%; Other, 4.7%.

AUSTIN (964,177, part [63,623] in Williamson County) county seat and state capital; state and federal payrolls, IRS center, high-tech industries, healthcare/hospitals, including state institutions for blind, deaf, mental illnesses; popular retirement area. Anderson Mill, Del Valle, and Oak Hill are now part of Austin.

Other towns include: **Bee Cave** (9,028) retail, tourism, SpringFest in April; **Briarcliff** (2,133); **Creedmoor** (452); **Garfield** (2,932); **Hornsby Bend** (9,866); **Hudson Bend** (3,035); **Jonestown** (2,456) tourism, retail, commuters, Cajun Fest in April; **Lago Vista** (9,348); **Lakeway** (19,300) residential real estate, retail, tourism, lake activities; **Manchaca** (1,685); **Manor** (18,285); **Mustang Ridge** (966, partly in Caldwell County).

Also, **Pflugerville** (66,884) high-tech industries, agriculture, government/services, Deutschen Pfest in October; **Point Venture** (1,267); **Rollingwood** (1,440); **San Leanna** (514); **Steiner Ranch** (18,189); **Sunset Valley** (656); **The Hills** (2,535) residential community; **Volente** (542); **Webberville** (416); **Wells Branch** (13,837); **West Lake Hills** (3,322).

Also, part [8,447] of **Cedar Park**, part [9,997] of Leander, and part [1,779] of **Round Rock**, all mostly in Williamson County. Part [1,592] of **Elgin**, mostly in Bastrop County.

For explanation of sources, symbols, and abbreviations, see p. 207 and foldout map.

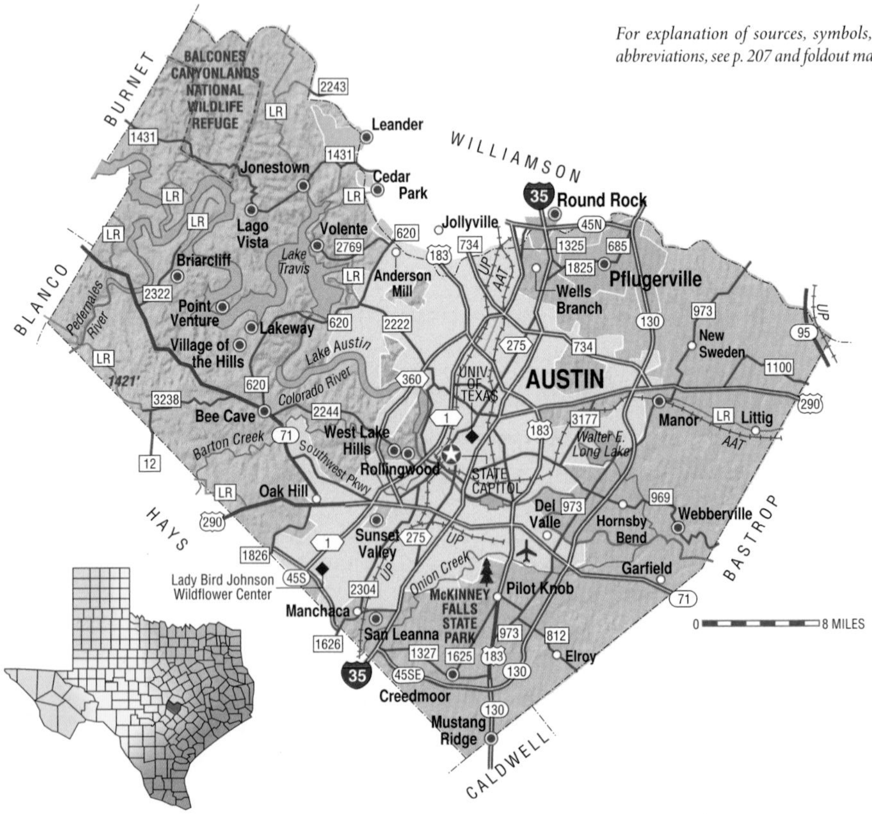

Trinity County

Physical Features: Heavily forested East Texas county of hills, between Neches and Trinity (Lake Livingston) rivers; rich alluvial soils, sandy upland; 67,910 acres in national forest.

Economy: Forestry, cattle, tourism, government/services.

History: Caddoes, reduced by disease in the late 1700s. Kickapoo, Alabama, and Coushatta in area when Anglo-Americans settled in the 1840s. Named for river; county created in 1850 out of Houston County, organized the same year.

Recreation: Lake activities, fishing, hiking, hunting, national forest, historic site.

Minerals: Limited oil, gas, sand and gravel.

Agriculture: Beef cattle. Market value $8.2 million. Timber sales significant. Hunting leases, fishing.

Vital Statistics, annual: Births, 126; deaths, 253; marriages, 45; divorces, 26.

Race/Ethnicity: Anglo, 77.4%; Hispanic, 9.7%; Black, 8%; Asian, 0.2%; Other, 4.7%.

GROVETON (913) county seat; logging, government/services, recreation; museum, library; Bear Chase marathon in April.

TRINITY (2,377) government/services, steel fabrication, forest-industries center, commuters; hospital.

Other towns include: **Apple Springs** (350); **Centralia** (190); **Pennington** (67); **Sebastopol** (300) historic town; **Westwood Shores** (1,455).

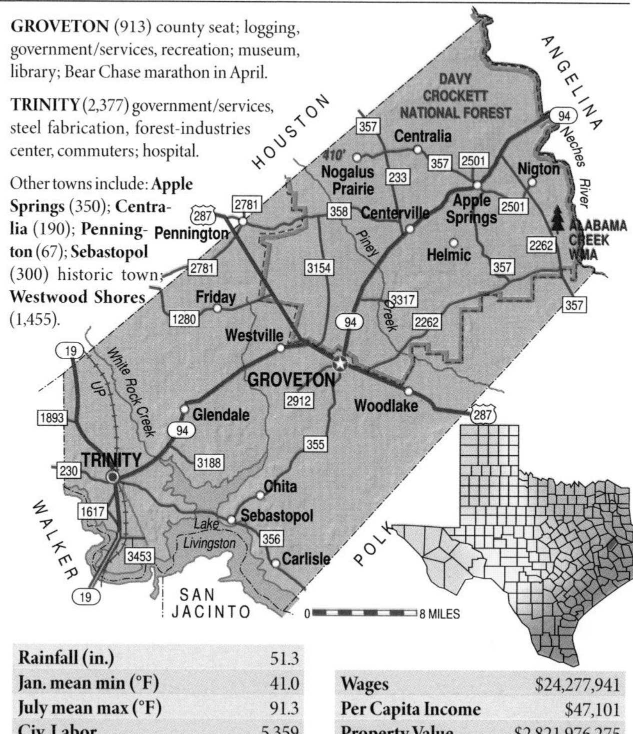

Population	13,827
Change from 2010	–5.2%
Area (sq. mi.)	714.0
Land Area (sq. mi.)	693.6
Altitude (ft.)	131–410

Rainfall (in.)	51.3
Jan. mean min (°F)	41.0
July mean max (°F)	91.3
Civ. Labor	5,359
Unemployed	5.2%

Wages	$24,277,941
Per Capita Income	$47,101
Property Value	$2,821,976,275
Retail Sales	$94,794,092

Tyler County

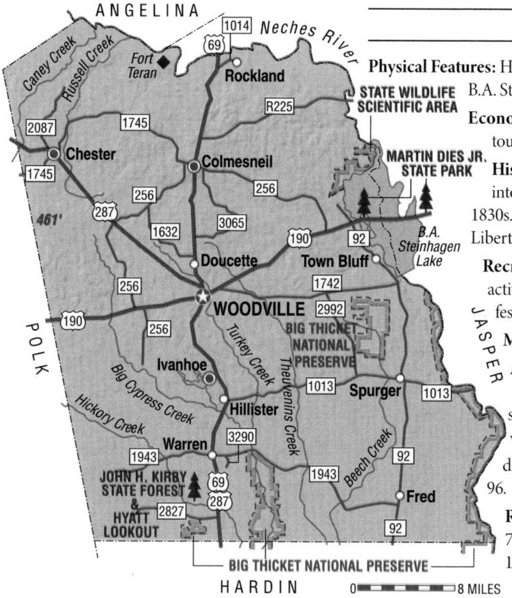

Physical Features: Hilly East Texas county; densely timbered; drains to Neches River; B.A. Steinhagen Lake; Big Thicket is unique plant and animal area.

Economy: Lumbering, government/services, some manufacturing, tourism, hunting leases.

History: Caddoan area. Cherokees, Alabama, and Coushatta pushed into area from U.S. South in the 1820s. Anglo-Americans settled in the 1830s. Named for U.S. President John Tyler; county created in 1846 from Liberty County, organized the same year.

Recreation: Big Thicket National Preserve; Heritage Village; lake activities; Allan Shivers Museum; state forest; historic sites; dogwood festival in spring; Western Weekend in March; county fair in October.

Minerals: Oil, natural gas.

Agriculture: Cattle, hay, nursery crops, blueberries, horses. Market value $14.9 million. Timber sales significant.

Vital Statistics, annual: Births, 201; deaths, 322; marriages, 85; divorces, 96.

Race/Ethnicity: Anglo, 77.3%; Hispanic, 7.7%; Black, 10.3%; Asian, 0.5%; Other, 4.2%.

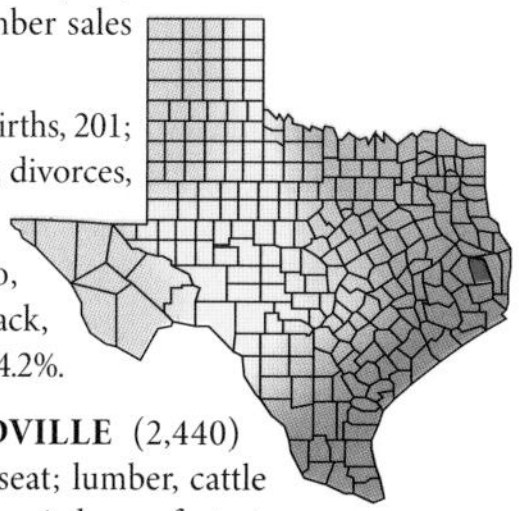

WOODVILLE (2,440) county seat; lumber, cattle market, varied manufacturing, tourism; hospital, prison.

Other towns include: **Chester** (277); **Colmesneil** (551); **Doucette** (160); **Fred** (300); **Hillister** (250); **Ivanhoe** (1,372) **Spurger** (590); **Warren** (847).

Population	20,077
Change from 2010	–7.8%
Area (sq. mi.)	935.6
Land Area (sq. mi.)	924.5
Altitude (ft.)	50–461
Rainfall (in.)	59.1
Jan. mean min (°F)	39.9

July mean max (°F)	90.6
Civ. Labor	7,167
Unemployed	6.0%
Wages	$45,086,491
Per Capita Income	$41,613
Property Value	$3,825,469,177
Retail Sales	$173,277,324

Upshur County

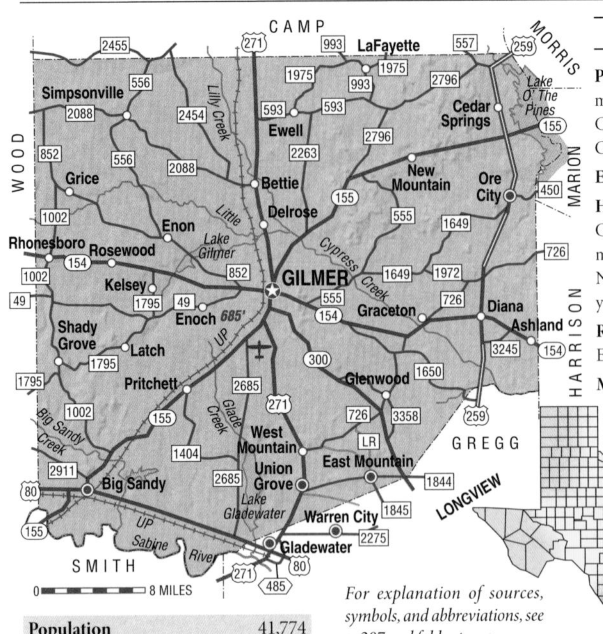

For explanation of sources, symbols, and abbreviations, see p. 207 and foldout map.

Physical Features: East Texas county; rolling to hilly, more than half forested; drains to Sabine River, Little Cypress Creek, Lake O' the Pines, Lake Gilmer, Lake Gladewater.

Economy: Manufacturing, oil, gas, agribusiness, timber.

History: Caddoes; reduced by epidemics in the 1700s. Cherokees in area in the 1820s. Anglo-American settlement in the mid-1830s. County created from Harrison, Nacogdoches counties in 1846, organized the same year; named for U.S. Secretary of State A.P. Upshur.

Recreation: Scenic trails, hunting, fishing, fall foliage, East Texas Yamboree in October at Gilmer.

Minerals: Oil, gas, sand, gravel.

Agriculture: Dairies, cattle, hay, vegetable crops, poultry. Market value $40.7 million. Timber a major product.

Vital Statistics, annual: Births, 489; deaths, 556; marriages, 162; divorces, 150.

Race/Ethnicity: Anglo, 76.5%; Hispanic, 9.7%; Black, 7.1%; Asian, 0.4%; Other, 6.2%.

GILMER (4,894) county seat; agriculture, communications, electric power; museum; trails, parks; site of Cherokee village.

Other towns include: **Big Sandy** (1,263); **Diana** (585); **East Mountain** (922); **Ore City** (1,142); **Union Grove** (453). Part [2,369] of **Gladewater** (6,341 total, rest in Gregg County).

Population	41,774
Change from 2010	6.3%
Area (sq. mi.)	592.6
Land Area (sq. mi.)	583.0
Altitude (ft.)	228–685
Rainfall (in.)	47.9
Jan. mean min (°F)	34.0
July mean max (°F)	91.1

Civ. Labor	17,822
Unemployed	4.3%
Wages	$92,398,460
Per Capita Income	$43,308
Property Value	$4,497,983,028
Retail Sales	$320,704,282

Upton County

Physical Features: Western county; north flat, south rolling, hilly; limestone, sandy loam soils, drains to creeks.

Economy: Oil, wind turbines, farming, ranching.

History: Apache and Comanche area until the tribes were removed by the U.S. Army in the 1870s. Sheep and cattle ranching developed in the 1880s. Oil discovered in 1925. County created in 1887 from Tom Green County; organized in 1910; the name honors brothers John and William Upton, Confederate colonels.

Recreation: Historic sites, Mendoza Trail museum, scenic areas, dinosaur tracks west of McCamey.

Minerals: Oil, natural gas.

Agriculture: Cotton, sheep, goats, cattle, watermelons, pecans. Extensive irrigation. Market value $19.1 million.

Vital Statistics, annual: Births, 40; deaths, 44; marriages, 18; divorces, 20.

Race/Ethnicity: Anglo, 39.8%; Hispanic, 54.3%; Black, 1.8%; Asian, 0.1%; Other, 3.9%.

RANKIN (759) county seat, oil, ranching, farming; hospital; Barbados cookoff in May.

McCAMEY (1,825) government/services, wind and solar power, oil; hospital; Wind Energy cookoff and festival in September.

Other town: **Midkiff** (182).

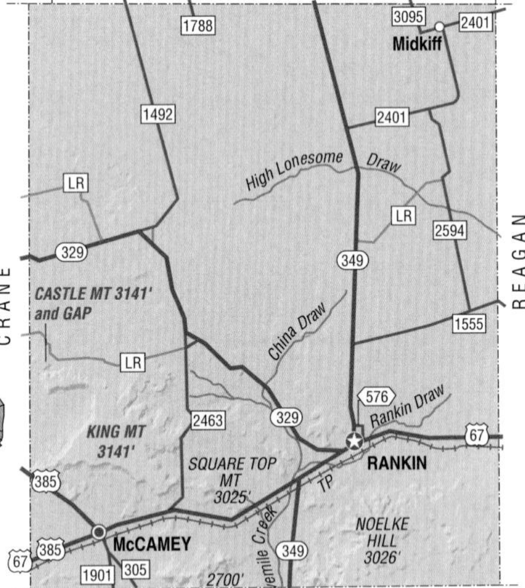

Population	3,265
Change from 2010	–2.7%
Area (sq. mi.)	1,241.5
Land Area (sq. mi.)	1,241.3

Altitude (ft.)	2,310–3,141
Rainfall (in.)	14.8
Jan. mean min (°F)	34.7
July mean max (°F)	95.9
Civ. Labor	2,349

Unemployed	2.7%
Wages	$58,800,536
Per Capita Income	$61,595
Property Value	$15,019,707,748
Retail Sales	$35,662,825

Uvalde County

Physical Features: Edwards Plateau, rolling hills below escarpment; spring-fed Sabinal, Frio, Leona, Nueces rivers; cypress, cedar, other trees, including maple groves.

Economy: Agribusinesses, hunting leases, light manufacturing, tourism.

History: Mission Nuestra Señora de la Candelaria founded in 1762 for Lipan Apaches near present-day Montell; Comanches harassed mission. U.S. military outpost established in 1849. County created from Bexar in 1850; re-created and organized in 1856; named for 1778 governor of Coahuila, Juan de Ugalde, with name Anglicized.

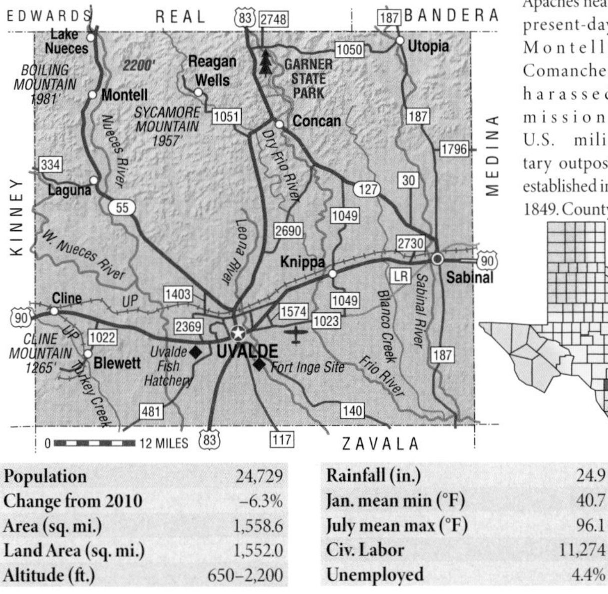

Recreation: Deer, turkey hunting; Garner State Park; water activities on rivers; John Nance Garner museum; Uvalde Memorial Park; scenic trails, historic sites.

Minerals: Asphalt, stone, sand, gravel.

Agriculture: Cattle, vegetables, corn, cotton, sorghum, sheep, goats, hay, wheat. Substantial irrigation. Market value $87.1 million.

Vital Statistics, annual: Births, 386; deaths, 328; marriages, 152; divorces, 5.

Race/Ethnicity: Anglo, 26.9%; Hispanic, 70.5%; Black, 0.4%; Asian, 0.6%; Other, 1.5%.

UVALDE (15,312) county seat; vegetable, wool, mohair processing, tourism; opera house; junior college, A&M research center; hospital; Fort Inge Day in April.

Sabinal (1,401) farm, ranch center, tourism, retirement area.

Other towns include: **Concan** (500); **Knippa** (808); **Utopia** (210) resort; **Uvalde Estates** (2,388).

Population	24,729
Change from 2010	–6.3%
Area (sq. mi.)	1,558.6
Land Area (sq. mi.)	1,552.0
Altitude (ft.)	650–2,200
Rainfall (in.)	24.9
Jan. mean min (°F)	40.7
July mean max (°F)	96.1
Civ. Labor	11,274
Unemployed	4.4%
Wages	$108,703,507
Per Capita Income	$53,257
Property Value	$5,296,409,657
Retail Sales	$481,098,078

Val Verde County

Physical Features: Southwestern county bordering Mexico, rolling, hilly; brushy; Devils, Pecos rivers, Rio Grande and Amistad Reservoir; limestone, alluvial soils.

Economy: Agribusiness, tourism, trade center, military, Border Patrol, hunting leases, fishing.

History: Apaches, Coahuiltecans, Jumanos present when Spanish came through in the late 1500s. Comanches arrived later. U.S. military outpost established in 1850s to protect settlers. Only county named for Civil War battle; Val Verde means green valley. Created in 1885 from Crockett, Kinney, Pecos counties, organized the same year.

Recreation: Gateway to Mexico; deer hunting, fishing; Amistad lake activities; two state parks; Langtry restoration of Judge Roy Bean's saloon; ancient pictographs; San Felipe Springs; winery.

Minerals: Production sand and gravel, gas, oil.

Agriculture: Sheep, Angora goats, meat goats (second in numbers); cattle; minor irrigation. Market value $9.4 million.

Vital Statistics, annual: Births, 732; deaths, 570; marriages, 344; divorces, 113.

Race/Ethnicity: Anglo, 16.5%; Hispanic, 80.3%; Black, 1.1%; Asian, 0.7%; Other, 1.4%.

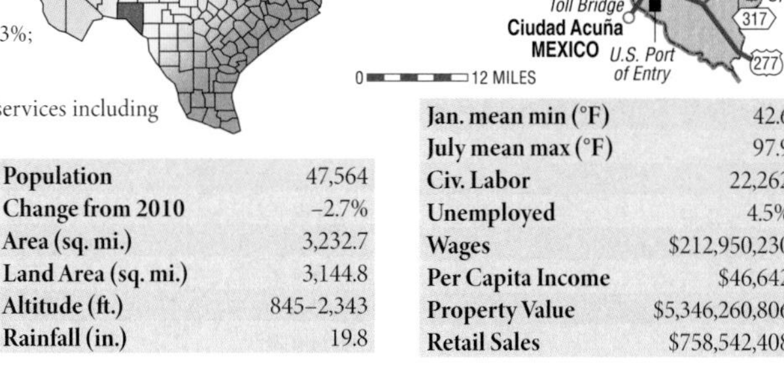

DEL RIO (34,584) county seat; government/services including federal agencies/military, agribusiness, tourism; hospital, extension colleges; Fiesta de Amistad in October.

Laughlin Air Force Base (1,989).

Other towns and places include: **Cienegas Terrace** (2,342); **Comstock** (344); **Langtry** (30); **Val Verde Park** (3,740).

Population	47,564
Change from 2010	–2.7%
Area (sq. mi.)	3,232.7
Land Area (sq. mi.)	3,144.8
Altitude (ft.)	845–2,343
Rainfall (in.)	19.8
Jan. mean min (°F)	42.6
July mean max (°F)	97.9
Civ. Labor	22,262
Unemployed	4.5%
Wages	$212,950,230
Per Capita Income	$46,642
Property Value	$5,346,260,806
Retail Sales	$758,542,408

Van Zandt County

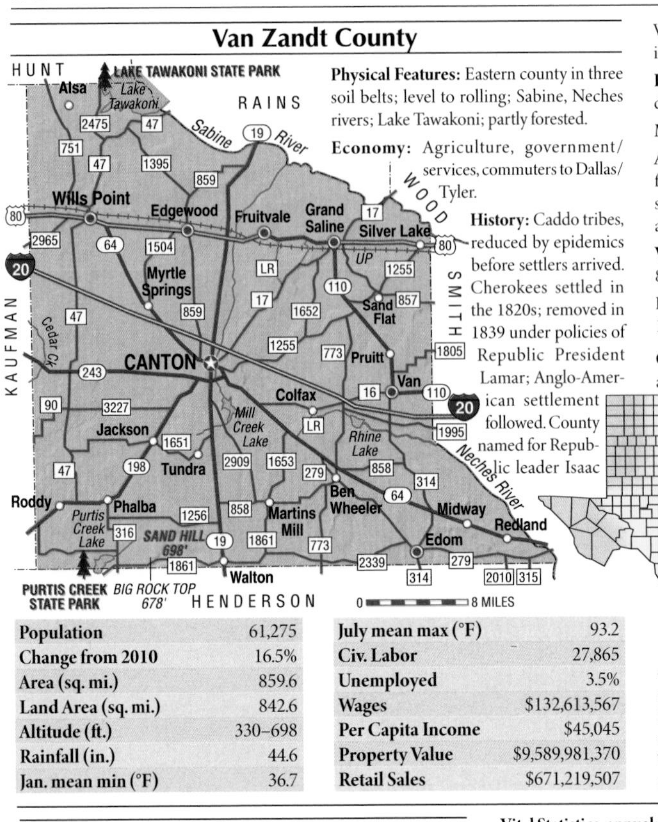

Physical Features: Eastern county in three soil belts; level to rolling; Sabine, Neches rivers; Lake Tawakoni; partly forested.

Economy: Agriculture, government/services, commuters to Dallas/Tyler.

History: Caddo tribes, reduced by epidemics before settlers arrived. Cherokees settled in the 1820s; removed in 1839 under policies of Republic President Lamar; Anglo-American settlement followed. County named for Republic leader Isaac Van Zandt; created from Henderson County in 1848, organized the same year.

Recreation: Canton First Monday trade days, lake activities, state parks, historic sites.

Minerals: Oil, gas.

Agriculture: Nurseries, beef cattle, hay and foliage, dairies, vegetables. First in nursery stock acreage in the open and in sweet potato acreage. Market value $104.6 million.

Vital Statistics, annual: Births, 575; deaths, 835; marriages, 309; divorces, 200.

Race/Ethnicity: Anglo, 80.6%; Hispanic, 11.9%; Black, 2.5%; Asian, 0.5%; Other, 4.5%.

CANTON (4,312) county seat; tourism, agribusiness, commuters; museums, bluegrass festival in June.

WILLS POINT (3,863) government/services, retail, tourism, commuters to Dallas and Tyler; depot museum, bluebird festival in April.

Other towns include: **Ben Wheeler** (2,026); **Edgewood** (1,592) commuters, heritage park, antiques; **Edom** (349) arts and crafts; **Fruitvale** (490); **Grand Saline** (3,165) salt plant, agriculture, medical services/hospital, Salt Palace museum, salt prairie marsh, birding, Salt Festival in September; **Van** (2,745) oil center, hay, cattle, oil festival in October.

Population	61,275
Change from 2010	16.5%
Area (sq. mi.)	859.6
Land Area (sq. mi.)	842.6
Altitude (ft.)	330–698
Rainfall (in.)	44.6
Jan. mean min (°F)	36.7
July mean max (°F)	93.2
Civ. Labor	27,865
Unemployed	3.5%
Wages	$132,613,567
Per Capita Income	$45,045
Property Value	$9,589,981,370
Retail Sales	$671,219,507

Victoria County

Physical Features: Rolling prairies, intersected by many streams; sandy loams, clays, alluvial soils.

Economy: Petrochemical plants, government/services, oil, manufacturing, agribusiness, tourism, healthcare.

History: Karankawas and other tribes in the area when Spanish explored in 1528. Comanches, Tawakonis arrived later. La Salle's camp on Garcitas Creek 1685–1687. Spanish ranching developed in the 1750s. Anglo-Americans arrived after 1836. An original county, created in 1836 from Mexican municipality named for President Guadalupe Victoria of Mexico.

Recreation: Fishing, hunting; saltwater activities, historic homes, sites, riverside park, Coleto Creek Reservoir and park, zoo, Czech festival in September at Victoria.

Minerals: Oil, gas, sand, gravel.

Agriculture: Corn, beef cattle, grain sorghums, cotton, rice, soybeans. Market value $58.4 million.

Vital Statistics, annual: Births, 1,166; deaths, 1,036; marriages, 283; divorces, 334.

Race/Ethnicity: Anglo, 43.1%; Hispanic, 47%; Black, 5.7%; Asian, 1.5%; Other, 2.7%.

VICTORIA (65,377) county seat; petrochemicals, government/services, hospitals/healthcare, retail, oil, manufacturing, agribusiness, tourism; Victoria College, University of Houston at Victoria; community theater, symphony, museums.

Other towns include: **Bloomington** (1,321); **Inez** (2,385); **Nursery** (600); **Placedo** (443); **Telferner** (700); **Quail Creek** (1,454).

For explanation of sources, symbols, and abbreviations, see p. 207 and foldout map.

Population	90,964
Change from 2010	4.8%
Area (sq. mi.)	888.8
Land Area (sq. mi.)	882.1
Altitude (ft.)	sea level–230
Rainfall (in.)	40.4
Jan. mean min (°F)	45.5
July mean max (°F)	94.1
Civ. Labor	41,365
Unemployed	4.2%
Wages	$519,814,136
Per Capita Income	$58,479
Property Value	$11,990,976,428
Retail Sales	$2,142,479,471

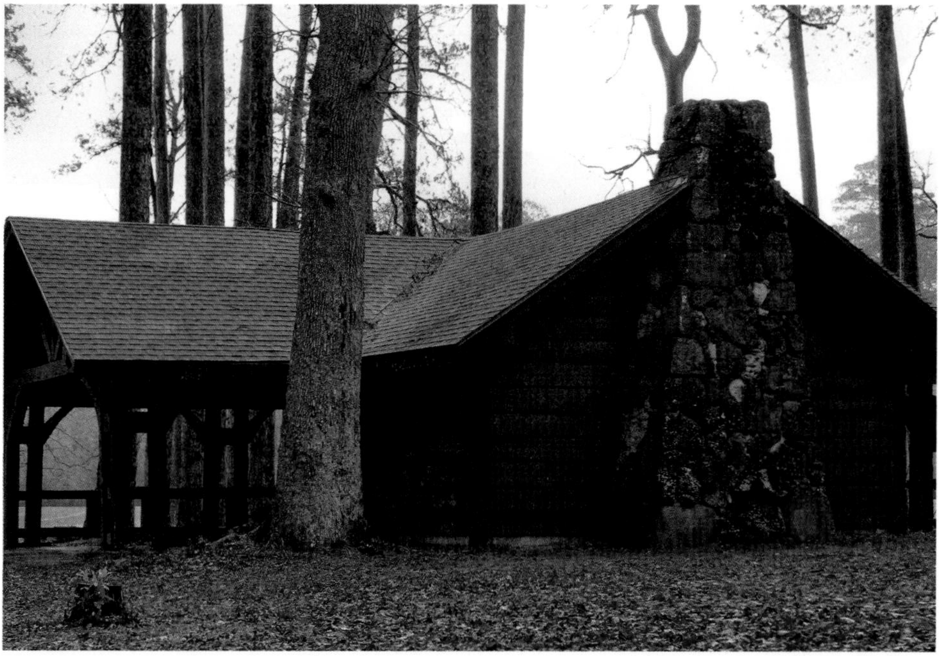

The Double Lake Recreation Area in Sam Houston National Forest. Photo by Larry D. Moore, CC by SA 4.0

Walker County

Physical Features: South central county north of Houston of rolling hills; more than 70% forested; national forest; San Jacinto, Trinity rivers; Lake Livingston, Lake Conroe.

Economy: State employment in prison system, education.

History: Coahuiltecans, Bidais in area when Spanish explored around 1690. Later, area became trading ground for many Indian tribes. Anglo-Americans settled in the 1830s. Antebellum slaveholding area. County created in 1846 from Montgomery County and organized the same year; first named for U.S. Secretary of the Treasury R.J. Walker; renamed 1863 for Texas Ranger Capt. S.H. Walker.

Recreation: Fishing, hunting, lake activities; Sam Houston museum, homes, grave; prison museum; other historic sites, state park, Sam Houston National Forest; Sam Houston folk festival in spring.

Minerals: Clays, natural gas, oil, sand and gravel, stone.

Agriculture: Cattle, nursery plants, poultry, cotton, hay. Market value $33.8 million. Timber sales substantial.

Vital Statistics, annual: Births, 640; deaths, 672; marriages, 385; divorces, 210.

Race/Ethnicity: Anglo, 52.1%; Hispanic, 21.7%; Black, 21.4%; Asian, 1.5%; Other, 3.3%.

HUNTSVILLE (46,288) county seat; state prison system, Sam Houston State University, forest products, varied manufacturing; hospital; museums, arts center.

Other towns include: **Dodge** (150); **New Waverly** (966); **Riverside** (553).

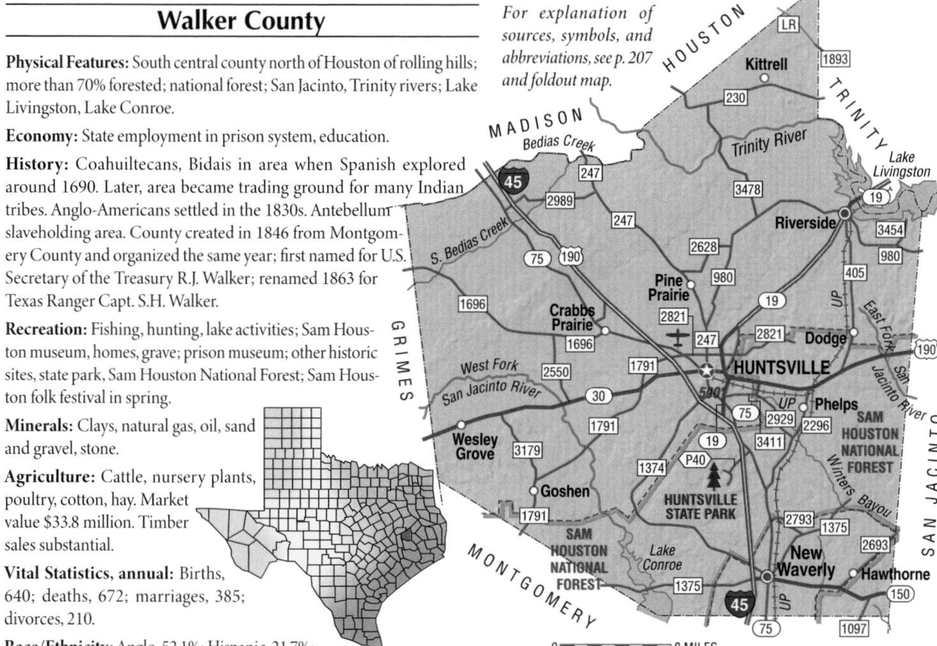

Population	77,977
Change from 2010	14.9%
Area (sq. mi.)	801.5
Land Area (sq. mi.)	784.2
Altitude (ft.)	131–500
Rainfall (in.)	51.3
Jan. mean min (°F)	41.0

July mean max (°F)	91.3
Civ. Labor	23,957
Unemployed	4.7%
Wages	$314,968,628
Per Capita Income	$33,345
Property Value	$9,322,807,719
Retail Sales	$949,980,663

Waller County

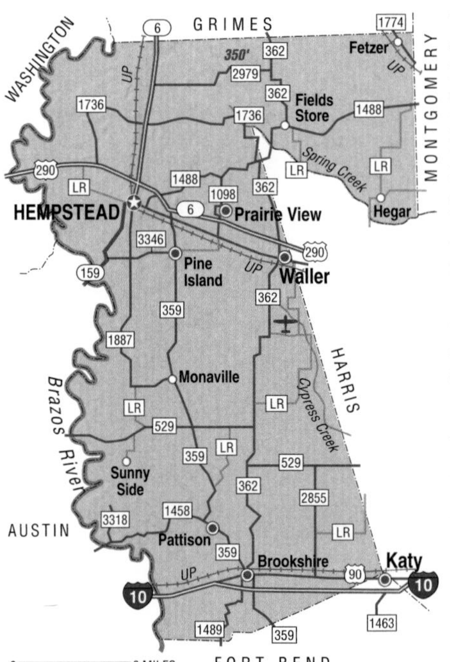

Physical Features: Southeastern county west of Houston on rolling prairie; drains to Brazos; alluvial soils; about 20 percent forested.

Economy: Agribusiness, education, equine-related businesses, part of Houston metropolitan area.

History: Bidais Indians reduced to about 100 when Anglo-Americans settled in 1820s. Antebellum slaveholding area. County named for Edwin Waller, Republic leader; created in 1873 from Austin, Grimes counties, organized the same year.

Recreation: Fishing, hunting; historic sites; museum.

Minerals: Oil, gas.

Agriculture: Cattle, hay, rice, greenhouse nurseries, turf grass. 10,000 acres irrigated. Market value $102.4 million. Some timber marketed.

Vital Statistics, annual: Births, 689; deaths, 457; marriages, 288; divorces, 68.

Race/Ethnicity: Anglo, 41.4%; Hispanic, 32.5%; Black, 21.3%; Asian, 1.4%; Other, 3.4%.

HEMPSTEAD (6,028) county seat; varied manufacturing, commuting to Houston, agribusiness center, large vegetable market; watermelon fest in July.

PRAIRIE VIEW (6,843) home of Prairie View A&M University.

Other towns include: **Brookshire** (5,501); **Pattison** (594); **Pine Island** (1,161); **Waller** (2,796, partly in Harris County) agriculture, education, construction.

Population	59,781
Change from 2010	38.4%
Area (sq. mi.)	517.8
Land Area (sq. mi.)	513.4
Altitude (ft.)	100–350

Rainfall (in.)	43.9
Jan. mean min (°F)	42.9
July mean max (°F)	93.4
Civ. Labor	25,450
Unemployed	4.3%

Wages	$354,105,376
Per Capita Income	$49,404
Property Value	$16,363,626,187
Retail Sales	$705,606,191

Ward County

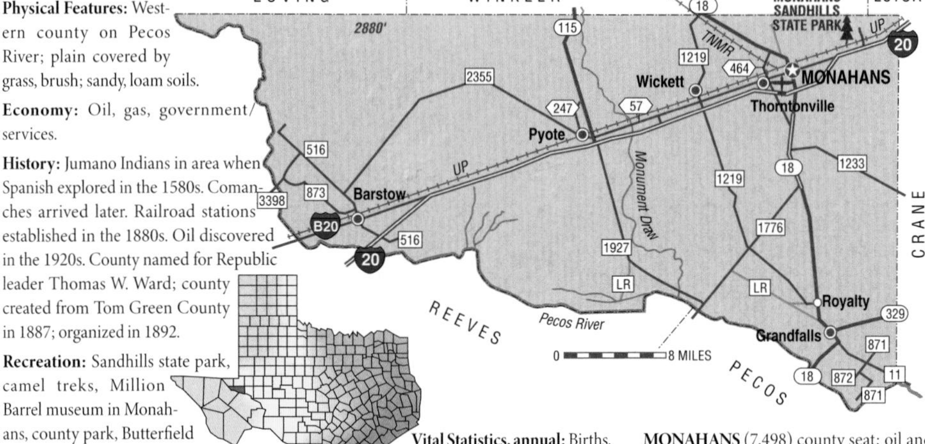

Physical Features: Western county on Pecos River; plain covered by grass, brush; sandy, loam soils.

Economy: Oil, gas, government/services.

History: Jumano Indians in area when Spanish explored in the 1580s. Comanches arrived later. Railroad stations established in the 1880s. Oil discovered in the 1920s. County named for Republic leader Thomas W. Ward; county created from Tom Green County in 1887; organized in 1892.

Recreation: Sandhills state park, camel treks, Million Barrel museum in Monahans, county park, Butterfield stagecoach festival in July.

Minerals: Oil, gas, caliche, sand, gravel.

Agriculture: Beef cattle, greenhouse crops, alfalfa, horses. Market value $19.1 million. Hunting leases important.

Vital Statistics, annual: Births, 183; deaths, 134; marriages, 73; divorces, 38.

Race/Ethnicity: Anglo, 38.7%; Hispanic, 54.3%; Black, 3.6%; Asian, 0.6%; Other, 2.8%.

MONAHANS (7,498) county seat; oil and gas, tourism, ranching; hospital, Odessa College extension.

Other towns include: **Barstow** (257); **Grandfalls** (330); **Pyote** (72); **Southwest Sandhill** (1,136); **Thorntonville** (546); **Wickett** (410).

Population	11,194
Change from 2010	5.0%
Area (sq. mi.)	835.8
Land Area (sq. mi.)	835.6
Altitude (ft.)	2,400–2,880

Rainfall (in.)	13.8
Jan. mean min (°F)	28.8
July mean max (°F)	97.3
Civ. Labor	6,183
Unemployed	3.7%

Wages	$108,663,458
Per Capita Income	$55,099
Property Value	$6,638,758,950
Retail Sales	$187,778,708

Washington County

Physical Features: South central county in Brazos valley; rolling prairie of sandy loam, alluvial soils.

Economy: Agribusiness, oil, tourism, manufacturing, government/services.

History: Coahuiltecan tribes and Tonkawas in area when Anglo-American settlers arrived in 1821. Antebellum slaveholding area. Germans arrived around 1870. County named for George Washington; an original county, created in 1836, organized in 1837.

Recreation: Historic sites, including Chappell Hill Historical Society Museum, Washington-on-the-Brazos, Texas Baptist Historical Museum, Star of republic Museum; wildflowers, Somerville Lake, fishing, hunting, birding, antique rose nursery; Bluebonnet Festival in April, Brenham Maifest in May, Scarecrow Festival in October, Washington County Fair in September.

Minerals: Oil, gas, and stone.

Agriculture: Cattle, poultry, dairy products, hogs, horses, hay, corn, sorghum, cotton, small grains, nursery crops, and honey.

Vital Statistics, annual: Births, 365; deaths, 479; marriages, 164; divorces, 92.

Race/Ethnicity: Anglo, 61.5%; Hispanic, 17.9%; Black, 15.5%; Asian, 1.5%; Other, 3.5%.

BRENHAM (18,117) county seat; Blue Bell creamery, retail, tourism; hospital; Blinn College; Maifest.

Other towns include: **Burton** (283) agriculture, tourism, national landmark cotton gin, festival in April; **Chappell Hill** (750) agriculture, industrial, tourism, museum, historic homes; **Washington** (100) site of signing of Texas Declaration of Independence.

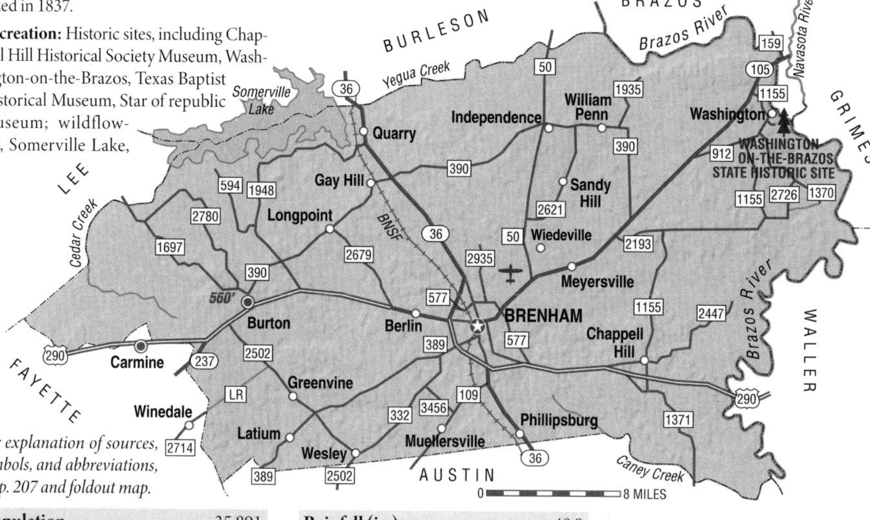

For explanation of sources, symbols, and abbreviations, see p. 207 and foldout map.

Population	35,891
Change from 2010	6.4%
Area (sq. mi.)	621.8
Land Area (sq. mi.)	604.0
Altitude (ft.)	150–560

Rainfall (in.)	48.0
Jan. mean min (°F)	41.3
July mean max (°F)	93.2
Civ. Labor	15,256
Unemployed	4.0%

Wages	$202,513,784
Per Capita Income	$61,295
Property Value	$11,685,910,332
Retail Sales	$615,005,915

Corrals at the Washington on the Brazos State Historic Site. Photo by Reading, CC by SA 4.0

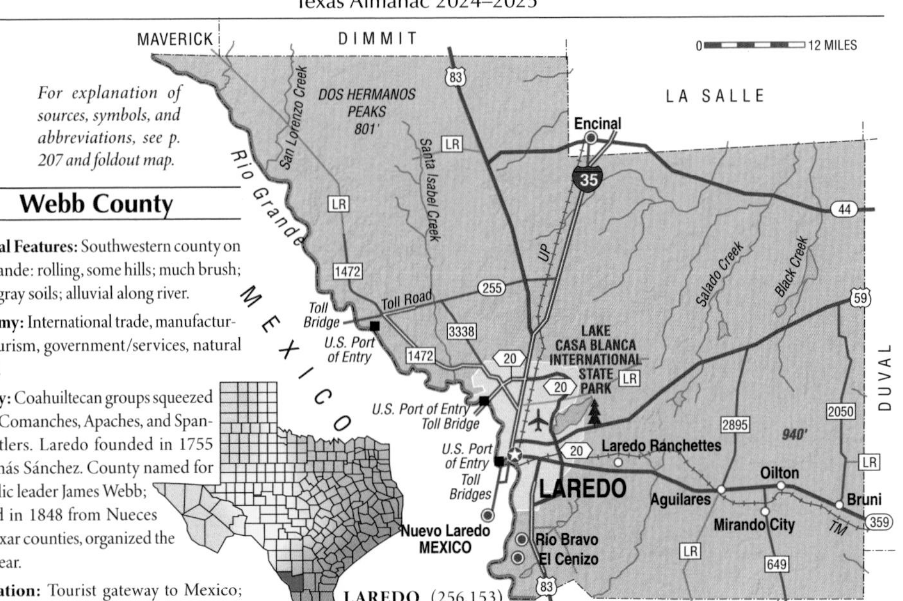

For explanation of sources, symbols, and abbreviations, see p. 207 and foldout map.

Webb County

Physical Features: Southwestern county on Rio Grande: rolling, some hills; much brush; sandy, gray soils; alluvial along river.

Economy: International trade, manufacturing, tourism, government/services, natural gas, oil.

History: Coahuiltecan groups squeezed out by Comanches, Apaches, and Spanish settlers. Laredo founded in 1755 by Tomás Sánchez. County named for Republic leader James Webb; created in 1848 from Nueces and Bexar counties, organized the same year.

Recreation: Tourist gateway to Mexico; hunting, fishing; Lake Casa Blanca park, water recreation; historic sites; Museum of Republic of the Rio Grande; Fort McIntosh; minor league baseball; Washington's Birthday celebration.

Minerals: Natural gas, oil, coal.

Agriculture: Onions, melons, nursery crops, cattle, horses, goats. About 2,500 acres irrigated. Market value $28.4 million. Mesquite sold. Hunting leases important.

Vital Statistics, annual: Births, 4,344; deaths, 2,182; marriages, 1,456; divorces, 16.

Race/Ethnicity: Anglo, 3.6%; Hispanic, 95.2%; Black, 0.3%; Asian, 0.5%; Other, 0.4%.

LAREDO (256,153) county seat; international trade, retail center, government/services; rail, highway gateway to Mexico; junior college, Texas A&M International University, community college; hospitals; entertainment/sports arena; "El Grito" on Sept. 15; Jalapeño festival in February.

Other towns and places include: **Bruni** (376); **El Cenizo** (2,506); **Mirando City** (189); **Oilton** (108); **Rio Bravo** (4,400).

Population	267,945
Change from 2010	7.0%
Area (sq. mi.)	3,375.6

Land Area (sq. mi.)	3,361.5
Altitude (ft.)	310–940
Rainfall (in.)	19.7
Jan. mean min (°F)	48.8
July mean max (°F)	100.1
Civ. Labor	117,364
Unemployed	4.1%
Wages	$1,202,978,176
Per Capita Income	$40,850
Property Value	$38,357,942,835
Retail Sales	$4,505,784,858

Part of the old Route 66 runs through Shamrock in Wheeler County. Photo by Eric Shaw White, CC by SA 3.0

Wharton County

Physical Features: Gulf prairie; bisected by the Colorado River; alluvial, black, sandy loam soils.

Economy: Oil, agribusiness, hunting, manufacturing, government/services.

History: Karankawas in area until the 1840s. Anglo-American colonists settled in 1823. Czechs, Germans arrived in 1880s. Mexican migration increased after 1950. County named for John A. and William H. Wharton, brothers active in Texas Revolution; created in 1846 from Jackson, Matagorda, Colorado counties, organized the same year.

Recreation: Waterfowl hunting, fishing, big-game, birding; museums; riverfront park at Wharton; historic sites; old Plaza Theater at Wharton.

Minerals: Oil, gas.

Agriculture: Rice (first in acreage); cotton, milo, corn, sorghum, soybeans; 72,000 acres irrigated. Also, eggs, nurseries/turf grass (first in value of sales), cattle, aquaculture. Market value $208.5 million.

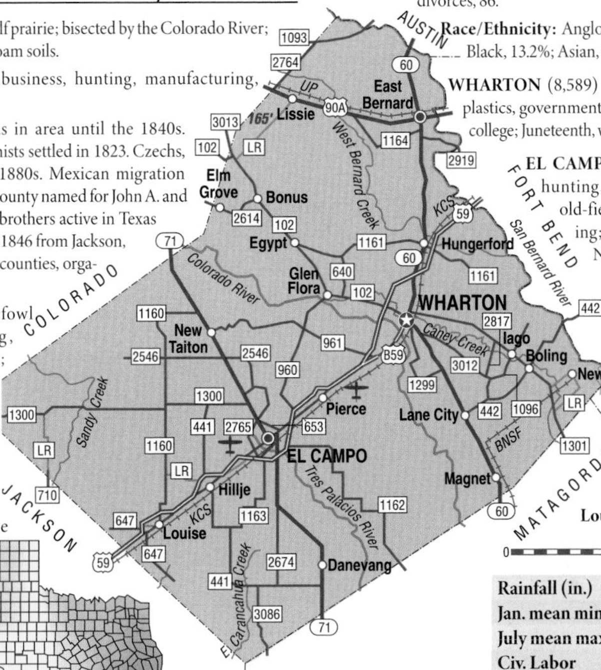

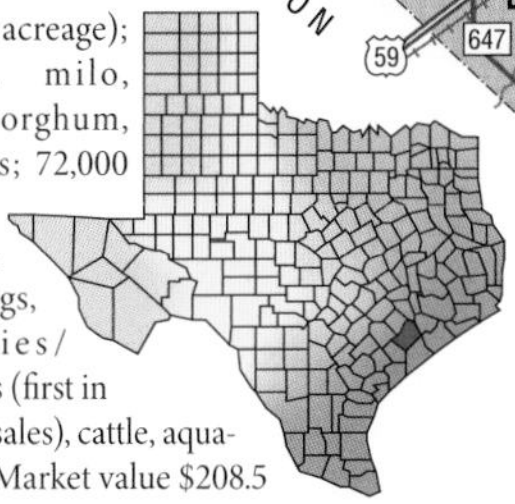

Vital Statistics, annual: Births, 543; deaths, 537; marriages, 198; divorces, 86.

Race/Ethnicity: Anglo, 43.6%; Hispanic, 40.8%; Black, 13.2%; Asian, 0.4%; Other, 2%.

WHARTON (8,589) county seat; health care, plastics, government/services; hospitals, junior college; Juneteenth, wine/arts festival in October.

EL CAMPO (12,290) agribusiness, hunting, varied manufacturing, old-field services, rice processing; hospital; Polka Expo in November.

Other towns include: **Boling** (1,148); **Danevang** (61); **East Bernard** (2,248) commuters, agribusiness, retail, kolache-klobase festival in June; **Glen Flora** (210); **Hungerford** (92); **Lane City** (111); **Louise** (1,061); **Pierce** (51).

Population	41,721
Change from 2010	1.1%
Area (sq. mi.)	1,094.4
Land Area (sq. mi.)	1,086.2
Altitude (ft.)	50–165

Rainfall (in.)	49.6
Jan. mean min (°F)	44.5
July mean max (°F)	94.5
Civ. Labor	21,416
Unemployed	3.8%
Wages	$193,474,607
Per Capita Income	$52,948
Property Value	$8,280,663,718
Retail Sales	$1,078,884,971

Wheeler County

Physical Features: Panhandle county adjoining Oklahoma. Plain, on edge of Caprock; Red River, Sweetwater Creek; some canyons; red sandy loam, black clay soils.

Economy: Oil, gas, agribusiness, tourism.

History: Apaches, displaced by Kiowas and Comanches around 1700. Fort Elliott established in 1875 after Indians forced into Oklahoma. Ranching began in the late 1870s. Oil boom in the 1920s. County named for pioneer jurist R.T. Wheeler; county created from Bexar, Young districts in 1876; organized in 1879.

Recreation: Pioneer West museum at Shamrock; historic sites; Old Mobeetie jail, trading post, Fort Elliott.

Minerals: Oil, natural gas.

Agriculture: Fed beef, cow-calf and stocker cattle, swine, horses; wheat, rye, grain sorghum, cotton. Market value $70.6 million.

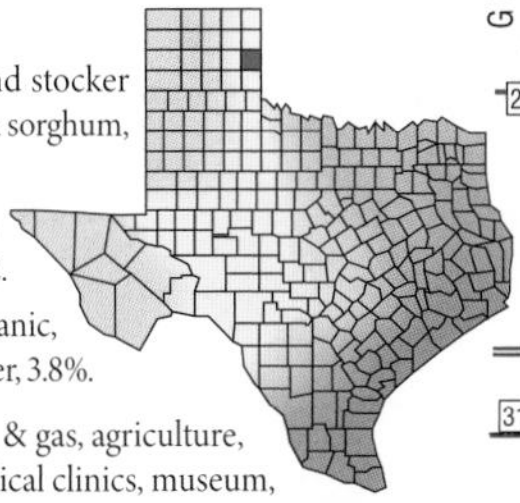

Vital Statistics, annual: Births, 45; deaths, 71; marriages, 41; divorces, 2.

Race/Ethnicity: Anglo, 69.5%; Hispanic, 24.6%; Black, 1.6%; Asian, 0.5%; Other, 3.8%.

WHEELER (1,462) county seat; oil & gas, agriculture, government/services; hospital, medical clinics, museum, library, aquatics center.

SHAMROCK (1,773) tourism, agribusiness antiques shops; hospital, library, old Route 66 sites; St. Patrick's Day event.

Other towns include: **Allison** (188); **Briscoe** (135); **Mobeetie** (86).

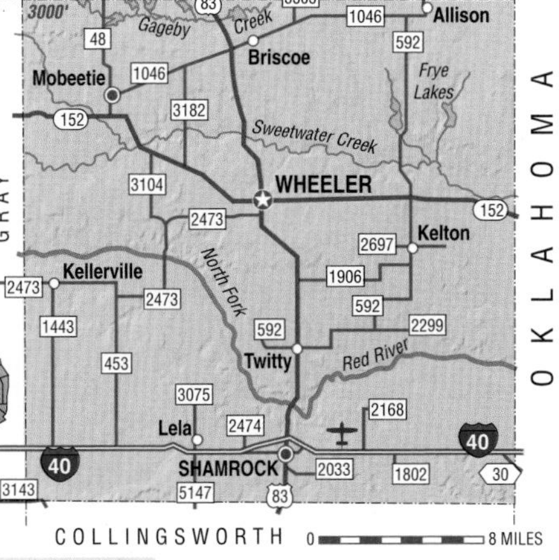

Population	4,927
Change from 2010	–8.9%
Area (sq. mi.)	915.5
Land Area (sq. mi.)	914.5
Altitude (ft.)	2,005–3,000

Rainfall (in.)	25.3
Jan. mean min (°F)	25.3
July mean max (°F)	91.9
Civ. Labor	1,989
Unemployed	3.9%

Wages	$19,773,471
Per Capita Income	$49,906
Property Value	$2,460,362,106
Retail Sales	$72,715,868

The Grand Theater in Electra was built in 1919. Photo by Renelibrary, CC by SA 4.0

Wichita County

Physical Features: Northwest county in prairie bordering Oklahoma; drained by Red, Wichita rivers; North Fork Buffalo Creek Reservoir, Lake Wichita; sandy, loam soils.

Economy: Manufacturing, retail trade center, air base, government/services, agriculture.

History: Wichitas and other Caddoan tribes in the area in the 1700s; later, Comanches, Apaches also present until the 1850s. Anglo-American settlement increased after 1870. County named for tribe; created from Young Territory in 1858; organized in 1882.

Recreation: Museums; historic sites; Texas-Oklahoma High School Oil Bowl football game; collegiate activities; water sports; Ranch Round-up in July, Fiestas Patrias parade in September.

Minerals: Oil.

Agriculture: Beef cattle, horticulture, wheat, hay. Seventy-five percent of hay irrigated; 10% of wheat/cotton. Market value $33.8 million.

Vital Statistics, annual: Births, 1,534; deaths, 1,637; marriages, 772; divorces, 328.

For explanation of sources, symbols, and abbreviations, see p. 207 and foldout map.

Race/Ethnicity: Anglo, 61.6%; Hispanic, 19.9%; Black, 10.3%; Asian, 2%; Other, 6.1%.

WICHITA FALLS (102,988) county seat; distribution center for large area of Texas and Oklahoma, government/services, varied manufacturing, oil-field services; hospitals, including North Texas state hospital; Midwestern State University, vocational-technical training center; hiking trails; Hotter'n Hell bicycle race in August; Sheppard Air Force Base.

Other cities include: **Burkburnett** (10,975) some manufacturing, Trails and Tales of Boomtown USA display and tours; **Cashion** (288); **Electra** (2,282) oil, agriculture, manufacturing, commuters to Wichita Falls, hospital, goat barbecue in May; **Iowa Park** (6,547) manufacturing, prison, Parkfest in May; **Kamay** (640); **Pleasant Valley** (356).

Population	130,069
Change from 2010	-1.1%
Area (sq. mi.)	633.1
Land Area (sq. mi.)	627.8
Altitude (ft.)	912–1240
Rainfall (in.)	27.9
Jan. mean min (°F)	31.8
July mean max (°F)	95.3
Civ. Labor	55,458
Unemployed	3.9%
Wages	$687,030,671
Per Capita Income	$50,210
Property Value	$12,661,914,147
Retail Sales	$2,122,897,252

Wilbarger County

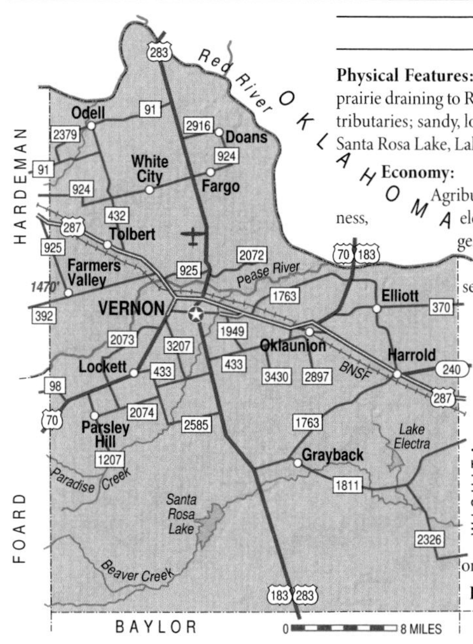

Physical Features: Gently rolling prairie draining to Red, Pease rivers, tributaries; sandy, loam, waxy soils; Santa Rosa Lake, Lake Electra.

Economy: Agribusiness, electricity generating plant, government/services.

History: Anglo-American settlement developed after removal of the Comanches into the Indian Territory in 1875. County named for pioneers Josiah and Mathias Wilbarger; created from the Bexar District in 1858 and organized in 1881.

Recreation: Doan's Crossing, on route of cattle drives; Waggoner Ranch, other historic sites; hunting, fishing; Red River Valley Museum; Santa Rosa roundup in May.

Minerals: Oil.

Agriculture: Wheat, cattle, cotton, alfalfa, peanuts; 15,000 acres irrigated. Market value $51.9 million.

Vital Statistics, annual: Births, 134; deaths, 209; marriages, 90; divorces, 33.

Race/Ethnicity: Anglo, 54.4%; Hispanic, 29%; Black, 7.9%; Asian, 4.4%; Other, 4.4%.

VERNON (10,045) county seat; government/services, agribusiness, manufacturing, electricity-generating plant; college; state hospital/mental health center, private hospital, prison; museums; vintage car show in August.

Other towns include: **Harrold** (129); **Lockett** (357) A&M extension center; **Odell** (100); **Oklaunion** (77).

Population	12,731
Change from 2010	–5.9%
Area (sq. mi.)	977.9
Land Area (sq. mi.)	970.8
Altitude (ft.)	1,030–1,470
Rainfall (in.)	28.4
Jan. mean min (°F)	30.2
July mean max (°F)	95.4
Civ. Labor	4,832
Unemployed	4.9%
Wages	$65,471,722
Per Capita Income	$59,952
Property Value	$2,861,462,356
Retail Sales	$328,500,842

Willacy County

Physical Features: Flat coastal prairie sloping toward Gulf; alluvial, sandy, marshy soils; Padre Island; La Sal Vieja, salt lake; wildlife refuge.

Economy: Agribusiness, oil, government/services.

History: Coahuiltecan area when Spanish explored in the 1500s. Spanish ranching began in the 1790s. County named for legislator John G. Willacy; created in 1911 from Cameron, Hidalgo counties, organized in 1912; reorganized in 1921 after most of its territory was given over to the newly created Kenedy County.

Recreation: Fresh and saltwater fishing, hunting of deer, turkey, dove; mild climate attracts many winter tourists.

Minerals: Oil, natural gas.

Agriculture: Cotton, sorghum, corn, vegetables, sugar cane, watermelon; 20% of cropland irrigated. Livestock includes cattle, horses, goats, hogs. Market value $88.1 million.

Vital Statistics, annual: Births, 226; deaths, 253; marriages, 59; divorces, 39.

Race/Ethnicity: Anglo, 9%; Hispanic, 87.3%; Black, 2.2%; Asian, 0.8%; Other, 0.7%.

RAYMONDVILLE (10,510) county seat; agribusiness, oil, food processing, tourism, enterprise zone, prison; museum; Wild in Willacy Boot Fest in October.

Other towns include: **Lasara** (857); **Lyford** (2,210); **Port Mansfield** (168) charter fishing, bait and tackle, ecotourism/birding, nature trail, fishing tournament in July; **San Perlita** (531); **Sebastian** (1,331).

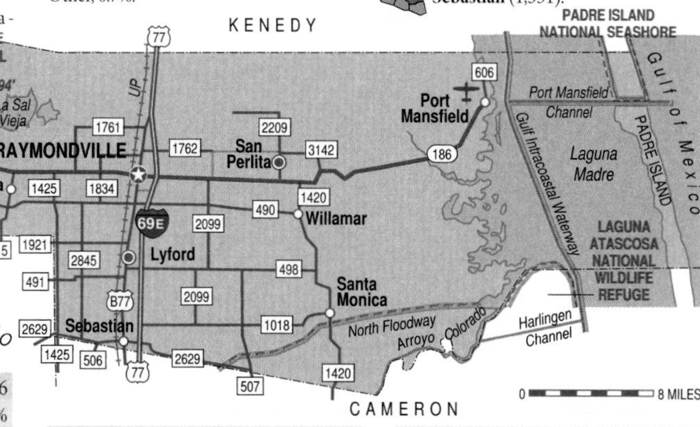

Population	20,316
Change from 2010	–8.2%
Area (sq. mi.)	784.3
Land Area (sq. mi.)	590.6
Altitude (ft.)	sea level–94
Rainfall (in.)	25.5
Jan. mean min (°F)	49.9
July mean max (°F)	96.8
Civ. Labor	7,227
Unemployed	8.2%
Wages	$51,207,496
Per Capita Income	$37,792
Property Value	$2,870,208,984
Retail Sales	$111,382,322

Williamson County

Physical Features: Central county near Austin. Level to rolling; mostly Blackland soil, some loam, sand; drained by San Gabriel River and tributaries; Granger Lake, Lake Georgetown.

Economy: Agribusinesses, varied manufacturing, education center, government/services; the county is part of Austin metropolitan area.

History: Tonkawa area; later, other tribes moved in. Comanches raided until the 1860s. Anglo-American settlement began in the late 1830s. County named for Robert M. Williamson, pioneer leader; created from Milam County and organized in 1848.

Recreation: Lake recreation; Inner Space Cavern; historic sites; deer hunting, fishing; Gov. Dan Moody Museum at Taylor; San Gabriel Park; old settlers park; walking tours, rattlesnake sacking, barbecue cookoff, frontier days in summer; Round Rock minor league baseball; Cedar Park Center, home of Austin Spurs NBA developmental basketball team and the Texas Stars AHL hockey team.

Minerals: Building stone, sand and gravel.

Agriculture: Corn, cattle, sorghum, cotton, wheat, hay, nursery crops. Market value $114.9 million.

Vital Statistics, annual: Births, 6,863; deaths, 3,683; marriages, 2,551; divorces, 798.

Race/Ethnicity: Anglo, 55.2%; Hispanic, 24.2%; Black, 6.3%; Asian, 8.9%; Other, 5.4%.

GEORGETOWN (75,420) county seat; education, health, government/services, manufacturing, retail; hospital; Southwestern University; Red Poppy festival in April.

ROUND ROCK (123,876, part [1,905] in Travis County) semiconductor, varied manufacturing, tourism and distribution center; hospital; Texas Baptist Children's Home.

CEDAR PARK (78,693, part [7,325] in Travis County) energy equipment manufacturing, millwork, concrete production, commuting to Austin; hospital, community college extension; steam-engine train; Cedar Fest in the spring.

Leander (67,124, part [9,997] in Travis County) varied manufacturing, government/services, community college campus, Old Town street festival in June, Leanderthal Lady prehistoric site.

Taylor (16,807) varied manufacturing, wholesale, transportation, government/services; hospital, college extension campuses, museum, parks; Blackland Prairie Day in May.

Other towns include: **Bartlett** (1,643, partly in Bell County) cotton, corn production, commuters, prison, first rural electrification in nation in 1933, clinic, library; **Brushy Creek** (22,972); **Coupland** (290); **Florence** (1,201).

Also, **Granger** (1,193); **Hutto** (30,855) agriculture, manufacturing, government/services, commuters to Austin, museum, Olde Tyme Days in October; **Jarrell** (2,111); **Jollyville** (18,409, partly in Travis County); **Liberty Hill** (6,801) artisans center; **Schwertner** (175); **Thrall** (860); **Walburg** (277); **Weir** (714).

Also, part [63,623] of **Austin**.

Population	643,026
Change from 2010	52.1%
Area (sq. mi.)	1,134.4
Land Area (sq. mi.)	1,118.3
Altitude (ft.)	400–1,360

Rainfall (in.)	37.1
Jan. mean min (°F)	38.1
July mean max (°F)	94.9
Civ. Labor	364,532
Unemployed	2.9%

Wages	$3,803,890,625
Per Capita Income	$62,931
Property Value	$159,572,227,878
Retail Sales	$12,340,863,457

For explanation of sources, symbols, and abbreviations, see p. 207 and foldout map.

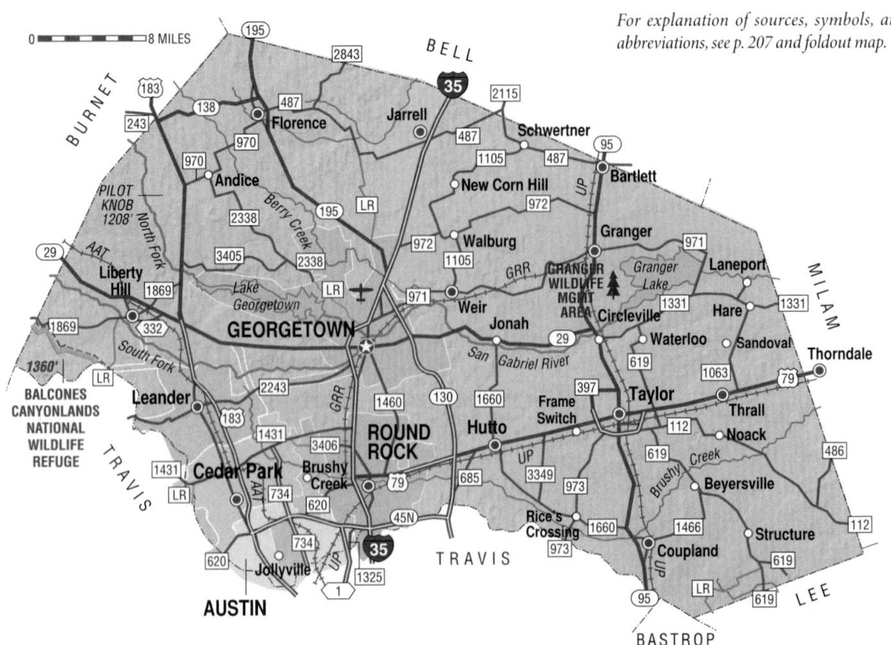

Wilson County

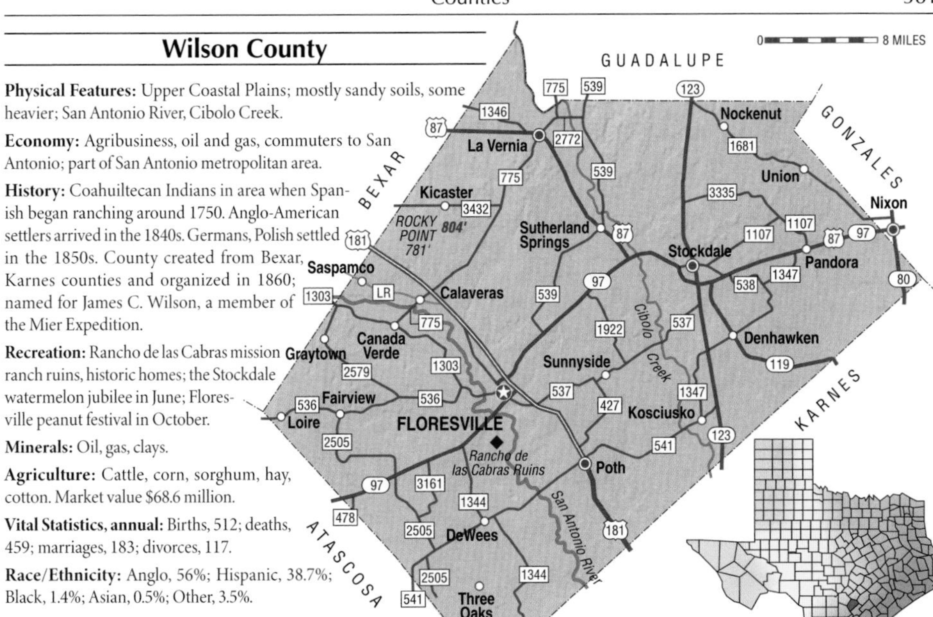

For explanation of sources, symbols, and abbreviations, see p. 207 and foldout map.

Physical Features: Upper Coastal Plains; mostly sandy soils, some heavier; San Antonio River, Cibolo Creek.

Economy: Agribusiness, oil and gas, commuters to San Antonio; part of San Antonio metropolitan area.

History: Coahuiltecan Indians in area when Spanish began ranching around 1750. Anglo-American settlers arrived in the 1840s. Germans, Polish settled in the 1850s. County created from Bexar, Karnes counties and organized in 1860; named for James C. Wilson, a member of the Mier Expedition.

Recreation: Rancho de las Cabras mission ranch ruins, historic homes; the Stockdale watermelon jubilee in June; Floresville peanut festival in October.

Minerals: Oil, gas, clays.

Agriculture: Cattle, corn, sorghum, hay, cotton. Market value $68.6 million.

Vital Statistics, annual: Births, 512; deaths, 459; marriages, 183; divorces, 117.

Race/Ethnicity: Anglo, 56%; Hispanic, 38.7%; Black, 1.4%; Asian, 0.5%; Other, 3.5%.

FLORESVILLE (7,554) county seat; government/services, distribution, retail trade; hospital; parks.

Other towns include: **La Vernia** (1,154); **Pandora** (110); **Poth** (1,866) agriculture, commuting to San Antonio, bicycle ride in April; **Stockdale** (1,435) agriculture, commuting to San Antonio, museum, nature center; **Sutherland Springs** (420).

Population	51,257
Change from 2010	19.4%
Area (sq. mi.)	808.4

Land Area (sq. mi.)	803.7
Altitude (ft.)	300–804
Rainfall (in.)	31.6
Jan. mean min (°F)	40.9

July mean max (°F)	95.7
Civ. Labor	25,982
Unemployed	3.3%
Wages	$116,102,708
Per Capita Income	$55,762
Property Value	$8,278,154,634
Retail Sales	$627,420,855

Winkler County

Physical Features: Western county adjoining New Mexico on plains, partly sandy hills.

Economy: Oil and natural gas, ranching, prison, some farming.

History: Apache area until arrival of Comanches in the 1700s. Anglo-Americans began ranching in the 1880s. Oil discovered in 1926. Mexican migration increased after 1960. County named for Confederate Col. C.M. Winkler; created from Tom Green County in 1887; organized in 1910.

Recreation: Part of Monahans Sandhills State Park; Roy Orbison museum; Wink Sink, large sinkhole.

Minerals: Oil, gas.

Agriculture: Beef cattle. Market value $3.4 million.

Vital Statistics, annual: Births, 98; deaths, 89; marriages, 46; divorces, 15.

Race/Ethnicity: Anglo, 34.7%; Hispanic, 60.7%; Black, 1.8%; Asian, 1%; Other, 1.8%.

KERMIT (6,016) county seat; oil, gas, ranching, some farming; hospital; Celebration Days in September.

Wink (882) oil, gas, ranching.

Population	7,415
Change from 2010	4.3%
Area (sq. mi.)	841.3

Land Area (sq. mi.)	841.1
Altitude (ft.)	2,665–3,400
Rainfall (in.)	11.4
Jan. mean min (°F)	31.5
July mean max (°F)	97.1

Civ. Labor	3,977
Unemployed	3.9%
Wages	$74,490,229
Per Capita Income	$66,180
Property Value	$5,103,788,444
Retail Sales	$160,775,420

Wise County

Physical Features: Northwest county of rolling prairie, some oaks; clay, loam, sandy soils; Lake Bridgeport, Eagle Mountain Lake.

Economy: Petroleum, sand and gravel, agribusiness, many residents work in Fort Worth.

History: Caddo Indian groups. Delaware tribe present when Anglo-Americans arrived in the 1850s. County created in 1856 from Cooke County, organized the same year; named for Virginian, U.S. Sen. Henry A. Wise, who favored annexation of Texas.

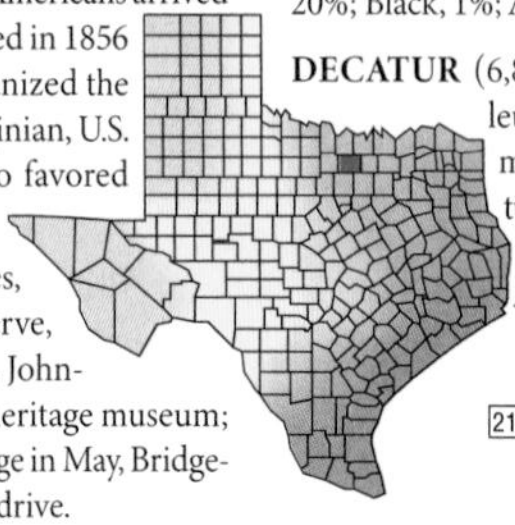

Recreation: Lake activities, hunting, exotic deer preserve, historical sites, Lyndon B. Johnson National Grassland, heritage museum; Decatur food truck challenge in May, Bridgeport Christmas in July toy drive.

Population	71,714
Change from 2010	21.3%
Area (sq. mi.)	922.6
Land Area (sq. mi.)	904.4
Altitude (ft.)	649–1,180
Rainfall (in.)	33.3
Jan. mean min (°F)	32.8
July mean max (°F)	94.1
Civ. Labor	34,311
Unemployed	3.5%
Wages	$319,893,100
Per Capita Income	$53,871
Property Value	$14,904,546,683
Retail Sales	$1,068,071,589

Minerals: Gas, oil, sand, gravel.

Agriculture: Beef cattle, hay, dairies, horses, wheat, goats. Market value $46.3 million.

Vital Statistics, annual: Births, 771; deaths, 784; marriages, 345; divorces, 297.

Race/Ethnicity: Anglo, 73.6%; Hispanic, 20%; Black, 1%; Asian, 0.5%; Other, 5%.

DECATUR (6,875) county seat; petroleum center, dairying, cattle marketing, some manufacturing; hospital.

BRIDGEPORT (5,972) trade center for lake resort, oil and gas production, manufacturing, prison release facility; time-share housing, art community.

Other towns include: **Alvord** (1,433); **Aurora** (1,449) sand and gravel, manufacturing, equestrian center, "alien crash" site; **Boyd** (1,481); **Chico** (996); **Greenwood** (76); **Lake Bridgeport** (349); **Newark** (1,149); **New Fairview** (1,438); **Paradise** (522); **Pecan Acres** (4,250); **Rhome** (1,737); **Runaway Bay** (1,659) tourism, fishing, boating, golf club, Firecracker Scramble in July; **Slidell** (175).

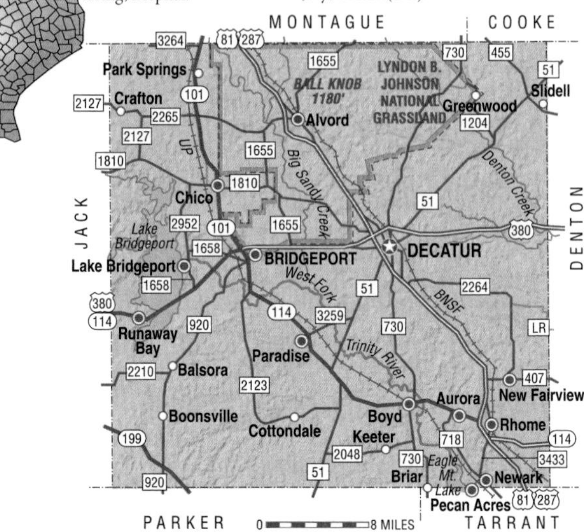

R.C. Mount House outside Chico is a Texas Historic Landmark Photo by Renelibrary, CC by SA 4.0

Wood County

Physical Features: Hilly northeastern county almost half forested; sandy to alluvial soils; drained by Sabine and tributaries; Lake Fork Reservoir, Lake Quitman, Lake Winnsboro, Lake Hawkins, Holbrook Lake.

Economy: Agribusiness, oil, gas, tourism.

History: Caddos, reduced by disease. Anglo-American settlement developed in the 1840s. County created from Van Zandt County in 1850, organized the same year; named for Gov. George T. Wood.

Recreation: Autumn trails; lake activities; hunting, fishing, birding; Gov. Hogg shrine and museum; historic sites; scenic drives; Mineola depot.

Minerals: Gas, oil, sand, gravel.

Agriculture: Cattle, dairies, poultry, forages, vegetables, nurseries. Market value $127.5 million. Timber production significant.

Vital Statistics, annual: Births, 362; deaths, 754; marriages, 191; divorces, 151.

Race/Ethnicity: Anglo, 80.1%; Hispanic, 10.9%; Black, 3.7%; Asian, 0.5%; Other, 4.8%.

QUITMAN (1,991) county seat; tourism, food processing, some manufacturing; hospital; botanical gardens.

MINEOLA (4,949) agriculture, railroad center (Amtrak), oil and gas, heritage and nature tourism; museum, library; nature preserve; Ironhorse Festival in September.

WINNSBORO (3,527, partly in Franklin County) poultry production, dairies, distribution, prison; hospital; arts center.

Other towns include: **Alba** (783, partly in Rains County); **Golden** (398) Sweet Potato festival in October; **Hawkins** (1,314) petroleum, water bottling, Jarvis Christian College, oil festival in October; **Holly Lake Ranch** (3,031); **Yantis** (414).

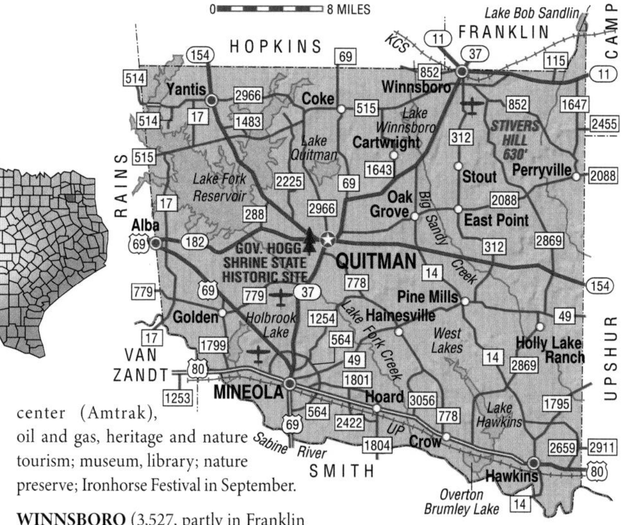

Population	45,875
Change from 2010	9.3%
Area (sq. mi.)	695.7

Land Area (sq. mi.)	645.2
Altitude (ft.)	270–630
Rainfall (in.)	46.5
Jan. mean min (°F)	35.3
July mean max (°F)	91.9
Civ. Labor	18,256
Unemployed	4.5%
Wages	$127,224,322
Per Capita Income	$47,546
Property Value	$7,395,177,514
Retail Sales	$652,795,080

Yoakum County

Physical Features: Western county is level to rolling; playas, draws; sandy, loam, chocolate soils.

Economy: Oil and gas, agriculture.

History: Comanche hunting area. Anglo-Americans began ranching in the 1890s. Oil discovered in 1936. Mexican migration increased in the 1950s. County named for Henderson Yoakum, pioneer historian; created from Bexar District in 1876; organized in 1907.

Recreation: Tsa Mo Ga museum at Plains; Plains watermelon roundup on Labor Day weekend.

Minerals: Oil, natural gas.

Agriculture: Cotton, peanuts (third in acreage), sorghum, wheat, watermelons, cattle. Some 90,000 acres irrigated. Market value $100.2 million.

Vital Statistics, annual: Births, 143; deaths, 91; marriages, 45; divorces, 30.

Race/Ethnicity: Anglo, 32.3%; Hispanic, 64.6%; Black, 0.7%; Asian, 0.6%; Other, 1.8%.

PLAINS (1,351) county seat; oil, agribusiness center.

DENVER CITY (4,390) center for oil, agriculture activities in two counties; hospital/medical services, library, museum; Annie Armstrong dugout shelter.

Population	7,607
Change from 2010	–3.5%
Area (sq. mi.)	799.7
Land Area (sq. mi.)	799.7
Altitude (ft.)	3,400–3,891
Rainfall (in.)	16.2

Jan. mean min (°F)	26.2
July mean max (°F)	91.9
Civ. Labor	3,286
Unemployed	4.0%
Wages	$58,478,297
Per Capita Income	$51,954

Property Value	$4,225,313,256
Retail Sales	$98,725,692

The old Nelson Realty building in Newcastle. Photo by Renelibrary, CC by SA 4.0

Young County

Physical Features: Hilly, broken; drained by Brazos and tributaries; Possum Kingdom Lake, Lake Graham.

Economy: Oil, agribusiness, tourism, hunting leases.

History: U.S. military outpost established in 1851. Site of Brazos Indian Reservation from 1854–1859 with Caddoes, Wacos, and other tribes. Anglo-American settlers arrived in the 1850s. County named for early Texan, Col. W.C. Young; created from Bosque and Fannin counties, and organized in 1856; reorganized in 1874.

Recreation: Lake activities; hunting; Fort Belknap; marker at oak tree in Graham where ranchers formed forerunner of Texas and Southwestern Cattle Raisers Association.

Minerals: Oil, gas, sand, and gravel.

Agriculture: Beef cattle; wheat is the chief crop, also hay, cotton, pecans, nursery plants. Market value $21.7 million.

Vital Statistics, annual: Births, 196; deaths, 333; marriages, 79; divorces, 54.

Race/Ethnicity: Anglo, 75%; Hispanic, 19.6%; Black, 1%; Asian, 0.5%; Other, 3.9%.

GRAHAM (8,765) county seat; oil and gas production, agriculture, tourism, government/services; hospital; old post office museum and art center; Crawfish and Cannons in April.

Other towns include: **Loving** (95); **Newcastle** (531) old coal-mining town; **Olney** (3,019) aluminum, varied manufacturing, hospital, Amputee Dove Hunt in September; **South Bend** (100).

Population	17,977
Change from 2010	-3.1%
Area (sq. mi.)	930.9
Land Area (sq. mi.)	914.5
Altitude (ft.)	995–1,522

Rainfall (in.)	29.3
Jan. mean min (°F)	31.8
July mean max (°F)	95.4
Civ. Labor	8,083
Unemployed	3.4%

Wages	$102,737,381
Per Capita Income	$58,602
Property Value	$3,222,474,261
Retail Sales	$348,462,582

Zapata County

Physical Features: South Texas county of rolling, brushy topography; broken by tributaries of Rio Grande; Falcon Reservoir.

Economy: Natural gas and oil production and services, wind farms, banking, tourism/Falcon Reservoir activities.

History: Coahuiltecan Indians in area when the ranch settlement of Nuestra Señora de los Dolores was established in 1750. Anglo-American migration increased after 1980. County named for Col. Antonio Zapata, pioneer rancher; created and organized in 1858 from Starr, Webb counties.

Recreation: Lake, state park, hunting, fishing, bird watching, golfing, Dolores Hacienda site, rock hunting, Los Corralitos Ranch, Trevino-Uribe Fort.

Minerals: Natural gas, caliche.

Agriculture: Beef cattle, sorghum, meat goats. Market value $6.3 million. Hunting/wildlife leases important.

Vital Statistics, annual: Births, 207; deaths, 127; marriages, 37; divorces, NA.

Race/Ethnicity: Anglo, 5.7%; Hispanic, 93.6%; Black, 0.1%; Asian, 0.1%; Other, 0.5%.

ZAPATA (4,928) county seat; tourism, agribusiness, oil, retirement center; clinic; fajita cook-off in November.

Other towns include: **Falcon Lake Estates** (896); **Lopeño** (42); **Medina** (5,004); **San Ygnacio** (582) historic buildings, museum.

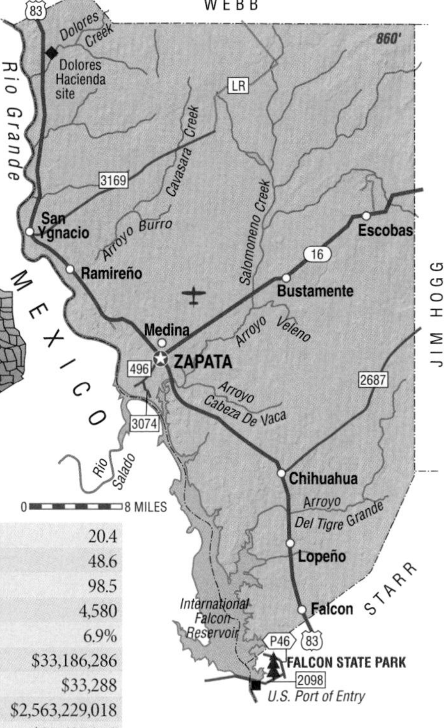

Population	13,908
Change from 2010	–0.8%
Area (sq. mi.)	1,058.0
Land Area (sq. mi.)	998.4
Altitude (ft.)	301–860

Rainfall (in.)	20.4
Jan. mean min (°F)	48.6
July mean max (°F)	98.5
Civ. Labor	4,580
Unemployed	6.9%
Wages	$33,186,286
Per Capita Income	$33,288
Property Value	$2,563,229,018
Retail Sales	$83,637,010

Zavala County

Physical Features: Southwestern county near Mexican border; rolling plains broken by much brush; Nueces, Leona, other streams; Upper Nueces Reservoir.

Economy: Agribusiness, food packaging, leading county in Winter Garden truck-farming area, government/services.

History: Coahuiltecan area; Apaches, Comanches arrived later. Ranching developed in the late 1860s. County created from Maverick and Uvalde counties in 1858; organized in 1884; named for Texas Revolutionary leader Lorenzo de Zavala.

Recreation: Hunting, fishing; spinach festival in November.

Minerals: Oil, natural gas.

Agriculture: Cattle, grains, vegetables, cotton, pecans. About 30,000 acres irrigated. Market value $66.6 million. Hunting leases important.

Vital Statistics, annual: Births, 145; deaths, 156; marriages, 30; divorces, NA.

Race/Ethnicity: Anglo, 5.9%; Hispanic, 92.5%; Black, 0.7%; Asian, 0.2%; Other, 0.7%.

CRYSTAL CITY (6,335) county seat; agribusiness, food processing, oil-field services; site of World War II detention center. Home of Popeye statue.

Other towns include: **Batesville** (1,090); **Chula Vista** (625); **La Pryor** (973).

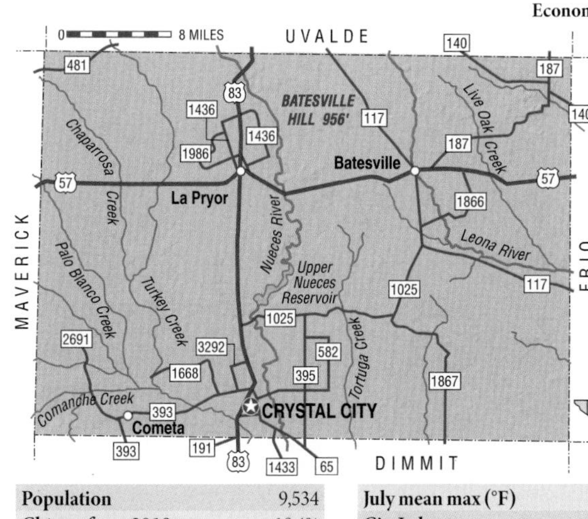

Population	9,534
Change from 2010	–18.4%
Area (sq. mi.)	1,301.7
Land Area (sq. mi.)	1,297.4
Altitude (ft.)	540–956
Rainfall (in.)	19.5
Jan. mean min (°F)	45.9

July mean max (°F)	97.6
Civ. Labor	3,395
Unemployed	8.6%
Wages	$33,793,552
Per Capita Income	$43,868
Property Value	$3,464,692,601
Retail Sales	$67,177,968

THE GREAT TEXAS LAND RUSH

We'd like to extend a big ***Thank You!*** to everyone who has adopted a town or county since our last edition. Adopters have their names and messages displayed on www.TexasAlmanac.com and a certificate to display in their homes.

Now available for adoption: lakes, colleges, and universities.

Go to www.GreatTexasLandRush.com and support the *Texas Almanac* today!

THE GREAT TEXAS LAND RUSH
STAKE YOUR CLAIM

Abbott — The Gayle Family
Abilene — Jane and Eileen Suggs
Abilene — Tasha Rose Williams
Ables Springs — Antonio Maffei
Acme — Richard D. Henize
Ad Hall — Henry D. Hall Jr.
Agua Nueva — Mr. A.C. Jones IV, Jones Ranch LLC
Alamo — Yolanda Katherine Lopez Parker
Aledo — Magnus Research Group
Alexander — John Lea
Alice — David Rice
Allison — Randy Hankins
Alpine — Larry Winn
Amarillo — Joseph & Mary Hughes
Ambrose — Ambrose Archer Wuebel
Amy — Amy Ivy
Anadarko — Ricardo Cruz
Andice — The Lucero and Feldhege Family
Anneville — John Misner
Armstrong County — Bryan Thompson
Arneckeville — Ashley DeAtley
Arvana — Andrew Moore
Austin — Corrine B. Richardson
Austwell — Humberto Gonzales Guerra
Azle — DeAnn Dunaway
Backbone Valley — Brandon Cate
Balch Springs — Josh Balch
Balcones Heights — Matt Murphy
Ballard — Michelle Ballard
Balmorhea — Blue Barrel Consulting
Bastrop — Debra DeWitt Jordan
Beattie — John Beatty
Bedford — Linda J. Dennis
Beeville — Carolyn Miakashi
Belleview — Karl Duncan
Ben Arnold — Jeanne, Danny, Vickie, and Angie Matous
Benbrook — Magnus Research Group
Bennett — Paige Nash
Big Spring — Caroline Reaves-Powers
Black Jack — Edwin Holly Toran Jr.
Bloomburg — Kathryn Hurt (Peacock)
Bolivar Peninsula — Sue Kirkpatrick
Bovine Bend — Allens Creek Storage
Brodie — Tyler Seveson
Brooke — Brooke G.
Brushie Prairie — Morgan Putman
Buckeye — Linda Irene Alaniz Garcia LaMotte
Buda — John & Sakiko Willis
Buffalo — Susan Pense, President of the Buffalo Chamber of Commerce
Buffalo Gap — John Layne Entertainment LLC
Byers — TFR Bronzes
Cain City — Katrina Cain
Calliham — Christine Stephenson Forrest
Cameron — The Matous Kids
Cameron County — Weird Austin Productions
Cameron County — Amanda L. Clements
Canadian — Sulaimaan Bhatti
Candelaria — Corinne S. Candelaria
Centerville — Teresa Berryman Johnson
Chancey — Heather Moody
Chico — Martha Anne "Marti" Moser
Christoval — John Lea
Cistern — Kevin and Debra DeWitt Jordan
Clairemont — Michael L. Upchurch
Clay County — TFR Bronzes
Cloud — The Texas Telegram Telegraph and Donald Lyles
Cochran — C C Slaughter Farms
Coldspring — Edward A. Jones
College Station — Kasen Hobson
Comanche — Lezlee Liljenberg
Corpus Christi — Manuel G. Pena
Corpus Christi — Steven and Jaci Weston
Corrigan — Sally Cockrell Carter
Crabapple — John Lea
Crane — DG Smith CHS, Since 1929
Creamlevel — Jane Hill Bonham
Creedmoor — Peter Pehl II
Crews — Sinikka Nielsen Melvin
Crockett — A Downes Descendent
Culberson — Spoiled By Jesus Ministries
Cut And Shoot — Zander Parker
Daingerfield — Tony and Aretha Evans
Dale — Emilie Jones Siarkiewicz
Denton — John Jenkins
Denton — Alan Berggren
Diddy Wa Diddy — Kristoff Storm
Ding Dong — Eric the cat
Doak Springs — Rachel M. Anderson
Dobyville — Steve Leftwich
Double Horn — The Maxwell Family
Dreyer — Allan Rhys Dreyer
Dubina — Ronnie Martin Janecka
Dublin — Carol Faris Gordy
Duffau — Kathy Glasscock Bahlmann
Eagle Pass — Walter Pophin
East Sweden — Mandie de Leon
Easterly — Ivy Easterly
Ecleto — Eduardo Mendoza
Edna — Elizabeth Mesa
Egypt — Jackson Family
El Campo — James W. McClure, Jr.
Elliott — Al & Barbara Elliott
Elliott's Ferry — Dolly Anna Ruth Elliott-Hames-Hubbard
El Paso — The Rodeo Parade LLC
Emille — Callie Young
Erath — Carol Faris Gordy
Erin — Erin McKool
Exray — Angela Little Bozarth
Fairview — Annette Tillman Williams
Fayette County — Cathy Mace Frietsch
Fayetteville — Linda J. Dennis
Fodice — Baker Wilbanks Lyle Family
Fort Davis — Dr. Billy Ingram
Fort Elliott — Al & Barbara Elliott
Fosterville — Alexis Bartleet
Fredericksburg — Liebeskind, A Children's Boutique
Freeneytown — George Edward Freeney Jr.
Freeport — Koressa Gregory
Frenstat — Elizabeth Hubenak
Fruitvale — R&B
Gilleland Creek — The fifth generation Texans and the oldest children Gary Gilleland
Gillespie County — Friends of Gillespie County Country Schools, Inc.
Gilmer — Ann Stembridge Bates
Gladewater — Walker Manor Bed & Breakfast
Gladstell — William D. Smith Jr.
Gladys — Glover Family Alliance, LLC
Goldsmith — Mike Goldsmith
Goldthwaite — Kerry Reed Jones
Goliad — Samantha McMillan
Grapeland — Danalee Herring
Grapevine — M.E. & Barbara Musgrove
Greta — Lisa Ann Byrd Putnam
Groom — Tom and Connie Britten
Guajillo — Dolores Pompa
Gum Island — Bubblegum Boys Fantasy Football League
Hail — Rachel VanRoekel
Happy — Mike Kaminski
Harlingen — Liza M. Saldana
Harlow — Matthew and Alicia Robinson
Harris County — The Hughes Family
Helotes — Edna Marnock Smith
Hemming — Glen & Ellen McBride
Hicks — Carole Hicks Welker
Highland Village — John and Jerri Lynn Randall III
Hillsboro — Brian Thompson
Hobart — Michael S. Goodrich
Hochheim — Betty Raetzsch-Saenz
Holliday — Michelle Pounds
Honey Grove — The Pinckards
Hopkinsville — Larry Johnson
Irving — Irving Heritage Society
Ivan — Ivan Albert Palacios
Ivy — Ivy Easterly
Jardin — Angels Under Cover
Jefferson — Crystal Storm Ortiz
Katemcy — John Beatty
Katy — ssteezybreezyy
Kenney — Bill Kenney Productions
Killeen — Zachary Tomaka
Kirk — Robert E. & Judy D. Kirk
Kolls — Tyler Severson
Kolls — Adam M.F. Kolls
Kopperl — Shannon Watts
Kosciusko — Peggy Kotara-Spore
Kyle — Carol
Kyote — K. Jenschke
La Bahia — Martin P. Eustis

Ladonia — Jody & Kristina Rowell
Lago Vista — Ender Guardian
La Grange — Texas Heroes Museum
Lake Dunlap — L.C. and Tiffiny Fuller
Lake Worth — Jesse Vasquez Jr.
La Marque — Joseph and Sarah Lowry
Lancaster — Tony & Aretha Evans
Lanely — Robert Steven Lane
Lantana — Koen & Nyle Vautherot
Laredo — Koressa Gregory
Lautz — Lindsay Allan Lautz
Lime City — A-No-1
Lincoln — Demetria Anderson Cooper
Little New York — Nichole
Livingston — Trisha Barton & Family
Lodi — Susan Stanelle
Loebau — Chad Kunkel and Loebau Store
Long Branch — Willie L (Castleberry) McDaniel
Los Ojuelos — Dolores Pompa
Lovelady — Anne Toney
Loveless — Cailín Heffernan & Henry Aronson
Lyles — Private Collection of Robert Lee Matta Family
Macdona — Harding Macdona
Magnolia — Josey Reynolds & Helen Vandergriff
Manor — Robert Battaile
Mansfield — Kimberly Roe Yuhasz
Mantua — Amanda McAdams
Marfa — La República De Texas
Marjorie — Karen Slagle
Mart — The Agape Home LLC
Martha — Leo Brown
Martha — Leo & Kim Brown
Matagorda — Sharon Wyatt
McAdoo — William Blake Vejar
McGirk — John and Terry McLaughlin
McKay — Shar McKay
Melvin — Cody E. Neal and Clayton J. Neal
Mentz — David and Jane Braden
Mercedes — 5
Meridian — Don and Sylvia Hartless
Middleton — Teresa Berryman Johnson
Midland — Edward The Who
Midland — Samuel John Jobe
Mifflin — Amanda Kowalski
Mims Chapel — Mara Lee Moats
Mineola — Jennifer Flynt
Mingus — Janet Lynn Gatejen and Timothy Patrick Grieve
Mission Valley — Chad Sherman
Mont — David Blackburn
Moravia — Eric and Teri Blahuta
Morgan's Point — Claude Hunter
Mullin — Grosenbacher Farm & Ranch
Mutt and Jeff — One Step Past
Nameless — Chris Parker
Natalie — Natalie
Needville — Regina Rash
New Braunfels — McKenna Beseda
New Harp — Randell Johnson + Janet Johnson
New Sweden — Betty Saenz
North Elm — Sammy Blocker
North Waco — Walter Pophin
Oak Point — Dena Meek
Oakalla — Wanda Williams Langford
Oatmeal — Rob Pantzer
O'Donnell — TTM
Oilton — 24X IAM. Isaac Austin McMahan
Old San Antonio — Monica L. Rollins
Old Troy — Troy Armstrong-Meyer
Onalaska — Jesus G. Mora & Family
Oplin — Cody and Tami Miller
Orange — John Lea
Orange Grove — Mr. & Mrs Albert Sanchez Jr.
Otis Chalk — Albert Chalk McGehee Jr.
Ovalo — John Lea
Pampa — Mary Eloise Batts
Pancake — Michael S. Ward
Panorama Village — Rick and Jeanie Rose
Paris — Hezzie Paget
Park — The Crouse Family
Pattison — Mary Obois
Peach — James and Cindy Palomo
Pecos — Brian Thompson
Peerless — Laura Lindley
Petty — Matt and Aron Allee
Pioneer — Laura Molloy
Poolville — Turner Ranch
Postoak — The Sparkman Family
Quakertown — Christina Rene Gonzales
Ratibor — Hunter's Creek Land & Cattle
Red Star — Jody Wilkerson
Refugio — Lisa Ann Byrd Putnam
Reno — William S. Heuberger
Riceville — Sheri Cortez
Richmond — Matthew Driggers
Rockport — John David Kroll
Rockville — Dave McMullen
Rockwall — Cindy Palomo
Rocky Well — Claude Hunter
Roganville — Prewitt Reunion
Rosebud — Vickie Matous Eberth
Rosenberg — Danny M. Diaz
Round Rock — Nola Stover Beck
Round Top — Vicki Wallace and John Callaway
Roundtree — James Roundtree
Rusk — The Rev. Dr. T. Randall Smith
Sabinal — Maria Sicily Guido
Saint Jo — Richard and Hollis Notgrass
Sam Fordyce — Thomas G Fordyce
San Angelo — Larry Winn
Sanco — T Farm & Ranch (Cody & Jennifer)
San Fernando de Bexar — Yolanda Katherine Lopez Parker
San Geronimo — Four Leaf Spice Company
San Ignacio de Loyola — Yolanda Katherine Lopez Parker
San Luis — Christopher Davis & Amy Davis
San Marcos — Richard Germer
San Saba — Carl Carter
Sand Hill — The Stargell Family
Sarahville de Viesca — Rancho Viesca/ Mark M. Ellison
Saspamco — Murillo Family
Schulenburg — ESG Natural Resources LLC
Scottsville — Scott Owens
Seymour — Whiteside Museum of Natural History
Shelby County — Wayne Adams
Sierra Blanca — Guillermina Gonjon
Slaughter — Descendants of J.M. and Mattie Lee King
Socorro — Celina Padilla
Sonora — Edward A. Jones
South Padre Island — Ivy Easterly
Spanish Fort — David Lee Ballinger
Sprinkle — Audrina Torres
Sterley — Nancy D. Henderson
Stockard — Dan R. Stockard
Styx — Paul Godwin
Sugar Land — Regina Rash
Sugar Land — Richard Germer
Tell — Jeanette Hightower Whitehead
The Woodlands — Lauren Doss
Thornton — For Elisea Lopez Villa
Thrift — Cynthia, Ivy, and Roy Wood
Tiki Island — Kevin King
Tilden — Anne Evelyn Swenson
Tivett — Tim & Evelyn Killion
Todd City — Elizabeth Todd Sampley
Tolar — Hugo Nicolas Sibrian
Tom Bean — Bobby Glen Yowell Jr.
Travis County — Weird Austin Productions
Tucker — Officials of Tucker Land, Anderson County
Turkey — Jim Gatlin family
Turnbaugh Corner — The Turnbaugh Family of Pittsburgh, Pennsylvania
Tuscaloosa — Scotty Good
Utopia — Angela Durbon
Uvalde — Dennis Clark
Uvalde County — Dennis Clark
Van Alstyne — Dr. Susana E. Mendez, OMD, MBA, ABMPP, CAS, L.AC, LCDC, MAC
Van Alstyne — Amanda McAdams
Waco — Mark Browning
Waco — William Heck
Walburg — Phillip Theodore Schneider
Walker Station — Marcella Dean
Warren City — P.R. Davis Enterprises, Go Local 4it.
Weatherford — Matthew Lindsey
Weeping Mary — John Lea
White City — Calvary Bible Church on the Divide
White Settlement — Mike Arnold Jr.
Whiteflat — The Jack Spray Family
Whitewright — Molly Malinda M. Reed
Wichita Falls — Christine Stephenson Forrest
Williamson County — Waylon and Wyatt Fowles
Willis — Therese Palermo & Bernie Hughes
Wills Point — Dakota DeBoard
Wimberley — Margaux Vautherot
Winchester — Lone Star Back Roads, LLC
Word — Nola Stover Beck
Worthy — Yolanda Katherine Lopez Parker
Yarboro — Frank and Dorothy Wichmann Family
Yowell — Charlotte Yowell
Zipp City — The Williams Family
Zita — J. R.
Zodiac — Jessica Pitman
Zorn — David B. Zorn

THE GREAT TEXAS LAND RUSH STAKE YOUR CLAIM

POPULATION

POPULATION 2020 & 2021

TEN LARGEST U.S. METRO AREAS

SPECIAL THANKS TO JOHNNY CARRABBA FAMILY OF RESTAURANTS
FOR SPONSORING THIS CHAPTER OF THE TEXAS ALMANAC

A BARGE OF TOURISTS ON THE SAN ANTONIO RIVERWALK.
PHOTO BY CAROL M. HIGHSMITH, PUBLIC DOMAIN.

Population 2020 and 2021

Population: Numbers in parentheses are from the 2020 U.S. census. The Census Bureau counts only incorporated cities and a few unincorporated towns called Census Designated Places. Names of the incorporated cities are in capital letters, e.g., "ABBOTT".

Population figures at the far right for incorporated cities and CDPs are U.S. Census or American Community Survey (ACS) estimates for 2021. The population figure given for other towns is an estimate received from local officials through a Texas Almanac survey.

When no 2020 census was conducted for a newly incorporated city, these places show "(nc)" for "not counted" in place of a 2020 population figure.

Location: The county in which the town is located follows the name of the town. If more than one county is listed, the town is principally in the first-named county, e.g., "ABERNATHY, Hale, Lubbock".

Businesses: The number following the county name indicates the number of active sales tax permit holders as of July 2023 as reported by the state comptroller.

For example, "ABBOTT, Hill, 33" means Abbott in Hill County had 33 businesses.

Post Offices: Places with post offices, as of July 2023, are marked with an asterisk (*), e.g., "*Afton".

Town, County . . . . Pop. 2021

A

*ABBOTT, Hill, 33 (352) 357
*ABERNATHY, Hale, Lubbock, 100 (2,865) 2,804
*ABILENE, Taylor, Jones, 4,199 (125,182) 125,070
Ables Springs, Kaufman 20
Abner, Kaufman 75
Abram, Hidalgo (1,108) 1,671
Acala, Hudspeth (11) 36
*Ace, Polk, 2 40
*ACKERLY, Dawson, Martin, 19 (264) 265
Acme, Hardeman 7
Acton, Hood, 5 1,129
Acuff, Lubbock, 1 152
Acworth, Red River 50
Adams Gardens, Cameron 350
Adams Store, Panola 12
Adamsville, Lampasas 75
Addicks, Harris . . . . . . [part of Houston]
Addielou, Red River 31
*ADDISON, Dallas, 1,381 (16,661) 17,012
Adell, Parker 100
*Adkins, Bexar, 242 400
Admiral, Callahan 18
Adobes, Presidio 5
*ADRIAN, Oldham, 8 (128) 129
Advance, Parker 100
*Afton, Dickens, 4 15
Agnes, Parker 60
*AGUA DULCE, Nueces, 18 (685) . . . 688
Agua Dulce, El Paso (3,218) 2,633
Agua Nueva, Jim Hogg 5
Aguilares, Webb (6) 6
*Aiken, Floyd, 1 52
Aiken, Shelby 150
Aikin Grove, Red River 15
Airport Heights, Starr (151) 146
Airport Road Addition, Brooks, (96) 152
Airville, Bell 65
Alabama-Coushatta, Polk 572
*ALAMO, Hidalgo, 745 (19,493) . . 20,017
Alamo Alto, El Paso 19
Alamo Beach, Calhoun (254) 454
ALAMO HEIGHTS, Bexar, 99 (7,357) 7,392
Alanreed, Gray, 2 (23) 50
Alazan, Nacogdoches 100
*ALBA, Wood, Rains, 125 (473) 483
*ALBANY, Shackelford, 117 (1,854) 1,927
Albert, Gillespie 25
Albion, Red River 52
Alderbranch, Anderson 3
Aldine, Harris (15,999) 15,887
*ALEDO, Parker, 606 (4,858) 5,380
Aleman, Hamilton 50
Alexander, Erath 40
Aley, Henderson 45
Alfred, Jim Wells (82) 274
Algerita, San Saba 10
Algoa, Galveston, 4 135
*ALICE, Jim Wells, 787 (17,891) . . . 17,761
Alice Acres, Jim Wells (465) 241
*Alief, Harris . . . . [part of Houston]
Allamoore, Hudspeth, 4 10
*ALLEN, Collin, 3,048 (104,627) 106,874
Allenfarm, Brazos 35
Allenhurst, Matagorda 72
Allen's Chapel, Fannin 30
Allen's Point, Fannin 40
Allentown, Angelina 800
Alleyton, Colorado, 30 165
*Allison, Wheeler, 5 (125) 188
Allmon, Floyd 24
Allred, Yoakum 90
ALMA, Ellis (373) 392
Almira, Cass 30
*ALPINE, Brewster, 400 (6,035) 5,815
Alsa, Van Zandt 30
*Altair, Colorado, 8 30
*ALTO, Cherokee, 80 (1,027) 1,033
Alto Bonito Heights, Starr (296) 387
Altoga, Collin 137
ALTON, Hidalgo, 305 (18,198) . . . 18,860
Alum Creek, Bastrop 70
*ALVARADO, Johnson, 635 (4,739) 5,111
*ALVIN, Brazoria, 1,365 (27,098) . . 27,576
*ALVORD, Wise, 104 (1,351) 1,433
Amada Acres, Starr (79) 79
Amargosa, Jim Wells (305) 125
*AMARILLO, Potter, Randall, 7,039 (200,393) 201,234
Amaya, Zavala (108) 51
Ambia, Lamar 16
Ambrose, Grayson, 1 90
AMES, Liberty, 2 (937) 1,009
Ames, Coryell 10
*AMHERST, Lamb, 16 (678) 664
Amherst, Lamar 125
Amistad, Val Verde (24) 51
Ammannsville, Fayette 137
Amphion, Atascosa 26
Amsterdam, Brazoria, 1 193
Anacua, Starr (24) 24
Anadarko, Rusk 30
*ANAHUAC, Chambers, 132 (1,980) 1,962
Anchor, Brazoria 150
*ANDERSON, Grimes, 133 (193) . . . 195
Anderson Mill, Williamson, Travis . . . . [part of Austin]
Ander-Weser-Kilgore, Goliad 322
Andice, Williamson 300
*ANDREWS, Andrews, 673 (13,487) 13,370
*ANGLETON, Brazoria, 749 (19,429) 19,401
ANGUS, Navarro, 1 (444) 457
*ANNA, Collin, 516 (16,896) 20,243
Annaville, Nueces . . . . [part of Corpus Christi]
ANNETTA, Parker, 6 (3,041) 3,153

The Crockett Street entertainment district in downtown Beaumont features five historic buildings. Photo by Nicholas Henderson, Flickr, CC 2.0

Town, County	Pop. 2021
ANNETTA NORTH, Parker, 1 (554)	572
ANNETTA SOUTH, Parker, 1 (621)	637
*ANNONA, Red River, 11 (184)	183
*ANSON, Jones, 115 (2,294)	2,347
Antelope, Jack	65
ANTHONY, El Paso (Dona Ana Co., NM), 136 (3,671)	3,665
Antioch, Delta	10
Antioch, Madison	15
Antioch, Cass	45
Antioch Colony, Hays	25
*ANTON, Hockley, 31 (907)	883
APPLEBY, Nacogdoches (552)	548
*Apple Springs, Trinity, 25	350
*AQUILLA, Hill, 26 (101)	104
*ARANSAS PASS, San Patricio, Aransas, 433 (7,941)	8,011
Arbala, Hopkins	41
Arcadia, Shelby, 1	35
*ARCHER CITY, Archer, 70 (1,601)	1,584
ARCOLA, Fort Bend, 81 (2,034)	2,156
Arden, Irion	7
Argo, Titus	90
*ARGYLE, Denton, 592 (4,403)	4,707
*ARLINGTON, Tarrant, 9,842 (394,266)	392,786
Armstrong, Kenedy, 3	4
Armstrong, Bell	25
Arneckeville, DeWitt	50
Arnett, Hockley	5
Arnett, Coryell	15
*ARP, Smith, 89 (892)	926
Arroyo City, Cameron, 1	600
Arroyo Colorado Estates, Cameron, (833)	982
Arroyo Gardens, Cameron (420)	167
*Art, Mason, 4	14
Artesia Wells, La Salle	35
*Arthur City, Lamar, 24	180
Arvana, Dawson	8
Asa, McLennan	46
Ash, Houston	19
Ashby, Matagorda	60
*ASHERTON, Dimmit, 27 (722)	718
Ashland, Upshur	45

Town, County	Pop. 2021
Ashtola, Donley	20
Ashwood, Matagorda	132
Asia, Polk	83
*ASPERMONT, Stonewall, 57 (789)	759
Atascocita, Harris, 66 (88,174)	84,222
*Atascosa, Bexar, 121	600
Ater, Coryell	12
*ATHENS, Henderson, 842 (12,857)	12,890
*ATLANTA, Cass, 270 (5,433)	5,409
Atlas, Lamar	28
Atoy, Cherokee	50
*AUBREY, Denton, 769 (5,006)	6,490
Augusta, Houston	40
AURORA, Wise, 28 (1,390)	1,449
*AUSTIN, Travis, Williamson, 42,140 (961,855)	964,177
Austonio, Houston	37
*AUSTWELL, Refugio, 9 (118)	118
Authon, Parker	15
*Avalon, Ellis, 5	400
*AVERY, Red River, 37 (421)	426
*AVINGER, Cass, 63 (371)	373
Avoca, Jones, 6	121
*Axtell, McLennan, 53	300
*AZLE, Tarrant, Parker, 931 (13,369)	13,518

B

Town, County	Pop. 2021
Back, Gray	6
*Bacliff, Galveston, 181 (9,677)	10,567
*Bagwell, Red River, 9	150
*BAILEY, Fannin, 4 (220)	231
BAILEY'S PRAIRIE, Brazoria, 3 (775)	781
Baileyville, Milam	32
Bainer, Lamb	10
Bainville, Karnes	8
*BAIRD, Callahan, 99 (1,479)	1,498
Baker, Floyd	28
Bakersfield, Pecos, 1	9
*BALCH SPRINGS, Dallas, 620 (27,685)	27,160
BALCONES HEIGHTS, Bexar, 81 (2,746)	2,725
Bald Hill, Angelina	100
Bald Prairie, Robertson	40

Town, County	Pop. 2021
*BALLINGER, Runnels, 193 (3,619)	3,580
*BALMORHEA, Reeves, 40 (408)	398
Balsora, Wise	50
B and E, Starr (489)	177
*BANDERA, Bandera, 501 (829)	839
Bandera Falls, Bandera	90
*BANGS, Brown, 59 (1,540)	1,542
*Banquete, Nueces, 12 (745)	425
Barbarosa, Guadalupe	46
Barclay, Falls	58
*BARDWELL, Ellis, 4 (625)	637
*Barker, Harris, 1	2,500
*Barksdale, Edwards, 11 (91)	24
Barnes, Polk	75
*Barnhart, Irion, 10	110
Barnum, Polk	50
Barrera, Starr (122)	329
Barrett, Harris (5,223)	3,668
*BARRY, Navarro, 32 (220)	223
*BARSTOW, Ward, 15 (265)	257
*BARTLETT, Williamson, Bell, 72 (1,633)	1,643
Barton Corners, Lipscomb	4
Barton Creek, Travis (3,356)	3,183
BARTONVILLE, Denton, 89 (1,725)	1,771
Barwise, Floyd	16
*Basin, Brewster	30
Bassett, Bowie	100
*BASTROP, Bastrop, 1,138 (9,688)	10,434
Bateman, Bastrop	12
*Batesville, Zavala, 13 (787)	1,090
Batesville, Red River	14
*Batson, Hardin, 34	140
Battle, McLennan	100
Baxter, Henderson	150
*BAY CITY, Matagorda, 653 (18,061)	17,882
Baylor Lake, Childress	50
BAYOU VISTA, Galveston, 15 (1,763)	1,755
*BAYSIDE, Refugio, 7 (275)	275
*BAYTOWN, Harris, Chambers, 2,578 (83,701)	82,480
BAYVIEW, Cameron, 18 (475)	501
Bazette, Navarro	30

Town, County	Pop. 2021
BEACH CITY, Chambers, 48 (3,221)	3,208
BEAR CREEK, Hays, 1 (397)	418
Bear Creek Ranch, Dallas (1,787)	2,247
*BEASLEY, Fort Bend, 61 (608)	599
Beattie, Comanche	48
*BEAUMONT, Jefferson, 3,953 (115,282)	112,556
Beauxart Gardens, Jefferson, (1,064)	864
Beaver Creek, Burleson (910)	1,176
Beaver Dam, Bowie	10
Bebe, Gonzales, 2	42
Becker, Kaufman	300
*BECKVILLE, Panola, 48 (722)	736
Becton, Lubbock	62
*BEDFORD, Tarrant, 1,340 (49,928)	49,187
*BEDIAS, Grimes, 67 (361)	370
BEE CAVE, Travis, 416 (9,144)	9,028
Bee House, Coryell	15
*BEEVILLE, Bee, 544 (13,669)	13,641
Belcherville, Montague	25
Belfalls, Bell	30
Belgrade, Newton	20
Belk, Lamar	58
*BELLAIRE, Harris, 643 (17,202)	16,983
Bell Branch, Ellis	125
*BELLEVUE, Clay, 34 (289)	289
*BELLMEAD, McLennan, 176 (10,494)	10,575
*BELLS, Grayson, 101 (1,521)	1,540
*BELLVILLE, Austin, 408 (4,206)	4,108
Belmena, Milam	15
Belmont, Gonzales, 2	55
Belott, Houston	101
Belterra, Hays (6,170)	7,736
*BELTON, Bell, 1,162 (23,054)	23,845
Ben Arnold, Milam (117)	49
*BENAVIDES, Duval, 20 (1,183)	1,195
*Ben Bolt, Jim Wells, 7 (1,662)	1,555
*BENBROOK, Tarrant, 658 (24,520)	24,605
Benchley, Robertson, Brazos	110
*Bend, San Saba, Lampasas, 3	115
*Ben Franklin, Delta, 3	60
Ben Hur, Limestone	42
*BENJAMIN, Knox, 10 (196)	200
Benjamin Perez, Starr (29)	121
Bennett, Parker	120
Benoit, Runnels	10
Bentonville, Jim Wells, 1	15
*Ben Wheeler, Van Zandt, 179 (456)	2,026
*Berclair, Goliad, 3	253
Berea, Houston	41
Berea, Marion	200
Bergheim, Kendall, 29	1,213
Berlin, Washington	40
Bernardo, Colorado	155
BERRYVILLE, Henderson, 1 (824)	852
*BERTRAM, Burnet, Williamson, 193 (1,616)	1,764
Bessmay, Jasper	400
Best, Reagan	2
Bethany, Panola	50
Bethel, Runnels	20
Bethel, Anderson	75

Town, County	Pop. 2021
Bethel, Henderson	125
Bethlehem, Upshur	75
Bettie, Upshur	110
Beulah, Limestone	12
BEVERLY HILLS, McLennan, 41 (1,878)	1,876
BEVIL OAKS, Jefferson, 4 (1,089)	1,058
Bevilport, Jasper	12
Beyersville, Williamson	80
Biardstown, Lamar	75
*Bigfoot, Frio, 20 (480)	1,390
Big Hill, Limestone	9
*BIG LAKE, Reagan, 167 (2,965)	2,850
*BIG SANDY, Upshur, 149 (1,231)	1,263
*BIG SPRING, Howard, 921 (26,144)	25,735
Big Thicket Estates, Liberty, Polk, (514)	615
Big Valley, Mills	35
*BIG WELLS, Dimmit, 13 (483)	487
Biloxi, Newton	75
Birch, Burleson	200
Birome, Hill	30
Birthright, Hopkins	100
Biry, Medina	24
*BISHOP, Nueces, 69 (3,174)	3,155
BISHOP HILLS, Potter (211)	207
*Bivins, Cass, 14 (153)	154
Bixby, Cameron (352)	412
Black, Parmer	100
Blackfoot, Anderson	50
Black Hill, Atascosa	60
Black Hills, Navarro	80
Black Jack, Robertson	45
Black Jack, Cherokee	47
Black Oak, Hopkins	150
*BLACKWELL, Nolan, Coke, 28 (258)	254
Blair, Taylor	25
Blanchard, Polk	500
*BLANCO, Blanco, 381 (1,682)	1,780
Blanconia, Bee, Refugio	100
Bland Lake, San Augustine	80
*BLANKET, Brown, 31 (369)	369
Blanton, Hill	5

Town, County	Pop. 2021
Bleakwood, Newton	450
*Bledsoe, Cochran (56)	132
*Bleiblerville, Austin, 5	125
*Blessing, Matagorda, 43 (856)	249
Blevins, Falls	36
Blewett, Uvalde	7
Blodgett, Titus	60
*BLOOMBURG, Cass, 17 (321)	324
*BLOOMING GROVE, Navarro, 31 (857)	878
*Bloomington, Victoria, 29 (2,082)	1,321
*BLOSSOM, Lamar, 86 (1,402)	1,401
Blue, Lee	75
Blueberry Hill, Bee (844)	688
*Bluegrove, Clay, 1	135
BLUE MOUND, Tarrant, 47 (2,393)	2,359
*BLUE RIDGE, Collin, 124 (1,180)	1,187
Bluetown, Cameron, 1 (491)	458
*Bluff Dale, Erath, 59 (151)	82
*Bluffton, Llano, 7	75
*BLUM, Hill, 45 (383)	388
Bluntzer, Nueces	150
Boca Chica Village, Cameron	34
*BOERNE, Kendall, 2,153 (17,850)	19,109
*BOGATA, Red River, 66 (1,074)	1,089
Bois d'Arc, Anderson	25
Bois d'Arc, Rains	6
Bold Springs, Polk	100
Boles Home, Hunt	100
*Boling, Wharton, 70 (930)	1,148
Bolivar, Denton	140
Bolivar Peninsula, Galveston, (2,769)	2,829
Bomarton, Baylor	15
Bonami, Jasper	12
Bonanza, Hopkins	26
Bonanza Hills, Webb (61)	54
*BONHAM, Fannin, 461 (10,408)	10,559
Bonita, Montague	25
BONNEY, Brazoria (180)	183
Bonnie View, Refugio	97

Ten Largest U.S. Metro Areas

Rank	Metro Area	2020 U.S. Census
1.	New York-Newark-Jersey City (NY-NJ-PA)	20,140,470
2.	Los Angeles-Long Beach-Anaheim (CA)	13,200,998
3.	Chicago-Naperville-Elgin (IL-IN-WI)	9,618,502
4.	**Dallas-Fort Worth-Arlington (TX)**	**7,637,387**
5.	**Houston-The Woodlands-Sugar Land (TX)**	**7,122,240**
6.	Washington-Arlington-Alexandria (DC-VA-MD-WV)	6,385,162
7.	Philadelphia-Camden-Wilmington (PA-NJ-DE-MD)	6,245,051
8.	Miami-Ft. Lauderdale-Pompano Beach (FL)	6,138,333
9.	Atlanta-Sandy Springs-Alpharetta (GA)	6,089,815
10.	Boston-Cambridge-Newton (MA-NH)	4,948,203

Source: U.S. Census

Town, County	Pop. 2021
Bonus, Wharton	44
*Bon Wier, Newton, 15	375
*BOOKER, Lipscomb, Ochiltree, 58 (1,437)	1,365
Boonsville, Wise	52
Booth, Fort Bend, 1	50
Bootleg, DeafSmith	10
Borden, Colorado	20
*BORGER, Hutchinson, 431 (12,551)	12,419
Bosqueville, McLennan	200
Boston, Bowie, 1	[part of New Boston]
Botines, Webb (149)	17
*BOVINA, Parmer, 47 (1,699)	1,703
Bowers City, Gray	10
*BOWIE, Montague, 419 (5,448)	5,534
Bowman, Archer	300
Bowser, San Saba	20
Box Canyon, Val Verde (29)	90
Box Church, Limestone	45
Boxelder, Red River	100
Boxwood, Upshur	20
Boyce, Ellis	125
*BOYD, Wise, 194 (1,416)	1,481
Boyd, Fannin	105
*Boys Ranch, Oldham, 2 (173)	150
Boz-Bethel, Ellis	100
Bozar, Mills	9
Brachfield, Rusk	40
Bracken, Comal, 10	95
*BRACKETTVILLE, Kinney, 85 (1,341)	1,400
Brad, Palo Pinto	16
Bradford, Anderson	60
Bradshaw, Taylor	61
*BRADY, McCulloch, 249 (5,118)	5,032
Branch, Collin	530
Branchville, Milam	127
*Brandon, Hill, 1	75
*Brashear, Hopkins, 25	280
*BRAZORIA, Brazoria, 311 (2,866)	2,845
Brazos, Palo Pinto (112)	173
BRAZOS COUNTRY, Austin, (514)	510
Brazos Point, Bosque	20
Brazosport, Brazoria	60,138
*BRECKENRIDGE, Stephens, 336 (5,187)	5,244
*BREMOND, Robertson, 62 (858)	854
*BRENHAM, Washington, 1,259 (17,369)	18,117
Breslau, Lavaca	65
Briar, Tarrant, Wise, Parker, (7,035)	5,635
BRIARCLIFF, Travis, 23 (2,062)	2,133
BRIAROAKS, Johnson, 2 (507)	508
Brice, Hall, Briscoe	20
*BRIDGE CITY, Orange, 243 (9,546)	9,519
*BRIDGEPORT, Wise, 401 (5,923)	5,972
Bridges Chapel, Titus	60
*Briggs, Burnet, 13 (101)	18
Bright Star, Rains	25
Brinker, Hopkins	100
*Briscoe, Wheeler, 6	135
Bristol, Ellis (714)	504
*BROADDUS, San Augustine, 25 (184)	186
Broadway, Lamar	25
BROCK, Parker, 57 (nc)	967
Brock Junction, Parker	100
Bronco, Yoakum	30
*Bronson, Sabine, 25	377
*BRONTE, Coke, 48 (933)	945
*Brookeland, Sabine, 80	300
*Brookesmith, Brown, 7	61
Brooks, Panola	40
Brookshier, Runnels	15
*BROOKSHIRE, Waller, 447 (5,066)	5,501
BROOKSIDE VILLAGE, Brazoria, 21 (1,548)	1,552
*Brookston, Lamar, 32 (91)	45
Broom City, Anderson	20
BROWNDELL, Jasper, 3 (160)	157
*BROWNFIELD, Terry, 286 (8,936)	8,916
Browning, Smith	25
*BROWNSBORO, Henderson, 129 (1,212)	1,229
Brownsboro, Caldwell	50
*BROWNSVILLE, Cameron, 6,417 (186,738)	187,831
*BROWNWOOD, Brown, 798 (18,862)	18,770
Broyles Chapel, Anderson	60
*BRUCEVILLE-EDDY, McLennan, Falls, 107 (1,413)	1,426
Brumley, Upshur	75
Brundage, Dimmit (12)	12
*Bruni, Webb, 10 (251)	376
Brushie Prairie, Navarro	35
Brushy Creek, Williamson, (22,519)	22,972
Brushy Creek, Anderson	125
*BRYAN, Brazos, 2,889 (83,980)	86,866
Bryans Mill, Cass	150
Bryarly, Red River	3
Bryce, Rusk	15
*BRYSON, Jack, 20 (430)	447
*Buchanan Dam, Llano, 90 (1,508)	1,344
Buchanan Lake Village, Llano (720)	654
Buchel, DeWitt	45
Buckeye, Matagorda	16
*BUCKHOLTS, Milam, 35 (365)	372
Buckhorn, Austin	50
Buckhorn, Newton	80
Buckner, Parker	10
*BUDA, Hays, 1,169 (15,108)	15,643
Buena Vista, Starr (93)	73
Buena Vista, Shelby	20
*BUFFALO, Leon, 186 (1,767)	1,789
*BUFFALO GAP, Taylor, 60 (543)	569
Buffalo Mop, Limestone	21
BUFFALO SPRINGS, Lubbock, 3 (468)	459
Buffalo Springs, Clay	45
Buford, Mitchell	30
Bugscuffle, Rusk	12
Bula, Bailey	35
Bulcher, Cooke	3
*BULLARD, Smith, Cherokee, 340 (3,318)	3,706
Bull Run, Newton	90
*BULVERDE, Comal, Bexar, 569 (5,692)	5,996
*Buna, Jasper, 228 (2,137)	1,689
Buncombe, Panola	95
Bunger, Young	24
BUNKER HILL VILLAGE, Harris, 3 (3,822)	3,761
Bunyan, Erath	20
*BURKBURNETT, Wichita, 214 (10,939)	10,975
BURKE, Angelina, 19 (691)	692
*Burkett, Coleman, 2	90
*Burkeville, Newton, 19	603
Burleigh, Austin	150
*BURLESON, Johnson, Tarrant, 2,014 (47,641)	51,618
*Burlington, Milam, 15 (81)	81
*BURNET, Burnet, 658 (6,436)	6,676
Burns, Bowie	400
Burns City, Cooke	45
Burrantown, Houston	70
*BURTON, Washington, 120 (297)	283
*Bushland, Potter, 21 (2,234)	2,581
Bustamante, Zapata	10
Busterville, Hockley	6
Butler, Bastrop	40
Butler, Freestone	67
Butterfield, El Paso (100)	110
*BYERS, Clay, 13 (454)	453
*BYNUM, Hill, 13 (171)	172
Byrd, Ellis	30
Byrdtown, Lamar	22

C

Town, County	Pop. 2021
*CACTUS, Moore, 42 (3,057)	3,050
*Caddo, Stephens, 8	70
*CADDO MILLS, Hunt, 279 (1,495)	2,321
Cade Chapel, Navarro, Freestone	25
Cade Lakes, Burleson (507)	361
Cadiz, Bee	15
Calallen, Nueces	[part of Corpus Christi]
Calaveras, Wilson, Bexar	100
*CALDWELL, Burleson, 407 (3,993)	4,109
Caledonia, Rusk	75
Calf Creek, McCulloch	23
Calina, Limestone	10
*Call, Newton, 14	493
Callender Lake, Van Zandt (1,090)	884
*Calliham, McMullen, 8	100
CALLISBURG, Cooke, 5 (321)	320
Call Junction, Jasper	50
*CALVERT, Robertson, 68 (962)	962
Camargito, Starr (324)	286
*Camden, Polk	1,200
*CAMERON, Milam, 236 (5,306)	5,352
Cameron Park, Cameron (6,099)	5,464
Camilla, San Jacinto	200
Camp Air, Mason	12
*CAMPBELL, Hunt, 101 (542)	554
*Campbellton, Atascosa, 4	350
Camp Creek Lake, Robertson	350
Campo Verde, Starr (111)	176
Camp Ruby, Polk	35
Camp San Saba, McCulloch	36
Camp Seale, Polk	53

Town, County	Pop. 2021
Camp Springs, Scurry	10
Camp Swift, Bastrop (7,943)	6,901
Camp Switch, Gregg	70
Campti, Shelby	25
Camp Verde, Kerr, 4	41
*CAMP WOOD, Real, 43 (517)	508
Canada Verde, Wilson	40
*CANADIAN, Hemphill, 201 (2,339)	2,248
Candelaria, Presidio	55
CANEY CITY, Henderson, 2 (187)	188
Cannon, Grayson	50
*CANTON, Van Zandt, 984 (4,229)	4,312
Cantu Addition, Brooks (191)	191
*Canutillo, El Paso, 396 (6,212)	6,393
*CANYON, Randall, 613 (14,836)	15,221
Canyon City, Comal	800
Canyon Creek, Hood (1,249)	969
*Canyon Lake, Comal, 723 (31,124)	30,641
Cape Royale, San Jacinto (657)	416
Caplen, Galveston	60
Capps Corner, Montague	30
Cap Rock, Crosby	6
Caps, Taylor	300
Caradan, Mills	20
Carancahua, Jackson	375
*CARBON, Eastland, 16 (281)	286
Carbondale, Bowie	10
Carey, Childress	25
Carlisle, Trinity	110
Carlos, Grimes, 1	60
*Carlsbad, Tom Green, 24 (622)	613
CARL'S CORNER, Hill, 1 (201)	209
Carlson, Travis	20
*Carlton, Hamilton, 7 (102)	12
*CARMINE, Fayette, 88 (244)	244
Carmona, Polk	50
Caro, Nacogdoches	70
Carrizo Hill, Dimmit (550)	1,076
*CARRIZO SPRINGS, Dimmit, 237 (4,892)	4,833
Carroll, Smith	60
Carroll Springs, Anderson, Henderson	20
*CARROLLTON, Dallas, Denton, 4,932 (133,434)	133,251
Carson, Fannin	22
Carta Valley, Edwards	12
Carter, Parker (1,637)	1,467
Carterville, Cass	39
*CARTHAGE, Panola, 525 (6,569)	6,533
Cartwright, Wood	144
Casa Blanca, Starr (65)	65
Casa Piedra, Presidio	8
Casas, Starr (29)	29
Cash, Hunt	56
CASHION, Wichita (286)	288
*Cason, Morris	173
Cass, Cass	100
Cassie, Burnet	496
Cassin, Bexar	200
*Castell, Llano, 8	72
CASTLE HILLS, Bexar, 80 (3,978)	3,947
Castolon, Brewster	8

Town, County	Pop. 2021
*CASTROVILLE, Medina, 330 (2,954)	3,005
Catarina, Dimmit, 6 (70)	84
*Cat Spring, Austin, 73	200
Caviness, Lamar	90
Cawthon, Brazos	75
Cayote, Bosque	75
*Cayuga, Anderson, 2	137
Cedar Bayou, Harris	1,555
*Cedar Creek, Bastrop, 341 (3,154)	4,076
*CEDAR HILL, Dallas, Ellis, 1,285 (49,148)	48,557
Cedar Hill, Floyd	24
Cedar Lake, Matagorda	160
*Cedar Lane, Matagorda, 1	300
*CEDAR PARK, Williamson, Travis, 2,794 (77,595)	78,693
Cedar Point, Polk (851)	425
Cedar Shores, Bosque	270
Cedar Springs, Falls	90
Cedar Springs, Upshur	100
Cedarvale, Kaufman	50
Cedar Valley, Bell	14
Cee Vee, Cottle, 2	45
Cego, Falls	42
Cele, Travis	20
*CELESTE, Hunt, 72 (809)	822
*CELINA, Collin, Denton, 598 (16,739)	23,811
*CENTER, Shelby, 443 (5,221)	5,133
Center, Limestone	76
Center City, Mills, Hamilton	27
Center Grove, Houston	39
Center Grove, Titus	35
Center Hill, Houston	105
Center Plains, Swisher	20
*Center Point, Kerr, 100 (1,263)	1,759
Center Point, Camp	41
Center Point, Upshur	50
Centerview, Leon	20
*CENTERVILLE, Leon, 93 (905)	921
Centerville, Trinity	60
Central, Angelina	1,400
Central Gardens, Jefferson (4,373)	3,377
Central Heights, Nacogdoches	300
Central High, Cherokee	30
*Centralia, Trinity	190
Cesar Chavez, Hidalgo (1,608)	1,174
Cestohowa, Karnes, 1	110
Chalk, Cottle	17
Chalk Hill, Rusk	200
Chalk Mountain, Erath, Somervell, 1	25
Chambliss, Collin	29
Champion, Nolan	10
Champions, Harris	21,250
Chances Store, Burleson	15
*CHANDLER, Henderson, 222 (3,275)	3,400
Chaney, Eastland	35
*Channelview, Harris, 638 (45,688)	42,394
*CHANNING, Hartley, 8 (281)	266
Chaparrito, Starr (142)	152
Chapeno, Starr (42)	16
Chapman, Rusk	20
*Chapman Ranch, Nueces	200
Chappel, San Saba	25

Town, County	Pop. 2021
*Chappell Hill, Washington, 115	750
Charco, Goliad	96
Charleston, Delta, Hopkins	150
Charlie, Clay	70
*CHARLOTTE, Atascosa, 46 (1,524)	1,554
*Chatfield, Navarro, 9	40
Cheapside, Gonzales, DeWitt	5
Cheek, Jefferson	1,096
Cheneyboro, Navarro	100
*Cherokee, San Saba, 14	175
Cherry Spring, Gillespie	75
*CHESTER, Tyler, 11 (270)	277
Chesterville, Colorado, 1	30
*CHICO, Wise, 89 (946)	996
*Chicota, Lamar, 1	150
Chihuahua, Zapata	77
*CHILDRESS, Childress, 191 (5,737)	5,844
*CHILLICOTHE, Hardeman, 20 (549)	554
*Chilton, Falls, 24 (776)	988
*CHINA, Jefferson, 27 (1,260)	1,240
CHINA GROVE, Bexar, 39 (1,141)	1,133
China Grove, Scurry	15
*China Spring, McLennan, 151 (1,436)	1,342
Chinati, Presidio	8
Chinquapin, Matagorda	6
*CHIRENO, Nacogdoches, 23 (370)	369
Chita, Trinity	81
Choate, Karnes	30
Chocolate Bayou, Brazoria	60
Choice, Shelby	35
*Chriesman, Burleson, 1	30
*CHRISTINE, Atascosa, 7 (337)	344
*Christoval, Tom Green, 59 (482)	299
Chula Vista, Maverick (5,100)	212
Chula Vista, Cameron (257)	3,586
Chula Vista, Zavala (307)	625
Church Hill, Rusk	20
Churchill, Brazoria	90
*CIBOLO, Guadalupe, 623 (32,276)	33,475
Cienegas Terrace, Val Verde, (3,025)	2,342
Cinco Ranch, Fort Bend, Harris, (16,899)	18,399
Cipres, Hidalgo	20
Circle, Lamb	6
Circle Back, Bailey	8
Circle D-KC Estates, Bastrop, (2,588)	2,450
Circleville, Williamson	50
*CISCO, Eastland, 201 (3,883)	3,883
Cistern, Fayette, 1	137
Citrus City, Hidalgo (3,291)	2,941
Citrus Grove, Matagorda	30
Clairemont, Kent	12
Clairette, Erath	55
Clara, Wichita	100
Clardy, Lamar	160
*CLARENDON, Donley, 122 (1,877)	1,867
Clareville, Bee	25
Clark, Liberty	75

Town, County	Pop. 2021
Clarkson, Milam	10
*CLARKSVILLE, Red River, 158 (2,857)	2,790
CLARKSVILLE CITY, Gregg, Upshur, 5 (780)	780
*CLAUDE, Armstrong, 60 (1,186)	1,184
Clauene, Hockley	10
Clawson, Angelina	1,500
Clay, Burleson (139)	139
Clays Corner, Parmer	15
*Clayton, Panola, 2	125
Claytonville, Swisher	85
Clear Creek, Burnet	78
CLEAR LAKE SHORES, Galveston, 63 (1,258)	1,263
*CLEBURNE, Johnson, 1,415 (31,352)	31,999
Clegg, Live Oak	125
Clemville, Matagorda, 1	25
Cleo, Kimble	3
*CLEVELAND, Liberty, 1,133 (7,471)	7,999
Cleveland, Austin	125
Cliffside, Potter	206
*CLIFTON, Bosque, 303 (3,465)	3,488
Climax, Collin	82
Cline, Uvalde	15
*CLINT, El Paso, 117 (923)	930
Clinton, Hunt	150
Close City, Garza	65
Cloverleaf, Harris, 1 (24,100)	25,576
*CLUTE, Brazoria, 347 (10,604)	10,593
*CLYDE, Callahan, 259 (3,811)	3,923
*COAHOMA, Howard, 43 (945)	914
Coble, Hockley	11
Cochran, Austin	200
COCKRELL HILL, Dallas, 49 (3,815)	3,719
COFFEE CITY, Henderson, 6 (249)	244
Coffeeville, Upshur	50
Cofferville, Lamb	4
Coit, Limestone	25
Coke, Wood	53
*COLDSPRING, San Jacinto, 176 (819)	777
*COLEMAN, Coleman, 246 (3,912)	3,917
Colfax, Van Zandt	94
Colita, Polk, Trinity	50
College Hill, Bowie	40
College Mound, Kaufman	500
*Collegeport, Matagorda	80
*COLLEGE STATION, Brazos, 3,020 (120,511)	120,019
*COLLEYVILLE, Tarrant, 1,014 (26,057)	25,986
*COLLINSVILLE, Grayson, 94 (1,866)	1,931
*COLMESNEIL, Tyler, 48 (542)	551
Colony, Rains	35
Colorado Acres, Webb (127)	74
*COLORADO CITY, Mitchell, 220 (3,991)	4,391
Coltharp, Houston	40
Colton, Travis	50
*COLUMBUS, Colorado, 380 (3,699)	3,587
*COMANCHE, Comanche, 284 (4,211)	4,235
*COMBES, Cameron, 20 (2,999)	3,040
COMBINE, Kaufman, Dallas, 56 (2,245)	2,358
Cometa, Zavala	10
*Comfort, Kendall, 317 (2,211)	1,955
*COMMERCE, Hunt, 264 (9,090)	8,828
*COMO, Hopkins, 35 (728)	732
*Comstock, Val Verde, 8	344
Comyn, Comanche	30
*Concan, Uvalde, 67	500
*Concepcion, Duval, 4 (42)	19
Concord, Rusk	23
*Concord, Leon	28
Concord, Cherokee	50
Concord, Madison	50
Concrete, DeWitt	46
Cone, Crosby, 1	50
Conlen, Dallam	14
Connor, Madison	20
*CONROE, Montgomery, 5,017 (89,956)	94,400
Content, Bell	25
*CONVERSE, Bexar, 888 (27,466)	28,643
Conway, Carson	20
Cooks Point, Burleson	60
*Cookville, Titus, 37	105
COOL, Parker (211)	214
*COOLIDGE, Limestone, 12 (778)	777
*COOPER, Delta, 90 (1,911)	1,951
Cooper, Houston	27
Copano Village, Aransas	210
*Copeville, Collin, 4	243
*COPPELL, Dallas, Denton, 1,438 (42,983)	42,221
*COPPERAS COVE, Coryell, 745 (36,670)	37,041
COPPER CANYON, Denton, 26 (1,731)	1,759
Corbet, Navarro	80
Cordele, Jackson	51
CORINTH, Denton, 481 (22,634)	22,690
Corinth, Jones	10
Corinth, Leon	50
Corley, Bowie	35
Cornersville, Hopkins	200
Cornett, Cass	30
Cornudas, Hudspeth	5
*CORPUS CHRISTI, Nueces, 9,037 (317,863)	317,773
CORRAL CITY, Denton, (33)	36
*CORRIGAN, Polk, 74 (1,477)	1,480
*CORSICANA, Navarro, 1,089 (25,109)	25,203
Coryell City, Coryell	70
*Cost, Gonzales, 17	84
Cotton Center, Fannin	33
*Cotton Center, Hale, 5	300
Cottondale, Wise	300
Cotton Gin, Freestone	28
Cotton Patch, DeWitt, 1	11
COTTONWOOD, Kaufman, 1 (181)	194
Cottonwood, Somervell	24
Cottonwood, Madison	40
Cottonwood, Callahan	150

The dog park at Veteran's Memorial Park in Cedar Park. Photo by Tap, CC by SA 3.0

Town, County	Pop. 2021
COTTONWOOD SHORES, Burnet, 48 (1,403)	1,512
*COTULLA, La Salle, 208 (3,718)	3,725
Couch, Karnes	10
Coughran, Atascosa	20
Country Acres, San Patricio (163)	208
County Line, Rains	40
County Line, Lubbock	59
*COUPLAND, Williamson, 48 (289)	290
Courtney, Grimes	60
COVE, Chambers, 41 (525)	559
Cove Springs, Cherokee	49
*COVINGTON, Hill, 32 (261)	270
Cox, Upshur	30
*Coyanosa, Pecos, 11 (155)	165
Coy City, Karnes	30
Coyote Acres, Jim Wells (570)	894
COYOTE FLATS, Johnson (345)	349
Crabbs Prairie, Walker	240
Craft, Cherokee	21
Crafton, Wise	100
*CRANDALL, Kaufman, 174 (3,860)	4,278
*CRANE, Crane, 128 (3,478)	3,484
*CRANFILLS GAP, Bosque, 16 (277)	282
*CRAWFORD, McLennan, 74 (887)	903
Creath, Houston	20
Crecy, Trinity	15
CREEDMOOR, Travis, 42 (458)	452
Crescent Heights, Henderson	180
*CRESSON, Hood, Johnson, Parker, 141 (1,349)	1,849
Crews, Runnels	30
Crisp, Ellis	115
*CROCKETT, Houston, 368 (6,332)	6,406
*Crosby, Harris, 734 (3,417)	1,823
*CROSBYTON, Crosby, 61 (1,492)	1,488
Cross, McMullen	25
Cross, Grimes	53
Cross Cut, Brown, 1	22
Cross Mountain, Bexar (3,944)	4,443
*CROSS PLAINS, Callahan, 78 (899)	926
CROSS ROADS, Denton, 182 (1,744)	1,817
Cross Roads, Milam	35
Cross Roads, Madison	75
Cross Roads, Henderson	160
Crossroads, Delta	20
Crossroads, Hopkins	50
Crossroads, Cass	60
Crossroads, Harrison	100
CROSS TIMBER, Johnson (362)	397
Croton, Dickens	7
Crow, Wood	178
*CROWELL, Foard, 45 (769)	749
*CROWLEY, Tarrant, 598 (18,070)	19,333
Crown, Atascosa	10
Cruz Calle, Duval	12
Cryer Creek, Navarro	15
Crystal Beach, Galveston, 122	800
*CRYSTAL CITY, Zavala, 142 (6,354)	6,335
Crystal Falls, Stephens	10
Crystal Lake, Anderson	12
Cuadrilla, El Paso	67
*CUERO, DeWitt, 374 (8,128)	8,235
Cuevitas, Hidalgo (33)	679
*CUMBY, Hopkins, 70 (679)	695
Cumings, Fort Bend (2,207)	1,642
Cundiff, Jack	45
*CUNEY, Cherokee, 5 (116)	113
*Cunningham, Lamar, 1	110
Currie, Navarro	25
Curtis, Jasper	150
*CUSHING, Nacogdoches, 62 (557)	558
Cusseta, Cass	30
*CUT AND SHOOT, Montgomery, 17 (1,087)	1,139
Cuthand, Red River	116
Cyclone, Bell	47
Cypress, Franklin	20
Cypress Creek, Kerr	200
*Cypress, Harris, 5,290	120,000
Cypress Mill, Blanco, 2	200
D	
Dacosta, Victoria	89
Dacus, Montgomery	190
Daffan, Travis	500
*DAINGERFIELD, Morris, Titus, 136 (2,522)	2,510
*DAISETTA, Liberty, 18 (923)	992
Dalby Springs, Bowie	75
*Dale, Caldwell, 138	300
*DALHART, Dallam, Hartley, 375 (8,447)	8,347
*Dallardsville, Polk	350
*DALLAS, Dallas, Collin, Denton, 43,940 (1,304,379)	1,288,457
Dalton, Cass	50
DALWORTHINGTON GARDENS, Tarrant, 43 (2,293)	2,273
*Damon, Brazoria, 59 (436)	154
*DANBURY, Brazoria, 74 (1,671)	1,655
*Danciger, Brazoria	90
*Danevang, Wharton, 3	61
Daniels, Panola	75
Danville, Gregg, Rusk	200
Darby Hill, San Jacinto	25
Darco, Harrison	10
Darden, Polk	320
*DARROUZETT, Lipscomb, 14 (309)	302
Datura, Limestone	2
*Davilla, Milam, 1	191
Davis, Atascosa, 1	8
Davis Prairie, Limestone	17
*Dawn, DeafSmith, 4	52
*DAWSON, Navarro, 27 (815)	835
*DAYTON, Liberty, 621 (8,777)	9,134
DAYTON LAKES, Liberty (45)	50
Deadwood, Panola	106
DEAN, Clay, 1 (488)	493
Dean, Hockley	20
*Deanville, Burleson, 2 (63)	200
*DeBerry, Panola, 36	200
*DECATUR, Wise, 776 (6,538)	6,875
Decker Prairie, Montgomery	2,000
DeCORDOVA, Hood (3,007)	3,104

A panorama of the Dallas skyline, through a window at the Perot Museum of Nature and Science. Photo by Jonathan Cutrer, jcutrer.com

Town, County	Pop. 2021
*DEER PARK, Harris, 800 (34,495)	33,676
Deerwood, Montgomery (1,745)	1,522
*DE KALB, Bowie, 119 (1,527)	1,511
*DE LEON, Comanche, 125 (2,258)	2,282
Delhi, Caldwell	150
Delia, Limestone	20
*DELL CITY, Hudspeth, 18 (245)	367
Del Mar Heights, Cameron (78)	79
*Delmita, Starr, 4 (186)	132
Delray, Panola	45
*DEL RIO, Val Verde, 943 (34,673)	34,584
Delrose, Upshur	35
Del Sol, San Patricio (333)	256
*Del Valle, Travis, 376	12
Demi-John, Brazoria	300
Democrat, Mills, Comanche	8
Denhawken, Wilson	52
*DENISON, Grayson, 997 (24,479)	25,179
Denning, San Augustine	100
*Dennis, Parker, 3 (727)	727
Denson Springs, Anderson	60
*DENTON, Denton, 3,941 (139,869)	148,146
Denton, Callahan	6
*DENVER CITY, Yoakum, Gaines, 214 (4,470)	4,390
*DEPORT, Lamar, Red River, 20 (550)	551
Derby, Frio	50
*Desdemona, Eastland, 7	180
Desert, Collin	35
*DeSOTO, Dallas, 1,181 (56,145)	55,729
*DETROIT, Red River, 46 (704)	707
*DEVERS, Liberty, 21 (361)	389
*DEVINE, Medina, 299 (4,324)	4,410
Dew, Freestone	150
DeWees, Wilson	60
Deweesville, Karnes	12
*Deweyville, Newton, 4 (571)	519
Dewville, Gonzales	30
Dexter, Cooke	12
*D'Hanis, Medina, 38 (785)	615
Dial, Fannin	76
Dialville, Cherokee	200
*Diana, Upshur, 121	585
*DIBOLL, Angelina, 126 (4,457)	4,449
Dicey, Parker	40
*DICKENS, Dickens, 8 (219)	404
*DICKINSON, Galveston, 842 (20,847)	21,697
*Dike, Hopkins, 23	170
*DILLEY, Frio, 129 (3,274)	3,310
Dilworth, Gonzales	18
Dilworth, Red River	25
*Dime Box, Lee, 47 (207)	236
*DIMMITT, Castro, 130 (4,171)	4,167
Dimple, Red River	60
Dinero, Live Oak, 1	344
Ding Dong, Bell	301
Direct, Lamar	85
Dirgin, Rusk	50
DISH, Denton, 1 (437)	437
Divide, Kerr	50
Divot, Frio, 1	30

Town, County	Pop. 2021
Dixie, Grayson	17
Dixon, Hunt	31
Dixon-Hopewell, Houston	10
Doak Springs, Lee	50
Doans, Wilbarger	20
*Dobbin, Montgomery, 1	310
Dobrowolski, Atascosa	10
Dodd, Castro	12
*DODD CITY, Fannin, 26 (369)	380
*Dodge, Walker, 4	150
*DODSON, Collingsworth (93)	91
Dodson Prairie, Palo Pinto	18
Doffing, Hidalgo (5,618)	5,396
Dog Ridge, Bell	215
Dogwood City, Smith	800
Dolen, Liberty	75
DOMINO, Cass, 1 (71)	74
*Donie, Freestone, 14	250
*DONNA, Hidalgo, 780 (16,797)	16,821
*Doole, McCulloch	74
Doolittle, Hidalgo (4,061)	6,253
DORCHESTER, Grayson, 1 (69)	69
Dorras, Stonewall, Fisher	20
Doss, Cass	15
*Doss, Gillespie, 10	100
Dot, Falls	17
Dotson, Panola	35
Double Bayou, Chambers	200
DOUBLE OAK, Denton, 85 (3,054)	3,054
DOUBLE HORN, Burnet (nc)	264
*Doucette, Tyler, 1	160
Dougherty, Rains	40
*Dougherty, Floyd, 3	91
*Douglass, Nacogdoches, 31	380
*DOUGLASSVILLE, Cass, 11 (211)	213
Downing, Comanche	30
Downsville, McLennan	150
Downtown Texas, Milam	34
Doyle, San Patricio	243
Doyle, Limestone	50
Dozier, Collingsworth	4
Drane, Navarro	16
Drasco, Runnels	15
Draw, Lynn	18
Dreka, Shelby	30
Dresden, Navarro	25
Dreyer, Gonzales	20
*Driftwood, Hays, 186 (106)	87
*DRIPPING SPRINGS, Hays, 1,019 (4,650)	5,787
*DRISCOLL, Nueces, 21 (680)	673
Drop, Denton	90
*Dryden, Terrell, 2	13
Dubina, Fayette	272
*DUBLIN, Erath, 267 (3,359)	3,433
Dudley, Callahan	25
Duffau, Erath	76
*DUMAS, Moore, 447 (14,501)	14,290
Dumont, King, Dickens, 1	19
Dunbar, Rains	40
*DUNCANVILLE, Dallas, 1,106 (40,706)	39,797
Dundee, Archer, 1	12
Dunlap, Cottle	10
Dunlap, Travis	80
Dunlay, Medina, 2	145

Town, County	Pop. 2021
Dunn, Scurry	75
Duplex, Fannin	25
Durango, Falls	54
Duren, Mills	15
Duster, Comanche	25
Dye, Montague	30

E

Town, County	Pop. 2021
Eagle, Chambers	30
*EAGLE LAKE, Colorado, 132 (3,442)	3,484
Eagle Mountain, Tarrant	[part of Saginaw]
*EAGLE PASS, Maverick, 1,241 (28,130)	28,596
*EARLY, Brown, 208 (3,087)	3,145
*EARTH, Lamb, 31 (901)	901
East Afton, Dickens	13
East Alto Bonito, Starr (905)	551
*EAST BERNARD, Wharton, 153 (2,218)	2,248
East Caney, Hopkins	100
East Columbia, Brazoria (128)	178
East Delta, Delta	60
East Direct, Lamar	48
Easter, Castro	26
Easterly, Robertson	61
Eastgate, Liberty	200
East Hamilton, Shelby	25
*EASTLAND, Eastland, 223 (3,609)	3,621
East Lopez, Starr (136)	199
EAST MOUNTAIN, Upshur, 3 (899)	922
EASTON, Gregg, Rusk (499)	763
East Point, Wood	40
East Sweden, McCulloch	40
EAST TAWAKONI, Rains, 9 (824)	850
Ebenezer, Jasper	50
Ebenezer, Camp	55
Echo, Coleman	6
Ecleto, Karnes	22
*ECTOR, Fannin, 20 (737)	497
*EDCOUCH, Hidalgo, 97 (2,732)	2,720
*EDEN, Concho, 62 (1,100)	1,543
Eden, Nacogdoches	100
Edgar, DeWitt	8
Edge, Brazos	10
EDGECLIFF VILLAGE, Tarrant, 26 (3,788)	3,761
Edgewater Estates, San Patricio, (71)	160
*EDGEWOOD, Van Zandt, 149 (1,530)	1,592
Edgeworth, Bell	15
Edhube, Fannin	40
*EDINBURG, Hidalgo, 2,828 (100,243)	102,483
*EDMONSON, Hale, 3 (86)	86
*EDNA, Jackson, 310 (5,987)	5,944
Edna Hill, Erath	32
EDOM, Van Zandt, 18 (339)	349
*Edroy, San Patricio, 1 (422)	285
Egan, Johnson, 1	133
*Egypt, Wharton, 4	26
Eidson Road, Maverick (9,461)	9,743
Elam Springs, Upshur	50
Elbert, Throckmorton, 4 (29)	8

Town, County	Pop. 2021
Elbow, Howard	10
El Brazil, Starr (53)	38
El Camino Angosto, Cameron, (186)	186
*EL CAMPO, Wharton, 660 (12,350)	12,290
El Castillo, Starr (219)	103
El Cenizo, Starr (273)	2,506
EL CENIZO, Webb, 13 (2,540)	328
El Centro, Starr	50
El Chaparral, Starr (467)	339
*ELDORADO, Schleicher, 90 (1,574)	1,585
Eldorado Center, Navarro	20
Eldridge, Colorado	10
*ELECTRA, Wichita, 79 (2,292)	2,282
Elevation, Milam	12
*ELGIN, Bastrop, 659 (9,784)	10,549
Elias-Fela Solis, Starr (17)	17
Eliasville, Young, 2	100
*El Indio, Maverick (182)	182
Elk, McLennan	150
*ELKHART, Anderson, 99 (1,287)	1,277
EL LAGO, Harris, 56 (3,090)	3,006
*ELLINGER, Fayette, 18 (nc)	286
Elliott, Wilbarger	50
Elliott, Robertson	55
*Elmaton, Matagorda, 3	160
Elm Creek, Maverick (2,884)	3,902
*ELMENDORF, Bexar, 156 (1,862)	2,029
El Mesquite, Starr (50)	50
Elm Grove, San Saba	15
Elm Grove, Cherokee	50
Elm Grove, Wharton	76
Elm Grove Camp, Guadalupe	88
*Elm Mott, McLennan, 128	300
*Elmo, Kaufman (803)	1,065
Elmont, Grayson	15
Elm Ridge, Milam	25
Elmwood, Anderson	15
Eloise, Falls	19
El Oso, Karnes	35
*EL PASO, El Paso, 17,716 (678,815)	678,415
El Quiote, Starr (226)	146
El Rancho Vela, Starr (254)	266
El Refugio, Starr (407)	757
Elroy, Travis, 1	125
*ELSA, Hidalgo, 196 (5,668)	5,680
El Sauz, Starr, 1	50
El Socio, Starr (104)	17
Elton, Dickens	4
El Toro, Jackson	136
Elwood, Madison	50
Elwood, Fannin	31
*Elysian Fields, Harrison, 3	500
Emberson, Lamar	80
Emerald Bay, Smith (1,146)	1,292
EMHOUSE, Navarro (187)	192
Emmett, Navarro	100
*EMORY, Rains, 257 (1,251)	1,291
Encantada-Ranchito El Calaboz, Cameron (1,981)	1,362
ENCHANTED OAKS, Henderson, 1 (347)	354
*ENCINAL, La Salle, 42 (540)	539
*Encino, Brooks, 6 (109)	71
*Energy, Comanche, 3	70
Engle, Fayette	141
English, Red River	100
*Enloe, Delta, 1	90
*ENNIS, Ellis, 862 (20,159)	21,210
Enoch, Upshur	25
*Enochs, Bailey	80
Enon, Upshur	204
*Eola, Concho, 5	215
Eolian, Stephens	9
*Era, Cooke, 7	150
Ericksdahl, Jones	35
Erin, Jasper	70
Erna, Menard, Mason	27
Erwin, Grimes	52
Escobares, Starr, 3 (2,588)	2,569
Escobar I, Starr	352
Escobas, Zapata	2
Eskota, Fisher	32
Esperanza, Hudspeth	75
Espey, Atascosa	55
Estacado, Lubbock, Crosby	32
*ESTELLINE, Hall, 4 (121)	124
Estes, Aransas	300
Ethel, Grayson	40
*Etoile, Nacogdoches, 21	700
Eugenio Saenz, Starr (182)	266
Eula, Callahan	125
*EULESS, Tarrant, 1,623 (61,032)	60,500
Eulogy, Bosque	10
EUREKA, Navarro (313)	321
Eureka, Franklin	18
*EUSTACE, Henderson, 129 (1,137)	1,153
*Evadale, Jasper, 26 (1,246)	1,168
*EVANT, Coryell, Hamilton, 38 (455)	454
Evergreen, Starr (80)	34
Evergreen, San Jacinto	100
EVERMAN, Tarrant, 99 (6,154)	6,067
Ewell, Upshur	20
Ezzell, Lavaca	55

F

Town, County	Pop. 2021
*Fabens, El Paso, 127 (7,498)	5,460
Fabrica, Maverick (772)	1,147
FAIRCHILDS, Fort Bend, 2 (864)	921
*FAIRFIELD, Freestone, 268 (2,850)	2,896
Fairland, Burnet	340
Fairlie, Hunt	80
Fairmount, Sabine	1,500
Fair Oaks, Limestone, 25	15
FAIR OAKS RANCH, Bexar, Comal, Kendall, 164 (9,833)	10,505
Fair Play, Panola	80
FAIRVIEW, Collin, 275 (10,372)	10,683
Fairview, Howard	5
Fairview, Cass	20
Fairview, Hockley	20
Fairview, Hood	30
Fairview, Armstrong	10
Fairview, Wilson	95
Fairview, Gaines	160
Fairy, Hamilton, 1	40
Falconaire, Starr (92)	18
*Falcon Heights, Starr, 4 (18)	18
Falcon Lake Estates, Zapata (962)	896
Falcon Mesa, Zapata (523)	90
Falcon Village, Starr (3)	3
*FALFURRIAS, Brooks, 173 (4,609)	4,787
Fallon, Limestone	100
*FALLS CITY, Karnes, 56 (514)	544
Falman, San Patricio (60)	7
Famuliner, Cochran	5
Fannett, Jefferson, 6 (2,363)	2,290
*Fannin, Goliad, 8	359
Fargo, Wilbarger	169
Farmers Academy, Titus	75
*FARMERS BRANCH, Dallas, 1,384 (35,991)	36,442
Farmers Valley, Wilbarger	30
*FARMERSVILLE, Collin, 337 (3,612)	3,808
Farmington, Grayson	40
*Farnsworth, Ochiltree, 4 (95)	25
Farrar, Limestone	51
Farrsville, Newton	152
*FARWELL, Parmer, 73 (1,425)	1,389
Fashing, Atascosa, 1	35
*FATE, Rockwall, 275 (17,958)	21,013
Faught, Lamar	25
Faulkner, Lamar	10
Fawil, Newton	183
*FAYETTEVILLE, Fayette, 116 (246)	246
Faysville, Hidalgo	500
Fedor, Lee	92
*Fentress, Caldwell, 15	380
Fernando Salinas, Starr (25)	25
*FERRIS, Ellis, 210 (2,788)	2,857
Fetzer, Waller	150
Fields Store, Waller	500
*Fieldton, Lamb	20
Fife, McCulloch	32
Fifth Street, Fort Bend (2,284)	1,397
Files Valley, Hill	60
Fincastle, Henderson	75
Finney, Hale	18
*Fischer, Comal, 68	400
Fisk, Coleman	40
Five Points, Ellis	25
Flaccus, Karnes	15
Flagg, Castro	26
*Flat, Coryell (157)	610
Flat Fork, Shelby	10
*FLATONIA, Fayette, 155 (1,308)	1,336
Flat Prairie, Trinity	33
Flats, Rains	40
Flat Top, Stonewall	5
*Flint, Smith, 384	2,500
Flo, Leon	12
Flomot, Motley, 4	181
Flora, Hopkins	20
Flor del Rio, Starr (101)	101
*FLORENCE, Williamson, 180 (1,171)	1,201
*FLORESVILLE, Wilson, 652 (7,203)	7,554
Florey, Andrews	25
Flour Bluff, Nueces	[part of Corpus Christi]
Flowella, Brooks (117)	19
Flower Hill, Colorado	20

Town, County	Pop. 2021
*FLOWER MOUND, Denton, 2,199 (75,956)	77,243
Floyd, Hunt	90
*FLOYDADA, Floyd, 119 (2,675)	2,654
*Fluvanna, Scurry, 16 (78)	84
*Flynn, Leon, 3	81
Foard City, Foard	10
Fodice, Houston	49
*FOLLETT, Lipscomb, 20 (373)	362
Folsom, Shelby	30
Ford, DeafSmith	25
Fords Corner, San Augustine	30
Fordtran, Victoria	18
Forest, Cherokee	85
*Forestburg, Montague, 21	50
Forest Chapel, Lamar	105
Forest Glade, Limestone	340
Forest Grove, Milam	60
Forest Heights, Orange (1,329)	1,600
FOREST HILL, Tarrant, 401 (13,955)	13,818
Forest Hill, Wood	30
Forest Hill, Lamar	50
*FORNEY, Kaufman, 1,419 (23,455)	27,256
*Forreston, Ellis, Navarro, 6	400
*FORSAN, Howard, 9 (225)	219
Fort Bliss, El Paso, 63 (11,260)	14,226
Fort Cavazos, Bell, Coryell, 147 (28,295)	24,781
Fort Clark Springs, Kinney (1,215)	1,338
*Fort Davis, Jeff Davis, 103 (1,024)	1,012
*Fort Hancock, Hudspeth, 20 (1,052)	990
*Fort McKavett, Menard, 6	50
Fort Parker, Limestone	2
Fort Parker State Park, Limestone	30
Fort Sherman, Titus	200
Fort Spunky, Hood	15
*FORT STOCKTON, Pecos, 381 (8,466)	8,423
*FORT WORTH, Tarrant, Denton, Parker, Wise, 22,723 (918,915)	935,508
Foster, Terry	6
Fostoria, Montgomery	586
Fouke, Wood	30
Four Corners, Fort Bend, (12,103)	11,133
Four Corners, Chambers	18
Four Corners, Brazoria	60
Four Corners, Montgomery	500
Four Points, Webb (10)	10
Fowlerton, La Salle, 5 (73)	66
Frame Switch, Williamson	25
*Francitas, Jackson, 1	125
Frankel City, Andrews	2
Frankell, Stephens	8
*FRANKLIN, Robertson, 161 (1,614)	1,670
*FRANKSTON, Anderson, 148 (1,126)	1,114
*Fred, Tyler, 12	300
*FREDERICKSBURG, Gillespie, 1,598 (10,875)	11,072
*Fredonia, Mason, San Saba, 8	55
Freedom, Rains	32
*FREEPORT, Brazoria, 411 (10,696)	10,594
*FREER, Duval, 106 (2,461)	2,472
Freestone, Freestone	100
Frelsburg, Colorado	75
Frenstat, Burleson	50
*Fresno, Fort Bend, 370 (24,486)	23,921
Fresno, Collingsworth	10
Freyburg, Fayette	148
Friday, Trinity	70
Friendship, Upshur	25
Friendship, Dawson	40
Friendship, Smith	200
Friendship Village, Bowie	200
*FRIENDSWOOD, Galveston, Harris, 1,581 (41,213)	41,004
Frio Town, Frio	9
*FRIONA, Parmer, 129 (4,171)	4,144
*FRISCO, Collin, Denton, 6,466 (200,509)	210,719
*FRITCH, Hutchinson, Moore, 93 (1,859)	1,851
Frog, Kaufman	90
Fronton, Starr (172)	249
Fronton Ranchettes, Starr (174)	155
*FROST, Navarro, 40 (620)	636
Fruitland, Montague	20
*FRUITVALE, Van Zandt, 24 (476)	490
Frydek, Austin, 1	900
Fulbright, Red River	150
*FULSHEAR, Fort Bend, 582 (16,856)	25,169
*FULTON, Aransas, 64 (1,523)	1,549
Funston, Jones	26
Furrh, Panola	40

G

Town, County	Pop. 2021
Gadston, Lamar	35
*Gail, Borden, 8 (249)	173
*GAINESVILLE, Cooke, 954 (17,394)	17,576
Galena, Smith	50
*GALENA PARK, Harris, 131 (10,740)	10,461
Galilee, Smith	150
*GALLATIN, Cherokee, 4 (321)	326
Galloway, Panola	71
*GALVESTON, Galveston, 1,940 (53,695)	53,219
*GANADO, Jackson, 114 (1,975)	1,982
Garceño, Starr (440)	340
*Garciasville, Starr, 4 (43)	60
*Garden City, Glasscock, 42 (334)	262
*Gardendale, Ector, 99 (2,020)	1,268
Gardendale, La Salle	80
GARDEN RIDGE, Comal, 126 (4,186)	4,335
Garden Valley, Smith, 1	150
Garfield, Travis, 3 (1,825)	2,932
Garfield, DeWitt	16
*GARLAND, Dallas, 5,980 (246,018)	242,035
Garland, Bowie	45
Garner, Parker (397)	386
Garner State Park, Uvalde	50
GARRETT, Ellis, 3 (829)	854
Garretts Bluff, Lamar	25
*GARRISON, Nacogdoches, 67 (789)	793
*Garwood, Colorado, 39 (510)	408
*GARY, Panola, 43 (335)	338
Garza-Salinas II, Starr (651)	579
Gastonia, Kaufman	100
*GATESVILLE, Coryell, 468 (16,135)	16,854
*Gause, Milam, 23 (275)	234
Gay Hill, Washington	40
Geneva, Sabine	200
Geneview, Stonewall	3
Gentry's Mill, Hamilton	20
George's Creek, Somervell, Johnson, Hood	43
*GEORGETOWN, Williamson, 3,167 (67,176)	75,420
*GEORGE WEST, Live Oak, 201 (2,171)	2,192
Georgia, Lamar	55
Germany, Houston	23
Geronimo, Guadalupe, 10 (1,097)	984
GHOLSON, McLennan, 6 (1,250)	1,262
Gibtown, Jack	20
*GIDDINGS, Lee, 411 (4,969)	5,067
Gilchrist, Galveston, 12	300
*Gillett, Karnes, 12	120
Gilliland, Knox	20
*GILMER, Upshur, 609 (4,843)	4,894
Gilpin, Dickens	2
Ginger, Rains	70
*Girard, Kent, 1 (53)	20
Girvin, Pecos, 3	20
Gist, Jasper	20
Givens, Lamar	135
*GLADEWATER, Gregg, Upshur, 393 (6,134)	6,137
Glaze City, Gonzales	10
Glazier, Hemphill (60)	60
Gleckler, Lavaca	78
Glen Cove, Coleman	40
Glendale, Trinity	175
Glenfawn, Rusk	100
*Glen Flora, Wharton, 9	210
Glenn, Dickens	4
GLENN HEIGHTS, Dallas, Ellis, 203 (15,819)	17,127
Glenrio, DeafSmith	10
*GLEN ROSE, Somervell, 329 (2,659)	2,848
Glenwood, Upshur	150
Glidden, Colorado, 3 (741)	650
Globe, Lamar	60
Glory, Lamar	30
*Gober, Fannin, 1	146
*GODLEY, Johnson, 195 (1,450)	1,858
*Golden, Wood, 2	398
Goldfinch, Frio	35
*Goldsboro, Coleman, 1	15
*GOLDSMITH, Ector, 25 (236)	228
*GOLDTHWAITE, Mills, 146 (1,738)	1,715
*GOLIAD, Goliad, 241 (1,620)	1,624
GOLINDA, Falls, McLennan, 4 (618)	667
Golly, DeWitt	41
Gomez, Terry	6
*GONZALES, Gonzales, 413 (7,165)	7,098
Goober Hill, Shelby	30
Goodland, Bailey	10

Town, County	Pop. 2021
Goodlett, Hardeman	80
GOODLOW, Navarro, 2 (178)	180
Good Neighbor, Hopkins	40
Goodnight, Armstrong	20
*GOODRICH, Polk, 47 (248)	258
Goodsprings, Rusk	40
Goodwill, Burleson	12
Goodwin, San Augustine	70
*GORDON, Palo Pinto, 41 (470)	474
*Gordonville, Grayson, 50	165
*GOREE, Knox, 5 (158)	162
*GORMAN, Eastland, 49 (976)	990
Goshen, Walker	250
Gould, Cherokee	20
*Gouldbusk, Coleman, 7	70
Graceton, Upshur	100
*GRAFORD, Palo Pinto, 117 (669)	685
*GRAHAM, Young, 616 (8,732)	8,765
Graham, Garza	60
*GRANBURY, Hood, 1,929 (10,958)	11,424
Grand Acres, Cameron	43
Grand Bluff, Panola	115
*GRANDFALLS, Ward, 13 (340)	330
*GRAND PRAIRIE, Dallas, Tarrant, Ellis, 4,943 (196,100)	197,347
*GRAND SALINE, Van Zandt, 193 (3,107)	3,165
*GRANDVIEW, Johnson, 233 (1,879)	1,889
Grandview, Dawson	8
Grandview, Gray	13
*GRANGER, Williamson, 71 (1,183)	1,193
Grangerland, Montgomery, 4 (754)	850
GRANITE SHOALS, Burnet, 82 (5,129)	5,222
GRANJENO, Hidalgo (283)	287
Grape Creek, Tom Green, 2 (3,594)	4,024
*GRAPELAND, Houston, 128 (1,465)	1,493
*GRAPEVINE, Tarrant, 2,559 (50,631)	50,872
Grassland, Lynn	40
Gray, Marion	12
Grayback, Wilbarger	10
GRAYS PRAIRIE, Kaufman (325)	347
Graytown, Wilson, Bexar	85
Green, Karnes	50
Green Hill, Titus	80
Green Lake, Calhoun	51
Greenpond, Hopkins	150
Green's Creek, Erath	75
Green Valley, Denton	100
Green Valley Farms, Cameron, (655)	244
Greenview, Hopkins	25
*GREENVILLE, Hunt, 1,156 (28,164)	29,578
Greenvine, Washington	35
Greenwood, Red River	20
*Greenwood, Wise	76
Greenwood, Hopkins	100
Greenwood, Midland	2,000
*GREGORY, San Patricio, 57 (1,740)	1,740
Gresham, Smith	1,000
GREY FOREST, Bexar, 4 (492)	489
Gribble Springs, Denton	55
Grice, Upshur	20
Griffith, Cochran	12
Grigsby, Shelby	15
Grit, Mason	15
*GROESBECK, Limestone, 194 (3,631)	3,645
*GROOM, Carson, 36 (552)	547
Grosvenor, Brown	24
*GROVES, Jefferson, 284 (17,335)	16,915
*GROVETON, Trinity, 87 (918)	913
Grow, King	9
Gruenau, DeWitt	18
Gruene, Comal	[part of New Braunfels]
*GRUVER, Hansford, 45 (1,130)	1,108
Guadalupe, Victoria	70
Guadalupe-Guerra, Starr (60)	51
Guadalupe Station, Culberson	10
*Guerra, Jim Hogg (3)	3
Gum Springs, Cass	59
GUN BARREL CITY, Henderson, 343 (6,190)	6,378
Gunsight, Stephens	6
*GUNTER, Grayson, 129 (2,060)	2,255
Gus, Burleson	50
*GUSTINE, Comanche, 13 (392)	402
*Guthrie, King, 9 (151)	164
Gutierrez, Starr (69)	9
*Guy, Fort Bend, 19	239
Guys Store, Leon	20
H	
Haciendito, Presidio	10
HACKBERRY, Denton (2,973)	2,961
Hackberry, Edwards	3
Hackberry, Lavaca	40
Hackberry, Garza	5
Hackberry, Cottle	30
Hagansport, Franklin	40
Hagerville, Houston	70
Hail, Fannin	30
Hainesville, Wood, 1	95
*HALE CENTER, Hale, 44 (2,062)	2,015
Halfway, Hale	165
Hall, San Saba	25
*HALLETTSVILLE, Lavaca, 315 (2,731)	2,742
Halls Bluff, Houston	67
HALLSBURG, McLennan (419)	433
*HALLSVILLE, Harrison, 231 (4,277)	4,528
*HALTOM CITY, Tarrant, 1,323 (46,073)	45,746
Hamby, Taylor	100
*HAMILTON, Hamilton, 204 (2,895)	2,871
*HAMLIN, Jones, Fisher, 68 (1,831)	1,879
Hammond, Robertson	44
Hamon, Gonzales, 1	20
*Hamshire, Jefferson, 40 (962)	1,420
Hancock, Dawson	20
Hancock, Comal	1,000
*Hankamer, Chambers, 22	226
Hannibal, Erath	25
Hanover, Milam	25
*HAPPY, Swisher, Randall, 41 (602)	613
Happy Union, Hale	25
Happy Valley, Taylor	12
Harbin, Erath	21
*HARDIN, Liberty, 5 (768)	811
Harding Gill Tract, Hidalgo (21)	21
Hare, Williamson	60
*Hargill, Hidalgo, 5 (800)	1,094
*HARKER HEIGHTS, Bell, 726 (33,097)	33,560
Harkeyville, San Saba	12
*Harleton, Harrison, 32	390
*HARLINGEN, Cameron, 2,522 (71,829)	71,925
Harmon, Lamar	12
Harmony, Kent	10
Harmony, Grimes	12
Harmony, Floyd	42
Harmony, Nacogdoches	50
*Harper, Gillespie, 117 (1,332)	1,203
Harpersville, Stephens	5
Harrison, McLennan	100
Harrold, Wilbarger, 4 (87)	129
*HART, Castro, 26 (869)	882
Hartburg, Newton	893
Hart Camp, Lamb	4
*Hartley, Hartley, 32 (382)	368
Harvard, Camp	48
Harvey, Brazos	1,000
Harwell Point, Burnet	138
*Harwood, Gonzales, 41 (120)	36
*HASKELL, Haskell, 125 (3,089)	3,046
Haslam, Shelby	100
*HASLET, Tarrant, 678 (1,952)	2,371
Hasse, Comanche	50
Hatchel, Runnels	6

The Haltom City watertower. Photo by Wil C. Fry, Flickr, CC by NC ND 2.0

Town, County	Pop. 2021
Hatchettville, Hopkins	20
Havana, Hidalgo (361)	252
HAWK COVE, Hunt (452)	462
*HAWKINS, Wood, 157 (1,274)	1,314
*HAWLEY, Jones, 75 (545)	566
Hawthorne, Walker	100
Haynesville, Wichita	65
HAYS, Hays (227)	240
Hazeldell, Comanche	12
H. Cuellar Estates, Starr (11)	85
*HEARNE, Robertson, 209 (4,544)	4,531
Heartland, Kaufman, 80 (8,509)	7,114
HEATH, Rockwall, Kaufman, 280 (9,769)	10,266
*Hebbronville, Jim Hogg, 121 (4,101)	4,283
HEBRON, Denton (803)	803
Heckville, Lubbock	91
*HEDLEY, Donley, 19 (275)	278
Hedwigs Hill, Mason	12
HEDWIG VILLAGE, Harris, 44 (2,370)	2,328
Hefner, Knox	3
Hegar, Waller	100
Heidelberg, Hidalgo (1,507)	2,011
*Heidenheimer, Bell, 6	224
Helena, Karnes	35
Helmic, Trinity	86
*HELOTES, Bexar, 765 (9,030)	9,178
*HEMPHILL, Sabine, 218 (1,029)	1,008
*HEMPSTEAD, Waller, 420 (5,430)	6,028
*HENDERSON, Rusk, 786 (13,271)	13,502
Henkhaus, Lavaca	88
Henly, Hays	140
*HENRIETTA, Clay, 147 (3,111)	3,102
Henry's Chapel, Cherokee	75
*HEREFORD, DeafSmith, 456 (14,972)	14,779
Hermits Cove, Rains	40
*Hermleigh, Scurry, 29 (383)	428
Hester, Navarro	35
*HEWITT, McLennan, 388 (16,026)	16,131
*Hext, Menard, 1	75
HICKORY CREEK, Denton, 137 (4,718)	5,244
Hickory Creek, Houston	31
Hickory Creek, Hunt	40
*HICO, Hamilton, 213 (1,335)	1,343
*HIDALGO, Hidalgo, 575 (13,964)	14,239
HIDEAWAY, Smith, 50 (3,201)	3,251
Higginbotham, Gaines	21
*HIGGINS, Lipscomb, 14 (356)	345
High, Lamar	14
Highbank, Falls	20
High Hill, Fayette	176
*High Island, Galveston, 9	300
Highland, Erath, 1	60
HIGHLAND HAVEN, Burnet, 4 (418)	418
HIGHLAND PARK, Dallas, 66 (8,864)	8,747
*Highlands, Harris, 194 (8,612)	7,714
HIGHLAND VILLAGE, Denton, 546 (15,899)	15,952
Hightower, Liberty	225
HILL COUNTRY VILLAGE, Bexar, 30 (942)	940
Hillcrest, Colorado	25
HILLCREST VILLAGE, Brazoria, (705)	693
*Hillister, Tyler, 11	250
Hillje, Wharton, 1	51
Hills, Lee	20
*HILLSBORO, Hill, 410 (8,221)	8,305
Hillside Acres, Webb (3)	3
Hilltop, Frio (356)	209
Hilltop, Starr (120)	204
*Hilltop Lakes, Leon, 27 (1,385)	713
HILSHIRE VILLAGE, Harris, 2 (816)	806
Hinckley, Lamar	40
Hindes, Atascosa	14
Hinkles Ferry, Brazoria	100
Hiram, Kaufman	75
*HITCHCOCK, Galveston, 220 (7,301)	7,408
Hitchland, Hansford	15
Hix, Burleson	35
Hoard, Wood	45
Hobbs, Fisher	32
Hobson, Karnes, 18	135
Hochheim, DeWitt	70
*Hockley, Harris, 480	400
Hodges, Jones	150
Hogansville, Rains	300
Hogg, Burleson	20
Holiday Beach, Aransas (526)	353
HOLIDAY LAKES, Brazoria, 6 (991)	1,022
*HOLLAND, Bell, 70 (1,075)	1,086
Holland Quarters, Panola	40
*HOLLIDAY, Archer, 66 (1,524)	1,570
Holly, Houston	95
Holly Grove, Polk	20
Holly Lake Ranch, Wood, 47 (2,951)	2,482
Holly Springs, Jasper, Newton	50
HOLLYWOOD PARK, Bexar, 37 (3,130)	3,106
Holman, Fayette	101
Homer, Angelina	475
Homestead Meadows North, El Paso (5,210)	6,521
Homestead Meadows South, El Paso (7,142)	7,981
*HONDO, Medina, 393 (8,289)	8,387
*HONEY GROVE, Fannin, 112 (1,715)	1,753
Honey Island, Hardin	200
Hood, Cooke	13
Hooker Ridge, Rains	250
*HOOKS, Bowie, 80 (2,518)	2,514
Hoover, Gray	5
Hoover, Lamar	20
Hope, Lavaca	45
Hopewell, Houston	22
Hopewell, Franklin	50
Hopewell, Red River	152
Hopewell, Lamar	90
Hopewell, Smith	45
HORIZON CITY, El Paso, 403 (22,489)	23,162
Hornsby Bend, Travis (12,168)	9,866
Horseshoe Bend, Cooke (949)	642
HORSESHOE BAY, Llano, Burnet, 173 (4,257)	4,490
Hortense, Polk	20
Horton, Delta	40
Horton, Panola	200
*HOUSTON, Harris, Fort Bend, Montgomery, 95,232 (2,304,580)	2,288,250
Howard, Ellis	60
HOWARDWICK, Donley, 7 (370)	371
*HOWE, Grayson, 114 (3,571)	3,615
Howland, Lamar	65
Hoxie, Williamson	60
Hoyte, Milam	20
Hub, Parmer	25
*HUBBARD, Hill, 76 (1,394)	1,402
Hubbard, Bowie	350
Huber, Shelby	15
Huckabay, Erath (268)	319
HUDSON, Angelina, 5 (4,849)	4,986
Hudson Bend, Travis (4,005)	3,035
HUDSON OAKS, Parker, 223 (2,174)	2,478
Huffines, Cass	140
*Huffman, Harris, 324	15,000
Hufsmith, Harris	500
*HUGHES SPRINGS, Cass, 136 (1,575)	1,543
*Hull, Liberty, 37 (522)	475
*HUMBLE, Harris, 4,133 (16,795)	16,396
*Hungerford, Wharton, 13 (390)	92
*Hunt, Kerr, 44	708
Hunter, Comal	40
HUNTERS CREEK VILLAGE, Harris (4,385)	4,314
*HUNTINGTON, Angelina, 153 (2,025)	2,019
Huntoon, Ochiltree	22
*HUNTSVILLE, Walker, 1,406 (45,941)	46,288
Hurley, Wood	30
Hurlwood, Lubbock	152
Hurnville, Clay	10
*HURST, Tarrant, 1,590 (40,413)	40,055
Hurstown, Shelby	20
Hurst Springs, Coryell	10
*HUTCHINS, Dallas, 157 (5,607)	5,566
*HUTTO, Williamson, 1,061 (27,577)	30,855
HUXLEY, Shelby, 1 (361)	359
*Hye, Blanco, 25	72
Hylton, Nolan	6

I

Town, County	Pop. 2021
Iago, Wharton, 2 (148)	17
Ida, Grayson	30
*IDALOU, Lubbock, 115 (2,193)	2,152
Iglesia Antigua, Cameron (415)	121
Ike, Ellis	50
Illinois Bend, Montague	40
IMPACT, Taylor (22)	20
*Imperial, Pecos, 8 (294)	245
Inadale, Scurry	12

Town, County	Pop. 2021
Independence, Washington, 1	140
India, Ellis	30
Indian Creek, Brown	28
Indian Creek, Smith	300
Indian Gap, Hamilton	35
Indian Hill, Newton	7
Indian Hills, Hidalgo (2,694)	2,454
INDIAN LAKE, Cameron, 2 (839)	851
Indianola, Calhoun	200
Indian Rock, Upshur	45
Indian Springs, Polk (892)	684
Indio, Starr (65)	65
Indio, Presidio	5
*INDUSTRY, Austin, 38 (268)	273
*Inez, Victoria, 103 (2,641)	2,385
*INGLESIDE, San Patricio, 216 (9,519)	9,898
INGLESIDE ON THE BAY, San Patricio, 1 (614)	608
*INGRAM, Kerr, 171 (1,787)	1,813
*IOLA, Grimes, 75 (311)	322
IOWA COLONY, Brazoria, 59 (8,154)	10,883
*IOWA PARK, Wichita, 234 (6,535)	6,547
*Ira, Scurry, 16	250
*IRAAN, Pecos, 63 (1,055)	1,037
*IREDELL, Bosque, 33 (305)	310
Ireland, Coryell	60
*Irene, Hill, 2	170
Ironton, Cherokee	110
*IRVING, Dallas, 6,757 (256,684)	254,198
Isla, Sabine	350
Israel, Polk	25
*ITALY, Ellis, 88 (1,926)	1,981
*ITASCA, Hill, 74 (1,562)	1,625
Ivan, Stephens	15
IVANHOE, Tyler, 24 (1,327)	1,372
*Ivanhoe, Fannin	110
Izoro, Lampasas, Coryell	17

J

Town, County	Pop. 2021
JACINTO CITY, Harris, 89 (9,613)	9,378
*JACKSBORO, Jack, 248 (4,184)	4,209
Jackson, Van Zandt	25
Jackson, Shelby	50
*JACKSONVILLE, Cherokee, 815 (13,997)	14,074
Jacobia, Hunt	60
Jakes Colony, Guadalupe	95
JAMAICA BEACH, Galveston, 22 (1,078)	1,072
James, Shelby	75
Jamestown, Smith	75
Jamestown, Newton	196
Jardin de San Julian, Starr (23)	23
*JARRELL, Williamson, 327 (1,753)	2,111
*JASPER, Jasper, 503 (6,884)	7,285
*JAYTON, Kent, 18 (511)	503
Jean, Young	110
*JEFFERSON, Marion, 269 (1,875)	1,849
Jenkins, Morris	350
Jennings, Lamar	85
*Jermyn, Jack, 2	75
JERSEY VILLAGE, Harris, 300 (7,921)	7,731
*JEWETT, Leon, 93 (793)	797
JF Villarreal, Starr (82)	324
Jiba, Kaufman	50
*JOAQUIN, Shelby, 73 (734)	728
Joe Lee, Bell	8
*JOHNSON CITY, Blanco, 272 (1,627)	1,717
Johnsville, Erath	45
Johntown, Red River	175
*Joinerville, Rusk	140
Joliet, Caldwell	70
JOLLY, Clay, 1 (172)	173
Jollyville, Williamson, Travis	18,409
Jonah, Williamson	60
*Jonesboro, Coryell, Hamilton, 27	125
JONES CREEK, Brazoria, 19 (1,975)	1,959
Jones Prairie, Milam	20
JONESTOWN, Travis, 138 (2,365)	2,456
*Jonesville, Harrison, 1	70
Joplin, Jack	15
Joppa, Burnet	84
Jordans Store, Shelby	20
*JOSEPHINE, Collin, 52 (2,119)	4,565
*JOSHUA, Johnson, 435 (7,891)	8,098
Josserand, Trinity	29
Jot-Em-Down, Delta, Hunt	8
*JOURDANTON, Atascosa, 194 (4,094)	4,127
Joy, Clay	110
Jozye, Madison	36
Juarez, Cameron (642)	1,948
Jud, Haskell	60
*Judson, Gregg, 3	1,057
Juliff, Fort Bend	100
Jumbo, Panola	60
*JUNCTION, Kimble, 213 (2,451)	2,494
Justiceburg, Garza, 10	45
*JUSTIN, Denton, 461 (4,409)	5,031

K

Town, County	Pop. 2021
Kalgary, Crosby	2
*Kamay, Wichita, 5	640
Kamey, Calhoun	25
Kanawha, Red River	90
*Karnack, Harrison, 41	350
*KARNES CITY, Karnes, 133 (3,111)	3,270
Karon, Live Oak	25
Katemcy, Mason	80
*KATY, Harris, Waller, Fort Bend, 9,903 (21,894)	24,005
*KAUFMAN, Kaufman, 566 (6,797)	7,379
K-Bar Ranch, Jim Wells (375)	456
Keechi, Leon	15

CITIES & TOWNS

The Jamaica Beach City Hall and emergency services building. Photo by Whisper to me, Public Domain

Town, County	Pop. 2021
*KEENE, Johnson, 81 (6,387)	6,346
Keeter, Wise	250
Keith, Grimes	50
*KELLER, Tarrant, 1,411 (45,776)	45,397
Kellerville, Wheeler	15
Kellogg, Hunt	20
Kellyville, Marion	75
Kelsey, Upshur	50
Kelton, Wheeler	34
*KEMAH, Galveston, 415 (1,807)	1,803
*KEMP, Kaufman, 238 (1,129)	1,178
Kemper City, Victoria	16
*KEMPNER, Lampasas, 176 (1,146)	1,182
*Kendalia, Kendall, 18	149
*KENDLETON, Fort Bend, 7 (343)	342
*KENEDY, Karnes, 201 (3,473)	3,626
KENEFICK, Liberty, 3 (615)	668
*KENNARD, Houston, 30 (272)	280
*KENNEDALE, Tarrant, 371 (8,517)	8,463
*Kenney, Austin, 4	957
Kenser, Hunt	100
Kensing, Delta	30
Kent, Culberson, 3	30
Kentucky Town, Grayson	20
*KERENS, Navarro, 78 (1,505)	1,505
*KERMIT, Winkler, 248 (6,267)	6,016
Kerrick, Dallam, 1	35
*KERRVILLE, Kerr, 1,578 (24,278)	24,477
Kerrville South, Kerr	6,600
Key, Dawson	10
Kiam, Polk	24
Kicaster, Wilson	190
Kickapoo Indian Reservation, Maverick	366
*Kildare, Cass	104
*KILGORE, Gregg, Rusk, 955 (13,376)	13,383
*KILLEEN, Bell, 3,047 (153,095)	156,261
King, Coryell	30
King Ranch Headquarters, Kleberg	191
*KINGSBURY, Guadalupe, 83 (132)	134
*Kingsland, Llano, 275 (7,028)	6,917
Kingston, Hunt	140
*KINGSVILLE, Kleberg, 644 (25,402)	25,069
Kingtown, Nacogdoches	300
Kingwood, Harris, Montgomery, 1,455	[part of Houston]
Kinkler, Lavaca	75
Kiomatia, Red River	50
KIRBY, Bexar, 85 (8,142)	8,100
*KIRBYVILLE, Jasper, 170 (2,036)	2,003
Kirk, Limestone	10
Kirkland, Childress, Hardeman	25
Kirtley, Fayette	93
*KIRVIN, Freestone, 4 (101)	103
Kittrell, Walker	126
Klein, Harris, 58	45,000
Klondike, Dawson	50
*Klondike, Delta, 9	175
Klump, Washington	20
Knapp, Scurry	10
*Knickerbocker, Tom Green, 3	94
*Knippa, Uvalde, 19 (606)	808
Knobbs Springs, Lee	20
KNOLLWOOD, Grayson, 3 (764)	776
*Knott, Howard, 8	200
*KNOX CITY, Knox, 49 (1,065)	1,052
Koerth, Lavaca	45
Kokomo, Eastland	25
Komensky, Lavaca	75
*Kopperl, Bosque, 23 (164)	121
Kosciusko, Wilson	390
*KOSSE, Limestone, 37 (458)	454
*KOUNTZE, Hardin, 208 (1,981)	2,163
*KRESS, Swisher, 23 (596)	608
KRUGERVILLE, Denton, 69 (1,766)	1,920
*KRUM, Denton, 266 (5,483)	5,823
*KURTEN, Brazos, 4 (395)	406
*KYLE, Hays, 1,315 (45,697)	51,789
Kyote, Atascosa	34
L	
LaBelle, Jefferson	40
*La Blanca, Hidalgo, 21 (2,078)	3,304
La Carla, Starr (55)	82
La Casita, Starr (139)	139
Laceola, Madison	10
La Chuparosa, Starr (74)	74
Lackland Air Force Base, Bexar, 32 (9,467)	7,417
La Coma, Webb (7)	34
La Coma Heights, (nc)	110
*LA COSTE, Medina, 47 (1,077)	1,107
Lacy, Trinity	44
LACY-LAKEVIEW, McLennan, 63 (6,988)	7,090
*LADONIA, Fannin, 26 (597)	612
La Escondida, Starr (183)	242
La Esperanza, Starr (217)	64
LaFayette, Upshur	80
*LA FERIA, Cameron, 253 (6,817)	6,814
La Feria North, Cameron (225)	219
Lagarto, Live Oak	735
La Gloria, Jim Wells	70
La Gloria, Starr	150
Lago, Cameron (161)	86
Lago Vista, Starr (133)	9,348
*LAGO VISTA, Travis, 367 (8,896)	91
*LA GRANGE, Fayette, 562 (4,391)	4,423
*LA GRULLA, Starr, 7 (1,222)	1,207
Laguna, Uvalde	8
Laguna Heights, Cameron, 19 (962)	1,521
Laguna Park, Bosque, 12 (1,372)	1,520
Laguna Seca, Hidalgo (232)	239
LAGUNA VISTA, Cameron, 68 (3,520)	3,605
Laguna Vista, Burnet	94
La Homa, Hidalgo (11,267)	11,924
*Laird Hill, Rusk, 1	300
La Isla, El Paso	27
Lajitas, Brewster, 6	75
*LA JOYA, Hidalgo, 105 (4,457)	4,587
La Junta, Parker	300
Lake Arrowhead, Clay	250
LAKE BRIDGEPORT, Wise, 2 (339)	349
Lake Brownwood, Brown (1,462)	1,595
Lake Bryan, Brazos (2,060)	1,555
Lake Cherokee, Rusk (2,980)	3,336
Lake Cisco, Eastland	300
LAKE CITY, San Patricio, 7 (447)	458
Lake Colorado City, Mitchell (636)	752
*Lake Creek, Delta, Lamar, 3	55
*LAKE DALLAS, Denton, 235 (7,708)	7,722
Lake Dunlap, Guadalupe (1,981)	1,412
Lakehills, Bandera, 111 (5,295)	5,499
*LAKE JACKSON, Brazoria, 773 (28,177)	27,879
Lake Kiowa, Cooke, 33 (2,254)	2,409
Lake Leon, Eastland	75
Lake Medina Shores, Bandera, (1,110)	696
Lake Meredith Estates, Hutchinson, (338)	173
Lake Murvaul, Panola	300
Lake Nueces, Uvalde	60
LAKEPORT, Gregg, 12 (976)	972
Lakeshore Gardens-Hidden Acres, San Patricio (637)	337
LAKESIDE, San Patricio (338)	347
LAKESIDE, Tarrant, 37 (1,649)	1,624
LAKESIDE CITY, Archer, 7 (1,082)	1,150
Lakeside Village, Bosque	226
LAKE TANGLEWOOD, Randall, (686)	706
Lake Victor, Burnet	265
*LAKEVIEW, Hall, 3 (60)	60
Lake View, Val Verde (197)	176
Lakeview, Lynn	15
Lakeview, Floyd	39
Lakeview, Orange	75
*LAKEWAY, Travis, 682 (19,189)	19,300
Lakewood Harbor, Bosque	250
LAKEWOOD VILLAGE, Denton, 9 (635)	660
*LAKE WORTH, Tarrant, 268 (4,711)	4,674
La Loma de Falcon, Starr (72)	72
Lamar, Aransas, Refugio, 1 (724)	1,328
*LA MARQUE, Galveston, 380 (18,030)	18,697
Lamasco, Fannin	32
*LAMESA, Dawson, 344 (8,674)	8,751
La Minita, Starr (129)	81
Lamkin, Comanche (46)	17
La Moca Ranch, Webb (25)	44
*LAMPASAS, Lampasas, 511 (7,291)	7,517
Lanark, Cass	30
*LANCASTER, Dallas, 822 (41,275)	40,728
*Lane City, Wharton, 7	111
Lanely, Freestone	27
Laneport, Williamson	40
*Laneville, Rusk, 12	169
*Langtry, Val Verde	30
Lanier, Cass	80
Lannius, Fannin	79
Lantana, Denton, 216 (10,785)	11,559
La Paloma, Cameron (3,218)	3,138
La Paloma Addition, San Patricio, (314)	298

Town, County	Pop. 2021
La Paloma-Lost Creek, Nueces, (1,359)	670
La Paloma Ranchettes, Starr (329)	31
La Parita, Atascosa	48
*LA PORTE, Harris, 1,091 (35,124)	35,964
La Presa, Webb (241)	203
*La Pryor, Zavala, 32 (1,294)	973
La Puerta, Starr (638)	669
*LAREDO, Webb, 7,732 (255,205)	256,153
Laredo Ranchettes, Webb (21)	21
Laredo Ranchettes West, Webb (5)	5
La Reforma, Starr	20
Lariat, Parmer	100
La Rosita, Starr (82)	100
*Larue, Henderson, 40	250
*LaSalle, Jackson, 2	110
Lasana, Cameron (104)	83
*Lasara, Willacy, 7 (909)	857
Las Escobas, Starr	5
Las Haciendas, Webb (2)	2
Las Lomas, Starr (3,054)	1,882
Las Lomitas, Jim Hogg (235)	90
Las Palmas, Zapata (59)	47
Las Palmas II, Cameron (891)	1,128
Las Pilas, Webb (7)	7
Las Quintas Fronterizas, Maverick, (2,326)	1,062
Lassater, Marion, 1	60
Las Yescas, Cameron	221
Latch, Upshur	50
Latex, Harrison	75
*LATEXO, Houston, 4 (232)	242
La Tina Ranch, Cameron (687)	844
Latium, Washington	30
Laughlin Air Force Base, Val Verde, 8 (1,673)	1,989
Laurel, Newton	357
Laureles, Cameron (4,111)	3,691
Lavender, Limestone	30
*LA VERNIA, Wilson, 443 (1,077)	1,154
La Victoria, Starr (176)	188
*LA VILLA, Hidalgo, 18 (2,804)	2,712
*LAVON, Collin, 184 (4,469)	5,342
*LA WARD, Jackson, 8 (176)	189
*LAWN, Taylor, 13 (311)	312
Lawrence, Kaufman	259
*Lazbuddie, Parmer, 5	248
*LEAGUE CITY, Galveston, Harris, 2,164 (114,392)	115,595
Leagueville, Henderson	50
*LEAKEY, Real, 111 (315)	333
*LEANDER, Williamson, 1,856 (59,202)	67,124
LEARY, Bowie, 2 (433)	439
*Ledbetter, Fayette, Lee, 33	83
Leedale, Bell	24
*Leesburg, Camp, 16	128
*Leesville, Gonzales, 6	152
*LEFORS, Gray, 6 (420)	412
*Leggett, Polk, 4	500
Lehman, Cochran	6
Leigh, Harrison	60
Lela, Wheeler	135
*Lelia Lake, Donley, 2 (51)	55
*Leming, Atascosa, 8 (841)	549
*Lenorah, Martin, 14	83
Lenz, Karnes	50
Leo, Lee	10
Leo, Cooke	20
*LEONA, Leon, 13 (151)	157
*LEONARD, Fannin, 149 (1,987)	2,039
Leon Junction, Coryell	50
Leon Springs, Bexar	[part of San Antonio]
*LEON VALLEY, Bexar, 181 (11,542)	11,463
*LEROY, McLennan, 5 (354)	354
Lesley, Hall	25
*LEVELLAND, Hockley, 496 (12,652)	12,665
Leverett's Chapel, Rusk	400
Levi, McLennan	50
Levita, Coryell	70
*LEWISVILLE, Denton, 3,756 (111,822)	112,944
*LEXINGTON, Lee, 121 (1,217)	1,231
*LIBERTY, Liberty, 546 (8,279)	8,539
Liberty, Milam	40
Liberty, Newton	128
Liberty, Lubbock	228
Liberty City, Gregg, 2 (2,721)	2,160
*LIBERTY HILL, Williamson, 775 (3,646)	6,801
Liberty Hill, Milam	25
Liberty Hill, Houston	73
Lilbert, Nacogdoches	100
*Lillian, Johnson, 8	1,160
*Lincoln, Lee, 20	336
*LINDALE, Smith, 544 (6,059)	6,313
*LINDEN, Cass, 93 (1,825)	1,786
Lindenau, DeWitt	50
Lindendale, Kendall	70
*LINDSAY, Cooke, 28 (1,045)	1,069
Lindsay, Reeves (452)	905
*Lingleville, Erath, 3 (166)	269
*Linn, Hidalgo, 8 (733)	613
Linn Flat, Nacogdoches	60
Linwood, Cherokee	40
*LIPAN, Hood, 117 (505)	520
*Lipscomb, Lipscomb, 3 (66)	34
*Lissie, Wharton, 2	72
Littig, Travis	35
Little Cypress, Orange (1,968)	2,173
*LITTLE ELM, Denton, 1,046 (46,453)	51,042
*LITTLEFIELD, Lamb, 161 (5,943)	5,871
Little Hope, Wood	25
Little Midland, Burnet	82
Little New York, Gonzales	15
*LITTLE RIVER-ACADEMY, Bell, 49 (1,992)	1,989
Lively, Kaufman	50
LIVE OAK, Bexar, 373 (15,781)	15,840
*LIVERPOOL, Brazoria, 26 (475)	494
*LIVINGSTON, Polk, 1,014 (5,640)	5,829
*LLANO, Llano, 314 (3,325)	3,347
Llano Grande, Hidalgo (2,952)	2,103
Locker, San Saba	16
Lockett, Wilbarger (173)	357
Lockettville, Hockley	20
*LOCKHART, Caldwell, 567 (14,379)	14,844
*LOCKNEY, Floyd, 54 (1,498)	1,481
Locust, Grayson	118
*Lodi, Marion	175
Loebau, Lee	35
Logan, Panola	40
LOG CABIN, Henderson, 7 (678)	749
*Lohn, McCulloch, 8	149
Loire, Wilson, Atascosa	50
Lois, Cooke	10
*Lolita, Jackson, 27 (519)	715
Loma Alta, McMullen	25
Loma Alta, Val Verde	30
Loma Grande, Zavala (135)	165
Loma Linda, San Patricio (149)	125
Loma Linda East, Jim Wells (305)	23
Loma Linda East, Starr (67)	67
Loma Linda West, Starr (98)	96
Loma Vista, Starr (117)	37
Lomax, Howard	25
*LOMETA, Lampasas, 50 (753)	766
*London, Kimble, 16	180
Lone Camp, Palo Pinto	110
Lone Cedar, Ellis	18
Lone Grove, Llano	50
*LONE OAK, Hunt, 78 (643)	725
Lone Oak, Colorado	50
Lone Pine, Houston	81
*LONE STAR, Morris, 59 (1,400)	1,407
Lone Star, Cherokee	20
Lone Star, Lamar	35
Lone Star, Floyd	42
*Long Branch, Panola, 12	150
Long Lake, Anderson	30
Long Mott, Calhoun	76
Longoria, Starr (81)	58
Longpoint, Washington	30
*LONGVIEW, Gregg, Harrison, 3,963 (81,638)	81,762
Longworth, Fisher	47
Looneyville, Nacogdoches	50
*Loop, Gaines, 8 (216)	190
*Lopeño, Zapata, 2 (70)	42
Lopezville, Hidalgo (2,367)	1,683
*LORAINE, Mitchell, 12 (504)	550
*LORENA, McLennan, 272 (1,785)	1,791
*LORENZO, Crosby, 29 (964)	964
Los Altos, Webb (175)	113
Los Alvarez, Starr (247)	190
Los Angeles, La Salle	15
Los Angeles Subdivision, Willacy, (108)	366
Los Arcos, Webb (83)	35
Los Arrieros, Starr (43)	43
Los Barreras, Starr (278)	408
Los Centenarios, Webb (49)	49
Los Corralitos, Webb (36)	36
*Los Ebanos, Hidalgo, 3 (239)	42
Los Ebanos, Starr (281)	666
Los Escondidos, Burnet	80
*LOS FRESNOS, Cameron, 437 (8,114)	8,152
Los Fresnos, Webb (71)	218
Los Huisaches, Webb (15)	38
*LOS INDIOS, Cameron, 12 (1,008)	1,012
Los Lobos, Zapata (7)	7
Los Minerales, Webb (30)	30

Town, County	Pop. 2021
Los Nopalitos, Webb (49)	49
Losoya, Bexar	500
Lost Creek, Travis (1,276)	1,157
Lost Prairie, Limestone	2
Los Veteranos I, Webb (0)	42
Los Veteranos II, Webb (11)	25
LOS YBANEZ, Dawson (28)	22
*LOTT, Falls, 88 (644)	668
*Louise, Wharton, 66 (889)	1,061
Lovelace, Hill	30
*LOVELADY, Houston, 61 (570)	587
*Loving, Young, 7 (143)	95
*Lowake, Concho, 2	40
LOWRY CROSSING, Collin, 1 (1,689)	1,695
Loyal Valley, Mason	52
Loyola Beach, Kleberg	185
*Lozano, Cameron, 1 (174)	174
*LUBBOCK, Lubbock, 8,657 (257,141)	260,993
LUCAS, Collin, 191 (7,612)	8,029
Luckenbach, Gillespie	25
*LUEDERS, Jones, 10 (258)	261
Luella, Grayson	639
*LUFKIN, Angelina, 2,060 (34,143)	34,074
*LULING, Caldwell, 274 (5,599)	5,518
*LUMBERTON, Hardin, 573 (13,554)	13,802
Lums Chapel, Lamb	6
Luther, Howard	3
Lutie, Collingsworth	10
Lydia, Red River	109
*LYFORD, Willacy, 69 (2,249)	2,210
Lynn Grove, Grimes	25
*Lyons, Burleson, 4 (236)	505
*LYTLE, Atascosa, Medina, Bexar, 224 (2,914)	2,965
Lytton Springs, Caldwell, 1	300
M	
*MABANK, Kaufman, Henderson, 409 (4,050)	4,562
Mabelle, Baylor	9
Mabry, Red River	60
*Macdona, Bexar, 1 (464)	466
Macon, Franklin	21
Macune, San Augustine	50
*MADISONVILLE, Madison, 259 (4,420)	4,565
Madras, Red River	61
Magnet, Wharton	42
*MAGNOLIA, Montgomery, 2,266 (2,359)	2,635
Magnolia, San Jacinto	150
Magnolia Beach, Calhoun (217)	108
Magnolia Springs, Jasper, 2	20
Maha, Travis	200
Mahl, Nacogdoches	150
Mahomet, Burnet	97
Majors, Franklin	13
*MALAKOFF, Henderson, 179 (2,179)	2,219
Mallard, Montague	12
*MALONE, Hill, 18 (237)	240
Malta, Bowie	350
Malvern, Leon	12
Mambrino, Hood	74
*Manchaca, Travis, 165 (2,266)	1,685
Manchester, Red River	185
Mangum, Eastland	15
Manheim, Lee	50
Mankin, Henderson	30
Mankins, Archer	10
*MANOR, Travis, 657 (13,652)	18,285
*MANSFIELD, Tarrant, Johnson, Ellis, 2,347 (72,602)	74,368
Manuel Garcia, Starr (204)	282
Manuel Garcia II, Starr (62)	62
*MANVEL, Brazoria, 517 (9,992)	12,355
Maple, Red River	30
Maple, Bailey, 1	40
Maple Springs, Titus	25
Mapleton, Houston	32
*Marathon, Brewster, 30 (410)	427
*MARBLE FALLS, Burnet, 872 (7,037)	7,227
*MARFA, Presidio, 208 (1,788)	1,750
Margaret, Foard, Hardeman	50
Marie, Runnels	10
*MARIETTA, Cass, 7 (115)	113
*MARION, Guadalupe, 206 (1,034)	1,044
*Markham, Matagorda, 21 (908)	983
Markley, Young	25
*MARLIN, Falls, 164 (5,462)	5,543
Marlow, Milam	45
*MARQUEZ, Leon, 48 (181)	182
Mars, Van Zandt, Henderson	20
*MARSHALL, Harrison, 1,014 (23,392)	22,662
Marston, Polk	25
*MART, McLennan, 71 (1,748)	1,791
*MARTINDALE, Caldwell, 83 (1,253)	1,209
Martinez, Starr (42)	42
Martins Mill, Van Zandt	158
Martin Springs, Hopkins	200
*Martinsville, Nacogdoches	350
Marvin, Lamar	48
Maryetta, Jack	7
*Maryneal, Nolan, 4	50
Marysville, Cooke	12
*MASON, Mason, 216 (2,121)	2,119
Massey Lake, Anderson	30
Masterson, Moore, 2	2
*MATADOR, Motley, 37 (569)	571
*Matagorda, Matagorda, 53 (313)	431
*MATHIS, San Patricio, 208 (4,333)	4,354
Matthews, Colorado	20
*MAUD, Bowie, 55 (977)	975
*Mauriceville, Orange, 13 (2,983)	2,597
Maverick, Runnels	35
Maxdale, Bell	25
Maxey, Lamar	70
*Maxwell, Caldwell, 62	500
*May, Brown, 33 (277)	226
*Maydelle, Cherokee, 2	250
Mayfield, Hill	25
Mayfield, Hale	26
Mayflower, Newton	50
Maynard, San Jacinto	90
*MAYPEARL, Ellis, 55 (939)	944
Maysfield, Milam	140
*McAdoo, Dickens, 2	75
*McALLEN, Hidalgo, 5,797 (142,210)	143,920
McBeth, Brazoria	20
*McCAMEY, Upton, 81 (1,831)	1,825
*McCaulley, Fisher, 4 (79)	36
McClanahan, Falls	30
McCook, Hidalgo, 1	50
McCoy, Floyd	20
McCoy, Kaufman	20
McCoy, Atascosa, 7	30
McCoy, Panola	30
McCoy, Red River	175
*McDade, Bastrop, 66 (720)	1,376
*McFaddin, Victoria, 1	50
McGirk, Hamilton, Mills	18
*McGREGOR, McLennan, 300 (5,321)	5,522
*McKINNEY, Collin, 5,699 (195,308)	202,690
McKinney Acres, Andrews (852)	842
*McLEAN, Gray, 32 (665)	654
McLENDON-CHISHOLM, Rockwall (3,562)	4,206
*McLeod, Cass, 4 (311)	305
McMahan, Caldwell, 3	90
McMillin, San Saba	15
McNair, Harris	2,039
McNary, Hudspeth	100
McNeil, Caldwell	50
*McQueeney, Guadalupe, 69 (2,397)	2,536
*MEADOW, Terry, 28 (601)	592
Meadow Grove, Bell	22
MEADOWLAKES, Burnet, 39 (1,907)	1,922
MEADOWS PLACE, Fort Bend, 99 (4,767)	4,671
Mecca, Madison, Grimes	48
Medicine Mound, Hardeman	25
Medill, Lamar	50
Medina, Zapata (3,953)	5,004
*Medina, Bandera, 53	850
Meeker, Jefferson	2,280
Meeks, Bell	6
*MEGARGEL, Archer, 11 (174)	177
*MELISSA, Collin, 366 (13,901)	16,983
Melrose, Nacogdoches	400
*MELVIN, McCulloch, 6 (123)	124
*MEMPHIS, Hall, 60 (2,048)	2,055
*MENARD, Menard, 82 (1,348)	1,355
Mendoza, Caldwell	100
Menlow, Hill	12
*Mentone, Loving, 19 (22)	8
Mentz, Colorado	100
*MERCEDES, Hidalgo, 672 (16,258)	16,312
Mercury, McCulloch	166
*Mereta, Tom Green, 5	131
*MERIDIAN, Bosque, 125 (1,396)	1,407
*Merit, Hunt, 1	225
*MERKEL, Taylor, 136 (2,471)	2,457
Merle, Burleson	10
Merriman, Eastland	14
*MERTENS, Hill, 6 (144)	149
*MERTZON, Irion, 65 (747)	771
*MESQUITE, Dallas, Kaufman, 3,129 (150,108)	147,691

Town, County	Pop. 2021
Mesquite, Starr (479)	181
Metcalf Gap, Palo Pinto	6
*MEXIA, Limestone, 336 (6,893)	6,876
Meyersville, Washington	15
*Meyersville, DeWitt, 16	110
*MIAMI, Roberts, 29 (539)	521
Mico, Medina, 63	107
Midcity, Lamar	50
Middleton, Leon	26
*Midfield, Matagorda, 13 (356)	58
*Midkiff, Upton, 20	182
*MIDLAND, Midland, Martin, 6,228 (132,524)	131,325
*MIDLOTHIAN, Ellis, 1,294 (35,125)	37,053
*MIDWAY, Madison, Montgomery, 33 (173)	184
Midway, Limestone	9
Midway, Dawson	12
Midway, Upshur	20
Midway, Jim Wells	24
Midway, Van Zandt	31
Midway, Red River	40
Midway, Fannin	51
Midway, Titus	110
Midway, Polk	525
Midway North, Hidalgo (4,232)	3,573
Midway South, Hidalgo (2,307)	2,563
Midyett, Panola	150
Miguel Barrera, Starr (132)	137
Mikes, Starr (942)	1,394
Mikeska, Live Oak	10
Mila Doce, Hidalgo (6,162)	7,047
*Milam, Sabine, 22 (1,355)	1,697
*MILANO, Milam, 41 (390)	398
Milburn, McCulloch	8
MILDRED, Navarro, 1 (399)	413
*MILES, Runnels, 61 (875)	907
*MILFORD, Ellis, 23 (722)	730
Mill Creek, Washington	40
Miller Grove, Hopkins	115
MILLERS COVE, Titus, 2 (71)	72
*Millersview, Concho, 7	80
Millett, La Salle	60
Millheim, Austin	170
*Millican, Brazos, 6	240
*MILLSAP, Parker, 124 (370)	386
Milo Center, DeafSmith	5
Milton, Lamar	50
Mims, Brazoria	160
*Minden, Rusk, 2	150
*MINEOLA, Wood, 517 (4,823)	4,949
Mineral, Bee, 3	65
*MINERAL WELLS, Palo Pinto, Parker, 694 (14,820)	14,902
Minerva, Milam	100
Mings Chapel, Upshur	50
*MINGUS, Palo Pinto, 34 (223)	230
Minter, Lamar	78
Mi Ranchito Estate, Starr (409)	921
Mirando City, Webb, 11 (222)	189
*MISSION, Hidalgo, 2,976 (85,778)	86,223
Mission Bend, Fort Bend, Harris, (36,914)	38,772
Mission Valley, Victoria	225
*MISSOURI CITY, Fort Bend, Harris, 2,521 (74,259)	74,850
Mixon, Cherokee	50
*MOBEETIE, Wheeler, 11 (87)	86
MOBILE CITY, Rockwall (142)	145
Moffat, Bell	1,406
Moffett, Angelina	100
Moline, Lampasas	32
*MONAHANS, Ward, 415 (7,836)	7,498
Monaville, Waller, 1	180
Monkstown, Fannin	35
Monroe, Rusk	96
Monroe City, Chambers	5
Mont, Lavaca	30
*Montague, Montague, 30 (261)	248
*Montalba, Anderson, 24	110
*MONT BELVIEU, Chambers, 185 (7,654)	8,337
Monte Alto, Hidalgo, 36 (1,930)	2,136
Monte Grande, Cameron	97
Montell, Uvalde	20
*MONTGOMERY, Montgomery, 1,855 (1,948)	2,321
Monthalia, Gonzales	32
Monticello, Titus	20
*MOODY, McLennan, 115 (1,376)	1,411
*Moore, Frio, 27 (610)	122
Moore's Crossing, Travis	25
MOORE STATION, Henderson, (160)	159
Mooreville, Falls	96
Mooring, Brazos	80
Moraida, Starr (229)	229
Morales, Jackson	72
Morales-Sanchez, Zapata (46)	46
*MORAN, Shackelford, 11 (226)	236
Moravia, Lavaca, 1	165
*MORGAN, Bosque, 39 (454)	457
Morgan Creek, Burnet	126
Morgan Farm Area, San Patricio, (573)	370
*Morgan Mill, Erath, 4	206
MORGAN'S POINT, Harris, 9 (273)	271
MORGAN'S POINT RESORT, Bell, 14 (4,636)	4,713
Morning Glory, El Paso (522)	494
*Morse, Hansford, 4 (157)	251
*MORTON, Cochran, 37 (1,690)	1,668
Morton, Harrison	75
Morton Valley, Eastland	46
*Moscow, Polk, 15	170
Mosheim, Bosque (48)	18
Moss Bluff, Liberty	65
Moss Hill, Liberty, 3	180
Mostyn, Montgomery	90
*MOULTON, Lavaca, 66 (854)	861
*Mound, Coryell, 1 (174)	214
Mound City, Anderson, Houston	25
MOUNTAIN CITY, Hays, 12 (622)	656
*Mountain Home, Kerr, 51	96
Mountain Peak, Ellis	300

Midlothian is home to three different cement production facilities. Photo by Nicholas Henderson, Flickr, CC 2.0

Town, County	Pop. 2021
Mountain Springs, Cooke	600
Mount Bethel, Panola	65
*MOUNT CALM, Hill, 23 (282)	290
*MOUNT ENTERPRISE, Rusk, 77 (505)	504
Mount Haven, Cherokee	30
Mount Hermon, Shelby	80
Mount Olive, Lavaca	50
*MOUNT PLEASANT, Titus, 855 (16,047)	16,079
Mount Rose, Falls	15
Mount Selman, Cherokee	325
Mount Sylvan, Smith	181
*MOUNT VERNON, Franklin, 174 (2,491)	2,477
Mount Vernon, Houston	43
Mozelle, Coleman	15
Muellersville, Washington	20
*MUENSTER, Cooke, 147 (1,536)	1,580
Mulberry, Fannin	141
Muldoon, Fayette, 17	95
*MULESHOE, Bailey, 203 (5,160)	5,090
*MULLIN, Mills, 19 (130)	131
Mullins Prairie, Fayette	107
*Mumford, Robertson, 2	170
*MUNDAY, Knox, 52 (1,246)	1,240
Munger, Limestone	5
Mungerville, Dawson	20
Muniz, Hidalgo (1,593)	1,070
*MURCHISON, Henderson, 97 (516)	523
Murillo, Hidalgo (9,158)	8,989
MURPHY, Collin, 546 (21,013)	21,219
Murray, Young	29
Murvaul, Panola	150
MUSTANG, Navarro (0)	21
Mustang, Denton	25
Mustang Mott, DeWitt	20
MUSTANG RIDGE, Travis, Caldwell, 10 (944)	966
*Myra, Cooke, 2 (202)	382
Myrtle Springs, Van Zandt (954)	549

N

Town, County	Pop. 2021
*NACOGDOCHES, Nacogdoches, 1,631 (32,147)	32,118
*Nada, Colorado, 8 (231)	262
*NAPLES, Morris, 68 (1,387)	1,391
Narciso Pena, Starr (32)	32
Naruna, Burnet	95
*NASH, Bowie, 111 (3,814)	3,831
Nash, Ellis	40
NASSAU BAY, Harris, 54 (5,347)	5,213
Nat, Nacogdoches	50
*NATALIA, Medina, 116 (1,202)	1,271
NAVARRO, Navarro, 1 (232)	235
Navarro Mills, Navarro	90
*NAVASOTA, Grimes, 530 (7,643)	8,068
Navidad, Jackson	227
*NAZARETH, Castro, 31 (310)	312
Necessity, Stephens	10
Nechanitz, Fayette	57
*Neches, Anderson, 2 (266)	190
*NEDERLAND, Jefferson, 707 (18,856)	18,331
Needmore, Terry	7
Needmore, Bailey	20
*NEEDVILLE, Fort Bend, 276 (3,089)	3,062
Negley, Red River	136
Neinda, Jones	21
Nell, Live Oak	60
Nelson City, Kendall	50
Nelsonville, Austin	200
Nelta, Hopkins	36
*Nemo, Somervell, 22	56
Nesbitt, Harrison (273)	179
Netos, Starr (18)	18
Neuville, Shelby	65
*NEVADA, Collin, 159 (1,314)	1,331
*NEWARK, Wise, 70 (1,096)	1,149
*New Baden, Robertson, 2	150
NEW BERLIN, Guadalupe, 6 (656)	679
New Bielau, Colorado	30
*NEW BOSTON, Bowie, 244 (4,612)	4,579
*NEW BRAUNFELS, Comal, Guadalupe, 4,405 (90,403)	98,857
New Bremen, Austin	125
Newburg, Comanche	32
Newby, Leon	40
*New Caney, Montgomery, 674	6,800
*NEWCASTLE, Young, 18 (526)	531
NEW CHAPEL HILL, Smith (620)	626
New Colony, Bell	12
New Colony, Cass	65
New Corn Hill, Williamson	475
New Davy, DeWitt	20
*NEW DEAL, Lubbock, 16 (730)	729
NEW FAIRVIEW, Wise, 1 (1,386)	1,438
New Falcon, Zapata, 1 (117)	117
Newgulf, Wharton	10
New Harmony, Shelby	40
New Harmony, Smith	350
NEW HOME, Lynn, 19 (326)	335
NEW HOPE, Collin (661)	664
New Hope, Jones	9
New Hope, Wood	15
New Hope, Cherokee	50
New Hope, San Augustine	75
New Hope, Smith	75
Newlin, Hall	27
*NEW LONDON, Rusk, 8 (958)	958
New Lynn, Lynn	4
New Moore, Lynn	10
New Mountain, Upshur	20
Newport, Clay, Jack, 1	75
New Salem, Rusk	55
New Salem, Palo Pinto	89
Newsome, Camp	113
*NEW SUMMERFIELD, Cherokee, 24 (843)	859
New Sweden, Travis	60
New Taiton, Wharton	10
*NEWTON, Newton, 78 (1,633)	1,991
*New Ulm, Austin, 73 (285)	391
*NEW WAVERLY, Walker, 182 (914)	966
New Wehdem, Austin	414
New Willard, Polk	160
New York, Henderson	60
NEYLANDVILLE, Hunt (67)	68
NIEDERWALD, Hays, Caldwell, 37 (668)	671
Nigton, Trinity	87
Nimrod, Eastland	45
Nina, Starr (124)	623
Nineveh, Leon	50
Nix, Lampasas	14
*NIXON, Gonzales, Wilson, 71 (2,341)	2,355
Noack, Williamson	70
Nobility, Fannin	100
Noble, Lamar	14
Nockernut, Wilson	20
*NOCONA, Montague, 166 (3,002)	3,059
Nocona Hills, Montague (637)	578
Nogalus Prairie, Trinity	109
*Nolan, Nolan, 1	60
*NOLANVILLE, Bell, 97 (5,917)	6,249
*NOME, Jefferson, 27 (469)	453
Noodle, Jones	40
NOONDAY, Smith, 7 (612)	616
Nopal, DeWitt, Gonzales	25
*NORDHEIM, DeWitt, 26 (336)	330
Norman, Williamson	40
Normandy, Maverick (54)	39
*NORMANGEE, Leon, Madison, 87 (495)	506
*Normanna, Bee, 4 (98)	80
Norse, Bosque	110
North Alamo, Hidalgo (3,722)	4,080
NORTH CLEVELAND, Liberty, (225)	246
North Escobares, Starr (162)	174
Northfield, Motley, 3	15
NORTHLAKE, Denton, 219 (5,201)	6,829
North Pearsall, Frio (739)	1,022
*NORTH RICHLAND HILLS, Tarrant, 1,763 (69,917)	70,209
Northridge, Starr	91
Northrup, Lee	86
North San Pedro, Nueces (735)	752
North Star, Archer	10
*North Zulch, Madison, 44	600
Norton, Runnels, 5	50
*Notrees, Ector	20
*NOVICE, Coleman, 3 (122)	121
Novice, Lamar	35
Noxville, Kimble	3
Nugent, Jones	50
Nunelee, Fannin	90
*Nursery, Victoria, 5	600

O

Town, County	Pop. 2021
Oakalla, Burnet, 2	99
Oakdale, Polk	25
Oak Forest, Gonzales	24
OAK GROVE, Kaufman (617)	670
Oak Grove, Colorado	40
Oak Grove, Wood	140
Oak Grove, Bowie	90
Oak Hill, Rusk	200
Oak Hill, Travis, 1	[part of Austin]
*Oakhurst, San Jacinto, 15 (148)	21
Oak Island, Chambers (371)	374
Oakland, Van Zandt	26
Oakland, Cherokee	50
Oakland, Colorado, Lavaca, 2	80
OAK LEAF, Ellis, 27 (1,552)	1,616
OAK POINT, Denton, 150 (4,357)	5,557

CITIES & TOWNS

Town, County	Pop. 2021
OAK RIDGE, Cooke, 2 (242)	253
OAK RIDGE, Kaufman (771)	887
Oak Ridge, Grayson	161
Oak Ridge, Nacogdoches	225
OAK RIDGE NORTH, Montgomery, 82 (3,057)	3,032
Oak Trail Shores, Hood (2,979)	2,778
OAK VALLEY, Navarro (406)	418
Oakville, Live Oak, 9	260
*OAKWOOD, Leon, 58 (389)	394
Oatmeal, Burnet	74
*O'BRIEN, Haskell, 2 (91)	92
Ocee, McLennan	84
Odds, Limestone	24
Odell, Wilbarger	100
*ODEM, San Patricio, 103 (2,255)	2,265
*ODESSA, Ector, Midland, 5,496 (114,428)	112,483
*O'DONNELL, Lynn, Dawson, 30 (704)	726
Oenaville, Bell	108
O'Farrell, Cass	20
Ogburn, Wood	10
*OGLESBY, Coryell, 29 (441)	434
*Oilton, Webb, 8 (270)	108
Oklahoma, Montgomery, 1	800
Oklahoma Flat, Hockley	4
Oklahoma Lane, Parmer	25
*Oklaunion, Wilbarger, 3 (88)	77
Okra, Eastland	20
Ola, Kaufman	65
Old Boston, Bowie	100
Old Center, Panola	83
Old Dime Box, Lee	225
*Olden, Eastland, 2	113
Oldenburg, Fayette	92
Old Escobares, Starr	106
*Old Glory, Stonewall, 6	100
Old Midway, Leon	12
*Old Ocean, Brazoria, 8	150
OLD RIVER-WINFREE, Chambers, 37 (1,315)	1,310
Old Salem, Bowie	50
Old Union, Limestone	25
Old Union, Bowie	100
Oletha, Limestone	53
Olfen, Runnels	35
Olin, Hamilton	15
Olivarez, Hidalgo (4,248)	7,213
Olivia, Calhoun, 1	215
Olivia Lopez de Gutierrez, Starr, (49)	570
Ollie, Polk	5
*Olmito, Cameron, 91 (1,021)	901
Olmito and Olmito, Starr (276)	337
Olmos, Guadalupe	65
OLMOS PARK, Bexar, 40 (2,180)	2,162
*OLNEY, Young, 122 (3,007)	3,019
*OLTON, Lamb, 71 (1,989)	1,967
*OMAHA, Morris, 61 (936)	936
Omen, Smith	150
*ONALASKA, Polk, 126 (3,020)	3,143
Onion Creek, Travis	[part of Austin]
Opdyke, Hockley	50
OPDYKE WEST, Hockley (220)	217
Oplin, Callahan	75
O'Quinn, Fayette	191
Oran, Palo Pinto	61
*ORANGE, Orange, 1,069 (19,324)	19,169
Orangedale, Bee	40
*Orangefield, Orange, 7	725
*ORANGE GROVE, Jim Wells, 158 (1,165)	1,183
Orangeville, Fannin	60
Orason, Cameron (88)	557
*ORCHARD, Fort Bend, 17 (313)	315
*ORE CITY, Upshur, 71 (1,108)	1,142
Orient, Tom Green	57
*Orla, Reeves, 43	80
Osage, Coryell	30
Osage, Colorado	10
Oscar, Bell	58
Osceola, Hill	95
Otey, Brazoria	31
Ottine, Gonzales	80
Otto, Falls	48
*Ovalo, Taylor, 22	225
*OVERTON, Rusk, Smith, 135 (2,275)	2,274
OVILLA, Ellis, Dallas, 131 (4,304)	4,349
Owens, Crosby	4
Owens, Brown	16
Owentown, Smith	100
Owl Creek, Bell	130
Owl Ranch, Jim Wells (189)	196
Oxford, Llano	18
OYSTER CREEK, Brazoria, 32 (1,173)	1,186
*Ozona, Crockett, 160 (2,663)	2,343

P

Town, County	Pop. 2021
Pablo Pena, Starr (80)	362
Pacio, Delta	35
Padgett, Young	18
*PADUCAH, Cottle, 41 (1,063)	1,060
*Paige, Bastrop, 115 (278)	142
Paint Creek, Haskell	150
*PAINT ROCK, Concho, 15 (237)	350
Paisano Park, San Patricio (96)	41
*PALACIOS, Matagorda, 182 (4,395)	4,418
*PALESTINE, Anderson, 974 (18,544)	18,756
PALISADES, Randall (268)	275
Palito Blanco, Jim Wells	750
*PALMER, Ellis, 121 (2,393)	2,461
Palmer, Cameron (1,082)	1,515
PALMHURST, Hidalgo, 128 (2,601)	2,602
PALM VALLEY, Cameron, 3 (1,413)	1,398
PALMVIEW, Hidalgo, 519 (15,830)	15,884
Palmview South, Hidalgo (2,008)	2,486
Palo Blanco, Starr (238)	45
Paloduro, Armstrong	10
Paloma Creek, Denton (3,177)	3,347
Paloma Creek South, Denton, (9,539)	7,896
*Palo Pinto, Palo Pinto, 34 (276)	173
Paluxy, Hood, Erath	36
*PAMPA, Gray, 630 (16,867)	16,474
Pancake, Coryell	11
Pandale, Val Verde	25
*Pandora, Wilson	110
*PANHANDLE, Carson, 95 (2,378)	2,337
*Panna Maria, Karnes, 4	45
*Panola, Panola, 1	305
PANORAMA VILLAGE, Montgomery, 6 (2,515)	2,547
*PANTEGO, Tarrant, 332 (2,568)	2,528
Panther Junction, Brewster	130
Papalote, Bee, 1	75
*PARADISE, Wise, 151 (475)	522
*PARIS, Lamar, 1,129 (24,476)	24,407
Park, Fayette	25
PARKER, Collin, 88 (5,462)	5,833
Parker, Johnson	93
Park Springs, Wise	90
Parsley Hill, Wilbarger	25
Parvin, Denton	44
*PASADENA, Harris, 3,417 (151,950)	148,626
Patillo, Erath	10
Patman Switch, Cass	40
Patonia, Polk	15
Patricia, Dawson	50
Patroon, Shelby	25
*PATTISON, Waller, 71 (547)	594
PATTON VILLAGE, Montgomery, 3 (1,647)	1,730
Pattonfield, Upshur	20
*Pattonville, Lamar, 21	180
Pawelekville, Karnes, 1	110
*Pawnee, Bee, 8 (140)	85
Paxton, Shelby	50
Paynes Corner, Gaines	18
PAYNE SPRINGS, Henderson, 4 (741)	750
Peach Creek, Brazos	150
Peacock, Stonewall	100
Peadenville, Palo Pinto	15
Pearl, Coryell	50
*PEARLAND, Brazoria, Harris, Fort Bend, 3,716 (125,828)	125,990
Pearl City, DeWitt	4
*PEARSALL, Frio, 262 (7,325)	7,637
Pearson, Medina	24
Pearsons Chapel, Houston	95
Pear Valley, McCulloch	37
*PEASTER, Parker, 2 (nc)	642
Pecan Acres, Tarrant, Wise, (4,808)	4,250
*PECAN GAP, Delta, Fannin, 6 (178)	181
Pecan Grove, Fort Bend (22,782)	19,944
PECAN HILL, Ellis (735)	740
Pecan Plantation, Hood (6,236)	6,607
Pecan Wells, Hamilton	6
*PECOS, Reeves, 445 (12,916)	12,673
Peeltown, Kaufman	75
Peerless, Hopkins	90
Peggy, Atascosa, 1	22
Pelham, Navarro	75
PELICAN BAY, Tarrant, 4 (2,049)	2,236
Pena, Starr (73)	87
*Pendleton, Bell, 5 (845)	791
*PENELOPE, Hill, 8 (180)	182
*PEÑITAS, Hidalgo, 194 (6,460)	6,399
*Pennington, Trinity, Houston, 8	67
*Penwell, Ector, 6	41
Peoria, Hill, 1	105

The Parker House Ranching Museum in Odessa was first opened in 1996 and is free to the public. Photo by Diann Bayes, Flickr, CC by NC ND 2.0

Town, County	Pop. 2021
*Pep, Hockley	30
Percilla, Houston	95
Perezville, Hidalgo (2,685)	2,577
Pernitas Point, Live Oak, Jim Wells	274
*Perrin, Jack, 42 (346)	54
Perry, Falls	76
*PERRYTON, Ochiltree, 404 (8,492)	8,289
Perryville, Wood	35
Personville, Limestone	50
Pert, Anderson	20
Peters, Austin	150
*PETERSBURG, Hale, Floyd, 29 (1,014)	982
Peter's Prairie, Red River	40
Petersville, DeWitt	38
*PETROLIA, Clay, 14 (514)	516
PETRONILA, Nueces, 1 (89)	87
Petteway, Robertson	25
Pettibone, Milam	25
Pettit, Hockley	30
*Pettus, Bee, 16 (449)	640
*Petty, Lamar, 12 (140)	160
Petty, Lynn	8
Peyton, Blanco	30
*PFLUGERVILLE, Travis, 2,430 (65,191)	66,884
Phalba, Van Zandt	73
*PHARR, Hidalgo, 1,877 (79,715)	79,697
Phelps, Walker	98
Phillipsburg, Washington	75
Pickens, Henderson	20
Pickett, Navarro	30
*Pickton, Hopkins, 21	300
Pidcoke, Coryell	50
Piedmont, Upshur	20
Piedmont, Grimes	50
*Pierce, Wharton, 3	51
Pike, Collin	47
Pilgrim, Gonzales	22
Pilgrim Rest, Rains	72
Pilot Grove, Grayson	48
Pilot Knob, Travis	500
*PILOT POINT, Denton, 316 (4,381)	4,651
Pine, Camp	78
Pine Branch, Red River	40
Pinebrook, Grimes (485)	63
PINE FOREST, Orange, 9 (499)	503
Pine Forest, Hopkins	100
Pine Grove, Cherokee	30
Pine Grove, Newton	180
Pine Harbor, Marion (785)	809
Pinehill, Rusk	70
*Pinehurst, Montgomery (5,195)	2,216
PINEHURST, Orange, 268 (2,232)	4,727
PINE ISLAND, Waller, 1 (1,077)	1,161
Pine Island, Jefferson	350
*PINELAND, Sabine, 34 (888)	899
Pine Mills, Wood	75
Pine Prairie, Walker	450
Pine Springs, Culberson	20
Pine Springs, Smith	150
Pineview, Wood	10
Pinewood Estates, Hardin (1,641)	1,407
Piney, Austin	60
PINEY POINT VILLAGE, Harris, 4 (3,128)	3,072
Pin Hook, Lamar	48
Pioneer, Eastland	20
*Pipe Creek, Bandera, 185	130
Pitner Junction, Rusk	20
*PITTSBURG, Camp, 359 (4,335)	4,374
*Placedo, Victoria, 13 (625)	443
Placid, McCulloch	32
Plain, Houston	30
*PLAINS, Yoakum, 68 (1,355)	1,351
*PLAINVIEW, Hale, 765 (20,187)	19,739
*PLANO, Collin, Denton, 10,422 (285,494)	288,253
*Plantersville, Grimes, 187 (464)	473
Plaska, Hall	20
PLEAK, Fort Bend, 4 (971)	1,031
Pleasant Farms, Ector	800
Pleasant Grove, Limestone	20
Pleasant Grove, Wood	30
Pleasant Grove, Falls	35
Pleasant Grove, Upshur	35
Pleasant Hill, Polk (610)	1,060
Pleasant Hill, Eastland	15
Pleasant Hill, Yoakum	30
Pleasant Hill, Nacogdoches	250
*PLEASANTON, Atascosa, 579 (10,648)	10,780
PLEASANT VALLEY, Wichita, 1 (357)	356

Town, County	Pop. 2021
Pleasant Valley, Garza	5
*Pledger, Matagorda, 2	265
Pluck, Polk	53
*Plum, Fayette (366)	582
PLUM GROVE, Liberty, 2 (1,245)	1,344
Pluto, Ellis	30
POETRY, Hunt, Kaufman	90
*POINT, Rains, 86 (745)	765
*POINT BLANK, San Jacinto, 63 (643)	663
*POINT COMFORT, Calhoun, 24 (603)	583
Point Enterprise, Limestone	200
POINT VENTURE, Travis, 3 (1,260)	1,267
Polar, Kent	15
*Pollok, Angelina, 79	400
*PONDER, Denton, 142 (2,442)	2,429
Ponta, Cherokee	50
*Pontotoc, Mason, 11	125
Poole, Rains	20
*Poolville, Parker, 130	520
Port Acres, Jefferson, 3	[part of Port Arthur]
Port Alto, Calhoun	45
*PORT ARANSAS, Nueces, 394 (2,904)	3,105
*PORT ARTHUR, Jefferson, 1,112 (56,039)	55,724
*Port Bolivar, Galveston, 38	700
*Porter, Montgomery, 868	4,200
Porter Heights, Montgomery, (1,903)	1,167
Porter Springs, Houston	50
*PORT ISABEL, Cameron, 296 (5,028)	5,094
*PORTLAND, San Patricio, 468 (20,383)	20,536
*PORT LAVACA, Calhoun, 508 (11,557)	11,259
Port Mansfield, Willacy, 21 (319)	132
*PORT NECHES, Jefferson, 315 (13,692)	13,416
*Port O'Connor, Calhoun, 98 (954)	1,084
Port Sullivan, Milam, Robertson	15
Porvenir, Presidio	3
Posey, Hopkins	12
Posey, Lubbock	225
*POST, Garza, 169 (4,790)	4,791
Post Oak, Blanco	10
Post Oak, Lee	100
Postoak, Lamar	65
Postoak, Jack, Clay	20
POST OAK BEND, Kaufman (683)	762
Post Oak Point, Austin	60
*POTEET, Atascosa, 241 (2,795)	2,880
*POTH, Wilson, 40 (1,819)	1,866
Potosi, Taylor, 1 (3,947)	4,720
*POTTSBORO, Grayson, 277 (2,488)	2,613
Pottsville, Hamilton, 2	105
*Powderly, Lamar, 84 (1,261)	1,247
*POWELL, Navarro, 15 (99)	101
*POYNOR, Henderson, 5 (287)	288
Prado Verde, El Paso (209)	438
Praesel, Milam (446)	63
Praha, Fayette	90
Prairie Chapel, McLennan	35
Prairie Dell, Bell	34
Prairie Hill, Washington	20
*Prairie Hill, Limestone, 7	150
*Prairie Lea, Caldwell, 5	320
Prairie Point, Cooke	22
*PRAIRIE VIEW, Waller, 46 (8,184)	6,843
Prairieville, Kaufman	75
*PREMONT, Jim Wells, 75 (2,455)	2,441
*PRESIDIO, Presidio, 101 (3,264)	3,301
Preston, Grayson, 1 (2,101)	2,217
*Price, Rusk, 1	275
*Priddy, Mills, 9 (150)	160
PRIMERA, Cameron, 1 (5,257)	5,303
Primrose, Van Zandt	26
*PRINCETON, Collin, 603 (17,027)	20,046
Pringle, Hutchinson, 1	20
Pritchett, Upshur	125
*Proctor, Comanche, 6 (93)	57
*PROGRESO, Hidalgo, 37 (4,807)	4,904
PROGRESO LAKES, Hidalgo, 15 (257)	259
Progress, Bailey	49
Prospect, Rains	40
*PROSPER, Collin, Denton, 1,193 (30,174)	34,136
PROVIDENCE VILLAGE, Denton, 99 (7,691)	7,812
Providence, Floyd	78
Providence, Polk	350
Pruitt, Cass	25
Pruitt, Van Zandt	45
Pueblo East, Webb (1)	1
Pueblo Nuevo, Webb (432)	632
Puerto Rico, Hidalgo	50
Pullman, Potter	31
Pumphrey, Runnels	15
Pumpkin, San Jacinto	100
Pumpville, Val Verde	25
Punkin Center, Eastland	12
Punkin Center, Dawson	8
*Purdon, Navarro, 32	133
Purley, Franklin	100
*Purmela, Coryell, 12	50
Pursley, Navarro	40
Purves, Erath	50
*PUTNAM, Callahan, 4 (63)	65
*PYOTE, Ward, 16 (72)	72

Q

Town, County	Pop. 2021
*Quail, Collingsworth, 2 (17)	25
Quail Creek, Victoria (1,800)	1,454
*QUANAH, Hardeman, 117 (2,279)	2,272
Quarry, Washington	60
Quarterway, Hale	24
*QUEEN CITY, Cass, 105 (1,397)	1,409
*Quemado, Maverick, 21 (162)	112
Quesada, Starr (7)	57
Quicksand, Newton	50
Quihi, Medina	125
*QUINLAN, Hunt, 384 (1,414)	1,455
QUINTANA, Brazoria, 5 (26)	25
*QUITAQUE, Briscoe, Floyd, 23 (342)	334
*QUITMAN, Wood, 253 (1,942)	1,991

R

Town, County	Pop. 2021
Rabbs Prairie, Fayette	79
Raccoon Bend, Austin	775
Rachal, Brooks, 1	36
Radar Base, Maverick (93)	86
Radium, Jones	10
Rafael Pena, Starr (16)	16
Ragtown, Lamar	30
*Rainbow, Somervell, 32	121
Raisin, Victoria	85
Raleigh, Navarro	40
*RALLS, Crosby, 50 (1,665)	1,639
Ramireno, Zapata (6)	6
Ramirez, Duval	42
Ramirez-Perez, Starr (66)	66
Ramos, Starr (144)	54
Ranchette Estates, Willacy (106)	175
Ranchitos Del Norte, Starr (214)	370
Ranchitos East, Webb (189)	316
Ranchitos Las Lomas, Webb (167)	319
Rancho Alegre, Jim Wells (1,415)	1,561
Rancho Banquete, Nueces (459)	517
Rancho Chico, San Patricio (387)	324
Ranchos Penitas West, Webb (466)	519
RANCHO VIEJO, Cameron, 55 (2,838)	2,856
Rancho Viejo, Starr (233)	280
Rand, Kaufman (1,280)	70
Randado, Jim Hogg, Zapata (2,300)	6
*Randolph, Fannin, 6 (255)	600
Randolph Air Force Base, Bexar, 16 (780)	1,842
*RANGER, Eastland, 90 (1,189)	2,276
RANGERVILLE, Cameron (197)	197
*RANKIN, Upton, 44 (nc)	759
Rankin, Ellis	10
RANSOM CANYON, Lubbock, 40 (nc)	1,170
Ratamosa, Cameron (nc)	88
*Ratcliff, Houston, 3	106
Ratibor, Bell	22
Rattan, Delta	10
*RAVENNA, Fannin, 25 (175)	183
Rayburn, Liberty	60
Rayland, Foard	30
*RAYMONDVILLE, Willacy, 238 (10,236)	10,510
Ray Point, Live Oak	200
*Raywood, Liberty, 17	231
Razor, Lamar	20
*Reagan, Falls, 5	300
Reagan Wells, Uvalde	30
Reagor Springs, Ellis	250
*Realitos, Duval, 5 (121)	84
Red Bank, Bowie	125
Red Bluff, Reeves	40
Red Bluff, Jackson	45
Redfield, Nacogdoches (392)	117
Redford, Presidio, 2 (43)	43
Red Hill, Limestone	20
Red Hill, Cass	28
Red Lake, Freestone	50
Redland, Angelina (1,088)	1,319
Redland, Leon	35
Redland, Van Zandt	45
RED LICK, Bowie (946)	937

Town, County	Pop. 2021
*RED OAK, Ellis, Navarro, 630 (14,222)	15,364
Red Ranger, Bell	30
*Red Rock, Bastrop, 64 (410)	397
Red Springs, Baylor	42
Red Springs, Smith	350
Redtown, Anderson	30
Redtown, Angelina	500
*REDWATER, Bowie, 7 (853)	851
Redwood, Guadalupe (4,003)	3,353
Reeds Settlement, Red River	50
Reedville, Caldwell	520
Reese, Cherokee	75
Refuge, Houston	20
*REFUGIO, Refugio, 149 (2,712)	2,790
Regency, Mills	25
Regino Ramirez, Starr (120)	18
Rehburg, Washington	20
Reid Hope King, Cameron (667)	814
Reilly Springs, Hopkins	75
Rek Hill, Fayette	168
*REKLAW, Cherokee, Rusk, 24 (332)	333
Relampago, Hidalgo (129)	432
Rendon, Tarrant, 2 (13,533)	14,597
RENO, Lamar, 92 (3,454)	3,460
RENO, Parker, Tarrant (2,878)	3,100
RETREAT, Navarro (410)	432
Retreat, Grimes	25
Retta, Tarrant, Johnson	[part of Fort Worth]
Reynard, Houston	75
Rhea, Parmer	98
Rhineland, Knox	120
*RHOME, Wise, 236 (1,630)	1,737
Rhonesboro, Upshur	40
Ricardo, Kleberg, 2 (1,075)	1,041
*RICE, Navarro, 77 (1,203)	1,236
Rice's Crossing, Williamson	130
Rice Tracts, Cameron (733)	918
*Richards, Grimes, 37 (184)	136
*RICHARDSON, Dallas, Collin, 4,517 (119,469)	116,382

Town, County	Pop. 2021
*RICHLAND, Navarro, 16 (255)	265
Richland, Rains	50
*RICHLAND HILLS, Tarrant, 353 (8,621)	8,484
*RICHLAND SPRINGS, San Saba, 26 (244)	249
*RICHMOND, Fort Bend, 3,829 (11,627)	12,233
RICHWOOD, Brazoria, 99 (4,781)	4,761
Riderville, Panola	50
Ridge, Mills	25
Ridge, Robertson	67
Ridgeway, Hopkins	54
Ridings, Fannin	200
*RIESEL, McLennan, 76 (1,062)	1,071
Rincon, Starr	5
Ringgold, Montague, 3 (146)	171
RIO BRAVO, Webb, 15 (4,450)	4,400
*Rio Frio, Real, 16	50
*RIO GRANDE CITY, Starr, 796 (15,317)	15,670
Rio Grande Village, Brewster	12
*RIO HONDO, Cameron, 121 (2,021)	2,018
*Riomedina, Medina, 22	60
Rios, Duval	75
*RIO VISTA, Johnson, 73 (1,008)	1,078
*RISING STAR, Eastland, 63 (756)	766
Rita, Burleson	50
Rivera, Starr	182
Riverby, Fannin	8
River Crest Estates, Angelina	150
Rivereno, Starr (62)	62
River Hill, Panola	125
RIVER OAKS, Tarrant, 160 (7,646)	7,524
Rivers End, Brazoria	90
*RIVERSIDE, Walker, 8 (522)	553
*Riviera, Kleberg, 54 (609)	675
Riviera Beach, Kleberg, 1	155
Roach, Cass	50
ROAD RUNNER, Cooke (766)	779

Town, County	Pop. 2021
Roane, Navarro	120
*ROANOKE, Denton, 658 (9,665)	9,878
Roans Prairie, Grimes, 1	64
*ROARING SPRINGS, Motley, 12 (217)	214
Robbins, Leon	20
*ROBERT LEE, Coke, 55 (1,027)	1,022
Robertson, Crosby	10
ROBINSON, McLennan, 312 (12,443)	12,755
*ROBSTOWN, Nueces, 552 (10,143)	10,157
*ROBY, Fisher, 29 (591)	594
*Rochelle, McCulloch, 18 (169)	214
*ROCHESTER, Haskell, 14 (248)	248
Rock Bluff, Burnet	90
Rock Creek, Somervell	70
*ROCKDALE, Milam, 331 (5,323)	5,398
Rockett, Ellis	300
Rockford, Lamar	30
Rockhouse, Austin, Fayette	100
*Rock Island, Colorado, 2 (228)	447
Rockland, Tyler	98
Rockne, Bastrop	190
*ROCKPORT, Aransas, 883 (10,070)	10,436
*ROCKSPRINGS, Edwards, 62 (874)	874
*ROCKWALL, Rockwall, 2,203 (47,251)	49,669
Rockwell Place, Randall (1,811)	1,445
*Rockwood, Coleman, 1	53
Rocky Branch, Morris	135
Rocky Creek, Blanco	20
ROCKY MOUND, Camp (78)	83
Rocky Point, Burnet	152
Roddy, Van Zandt	29
Rodney, Navarro	15
Roeder, Titus	75
Roganville, Jasper	70
*ROGERS, Bell, 74 (1,113)	1,104
Rogers, Taylor	151
Rolling Hills, Potter	1,000

The City Hall in Premont. Photo by Larry D. Moore, CC by SA 4.0

Town, County	Pop. 2021
Rolling Meadows, Gregg	362
ROLLINGWOOD, Travis, 31 (1,467)	1,440
Roma Creek, Starr	325
*ROMA-Los Saenz, Starr, 335 (11,561)	11,505
ROMAN FOREST, Montgomery, 7 (1,781)	1,874
*Romayor, Liberty, 1	135
*Roosevelt, Kimble, 3	14
Roosevelt, Lubbock	362
*ROPESVILLE, Hockley, 46 (430)	418
Rosalie, Red River	100
*Rosanky, Bastrop, 27 (1,473)	1,488
*ROSCOE, Nolan, 61 (1,271)	1,244
*ROSEBUD, Falls, 72 (1,296)	1,345
ROSE CITY, Orange, 6 (326)	330
Rose Hill, San Jacinto	30
Rose Hill, Harris	3,500
ROSE HILL ACRES, Hardin, 2 (325)	328
*ROSENBERG, Fort Bend, 1,611 (38,282)	39,468
Rosevine, Sabine	50
Rosewood, Upshur	100
*Rosharon, Brazoria, 567 (1,362)	1,721
Rosita, Maverick (3,501)	3,799
Rosita, Duval	25
*ROSS, McLennan, 7 (245)	251
*ROSSER, Kaufman, 12 (301)	322
*Rosston, Cooke, 5	75
Rossville, Atascosa	200
*ROTAN, Fisher, 60 (1,332)	1,349
Rough Creek, San Saba	8
Round House, Navarro	40
*ROUND MOUNTAIN, Blanco, 40 (101)	104
Round Mountain, Travis	59
Round Prairie, Navarro	40
*ROUND ROCK, Williamson, Travis, 5,021 (119,468)	123,876
Round Timber, Baylor	2
*ROUND TOP, Fayette, 212 (87)	93
Roundup, Hockley	20
Rowden, Callahan	15
*Rowena, Runnels, 23 (305)	197
*ROWLETT, Dallas, Rockwall, 1,513 (62,535)	63,671
*ROXTON, Lamar, 19 (548)	546
Royalty, Ward	27
*ROYSE CITY, Rockwall, Collin, 798 (13,508)	15,978
Rucker, Comanche	28
Rugby, Red River	24
Ruidosa, Presidio	18
*RULE, Haskell, 18 (561)	568
Rumley, Lampasas	30
RUNAWAY BAY, Wise, 40 (1,546)	1,659
*RUNGE, Karnes, 26 (892)	963
Rural Shade, Navarro	30
*RUSK, Cherokee, 233 (5,285)	5,537
Russell, Leon	27
Rutersville, Fayette	137
Ruth Springs, Henderson	120
*Rye, Liberty, 4	150
S	
Sabanno, Eastland	12
*SABINAL, Uvalde, 66 (1,364)	1,401
*Sabine Pass, Jefferson, 20	[part of Port Arthur]
SACHSE, Dallas, Collin, 589 (27,103)	29,042
*Sacul, Nacogdoches, 3	150
*SADLER, Grayson, 26 (336)	337
Sagerton, Haskell, 1	171
*SAGINAW, Tarrant, 556 (23,890)	24,011
St. Francis, Potter	30
*ST. HEDWIG, Bexar, 96 (2,227)	2,258
*SAINT JO, Montague, 68 (881)	901
St. John Colony, Caldwell	150
St. Lawrence, Glasscock	90
St. Mary's Colony, Bastrop	50
ST. PAUL, Collin, 36 (992)	994
St. Paul, San Patricio (608)	1,318
*SALADO, Bell, 452 (2,394)	2,391
Salem, Cherokee	20
Salem, Grimes	54
Salem, Newton	218
Salesville, Palo Pinto	88
Salida del Sol Estates, Hidalgo, (6,496)	5,430
Saline, Menard	70
*Salineño, Starr, 1 (176)	71
Salineño North, Starr (117)	115
Salmon, Anderson	20
Salt Flat, Hudspeth, 4	8
Salt Gap, McCulloch	25
*Saltillo, Hopkins, 22	200
Samaria, Navarro	90
Sammy Martinez, Starr (123)	126
*Samnorwood, Collingsworth (24)	31
Sample, Gonzales	16
Sam Rayburn, Jasper, 2 (1,273)	1,100
*SAN ANGELO, Tom Green, 3,642 (99,893)	99,667
*SAN ANTONIO, Bexar, 44,623 (1,434,625)	1,451,853
San Antonio Prairie, Burleson	20
*SAN AUGUSTINE, San Augustine, 144 (1,920)	1,854
*SAN BENITO, Cameron, 922 (24,861)	24,780
San Carlos, Hidalgo, 1 (3,087)	4,177
San Carlos, Starr	10
San Carlos I, Webb (187)	248
San Carlos II, Webb (220)	251
Sanco, Coke	15
SANCTUARY, Parker, 5 (337)	347
Sand Branch, Dallas	400
*Sanderson, Terrell, 32 (664)	664
Sand Flat, Van Zandt	25
Sand Flat, Leon	32
Sand Flat, Rains	45
Sand Flat, Smith	100
Sand Flat, Johnson	133
Sand Hill, Upshur	75
Sandhill, Floyd	33
*Sandia, Jim Wells, 72 (326)	382
*SAN DIEGO, Duval, Jim Wells, 111 (3,748)	3,755
Sandlin, Stonewall	3
Sandoval, Starr (37)	37
Sandoval, Williamson	60
Sand Springs, Howard (878)	953
Sandusky, Grayson	15
Sandy, Limestone	5
Sandy, Blanco	150
SANDY OAKS, Bexar (5,075)	5,133
Sandy Harbor, Llano	85
Sandy Hill, Washington	50
Sandy Hollow-Escondidas, Nueces, (342)	571
SANDY POINT, Brazoria, 2 (207)	212
*SAN ELIZARIO, El Paso, 152 (10,116)	10,093
*SAN FELIPE, Austin, 11 (691)	688
San Fernando, Starr (49)	49
*SANFORD, Hutchinson, 5 (132)	134
San Gabriel, Milam, Williamson	70
*SANGER, Denton, 495 (8,839)	9,380
*San Isidro, Starr, 6 (187)	182
San Jose, Duval	15
*SAN JUAN, Hidalgo, 709 (35,294)	35,577
San Juan, Starr (203)	69
SAN LEANNA, Travis (522)	514
San Leon, Galveston, 125 (6,135)	5,144
*SAN MARCOS, Hays, Caldwell, Guadalupe, 2,486 (67,553)	68,580
SAN PATRICIO, San Patricio (384)	393
San Pedro, Cameron (442)	209
*SAN PERLITA, Willacy, 6 (538)	531
San Roman, Starr	5
*SAN SABA, San Saba, 202 (3,117)	3,151
SANSOM PARK, Tarrant, 48 (5,454)	5,388
*SANTA ANNA, Coleman, 68 (1,014)	1,022
Santa Anna, Starr (12)	11
Santa Catarina, Starr	15
SANTA CLARA, Guadalupe, 1 (778)	771
Santa Cruz, Starr (74)	500
*Santa Elena, Starr, 9	35
*SANTA FE, Galveston, 486 (12,735)	12,783
*Santa Maria, Cameron, 1 (651)	618
Santa Monica, Willacy (86)	10
Santa Rita Ranch, Williamson, (3,152)	3,410
*SANTA ROSA, Cameron, 56 (2,450)	2,423
Santa Rosa, Starr (265)	324
Santel, Starr (24)	12
*Santo, Palo Pinto, 65 (347)	308
*San Ygnacio, Zapata, 11 (504)	582
*Saragosa, Reeves, 1	185
*Saratoga, Hardin, 8	1,000
Sardis, Ellis	60
Sargent, Matagorda, 33 (1,212)	1,319
*Sarita, Kenedy, 10 (205)	164
Saron, Trinity	6
Saspamco, Wilson	300
*Satin, Falls, 3	86
Sattler, Comal, 3	2,500
Saturn, Gonzales	15
Savannah, Denton, 71 (6,529)	6,565
*SAVOY, Fannin, 36 (712)	732
Scenic Oaks, Bexar (10,458)	9,136
Schattel, Frio	30

Town, County	Pop. 2021
*SCHERTZ, Guadalupe, Comal, Bexar, 1,251 (42,002)	42,622
Schicke Point, Calhoun	70
Schroeder, Goliad	347
*SCHULENBURG, Fayette, 264 (2,633)	2,669
Schumansville, Guadalupe	678
Schwab City, Polk	120
*Schwertner, Williamson, 3	175
Scissors, Hidalgo (3,758)	4,052
*SCOTLAND, Archer, 15 (413)	419
*SCOTTSVILLE, Harrison, 5 (334)	338
Scranton, Eastland	40
Scrappin Valley, Newton	25
*Scroggins, Franklin, 37	150
*SCURRY, Kaufman, 116 (688)	732
*SEABROOK, Harris, 481 (13,618)	13,560
*SEADRIFT, Calhoun, 69 (995)	999
*SEAGOVILLE, Dallas, 499 (18,446)	18,805
*SEAGRAVES, Gaines, 70 (2,153)	2,185
Seale, Robertson	60
*SEALY, Austin, 535 (6,839)	6,775
Seaton, Bell	60
Seawillow, Caldwell	75
*Sebastian, Willacy, 25 (1,684)	1,331
Sebastopol, Trinity	300
Seco Mines, Maverick (572)	1,064
Security, Montgomery	200
Sedalia, Collin	24
Segno, Polk	80
Segovia, Kimble	12
*SEGUIN, Guadalupe, 1,691 (29,433)	30,902
Seis Lagos, Collin (1,450)	1,122
Sejita, Duval	24
Selden, Erath	55
Selfs, Fannin	30
SELMA, Bexar, Guadalupe, Comal, 453 (10,952)	11,619
*SEMINOLE, Gaines, 643 (6,988)	7,026
Sempronius, Austin	25
Senate, Jack	20
Serbin, Lee	109
Serenada, Williamson (2,098)	1,668
Seth Ward, Hale (1,603)	1,849
SEVEN OAKS, Polk, 1 (68)	69
Seven Pines, Gregg, Upshur	50
SEVEN POINTS, Henderson, 104 (1,370)	1,402
Seven Sisters, Duval	25
Sexton, Sabine	29
*SEYMOUR, Baylor, 135 (2,575)	2,584
Shadybrook, Cherokee (2,400)	2,191
Shady Grove, Cherokee	30
Shady Grove, Upshur	40
Shady Grove, Panola	45
Shady Grove, Houston	83
Shady Grove, Smith	250
Shady Grove, Burnet	114
Shady Hollow, Travis (4,822)	4,587
Shady Oaks, Henderson	300
SHADY SHORES, Denton, 56 (2,764)	2,849
Shafter, Presidio, 1	57
*SHALLOWATER, Lubbock, 158 (2,964)	2,940
*SHAMROCK, Wheeler, 118 (1,789)	1,773
Shangri La, Burnet	108
Shankleville, Newton	35
Shannon, Clay	20
Sharp, Milam	52
SHAVANO PARK, Bexar, 124 (3,524)	3,569
Shawnee Prairie, Angelina, 1	20
Shaws Bend, Colorado	100
*Sheffield, Pecos, 8 (174)	40
Shelby, Austin, 2	300
*Shelbyville, Shelby, 40 (100)	199
Sheldon, Harris (2,361)	2,176
SHENANDOAH, Montgomery, 344 (3,499)	3,593
Shep, Taylor	25
*SHEPHERD, San Jacinto, 130 (2,105)	2,045
*Sheridan, Colorado, 25 (520)	398
*SHERMAN, Grayson, 1,567 (43,645)	44,873
Sherry, Red River	15
Sherwood, Irion, Tom Green, 2	170
Sherwood Shores, Grayson (1,165)	778
Sherwood Shores, Bell	774
Sherwood Shores, Burnet	920
Shields, Coleman	8
Shiloh, Leon	30
Shiloh, Limestone	250
*SHINER, Lavaca, 184 (2,127)	2,154
Shirley, Hopkins	20
*Shiro, Grimes, 9 (201)	75
Shive, Hamilton	60
SHOREACRES, Harris, 25 (1,566)	1,530
Short, Shelby	15
Shovel Mountain, Burnet	148
*Sidney, Comanche, 7	148
Sienna Plantation, Fort Bend, (20,204)	22,980
*Sierra Blanca, Hudspeth, 35 (315)	676
Siesta Acres, Maverick (1,866)	1,687
Siesta Shores, Zapata (1,450)	1,715
Silas, Shelby	75
Siloam, Bowie	50
*SILSBEE, Hardin, 471 (6,935)	6,851
*Silver, Coke	34
Silver City, Milam	25
Silver City, Red River	25
Silver City, Navarro	100
Silver Creek Village, Burnet	300
Silver Lake, Van Zandt	42
*SILVERTON, Briscoe, 40 (629)	613
Silver Valley, Coleman	15
Simmons, Live Oak	65
*Simms, Bowie, 29	300
Simms, DeafSmith	6
*SIMONTON, Fort Bend, 31 (647)	642
Simpsonville, Matagorda	6
Simpsonville, Upshur	100
Sinclair City, Smith	50
Singleton, Grimes, 2	45
*SINTON, San Patricio, 264 (5,504)	5,562
Sipe Springs, Comanche	70
Sisterdale, Kendall, 3	110
Sivells Bend, Cooke	36
Six Mile, Calhoun	300
Skeeterville, San Saba	10
*SKELLYTOWN, Carson, 6 (394)	394
*Skidmore, Bee, 32 (863)	1,265
Slate Shoals, Lamar	10
*SLATON, Lubbock, 190 (5,858)	5,811
Slayden, Gonzales	10
Slide, Lubbock	245
*Slidell, Wise, 3	175
Sloan, San Saba	30
Slocum, Anderson	150
Smetana, Brazos	80
*SMILEY, Gonzales, 24 (475)	480
Smithland, Marion, Cass	179
Smith Point, Chambers, 1	180
Smithson Valley, Comal	1,000
*SMITHVILLE, Bastrop, 355 (3,922)	4,047
Smithwick, Burnet	102
*SMYER, Hockley, 11 (441)	433
Smyrna, Rains	25
Smyrna, Cass	215
*SNOOK, Burleson, 22 (506)	519
Snow Hill, Collin	23
Snow Hill, Upshur	75
*SNYDER, Scurry, 569 (11,438)	11,264
*SOCORRO, El Paso, 487 (34,306)	36,236
Soldier Mound, Dickens	10
Solis, Cameron (722)	844
*SOMERSET, Bexar, 101 (1,756)	1,765
*SOMERVILLE, Burleson, 139 (1,312)	1,329
Sommer's Mill, Bell	27
*SONORA, Sutton, 169 (2,502)	2,462
Sonterra, Williamson (7,679)	6,765
*SOUR LAKE, Hardin, 151 (1,773)	1,792
South Alamo, Hidalgo (3,414)	3,228
*South Bend, Young, 2	100
South Bosque, McLennan	1,523
South Brice, Hall	19
South Fork Estates, Jim Hogg (136)	38
SOUTH FRYDEK, Austin (207)	210
*SOUTH HOUSTON, Harris, 606 (16,153)	15,878
*SOUTHLAKE, Tarrant, Denton, 1,721 (31,265)	31,105
Southland, Garza, 2	157
South La Paloma, Jim Wells (347)	790
*SOUTHMAYD, Grayson, 5 (978)	1,013
SOUTH MOUNTAIN, Coryell, (411)	402
*SOUTH PADRE ISLAND, Cameron, 461 (2,066)	2,061
*South Plains, Floyd	67
South Point, Cameron (1,014)	947
South Purmela, Coryell	10
South Shore, Bell	60
SOUTHSIDE PLACE, Harris, 4 (1,835)	1,826
South Sulphur, Hunt	60
South Toledo Bend, Newton (434)	337
Southton, Bexar	113
Southwest Sandhill, Ward (1,666)	1,136
*Spade, Lamb, 1 (71)	55
Spanish Fort, Montague	50
Sparenberg, Dawson	40
Sparks, El Paso (4,760)	5,169

Town, County	Pop. 2021
Sparks, Bell	40
Speaks, Lavaca, 1	60
*SPEARMAN, Hansford, 119 (3,171)	3,087
Speegleville, McLennan, 2	1,655
*Spicewood, Burnet, 578	4,000
Spider Mountain, Burnet	92
*SPLENDORA, Montgomery, 271 (1,683)	1,780
SPOFFORD, Kinney (41)	47
Spraberry, Midland	46
*Spring, Harris, 8,754 (62,559)	62,569
*SPRING BRANCH, Comal, 769 (206)	221
Spring Creek, San Saba	20
Spring Creek, Hutchinson	20
Springdale, Cass	55
Springfield, Anderson	30
Spring Gardens, Nueces (497)	489
Spring Hill, San Jacinto	38
Spring Hill, Navarro	60
Spring Hill, Bowie	100
*SPRINGLAKE, Lamb, 10 (145)	140
*SPRINGTOWN, Parker, 596 (3,064)	3,355
Spring Valley, McLennan, 15	400
SPRING VALLEY VILLAGE, Harris (4,229)	4,217
*SPUR, Dickens, 56 (863)	740
*Spurger, Tyler, 28	590
Stacy, McCulloch	20
Staff, Eastland	65
*STAFFORD, Fort Bend, Harris, 1,643 (17,666)	17,364
Stag Creek, Comanche	45
STAGECOACH, Montgomery, 15 (580)	588
Stairtown, Caldwell	35
Staley, San Jacinto	30
*STAMFORD, Jones, Haskell, 131 (2,907)	2,977
Stampede, Bell	6
Stamps, Upshur	45
*STANTON, Martin, 172 (2,657)	2,649
*Staples, Guadalupe, 8 (193)	188
*Star, Mills, 2	97
STAR HARBOR, Henderson (482)	501
Star Route, Cochran	15
Starrville, Smith	75
Startzville, Comal, 3	7,000
Steele Hill, Dickens	4
Steiner Ranch, Travis (16,713)	18,189
Stephens Creek, San Jacinto	385
*STEPHENVILLE, Erath, 1,110 (20,897)	21,199
Sterley, Floyd	31
*STERLING CITY, Sterling, 57 (1,121)	1,122
Stewards Mill, Freestone	22
Stewart, Rusk	15
Stiles, Reagan	4
Stillwell Store, Brewster	2
*STINNETT, Hutchinson, 65 (1,650)	1,638
Stith, Jones	50
*STOCKDALE, Wilson, 125 (1,413)	1,435
Stockman, Shelby	55
STOCKTON BEND, Hood (380)	397
Stoneburg, Montague	51
Stoneham, Grimes	15
*Stonewall, Gillespie, 71 (451)	512
Stony, Denton	25
Stout, Wood	302
*Stowell, Chambers, 9 (1,743)	2,085
Stranger, Falls	12
*STRATFORD, Sherman, 74 (1,939)	1,953
Stratton, DeWitt	25
*STRAWN, Palo Pinto, 36 (540)	549
Streeter, Mason	85
*STREETMAN, Freestone, 68 (248)	255
String Prairie, Bastrop, 1	40
Stringtown, Newton	20
Structure, Williamson	50
Stubblefield, Houston	15
Stubbs, Kaufman	50
Study Butte, Brewster (200)	172
Sturgeon, Cooke	10
Styx, Kaufman	50
Sublime, Lavaca, 3	75
*SUDAN, Lamb, 30 (940)	939
Sugar Hill, Titus	90
*SUGAR LAND, Fort Bend, 5,556 (111,026)	109,373
Sugar Valley, Matagorda	45
*SULLIVAN CITY, Hidalgo, 93 (3,908)	3,905
*Sulphur Bluff, Hopkins, 7	280
*SULPHUR SPRINGS, Hopkins, 902 (15,941)	15,995
Summerfield, Castro, Parmer, 2 (34)	34
Summerville, Gonzales, 1	45
*Sumner, Lamar, 76	95
*SUNDOWN, Hockley, 46 (1,283)	1,265
Sunny Side, Waller	250
Sunnyside, Castro	64
Sunnyside, Wilson	100
SUNNYVALE, Dallas, 261 (7,893)	8,062
*SUNRAY, Moore, 59 (1,707)	1,702
Sunrise, Falls	200
*SUNRISE BEACH VILLAGE, Llano, 32 (739)	766
Sunrise Shores, Henderson (598)	536
*Sunset, Montague, Wise, 61 (543)	520
Sunset, Starr (34)	59
Sunset Acres, Webb (4)	17
Sunset Oaks, Burnet	198

The Newman House in Sweetwater, built in the Tudor Revival style in 1925, is on the National Register of Historic Places. Photo by Larry D. Moore, CC by SA 4.0

Town, County	Pop. 2021
SUNSET VALLEY, Travis, 139 (683)	656
SUN VALLEY, Lamar, 1 (70)	71
SURFSIDE BEACH, Brazoria, 35 (640)	656
*Sutherland Springs, Wilson, 15	420
Swamp City, Gregg	8
Swan, Smith	150
*SWEENY, Brazoria, 148 (3,626)	3,591
Sweet Home, Lee, 7	30
Sweet Home, Guadalupe	294
*Sweet Home, Lavaca	360
Sweet Union, Cherokee	40
*SWEETWATER, Nolan, 411 (10,622)	10,513
Swenson, Stonewall	80
Swift, Nacogdoches	210
Swiss Alp, Fayette	17
Sylvan, Lamar	68
*Sylvester, Fisher, 1 (52)	40

T

Town, County	Pop. 2021
Tabor, Brazos	150
Tadmor, Houston	67
*TAFT, San Patricio, 115 (2,801)	2,818
Taft Southwest, San Patricio, (1,296)	1,537
*TAHOKA, Lynn, 99 (2,375)	2,390
*TALCO, Titus, 33 (494)	488
*Talpa, Coleman, 13	127
TALTY, Kaufman, 2 (2,500)	2,710
Tamina, Montgomery	900
Tanglewood, Lee	60
Tanquecitos South Acres, Webb, (229)	199
Tanquecitos South Acres II, Webb, (60)	60
Tarkington Prairie, Liberty	300
*Tarpley, Bandera, 4	30
*Tarzan, Martin, 7	30
Tascosa Hills, Potter	90
*TATUM, Rusk, Panola, 97 (1,342)	1,340
*TAYLOR, Williamson, 653 (16,267)	16,807
TAYLOR LAKE VILLAGE, Harris, 20 (3,704)	3,617
TAYLOR LANDING, Jefferson, 1 (278)	278
Taylorsville, Caldwell	35
Taylor Town, Lamar	40
Tazewell, Hopkins	20
*TEAGUE, Freestone, 162 (3,384)	3,447
Teaselville, Smith, 1	150
*TEHUACANA, Limestone, 9 (228)	224
Telegraph, Kimble	3
*Telephone, Fannin, 26	210
*Telferner, Victoria, 9	700
Telico, Ellis, Navarro	115
*Tell, Childress, Cottle, Hall	20
*TEMPLE, Bell, 2,513 (82,073)	85,416
*TENAHA, Shelby, 51 (989)	991
Tenmile, Dawson	30
*Tennessee Colony, Anderson, 35	300
*Tennyson, Coke, 2	46
*Terlingua, Brewster, 85 (78)	127
*TERRELL, Kaufman, 1,081 (17,465)	18,567
TERRELL HILLS, Bexar, 28 (5,045)	5,037
Terry Chapel, Falls	30
Terryville, DeWitt	40
*TEXARKANA, Bowie (Miller Co., Ark.), 1,719 (36,193)	36,017
*TEXAS CITY, Galveston, 1,055 (51,898)	54,247
TEXHOMA, Sherman (Texas Co., Okla.), 8 (258)	259
*TEXLINE, Dallam, 30 (448)	460
Texroy, Hutchinson	50
Thalia, Foard	50
*THE COLONY, Denton, 1,075 (44,534)	45,000
Thedford, Smith	65
The Grove, Coryell	100
THE HILLS, Travis, 43 (2,613)	2,535
The Homesteads, Johnson, (3,890)	3,626
Thelma, Limestone	20
Thelma, Bexar	150
Theon, Williamson	30
Thermo, Hopkins	56
*The Woodlands, Montgomery, 2,934 (114,436)	115,716
*Thicket, Hardin, 9	306
*Thomaston, DeWitt, 1	45
*THOMPSONS, Fort Bend, 4 (156)	163
Thompsonville, Jim Hogg (26)	216
Thompsonville, Gonzales	30
Thornberry, Clay	75
*THORNDALE, Milam, 83 (1,263)	1,287
*THORNTON, Limestone, 30 (421)	415
THORNTONVILLE, Ward (561)	546
Thorp Spring, Hood	222
*THRALL, Williamson, 53 (816)	860
Three League, Martin	20
Three Oaks, Wilson	150
*THREE RIVERS, Live Oak, 152 (1,474)	1,562
Three States, Cass	45
*THROCKMORTON, Throckmorton, 49 (727)	749
Thunderbird Bay, Brown (764)	760
Thurber, Erath	48
Tidwell, Hunt	50
Tierra Bonita, Cameron (179)	57
Tierra Dorada, Starr (29)	29
Tierra Grande, Nueces (303)	185
Tierra Verde, Nueces (298)	232
Tigertown, Lamar	400
TIKI ISLAND, Galveston, 16 (1,106)	1,103
*Tilden, McMullen, 47 (190)	227
Tilmon, Caldwell	60
TIMBERCREEK CANYON, Randall (430)	445
Timberwood, Bexar (35,217)	33,506
*TIMPSON, Shelby, 90 (989)	991
Tin Top, Parker	500
*TIOGA, Grayson, 57 (1,142)	1,192
TIRA, Hopkins (319)	327
*Tivoli, Refugio, 19 (419)	645
TOCO, Lamar, 1 (91)	91
Todd City, Anderson	10
TODD MISSION, Grimes, 45 (121)	124
Tokio, Terry, 1	6
Tokio, McLennan	250
*TOLAR, Hood, 100 (941)	989
Tolbert, Wilbarger	15
Tolette, Lamar	40
Tolosa, Kaufman, Henderson	65
*TOMBALL, Harris, 3,141 (12,341)	12,810
*TOM BEAN, Grayson, 30 (930)	933
Tomlinson Hill, Falls	64
TOOL, Henderson, 83 (2,175)	2,212
Topsey, Coryell	35
*Tornillo, El Paso, 26 (1,432)	1,360
Tours, McLennan	130
*Tow, Llano, 20 (226)	162
Town Bluff, Tyler	429
*TOYAH, Reeves, 5 (61)	61
*Toyahvale, Reeves, 2	60
Tradewinds, San Patricio (160)	273
Travis, Falls, 2	48
Travis Ranch, Kaufman (7,324)	8,201
Trawick, Nacogdoches	375
Treasure Island, Brazoria	152
Treasure Island, Guadalupe	172
*TRENT, Taylor, 14 (295)	293
*TRENTON, Fannin, 107 (743)	773
Trickham, Coleman	29
Trimmer, Bell	390
*TRINIDAD, Henderson, 59 (860)	861
*TRINITY, Trinity, 217 (2,343)	2,377
TROPHY CLUB, Denton, 297 (13,688)	13,745
*TROUP, Smith, Cherokee, 190 (2,006)	2,039
Trout Creek, Newton	70
*TROY, Bell, 133 (2,375)	2,468
Truby, Jones	26
Trumbull, Ellis	100
Truscott, Knox, 6	50
Tucker, Anderson	175
*Tuleta, Bee, 12 (231)	289
*TULIA, Swisher, 142 (4,473)	4,474
Tulip, Fannin	10
Tulsita, Bee (31)	31
Tundra, Van Zandt	34
Tunis, Burleson (90)	16
*TURKEY, Hall, 26 (317)	326
Turlington, Freestone	27
Turnersville, Travis	90
Turnersville, Coryell	125
*Turnertown-Selman City, Rusk	271
Turtle Bayou, Chambers	55
*TUSCOLA, Taylor, 167 (850)	847
Tuxedo, Jones	42
Twichell, Ochiltree	22
Twitty, Wheeler	12
*TYE, Taylor, 59 (1,176)	1,192
*TYLER, Smith, 5,596 (105,995)	107,192
*Tynan, Bee, 6 (254)	268
Type, Williamson, Bastrop	40

Town, County . . . . Pop. 2021

U

UHLAND, Hays, Caldwell, 26 (1,588). 1,667
*Umbarger, Randall, 7 (123) 72
UNCERTAIN, Harrison, 6 (85). 88
Union, Terry 8
Union, Scurry 20
Union, Wilson. 52
UNION GROVE, Upshur (441) 453
Union Grove, Bell 12
Union High, Navarro 30
Union Hill, Denton 25
UNION VALLEY, Hunt (370). 398
Unity, Lamar 60
*UNIVERSAL CITY, Bexar, 584 (19,720). 19,808
UNIVERSITY PARK, Dallas, 136 (25,278). 24,849
Upper Meyersville, DeWitt 33
Upshaw, Nacogdoches 400
Upton, Bastrop 25
Urbana, San Jacinto 15
Utley, Bastrop 30
*Utopia, Uvalde, 61 (225) 210
*UVALDE, Uvalde, 639 (15,217) . . 15,312
Uvalde Estates, Uvalde (1,879). 2,388

V

Valdasta, Collin 82
*VALENTINE, Jeff Davis, 6 (73) 108
*Valera, Coleman, 2 (94). 18
Valle de Oro, Potter, 5 250
Valle Hermoso, Starr (93) 93
Valle Vista, Starr (545) 699
Valley Creek, Fannin 110
*VALLEY MILLS, Bosque, McLennan, 131 (1,229). 1,243
*Valley Spring, Llano, 3 50
*VALLEY VIEW, Cooke, 153 (737). . . 759
Valley View, Runnels 10
Valley View, Upshur 75
Valley View, Wichita. 210
Valley Wells, Dimmit 21
Val Verde, Milam 25
Val Verde Park, Val Verde (2,332) . . . 3,740
*VAN, Van Zandt, 151 (2,664) 2,745
*VAN ALSTYNE, Grayson, 336 (4,369). 5,165
Vance, Real, 1 20
*Vancourt, Tom Green, 6 131
Vandalia, Red River 35
*Vanderbilt, Jackson, 12 (409) 492
*Vanderpool, Bandera, 16. 20
Vandyke, Comanche. 20
*VAN HORN, Culberson, 101 (1,941). 1,946
*Van Vleck, Matagorda, 47 (1,923). . 1,054
Vasco, Delta. 20
Vashti, Clay 70
Vattmann, Kleberg 25
Vaughan, Hill. 75
Veach, San Augustine 12
Vealmoor, Howard 5
*VEGA, Oldham, 54 (879) 869
*VENUS, Johnson, 227 (4,361) 5,727
Vera, Knox. 30
Verdi, Atascosa, 1 110
Verhalen, Reeves, 1 12
*Veribest, Tom Green, 5 115
*VERNON, Wilbarger, 361 (10,078). 10,045
Verona, Collin 34
Vessey, Red River 15
Viboras, Starr. 15
Vick, Concho 20
*VICTORIA, Victoria, 3,002 (65,534). 65,377
Victoria, Limestone 25
Victoria Vera, Starr (93) 34
Victory City, Bowie 350
*VIDOR, Orange, 556 (9,789). 9,712
Vienna, Lavaca 40
View, Taylor 350
Vigo Park, Swisher. 36
Villa del Sol, Cameron (153) 451
*Village Mills, Hardin, 29 200
Villa Pancho, Cameron (467) 343
Villarreal, Starr (112) 17
Villa Verde, Hidalgo (711). 74
Vincent, Howard 10
Vineyard, Jack 19
VINTON, El Paso, 76 (2,684) 2,769
Violet, Nueces 160
Vistula, Houston 21
*Voca, McCulloch, 18 56
VOLENTE, Travis, 26 (561) 542
Volga, Houston 9
*VON ORMY, Bexar, 184 (1,174). . . 1,177
Voss, Coleman, 6 20
*Votaw, Hardin, 3 160
Vsetin, Lavaca 45

W

*WACO, McLennan, 4,972 (138,486). 139,594
*Wadsworth, Matagorda, 12 (302) . . . 507
*WAELDER, Gonzales, 44 (933) 941
Wagner, Hunt 75
Waka, Ochiltree, 3 (50). 114
Wakefield, Polk 25
WAKE VILLAGE, Bowie, 109 (5,945). 5,897
*Walburg, Williamson, 1 277
Walcott, Deaf Smith 5
Waldeck, Fayette 34
Waldrip, McCulloch. 15
Walhalla, Fayette 38
*Wall, Tom Green, 14 329
Wallace, Van Zandt 70
*WALLER, Waller, Harris, 521 (2,682). 2,796
*WALLIS, Austin, 126 (1,292) 1,296
*Wallisville, Chambers, 41 300
Walnut Bend, Cooke 45
Walnut Grove, Panola. 125
*WALNUT SPRINGS, Bosque, 55 (795). 815
Walton, Van Zandt 60
Wamba, Bowie 430
Waneta, Houston 19
Waples, Hood 155
*Warda, Fayette, 4 121
Ward Creek, Bowie 10
*Waring, Kendall, 8 73
*Warren, Tyler, 54 (677) 847
WARREN CITY, Gregg, Upshur, 1 (319). 321
Warrenton, Fayette, 7 186
Warsaw, Kaufman 100
Washburn, Armstrong, 2 (116) 227
*Washington, Washington, 52 100
*WASKOM, Harrison, 103 (1,910). . 1,946
Wastella, Nolan 12
*WATAUGA, Tarrant, 573 (23,650). 23,313
Waterloo, Williamson. 70
Waterman, Shelby 40
*Water Valley, Tom Green, 7 203
Watson, Burnet 50
Watt, Limestone. 25
Waverly, San Jacinto, Walker 200
*WAXAHACHIE, Ellis, 1,868 (41,140). 43,368
Wayne, Cass 15
Wayside, Armstrong, 3 25
Wayside, Roberts. 40
Wealthy, Leon 12
*WEATHERFORD, Parker, 2,657 (30,854). 33,710
Weatherly, Hall 8
Weaver, Hopkins 35
WEBBERVILLE, Travis, 12 (394). . . . 416
Webbville, Coleman. 15
*WEBSTER, Harris, 1,196 (12,499). 12,193
Weches, Houston. 46
Weedhaven, Jackson. 35
Weeping Mary, Cherokee 85
*Weesatche, Goliad, 2 411
*WEIMAR, Colorado, 190 (2,076). . 2,074
*WEINERT, Haskell, 4 (172). 175
*WEIR, Williamson, 11 (699) 714
Wiess Bluff, Jasper 60
*Welch, Dawson, 7 (234). 210
Welcome, Austin 300
Weldon, Houston. 131
Welfare, Kendall 10
*Wellborn, Brazos, 1 400
*WELLINGTON, Collingsworth, 69 (1,896). 1,867
*WELLMAN, Terry, 8 (230) 224
*WELLS, Cherokee, 18 (853) 867
Wells, Lynn 10
Wells Branch, Travis (14,000) 13,837
*WESLACO, Hidalgo, 1,390 (40,160). 41,024
Wesley, Washington, Austin. 65
Wesley Grove, Walker. 25

CITIES & TOWNS

Town, County	Pop. 2021
*WEST, McLennan, 252 (2,531)	2,557
West Alto Bonito, Starr (615)	493
*WESTBROOK, Mitchell, 14 (201)	224
*WEST COLUMBIA, Brazoria, 213 (3,644)	3,611
Westcott, San Jacinto	55
Westdale, Jim Wells (325)	82
Western Lake, Parker (1,762)	1,192
*Westhoff, DeWitt, 9	410
WESTLAKE, Tarrant, Denton, 113 (1,623)	1,683
*WEST LAKE HILLS, Travis, 457 (3,444)	3,322
West Livingston, Polk (8,156)	7,295
West Mineola, Wood	20
*Westminster, Collin, 1 (1,035)	1,006
West Mountain, Upshur	325
West Odessa, Ector, 1 (33,340)	31,927
*WESTON, Collin, 2 (283)	299
WESTON LAKES, Fort Bend, 11 (3,853)	4,061
WEST ORANGE, Orange, 80 (3,459)	3,433
Westover, Baylor	18
WESTOVER HILLS, Tarrant, 3 (641)	641
Westphalia, Falls, 1	186
West Point, Fayette, 33	213
West Sharyland, Hidalgo (2,004)	1,428
West Sinton, San Patricio	150
WEST TAWAKONI, Hunt, 40 (1,895)	1,932
WEST UNIVERSITY PLACE, Harris, 37 (14,955)	14,724
Westville, Trinity	46
Westway, El Paso (3,811)	3,726
Westway, DeafSmith	15
Westwood Shores, Trinity (1,239)	1,455
WESTWORTH VILLAGE, Tarrant, 68 (2,585)	2,602
*WHARTON, Wharton, 423 (8,627)	8,589
Wheatland, Tarrant, Parker	175
*WHEELER, Wheeler, 80 (1,487)	1,462
Wheeler Springs, Houston	89
*Wheelock, Robertson, 1	225
White City, San Augustine	20
White City, Wilbarger	40
*WHITE DEER, Carson, 36 (918)	904
*WHITEFACE, Cochran, 10 (375)	371
Whiteflat, Motley	4
Whitehall, Grimes	30
White Hall, Bell	262
*WHITEHOUSE, Smith, 381 (8,257)	8,734
*WHITE OAK, Gregg, 206 (6,225)	6,169
White Oak, Titus	60
White River Lake, Crosby	83
White Rock, San Augustine	60
White Rock, Hunt	60
White Rock, Robertson	80
White Rock, Red River	90
*WHITESBORO, Grayson, 342 (4,074)	4,217
*WHITE SETTLEMENT, Tarrant, 205 (18,269)	18,084
White Star, Motley	6
Whiteway, Hamilton	8
*WHITEWRIGHT, Grayson, Fannin, 165 (1,725)	1,753
*Whitharral, Hockley, 3 (119)	73
Whitman, Washington	25
*WHITNEY, Hill, 332 (1,992)	2,033
Whitsett, Live Oak, 15	200
Whitson, Coryell	50
*Whitt, Parker, 2	38
Whon, Coleman	35
*WICHITA FALLS, Wichita, 3,072 (102,316)	102,988
*WICKETT, Ward, 24 (422)	410
Wied, Lavaca	65
Wiedeville, Washington	35
*Wiergate, Newton, 2	350
Wigginsville, Montgomery	100
Wilcox, Burleson	39
Wilderville, Falls	45
*Wildorado, Oldham, 9 (201)	150
Wild Peach, Brazoria (2,329)	2,134
Wildwood, Hardin, 1 (1,121)	732
Wilkins, Upshur	75
William Penn, Washington	40
*WILLIS, Montgomery, 1,004 (6,431)	6,710
Willow City, Gillespie, 10	22
Willow Grove, McLennan (2,082)	2,231
WILLOW PARK, Parker, 210 (4,936)	5,194
Willow Springs, Rains	25
Willow Springs, Fayette	74
*WILLS POINT, Van Zandt, 460 (3,747)	3,863
*WILMER, Dallas, 123 (4,974)	5,332
Wilmeth, Runnels	15
*WILSON, Lynn, 34 (434)	444
Wilson, Falls	42
*WIMBERLEY, Hays, 890 (2,839)	2,877
Winchell, Brown	20
Winchester, Fayette, 5	232
WINDCREST, Bexar, 293 (5,865)	5,828
Windemere, Travis	1,184
*WINDOM, Fannin, 13 (189)	196
*WINDTHORST, Archer, 47 (342)	344
Winedale, Fayette, Washington	67
*WINFIELD, Titus, 15 (422)	422
*Wingate, Runnels, 11 (83)	113
*WINK, Winkler, 39 (915)	882
Winkler, Navarro, Freestone	26
*Winnie, Chambers, 274 (3,162)	2,366
*WINNSBORO, Wood, Franklin, 344 (3,455)	3,527
*WINONA, Smith, 74 (623)	643
Winter Haven, Dimmit	123
*WINTERS, Runnels, 92 (2,345)	2,365
Witting, Lavaca	90
WIXON VALLEY, Brazos (228)	232
Wizard Wells, Jack	69
*Woden, Nacogdoches, 2	400
*WOLFE CITY, Hunt, 78 (1,399)	1,406
*WOLFFORTH, Lubbock, 300 (5,521)	6,008
Womack, Bosque	25
Woodbine, Cooke	250
WOODBRANCH, Montgomery, (1,330)	1,420
Woodbury, Hill	45
WOODCREEK, Hays, 8 (1,770)	1,804
Wooded Hills, Johnson	580
Wood Hi, Victoria	35
*Woodlake, Trinity, 1	180
Woodland, Red River	128
*Woodlawn, Harrison, 5	550
WOODLOCH, Montgomery, (186)	184
Woodrow, Lubbock	2,034
Woodrow, Fort Bend	190
Woods, Panola	65
*WOODSBORO, Refugio, 59 (1,319)	1,299
*WOODSON, Throckmorton, 9 (219)	229
Wood Springs, Smith	200
*WOODVILLE, Tyler, 272 (2,403)	2,440
Woodville, Cherokee	20
Woodward, La Salle	6
WOODWAY, McLennan, 307 (9,383)	9,474
Woosley, Rains	47
*WORTHAM, Freestone, 40 (980)	1,002
Worthing, Lavaca	55
Wright City, Smith	172
Wrightsboro, Gonzales	10
Wyldwood, Bastrop (3,694)	3,718
*WYLIE, Collin, Rockwall, Dallas, 1,532 (57,526)	59,394
Wylie, Taylor	[part of Abilene]
Y	
*Yancey, Medina, 19 (300)	384
*YANTIS, Wood, 128 (405)	414
Yard, Anderson	50
Yarrellton, Milam	35
Yellowpine, Sabine	97
*YOAKUM, Lavaca, DeWitt, 295 (5,908)	5,923
*YORKTOWN, DeWitt, 149 (1,810)	1,811
Youngsport, Bell	49
Yowell, Delta, Hunt	30
Ysleta del Sur Pueblo, El Paso, 1	350
Yznaga, Cameron (108)	78
Z	
Zabcikville, Bell	76
*Zapata, Zapata, 307 (5,383)	4,928
Zapata Ranch, Willacy (87)	225
Zarate, Starr (79)	79
*ZAVALLA, Angelina, 54 (603)	607
*Zephyr, Brown, 28 (179)	198
Zimmerscheidt, Colorado	50
Zion Hill, Guadalupe	595
Zipperlandville, Falls	22
Zorn, Guadalupe	287
Zuehl, Guadalupe (399)	375
Zunkerville, Karnes	15

ELECTIONS

SPECIAL THANKS TO TEXAS CAPITAL BANK
FOR SPONSORING THIS CHAPTER OF THE TEXAS ALMANAC

PHOTO BY MIGUEL GUTIERREZ JR., THE TEXAS TRIBUNE

TEXAS TRIBUNE REPORTS: POLITICS

by Matthew Watkins, Managing Editor for News and Politics

THE TEXAS TRIBUNE

Texas has been dominated by Republicans for decades. But that one-party rule hasn't prevented political conflict from being a defining feature of how the state is run. The Republicans in power have long fought with one another, with the leaders of more liberal cities, and with different factions of the GOP.

WHO HOLDS THE POWER?

In Texas, the three most powerful positions are governor, lieutenant governor, and House speaker. The governor, of course, is the top office. The governor appoints boards and commissioners that oversee virtually all the state agencies, they issue and sign executive orders and disaster proclamations, and they enjoy the ability to attract the most attention and drive the agenda for state government. But the state Constitution's authors were wary of concentrating too much power in one place, so they limited the governor's power in some ways. Most state agency heads don't directly work for the governor; they work for boards and commissions appointed by them. The governor can't hire or fire those employees and doesn't control their budgets. The governor has to use the prominence of their position and their relationships with appointees to exert influence.

The lieutenant governor is elected separately from the governor. That position takes over the governor's responsibilities when the governor is out of state, and is next in line to take office if the governor steps down. But the lieutenant governor's real power comes from their responsibility of presiding over the Texas Senate. The lieutenant governor appoints senators to committees and controls which bills, including the state budget, reach the Senate floor and when. Because of that, the position wields immense power over the Senate, and has a secondary ability to influence the state agencies, universities, and other areas of the state that might be influenced by laws the Texas Legislature passes. It has long been said that the lieutenant governor's office is where the true power in Texas lies, and at least during the 140 days the Legislature is in session, that might be true.

The House speaker presides over the Texas House. The position also appoints committee members and has significant control over the actions of the House. But the speaker is elected by the House members, and is thus vulnerable to being unseated by a majority of them if they dislike how the chamber is run. That often means the House speaker must be more responsive to their wishes and demands, compared with the lieutenant governor, who is elected by the people of Texas and therefore doesn't owe their job to the senators.

A DELICATE BALANCE

Often, the ability to get things done can depend on the ability of those three leaders to get along. This was on display during the 2023 regular session of the Legislature, when lawmakers were in agreement that they wanted to cut property taxes, but Gov. Greg Abbott, House Speaker Dade Phelan, and Lt. Gov. Dan Patrick were in open conflict about how to do it. Ultimately, they couldn't come to an agreement during the regular session and lawmakers were called into a special legislative session to figure out a deal.

Often driving that conflict is the fact that the Republican Party is split into factions. There is a hardline conservative group that fiercely supports former President Donald Trump, pushes strong social conservative positions, and opposes any kind of compromise with Democrats. Patrick is often considered a leading member of that group. There is a more traditional faction that pushes conservative views on issues like guns, abortion, and other social issues, too, but often focuses more on economic development and business issues. Many see Phelan aligned with that group, as he is known to cooperate some with Democrats in the way he governs the House. Abbott often balances between those two factions, gaining support and, at times, skepticism from either side, though he often polls as one of the state's most popular Republicans.

Republican voters and officials in Texas often cite border security as one of their top priorities. They often push pro-gun policies, fight what they consider "woke" agendas in schools and universities, and are largely supportive of the state's oil and gas industry. They often clash with big-city mayors, who in cities like Austin, Houston, Dallas, and San Antonio are more often aligned with the politics of the Democratic Party.

2022 Gubernatorial Election Results by County

Source: Texas Secretary of State.

Below are the official results by county for the race of governor. Listed are the leading candidates: Beto O'Rourke for the Democratic Party, Greg Abbott for the Republican Party, Mark Tippetts for the Libertarian Party, and Delilah Barrios for the Green Party.

The total number of votes counted in the governor race, 8,102,908, was 47.79% of the registered voters. The voting-age population in November 2022 was estimated at 21,866,700. The statewide turnout in the previous presidential election in 2020 was 66.73% of the registered voters.

For historical election results, including presidential races since 1848, senator and primary races since 1906, governor races since 1845, and prohibition elections since 1854, see the "Elections" section at texasalmanac.com.

County	Registered Voters	Turnout %	Governor							
			Abbott	%	O'Rourke	%	Tippetts	%	Barrios	%
Statewide	**17,672,143**	**47.79%**	**4,437,099**	**54.76%**	**3,553,656**	**43.86%**	**81,932**	**1.01%**	**28,584**	**0.35%**
Anderson	29,494	51.18%	11,762	81.43%	2,545	17.62%	105	0.73%	33	0.23%
Andrews	10,369	38.68%	3,302	86.24%	479	12.51%	29	0.76%	16	0.42%
Angelina	54,088	47.05%	19,142	77.83%	5,174	21.04%	186	0.76%	93	0.38%
Aransas	18,821	53.86%	7,581	78.63%	1,924	19.96%	99	1.03%	33	0.34%
Archer	6,557	60.18%	3,498	90.90%	315	8.19%	32	0.83%	3	0.08%
Armstrong	1,445	65.82%	833	92.25%	60	6.64%	9	1.00%	1	0.11%
Atascosa	29,927	44.11%	8,801	69.30%	3,709	29.21%	114	0.90%	72	0.57%
Austin	20,848	55.74%	9,209	82.19%	1,873	16.72%	100	0.89%	21	0.19%
Bailey	3,501	43.70%	1,105	82.90%	213	15.98%	9	0.68%	6	0.45%
Bandera	17,963	60.53%	8,527	81.36%	1,816	17.33%	105	1.00%	28	0.27%
Bastrop	55,779	54.10%	16,707	57.15%	12,007	41.07%	371	1.27%	133	0.45%
Baylor	2,381	57.00%	1,183	90.51%	105	8.03%	17	1.30%	2	0.15%
Bee	15,744	42.77%	4,347	67.84%	1,976	30.84%	55	0.86%	30	0.47%
Bell	227,727	41.44%	51,888	59.01%	34,785	39.56%	888	1.01%	363	0.41%
Bexar	1,230,662	45.93%	221,993	41.05%	311,023	57.52%	5,127	0.95%	2,549	0.47%
Blanco	10,137	68.81%	5,142	75.91%	1,522	22.47%	89	1.31%	20	0.30%
Borden	462	72.37%	306	96.53%	9	2.84%	2	0.63%	0	0.00%
Bosque	13,079	59.43%	6,278	84.07%	1,099	14.72%	68	0.91%	17	0.23%
Bowie	60,986	45.27%	20,206	76.03%	6,060	22.80%	209	0.79%	97	0.36%
Brazoria	234,988	48.49%	64,938	59.07%	43,364	39.44%	1,236	1.12%	376	0.34%
Brazos	126,123	50.54%	35,768	59.66%	23,103	38.53%	881	1.47%	181	0.30%
Brewster	7,513	54.03%	2,014	53.52%	1,678	44.59%	53	1.41%	18	0.48%
Briscoe	994	60.16%	539	91.05%	49	8.28%	2	0.34%	2	0.34%
Brooks	5,152	41.56%	785	39.09%	1,204	59.96%	9	0.45%	10	0.50%
Brown	24,674	52.09%	10,853	88.34%	1,308	10.65%	93	0.76%	31	0.25%
Burleson	12,901	53.86%	5,506	82.03%	1,142	17.01%	53	0.79%	10	0.15%
Burnet	36,364	60.41%	16,505	78.18%	4,337	20.54%	220	1.04%	43	0.20%
Caldwell	25,248	47.07%	6,351	55.92%	4,790	42.17%	140	1.23%	77	0.68%
Calhoun	12,874	44.94%	4,228	75.61%	1,292	23.10%	53	0.95%	19	0.34%
Callahan	10,020	54.44%	4,770	90.58%	444	8.43%	37	0.70%	15	0.28%
Cameron	227,694	35.06%	34,290	44.48%	41,667	54.05%	572	0.74%	553	0.72%
Camp	8,041	52.07%	3,082	77.38%	863	21.67%	26	0.65%	10	0.25%
Carson	4,162	59.73%	2,177	90.94%	183	7.64%	31	1.29%	3	0.13%
Cass	21,145	49.27%	8,415	84.41%	1,460	14.65%	71	0.71%	18	0.18%
Castro	3,637	43.04%	1,226	82.12%	239	16.01%	17	1.14%	11	0.74%
Chambers	33,155	48.12%	12,964	82.38%	2,559	16.26%	183	1.16%	28	0.18%
Cherokee	30,080	49.76%	12,023	83.01%	2,323	16.04%	105	0.72%	32	0.22%
Childress	3,675	49.24%	1,562	89.21%	162	9.25%	20	1.14%	7	0.40%
Clay	8,066	57.74%	4,052	90.31%	393	8.76%	34	0.76%	8	0.18%
Cochran	1,738	37.68%	506	82.14%	95	15.42%	10	1.62%	2	0.32%
Coke	2,265	61.76%	1,260	90.71%	114	8.21%	11	0.79%	4	0.29%
Coleman	5,986	56.46%	2,942	90.83%	269	8.31%	18	0.56%	10	0.31%
Collin	693,753	54.83%	198,236	54.34%	161,737	44.34%	3,875	1.06%	838	0.23%
Collingsworth	1,858	50.41%	845	91.35%	75	8.11%	5	0.54%	0	0.00%
Colorado	14,345	54.22%	6,084	80.63%	1,395	18.49%	50	0.66%	17	0.23%
Comal	130,109	59.78%	54,503	72.90%	19,195	25.67%	882	1.18%	161	0.22%
Comanche	9,832	51.13%	4,203	87.09%	567	11.75%	47	0.97%	9	0.19%
Concho	1,731	56.26%	818	86.74%	109	11.56%	12	1.27%	4	0.42%

Gubernatorial Vote 2022

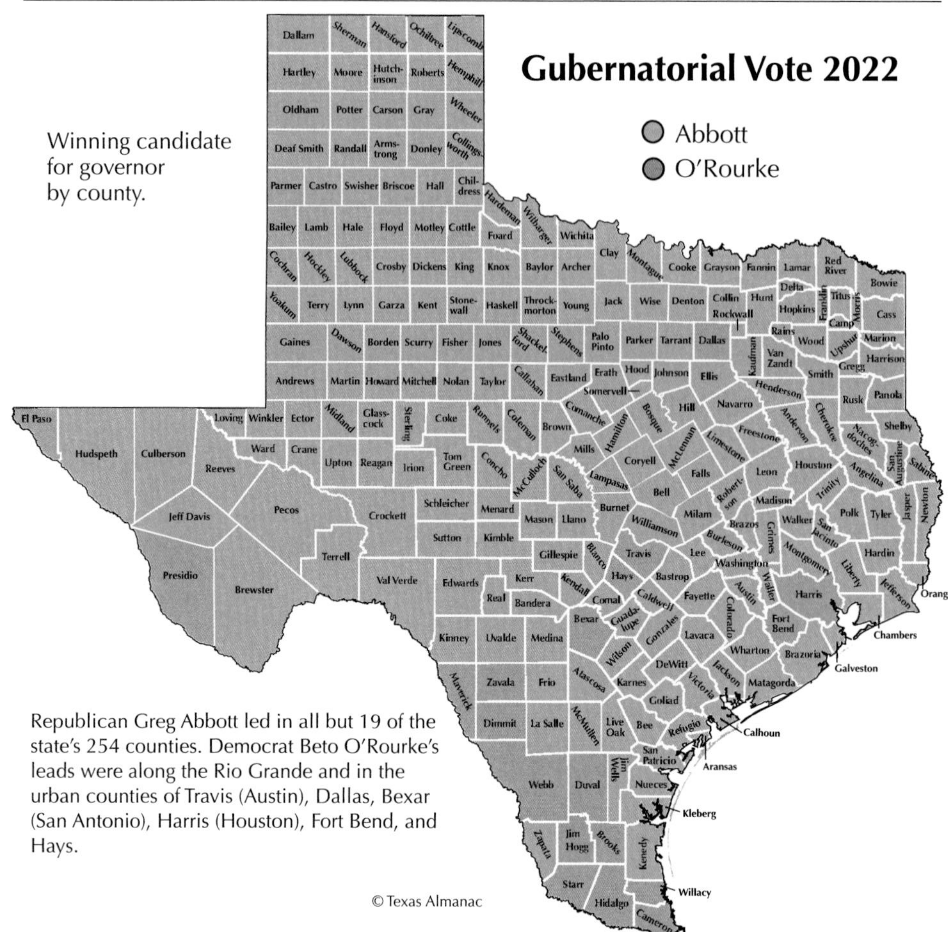

Winning candidate for governor by county.

Republican Greg Abbott led in all but 19 of the state's 254 counties. Democrat Beto O'Rourke's leads were along the Rio Grande and in the urban counties of Travis (Austin), Dallas, Bexar (San Antonio), Harris (Houston), Fort Bend, and Hays.

County	Registered Voters	Turnout %	Governor							
			Abbott	%	O'Rourke	%	Tippetts	%	Barrios	%
Cooke	28,699	55.56%	12,815	83.62%	2,308	15.06%	170	1.11%	32	0.21%
Coryell	42,839	39.49%	11,652	71.19%	4,450	27.19%	194	1.19%	67	0.41%
Cottle	956	55.09%	453	88.13%	54	10.51%	7	1.36%	0	0.00%
Crane	2,670	45.10%	983	85.70%	150	13.08%	8	0.70%	6	0.52%
Crockett	2,260	58.23%	964	75.73%	276	21.68%	18	1.41%	14	1.10%
Crosby	3,525	37.21%	990	78.95%	255	20.33%	6	0.48%	3	0.24%
Culberson	1,599	48.33%	391	53.13%	328	44.57%	6	0.82%	10	1.36%
Dallam	2,898	38.90%	958	91.24%	78	7.43%	9	0.86%	5	0.48%
Dallas	1,420,223	46.15%	224,684	35.93%	392,634	62.78%	5,824	0.93%	2,022	0.32%
Dawson	6,919	38.06%	2,088	82.99%	402	15.98%	17	0.68%	9	0.36%
Deaf Smith	8,764	35.40%	2,281	77.40%	635	21.55%	15	0.51%	16	0.54%
Delta	3,975	53.09%	1,711	84.41%	295	14.55%	14	0.69%	7	0.35%
Denton	606,275	54.63%	177,017	55.70%	136,389	42.92%	3,519	1.11%	771	0.24%
DeWitt	12,174	53.87%	5,151	84.99%	878	14.49%	23	0.38%	9	0.15%
Dickens	1,370	58.16%	684	86.47%	98	12.39%	8	1.01%	1	0.13%
Dimmit	6,982	42.87%	1,080	37.55%	1,757	61.09%	17	0.59%	22	0.76%
Donley	2,225	55.60%	1,084	90.94%	97	8.14%	7	0.59%	4	0.34%
Duval	8,129	46.65%	1,600	43.53%	2,018	54.90%	19	0.52%	39	1.06%
Eastland	12,282	53.17%	5,468	88.91%	634	10.31%	38	0.62%	9	0.15%
Ector	83,323	32.11%	19,212	75.49%	5,950	23.38%	209	0.82%	75	0.29%
Edwards	1,461	58.02%	712	87.47%	99	12.16%	3	0.37%	0	0.00%
Ellis	131,057	34.15%	45,564	67.23%	21,338	31.49%	682	1.01%	177	0.26%
El Paso	506,554	53.34%	57,573	34.80%	105,156	63.56%	1,481	0.90%	1,207	0.73%

County	Registered Voters	Turnout %	Governor							
			Abbott	%	O'Rourke	%	Tippetts	%	Barrios	%
Erath	24,860	55.20%	10,956	83.54%	1,976	15.07%	133	1.01%	47	0.36%
Falls	10,302	47.73%	3,480	74.00%	1,168	24.84%	46	0.98%	9	0.19%
Fannin	23,363	51.87%	9,694	83.10%	1,831	15.70%	107	0.92%	30	0.26%
Fayette	17,810	60.49%	8,649	82.37%	1,748	16.65%	81	0.77%	19	0.18%
Fisher	2,681	54.56%	1,172	83.65%	210	14.99%	14	1.00%	5	0.36%
Floyd	3,669	41.70%	1,250	85.21%	201	13.70%	12	0.82%	4	0.27%
Foard	824	67.56%	452	85.44%	69	13.04%	6	1.13%	2	0.38%
Fort Bend	521,611	49.68%	117,249	46.89%	129,116	51.63%	2,518	1.01%	1,153	0.46%
Franklin	7,228	56.02%	3,369	86.01%	512	13.07%	28	0.71%	7	0.18%
Freestone	12,749	54.21%	5,600	84.07%	991	14.88%	56	0.84%	14	0.21%
Frio	9,114	42.23%	1,872	50.21%	1,791	48.04%	25	0.67%	28	0.75%
Gaines	9,897	43.43%	3,761	91.44%	311	7.56%	30	0.73%	11	0.27%
Galveston	235,262	49.24%	68,822	62.15%	40,229	36.33%	1,315	1.19%	360	0.33%
Garza	2,659	47.10%	1,056	88.00%	135	11.25%	7	0.58%	1	0.08%
Gillespie	21,123	65.80%	10,801	80.67%	2,421	18.08%	133	0.99%	23	0.17%
Glasscock	813	71.59%	542	94.76%	27	4.72%	2	0.35%	1	0.17%
Goliad	5,771	60.79%	2,664	79.14%	663	19.70%	25	0.74%	13	0.39%
Gonzales	12,685	45.04%	4,369	78.49%	1,129	20.28%	40	0.72%	27	0.49%
Gray	12,611	47.56%	5,013	90.19%	478	8.60%	47	0.85%	20	0.36%
Grayson	92,038	50.70%	34,903	77.58%	9,563	21.26%	397	0.88%	122	0.27%
Gregg	73,931	47.21%	24,223	72.93%	8,662	26.08%	236	0.71%	84	0.25%
Grimes	19,170	50.86%	7,607	80.65%	1,732	18.36%	74	0.78%	19	0.20%
Guadalupe	119,523	50.26%	36,882	64.48%	19,356	33.84%	733	1.28%	215	0.38%
Hale	18,458	36.53%	5,094	80.49%	1,165	18.41%	52	0.82%	16	0.25%
Hall	1,832	49.91%	772	88.03%	94	10.72%	8	0.91%	3	0.34%
Hamilton	5,964	60.44%	3,006	86.48%	433	12.46%	30	0.86%	5	0.14%
Hansford	2,970	53.71%	1,419	93.23%	91	5.98%	7	0.46%	5	0.33%
Hardeman	2,459	41.72%	866	87.92%	114	11.57%	3	0.30%	2	0.20%
Hardin	41,408	48.17%	17,447	88.88%	2,035	10.37%	129	0.66%	14	0.07%
Harris	2,568,463	44.38%	490,261	44.47%	595,653	54.03%	11,812	1.07%	4,526	0.41%
Harrison	45,789	48.67%	16,472	77.13%	4,688	21.95%	137	0.64%	53	0.25%
Hartley	2,682	60.10%	1,463	92.95%	96	6.10%	12	0.76%	3	0.19%
Haskell	3,375	51.88%	1,465	87.72%	191	11.44%	6	0.36%	4	0.24%
Hays	167,750	55.87%	39,085	43.58%	48,970	54.60%	1,267	1.41%	351	0.39%
Hemphill	2,303	61.50%	1,198	88.02%	138	10.14%	20	1.47%	5	0.37%
Henderson	58,253	51.45%	22,909	81.81%	4,798	17.13%	243	0.87%	49	0.17%
Hidalgo	416,978	34.81%	56,783	40.22%	82,671	58.55%	837	0.59%	895	0.63%
Hill	25,006	47.06%	9,418	82.72%	1,830	16.07%	109	0.96%	24	0.21%
Hockley	13,510	42.73%	4,690	84.79%	786	14.21%	39	0.71%	14	0.25%
Hood	48,651	58.32%	22,596	82.99%	4,301	15.80%	281	1.03%	47	0.17%
Hopkins	24,724	52.54%	10,223	82.77%	1,999	16.18%	102	0.83%	27	0.22%
Houston	13,472	55.48%	5,726	79.70%	1,399	19.47%	44	0.61%	15	0.21%
Howard	16,934	40.67%	5,367	81.71%	1,077	16.40%	82	1.25%	40	0.61%
Hudspeth	2,097	43.52%	606	66.89%	270	29.80%	11	1.21%	18	1.99%
Hunt	64,334	49.59%	23,744	77.75%	6,422	21.03%	292	0.96%	77	0.25%
Hutchinson	13,333	47.66%	5,437	89.69%	540	8.91%	72	1.19%	12	0.20%
Irion	1,229	59.55%	618	88.92%	70	10.07%	7	1.01%	0	0.00%
Jack	5,603	57.06%	2,744	91.68%	227	7.58%	19	0.63%	3	0.10%
Jackson	9,552	50.18%	4,013	87.30%	550	11.96%	26	0.57%	8	0.17%
Jasper	23,739	49.91%	9,701	85.25%	1,601	14.07%	59	0.52%	15	0.13%
Jeff Davis	1,584	68.45%	641	61.05%	374	35.62%	30	2.86%	5	0.48%
Jefferson	147,873	44.33%	34,988	56.02%	26,641	42.66%	539	0.86%	265	0.42%
Jim Hogg	3,702	43.51%	650	42.15%	876	56.81%	6	0.39%	10	0.65%
Jim Wells	26,593	37.37%	5,063	53.05%	4,375	45.85%	58	0.61%	47	0.49%
Johnson	116,736	49.63%	42,954	76.89%	12,266	21.96%	520	0.93%	107	0.19%
Jones	10,294	49.58%	4,349	87.12%	581	11.64%	52	1.04%	9	0.18%
Karnes	8,351	47.38%	3,007	78.76%	776	20.32%	25	0.65%	10	0.26%
Kaufman	93,515	47.74%	28,306	66.09%	14,024	32.74%	379	0.88%	111	0.26%
Kendall	36,571	63.89%	17,719	78.55%	4,506	19.98%	269	1.19%	54	0.24%
Kenedy	301	57.09%	109	71.24%	42	27.45%	1	0.65%	1	0.65%
Kent	588	61.08%	312	89.14%	34	9.71%	2	0.57%	2	0.57%

County	Registered Voters	Turnout %	Governor							
			Abbott	%	O'Rourke	%	Tippetts	%	Barrios	%
Kerr	39,036	60.10%	17,524	77.95%	4,648	20.68%	249	1.11%	55	0.24%
Kimble	3,174	61.13%	1,666	88.81%	188	10.02%	16	0.85%	6	0.32%
King	158	67.76%	100	97.09%	3	2.91%	0	0.00%	0	0.00%
Kinney	2,183	56.43%	907	75.96%	258	21.61%	15	1.26%	8	0.67%
Kleberg	18,605	43.17%	4,074	53.40%	3,463	45.39%	49	0.64%	37	0.48%
Knox	2,176	49.31%	889	85.48%	140	13.46%	5	0.48%	6	0.58%
Lamar	32,359	49.58%	12,521	81.61%	2,657	17.32%	126	0.82%	24	0.16%
Lamb	7,864	40.62%	2,628	85.32%	419	13.60%	21	0.68%	12	0.39%
Lampasas	15,904	54.23%	6,625	80.29%	1,502	18.20%	78	0.95%	43	0.52%
La Salle	4,311	34.49%	761	52.96%	662	46.07%	5	0.35%	9	0.63%
Lavaca	13,986	60.55%	7,380	89.90%	759	9.25%	49	0.60%	19	0.23%
Lee	11,539	56.34%	5,108	81.31%	1,095	17.43%	53	0.84%	18	0.29%
Leon	11,896	59.30%	6,082	88.62%	698	10.17%	57	0.83%	18	0.26%
Liberty	49,826	41.29%	16,080	81.25%	3,488	17.62%	167	0.84%	56	0.28%
Limestone	13,952	51.18%	5,390	78.67%	1,366	19.94%	63	0.92%	32	0.47%
Lipscomb	1,901	54.37%	894	91.50%	69	7.06%	12	1.23%	2	0.20%
Live Oak	7,677	53.55%	3,424	85.60%	545	13.63%	23	0.58%	8	0.20%
Llano	17,557	65.60%	8,977	81.39%	1,920	17.41%	111	1.01%	16	0.15%
Loving	109	74.53%	70	88.61%	6	7.59%	2	2.53%	1	1.27%
Lubbock	187,728	46.94%	58,163	69.43%	24,497	29.24%	891	1.06%	208	0.25%
Lynn	4,098	43.87%	1,502	86.97%	196	11.35%	19	1.10%	10	0.58%
Madison	8,148	51.08%	3,272	83.75%	595	15.23%	34	0.87%	4	0.10%
Marion	7,630	49.57%	2,557	77.44%	700	21.20%	34	1.03%	10	0.30%
Martin	3,350	59.71%	1,341	88.93%	149	9.88%	12	0.80%	6	0.40%
Mason	3,184	49.89%	1,703	85.53%	268	13.46%	16	0.80%	4	0.20%
Matagorda	21,681	45.53%	7,350	75.61%	2,273	23.38%	69	0.71%	29	0.30%
Maverick	34,073	46.43%	3,862	40.30%	5,555	57.97%	67	0.70%	98	1.02%
McCulloch	5,396	64.48%	2,221	86.66%	314	12.25%	21	0.82%	7	0.27%
McLennan	154,088	46.94%	47,875	65.95%	23,765	32.74%	735	1.01%	184	0.25%
McMullen	660	28.87%	343	92.20%	28	7.53%	1	0.27%	0	0.00%
Medina	35,611	50.12%	12,601	72.56%	4,591	26.44%	114	0.66%	54	0.31%
Menard	1,420	56.00%	659	85.03%	110	14.19%	5	0.65%	1	0.13%
Midland	96,512	44.83%	32,389	80.87%	7,154	17.86%	398	0.99%	112	0.28%
Milam	16,380	52.74%	6,717	80.37%	1,559	18.65%	64	0.77%	18	0.22%
Mills	3,455	63.26%	1,894	89.30%	198	9.34%	23	1.08%	6	0.28%
Mitchell	4,469	41.45%	1,576	88.49%	185	10.39%	15	0.84%	5	0.28%
Montague	14,661	55.62%	7,004	89.20%	765	9.74%	66	0.84%	17	0.22%
Montgomery	409,759	52.85%	152,694	73.39%	52,654	25.31%	2,206	1.06%	455	0.22%
Moore	9,941	38.07%	3,081	85.51%	479	13.29%	27	0.75%	14	0.39%
Morris	8,708	47.94%	3,041	76.10%	921	23.05%	19	0.48%	14	0.35%
Motley	822	62.45%	482	95.63%	18	3.57%	4	0.79%	0	0.00%
Nacogdoches	39,321	50.86%	13,248	69.91%	5,480	28.92%	182	0.96%	30	0.16%
Navarro	31,135	47.31%	10,830	76.63%	3,157	22.34%	100	0.71%	43	0.30%
Newton	9,376	48.52%	3,660	83.70%	689	15.76%	16	0.37%	8	0.18%
Nolan	8,751	44.11%	3,093	81.33%	647	17.01%	41	1.08%	20	0.53%
Nueces	213,925	43.89%	47,567	53.27%	40,474	45.32%	836	0.94%	424	0.47%
Ochiltree	5,135	43.66%	1,975	92.90%	135	6.35%	10	0.47%	6	0.28%
Oldham	1,318	61.45%	710	92.21%	50	6.49%	7	0.91%	3	0.39%
Orange	55,008	47.71%	21,153	84.28%	3,722	14.83%	168	0.67%	53	0.21%
Palo Pinto	19,390	51.00%	7,896	83.21%	1,486	15.66%	83	0.87%	24	0.25%
Panola	17,176	50.02%	7,039	84.67%	1,213	14.59%	46	0.55%	13	0.16%
Parker	115,621	57.08%	52,523	82.80%	10,123	15.96%	670	1.06%	113	0.18%
Parmer	4,452	41.19%	1,546	87.44%	202	11.43%	10	0.57%	10	0.57%
Pecos	8,210	46.16%	2,548	69.20%	1,043	28.33%	51	1.39%	40	1.09%
Polk	42,228	42.01%	13,377	79.74%	3,229	19.25%	137	0.82%	33	0.20%
Potter	58,048	40.05%	16,082	73.75%	5,361	24.58%	266	1.22%	87	0.40%
Presidio	4,399	41.71%	561	32.54%	1,133	65.72%	14	0.81%	16	0.93%
Rains	8,775	59.16%	4,339	87.01%	596	11.95%	41	0.82%	11	0.22%
Randall	95,933	52.40%	39,243	81.72%	8,228	17.13%	442	0.92%	98	0.20%
Reagan	1,816	41.53%	616	86.03%	90	12.57%	4	0.56%	6	0.84%
Real	2,716	62.81%	1,337	85.21%	218	13.89%	10	0.64%	2	0.13%

County	Registered Voters	Turnout %	Governor							
			Abbott	%	O'Rourke	%	Tippetts	%	Barrios	%
Red River	8,621	51.82%	3,482	81.47%	764	17.88%	20	0.47%	8	0.19%
Reeves	7,486	29.77%	1,341	61.60%	801	36.79%	16	0.73%	19	0.87%
Refugio	4,913	49.26%	1,658	71.59%	639	27.59%	12	0.52%	7	0.30%
Roberts	699	66.97%	430	96.85%	7	1.58%	5	1.13%	1	0.23%
Robertson	12,001	51.53%	4,643	77.16%	1,293	21.49%	62	1.03%	19	0.32%
Rockwall	79,059	55.75%	30,211	70.47%	12,132	28.30%	447	1.04%	81	0.19%
Runnels	6,723	49.57%	2,924	90.41%	277	8.57%	29	0.90%	4	0.12%
Rusk	32,951	49.30%	12,762	81.66%	2,697	17.26%	117	0.75%	49	0.31%
Sabine	8,215	52.95%	3,755	90.16%	385	9.24%	20	0.48%	5	0.12%
San Augustine	6,052	49.13%	2,288	79.86%	546	19.06%	27	0.94%	4	0.14%
San Jacinto	19,809	50.11%	7,882	82.54%	1,540	16.13%	95	0.99%	30	0.31%
San Patricio	44,067	42.47%	12,028	67.20%	5,643	31.53%	142	0.79%	83	0.46%
San Saba	3,780	59.38%	1,947	89.93%	200	9.24%	16	0.74%	2	0.09%
Schleicher	1,700	61.20%	834	82.74%	159	15.77%	8	0.79%	7	0.69%
Scurry	9,315	46.17%	3,607	87.38%	480	11.63%	29	0.70%	12	0.29%
Shackelford	2,329	55.12%	1,148	92.66%	81	6.54%	8	0.65%	2	0.16%
Shelby	15,922	45.22%	5,846	84.33%	1,045	15.08%	32	0.46%	9	0.13%
Sherman	1,380	54.17%	665	93.93%	35	4.94%	7	0.99%	1	0.14%
Smith	153,936	51.51%	56,608	74.27%	18,763	24.62%	648	0.85%	184	0.24%
Somervell	6,995	59.89%	3,430	84.90%	553	13.69%	49	1.21%	6	0.15%
Starr	34,065	32.96%	4,460	40.12%	6,455	58.06%	62	0.56%	139	1.25%
Stephens	5,712	50.33%	2,511	91.48%	217	7.91%	16	0.58%	1	0.04%
Sterling	775	58.11%	423	94.42%	20	4.46%	3	0.67%	2	0.45%
Stonewall	929	61.55%	492	87.08%	70	12.39%	2	0.35%	1	0.18%
Sutton	2,333	52.04%	970	83.48%	178	15.32%	8	0.69%	6	0.52%
Swisher	3,853	45.20%	1,399	83.97%	238	14.29%	19	1.14%	9	0.54%
Tarrant	1,260,870	49.13%	303,600	51.34%	279,423	47.25%	6,443	1.09%	1,801	0.30%
Taylor	86,089	48.59%	30,030	76.12%	8,888	22.53%	409	1.04%	119	0.30%
Terrell	629	69.38%	326	76.53%	94	22.07%	4	0.94%	0	0.00%
Terry	6,354	42.65%	2,167	83.67%	377	14.56%	26	1.00%	19	0.73%
Throckmorton	1,218	56.48%	612	91.75%	51	7.65%	4	0.60%	0	0.00%
Titus	17,740	43.63%	5,701	77.86%	1,535	20.96%	70	0.96%	16	0.22%
Tom Green	70,922	47.44%	23,873	74.96%	7,516	23.60%	326	1.02%	116	0.36%
Travis	886,480	53.92%	119,321	25.89%	334,667	72.61%	5,506	1.19%	1,327	0.29%
Trinity	11,650	46.79%	4,465	83.60%	825	15.45%	42	0.79%	9	0.17%
Tyler	14,510	51.99%	6,343	87.54%	816	11.26%	69	0.95%	14	0.19%
Upshur	28,969	51.50%	12,270	86.00%	1,856	13.01%	121	0.85%	19	0.13%
Upton	2,152	51.86%	908	85.82%	124	11.72%	12	1.13%	14	1.32%
Uvalde	17,462	47.08%	4,779	60.14%	3,048	38.36%	65	0.82%	43	0.54%
Val Verde	29,351	33.91%	5,530	58.16%	3,814	40.11%	73	0.77%	86	0.90%
Van Zandt	39,954	53.20%	17,773	87.21%	2,414	11.85%	141	0.69%	37	0.18%
Victoria	56,411	46.88%	18,519	73.23%	6,452	25.51%	190	0.75%	122	0.48%
Walker	36,058	50.65%	12,309	70.78%	4,861	27.95%	166	0.95%	52	0.30%
Waller	37,595	46.39%	11,381	68.13%	5,100	30.53%	170	1.02%	50	0.30%
Ward	6,914	38.12%	2,065	82.01%	418	16.60%	26	1.03%	8	0.32%
Washington	24,644	58.79%	10,965	78.48%	2,824	20.21%	155	1.11%	25	0.18%
Webb	143,148	32.31%	16,409	36.70%	27,156	60.73%	350	0.78%	797	1.78%
Wharton	25,890	48.72%	9,354	76.96%	2,697	22.19%	72	0.59%	28	0.23%
Wheeler	3,344	52.56%	1,569	93.06%	103	6.11%	13	0.77%	1	0.06%
Wichita	78,794	42.60%	23,328	73.75%	7,824	24.74%	358	1.13%	113	0.36%
Wilbarger	8,360	40.65%	2,606	82.68%	517	16.40%	21	0.67%	8	0.25%
Willacy	11,728	34.50%	1,656	43.13%	2,138	55.68%	32	0.83%	13	0.34%
Williamson	415,096	56.72%	111,488	49.43%	110,242	48.88%	3,161	1.40%	608	0.27%
Wilson	37,022	54.28%	14,952	76.81%	4,317	22.18%	141	0.72%	55	0.28%
Winkler	3,984	34.45%	1,130	85.54%	177	13.40%	10	0.76%	4	0.30%
Wise	49,888	53.32%	21,979	85.12%	3,538	13.70%	249	0.96%	52	0.20%
Wood	32,804	56.48%	15,678	86.27%	2,331	12.83%	141	0.78%	23	0.13%
Yoakum	4,264	39.78%	1,427	87.22%	190	11.61%	13	0.79%	6	0.37%
Young	11,884	54.32%	5,498	88.76%	630	10.17%	51	0.82%	10	0.16%
Zapata	7,886	44.87%	1,817	52.77%	1,585	46.04%	18	0.52%	23	0.67%
Zavala	7,817	32.31%	780	31.84%	1,642	67.02%	4	0.16%	24	0.98%

General Election, 2022

Source: Texas Secretary of State.

Below are the official voting results for the general election held November 8, 2022, as canvassed by the State Canvassing Board.

Federal races include the House of Representatives elections. Statewide races include lieutenant general, attorney general, comptroller of public accounts, commissioner of the General Land Office, commissioner of agriculture, railroad commissioner, the Texas Supreme Court, and the courts of criminal appeals. District races include the state senate, state board of education, the state House of Representatives, judges for the court of appeals, and district judges. Races with a single candidate are omitted. Historical entries can be found at our website, texasalmanac.com.

Abbreviations used are (Dem.) Democrat, (Rep.) Republican, (Lib.) Libertarian, (Ind.) Independent and (W-I) Write-in.

Federal Races

U.S. House of Representatives

(See map of districts on p. 526.)

District 1

Candidate	Votes	Percent
Nathaniel Moran (Rep.)	183,224	78.08%
Jrmar (J.J.) Jefferson (Dem.)	51,438	21.92%
Total Votes	234,662	

District 2

Candidate	Votes	Percent
Dan Crenshaw (Rep.)	151,791	65.91%
Robin Fulford (Dem.)	78,496	34.09%
Total Votes	230,287	

District 3

Candidate	Votes	Percent
Keith Self (Rep.)	164,240	60.55%
Sandeep Srivastava (Dem.)	100,121	36.91%
Christopher Claytor (Lib.)	6,895	2.54%
Total Votes	271,256	

District 4

Candidate	Votes	Percent
Pat Fallon (Rep.)	170,781	66.71%
Iro Omere (Dem.)	79,179	30.93%
John Simmons (Lib.)	6,049	2.36%
Total Votes	256,009	

District 5

Candidate	Votes	Percent
Lance Gooden (Rep.)	135,595	63.97%
Tartisha Hill (Dem.)	71,930	33.93%
Kevin A. Hale (Lib.)	4,293	2.03%
Ruth Torres (W-I)	147	0.07%
Total Votes	211,965	

District 7

Candidate	Votes	Percent
Lizzie Fletcher (Dem.)	115,994	63.79%
Johnny Teague (Rep.)	65,835	36.21%
Total Votes	181,829	

District 8

Candidate	Votes	Percent
Morgan Luttrell (Rep.)	153,127	68.07%
Laura Jones (Dem.)	68,715	30.54%
Roy Eriksen (Lib.)	3,126	1.39%
Total Votes	224,968	

District 9

Candidate	Votes	Percent
Al Green (Dem.)	125,446	76.68%
Jimmy I. Leon (Rep.)	38,161	23.32%
Total Votes	163,607	

District 10

Candidate	Votes	Percent
Michael McCaul (Rep.)	159,469	63.3%
Linda Nuno (Dem.)	86,404	34.3%
Bill Kelsey (Lib.)	6,064	2.41%
Total Votes	251,937	

District 12

Candidate	Votes	Percent
Kay Granger (Rep.)	152,953	64.27%
Trey J. Hunt (Dem.)	85,026	35.73%
Total Votes	237,979	

District 13

Candidate	Votes	Percent
Ronny Jackson (Rep.)	161,767	75.35%
Kathleen Brown (Dem.)	52,910	24.65%
Total Votes	214,677	

District 14

Candidate	Votes	Percent
Randy Weber (Rep.)	149,543	70.16%
Mikal Williams (Dem.)	63,606	29.84%
Total Votes	213,149	

District 15

Candidate	Votes	Percent
Monica De La Cruz (Rep.)	80,978	53.31%
Michelle Vallejo (Dem.)	68,097	44.83%
Ross Lynn Leone, Jr. (Lib.)	2,814	1.85%
Total Votes	151,889	

District 16

Candidate	Votes	Percent
Veronica Escobar (Dem.)	95,510	63.46%
Irene Armendariz Jackson (Rep.)	54,986	36.54%
Total Votes	150,496	

District 17

Candidate	Votes	Percent
Pete Sessions (Rep.)	144,408	66.48%
Mary Jo Woods (Dem.)	72,801	33.52%
Total Votes	217,209	

District 18

Candidate	Votes	Percent
Sheila Jackson Lee (Dem.)	110,511	70.72%
Carmen Maria Montiel (Rep.)	40,941	26.2%
Phil Kurtz (Lib.)	2,050	1.31%
Vince Duncan (Ind.)	2,766	1.77%
Total Votes	156,268	

District 19

Candidate	Votes	Percent
Jodey C. Arrington (Rep.)	152,321	80.3%
Nathan Lewis (Ind.)	37,360	19.7%
Total Votes	189,681	

District 20

Candidate	Votes	Percent
Joaquin Castro (Dem.)	115,352	68.42%
Kyle Sinclair (Rep.)	53,226	31.57%
Adam Jonasz (W-I)	21	0.01%
Total Votes	168,599	

District 21

Candidate	Votes	Percent
Chip Roy (Rep.)	207,426	62.84%
Claudia Andreana Zapata (Dem.)	122,655	37.16%
Total Votes	330,081	

District 22

Candidate	Votes	Percent
Troy E. Nehls (Rep.)	150,014	62.19%
Jamie Kaye Jordan (Dem.)	85,653	35.51%
Joseph Leblanc (Lib.)	5,378	2.23%
Jim Squires (W-I)	170	0.07%
Total Votes	241,215	

District 23

Candidate	Votes	Percent
Tony Gonzales (Rep.)	116,649	55.87%
John Lira (Dem.)	80,947	38.77%
Frank Lopez Jr. (Ind.)	11,180	5.36%
Total Votes	208,776	

District 24

Candidate	Votes	Percent
Beth Van Duyne (Rep.)	177,947	59.75%
Jan McDowell (Dem.)	119,878	40.25%
Total Votes	297,825	

District 26

Candidate	Votes	Percent
Michael C. Burgess (Rep.)	183,639	69.29%
Mike Kolls (Lib.)	81,384	30.71%
Total Votes	265,023	

District 27

Michael Cloud (Rep.) 133,416 64.44%
Maclovio Perez Jr. (Dem.) 73,611 35.56%
Total Votes 207,027

District 28

Henry Cuellar (Dem.) 93,803 56.65%
Cassy Garcia (Rep.) 71,778 43.35%
Total Votes 165,581

District 29

Sylvia Garcia (Dem.) 71,837 71.41%
Robert Schafranek (Rep.) 28,765 28.59%
Total Votes 100,602

District 30

Jasmine Crockett (Dem.) 134,876 74.72%
James Rodgers (Rep.) 39,209 21.72%
Phil Gray (Lib.) 1,870 1.04%
Zachariah Manning (Ind.) 3,820 2.12%
Debbie Walker (W-I) 738 0.41%
Total Votes 180,513

District 32

Colin Allred (Dem.) 116,005 65.36%
Antonio Swad (Rep.) 61,494 34.64%
Total Votes 177,499

District 33

Marc Veasey (Dem.) 82,081 71.98%
Patrick David Gillespie (Rep.) 29,203 25.61%
Ken Ashby (Lib.) 2,746 2.41%
Total Votes 114,030

District 34

Vicente Gonzalez (Dem.) 70,896 52.73%
Mayra Flores (Rep.) 59,464 44.23%
Chris Royal (Ind.) 4,079 3.03%
Total Votes 134,439

District 35

Greg Casar (Dem.) 129,599 72.58%
Dan McQueen (Rep.) 48,969 27.42%
Total Votes 178,568

District 36

Brian Babin (Rep.) 145,599 69.46%
Jon Haire (Dem.) 64,016 30.54%
Total Votes 209,615

District 37

Lloyd Doggett (Dem.) 219,358 76.76%
Jenny Garcia Sharon (Rep.) 59,923 20.97%
Clark Patterson (Lib.) 6,332 2.22%
Sherri Lynn Taylor (W-I) 176 0.06%
Total Votes 285,789

District 38

Wesley Hunt (Rep.) 163,597 62.95%
Duncan F. Klussmann (Dem.) 92,302 35.52%
Joel Dejean (Ind.) 3,970 1.53%
Total Votes 259,869

State Races

Lieutenant Governor

Dan Patrick (Rep.) 4,317,692 53.75%
Mike Collier (Dem.) 3,492,544 43.48%
Shanna Steele (Lib.) 222,208 2.77%
Total Votes 8,032,444

Attorney General

Ken Paxton (Rep.) 4,278,986 53.42%
Rochelle Mercedes Garza (Dem.) 3,497,267 43.66%
Mark Ash (Lib.) 233,750 2.92%
Total Votes 8,010,003

Comptroller of Public Accounts

Glenn Hegar (Rep.) 4,496,319 56.39%
Janet T. Dudding (Dem.) 3,265,069 40.95%
V. Alonzo Echevarria-Garza (Lib.) 212,205 2.66%
Total Votes 7,973,593

Commissioner of the General Land Office

Dawn Buckingham (Rep.) 4,463,452 56.15%
Jay Kleberg (Dem.) 3,350,291 42.15%
Alfred Molison, Jr. (Lib.) 133,034 1.67%
Carrie Evelyn Menger (W-I) 1,812 0.02%
Total Votes 7,948,589

Commissioner of Agriculture

Sid Miller (Rep.) 4,480,186 56.33%
Susan Hays (Dem.) 3,473,603 43.67%
Total Votes 7,953,789

Railroad Commissioner

Wayne Christian (Rep.) 4,401,187 55.37%
Luke Warford (Dem.) 3,222,305 40.54%
Jaime Andres Diez (Lib.) 239,489 3.01%
Hunter Wayne Crow (Green) 85,570 1.08%
Total Votes 7,948,551

Supreme Court

Justice, Place 3

Debra Lehrmann (Rep.) 4,475,136 56.17%
Erin A. Nowell (Dem.) 3,330,529 41.8%
Thomas Edward Oxford (Lib.) 162,036 2.03%
Total Votes 7,967,701

Justice, Place 5

Rebeca Huddle (Rep.) 4,530,668 57.08%
Amanda Reichek (Dem.) 3,406,054 42.92%
Total Votes 7,936,722

Justice, Place 9

Evan Young (Rep.) 4,474,900 56.41%
Julia Maldonado (Dem.) 3,458,103 43.59%
Total Votes 7,933,003

Court of Criminal Appeals

Judge, Place 5

Scott Walker (Rep.) 4,513,500 56.94%
Dana Huffman (Dem.) 3,413,071 43.06%
Total Votes 7,926,571

Judge, Place 6

Jesse F. McClure, III (Rep.) 4,526,307 57.22%
Robert Johnson (Dem.) 3,383,705 42.78%
Total Votes 7,910,012

District Races

State Board of Education

Member, District 1

Melissa N. Ortega (Dem.) 247,093 55.79%
Michael Travis Stevens (Rep.) 195,794 44.21%
Total Votes 442,887

Member, District 2

L.J. Francis (Rep.) 194,976 50.18%
Victor Perez (Dem.) 193,578 49.82%
Total Votes 388,554

Member, District 3

Marisa B. Perez-Diaz (Dem.) 258,122 54.92%
Ken Morrow (Rep.) 211,906 45.08%
Total Votes 470,028

Member, District 5

Rebecca Bell-Metereau (Dem.) 419,391 63.82%
Perla Muñoz Hopkins (Rep.) 237,773 36.18%
Total Votes 657,164

Member, District 6

Will Hickman (Rep.) 364,447 60.25%
Michelle Palmer (Dem.) 240,384 39.74%
Rebekah Plourde (W-I) 59 0.01%
Total Votes 604,890

Member, District 7

Julie Pickren (Rep.) .... 346,419 .... 60.56%
Dan Hochman (Dem.) .... 213,742 .... 37.37%
Alan Pyeatt (Lib.) .... 11,835 .... 2.07%
Total Votes 571,996

Member, District 8

Audrey Young (Rep.) .... 313,220 .... 71.38%
Rhett Rosenquest Smith (Lib.) .... 125,616 .... 28.62%
Total Votes 438,836

Member, District 11

Patricia Pat Hardy (Rep.) .... 390,046 .... 63.28%
Luis Miguel Sifuentes (Dem.) .... 226,183 .... 36.69%
Kathi Arocha (W-I) .... 176 .... 0.03%
Total Votes 616,405

Member, District 12

Pam Little (Rep.) .... 400,089 .... 61.03%
Alex Cornwallis (Dem.) .... 236,589 .... 36.09%
Christy Mowrey (Lib.) .... 18,671 .... 2.85%
Rosiland Davis (W-I) .... 219 .... 0.03%
Total Votes 655,568

Member, District 13

Aicha Davis (Dem.) .... 275,226 .... 72.27%
Kathryn Monette (Rep.) .... 105,595 .... 27.73%
Total Votes 380,821

Member, District 14

Evelyn Brooks (Rep.) .... 399,567 .... 64.73%
Tracy Fisher (Dem.) .... 217,669 .... 35.27%
Total Votes 617,236

State Senator

District 2

Bob Hall (Rep.) .... 172,713 .... 61.9%
Prince S. Giadolor (Dem.) .... 106,309 .... 38.1%
Total Votes 279,022

District 3

Robert Nichols (Rep.) .... 213,288 .... 77.41%
Steve Russell (Dem.) .... 58,285 .... 21.16%
Desarae Lindsey (Lib.) .... 3,941 .... 1.43%
Total Votes 275,514

District 4

Brandon Creighton (Rep.) .... 202,341 .... 69.94%
Misty Bishop (Dem.) .... 86,946 .... 30.06%
Total Votes 289,287

District 5

Charles Schwertner (Rep.) .... 192,146 .... 71.57%
Tommy Estes (Lib.) .... 76,317 .... 28.43%
Total Votes 268,463

District 8

Angela Paxton (Rep.) .... 187,754 .... 57.69%
Jonathan Cocks (Dem.) .... 128,399 .... 39.45%
Edward Kless (Lib.) .... 9,293 .... 2.86%
Total Votes 325,446

District 9

Kelly Hancock (Rep.) .... 166,864 .... 60.05%
Gwenn Burud (Dem.) .... 111,019 .... 39.95%
Total Votes 277,883

District 12

Tan Parker (Rep.) .... 213,018 .... 61.44%
Francine Ly (Dem.) .... 133,679 .... 38.56%
Total Votes 346,697

District 14

Sarah Eckhardt (Dem.) .... 265,094 .... 82.23%
Steven E. Haskett (Lib.) .... 57,305 .... 17.77%
Total Votes 322,399

District 15

John Whitmire (Dem.) .... 159,125 .... 65.33%
George Brian Vachris (Rep.) .... 84,437 .... 34.67%
Total Votes 243,562

District 16

Nathan Johnson (Dem.) .... 118,663 .... 61.95%
Brandon Copeland (Rep.) .... 72,885 .... 38.05%
Total Votes 191,548

District 17

Joan Huffman (Rep.) .... 179,653 .... 65.33%
Titus Benton (Dem.) .... 95,320 .... 34.67%
Total Votes 274,973

District 18

Lois W. Kolkhorst (Rep.) .... 186,367 .... 66.17%
Josh Tutt (Dem.) .... 95,287 .... 33.83%
Total Votes 281,654

District 19

Roland Gutierrez (Dem.) .... 117,491 .... 55.39%
Robert Garza (Rep.) .... 94,613 .... 44.61%
Total Votes 212,104

District 20

Juan Chuy Hinojosa (Dem.) .... 102,280 .... 59.18%
Westley Wright (Rep.) .... 70,536 .... 40.82%
Total Votes 172,816

District 21

Judith Zaffirini (Dem.) .... 129,832 .... 61.56%
Julie Dahlberg (Rep.) .... 75,799 .... 35.94%
Arthur DiBianca (Lib.) .... 5,282 .... 2.5%
Total Votes 210,913

District 22

Brian Birdwell (Rep.) .... 190,988 .... 74.26%
Jeremy Schroppel (Lib.) .... 66,204 .... 25.74%
Total Votes 257,192

District 24

Pete Flores (Rep.) .... 187,598 .... 64.32%
Kathy Jones-Hospod (Dem.) .... 104,063 .... 35.68%
Total Votes 291,661

District 25

Donna Campbell (Rep.) .... 243,966 .... 62.83%
Robert Walsh (Dem.) .... 144,350 .... 37.17%
Total Votes 388,316

District 26

José Menéndez (Dem.) .... 140,799 .... 66.55%
Ashton Murray (Rep.) .... 70,773 .... 33.45%
Total Votes 211,572

District 27

Morgan Lamantia (Dem.) .... 88,037 .... 50.19%
Adam Hinojosa (Rep.) .... 87,378 .... 49.81%
Total Votes 175,415

District 29

César J. Blanco (Dem.) .... 111,638 .... 64.09%
Derek L. Zubeldia (Rep.) .... 62,544 .... 35.91%
Total Votes 174,182

State Representative

District 4

Keith Bell (Rep.) .... 42,041 .... 77.26%
Matt Savino (Lib.) .... 12,374 .... 22.74%
Total Votes 54,415

District 6

Matt Schaefer (Rep.) .... 43,841 .... 73.29%
Cody J. Grace (Dem.) .... 15,975 .... 26.71%
Total Votes 59,816

District 8

Cody Harris (Rep.) .... 46,526 .... 87.99%
R. Edwin Adams (Lib.) .... 6,350 .... 12.01%
Total Votes 52,876

District 9

Trent Ashby (Rep.) .... 52,178 .... 82.37%
Jason Rogers (Dem.) .... 11,171 .... 17.63%
Total Votes 63,349

District 13

Angelia Orr (Rep.) .... 41,423..........77.5%
Cedric Davis Sr (Dem.) .... 12,027..........22.5%
Total Votes 53,450

District 14

John Raney (Rep.) .... 29,868........68.09%
Jeff Miller (Lib.)...................................... 13,995........31.91%
Total Votes 43,863

District 15

Steve Toth (Rep.) .... 47,021........65.67%
Kristin Johnson (Dem.)........................... 24,578........34.33%
Total Votes 71,599

District 17

Stan Gerdes (Rep.) .... 39,092........64.21%
Madeline Eden (Dem.)........................... 19,404........31.87%
Linda Curtis (Ind.) .... 2,388..........3.92%
Total Votes 60,884

District 19

Ellen Troxclair (Rep.).............................. 70,492........72.65%
Pam Baggett (Dem.) .... 26,533........27.35%
Total Votes 97,025

District 20

Terry M. Wilson (Rep.)........................... 49,345........59.08%
Raul Camacho (Dem.) .... 34,175........40.92%
Total Votes 83,520

District 22

Christian "Manuel" Hayes (Dem.)........... 21,399........56.49%
Jacorion Randle (Rep.)........................... 16,484........43.51%
Total Votes 37,883

District 23

Terri Leo-Wilson (Rep.).......................... 35,559........63.78%
Keith G. Henry (Dem.)............................ 20,192........36.22%
Total Votes 55,751

District 24

Greg Bonnen (Rep.)................................ 47,240........68.01%
Michael J Creedon (Dem.) .... 20,842........30.01%
Ryan L. Mccamy (Lib.)............................. 1,374..........1.98%
Total Votes 69,456

District 26

Jacey Jetton (Rep.).................................. 37,376........60.67%
Daniel Lee (Dem.) .... 24,230........39.33%
Total Votes 61,606

District 27

Ron Reynolds (Dem.).............................. 40,668........70.27%
Sohrab Gilani (Rep.) .... 17,206........29.73%
Total Votes 57,874

District 28

Gary Gates (Rep.) .... 40,240........61.56%
Nelvin J. Adriatico (Dem.)....................... 25,124........38.44%
Total Votes 65,364

District 31

Ryan Guillen (Rep.) .... 34,806........71.24%
Martha M. Gutierrez (Dem.) .... 14,054........28.76%
Total Votes 48,860

District 33

Justin Holland (Rep.)............................... 44,031........65.11%
Graeson Lynskey (Dem.)......................... 23,597........34.89%
Total Votes 67,628

District 34

Abel Herrero (Dem.)................................ 22,231........57.65%
Carolyn Vaughn (Rep.)............................ 16,333........42.35%
Total Votes 38,564

District 35

Oscar Longoria (Dem.) .... 15,569........64.18%
Oscar Rosa (Rep.) .... 8,690........35.82%
Total Votes 24,259

District 37

Janie Lopez (Rep.).................................... 20,437........51.83%
Luis Villarreal Jr. (Dem.) .... 18,995........48.17%
Total Votes 39,432

District 39

Armando "Mando" Martinez (Dem.)....... 19,027........64.69%
Jimmie Garcia (Rep.) .... 10,385........35.31%
Total Votes 29,412

District 41

Bobby Guerra (Dem.) .... 22,352........56.97%
John (Doc) Robert Guerra (Rep.)............. 16,883........43.03%
Total Votes 39,235

District 42

Richard Peña Raymond (Dem.).............. 24,075........71.21%
Joe Brennan (Rep.)..................................... 9,734........28.79%
Total Votes 33,809

District 44

John Kuempel (Rep.)............................... 42,558..........69.3%
Robert M. Bohmfalk (Dem.).................... 18,857..........30.7%
Total Votes 61,415

District 45

Erin Zwiener (Dem.) .... 39,078........59.24%
Michelle M. Lopez (Rep.) .... 26,888........40.76%
Total Votes 65,966

District 46

Sheryl Cole (Dem.) .... 47,273........75.48%
Sam Strasser (Rep.) .... 13,628........21.76%
Thomas Kost (Lib.) .... 1,726..........2.76%
Total Votes 62,627

District 47

Vikki Goodwin (Dem.)............................. 51,045........61.27%
Rob Mccarthy (Rep.)............................... 32,272........38.73%
Total Votes 83,317

District 48

Donna Howard (Dem.)............................ 64,039........79.57%
Daniel Jerome Mccarthy (Lib.) .... 16,439........20.43%
Total Votes 80,478

District 49

Gina Hinojosa (Dem.) .... 68,786........83.44%
Katherine Griffin (Rep.)........................... 11,882........14.41%
J. David Roberson (Lib.)............................ 1,768..........2.14%
Total Votes 82,436

District 50

James Talarico (Dem.)............................. 36,881........76.85%
Victor Johnson (Rep.)................................ 9,718........20.25%
Ted Brown (Lib.) .... 1,392...........2.9%
Total Votes 47,991

District 51

Maria Luisa "Lulu" Flores (Dem.)............ 42,393........84.43%
Robert Reynolds (Rep.) .... 7,818........15.57%
Total Votes 50,211

District 52

Caroline Harris (Rep.).............................. 43,498........55.94%
Luis Echegaray (Dem.) .... 34,256........44.06%
Total Votes 77,754

District 53

Andrew S. Murr (Rep.)............................ 63,034........79.83%
Joe P. Herrera (Dem.).............................. 15,926........20.17%
Total Votes 78,960

District 54

Brad Buckley (Rep.) .... 24,729........62.99%
Jonathan Hildner (Dem.)......................... 14,531........37.01%
Total Votes 39,260

District 55

Hugh D. Shine (Rep.).............................. 28,868........61.06%
Tristian T.d. Sanders (Dem.)..................... 18,409........38.94%
Total Votes 47,277

District 56

Charles Doc Anderson (Rep.).................. 43,026........70.15%
Erin Shank (Dem.).................................... 18,306........29.85%
Total Votes 61,332

District 57

Richard Hayes (Rep.) .... 39,934 .... 65.29%
Darren Hamilton (Lib.) .... 21,227 .... 34.71%
Total Votes 61,161

District 61

Frederick Frazier (Rep.) .... 40,073 .... 58.26%
Sheena King (Dem.) .... 28,709 .... 41.74%
Total Votes 68,782

District 63

Ben Bumgarner (Rep.) .... 35,965 .... 55.93%
H. Denise Wooten (Dem.) .... 28,342 .... 44.07%
Total Votes 64,307

District 65

Kronda Thimesch (Rep.) .... 42,934 .... 59.79%
Brittney Verdell (Dem.) .... 28,878 .... 40.21%
Total Votes 71,812

District 66

Matt Shaheen (Rep.) .... 42,795 .... 60.42%
Jesse Ringness (Dem.) .... 28,039 .... 39.58%
Total Votes 70,834

District 67

Jeff Leach (Rep.) .... 38,828 .... 59.2%
Kevin Morris (Dem.) .... 26,760 .... 40.8%
Total Votes 65,588

District 69

James B. Frank (Rep.) .... 40,299 .... 79.13%
Walter Coppage (Dem.) .... 9,528 .... 18.71%
Michael Neumann (Lib.) .... 1,100 .... 2.16%
Total Votes 50,927

District 70

Mihaela Elizabeth Plesa (Dem.) .... 29,660 .... 50.73%
Jamee Jolly (Rep.) .... 28,801 .... 49.27%
Total Votes 58,461

District 71

Stan Lambert (Rep.) .... 42,857 .... 81%
Linda Goolsbee (Dem.) .... 10,055 .... 19%
Total Votes 52,912

District 73

Carrie Isaac (Rep.) .... 67,491 .... 70.35%
Justin Calhoun (Dem.) .... 28,441 .... 29.65%
Total Votes 95,932

District 74

Eddie Morales (Dem.) .... 21,112 .... 55.67%
Katherine Parker (Rep.) .... 16,813 .... 44.33%
Total Votes 37,925

District 75

Mary E. González (Dem.) .... 19,371 .... 75.91%
Jonathan Mullins (Lib.) .... 6,148 .... 24.09%
Total Votes 25,519

District 76

Suleman Lalani (Dem.) .... 28,312 .... 57.26%
Dan Mathews (Rep.) .... 21,131 .... 42.74%
Total Votes 49,443

District 85

Stan Kitzman (Rep.) .... 49,359 .... 73.82%
Larry E. Baggett (Dem.) .... 16,201 .... 24.23%
Michael L. Miller (Lib.) .... 1,308 .... 1.96%
Total Votes 66,868

District 87

Four Price (Rep.) .... 32,924 .... 87.08%
Nick Hearn (Lib.) .... 4,887 .... 12.92%
Total Votes 37,811

District 92

Salman Bhojani (Dem.) .... 20,182 .... 58.01%
Joe F. Livingston (Rep.) .... 14,610 .... 41.99%
Total Votes 34,792

District 93

Nate Schatzline (Rep.) .... 34,991 .... 59.93%
K.C. Chowdhury (Dem.) .... 23,399 .... 40.07%
Total Votes 58,390

District 94

Tony Tinderholt (Rep.) .... 35,092 .... 56.63%
Dennis Sherrard (Dem.) .... 26,879 .... 43.37%
Total Votes 61,971

District 95

Nicole Collier (Dem.) .... 28,400 .... 74.88%
Taylor Mondick (Rep.) .... 9,529 .... 25.12%
Total Votes 37,929

District 97

Craig Goldman (Rep.) .... 37,439 .... 58.2%
Laurin Mclaurin (Dem.) .... 26,890 .... 41.8%
Total Votes 64,329

District 98

Giovanni Capriglione (Rep.) .... 52,385 .... 66.27%
Shannon Elkins (Dem.) .... 26,665 .... 33.73%
Total Votes 79,050

District 99

Charlie Geren (Rep.) .... 33,211 .... 61.84%
Mimi Coffey (Dem.) .... 20,490 .... 38.16%
Total Votes 53,701

District 100

Venton C. Jones (Dem.) .... 23,567 .... 85.09%
Joe Roberts (Lib.) .... 4,131 .... 14.91%
Total Votes 27,698

District 102

Ana-Maria Ramos (Dem.) .... 23,068 .... 62.22%
Susan Fischer (Rep.) .... 14,007 .... 37.78%
Total Votes 37,075

District 103

Rafael M. Anchía (Dem.) .... 26,783 .... 75.52%
Alejandro Arrieta (Ind.) .... 8,681 .... 24.48%
Total Votes 35,464

District 105

Terry Meza (Dem.) .... 17,064 .... 55.8%
Allan E. Meagher (Rep.) .... 13,519 .... 44.2%
Total Votes 30,583

District 107

Victoria Neave Criado (Dem.) .... 18,702 .... 72.88%
Shane D. Newsom (Lib.) .... 6,960 .... 27.12%
Total Votes 25,662

District 108

Morgan Meyer (Rep.) .... 49,755 .... 56.45%
Elizabeth Ginsberg (Dem.) .... 38,390 .... 43.55%
Total Votes 88,145

District 111

Yvonne Davis (Dem.) .... 37,610 .... 79.12%
Benny Flores Yrigollen (Rep.) .... 9,927 .... 20.88%
Total Votes 47,537

District 112

Angie Chen Button (Rep.) .... 37,566 .... 54.83%
Elva Curl (Dem.) .... 30,946 .... 45.17%
Total Votes 68,512

District 114

John Bryant (Dem.) .... 36,948 .... 66.01%
Sarah Lamb (Rep.) .... 19,028 .... 33.99%
Total Votes 55,976

District 115

Julie Johnson (Dem.) .... 30,085 .... 56.7%
Melisa Denis (Rep.) .... 22,973 .... 43.3%
Total Votes 53,058

District 117

Philip Cortez (Dem.) .... 27,821 .... 62.6%
Aaron Schwope (Rep.) .... 16,620 .... 37.4%
Total Votes 44,441

District 118

John Lujan (Rep.) .... 26,357 .... 51.84%

Frank Ramirez (Dem.) .... 24,488 .... 48.16%
Total Votes 50,845

District 119

Elizabeth "Liz" Campos (Dem.) .... 29,253 .... 78.02%
Arthur M. Thomas IV (Lib.) .... 8,243 .... 21.98%
Total Votes 37,496

District 120

Barbara Gervin-Hawkins (Dem.) .... 26,413 .... 67.5%
Ronald Payne (Rep.) .... 12,718 .... 32.5%
Total Votes 39,131

District 121

Steve Allison (Rep.) .... 42,469 .... 55.02%
Becca Moyer Defelice (Dem.) .... 34,721 .... 44.98%
Total Votes 77,190

District 122

Mark Dorazio (Rep.) .... 47,804 .... 56.02%
Angi Aramburu (Dem.) .... 35,105 .... 41.14%
Stephanie Berlin (Lib.) .... 2,420 .... 2.84%
Total Votes 85,329

District 123

Diego Bernal (Dem.) .... 34,414 .... 66.76%
Charlotte Valdez (Rep.) .... 17,138 .... 33.24%
Total Votes 51,552

District 124

Josey Garcia (Dem.) .... 23,633 .... 66.99%
Johnny Arredondo (Rep.) .... 11,643 .... 33.01%
Total Votes 35,276

District 125

Ray Lopez (Dem.) .... 34,762 .... 62.41%
Carlos Antonio Raymond (Rep.) .... 20,933 .... 37.59%
Total Votes 55,695

District 128

Briscoe Cain (Rep.) .... 32,465 .... 70.49%
Charles "Chuck" Crews (Dem.) .... 13,594 .... 29.51%
Total Votes 46,059

District 129

Dennis Paul (Rep.) .... 39,062 .... 60.79%
Kat Marvel (Dem.) .... 25,194 .... 39.21%
Total Votes 64,256

District 131

Alma A. Allen (Dem.) .... 25,066 .... 80.52%
Gerry Monroe (Rep.) .... 6,063 .... 19.48%
Total Votes 31,129

District 132

Mike Schofield (Rep.) .... 36,322 .... 59.74%
Cameron "Cam" Campbell (Dem.) .... 24,483 .... 40.26%
Total Votes 60,805

District 133

Mano Deayala (Rep.) .... 36,849 .... 61.44%
Mohamad Maarouf (Dem.) .... 21,826 .... 36.39%
James Patrick Harren (Lib.) .... 1,297 .... 2.16%
Total Votes 59,972

District 134

Ann Johnson (Dem.) .... 49,688 .... 61.56%
Ryan McConnico (Rep.) .... 29,968 .... 37.13%
Carol Unsicker (Lib.) .... 1,058 .... 1.31%
Total Votes 80,714

District 135

Jon Rosenthal (Dem.) .... 23,354 .... 57.62%
Mike May (Rep.) .... 17,178 .... 42.38%
Total Votes 40,532

District 136

John H. Bucy III (Dem.) .... 36,137 .... 61.32%
Michelle Evans (Rep.) .... 21,240 .... 36.04%
Burton Culley (Lib.) .... 1,552 .... 2.63%
Total Votes 58,929

District 137

Gene Wu (Dem.) .... 14,451 .... 76.02%
Lee Sharp (Lib.) .... 4,559 .... 23.98%
Total Votes 19,010

District 138

Lacey Hull (Rep.) .... 32,395 .... 57.09%
Stephanie Morales (Dem.) .... 24,353 .... 42.91%
Total Votes 56,748

District 145

Christina Morales (Dem.) .... 32,292 .... 71.33%
Michael Mabry (Rep.) .... 12,979 .... 28.67%
Total Votes 45,271

District 148

Penny Morales Shaw (Dem.) .... 20,456 .... 55.52%
Kay Smith (Rep.) .... 15,691 .... 42.59%
Grizzle Trojacek (Lib.) .... 697 .... 1.89%
Total Votes 36,844

District 149

Hubert Vo (Dem.) .... 19,034 .... 59.84%
Lily Truong (Rep.) .... 11,975 .... 37.65%
Braxton Bogue (Lib.) .... 799 .... 2.51%
Total Votes 31,808

Texas Election Turnout by Voting Age Population

Year	2020	2016	2012	2008	2004	2000	1996	1992	1988	1984	1980	1976
Major Candidates	Biden/ Trump	Trump/ Clinton	Obama/ Romney	Obama/ McCain	Bush/Kerry	Bush/Gore	Clinton/ Dole	Clinton/ Bush/Perot	Bush/ Dukakis	Reagan/ Mondale	Reagan/ Carter	Carter/ Ford
Percent of VAP that voted	52.4	46.5	43.7	45.6	46.1	44.3	41.0	47.6	44.3	47.6	45.6	46.1
Percent of registered voters that voted	66.7	58.6	59.5	56.6	51.8	53.2	72.9	66.2	68.3	68.4	64.8	66.6

Sources: Federal Election Commission and the Texas Secretary of State office.

The **voting age population (VAP)** refers to the total number of persons of voting age regardless of citizenship, military status, felony conviction or mental state. The Bureau of the Census is the source for the VAP estimates.

Since the National Voter Registration Act of 1993, non-voters cannot be removed from registration rolls of a county until two federal elections have been held. So, for instance, if a person moved in December 2016 from one county to another, that person could be counted as a non-voter in the previous county of residence through the general election of November 2020. These are called "suspense voters" on county rolls and have affected the statistical reports of the percentage of registered voters participating in elections.

The presidential elections have a larger voter turnout than off-year and state elections.

District 150

Valoree Swanson (Rep.) 34,842 60.7%
Ginny Brown Daniel (Dem.) 22,558 39.3%
Total Votes 57,400

Courts of Appeals

1st District

Chief Justice

Terry Adams (Rep.) 820,060 50.77%
Julie Countiss (Dem.) 756,501 46.84%
Ted Wood (Ind.) 38,560 2.39%
Total Votes 1,615,121

Justice, Place 4

April Farris (Rep.) 841,506 52.2%
Mike Engelhart (Dem.) 770,499 47.8%
Total Votes 1,612,005

2nd District

Justice, Place 3

Elizabeth Kerr (Rep.) 654,798 60.82%
Delonia A. Watson (Dem.) 421,853 39.18%
Total Votes 1,076,651

3rd District

Justice, Place 4

Rosa Lopez Theofanis (Dem.) 558,955 52.63%
Lesli R. Fitzpatrick (Rep.) 503,131 47.37%
Total Votes 1,062,086

4th District

Justice, Place 6

Irene Rios (Dem.) 410,773 50.64%
Todd McCray (Rep.) 400,399 49.36%
Total Votes 811,172

Justice, Place 7—Unexpired Term

Lori I. Valenzuela (Rep.) 409,842 50.58%
Rebecca "Beckie" Palomo (Dem.) 400,505 49.42%
Total Votes 810,347

5th Court Of Appeals District

Justice, Place 4

Maricela Moore (Dem.) 572,345 50.82%
Emily A. Miskel (Rep.) 553,846 49.18%
Total Votes 1,126,191

Justice, Place 7

Nancy Kennedy (Dem.) 574,887 51.08%
Kristina Williams (Rep.) 550,649 48.92%
Total Votes 1,125,536

8th Court Of Appeals District

Justice, Place 2—Unexpired Term

Lisa Soto (Dem.) 111,838 60.39%
Jeff Alley (Rep.) 73,367 39.61%
Total Votes 185,205

9th Court Of Appeals District

Justice, Place 2

Jay Wright (Rep.) 285,428 75.75%
Bob Mabry (Dem.) 91,397 24.25%
Total Votes 376,825

13th Court Of Appeals District

Justice, Place 3

Aaron Peña (Rep.) 225,339 52.57%
Leticia Hinojosa (Dem.) 203,288 47.43%
Total Votes 428,627

14th Court Of Appeals District

Justice, Place 2

Kevin Jewell (Rep.) 835,179 51.95%
Cherí C. Thomas (Dem.) 772,544 48.05%
Total Votes 1,607,723

Justice, Place 9

Randy Wilson (Rep.) 849,980 52.91%
William Demond (Dem.) 756,443 47.09%
Total Votes 1,606,423

District Judges

40th Judicial District

Bob Carroll (Rep.) 46,732 71%
Rwan "Ro" Hardesty (Dem.) 19,085 29%
Total Votes 65,817

44th Judicial District

Veretta Frazier (Dem.) 378,705 61.58%
Ashley Wysocki (Rep.) 236,287 38.42%
Total Votes 614,992

45th Judicial District

Mary Lou Alvarez (Dem.) 294,087 56.46%
Patricia Jay (Rep.) 226,797 43.54%
Total Votes 520,884

55th Judicial District

Latosha Lewis Payne (Dem.) 548,194 51.17%
Nile Copeland (Rep.) 523,089 48.83%
Total Votes 1,071,283

113th Judicial District

Rabeea Collier (Dem.) 551,221 51.51%
Nathan J. Milliron (Rep.) 518,974 48.49%
Total Votes 1,070,195

269th Judicial District

Cory Don Sepolio (Dem.) 540,755 51.15%
Bruce Bain (Rep.) 516,472 48.85%
Total Votes 1,057,227

270th Judicial District

Dedra Davis (Dem.) 537,418 50.74%
Michael Landrum (Rep.) 521,801 49.26%
Total Votes 1,059,219

280th Judicial District

Damiane "Dianne" Curvey (Dem.) 535,258 50.7%
Rose Cardenas (Rep.) 520,390 49.3%
Total Votes 1,055,648

281st Judicial District

Christine Weems (Dem.) 542,820 51.33%
Michelle Fraga (Rep.) 514,774 48.67%
Total Votes 1,057,594

285th Judicial District

Nadine Melissa Nieto (Dem.) 295,361 56.91%
Mark Thompson (Rep.) 223,595 43.09%
Total Votes 518,956

288th Judicial District

Cynthia Marie Chapa (Dem.) 299,266 57.69%
Art Rossi (Rep.) 219,477 42.31%
Total Votes 518,743

295th Judicial District

Donna Roth (Dem.) 545,117 51.58%
Malcolm Whittaker (Rep.) 511,686 48.42%
Total Votes 1,056,803

301st Judicial District

Mary Brown (W-I) 61,375 53.66%
Earl Jackson (W-I) 33,303 29.12%
Michelle McKinney (W-I) 19,693 17.22%
Total Votes 114,371

303rd Judicial District

Ladeitra Adkins (Dem.) 370,012 60.17%
Rhonda Hunter (Rep.) 244,897 39.83%
Total Votes 614,909

308th Judicial District

Gloria López (Dem.) 549,939 51.98%
Todd Frankfort (Rep.) 507,966 48.02%
Total Votes 1,057,905

309th Judicial District

Linda Marie Dunson (Dem.) 546,350 51.78%
Jesus Guillen (Rep.) 508,851 48.22%
Total Votes 1,055,201

310th Judicial District

Sonya Leah Heath (Dem.) 548,550 52.03%
Andrew Michael Bayley (Rep.) 505,741 47.97%
Total Votes 1,054,291

311th Judicial District

Germaine Ja'net Tanner (Dem.) 539,107 51.22%
Gardner Eastland (Rep.) 513,442 48.78%
Total Votes 1,052,549

312th Judicial District

Teresa J. Waldrop (Dem.) 550,370 52.27%
Quyen Pham (Rep.) 502,627 47.73%
Total Votes 1,052,997

313th Judicial District

Natalia Oakes (Dem.) 541,754 51.46%
Rachel Leal-Hudson (Rep.) 510,998 48.54%
Total Votes 1,052,752

314th Judicial District

Michelle Moore (Dem.) 547,200 51.94%
Cindy Hide (Rep.) 506,239 48.06%
Total Votes 1,053,439

315th Judicial District

Leah Shapiro (Dem.) 542,729 51.54%
Maria Valeria Brock (Rep.) 510,394 48.46%
Total Votes 1,053,123

317th Judicial District

Gordon Friesz (Rep.) 33,847 54.97%
Chelsie Ramos (Dem.) 27,728 45.03%
Total Votes 61,575

323rd Judicial District

Alex Kim (Rep.) 309,501 53.49%
Frank Adler (Dem.) 269,076 46.51%
Total Votes 578,577

324th Judicial District

Beth A. Poulos (Rep.) 310,675 53.72%
Crystal Gayden (Dem.) 267,647 46.28%
Total Votes 578,322

328th Judicial District

Monica Rawlins (Dem.) 121,528 50.11%
Walter Armatys (Rep.) 120,984 49.89%
Total Votes 242,512

428th Judicial District

Joe Pool (Dem.) 43,942 50.55%
Bill Henry (Rep.) 42,983 49.45%
Total Votes 86,925

437th Judicial District

Joel Perez (Dem.) 289,246 55.64%
Melisa Skinner (Rep.) 230,644 44.36%
Total Votes 519,890

455th Judicial District

Laurie Eiserloh (Dem.) 318,646 72.01%
Cleve W. Doty (Rep.) 123,852 27.99%
Total Votes 442,498

458th Judicial District

Chad Bridges (Rep.) 121,380 50.08%
Stephen Longoria (Dem.) 120,973 49.92%
Total Votes 242,353

482nd Judicial District

Veronica Monique Nelson (Dem.) 540,103 51.02%
Maritza Antu (Rep.) 518,523 48.98%
Total Votes 1,058,626

485th Judicial District

Steven Jumes (Rep.) 310,017 53.59%
John Brender (Dem.) 268,463 46.41%
Total Votes 578,480

County Criminal Courts

Bexar County

Criminal District Attorney

Joe Gonzales (Dem.) 296,379 56.14%
Marc Lahood (Rep.) 231,556 43.86%
Total Votes 527,935

Dallas County

Criminal District Attorney

John Creuzot (Dem.) 368,057 59.47%
Faith Johnson (Rep.) 250,880 40.53%
Total Votes 618,937

Galveston County

Criminal District Attorney

Jack Roady (Rep.) 71,881 65.6%
Rachel Dragony (Dem.) 37,687 34.4%
Total Votes 109,568

Hays County

Criminal District Attorney

Kelly Higgins (Dem.) 46,609 53.14%
David Puryear (Rep.) 41,103 46.86%
Total Votes 87,712

Hidalgo County

Criminal District Attorney

Toribio "Terry" Palacios (Dem.) 83,998 60.76%
Juan Tijerina (Rep.) 54,249 39.24%
Total Votes 138,247

McLennan County

Criminal District Attorney

Josh Tetens (Rep.) 49,267 68.94%
Aubrey Robertson (Dem.) 22,195 31.06%
Total Votes 71,462

Tarrant County

Criminal District Judge #4

Andy Porter (Rep.) 310,949 53.69%
Sam Williams (Dem.) 268,167 46.31%
Total Votes 579,116

Criminal District Attorney

Phil Sorrells (Rep.) 309,730 53.24%
Tiffany D. Burks (Dem.) 272,066 46.76%
Total Votes 581,796

Texas Primary Elections, 2022

Source: Texas Secretary of State.

Following are the official results for the contested races in the Democratic and Republican primaries held March 1, 2022. Included are selected federal, statewide, and selected district races. Runoffs were held on May 24.

Some data was omitted for space, including the Democratic Texas House of Representatives, judges in the Court of Appeals, district-level races, some races in which only a single candidate was running, select races in the US House of Representatives, and some party propositions.

For full and historical election results, see texasalmanac.com.

Democratic Primary

Federal Races

U.S. House of Representatives

District 1

Candidate	Votes	Percent
Jrmar (JJ) Jefferson	7,411	45.46%
Victor D. Dunn	4,554	27.93%
Stephen Kocen	2,457	15.07%
Gavin Dass	1,881	11.54%
Total Votes	16,303	

District 2

Candidate	Votes	Percent
Robin Fulford	17,160	100%

District 3

Candidate	Votes	Percent
Sandeep Srivastava	13,865	61.91%
Doc Shelby	8,531	38.09%
Total Votes	22,396	

District 4

Candidate	Votes	Percent
Iro Omere	16,404	100%

District 5

Candidate	Votes	Percent
Tartisha Hill	10,689	52.67%
Kathleen Cordelia Bailey	9,605	47.33%
Total Votes	20,294	

District 7

Candidate	Votes	Percent
Lizzie Fletcher	29,579	100%

District 8

Candidate	Votes	Percent
Laura Jones	14,496	100%

District 9

Candidate	Votes	Percent
Al Green	42,782	100%

District 10

Candidate	Votes	Percent
Linda Nuno	20,537	100%

District 12

Candidate	Votes	Percent
Trey J. Hunt	20,561	100%

District 13

Candidate	Votes	Percent
Kathleen Brown	10,807	100%

District 14

Candidate	Votes	Percent
Mikal Williams	10,691	50.17%
Eugene Howard	10,619	49.83%
Total Votes	21,310	

District 15

Candidate	Votes	Percent
Ruben Ramirez	9,221	28.27%
Michelle Vallejo	6,570	20.14%
John Villarreal Rigney	6,268	19.22%
Eliza Alvarado	5,398	16.55%
Vanessa Stephanie Tijerina	3,470	10.64%
Julio Garza	1,693	5.19%
Total Votes	32,620	

District 16

Candidate	Votes	Percent
Veronica Escobar	30,954	87.96%
Dmb Deliris Montanez Berrios	4,235	12.04%
Total Votes	35,189	

District 17

Candidate	Votes	Percent
Mary Jo Woods	17,085	100%

District 18

Candidate	Votes	Percent
Sheila Jackson Lee	35,194	100%

District 20

Candidate	Votes	Percent
Joaquin Castro	33,214	100%

District 21

Candidate	Votes	Percent
Claudia Andreana Zapata	16,604	47.23%
Ricardo Villarreal	9,590	27.28%
Coy Gee Branscum II	3,157	8.98%
David Anderson Jr.	3,038	8.64%
Scott William Sturm	1,865	5.30%
Cherif Gacis	902	2.57%
Total Votes	35,156	

District 22

Candidate	Votes	Percent
Jamie Kaye Jordan	20,818	100%

District 23

Candidate	Votes	Percent
John Lira	19,816	55.85%
Priscilla Golden	15,664	44.15%
Total Votes	35,480	

District 24

Candidate	Votes	Percent
Jan McDowell	11,467	39.30%
Derrik T. Gay	9,571	32.80%
Kathy Fragnoli	8,139	27.90%
Total Votes	29,177	

District 27

Candidate	Votes	Percent
Maclovio Perez Jr.	13,044	59.11%
Anthony J. Tristan	5,733	25.98%
Victor Melgoza	3,289	14.91%
Total Votes	22,066	

District 28

Candidate	Votes	Percent
Henry Cuellar	23,988	48.66%
Jessica Cisneros	22,983	46.62%
Tannya Judith Benavides	2,324	4.71%
Total Votes	49,295	

District 29

Candidate	Votes	Percent
Sylvia Garcia	19,402	100%

District 30

Candidate	Votes	Percent
Jasmine Crockett	26,798	48.47%
Jane Hope Hamilton	9,436	17.07%
Keisha Williams-Lankford	4,323	7.82%
Barbara Mallory Caraway	4,277	7.74%
Abel Mulugheta	3,284	5.94%
Roy Williams Jr.	2,746	4.97%
Vonciel Jones Hill	1,886	3.41%
Jessica Mason	1,858	3.36%
Arthur Dixon	677	1.22%
Total Votes	55,285	

District 32

Candidate	Votes	Percent
Colin Allred	31,805	100%

District 33

Candidate	Votes	Percent
Marc Veasey	16,806	69.51%
Carlos Quintanilla	7,373	30.49%
Total Votes	24,179	

District 34

Candidate	Votes	Percent
Vicente Gonzalez	23,531	64.77%
Laura Cisneros	8,456	23.28%
Beatriz Reynoso	1,287	3.54%
William Thompson	1,085	2.99%
Filemon Meza	920	2.53%
Diego Zavala	718	1.98%
Osbert Rodriguez Haro	331	0.91%
Total Votes	36,328	

District 35

Greg Casar .... 25,505 .... 61.12%
Eddie Rodriguez .... 6,526 .... 15.64%
Rebecca Viagran .... 6,511 .... 15.60%
Carla-Joy Sisco .... 3,190 .... 7.64%
Total Votes 41,732

District 36

Jon Haire .... 16,589 .... 100%

District 37

Lloyd Doggett .... 60,007 .... 79.27%
Donna Imam .... 13,385 .... 17.68%
Chris Jones .... 1,503 .... 1.99%
Quinton "Q" Beaubouef .... 804 .... 1.06%
Total Votes 75699

District 38

Diana Martinez Alexander .... 9,861 .... 44.60%
Duncan F. Klussmann .... 8,698 .... 39.34%
Centrell Reed .... 3,550 .... 16.06%
Total Votes 22,109

State Races

Governor

Beto O'Rourke .... 983,182 .... 91.41%
Joy Diaz .... 33,622 .... 3.13%
Michael Cooper .... 32,673 .... 3.04%
Rich Wakeland .... 13,237 .... 1.23%
Inocencio (Inno) Barrientez .... 12,887 .... 1.20%
Total Votes 1,075,601

Lieutenant Governor

Mike Collier .... 422,379 .... 41.72%
Michelle Beckley .... 304,799 .... 30.10%
Carla Brailey .... 285,342 .... 28.18%
Total Votes 1,012,520

Attorney General

Rochelle Mercedes Garza .... 438,134 .... 42.97%
Joe Jaworski .... 202,140 .... 19.82%
Lee Merritt .... 198,108 .... 19.43%
Mike Fields .... 125,373 .... 12.30%
S. "Tbone" Raynor .... 55,944 .... 5.49%
Total Votes 1,019,699

Comptroller of Public Accounts

Janet T. Dudding .... 454,338 .... 46.29%
Angel Luis Vega .... 338,877 .... 34.53%
Tim Mahoney .... 188,250 .... 19.18%
Total Votes 981,465

Commissioner of the General Land Office

Sandragrace Martinez .... 313,780 .... 31.80%
Jay Kleberg .... 257,034 .... 26.05%
Jinny Suh .... 216,238 .... 21.91%
Michael Lange .... 199,764 .... 20.24%
Total Votes 986,816

Commissioner of Agriculture

Susan Hays .... 814,283 .... 82.77%
Ed Ireson .... 169,503 .... 17.23%
Total Votes 983,786

Railroad Commissioner

Luke Warford .... 916,650 .... 100%

Supreme Court

Justice, Place 3

Erin A. Nowell .... 914,184 .... 100%

Justice, Place 5

Amanda Reichek .... 913,836 .... 100%

Justice, Place 9

Julia Maldonado .... 922,595 .... 100%

Court of Criminal Appeals

Justice, Place 5

Dana Huffman .... 911,472 .... 100%

Justice, Place 6

Robert Johnson .... 906,119 .... 100%

District Races

State Board Of Education

District 5

Melissa N. Ortega .... 42,374 .... 46.12%
Laura Marquez .... 32,504 .... 35.37%
Omar Yanar .... 17,008 .... 18.51%
Total Votes 91,886

District 2

Victor Perez .... 21,702 .... 29.58%
Pete Garcia .... 17,856 .... 24.34%
Thomas Garcia .... 15,331 .... 20.89%
Michael Vargas .... 14,510 .... 19.78%
Wayne Raasch .... 3,974 .... 5.42%
Total Votes 73,373

District 3

Marisa B. Perez-Diaz .... 77,509 .... 100%

District 4

Coretta Mallet-Fontenot .... 28,917 .... 38.61%
Staci Childs .... 21,064 .... 28.12%
Marvin Johnson .... 11,176 .... 14.92%
Theldon Branch .... 8,254 .... 11.02%
Larry McKinzie .... 5,490 .... 7.33%
Total Votes 74,901

District 5

Rebecca Bell-Metereau .... 91,899 .... 73.73%
Juan Juárez .... 24,667 .... 19.79%
Kevin Guico .... 8,077 .... 6.48%
Total Votes 124,643

District 6

Michelle Palmer .... 53,055 .... 100%

District 7

Dan Hochman .... 58,897 .... 100%

District 11

Luis Miguel Sifuentes .... 25,401 .... 47.24%
James Whitfield .... 18,104 .... 33.67%
"DC" Caldwell I .... 10,261 .... 19.08%
Total Votes 53,766

District 12

Alex Cornwallis .... 28,985 .... 51.4%
Roberto Velasco .... 27,403 .... 48.6%
Total Votes 56,388

District 13

Aicha Davis .... 87,947 .... 100%

District 14

Tracy Fisher .... 40,860 .... 100%

State Senator

District 2

Prince S. Giadolor .... 25,594 .... 100%

District 3

Steve Russell .... 18,205 .... 100%

District 4

Misty Bishop .... 19,292 .... 100%

District 6

Carol Alvarado .... 23,408 .... 100%

District 8

Jonathan Cocks .... 24,775 .... 100%

District 9

Gwenn Burud .... 23,474 .... 100%

District 10

Beverly Powell .... 27,486 .... 100%

District 12

Francine Ly .... 21,951 .... 73%

Ferdi Mongo .... 8,015 .... 26.75%
Total Votes 29,966

District 13

Borris L. Miles .... 45,597 .... 100%

District 14

Sarah Eckhardt .... 77,309 .... 100%

District 15

John Whitmire .... 26,286 .... 58.44%
Molly Cook .... 18,695 .... 41.56%
Total Votes 44,981

District 16

Nathan Johnson .... 31,323 .... 100%

District 17

Titus Benton .... 11,958 .... 51.21%
Miguel Gonzalez .... 11,393 .... 48.79%
Total Votes 23,351

District 18

Josh Tutt .... 22,617 .... 100.00%

District 19

Roland Gutierrez .... 36,159 .... 100%

District 20

Juan "Chuy" Hinojosa .... 36,830 .... 100%

District 21

Judith Zaffirini .... 47,076 .... 100%

District 23

Royce West .... 63,371 .... 100%

District 24

Kathy Jones-Hospod .... 20,753 .... 80%
Jeremy Kohlwes .... 5,208 .... 20.06%
Total Votes 25,961

District 25

Robert Walsh .... 35,192 .... 100%

District 26

José Menéndez .... 41,833 .... 100%

District 27

Morgan Lamantia .... 13,531 .... 33.74%
Sara Stapleton-Barrera .... 13,101 .... 32.67%
Alex Dominguez .... 10,163 .... 25.34%
Salomon Torres .... 3,312 .... 8%
Total Votes 40,107

District 29

César J. Blanco .... 35,195 .... 100%

Democratic Runoff

Federal Races

U.S. Representatives

District 1

Jrmar (J.J.) Jefferson .... 5,607 .... 75.87%
Victor D. Dunn .... 1,783 .... 24.13%
Total Votes 7,390

District 15

Michelle Vallejo .... 6,079 .... 50.12%
Ruben Ramirez .... 6,049 .... 49.88%
Total Votes 12,128

District 21

Claudia Andreana Zapata .... 13,886 .... 63.46%
Ricardo Villarreal .... 7,996 .... 36.54%
Total Votes 21,882

District 24

Jan McDowell .... 7,118 .... 51.19%
Derrik T. Gay .... 6,788 .... 48.81%
Total Votes 13,906

District 28

Henry Cuellar .... 22,895 .... 50.31%
Jessica Cisneros .... 22,614 .... 49.69%
Total Votes 45,509

District 30

Jasmine Crockett .... 17,462 .... 60.57%
Jane Hope Hamilton .... 11,369 .... 39.43%
Total Votes 28,831

District 38

Duncan F. Klussmann .... 6,449 .... 61.07%
Diana Martinez Alexander .... 4,111 .... 38.93%
Total Votes 10,560

State Races

Lieutenant Governor

Mike Collier .... 265,345 .... 54.82%
Michelle Beckley .... 218,727 .... 45.18%
Total Votes 484,072

Attorney General

Rochelle Mercedes Garza .... 305,168 .... 62.67%
Joe Jaworski .... 181,744 .... 37.33%
Total Votes 486,912

Comptroller of Public Accounts

Janet T. Dudding .... 292,069 .... 61.41%
Angel Luis Vega .... 183,533 .... 38.59%
Total Votes 475,602

Commissioner of the General Land Office

Jay Kleberg .... 254,273 .... 52.95%
Sandragrace Martinez .... 225,964 .... 47.05%
Total Votes 480,237

District Races

State Board Of Education

Member, District 1

Melissa N. Ortega .... 32,123 .... 57.47%
Laura Marquez .... 23,776 .... 42.53%
Total Votes 55,899

Member, District 2

Victor Perez .... 20,769 .... 56.10%
Pete Garcia .... 16,252 .... 43.90%
Total Votes 37,021

Member, District 4

Staci Childs .... 20,160 .... 58.05%
Coretta Mallet-Fontenot .... 14,566 .... 41.95%
Total Votes 34,726

State Senator

District 27

Morgan Lamantia .... 14,288 .... 56.89%
Sara Stapleton-Barrera .... 10,825 .... 43.11%
Total Votes 25,113

Republican Primary

Federal Races

U.S. Representatives

District 1

Nathaniel Moran .... 51,312 .... 63%
Joe McDaniel .... 19,708 .... 24.20%
Aditya "A.D." Atholi .... 6,186 .... 7.60%
John Porro .... 4,238 .... 5.20%
Total Votes 81,444

District 2

Dan Crenshaw .... 45,863 .... 74.47%
Jameson Ellis .... 10,195 .... 16.55%
Martin Etwop .... 2,785 .... 4.52%
Milam Langella .... 2,741 .... 4.45%
Total Votes 61,584

District 3

Van Taylor .... 31,489 .... 48.84%

Keith Self .... 17,058 .... 26.46%
Suzanne Harp .... 13,375 .... 20.75%
Rickey Williams .... 1,731 .... 2.68%
Jeremy D. Ivanovskis .... 818 .... 1.27%
Total Votes 64,471

District 4

Pat Fallon .... 41,297 .... 58.96%
Dan Thomas .... 21,168 .... 30.22%
John E. Harper .... 7,576 .... 10.82%
Total Votes 70,041

District 5

Lance Gooden .... 47,692 .... 100%

District 6

Jake Ellzey .... 38,683 .... 71.20%
James Buford .... 8,636 .... 15.90%
Bill Payne .... 7,008 .... 12.90%
Total Votes 54,327

District 7

Johnny Teague .... 9,293 .... 42.99%
Tim Stroud .... 6,346 .... 29.36%
Tina Blum Cohen .... 1,792 .... 8.29%
Lance Stewart .... 1,764 .... 8.16%
Rudy A. Atencio .... 1,024 .... 4.74%
Laique Rehman .... 977 .... 4.52%
Benson Gitau .... 422 .... 1.95%
Total Votes 21,618

District 8

Morgan Luttrell .... 34,271 .... 52.15%
Christian Collins .... 14,659 .... 22.31%
Jonathan Hullihan .... 8,296 .... 12.62%
Dan McKaughan .... 1,585 .... 2.41%
Candice C. Burrows .... 1,519 .... 2.31%
Jessica Wellington .... 1,550 .... 2.36%
Jonathan A. Mitchell .... 791 .... 1.20%
Chuck Montgomery .... 1,169 .... 1.78%
Michael Philips .... 871 .... 1.33%
Betsy Bates .... 712 .... 1.08%
Taylor M. Whichard IV .... 295 .... 0.45%
Total Votes 65,718

District 9

Jimmy I. Leon .... 10,503 .... 100%

District 10

Michael McCaul .... 63,920 .... 100%

District 11

August Pfluger .... 61,479 .... 100%

District 12

Kay Granger .... 46,779 .... 75.21%
Ryan J. Catala .... 8,759 .... 14.08%
Alysia Rieg .... 6,662 .... 10.71%
Total Votes 62,200

District 13

Ronny Jackson .... 71,554 .... 100%

District 14

Randy Weber .... 58,439 .... 89.26%
Keith Casey .... 5,178 .... 7.91%
Ruben Landon Dante .... 1,854 .... 2.83%
Total Votes 65,471

District 15

Monica De La Cruz .... 16,835 .... 56.52%
Mauro Garza .... 4,544 .... 15.25%
Sara Canady .... 2,741 .... 9.20%
Ryan Krause .... 2,728 .... 9.16%
Steve Schmuker Jr. .... 1,064 .... 3.57%
John C. Lerma .... 658 .... 2.21%
Aizar Cavazos .... 504 .... 1.69%
Angela Juarez .... 416 .... 1.40%
Vangela Churchill .... 298 .... 1%
Total Votes 29,788

District 16

Irenearmendariz Jackson .... 12,623 .... 100%

District 17

Pete Sessions .... 48,222 .... 69.95%
Paulette Carson .... 7,246 .... 10.51%
Jason "Stormchaser" Nelson .... 8,371 .... 12.14%
Rob Rosenberger .... 5,100 .... 7.40%
Total Votes 68,939

District 18

Carmen Maria Montiel .... 11,087 .... 100%

District 19

Jodey C. Arrington .... 68,503 .... 100%

District 20

Kyle Sinclair .... 15,938 .... 100%

District 21

Chip Roy .... 78,087 .... 83.23%
Robert Lowry .... 7,642 .... 8.15%
Dana Zavorka .... 4,206 .... 4.48%
Michael Alexander French .... 3,886 .... 4.14%
Total Votes 93,821

District 22

Troy E. Nehls .... 50,281 .... 87.20%
Gregory Jonathan Thorne .... 7,378 .... 12.80%
Total Votes 57,659

District 23

Alma Arredondo-Lynch .... 7,261 .... 15.22%
Alía Garcia .... 3,235 .... 6.78%
Tony Gonzales .... 37,212 .... 78%
Total Votes 47,708

District 24

Beth Vanduyne .... 61,768 .... 85.04%
Nate Weymouth .... 10,868 .... 14.96%
Total Votes 72,636

District 25

Roger Williams .... 69,418 .... 100%

District 26

Michael C. Burgess .... 42,006 .... 66.84%
Vincent Gallo .... 6,437 .... 10.24%
Brian Brazeal .... 5,892 .... 9.38%
Isaac Smith .... 5,085 .... 8.09%
Raven Harrison .... 3,427 .... 5.45%
Total Votes 62,847

District 27

Michael Cloud .... 45,741 .... 72.47%
A.J. Louderback .... 7,704 .... 12.21%
Chris Mapp .... 4,542 .... 7.20%
Andrew Alvarez .... 2,648 .... 4.20%
Eric Mireles .... 2,478 .... 3.93%
Total Votes 63,113

District 28

Cassy Garcia .... 5,923 .... 23.55%
Sandra Whitten .... 4,534 .... 18.02%
Steven Fowler .... 3,388 .... 13.47%
Willie Vasquez Ng .... 3,358 .... 13.35%
Ed Cabrera .... 3,343 .... 13.29%
Eric Hohman .... 2,988 .... 11.88%
Rolando Rodriguez .... 1,622 .... 6.45%
Total Votes 25,156

District 29

Robert Schafranek .... 3,299 .... 39.35%
Julio Garza .... 2,629 .... 31.36%
Jaimy Blanco .... 2,212 .... 26.38%
Lulite Ejigu .... 244 .... 2.91%
Total Votes 8,384

District 30

James "J. Frank" Harris .... 3,952 .... 32.91%
James Rodgers .... 3,754 .... 31.26%
Kelvin Goodwin-Castillo .... 2,023 .... 16.85%
Lizbeth Diaz .... 1,416 .... 11.79%
Dakinya "Kinya" Jefferson .... 703 .... 5.85%
Angeigh J. Roc'Ellerpitts .... 160 .... 1.33%
Total Votes 12,008

District 31

John Carter .... 50,887 .... 71.08%
Mike Williams .... 14,115 .... 19.72%
Abhiram Garapati .... 6,590 .... 9.20%
Total Votes 71,592

District 32

Antonio Swad .... 8,962 .... 40.30%
Justin Webb .... 4,007 .... 18.02%
Nathan Davis .... 3,549 .... 15.96%
Darrell Day .... 2,321 .... 10.44%
Brad Namdar .... 2,270 .... 10.21%
Ee Okpa .... 1,128 .... 5.07%
Total Votes 22,237

District 33

Patrick David Gillespie .... 5,709 .... 63.48%
Robert Mac Glaflin .... 3,284 .... 36.52%
Total Votes 8,993

District 34

Mayra Flores .... 9,490 .... 60.35%
Frank McCaffrey .... 3,444 .... 21.90%
Gregory Scott Kunkle Jr. .... 1,677 .... 10.66%
Juana Cantu-Cabrera .... 1,115 .... 7.09%
Total Votes 15,726

District 35

Dan McQueen .... 2,900 .... 21.28%
Michael Rodriguez .... 2,034 .... 14.93%
Bill Condict .... 1,529 .... 11.22%
Marilyn Jackson .... 1,473 .... 10.81%
Dan Sawatzki .... 1,414 .... 10.38%
Jennifer Sundt .... 1,299 .... 9.53%
Sam Montoya .... 1,227 .... 9.01%
Alejandro Ledezma .... 833 .... 6.11%
Jenai Aragona .... 589 .... 4.32%
Asa George Kent Palagi .... 327 .... 2.40%
Total Votes 13,625

District 36

Brian Babin .... 59,381 .... 100%

District 37

Jenny Garcia Sharon .... 9,087 .... 46.77%
Rod Lingsch .... 5,403 .... 27.81%
Jeremiah Diacogiannis .... 4,938 .... 25.42%
Total Votes 19,428

District 38

Wesley Hunt .... 35,291 .... 55.32%
Mark Ramsey .... 19,352 .... 30.33%
David Hogan .... 3,125 .... 4.90%
Roland Lopez .... 2,048 .... 3.21%
Brett Guillory .... 1,416 .... 2.22%
Jerry Ford .... 997 .... 1.56%
Richard Welch .... 633 .... 0.99%
Alex Cross .... 460 .... 0.72%
Damien Matthew Peter Mockus .... 249 .... 0.39%
Phil Covarrubias .... 228 .... 0.36%
Total Votes 63,799

State Race

Governor

Greg Abbott .... 1,299,059 .... 66.48%
Allen B. West .... 239,557 .... 12.26%
Don Huffines .... 234,138 .... 11.98%
Chad Prather .... 74,173 .... 3.80%
Rick Perry .... 61,424 .... 3.14%
Kandy Kaye Horn .... 23,605 .... 1.21%
Paul Belew .... 11,387 .... 0.58%
Danny Harrison .... 10,829 .... 0.55%
Total Votes 1,954,172

Lieutenant Governor

Dan Patrick .... 1,425,717 .... 76.61%
Daniel Miller .... 127,735 .... 6.86%
Trayce Bradford .... 120,514 .... 6.48%
Aaron Sorrells .... 73,031 .... 3.92%
Zach Vance .... 70,863 .... 3.81%
Todd M. Bullis .... 43,097 .... 2.32%
Total Votes 1,860,957

Attorney General

Ken Paxton .... 823,199 .... 42.71%
George P. Bush .... 439,240 .... 22.79%
Eva Guzman .... 337,761 .... 18%
Louie Gohmert .... 327,257 .... 16.98%
Total Votes 1,927,457

Comptroller of Public Accounts

Glenn Hegar .... 1,386,782 .... 81.69%
Mark V. Goloby .... 310,829 .... 18.31%
Total Votes 1,697,611

Commissioner of the General Land Office

Dawn Buckingham .... 679,125 .... 42%
Tim Westley .... 239,473 .... 14.78%
Jon Spiers .... 203,879 .... 12.58%
Don W. Minton .... 171,001 .... 10.55%
Victor Avila .... 121,998 .... 7.53%
Weston Martinez .... 107,219 .... 6.62%
Rufus Lopez .... 49,475 .... 3.05%
Ben Armenta .... 48,029 .... 2.96%
Total Votes 1,620,199

Commissioner of Agriculture

Sid Miller .... 992,330 .... 58.48%
James White .... 528,434 .... 31.14%
Carey A. Counsil .... 176,083 .... 10.38%
Total Votes 1,696,847

Railroad Commissioner

Sarah Stogner .... 244,949 .... 14.96%
Wayne Christian .... 775,679 .... 47.37%
Tom Slocum Jr. .... 234,439 .... 14.32%
Marvin “Sarge” Summers .... 194,099 .... 11.85%
Dawayne Tipton .... 188,428 .... 11.51%
Total Votes 1,637,594

Supreme Court

Justice, Place 3

Debra Lehrmann .... 1,535,581 .... 100%

Justice, Place 5

Rebeca Huddle .... 1,519,069 .... 100%

Justice, Place 9

Evan Young .... 860,852 .... 54.86%
David J. Schenck .... 708,359 .... 45.14%
Total Votes 1,569,211

Judge, Court of Criminal Appeals Place 2

Mary Lou Keel .... 1,485,583 .... 100%

Judge, Court of Criminal Appeals Place 5

Scott Walker .... 884,160 .... 56.62%
Clint Morgan .... 677,504 .... 43.38%
Total Votes 1,561,664

Judge, Court of Criminal Appeals Place 6

Jesse F. McClure, III .... 1,474,886 .... 100%

District Races

State Board of Education

Member, District 1

Michael “Travis” Stevens .... 39,865 .... 63.64%
Lani Popp .... 22,772 .... 36.36%
Total Votes 62,637

Member, District 2

L.J. Francis .... 38,009 .... 57.49%
Hilda Garza Deshazo .... 28,105 .... 42.51%
Total Votes 66,114

Member, District 3

Ken Morrow .... 42,291 .... 55.88%
Lana Jean Holland .... 33,393 .... 44.12%
Total Votes 75,684

Member, District 5

Mark Loewe .... 39,106 .... 53.51%
Robert Morrow .... 33,975 .... 46.49%
Total Votes 73,081

Member, District 6

Will Hickman .... 81,302 .... 64.91%
Mike Wolfe .... 43,944 .... 35.09%
Total Votes 125,246

Member, District 7

Julie Pickren .... 66,229 .... 50.52%
Michael Barton .... 41,349 .... 31.54%
Danny Surman .... 19,096 .... 14.57%
Abolaji Tijani "Ayo" Ayobami .... 4,415 .... 3.37%
Total Votes 131,089

Member, District 8

Audrey Young .... 94,705 .... 100%

Member, District 9

Keven M. Ellis .... 135,023 .... 100%

Member, District 10

Tom Maynard .... 168,646 .... 100%

Member, District 11

Patricia "Pat" Hardy .... 84,028 .... 58.92%
Joshua Tarbay .... 29,554 .... 20.72%
Rebecca Garcia .... 17,260 .... 12.10%
"D.C." Caldwell .... 11,781 .... 8.26%
Total Votes 142,623

Member, District 12

Pam Little .... 121,622 .... 100%

Member, District 13

Kathryn Monette .... 9,111 .... 30%
A. Denise Russell .... 8,910 .... 29.34%
Natalie Kohn .... 7,082 .... 23.32%
Ajua Mason .... 5,267 .... 17.34%
Total Votes 30,370

Member, District 14

Evelyn Brooks .... 77,805 .... 57.22%
Sue Melton-Malone .... 58,161 .... 42.78%
Total Votes 135,966

Member, District 15

Aaron Kinsey .... 83,096 .... 52.23%
Jay Johnson .... 75,997 .... 47.77%
Total Votes 159,093

State Senators

District 1

Bryan Hughes .... 88,469 .... 100%

District 2

Bob Hall .... 57,489 .... 100%

District 3

Robert Nichols .... 88,368 .... 100%

District 4

Brandon Creighton .... 74,399 .... 100%

District 5

Charles Schwertner .... 72,796 .... 100%

District 7

Paul Bettencourt .... 58,512 .... 100%

District 8

Angela Paxton .... 46,355 .... 65.15%
Matt Rostami .... 24,794 .... 34.85%
Total Votes 71,149

District 9

Kelly Hancock .... 55,084 .... 100%

District 10

Phil King .... 52,008 .... 75.59%
Warren V. Norred .... 16,797 .... 24.41%
Total Votes 68,805

District 11

Mayes Middleton .... 42,083 .... 62.77%
Bob Mitchell .... 10,322 .... 15.40%
Robin Armstrong .... 9,638 .... 14.38%
Bianca Gracia .... 4,996 .... 7.45%
Total Votes 67,039

District 12

Tan Parker .... 53,212 .... 71.07%
Chris Russell .... 21,657 .... 28.93%
Total Votes 74,869

District 15

George Brian Vachris .... 23,261 .... 100%

District 16

Brandon Copeland .... 21,587 .... 100%

District 17

Joan Huffman .... 58,841 .... 100%

District 18

Lois W. Kolkhorst .... 72,214 .... 100%

District 19

Robert Garza .... 27,135 .... 100%

District 20

Westley Wright .... 16,232 .... 73.15%
Johnny Partain .... 5,959 .... 26.85%
Total Votes 22,191

District 21

Julie Dahlberg .... 24,855 .... 100%

District 22

Brian Birdwell .... 69,270 .... 100%

District 24

Pete Flores .... 38,342 .... 46.06%
Raul Reyes .... 27,243 .... 32.73%
Lamar Lewis .... 17,650 .... 21.21%
Total Votes 83,235

District 25

Donna Campbell .... 73,769 .... 79.46%
Channon Cain .... 19,071 .... 20.54%
Total Votes 92,840

District 26

Ashton Murray .... 22,442 .... 100%

District 27

Adam Hinojosa .... 13,351 .... 50.98%
Raul Torres .... 9,062 .... 34.60%
Isreal Salinas .... 3,777 .... 14.42%
Total Votes 26,190

District 28

Charles Perry .... 79,494 .... 100%

District 29

Derek L. Zubeldia .... 16,206 .... 100%

District 30

Drew Springer .... 69,958 .... 100%

District 31

Kevin Sparks .... 45,867 .... 54.88%
Tim Reid .... 19,039 .... 22.78%
Stormy Bradley .... 13,573 .... 16.24%
Jesse Quackenbush .... 5,101 .... 6.10%
Total Votes 83,580

State Representative

District 1

Gary Vandeaver .... 13,279 .... 62.88%
George Lavender .... 6,115 .... 28.96%
Ray Null .... 1,723 .... 8.16%
Total Votes 21,117

District 2

Bryan Slaton .... 16,609 .... 82.37%
Clyde Bostick .... 3,555 .... 17.63%
Total Votes 20,164

District 3

Cecil Bell Jr. .... 14,080 .... 67.19%
Kelly McDonald .... 6,877 .... 32.81%
Total Votes 20,957

District 4

Keith Bell .... 14,336 .... 100%

District 5

Cole Hefner .... 20,202 .... 80.95%
Dewey R. Collier .... 4,753 .... 19.05%
Total Votes 24,955

District 6

Matt Schaefer .... 17,994 .... 88.88%
Charles Turner .... 2,251 .... 11.12%
Total Votes 20,245

District 7

Jay Dean .... 16,300 .... 100%

District 8

Cody Harris .... 20,433 .... 100%

District 9

Trent Ashby .... 23,629 .... 100%

District 10

Brian Harrison .... 13,325 .... 100%

District 11

Travis Clardy .... 13,828 .... 52.76%
Rachel Hale .... 5,459 .... 20.83%
Greg Caldwell .... 3,785 .... 14.44%
Mark Williams .... 3,139 .... 11.98%
Total Votes 26,211

District 12

Kyle Kacal .... 11,675 .... 46.97%
Ben Bius .... 10,392 .... 41.81%
Joshua Hamm .... 2,791 .... 11.23%
Total Votes 24,858

District 13

Angelia Orr .... 10,177 .... 51.28%
Dennis D. Wilson .... 9,669 .... 48.72%
Total Votes 19,846

District 14

John Raney .... 7,235 .... 57.20%
John Harvey Slocum .... 5,414 .... 42.80%
Total Votes 12,649

District 15

Steve Toth .... 13,984 .... 69.22%
Maris Blair .... 6,218 .... 30.78%
Total Votes 20,202

District 16

Will Metcalf .... 20,952 .... 100%

District 17

Stan Gerdes .... 6,277 .... 29.96%
Paul Pape .... 5,811 .... 27.73%
Tom Glass .... 5,377 .... 25.66%
Trey Rutledge .... 2,122 .... 10.13%
Jen Bezner .... 1,365 .... 6.51%
Total Votes 20,952

District 18

Ernest Bailes .... 12,742 .... 56.18%
Janis Holt .... 5,995 .... 26.43%
Ronnie "Bubba" Tullos .... 2,631 .... 11.60%
Stephen A. Missick .... 1,313 .... 5.79%
Total Votes 22,681

District 19

Justin Berry .... 11,523 .... 35.43%
Ellen Troxclair .... 12,435 .... 38.24%
Nubia Devine .... 7,072 .... 21.75%
Perla Hopkins .... 1,490 .... 4.58%
Total Votes 32,520

District 20

Terry M. Wilson .... 16,145 .... 100%

District 21

Dade Phelan .... 20,512 .... 100%

District 22

Jacorion Randle .... 5,119 .... 100%

District 23

Patrick Gurski .... 5,236 .... 31.39%
Terri Leo-Wilson .... 4,690 .... 28.12%
Gina D. Smith .... 3,084 .... 18.49%
Abel Longoria .... 3,670 .... 22%
Total Votes 16,680

District 24

Greg Bonnen .... 17,552 .... 100%

District 25

Cody Thane Vasut .... 13,695 .... 100%

District 26

Jacey Jetton .... 10,401 .... 100%

District 27

Sohrab Gilani .... 4,016 .... 100%

District 28

Gary Gates .... 10,655 .... 75.23%
Robert Boettcher .... 3,508 .... 24.77%
Total Votes 14,163

District 29

Ed Thompson .... 13,295 .... 100%

District 30

Geanie W. Morrison .... 20,079 .... 100%

District 31

Ryan Guillen .... 7,544 .... 56.64%
Mike Monreal .... 4,539 .... 34.08%
Alena Berlanga .... 1,237 .... 9.29%
Total Votes 13,320

District 32

Todd Hunter .... 14,759 .... 100%

District 33

Justin Holland .... 11,821 .... 69.23%
Dennis London .... 4,413 .... 25.84%
Scott R. Lamarca .... 841 .... 4.93%
Total Votes 17,075

District 34

Carolyn Vaughn .... 4,835 .... 72.25%
James Hernandez .... 1,857 .... 27.75%
Total Votes 6,692

District 35

Oscar Rosa .... 1,681 .... 100%

District 37

Janie Lopez .... 4,744 .... 69.35%
George Rivera .... 2,097 .... 30.65%
Total Votes 6,841

District 39

Jimmie Garcia .... 2,455 .... 100%

District 41

John (Doc) Robert Guerra .... 4,519 .... 100%

District 42

Joe Brennan .... 1,897 .... 100%

District 43

J.M. Lozano .... 11,581 .... 100%

District 44

John Kuempel .... 16,406 .... 100%

District 45

Michelle M. Lopez .... 8,159 .... 100%

District 46

Sam Strasser .... 3,149 .... 100%

District 47

Rob Mccarthy .... 8,463 .... 100%

District 49

Katherine Griffin .... 2,889 .... 100%

District 50

Victor Johnson .... 2,396 .... 100%

District 51

Robert Reynolds .... 1,615 .... 100%

District 52

Patrick Mcguinness .... 5,721 .... 35.12%
Caroline Harris .... 5,110 .... 31.37%
Nelson Jarrin .... 4,198 .... 25.77%
Jonathan Schober .... 1,261 .... 7.74%
Total Votes 16290

District 53

Andrew S. Murr .... 21,326 .... 63.35%
Wesley "Wes" Virdell .... 12,339 .... 36.65%
Total Votes 33,665

District 54

Brad Buckley .... 8,857 .... 100%

District 55

Hugh D. Shine .... 10,301 .... 100%

District 56

Charles Doc Anderson .... 17,837 .... 100%

District 57

Richard Hayes .... 7,151 .... 57.50%
Matthew Poole .... 3,565 .... 28.66%
Matthew E. Haines .... 1,721 .... 13.84%
Total Votes 12,437

Republican Runoff

Federal Races

U.S. House of Representatives

District 7

Johnny Teague .... 9,152 .... 63.60%
Tim Stroud .... 5,239 .... 36.40%
Total Votes 14,391

District 28

Cassy Garcia .... 8,485 .... 56.95%
Sandra Whitten .... 6,413 .... 43.05%
Total Votes 14,898

District 29

Robert Schafranek .... 2,875 .... 60.73%
Julio Garza .... 1,859 .... 39.27%
Total Votes 4,734

District 30

James Rodgers .... 3,090 .... 56.92%
James "J. Frank" Harris .... 2,339 .... 43.08%
Total Votes 5,429

State Races

Attorney General

Ken Paxton .... 633,223 .... 67.96%
George P. Bush .... 298,577 .... 32.04%
Total Votes 931,800

Commissioner of the General Land Office

Dawn Buckingham .... 595,554 .... 68.78%
Tim Westley .... 270,365 .... 31.22%
Total Votes 865,919

Railroad Commissioner

Wayne Christian .... 574,573 .... 65.04%
Sarah Stogner .... 308,859 .... 34.96%
Total Votes 883,432

District Races

State Board of Education

Member, District 13

Kathryn Monette .... 9,915 .... 64.67%
A. Denise Russell .... 5,416 .... 35.33%
Total Votes 15,331

State Senator

District 24

Pete Flores .... 28,116 .... 59.15%
Raul Reyes .... 19,417 .... 40.85%
Total Votes 47,533

State Representatives

District 12

Kyle Kacal .... 9,366 .... 57.91%
Ben Bius .... 6,806 .... 42.09%
Total Votes 16,172

District 17

Stan Gerdes .... 6,591 .... 51.24%
Paul Pape .... 6,271 .... 48.76%
Total Votes 12,862

District 19

Ellen Troxclair .... 12,573 .... 56.51%
Justin Berry .... 9,677 .... 43.49%
Total Votes 22,250

District 23

Terri Leo-Wilson .... 5,224 .... 57.67%
Patrick Gurski .... 3,835 .... 42.33%
Total Votes 9,059

Political Party Organizations

Democratic State Executive Committee

txdemocrats.org
Chairman: Gilberto Hinojosa
P.O. Box 15707, Austin 78761

Republican State Executive Committee

texasgop.org
Chairman: Allen West
P.O. Box 2206, Austin 78768

Libertarian State Executive Committee

lptexas.org
Chair: Whitney Bilyeu
100 Congress Ave., Ste. 2000, Austin 78701

Green State Executive Committee

txgreens.org
Co-Chairs: Alfred Molison and Laura Palmer
P.O. Box 271080, Houston 77277

GOVERNMENT

REPORT ON THE 88TH LEGISLATURE

HISTORICAL DOCUMENTS & CHIEF OFFICIALS

STATE GOVERNMENT FINANCIALS

STATE EXECUTIVE, LEGISLATIVE, & JUDICIAL OFFICIALS

STATE AGENCIES, BOARDS, & COMMISSIONS

LOCAL & COUNTY OFFICIALS

FEDERAL OFFICIALS & MILITARY BASES

Opening day in the 88th Legislature. Photo by Evan L'Roy for The Texas Tribune

Report on the 88th Legislature

By Carolyn Barta

The Texas Legislature rarely meets without generating some drama, and 2023 gatherings were no exception. Yet, despite intrigue aplenty in the 88th biennial session and subsequent special sessions, lawmakers were able to pass the largest two-year budget ever and, in a second special session, a record-breaking property tax cut.

The usual chaotic end to the 140-day regular session was complicated by the unexpected delivery of 20 articles of impeachment by a House investigative committee against Atty. Gen. Ken Paxton. Two days before adjournment sine die May 29, 2023, the Republican-dominated Texas House voted overwhelmingly (121 to 23) to impeach the embattled 3-term Republican state official, long mired in legal and ethical challenges. His fate would depend on a later Senate trial.

Before that, the House voted to expel State Rep. Bryan Slaton, R-Royse City, after an internal investigation determined he had engaged in inappropriate sexual conduct with a 19-year-old aide after furnishing her with alcohol.

Both actions were historic. Only one statewide elected official had ever been impeached and removed from office, Gov. James Ferguson more than 100 years before. Slaton was the first House member ousted since 1927.

From the January opening gavel, the 140-day session was destined to be historic for another reason — an embarrassment of riches. Lawmakers could address spending needs with a stunning $32.7 billion budget surplus, attributed to Texas' rapid economic rebound from COVID-19, inflation, and GOP leaders' hoarding of federal pandemic aid.

Republican leaders vowed to return much of the surplus to property owners and, after a months-long stalemate between the House and Senate, finally delivered an $18 billion tax cut deal, which primary author Sen. Paul Bettencourt, R-Houston, called a "Texas-sized tax cut."

Lawmakers also were called upon to respond to the worst school shooting in Texas history — the tragic mass killing of 19 students and two teachers at a Uvalde elementary school on May 24, 2022.

The pot, as usual, was stirred by partisan politics. Republican dominance — 85–64 in the House and 19–12 in the Senate, along with a Republican governor, lieutenant governor and House speaker — guaranteed that controversial super-conservative policy proposals would be offered to maintain Texas' national reputation as a flagship red state.

But divisiveness and infighting prevailed. Differences between the two houses stymied passage of top priority bills of Gov. Greg Abbott and Lt. Gov. Dan Patrick, the Senate's presiding officer and second-most-powerful statewide elected official. Open sniping developed between the lieutenant governor and the House speaker — Rep. Dade Phelan, R-Beaumont — elected by the chamber's membership.

Republicans campaigned on promises of property tax relief in the face of escalating property values but split over differing plans. The House, led by Phelan, wanted to spread the relief among all landowners — homeowners and business and commercial property owners — by providing state funds to lower local property tax rates through "rate compression." The Senate accepted rate compression but also insisted on raising homestead exemptions from $40,000 to $100,000, which Patrick championed to help residential homeowners more.

Abbott stayed mostly mute during the fight between the chambers, finally siding with the House plan. When no plan passed, Abbott promised to keep lawmakers in Austin all summer, if needed, to address property taxes and his other priorities.

During the first 30-day special session in June, the governor tried to force delivery of a property tax bill by vetoing an unheard-of 70-plus bills, the second-highest number behind 82 vetoed by Gov. Rick Perry in 2001. Most of Abbott's vetoes were Senate bills, and Patrick argued they were not vetoed for policy reasons. To be sure, the governor said the bills could wait until lawmakers figured out property taxes.

Midway through Abbott's second called overtime session, the Senate and House reached the $18 billion compromise, which included more than $5 billion approved for property tax relief in 2019 and $12.6 billion to reduce the school property tax rate by 10.7 cents per $100 valuation. All three leaders claimed victory.

Under the deal, homeowners would have $100,000 of the value of their house not subjected to school property taxes, pleasing Patrick since the higher homestead exemptions would provide more relief for homes of modest values. But business also got a break, pleasing Phelan and Abbott. Non-homesteaded residential and commercial properties valued at $5 million or less would get a temporary cap of 20% on appraisal increases for three years, and franchise taxes for small businesses would be cut.

The state would send $12 billion to school districts over two years to offset a reduction in school district maintenance and operations taxes. Absent was any targeted relief for renters or increase in teacher pay, although Patrick and other Republicans promised teacher pay would be taken up in a fall special session. Abbott signed the bill, and parts of the plan would be put in a constitutional amendment election in November.

Abbott's other top priority was to provide state funds for "school choice." At events across the state, he promoted access to an "education savings account" for parents to use for private schools or home-schooling. Democrats and rural Republicans balked for fear money would be siphoned from public schools.

With the extraordinary $32.7 billion budget surplus, some lawmakers were optimistic early that big issues facing public schools could be addressed. But clashing political ideologies, the fight over school vouchers, and squabbles between the Senate and House thwarted passage of bills that could have sent billions to public education. Among the disappointments at regular session's end was the failure to increase the per-student allotment and pass teacher pay raises to address a critical teacher shortage.

Much of the regular session's focus was on issues evolving from broad cultural wars sweeping the nation. Texas joined 17 other states restricting transgender minors from accessing puberty blockers and hormone therapies. Laws were passed to require college athletes to compete on sports teams that align with their sex assigned at birth, to prohibit sexualized performances and drag shows in the presence of minors, and to ban sexually explicit books in school libraries.

Members also debated various religion-based bills, such as allowing schools to hire chaplains, setting aside time for Bible reading and prayer, and requiring schools to display the 10 Commandments.

The Paxton drama and disputes over social issues obscured more monumental actions taken during the regular session, including passage of the largest-ever budget bill, topping $300 billion for the first time.

Here is an expanded look.

Budget: The two-year appropriations bill, the only act the Legislature is constitutionally required to pass, topped out at an unheard-of $321.3 billion. It allocated significant funds for tax cuts, improving mental health access, pay raises for state employees and retired teachers, border security, state parks expansions, the state's energy grid, infrastructure for broadband and water, and higher education. Some $4 billion was set aside to increase teacher pay and school funding, but only if private school vouchers were passed.

The budget allocated more than $5 billion for border security, including $1 million for a border wall, almost $1.4 billion for Abbott to use at his discretion for border operations, and nearly $750 million to the Texas Department of Public Safety for border security.

Other expenditures included $1 billion for a new state water fund to jumpstart massive water supply projects and fix aging water infrastructure and $1 billion in park funding, both contingent on voter approval in November. Some $3 billion would be poured into state behavioral health services, most to renovate or build new mental health state hospitals. Lawmakers appropriated $18 million for opioid overdose prevention, education, and overdose reversal medication.

The budget left $10.7 billion in the general fund and $27 billion in the Rainy Day Fund.

Higher Ed: The Legislature approved a $700 million investment in higher education to allow universities to keep tuition flat for the next two years, but approval was tied to the dismantling of diversity, equity, and inclusion (DEI) offices and revoking or limiting tenure. DEI programs were halted. Unable to eliminate tenure, which offers job protection and academic freedom to professors, legislators made it easier to fire faculty for reasons such as "professional incompetence" or "conduct involving moral turpitude."

Guns: Lawmakers declined to significantly restrict gun purchase and carry in the aftermath of the deadly Uvalde school attack. Uvalde parents and their supporters urged members to raise the minimum age to own a semi-automatic assault rifle, which would have prevented the teenage gunman in Uvalde from legally purchasing his weapons.

Instead, they passed a law requiring school districts to have a safety guard at every school, which some regarded as a little-funded mandate with the money provided. The rare bills limiting access to guns (1) closed a loophole in state law that allowed people with serious mental health issues as juveniles to legally purchase firearms and (2) required courts to report certain involuntary mental health hospitalizations to the federal gun background check system.

Border security: Bills passed would give federal Border Patrol agents arrest, search, and seizure authority if a border crime warrants felony charges; compensate farmers and ranchers for property damage caused by border-related crimes; and give the governor power to develop a border security plan in an interstate compact. Abbott wanted more action on border control, including increased penalties for human smuggling and operating a stash house.

Shoring up the power grid: A fund was created to encourage construction of gas-fueled power plants even though many failed dramatically in the deadly 2021 winter storm, when millions were without power for days. But how electricity is created and sold in the Texas market was not changed.

Expanding broadband: A $1.5 billion infrastructure fund was set up to expand internet availability, as 7 million people in Texas lack access to service. It requires voter approval.

Preempting local regulations: Sweeping legislation referred to as the "Death Star" bill bars cities and counties from issuing local ordinances that go beyond what's allowed under state law in areas including land use, labor, finance, environment, agriculture, public health, and more. Local officials argued their communities would be prevented from enacting regulations tailored to their specific needs. Houston wasted no time in filing suit.

Other bills passed would:

- Combat a growing fentanyl crisis by allowing people to be prosecuted for murder who manufacture or distribute fentanyl illegally in cases that lead to death.
- Extend postpartum Medicaid benefits for low-income mothers from two months to a full year, to stem the rise in maternal deaths.
- Restore election fraud to a felony, after it was made a misdemeanor two years before.

High-profile bills that failed:

- Prison air conditioning: A bill to spend more than a half-billion to air-condition state prisons was stymied despite a study that found 13% of Texas prison deaths (271) between 2001 and 2019 may have been attributed to extreme Texas heat in prisons without air con.
- Casinos: The push to legalize casino gambling attracted public interest early, but the primary casino proposal fell short of votes.
- Restricting foreign land ownership of agricultural land, timberland, and oil and gas rights by entities associated with any country that posed a risk to U.S. national interests.
- Permanent adoption of Daylight Saving Time.

Impeachment

The Texas Senate voted on September 16, 2023, after a 10-day trial, to acquit Atty. Gen. Ken Paxton on 16 articles of impeachment. Twenty-one senators had to approve at least one article to convict and remove him from office. Separately, senators voted to dismiss four other articles. The Senate, unlike the House, voted largely along party lines. The closest votes were 14 to convict and 16 for acquittal – the outcome on 12 articles. Only two Republicans sided with the chamber's 12 Democrats. Paxton's wife, Sen. Angela Paxton, R-McKinney, was present but not allowed to vote.

An outspoken ally of President Trump, Paxton sued the Biden administration multiple times, spearheaded a lawsuit to overturn the 2020 presidential election and built a reputation as a Christian conservative and family values Republican. House impeachment managers charged him with abuse of office, bribery, dereliction of duty, and obstruction of justice. They claimed he used his office to benefit Austin real estate investor Nate Paul, a campaign donor who facilitated the A-G's alleged extramarital affair with a woman identified as Laura Olson, a former Senate aide hired by Paul. None of those three testified.

Lt. Gov. Dan Patrick presided as trial judge. Both sides employed high-profile Texas lawyers. House managers questioned 13 witnesses, the defense only four but conducted tough cross-examinations. Prosecutors built their case on the testimony of senior staff members in the A-G's office who went to the FBI in September 2020 with allegations that Paxton was engaging in conduct that could be illegal. Defense lawyer Tony Buzbee maintained the House managers failed to prove beyond a reasonable doubt any of their charges.

Four of the whistleblowers sued Paxton claiming wrongful termination and agreed to a $3.3 million settlement. The agency's request for state funds for that payout triggered the inquiry by the House Committee on General Investigating, chaired by Rep. Andrew Murr, R-Junction, who then headed the House managers team.

Paxton, a former state representative and senator serving his third term as attorney general, was returned to office as the state's top lawyer. But he still faces securities fraud charges in state court, an FBI investigation, and a state bar complaint. And the Legislature still faces another potential special session to consider school choice.

Carolyn Barta is a former political writer for The Dallas Morning News *and retired journalism professor at Southern Methodist University.* ☆

The impeachment trial of AG Ken Paxton began September 5, 2023. Photo by Bob Daemmrich for The Texas Tribune

Declaration of Independence of the Republic of Texas

The Declaration of Independence of the Republic of Texas was adopted in general convention at Washington-on-the-Brazos, March 2, 1836.

Richard Ellis, president of the convention, appointed a committee of five to write the declaration for submission to the convention. However, there is much evidence that George C. Childress, one of the members, wrote the document with little or no help from the other members. Childress is therefore generally accepted as the author.

The text of the declaration is followed by the names of the signers of the document. The names are presented here as the signers actually signed the document.

Our thanks to the staff of the Texas State Archives for furnishing a photocopy of the signatures.

UNANIMOUS

Declaration of Independence,

BY THE
DELEGATES OF THE PEOPLE OF TEXAS,
IN GENERAL CONVENTION,
AT THE TOWN OF WASHINGTON,
ON THE SECOND DAY OF MARCH, 1836.

WHEN A GOVERNMENT has ceased to protect the lives, liberty and property of the people from whom its legitimate powers are derived, and for the advancement of whose happiness it was instituted; and so far from being a guarantee for the enjoyment of those inestimable and inalienable rights, becomes an instrument in the hands of evil rulers for their oppression; when the Federal Republican Constitution of their country, which they have sworn to support, no longer has a substantial existence, and the whole nature of their government has been forcibly changed without their consent, from a restricted federative republic, composed of sovereign states, to a consolidated central military despotism, in which every interest is disregarded but that of the army and the priesthood — both the eternal enemies of civil liberty, and the ever-ready minions of power, and the usual instruments of tyrants; When long after the spirit of the Constitution has departed, moderation is at length, so far lost, by those in power that even the semblance of freedom is removed, and the forms, themselves, of the constitution discontinued; and so far from their petitions and remonstrances being regarded, the agents who bear them are thrown into dungeons; and mercenary armies sent forth to force a new government upon them at the point of the bayonet. When in consequence of such acts of malfeasance and abdication, on the part of the government, anarchy prevails, and civil society is dissolved into its original elements: In such a crisis, the first law of nature, the right of self-preservation — the inherent and inalienable right of the people to appeal to first principles and take their political affairs into their own hands in extreme cases — enjoins it as a right towards themselves and a sacred obligation to their posterity, to abolish such government and create another in its stead, calculated to rescue them from impending dangers, and to secure their future welfare and happiness.

Nations, as well as individuals, are amenable for their acts to the public opinion of mankind. A statement of a part of our grievances is, therefore, submitted to an impartial world, in justification of the hazardous but unavoidable step now taken of severing our political connection with the Mexican people, and assuming an independent attitude among the nations of the earth.

The Mexican government, by its colonization laws, invited and induced the Anglo-American population of Texas to colonize its wilderness under the pledged faith of a written constitution, that they should continue to enjoy that constitutional liberty and republican government to which they had been habituated in the land of their birth, the United States of America. In this expectation they have been cruelly disappointed, inasmuch as the Mexican nation has acquiesced in the late changes made in the government by General Antonio Lopez de Santa Anna, who, having overturned the constitution of his country, now offers us the cruel alternative either to abandon our homes, acquired by so many privations, or submit to the most intolerable of all tyranny, the combined despotism of the sword and the priesthood.

It has sacrificed our welfare to the state of Coahuila, by which our interests have been continually depressed, through a jealous and partial course of legislation carried on at a far distant seat of government, by a hostile majority, in an unknown tongue; and this too, notwithstanding we have petitioned in the humblest terms, for the establishment of a separate state government, and have, in accordance with the provisions of the national constitution, presented the general Congress, a republican constitution which was without just cause contemptuously rejected.

It incarcerated in a dungeon, for a long time, one of our citizens, for no other cause but a zealous endeavor to procure the acceptance of our constitution and the establishment of a state government.

It has failed and refused to secure on a firm basis, the right of trial by jury; that palladium of civil liberty, and only safe guarantee for the life, liberty, and property of the citizen.

It has failed to establish any public system of education, although possessed of almost boundless resources (the public domain) and, although, it is an axiom, in political science, that unless a people are educated and enlightened it is idle to expect the continuance of civil liberty, or the capacity for self-government.

It has suffered the military commandants stationed among us to exercise arbitrary acts of oppression and tyranny; thus trampling upon the most sacred rights of the citizen and rendering the military superior to the civil power.

It has dissolved by force of arms, the state Congress of Coahuila and Texas, and obliged our representatives to fly for their lives from the seat of government; thus depriving us of the fundamental political right of representation.

It has demanded the surrender of a number of our citizens, and ordered military detachments to seize and carry them into the Interior for trial; in contempt of the civil authorities, and in defiance of the laws and constitution.

It has made piratical attacks upon our commerce; by commissioning foreign desperadoes, and authorizing them to seize our vessels, and convey the property of our citizens to far distant ports of confiscation.

It denies us the right of worshipping the Almighty according to the dictates of our own consciences, by the support of a national religion calculated to promote the temporal interests of its human functionaries rather than the glory of the true and living God.

It has demanded us to deliver up our arms; which are essential to our defense, the rightful property of freemen, and formidable only to tyrannical governments.

It has invaded our country, both by sea and by land, with intent to lay waste our territory and drive us from our homes; and has now a large mercenary army advancing to carry on against us a war of extermination.

It has, through its emissaries, incited the merciless savage, with the tomahawk and scalping knife, to massacre the inhabitants of our defenseless frontiers.

It hath been, during the whole time of our connection with it, the contemptible sport and victim of successive military revolutions and hath continually exhibited every characteristic of a weak, corrupt and tyrannical government.

These, and other grievances, were patiently borne by the people of Texas until they reached that point at which forbearance ceases to be a virtue. We then took up arms in defense of the national constitution. We appealed to our Mexican brethren for assistance. Our appeal has been made in vain. Though months have elapsed, no sympathetic response has yet been heard from the Interior. We are, therefore, forced to the melancholy conclusion that the Mexican people have acquiesced in the destruction of their liberty, and the substitution therefor of a military government — that they are unfit to be free and incapable of self-government.

The necessity of self-preservation, therefore, now decrees our eternal political separation.

We, therefore, the delegates, with plenary powers, of the people of Texas, in solemn convention assembled, appealing to a candid world for the necessities of our condition, do hereby resolve and DECLARE *that our political connection with the Mexican nation has forever ended; and that the people of Texas do now constitute a* FREE, SOVEREIGN *and* INDEPENDENT REPUBLIC, *and are fully invested with all the rights and attributes which properly belong to the independent nations; and, conscious of the rectitude of our intentions, we fearlessly and confidently commit the issue to the decision of the Supreme Arbiter of the destinies of nations.*

RICHARD ELLIS, president of the convention and Delegate from Red River.

Charles B Stewart

Thos Barnett
John S.D. Byrom

Franco Ruiz
J. Antonio Navarro
Jesse B. Badgett
Wm D. Lacey
William Menefee
Jno Fisher
Mathew Caldwell
William Mottley
Lorenzo de Zavala
Stephen H. Everitt
Geo W Smyth

Elijah Stapp
Claiborne West

Wm B Scates

M.B. Menard
A.B. Hardin
J.W. Bunton
Thos J. Gasley
R. M. Coleman
Sterling C. Robertson
Benj Briggs Goodrich
G.W. Barnett
James G. Swisher
Jesse Grimes
S. Rhoads Fisher
John W. Moore
John W. Bower
Saml A Maverick from Bejar
Sam P. Carson
A. Briscoe
J.B. Woods
Jas Collinsworth
Edwin Waller
Asa Brigham
Geo. C. Childress
Bailey Hardeman
Rob. Potter

Thomas Jefferson Rusk
Chas. S. Taylor
John S. Roberts

Robert Hamilton
Collin McKinney
Albert H Latimer
James Power

Sam Houston
David Thomas

Edwd Conrad
Martin Parmer
Edwin O. LeGrand
Stephen W. Blount
Jas Gaines
Wm Clark, Jr
Sydney O. Penington
Wm Carrol Crawford
Jno Turner

Test. H.S. Kimble, Secretary

Documents Concerning the Annexation of Texas to the United States

For an overview of the subject, please see these discussions: The New Handbook of Texas, Texas State Historical Association, Austin, 1996; Vol. 1, pages 192–193. On the web: www.tshaonline.org/handbook/entries/annexation. Also see, the Texas State Library and Archives website: www.tsl.texas.gov/ref/abouttx/annexation/index.html and the Texas Almanac website: www.texasalmanac.com/articles/annexation-and-statehood.

Joint Resolution for Annexing Texas to the United States

Resolved

by the Senate and House of Representatives of the United States of America in Congress assembled,

That Congress doth consent that the territory properly included within and rightfully belonging to the Republic of Texas, may be erected into a new State to be called the State of Texas, with a republican form of government adopted by the people of said Republic, by deputies in convention assembled, with the consent of the existing Government in order that the same may by admitted as one of the States of this Union.

2. And be it further resolved, That the foregoing consent of Congress is given upon the following conditions, to wit:

First, said state to be formed, subject to the adjustment by this government of all questions of boundary that may arise with other government,

—and the Constitution thereof, with the proper evidence of its adoption by the people of said Republic of Texas, shall be transmitted to the President of the United States, to be laid before Congress for its final action on, or before the first day of January, one thousand eight hundred and forty-six.

Second, said state when admitted into the Union, after ceding to the United States all public edifices, fortifications, barracks, ports and harbors, navy and navy yards, docks, magazines and armaments, and all other means pertaining to the public defense, belonging to the said Republic of Texas, shall retain funds, debts, taxes and dues of every kind which may belong to, or be due and owing to the said Republic;

and shall also retain all the vacant and unappropriated lands lying within its limits, to be applied to the payment of the debts and liabilities of said Republic of Texas, and the residue of said lands, after discharging said debts and liabilities, to be disposed of as said State may direct; but in no event are said debts and liabilities to become a charge upon the Government of the United States.

Third — New States of convenient size not exceeding four in number, in addition to said State of Texas and having sufficient population, may, hereafter by the consent of said State, be formed out of the territory thereof, which shall be entitled to admission under the provisions of the Federal Constitution;

and such states as may be formed out of the territory lying south of thirty-six degrees thirty minutes north latitude, commonly known as the Missouri Compromise Line, shall be admitted into the Union, with or without slavery, as the people of each State, asking admission shall desire;

and in such State or States as shall be formed out of said territory, north of said Missouri Compromise Line, slavery, or involuntary servitude (except for crime) shall be prohibited.

3. And be it further resolved, That if the President of the United States shall in his judgment and discretion deem it most advisable, instead of proceeding to submit the foregoing resolution of the Republic of Texas, as an overture on the part of the United States for admission, to negotiate with the Republic; then,

Be it resolved, That a State, to be formed out of the present Republic of Texas, with suitable extent and boundaries, and with two representatives in Congress, until the next appointment of representation, shall be admitted into the Union, by virtue of this act, on an equal footing with the existing States, as soon as the terms and conditions of such admission, and the cession of the remaining Texian territory to the United States shall be agreed upon by the governments of Texas and the United States:

And that the sum of one hundred thousand dollars be, and the same is hereby, appropriated to defray the expenses of missions and negotiations, to agree upon the terms of said admission and cession, either by treaty to be submitted to the Senate, or by articles to be submitted to the two houses of Congress, as the President may direct.

Approved, March 1, 1845.

Source: Peters, Richard, ed., The Public Statutes at Large of the United States of America, v.5, pp. 797–798, Boston, Chas. C. Little and Jas. Brown, 1850.

Twenty-Ninth Congress: Session 1 — Resolutions [No. 1.] Joint Resolution for the Admission of the State of Texas into the Union

Whereas

the Congress of the United States, by a joint resolution approved March the first, eighteen hundred and forty-five, did consent that the territory properly included within, and rightfully belonging to, the Republic of Texas, might be erected into a new State, to be called _The State of Texas,_ with a republican form of government, to be adopted by the people of said republic, by deputies in convention assembled, with the consent of the existing government, in order that the same might be admitted as one of the States of the Union;

which consent of Congress was given upon certain conditions specified in the first and second sections of said joint resolution;

and whereas the people of the said Republic of Texas, by deputies in convention assembled, with the consent of the existing government, did adopt a constitution, and erect a new State with a republican form of government, and, in the name of the people of Texas, and by their authority, did ordain and declare that they assented to and accepted the proposals, conditions, and guaranties contained in said first and second sections of said resolution:

and whereas the said constitution, with the proper evidence of its adoption by the people of the Republic of Texas, has been transmitted to the President of the United States and laid before Congress, in conformity to the provisions of said joint resolution:

Therefore—

Resolved by the Senate and House of Representatives of the United States of America in Congress assembled, That the State of Texas shall be one, and is hereby declared to be one, of the United States of America, and admitted into the Union on an equal footing with the original States in all respects whatever.

Sec. 2. And be it further resolved, That until the representatives in Congress shall be apportioned according to an actual enumeration of the inhabitants of the United States, the State of Texas shall be entitled to choose two representatives.

Approved, December 29, 1845.

Source: Minot, Geo., ed., Statutes at Large and Treaties of the United States of America from Dec. 1, 1845, to March 3, 1851, V. IX, p. 108

Constitution of Texas

The complete official text of the Constitution of Texas, including the original document, which was adopted Feb. 15, 1876, plus all amendments approved since then, is available on the State of Texas website:

statutes.capitol.texas.gov/

An index and search features at that website allow exploration of the 17 Articles and subsequent Sections of the Constitution, along with other Texas Statutes.

For election information, upcoming elections, amendment or other election votes, and voter registration information, go to:

www.sos.state.tx.us/elections/index.shtml

According to the **Legislative Reference Library of Texas**, "The Texas Constitution is one of the longest in the nation and is still growing. As of 2019 (the 86th Legislature), the Texas Legislature has proposed a total of 690 amendments. Of these, 507 have been adopted, and 180 have been defeated by Texas voters. Thus, the Texas Constitution has been amended 507 times since its adoption in 1876."

Amending the Texas Constitution requires a two-thirds favorable vote by both the Texas House of Representatives and the Texas Senate, followed by a majority vote of approval by voters in a statewide election.

Prior to 1973, amendments to the constitution could not be submitted by a special session of the Legislature. But the constitution was amended in 1972 to allow submission of amendments if the special session was opened to the subject by the governor.

Constitutional amendments are not subject to a gubernatorial veto. Once submitted, voters have the final decision on whether to change the constitution as proposed.

For more information on bills and constitutional amendments, see the Legislative Reference Library of Texas website:

lrl.texas.gov/

Amendments, 2021

The following 8 amendments were submitted to voters by the 87th Legislature in an election on Nov. 2, 2021.

HJR 99: Proposing a constitutional amendment authorizing a county to finance the development or redevelopment of transportation or infrastructure in unproductive, underdeveloped, or blighted areas in the county; authorizing the issuance of bonds and notes. **Adopted.**

Votes for: 931,447; Votes against: 557,093

HJR 125: Proposing a constitutional amendment to allow the surviving spouse of a person who is disabled to receive a limitation on the school district ad valorem taxes on the spouse's residence homestead if the spouse is 55 years of age or older at the time of the person's death. **Adopted.**

Votes for: 1,285,384; Votes against: 190,109

HJR 143: Proposing a constitutional amendment authorizing the professional sports team charitable foundations of organizations sanctioned by certain professional associations to conduct charitable raffles at rodeo venues. **Adopted.**

Votes for: 1,242,625; Votes against: 239,783

HJR 165: Proposing a constitutional amendment providing additional powers to the State Commission on Judicial Conduct with respect to candidates for judicial office. **Adopted.**

Votes for: 852,336; Votes against: 586,686

SJR 19: Proposing a constitutional amendment establishing a right for residents of certain facilities to designate an essential caregiver for in-person visitation. **Adopted.**

Votes for: 1,293,922; Votes against: 178,665

SJR 27: Proposing a constitutional amendment to prohibit this state or a political subdivision of this state from prohibiting or limiting religious services of religious organizations. **Adopted.**

Votes for: 925,447; Votes against: 557,093

SJR 35: Proposing a constitutional amendment authorizing the legislature to provide for an exemption from ad valorem taxation of all or part of the market value of the residence homestead of the surviving spouse of a member of the armed services of the United States who is killed or fatally injured in the line of duty. **Adopted.**

Votes for: 1,291,920; Votes against: 180,179

SJR 47: Proposing a constitutional amendment changing the eligibility requirements for certain judicial offices. **Adopted.**

Votes for: 845,030; Votes against: 592,585

Amendments, 2023

The following 14 amendments will be submitted to voters by the 88th Legislature in an election on Nov. 7, 2023.

HJR 2: Proposing a constitutional amendment to provide a cost-of-living adjustment to certain annuitants of the Teacher Retirement System of Texas.

HJR 2: Proposing a constitutional amendment to establish a temporary limit on the maximum appraised value of real property other than a residence homestead for ad valorem tax purposes; to increase the amount of the exemption from ad valorem taxation by a school district applicable to residence homesteads from $40,000 to $100,000; to adjust the amount of the limitation on school district ad valorem taxes imposed on the residence homesteads of the elderly or disabled to reflect increases in certain exemption amounts; to except certain appropriations to pay for ad valorem tax relief from the constitutional limitation on the rate of growth of appropriations; and to authorize the legislature to provide for a four-year term of office for a member of the board of directors of certain appraisal districts.

HJR 3: The constitutional amendment relating to the Texas University Fund, which provides funding to certain institutions of higher education to achieve national prominence as major research universities and drive the state economy.

SJR 32: Proposing a constitutional amendment to permit conservation and reclamation districts in El Paso County to issue bonds supported by ad valorem taxes to fund the development and maintenance of parks and recreational facilities.

SJR 64: The constitutional amendment authorizing a local option exemption from ad valorem taxation by a county or municipality of all or part of the appraised value of real property used to operate a child-care facility.

SJR 74: The constitutional amendment providing for the creation of the centennial parks conservation fund to be used for the creation and improvement of state parks.

SJR 75: The constitutional amendment creating the Texas water fund to assist in financing water projects in this state.

SJR 87: The constitutional amendment to authorize the legislature to exempt from ad valorem taxation equipment or inventory held by a manufacturer of medical or biomedical products to protect the Texas healthcare network and strengthen our medical supply chain.

SJR 93: The constitutional amendment providing for the creation of the Texas energy fund to support the construction, maintenance, modernization, and operation of electric generating facilities.

HJR 107: The constitutional amendment to increase the mandatory age of retirement for state justices and judges.

HJR 125: The constitutional amendment creating the broadband infrastructure fund to expand high-speed broadband access and assist in the financing of connectivity projects.

HJR 126: The constitutional amendment protecting the right to engage in farming, ranching, timber production, horticulture, and wildlife management.

HJR 132: The constitutional amendment prohibiting the imposition of an individual wealth or net worth tax, including a tax on the difference between the assets and liabilities of an individual or family.

HJR 134: The constitutional amendment providing for the abolition of the office of county treasurer in Galveston County. ☆

Early Leaders of Texas

The presidents of the Republic of Texas and the state's first Governor, from top left: **David G. Burnet**, provisional president; **Sam Houston**, second and fourth presidents; **Mirabeau B. Lamar**, third president.

Second row, left: **Anson Jones**, the Republic's last president; and **J. Pinckney Henderson**, the Lone Star State's first governor.

Texas' Chief Governmental Officials

On this and the following pages are lists of the principal administrative officials who have served the Republic and State of Texas with dates of their tenures of office. In a few instances, there are disputes as to the exact dates of tenures. Dates listed here are those that appear the most authentic.

★ ★ ★ ★ ★ ★ ★

Governors and Presidents

Spanish Royal Governors

(Some authorities would include Texas under administrations of several earlier Spanish governors. The late Dr. C.E. Castañeda, Latin-American librarian of The University of Texas and authority on the history of Texas and the Southwest, would include the following four: Francisco de Garay, 1523–1526; Pánfilo de Narváez, 1526–28; Nuño de Guzmán, 1528–1530; and Hernando de Soto, 1538–1543.)

Domingo Terán de los Rios 1691–1692
Gregorio de Salinas Varona 1692–1697
Francisco Cuerbo y Valdés 1698–1702
Mathías de Aguirre 1703–1705
Martín de Alarcón 1705–1708
Simón Padilla y Córdova 1708–1712
Pedro Fermin de Echevers y Subisa 1712–1714
Juan Valdéz 1714–1716
Martín de Alarcón 1716–1719
José de Azlor y Virto de Vera, Marqués de San Miguel de Aguayo 1719–1722
Fernando Pérez de Almazán 1722–1727
Melchor de Mediavilla y Azcona 1727–1731
Juan Antonio Bustillo y Ceballos 1731–1734
Manuel de Sandoval 1734–1736
Carlos Benites Franquis de Lugo 1736–1737
Joseph Fernández de Jáuregui y Urrutia 1737–1737
Prudencio de Orobio y Basterra 1737–1741
Tomás Felipe Winthuisen (or Winthuysen) 1741–1743
Justo Boneo y Morales 1743–1744
Francisco García Larios 1744–1748
Pedro del Barrio Junco y Espriella 1748–1750
Jacinto de Barrios y Jáuregui 1751–1759
Angel de Martos y Navarrete 1759–1767
Hugo Oconór 1767–1770
Juan María Vicencio, Barón de Ripperdá 1770–1778
Domingo Cabello y Robles 1778–1786
Rafael Martínez Pacheco 1787–1790
Manuel Muñoz 1790–1799
Juan Bautista de Elguezábal 1799–1805
Antonio Cordero y Bustamante 1805–1808
Manuel María de Salcedo 1808–1813
(Mexico's War of Independence 1810–1812 created governmental instability.)

Juan Bautista de las Casas................................1811–1811
(Revolutionary governor)
Cristóbal Domínguez, Benito de Armiñan, Mariano Varela, Juan Ignacio Pérez, Manuel Pardo *(ad interim)*............................1813–1817
Antonio María Martínez................................1817–1821

Governors Under Mexican Rule

The first two governors under Mexican rule, Trespalacios and García, were of Texas only as Texas was then constituted. Beginning with Gonzáles, 1824, the governors were for the joint State of Coahuila y Texas.

José Felix Trespalacios................................1822–1823
Luciano García................................1823–1824
Rafael Gonzáles................................1824–1826
Victor Blanco................................1826–1827
José María Viesca................................1827–1830
Ramón Eca y Músquiz................................1830–1831
José María Letona................................1831–1832
Ramón Eca y Músquiz................................1832–1832
Juan Martín de Veramendi................................1832–1833
Juan José de Vidáurri y Villasenor................................1833–1834
Juan José Elguezábal................................1834–1835
José María Cantú................................1835–1835
Agustín M. Viesca................................1835–1835
Marciel Borrego................................1835–1835
Ramón Eca y Músquiz................................1835–1835

Provisional Colonial Governor, Before Independence

Henry Smith (Impeached)...........................1835–Jan. 1836
(James W. Robinson served as acting governor after Smith was impeached.)

Presidents of the Republic of Texas

David G. Burnet........Mar. 16, 1836–Oct. 22, 1836
(provisional)
Sam Houston........Oct. 22, 1836–Dec. 10, 1838
Mirabeau B. Lamar........Dec. 10, 1838–Dec. 13, 1841
Sam Houston........Dec. 13, 1841–Dec. 9, 1844
Anson Jones........Dec. 9, 1844–Feb. 19, 1846

Governors Since Annexation

Abbrevations: (D) Democrat, (R) Republican, (I) Independent. Many of the early Governors ran with no party affiliation.

J. Pinckney Henderson................Feb. 19, 1846–Dec. 21, 1847
(Albert C. Horton served as acting governor while Henderson was away in the Mexican War.)
George T. Wood........................Dec. 21, 1847–Dec. 21, 1849
Peter Hansbrough Bell................Dec. 21, 1849–Nov. 23, 1853
(Resigned to enter U.S. House of Representatives.)
J. W. Henderson........................Nov. 23, 1853–Dec. 21, 1853
Elisha M. Pease........................Dec. 21, 1853–Dec. 21, 1857
Hardin R. Runnels (D)................Dec. 21, 1857–Dec. 21, 1859
Sam Houston..........................Dec. 21, 1859–Mar. 16, 1861
(Resigned because of state's secession from the Union.)
Edward Clark..........................Mar. 16, 1861–Nov. 7, 1861
Francis R. Lubbock......................Nov. 7, 1861–Nov. 5, 1863
(Resigned to enter Confederate Army.)
Pendleton Murrah......................Nov. 5, 1863–June 17, 1865
(Fled to Mexico upon the fall of Confederacy. Lt. Gov. Fletcher S. Stockdale briefly acted as governor after Murrah's departure.)
Andrew J. Hamilton....................June 17, 1865–Aug. 9, 1866
(Hamilton received a commission as "military governor of Texas" from President Abraham Lincoln on Nov. 14, 1862. He appears to have served in that capacity continuously until his "reappointment" as "provisional governor" by President Andrew Johnson on June 17, 1865. Apparently Johnson used the term "reappointment" because Hamilton was already serving as military governor.)
James W. Throckmorton...............Aug. 9, 1866–Aug. 8, 1867
Elisha M. Pease (R).....................Aug. 8, 1867–Sept. 30, 1869
(Appointed under martial law after Throckmorton was removed on July 30, 1867, by Gen. Philip Sheridan. Pease formally took possession of the office on Aug. 8. He resigned and vacated the office Sept. 30, 1869, but no successor was named until Jan. 8, 1870. Some historians extend Pease's term to that date, but in reality Texas was without a head of governemnt for that period.)
Edmund J. Davis (R).....................Jan. 8, 1870–Jan. 15, 1874
(Appointed provisional governor after being elected.)
Richard Coke (D)........................Jan. 15, 1874–Dec. 1, 1876
(Resigned to enter U.S. Senate.)
Richard B. Hubbard (D)................Dec. 1, 1876–Jan. 21, 1879
Oran M. Roberts (D)...................Jan. 21, 1879–Jan. 16, 1883
John Ireland (D)........................Jan. 16, 1883–Jan. 18, 1887
Lawrence Sullivan Ross (D)...........Jan. 18, 1887–Jan. 20, 1891
James Stephen Hogg (D)................Jan. 20, 1891–Jan. 15, 1895
Charles A. Culberson (D)...............Jan. 15, 1895–Jan. 17, 1899
Joseph D. Sayers (D)....................Jan. 17, 1899–Jan. 20, 1903
S. W. T. Lanham (D)....................Jan. 20, 1903–Jan. 15, 1907
Thos. Mitchell Campbell (D)...........Jan. 15, 1907–Jan. 17, 1911
Oscar Branch Colquitt (D).............Jan. 17, 1911–Jan. 19, 1915
James E. Ferguson (D)................Jan. 19, 1915–Sept. 25, 1917
(Impeached in August 1917. Lt. Gov. Hobby served as acting governor during the impeachment proceedings. Ferguson was removed from office Sept. 25.)
William Pettus Hobby (D)............Aug. 25, 1917–Jan. 18, 1921
Pat Morris Neff (D).....................Jan. 18, 1921–Jan. 20, 1925
Miriam A. Ferguson (D)...............Jan. 20, 1925–Jan. 17, 1927
Dan Moody (D)..........................Jan. 17, 1927–Jan. 20, 1931
Ross S. Sterling (D).....................Jan. 20, 1931–Jan. 17, 1933
Miriam A. Ferguson (D)................Jan. 17, 1933–Jan. 15, 1935
James V. Allred (D)......................Jan. 15, 1935–Jan. 17, 1939
W. Lee O'Daniel (D).....................Jan. 17, 1939–Aug. 4, 1941
(Resigned to enter U.S. Senate.)
Coke R. Stevenson (D)..................Aug. 4, 1941–Jan. 21, 1947
Beauford H. Jester (D).................Jan. 21, 1947–July 11, 1949
(Died in office. Succeeded by Lt. Gov. Shivers.)
Allan Shivers (D).......................July 11, 1949–Jan. 15, 1957
Price Daniel (D)........................Jan. 15, 1957–Jan. 15, 1963
John Connally (D)......................Jan. 15, 1963–Jan. 21, 1969
Preston Smith (D).......................Jan. 21, 1969–Jan. 16, 1973
Dolph Briscoe (D)......................Jan. 16, 1973–Jan. 16, 1979
(Effective in 1975, the term of office was increased from 2 to 4 years.)
William P. Clements (R)...............Jan. 16, 1979–Jan. 18, 1983
Mark White (D).........................Jan. 18, 1983–Jan. 20, 1987
William P. Clements (R)...............Jan. 20, 1987–Jan. 15, 1991
Ann W. Richards (D)....................Jan. 15, 1991–Jan. 17, 1995
George W. Bush (R)....................Jan. 17, 1995–Dec. 21, 2000
(Resigned to become U.S. president.)
Rick Perry (R)..........................Dec. 21, 2000–Jan. 20, 2015
Greg Abbott (R)..............................Jan. 20, 2015–present

★★★★★★★

Vice Presidents and Lieutenant Governors

Vice Presidents of the Republic

Lorenzo de Zavala.....................Mar. 16, 1836–Oct, 17, 1836
(Provisional.)
Mirabeau B. Lamar....................Oct. 22, 1836–Dec.10, 1838
David G. Burnet........................Dec. 10, 1838–Dec.13, 1841
Edward Burleson........................Dec. 13, 1841–Dec. 9, 1844
Kenneth L. Anderson....................Dec. 9, 1844–July 3, 1845
(Died in office.)

Lieutenant Governors

Albert C. Horton (D) ....May 2, 1846–Dec. 21, 1847
John A. Greer (D) ....Dec. 21, 1847–Dec. 22, 1851
J. W. Henderson (D)....................Dec. 22, 1851–Nov. 23, 1853
(Briefly succeeded to governorship when Gov. Bell resigned to enter U.S. House of Representatives.)
D. C. Dickson (D)......................Dec. 21, 1853–Dec. 21, 1855
H. R. Runnels (D)......................Dec. 21, 1855–Dec. 21, 1857
F. R. Lubbock (D)......................Dec. 21, 1857–Dec. 21, 1859
Edward Clark (I).......................Dec. 21, 1859–Mar. 16, 1861
(Succeeded Gov. Sam Houston when Houston refused to take oath to Confederacy.)
John M. Crockett (D).................... Nov. 7, 1861–Nov. 5, 1863
Fletcher S. Stockdale (D)................ Nov. 7, 1863–June 17, 1865
(Fall of Confederacy.)
George W. Jones (D)....................Aug. 9, 1866–July 30, 1867
(Jones was removed by Gen. Philip Sheridan.)
J. W. Flanagan (R)... 1869
(Elected in 1869, Flanagan was appointed U.S. senator and was never inaugurated as lt. governor.)
R. B. Hubbard (D)........................Jan. 15, 1873–Dec. 1, 1876
(Succeeded Gov. Richard Coke when he resigned to become U.S. senator.)
J. D. Sayers (D)............................Jan. 21, 1879–Jan. 18, 1881
L. J. Storey (D)............................Jan. 18, 1881–Jan. 16, 1883
Marion Martin (D) .... Jan. 16, 1883–Jan. 20, 1885
Barnett Gibbs (D)....................... Jan. 20, 1885–Jan. 19, 1887
T. B. Wheeler (D)........................ Jan. 19, 1887– Jan. 21, 1891
George C. Pendleton (D) ....Jan. 21, 1891–Jan. 17, 1893
M. M. Crane (D) ....Jan. 17, 1893–Jan. 15, 1895
George T. Jester (D)......................Jan. 15, 1895–Jan. 17, 1899
J. N. Browning (D) ....Jan. 17, 1899– Jan. 20, 1903
George D. Neal (D) ....Jan. 20, 1903–Jan. 15, 1907
A. B. Davidson (D) ....Jan. 15, 1907–Jan. 21, 1913
Will H. Mayes (D).......................Jan. 21, 1913–Aug. 14, 1914
(resigned)
William P. Hobby (D)..................Jan. 19, 1915–Aug. 25, 1917
(Served as acting governor during the impeachment of Gov. Jim Ferguson. Took oath as governor after Ferguson was removed from office Sept. 25.)
W. A. Johnson (D)...................... Sept. 29, 1917–Jan. 18, 1921
(Selected as president of the state Senate and acting lt. governor, serving Hobby's unexpired term. He was then elected statewide to the office in 1918.)
Lynch Davidson (D) .... Jan. 18, 1921–Jan. 16, 1923
T. W. Davidson (D) .... Jan. 16, 1923–Jan. 20, 1925
Barry Miller (D)......................... Jan. 20, 1925–Jan. 20, 1931
Edgar E. Witt (D) ....Jan. 20, 1931–Jan. 15, 1935
Walter Woodul (D) ....Jan. 15, 1935–Jan. 17, 1939
Coke R. Stevenson (D)..................Jan. 17, 1939–Aug. 4, 1941
(Became governor upon resignation of Gov. W. Lee O'Daniel to become U.S. senator.)
John Lee Smith (D) .... Jan. 19, 1943–Jan. 21, 1947
Allan Shivers (D)........................ Jan. 21, 1947–July 11, 1949
(Shivers succeeded to the governorship on death of Gov. Beauford H. Jester.)
Ben Ramsey (D)........................ Jan. 16, 1951–Sept. 18, 1961
(Ramsey resigned to become a member of the Texas Railroad Commission.)
Preston Smith (D)....................... Jan. 15, 1963–Jan. 21, 1969
Ben Barnes (D).......................... Jan. 21, 1969–Jan. 16, 1973
William P. Hobby Jr. (D)................ Jan. 16, 1973–Jan. 15, 1991
Robert D. Bullock (D).................. Jan. 15, 1991–Jan. 19, 1999
Rick Perry (R) ....Jan. 19, 1999–Dec. 21, 2000
Bill Ratliff (R) ....Dec. 28, 2000–Jan. 14, 2003
(Elected by state Senate when Perry succeeded to governorship.)
David Dewhurst (R) .... Jan. 21, 2003–Jan. 20, 2015
Dan Patrick (R) ....Jan. 20, 2015–present

★ ★ ★ ★ ★ ★ ★ ★

Secretaries of State Of the Republic

Raines Yearbook for Texas, 1901, gives the following record of Secretaries of State during the era of the Republic of Texas:

Under David G. Burnet: Samuel P. Carson, James Collingsworth, and W. H. Jack.

Under Sam Houston (first term): Stephen F. Austin, 1836. J. Pinckney Henderson and Dr. Robert A. Irion, 1837–1838.

Under Mirabeau B. Lamar: Bernard Bee appointed Dec. 16, 1838; James Webb appointed Feb. 6, 1839; D. G. Burnet appointed Acting Secretary of State, May 31, 1839; N. Amory appointed Acting Secretary of State, July 23, 1839; D. G. Burnet appointed Acting Secretary of State, Aug. 5, 1839; Abner S. Lipscomb appointed Secretary of State, Jan. 31, 1840, and resigned Jan. 22, 1841; Joseph Waples appointed Acting Secretary of State, Jan. 23, 1841, and served until Feb. 8, 1841; James S. Mayfield appointed Feb. 8, 1841; Joseph Waples appointed April 30, 1841, and served until May 25, 1841; Samuel A. Roberts appointed May 25, 1841; reappointed Sept. 7, 1841.

Under Sam Houston (second term): E. Lawrence Stickney, Acting Secretary of State until Anson Jones was appointed Dec. 13, 1841. Jones served as Secretary of State throughout this term except during the summer and part of this term of 1842, when Joseph Waples filled the position as Acting Secretary of State.

Under Anson Jones: Ebenezer Allen served from Dec. 10, 1844, until Feb. 5, 1845, when Ashbel Smith became Secretary of State. Allen was again named Acting Secretary of State, March 31, 1845, and later named Secretary of State.

In addition to the above, documents in the Texas State Archives indicate that **Joseph C. Eldredge**, Chief Clerk of the State Department during much of the Republic's existence, signed a number of documents in the absence of the office-holder in the capacity of "Acting Secretary of State."

State Secretaries of State

Charles Mariner ....Feb. 20, 1846–May 4, 1846
David G. Burnet...........................May 4, 1846–Jan. 1, 1848
Washington D. Miller ....Jan. 1, 1848–Jan. 2, 1850
James Webb ....Jan. 2, 1850–Nov. 14, 1851
Thomas H. Duval......................Nov. 14, 1851–Dec. 22, 1853
Edward Clark .... Dec. 22, 1853–Dec. 1857
T. S. Anderson.............................Dec. 1857–Dec. 27, 1859
E. W. Cave ....Dec. 27, 1859–Mar. 16, 1861
Bird Holland .... Mar. 16, 1861–Nov. 1861
Charles West ....Nov. 1861–Sept. 1862
Robert J. Townes .... Sept. 1862–May 2, 1865
Charles R. Pryor............................May 2, 1865–Aug. 1865
James H. Bell ....Aug. 1865–Aug. 1866
John A. Green ....Aug. 1866–Aug. 1867
D. W. C. Phillips............................... Aug. 1867–Jan. 1870
J. P. Newcomb ....Jan. 1, 1870–Jan. 17, 1874
George Clark.............................Jan. 17, 1874–Jan. 27, 1874
A. W. DeBerry........................... Jan. 27, 1874–Dec. 1, 1876
Isham G. Searcy..........................Dec. 1, 1876–Jan. 23, 1879
J. D. Templeton.......................... Jan. 23, 1879–Jan. 22, 1881
T. H. Bowman........................... Jan. 22, 1881–Jan. 18, 1883

J. W. Baines .... Jan. 18, 1883–Jan. 21, 1887
John M. Moore .... Jan. 21, 1887–Jan. 22, 1891
George W. Smith .... Jan. 22, 1891–Jan. 17, 1895
Allison Mayfield .... Jan. 17, 1895–Jan. 5, 1897
J. W. Madden .... Jan. 5, 1897–Jan. 18, 1899
D. H. Hardy .... Jan. 18, 1899–Jan. 19, 1901
John G. Tod .... Jan. 19, 1901–Jan., 1903
J. R. Curl .... Jan. 1903–April 1905
O. K. Shannon .... April 1905–Jan. 1907
L. T. Dashiel .... Jan. 1907–Feb. 1908
W. R. Davie .... Feb. 1908–Jan. 1909
W. B. Townsend .... Jan. 1909–Jan. 1911
C. C. McDonald .... Jan. 1911–Dec. 1912
J. T. Bowman .... Dec. 1912–Jan. 1913
John L. Wortham .... Jan. 1913–June 1913
F. C. Weinert .... June 1913–Nov. 1914
D. A. Gregg .... Nov. 1914–Jan. 1915
John G. McKay .... Jan. 1915–Dec. 1916
C. J. Bartlett .... Dec. 1916–Nov. 1917
George F. Howard .... Nov. 1917–Nov. 1920
C. D. Mims .... Nov. 1920–Jan. 1921
S. L. Staples .... Jan. 1921–Aug. 1924
J. D. Strickland .... Sept. 1924–Jan. 1, 1925
Henry Hutchings .... Jan. 1, 1925–Jan. 20, 1925
Mrs. Emma G. Meharg .... Jan. 20, 1925–Jan. 1927
Mrs. Jane Y. McCallum .... Jan. 1927–Jan. 1933
W. W. Heath .... Jan. 1933–Jan. 1935
Gerald C. Mann .... Jan. 1935–Aug. 31, 1935
R. B. Stanford .... Aug. 31, 1935–Aug. 25, 1936
B. P. Matocha .... Aug. 25, 1936–Jan. 18, 1937
Edward Clark .... Jan. 18, 1937–Jan. 1939
Tom L. Beauchamp .... Jan. 1939–Oct. 1939
M. O. Flowers .... Oct. 26, 1939–Feb. 25, 1941
William J. Lawson .... Feb. 25, 1941–Jan. 1943
Sidney Latham .... Jan. 1943–Feb. 1945
Claude Isbell .... Feb. 1945–Jan. 1947
Paul H. Brown .... Jan. 1947–Jan. 19, 1949
Ben Ramsey .... Jan. 19, 1949–Feb. 9, 1950
John Ben Shepperd .... Feb. 9, 1950–April 30, 1952
Jack Ross .... April 30, 1952–Jan. 9, 1953
Howard A. Carney .... Jan. 9, 1953–Apr. 30, 1954
C. E. Fulgham .... May 1, 1954–Feb. 15, 1955
Al Muldrow .... Feb. 16, 1955–Nov. 1, 1955
Tom Reavley .... Nov. 1, 1955–Jan. 16, 1957
Zollie Steakley .... Jan. 16, 1957–Jan. 2, 1962
P. Frank Lake .... Jan. 2, 1962–Jan. 15, 1963
Crawford C. Martin .... Jan. 15, 1963–Mar. 12, 1966
John L. Hill .... Mar. 12, 1966–Jan. 22, 1968
Roy Barrera .... Mar. 7, 1968–Jan. 23, 1969
Martin Dies Jr. .... Jan. 23, 1969–Sept. 1, 1971
Robert D. (Bob) Bullock .... Sept. 1, 1971–Jan. 2, 1973
V. Larry Teaver Jr. .... Jan. 2, 1973–Jan. 19, 1973
Mark W. White Jr. .... Jan. 19, 1973–Oct. 27,1977
Steven C. Oaks .... Oct. 27, 1977–Jan. 16, 1979
George W. Strake Jr. .... Jan. 16, 1979–Oct. 6, 1981
David A. Dean .... Oct. 22, 1981–Jan. 18, 1983
John Fainter .... Jan. 18, 1983–July 31, 1984
Myra A. McDaniel .... Sept. 6, 1984–Jan. 26, 1987
Jack Rains .... Jan. 26, 1987–June 15, 1989
George Bayoud Jr. .... June 19, 1989–Jan. 15, 1991
John Hannah Jr. .... Jan. 17, 1991–Mar. 11, 1994
Ronald Kirk .... April 4, 1994–Jan. 10, 1995
Antonio O. "Tony" Garza Jr. .... Jan. 18, 1995–Dec. 2, 1997
Alberto R. Gonzales .... Dec. 2, 1997–Jan. 10, 1999
Elton Bomer .... Jan. 11, 1999–Dec. 31, 2000
Henry Cuellar .... Jan. 2, 2001–Oct. 5, 2001
Gwyn Shea .... Jan. 2, 2002–Aug. 4, 2003
Geoff Connor .... Sept. 26, 2003–Jan. 1, 2005
J. Roger Williams .... Jan. 1, 2005–July 1, 2007
Phil Wilson .... July 1, 2007–July 6, 2008

The Capitals of Texas

The capitals of the six nations that have ruled Texas have been:

Spain: Valladolid (before 1551) and Madrid

France: Paris

Mexico: Mexico City, D.F.

Republic Of Texas: San Felipe de Austin, Washington-on-the-Brazos, Harrisburg, Galveston Island, Velasco, Columbia, Houston, and Austin

United States: Washington, D.C.

Confederate States Of America: Montgomery, Alabama and Richmond, Virginia

Learn more at TexasAlmanac.com

Esperanza (Hope) Andrade .... July 23, 2008–Nov. 23,2012
John T. Steen Jr. .... Nov. 27, 2012–Jan. 7, 2014
Nandita Berry .... Jan. 7, 2014–Jan 21, 2015
Carlos H. Cascos .... Jan 21, 2015–Jan 5, 2017
Rolando B. Pablos .... Jan 5, 2017–Dec. 17, 2018
David Whitley .... Dec. 17, 2018–May 27, 2019
(Senate refused to confirm)
Ruth Ruggero Hughs .... Aug. 19, 2019–May 31, 2021
(Resigned)
John B. Scott .... Oct. 21,2021–Dec. 31, 2022
Jane Nelson .... Jan. 5, 2023–present

★ ★ ★ ★ ★ ★ ★

Attorneys General of the Republic

David Thomas and Peter W. Grayson .... Mar. 2–Oct. 22, 1836
J. Pinckney Henderson, Peter W. Grayson,
John Birdsall, and A.S. Thurston 1836–1838
J.C. Watrous .... Dec. 1838–June 1, 1840
Joseph Webb and F.A. Morris 1840–1841
George W. Terrell, Ebenezer Allen 1841–1844
Ebenezer Allen 1844–1846

State Attorneys General

Volney E. Howard (D) .... Feb. 21, 1846–May 7, 1846
John W. Harris (D) .... May 7, 1846–Oct. 31, 1849
Henry P. Brewster .... Oct. 31, 1849–Jan. 15, 1850
A. J. Hamilton .... Jan. 15, 1850–Aug. 5, 1850
(The first few attorneys general held office by appointment of the governor. The office was made elective in 1850 by constitutional amendment. Ebenezer Allen was the first elected attorney general.)
Ebenezer Allen .... Aug. 5, 1850–Aug. 2, 1852
Thomas J. Jennings .... Aug. 2, 1852–Aug. 4, 1856
James Willie .... Aug. 4, 1856–Aug. 2, 1858
Malcolm D. Graham (D) .... Aug. 2, 1858–Aug. 6, 1860
George M. Flournoy (D) .... Aug. 6, 1860–Jan. 15, 1862
N. G. Shelley (D) .... Feb. 3, 1862–Aug. 1, 1864
B. E. Tarver (D) .... Aug. 1, 1864–Dec. 11, 1865
Wm. Alexander (Unionist) .... Dec. 11, 1865–June 25, 1866
W. M. Walton (D) .... June 25, 1866–Aug. 27, 1867
Wm. Alexander (R) .... Aug. 27, 1867–Nov. 5, 1867
Ezekiel B. Turner (I) .... Nov. 5, 1867–July 11, 1870
Wm. Alexander (R) .... July 11, 1870–Jan. 27, 1874
George Clark (D) .... Jan. 27, 1874–Apr. 25, 1876
H. H. Boone (D) .... Apr. 25, 1876–Nov. 5, 1878
George McCormick .... Nov. 5, 1878–Nov. 2, 1880
J. H. McLeary (D) .... Nov. 2, 1880–Nov. 7, 1882
John D. Templeton (D) .... Nov. 7, 1882–Nov. 2, 1886
James S. Hogg (D) .... Nov. 2, 1886–Nov. 4, 1890

C. A. Culberson (D)....................Nov. 4, 1890–Nov. 6, 1894
M. M. Crane (D)....................Nov. 6, 1894–Nov. 8, 1898
Thomas S. Smith (D)....................Nov. 8, 1898–Mar. 15,1901
C. K. Bell (D)....................Mar. 20, 1901–Jan. 1904
R. V. Davidson (D)....................Jan. 1904–Dec. 31, 1909
Jewel P. Lightfoot (D)....................Jan. 1, 1910–Aug. 31, 1912
James D. Walthall (D)....................Sept. 1, 1912–Jan. 1, 1913
B. F. Looney (D)....................Jan. 1, 1913–Jan., 1919
C. M. Cureton (D)....................Jan. 1919–Dec. 1921
W. A. Keeling (D)....................Dec. 1921–Jan. 1925
Dan Moody (D)....................Jan. 1925–Jan. 1927
Claude Pollard (D)....................Jan. 1927–Sept. 1929
R. L. Bobbitt (D)....................Sept. 1929–Jan. 1931
(Appointed)
James V. Allred (D)....................Jan. 1931–Jan. 1935
William McCraw (D)....................Jan. 1935–Jan. 1939
Gerald C. Mann (D)....................Jan. 1939–Jan. 1944
(Resigned)
Grover Sellers (D)....................Jan. 1944–Jan. 1947
Price Daniel (D)....................Jan. 1947–Jan. 1953
John Ben Shepperd (D)....................Jan. 1953–Jan. 1, 1957
Will Wilson (D)....................Jan. 1, 1957–Jan. 15, 1963
Waggoner Carr (D)....................Jan. 15, 1963–Jan. 1, 1967
Crawford C. Martin (D)....................Jan. 1, 1967–Dec. 29, 1972
John Hill (D)....................Jan. 1, 1973–Jan. 16, 1979
Mark White (D)....................Jan. 16, 1979–Jan. 18, 1983
Jim Mattox (D)....................Jan. 18, 1983–Jan. 15, 1991
Dan Morales (D)....................Jan. 15, 1991–Jan. 13, 1999
John Cornyn (R)....................Jan. 13, 1999–Dec. 2, 2002
Greg Abbott (R)....................Dec. 2, 2002–Jan. 20, 2015
Ken Paxton (R)....................Jan. 20, 2015–present

★★★★★★★

Treasurers of the Republic

Asa Brigham....................1838–1840
James W. Simmons....................1840–1841
Asa Brigham....................1841–1844
Moses Johnson....................1844–1846

State Treasurers

James H. Raymond....................Feb. 24, 1846–Aug. 2, 1858
C.H. Randolph....................Aug. 2, 1858–June 1865
(Randolph fled to Mexico upon collapse of Confederacy. No exact date is available for his departure from office or for Harris' succession to the post. It is believed Harris took office Oct. 2, 1865.)
Samuel Harris....................Oct. 2, 1865–June 25, 1866
W.M. Royston....................June 25, 1866–Sept. 1, 1867
John T. Allan....................Sept. 1, 1867–Jan. 1869
George W. Honey....................Jan. 1869–Jan. 1874
(Honey was removed from office for a short period in 1872 and B. Graham served in his place.)
B. Graham *(short term)*....................beginning May 27, 1872
A. J. Dorn....................Jan. 1874–Jan. 1879
F. R. Lubbock....................Jan. 1879–Jan. 1891
W. B. Wortham....................Jan. 1891–Jan. 1899
John W. Robbins....................Jan. 1899–Jan. 1907
Sam Sparks....................Jan. 1907–Jan. 1912
J. M. Edwards....................Jan. 1912–Jan. 1919
John W. Baker....................Jan. 1919–Jan. 1921
G. N. Holton....................July 1921–Nov. 21, 1921
C. V. Terrell....................Nov. 21, 1921–Aug. 15, 1924
S. L. Staples....................Aug. 16, 1924–Jan. 15, 1925
W. Gregory Hatcher....................Jan. 16, 1925–Jan. 1, 1931
Charley Lockhart....................Jan. 1, 1931–Oct. 25, 1941
Jesse James....................Oct. 25, 1941–Sept. 29, 1977
Warren G. Harding....................Oct. 7, 1977–Jan. 3, 1983
Ann Richards....................Jan. 3, 1983–Jan. 2, 1991
Kay Bailey Hutchison....................Jan. 2, 1991–June 1993
Martha Whitehead....................June 1993–Aug. 1996

The office of treasurer was eliminated by constitutional amendment in an election Nov. 7, 1995, effective the last day of August 1996.

Railroad Commissioners

After the first three names in the following list, each commissioner's name is followed by a surname in parentheses. The name in parentheses is the name of the commissioner whom that commissioner succeeded.

John H. Reagan....................June 10, 1891–Jan. 20, 1903
L. L. Foster....................June 10, 1891–April 30, 1895
W. P. McLean....................June 10, 1891–Nov. 20, 1894
L. J. Storey (McLean)....................Nov. 21, 1894–Mar. 28,1909
N. A. Stedman (Foster)....................May 1, 1895–Jan. 4, 1897
Allison Mayfield (Stedman)....................Jan. 5, 1897–Jan. 23, 1923
O. B. Colquitt (Reagan)....................Jan. 21, 1903–Jan. 17, 1911
William D. Williams (Storey)....................April 28, 1909–Oct. 1, 1916
John L. Wortham (Colquitt)....................Jan. 21, 1911–Jan. 1, 1913
Earle B. Mayfield (Wortham)....................Jan. 2, 1913–Mar. 1, 1923
Charles Hurdleston (Williams)....................Oct. 10, 1916–Dec. 31,1918
Clarence Gilmore (Hurdleston)....................Jan. 1, 1919–Jan. 1, 1929
N. A. Nabors (A. Mayfield)....................Mar. 1, 1923–Jan. 18, 1925
William Splawn (E. Mayfield)....................Mar. 1, 1923–Aug. 1, 1924
C. V. Terrell (Splawn)....................Aug. 15, 1924–Jan. 1, 1939
Lon A. Smith (Nabors)....................Jan. 29, 1925–Jan. 1, 1941
Pat M. Neff (Gilmore)....................Jan. 1, 1929–Jan. 1, 1933
Ernest O. Thompson (Neff)....................Jan. 1, 1933–Jan. 8, 1965
G. A. (Jerry) Sadler (Terrell)....................Jan. 1, 1939–Jan. 1, 1943
Olin Culberson (Smith)....................Jan. 1, 1941–June 22, 1961
Beauford Jester (Sadler)....................Jan. 1, 1943–Jan. 21, 1947
William J. Murray Jr. (Jester)....................Jan. 21, 1947–Apr. 10, 1963
Ben Ramsey (Culberson)....................Sept. 18, 1961–Dec. 31, 1976
Jim C. Langdon (Murray)....................May 28, 1963–Dec. 31, 1977
Byron Tunnell (Thompson)....................Jan. 11, 1965–Sept. 15, 1973
Mack Wallace (Tunnell)....................Sept. 18, 1973–Sept. 22, 1987
Jon Newton (Ramsey)....................Jan. 10, 1977–Jan. 4, 1979
John H. Poerner (Langdon)....................Jan. 2, 1978–Jan. 1, 1981
James E. Nugent (Newton)....................Jan. 4, 1979–Jan. 3,1995
Buddy Temple (Poerner)....................Jan. 2, 1981–Mar. 2, 1986
Clark Jobe (Temple)....................Mar. 3, 1986–Jan. 5, 1987
John Sharp (Jobe)....................Jan. 6, 1987–Jan. 2, 1991
Kent Hance (Wallace)....................Sept. 23, 1987–Jan. 2, 1991
Robert Krueger (Hance)....................Jan. 3, 1991–Jan. 22, 1993
(Krueger resigned when Gov. Ann Richards appointed him interim U.S. senator on the resignation of Sen. Lloyd Bentsen.)
Lena Guerrero (Sharp)....................Jan. 23, 1991–Sept. 25, 1992
James Wallace (Guerrero)....................Oct. 2, 1992–Jan. 4, 1993
Barry Williamson (Wallace)....................Jan. 5, 1993–Jan. 4, 1999
Mary Scott Nabers (Krueger)....................Feb. 9, 1993–Dec. 9, 1994
Carole K. Rylander (Nabers)....................Dec. 10, 1994–Jan. 4, 1999
Charles Matthews (Nugent)....................Jan. 3, 1995–Jan. 31, 2005
Antonio Garza (Williamson)....................Jan. 4, 1999–Nov. 18, 2002
Michael Williams (Rylander)....................Jan. 4, 1999–Mar. 31, 2011
Victor G. Carrillo (Garza)....................Feb. 19, 2003–Jan. 3, 2011
Elizabeth A. Jones (Matthews)....................Feb. 2, 2005–Feb. 28, 2012
David Porter (Carrillo)....................Jan. 5, 2011–Jan. 2, 2017
Barry T. Smitherman (Williams)....................July 8, 2011–Jan. 2, 2015
Buddy Garcia (Jones)....................April 16, 2012–Dec. 7, 2012
(Appointed by Gov. Perry.)
Ryan Sitton (Smitherman)....................Jan 5, 2015–Jan. 4, 2021
Christi Craddick (Garcia)....................Dec. 17, 2012–present
Wayne Christian (Porter)....................Jan 9, 2017–present
Jim Wright (Sitton)....................Jan. 4, 2021–present

★ ★ ★ ★ ★ ★ ★

Comptrollers of Public Accounts For the Republic

John H. Money.........................Dec. 30, 1835–Jan. 17, 1836
H. C. Hudson............................Jan. 17, 1836–Oct. 22, 1836
Elisha M. Pease.................................June 1837–Dec. 1837
F. R. Lubbock.................................. Dec. 1837–Jan. 1839
Jas. W. Simmons........................Jan. 15, 1839–Sept. 30, 1840
Jas. B. Shaw............................Sept. 30, 1840–Dec. 24, 1841
F. R. Lubbock............................Dec. 24, 1841–Jan. 1, 1842
Jas. B. Shaw................................Jan. 1, 1842–Jan. 1, 1846

State Comptrollers of Public Accounts

Jas. B. Shaw..............................Feb. 24, 1846–Aug. 2, 1858
Clement R. Johns.........................Aug. 2, 1858–Aug. 1, 1864
Willis L. Robards........................Aug. 1, 1864–Oct. 12, 1865
Albert H. Latimer......................Oct. 12, 1865–Mar. 27, 1866
Robert H. Taylor...................... Mar. 27, 1866–June 25, 1866
Willis L. Robards......................June 25, 1866–Aug. 27, 1867
Morgan C. Hamilton...................Aug. 27, 1867–Jan. 8, 1870
A. Bledsoe................................Jan. 8, 1870–Jan. 20, 1874
Stephen H. Darden......................Jan. 20, 1874–Nov. 2, 1880
W. M. Brown........................... Nov. 2, 1880–Jan. 16, 1883
W. J. Swain.............................. Jan. 16, 1883–Jan. 18, 1887
John D. McCall......................... Jan. 18, 1887–Jan. 15, 1895
R. W. Finley............................. Jan. 15, 1895–Jan. 15, 1901
R. M. Love.................................Jan. 15, 1901–Jan. 1903
J. W. Stephen....................................Jan. 1903–Jan. 1911
W. P. Lane....................................... Jan. 1911–Jan. 1915
H. B. Terrell.....................................Jan. 1915–Jan. 1920
M. L. Wiginton..................................Jan. 1920–Jan. 1921
Lon A. Smith....................................Jan. 1921–Jan. 1925
S. H. Terrell.....................................Jan. 1925–Jan. 1931
Geo. H. Sheppard..........................Jan., 1931–Jan. 17, 1949
Robert S. Calvert...........................Jan. 17, 1949–Jan., 1975
Robert D. (Bob) Bullock......................Jan. 1975–Jan. 3, 1991
John Sharp................................Jan. 3, 1991–Jan. 2, 1999
Carole Keeton Strayhorn.................Jan. 2, 1999–Jan. 1, 2007
Susan Combs..............................Jan. 1, 2007–Jan. 1, 2015
Glenn Hegar.................................. Jan. 2, 2015–present

★ ★ ★ ★ ★ ★ ★

U.S. Senators from Texas

U.S. Senators were selected by the legislatures of the states until the U.S. Constitution was amended in 1913 to require popular elections. In Texas, the first Senator chosen by the voters in a general election was Charles A. Culberson in 1916. Because of political pressures, however, the rules of the Democratic Party of Texas were changed in 1904 to require that all candidates for office stand before voters in the primary. Consequently, Texas' Senators faced voters in 1906, 1910 and 1912 before the U.S. Constitution was changed.

Following is the succession of Texas representatives in the United States Senate since the annexation of Texas to the Union in 1845:

Houston Succession

Sam Houston (I)........................Feb. 21, 1846–Mar. 4, 1859
John Hemphill (D).......................Mar. 4, 1859–July 11, 1861
Louis T. Wigfall and W. S. Oldham took their seats in the Confederate Senate, Nov. 16, 1861, and served until the Confederacy collapsed. After that event, the State Legislature on Aug. 21, 1866, elected David G. Burnet and Oran M. Roberts to the U.S. Senate, anticipating immediate readmission to the Union, but they were not allowed to take their seats.
Morgan C. Hamilton (R)..............Feb. 22, 1870–Mar. 3, 1877
Richard Coke (D)........................Mar. 4, 1877–Mar. 3, 1895
Horace Chilton (D).....................Mar. 3, 1895–Mar. 3, 1901
Joseph W. Bailey (D)....................Mar. 3, 1901–Jan. 8, 1913
(Resigned.)
Rienzi Melville Johnston (D).............Jan. 8, 1913–Feb. 3, 1913
(Appointed to fill vacancy.)
Morris Sheppard (D)....................Feb. 13, 1913–Apr. 9, 1941
(Died in office)
Andrew J. Houston (D)............................June 2–26, 1941
(Appointed to fill vacancy; died in office.)
W. Lee O'Daniel (D)....................Aug. 4, 1941–Jan. 3, 1949
Lyndon B. Johnson (D)..................Jan. 3, 1949–Jan. 20, 1961
(Resigned to become U.S. vice president.)
William A. Blakley (D).................Jan. 20, 1961–June 15, 1961
(Appointed to fill vacancy.)
John G. Tower (R).......................June 15, 1961–Jan. 21, 1985
Phil Gramm (R).........................Jan. 21, 1985–Dec. 2, 2002
John Cornyn (R)............................ Dec. 2, 2002–present

Rusk Succession

Thomas J. Rusk (D).................... Feb 21, 1846–July 29, 1857
(Died in office.)
J. Pinckney Henderson (D)............. Nov. 9, 1857–June 4, 1858
(Died in office.)
Matthias Ward (D).....................Sept. 29, 1858–Dec. 5, 1859
(Appointed to fill vacancy.)
Louis T. Wigfall (D)....................Dec. 5, 1859–Mar. 23, 1861
(Succession was broken by secession. See note above under Houston Succession.)
James W. Flanagan (R).................Feb. 22, 1870–Mar. 3, 1875
Samuel B. Maxey (D)....................Mar. 3, 1875–Mar. 3, 1887
John H. Reagan (D)....................Mar. 3, 1887–June 10, 1891
(Resigned to head Texas Railroad Commission.)
Horace Chilton (D).....................Dec. 7, 1891–Mar. 30,1892
(Appointed to fill vacancy.)
Roger Q. Mills (D)..................... Mar. 30, 1892–Mar. 3, 1899
Charles A. Culberson (D)...............Mar. 3, 1899–Mar. 4, 1923
Earle B. Mayfield (D)...................Mar. 4, 1923–Mar. 4, 1929
Tom Connally (D)........................Mar. 4, 1929–Jan. 3, 1953
Price Daniel (D)..........................Jan. 3, 1953–Jan. 15, 1957
(Resigned to become governor.)
William A. Blakley (D)................. Jan. 15, 1957–Apr. 27, 1957
(Appointed to fill vacancy.)
Ralph W. Yarborough (D).............Apr. 27, 1957–Jan. 12, 1971
Lloyd Bentsen (D)......................Jan. 12, 1971–Jan. 20, 1993
(Resigned to become U.S. Secretary of Treasury.)
Robert Krueger (D)...................Jan. 20, 1993–June 14, 1993
(Appointed to fill vacancy.)
Kay Bailey Hutchison (R)............. June 14, 1993–Jan. 20, 2013
Ted Cruz (R)................................Jan. 20, 2013–present

★ ★ ★ ★ ★ ★ ★

General Land Office Commissioners For the Republic

John P. Borden........................ Aug. 23, 1837–Dec. 12, 1840
H. W. Raglin........................... Dec. 12, 1840–Jan. 4, 1841
Thomas William Ward................ Jan. 4, 1841–Mar. 20, 1848
(Part of term after annexation.)

State Land Commissioners

George W. Smyth.......................Mar. 20, 1848–Aug. 4, 1851
Stephen Crosby......................... Aug. 4, 1851–Mar. 1, 1858
Francis M. White........................Mar. 1, 1858–Mar. 1, 1862
Stephen Crosby..........................Mar. 1, 1862–Sept. 1, 1865

House Speaker Dade Phelan recording a vote in the Texas House of Representatives. Photo by Evan L'Roy for the Texas Tribune

Francis M. White........................Sept. 1, 1865–Aug. 7, 1866
Stephen Crosby........................Aug. 7, 1866–Aug. 27, 1867
Joseph Spence........................Aug. 27, 1867–Jan. 19, 1870
Jacob Kuechler........................Jan. 19, 1870–Jan. 20, 1874
J. J. Groos........................Jan. 20, 1874–June 15, 1878
W. C. Walsh........................July 30, 1878–Jan. 10, 1887
R. M. Hall........................Jan. 10, 1887–Jan. 16, 1891
W. L. McGaughey........................Jan. 16, 1891–Jan. 26, 1895
A. J. Baker........................Jan. 26, 1895–Jan. 16, 1899
George W. Finger........................Jan. 16, 1899–May 4, 1899
Charles Rogan........................May 11, 1899–Jan. 10, 1903
John J. Terrell........................Jan. 10, 1903–Jan. 11, 1909
J. T. Robison........................Jan, 1909–Sept. 11, 1929
J. H. Walker........................Sept. 11, 1929–Jan., 1937
William H. McDonald........................Jan 1937–Jan. 1939
Bascom Giles........................Jan. 1939–Jan. 5, 1955
J. Earl Rudder........................Jan. 5, 1955–Feb. 1, 1958
Bill Allcorn........................Feb. 1, 1958–Jan. 1, 1961
Jerry Sadler........................Jan. 1, 1961–Jan. 1, 1971
Bob Armstrong........................Jan. 1, 1971–Jan. 1, 1983
Garry Mauro........................Jan. 1, 1983–Jan. 7, 1999
David Dewhurst........................Jan. 7, 1999–Jan. 3, 2003
Jerry Patterson........................Jan. 3, 2003–Jan. 2, 2015
George P. Bush........................Jan. 2, 2015–Jan. 10, 2023
Dawn Buckingham........................Jan. 10, 2023–present

★ ★ ★ ★ ★ ★ ★

Speakers of the House For the Republic

Speaker	Term	Congress
Ira Ingram	1836–37	1st
Branch Tanner Archer	1837	2nd
Joseph Rowe	1838	2nd
John M. Hansford	1838–39	3rd
David Spangler Kaufman	1840–41	4th, 5th
Kenneth L. Anderson	1841–42	6th
Nicholas H. Darnell	1842–43	7th
Richardson A. Scurry	1843–44	8th
John M. Lewis	1844–45	9th

State Speakers of the House

Speaker, Residence	Term	Leg.
William E. Crump (D), Bellville	1846	1st
John Brown (D), Brownsboro	1846	1st
Edward T. Branch (D), Liberty	1846	1st
William H. Bourland (D), Paris	1846	1st
Stephen W. Perkins (D), Columbia	1846	1st
James W. Henderson (D), Houston	1847–48	2nd
Charles G. Keenan (D), Huntsville	1849–51	3rd
David C. Dickson (D), Anderson	1851–53	4th
Hardin R. Runnels (D), Boston	1853–55	5th
Hamilton P. Bee (D), Laredo	1855–57	6th
William S. Taylor (D), Larissa	1857–58	7th
Matt F. Locke (D), Lafayette	1858–59	7th
Marion DeKalb Taylor (D), Jefferson	1859–61	8th
Constantine W. Buckley (D), Richmond	1861	9th
Nicholas H. Darnell (D), Dallas	1861–62	9th
Constantine W. Buckley (D), Richmond	1863	9th
Marion DeKalb Taylor (D), Jefferson	1863–65	10th
Nathaniel M. Burford (Unionist), Dallas	1866	11th
(Vacant under Congressional Reconstruction and military administration, 1867-1870)		
Ira H. Evans (R), Corpus Christi	1870–71	12th
William H. Sinclair (R), Galveston	1871–73	12th
Marion DeKalb Taylor (D), Jefferson	1873–74	13th
Guy M. Bryan (D), Galveston	1874–76	14th
Thomas R. Bonner (D), Tyler	1876–79	15th
John H. Cochran (D), Dallas	1879–81	16th
George R. Reeves (D), Pottsboro	1881–83	17th
Charles R. Gibson (D), Waxahachie	1883–85	18th
Lafayette L. Foster (D), Groesbeck	1885–87	19th
George C. Pendleton (D), Belton	1887–89	20th
Frank P. Alexander (D), Greenville	1889–91	21st
Robert T. Milner (D), Henderson	1891–93	22nd
John H. Cochran (D), Dallas	1893–95	23rd
Thomas Slater Smith (D), Hillsboro	1895–97	24th

Speaker, Residence	Term	Leg.
L. Travis Dashiell (D), Jewett	1897–99	25th
J. S. Sherrill (D), Greenville	1899–1901	26th
Robert E. Prince (D), Corsicana	1901–03	27th
Pat M. Neff (D), Waco	1903–05	28th
Francis W. Seabury (D), Rio Grande City	1905–07	29th
Thomas B. Love (D), Lancaster	1907–09	30th
Austin M. Kennedy (D), Waco	1909	31st
(Resigned during 31st session)		
John W. Marshall (D), Whitesboro	1909–11	31st
Sam Rayburn (D), Bonham	1911–13	32nd
Chester H. Terrell (D), San Antonio	1913–15	33rd
John W. Woods (D), Rotan	1915–17	34th
Franklin O. Fuller (D), Coldspring	1917–19	35th
R. Ewing Thomason (D), El Paso	1919–21	36th
Charles G. Thomas (D), Lewisville	1921–23	37th
Richard E. Seagler (D), Palestine	1923–25	38th
R. Lee Satterwhite (D), Amarillo	1925–27	39th
Robert L. Bobbitt (D), Laredo	1927–29	40th
W. S. Barron (D), Bryan	1929–31	41st
Fred H. Minor (D), Denton	1931–33	42nd
Coke R. Stevenson (D), Junction	1933–37	43rd–44th
Robert W. Calvert (D), Hillsboro	1937–39	45th
R. Emmett Morse (D), Houston	1939–41	46th
Homer L. Leonard (D), McAllen	1941–43	47th
Price Daniel (D), Liberty	1943–45	48th
Claud H. Gilmer (D), Rocksprings	1945–47	49th
William O. Reed (D), Dallas	1947–49	50th
Durwood Manford (D), Smiley	1949–51	51st
Reuben Senterfitt (D), San Saba	1951–55	52nd–53rd
Jim T. Lindsey (D), Texarkana	1955–57	54th
Waggoner Carr (D), Lubbock	1957–61	55th–56th
James A. Turman (D), Gober	1961–63	57th
Byron M. Tunnell (D), Tyler	1963–65	58th
Ben Barnes (D), De Leon	1965–69	59th–60th
Gus F. Mutscher (D), Brenham	1969–72	61st–62nd
(Resigned during 62nd session)		
Rayford Price (D), Palestine	1972–73	62nd
Price Daniel Jr. (D), Liberty	1973–75	63rd
Bill Clayton (D), Springlake	1975–83	64th–67th
Gib Lewis (D), Fort Worth	1983–93	68th–72nd
Pete Laney (D), Hale Center	1993–2003	73rd–77th
Tom Craddick (R), Midland	2003–09	78th–80th
Joe Straus (R), San Antonio	2009–19	81st–85th
Dennis Bonnen (R), Angleton	2019–21	86th
Dade Phelan (R), Beaumont	2021–present	87th

★ ★ ★ ★ ★ ★ ★

Chief Justice of the Supreme Court Republic of Texas

James Collinsworth.................... Dec. 16, 1836–July 23, 1838

John Birdsall ....Nov. 19–Dec. 12, 1838

(Senate refused to confirm)

Thomas J. Rusk..........................Dec. 12, 1838–Dec. 5, 1840

John Hemphill ....Dec. 5, 1840–Dec. 29, 1845

Under Constitutions of 1845 and 1861

John Hemphill ....Mar. 2, 1846–Oct. 10, 1858
Royall T. Wheeler..........................Oct. 11, 1858–April 1864
Oran M. Roberts.........................Nov. 1, 1864–June 30, 1866

Under Constitution of 1866 (Presidential Reconstruction)

George F. Moore ....Aug. 16, 1866–Sept. 10, 1867
(Removed under Congressional Reconstruction by military authorities who appointed members of the next court.)

Under Constitution of 1866 (Congressional Reconstruction)

Amos Morrill.............................Sept. 10, 1867–July 5, 1870

Under Constitution of 1869

Lemuel D. Evans ....July 5, 1870–Aug. 31, 1873
Wesley Ogden...........................Aug. 31, 1873–Jan. 29, 1874
Oran M. Roberts......................... Jan. 29, 1874–Apr. 18, 1876

Under Constitution of 1876

Oran M. Roberts..........................Apr. 18, 1876–Oct. 1, 1878
George F. Moore .... Nov. 5, 1878–Nov. 1, 1881
Robert S. Gould..........................Nov. 1, 1881–Dec. 23, 1882
Asa H. Willie ....Dec. 23, 1882–Mar. 3, 1888
John W. Stayton ....Mar. 3, 1888–July 5, 1894
Reuben R. Gaines..........................July 10, 1894–Jan. 5, 1911
Thomas J. Brown.......................... Jan. 7, 1911–May 26, 1915
Nelson Phillips...........................June 1, 1915–Nov. 16, 1921
C. M. Cureton.............................Dec. 2, 1921–Apr. 8, 1940
Hortense Sparks Ward...................Jan. 8, 1925–May 23, 1925
(Mrs. Ward headed a special Supreme Court to hear one case in 1925.)
W. F. Moore .... Apr. 17, 1940–Jan. 1, 1941
James P. Alexander.......................... Jan. 1, 1941–Jan. 1, 1948
J. E. Hickman...............................Jan. 5, 1948–Jan. 3, 1961
Robert W. Calvert......................... Jan. 3, 1961–Oct. 4, 1972
Joe R. Greenhill .... Oct. 4, 1972–Oct. 25, 1982
Jack Pope ....Nov. 29, 1982–Jan. 5, 1985
John L. Hill Jr...............................Jan. 5, 1985–Jan. 4, 1988
Thomas R. Phillips........................Jan. 4, 1988–Sept. 3 2004
Wallace B. Jefferson.....................Sept. 14, 2004–Oct. 1, 2013
Nathan L. Hecht..............................Oct. 1, 2013–present

★ ★ ★ ★ ★ ★ ★

Presiding Judges, Court of Appeals (1876–1891) and Court of Criminal Appeals (1891–present)

Mat D. Ector............................ May 6, 1876–Oct. 29, 1879
John P. White........................... Nov. 9, 1879–Apr. 26, 1892
James M. Hurt........................... May 4, 1892–Dec. 31, 1898
W. L. Davidson..........................Jan. 2, 1899–June 27, 1913
A. C. Prendergast.......................June 27, 1913–Dec. 31, 1916
W. L. Davidson............................Jan. 1, 1917–Jan. 25, 1921
Wright C. Morrow.......................Feb. 8, 1921–Oct. 16, 1939
Frank Lee Hawkins...................... Oct. 16, 1939–Jan. 2, 1951
Harry N. Graves..........................Jan. 2, 1951–Dec. 31, 1954
W. A. Morrison............................ Jan. 1, 1955–Jan. 2, 1961
Kenneth K. Woodley....................... Jan. 3, 1961–Jan. 4, 1965
W. T. McDonald..........................Jan. 4, 1965–June 25, 1966
W. A. Morrison...........................June 25, 1966–Jan. 1, 1967
Kenneth K. Woodley....................... Jan. 1, 1967–Jan. 1, 1971

John F. Onion Jr. .... Jan. 1, 1971–Jan. 1, 1989
Michael J. McCormick .... Jan. 1, 1989–Jan. 1, 2001
Sharon Keller .... Jan. 1, 2001–present

★ ★ ★ ★ ★ ★ ★

Administrators of Public Education, Superintendents of Public Instruction

Pryor Lea .... Nov. 10, 1866–Sept. 12, 1867
Edwin M. Wheelock .... Sept. 12, 1867–May 6, 1871
Jacob C. DeGress .... May 6, 1871–Jan. 20, 1874
O. H. Hollingsworth .... Jan. 20, 1874–May 6, 1884
B. M. Baker .... May 6, 1884–Jan. 18, 1887
O. H. Cooper .... Jan 18, 1887–Sept. 1, 1890
H. C. Pritchett .... Sept. 1, 1890–Sept. 15, 1891
J. M. Carlisle .... Sept. 15, 1891–Jan. 10, 1899
J. S. Kendall .... Jan. 10, 1899–July 2, 1901
Arthur Lefevre .... July 2, 1901–Jan. 12, 1905
R. B. Cousins .... Jan. 12, 1905–Jan. 1, 1910
F. M. Bralley .... Jan. 1, 1910–Sept. 1, 1913
W. F. Doughty .... Sept. 1, 1913–Jan. 1, 1919
Annie Webb Blanton .... Jan. 1, 1919–Jan. 16, 1923
S. M. N. Marrs .... Jan. 16, 1923–April 28, 1932
C. N. Shaver .... April 28, 1932–Oct. 1, 1932
L. W. Rogers .... Oct. 1, 1932–Jan. 16, 1933
L. A. Woods .... Jan. 16, 1933–1951

The office of State Superintendent of Public Instruction was abolished by the **Gilmer-Aikin Laws of 1949** and the office of Commissioner of Education was created. The Commissioner is appointed by the State Board of Education, (also created by the Gilmer-Aikin Laws) the members of which are elected by the people.

State Commissioners of Education

J. W. Edgar .... May 31, 1951–June 30, 1974
Marlin L. Brockette .... July 1, 1974–Sept. 1, 1979
Alton O. Bowen .... Sept. 1, 1979–June 1, 1981
Raymon Bynum .... June 1, 1981–Oct. 31, 1984
W. N. Kirby .... April 13, 1985–July 1, 1991
Lionel R. Meno .... July 1, 1991–Mar. 1, 1995
Michael A. Moses .... Mar. 9, 1995–Aug. 18, 1999
Jim Nelson .... Aug. 18, 1999–Mar. 25, 2002
Felipe Alanis .... Mar. 25, 2002–July 31, 2003
Shirley J. Neeley .... Jan. 12, 2004–July 1, 2007
Robert Scott .... July 1, 2007–July 2, 2012
Michael Williams .... Sept. 1, 2012–Dec. 31, 2015
Mike Morath .... Jan. 4, 2016–present

★ ★ ★ ★ ★ ★ ★

State Commissioners of Agriculture

Robert Teague Milner 1907–1908
Edward Reeves Kone 1908–1914
Fred Davis 1915–1920
George B. Terrell 1921–1930
James E. McDonald 1931–1950
John C. White 1951–1977
Reagan V. Brown 1977–1982
Jim Hightower 1983–1990
Rick Perry 1991–1998
Susan Combs 1999–2006
Todd Staples 2007–2015
Sid Miller 2015–present

Cecilia Abbott.

Photo courtesy of the Office of the First Lady.

First Ladies of Texas

Martha Evans Gindratt Wood 1847–1849
Bell Administration 1849–1853
(Gov. Peter Hansbrough Bell was not married while in office.)
Lucadia Christiana Niles Pease 1853–57; 1867–69
Runnels Administration 1857–1859
(Gov. Hardin R. Runnels never married.)
Margaret Moffette Lea Houston 1859–1861
Martha Evans Clark 1861
Adele Barron Lubbock 1861–1863
Susie Ellen Taylor Murrah 1863–1865
Mary Jane Bowen Hamilton 1865–1866
Annie Rattan Throckmorton 1866–1867
Ann Elizabeth Britton Davis 1870–1874
Mary Home Coke 1874–1876
Janie Roberts Hubbard 1876–1879
Frances Wickliff Edwards Roberts 1879–1883
Anne Maria Penn Ireland 1883–1887
Elizabeth Dorothy Tinsley Ross 1887–1891
Sarah Stinson Hogg 1891–1895
Sally Harrison Culberson 1895–1899
Orlene Walton Sayers 1899–1903
Sarah Beona Meng Lanham 1903–1907
Fannie Brunner Campbell 1907–1911
Alice Fuller Murrell Colquitt 1911–1915
Miriam A. Wallace Ferguson 1915–1917
(Miriam A. Wallace Ferguson was Mistress of the Mansion while her husband, James E. Ferguson, was governor, 1915–1917. She served as both Governor and Mistress of the Mansion, 1925–1927 and 1933–1935.)
Willie Cooper Hobby 1917–1921
Myrtle Mainer Neff 1921–1925
Mildred Paxton Moody 1927–1931
Maud Gage Sterling 1931–1933
Jo Betsy Miller Allred 1935–1939
Merle Estella Butcher O'Daniel 1939–1941
Fay Wright Stevenson 1941–1942
(Died in the Governor's Mansion on Jan. 3, 1942.)
Edith Will Scott Stevenson 1942–1946
(Mother of Gov. Coke R. Stevenson and Mistress of the Mansion upon the death of the governor's wife.)
Mabel Buchanan Jester 1946–1949
Marialice Shary Shivers 1949–1957
Jean Houston Baldwin Daniel 1957–1963
Idanell Brill Connally 1963–1969
Ima Mae Smith 1969–1973
Betty Jane Slaughter Briscoe 1973–1979
Rita Crocker Bass Clements 1979–1983
Linda Gale Thompson White 1983–1987
Rita Crocker Bass Clements 1987–1991
Richards Administration 1991–1995
(Gov. Ann Richards was not married while in office.)
Laura Welch Bush 1995–2000
Anita Thigpen Perry 2000–2015
Cecilia Abbott 2015–present

State Government

Texas state government is divided into executive, legislative, and judicial branches under the Texas Constitution adopted in 1876.

The chief executive is the Governor, whose term is for four years. Other elected state officials with executive responsibilities include the Lieutenant Governor, Attorney General, Comptroller of Public Accounts, Commissioner of the General Land Office, and Commissioner of Agriculture. The terms of those officials are also four years.

The Secretary of State and the Commissioner of Education are appointed by the Governor.

Except for making numerous appointments and calling special sessions of the Legislature, the Governor's powers are limited in comparison with those in most states.

The Governor's office welcomes comments and concerns, which are relayed to government officials who may offer assistance. **Send a message through the webform at:**

https://gov.texas.gov/contact

Or call the **Citizen's Opinion Hotline:**

1 (800) 843-5789

Government Financials

Taxes are the state government's primary source of income. On this and the following pages are summaries of state revenues and expenditures, tax collections, tax revenue by type of tax, a summary of the state budgets for the 2020–2021 and 2022–2023 bienniums, Texas Lottery income and expenditures, and the amount of federal payments to state agencies. **Totals may not sum due to rounding.**

Notable figures from the table below: "Sales of Goods and Services" increased by 102.1% in 2021. "Federal Income" increased 77.7% to $103.3 billion in 2021 from $58.1 billion in 2020. "Land Income" increased by 100.6% in 2022.

State Revenues by Source and Expenditures by Function, Total of All Funds
Amounts (in $ Millions) and Percent Change from Previous Year

Revenues by Source	2022	%	2021	%	2020	%	2019	%	2018	%
Tax Collections	79,978	25.9	63,538	10.7	57,380	–3.4	59,381	6.8	55,585	12.0
Federal Income	73,482	–28.8	103,251	77.7	58,117	38.7	41,904	5.8	39,618	3.3
Licenses, Fees, Permits, Fines, and Penalties	6,829	5.2	6,492	4.0	6,241	–4.6	6,542	1.0	6,477	3.5
State Health Service Fees and Rebates	10,763	48.6	7,242	–3.4	7,497	5.8	7,088	–6.7	7,599	13.4
Net Lottery Proceeds	3,058	3.5	2,955	23.5	2,392	–4.7	2,510	12.6	2,229	8.5
Land Income	4,319	100.6	2,153	19.0	1,809	–19.6	2,251	9.2	2,061	21.6
Interest and Investment Income	2,660	22.0	2,181	–13.8	2,529	1.0	2,504	35.4	1,849	9.3
Settlements of Claims	742	–3.1	766	22.7	624	–3.4	647	18.8	544	3.2
Escheated Estates	1,012	27.7	793	10.8	715	3.2	693	9.0	636	–35
Sales of Goods and Services	468	–9.2	515	102.1	255	–8.6	279	–2.2	285	–7.5
Other Revenues	21,649	–0.8	21,816	443.2	4,016	–3.0	4,142	26.2	3,282	10.4
Total Net Revenues	**204,960**	**–3.2**	**211,701**	**49.5**	**141,576**	**10.7**	**127,941**	**6.5**	**120,166**	**8.1**
Expenditures by Function	**2022**	**%**	**2021**	**%**	**2020**	**%**	**2019**	**%**	**2018**	**%**
General Government	11,178	9.4	10,215	63.6	3,714	5.4	3,522	4.1	3,384	3.2
Education	49,662	10.3	45,025	4.8	42,869	13.9	37,653	2.4	36,783	3.6
Employee Benefits	10,537	8.0	9,756	49.0	4,972	0.2	4,961	4.2	4,760	0.1
Health and Human Services	76,678	–17.6	93,045	38.5	57,197	10.3	51,873	2.9	50,421	2.7
Public Safety and Corrections	5,998	25.4	4,782	–2.0	4,877	–6.1	5,193	–3.4	5,375	9.1
Transportation	12,506	–3.1	12,900	2.0	12,647	20.5	10,494	5.5	9,952	–3
Natural Resources/Recreational Services	4,148	10.2	3,766	17.2	3,116	10.8	2,812	2.4	2,746	34.2
Regulatory Agencies	370	3.6	357	7.4	331	–1.5	336	7.5	312	–10.7
Lottery Winnings Paid*	752	–1.9	767	29.4	541	–20.9	684	9.0	628	12.7
Debt Service – Interest	1,105	–20.6	1,392	–19.3	1,661	1.0	1,645	3.3	1,593	26.8
Capital Outlay	1,546	14.5	1,350	11.7	1,192	40.2	851	42.1	599	–2.4
Total Net Expenditures	**174,481**	**–4.8**	**183,355**	**27.4**	**133,118**	**10.9**	**120,025**	**3.0**	**116,554**	**3.5**

* Does not include payments made by retailers.

All amounts rounded. Revenue and expenditures exclude trust funds. Fiscal years end August 31.

Source: 2021 State of Texas Annual Cash Report and 2022 State of Texas Annual Cash Report, Comptroller of Public Accounts.

Governor Greg Abbott
P.O. Box 12428
Austin 78711
(512) 463-2000
gov.texas.gov/
Salary: $153,750

Lt. Governor Dan Patrick
P.O. Box 12068
Austin 78711
(512) 463-0001
www.ltgov.texas.gov/
Salary: Same as Senator when serving as President of the Senate, same as Governor when serving as Governor.

Attorney General
Ken Paxton
P.O. Box 12548
Austin 78711
(512) 463-2100
www.texasattorneygeneral.gov/
Salary: $153,750

Comptroller of Public Accounts
Glenn Hegar
P.O. Box 13528
Austin 78711
(512) 463-4600
comptroller.texas.gov/
Salary: $153,750

Texas Land Commissioner
Dawn Buckingham, M.D.
P.O. Box 12873
Austin 78711
(512) 463-5256
www.glo.texas.gov
Salary: $140,938

Agriculture Commissioner
Sidney C. Miller
P.O. Box 12847
Austin 78711
(512) 463-7476
www.texasagriculture.gov
Salary: $140,938

Secretary of State
Jane Nelson
P.O. Box 12697
Austin 78711
(512) 463-5770
www.sos.state.tx.us
Salary: $197,415

Education Commissioner
Michael H. Morath
1701 N. Congress Ave.
Austin 78701
(512) 463-8985
tea.texas.gov/
Salary: $220,375

State Government Budget Summary, 2024–2025 Biennium

Source: Legislative Budget Board; www.lbb.state.tx.us.

The Legislative Budget Board's (LBB) baseline appropriations for state government operations for the 2024–2025 biennium total $321.3 billion from All Funds functions of state government. The funding is a $18.0 billion, or 6.0%, increase from the 2022–2023 biennial level of $303.3 billion.

General Revenue Funds, including funds dedicated within the General Revenue Fund, total $144.1 billion for the 2024–2025 biennium, an increase of $13.7 billion, or 10.5%, from the adjusted 2022–2023 biennial spending level of $130.4 billion. The table below details the difference in spending by article.

General Revenue Funds, by Article

Article (Governmental Division)	Estimated/ Budgeted 2022–2023	2024–2025 Budget	Biennial Change	Percentage Change
Art. I: General Government	$ 10,845.8	$ 9,334.1	– $ 1,511.7	–13.9%
Art. II: Health and Human Services	39,015.2	42,862.1	3,846.9	9.9%
Art. III: Agencies of Education	62,752.0	72,006.6	9,254.6	14.8%
Public Education	41,454.6	50,402.9	8,948.3	21.6%
Higher Education	21,297.4	21,603.7	306.3	1.4%
Art. IV: The Judiciary	597.7	860.3	262.6	43.9%
Art. V: Public Safety & Criminal Justice	12,645.8	13,364.7	718.9	5.7%
Art. VI: Natural Resources	3,294.4	3,486.4	192.0	5.8%
Art. VII: Business & Economic Dev.	508.1	1,292.5	784.4	154.4%
Art. VIII: Regulatory	311.2	434.1	122.9	39.5%
Art. IX: General Provisions	—	—	—	—
Art. X: The Legislature	433.4	489.6	56.2	13.0%
Total, All Articles	**$ 130,403.6**	**$ 144,130.4**	**$ 13,726.8**	**10.5%**

Totals may not sum due to rounding. All dollar figures in millions.

Source: Summary of Conference Committee Report on House Bill 1: Highlights of the Appropriations for the 2024–25 Biennium, May 2023

State Tax Collections 2002–2022

FY	State Tax Collections (in millions)	Resident Population	Per Capita Tax Collections	Taxes as % of Personal Income
2022	$ 77,210.7	29,805,197	$ 2,088	4.3%
2021	61,473.5	29,484,994	2,591	4.0%
2020	57,379.8	29,293,475	1,959	3.6%
2019	59,380.7	28,950,175	2,051	4.1%
2018	55,584.8	28,668,600	1,939	4.0%
2017	49,643.4	28,255,300	1,757	3.8%
2016	48,476.2	27,845,500	1,741	3.8%
2015	51,683.1	27,389,200	1,887	4.0%
2014	50,992.6	26,788,600	1,896	4.3%
2013	47,781.0	26,399,510	1,810	4.2%
2012	44,079.1	26,005,770	1,695	4.0%
2011	38,856.2	25,592,790	1,518	3.8%
2010	35,368.9	25,191,450	1,404	3.7%
2009	37,822.5	24,737,000	1,529	4.1%
2008	41,357.9	24,250,000	1,705	4.3%
2007	36,955.6	23,778,000	1,554	4.3%
2006	33,544.5	23,339,000	1,437	4.1%
2005	29,838.3	22,808,000	1,308	4.0%
2004	27,913.0	22,409,000	1,246	4.1%
2003	26,126.7	22,052,000	1,185	4.1%
2002	$ 26,279.1	21,673,000	$ 1,213	4.2%

Sources: 2022 State of Texas Annual Cash Report; historic data collected from older reports.

Tax Revenues, 2021–2022

Type of Tax	FY 2021	Change	FY 2022	Change
Sales	$ 31,019.6	5.6%	$ 42,971.9	19.3%
Motor Vehicle Sales/ Rentals*	5,730.9	19.0%	6,449.1	12.5%
Motor Fuels	3,596.9	2.0%	3,783.9	5.2%
Franchise	4,529.8	2.5%	5,672.9	25.2%
Oil Production	3,449.1	6.8%	6,361.7	84.4%
Insurance	2,699.6	–1.5%	3,121.9	15.6%
Cigarette & Tobacco	1,397.3	7.6%	1,210.7	-13.4%
Natural Gas Production	1,568.5	69.5%	4,469.9	185%
Alcoholic Beverages	1,257.4	11.7%	1,644.0	30.7%
Hotel	487.8	3.6%	699.9	43.5%
Utility	538.8	12.7%	556.7	3.3%
Other Taxes	197.5	–21.8%	268.1	35.7%
Total	**$ 61,473.5**	7.1%	**$ 77,210.7**	25.6%

Totals may not sum due to rounding.
All dollar figures in millions.
*Includes tax on manufactured housing sales.

Source: 2022 State of Texas Annual Cash Report.

Federal Revenue by Agency

Texas received $72.8 billion in federal funds during fiscal 2022, an decrease of $9.2 billion, or 11.2% from fiscal 2021. Federal funds accounted for 39.7% of total net revenue, the second-largest source of revenue in fiscal 2022.

	FY 2019	FY 2020	FY 2021	FY 2022
Health and Human Services	$ 27,279.5	$ 32,103.8	$ 34,764.0	$ 42,026.0
Texas Education Agency	5,608.0	5,226.7	6,317.4	12,104.8
Texas Dept. of Transportation	4,026.4	5,217.4	5,504.6	4,523.3
Texas Division of Emergency Management	—	625.3	7,481.4	3,487.3
Texas Workforce Commission	1,427.9	2,384.8	4,715.6	3,485.7
Texas Dept. of Housing & Community Affairs	242.0	280.7	2,223.5	2,167.2
General Land Office	413.0	925.8	1,110.5	1,462.9
Department of State Health Services	285.4	361.6	616.3	967.7
Dept. of Agriculture	638.6	742.0	1,251.3	813.1
All other Agencies	1,983.5	10,248.7	17,955.4	1,700.8
Total	**$ 41,904.5**	**$ 58,116.8**	**$ 81,940.1**	**$ 72,738.7**

Totals may not sum due to rounding. All figures in millions.

Source: 2022 State of Texas Annual Cash Report

Texas Lottery

Source: Texas Lottery Commission; www.txlottery.org/

The State Lottery Act was passed by the Texas Legislature in July 1991. Texas voters approved a constitutional amendment authorizing a state lottery in an election on Nov. 5, 1991, by a vote of 1,326,154 to 728,994. Since the first ticket was sold on May 29, 1992, the Texas Lottery® has generated $132.1 billion in total sales, $37.3 billion in revenue for the state, and $81.9 billion in prizes have been distributed to players through June 2023.

Since 1997, the Texas Lottery has contributed $31.4 billion to the Foundation School Fund, which supports public education. Before September 1997, revenues were only deposited in the General Revenue Fund.

As authorized by the state Legislature, certain Texas Lottery revenues have been earmarked to benefit state programs, including the Fund for Veterans Assistance, which is administered by the Texas Veterans Commission. Sales and unclaimed prizes from the veterans' designated scratch-off games have totaled $217.0 million since 2010.

Other Texas Lottery funds, such as unclaimed prizes, contribute to other causes and programs as authorized by the Texas Legislature.

Distribution of Texas Lottery proceeds for fiscal year 2022:

- 67.5% to prizes paid
- 23.8% to the Foundation School Fund
- 5.0% to retailer commissions
- 3.1% for lottery administration
- 0.3% to the Texas Veterans Commission. ☆

Texas Lottery Financial Data
Start-up to Aug. 31, 2022

Period	Sales	Value of Prizes Won	Retailer Comm-issions	Revenue to State of Texas*
FY 2022	$8,296.9	$5,599.7	$415.4	$1,998.4
FY 2021	8,107.2	5,418.3	405.8	1,998.3
FY 2020	6,704.0	4,442.4	335.6	1,683.7
FY 2019	6,251.5	4,056.5	313.1	1,636.6
FY 2018	5,626.8	3,666.1	281.5	1,450.5
FY 2017	5,077.5	3,257.4	253.9	1,334.0
FY 2016	5,067.5	3,186.4	253.5	1,392.3
FY 2015	4,529.7	2,858.3	226.7	1,242.7
FY 2014	4,384.6	2,741.2	219.5	1,220.7
FY 2013	4,376.3	2,767.4	218.9	1,214.1
FY 2012	4,190.8	2,632.6	209.8	1,155.5
FY 2011	3,811.3	2,387.2	190.8	1,023.8
FY 2010	3,738.4	2,300.2	187.3	1,063.1
FY 2009	3,720.1	2,299.8	186.1	1,062.2
FY 2008	3,671.5	2,281.1	183.8	1,034.9
FY 2007	3,774.2	2,315.3	188.8	1,093.0
FY 2006	3,774.7	2,310.6	188.8	1,090.3
FY 2005	3,662.5	2,228.0	183.2	1,070.3
FY 2004	3,487.9	2,068.6	174.4	1,051.0
FY 2003	3,130.7	1,845.2	156.6	949.1
FY 2002	2,966.3	1,715.4	148.4	928.9
FY 2001	2,825.3	1,643.2	141.3	864.0
FY 2000	2,657.3	1,508.8	133.0	862.8
FY 1999	2,571.6	1,329.0	128.8	953.4
FY 1998	3,090.0	1,648.1	154.6	1,097.8
FY 1997	3,745.5	2,151.7	187.4	1,182.8
FY 1996	3,432.3	1,951.1	171.7	1,098.3
FY 1995	3,036.5	1,689.3	151.8	1,015.0
FY 1994	2,760.2	1,528.7	138.0	927.7
FY 1993	1,856.1	981.7	92.8	656.8
Start up to FY 1992	591.6	268.9	29.6	250.0
Total	**$124,916.8**	**$77,078.2**	**$6,250.9**	**$35,602.0**

All figures in millions.
*Revenue to the state presented on an accrual basis.

Source: Texas Lottery Commission Summary Financial Report

House Speaker Dade Phelan gavels the House into session on the first day of the second special session on June 28, 2023. Photo by Evan L'Roy, The Texas Tribune

Texas' 88th Legislature

The Texas Legislature has **181 members: 31 in the Senate** and **150 in the House of Representatives**. Regular sessions convene on the second Tuesday of January in odd-numbered years, but the governor may call special sessions. Article III of the Texas Constitution deals with the legislative branch. On the web: capitol.texas.gov.

The following lists are of members of the **88th Legislature**, which convened for its Regular Session on Jan. 10, 2023, and adjourned on May 29, 2023. **See page 444 to read our report on this year's session**. The 89th Legislature is scheduled to convene on Jan. 14, 2025, and adjourn June 2, 2025.

Salary: The salary of all members of the Legislature, both Senators and Representatives, is $7,200 per year and $124 per diem during legislative sessions; mileage allowance at same rate provided by law for state employees. The per diem payment applies during each regular and special session of the Legislature.

State Senate

All thirty-one members of the State Senate are elected to four-year, overlapping terms. **Senatorial Districts** include one or more whole counties; some counties have more than one Senator.

The address of Senators is Texas Senate, P.O. Box 12068, Austin 78711-2068; phone (512) 463-0200; Fax: (512) 463-0326. On the web: senate.texas.gov.

President of the Senate: Lt. Gov. Dan Patrick; **President Pro Tempore:** Kelly Hancock (R-North Richland Hills); **Secretary of the Senate:** Patsy Spaw; **Sergeant-at-Arms:** Austin Osborn.

Texas State Senators

District, Member, Party-Hometown, Occupation

1. Bryan Hughes, R-Mineola; attorney.
2. Bob Hall, R-Edgewood; retired military.
3. Robert Nichols, R-Jacksonville; engineer.
4. Brandon Creighton, R-Conroe; attorney.
5. Charles Schwertner, R-Georgetown; surgeon.
6. Carol Alvarado, D-Houston; small-business owner.
7. Paul Bettencourt, R-Houston; tax advisor.
8. Angela Paxton, R-McKinney; consultant, former educator.
9. Kelly Hancock, R-North Richland Hills; business owner.
10. Phil King, R-Weatherford; attorney.
11. Mayes Middleton, R-Galveston; oil and gas.
12. Tan Parker, R-Flower Mound; businessman.
13. Borris L. Miles, D-Houston; insurance and real estate developer.
14. Sarah Eckhardt, D-Austin; attorney.
15. John Whitmire, D-Houston; attorney.
16. Nathan Johnson, D-Dallas; attorney.
17. Joan Huffman, R-Houston; attorney.
18. Lois W. Kolkhorst, R-Brenham; business owner.
19. Roland Gutierrez, D-San Antonio; attorney.
20. Juan "Chuy" Hinojosa, D-McAllen; attorney.
21. Judith Zaffirini, D-Laredo; communications specialist, former educator.
22. Brian Birdwell, R-Granbury; retired military.
23. Royce West, D-Dallas; attorney.
24. Pete Flores, R-Pleasanton; retired game warden.
25. Donna Campbell, R-New Braunfels; physician.
26. José Menéndez, D-San Antonio; businessman.
27. Morgan LaMantia, D-South Padre Island; attorney.
28. Charles Perry, R-Lubbock; certified public accountant.
29. César Blanco, D-El Paso; consultant.
30. Drew Springer, R-Muenster; financial services.
31. Kevin Sparks, R-Midland; oil and gas operator.

House of Representatives

This is a list of the 150 current members of the House of Representatives. They were elected for two-year terms from the districts shown below. Representatives and senators receive the same salary.

The address of all Representatives is House of Representatives, P.O. Box 2910, Austin, 78768–2910; phone: (512) 463–1000; Fax: (512) 463–5896. On the web: house.texas.gov

Speaker: Dade Phelan (R-Beaumont); **Chief Clerk:** Stephen Brown; **Sergeant-at-Arms:** Kara Coffee.

Texas State Representatives

District, Member, Party-Hometown, Occupation

1. Gary VanDeaver, R-New Boston; retired educator.
2. Vacant.
3. Cecil Bell, Jr., R-Magnolia; contractor.
4. Keith Bell, R-Forney; electrical contractor.
5. Cole Hefner, R-Mount Pleasant; insurance agent.
6. Matt Schaefer, R-Tyler; attorney.
7. Jay Dean, R-Longview; self-employed.
8. Cody Harris, R-Palestine; ranch broker.
9. Trent Ashby, R-Lufkin; title insurance executive.
10. Brian Harrison, R-Midlothian; consultant.
11. Travis Clardy, R-Nacogdoches; attorney.
12. Kyle Kacal, R-College Station; rancher.
13. Angelia Orr, R-Hillsboro; asset manager.
14. John Raney, R-Bryan; bookstore owner.
15. Steve Toth, R-The Woodlands; business owner.
16. Will Metcalf, R-Conroe; banker.
17. Stan Gerdes, R-Smithville; consultant.
18. Ernest Bailes, R-Shepherd; self-employed.
19. Ellen Troxclair, R-Lakeway; self-employed.
20. Terry M. Wilson, R-Marble Falls; retired military.
21. Dade Phelan, R-Beaumont; real estate developer.
22. Christian Manuel, D-Beaumont; state employee.
23. Terri Leo-Wilson, R-Galveston; retired teacher.
24. Greg Bonnen, R-Friendswood; neurosurgeon.
25. Cody Vasut, R-Angleton; attorney.
26. Jacey Jetton, R-Sugar Land; business owner.
27. Ron Reynolds, D-Missouri City; attorney.
28. Gary Gates, R-Richmond; real estate, property management.
29. Ed Thompson, R-Pearland; insurance agent.
30. Geanie W. Morrison, R-Victoria; state representative.
31. Ryan Guillen, R-Rio Grande City; investor, rancher.
32. Todd Hunter, R-Corpus Christi; attorney.
33. Justin Holland, R-Heath; real estate broker.
34. Abel Herrero, D-Robstown; attorney.
35. Oscar Longoria, D-Peñitas; attorney.
36. Sergio Muñoz, Jr., D-Palmview; attorney.
37. Janie Lopez, R-San Benito; mental health professional.
38. Erin Gámez, D-Brownsville; attorney.
39. Armando "Mando" Martinez, D-Weslaco; contractor.
40. Terry Canales, D-Edinburg; attorney.
41. R. D. "Bobby" Guerra, D-Mission; attorney.
42. Richard Peña Raymond, D-Laredo; mediator.
43. J. M. Lozano, R-Kingsville; businessman.
44. John Kuempel, R-Seguin; salesman.
45. Erin Zwiener, D-Driftwood; writer.
46. Sheryl Cole, D-Austin; attorney, CPA.
47. Vikki Goodwin, D-Austin; real estate broker.
48. Donna Howard, D-Austin; community advocate.
49. Gina Hinojosa, D-Austin; attorney.
50. James Talarico, D-Austin; nonprofit director.
51. Lulu Flores, D-Austin; attorney.
52. Caroline Harris, R-Round Rock; policy advisor
53. Andrew Murr, R-Junction; attorney, rancher.
54. Brad Buckley, R-Salado; veterinarian.
55. Hugh D. Shine, R-Temple; financial advisor.
56. Charles "Doc" Anderson, R-Waco; retired veterinarian.
57. Richard Hayes, R-Denton; attorney.
58. DeWayne Burns, R-Cleburne; investor, farmer, rancher.
59. Shelby Slawson, R-Stephenville; attorney.
60. Glenn Rogers, R-Graford; veterinarian, rancher.
61. Frederick Frazier, R-McKinney; police officer.
62. Reggie Smith, R-Van Alstyne; attorney.
63. Benjamin Bumgarner, R-Flower Mound; self-employed.
64. Lynn Stucky, R-Denton; veterinarian.
65. Kronda Thimesch, R-Carrollton; business owner.
66. Matt Shaheen, R-Plano; technology executive.
67. Jeff Leach, R-Allen; attorney.
68. David Spiller, R-Jacksboro; attorney.
69. James B. Frank, R-Wichita Falls; business owner.
70. Mihaela Plesa, D-Dallas; fashion merchandising and design.
71. Stan Lambert, R-Abilene; retired banker.
72. Drew Darby, R-San Angelo; attorney, businessman.
73. Carrie Isaac, R-Dripping Springs; consultant.
74. Eddie Morales, Jr., D-Eagle Pass; attorney.
75. Mary González, D-Clint; consultant, professor.
76. Suleman Lalani, D-Sugar Land; physician.
77. Evelina "Lina" Ortega, D-El Paso; attorney.
78. Joseph Moody, D-El Paso; attorney.
79. Claudia Ordaz, D-El Paso, self-employed.
80. Tracy O. King, D-Uvalde; businessman.
81. Brooks Landgraf, R-Odessa; attorney, rancher.
82. Tom Craddick, R-Midland; business development manager.
83. Dustin Burrows, R-Lubbock; attorney.
84. Carl H. Tepper, R-Lubbock; commercial real estate.
85. Stan Kitzman, R-Pattison; small-business owner.
86. John T. Smithee, R-Amarillo; attorney.
87. Four Price, R-Amarillo; attorney.
88. Ken King, R-Canadian; oil & gas service executive.

89. Candy Noble, R-Lucas.
90. Ramón Romero, Jr., D-Fort Worth; CEO.
91. Stephanie Klick, R-Fort Worth; registered nurse.
92. Salman Bhojani, D-Euless; attorney, real estate investor.
93. Nate Schatzline, R-Fort Worth; operations director, pastor.
94. Tony Tinderholt, R-Arlington; retired military.
95. Nicole Collier, D-Fort Worth; attorney.
96. David Cook, R-Mansfield; attorney.
97. Craig Goldman, R-Fort Worth; real estate, investments.
98. Giovanni Capriglione, R-Southlake; small-business owner.
99. Charlie Geren, R-River Oaks; restaurant owner, rancher.
100. Venton Jones, D-Dallas; nonprofit CEO.
101. Chris Turner, D-Grand Prairie; communications consultant.
102. Ana-Maria Ramos, D-Richardson; attorney, professor.
103. Rafael Anchía, D-Dallas; attorney.
104. Jessica González, D-Dallas; attorney.
105. Terry Meza, D-Irving; attorney.
106. Jared Patterson, R-Frisco; energy services.
107. Victoria Neave Criado, D-Dallas; attorney.
108. Morgan Meyer, R-University Park; attorney.
109. Carl O. Sherman, Sr., D-DeSoto; pastor, businessman.
110. Toni Rose, D-Dallas; independent contractor.
111. Yvonne Davis, D-Dallas; small-business owner.
112. Angie Chen Button, R-Richardson; marketing.
113. Rhetta Bowers, D-Rowlett; educator.
114. John Bryant, D-Dallas; attorney.
115. Julie Johnson, D-Farmers Branch; attorney.
116. Trey Martinez Fischer, D-San Antonio; contractor.
117. Philip Cortez, D-San Antonio; public relations.
118. John Lujan, R-San Antonio; small-business owner.
119. Liz Campos, D-San Antonio; self-employed.
120. Barbara Gervin-Hawkins, D-San Antonio; education.
121. Steve Allison, R-San Antonio; attorney.
122. Mark Dorazio, R-San Antonio; self-employed.
123. Diego Bernal, D-San Antonio; attorney.
124. Josey Garcia, D-San Antonio; retired military.
125. Ray Lopez, D-San Antonio.
126. Sam Harless, R-Spring; automobile dealer.
127. Charles Cunningham, R-Humble; retired businessman.
128. Briscoe Cain, R-Deer Park; attorney.
129. Dennis Paul, R-Houston; engineer.
130. Tom Oliverson, R-Cypress; anesthesiologist.
131. Alma Allen, D-Houston; educational consultant.
132. Mike Schofield, R-Katy; attorney.
133. Mano DeAyala, R-Houston; attorney.
134. Ann Johnson, D-Houston; attorney.
135. Jon E. Rosenthal, D-Houston; engineer.
136. John H. Bucy, III, D-Austin; small-business owner.
137. Gene Wu, D-Houston; attorney.
138. Lacey Hull, R-Houston; consultant.
139. Jarvis Johnson, D-Houston; business owner.
140. Armando Walle, D-Houston; legal assistant.
141. Senfronia Thompson, D-Houston; attorney.
142. Harold Dutton, Jr., D-Houston; attorney.
143. Ana Hernandez, D-Houston; attorney.
144. Mary Ann Perez, D-Houston; insurance agent.
145. Christina Morales, D-Houston; funeral director.
146. Shawn Thierry, D-Houston; attorney.
147. Jolanda "Jo" Jones, D-Houston; attorney.
148. Penny Morales Shaw, D-Houston; attorney.
149. Hubert Vo, D-Houston; businessman.
150. Valoree Swanson, R-Spring; businesswoman. ☆

Texas House of Representatives, 88th Legislature

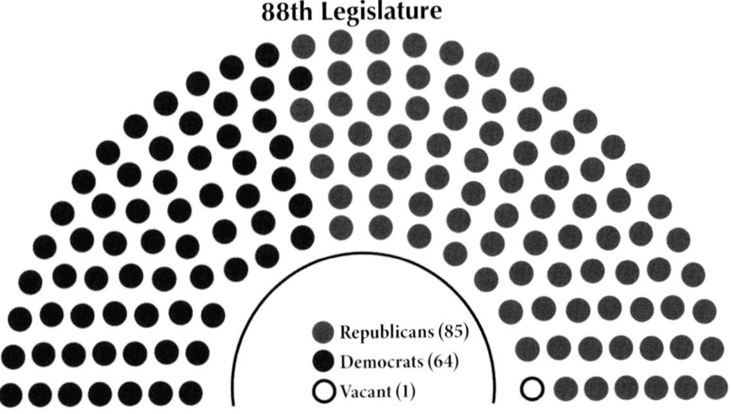

Texas Supreme Court, 2023. Top row, left to right: Justice Huddle, Justice Busby, Justice Devine, Justice Blacklock, Justice Bland, and Justice Young. Front row, left to right: Justice Lehrmann, Chief Justice Hecht, and Justice Boyd.

Texas State Judiciary

The judiciary of the state consists of nine justices of the Supreme Court of Texas; nine judges of the Court of Criminal Appeals; 80 justices of the 14 Courts of Appeals; 459 judges of the State District Courts; 13 judges of the Criminal District Courts; 527 County Court judges; 805 Justice Court judges; and more than 1,200 Municipal Court judges in 944 cities.

Since 1876, judges at all levels are elected by voters in partisan elections. The Judicial Campaign Fairness Act was added to the Texas Election Code in 1995 by the 74th Legislature and limits individual campaign contributions to $5,000 for a statewide judicial office and $1,000–$5,000 for other judicial offices, depending on judicial district population. The exception is law firms, for which a $50 limit is set.

In addition to its system of formal courts, the State of Texas has established 18 **Alternative Dispute Resolution Centers**. The centers are headed by a director and help ease the caseload of Texas courts by using mediation, arbitration, negotiation, and moderated settlement conferences to handle disputes.

Centers are located in Amarillo, Austin, Beaumont, Bryan–College Station, Conroe, Corpus Christi, Dallas, Denton, El Paso, Fort Worth, Houston, Kerrville, Lubbock, Paris, Richmond, San Antonio, San Marcos, and Waco.

(The list of U.S. District Courts in Texas can be found in the Federal Government section, page 531.)

State Higher Courts

The state's higher courts include the Supreme Court, the Court of Criminal Appeals, the Courts of Appeals, and District Courts. Justices of the Supreme Court, Court of Criminal Appeals, and Courts of Appeals are elected to six-year, overlapping terms. District Court judges are elected to four-year terms.

Base annual judicial salaries as set by the 86th Legislature are: Supreme Court and Court of Criminal Appeals chief justices, $170,500, justices, $168,000; Court of Appeals chief justices, $156,500; justices, $154,000. Court of Appeals justices also may receive additional compensation paid by counties for extra judicial service, not to exceed $9,000 per year.

District Court judges receive $140,000 from the state. They may receive additional compensation paid by counties, not to exceed $18,000 per year.

The justices listed below are current as of August 2023. Notations in parentheses are term of office expiration dates. Elsewhere in this section are lists of District Court judges by district number, district court numbers in each county, and county court judges.

Supreme Court

Chief Justice, Nathan L. Hecht (12/31/26). **Justices**: Jimmy Blacklock (12/31/24); Jane Bland (12/31/24); Jeff Boyd (12/31/26); Brett Busby (12/31/26); John Phillip Devine (12/31/24); Rebeca Huddle (12/31/28); Debra Lehrmann (12/31/28); and Evan A. Young (12/31/2028).

Clerk of Court, Blake A. Hawthorne. Location of court, Austin. Web: www.txcourts.gov/supreme.

Court of Criminal Appeals

Presiding Judge, Sharon Keller (12/31/24). **Judges**: Barbara Parker Hervey (12/31/24); Mary Lou Keel (12/31/28); Jesse F. McClure III (12/31/28); David Newell (12/31/26); Bert Richardson (12/31/26); Michelle Slaughter (12/31/24); Scott Walker (12/31/28); and Kevin Patrick Yeary (12/31/26). **State Prosecuting Attorney**, Stacey M. Soule.

Clerk of Court, Deanna Williamson. Location of court, Austin. Web: www.txcourts.gov/cca.

Courts of Appeals

These courts have jurisdiction within their respective supreme judicial districts. A constitutional amendment approved in 1978 raised the number of associate justices for Courts of Appeals where needed. Judges are elected from the district for six-year terms. An amendment adopted in 1980 changed the name of the old Courts of Civil Appeals to the Courts of Appeals and changed the jurisdiction of the courts. Terms end on 12/31 of the year in parentheses.

First District, Houston§: Chief Justice Terry Adams (2028). **Justices:** Julie Countiss (2024); April L. Farris (2028); Gordon Goodman (2024); Amparo M. Guerra (2026); Richard Hightower (2024); Peter Kelly (2024); Sarah Beth Landau (2024); and Veronica Rivas-Malloy (2026). **Clerk of Court,** Deborah M. Young. **Counties in the First District:** Austin, Brazoria, Chambers, Colorado, Fort Bend, Galveston, Grimes, Harris, Waller, Washington.

Second District, Fort Worth: Chief Justice Bonnie Sudderth (2028). **Justices:** Dabney Bassel (2024); J. Wade Birdwell (2024); Elizabeth Kerr (2028); Brian Walker (2026); Mike Wallach (2024); Dana Womack (2026). **Clerk of Court,** Debra Spisak. **Counties in the Second District:** Archer, Clay, Cooke, Denton, Hood, Jack, Montague, Parker, Tarrant, Wichita, Wise, Young.

Third District, Austin: Chief Justice Darlene Byrne (2026). **Justices:** Thomas J. Baker (2024); Chari L. Kelly (2024); Edward Smith (2024); Rosa Lopez Theofanis (2028); and Gisela D. Triana (2024). **Clerk of Court,** Jeffrey D. Kyle. **Counties in the Third District:** Bastrop, Bell, Blanco, Burnet, Caldwell, Coke, Comal, Concho, Fayette, Hays, Irion, Lampasas, Lee, Llano, McCulloch, Milam, Mills, Runnels, San Saba, Schleicher, Sterling, Tom Green, Travis, Williamson.

Fourth District, San Antonio: Chief Justice Rebeca C. Martinez (2026). **Justices:** Patricia O'Connell Alvarez (2024); Luz Elena D. Chapa (2024); Irene Rios (2028); Liza A. Rodriguez (2024); Lori I. Valenzuela (2026); and Beth Watkins (2024). **Clerk of Court,** Michael A. Cruz. **Counties in the Fourth District:** Atascosa, Bandera, Bexar, Brooks, Dimmit, Duval, Edwards, Frio, Gillespie, Guadalupe, Jim Hogg, Jim Wells, Karnes, Kendall, Kerr, Kimble, Kinney, La Salle, Mason, Maverick, McMullen, Medina, Menard, Real, Starr, Sutton, Uvalde, Val Verde, Webb, Wilson, Zapata, Zavala.

Fifth District, Dallas: Chief Justice Robert D. Burns, III (2024). **Justices:** Cory L. Carlyle (2024); Dennise Garcia (2026); Bonnie Lee Goldstein (2026); Nancy Kennedy (2028); Emily Miskel (2024); Ken Molberg (2024); Erin A. Nowell (2024); Robbie Partida-Kipness (2024); Bill Pedersen, III (2024); Amanda L. Reichek (2024); and Craig Smith (2026). **Clerk of Court,** Ruben Morin. **Counties in the Fifth District:** Collin, Dallas, Grayson, Hunt, Kaufman, Rockwall.

Sixth District, Texarkana: Chief Justice Scott E. Stevens (2028). **Justices:** Jeff Rambin (2024) and Charles van Cleef (2028). **Clerk of Court,** Debbie Autrey. **Counties in the Sixth District:** Bowie, Camp, Cass, Delta, Fannin, Franklin, Gregg, Harrison, Hopkins, Hunt, Lamar, Marion, Morris, Panola, Red River, Rusk, Titus, Upshur, Wood.

Seventh District, Amarillo: Chief Justice Brian Quinn (2026). **Justices:** Lawrence M. Doss (2028); Judy C. Parker (2024); and Alex L. Yarbrough (2026). **Clerk of Court,** Bobby Ramirez. **Counties in the Seventh District:** Armstrong, Bailey, Briscoe, Carson, Castro, Childress, Cochran, Collingsworth, Cottle, Crosby, Dallam, Deaf Smith, Dickens, Donley, Floyd, Foard, Garza, Gray, Hale, Hall, Hansford, Hardeman, Hartley, Hemphill, Hockley, Hutchinson, Kent, King, Lamb, Lipscomb, Lubbock, Lynn, Moore, Motley, Ochiltree, Oldham, Parmer, Potter, Randall, Roberts, Sherman, Swisher, Terry, Wheeler, Wilbarger, Yoakum.

Eighth District, El Paso: Chief Justice Yvonne T. Rodriguez (2026). **Justices:** Gina M. Palafox (2028) and Lisa Soto (2026). **Clerk of Court,** Elizabeth G. Flores. **Counties in the Eighth District:** Andrews, Brewster, Crane, Crockett, Culberson, El Paso, Hudspeth, Jeff Davis, Loving, Pecos, Presidio, Reagan, Reeves, Terrell, Upton, Ward, Winkler.

Ninth District, Beaumont: Chief Justice Scott Golemon (2026). **Justices:** Hollis Horton (2024); Leanne Johnson (2024); and Jay Wright (2028). **Clerk of Court,** Carly Latiolais. **Counties in the Ninth District:** Hardin, Jasper, Jefferson, Liberty, Montgomery, Newton, Orange, Polk, San Jacinto, Tyler.

Tenth District, Waco: Chief Justice Tom Gray (2024). **Justices:** Matt Johnson (2026) and Steven Lee Smith (2028). **Clerk of Court,** Nita Whitener. **Counties in the Tenth District:** Bosque, Brazos, Burleson, Coryell, Ellis, Falls, Freestone, Hamilton, Hill, Johnson, Leon, Limestone, Madison, McLennan, Navarro, Robertson, Somervell, Walker.

Eleventh District, Eastland: Chief Justice John M. Bailey (2024). **Justices:** W. Stacy Trotter (2028) and Bruce Williams (2026). **Clerk of Court,** Marla Hanks. **Counties in the Eleventh District:** Baylor, Borden, Brown, Callahan, Coleman, Comanche, Dawson, Eastland, Ector, Erath, Fisher, Gaines, Glasscock, Haskell, Howard, Jones, Knox, Martin, Midland, Mitchell, Nolan, Palo Pinto, Scurry, Shackelford, Stephens, Stonewall, Taylor, Throckmorton.

Twelfth District, Tyler: Chief Justice James T. Worthen (2026). **Justices:** Brian Hoyle (2026) and Greg Neeley (2024). **Clerk of Court,** Katrina McClenny. **Counties in the Twelfth District:** Anderson, Angelina, Cherokee, Gregg, Henderson, Houston, Nacogdoches, Rains, Rusk, Sabine, San Augustine, Shelby, Smith, Trinity, Upshur, Van Zandt, Wood.

Thirteenth District, Corpus Christi: Chief Justice Dori Contreras (2024). **Justices:** Gina M. Benavides (2024); Nora L. Longoria (2024); Lionel Aron Peña, Jr. (2028); Clarissa Silva (2026); and Jaime E. Tijerina (2024). **Clerk of Court,** Kathy S. Mills. **Counties in the Thirteenth District:** Aransas, Bee, Calhoun, Cameron, DeWitt, Goliad, Gonzales, Hidalgo, Jackson, Kenedy, Kleberg, Lavaca, Live Oak, Matagorda, Nueces, Refugio, San Patricio, Victoria, Wharton, Willacy.

Fourteenth District, Houston†: Chief Justice Tracy Christopher (2026). **Justices:** Frances Bourliot (2024); Meagan Hassan (2024); Kevin Jewell (2028); Margaret "Meg" Poissant (2024); Charles A. Spain (2024); Randy Wilson (2028); Ken Wise (2026); and Jerry Zimmerer (2024). **Clerk of Court,** Deborah M. Young. **Counties in the Fourteenth District:** Austin, Brazoria, Chambers, Colorado, Fort Bend, Galveston, Grimes, Harris, Waller, Washington. ☆

§*The location of the First Court of Appeals was changed from Galveston to Houston by the 55th Legislature, with the provision that all cases originated in Galveston County be tried in that city and with the further provision that any case may, at the discretion of the court, be tried in either city.*

†*Because of the heavy workload of the Houston-area Court of Appeals, the 60th Legislature in 1967 provided for the establishment of a Fourteenth Appeals Court in Houston.*

District Judges in Texas

Below are the names of all district judges in Texas, as of July 2023, listed in district court order. To determine which judges have jurisdiction in specific counties, refer to the Texas Courts by County table, on pages 472–473.

Dist	Judge
1	Craig M. Mixson (R)
1-A	Delinda Gibbs-Walker (R)
2	R. Chris Day (R)
3	Mark A. Calhoon (R)
4	J. Clay Gossett (R)
5	Bill Miller (R)
6	Wes Tidwell (R)
7	Kerry L. Russell (R)
8	Eddie Northcutt (R)
9	Phil A. Grant (R)
10	Kerry Neves (R)
11	Kristen B. Hawkins (D)
12	David W. Moorman (R)
13	James E. Lagomarsino (R)
14	Eric V. Moyé (D)
15	Jim Fallon (R)
16	Sherry Shipman (R)
17	Melody Wilkinson (R)
18	Sydney B. Hewlett (R)
19	Thomas West (R)
20	John W. Youngblood (R)
21	Carson Campbell (R)
22	Bruce Boyer (R)
23	Ben Hardin (R)
24	Jack W. Marr (R)
25	William D. Old, III (R)
25-A	Jessica R. Crawford (R)
26	Donna King (R)
27	John Gauntt (R)
28	Nanette Hasette (D)
29	Michael Moore (R)
30	Jeff McKnight (R)
31	Steven R. Emmert (R)
32	Glen N. Harrison (R)
33	Allan Garrett (R)
34	William E. Moody (D)
35	Michael L. Smith (R)
36	Starr Bauer (R)
37	Nicole Garza (D)
38	Camile G. DuBose (R)
39	Shane Hadaway (R)
40	Bob Carroll (R)
41	Anna Perez (D)
42	James Eidson (R)
43	Craig Towson (R)
44	Veretta Frazier (D)
45	Mary Lou Alvarez (D)
46	Cory Curtis (R)
47	Dee Johnson (R)
48	Christopher Taylor (R)
49	Joe Lopez (D)
50	Jennifer A. Habert (R)
51	Carmen Symes Dusek (R)
52	Trent D. Farrell (R)
53	Maria Cantu Hexel (D)
54	Susan Kelly (R)
55	Latosha L. Payne (D)
56	Lonnie Cox (R)
57	Toni Arteaga (D)
58	Kent Walston (D)
59	Larry Phillips (R)
60	Justin Sanderson (D)
61	Fredericka Phillips (D)
62	Will Biard (R)
63	Roland Andrade (R)
64	Danah Zirpoli (R)
65	Yahara Lisa Gutierrez (D)
66	A. Lee Harris (R)
67	Donald J. Cosby (R)
68	Martin Hoffman (D)
69	Kimberly Allen (R)
70	Denn Whalen (R)
71	Brad Morin (R)
72	John Grace (R)
73	David A. Canales (D)
74	Gary Coley (R)
75	Mark Morefield (R)
76	Angela Saucier (R)
77	Patrick Simmons (R)
78	Meredith Kennedy (R)
79	Richard Terrell (D)
80	Jeralynn Manor (D)
81	Lynn Ellison (R)
82	Bryan F. Russ, Jr. (R)
83	Robert E. Cadena (R)
84	Curtis W. Brancheau (R)
85	Kyle Hawthorne (R)
86	Casey Blair (R)
87	Amy Thomas Ward (R)
88	Earl Stover, III (R)
89	Charles M. Barnard (R)
90	Stephen Bristow (R)
91	Steven R. Herod (R)
92	Luis M. Singleterry (D)
93	Fernando Mancias (D)
94	Bobby Galvan (D)
95	Monica Purdy (D)
96	Pat Gallagher (R)
97	Jack McGaughey (R)
98	Rhonda Hurley (D)
99	Phillip Hays (R)
100	Stuart Messer (R)
101	Staci Williams (D)
102	Jeff M. Addison (R)
103	Janet Leal (D)
104	Jeff Propst (R)
105	Jack W. Pulcher (R)
106	Reed Filley (R)
107	Benjamin Euresti, Jr. (D)
108	Doug Woodburn (R)
109	John L. Pool (R)
110	Bill Smith (R)
111	Monica Zapata Notzon (D)
112	Pete Gomez, Jr. (D)
113	Rabeea Collier (D)
114	Austin Reeve Jackson (R)
115	Dean Fowler (R)
116	Tonya Parker (D)
117	Susan Barclay (R)
118	R. Shane Seaton (R)
119	Ben Woodward (R)
120	Maria Salas-Mendoza (D)
121	Trey Didway (R)
122	Jeth Jones, II (R)
123	LeAnn Kay Rafferty (R)
124	F. Alfonso Charles (R)
125	Kyle Carter (D)
126	Aurora Martinez Jones (D)
127	R.K. Sandill (D)
128	Courtney Arkeen (R)
129	Michael Gomez (D)
130	Denise M. Fortenberry (R)
131	Norma Gonzales (D)
132	Dana Cooley (R)
133	Jaclanel McFarland (D)
134	Dale B. Tillery (D)
135	Stephen Williams (R)
136	Baylor Wortham (D)
137	Trey McClendon (R)
138	Gabby Garcia (D)
139	Bobby Flores (D)
140	Douglas H. Freitag (R)
141	John P. Chupp (R)
142	David G. Rogers (R)
143	Michael Swanson (R)
144	Michael Mery (D)
145	Jeff Davis (R)
146	Jack Jones (R)
147	Clifford A. Brown (D)
148	David Klein (R)
149	Jessica Pulcher (R)
150	Monique Diaz (D)
151	Mike Engelhart (D)
152	Robert Schaffer (D)
153	Susan McCoy (R)
154	Scott Say (R)
155	Jeff Steinhauser (R)
156	Patrick L. Flanigan (R)
157	Tanya Garrison (D)
158	Steve Burgess (R)
159	Todd Kassaw (R)
160	Aiesha Redmond (D)
161	Justin Low (R)
162	Ashley Wysocki (R)
163	Rex Wayne Peveto (R)
164	Cheryl E. Thornton (D)
165	Ursula A. Hall (D)
166	Laura Salinas (D)
167	Dayna Blazey (D)
168	Marcos Lizarraga (D)
169	Cari L. Starritt-Burnett (R)
170	Jim Meyer (R)
171	Bonnie Rangel (D)
172	Mitch Templeton (R)
173	Dan Moore (R)
174	Hazel B. Jones (D)
175	Catherine Torres-Stahl (D)
176	Nikita Harmon (D)
177	Robert Johnson (D)
178	Kelli Johnson (D)
179	Ana Martinez (D)
180	Tami C. Pierce (R)
181	Titiana D. Frausto (R)
182	Danny Lacayo (D)
183	Kristin M. Guiney (R)
184	Kat Thomas (D)
185	Andrea Beall (D)
186	Kristina Escalona (D)
187	Stephanie R. Boyd (D)
188	Scott Novy (R)
189	Tami Craft (D)
190	Beau Miller (D)
191	Gena Slaughter (D)
192	Maria Aceves (D)
193	Bridgett Whitmore (D)
194	Ernest B. White, III (D)
195	Hector Garza (D)
196	Andrew Bench (R)
197	Adolfo Cordova (D)
198	Pat Maguire (R)
199	Angela Tucker (R)

Dist	Judge
200	Jessica Mangrum (D)
201	Amy Clark Meachum (D)
202	John Tidwell (R)
203	Rocky Jones (D)
204	Tammy Kemp (D)
205	Francisco X. Dominguez (D)
206	Rose Guerra Reyna (D)
207	Tracie Wright-Reneau (R)
208	Beverly Armstrong (D)
209	Brian E. Warren (D)
210	Alyssa G. Perez (D)
211	Brody Shanklin (R)
212	Patricia V. Grady (R)
213	Christopher R. Wolfe (R)
214	Inna Klein (R)
215	Elaine H. Palmer (D)
216	Albert D. Patillo, III (R)
217	Robert K. Inselmann, Jr. (R)
218	Russell Wilson (R)
219	Jennifer Edgeworth (R)
220	Shaun Carpenter (R)
221	Lisa B. Michalk (R)
222	Roland Saul (R)
223	Phil Vanderpool (R)
224	Marisa Flores (D)
225	Christine Vasquez Hortick (D)
226	Velia J. Meza (D)
227	Christine Del Prado (D)
228	Frank Aguilar (D)
229	Balde Garza (D)
230	Chris Morton (D)
231	Jesse Nevarez, Jr. (R)
232	Josh Hill (D)
233	Kenneth E. Newell (R)
234	Lauren Reeder (D)
235	Janelle M. Haverkamp (R)
236	Tom Lowe (R)
237	Les Hatch (R)
238	Elizabeth Leonard (R)
239	Greg Hill (R)
240	Surendran K. Pattel (D)
241	Debbie Gunter (R)
242	Kregg Hukill (R)
243	Selena N. Solis (D)
244	Lori Ruiz-Crutcher (R)
245	Angela Lancelin (D)
246	Angela Graves-Harrington (D)
247	Janice Berg (D)
248	Hilary Unger (D)
249	Tiffany Strother (R)
250	Karin Crump (D)
251	Ana Estevez (R)
252	Raquel West (D)
253	Chap B. Cain, III (R)
254	Kim Brown (D)
255	Vonda Bailey (D)
256	Sandre Streete (D)
257	Sandra Peake (D)
258	Travis Kitchens (R)
259	Brooks H. Hagler (D)
260	Steve Parkhurst (R)
261	Daniela Deseta Lyttle (D)
262	Lori C. Gray (D)
263	Melissa Marie Morris (D)
264	Paul LePak (R)
265	Jennifer Bennett (D)
266	Jason Cashon (R)
267	Julie Bauknight (R)
268	Steve Rogers (R)
269	Cory Sepolio (D)
270	Dedra Davis (D)
271	Brock Smith (R)

Dist	Judge
272	John Brick (R)
273	James A. Payne, Jr. (R)
274	Gary L. Steel (R)
275	Marla Cuellar (D)
276	Michael P. Kopech (R)
277	Stacey Mathews (R)
278	Hal R. Ridley (R)
279	Randy Shelton (D)
280	Dianne Curvey (D)
281	Christine Weems (D)
282	Amber Givens (D)
283	Lela D. Mays (D)
284	Kristin Bays (R)
285	Nadine Melissa Nieto (D)
286	Pat Phelan (R)
287	Kathryn Gurley (R)
288	Cynthia Marie Chapa (D)
289	Rose Soza (D)
290	Jennifer Peña (D)
291	Stephanie Huff (D)
292	Brandon Birmingham (D)
293	Maribel Flores (D)
294	Chris Martin (R)
295	Donna Roth (D)
296	John Roach, Jr. (R)
297	David Hagerman (R)
298	Emily G. Tobolowsky (D)
299	Karen Sage (D)
300	Chad Bradshaw (R)
301	Mary Brown (D)
302	Sandra Jackson (D)
303	Ladeitra Adkins (D)
304	Andrea Lane (D)
305	Cheryl Lee Shannon (D)
306	Anne Darring (R)
307	Tim Womack (R)
308	Gloria Lopez (D)
309	Linda Marie Dunson (D)
310	Sonya Leah Heath (D)
311	Germaine Tanner (D)
312	Teresa J. Waldrop (D)
313	Natalia Oakes (D)
314	Michelle Moore (D)
315	Leah Shapiro (D)
316	James Mosley (R)
317	Gordon Friesz (R)
318	David W. Lindemood (R)
319	David Stith (R)
320	Steven Denny (R)
321	Robert Wilson (R)
322	James B. Munford (R)
323	Alex Kim (R)
324	Beth A. Poulos (R)
325	Cynthia Terry (R)
326	Paul Rotenberry (R)
327	Monique Velarde Reyes (D)
328	Monica Rawlins (D)
329	Randy M. Clapp (R)
330	Andrea Plumlee (D)
331	Chantal Melissa Eldridge (D)
332	Mario E. Ramirez, Jr. (D)
333	Brittanye Morris (D)
334	Dawn Deshea Rogers (D)
335	Reva Towslee-Corbett (R)
336	Laurine J. Blake (R)
337	Colleen Gaido (D)
338	Ramona Franklin (D)
339	Te'iva Bell (D)
340	Jay Weatherby (R)
341	Beckie Palomo (D)
342	Kimberly Fitzpatrick (R)
343	Janna Whatley (R)

Dist	Judge
344	Randy McDonald (R)
345	Jan Soifer (D)
346	Patricia Baca (D)
347	Missy Medary (R)
348	Megan Fahey (R)
349	Pam Foster Fletcher (R)
350	Thomas Wheeler (R)
351	Nata Cornelio (D)
352	Josh Burgess (R)
353	Madeleine Connor (D)
354	Kelli Aiken (R)
355	Bryan Bufkin (R)
356	Steven Thomas (R)
357	Juan A. Magallanes (D)
358	John F. Shrode (R)
359	Kathleen A. Hamilton (R)
360	Patricia Baca Bennett (R)
361	David Hilburn (R)
362	Bruce McFarling (R)
363	Tracy Holmes (D)
364	Billy Eichman (R)
365	Amado Abascal (D)
366	Tom Nowak (R)
367	Brent Hill (R)
368	Sarah Bruchmiller (R)
369	C. Michael Davis (R)
370	Noe Gonzalez (D)
371	Ryan Hill (R)
372	Julie Lugo (R)
377	Eli Garza (R)
378	Doug Wallace (R)
379	Ron Rangel (D)
380	Ben N. Smith (R)
381	Jose L. Garza (D)
382	Brett Hall (R)
383	Lyda Ness Garcia (D)
384	Patrick M. Garcia (D)
385	Leah G. Robertson (R)
386	Jackie Valdez (D)
387	Janet Buening Heppard (D)
388	Marlene Gonzalez (D)
389	Letty Lopez (D)
390	Julie H. Kocurek (D)
391	Brad Goodwin (R)
392	Scott McKee (R)
393	Doug Robison (R)
394	Roy B. Ferguson (D)
395	Ryan D. Larson (R)
396	George Gallagher (R)
397	Brian Keith Gary (R)
398	Keno Vasquez (D)
399	Frank J. Castro (D)
400	Tameika Carter (D)
401	George Flint (R)
402	J. Brad McCampbell (R)
403	Brandy Mueller (D)
404	Ricardo M. Adobbati (D)
405	Jared Robinson (R)
406	Oscar J. Hale, Jr. (D)
407	Tina Torres (D)
408	Angelica Jimenez (D)
409	Sam Medrano, Jr. (D)
410	Jennifer Robin (R)
411	John Wells (R)
412	Justin R. Gilbert (R)
413	William C. Bosworth, Jr. (R)
414	Vicki Menard (R)
415	Graham Quisenberry (R)
416	Andrea Thompson (R)
417	Cyndi Wheless (R)
418	Tracy A. Gilbert (R)
419	Catherine A. Mauzy (D)

Dist	Judge
420	Ed Klein (R)
421	Chris Schneider (R)
422	Shelton Gibbs, IV (R)
423	Chris Duggan (D)
424	Evan Stubbs (R)
425	Betsy F. Lambeth (R)
426	Steve Duskie (R)
427	Tamara Needles (D)
428	Joe Pool (D)
429	Jill R. Willis (R)
430	Israel Ramon (D)
431	Jim Johnson (R)
432	Ruben Gonzalez, Jr. (R)
433	Dib Waldrip (R)
434	Christian Becerra (D)
435	Patty Maginnis (R)
436	Cruz Shaw (D)
437	Joel Perez (D)
438	Rosie Alvarado (D)
439	David Rakow (R)
440	Grant Kinsey (R)
441	Jeff Robnett (R)
442	Tiffany Haertling (R)
443	Cindy Ermatinger (R)
444	David A. Sanchez (D)
445	Gloria M. Rincones (D)

Dist	Judge
446	Sara Kate Billingsley (R)
448	Sergio H. Enriquez (D)
449	Renee Rodriguez-Betancourt (D)
450	Brad Urrutia (D)
451	Kirsten Cohoon (R)
452	Robert Hofmann (R)
453	Sherri Tibbe (D)
454	Danny Kindred (R)
455	Laurie Eiserloh (D)
456	Heather Hines Wright (R)
457	Vince Santini (R)
458	Chad Bridges (R)
459	Maya Guerra Gamble (D)
460	Selena Alvarenga (D)
461	Patrick Bulanek (R)
462	Lee Ann Breading (R)
464	Joe Ramirez (D)
466	Stephanie Bascon (R)
467	Derbha Jones (R)
468	Lindsey Wynne (R)
469	Piper McCraw (R)
470	Brook Fulks (R)
471	Andrea Bouressa (R)
474	Alan Bennett (R)
475	Taylor Heaton (R)
476	Ysmael D. Fonseca (R)

Dist	Judge
478	Wade Faulkner (R)
480	Scott K. Field (R)
481	Crystal Edmonson Levonius (R)
482	Veronica M. Nelson (D)
483	Tanner Neidhardt (R)
484	Adela Kowalski-Garza (D)
485	Steven Jumes (R)
505	Kali Morgan (D)
506	Gary W. Chaney (R)
507	Julia Maldonado (D)

Criminal District Courts	
Dallas 1	Tina Yoo Clinton (D)
Dallas 2	J.J. Koch (R)
Dallas 3	Audra LaDawn Riley (D)
Dallas 4	Dominique Collins (D)
Dallas 5	Carter Thompson (D)
Dallas 6	Jeanine Howard (D)
Dallas 7	Chika Anyiam (D)
El Paso	Diane Navarette (D)
Jefferson	Johnny Stevens (D)
Tarrant 1	Elizabeth Beach (R)
Tarrant 2	Wayne Francis Salvant (R)
Tarrant 3	Douglas A. Allen (R)
Tarrant 4	Mike Thomas (R)

Administrative Judicial Regions of Texas

There are 11 administrative judicial regions in the state for administrative purposes. Presiding Judges are appointed by the Governor to four-year terms. They must be active or retired region judges or active or retired appellate judges with judicial experience in a region court. They receive extra compensation of $5,000, paid by counties in the administrative region.

The Presiding Judge convenes an annual conference of judges in the administrative region to consult on business in the courts and to adopt rules for administering cases in the region.

The Presiding Judge may assign active or retired region judges residing within the administrative region to any of its region courts. The Presiding Judge of one administrative region may request the Presiding Judge of another administrative region to assign a judge from that region to sit in a region court in the requesting Judge's administrative region.

The Chief Justice of the Supreme Court of Texas convenes an annual conference of the 11 Presiding Judges to determine the need for assignment of judges and to promote the uniform administration of the assignments. The Chief Justice can assign judges of one administrative region for service in another region. Terms end in the year in parentheses.

First Region: Ray Wheless, McKinney (2026): Collin, Dallas, Ellis, Fannin, Grayson, Kaufman, Rockwall.

Second Region: Robert H. Trapp, Conroe (2026): Angelina, Bastrop, Brazos, Burleson, Chambers, Grimes, Hardin, Jasper, Jefferson, Lee, Liberty, Madison, Montgomery, Newton, Orange, Polk, San Jacinto, Trinity, Tyler, Walker, Waller, Washington.

Third Region: Dibrell "Dib" Waldrip, New Braunfels (2024): Austin, Bell, Blanco, Bosque, Burnet, Caldwell, Colorado, Comal, Comanche, Coryell, Falls, Fayette, Gonzales, Guadalupe, Hamilton, Hays, Hill, Lampasas, Lavaca, Llano, McLennan, Milam, Navarro, Robertson, San Saba, Travis, Williamson.

Fourth Region: Sid Harle, San Antonio (2025): Aransas, Atascosa, Bee, Bexar, Calhoun, De Witt, Dimmit, Frio, Goliad, Jackson, Karnes, La Salle, Live Oak, Maverick, McMullen, Refugio, San Patricio, Victoria, Webb, Wilson, Zapata, Zavala.

Fifth Region: Missy Medary, Corpus Christi (2023): Brooks, Cameron, Duval, Hidalgo, Jim Hogg, Jim Wells, Kenedy, Kleberg, Nueces, Starr, Willacy.

Sixth Region: Stephen B. Ables, Kerrville (2024): Bandera, Brewster, Crockett, Culberson, Edwards, El Paso, Gillespie, Hudspeth, Jeff Davis, Kendall, Kerr, Kimble, Kinney, Mason, McCulloch, Medina, Menard, Pecos, Presidio, Reagan, Real, Sutton, Terrell, Upton, Uvalde, Val Verde.

Seventh Region: Dean Rucker, Midland (2023): Andrews, Borden, Brown, Callahan, Coke, Coleman, Concho, Crane, Dawson, Ector, Fisher, Gaines, Garza, Glasscock, Haskell, Howard, Irion, Jones, Kent, Loving, Lynn, Martin, Midland, Mills, Mitchell, Nolan, Reeves, Runnels, Schleicher, Scurry, Shackelford, Sterling, Stonewall, Taylor, Throckmorton, Tom Green, Ward, Winkler.

Eighth Region: David Evans, Fort Worth (2026): Archer, Clay, Cooke, Denton, Eastland, Erath, Hood, Jack, Johnson, Montague, Palo Pinto, Parker, Somervell, Stephens, Tarrant, Wichita, Wise, Young.

Ninth Region: Ana Estevez, Amarillo (2024): Armstrong, Bailey, Baylor, Briscoe, Carson, Castro, Childress, Cochran, Collingsworth, Cottle, Crosby, Dallam, Deaf Smith, Dickens, Donley, Floyd, Foard, Gray, Hale, Hall, Hansford, Hardeman, Hartley, Hemphill, Hockley, Hutchinson, King, Knox, Lamb, Lipscomb, Lubbock, Moore, Motley, Ochiltree, Oldham, Parmer, Potter, Randall, Roberts, Sherman, Swisher, Terry, Wheeler, Wilbarger, Yoakum.

Tenth Region: Alfonso Charles, Longview (2026): Anderson, Bowie, Camp, Cass. Cherokee, Delta, Franklin, Freestone, Gregg, Harrison, Henderson, Hopkins, Houston, Hunt, Lamar, Leon, Limestone, Marion, Morris, Nacogdoches, Panola, Rains, Red River, Rusk, Sabine, San Augustine, Shelby, Smith, Titus, Upshur, Van Zandt, Wood.

Eleventh Region: Susan Brown, Houston (2026): Brazoria, Fort Bend, Galveston, Harris, Matagorda, Wharton.☆

Texas Courts by County

Below are listed the state district court or courts, court of appeals district, administrative judicial district, and U.S. judicial district for each county in Texas as of July 2023. For the names of the state district court judges, see the table by district number beginning on page 469. For more information about the state Court of Appeals Districts, see page 468; Administrative Judicial Regions are on page 471. More about the U.S. Judicial Districts is found on pages 531–533. Lists of County judges are found on pages 505–507 and 513–518.

County	State Dist. Court(s)	Ct. of Appeals Dist	Adm. Jud. Reg.	U.S. Jud. Dist.
Anderson	3, 87, 349, 369	12	10	E-Tyler
Andrews	109	8	7	W-Midland
Angelina	159, 217	12	2	E-Lufkin
Aransas	36, 156, 343	13	4	S-C.Christi
Archer	97	2	8	N-W. Falls
Armstrong	47	7	9	N-Amarillo
Atascosa	81, 218	4	4	W-San Ant.
Austin	155	1, 14	3	S-Houston
Bailey	287	7	9	N-Lubbock
Bandera	198	4	6	W-San Ant.
Bastrop	21, 335, 423	3	2	W-Austin
Baylor	50	11	9	N-W. Falls
Bee	36, 156, 343	13	4	S-C. Christi
Bell	27, 146, 169, 264, 426, 478	3	3	W-Waco
Bexar	37, 45, 57, 73, 131, 144, 150, 166, 175, 186, 187, 224, 225, 226, 227, 285, 288, 289, 290, 379, 386, 399, 407, 408, 436, 437, 438	4	4	W-San Ant.
Blanco	33, 424	3	3	W-Austin
Borden	132	11	7	N-Lubbock
Bosque	220	10	3	W-Waco
Bowie	5, 102, 202	6	10	E-Texark
Brazoria	149, 239, 300, 412, 461	1, 14	11	S-Galves
Brazos	85, 272, 361	10	2	S-Houston
Brewster	394	8	6	W-Pecos
Briscoe	110	7	9	N-Amarillo
Brooks	79	4	5	S-C. Christi
Brown	35	11	7	N-S. Angelo
Burleson	21, 335	10	2	W-Austin
Burnet	33, 424	3	3	W-Austin
Caldwell	22, 207, 421	3	3	W-Austin
Calhoun	24, 135, 267	13	4	S-Victoria
Callahan	42	11	7	N-Abilene
Cameron	103, 107, 138, 197, 357, 404, 444, 445, 484	13	5	S-Brownsville
Camp	76, 276	6	10	E-Marshall
Carson	100	7	9	N-Amarillo
Cass	5	6	10	E-Marshall
Castro	64, 242	7	9	N-Amarillo
Chambers	253, 344	1, 14	2	S-Galves
Cherokee	2, 369	12	10	E-Tyler
Childress	100	7	9	N-Amarillo
Clay	97	2	8	N-W. Falls
Cochran	286	7	9	N-Lubbock
Coke	51	3	7	N-S. Angelo
Coleman	42	11	7	N-S. Angelo
Collin	199, 219, 296, 366, 380, 401, 416, 417, 428, 429, 468, 469, 470, 471	5	1	E-Sherman
Collingsworth	100	7	9	N-Amarillo
Colorado	25, 25-A	1, 14	3	S-Houston
Comal	22, 207, 274, 433, 463, 466	3	3	W-San Ant.
Comanche	220	11	3	N-Ft. Worth
Concho	119	3	7	N-S. Angelo
Cooke	235	2	8	E-Sherman
Coryell	52, 440	10	3	W-Waco
Cottle	50	7	9	N-W. Falls
Crane	109	8	7	W-Midland
Crockett	112	8	6	N-S. Angelo
Crosby	72	7	9	N-Lubbock
Culberson	205, 394	8	6	W-Pecos
Dallam	69	7	9	N-Amarillo
Dallas	14, 44, 68, 95, 101, 116, 134, 160, 162, 191, 192, 193, 194, 195, 203, 204, 254, 255, 256, 265, 282, 283, 291, 292, 298, 301, 302, 303, 304, 305, 330, 363, Cr. 1, Cr. 2, Cr. 3, Cr. 4, Cr. 5, Cr. 6, Cr. 7,	5	1	N-Dallas
Dawson	106	11	7	N-Lubbock
Deaf Smith	222	7	9	N-Amarillo
Delta	8, 62	6	10	E-Sherman
Denton	16, 158, 211, 362, 367, 393, 431, 442, 462, 467, 481	2	8	E-Sherman
DeWitt	24, 135, 267	13	4	S-Victoria
Dickens	110	7	9	N-Lubbock
Dimmit	293, 365	4	4	W-San Ant.
Donley	100	7	9	N-Amarillo
Duval	229	4	5	S-C. Christi
Eastland	91	11	8	N-Abilene
Ector	70, 161, 244, 358, 446	11	7	W-Midland
Edwards	452	4	6	W-Del Rio
Ellis	40, 378, 443	10	1	N-Dallas
El Paso	34, 41, 65, 120, 168, 171, 205, 210, 243, 327, 346, 383, 384, 388, 409, 448, Cr. 1	8	6	W-El Paso
Erath	266	11	8	N-Ft. Worth
Falls	82	10	3	W-Waco
Fannin	336	6	1	E-Sherman
Fayette	155	3	3	S-Houston
Fisher	32	11	7	N-Abilene
Floyd	110	7	9	N-Lubbock
Foard	46	7	9	N-W. Falls
Fort Bend	240, 268, 328, 387, 400, 434, 458, 505	1, 14	11	S-Houston
Franklin	8, 62	6	10	E-Texark
Freestone	77, 87	10	10	W-Waco
Frio	81, 218	4	4	W-San Ant.
Gaines	106	11	7	N-Lubbock
Galveston	10, 56, 122, 212, 306, 405	1, 14	11	S-Galves
Garza	106	7	7	N-Lubbock
Gillespie	216	4	6	W-Austin
Glasscock	118	11	7	N-S. Angelo
Goliad	24, 135, 267	13	4	S-Victoria
Gonzales	25, 25-A	13	3	W-San Ant.
Gray	31, 223	7	9	N-Amarillo
Grayson	15, 59, 397	5	1	E-Sherman
Gregg	124, 188, 307	6, 12	10	E-Tyler
Grimes	12, 506	1, 14	2	S-Houston
Guadalupe	25, 25-A, 274, 456	4	3	W-San Ant.
Hale	64, 242	7	9	N-Lubbock
Hall	100	7	9	N-Amarillo
Hamilton	220	10	3	W-Waco
Hansford	84	7	9	N-Amarillo
Hardeman	46	7	9	N-W. Falls
Hardin	88, 356	9	2	E-B'mont
Harris	11, 55, 61, 80, 113, 125,127, 129, 133, 151, 152, 157, 164, 165, 174, 176, 177, 178, 179, 180, 182, 183, 184, 185, 189, 190, 208, 209, 215, 228, 230, 232, 234, 245, 246, 247, 248, 257, 262, 263, 269, 270, 280, 281, 295, 308, 309, 310, 311, 312, 313, 314, 315, 333, 334, 337, 338, 339, 351, 507, 482	1, 14	11	S-Houston
Harrison	71	6	10	E-Marshall
Hartley	69	7	9	N-Amarillo
Haskell	39	11	7	N-Abilene
Hays	22, 207, 274, 428, 453, 483	3	3	W-Austin
Hemphill	31	7	9	N-Amarillo
Henderson	3, 173, 392	12	10	E-Tyler
Hidalgo	92, 93, 139, 206, 275, 332, 370, 389, 398, 430, 449, 464, 476	13	5	S-McAllen
Hill	66	10	3	W-Waco
Hockley	286	7	9	N-Lubbock

County	State Dist. Court(s)	Ct. of Appeals Dist	Adm. Jud. Reg.	U.S. Jud. Dist.
Hood	355	2	8	N-Ft. Worth
Hopkins	8, 62	6	10	E-Sherman
Houston	3, 349	12	10	E-Lufkin
Howard	118	11	7	N-Abilene
Hudspeth	205, 394	8	6	W-Pecos
Hunt	196, 354	5, 6	10	N-Dallas
Hutchinson	84, 316	7	9	N-Amarillo
Irion	51	3	7	N-S. Angelo
Jack	271	2	8	N-Ft. Worth
Jackson	24, 135, 267	13	4	S-Victoria
Jasper	1, 1-A	9	2	E-B'mont
Jeff Davis	394	8	6	W-Pecos
Jefferson	58, 60, 136, 172, 252, 279, 317, Cr. 1	9	2	E-B'mont
Jim Hogg	229	4	5	S-Laredo
Jim Wells	79	4	5	S-C. Christi
Johnson	18, 249, 413	10	8	N-Dallas
Jones	259	11	7	N-Abilene
Karnes	81, 218	4	4	W-San Ant.
Kaufman	86, 422	5	1	N-Dallas
Kendall	451	4	6	W-San Ant.
Kenedy	105	13	5	S-C. Christi
Kent	39	7	7	N-Lubbock
Kerr	198, 216	4	6	W-San Ant.
Kimble	452	4	6	W-Austin
King	50	7	9	N-W. Falls
Kinney	63	4	6	W-Del Rio
Kleberg	105	13	5	S-C. Christi
Knox	50	11	9	N-W. Falls
Lamar	6, 62	6	10	E-Sherman
Lamb	154	7	9	N-Lubbock
Lampasas	27	3	3	W-Austin
La Salle	81, 218	4	4	S-Laredo
Lavaca	25, 25-A	13	3	S-Victoria
Lee	21, 335	3	2	W-Austin
Leon	87, 278, 369	10	10	W-Waco
Liberty	75, 253	9	2	E-B'mont
Limestone	77, 87	10	10	W-Waco
Lipscomb	31	7	9	N-Amarillo
Live Oak	36, 156, 343	13	4	S-C. Christi
Llano	33, 424	3	3	W-Austin
Loving	143	8	7	W-Pecos
Lubbock	72, 99, 137, 140, 237, 364	7	9	N-Lubbock
Lynn	106	7	7	N-Lubbock
Madison	12, 278	10	2	S-Houston
Marion	115, 276	6	10	E-Marshall
Martin	118	11	7	W-Midland
Mason	452	4	6	W-Austin
Matagorda	23, 130	13	11	S-Galves
Maverick	293, 365	4	4	W-Del Rio
McCulloch	452	3	6	W-Austin
McLennan	19, 54, 74, 170, 414, 474	10	3	W-Waco
McMullen	36, 156, 343	4	4	S-Laredo
Medina	454	4	6	W-San Ant.
Menard	452	4	6	N-S. Angelo
Midland	142, 238, 318, 385, 441	11	7	W-Midland
Milam	20	3	3	W-Waco
Mills	35	3	7	N-S. Angelo
Mitchell	32	11	7	N-Abilene
Montague	97	2	8	N-W. Falls
Montgomery	9, 221, 284, 359, 410, 418, 435, 457	9	2	S-Houston
Moore	69	7	9	N-Amarillo
Morris	76, 276	6	10	E-Marshall
Motley	110	7	9	N-Lubbock
Nacogdoches	145, 420	12	10	E-Lufkin
Navarro	13	10	3	N-Dallas
Newton	1, 1-A	9	2	E-B'mont
Nolan	32	11	7	N-Abilene
Nueces	28, 94, 105, 117, 148, 214, 319, 347	13	5	S-C. Christi
Ochiltree	84	7	9	N-Amarillo
Oldham	222	7	9	N-Amarillo
Orange	128, 163, 260	9	2	E-B'mont
Palo Pinto	29	11	8	N-Ft. Worth
Panola	123	6	10	E-Tyler
Parker	43, 415	2	8	N-Ft. Worth
Parmer	287	7	9	N-Amarillo
Pecos	83, 112	8	6	W-Pecos
Polk	258, 411	9	2	E-Lufkin

County	State Dist. Court(s)	Ct. of Appeals Dist	Adm. Jud. Reg.	U.S. Jud. Dist.
Potter	47, 108, 181, 251, 320	7	9	N-Amarillo
Presidio	394	8	6	W-Pecos
Rains	8, 354	12	10	E-Tyler
Randall	47, 181, 251	7	9	N-Amarillo
Reagan	112	8	6	N-S. Angelo
Real	38	4	6	W-San Ant.
Red River	6, 102	6	10	E-Texark
Reeves	143	8	7	W-Pecos
Refugio	24, 135, 267	13	4	S-Victoria
Roberts	31	7	9	N-Amarillo
Robertson	82	10	3	W-Waco
Rockwall	382, 439	5	1	N-Dallas
Runnels	119	3	7	N-S. Angelo
Rusk	4	6, 12	10	E-Tyler
Sabine	1, 273	12	10	E-Lufkin
San Augustine	1, 273	12	10	E-Lufkin
San Jacinto	258, 411	9	2	S-Houston
San Patricio	36, 156, 343	13	4	S-C. Christi
San Saba	33, 424	3	3	W-Austin
Schleicher	51	3	7	N-S. Angelo
Scurry	132	11	7	N-Lubbock
Shackelford	259	11	7	N-Abilene
Shelby	123, 273	12	10	E-Lufkin
Sherman	69	7	9	N-Amarillo
Smith	7, 114, 241, 321, 475	12	10	E-Tyler
Somervell	18, 249	10	8	W-Waco
Starr	229, 381	4	5	S-McAllen
Stephens	90	11	8	N-Abilene
Sterling	51	3	7	N-S. Angelo
Stonewall	39	11	7	N-Abilene
Sutton	112	4	6	N-S. Angelo
Swisher	64, 242	7	9	N-Amarillo
Tarrant	17, 48, 67, 96, 141, 153, 213, 231, 233, 236, 297, 322, 323, 324, 325, 342, 348, 352, 360, 371, 372, 396, 432, 485, Cr. 1, Cr. 2, Cr. 3, Cr. 4	2	8	N-Ft. Worth
Taylor	42, 104, 326, 350	11	7	N-Abilene
Terrell	63, 83	8	6	W-Del Rio
Terry	121	7	9	N-Lubbock
Throckmorton	39	11	7	N-Abilene
Titus	76, 276	6	10	E-Texark
Tom Green	51, 119, 340, 391	3	7	N-S. Angelo
Travis	53, 98, 126, 147, 167, 200, 201, 250, 261, 299, 331, 345, 353, 390, 403, 419, 427, 450, 455, 459, 460	3	3	W-Austin
Trinity	258, 411	12	2	E-Lufkin
Tyler	1-A, 88	9	2	E-Lufkin
Upshur	115	6, 12	10	E-Marshall
Upton	112	8	6	W-Midland
Uvalde	38	4	6	W-Del Rio
Val Verde	63, 83	4	6	W-Del Rio
Van Zandt	294	12	10	E-Tyler
Victoria	24, 135, 267, 377	13	4	S-Victoria
Walker	12, 278	10	2	S-Houston
Waller	506	1, 14	2	S-Houston
Ward	143	8	7	W-Pecos
Washington	21, 335	1, 14	2	W-Austin
Webb	49, 111, 341, 406	4	4	S-Laredo
Wharton	23, 329	13	11	S-Houston
Wheeler	31	7	9	N-Amarillo
Wichita	30, 78, 89	2	8	N-W. Falls
Wilbarger	46	7	9	N-W. Falls
Willacy	197	13	5	S-Brownsville
Williamson	26, 277, 368, 395, 425, 480	3	3	W-Austin
Wilson	81, 218	4	4	W-San Ant.
Winkler	109	8	7	W-Pecos
Wise	271	2	8	N-Ft. Worth
Wood	402	6, 12	10	E-Tyler
Yoakum	121	7	9	N-Lubbock
Young	90	2	8	N-W. Falls
Zapata	49	4	4	S-Laredo
Zavala	293, 365	4	4	W-Del Rio

Texas State Agencies

The following pages contain information about several of the many state agencies in Texas. Information was supplied to the Texas Almanac by the agencies, their websites, and from news reports. For more information about state agencies, boards, and commissions, go to: www.tsl.texas.gov/apps/lrs/agencies/index.html.

Texas Commission on Environmental Quality

Source: Texas Commission on Environmental Quality; www.tceq.texas.gov

The Texas Commission on Environmental Quality (TCEQ) is the state's leading environmental agency. The TCEQ works to protect Texas' human and natural resources in a manner consistent with sustainable economic development. The agency has about 2,700 employees; of those, about 800 work in the 16 regional offices.

One of the TCEQ's major functions is issuing permits and other authorizations for the control of air pollution, the safe operation of water and wastewater utilities, and the management of hazardous and nonhazardous waste.

The agency promotes voluntary compliance with environmental laws through pollution prevention programs, regulatory workshops, and assistance to businesses and local governments. When environmental laws are violated, the TCEQ has the authority to levy penalties as much as $25,000 a day per violation for administrative cases. In a typical year, the agency conducts more than 105,000 investigations at regulated entities for compliance with state and federal laws and receives about 4,000 complaints.

Office of Air

Texas is home to some of the largest U.S. cities, with several metropolitan populations of greater than 1 million people. With these concentrated populations, vehicular traffic and other emissions can create air quality issues among the most challenging in the country.

The state has a fast-growing population, a large industrial base concentrated along the Gulf Coast, and an oil and gas industry expanding throughout much of the state. The TCEQ conducts survey activities along with targeted and/or specialized monitoring activities to evaluate changing air quality conditions across the state.

The TCEQ measures air quality across the state for compliance with federal standards, as well as for localized compounds of concern. Texas' air toxic monitoring network is one of the most comprehensive in the country with more than 80 monitoring sites located across the state.

The TCEQ is responsible for developing a state implementation plan to bring metropolitan areas into compliance with federal air quality standards, such as the ozone standard. The leading areas of concern for ozone issues are the Houston-Galveston-Brazoria and Dallas–Fort Worth areas.

Office of Water

The TCEQ preserves and improves the quality of the state's surface waters by establishing surface water quality standards; monitoring, assessing, and reporting conditions; and implementing plans to reduce pollution and improve water quality. It protects surface water users through the water rights permitting process and the watermaster programs.

The TCEQ is also responsible for most state and federal regulatory programs that protect groundwater, administers permits for the discharge of wastewater and stormwater, and conducts Section 401 certifications of federal permits.

The agency enforces the federal Safe Drinking Water Act, oversees the protection of the state's approximately 7,000 public water systems providing drinking water to roughly 27 million customers, and has general supervision of water districts.

Office of Waste

Waste management projects at the TCEQ include Superfund projects, pesticide collections, and permits and authorizations for municipal and industrial waste management. Another major cleanup program focuses on leaking petroleum storage tanks. In 2019, there were 55 Superfund sites in the state, and work continues at another 1,344 sites.

The TCEQ issues permits and other authorizations for municipal and industrial waste management, including landfills and storage, processing, and recycling operations. In addition, the safe recycling of both municipal and industrial waste streams is encouraged.

The TCEQ also regulates the disposal of radioactive material, with the exception of naturally occurring radioactive material (NORM) generated as a result of oil and gas exploration. This includes the regulation of the receipt, processing, storage, and disposal of by-product and low-level radioactive waste, the licensing of uranium and thorium recovery facilities, decommissioning of inactive uranium-recovery facilities, permitting for underground injection control, and legacy radioactive material disposal sites.

Help With Understanding Environmental Rules

The TCEQ offers services to anyone interested in environmental stewardship and navigating TCEQ's programs and regulatory requirements. Staff members host workshops on recycling and disposal opportunities, and on regulatory and pollution prevention topics.

The TCEQ also offers free compliance assistance to thousands of small businesses and local governments each year. Contact the TCEQ at PO Box 13087, Austin, 78711; (512) 239–1000. ☆

Health and Human Services

Source: Texas Health and Human Services, hhs.texas.gov

Texas Health and Human Services (HHS) is the oversight agency for the state's health and human services system. HHS also administers state and federal programs that provide financial, health, and social services to Texans. Executive Commissioner Cecile Erwin Young was appointed on Aug. 14, 2020.

In 2003, the 78th Texas Legislature mandated an unprecedented transformation of the state's health and human services system, blending 12 agencies into five. The system transformed again in 2017, with the goal of removing bureaucratic silos, creating clear lines of accountability, and making it easier for people to find out about services or benefits they might qualify for.

Today's HHS consists of only two agencies: Texas Health and Human Services Commission (HHSC) and the Texas Department of State Health Services (DSHS). The executive commissioner is appointed by the governor and confirmed by the Senate. The Department of Family and Protective Services is an independent agency under the HHSC umbrella.

HHS is located at 4601 Guadalupe St., Austin, 78711–3247; Phone: (512) 424–6500; TTY: (512) 424–6597.

Health and Human Services Commission

The HHSC oversees the licensing and credentialing of facilities for long-term care, including nursing homes and assisted living; licenses child care providers; and manages daily operations at state-supported hospitals and living centers.

It also delivers benefits and services such as Medicaid, SNAP food benefits, and TANF cash assistance; services for women and people with special health needs; long-term care for the aging and those with disabilities; and behavioral health services.

Department of State Health Services

DSHS serves as the public health authority for Texas, providing vital statistics and health data to the public, leading the public-health response in times of disaster or outbreaks, and administering chronic and infectious disease prevention and testing. The department also licenses and regulates facilities on topics including youth camps and mobile food establishments. It is led by Commissioner of Public Health Dr. Jennifer Shuford.

The client services DSHS previously provided were transferred to HHSC in 2016.

Department of Family and Protective Services

The Department of Family and Protective Services (DFPS) works to protect children and vulnerable adults through prevention programs, investigations, and services and referrals. DFPS has five major programs:

- Adult Protective Services
- Child Protective Services
- Investigations
- Prevention and Early Intervention
- Statewide Intake

To report abuse, neglect, or exploitation of children, the elderly or people with disabilities, call 1-800-252-5400 or report online at www.txabusehotline.org. For emergencies call 911.

DFPS headquarters address: 4900 N. Lamar Blvd., Austin, 78751; Mailing address: PO Box 149030, Austin, 78714-9030; https://www.dfps.texas.gov/.

Other HHSC Programs

The Family Violence program offers emergency shelter and services to victims and their children.

The Disaster Assistance program processes grant applications for victims of presidentially declared disasters, such as tornados, floods, and hurricanes.

As of 2017, the HHS no longer provides refugee resettlement services. Nonprofit agencies, including U.S. Committee for Refugees and Immigrants (USCRI), have stepped in to provide health services for these groups.☆

Major HHS Programs at a Glance

The **Medicaid** program provides healthcare coverage for one out of every three children in Texas, pays for half of all births, and accounts for 25 percent of the state's total budget. In 2018, an average of 4 million Texans received healthcare coverage through Medicaid.

The Children's Health Insurance Program (CHIP) is designed for families who earn too much money to qualify for Medicaid yet cannot afford private insurance.

The Temporary Assistance for Needy Families (TANF) program provides basic financial assistance for needy children and the parents or caretakers with whom they live. As a condition of eligibility, caretakers must sign and abide by a personal-responsibility agreement. Time limits for benefits have been set by both state and federal welfare-reform legislation.

SNAP food benefits, formerly known as food stamps, is a federally funded program that assists low-income families, the elderly, and single adults obtain a nutritionally adequate diet.

Both SNAP and TANF benefits are delivered via the electronic benefit transfer (EBT) system, through which clients access benefits at about 12,000 retail locations statewide with the Lone Star card. Information about Medicaid, CHIP, and other health and human services programs can be found at www.211texas.org, or by calling **2-1-1**, a toll-free local resource for information on HHS programs.

The General Land Office

Source: General Land Office of Texas, glo.texas.gov

The Texas General Land Office (GLO) is one of the oldest governmental entities in the state, dating back to the Republic of Texas. The first General Land Office was established in 1836 by the Republic's constitution, and the first Texas Congress enacted the provision into law in 1837. The GLO was established to oversee distribution of public lands, register titles, issue patents on land, and maintain records of land granted.

In the early years of statehood, beginning in 1845, Texas established the precedent of using its vast public domain for public benefit. The first use was to sell or trade land to eliminate the huge debt remaining from Texas' War for Independence and the early years of the Republic.

Texas also gave away land to settlers as homesteads; to veterans as compensation for service; for internal improvements, including building railroads, shipbuilding, and improving rivers for navigation; and to build the state Capitol.

The public domain was closed in 1898 when the Texas Supreme Court declared there was no more vacant and unappropriated land in Texas. In 1900, all remaining unappropriated land was set aside by the Legislature to benefit public schools.

Today, 13 million acres of land and minerals, owned by the Permanent School Fund, the Permanent University Fund, various other state agencies, and the Veterans Land Board, are managed by the GLO and the Commissioner of the Texas General Land Office.

Historic Distribution of the Public Lands of Texas

PURPOSE	ACRES
Settlers	**68,027,108**
Spain and Mexico	24,583,923
Spanish and Mexican Grants south of the Nueces River, recognized by Act of Feb. 10, 1852	3,741,241
Headrights	30,360,002
Republic colonies	4,494,806
Preemption land	4,847,136
Military	**9,874,262**
Bounty	5,354,250
Battle donations	1,162,240
Veterans donations	1,377,920
Confederate	1,979,852
Improvements	**37,155,714**
Road	27,716
Navigation	4,261,760
Irrigation	584,000
Ships	17,000
Manufacturing	111,360
Railroads	32,153,878
Education	**52,329,168**
University, public school, and eleemosynary institutions	52,329,168
Total of distributed lands	**167,386,252**

This includes over 4 million acres of submerged coastal lands, which consist of bays, inlets, and the area from the Texas shoreline to the three-marine-league line (10.36 miles) in the Gulf of Mexico. It is estimated that more than 1 million acres make up the public domain of the state's riverbeds and another 1.7 million acres are excess lands belonging to the Permanent School Fund.

The GLO is the steward of the Texas Gulf Coast, serving as the premier state agency for protecting and renourishing the coast and fighting coastal erosion. In 1999, the Legislature created the Coastal Erosion Planning and Response Act and put the GLO in charge of facilitating restoration and preservation of eroding beaches, dunes, wetlands, and other bay shorelines along the Texas coast.

The Permanent School Fund owns mineral rights alone in almost 7.4 million acres covered under the Relinquishment Act, the Free Royalty Act, and the various sales acts, and it has outright ownership to about 747,522 upland acres, mostly west of the Pecos River.

Texas Veterans Land Board Programs

The Veterans Land Board (VLB) was formally established by the Legislature to administer benefits for Texas Veterans in 1946, with the first loan made in 1949.

Since then, the programs have evolved to include low-interest land, housing, and home improvement loans. VLB has funded more than 220,000 loans amounting to more than $11 billion for Texas veterans, military members, and their families since its inception.

VLB strives to offer the best benefits program in the nation and works to ensure that Texas veterans are aware of these benefits.

In a joint effort with the Texas Veterans Commission, the VLB operates the Texas Veterans Call Service Center to connect veterans, military members, and their families with the benefits and services they need. For more information, contact VLB at 1-800-252-VETS (8387) or https://vlb.texas.gov/

Texas State Veterans

In 1997, the 75th Legislature approved legislation authorizing the Veterans Land Board to construct and operate Texas State Veterans Homes under a cost-sharing program with the U.S. Department of Veterans Affairs (USDVA). The homes provide affordable, quality, long-term care for Texas' veterans.

The VLB owns and operates several cemeteries under USDVA guidelines. The USDVA funds the design and construction of the cemeteries, but the land must be donated.

The Alamo

In 2011, the 82nd Legislature granted authority over the Alamo to the GLO. The Alamo hosts millions of visitors from around the world each year. UNESCO designated the Alamo and four other Spanish missions in San Antonio as U.S. World Heritage sites in 2015. ☆

The lighthouse at Port Isabel. Photo by the Texas Historical Commission

Texas Historical Commission

The Texas Historical Commission protects and preserves the state's historic and prehistoric resources. The Texas State Legislature established the Texas State Historical Survey Committee in 1953 to identify important historic sites across the state. (For a comprehensive list of state historic sites, check out pages 159–162 in the Recreation chapter.)

The Texas Legislature changed the agency's name to the Texas Historical Commission in 1973 and increased its mission and its protective powers. Today the agency's concerns include archaeology, architecture, community heritage development, historic sites, history programs, and education. The commission:

- Works with communities and individuals to help identify important historic resources and develop a plan to preserve them.
- Provides leadership and training to county historical commissions, heritage organizations, and museums in Texas' 254 counties.
- Helps protect Texas' diverse architectural heritage, including historic county courthouses.
- Partners with communities to stimulate tourism and economic development.
- Assists Texas cities in the revitalization of their historic downtowns through the Texas Main Street Program.
- Administers the state's historical marker program, which has around 15,000 markers across the state.
- Consults with citizens and groups to nominate properties as Recorded Texas Historic Landmarks, State Archeological Landmarks, and to the National Register of Historic Places.
- Operates 20 state historic sites including house museums, military forts, and archeological sites.
- Works with property owners to save archeological sites on private land and ensures archeological sites are protected as land is developed for highways and other public construction projects.

Mailing address: PO Box 12276, Austin 78711–2276; (512) 463–6100; www.thc.texas.gov.

Railroad Commission of Texas

The Railroad Commission of Texas has primary regulatory jurisdiction over the oil and natural gas industry, pipeline transporters, the natural gas and hazardous liquid pipeline industry, natural gas utilities, the liquefied petroleum gas (LP-gas) industry, rail industry, and coal and uranium surface mining operations. It also promotes the use of LP-gas as an alternative fuel in Texas through research and education.

The commission exercises its statutory responsibilities under provisions of the Texas Constitution, the Texas Natural Resources Code, the Texas Water Code, the Texas Utilities Code, the Coal and Uranium Surface Mining and Reclamation Acts, the Pipeline Safety Acts, and the Railroad Safety Act.

The commission has regulatory and enforcement responsibilities under federal law, including the Federal Railroad Safety Act, the Local Rail Freight Assistance Act, the Surface Coal Mining Control and Reclamation Act, the Pipeline Safety Acts, the Resource Conservation Recovery Act, and the Clean Water Act.

The Railroad Commission was established by the Texas Legislature in 1891 and given jurisdiction over rates and operations of railroads, terminals, wharves, and express companies. In 1917, the legislature declared pipelines to be common carriers and gave the commission regulatory authority over them. It was also given the responsibility to administer conservation laws relating to oil and natural gas production.

The Railroad Commission exists to protect the environment, public safety, and the rights of mineral interest owners; to prevent waste of natural resources; and to assure fair and equitable utility rates in those industries over which it has authority. Mailing address: PO Box 12967, Austin 78711–2967; (512) 463–7158; www.rrc.state.tx.us.

Texas Department of Juvenile Justice

The Texas Department of Juvenile Justice was created on Dec. 1, 2011, by Senate Bill 653, 82nd Legislature. Its creation abolished both the Texas Youth Commission and the Texas Juvenile Probation Commission.

The agency's executive director is Shandra Carter, and it has a 13-member commission who are appointed to six-year terms. It is chaired by Scott Matthew of Georgetown.

The **Texas Youth Commission (TYC)** had operated correctional facilities and halfway houses for serious youth offenders. In 2007, widespread sexual and physical abuse was uncovered at many of its facilities. After a number of supervisors were dismissed, the entire TYC board resigned on March 15, 2007, and their powers were transferred to a conservator. The 80th Texas Legislature approved a bill to overhaul the troubled agency.

The **Texas Department of Juvenile Justice** is a unified state juvenile justice agency that works in partnership with local county governments, courts, and communities to promote public safety by providing services to youth from initial contact through end of supervision. Its expressed goals are to:

- Support development of county-based programs and services for youth and families that reduce the need for out-of-home placement;
- Seek alternatives to placing youthful offenders in secure state facilities, while also addressing treatment of youth and protecting the public;
- Locate facilities as geographically close as possible to workforce and other services, and support youths' connection to their families;
- Encourage regional and county collaboration;
- Enhance the continuity of care throughout the juvenile justice system; and
- Use secure facilities of a size that supports effective youth rehabilitation and public safety.

The agency is located at 1711 San Jacinto Blvd., Austin 78701. Mailing Address: PO Box 12757, Austin 78711–2757; (512) 490–7130; www.tjjd.texas.gov/.

Texas Workforce Commission

The Texas Workforce Commission (TWC) is the state government agency charged with overseeing and providing workforce development services to employers and job seekers of Texas. It is led by three appointed commissioners, representing the public (Chairman Bryan Daniel), labor (Alberto Treviño III), and employers (Aaron Demerson).

For employers, TWC offers recruiting, retention, training and retraining, outplacement services, and information on labor law and labor market statistics.

For job seekers, TWC offers career development information, job search resources, training programs, and, as appropriate, unemployment benefits. While targeted populations receive intensive assistance to overcome barriers to employment, all Texans can benefit from the services offered by TWC and its network of workforce partners.

The Texas Workforce Commission is part of a local and state network dedicated to developing the workforce of Texas. The network is composed of the statewide efforts of the commission coupled with planning and service provision on a regional level by 28 local workforce boards. This network gives customers access to local workforce solutions and statewide services in a single location — Texas Workforce Centers.

Primary services of the Texas Workforce Commission and its network partners are funded by federal tax revenue and are generally free to all Texans.

Job searchers and employeers can connect through https://www.workintexas.com

Mailing address: 101 E. 15th Street, Austin 78778; (512) 463–2222; www.twc.state.tx.us. ☆

Texas State Boards and Commissions

Following is a list of appointees to state boards and commissions, as well as names of other state officials, revised to **July 2023**. Information includes, where available, (1) date of creation; (2) whether the position is elective or appointive; (3) length of term; (4) compensation, if any; (5) number of members; (6) names of appointees, their hometowns, and expiration of terms. In some instances the date of term expiration has passed; in such cases, no new appointment had been made by press time, and the official is continuing to fill the position until a successor is named. Most positions marked "apptv." are appointed by the Governor. Where otherwise, appointing authority is given. Most advisory boards are not listed. Salaries for commissioners and administrators are those that were authorized by the appropriations bill passed by the 87th Legislature for the 2022–2023 biennium. They are "not-to-exceed" salaries: maximum authorized salaries for the positions. Actual salaries may be less than those stated here.

Accountancy, Texas State Board of Public: (1945 with 2-yr. terms; reorganized 1959 as 9-member board with 6-yr. overlapping terms; number of members increased to 12 in 1979; increased to 15 in 1989); per diem and expenses: Presiding Officer Debra D. Seefeld, Montgomery (1/31/25); Susan I. Adams, Colleyville (1/31/27); Kimberly D. "Kim" Crawford, Arlington (1/31/29); Olivia Espinoza-Riley, Addison (1/31/27); Renee D. Foshee, San Marcos (1/31/27); Himesh M. Gandhi, Sugar Land (1/31/25); Ray R. Garcia, Houston (1/31/27); Jamie D. Grant, Arlington (1/31/23); Jill A. Holup, Austin (1/31/25); Kevin J. Koch, Temple (1/31/25); Sherri B. Merket, Midland (1/31/29); Thomas M. Neuhoff, Tyler (1/31/29); Jeannette P. Smith, Mission (1/31/25); Sheila M. Vallés-Pankratz, Mission (1/31/27); Susan M. Warren, Georgetown (1/31/29). Exec. Dir. William Treacy ($200,000), 505 E. Huntland Dr., Ste. 380, Austin 78752-3757; (512) 305–7800.

Acupuncture Examiners, Texas State Board of: (1993); apptv.; 6-yr.; per diem; 9 members: Presiding Officer Donna S. Guthery, Bellaire (1/31/23); Elisabeth Lee "Ellee" Carlson, Garland (1/31/25); Sheri J. Davidson, Houston (1/31/25); Maria M. Garcia, Plano (1/31/27); Samantha A. Gonzalez, San Antonio (1/31/27); Mary E. Hebert, Nacogdoches (1/31/25); Grant E. Weidler, Spring (1/31/23); Rey Ximenes, Spicewood (1/31/27); 1 vacancy. Exec. Dir. Stephen Brint Carlton, 1801 Congress Ave., Ste. 9.200, Austin 78701; (512) 305–7010.

Adjutant General's Dept. (See Military Dept., Texas.)

Administrative Hearings, State Office of: (1991); apptv.; 2-yr.; 1 member: Chief Admin. Law Judge Kristofer Monson, Driftwood (5/15/24) ($180,000), 300 W. 15th St., Ste. 504, Austin 78701; (512) 475–4993.

Affordable Housing Corporation, Texas State: (1994); 6 yrs.; 5 members: Chair Bill Dietz, Waco (2/1/25); Valerie V. Cardenas, San Juan (2/1/25); Courtney Johnson Rose, Missouri City (2/1/27); Andy Williams, Fort Worth (2/1/23); Lemuel Williams, Austin (2/1/27). Pres. David Long, 6701 Shirley Ave., Austin 78752; (512) 477–3555.

Aging and Disability Services Council, Department of (DADS): Est. 2003 by the 78th Legislature; later abolished by 84th Legislature (Senate Bill 200) effective 9/1/2017 and services merged into Texas Health and Human Services Commission.

Alcoholic Beverage Commission, Texas: (1935 as Liquor Control Board; name changed in 1970); apptv.; 6-yr; per diem and expenses; administrator apptd. by commission; 5 members: Chair Kevin J. Lilly, Houston (11/15/27); M. Scott Adkins, El Paso (11/15/23); Jason E. Boatright, Dallas (11/15/23); Hasan K. Mack, Austin (11/15/25); Deborah Gray Marino, San Antonio (11/15/25). Exec. Dir. Thomas Graham ($200,000), 5806 Mesa Dr., PO Box 13127, Austin 78711; (512) 206–3333.

Alzheimer's Disease and Related Disorders, Texas Council on: (1987); apptv.; 2-yr.; 15 members (3 ex officio; 12 appointed by Gov., Lt. Gov., and House Speaker): Chair Marc Diamond, Dallas (8/31/25); Byron Cordes, San Antonio (8/31/23); Laura DeFina, Richardson (8/31/25); Joe A. Evans Jr., Beaumont (8/31/27); Vaunette Fay, Houston (8/31/21); Ana Guerrero Gore, Galveston (8/31/21); Char Hu, Dallas (8/31/23); Eddie L. Patton Jr., Houston (8/31/27); Mary Ellen Quiceno, Galveston (8/31/23); Sudha Seshadri, San Antonio (8/31/19); Terrence Sommers, Amarillo (8/31/23); Angela Turner, Normangee (8/31/2025). Ex officio members include 1 from Texas Dept. of State Health Services and 2 from Texas Health and Human Services Commission. 1100 W. 49th St., PO Box 149347, Austin 78714-9347; (800) 242–3399.

Angelina & Neches River Authority: (1935 as Sabine-Neches Conservation Dist.; reorganized in 1950 and name changed to Neches River Conservation Dist.; changed to present name in 1977); apptv.; expenses; 6-yr.; 9 members: Pres. Joseph L. "Jody" Anderson, Lufkin (9/5/25); Kimberly M. "Kim" Childs, Nacogdoches (9/5/25); Erin Holloway, Arp (9/5/2027); Robert E. "Eddie" Hopkins, Jasper (9/5/23); Donnie R. Kee, Lufkin (9/5/23); Virginia "Ginger" Lymbery, Lufkin (9/5/23); Dale Morton, Nacogdoches (9/5/27); Thomas R. "Tom" Murphy, Crockett (9/5/25); Francis G. Spruiell, Center (9/5/27). Gen. Mgr. Kelley Holcomb, 2901 N. John Redditt Dr., Lufkin 75904; (936) 632–7795.

Animal Health Commission, Texas: (1893 as Texas Livestock Sanitary Commission; name changed in 1959; members increased to 9 in 1973; raised to current number in 1983); apptv.; per diem and expenses; 6-yr.; 13 members: Chair Coleman Locke, Wharton (9/6/27); Ali Broyles, Weatherford (9/6/27); Jimmie Ruth Evans, San Antonio (9/6/25); Melanie Johnson, Houston (9/6/25); Kenneth "Ken" Jordan, San Saba (9/6/27); Barret J. Klein, Boerne (9/6/25); Joe Leathers, Guthrie (9/6/25); Thomas "Tommy" Oates, Huntsville (9/6/25); Joseph G. "Joe" Osterkamp, Muleshoe (9/6/23); Wendee L. Payne, Lubbock (9/6/23); Keith M. Staggs, Gonzales (9/6/23); Benjamin Turner, Kingsville (9/6/27); Leo Vermedahl, Dalhart (9/6/23). Exec. Dir. Andy Schwartz ($155,814), 2105 Kramer Ln., PO Box 12966, Austin 78711-2966; (512) 719–0700.

Appraiser Licensing & Certification Board, Texas: (1991); 6-yr.; apptv.; per diem on duty; 9 members; 1 ex officio: Texas General Land Office; 8 apptd: Chair Sara Oates, Austin (1/31/25); R. Chance Bolton, Bee Cave (1/31/27); Rolando Castro, Cypress (1/31/29); John H. Eichelberger, Houston (1/31/29); Paola Escalante-Castillo, Weslaco (1/31/27); Martha Gayle Reid Lynch, El Paso (1/31/27); Stephanie Robinson, McKinney (1/31/25); Lisa Sprinkle, El Paso (1/31/25). Comm. Chelsea Buchholtz, PO Box 12188, Austin 78711-2188; (512) 936–3001.

Architectural Examiners, Texas Board of: (1937 as 3-member board; raised to 6 members in 1951 and to 9 in 1977); apptv.; 6-yr.; per diem and expenses. Chair Debra Dockery, San Antonio (1/31/23); Tim A. Bargainer, Georgetown (1/31/25); Darren L. James, Lewisville (1/31/25); Rosa G. Salazar, Lubbock (1/31/23); Joyce J. Smith, Burnet (1/31/23); Fernando Trevino, San Antonio (1/31/25); Jennifer Walker, Lampasas (1/31/27); Bob Wetmore, Austin (1/31/27); 1 vacancy. Exec. Dir. Julie Hildebrand ($170,145), 505 E. Huntland Dr., Ste. 350, PO Box 12337, Austin 78711; (512) 305–9000.

Arts, Texas Commission on the: (1965 as Texas Fine Arts Commission; name changed to Texas Commission on the Arts and Humanities in 1971; to present form in 1979); apptv.; 6-yr.; expenses; 9 members: Chair Dale W. Brock, Fort Worth (8/31/23); Theresa W. Chang, Houston (8/31/25); Diane Milliken Garza, Brownsville (8/31/27); Adrian Guerra, Roma

(8/31/23); Mary Ann Apap Heller, Austin (8/31/25); Patty Nuss, Corpus Christi (8/31/23); Karen Partee, Marshall (8/31/25); Marci Roberts, Marathon (8/31/27); 1 vacancy. Exec. Dir. Gary Gibbs ($129,927), 920 Colorado St., Ste. 501, PO Box 13406, Austin 78711-3406; (512) 463–5535.

Assistive and Rehabilitative Services, Department of: (2004); apptv.; 6-yr.; 9 members: Department was dissolved in September 2016 and programs were transferred to Texas Workforce Commission.

Athletic Trainers, Advisory Board of: (1971 as Texas Board of Athletic Trainers; name changed in 1975); expenses; 6-yr.; 5 members: Presiding Officer Britney Webb, San Marcos (1/31/27); Michael Fitch, Dallas (1/31/29); Ronald Hebert III, Cypress (1/31/27); David Schmidt, San Antonio (1/31/29); David Weir, College Station (1/31/25). PO Box 12157, Austin 78711; (512) 463–6599.

Auditor's Office, State: (1929); 2-yr.; apptd. by Legislative Audit Committee, a joint Senate-House committee: State Auditor Lisa R. Collier ($220,000), 1501 Congress Ave., PO Box 12067, Austin 78711-2067; (512) 936–9500.

Autism and Pervasive Developmental Disorders, Texas Council on: (1987); abolished by the 84th Legislature in 2015. Duties transferred to Texas Health and Human Services Commission.

Banking, Texas Department of: (1923); 2-yr.; apptd. by State Finance Commission; Comm. Charles G. Cooper ($254,850); 2601 N. Lamar Blvd., Austin 78705; (512) 475–1300. (See also Finance Commission of Texas.)

Barbering and Cosmetology Advisory Board: (1929 as 3-member Texas Board of Barber Examiners; members increased in 1975; name changed in 2005 to Advisory Board on Barbering and functions transferred to Texas Dept. of Licensing & Regulation; name changed to present form in 2022 when consolidated with Advisory Board on Cosmetology); 6-yr.; 9 members: Presiding Officer Mary Paschal-Lindsay, Houston (1/31/25); Aurora Farthing, Lubbock (1/31/27); Salvador Flores, McAllen (1/31/25); Naylan Holman, Plano (1/31/29); Natalie Inderman, Lubbock (1/31/29); Ron Jemison Jr., Houston (1/31/27); Le'Detrick Leonard, Austin (1/31/25); Darren Peterson, Lakeway (1/31/27); Laura Valdez, Austin (1/31/29). PO Box 12157, Austin 78711; (512) 463–6599.

Bar of Texas, State: (1939 as administrative arm of Supreme Court); 46 directors, 36 elected by membership, 6 apptd by Texas Supreme Court, 4 by bar president; 3-yr. terms; also 14 ex officio members, including immediate past chair and out-of-state members; expenses paid from dues collected from membership. Chair Chad Baruch, Texas Law Center, 1414 Colorado St., Austin 78701; (512) 427–1463.

Behavioral Health Executive Council, Texas: (2019, created by Legislature to comprise 4 existing Boards of Examiners); 6-yr. for presiding member, 2-yr. for others; 9 members: Presiding Member Gloria Canseco, San Antonio (2/1/25); John K. Bielamowicz, Waxahachie (2/1/22); Brian C. Brumley, Sumner (2/1/23); Mark E. Cartwright, Frisco (2/1/23); Steven Hallbauer, Rockwall (2/1/23); Asia Rodgers, Fort Worth (2/1/24); Anthony C. Scoma, Austin (2/1/27); Jeanene L. Smith, Austin (2/1/22); Christopher S. Taylor, Dallas (2/1/22). Exec. Dir. Darrel D. Spinks ($175,000), 1801 Congress Ave., Ste. 7.300, Austin 78701; (512) 305–7700.

Blind, Texas Commission for the: as of September 2016 the commission was incorporated into the Texas Workforce Commission.

Blind and Visually Impaired, Texas School for the: (1979); apptv.; 6-yr.; expenses; 9 members: Pres. Lee Sonnenberg, Lubbock (1/31/25); Dan Brown, Pflugerville (1/31/23); Maghan Gautney, Anna (1/31/27); Michael Hanley, Leander (1/31/23); Beth Jones, Anna (1/31/25); Brenda Lee, Brownwood (1/31/27); Julie Prause, Columbus (1/31/23); Elaine Robertson, Katy (1/31/25); Ernest Worthington, Lancaster (1/31/27). Supt. Emily Coleman ($159,993), 1100 W. 45th St., Austin 78756; (512) 454–8631.

Bond Review Board, Texas: (1987); composed of Gov., Lt. Gov., House Speaker, and Comptroller. Exec. Dir. Rob Latsha ($127,500); 300 W. 15th St., Ste. 409, PO Box 13292, Austin 78711-3292; (512) 463–1741.

Brazos River Authority: (1929 as Brazos River Conservation and Reclamation District; name changed to present form in 1953); apptv.; 6-yr; expenses; 21 members: Presiding Officer Cynthia A. Flores, Round Rock (2/1/27); Thomas Abraham, Sugar Land (2/1/25); Gary Boren, Lubbock (2/1/25); Mike Fernandez, Abilene (2/1/25); Christine Giese, Brenham (2/1/27); Jennifer "Jen" Henderson, Round Rock (2/1/29); Rick Huber, Granbury (2/1/27); Helen Jimenez, Richmond (2/1/27); Judy Ann Krohn, Georgetown (2/1/29); Traci Garrett LaChance, Danbury (2/1/29); Jim Lattimore Jr., Graford (2/1/25); Wesley D. Lloyd, Waco (2/1/25); John H. Luton, Granbury (2/1/27); Anthony Mbroh, Dallas (2/1/25); Austin Ruiz, Harker Heights (2/1/27); David Savage, Katy (2/1/25); Jarrod D. Smith, Danbury (2/1/29); W. Wintford "Ford" Taylor III, Waco (2/1/27); R. Wayne Wilson, Bryan (2/1/29); 2 vacancies. Gen. Mgr. David Collinsworth, 4600 Cobbs Dr., PO Box 7555, Waco 76714; (254) 761–3100.

Canadian River Compact Commission: (1951, negotiates with New Mexico and Oklahoma regarding waters of the Canadian); apptv.; 6-yr.; Comm. Roger S. Cox (12/31/27), PO Box 1750, Amarillo 79105-1750; (806) 242–9651.

Canadian River Municipal Water Authority: (1953); 2-yr.; 17 members apptd. by member cities: Pres. Richard Ellis, Levelland; Jerry Carlson, Pampa; Jim Collins, Lubbock; Tyke Dipprey, Plainview; Rickey Dunn, Brownfield; Charles Gillingham, Borger; Ryan Hall, Levelland; Bill Hallerberg, Amarillo; Jay House, Lubbock; Jay Dee House, Tahoka; Glendon Jett, Borger; Cris Norris, Lamesa; Virginio Ortega, Plainview; Mac Smith, Pampa; Roy Urrutia, Amarillo; Charlie Vaughn, O'Donnell; Chad Wilson, Slaton. Gen. Mgr. Drew Satterwhite, 9875 Water Authority Rd., PO Box 9, Sanford 79078; (806) 865–3325.

Cancer Prevention & Research Institute of Texas: (1985 as Texas Cancer Council; name changed in 2007); apptv.; 6-yr.; expenses; 9 members, 3 each apptd. by Gov., Lt. Gov., and House Speaker: Presiding Officer Mahendra C. Patel, San Antonio (1/31/27); David A. Cummings, San Angelo (1/31/29), Ambrosio Hernandez, Pharr (1/31/25); Donald "Dee" Margo, El Paso (1/31/27); Will Montgomery, Dallas (1/31/23); Cindy Barberio Payne, Spring Branch (1/31/25); William Rice, Austin (1/31/25); Craig Rosenfeld, Dallas (1/31/17); 1 vacancy. CEO Wayne Roberts ($281,875), 1701 Congress Ave., Ste. 6-127, PO Box 12097, Austin 78711; (512) 463–3190.

Cardiovascular Disease and Stroke, Texas Council on: (1999); apptv.; 6-yr.; 14 members: 3 ex officio: 1 each from Texas Workforce Commission, Health and Human Services Commission, Texas Dept. of State Health Services; 11 apptd.: Chair Suzanne Hildebrand, Live Oak (2/1/25); Elie Balesh, Houston (2/1/25); Stanley M. Duchman, Houston (2/1/27); Janet Hall Hewlett, Florence (2/1/23); Samantha Kersey, Dickinson (2/1/25); Sherron Meeks, Odessa (2/1/27); J. Neal Rutledge, Austin (2/1/23); Kyle Sheets, Ovalo (2/1/23); E'Loria Simon-Campbell, Houston (2/1/25); Marcie Wilson, Lakeway (2/1/27); 1 vacancy. PO Box 149347, Austin 78714-9347; (512) 776–7111.

Cemetery Committee, Texas State: (1997); apptv.; 6-yr.; 3 members: Chair Thomas N. "Tom" Sellers, Austin (2/1/27); James L. "Jim" Bayless Jr., Austin (2/1/23); Carolyn Hodges, Houston (2/1/25). Admin. Nathan Stephens, 909 Navasota St., Austin 78702; (512) 463–6600.

Central Colorado River Authority **(See Colorado River Authority, Central.)**

Chemist, Office of the Texas State: (1911); ex officio, indefinite term: State Chemist Tim Herrman, 445 Agronomy Rd., PO Box 3160, College Station 77841-3160; (979) 845–1121.

Chiropractic Examiners, Texas Board of: (1949); apptv.; 6-yr.; expenses; 9 members: Pres. Mark Bronson, Fort Worth (2/1/27);

The entrance to the Texas State Cemetery. Photo by xvla, Flickr, CC by 2.0

Sarah Abraham, Sugar Land (2/1/27); Brandon Allen, Austin (2/1/25); Nicholas Baucum, Corpus Christi (2/1/27); Michael P. Henry, Austin (2/1/25); Josh Hollub, Houston (2/1/29); Matthew Mix, Bastrop (2/1/29); Mindy Neal, Bovina (2/1/29); Scott Wofford, Abilene (2/1/25). Exec. Dir. Patrick Fortner ($100,830), 1801 Congress Ave., Ste. 10.500, Austin 78701-1319; (512) 305–6700.

Civil Commitment Office, Texas: (2011 as Office of Violent Sex Offender Management; took present name in 2015); apptv.; 6-yr.; 5 members: Chair Christy Jack, Fort Worth (2/1/29); Jose Aliseda, Beeville (2/1/25); Roberto Dominguez, Mission (2/1/29); Rona Stratton Gouyton, Fort Worth (2/1/27); Kathryn E. "Katie" McClure, Kingwood (2/1/27). Exec. Dir. Marsha McLane, 4616 W. Howard Ln., Bldg. 2, Ste. 350, Austin 72728; (512) 341–4421.

Coastal Water Authority: (1967 as Coastal Industrial Water Authority; name changed in 1985); 2-yr.; per diem and expenses; 7 members; 4 apptd. by Houston mayor; 3 by Gov.: Pres. D. Wayne Klotz, Houston (3/31/23); Tony L. Council, Houston (3/31/23); Thomas A. "Tom" Reiser, Houston (4/1/19); Jon M. "Mark" Sjolander, Dayton (4/1/24); Joseph G. Soliz, Houston (3/31/18); Douglas E. Walker, Beach City (4/1/19); Giti Zarinkelk, Houston (3/31/18). Exec. Dir. Greg Olinger, 1801 Main St., Ste. 800, Houston 77002; (713) 658–9020.

Colorado River Authority, Central: (1935); Abolished December 1, 2017 by 85th Legislature. All assets were transferred to Coleman County.

Colorado River Authority, Lower: (1934 as 9-member board; members increased in 1951 and 1975); apptv.; 6-yr.; per diem on duty; 15 members: Chair Timothy Timmerman, Austin (2/1/25); Michael L. "Mike" Allen, Kerrville (2/1/25); Matthew L. "Matt" Arthur, La Grange (2/1/27); Melissa K. Blanding, Driftwood (2/1/27); Stephen F. Cooper, El Campo (2/1/29); Joseph M. "Joe" Crane, Bay City (2/1/27); Carol Freeman, Llano (2/1/27); Thomas L. "Tom" Kelley, Eagle Lake (2/1/29); Robert "Bobby" Lewis, Elgin, (2/1/25); Thomas Michael Martine, Cypress Mill (2/1/25); Hatch C. Smith Jr., Boerne (2/1/29); Margaret D. "Meg" Voelter, Austin (2/1/25); Martha Leigh M. Whitten, San Saba (2/1/27); David Willmann, Llano (2/1/29); Nancy Eckert Yeary, Lampasas (2/1/29). Gen. Mgr. Phil Wilson, 3700 Lake Austin Blvd., PO Box 220, Austin 78767; (512) 578–3200.

Colorado River Authority, Upper: (1935 as 9-member board; reorganized in 1965); apptv.; 6-yr.; per diem and expenses; 9 members: Chair Nancy Blackwell, Ballinger (2/1/27); Reese Braswell, Bronte (2/1/27); Erica Hall, Abilene (2/1/27); Fred Hernandez Jr., San Angelo (2/1/25); Leslie Lasater, San Angelo (2/1/27); Tanner Mahan, Menard (2/1/23); Kathryn Mews, Menard (2/1/23); Hugh "Che" Stone, San Angelo (2/1/23); Mason Vaughan, Eldorado (2/1/25). Director Scott McWilliams, 512 Orient, San Angelo 76903; (325) 655–0565.

Consumer Credit Commissioner, Texas Office of: Comm. Leslie L. Pettijohn ($203,840), 2601 N. Lamar Blvd., Austin 78705; (512) 936–7600. Consumer Help Line: (800) 538–1579.

Cosmetology, Advisory Board on: (See Barbering and Cosmetology Advisory Board.)

Counselors, Texas State Board of Examiners of Professional: (1981); apptv.; 6-yr.; expenses; 9 members: Chair Steven Hallbauer, Rockwall (2/1/23); Carmelia "Lia" Amuna, Killeen (2/1/27); Loretta J. Bradley, Lubbock (2/1/27); Brenda S. Compagnone, San Antonio (2/1/25); Vanessa Hall, Tomball (2/1/25); Garrett A. Nerren, Dallas (2/1/25); Roy Smith, Midland (2/1/23); Carolyn Janie Stubblefield, Dallas (2/1/23); Christopher S. Taylor, Dallas (2/1/27). Admin. Cristina De Luna, 1801 Congress Ave., Ste. 7.300, Austin 78701; (512) 305–7700.

County and District Retirement System, Texas: (See Retirement System, Texas County and District.)

Court Administration, Office of: (1985); apptd. by State Supreme Court chief justice; 1 member who also serves as executive director of the Texas Judicial Council: Admin. Dir. Megan LaVoie ($211,500), 205 W. 14th St., Ste. 600, PO Box 12066, Austin 78711-2066; (512) 463–1625.

Court Interpreters Advisory Board, Licensed: Apptv. by Texas Supreme Court; part of Judicial Branch Certification Commission; staggered terms; 6-yr., 5 members: Presiding Officer Laura Angelini, San Antonio (2/1/27); Cynthia de Peña, McAllen (2/1/23); Luis Garcia, Keller (2/1/27); Robert Richter Jr., Houston (2/1/19); Melissa Wallace, San Antonio (2/1/19). 205 W. 14th St., Ste. 600, PO Box 12066, Austin 78711-2066; (512) 475–4368.

Court Reporters Certification Advisory Board: Apptv. by Texas Supreme Court; part of Judicial Branch Certification Commission; staggered terms; 6-yr., 7 members: Presiding Officer Catherine Torres-Stahl, San Antonio (2/1/29); Mellony Ariail, Weatherford (2/1/29); Janice Eidd-Meadows, Tyler (12/31/27); Shari Krieger, Mansfield (2/1/27); Molly Pela, Houston (2/1/19); Whitney Alden Riley, Boerne (2/1/19); Kim Tindall, San Antonio (2/1/23). 205 W. 14th St., Ste. 600, PO Box 12066, Austin 78711-2066; (512) 475–4368.

Credit Union Commission: (1949 as 3-member Credit Union Advisory Commission; name changed and members increased to 6 in 1969; increased again in 1981); apptv.; 6-yr.; expenses; 9 members: Chair James L. "Jim" Minge, Arlington (2/15/23); Elizabeth L. "Liz" Bayless, Austin (2/15/25); David Bleazard, Katy (2/15/27); Karyn C. Brownlee, Coppell (2/15/23); Kay Rankin-Swan, Monahans (2/15/25); David F. Shurtz, Hudson Oaks (2/15/25); Beckie Stockstill Cobb, Deer Park (2/15/27); 2 vacancies. Comm. Michael S. Riepen ($200,000), 914 E. Anderson Ln., Austin 78752; (512) 837–9236.

Crime Stoppers Council, Texas: (1981); apptv.; 4-yr.; per diem and expenses; 5 members: Chair Greg New, Waxahachie (9/1/24); Lauren Day, Austin (9/1/24); Perry Gilmore, Amarillo (9/1/25); Carlo Hernandez, Brownsville (9/1/25); Stephanie Vanskike, Beaumont (9/1/24). www.the texascrimestoppers.org.

Crime Victims' Institute: (1995 as function of attorney general's office; transferred to Sam Houston State University in 2003); apptv.; 2-yr.; 10 members: Lee Ann Breading, Denton (1/31/25); Abigail Brookshire, Midlothian (1/31/25); Libby Hamilton, Round Rock (1/31/25); Joan Huffman, Houston (1/31/25); Emmitt Jackson, Argyle (1/31/25); Andrew Murr, Junction (1/31/25); Brandi Reed, Amarillo (1/31/25); David E. Schwartz, Bellaire (1/31/24); Hector Villarreal, Alice (1/31/24); Erleigh Wiley, Forney (1/31/25). Dir. Mary Breaux, 816 17th St., PO Box 2180, Huntsville 77341-2180; (936) 294–3100.

Criminal Justice, Texas Department of: (1989, assumed duties of former Department of Corrections, Adult Probation Commission, and Board of Pardons and Paroles); apptv; 6-yr.; expenses; 9 members: Chair Patrick L. O'Daniel, Austin (2/1/23); Rodney Burrow, Pittsburg (2/1/27); Molly Francis, Dallas (2/1/25); Faith Johnson, Dallas (2/1/25); Larry Miles, Amarillo (2/1/23); Eric Nichols, Austin (2/1/27); Derrelynn Perryman, Fort Worth (2/1/27); Sichan Siv, San Antonio (2/1/25); 1 vacancy. Exec. Dir. Bryan Collier ($275,501), PO Box 99, Huntsville 77342-0099; (936) 295–6371.

Deaf, Texas School for the: (1979); apptv.; 6-yr.; expenses; 9 members: Pres. Shawn P. Saladin, Edinburg (1/31/23); Sha Cowan, Dripping Springs (1/31/23); Christopher Moreland, New Braunfels (1/31/23); Darlene "DJ" Nobles, Waco (1/31/27); David Saunders, Waxahachie (1/31/25); Kathy Sellers, Kosse (1/31/27); Keith Sibley, Bedford (1/31/25); Heather Withrow, Austin (1/31/25); 1 vacancy. Supt. Claire Bugen ($171,688), 1102 S. Congress Ave., Austin 78704; (512) 462–5353.

Demographic Center, Texas: (2001); created by 77th Legislature; State Demographer Lloyd B. Potter, 501 W. César Chávez Blvd., San Antonio 78207-4415; (210) 458–6543.

Dental Examiners, Texas State Board of: (1919 as 6-member board; increased to 9 members in 1971; increased to 12 in 1981; increased to 15 in 1991; sunsetted in 1994; reconstituted with 18 members in 1995; reduced to present number in 2005); apptv.; 6-yr.; per diem and expenses; 11 members: Presiding Officer David H. Yu, Austin (2/1/25); Linda Treviño Burke, Harlingen (2/1/25); Ricky Garcia, Pasadena (2/1/27); Bryan Henderson II, Dallas (2/1/23); Lorie Jones, Magnolia (2/1/23); Yvonne E. Maldonado, El Paso (2/1/27); Robert G. McNeill, Dallas (2/1/27); Margo Y. Melchor, Houston (2/1/27); Lois M. Palermo, League City (2/1/27); Jorge Quirch, Missouri City (2/1/23); Kathryn Sisk, Spring Branch (2/1/23). Exec. Dir. Casey Nichols ($127,435), 1801 Congress Ave., Ste. 8.600, Austin 78701; (512) 463–6400.

Diabetes Council, Texas: (1983; with 5 ex officio and 6 public members serving 2-yr. terms; changed in 1987 to 3 ex officio and 8 public members; changed to present in 1991; term length changed from 4 to 6 years in 1997); 6-yr.; 16 members: 11 apptv.: Acting Chair Stephen Ponder, Belton (2/1/25); Gary Francis, San Antonio (2/1/27); Dirrell Jones, Farmers Branch (2/1/25); Aida "Letty" Moreno-Brown, El Paso (2/1/27); Ninfa Peña-Purcell, College Station (2/1/27); Jason Ryan, Houston (2/1/25); Maryanne Strobel, Cypress (2/1/27); Christine Wicke, McKinney (2/1/25); 3 vacancies. The 5 ex officio members include 1 each from Texas Workforce Commission, Texas Health and Human Services Commission, Texas Dept. of State Health Services, Employees Retirement System, and Teacher Retirement System. Coord. Julie Kepelsen, 1100 W. 49th St., PO Box 149347, Austin 78756; (512) 776–2834.

Dietitians, State Board of Examiners of: All duties transferred to the Texas Department of Licensing and Regulation. Abolished in 2015 by the 84th Legislature, S.B. 202.

Disabilities, Governor's Committee on People with: (1949 as Gov.'s Committee on Employment of the Handicapped; re-created in 1983 as Gov.'s Committee for Disabled Persons; given current name and expanded duties in 1991); apptv.; 2-yr. and at pleasure of Gov.; 12 members: Chair Richard Martinez, San Antonio (2/1/24); Kori A. Allen, McKinney (2/1/24); Ellen M. Bauman, Joshua (2/1/23); Evelyn Cano, Pharr (2/1/24); Elyse L. Lieberman, Victoria (2/1/23); Eric N. Lindsay, San Antonio (2/1/23); Jose J. "Joseph" Muñiz, Harlingen (2/1/24); Kristie L. Orr, College Station (2/1/23); Dylan M. Rafaty, Plano (2/1/23); Emma F. Rudkin, Boerne (2/1/24); Benjamin Willis (2/1/24); Kristopher A.W. "Kris" Workman, Sutherland Springs (2/1/23). Exec. Dir. Ron Lucey, 1100 San Jacinto Blvd., Austin 78701; (512) 463–5739; 7-1-1 TDD.

Disabilities, Texas Council for Developmental: (1971); apptv.; 6-yr.; 27 members; 19 apptv.: Chair Mary Durheim, Spring (2/1/23); Ronald "Ronnie" Browning, Spring (2/1/23); Deborah "Debbie" Carlisle, San Antonio (2/1/27); William "Bill" Coorsh, Houston (2/1/27); Gladys Cortez, McAllen (2/1/23); Kyle Cox, College Station (2/1/27); Maverick Crawford III, San Antonio (2/1/25); Andrew "Andy" Crim, Fort Worth (2/1/25); Juan Carlos Lopez, Edinburg (2/1/23); Scott McAvoy, Cedar Park (2/1/27); Amanda Miles, Alvin (2/1/25); Angela "Angie" Panciza, Houston (2/1/27); Michael Peace, Poteet (2/1/25); Robert Schier III, Elgin (2/1/23); Eric Shahid, Somerville (2/1/25); Meredith Silcox, Splendora (2/1/27); Lora Taylor, Houston (2/1/25); John Thomas, Weatherford (2/1/27); Kimberly Torres, Houston (2/1/25). 8 ex officio members from various state agencies. Exec. Dir. Beth Stalvey ($154,076), 6201 E. Oltorf St., Ste. 600, Austin 78741-7509; (512) 437–5432.

Disabilities, Texas Council on Purchasing from People with: Duties transferred to Texas Workforce Commission in 2015. Abolished by the legislature in 2015.

Disabilities, Texas Office for Prevention of Developmental: Abolished in 2017.

Education, State Board of: (1866; re-created in 1928 and re-formed in 1949 by Gilmer-Aikin Act to consist of 21 elective members from districts co-extensive with 21 congressional districts at that time; increased to 24 with congressional redistricting in 1971; increased to 27 with congressional redistricting in 1981; reorganized by special legislative session as 15-member apptv. board in 1984; became elective board again in 1988); expenses; 4-yr.; 15 members: Dist. 1: Melissa N. Ortega (D), El Paso (1/1/25); Dist. 2: LJ Francis (R), Corpus Christi (1/1/27); Dist. 3: Marisa B. Perez-Diaz (D), Converse (1/1/25); Dist. 4: Staci Childs (D), Houston (1/1/25); Dist. 5: Rebecca Bell-Metereau (D), San Marcos (1/1/27); Dist. 6: Will Hickman (R), Houston (1/1/27); Dist. 7: Julie Pickren (R), Pearland (1/1/27); Dist. 8: Audrey Young (R), Trinity (1/1/27); Dist. 9: Chair Keven Ellis (R), Lufkin (1/1/27); Dist. 10: Tom Maynard (R), Florence (1/1/25); Dist. 11: Patricia Hardy (R), Fort Worth (1/1/25); Dist. 12: Pam Little (R), Fairview (1/1/25); Dist. 13: Aicha Davis (D), Dallas (1/1/27); Dist. 14: Evelyn Brooks (R), Frisco (1/1/27); Dist. 15: Aaron Kinsey (R), Midland (1/1/25). c/o Texas Education Agency, 1701 Congress Ave., Austin 78701; (512) 463–9007.

Education Agency, Texas: (1949, established by Gilmer-Aikin Act, replacing office led since 1866 by State Superintendent of Public Instruction); presently led by Commissioner of Education, apptd.

by Gov. since 1995; 4-yr.: Comm. Mike Morath ($220,375 plus supplement), 1701 Congress Ave., Austin 78701; (512) 463–9734.

Education Board, Southern Regional: (1969); apptv.; 4-yr.; 5 members: Gov. Greg Abbott (ex officio, 1/20/27); Kendall Baker, Houston (6/30/23); Harrison Keller, Austin (6/30/25); Mike Morath, Austin (6/30/26); Larry Taylor, Friendswood (6/30/24). Pres. Stephen L. Pruitt, 592 10th St. NW, Atlanta, GA 30318; (404) 875–9211.

Educator Certification, State Board for: (1995); apptv.; 6-yr.; expenses; 15 members; 4 ex officio: rep. of Comm. of Education, rep. of Comm. of Higher Education, rep. of alternative certification program, dean of a college of education; 11 apptv.: Chair Jean Streepey, Dallas (2/1/25); Bob Brescia, Odessa (2/1/29); Tommy L. Coleman, Beaumont (2/1/25); Julia Dvorak, Pflugerville (2/1/25); Cristina Galindo, Houston (2/1/27); Bena Glasscock, Adrian (2/1/27); Rex Gore, Austin (2/1/27); Courtney Boswell MacDonald, Kerrville (2/1/29); Michael D. McFarland, Crowley (2/1/27); Scott Muri, Odessa (2/1/29); Josue Tamarez Torres, Forney (2/1/25). 1701 Congress Ave., 5th Fl., Austin 78701-1494; (512) 936–8400.

Edwards Aquifer Authority: (1993); 4-yr.; expenses; 17 members (2 apptv. and 15 elected from single-member districts). Apptv. members: Fohn Bendele, Medina & Uvalde Cos. (12/1/24); Gary Middleton, South Central Texas Water Advisory Committee (12/1/24). Elected members: Dist. 1: Carol Patterson, Bexar Co. (12/1/26); Dist. 2: Byron Miller, Bexar Co. (12/1/24); Dist. 3: Abelardo A. "Abe" Salinas III, Bexar Co. (12/1/26); Dist. 4: Benjamin Youngblood III, Bexar Co. (12/1/24); Dist. 5: Randall Perkins, Bexar Co. (12/1/26); Dist. 6: Deborah Carington, Bexar Co. (12/1/24); Dist. 7: Chair Enrique Valdivia, Bexar Co. (12/1/26); Dist. 8: Kathleen Krueger, Comal Co. (12/1/24); Dist. 9: Matthew Hoyt, Comal & Guadalupe Cos. (12/1/26); Dist. 10: Austin Bodin, Hays Co. (12/1/26); Dist. 11: Rachel Allyn Sanborn, Hays & Caldwell Cos. (12/1/26); Dist. 12: Scott Yanta, Medina Co. (12/1/24); Dist. 13: Russell Persyn, Medina & Atascosa Cos. (12/1/26); Dist. 14: Donald W. Baker, Uvalde Co. (12/1/24); Dist. 15: Rader Gilleland, Uvalde Co. (12/1/26). Gen. Mgr. Roland Ruiz, 900 E. Quincy St., San Antonio 78215; (210) 222–2204.

Emergency Communications, Commission on State: (1985 as 17-member Advisory Commission on State Emergency Communications; name changed and members reduced to 12 in 2000); apptv.; 4-yr.; expenses; 12 members, 3 ex officio: reps. of Dept. of State Health Services, Public Utility Commission, and Dept. of Information Resources; 9 apptd.: Presiding Officer James Beauchamp, Midland (9/1/25); Sue A. Brannon, Midland (9/1/23); Edwina Lane, Savoy (9/1/23); Lucille Maes, Angleton (9/1/25); Jack D. Miller, Denton (9/1/21); Clinton Sawyer, Amherst (9/1/25); Catherine A. "Cathy" Skurow, Portland (9/1/23); Larry L. "Chip" VanSteenberg, Conroe (9/1/27); Von C. Washington Sr., El Paso (9/1/27). Exec. Dir. Kelli Merriweather ($140,698), 1801 Congress Ave., Ste. 11.100, Austin 78701; (512) 305–6911.

Emergency Management, Texas Division of: (1951 as Division of Defense and Disaster Relief; incorporated into Dept. of Public Safety in 1963; took current name in 2009; became component of Texas A&M University System in 2019) Chief W. Nim Kidd, 2883 Hwy. 71 E., Austin 78617; (512) 424–2208.

Emergency Services Retirement System, Texas: (See Retirement System, Texas Emergency Services.)

Employees Retirement System of Texas: (See Retirement System of Texas, Employees.)

Engineers and Land Surveyors, Texas Board of Professional: (1937 as 6-member Texas State Board of Registration for Professional Engineers; members increased to 9 in 1981; name changed to Texas Board of Professional Engineers in 1997, took current name in 2019 when merged with Texas Board of Professional Land Surveying); apptv.; per diem and expenses; 6-yr.; 10 members, inc. 1 rep from General Land Office with unlimited term (Mark Neugebauer, Round Rock); 9 termed members: Chair Sina K. Nejad, Beaumont (9/26/25); Ademola Adejokun, Arlington (9/26/23); Albert Cheng, Houston (9/26/27); Karen A. Friese, Austin (9/26/27); Coleen Johnson, Leander (9/26/25); Marguerite McClinton Stoglin, Grand Prairie (9/26/25); Catherine Norwood, Midland (9/26/27); Rolando Rubiano, Harlingen (9/26/23); Kiran Shah, Richmond (9/26/23). Exec. Dir. Lance Kinney ($201,531), 1917 S. Interstate 35, Austin 78741; (512) 440–7723.

Environmental Quality, Texas Commission on: (1913 as State Board of Water Engineers; name changed in 1962 to Texas Water Commission; reorganized and name changed in 1965 to Water Rights Commission; reorganized and name changed back to Texas Water Commission in 1977 to perform judicial function for the Texas Dept. of Water Resources; name changed to Texas Natural Resource Conservation Commission in 1993; changed to present form in 2002); apptv.; 6-yr.; 3 members full-time ($201,000): Chair Jon Niermann, Austin (8/31/27); Bobby Janecka, Austin (8/31/25); Emily Lindley, Austin (8/31/23). Interim Exec. Dir. Kelly Keel ($197,500), 12100 Park 35 Circle, PO Box 13087, Austin 78711-3087; (512) 239–1000.

Ethics Commission, Texas: (1991); apptv.; 4-yr.; 8 members: 4 apptd. by Gov., 2 by Lt. Gov., 2 by House Speaker: Chair Randall H. Erben, Austin (11/19/21); Chad M. Craycraft, Dallas (11/19/23); Chris Flood, Houston (11/19/19); Mary K. "Katie" Kennedy, Houston (11/19/23); Patrick W. Mizell, Houston (11/19/21); Richard S. Schmidt, Corpus Christi (11/19/21); Joseph O. Slovacek, Houston (11/19/21); Steven D. Wolens, Dallas (11/19/19). Exec. Dir. J.R. Johnson ($139,097), 201 E. 14th St., 10th Fl., PO Box 12070, Austin 78711-2070; (512) 463–5800. Disclosure Filing Fax: (512) 463–8808.

Facilities Commission, Texas: (2007; formerly Texas Building and Procurement Commission); apptv.; 6-yr.; 7 members: Chair Brian Bailey, Austin (1/31/27); Eddy Betancourt, Mission (1/31/29); Danny Signorelli, The Woodlands (1/31/29); C. Price Wagner, Dallas (1/31/25); 3 vacancies. Exec. Dir. Mike Novak ($177,982), 1711 San Jacinto Blvd., PO Box 13047, Austin 78711-3047; (512) 463–3446.

Family and Protective Services, Department of: (1991 as Dept. of Protective and Regulatory Services; reorganized to present form in 2004); apptv.; 6-yr.; 9 members: Chair Bonnie Hellums, Houston (2/1/23); Connie Almeida, Richmond (2/1/27); Omedi "Dee Dee" Cantu Arismendez, Alice (2/1/27); Liesa Hackett, Huntsville (2/1/23); Greg Hamilton, Hutto (2/1/27); Cortney Jones, Austin (2/1/25); Matt Kouri, Austin (2/1/23); Julie Krawczyk, Garland (2/1/25); Enrique Mata, El Paso (2/1/25). Comm. Stephanie Muth ($235,500), 4900 N. Lamar Blvd., PO Box 149030, Austin 78714-9030; (512) 929–6900. Abuse Hotline: (800) 252–5400. Ombudsman Hotline: (800) 720–7777.

Film Commission, Texas: (1971, became part of the Economic Development and Tourism Division in office of Gov. in 2015); Dir. Stephanie Whallon ($111,961), 1100 San Jacinto Blvd., Ste. 3.410, PO Box 12428, Austin 78711; (512) 463–9200.

Finance Commission of Texas: (1923 as Banking Commission; reorganized as Finance Commission in 1943 with 9 members; members increased to 12 in 1983; changed back to 9 members in 1989; increased to 11 in 2009); apptv.; 6-yr.; per diem and traveling expenses; Chair Phillip A. Holt, Bonham (2/1/28); Robert "Bob" Borochoff, Houston (2/1/28); Hector J. Cerna, Eagle Pass (2/1/26); Glen Martin "Marty" Green, Dallas (2/1/28); William M. "Will" Lucas, Center (2/1/24); Sharon McCormick, Frisco (2/1/26); Roselyn "Rosie" Morris, San Marcos (2/1/26); Vince E. Puente Sr., Fort Worth (2/1/24); Debbie Scanlon, Missouri City (2/1/28); Laura Nassri Warren, Palmhurst (2/1/26). Exec. Dir. Charles G. Cooper ($254,850), 2601 N. Lamar Blvd., Austin 78705; (512) 936–6222. (See also Banking, Texas Department of.)

Fire Protection, Texas Commission on: (1991; formed by consolidation of Fire Dept. Emergency Board and Commission on Fire Protection Personnel Standards and Education); apptv.; 6-yr.; expenses; 13 members: Presiding Officer J.P. Steelman, Longview (2/1/23); Christopher G. Cantu, Round Rock (2/1/27); David Coatney, College Station (2/1/27); Sue De Villez, Georgetown (2/1/25); Michael Glynn, Roanoke (2/1/27); Paul Hamilton, Amarillo (2/1/25); Mike Jones, Burleson (2/1/23); Clyde Loll, Huntsville (2/1/27); Bob D. Morgan, Fort Worth (2/1/23); Mala Sharma, Houston (2/1/23); Tim Smith, Lubbock (2/1/27); Kelly Vandygriff, Abernathy (2/1/25); Rusty Wilson, Mesquite (2/1/25). Chief Mike Wisko ($123,883), 1701 Congress Ave., Ste. 1-105, PO Box 2286, Austin 78768-2286; (512) 936–3838.

Forensic Science Commission, Texas: (2005); apptv.: 2-yr.; 9 members: 4 apptd. by Gov., 3 by Lt. Gov., and 2 by Atty. Gen.: Presiding Officer Jeffrey J. Barnard, Dallas (9/1/23); Patrick Buzzini, Spring (9/1/24); Michael Coble, Fort Worth (2/1/24); Mark Daniel, Fort Worth (9/1/23); Nancy Downing, Bryan (9/1/24); Jasmine Drake, Conroe (9/1/24); Sarah Kerrigan, The Woodlands, (9/1/23); Jarvis Parsons, Bryan (9/1/2023); 1 vacancy. Coord. Kathryn Adams, 1700 Congress Ave., Ste. 445, Austin 78701; (888) 296–4232.

Funeral Service Commission, Texas: (1903 as State Board of Embalming; 1935 as State Board of Funeral Directors and Embalmers; name changed to present form in 1987); apptv.; per diem and expenses; 6-yr.; 7 members: Presiding Officer Larry Allen, Mesquite (2/1/27); Timothy Brown, McAllen (2/1/27); Kevin Combest, Lubbock (2/1/25); Dianne Hefley, Amarillo (2/1/23); Eric Opiela, Austin (2/1/25); Jonathan Scepanski, McAllen (2/1/25); Kristin Tips, San Antonio (2/1/23). Exec. Dir. James White ($101,000), 1801 Congress Ave., Ste. 11.800, Austin 78701; (512) 936–2474.

Geoscientists, Texas Board of Professional: (2001); apptv.; expenses; 3-yr.; 9 members (6 professional geoscientists, 3 public members): Chair Becky L. Johnson, Fort Worth (2/1/23); Bereket M. Derie, Georgetown (2/1/27); Margon Dillard, Richmond (2/1/25); Steven Fleming, Shavano Park (2/1/27); Edward F. Janak Jr., Fredericksburg (2/1/25); W. David Prescott II, Amarillo (2/1/25); Brandon Stowers, Denton (2/1/23); LaFawn Thompson, New Braunfels (2/1/27); Mark N. Varhaug, Dallas (2/1/23). Exec. Dir. Rene D. Truan ($109,157), 1801 Congress Ave., Ste. 7.800, PO Box 13225, Austin 78711; (512) 936–4408.

Guadalupe-Blanco River Authority: (1935); apptv.; per diem and expenses on duty; 6-yr.; 9 members: Chair Dennis L. Patillo, Victoria (2/1/27); Robert E. Blaschke, Woodsboro (2/1/29); William Carbonara, Cuero (2/1/25); James P. Cohoon, Boerne (2/1/27); John P. Cyrier, Lockhart (2/1/29); Steve Ehrig, Gonzales (2/1/25); Don Meador, San Marcos (2/1/25); Sheila L. Old, Seguin (2/1/27); Emanuel Valdez, New Braunfels (2/1/29). Gen. Mgr. Darrell Nichols, 2225 E. Common St., New Braunfels; (830) 379–5822.

Guadalupe River Authority, Upper: (1939); apptv.; 6-yr.; 9 members: Pres. Diane L. McMahon, Kerrville (2/1/27); Aaron C. Bulkley, Hunt (2/1/25); Austin Dickson, Kerrville (2/1/27); Dick Eastland, Hunt (2/1/25); Frances Lovett, Center Point (2/1/25); William R. Rector, Kerrville (2/1/29); Blake W. Smith, Hunt (2/1/27); Maggie Snow, Kerrville (2/1/29); Jeanne Stacy, Ingram (2/1/29). Gen. Mgr. Tara Bushnoe, 125 Lehmann Dr., Ste. 100, Kerrville 78028; (830) 896–5445.

Guaranteed Student Loan Corporation, Texas: (1979 as nonprofit corp.); as of July 21, 2019, the organization is named Trellis Company.

Guardianship Certification Advisory Board: Apptv. by Texas Supreme Court; part of Judicial Branch Certification Commission; staggered terms; 6-yr., 5 members: Presiding Officer Jamie MacLean, Austin (2/1/27); Jason S. Armstrong, Lufkin (2/1/19); Gladys Burwell, Friendswood (2/1/19); Leonard James, Spring (2/1/23); Chris Wilmoth, Dallas (2/1/27). 205 W. 14th St., Ste. 600, PO Box 12066, Austin 78711-2066; (512) 475–4368.

Gulf Coast Authority: (1969); apptv.; 2-yr.; per diem, expenses on duty; 9 members: 3 apptd. by Gov., 3 by County Commissioners Courts of counties in district, 3 by Mayors Councils of cities in district. Chair Franklin D. R. Jones Jr., Harris Co. (8/31/21); Amber Batson, Harris Co. (8/31/23); Billy J. Enochs, Galveston Co. (8/31/21); Stephanie Farner, Chambers Co. (8/31/24); Lamont E. Meaux, Chambers Co. (8/31/24); Jackie Peden, Galveston Co. (8/31/23); Mark Schultz, Chambers Co. (8/31/20); Kevin Scott, Galveston Co. (8/31/24); Robert Swanson, Harris Co. (8/31/24). Gen. Mgr. Elizabeth Fazio Hale, 910 Bay Area Blvd., Houston 77058; (281) 488–4115.

Gulf States Marine Fisheries Commission: (1949 with members from Texas, Alabama, Florida, Louisiana and Mississippi); apptv.; 3-yr.; 3 Texas members: 2 ex officio: Texas Parks and Wildlife Dept. exec. dir. and 1 member of Legislature; 1 apptd. by Gov.: Douglas W. "Doug" Boyd, Boerne (3/17/23). Exec. Dir. David M. Donaldson, 2404 Government St., Ocean Springs, MS 39564; (228) 875–5912.

Health and Human Services Commission, Texas: (1939 as Dept. of Public Welfare; changed to Texas Dept. of Human Resources in 1977; changed to Texas Dept. of Human Services in 1985; changed to present name in 1992). Exec. Comm. Cecile Erwin Young ($290,258), 4601 W. Guadalupe St., PO Box 13247, Austin 78711-3247; (512) 424–6500.

Health Coordinating Council, Texas Statewide: (1977); apptv.; 6-yr.; 17 members (4 ex officio; 13 apptd. by Gov.): Chair Elizabeth Protas, League City (8/31/23); Carol Boswell, Andrews (8/31/27); Chelsea Elliott, Austin (8/31/23); Kimberley Haynes, Leander (8/31/25); Ken Holland, Huntsville (8/31/27); Emily Hunt, Houston (8/31/23); Quincy C. Moore III, Cypress (8/31/25); Tamara Rhodes, Fort Worth (8/31/27); Melinda Rodriguez, San Antonio (8/31/27); Cheryl T. Sparks, Big Spring (8/31/25); Cheletta Watkins, Forney (8/31/25); D. Bailey Wynne, Dallas (8/31/23); Yasser Zeid, Longview (8/31/27). Ex-officio members include 1 each from Texas Dept. of State Health Services and Texas Higher Education Coordinating Board, and 2 from Texas Health and Human Services Commission. Interim Dir. Chris Aker, PO Box 149347, Austin, TX 78714-9347; (512) 776–6541.

Health Professions Council: (1993); ex officio; 13 members: 1 from Gov.'s office, 1 from the Atty. Gen.'s office, and 1 each from the following 11 regulating agencies: Texas Board of Chiropractic Examiners, Texas State Board of Dental Examiners, Texas Medical Board, Texas Board of Nursing, Texas Optometry Board, Texas State Board of Pharmacy, Executive Council of Physical Therapy and Occupational Therapy Examiners, Texas Behavioral Health Executive Council, Texas State Board of Veterinary Medical Examiners, Texas Funeral Service Commission, Texas Health and Human Services Commission. Admin. Officer John Monk ($140,316), 1801 Congress Ave., Ste. 10.300, Austin 78701; (512) 305–8550.

Health Services, Texas Department of State: (2003, merging Texas Dept. of Health, Texas Dept. of Mental Health and Mental Retardation, Texas Health Care Information Council, Texas Comm. on Alcohol and Drug Abuse); Comm. Jennifer Shuford ($271,083), 1100 W. 49th St., PO Box 149347, Austin 78714-9347; (512) 776–7111.

Health Services Authority, Texas: (2007); apptv.; 2-yr.; expenses; 2 ex officio plus 12 apptd. members: Chair Shannon Calhoun, Goliad (6/15/23); Paula Anthony-McMann, Tyler (6/15/23); Victoria Ai Linh Bryant, Houston (6/15/23); Salil Deshpande, Houston (6/15/23); Kenneth James, Volente (6/15/23); Jerome Lisk, Tyler (6/15/23); Leticia Rodriguez, Monahans (6/15/23); Jonathan Sandstrom Hill, Lakeway (6/15/23); Siobhan Shahan, Amarillo (6/15/23); Cynthia Stinson, Lumberton (6/15/23); Carlos Vital, Friendswood (6/15/23); 1 vacancy. 901 S. MoPac Blvd., Bldg. 1, Ste. 300, Austin 78746; (512) 329–2730.

Health Services Council, Texas Department of State: (1975); Abolished August 31, 2016.

Hearing Instruments, State Committee of Examiners in the Fitting and Dispensing of: (1969); Abolished by the 84th Legislature, S.B 202. As of Oct. 1, 2016, all duties transferred to the Texas Department of Licensing and Regulation.

Higher Education Coordinating Board, Texas: (1953 as temporary board; became permanent 15-member Texas Commission on Higher Education in 1955; changed to Texas College and University Systems Coordinating Board in 1965; name and membership changed to present form in 1987); apptv.; 6-yr.; expenses; 9 members, plus 1 ex officio student rep. serving 1-yr.: Chair Fred Farias III, McAllen (8/31/25); S. Javaid Anwar, Midland (8/31/27); Richard L. Clemmer, Austin (8/31/23); Emma W. Schwartz, El Paso (8/31/25); Donna N. Williams, Arlington (8/31/23); Welcome W. Wilson Jr., Houston (8/31/23); Daniel Wong, Missouri City (8/31/27); 2 vacancies. Comm. of Higher Education Harrison Keller ($299,813), 1801 Congress Ave, Ste. 12.200, PO Box 12788, Austin 78711-2788; (512) 427-6566.

Higher Education Tuition Board, Texas Prepaid: (1995); apptv.; expenses; 6 members, plus 1 ex officio chair: State Comptroller; 2 apptd. by Gov. and 4 by Lt. Gov. Members: Sarina Lora Davidson, Fort Worth (2/1/29); Michele Purgason, Arlington (2/1/23); Ben Streusand, Spring (2/1/13); Judy Trevino, San Antonio (2/1/27); Jarrod Winkcompleck, Austin (2/1/23); Deborah Zuloaga, El Paso (2/1/19). c/o Educational Opportunities and Investment Division, Comptroller of Public Accounts, PO Box 13528, Austin 78711-3528; (800) 445-4723.

Historian, Texas State: (2005); apptv.; 2-yr.; Monte L. Monroe, Lubbock (9/30/24).

Historical Commission, Texas: (1953); apptv.; expenses; 6-yr.; 15 members: Chair John L. Nau III, Houston (2/1/27); Donna Bahorich, Houston (2/1/25); Earl Broussard, Austin (2/1/23); Jim Bruseth, Austin (2/1/25); Monica Zárate Burdette, Rockport (2/1/27); John W. Crain, Dallas (2/1/25); Garrett Donnelly, Midland (2/1/23); Renee Dutia, Dallas (2/1/25); Lilia Garcia, Raymondville (2/1/27); David Gravelle, Dallas (2/1/27); Laurie Limbacher, Austin (2/1/23); Catherine McKnight, Dallas (2/1/23); Tom Perini, Buffalo Gap (2/1/27); Gilbert E. Peterson, Alpine (2/1/25); Daisy Sloan White, College Station (2/1/23). Exec. Dir. Mark Wolfe ($161,027), 1511 Colorado St., PO Box 12276, Austin 78711; (512) 463-6100.

Holocaust, Genocide, and Antisemitism Advisory Commission, Texas: (2009 as Texas Holocaust and Genocide Commission; took present name and membership in 2021); apptv.; 6-yr.; 9 members: Chair Kenneth E. Goldberg, Dallas (2/1/29); Jeffrey L. Beck, Dallas (2/1/29); Ilan S. Emanuel, Corpus Christi (2/1/27); Lucy Taus Katz, Austin (2/1/25); Ira M. Mitzner, Houston (2/1/27); Providence Nkurunziza, Fort Worth (2/1/25); Sandra Hagee Parker; 2 vacancies. Exec. Dir. Joy Nathan ($95,989), PO Box 12276, Austin 78711-2276; (512) 463-5108.

Housing and Community Affairs, Texas Department of: (1979 as Texas Housing Agency; merged with Department of Community Affairs and name changed in 1991); apptv.; expenses; 6-yr.; 7 members: Chair Leo Vasquez, Houston (1/31/23); Anna Maria Farias, San Antonio (1/31/27); Holland Harper, Paris (1/31/29); Kenny Marchant, Coppell (1/31/25); Ajay Thomas, Austin (1/31/25); 2 vacancies. Exec. Dir. Bobby Wilkinson ($192,299), 221 E. 11th St., PO Box 13941, Austin 78711-3941; (512) 475-3800.

Human Rights, Texas Commission on: (2004 as part of the Texas Workforce Commission's Civil Rights Division); as of September 1, 2015, the duties and authority of the commission were transferred to the Texas Workforce Commissioners.

Indigent Defense Commission, Texas: (2001 as Texas Task Force on Indigent Defense, took present name and form in 2011); 13 members: 8 ex officio: Chief Justice of Supreme Court and 3 other judges, 2 reps. from Texas Senate, 2 from House of Reps.; 5 apptd., 2-yr.: Alex Bunin, Houston (2/1/23); Valerie Covey, Georgetown (2/1/22); Richard Evans, Bandera (2/1/22); Missy Medary, Corpus Christi (2/1/22); Gonzalo Rios, San Angelo (2/1/23). Interim Exec. Dir. Scott Ehlers, 209 W. 14th St., Rm. 202, Austin 78701; (512) 936-6994. Toll-free: (866) 499-0656.

Industrialized Building Code Council, Texas: (1973); apptv.; 2-yr.; 12 members: Presiding Officer Scott A. McDonald III, Keller (2/1/23); Suzanne R. Arnold, Garland (2/1/24); Devin Duvak, Burleson (2/1/23); Janet Hoffman, Galveston (2/1/24); Otis W. Jones Jr., Houston (2/1/23); Binoy J. Kurien, Pearland (2/1/23); Edwin O. Lofton Jr., Horseshoe Bay (2/1/24); Edward Martin Jr., Austin (2/1/23); John D. Scholl, Claude (2/1/24); Stephen Shang, Austin (2/1/23); William F. "Dubb" Smith III, Dripping Springs (2/1/24); 1 vacancy; c/o Texas Dept. of Licensing and Regulation, PO Box 12157, Austin 78711; (512) 539-5735.

Information Resources, Texas Department of: (1981 as Automated Information and Telecommunications Council; name changed to current in 1990); 6-yr.; expenses; 10 members: 3 ex officio, reps of Dept. of Insurance, Dept. of Transportation, and Texas Health and Human Services Commission; 7 apptv.: Chair Ben Gatzke, Fort Worth (2/1/29); Jeffrey W. Allison, Houston (2/1/27); Mike Bell, Spring (2/1/29); Christopher "Stephen" Franke, Dallas (2/1/27); Stacey Napier, Austin (2/1/25); Jeffrey Tayon, Houston (2/1/27); Kara Thompson, Austin (2/1/25). Exec. Dir. Amanda Crawford ($194,182), 300 W.15th St., Ste. 1300, PO Box 13564, Austin 78711-3564; (512) 475-4700.

Injured Employee Counsel, Office of: (2005); apptv.; 2-yr.; 1 member: Public Counsel Dirk Johnson ($151,048), 1601 Congress Ave., Austin 78701; (866) 393-6432.

Insurance, Texas Dept. of: (1876 as Dept. of Insurance; changed to Dept. of Agriculture, Insurance, Statistics and History in 1887; to Dept. of Insurance and Banking in 1907; to present name in 1923); Commissioner (apptv.; Cassie Brown, 2/1/23; $217,139), 1601 Congress Ave., PO Box 12030, Austin 78711-2030; (512) 676-6000.

Insurance Counsel, Office of Public: (See Public Insurance Counsel, Office of.)

Interstate Commission for Adult Offender Supervision: (1937 as Interstate Compact for the Supervision of Parolees and Probationers; took present name in 2000); 50 member states; apptv.: Pam Alexander-Schneider, Lubbock (2/1/27). Compact Admin. for Texas Rene Hinojosa ($169,380). Chair Mary Kay Hudson, 3070 Lake Crest Circle, Ste. 400-264, Lexington, KY 40513; (859) 721-1050.

Interstate Mining Compact Commission: (1970); 24 member states, plus 2 associate member states; ex officio or apptv., according to gov's. choice; Texas reps. are appointed from the Texas Railroad Commission: Jim Wright. Exec. Dir. Tom Clarke, 437 Carlisle Dr., Ste. A, Herndon, VA 20170; (703) 709-8654.

Interstate Oil & Gas Compact Commission: (1935); 30 member states, plus 8 associate member states; ex officio or apptv., according to gov's. choice; per diem and expenses. Official rep. for Texas: Wayne Christian. Exec. Dir. Lori Wrotenbery, 900 NE 23rd St., Oklahoma City, OK 73105; (405) 522-8380.

Jail Standards, Texas Commission on: (1975); apptv.; 6-yr.; expenses; 9 members: Chair Bill Stoudt, Longview (1/31/25); Patricia M. Anthony, Garland (1/31/25); Raul "Pinky" Gonzales, Refugio (1/31/27); Duane Lock, Southlake (1/31/29); Monica H. McBride, Alpine (1/31/25); Ben Perry, Waco (1/31/29); Esmaeil Porsa, Parker (1/31/29); Ross Garrick Reyes, Melissa (1/31/27); Kelly Rowe, Lubbock (2/1/27). Exec. Dir. Brandon Wood ($121,020), 300 W. 15th St., Ste. 503, PO Box 12985, Austin 78711-2985; (512) 463-5505.

Judicial Branch Certification Commission: (2015); apptv.; 6-yr.; 9 members, inc. 4 apptd by Supreme Court and 5 judges: Chair Sid L. Harle, San Antonio (2/1/29); Velma Arellano, Corpus Christi (2/1/27); Mark P. Blenden, Bedford (2/1/29); Don D. Ford III,

Houston (2/1/19); Glen Harrison, Sweetwater (2/1/27); Ann Murray Moore, Edinburg (2/1/27); William C. Sowder, Lubbock (2/1/27); Polly Jackson Spencer, San Antonio (2/1/19); Victor Villarreal, Laredo (2/1/29). 205 W. 14th St., Ste. 600, PO Box 12066, Austin 78711-2066; (512) 475–4368.

Judicial Compensation Commission: (2007); apptv.; 6-yr.; expenses; 9 members: Chair Scott J. Salmans, McGregor (2/1/27); Carlos Amaral, Plano (2/1/25); Cindy Olson Bourland, Round Rock (2/1/25); JJ Clemence, Sugar Land (2/1/27); Conrith Warren Davis, Sugar Land (2/1/23); Tony Fidelie Jr., Wichita Falls (2/1/27); Phil Wayne Johnson, Lubbock (2/1/23); Linda W. Kinney, Comfort (2/1/23); Curt Nelson, San Antonio (2/1/25). 205 W. 14th St., PO Box 12066, Austin 78711-2066; (512) 463–1625.

Judicial Conduct, State Commission on: (1965 as 9-member Judicial Qualifications Commission; name changed to present in 1977); expenses; 6-yr.; 13 members: 6 apptd. by Supreme Court; 2 by State Bar; 5 by Gov.: Chair Gary L. Steel, Seguin (11/19/23); Ronald E. Bunch, Waxahachie (11/19/23); Valerie Ertz, Dallas (11/19/23); Janis Holt, Silsbee (11/19/25); Andrew M. "Andy" Kahan, Houston (11/19/27); Wayne Money, Greenville (11/19/27); Clifton Roberson, Tyler (11/19/25); Tano E. Tijerina, Laredo (11/19/23); Carey F. Walker, Fort Worth (11/19/27); Kathy P. Ward, Plano (11/19/27); Ken Wise, Houston (11/19/25); 2 vacancies. Exec. Dir. Jacqueline Habersham ($135,149), 300 W. 15th St., PO Box 12265, Austin 78711; (512) 463–5533.

Judicial Council, Texas: (1929 as Texas Civil Judicial Council; name changed in 1975); 6-yr.; expenses; 22 members: 16 ex officio and 6 apptd. from general public: Legislative Members: Brandon Creighton, Conroe; Jeff Leach, Allen; Reggie Smith, Sherman; Judith Zaffirini, Laredo. Judicial Members: Chair Nathan L. Hecht, Dallas (12/31/26); Bill Gravell Jr., Round Rock (2/1/23); Sharon Keller, Dallas (12/31/24); Claudia Laird, Conroe (2/1/25); Missy Medary, Corpus Christi (2/1/25); Emily Miskel, McKinney (2/1/23); Valencia Nash, Dallas (2/1/25); Kathleen Person, Temple (2/1/23); Sherry Radack, Houston (2/1/23); Maggie Sawyer, Brady (2/1/23); Edward J. Spillane III, College Station (2/1/25); Ken Wise, Houston (2/1/25). Citizen Members: Zina Bash, Austin (6/30/27); Kevin Bryant, Dallas (6/30/23); Jennifer Caughey, Houston (6/30/27); Sonia Clayton, Houston (6/30/25); Jon Gimble, Waco (6/30/25); Rachel Racz, Fort Worth (6/30/23). Exec. Dir. Megan LaVoie, 205 W. 14th St., Ste. 600, PO Box 12066, Austin 78711-2066; (512) 463–1625.

Judicial Districts Board: (1985); 13 ex officio members (term in other office); 1 apptv. (4 yrs.); ex officio: Chief Justice of Texas Supreme Court; Presiding Judge, Court of Criminal Appeals; Presiding Judge of each of 11 Administrative Judicial Districts; Gov. apptee.: Thomas Phillips, West Lake Hills (12/31/26). 205 W. 14th St., Austin 78701.

Juvenile Justice Department, Texas: (2011, combining the Texas Youth Commission and Texas Juvenile Probation Commission); apptv.; 6-yr.; expenses; 13 members: Chair David "Scott" Matthew, Georgetown (2/1/25); Edeska Barnes Jr., Jasper (2/1/27); James Castro, Bergheim (2/1/23); Mona Lisa Chambers, Houston (2/1/25); Pama Hencerling, Victoria (2/1/23); Pat Sabala Henry, Morton (2/1/23); Ann Lattimore, Cedar Park (2/1/27); Melissa Martin, Deer Park (2/1/25); Allison Palmer, San Angelo (2/1/23); Cynthia "Cyndi" Wheless, McKinney (2/1/27); 3 vacancies. Exec. Dir. Shandra Carter ($216,725), 1711 San Jacinto Blvd., PO Box 12757, Austin 78711-2757; (512) 490–7130. Abuse Hotline: (866) 477–8354.

Land Board, School: (1939); 2-yr.; per diem and expenses; 5 members: 1 ex officio: Comm. of General Land Office; 4 apptd.: 1 by Atty. Gen. and 3 by Gov.; ex officio chair: Dawn Buckingham; members: Gilbert Burciaga, Austin (8/29/23); Marcella Burke, Houston (8/29/23); James B. "Brad" Curlee, Round Rock (8/29/23); Michael A. Neill, Athens (8/29/23). c/o General Land Office, 1700 Congress Ave., PO Box 12873, Austin 78711-2873; (512) 463–5001.

Land Board, Veterans: (1949 as 3-member ex officio board; reorganized 1956); 4-yr.; per diem and expenses; 3 members: 1 ex officio chair: Comm. of General Land Office; 2 apptd.: Rothfelder, New Braunfels (12/29/24); Judson Scott, Bee Cave (12/29/26). Exec. Sec. Tony Dale, 1700 Congress Ave., PO Box 12873, Austin 78711-2873; (512) 463–5001.

Land Surveying, Texas Board of Professional: (See Engineers and Land Surveyors, Texas Board of Professional.)

Lavaca-Navidad River Authority: (1954 as 7-member Jackson County Flood Control District; reorganized as 9-member board in 1959; name changed to present form in 1969); apptv.; 6-yr.; per diem and expenses; 9 members: Pres. Jerry Adelman, Palacios (5/1/23); Callaway Aimone, Edna (5/1/25); Sandra "Sandy" Johs, La Ward (5/1/27); Lee Kucera, Edna (5/1/23); Michael "Vance" Mitchell, Lolita (5/1/27); Terri Parker, Ganado (5/1/23); Leonard Steffek, Edna (5/1/25); Jennifer Storz, Edna (5/1/27); Charles Taylor, Cape Carancahua (5/1/25). Gen. Mgr. Patrick Brzozowski, 4631 FM 3131, PO Box 429, Edna 77957; (361) 782–5229.

Law Enforcement, Texas Commission on: (1965 as Texas Commission on Law Enforcement Officer Standards & Education; changed name to present form in 2014); apptv.; 6-yr.; expenses; 9 members: Presiding Officer Kim Lemaux, Arlington (8/30/27); Janna Atkins, Abilene (8/30/23); Patricia Burruss, Olmito (8/30/25); Martina Lemond Dixon, Kingwood (8/30/23); Michael Griffis, Odessa (8/30/25); Jason D. Hester, Lago Vista (8/30/25); Ron E. Hood, Dripping Springs (8/30/23); Mario Lizcano Jr., Pharr (8/30/27); 1 vacancy. Interim Exec. Dir. John P. Beauchamp ($136,649), 6330 E. Hwy. 290, Ste. 200, Austin 78723; (512) 936–7700.

Law Examiners, Texas Board of: (1919); 9 attorneys apptd. by Supreme Court biennially for 6-year terms expiring in odd-numbered years. Chair Augustin Rivera Jr., Corpus Christi (9/30/29); Barbara Ellis, Austin (9/30/25); Teresa Ereon Giltner, Dallas (9/30/29); C. Alfred Mackenzie, Waco (9/30/29); Dwaine M. Massey, Houston (9/30/25); Anna M. McKim, Lubbock (9/30/27); Harold "Al" Odom, Houston (9/30/27); Cynthia Eva Hujar Orr, San Antonio (9/30/27); Carlos R. Soltero, Austin (9/30/25). Exec. Dir. Nahdiah Hoang, 205 W. 14th St., PO Box 13486, Austin 78711-3486; (512) 463–1621.

Law Library, Texas State: (1971); ex officio; expenses; 3 members: reps. of Atty. Gen., Chief Justice of Supreme Court, Presiding Judge of Court of Criminal Appeals. Dir. Amy Small ($101,000), 205 W. 14th St., PO Box 12367, Austin 78711-2367; (512) 463–1722.

Legislative Budget Board: (1949); 10 members; 5 ex officio: Lt. Gov.; House Speaker; Chair, Senate Finance Comm.; Chair, House Appropriations Comm.; Chair, House Ways and Means Comm.; 5 other members of Legislature. Dir. Jerry McGinty ($220,000), 1501 Congress Ave., PO Box 12666, Austin 78711; (512) 463–1200.

Legislative Council, Texas: (1949); 14 ex officio members: Lt. Gov.; House Speaker; 6 senators apptd. by Lt. Gov.; 5 representatives by Speaker; Chair, House Administration Committee. Exec. Dir. Jeff Archer ($220,000), 1501 Congress Ave., PO Box 12128, Austin 78711-2128; (512) 463–1155.

Legislative Redistricting Board: (1951); 5 ex officio members: Lt. Gov., House Speaker, Atty. Gen., Comptroller of Public Accounts, Comm. of General Land Office; PO Box 12128, Austin 78711-2128; (512) 463–6622.

Legislative Reference Library of Texas: (1909); 3 ex officio members: Lt. Gov., House Speaker, Chair of House Appropriations Comm.; 3 Legislative members; indefinite term. Dir. Mary Camp ($165,000), 1100 Congress Ave., Rm. 2N.3, Austin 78701; (512) 463–1252.

Librarian, State: (1839; present office est. 1909); apptv., indefinite term: Gloria Meraz ($148,197), PO Box 12927, Austin 78711-2927; (512) 463–5455.

Library and Archives Commission, Texas State: (1909 as 5-member Library and State Historical Commission; name changed to present form in 1979); apptv.; per diem and expenses on duty; 6-yr.; 7 members: Chair Martha Wong, Houston (9/28/27); David C. Garza, Brownsville (9/28/25); David Iglesias, Tyler (9/28/27); Arthur T. "Art" Mann, Hillsboro (9/28/23); Nancy Painter Paup, Fort Worth (9/28/27); Bradley S. "Brad" Tegeler, Austin (9/28/25); Darryl Tocker, Austin (9/28/23). Dir. and Librarian Gloria Meraz ($148,197), 1201 Brazos St., PO Box 12927, Austin 78711-2927; (512) 463–5474.

Licensing and Regulation, Texas Department of: (1989); apptv.; 6-yr.; expenses; 7 members: Chair Rick Figueroa, Brenham (2/1/21); Thomas F. Butler, Deer Park (2/1/25); Gerald R. Callas, Beaumont (2/1/23); Helen Callier, Kingwood (2/1/21); Nora Castañeda, Harlingen (2/1/25); Joel Garza, Pearland (2/1/21); Gary Wesson, Richmond (2/1/23). Exec. Dir. Brian E. Francis ($185,250), 920 Colorado St., PO Box 12157, Austin 78711; (512) 463–6599.

Lottery Commission, Texas: (1993); 6-yr.; apptv.; expenses; 5 members: Chair Robert G. Rivera, Dallas (2/1/27); Cindy Lyons Fields, El Paso (2/1/23); Mark A. Franz, Austin (2/1/25); Erik C. Saenz, Houston (2/1/23); Jamey Steen, Houston (2/1/25). Exec. Dir. Gary Grief ($213,344), 1801 Congress Ave., Ste. 6.403, PO Box 16630, Austin 78761-6630; (512) 344–5000.

Lower Colorado River Authority (See Colorado River Authority, Lower.)

Lower Concho River Water and Soil Conservation Authority (See Concho River Water and Soil Conservation Authority, Lower.)

Lower Neches Valley Authority (See Neches Valley Authority, Lower.)

Manufactured Housing Division: (1995, part of Texas Dept. of Housing and Community Affairs); apptv.; 6-yr.; 5 members: Chair Ronnie Richards, Clear Lake Shores (1/31/29); Jason R. Denny, Austin (1/31/25); Joe Gonzalez, Round Rock (1/31/27); Sylvia L. Guzman, Spring (1/31/25); Keith C. Thompson, Lubbock (1/31/29). Exec. Dir. Jim R. Hicks, 1801 Congress Ave., Ste. 11.400, PO Box 12489, Austin 78711-2489; (512) 475–2200.

Marriage and Family Therapists, Texas State Board of Examiners of: (1991); apptv.; 6-yr.; per diem and transportation expenses; 9 members: Presiding Member Lisa V. Merchant, Clyde (2/1/23); Russell F. "Russ" Bartee, Fort Worth (2/1/25); Jodie Elder, Dallas (2/1/27); George F. Francis IV, Georgetown (2/1/23); Evelyn Husband-Thompson, Houston (2/1/27); Daniel W. Parrish, DeSoto (2/1/25); Anthony C. Scoma, Austin (2/1/27); Jeanene L. Smith, Austin (2/1/25); Richmond E. Stoglin, Arlington (2/1/23). Board Admin. Sarah Faszholz ($72,000), 1801 Congress Ave., Ste. 7.300, Austin 78701; (512) 305–7700.

Medical Board, Texas: (1907 as 11-member Texas State Board of Medical Examiners; members increased to 12 in 1931, 15 in 1981,18 in 1993 and 19 in 2003; changed to present name in 2005 by Senate Bill 419); apptv.; 6-yr.; per diem on duty; 19 members, inc. 12 doctors: Pres. Sherif Z. Zaafran, Houston (4/13/27); Devinder S. Bhatia, Houston (4/13/25); George L. De Loach, Livingston (4/13/23); James S. Distefano, College Station (4/13/25); Kandace B. Farmer, Highland Village (4/13/27); Robert D. Martinez, Mission (4/13/25); Jayaram B. Naidu, Odessa (4/13/27); Satish Nayak, Andrews (4/13/25); Manuel "Manny" Quinones Jr., San Antonio (4/13/23); Jason K. Tibbels, Bridgeport (4/13/25); David G. Vanderweide, League City (4/13/23); 1 vacancy. 7 Public Members: Sharon J. Barnes, Rosharon (4/13/23); Michael E. Cokinos, Houston (4/13/27); Robert Gracia, Richmond (4/13/23); Tomeka M. Herod, Allen (4/13/25); LuAnn Morgan, Midland (4/13/27); Ebony V. Todd, Fort Cavazos (4/13/27); 1 vacancy. Exec. Dir. Stephen Brint Carlton ($165,315), 1801 Congress Ave., Ste. 9.200, PO Box 2018, Austin 78768-2018; (512) 305–7010. Consumer Complaint Hotline: (800) 201–9353.

Medical Physicists, Texas Board of Licensure for Professional: (1991); abolished by the Legislature in 2015. All duties transferred to the Texas Medical Board.

Medical Radiologic Technology, Texas Board of: (2015); apptv.; 6-yr.; 9 members: Presiding Officer Faraz Khan, Houston (2/1/25); Nicholas Beckmann, Houston (2/1/27); Jennifer Brandt, Fort Worth (2/1/23); Linda Brown, Port Neches (2/1/23); Regan Landreth, Georgetown (2/1/25); Shannon Lutz, Cypress (2/1/23); Scott Morren, Anton (2/1/27); Shaila D. Parker, Dallas (2/1/27); Carol Waddell, West (2/1/25). Exec. Dir. Stephen Brint Carlton, 1801 Congress Ave., Ste. 9.200, Austin 78701; (512) 305–7010.

Midwifery Board, Texas: (1999); abolished by the Legislature in 2015. All duties transferred to the Texas Department of Licensing and Regulation.

Military Dept., Texas: (1836 by Republic of Texas; Adjutant General's Dept. established 1905, renamed 2013); apptv.; commanded by Adjutant General, Maj. Gen. Thomas Suelzer ($191,357); assisted by Army National Guard Brig. Gen. Monie R. Ulis; Air National Guard Brig. Gen. Andrew Camacho; State Air Guard Maj. Gen. Anthony Woods. Officers serve at the pleasure of the Gov.; c/o Camp Mabry, 2200 W. 35th St., Bldg. 1, PO Box 5218, Austin 78703; (512) 782–5001.

Military Preparedness Commission, Texas: (2003); apptv.; 6-yr.; 3 ex-officio members (1 Senator, 1 House Representative, 1 General); 13 apptv.: Chair Kevin Pottinger, Fort Worth (2/1/27); Mike Boyd, San Angelo (2/1/25); Garry Bradford, Corpus Christi (2/1/25); Darrell Coleman, Wichita Falls (2/1/25); Tom Duncavage, Houston (2/1/29); Todd Fox, Killeen (2/1/25); Dennis Lewis, Texarkana (2/1/27); Benjamin Miranda, El Paso (2/1/29); Kenneth Sheets, Mesquite (2/1/27); Annette Sobel, Lubbock (2/1/29); Timothy Strawther, San Antonio (2/1/29); Michael Bob Starr, Abilene (2/1/29); Shannalea Taylor, Del Rio (2/1/27). Dir. Keith Graf, PO Box 12428, Austin 78711; (512) 475–1475.

Motor Vehicles, Texas Department of: (2009); apptv.; 6-yr.; 9 members: Chair Charles Bacarisse, Houston (2/1/25); Christian Alvarado, Austin (2/1/27); Stacey Gillman, Houston (2/1/25); Brett Graham, Denison (2/1/23); Tammy McRae, Conroe (2/1/25); Sharla Omumu, Cypress (2/1/27); John M. Prewitt, Cypress (2/1/23); Paul Scott, Lubbock (2/1/23); 1 vacancy. Exec. Dir. Daniel Avitia ($210,850), 4000 Jackson Ave., Austin 78731; (512) 465–3000.

Municipal Retirement System, Texas (See Retirement System, Texas Municipal.)

Music Office, Texas: (1990, became part of the Office of Gov. in 1991); Dir. Brendon Anthony, 1100 San Jacinto Blvd., Ste. 3.418, PO Box 12428, Austin 78711; (512) 463–6666.

Neches River Municipal Water Authority, Upper: (1953 as 9-member board; members decreased to 3 in 1959); apptv.; 6-yr.; 3 members: Pres. Jay Herrington, Palestine (2/1/27); Joe Crutcher, Palestine (2/1/23); Paul Morris, Palestine (2/1/25). Gen. Mgr. Monty D. Shank, 210 FM 1892 (Frankston), PO Box 1965, Palestine 75802; (903) 876–2237.

Neches Valley Authority, Lower: (1933); apptv.; per diem and expenses on duty; 6-yr.; 9 members: Pres. William D. "Bill" Voigtman, Silsbee (7/28/23); Lonnie B. Grissom, Woodville (7/28/27); Kal A. Kincaid, Beaumont (7/28/23); Steve Lucas, Beaumont (7/28/25); Clint A. Mitchell, Nederland (7/28/23); Ivy Pate, Beaumont (7/28/27); James M. Scott, Beaumont (7/28/25); Charles "Caleb" Spurlock, Woodville (7/28/25); Jeanie Turk, Sour Lake (7/28/27). Gen. Mgr. Scott Hall, 7850 Eastex Fwy., PO Box 5117, Beaumont 77726-5117; (409) 892–4011.

North Texas Tollway Authority: (1997); 2-yr.; 9 members, 8 apptd. by 4 counties (Collin, Dallas, Denton, Tarrant), 1 by Gov.: Chair

Texas Parks and Wildlife Department celebrated its 100th anniversary in 2023.

Marcus Knight, Lancaster; Lynn Gravley, Gunter; Mojy Haddad, Arlington; Pete Kamp, Denton; Scott D. Levine, Parker; John Mahalik, Carrollton; George "Tex" Quesada, Dallas; Glen Whitley, Fort Worth; Jane Willard, Celina. Exec. Dir. James Hofmann, PO Box 260928, Plano 75026-0928; ((817) 731–6882).

Nueces River Authority: (1953 as Nueces River Conservation and Reclamation District; name changed to present form in 1971); apptv.; 6-yr.; per diem and expenses; 21 members: Pres. Dan Leyendecker, Corpus Christi (2/1/25); Alston Beinhorn, Catarina (2/1/23); Jane D. Bell, Corpus Christi (2/1/25); Allan P. Bloxsom III, Boerne (2/1/27); Dane Brunn, Corpus Christi (2/1/25); Eric Burnett, Portland (2/1/27); Ross G. Cansino, George West (2/1/27); Marshall E. Davidson, Ingleside (2/1/23); Chad H. Foster Jr., Uvalde (2/1/23); Annelise V. Gonzalez, San Antonio (2/1/23); Debra Y. Hatch, Corpus Christi (2/1/23); Karin E. Knolle, Sandia (2/1/27); Stacy Meuth, Floresville (2/1/27); Elizabeth Perez-Aliseda, Beeville (2/1/27); David Purser, Karnes City (2/1/25); Armandina "Dina" Ramirez, Karnes City (2/1/25); Tomas Ramirez III, Devine (2/1/21); William J. "Bill" Schuchman, Jourdanton (2/1/23); Anita Shackelford, Leakey (2/1/25); Howard A. "Tony" Wood, Corpus Christi (2/1/23); 1 vacancy. Exec. Dir. John J. Byrum II, 539 Hwy. 83 S., Uvalde 78801; (830) 278–6810.

Nursing, Texas Board of: (1909 as 5-member Texas Board of Nurse Examiners; members increased to 6 in 1931 and to 9 in 1981; name changed to present and members increased to 13 in 2007); apptv.; per diem and expenses; 6-yr.; 13 members: Pres. Kathy Shipp, Lubbock (1/31/23); Daryl Chambers, Grand Prairie (1/31/27); Laura Disque, Pharr (1/31/25); Allison P. Edwards, Bellaire (1/31/27); Carol Kay Hawkins, San Antonio (1/31/25); Mazie Mathews Jamison, Dallas (1/31/23); Kenneth D. "Ken" Johnson, San Angelo (1/31/27); Kathy Leader-Horn, Granbury (1/31/27); Melissa Schat, Granbury (1/31/25); Tyrone Sharp, Houston (1/31/23); Rickey "Rick" Williams, Killeen (1/31/25); Kimberly "Kim" Wright, Big Spring (1/31/23); 1 vacancy. Exec. Dir. Katherine A. Thomas ($169,537), 1801 Congress Ave., Ste. 10.200, Austin 78701; (512) 305–7400.

Occupational Therapy Examiners, Texas Board of: (1983 as 6-member board; increased to 9 in 1999); apptv.; 6-yr.; per diem and expenses; 9 members: Chair Stephanie Johnston, Magnolia (2/1/27); Estrella Barrera, Austin (2/1/29); Jacob Boggus, Harlingen (2/1/27); Blanca Cardenas, Mission (2/1/29); Jennifer Clark, Iola (2/1/25); Karen Gardner, Brenham (2/1/23); Eddie Jessie, Houston (2/1/25); Sally Harris King, Houston (2/1/27); Todd Novosad, Bee Cave (2/1/25). Exec. Dir. Ralph Harper, 1801 Congress Ave., Ste. 10.900, Austin 78701; (512) 305–6900.

Offenders with Medical or Mental Impairments, Texas Correctional Office on: apptv.; 6-yr.; 21 members: 11 ex officio from various state agencies; 10 apptd. by Gov.: Chair Robb Catalano, Fort Worth (2/1/25); Sanjay Adhia, Sugar Land (2/1/27); Allan Cain, Carthage (2/1/23); James B. Eby, Wichita Falls (2/1/25); Matthew Faubion, San Antonio (2/1/23); Scott MacNaughton, San Antonio (2/1/23); Trenton R. Marshall, Burleson (2/1/25); Casey O'Neal, Austin (2/1/25); Denise Oncken, Houston (2/1/27); Rogelio Rodriguez, El Paso (2/1/27). Dir. April Zamora ($146,085), 4616 W. Howard Ln., Ste. 200, Austin 78728; (512) 671–2134.

One-Call Board of Texas: (1997; created by the Underground Facility Damage Prevention and Safety Act and serves as the board for the Texas Underground Facility Notification Corp.); apptv.; 3-yr.; 12 members: Chair Robert DeLeon, Corpus Christi (8/31/25); Robert Bridge, Normanna (8/31/24); Joe Canales, Austin (8/31/25); Joseph Costa, DeSoto (8/31/23); Derek Delgado, Pasadena (8/31/25); Sandy Galvan, San Antonio (8/31/25); Richard "Rich" Gann, Sugar Land (8/31/24); William Geise, Austin (8/31/23); Marcela Navarrete, El Paso (8/31/24); Christopher Nowak, Houston (8/31/23); Manish Seth, Missouri City (8/31/24); George Spencer, Austin (8/31/23). Exec. Dir. Don Ward, 9415 Burnet Rd., Ste. 311, PO Box 9764, Austin 78766; (512) 467–2850.

Optometry Board, Texas: (1921 as 6-member State Board of Examiners in Optometry; name and number of members changed to present in 1981); apptv.; per diem; 6-yr.; 9 members: Chair Mario Gutierrez, San Antonio (1/31/23); Judith Chambers, Austin (1/31/25); John Todd Cornett, Amarillo (1/31/25); Ron Hopping, Houston (1/31/27); Carey A. Patrick, Allen (1/31/27); Rene Peña, El Paso (1/31/27); Meghan Schutte, Austin (1/31/25); Ty Sheehan, San Antonio (1/31/23); Bill Thompson, Richardson (1/31/23). Exec. Dir. Janice McCoy ($91,324), 1801 Congress Ave., Ste. 9.300, Austin 78701-1319; (512) 305–8500.

Pardons and Paroles, Texas Board of: (1893 as Board of Pardon Advisers; changed in 1936 to Board of Pardons and Paroles with 3 members; members increased to 6 in 1983; made a division of the Texas Dept. of Criminal Justice in 1990); apptv.; 6-yr.; 7 members (chairman, $176,300; members, $125,000 each): Chair David G. Gutiérrez, Salado (2/1/27); Elodia Brito, Amarillo (2/1/29); Carmella Jones, Eastland (2/1/25); Brian Long, Kilgore (2/1/29); Marsha Moberley, Cedar Park (2/1/25); Linda Molina, San Antonio (2/1/27); Ed Robertson, Pflugerville

(2/1/27). Parole Commissioners: Michael Adams, Huntsville; Richard Aiello, Austin; Jacqueline Bishop, Huntsville; Edward Davila, Amarillo; Lee Anne Eck-Massingill, Gatesville; Ira Evans, Angleton; Mary J. Farley, Austin; Sandra Fletcher, Angleton; Troy Fox, Austin; Raymond Gonzalez, San Antonio; James Paul Kiel, Palestine; Jeffrey Marton, Amarillo; Anthony Ramirez, San Antonio; Alfredo Salcido, Huntsville; Roel Tejada, Gatesville. Gen. Counsel Bettie L. Wells ($145,000), 8610 Shoal Creek Blvd., PO Box 13401, Austin 78711-3401; (512) 406–5452.

Parks and Wildlife Commission, Texas: (1963 as 3-member board; members increased to 6 in 1971 and to 9 in 1983); apptv.; expenses; 6-yr.; 9 members: Chair Arch H. "Beaver" Aplin III, Lake Jackson (2/1/23); James E. Abell, Kilgore (2/1/25); Oliver J. Bell, Cleveland (2/1/29); Paul L. Foster, El Paso (2/1/27); Anna B. Galo, Laredo (2/1/27); Jeffery D. Hildebrand, Houston (2/1/25); Robert L. "Bobby" Patton Jr., Fort Worth (2/1/25); Travis B. "Blake" Rowling, Dallas (2/1/27); Dick Scott, Wimberley (2/1/29). Exec. Dir. David Yoskowitz ($215,412), 4200 Smith School Rd., Austin 78744; (512) 389–4800.

Pecos River Compact Commission: (1942, negotiates with New Mexico regarding waters of the Pecos); apptv.; 6-yr.; salary and expenses. Comm. Frederic "Rick" Tate (1/23/23), PO Box 969, Marfa 79843; (432) 729–3225.

Pension Review Board, Texas: (1979); apptv.; 6-yr.; 7 members: Chair Stephanie Leibe, Austin (1/31/27); Keith Brainard, Georgetown (1/31/25); Marcia Dush, Austin (1/31/25); Christopher Gonzales, Cypress (1/31/27); Robert D. "Rob" Ries, Austin (1/31/23); Christopher Zook, Houston (1/31/27); 1 vacancy. Exec. Dir. Amy Cardona ($126,730), 300 W. 15th St., Ste. 406, PO Box 13498, Austin 78711-3498; (512) 463–1736.

Pharmacy, Texas State Board of: (1907 as 6-member board; members increased to current number in 1981); apptv.; 6-yr.; 11 members: Pres. Julie Spier, Katy (8/31/23); Rick Fernandez, Northlake (8/31/23); Daniel Guerrero, San Marcos (8/31/23); Lori Henke, Amarillo (8/31/23); Donnie Lewis, Athens (8/31/25); Bradley A. Miller, Austin (8/31/25); Donna Montemayor, San Antonio (8/31/25); Ian Shaw, Dallas (8/31/27); Suzette Tijerina, Castle Hills (8/31/27); Rick Tisch, Spring (8/31/25); Jenny Downing Yoakum, Kilgore (8/31/27). Exec. Dir. Ann Driscoll ($88,493), 1801 Congress Ave., Ste. 13.100, Austin 78701-1319; (512) 305–8000. Consumer complaints: (800) 821–3205.

Physical Therapy and Occupational Therapy Examiners, Executive Council of: (1971); apptv.; 2-yr.; expenses; 5 members: Presiding Officer Manoranjan "Mano" Mahadeva, Frisco (2/1/23); Harvey Aikman, Mission (2/1/27); Donivan Hodge, Spicewood (2/1/23); Eddie Jessie, Houston (2/1/25); Stephanie Johnston, Magnolia (2/1/27). Exec. Dir. Ralph Harper ($100,893), 1801 Congress Ave., Ste. 10.900, Austin 78701-3942; (512) 305–6900.

Physical Therapy Examiners, Texas Board of: (1971); apptv.; 6-yr.; expenses; 9 members: Chair Harvey Aikman, Mission (1/31/27); Glenda Clausell, Houston (1/31/27); Jacob Delgado, Hewitt (1/31/25); Manuel "Tony" Domenech, Austin (1/31/23); Donivan Hodge, Spicewood (1/31/23); Liesl Olson, Lubbock (1/31/27); Omar Palomin, McAllen (1/31/23); Kathryn "Kate" Roby, Temple (1/31/25); Melissa Skillern, Manvel (1/31/25). Exec. Dir. Ralph Harper, 1801 Congress Ave., Ste. 10.900, Austin 78701; (512) 305–6900.

Physician Assistant Board, Texas: (1993 as Physician Assistant Advisory Council; changed to present name in 1995); apptv.; 6-yr.; 13 members: Chair Karrie Lynn Crosby, Robinson (2/1/27); Clay P. Bulls, Abilene (2/1/27); Jennifer L. Clarner, Austin (2/1/23); Victor S. Ho, Houston (2/1/27); Lawrence G. "Larry" Hughes, Frisco (2/1/25); Sandra Longoria, Harlingen (2/1/25); Cameron J. McElhany, Austin (2/1/23); Melinda Ann Moore Gottschalk, Round Rock (2/1/25); Gregory Rowin, Harlingen (2/1/23); Andrew Sauer, Amarillo (2/1/27); Lali Shipley, Austin (2/1/27); 2 vacancies. Exec. Dir. Stephen Brint Carlton, 1801 Congress Ave., Ste. 9.200, Austin 78701; (512) 305–7010. Consumer Complaints: (800) 201–9353.

Plumbing Examiners, Texas State Board of: (1947 as 6-member board; members increased to 9 in 1981); apptv.; expenses; 6-yr.; Chair Frank S. Denton, Conroe (9/5/25); James "Ron" Ainsworth, Midland (9/5/23); Darrin Black, Abilene (9/5/27); Milton Gutierrez, Round Rock (9/5/27); William "Bill" Klock, Houston (9/5/23); Thomas "Justin" MacDonald, Kerrville (9/5/25); Thomas "Tommy" Rice Jr., Houston (9/5/27); Norma Yado, McAllen (9/5/28); David "Dave" Yelovich, Friendswood (9/5/25). Exec. Dir. Lisa G. Hill ($120,586), 929 E. 41st St., PO Box 4200, Austin 78765-4200; (512) 936–5200.

Podiatric Medical Examiners Advisory Board: (1923 as 6-member State Board of Chiropody Examiners; name changed to State Board of Podiatry Examiners in 1967; made 9-member board in 1981; name changed to present form in 1996; in 2017 the licensing and regulation of the practice of Podiatry transferred to the Texas Department of Licensing and Regulation); apptv.; 6-yr.; expenses; 9 members: Presiding Officer Travis A. Motley, Fort Worth (2/1/23); Cory Brown, Abilene (2/1/23); Leslie Campbell, Allen (2/1/27); Maria "Yvette" Hernandez, Rio Grande City (2/1/23); Kristin Lea Luckey, Harlingen (2/1/27); James Michael Lunsford, Austin (2/1/25); Joe E. Martin, College Station (2/1/25); Renee K. Pietzsch, Georgetown (2/1/27); Cirenia Hernandez Terrazas, Austin (2/1/25). PO Box 12157, Austin 78711; (512) 463–6599.

Port Freeport Commission: (1925); 6-yr.; 6 elected members: Chair Ravi K. Singhania, Brazosport (5/31/25); Dan Croft, Jones Creek (5/31/25); Barbara Fratila, Lake Jackson (5/31/29); Rob Giesecke, Damon (5/31/27); Kim Kincannon, West Columbia (5/31/29); Rudy Santos, Angleton (5/31/27). Exec. Dir. Phyllis Saathoff, 1100 Cherry St., Freeport 77541; (979) 233–2667.

Prepaid Higher Education Tuition Board, Texas (See Higher Education Tuition Board, Texas Prepaid.)

Preservation Board, State: (1983); 2-yr.; 6 members (3 ex officio: Gov., Lt. Gov., House Speaker); 3 apptv.: 1 apptd. by Gov.: Alethea Swann Bugg, San Antonio (2/1/25); 1 senator apptd. by Lt. Gov.; 1 representative by Speaker. Exec. Dir. Rod Welsh ($175,990), 201 E. 14th St., PO Box 13286, Austin 78711; (512) 463–5495.

Prison Board (See Criminal Justice, Texas Dept. of.)

Private Security Advisory Committee, Texas: (1969 as Board of Private Investigators and Private Security Agencies; reorganized in 1998 as Texas Comm. on Private Security; re-established in 2004 as a bureau of the Texas Dept. of Public Safety named Texas Private Security Board and in 2020 took its current name); apptv.; expenses; 6-yr.; 8 members (1 ex officio: Dir., Dept. of Public Safety); 7 apptd.: Chair Patricia James, Houston (1/31/27); D. Wade Hayden, San Antonio (1/31/25); John Helweg, Houston (1/31/27); Debbra Ulmer, Houston (1/31/25); 3 vacancies. Service Dir. Chris Sims ($135,960), 6100 Guadalupe St., PO Box 4087, Austin 78773-0001; (512) 424–7293.

Prosecuting Attorney, State: (1923) apptd. by Court of Criminal Appeals: Stacey M. Soule ($154,000), 209 W. 14th St., PO Box 13046, Austin 78711-3046; (512) 463–1660.

Psychologists, Texas State Board of Examiners of: (1969 as 6-member board; members increased to 9 in 1981); apptv.; 6-yr.; per diem and expenses; 9 members: Presiding Member John K. Bielamowicz, Waxahachie (10/31/27); Herman Adler, Houston (10/31/23); Jamie Becker, Plano (10/31/25); Ryan T. Bridges, Houston (10/31/23); Jeanette Deas Calhoun, Tyler (10/31/25); Mark E. Cartwright, Dallas (5/31/27); Roxana I. Lambdin, Kerrville (10/31/27); Sangeeta Singg, San Angelo (10/31/25); Andoni Zagouris, Kingsland (10/31/23). Board Admin. Diane Moore ($60,000), 1801 Congress Ave., Ste. 7.300, Austin 78701; (512) 305–7700.

Public Finance Authority, Texas: (1984, assumed duties of Texas Building Authority); apptv.; per diem and expenses; 6-yr.; 7 members: Chair Billy M. Atkinson Jr., Sugar Land (2/1/23); Lance S. Etcheverry, Dallas (2/1/25); Larry G. Holt, Bryan (2/1/27);

Ramon Manning, Houston (2/1/27); Shanda Perkins, Burleson (2/1/25); Jay A. Riskind, Austin (2/1/23); Ben Streusand, Spring (2/1/25). Exec. Dir. Lee Deviney ($200,000), 300 W. 15th St., Ste. 411, PO Box 12906, Austin 78711-2906; (512) 463–5544.

Public Insurance Counsel, Office of: (1991). Public Counsel (apptv.; 2-yr.) David Bolduc ($149,976), (2/1/25), 1601 Congress Ave., Ste. 3.500, Austin 78701; (512) 322–4143.

Public Safety Commission: (1935 with 3 members; members increased to 5 in 2007); apptv.; expenses; 6-yr.; 5 members: Chair Steven P. Mach, Houston (1/1/28); Nelda L. Blair, Conroe (1/1/26); Larry B. Long, Dallas (1/1/28); Steve H. Stodghill, Dallas (1/1/24); Dale Wainwright, Austin (1/1/24). Dir. of Texas Dept. of Public Safety Steven C. McCraw ($299,813), 5805 N. Lamar Blvd., PO Box 4087, Austin 78773-0001; (512) 424–2000.

Public Utility Commission of Texas: (1975); apptv.; 6-yr.; 3 members ($201,000): Interim Chair Kathleen Jackson, Beaumont (9/1/27); Lori Cobos, Austin (9/1/21); Jimmy Glotfelty, Houston (9/1/25); Will McAdams, Austin (9/1/25); 1 vacancy. Exec. Dir. Thomas Gleeson ($200,000), 1701 Congress Ave., 7th Fl., PO Box 13326, Austin 78711-3326; (512) 936–7000.

Public Utility Counsel, Office of: (1983); apptv.; 2-yr.; Public Counsel: Courtney K. Hjaltman ($165,000), (2/1/25), 1701 Congress Ave., Ste. 9-180, PO Box 12397, Austin 78711-2397; (512) 936–7500.

Racing Commission, Texas: (1986); apptv.; 6-yr.; per diem and expenses; 9 members; 2 ex officio: Chair, Public Safety Comm. and Comm. of Agriculture; 7 apptv.: Chair Robert C. Pate, Corpus Christi (2/1/29); Rebecca Contreras, Hutto (2/1/25); Margaret Martin, Boerne (2/1/27); Constance McNabb, Montgomery (2/1/27); Michael Moore, Fort Worth (2/1/29); A.J. Waight, Willow City (2/1/27); 1 vacancy. Exec. Dir. Amy F. Cook ($130,000), 1801 Congress Ave., Ste. 7.600, PO Box 12080, Austin 78711-2080; (512) 833–6699.

Radiation Advisory Board, Texas: (1961); apptv.; 6-yr.; 18 members: Roland Benke, Austin (4/16/27); Michael Britt, New Braunfels (4/16/25); Charles Cavnor, Little Elm (4/16/25); John Hageman, San Antonio (4/16/23); Mark Harvey, Houston (4/16/27); Lisa Masters, San Antonio (4/16/27); Darlene Metter, San Antonio (4/16/25); Sanjay Narayan, Dallas (4/16/27); William Pate, League City (4/16/25); Kenneth "Ken" Peters, Granbury (4/16/25); Doug Posey, Corpus Christi (4/16/23); Gerald T. "Tim" Powell, Bay City (4/16/27); Kevin L. Raabe, Floresville (4/16/23); Robert "Bob" Redweik, Tomball (4/16/25); Darshan J. Sachde, Austin (4/16/25); Mark Silberman, Austin (4/16/23); Lynn Slaney Silguero, Frisco (4/16/23); Simon Trubek, Austin (4/16/27). 8407 Wall St., PO Box 149347, Austin 78714-9347; (512) 942–9238.

Radioactive Waste Disposal Compact Commission, Texas Low-Level: (1993); apptv.; 6-yr.; expenses; 6 Texas members, plus 2 members from Vermont; Texas apptees.: Chair Brandon T. Hurley, Grapevine (8/31/25); Lisa Edwards, Granbury (8/31/23); Linda Morris, Waco (8/31/27); Jeff Mundy, Austin (8/31/25); Sumana Nayak, Andrews (8/31/27); John M. Salsman, Driftwood (8/31/23). Exec. Dir. Stephen Raines, 1502 West Ave., Austin 78701; (737) 300–2154.

Railroad Commission of Texas: (1891); elective; 6-yr.; 3 members, $140,937 each: Wayne Christian (12/31/28); Christi Craddick (12/31/24); Jim Wright (12/31/26). Exec. Dir. Wei Wang ($251,652), 1701 Congress Ave., PO Box 12967, Austin 78711-2967; (512) 463–7158.

Real Estate Commission, Texas: (1949 as 6-member board; members increased to current number in 1979); apptv.; per diem and expenses; 6-yr.; 9 members: Chair R. Scott Kesner, El Paso (1/31/25); Stuart Bernstein, Austin (1/31/29); Chance Brown, Cypress (1/31/29); Jason Hartgraves, Addison (1/31/25); Leslie Lerner, Houston (1/31/27); Renee Harvey Lowe, Clarksville (1/31/29); Benjamin "Ben" Peña, Bayview (1/31/27); Barbara Russell, Denton (1/31/25); Mark Woodroof, Houston (1/31/27). Exec. Dir. Chelsea Buchholtz ($200,582), 1700 Congress Ave., Ste. 400, PO Box 12188, Austin 78711-2188; (512) 936–3000.

Real Estate Research Center, Texas: (1971); apptv.; 6-yr.; 10 members; 1 ex officio: rep. of Texas Real Estate Commission; 9 apptv.: Chair W. Douglas Jennings, Fort Worth (1/31/27); Troy C. Alley Jr., DeSoto (1/31/23); Russell L. Cain, Port Lavaca (1/31/23); Doug Foster, San Antonio (1/31/27); Vicki Fullerton, The Woodlands (1/31/25); Patrick Geddes, Dallas (1/31/23); Besa Martin, Boerne (1/31/27); Rebecca "Becky" Vajdak, Temple (1/31/25); 1 vacancy. Exec. Dir. Gary Maler, 1700 Research Pkwy., Ste. 200, Texas A&M University, 2115 TAMU, College Station 77843-2115; (979) 845–2031.

Redistricting Board, Legislative (See Legislative Redistricting Board.)

Red River Authority of Texas: (1959); apptv.; 6-yr.; per diem and expenses; 9 members: Pres. Jerry Bob Daniel, Truscott (8/11/27); Mary Lou Bradley, Memphis (8/11/25); Jerry Dan Davis, Wellington (8/11/23); Tonya D. Detten, Panhandle (8/11/25); Conrad J. Masterson Jr., Cee Vee (8/11/27); Michael R. Sandefur, Texarkana (8/11/23); Stephen A. Thornhill, Denison (8/11/25); Joe L. Ward, Telephone (8/11/23); 1 vacancy. Gen. Mgr. Randall W. Whiteman, 3000 Hammon Rd., PO Box 240, Wichita Falls 76307; (940) 723–8697.

Red River Compact Commission: (1949, negotiates with Oklahoma, Arkansas and Louisiana regarding waters of the Red); apptv.; 6-yr.; salary and expenses. Comm. Robin Phillips, Sherman (2/1/29), 300 N. Travis St., Sherman 75090; (903) 870–0070.

Rehabilitation Council of Texas: (1973); apptv.; 3-yr.; at least 15 members: Christopher M. "Mark" Baird, San Angelo (10/29/24); Glenda J. Born, Austin (10/29/24); Amanda Bowdoin, Forney (10/29/23); Jennifer Clouse, Temple (2/25/23); Lisa Cowart, Sour Lake (10/29/24); Michele L. Dobbins, Pasadena (10/29/24); Cheryl A. Fuller, Austin; Lindsey Geeslin, Lorena (10/29/23); Gennadiy Goldenshteyn, Dallas (2/25/23); April Pollreisz, Amarillo (10/29/24); Joe Powell, Irving (10/29/24); Emily Robinson, Pflugerville (10/29/23); Rodrick Robinson, McKinney (10/29/23); Peggy Schmidt, Lucas (10/29/25); Daniel W. Solcher, Allen (10/29/25); Karen Stanfill, Houston (10/29/25); James E. Williams Jr., Leander (10/29/24). 101 E. 15th St., Rm. 144T, Austin 78778-0001; (512) 936–3445.

Respiratory Care Board: (2015); apptv.; 6-yr.; 9 members: Presiding Officer Latana T. Jackson, Cedar Hill (2/1/23); Samuel L. Brown Jr., Marshall (2/1/25); Tim R. Chappell, Plano (2/1/27); Sam Gregory "Gregg" Marshall, Round Rock (2/1/27); Debra E. Patrick, McKinney (2/1/25); Shad J. Pellizzari, Cedar Park (2/1/23); Kandace D. "Kandi" Pool, San Angelo (2/1/27); Hammad Nasir Qureshi, Tomball (2/1/25); Sonia K. Sanderson, Beaumont (2/1/23). Exec. Dir. Stephen Brint Carlton, 1801 Congress Ave., Ste. 9.200, PO Box 2018, Austin 78768; (512) 305–7010.

Retirement System, Texas County & District: (1967); apptv.; 6-yr.; 9 members: Chair Mary Louise Nicholson, Fort Worth (12/31/23); Tammy Biggar, Bonham (12/31/25); Chris Davis, Alto (12/31/27); Sammy Farias, Beeville (12/31/27); Susan Fletcher, Frisco (12/31/23); Deborah Hunt, Georgetown (12/31/27); Kara Sands, Corpus Christi (12/31/23); Chris Taylor, Fort Worth (12/31/25); Holly Williamson, Houston (12/31/25). Exec. Dir. Amy Bishop, 901 S. MoPac Expwy., Bldg. IV, Ste. 500, Austin 78746; (512) 328–8889.

Retirement System, Texas Emergency Services: (1977; formerly the Fire Fighters' Relief and Retirement Fund); apptv.; expenses; 6-yr.; 9 members: Chair Pilar Rodriguez, Edinburg (9/1/27); Nathan Douglas, Seabrook (9/1/25); Matthew "Matt" Glaves, Alvin (9/1/25); Edward J. Keenan, Houston (9/1/23); Brad Landi, Austin (9/1/27); Jerry Romero, El Paso (2/1/25); Rodney Alan Ryalls, Burkburnett (9/1/23); Brian Smith, Austin (9/1/27);

Stephanie Lynn Wagner, Wimberley (9/1/23). Exec. Dir. Tiffany White ($100,000), PO Box 12577, Austin 78711; (512) 936-3372.

Retirement System, Texas Municipal: (1947); apptv.; 6-yr.; expenses; 6 members: Chair Bob Scott, Prosper (2/1/25); Anali Alanis, Pharr (2/1/27); Jesús Garza, Victoria (2/1/23); Johnny Huizar, Pleasanton (2/1/23); David Landis, Perryton (2/1/27); Bill Philibert, Deer Park (2/1/25); . Exec. Dir. David Wescoe, 2717 Perseverance Dr., Ste. 300, PO Box 149153, Austin 78714-9153; (512) 476-5576.

Retirement System of Texas, Employees: (1949); apptv.; 6-yr.; 6 members: 1 apptd. by Gov., 1 by Chief Justice of State Supreme Court, 1 by House Speaker; 3 elected by ERS members: Chair James "Jim" Kee, San Antonio (8/31/26); Brian R. Barth, Austin (8/31/25); Neika Clark, Houston (8/31/27); I. Craig Hester, Austin (8/31/28); Catherine Melvin, Austin (8/31/23); John R. Rutherford, Houston (8/31/24). Exec. Dir. Porter Wilson ($348,519), 200 E. 18th St., PO Box 13207, Austin 78711-3207; (877) 275-4377.

Retirement System of Texas, Teacher: (1937 as 6-member board; members increased to 9 in 1973); 6-yr.; expenses; 9 members; 2 apptd. by State Board of Education, 3 by Gov., 4 by Gov. after being nominated by popular ballot of retirement system members: Chair Jarvis V. Hollingsworth, Missouri City (8/31/23); Brittny Allred, Dallas (8/31/27); Michael Ball, Argyle (8/31/25); David Corpus, Humble (8/31/25); John Elliott, Austin (8/31/27); James Dick Nance, Hallettsville (8/31/23); Nanette Sissney, Whitesboro (8/31/23); Robert H. Walls Jr., San Antonio (8/31/25); Elvis Williams, Fair Oaks Ranch (8/31/27). Exec. Dir. Brian Guthrie ($500,000), 1000 Red River St., Austin 78701-2698; (512) 542-6400.

Rio Grande Compact Commission: (1929, negotiates with Colorado and New Mexico regarding waters of the Rio Grande); apptv.; 6-yr.; salary and expenses; Comm. Robert S. "Bobby" Skov, Fabens (6/9/25), 401 E. Franklin Ave. Ste. 560, El Paso 79901-1212; (915) 764-0014.

Risk Management, State Office of: apptv.; 2-yr.; 5 members: Chair Lloyd M. Garland, Lubbock (2/1/25); William Brown, San Antonio (2/1/27); Ricardo "Rick" Galindo III, San Antonio (2/1/25); Tomas Gonzalez, El Paso (2/1/23); Gerald Ladner Sr., Austin (2/1/27). Exec. Dir. Stephen Vollbrecht ($150,563), 300 W. 15th St., 6th Fl., PO Box 13777, Austin 78711-3777; (512) 475-1440.

Sabine River Authority of Texas: (1949); apptv.; per diem and expenses; 6-yr.; 9 members: Pres. Janie Walenta, Quitman (7/6/23); Thomas "Tom" Beall, Milam (7/6/23); Elton Brock, Marshall (7/6/27); Jeffrey D. "Jeff" Jacobs, Rockwall (7/6/25); Joshua A. "Josh" McAdams, Center (7/6/25); Darrin R. Rudolph, Longview (7/6/27); Jeanette Sterner, Holly Lake Ranch (7/6/27); Cliff Todd, Long Branch (7/6/23); Kevin M. Williams, Orange (7/6/25). Gen. Mgr. David Montagne, PO Box 579, Orange 77631-0579; (409) 746-2192.

Sabine River Compact Commission: (1953, negotiates with Louisiana regarding the waters of the Sabine); apptv.; 6-yr.; salary and expenses; 2 commissioners: Connie Wade Gipson, Longview (7/12/28); Michael H. Lewis, Newton (7/12/25); c/o PO Box 13087, Austin 78711-3087; (512) 239-4696.

San Antonio River Authority: (1937); elective; 6-yr.; 12 members: Chair Jim Campbell, Bexar Co. (11/2/27); Dominic Carvajal, Wilson Co. (11/2/27); Alicia L. Cowley, Goliad Co. (11/2/27); James Fuller, Goliad Co. (11/4/25); Lourdes Galvan, Bexar Co. (11/4/25); Derek J. Gaudlitz, Wilson Co. (11/2/28); Jerry G. Gonzales, Bexar Co. (11/4/25); Michael W. Lackey, Bexar Co. (11/2/27); Hector R. Morales, Bexar Co. (11/7/23); Gaylon J. Oehlke, Karnes Co. (11/4/25); Deb B. Prost, Bexar Co. (11/7/23); H.B. "Trip" Ruckman III, Karnes Co. (11/2/27). Gen. Mgr. Derek Boese, 100 E. Guenther St., San Antonio 78204; (210) 227-1373.

San Jacinto River Authority: (1937); apptv.; expenses while on duty; 6-yr.; 7 members: Pres. Ronnie Anderson, Mont Belvieu (10/16/27); Ed Boulware, Montgomery (10/16/23); Stacey Buick, Montgomery (10/16/27); William "Wil" Faubel, Montgomery (10/16/25); Stephanie Johnson, Montgomery (10/16/25); Mark Micheletti, Kingwood (10/16/23); Ricardo "Rick" Mora, The Woodlands (10/16/25). Interim Gen. Mgr. Ed Shackelford, 1577 Dam Site Rd., PO Box 329, Conroe 77305; (936) 588-3111.

Savings and Mortgage Lending, Department of: (1961); commissioner apptd. by State Finance Commission. Comm. Hector Retta ($200,004), 2601 N. Lamar Blvd., Ste. 201, Austin 78705; (512) 475-1350.

School Land Board (See Land Board, School.)

School Safety Center, Texas: (2001); apptv.; 2-yr.; 5 ex officio members from the Texas Higher Education Coord. Board, Texas Education Agency, Health and Human Services Comm., Attorney General's office, and the Texas Juvenile Justice Dept.; 12 apptd. members: Chair Craig Bessent, Abilene (2/1/22); Bill Avera, Jacksonville (2/1/22); Kerri Brady, Georgetown (2/1/22); Melissa Dunbar, Center Point (2/1/25); Edwin S. Flores, Dallas (2/1/25); Bryan Hedrick, Hereford (2/1/22); James M. Mosley, Borger (2/1/25); Teresa K. Oldham, Jarrell (2/1/22); Noe E. Perez, Laguna Vista (2/1/25); Michael L. Slaughter, Wylie (2/1/25); Jill M.Tate, Colleyville (2/1/25); Alan Trevino, Burnet (2/1/22). Dir. Kathy Martinez-Prather, 601 University Dr., San Marcos 78666; (512) 245-8082.

Securities Board, Texas State: (1957, the outgrowth of several amendments to the Texas Securities Act, originally passed in 1913); expenses; 6-yr.; 5 members: Chair E. Wally Kinney, Comfort (1/20/25); Robert Belt, Houston (1/20/23); Kenny Koncaba, Friendswood (1/20/23); Ejike E. Okpa, Dallas (1/20/27); Melissa Tyroch, Belton (1/20/25). Comm. Travis J. Iles ($172,087), 208 E. 10th St., PO Box 13167, Austin 78711-3167; (512) 305-8300.

Sex Offender Treatment, Council on: (1983); apptv.; expenses; 6-yr.; 7 members: Presiding Officer Aaron Paul Pierce, Temple (2/1/23); Elizabeth Cox, San Antonio (2/1/25); Ezio Leite, North Richland Hills (2/1/27); Jarrett Lujan, Marfa (2/1/27); Emily Orozco-Crousen, Abilene (2/1/27); Andrea Ortiz, Dallas (2/1/29); Tiffany Strother, Godley (2/1/25). Exec. Dir. Pamela Adams, c/o Texas Dept. of State Health Services, PO Box 149347, Austin 78714-9347; (512) 438-5446.

Skill Standards Board, Texas: (1995); abolished and its powers and duties were transferred to the Texas Workforce Investment Council on September 1, 2015.

Social Worker Examiners, Texas State Board of: (1993); apptv.; 6-yr.; per diem and travel expenses; 9 members: Presiding Member Brian C. Brumley, Sumner (2/1/27); Katie Andrade, Mount Pleasant (2/1/27); Megan Marie Graham, Houston (2/1/23); Audrey Ramsbacher, San Antonio (2/1/23); Asia Rodgers, Fort Worth (2/1/25); Dolores Saenz-Davila, McAllen (2/1/25); Jennifer Swords, Fort Worth (2/1/25); 2 vacancies. Admin. Sarah Faszholz ($72,000), 1801 Congress Ave., Ste. 7.300, Austin 78701; (512) 305-7700.

Soil & Water Conservation Board, Texas State: (1939); 2-yr.; 7 members: 2 apptd. by Gov.; 5 elected by district directors: Chair David Basinger, Deport (5/1/24); Marty H. Graham, Rocksprings (5/5/24); Scott Buckles, Stratford (5/7/25); José Dodier Jr., Zapata (5/7/25); Barry Mahler, Iowa Park (5/7/25); Gov. Apptees.: Tina Y. Buford, Harlingen (2/1/24); 1 vacancy. Exec. Dir. Rex Isom ($150,283), 1497 Country View Ln., Temple 76504; (254) 773-2250.

Special Education, Continuing Advisory Committee for: (1997); apptv.; 4-yr.; 17 members: Shemica S. Allen, Allen (2/1/23); Aaron Bangor, Austin (2/1/24); Teresa Bronsky, Plano (2/1/23); Claudia Cavazos, Pearland (2/1/24); Marissa Esquivel, Beeville (2/1/24); April Estrada, Wylie (2/1/24); Barbie Ezell, Portland (2/1/24); Sheryl Kubala, Austin (2/1/24); Amy Litzinger, Austin (2/1/23); Diana Nelson, Martindale (2/1/24); Susan Nichols, Carrollton (2/1/23); Jen Stratton, Austin (2/1/23); Agata K.

"Agatha" Thibodeaux, Katy (2/1/23); Laura Villarreal, Universal City (2/1/23); Jo Ann Garza Wofford, New Braunfels (2/1/23); 2 vacancies. c/o Texas Education Agency, 1701 Congress Ave., Austin 78701; (512) 463–9734; Parent Information Line: (800) 252–9668.

Speech Language Pathologists and Audiologists Advisory Board: (2015); apptv.; 6-yr.; 9 members: Presiding Officer Sherry Sancibrian, Lubbock (9/1/27); Chereece Andrews, Houston (9/1/27); Cheval Bryant, Sugar Land (9/1/25); Tammy Camp, Shallowater (9/1/23); Kristina Kelley, Dallas (9/1/23); Cristen Plummer-Culp, Round Rock (9/1/25); Stacy Poteet, Lubbock (9/1/27); Kimberly Ringer, Pflugerville (9/1/23); Elizabeth Sterling, Austin (9/1/25). PO Box 12157, Austin 78711; (512) 463–6599.

State-Federal Relations, Texas Office of: (1971); apptv., indefinite term: Dir. Wes Hambrick, 660 Pennsylvania Ave. SE, Ste. 203, Washington, DC 20003; (202) 638–3927.

Sulphur River Basin Authority: (1985); apptv.; 6-yr.; 7 members: Chair Chris Spencer, Hughes Springs (2/1/23); Gary Cheatwood, Bogata (2/1/23); Emily Glass, Sulphur Springs (2/1/27); Reeves Hayter, Paris (6/15/25); Kirby Hollingsworth, Mount Vernon (2/1/27); Wallace E. "Wally" Kraft II, Paris (2/1/25); Kelly Mitchell, Texarkana (2/1/23). Admin. Nancy Rose, 911 N. Bishop St., Ste. C104, Wake Village 75501; (903) 223–7887.

Sunset Advisory Commission, Texas: (1977); 12 members: 5 members of House of Representatives, 5 members of Senate, 1 public member apptd. by Speaker, 1 public member by Lt. Gov.; 2-yr.; expenses. Public members: Jeff Austin III, Jacksonville (9/1/23); James "Jim" Lee, Houston (9/1/23). Acting Dir. Brian Francis ($190,000), 1501 Congress Ave., 6th Fl., PO Box 13066, Austin 78711; (512) 463–1300.

Teacher Retirement System (See Retirement System of Texas, Teacher.)

Texas A&M University System Board of Regents: (1875); apptv.; 6-yr.; expenses; 9 members: Chair Bill Mahomes, Dallas (2/1/27); Robert L. Albritton, Fort Worth (2/1/27); David Baggett, Houston (2/1/29); John Bellinger, San Antonio (2/1/29); James R. "Randy" Brooks, San Angelo (2/1/27); Jay Graham, Houston (2/1/25); Michael A. "Mike" Hernandez III, Fort Worth (2/1/25); Michael J. Plank, Houston (2/1/25); Sam Torn, Houston (2/1/29). Chancellor John Sharp, 301 Tarrow St., College Station 77840-7896; (979) 458–7700.

Texas Southern University Board of Regents: (1947); apptv.; expenses; 6-yr.; 9 members: Chair Albert H. Myres, Houston (2/1/25); Caroline Baker Hurley, Houston (2/1/27); James M. Benham, College Station (2/1/29); Richard A. Johnson III, Houston (2/1/29); Pamela A. Medina, Houston (2/1/25); Stephanie D. Nellons-Paige, Houston (2/1/25); Marilyn A. Rose, Houston (2/1/27); Brandon L. Simmons, Houston (2/1/29); 1 vacancy. Acting CEO Dakota Doman, 3100 Cleburne St., Houston 77004; (713) 313–7992.

Texas State Technical College Board of Regents: (1960 as Board of the Texas State Technical Institute; changed to present name in 1991); apptv.; expenses; 6-yr.; 9 members: Chair Tiffany Tremont, New Braunfels (8/31/23); Tony Abad, Waco (8/31/27); Curtis Cleveland, Waco (8/31/27); Lizzy de la Garza Putegnat, Harlingen (8/31/27); Keith Honey, Longview (8/31/25); Charles "Pat" McDonald, Richmond (8/31/23); Robert J. "Robb" Misso III, Cedar Park (8/31/23); Kathy Stewart, San Angelo (8/31/25); Ron Widup, Arlington (8/31/25). Chancellor Mike Reeser, 3801 Campus Dr., Waco 76705; (254) 799–3611.

Texas State University System Board of Regents, The: (1911 as Board of Regents of State Teachers Colleges; name changed in 1965 to Board of Regents of State Senior Colleges; changed to present form in 1975); apptv.; per diem and expenses; 6-yr.; 9 members: Chair Duke Austin, Houston (2/1/23); Charlie Amato, San Antonio (2/1/25); Sheila Faske, Rose City (2/1/27); Dionicio "Don" Flores, El Paso (2/1/25); Russell Gordy, Houston (2/1/29); Stephen Lee, Beaumont (2/1/27); Tom Long, Frisco (2/1/29); William F. Scott, Nederland (2/1/25); Alan L. Tinsley, Madisonville (2/1/27). Chancellor Brian McCall, 601 Colorado St., Austin 78701-2904; (512) 463–1808.

Texas Tech University System Board of Regents: (1923); apptv.; expenses; 6-yr.; 9 members: Chair Mark Griffin, Lubbock (1/31/25); Arcilia Acosta, Dallas (1/31/27); Cody Campbell, Fort Worth (1/31/27); Clay Cash, Lubbock (1/31/29); Tim Culp, Midland (1/31/29); Pat Gordon, El Paso (1/31/27); Ginger Kerrick Davis, Webster (1/31/25); Shelley Sweatt, Wichita Falls (1/31/29); Dusty Womble, Lubbock (1/31/25). Chancellor Tedd L. Mitchell, 1508 Knoxville Ave., Ste. 302, PO Box 42011, Lubbock 79409-2011; (806) 742–2161.

Texas Woman's University Board of Regents: (1901); apptv.; expenses; 6-yr.; 9 members: Chair Stacie D. McDavid, Fort Worth (2/1/25); Bernadette C. Coleman, Denton (2/1/23); Bob Hyde, Irving (2/1/25); Jill Jester, Denton (2/1/23); Janelle Shepard, Weatherford (2/1/27); Mary P. Wilson, Austin (2/1/25); Crystal Wright, Houston (2/1/27); Kathleen Wu, Dallas (2/1/23); 1 vacancy. Chancellor Carine M. Feyten, 304 Administration Dr., PO Box 425589, Denton 76204; (940) 898–2000.

Transportation Commission, Texas: (1917 as State Highway Commission; merged with Mass Transportation Commission and name changed to State Board of Highways and Public Transportation in 1975; merged with Texas Dept. of Aviation and Texas Motor Vehicle Commission and name changed to present form in 1991); governs the Texas Department of Transportation; apptv.; 6-yr.; 5 members: Chair J. Bruce Bugg Jr., San Antonio (2/1/27); Steven D. Alvis, Hockley (2/1/29); W. Alvin New, Christoval (2/1/27); Alejandro G. "Alex" Meade III, Mission (2/1/25); Robert C. Vaughn, Dallas (2/1/25). Exec. Dir. Marc D. Williams ($344,000), 125 E. 11th St., Austin 78701; (512) 463–8588.

Trinity River Authority: (1955); apptv.; per diem and expenses; 6-yr.; 25 members: Pres. Tommy G. Fordyce, Huntsville (3/15/25); Cathy Altman, Midlothian (3/15/23); Henry Borbolla III, Fort Worth (3/15/25); C. Cole Camp, Arlington (3/15/25); Megan W. Deen, Fort Worth (3/15/23); Benny L. Fogleman, Livingston (3/15/27); Lisa A. Hembry, Dallas (3/15/23); Jerry F. House, Leona (3/15/23); John W. Jenkins, Hankamer (3/15/27); Margaret S.C. Keliher, Dallas (3/15/27); David B. Leonard, Liberty (3/15/25); Victoria K. Lucas, Terrell (3/15/23); D. Joe McCleskey, Apple Springs (3/15/23); Robert F. McFarlane, Palestine (3/15/27); Lewis H. McMahan, Dallas (3/15/25); Steven L. Roberts, Coldspring (3/15/23); William O. Rodgers, Fort Worth (3/15/27); Amir A. Rupani, Dallas (3/15/25); Kathryn L. Sanders, Athens (3/15/25); C. Dwayne Somerville, Mexia (3/15/25); Frank H. Steed Jr., Kerens (3/15/27); Frederick C. Tate, Colleyville (3/15/27); Brenda K. Walker, Palestine (3/15/25); David G. Ward, Madisonville (3/15/23); Gregory S. Wassberg, Grapeland (3/15/27). Gen. Mgr. J. Kevin Ward, 5300 S. Collins St., PO Box 60, Arlington 76004; (817) 467–4343.

Tuition Board, Texas Prepaid Higher Education (See Higher Education Tuition Board, Texas Prepaid.)

University Lands, Board for Lease of: (1929 as 3-member board; members increased to 4 in 1985); 2-yr.; 4 members: Comm. of General Land Office, 2 members of Board of Regents of The University of Texas, 1 of Board of Regents of Texas A&M University. Ex officio Chair Dawn Buckingham; Christina Melton Crain, Dallas (2/1/25); Mike Hernandez III, Fort Worth (2/1/25); Nolan Perez, Harlingen (2/1/27). CEO: William R. "Billy" Murphy Jr., 825 Town and Country Ln., Ste. 1100, Houston 77024; (713) 352–3808.

University of Houston System Board of Regents: (1963); apptv.; expenses; 6-yr.; 9 members: Chair Tilman J. Fertitta, Houston (8/31/27); Durga D. Agrawal, Houston (8/31/25); Doug H. Brooks, Plano (8/31/23); Alonzo Cantu, McAllen (8/31/25); Gregory C. King, San Antonio (8/31/23); Beth Madison,

Houston (8/31/27); John A. McCall Jr., Crockett (8/31/25); Jack B. Moore, Houston (8/31/23); Ricky Raven, Sugar Land (8/31/27). Chancellor Renu Khator, 4800 Calhoun Rd., Houston 77004; (832) 842–3444.

University of North Texas System Board of Regents: (1949); apptv.; 6-yr.; expenses; 9 members: Chair Laura Wright, Dallas (5/22/27); Melisa Denis, Southlake (5/22/25); Mary Denny, Aubrey (5/22/23); Daniel Feehan, Fort Worth (5/22/25); Milton B. Lee II, San Antonio (5/22/23); Ashok "A.K." Mago, Dallas (5/22/27); Carlos Munguia, University Park (5/22/23); Lindy Rydman, Houston (5/22/27); John Scott Jr., Keller (5/22/25). Chancellor Michael R. Williams, 1901 Main St., Dallas 75201; (214) 571–4800.

University of Texas System Board of Regents: (1881); apptv.; expenses; 6-yr.; 9 members: Chair Kevin P. Eltife, Tyler (2/1/27); Christina Melton Crain, Dallas (2/1/25); Robert P. Gauntt, Austin (2/1/29); Jodie Lee Jiles, Houston (2/1/25); Janiece Longoria, Houston (2/1/29); Nolan Perez, Harlingen (2/1/27); Stuart W. Stedman, Houston (2/1/27); Kelcy L. Warren, Dallas (2/1/25); James C. "Rad" Weaver, San Antonio (2/1/29). Chancellor James B. Milliken, 210 W. Seventh St., Austin 78701-2982; (512) 499–4200.

Upper Colorado River Authority (See Colorado River Authority, Upper.)

Upper Guadalupe River Authority (See Guadalupe River Authority, Upper.)

Upper Neches River Municipal Water Authority (See Neches River Municipal Water Authority, Upper.)

Utility Commission, Public (See Public Utility Commission.)

Veterans Commission, Texas: (1927 as Veterans State Service Office; reorganized as Veterans Affairs Commission in 1947 with 5 members; name changed to present form in 1985); apptv.; 6-yr.; per diem while on duty and expenses; 5 members: Chair Laura Koerner, Fair Oaks Ranch (12/31/23); Kevin Barber, Houston (12/31/27); Mary Dale, Cedar Park (12/31/25); Mike Hernandez, Abilene (12/31/25); Kimberlee Shaneyfelt, Dallas (12/31/23). Exec. Dir. Thomas P. Palladino ($151,123), PO Box 12277, Austin 78711-2277; (512) 463–6564.

Veterans Land Board (See Land Board, Veterans.)

Veterinary Medical Examiners, Texas Board of: (1911; revised 1953; made 9-member board in 1981); apptv.; expenses on duty; 6-yr.; 9 members: Pres. Steven Golla, New Braunfels (8/26/27); Sue Allen, Waco (8/26/25); Sandra "Lynn" Criner, Needville (8/26/27); Samantha Mixon, Boerne (8/26/23); Raquel Olivier, Houston (8/26/23); Keith Pardue, Austin (8/26/27); Randall Skaggs, Perryton (8/26/23); Michael White, Conroe (8/26/25); Victoria Whitehead, Lubbock (8/26/25). Exec. Dir. Brittany Sharkey ($113,412), 1801 Congress Ave., Ste. 8.800, Austin 78701; (512) 305–7555.

Water Development Board, Texas: (1957; legislative function for the Texas Dept. of Water Resources, 1977); apptv.; per diem and expenses; 6-yr.; 3 members: Chair Brooke T. Paup, Austin (2/1/25); George B. Peyton V, Austin (2/1/27); L'Oreal Stepney, Pflugerville (2/1/29). Exec. Admin. Jeff Walker ($199,582), 1700 Congress Ave., PO Box 13231, Austin 78711-3231; (512) 463–7847.

Women, Governor's Commission for: (1967); apptv.; 2-yr; up to 15 members: Chair Nathali Parker, New Braunfels (12/31/23); Gina Bellinger, San Antonio (12/31/23); Gita Bolt, Houston (12/31/23); Ashley Cash, Lubbock (12/31/23); Denise Castillo-Rhodes, Houston (12/31/23); Cynthia Conroy, El Paso (12/31/23); Sasha Crane, McAllen (12/31/23); Maru De La Paz, Harlingen (12/31/23); Amy Henderson, Amarillo (12/31/23); Lorena Junco Margain, Austin (12/31/23); Jinous Rouhani, Austin (12/31/23); Catherine Susser, Dallas (12/31/23); Patsy Wesson, Fort Worth (12/31/23); Laura Koenig Young, Tyler (12/31/23). Exec. Dir. Christina McKinney, 1100 San Jacinto Blvd., Rm. 2.256, PO Box 12428, Austin 78711; (512) 475–2615.

Workers' Compensation, Commissioner of: (1991; functions transferred to the Texas Dept. of Insurance Division of Workers' Compensation in 2005); apptv.; 2-yr.; Comm. Jeff Nelson ($169,111), (2/1/23), 1601 Congress Ave., Austin 78701; (800) 252–7031.

Workforce Commission, Texas: (1936 as Texas Employment Commission; name changed 1995); apptv.; 6-yr.; 3 members ($201,000): Chair Bryan Daniel, Georgetown (2/1/25); Aaron Demerson, Austin (2/1/27); Alberto Treviño, Harlingen (2/1/29). Exec. Dir. Ed Serna ($200,494), 101 E. 15th St., Austin 78778; (512) 463–2222.

Workforce Investment Council, Texas: (1993); apptv.; 19 members: 5 ex officio members (representing Economic Development and Tourism Office, Higher Education Coord. Board, Texas Education Agency, Texas Health and Human Services Comm., Texas Workforce Comm.); 14 apptd.: Chair Rick Rhodes, Austin (9/1/23); Paloma Ahmadi, Shavano Park (9/1/27); Joe Arnold, Muldoon (9/1/27); Jesse Gatewood, Corpus Christi (9/1/23); Lindsey Geeslin, Waco (9/1/27); Lauren Gore, Houston (9/1/25); Thomas Halbouty, Southlake (9/1/25); John Martin, San Antonio (9/1/23); Wayne Oswald, Houston (9/1/27); Paul Puente, Houston (9/1/27); Richard Rhodes, Austin (9/1/25); Brandon Willis, Beaumont (9/1/25); 2 vacancies. Dir. Kaki Leyens, 1100 San Jacinto Blvd., Ste. 1.100, Austin 78701; (512) 936–8100. ☆

The entrance to Texas Southern University in Houston. Photo by 2C2K Photography, Flickr, CC 2.0

Local Government

Texas has **254 counties**, a number that has not changed since 1931 when Loving County was organized. Loving has a population of 57, according to the 2021, U.S. Census estimate, compared with 164 in 1970 and a peak of 285 in 1940. It is the **least-populous county** in Texas. In contrast, Harris County has **the most residents** in Texas, with a 2021 population estimate of **4,728,030**.

Counties range in area from Rockwall's 148.7 square miles to the 6,192.8 square miles in Brewster, which is equal to the combined area of the states of Connecticut and Rhode Island.

The Texas Constitution makes a county a legal subdivision of the state. Each county has a **commissioners court**. It consists of four commissioners, each elected from a commissioner's precinct, and a county judge elected from the entire county. In smaller counties, the county judge retains judicial responsibilities in probate and insanity cases. **For names of county and district officials, see tables on pages 513–524.**

There are **1,226 incorporated municipalities** in Texas that range in size from 12 residents in Los Ybanez to Houston's 2,293,288, according to the American Community Survey 2021 estimates. More than 80 percent of the state's population lives in cities and towns, meeting the U.S. Census Bureau definition of urban areas.

Texas had **356 incorporated towns with more than 5,000 population**, according to the American Community Survey 2021 estimates. Under law, these cities may adopt their own charters (called home rule) by a majority vote. Cities of fewer than 5,000 may be chartered only under the general law.

Some home-rule cities may have fewer than 5,000 residents because population has declined since adopting home-rule charters.

Mayors and City Managers of Texas Cities

This list was compiled from online sources and phone calls. It includes the name of each city's mayor, as well as the name of the city manager, city administrator, city coordinator, or other managing executive for municipalities having that form of government. **Home-rule cities are marked in this list by a single-dagger symbol (†) after the name.**

A

Abbott . . . . Anthony R. Pustejovsky
Abernathy . . . . Ron Johnson
City Mgr., Delano Smith
Abilene † . . . . Weldon W. Hurt
City Mgr., Robert Hanna
Ackerly . . . . Scott Ragle
Addison † . . . . Bruce Arfsten
City Mgr., David Gaines
Adrian . . . . Maggie Gruhlkey
Agua Dulce . . . . John Howard
Alamo † . . . . Diana Martinez
City Mgr., Robert L. Salinas
Alamo Heights † . . . . Bobby Rosenthal
City Mgr., Buddy Kuhn
Alba . . . . Don Heinert
Albany . . . . Rodney Alexander
City Mgr., Billy Holson
Aledo † . . . . Nick Stanley
City Mgr., Noah A. Simon
Alice † . . . . Cynthia Carrasco
City Mgr., Michael Esparza
Allen † . . . . Ken Fulk
City Mgr., Eric Ellwanger
Alma . . . . Renee Jones
City Admin., Linda Blazek
Alpine † . . . . Catherine Eaves
City Mgr., Megan Antrim
Alto . . . . Jimmy Allen
Alton † . . . . Salvador Vela
City Mgr., Jeff Underwood
Alvarado . . . . Jacob Wheat
City Mgr., Paul DeBuff
Alvin † . . . . Gabe Adame
City Mgr., Junru Roland
Alvord . . . . Caleb Caviness
City Admin., Troy Gregg
Amarillo † . . . . Cole Stanley
City Mgr., Jared Miller
Ames . . . . Barbara L. Domain
Amherst . . . . Clinton Sawyer
Anahuac . . . . Danny Thompson
City Admin., Kenneth Kathan
Anderson . . . . Marc Benton
Andrews † . . . . Flora Braly
City Mgr., Steve Eggleston
Angleton † . . . . John Wright
City Mgr., Chris Whittaker
Angus . . . . Julie Humphries
Anna † . . . . Nate Pike
City Mgr., Ryan Henderson, Interim
Annetta . . . . Sandy Roberts
City Admin., Jamee Long
Annetta North . . . . Robert Schmidt
Annetta South . . . . Charles Marsh
Annona . . . . George English, Sr.
Anson † . . . . Sara Alfaro
City Mgr., Sonny Campbell
Anthony . . . . Anthony David Turner
Anton . . . . Blake Cate
City Mgr., Mike Sea
Appleby . . . . Tom Bush
City Mgr., Kevin Pierce
Aquilla . . . . James Hamner, Sr.
Aransas Pass † . . . . Ram Gomez
City Mgr., Gary Edwards
Archer City . . . . Jake Truette
City Mgr., George Huffman
Arcola . . . . Fred A. Burton
City Admin., Annette Guajardo
Argyle . . . . Rick Bradford
Town Admin., Erika McComis
Arlington † . . . . Jim Ross
City Mgr., Trey Yelverton
Arp . . . . Dennis Ford
Asherton . . . . Alex Bustamante, Jr.
Aspermont . . . . Steven Ellis
City Admin., Lorenzo Calamaco
Athens † . . . . Aaron (Bubba) Smith
City Mgr., Elizabeth Borstad
Atlanta † . . . . James Brooks
City Mgr., David Cockrell
Aubrey . . . . Chris Rich
Town Admin., Charles Kreidler
Aurora . . . . Bryan Dolan
City Admin., Cori Reaume, Interim
Austin † . . . . Kirk Watson
City Mgr., Jesús Garza, Interim
Austwell . . . . Andrew Biery
Avery . . . . Alex Ackley
Avinger . . . . Marvin Parvino
Azle † . . . . Alan Brundrett
City Mgr., Tom Muir

B

Bailey . . . . Kenneth Burks
Bailey's Prairie . . . . Tammy Mutina
Baird . . . . Jim Dobbs
City Admin., Lori Higgins
Balch Springs † . . . . Carrie Gordon
City Mgr., Susan Cluse
Balcones Heights . . . . Suzanne de Leon
City Admin., Gilbert Perales
Ballinger † . . . . Dawni Seymore
City Mgr., Brian Frieda
Balmorhea . . . . John L. Davis
Bandera . . . . Rebeca Gibson
City Admin., (vacant)
Bangs . . . . Steve Whittenberg
Bardwell . . . . Jodie Odlozil
Barry . . . . Charles Worsham
Barstow . . . . Olga Abila
Bartlett . . . . Chad Mees
City Admin., Joseph Resendez
Bartonville . . . . Jaclyn Carrington
Town Admin., Thad Chambers
Bastrop † . . . . Lyle Nelson
City Mgr., Sylvia Carrillo
Bay City † . . . . Robert Nelson
City Mgr., Shawna Burkhart
Bayou Vista . . . . Paula Eshelman
City Admin., Lillian Salinas
Bayside . . . . Sharon Scott

Street art in Brenham: Lady and Bear, painted by Michael C. Rodriguez. Photo by Wally Gobetz, Flickr, CC by NC-ND 2.0

Baytown † ... Brandon Capetillo
City Mgr., Rick Davis
Bayview ... Gary E. Paris
Beach City ... Ken Pantin
Bear Creek ... Mark Bohm
Beasley ... Kenneth Reid
Beaumont † ... Roy West
City Mgr., Kenneth R. Williams
Beckville ... Andrew Nixon
Bedford † ... Michael Boyter
City Mgr., Jimmy Stathatos
Bedias ... Gwen Boullion
Bee Cave † ... Kara King
City Mgr., Clint Garza
Beeville † ... Brian Watson
City Mgr., John Benson
Bellaire † ... Andrew S. Friedberg
City Mgr., Sharon Citino
Bellevue ... Robert Ratliff
Bellmead † ... Travis Gibson
City Mgr., Yousry (Yost) Zakhary
Bells ... Joe Paul Smith
City Admin., Beth Woodson
Bellville ... James Harrison
City Admin., Shawn Jackson
Belton † ... David K. Leigh
City Mgr., Sam A. Listi
Benavides ... Ramiro Saenz
Benbrook † ... Jason Ward
City Mgr., Andy Wayman
Benjamin ... Shelby Russell
Berryville ... Sue Morgan
Bertram ... Mike Dickinson
Beverly Hills ... David Gonzales
Bevil Oaks ... Barbara Emmons
Big Lake ... David Melms
Big Sandy ... Linda Baggett
City Admin., Laura Rex
Big Spring † ... Robert Moore
City Mgr., Todd Darden
Big Wells ... Robert D. Juarez, Jr.
Bishop ... Noel Barrera Lopez
Bishop Hills ... Betty Benham
Blackwell ... Laura Rozzlle
Blanco ... Mike Arnold
City Admin., Warren Escovy
Blanket ... B.J. McGinnis
Bloomburg ... Delores Simmons
Blooming Grove ... William Carroll
Blossom ... Jeff Stover
Blue Mound ... Darlene Copeland
Blue Ridge ... Rhonda Williams
Blum ... Chryle Hackler
Boerne † ... Frank Ritchie
City Mgr., Ben Thatcher
Bogata ... Larry Hinsley
Bonham † ... H.L. Compton
City Mgr., Sean Pate
Bonney ... Raymond Cantu
Booker ... Stephen Skipper
Borger † ... Karen Felker
City Mgr., Garrett Spradling
Bovina ... Frank Gonzalez, Jr.
City Mgr., Cesar Marquez
Bowie † ... Gaylynn Burris
City Mgr., Bert Cunningham
Boyd ... Rodney Holmes
City Admin., William Taylor
Brackettville ... Eric J. Martinez
City Admin., Nora Y. Rivas
Brady † ... Aaron Garcia
City Mgr., Erin Corbell
Brazoria ... Philip Ray
City Mgr., Sheila Williams
Brazos Country ... Bob Ray
Breckenridge † ... Bob Sims
City Mgr., Cynthia Northrop
Bremond ... Rick Swick
Brenham † ... Atwood C. Kenjura
City Mgr., Carolyn D. Miller
Briarcliff ... Al Hostetler
City Admin., Aaron Johnson
Briaroaks ... Howard Bogart
Bridge City † ... David Rutledge
City Mgr., Mike Lund, Interim
Bridgeport † ... Randy Singleton
City Mgr., Mike Murray
Broaddus ... Shirley Parker
Brock ... Jay Hamilton
Bronte ... Paul Gohman
Brookshire ... Darrell Branch
City Admin., Mike Barnes, Interim
Brookside Village ... Glenda Hundl
Browndell ... Tinacy Brooks
Brownfield † ... Tom Hesse
City Mgr., Jeff Davis
Brownsboro ... Dusty Wise
Brownsville † ... John Cowen, Jr.
City Mgr., Helen Ramirez
Brownwood † ... Stephen E. Haynes
City Mgr., Emily Crawford
Bruceville-Eddy ... Linda Owens
City Admin., Kent Manton
Bryan † ... Bobby Gutierrez
City Mgr., Kean Register
Bryson ... Lutitia Ford
Buckholts ... Teresa Eaton
Buda † ... Lee Urbanovsky
City Mgr., Micah Grau
Buffalo ... Jerrod Jones
Buffalo Gap ... David L. Perry
Buffalo Springs ... Dennis Waldrop
Bullard ... Shirley Coe
City Mgr., David Hortman
Bulverde † ... Bill Krawietz
City Mgr., Charles West
Bunker Hill Village ... Robert P. Lord
City Admin., Gerardo Barrera
Burkburnett † ... Lori Kemp
City Mgr., Fred Tillman, Interim
Burke ... John Thomas Jones
Burleson † ... Chris Fletcher
City Mgr., Bryan Langley
Burnet † ... Gary Wideman
City Mgr., David Vaughn
Burton ... Karen Buck
Byers ... Norrieca Dalton

Bynum . . . . Rachel McCurlie

C

Cactus. . . . . Socorro Marquez
City Mgr., Aldo Gallegos
Caddo Mills . . . . Chris Davies
City Mgr., Matt McMahan
Caldwell . . . . Janice Easter
City Admin., Camden White
Callisburg . . . . Nathan Caldwell
Calvert . . . . Layla H. Wright
City Admin., Phyllis Sabo
Cameron †. . . . . Bill Harris
City Mgr., Ricky Tow
Campbell . . . . Terry Trapp
Camp Wood . . . . Juan (Mafy) Gomez
Canadian . . . . Terrill Bartlett
City Mgr., Joe Jarosek
Caney City . . . . Steve Pine
Canton . . . . Lou Ann Everett
City Mgr., Lonny Cluck
Canyon †. . . . . Gary Hinders
City Mgr., Joe Price
Carbon . . . . Corey Hull
Carl's Corner . . . . Susan Ezell
Carmine . . . . Wade Eilers
Carrizo Springs †. . . . . Oscar Puente
City Mgr., Chris A. Castaneda
Carrollton †. . . . . Steve Babick
City Mgr., Erin Rinehart
Carthage †. . . . . Olin Joffrion
City Mgr., Stephen K. Williams
Cashion . . . . Debra Carr
Castle Hills . . . . JR Trevino
City Mgr., Ryan Rapelye
Castroville . . . . Darrin Schroeder
City Admin., Scott Dixon
Cedar Hill †. . . . . Stephen Mason
City Mgr., Greg Porter
Cedar Park † . . . . Jim Penniman-Morin
City Mgr., Brenda Eivens
Celeste . . . . Shaunna Cole
Celina †. . . . . Ryan Tubbs
City Mgr., Karla Stovall, Interim
Center †. . . . . David Chadwick
City Mgr., Chad Nehring
Centerville . . . . Noal Ray Goolsby
Chandler. . . . . Cy Ditzler
City Admin., John Whitsell
Channing . . . . Troy Williams
Charlotte . . . . Stephen Porter
Chester . . . . Robert Poynter
Chico . . . . Colleen Self
Childress † . . . . Cary Preston
City Mgr., Kevin Hodges
Chillicothe . . . . Cathy Young
China . . . . Matt Lopez
China Grove . . . . Mary A. Hajek
City Admin., Susan Conaway
Chireno . . . . Susan Higginbotham
City Admin., Steven Spencer
Christine . . . . Jerry Flores
Cibolo †. . . . . Mark Allen
City Mgr., Wayne Reed
Cisco †. . . . . Stephen Forester
City Mgr., Darwin Archer
Clarendon . . . . Jacob Fangman
City Admin., David Dockery
Clarksville . . . . Ann Rushing
City Mgr., Deana Smith
Clarksville City . . . . Joe B. Spears
City Mgr., Matt Maines
Claude . . . . Joe Minkley
City Admin., Howard Heath
Clear Lake Shores . . . . . Randy Chronister
City Admin., Brad Goudie
Cleburne †. . . . . Scott Cain
City Mgr., Steve Polasek
Cleveland † . . . . Danny Lee
City Mgr., Scott Swigert
Clifton . . . . Richard Spitzer
City Admin., David McDowell
Clint . . . . Ramon Cano
Clute †. . . . . Calvin Shiflet
City Mgr., CJ Snipes
Clyde . . . . Rodger Brown
City Admin., Christopher McGuire
Coahoma . . . . Jay Holt
Cockrell Hill . . . . Luis D. Carrera
City Admin., Bret Haney
Coffee City . . . . Jeff Blackstone
Coldspring . . . . John Benestante
Coleman †. . . . . Tommy Sloan
City Mgr., Diana Lopez
College Station † . . . . Karl Mooney
City Mgr., Bryan Woods
Colleyville † . . . . Bobby Lindamood
City Mgr., Jerry Ducay
Collinsville . . . . Derek M. Kays
City Admin., Dannielle Talley
Colmesneil . . . . Duane Crews
Colorado City †. . . . . Ruben Hurt
City Mgr., Donna Madrid
Columbus . . . . Lori An Gobert
City Mgr., Donald Warschak
Comanche. . . . . Mary A. Boyd
Combes. . . . . Silvestre (Silver) Garcia
Town Admin., Aida Gutierrez
Combine . . . . Tim Ratcliff
City Mgr., Jack Gilbert
Commerce † . . . . Teddy Reel
City Mgr., Howdy Lisenbee
Como . . . . Jerry Radney
Conroe †. . . . . Jody Czajkoski
City Admin., Gary Scott
Converse †. . . . . Alfred (Al) Suarez
City Mgr., Ronnie Guest
Cool . . . . Dorothy Hall
Coolidge . . . . Tonia Bruckner
Cooper . . . . Darren Braddy
Coppell †. . . . . Wes Mays
City Mgr., Mike Land
Copperas Cove † . . . . Dan Yancey
City Mgr., Ryan Haverlah
Copper Canyon . . . . Ron Robertson
Town Admin., Donna Welsh
Corinth †. . . . . Bill Heidemann
City Mgr., Scott Campbell
Corpus Christi † . . . . Paulette M. Guajardo
City Mgr., Peter Zanoni
Corral City . . . . Jamie Sue Harris
Corrigan . . . . Johnna Gibson
City Mgr., Darrian Hudman
Corsicana † . . . . Mike Fletcher
City Mgr., Connie Standridge
Cottonwood . . . . Karen Deloney
Cottonwood Shores . . . . Jared Dodd
City Admin., J.C. Hughes
Cotulla . . . . Javier Garcia
City Admin., David Wright
Coupland . . . . Jack R. Piper
Cove . . . . Leroy Stevens
Covington . . . . Curtis Wood
Coyote Flats . . . . Doug Peterson
Crandall . . . . David Lindsey
City Mgr., Jerry Dean
Crane . . . . Manuel Cadena, Jr.
City Admin., Dru Gravens
Cranfills Gap . . . . David D. Witte
Crawford . . . . Brian Porter
City Mgr., Brian Bolfing
Creedmoor . . . . Fran Klestinec
City Admin., Robert Wilhite
Cresson. . . . . Teena Conway
Crockett † . . . . Ianthia Fisher
City Admin., John Angerstein
Crosbyton . . . . Dusty Cornelius
City Admin., Amy Wallace
Cross Plains . . . . Gary Moses
City Admin., Debbie Gosnell
Cross Roads . . . . T. Lynn Tompkins, Jr.
Town Admin., Kristi Gilbert
Cross Timber . . . . Patti Meier
Crowell . . . . Ronnie Allen
Crowley † . . . . Billy P. Davis
City Mgr., Robert Loftin
Crystal City †. . . . . Frank Moreno, Jr.
City Mgr., Felix Benavides
Cuero † . . . . Sara Post-Meyer
City Mgr., Wayne Berger
Cumby . . . . Amber Hardy
Cuney . . . . Oscar Birdow
Cushing . . . . Robert Sides
Cut and Shoot . . . . Nyla Akin Dalhaus

D

Daingerfield †. . . . . Wade Kerley
City Mgr., Keith Whitfield
Daisetta . . . . Eric Thaxton
Dalhart †. . . . . Justin Moore
City Mgr., Stacey Norris
Dallas †. . . . . Eric Johnson
City Mgr., T.C. Broadnax
Dalworthington Gardens. . . Laurie Bianco
City Admin., Lola Smith,
Danbury . . . . Sue Powell
Darrouzett . . . . Alan Meier
City Mgr., (vacant)
Dawson. . . . . Stephen Sanders
Dayton † . . . . Martin Mudd
City Mgr., Kimberly Judge
Dayton Lakes . . . . Justin McCormick
Dean . . . . Steve L. Sicking
Decatur †. . . . . Mike McQuiston
City Mgr., Nate Mara
DeCordova . . . . Dave Hanson
Deer Park † . . . . Jerry Mouton, Jr.
City Mgr., James J. Stokes
De Kalb . . . . Lowell Walker
De Leon † . . . . Jan Grisham
City Admin., David Denman
Dell City . . . . Deborah Berry
Del Rio † . . . . Alvaro (Al) Arreola
City Mgr., John A. Sheedy, IV
Denison † . . . . Janet Gott
City Mgr., Bobby Atteberry, Interim
Dennis . . . . James Synowsky
Denton † . . . . Gerard Hudspeth
City Mgr., Sara Hensley
Denver City †. . . . . Tommy Hicks
City Mgr., Stan David
Deport . . . . Patrick Watson

DeSoto † . . . . Rachel L. Proctor
City Mgr., Brandon Wright
Detroit . . . . Kenneth Snodgrass
Devers . . . . Steven Horelica
Devine . . . . Butch Cook
City Admin., Dora V. Rodriguez, Interim
Diboll † . . . . Trey Wilkerson
City Mgr., Jason A. Arnold
Dickens . . . . David Warren
Dickinson † . . . . Sean Skipworth
City Mgr., Theo Melancon
Dilley . . . . Mary Ann Obregon
City Admin., Henry Arredondo
Dimmitt † . . . . Scott Sheffy
City Mgr., Daniel Jackson
Dish . . . . William Sciscoe
Dodd City . . . . Timothy Davis
Dodson . . . . Steve Kane
Domino . . . . Moria White
Donna † . . . . Rick Morales
City Mgr., Carlos Yerena
Dorchester . . . . David Smith
Double Horn . . . . Cathy Sereno
Double Oak . . . . Patrick Johnson
Douglassville . . . . Douglass Heath
Dripping Springs . . . . Bill Foulds, Jr.
City Admin., Michelle Fischer
Driscoll . . . . Mark Gonzalez
Dublin . . . . David Leatherwood
City Mgr., Bobby Mendez
Dumas † . . . . Bob Brinkmann
City Mgr., Ray Resendez
Duncanville † . . . . Barry L. Gordon
City Mgr., Robert D. Brown, Jr.

E

Eagle Lake . . . . Timothy L. Kelley
City Mgr., Charles (Tink) Jackson
Eagle Pass † . . . . Rolando Salinas, Jr.
City Mgr., Ivan Morua
Early . . . . Robert Mangrum
City Admin., Tony Aaron
Earth . . . . Guillermo (William) Flores
East Bernard . . . . Marvin R. Holub
Eastland † . . . . Larry Vernon
City Mgr., John (JJ) Oznick, Jr.
East Mountain . . . . Marc Covington
Easton . . . . Walter Ward
City Admin., Leah Robertson
East Tawakoni . . . . Holly Calhoun
Ector . . . . Jerry M. Newell
Edcouch . . . . Virginio Gonzalez, Jr.
City Mgr., Victor Hugo de la Cruz
Eden . . . . Agapito Torres
City Admin., Laura Beeson
Edgecliff Village . . Dennis (Mickey) Rigney
City Admin., Veronica Gamboa
Edgewood . . . . Stevan Steadham
City Admin., Petra Marley
Edinburg † . . . . Ramiro Garza, Jr.
City Mgr., Myra L. Ayala
Edmonson . . . . Tom Crawford
Edna † . . . . Lance Smiga
City Mgr., Gary Broz
Edom . . . . Barbara Crow
El Campo † . . . . Chris Barbee
City Mgr., Courtney Sladek
El Cenizo . . . . Carina Hernandez
City Admin., Jaime Montes
Eldorado . . . . George Arispe
Electra † . . . . Lynda Lynn
City Admin., Steve Bowlin
Elgin † . . . . Theresa McShan
City Mgr., Thomas Mattis
Elkhart . . . . Jennifer McCoy
El Lago . . . . Shawn Findley
Ellinger . . . . Matt Mikulenka
Elmendorf . . . . Michael J. Gonzales
City Admin., Cody Dailey
El Paso † . . . . Oscar Leeser
City Mgr., Cary Westin, Interim
Elsa † . . . . Alonzo R. Perez
City Mgr., JJ Ybarra
Emhouse . . . . Jimmy Barkley
Emory . . . . Earl Hill, III
City Admin., Angie Allen
Enchanted Oaks . . . . Natalie Oñate
Encinal . . . . Esmeralda Yanet Arce
City Mgr., Velma Davila
Ennis † . . . . Angeline Juenemann
City Mgr., Marty Nelson
Escobares . . . . Ivan Escobar
Estelline . . . . Jeff Jones
Euless † . . . . Linda Martin
City Mgr., Loretta Getchell
Eureka . . . . Tammy Cantrell
Eustace . . . . Dustin Shelton
Evant . . . . Charles Weeks
Everman † . . . . Ray Richardson
City Mgr., Craig Spencer

F

Fairchilds . . . . Lance Bertolino
Fairfield . . . . Kenneth Hughes
City Admin., Nate Smith
Fair Oaks Ranch † . . . . Greg Maxton
City Mgr., Scott Huizenga, Interim
Fairview † . . . . Henry Lessner
Town Mgr., Julie Couch
Falfurrias . . . . Justo Ramirez
City Admin., Andy Garcia
Falls City . . . . Brent Houdmann
Farmers Branch † . . . . Terry Lynne
City Mgr., Ben Williamson
Farmersville . . . . Bryon Wiebold
City Mgr., Ben White
Farwell . . . . Stephen Schilling
Fate † . . . . David Billings
City Mgr., Michael Kovacs
Fayetteville . . . . Mike Stroup
Ferris . . . . Fred Pontley
City Mgr., Brooks Williams
Flatonia . . . . Dennis Gessaman
City Mgr., Sonya Bishop
Florence . . . . Mary Condon
Floresville † Cecelia (Cissy) Gonzalez-Dippel
City Mgr., Andy Joslin
Flower Mound † . . . . Derek France
Town Mgr., James Childers
Floydada . . . . Bobby Gilliland
City Mgr., Darrell Gooch
Follett . . . . Lynn Blau
City Mgr., John D. Butler
Forest Hill † . . . . . . Stephanie Boardingham
City Mgr., Venus Wehle, Interim
Forney † . . . . Jason Roberson
City Mgr., Charles Daniels
Forsan . . . . Steve Park
Fort Stockton † . . . . Paul Casias
City Mgr., Frank Rodriguez, III
Fort Worth † . . . . Mattie Parker
City Mgr., David Cooke
Franklin . . . . Molly Hedrick
Frankston . . . . Tommy Carr
Fredericksburg † . . . . Jeryl Hoover
City Mgr., Clinton Bailey
Freeport † . . . . Brooks Bass
City Mgr., Tim Kelty
Freer . . . . Martin Martinez
Friendswood † . . . . Mike Foreman
City Mgr., Morad Kabiri
Friona . . . . Greg Lewellen
City Mgr., Leander (Lee) Davila
Frisco † . . . . Jeff Cheney
City Mgr., Wes Pierson
Fritch . . . . Billy Robbins
City Mgr., Brent Sheets
Frost . . . . Scott Dowdle
Fruitvale . . . . Vicki Ferguson
Fulshear † . . . . Aaron Groff
City Mgr., Jack Harper
Fulton . . . . Kelli Cole

G

Gainesville † . . . . Tommy Moore
City Mgr., Barry Sullivan
Galena Park † . . . . Esmeralda Moya
Gallatin . . . . Kathy Dethlefs
Galveston † . . . . Craig Brown
City Mgr., Brian Maxwell
Ganado . . . . Clinton Tegeler
Garden Ridge . . . . Robb Erickson
City Admin., Nancy Cain
Garland † . . . . Scott LeMay
City Mgr., Judson Rex
Garrett . . . . Matt Newsom
Garrison . . . . Keith Yarbrough
City Supt., Jack Brown
Gary . . . . Billy Anderson, II
Gatesville † . . . . Gary Chumley
City Mgr., Scott Albert
Georgetown † . . . . Josh Schroeder
City Mgr., David Morgan
George West † . . . . Andrew Garza
City Mgr., Shirley Holm, Interim
Gholson . . . . Taylor Jackson
Giddings † . . . . Joel Lopez
City Mgr., Spencer Schneider
Gilmer † . . . . Tim Marshall
City Mgr., Greg Hutson
Gladewater † . . . . Scott E. Owens
City Mgr., Charlie Smith, Interim
Glenn Heights † . . . . Sonja A. Brown
City Mgr., Keith Moore, Interim
Glen Rose . . . . Joe Boles
City Admin., Michael Leamons
Godley . . . . Acy McGehee
City Admin., David J. Wallis
Goldsmith . . . . Richard Bradley
City Mgr., Bennie Cope
Goldthwaite . . . . J. Wilson
City Mgr., Robert E. Lindsey, III
Goliad . . . . Brenda Moses
Golinda . . . . Joyce Farar
Gonzales † . . . . S.H. (Steve) Sucher
City Mgr., Tim Crow
Goodlow . . . . John Moss, Sr.
Goodrich . . . . Kelly Nelson
Gordon . . . . Roger Keck
Goree . . . . Randy Hibdon

Gorman † . . . . .David Perry
Graford . . . . Janet Francies
Graham † . . . . Alex Heartfield
City Mgr., Eric Garretty
Granbury † . . . . Jim Jarratt
City Mgr., Chris Coffman
Grandfalls . . . . Jim Cahill
Grand Prairie † . . . . Ron Jensen
City Mgr., Steve Dye
Grand Saline . . . . Jeremy Gunnels
City Admin., Dana Clair
Grandview . . . . .William Houston
City Mgr., Katherine Reading, Interim
Granger . . . . .Monica Stojanik
City Admin., Christy Cavness Bradshaw
Granite Shoals † . . . . .Kiel Arnone
City Mgr., Peggy Smith
Granjeno . . . . .Yvette Cabrera
Grapeland . . . . .Mitchell Woody
Grapevine † . . . . .William D. Tate
City Mgr., Bruno Rumbelow
Grays Prairie . . . . Lorenzo Garza, Jr.
Greenville † . . . . .Jerry Ransom
City Mgr., Summer Spurlock
Gregory . . . . .Jeronimo B. Garcia
City Admin., Tony Cano
Grey Forest . . . Amanda (Mandie) Waldrop
Groesbeck . . . . Matthew Dawley
City Admin., Chris Henson
Groom .Tim Case
Groves † . . . . .Chris Borne
City Mgr., Lance Billeaud, Interim
Groveton . . . . Tommy Walton
Gruver . . . . Steven Davis
City Mgr., Johnnie Williams
Gun Barrel City † . . . .(vacant)
City Mgr., Mickie Raney, Interim
Gunter . . . . Karen Souther
City Mgr., Jeff Gibson, Interim
Gustine . . . . Ken Huey

H

Hackberry . . . . Ronald Austin
City Admin., Brenda Lewallen
Hale Center . . . . W.H. Johnson
City Mgr., Mike Cypert
Hallettsville . . . . .Alice Jo Summers
City Admin., Grace Ward
Hallsburg . . . . .Mike Glockzin
Hallsville . . . . Jesse Casey
Haltom City † . . . . .An Truong
City Mgr., Rex L. Phelps
Hamilton . . . . .Rodney Craddick
City Admin., Ryan Polster
Hamlin . . . . Curtis Collins
City Admin., Bobby Evans
Happy . . . . Sara Tirey
Hardin . . . . .Harry Johnson
Harker Heights † . . . . . .Michael Blomquist
City Mgr., David R. Mitchell
Harlingen † . . . . Norma Sepulveda
City Mgr., Gabriel Gonzalez
Hart . . . . Eliazar Castillo
City Admin., Adrian Rosas
Haskell . . . . .Alberto Alvarez, Jr.
City Admin., Winston Stephens, Interim
Haslet . . . . Gary Hulsey
Hawk Cove . . . . .Darren Evans
City Admin., Rhonda McKeehan
Hawkins . . . . Susan Hubbard
Hawley . . . . Billy Richardson
Hays . . . . .Billy Maphies

Hearne † . . . . Ruben Gomez
City Mgr., Alonzo Echavarria-Garza
Heath † . . . . Kelson Elam
City Mgr., Aretha L. Adams
Hebron . . . . Kelly Clem
Hedley . . . . .Carrie Butler
Hedwig Village . . . . Tom Jinks
City Admin., Wendy Baimbridge
Helotes . . . . .Rich Whitehead
City Admin., Marian Mendoza
Hemphill . . . . Robert Hamilton
City Mgr., Thad Smith
Hempstead † . . . . Erica Gillum
Henderson † . . . . John (Buzz) Fullen
City Mgr., Jay Abercrombie
Henrietta . . . . Roy L. Boswell
City Admin., (vacant)
Hereford † . . . . Cathy Bunch
City Mgr., Steve Bartels
Hewitt † . . . . .Steve Fortenberry
City Mgr., Bo Thomas
Hickory Creek . . . . Lynn Clark
Town Admin., John Smith
Hico . . . . .Eddie Needham
City Admin., Andy Wolfe
Hidalgo † . . . . Sergio Coronado
City Mgr., Julian Gonzalez
Hideaway . . . . James K. Brown, Jr.
Higgins . . . . .Mark McKnight
City Mgr., (vacant)
Highland Haven . . . . Olan Kelley
Highland Park † . . . . .Will C. Beecherl
Town Admin., Bill Lindley
Highland Village † . . . . . . Daniel Jaworski
City Mgr., Paul Stevens
Hill Country Village Gabriel Durand-Hollis
City Admin., Frank Morales
Hillcrest Village . . . . Tom Wilson
Hillsboro † . . . . Andrew L. Smith
City Mgr., Megan Henderson
Hilshire Village . . . Robert (Bob) Buesinger
City Admin., (vacant)
Hitchcock † . . . . Chris Armacost
City Admin., Marie Gelles
Holiday Lakes . . . . Norman Schroeder
Holland . . . . Johnny Kallus
Holliday . . . . Allen Moore
Hollywood Park . . . . .Sean Moore
Hondo † . . . . John McAnelly
City Mgr., Robert Herrera, Interim
Honey Grove . . . . Claude Caffee
Hooks . . . . Mark Reiter
Horizon City † . . . . .Andres Renteria
Horseshoe Bay † . . . . . Cynthia Clinesmith
City Mgr., Jeff Koska
Houston † . . . . .Sylvester Turner
Howardwick . . . . Tony Clemishire
Howe . . . . Karla McDonald
City Admin., Jeff Stanley
Hubbard . . . . .Mary Alderman
City Mgr., Jason Patrick
Hudson . . . . .Robert Smith
City Admin., James Freeman
Hudson Oaks . . . . .Tom Fitzpatrick
City Admin., Sterling Naron
Hughes Springs . . . . James Samples
City Mgr., Stephen Barnes
Humble † . . . . Norman Funderburk
City Mgr., Jason Stuebe
Hunters Creek Village . . . . .Jim Pappas
City Admin., Tom Fullen

Huntington . . . . Todd Ricks
City Admin., Bill Stewart
Huntsville † . . . . .Andy Brauninger
City Mgr., Aron Kulhavy
Hurst † . . . . Henry Wilson
City Mgr., Clay Caruthers
Hutchins . . . . .Mario Vasquez
City Admin., James Quin
Hutto † . . . . Mike Snyder
City Mgr., James Earp
Huxley . . . . Larry Vaughn

I

Idalou . . . . Russ Perkins
City Admin., Suzette Williams
Impact . . . . Trevor Dickson
Indian Lake . . . . James Chambers
Industry . . . . Mable Meyers
Ingleside † . . . . .Oscar Adame
City Mgr., Brenton Lewis
Ingleside on the Bay . . . . .Jo Ann Ehmann
Ingram . . . . .Claud Jordan
Iola . . . . .Christina Stover
Iowa Colony † . . . . Wil Kennedy
City Mgr., Robert Hemminger
Iowa Park † . . . . Ray Schultz
City Mgr., Jerry Flemming
Iraan . . . . .Karina Browning
Iredell . . . . Joel Wellborn
Irving † . . . . .Rick Stopfer
City Mgr., Chris Hillman
Italy . . . . .Bryant Cockran
City Admin., Shawn Holden
Itasca . . . . .James Bouldin
City Admin., CinDee Garrett
Ivanhoe . . . . Skip Blackstone

J

Jacinto City † . . . . .Ana Diaz
City Mgr., Lon Squyres
Jacksboro . . . . Craig Fenter
City Mgr., Michael R. Smith
Jacksonville † . . . . Randy Gorham
City Mgr., James Hubbard
Jamaica Beach . . . . Sharon Bower
City Admin., (vacant)
Jarrell . . . . Patrick Sherek
City Mgr., Grace Matlock, Interim
Jasper † . . . . Anderson Land
City Mgr., Denise Kelley
Jayton . . . . .George Chisum
Jefferson . . . . Rob Baker
Jersey Village † . . . . Bobby Warren
City Mgr., Austin Bleess
Jewett . . . . John Sitton
Joaquin . . . . Frank Cooper
Johnson City . . . . Stephanie Fisher
Jolly . . . . D. LeAnn Skinner
Jones Creek . . . . .Terry Jeffers
Jonestown . . . . Paul Johnson
City Admin., Steve Jones
Josephine . . . . .Jason Turney
City Admin., Lisa Palomba
Joshua † . . . . Scott Kimble
City Mgr., Mike Peacock
Jourdanton . . . . .Robert A. Williams
City Mgr., Bobby J. Martinez
Junction . . . . Russell Hammonds
Justin † . . . . .James Clark
City Mgr., Jarrod Greenwoods

K

Karnes City . . . . Leroy T. Skloss
City Mgr., Veronica Butler, Interim

Katy † . . . . William H. (Dusty) Thiele
City Admin., Byron J. Hebert

Kaufman † . . . . Jeff Jordan
City Mgr., Mike Holder

Keene † . . . . Lisa Parrish
City Mgr., Bernie Parker

Keller † . . . . Armin Mizani
City Mgr., Mark Hafner

Kemah . . . . Robin Collins
City Admin., (vacant)

Kemp . . . . Christi Neal
City Admin., Regina Kiser

Kempner . . . . John (JW) Wilkerson
City Mgr., Heriberto Rodriguez

Kendleton . . . . Darryl K. Humphrey, Sr.

Kenedy . . . . Brandon Briones
City Mgr., (vacant)

Kenefick . . . . Martin (Marty) Wells

Kennard . . . . Jesse Stephens
City Admin., April Wright

Kennedale † . . . . Jan Joplin
City Mgr., Darrell Hull

Kerens . . . . Jeffrey Saunders

Kermit † . . . . David Holbrook
City Mgr., Frankie Davis

Kerrville † . . . . Judy Eychner
City Mgr., E.A. Hoppe

Kilgore † . . . . Ronnie E. Spradlin, III
City Mgr., Josh Selleck

Killeen † . . . . Debbie Nash-King
City Mgr., Kent Cagle

Kingsbury . . . . Shirley Nolen

Kingsville † . . . . Sam R. Fugate
City Mgr., Mark McLaughlin

Kirby † . . . . Janeshia A. Grider
City Mgr., (vacant)

Kirbyville . . . . Frank George

Kirvin . . . . J.W. Walthall

Knollwood . . . . Rosalie Dunn

Knox City . . . . Gene Ward
City Admin., Brian Barboza

Kosse . . . . Brooks Valls

Kountze . . . . Fred Williams
City Admin., Roderick Hutto

Kress . . . . Johnny Taylor

Krugerville . . . . Jeff Parrent

Krum † . . . . Rhonda Harrison

Kurten . . . . Chris Court

Kyle † . . . . Travis Mitchell
City Mgr., Bryan Langley

L

La Coste . . . . Andy Keller
City Admin., Darrell Rawlings

Lacy Lakeview † . . . . A. Niecey Payne
City Mgr., Calvin Hodde

Ladonia . . . . Patricia Harrod

La Feria † . . . . Olga H. Maldonado
City Mgr., Jaime S. Sandoval

Lago Vista † . . . . Ed Tidwell
City Mgr., Tracie Hlavinka

La Grange † . . . . Jan Dockery
City Mgr., Fred Bell

La Grulla . . . . Laura Patricia Solis

Laguna Vista † . . . . Michael Carter
City Mgr., Rendie Gonzales

La Joya † . . . . Isidro Casanova
City Admin., (vacant)

Lake Bridgeport . . . . Nick Bilby

Lake City . . . . Shannan Smith

Lake Dallas † . . . . Andi Nolan
City Mgr., Kandace Lesley

Lake Jackson † . . . . Gerald Roznovsky
City Mgr., Modesto Mundo

Lakeport . . . . Johnny Sammons

Lakeside (San Patricio Co.) . . . . Jeff Mason

Lakeside (Tarrant Co.) . . . . . Patrick Jacob
Town Admin., Norman Craven

Lakeside City . . . . Cory Glassburn
City Admin., John Strenski

Lake Tanglewood . . . . Tiffany Rogers

Lakeview . . . . Kelly Clark

Lakeway † . . . . Thomas Kilgore
City Mgr., Joseph Molis

Lakewood Village . . . . Mark Vargus
Town Admin., Linda Ruth

Lake Worth † . . . . Walter Bowen
City Mgr., Stacey Almond

La Marque † . . . . Keith Bell
City Mgr., Cesar Garcia

Lamesa † . . . . Josh Stevens
City Mgr., Joe Hines

Lampasas † . . . . Herb Pearce
City Mgr., Finley DeGraffenried

Lancaster † . . . . Clyde C. Hairston
City Mgr., Opal Mauldin-Jones

La Porte † . . . . Louis R. Rigby
City Mgr., Corby Alexander

Laredo † . . . . Victor D. Treviño
City Mgr., Joseph Neeb

Latexo . . . . Robert Hernandez

La Vernia . . . . Martin Poore
City Admin., Yvonne Griffin

La Villa . . . . Alma Moron

Lavon . . . . Vicki Sanson
City Admin., Kim Dobbs

La Ward . . . . Richard Koch

Lawn . . . . Veronica Burleson

League City † . . . . Nick Long
City Mgr., John Baumgartner

Leakey . . . . Hazel Pendley

Leander † . . . . Christine DeLisle
City Mgr., Rick Beverlin

Leary . . . . B.J. Martin
City Admin., Randy Mansfield

Lefors . . . . Michael Ray

Leona . . . . Ernest (Bubba) Oden

Leonard . . . . Michael Pye
City Admin., George Evanko

Leon Valley † . . . . Chris Riley
City Mgr., Crystal Caldera

Leroy . . . . Ernest Moravec

Levelland † . . . . Barbra Pinner
City Mgr., Brandon Anderson

Lewisville † . . . . TJ Gilmore
City Mgr., Claire Powell

Lexington . . . . Allen Retzlaff

Liberty † . . . . Carl Pickett
City Mgr., Tom Warner

Liberty Hill . . . . Liz Branigan
City Admin., Paul Brandenburg

Lindale † . . . . Jeff Daugherty
City Mgr., Carolyn Caldwell

Linden . . . . Lynn Reynolds
City Admin., Lee Elliott

Lindsay . . . . Scott Neu

Lipan . . . . Mike Stowe

Little Elm † . . . . Curtis J. Cornelious
Town Mgr., Matt Mueller

Littlefield † . . . . Eric Turpen
City Mgr., Mitch Grant

Little River-Academy . Domingo Montalbo

Live Oak † . . . . Mary M. Dennis
City Mgr., Glen A. Martel

Liverpool . . . . Ric Bogue

Livingston . . . . Judy B. Cochran
City Mgr., Bill Wiggins

Llano . . . . Marion Bishop
City Mgr., Marty Mangum

Lockhart † . . . . Lew White
City Mgr., Steve Lewis

Lockney . . . . Aaron Wilson
City Mgr., G.A. (Buster) Poling, Jr.

Log Cabin . . . . Jennifer Williams

Lometa . . . . Stephen Brister Hicks

Lone Oak . . . . Douglas E. Williams

Lone Star . . . . Brianna McClain

Longview † . . . . Andy Mack
City Mgr., Rolin C. McPhee

Loraine . . . . Suzanna Epperson

Lorena . . . . Tommy Ross
City Mgr., Kevin Neal

Lorenzo . . . . Tim Tiner
City Admin., Michael Chambers

Los Fresnos † . . . . Alejandro Flores
City Mgr., Mark Milum

Los Indios . . . . Jaime Gonzalez
City Admin., Jared Hockema

Los Ybanez . . . . Mary A. Ybanez
City Mgr., John Castillo

Lott . . . . Sue Tacker

Lovelady . . . . William B. Shoemaker

Lowry Crossing . . . . Bob Petitt
City Admin., Janis Cable

Lubbock † . . . . Tray Payne
City Mgr., W. Jarrett Atkinson

Lucas † . . . . Jim Olk
City Mgr., Joni Clarke

Lueders . . . . Benny Jarvis

Lufkin † . . . . Mark Hicks
City Mgr., Kevin Gee

Luling † . . . . CJ Watts
City Mgr., Mark Mayo

Lumberton † . . . . Don Surratt
City Mgr., Steve Clark

Lyford . . . . Jose G. (Wally) Solis

Lytle . . . . Ruben Gonzalez
City Admin., Matthew Dear

M

Mabank . . . . Randy Teague
City Admin., Bryant Morris

Madisonville . . . . Bill Parten
City Mgr., Fabrice Kabona

Magnolia . . . . Todd Kana
City Admin., Don Doering

Malakoff . . . . Nicole Mason-Driver
City Admin., Tim Whitley

Malone . . . . James Lucko

Manor † . . . . Christopher Harvey
City Mgr., Scott Moore

Mansfield † . . . . Michael Evans
City Mgr., Joe Smolinski

Manvel † . . . . Dan Davis
City Mgr., Kyle J. Jung

Marble Falls † . . . . Dave Rhodes
City Mgr., Mike Hodge

The tornado memorial in Lubbock, built in remembrance of the two tornadoes that struck the city on May 11, 1970. Photo by Larry Syverson, Flickr, CC by 2.0

Marfa . . . . .Manuel V. Baeza
City Admin., Amanda Roane
Marietta . . . .(vacant)
City Mgr., Charles Elliott
Marion . . . . Victor A. Contreras
Marlin † . . . . Susan R. Byrd
City Mgr., Cedric Davis, Sr.
Marquez . . . . Stynette Clary
City Mgr., Lauren Powers
Marshall † . . . . .Amy Ware
City Mgr., Terrell Smith
Mart . . . . Robert Kaiser
Martindale . . . . .Katherine Glaze
City Admin., Jared Anable
Mason . . . . Frank Bartlett
City Admin., John Palacio
Matador . . . . Pat Smith
Mathis † . . . . Ciri Villarreal
City Mgr., Michael Barrera
Maud . . . . Jimmy Clary
Maypearl . . . . Chance Lynch
McAllen † . . . . .Javier Villalobos
City Mgr., Roel Roy Rodriguez
McCamey . . . . .Pedro (Pete) Rosales
McGregor † . . . . James S. Hering
City Mgr., Kevin Evans
McKinney † . . . . George Fuller
City Mgr., Paul Grimes
McLean . . . . Tanner Hess
McLendon-Chisholm . . . . Keith Short
City Admin., Konrad Hildebrandt
Meadow . . . . .Natalie Howard
City Admin., Terri McClanahan
Meadowlakes . . . . .Mark Bentley
City Mgr., Johnnie Thompson
Meadows Place . . . . . Charles D. Jessup, IV
City Admin., Nick Haby
Megargel . . . . .Randall Williams
Melissa † . . . . Jay Northcut
City Mgr., Jason Little
Melvin . . . . Gary Adams
Memphis . . . . .Joe Davis
Menard . . . . .Barbara Hooten
City Admin., Don Kerns
Mercedes † . . . . .Oscar D. Montoya, Sr.
City Mgr., Alberto Perez
Meridian . . . . .Ryan Nieuwenhuis
City Admin., Marie Garland
Merkel . . . . .Mary Schrampfer
City Mgr., Evelyn Morse, Interim
Mertens . . . . .Amber Phillips
Mertzon . . . . Aubrey Stewart
City Admin., Michele Wardlaw
Mesquite † . . . . Daniel Alemán, Jr.
City Mgr., Cliff Keheley
Mexia † . . . . Geary Smith
City Mgr., Jeff Arnswald
Miami . . . . .Chad Breeding
Midland † . . . . .Lori Blong
City Mgr., Morris Williams, Interim
Midlothian † . . . . Justin Coffman
City Mgr., Chris Dick
Midway . . . . Brenda Ford
Milano . . . . Karl Westbrook
Mildred . . . . Bryan Roach
Miles . . . . Tammy Pitt
Milford . . . . .Bruce Perryman
Miller's Cove . . . . Willie B. Garrett
Millsap . . . . Jamie French
City Mgr., Ashley Davis
Mineola . . . . Jayne Lankford
City Mgr., Mercy L. Rushing
Mineral Wells † . . . . .Regan Johnson
City Mgr., Dean Sullivan
Mingus . . . . .Vincent Huckaba
Mission † . . . . Norie Gonzalez Garza
City Mgr., Randy Perez
Missouri City † . . . . .Robin J. Elackatt
City Mgr., Angel L. Jones
Mobeetie . . . . John Charles Helton, Jr.
Mobile City . . . . .Kenny Phillips
Monahans † . . . . .Adam Steen
City Mgr., Rex M. Thee
Mont Belvieu † . . . . Joey McWilliams
City Mgr., Brian Winningham
Montgomery . . . . Byron Sanford
City Admin., Gary Palmer
Moody . . . . Charleen Dowell
City Admin., Keith Fisher
Moore Station . . . . Charles Anderson
Moran . . . . Tyler George
Morgan . . . . Jonathan W. Croom, II
Morgan's Point . . . . Michel J. Bechtel
City Admin., Brian Schneider
Morgan's Point Resort . . . . . Dennis Green
City Mgr., Dalton Rice
Morton . . . . Richard Levitt
City Mgr., Veronica Olguin
Moulton . . . . Mark Zimmerman
City Admin., LuAnn D. Rogers
Mountain City . . . . Ralph McClendon
City Admin., Tiffany Curnutt
Mount Calm . . . . Jimmy Tucker
Mount Enterprise . . . . Jim Reese
Mount Pleasant † . . . . Tracy Craig, Sr.
City Mgr., Ed Thatcher
Mount Vernon . . . . Brad Hyman
City Admin., Craig Lindholm, Interim
Muenster . . . . .Tim Felderhoff
City Admin., Adam Deweber
Muleshoe † . . . . .Colt Ellis
City Mgr., Ramon Sanchez
Mullin . . . . Dexter Morris, Acting
Munday . . . . Bob Bowen
City Admin., David Trevino
Murchison . . . . .Brad Gray, Acting
Murphy † . . . . .Scott Bradley
City Mgr., Mike Castro
Mustang Ridge . . . . .David Bunn

N

Nacogdoches † . . . . Randy Johnson
City Mgr., Keith Kiplinger, Interim
Naples . . . . .Bryan Tefteller
Nash . . . . Robert Bunch
City Admin., Doug Bowers
Nassau Bay † . . . . Phil Johnson
City Mgr., (vacant)
Natalia . . . . .Samuel Bluemel, Jr.
City Admin., Nichole Bermea, Interim
Navarro . . . . Vickie Lynn Farmer
Navasota † . . . . William A. (Bert) Miller, III
City Mgr., Jason B. Weeks
Nazareth . . . . .Marlin Durbin
City Mgr., Lacey Farris

Nederland † . . . . . Don Albanese
City Mgr., Christopher Duque
Needville . . . . . Chad Nesvadba
Nevada . . . . . Ben Ponce
Newark . . . . . Crystal Cardwell
New Berlin . . . . . Walter Williams
City Admin., Mindy Paxton
New Boston . . . . . Ronald Humphrey
City Admin., Wayne Dial
New Braunfels † . . . . . Neal Linnartz
City Mgr., Robert Camareno
Newcastle . . . . . Adrian Ontiveroz
New Chapel Hill . . . . . Riley Harris
New Deal . . . . . John Salter
New Fairview . . . . . John Taylor
City Admin., John Cabrales, Jr.
New Home . . . . . Brad Emert
New Hope . . . . . Andy Reitinger
New London . . . . . Dale McNeel
New Summerfield . . . . . Jane Barrow
Newton . . . . . Mark Bean
City Admin., Donald H. Meek
New Waverly . . . . . Nathaniel James
Neylandville . . . . . Kathy Wilson
Niederwald . . . . . Charles Bisson
City Admin., Richard L. Crandal, Jr.
Nixon . . . . . Dorothy Riojas
City Mgr., Harold D. Rice
Nocona . . . . . Robert H. Fenoglio
City Mgr., Lynn Henley
Nolanville † . . . . . Andy Williams
City Mgr., Kara Escajeda
Nome . . . . . Kerry Abney
Noonday . . . . . Mike Turman
Nordheim . . . . . Katherine Payne
Normangee . . . . . Troy Noey
North Cleveland . . . . . Bob Bartlett
Northlake † . . . . . David Rettig
Town Mgr., Drew Corn
North Richland Hills † . . . . Oscar Trevino
City Mgr., Mark Hindman
Novice . . . . . Bobby Green

O

Oak Grove . . . . . Jeffrey Davis
Oak Leaf . . . . . Tom Leverentz
Oak Point . . . . . Dena Meek
City Mgr., Stephen Ashley
Oak Ridge (Cooke Co.) . . . . Chad Ramsey
Oak Ridge (Kaufman Co.) . . . . . Al Rudin
Oak Ridge North . . . . . Paul Bond
City Mgr., Heather Neeley
Oak Valley . . . . . Jarrett Greer
Oakwood . . . . . Jacquelyn Morrow
O'Brien . . . . . Chris Casillas
Odem . . . . . David Bargas Maldonado
Odessa † . . . . . Javier Joven
City Mgr., Agapito Bernal, Interim
O'Donnell . . . . . Kim Parker
Oglesby . . . . . Bruce Pomerenke
Old River-Winfree . . . . . Joe Landry
Olmos Park . . . . . Deanna Rickabaugh
City Mgr., Celia DeLeon
Olney † . . . . . Rue Rogers
City Admin., Arpegea Pagsuberon
Olton . . . . . Mark McFadden
City Admin., Keeley Adams
Omaha . . . . . Ernest Paul Pewitt
Onalaska . . . . . James Arnett
City Admin., Angela Stutts
Opdyke West . . . . . Wayne Riggins
Orange † . . . . . Larry Spears
City Mgr., Mike Kunst
Orange Grove . . . . . Carl Srp
City Admin., Todd Wright
Orchard . . . . . Rod Pavlock
Ore City . . . . . Angie Edwards
Overton . . . . . Curtis Gilbert
City Mgr., Shane West
Ovilla . . . . . Richard Dormier
City Mgr., David D. Henley
Oyster Creek . . . . . Justin Mills

P

Paducah . . . . . Rodger Brannen
Paint Rock . . . . . Frances Maupin
Palacios † . . . . . Jim Gardner
City Mgr., Cynthia Raleigh
Palestine † . . . . . Mitchell Jordan
City Mgr., Teresa Herrera
Palisades . . . . . Jerry Lane
Palmer . . . . . Kenneth Bateman
City Admin., Alicia Baran
Palmhurst . . . . . Fred del Barrio
City Mgr., Lori A. Lopez
Palm Valley . . . . . Michael Galvan
Palmview † . . . . . Ricardo Villareal
City Mgr., Michael Leo
Pampa † . . . . . Lance DeFever
City Mgr., Shane Stokes
Panhandle . . . . . Doyle Robinson
City Mgr., Terry Coffee
Panorama Village . . . . . Lynn Scott
Pantego . . . . . Russ Brewster
City Mgr., Joe Ashton
Paradise . . . . . Amanda Black
Paris † . . . . . Reginald B. Hughes
City Mgr., Grayson Path
Parker . . . . . Lee Pettle
City Admin., Luke Olson
Pasadena † . . . . . Jeff A. Wagner
Pattison . . . . . Joe Garcia
Patton Village . . . . . Scott Anderson
Payne Springs . . . . . Andrea Miller
Pearland † . . . . . Kevin Cole
City Mgr., Clay Pearson
Pearsall † . . . . . Ben T. Briscoe
City Mgr., Federico Reyes
Peaster . . . . . Don Smelley
Pecan Gap . . . . . Cole Hoskison
Pecan Hill . . . . . Don Schmerse
Pecos † . . . . . Teresa Winkles
City Mgr., Charles Lino
Pelican Bay . . . . . Tamra Olague
Penelope . . . . . Phillip Esparza
Peñitas † . . . . . Ramiro Loya
City Mgr., Humberto Garza
Perryton . . . . . Kerry Symons
City Mgr., David Landis
Petersburg . . . . . Thomas Roden
City Mgr., Mario Martinez
Petrolia . . . . . Troy Inman
Petronila . . . . . Todd Wright
Pflugerville † . . . . . Victor Gonzales
City Mgr., Sereniah Breland
Pharr † . . . . . Ambrosio (Amos) Hernandez
City Mgr., Anali Alaniz, Interim
Pilot Point † . . . . . Elisa Beasley
City Mgr., Britt M. Lusk
Pine Forest . . . . . Cathy Nagel
Pinehurst . . . . . Sarah McClendon
City Admin., Jerry Hood
Pine Island . . . . . Steve Nagy
Pineland . . . . . Joe Lane
Piney Point Village . . . . . Mark Kobelan
City Admin., Bobby Pennington
Pittsburg † . . . . . David Abernathy
City Mgr., Clint Hardeman
Plains . . . . . Robert Whitfield
City Admin., Steve Vasquez
Plainview † . . . . . Charles Starnes
City Mgr., Jeffrey Snyder
Plano † . . . . . John B. Muns
City Mgr., Mark D. Israelson
Plantersville . . . . . Karen Hale
Pleak . . . . . Larry Bittner
Pleasanton † . . . . . Clinton J. Powell
City Mgr., Johnny Huizar
Pleasant Valley . . . . . Jerry Gholson
Plum Grove . . . . . Mary Arrendell
Poetry . . . . . Tara Senkevech
Point . . . . . Dustin Briggs
Point Blank . . . . . Mark T. Wood
City Mgr., Kelly Hoot
Point Comfort . . . . . Stephen Lambden
City Admin., Tammy Soliz
Point Venture . . . . . (vacant)
Ponder . . . . . Matthew Poole
Port Aransas † . . . . . Wendy Moore
City Mgr., David Parsons
Port Arthur † . . . . . Thurman Bill Bartie
City Mgr., Ron Burton
Port Isabel † . . . . . Martin Cantu, Jr.
City Mgr., Jared Hockema
Portland † . . . . . Cathy Skurow
City Mgr., Randy Wright
Port Lavaca † . . . . . Jack Whitlow
City Mgr., Joanna P. (Jody) Weaver
Port Neches † . . . . . Glenn Johnson
City Mgr., André Wimer
Post . . . . . Marvin Self
City Mgr., J. Rhett Parker
Post Oak Bend . . . . . Mike Parker
Poteet . . . . . Denise Leal Sanchez
City Admin., Melissa Popham
Poth . . . . . Chrystal Eckel
Pottsboro . . . . . Frank Budra
City Mgr., Kacie Galyon
Powell . . . . . Clay Jackson
Poynor . . . . . Dannie Smith
Prairie View † . . . . Ron Leverett Carl Jones, Interim
Premont . . . . . Priscilla Vargas
Presidio . . . . . John Ferguson
City Admin., Pablo E. Rodriguez
Primera . . . . . Pat Patterson
City Admin., Celina Gonzales
Princeton . . . . . Brianna Chacón
City Mgr., Derek Borg
Progreso . . . . . Gerardo Alanis
City Admin., Alfredo Espinosa
Progreso Lakes . . . . . Harold Seiver
Prosper † . . . . . David F. Bristol
Town Mgr., Mario Canizares
Providence Village † . . . . . Linda Inman
Town Mgr., Brian Roberson
Putnam . . . . . Hubert Donaway
Pyote . . . . . Abigail Pritchard

Q

Quanah † . . . . . Kathy Butler
City Admin., Paula Wilson
Queen City . . . . . Harold Martin

Quinlan . . . . Jacky Goleman
City Admin., John Adel
Quintana . . . . Shari Wright
City Admin., Tammi Cimiotta
Quitaque . . . . Phil Barefield
City Mgr., Maria Merrell
Quitman . . . . Randy Dunn
City Admin., James Attaway

R

Ralls . . . . Terry Hitt
City Admin., Kim Perez
Rancho Viejo . . . . Maribel B. Guerrero
Town Admin., Fred Blanco
Ranger † . . . . Terry Robinson
City Mgr., Savannah Fortenberry
Rangerville . . . . Wayne Halbert
Rankin . . . . Brandon Brown
Ransom Canyon . . . . Jana Trew
City Admin., Maria Elena Quintanilla
Ravenna . . . . Joe Passanisi
Raymondville † . . . . Gilbert Gonzales
City Mgr., Antonio (Tony) Chavez
Red Lick . . . . Michael Peek
Red Oak † . . . . Mark Stanfill
City Mgr., Todd Fuller
Redwater . . . . Clay Parker
City Admin., Dessie Whelchel
Refugio . . . . Wanda Dukes
Reklaw . . . . Bob Parrott
Reno (Lamar Co.) . . . . Stacey Nichols
Reno (Parker Co.) . . . . Hector Bas
City Admin., (vacant)
Retreat . . . . Janice Barfknecht
Rhome . . . . Patricia Mitchell
City Admin., Amanda DeGan
Rice . . . . J. Nicole Jackson
City Admin., Vicki Fisher
Richardson † . . . . Robert (Bob) Dubey
City Mgr., Don Magner
Richland . . . . Kenneth Guard
Richland Hills † . . . . Edward Lopez
City Mgr., Candice Edmondson
Richland Springs . . . . Johnie Reeves
Richmond † . . . . Rebecca (Becky) Haas
City Mgr., Terri Vela
Richwood † . . . . Michael Durham
City Mgr., Eric Foerster
Riesel . . . . Marshall Shaw
Rio Bravo † . . . . Gilberto Aguilar, Jr.
City Admin., Jesus Olivares
Rio Grande City † . . . . Joel Villarreal
Rio Hondo . . . . . . Gustavo (Gus) Olivares
City Admin., Ben Medina
Rio Vista . . . . Jeff Faraizl
Rising Star . . . . Jimmy L. Carpenter
City Admin., Jan Clark
River Oaks † . . . . Darren Houk
City Admin., Marvin Gregory
Riverside . . . . John LeMaire
Road Runner . . . . David Ortega, Jr.
Roanoke † . . . . Scooter Gierisch
City Mgr., Cody Petree
Roaring Springs . . . . Jeff Thacker
Robert Lee . . . . Jason Moran
City Supt., Kimble Middleton
Robinson † . . . . Bert Echterling
City Mgr., Craig Lemin
Robstown † . . . . Gilbert Gomez
Roby . . . . Eli Sepeda
City Mgr., Jack W. Brown

Rochester . . . . Marvin Stegemoeller
City Admin., Gail Nunn
Rockdale † . . . . Brett Boren
City Mgr., Barbara Holly
Rockport † . . . Lowell Timothy (Tim) Jayroe
City Mgr., Vanessa Shrauner
Rocksprings . . . . LaWanda Goller
Rockwall † . . . . Trace Johannesen
City Mgr., Mary Smith
Rocky Mound . . . . Noble T. Smith
Rogers . . . . Jeff Watson
City Admin., Tammy Cockrum
Rollingwood . . . . Gavin Massingill
City Admin., Ashley Wayman
Roma † . . . . Jaime Escobar, Jr.
City Mgr., Alejandro Barrera
Roman Forest . . . . Chris Parr
City Admin., Timothy J. Underwood
Ropesville . . . . Brenda Rabel
City Admin., Susan Thompson
Roscoe . . . . David Ralph
City Mgr., Jack Brown, Interim
Rosebud . . . . Marlene Zipperlen
City Admin., Kenny Ray Murray
Rose City . . . . Tony Wilcoxson
Rose Hill Acres . . . . David Lang
Rosenberg † . . . . Kevin Raines
City Mgr., John Maresh
Ross . . . . Jim Jaska
Rosser . . . . Shannon R. Corder
Rotan . . . . Zachary Johnson
City Mgr., Carla Thornton
Round Mountain . . . . Alvin Gutierrez
Round Rock † . . . . Craig Morgan
City Mgr., Laurie Hadley
Round Top . . . . Mark Massey
Rowlett † . . . . Blake Margolis
City Mgr., Brian Funderburk
Roxton . . . . Paul Helms
City Mgr., Janet Wheeler
Royse City † . . . . Clay Ellis
City Mgr., Carl Alsabrook
Rule . . . . Delle Watkins
Runaway Bay . . . . Herman White
Runge . . . . Homer Lott, Jr.
Rusk † . . . . Ben Middlebrooks
City Mgr., Amanda Hilll

S

Sabinal . . . . Charles D. Story
Sachse † . . . . Jeff Bickerstaff
City Mgr., Gina Nash
Sadler . . . . Jackie Moss
City Admin., Jaime Vannoy
Saginaw † . . . . Todd Flippo
City Mgr., Gabriel Reaume
Saint Hedwig . . . . Dee Grimm
City Mgr., Maria Hernandez
Saint Jo . . . . Shawn Armstrong
Salado . . . . Michael Coggin
Village Admin., Don Ferguson
San Angelo † . . . . Brenda Gunter
City Mgr., Daniel Valenzuela
San Antonio † . . . . Ron Nirenberg
City Mgr., Erik Walsh
San Augustine . . . . Leroy Hughes
City Mgr., Jeaneyse Mosby
San Benito † . . . . Ricardo (Rick) Guerra
City Mgr., Manuel De La Rosa
Sanctuary . . . . Megg Galloway

San Diego . . . . . Araseli Sally Lichtenberger
City Dir., Aleida L. Luera
Sandy Oaks . . . . Michael Martinez, Jr.
Sandy Point . . . . Charles J. Waller, Jr.
San Elizario . . . . Isela Reyes
San Felipe . . . . Bobby Byars
Sanford . . . . Dallis Shelton
Sanger † . . . . Thomas Muir
City Mgr., John Noblitt
San Juan † . . . . Mario Garza
City Mgr., Benjamin Arjona
San Leanna . . . . Molly Quirk
City Admin., Rebecca Howe
San Marcos † . . . . Jane Hughson
City Mgr., Stephanie Reyes
San Patricio . . . . Jackie Hale
San Perlita . . . . George M. Guadiana
San Saba . . . . Ken Jordan
City Mgr., Scott Edmonson
Sansom Park . . . . Jim Barnett, Jr.
City Admin., Angela Winkle
Santa Anna . . . . Kevin Morris
Santa Clara . . . . Jeff Hunt
Santa Fe † . . . . Bill Pittman
City Mgr., Alun Thomas
Santa Rosa . . . . Fermin Munoz
Savoy . . . . Joe Petree
Schertz † . . . . Ralph Gutierrez
City Mgr., Steve Williams
Schulenburg . . . . Connie Koopmann
City Admin., Tami Walker
Scotland . . . . Ron Hoff
Scottsville . . . . Kerry L. Cade
Scurry . . . . Johnny Blazek
Seabrook † . . . . Thom Kolupski
City Mgr., Gayle Cook
Seadrift . . . . Elmer DeForest
Seagoville † . . . . . Lackey Stepper Sebastian
City Mgr., Patrick Stallings
Seagraves . . . . Rick Dollahan
Sealy † . . . . Carolyn Bilski
City Mgr., Kimbra Hill
Seguin † . . . . Donna Dodgen
City Mgr., Steve Parker
Selma . . . . Tom Daly
City Admin., Johnny Casias
Seminole † . . . . Chet Clark
City Admin., Mary Furlow
Seven Oaks . . . . Anna Wallace
Seven Points . . . . Skippy Waters
Seymour . . . . Mark McCord
City Admin., Jeff Brasher
Shady Shores . . . . Cindy Aughinbaugh
Shallowater . . . . Royking Potter
City Mgr., Russel Moses
Shamrock . . . . Lynn Ramsey
City Mgr., Troy Potts
Shavano Park . . . . Bob Werner
City Mgr., Bill Hill
Shenandoah . . . . John Escoto
City Admin., Kathie Reyer
Shepherd . . . . Charles Minton
Sherman † . . . . David Plyler
City Mgr., Robby Hefton
Shiner . . . . Fred Hilscher
Shoreacres . . . . David Jennings
City Mgr., Troy Harrison
Silsbee † . . . . Danny Reneau
City Mgr., DeeAnn Zimmerman
Silverton . . . . Lane B. Garvin
City Admin., James Fisher, Interim
Simonton . . . . Laurie Boudreaux
City Admin., Jennifer Jones Ward

Sinton † . . . . . Edward Adams
City Mgr., John D. Hobson
Skellytown . . . . . Amanda Dickerson
Slaton † . . . . . Clifton Shaw
City Admin., Wade Wilson
Smiley . . . . . Lisa Benavides
Smithville . . . . . Sharon Foerster
City Mgr., Robert Tamble
Smyer . . . . . Joe Riddle
Snook . . . . . Frank Fields
City Admin., David Junek
Snyder † . . . . . Stephanie Ducheneaux
City Mgr., Eli Torres, Interim
Socorro † . . . . . Ivy Avalos
City Mgr., Adriana Rodarte
Somerset . . . . . Lydia P. Hernandez
City Admin., Omar H. Pachecano
Somerville . . . . . Tommy Thompson
City Admin., Danny Segundo
Sonora . . . . . Juanita Gomez
City Mgr., Arturo Fuentes
Sour Lake . . . . . Bruce Robinson
City Mgr., Jack Provost
South Frydek . . . . . Laura Meyer
South Houston . . . . . Joe Soto
Southlake † . . . . . John Huffman
City Mgr., Shana K. Yelverton
Southmayd . . . . . David Turner
South Mountain . . . . . (vacant)
South Padre Island † . . . . Patrick McNulty
City Mgr., Randy Smith
Southside Place . . . . . Andy Chan
City Mgr., David Moss
Spearman . . . . . Tobe Shields
City Mgr., Justin Parker
Splendora . . . . . Dorothy Welch
Spofford . . . . . Pablo Resendez
Spring Branch . . . . . James Mayer
Springlake . . . . . Gaylon Conner
Springtown . . . . . Greg Hood
City Admin., David Miller
Spring Valley . . . . . Marcus Vajdos
City Admin., (vacant)
Spur . . . . . Louise Jones
Stafford † . . . . . Ken Mathew
Stagecoach . . . . . Galen Mansee
Stamford † . . . . . James M. Decker
City Mgr., Alan Plumlee
Stanton . . . . . Sally Poteet
City Admin., Jessie Montez
Staples . . . . . Ronnie Clark
Star Harbor . . . . . Richard Haley
City Admin., Adabeth Shumate
Stephenville † . . . . . Doug Svien
City Mgr., Jason King
Sterling City . . . . . Lane Horwood
Stinnett . . . . . Colin Locke
City Admin., Stacie Miller
Stockdale . . . . . Ray Wolff
City Mgr., Banks Akin
Stockton Bend . . . . . Edward Reiter
St. Paul . . . . . David Gensler
Stratford . . . . . Greg Wright
City Admin., Tommy Bogart
Strawn . . . . . Tye Jackson
City Admin., Danny Miller
Streetman . . . . . Johnny A. Robinson
Sudan . . . . . Michael Williamson
Sugar Land † . . . . . Joe R. Zimmerman
City Mgr., Mike Goodrum
Sullivan City † . . . . . Alma D. Salinas
City Mgr., Ana M. Mercado
Sulphur Springs † . . . . . John A. Sellers
City Mgr., Marc Maxwell
Sundown . . . . . Jonathan Strickland
City Admin., Billy Hernandez
Sunnyvale † . . . . . Saji George
Town Mgr., Jeff Jones
Sunray . . . . . Bruce Broxson
City Mgr., K.J. Perry
Sunrise Beach Village . . . . Chellie Stewart
Sunset Valley . . . . . Marc Bruner
City Admin., Matt Lingafelter
Sun Valley . . . . . Tom Wagnon
Surfside Beach . . . . . Gregg Bisso
Sweeny † . . . . . Dusty Hopkins
City Mgr., Lindsay Koskiniemi
Sweetwater † . . . . . Jim McKenzie
City Mgr., David A. Vela

T

Taft . . . . . Randy Powell
City Mgr., William Linn
Tahoka . . . . . John B. Baker
City Admin., Julie Arrington
Talco . . . . . Shirley Caruthers
Talty . . . . . Frank Garrison
City Mgr., James Stroman
Tatum . . . . . Don Hall
Taylor † . . . . . Brandt Rydell
City Mgr., Brian LaBorde
Taylor Lake Village . . . . . Jon Keeney
City Admin., Stacey Fields
Taylor Landing . . . . . John Durkay
Teague . . . . . David Huffman
City Admin., Theresa Bell
Tehuacana . . . . . Janis Johnson
Temple † . . . . . Tim Davis
City Mgr., Brynn Myers
Tenaha . . . . . O'Neal Jones, Jr.
City Admin., Amanda Treat-Brock
Terrell † . . . . . Rick Carmona
City Mgr., Mike Sims
Terrell Hills † . . . . . John Low
City Mgr., William Foley
Texarkana † . . . . . Bob Bruggeman
City Mgr., David Orr
Texas City † . . . . . Dedrick D. Johnson, Sr.
Texhoma . . . . . Lazaro Salamanca
Texline . . . . . Jeff Finnegan
City Mgr., Marcia French
The Colony † . . . . . Richard Boyer
City Mgr., Troy Powell
The Hills (Village of) . . . . . Greg Wharton
City Mgr., Dean Huard
Thompsons . . . . . Freddie Newsome
Thorndale . . . . . George Galbreath, Jr.
City Admin., Raymond Miller, Jr.
Thornton . . . . . Charles (Chuck) Robinson
City Mgr., Victoria Winstead
Thorntonville . . . . . Bryan Mann
Thrall . . . . . Troy Marx
Three Rivers . . . . . Felipe Q. Martinez
City Admin., Thomas Salazar
Throckmorton . . . . . Will Carroll
Tiki Island . . . . Vernon (Goldie) Teltschick
Timbercreek Canyon . . . . . Brian Giffin
City Mgr., Amber Gerber
Timpson . . . . . Debra Smith
Tioga . . . . . Craig Jezek
Tira . . . . . Allen Joslin
Toco . . . . . Christopher Gray
Todd Mission . . . . . George C. Coulam
City Mgr., Neal Wendele
Tolar . . . . . Matt Hutsell
Tom Bean . . . . . Daniel Harrison
Tomball † . . . . . Lori Klein Quinn
City Mgr., David Esquivel
Tool . . . . . Tommy Lawhon
City Admin., Julius Kizzee
Toyah . . . . . Gordon Hoyt
Trent . . . . . Leanna West
Trenton . . . . . Rodney Alexander
Trinidad . . . . . Leslie Parker
City Admin., Terri R. Newhouse
Trinity . . . . . Billy Goodin
City Mgr., Tim King
Trophy Club † . . . . . Jeannette Tiffany
Town Mgr., Patrick Arata, Interim
Troup . . . . . Jeff Hale
City Mgr., Gene Cottle
Troy . . . . . Michael Morgan
City Admin., Gary O. Smith
Tulia † . . . . . Dusty George
City Mgr., B.J. Potts
Turkey . . . . . Christy Yates
City Mgr., Larry Plumlee
Tuscola . . . . . Joe Quick
City Admin., Genny Abercrombie
Tye . . . . . Nancy Moore
Tyler † . . . . . Don Warren
City Mgr., Edward Broussard

U

Uhland . . . . . Lacee Duke
City Admin., Karen Gallaher
Uncertain . . . . . Judye Patterson
Union Grove . . . . Mallory Dippold Shelton
Union Valley . . . . . Craig Waskow
Universal City † . . . . . John Williams
City Mgr., Kim Turner
University Park † . . . . . Thomas H. Stewart
City Mgr., Robbie Corder
Uvalde † . . . . . Don McLaughlin
City Mgr., Vince DiPiazza

V

Valentine . . . . . Summer Webb
Valley Mills . . . . . Ray Bickerstaff
Valley View . . . . . Janson Bewley
Van . . . . . Tammy Huff
City Mgr., (vacant)
Van Alstyne † . . . . . Jim Atchison
City Mgr., Lane Jones
Van Horn . . . . . Duane (Toto) Corrales
City Admin., Mark A. Cabezuela
Vega . . . . . Roudy Blasingame
Venus . . . . . Alejandro Galaviz
City Admin., Tonya Roberts
Vernon † . . . . . Pam Gosline
City Mgr., Darell Kennon
Victoria † . . . . . Jeff Bauknight
City Mgr., Jesús A. Garza
Vidor † . . . . . Misty Songe
City Mgr., Robbie Hood
Vinton . . . . . Rachel Quintana
Village Admin., Andrea Carrillo
Volente . . . . . Tom Blauvelt
City Admin., Lacie Hale
Von Ormy . . . . . Casey Homer
City Admin., Valerie Michelle Naff

The historic Cortez Hotel in Weslaco opened in 1928. Photo by C Hanchey, Flickr, CC by NC 2.0

W

Waco † . . . . Dillon Meek
City Mgr., Bradley Ford
Waelder . . . . Roy Tovar
City Mgr., James L. Wright
Wake Village † . . . . Sheryl Collum
City Admin., Jim Roberts
Waller . . . . Danny Marburger
Wallis . . . . Preston Little
Walnut Springs . . . . Sammy Ortega
Warren City . . . . Ricky Wallace
Waskom . . . . Jesse Moore
Watauga † . . . . Arthur L. Miner
City Mgr., Joshua Jones
Waxahachie † . . . . David Hill
City Mgr., Michael Scott
Weatherford † . . . . Paul Paschall
City Mgr., James Hotopp
Webberville . . . . Hector Gonzales
Webster † . . . . Donna Rogers
City Mgr., Michael K. Ahrens
Weimar . . . . Milton R. Koller
City Mgr., Mike Barrow
Weinert . . . . David Caldwell
Weir . . . . Alber Walther
Wellington . . . . Larry Adams
City Mgr., Jon Sessions
Wellman . . . . Eddie Garza
Wells . . . . Tony McKnight
Weslaco † . . . . David Suarez
City Mgr., Martin Garza
West . . . . Tommy Muska
City Admin., Shelly Nors
Westbrook . . . . John Manning
West Columbia . . . . . Laurie B. Kincannon
City Mgr., Debbie Sutherland
Westlake . . . . Sean Kilbride
Town Mgr., Wade Carroll
West Lake Hills . . . . Linda Anthony
City Admin., Trey Fletcher
Weston . . . . Jery Randall
Weston Lakes . . . . Bob Wall
West Orange † . . . . Randy Branch
Westover Hills . . . . Kelly Thompson
West Tawakoni . . . . Jim Turnipseed
City Admin., Anette Lemons
West University Place † . . . . Susan Sample
City Mgr., Dave Beach
Westworth Village . . . . L. Kelly Jones
City Admin., Brandy Barrett
Wharton † . . . . Tim Barker
City Mgr., Joseph R. Pace
Wheeler . . . . Dan Sams
White Deer . . . . Robert Peets
City Supt., Anthony Scott
Whiteface . . . . James Solis
Whitehouse † . . . . James Wansley
City Mgr., Leslie Black
White Oak † . . . . Kyle Kutch
City Coord., Jimmy Purcell
Whitesboro . . . . David Blaylock
City Admin., Michael Marter
White Settlement † . Amber Munoz, Acting
City Mgr., Jeff James
Whitewright . . . . Tona Shiplet
Whitney . . . . Janice Sanders
Wichita Falls † . . . . Stephen Santellana
City Mgr., Darron Leiker
Wickett . . . . Xavier Estrada
Willis † . . . . Leonard Reed
City Mgr., Sheyi I. Ipaye
Willow Park . . . . Doyle Moss
City Admin., Bryan Grimes
Wills Point . . . . Mark Turner
City Admin., Pam Pearson
Wilmer . . . . Sheila Petta
City Admin., Rona Stringfellow
Wilson . . . . Randy Dunn
Wimberley . . . . Gina Fulkerson
City Admin., Timothy Patek
Windcrest † . . . . Dan Reese
City Mgr., Rafael Castillo
Windom . . . . Liena Fox
Windthorst . . . . Justin Keener
Winfield . . . . Debbie Cruitt
Wink . . . . Eric Hawkins
Winnsboro . . . . Andrea Newsom
City Admin., Makenzie Lyons
Winona . . . . Rachel Moreno
Winters . . . . Mark Burkhart
Wixon Valley . . . . James (Jim) Soefje
Wolfe City . . . . Jamie Moore
Wolfforth . . . . Charles Addington, II
City Mgr., Randy Criswell
Woodbranch Village . . . . Mike Tyson
Woodcreek . . . . Jeff Rasco
City Mgr., Kevin Rule
Woodloch . . . . Donald Nichols
Woodsboro . . . . Kay Roach
Woodson . . . . Bobby Mathiews
Woodville . . . . Amy Bythewood
City Admin., Mandy K. Risinger
Woodway † . . . . Amine Quorzal
City Mgr., Shawn Oubre
Wortham . . . . Pellie Goolsby
Wylie † . . . . Matthew Porter
City Mgr., Brent Parker

Y

Yantis . . . . John D. (Trey) Norris, III
Yoakum † . . . . Michael Brandt
City Mgr., Kevin Coleman
Yorktown . . . . Bill Baker
City Mgr., Michele Warwas

Z

Zavalla . . . . Brenda Cox

The Wood County Court House in Quitman was built in 1925 and became a Texas Historic Landmark in 2003. Photo by Larry D. Moore, CC by SA 3.0

County Courts

Each Texas county has one county court created by the Texas Constitution — a constitutional county court — which is presided over by the county judge (see table beginning on page 513 for a list of county judges). In more populated counties, the Legislature has created statutory county courts, including courts at law, probate courts, juvenile courts, domestic relations courts, and criminal courts at law. Following is a list of statutory county courts and judges, as reported in the Texas Judicial Directory as of July 2023. Other courts with jurisdiction in each county can be found on pages 472–473. Other county and district officials can be found on pages 513–524.

Anderson: Court at Law, Brendan Jeffrey Doran.

Angelina: Court at Law No. 1, Joe Lee Register; No. 2, Clyde M. Herrington.

Aransas: Court at Law, Richard Bianchi.

Atascosa: Court at Law, Bob Brendel

Austin: Court at Law, Daniel W. Leedy.

Bastrop: Court at Law, M. Benton Eskew.

Bell: Court at Law No. 1, Jeanne Parker; No. 2, John Michael Mischtian; No. 3, Rebecca DePew.

Bexar: Court at Law No. 1, Helen Petry Stowe; No. 2, Grace M. Uzomba; No. 3, David J. Rodriguez; No. 4, Alfredo Ximenez; No. 5, John Amos Longoria; No. 6, Wayne A. Christian; No. 7, Michael DeLeon; No. 8, Mary D. Roman; No. 9, Gloria Saldana; No. 10, J. Frank Davis; No. 11, Carl T. Stolhandske; No. 12, Yolanda Huff; No. 13, Rosie Gonzalez; No. 14, Carlo R. Key; No. 15, Melissa Vara. **Probate Court**, No. 1, Oscar Kazen; No. 2, Veronica Vasquez.

Bosque: Court at Law, Luke A. Giesecke.

Bowie: Court at Law, Craig L. Henry.

Brazoria: Court at Law No. 1 & **Probate Court**, Courtney T. Gilbert; No. 2 & **Probate Court**, Marc W. Holder; No. 3 & **Probate Court**, Jeremy E. Warren; No. 4 & **Probate Court**, Lori L. Rickert.

Brazos: Court at Law No. 1, Amanda S. Matzke; No. 2, James White Locke.

Brown: Court at Law, Sam Clifton Moss.

Burnet: Court at Law, Linda M. Bayless.

Caldwell: Court at Law, Barbara L. Molina.

Calhoun: Court at Law, Alex R. Hernandez.

Cameron: Court at Law No. 1, Arturo A. McDonald Jr.; No. 2, Laura Betancourt; No. 3, David Gonzales III; No. 4, Sheila Garcia Bence; No. 5, Estela Chavez-Vasquez.

Cass: Court at Law, Donald W. Dowd.

Cherokee: Court at Law, Janice C. Stone.

Collin: Court at Law No. 1, Corinne Ann Mason; No. 2, Barnett Walker; No. 3, Lance S. Baxter; No. 4, David D. Rippel; No. 5, Dan K. Wilson; No. 6, Jay A. Bender; No. 7, David Waddill. **Probate Court**, Weldon S. Copeland Jr.

Comal: Court at Law No. 1, Randy C. Gray; No. 2 Charles A. Stephens II; No. 3, Deborah Wigington.

Cooke: Court at Law, John H. Morris.

Coryell: Court at Law, John R. Lee.

Dallas: Court at Law No. 1, D'Metria Benson; No. 2, Melissa Bellan; No. 3, Sally L. Montgomery; No. 4, Paula Rosales; No. 5, Mark Greenberg. **Criminal Court** No. 1, Dan Patterson; No. 2, Julia Hayes; No. 3,

Audrey Moorhead; No. 4, Nancy Cutler Mulder; No. 5, Lisa Green; No. 6, Angela M. King; No. 7, Remeko Tranisha Edwards; No. 8, Carmen P. White; No. 9, Peggy Hoffman; No. 10, Etta J. Mullin; No. 11, Shequitta Kelly. **Probate Court** No. 1, Brenda Hull Thompson; No. 2, Ingrid Michelle Warren; No. 3, Margaret R. Jones-Johnson.

Denton: Court at Law No. 1 & **Juvenile Court**, Kimberly McCary; No. 2, Robert Ramirez. **Criminal Court at Law** No. 1, David W. Jahn; No. 2, Susan Piel; No. 3, Forrest Beadle; No. 4, Chance Oliver; No. 5, Charles (Coby) Waddill. **Probate Court**, Bonnie J. Robison.

Ector: Court at Law No. 1, Brooke Hendricks; No. 2, Christopher M. Clark.

Ellis: Court at Law No. 1, Jim Chapman; No. 2, A. Gene Calvert Jr.

El Paso: Court at Law No. 1, Ruth Reyes; No. 2, Julie Gonzalez; No. 3, Javier Alvarez; No. 4, Alejandro Gonzalez; No. 5, Jesus Rodriguez; No. 6, M. Sue Kurita; No. 7, Ruben Morales. **Criminal Court at Law** No. 1, Alma R. Trejo; No. 2, Robert S. Anchondo; No. 3, Carlos Carrasco; No. 4, Jessica Vazquez. **Probate Court** No. 1, Patricia B. Chew; No. 2, Eduardo Gamboa.

Erath: Court at Law, Blake B. Thompson.

Fannin: Court at Law, Charles Butler.

Fisher: Multicounty **Court at Law**, David C. Hall (also Mitchell and Nolan Counties)

Fort Bend: Court at Law No. 1, Christopher G. Morales; No. 2, Jeffery A. McMeans; No. 3, Juli Mathew; No. 4, Toni M. Wallace; No. 5, Teana V. Watson; No. 6, Sherman Hatton, Jr.

Galveston: Court at Law No. 1, John Grady; No. 2, Kerri M. Foley; No. 3, Jack Ewing. **Probate Court**, Kimberly A. Sullivan.

Gillespie: Court at Law, Christopher G. Nevins

Grayson: Court at Law No. 1, James C. Henderson; No. 2, Carol M. Siebman.

Gregg: Court at Law No. 1, R. Kent Phillips. No. 2, Vincent L. Dulweber.

Grimes: Court at Law, Tuck Moody McLain

Guadalupe: Court at Law No. 1, Bill Squires; No. 2, Kirsten Legore.

Harris: Civil **Court at Law** No. 1, Vacant; No. 2, Jim F. Kovach; No. 3, LaShawn A. Williams; No. 4, Lesley Briones. County **Criminal Court at Law** No. 1, Alex Salgado; No. 2, Ronnisha Bowman; No. 3, Erica Hughes; No. 4, Shannon Baldwin; No. 5, David M. Fleischer; No. 6, Kelley Andrews; No. 7, Andrew A. Wright; No. 8, Franklin Bynum; No. 9, Toria J. Finch; No. 10, Lee Harper Wilson; No. 11, Sedrick T. Walker II; No. 12, Genesis Draper; No. 13, Raul Rodriguez; No. 14, David L. Singer; No. 15, Tonya Jones; No. 16, Darrell William Jordan. **Probate Court** No. 1, Jerry W. Simoneaux; No. 2, Michael B. Newman; No. 3, Jason Cox; No. 4, James Horwitz.

Harrison: Court at Law, Joe M. Black IV.

Hays: Court at Law No. 1, Robert E. Updegrove; No. 2, Chris Johnson; No. 3, Dan O'Brien.

Henderson: Court at Law No 1, Scott S. Williams; No 2, Nancy Adams Perryman.

Hidalgo: Court at Law No. 1, Rodolfo Gonzalez; No. 2, Jaime Palacios; No. 4, Federico Garza Jr.; No. 5, Arnoldo Cantu; Jr. No. 6, Albert Garcia; No. 7, Sergio Valdez; No. 8, Omar Maldonado, No. 9, Patricia O'Caña-Oliveres; No. 10 Armando J. Marroquin. **Probate Court**, JoAnne Garcia.

Hill: Court at Law, Matthew S. Crain.

Hood: Court at Law, Vincent Messina.

Hopkins: Court at Law, Nicholas C. Harrison.

Houston: Court at Law, Sarah Tunnell Clark.

Hunt: Court at Law No. 1, Timothy S. Linden; No. 2, Joel D. Littlefield.

Jefferson: Court at Law No. 1, Gerald W. Eddins; No. 2, Terrence L. Holmes; No. 3, Clint M. Woods.

Jim Wells: Court at Law, Michael Ventura Garcia

Johnson: Court at Law No. 1, Robert B. Mayfield III; No. 2, F. Steven McClure.

Kaufman: Court at Law No. 1, Tracy Gray; No. 2, Bobby L. Rich, Jr.

Kerr: Court at Law, Susan F. Harris.

Kleberg: Court at Law, Jamie E. Carrillo.

Lamar: Court at Law, Bill H. Harris.

Liberty: Court at Law, Thomas A. Chambers; No. 2, Wesley N Hinch.

Lubbock: Court at Law No. 1, Mark J. Hocker; No. 2, Drue A. Farmer; No. 3, Benjamin Webb.

McLennan: Court at Law No. 1, Vikram Deivanayagam; No. 2, T. Bradley Cates.

Medina: Court at Law, Mark Cashion.

Midland: Court at Law No. 1, K. Kyle Peeler; No. 2, Marvin L. Moore.

Mitchell: Multicounty **Court at Law**, David C. Hall. (also Fisher and Nolan Counties)

Montgomery: Court at Law No. 1, Dennis D. Watson; No. 2, Claudia L. Laird; No. 3, Amy Tucker; No. 4, Mary Ann Turner; No. 5, Keith Mills Stewart.

Moore: Court at Law, Jerod Pingelton.

Nacogdoches: Court at Law, John A. (Jack) Sinz.

Navarro: Court at Law, Amanda D. Putman.

Nolan: Multicounty **Court at Law**, David C. Hall. (also Fisher and Mitchell Counties)

Nueces: Court at Law No. 1, Robert J. Vargas; No. 2, Lisa Elisabet Gonzales; No. 3, Deeanne Galvan; No. 4, Mark H. Woerner; No. 5, Timothy J. McCoy.

Orange: Court at Law No. 1, Mandy White-Rogers; No 2, Troy Johnson.

Panola: Court at Law, Terry D. Bailey.

Parker: Court at Law No. 1, Jerry D. Buckner; No. 2, Lynn Marie Johnson.

Polk: Court at Law, Tom Brown.

Potter: Court at Law No. 1, Walt Weaver; No. 2, Matt Hand.

Randall: Court at Law No. 1, James W. Anderson. No. 2, Matthew Martindale.

Reeves: Court at Law, Scott W. Johnson.

Rockwall: Court at Law No. 1, Brian Williams; No. 2 Stephani Woodward.

Rusk: Court at Law, Chad W. Dean.

San Patricio: Court at Law, M. Elizabeth Welborn.

Smith: Court at Law No. 1, Jason A. Ellis; No. 2, Taylor Heaton. No. 3, Floyd Thomas Getz.

Starr: Court at Law, Orlando Rodriguez.

Tarrant: Court at Law No. 1, Donald R. Pierson; No. 2, Jennifer Rymell; No. 3, Mike Hrabal. **Criminal Court at Law** No. 1, David Cook; No. 2, Carey F. Walker; No. 3, Bob McCoy; No. 4, Deborah L. Nekhom; No. 5, Jamie Cummings; No. 6, Molly S. Jones; No. 7, Cheril S. Hardy; No. 8, Charles L. Vanover; No. 9, Brent A. Carr; No. 10, Phil A. Sorrels. **Probate Court** No. 1, Christopher W. Ponder; No. 2, Brooke Ulrickson Allen.

Taylor: Court at Law No. 1, Robert Harper; No. 2, Harriett L. Haag.

Tom Green: Court at Law No. 1, Charles (Ben) Nolen; No. 2, Penny Anne Roberts.

Travis: Court at Law No. 1, J. Todd T. Wong; No. 2, Eric M. Shepperd; No. 3, John H. Lipscombe; No. 4, Dimple Malhotra; No. 5, Nancy Hohengarten; No. 6, Brandy Mueller; No. 7, Elisabeth A. Earle; No. 8, Carlos H. Barrera; No. 9, Kim Williams. **Probate Court**, Guy Herman.

Val Verde: Court at Law, Sergio J. Gonzalez.

Van Zandt: Court at Law, Joshua Wintters.

Victoria: Court at Law No. 1, Travis H. Ernst; No. 2, Daniel F. Gilliam.

Walker: Court at Law, Tracy M. Sorensen.

Waller: Court at Law, Carol A. Chaney.

Washington: Court at Law, Eric Thomas Berg.

Webb: Court at Law No. 1, Hugo D. Martinez; No. 2, Victor G. Villarreal.

Wichita: Court at Law No. 1, Gary Wayne Butler; No. 2, Greg King.

Williamson: Court at Law No. 1, Brandy Hallford; No. 2, Laura B. Barker; No. 3, Doug Arnold; No. 4, John B. McMaster.

Wise: Court at Law No. 1, Greg Lowery; No. 2, Stephen J. Wren. ☆

Regional Councils of Government

Source: Texas Association of Regional Councils; www.txregionalcouncil.org/

The concept of regional planning and cooperation, fostered by enabling legislation in 1965, has spread across Texas since organization of the **North Central Texas Council of Governments** in 1966.

Regional councils are voluntary associations of local governments that deal with problems and planning needs that cross the boundaries of individual local governments or that require regional attention.

These concerns include criminal justice, emergency communications, job-training programs, solid-waste management, transportation, and water-quality management. The councils make recommendations to member governments and may assist in implementing the plans. Financing is provided by local, state, and federal governments.

The **Texas Association of Regional Councils** is at 701 Brazos, Ste. 780, Austin 78701; (512) 478-4715. Following is a list of the 24 regional councils, member counties, executive director, and contact information:

1. **Panhandle Regional Planning Commission** (Armstrong, Briscoe, Carson, Castro, Childress, Collingsworth, Dallam, Deaf Smith, Donley, Gray, Hall, Hansford, Hartley, Hemphill, Hutchinson, Lipscomb, Moore, Ochiltree, Oldham, Parmer, Potter, Randall, Roberts, Sherman, Swisher, and Wheeler) Dustin Meyer, P.O. Box 9257, Amarillo 79105-9257; (806) 372-3381; www.theprpc.org.
2. **South Plains Association of Governments** (Bailey, Cochran, Crosby, Dickens, Floyd, Garza, Hale, Hockley, King, Lamb, Lubbock, Lynn, Motley, Terry, and Yoakum) Tim Pierce, P.O. Box 3730, Lubbock 79452-3730; (806) 762-8721; www.spag.org.
3. **Nortex Regional Planning Commission** (Archer, Baylor, Clay, Cottle, Foard, Hardeman, Jack, Montague, Wichita, Wilbarger, and Young) Dennis Wilde, P.O. Box 5144, Wichita Falls 76307-5144; (940) 322–5281; www.nortexrpc.org.
4. **North Central Texas Council of Governments** (Collin, Dallas, Denton, Ellis, Erath, Hood, Hunt, Johnson, Kaufman, Navarro, Palo Pinto, Parker, Rockwall, Somervell, Tarrant, and Wise) R. Michael Eastland, P.O. Box 5888, Arlington 76005-5888; (817) 640–3300; www.nctcog.org.
5. **Ark-Tex Council of Governments** (Bowie, Cass, Delta, Franklin, Hopkins, Lamar, Morris, Red River, and Titus) Chris Brown, 4808 Elizabeth St., Texarkana, Texas 75503; (903) 832–8636; www.atcog.org.
6. **East Texas Council of Governments** (Anderson, Camp, Cherokee, Gregg, Harrison, Henderson, Marion, Panola, Rains, Rusk, Smith, Upshur, Van Zandt, and Wood) David Cleveland, 3800 Stone Rd., Kilgore 75662-6297; (903) 218–6400; www.etcog.org.
7. **West Central Texas Council of Governments** (Brown, Callahan, Coleman, Comanche, Eastland, Fisher, Haskell, Jones, Kent, Knox, Mitchell, Nolan, Runnels, Scurry, Shackelford, Stephens, Stonewall, Taylor, and Throckmorton) Joe Rogers, 3702 Loop 322, Abilene 79602-7300; (325) 672–8544; www.wctcog.org.
8. **Rio Grande Council of Governments** (Brewster, Culberson, El Paso, Hudspeth, Jeff Davis, Presidio, and Doña Ana County, N.M.) Annette Gutierrez, 8037 Lockheed Dr., Ste. 100, El Paso 79925; (915) 533–0998; www.riocog.org.
9. **Permian Basin Regional Planning Commission** (Andrews, Borden, Crane, Dawson, Ector, Gaines, Glasscock, Howard, Loving, Martin, Midland, Pecos, Reeves, Terrell, Upton, Ward, and Winkler) Virginia Belew, PO Box 60660, Midland 79711-0660; (432) 563–1061; www.pbrpc.org.

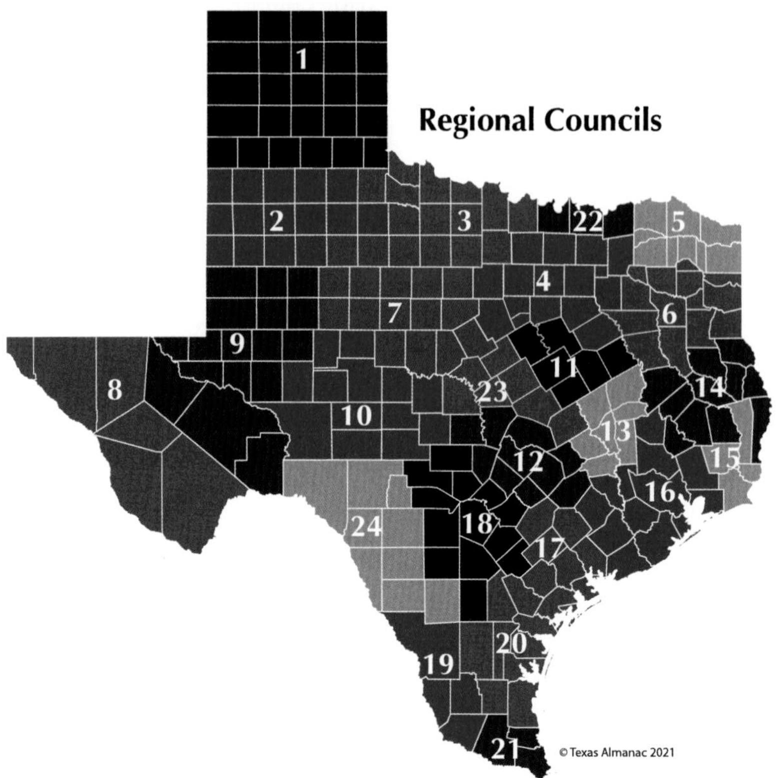

10. **Concho Valley Council of Governments** (Coke, Concho, Crockett, Irion, Kimble, Mason, McCulloch, Menard, Reagan, Schleicher, Sterling, Sutton, and Tom Green) John Austin Stokes, 2801 W. Loop 206, Ste. A, San Angelo 76904; (325) 944–9666; www.cvcog.org.

11. **Heart of Texas Council of Governments** (Bosque, Falls, Freestone, Hill, Limestone, and McLennan) Russell Devorsky, 1514 S. New Road, Waco 76711; (254) 292–1800; www.hotcog.org.

12. **Capital Area Council of Governments** (Bastrop, Blanco, Burnet, Caldwell, Fayette, Hays, Lee, Llano, Travis, and Williamson) Betty Voights, 6800 Burleson Rd., Bldg. 310, Ste. 165, Austin 78744; (512) 916–6018; www.capcog.org.

13. **Brazos Valley Council of Governments** (Brazos, Burleson, Grimes, Leon, Madison, Robertson, and Washington) Michael Parks, P.O. Drawer 4128, Bryan 77805–4128; (979) 595–2800; www.bvcog.org.

14. **Deep East Texas Council of Governments** (Angelina, Houston, Nacogdoches, Newton, Polk, Sabine, San Augustine, San Jacinto, Shelby, Trinity, and Tyler) Lonnie Hunt, 1405 Kurth Dr., Lufkin, 75904; (963) 634–2247; www.detcog.gov.

15. **South East Texas Regional Planning Commission** (Hardin, Jasper, Jefferson, and Orange) Shanna Burke, 2210 Eastex Fwy., Beaumont 77703; (409) 899–8444; www.setrpc.org.

16. **Houston-Galveston Area Council** (Austin, Brazoria, Chambers, Colorado, Fort Bend, Galveston, Harris, Liberty, Matagorda, Montgomery, Walker, Waller, and Wharton) Chuck Wemple, 3555 Timmons Ln., Ste. 120, Houston 77227–2777; (713) 993–4514; www.h-gac.com.

17. **Golden Crescent Regional Planning Commission** (Calhoun, DeWitt, Goliad, Gonzales, Jackson, Lavaca, and Victoria) Michael Ada, 1908 N. Laurent, Ste. 600, Victoria 77901; (361) 578–1587; www.gcrpc.org.

18. **Alamo Area Council of Governments** (Atascosa, Bandera, Bexar, Comal, Frio, Gillespie, Guadalupe, Karnes, Kendall, Kerr, McMullen, Medina, and Wilson) Diane Rath, 2700 NE Loop 410, Ste. 101, San Antonio 78217; (210) 362–5200; www.aacog.com.

19. **South Texas Development Council** (Jim Hogg, Starr, Webb, and Zapata) Juan Rodriguez, 1002 Dicky Lane, Laredo 78044–2187; (956) 722–3995; www.stdc.cog.tx.us.

20. **Coastal Bend Council of Governments** (Aransas, Bee, Brooks, Duval, Jim Wells, Kenedy, Kleberg, Live Oak, Nueces, Refugio, and San Patricio) John P. Buckner, 2910 Leopard St, Corpus Christi 78408; (361) 883–5743; coastalbendcog.org.

21. **Lower Rio Grande Valley Development Council** (Cameron, Hidalgo, and Willacy) Manny Cruz, 301 W. Railroad St., Weslaco 78596; (956) 682–3481; www.lrgvdc.org.

22. **Texoma Council of Governments** (Cooke, Fannin, and Grayson) Eric Bridges, 1117 Gallagher Dr., Ste. 470, Sherman 75090; (903) 813–3514; www.tcog.com.

23. **Central Texas Council of Governments** (Bell, Coryell, Hamilton, Lampasas, Milam, Mills, and San Saba) Jim Reed, P.O. Box 729, Belton 76513–0729; (254) 770–2210; www.ctcog.org.

24. **Middle Rio Grande Development Council** (Dimmit, Edwards, Kinney, La Salle, Maverick, Real, Uvalde, Val Verde, and Zavala) Nick Gallegos, 307 W. Nopal, Carrizo Springs 78834; (830) 876–3533; www.mrgdc.org. ☆

County Tax Appraisers

Source: https://comptroller.texas.gov/taxes/property-tax/county-directory

County tax appraisers can answer questions about property values, tax exemptions, protests and appeals, and appraisal methodology. The following list includes the mailing address and phone number for each appraiser and is current to July 2023.

Anderson: Adrienne Polk, P.O. Box 279, Palestine 75802

Andrews: Susan Brewer, 600 N. Main St., Andrews 79714

Angelina: Tim Chambers, P.O. Box 2357, Lufkin 75902

Aransas: Mike Soto, 11 Hwy 35 N., Rockport 78382

Archer: Kimbra York, P.O. Box 1141, Archer City 76351

Armstrong: Marissa Clement, P.O. Box 149, Claude 79019

Atascosa: Michelle L. Berdeaux, P.O. Box 600, Pleasanton 78065

Austin: Greg Cook, 906 E. Amelia St., Bellville 77418

Bailey: Jessica Rivera, 302 Main St., Muleshoe 79347

Bandera: Dustin Vernor, P.O. Box 1119, Bandera 78003

Bastrop: Faun Cullens, P.O. Box 578, Bastrop 78602

Baylor: Mitzi Welch, 211 N. Washington St., Seymour 76380

Bee: Richard Petree, 401 N. Washington St., Beeville 78102

Bell: Billy White, P.O. Box 390, Belton 76513

Bexar: Michael Amezquita, P.O. Box 830248, San Antonio 78283

Blanco: Candice Fry, P.O. Box 338, Johnson City 78636

Borden: Tracy Cooley, P.O. Box 298, Gail 79738

Bosque: Christopher Moser, P.O. Box 393, Meridian 76665

Bowie: Mike Brower, P.O. Box 6527, Texarkana 75505

Brazoria: Marcel Pierel III, 500 N. Chenango St., Angleton 77515

Brazos: Dana Horton, 4051 Pendleton Dr., Bryan 77802

Brewster: Denise Flores, 107 W. Avenue E, Alpine 79830

Briscoe: Theresa Clinton, P.O. Box 728, Silverton 79257

Brooks: Daniel Garcia, P.O. Drawer A, Falfurrias 78355

Brown: Brett McKibben, 403 Fisk Ave., Brownwood 76801

Burleson: Tonya Barnes, P.O. Box 1000, Caldwell 77836

Burnet: Stan Hemphill, P.O. Box 908, Burnet 78611

Caldwell: Shanna Ramzinski, P.O. Box 900, Lockhart 78644

Calhoun: Jesse Hubbell, P.O. Box 49, Port Lavaca 77979

Callahan: Mathew Walker, 302 Chestnut St., Baird 79504

Cameron: Richard Molina, P.O. Box 1010, San Benito 78586

Camp: Jan Tinsley, 143 Quitman St., Pittsburg 75686

Carson: Shannon Hensley, P.O. Box 970, Panhandle 79068

Cass: Lacy Hicks, 502 N. Main St., Linden 75563

Castro: Steven Cole Pierce, 204 S.E. 3rd St., Dimmitt 79027

Chambers: Mitchell McCullough, P.O. Box 1520, Anahuac 77514

Cherokee: J.L. Flowers, P.O. Box 494, Rusk 75785

Childress: Twila Butler, 1710 Ave. F NW, Childress 79201

Clay: Lisa Murphy, P.O. Box 108, Henrietta 76365

Cochran: David Greener, 109 S.E. First St., Morton 79346

Coke: Luke Robbins, P.O. Box 2, Robert Lee 76945

Coleman: Eva Bush, P.O. Box 914, Coleman 76834

Collin: Marty Wright, 250 W. Eldorado Pkwy., McKinney 75069

Collingsworth: Brittany Warren, 800 West Ave., Box 9, Wellington, 79095

Colorado: Mark Price, P.O. Box 10, Columbus 78934

Comal: Jeffrey Booker, 900 S. Seguin Ave., New Braunfels 78130

Comanche: JoAnn Hohertz, 8 Huett Cir., Comanche 76442

Concho: D'Andra Warlick, P.O. Box 68, Paint Rock 76866

Cooke: Doug Smithson, 201 N. Dixon St., Gainesville 76240

Coryell: Mitch Fast, 705 E. Main St., Gatesville 76528

Cottle: Nakia Hargrave, P.O. Box 459, Paducah 79248

Crane: Byron Bitner, 511 W. 8th St., Crane 79731

Crockett: Janet M. Thompson, P.O. Box 1569, Ozona 76943

Crosby: Crystal Hill, P.O. Box 505, Crosbyton 79322

Culberson: Maricel G. Gonzalez, P.O. Box 550, Van Horn 79855

Dallam: Holly McCauley, P.O. Box 579, Dalhart 79022

Dallas: Kenneth Nolan, 2949 N. Stemmons Fwy., Dallas 75247

Dawson: Norma J. Brock, P.O. Box 797, Lamesa 79331

Deaf Smith: Danny Jones, P.O. Box 2298, Hereford 79045

Delta: Kim Gregory, P.O. Box 47, Cooper 75432

Denton: Don Spencer, P.O. Box 2816, Denton 76202

DeWitt: Denise Moore, 103 E. Bailey St., Cuero 77954

Dickens: Vonda Brendle, P.O. Box 180, Dickens 79229

Dimmit: Norma Carrillo, 203 W. Houston St., Carrizo Springs 78834

Donley: Paula Lowrie, P.O. Box 1220, Clarendon 79226

Duval: Raul Garcia, P.O. Box 809, San Diego 78384

Eastland: Randy Clark, P.O. Box 914, Eastland 76448

Ector: Anita Campbell, 1301 E. 8th St., Odessa 79761

Edwards: Renn Rudasill Riley, P.O. Box 858, Rocksprings 78880

Ellis: Kathy Rodrigue, P.O. Box 878, Waxahachie 75165

El Paso: Dinah Kilgore, 5801 Trowbridge Dr., El Paso 79925

Erath: Jerry D. Lee, 1195 W. South Loop, Stephenville 76401

Falls: Martha Davis, 403 Craik St., Marlin 76661

Fannin: Tylene Gamble, 831 W. State Hwy. 56, Bonham 75418

Fayette: Richard Moring, P.O. Box 836, La Grange 78945

Fisher: Holli Bufkin, P.O. Box 516, Roby 79543

Floyd: Jim Finley, P.O. Box 249, Floydada 79235

Foard: Holly Morton, P.O. Box 419, Crowell 79227

Fort Bend: Jordan Wise, 2801 B.F. Terry Blvd., Rosenberg 77471

Franklin: Russell McCurdy, P.O. Box 720, Mount Vernon 75457

Freestone: Don Awalt, 218 N. Mount St., Fairfield 75840

Frio: Edward Garza, P.O. Box 1129, Pearsall 78061

Gaines: Gayla Harridge, P.O. Box 490, Seminole 79360

Galveston: Krystal McKinney, 9850 Emmett F. Lowry Expwy., Texas City 77591

Garza: Allisha Belongia, P.O. Drawer F, Post 79356

Gillespie: Scott Fair, 1159 S. Milam St., Fredericksburg 78624

Glasscock: Scott Smetana, P.O. Box 155, Garden City 79739

Goliad: Robert Ckodre, P.O. Box 34, Goliad 77963

Gonzales: John Liford, P.O. Box 867, Gonzales 78629

Gray: Tyson Paronto, P.O. Box 836, Pampa 79066

Grayson: Shawn D. Coker, 515 N. Travis St., Sherman 75090

Gregg: Mark Cormier, 4367 W. Loop 281, Longview 75604

Grimes: Mark Boehnke, P.O. Box 489, Anderson 77830

Guadalupe: Peter Snaddon, 3000 N. Austin St., Seguin 78155

Hale: Andrew Moritz, P.O. Box 29, Plainview 79073

Hall: Gina Chavira, 512 W. Main St., Memphis 79245

Hamilton: Codi Ann McCarn, 119 E. Henry St., Hamilton 76531

Hansford: Brandi Thompson, 709 W. 7th Ave., Spearman 79081

Hardeman: Jordan Light, P.O. Box 388, Quanah 79252

Hardin: Angela Waldrep, P.O. Box 670, Kountze 77625

Harris: Roland Altinger, P.O. Box 920975, Houston 77292

Harrison: Robert Lisman, P.O. Box 818, Marshall 75671

Hartley: Juan Salazar, P.O. Box 405, Hartley 79044

Haskell: Jamie Ferguson, P.O. Box 467, Haskell 79521

Hays: Laura Raven, 21001 N. IH-35, Kyle 78640

Hemphill: Pam Scates, 223 Main St., Canadian 79014

Henderson: Bill Jackson, P.O. Box 430, Athens 75751

Hidalgo: Rolando Garza, P.O. Box 208, Edinburg 78540

Hill: Mike McKibben, P.O. Box 416, Hillsboro 76645

Hockley: Lorie Marquez, P.O. Box 1090, Levelland 79336

Hood: Richard Petree, P.O. Box 819, Granbury 76048

Hopkins: Cathy N. Singleton, P.O. Box 753, Sulphur Springs 75482

Houston: Carey Minter, P.O. Box 112, Crockett 75835

Howard: Richard Petree, P.O. Drawer 1151, Big Spring 79720

Hudspeth: Adolfo Ramirez, P.O. Box 429, Sierra Blanca 79851

Hunt: Brent South, P.O. Box 1339, Greenville 75403

Hutchinson: Joe Raper, P.O. Box 5065, Borger 79008

Irion: Byron Bitner, P.O. Box 980, Mertzon 76941

Jack: Chase Lewis, P.O. Box 958, Jacksboro 76458

Jackson: Damon D. Moore, 404 N. Allen St., Edna 77957

Jasper: Lori Barnett, 137 N. Main St., Jasper 75951

Jeff Davis: Gary Zeitler, P.O. Box 373, Fort Davis 79734

Jefferson: Angela Bellard, P.O. Box 21337, Beaumont 77720

Jim Hogg: Jorge Arellano, P.O. Box 459, Hebbronville 78361

Jim Wells: G. Carlos Rodriguez Jr., P.O. Box 607, Alice 78333

Johnson: Jim Hudspeth, 109 N. Main St., Cleburne 76033

Jones: Kim McLemore, P.O. Box 348, Anson 79501

Karnes: Brian Stahl, 915 S. Panna Maria Ave., Karnes City 78118

Kaufman: Sarah Curtis, P.O. Box 819, Kaufman 75142

Kendall: Nelia McNeal, 118 Market Ave., Boerne 78006

Kenedy: Thomas G. Denney, P.O. Box 39, Sarita 78385

Kent: Cindy Watson, P.O. Box 68, Jayton 79528

Kerr: Sharon Constantinides, P.O. Box 294387, Kerrville 78029

Kimble: Kenda McPherson, P.O. Box 307, Junction 76849

King: Kala Briggs, P.O. Box 117, Guthrie 79236

Kinney: Todd Tate, P.O. Box 1377, Brackettville 78832

Kleberg: Tina Flores, P.O. Box 1027, Kingsville 78363

Knox: Mitzi Welch, P.O. Box 47, Benjamin 79505

Lamar: Stephanie Lee, P.O. Box 400, Paris 75461

Lamb: Lesa Kloiber, P.O. Box 950, Littlefield 79339

Lampasas: Susan Jones, P.O. Box 175, Lampasas 76550

La Salle: Bobby Peregoy, P.O. Box 1530, Cotulla 78014

Lavaca: Pamela Lathrop, P.O. Box 386, Hallettsville 77964

Lee: James Orr, 898 E. Richmond St., Giddings 78942

Leon: Jeff Beshears, P.O. Box 536, Centerville 75833

Liberty: Lana McCarty, P.O. Box 10016, Liberty 77575

Limestone: Terri Lenamon, 303 S. Waco St., Groesbeck 76642

Lipscomb: Angela Peil, P.O. Box 128, Darrouzett 79024

Live Oak: Irene Gonzales, P.O. Box 2370, George West 78022

Llano: Scott Dudley, 103 E. Sandstone St., Llano 78643

Loving: Sherlene Burrows, P.O. Box 352, Mentone 79754

Lubbock: Tim Radloff, P.O. Box 10542, Lubbock 79408

Lynn: Ryan Nichols, P.O. Box 789, Tahoka 79373

Madison: Matt Newton, P.O. Box 1328, Madisonville 77864

Marion: Anna Lummus, 801 N. Tuttle St., Jefferson 75657

Martin: Marsha Graves, P.O. Box 1349, Stanton 79782

Mason: Christel B. Lively, P.O. Box 1119, Mason 76856

Matagorda: Vince Maloney, 2225 Ave. G, Bay City 77414

Maverick: Raul Fuentes, P.O. Box 2628, Eagle Pass 78853

McCulloch: Zane Brandenberger, 306 W. Lockhart St., Brady 76825

McLennan: Joe Don Bobbitt, 315 S. 26th St., Waco 76710

McMullen: Blaine Patterson, P.O. Box 338, Tilden 78072

Medina: Johnette Dixon, 1410 Ave. K, Hondo 78861

Menard: Kayla Wagner, P.O. Box 1008, Menard 76859

Midland: Jerry Bundick, P.O. Box 908002, Midland 79703

Milam: Leslie Sootoo, P.O. Box 769, Cameron 76520

Mills: Richard Petree, P.O. Box 565, Goldthwaite 76844

Mitchell: John Stewart, 2112 Hickory St., Colorado City 79512

Montague: Kim Haralson, P.O. Box 121, Montague 76251

Montgomery: Janet Jennings-Doyle, P.O. Box 2233, Conroe 77305

Moore: Samantha Trujillo, P.O. Box 717, Dumas 79029

Morris: Summer Golden, P.O. Box 563, Daingerfield 75638

Motley: Jim Finley, P.O. Box 249, Floydada 79235

Nacogdoches: Jason Malott, 216 W. Hospital St., Nacogdoches 75961

Navarro: Bud Black, P.O. Box 3118, Corsicana 75110

Newton: Margie L. Herrin, 109 Court St., Newton 75966

Nolan: Stephanie Bock, P.O. Box 1256, Sweetwater 79556

Nueces: Ramiro Canales, 201 N. Chaparral St., Corpus Christi 78401

Ochiltree: Julia Mendez, 825 S. Main St., Perryton 79070

Oldham: Leann Voyles, P.O. Box 310, Vega 79092

Orange: Scott Overton, P.O. Box 457, Orange 77631

Palo Pinto: Donna Epperson, P.O. Box 250, Palo Pinto 76484

Panola: Michael Douglas McPhail, 1736 Ballpark Dr., Carthage 75633

Parker: Rick Armstrong, 1108 Santa Fe Dr., Weatherford 76086

Parmer: Jill Timms, P.O. Box 56, Bovina 79009

Pecos: Sam Calderon III, P.O. Box 237, Fort Stockton 79735

Polk: Chad Hill, 114 Matthews St., Livingston 77351

Potter: Jeff Dagley, P.O. Box 7190, Amarillo 79110

Presidio: Cynthia Ramirez, P.O. Box 879, Marfa 79843

Rains: Sherri McCall, P.O. Box 70, Emory 75440

Randall: Jeff Dagley, P.O. Box 7190, Amarillo 79110

Reagan: Jacquelyn Botello, P.O. Box 8, Big Lake 76932

Real: Juan Saucedo, P.O. Box 158, Leakey 78873

Red River: Brandi Clark, P.O. Box 461, Clarksville 75426

Reeves: Shawn Davis, P.O. Box 1229, Pecos 79772

Refugio: Phillip Gonzales, P.O. Box 156, Refugio 78377

Roberts: Hether Williams, P.O. Box 458, Miami 79059

Robertson: Nancy Commander, P.O. Box 998, Franklin 77856

Rockwall: Kevin Passons, 841 Justin Rd., Rockwall 75087

Runnels: PaulScott Randolph, P.O. Box 524, Ballinger 76821

Rusk: Weldon Cook, P.O. Box 7, Henderson 75652

Sabine: Tina Ford, P.O. Box 137, Hemphill 75948

San Augustine: Evelyn Watts, 122 N. Harrison St., San Augustine 75972

San Jacinto: Troy Carlson, P.O. Box 1170, Coldspring 77331

San Patricio: Robert Cenci, P.O. Box 938, Sinton 78387

San Saba: Patricia Turner, 601 W. Wallace St., San Saba 76877

Schleicher: Greg Kelly, P.O. Box 936, Eldorado 76936

Scurry: Jackie Martin, 2612 College Ave., Snyder 79549

Shackelford: Clayton Snyder, P.O. Box 2247, Albany 76430

Shelby: Robert N. Pigg, 724 Shelbyville St., Center 75935

Sherman: Courtney Copley, P.O. Box 239, Stratford 79084

Smith: Carol Dixon, 245 South S.E. Loop 323, Tyler 75702

Somervell: Wes Rollen, 112 Allen Dr., Glen Rose 76043

Starr: Rosalva Guerra, 100 N. FM 3167, Rio Grande City 78582

Stephens: Gary Zeitler, P.O. Box 351, Breckenridge 76424

Sterling: Priscilla Glass, P.O. Box 28, Sterling City 76951

Stonewall: Debra Smith, P.O. Box 308, Aspermont 79502

Sutton: Mary Bustamante, 300 E. Oak St., Sonora 76950

Swisher: Andrew Moritz, P.O. Box 8, Tulia 79088

Tarrant: Jeff Law, 2500 Handley-Ederville Rd., Fort Worth 76118

Taylor: Gary Earnest, P.O. Box 1800, Abilene 79604

Terrell: Blain Chriesman, P.O. Box 747, Sanderson 79848

Terry: Eddie Olivas, P.O. Box 426, Brownfield 79316

Throckmorton: DeDe Smith, P.O. Box 788, Throckmorton 76483

Titus: Shirley Dickerson, P.O. Box 528, Mount Pleasant 75456

Tom Green: Tyler Johnson, 2302 Pulliam St., San Angelo 76905

Travis: Marya Crigler, P.O. Box 149012, Austin 78714

Trinity: Gary Gallant, P.O. Box 950, Groveton 75845

Tyler: David Luther, P.O. Drawer 9, Woodville 75979

Upshur: Amanda Thibodeaux, 105 Diamond Loch, Gilmer 75644

Upton: Linda Zarate, P.O. Box 1110, McCamey 79752

Uvalde: Roberto Valdez, 209 N. High St., Uvalde 78801

Val Verde: Jacqueline Casanova, 417 W. Cantu Rd., Del Rio 78840

Van Zandt: Emily Reeves, P.O. Box 926, Canton 75103

Victoria: Keri Woodcliffe, 2805 N. Navarro St., Victoria 77901

Walker: Stacey Poteete, P.O. Box 1798, Huntsville 77342

Waller: Becky Gurrola, P.O. Box 887, Hempstead 77445

Ward: Norma Valdez, P.O. Box 905, Monahans 79756

Washington: Dyann White, P.O. Box 681, Brenham 77834

Webb: Bobby Peregoy, 3302 Clark Blvd., Laredo 78043

Wharton: Brian Niemeier, 308 E. Milam, Wharton 77488

Wheeler: Kimberly Morgan, P.O. Box 1200, Wheeler 79096

Wichita: Lisa Stephens-Musick, P.O. Box 5172, Wichita Falls 76307

Wilbarger: Sandy Burkett, P.O. Box 1519, Vernon 76385

Willacy: Agustin Lopez, 688 FM 3168, Raymondville 78580

Williamson: Alvin Lankford, 625 FM 1460, Georgetown 78626

Wilson: Jennifer Coldewey, 1611 Railroad St., Floresville 78114

Winkler: Rhonda Shaw, P.O. Box 1219, Kermit 79745

Wise: Deidra Deaton, 400 E. Business 380, Decatur 76234

Wood: Tracy Nichols, P.O. Box 1706, Quitman 75783

Yoakum: Brooks Barrett, P.O. Box 748, Plains 79355

Young: Jesse Blackmon, P.O. Box 337, Graham 76450

Zapata: Amada Gonzalez, 200 E. 7th Ave., Zapata 78076

Zavala: Yolanda Lavenant, 323 W. Zavala, Crystal City 78839 ☆

Wet-Dry Counties

Source: Texas Alcoholic Beverage Commission, www.tabc.texas.gov

Although the laws regulating the alcoholic beverage industry are consistent statewide, the Alcoholic Beverage Code allows for local-option elections to determine the types of alcoholic beverages that may be sold and how they can be sold.

Elections can be held by counties, cities, or individual justice of the peace precincts. In the time since our last edition went to press, four counties have moved from Part Wet to Wet: Crane, Kerr, Mason, and Wilson.

As of June 2023, there were 59 completely wet counties in Texas and 5 completely dry counties.

Over time, Texas has been getting "wetter." In 2003, there were 35 completely wet counties and 51 completely dry. In 1995, there were 53 dry counties, and in 1986, there were 62 dry counties. The list below reflects the wet, part wet, and dry coding on the map.

Counties where all alcoholic beverage sales are legal everywhere (59): Aransas, Austin, Bexar, Brazos, Brewster, Brooks, Burnet, Cameron, Childress, Clay, Collingsworth, Colorado, Comal, Cottle, Crane, Crosby, Culberson, Dimmit, Donley, Duval, Ector, El Paso, Fayette, Fisher, Fort Bend, Goliad, Gonzales, Guadalupe, Hidalgo, Hudspeth, Jim Hogg, Kendall, Kenedy, Kerr, Kinney, Kleberg, La Salle, Mason, Midland, Mitchell, Nolan, Nueces, Ochiltree, Presidio, San Saba, Scurry, Sherman, Starr, Sutton, Val Verde, Victoria, Waller, Washington, Webb, Wharton, Wilbarger, Wilson, Zapata, Zavala.

Counties that are partially wet (191): Anderson, Andrews, Angelina, Archer, Armstrong, Atascosa, Bailey, Bandera, Bastrop, Baylor, Bee, Bell, Blanco, Bosque, Bowie, Brazoria, Briscoe, Brown, Burleson, Caldwell, Calhoun, Callahan, Camp, Carson, Cass, Castro, Chambers, Cherokee, Cochran, Coke, Coleman, Collin, Comanche, Concho, Cooke, Coryell, Crockett, Dallam, Dallas, Dawson, Deaf Smith, Delta, Denton, DeWitt, Dickens, Eastland, Edwards, Ellis, Erath, Falls, Fannin, Floyd, Foard, Franklin, Freestone, Frio, Gaines, Galveston, Garza, Gillespie, Glasscock, Gray, Grayson, Gregg, Grimes, Hale, Hall, Hamilton, Hansford, Hardeman, Hardin, Harris, Harrison, Hartley, Haskell, Hays, Hemphill, Henderson, Hill, Hockley, Hood, Hopkins, Houston, Howard, Hunt, Hutchinson, Irion, Jack, Jackson, Jasper, Jeff Davis, Jefferson, Jim Wells, Johnson, Jones, Karnes, Kaufman, Kimble, King, Knox, Lamar, Lamb, Lampasas, Lavaca, Lee, Leon, Liberty, Limestone, Lipscomb, Live Oak, Llano, Loving, Lubbock, Lynn, Madison, Marion, Martin, Matagorda, Maverick, McCulloch, McLennan, McMullen, Medina, Menard, Milam, Mills, Montague, Montgomery, Moore, Morris, Motley, Nacogdoches, Navarro, Newton, Oldham, Orange, Palo Pinto, Panola, Parker, Parmer, Pecos, Polk, Potter, Rains, Randall, Reagan, Real, Red River, Reeves, Refugio, Robertson, Rockwall, Runnels, Rusk, Sabine, San Augustine, San Jacinto, San Patricio, Schleicher, Shackelford, Shelby, Smith, Somervell, Stephens, Sterling, Stonewall, Swisher, Tarrant, Taylor, Terrell, Terry, Titus, Tom Green, Travis, Trinity, Tyler, Upshur, Upton, Uvalde, Van Zandt, Walker, Ward, Wheeler, Wichita, Willacy, Williamson, Winkler, Wise, Wood, Yoakum, Young.

Counties where no sales of alcoholic beverages are legal anywhere (4): Borden, Kent, Roberts, Throckmorton. ☆

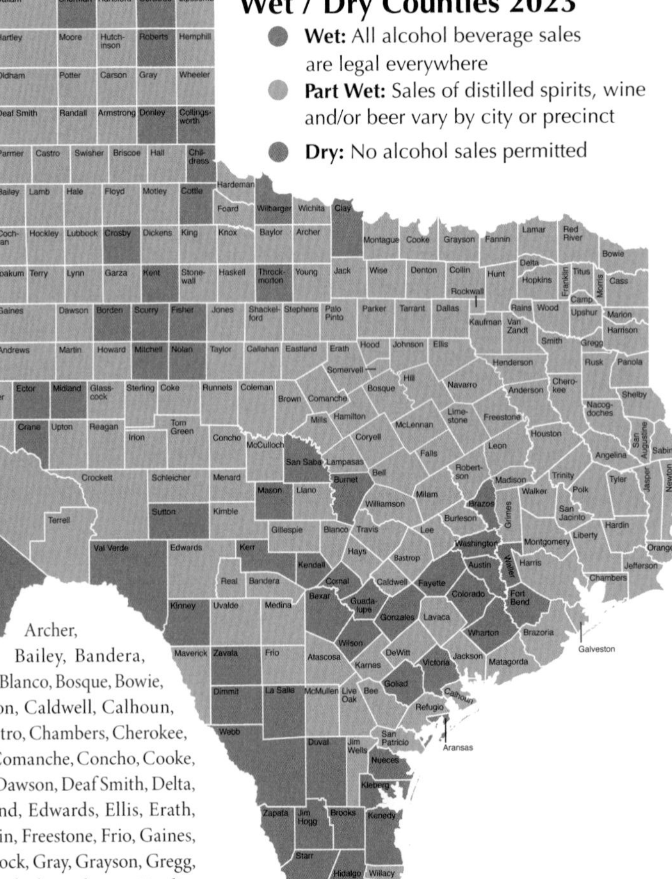

Texas County and District Officials – Table No. 1

County Seats, County Judges, County Clerks, County Attorneys, County Treasurers, Tax Assessors–Collectors, and Sheriffs

See Table No. 2 on **pages 519–524** for District Clerks, District Attorneys, and County Commissioners. Judges in county courts at law, as well as probate courts, juvenile/domestic relations courts, county criminal courts, and county criminal courts of appeal, are on **pages 505–507**. The officials listed here are elected by popular vote. If no county attorney is listed, the district attorney, whose name is listed in Table No. 2, assumes the duties of that office.

County	County Seat	County Judge	County Clerk	County Attorney	County Treasurer	Assessor–Collector	Sheriff
Anderson	Palestine	Carey McKinney	Mark Staples		Tara Holliday	Margie Grissom	W.R. (Rudy) Flores
Andrews	Andrews	Charlie Falcon	Vicki Scott	Sean Galloway	*Office abolished 11-5-1985.*	Robin Harper	Rusty Stewart
Angelina	Lufkin	Keith Wright	Amy Fincher	Cary Kirby	Jill Brewer	Billie Page	Tom Selman
Aransas	Rockport	Ray A. Garza	Misty R.F. Kimbrough	Amanda Oster	Alma Cartwright	Anna Marshall	William (Bill) Mills
Archer	Archer City	Randall C. Jackson	Karren Winter	David Levy	Patricia A. Vieth	Dawn Vieth	Jack Curd
Armstrong	Claude	Adam Ensey	Tawnee Blodgett		Susan Overcast McGrath	Jamie Craig	Melissa Anderson
Atascosa	Jourdanton	Weldon Cude	Theresa Carrasco	Lucinda A. Vickers	Laura Pawelek	Loretta Holley	David Soward
Austin	Bellville	Tim Lapham	Andrea Cardenas		Bryan Haevischer	Kim Rinn	Jack Brandes
Bailey	Muleshoe	Basil Nash	Irene Espinoza	Michaela Kee	Shonda L. Black	Maria Gonzalez	Richard Wills
Bandera	Bandera	Richard Evans	Tandie Mansfield	Janna Lindig	Beverly Schmidt	Rebekah (Reba) Dolphus	Dan Butts
Bastrop	Bastrop	Gregory Klaus	Krista Bartsch		Brittney Ross	Ellen Owens	Maurice Cook
Baylor	Seymour	Rusty A. Stafford	Chris Jakubicek	Cindy Ayres	Kevin Hostas	Jeanette Holub	Sam Mooney
Bee	Beeville	George (Trace) Morill, III	Michele Bridge	Mike Knight	*Office abolished 11-2-1982.*	Michelle Matus	Alden E. Southmayd, III
Bell	Belton	David Blackburn	Shelley Coston	James E. Nichols	Gaylon Evans	Shay Luedeke	Eddy Lange
Bexar	San Antonio	Peter Sakai	Lucy Adame-Clark	*Office abolished.*	*Office abolished 11-5-1985.*	Albert Uresti	Javier Salazar
Blanco	Johnson City	Brett Bray	Laura Walla	Deborah Earley	Camille Swift	Kristen Spies	Don Jackson
Borden	Gail	Shane Walker	Jana Underwood	Marlo Holbrooks	Shawna Gass	Benny Allison	Benny Allison
Bosque	Meridian	Cindy Vanlandingham	Tabatha Ferguson	Natalie Koehler	Pam Browning	Arlene Swiney	Trace Hendricks
Bowie	New Boston	Bobby Howell	Tina Petty		Donna Burns	Josh Davis	Jeff Neal
Brazoria	Angleton	L.M. (Matt) Sebesta, Jr.	Joyce Hudman		Angela Dees	Kristin R. Bulanek	Bo Stallman
Brazos	Bryan	Duane Peters	Karen McQueen	Earl Gray	Laura Taylor Davis	Kristeen Roe	Wayne Dicky
Brewster	Alpine	Greg P. Henington	Sarah Vasquez	J. Steve Houston	Julie K. Morton	Sylvia Vega	Ronny Dodson
Briscoe	Silverton	Rank Cogdell	Amy Fuston	(vacant)	Mary Jo Brannon	Jon Etta Ziegler	Garrett Davis
Brooks	Falfurrias	Eric Ramos	Elvaray B. Silvas	David T. Garcia	Alan Hernandez	Urbino (Benny) Martinez	Urbino (Benny) Martinez
Brown	Brownwood	Shane Britton	Sharon Ferguson	Jennifer Broughton	Ann Krpoun	Christine Pentecost	Vance W. Hill
Burleson	Caldwell	Keith Schroeder	Anna L. Schielack	Susan Deski	Stephanie Smith	Jessica Lucero	Gene Hermes
Burnet	Burnet	James Oakley	Vicinta Stafford	Eddie Arredondo	Karrie Crownover	Sheri Frazier	Calvin Boyd
Caldwell	Lockhart	Hoppy Haden	Teresa Rodriguez		Angela Meuth Rawlinson	Darla Law	Mike Lane
Calhoun	Port Lavaca	Richard H. Meyer	Anna Goodman		Rhonda Kokena	Kerri Boyd	Bobbie Vickery
Callahan	Baird	Nicki Harle	Nicole Crocker	Shane Deel	Amber Douglas	Tammy Walker	Eric Pechacek
Cameron	Brownsville	Eddie Treviño, Jr.	Sylvia Garza-Perez	Luis V. Saenz	David A. Betancourt	Antonio (Tony) Yzaguirre, Jr.	Eric Garza
Camp	Pittsburg	A.J. Mason	Sandra Knight	James (Jas) W. Wallace, III	Kim Pittman	Missy Huffman	John Cortelyou
Carson	Panhandle	Dan Looten	Gayla Cates	Scott Sherwood	Denise Salzbrenner	Ashley Montgomery	Tam Terry
Cass	Linden	Travis Ransom	Amy L. Varnell		Melissa Shores	Angela Young	Larry Rowe
Castro	Dimmitt	Mandy Gfeller	JoAnna Blanco	Shalyn Hamlin	Elaine D. Flynt	Connie Gilbreath	Salvador Rivera
Chambers	Anahuac	Jimmy Sylvia	Heather Hawthorne	Ashley Cain Land	Nicole M. Whittington	Laurie G. Payton	Brian C. Hawthorne
Cherokee	Rusk	Chris Davis	Laverne Lusk	Dana Young	Erin Curtis	Shonda McCutcheon Potter	Brent Dickson

County	County Seat	County Judge	County Clerk	County Attorney	County Treasurer	Assessor–Collector	Sheriff
Childress	Childress	Kim Jones	Barbara Spitzer	Greg Buckley	Brenda Overstreet	Kathy Dobbs	Matthew Bradley
Clay	Henrietta	Mike Campbell	Sasha Kelton	Seth C. Slagle	Danja Bloodworth	Patti Jackson	Sidney (Kirk) Horton
Cochran	Morton	Pat Sabala Henry	Lisa Smith	Amanda Martin	Tommy Smith	Dixie Mendoza	Jorge De La Cruz
Coke	Robert Lee	Hal Spain	Jennifer Burdett	Nicholas (Nick) E. Arrott, II	Therese Emert	Josie Dean	Wayne McCutchen
Coleman	Coleman	Billy D. Bledsoe	Stacey Mendoza	Hayden J. Wise	Jeana Farrow	Jamie Dodgen	Les Cogdill
Collin	McKinney	Chris Hill	Stacey Kemp			Kenneth Maun	Jim Skinner
Collingsworth	Wellington	Scot Martindale	Jackie Johnson	Gaylon Davis	Gina Harris	Sharon Chism	Kent Riley
Colorado	Columbus	Ty Prause	Kimberly Menke	Jay E. Johannes	Joyce Guthmann	Erica Kollaja	R.H. (Curly) Wied
Comal	New Braunfels	Sherman Krause	Bobbie Koepp		Renee Couch	Kristen H. Hoyt	Mark Reynolds
Comanche	Comanche	Stephanie L. Davis	Ruby Lesley	Craig Willingham	Patsy Phifer	Grace Everhart	Chris Pounds
Concho	Paint Rock	David Dillard	Amber Hall	Ginger Treadwell	Jenifer Gierisch	Chad Miller	Chad Miller
Cooke	Gainesville	John O. Roane	Pam Harrison	Edmund J. Zielinski	Patty Brennan	Brandy Ann Carr	Ray Sappington
Coryell	Gatesville	Roger A. Miller	Jennifer Newton	Brandon Belt	Randi McFarlin	Justin K. Carothers	Scott Williams
Cottle	Paducah	Karl Holloway	Vickey Wederski	Greg Buckley	Crystal Tucker	Nakia Hargrave	Mark Box
Crane	Crane	Roy Hodges	Janie Macias Hodges	Austin Rawls	Syndi Cadena	Judy Crumrine	Andrew Aguilar
Crockett	Ozona	Frank Tambunga	Ninfa Preddy	Jody K. Upham	Laura Conner	Michelle M. Medley	Antonio Alejandro, III
Crosby	Crosbyton	Rusty Forbes	Tammy Marshall	Michael Sales	Debra Riley	Michele Cook	Ethan Villanueva
Culberson	Van Horn	Carlos G. Urias	Linda McDonald	Stephen Mitchell	Adrian Hinojos	Jose Morales	Oscar Carrillo
Dallam	Dalhart	Wes Ritchey	Terri Banks	Whitney Hill	Kenda McKay	Jami Parr	Shane Stevenson
Dallas	Dallas	Clay Jenkins	John F. Warren		Pauline Medrano	John R. Ames	Marian Brown
Dawson	Lamesa	Foy O'Brien	Clare Christy	Steven B. Payson	Terri Stahl	Cheryl Miller	Matt Hogg
Deaf Smith	Hereford	D.J. Wagner	Rachel Garman		Brooke Fuentes	Teresa Garth	J. Dale Butler
Delta	Cooper	Tanner Crutcher	Janice Roberts	Jay Garrett	Debbie Huie	Dawn Stewart	Charla Singleton
Denton	Denton	Andy Eads	Juli Luke		Cindy Yeatts Brown	Michelle French	Tracy Murphree
DeWitt	Cuero	Daryl L. Fowler	Natalie Carson	A. Jay Condie	Carol Ann Martin	Ashley D. Mraz	Carl Bowen
Dickens	Dickens	Kevin Brendle	Danay Carnes	Aaron Clements	Brandi Abbott	Rebecca Haney	Terry Braly
Dimmit	Carrizo Springs	Martha Alicia Gomez Ponce	Mario Z. Garcia	Daniel M. Gonzalez	Oscar Ortiz	Mary E. Sandoval	Robert Mendoza
Donley	Clarendon	John C. Howard	Vicky Tunnell	Landon Lambert	Wanda Smith	Kristy Christopher	Charles (Butch) Blackburn
Duval	San Diego	Arnoldo Cantu	Sally Lichtenberger	Baldemar Gutierrez	Sylvia Lazo	Roberto Elizondo	Romeo R. Ramirez
Eastland	Eastland	David Hullum	Cathy Jentho		Christina Dodrill	Andrea May	Jason Weger
Ector	Odessa	Dustin Fawcett	Jennifer Martin	Lee McClendon	Cleopatra Anderson-Callaway	Lindy Wright	Mike Griffis
Edwards	Rocksprings	Souli Asa Shanklin	Olga Lydia Reyes	Allen Ray Moody	Lupe S. Enriquez	Lorri Garcia Ruiz	James W. Guthrie
Ellis	Waxahachie	Todd Little	Krystal Valdez	Ann Montgomery	Cheryl Chambers	Richard Rozier	Brad Norman
El Paso	El Paso	Ricardo A. Samaniego	Delia Briones	Jo Anne Bernal	*Office abolished 1989.*	Ruben P. Gonzalez	Richard Wiles
Erath	Stephenville	Brandon J. Huckabee	Gwinda Jones	Lisa Pence	Angie Shawver	Jennifer Carey	Matt Coates
Falls	Marlin	Jay Elliott	Elizabeth Perez	Kathryn (Jody) Gilliam	Sheryl Pringle	Kayci Nehring	Joe Lopez
Fannin	Bonham	Newt Cunningham	Tammy Biggar	Richard E. Glaser	David E. Woodson	Gail Young	Mark Johnson
Fayette	La Grange	Dan Mueller	Brenda Fietsam	Peggy Supak	*Office abolished 11-3-87.*	Sylvia Mendoza	Keith Korenek
Fisher	Roby	Ken Holt	Pat Thomson	Michael Hall	Jeanna Parks	Jonnye Lu Gibson	Randy Ford
Floyd	Floydada	Marty Lucke	Ginger Morgan	Lex Herrington	Lori Morales	Delia Suarez	Paul Raissez
Foard	Crowell	Mark Christopher	Debra Hopkins	Marshall Capps	Darcy Moore	Mike Brown	Mike Brown
Fort Bend	Richmond	KP George	Laura Richard	Bridgette Smith-Lawson	Bill Rickert	Carmen P. Turner	Eric Fagan
Franklin	Mount Vernon	Scott Lee	Brook Bussell	Landon Ramsay	Paris Tillery	Melissa McSwain Clawson	Ricky Jones

County	County Seat	County Judge	County Clerk	County Attorney	County Treasurer	Assessor–Collector	Sheriff
Freestone	Fairfield	Linda K. Grant	Renee Reynolds	Brian Evans	Jeannie Keeney	Daniel M. Ralstin	Jeremy Shipley
Frio	Pearsall	Rochelle Lozano Camacho	Aaron Tomas Ibarra	Joseph Sindon	Pete Jasso Martinez	Anna L. Alaniz	Michael (Mike) Morse
Gaines	Seminole	Cindy Therwhanger	Terri Berry	Joe H. Nagy, Jr.	Michael Lord, Jr.	Susan Shaw	Ronny Pipkin
Galveston	Galveston	Mark Henry	Dwight D. Sullivan		Hank Dugie	Cheryl E. Johnson	Henry A. Trochesset
Garza	Post	Lee Norman	Terri Laurence	Ted Weems	LuAnne Terry	Nancy Wallace	Terry Morgan
Gillespie	Fredericksburg	Daniel Jones	Lindsey Brown	Steven A. Wadsworth	Dana Smith	Vicki J. Schmidt	Buddy Mills
Glasscock	Garden City	Billy Ray Reynolds	Rebecca Batla	Hardy Wilkerson	Vikki Calloway	Tina Flores	Keith Burnett
Goliad	Goliad	Mike Bennett	Vickie Quinn	Tim Poynter, pro tem	Christina Hernandez	Michelle Garcia	Roy Boyd
Gonzales	Gonzales	Patrick C. Davis	Lona Ackman	Paul Watkins	Sheryl Barborak	Crystal Cedillo	Keith Schmidt
Gray	Pampa	Chris Porter	Jeanne Horton	Josh Seabourn	Elaine Morris	Gaye Whitehead	Michael Ryan
Grayson	Sherman	Bruce Dawsey	Deana Patterson		Gayla Hawkins	Bruce Stidham	Tom Watt
Gregg	Longview	Bill Stoudt	Michelle Gilley		*Office abolished 1-1-88.*	Michelle Terry	Maxey Cerliano
Grimes	Anderson	Joe Fauth, III	Vanessa Burzynski	Jon C. Fultz	Tom Maynard	Mary Ann Waters	Donald G. Sowell
Guadalupe	Seguin	Kyle Kutscher	Teresa Kiel	Dave Willborn	Linda Douglass	Daryl John	Arnold S. Zwicke
Hale	Plainview	David Mull	Christine Reyna	Jim Tirey	Ida A. Tyler	Roland Nash	David Cochran
Hall	Memphis	Ray Powell	Kaci Mills	Harley Caudle	Janet Bridges	Teresa Altman	Tom Heck
Hamilton	Hamilton	James Yates	Cynthia K. Puff	Mark Henkes	Tonya Cox	Terry Payne Short	Justin Caraway
Hansford	Spearman	Tim Glass	Janet Torres	Cheryl Nelson	Cindy Lopez	Linda Cummings	Robert Mahaffee
Hardeman	Quanah	Ronald Ingram	Stella Doyal	Stanley Watson	Traysha Newsom	Jan Evans	Pat Laughery
Hardin	Kountze	Wayne McDaniel	Connie Becton	Matthew Minick	Deborah McWilliams	Shirley Cook	Mark Davis
Harris	Houston	Lina Hidalgo	Teneshia Hudspeth	Christian D. Menefee	Carla L. Wyatt	Ann Harris Bennett	Ed Gonzalez
Harrison	Marshall	Chad Sims	Liz James		Sherry Rushing	Veronica King	Brandon (BJ) Fletcher
Hartley	Channing	Ronnie Gordon	Melissa Mead	Robert Elliott	Dinkie Parman	Chanze Fowler	Chanze Fowler
Haskell	Haskell	Kenny Thompson	Belia Abila	Kris Fouts	Stacia Leach	Connie Benton	David Halliburton
Hays	San Marcos	Ruben Becerra	Elaine Cárdenas		Daphne Tenorio	Jenifer O'Kane	Gary Cutler
Hemphill	Canadian	Lisa Johnson	Sylvia Guerrero	Kyle Miller	Kay Smallwood	Chris Jackson	Brent Clapp
Henderson	Athens	Wade McKinney	Mary Margaret Wright	Clint Davis	Michael Bynum	Peggy Goodall	Botie Hillhouse
Hidalgo	Edinburg	Richard F. Cortez	Arturo Guajardo, Jr.		Lita Leo	Pablo (Paul) Villarreal, Jr.	J.E. (Eddie) Guerra
Hill	Hillsboro	Justin Lewis	Nicole Tanner	David Holmes	Rachel Parker	Krissi Hightower	Rodney B. Watson
Hockley	Levelland	Sharla Baldridge	Jennifer Nicole Palermo	Anna Hord	Kelli Martin	Debra C. Bramlett	Ray Scifres
Hood	Granbury	Ron Massingill	Katie Lang	Matthew A. Mills	Leigh Ann McCoy	Andrea Ferguson	Roger Deeds
Hopkins	Sulphur Springs	Robert Newsom	Tracy Smith	Dusty Rabe	Danny Davis	Debbie Pogue Mitchell	Lewis Tatum
Houston	Crockett	Jim L. Lovell	Terri Meadows	Daphne Lynette Session	Janis Omelina	Laronica Wooten Smith	Randy Hargrove
Howard	Big Spring	Randy Johnson	Brent Zitterkopf	Joshua Hamby	Sharon Adams	Tiffany Sayles	Stan Parker
Hudspeth	Sierra Blanca	Joanna (Jojo) Mackenzie	Brenda Sanchez	?? (vacant)	Blanca Rosa Santana	Patricia Rose	Arvin West
Hunt	Greenville	Bobby W. Stovall	Becky Landrum	G. Calvin Grogan	Brittni Turner	Randy L. Wineinger	Terry Jones
Hutchinson	Stinnett	Cindy Irwin	Kelly Ratliff	Craig Jones	Amy Back	Carrie Kimmell	Blaik Kemp
Irion	Mertzon	Molly Criner	Shirley Graham	James Ridge	Carolyn Huelster	Joyce Gray	W.A. Estes
Jack	Jacksboro	Brian Keith Umphress	Vanessa James	Michael Brad Dixon	Brad Campsey	Sharon Robinson	Thomas Spurlock
Jackson	Edna	Jill S. Sklar	Katherine R. Brooks		Mary Horton	Monica Foster	Kelly Janicka
Jasper	Jasper	Mark Allen	Holly Thomas		Rene Kelley-Ellis	Bobby Biscamp	Mitchel Newman
Jeff Davis	Fort Davis	Curtis Evans	Jennifer Wright	Teresa L. Todd	Dawn Kitts	William (Bill) Kitts	William (Bill) Kitts
Jefferson	Beaumont	Jeff Branick	Roxanne Acosta-Hellberg		Tim Funchess	Allison Nathan Getz	Zena Stephens
Jim Hogg	Hebbronville	Juan Carlos Guerra	Zonia G. Morales	Rodolfo Gutierrez	Gloria (Gigi) Benavides	Norma Liza S. Hinojosa	Erasmo Alarcon, Jr.

County	County Seat	County Judge	County Clerk	County Attorney	County Treasurer	Assessor–Collector	Sheriff
Jim Wells	Alice	Pedro (Pete) Trevino, Jr.	J.C. Perez, III	Michael Guerra	Mark Dominguez	Mary Lozano	Danny Bueno
Johnson	Cleburne	Christopher Boedeker	April Long	Bill Moore	Kathy Blackwell	Scott Porter	Adam King
Jones	Anson	Dale Spurgin	LeeAnn Jennings	Chad Cowan	Kristian Smith	Gloria Little	Danny Jimenez
Karnes	Karnes City	Wade J. Hedtke	Carol Swize	David Chapman	Vi Swierc	Tammy Braudaway	Dwayne Villanueva
Kaufman	Kaufman	Jakie Allen	Laura Hughes		Chuck Mohnkern	Teressa Floyd	Bryan W. Beavers
Kendall	Boerne	Shane Stolarczyk	Denise Maxwell		Sheryl D'Spain	James Hudson	Al Auxier
Kenedy	Sarita	Charles Burns	Veronica Vela	Allison Strauss	Cynthia M. Salinas	Irma G. Longoria	Ramon Salinas, III
Kent	Jayton	Layne Coulter	Craig Harrison	Katie Lackey	Christy Long	William Scogin	William Scogin
Kerr	Kerrville	Rob Kelly	Jackie (JD) Dowdy	Heather Stebbins	Tracy Soldan	Bob Reeves	Larry L. Leitha
Kimble	Junction	Harold (Hal) Rose	Karen E. Page	Andrew James Heap	Billie Stewart	Allen Castleberry	Allen Castleberry
King	Guthrie	Duane Lee Daniel	Jammye D. Timmons	George (Trey) Poage	Maggie Oliver	Amy McCauley	Michael R. McWhirter
Kinney	Brackettville	John Paul Schuster	Rick Alvarado	Brent Smith	Diana Gutierrez	Martha Peña-Padron	Brad Coe
Kleberg	Kingsville	Rudy Madrid	Salvador (Sonny) Barrera, III	Kira Talip Sanchez	Priscilla Alaniz Cantu	Maria Victoria Valadez	Richard Kirkpatrick
Knox	Benjamin	Stan Wojcik	Lisa Cypert	Lina Reyes Trevino	Julie Bradley	Penny Eaton	Bridger Bush
Lamar	Paris	Brandon Bell	Ruth Sisson	Gary Young	Camey Boyer	Haskell Maroney	Scott Cass
Lamb	Littlefield	James M. DeLoach	Tonya Ritchie	Rickie Redman	Jerry Yarbrough	Tammy Kirkland	Gary Maddox
Lampasas	Lampasas	Randall J. Hoyer	Dianne Miller	John K. Greenwood	Melissa Karcher	Betty Salinas	Jesus (Jess) G. Ramos
La Salle	Cotulla	Leodoro Martinez, III	Sonia Maldonado	Elizabeth Martinez	Maria Perez	Dora A. Gonzales	Anthony Zertuche
Lavaca	Hallettsville	Keith Mudd	Barbara K. Steffek	Kyle A. Denney	Karen Bludau	Deborah A. Sevcik	Micah Harmon
Lee	Giddings	Frank J. Malinak	Sharon Blasig	Martin Placke	Melinda (Lyndy) Krause	David Matthijetz	Casey Goetz
Leon	Centerville	Byron Ryder	Christie Wakefield	Keith Cook	Brandi S. Hill	Robin Shafer	Kevin Ellis
Liberty	Liberty	Jay H. Knight	Lee Haidusek Chambers	Matthew Poston	Kim Harris	Richard Brown	Robert (Bobby) Rader
Limestone	Groesbeck	Richard Duncan	Kerrie Cobb	William Roy DeFriend	Carol Pickett	Stacy L. Hall	Murray Agnew
Lipscomb	Lipscomb	Dori Artis	Kim Blau	Matthew D. Bartosiewicz	Kimberly L. Long	Gailan Winegarner	Ty Lane
Live Oak	George West	James Liska	Donna VanWay	Dwayne McWilliams	Kitley Moffatt-Wasicek	Deanna Atkinson	Larry Busby
Llano	Llano	Ron Cunningham	Marci Hadeler	Dwain K. Rogers	Cheryl Regmund	Kris Fogelberg	Bill Blackburn
Loving	Mentone	Skeet Lee Jones	Mozelle Carr	Steve Simonsen	Regina Wilkinson	Chris H. Busse	Chris H. Busse
Lubbock	Lubbock	Curtis Parrish	Kelly Pinion		Chris Winn	Ronnie Keister	Kelly S. Rowe
Lynn	Tahoka	Mike Braddock	Karen Strickland	Rebekah Filley	Amy Schuknecht	Donna Willis	Wanda Mason
Madison	Madisonville	Clark Osborne	Adrian Lawson		Judi Delesandri	Karen M. Lane	Bobby Adams
Marion	Jefferson	Leward J. LaFleur	Kim Wise	Angela Smoak	B.J. Westbrook	Karen Jones	David Capps
Martin	Stanton	Bryan Cox	Linda Gonzales	James Napper	Cynthia O'Donnell	Kathy Hull	Brad Ingram
Mason	Mason	Sheree Hardin	Pam Beam	Rebekah Whitworth	Ally Yonker	Joe Lancaster	Joe Lancaster
Matagorda	Bay City	Bobby Seiferman	Stephanie Wurtz	Jennifer Kim Chau	Loretta K. Griffin	Becky Cook	Frank D. Osborne
Maverick	Eagle Pass	Ramsey English Cantú	Sara Montemayor	Jaime (AJ) Iracheta	Rito Valdez	Asalia Casares	Tom Schmerber
McCulloch	Brady	Frank Trull	Christine Jones	Greg Torres	Mikkie Williams	Silvia Campos	Matt Andrews
McLennan	Waco	Scott Felton	Andy Harwell		Bill Helton	Randy H. Riggs	Parnell McNamara
McMullen	Tilden	James E. Teal	Mattie S. Sadovsky	Kimberly Kreider-Dusek	Jill Atkinson	Bessilia (Bessie) Guerrero	Emmett Shelton
Medina	Hondo	Keith Lutz	Gina Champion		Debbie Southwell	Melissa Lutz	Randy Brown
Menard	Menard	Brandon Corbin	Christy Eggleston	Luke Davis	Tami Russell	Tim Powell	Buck Miller
Midland	Midland	Terry Johnson	Alison Haley	Russell Malm	Sara Gray	Karen Hood	David Criner
Milam	Cameron	Bill Whitmire	Jodi Morgan	Bill Torrey	Linda Acosta	Sherry Mueck	Mike Clore
Mills	Goldthwaite	Jett J. Johnson	Sonya Scott	Gerald Hale	Summer Campbell	Lori King	Clint Hammonds

County	County Seat	County Judge	County Clerk	County Attorney	County Treasurer	Assessor–Collector	Sheriff
Mitchell	Colorado City	Mike Redwine	Carla Kern	Sterling T. Burleson, II	Jennifer Rivera	Teresa Hughes	Patrick Toombs
Montague	Montague	Kevin Benton	Kim Jones	Clay V. Riddle	Jennifer Fenoglio	Kathryn Phillips	Marshall Thomas
Montgomery	Conroe	Mark J. Keough	L. Brandon Steinmann	B.D. Griffin	Melanie Bush	Tammy J. McRae	Rand Henderson
Moore	Dumas	Rowdy Rhoades	Brenda McKanna	Scott Higginbotham	Kara Milligan	Chris A. Rivera	Morgan W. Hightower
Morris	Daingerfield	Doug Reeder	Brittany Andrews	Ricky Shelton	Molly Cummings	Kim Thomasson	Jack Martin
Motley	Matador	James B. (Jim) Meador	D'anna Russell	Tom Edwards	Misty Jones	Ronda Miller	Robert Fisk
Nacogdoches	Nacogdoches	Greg Sowell	Sandra (Sandy) Yates	John Fleming	Denise Baublet	Kim Morton	Jason Bridges
Navarro	Corsicana	H.M. Davenport, Jr.	Sherry Dowd		Ryan Douglas	Mike Dowd	Elmer Tanner
Newton	Newton	Ronald J. Cochran	Sandra K. Duckworth		Ginger Sims	Melissa J. Burks	Robert Burby
Nolan	Sweetwater	Whitley May	Sharla Keith	Samantha Morrow	Jeanne Wells	Kathy Bowen	David Warren
Nueces	Corpus Christi	Connie Scott	Kara Sands	Jenny P. Dorsey	*Office abolished 11-3-87.*	Kevin Kieschnick	J.C. Hooper
Ochiltree	Perryton	Charles E. Kelly	Sandra Limas	Jose N. Meraz	Tambra J. Kile	Linda Womble	Terry Bouchard
Oldham	Vega	Shawn Ballew	Darla Lookingbill	Kent Birdsong	Rebecca Hatfield	Linda Brown	Brent Warden
Orange	Orange	John Gothia	Brandy Robertson	John Kimbrough	Christy Khoury	Karen Fisher	Jimmy Lane Mooney
Palo Pinto	Palo Pinto	Shane Long	Janette K. Green	Maegan Kostiha	Deanna Copeland	Stacy L. Choate	Brett E. McGuire
Panola	Carthage	Rodger McLane	Bobbie Davis		Joni Reed	Holly Gibbs	Cutter Clinton
Parker	Weatherford	Pat Deen	Lila Deakle	John Forrest	Becky McCullough	Jenny Gentry	Russ Authier
Parmer	Farwell	Isabel (Izzy) Carrasco	Susie Spring	Jeff W. Actkinson	Sharon May	Awyna Sanchez	Eric Geske
Pecos	Fort Stockton	Joe Shuster	Liz Chapman	Frank Lacy	Sonia Murphy	Santa Acosta	Thomas J. (TJ) Perkins
Polk	Livingston	Sydney Murphy	Schelana Hock		Terri Williams	Leslie Jones Burks	Byron A. Lyons
Potter	Amarillo	Nancy Tanner	Julie Smith	Scott Brumley	Brooke Graves	Sherri Aylor	Brian Thomas
Presidio	Marfa	Jose Portillo, Jr.	Florcita Zubia	Rod Ponton	Frances Garcia	Natalia Williams	Danny Dominguez
Rains	Emory	Linda Wallace	Mandy Sawyer	Robert Vititow	Teresa Northcutt	Sheila Floyd	Michael Hopkins
Randall	Canyon	Christy Dyer	Susan Allen		Angie Parker	Christina McMurray	Christopher Forbis
Reagan	Big Lake	Jim O'Bryan	Tammy Hodge	Michele Dodd	Leticia Quiñonez	Cynthia Aguilar	Jeff N. Garner
Real	Leakey	Bella A. Rubio	D'Ann Green	Bobby Jack Rushing	Jennifer Manchester	Terrie Pendley	Nathan T. Johnson
Red River	Clarksville	Robert Bridges	Shawn Weemes	Val Varley	Lorena De la Torre	Tonya R. Martin	Jimmy Caldwell
Reeves	Pecos	Leo Hung	Evangelina (Yvonne) Abila	Alva Alvarez	Zulema E. Rodriguez	Rosemary Chabarria	Arturo (Art) Granado
Refugio	Refugio	Jhiela (Gigi) Poynter	Ida Ramirez	Deborah A. Bauer	Rita Trojcak	Ida Turner	Raul (Pinky) Gonzales
Roberts	Miami	Mitchell D. Locke	Toni Rankin	William P. Weiman	Amy Tennant	Hether Williams	Bruce Skidmore
Robertson	Franklin	Joe David Scarpinato	Stephanie M. Sanders	W. Coty Siegert	Melinda Turner	Michael (Duba) Brewer	Gerald Yezak
Rockwall	Rockwall	Frank New	Jennifer Fogg		David Peek	Kim Sweet	Terry Garrett
Runnels	Ballinger	Julia Miller	Jennifer Hoffpauir	Ben Clayton	Laura Pospichal	Robin Burgess	Carl L. Squyres
Rusk	Henderson	Joel Hale	Trudy McGill	Micheal E. Jimerson	Andy Vinson	Nesha Partin	Johnwayne Valdez
Sabine	Hemphill	Daryl Melton	Jamie Clark	Robert G. Neal, Jr.	Tricia Jacks	Martha M. Stone	Thomas N. Maddox
San Augustine	San Augustine	Jeff Boyd	Margo Noble	Jon Bates	Pam Smith	Regina Barthol	Robert Cartwright
San Jacinto	Coldspring	Fritz Faulkner	Dawn Wright		Dianna (Dee Dee) Adams	Betty Davis	Greg Capers
San Patricio	Sinton	David Krebs	Gracie Alaniz-Gonzales	Tamara Cochran-May	Denise Janak	Marcela Thormaehlen	Oscar Rivera
San Saba	San Saba	Jody Fauley	Kim Wells	Randall Robinson	Lois VanBeck	David Jenkins	David Jenkins
Schleicher	Eldorado	Charlie Bradley	Mary Ann Gonzalez	Clint T. Griffin	Jennifer L. Henderson	Vanessa Covarrubiaz	Jason Chatham
Scurry	Snyder	Dan Hicks	Melody Appleton	Michael Hartman	Kirsta Koennecke	Jana Young	Trey Wilson
Shackelford	Albany	John Viertel	Cheri Hawkins	Rollin Rauschl	Tammy Brown	Edward A. Miller	Edward A. Miller
Shelby	Center	Allison Harbison	Jennifer Fountain	John Price	Ann Blackwell	Debora Riley	Kevin Windham
Sherman	Stratford	Terri Beth Carter	Laura Rogers	Erin Lands Anchondo	Alicia Law	Kalee Flippin	Ted Allen

County	County Seat	County Judge	County Clerk	County Attorney	County Treasurer	Assessor–Collector	Sheriff
Smith	Tyler	Neal Franklin	Karen Phillips		Kelli R. White	Gary Barber	Larry Smith
Somervell	Glen Rose	Danny L. Chambers	Michelle Reynolds	Trey Brown	Valerie Williams	April Campos	Alan West
Starr	Rio Grande City	Eloy Vera	Humberto Gonzalez	Rene Montalvo	Romeo Gonzalez	Ameida Salinas	Rene (Orta) Fuentes
Stephens	Breckenridge	Michael Roach	Jackie Ensey	Gary Trammel	Sharon Trigg	Christie Latham	Kevin Roach
Sterling	Sterling City	Deborah Horwood	Jerri McCutchen	Lilli Hensley	Rhea McGinnis	Ellen Clark	Russell Irby
Stonewall	Aspermont	Ronnie Moorhead	Holly McLaury	Riley Branch	Anya Mullen	Lacy English	William (Bill) Mullen
Sutton	Sonora	Joseph Harris	Pam Thorp	Dawn Cahill	Janell Martin	Kathy Sanchez Marshall	DuWayne Castro
Swisher	Tulia	Harold Keeter	C.J. Chasco	J. Michael Criswell	Jolina Flowers	Deborah Lemons	Jim McCaslin
Tarrant	Fort Worth	Tim O'Hare	Mary Louise Nicholson		*Office abolished 4-2-83.*	Wendy Burgess	Bill E. Waybourn
Taylor	Abilene	Phil Crowley	Brandi DeRemer		Lesa Hart Crosswhite	Kay Middleton	Ricky Bishop
Terrell	Sanderson	Dale Lynn Carruthers	Raeline Thompson	Kenneth D. Bellah	Rebecca Luevano	Thaddeus C. (Thad) Cleveland	Thaddeus C. (Thad) Cleveland
Terry	Brownfield	Tony Serbantez	Kim Carter	Jo'Shae Ferguson-Worley	Andrea Perry	Rexann W. Furlow	Timothy Click
Throckmorton	Throckmorton	Caleb Hodges	Dianna Moore	Kris Fouts	Michelle Clark	Doc Wigington	Doc Wigington
Titus	Mount Pleasant	Kent Cooper	Leslie Brosnan	John Mark Cobern	Dana Wallace-Applewhite	Melissa Stevens	Tim C. Ingram
Tom Green	San Angelo	Lane Carter	Christina Ubando	Chris Taylor	Dianna Spieker	Becky Robles	J. Nick Hanna
Travis	Austin	Andy Brown	Dyana Limon-Mercado	Delia Garza	Dolores Ortega Carter	Bruce Elfant	Sally Hernandez
Trinity	Groveton	Danny Martin	Shasta Bergman	Colton Hay	Orrin Hargrave	Nancy Shanafelt	Woody Wallace
Tyler	Woodville	Milton Powers	Donece Gregory		Leann Monk	Lynnette Cruse	Bryan Weatherford
Upshur	Gilmer	Todd Tefteller	Terri Ross		Brandy Vick	Luana Howell	Larry Webb
Upton	Rankin	Dusty W. Kilgore	LaWanda McMurray	Paige Skehan	Vivian Venegas	Monica Zarate	William Mitch Upchurch
Uvalde	Uvalde	William R. Mitchell	Donna M. Williams	John Dodson	Joni Deorsam	Rita C. Verstuyft	Ruben Nolasco
Val Verde	Del Rio	Lewis Owens	Teresa Esther Chapoy	David E. Martinez	Aaron D. Rodriguez	Elodia Garcia	Joe Frank Martinez
Van Zandt	Canton	Andy Reese	Susan Strickland		Kenny Edwards	Misty Stanberry	Joe Carter
Victoria	Victoria	Ben Zeller	Heidi Easley		Paige Foster	Ashley Hernandez	Justin Marr
Walker	Huntsville	Colt Christian	Kari French		Amy Klawinsky	Diana L. McRae	Clint McRae
Waller	Hempstead	Carbett (Trey) J. Duhon, III	Debbie Hollan	Elton Mathis	Joan Sargent	Ellen C. Shelburne	Troy Guidry
Ward	Monahans	Greg M. Holly	Denise Valles	Alan Nicholas	Carleigh Ennis	Vicki Heflin	Frarin Valle
Washington	Brenham	John Durrenberger	Beth A. Rothermel	Renee Ann Mueller	Peggy Kramer	Cheryl Gaskamp	Otto H. Hanak
Webb	Laredo	Tano E. Tijerina	Margie Ramirez Ibarra	Marco A. Montemayor	Raul Reyes	Patricia Barrera	Martin Cuellar
Wharton	Wharton	Phillip Spenrath	Barbara Svatek	G.A. (Trey) Maffett	Audrey Scearce	Cindy Hernandez	Shannon Srubar
Wheeler	Wheeler	Pat McDowell	Margaret Dorman	Leslie Timmons	Renee Warren	Cindy Brown	Johnny Carter
Wichita	Wichita Falls	Jim Johnson	Annette Stanley		Stephen Jones	Tommy Smyth	David Duke
Wilbarger	Vernon	Greg Tyra	Jana Kennon	Cornell Curtis	Joann Carter	Tissha Taylor	Brian Fritze
Willacy	Raymondville	Aurelio (Keter) Guerra	Susana R. Garza	Annette C. Hinojosa	Ruben Cavazos	Elizabeth Barnhart	Jose Salazar
Williamson	Georgetown	Bill Gravell, Jr.	Nancy E. Rister	Doyle (Dee) Hobbs, Jr.	D. Scott Heselmeyer	Larry Gaddes	Mike Gleason
Wilson	Floresville	Henry L. (Hank) Whitman, Jr.	Genevieve Martinez	Tom Caldwell	Christina Mutz	Dawn Polasek Barnett	Jim Stewart
Winkler	Kermit	Charles M. Wolf	Pam Greene	Thomas Duckworth, Jr.	Susan Willhelm	Minerva Soltero	Darin Mitchell
Wise	Decatur	J.D. Clark	Blanca Tuma	Che Rotramble	Katherine Hudson	Monte Shaw	Lane Akin
Wood	Quitman	Kevin White	Kelley Price		Daphne Carter	Carol Taylor	Kelly Cole
Yoakum	Plains	Michael C. Ybarra	Summer Lovelace		Darla Welch	Ann Saxon	David Bryant
Young	Graham	Edwin S. (Win) Graham, IV	Ann Ford	Chris Baran	Kathy Mishler	Christy Centers	Travis Babcock
Zapata	Zapata	Joe Rathmell	Mary Jayne Villarreal-Bonoan	Said Alfonso Figueroa	Romeo Salinas	Delia Mendoza	Raymundo Del Bosque
Zavala	Crystal City	Cindy Martínez-Rivera	Michelle B. Urrabazo	Eduardo Serna	Elizabeth Tovar	Rosario (Chari) Benavidez	Eusevio Salinas

Texas County and District Officials — Table No. 2

District Clerks, District Attorneys, and County Commissioners

See Table No. 1 on **pages 513–518** for County Seats, County Judges, County Clerks, County Attorneys, County Treasurers, Tax Assessors-Collectors, and Sheriffs. Judges in county courts at law, as well as probate courts, juvenile/domestic relations courts, county criminal courts, and county criminal courts of appeal, are on pages **505–507**. If more than one district attorney is listed for a county, the district court number is noted in parentheses after each attorney's name. The officials listed here are elected by popular vote. If no district attorney is listed, the county attorney, whose name is listed in Table No. 1, assumes the duties of that office.

County	District Clerk	District Attorney	Comm. Precinct 1	Comm. Precinct 2	Comm. Precinct 3	Comm. Precinct 4
Anderson	Teresia Coker	Allyson Mitchell	Greg Chapin	Rashad Mims	Kenneth Dickson	Joey Hill
Andrews	Sherry Dushane	Sean Galloway	Kerry Pack	Mark Savell	Jeneane Anderegg	Jim Waldrop
Angelina	Reba Squyres	Janet Cassels	Kent Walker	Kermit Kennedy	Terry Pitts	Kenneth Jeffrey
Aransas	Pam Heard		Jack Chaney	Leslie (Bubba) Casterline	Pat Rousseau	Bob Dupnik
Archer	Lori Rutledge	Casey Hall	Wade Scarbrough	Darin Wolf	Pat Martin, III	Todd Herring
Armstrong	Tawnee Blodgett	Randall C. Sims	Shawn Smith	Clint Cornell	Robert Harris	Joe Neely
Atascosa	Margaret E. Littleton	Audrey Gossett Louis	Mark Gillespie	Mark Bowen	Eliseo Perez	Kennard (Bubba) Riley
Austin	Sue Murphy	Travis J. Koehn	Mark Lamp	Robert (Bobby) Rinn	Leroy Cerny	Chip Reed
Bailey	Becky Espinoza	Jackie R. Claborn, II	Gary Don Gartin	Mike Slayden	Cody Black	Jim Daniel
Bandera	Tammy Kneuper	Stephen Harpold	Bruce Eliker	Greg P. Grothues	Jack Moseley	Jordan (Jody) Rutherford
Bastrop	Sarah Loucks	Bryan Goertz	Mel Hamner	Clara Beckett	Mark Meuth	David Glass
Baylor	Chris Jakubicek	Hunter Brooks	Rick Gillispie	Larry Elliott	Reed Slaggle	Jim Stout
Bee	Zenaida Silva	Jose Aliseda	Kristofer Linney	Dennis DeWitt	Sammy G. Farias	Tino Olivares
Bell	Joanna Staton	Henry Garza	Russell Schneider	Bobby Whitson	Bill Schumann	Louie Minor
Bexar	Gloria A. Martinez	Joe Gonzales	Rebeca Clay-Flores	Justin Rodriguez	Grant Moody	Tommy Calvert
Blanco	Celia Doyle	Wiley B. (Sonny) McAfee	Tommy Weir	Emil Ray Uecker	Chris Liesmann	Charles Riley
Borden	Jana Underwood	Ben R. Smith	Norman (Jibber) Herridge	Randy Adcock	Ernest Reyes	Greg Stansell
Bosque	Juanita Miller	Adam Sibley	Billy Hall	Terry Townley	Larry (Shotgun) Philipp	Ronny Liardon
Bowie	Lori Caraway	Jerry Rochelle	Sammy Stone	Tom Whitten	James Strain	Mike Carter
Brazoria	Cassandra Tigner	Tom Selleck	Donald (Dude) Payne	Ryan Cade	Stacy Adams	David Linder
Brazos	Gabriel Garcia	Jarvis Parsons	Steve Aldrich	Russ Ford	Nancy Berry	Irma Cauley
Brewster	Sarah Fellows Martinez	Ori T. White	Jim Westermann	Sara Allen Colando	Ruben Ortega	Mo Morrow
Briscoe	Amy Fuston	Emily Teegardin	Ken Wood	Jack Wellman	Danny Francis	John Burson
Brooks	Elvaray B. Silvas	Carlos Omar Garcia	Eduardo (Eddy) Garza	Rolando Gutierrez	Horacio Villareal, III	Ernesto (Pepe) Williams
Brown	Cheryl Jones	Micheal Murray	Gary Worley	Joel Kelton	Wayne Shaw	Larry Traweek
Burleson	Dana Fritsche	Susan Deski	Dwayne Faust	Vincent Svec, Jr.	David Hildebrand	Robert (Bobby) Urbanovsky
Burnet	Casie Walker	Wiley B. (Sonny) McAfee	Jim Luther, Jr.	Damon Beierle	Billy Wall	Joe Don Dockery
Caldwell	Juanita Allen	Fred Weber	B.J. Westmoreland	Rusty Horne	Edward (Ed) Theriot	Dyral Thomas
Calhoun	Anna Kabela	Dan Heard	David Hall	Vern Lyssy	Joel Behrens	Gary Reese
Callahan	Sharon Owens	Shane Deel	Ashley McGowen	Bryan Farmer	Tom Windham	Erwin Clark
Cameron	Laura Perez-Reyes	Luis V. Saenz	Sofia C. Benavides	Joey Lopez	David A. Garza	Gus Ruiz
Camp	Kelly Gunn	David Colley	George French	Tommy Rozell	Perry Weeks	Steve Lindley
Carson	Gayla Cates	Luke M. Inman	Mike Britten	James Martin	Mike Jennings	Kevin Howell
Cass	Jamie Albertson	Courtney Shelton	Brett Fitts	Kevin Young	Paul Cothren	Darrell Godwin
Castro	JoAnna Blanco	Shalyn Hamlin	Paul Ramirez	Tim Elliott	Michael Goolsby	Ralph Brockman
Chambers	Patti L. Henry	Cheryl Swope Lieck	Jimmy Gore	Kenneth Mark Tice	Tommy Hammond	Ryan J. Dagley
Cherokee	Alison Dotson	Elmer Beckworth	Kelly Traylor	Steven Norton	Patrick Reagan	Billy McCutcheon
Childress	Barbara Spitzer	Luke Inman	Jeremy Hill	Mark Ross	Kevin Hackler	Rick Elliot

County	District Clerk	District Attorney	Comm. Precinct 1	Comm. Precinct 2	Comm. Precinct 3	Comm. Precinct 4
Clay	Marianne Bowles	Casey Hall	Richard Lowery	Jack Pickett	Retta Collins	Chase Broussard
Cochran	Lisa Smith	Angela Overman	Timothy Roberts	Matt Evans	Eric Silhan	Reynaldo Morin
Coke	Jennifer Burdett	Allison Palmer	Donald Robertson	Paul Williams	Marshall Millican	Joe Sefcik
Coleman	Darlene Huddle-Boyd	Heath Hemphill	Matt Henderson	Jim Rice	Scotty Lawrence	Alan Davis
Collin	Michael Gould	Greg Willis	Susan Fletcher	Cheryl Williams	Darrell Hale	Duncan Webb
Collingsworth	Jackie Johnson	Luke M. Inman	Farris Nation	James Ellis	Joel Sherwood	Richard Johnson
Colorado	Valerie Harmon	Jay E. Johannes	Doug Wessels	Ryan Brandt	Keith Neuendorff	Darrell Gertson
Comal	Heather Kellar	Jennifer Tharp	Donna Eccleston	Scott Haag	Kevin Webb	Jen Crownover
Comanche	Brandy Jones	Adam Sibley	Gary (Corky) Underwood	Russell Gillette	Sherman Sides	Jimmy Dale Johnson
Concho	Amber Hall	John Best	Trey Bradshaw	Eric Gully	Gary Gierisch	Keith Dillard
Cooke	Marci A. Gilbert	John Warren	Gary Hollowell	Jason Snuggs	Adam Arendt	Matt Sicking
Coryell	Becky Moore	Dusty Boyd	Kyle Matthews	Scott Weddle	Ryan Basham	Keith Taylor
Cottle	Vickey Wederski	Hunter Brooks	Arty Tucker	Steven Beck, Jr.	Harvey Truelock	John B. Brothers
Crane	Janie Macias Hodges	Amanda Navarette	Manuella Kirkpatrick	Dennis Young	Domingo Escobedo	Danny Castro
Crockett	Ninfa Preddy	Laurie English	Elsa Fierro	G.L. Bunger, V	Wesley Bean	Mike Medina, Jr.
Crosby	Shari Smith	Michael Sales	Larry McCauley	Frank Mullins	Donald Kirksey	Kevin Langdon
Culberson	Linda McDonald	Bill D. Hicks	Frank Franco	Raul Rodriguez	Gilda Morales	Adrian Norman
Dallam	Terri Banks	Erin Lands Anchondo	Carl McCarty	Corey Crabtree	Levi James	Floyd French
Dallas	Felicia Pitre	John Creuzot	Theresa Daniel	Andy Sommerman	John Wiley Price	Elba Garcia
Dawson	Adreana Gonzalez	Philip Mack Furlow	Mark Shofner	Ryan Webb	Nicky Goode	Russell Cox
Deaf Smith	Elaine Gerber	Chris Strowd	Chris Kahlich	Jerry O'Connor	Mike Brumley	Dale Artho
Delta	Janice Roberts	Will Ramsay	Morgan Baker	Jimmy Sweat	Anthony Roberts	Mark Brantley
Denton	David Trantham	Paul Johnson	Ryan Williams	Kevin Falconer	Bobbie J. Mitchell	Dianne Edmondson
DeWitt	Esther Ruiz	Robert C. Lassmann	Curtis G. Afflerbach	James B. Pilchiek, Sr.	James Kaiser	Brian Carson
Dickens	Danay Carnes	Emily Teegardin	Dennis Wyatt	Mike Smith	Charles Morris	Greg Arnold
Dimmit	Maricela G. Gonzalez	Roberto Serna	Jose A. Urenda	Alonso G. Carmona	Juan Carmona	Valerie Rubalcaba
Donley	Fay Vargas	Luke M. Inman	Mark White	Daniel Ford	Neil Koetting	Dan Sawyer
Duval	Rachel S. Vela	G. Allen Ramirez	Pete Guerra	Adalberto (Chaico) Vera	Marla Garza	Marty Perez
Eastland	Chelsea Henry	Brad Stephenson	Andy Maxwell	James Crenshaw	Ronnie Wilson	Robert Rains
Ector	Clarissa Webster	Dusty Gallivan	Mike Gardner	Greg Simmons	Don Stringer	Billy Hall
Edwards	Olga Lydia Reyes	Tonya Ahlschwede	Marty H. Graham	Steve Smith	Matt Fry	Mike Grooms
Ellis	Melanie Reed	Ann Montgomery	Randy Stinson	Lane Grayson	Paul Perry	Kyle Butler
El Paso	Norma Favela Barceleau	Bill D. Hicks	Carlos Leon	David Stout	Iliana Holguin	Sergio Coronado
Erath	Wanda Greer	Alan Nash	Dee Stephens	Albert Ray	Joe Brown	Jim Buck
Falls	Laurie Smith	Kathryn (Jody) Gilliam	Milton Albright	F.A. Green	Jason Willberg	Nita Wuebker
Fannin	April Gibbs	Richard E. Glaser	Edwina Lane	A.J. Self	Jerry Magness	Doug Kopf
Fayette	Linda Svrcek	Peggy Supak	Jason McBroom	Luke Sternadel	Harvey Berckenhoff	Drew Brossmann
Fisher	Gina Pasley	Richard Thompson	Gordon Pippin	Dexter Elrod	Preston Martin	Micah Evans
Floyd	Patty Davenport	Emily Teegardin	Tanner R. Smith	Clint Bigham	Nathan Johnson	David Martinez
Foard	Debra Hopkins	John Staley Heatly	Ricky Hammonds	Rockne Wisdom	Larry Wright	Anthony Hinsley
Fort Bend	Beverley McGrew Walker	Brian Middleton	Vincent Morales, Jr.	Grady Prestage	Andy Meyers	Dexter L. McCoy
Franklin	Ellen Jaggers	Will W. Ramsay	Jerry Cooper	Toby Godfrey	Charlie Emerson	Scott Smith
Freestone	Teresa Black	Brian Evans	Andy Bonner	Will McSwane	Lloyd Lane	Clyde Ridge, Jr.

County	District Clerk	District Attorney	Comm. Precinct 1	Comm. Precinct 2	Comm. Precinct 3	Comm. Precinct 4
Frio	Ofilia M. Trevino	Audrey Gossett Louis	Joe Vela	Mario Martinez	Raul Carrizales	Danny Cano
Gaines	Susan Murphree	Philip Mack Furlow	Brian Rosson	Josh Elder	David Murphree	Biz Houston
Galveston	John D. Kinard	Jack Roady	Darrell Apffel	Joe Giusti	Stephen D. Holmes	Robin Armstrong
Garza	Terri Laurence	Philip Mack Furlow	Jeff Williams	Kim Wilks	Ted Brannon	Giles W. Dalby, Jr.
Gillespie	Jan Davis	Lucy Wilke	Charles Olfers	Keith Kramer	Dennis Neffendorf	Don Weinheimer
Glasscock	Rebecca Batla	Joshua Hamby	Charles Gully	Mark Halfmann	Brian Frerich	John Seidenberger
Goliad	Vickie Quinn	Rob Lassmann	Kenneth Edwards	David Young	Kirby Brumby	Kevin Fagg
Gonzales	Janice Sutton		K.O. (Dell) Whiddon	Donnie R. Brzozowski	Kevin T. La Fleur	Collie Boatright
Gray	Phyllis Carroll	Franklin McDonough	Logan Hudson	Lake Arrington	John Mark Baggerman	Jeff Haley
Grayson	Kelly Ashmore	J. Brett Smith	Jeff Whitmire	Art Arthur	Phyllis James	Matt Hardenburg
Gregg	Trey Hattaway	John Moore	Ronnie L. McKinney	Ray Bostick. Jr.	Floyd Wingo	Danny Craig, Sr.
Grimes	Diane Leflore	Andria Bender	Chad Mallett	David Tullos	Barbara Walker	Phillip Cox
Guadalupe	Linda Balk		Greg Seidenberger	Drew Engelke	Michael Carpenter	Stephen Germann
Hale	Carla Cannon	Wally Hatch	Harold King	Jerry Bright	Vickie Milner	Benny Cantwell
Hall	Kaci Mills	Luke M. Inman	Ronny Wilson	Terry Lindsey	Gary Proffitt	Troy Glover
Hamilton	Sandy Layhew	Adam Sibley	Johnny Wagner	Keith Allen Curry	Lloyd Huggins	Dickie Clary
Hansford	Janet Torres	Mark Snider	Ira G. (Butch) Reed	Robert Whitaker	Tim Stedje	Wylee Maupin
Hardeman	Stella Doyal	Staley Heatly	Chris Call	Haden Braziel	Barry Haynes	Rodney Foster
Hardin	Dana Hogg	Rebecca Walton	L.W. Cooper, Jr.	Chris Kirkendall	Amanda Young	Ernie Koch
Harris	Marilyn Burgess	Kim Ogg	Rodney Ellis	Adrian Garcia	Tom S. Ramsey	Lesley Briones
Harrison	Sherry Griffis	Reid McCain	William D. Hatfield	Zephaniah Timmins	Phillip Mauldin	Jay Ebarb
Hartley	Melissa Mead	Erin Lands Anchondo	David Vincent	David Spinhirne	Chad Hicks	Robert (Butch) Owens
Haskell	Cynthia Jones	Mike Fouts	Jerry Don Garcia	Bill Steele	Matt Sanders	Russell Beakley
Hays	Avrey Anderson	Kelly Higgins	Debbie Ingalsbe	Michelle Cohen	Lon Shell	Walt Smith
Hemphill	Sylvia Guerrero	Franklin McDonough	Dawn E. Webb	Tim Alexander	Curt McPherson	Nicholas Thomas
Henderson	Betty Herriage	Jenny Palmer	Wendy Spivey	Scott Tuley	Charles (Chuck) McHam	Mark Richardson
Hidalgo	Laura Hinojosa	Ricardo Rodriguez, Jr.	David L. Fuentes	Eduardo (Eddie) Cantu	Everardo (Ever) Villareal	Ellie Torres
Hill	Marchel Eubank	Mark Pratt	Jim Holcomb	Larry Crumpton	Scotty Hawkins	Martin Lake
Hockley	Oralie Gutierrez	Angela L. Overman	Alan Wisdom	Larry Carter	Seth Graf	Tommy Clevenger
Hood	Tonna Trumble Hitt	Ryan Sinclair	Kevin Andrews	Nannette Samuelson	Jack Wilson	Dave Eagle
Hopkins	Cheryl Fulcher	Will Ramsay	Mickey Barker	Greg Anglin	Wade Bartley	Joe Price
Houston	Laura Goolsby	Donna Gordon Kaspar	Gary Lovell	Willie Kitchen	Gene Stokes	Jimmy Henderson
Howard	Joanna Gonzales	Joshua Hamby	Eddilisa Ray	Cash Berry	Jimmie Long	Doug Wagner
Hudspeth	Brenda Sanchez	Bill D. Hicks	Andrew Virdell	Sergio Quijas	Johny Sheets	Canuto Mariscal
Hunt	Susan Spradling	Noble D. Walker	Mark Hutchins	David Monroe	Phillip Martin	Steven Harrison
Hutchinson	Tammy McBrayer	Mark Snider	Gary Alexander	Dwight Kirksey	Ben Bentley	Chris Prock
Irion	Shirley Graham	Allison Palmer	Tia Paxton	Jeff Davidson	John Nanny	Bill (Beaver) McManus, III
Jack	Tracie Pippin	James Stainton	Gary Oliver	Kenny Salazar	Henry Birdwell, Jr.	Terry Ward
Jackson	Sharon Mathis	Pam Guenther	Wayne Hunt	Wayne Bubela	Glenn Martin	Dennis Karl
Jasper	Rosa Norsworthy	Anne Pickle	Seth Martindale	Kevin Holloway	Willie Stark	Dennis Marks
Jeff Davis	Jennifer Wright	Ori T. White	Jody Adams	Roy Hurley	John Davis	Royce Laskoskie
Jefferson	Jamie Smith	Keith Giblin	Vernon Pierce	Cary Erickson	Michael Sinegal	Everette (Bo) Alfred
Jim Hogg	Zonia G. Morales	Gocha A. Ramirez	Antonio (Tony) Flores, III	Abelardo Alaniz	Sandalio Ruiz	Cynthia Guerra Betancourt
Jim Wells	R. David Guerrero	Carlos Omar Garcia	Margie H. Gonzalez	Ventura Garcia	Renee Kirchoff Chapa	Wicho Gonzalez

County	District Clerk	District Attorney	Comm. Precinct 1	Comm. Precinct 2	Comm. Precinct 3	Comm. Precinct 4
Johnson	David Lloyd	Dale Hanna	Rick Bailey	Kenny Howell	Mike White	Larry Woolley
Jones	Lacey Hansen	Joe Edd Boaz	Roy Spalding	Lonnie Vivian	Ross Davis	Joel Spraberry
Karnes	Denise Rodriguez	Audrey Gossett Louis	Shelby Dupnik	Benny Lyssy	James Rosales	Wesley Gisler
Kaufman	Rhonda Hughey	Erleigh Norville Wiley	Mike Hunt	Skeet Phillips	Terry Barber	Tommy Moore
Kendall	Susan Jackson	Nicole S. Bishop	Christina Bergmann	Andra M. Wisian	Richard Chapman	Chad Carpenter
Kenedy	Veronica Vela	John T. Hubert	Joe Recio	Israel Vela, Jr.	Sarita Armstrong Hixon	Jose Salazar
Kent	Craig Harrison	Mike Fouts	Roy W. Chisum	Don Long	Daryl Ham	Robert Graham
Kerr	Dawn Lantz	Stephen Harpold (198th); Lucy Wilke (216th)	Harley David Belew	Rich Paces	Jonathan Letz	Don Harris
Kimble	Karen E. Page	Tonya Ahlschwede	Brayden Schulze	Kelly Simon	Dennis Dunagan	Kenneth Hoffman
King	Jammye D. Timmons	Hunter Brooks	Reggie Hatfield	Chris McCauley	Dwayne Green	Jay Hurt
Kinney	Rick Alvarado	Suzanne West	Mark Frerich	Joe Montalvo	Dennis Dodson	Tim Ward
Kleberg	Jennifer Whittington	John T. Hubert	David Rosse	Chuck Schultz	Jerry Martinez	Marcus Salinas
Knox	Lisa Cypert	Hunter Brooks	Johnny McCown	Kim Sealy	Ray Herring	Nathan Urbanczyk
Lamar	Shawntel Golden	Gary Young	Alan Skidmore	Lonnie Layton	Ronnie Bass	Kevin Anderson
Lamb	Debbie Long	Rickie Redman	Cory DeBerry	Kent Lewis	Danny Short	Lee Logan
Lampasas	Edith Wagner Harrison	John K. Greenwood	Bobby Carroll	Jamie Smart	Lewis Bridges	Mark Rainwater
La Salle	Sonia Maldonado	Audrey Gossett Louis	Noel Niavez	Joaquin Alba	Erasmo Ramirez, Jr.	Raul Ayala
Lavaca	Lori A. Wenske	Kyle A. Denney	Edward Pustka	Wayne Faircloth	Kenny Siegel	Dennis W. Kocian
Lee	Lisa Teinert	Martin Placke	Mark Matthijetz	Richard Wagner	Alan Turner	Steven Knobloch
Leon	Cassandra Noey	James (Caleb) Henson	Joey Sullivan	Newman Paul Bing	Kyle Workman	Thomas J. Foley
Liberty	Delia Sellers	Jennifer L. Bergman	Bruce Karbowski	Greg Arthur	David S. Whitmire	Leon Wilson
Limestone	Carol Jenkins	William Roy DeFriend	Bill David Sadler	Micah Anderson	Stephen Friday	Bobby Forrest
Lipscomb	Kim Blau	Franklin McDonough	Juan Cantu	Merle Miller	Scotty Schilling	Dan Cockrell
Live Oak	Melanie Matkin	Jose Aliseda	Richard Lee	Randy Kopplin	Mitchell Williams	Lucio Morin
Llano	Ashley Inge	Wiley B. (Sonny) McAfee	Peter R. Jones	Linda Raschke	Mike Sandoval	Jerry Don Moss
Loving	Mozelle Carr	Randall (Randy) Reynolds	Harlan Hopper	Ysidro (Joe) Renteria	Raymond W. King	Brad Cook
Lubbock	Sara L. Smith	K. Sunshine Stanek	Terence Kovar	Jason Corley	Gilbert A. Flores	Jordan Rackler
Lynn	Courtney Odom	Philip Mack Furlow	Mark Woodley	John Hawthorne	Don Blair	Larry Durham
Madison	Rhonda Savage	Courtney Cain	Ken Starr	Carl Wiseman	Carl L. Cannon	David Pohorelsky
Marion	Susan Anderson	Angela Smoak	J.R. Ashley	Jacob Pattison	Ralph Meisenheimer	Gered Lee
Martin	Linda Gonzales	Joshua hamby	Kenny Stewart	Auggie Ramos	Bobby Holland	Koy Blocker
Mason	Pam Beam	Tonya Ahlschwede	Reggie Loeffler	Fred Estes	Buddy Schuessler	Dave Underwood
Matagorda	Janice L. Hawthorne	Steven Reis	Edward (Bubba) Cook	Mike Estlinbaum	Troy Shimek	Charles (Bubba) Frick
Maverick	Leopoldo Vielma	Roberto Serna	Gerardo (Jerry) Morales	Rosanna (Roxi) Rios	Olga Ramos	Roberto Ruiz
McCulloch	Michelle Pitcox	Tonya Ahlschwede	Carol Anderson	Randy Deans	Jason Behrens	Don Bratton
McLennan	Jon Gimble	Josh Tetens	Jim Smith	Patricia Miller	Will Jones	Ben Perry
McMullen	Mattie S. Sadovsky	Jose Aliseda	Larry Garcia	Murray Swaim	Scotty McClaugherty	Max Quintanilla, Jr.
Medina	Cindy Fowler	Mark P. Haby	Tim Neuman	Larry Sittre	David Lynch	Daniel Lawler
Menard	Christy Eggleston	Tonya Ahlschwede	Frank Davis	Jay Cunningham	Ed Keith	Tyler Wright
Midland	Alex (Lex) Archuleta	Laura A. Noldolf	Scott Ramsey	Jeff Somers	Luis Sánchez	Dianne Anderson
Milam	Karen Berry	Bill Torrey	Henry (Hub) Hubnik	James Denman	Art Neal	Wesley Payne
Mills	Sonya Scott	Micheal Murray	Mike Wright	Robert Head	Dale Partin	Jason Williams

County	District Clerk	District Attorney	Comm. Precinct 1	Comm. Precinct 2	Comm. Precinct 3	Comm. Precinct 4
Mitchell	Belinda Blassingame	Ricky Thompson	Dennis Jones	Jeremy Strain	Jesse Munoz	Ricky Bailey
Montague	Robin Woods	Casey Hall	Roy Darden	Mike Mayfield	Mark Murphey	Bob Langford
Montgomery	Melisa Miller	Brett Ligon	Robert C. Walker	Charlie Riley	James Noack	Matt Gray
Moore	Mayra Rivero	Erin Lands Anchondo	Daniel Garcia	Miles Mixon	Dee Vaughan	Colt Farni
Morris	Gwen Ashworth	Ricky Shelton	Greg Frazier	Kerry McCoy	Michael Clair	Todd Freeman
Motley	D'anna Russell	Emily Teegardin	Douglas Campbell	Roegan Cruse	Franklin Jameson	Timmy Brooks
Nacogdoches	Loretta Cammack	Andrew Jones	Jerry Don Williamson	Sandy McCorvey	Robin Dawley	Mark Harkness
Navarro	Joshua B. Tackett	William Thompson	Jason Grant	Eddie Perry	Eddie Moore	David Brewer
Newton	Nikki Windham	Courtney Tracy Ponthier	Danny Bentsen	Phillip A. White	Gary Fomby	Leanord (Bubba) Powell
Nolan	Jamie Clem	Richard Thompson	Terry Willman	Seth Mahaffey	Tommy White	Henry Ortega, Jr.
Nueces	Anne Lorentzen	Mark A. Gonzalez	Robert Hernandez	Joe A. (JAG) Gonzalez	John Marez	Brent Chesney
Ochiltree	Shawn Bogard	Jose N. Meraz	Duane Pshigoda	Joe Johnson	JW DeWitt	Kevin Walker
Oldham	Darla Lookingbill		Quincy Taylor	Jim Watkins	Roger Morris	Daniel Gruhlkey
Orange	Anne Reed	John Kimbrough	Johnny Trahan	Chris Sowell	Kirk Roccaforte	Robert Viator
Palo Pinto	Jonna Banks	Kriste Burnett	Gary Glover	Mike Reed	Mike Pierce	Jeff Fryer
Panola	Lindsey Smith	Danny Buck Davidson	Billy Alexander	David A. Cole	Craig M. Lawless	Dale LaGrone
Parker	Sharena Gilliland	Jeff Swain	George Conley	Jacob Holt	Larry Walden	Mike Hale
Parmer	Sandra Warren	Jackie R. Claborn, II	Kirk Frye	Charles Wilkins	Kenny White	Casey Russell
Pecos	Darla Cude	Ori T. White (83rd); Laurie English (112th)	Tom Chapman	Robert Gonzales	Mickey Jack Perry	Nathan Reeves
Polk	Bobbye Richards	Shelly Bush-Sitton	Guylene Robertson	Mark DuBose	Milt Purvis	Jerry Cassity
Potter	Stephnie Menke	Randall Sims	H.R. Kelly	Blair Schaffer	John Coffee	Warren Coble, Sr.
Presidio	Florcita Zubia	Ori T. White	Brenda Silva Bentley	Margarito Hernandez	Jose Cabezuela	David Beebe
Rains	Laura Pate	Robert Vititow	Jeremy Cook	Mike Willis	Korey Young	Lori Northcutt
Randall	Joel Forbis	Robert Love	Rusty Carnes	Eric Barry	Bob Robinson	Tam Boatler
Reagan	Tammy Hodge	Laurie English	Mike Vargas	Tim Sellman	Tommy Holt	Mary Loftin
Real	D'Ann Green	Christina Mitchell Busbee	Brad Hart	Shawn D. Gray	Ramon Ybarra	Charles E. Hunger
Red River	Brenna Williams	Val Varley	Donnie Gentry	David Hutson	Jeff Moore	Bruce Emery
Reeves	Julia Perez	Randall W. Reynolds	Rojelio Alvarado	Israel Campos	Paul Hinojos	Tony Trujillo
Refugio	Sylvia M. Lopez	Robert C. Lassmann	Roy Payne	Stanley Tuttle	Gary Lee Wright	Blaine Wolfshohl
Roberts	Toni Rankin	Franklin McDonough	Cleve Wheeler	William Gill	Kelly Flowers	James F. Duvall
Robertson	Barbara W. Axtell	W. Coty Siegert	Ty Rampy	Donald Threadgill	Chuck Hairston	James Taylor
Rockwall	Lea Carlson	Kenda Culpepper	Cliff Sevier	Dana Macalik	Dennis Bailey	John Stacy
Runnels	Tammy Burleson	John Best	Carl King	Chris Ocker	Brandon Poehls	Juan Ornelas
Rusk	Terri Pirtle Willard	Micheal E. Jimerson	Randy Gaut	Robert Kuykendall	Greg Gibson	Bennie Whitworth
Sabine	Lisa Pitre	Paul A. Robbins	Brent Cox	Keith Nabours	Stanley Jacks	James Lowe
San Augustine	Jeanette Bryan	Paul A. Robbins	Tommy Pickard	Daniel Holman	Joey Holloway	Steve Bryan
San Jacinto	Tammy Currie	Todd Dillon	Laddie McAnally	Donny Marrs	David Brandon	Mark Nettuno
San Patricio	Heather B. Marks	Samuel B. Smith	Sonia Lopez	Tom Yardley	Lilly Wilkinson	Howard Gillespie
San Saba	Kim Wells	Wiley B. (Sonny) McAfee	James Lebow	Mike Poe	Kenley Kroll	Greg McGregor
Schleicher	Mary Ann Gonzalez	Allison Palmer	Gary Gibson	Steve Nelson	Kirk Griffin	Chris Meador
Scurry	Candace Jones	Ben Smith	Terry D. Williams	Doug Scott	Shawn McCowen	Jeff Mitchell
Shackelford	Cheri Hawkins	Joe Edd Boaz	Steve Riley	Ace Reames	Lanham Martin	Cody Jordan
Shelby	Lori Oliver	Karren Price	Roscoe McSwain	Jimmy Lout	Stevie Smith	Tom Bellmyer

County	District Clerk	District Attorney	Comm. Precinct 1	Comm. Precinct 2	Comm. Precinct 3	Comm. Precinct 4
Sherman	Laura Rogers	Erin Lands Anchondo	Dan Law	Terry Mathews	Jeff Crippen	David Davis
Smith	Penny Clarkston	Jacob Putman	Pam Frederick	John Moore	Terry Lee Phillips	Ralph Caraway, Sr.
Somervell	Virginia Dickson	Dale Hanna	Jeff Harris	Richard Talavera	Tammy Ray	Wade Busch
Starr	Orlando Velasquez	Gocha A. Ramirez	Jose Francisco (Kiki) Perez	Raul (Roy) Peña, III	Eloy Garza	Ruben D. Saenz
Stephens	Christie Coapland	Dee Hudson Peavy	David Fambro	Mark McCullough	William H. Warren	Eric O'Dell
Sterling	Jerri McCutchen	Allison Palmer	Ross Copeland	Edward Michulka, Jr.	Tommy Wright, Jr.	Reed Stewart
Stonewall	Holly McLaury	Mike Fouts	Charles (Shorty) Martin	Gerry Messick	Billy Kirk Meador	Gary Myers
Sutton	Pam Thorp	Laurie K. English	Lee C. Bloodworth	Bob Brockman	Carl Teaff	Harold Martinez
Swisher	C.J. Chasco	J. Michael Criswell	Lloyd Rahlfs	Danny Morgan	Joe Murrell	Larry Buske
Tarrant	Thomas A. Wilder	Phil Sorrells	Roy Charles Brooks	Alisa Simmons	Gary Fickes	Manny Ramirez
Taylor	Tammy Robinson	James Hicks	Randall D. Williams	Kyle Kendrick	Brad Birchum	Chuck Statler
Terrell	Raeline Thompson	Suzanne West	Adam Johnson	Lupe Garza	Arnulfo Serna	Gene Chavez
Terry	Tiffany O'Briant	Jo'Shae Ferguson-Worley	Mike Swain	Richard Cavazos	Martin Lefevere	Ernesto Elizardo
Throckmorton	Dianna Moore	Mike Fouts	Casey Wells	Kasey Hibbitts	Greg Brockman	Klay Mitchell
Titus	Marcus Carlock	David Colley	Jeff Parchman	Joe D. Mitchell	Dana Applewhite	Jimmy Parker
Tom Green	Anthony Joseph Monico	Allison Palmer (51st); John H. Best (119th)	Ralph Hoelscher	Sammy Farmer	Rick Bacon	Shawn Nanny
Travis	Velva L. Price	José Garza	Jeff Travillion	Brigid Shea	Ann Howard	Margaret Gómez
Trinity	Jillian Steptoe	Bennie L. Schiro	Tommy Park	Mike Loftin	Neal Smith	Steven Truss
Tyler	Pamela Reneé Crews	Lucas Babin	Joe Blacksher	Doug Hughes	Mike Marshall	Charles (Buck) Hudson
Upshur	Nicole Hernandez	Billy Byrd	Gene Dolle	Dustin Nicholson	Michael Ashley	Jay Miller
Upton	LaWanda McMurray	Laurie English	Pete Jackson	Cody Owens	Mike Smart	Cody Zamora
Uvalde	Christina J. Ovalle	Christina Mitchell Busbee	John Yeackle	Mariano Pargas, Jr.	Jerry W. Bates	Ronald (Ronnie) Garza
Val Verde	Jo Ann Cervantes	Suzanne West	Martin Wardlaw	Juan Carlos Vazquez	Robert Beau Nettleton	Gustavo (Gus) Flores
Van Zandt	Karen L. Wilson	Tonda Curry	Chad LaPrade	Virgil Melton, Jr.	Keith Pearson	Brandon Barton
Victoria	Kim Plummer	Constance Filley Johnson	Danny Garcia	Jason Ohrt	Gary Burns	Kenneth Saxton
Walker	Leslie Woolley	Will Durham	Danny Kuykendall	Ronnie White	Bill Daugette	Brandon Decker
Waller	Liz Pirkle	Elton Mathis	John A. Amsler	Walter E. Smith	Kendric D. Jones	Justin Beckendorff
Ward	Valerie Romo	Randall W. Reynolds	Tino Sanchez	Larry Hanna	Dexter Nichols	Eddie Nelms
Washington	Tammy Brauner	Julie Renken	Don Koester	Candice Bullock	Kirk Hanath	Dustin Majewski
Webb	Esther Degollado	Isidro R. (Chilo) Alaniz	Jesse Gonzalez	Rosaura (Wawi) Tijerina	John Galo	Ricardo A. Jaime
Wharton	Kendra Charbula	Dawn Elizabeth Allison	Richard Zahn	Bud Graves	Steven Goetsch	Doug Mathews
Wheeler	Sherri Jones	Franklin McDonough	Jackie Don May, Jr.	Phillip Gaines	David Simpson	John Walker
Wichita	Leslee Mannon	John Gillespie	Mark Beauchamp	Mickey Fincannon	Barry Mahler	Jeff Watts
Wilbarger	Brenda Peterson	Staley Heatly	Billy Taylor	Phillip Graf	Scott Inglish	Josh Patterson
Willacy	Isabel Adame	Annette C. Hinojosa	Eliberto (Beto) Guerra	Mario Tijerina	Henry De La Paz	Ernie Garcia
Williamson	Lisa David	Shawn Dick	Terry Cook	Cynthia Long	Valerie Covey	Russ Boles
Wilson	Deborah Bryan	Audrey Gossett Louis	Gary Martin	Russell A. King	Jeffery Pierdolla	John (Scott) Akin
Winkler	Geneva Baker	Amanda Navarette	Billy J. Stevens	Robbie Wolf	Victor Berzoza	Billy Ray Thompson
Wise	Loucrecia Biggerstaff	James Stainton	Biff Hayes	Kevin D. Burns	Danny Lambert	Colby Shawn
Wood	Suzy Wright	Angela Albers	Virgil Holland	Jerry Gaskill	Mike Simmons	Russell Acker
Yoakum	Sandra Roblez	Bill Helwig	Woodson W. Lindsey	Ray Marion	Tommy Box	Tim Addison
Young	Jamie Freeze Land	Dee Peavy	Stacy Creswell	Scott Shook	Stacey Rogers	Jimmy Wiley
Zapata	Dora Martinez Castañon	Isidro R. (Chilo) Alaniz	Paco Mendoza	Olga M. Elizondo	Jose A. Solis	Norberto Garza
Zavala	Rachel Ramirez	Robert Serna	Joe Cruz	Raul Gomez	Jesse Gonzalez	Florencio (Flo) Melendrez

Texans in Congress

Besides the two members of the U.S. Senate allocated to each state, Texas was allocated 38 members in the U.S. House of Representatives for the 118th Congress. The term of office for members of the House is two years; the terms of all members will expire in January 2025. Senators serve six-year terms. Sen. John Cornyn's term will end in 2027. Sen. Ted Cruz's term will end in 2025.

Addresses and phone numbers of the lawmakers' Washington and district offices are below, as well as the committees on which they serve. Washington zip codes are 20515 for members of the House and 20510 for senators. The telephone area code for Washington is 202.

In 2023, members of Congress received a salary of $174,000. Members in leadership positions received $193,400.

U.S. Senate

(Total members 100; Republicans 49, Democrats 48, Independents 3.)

CORNYN, John. Republican (Home: Austin); Washington Office: 517 HSOB; (202) 224-2934. www.cornyn.senate.gov.

Texas Offices: 221 W. 6th, Ste. 1530, Austin 78701, (512) 469-6034; 5001 Spring Valley, Ste. 1125 E, Dallas 75244, (972) 239-1310; 6770 W. Expressway 83, Ste 302, Harlingen 78552, (956) 423-0162; 5300 Memorial Dr., Ste. 710, Houston 77007, (713) 572-3337; 1500 Broadway, Ste. 1230, Lubbock 79401, (806) 472-7533; 600 Navarro, Ste. 210, San Antonio 78205, (210) 224-7485; 100 E. Ferguson, Ste. 1004, Tyler 75702, (903) 593-0902.

John Cornyn

Committees: Finance, Judiciary, Select Committee on Intelligence, Caucus on International Narcotics Control.

CRUZ, Ted. Republican (Home: Houston); Washington Office: 404 RSOB; (202) 224-5922. www.cruz.senate.gov.

Ted Cruz

Texas Offices: 300 E. 8th, Ste. 961, Austin 78701, (512) 916-5834; 3626 N. Hall, Ste. 410, Dallas 75219, (214) 599-8749; 1919 Smith, Ste. 9047, Houston 77002, (713) 718-3057; 200 S. 10th, Ste. 1603, McAllen 78501, (956) 686-7339; 9901 IH-10W, Ste. 950, San Antonio 78230, (210) 340-2885; 305 S. Broadway, Ste. 501, Tyler 75702, (903) 593-5130.

Committees: Foreign Relations; Commerce, Science and Transportation; Judiciary; Rules and Administration.

U.S. House of Representatives

(Total districts 435; Republicans 222, Democrats 212, 1 vacant. Texas delegation of 38; 25 Republicans, 13 Democrats.)

District 1 — MORAN, Nathaniel, R-Tyler; Washington Office: 1541 LHOB; (202) 225-3035. District Offices: 100 N. Bolivar, Marshall 75671, (903) 561-6349; 2500 N. Robison Rd., Ste. 190, Texarkana 75501, (903) 561-6349; 101 E Methvin, Ste. 302, Longview 75601, (903) 561-6349; 1121 ESE Loop 323, Ste. 206, Tyler 75701, (903) 561-6349. Committees: Education and the Workforce, Foreign Affairs, Judiciary.

District 2 — CRENSHAW, Dan, R-Kingwood; Washington Office: 248 CHOB; (202) 225-6565. District Offices: 1849 Kingwood Dr., Ste. 100, Kingwood 77339, (713) 860-1330; 2829 Technology Forest, Ste. #280, The Woodlands 77381, (281) 640-7720. Committees: Energy and Commerce, Intelligence.

District 3 — SELF, Keith, R-McKinney; Washington Office: 1113 LHOB; (202) 225-4201. District Offices: 4500 W. Eldorado Pkwy, Ste. 3500, McKinney 75070, (972) 202-4150; PO Box 1470, Greenville,75403, (903) 458-7037. Committees: Foreign Affairs, Veterans' Affairs.

District 4 — FALLON, Pat, R-Sherman; Washington Office, 2416 RHOB; (202) 225-6673: District Offices: 6531 Horizon, Ste. A, Rockwall 75032, (972) 771-0100; 100 W. Houston, Ste. 14, Sherman 75090, (903) 820-5170; 15 James Carlow, New Boston 75570, (903) 716-7500. Committees: Armed Services, Oversight and Accountability.

District 5 — GOODEN, Lance, R-Terrell; Washington Office: 2431 RHOB; (202) 225-3484. District Office: 220 Burnett Trail, Canton 75103, (903) 502-5300. Committees: Judiciary, Transportation and Infrastructure.

District 6 — ELLZEY, Jake, R-Midlothian; Washington Office: 1721 LHOB; (202) 225-2002. District Offices: 2001 Bates, Ste. 100, Waxahachie 75167, (469) 550-7150; 122 N. Beaton, Corsicana 75110, (903) 602-7860. Committees: Appropriations, Small Business.

District 7 — FLETCHER, Lizzie, D-Houston; Washington Office: 346 CHOB; (202) 225-2571; District Offices: 3700 Buffalo Speedway, Ste. 610, Houston 77098, (713) 353-8680; 1600 Highway 6, Ste. 455, Sugar Land 77478, (713) 353-8680. Committee: Energy and Commerce.

District 8 — LUTTRELL, Morgan, R-Magnolia; Washington Office: 1320 LHOB; (202) 225-4901. District Office: 18230 FM 1488, Ste. 308, Magnolia 77354; (281) 305-7890. Committees: Armed Services, Homeland Security, Veterans' Affairs.

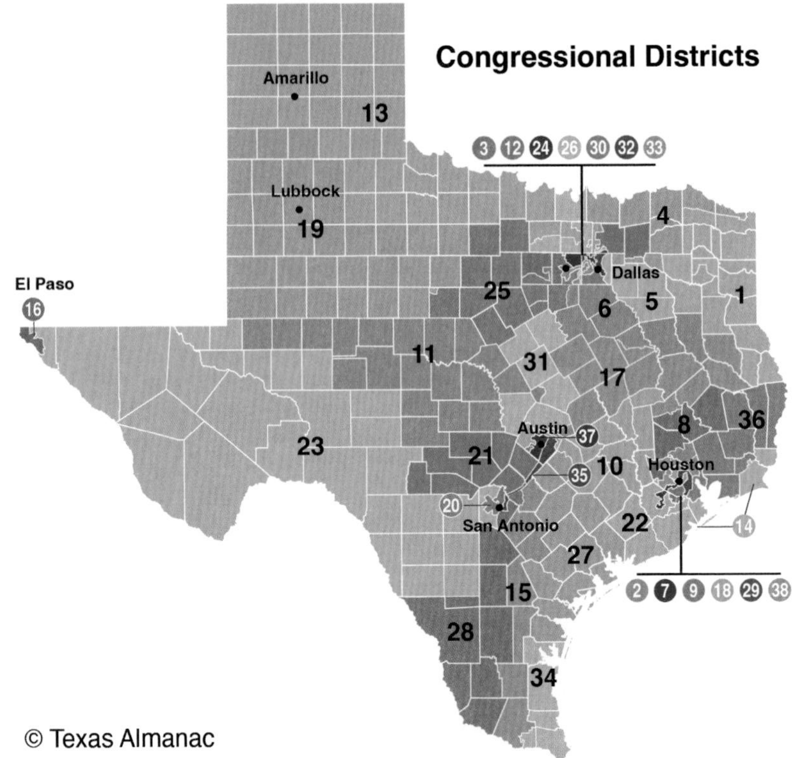

District 9 — GREEN, Al, D-Houston; Washington Office: 2347 RHOB; (202) 225–7508; District Offices: 3003 South Loop West, Ste. 460, Houston 77054, (713) 383–9234; 2440 Texas Parkway, Ste. 115, Missouri City 77489, (713) 383–9234. Committee: Financial Services.

District 10 — McCAUL, Michael, R-West Lake Hills; Washington Office: 2300 RHOB; (202) 225–2401. District Offices: 175 Century Square Drive, Ste. 210, College Station 77840, (979) 431–6480; 11614 FM 2244, Ste. 160, Austin 78738, (512) 473–2357. Committees: Foreign Affairs, Homeland Security.

District 11— PFLUGER, August, R-San Angelo; Washington Office: 1124 LHOB; (202) 225–3605. District Offices: 6 Desta Dr., Ste. 2000, Midland 79705, (432) 687–2390; 501 Center Ave., Brownwood 76801, (325) 646–1950; 104 W. Sandstone, Llano 78643, (325) 247–2826; 1010 E 8th St., Odessa 79761, (432) 331–9667; 135 W. Twohig, Ste. B, San Angelo 76903, (325) 659–4010; 505 E Jasper Drive, Killeen 76541, (254) 669–6570. Committees: Homeland Security, Energy and Commerce.

District 12 — GRANGER, Kay, R-Fort Worth; Washington Office: 2308 RHOB; (202) 225–5071; District Office: 1701 River Run Rd., Ste. 407, Fort Worth 76107, (817) 338–0909. Committee: Appropriations.

District 13 — JACKSON, Ronny, R-Amarillo; Washington Office: 446 CHOB; (202) 225–3706; District Offices: 620 S. Taylor, Ste. 200, Amarillo 79101, (806) 641–5600; 2525 Kell Blvd., Ste. 406, Wichita Falls 76308, (940) 285–8000. Committees: Agriculture, Armed Services, Foreign Affairs, Select Subcommittee on the Coronavirus Pandemic.

District 14 — WEBER, Randy, R-Friendswood; Washington Office: 107 CHOB; (202) 225–2831. District Offices: 350 Pine, Ste. 1450, Beaumont 77701, (409) 835–0108; 122 West Way, Ste. 301, Lake Jackson 77566, (979) 285–0231; 174 Calder Rd., Ste. 600, League City 77573, (281) 316–0231. Committees: Energy and Commerce, Science, Space, and Technology.

District 15 — DE LA CRUZ, Monica, R-Edinburg; Washington Office: 1415 LHOB; (202) 225–9901. District Offices: 1400 N McColl Rd., Ste. 103, McAllen 78504, (956) 800–6069; 211 W Court St, Seguin 78155, (830) 463–0800. Committees: Agriculture, Financial Services.

District 16 — ESCOBAR, Veronica, D-El Paso; Washington Office: 2448 RHOB; (202) 225–4831. District Office: 221 N. Kansas, Ste. 1500, El Paso 79901, (915) 541–1400. Committees: Armed Services, Judiciary, Ethics.

District 17 — SESSIONS, Pete, R-Waco; Washington Office: 2204 RHOB; (202) 225–6105; District Offices: 400 Austin Ave., Ste. 302, Waco 76701, (254) 633–4500; 901 Normal Park Drive Ste. 208, Huntsville 77320 (936) 755–7770; 3034 Raguet St, Nacogdoches 75965–2852, (936) 585–7959; 300 E Shepherd Avenue, Ste. 210, Lufkin 75902, (936) 219–6450. Committees: Financial Services, Oversight and Accountability.

District 18 — JACKSON LEE, Sheila, D-Houston; Washington Office: 2314 RHOB; (202) 225–3816; District Offices: 1919 Smith, Ste. 1180, Houston 77002, (713) 655–0050; 420 W. 19th St., Houston 77008, (713) 861–4070;

6719 W. Montgomery, Ste. 204, Houston 77091, (713) 691–4882; 4300 Lyons Ave., Houston 77020, (713) 227–7740. Committees: Budget, Homeland Security, Judiciary.

District 19 — ARRINGTON, Jodey, R-Lubbock; Washington Office: 1107 LHOB; (202) 225–4005. District Offices: 500 Chestnut St., Abilene 79602, (325) 675–9779; 1312 Texas Ave., Ste. 219, Lubbock 79401, (806) 763–1611. Committee: Budget; Ways and Means.

District 20 — CASTRO, Joaquin, D-San Antonio; Washington Office: 2241 RHOB; (202) 225–3236. District Office: 727 E. Cesar E. Chavez Blvd., Ste. B-128, San Antonio 78206, (210) 348–8216. Committees: Intelligence; Foreign Affairs.

District 21 — ROY, Chip S., R-Dripping Springs; Washington Office: 103 CHOB; (202) 225–4236. District Office: 16414 San Pedro Ave, Ste. 817, San Antonio 78232, (210) 821–5024; 5900 Southwest Parkway, Bldg 5, Ste. 520, Austin 78735, (512) 871–5959; 125 Lehmann Drive, Ste. 201, Kerrville 78028, (830) 896–0154. Committees: Budget, Judiciary, Rules.

District 22 — NEHLS, Troy E., R-Richmond; Washington Office: 1104 LHOB; (202) 225–5951. District Office: 6510 FM 359 S., Ste. 210, Fulshear 77441, (346) 762–6600. Committees: Judiciary, Transportation and Infrastructure.

District 23 — GONZALES, Tony, R-San Antonio; Washington Office: 2244 RHOB; (202) 225–4511. District Offices: 4372 N. Loop 1604 W, Ste. 205, San Antonio 78249, (210) 806–9920 (appt. only); 712 E. Gibbs, Ste. 101, Del Rio 78840, (830) 308–6200; 103 W. Callaghan, Fort Stockton 79735, (432) 299–6200; 10167 Socorro Rd., Socorro 79927, (915) 990–1500 (appt only). Committees: Appropriations, Homeland Security.

District 24 — VAN DUYNE, Beth, R-Irving; Washington Office: 1725 LHOB; (202) 225–6605. District Office:14951 Dallas Pkwy. Unit 830, Dallas 75254, (972) 966–5500. Committees: Small Business, Ways and Means.

District 25 — WILLIAMS, Roger, R-Willow Park; Washington Office: 2336 RHOB; (202) 225–9896. District Offices:1000 Ballpark Way, Ste. 310, Arlington 76011, (682) 218–5965; 115 S. Main, Ste. 206, Cleburne 76033, (817) 774–2575. Committees: Financial Services; Small Business.

District 26 — BURGESS, Michael, R-Lewisville; Washington Office: 2161 RHOB; (202) 225–7772. District Office: 2000 S. Stemmons Fwy., Ste. 200, Lake Dallas 75065, (972) 497–5031. Committees: Budget; Energy and Commerce; Rules.

District 27 — CLOUD, Michael, R-Victoria; Washington Office: 171 CHOB; (202) 225–7742. District Offices:555 N. Carancahua St. Tower II, Ste. 980, Corpus Christi 78401, (361) 884–2222; 111 N. Glass St, Ste. 102, Victoria 77901, (361) 894–6446. Committees: Appropriations, Select Subcommittee on the Coronavirus Pandemic.

District 28 — CUELLAR, Henry, D-Laredo; Washington Office: 2372 RHOB; (202) 225–1640. District Offices: 602 E. Calton Rd., Laredo 78041, (956) 725–0639; 1145 E. Commerce, Ste. 205, San Antonio 78205, (210) 271–2851; 100 N. FM 3167, Rio Grande City 78582, (956) 487–5603. Committee: Appropriations.

District 29 — GARCIA, Sylvia, D-Houston; Washington Office: 2419 RHOB; (202) 225–1688; District Office: 11811 East Fwy., Ste. 430, Houston 77029, (832) 325–3150. Committees: Financial Services, Select Subcommittee on the Weaponization of the Fed Govt.

District 30 — CROCKETT, Jasmine, D-Dallas; Washington Office: 1616 LHOB; (202) 225–8885. District Office: 1825 Market Center Blvd., Ste. 440, Dallas 75207, (214) 922–8885. Committees: Agriculture, Oversight and Accountability.

District 31 — CARTER, John, R-Round Rock; Washington Offices: 2208 RHOB; (202) 225–3864. District Offices: 2180 N. Main, Ste. I-10, Belton 76513, (254) 933–1392; 4411 S. I-35, Ste. 115, Georgetown 78626, (512) 591–9061. Committee: Appropriations.

District 32 — ALLRED, Colin, D-Dallas; Washington Office: 348 CHOB; (202) 225–2231; District Office: 100 N. Central Expressway, Ste. 602, Richardson, 75080, (972) 972–7949. Committees: Foreign Affairs, Select Subcommittee on the Weaponization of the Fed Govt, Transportation and Infrastructure.

District 33 — VEASEY, Marc, D-Fort Worth; Washington Office: 2348 RHOB; (202) 225–9897. District Offices: 1881 Sylvan Ave., Ste 108, Dallas 75208, (214) 741–1387; 6707 Brentwood Stair Rd., Ste. 200, Fort Worth 76112, (817) 920–9086. Committees: Armed Services; Energy and Commerce.

District 34 — GONZALEZ, Vicente, D-McAllen; Washington Office: 154 CHOB; (202) 225–2531. District Offices: 835 E. Levee St., 6th Floor, Brownsville 78520, 956-682–5545; 100 W. King Ave., Ste. 106, Kingsville 78363, 956-682–5545; 255 S. Kansas Ave, Weslaco 78596, 956-682–5545. Committee: Financial Services

District 35 — CASAR, Greg, D-Austin; Washington Office: 1339 LHOB; (202) 225–5645. District Office: (512) 691–1200. Committees: Agriculture, Oversight and Accountability

District 36 — BABIN, Brian, R-Woodville; Washington Office: 2236 RHOB; (202) 225–1555. District Offices: 203 Ivy Ave., Ste 600, Deer Park 77536, (832) 780–0966; 769 S. Main, Lumberton 77657, (409) 883–8075; 100 W. Bluff Dr., Woodville 75979, (409) 331–8066. Committees: Transportation and Infrastructure; Science, Space and Technology.

District 37 — DOGGETT, Lloyd, D-Austin; Washington Office: 2307 RHOB; (202) 225–4865. District Office: 300 E. 8th, 7th Fl., Austin 78701, (512) 916–5921. Committees: Budget, Joint Committee on Taxation, Ways and Means.

District 38 — HUNT, Wesley, R-Houston; Washington Office: 1520 LHOB; (202) 225–5646. District Offices: 5599 San Felipe St., Ste. 950, Houston, 77056, (832) 357–0555; 990 Village Square Dr., Ste. G-900, Tomball 77375, (346) 246–7355. Committees: Natural Resources, Judiciary, Small Business. ☆

U.S. Tax Collections in Texas

(in thousands) *Information for fiscal years furnished by the Internal Revenue Service.*

Fiscal Year	Individual Income and Employment Taxes	Corporation Income Taxes	Estate Taxes	Gift Taxes	Excise Taxes	TOTAL U.S. Taxes Collected in Texas
2022	$ 332,138,185	$ 36,394,970	$ 2,108,978	$ 349,218	$ 21,053,057	$ 400,867,645
2021	261,047,291	27,143,965	1,996,227	259,352	17,143,535	312,071,886
2020	239,159,253	14,508,511	1,023,884	113,036	17,291,862	275,485,613
2019	245,361,121	18,470,193	1,620,965	148,057	22,661,021	292,330,171
2018	240,169,156	15,756,288	1,395,067	135,733	22,592,120	280,048,364
2017	225,236,761	22,939,596	1,314,828	123,822	21,340,788	270,955,237
2016	218,950,277	19,021,716	1,318,116	140,191	21,698,393	261,138,693
2015	226,945,577	32,083,819	1,167,572	115,516	19,591,942	279,904,425
2014	211,993,178	32,585,544	1,557,068	89,865	19,110,528	265,336,183
2013	195,542,035	33,933,242	890,069	596,861	18,950,003	249,912,209
2012	171,880,127	27,984,282	796,227	180,060	18,619,137	219,459,878
2011	160,086,749	21,880,905	117,936	359,987	15,850,240	198,295,817
2010	147,748,859	24,991,374	1,210,600	287,181	14,904,099	189,142,112
2009	158,798,111	24,235,172	1,780,030	242,918	15,465,279	200,521,512
2008	178,761,539	39,971,658	1,549,767	243,043	15,150,053	235,676,058

Federal Funds Distribution in Texas

	2021		2022
Total all	**$ 349.7 billion**		**$ 277.6 billion**
Direct payments	$ 154.3 billion	Direct payments	$ 130.4 billion
Grants	113.0 billion	Grants	72.3 billion
Contracts	55.1 billion	Contracts	67.4 billion
Loans	21.8 billion	Other financial assistance	7.2 billion
Other financial assistance	5.5 billion	Loans	254.1 million
Top 5 by program			
Social Security retirement	$ 58.7 billion	Social Security retirement	$ 64.0 billion
Medical assistance	34.1 billion	Medical assistance	38.0 billion
Coronavirus Relief Fund	26.3 billion	Veterans compensation	13.9 billion
Education stabilization	23.7 billion	SNAP	11.5 billion
Paycheck Protection	22.4 billion	Social Security disability	9.1 billion
Top 5 by agency			
Social Security Administration	$ 79.4 billion	Social Security Administration	$ 85.6 billion
Department of Health and Human Svs	64.5 billion	Department of Health and Human Svs	59.2 billion
Department of Defense	36.4 billion	Department of Defense	46.8 billion
Department of the Treasury	31.0 billion	Department of Veterans Affairs	32.1 billion
Department of Education	30.9 billion	Department of Agriculture	20.7 billion

Information for fiscal years from USAspending.gov

Federal Funds Distribution to States, trailing 12 months

Rank	State	Total	Per Capita	Rank	State	Total	Per Capita
1	California	$ 361.2 billion	$ 9,136	11	South Carolina	107.7 billion	21,429
2	**Texas**	**246.3 billion**	**8,702**	12	Connecticut	100.4 billion	27,995
3	Florida	240.2 billion	11,449	13	Ohio	100.1 billion	8,587
4	Pennsylvania	221.8 billion	17,324	14	Michigan	97.1 billion	9,750
5	New York	214.4 billion	10,800	15	Arizona	95.2 billion	13,567
6	Minnesota	183.5 billion	32,908	16	Wisconsin	93.9 billion	16,201
7	Indiana	162.4 billion	24,358	17	Tennessee	92.0 billion	13,694
8	Virginia	159.3 billion	18,807	18	Maryland	89.5 billion	14,783
9	Illinois	139.8 billion	10,917	19	North Carolina	87.9 billion	8,553
10	Kentucky	135.8 billion	30,496	20	Massachusetts	82.2 billion	11,976

Source: USAspending.gov

Major Military Installations

Below are listed the major military installations in Texas in 2023. "Civilian" refers to Department of Defense and contractor personnel. In October 2010, Fort Sam Houston, Lackland AFB, and Randolph AFB were merged into Joint Base San Antonio under the jurisdiction of the U.S. Air Force 502nd Air Base Wing.

U.S. Navy

Naval Air Station Corpus Christi

Location: Corpus Christi (est. 1941)

Address: NAS Corpus Christi, 11001 D St., Corpus Christi 78418

Main phone number: (361) 961–2811

Personnel: 1,369 active-duty; 395 reserve; 710 civilians.

Major units: Naval Air Training Command Headquarters; Training Air Wing 4; Marine Aviation Training Support Group; Coast Guard Air Group; Corpus Christi Army Depot (est. 1961).

Naval Air Station–Joint Reserve Base Fort Worth

Location: westside Fort Worth (est. 1994)

Address: NAS-JRB, 1510 Chennault Ave., Fort Worth 76113

Main phone number: (817) 782–3058

Personnel: Active-duty: 2 Army; 232 Navy; 487 Marines; 159 Air Force. Reserve: 605 Army; 2,074 Navy; 1,366 Marines; 975 Air Force. 1,709 Air National Guard; 892 civilians.

Major units: Navy Fleet Logistics Support Squadron 59; 8th Marine Corps District; Marine Air Group 41; 14th Marine Regiment; Marine Aviation Logistics Squadron 41; Marine Fighter Attack Squadron 112; 136th Airlift Wing, Texas Air National Guard; U.S. Army 90th Aviation Support Battalion; 10th Air Force, 301st Fighter Wing, Air Force Reserve.

Naval Air Station Kingsville

Location: Kingsville (est. 1942)

Address: NAS Kingsville 78363

Main phone number: (361) 516–6136

Personnel: 363 active-duty; 159 reserve; 243 civilians.

Major units: Training Air Wing Two; Training Squadrons 21 and 22; Naval Auxiliary Landing Field Orange Grove; McMullen Target Range, Escondido Ranch.

U.S. Army

Fort Bliss

Location: El Paso (est. 1849)

Address: 1741 Marshall Rd., Fort Bliss 79916

Main phone number: (915) 568–2121

Personnel: 25,546 active-duty; 260 reserve; 5,660 civilians.

Major units: 1st Armored Division; 32nd Air and Missile Defense Command; 15th Sustainment Brigade; 5th Armored Brigade; Air Defense Artillery School; 11th Air Defense Artillery Brigades; Joint Task Force North; 204th Military Intelligence Battalion; 212th Fires Brigade; 402nd Field Artillery Brigade; Biggs Army Airfield (est. 1916).

Fort Cavazos

Location: Killeen (est. 1942)

Address: Fort Cavazos 76544

Main phone number: (254) 286–5139

Personnel: 36,391 active-duty; 805 reserve; 6,915 civilians.

Major units: III Corps, Headquarters Command; First Army Division West; 1st Cavalry Division; 13th Sustainment Command; 89th Military Police Brigade; 3rd Cavalry Regiment; 41st Fires Brigade; 504th Battlefield Surveillance Brigade; Army Operational Test Command; Darnell Army Medical Center.

Red River Army Depot

Location: 18 miles west of Texarkana (est. 1941)

Address: Red River Army Depot, Texarkana 75507

Main phone number: (903) 334–2141

Personnel: 19 active-duty; 93 reserve; 3,059 civilians.

Major unit: Defense Distribution Center; U.S. Army Tank-Automotive and Armaments Command.

U.S. Air Force

Joint Base San Antonio (Fort Sam Houston, Lackland AFB, and Randolph AFB)

Location: San Antonio (est. 2010)

Address: 2080 Wilson Road, JBSA-Fort Sam Houston 78234-5004

Main phone number: (210) 221–5453

Personnel: 65,000 active-duty; 5,400 reserve; 25,000 civilians

Major units: 502nd Air Base Wing; 59th Medical Wing; 37th and 12th Training Wing; 616th Operations Center; 67th and 688th Cyberspace Wing; 350th Spectrum Warfare Wing; 22nd, 10th, and 4th Air Force Reserves; Texas Air Guard 149th Fighter Wing; US Army Medical Command; US Army Veterinary Corps; 7th Signal Command; 470th Military Intelligence Brigade.

Dyess Air Force Base

Location: Abilene (est. 1942 as Tye Army Airfield, closed at end of World War II, re-established in 1956)

Address: Dyess Air Force Base, 79607

Main phone number: (325) 696–3113

Personnel: 4,221 active-duty; 425 reserve; 710 civilians.

Major units: 7th Bomb Wing (Air Combat Command); 317th Airlift Group.

Goodfellow Air Force Base

Location: San Angelo (est. 1940)

Address: Goodfellow AFB, San Angelo 76908

Main phone number: (325) 654–3876

Personnel: 3,195 active-duty; 29 reserve; 635 civilians.

Major units: 17th Training Wing; 517th Training Squadron; 17th Medical Group; 17th Mission Support Group.

Laughlin Air Force Base

Location: Del Rio (est. 1942).
Address: Laughlin Air Force Base, 78843
Main phone number: (830) 298–3511
Personnel: 1,288 active-duty; 82 reserve; 1,108 civilians.
Major unit: 47th Flying Training Wing.

Sheppard Air Force Base

Location: Wichita Falls (est. 1941).
Address: Sheppard Air Force Base, 76311
Main phone number: (940) 676–2511
Personnel: 5,973 active-duty; 131 reserve; 1,603 civilians.
Major units: 82nd Training Wing; 80th Flying Training Wing; NCO Academy.

Texas Military Forces

Tracing their history to early frontier days, the Texas Military Forces are organized into the **Texas Army National Guard, Texas Air National Guard,** and the **Texas State Guard**.

The **governor** is commander-in-chief of the Texas Military Forces. This command function is exercised through the adjutant general appointed by the governor and approved by federal and state legislative authority. Major General Thomas Suelzer has served as the current adjutant general since 2022.

When not in active federal service, Camp Mabry serves as the administative and storage headquarters. Camp Mabry was established in the early 1890s as a summer encampment of the Texas Volunteer Guard, a forerunner of the Texas National Guard. The name honors Woodford Haywood Mabry, adjutant general from 1891–1898.

The State Guard, an all-volunteer backup force, was created by the Legislature in 1941. It became an active element of the state military forces in 1965 with a mission of reinforcing the National Guard in emergencies and replacing National Guard units called into federal service. The State Guard had a membership of approximately 1,678 personnel in 2017.

The Army National Guard is available for state and national emergencies and has been used extensively during natural disasters. There were 18,160 Texans serving in the Texas Army National Guard in 2017.

When the military forces were reorganized following World War II, the Texas Air National Guard was added. Its units augment major Air Force commands. There were 3,170 service members in the Air National Guard in 2017.

When called into active federal service, National Guard units come within the chain of command of the Army and Air Force units.

Camp Mabry

Location: Austin, just west of MoPac Blvd.
Address: Box 5218, Austin 78763
Main phone number: (512) 465–5101
Web site: https://tmd.texas.gov/
Adjutant General of Texas: Maj. General Thomas Suelzer
Major units: Joint Force Headquarters, the Standing Joint Interagency Task Force, the 36th Infantry Division, the 147th Reconnaissance Wing, 149th Fighter Wing, and the 136th Airlift Wing. Texas Air National Guard.
Texas Military Forces Museum: open Wednesday–Sunday, 10 a.m. to 4 p.m.☆

Presidential Medal of Freedom

President Joe Biden bestowed Presidential Medals of Freedom to two Texans in 2022: **Juliet V. García** and **Simone Biles**.

Juliet García was born the middle of three children in Brownsville and earned her bachelor's and master's degrees at the U. of Houston and a Ph.D. at UT Austin. She became the first Mexican–American female to head a U.S. college or university when she was appointed president at Texas Southmost College in 1986. García led the joint institution when TSC merged with UT Brownsville in 1991 and stayed on as president of UTB when the two split in 2011. She currently serves as a senior advisor to the University of Texas System.

Simone Biles was born in Columbus, Ohio and moved to Spring as a child with her three siblings to live with their maternal grandfather. She is an artistic gymnast who has earned seven Olympic medals (four golds) and 25 World Championship medals (19 golds) in her career so far. Biles testified to the Senate Judicial Committee in 2021 during the investigation into abuse in the USA Gymnastics and U.S. Olympic systems. She is the youngest person to win the Presidential Medal of Freedom.

Juliet García (top) and Simone Biles (bottom) receiving the Presidential Medal of Freedom, July 7, 2022. Photos by the White House, Public Domain

Federal Courts in Texas

Source: The following list of U.S. appeals and district court judges and officials was compiled from court websites.

Texas is divided into four federal judicial districts, each of which is comprised of several divisions. Appeal from all Texas federal courts is to the U.S. Fifth Circuit Court of Appeals in New Orleans.

U.S. Court of Appeals, Fifth Circuit

The Fifth Circuit is composed of Louisiana, Mississippi, and Texas. Sessions are held in each of the states at least once a year and may be scheduled at any location having adequate facilities. U.S. circuit judges are appointed for life and received a salary of $246,600 in 2023.

Circuit Judges:

- Chief Judge, Priscilla Richman, Austin.
- Andrew S. Oldham, Austin.
- Stuart Kyle Duncan, Baton Rouge, La.
- Catharina Haynes, James C. Ho, and Don R. Willett, Dallas.
- Jennifer Walker Elrod, Edith H. Jones, and Jerry E. Smith, Houston.
- James E. Graves Jr., Leslie H. Southwick, and Cory T. Wilson, Jackson, Miss.
- Dana M. Douglas, Kurt D. Engelhardt, and Stephen A. Higginson, New Orleans, La.
- Carl E. Stewart, Shreveport, La.

Senior Judges: James L. Dennis, Baton Rouge, La.; Patrick E. Higginbotham, Dallas; Carolyn Dineen King, Houston; Rhesa H. Barksdale and E. Grady Jolly, Jackson, Miss.; W. Eugene Davis and John M. Duhé Jr., New Iberia, La.; Edith Brown Clement, New Orleans, La.; Jacques L. Wiener Jr., Shreveport, La.

Clerk of Court: Lyle W. Cayce, New Orleans, La.

U.S. District Courts

U.S. district judges are appointed for life and received a salary in 2023 of $232,600.

Northern Texas District

www.txnd.uscourts.gov

District Judges:

- Chief Judge, David C. Godbey, Dallas
- Matthew J. Kacsmaryk, Amarillo.
- Jane J. Boyle, Ada Brown, Ed Kinkeade, Sam A. Lindsay, Karen Gren Scholer, and Brantley Starr, Dallas.
- Reed O'Connor and Mark T. Pittman, Fort Worth.
- James Wesley Hendrix, Lubbock.

Senior Judges: A. Joe Fish, Sidney A. Fitzwater, and Barbara M.G. Lynn, Dallas; Terry R. Means, Fort Worth; Sam R. Cummings, Lubbock.

Clerk of District Court: Karen Mitchell, Dallas.

U.S. Attorney: Leigha Simonton.

Federal Public Defender: Jason Hawkins.

U.S. Marshal: (vacant).

Bankruptcy Judges: Chief Judge, Stacey G.C. Jernigan, Dallas. Judges Scott W. Everett and Michelle V. Larson, Dallas; Edward L. Morris and Mark X. Mullin, Fort Worth; Robert L. Jones, Lubbock.

Following are the divisions of the Northern District and the counties in each division:

Abilene Division

Callahan, Eastland, Fisher, Haskell, Howard, Jones, Mitchell, Nolan, Shackelford, Stephens, Stonewall, Taylor, and Throckmorton. **Magistrate Judge:** John R. Parker. **Courtroom Deputy:** Jennifer Chittum.

Amarillo Division

Armstrong, Briscoe, Carson, Castro, Childress, Collingsworth, Dallam, Deaf Smith, Donley, Gray, Hall, Hansford, Hartley, Hemphill, Hutchinson, Lipscomb, Moore, Ochiltree, Oldham, Parmer, Potter, Randall, Roberts, Sherman, Swisher, and Wheeler. **Magistrate Judge:** Lee Ann Reno. **Courtroom Deputy:** Christopher Kordes.

Dallas Division

Dallas, Ellis, Hunt, Johnson, Kaufman, Navarro, and Rockwall. **Magistrate Judges:** David L. Horan, Irma Carrillo Ramirez, Rebecca Rutherford, and Renee H. Toliver. **Courtroom Deputies:** Marie Gonzales, Lavenia Price, Shakira Todd, and Mervin Wright.

Fort Worth Division

Comanche, Erath, Hood, Jack, Palo Pinto, Parker, Tarrant, and Wise. **Magistrate Judges:** Jeffrey L. Cureton and Hal R. Ray Jr. **Courtroom Deputies:** Julie Harwell and Elsherie Moore.

Lubbock Division

Bailey, Borden, Cochran, Crosby, Dawson, Dickens, Floyd, Gaines, Garza, Hale, Hockley, Kent, Lamb, Lubbock, Lynn, Motley, Scurry, Terry, and Yoakum. **Magistrate Judge:** D. Gordon Bryant Jr. **Courtroom Deputy:** Zelma Zertuche.

San Angelo Division

Brown, Coke, Coleman, Concho, Crockett, Glasscock, Irion, Menard, Mills, Reagan, Runnels, Schleicher, Sterling, Sutton, and Tom Green. **Magistrate Judge:** John R. Parker. **Division Manager:** Erik Paltrow.

Wichita Falls Division

Archer, Baylor, Clay, Cottle, Foard, Hardeman, King, Knox, Montague, Wichita, Wilbarger, and Young. **Magistrate Judge:** Hal R. Ray Jr.

Western Texas District

www.txwd.uscourts.gov

District Judges:

- Chief Judge, Alia Moses, Del Rio.
- Robert Pitman, Austin.
- Kathleen Cardone, El Paso.
- David Counts, Midland.
- Fred Biery, Orlando L. Garcia, Jason Pulliam, and Xavier Rodriguez, San Antonio.

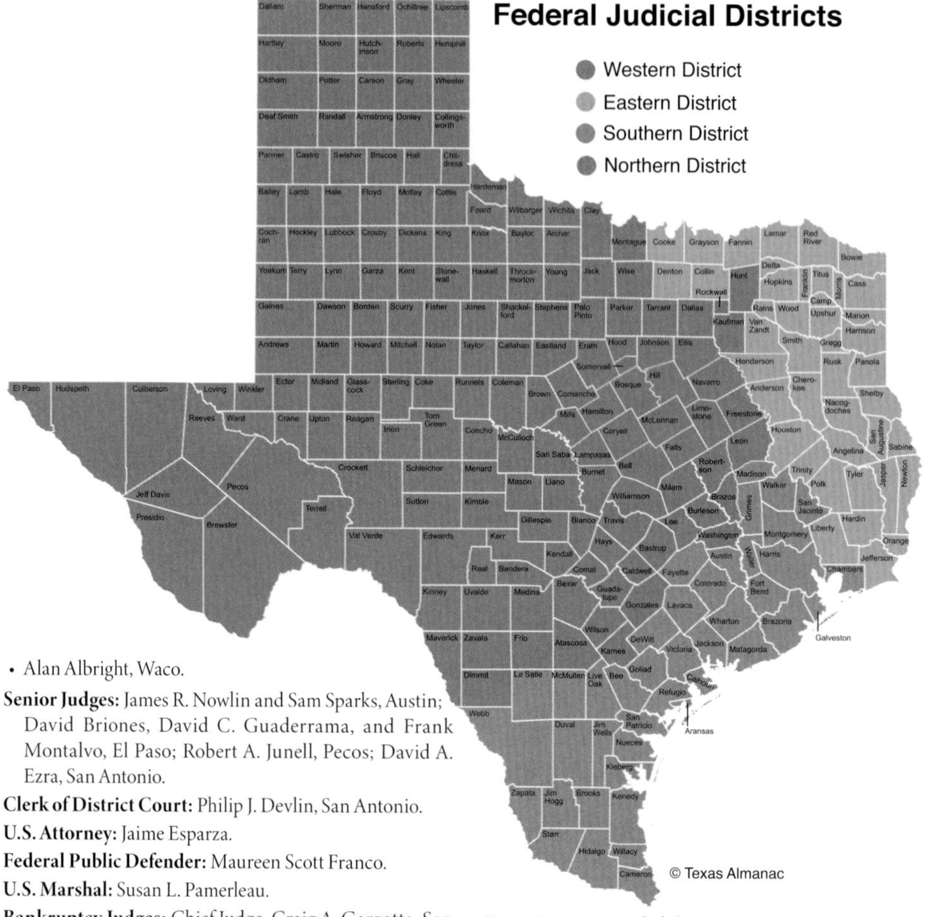

• Alan Albright, Waco.

Senior Judges: James R. Nowlin and Sam Sparks, Austin; David Briones, David C. Guaderrama, and Frank Montalvo, El Paso; Robert A. Junell, Pecos; David A. Ezra, San Antonio.

Clerk of District Court: Philip J. Devlin, San Antonio.

U.S. Attorney: Jaime Esparza.

Federal Public Defender: Maureen Scott Franco.

U.S. Marshal: Susan L. Pamerleau.

Bankruptcy Judges: Chief Judge, Craig A. Gargotta, San Antonio. Judges, H. Christopher Mott and Shad M. Robinson, Austin; Ronald B. King and Michael M. Parker, San Antonio.

Following are the divisions of the Western District and the counties in each division.

Austin Division

Bastrop, Blanco, Burleson, Burnet, Caldwell, Gillespie, Hays, Kimble, Lampasas, Lee, Llano, Mason, McCulloch, San Saba, Travis, Washington, and Williamson. **Magistrate Judges:** Susan Hightower, Dustin M. Howell, and Mark Lane. **Courtroom Deputies:** Samantha Landeros, Laura Thomson, and Celine Valverde.

Del Rio Division

Edwards, Kinney, Maverick, Terrell, Uvalde, Val Verde, and Zavala. **Magistrate Judges:** Matthew H. Watters and Collis White. **Courtroom Deputies:** Mary Cienega and Carmen Levrie.

El Paso Division

El Paso, Hudspeth. **Magistrate Judges:** Anne T. Berton, Robert F. Castañeda, Leon Schydlower, and Miguel A. Torres. **Courtroom Deputies:** Veronica Medina, Veronica Montoya, Fidel Morales, and Cecie Rodriguez.

Fort Cavazos Division

Fort Cavazos Military Reservation. **Courtroom Deputy:** Michelle Ortiz.

Midland–Odessa Division

Andrews, Crane, Ector, Martin, Midland, and Upton. Court for the Midland-Odessa Division is held at Midland, but may, at the discretion of the court, be held in Odessa. **Magistrate Judge:** Ronald C. Griffin. **Courtroom Deputy:** Monica Ramirez.

Pecos Division

Brewster, Culberson, Jeff Davis, Loving, Pecos, Presidio, Reeves, Ward, and Winkler. **Magistrate Judge:** David B. Fannin, Alpine. **Courtroom Deputy:** Yvette Lujan.

San Antonio Division

Atascosa, Bandera, Bexar, Comal, Dimmit, Frio, Gonzales, Guadalupe, Karnes, Kendall, Kerr, Medina, Real, and Wilson. **Magistrate Judges:** Henry J. Bemporad, Elizabeth S. "Betsy" Chestney, and Richard B. Farrer, San Antonio. **Courtroom Deputies:** Amy Jackson, Valeria Sandoval, and Crystal Sosa.

Waco Division

Bell, Bosque, Coryell, Falls, Freestone, Hamilton, Hill, Leon, Limestone, McLennan, Milam, Robertson, and Somervell. **Magistrate Judges:** Derek T. Gilliland and Jeffrey C. Manske. **Courtroom Deputies:** Melissa Copp and Abigail Ernstes.

Eastern Texas District

www.txed.uscourts.gov

District Judges:

- Chief Judge, Rodney Gilstrap, Marshall.
- Ron Clark, Marcia A. Crone, and Michael J. Truncale, Beaumont.
- Sean D. Jordan and Richard Schell, Plano.
- Amos L. Mazzant III, Sherman.
- Robert W. Schroeder III, Texarkana.
- J. Campbell Barker and Jeremy D. Kernodle, Tyler.

Clerk of District Court: David A. O'Toole, Tyler.

U.S. Attorney: Damien Diggs.

Federal Public Defender: John D. McElroy.

U.S. Marshal: John M. Garrison.

Bankruptcy Judges: Chief Judge, Brenda T. Rhoades, Plano; Judge, Joshua P. Searcy, Tyler.

Following are the divisions of the Eastern District and the counties in each division:

Beaumont Division

Hardin, Jasper, Jefferson, Liberty, Newton, and Orange. Magistrates: Zack Hawthorn and Christine L. Stetson. **Courtroom Deputies:** Tonya Piper and Sherre White.

Lufkin Division

Angelina, Houston, Nacogdoches, Polk, Sabine, San Augustine, Shelby, Trinity, and Tyler. **Deputy-in-charge:** Brandy Fairley.

Marshall Division

Camp, Cass, Harrison, Marion, Morris, and Upshur. Magistrate: Roy Payne. **Courtroom Deputy:** Becky Andrews.

Sherman Division

Collin, Cooke, Delta, Denton, Fannin, Grayson, Hopkins, and Lamar. Magistrates: Aileen Goldman Durrett, Sherman, and Kimberly C. Priest Johnson, Plano. **Courtroom Deputies:** Maria Cox and Karen Lee.

Texarkana Division

Bowie, Franklin, Red River, and Titus. Magistrate: Boone Baxter. **Courtroom Deputy:** Nicole Peavy.

Tyler Division

Anderson, Cherokee, Gregg, Henderson, Panola, Rains, Rusk, Smith, Van Zandt, and Wood. Magistrates: John D. Love and K. Nicole Mitchell. **Courtroom Deputies:** Sharon Baum and Lisa Hardwick.

Southern Texas District

www.txs.uscourts.gov

District Judges:

- Chief Judge, Randy Crane, McAllen.
- Rolando Olvera and Fernando Rodriguez Jr., Brownsville.
- David S. Morales, Nelva Gonzales Ramos, and Drew B. Tipton, Corpus Christi.
- Jeffrey V. Brown, Galveston.
- Alfred H. Bennett, Keith P. Ellison, Charles Eskridge, Andrew S. Hanen, George C. Hanks Jr., Lynn N. Hughes, and Lee H. Rosenthal, Houston.
- Marina Garcia Marmolejo and Diana Saldaña, Laredo.
- Micaela Alvarez and Ricardo H. Hinojosa, McAllen.

Senior Judges: Janis Graham Jack, Corpus Christi; David Hittner, Kenneth M. Hoyt, Sim Lake, Gray H. Miller, and Ewing Werlein Jr., Houston; John D. Rainey, Victoria.

Clerk of Court: Nathan Ochsner, Houston.

U.S. Attorney: Alamdar Hamdani.

Federal Public Defender: Marjorie A. Meyers.

U.S. Marshal: T. Michael O'Connor.

Bankruptcy Judges: Chief Judge, Eduardo V. Rodriguez, McAllen. Judges, Marvin Isgur, David R. Jones, Christopher M. Lopez, and Jeffrey P. Norman, Houston.

Following are the divisions of the Southern District and the counties in each division:

Brownsville Division

Cameron and Willacy. **Magistrate Judges:** Karen Betancourt and Ignacio Torteya III. **Deputy-in-charge:** Rosy D'Venturi.

Corpus Christi Division

Aransas, Bee, Brooks, Duval, Jim Wells, Kenedy, Kleberg, Live Oak, Nueces, and San Patricio. **Magistrate Judges:** Julie K. Hampton, Jason B. Libby, and Mitchel Neurock. **Deputy-in-charge:** Amanda Otto.

Galveston Division

Brazoria, Chambers, Galveston, and Matagorda. **Magistrate Judge:** Andrew M. Edison. **Deputy-in-charge:** Lucia Smith.

Houston Division

Austin, Brazos, Colorado, Fayette, Fort Bend, Grimes, Harris, Madison, Montgomery, San Jacinto, Walker, Waller, and Wharton. **Magistrate Judges:** Peter Bray, Christina A. Bryan, Yvonne Y. Ho, Dena Hanovice Palermo, and Sam S. Sheldon. **Deputy-in-charge:** Darlene Hansen.

Laredo Division

Jim Hogg, La Salle, McMullen, Webb, and Zapata. **Magistrate Judges:** Christopher A. dos Santos, John A. Kazen, and Diana Song Quiroga. **Deputy-in-charge:** Aimee Veliz.

McAllen Division

Hidalgo and Starr. **Magistrate Judges:** Juan F. Alanis, J. Scott Hacker, and Nadia S. Medrano. **Deputy-in-charge:** Velma T. Barrera.

Victoria Division

Calhoun, DeWitt, Goliad, Jackson, Lavaca, Refugio, and Victoria. **Deputy-in-charge:** Lana Reimann. ☆

LAW ENFORCEMENT

CRIME REPORTING IN TEXAS

CRIME PROFILE OF TEXAS COUNTIES, 2021

TEXAS JAILS & PRISONS

CORRECTIONAL INSTITUTIONS IN TEXAS, 2023

Crime Reporting in Texas

Source: Texas Department of Public Safety, Austin www.dps.texas.gov; Gun Violence Archive, https://www.gunviolencearchive.org/

The crime statistics in this chapter are all thanks to the **Uniform Crime Reporting (UCR)** programs used by law enforcement agencies in Texas, and nationwide. The first of these programs in the United States was the Committee on Uniform Crime Records, developed by the International Association of Chiefs of Police (IACP) in the 1920s. The first IACP crime collection program, in 1930, was voluntary, and gathered information from 400 police agencies in 43 states. The FBI was authorized as the national clearinghouse for the information collected by that program. In 2021, 1,248 Texas law enforcement agencies submitted crime data to the UCR program.

UCR programs collect data on a summary basis, which provides reliable information about crime, but has many limitations. In 1985 Texas began using the **Incident Based Reporting (IBR)** system, whereby crime data is collected electronically, and includes the circumstances of each incident. The national system, called NIBRS, has been slow to grow, but state programs and the FBI have worked in partnership to assist in the transition.

Texas Crime Rate* by Offense

Crime	2020	2021	% Change
Aggravated Assault	299.8	307.8	3.2%
Robbery	91.1	75.6	–16.6%
Rape	45.4	49.7	10.0%
Murder	6.6	7.0	7.1%
Violent Crime Total	**442.9**	**440.0**	**–0.1%**
Larceny-Theft	1,571.6	1,501.3	–3.9%
Burglary	367.9	324.4	–11.3%
Motor Vehicle Theft	284.4	297.0	5.0%
Property Crime Total	**2,223.9**	**2,122.8**	**–4.0%**
Family Violence	728.4	783.0	8.1%
Sexual Assault	57.8	62.4	8.6%
Hate Crime	1.9	1.7	–7.6%
State Mandated Reporting Total	**788.1**	**847.2**	**8.1%**
Total	**3,454.8**	**3,410.0**	**–0.7%**

*Crime rate is based on the FBI's 2021 estimated population of 28,927,914

Source: "2021 Crime in Texas" TDPS

Texas first adopted the Uniform Crime Report in 1976, and the Department of Public Safety accepted the responsibility of collecting, validating, and tabulating reports from across the state. The Uniform Crime Reporting Section, created specifically for this purpose, is part of the Crime Records Service division of the department.

The state became certified to collect NIBRS data in 1998, and in 2015, House Bill 11 set a goal to transition all of Texas to NIBRS by September 1, 2019. About 550 agencies met that goal. In 2021, a total of 1,014 agencies in Texas had adopted NIBRS methodology, representing **98% of the jurisdictional population of the state**.

Crime in Texas: 2021

In Texas, the Department of Public Safety collects data for the national UCR program from police, sheriff's offices, and its own officers. Data are estimated for non-reporting agencies and those that did not have 12 months of data.

Agencies that contributed data for the "2021 Crime in Texas" report include: 57 college and university police departments, 51 independent school district and zero population police departments, 222 county sheriff's offices, and 661 city police departments. (However, only 1,001 agencies contributed to the data in the "Crime Profile of Texas Counties, 2021" table on page 537.)

Previous crime index reports included seven major crime categories. The 2021 report is the first to include three state-mandated crimes in the crime rate: family violence, sexual assault, and hate crimes. Other crime reports in the index are designated as either violent crimes (murder, rape, robbery, and aggravated assault) or property crime (burglary, larceny-theft, and motor vehicle theft).

The facts listed in this chapter scratch the surface of the information available in the "2021 Crime in Texas" report.

Crime Rate by Offense

The 2021 state-mandated reporting crime rate increased 7.5% from 2020, the violent crime rate decreased 0.6% from 2020, and the property crime rate decreased 4.5% from 2020.

Robbery (–16.6%) and burglary (–11.3%) showed the largest decreases. Rape had the largest increase (10.0%), followed by sexual assault (8.6%) and family violence (8.1%).

The estimated value of property stolen during the commission of index crimes in 2021 was more than $1.5 billion, and about 44.0% of that property was recovered within the same year.

Crime Volume by Offense

During 2021, there was a reported total of 1,006,887 index offenses in Texas. This represents a crime-volume decrease of 0.7% when compared to 1,014,368 reported offenses in 2020. The crime volume in three of the four largest cities also decreased year over year.

In 2021, there were 3,410.0 index crimes per 100,000 people, compared with 3,454.8 in 2020, according to data compiled by the Department of Public Safety's Uniform Crime Reporting (UCR) program. The 2021 crime rate is based on the FBI's estimated population of the state: 28,927,914.

Non-Index Crimes

Arson

The reported number of arsons committed in Texas in 2021 was 2,921, an increase of 23.5% from 2019. Communities of more than 100,000 reported the highest volume of arsons (2,242), but communities of fewer than 2,500 combined for the highest rate (21.3 per 100,000 people).

Hate Crimes

There were 641 hate crime incidents reported in Texas in 2021, a decrease of 7.6% from 2020. Broken down by bias motivation, 61.1% of incidents were motivated by race or ethnicity, 26.3% by sexual orientation, 10.0% by religion, and 2.6% by disability. In 32.7% of the offenses the offender was a stranger to the victim, and in 27.5% the relationship was unknown.

Driving Under the Influence

The number of arrests for operating a motor vehicle while mentally or physically impared totalled 62,749 in 2021, with 18.8% of those aged 25–29, 16.9% aged 20–24, and 3.2% between the ages 15 to 19. The majority of people arrested were male (75.5%).

Mass Shootings

The 2021 crime report did not address mass shootings. According to the Gun Violence Archive, a non-profit that documents gun violence and gun crime in the U.S., Texas had 57 mass shootings (defined as incidents where "four or more people are shot or killed in a single incident, not including the shooter") in 2021, resulting in 234 injuries and 67 deaths.

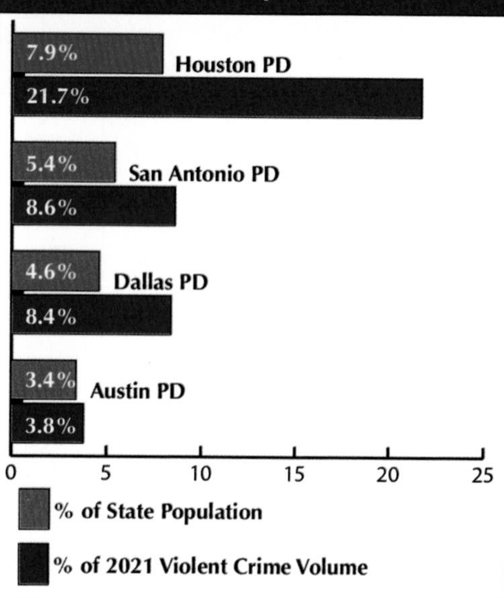

Law Enforcement Assaults and Deaths

Assaults on law enforcement personnel decreased 0.6% in 2021 to 5,228 from 5,261 in 2020. Of those assaults, 55% resulted in minor or non-serious injuries. The largest number of assaults occurred while officers were responding to a disturbance call. Eight law officers were killed in the line of duty in 2021, and another two died in duty-related vehicle crashes. ☆

Texas Crime Volume by Offense

Crime	2017	2018	2019	2020	2021	2020-2021 % Change	2017-2021 % Change
Aggravated Assault	75,347	74,165	75,595	88,030	90,876	3.2%	20.6%
Robbery	32,120	28,273	28,854	26,750	22,320	–16.6%	–30.5%
Rape	14,332	14,891	14,656	13,327	14,671	10.1%	2.4%
Murder	1,412	1,324	1,403	1,927	2,064	7.1%	46.2%
Violent Crime Total	**123,211**	**118,653**	**120,508**	**130,034**	**129,931**	**–0.1%**	**5.5%**
Larceny-Theft	133,145	117,513	112,405	108,015	95,800	–11.3%	–28.0%
Burglary	518,414	491,028	496,279	461,421	443,309	–3.9%	–14.5%
Motor Vehicle Theft	67,285	69,730	76,687	83,504	87,703	5.0%	30.3%
Property Crime Total	**718,844**	**678,271**	**685,371**	**652,940**	**626,812**	**–4.0%**	**–12.8%**
Family Violence	195,315	190,851	196,902	213,875	231,207	8.1%	18.4%
Sexual Assault	18,559	20,105	19,280	16,969	18,429	8.6%	–0.7%
Hate Crime	190	380	407	550	508	–7.6%	167.4%
State Mandated Reporting Total	**214,064**	**211,336**	**216,589**	**231,394**	**250,144**	**8.1%**	**16.9%**
Total	**1,056,119**	**1,008,260**	**1,022,468**	**1,014,368**	**1,006,887**	**–0.7%**	**–4.7%**

Highest number of reports for each type of crime are highlighted in yellow.

Source: "2021 Crime in Texas" TDPS

Crime Profile of Texas Counties, 2021

	No. Agencies Reporting	Murder	Rape	Robbery	Assault	Burglary	Larceny-Theft	Auto Theft	Total Index Crimes	Crime Rate per 100,000
Anderson	2	1	12	6	83	97	321	37	557	2,949.3
Andrews	1	0	8	2	44	36	164	29	283	1,925.3
Angelina	7	5	35	23	212	324	1,108	149	1,856	2,303.5
Aransas	2	3	15	5	69	154	477	48	771	3,961.0
Archer	1	0	0	0	1	2	3	2	8	467.6
Armstrong	1	0	0	0	0	0	3	2	5	270.7
Atascosa	6	9	2	8	121	161	641	130	1,072	2,040.2
Austin	5	1	9	6	37	54	148	39	294	985.4
Bailey	2	0	0	0	6	6	21	2	35	531.3
Bandera	1	3	2	1	27	41	90	22	186	775.6
Bastrop	5	1	46	20	265	216	747	161	1,456	1,554.6
Baylor	2	0	0	0	2	4	7	6	19	548.3
Bee	2	0	8	6	94	152	327	48	635	1,968.7
Bell	11	27	201	145	1,018	1,034	4,198	743	7,366	1,996.3
Bexar	28	186	1,244	1,842	8,967	9,041	50,967	10,061	82,308	4,027.3
Blanco	2	1	4	4	19	38	68	5	139	1,380.1
Borden	1	0	0	0	1	4	7	2	14	1,983.0
Bosque	4	0	2	0	15	45	65	11	138	747.4
Bowie	7	21	70	41	307	248	1,387	212	2,286	2,511.4
Brazoria	21	8	133	89	587	658	4,001	465	5,941	1,543.3
Brazos	4	10	140	69	360	603	3,074	352	4,608	1,967.1
Brewster	3	1	2	0	8	25	20	13	69	754.7
Briscoe	1	0	0	0	0	2	7	0	9	616.9
Brooks	2	0	1	0	10	14	19	3	47	684.0
Brown	3	0	35	9	114	180	512	43	893	2,500.0
Burleson	3	0	5	2	31	37	52	17	144	780.0
Burnet	5	2	37	4	81	106	308	55	593	1,269.3
Caldwell	3	6	7	1	43	46	169	60	332	781.5
Calhoun	4	0	10	1	44	50	120	18	243	1,262.5
Callahan	2	0	1	0	9	11	15	14	50	493.6
Cameron	16	18	185	213	1,205	1,064	5,886	423	8,994	2,163.1
Camp	2	1	6	2	19	38	85	10	161	1,238.7
Carson	2	0	0	0	0	2	4	5	11	190.8
Cass	5	1	13	1	40	87	157	57	356	1,222.0
Castro	2	0	2	1	7	8	15	10	43	592.8
Chambers	3	2	19	11	100	121	508	105	866	2,058.8
Cherokee	4	5	23	8	132	154	430	67	819	1,562.6
Childress	2	0	1	1	11	13	17	4	47	663.8
Clay	1	0	3	0	8	25	28	14	78	748.1
Cochran	1	0	1	0	8	11	9	1	30	1,054.9
Coke	1	0	0	0	2	12	14	5	33	1,002.7
Coleman	2	0	0	0	7	31	17	7	62	1,202.9
Collin	17	20	300	132	758	1,192	8,384	928	11,714	1,196.9
Collingsworth	1	0	0	0	2	2	4	2	10	353.2
Colorado	3	3	6	5	16	45	135	33	243	1,374.0
Comal	4	1	52	37	257	348	1,367	277	2,339	1,264.0
Comanche	3	1	9	2	17	32	107	14	182	1,338.9
Concho	1	0	0	0	5	2	1	0	8	294.4
Cooke	2	0	23	8	88	117	381	58	675	1,681.9
Coryell	3	0	47	12	105	164	593	74	995	1,295.7
Cottle	0	NR	NR	NR	NR	NR	NR	NR	NR	NR

NR = Not Reported

Source: "2021 Crime in Texas," TDPS.

Crime Profile of Texas Counties, 2021

	No. Agencies Reporting	Murder	Rape	Robbery	Assault	Burglary	Larceny-Theft	Auto Theft	Total Index Crimes	Crime Rate per 100,000
Crane	2	0	1	0	2	0	6	5	14	294.2
Crockett	1	0	1	0	2	25	7	1	36	1,040.5
Crosby	1	0	0	0	4	14	7	6	31	2,838.8
Culberson	0	NR	NR	NR	NR	NR	NR	NR	NR	NR
Dallam	2	1	4	0	22	31	75	32	165	1,684.4
Dallas	33	301	1,159	3,399	10,624	11,097	52,904	17,358	96,842	3,305.3
Dawson	1	0	2	0	1	20	25	8	56	1,581.0
Deaf Smith	2	0	3	2	47	59	179	26	316	1,757.3
Delta	1	0	1	0	2	11	7	1	22	414.6
Denton	25	10	376	146	770	908	6,659	966	9,835	1,365.1
DeWitt	2	1	10	2	88	27	134	32	294	1,861.2
Dickens	0	NR	NR	NR	NR	NR	NR	NR	NR	NR
Dimmit	0	NR	NR	NR	NR	NR	NR	NR	NR	NR
Donley	1	0	0	0	4	15	10	6	35	1,081.9
Duval	2	0	2	0	15	31	53	38	139	1,827.7
Eastland	5	0	14	0	33	81	116	27	271	1,659.8
Ector	6	13	73	105	545	536	2,083	434	3,789	2,206.6
Edwards	1	0	0	0	0	7	3	5	15	790.7
Ellis	9	5	69	31	209	277	1,673	234	2,498	1,347.0
El Paso	11	36	426	254	1,382	1,361	7,354	1,093	11,906	1,422.9
Erath	4	1	34	3	31	89	252	17	427	984.8
Falls	2	0	3	2	12	33	9	9	68	1,234.1
Fannin	4	2	13	4	42	35	98	17	211	859.9
Fayette	4	2	12	0	36	39	161	24	274	1,079.0
Fisher	0	NR	NR	NR	NR	NR	NR	NR	NR	NR
Floyd	3	0	5	0	18	19	31	11	84	1,514.1
Foard	1	0	0	0	0	0	0	0	0	0
Fort Bend	12	24	228	241	1,093	1,182	6,904	751	10,423	1,269.5
Franklin	2	0	8	0	17	36	43	9	113	1,128.0
Freestone	4	1	4	1	37	59	107	17	226	1,148.1
Frio	1	1	3	2	20	69	65	20	180	1,670.4
Gaines	2	0	2	2	16	30	92	13	155	806.8
Galveston	13	28	250	117	591	880	4,465	753	7,084	1,972.0
Garza	1	0	3	0	2	9	15	0	29	472.5
Gillespie	2	1	17	2	9	42	99	7	177	657.8
Glasscock	1	0	0	0	0	6	9	2	17	1,174.8
Goliad	1	0	1	3	9	122	46	7	188	2,476.6
Gonzales	4	0	12	3	172	41	107	25	360	1,962.9
Gray	2	3	9	3	55	90	274	24	458	2,143.7
Grayson	13	2	88	22	304	458	1,117	249	2,240	1,711.8
Gregg	7	12	94	55	302	528	2,039	345	3,375	2,573.1
Grimes	3	2	15	8	48	108	140	37	358	1,208.1
Guadalupe	4	2	30	18	93	202	958	167	1,470	1,327.5
Hale	3	0	9	10	105	137	338	58	657	2,829.9
Hall	2	0	1	0	5	9	8	4	27	983.6
Hamilton	4	0	0	0	7	14	21	6	48	566.0
Hansford	2	0	0	0	1	3	9	1	14	269.4
Hardeman	1	1	0	1	2	2	19	0	25	763.8
Hardin	5	1	27	4	41	98	219	83	473	814.3
Harris	42	629	2,648	9,838	26,833	23,068	107,646	24,153	194,815	4,068.0
Harrison	4	4	9	20	155	233	562	124	1,107	1,733.6

NR = Not Reported

Source: "2021 Crime in Texas", TDPS.

Crime Profile of Texas Counties, 2021

	No. Agencies Reporting	Murder	Rape	Robbery	Assault	Burglary	Larceny-Theft	Auto Theft	Total Index Crimes	Crime Rate per 100,000
Hartley	1	0	0	0	1	5	3	4	13	465.9
Haskell	2	0	3	0	7	8	16	6	40	708.2
Hays	5	5	166	64	481	508	2,563	334	4,121	1,653.0
Hemphill	1	0	0	0	0	1	13	1	15	401.3
Henderson	12	2	31	12	94	129	291	82	641	791.6
Hidalgo	21	30	423	247	1,770	1,584	10,825	849	15,728	1,828.7
Hill	4	1	26	10	53	78	304	61	533	1,505.2
Hockley	3	0	12	4	111	105	203	33	468	2,061.5
Hood	2	0	9	4	52	83	585	53	786	1,244.2
Hopkins	2	2	11	2	40	39	90	34	218	602.2
Houston	3	0	9	1	28	67	134	23	262	262
Howard	2	6	8	21	196	214	600	99	1,144	3,148.3
Hudspeth	1	0	3	0	9	1	2	1	16	317.6
Hunt	5	3	42	39	430	305	819	217	1,855	1,969.5
Hutchinson	3	0	20	2	21	90	185	35	353	1,736.8
Irion	1	0	0	0	1	8	8	3	20	1,296.2
Jack	2	0	5	0	6	17	15	7	50	557.4
Jackson	3	3	5	2	28	38	61	23	160	1,082.3
Jasper	2	1	11	13	58	212	397	44	736	2,232.9
Jeff Davis	1	0	0	0	3	0	1	1	5	228.7
Jefferson	7	23	177	336	1,388	1,307	3,678	673	7,582	3,064.5
Jim Hogg	1	0	0	0	9	17	15	8	49	956.7
Jim Wells	2	2	28	14	141	246	622	64	1,117	3,163.0
Johnson	9	6	121	26	392	266	1,651	252	2,714	1,434.9
Jones	3	0	4	0	12	24	42	7	89	802.1
Karnes	3	0	6	1	29	41	113	9	199	1,285.8
Kaufman	10	9	60	34	233	282	1,127	218	1,963	1,342.9
Kendall	2	1	12	1	28	76	259	58	435	920.5
Kenedy	1	0	0	0	1	3	0	5	9	2,419.4
Kent	0	NR	NR	NR	NR	NR	NR	NR	NR	NR
Kerr	4	1	30	3	98	95	354	52	633	1,201.8
Kimble	2	0	0	0	4	3	2	1	10	230.8
King	1	0	0	0	0	0	0	0	0	0
Kinney	0	NR	NR	NR	NR	NR	NR	NR	NR	NR
Kleberg	2	8	13	8	120	99	484	33	765	2,560.8
Knox	1	0	1	0	2	2	5	0	10	893.7
Lamar	4	4	44	10	202	195	524	94	1,073	2,171.4
Lamb	4	0	7	1	15	48	60	15	146	1,396.5
Lampasas	3	0	5	0	39	34	182	17	277	1,371.2
La Salle	1	0	0	1	15	17	22	5	60	868.7
Lavaca	4	1	3	0	24	37	72	17	154	768.1
Lee	2	1	11	5	18	35	116	23	209	1,302.9
Leon	2	0	1	0	15	42	74	16	148	952.5
Liberty	3	3	45	9	105	147	440	244	993	1,183.7
Limestone	3	0	19	2	47	88	173	24	353	1,528.8
Lipscomb	1	0	0	0	1	6	17	2	26	848.6
Live Oak	0	NR	NR	NR	NR	NR	NR	NR	NR	NR
Llano	3	0	5	3	19	67	139	27	260	1,391.3
Loving	1	0	1	0	2	1	16	0	20	10,256.4
Lubbock	10	27	304	393	2,252	2,342	7,181	1,234	13,733	4,394.0
Lynn	2	0	5	0	9	14	18	5	51	972.0

NR = Not Reported

Source: "2021 Crime in Texas," TDPS.

Crime Profile of Texas Counties, 2021

	No. Agencies Reporting	Murder	Rape	Robbery	Assault	Burglary	Larceny-Theft	Auto Theft	Total Index Crimes	Crime Rate per 100,000
Madison	2	0	6	2	21	23	57	18	127	890.0
Marion	1	1	1	0	33	40	49	10	134	1,696.0
Martin	2	0	3	2	20	30	101	0	156	2,657.6
Mason	1	0	0	0	4	3	7	1	15	346.0
Matagorda	5	2	43	7	161	175	657	88	1,133	3,116.1
Maverick	1	0	2	8	43	212	443	71	779	2,613.5
McCulloch	2	2	1	0	12	77	47	21	160	2,076.3
McLennan	12	19	190	161	911	1,202	4,573	595	7,651	3,071.0
McMullen	0	NR	NR	NR	NR	NR	NR	NR	NR	NR
Medina	5	2	11	2	68	82	391	78	634	1,252.7
Menard	0	NR	NR	NR	NR	NR	NR	NR	NR	NR
Midland	3	18	158	43	539	369	2,125	420	3,672	2,057.3
Milam	4	1	5	2	44	85	167	38	342	1,397.8
Mills	1	0	4	0	7	33	8	0	52	1,088.1
Mitchell	0	NR	NR	NR	NR	NR	NR	NR	NR	NR
Montague	2	0	9	3	20	81	115	11	239	1,518.2
Montgomery	15	17	175	118	966	1,177	5,768	962	9,183	1,454.0
Moore	4	2	15	1	55	53	259	38	423	1,912.5
Morris	2	0	0	3	7	13	32	10	65	1,692.7
Motley	1	0	0	0	0	3	0	2	5	427.0
Nacogdoches	5	6	18	5	85	154	684	68	1,020	1,590.9
Navarro	7	2	44	15	155	164	574	87	1,041	2,062.3
Newton	2	0	2	1	6	20	43	7	79	599.3
Nolan	3	0	1	1	8	16	34	2	62	1,494.0
Nueces	4	20	265	481	2,145	1,866	7,909	1,050	13,736	3,836.0
Ochiltree	2	0	6	0	34	42	63	5	150	1,587.5
Oldham	1	0	0	1	0	2	2	0	5	235.5
Orange	6	5	34	17	140	317	676	168	1,357	1,662.1
Palo Pinto	2	1	16	3	27	170	320	58	595	2,029.2
Panola	3	2	4	2	65	80	285	39	477	2,107.9
Parker	4	5	70	16	147	396	1,187	180	2,001	1,420.7
Parmer	4	0	3	0	6	12	26	15	62	662.6
Pecos	1	0	1	0	5	14	33	9	62	740.3
Polk	4	8	22	7	79	144	487	98	845	1,585.9
Potter	4	21	156	185	1,198	1,341	4,722	892	8,515	3,976.2
Presidio	2	0	0	0	1	0	2	0	3	114.7
Rains	2	0	0	0	9	6	10	2	27	214.2
Randall	3	1	21	5	47	79	292	55	500	1,231.0
Reagan	1	0	2	1	0	4	20	4	31	806.0
Real	1	0	1	0	4	93	21	5	124	3,661.1
Red River	2	0	5	0	18	27	27	8	85	969.5
Reeves	2	2	6	1	52	24	95	9	189	1,770.5
Refugio	3	2	0	2	3	25	34	29	95	1,404.9
Roberts	1	0	0	0	0	0	0	0	0	0
Robertson	5	2	10	4	36	59	89	23	223	1,308.3
Rockwall	5	0	38	5	80	126	897	91	1,237	1,179.1
Runnels	4	0	5	1	18	51	42	10	127	1,234.6
Rusk	5	5	21	10	142	175	551	97	1,001	1,969.2
Sabine	3	0	9	0	13	15	48	7	92	1,004.4
San Augustine	2	0	2	1	13	95	49	13	173	2,133.7
San Jacinto	0	NR	NR	NR	NR	NR	NR	NR	NR	NR

NR = Not Reported

Source: "2021 Crime in Texas," TDPS.

Crime Profile of Texas Counties, 2021

	No. Agencies Reporting	Murder	Rape	Robbery	Assault	Burglary	Larceny-Theft	Auto Theft	Total Index Crimes	Crime Rate per 100,000
San Patricio	6	2	25	14	63	118	556	43	821	2,125.8
San Saba	1	0	0	0	5	2	14	6	27	861.2
Schleicher	1	0	0	0	2	4	7	0	13	487.1
Scurry	2	2	12	1	134	76	182	25	432	2,622.8
Shackelford	1	0	0	0	1	2	8	0	11	337.5
Shelby	3	2	1	2	29	71	185	27	317	1,349.7
Sherman	0	NR	NR	NR	NR	NR	NR	NR	NR	NR
Smith	9	10	101	66	650	647	3,065	436	4,975	2,126.3
Somervell	1	0	0	0	4	26	40	0	70	768.0
Starr	6	0	15	3	90	172	283	48	611	955.5
Stephens	2	0	6	0	18	20	72	16	132	1,432.8
Sterling	1	0	0	0	0	5	1	2	8	605.1
Stonewall	0	NR	NR	NR	NR	NR	NR	NR	NR	NR
Sutton	2	0	2	0	5	9	7	4	27	735.7
Swisher	2	0	6	2	22	41	68	8	147	2,473.5
Tarrant	40	166	1,260	1,227	6,497	6,479	35,903	6,788	58,320	2,808.3
Taylor	5	7	132	83	409	568	1,995	219	3,413	2,365.9
Terrell	1	0	0	0	0	0	0	0	0	0
Terry	2	0	5	5	29	36	70	17	162	1,348.4
Throckmorton	1	0	2	0	6	0	2	0	10	685.9
Titus	2	0	26	9	94	95	356	43	623	1,908.2
Tom Green	3	6	74	46	268	514	2,030	254	3,192	2,664.9
Travis	18	91	726	1,073	4,111	5,649	28,896	5,236	45,782	3,355.3
Trinity	2	0	1	1	12	47	44	17	122	1,021.0
Tyler	3	4	2	2	23	87	105	38	261	1,222.0
Upshur	4	5	30	5	58	160	243	43	544	1,407.7
Upton	1	0	0	0	1	3	7	3	14	387.1
Uvalde	3	1	10	10	70	109	569	58	827	3,120.0
Val Verde	1	0	11	2	39	63	48	14	177	1,377.5
Van Zandt	5	3	7	7	66	152	125	27	387	723.4
Victoria	2	5	83	45	345	419	1,421	125	2,443	2,668.9
Walker	3	2	51	20	213	168	724	134	1,312	1,826.1
Waller	7	2	22	17	138	141	336	62	718	1,272.2
Ward	2	0	17	5	22	67	166	45	322	2,652.8
Washington	2	0	10	6	117	55	225	31	444	1,246.2
Webb	5	13	108	98	642	439	2,657	261	4,218	1,544.6
Wharton	4	5	13	16	163	137	590	73	997	2,413.5
Wheeler	1	0	2	0	5	6	6	1	20	634.1
Wichita	7	13	151	56	452	694	2,359	427	4,152	3,145.0
Wilbarger	2	0	3	6	36	31	103	18	197	1,597.0
Willacy	3	0	8	5	102	43	152	16	326	1,799.5
Williamson	14	14	194	68	460	838	5,790	528	7,892	1,345.5
Wilson	3	0	21	3	47	91	225	41	428	880.6
Winkler	3	0	2	1	11	51	48	10	123	1,557.9
Wise	5	5	34	6	71	32	320	22	490	683.5
Wood	6	1	11	6	40	127	213	32	430	914.9
Yoakum	2	0	4	2	12	12	53	10	93	1,068.4
Young	3	0	10	3	29	25	74	15	156	883.1
Zapata	1	0	0	0	10	21	37	1	69	491.5
Zavala	1	0	12	0	22	14	20	10	78	1,711.7
TOTALS	**1,001**	**2,064**	**14,666**	**22,320**	**90,867**	**95,765**	**443,258**	**87,689**	**756,629**	—

NR = Not Reported

Source: "2021 Crime in Texas," TDPS.

Texas Jails and Prisons

Sources: Texas Department of Criminal Justice, www.tdcj.texas.gov, Windham School District, wsdtx.org/

The **Texas Board of Criminal Justice** is composed of nine non-salaried members who are appointed by the governor for staggered six-year terms. The board employs the **Texas Department of Criminal Justice** (TDCJ) executive director, sets rules and policies that guide the agency, and considers other agency actions at its meetings. (See page 482 in Texas State Boards and Commissions for more.) In addition, the board appoints an inspector general, a director of internal audits, a director of state counsel for offenders, and a prison rape elimination act ombudsman.

Board members serve in a separate capacity as the Board of Trustees for the **Windham School District** by hiring a superintendent and providing similar oversight. The Windham School District serves TDCJ inmates at 89 sites, and offers both academic and career and technical programs. The school district is a separate entity primarily funded through the Texas Education Agency (TEA).

Texas Department of Criminal Justice

The TDCJ executive director is responsible for the administration and enforcement of statutes relative to the criminal justice system. The agency is split into 16 divisions under three categories: offender management, programs, and support services.

The four divisions classified as offender management include:

- **Correctional Institutions Division (CID):** responsible for the confinement of adult felony offenders who are sentenced to incarceration in Texas. (More about this division on the next page.)
- **Private Facility Contract Monitoring/Oversight Division (PFCMOD):** responsible for oversight and monitoring contracts for privately operated secure facilities and community-based facilities, including substance abuse treatment services.
- **Parole Division:** supervises all offenders released on parole or mandatory supervision, conducts release and transition planning, and verifies compliance with statutory provisions of release. In addition, this division contracts for electronic monitoring and processing responses to violations, administers programs and services through District Resource Centers and Parole Offices, and coordinates the Interstate Compact for Adult Offender Supervision. In 2022 there were 67 district parole offices.
- **Community Justice Assistance Division (CJAD):** administers adult probation in partnership with community supervision and corrections departments (CSCD). CJAD is responsible for the distribution of formula and grant funds; the development and enforcement of standards, including best-practice treatment standards; conducting program and fiscal audits; providing training and certification of community supervision officers; and more.

Programs encompass three divisions: **Rehabilitation Programs** (coordinates inmate programs), **Re-entry and Integration Programs** (operates a three-phase program for community re-entry, aimed at reducing recidivisim) and **Victim Services** (provides personal services to victims of crime and their families).

The divisions operating as Support Services deal with the day-to-day operation of the TDCJ. They include: Office of the General Counsel, Office of the Chief of Staff, Office of Emergency Management, Training and Leader Development, Health Services, Human Resources, Research and Development, and the Administrative Review and Risk Management.

The final four divisions operate in coordination with the TDCJ Chief Financial Officer: Business and Finance, Information Technology, Manufacturing, Agribusiness and Logistics, and Facilities.

Texas Department of Criminal Justice Operating Budget FY 2022

Budget Item	Total, All Funds* ($ in millions)	Percent of Total*
A: Provide Prison Diversions	$247.4	7.4%
B: Special Needs Inmates	$27.8	0.8%
C: Incarcerate Inmates	$2,884.3	83.3%
D: Board of Pardons and Paroles	$28.8	0.8%
E: Operate Parole System	$184.7	5.4%
F: Indirect Administration	$80.1	2.4%
TOTAL	$3,413.2	100%

* Figures are rounded and may not equal totals.

Source: TDCJ Annual Review for FYE 2022

On-Hand Inmate Profile Fiscal Year 2022

Sex – Ethnicity – Age	
Male: 92.5%	Hispanic: 33.3%
Black: 32.5%	Other: 0.6%
White: 33.5%	Average age: 40.9
Average Sentences	
Prison: 20.7 years	State jail: 1.2 years
Average Part of Sentence Served	
Prison: *61.8%	State jail: *99.7%
Education	
Average IQ	90.2
Offence	
Violent: 62.3%	Drug: 14.5%
Property: 8.7%	Other: 14.5%

* Based on offenders released in FY 2022

Source: TDCJ Statistical Report FYE 2022

Correctional Institutions Division

In addition to the incarceration of offenders, the CID has support functions, including: classification and records; counsel substitute; laundry, food and supply; offender transportation; and correctional training and staff development. As of July 2023, there were 89 state-operated facilities, including state prisons (59) and jails (13), psychiatric facilities (4), pre-release facilities (3), substance abuse felony punishment facilities (4), intermediate sanction facilities (2), a geriatric facility (1), medical facilities (2), and the Developmental Disability Program facility (1).

The table below lists all of the TDCJ correctional institutions in the state alphabetically by county. It includes both those operated by the CID as well as privately-operated facilities.

The town listed is the nearest one to the facility, although the unit may actually be in another county. For instance, the Middleton Transfer Facility is in Jones County, but the nearest city is Abilene, which is in Taylor County. ☆

On-Hand Population
As of Aug. 31, 2022

Prisoners	
Prison	116,684
State Jails	2,576
SAFP (Substance Abuse)	2,716
TOTAL	**121,976**
Supervision	
Parole	81,113
Discretionary Mandatory Supervision	17,296
Mandatory Supervision	4,357
TOTAL	**102,766**
Probation	
Community Supervision Placements*	360,186

*Total adults on direct, indirect, and pretrial supervision, minus transfers

Source: TDCJ Statistical Report FYE 2022

Correctional Institutions in Texas 2023

County	Unit	Nearest Town	Max. Capacity, Gender	Employees	Type*/Operator**
Anderson	Beto	Tennessee Colony	3,471 Male	472	Prison (CID)
Anderson	Coffield	Tennessee Colony	4,139 Male	518	Prison (CID)
Anderson	Michael	Tennessee Colony	2,552 Male	504	Prison (CID)
Anderson	Powledge	Palestine	1,137 Male	290	Prison (CID)
Angelina	Diboll	Diboll	518 Male	136	Private Prison (MTC)
Angelina	Duncan	Diboll	606 Male	139	Geriatric (CID)
Bee	Garza West	Beeville	2,278 Male	401	Prison (CID)
Bee	McConnell	Beeville	2,956 Male	473	Prison (CID)
Bexar	Dominguez	San Antonio	2,276 Male	382	State Jail (CID)
Bowie	Telford	New Boston	2,019 Male	449	Prison (CID)
Brazoria	Clemens	Brazoria	1,536 Male	348	Prison (CID)
Brazoria	Memorial	Rosharon	1,610 Male	567	Prison (CID)
Brazoria	Ramsey	Rosharon	1,891 Male	429	Prison (CID)
Brazoria	Stringfellow	Rosharon	1,531 Male	313	Prison (CID)
Brazoria	Terrell	Rosharon	1,603 Male	466	Prison (CID)
Brazos	Hamilton	Bryan	1,166 Male	256	Pre-Release (CID)
Brown	Havins	Brownwood	596 Male	181	Pre-Release (CID)
Burnet	Halbert	Burnet	612 Female	135	SAFPF (CID)
Caldwell	Coleman	Lockhart	1,000 Female	204	Private Prison (MTC)
Cherokee	Hodge	Rusk	989 Male	333	DDP (CID)
Cherokee	Skyview	Rusk	562 Male/Female	318	Psychiatric (CID)
Childress	Roach	Childress	1,384 Male	289	Prison (CID)
Coryell	Crain	Gatesville	2,115 Female	711	Prison (CID)
Coryell	Hilltop	Gatesville	553 Female	268	Prison (CID)
Coryell	Hughes	Gatesville	2,984 Male	515	Prison (CID)
Coryell	Mountain View	Gatesville	645 Female	300	Prison (CID)
Coryell	Murray	Gatesville	1,264 Female	341	Prison (CID)

* **Facility type abbreviations:** SAFPF (Substance Abuse Felony Punishment Facility); ISF (Intermediate Sanction Facility); DDP (Developmentally Disabled Program)

** **Operator abbreviations:** CID (TDCJ Correctional Institutions Division); MTC (Management and Training Corporation)

Source: TDCJ Unit Directory

Correctional Institutions in Texas 2023

County	Unit	Nearest Town	Max. Capacity, Gender	Employees	Type*/Operator**
Coryell	Woodman	Gatesville	900 Female	270	State Jail (CID)
Dallas	Hutchins	Dallas	2,276 Male	399	State Jail (CID)
Dawson	Smith	Lamesa	1,596 Male	252	Prison (CID)
DeWitt	Stevenson	Cuero	1,384 Male	272	Prison (CID)
Duval	Glossbrenner	San Diego	612 Male	123	SAFPF (CID)
El Paso	Sanchez	El Paso	1,100 Male	287	State Jail (CID)
Falls	Hobby	Marlin	1,384 Female	299	Prison (CID)
Falls	Marlin	Marlin	606 Female	126	Prison (CID)
Fannin	Cole	Bonham	900 Male	226	State Jail (CID)
Fannin	Moore, C.	Bonham	1,224 Male	245	Prison (CID)
Fort Bend	Jester III	Richmond	1,131 Male	288	Prison (CID)
Fort Bend	Scott	Richmond	550 Male	433	Psychiatric (CID)
Fort Bend	Vance	Richmond	378 Male	116	Prison (CID)
Freestone	Boyd	Teague	1,372 Male	298	Prison (CID)
Frio	Briscoe	Dilley	376 Male	233	Prison (CID)
Galveston	Hospital Galveston	Galveston	365 Male/Female	496	Medical (CID)
Galveston	Young	Dickinson	455 Female	302	Medical (CID)
Gray	Baten	Pampa	188 Male	29	ISF (CID)
Gray	Jordan	Pampa	1,008 Male	289	Prison (CID)
Grimes	Luther	Navasota	1,316 Male	323	Prison (CID)
Grimes	Pack	Navasota	1,478 Male	334	Prison (CID)
Hale	Formby	Plainview	1,100 Male	278	State Jail (CID)
Hale	Wheeler	Plainview	576 Male	127	State Jail (CID)
Harris	Kegans	Houston	657 Male	155	ISF (CID)
Harris	Lychner	Humble	2,276 Male	413	State Jail (CID)
Hartley	Dalhart	Dalhart	780 Male	237	Prison (CID)
Hays	Kyle	Kyle	520 Male	117	Private Prison (MTC)
Hidalgo	Lopez	Edinburg	1,100 Male	257	State Jail (CID)
Hidalgo	Segovia	Edinburg	1,224 Male	233	Pre-Release (CID)
Houston	Wainwright	Lovelady	2,143 Male	423	Prison (CID)
Jack	Lindsey	Jacksboro	839 Male	202	State Jail (MTC)
Jasper	Goodman	Jasper	68 Male	155	Prison/ISF (CID)
Jefferson	Gist	Beaumont	2,276 Male	368	State Jail (CID)
Jefferson	LeBlanc	Beaumont	1,224 Male	248	Pre-Release (CID)
Jefferson	Stiles	Beaumont	2,887 Male	495	Prison (CID)
Johnson	Estes	Venus	1,040 Male	191	Private Prison (MTC)
Jones	Middleton	Abilene	2,128 Male	504	Prison (CID)
Jones	Robertson	Abilene	2,978 Male	513	Prison (CID)
Karnes	Connally	Kenedy	2,092 Male	354	Prison (CID)
La Salle	Cotulla	Cotulla	606 Male	99	Prison (CID)
Liberty	Bell	Cleveland	520 Male	134	Private Prison (MTC)
Liberty	Henley	Dayton	576 Female	124	State Jail (CID)
Liberty	Hightower	Dayton	1,384 Male	335	Prison (CID)
Liberty	Plane/Santa Maria Baby Bonding	Dayton	2,075 Female	418	State Jail (CID)

* **Facility type abbreviations:** SAFPF (Substance Abuse Felony Punishment Facility); ISF (Intermediate Sanction Facility); DDP (Developmentally Disabled Program)

** **Operator abbreviations:** CID (TDCJ Correctional Institutions Division); MTC (Management and Training Corporation)

Source: TDCJ Unit Directory

Correctional Institutions in Texas 2023

County	Unit	Nearest Town	Max. Capacity, Gender	Employees	Type*/Operator**
Lubbock	Montford/West Texas Hospital	Lubbock	1,044 Male	591	Psychiatric (CID)
Madison	Ferguson	Midway	2,096 Male	364	Prison (CID)
Medina	Ney	Hondo	576 Male	134	Prison (CID)
Medina	Torres	Hondo	1,384 Male	298	Prison (CID)
Mitchell	Wallace/San Angelo Work Camp	Colorado City	1,448 Male	255	Prison (CID)
Pecos	Fort Stockton	Fort Stockson	606 Male	114	Prison (CID)
Pecos	Lynaugh	Fort Stockton	1,416 Male	289	Prison (CID)
Polk	Polunsky	Livingston	2,984 Male	554	Prison (CID)
Potter	Clements	Amarillo	2,932 Male	590	Prison (CID)
Rusk	Bradshaw	Henderson	768 Male	266	State Jail (MTC)
Rusk	East Texas	Henderson	1,060 Male/Female	493	Multi-Use (MTC)
Rusk	Moore, B.	Overton	500 Male	109	Private Prison (MTC)
San Saba	San Saba	San Saba	606 Female	135	Prison (CID)
Scurry	Daniel	Snyder	504 Male	224	Prison (CID)
Stephens	Sayle	Breckenridge	632 Male	146	SAFPF (CID)
Swisher	Mechler	Tulia	606 Male	117	Prison (CID)
Travis	Travis County	Austin	1,161 Male	264	State Jail (CID)
Tyler	Lewis	Woodville	2,130 Male	371	Prison (CID)
Walker	Byrd	Huntsville	1,365 Male	282	Prison (CID)
Walker	Ellis	Huntsville	2,073 Male	400	Prison (CID)
Walker	Estelle	Huntsville	3,480 Male	755	Prison (CID)
Walker	Goree	Huntsville	1,321 Male	315	Prison (CID)
Walker	Holliday	Huntsville	2,128 Male	435	Prison (CID)
Walker	Huntsville	Huntsville	1,705 Male	446	Prison (CID)
Walker	Wynne	Huntsville	2,621 Male	480	Prison (CID)
Wichita	Allred	Iowa Park	3,708 Male	687	Prison (CID)
Willacy	Willacy County	Raymondville	1,069 Male	183	State Jail (MTC)
Wise	Bridgeport	Bridgeport	520 Male	117	Private Prison (MTC)
Wood	Johnston	Winnsboro	612 Male	160	SAFPF (CID)
Walker	Wynne	Huntsville	2,621 Male	697	Prison (CID)
Wichita	Allred	Iowa Park	3,722 Male	939	Prison (CID)
Willacy	Willacy County	Raymondville	1,069 Male	183	State Jail (La Salle)
Wise	Bridgeport	Bridgeport	520 Male	117	Private Prison (MTC)
Wood	Johnston	Winnsboro	612 Male	160	SAFPF (CID)

* **Facility type abbreviations:** SAFPF (Substance Abuse Felony Punishment Facility); ISF (Intermediate Sanction Facility); DDP (Developmentally Disabled Program)

** **Operator abbreviations:** CID (TDCJ Correctional Institutions Division); MTC (Management and Training Corporation)

Source: TDCJ Unit Directory

Federal Prisons

The Federal Bureau of Prisons (BOP) operates 11 prisons and four offices in the state of Texas. Recent data shows 16,147 federal inmates confined to the following locations in Texas:

- Bastrop Federal Correction Institution
- Beaumont Federal Correction Complex
- Big Spring Federal Correction Institution
- Bryan Federal Prison Camp – Female
- Carswell Federal Medical Center – Female
- Fort Worth Federal Medical Center
- Houston Federal Detention Center – Female
- La Tuna Federal Correction Institution
- Seagoville Federal Correction Institution
- Texarkana Federal Correction Institution
- Three Rivers Federal Correction Institution

Currently, Texas is home to about 11.3% of the total 143,493 inmates in BOP-managed institutions nationwide.

Source: https://www.bop.gov

CULTURE & THE ARTS

MUSEUMS, TEXAS MEDAL OF THE ARTS

STATE ARTISTS, POETS & HISTORIANS

FILM & TELEVISION, HOLIDAYS, RELIGION & MORE...

SPECIAL THANKS TO THE ALAMO EXHIBIT
FOR SPONSORING THIS CHAPTER OF THE TEXAS ALMANAC

Texas Museums of Art, Science, History

Listed below are links to the websites of Texas museums. Where required, some have indication of the area of emphasis of the exhibits.

Abilene

Frontier Texas! (history) frontiertexas.com

The Grace Museum (art, history) thegracemuseum.org

National Center for Children's Illustrated Literature (art) nccil.org

Addison

Cavanaugh Flight Museum cavflight.org

Albany

Old Jail Art Center (art) theojac.org

Alpine

Museum of the Big Bend (history) museumofthebigbend.com

Amarillo

Amarillo Museum of Art amoa.org

American Quarter Horse Hall of Fame & Museum aqha.com/museum

Don Harrington Discovery Center (science, children's) discoverycenteramarillo.org

Texas Pharmacy Museum ttuhsc.edu/pharmacy/museum

Angleton

Brazoria County Historical Museum brazoriacountytx.gov/departments/museum

Austin

Blanton Museum of Art blantonmuseum.org

Bullock Texas State History Museum thestoryoftexas.com

The Contemporary Austin (art) thecontemporaryaustin.org

Elisabet Ney Museum (art, history) austintexas.gov/elisabetney

French Legation Museum (history) thc.texas.gov/historic-sites/french-legation-state-historic-site

Harry Ransom Center (history, literature) hrc.utexas.edu

Lady Bird Johnson Wildflower Center wildflower.org

Lyndon B. Johnson Presidential Library lbjlibrary.org

Mexic-Arte Museum (art) mexic-artemuseum.org

O. Henry Museum (history) austintexas.gov/department/o-henry-museum

Pioneer Farms pioneerfarms.org

Texas Capitol Visitors Center (history) tspb.texas.gov/prop/tcvc/cvc/cvc.html

Texas Memorial Museum (history, natural history) tmm.utexas.edu

Texas Military Forces Museum texasmilitaryforcesmuseum.org

Texas Music Museum texasmusicmuseum.org

Thinkery (children's) thinkeryaustin.org

Umlauf Sculpture Garden & Museum umlaufsculpture.org

Wild Basin Wilderness Preserve stedwards.edu/centers-institutes/wild-basin-creative-research-center

Women & Their Work (art) womenandtheirwork.org

Bay City

Matagorda County Museum (history) cityofbaycity.org/389/Museum

Beaumont

Art Museum of Southeast Texas amset.org

Edison Museum (science) edisonmuseum.org

Fire Museum of Texas firemuseumoftexas.com

Spindletop/Gladys City Boomtown (history) lamar.edu/spindletop-gladys-city

Texas Energy Museum (history) texasenergymuseum.org

Beeville

Beeville Art Museum bamtexas.org

Belton

Bell County Museum (history) bellcountymuseum.org

Bellville

Austin County Jail Museum austincounty.com/page/austin.Museum

Big Spring

Heritage Museum of Big Spring bigspringtxhistorymuseum.com

Bonham

Fannin County Museum of History fannincountymuseum.org

Fort Inglish Village (history) visitbonham.com/things-to-see/fort-inglish-village

Sam Rayburn Library and Museum cah.utexas.edu/museums/rayburn.php

Borger

Hutchinson County Historical Museum hutchinsoncountymuseum.org

Brownsville

Brownsville Heritage Museum brownsvillehistory.org/heritage-museum.html

Brownsville Museum of Fine Art bmfa.us

Children's Museum of Brownsville cmofbrownsville.org

Costumes of the Americas Museum (folk art) visitbtx.com/members/costumes-of-the-americas-museum

RGV Commemorative Air Force Museum (history) rgvcaf.org/museum.html

Stillman House Museum (history) www.brownsvillehistory.org/stillman-house-museum.html

Brownwood

Brown County Museum of History browncountymuseum.org

Lehnis Railroad Museum (history) brownwoodtexas.gov/228/Lehnis-Railroad-Museum

Bryan-College Station

Brazos Valley African American Museum (history) bvaam.org

Brazos Valley Museum of Natural History brazosvalleymuseum.org

Children's Museum of the Brazos Valley cmbv.org

George H.W. Bush Presidential Library bush41.org

University Art Galleries uart.tamu.edu

Buffalo Gap

Taylor County History Center taylorcountyhistorycenter.org

Burton

Texas Cotton Gin Museum (history) texascottonginmuseum.org

Canadian

The Citadelle Art Museum thecitadelle.org

River Valley Pioneer Museum rivervalleymuseum.org

Canyon
Panhandle-Plains Historical Museum panhandleplains.org

Carthage
Texas Country Music Hall of Fame & the Tex Ritter Museum tcmhof.com

Clarendon
Saints' Roost Museum (history) saintsroostmuseum.com

Clifton
Bosque Museum (history) bosquemuseum.org

Conroe
Heritage Museum of Montgomery County heritagemuseum.us

Corpus Christi
Art Museum of South Texas artmuseumofsouthtexas.org

Corpus Christi Museum of Science and History ccmuseum.com

Texas State Aquarium texasstateaquarium.org

Texas State Museum of Asian Cultures texasasianculturesmuseum.org

USS Lexington Museum (history) usslexington.com

Corsicana
The Pearce Museum (art, history) pearcemuseum.com

Cotulla
Brush Country Museum (history) texastimetravel.com/directory/brush-country-museum

Dalhart
XIT Museum (history) xitmuseum.org

Dallas
African American Museum (history) aamdallas.org

Crow Museum of Asian Art crowcollection.org

Dallas Heritage Village texastimetravel.com/directory/dallas-heritage-village-old-city-park

Dallas Historical Society (Fair Park) dallashistory.org

Dallas Museum of Art dma.org

Frontiers of Flight Museum flightmuseum.com

George W. Bush Presidential Library georgewbushlibrary.smu.edu

Meadows Museum (art) meadowsmuseumdallas.org

Nasher Sculpture Center nashersculpturecenter.org

Perot Museum of Nature and Science perotmuseum.org

The Sixth Floor Museum (history) jfk.org

Denison
Red River Railroad Museum redriverrailmuseum.org

Denton
Courthouse-on-the-Square Museum dentoncounty.gov/Facilities/Facility/Details/Courthouseonthe Square-Museum-11

Denton Firefighters' Museum discoverdenton.com/listing/denton-firefighters-museum/455

University of North Texas Art Galleries galleries.cvad.unt.edu

Dublin
Dublin Bottling Works (history) dublinbottlingworks.com

Dublin Rodeo Heritage Museum rodeoheritagemuseum.org

Dumas
Window on the Plains Museum (history, art) dumasmuseumandartcenter.org

Edgewood
Heritage Park Museum of East Texas heritageparkmuseumofetx.org

Edinburg
Museum of South Texas History mosthistory.org

El Campo
El Campo Museum of Natural History museumsusa.org/museums/info/15689

El Paso
Centennial Museum/Chihuahuan Desert Gardens utep.edu/centennial-museum

El Paso Museum of Archaeology archaeology.elpasotexas.gov

El Paso Museum of Art epma.art

El Paso Museum of History history.elpasotexas.gov

Fort Davis
Chihuahuan Desert Research Institute cdri.org

Fort Stockton
Annie Riggs Museum (history) annieriggsmuseum.org

Fort Worth
Amon Carter Museum of American Art cartermuseum.org

Cattle Raisers Museum (history) cattleraisersmuseum.org

Fort Worth Museum of Science and History fwmuseum.org

Kimbell Art Museum kimbellart.org

Log Cabin Village (history) logcabinvillage.org

Modern Art Museum of Fort Worth themodern.org

National Cowgirl Museum and Hall of Fame cowgirl.net

Sid Richardson Museum (art) sidrichardsonmuseum.org

Texas Civil War Museum texascivilwarmuseum.com

Fredericksburg
National Museum of the Pacific War pacificwarmuseum.org

Pioneer Museum of Fredericksburg pioneermuseum.net

Frisco
Museum of the American Railroad historictrains.org

National Videogame Museum nvmusa.org

Galveston
The Bryan Museum (art, history) thebryanmuseum.org

Galveston Children's Museum galvestoncm.org

Moody Mansion (history) moodymansion.org

Offshore Energy Center/Ocean Star (science, industry) energyeducation.org/museum

Texas Seaport Museum and Tallship "Elissa" galvestonhistory.org/sites/1877-tall-ship-elissa-at-the-galveston-historic-seaport

Gilmer
Flight of Phoenix Aviation Museum flightofthephoenix.org

Greenville
Audie Murphy/American Cotton Museum (history) cottonmuseum.com

Henderson
Depot Museum (history) depotmuseum.com

Houston
Blaffer Art Museum, University of Houston blafferartmuseum.org

Children's Museum of Houston cmhouston.org

Contemporary Arts Museum Houston camh.org

Czech Center Museum Houston (history) czechcenter.org

The Health Museum

thehealthmuseum.org

Houston Center for Contemporary Craft crafthouston.org

Houston Center for Photography hcponline.org

Houston Fire Museum (history) houstonfiremuseum.org

Houston Museum of Natural Science hmns.org

Lawndale Art Center lawndaleartcenter.org

Lone Star Flight Museum lonestarflight.org

The Menil Collection (art) menil.org

Museum of Fine Arts, Houston mfah.org

The Printing Museum printingmuseum.org

San Jacinto Museum of History sanjacinto-museum.org

Space Center Houston spacecenter.org

Huntsville

Sam Houston Memorial Museum and Republic of Texas Presidential Library samhoustonmemorial museum.com

Texas Prison Museum txprisonmuseum.org

Kerrville

The Museum of Western Art museumofwesternart.com

Kilgore

East Texas Oil Museum easttexasoilmuseum.kilgore.edu

Lake Jackson

Lake Jackson Historical Museum ljhistory.org

Laredo

Lamar Bruni Vergara Planetarium tamiu.edu/planetarium

Republic of the Rio Grande Museum (history) republicoftheriogrande.org

League City

Butler Longhorn Museum butlerlonghornmuseum.com

West Bay Common School Children's Museum (history) oneroomschoolhouse.org

Longview

Longview Museum of Fine Arts lmfa.org

Lubbock

FiberMax Center for Discovery: Agriculture agriculturehistory.org

Buddy Holly Center (history, music) buddyhollycenter.org

Museum of Texas Tech University (art, humanities, science) depts.ttu.edu/museumttu

National Ranching Heritage Center ranchingheritage.org

Science Spectrum sciencespectrum.org

Lufkin

Naranjo Museum of Natural History naranjomuseum.org

Texas Forestry Museum treetexas.com

Marfa

The Chinati Foundation (art) chinati.org

Marshall

Harrison County Historical Museum texastimetravel.com/directory/harrison-county-historical-museum-historic

Michelson Museum of Art michelsonmuseum.org

McAllen

International Museum of Art & Science theimasonline.org

McKinney

Heard Natural Science Museum & Wildlife Sanctuary heardmuseum.org

Midland

Museum of the Southwest (art, science, children's) museumsw.org

Petroleum Museum petroleummuseum.org

Nacogdoches

Millard's Crossing Historic Village mchvnac.com

New Braunfels

McKenna Children's Museum mckennakids.org

Sophienburg Museum & Archives (history) www.sophienburg.com

Odessa

Ellen Noël Art Museum noelartmuseum.org

The Presidential Archives and Leadership Library texastimetravel.com/directory/presidential-archives-and-leadership-library

Orange

Stark Museum of Art starkmuseum.org

Panhandle

Carson County Square House Museum (history, art) squarehousemuseum.weebly.com

Perryton

Museum of the Plains (history) museumoftheplains.com

Plano

Heritage Farmstead Museum heritagefarmstead.org

Port Arthur

Museum of the Gulf Coast (history) museumofthegulfcoast.org

Port Lavaca

Calhoun County Museum (history) calhouncountymuseum.org

Richmond

George Ranch Historical Park georgeranch.org

Rockport

Texas Maritime Museum texasmaritimemuseum.org

Rosenberg

The Black Cowboy Museum blackcowboymuseum.org

Rosenberg Railroad Museum rosenbergrrmuseum.org

Round Top

Henkel Square Market (history) henkelsquareroundtop.com

Winedale Historical Complex briscoecenter.org/winedale/

San Angelo

Miss Hattie's Bordello Museum (history) misshatties.com

San Angelo Museum of Fine Arts samfa.org

San Antonio

The Alamo thealamo.org

Briscoe Western Art Museum briscoemuseum.org

Holocaust Memorial Museum of San Antonio hmmsa.org

Institute of Texan Cultures (history) texancultures.com

McNay Art Museum mcnayart.org

San Antonio Art League & Museum saalm.org

San Antonio Museum of Art samuseum.org

The Witte Museum (science, history) wittemuseum.org

San Marcos

LBJ Museum San Marcos (history) lbjmuseum.com

The Wittliff Collections (art) thewittliffcollections.txstate.edu

Sarita

Kenedy Ranch Museum of South Texas kenedy.org/museum

Schulenburg

Stanzel Model Aircraft Museum stanzelmuseum.org

Serbin

Texas Wendish Heritage Museum texaswendish.org/museum

Sherman

Sherman Jazz Museum shermanjazzmuseum.com

The Sherman Museum (history) theshermanmuseum.org

Snyder

Scurry County Museum (history) scurrycountymuseum.org

Sulphur Springs

Southwest Dairy Museum and Education Center southwestdairyfarmers.com

Teague

The Burlington-Rock Island Railroad Museum therailroadmuseum.com

Temple

Czech Heritage Museum czechheritagemuseum.org

Railroad and Heritage Museum templerrhm.org

Texarkana

Museum of Regional History texarkanamuseum.org

The Woodlands

The Woodlands Children's Museum woodlandschildrensmuseum.org

Thurber

W.K. Gordon Museum and Research Center for Industrial History of Texas tarleton.edu/gordoncenter

Tyler

Discovery Science Place discoveryscienceplace.org

Historic Aviation Memorial Museum tylerhamm.com

Smith County Historical Museum smithcountyhistoricalsociety.org/museum

Tyler Museum of Art tylermuseum.org

Victoria

Children's Discovery Museum cdmgoldencrescent.com

Museum of the Coastal Bend (history) museumofthecoastalbend.org

The Nave Museum (art) navemuseum.com

Waco

Dr Pepper Museum (history) drpeppermuseum.com

Martin Museum of Art martinmuseum.artsandsciences.baylor.edu

Mayborn Museum (history, science) mayborn.web.baylor.edu

Texas Ranger Hall of Fame and Museum texasranger.org

Texas Sports Hall of Fame tshof.org

Washington

Star of the Republic Museum (history) texastimetravel.com/directory/star-republic-museum

Weatherford

Museum of the Americas (history, folk art) museumoftheamericas.com

The National Vietnam War Museum nationalvnwarmuseum.org

Wharton

20th Century Technology Museum 20thcenturytech.com

White Settlement

White Settlement Historical Museum wsmuseum.com

Wichita Falls

Kell House Museum (history) kellhouseheritagecenter.org

Museum of North Texas History museumofnorthtexashistory.org

Professional Wrestling Hall of Fame & Museum pro-wrestling-hall-of-fame-museum.business.site

Wichita Falls Museum of Art wfma.msutexas.edu

Yoakum

Yoakum Heritage Museum yoakumareachamber.com/visit-yoakum/experience-history

Public Libraries in Texas

Source: Library Development Division of the Texas State Library and Archives in Austin.

Texas public libraries continue to strive to meet the education and information needs of Texans by providing library services of high quality with often-times-limited resources.

Each year, services provided by public libraries increase, with more visits to public libraries and higher attendance in library programs.

The challenges facing public libraries in Texas are many and varied. The costs for providing electronic and online sources, in addition to traditional services, are growing faster than budgets.

Urban libraries are trying to serve growing populations, while libraries in rural areas are trying to serve remote populations and provide distance learning where possible.

National rankings of public libraries are published by the Institute of Museum and Library Services at imls.gov/research-evaluation/data-collection/public-libraries-survey.

When comparing Texas statistics to those nationally, Texas continues to rank below most of the other states in most categories, with the exception of public use of internet terminals.

Complete statistical information on public libraries is available on the Texas State Library's website: tsl.texas.gov/landing/statistics.html. There is also a listing of libraries at: tsl.texas.gov/texshare/libsearch. ☆

Texas Institute of Letters Awards

Each year since 1939, the **Texas Institute of Letters** (texasinstituteofletters.org) has honored outstanding literature and journalism that is either by Texans or about Texas subjects.

Awards have been made for fiction, nonfiction, Southwest history, general information, magazine and newspaper journalism, children's books, translation, poetry, and book design.

The awards for book design and translation are awarded biyearly.

The awards of recent years are listed below; see previous recipients at tshaonline.org.

2023

Best Book of Fiction: Rudy Ruiz, *Valley of Shadows*

Best First Book of Fiction: Ramona Reeves, *It Falls Gently All Around and Other Stories*

Best Book of Nonfiction: Kirk Wallace Johnson, *The Fishermen and the Dragon*

Best Book of Poetry: Jasminne Mendez, *City without Altar*

Best First Book of Poetry: Laura Villareal, *Girl's Guide to Leaving*

Most Significant Scholarly Book: Sam W. Haynes, *Unsettled Land: From Revolution to Republic, the Struggle for Texas*

Best Young Adult Book: Guadalupe García McCall, *Echoes of Grace*

Best Middle Grade Book: Rebecca Balcárcel, *Shine On, Luz Véliz!*

Best Picture Book: Xelena Gonzalez, Adriana M. Garcia, *Where Wonder Grows*

Best Design of a Trade Book: Jennifer Sperry Steinorth, *Her Read* (found poetry of *The Meaning of Art* by Herbert Read)

Best Translation of a Book: David Bowles, translator of *The Sea-Ringed World: Sacred Stories of the Americas* by María García Esperón

Best Short Story: Bret Anthony Johnston, "Playing the Ghost"

Best Short Nonfiction: Gus Bova, "Uvalde Vive"

Lon Tinkle Award (for career): Beverly Lowry

2022

Best Book of Fiction: Heath Dollar, *Old Country Fiddle: Stories*

Best First Book of Fiction: Babette Fraser Hale, *A Wall of Bright Dead Feathers*

Best Book of Nonfiction: Lise Olsen, *Code of Silence*

Best Book of Poetry: Rodney Gomez, *Arsenal with Praise Song*

Best First Book of Poetry: César Leonardo de León, *Speaking with Grackles by Soapberry Trees*

Most Significant Scholarly Book: Nicholas Keefauver Roland, *Violence in the Hill Country: The Texas Frontier in the Civil War Era*

Best Young Adult Book: David Bowles & Raúl the Third, *Clockwork Curandera*

Best Middle Grade Book: Varian Johnson, *Playing the Cards You're Dealt*

Best Picture Book: Divya Srinivasan, *What I Am*

Best Short Story: Dagoberto Gilb, "Two Red Foxes"

Best Short Nonfiction: Skip Hollandsworth, "The Notorious Mrs. Mossler"

Lon Tinkle Award (for career): Celeste Bedford Walker

2021

Bryan Washington: *Memorial: A Novel*

Marisol Cortez: *Luz at Midnight*

Joe Holley: *Sutherland Springs*

Chera Hammons: *Maps of Injury*

David Meischen: *Anyone's Son*

Miguel Angel González-Quiroga: *War and Peace on the Rio Grande Frontier: 1830-1880*

Darcie Little Badger: *Elatsoe*

Francisco Stork: *Illegal*

Christina Soontornvat: *A Wish in the Dark*

Jerome Pumphrey and Jarrett Pumphrey: *The Old Truck*

Mary Ann Jacob: designer of *Daddy-O's Book of Big-Ass Art*, by Bob "Daddy-O" Wade

David Meischen: "Crossing the Light," *Storylandia*

ire'ne lara silva: "A Place Before Words," *Texas Highways*

Cyrus Cassells: translator of *Still Life with Children: Selected Poems of Francesc Parcerisas*

Lon Tinkle Award (for career): Benjamin Alire Sáenz

2020

Oscar Cásares: *Where We Come From*

Bryan Washington: *Lot: Stories*

Holly George-Warren: *Janis: Her Life and Music*

Ron Tyler: *The Art of Texas: 250 Years*

Naomi Shihab Nye: *The Tiny Journalist*

Lupe Mendez: *Why I Am Like Tequila* (Aquarius Press)

Sergio Troncoso: "Rosary on the Border" in *A Peculiar Kind of Immigrant's Son*

Skip Hollandsworth: "Sabika's Story," in *Texas Monthly*

Rebecca Balcárcel: *The Other Half of Happy*

Rubén Degollado: *Throw: A Novel*

José M. Hernández: *The Boy Who Touched the Stars*

Lon Tinkle Award (for career): John Rechy

2019

Ben Fountain: *Beautiful Country Burn Again: Democracy, Rebellion, and Revolution*

Natalia Sylvester: *Everyone Knows You Go Home*

Stephen Markley: *Ohio*

Tarfia Faizullah: *Registers of Illuminated Villages*

Megan Peak: *Girldom*

Brent Nongbri: *God's Library: The Archaeology of the Earliest Christian Manuscripts*

David Bowles: *The Feathered Serpent, Dark Heart of Sky: Myths of Mexico* and *They Call Me Güero*

Varian Johnson: *The Parker Inheritance*

Chris Barton: *What Can You Do with a Voice Like That?*

Clay Reynolds: "Railroad Man," *New Madrid*, and "Autumn Moon," *New Texas*

Lon Tinkle Award (for career): Naomi Shihab Nye

2018

Jan Reid: *Sins of the Younger Sons*

Chanelle Benz: *The Man Who Shot Out My Eye is Dead*

Roger D. Hodge: *Texas Blood: Seven Generations Among the Outlaws, Ranchers, Indians, Missionaries, Soldiers, and Smugglers of the Borderlands*

Jerry D. Thompson: *Tejano Tiger: José de los Santos Benavides and the Texas-Mexico Borderlands, 1823–1891*

Sasha Pimentel: *For Want of Water: and other poems*

Vanessa Villarreal: *Beast Meridian*

Brett Anthony Johnston: "Miss McElroy," *Ecotone*

Rose Cahalan: "Ride Like a Girl," *Texas Observer*

Michael Merschel: *Revenge of the Star Survivors*

Francisco X. Stork: *Disappeared*

Xelena González and Adriana M. Garcia: *All Around Us*

Philip Boehm: translator of *Chasing the King of Hearts,* by Hanna Krall

Mary Ann Jacob: designer, *The Nueces River, Rio Escondido,* by Margie Crisp and William B. Montgomery

Lon Tinkle Award (for career): Sandra Cisneros

2017

Paulette Jiles: *News of the World*

Amy Gentry: *Good as Gone*

Skip Hollandsworth: *The Midnight Assassin*

Max Krochmal: *Blue Texas: The Making of a Multiracial Democratic Coalition in the Civil Rights Era*

Bruce Bond: *Gold Bee*

Miriam Bird Greenberg: *In the Volcano's Mouth*

Stephen Harrigan: "Off Course," *Texas Monthly*

David Meischen: "Cicada Song," *Salamander*

Kathi Appelt and Alison McGhee: *Maybe a Fox*

Phillippe Diederich: *Playing for the Devil's Fire*

Dianna Hutts Aston: *A Beetle Is Shy*

Kristie Lee: *From Tea Cakes to Tamales*

Lon Tinkle Award (for career): Pat Mora

2016

Antonio Ruiz-Camacho: *Barefoot Dogs*

Mary Helen Specht: *Migratory Animals*

Jan Jarboe Russell: *The Train to Crystal City*

Andrew Torget III: *Seeds of Empire*

Laurie Ann Guerrero: *A Crown for Gumecindo*

J. Scott Brownlee: *Requiem for Used Ignition Cap*

W.K. Stratton: "My Brother's Secret," *Texas Monthly*

Brian Van Reet: "The Chaff," *Iowa Review*

Don Tate: *The Remarkable Story of George Moses Horton: Poet*

Brian Yansky: *Utopia, Iowa*

Pat Mora: *The Remembering Day/El dia de los muertos*

Andrea Caillouet: *The Luck Archive: Exploring Belief, Superstition, and Tradition*

Marian Schwartz: translator of *Anna Karenina,* by Leo Tolstoy

Lon Tinkle Award (for career): Sarah Bird

2015

Elizabeth Crook: *Monday, Monday*

Michael Morton: *Getting Life: An Innocent Man's 25-Year Journey from Prison to Peace*

Merritt Tierce: *Love Me Back*

Lawrence T. Jones: *Lens on the Texas Frontier*

Katherine Hoerth: *Goddess Wears Cowboy Boots*

Brian Van Reet: "Eat the Spoil," in *Missouri Review*

Chloe Honum: *The Tulip-Flame*

Pamela Colloff: "The Witness," *Texas Monthly*

Bill Wittliff and Ellen McKie: *The Devil's Backbone,* written by Bill Wittliff, illustrated by Jack Unruh

Nikki Lofton: *Nightingale's Nest*

Glaudia Guadalupe Martinez: *Pig Park*

Pat Mora and Lilbby Martinez: *I Pledge Allegiance*

Lon Tinkle Award (for career): Lawrence Wright

2014

Tom Zigal: *Many Rivers to Cross*

John Talifarro: *All The Great Prizes: The Life of John Hay from Lincoln to Roosevelt*

Lawrence Wright: *Going Clear: Scientology, Hollywood, and the Prison of Belief*

Nan Cuba: *Body and Bread*

Raúl Coronado: *A World Not to Come: A History of Latino Writing and Print Culture*

Pattiann Rogers: *Holy Heathen Rhapsody*

Bret Anthony Johnston: "To a Good Home," *Virginia Quarterly Review*

Sasha West: *Failure And I Bury The Body*

John MacCormack: "Life On The Shale," *San Antonio Express-News,* series

Lindsay Starr: *Two Prospectors: The Letters of Sam Shepard and Johnny Dark*

Xavier Garza: *Maximilian and the Mystery of the Bingo Rematch*

Kathi Appelt: *The True Blue Scouts of Sugar Man Swamp*

David Bowles: *Flower, Song, Dance: Aztec and Mayan Poetry*

Lon Tinkle Award (for career): Jan Reid

2013

Ben Fountain: *Billy Lynn's Long Halftime Walk*

Margie Crisp: *River of Contrasts*

Kevin Grauke: *Shadows of Men*

Kate Sayen Kirkland: *Captain James A. Baker of Houston: 1857–1941*

Ken Fontenot: *Kingdom of Birds*

James Sanderson: "Bankers," in *Descant*

Kathleen Winter: *Nostalgia for the Criminal Past*

Mellissa Del Bosque: "The Deadliest Place in Mexico," *The Texas Observer,* February, 12, 2012

Kristina Kachele: *In the Country of Empty Crosses,* written by Arturo Madrid

Donna Rubin: *Log Cabin Kitty*

Melodie Cuate: *Journey to Plum Creek*

Lon Tinkle Award (for career): Stephen Harrigan

2012

Stephen Harrigan: *Remember Ben Clayton*

Steven Fenberg: *Unprecedented Power: Jesse Jones, Capitalism, and the Common Good*

Siobhan Fallon: *You Know When the Men Are Gone*

Christopher Long: *The Looshaus*

Jennifer Grotz: *The Needle*

Bret Anthony Johnston: "Paradeability," *American Short Fiction*

Jose Antonio Rodriguez: *The Shallow End of Sleep*

Skip Hollandsworth: "The Lost Boys," *Texas Monthly,* April 2011

Jordan Smith: "The Science of Injustice," *Austin Chronicle,* August 19, 2011

Barbara Werden and Lindsay Starr: *Lone Star Law,* written by Michael Ariens

Dave Oliphant: *After-Dinner Declarations* by Nicanor Parra

Elaine Scott: *Space, Stars and the Beginning of Time*

J.L. Powers: *This Thing Called the Future*

Lon Tinkle Award (for career): Gary Cartwright

Austin native David Ramirez plays in a theater in Dallas on February 25, 2023. Photo by Rusty Shacklefort.

State Cultural Agencies Assist the Arts

Source: Principally the Texas Commission on the Arts, along with other state cultural agencies.

Culture in Texas, as in any market, is a mixture of activity generated by both the commercial and the nonprofit sectors. The commercial sector encompasses Texas-based profit-making businesses, including commercial recording artists, nightclubs, record companies, private galleries, assorted boutiques that carry fine art collectibles, and private dance and music halls. Texas also has extensive cultural resources offered by nonprofit organizations that are engaged in charitable, educational, and humanitarian activities.

The Legislature has authorized five state agencies to administer cultural services and funds for the public good. The agencies are:

- Texas Commission on the Arts
- Texas Film Commission
- Texas Historical Commission
- Texas State Library and Archives Commission
- The State Preservation Board

Although not a state agency, another organization that provides cultural services to the citizens of Texas is Humanities Texas.

The Commission on the Arts was established in 1965 to develop a receptive climate for the arts through the conservation and advancement of Texas' rich and diverse arts and cultural industries.

The Texas Commission on the Arts' goals are:

- Provide grants for the arts and cultural industries in Texas.
- Provide the financial, human, and technical resources necessary to ensure viable arts and cultural communities.
- Promote widespread attendance at arts and cultural performances and exhibitions in Texas.
- Ensure access to arts in Texas through marketing, fund raising, and cultural tourism.

The commission is responsible for several initiatives including:

- Arts Education: programs that serve the curricular and training needs of the state's school districts, private schools, and home schools.
- Marketing and Public Relations: marketing and fund-raising expertise to generate funds for agency operations and increase visibility of the arts in Texas.
- Cultural Tourism: programs that develop and promote tourism destinations featuring the arts.

Information on programs is available on the Texas Commission on the Arts at arts.texas.gov. ☆

Performing Arts Organizations: Dance, Music, Theater

The Texas Commission on the Arts provides a listing of performing arts companies and artists in Texas at www.arts.texas.gov/artroster/roster/show/all. There are links arranged by category: dance, theater, music, etc.

There is also https://www.arts.texas.gov/resources/art-in-communities, which provides more information about community arts programs, as well as swpap.org, which displays performing arts organizations by city.

Texas Medal of the Arts Awards

Source: Texas Commission on the Arts.

The Texas Medals of the Arts are presented to artists and arts patrons with Texas ties. The awards are administered by the Texas Cultural Trust Council.

The council was established to raise money and awareness for the Texas Cultural Trust Fund, which was created by the Legislature in 1993 to support cultural arts in Texas (txculturaltrust.org).

The medals, awarded every two years, were first presented in 2001. A concurrent proclamation by the state Senate and House of Representatives honors the recipients, and the governor presents the awards in Austin. ☆

2023

Lifetime Achievement Award: Carole Cook, Abilene, musical theater.
Architecture: Miró Rivera Architects: Juan Miró and Miguel Rivera, Austin.
Arts in Health: Center for Performing Arts Medicine, Houston Methodist.
Dance: Septime Webre, Brownsville.
Fashion: Lela Rose, Dallas.
Film/Actor: Luke Wilson, Dallas.
Film/Producer: Taylor Sheridan.
Literary Arts: Benjamin Alire Sáenz, El Paso.
Music: Christopher Cross, San Antonio.
Music/Songwriter: Miranda Lambert, Lindale.
Visual Arts: Deborah Roberts, Austin.

2021

Canceled due to COVID-19.

2019

Design: Brandon Maxwell, Longview, fashion designer, photographer.
Music: Boz Scaggs, Plano, singer/songwriter.
Visual arts: Trenton Doyle Hancock, Houston and Paris, TX, artist.
Music Ensemble: Conspirare, Austin, choral ensemble.
Literary: Stephen Harrigan, Austin, Abilene, and Corpus Christi, author, journalist.
Film: Matthew McConaughey, Austin, Uvalde, and Longview, actor.
Multimedia: Mark Seliger, Amarillo and Houston, photographer.
Theater: Jennifer Holliday, Houston, singer, actor.
Arts education: Vidal M. Treviño School of Communications and Fine Arts, Laredo.
Architecture: Elaine Molinar, El Paso, and Craig Dykers, San Antonio.

2017

Lifetime Achievement Award: Kenny Rogers of Houston.
Multimedia: Kris Kristofferson, Brownsville.
Music: Yolanda Adams, Houston.
Visual arts: Leo Villareal, El Paso, artist.
Dance: Lauren Anderson, Houston.
Literary: John Phillip Santos, San Antonio.
Film: Janine Turner, Euless, actor.
Journalism: Scott Pelley, San Antonio, news broadcaster.
Television: Jaclyn Smith, Houston, actor.
Theater: Renée Elise Goldsberry, Houston.
Arts education: Dallas Black Dance Theatre.
Architecture: Frank Welch, Dallas.
Individual arts patron: Lynn Wyatt, Houston.
Corporate arts patrons: John Paul and Eloise DeJoria, Austin.
Foundation arts patron: Tobin Endowment, San Antonio.

2015

Lifetime Achievement Award: The Gatlin Brothers of Seminole, Abilene, and Odessa.
Multimedia: Emilio Nicolas Sr. of San Antonio, for work as broadcaster.
Music: T Bone Burnett of Fort Worth.
Visual arts: Rick Lowe of Houston, artist.
Dance: Kilgore Rangerettes.
Literary: Lawrence Wright, Austin and Dallas.
Film: Jamie Foxx, Terrell, actor.
Television: Dan Rather, Wharton, news broadcaster.
Television: Chandra Wilson, Houston, actor.
Theater: Robert Schenkkan, Austin.
Arts education: Booker T. Washington High School for the Performing and Visual Arts, Dallas.
Architecture: Charles Renfro, Houston.
Individual arts patron: Margaret McDermott, Dallas.
Corporate arts patron: Dr Pepper Snapple Group, Plano.
Standing Ovation Award: Ruth Altshuler of Dallas.

2013

Multimedia: Eva Longoria of Corpus Christi, for work as actress, author, and philanthropist.
Music: Steve Miller of Dallas.
Visual arts: James Surls, Splendora, artist.
Dance: Houston Ballet.
Television/Film: Ricardo Chavira, San Antonio, actor.
Theater arts: Joe Sears and Jaston Williams, Austin *(Greater Tuna* fame).
Arts education: Big Thought / Gigi Antoni, Dallas.
Individual arts patron: Gene Jones and Charlotte Jones Anderson, Dallas.
Foundation arts patron: Kimbell Arts Foundation, Fort Worth.
Corporate arts patron: Texas Monthly.

2011

Lifetime Achievement Award: Barbara Smith Conrad from Center Point near Pittsburg, operatic mezzo-soprano and civil rights icon.
Music: ZZ Top of Houston, legendary band that sold over 50 million albums.
Literary: Robert M. Edsel, Dallas, author and founder/president of the Monuments Men Foundation for the Preservation of Art.
Visual arts: James Drake, Lubbock, artist.
Television: Bob Schieffer, Fort Worth, CBS news anchor.
Theater arts: Alley Theatre, Houston.
Multimedia: Ray Benson, Austin, front man for Asleep at the Wheel and co-writer of the play *A Ride with Bob* based on the life of Bob Wills.
Film: Marcia Gay Harden, UT-Austin graduate, Oscar-winning actress.
Film: Bill Paxton, Fort Worth, four-time Golden Globe nominee.
Arts education: Tom Staley, director of the Harry Ransom Center at UT-Austin.
Individual arts patron: Ernest and Sarah Butler of Austin, major donors to Austin arts groups.
Corporate arts patron: H-E-B, grocer with a long history of supporting the arts throughout Texas.

2009

A Standing Ovation Award was presented to former First Lady Laura Bush of Midland and Dallas.
Lifetime Achievement Award: posthumously to artist Robert Rauschenberg, born in Port Arthur.
Music: Clint Black of Katy, country music singer/songwriter.
Literary: T.R. Fehrenbach of San Antonio. Mr. Fehrenbach,

born in San Benito, is the author of 18 nonfiction books, including *Lone Star: A History of Texas and Texans.*

Visual arts: Keith Carter of Beaumont, photographer.

Theater arts: Betty Buckley of Fort Worth, Tony Award winner and film actress.

Multimedia: *Austin City Limits,* the 30-year television series.

Film: Robert Rodriguez of Austin. Mr. Rodriguez, born in San Antonio, is a film director and writer.

Architecture: David Lake of Austin and Ted Flato of Corpus Christi, both now working in San Antonio.

Arts education: Pianist James Dick of Round Top, founder of the International Festival-Institute there.

Individual arts patron: Edith O'Donnell of Dallas.

Corporate arts patron: Anheuser-Busch of St. Louis and Houston.

2007

Lifetime Achievement Award: Broadcast newsman Walter Cronkite of Houston.

Music: Ornette Coleman of Fort Worth, jazz saxophonist.

Dance: Alvin Ailey American Dance Theater. The late Alvin Ailey, born in Rogers, was a creator of African American dance works.

Literary: writer Sandra Brown of Waco.

Visual arts: Jesús Moroles of Corpus Christi/Rockport, sculptor.

Theater arts: actress Judith Ivey of El Paso.

Multimedia: Bill Wittliff of Taft and Austin, publisher, writer, photographer, director, producer.

Arts education: Paul Baker of Hereford/Waelder. Headed drama departments at Baylor and Trinity universities.

Individual arts patron: Diana and Bill Hobby of Houston.

Corporate arts patron: Neiman Marcus, Dallas.

Foundation arts patron: Sid W. Richardson Foundation of Fort Worth.

2006

Lawrence Wright: *The Looming Tower: Al-Qaeda and the Road to 9/11*

Cormac McCarthy: *The Road*

Dominic Smith: *The Mercury Visions of Louis Daguerre*

Marian Schwartz: translator of *White on Black* by Ruben Gallego

Tony Freemantle: "The Gulf Coast Revisited" in the *Houston Chronicle*

Mary Ann Jacob: *Timeless Texas*

John Sprong: "The Good Book and the Bad Book" in *Texas Monthly*

Mark Wisniewski: "Prisoners of War"

Tim Tingle: *Crossing Bok Chitto: A Choctaw Tale of Friendship and Freedom*

Heather Hepler: *Scrambled Eggs at Midnight*

Jerry Thompson: *Civil War to the Bloody End: The Life and Times of Major Samuel P. Heintzelman*

Christopher Bakken: *Goat Funeral*

Lon Tinkle Award (for career): William D. Wittliff

Special Citation: Allen Maxwell

2005

Lifetime Achievement Award: singer Vikki Carr of El Paso.

Television/theater: actress Phylicia Rashad of Houston.

Music: singer/songwriter Lyle Lovett of Klein.

Dance: Ben Stevenson of Houston and Fort Worth.

Literary arts: Naomi Shihab Nye of San Antonio.

Visual arts: Jose Cisneros of El Paso.

Theater: Robert Wilson of Waco.

Arts education: Ginger Head-Gearheart of Fort Worth, advocate of arts education in public schools.

Individual arts patrons: Joe R. and Teresa Lozano Long of Austin, philanthropists.

Foundation arts patron: Nasher Foundation/Dallas.

2004

Steven Mintz: *Huck's Raft*

Laurie Lynn Drummond: *Anything You Say Can and Will Be Held Against You*

Bret Anthony Johnston: *Corpus Christi*

William Wenthe: *Not Till We Are Lost*

Andres Resendez: *Changing National Identities at the Frontier: Texas and New Mexico, 1800–1850*

Philip Boehm: translator of *Death in Danzig* by Stefan Chwin

Mike Nichols: *Balaam Gimble's Gumption*

Ben Fountain: "Bouki and the Cocaine"

Zanto Peabody: "The Search for Eddie Peabody" in the *Houston Chronicle*

DJ Stout and Julie Savasky: *Maps of the Imagination*

Lawrence Wright: "The Kingdom of Silence" in the *New Yorker*

Diane Stanley: *Jack and the Beanstalk*

Susan Abraham and Denise Gonzales: *Cecilia's Year*

Lon Tinkle Award (for career): T.R. Fehrenbach

2003

Lifetime Achievement: John Graves of Glen Rose, author of *Goodbye to A River.*

Media-film/television acting: Fess Parker of Fort Worth.

Music: country singer Charley Pride of Dallas.

Dance: Tommy Tune of Wichita Falls and Houston.

Theater: Enid Holm of Odessa, actress and former executive director of Texas Nonprofit Theatres.

Literary arts: Sandra Cisneros of San Antonio.

Visual arts: sculptor Glenna Goodacre of Dallas.

Folk arts: Tejano singer Lydia Mendoza of San Antonio.

Architecture: State Capitol Preservation Project of Austin, headed by Dealey Herndon.

Arts education: theater teacher Marca Lee Bircher, Dallas.

Individual arts patron: philanthropist Nancy B. Hamon of Dallas.

Corporate arts patron: Exxon/Mobil based in Irving.

Foundation arts patron: Houston Endowment Inc.

2002

Kathi Appelt: *Where, Where Is Swamp Bear?*

Carolee Dean: *Comfort*

Juan Rulfo: *Pedro Paramo*

Ben Fountain III: "Near-Extinct Birds of the Central Cordillera"

Mark Lisheron and Bill Bishop: "Cities of Ideas" in the *Austin American-Statesman*

Lawrence Wright: "The Man Behind Bin Laden" in the *New Yorker*

Dan Rifenburgh: *Advent*

Reginald Gibbons: *It's Time*

Kinky Friedman: *Meanwhile Back at the Ranch*

Michael Gagarin: *Antiphon the Athenian: Oratory, Law, and Justice in the Age of the Sophists*

Ray Gonzalez: *The Underground Heart: A Return to a Hidden Landscape*

Lisa Schamess: *Borrowed Light*

Rick Bass: *Hermit's Story*

Lon Tinkle Award (for career): Shelby Hearon

(In 1983, The Texas Almanac was honored with a Special Citation.)

2001

Lifetime Achievement: Van Cliburn of Fort Worth.

Film: actor Tommy Lee Jones of San Saba.

Music: singer-songwriter Willie Nelson of Austin.

Dance: Debbie Allen of Houston, choreographer, director, actress and composer.

Theater: *Texas* musical-drama producer Neil Hess of Amarillo.

Literary arts: playwright Horton Foote of Wharton.

Visual arts: muralist John Biggers of Houston.

Folk arts: musician brothers Santiago Jimenez Jr. and Flaco Jimenez of San Antonio.

Architecture: restoration architect Wayne Bell of Austin.

Arts education: theater arts director Gilberto Zepeda Jr. of Pharr.

Individual arts patron: philanthropist Jack Blanton of Houston.

Corporate arts patron: SBC Communications Inc. of San Antonio.

Foundation arts patron: Meadows Foundation of Dallas.☆

State Artists of Texas

Sources: Texas State Library and Archives; Texas Commission on the Arts; The Dallas Morning News.

Since 2001, a committee of seven members appointed by the governor, lieutenant governor, and speaker of the House of Representatives selects the poet laureate, state artists, and state musician based on recommendations from the Texas Commission on the Arts.

Previously, the Legislature made the nominations.

The state historian is appointed by the governor and is recommended by both the Texas State Historical Association and the Texas Historical Commission. ☆

Years	Artist, Hometown/Residence
1971-72	Joe Ruiz Grandee, Arlington
1972-73	Melvin C. Warren, Clifton
1973-74	Ronald Thomason, Weatherford A.C. Gentry Jr., Tyler, alternate
1974-75	Joe Rader Roberts, Dripping Springs Bette Lou Voorhis, Austin, alternate
1975-76	Jack White, New Braunfels
July 4, 1975 –July 4, 1976	Robert Summers, Glen Rose Bicentennial Artist
1976-77	James Boren, Clifton Kenneth Wyatt, Lubbock, alternate
1977-78	Edward "Buck" Schiwetz, DeWitt County Renne Hughes, Tarrant County, alternate
1978-79	Jack Cowan, Rockport Gary Henry, Palo Pinto County, alternate Joyce Tally, Caldwell County, alternate
1979-80	Dalhart Windberg, Travis County Grant Lathe, Canyon Lake, alternate
1980-81	Harry Ahysen, Huntsville Jim Reno, Simonton, alternate
1981-82	Jerry Newman, Beaumont Raul Guiterrez, San Antonio, alternate
1982-83	Dr. James H. Johnson, Bryan Armando Hinojosa, Laredo, alternate
1983-84	Raul Gutierrez, San Antonio James Eddleman, Lubbock, alternate
1984-85	Covelle Jones, Lubbock Ragan Gennusa, Austin, alternate
1986-87	Chuck DeHaan, Graford
1987-88	Neil Caldwell, Angleton Rey Gaytan, Austin, alternate
1988-89	George Hallmark, Walnut Springs Tony Eubanks, Grapevine, alternate

Year	Two-dimensional	Three-dimensional
1990-91	Mondel Rogers, Sweetwater	Ron Wells, Cleveland
1991-92	Woodrow Foster, Center	Kent Ullberg, Corpus Christi
	Harold Phenix, Houston, alternate	Mark Clapham, Conroe, alternate
1993-94	Roy Lee Ward, Hunt	James Eddleman, Lubbock
1994-95	Frederick Carter, El Paso	Garland A. Weeks, Wichita Falls
1998-99	Carl Rice Embrey, San Antonio	Edd Hayes, Humble
2000-02	Vacant	
2003	Ralph White, Austin	Dixie Friend Gay, Houston
2004	Sam Caldwell, Houston	David Hickman, Dallas
2005	Kathy Vargas, San Antonio	Sharon Kopriva, Houston
2006	George Boutwell, Bosque County	James Surls, Athens
2007	Lee Herring, Rockwall	David Keens, Arlington
2008	Janet Eager Krueger, Encinal	Damian Priour, Austin
2009	René Alvarado, San Angelo	Eliseo Garcia, Farmers Branch
2010	Marc Burckhardt, Austin	John Bennett, Fredericksburg
2011	Melissa Miller, Austin	Jesús Moroles, Rockport
2012	Karl Umlauf, Waco	Bill FitzGibbons, San Antonio
2013	Jim Woodson, Waco, Fort Worth	Joseph Havel, Houston
2014	Julie Speed, Austin, Marfa	Ken Little, Canyon, San Antonio
2015	Vincent Valdez, San Antonio	Margo Sawyer, Houston, Elgin
2016	Dornith Doherty, Houston, Southlake	Dario Robleto, San Antonio, Houston
2017	Kermit Oliver, Refugio, Houston, Waco	Beverly Penn, San Marcos
2018	Sedrick Huckaby, Fort Worth	Beili Liu, Austin
2019	Mary McCleary, Nacogdoches	Rick Lowe, Houston
2020	Earlie Hudnall Jr., Houston	Gabriel Dawe, Dallas
2021	Annette Lawrence, Denton	Jennifer Ling Datchuk, San Antonio
2022	Celia Álvarez Muñoz, El Paso, Arlington	Jesse Lott, Houston
2023	Gaspar Enriquez, El Paso	James Watkins, Lubbock
2024	Michael Ray Charles, Houston	Diana Kersey, Lubbock, San Antonio

State Historians of Texas

Year	Historian, College
2007-09	Jesús de la Teja, Texas State Univ.
2009-12	Light Cummins, Austin College
2012-16	Bill O'Neal, Panola College
2016-18	Vacant
2018-24	Monte Monroe, Texas Tech Univ.

State Musicians of Texas

Year	Artist, Hometown/Residence
2003	James Dick, Round Top
2004	Ray Benson, Austin
2005	Johnny Gimble, Tyler
2006	Billy Joe Shaver, Waco
2007	Dale Watson, Pasadena/Austin
2008	Shelley King, Austin
2009	Willie Nelson, Abbott/Austin
2010	Sara Hickman, Austin
2011	Lyle Lovett, Klein
2012	Billy Gibbons (ZZ Top), Houston
2013	Craig Hella Johnson, Austin
2014	Flaco Jiménez, San Antonio
2015	Jimmie Vaughn, Dallas/Austin
2016	Joe Ely, Lubbock, Austin
2017	George Strait, Poteet/San Antonio
2018	Marcia Ball, Orange/Austin
2019	Little Joe Hernandez, Temple/San Antonio
2020	Emily Gimble, Austin
2021	Leon Bridges, Fort Worth
2022	Eva Ybarra, San Antonio
2023	Gary Clark, Jr., Austin
2024	Kelly Clarkson, Fort Worth, Burleson

Poets Laureate of Texas

Years	Poet, Hometown/Residence
1962	Marvin Davis Winsett, Dallas
1963	Gwendolyn Bennett Pappas, Houston Vassar Miller, Houston, alternate
1964-65	Jenny Lind Porter, Austin Edith Rayzor Canant, Texas City, alt.
1966	Bessie Maas Rowe, Port Arthur Grace Marie Scott, Abilene, alternate
1967	William E. Bard, Dallas Bessie Maas Rowe, Port Arthur, alt.
1968	Kathryn Henry Harris, Waco Sybil Leonard Armes, El Paso, alt.
1969-70	Anne B. Marely, Austin Rose Davidson Speer, Brady, alt.
1970-71	Mrs. Robby K. Mitchell, McKinney Faye Carr Adams, Dallas, alternate
1971-72	Terry Fontenot, Port Arthur Faye Carr Adams, Dallas, alternate
1972-73	Mrs. Clark Gresham, Burkburnett Marion McDaniel, Sidney, alternate
1973-74	Violette Newton, Beaumont Stella Woodall, San Antonio, alternate
1974-75	Lila Todd O'Neil, Port Arthur C.W. Miller, San Antonio, alternate
1975-76	Ethel Osborn Hill, Port Arthur Gene Shuford, Denton, alternate
1976-77	Florice Stripling Jeffers, Burkburnett Vera L. Eckert, San Angelo, alternate
1977-78	Ruth Carruth, Vernon Joy Gresham Hagstrom, Burkburnett, alter-nate.
1978-79	Patsy Stodghill, Dallas Dorothy B. Elfstroman, Galveston, alt.
1979-80	Dorothy B. Elfstroman, Galveston Ruth Carruth, Vernon, alternate
1980-81	Weems S. Dykes, McCamey Mildred Crabree Speer, Amarillo, alt.
1981-82	Vacant
1982-83	William D. Barney, Fort Worth Vassar Miller, Houston, alternate
1983-87	Vacant
1987-88	Ruth E. Reuther, Wichita Falls
1988-89	Vassar Miller, Houston
1989-93	Vacant
1993-94	Mildred Baass, Victoria
1994-99	Vacant
2000	James Hoggard, Wichita Falls
2001	Walter McDonald, Lubbock
2002	Vacant
2003	Jack Myers, Mesquite
2004	Cleatus Rattan, Cisco
2005	Alan Birkelbach, Plano
2006	Red Steagall, Fort Worth
2007	Steven Fromholz, Kopperl, Sugar Land
2008	Larry Thomas, Houston
2009	Paul Ruffin, Huntsville
2010	Karla K. Morton, Denton, Fort Worth
2011	David M. Parsons, Conroe
2012	Jan Seale, McAllen
2013	Rosemary Catacalos, San Antonio
2014	Dean Young, Austin
2015	Carmen Tafolla, San Antonio
2016	Laurie Ann Guerrero, San Antonio
2017	Jenny Browne, San Antonio
2018	Carol Coffee Reposa, San Antonio
2019	Carrie Fountain, Austin
2020	Emmy Pérez, McAllen
2021	Cyrus Cassells, Austin
2022	Lupe Mendez, Galveston, Houston, Rio Grande Valley
2023	ire'ne lara silva, Edinburg
2024	Amanda Johnston, Austin

Philosophical Society of Texas Awards of Merit

The Philosophical Society of Texas established the Award of Merit in 2000.

The categories were expanded in 2012 to separate categories, one for fiction and one for nonfiction.

In 2015, an award for poetry was introduced.

The book must be about Texas or the author must have been born in or have resided within the boundaries claimed by the Republic of Texas in 1836. ☆

Year	Category	Award
2006		Mavis P. Kelsey Sr. and Robin Brandt Hutchinon, *Engraved Prints of Texas, 1554–1900*, Texas A&M University Press, 2005
2007		Richard B. McCaslin, *At the Heart of Texas, 100 Years of the Texas State Historical Association, 1897–1997*, Texas State Historical Association Press, 2006.
2008		Stephen Fox, *The Country Houses of John F. Staub*, Texas A&M University Press, 2007.
2009		Pekka Hämäläinen, *The Comanche Empire*, Yale University Press, 2008.
2010		Emilio Zamora, *Claiming Rights and Righting Wrongs in Texas: Mexican Workers and Job Politics During World War II*, Texas A&M University Press, 2009.
2011		Dan K. Utley and Cynthia J. Beeman, *History Ahead: Stories beyond the Texas Roadside Markers*, Texas A&M University Press, 2011.
2012	Fiction	Gerald Duff, *Blue Sabine*, Moon City Press, 2011.
	Non-fiction	Michael Berryhill, *The Trails of Eroy Brown: The Murder Case that Shook the Texas Prison System*, University of Texas Press, 2011.
2013	Fiction	Ben Rehder, *The Chicken Hanger: A Novel*, Texas Christian University Press, 2012.
	Non-fiction	Jan Reid, *Let the People In: The Life and Times of Ann Richards*, UT Press, 2012.
2014	Fiction	Thomas Zigal, *Many Rivers to Cross*, Texas Christian University Press, 2013.
	Non-fiction	Raúl Coronado, *A World Not to Come: A History of Latino Writing and Print Culture*, Harvard University Press, 2013.
2015	Fiction	Sara Bird, *Above the East China Sea*, Knopf, 2014.
	Fiction	James Magnuson, *Famous Writers I have Known: A Novel*, W.W. Norton & Company, 2014.
	Non-fiction	Katie Robinson Edwards, *Midcentury Modern Art in Texas*, University of Texas Press, 2014.
	Poetry	Christian Wiman, *Once in the West*, Farrar, Straus and Giroux, 2014.
2016	Fiction	Sanderia Faye, *Mourner's Bench*, University of Arkansas Press, 2015.
	Non-fiction	Ron J. Jackson Jr. and Lee Spencer White, *Joe: The Slave Who Became an Alamo Legend*, University of Oklahoma Press, 2015.
	Poetry	James Hoggard, *New and Selected Poems*, TCU Press, 2015.
2017	Fiction	Dominic Smith, *The Last Painting of Sara de Vos*, 2016.
	Non-fiction	Kenneth Hafertepe, *The Material Culture of German Texans*, 2016.
	Poetry	Jonathan Fink, *Barbarossa*, 2016.
2018	Fiction	Chanelle Benz, *The Man Who Shot Out My Eye Is Dead*, 2017.
	Non-fiction	Andrew Sansom and William E. Reaves, *Of Texas Rivers and Texas Art*, 2017.
	Poetry	Dan Williams, *Past Purgatory, A Distant Paradise*, 2017.
2019	Fiction	Elizabeth Crook, *The Which Way Tree*, 2018.
	Non-fiction	Andrew Saansom, *Seasons at Selah: The Legacy of the Bamberger Ranch Preserve*, 2018.
	Poetry	Megan Peak, *Girldom*, 2018.
2020	Fiction	Leila Meachan, *Dragonfly*, 2019.
	Non-fiction	Stephen Harrigan, *Big Wonderful Thing: A History of Texas*, 2019.
	Poetry	Edward Vidaurre, *JazzHouse*, 2019.
2021	Fiction	Paulette Jiles, *Simon the Fiddler*, 2020.
	Non-fiction	Gregg Cantrell, *The People's Revolt: Texas Populists and the Roots of American Liberalism*, 2020.
	Poetry	Matt Morton, *Improvisation Without Accompaniment*, 2020.
2022	Fiction	Jan Reid, *The Song Leader*, 2021.
	Non-fiction	James E. Crisp, *Inside the Texas Revolution: The Enigmatic Memoir of Herman Ehrenberg*, 2021.
	Poetry	César Leonardo de León, *Speaking with Grackles by Soapberry Trees*, 2021.

Recent Movies Made in Texas

Sources: Texas Film Commission.

Following is a partial list of recent major productions filmed in Texas in descending order by date. The date is for the year of release of the film, while actual location shots occurred earlier.

Location information is from the Texas Film Commission and other sources.

The totals are not comprehensive. "Television series" includes miniseries. Not included are short films, T.V. movies and specials, single episodes or segments of television shows, or music videos. Some of the major artists who worked on the project are listed in the column at far right. An asterisk (*) signifies the artist has a Texas connection. ☆

Year	Movie	Locations	Artists
2023	**80 for Brady**	Houston	Jane Fonda, Lily Tomlin, Rita Moreno (actors)
2023	**Caddo Lake**	Karnack	M. Night Shyamalan (producer)
2023	**Chocolate Lizards**	Abilene, Bartlett, Elgin, Georgetown, Hutto, Pflugerville, Round Rock, Schwertner, Taylor	Carrie-Anne Moss, Thomas Haden Church*, Bruce Dern (actors)
2023	**Happiness for Beginners**	Austin	Ellie Kemper, Luke Grimes (actors)
2023	**Home Free**	Austin, San Marcos	John Karna* (actor)
2023	**Hypnotic**	Austin, Georgetown, Manor, Taylor	Robert Rodriguez* (director), Ben Affleck (actor)
2023	**Kasi**	Houston, League City, Pearland, Rosharon	Lakisha R. Lemons* (director)
2023	**The Long Game**	Bastrop, Lockhart, San Marcos, Smithville	Dennis Quaid, Cheech Marin, Brett Cullen* (actors)
2023	**Spy Kids 5: Armageddon**	Austin	Robert Rodriguez* (Director); Gina Rodriguez, Zachary Levi Pugh (actors)
2022	**Blood Relatives**	Austin, Taylor	Noah Segan (director, actor), Victoria Moroles*, Akasha Villalobos* (actors)
2022	**Bull Shark**	Pilot Point, Sanger, Tioga, Valley View	Billy Blair* (actor)
2022	**Conception**	Houston	Tarun Verma (director), Anjel GoldMine* (actor)
2022	**Facing Nolan**	Alvin, Arlington, Austin, Dallas, Fort Worth, Georgetown, Houston, Irving, Junction, Refugio, Round Rock, Three Rivers	Nolan Ryan* (subject of documentary)
2022	**Free Dead or Alive**	Alpine, Austin, Buda, Lajitas, Terlingua	Patricia Velasquez, Robert LaSado (actors)
2022	**Going Varsity in Mariachi**	Edinburg, McAllen, San Antonio	Sam Osborn, Alejandra Vasquez* (directors)
2022	**Hip Hop Christmas Wedding**	Houston	Greg Carter* (director); Ne-Yo, Serayah (actors)
2022	**Look Both Ways**	Austin, Lockhart	Luke Wilson* (actor)
2022	**The Pro Bono Watchman**	Austin, Bastrop	Mike Gassaway (actor)
2022	**Storage Locker**	Austin, Elgin	Allen Danziger (actor)
2022	**What Remains**	Amarillo, Canyon, Claude	Anne Heche, Kellan Lutz (actors)
2022	**You Are Not Alone**	Austin	Dr. Andrew Shea* (director), Cindy McCreery* (writer)
2021	**Hip Hop Family Christmas**	Houston	Greg Carter* (director); Ne-Yo, Serayah (actors)
2021	**On Guard: A Story of American Youth**	El Paso	Allen Otto* (director)

Number of Production Projects in Texas by Year

	2022	2021	2020	2019	2018	2017	2016	2015	2014	2011	2010
Feature Films	13	20	16	21	18	19	24	14	26	16	38
TV Series	20	35	20	39	26	23	15	20	14	15	17
Total	**33**	**55**	**36**	**60**	**44**	**42**	**39**	**34**	**40**	**31**	**55**

Sources: Texas Film Commission and the Motion Picture Association of America.

Television series that were recently produced in Texas include *Fear the Walking Dead* seasons 6 and 7, *Real Housewives of Dallas* season 5, *Castlevania* season 4, *Masters of the Universe: Revelation, Magnolia Table* seasons 1-6, and some syndicated programs, in addition to the long-running *Austin City Limits.*

Film and Television Work in Texas

Source: Texas Film Commission at gov.texas.gov/film/

For almost a century, Texas has been one of the nation's top filmmaking states, after California and New York. More than 1,600 films have been made in Texas since 1910, including *Wings*, the first film to win an Academy Award for Best Picture, which was made in San Antonio in 1927.

Texas' attractions to filmmakers are its diverse locations, abundant sunshine and moderate winter weather, and a variety of support services. The economic benefits of hosting on-location filming over the past decade are estimated at more than $3 billion. Besides salaries paid to locally hired technicians and actors, as well as fees paid to location owners, the production companies do business with hotels, car rental agencies, lumberyards, restaurants, grocery stores, utilities, security services, and florists.

All types of projects come to Texas besides films, including television features and news organizations, commercials, corporate films, and game videos.

Many projects made in Texas originate in California studios, but Texas is also the home of many independent filmmakers who make films outside the studio system. Some films and television shows made in Texas have become icons. *Giant*, John Wayne's *The Alamo*, and the long-running TV series *Dallas* all made their mark on the world's perception of Texas.

The Texas Film Commission, a division of the Office of the Governor, markets to Hollywood Texas' locations, support services, and workforce availability. The legislature funded the Texas Moving Image Incentive Program with $22 million in the 2018–2019 biennium.

The commission's free services include location research, employment referrals for production assistants, red-tape-cutting, and information on weather, travel, and other topics affecting production. ☆

Regional Commissions

Amarillo Film Commission

Sherman Bass, Film Commissioner
Amarillo Film Office / Visit Amarillo
1000 S. Polk
Amarillo 79101
(806) 342-2017 (O)
(806) 414-2576 (C)
sherman@visitamarillo.com
www.visitamarillo.com/media/film

Austin Film Commission

Brian Gannon, Director
111 Congress Ave., Suite 700
Austin 78701
(800) 926-2282 ext. 7230
(512) 583-7230
(512) 583-7282 (fax)
bgannon@austintexas.org
www.austinfilmcommission.com

Brownsville Border Film Commission

Adalberto Guzman, Creative Services Manager
City of Brownsville
650 Ruben M. Torres Sr. Blvd.
Brownsville 78521
(956) 547-6505
adalberto.guzman@brownsvilletx.gov
www.filmbtx.com

Conroe Film Commission

Jodi Willard, Marketing Manager
Visit Conroe
300 West Davis St., Suite 520
Conroe 77301
(936) 522-3502
(877) 426-6763
jodi@visitconroe.com
www.visitconroe.com

Corpus Christi Film Commission

Mary Herrera, Administrative Assistant
Visit Corpus Christi
400 Mann Street, Ste. 1100
Corpus Christi 78401
(361) 881-1888
mary@visitcorpuschristi.com
www.visitcorpuschristi.com

Dallas Film & Creative Industries Office

Tony Armer, Commissioner
1807 Ross Ave., Ste 450
Dallas 75201
(469) 394-6331 (C)
(214) 571-1050 (O)
info@dallascreates.org
tony.armer@dallascreates.org
www.dallascreates.org

El Paso Film and Creative Industries Commission

Drew Mayer-Oakes, Commissioner
Destination El Paso
One Civic Center Plaza
El Paso 79901
(915) 534-0698 (O)
(915) 892-2783 (C)
film@destinationelpaso.com
www.visitelpaso.com/creativelpaso

Fort Worth Film Commission

Jessica Christopherson, Director
Taylor Hardy, Film & Marketing Director
111 W. 4th St., Suite 200
Fort Worth 76102
(817) 698-7842
(800) 433-5747
jessicachristopherson@fortworth.com
taylorhardy@fortworth.com
www.filmfortworth.com

Houston Film Commission

Alfred Cervantes, Executive Director
701 Avenida de las Americas, Suite 200
Houston 77010
(713) 853-8957
(713) 223-3816 (fax)
acervantes@houstonfilmcommission.com
www.houstonfilmcommission.com

San Antonio Film Commission

Kimberly LeBlanc, Film & Music Commissioner
115 Plaza De Armas, Suite 102
San Antonio 78205
(210) 207-6730
kimberly.leblanc@sanantonio.gov
filmsa@filmsanantonio.com
www.filmsanantonio.com

South Padre Island Film Commission

Blake Henry, Director
7355 Padre Boulevard
South Padre Island 78597
(956) 761-8388
(956) 761-8106
blake@sopadre.com
www.sopadre.com

Holidays, Anniversaries, and Festivals, 2024–2025

Below are listed the principal federal and state government holidays; Christian, Jewish, and Islamic holidays and festivals; and special recognition days for 2024 and 2025.

Technically, the United States does not observe national holidays. Each state has jurisdiction over its holidays, which are usually designated by its legislature.

This list was compiled partially from the Texas Government Code, the U.S. Office of Personnel Management, and *Astronomical Phenomena 2024* and *Astronomical Phenomena 2025*, which are published jointly by the U.S. Naval Observatory and the United Kingdom Hydrographic Office.

See the footnotes for explanations of the symbols. ☆

2024		
New Year's Day	§	**Mon., Jan. 1**
Epiphany		Sat., Jan. 6
Sam Rayburn Day	‡	Sat., Jan. 6
Martin Luther King Jr. Day	§	**Mon., Jan. 15**
Confederate Heroes' Day	§	Fri., Jan. 19
Valentine's Day		Wed., Feb. 14
Ash Wednesday		Wed., Feb. 14
Presidents' Day	§	**Mon., Feb. 19**
Texas Independence Day	§	Sat., Mar. 2
Ramadan, first day of		Sun., Mar. 10
Palm Sunday		Sun., Mar. 24
Good Friday	§	Fri., Mar. 29
César Chávez Day	§	Sun., Mar. 31
Easter Day		Sun., Mar. 31
Former Prisoners of War Day	‡	Tue., Apr. 9
San Jacinto Day	§	Sun., Apr. 21
Passover (Pesach), first day of		Mon., Apr. 22
Ascension Day		Thu., May 9
Mother's Day		Sun., May 12
Armed Forces Day		Sat., May 18
Whit Sunday — Pentecost		Sun., May 19
Trinity Sunday		Sun., May 26
Memorial Day	§	**Mon., May 27**
Shavuot (Feast of Weeks)		Tue., June 11
Flag Day (U.S.)		Fri., June 14
Father's Day		Sun., June 16
Emancipation Day in Texas (Juneteenth)	§	**Wed., June 19**
Independence Day	§	**Thu., July 4**
Islamic New Year		Sun., July 7
Lyndon Baines Johnson Day	§	Tue., Aug. 27
Labor Day	§	**Mon., Sept. 2**
Grandparents Day		Sun., Sept. 8
Rosh Hashanah (Jewish New Year)		Wed., Oct. 2
Yom Kippur (Day of Atonement)		Sat., Oct. 12
Columbus Day	‡	**Mon., Oct. 14**
Sukkot (Tabernacles), first day of		Wed., Oct. 16
Halloween		Thu., Oct. 31
Father of Texas Day	‡	Sun., Nov. 3
General Election Day	§	Tue., Nov. 5
Veterans Day	§	**Mon., Nov. 11**
Thanksgiving Day	§	**Thu., Nov. 28**
First Sunday in Advent		Sun., Dec. 1
Christmas Day	§	**Wed., Dec. 25**
Hanukkah, first day of		Thur., Dec. 26

2025		
New Year's Day	§	**Wed., Jan. 1**
Epiphany		Mon., Jan. 6
Sam Rayburn Day	‡	Mon., Jan. 6
Confederate Heroes' Day	§	Sun., Jan. 19
Martin Luther King Jr. Day	§	**Mon., Jan. 20**
Valentine's Day		Fri., Feb. 14
Presidents' Day	§	**Mon., Feb. 17**
Ramadan, first day of		Fri., Feb. 28
Texas Independence Day	§	Sun., Mar. 2
Ash Wednesday		Wed., Mar. 5
César Chávez Day	§	Mon., Mar. 31
Former Prisoners of War Day	‡	Wed., Apr. 9
Passover (Pesach), first day of		Sat., Apr. 12
Palm Sunday		Sun., Apr. 13
Good Friday	§	Fri., Apr. 18
Easter Day		Sun., Apr. 20
San Jacinto Day	§	Mon., Apr. 21
Mother's Day		Sun., May 11
Armed Forces Day		Sat., May 17
Memorial Day	§	**Mon., May 26**
Ascension Day		Thu., May 29
Shavuot (Feast of Weeks)		Sun., June 1
Whit Sunday — Pentecost		Sun., June 8
Flag Day (U.S.)		Sat., June 14
Trinity Sunday		Sun., June 15
Father's Day		Sun., June 15
Emancipation Day in Texas (Juneteenth)	§	**Thu., June 19**
Islamic New Year		Thu., June 26
Independence Day	§	**Fri., July 4**
Lyndon Baines Johnson Day	§	Wed., Aug. 27
Labor Day	§	**Mon., Sep. 1**
Grandparents Day		Sun., Sep. 7
Rosh Hashanah (Jewish New Year)		Mon., Sep. 22
Yom Kippur (Day of Atonement)		Thurs., Oct. 2
Sukkot (Tabernacles), first day of		Mon., Oct. 6
Columbus Day	‡	**Mon., Oct. 13**
Halloween		Fri., Oct. 31
Father of Texas Day	‡	Mon., Nov. 3
General Election Day	§	Tue., Nov. 4
Veterans Day	§	**Tue., Nov. 11**
Thanksgiving Day	§	**Thu., Nov. 27**
First Sunday in Advent		Sun., Nov. 30
Hanukkah, first day of		Sun., Dec. 14
Christmas Day	§	**Thu., Dec. 25**

Federal legal public holidays are shown in bold. If the holiday falls on a Sunday, the following Monday may be treated as a holiday. If the holiday falls on a Saturday, the preceding Friday may be treated as a holiday.

§ **State holiday in Texas**. For state employees, the Friday after Thanksgiving Day, Dec. 24, and Dec. 26 are also holidays. **Optional holidays** are César Chávez Day, Good Friday, Rosh Hashanah, and Yom Kippur. **Partial-staffing holidays** are Confederate Heroes Day, Texas Independence Day, San Jacinto Day, Emancipation Day in Texas, and Lyndon Baines Johnson Day. State offices will be open on optional holidays and partial-staffing holidays.

‡ **State Recognition Days**, as designated by the Texas Legislature.

Notes on holidays:

- Confederate Heroes Day combines the birthdays of Robert E. Lee (Jan. 19) and Jefferson Davis (June 3).
- Presidents' Day combines the birthdays of George Washington (Feb. 22) and Abraham Lincoln (Feb. 12).
- Jewish and Islamic holidays are tabular, meaning they begin at sunset on the previous evening.
- Between 1939 and 1957, Texas observed Thanksgiving Day on the last Thursday in November. As a result, in a November having five Thursdays, Texas celebrated national Thanksgiving on the fourth Thursday and Texas Thanksgiving on the fifth Thursday. In 1957, Texas changed the state observance to coincide with the national holiday.

Religious Affiliation Change: 2010 to 2020

Source: "2020 U.S. Religion Census" and "2010 U.S. Religion Census," www.usreligioncensus.org

The "2020 U.S. Religion Census" had the participation of more than 161 million individuals and 350,000 congregations, making it the most inclusive report of its kind to date. Texas continues to be one of the nation's more "religious" states, with 55.1% of the population adherents to a religion. For the population of the U.S. as a whole, 48.7% are adherents to a religion.

The census, sponsored by the Association of Statisticians of American Religious Bodies, is the only U.S. survey to report religious membership down to the county level, as well as at the state level. The census relies on self-reports from congregations for membership numbers.

According to the survey: "Exact definitions of 'congregations' and 'adherents' vary by religious body. Congregations may be parishes, churches, synagogues, mosques, temples, or another site where a religious body has regularly scheduled worship services. Adherents generally are members, children who are not members, and others who are not members but are considered participants in the congregation."

The populations of both adherents and non-adherents in Texas have grown since the 2010 survey. Adherents in 2020 totaled 16,045,479, a 14.7% increase over 2010 adherents of 13,994,564. Those unclaimed by any faith in 2020 grew 17.5% to 13,100,026 from the 2010 total of 11,150,997.

Areas of Greatest Change

The Catholic Church in Texas had the greatest increase in adherents between 2010 and 2020. Growth of 1,231,642 represents a 26.4% increase. Despite this increase, Texas remains the state with the third-largest number of Catholics.

Non-denominational Christian churches also showed significant growth in adherents since 2010. According to the 2020 survey, people claiming this faith have increased by 859,244 or 55.6%.

Baptist adherents as a group declined by only 3.2% in the ten-year span, and the Southern Baptist Convention saw the largest drop in membership, losing 401,356 or 10.8%. However, it is possible that many of these adherents now attend services with the National Missionary Baptist Convention of America. The group's 875 congregations attracted 260,915 new members since 2010, a 766.5% increase.

The Muslim population of Texas experienced a decline of 25.8% since 2010. The loss of 108,763 members dropped Texas in the state rankings from first in 2010 to fifth in 2020.

The United Methodist Church, while remaining the fourth-largest religious body in the state (see the table in green, below), lost 9.3% of its members between 2010 and 2020. ☆

According to the *2020 U.S. Religion Census,* Texas ranks:

— **First** in number of Baptists, with 3,836,478.

— **First** in number belonging to nondenominational Christian churches, with 2,405,786.

— **Third**, behind California and New York in number of Catholics.

— **Fourth** in number of Hindus.

— **Fourth** in number of Buddhists.

— **Fifth** in number of Muslims.

— **Fifth** in number of Mormons.

Largest Religious Bodies	Adherents	Share of Texas Population	Share of Texas' Adherents
Catholic Church	5,905,142	20.26%	36.80%
Southern Baptist Convention	3,319,962	11.39%	20.69%
Non-denominational Christian Churches	2,405,786	8.25%	14.99%
United Methodist Church	938,399	3.22%	5.85%
Church of Jesus Christ of Latter-day Saints	362,037	1.24%	2.26%
Jehovah's Witnesses	317,698	1.09%	1.98%
Muslim Estimate	313,209	1.07%	1.95%
Churches of Christ	312,132	1.07%	1.95%
Assemblies of God	296,826	1.02%	1.85%
National Missionary Baptist Convention, Inc.	294,954	1.01%	1.84%
Episcopal Church	134,318	0.46%	0.84%
Lutheran Church–Missouri Synod	112,900	0.39%	0.70%
Unclaimed by any faith	13,100,026	44.94%	—

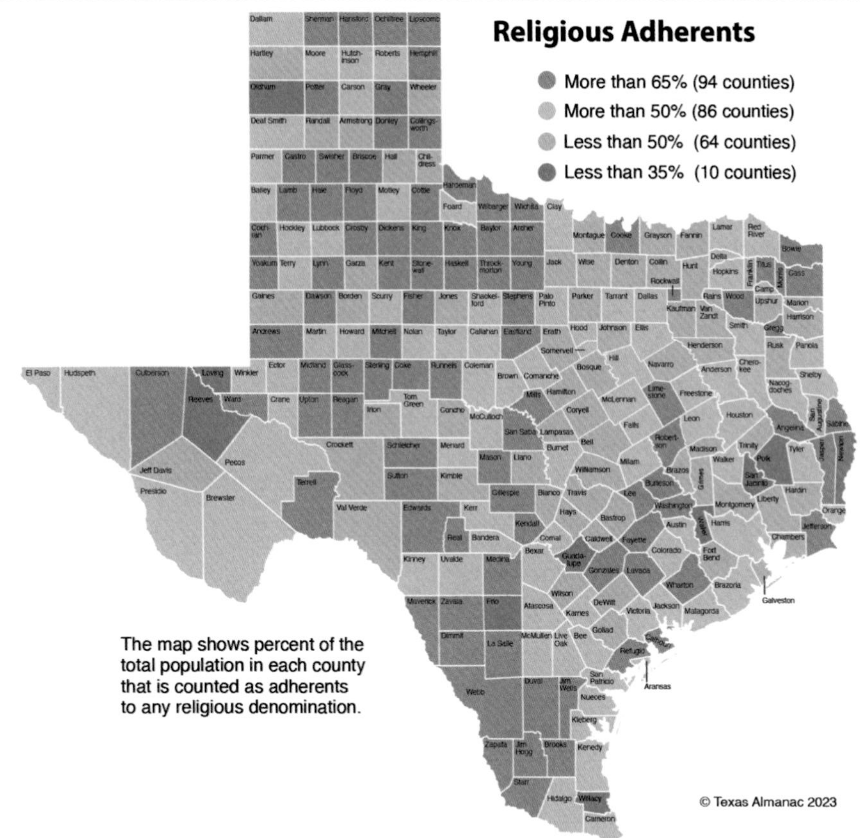

Numbers of Members Statewide by Denomination

	Adherents 2010	Change	Adherents 2020
Adventist	**74,120**	**+ 25,881**	**100,001**
Advent Christian Church (2 congregations)	—		95
Church of God General Conference (1 congregation)	65		38
General Conference of the Church of God (Seventh Day) (64 congregations)	—		—
Seventh–day Adventist Church (412 congregations)	74,055		99,868
United Church of God (12 congregations)	—		—
Anglican/Episcopal	**148,439**	**–14,121**	**134,318**
Anglican Catholic Church (4 congregations)	—		—
Anglican Church in North America (104 congregations)	—		—
Episcopal Church (353 congregations)	148,439		134,318
Intl Communion of the Charismatic Episcopal Church (1 congregation)	—		—
Reformed Episcopal Church (13 congregations)	—		—
Baha'i Faith (67 congregations)	**13,235**	**+ 1,169**	**14,404**
Baptist	**3,961,657**	**–125,179**	**3,836,478**
Alliance of Baptists (11 congregations)	—		—
American Baptist Association (147 congregations)	39,354		27,422
American Baptist Churches in the U.S.A. (14 congregations)	7,172		4,537
Association of Reformed Baptist Churches of America (6 congregations)	—		—
Baptist Missionary Association of America (394 congregations)	—		—
Converge Worldwide (18 congregations)	1,320		—
Full Gospel Baptist Church Fellowship (157 congregations)	—		27,088
General Association of General Baptists (6 congregations)	—		4,060
General Association of Regular Baptist Churches (5 congregations)	—		—
International Churches of Christ (11 congregations)	2,857		4,020

	Adherents 2010	Change	Adherents 2020
National Association of Free Will Baptists (42 congregations)	3,111		1,449
National Baptist Convention of America Intl, Inc. (104 congregations)	89,050		66,790
National Baptist Convention, USA, Inc. (94 congregations)	59,529		79,088
National Missionary Baptist Convention of America (875 congregations)	34,039		294,954
North American Baptist Conference (13 congregations)	1,157		—
Primitive Baptists Associations (49 congregations)	—		4,291
Progressive National Baptist Convention, Inc. (9 congregations)	2,683		2,778
Seventh Day Baptist General Conf. of the U.S. and Canada (2 congregations)	67		39
Southern Baptist Convention (7,935 congregations)	3,721,318		3,319,962
Sovereign Grace Churches (8 congregations)	—		—
Buddhism	**66,116**	**- 5,234**	**60,882**
Buddhism, Mahayana (41 congregations)	49,874		26,714
Buddhism, Theravada (41 congregations)	13,461		23,373
Buddhism, Vajrayana (16 congregations)	2,781		10,795
(Catholic Liturgical) Catholic Church (1,342 congregations)	**4,673,500**	**+ 1,231,642**	**5,905,142**
(Christian Scientist) Church of Christ, Scientist (10 congregations)	**—**		**—**
(Churches of Christ) United Church of Christ (54 congregations)	**17,464**	**- 7,314**	**10,150**
Hinduism	**60,725**	**+ 16,351**	**77,076**
Hindu, Traditional Temples (37 congregations)	—		77,076
Hinduism: Hindu Post Renaissance	968		—
Hinduism: Hindu Renaissance	98		—
Hinduism: Indian–American Hindu Temple Associations	36,550		—
Hinduism: Traditional Hindu Temples	23,109		—
Holiness	**85,204**	**- 13,068**	**72,136**
Bible Methodist Connection of Churches (4 congregations)	—		—
Christian and Missionary Alliance (46 congregations)	5,465		4,731
Church of Christ (Holiness) U.S.A (5 congregations)	—		—
Church of God (Anderson, Indiana) (66 congregations)	3,990		8,860
Church of the Nazarene (323 congregations)	44,836		44,112
Churches of Christ in Christian Union (4 congregations)	—		—
Free Methodist Church–USA (18 congregations)	1,864		751
Missionary Church, The (26 congregations)	3,119		4,057
Salvation Army (55 congregations)	23,761		8,137
Wesleyan Church (19 congregations)	2,169		1,488
(Islam) Muslim Estimate (225 congregations)	**421,972**	**- 108,763**	**313,209**
Jain (4 congregations)	**—**		**—**
Jehovah's Witnesses (1,191 congregations)	**—**	**+ 317,698**	**317,698**
Judaism	**60,645**	**- 3,504**	**57,141**
Conservative Judaism (15 congregations)	17,889		17,513
Orthodox Judaism (18 congregations)	8,410		8,110
Reconstructionist Judaism (2 congregations)	356		140
Reform Judaism (29 congregations)	33,990		31,378
Latter-day Saints (Mormonism)	**300,591**	**+ 61,446**	**362,037**
Church of Jesus Christ (Bickertonite) (1 congregation)	—		—
Church of Jesus Christ of Latter–day Saints (731 congregations)	296,141		362,037
Community of Christ (31 congregations)	4,450		—
Liberal	**8,107**	**+ 2,520**	**10,627**
American Ethical Union (1 congregation)	—		—
Unitarian Universalist Association (46 congregations)	8,107		10,627
Lutheran	**272,066**	**- 61,960**	**210,106**
Association of Free Lutheran Congregations (6 congregations)	—		281
Church of the Lutheran Brethren of America	72		—
Church of the Lutheran Confession (2 congregations)	—		—
Evangelical Lutheran Church in America (308 congregations)	111,647		77,170
Evangelical Lutheran Synod (4 congregations)	75		247
Lutheran Church–Missouri Synod (LCMS) (371 congregations)	132,508		112,900
Lutheran Congregations in Mission for Christ (53 congregations)	20,936		11,382

	Adherents 2010	Change	Adherents 2020
North American Lutheran Church (35 congregations)	—		—
Wisconsin Evangelical Lutheran Synod (39 congregations)	6,828		8,126
Mennonite/Amish	**3,436**	**+ 1,853**	**5,289**
Amish Groups, undifferentiated (1 congregation)	52		59
Beachy Amish Mennonite Churches (2 congregations)	265		152
Church of God in Christ, Mennonite (11 congregations)	1,068		1,495
Conservative Mennonite Conference (2 congregations)	106		71
Eastern Pennsylvania Mennonite Church (2 congregations)	—		1,221
Maranatha Amish Mennonite (1 congregation)	—		141
Mennonite Brethren Churches, U.S. Conference of (11 congregations)	403		588
Mennonite Church, USA (25 congregations)	1,233		1,259
Unaffiliated Amish–Mennonite (Conservative) (2 congregations)	309		303
Methodist	**1,135,595**	**– 107,848**	**1,027,747**
African Methodist Episcopal Church (227 congregations)	43,839		47,550
African Methodist Episcopal Zion Church (8 congregations)	1,327		1,108
Christian Methodist Episcopal Church (212 congregations)	37,986		38,645
Congregational Methodist Church (39 congregations)	2,396		—
Evangelical Covenant Church (18 congregations)	1,393		2,045
Evangelical Free Church of America (70 congregations)	13,486		—
Evangelical Methodist Church (14 congregations)	—		—
United Methodist Church (1,758 congregations)	1,035,168		938,399
Unity of the Brethren (24 congregations)	—		—
Orthodox	**32,453**	**+ 23,325**	**55,778**
America, Canada and Europe Reg. Malankara Syriac Knanaya Arch. (3 congr.)	—		810
Antiochian Orthodox Christian Archdiocese of North America (22 congr.)	5,348		6,093
Armenian Apostolic Orthodox Church (C. of Etchmiadzin) (4 congregations)	515		1,030
Coptic Orthodox Church in North America (24 congregations)	3,866		10,519
Eritrean Orthodox Churches (7 congregations)	1,000		4,042
Ethiopian Orthodox Church in the United States of America (17 congr.)	—		8,087
Greek Orthodox Archdiocese of America (16 congregations)	12,167		11,904
Malankara Archdiocese of the Syrian Orthodox Church in N. A. (6 congr.)	1,260		1,838
Malankara Orthodox Syrian Church (17 congregations)	2,433		5,461
Orthodox Church in America, The (18 congregations)	2,657		2,557
Russian Orthodox Church Outside of Russia, The (8 congregations)	1,022		1,673
Serbian Orthodox Church in North and South America (4 congregations)	1,375		1,214
Syrian (Syriac) Orthodox Church of Antioch (3 congregations)	210		180
The Romanian Orthodox Metropolia of the Americas (3 congregations)	600		370
Pentecostal	**454,628**	**+ 42,038**	**496,666**
Apostolic Faith Mission of Portland, Oregon (3 congregations)	135		—
Assemblies of God, General Council of the (1,432 congregations)	275,565		296,826
Association of Vineyard Churches (29 congregations)	8,527		5,998
Bible Way Church of Our Lord Jesus Christ World Wide, Inc. (3 congr.)	—		340
Calvary Chapel (11 congregations)	—		—
Christian Congregation in North America (6 congregations)	—		—
Church of God (Cleveland, Tennessee) (254 congregations)	47,709		35,397
Church of God in Christ (373 congregations)	77,545		92,815
Church of God of Prophecy (86 congregations)	3,610		—
Church of God of the Apostolic Faith, Inc. (17 congregations)	—		—
Church of Our Lord Jesus Christ of the Apostolic Faith (33 congregations)	—		4,246
Church of the Living God (Christian Workers for Fellowship) (25 congr.)	—		—
Congregational Holiness Church (5 congregations)	1,280		—
Elim Fellowship (3 congregations)	—		—
Full Gospel Christian Assemblies International (72 congregations)	—		37,080
International Church of the Foursquare Gospel (71 congregations)	11,047		21,366
International Pentecostal Holiness Church	15,576		—
Open Bible Churches (3 congregations)	148		142
Pentecostal Assemblies of the World (7 congregations)	—		2,456

	Adherents 2010	Change	Adherents 2020
Pentecostal Church of God (116 congregations)	13,486		—
United Pentecostal Church International (735 congregations)	—		—
Presbyterian/Reformed	**183,290**	**– 71,309**	**111,981**
Associate Reformed Presbyterian Church (General Synod) (3 congregations)	223		—
Cumberland Presbyterian Church (37 congregations)	6,355		7,173
Cumberland Presbyterian Church in America (19 congregations)	—		2,236
ECO: A Covenant Order of Evangelical Presbyterians (37 congregations)	—		—
Evangelical Presbyterian Church (1981) (25 congregations)	2,883		—
Orthodox Presbyterian Church (21 congregations)	824		—
Presbyterian Church (U.S.A.) (417 congregations)	155,046		81,282
Presbyterian Church in America (100 congregations)	17,959		21,290
Reformed Presbyterian Church of North America (Covenanters) (3 congr.)	—		95
Quakers	**2,892**	**– 1,151**	**1,741**
Charis Fellowship (2 congregations)	—		—
Church of the Brethren (1 congregation)	118		26
Evangelical Friends Church International (9 congregations)	1,845		985
Friends General Conference (18 congregations)	929		718
Friends United Meeting (1 congregation)	—		11
Old German Baptist Brethren Church, New Conference	—		1
Reformed/Congregational	**1,957**	**+ 240**	**2,197**
Christian Reformed Church in North America (19 congregations)	1,416		1,386
Communion of Reformed Evangelical Churches (3 congregations)	—		—
Conservative Congregational Christian Conference (2 congregations)	29		230
Evangelical Association of Reformed and Congr. Christian Churches (7 congr.)	—		—
Reformed Church in America (14 congregations)	512		581
Restorationists	**466,024**	**– 47,807**	**418,217**
Christian Church (Disciples of Christ) (357 congregations)	74,817		65,650
Christian Churches and Churches of Christ (118 congregations)	40,078		40,435
Churches of Christ (1897 congregations)	351,129		312,132
(Sikh) American Sikh Council (20 congregations)	**—**		**—**
Unity Churches, Association of (41 congregations)	**—**		**—**
(Zoroastrian) Federation of Zoroastrian Associations of North America (3 congr.)	**1,095**	**– 1,095**	**—**
Unclassified	**—**		**—**
Agape Christian Fellowship (1 congregation)	—		30
Apostolic Christian Church of America (4 congregations)	46		79
Apostolic Christian Faith (2 congregations)	—		12
Biblical Mennonite Alliance (1 congregation)	—		43
Chabad Judaism (43 congregations)	—		—
Christadelphians (16 congregations)	—		—
Christian Brethren (Plymouth Brethren) (42 congregations)	—		—
Grace Gospel Fellowship (4 congregations)	—		—
Hindu Yoga and Meditation (81 congregations)	—		35,077
Independent Judaism (1 congregation)	—		20
Malankara Mar Thoma Church (8 congregations)	—		1,391
Nationwide Fellowship Mennonite Churches (2 congregations)	—		157
New Apostolic Church USA (8 congregations)	—		—
Non-denominational Christian Churches (4,212 congregations)	1,546,542	859,244	2,405,786
Unaffiliated Conservative Mennonite (1 congregation)	—		30
Unaffiliated Conservative Mennonite (Grandview fellowship) (2 congr.)	—		140
United House of Prayer (1 congregation)	—		100
Universal Fellowship of Metropolitan Community Churches (13 congr.)	2,765		1,498
Vedanta Society (3 congregations)	—		—
Statewide Totals	**13,994,564**	**+ 2,050,915**	**16,045,479**
Unclaimed (not counted as adherent to religion)	**11,150,997**	**+ 1,949,029**	**13,100,026**

Note: Some religious bodies with no adherents in Texas have been omitted from this table due to space limitations.

Source: U.S. Religion Census, 2020 and U.S. Religion Census, 2010, both conducted by the Association of Statisticians of American Religious Bodies.

HEALTH & SCIENCE

TEXAS TRIBUNE REPORTS: HEALTH

VITAL STATISTICS

HONORED SCIENTISTS

MENTAL HEALTH & SUBSTANCE ABUSE

TEXAS TRIBUNE REPORTS: HEALTH

By The Texas Tribune Health Reporting Team

THE TEXAS TRIBUNE

On June 14, 2023, Texas became the last state in the country to allow its COVID-19 public health emergency to expire. Gov. Greg Abbott had allowed it to remain in place longer than other places because he wanted to restrict local authorities' ability to issue mask mandates or other public health initiatives, and the statewide emergency gave him the power to do so. More than 92,000 people in Texas died with COVID during the public emergency. But in addition to the human toll, the pandemic revealed a number of issues and challenges facing the health care system in Texas. Here's an overview of some key health care issues in Texas:

A STAFFING SHORTAGE

A staffing crisis is playing out at hospitals all across the United States as medical professionals are leaving the field due to burnout, violent attacks against medical workers have increased, and the workload has increased because of the pandemic.

According to the Texas Hospital Association, that problem is especially acute among nurses. Vacancy rates for nurses have surpassed 5%, and median turnover rates are just under 20%. Rural areas have a shortage of doctors and nurses, one contributing factor that has led to hospitals closing and rural residents being underserved by the medical field.

In 2023, the Legislature sought to address the shortages by passing a law that establishes scholarships, grants, and loan repayment programs to support nursing students and faculty.

DRUG ADDICTION

State leaders and law enforcement officials have been raising the alarm for years about fentanyl in the state. The illicit use of fentanyl began increasing in Texas around 2015, quickly sparking a crisis. Obtained with a doctor's prescription, the synthetic opioid can be an effective pain reliever. But there's been a rise both in the illegal use of the drug and now the manufacturing of counterfeit prescription drugs that contain fentanyl but are packaged to look like something else, in an effort to cause addiction and generate repeat buyers.

Opioids, including heroin, prescription pills, and fentanyl, have caused the most overdose deaths in Texas, according to a Texas Health and Human Services report that studied death certificate data from 2010 to 2019. And because opioids are often mixed with other drugs, there's been a rise in deaths known as polysubstance overdoses. The most recent state data show those deaths reaching a rate of four per 100,000 people in 2019.

Texas lawmakers have recently tried to tackle the state's overdose problem by aggressively attacking fentanyl distribution and use by means of enforcement and awareness.

ABORTION

Abortion in Texas has been illegal for more than a year. The number of monthly abortions in Texas has dropped into the low single digits. Supporters of a ban have celebrated it. There have been sporadic reports of women nearly dying from pregnancy complications, or dying after having to travel out of state for abortions, or facing million-dollar lawsuits for helping friends acquire abortion medication.

In response to the new landscape, lawmakers in 2023 prioritized several women's health issues. They eliminated sales tax on diapers, menstrual supplies, and many pregnancy-related supplies. They also extended Medicaid coverage for moms, from two months to a year after childbirth.

MENTAL HEALTH

After several mass shootings in recent years, lawmakers have highlighted a need to boost mental health services in the state. Texas ranks dead last when it comes to access to children's mental health services and 33rd for adult care, according to Mental Health America, a nonprofit advocacy group. Recently, 98% of Texas' 254 counties were wholly or partially designated by the federal government as "mental health professional shortage areas."

The workforce issues reach the highest levels of the mental health system. In May, Texas couldn't use over 700 of its 2,911 funded state psychiatric hospital beds due to workforce shortages. At the end of 2022, state hospitals had 5,987 full-time employees, a drop from the 7,409 full-time employees in 2019. Lawmakers responded by boosting mental health funding by around $1 billion during the 2023 legislative session.

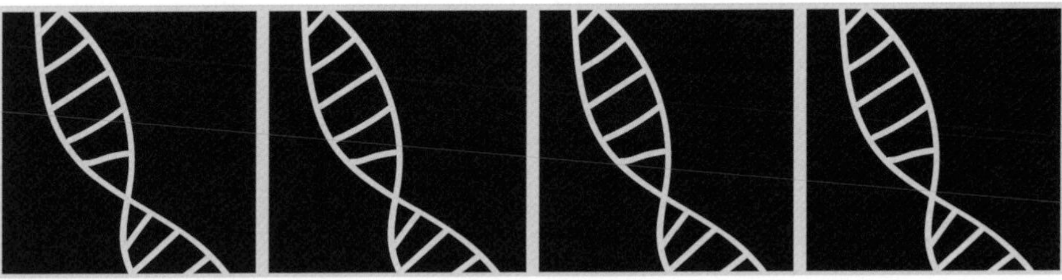

COVID-19 in Texas Vital Statistics

Texas Department of State Health Services: Vital Statistics and Center for Health Statistics.

Heart disease and cancer remained the major causes of death in 2020, the latest year for which statistical breakdowns were available from the Center for Health Statistics, Texas Department of State Health Services. COVID-19 claimed the third most deaths at 31,281.

Of the 249,256 deaths, heart disease claimed 49,901 lives and cancer claimed 41,695 lives. These two diseases have been the leading causes of death in Texas and the nation since 1950. COVID-19 ranked third with 31,281 deaths. These three diseases accounted for nearly half, 49.3%, of all Texas resident deaths in 2020.

The number of babies born to Texas mothers in 2020 was 368,317, a decrease from 377,710 in 2019. The state's birth rate in 2020 was 12.5 per 1,000 population, down slightly from 13 in 2019. In 1960, the figure was 25.7.

In 2021, the number of induced abortions decreased to 53,572 from 2020's count of 56,358. The highest number of induced abortions was 81,591 in 2008. ☆

Healthcare and Deaths in Texas Counties

County	2022 Physicians	2021 Hospital Beds	2020 Total Deaths	2020 Fertility rate†	2021 Abortions
Statewide Total	**23,424**	**87,386**	**249,256**	**62.7**	**53,572**
Anderson	32	160	735	73.6	40
Andrews	9	34	153	79.1	3
Angelina	86	478	1,155	66.9	97
Aransas	10	0	435	58.8	23
Archer	0	0	87	53.1	1
Armstrong	0	0	38	65.8	0
Atascosa	13	67	572	71.1	75
Austin	7	32	323	65.8	25
Bailey	2	25	70	95.4	4
Bandera	5	0	312	58.5	16
Bastrop	26	15	824	71.1	143
Baylor	6	25	69	73.7	1
Bee	11	69	321	67.9	44
Bell	314	1,207	2,818	76.7	893
Bexar	1,774	8,031	16,664	60.8	5,180
Blanco	4	0	133	50.6	17
Borden	0	0	—	53.8	0
Bosque	11	25	332	63.4	7
Bowie	104	868	1,228	64.6	99
Brazoria	234	287	2,868	62.3	620
Brazos	219	661	1,341	42.9	330
Brewster	10	25	103	51.8	4
Briscoe	0	0	28	59.7	1
Brooks	1	0	117	86.5	5
Brown	30	188	671	56.1	17
Burleson	4	25	255	65.2	17
Burnet	46	71	591	59.2	57
Caldwell	13	59	482	67.9	85
Calhoun	18	25	252	71.9	14
Callahan	1	0	232	57.6	4
Cameron	272	1,420	4,220	72.6	417
Camp	8	25	199	72.1	19
Carson	0	0	97	42.2	1
Cass	8	0	528	61.5	17
Castro	3	17	87	74	0
Chambers	5	44	385	65	57
Cherokee	39	385	684	79.5	40

County	2022 Physicians	2021 Hospital Beds	2020 Total Deaths	2020 Fertility rate†	2021 Abortions
Childress	10	39	86	65.8	1
Clay	4	25	147	51.3	2
Cochran	0	18	37	78.7	1
Coke	0	0	62	65.9	0
Coleman	5	25	152	63.9	3
Collin	1,121	2,934	5,692	52.5	1,447
Collingsworth	1	13	48	59.6	0
Colorado	16	65	305	74.3	20
Comal	104	332	1,611	59.2	228
Comanche	11	25	238	68	4
Concho	3	18	34	66.6	4
Cooke	18	78	485	72	26
Coryell	17	25	611	51.6	106
Cottle	0	0	35	59.4	1
Crane	2	25	48	73.2	6
Crockett	1	0	61	63.8	4
Crosby	1	2	97	69	5
Culberson	2	14	36	84.7	0
Dallam	1	0	79	124	0
Dallas	2,616	8,633	19,989	65.5	6,867
Dawson	6	23	192	88.1	3
Deaf Smith	5	42	200	88.1	14
Delta	0	0	90	76.6	2
Denton	529	1,589	4,822	51.3	1
DeWitt	15	49	304	76	1,253
Dickens	0	0	41	55.9	0
Dimmit	6	48	106	70.1	10
Donley	1	0	55	57.5	1
Duval	0	0	137	73.5	11
Eastland	7	52	279	67.4	13
Ector	102	652	1,623	85.2	139
Edwards	2	0	34	77.6	0

Physicians – All M.D.s and D.O.s. in direct patient care.
Hospital Beds – Beds not including military and veteran's hospitals, nor beds in hospitals that were not in compliance with state regulations.
†Fertility rate figured per 1,000 women ages 15-44, 2017-2020.
*"Other" signifies abortions performed in Texas but county of residence unknown, plus abortions obtained outside the state by Texas residents.

County	2022 Physicians	2021 Hospital Beds	2020 Total Deaths	2020 Fertility rate†	2021 Abortions
Ellis	114	235	1,668	62.3	285
El Paso	534	2,732	8,393	66.2	29
Erath	24	98	365	45.1	54
Falls	2	36	199	53.6	17
Fannin	10	25	493	61.8	25
Fayette	12	65	378	59.6	24
Fisher	3	14	70	64.3	2
Floyd	6	25	109	71.4	3
Foard	0	0	31	61.6	0
Fort Bend	609	1,197	4,545	55.7	1,359
Franklin	3	0	159	66.7	4
Freestone	6	37	281	66.7	14
Frio	9	22	190	75	28
Gaines	8	104	167	107.5	1
Galveston	245	1,074	3,338	59.1	563
Garza	0	0	67	62.8	0
Gillespie	33	84	389	67.1	15
Glasscock	0	0	10	70.8	0
Goliad	0	0	75	55.7	4
Gonzales	10	33	258	75.8	17
Gray	10	109	294	71.9	2
Grayson	118	725	1,787	64.8	126
Gregg	151	316	1,630	67.8	173
Grimes	15	25	355	70.1	38
Guadalupe	77	153	1,377	55.6	208
Hale	20	88	454	68.5	21
Hall	0	0	53	46.9	1
Hamilton	9	25	122	65.1	4
Hansford	2	14	54	74.4	0
Hardeman	2	24	75	54.2	5
Hardin	10	4	666	65	45
Harris	4,607	16,072	32,812	65.2	14,122
Harrison	14	574	769	61.1	71
Hartley	8	21	53	86.7	1
Haskell	3	25	84	50.5	1
Hays	165	383	1,340	48.5	566
Hemphill	6	74	24	51.9	0
Henderson	42	127	1,320	67.7	61
Hidalgo	538	2,356	7,239	75.4	1,050
Hill	9	25	526	65.3	35
Hockley	9	48	324	63.4	10
Hood	40	73	900	62.2	27
Hopkins	15	96	523	67.7	21
Houston	9	25	355	62.3	14
Howard	15	146	466	71	21
Hudspeth	1	0	39	42.7	0
Hunt	46	235	1,163	63.8	97
Hutchinson	9	25	315	66.8	3
Irion	0	0	19	66.4	3
Jack	9	17	104	62	3
Jackson	9	25	183	82.7	14
Jasper	13	59	531	67.5	32
Jeff Davis	1	0	29	57.2	0
Jefferson	175	1,335	2,958	70.8	492
Jim Hogg	0	0	60	68.4	7
Jim Wells	16	135	494	68	40
Johnson	67	232	1,830	63.9	169
Jones	4	45	262	63.6	9
Karnes	6	25	189	68.9	10
Kaufman	42	396	1,274	67	246
Kendall	46	0	455	48.9	29
Kenedy	0	0	—	36.4	0
Kent	0	0	17	54.1	0
Kerr	53	344	830	62.2	51
Kimble	2	15	65	81.5	5
King	0	0	—	68.6	0
Kinney	0	0	47	65.7	2
Kleberg	17	96	347	56.6	49
Knox	1	25	75	71.7	2
Lamar	36	154	786	69.6	10
Lamb	4	75	224	73.4	36
Lampasas	11	25	285	57.8	3
La Salle	2	0	78	70.3	14
Lavaca	10	48	319	71.9	9
Lee	6	0	226	70.7	22
Leon	2	0	251	74.3	10
Liberty	28	45	885	68.2	117
Limestone	16	78	338	67.9	23
Lipscomb	0	0	33	73.2	0
Live Oak	0	0	156	73.6	11
Llano	14	27	377	66.8	17
Loving	0	0	—	—	1
Lubbock	274	1,473	3,470	55.3	174
Lynn	5	24	93	72.5	1
Madison	7	25	168	63.8	15
Marion	2	0	182	60.4	8
Martin	3	18	66	85.3	4
Mason	1	0	48	78.6	4
Matagorda	20	75	467	60.4	46
Maverick	25	105	688	77.4	60
McCulloch	5	25	124	54.5	5
McLennan	243	593	2,742	81.4	313
McMullen	0	0	18	89	0
Medina	20	25	521	67.5	48
Menard	1	0	41	62.5	3
Midland	102	684	1,312	80	149

Physicians – All M.D.s and D.O.s. in direct patient care.
Hospital Beds – Beds not including military and veteran's hospitals, nor beds in hospitals that were not in compliance with state regulations.
†Fertility rate figured per 1,000 women ages 15-44, 2017-2020.
*"Other" signifies abortions performed in Texas but county of residence unknown, plus abortions obtained outside the state by Texas residents.

County	2022 Physicians	2021 Hospital Beds	2020 Total Deaths	2020 Fertility rate†	2021 Abortions
Milam	9	0	307	65.5	23
Mills	3	0	78	47.4	1
Mitchell	5	25	92	78.7	5
Montague	8	22	373	63.1	17
Montgomery	609	2,373	4,672	62.4	759
Moore	13	25	192	96.6	5
Morris	2	0	194	69.5	12
Motley	0	0	23	71.6	0
Nacgdoches	57	392	758	52.3	78
Navarro	22	162	634	73.5	60
Newton	3	0	213	57.1	12
Nolan	10	86	229	76.9	4
Nueces	367	2,011	3,787	60.6	575
Ochiltree	6	25	102	70.3	2
Oldham	0	0	20	54.4	0
Orange	20	0	1,151	68.3	106
Palo Pinto	15	74	456	68.5	16
Panola	4	42	378	65.5	14
Parker	65	129	1,418	61.2	95
Parmer	3	25	114	88.7	0
Pecos	8	39	193	78.4	10
Polk	27	66	822	69	40
Potter	147	1,090	1,638	72	21
Presidio	3	0	64	85.6	4
Rains	1	0	193	66	7
Randall	39	0	1,403	56.4	11
Reagan	1	7	34	82.5	3
Real	0	0	73	68.1	4
Red River	2	0	256	64.7	9
Reeves	6	25	151	87.2	4
Refugio	3	20	110	60.9	5
Roberts	0	0	12	50.2	0
Robertson	0	0	235	70	17
Rockwall	102	236	751	53.4	118
Runnels	7	50	163	66.3	5
Rusk	43	96	682	65.9	33
Sabine	3	25	190	72.3	9
S. Augustine	2	18	173	70.5	8
San Jacinto	3	0	379	63.6	22
San Patricio	19	0	770	70.8	75
San Saba	1	0	100	71.9	2
Schleicher	0	14	28	43.4	0
Scurry	12	25	223	75.5	10
Shackelford	1	0	51	63.5	4
Shelby	4	0	330	73.9	28
Sherman	0	0	28	90.5	1
Smith	282	1,369	2,726	63.3	305
Somervell	8	16	113	48.7	7

County	2022 Physicians	2021 Hospital Beds	2020 Total Deaths	2020 Fertility rate†	2021 Abortions
Starr	18	48	717	87.7	54
Stephens	5	40	144	70.8	2
Sterling	0	0	14	68.7	1
Stonewall	1	20	28	56.9	1
Sutton	2	12	49	65.3	3
Swisher	2	20	116	63.8	1
Tarrant	1,816	6,595	16,364	60.4	4,222
Taylor	123	946	1,631	66.4	133
Terrell	0	0	14	64.7	5
Terry	5	45	175	87.2	0
Throckmorton	1	14	17	69.5	0
Titus	29	174	341	70.9	28
Tom Green	118	732	1,430	62.6	88
Travis	1,413	3,666	6,967	51	3,340
Trinity	3	0	253	61.1	8
Tyler	5	49	322	66.8	23
Upshur	7	0	556	63.7	14
Upton	0	29	44	69.4	3
Uvalde	15	25	328	75.3	37
Val Verde	22	97	570	81.2	64
Van Zandt	9	0	835	64.4	49
Victoria	86	712	1,036	66.9	116
Walker	39	123	672	42.2	103
Waller	6	0	457	53.1	90
Ward	2	25	134	86.5	2
Washington	29	60	479	58.9	42
Webb	125	574	2,182	78.8	296
Wharton	23	49	537	72.8	64
Wheeler	4	41	71	61.3	1
Wichita	125	528	1,637	62.8	100
Wilbarger	6	128	209	63.7	6
Willacy	7	0	253	66.8	18
Williamson	526	999	3,683	53.6	834
Wilson	17	44	459	58.6	60
Winkler	3	19	89	81.4	1
Wise	37	150	784	61.8	46
Wood	22	50	754	58.9	23
Yoakum	5	24	91	91.9	14
Young	15	50	333	66.5	8
Zapata	0	0	127	76.1	15
Zavala	1	0	156	68.6	17
Other*	–	–	–	–	1,116

Physicians – All M.D.s and D.O.s. in direct patient care.
Hospital Beds – Beds not including military and veteran's hospitals, nor beds in hospitals that were not in compliance with state regulations.
†Fertility rate figured per 1,000 women ages 15-44, 2017-2020.
*"Other" signifies abortions performed in Texas but county of residence unknown, plus abortions obtained outside the state by Texas residents.

A groom adjusts his new husband's bowtie at their wedding in Austin on November 28, 2015. Photo by Zachary Hunt.

Marriage and Divorce

Source: Statistical Abstracts of the United States, National Vital Statistics System, Centers for Disease Control and Prevention.

These charts are for certain years, including 1946, when there was a significant increase in marriages after World War II as well as a significant increase in divorces. Also included are the years 1979-81 when the marriage and divorce rates reached another peak. ☆

Texas

Year	Total Marriages	Marriage Rate*	Total Divorces	Divorce Rate*
2021	171,353	5.8	41,638	1.4
2020	157,628	5.3	44,315	1.5
2019	137,572	4.9	61,206	2.1
2018	130,529	6.1	75,389	2.6
2017	203,767	7.1	136,717	2.2
2010	174,171	6.9	82,098	3.3
2005	169,300	7.4	74,000	3.2
2000	196,400	9.6	85,200	4.2
1995	188,500	10.1	98,400	5.3
1990	182,800	10.5	94,000	5.5
1985	213,800	13.1	101,200	6.2
1981	**194,800**	**13.2**	**101,900**	**6.9**
1980	**181,800**	**12.8**	**96,800**	**6.8**
1979	**172,800**	**12.9**	**92,400**	**6.9**
1975	153,200	12.5	76,700	6.3
1970	139,500	12.5	51,500	4.6
1960	91,700	9.6	34,732	3.6
1950	89,155	11.6	37,400	4.9
1946	**143,092**	**20.5**	**57,112**	**8.4**
1940	86,500	13.5	27,500	4.3

**Rate per 1,000 population.*
Totals and rates for marriages 2020-2021 and divorces 2018-2021 are based on Texas' estimated population total.

United States

Year	Total Marriages	Marriage Rate*	Total Divorces†	Divorce Rate*
2021	1,985,072	6.0	689,308	2.5
2020	1,676,911	5.1	630,505	2.3
2019	2,015,603	6.1	746,971	2.7
2018	2,132,853	6.5	782,038	2.9
2017	2,236,496	6.9	787,251	2.9
2016	2,251,411	7.0	776,288	3.0
2015	2,221,579	6.9	800,909	3.1
2010	2,096,000	6.8	872,000	3.6
2005	2,230,000	7.5	847,000	3.6
2000	2,329,000	8.2	944,000	4.0
1995	2,336,000	8.9	1,169,000	4.4
1990	2,443,000	9.8	1,182,000	4.7
1985	2,425,000	10.2	1,187,000	5.0
1981	**2,422,100**	**10.6**	**1,213,000**	**5.3**
1980	**2,390,300**	**10.6**	**1,189,000**	**5.2**
1979	**2,331,300**	**10.6**	**1,181,000**	**5.4**
1970	2,159,000	10.6	708,000	3.5
1960	1,523,381	8.5	393,000	2.2
1950	1,667,231	11.1	385,144	2.6
1946	**2,291,045**	**16.4**	**610,000**	**4.3**
1940	1,595,879	12.1	264,000	2.0

†Since 2000, the total number of divorces does not include four to six states, including California.

Texans in the National Academy of Sciences

Source: National Academy of Sciences.

The National Academy of Sciences is a private organization of researchers dedicated to the furtherance of science and its use for the general welfare. A total of 165 scientists who have had positions with Texas institutions have been named members or associates.

Established by congressional acts of incorporation, which were signed by President Lincoln in 1863, the academy acts as official adviser to the federal government in matters of science and technology. Election to the academy is one of the highest honors that can be accorded a scientist. As of July 2023, the number of active members was 3,182.

Elected from Texas in 2021 and 2022 were Anthony Di Fiore and Jonathan L. Sessler of the University of Texas at Austin; Stephen A. Fuselier at the Southwest Research Institute; and Donald W. Hilgemann, Margaret A. Phillips, and Jonathan C. Cohen of the University of Texas Southwestern Medical Center.

In 1931, Robert Moore (UT-Austin 1920–69) and Hermann Muller (Rice 1915-18, UT-Austin 1920–32) became the first scientists from Texas institutions elected to the academy. ☆

Academy Member	Affiliation	Elected
Perry L. Adkisson †	Texas A&M	1979
Richard W. Aldrich	UT-Austin	2008
James P. Allison	UT-MD Anderson Cancer	1997
Abram Amsel †	UT-Austin	1992
Neal R. Amundson †	University of Houston	1992
Leif Andersson	Texas A&M	2012
Dora E. Angelaki	Baylor Medical	2014
Charles J. Arntzen	Texas A&M	1983
David H. Auston	Rice	1991
Paul F. Barbara †	UT-Austin	2006
Allen J. Bard	UT-Austin	1982
Bonnie Bartel	Rice	2016
D.H.R. Barton †	Texas A&M	1970
Frederic C. Bartter †	UT-Health Science at San Antonio	1979
John D. Baxter †	Houston Methodist Research Institute	2003
Arthur L. Beaudet	Baylor Medical	2011
Hugo Bellen	Baylor College of Medicine	2020
Brian J.L. Berry	UT-Dallas	1975
Bruce Beutler †	UT-Southwestern Medical	2008
Lewis R. Binford	Southern Methodist University	2001
R.H. Bing †	UT-Austin	1965
Harold C. Bold †	UT-Austin	1973
Norman E. Borlaug	Texas A&M	1968
Maurice S. Brookhart	University of Houston	2001
Michael S. Brown	UT-Southwestern Medical	1980
James J. Bull	UT-Austin	2016
Karl W. Butzer †	UT-Austin	1996
Horace R. Byers †	Texas A&M	1952
Luis A. Caffarelli	UT-Austin	1991
C. Thomas Caskey †	Baylor Medical	1993
Joseph W. Chamberlain †	Rice	1965
Zhijian (James) Chen	UT-Southwestern Medical	2014
Wah Chiu	Baylor Medical	2012
C.W. Chu	University of Houston	1989
Melanie H. Cobb	UT-Southwestern Medical	2006
Jonathan C. Cohen	UT-Southwestern Medical	2022
Neal G. Copeland	Houston Methodist Research Institute	2009
F. Albert Cotton †	Texas A&M	1967
Robert F. Curl Jr. †	Rice	1997
Marcetta Darensbourg	Texas A&M	2017
Russell A. DeBose-Boyd	UT-Southwestern Medical	2023
Johann Deisenhofer	UT-Southwestern Medical	1997
Ronald A. DePinho	UT-MD Anderson Cancer	2012
Gerard H. de Vaucouleurs †	UT-Austin	1986
Ronald DeVore	Texas A&M	2017
Bryce DeWitt †	UT-Austin	1990
Robert E. Dickinson	UT-Austin	1988
Anthony Di Fiore	UT-Austin	2021
Richard A. Dixon	University of North Texas	2007
Stephen J. Elledge	Baylor Medical	2003
Ronald W. Estabrook †	UT-Southwestern Medical	1979
Mary K. Estes	Baylor Medical	2007
Karl Folkers †	UT-Austin	1948
Marye Anne Fox	UT-Austin	1994
Katherine Freese	UT-Austin	2020
Stephen A. Fuselier	Southwest Research Institute	2021
David L. Garbers †	UT-Southwestern Medical	1993
Wilson S. Geisler	UT-Austin	2008
Quentin H. Gibson	Rice	1982
Alfred G. Gilman †	UT-Southwestern Medical	1985
Joseph L. Goldstein	UT-Southwestern Medical	1980
John B. Goodenough †	UT-Austin	2012
Cameron M. Gordon	UT-Austin	2023
William E. Gordon	Rice	1968
Verne E. Grant †	UT-Austin	1968
Jan-Ake Gustafsson	University of Houston	2002
Norman Hackerman †	Robert A. Welch Foundation	1971
Naomi J. Halas	Rice	2013
Carl G. Hartman †	UT-Austin	1937
Luis Herrera-Estrella	Texas Tech	2003
Dudley Herschbach	Texas A&M	1967
Donald W. Hilgemann	UT-Southwestern Medical	2021
David M. Hillis	UT-Austin	2008
Helen H. Hobbs	UT-Southwestern Medical	2007
Lora V. Hooper	UT-Southwestern Medical	2015
A. James Hudspeth	UT-Southwestern Medical	1991
Thomas J.R. Hughes	UT-Austin	2009
Nancy A. Jenkins	UT-MD Anderson Cancer	2008
V. Craig Jordan	UT-MD Anderson Cancer	2009
Robert C. Kennicutt, Jr.	Texas A&M	2006
James L. Kinsey †	Rice	1991
Mark Kirkpatrick	UT-Austin	2020
Steven A. Kliewer	UT-Southwestern Medical	2015
Ernst Knobil †	UT-Houston Health Science	1986
Jay K. Kochi †	University of Houston	1982
John Kormendy †	UT-Austin	2020
P. Kusch †	UT-Dallas	1956
Alan M. Lambowitz	UT-Austin	2004
Neal F. Lane	Rice	2009
David M. Lee	Texas A&M	1991
Beth Levine †	UT-Southwestern Medical	2013
Herbert Levine	Rice	2011
Gardner Lindzey †	UT-Austin	1989
Gigi Lozano	UT-MD Anderson Cancer	2017
Alan G. MacDiarmid †	UT-Dallas	2002
Allan H. MacDonald	UT-Austin	2010
David J. Mangelsdorf	UT-Austin	2008
John L. Margrave †	Rice	1974
Martin M. Matzuk	Baylor Medical	2014
S.M. McCann †	UT-Southwestern Medical	1983
Steven L. McKnight	UT-Southwestern Medical	1992
David J. Meltzer	Southern Methodist University	2009
Robert Moore †	UT-Austin	1931
Nancy A. Moran	UT-Austin	2004
Sean J. Morrison	UT-Southwestern Medical	2020
Hermann Muller †	Rice, UT-Austin	1931
Hans J. Muller-Eberhard †	UT-Houston Health Science	1974
Ferid Murad	UT-Houston Health Science	1997

† – Deceased
UT – University of Texas

Academy Member	Affiliation	Elected
Jack Myers †	UT-Austin	1975
Kyriacos C. Nicolaou	Rice	1996
Robert N. Noyce †	SEMATECH/Austin	1980
David R. Nygren	UT-Arlington	2000
Eric N. Olson	UT-Southwestern Medical	2000
Bert W. O'Malley	Baylor Medical	1992
Jose N. Onuchic	Rice	2006
Kim Orth	UT-Southwestern Medical	2020
Theophilus S. Painter †	UT-Austin	1938
Duojia Pan	UT-Southwestern Medical	2023
Luis F. Parada	UT-Southwestern Medical	2011
John Patterson †	UT-Austin	1941
Margaret A. Phillips	UT-Southwestern Medical	2021
Kenneth L. Pike †	Summer Institute of Linguistics	1985
Helen Piwnica-Worms	UT-MD Anderson Cancer	2023
William H. Press	UT-Austin	1994
Darwin J. Prockop	Texas A&M	1991
Lester J. Reed †	UT-Austin	1973
Peter M. Rentzepis	Texas A&M	1978
Rebecca Richards-Kortum	Rice	2015
Ignacio Rodriguez-Iturbe †	Texas A&M	2010
Michael K. Rosen	UT-Southwestern Medical	2020
A. Catharine Ross	Texas A&M	2003
Peter J. Rossky	UT-Austin	2011
David W. Russell	UT-Southwestern Medical	2006
Marlan O. Scully	Texas A&M	2001
Jonathan L. Sessler	UT-Austin	2021
Richard E. Smalley †	Rice	1990
Esmond E. Snell †	UT-Austin	1955

Academy Member	Affiliation	Elected
Richard C. Starr †	UT-Austin	1976
Patrick Stover	Texas A&M	2016
Thomas Südhof	UT-Southwestern Medical	2002
Max D. Summers	Texas A&M	1989
John Suppe	University of Houston	1995
Harry L. Swinney	UT-Austin	1992
Joseph S. Takahashi	UT-Southwestern Medical	2003
John T. Tate	UT-Austin	1969
Karen K. Uhlenbeck	UT-Austin	1986
Jonathan W. Uhr	UT-Southwestern Medical	1984
Roger H. Unger †	UT-Southwestern Medical	1986
H.S. Vandiver †	UT-Austin	1934
Moshe Y. Vardi	Rice	2015
Ellen S. Vitetta	UT-Southwestern Medical	1994
Salih J. Wakil †	Baylor Medical	1990
Xiaodong Wang	UT-Southwestern Medical	2004
Steven Weinberg †	UT-Austin	1972
D. Fred Wendorf †	Southern Methodist University	1987
John Archibald Wheeler †	UT-Austin	1952
Roger J. Williams †	UT-Austin	1946
Jean D. Wilson †	UT-Southwestern Medical	1983
Peter G. Wolynes	Rice	1991
James E. Womack	Texas A&M	1999
Richard D. Wood	UT-MD Anderson Cancer	2023
Karen L. Wooley	Texas A&M	2020
Masahi Yanagisawa	UT-Southwestern Medical	2003
Clarence Zener †	Texas A&M	1959
Huda Y. Zoghbi	Baylor Medical	2004

† – Deceased
UT – University of Texas

Science Research Funding at Universities

The following chart shows funding for research and development by source at universities in Texas, in order of total R&D funding. Colleges and universities not listed received less. The figures are from the National Science Foundation's Higher Education Research and Development Survey (HERDS) and are for fiscal year 2021. ☆

(Thousands of dollars)	All R&D expenditures	Federal Government	State/Local Government	Business	Nonprofit Organizations	Institutional Funds	All Other Sources
United States	$89,872,007	$49,228,127	$4,745,398	$22,481,841	$5,118,899	$5,604,133	$2,693,609
Texas (all colleges statewide)	**$6,855,976**	**$2,874,320**	**$930,778**	**$1,875,339**	**$478,606**	**$418,274**	**$278,659**
1. Texas A&M	1,147,720	528,057	198,483	313,192	32,978	45,135	29,875
2. UT–M.D. Anderson Cancer Center	1,124,971	217,073	293,325	233,279	211,849	32,741	136,704
3. UT–Austin	779,348	489,827	30,336	139,669	68,580	43,258	7,678
4. Baylor College of Medicine	716,976	365,472	34,447	239,079	29,465	48,513	—
5. UT–Southwestern Medical Center	632,134	257,611	68,114	151,111	38,886	52,491	63,921
6. UT–HSC, Houston	308,823	165,139	42,636	47,653	16,305	24,200	12,890
7. UT–HSC, San Antonio	219,734	106,824	25,110	51,848	10,085	25,548	319
8. Rice University	207,404	95,648	7,372	62,352	7,123	30,638	4,271
9. University of Houston	202,536	77,489	35,530	71,291	7,745	7,309	3,172
10. Texas Tech University	197,739	33,938	27,357	108,999	12,221	14,929	295
11. UT–Medical Branch	185,759	117,915	7,739	39,565	8,424	12,116	—
12. UT–San Antonio	145,362	42,952	17,629	67,130	5,196	9,854	2,601
13. UT–Arlington	126,477	46,946	19,262	49,685	3,006	6,131	1,447
14. UT–Dallas	122,825	58,249	11,065	29,308	6,581	17,622	—
15. UT–El Paso	109,410	43,930	19,841	34,866	994	3,441	6,338
16. University of North Texas, Denton	81,252	18,702	5,567	53,591	1,992	1,329	71
17. Texas State University	72,510	31,116	3,949	31,792	765	4,888	—
18. UT–Rio Grande Valley	58,187	13,018	6,945	29,053	265	8,701	205
19. University of North Texas, HSC	50,698	32,464	9,224	6,615	1,633	626	136
20. Baylor University	48,809	11,025	1,892	26,678	3,116	4,510	1,588
21. Southern Methodist University	41,960	17,886	1,039	18,643	2,072	2,144	176
22. Texas Tech University, HSC	41,583	12,148	16,670	8,153	342	1,268	3,002
23. Texas A&M–Corpus Christi	30,500	10,967	9,110	4,589	603	2,642	2,589
24. UT–HSC, Tyler	27,928	12,007	6,884	3,545	111	5,381	—
25. Texas A&M-Kingsville	23,578	9,265	4,652	3,614	353	5,468	226
26. Tarleton State University	17,729	4,620	3,749	8,949	263	148	—
27. Prairie View A&M University	17,582	9,566	4,041	3,421	115	439	—
28. Texas Christian University	15,336	4,448	438	8,684	1,670	23	73
29. Sam Houston State University	13,315	5,632	232	6,985	29	416	21
30. Texas Tech, HSC, El Paso	11,360	1,831	2,829	6,064	395	241	—

UT – University of Texas
HSC – Health Science Center

National Health Expenditures

GDP and Expenditures ($ billion)	2021	2020	2019	2018	2017	2000
Total Health Expenditures	**$4,255.1**	**$4,144.1**	**$3,795.4**	**$3,604.4**	**$3,446.5**	**$1,377.2**
Percent of GDP	18.3%	19.7%	17.7%	17.6%	17.7%	13.8%
Per capita amount (in dollars)	$12,914.0	$12,591.0	$11,582.0	$11,040.0	$10,611.0	$4,878.0
Personal health care expenditure	$3,553.4	$3,367.0	$3,173.1	$3,019.8	$2,903.8	$1,161.5
Cost of private insurance	$1,211.4	$1,145.1	$1,157.8	$1,129.8	$1,080.0	$52.3
Hospital care expenditures	$1,324.0	$1,267.8	$1,192.0	$1,122.7	$1,077.6	$415.5
Gross Domestic Product (GDP)	**$23,315.1**	**$21,060.5**	**$21,433.2**	**$20,533.1**	**$19,485.4**	**$9,952.0**

Source: U.S. Centers for Medicare and Medicaid Services.

Comparison of Vital Statistics

Data from 2021 with states that either border Texas or have large populations. ***Lowest and highest with number in bold.***

State/Country	Birthrate*	Death Rate*	Life Expectancy
Texas	12.7	9.1	76.5
Arkansas	11.9	13.2	73.8
California	10.7	8.5	79.0
Florida	9.9	12.0	77.5
Georgia	11.5	10.4	75.6
Louisiana	12.4	12.4	73.1
Michigan	10.4	11.7	76.0
New Hampshire	**8.7**	12.6	77.8
New Mexico	10.1	12.0	74.5
New York	10.6	9.1	77.7
Ohio	11.0	12.5	75.3
Oklahoma	12.1	12.8	74.1
Utah	**14.0**	**6.8**	78.6
West Virginia	9.6	**16.5**	72.8
United States	11.0	10.4	76.4
Afghanistan	34.8	12.1	**54.1**
Angola	**41.4**	7.8	62.5
Brazil	13.4	6.9	76.1
Canada	10.1	8.2	84.0
Germany	9.0	12.0	81.7
Italy	7.0	11.3	82.8
Japan	6.9	11.7	85.0
Monaco	**6.6**	10.9	**89.6**
Mexico	14.0	7.1	73.5
Qatar	9.3	**1.4**	80.0
Russia	9.2	**13.3**	72.7
South Sudan	37.1	9.2	59.7
United Kingdom	10.8	9.1	82.1
World	18.1	7.7	70.5

*Rates are number during one year per 1,000 persons. Sources: National Vital Statistics Report 2021; Centers for Disease Control and Prevention, National Center for Health Statistics, National Vital Statistics System 2018-2021; CIA World Factbook, 2023.

Life Expectancy at Birth for Texans by Group

Sex	All	Whites	Blacks	Hispanics
Total population	76.5	—	—	—
Males	73.7	—	—	—
Females	79.3	—	—	—

Source: Centers for Disease Control, National Vital Statistics Reports, Vol. 71, for 2020.

Texas Births by Race/Ethnicity and Sex

Race/Sex	2020	2019	2015	2000
All Races	368,317	377,710	403,439	363,325
All Male	188,551	193,032	205,972	185,591
All Female	179,766	184,678	197,467	177,734
White Total	118,242	122,424	136,663	142,553
White Male	60,995	62,729	69,935	72,972
White Female	57,247	59,695	66,728	69,581
Black Total	46,150	46,642	47,515	41,180
Black Male	23,421	23,808	24,140	21,128
Black Female	22,729	22,834	23,375	20,052
Hispanic Total	175,967	179,713	191,080	166,440
Hispanic Male	89,837	91,493	97,469	84,750
Hispanic Female	86,130	88,220	93,611	81,690
Other* Total	27,958	28,931	28,181	13,152
Other Male	14,298	15,002	14,428	6,741
Other Female	13,660	13,929	13,753	6,411

*Other includes births of unknown race/ethnicity.

Source: Texas Department of State Health Services.

Disposition of Bodies in Texas by Percent of Deaths*

Year	Burial	Cremation	Donation of Body	Removal from State/Other†
2020	46.1%	45.7%	1.5%	6.7%
2019	44.4%	48.0%	1.7%	5.9%
2018	43.6%	50.0%	1.5%	4.9%
2017	46.8%	43.9%	1.4%	7.9%
2001	75.5%	17.3%	0.8%	6.3%
1995	81.7%	11.6%	0.8%	5.8%
1989	83.7%	7.1%	0.7%	8.5%

*Resident Deaths: Deaths where decedent resided in Texas, regardless of where death occurred.

†Includes Removal from State, Entombment, Other, and Unknown.

Source: Texas Death Certificate Data; Texas Department of State Health Services, Center for Health Statistics.

Texan Nobel Prize Winners

Sources: The Nobel Foundation (nobelprize.org), Fort Worth Star-Telegram.

On November 27, 1895, Alfred Nobel signed his last will and testament, giving the largest share of his fortune to a series of prizes in physics, chemistry, physiology or medicine, literature and peace—the Nobel Prizes. In 1968, Sveriges Riksbank (Sweden's central bank) established The Sveriges Riksbank Prize in Economic Sciences in Memory of Alfred Nobel.

Between 1901 and 2022, the Nobel Prizes and the prize in economic sciences were awarded 615 times. Nobel Prizes have been awarded to individuals 959 times and organizations 30 times between 1901 and 2022. Of them, 92 were for economic sciences. A small number of individuals and organizations have been honored more than once, which means that 954 unique individuals and 27 unique organizations have received the Nobel Prize in total.

There are some years when the Nobel Prizes have not been awarded. The total number of times are 49. Several occurred during World Wars I (1914-1918) and II (1939-1945). In the statutes of the Nobel Foundation it says: "If none of the works under consideration is found to be of the importance indicated in the first paragraph, the prize money shall be reserved until the following year. If, even then, the prize cannot be awarded, the amount shall be added to the Foundation's restricted funds." ☆

Texan Nobel Prize Winners

Year	Name	Nobel Prize in
2019	John Goodenough	Chemistry
2018	James Allison	Physiology or Medicine
2017	Michael W. Young	Physiology or Medicine
2015	Aziz Sancar	Chemistry
2011	Bruce Beutler	Physiology or Medicine
2003	John Maxwell Coetzee	Literature
2000	Alan MacDiarmid	Chemistry
2000	Jack Kilby	Physics
1996	Robert F. Curl Jr.	Chemistry
1994	Alfred Gilman	Physiology or Medicine
1993	Russell Alan Hulse	Physics
1990	E. Donnall Thomas	Physiology or Medicine
1988	Johann Deisenhofer	Chemistry
1985	Michael S. Brown and Joseph Goldstein	Physiology or Medicine
1979	Steven Weinberg	Physics
1977	Ilya Prigogine	Chemistry
1970	Norman Borlaug	Peace
1946	Hermann Joseph Muller	Physiology or Medicine

Community Hospitals in Texas

Source: The Texas Hospital Association.

Of the 652 reporting hospitals in Texas in 2020, 528 were considered community hospitals.

A community hospital is defined as either a nonfederal, short-term general hospital or a special hospital whose facilities and services are available to the public. A hospital may include a nursing home-type unit and still be classified as short-term, provided that the majority of its patients are admitted to units where the average length of stay is less than 30 days.

- The 528 hospitals employed 371,350 full-time equivalent people (FTEs) with a payroll, including benefits, of more than $31.7 billion.
- These hospitals contained some 66,844 beds.
- The average length of stay was 5.3 days in 2017, compared to 6.8 days in 1975. This was less than the U.S. average of 5.5 days.
- The average cost per adjusted admission in Texas was $12,357 or $2,552 per day. This was 5.8 percent less than the U.S. average of $13,126.
- There were 2.7 million admissions in Texas, which accounted for 14.5 million inpatient days.
- There were 45.1 million outpatient visits in 2017, of which 11.9 million were emergency room visits.
- Of the FTEs working in community hospitals within Texas, there were 122,050 registered nurses and 7,700 licensed vocational nurses. ☆

Mental Health and Substance Abuse

Diagnosis of Adult Clients in Texas/United States: 2019–2020

Diagnosis	Texas clients	% of clients with diagnosis		Employed as % of known employment
		Texas	United States	Texas
Schizophrenia	43,991	19.6	13.9	12.0
Bipolar disorder	141,710	63.0	40.1	27.5
Other psychoses	660	0.3	2.2	20.0
All other diagnoses	3,958	1.8	36.9	32.2
No diagnosis/deferred	34,655	15.4	6.8	26.4
Total	**224,974**	**100.0**	**100.0**	**24.4**

Source: U.S. Department of Health and Human Services, Center for Mental Health Services, Uniform Reporting System, 2020.

Readmission Within 180 Days of Mental Health Treatment: 2019–2020

Age	Civil* Texas	Civil U.S.	States/Terr. reporting	Forensic* Texas	Forensic U.S.
In percent of clients.					
0 to 12	12.6%	15.6%	14%	—	1.4%
13 to 17	15.5	17.1	19	13.2%	11.5
18 to 20	12.7	19.6	31	4.3	7.4
21 to 64	18.1	20.3	49	6.7	10.1
65 to 74	14.8	20.1	38	5.0	13.7
75 and over	0.0	13.1	18	-	9.0
Total	**17.4**	**19.9**	**49**	**6.7**	**10.2**

*Forensic services are mental health services provided to persons directed into treatment by the criminal justice system; others are listed as "Civil." *Source: U.S. Department of Health and Human Services, Center for Mental Health Services,* Uniform Reporting System, 2020.

Substance Abuse Treatment in Texas: 2020

Facility operation	No.	%	Clients in treatment on March 31, 2020		
			No.	%	Clients under 18
Private nonprofit	199	39.1	7,254	26.8%	581
Private for-profit	257	50.5	14,723	54.4	512
Local/county/community	25	4.9	513	1.9	97
State	8	1.6	929	3.4	26
Federal	19	3.7	3,605	13.3	-
Tribal	1	0.2	54	0.2	-
Total	**509**	**100.0**	**27,078**	**100.0**	**1,216**
Problem treated	**No.**	**%**	**No.**	**%**	**...per 100,000 pop.**
Alcohol and drug abuse	216	42.4	5,405	23.5	25
Drug abuse only	252	49.5	14,121	61.4	64
Alcohol abuse only	194	38.1	3,483	15.1	16

Source: National Survey of Substance Abuse Treatment Services, 2020.

Estimated Use of Drugs in Texas and Bordering States: 2021

State	Any illicit drug	Marijuana	Other than marijuana[1]	Cigarettes	Binge alcohol[2]	Pain reliever misuse[4]
*Current users[3] as **percent of population, age 12+ years**. Selected states.*						
U.S. total	14.29%	18.74%	3.23%	15.59%	21.45%	3.11%
Texas	**8.51**	**12.65**	**2.13**	**14.36**	**22.16**	**2.86**
Arkansas	11.14	15.56	3.17	20.15	20.40	3.92
Louisiana	14.39	19.03	3.66	20.18	23.54	3.75
Oklahoma	17.29	24.16	3.10	19.03	20.76	3.16
New Mexico	20.15	22.78	4.08	16.39	22.06	2.90

[1]Marijuana users who have also used another drug are included. [2]Binge use is defined as drinking five or more drinks on the same occasion on at least one day in the past 30 days. [3]Used drugs at least once within month. [4]Within the last year. *Source: U.S. Substance Abuse and Mental Health Services Administration,* National Survey on Drug Use and Health, 2021.

State Institutions for Mental Health Services

Source: U.S. Department of Health and Human Services and the Texas Department of State Health Services.

Mental health services were provided to some 425,546 Texans in 2021 in various institutions, including community centers.

In 2004, the Texas Department of State Health Services was created (DSHS), bringing together:

- the Texas Department of Health,
- the Texas Department of Mental Health and Mental Retardation (MHMR),
- Commission on Alcohol and Drug Abuse,
- the Texas Health Care Information Council.

In 2016, Texas Health and Human Services was created by the Legislature with two agencies: the Texas Health and Human Services Commission (HHSC) and DSHS, with many direct client services transferred from DSHS to HHSC, including mental health services.

In 2021, state mental health agency expenditure was $1,207,619,240, with $779,283,528 for community services, according to the federal Uniform Reporting System for the states.

Hospitals for Persons with Mental Illness

Following is a list of the 11 state hospitals, the year each was founded, and number of beds in 2023, totaling 2,320.

Austin State Hospital — Austin; 1857; 263 beds.
Big Spring State Hospital — Big Spring; 1937; 180 beds.
El Paso Psychiatric Center — El Paso; 1974; 74 beds.
John S. Dunn Behavioral Sciences Center — Houston; 2022.
Kerrville State Hospital — Kerrville; 1950; 220 beds.
North Texas State Hospital — Wichita Falls (1922), 268 beds; and Vernon (1969), 294 beds.
Rio Grande State Center — Harlingen; 1962; 52 beds.
Rusk State Hospital — Rusk; 1919; 288 beds.
San Antonio State Hospital — San Antonio; 1892; 302 beds.
Terrell State Hospital — Terrell; 1885; 305 beds.
Waco Center for Youth — Waco; 1979; 74 beds.

Community Mental Health Centers

Following is a list of community mental health centers, the year each was founded, and the counties each serves.

Abilene — Betty Hardwick Center; 1971; Callahan, Jones, Shackelford, Stephens, and Taylor.
Amarillo — Texas Panhandle Centers; 1968; Armstrong, Carson, Collingsworth, Dallam, Deaf Smith, Donley, Gray, Hall, Hansford, Hartley, Hemphill, Hutchinson, Lipscomb, Moore, Ochiltree, Oldham, Potter, Randall, Roberts, Sherman, and Wheeler.
Austin — Integral Care; 1967; Travis.
Beaumont — Spindletop Center; 1967; Chambers, Hardin, Jefferson, and Orange.
Big Spring — West Texas Centers; 1997; Andrews, Borden, Crane, Dawson, Fisher, Gaines, Garza, Glasscock, Howard, Kent, Loving, Martin, Mitchell, Nolan, Reeves, Runnels, Scurry, Terrell, Terry, Upton, Ward, Winkler, and Yoakum.
Brownwood — Center for Life Resources; 1969; Brown, Coleman, Comanche, Eastland, McCulloch, Mills, and San Saba.
Bryan-College Station — MHMR Authority of Brazos Valley; 1972; Brazos, Burleson, Grimes, Leon, Madison, Robertson, and Washington.
Conroe — Tri-County Behavioral Healthcare; 1983; Liberty, Montgomery, and Walker.
Corpus Christi — Nueces Center for Mental Health & Intellectual Disabilities; 1970; Nueces.
Dallas — North Texas Behavioral Health Authority (NTBHA); 1967; Dallas, Ellis, Hunt, Kaufman, Navarro, and Rockwall.
Denton — Denton County MHMR Center; 1987; Denton.
Edinburg — Tropical Texas Behavioral Health; 1967; Cameron, Hidalgo, and Willacy.
El Paso — Emergence Health Network; 1968; El Paso.
Fort Worth — MHMR of Tarrant County; 1969; Tarrant.
Granbury — Pecan Valley Centers for Behavioral & Developmental HealthCare; 1977; Erath, Hood, Johnson, Palo Pinto, Parker, and Somervell.
Houston — The Harris Center for Mental Health and IDD; 1965; Harris.
Jacksonville — Anderson-Cherokee Community Enrichment Services (ACCESS); 1995; Anderson and Cherokee.
Kerrville — Hill Country Mental Health & Developmental Disabilities Centers; 1997; Bandera, Blanco, Comal, Edwards, Gillespie, Hays, Kendall, Kerr, Kimble, Kinney, Llano, Mason, Medina, Menard, Real, Schleicher, Sutton, Uvalde, and Val Verde.
Laredo — Border Region Behavioral Health Center; 1969; Jim Hogg, Starr, Webb, and Zapata.
Longview — Community Healthcore; 1970; Bowie, Cass, Gregg, Harrison, Marion, Panola, Red River, Rusk, and Upshur.
Lubbock — StarCare Specialty Health System; 1969; Cochran, Crosby, Hockley, Lubbock, and Lynn.
Lufkin — Burke Center; 1975; Angelina, Houston, Jasper, Nacogdoches, Newton, Polk, Sabine, San Augustine, San Jacinto, Shelby, Trinity, and Tyler.
Lytle — Camino Real Community Services; 1996; Atascosa, Dimmit, Frio, La Salle, Karnes, Maverick, McMullen, Wilson, and Zavala.
McKinney — LifePath Systems; 1986; Collin.
Midland — PermiaCare; 1969; Brewster, Culberson, Ector, Hudspeth, Jeff Davis, Midland, Pecos, and Presidio.
Plainview — Central Plains Center; 1969; Bailey, Briscoe, Castro, Floyd, Hale, Lamb, Motley, Parmer, and Swisher.
Portland — Coastal Plains Community Center; 1996; Aransas, Bee, Brooks, Duval, Jim Wells, Kenedy, Kleberg, Live Oak, and San Patricio.
Rosenberg — Texana Center; 1996; Austin, Colorado, Fort Bend, Matagorda, Waller and Wharton.
Round Rock — Bluebonnet Trails Community Services; 1997; Bastrop, Burnet, Caldwell, Fayette, Gonzales, Guadalupe, Lee, and Williamson.
San Angelo — MHMR Services for the Concho Valley; 1969; Coke, Concho, Crockett, Irion, Reagan, Sterling, and Tom Green.
San Antonio — The Center for Health Care Services; 1966; Bexar.
Sherman — Texoma Community Center; 1974; Cooke, Fannin, and Grayson.
Temple — Central Counties Services; 1967; Bell, Coryell, Hamilton, Lampasas, and Milam.
Terrell — Lakes Regional MHMR Center; 1996; Camp, Delta, Franklin, Hopkins, Lamar, Morris, and Titus.
Texas City — Gulf Coast Center; 1969; Brazoria and Galveston.
Tyler — Andrews Center Behavioral Healthcare System; 1970; Henderson, Rains, Smith, Van Zandt, and Wood.
Victoria — Gulf Bend Center; 1970; Calhoun, DeWitt, Goliad, Jackson, Lavaca, Refugio, and Victoria.
Waco — Heart of Texas Region MHMR Center; 1969; Bosque, Falls, Freestone, Hill, Limestone, and McLennan.
Wichita Falls — Helen Farabee Centers; 1969; Archer, Baylor, Childress, Clay, Cottle, Dickens, Foard, Hardeman, Haskell, Jack, King, Knox, Montague, Stonewall, Throckmorton, Wichita, Wilbarger, Wise, and Young. ☆

EDUCATION

TEXAS TRIBUNE REPORTS: EDUCATION

PUBLIC SCHOOLS

UIL & TEXAS HISTORY DAY WINNERS

COLLEGES & UNIVERSITIES

SPECIAL THANKS TO THE BRYAN MUSEUM
FOR SPONSORING THIS CHAPTER OF THE TEXAS ALMANAC

TEXAS TRIBUNE REPORTS: EDUCATION

THE TEXAS TRIBUNE

By Brian Lopez, K-12 Education Writer
and Matthew Watkins, Managing Editor for News and Politics

Texas has more than 5 million students enrolled in elementary and secondary schools across the state, and another 1.3 million enrolled in universities, community colleges, and medical schools. The state's schools are vital to lifting people out of poverty and building the workforce of the future. But many challenges exist. Here's a look at some of the top current issues in Texas schools.

EDUCATING A DIVERSE POPULATION

Texas public schools are more diverse than the population as a whole. Hispanic students make up a majority of the K-12 population, while 26.8% of students are white and 12.8% are Black. At the state's four-year universities, however, white students are the biggest demographic group, making up just under 40% of the student population. Hispanics make up 30%, and Black students make up 10.6% of the population.

One of the challenges is the struggle Texas schools face in educating vulnerable populations, which are disproportionately made up of students of color. More than three-fifths of Texas public school students are considered by the state to be economically disadvantaged. More than one-fifth have limited English proficiency. Only about 56% of students graduate from Texas high schools considered college ready in reading. For math, that number is only 46%.

Another challenge is cost. In 2022, the statewide average tuition and fees at a public four-year university in Texas were around $5,250 per semester. That is an increase of 33% in the past decade.

LEARNING LOSS

Two years of school disruptions due to COVID caused significant harm to students' learning, and the state has yet to recover. The number of students who were reading at grade level was 47% in 2019. In 2021, that number dropped to 43%. Math results were even worse. Half of Texas students were meeting grade level in math in 2019. By 2021, that number had dropped to 35%.

State officials have said that the negative impacts of COVID erased years of student growth in reading and math. Economically disadvantaged students suffered the worst effects, but state officials said the impacts of COVID learning loss were felt across income levels.

TEACHER SHORTAGE

Even before the COVID-19 pandemic, Texas was already facing a teacher shortage. Issues like low pay, working overtime, health worries during the pandemic, and being caught in the middle of Texas' culture wars have led more teachers to leave the profession. The TEA has noted that the state is struggling to fill its teacher vacancies. Retaining teachers has also become increasingly difficult, and schools are having to refill positions on a yearly basis.

An effort to give teachers raises was unsuccessful during the 2023 regular session of the Texas Legislature, but lawmakers are likely to reconsider those measures later in the year. Other bills to address the shortage also failed to pass.

SOCIAL ISSUES

School districts across the state have been embroiled in questions about what kind of books and lessons on the subject of race, gender, and sexuality are appropriate for school-aged students. In recent years, lawmakers have sought to limit the teaching of lessons that pertain to the idea of systemic racism or the role of racism in the state's and nation's histories. People pushing for the laws argue that, taken too far, those lessons can give students the impression certain students should feel guilty or inferior because of their race. Opponents say the lessons are simply trying to teach a more well-rounded version of history that is relevant to the state's diverse student population.

Library books have taken a particular focus, with some parents and politicians singling out books they feel are too graphic or sexual in nature. Many of those books have discussed LGBTQ issues that some parents feel are inappropriate for young students. Other parents and many authors have argued that such scrutiny amounts to censorship, and that those books can be helpful for LGBTQ students finding their identities.

Texas Public Schools

Sources: Reports and online directory of the Texas Education Agency, tea.texas.gov; reporting by the Texas Tribune, as well as "Texas Public Schools Explorer" at schools.texastribune.org; the Texas Permanent School Fund Annual Comprehensive Financial Report for 2021 and 2022; and the biannually produced "Summary of 2020–21 Conference Committee Report for HB1."

Enrollment in Texas public schools continues to rise. In the 2021–2022 school year, 5,427,370 students were enrolled. That's an increase of 1.04% over enrollment in the 2020–2021 school year, which saw the enrollment of 5,371,586 students, and a jump of 9.02% above enrollment from 2011–2012, when 4,978,120 students enrolled, according to the Texas Education Agency.

In Texas, there are 1,207 independent and common school districts and 185 charter operators. Independent school districts are administered by an elected board of trustees and deal directly with the Texas Education Agency. Common districts are supervised by elected county school superintendents and county trustees. Charter schools are discussed later in this article.

As of the 2021–2022 school year, there were 17 school districts with more than 50,000 students enrolled in their various schools; 26% of all students in Texas attend school in these large districts. By contrast, only 1.9% of Texas students are enrolled at the 407 smallest districts in Texas, each of which has fewer than 500 students enrolled.

5 Largest School Districts, by Enrollment (May 2023)

School District	County	Enrollment
Houston ISD	Harris	189,934
Dallas ISD	Dallas	141,169
Cypress-Fairbanks ISD	Harris	118,010
Northside ISD	Bexar	102,719
Katy ISD	Harris, Fort Bend, Waller	92,667

5 Smallest School Districts, by Enrollment (May 2023)

School District	County	Enrollment
San Vicente ISD	Brewster	12
Ramirez CSD	Duval	21
Doss Consolidated CSD	Gillespie	22
Divide ISD	Kerr	37
Lake Granbury Academy Charter School	Hood	41

Brief History of Public Education in Texas

Public education was one of the primary goals of the early settlers of Texas, who listed in the Texas Declaration of Independence the failure to provide education as one of their grievances against Mexico.

As early as 1838, President Mirabeau B. Lamar's message to the Republic of Texas Congress advocated setting aside public domain for public schools. His interest caused him to be called the "Father of Education in Texas." In 1839, Congress designated three leagues of land to support public schools for each Texas county and 50 leagues for a state university. In 1840, each county was allocated one more league of land.

The Republic, however, did not establish a public school system or a university. After Texas was admitted into the Union, the 1845 Texas State Constitution advocated public education, instructing the Legislature to designate at least 10% of the tax revenue for schools. Further delay occurred until Gov. Elisha M. Pease, on Jan. 31, 1854, signed the bill setting up the Texas public school system.

The public school system was made possible by setting aside $2 million out of $10 million Texas received for relinquishing its claim to land north and west of its present boundaries in the Compromise of 1850.

Early Funding and Administration Changes

During 1854, legislation provided for state apportionment of funds based upon an annual census. Also, railroads receiving grants were required to survey alternate sections to be set aside for public-school financing. The first school census that year showed 65,463 students; state fund apportionment was 62 cents per student.

When adopted in 1876, the present Texas Constitution provided: "All funds, lands, and other property heretofore set apart and appropriated for the support of public schools; all the alternate sections of land reserved by the state of grants heretofore made or that may hereafter be made to railroads, or other corporations, of any nature whatsoever; one half of the public domain of the state, and all sums of money that may come to the state from the sale of any portion of the same shall constitute a perpetual public school fund."

More than 52 million acres of the Texas public domain were allotted for school purposes. (See table "Distribution of the Public Lands of Texas" on page 476.)

In 1949, the Gilmer-Aikin Laws reorganized the state system of public schools by making sweeping changes in administration and financing. The Texas Education Agency, headed by the governor-appointed Commissioner of Education, administers the public-school system.

The policy-making body for public education is the 15-member State Board of Education, which is elected from separate districts for overlapping four-year terms. Current membership of the board is listed on page 482 in the State Government chapter.

Targeting Student Performance

The 68th Legislature passed one of the most historic education-reform bills of the past 50 years when lawmakers met in special session in the summer of 1984. House Bill 72 came in response to growing concern over deteriorating literacy among Texas' schoolchildren over two decades, reflected in students' scores on standardized tests.

Provisions of HB 72 raised teachers' salaries, but tied those raises to teacher performance. It also introduced more stringent teacher certification and initiated competency testing for teachers. Lawmakers also created the 22:1 class size ratio for kindergarten through fourth-grade classes and the no-pass, no-play rule.

Sweeping Reforms

In 1995, the 74th Legislature took on a monumental task and completely rewrote all the state's public education laws.

The Public Schools Reform Act of 1995 increased local control of public schools by limiting the Texas Education Agency to recommending and reporting on educational goals; overseeing charter schools; managing the permanent, foundation, and available school funds; administering an accountability system; creating and implementing the student testing program; recommending educator appraisal and counselor evaluation instruments; and developing plans for special, bilingual, compensatory, gifted and talented, vocational, and technology education.

It also reduced the authority of the State Board of Education. The goal was to return as much authority as possible to the local level. However, each subsequent legislature has reinstated some state-level control.

Financial Reform

In 2019, the 86th Legislature focused on school finances and taking some of the financial burden for public education off of property owners. Maintenance and operations (M&O) property taxes fund much of public education in Texas.

The $11.6 billion finance bill included $6.5 billion in new public education spending and $5.1 billion for lowering property tax bills. Its measures included increased per-student base funding by 20%, provided raises for teachers, funded free full-day pre-K for eligible 4-year-olds, and reduced the amount of money that wealthier school districts spent subsidizing poorer districts, a recapture program informally known as "Robin Hood."

The bill also offered $3,000 to $12,000 to districts providing merit-pay bonuses to their best teachers, and school administrators are required to use part of their funding to offer raises and benefits for teachers with more than five years of experience.

Social and Safety Concerns

In 2022, the 87th Legislature passed laws regulating how race, slavery, and history are taught in classes. Lawmakers took aim at "CRT," or "critical-race theory," which maintains that racism is baked into legal systems and is not limited to individual action alone. Although critical race theory is primarily taught at the university level, Senate Bill 3 restricts it at the public one, stating that a "teacher may not be compelled to discuss a widely debated and currently controversial issue of public policy or social affairs," with no definition of what a "controversial issue" might be.

Under House Bill 25, transgender athletes are required to play on teams that correspond to birth certificates issued on or near the time of their births. Under this law, modified birth certificates would only be accepted if they had been altered to fix clerical errors. According to Jamey Harrison, deputy director of the University Interscholastic League (UIL), schools that do not comply with these measures would face sanctions and forfeit competitions at minimum.

In 2023, the 88th Legislature approved House Bill 3, a school safety measure that requires an armed security officer at every Texas campus, offers mental health training for district employees who regularly interact with children, and creates regional safety teams that conduct intruder detection audits at least once a year. House Bill 3 also created a

Permanent School Fund

Year	Fund Value* (in millions)	Funds Distributed to Schools (in millions)
2022	$56,810.7	$2,142.3
2021	$55,624.1	$1,701.7
2020	$46,675.6	$1,701.7
2019	$46,500.4	$1,535.8
2018	$44,067.5	$1,235.8
2017	$41,418	$1,056.4
2016	$37,263.9	$1,056.4
2015	$33,833.5	$8,38.7
2014	$34,951.2	$8,38.7
2013	$27,277	$1,020.9
2012	$25,503	$1,020.9
2011	$24,091.6	$1,092.8
2010	$22,107.8	$60.7
2009	$20,545.3	$716.5
2008	$23,142.4	$716.5
2007	$25,311.8	$843.1
2006	$22,802.7	$841.9
2005	$21,354.3	$880
2004	$19,261.8	$825.1
2003	$18,037.3	—
2002	$17,047.2	—
2001	$19,021.8	—
2000	$22,275.6	—
1999	$19,615.7	$698.5
1998	$16,296.2	$661.9
1997	$15,496.6	$690.8
1996	$12,995.8	$692.7
1995	$12,273.2	$740
1994	$11,330.6	$737
1993	$11,822.5	$737.7
1992	$10,944.9	$739.5
1991	$10,227.8	$739.2
1990	$7,328.2	$700.3
1980	$2,464.6	$3
1970	$842.2	$287.2
1960	$425.8	$164.2
1950	$161.2	$94
1940	$68.3	$34.6
1930	$38.7	$27.3
1920	$25.7	$18.4
1910	$16.8	$5.9

*Prior to 1991, the PSF reported cash, bonds at par, and stock at book value. From 1991 to the present, the PSF has reported cash, bonds and stocks at fair value.

Texas School Enrollment and Expenditures per Student

School Year	Enrollment	Spending per student
2021–2022	5,427,370	—
2020–2021	5,371,586	$14,797
2019–2020	5,493,940	$14,058
2018–2019	5,431,910	$13,108
2017–2018	5,399,682	$12,861
2016–2017	5,343,893	$12,634
2015–2016	5,284,306	$12,264
2014–2015	5,232,065	$11,704
2013–2014	5,151,925	$10,971
2012–2013	5,058,939	$10,549
2011–2012	4,978,120	$10,556
2010–2011	4,912,385	$11,142
2009–2010	4,824,778	$11,543
2008–2009	4,728,204	$11,567
2007–2008	4,651,516	$10,162

Graduates and Dropouts

School Year	Graduates	*Dropouts
2020–2021	358,842	46,299
2019–2020	360,220	30,921
2018–2019	355,615	34,477
2017–2018	347,893	33,697
2016–2017	334,424	33,050
2015–2016	324,311	33,466
2014–2015	313,397	33,437
2013–2014	303,109	35,358
2012–2013	301,418	34,696
2011–2012	292,636	36,276
2010–2011	290,581	34,363
2009–2010	280,520	33,235
2008–2009	264,275	40,923
2007–2008	252,121	45,796
2006–2007	241,193	55,306

* Grades 7–12.

safety and security department within the Texas Education Agency. The Texas Education Agency was given the authority to compel school districts to formulate and follow active shooter protocols, with non-compliant districts put under state supervision. The Texas School Safety Center, a think tank located at Texas State University in San Marcos, was tasked with reviewing best practices for campus security every five years. House Bill 3 allocated $1.1 billion in funding to the Texas Education Agency for use in school safety grants, promising at least $15,000 per campus and $10 per student.

Charter Schools

Charter-school legislation in Texas provides for four types of charter schools: the home-rule school district charter, the campus or campus-program charter, the open-enrollment charter and a university-sponsored charter. A charter contract is typically granted for five years and can be revoked if the school violates its charter.

Since the inception of the charter school movement in Texas, the charter contracts have been granted by the State Board of Education (SBOE). However, Senate Bill (SB) 2, which passed during the 2013 legislative session, shifted the authority to grant a charter to the commissioner of education. The State Board of Education, however, may veto any of his selections.

As of the 2021–2022 school year, there were 185 active charter school districts in Texas. Since 1996, 342 charters have been approved and 158 have closed (including 38 closures due to the charter being revoked). So far, no district has created a home-rule charter, although citizens in Dallas ISD discussed it. There are 128 campus charter schools, which are created by school districts and overseen by each school district's board of trustees.

The most popular form of charter schools is the open-enrollment charter. These are public schools released from some Texas education laws and regulations. Many charter schools have focused efforts on educating young people who are at risk of dropping out of school or who have dropped out and then returned to school. During the 2021–2022 school year, there were 878 open-enrollment schools attended by 377,375 students, about 7.0% of the state's public school students.

The state also approves university-sponsored charters; 28 such schools are active and in operation, according to a search of TEA's online directory.

State Appropriations

For FY22–23, general revenue financing for public education totals $51.6 billion, an increase of $5.0 billion over the FY21–22 funding level. Most of the funding for public education comes through the Foundation School Program (FSP) system.

According to the Legislative Budget Board, supplemental appropriation for public education included:

- $600 million in federal funds from the American Rescue Plan Act to TEA to assist school districts in implementing school safety initiatives.
- $14.5 million to improve teacher and principal hiring and recruitment, mentoring, education preparation and program quality improvement, and retainment.
- $1 billion to the Teacher Retirement System of Texas.

Permanent School Fund

The Texas public school system was established and the Permanent School Fund (PSF or "the Fund") set up by the Fifth Legislature, Jan. 31, 1854. The 170-year-old PSF is

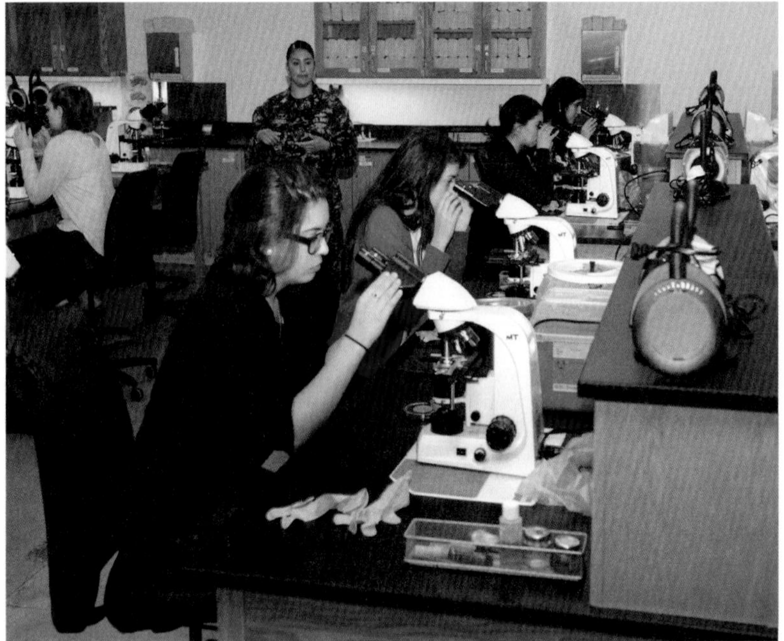

Hospital Corpsman 1st Class Elizabeth Sifuentes, a medical laboratory technician instructor at the Medical Education and Training Campus (METC), talks to students from John Marshall High School while they look through microscopes during a tour of METC at Joint Base San Antonio–Fort Sam Houston on March 2, 2017. The tour was conducted by METC's Navy service component, Navy Medicine Training Support Center, as part of their Science, Technology, Engineering and Mathematics (STEM) efforts. Photo by Jacquelyn D. Childs.

managed by the State Board of Education and is the largest educational endowment in the United States. It is invested in global markets and broadly diversified.

In 2021, the 87th Legislature passed SB 1232, which separated the Fund from the Texas Education Agency in 2023. The PSF then became a standalone entity known as the Texas Permanent School Fund Corporation.

Every year, a distribution is made from PSF to pay a portion of educational costs in each public school district. The amount distributed is subject to two constraints set in Article VII, Section 5 of the Texas Constitution:

The SBOE may not approve a distribution rate or transfer to the Available School Fund (ASF) that exceeds 6.0% of the average market value of the fund, excluding real property.

The total distributions over a 10-year period to the ASF may not exceed the total return on the PSF's investment assets over the same period.

The fund was first established in 1854 with $2.0 million. The funds distributed to schools that year was $40,587. By the year 1900 the fund had grown to $9.1 million. Funds distributed to schools in 1900 totalled $3.0 million. The PSF balance, as of Aug. 31, 2022, was $56.8 billion, an increase of $1.2 billion from the prior year.

The PSF also provides a guarantee for bonds issued by local school districts, allowing districts to pay lower interest rates. As of Aug. 31, 2022, PSF assets guaranteed $99.5 billion in school district bonds to 867 public school districts and $3.7 billion in charter district bonds to 31 charter districts. ☆

Public School Personnel and Salaries

Personnel Category*	Personnel 2020—2021	Personnel 2021—2022	% Change from Previous	Average Base Salaries 2020—2021	Average Base Salaries 2021—2022	% Change from Previous
Teachers	369,389	369,684	0.08%	$57,641	$58,887	2.16%
Campus Administration	22,378	23,929	6.93%	$83,423	$83,445	0.03%
Central Administration	8,657	9,049	4.53%	$109,661	$110,949	1.17%
Professional Support†	79,049	80,669	2.05%	$68,014	$69,473	2.15%
Total Professionals	**479,475**	**483,331**	**0.80%**	$61,494	$62,844	2.20%
Paraprofessionals	79,391	83,021	4.57%	$22,215	$23,063	3.82%
Auxiliary Staff	186,946	185,986	-0.51%	$28,812	$29,712	3.12%
Total Staff	**745,813**	**752,339**	**0.88%**	$49,120	$50,264	2.33%

*Personnel figures are full-time equivalent

†The Professional Support category includes supervisors, counselors, educational diagnosticians, librarians, nurses/physicians, therapists, and psychologists.

Source: TEA Staff Salary reports for 2018–2019 and 2019–2020

University Interscholastic League Winning Schools for the 2021–2022 and 2022–2023 School Years

Source: University Interscholastic League, uiltexas.org

The UIL Lone Star Cup is awarded annually to six high schools, one in each of the six UIL classifications, based on their team performance in district and state championships. The winning schools receive the UIL Lone Star Cup trophy and a $1,000 scholarship.

Lone Star Cup Champions						
YEAR	1A	2A	3A	4A	5A	6A
2022	Tilden McMullen County	Beckville	Lorena	Argyle	Lucas Lovejoy	Southlake Carroll
2023	Abbott	Mason	Lorena	Argyle	Dallas Highland Park	Southlake Carroll

The schools of individuals who won state championships in the academic, music, and the arts categories are listed first, then the winners in some sports categories. For other sports results, see page 181. An em-dash (—) in the box means there was no competition in that conference in that category for that year.

State Champions, Academics

YEAR	1A	2A	3A	4A	5A	6A
Overall State Meet Academic Champions						
2022	Nazareth	Sabine Pass	Gladewater-Sabine	Argyle	PSJA Southwest	Clements (Sugar Land)
2023	Nazareth	Sabine Pass	Gladewater-Sabine	Sulphur Springs	Argyle	Allen
Accounting						
2022	Happy	Vega	Central (Pollok)	Argyle	Friendswood	Cypress Woods
2023	Happy	Vega	Childress	Dallas Business & Management	Argyle	Mesquite
Calculator Applications						
2022	Knippa	Woodsboro	Sabine (Gladewater)	Big Spring	Sharyland Pioneer (Mission)	PSJA (San Juan)
2023	Newcastle	Woodsboro	Mission Collegiate	Big Spring	Wylie (Abilene)	North Shore (Houston)
Computer Applications						
2022	Happy	Vega	Chapel Hill (Mount Pleasant)	Melissa	Sharyland Pioneer (Mission)	Cypress Woods
2023	Rocksprings	Winters	Fairfield	Lindale	Melissa	Flower Mound (Lewisville)
Computer Science						
2022	Aspermont	San Augustine	Fairfield	School for Talented & Gifted (Dallas)	Heritage (Frisco)	Cypress Woods
2023	Aspermont	San Augustine	Brock	School for Talented & Gifted (Dallas)	Lebanon Trail (Frisco)	Clements (Fort Bend)
Current Issues						
2022	UT Tyler University Academy (Tyler)	Mason	London (Corpus Christi)	Wimberley	Cedar Park	Allen
2023	Gail Borden County	Mason	Mansfield Frontier	Burnet	Hays (Buda)	The Woodlands (Conroe)
Editorial Writing						
2022	Chireno	Farwell	Comanche	Lindale	Princeton	Mesquite
2023	San Isidro	Douglass	Gladewater Sabine	Stafford	Forney	Shadow Creek (Alvin)
Feature Writing						
2022	Savoy	Coleman	Wall	Lindale	Heritage (Frisco)	Waxahachie
2023	Gorman	Martins Mill	Buffalo	Sulphur Springs	Foster (Richmond)	Bellaire (Houston)
Headline Writing						
2022	Nazareth	Vega	Chapel Hill (Mt. Pleasant)	Hardin-Jefferson (Sour Lake)	Hendrickson (Pflugerville)	Waxahachie

YEAR	1A	2A	3A	4A	5A	6A
2023	Nazareth	Archer City	West	Sulphur Springs	Amarillo	United (Laredo)
			Informative Speaking			
2022	Blackwell	Shelbyville	Lago Vista	Terrell	Mount Pleasant	Hays (Buda)
2023	Lenora Grady	Shelbyville	Mount Pleasant Chapel Hill	La Vernia	Vela (Edinburg)	Plano West
			Journalism Team			
2022	Nazareth	Lovelady	Industrial (Vanderbilt)	Lindale	Cedar Park	Waxahachie
2023	Nazareth	Martin's Mill	White Oak	Sulphur Springs	Foster (Richmond)	Mesquite
			Lincoln-Douglas Debate			
2022	Blackwell	Mason	Grand Saline	La Vernia	Katy Jordan (Fulshear)	McNeil (Austin)
2023	Lometa	Chireno	Mount Pleasant Chapel Hill	La Vernia	A&M Consolidated (College Station)	Stevens (Northside)
			Literary Criticism			
2022	Graford	Groveton	Holliday	Argyle	Sulphur Springs	Midway (Waco)
2023	Baird	Groveton	New Waverly	Kaufman	Argyle	Memorial (Houston)
			Mathematics			
2022	Knippa	Woodsboro	Idalou	Big Spring	Highland Park (Dallas)	Clements (Sugar Land)
2023	Newcastle	Woodsboro	Mission Collegiate	School of Science and Engineering (Dallas)	Heritage (Frisco)	Highland Park (Dallas)
			News Writing			
2022	Chireno	Lovelady	Industrial (Vanderbilt)	Canyon	Princeton	Lamar (Houston)
2023	Nazareth	Muenster	White Oak	Canton	Weslaco East	Hebron (Lewisville)
			Number Sense			
2022	Jonesboro	Woodsboro	Idalou	Salado	Highland Park (Dallas)	Clements (Sugar Land)
2023	Jonesboro	Woodsboro	Mission Collegiate	School of Science and Engineering (Dallas)	Sharyland Pioneer	Cane (Klein)
			Persuasive Speaking			
2022	Lometa	Union Grove (Gladewater)	Holliday	Paris	Leander	Spring Woods (Houston)
2023	Lometa	Saratoga West Hardin	BASIS Shavano (San Antonio)	Canyon Randall	Hays (Buda)	Plano West
			Poetry Interpretation			
2022	Nazareth	Sundown	Lexington	Liberty	PSJA Southwest (Pharr)	Harlingen South
2023	Nazareth	Three Rivers	Edna	Tuloso-Midway (Corpus Christi)	Harlingen South	Cypress Park
			Prose Interpretation			
2022	Coolidge	Ropes (Ropesville)	Holliday	Tuloso-Midway (Corpus Christi)	Midlothian	Seven Lakes (Katy)
2023	Barksdale Nueces Canyon	Tioga	White Oak	Wimberley	Sharyland Pioneer	Harlingen
			Ready Writing			
2022	Irion County (Mertzon)	Martin's Mill	Paradise	Royal (Pattison)	Pine Tree (Longview)	Central (San Angelo)
2023	UT Tyler University Academy	Lindsay	Childress	Sulphur Springs	Ball (Galveston)	Allen
			Science			
2022	UT Tyler University Academy	Lindsay	BASIS Shavano (San Antonio)	Sunnyvale	Highland Park (Dallas)	Dulles (Sugar Land)
2023	Wheeler Kelton	Woodsboro	BASIS Shavano (San Antonio)	Gateway College Preparatory (Georgetown)	Rider (Wichita Falls)	Carnegie Vanguard (Houston)

YEAR	1A	2A	3A	4A	5A	6A
Social Studies						
2022	Moulton	Tioga	Llano	Burnet	Rouse (Leander)	Flower Mound
2023	Moulton	Tolar	Callisburg	Burnet	Cedar Park	Vista Ridge (Cedar Park)
Speech Team						
2022	Blackwell	Mason	Elysian Fields	Tuloso-Midway (Corpus Christi)	Mount Pleasant	Clements (Sugar Land)
2023	Lenorah Grady	Saratoga West Hardin	BASIS Shavano (San Antonio)	La Vernia	Hendrickson (Pflugerville)	Plano West
Spelling & Vocabulary						
2022	Moulton	Mason	Henrietta	Hudson (Lufkin)	Sherman	Allen
2023	Kennard	Crawford	Henrietta	Big Spring	Sherman	Bridgeland
Spelling & Vocabulary Team						
2022	Moulton	Sabine Pass	Henrietta	Giddings	Sulphur Springs	Allen
2023	Moulton	Crawford	Henrietta	Canton	Flour Bluff (Corpus Christi)	Allen

State Champions, Publications

YEAR	Yearbooks (Gold Awards)	Print Newspapers (Gold Awards)
2022	Aledo H.S., *Ledoian;* James Bowie H.S., *The Lone Star;* Kealing Middle School, *The Vespa;* McKinney H.S., *The Lion;* Pleasant Grove H.S., *The Hawk;* St. Mark's School of Texas, *Marksmen;* Texas H.S., *Tiger;* Vista Ridge H.S., *The Lonestar*	Episcopal School of Dallas, *Eagle Edition;* McCallum H.S., *The Shield;* Pleasant Grove H.S., *The Edge;* St. Mark's School of Texas, *The ReMarker;* Texas H.S., *Tiger Times.*
2023	James Bowie H.S., *Lone Star;* Round Rock H.S., *Dragon;* Pleasant Grove H.S., *The Hawk;* El Dorado H.S., *The Legend;* Episcopal School of Dallas, *Carillon;* Texas H.S., *Tiger;* Aledo H.S., *Ledoian;* Vista Ridge H.S., *The Lonestar.*	St. Mark's School of Texas, *The Remarker;* Texas H.S., *Tiger Times;* McCallum H.S., *The Shield;* Pleasant Grove H.S., *The Edge;* James Bowie H.S., *The Dispatch.*

State Champions, Music and Theater

YEAR	1A	2A	3A	4A	5A	6A
One-Act Play						
2022	Abbott	Mason	White Oak	Paris North Lamar	Boerne Champion	Fort Bend Bush
2023	Trinidad	Christoval	Mount Vernon	Randall (Canyon)	Harlingen South	Midland
Marching Band						
2022	Menard	Tenaha	Mineola	Argyle	Cedar Park	Hebron
2023	—	Shiner	—	Celina	—	Vandegrift

State Champions, Athletics

YEAR	1A	2A	3A	4A	5A	6A
Cross Country Team, Boys						
2022	Miller Grove (Cumby)	Poolville	Whitesboro	San Elizario	Grapevine	Carroll (Southlake)
2023	Saltillo	Plains	Lytle	Canyon	Grapevine	Carroll (Southlake)
Cross Country Individual, Boys						
2022	Guthrie	Brackett (Brackettville)	Poth	Athens	Grapevine	Vandegrift (Austin)
2023	Irion County (Mertzon)	Goldthwaite	Holliday	Diamond Hill-Jarvis (Fort Worth)	Monterey (Lubbock)	Vandegrift (Austin)
Cross Country Team, Girls						
2022	Imperial Buena Vista	Wellington	Holliday	Celina	Lovejoy (Lucas)	Flower Mound (Lewisville)
2023	Miller Grove	Hamilton	Whitesboro	Celina	Lovejoy (Lucas)	Flower Mound (Lewisville)
Cross Country Individual, Girls						
2022	Springlake (Earth)	Wellington	Holliday	Melissa	Randall (Canyon)	Flower Mound (Lewisville)
2023	Springlake (Earth)	Shelbyville	Pilot Point	Canyon	Georgetown	Flower Mound (Lewisville)
Golf Team, Boys						
2022	Jonesboro	Vega	Brock	Argyle	Anderson (Austin)	Westlake (Austin)
2023	Wildorado	Lindsay	Callisburg	Randall (Canyon)	Montgomery Lake Creek	Westlake (Austin)

YEAR	1A	2A	3A	4A	5A	6A
Golf Individual, Boys						
2022	Jonesboro	Morton	Lago Vista	Argyle	Anderson (Austin)	Plano West
2023	Wildorado	Lindsay	Orangefield	Wimberley	Texas (Texarkana)	Westlake (Austin)
Golf Team, Girls						
2022	Jonesboro	Vega	Brock	Argyle	Anderson (Austin)	Westlake (Austin)
2023	Garden City	Mason	Wall	Andrews	Alamo Heights (San Antonio)	Vandegrift (Austin)
Golf Individual, Girls						
2022	Fort Elliott (Briscoe)	Quanah	Columbus	Bullard	Lebanon Trail (Frisco)	Carroll (Southlake)
2023	Happy	Mason	Chapel Hill (Mount Pleasant)	Sunnyvale	Grapevine	Vandegrift (Austin)
Tennis, Team						
2022	—	—	—	Wimberley	Highland Park (Dallas)	Plano West
2023	—	—	—	Randall (Canyon)	Amarillo	Westwood (Round Rock)
Tennis, Boys Singles						
2022	Nueces Canyon (Barksdale)	Maud	Wall	Boerne	Kempner (Fort Bend)	Reagan (San Antonio)
2023	Utopia	Mason	London (Corpus Christi)	Anna	Kempner (Fort Bend)	Northside Harlan (San Antonio)
Tennis, Boys Doubles						
2022	Sterling City	Mason	Wall	Wimberley	Amarillo	Westwood (Round Rock)
2023	Menard	Mason	Vernon	Boerne	Amarillo	The Woodlands (Conroe)
Tennis, Girls Singles						
2022	Miami	Albany	Queen City	Argyle	Amarillo	Westwood (Round Rock)
2023	Runge	Port Aransas	Vernon	Taylor	Argyle	Bellaire (Houston)
Tennis, Girls Doubles						
2022	Knippa	Mason	Peaster	Tuloso-Midway (Corpus Christi)	Highland Park (Dallas)	Carroll (Southlake)
2023	Utopia	Mason	Vernon	Bullard	Amarillo	Memorial (Houston)
Tennis, Mixed Doubles						
2022	Utopia	Mason	Reagan County (Big Lake)	Hereford	Liberty (Frisco)	Plano West
2023	Irion County (Mertzon)	Mason	Vernon	Hereford	College Station	Plano West
Track & Field, Boys Team						
2022	Paducah	Shiner	Brock	La Vega (Waco)	Liberty (Frisco)	Summer Creek (Humble)
2023	Turkey Valley	Refugio	Brock	Wimberley	Marshall (Fort Bend)	Summer Creek (Humble)
Track & Field, Girls Team						
2022	Sands (Ackerly)	Panhandle	Yoe (Cameron)	Kennedale	Lancaster	DeSoto
2023	Sands (Ackerly)	Haskell	Randolph (Universal City)	Canyon	Marshall (Fort Bend)	Flower Mound (Lewisville)

Wrestling, Boys

2022

DIV	Weight Classes						
	106	113	120	126	132	138	145
5A	Tascosa (Amarillo)	Dumas	Creekview (Carrollton)	Randall (Canyon)	Jordan (Katy)	Lubbock	Dumas
6A	Martin (Arlington)	Ellison (Killeen)	Martin (Arlington)	Bryan	Eastwood (El Paso)	Allen	The Woodlands College Park (Conroe)
DIV	152	160	170	182	195	220	285
5A	Centennial (Frisco)	Caney Creek (Conroe)	Glenn (Leander)	Midlothian	Heritage (Frisco)	Lovejoy (Lucas)	Lovejoy (Lucas)
6A	Clear Lake (Houston)	Taylor (Katy)	Allen	New Braunfels	Plano West	Allen	Katy

2023

DIV	106	113	120	126	132	138	144
5A	Randall (Canyon)	Centennial (Burleson)	Uvalde	Dumas	Midlothian	Lancaster	Caprock (Amarillo)
6A	Timber Creek (Keller)	Martin (Arlington)	Allen	Martin (Arlington)	Eastwood (El Paso)	Westside (Houston)	Allen
DIV	150	157	165	175	190	215	285
5A	Dumas	Lubbock	Tascosa (Amarillo)	Melissa	Midlothian	Northwest	Lovejoy (Lucas)
6A	Montwood (El Paso)	Martin (Arlington)	Katy	Klein	Rockwall	Allen	Timber Creek (Keller)

Wrestling, Girls

2022

DIV	Weight Classes				
	95	102	110	119	128
5A	A&M Consolidated (College Station)	Randall (Canyon)	Lovejoy (Lucas)	Caprock (Amarillo)	Foster (Richmond)
6A	Heath (Rockwall)	The Woodlands College Park (Conroe)	Carroll (Southlake)	Bowie (Austin)	Rockwall
DIV	138	148	165	185	215
5A	Memorial (McAllen)	Caprock (Amarillo)	Azle	Randall (Canyon)	Kingwood Park (Humble)
6A	Vista Ridge (Cedar Park)	Smithson Valley (Comal)	Allen	Pharr-San Juan-Alamo	Woodlands College Park (Conroe)

2023

DIV	100	107	114	120	126	132
5A	Hanks (El Paso)	Grapevine	Ellison (Killeen)	Carroll (Corpus Christi)	Foster (Richmond)	Chapin (El Paso)
6A	Franklin (El Paso)	Conroe (The Woodlands)	Lake Highlands (Richardson)	Eastwood (El Paso)	Bowie (Austin)	Martin (Arlington)
DIV	138	145	152	165	185	235
5A	Memorial (McAllen)	Azle	Friendswood	Memorial (Frisco)	Lubbock	Andress (El Paso)
6A	Conroe (Woodlands College Park)	Euless (Trinity)	Allen	Frenship (Wolfforth)	Oak (Klein)	El Paso Americas

State and National History Day Contests, 2022–2023

TEXAS HISTORY DAY

Each year thousands of students, encouraged by teachers and parents statewide, participate in the National History Day program in Texas. Texas History Day, an affiliate of NHD, is a highly regarded academic program for 6th through 12th grade students. Students that place first or second at the state contest get the chance to compete in the national contest in Washington, D.C. Learn more at **texashistoryday.com.**

State History Day Winners 2022

Theme: Debate and Diplomacy in History

	Junior	Senior
	Documentaries	
Individual	**1st** *Diplomacy: The Key to Preventing Nuclear War,* Legacy M.S. (Selma)	**1st** *Communist in the Cornfields: Roswell Garst's Citizen Diplomacy,* Livingston H.S.
	2nd *Borders Divide, Waters Unite: The Indus Waters Treaty,* E.F. Green Junior School (Baytown)	**2nd** *This Is Not Your War, Soul Brother: Muhammad Ali's Debate Over Force Diplomacy During the Vietnam War,* Goose Creek Memorial (Baytown)
Group	**1st** *America's Secret: The Debate, Failure, and Consequences of Japanese Internment,* North Belton M.S. (Temple)	**1st** *The Small Ball That Moved the Big World: How a Game of Ping Pong Forever Changed U.S.-China Relations,* Jasper H.S. (Plano)
	2nd *A Race to Ratification: The Road to the Perfect 36,* E.F. Green Junior School (Baytown)	**2nd** *The Multiplex of Mental Health: The Various Debates and Diplomatic Reforms in Regards to Mental Health,* New Caney H.S.
	Exhibits	
Individual	**1st** *A Broken Peace: The Treaty of Versailles,* Sartartia M.S. (Sugar Land)	**1st** *Debate and Diplomacy: Perspectives on the Annexation of the Republic of Texas,* Bryan Collegiate H.S.
	2nd *A Desire Sparks Conflict,* Lewis M.S. (Houston)	**2nd** *The Irish Troubles: The Long Debate Over Ireland's Identity,* New Caney H.S.
Group	**1st** *Brown v. Board of Education: Separate Is Not Equal,* Gentry J.H. (Baytown)	**1st** *The Game That Changed the World: How Ping-Pong Diplomacy Salvaged International Relations Between the United States and the People's Republic of China,* IMPACT Early College H.S. (Baytown)
	2nd *Laundry-Folders, Diaper-Changers, Dinner-Makers: The Women Who First Pushed for a Diplomatic End to the Vietnam War,* Sudie L. Williams TAG Academy (Dallas)	**2nd** *"A System Totally Alien to Our Ideals": The Debate and Diplomacy that Dismantled the Apartheid System in South Africa,* Health Careers H.S. (San Antonio)
	Performances	
Individual	**1st** *Debate and Diplomacy: President Nixon's Trip to China,* Macario Garcia M.S. (Richmond)	**1st** *Pleading for my People: The Truth Behind Debate and Diplomacy,* Plano SR H.S.
	2nd *The Coming of My People—The Civil Rights Act of 1964,* Stovall M.S. (Houston)	**2nd** *Marsha P. Johnson: In the Fight for Life,* Nimitz H.S. (Humble)
Group	**1st** *Treaty of New Echota: Reaping the Sewn,* C.M. Rice M.S. (Plano)	**1st** *Women's Suffrage,* Veterans Memorial Early College H.S. (Brownsville)
	2nd *Cuban Missile Crisis,* Woodcreek J.H. (Katy)	**2nd** *Operation Ortsac: The Operation that Propelled Backdoor Diplomacy,* Plano East SR H.S. (Plano)
	Websites	
Individual	**1st** *The 1959 Soviet-American Exhibitions: Cultural Diplomacy Sparks a Debate in the Kitchen,* Dripping Springs M.S.	**1st** *The Marshall Plan: American Foreign Diplomacy from Post-World War II Europe's Ashes,* Jasper H.S. (Plano)
	2nd *The Seneca Falls Convention: The First Diplomatic Women's Rights Gathering,* East Central Heritage M.S. (St. Hedwig)	**2nd** *The Sykes-Picot Agreement: Blood-Stained Hands—The World's Worst Diplomatic Disaster,* Saint Mary's Hall (San Antonio)
Group	**1st** *Yellow Rain: A Test in Diplomacy and a Debate Between Powers,* Hornedo M.S. (El Paso)	**1st** *Conservation Controversy: The Negotiations on Preserving Natural Lands That Brought About the Birth of the National Park Service,* Northstar School (Mansfield)
	2nd *International Space Station: One Giant Leap for Diplomacy,* Kimbrough M.S. (Mesquite)	**2nd** *When Nobody Is the Good Guy: Operation Condor,* Plano East S.R. H.S.
	Papers	
Individual	**1st** *The Chinese Rites Controversy and Its Impact on Western Relations with China,* Lively M.S. (Austin)	**1st** *English Diplomacy via German Relativity: The 1919 Eclipse Expedition to Show "Light-Rays, When Near the Sun, DO NOT GO STRAIGHT,"* Plano East S.R. H.S. (Richardson)
	2nd *Diplomacy in the Nuclear Age,* Canyon Ridge M.S. (Austin)	**2nd** *The Jordan-Israel Peace Treaty of 1994: A "Watershed" Diplomacy,* Greenhill School (Dallas)

National History Day 2022

1st Place Senior Individual Documentary	1st Place Senior Group Documentary	1st Place Junior Group Exhibit
Communist in the Cornfields: Roswell Garst's Citizen Diplomacy, Livingston H.S.	*The Small Ball That Moved the Big World: How a Game of Ping Pong Forever Changed U.S.-China Relations,* Jasper H.S.	*Laundry-Folders, Diaper-Changers, Dinner-Makers: The Women Who First Pushed for a Diplomatic End to the Vietnam War,* Sudie L. Williams TAG (Dallas)

State History Day Winners 2023

Theme: Frontiers in History: People, Places, Ideas

	Junior	Senior
Documentaries		
Individual	**1st** *Fritz Harber: The Good, the Bad, the Ugly,* Quail Valley M.S. (Missouri City)	**1st** *Cotton: Pushing Humans to New Frontiers,* Debakey H.S. for Health Professions (Houston)
	2nd *Anna May Wong: The Toll of Stardom,* Canyon Ridge M.S. (Austin)	**2nd** *Image Is Everything: Richard Nixon's New Political Frontier,* Livingston
Group	**1st** *Perseverance, Bravery, and Breaking the Frontier: The Story of Virginia Hall,* North Belton M.S. (Temple)	**1st** *Jack Kilby and the Circuit That Conquered the World,* Plano East S.R. H.S. (Murphy)
	2nd *Exploring the Final Frontier: A Race to Space,* North Belton M.S. (Temple)	**2nd** *John Webber and the Underground Railroad,* Donna
Exhibits		
Individual	**1st** *National Association Opposed to Women Suffrage,* Cedar Bayou J.H. (Baytown)	**1st** *Window to the Universe: How the Hubble Space Telescope Revolutionized the Study of Astronomy,* New Caney
	2nd *Judge Reynaldo Garza: First Hispanic Federal Judge,* Stell M.S. (Brownsville)	**2nd** *A New Age of Politics: Barbara Jordan's Influence on the Exposure of African American Female Representation in Government,* Odyssey Academy—Bay Area (League City)
Group	**1st** *Got Safe Milk?,* E.F. Green Junior School (Baytown)	**1st** *The Hidden Bomber of WWII: Outwitting the Enigma Code,* Veterans Memorial Early College H.S. (Brownsville)
	2nd *Me for Ma: A Frontier for Women in Politics,* North Belton M.S. (Temple)	**2nd** *The Sky's the Limit: How the Mayo Clinic Aero Medical Unit Brought Military Aviation and Medicine to New Heights,* Health Careers H.S. (San Antonio)
Performances		
Individual	**1st** *Alexander Fleming and the Discovery of Penicillin,* Stillman M.S. (Brownsville)	**1st** *The Secret Weapon: How Radar Changed the Course of World War II,* I.M. Terrell Academy for STEM and VPA (Fort Worth)
	2nd *Hitchcock: The Making of Psycho and Pioneering Hollywood Cinema,* Odyssey Academy—Bay Area (League City)	**2nd** *Reporting Live: Integration in the States,* Nimitz H.S. (Humble)
Group	**1st** *Is There a Doctor in the House: The Tale of Dr. Sara Josephine Baker and Typhoid Mary,* Atlas Academy (Waco)	**1st** *A Reborn Nation: Exploring Post-Colonialism in Free Algeria,* Plano East S.R. H.S.
	2nd *Mission Impossible: Cabeza de Vaca y la Nueva Frontera,* Marathon	**2nd** *Falls and Frontiers,* Veterans Memorial Early College H.S. (Brownsville)
Websites		
Individual	**1st** *Nuclear Fission and the Atomic Bomb,* Austin Classical School (Austin)	**1st** *Power for the People: How LBJ Tamed the Frontiers of Texas Hill Country Electrification,* Dripping Springs
	2nd *The North Atlantic Treaty Organization: Uniting as a New Frontier,* E.F. Green Junior School (Baytown)	**2nd** *Reform and Opening-Up: Deng Xiaoping's Magnum Opus Pushes China's Economic Frontier,* Jasper H.S. (Plano)
Group	**1st** *The Light in the Darkness: The Frontier of Electrifying Rural America,* Livingston	**1st** *A Time for Greatness: JFK's New Frontier and a Revitalized America,* William B. Travis H.S. (Richmond)
	2nd *Project Echo—The Satellite That Changed the World,* Canyon Ridge M.S. (Austin)	**2nd** *The New American Women: From Flappers to Feminism,* New Caney
Papers		
Individual	**1st** *A "Social Frontier": Boy Scouts, Progressive Education and the Turner Thesis,* Lively M.S. (Austin)	**1st** *Frontiers in History: African Americans' Struggle for Equality,* Chaparral H.S. (Harker Heights)
	2nd *Booker T. Washington v. W.E.B. Du Bois: Frontiers in Black Upward Mobility, Civil Rights, and Economic Stability; Challenging Conventional Thinking in America,* E.F. Green Junior School (Baytown)	**2nd** *Reconstructing the Myth: The Transcontinental Railroad and the Chinese Laborers,* Westwood H.S. (Austin)

National History Day 2023

1st Place Junior Paper	**2nd Place** Senior Individual Exhibit	**2nd Place** Senior Individual Website
A "Social Frontier": Boy Scouts, Progressive Education and the Turner Thesis, Lively M.S. (Austin)	*Window to the Universe: How the Hubble Space Telescope Revolutionized the Study of Astronomy,* New Caney H.S.	*Power for the People: How LBJ Tamed the Frontiers of Texas Hill Country Electrification,* Dripping Springs H.S.

Colleges and Universities

Sources: Texas Higher Education Coordinating Board; highered.texas.gov; 2022-2023 Governor's Budget; "Summary of Higher Education Legislation: 87th Texas Legislature, 2021"; Legislative Budget Board, "Summary of 2020–21 Conference Committee Report for HB1"

Enrollment in Texas public, independent, career, and private colleges and universities in fall 2021 totaled 1,489,215 students, a decrease of 7,342 students, –0.5%, from the fall 2020 enrollment of 1,496,557.

Enrollment in fall 2021 in the 37 public universities was 665,213, a 0.3% decrease from 2020's enrollment of 667,046. Health-related institutions had enrollment in 2021 of 31,548, a 3.3% increase from fall 2020 (30,533).

The state's public community colleges and Texas State Technical College System, which offer two-year degree programs, reported fall 2021 enrollments totaling 665,364 students, a decrease of 1.2% from enrollment of 673,605 reported in fall 2020.

Enrollment for fall 2021 at independent and career colleges and universities was 126,607 students, up slightly from the 124,888 students enrolled in fall 2020.

Cost of Public Higher Education in Texas

	2-Year Schools (82)		4-Year Schools (37)	
	2019	2020	2019	2020
Average Tuition and Fees	$2,760	$2,772	$8,059	$9,844
Average Debt	$15,422	$15,625	$25,374	$25,101
% of Students with Debt	28.9%	28.5%	57.7%	56.4%

Brief History of Higher Education in Texas

The first permanent institutions of higher education established in Texas were church-supported schools, although there were some earlier efforts:

Rutersville University was established in 1840 by Methodist minister Martin Ruter in Fayette County and was the predecessor of Southwestern University in Georgetown, which was established in 1843; Baylor University, now at Waco, was established in 1845 at Independence, Washington County, by the Texas Union Baptist Association; and Austin College, now at Sherman, was founded in 1849 at Huntsville by the Brazos Presbytery of the Old School Presbyterian Church.

Other historic Texas schools of collegiate rank included:

Larissa College, 1848, at Larissa, Cherokee County; McKenzie College, 1841, Clarksville, Red River County; Chappell Hill Male and Female Institute, 1850, Chappell Hill, Washington County; Soule University, 1855, Chappell Hill; Johnson Institute, 1852, Driftwood, Hays County; Nacogdoches University, 1845, Nacogdoches; Salado College, 1859, Salado, Bell County.

Add-Ran College, established in 1873 at Thorp Spring, Hood County, was the predecessor of present-day Texas Christian University, Fort Worth.

Texas A&M University and The University of Texas

The Agricultural and Mechanical College of Texas (now Texas A&M University), authorized by the Legislature in 1871, opened its doors in 1876 to become the first publicly supported institution of higher education in Texas.

In 1881, Texans established The University of Texas in Austin, with a medical branch in Galveston. The Austin institution opened Sept. 15, 1883, and the Galveston school opened in 1891.

First College for Women

In 1901, the 27th Legislature established the Girls Industrial College, which began classes at its campus in Denton in 1903. A campaign to establish a state industrial college for women was led by the State Grange and Patrons of Husbandry.

A bill was signed into law on April 6, 1901, creating the college. It was charged with a dual mission, which continues to guide the university today, to provide a liberal arts education and to prepare young women with a specialized education "for the practical industries of the age."

In 1905, the name of the college was changed to the College of Industrial Arts; in 1934, it was changed to Texas State College for Women.

Since 1957, the institution, which is now the largest university principally for women in the United States, has been the Texas Woman's University.

Historic, Primarily Black Colleges

A number of Texas schools were established primarily for blacks, although collegiate racial integration has long been the status quo. Title III of the Higher Education Act of 1965 established the term Historically Black College/University (HBCU), defined as a school of higher learning that was established and accredited before the 1964 Civil Rights Act and was dedicated to educating African Americans.

Today there are nine HBCUs in Texas: state-supported Prairie View A&M University (originally established as Alta Vista Agricultural College in 1876), Prairie View; St. Philip's College, San Antonio; Texas Southern University, Houston; privately supported Huston-Tillotson University, Austin; Jarvis Christian College, Hawkins; Southwestern Christian College, Terrell; Wiley College, Marshall; Paul Quinn College, originally located in Waco, now in Dallas; and Texas College, Tyler.

Predominantly black colleges that are important in the history of higher education in Texas, but which have ceased operations, include Bishop College, established in Marshall in 1881, then moved to Dallas; Mary Allen College, established in Crockett in 1886; and Butler College, originally named the Texas Baptist Academy, in 1905 in Tyler.

Hispanic-Serving Institutions

Title V of the Higher Education Act of 2008 established grant programs for public colleges that qualify as

Hispanic-Serving Institutions (HSIs). An HSI is defined as a not-for-profit institution of higher learning with a full-time equivalent undergraduate student enrollment that is at least 25% Hispanic.

According to the Hispanic Association of Colleges & Universities, Texas has 63 HSIs, including many community colleges, operating today.

State Appropriations

The biennial All Funds budget for higher education totaled $22.5 billion for FY22–23, a decrease of 7.5% from the FY20–21 funding level ($24.3 billion). This amount represents about 8.9% of the total general revenue budget. This decrease is due to the Texas Department of Emergency Management's receipt of $2.7 billion in one-time COVID-19 federal funding in FY20-21.

The General Revenue budget for higher education increased from $14.9 billion in FY20-21 to $15.7 billion in FY22-23, an increase of approximately 5.3%. Rates for all of the higher education formulas were increased over the FY20-21 rates.

The general revenue funds increase includes:

- $175 million of pandemic-inspired Governor's Emergency Education Relief Fund (GEER) funding for student financial aid, improvements in online learning, and enhanced data infrastructure capabilities. This included $57 million to existing state financial aid programs, $46.5 million in emergency student support, $46.5 million in financial aid for upskilling and reskilling displaced workers, and $10 million to improve the quality of online learning;
- $62.2 million to recruit world-class researchers to Texas universities;
- $271.2 million for the Texas Guaranteed Tuition Program;
- $45 million to Texas A&M University at Galveston for dock and other infrastructure improvements;
- $110 million for TEXAS Grants, Tuition Equalization Grants, and Texas Equal Opportunity Grants;
- $48.6 million for Graduate Medical Education expansion, which maintains a 1.1 to 1 ratio of first-year residency positions to medical school graduates. ☆

Top 5 Undergrad Majors at Public Universities, 2020

1. Business, Management, Marketing, and Related Support Services (21,122 students)
2. Health Professions and Related Programs (11,885 students)
3. Multi/Interdisciplinary Studies (11,090 students)
4. Engineering (9,473 students)
5. Biological and Biomedical Sciences (7,517 students)

Source: Texas Public Higher Education Almanac 2020

Universities and Colleges

Sources: Texas Higher Education Coordinating Board (highered.texas.gov and txhighereddata.org) and individual institutions. Dates of establishment may differ from Brief History on page 594 because schools use the date when authorization was given rather than date of first classes.

Higher-Education Systems

System	Abbreviation	Location	Founded	Leader	Number of Faculty		Enrollment	
					2020	2021	Fall Term, 2020	Fall Term, 2021
Alamo Colleges District	ACD	San Antonio	1978	Dr. Mike Flores	2,108	2,063	68,319	63,999
Howard County Junior College District	HCJCD	Big Spring	1946	Dr. Cheryl T. Sparks	157	174	3,764	3,951
Lone Star College System	LSC	The Woodlands	1973	Dr. Stephen C. Head	3,496	3,351	70,694	72,036
Texas A&M University System	TAMUS	College Station	1948	Dr. John Sharp	7,023	10,080	152,200	151,824
Texas State University System	TSUS	Austin	1911	Dr. Brian McCall	3,920	3,965	87,084	86,442
Texas Tech University System	TTUS	Lubbock	1996	Dr. Tedd L. Mitchell	2,412	8,333	61,353	61,346
University of Houston System	UHS	Houston	1977	Dr. Renu Khator	3,475	3,453	76,283	75,525
University of North Texas System	UNTS	Dallas	1999	Dr. Michael R. Williams	1,964	4,285	47,146	48,810
University of Texas System	UTS	Austin	1883	Dr. James B. Milliken	44,513	40,678	258,699	242,533

Public Universities

Institution	System	Location	Founded	Leader	Number of Faculty		Enrollment	
					2020	2021	Fall Term, 2020	Fall Term, 2021
Angelo State University	TTUS	San Angelo	1928	Lt. Gen. Ret. Ronnie D. Hawkins Jr.	427	452	10,489	10,485
Dallas College	—	Dallas	1966	Dr. Justin Lonon	2,083	2,443	57,601	61,925
Lamar University	TSUS	Beaumont	1923	Dr. Jaime R. Taylor	570	558	15,799	15,687
Midwestern State University	TTUS	Wichita Falls	1922	Dr. Keith Lamb	347	346	5,387	5,387
Prairie View A&M University	TAMUS	Prairie View	1876	Dr. Tomikia P. LeGrande	474	491	9,248	9,353
Sam Houston State University	TSUS	Huntsville	1879	Dr. Alisa White	979	970	21,650	21,219
Stephen F. Austin State University	UTS	Nacogdoches	1923	Dr. Steve Westbrook	730	758	12,488	11,888
Sul Ross State University	TSUS	Alpine	1917	Dr. J. Carlos Hernández	119	138	1,557	1,485
Sul Ross State University Rio Grande College	TSUS	Del Rio	1973	Dr. Robert Muñoz	39	40	916	840
Tarleton State University	TAMUS	Stephenville	1899	Dr. James Hurley	712	683	14,022	13,995
Texas A&M International University	TAMUS	Laredo	1970	Dr. Pablo Arenaz	347	365	8,270	8,145
Texas A&M University	TAMUS	College Station	1876	General (Ret.) Mark A. Welsh III	2,594	2,507	65,272	66,057
Texas A&M University–Central Texas	TAMUS	Killeen	2009	Dr. Marc A. Nigliazzo	159	178	2,339	2,218
Texas A&M University–Commerce	TAMUS	Commerce	1889	Dr. Mark J. Rudin	536	557	11,624	10,966
Texas A&M University–Corpus Christi	TAMUS	Corpus Christi	1973	Dr. Kelly M. Miller	658	642	10,820	10,762
Texas A&M University at Galveston	TAMUS	Galveston	1962	Col. Michael E. Fossum USAFR Ret.	136	124	1,653	2,168
Texas A&M University–Kingsville	TAMUS	Kingsville	1925	Dr. Robert H. Vela Jr.	460	437	6,915	6,375
Texas A&M University–San Antonio	TAMUS	San Antonio	2009	Dr. Linda Schott	329	369	6,741	6,858
Texas A&M University–Texarkana	TAMUS	Texarkana	1971	Dr. Ross C. Alexander	163	177	2,161	2,078
Texas Southern University	—	Houston	1926	Dr. Mary Evans Sias	618	642	7,015	7,524
Texas State University	TSUS	San Marcos	1903	Dr. Kelly R. Damphousse	1,795	1,811	37,812	37,864
Texas Tech University	TTUS	Lubbock	1923	Dr. Lawrence Schovanec	1,638	1,632	39,574	39,451
Texas Woman's University	—	Denton	1901	Dr. Carine M. Feyten	941	894	16,032	15,828
University of Houston	UHS	Houston	1927	Dr. Renu Khator	2,079	2,050	47,060	46,971
University of Houston–Clear Lake	UHS	Houston	1974	Dr. Richard Walker	483	493	9,053	9,279
University of Houston–Downtown	UHS	Houston	1948	Dr. Loren J. Blanchard	711	697	15,239	15,077
University of Houston–Victoria	UHS	Victoria	1973	Dr. Robert K. "Bob" Glenn	202	213	4,931	4,198
University of North Texas	UNTS	Denton	1890	Dr. Neal J. Smatresk	1,691	1,688	40,653	42,168
University of North Texas at Dallas	UNTS	Dallas	2000	Robert Mong	273	268	4,164	4,186
University of Texas at Arlington, The	UTS	Arlington	1895	Dr. Jennifer Cowley	1,362	1,392	42,733	41,515
University of Texas at Austin, The	UTS	Austin	1883	Dr. Jay Hartzell	2,864	2,898	50,282	51,786
University of Texas at Dallas, The	UTS	Richardson	1961	Dr. Richard C. Benson	1,249	1,266	28,669	29,696
University of Texas at El Paso, The	UTS	El Paso	1913	Dr. Heather Wilson	1,056	1,081	24,867	24,003
University of Texas of the Permian Basin, The	UTS	Odessa	1969	Dr. Sandra K. Woodley	4,272	260	5,530	5,043
University of Texas Rio Grande Valley, The	UTS	Edinburg	1973	Dr. Guy Bailey	1,358	1,419	32,220	31,718

Institution	System	Location	Founded	Leader	Number of Faculty		Enrollment	
					2020	2021	Fall Term, 2020	Fall Term, 2021
University of Texas at San Antonio, The	UTS	San Antonio	1969	Dr. Taylor Eighmy	1,306	1,314	34,402	34,177
University of Texas at Tyler, The	UTS	Tyler	1971	Dr. Kirk A. Calhoun	458	460	9,408	9,218
West Texas A&M University	TAMUS	Canyon	1910	Dr. Walter Wendler	455	466	10,051	9,545

Independent Senior Colleges or Universities

Institution	Location	Founded	Affiliation	Leader	Enrollment	
					Fall Term, 2021	Fall Term, 2022
Abilene Christian University	Abilene	1906	Church of Christ	Dr. Phil Schubert	4,863	4,920
Amberton University	Garland, Frisco	1971	Evangelical Christianity	Dr. Melinda H. Reagan	1,102	803
Arlington Baptist University	Arlington	1939	Baptist	Dr. Clifton McDaniel	—	—
Austin College	Sherman	1849	Presbyterian USA	Dr. Steven P. O'Day	1,302	1,228
Baylor University	Waco	1845	Southern Baptist	Dr. Linda A. Livingstone	19,297	20,626
Concordia University Texas	Austin	1926	Lutheran Church–Missouri Synod	Dr. Donald Christian	2,259	2,216
Criswell College	Dallas	1971	Baptist	Dr. Barry Creamer	—	—
Dallas Baptist University	Dallas	1898	Baptist	Dr. Adam C. Wright	4,247	4,366
Dallas Christian College	Dallas	1950	Christian	Dr. Brian D. Smith	—	—
East Texas Baptist University	Marshall	1913	Baptist	Dr. J. Blair Blackburn	1,777	1,764
Hardin-Simmons University	Abilene	1891	Southern Baptist	Eric I. Bruntmyer	2,132	1,933
Houston Christian University	Houston	1960	Baptist	Dr. Robert B. Sloan Jr.	3,963	4,120
Howard Payne University	Brownwood	1889	Baptist	Dr. Cory Hines	1,062	912
Huston-Tillotson University	Austin	1952	United Church of Christ and United Methodist	Dr. Melva K. Williams	1,070	1,001
Jarvis Christian College	Hawkins	1912	Disciples of Christ	Dr. Lester Newman	627	721
LeTourneau University	Longview	1946	Evangelical Christianity	Dr. Dale A. Lunsford	2,860	2,940
Lubbock Christian University	Lubbock	1957	Church of Christ	Dr. Scott McDowell	1,664	1,661
McMurry University	Abilene	1923	United Methodist	Dr. Sandra S. Harper	1,094	1,145
Our Lady of the Lake University of San Antonio	San Antonio	1895	Roman Catholic	Dr. Abel Antonio Chávez	2,771	2,550
Paul Quinn College	Dallas	1872	African Methodist Episcopal Church	Dr. Michael J. Sorrell	468	382
Rice University	Houston	1891	—	Dr. Reginald DesRoches	7,546	8,170
St. Edward's University	Austin	1885	Roman Catholic	Dr. Montserrat Fuentes	3,591	3,577
St. Mary's University of San Antonio	San Antonio	1852	Roman Catholic	Dr. Thomas J. Mengler J.D.	2,748	3,419
Schreiner University	Kerrville	1923	Presbyterian U.S.A.	Dr. Charlie McCormick	1,244	1,103
Southern Methodist University	Dallas	1911	United Methodist	Dr. R. Gerald Turner	12,373	12,385
South Texas College of Law	Houston	1923	—	Michael F. Barry	999	975
Southwestern Adventist University	Keene	1893	Seventh-Day Adventist	Dr. Ken Shaw	768	867
Southwestern Assemblies of God University	Waxahachie	1927	Assemblies of God	Dr. Kermit S. Bridges	2,003	1,573
Southwestern Christian College	Terrell	1948	Church of Christ	Dr. Ervin D. Seamster Jr.	80	115
Southwestern University	Georgetown	1840	United Methodist	Dr. Laura Skandera Trombley	1,505	1,500
Texas Christian University	Fort Worth	1873	Disciples of Christ	Dr. Victor J. Boschini Jr.	11,328	11,878
Texas College	Tyler	1894	Christian Methodist Episcopal	Dr. Dwight J. Fennell	763	737
Texas Lutheran University	Seguin	1891	Evangelical Lutheran	Dr. Debbie Cottrell	1,498	1,435
Texas Wesleyan University	Fort Worth	1891	United Methodist	Dr. Frederick G. Slabach	2,495	2,603
Trinity University	San Antonio	1869	Presbyterian U.S.A.	Dr. Vanessa B. Beasley	2,677	2,745

Institution	Location	Founded	Affiliation	Leader	Enrollment	
					Fall Term, 2021	Fall Term, 2022
University of Dallas	Irving	1956	Roman Catholic	Dr. Jonathan J. Sanford	2,489	2,538
University of the Incarnate Word	San Antonio	1881	Roman Catholic	Dr. Thomas M. Evans	7,103	6,891
University of Mary Hardin-Baylor	Belton	1845	Baptist	Dr. Randy O'Rear	3,876	3,732
University of St. Thomas	Houston	1947	Roman Catholic	Dr. Richard Ludwick	3,681	3,848
Wayland Baptist University	Plainview	1910	Southern Baptist	Dr. Bobby Hall	2,957	2,563
Wiley College	Marshall	1873	United Methodist	Dr. Herman J. Felton Jr.	606	665

Public Medical School or Health Science Center

Institution	System	Location	Founded	Leader	Enrollment	
					Fall Term, 2020	Fall Term, 2021
Sam Houston State University Medical School	—	Conroe	2019	Dr. Thomas Mohr	75	185
Texas A&M University Health Science Center	TAMUS	Bryan	1948	Dr. Jon Mogford	3,084	3,304
Texas Tech University Health Sciences Center	TTUS	Lubbock	1972	Dr. Lori Rice-Spearman	5,128	5,238
Texas Tech University Health Sciences Center El Paso	TTUS	El Paso	2013	Dr. Richard Lange	775	785
University of Houston Medical School	UHS	Houston	2019	Dr. Stephen J. Spann	30	60
University of North Texas Health Science Center at Fort Worth	UNTS	Fort Worth	1966	Dr. Michael R. Williams	2,329	2,456
University of Texas at Austin Dell Medical School	UTS	Austin	2012	Dr. Clay Johnston	194	197
University of Texas Health Science Center at Houston, The	UTS	Houston	1972	Dr. Giuseppe N. Colasurdo	5,611	5,758
University of Texas Health Science Center at San Antonio, The	UTS	San Antonio	1968	Dr. William L. Henrich	3,439	3,463
University of Texas M.D. Anderson Cancer Center, The	UTS	Houston	1941	Dr. Peter W.T. Pisters	376	358
University of Texas Medical Branch at Galveston, The	UTS	Galveston	1891	Dr. Charles P. Mouton	3,398	3,377
University of Texas Rio Grande Valley Medical School	UTS	Edinburg	2013	Dr. Michael B. Hocker	221	222

Institution	System	Location	Founded	Leader	Enrollment	
					Fall Term, 2020	Fall Term, 2021
University of Texas Southwestern Medical Center, The	UTS	Dallas	1943	Dr. Daniel K. Podolsky	2,299	2,308
University of Texas at Tyler Health Science Center, The	UTS	Tyler	1971	Dr. Kirk A. Calhoun	88	113

Independent Medical, Dental, or Chiropractic School

Institution	Location	Founded	Leader	Enrollment	
				Fall Term, 2021	Fall Term, 2022
Baylor College of Medicine	Houston	1903	Dr. Paul Klotman	1,596	1,586
Parker University	Dallas	1982	Dr. William E. Morgan	1,653	1,880
Texas Chiropractic College	Pasadena	1908	Dr. Stephen A. Foster	255	258

Public Community Colleges

Institution	System	Location	Founded	Leader	Number of Faculty		Enrollment	
					2020	2021	Fall Term, 2020	Fall Term, 2021
Alamo Colleges—Northeast Lakeview College	ACD	Universal City	2007	Dr. Veronica Garcia	160	189	6,657	6,704
Alamo Colleges—Northwest Vista College	ACD	San Antonio	1995	Ms. Debi Gaitan	544	532	18,542	16,604
Alamo Colleges—Palo Alto College	ACD	San Antonio	1983	Dr. Robert Garza	269	270	11,193	10,559
Alamo Colleges—St. Philip's College	ACD	San Antonio	1898	Dr. Adena Williams Loston	447	441	12,696	12,455
Alamo Colleges—San Antonio College	ACD	San Antonio	1925	Dr. Naydeen González-De Jesús	688	631	19,231	17,677
Alvin Community College	—	Alvin	1949	Dr. Robert Exley	323	329	5,591	4,970
Amarillo College	—	Amarillo	1929	Denese Skinner	402	412	9,102	9,140
Angelina College	—	Lufkin	1968	Dr. Michael J. Simon	265	243	4,073	4,249
Austin Community College	—	Austin	1972	Dr. Russell Lowery-Hart	1,886	1,922	36,868	32,890
Blinn College	—	Brenham	1883	Dr. Mary Hensley	665	697	17,955	17,077
Brazosport College	—	Lake Jackson	1967	Dr. Vincent R. Solis	180	179	3,829	3,914
Central Texas College	—	Killeen	1965	Dr. Jim Yeonopolus	582	575	7,649	6,641
Cisco College	—	Cisco	1909	Dr. Thad J. Anglin	179	187	3,251	3,090
Clarendon College	—	Clarendon	1898	Texas D. Buckhaults	74	73	1,417	1,401
Coastal Bend College	—	Beeville	1966	Dr. Justin Hoggard	183	184	4,105	3,927
College of the Mainland	—	Texas City	1967	Dr. Warren Nichols	263	258	4,335	4,133
Collin County Community College District	—	McKinney	1985	Dr. H. Neil Matkin	1,408	1,461	34,491	32,603
Del Mar College	—	Corpus Christi	1935	Dr. Mark Escamilla	517	513	10,678	10,395
El Paso Community College	—	El Paso	1969	Dr. William Serrata	1,234	1,269	25,303	23,824
Frank Phillips College	—	Borger	1948	Dr. Glendon Forgey	89	82	1,540	1,583
Galveston College	—	Galveston	1967	Dr. W. Myles Shelton	96	105	2,060	1,870
Grayson College	—	Denison	1963	Dr. Jeremy McMillen	202	207	4,032	3,865
Hill College	—	Hillsboro	1923	Dr. Thomas Mills	203	196	4,038	3,826
Houston Community College	—	Houston	1971	Dr. Cesar Maldonado	2,296	2,358	38,020	38,861
Howard College	HCJCD	Big Spring	1945	Dr. Cheryl T. Sparks	140	157	3,696	3,895
Kilgore College	—	Kilgore	1935	Dr. Cory Hines	256	260	5,089	5,081
Lamar Institute of Technology	TSUS	Beaumont	1923	Dr. Sidney Valentine	183	202	4,402	4,470
Lamar State College–Orange	TSUS	Orange	1969	Dr. Thomas Johnson	112	116	2,382	2,353
Lamar State College–Port Arthur	TSUS	Port Arthur	1909	Dr. Betty J. Reynard	123	130	2,566	2,524
Laredo College	—	Laredo	1947	Dr. Minita Ramirez	264	285	5,236	9,968
Lee College	—	Baytown	1934	Dr. Lynda Villanueva	388	361	4,271	7,159
Lone Star College–CyFair	LSC	Houston	2003	Dr. Valerie Jones	897	870	20,559	19,930
Lone Star College–Houston North	LSC	The Woodlands	2017	Dr. Stephen C. Head	—	—	1,875	2,094
Lone Star College–Kingwood	LSC	Humble	1984	Dr. Melissa N. Gonzalez	513	500	10,372	10,272

Institution	System	Location	Founded	Leader	Number of Faculty		Enrollment	
					2020	2021	Fall Term, 2020	Fall Term, 2021
Lone Star College–Montgomery	LSC	Conroe	1995	Dr. Rebecca L. Riley	597	617	13,269	13,226
Lone Star College–North Harris	LSC	Houston	1973	Dr. Archie L. Blanson	651	555	10,125	9,891
Lone Star College–Tomball	LSC	Tomball	1986	Dr. Lee Ann Nutt	343	346	5,763	6,731
Lone Star College–University Park	LSC	Houston	2012	Dr. Shah Ardalan	495	463	8,731	9,892
McLennan Community College	—	Waco	1965	Dr. Johnette McKown	422	426	7,742	7,329
Midland College	—	Midland	1972	Dr. Steve Thomas	255	244	4,763	5,045
Navarro College	—	Corsicana	1946	Dr. Kevin G. Fegan	417	366	7,065	6,456
North Central Texas College	—	Gainesville	1924	Dr. Brent Wallace	445	432	8,191	7,574
Northeast Texas Community College	—	Mount Pleasant	1984	Dr. Ron Clinton	163	163	2,758	2,823
Odessa College	—	Odessa	1946	Dr. Gregory Williams	261	291	6,978	7,943
Panola College	—	Carthage	1947	Dr. Gregory S. Powell	141	140	2,529	2,475
Paris Junior College	—	Paris	1924	Dr. Pamela Anglin	178	184	4,386	4,297
Ranger College	—	Ranger	1926	Derrick Worrells	135	136	2,304	2,262
San Jacinto College	—	Pasadena, La Porte, Houston	1961	Dr. Brenda Lang Hellyer	1,296	1,210	31,110	31,577
South Plains College	—	Levelland	1957	Dr. Robin Satterwhite	369	371	8,867	8,925
South Texas College	—	McAllen	1993	Dr. Ricardo Solis	1,119	1,140	27,710	28,184
Southwest Collegiate Institute for the Deaf	HCJCD	Big Spring	1979	Dr. Cheryl T. Sparks	17	17	68	56
Southwest Texas Junior College	—	Uvalde	1946	Dr. Hector Gonzales	219	231	6,376	5,594
Tarrant County College	—	Fort Worth	1965	Dr. Elva Concha LeBlanc	2,440	2,416	43,000	36,264
Temple College	—	Temple	1926	Dr. Christy Ponce	230	216	4,507	3,959
Texarkana College	—	Texarkana	1927	Dr. Jason Smith	213	201	3,810	3,573
Texas Southmost College	—	Brownsville	1926	Dr. Jesús Roberto Rodriguez	248	277	8,777	7,527
Texas State Technical College	—	Waco	1965	Dr. Michael L. Reeser	601	612	13,756	16,471
Trinity Valley Community College	—	Athens	1946	Dr. Jason Morrison	266	288	5,673	5,426
Tyler Junior College	—	Tyler	1926	Dr. L. Michael Metke	589	609	11,726	11,898
Vernon College	—	Vernon	1970	Dr. Dusty R. Johnston	142	148	2,773	2,358
Victoria College	—	Victoria	1925	Dr. Jennifer Kent	191	180	3,212	3,125
Weatherford College	—	Weatherford	1869	Dr. Tod Allen Farmer	309	304	5,390	5,645
Western Texas College	—	Snyder	1969	Dr. Barbara Beebe	81	83	1,442	1,430
Wharton County Junior College	—	Wharton	1946	Dr. Betty A. McCrohan	289	301	6,099	5,479

Independent Junior Colleges

Institution	Location	Affiliation	Founded	Leader	Enrollment	
					Fall Term, 2021	Fall Term, 2022
Jacksonville College	Jacksonville	Baptist Missionary Alliance	1899	Dr. John Mann	485	483

BUSINESS

TEXAS: THE ENERGY STATE

ECONOMY & EMPLOYMENT

BANKING, INSURANCE, CONSTRUCTION

COMMERCIAL FISHING & TOURISM

ELECTRIC GRIDS, OIL, GAS

MINERALS & MEDIA

TEXAS: THE ENERGY STATE

by Nora Ankrum

TEXAS ENERGY

WHERE WE STARTED . . .

AND WHERE WE ARE TODAY

Texas' first major oil discovery was an accident.

In 1894, drillers looking for water in Corsicana found black gold instead, and Texas' first boom town was born (Davenport, 2014). The petroleum industry, well into its fourth decade, was already established and flourishing outside Texas (Yergin, 1991). Concentrated in the Northeast, the industry was driven largely by demand for kerosene — a fuel used for lighting in the era before electrification. John D. Rockefeller had already built his Standard Oil empire and was, in fact, soon to retire (Poole, n.d.). Ohio that year produced more than 16 million barrels of oil (Weeks, 1895).

By contrast, Texas produced 60 barrels that year, according to the 1894–1895 annual report of the U.S. Geological Survey. In 1896, Corsicana produced 1,450 barrels, enough to flood Texas' limited market, which lacked infrastructure for processing and transporting large quantities of oil (Smith, 1952). Stuck with product they could not sell, producers were sometimes forced to discard it, simply pouring the precious liquid on the ground. Remote, largely undeveloped, and punishingly hot, Texas seemed an unlikely competitor in the oil game. Texas' geological advantages remained largely a mystery at the time. Most people did not yet understand that salt domes, plentiful along the Gulf Coast, often hid enormous pockets of oil underneath (Miller, 2021).

In 1901, the discovery of oil just south of Beaumont — at "the Hill," a salt dome known to smell of sulfur — changed everything (Yergin, 1991). Shooting 100 feet into the air, the gusher on the Hill, thereafter known as Spindletop, was unlike anything before it (Ramos, 2000; House, 1946). Flowing at an estimated rate of nearly 100,000 barrels a day, it produced more than the combined output of all U.S. oil wells at that time and introduced a new era of oil discovery throughout the Southwest (History.com Editors, 2019; Yergin, 1991). Befitting its name, Spindletop spun the industry in a new direction, ultimately pulling it, like a golden thread, to Texas — where it remains tightly wound to this day.

Ill-suited for kerosene, Texas oil was considered poor quality (Yergin, 1991). But at the dawn of the automobile age, the plentiful crude now found in Texas' Gulf Coast oil fields proved well-suited to the new gas-powered engines that had entered the American market (Library of Congress, n.d.). Rapid growth of the automobile industry catapulted Texas hydrocarbons to the center of modern life, not just in the mundane affairs of households and businesses but in the balance of world power. In World War I, the Allies were said to have "floated to victory upon a wave of oil" (Yergin, 1991, p. 167) as cars, trucks, tanks, and planes were deployed into battle for the first time. Oil proved indispensable in World War II, during which the U.S. produced about 60% of global supply (Martin, 2018). Many petroleum industry workers were exempted from the draft as the U.S. dramatically increased oil production to keep pace with demand, and 80% of that increase came from Texas. In total, Texas went from producing 34% of U.S. oil in 1942 to 44% in 1945 (Railroad Commission of Texas, n.d.; U.S. Energy Information Administration, 2023, August).

ELECTRICITY COMES TO TEXAS

Along with the automobile, another invention — the lightbulb — redefined Americans' relationship to energy. Together, these two innovations spurred massive infrastructure projects that Americans still depend on today: roadways and highways, power plants, and electric distribution systems. In Texas, electrification drove economic expansion alongside growth of the oil industry. Galveston was the first Texas city to build an electric power plant and, in 1883, install electric lighting (Anonymous, 1976; Minton, 2020). Known as the Wall Street of the Southwest, Galveston was among the wealthiest U.S. cities per capita at the time (Hartman, 1995; Burka, 1983). The country's first central power plant, the coal-fired Pearl Street Station in Manhattan, had begun operation only the year before (M. W., 2014).

Santa Rita #1 sat atop the first well to produce oil on University Lands, the 2 million acres of West Texas scrub set aside by the Texas Legislature in 1876 to support The University of Texas.

Prints and Photographs Collection, di_02266, The Dolph Briscoe Center for American History, The University of Texas at Austin

As cities electrified, rural areas lagged behind, mirroring a pattern of disparity that persists globally today (Wallace, 2016). Currently, 13% of the world lacks access to electricity, a critical component of human development and wellbeing (Ritchie & Roser, 2022). At the dawn of the 20th century, 60% of Americans lived in rural areas, as did most Texans (83%) (U.S. Census Bureau, 1995; Barr, 1995). The electric grid — what we understand today as a system of interconnected transmission lines that conduct electricity from power plants to consumers — was in its infancy. Power companies that built transmission lines were reluctant to invest in rural areas, considering the costs too high (Malone, n.d.). By the 1930s, only 10% of American farms had electricity; in Texas, the percentage was just 2.3% (Davis, 1976). Where utilities did provide service, such as in San Marcos and Kerrville, they often sold electricity at exorbitant prices (Bryce, 2020).

President Franklin D. Roosevelt viewed the situation as a crisis. "Electricity is a modern necessity of life, not a luxury," he declared (The American Presidency Project, n.d.). Texas Congressman Sam Rayburn, citing the plight of the "unwilling servants of the washtub and water pump" in his home state, helped develop federal legislation to address the problem (Anderson, n.d.). His Rayburn-Wheeler Act, also known as the Public Utility Holding Company Act of 1935 (PUHCA), helped prevent electric utilities from engaging in harmful business practices like price inflation. Rayburn also helped create a separate piece of Roosevelt's New Deal, the Rural Electrification Act (REA) of 1936. The law, which supported electrification projects through low-interest loans, helped spur a dramatic expansion in access to electric power. By the time Rayburn died in 1961, 97% of rural American farms had electricity (Thompson, 2016).

Too sparsely populated to meet REA requirements, the Texas Hill Country nearly missed out on this opportunity (Kelly, 2007). Long before he would become president, Lyndon B. Johnson, campaigning for Congress in 1937, played a pivotal role in bringing electric power to the region. Going door to door, he persuaded Hill Country farmers to join the newly formed Pedernales Electric Cooperative (PEC). Today, visitors to the Johnson City headquarters of the PEC — now the largest electric cooperative in the U.S. — can read on a state historical marker what happened next: After failing to persuade the head of the REA to loan funds to the PEC, Johnson lobbied Roosevelt himself (Anderson, 2018). Convinced, Roosevelt directed the REA to loan the PEC $3.3 million, enough money to build more than 1,700 miles of power lines. It would be the administration's largest-ever allotment (Pedernales Electric Cooperative, n.d.).

Rayburn and Johnson both would later cite their contributions to rural electrification among their proudest achievements (Anderson, n.d.; Kelly, 2007). Texas, being largely rural, was well-positioned to benefit from the New Deal's electricity reforms. These policies enabled a rapid improvement in living standards, helping lay the groundwork for American prosperity in the years after World War II and shift economic and political power to favor development of western and southern states (Bryce, 2020). Farmers saw huge productivity gains through access to refrigeration, milking machines, food processing equipment, and other innovations enabled by electrification (Bryce, 2020; Lewis & Severnini, 2020).

President Franklin D. Roosevelt (center) signs the Rural Electrification Act with Representative John E. Rankin (left) and Senator George W. Norris (right) on May 13, 1935.

Photo by the U.S. Government, Public Domain

Electrification also paved the way for air-conditioning, without which "the Sunbelt as we know it would not exist," writes Daniel Yergin in *The Quest* (2011, p. 634). Air conditioners evolved quickly from a luxury to a necessity in southern cities like Houston, proclaimed for many years to be "the air-conditioning capital of the world" (Gray, 2012; Rimer, 1998). Air-conditioning, writes Yergin, "made it possible for Houston to shed the indolent, oppressive swampy mugginess of its summer and become the 'oil capital of the world' and, eventually, the fourth-largest U.S. city" (Yergin, 2011, p. 634).

HOUSTON CHARGES IN

Today, Houston is more commonly described as the "energy" capital, reflecting its diversification into virtually every aspect of the energy industry, including alternatives to oil and gas (Greater Houston Partnership, n.d.). Driven by innovation and the imperative to address the challenges of climate change, the global energy system is undergoing dramatic change. To put a finer point on the message that Houston is changing with it, city leaders have sought in recent years to further revise Houston's moniker to "energy transition" capital of the world (Houston Energy Transition Initiative, 2022). According to energy executive Bobby Tudor, chair of the Houston Energy Transition Initiative (HETI), the oil and gas industry isn't going away, but it is "not likely to be the same engine for growth" as in the past (Mistretta, 2021).

This careful reframing reflects the strength of the oil and gas industry's deep ties not just to Texas' economy but its image and identity. Texas occupies a unique place in the popular imagination, in no small part because of oil. As Texas journalist Lawrence Wright has said, "Everyone in the world has an impression of Texas" (Cruz, 2018). A proliferation of Hollywood Westerns in the 1930s and 1940s helped to shape this impression, dramatizing the life of the Texas cowboy. Meanwhile, a different drama unfolded beyond Hollywood's gaze. Texas' first generation of oil tycoons was full of larger-than-life characters who left humble beginnings behind when they made good in the oil patch (Burrough, 2009). They tossed silver dollars at passersby, bought their own islands, and hosted parties that lasted for days — and they leveraged their considerable wealth to establish Texas' influence on the national stage.

As Bryan Burrough recounts in *The Big Rich* (2009), future President Lyndon B. Johnson began his political ascent in this era, aided in part by cash from Texas oilmen. Also during this time, Houston's business elite began lobbying, successfully, for federal policies to support the petroleum industry, and Texas oil billionaire Roy Cullen began sending cash to far-flung election campaigns outside Texas. In the 1952 presidential election season, he was the single largest American donor. Burrough writes that this election marked "the dawning of a new age, one in which American political power, heretofore centered in the Northeast, began to flow... into the West and the Southwest, especially to Texas" (p. 220).

People outside the state remained largely unaware of Texas' wealth until 1948, when a pair of articles in *Fortune* and *Life* magazines explored "a new crop of super rich" composed of milkmen, dry cleaners, and farmers turned multimillionaires (Burrough, 2009; LIFE, 1948, p. 23). The April 5 issue of *Life*, featuring a surreptitiously snapped photo of oilman H.L. Hunt — with the caption "Is this the richest man in the U.S.?" — changed Texas' image practically overnight. According to Burrough, "the story of Texas Oil... can be divided into halves, the anonymity of the pre-1948 years, and everything after" (2009, p. 166).

Americans thereafter would prove endlessly fascinated with Texas oil wealth — a notion now superimposed on the image of the Texas cowboy — which inspired countless writers and journalists to travel to the state and dissect its mystique. Notably, the Texas story — with its themes of excess, swagger, and rugged independence — became so ingrained in the public consciousness that David Jacobs, the L.A.-based creator of the wildly popular TV show *Dallas*, did not even visit the state before shooting the pilot episode (though he had once driven through it on a camping trip many years prior). "When I got down there, I realized I'd really been writing *Houston*," he later told *Texas Monthly* reporter Max Marshall. "Houston was the oil town; I didn't know that Dallas was the banking town" (Marshall, 2018). Premiering in April 1978, *Dallas* featured famously outlandish plotlines about a family of Texas oil billionaires, including the scheming anti-hero J.R. Ewing. The show became a worldwide pop culture phenomenon, broadcasting in more than 130 countries (Britannica, n.d.).

"WITS AND GUMPTION"

Although cautionary of the dangers of excess, the archetypal story of Texas oil wealth has an innate rags-to-riches appeal. In theory, anyone with "wits and gumption" (Gold, 2023) could strike it rich in the oil patch. But in reality, not everyone had this opportunity. At Spindletop, the only jobs available to members of Beaumont's Black community "were the kinds of lowly labor tangential to the process of oil production and therefore shut out of its profits" (Bohne, n.d.). Discrimination persisted as the industry expanded and professionalized. In the post-Depression era, job opportunities for minorities in Gulf Coast refineries were rare and limited largely to the lowest-paying positions; promotions to skilled positions were not accompanied by the pay raises and new job classifications afforded to white workers (Zamora, 1992). Edna Ferber was one of many midcentury writers drawn to Texas. In 1952, her novel *Giant* — later made into a film featuring James Dean as Jett Rink, a Texas ranch hand turned oil tycoon — was unusual in that it shed light on racism toward Mexican Americans in Texas (Agresta, 2018, Castillo, 2015).

Today, racial disparities can be found throughout the energy system. Reflective of national trends, people of color in Texas experience energy poverty (difficulties meeting their energy needs) at higher than average rates (American Council for an Energy-Efficient Economy, 2020; Drehobl, Ross & Ayala, 2020; Southeast Energy Efficiency Alliance & Texas Energy Poverty Research Institute, 2023). At the same time, they are more likely to work and live in fenceline communities (communities near polluting commercial facilities such as power plants and refineries) and to be exposed to health risks associated with pollutants from oil and gas facilities (Fleishman & Franklin, 2017; Kowalski, 2019; The Source, 2022; U.S. Environmental Protection Agency, n.d.-b).

Known as the "father of environmental justice" for his pioneering research and advocacy in this field, Robert Bullard, a distinguished professor at Texas Southern University, has been instrumental in raising awareness of racial disparities both nationally and in Texas, particularly in Gulf Coast communities with a high concentration of

U.S. theatrical poster for the film Giant *(1956).*

Poster designed by Bill Gold, Image in the Public Domain

A BRIEF HISTORY OF WIND POWER

Before the oil rig, there was the windmill. Used to pump clean water from aquifers below ground, windmills were once a central feature of Texas life, particularly in the arid West (Galbraith & Price, 2013). Recounting regional folk expressions in his 1931 book *The Great Plains*, Texas historian Walter Prescott Webb wrote "no woman should live in this country who cannot climb a windmill tower or shoot a gun" (p. 320).

The use of wind energy dates back to ancient times. As early as 5000 BCE, people were harnessing the wind to sail boats along the Nile River (U.S. Energy Information Administration, n.d.-b). Windmills first appeared in China and the Middle East around 200 BCE, where they were used for pumping water and milling grain. Estimated to be 1,000 years old, ancient Persian windmills used for grinding flour are still operating in Iran today (Carter, 2017).

Left: Settlers moving west relied on windmills like this for clean water.

Right: Today's wind turbines generate electricity that is transmitted to consumers across the state.

America's early settlers were familiar with windmills from Europe, where the technology had been in use since the Middle Ages (Welborn, 1976; Lienhard, n.d.). However, European designs proved ill-suited to conditions on the Great Plains, rendering much of this vast western territory — dubbed the Great American Dessert — unfit for cultivation (Welborn, 1976; Ross, 2018). In Texas' sparsely settled West, locals would convey the region's unforgiving conditions through the ominous names they gave its features: Bone Springs, Devil's Den, Robber's Roost (Alexander, 1975). Without windmills to pump water from underground, settlers made due living near creeks and rivers or relying on water wells, from which water would be hauled one bucket at a time.

Things changed in 1854, with the invention of an American windmill that could turn direction to face the wind (Galbraith & Price, 2013). A popular item in mail-order catalogues, this new model spread across the West, where it was "often among a homesteader's most prized possessions" (National Park Service, n.d.). As Kate Galbraith and Asher Price recount in their book, *The Great Texas Wind Rush*, Texas dominated the U.S. windmill market. Both rural and city dwellers depended on windmills for clean drinking water. Before it became an oil and gas hub, Midland had so many windmills it was known as Windmill Town (Leffler, 1952).

Windmills bolstered the Texas economy by enabling the westward expansion of ranching and small-scale farming, allowing access to clean water in environs otherwise inhospitable to cattle and crops (Galbraith & Price, 2013). Windmills also supported the westward expansion of the railroad, providing a means of sourcing the clean water locomotives needed to generate steam. Railroad expansion in turn helped Houston to evolve, by the 1890s, into the "Manchester of America" — home to more rail lines than any other U.S. city at the time (Klineberg, 2020, p. 18). These railways were so emblematic of Houston's early ambitions that the city's official seal today still features a locomotive (not an oil rig) in the center.

The locomotive, along with the commercial activity and acumen it facilitated, was instrumental in preparing Houston to take advantage of the Texas oil boom. By the time oil was discovered at Spindletop in 1901, "Houston was prepared to extract, refine, and ship [it] to all corners of the earth," writes Stephen L. Klineberg in *Prophetic City*. "Houston had the lumber for the oil barrels, the banks with the money, the railroads, and the infrastructure" (p. 22).

In the early 20th century, rural Texans began using windmill technology to generate modest amounts of electricity for nighttime lighting and listening to the radio (Galbraith & Price, 2013). "Wind chargers" could be found in mail-order catalogues, but many people built their own, particularly in the post-World War I years, which gave rise to clever new designs inspired by aircraft propellers (p. 34). Most cities had centralized power systems by this time, but rural Texans were left to fend for themselves until the New Deal legislation of the 1930s expanded access to electricity. Windmills, once so common on the Texas landscape, gradually disappeared after that. However, they have since staged a comeback. Today, Texas has 18,552 active wind turbines producing electricity, with more on the way (Hoen et al., 2023; Kennedy, 2023).

Author's Note: I'd like to give a special thanks to Kate Galbraith and Asher Price and their book The Great Texas Wind Rush: How George Bush, Ann Richards, and a Bunch of Tinkerers Helped the Oil and Gas State Win the Race to Wind Power, *which informed much of this section.*

Black and Hispanic households and petrochemical refineries (Buckley, 2022; Bullard & Hadayia, 2022; Mock, 2017). This work has paved the way for federal policies and funding to ensure that as the energy system changes, the benefits are shared equitably and vulnerable groups are protected (The White House, n.d.).

In 2021, the Department of Energy (DOE) appointed Shalanda Baker to be the first-ever deputy director for energy justice (U.S. Department of Energy, 2021). Growing up in Texas, Baker experienced energy disparities first-hand (Baker, 2021). In her mother's Austin apartment, winters were cold; she and her sister "layered on blankets and clothing" to stay warm at night; in the summer, the family escaped to the library to stay cool. Meanwhile, her father worked in the energy industry in Port Arthur. It was a good living, she says; but in the housing project where he lived, separated by only a metal fence from one of the world's largest oil refineries, his community lived with daily exposure to industrial pollution. In her new role at the DOE, Baker will be working to make sure marginalized communities have access to the benefits of clean energy technologies and have a voice in major decisions that affect them, such as siting of large-scale energy facilities (U.S. Department of Energy, 2021).

LAND OF BOOMS, BUSTS, AND PLOT TWISTS

By the time *Dallas* premiered in 1978, a fundamental shift was underway. H. L. Hunt and many of his contemporaries were now gone, replaced by a new, "dull" breed of super-rich — "a parade of pedestrian types who have cornered the market on faucets and tire treads," lamented *Texas Monthly* writer Bill Porterfield (1975, p. 64). Into this void stepped the colorful Ewings. But as J.R.'s star rose, U.S. oil production fell, reversing a century of steady growth (U.S. Energy Information Administration, 2023, August; Railroad Commission of Texas, n.d.). Meanwhile, supply disruptions from the Middle East drove fuel shortages, spiked prices, shocked the economy, and painfully demonstrated the downsides of oil dependence (Corbett, 2013; Graefe, 2013). For the first time, the U.S. did not have the spare capacity to compensate for a shortfall (Ross, 2013).

Inspiring new policies to support conservation, efficiency, and research, the crisis helped lay the groundwork for energy innovations that would later emerge (Breakthrough Staff, 2012; Ross, 2013). But it also set the stage for a brutal oil bust. In Texas, high oil prices created overnight millionaires, triggered a drilling spree among independent producers, and fueled construction of new housing and high-rises (Livingston, 2020). But eventually, the market adjusted: Demand for oil gradually subsided, global supply rose, and in 1986, oil prices took a dramatic plunge when Saudi Arabia and some of its neighbors, after several years of curtailing output, increased production (Gately, Adelman, & Griffin, 1986).

Price volatility has been a signature feature of the oil market since its earliest days. Spindletop's boom gave way to a bust when overproduction drove oil prices too low for producers to recoup their costs, echoing the experiences of Pennsylvania drillers 30 years prior (Burnett, 2001; Hart, 2017). Texas has seen many cycles of boom and bust, but the 1980s downturn hit the state particularly hard. The impacts rippled through the economy, from real estate and banking institutions to restaurants and car dealerships, vaporizing nearly a quarter of a million jobs in Houston alone (Livingston, 2020). Few went unscathed — even the former Texas governor, John Connally, was forced to sell his possessions in what was described as the "Super Bowl of auctions."

The crisis prompted local and state actions to reduce economic dependence on oil and gas. Houston over time diversified its economy, expanding its manufacturing, chemicals, and health industries (Federal Reserve Bank of Dallas, 2018a). Meanwhile, the state legislature in 1988 amended the Texas constitution to create the Economic Stabilization Fund (aka, the Rainy Day Fund), to which a portion of the state's severance tax is now allocated each year (Costello, Green & Graves, 2016).

Texas is one of a handful of states with substantial revenue from severance taxes (taxes on natural resource extraction) (Urban Institute, 2023). The Legislature established Texas' first oil production tax in 1905, followed by the natural gas production tax in 1931 (Texas Comptroller of Public Accounts, n.d.-a). Although these revenues have benefited the state treasury, they have also proven fickle. According to the Texas Comptroller, annual changes in this revenue source since 1997 have ranged from 116% to –53% (Falconnier & Julot, 2023). The Rainy Day Fund has reduced the state's dependence on this source of funding for everyday expenses while acting as a savings account for emergencies.

By the time the *Dallas* series finale aired in 1991, much had changed. NASA scientist James Hansen had delivered congressional testimony warning of climate change caused by fossil fuel combustion, elevating the issue to national policy debate in 1988 (Shabecoff,

A carefully restored old Sinclair gasoline station in Snyder, the seat of Scurry County.

Photo by Carol M. Highsmith, Public Domain

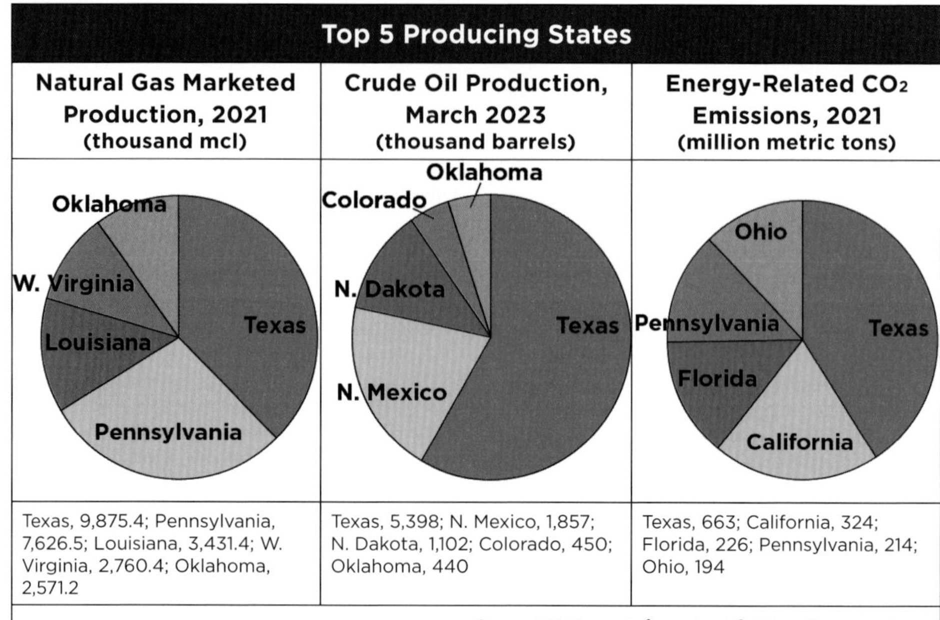

1988). In 1992, the U.S. would become a founding member of the United Nations Framework on Climate Change, pledging to prevent "dangerous human interference with the climate system" (Holthaus, 2018; United Nations, n.d.-b). Meanwhile, oil production in Texas had fallen by nearly half since its peak in 1972 (Railroad Commission of Texas, n.d.).

At the dawn of the new millennium, global "peak oil" predictions were abundant and renewable energy was growing in popularity (Geewax, 2014; Farhar, 1999). In his Epilogue to *The Big Rich*, published in 2009, Burrough observed that in Texas, oil no longer dominated the zeitgeist. "Houston and much of Texas is booming today not because of the oil beneath its dirt," he wrote, "but the expertise its engineers and executives have built over the years" (pp. 434–435). In 2010, actor Larry Hagman reprised his role as J.R. Ewing for a solar power commercial in which he declared oil "too dirty" (Sönke Wortmann Offiziell, 2013). Sliding a tan cowboy hat onto his head, he said, "I quit it years ago."

A LAND OF PLENTY

Unlike J.R., Texas did not quit oil. Experimentation with drilling techniques continued in Texas through the 1970s, 1980s, and 1990s, buoyed by federal subsidies and tax credits, private investment, and the perseverance of one Texan in particular: George Mitchell of Mitchell Energy (Trembath et al., 2012; Yergin, 2020). His stubborn, two-decade quest to profitably unlock natural gas from shale rock led to major breakthroughs in hydraulic fracturing ("fracking") and horizontal drilling in the late 1990s and early 2000s. These innovations reversed decades of stagnating output (first in natural gas, 2008; then in oil, 2010), catching the industry — and the world — by surprise (U.S. Energy Information Administration, 2023, August; Yergin, 2020). (For more on Mitchell and the shale boom, see *How an Invisible Gas Stole the Spotlight*, p. 613.) In recent years, production has risen to unprecedented heights. The U.S. now produces more oil and gas than any other country, much of it from Texas (Fiscal Notes staff, 2022; U.S. Energy Information Administration, 2019, 2023).

Home to more than half of the country's petroleum engineers, Texas truly is oil country (U.S. Bureau of Labor Statistics, 2022). In total, some 440,000 Texans work in the oil and gas industry (Texas Oil & Gas Association, 2023). A third of U.S. petroleum refineries, where crude oil is turned into products such as gasoline and asphalt, are concentrated along Texas' Gulf Coast (Greater Houston Partnership, 2021; U.S. Energy Information Administration, 2023, June). In 2022, Texas produced 1.8 billion barrels of crude oil — 42% of the U.S. total (U.S. Energy Information Administration, 2023, June). As the top oil- and gas-producing state of the world's top oil- and gas-producing country, Texas is a major player in the global energy system (U.S. Energy Information Administration, 2022a; 2022b; 2021; 2023, May). According to the Dallas Federal Reserve, "If Texas were a country, its current oil production would rank fourth globally, behind the U.S., Russia, and Saudi Arabia" (Slijk & Philips, 2021).

Texas' abundance of oil and gas is a gift of geology. Under Texans' feet lies a bounty of fossil fuels — primarily oil and natural gas, but some coal as well (U.S. Energy Information Administration, 2023, June). Having started out over 200 million years ago as plants and algae, these hydrocarbons have been transformed by time, heat, and pressure into a substance powerful enough to propel rockets into space (Clark, 2018). Enormous amounts of energy can be obtained by burning fossil fuels, which we use to run our cars and trucks, power the electric grid, and heat our homes and businesses. Fossil fuels are tremendously valuable in manufacturing as well, particularly for process heating, which enables transformation of raw materials into products like cement, iron, and glass (Office of Energy Efficiency & Renewable Energy, n.d.-b).

Burning fossil fuels releases carbon dioxide (CO_2), the greenhouse gas primarily responsible for climate change (U.S. Environmental Protection Agency, n.d.-a). Spanning eight unique climate zones, from arid deserts to humid subtropics, Texas experiences a wide variety of weather extremes — hurricanes, flooding, droughts, wildfires, and freezes — made more frequent and severe by climate change (Wasson, 2021; NASA, 2023; United Nations, n.d.-a). Analyses in recent years have found that Texas is the most natural disaster-prone state in the U.S. and has the highest number of extreme weather events costing more than $1 billion (Hubbard, 2021; Universal Ecological Fund, n.d.).

Hurricane Harvey in 2017 and Winter Storm Uri in 2021 are estimated to have cost $125 billion and $195 billion, respectively, placing them among the most costly natural disasters in U.S. history (National Oceanic and Atmospheric Association, n.d.; City of Austin, n.d.). In both events, socially vulnerable groups were the most impacted. During Hurricane Harvey, Houston's Black residents were the most likely to experience a flooded home, damaged vehicle, or lost income (Priest & Elliott, 2023). In the winter storm, communities of color were four times more likely than white communities to experience a power outage (Carvallo, Hsu, Shah & Taneja, 2021).

Texas is not only vulnerable to climate change but a key source of the greenhouse gases that cause it. Partly because so much of the world's oil and gas is extracted and processed in the state, Texas is the country's largest emitter of CO_2, releasing 663.5 million metric tons into the atmosphere in 2021 — nearly twice that of California, the second-largest emitter (U.S. Energy Information Administration, n.d.-a). In turn, the U.S. emits more CO_2 than any other country, with the exception of China (Crippa et al., 2022).

Just as Texas is naturally plentiful in fossil fuels, it also has an abundance of wind and sunshine. Currently the No. 2 producer of solar power in the U.S., Texas is projected to rank No. 1 by 2024, surpassing California in solar capacity (U.S. Energy Information Administration, 2023, July). Texas is the #1 producer of wind power and currently produces more than a quarter of the U.S. total (U.S. Energy Information Administration, 2023, June). (For more on wind in Texas, see "A Brief History of Wind Power," p. 607).

LONE STAR STATE OF MIND

Texas' leadership in renewable energy has been enabled not only by its abundance of wind and solar power but by the design of its electric grid and energy market. Texas is unique in that it has an electric grid all to itself. Much of the U.S. is served by the Western Interconnection, powering roughly the western half of the U.S., and the Eastern Interconnection, powering the remaining eastern half. Alaska and Hawaii each have several small grids (U.S. Environmental Protection Agency, n.d.-c). By contrast, the Texas Interconnection serves 90% of the state's load, providing power for 26 million people (Cohn, 2022; Electric Reliability Council of Texas, 2023, February). (The Western and Eastern interconnections serve the remaining 10% of Texas, comprising areas along the state's perimeter.)

This arrangement reflects decisions made in the early years of electrification. In 1935, as part of PUHCA, the Federal Power Act was amended to allow federal regulation of electric utilities operating in interstate commerce (Cohn, 2022). To avoid this federal oversight, most Texas utilities opted to limit their service territories to within state lines (while maintaining some cross-state interconnections for emergency use). Today, electricity transmission within the Texas Interconnection — operated by the Electric Reliability Council of Texas (ERCOT) — remains largely free from Federal Energy Regulatory Commission (FERC) oversight, though with some exceptions (e.g., pertaining to grid reliability) (Berman & Todderud, 2021).

This independence has been popularly touted as a function of Texas exceptionalism, reflecting a Lone Star ethos of stubborn self-reliance. An ERCOT chairman once joked at a board meeting that "FERC is a four-letter dirty word around

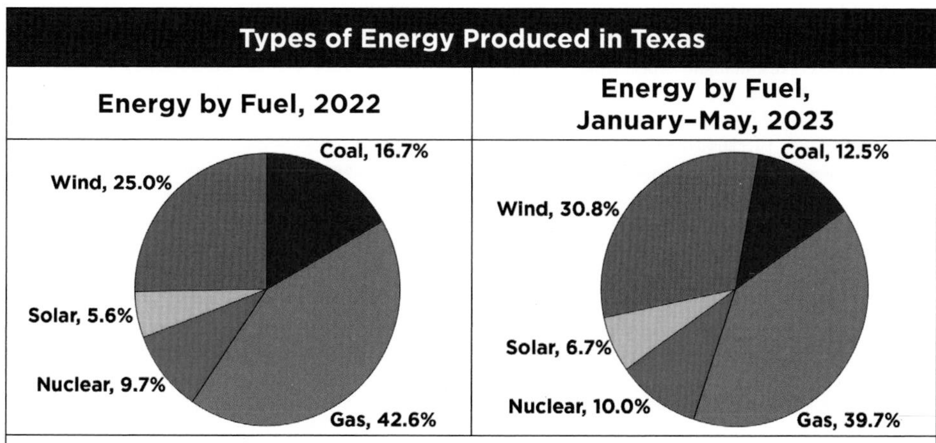

The Webberville Solar Farm near Austin, as seen from above. Photo by The tdog, Public Domain

here" (Klump, 2017). But Texas utilities were not alone in attempts to avoid interstate commerce. According to a Baker Institute report, utilities elsewhere in the U.S. attempted the same strategy but ultimately failed for lack of Texas' scale and resource abundance (Cohn, 2022). The report finds that despite rhetoric to the contrary, "business and technical" considerations have played a larger role than ideology in the commitment to isolation, and that this commitment may warrant reassessment given technological advances and other factors.

Although pragmatism may have played a bigger part than patriotism, the story of Texas' grid has not lacked for cowboy antics, as reflected in a 1970s kerfuffle dubbed the Midnight Connection (Cudahy, 1995). As the story goes, a holding company, the Central and Southwest Corporation (CSW), wanted for financial reasons to physically connect its Texas utilities to its utilities in Oklahoma. Other Texas utilities objected to the idea for fear the cross-state connection would subject them to federal regulation — but CSW was undeterred.

On May 4, 1976, CSW dispatched "an unknown trooper" to a Texas substation where, with the flip of a switch, electrons were sent across the state line to Oklahoma (Cudahy, 1995, p. 58). CSW attorney Richard D. Cudahy later recounted that "Like commandos operating far behind enemy lines, CSW caused power from deep in the heart of Texas to flow for several hours into interstate commerce" (p. 58). In response, two large Texas electric companies abruptly disconnected from the grid to avoid sending power out of state. This action prompted accusations of jeopardizing grid reliability, drawing several more utilities into the disagreement and triggering a protracted legal dispute that became a "watershed for the electric power industry" (p. 56). Ultimately, the proceedings allowed for unsynchronized DC interstate connections but largely maintained grid participants' freedom from federal regulation (Cohn, 2022).

THE GROWTH OF RENEWABLES

This autonomy helped lay the groundwork for Texas to become an unlikely frontrunner in renewable energy, beginning with policy changes in the 1990s. At that time, California had the most wind power in the country; meanwhile, Texas was one of several states focusing on electricity market reform, enabled by a series of federal policy changes meant to encourage competition and lower costs (Galbraith & Price, 2013). The Texas reforms famously began with musings sketched on a cocktail napkin by Texas Sen. David Sibley, Rep. Steve Wolens, and Pat Wood, chair of the Public Utility Commission of Texas (PUCT) (Weber, 2021). These musings — the basis of legislation that became state law in 1999 — evolved into a novel blueprint for allowing consumers to shop for electricity providers in a retail market. Sibley likened this freedom of choice to the simple beauty of shopping for a can of beans.

Before the law's passage, in anticipation of pushback from politically powerful monopoly utilities, Sibley and Wolens built broad support for the measure, lining up a "Rubik's cube of interests" across party lines (Galbraith & Price, 2013, p. 132). Crucially, environmental groups supported the measure, in part because it included a renewable portfolio standard (RPS). This measure mandated the addition of 2,000 megawatts of renewable energy to the state's grid by 2009. Signed by Gov. George W. Bush in 1999 with little fanfare about the RPS, the law quietly opened the door to wind power.

These changes stimulated development of wind energy with far more success than anticipated (Yergin, 2011). In 2006, Texas surpassed California to become the state with the most wind power. As Kate Galbraith and Asher Price recount in their book, *The Great Texas Wind Rush*, "projects were racing ahead so fast that towers and blades lay along… farm roads like wood waiting to be stacked" (p. 143). Pretty soon, the existing transmission lines could not accommodate all of the new electrons flowing from West Texas wind farms to the state's far-flung population centers. As a result, the Texas Legislature passed a law in 2005 directing the PUCT to develop a plan for expanding transmission capacity. In 2008, construction began on the Competitive Renewable Energy Zone (CREZ) transmission lines.

Elsewhere in the U.S., which has a patchwork of regulatory regimes across different states, transmission planning can be painstaking and protracted, often pitting stakeholders against one another (U.S. Department of Energy, 2022). By comparison, the relative autonomy of Texas' grid allows for a more streamlined process. The CREZ buildout did encounter some delays and cost overruns, due to the PUCT's efforts to accommodate concerns of landowners with properties impacted by the construction (Galbraith, 2011). Nonetheless, as the project progressed, FERC Chair Jon Wellinghoff said in 2011 that its speed was likely unprecedented. The project was complete by early 2014 (Titus, 2011).

The new transmission capacity and competitive power market facilitated rapid growth of wind and solar power, vaulting Texas far ahead of the rest of the country in renewable power generation. In 2022, Texas generated as much electricity from renewables as the next three top producers combined (California, Iowa, and Oklahoma) (Gearino, 2023). Wind and solar have reduced wholesale electricity costs for Texans — saving an estimated $31.5 billion between 2010 and 2022 — and have served as a hedge against volatile natural gas prices, helping to limit electricity cost increases when natural gas prices spike (Rhodes, 2023; Rhodes, 2022). They also helped to limit air pollution, save more than 8 trillion gallons of water, and avoid 588 million tons of CO_2 emissions between 2010 and August 2022 (Rhodes, 2022).

Despite the CREZ lines' success, Texas still sometimes has more renewable power than the grid can handle. Akin to early drillers in Corsicana forced to throw away surplus oil, wind producers must sometimes disengage generators on windy days, to avoid overloading the grid (Carver, 2022). ERCOT curtailed 5% and 9%, respectively, of available wind and solar generation in 2022 (U.S. Energy Information Association, 2023 July). Advanced battery technology can help with this problem, allowing for storage of surplus power until it's needed. Currently at the center of a "battery rush," Texas accounted in 2022 for nearly a third of new grid-scale energy storage in the U.S. (Groom & Kearney, 2023). Companies are building battery plants in Texas because they believe they can profit from selling stored electricity back into the grid, particularly when demand outstrips supply, such as when more air conditioners are running in the summer or when extreme weather events cause power plant failures.

Formerly an obscure topic, grid reliability has become a subject of deep concern and heightened anxiety for Texans in the wake of Winter Storm Uri in February 2021. The catastrophic storm blanketed the state in freezing weather for days, triggering widespread blackouts. More than 240 people died (Svitek, 2022). The weather caused equipment failures across every generation type, including renewables, nuclear, and coal. Texas' primary source of electricity, natural gas, was hit hardest as snow and ice shut down well sites and power plants (Golding, 2023; UT Energy Institute, 2021). In the aftermath, state lawmakers passed measures to enhance weatherization of critical infrastructure and improve market design, and the Department of Energy recently announced plans to give Texas $60.6 million to enhance grid resilience and power sector reliability (Penrod, 2021; Foxhall, 2023).

Nonetheless, Texas grid operators and policymakers continue to draw scrutiny as high demand and extreme temperatures test the grid (Weber, 2023; Wolf, 2023). Observers have called for a fresh examination of the case for Texas' grid isolation, arguing that interstate connections today would not only improve reliability but bring cash to energy-abundant Texas, which would be well-positioned to sell electricity to other states (Oxner, 2022). Meanwhile, federal lawmakers and FERC are exploring steps to force more grid connections between states, including Texas (DiNatale & Osborne, 2023).

SWAGGERING TO 2050

The summer of 2023 was the planet's hottest on record (Paddison, 2023). The high temperatures were dangerous for people without means to stay cool, driving up the number of heat-related deaths across Texas (Goodman, 2023; Nguyen, 2023). Even in Houston, where air-conditioning is nearly ubiquitous, 23,000 households — largely concentrated in the city's low-income communities — lack this basic necessity (Bruess, 2023). Texans who did have air-conditioners (and could afford to run them), relied on them to stay comfortable, driving up demand for electricity. Peak demand broke previous records 10 times between July and August (ERCOT, 2023, August). In midsummer, energy analysts noted that battery storage and renewables — which hit record output in June, at 31,498 megawatts — were helping to prevent blackouts as older thermal plants experienced outages (Proffer, 2023; Nilsen, 2023). Nonetheless, tight margins prompted ERCOT to issue repeated appeals to conserve electricity.

The global average temperature today is about 1.1 degrees Celsius higher than in the pre-Industrial period, and it will continue to rise, increasing the intensity and frequency of heat waves and other climate impacts (Intergovernmental Panel on Climate Change, 2023). To halt this upward trajectory, governments and businesses around the world have begun setting targets for bringing greenhouse gas emissions down to net-zero by 2050 (Net Zero Tracker, n.d.). In the U.S., the national strategy for reaching net-zero is laid out in the Federal Sustainability Plan, which was initiated in 2021 (The White House, 2021).

Several of the world's largest oil and gas companies have also announced net-zero goals, pledging to "help accelerate the energy transition through deep reductions in greenhouse gases" (Oil and Gas Climate Initiative, 2021). Among the companies are ExxonMobil and Chevron, both of which have ties to Texas' earliest oil fields. In Corsicana, the J.S. Cullinan Company — the first refinery west of the Mississippi — helped create a market for Texas oil (Stringer, 1952). After many iterations, it would become ExxonMobil (Stiles, Linsley, & Rienstra, 2008). Two companies born at Spindletop, Gulf Oil and the Texas Oil Co. (later Texaco), would become Chevron.

Electrification — the replacement of fossil fuel-dependent technologies with alternatives powered by electricity — will play an important role in this transition (Huismans & Voswinkel, 2023). Roads will have more electric-powered vehicles, for example (Popovich & Plumer, 2023). More efficient use of electricity (enabled by weatherization, for example) will also play a part, as will demand-response programs (enabling people to respond to grid conditions by reducing or shifting energy use). In turn, electricity must come from emissions-free sources. These changes will require major investment in grid modernization and expansion, a transformational undertaking reminiscent of the New Deal era, when much of the infrastructure Americans rely on today was first built (Klein, 2022).

Texas is in many respects ready to take on this challenge. Natural gas is the state's largest single source of electricity, accounting in 2022 for 43% of the state's generation mix (ERCOT, 2023, March). Although not an emissions-free source, plentiful natural gas — along with wind — has reduced Texas' reliance on coal, which is more polluting and has a bigger carbon footprint (U.S. Energy Information Administration, 2023, June). Meanwhile, solar and wind together accounted for 31% of generation in 2022 and were projected to overtake natural gas in 2023 (ERCOT, 2023, March; U.S. Energy Information Administration, 2022). Nationwide, projections show that additions of wind and solar over the next decade will be concentrated largely in Texas (U.S. Energy Information Administration, 2023, July).

However, inadequate transmission capacity threatens to limit the benefits of this growth (Peters, 2023; Reed, 2020). The U.S. has a backlog of power producers and storage providers waiting to be connected to the grid, with wait times on the rise (Wesoff & Olano, 2023; Lawrence Berkeley National Lab, 2023). Despite relatively low wait times and the highest project completion rate, Texas has the longest queue (Americans for a Clean Energy Grid, 2023; Wesoff & Olano, 2023). Meanwhile, grid congestion in Texas doubled between 2020 and 2021 (Americans for a Clean Energy Grid, 2023). Efforts are underway to ease these problems. Nationally, FERC in 2023 approved a new rule — one of the largest in the agency's history — to speed up the interconnection process (Downing, 2023). ERCOT, meanwhile, has $10.3 billion worth of transmission improvement projects planned for completion by 2028 (ERCOT, 2022).

Research to support innovation will also play a key role in the transition, because some of the technologies required for reaching net-zero are still in development or are not yet commercially competitive (International Energy Agency, 2023). In Texas, which is among the world's largest producers of hydrogen (a fuel widely used in industrial processes), there is strong interest in clean hydrogen research (Gee et al., 2022). Most hydrogen is produced using a CO_2-emitting process called steam methane reforming. Alternative methods can substantially shrink the large CO_2 footprint of Texas' industrial sector, which is difficult to decarbonize.

Carbon capture, utilization, and storage (CCUS) technologies are another key area of research interest in Texas, where repurposed pipeline and storage facilities, as well as depleted oil and gas reservoirs, might be exploited to capture, transport, and store CO_2 that would otherwise be released into the atmosphere (Hannis et al., 2017; Wilson, 2021). As with hydrogen, CCUS technologies can help limit emissions in hard-to-abate sectors while leveraging the capabilities of Texas' workforce (Gee et al., 2022).

Geothermal technologies — which can generate emissions-free electricity using heat abundant far beneath the ground — also show promise (Beard & Jones, 2023). Geothermal power can supply emissions-free high heat for industrial applications, and the expertise of Texas' workforce — particularly with regard to knowledge of the subsurface — likely confers Texas with a competitive advantage, as does the potential to repurpose oil and gas wells for geothermal production (Gee et al., 2022). These factors have drawn a growing number of geothermal startup companies to Texas (Lewis, 2023).

In 2022, researchers published a report analyzing several potential strategies for reaching net-zero in Texas (Gee et al., 2022). To their surprise, all of the strategies they examined (which included various combinations of electrification, clean hydrogen, and carbon capture, among other things) proved more economically advantageous than maintaining the status quo (Cockrell School of Engineering, 2022). Echoing the position of HETI's leaders, who say the transition presents opportunity for "massive economic growth," the researchers found that net-zero efforts benefit the economy through job creation, as well as through the public health benefits of a cleaner environment: Getting to net-zero won't be easy, they wrote — but it looks to be lucrative (Worland, 2023; Gee et al., 2022).

The report points to a variety of factors in Texas' favor, including its history of implementing energy solutions quickly and at scale. This factor is key given the scope and complexity of energy projects, and the imperative to meet net-zero quickly. As energy analyst Daniel Yergin has described it, "The objective of this transition is not just to bring on new energy sources, but to entirely change the energy foundations of what today is a $100 trillion global economy — and do so in little more than a quarter century" (Yergin, 2022). As these changes unfold, global energy supply will also need to keep pace with growing demand.

The challenge is enormous. In this respect, it is very Texan. The Texas net-zero report concludes that "Texas is uniquely positioned to lead the world in the transition to a carbon-neutral energy economy" (Gee et al., 2022, p. 7). Texas may not be accustomed to a carbon-neutral economy, but it is accustomed to being a leader. If summer 2023 was any indication, Texas may sweltering on the path to net-zero. But it will also be swaggering.

About the Author: *Nora Ankrum is a research project manager and external relations coordinator at the Energy Institute at the University of Texas at Austin, where she supports the Institute's work facilitating collaboration on energy-related initiatives and research. She brings to this role more than 15 years of experience as a professional communicator, much of it spent as an editor and journalist reporting on issues pertaining to energy research and policy. She is passionate about exploring and understanding the impacts that energy systems, policies, and innovations have on everyday life. Ankrum has a Bachelor of Arts in English from the University of Texas at Austin, and a Master of Public Affairs from the LBJ School of Public Affairs.*

LNG tanker Symphonic Breeze *is 289.7 meters long (about 950.5 ft.) and can carry 145,394 cubic meters of liquid natural gas. The largest LNG tankers in the world today can reach 1,132 ft. and carry 266,000 cubic meters of LNG. Photo by Garry Chapple, Pixabay*

HOW AN INVISIBLE GAS STOLE THE SPOTLIGHT

Emanating mysteriously from cracks and crevices in the earth, natural gas managed to capture the human imagination long before we had means to recover it from deep underground. In antiquity, our earliest encounters with this invisible, odorless substance — often through natural gas seepages fueling perceived "eternal" flames — inspired religious devotion and cultural mythmaking throughout Europe, India, Indonesia, and the Middle East (White, 1921, pp. 171–186). Humans since then have demonstrated considerable ingenuity in putting this resource to work. As early as 500 BCE, people in China were using natural gas to cook food and desalinate seawater. To transport gas from place to place, they fashioned pipes out of bamboo (Etiope, 2015).

Technological advancements have vastly expanded our access to natural gas and our ability to make use of it. Today, the majority of U.S. households use natural gas for heating, and nearly half use it for cooking (U.S. Energy Information Administration, 2023, March). Thanks to the shale boom, natural gas has replaced coal to become the largest single source of electricity in the U.S., accounting for nearly 40% of generation (U.S. Energy Information Administration, 2020; 2023, February). Much of that gas, along with the key innovation that enabled the boom, comes from Texas (Fiscal Notes staff, 2022).

THE "SHALE GALE"

Galveston-born George Mitchell spent the 1980s and 1990s searching for a way to liberate natural gas trapped in the microscopic pores of dense shale rock (Yergin, 2020). Conventional wisdom held that such a feat was unlikely, or at least unlikely to turn a profit, and people thought Mitchell Energy was throwing away its money. But in 1998, after years of failed experiments in the Dallas/Fort Worth area's Barnett Shale, Mitchell's employees had a breakthrough. Their innovation — a novel method of an existing drilling technique called hydraulic fracturing ("fracking") — quietly proved naysayers wrong and eventually unlocked an unprecedented bounty of both gas and oil from shale plays across the country.

Further experimentation demonstrated that combining the new technique with horizontal drilling improved output, and this development caught the attention of independent exploration and production companies (Yergin, 2020). Fanning out across shale plays in Texas and across the U.S., the companies knocked on doors of farmers and ranchers, asking to lease their land so they could put these new techniques into practice. In 2008, ten years after Mitchell Energy's discovery, U.S. natural gas output began to climb. Conjuring images of America's frontier days, boomtowns now sprang up across the U.S., as oil and gas majors joined the independents (Yergin, 2020). Known by many names — the "fracking boom," the "shale gale," America's "energy renaissance" — this new era was transformational, reshaping the global energy landscape.

Spanning eastern New Mexico and much of West Texas, the 75,000-square-mile Permian Basin is one of the country's oldest oil- and gas-producing regions (Federal Reserve Bank of Dallas, 2023). Since 2010, oil and gas output have climbed dramatically in the region, and today the Permian is the largest petroleum-producing basin in the country, accounting for 17% of U.S. natural gas production and 43% of U.S. oil production (U.S. Energy Information Administration, 2022, September). The shale boom has been credited with giving the Permian a second life after many years of decline, but it has also brought challenges, including price slumps in late 2014 and 2020 (Thompson, 2022). The first slump triggered the region's worst bust since the 1980s, kicking off a wave of bankruptcies (Federal Reserve Bank of Dallas, 2023). In the Permian's Midland-Odessa area, the unemployment rate doubled, and net migration went negative (Federal Reserve Bank of Dallas, 2018).

Nonetheless, each bust has been followed by a hearty rebound. In a dispatch from West Texas in 2019, *The Wall Street Journal* reported, "The brisket is scarce, the 'man-camps' are full, and oil workers with no time to spare pay $75 to skip the line at the barber shop" (Matthews & Elliott, 2019). In that year, the U.S. became a net total energy exporter for the first time in nearly seven decades (U.S. Energy Information Administration, 2022, April). Industry growth in the region today is strong but more gradual than before, due in part to pressure on companies to share profits with investors rather than use earnings to drill more (Domonoske, 2023). Analysts suggest this tempered growth may in turn temper the impacts of the next slump.

In 2021, Texas produced 25% of U.S. natural gas, making it the largest producer in the country (Fiscal Notes staff, 2022). In turn, the U.S. is now the largest producer in the world (U.S. Energy Information Administration, 2019). This role has powerful geopolitical implications. Crucially, U.S. natural gas has helped blunt the effects on Europe of Russia's war in Ukraine. After its invasion of Ukraine in February 2022, Russia — the world's second-largest natural gas producer — dramatically curtailed gas supply to import-dependent European countries, putting them in danger of energy shortages during the cold winter months (U.S. Energy Information Administration, 2019; Abnett, 2022). But the feared shortages never materialized, thanks in part to ample supply from the U.S. (Lefebvre, 2023; Oltermann, Henley, Chrisafis, Jones, & Walker, 2023)

The U.S. more than doubled its liquified natural gas (LNG) exports to Europe in 2022 (Morenne, Cole, DeLorenzo, 2023). Many of the tankers carrying that gas, enough per ship to heat at least 43,000 homes for a year, departed from Texas LNG terminals along the Gulf of Mexico. These exports contributed to record profits for American oil and gas companies, representing a substantial boon to Texas, home to more than a third of U.S. oil and gas sector employees (McCormick, 2022).

In the 20th century, oil played a decisive role in the outcomes of two world wars and gave the Organization of the Petroleum Exporting Countries (OPEC) — whose members hold more than 80% of the world's proven oil reserves — powerful leverage over the global economy (Ellerbeck, 2022). The events of 2022 showed that natural gas, long considered the "poor cousin of oil," could also play an outsized role in world affairs (Savcenko, 2023; Galbraith & Price, 2013, p.40).

NATURAL GAS EMERGES FROM OIL'S SHADOW

Commercial use of natural gas in the U.S. predates that of oil. Thanks to gaslight technology developed in England in the 1790s, "town gas" systems allowed U.S. cities throughout the 1800s to install street lighting for the first time (Energy Education, n.d.). These systems typically relied on what was then called "manufactured gas," derived from coal. In 1825 — more than three decades before Edwin Drake struck oil in Titusville, Pennsylvania — William Aaron Hart dug the first natural gas well in the U.S., allowing for nighttime illumination of a mill, several stores, and an inn in Fredonia, New York (Lash & Lash, 2014). Texas cities also adopted gas lighting systems, beginning with Galveston in 1856. The *San Antonio Express-News* and other local papers of the era commonly featured advisories warning people not to leave their gas porch lights on all night (Davila, 2019).

Gas lighting eventually gave way to electric lighting systems, but gas remained useful for heating and cooking, as well as for some industrial uses (Prindle, 1981). Nonetheless, the market for natural gas remained small. At the dawn of its oil boom, Texas didn't lack for natural gas, an inevitable byproduct of oil extraction. However, gas was costly and difficult to store and transport, making it a plentiful nuisance. Forced to use it or lose it, drillers opted largely for the latter, often setting in on fire or simply allowing it to vent into the atmosphere. Ultimately, Houston would emerge as the national hub of the interstate gas pipeline industry, but not until much later (Castaneda, 1990).

Due to concerns about energy security in the mid-1940s, the federal government encouraged installation of a pipeline network for natural gas, seen as a suitable oil substitute (Yergin, 1991). Technological advances in the 1920s had vastly improved pipeline technology, which was then put to use during World War II to build the Big Inch and Little Big Inch pipelines. These lines safely carried oil from Texas to the Northeast, bypassing the Atlantic shipping route where German submarines were known to sink U.S. oil tankers. The pipelines' strategic importance ultimately inspired the saying, "The war was won by an Inch" (Martin, 2018).

After the war, a federal report recommended converting these pipelines to natural gas transmission. The proposal sparked opposition from the railroad and coal industries, which balked at the prospect of Texas gas flowing to their

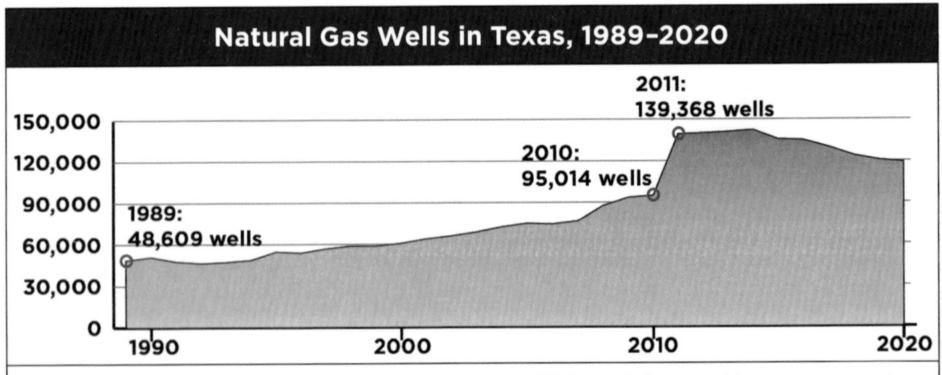

Source: U.S. Energy Information Administration, www.eia.gov

Workers constructing the Big Inch pipeline using the roll-weld method, October 1942. Photo by John Vachon, Public Domain

customers in the Northeast, where coal-derived products kept people warm through the winter (Castaneda, 1990). But the idea had support from influential Texas figures, including George R. Brown. Later dubbed by *Texas Monthly* as "the most powerful man in Texas . . . the entire nation, and, by extension, the entire world," Brown was part of the "8F Crowd" (Hurt, 1976). From the 1930s through 1960s, this group of Texas business and political leaders, including future President Lyndon B. Johnson, would meet regularly in Texas' "secret capital" — Suite 8F of Houston's Lamar Hotel — to shape the state's economic and political future.

In the contest over the Big Inch and Little Big Inch pipelines, the Texans prevailed. In 1947, the lines were sold to Brown's Texas Eastern Transmission Company (Castaneda, 1990). That year, a third pipeline, owned by El Paso Natural Gas, created a westward route for Texas natural gas, ending in Los Angeles. These events brought an end to manufactured gas as a significant industry in the U.S. They also reduced American reliance on crude, as intended, saving 700,000 barrels a day by 1950 (Yergin, 1991). Soon, the headquarters of U.S. pipeline companies — initially spread throughout the southwestern states — coalesced in Houston, after which point, "Houston and the natural gas industry matured together" (Castaneda, 1990, p. 95).

By the 1970s, 90% of electricity in Texas came from natural gas (Galbraith & Price, 2013). But production began to slow, and power shortages during a winter freeze in 1973 demonstrated the dangers of overreliance on this resource. The episode — a "frantic" event for utilities and an embarrassing "blow . . . to state pride" — helped prompt the establishment in May 1973 of the Governor's Energy Advisory Council to "assist the Governor in avoiding a potential energy crisis" (Galbraith & Price, 2013, pp. 39, 40, & 42). The Arab oil embargo later that year, which quadrupled the price of oil, prompted similar scrutiny at the national level and spawned a wave of new legislation enacting the first efficiency standards for cars, buildings, and appliances (Union of Concerned Scientists, 2006; Halverson, Shui, Evans, 2009; Office of Energy Efficiency & Renewable Energy, n.d.-a). In Texas, one of the first actions of the governor's council was to commission a report, on the state's potential for wind energy, that would end up laying the groundwork for the Texas wind industry's remarkable success decades later (Galbraith & Price, 2013).

FROM THE EARTH TO THE AIR TO THE WATER

Today, natural gas provides nearly half of Texas' electricity, and wind provides another 20% (Electric Reliability Council of Texas, 2023, March). Advances in renewables and abundance of natural gas have allowed for less dependence on coal, in Texas and nationally (U.S. Energy Information Administration, 2021, June). Because natural gas power plants emit half the CO_2 of coal plants, this trend helped to lower the carbon footprint of electricity generation in the U.S. by 32% between 2005 and 2019 (Weissman, 2016).

Natural gas is sometimes called a "bridge fuel" because of its potential to replace dirtier resources while cleaner alternatives mature and become more economically competitive. Nonetheless, the amount of CO_2 emitted through natural gas combustion remains substantial, accounting in 2022 for 34% of total energy-related CO_2 emissions in the U.S. (U.S. Energy Information Administration, n.d.-c). Natural gas extraction is associated with other environmental challenges as well, such as air and water pollution, which can pose health dangers to nearby communities (National Institute of Environmental Health Sciences, n.d.; U.S. Environmental Protection Agency, 2016). Also, earthquake activity has been linked to fracking, particularly to wastewater disposal practices, and Texas has seen increased seismicity in recent years (Savvaidis, 2022). To better understand this phenomenon, the Texas Legislature has tasked the University of Texas' Bureau of Economic Geology with tracking and studying seismic activity. The bureau formed a research unit, TexNet, which began collecting data on earthquakes throughout the state in 2017 (Bureau of Economic Geology, n.d.).

Fracking is a water-intensive process, consuming fresh water and producing wastewater. Although it accounts for a small fraction of statewide water use (less than 1%), it can have outsized local impacts in drought-prone areas (The Academy of Medicine, Engineering and Science of Texas, 2017). Given that Texas' water supply is projected to fall increasingly short of demand in the coming decades, reaching a potential shortfall of 8.9 million acre-feet by 2070, fracking may exacerbate challenges related to water scarcity (Grubbs et al., 2019). In 2021, state lawmakers created the Texas Produced Water Consortium to study how water generated from oil and gas operations might be reused rather than disposed of (Texas Produced Water Consortium, 2022). West Texas wells are expected to produce 588 million gallons of this "produced water" over the next 38 years (Baddour, 2022). Just as natural gas — once considered a waste product of oil extraction — has proven valuable in its own right, this "produced water" may do the same. If so, it will be plentiful. West Texas wells are expected to produce 588 million gallons of produced water over the next 38 years (Baddour, 2022).

FLARING THE WEALTH

There are places in Texas where the nighttime sky glows bright with an orange haze. Natural gas, set aflame through a routine practice called flaring, imprints this signature on the horizon, sometimes visible for miles. It is a puzzling feature of life in oil country — the sight of one of the world's most valuable resources going up in smoke. This practice is as old as the industry itself. In Texas in the 1930s and 1940s, "Miles away from any major oil field, newspapers could be read easily at night by the light of these flares" (Prindle, 1981, p. 296). Flaring occurs for a variety of reasons; for example, if pipeline capacity is insufficient for the volume of gas recovered from a well, workers will flare the excess. Today, according to the World Bank, the amount of natural gas flared globally each year would be enough to power sub-Saharan Africa (The World Bank, n.d.-b).

Because natural gas is composed primarily of the potent greenhouse gas methane, flaring (which converts methane into water and CO_2) is considered better than venting (releasing the methane unchanged into the atmosphere) (U.S. Department of Energy, 2019). However, as emissions tracking efforts have improved, data have shown that flaring is less effective than previously assumed; in Texas and North Dakota, findings show that methane emissions from flaring are five times greater than previously estimated (Plant, et. al, 2022).

Wells, tanks, pipelines, and processing plants are prone to natural gas leaks (called "fugitive emissions"), another hidden contributor to methane emissions. New monitoring has shown that both intentional and unintentional venting of natural gas are much more common than previously understood (Charles, 2022; Perkins, 2019). Studies in the Permian Basin have found that methane emissions are at least two to three times higher than Environmental Protection Agency estimates, with most emissions coming from a small number of "super emitters" (Environmental Defense Fund, 2021; Yu et al., 2022; Chen et al., 2022).

According to the International Energy Agency, cutting methane emissions is both inexpensive and "one of the most effective ways to limit global warming and improve air quality in the near term" (International Energy Agency, 2023). Overall, the energy sector is responsible for about 40% of global methane emissions attributed to human activity. The U.S. is among the world's top five methane-emitting countries, and within the U.S., Texas is the top emitter (International Energy Agency, 2022; Cumpton & Agbo, 2023). Methane is not as abundant in the atmosphere as CO_2, but monitoring by the National Oceanic and Atmospheric Administration has recorded large methane increases in recent years (National Oceanic and Atmospheric Association, Office for Coastal Management, 2023).

In 2015, the World Bank launched the Zero Routine Flaring by 2030 Initiative (The World Bank, n.d.-a). The U.S., along with 33 other countries and 54 oil companies, has endorsed the initiative, which requires annual reporting of flaring data. In January 2023, ExxonMobil, which has endorsed the initiative, announced it had ended routine flaring at its 700 Permian Basin sites, a first step in its plan to reach the 2030 goal (McEwen, 2023; Valle, 2023). Nonetheless, current projections suggest overall flaring in the region is likely to increase in 2024 (Disavino, 2023).

Natural gas flaring in a West Texas oilfield. Photo by Jonathan Cutrer, jcutrer.com

REFERENCES

Abnett, K. (2022, June 23). A dozen EU countries affected by Russian gas cuts, EU climate chief says. *Reuters*. https://www.reuters.com/business/energy/russian-gas-cuts-have-hit-12-countries-eu-climate-chief-says-2022-06-23

The Academy of Medicine, Engineering and Science of Texas. (2017). *Environmental and community impacts of shale development in Texas*. https://tamest.org/wp-content/uploads/2017/07/Final-Shale-Task-Force-Report.pdf

Agresta, M. (2018, May). A new book takes a look at the legacy of 'Giant'. *Texas Monthly*. https://www.texasmonthly.com/arts-entertainment/giant-steps

Alexander, N. (1975). Running the Rio Grande canyons: Robert T. Hill on the Big Bend. *Southwest Review*, 60(2), pp. 128–142.

American Council for an Energy-Efficient Economy. (2020, September). Energy burdens in Houston. https://www.aceee.org/sites/default/files/pdfs/aceee-01_energy_burden_-_houston.pdf

The American Presidency Project. (n.d.) *Address at Barnesville, Georgia*: August 11, 1938 [Speech transcript]. UC Santa Barbara. https://www.presidency.ucsb.edu/documents/address-barnesville-georgia

Americans for a Clean Energy Grid. (2023, June). *Transmission planning and development regional report card*. https://www.cleanenergygrid.org/wp-content/uploads/2023/06/ACEG_Transmission_Planning_and_Development_Report_Card.pdf

Anderson, B. (2018). Lyndon B. Johnson and Hill Country electrification. *The Historical Marker Database*. https://www.hmdb.org/m.asp?m=126764

Anderson, P. E. (n.d.). Sam Rayburn and rural electrification. *East Texas History*. https://easttexashistory.org/items/show/73

Anonymous. (1976). Electrical Power. *Handbook of Texas Online*. Texas State Historical Association. www.tshaonline.org/handbook/entries/electrical-power

Augustine, C., Fisher, S., Ho, J., Warren, I., & Witter, E. (2023, January). *Enhanced geothermal shot analysis for the Geothermal Technologies Office*. National Renewable Energy Laboratory, NREL/TP-5700-84822. https://www.nrel.gov/docs/fy23osti/84822.pdf

Austin Energy. (n.d.). *A history of Austin Energy*. https://austinenergy.com/about/history

Baddour, D. (2022, September 2). Texas' oil and gas industry will produce "massive amount" of toxic wastewater with few reuse options, study finds. *The Texas Tribune*. https://www.texastribune.org/2022/09/02/texas-wastewater-oil-gas-reuse/

Baker, S. (2021, June 8). Statement of Shalanda H. Baker, nominee for the position of Director of the Office of Minority Economic Impact before the Committee on Energy and Natural Resources. United States Senate. https://www.energy.senate.gov/services/files/DC36B994-A873-4171-A3B5-D9333C4F1267

Barr, A. (1995, November 1). Late nineteenth-century Texas. *Handbook of Texas Online*. Texas State Historical Association. https://www.tshaonline.org/handbook/entries/late-nineteenth-century-texas#:~:text=Most%20Texans%20lived%20and%20labored,and%20beyond%20the%20Pecos%20River.

Beard, J., & Jones, B. (2023). *The future of geothermal in Texas: The coming century of growth & prosperity in the Lone Star State*. The Mitchell Foundation. https://energy.utexas.edu/research/geothermal-texas

Berman, S., & Todderud, E. (2021, February 22). FERC authority over ERCOT. *Lexology*. https://www.lexology.com/library/detail.aspx?g=047b0d6f-3530-4ecf-b533-9463566d81a1

Bohne, C. (n.d.). Jake Simmons Jr. and East Texas oil. *East Texas History*. https://easttexashistory.org/items/show/364

Bradley, V. (2022, July 6). History of the moonlight towers in Austin, TX. *ATXtoday*. https://atxtoday.6amcity.com/moonlight-tower-history-austin-tx

Breakthrough Staff. (2012, March 1). *US government role in shale gas fracking history: A response to our critics*. The Breakthrough Institute. https://thebreakthrough.org/issues/energy/us-government-role-in-shale-gas-fracking-history-a-response-to-our-critics

Britannica. (n.d.). *Dallas: American television series*. https://www.britannica.com/topic/Dallas-American-television-series

Bruess, E. (2023, August 9). How one map tells the story of Houston's heat inequity across vulnerable communities. *Houston Landing*. https://houstonlanding.org/how-one-map-tells-the-story-of-houstons-heat-inequity-across-vulnerable-communities/

Bryan, A., Hundertmark, T., Lueck, K., Morrison, J., Roen, W., Siccardo, G., & Tai, H. (2021, October 22). *Managing water and climate risk with renewable energy*. McKinsey & Company. https://www.mckinsey.com/industries/electric-power-and-natural-gas/our-insights/managing-water-and-climate-risk-with-renewable-energy

Bryce, R. (2020). *A question of power: Electricity and the wealth of nations*. PublicAffairs.

Buckley, C. (2022, September 12). At 75, the father of environmental justice meets the moment. *The New York Times*. https://www.nytimes.com/2022/09/12/climate/robert-bullard-environmental-justice.html

Bullard, R., & Hadayia, J. (2022, October 26). Opinion: Polluters keep forgetting, this ain't our first rodeo. *Houston Chronicle*. https://www.houstonchronicle.com/opinion/outlook/article/Opinion-oil-gas-polluters-environmental-activism-17534184.php

Bureau of Economic Geology. (n.d.). *Texas seismological network and seismology research (TexNet)*. https://www.beg.utexas.edu/texnet-cisr/texnet

Burka, P. (1983, December). Grande dame of the Gulf. *Texas Monthly*. https://www.texasmonthly.com/being-texan/grande-dame-of-the-gulf/

Burnett, J. (2001). A salute to 'the oil century'. *NPR*. https://legacy.npr.org/programs/atc/features/2001/mar/010307.spindletop.html

Burrough, B. (2009). *The big rich: The rise and fall of the greatest Texas oil fortunes*. The Penguin Press.

Carter, E. (2017, November 6). Nashtifan windmills. *Atlas Obscura*. https://www.atlasobscura.com/places/nashtifan-windmills

Carvallo, J. P., Hsu, F. C., Shah, Z., & Taneja, J. (2021, April 14). *Frozen out in Texas: Blackouts and inequity*. The Rockefeller Foundation. https://www.rockefellerfoundation.org/case-study/frozen-out-in-texas-blackouts-and-inequity

Carver, J. L. (2022, August 2). Why the Texas grid causes the High Plains to turn off its wind turbines. *The Texas Tribune*. https://www.texastribune.org/2022/08/02/texas-high-plains-wind-energy

Castaneda, C. J. (1990). The Texas-Northeast connection: The rise of the post-World War II gas pipeline industry. *The Houston Review*, 12(2), pp. 79-95. https://houstonhistorymagazine.org/wp-content/uploads/2014/02/12.2-The-Texas-Northeast-Connection-The-Rise-of-Post-World-War-II-Gas-Pipline-Industry-Christopher-J-Castaneda.pdf

Castillo, J. (2015, April 16). How '50s James Dean movie dared show racism against Mexican Americans. *NBC News*. https://www.nbcnews.com/news/latino/how-50s-james-dean-movie-dared-show-racism-against-mexican-n341501

Charles, D. (2022, February 3). A satellite finds massive methane leaks from gas pipelines. *NPR.* https://www.npr.org/2022/02/03/1077392791/a-satellite-finds-massive-methane-leaks-from-gas-pipelines

Chen, Y., Sherwin, E. D., Berman, E. S., Jones, B. B., Gordon, M. P., Wetherley, E. B., Kort, E. A., & Brandt, A. R. (2022). Quantifying regional methane emissions in the New Mexico Permian Basin with a comprehensive aerial survey. *Environmental Science & Technology,* 56(7), pp. 4317–4323.

City of Austin. (n.d.). *Year in review: Winter Storm Uri.* City of Austin 2021 Year in Review. https://data.austintexas.gov/stories/s/Year-in-Review-Winter-Storm-Uri/hpvi-b8ze

Clark, J. D. (2018). *Ignition! An Informal History of Liquid Rocket Propellants.* Rutgers University Press Classics.

Cohn, J. A. (2022, December 1). *Connecting past and future: A history of Texas' isolated power grid.* Baker Institute for Public Policy. https://www.bakerinstitute.org/research/connecting-past-and-future-history-texas-isolated-power-grid

Corbett, M. (2013, November 22). *Oil shock of 1973–74.* Federal Reserve History. https://www.federalreservehistory.org/essays/oil-shock-of-1973-74

Costello, TJ, Green, D., & Graves, P. (2016, September). The Texas Economic Stabilization Fund: Saving for rainy days. *FiscalNotes: A Review of the Texas Economy.* Texas Comptroller of Public Accounts. https://comptroller.texas.gov/economy/fiscal-notes/2016/september/rainy-day.php

Crippa, M., Guizzardi, D., Banja, M., Solazzo, E., Muntean, M., Schaaf, E., Pagani, F., Monforti-Ferrario, F., Olivier, J., Quadrelli, R., Risquez Martin, A., Taghavi-Moharamli, P., Grassi, G., Rossi, S., Jacome Felix Oom, D., Branco, A., San-Miguel-Ayanz, J., & Vignati, E. (2022). CO_2 emissions of all world countries. *EDGAR – Emissions Database for Global Atmospheric Research,* JRC/IEA/PBL 2022 Report, EUR 31182 EN, Publications Office of the European Union, Luxembourg. doi:10.2760/730164

Cruz, C. (2018, May 11). 'Texas is where everything comes to an end': Author Lawrence Wright on Texas' unique past — and its precarious future. *PacificStandard.* https://psmag.com/social-justice/author-lawrence-wright-on-texas-unique-past-and-its-precarious-future

Cudahy, R. D. (1995, Summer). The second battle of the Alamo: The midnight connection. *Natural Resources & Environment,* 10(1), pp. 56–61, 85–87.

Cumpton, G., & Agbo, C. (2023). *Mitigating methane in Texas: Reducing emissions, creating jobs, and raising standards.* Texas Climate Jobs Project. https://static1.squarespace.com/static/60e76bd34e5317302f87f357/t/645d1db644 53b27b47622494/1683824055315/TCJP+Methane+Report+2023.pdf

Davenport, H. M., Jr. (2014, December 1). Corsicana: Accidental birthplace of the oil industry. *Bullock Museum.* Bullock Texas State History Museum. https://www.thestoryoftexas.com/discover/texas-story-project/corsicana-oil-navarro-county

Davila, G. (2019, January 13). Gas lights now illuminate Peacock Alley. *San Antonio Heron.* https://saheron.com/gas-lights-now-illuminate-peacock-alley

Davis, N. G. (1976). Rural electrification. *Handbook of Texas Online.* Texas State Historical Association. https://www.tshaonline.org/handbook/entries/rural-electrification

DiNatale, S., & Osborne, J. (2023, August 4). Feds considering rules that would require Texas power grid to connect with others across state lines. *San Antonio Express-News.*

Disavino, S., (2023, May 23). U.S. Permian natgas flaring could rise in 2024, report shows. *Reuters.* https://www.reuters.com/business/energy/us-permian-natgas-flaring-could-rise-2024-report-shows-2023-05-23

Domonoske, C. (2023, June 9). America is going through an oil boom — and this time it's different. *NPR.* https://www.npr.org/2023/06/09/1179415899/oil-production-gas-prices-opec-climate-change-permian-basin-texas

Downing, J (2023, July 31). FERC updates interconnection queue process with Order 2023. *RTO Insider.* https://www.rtoinsider.com/51474-ferc-queue-reform-order-2023/

Drehobl, A., Ross, L., & Ayala, R. (2020, September). *How high are household energy burdens?* American Council for an Energy-Efficient Economy. https://www.aceee.org/sites/default/files/pdfs/u2006.pdf

ERCOT. (2022, December). *Report on existing and potential electric system constraints and needs.* https://www.ercot.com/files/docs/2022/12/22/2022_Report_on_Existing_and_Potential_Electric_System_Constraints_and_Needs.pdf

ERCOT. (2023, March 7). Energy by fuel for 2022 [Chart]. *Fuel Mix Report: 2022.* https://www.ercot.com/gridinfo/generation

ERCOT. (2023, August). *Fact sheet.* https://www.ercot.com/files/docs/2022/02/08/ERCOT_Fact_Sheet.pdf

ERCOT. (2023, August 30). *ERCOT expects tight grid conditions, requests conservation today from 6 p.m. to 9 p.m. CT* [News release]. https://www.ercot.com/news/release/2023-08-30-ercot-expects-tight

Ellerbeck, S. (2022, November 11). Explainer: What is OPEC? *World Economic Forum.* https://www.weforum.org/agenda/2022/11/oil-opec-energy-price

Energy Education. (n.d.). *Town gas.* https://energyeducation.ca/encyclopedia/Town_gas

Environmental Defense Fund. (2021). *PermianMAP Final Report.* Permian Methane Analysis Project. https://blogs.edf.org/energyexchange/wp-content/blogs.dir/38/files/2022/11/PermianMAPFinalReport.pdf

Etiope, G. (2015). *Natural gas seepage: The Earth's hydrocarbon degassing.* Springer International Publishing.

Falconnier, J., & Julot, M. (2023, March). Texas' rainy day fund projected to hit cap for first time. *FiscalNotes: A Review of the Texas Economy.* Texas Comptroller of Public Accounts. https://comptroller.texas.gov/economy/fiscal-notes/2023/mar/rainyday.php#

Farhar, B. C. (1999, July). *Willingness to pay for electricity from renewable resources: A review of utility market research.* National Renewable Energy Laboratory, U.S. Department of Energy. https://www.nrel.gov/docs/fy99osti/26148.pdf

Federal Reserve Bank of Dallas. (2018, December). Houston–The Woodlands–Sugar Land: Texas' Gulf Coast hub and nation's energy capital. *Special Report: At the Heart of Texas: Cities' Industry Clusters Drive Growth.* https://www.dallasfed.org/research/heart/houston

Federal Reserve Bank of Dallas. (2018, December). Midland-Odessa: Riding the oil booms, seeking fewer busts.*Special Report: At the Heart of Texas: Cities' Industry Clusters Drive Growth.* https://www.dallasfed.org/~/media/Documents/research/heart/midland.pdf

Federal Reserve Bank of Dallas. (2023). Permian Basin: History. *Energy in the Eleventh District.* https://www.dallasfed.org/research/energy11/permian#history

Fiscal Notes staff. (2022, September). Texas' energy profile. *FiscalNotes: A Review of the Texas Economy.* Texas Comptroller of Public Accounts. https://comptroller.texas.gov/economy/fiscal-notes/2022/sep/energy.php

Fleischman, L., & Franklin, M. (2017, November). *Fumes across the fence-line.* Clean Air Task Force. http://www.catf.us/wp-content/uploads/2017/11/CATF_Pub_FumesAcrossTheFenceLine.pdf

Foxhall, E. (2023, July 6). Texas gets $60 million in federal funds to strengthen power grid against extreme weather. *The Texas*

Tribune. https://www.texastribune.org/2023/07/06/texas-electricity-grid-federal-grant-extreme-weather/

Galbraith, K. (2011, August 24). Cost of Texas wind transmission lines nears $7 billion. *The Texas Tribune*. http://www.texastribune.org/texas-energy/energy/cost-texas-wind-transmission-lines-nears-7-billion.

Galbraith, K., & Price, A. (2013). *The great Texas wind rush: How George Bush, Ann Richards, and a bunch of tinkerers helped the oil and gas state win the race to wind power*. University of Texas Press.

Gately, D., Adelman, M. A., & Griffin, J. M. (1986). Lessons from the 1986 oil price collapse. *Brookings papers on economic activity*, 1986(2), 237–284. https://doi.org/10.2307/2534475

Gearino, D. (2023, March 9). One state generates much, much more renewable energy than any other — and it's not California. *Inside Climate News*. https://insideclimatenews.org/news/09032023/inside-clean-energy-texas-renewables

Gee, I. M., Glazer, Y. R., Rhodes, J. D., Deetjen, T. A., Webber, M. E., Choukulkar, A., Cote, B., Clack, C., & Lewandowski, B. (2022, April). *Don't mess with Texas: Getting the lone star state to net-zero by 2050*. The University of Texas at Austin, Vibrant Clean Energy, and University of Colorado Boulder. https://cockrell.utexas.edu/images/pdfs/UT_Texas_Net_Zero_by_2050_April2022_Full_Report.pdf

Geewax, M. (2014, October 17). Predictions of 'peak oil' production prove slippery. *NPR*. https://www.npr.org/2014/10/17/356713298/predictions-of-peak-oil-production-prove-slippery

Gold, R. (2023, February). Whatever happened to the old-fashioned Texas oilmen? *Texas Monthly*. https://www.texasmonthly.com/news-politics/what-happened-to-old-fashioned-texas-oilmen-oil-boom/

Golding, G. (2023, January 17). *Texas electrical grid remains vulnerable to extreme weather events*. Federal Reserve Bank of Dallas. https://www.dallasfed.org/research/economics/2023/0117

Goodman, J. D. (2023, July 13). In a Texas city, heat proved deadly even for those long used to it. *The New York Times*. https://www.nytimes.com/2023/07/13/us/texas-heat-deaths-webb-county.html

Gopal, A. (2023, July 2). Batteries and renewables are saving Texas during the heat wave. *Forbes*. https://www.forbes.com/sites/anandgopal/2023/07/02/batteries-and-renewables-are-saving-texas-in-the-heat-wave/?sh=352a0af421dd

Graefe, L. (2013, November 13). *Oil shock of 1978–79*. Federal Reserve History. https://www.federalreservehistory.org/essays/oil-shock-of-1978-79

Gray, L. (2012, June 22). Gray: 'Air-conditioning capital of the world.' *Chron*. https://www.chron.com/life/gray/article/Gray-Air-conditioning-capital-of-the-world-3653254.php

Greater Houston Partnership. (2021, April 14). Gulf Coast refining capacity. *Data, Insights & Analysis*. https://www.houston.org/houston-data/gulf-coast-refining-capacity

Greater Houston Partnership. (n.d.). *Energy*. https://www.houston.org/why-houston/industries/energy

Groom, N., & Kearney, L. (2023, May 21). Insight: Texas battery rush: Oil state's power woes fuel energy storage boom. *Reuters*. https://www.reuters.com/business/energy/texas-battery-rush-oil-states-power-woes-fuel-energy-storage-boom-2023-05-31

Grubbs, S., Halbrook, S., Donald, J., & Wright, B. (2019, April). Texas water: Planning for more. *FiscalNotes: A Review of the Texas Economy*. Texas Comptroller of Public Accounts. https://comptroller.texas.gov/economy/fiscal-notes/2019/apr/tx-water-planning.php

Halverson, M. A., Shui, B., & Evans, M. (2009, April). *Country report on building energy codes in the United States*. Pacific Northwest National Laboratory, U.S. Department of Energy. https://www.pnnl.gov/main/publications/external/technical_reports/PNNL-17979.pdf

Hannis, S., Lu, J., Chadwick, A., Hovorka, S., Kirk, K., Romanak, K., & Pearce, J. (2017). CO_2 storage in depleted or depleting oil and gas fields: What can we learn from existing projects? *Energy Procedia*, 114. doi.org/10.1016/j.egypro.2017.03.1707

Hart, A. (2017, December 27). The story of Texas' energy economy is a tale of booms and busts. *Texas Standard*. https://www.texasstandard.org/stories/the-story-of-texas-energy-economy-is-a-tale-of-booms-and-busts

Hartman, B. (1995, October 1). Strand. *Handbook of Texas Online*. Texas State Historical Association. https://www.tshaonline.org/handbook/entries/strand

History.com Editors. (2019, June 10). *Spindletop*. https://www.history.com/topics/landmarks/spindletop

Hoen, B., Diffendorfer, J., Rand, J., Kramer, L., Garrity, C., & Hunt, H. (2023, May). *US wind turbine database files*. Energy Technologies Area, Berkeley Lab. https://eta-publications.lbl.gov/publications/us-wind-turbine-database-files

Holthaus, E. (2018, June 22). James Hansen's legacy: Scientists reflect on climate change in 1988, 2018, and 2048. *Grist*. https://grist.org/article/james-hansens-legacy-scientists-reflect-on-climate-change-in-1988-2018-and-2048

House, B. (1946, July). Spindletop. *The Southwestern Historical Quarterly*, 50(1). https://www.jstor.org/stable/30237257

Houston Energy Transition Initiative. (2022, October). *Perspective on the energy transition capital of the world: Houston's opportunity to win by catalyzing capital formation*. Greater Houston Partnership. https://www.houston.org/sites/default/files/2022-10/HETI_Capital%20Formation%20Perspective.pdf

Hubbard, K. (2021, May 4). These are America's most disaster-prone states. *U.S. News & World Report*. https://www.usnews.com/news/best-states/slideshows/the-most-disaster-prone-states-in-the-us

Huismans, M., & Voswinkel, F. (n.d.). *Electrification*. International Energy Agency. https://www.iea.org/energy-system/electricity/electrification

Hurt, H. (1976). The most powerful Texans. *Texas Monthly*. https://www.texasmonthly.com/news-politics/the-most-powerful-texans

Intergovernmental Panel on Climate Change. (2023). Summary for policymakers. *Climate Change 2023: Synthesis Report*. https://www.ipcc.ch/report/ar6/syr/downloads/report/IPCC_AR6_SYR_SPM.pdf

International Energy Agency. (2022). *Overview*. Global Methane Tracker. https://www.iea.org/reports/global-methane-tracker-2022/overview

International Energy Agency. (2023, February 21). *Methane emissions remained stubbornly high in 2022 even as soaring energy prices made actions to reduce them cheaper than ever*. https://www.iea.org/news/methane-emissions-remained-stubbornly-high-in-2022-even-as-soaring-energy-prices-made-actions-to-reduce-them-cheaper-than-ever

International Energy Agency. (2023). *Innovation: Tracking*. https://www.iea.org/energy-system/decarbonisation-enablers/innovation#tracking

International Energy Agency. (n.d.). *Carbon capture, utilisation and storage*. https://www.iea.org/energy-system/carbon-capture-utilisation-and-storage

Kelly, J. (2007, January 5). Travel: Seeing how LBJ brought power to the people. *American Heritage*. https://www.americanheritage.com/node/132467

Kennedy, A. (2023, May 29). Mapped: Renewable energy and battery installations in the U.S. in 2023. *Elements*. https://elements.visualcapitalist.com/new-us-renewable-energy

Klein, E. (2022, September 20). Transcript: Ezra Klein interviews Jesse Jenkins. *The Ezra Klein Show*. https://www.nytimes.com/2022/09/20/podcasts/transcript-ezra-klein-interviews-jesse-jenkins.html

Klineberg, S. L. (2020). *Prophetic city: Houston on the cusp of a changing America*. Avid Reader Press.

Klump, E. (2017, November 30). In Texas, specter of FERC jurisdiction stirs concern. *E&E News*. https://www.eenews.net/articles/in-texas-specter-of-ferc-jurisdiction-stirs-concern/

Kowalski, K. M. (2019, December 11). Study: Black, low-income Americans face highest risk from power plant pollution. *Energy News Network*. https://energynews.us/2019/12/11/study-black-low-income-americans-face-highest-risk-from-power-plant-pollution

Lash, G. G., & Lash, E. P. (2014, August 29). *Early history of the natural gas industry, Fredonia, New York* [adapted from oral presentation]. American Association of Petroleum Geologists. https://www.searchanddiscovery.com/pdfz/documents/2014/70168lash/ndx_lash.pdf.html

Lawrence Berkeley National Lab. (2023, April 6). Grid connection requests grow by 40% in 2022 as clean energy surges, despite backlogs and uncertainty. *Electricity Markets & Policy*. https://emp.lbl.gov/news/grid-connection-requests-grow-40-2022-clean

Lefebvre, B. (2023, February 23). How American energy helped Europe best Putin. *Politico*. https://www.politico.com/news/2023/02/23/american-energy-europe-putin-00083750

Leffler, J. (1952). Midland, TX. *Handbook of Texas Online*. Texas State Historical Association. https://www.tshaonline.org/handbook/entries/midland-tx

Lewis, J., & Severnini, E. (2020, March). Short- and long-run impacts of rural electrification: Evidence from the historical rollout of the U.S. power grid. *Journal of Development Economics*, 143. https://doi.org/10.1016/j.jdeveco.2019.102412

Lewis, M. (2023, January 25). Here's why Texas is a geothermal sleeping giant. *Electrek*. https://electrek.co/2023/01/25/texas-geothermal-energy

Library of Congress. (n.d.). *Who invented the automobile?* Everyday Mysteries. https://www.loc.gov/everyday-mysteries/motor-vehicles-aeronautics-astronautics/item/who-invented-the-automobile

Lienhard, J. H. (n.d.). *Engines of our ingenuity, no. 1359: Windmills*. https://www.uh.edu/engines/epi1359.htm#:~:text=Today%20we're%20pretty%20sure,of%20the%20sometimes%20fickle%20winds

LIFE. (1948, April 5). Southwest has a new crop of super rich. *LIFE*, 24(14). https://books.google.com/books?id=ZEEEAAAAMBAJ&source=gbs_all_issues_r&cad=1, p. 23

Livingston, A. (2020, May 18). "All of the party was over": How the last oil bust changed Texas. *The Texas Tribune*. https://www.texastribune.org/2020/05/18/texas-oil-prices-1980s

Long, C. (1995, April 1). Moonlight towers. *Handbook of Texas Online*. Texas State Historical Association. https://www.tshaonline.org/handbook/entries/moonlight-towers

Malone, L. J. (n.d.) *Rural Electrification Administration*. Economic History Association. https://eh.net/encyclopedia/rural-electrification-administration

Marshall, M. (2018, October). 'Dallas' at 40: The inside story behind the show that changed Texas forever. *Texas Monthly*. https://www.texasmonthly.com/the-culture/dallas-at-40-the-inside-story-behind-the-show-that-changed-texas-forever

Martin, K. (2018, March 26). *The big inch: Fueling America's WWII effort*. National Institute of Standards and Technology. https://www.nist.gov/blogs/taking-measure/big-inch-fueling-americas-wwii-war-effort#:~:text=At%20the%20time%2C%20the%20U.S.,kilometers%20of%20ocean%20to%20Europe

Matthews, C. M., & Elliott, R. (2019, March 1). In this oil boom town, even a barber can make $180,000. *The Wall Street Journal*. https://www.wsj.com/articles/in-this-oil-boom-town-even-a-barber-can-make-180-000-11551436210

McCormick, M. (2022, November 5). US oil producers reap $200bn windfall from Ukraine war price surge. *Financial Times*. https://www.ft.com/content/0d84255c-84ba-4462-b80a-8593352852e2

McEwen, M. (2023, January 27). ExxonMobil ends routine flaring in Permian Basin. *MRT*. https://www.mrt.com/business/oil/article/exxonmobil-announces-end-routine-flaring-permian-17743775.php

Miller, J. (2021, April). *The salty history of East Texas lies underground*. Texas Co-op Power. https://texascooppower.com/the-salty-history-of-east-texas-lies-underground

Minton, L. (2020, August). Texas' electricity resources: Where power comes from — and how it gets to you. *FiscalNotes: A Review of the Texas Economy*. Texas Comptroller of Public Accounts. https://comptroller.texas.gov/economy/fiscal-notes/2020/august/ercot.php

Mistretta, A. J. (2021, June 29). *Bobby Tudor keynote presentation at Future of Global Energy Conference*. Greater Houston Partnership. https://www.houston.org/news/bobby-tudor-keynote-presentation-future-global-energy-conference

Mock, B. (2017, September 15). Harvey's poorest victims will never rebuild. They're getting evicted. *Mother Jones*. https://www.motherjones.com/environment/2017/09/harveys-poorest-victims-will-never-rebuild-theyre-getting-evicted

Morenne, B., Cole, D., & DeLorenzo, D. (2023, March 3). How gas from Texas becomes cooking fuel in France. *The Wall Street Journal*. https://www.wsj.com/articles/american-fracked-gas-ukraine-invasion-europe-import-9e5cc725

M.W. (2014). *The history of electrification: New York City historic power plants*. Edison Tech Center. https://edisontechcenter.org/NYC.html

NASA. (n.d.). *The effects of climate change*. Global Climate Change: Vital Signs of the Planet. https://climate.nasa.gov/effects

National Institute of Environmental Health Sciences. (n.d.) Hydraulic fracturing and health. https://www.niehs.nih.gov/health/topics/agents/fracking/index.cfm

National Oceanic and Atmospheric Administration. (2023, April 5). *Greenhouse gases continued to increase rapidly in 2022*. https://www.noaa.gov/news-release/greenhouse-gases-continued-to-increase-rapidly-in-2022

National Oceanic and Atmospheric Association, Office for Coastal Management. (n.d.). *Hurricane costs*. https://coast.noaa.gov/states/fast-facts/hurricane-costs.html

National Park Service. (n.d.). *Windmills on the American plains*. https://www.nps.gov/articles/windmills.htm

Net Zero Tracker. (n.d.) Data Explorer [Interactive database]. https://zerotracker.net/

Nguyen, R. (2023, August 21). 2023 becomes deadliest summer in last 5 years for heat-related deaths in Harris, Fort Bend counties. *ABC13 Eyewitness News*. https://abc13.com/texas-heat-related-deaths-2023-heat-wave-weather-forecast-harris-county-medical-examiners-office/13681774/

Nilsen, E. (July 28, 2023). Wind and solar are propping up the Texas power grid amid a brutally long heat wave. *CNN*. https://www.cnn.com/2023/07/28/business/texas-renewable-energy-heat-wave-climate/index.html

Office of Energy Efficiency & Renewable Energy. (n.d.). *Decarbonizing process heat: Industrial Efficiency & Decarbonization*

Office. https://www.energy.gov/eere/iedo/decarbonizing-process-heat

Office of Energy Efficiency & Renewable Energy. (n.d.). *History and impacts: Buildings: Appliance & equipment standards*. https://www.energy.gov/eere/buildings/history-and-impacts

Office of the Federal Chief Sustainability Officer. (n.d.). *Federal sustainability plan*. https://www.sustainability.gov/federalsustainabilityplan/index.html

Oil and Gas Climate Initiative. (2021, September). *OGCI strategy*. https://3971732.fs1.hubspotusercontent-na1.net/hubfs/3971732/OGCI-Strategy-September-2021.pdf

Oltermann, P., Henley, J., Chrisafis, A., Jones, S., & Walker, S. (2023, February 3). How Putin's plans to blackmail Europe over gas supply failed. *The Guardian*. https://www.theguardian.com/world/2023/feb/03/putin-russia-blackmail-europe-gas-supply-ukraine

Oppenheimer, M. (2014, February 13). Austin's moon towers, beyond 'Dazed and Confused'. *The New York Times*. https://www.nytimes.com/2014/02/16/travel/austins-moon-towers-beyond-dazed-and-confused.html?_r=0

Oxner, R. (2022, February 15). Texas could connect to national power grids without losing autonomy, former grid regulator says. *Texas Tribune*. https://www.texastribune.org/2022/02/14/texas-national-power-grids/

Paddison, L. (2023, September 6). The world has just experienced the hottest summer on record—by a significant margin. *CNN*. https://www.cnn.com/2023/09/06/world/hottest-summer-record-climate-intl/index.html

Pedernales Electric Cooperative. (n.d.). *The cooperative story*. https://www.pec.coop/about-us/cooperative-difference/cooperative-story

Penrod, E. (2021, June 4). Texas lawmakers approve bill mandating power plant weatherization, market reforms. *UtilityDive*. https://www.utilitydive.com/news/texas-lawmakers-approve-bill-mandating-power-plant-weatherization-market-r/601138

Perkins, S. (2019, July 19). Major U.S. cities are leaking methane at twice the rate previously believed. *Science*. https://www.science.org/content/article/major-us-cities-are-leaking-methane-twice-rate-previously-believed

Peters, K. (2023, July 10). Congested transmission lines cause renewable power to go to waste in Texas. *Ars Technica*. https://arstechnica.com/science/2023/07/congested-transmission-lines-cause-renewable-power-to-go-to-waste-in-texas/

Plant, G., Kort, E. A., Brandt, A. R., Chen, Y., Fordice, G., Gorchov Negron, A. M., Schwietzke, S., Smith, M., & Zavala-Araiza, D. (2022). Inefficient and unlit natural gas flares both emit large quantities of methane. *Science*, 377(6614), p. 1566-1571. https://www.energy.gov/fecm/articles/natural-gas-flaring-and-venting-regulations-report

Poole, K. (n.d.). Biography: John D. Rockefeller, Senior. American Experience. PBS. https://www.pbs.org/wgbh/americanexperience/features/rockefellers-john/

Popovich, N., & Plumer, B. (2023, April 14). A key part of America's plan to slash carbon emissions: Plug in (almost) everything. *The New York Times*. https://www.nytimes.com/interactive/2023/04/14/climate/electric-car-heater-everything.html

Porterfield, B. (1975, March). H.L. Hunt's Long Goodbye. *Texas Monthly*. https://www.texasmonthly.com/news-politics/h-l-hunts-long-goodbye/

Priest, A. A., & Elliott, J. R. (2023, May 23). The multiplicity of impact: How social marginalization compounds climate disasters. *Environmental Sociology*, 9(3), 269–283. https://doi.org/10.1080/23251042.2023.2215592

Prindle, D. F. (1981, January). The Texas Railroad Commission and the elimination of the flaring of natural gas, 1930–1949. *Southwestern Historical Quarterly*, 84(3), 293–308. https://texashistory.unt.edu/ark:/67531/metapth101225/m1/341/?q=prindle

Proffer, E. (2023, June 30). Renewable energy sets new record for electricity production in Texas. *KVUE*. https://www.kvue.com/article/tech/science/environment/renewable-energy-record-texas/269-6c1032eb-d8ce-4a9b-8059-1783b8ee6947

Railroad Commission of Texas. (n.d.). *Historical crude oil production and well counts*. https://www.rrc.texas.gov/oil-and-gas/research-and-statistics/production-data/historical-production-data/crude-oil-production-and-well-counts-since-1935

Ramos, M. G. (2000). Oil and Texas: A cultural history. *Texas Almanac*. https://www.texasalmanac.com/articles/oil-and-texas-a-cultural-history

Reed, C. (2020, September 25). *The grid is changing in Texas, but can we overcome transmission constraints?* Sierra Club Lone Star Chapter. https://www.sierraclub.org/texas/blog/2020/09/grid-changing-texas-can-we-overcome-transmission-constraints

Rhodes, J. (2023, March 23). *Update on wholesale market cost savings attributable to Texas renewables* [Memorandum]. IdeaSmiths. https://www.ideasmiths.net/wp-content/uploads/2023/03/ERCOT_2022_RE_wholesalecosts_update_memo.pdf

Rhodes, J. D. (2022, October). *The impact of renewables in ERCOT*. IdeaSmiths. https://www.ideasmiths.net/wp-content/uploads/2022/10/IdeaSmiths_CFT_ERCOT_RE_FINAL.pdf

Rimer, S. (1998, July 2). Houston journal; broiling on the outside, but, really, it's no sweat. *The New York Times*. https://www.nytimes.com/1998/07/02/us/houston-journal-broiling-on-the-outside-but-really-it-s-no-sweat.html

Ritchie, H., & Roser, M. (2022). *Access to energy*. Our World in Data. https://ourworldindata.org/energy-access#access-to-electricity

Ross, J. F. (2018, September 10). How the West was lost. *The Atlantic*. https://www.theatlantic.com/ideas/archive/2018/09/how-the-west-was-lost/569365/

Ross, M. L. (2013, October 15). How the 1973 oil embargo saved the planet. *Foreign Affairs*. https://www.foreignaffairs.com/articles/north-america/2013-10-15/how-1973-oil-embargo-saved-planet

Savcenko, K. (2023, April 12). *How the Russia-Ukraine war is turning natural gas into the 'new oil'*. S&P Global Commodity Insights. https://www.spglobal.com/commodityinsights/en/market-insights/blogs/natural-gas/041223-how-the-russia-ukraine-war-is-turning-natural-gas-into-the-new-oil

Savvaidis, A. (2022, December 31). *2022 biennial report on seismic monitoring and research in Texas*. Bureau of Economic Geology. https://www.beg.utexas.edu/files/texnet/2022%20Biennial%20Report%20on%20Seismic%20Monitoring%20and%20Research%20in%20Texas.pdf

Shabecoff, P. (1988, June 24). Global warming has begun, expert tells Senate. *The New York Times*. https://www.nytimes.com/1988/06/24/us/global-warming-has-begun-expert-tells-senate.html

Slijk, C., & Philips, K. R. (2021). *Once-oil-dependent Texas economy to keep growing as renewable energy expands*. Federal Reserve Bank of Dallas. https://www.dallasfed.org/research/swe/2021/swe2103/swe2103b

Smith, J. C. (1952). Corsicana oilfield. *Handbook of Texas Online*. Texas State Historical Association. https://www.tshaonline.org/handbook/entries/corsicana-oilfield

Sönke Wortmann Offiziell. (2013) *SolarWorld – Larry Hagman* [YouTube video]. https://www.youtube.com/watch?v=ccOS-UMvjolA

The derricks at Burkburnett in Wichita County on January 20, 1919. Photo by W. H. Raymond, Public Domain

The Source. (2022, July 7). Chronic air pollution in Harris County is one example of environmental inequality in Texas. *Texas Public Radio*. https://www.tpr.org/podcast/the-source/2022-07-07/pollution-in-harris-county-is-one-example-of-environmental-injustice-in-texas

Southeast Energy Efficiency Alliance & Texas Energy Poverty Research Institute. (2023, April 20). *Energy insecurity in the South*. https://storymaps.arcgis.com/stories/4377299f586a493984222bfc6ee84e60

Stiles, J., Linsley, J. W., & Rienstra, E. W. (2008). *Giant under the hill: A history of the Spindletop oil discovery at Beaumont, Texas, in 1901*. Texas State Historical Association.

Stringer, T. W. (1952). Cullinan, Joseph Stephen (1860–1937). *Texas Handbook Online*. Texas State Historical Association. https://www.tshaonline.org/handbook/entries/cullinan-joseph-stephen

Svitek, P. (2022, January 1). Texas puts final estimate of winter storm death toll at 246. *The Texas Tribune*. https://www.texastribune.org/2022/01/02/texas-winter-storm-final-death-toll-246

Texas Comptroller of Public Accounts. (n.d.-a). *History of natural gas and crude oil tax rates*. https://comptroller.texas.gov/taxes/natural-gas/cong-rate-history.php

Texas Comptroller of Public Accounts. (n.d.-b). *Texas water tour: Surface water*. https://comptroller.texas.gov/economy/economic-data/water/2022/surface.php

Texas Oil & Gas Association. (2023, January). *Annual energy & economic impact report: 2022*. https://docs.txoga.org/files/3473-2022-energy-economic-impact-report.pdf

Texas Produced Water Consortium. (2022). *Beneficial use of produced water in Texas: Challenges, opportunities and the path forward*. https://www.depts.ttu.edu/research/tx-water-consortium/downloads/22-TXPWC-Report-Texas-Legislature.pdf

Thompson, J. (2022). *Looking back: Shale oil boom gave Permian Basin a second life*. Federal Reserve Bank of Dallas. https://www.dallasfed.org/research/swe/2022/swe2201/swe2201a

Thompson, L. (2016, November 18). *Rural Electrification Administration (REA)* (1935). The Living New Deal. https://livingnewdeal.org/glossary/rural-electrification-administration-rea-1935

Titus, E. (2011, December 7). Jon Wellinghoff: The TT interview. *The Texas Tribune*. http://www.texastribune.org/texas-energy/energy/jon-wellinghoff-tt-interview

Trembath, A., Jenkins, J., Nordhaus, T., & Shellenberger, M. (2012, May). *Where the shale gas revolution came from*. Breakthrough Institute Energy & Climate Program. https://s3.us-east-2.amazonaws.com/uploads.thebreakthrough.org/legacy/blog/Where_the_Shale_Gas_Revolution_Came_From.pdf

Union of Concerned Scientists. (2006, July 25). *A brief history of US fuel efficiency standards*. https://www.ucsusa.org/resources/brief-history-us-fuel-efficiency

United Nations. (n.d.-a). *Causes and effects of climate change*. https://www.un.org/en/climatechange/science/causes-effects-climate-change

United Nations. (n.d.-b). *What is the United Nations Framework Convention on Climate Change?* https://unfccc.int/process-and-meetings/what-is-the-united-nations-framework-convention-on-climate-change

Universal Ecological Fund. (n.d.). *Extreme weather events by state*. https://feu-us.org/our-work/case-for-climate-action-us/maps-events-by-state

Urban Institute. (2023). *Severance Taxes*. State and Local Backgrounders. https://www.urban.org/policy-centers/cross-center-initiatives/state-and-local-finance-initiative/state-and-local-backgrounders/severance-taxes

U.S. Bureau of Labor Statistics. (2022, May). *Petroleum engineers: Occupational employment and wages, May 2022*. Occupational Employment and Wage Statistics. https://www.bls.gov/oes/current/oes172171.htm

U.S. Census Bureau. (1995, October). *Urban and rural population: 1900 to 1990* [Table]. https://www2.census.gov/programs-surveys/decennial/tables/1990/1990-urban-pop/urpop0090.txt

U.S. Department of Energy. (2019, June). *Natural gas flaring and venting: State and federal regulatory overview, trends, and impacts*. https://www.energy.gov/fecm/articles/natural-gas-flaring-and-venting-regulations-report

U.S. Department of Energy. (2021, February 23). *Creating equity in energy for people of color*. https://www.energy.gov/articles/creating-equity-energy-people-color

U.S. Department of Energy. (2022, April). *Queued up ... but in need of transmission*. https://www.energy.gov/sites/default/files/2022-04/Queued%20Up%E2%80%A6But%20in%20Need%20of%20Transmission.pdf

U.S. Department of the Interior. (1976). *Texas SP moonlight towers*. National Archives Catalog. https://catalog.archives.gov/id/40973789

U.S. Energy Information Administration. (2019, August 20). The U.S. leads global petroleum and natural gas production with record growth in 2018. *Today in Energy*. https://www.eia.gov/todayinenergy/detail.php?id=40973

U.S. Energy Information Administration. (2020, August 5). *More than 100 coal-fired plants have been replaced or converted to natural gas since 2011*. https://www.eia.gov/todayinenergy/detail.php?id=44636

U.S. Energy Information Administration. (2021, June 9). Electric power sector CO_2 emissions drop as generation mix shifts from coal to natural gas. *Today in Energy*. https://www.eia.gov/todayinenergy/detail.php?id=48296#

U.S. Energy Information Administration. (2021, October 6). *Consumption*. International Energy Outlook 2021. https://www.eia.gov/outlooks/ieo/narrative/consumption/sub-topic-01.php

U.S. Energy Information Administration. (2022, April). *The United States has been an annual net total energy exporter since 2019*. U.S. Energy Facts Explained. https://www.eia.gov/energyexplained/us-energy-facts/imports-and-exports.php

U.S. Energy Information Administration. (2022, September 30). Advances in technology led to record new well productivity in the Permian Basin in 2021. *Today in Energy*. https://www.eia.gov/todayinenergy/detail.php?id=54079

U.S. Energy Information Administration. (2022, December). *Short-term energy outlook*. https://www.eia.gov/outlooks/steo/outlook.php#issues2022

U.S. Energy Information Administration. (2022a). *What countries are the top producers and consumers of oil?* Frequently asked questions (FAQS). https://www.eia.gov/tools/faqs/faq.php?id=709&t=6

U.S. Energy Information Administration. (2022b). *Texas: Profile analysis.* https://www.eia.gov/state/analysis.php?sid=TX#18

U.S. Energy Information Administration. (2023, February). *What is U.S. electricity generation by energy source?* Frequently asked questions (FAQS). https://www.eia.gov/tools/faqs/faq.php?id=427&t=3

U.S. Energy Information Administration. (2023, March). *Fuels used and end uses in U.S. homes, by home size, 2020* [Table]. https://www.eia.gov/consumption/residential/data/2020/hc/pdf/HC%201.9.pdf

U.S. Energy Information Administration. (2023, May 1). The 10 largest oil producers and share of total world oil production in 2022 [Table]. *What countries are the top producers and consumers of oil?* Frequently Asked Questions (FAQS). https://www.eia.gov/tools/faqs/faq.php?id=709&t=6

U.S. Energy Information Administration. (2023, June 15). *Texas state energy profile.* https://www.eia.gov/state/print.php?sid=TX

U.S. Energy Information Administration. (2023, July). A case study of transmission limits on renewables growth in Texas. https://www.eia.gov/electricity/markets/quarterly/archive/2023/transmission_limits_07_2023.pdf

U.S. Energy Information Administration. (2023, August 31). *U.S. field production of crude oil (thousand barrels per day)* [Table]. Petroleum & Other Liquids. https://www.eia.gov/dnav/pet/hist/LeafHandler.ashx?n=pet&s=mcrfpus2&f=a

U.S. Energy Information Administration. (n.d.-a). *Rankings: Total carbon dioxide emissions, 2021 (million metric tons)* [Table]. Texas State Profile and Energy Estimates. https://www.eia.gov/state/rankings/?sid=TX#/series/226

U.S. Energy Information Administration. (n.d.-b). *Wind explained: History of wind power.* https://www.eia.gov/energyexplained/wind/history-of-wind-power.php

U.S. Energy Information Administration. (n.d.-c). *Energy and the environment explained.* https://www.eia.gov/energyexplained/energy-and-the-environment/where-greenhouse-gases-come-from.php

U.S. Environmental Protection Agency. (n.d.-a). *Global greenhouse gas emissions data.* https://www.epa.gov/ghgemissions/global-greenhouse-gas-emissions-data

U.S. Environmental Protection Agency. (n.d.-b). *Power plants and neighboring communities.* Clean Air Power Sector Programs. https://www.epa.gov/power-sector/power-plants-and-neighboring-communities#graphing

U.S. Environmental Protection Agency. (n.d.-c). *U.S. grid regions.* https://www.epa.gov/green-power-markets/us-grid-regions

UT Energy Institute. (2021, July). *The timeline and events of the February 2021 Texas electric grid blackouts.* https://energy.utexas.edu/sites/default/files/UTAustin%20%282021%29%20EventsFebruary2021TexasBlackout%2020210714.pdf

Valle, S. (2023, January 25). Exclusive: Exxon halts routine gas flaring in the Permian, wants others to follow. *Reuters.* https://www.reuters.com/business/energy/exxon-halts-routine-gas-flaring-permian-wants-others-follow-2023-01-24

Wallace, H. D., Jr. (2016, February 12). *Power from the people: Rural electrification brought more than lights.* O Say Can You See? Stories from the Museum. National Museum of American History. https://americanhistory.si.edu/blog/rural-electrification

Wasson, M. (2021, June 11). Driving across the Lone Star State? What do you see and feel? *Spectrum News 1.* https://spectrumlocalnews.com/tx/south-texas-el-paso/weather/2021/06/10/what-do-you-feel-and-see-driving-across-the-lone-star-state-

Weaver, C. (n.d.). *Moonlight towers – 1895.* AustinPostCard.com. https://www.austinpostcard.com/moontower.php

Webb, W. P. (1931). *The Great Plains.* University of Nebraska Press.

Weber, A. (2021, December 22). Here's how Texas lawmakers – and Enron – shaped the state's electrical market. *Texas Standard.* https://www.texasstandard.org/stories/heres-how-texas-lawmakers-and-enron-shaped-the-states-electrical-market

Weber, P. (2023, June 27). A blistering heat wave is turning up the pressure on Texas' power grid. *AP News.* https://apnews.com/article/texas-heat-wave-2023-power-grid-758daa1be9d472f85028ab12bdc263ca

Weeks, D. (1895). Petroleum. *Sixteenth Annual Report of the United States Geological Survey to the Secretary of the Interior, 1894–95,* 315–404.

Weissman, S. (2016, March). *Natural gas as a bridge fuel: Measuring the bridge.* Center for Sustainable Energy. https://energycenter.org/sites/default/files/docs/nav/policy/research-and-reports/Natural_Gas_Bridge_Fuel.pdf

Welborn, D. B. (1976). Windmills. *Handbook of Texas Online.* https://www.tshaonline.org/handbook/entries/windmills

Wesoff, E., & Olano, M. V. (2023, April 14). Chart: US clean energy backlog balloons to unprecedented 2 terawatts. *Canary Media.* https://www.canarymedia.com/articles/clean-energy/chart-us-clean-energy-backlog-balloons-to-unprecedented-2-terawatts

White, I. C. (1921). Important epochs in the history of petroleum and natural gas. *Bulletin of the Geological Society of America,* 32(1), pp. 171-186.

The White House. (2021, December). *Federal sustainability plan: Catalyzing America's clean energy industries and jobs.* https://www.sustainability.gov/pdfs/federal-sustainability-plan.pdf

The White House. (n.d.). *Justice40: A whole-of-government initiative.* https://www.whitehouse.gov/environmentaljustice/justice40

Wilson, A. (2021, December 17). Pipelines may find new life moving carbon dioxide. *Journal of Petroleum Technology.* https://jpt.spe.org/pipelines-may-find-new-life-moving-carbon-dioxide

Wolf, Z. B. (2023, June 22). Why we're talking about the Texas power grid again. *CNN.* https://www.cnn.com/2023/06/22/politics/texas-power-grid-heat-what-matters/index.html

The World Bank. (n.d.). *Gas flaring explained.* https://www.worldbank.org/en/programs/gasflaringreduction/gas-flaring-explained

The World Bank. (n.d.) *"Zero Routine Flaring by 2030" initiative endorsers.* https://www.worldbank.org/en/programs/zero-routine-flaring-by-2030/endorsers

Yergin, D. (1991). *The prize: The epic quest for oil, money & power.* Free Press.

Yergin, D. (2011). *The quest: Energy, security, and the remaking of the modern world.* Penguin Books.

Yergin, D. (2020). *The new map: Energy, climate, and the clash of nations.* Penguin Press.

Yu, J., Hmiel, B., Lyon, D. R., Warren, J., Cusworth, D. H., Duren, R. M., Chen, Y., Murphy, E. C., & Brandt, A. R. (2022). Methane emissions from natural gas gathering pipelines in the Permian Basin. *Environmental Science & Technology Letters,* 9(11), pp. 969–974

Zamora, E. (1992, January). The failed promise of wartime opportunity for Mexicans in the Texas oil industry. *The Southwestern Historical Quarterly,* 95(3), pp. 323–350. https://www.jstor.org/stable/30241385

Texas Economy Rebounds from COVID-19

Source: Excerpted from the State of Texas Annual Cash Report 2022, Comptroller of Public Accounts.

The Texas economy added 726,900 nonfarm jobs from August 2021 to August 2022, an increase of 5.7%, to reach 13,530,100 at the end of fiscal year 2022. Texas added more new jobs than any other state over those 12 months. Private-sector employment rose by 6.6% while government employment (federal, state and local) grew by 0.5%. The state's rate of job growth was the highest among all 50 states.

Texas Industry Performance

Employment in the goods-producing industries increased by 7.8% in fiscal 2022, while employment in the service-providing industries grew by 5.3%. Employment increased in all three of the goods-producing industries (mining and logging, manufacturing, and construction), led by a 21.1% gain in mining and logging. All of the service-providing industries also saw year-over-year growth in employment, with the largest percentage gains in the information (11%) and leisure and hospitality (10.1%) industries.

Mining and Logging

Mining industry employment peaked in December 2014 at 321,900 and then declined steadily, reaching a low of 204,200 in September 2016. Industry employment then grew consistently for more than two years to reach 255,500 in January 2019. Industry employment fell sharply in fiscal 2020, but began to recover in the early months of fiscal 2021 and has increased consistently since then. August 2022 mining employment was up by 21.1% (38,100) from the August 2021 level, but at 219,000 was still 14.3% below the January 2019 peak.

Manufacturing

The Texas manufacturing industry gained 51,000 jobs over the past year, an increase of 5.8%. Durable goods employment was up 30,300, with the largest increase in the fabricated metals manufacturing sector (15,700, 13.3%). That sector is closely associated with oil and natural gas exploration and production, and employment in the sector has been increasing along with that in the mining industry. Overall, durable goods employment increased by 5.5%. Nondurable-goods manufacturing employment grew by 20,700 (6.4%), with the largest increase

Consumer Spending

Consumer spending is a major component of the Texas economy. In fiscal 2016, for the first time since 2010, state sales tax collections fell (by 2.3%) from the previous year's total. The decline in state sales tax revenue was led by reduced collections from the oil and natural gas-related exploration and production sectors, but collections from the manufacturing, retail trade, information and real estate sectors also were down compared to 2015. Growth in sales tax collections resumed in 2017, with revenue up 2.3% over 2016. Sales tax revenue was up again in 2018, by 10.5% and by another 6.5% in 2019 to reach $34.0 billion. Despite economic disruptions resulting from the COVID-19 virus, 2020 sales tax collections managed a further increase of 0.2% from 2019, as increases in collections from the retail trade sector outweighed reduced collections from other sectors. Fiscal 2021 sales tax collections were up 5.6% from 2020 collections, with growth accelerating in the final three months of the fiscal year and continuing through fiscal 2022. Total sales tax collections increased by 19.3% from 2021 levels, with particularly strong growth in mining industry collections (up 103.2%).

The Consumer Confidence Index is a monthly measure of consumer optimism, an important factor affecting the sales of housing, automobiles and other major purchases. The index for the four-state West South Central (WSC) Region, which includes Texas, was down by 17.5% in fiscal 2022. The index for the nation as a whole was down 10.4%.

Gross Domestic Product in Current Dollars

Location	Millions of Dollars			Percent of U.S. Total			GDP* 2021	
	2022	2021	2020	2022	2021	2020	China	$24,861
United States	**$25,462,722**	**$23,315,081**	**$21,060,474**	**100%**	**100%**	**100%**	United States	21,132
1. California	3,598,103	3,373,241	3,020,173	14.1	14.5	14.3	India	9,279
2. Texas	**2,355,960**	**2,051,769**	**1,789,933**	**9.3**	**8.8**	**8.5**	Japan	5,126
3. New York	2,053,180	1,901,297	1,740,805	8.1	8.2	8.3	Germany	4,424
4. Florida	1,389,070	1,255,558	1,116,727	5.5	5.4	5.3	Russia	4,078
5. Illinois	1,033,310	945,674	856,943	4.1	4.1	4.1	Indonesia	3,246
6. Pennsylvania	923,089	844,497	771,613	3.6	3.6	3.7	United Kingdom	3,128
7. Ohio	822,670	756,617	684,383	3.2	3.2	3.2	France	3,048
8. Georgia	755,698	691,627	625,426	3.0	3.0	3.0	Brazil	3,028
9. New Jersey	745,422	682,946	620,086	2.9	2.9	2.9	Italy	2,668
10. North Carolina	730,072	662,121	598,916	2.9	2.8	2.8	Mexico	2,478

Source: Bureau of Economic Analysis.

**Estimated GDP in billions of U.S. dollars, from the World Factbook of the CIA.*

The value of Texas exports in calendar year 2014 was a record $289 billion, an increase of 3.3% from 2013. Those exports provided a substantial boost to manufacturing, notably for companies producing chemicals, computers and electronics, petroleum products, industrial machinery and transportation equipment. In 2015, the value of Texas exports fell sharply (to $251 billion, down 13.1%), hurt by falling oil prices and a stronger dollar. Texas exports continued to fall in 2016, down another 7.4%. However, Texas 2017 exports were up 13.5% from the 2016 level and increased by another 19.4% in 2018. Total 2019 exports were 4.8% higher than 2018 exports; however, in November 2019, Texas exports decreased on a year-over-year basis. As a result of the COVID-19 pandemic and a fall in oil prices, exports fell sharply in 2020, down 15.5% from 2019 (to $279 billion). Export growth resumed in 2021, up 34.4% from 2020 and reaching a new high of $375 billion. Through July, Texas exports are up a further 39% from the corresponding period of 2021. Texas remains the nation's leading exporting state, as it has been for more than a decade. Texas exports comprised 20% of total U.S. exports in 2021.

Construction

Construction employment increased by 50,000 (6.8%) in fiscal 2022 to reach 785,700 in August 2022. Employment in the construction of buildings sector increased by 2.6% (4,100) and heavy and civil engineering construction employment grew by 13.1% (20,600).

Total housing construction activity in 2022 was up from 2021. While single-family building permits issued in the year ending in July 2022, at 172,566, were down 0.7% from the same period one year earlier, building permits for multi-family units were up significantly (by 29.5% to 99,445). According to Multiple Listing Service data from the Texas A&M Real Estate Center, the median sales price for an existing Texas single-family home rose by 12.9% over the past year, from $310,000 in July 2021 to $350,000 in July 2022. In July 2022, Texas had a 2.4-month inventory of existing homes for sale, up from a 1.6-month inventory in July of 2021.

Professional and Business Services

Employment in the professional and business services industry increased by 122,600 (6.4%) in fiscal 2022. Employment changes varied considerably among industry sectors, with the largest increases in services to buildings and dwellings (10.4%) and employment services (12.6%). Total professional and business services employment was 2,035,100 in August 2022.

Education and Health Services

The education and health services industry, composed of the educational services and health care and social assistance sectors, gained 88,300 jobs in fiscal 2022, an increase of 5.1%. The relatively small educational services sector saw an increase of 33,500 jobs (15.1%). Employment in the much larger health care and social assistance sector grew by 3.6% (54,800 jobs). In all, Texas education and health services employment increased to 1,828,700 in August 2022.

Financial Activities

In fiscal 2022 overall employment in the financial activities industry grew by 7.5% (63,200 jobs). The finance and insurance sector grew by 24,700 (4.0%) while the real estate and rental and leasing sector grew by 38,500 (16.9%). Credit intermediation (which includes financial institutions such as banks) is the industry's largest sector, employing 289,400 as of August 2022. Total Texas financial activities industry employment reached 901,700 in that month.

> **For more information**
>
> For a more detailed overview of population, income, jobs, wages and education trends of Texas' 12 economic regions, visit: comptroller.texas. gov/economy/economic-data/regions

Trade, Transportation and Utilities

The trade, transportation and utilities industry, the state's largest employer with 20% of total nonfarm jobs in August 2022, gained 118,900 jobs (4.6%) over the year. Employment in all three industry sectors—retail trade, wholesale trade and transportation, warehousing and utilities—increased during fiscal 2022. Wholesale trade employment was up 5.8% (34,700); transportation, warehousing and utilities employment grew by 40,900 (6.4%); and employment in the retail trade sector increased by 43,300 (3.2%). In all, the trade, transportation and utilities industry provided 2,700,900 Texas jobs in August 2022.

Information

The information industry is a collection of diverse sectors, representing established sectors of the economy (newspaper publishing, data processing, television broadcasting and wired telephone services) as well as some newer sectors (cell phone service providers, Internet providers and software). The newspaper, periodical and book publishing sector saw the largest percentage increase in employment over the year (1,200 jobs, 8.8%). Total industry employment grew 11% (23,300) to reach 234,200 in August 2022.

Leisure and Hospitality

Employment in the leisure and hospitality industry increased by 133,400 (10.1%) over the fiscal year. The majority of the industry's job gains occurred in the food services and drinking places sector, which added 95,500 jobs (8.8%). The largest percentage gain was in the accommodations sector, which grew by 19.2% (21,400). Total leisure and hospitality employment in August 2022 was 1,453,600, representing about 11% of total Texas employment.

Other Services

The other services industry is a varied mix of business activities including repair and maintenance services; laundry services; organizations; religious organizations; political and civic organizations; funeral services; parking garages; beauty salons; and a wide range of personal services. Repair and maintenance services employment increased by 8.1%, the highest rate among other services sectors. In all, other services industry employment grew by 27,500 to reach 448,000 in August 2022.

Government Employment

Government employment grew by 10,600 (0.5%) over the year. Federal government employment increased by 800; local government employment increased by 11,300; and state government employment fell by 1,500. Total government employment in Texas was 1,995,500 in August 2022. ☆

Texas Gross Domestic Product, 2013–2022, by Industry (in Millions)

Industry	2013	2014	2015	2016	2017	2018	2019	2020	2021	2022
Agriculture, Forestry, Fishing/Hunting	$10,791	$10,282	$12,226	$9,233	$10,230	$9,708	$8,331	$8,017	$11,297	15,025
% change*	32.6	-4.7	18.9	-24.5	10.8	-5.1	-14.2	-3.8	40.9	33.0
Natural Resources and Mining	186,363	205,168	122,168	99,193	126,508	155,545	146,548	87,206	165,634	261,566
% change	16.8	10.1	-40.5	-18.8	27.5	23.0	-5.8	-40.5	89.9	57.9
Construction	67,580	74,099	79,037	82,320	84,308	86,145	92,380	91,178	93,563	100,095
% change	6.0	9.6	6.7	4.2	2.4	2.2	7.2	-1.3	2.6	7.0
Manufacturing	224,682	202,280	211,752	197,649	215,097	243,820	225,919	197,650	226,953	263,733
% change	8.4	-10.0	4.7	-6.7	8.8	13.4	-7.3	-12.5	14.8	16.2
Trade, Transportation, Utilities	275,667	288,344	302,797	304,213	311,287	330,020	345,816	341,136	391,081	442,835
% change	3.4	4.6	5.0	0.5	2.3	6.0	4.8	-1.4	14.6	13.2
Information	54,387	53,987	59,693	61,159	64,248	68,039	70,754	73,488	80,187	93,894
% change	9.7	-0.7	10.6	2.5	5.0	5.9	4.8	3.9	9.1	17.1
Financial Activities	211,070	231,362	242,781	262,841	274,787	300,218	319,015	348,732	373,860	404,858
% change	5.7	9.6	4.9	8.3	4.5	9.3	6.3	9.3	7.2	8.3
Professional and Business Services	157,731	170,298	178,778	182,265	194,363	209,697	226,592	221,921	253,731	283,932
% change	4.5	8	5.0	2.0	6.6	7.9	8.1	-2.1	14.3	11.9
Educational and Health Services	95,828	99,713	106,562	112,963	117,123	121,536	128,096	128,154	136,974	147,780
% change	3.5	4.1	6.9	6.0	3.7	3.8	5.4	0.0	6.9	7.9
Leisure and Hospitality Services	45,614	51,045	56,530	59,315	60,734	62,142	66,134	53,156	67,535	77,963
% change	4.8	11.9	10.7	4.9	2.4	2.3	6.4	-19.6	27.1	15.4
Other Private Services	28,969	31,278	32,230	32,583	33,291	35,179	37,311	35,818	38,683	42,625
% change	4.5	8.0	3.0	1.1	2.2	5.7	6.1	4.0	8.0	10.2
Government and Schools	156,504	161,444	168,943	175,281	181,258	187,348	191,861	203,466	212,271	222,878
% change	3.3	3.2	4.6	3.8	3.4	3.4	2.4	6.0	4.3	5.0
TOTAL	$1,515,196	$1,579,299	$1,573,498	$1,579,015	$1,673,234	$1,809,397	$1,858,757	$1,789,932	$2,051,769	$2,357,184
% change	6.6	4.2	-0.4	0.4	6.0	2.7	2.7	-3.7	14.6	14.9
TOTAL (in 2009 chained dollars)**	$1,484,700	$1,529,617	$1,605,902	$1,619,954	$1,659,453	$1,728,304	$1,779,781	$1,747,562	$1,815,064	$1,873,184
% change	4.5	3.0	5.0	0.9	2.4	4.1	3.0	-1.8	3.9	3.2

*Percent change from the previous year. **In 1996, the U.S. Department of Commerce introduced the chained-dollar measure. The new measure is based on the average weights of goods and services in successive pairs of years. It is "chained" because the second year in each pair, with its weights, becomes the first year of the next pair. *Source: 2022 Comprehensive Annual Financial Report for the State of Texas.*

Per Capita Income by County, 2021

Source: Bureau of Economic Analysis, U.S. Department of Commerce, 2021.

Below are listed data for 2021 for total personal income and per capita income by county. Total income is reported in millions of dollars. The middle column indicates the percent of change in total personal income from 2020 to 2021.

In the far right column is the county's rank in the state for per capita income. Midland County was first with $126,738. The lowest per capita income was in Zapata County at $33,288. ☆

Top Ten

County	Major Towns	PCI
1. Midland	Midland	$126,738
2. Glasscock	Garden City	124,963
3. Sherman	Stratford	122,945
4. Loving	Mentone	115,158
5. McMullen	Tilden	110,273
6. Lipscomb	Lipscomb, Booker	102,569
7. Borden	Gail	101,470
8. Kendall	Boerne	96,628
9. Shackelford	Albany	93,075
10. King	Guthrie	91,930

Lowest Ten

County	Major Towns	PCI
245. Cameron	Brownsville	$37,861
246. Willacy	Raymondville	37,792
247. Coryell	Gatesville	37,476
248. Garza	Post	36,426
249. Mitchell	Colorado City	35,417
250. Starr	Rio Grande City	34,933
251. Bee	Beeville	34,738
252. Hidalgo	McAllen	34,503
253. Walker	Huntsville	33,345
254. Zapata	Zapata	33,288

Location	Total Income ($ mil)	% Change 2020-21	Per Capita Income	Rank in State
United States	$21,804,788	2.4%	$64,143	—
Metropolitan	19,019,408	7.4%	66,392	—
Nonmetro	2,269,301	7.7%	49,962	—
Texas	$1,861,396	5.3%	$59,865	—
Metropolitan	1,612,565	8.8%	60,960	—
Nonmetro	155,117	9.0%	50,445	—
Anderson	$2,479	10.1%	$42,444	232
Andrews	976	6.3%	52,943	123
Angelina	3,994	8.4%	46,170	201
Aransas	1,468	8.7%	59,878	66
Archer	522	5.7%	60,101	63
Armstrong	113	4.9%	61,382	54
Atascosa	2,334	10.0%	46,737	194
Austin	1,771	6.6%	58,284	82
Bailey	353	3.8%	51,709	143
Bandera	1,266	8.2%	58,706	76
Bastrop	4,514	15.3%	44,230	216
Baylor	204	7.4%	58,779	75
Bee	1,074	5.4%	34,738	251
Bell	18,755	8.5%	49,405	170
Bexar	105,023	7.9%	51,780	140
Blanco	786	7.3%	66,088	39
Borden	62	37.0%	101,470	7
Bosque	942	10.4%	50,943	149
Bowie	4,425	6.9%	47,792	182
Brazoria	21,399	7.4%	56,360	92
Brazos	11,070	8.6%	46,702	196
Brewster	501	7.6%	53,014	120
Briscoe	83	27.7%	58,862	74
Brooks	304	7.0%	43,437	224
Brown	1,758	7.6%	46,028	205
Burleson	1,038	11.1%	57,482	84
Burnet	3,026	9.7%	59,381	70
Caldwell	1,948	14.0%	41,642	235
Calhoun	1,195	1.5%	60,589	61
Callahan	719	8.4%	50,963	148
Cameron	16,016	11.7%	37,861	245
Camp	589	10.3%	46,705	195
Carson	324	16.7%	56,357	93
Cass	1,317	7.1%	46,101	204
Castro	604	8.5%	81,900	12
Chambers	2,961	7.2%	60,591	60
Cherokee	2,216	9.2%	43,376	225
Childress	269	11.6%	39,953	240
Clay	533	5.8%	51,938	137
Cochran	157	32.0%	62,305	50
Coke	162	6.2%	48,804	174
Coleman	424	9.6%	54,822	104
Collin	85,436	10.2%	77,006	18
Collingsworth	142	11.9%	54,140	110
Colorado	1,222	8.6%	59,219	72
Comal	11,735	11.8%	67,063	35
Comanche	690	6.8%	50,112	162
Concho	129	11.2%	38,635	243
Cooke	2,526	8.5%	59,800	68
Coryell	3,157	8.2%	37,476	247
Cottle	102	21.2%	73,613	22
Crane	253	8.5%	54,119	111
Crockett	175	5.0%	57,013	87
Crosby	270	16.8%	52,897	124
Culberson	156	7.9%	71,297	28
Dallam	506	3.3%	70,511	30
Dallas	186,761	8.2%	72,218	26

Location	Total Income ($ mil)	% Change 2020-21	Per Capita Income	Rank in State
Dawson	573	4.9%	46,139	202
Deaf Smith	1,111	8.7%	60,615	59
Delta	256	10.0%	47,471	185
Denton	64,759	10.0%	68,773	33
De Witt	1,333	13.0%	66,916	36
Dickens	89	7.9%	50,869	152
Dimmit	473	9.6%	55,771	96
Donley	165	8.2%	50,574	156
Duval	506	9.4%	51,887	139
Eastland	1,186	12.1%	66,400	37
Ector	8,636	5.8%	53,610	114
Edwards	106	2.6%	73,981	21
Ellis	10,822	12.6%	53,393	115
El Paso	38,245	8.3%	44,064	217
Erath	2,035	6.4%	46,906	192
Falls	756	10.3%	43,658	222
Fannin	1,699	11.0%	46,449	199
Fayette	1,613	6.7%	65,339	44
Fisher	212	17.9%	57,245	85
Floyd	285	18.4%	53,292	116
Foard	66	11.4%	61,279	56
Fort Bend	56,488	8.2%	65,797	42
Franklin	543	10.8%	51,926	138
Freestone	870	9.2%	44,014	218
Frio	736	11.6%	39,898	241
Gaines	1,108	7.4%	50,616	155
Galveston	21,329	6.3%	60,071	64
Garza	214	12.3%	36,426	248
Gillespie	2,130	8.4%	78,039	15
Glasscock	144	17.0%	124,963	2
Goliad	401	9.2%	55,947	95
Gonzales	1,131	15.4%	57,578	83
Gray	1,048	6.1%	49,815	166
Grayson	7,253	10.5%	52,055	133
Gregg	6,577	6.3%	52,958	121
Grimes	1,269	8.9%	41,914	233
Guadalupe	9,240	8.0%	52,190	132
Hale	1,403	9.6%	43,543	223
Hall	139	28.5%	48,706	175
Hamilton	639	7.5%	77,672	16
Hansford	398	10.7%	77,093	17
Hardeman	195	6.8%	54,847	102
Hardin	2,994	4.9%	52,544	131
Harris	311,431	6.8%	65,869	40
Harrison	3,314	7.4%	47,928	181
Hartley	409	0.3%	75,790	19
Haskell	294	11.1%	54,321	109
Hays	14,327	14.4%	56,097	94
Hemphill	248	5.2%	75,731	20
Henderson	4,066	9.9%	48,594	176
Hidalgo	30,375	11.1%	34,503	252
Hill	1,822	9.8%	49,968	164
Hockley	1,123	6.8%	52,586	130
Hood	3,912	9.6%	60,912	58
Hopkins	1,871	10.5%	50,272	159
Houston	1,086	7.1%	48,835	173
Howard	1,741	6.5%	51,007	147

Location	Total Income ($ mil)	% Change 2020-21	Per Capita Income	Rank in State
Hudspeth	140	11.0%	42,500	231
Hunt	4,839	11.4%	46,801	193
Hutchinson	1,027	7.7%	50,130	161
Irion	123	11.1%	78,988	14
Jack	394	7.3%	45,263	212
Jackson	786	9.3%	51,971	135
Jasper	1,631	5.9%	49,475	169
Jeff Davis	116	8.9%	59,302	71
Jefferson	12,239	4.5%	48,243	178
Jim Hogg	208	9.8%	43,336	226
Jim Wells	1,977	7.8%	50,892	150
Johnson	9,667	12.1%	51,619	144
Jones	773	10.5%	38,914	242
Karnes	1,079	16.2%	73,144	24
Kaufman	7,809	14.8%	49,494	168
Kendall	4,521	8.2%	96,628	8
Kenedy	16	2.9%	47,141	189
Kent	42	7.9%	55,725	99
Kerr	3,264	8.0%	61,401	53
Kimble	237	8.6%	54,345	108
King	24	6.4%	91,930	10
Kinney	134	6.8%	42,929	229
Kleberg	1,404	7.7%	45,818	206
Knox	169	7.2%	50,320	158
Lamar	2,540	8.5%	50,699	154
Lamb	705	9.1%	54,689	105
Lampasas	1,302	8.1%	58,507	78
La Salle	351	15.2%	52,652	128
Lavaca	1,281	7.5%	62,375	49
Lee	1,003	4.9%	56,674	89
Leon	849	11.6%	53,179	119
Liberty	4,179	10.8%	42,813	230
Limestone	1,049	10.5%	47,439	186
Lipscomb	301	4.2%	102,569	6
Live Oak	525	8.6%	46,134	203
Llano	1,312	8.8%	59,689	69
Loving	7	1.8%	115,158	4
Lubbock	15,999	7.2%	50,881	151
Lynn	333	34.9%	58,496	79
McCulloch	345	7.7%	40,859	238
McLennan	13,027	9.0%	47,582	183
McMullen	67	25.3%	84,121	11
Madison	561	13.0%	57,094	86
Marion	459	7.3%	50,775	153
Martin	438	14.2%	38,448	244
Mason	225	7.9%	45,744	207
Matagorda	1,845	7.1%	49,512	167
Maverick	2,232	8.9%	110,273	5
Medina	2,603	9.3%	50,076	163
Menard	94	8.0%	47,390	187
Midland	21,288	13.3%	126,738	1
Milam	1,137	11.6%	45,286	211
Mills	232	5.8%	51,712	142
Mitchell	321	6.8%	35,417	249
Montague	933	7.6%	45,716	208
Montgomery	44,756	7.8%	68,974	32
Moore	1,196	11.6%	56,634	90

Location	Total Income ($ mil)	% Change 2020-21	Per Capita Income	Rank in State
Morris	568	7.7%	47,226	188
Motley	45	1.1%	41,754	234
Nacogdoches	2,991	10.0%	46,246	200
Navarro	2,445	10.6%	45,616	209
Newton	528	6.0%	43,123	228
Nolan	768	10.0%	52,629	129
Nueces	18,661	7.5%	52,852	126
Ochiltree	628	13.7%	64,247	45
Oldham	124	3.5%	72,126	27
Orange	4,145	4.2%	48,912	172
Palo Pinto	1,493	10.2%	52,042	134
Panola	1,208	10.3%	53,292	116
Parker	10,246	11.8%	65,358	43
Parmer	623	13.0%	63,512	46
Pecos	660	6.1%	43,661	221
Polk	2,491	7.6%	47,994	180
Potter	6,499	6.0%	55,764	97
Presidio	379	12.0%	61,776	51
Rains	520	9.4%	41,563	237
Randall	8,111	8.0%	56,381	91
Reagan	199	4.3%	61,077	57
Real	157	9.3%	55,449	100
Red River	622	9.4%	53,818	113
Reeves	765	8.1%	52,811	127
Refugio	368	10.3%	54,475	107
Roberts	45	3.1%	56,868	88
Robertson	897	12.6%	52,894	125
Rockwall	8,244	12.9%	70,833	29
Runnels	510	9.7%	51,307	146
Rusk	236,777	8.1%	44,874	215
Sabine	451	7.9%	44,900	214
San Augustine	401	11.2%	50,573	157
San Jacinto	1,296	8.1%	46,477	198
San Patricio	3,582	9.7%	51,392	145
San Saba	255	6.9%	43,735	220
Schleicher	126	3.7%	51,775	141
Scurry	793	4.8%	47,138	190
Shackelford	299	8.1%	93,075	9
Shelby	1,308	16.1%	54,640	106
Sherman	344	29.3%	122,945	3
Smith	14,299	9.4%	60,284	62
Somervell	519	10.6%	54,826	103

Location	Total Income ($ mil)	% Change 2020-21	Per Capita Income	Rank in State
Starr	2,307	11.2%	34,933	250
Stephens	445	8.0%	48,498	177
Sterling	91	9.9%	65,866	41
Stonewall	89	7.1%	73,182	23
Sutton	227	4.5%	68,431	34
Swisher	509	23.6%	72,623	25
Tarrant	125,334	8.6%	58,940	73
Taylor	8,358	13.9%	58,316	81
Terrell	46	8.7%	63,481	47
Terry	533	6.1%	45,353	210
Throckmorton	104	60.9%	69,390	31
Titus	1,497	10.3%	48,007	179
Tom Green	7,150	6.4%	59,877	67
Travis	106,641	11.2%	81,708	13
Trinity	651	7.8%	47,101	191
Tyler	835	6.1%	41,613	236
Upshur	1,809	8.3%	43,308	227
Upton	201	9.9%	61,595	52
Uvalde	1,317	10.0%	53,257	118
Val Verde	2,2187	9.6%	46,642	197
Van Zandt	2,7607	11.0%	45,045	213
Victoria	5,320	7.6%	58,479	80
Walker	2,6007	7.8%	33,345	253
Waller	2,9537	8.9%	49,404	171
Ward	617	6.8%	55,099	101
Washington	2,200	3.9%	61,295	55
Webb	10,945	9.9%	40,850	239
Wharton	2,209	9.8%	52,948	122
Wheeler	246	6.1%	49,906	165
Wichita	6,531	7.1%	50,210	160
Wilbarger	763	11.3%	59,952	65
Willacy	768	15.7%	37,792	246
Williamson	40,466	14.9%	62,931	48
Wilson	2,858	9.7%	55,762	98
Winkler	491	4.6%	66,180	38
Wise	3,863	11.4%	53,871	112
Wood	2,181	8.3%	47,546	184
Yoakum	395	4.9%	51,954	136
Young	1,053	9.8%	58,602	77
Zapata	463	11.7%	33,288	254
Zavala	418	8.2%	43,868	219

8 Largest States' Unemployment Rates

Rank	State	June 2022	June 2023	Annual Change
1	California	3.9%	4.6%	0.7%
2	**Texas**	**3.8%**	**4.1%**	**0.3%**
3	Florida	2.8%	2.6%	–0.2%
4	New York	4.1%	3.9%	–0.2%
5	Pennsylvania	4.3%	3.8%	–0.5%
6	Illinois	4.4%	4.0%	–0.4%
7	Ohio	3.9%	3.4%	–0.5%
8	Georgia	3.0%	3.2%	0.2%

Eight largest states by population. *Source: Bureau of Labor Statistics. August 2023.*

Average Work Hours and Earnings

Source: Texas Workforce Commission.

The following table compares the average weekly earnings, hours worked per week, and average hourly wage in Texas for production workers in selected industries in 2021 and 2022. ☆

Industry	Average Weekly Earnings		Average Weekly Hours		Average Hourly Earnings	
	2021	2022	2021	2022	2021	2022
Mining and Logging	$1,453.34	$1,617.00	49.0	50.0	$29.66	$32.34
Manufacturing						
Durable Goods	1,217.72	1,380.39	42.4	44.4	28.72	31.09
Fabricated Metal Product Mfg.	925.96	1,070.91	38.2	42.7	24.24	25.08
Nondurable Goods	829.77	866.36	40.3	42.2	20.59	20.53
Trade, Transportation, Utilities						
Wholesale Trade	1,049.60	1,148.32	40.0	39.9	26.24	28.78
Machinery, Equipment, Supplies	1,047.78	1,181.11	41.3	40.7	25.37	29.02
Retail Trade						
Auto Dealers/Parts	1,076.56	1,166.10	37.2	38.6	28.94	30.21
Building Material/Garden Equip.	763.34	642.96	37.2	35.9	20.52	17.91
Gasoline Stations	$495.36	$507.44	36.0	34.9	$13.76	$14.54

Employment in Texas by Industry

Source: Texas Workforce Commission. Additional information available at the website twc.texas.gov.

Employment in Texas reached 13,944,600 in June 2023, up 542,500 jobs since June 2022. The following table shows Texas Workforce Commission estimates of the nonagricultural labor force by industry for June 2023 and the percent change during the year in the number employed. ☆

Industry	Employment June 2023	Monthly Change	Annual Change	Annual % Change
Total Nonagricultural	13,944,600	31,100	542,500	4.0%
Private	11,898,500	28,300	485,400	4.3
Goods-Producing	1,987,200	17,500	85,600	4.5%
Mining & Logging (oil, gas)	222,100	400	24,100	12.2
Construction	809,500	11,000	30,500	3.9
Manufacturing	955,600	6,100	31,000	3.4
Service-Providing	11,957,400	13,600	456,900	4.0%
Trade, Transportation, Utilities	2,785,700	5,200	83,400	3.1
Information	245,500	2,500	16,200	7.1
Financial Activities	915,100	5,300	40,000	4.6
Professional & Business Services	2,141,600	-3,100	73,300	3.5
Education & Health Services	1,898,800	11,900	107,500	6.0
Leisure & Hospitality	1,450,700	-10,800	45,100	3.2
Other Services	473,900	-200	34,300	7.8
Government	2,046,100	2,800	57,100	2.9%

Help Wanted: Top Online Postings of Job Vacancies

Occupation	June 2023	July 2023	Employer	September 2023
Registered Nurses	30,567	29,460	HCA Healthcare, Inc.	8,029
Retail Salespersons	19,267	19,755	Sonic Corp.	4,548
First-Line Supervisors of Retail Sales Workers	15,865	16,465	Houston Methodist	4,131
Sales Rep., Wholesale & Manufacturing, Except Tech. & Scientific Products	15,771	16,005	McDonald's Corporation	3,475
Software Developers	13,225	12,966	Christus Health	2,642
Customer Service Representatives	12,415	12,449	Texas Health and Human Services	2,552
Fast Food and Counter Workers	11,368	11,918	Baylor Scott & White Health	2,505

Source: Texas Workforce Commission from Conference Board Help Wanted Online Data Series.

Largest Banks Operating in Texas by Asset Size

Source: Texas Department of Banking, December 31, 2018

Abbreviations: N.A. National Association.

	Name	City	Class	Assets (thousands of dollars)	Loans
1	Charles Schwab Bank SSB	Westlake	State	351,075,000	25,537,000
2	JP Morgan Chase Bank	New York NY	National	246,711,590	—
3	Bank of America	Charlotte NC	National	165,066,597	—
4	USAA Federal Savings Bank	San Antonio	National	121,715,724	38,358,368
5	Comerica Bank	Dallas	State	86,257,000	50,582,000
6	Wells Fargo Bank	San Francisco CA	National	81,141,105	—
7	BBVA USA	Birmingham AL	State	44,240,950	—
8	Frost Bank	San Antonio	State	44,092,014	17,889,863
9	Texas Capital Bank N.A.	Dallas	National	40,035,375	24,393,255
10	Prosperity Bank	El Campo	State	35,563,929	19,617,895
11	Charles Schwab Premier Bank SSB	Westlake	State	33,115,000	0
12	Independent Bank	McKinney	State	18,110,591	12,770,197
13	Citibank	Sioux Falls SD	National	14,290,000	—
14	Plains Capital Bank	University Park	State	14,229,718	7,290,482
15	Zions Bancoporation N.A.	Salt Lake City UT	National	12,993,040	—
16	First Financial Bank N.A.	Abilene	National	12,065,711	5,322,562
17	International Bank of Commerce	Laredo	State	10,556,686	5,709,148
18	Capital One	New Orleans LA	National	10,391,469	—
19	Woodforest National Bank	The Woodlands	National	9,792,477	4,868,649
20	Veritex Community Bank	Dallas	State	9,232,171	6,969,847
21	NexBank	Dallas	State	9,082,950	4,484,518
22	Truist Bank	Charlotte NC	State	7,572,143	—
23	Amarillo National Bank	Amarillo	National	7,400,429	5,158,468
24	BOKF	Tulsa OK	National	7,005,971	—
25	Southside Bank	Tyler	State	6,994,558	3,716,598
26	Allegiance Bank	Houston	State	6,423,375	4,659,169
27	Happy State Bank	Happy	State	6,326,783	3,429,087
28	TBK Bank SSB	Dallas	State	6,082,072	5,083,712
29	Cadence Bank N.A.	Birmingham AL	National	5,899,767	—
30	Regions Bank	Birmingham AL	State	5,401,441	—
31	Wells Fargo Bank South Central N.A.	Houston	National	5,262,057	340,038
32	Broadway National Bank	San Antonio	National	4,874,723	2,545,097
33	American National Bank of Texas	Terrell	National	4,448,694	2,406,771
34	Bancorp South Bank	Tupelo MS	State	4,433,845	—
35	CommunityBank of Texas N.A.	Beaumont	National	4,029,141	2,891,632
36	First National Bank Texas	Killeen	National	3,889,580	1,351,218
37	First United Bank & Trust	Durant OK	State	3,860,938	—
38	City Bank	Lubbock	State	3,730,641	2,242,676
39	Inwood National Bank	Dallas	National	3,667,073	1,967,049
40	TIB The Independent BankersBank	Farmers Branch	National	3,585,613	1,218,169
41	Texas Bank and Trust Company	Longview	State	3,580,389	2,484,802
42	VeraBank N.A.	Henderson	National	3,193,383	1,644,130
43	Spirit of Texas Bank SSB	College Station	State	3,166,882	2,430,939
44	First Bank & Trust	Lubbock	State	2,991,053	1,516,387
45	Guaranty Bank & Trust N.A.	Mount Pleasant	National	2,891,363	1,909,755
46	Lone Star National Bank	Pharr	National	2,737,786	1,302,827
47	Texas Exchange Bank SSB	Crowley	State	2,712,587	740,867
48	American Momentum Bank	College Station	State	2,700,117	1,822,788
49	Vantage Bank Texas	San Antonio	State	2,653,253	2,034,678
50	WestStar Bank	El Paso	State	2,520,224	1,587,625

Deposits/Assets of Commercial Banks by County

Source: Federal Reserve Bank of Dallas as of Dec. 31, 2018.

(in thousands of dollars)

County	Banks	Deposits	Assets
Andrews	2	$786,813	$891,775
Angelina	1	209,518	253,557
Atascosa	2	156,141	179,741
Austin	5	2,247,370	2,640,246
Bailey	1	82,066	95,914
Bandera	2	200,559	222,443
Bastrop	2	732,743	832,163
Baylor	1	144,154	164,051
Bee	1	394,903	434,881
Bell	4	3,272,585	3,878,149
Bexar	8	35,295,268	41,739,510
Blanco	1	103,668	118,188
Bosque	2	212,576	235,388
Bowie	2	403,265	457,687
Brazoria	7	1,064,722	1,202,395
Brazos	2	1,376,265	1,702,781
Briscoe	1	48,994	58,522
Brooks	1	70,721	78,668
Brown	2	597,258	692,419
Burleson	1	518,430	585,429
Burnet	1	216,982	246,255
Caldwell	2	299,387	337,880
Calhoun	1	288,038	317,838
Callahan	1	361,301	417,210
Cameron	4	2,035,806	2,399,293
Camp	1	456,470	574,188
Carson	1	31,919	35,898
Cass	2	418,016	485,983
Castro	1	1,108,104	1,315,753
Chambers	1	107,951	121,100
Cherokee	2	1,939,996	2,323,662
Childress	1	100,825	109,158
Coke	1	35,596	41,227
Coleman	2	146,726	164,425
Collin	4	15,351,268	19,740,097
Collingsworth	1	346,069	397,725
Colorado	4	429,944	509,599
Comanche	1	84,215	92,919
Concho	2	180,945	205,992
Cooke	2	1,105,043	1,257,696
Coryell	2	628,133	702,303
Cottle	1	45,174	49,436
Crockett	1	226,569	255,317
Crosby	2	744,025	854,498
Dallas	24	98,710,887	124,594,733
Dawson	1	317,970	350,327
Deaf Smith	1	148,705	169,091
Delta	2	70,832	82,931
Denton	4	1,014,778	1,154,602
DeWitt	2	373,066	426,164
Dickens	1	40,782	45,300
Dimmit	1	65,660	75,849
Donley	1	35,155	42,941
Duval	2	95,912	108,840
Ector	2	741,013	835,144
Edwards	1	69,285	79,024
Ellis	4	1,329,849	1,514,241
El Paso	2	1,762,700	2,069,095
Erath	1	80,827	90,526
Fannin	1	86,664	99,674
Fayette	4	1,234,697	1,386,252
Fisher	1	72,316	79,543
Floyd	1	98,753	110,149
Foard	1	35,591	39,756
Franklin	1	137,570	191,004
Frio	2	651,437	747,255
Galveston	4	2,443,359	2,818,052
Gillespie	1	856,602	1,027,574
Gonzales	1	358,672	405,478
Gray	1	46,957	55,419
Grayson	3	531,304	603,838
Gregg	3	2,738,363	3,154,115
Grimes	2	286,326	329,785
Guadalupe	3	740,993	840,515
Hale	1	28,433	41,842
Hall	1	52,154	60,348
Hansford	3	383,962	442,146
Hardeman	1	54,058	59,433
Harris	17	19,229,546	22,831,273
Harrison	1	196,806	219,573
Haskell	1	61,248	69,714
Henderson	2	511,511	574,094
Hidalgo	5	2,837,932	3,245,212
Hill	1	147,021	174,653
Hockley	2	169,732	189,546
Hood	2	552,532	621,225
Hopkins	2	1,287,599	1,468,635
Houston	3	149,554	171,239
Howard	1	355,314	392,240
Hunt	1	45,217	49,406
Irion	1	413,042	443,331
Jack	1	214,449	240,334
Jackson	1	52,037	55,733
Jasper	1	224,576	257,831
Jeff Davis	1	77,685	85,847
Jefferson	1	2,811,864	3,280,197
Jim Hogg	1	77,858	93,485
Johnson	1	183,874	202,974
Jones	1	57,552	62,995
Karnes	2	742,308	820,886
Kaufman	2	2,934,672	3,243,517
Kendall	1	131,506	147,556
Kerr	1	144,894	159,550
Kimble	2	104,219	114,513
Kleberg	1	439,043	528,374
Lamar	3	503,771	598,254
Lamb	1	1,232,126	1,401,066
Lampasas	1	120,111	137,448
La Salle	1	87,693	98,237
Lavaca	2	901,613	1,014,153
Lee	1	188,031	209,953
Leon	2	904,919	1,029,838
Liberty	1	265,398	307,164
Limestone	2	263,888	305,100
Live Oak	2	473,387	541,096
Llano	2	324,676	364,865
Lubbock	9	7,202,629	8,437,114
Lynn	1	48,239	53,804
Martin	1	204,361	223,418
Mason	2	139,674	170,695
McCulloch	2	246,566	275,947
McLennan	12	3,601,061	4,121,667

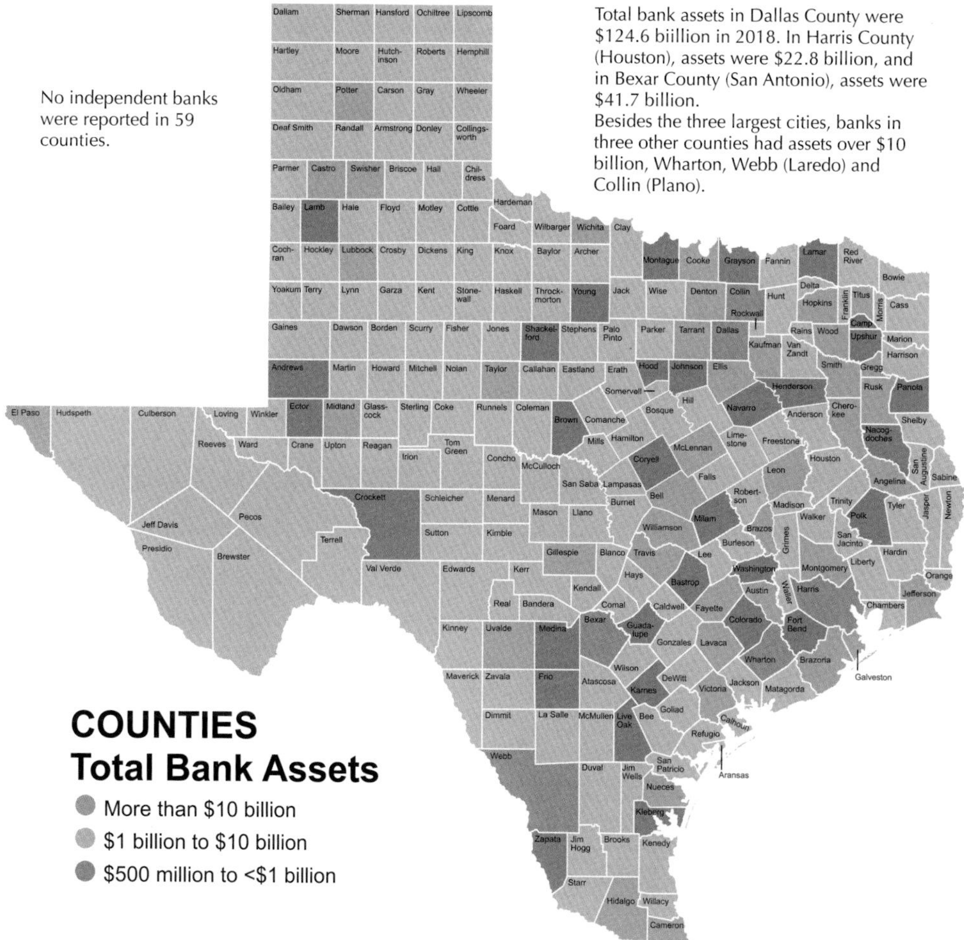

County	Banks	Deposits	Assets
Medina	3	544,978	615,950
Menard	1	31,988	36,668
Midland	5	4,546,544	5,152,536
Milam	3	753,409	865,275
Mills	1	284,812	315,242
Mitchell	1	113,904	125,272
Montague	1	600,346	694,569
Montgomery	1	5,338,201	5,923,725
Morris	2	174,566	229,772
Nacogdoches	1	649,877	727,918
Navarro	4	865,304	999,160
Nolan	2	266,816	296,100
Nueces	5	2,322,016	2,636,085
Ochiltree	1	150,362	172,423
Orange	1	190,459	208,340
Palo Pinto	1	90,435	105,391
Panola	2	473,116	603,570
Parker	2	533,691	592,673
Parmer	1	140,134	158,719
Pecos	2	352,805	388,375
Polk	3	719,847	843,224
Potter	3	4,930,457	5,774,064
Presidio	1	111,062	129,531
Randall	1	140,739	159,818

County	Banks	Deposits	Assets
Rockwall	1	56,079	62,457
Runnels	3	354,889	393,200
Rusk	2	2,463,609	2,805,100
Sabine	1	53,507	61,500
San Jacinto	2	147,118	162,736
San Patricio	1	126,919	142,889
San Saba	1	52,416	60,969
Schleicher	1	50,905	60,537
Scurry	2	217,249	246,149
Shackelford	1	516,595	592,295
Shelby	2	395,923	455,099
Sherman	1	211,463	244,798
Smith	4	5,420,176	7,478,325
Starr	1	71,385	84,166
Sterling	1	173,449	183,532
Stonewall	1	57,348	67,891
Sutton	1	340,941	423,400
Swisher	2	2,902,560	3,488,531
Tarrant	9	3,270,178	3,860,943
Taylor	3	6,407,214	7,846,262
Titus	2	1,963,071	2,367,052
Tom Green	1	235,462	270,620
Travis	3	242,106	315,275
Trinity	1	52,297	57,825

County	Banks	Deposits	Assets
Tyler	1	129,181	144,198
Upshur	2	510,368	587,879
Uvalde	1	1,589,321	1,734,034
Val Verde	1	23,455	28,288
Van Zandt	1	125,454	145,753
Walker	1	412,049	469,922
Ward	1	157,971	176,873
Washington	4	763,614	860,573
Webb	4	8,811,325	11,650,632
Wharton	3	18,334,982	23,884,829
Wheeler	1	66,550	75,402
Wichita	4	1,796,545	2,130,172
Wilbarger	1	248,340	294,284
Williamson	4	1,249,028	1,396,930
Wilson	1	41,929	51,535
Wise	2	240,164	279,433
Wood	2	1,551,311	2,052,193
Young	3	650,882	767,275
Zapata	2	378,887	513,078
Zavala	1	56,042	64,839

Texas Total Bank Resources and Deposits: 1905–2018

Source: Federal Reserve Bank of Dallas.

On Dec. 31, 2018, Texas had 409 national and state banks, the lowest number since our records began in 1905. In 1986, the number of independent banks in the state peaked at 1,972. In 2018, total assets were the highest ever at nearly $400 billion. Deposits peaked in 2018 at $328.9 billion.

Date	National Banks			State Banks			Combined Total		
	No. Banks	Assets (in thousands)	Deposits (in thousands)	No. Banks	Assets (in thousands)	Deposits (in thousands)	No. Banks	Assets (in thousands)	Deposits (in thousands)
Sept. 30, 1905	440	$ 189,484	$ 101,285	29	$ 4,341	$ 2,213	**469**	$ 193,825	$ 103,498
Nov. 10, 1910	516	293,245	145,249	621	88,103	59,766	**1,137**	381,348	205,015
Dec. 29, 1920	556	780,246	564,135	1,031	391,127	280,429	**1,587**	1,171,373	844,564
Dec. 31, 1930	560	1,028,420	826,723	655	299,012	231,909	**1,215**	1,327,432	1,058,632
Dec. 31, 1940	446	1,695,662	1,534,702	393	227,866	179,027	**839**	1,923,528	1,713,729
Dec. 31, 1950	442	6,467,275	6,076,006	449	1,427,680	1,338,540	**891**	7,894,955	7,414,546
Dec. 31, 1960	468	10,520,690	9,560,668	532	2,997,609	2,735,726	**1,000**	13,518,299	12,296,394
Dec. 31, 1970	530	22,087,890	18,384,922	653	8,907,039	7,958,133	**1,183**	30,994,929	26,343,055
Dec. 31, 1980	641	75,540,334	58,378,669	825	35,186,113	31,055,648	**1,466**	110,726,447	89,434,317
Dec. 31, 1985	1,058	144,674,908	111,903,178	878	64,349,869	56,392,634	**1,936**	209,024,777	168,295,812
Dec. 31, 1986	1,077	141,397,037	106,973,189	895	65,989,944	57,739,091	**1,972**	207,386,981	164,712,280
Dec. 31, 1987	953	135,690,678	103,930,262	812	54,361,514	47,283,855	**1,765**	190,052,192	151,214,117
Dec. 31, 1988	802	130,310,243	106,740,461	690	40,791,310	36,655,253	**1,492**	171,101,553	143,395,714
Dec. 31, 1989	687	133,163,016	104,091,836	626	40,893,848	36,652,675	**1,313**	174,056,864	140,744,511
Dec. 31, 1990	605	125,808,263	103,573,445	578	45,021,304	40,116,662	**1,183**	170,829,567	143,690,107
Dec. 31, 1993	502	139,409,250	111,993,205	510	44,566,815	39,190,373	**1,012**	183,976,065	151,183,578
Dec. 31, 1994	481	140,374,540	111,881,041	502	47,769,694	41,522,943	**983**	188,144,234	153,403,984
Dec. 31, 1995	456	152,750,093	112,557,468	479	49,967,946	42,728,454	**935**	202,718,039	155,285,922
Dec. 31, 1996	432	152,299,695	122,242,990	445	52,868,263	45,970,674	**877**	205,167,958	168,213,664
Dec. 31, 1997	417	180,252,942	145,588,677	421	54,845,186	46,202,808	**838**	235,098,128	191,791,485
Dec. 31, 1998	402	128,609,813	106,704,893	395	50,966,996	42,277,367	**797**	179,576,809	148,982,260
Dec. 31, 1999	380	128,878,607	99,383,776	373	52,266,148	42,579,986	**753**	181,144,755	141,963,762
Dec. 31, 2000	358	112,793,856	88,591,657	351	53,561,550	43,835,525	**709**	166,355,406	132,427,182
Dec. 31, 2001	342	85,625,768	72,812,548	344	59,047,520	47,843,799	**686**	144,673,288	120,656,347
Dec. 31, 2002	332	95,308,420	79,183,418	337	62,093,220	49,715,186	**669**	157,401,640	128,898,604
Dec. 31, 2003	316	75,003,613	62,567,943	337	61,448,617	49,790,333	**653**	136,452,230	112,358,276
Dec. 31, 2004	311	82,333,800	67,977,669	328	69,127,411	54,950,601	**639**	151,461,211	122,928,270
Dec. 31, 2005	302	96,505,262	77,688,463	324	76,697,256	61,257,128	**626**	173,202,518	138,945,591
Dec. 31, 2006	286	97,936,270	79,389,737	322	83,910,356	66,132,394	**608**	181,846,626	145,522,131
Dec. 31, 2007	282	107,260,539	83,637,302	330	154,283,181	114,537,280	**612**	261,543,720	198,174,582
Dec. 31, 2008	267	108,816,852	84,802,191	327	164,658,101	115,186,285	**594**	273,474,953	199,988,476
Dec. 31, 2009	263	153,639,579	109,552,071	318	162,958,865	120,962,911	**581**	316,598,444	230,514,982
Dec. 31, 2010	253	149,498,073	120,827,780	314	162,772,458	127,925,865	**567**	312,270,531	248,753,645
Dec. 31, 2011	250	159,621,331	129,799,399	302	169,525,070	137,180,187	**552**	329,146,401	266,979,586
Dec. 31, 2012	227	156,392,247	139,945,006	293	205,788,318	169,156,089	**520**	362,180,565	302,101,095
Dec. 31, 2013	211	138,785,446	118,373,970	283	216,540,710	181,010,324	**494**	355,326,156	299,384,294
Dec. 31, 2014	203	128,134,221	108,506,074	267	235,388,932	197,078,456	**470**	363,523,153	305,584,530
Dec. 31, 2015	195	117,391,368	99,420,411	252	246,932,641	204,350,121	**477**	364,324,009	303,770,532
Dec. 31, 2016	186	122,431,838	104,027,309	244	254,560,238	208,323,981	**430**	376,992,076	312,351,290
Dec. 31, 2017	183	133,291,358	111,896,128	240	259,417,028	212,732,825	**423**	392,708,386	324,628,953
Dec. 31, 2018	176	$137,477,382	$114,245,832	233	$262,400,881	$214,562,067	**409**	$399,878,263	$328,907,699

Texas State Banks

Consolidated Statement, Foreign and Domestic Offices, as of Dec. 31, 2018

Source: Federal Reserve Bank of Dallas

Number of Banks	233
(thousands of dollars)	
Assets	
Cash and balances due from banks:	
Non-interest-bearing balances and currency and coin	$ 4,962,045
Interest-bearing balances	13,098,333
Held-to-maturity securities	13,547,370
Available-for-sale securities	47,367,624
Equity securities not held for trading	54,182
Federal funds sold in domestic offices	1,365,496
Securities purchases under agreements to resell	11,642
Loans and lease financing receivables:	
Loans and leases held for sale	1,665,108
Loans and leases held for investment	163,989,470
Less: allowance for loan and lease losses	1,811,630
Loans and leases, net	162,177,840
Trading Assets	141,420
Premises and fixed assets	3,902,016
Other real estate owned	178,289
Investments in unconsolidated subsidiaries and associated companies	49,909
Direct/indirect investments in real estate ventures	12,944
Intangible assets	6,070,415
Other assets	7,796,248
Total Assets	**$ 262,400,881**
Liabilities	
Deposits:	
In domestic offices	$ 214,164,380
Non-interest-bearing	79,784,426
Interest-bearing	134,379,960
In foreign offices, edge & agreement subsidiaries and IBFs	497,687
Non-interest-bearing	264,633
Interest-bearing balances	233,054
Federal funds purchased and securities sold under agreements to repurchase:	
funds in domestic offices	451,840
securities sold under agreement to repurchase	2,280,725
Trading liabilities	299,103
Other borrowed money (mortgages/leases)	9,615,243
Subordinated notes and debentures	580,055
Other liabilities	2,000,675
Total Liabilities	$ 229,889,708
Equity Capital	
Perpetual preferred stock	$ 4,906
Common stock	482,034
Surplus (exclude surplus related to preferred stock)	16,457,220
Retained earnings	16,645,362
Accumulated other comprehensive income	–1,077,974
Other equity capital components	–7,519
Total bank equity capital	32,504,029
Minority interest in cons. subsidiaries	7,144
Total Equity Capital	$ 32,511,173
Total liabilities, minority interest and equity capital	**$ 262,400,881**

Texas National Banks

Consolidated Statement, Foreign and Domestic Offices, as of Dec. 31, 2018

Source: Federal Reserve Bank of Dallas

Number of Banks	176
(thousands of dollars)	
Assets	
Cash and balances due from banks:	
Non-interest-bearing balances and currency and coin	$ 2,708,378
Interest-bearing balances	9,238,424
Held-to-maturity securities	2,771,738
Available-for-sale securities	21,161,149
Equity securities not held for trading	37,944
Federal funds sold in domestic offices	3,375,562
Securities purchases under agreements to resell	125,000
Loans and lease financing receivables:	
Loans and leases held for sale	5,646,116
Loans and leases held for investment	87,674,263
Less: allowance for loan and lease losses	1,005,273
Loans and leases, net of allowance	86,668,990
Trading Assets	27,594
Premises and fixed assets	1,595,444
Other real estate owned	74,985
Investments in unconsolidated subsidiaries and associated companies	29,807
Direct/indirect investments in real estate ventures	2,099
Intangible assets	847,772
Other assets	3,166,380
Total Assets	**$ 137,477,382**
Liabilities	
Deposits:	
In domestic offices	$ 114,245,638
Non-interest-bearing	30,220,646
Interest-bearing	84,024,992
In foreign offices, edge & agreement subsidiaries and IBFs	0
Non-interest-bearing	0
Interest-bearing balances	0
Federal funds purchased and securities sold under agreements to repurchase:	
funds in domestic offices	792,297
securities sold under agreement to repurchase	883,402
Trading liabilities	21,011
Other borrowed money (mortgages/leases)	5,861,778
Subordinated notes and debentures	223,153
Other liabilities	975,172
Total Liabilities	$ 123,002,451
Equity Capital	
Perpetual preferred stock	$ 160,750
Common stock	357,986
Surplus (exclude surplus related to preferred stock)	4,607,653
Retained earnings	9,621,463
Accumulated other comprehensive income	– 278,689
Other equity capital components	– 7,973
Total bank equity capital	14,461,190
Minority interest in consolidated subsidiaries	13,741
Total Equity Capital	$ 14,474,937
Total liabilities, minority interest and equity capital	**$ 137,477,382**

Savings and Loan Associations in Texas

Source: Texas Department of Savings and Mortgage Lending.

This table includes all thrifts that are not also classified as banks under federal law: that is, it includes federal savings and loan associations and federal savings banks.

Year ending	Number of Inst.	Total Assets	Mortgage Loans	Cash/ Securities	Deposits	FHLB/ Borrowed Money	†Net Worth
		in thousands of dollars					
Dec. 31, 2018	5	$83,782,803	$6,020,272	$43,883,996	$73,570,292	$153,368	$8,284,160
Dec. 31, 2017	5	82,642,161	7,155,350	41,128,877	73,813,038	62,068	7,559,159
Dec. 31, 2016	6	80,671,509	48,621,797	29,471,795	73,504,651	349,316	7,166,859
Dec. 31, 2015	6	73,722,445	47,512,693	24,727,034	65,397,606	213,039	6,703,177
Dec. 31, 2014	8	71,253,195	45,943,853	29,164,768	62,899,043	379,957	6,470,089
Dec. 31, 2013	8	66,605,862	41,812,008	34,083,458	59,101,594	196,784	5,941,114
Dec. 31, 2012	12	64,448,340	41,967,892	20,925,955	57,004,423	579,846	5,645,916
Dec. 31, 2011	12	57,857,491	40,757,220	15,671,590	50,819,345	657,598	5,079,133
Dec. 31, 2010	19	53,980,441	17,005,657	14,230,550	46,935,007	987,211	4,840,466
Dec. 31, 2009	19	46,524,327	17,810,587	9,702,023	40,272,742	973,610	4,254,794
Dec. 31, 2008	22	87,572,855	49,816,471	31,763,898	52,606,655	27,137,730	6,582,759
Dec. 31, 2005	19	55,755,096	42,027,293	9,140,789	30,565,411	11,299,136	4,228,103
Dec. 31, 2000	25	55,709,391	43,515,610	1,512,444	28,914,234	17,093,369	4,449,097
Dec. 31, 1995	45	52,292,519	27,509,933	5,971,364	28,635,799	15,837,632	3,827,249
Dec. 31, 1994	50	50,014,102	24,148,760	6,790,416	29,394,433	15,973,056	3,447,110
Dec. 31, 1990 §	131	72,041,456	27,475,664	20,569,770	56,994,387	17,738,041	–4,566,656
Conservatorship	51	14,952,402	6,397,466	2,188,820	16,581,525	4,304,033	–6,637,882
Privately Owned	80	57,089,054	21,078,198	18,380,950	40,412,862	13,434,008	2,071,226
Dec. 31, 1989 §	196	90,606,100	37,793,043	21,218,130	70,823,464	27,158,238	–9,356,209
Conservatorship	81	22,159,752	11,793,445	2,605,080	25,381,494	7,103,657	–10,866,213
Privately Owned	115	68,446,348	25,999,598	18,613,050	45,441,970	20,054,581	1,510,004
Dec. 31, 1988	204	110,499,276	50,920,006	26,181,917	83,950,314	28,381,573	–4,088,355
Dec. 31, 1985	273	91,798,890	60,866,666	10,426,464	72,806,067	13,194,147	3,903,611
Dec. 31, 1980	318	$34,954,129	$27,717,383	$3,066,791	$28,439,210	$3,187,638	$1,711,201

Texas Savings Banks

Source: Texas Department of Savings and Mortgage Lending.

The savings bank charter was approved by the Legislature in 1993, and the first savings bank was chartered in 1994. Savings banks operate similarly to savings and loans associations in that they are housing-oriented lenders. Under federal law, a savings bank is categorized as a commercial bank and not a thrift. Therefore savings-bank information is also reported with state and national bank information.

Year ending	Number of Inst.	Total Assets	Mortgage Loans	Cash/ Securities	Deposits	FHLB/ Borrowed Money	†Net Worth
		in thousands of dollars					
Dec. 31, 2018	24	$24,434,061	$11,003,911	$9,104,353	$17,635,204	$3,653,055	$2,877,779
Dec. 31, 2017	24	22,355,393	10,721,196	7,199,404	16,479,408	3,194,283	2,462,036
Dec. 31, 2016	28	18,715,828	13,394,235	2,937,083	14,032,907	1,813,466	2,679,435
Dec. 31, 2015	28	13,790,890	10,291,788	2,597,416	10,218,604	1,199,403	2,202,693
Dec. 31, 2014	29	11,031,064	8,211,320	2,947,322	8,257,801	659,216	1,977,443
Dec. 31, 2013	30	10,194,983	7,148,798	3,389,771	7,739,381	499,261	1,812,736
Dec. 31, 2012	30	10,142,623	6,816,212	2,630,941	7,610,074	699,816	1,674,039
Dec. 31, 2011	30	9,530,011	6,132,972	2,650,324	7,247,147	568,547	1,543,269
Dec. 31, 2010	29	8,559,443	4,568,866	4,164,611	6,720,417	332,684	1,329,943
Dec. 31, 2009	29	8,372,892	4,283,372	1,237,215	6,330,896	307,494	1,201,409
Dec. 31, 2008	28	3,988,377	1,980,651	538,162	3,119,082	411,119	434,893
Dec. 31, 2007	26	9,967,678	6,471,833	1,027,709	6,162,709	2,328,467	1,372,231
Dec. 31, 2006	22	9,393,482	6,444,178	836,821	5,721,314	2,453,757	1,138,780
Dec. 31, 2005	19	8,720,497	5,605,678	985,535	5,308,639	1,967,673	1,352,882
Dec. 31, 2004	22	12,981,650	6,035,081	1,654,978	8,377,409	3,000,318	1,482,078
Dec. 31, 2003	23	17,780,413	8,396,606	3,380,565	11,901,441	3,315,544	2,422,317
Dec. 31, 2000	25	11,315,961	9,613,164	514,818	8,644,826	1,455,497	1,059,638
Dec. 31, 1995	13	7,348,647	5,644,591	1,106,557	4,603,026	2,225,793	519,827
Dec. 31, 1994	8	$6,347,505	$2,825,012	$3,139,573	$3,227,886	$2,628,847	$352,363

† Net worth includes permanent stock and paid-in surplus general reserves, surplus and undivided profits. § In 1989 and 1990, the Office of Thrift Supervision, U.S. Department of the Treasury, separated data on savings and loans (thrifts) into two categories: those under the supervision of the Office of Thrift Supervision (Conservatorship Thrifts) and those still under private management (Privately Owned).

Credit Unions: End of 2022

	# Credit Unions	Members	Surplus Funds	Savings	Loans	Assets
Texas	421	9.9 million	$35.7 billion	$127.3 billion	$109.8 billion	$151.5 billion
U.S.	4,759	130.2 million	$573.0 billion	$1,869.4 billion	$1,523.0 billion	$2,190.2 billion

Sources: Texas Credit Union Department and Credit Union National Association.

	U.S. Credit Union History				Texas Credit Union History			
Year	# Credit Unions	Members (million)	Savings ($ billion)	Loans ($ billion)	# Credit Unions	Members (million)	Savings ($ billion)	Loans ($ billion)
2022	4,857	136.5	$1,869.4	$1,523.0	420	10.3	$127,295	$109,786
2021	5,042	130.9	1,809.0	1,279.1	430	9.8	$121,066	$92,015
2020	5,206	125.7	1,605.8	1,187.3	435	9.6	$109,460	$86,157
2019	5,346	121.7	1,335.3	1,127.3	442	9.4	$94,398	$81,497
2018	5,489	117.5	1,234.8	1,058.9	454	9.0	$88,817	$78,088
2017	5,800	113.6	1,181.0	978.4	465	8.8	86.1	73.3
2016	6,022	109.2	1,114.4	889.5	471	8.5	81.7	68.1
2015	6,259	105.0	1.029.1	804.9	478	8.3	77.6	63.2
2014	6,513	101.5	971.2	728.9	490	8.2	73.2	NA
2013	6,795	98.4	930.0	659.4	503	8.1	70.1	55.0
2010	7,605	92.6	804.3	580.3	550	7.5	58.9	43.3
2005	9,198	87.0	591.4	474.2	625	6.8	40.2	32.7
2000	10,860	79.8	380.9	309.3	714	6.5	28.4	22.6
1995	12,230	69.3	278.8	198.4	819	5.4	20.3	14.7
1990	14,549	61.6	201.1	141.3	954	4.4	13.9	8.9
1980	21,465	43.9	61.7	48.7	1,379	3.2	4.8	3.7
1970	23,687	22.8	15.4	14.1	1,435	1.5	1.0	1.0
1960	20,094	12.0	4.8	4.4	1,159	0.7	0.3	0.3

Credit Unions in Texas

Source: Texas Credit Union Department, National Credit Union Administration, and Credit Union National Association.

Credit unions are chartered at federal and state levels. The National Credit Union Administration (NCUA) is the regulatory agency for the federal-chartered credit unions in Texas.

The Texas Credit Union Department is the regulatory agency for the state-chartered credit unions. It was established in 1969 as a separate agency by the 61st Legislature. In 2022, it supervised 171 active credit unions. These state-chartered credit unions served 4.0 million Texans and had approximately $57.0 billion in assets in 2022.

The department is supervised by the nine-member Texas Credit Union Commission, which is appointed by the governor to staggered terms of six years, with the terms of one-third of the members expiring Feb. 15 of each odd-numbered year.

The Texas Credit Union League was the state association for federal and state credit unions beginning in 1934. It is now called Cornerstone Credit Union League and includes Oklahoma and Arkansas. The league's address is 6801 Parkwood Blvd., Ste. 300, Plano 75024.The address for the Texas Credit Union Department is 914 East Anderson Lane, Austin 78752. Their website is cud.texas.gov. ☆

Comparison of Texas Credit Unions

as of Dec. 31, 2022

	State	Federal
No. of institutions	171	250
Total assets	$57.0 billion	$94.6 billion
Asset growth	1.5%	8.9%
Avg. asset size	$335.3 million	$378.2 million
Net Income	$541.5 million	$977.4 million

Source: Texas Credit Union Department.

Credit Outstanding by Lenders 2022

	U.S. Outstanding ($ billion)	Market Share
Banks/Savings Insti.	$2,032.2	41.5%
Finance Companies	$682.7	14.0%
Credit Unions	$636.7	13.0%
Federal Government*	$1,487.3	30.4%
Educational Insitutions*	$18.7	0.4%
Nonfinancial business	$35.8	0.7%
Total	$4,893.4	—

** Includes student loans.*

Source: Federal Reserve Board.

Insurance in Texas

Source: 2018 Annual Report, Texas Dept. of Insurance.

The Texas Department of Insurance reported that on Aug. 31, 2022, there were 3,439 entities licensed to handle insurance business in Texas and 850,846 agents and adjusters.

Under reforms in 1993-94, a three-member State Board of Insurance was replaced by the department, with a Commissioner of Insurance appointed by the governor for a two-year term in each odd-numbered year and confirmed by the Texas Senate.

On Sept. 1, 2005, legislation passed by the 79th Legislature took effect, transferring functions of the Texas Workers' Compensation Commission to the department and creating within it the Division of Worker's Compensation.

Also established was the office of Commissioner of Workers' Compensation, appointed by the governor, to enforce and implement the Texas Workers' Compensation Act.

Property/Casualty Filings in Texas

A single-form filing submission may contain multiple policy forms and endorsements.

Type form	2019	2020	2021	2022
Personal liability	42	25	38	17
Bond/miscellaneous	197	208	165	137
Certificate of insurance	6	5	1	3
Commercial automobile	345	253	305	307
Commercial property	178	258	305	152
General liability	649	796	1,031	434
Homeowners	188	208	195	172
Inland marine	100	256	231	106
Identity theft	4	2	1	1
Commercial multi-peril	566	697	752	416
Personal automobile	271	512	222	174
Professional liability	288	327	314	76
Workers' compensation	109	71	72	54
Cyber risk	19	29	28	5
Total filing submissions	**3,041**	**3,763**	**3,781**	**2,104**
Actual forms received	**26,744**	**25,941**	**20,860**	**14,199**

Inspection Operations in Texas

The inspections office of the Texas Department of Insurance oversees amusement rides for building code standards as well as commercial and residential buildings for windstorm compliance.

Windstorm operations	2019	2020	2021	2022
Applications processed	30,959	42,698	46,009	43,484
Inspections completed	4,050	3,352	3,055	2,914
Certificates of compliance	29,044	28,054	43,513	43,561
Amusement ride safety	**2019**	**2020**	**2021**	**2022**
Inspection certif. approved	9,946	4,869	4,534	4,970
Injuries reported	75	19	57	33
Non-compliant operators	159	120	—	19

Agent/adjuster licensing

Licenses, certificates, and registrations.

Agents / Adjusters	2019	2020	2021	2022
Life, accident, health	251,850	271,049	309,329	331,872
Property, casualty	146,289	149,153	158,331	166,618
Adjusters	153,413	154,106	158,771	180,386
Life only	47,995	57,405	73,086	85,480
Total, including other types	**671,383**	**704,697**	**776,947**	**850,846**

Premium Rates Compared

Auto Insurance: Average for Coverage by State, 2022

The U.S. average is $1,648. Ohio has the least expensive at $1,023. Most expensive states listed below:

1. Michigan $3,141
2. Louisiana $2,601
3.Nevada $2,402
4. Kentucky $2,368
5. DC $2,188
6. Florida $2,162
7. California $2,125
8. New York $2,062
9. Rhode Island $2,040
10. Connecticut $2,036
16. Texas $1,823

In dollars, twelve-month rates. Information not available from some states. Source: carinsurance.com.

Homeowners Insurance: Average Premiums by State, 2022

The national average rate was $2,777. Hawaii has the lowest home insurance rate at $582. Most expensive states listed below:

1. Oklahoma $5,317
2. Kansas $4,939
3. Nebraska $4,893
4. Arkansas $4,201
5. Texas $4,142
6. Kentucky $3,082
7. Mississippi $3,042
8. South Dakota $2,980
9. Colorado $2,964
10. Missouri $2,765

In dollars, twelve-month rates. $200,000 dwelling with $1,000 deductible and $100,000 liability. Source: insurance.com.

Texas Insurance Premiums, Payments				Capital/Surplus of Texas Companies
Year	Total Premiums	Claim Payments	Ratio	
2021	$212.4 billion	$164.6 billion	78.0	—
2020	$193.8 billion	$141.8 billion	73.0	—
2019	$182.3 billion	$141.3 billion	77.5	$1.3 trillion
2018	$175.8 billion	$134.2 billion	76.3	$1.2 trillion

Texas Top 5 Auto Insurers/2021		
Group	Premiums	% of market
Progressive	$3,795,014,379	16.1
State Farm	$3,357,021,890	14.2
Berkshire Hathaway	$3,254,006,880	13.8
Allstate Insurance	$2,717,999,925	11.5
USAA	$1,991,209,678	8.4
Texas Top 5 Homeowners Insurers/2021		
State Farm	$2,173,764,486	18.6
Allstate Insurance	$1,540,761,218	13.2
USAA	$1,195,853,586	10.2
Farmers Insurance	$1,102,529,452	9.4
Liberty Mutual	$1,097,495,627	9.4
Texas Top 5 Health Insurers/2021		
United Health	$19,589,773,756	21.2
Health Care Service Corp.	$17,332,461,411	18.8
Centene	$12,321,265,318	13.3
Elevance Health	$7,324,379,793	7.9
CVS	$4,903,269,470	5.3
Texas Top 5 Life Insurers/2021		
New York Life	$1,017,280,928	7.1
Northwestern Mutual	$810,141,664	5.7
Metropolitan	$784,576,358	5.5
Prudential of America	$651,529,323	4.6
Lincoln National	$643,241,172	4.5

Personal Auto/2021	
Companies in state	176
Groups in state	62
Policies (liability)	20,831,759
Total Premiums	$23,632,548,614
Homeowners Insurance/2021	
Companies in state	156
Groups in state	68
Homeowners	5,434,446
Dwelling	776,872
Tenants	2,251,544
Total Premiums	$11,702,515,570
Health Insurance/2021	
Companies in state	467
Groups in state	189
Insured Texans	23,842,828
Texans without insurance	5,224,044
Texas estimated pop.	29,066,872
Total Premiums	$92,434,575,678
Life Insurance/2021	
Companies in state	425
Groups in state	165
Total Premiums	$14,317,020,217

Ten-Year History, Number of Insurance Companies Operating in Texas										
	2008	2009	2010	2011	2012	2013	2014	2015	2016	2017
Life/Health										
Texas	170	161	161	157	153	149	146	145	145	140
Non-Texas	520	514	504	499	485	483	479	477	475	474
Non-U.S.	0	0	0	0	7	6	6	6	6	6
subtotal	690	675	665	656	645	638	638	628	626	620
Property/Casualty										
Texas	250	250	243	238	236	225	224	235	245	221
Non-Texas	942	948	948	947	935	948	946	952	940	941
Non-U.S.	0	0	0	0	18	17	16	15	16	17
subtotal	1,192	1,198	1,191	1,185	1,189	1,190	1,186	1,202	1,201	1,179
Other*										
Texas	348	353	350	332	324	301	303	295	298	295
Non-Texas	486	504	515	512	487	464	467	462	480	494
Non-U.S.	0	0	0	0	7	6	6	6	6	7
subtotal	834	857	865	844	818	771	776	763	784	796
Grand Total	**2,716**	**2,730**	**2,721**	**2,685**	**2,652**	**2,599**	**2,600**	**2,593**	**2,611**	**2,595**

**Other* includes: Nonprofit legal services corporations, third-party administrators, continuing care retirement communities, and health maintenance organizations.

Source for the information on this page: Texas Department of Insurance Annual Reports.

Construction

Texas Non-Residential Contract Awards

The chart below shows the total value of non-residential construction contract awards in Texas by month in billions of dollars. The change over the period from January 2018 to January 2019 was an increase of 21.9 percent.

Month	Total Awards
September 2015	$ 2.572
October 2015	3.261
November 2015	2.140
December 2015	1.697
January 2016	2.410
February 2016	1.469
March 2016	2.540
April 2016	1.840
May 2016	2.147
June 2016	2.455
July 2016	2.009
August 2016	2.373
September 2016	3.090
October 2016	2.517

Month	Total Awards
November 2016	1.803
December 2016	2.312
January 2017	2.952
February 2017	2.007
March 2017	2.447
April 2017	2.938
May 2017	3.561
June 2017	2.904
July 2017	3.415
August 2017	2.469
September 2017	2.345
October 2017	4.794
November 2017	2.152
December 2017	1.822

Month	Total Awards
January 2018	2.212
February 2018	1.938
March 2018	2.194
April 2018	1.689
May 2018	2.907
June 2018	4.517
July 2018	4.595
August 2018	2.192
September 2018	1.774
October 2018	1.834
November 2018	1.998
December 2018	2.567
January 2019	$ 2.697

Source: State Comptroller, 2019.

State Expenditures for Highways

The chart below shows net expenditures (excluding trusts) for state highway construction and maintenance by fiscal year and percent change from the previous year.

Year	Net Expenditures	Percent change
2007	$ 5,359,397,359	4.4
2008	$ 5,208,591,565	– 2.8
2009	$ 4,252,879,534	– 18.3
2010	$ 3,353,467,064	– 21.1
2011	$ 3,774,008,186	12.5
2012	$ 4,186,493,637	10.9
2013	$ 4,491,601,827	7.3
2014	$ 5,305,157,884	18.1
2015	$ 5,192,484,124	– 2.1
2016	$ 6,159,245,504	18.6
2017	$ 6,748,220,204	9.6
2018	$ 6,381,670,144	– 5.4

Source: Texas Annual Cash Reports.

Federal Funds for Highways

The chart below shows fiscal 2019 dispersement of Federal Highway Administration funds for construction and maintenance in thousands of dollars. The column at right shows dollars per capita.

State	Highway Funds	
	Total	Lane-miles
U.S. Total	$ 42,355,403	8,804,092
1. California	3,963,775	394,383
2. Texas	**3,790,154**	**679,917**
3. Florida	2,046,153	274,149
4. New York	1,812,763	239,763
5. Pennsylvania	1,771,931	251,271
6. Illinois	1,535,424	306,614
7. Ohio	1,447,596	262,377
8. Georgia	1,394,444	272,017
9. Michigan	1,137,059	256,207
10. North Carolina	1,126,340	227,544
11. Virginia	1,098,983	163,648

Source: Federal Highway Administration, 2019.

Texas Single-Family Building Permits

Year	No. of Dwelling Units		Avg. Value per Unit ($)	
	Units	% change	Value	% change
1980	67,870	–	$ 51,900	–
1981	66,161	– 2.5	55,700	7.3
1982	78,714	19.0	53,800	– 3.4
1983	103,252	31.2	63,400	17.8
1984	84,565	– 18.1	68,000	7.3
1985	67,964	– 19.6	71,000	4.4
1986	59,143	– 13.0	72,200	1.7
1987	43,975	– 25.6	77,700	7.6
1988	35,908	– 18.3	83,900	8.0
1989	36,658	2.1	90,400	7.7
1990	38,233	4.3	95,500	5.6
1991	46,209	20.9	92,800	– 2.8
1992	59,543	28.9	95,400	2.8
1993	69,964	17.5	96,400	1.0
1994	70,452	0.7	99,500	3.2
1995	70,421	0.0	100,300	0.8
1996	83,132	18.1	102,100	1.8
1997	82,228	– 1.1	108,900	6.7
1998	99,912	21.5	112,800	3.6
1999	101,928	2.0	118,800	5.3
2000	108,782	6.7	127,100	7.0
2001	111,915	2.9	124,700	– 1.9
2002	122,913	9.8	126,400	1.4
2003	137,493	11.9	128,800	1.9
2004	151,384	10.1	137,600	6.8
2005	166,203	9.8	144,300	4.9
2006	163,032	– 1.9	155,100	7.5
2007	120,366	– 26.2	169,000	9.0
2008	81,107	– 32.6	174,100	3.0
2009	68,230	– 15.9	167,900	– 3.6
2010	68,170	– 0.1	179,200	6.7
2011	67,254	– 1.3	191,100	6.6
2012	81,926	21.8	192,300	0.6
2013	93,478	14.1	197,500	2.7
2014	103,045	10.2	208,900	5.8
2015	105,448	2.3	217,100	3.9
2016	106,511	1.0	220,300	1.5
2017	116,766	9.6	$ 226,100	2.6

Real Estate Center at Texas A&M University, 2019.

Commercial Fishing in Texas

Total Texas coastwide landings in 2017 were more than 93.3 million pounds, valued at more than $236.9 million. Shrimp accounted for most of the weight and value of all seafood landed (see chart at bottom).

The Coastal Fisheries Division of the Texas Parks and Wildlife Department manages the marine fishery resources of Texas' four million acres of saltwater, including the bays and estuaries and out to nine nautical miles in the Gulf of Mexico.

The division works toward sustaining fishery populations at levels that are necessary to ensure replenishable stocks of commercially and recreationally important species.

It also focuses on habitat conservation and restoration and leads the agency research on all water-related issues, including assuring adequate in-stream flows for rivers and sufficient freshwater inflows for bays and estuaries. ☆

Leading U.S. Ports in 2021

Rank	Port	Value in Dollars (in millions)
1	New Bedford, MA	$569.7
2	Reedville, VA	466.5
3	Dutch Harbor, AK	249.0
4	Naknek, AK	245.2
5	Alaska Peninsula, AK	111.5
22	**Galveston, TX**	**62.8**

Source: National Ocean Economics Program, 2022.

Top Fishing Ports for Texas in 2021

Rank	Port	Dollars (millions)	Pounds (millions)
1	Galveston	$62.8	17.0
2	Brownsville-Port Isabel	50.1	16.4
3	Port Arthur	48.3	18.8
4	Palacios	48.1	17.1

Source: National Ocean Economics Program, 2022.

Landings by State 2021

Rank	States	Dollars (millions)	Pounds (millions)
	Total, U.S.	$5,446.3	5027.4
1	Alaska	$1,471.6	2381.4
2	Massachusetts	$712.2	181.8
3	Maine	$526.0	102.6
4	Virginia	$522.9	317.9
5	Louisiana	$334.5	702.3
6	Mississippi	$222.6	210.8
7	New Jersey	$222.2	150.6
8	**Texas**	**$209.3**	**69.3**

Source: National Marine Fisheries Service, 2022.

Texas Commercial Fishery Landings by Species

	2021		2017		2015	
Species	Pounds	Value	Pounds	Value	Pounds	Value
Shrimp, Brown	38,146,000	$102,552,105	49,857,425	$115,006,107	52,552,655	$96,897,374
Shrimp, White	25,106,879	74,581,315	28,914,208	74,195,669	16,644,175	45,591,742
Oyster, Eastern	5,653,022	31,212,919	3,503,518	20,403,679	1,582,685	8,232,088
Snapper, Red	2,699,553	12,646,666	2,212,786	9,881,455	2,151,587	9,387,187
Shrimp, marine, other	1,227,392	5,430,214	101,960	62,835	25,844	9,794
Crab, Blue	3,348,346	5,156,082	4,126,389	5,415,937	3,914,228	5,109,692
Drum, Black	1,050,140	1,621,538	1,926,052	2,457,801	1,812,617	2,003,383
Snapper, Vermilion	58,449	179,004	149.071	442.915	306,820	919,931
Croaker, Atlantic	101,260	1,098,639	87,768	766,557	90,084	745,8567
Total, including others	**78,012,064**	**$236,518,673**	**93,361,097**	**$236,992,832**	**80,356,029**	**$173,418,614**

Source: National Ocean Economics Program and National Marine Fisheries Service, 2022.

Tourism, Travel Impact Estimates by County, 2017

This analysis covers most travel in Texas including business, pleasure, shopping, to attend meetings and other destinations. **Spending** is all spending on goods and services by visitors at a destination. **Earnings** are wages and salaries of employees and income of proprietors of businesses that receive travel expenditures. Employment associated with these businesses are listed under **jobs**. **Local tax** receipts are from hotel taxes, local sales taxes, auto rental taxes, etc., as separate from state tax receipts, as well as spending by travel employees and property taxes attributable to travel businesses and employees. *Source: Office of the Governor, Economic Development and Tourism.*

County	Jobs	Spending	Earnings	Local Tax
		(in thousands)		
Anderson	681	$54,813	$14,056	$1,575
Andrews	433	29,194	6,705	752
Angelina	1,530	130,608	31,166	3,140
Aransas	1,288	102,093	33,087	3,397
Archer	9	1,864	172	17
Armstrong	8	1,226	95	6
Atascosa*	740	64,047	21,762	2,178
Austin	420	42,686	10,011	847
Bailey	73	4,441	1,298	132
Bandera	734	29,633	21,615	2,178
Bastrop	1,973	155,312	69,207	6,997
Baylor	28	6,299	772	72
Bee*	393	40,094	9,350	1,009
Bell	5,352	445,138	137,258	14,207
Bexar	69,220	7,106,223	2,398,606	314,164
Blanco	194	15,969	4,366	522
Borden	1	108	12	0
Bosque	200	16,614	8,002	692
Bowie	1,874	189,350	36,794	4,247
Brazoria	4,843	372,276	111,490	11,817
Brazos	6,162	479,396	151,433	17,196
Brewster	1,583	74,300	39,438	3,489
Briscoe	8	1,271	166	10
Brooks	77	12,926	1,903	235
Brown	642	50,158	16,441	1,827
Burleson	161	14,514	4,256	342
Burnet	1,130	82,449	32,877	3,425
Caldwell	213	33,108	8,582	788
Calhoun	393	42,702	10,801	1,504
Callahan	54	3,839	1,065	74
Cameron	9,571	801,598	212,848	27,058
Camp	86	15,975	1,693	127
Carson	22	5,837	414	27
Cass	270	20,510	5,267	463
Castro	21	2,502	447	32
Chambers	248	39,120	8,064	1,630
Cherokee	449	34,960	8,793	784
Childress	188	14,453	3,241	619

*Oil and gas production in recent years may affect travel impact estimates.

County	Jobs	Spending	Earnings	Local Tax
		(in thousands)		
Clay	44	20,575	778	56
Cochran	13	870	200	13
Coke	45	3,472	709	44
Coleman	80	6,742	1,518	154
Collin	15,658	1,500,619	645,351	66,202
Collingsworth	15	1,889	246	19
Colorado	507	55,988	13,652	1,195
Comal	4,690	405,262	148,845	15,611
Comanche	130	13,744	2,665	256
Concho	10	1,200	407	27
Cooke	577	60,728	16,502	1,792
Coryell	497	44,308	13,006	1,298
Cottle	10	1,677	181	12
Crane	36	3,322	626	85
Crockett	185	27,688	3,068	303
Crosby	25	1,609	442	30
Culberson	184	37,033	5,482	809
Dallam	283	14,121	6,144	618
Dallas	97,079	9,045,095	4,363,486	427,939
Dawson	210	17,710	3,443	373
Deaf Smith	178	16,175	3,605	461
Delta	14	1,515	311	21
Denton	6,806	713,091	245,921	27,936
DeWitt*	607	58,669	15,336	1,514
Dickens	7	483	137	11
Dimmit*	245	31,312	5,483	887
Donley	94	6,418	1,905	225
Duval	59	10,187	1,060	114
Eastland	245	16,171	4,416	555
Ector	2,522	425,258	86,756	14,726
Edwards	7	873	178	10
Ellis	1,256	167,432	47,721	5,452
El Paso	13,850	1,465,780	440,993	50,597
Erath	493	44,969	13,134	1,334
Falls	99	10,267	2,303	255
Fannin	119	14,966	2,640	310
Fayette	484	48,373	10,680	1,233
Fisher	7	992	167	13

*Oil and gas production in recent years may affect travel impact estimates.

Travel Impacts by Origin of Visitor, 2017

Origin	Spending ($Billions)	Earnings ($Billions)	Jobs (Thousand)	Tax Receipts ($Millions) Local	State	**Federal
Other U.S.	$28.1	$10.3	283.8	$783	$1,459	$1,754
International	$6.8	$1.9	62.6	$150	$344	$280
Texas	$29.7	$9.0	284.6	$595	$1,536	$1,414
All visitors	**$64.6**	**$21.2**	**631.0**	**$1,528**	**$3,338**	**$3,448**
Other Travel*	$10.2	$4.5	46.6	0	0	$1,106
Total Travel	**$74.7**	**$25.7**	**677.6**	**$1,528**	**$3,338**	**$4,554**

*Other Travel includes resident air travel, travel arrangement, and convention / trade shows.
**Federal includes motor vehicle fuel and airline ticket taxes, as well as income taxes attributable to travel industry income.
Source: Survey for the Office of Governor.

County	Jobs	Spending (in thousands)	Earnings	Local Tax
Floyd	32	4,916	685	46
Foard	4	370	94	8
Fort Bend	4,998	518,759	173,847	18,545
Franklin	112	9,456	1,770	200
Freestone	380	46,148	5,662	666
Frio*	375	34,848	8,474	1,004
Gaines	166	16,778	3,689	439
Galveston	10,840	989,973	289,894	40,726
Garza	102	9,724	2,923	225
Gillespie	1,001	102,974	30,436	4,688
Glasscock	3	258	44	2
Goliad	62	10,214	1,883	217
Gonzales*	217	28,781	5,255	680
Gray	537	42,017	13,062	1,246
Grayson	1,632	208,497	39,849	4,404
Gregg	2,586	219,822	60,375	6,303
Grimes	229	19,130	5,604	500
Guadalupe	2,002	165,633	70,231	6,524
Hale	703	48,242	12,610	1,382
Hall	13	2,283	311	34
Hamilton	56	6,171	1,365	160
Hansford	21	2,026	338	45
Hardeman	62	5,701	885	104
Hardin	493	43,916	10,275	1,138
Harris	109,463	12,165,938	5,247,543	594,078
Harrison	688	88,366	15,150	1,189
Hartley	12	1,053	205	15
Haskell	97	5,829	1,416	216
Hays	3,820	348,914	120,122	12,830
Hemphill	65	8,637	1,517	344

*Oil and gas production in recent years may affect travel impact estimates.

County	Jobs	Spending (in thousands)	Earnings	Local Tax
Henderson	496	110,527	21,561	1,980
Hidalgo	16,863	1,268,691	389,497	38,656
Hill	502	58,226	10,199	946
Hockley	347	24,281	6,627	548
Hood	532	63,134	17,087	1,951
Hopkins	532	66,320	13,099	1,230
Houston	237	32,484	5,913	433
Howard	862	114,305	19,329	3,079
Hudspeth	16	5,138	414	20
Hunt	826	108,037	30,989	2,747
Hutchinson	397	38,076	9,210	1,013
Irion	16	10,120	416	21
Jack	39	4,347	747	66
Jackson	102	11,836	2,443	252
Jasper	520	38,870	11,408	1,198
Jeff Davis	115	8,699	4,360	188
Jefferson	6,088	548,993	128,520	16,527
Jim Hogg	55	5,015	1,251	99
Jim Wells	736	66,125	16,358	1,251
Johnson	1,155	150,770	34,509	3,954
Jones	123	8,247	2,585	175
Karnes*	446	54,288	13,195	1,434
Kaufman	825	137,285	26,809	2,798
Kendall	1,276	87,004	32,197	2,814
Kenedy	13	829	320	13
Kent	7	714	142	7
Kerr	1,543	98,360	40,388	3,936
Kimble	138	16,466	2,580	388
King	0	43	7	0
Kinney	108	5,691	2,081	115

*Oil and gas production in recent years may affect travel impact estimates.

County	Jobs	Spending	Earnings	Local Tax
		(in thousands)		
Kleberg	524	57,610	14,091	1,539
Knox	18	2,760	375	29
La Salle*	595	37,187	14,650	1,745
Lamar	867	70,867	21,008	2,099
Lamb	101	12,804	1,905	175
Lampasas	164	15,165	3,361	402
Lavaca	143	16,967	4,178	450
Lee	207	24,239	6,297	513
Leon	247	32,534	5,156	630
Liberty	438	53,195	18,276	1,633
Limestone	132	18,430	2,810	405
Lipscomb	8	2,232	200	12
Live Oak*	261	35,765	5,181	710
Llano	2,202	106,885	47,838	4,136
Loving	1	44	7	0
Lubbock	8,672	757,603	279,900	25,832
Lynn	15	1,096	252	17
Madison	104	10,890	2,260	308
Marion	129	8,540	2,062	213
Martin	93	17,482	1,737	101
Mason	52	3,045	738	85
Matagorda	1,045	66,052	23,286	2,808
Maverick*	657	59,383	14,697	1,830
McCulloch	156	18,494	2,546	471
McLennan	5,772	556,876	149,083	16,348
McMullen*	13	1,960	468	19
Medina	379	43,673	8,968	768
Menard	14	2,612	305	25
Midland	3,687	544,447	104,044	16,187
Milam	314	28,447	6,931	627
Mills	21	2,784	492	56
Mitchell	62	9,703	1,863	242
Montague	287	18,370	5,146	493
Montgomery	7,133	632,996	311,864	31,168
Moore	389	42,936	7,343	1,287
Morris	43	5,510	995	79
Motley	5	736	101	7
Nacgdoches	1,120	78,953	21,569	2,620
Navarro	599	50,688	12,329	1,426
Newton	32	4,796	716	57
Nolan	399	25,312	9,195	1,235
Nueces	14,895	1,140,074	385,275	49,230
Ochiltree	196	18,856	3,658	527
Oldham	53	8,595	934	87
Orange	1,099	120,943	27,933	2,940
Palo Pinto	555	71,755	13,719	1,178
Panola	194	17,446	3,559	567
Parker	855	110,602	25,987	2,631
Parmer	39	4,856	731	64
Pecos	586	62,303	9,803	2,496
Polk	795	56,603	18,565	1,490
Potter	8,312	755,558	207,026	26,748
Presidio	79	15,432	2,947	655
Rains	92	8535	2,888	204
Randall	1,260	113,680	23,831	2,411
Reagan	172	11,551	3,030	160
Real	94	7,497	2,420	181
Red River	33	4,298	1,002	70
Reeves	1,342	120,899	25,076	5,471
Refugio	108	21,609	2,531	257
Roberts	2	1,004	43	2
Robertson	246	22,106	4,572	700
Rockwall	891	97,352	27,912	3,534
Runnels	82	6,898	1,441	126
Rusk	346	36,560	7,641	786
Sabine	117	12,601	2,428	139
S.Augustne	109	7,437	1,918	131
SanJacinto	151	11,857	2,774	158
SanPatricio	1,326	140,681	37,759	4,704
San Saba	74	4,489	1,025	101
Schleicher	7	457	130	9
Scurry	572	37,976	12,099	1,176
Shackelford	84	2,288	1,533	112
Shelby	527	34,918	8,878	893
Sherman	29	5,086	453	31
Smith	3,924	354,399	104,858	10,487
Somervell	156	17,600	4,252	608
Starr	245	27,636	5,628	632
Stephens	82	7,147	1,766	192
Sterling	16	2,356	226	16
Stonewall	20	1,057	280	17
Sutton	138	7,937	2,059	326
Swisher	44	3,536	860	68
Tarrant	76,486	5,613,557	4,283,738	345,928
Taylor	3,789	422,356	100,711	12,755
Terrell	14	1,098	199	8
Terry	201	11,335	3,480	411
Throckmrton	11	3,336	202	13

*Oil and gas production in recent years may affect travel impact estimates.

*Oil and gas production in recent years may affect travel impact estimates.

County	Jobs	Spending	Earnings	Local Tax
		(in thousands)		
Titus	518	55,034	11,298	1,326
Tom Green	3,354	218,875	77,976	6,920
Travis	56,325	5,666,532	2,009,187	267,471
Trinity	225	10,993	5,977	390
Tyler	140	10,935	2,415	235
Upshur	180	22,334	3,725	344
Upton	54	3,252	801	94
Uvalde	834	82,685	20,689	2,964
Val Verde	662	55,972	16,178	1,854
Van Zandt	485	51,397	10,934	1,004
Victoria	1,524	215,854	41,638	5,326
Walker	1,132	106,675	24,187	2,568
Waller	229	50,695	8,400	1,223
Ward	856	53,952	15,760	2,459
Washington	672	91,919	17,082	1,904

*Oil and gas production in recent years may affect travel impact estimates.

County	Jobs	Spending	Earnings	Local Tax
		(in thousands)		
Webb*	6,103	568,444	154,510	16,024
Wharton	484	41,084	9,963	1,292
Wheeler	155	19,477	3,033	409
Wichita	3,371	219,588	56,433	6,643
Wilbarger	255	22,532	5,211	705
Willacy	162	25,687	4,199	386
Williamson	5,620	627,148	176,440	21,953
Wilson*	395	34,179	10,101	850
Winkler	93	11,658	1,667	294
Wise	898	58,350	17,172	1,668
Wood	366	26,630	8,406	566
Yoakum	73	6,360	1,435	199
Young	313	23,258	7,276	666
Zapata	181	15,747	2,947	218
Zavala	45	7,351	902	80

*Oil and gas production in recent years may affect travel impact estimates.

Telecommunications Trends to High-Speed, Wireless

Sources: Federal Communications Commission and Public Utility Commission of Texas.

The chart below shows the move to wireless communications, and the decline in the number of telephone land lines in Texas and nationwide. The chart also shows the growth of high-speed Internet use in the state and in the United States.

	2021	2016	2013	2011	2009	2005
Mobile Wireless Telephone Subscribers						
Texas	30,510,000	28,840,000	24,890,000	23,482,000	21,008,000	14,424,000
U.S.	357,225,000	395,900,000	310,691,000	290,304,000	261,284,000	192,053,000
Local Telephone Wirelines/Landlines						
Texas	2,556,000	8,110,000	8,840,000	9,590,000	10,500,000	12,310,000
U.S.	45,765,000	121,331,000	133,233,000	143,319,000	152,945,000	157,041,487
Internet Connections						
Texas	45,432,000	30,171,000	23,612,000	17,487,000	7,484,000	2,943,000
U.S.	510,200,000	369,416,000	275,608,000	206,124,000	102,043,000	42,518,000

U.S. Internet Lines by Technology, 2021 (in thousands)

	aDSL	Cable Modem	Fiber	Satellite	Fixed Wireless	Mobile Wireless	Total
Texas	1,441	5,744	2,591	NA	412	35,023	45,432
U.S.	16,868	80,232	23,338	1,873	2,923	384,420	510,198

The chart below shows the percent of the population that in 2021 had access to advanced, high-quality voice, data, graphics, and video offerings. *Source: Federal Communications Commission 2022 Broadband Progress Report.*

Households with Access to Advanced Telecommunications (25 Mbps/3 Mbps)

Location	Total (2021)	Percent (2021)
Texas	8,558,000	84.0
U.S.	102,804,000	82.0

Texas Electric Grids: Demand and Capacity

- The Electric Reliability Council of Texas (ERCOT) operates the electric grid for 75% of the state.
- Part of the Panhandle, part of the South Plains, and a corner of Northeast Texas are under the Southwest Power Pool (SPP).
- El Paso and the far western corner of the Trans Pecos are under the Western Electric Coordinating Council (WECC).
- The southeast corner of Texas is under the SERC Reliability Corporation.

The councils were first formed in 1968 to ensure adequate bulk power supply.

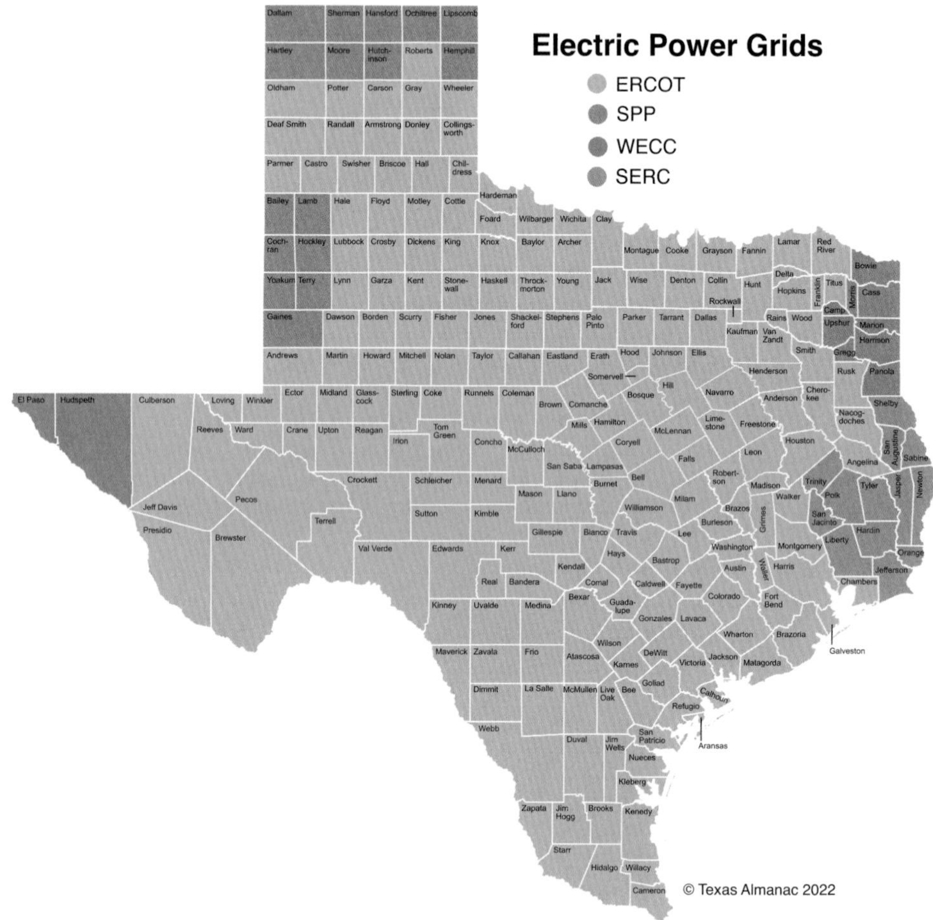

Texas' Installed Wind Capacity (MW)						
	2021	**2020**	**2015**	**2010**	**2005**	**2000**
U.S.	132,753	118,379	66,008	40,267	9,149	2,566
Texas	34,370	30,107	14,208	10,089	1,995	181
Share of U.S. Total	25.9%	25.4%	21.5%	25.1%	21.8%	7.1%

Sources: U.S. Energy Information Administration and the American Wind Energy Association

ERCOT Net Energy for Load, 2022 and 2021 (MWh)

	2022 Energy	Forecasted Energy	Difference	2021 Energy	Change from 2021	Change from 2021
Jan	33,399,763	33,434,286	– 0.10%	30,821,915	2,577,847	8.36%
Feb	31,278,988	29,318,272	6.69%	29,095,558	2,183,430	7.50%
Mar	30,456,522	30,811,374	– 1.15%	27,328,259	3,128,263	11.45%
Apr	30,789,882	30,794,640	– 0.02%	28,089,570	2,700,313	9.61%
May	38,535,175	35,460,197	8.67%	31,785,102	6,750,072	21.24%
Jun	42,039,496	39,832,001	5.54%	37,345,561	4,693,935	12.57%
Jul	45,986,059	42,870,876	7.27%	39,576,929	6,409,130	16.19%
Aug	43,001,722	43,830,180	– 1.89%	41,395,541	1,606,181	3.88%
Sep	37,422,408	37,740,895	– 0.84%	36,555,303	867,105	2.37%
Oct	32,178,969	34,123,473	– 5.70%	32,670,092	– 491,122	– 1.50%
Nov	31,208,957	31,125,399	0.27%	27,996,249	3,212,708	11.48%
Dec	33,785,716	33,991,441	– 0.61%	30,187,900	3,597,816	11.92%
Annual	430,083,656	423,333,035	1.59%	392,847,979	37,235,678	9.48%

Source: ERCOT 2022 Demand and Energy Report.

ERCOT Max 1-Hour Demand, 2022 and 2021 (MWh)

	2022 Demand	Forecasted Demand	Difference	2021 Demand	Change from 2021	Change from 2021	Max All Time	Max All Time Date
Jan	63,541	59,218	7.30%	58,606	4,935	8.42%	65,915	01/17/2018
Feb	68,968	59,429	16.05%	69,812	-844	-1.21%	69,812	02/14/2021
Mar	56,463	53,275	5.99%	45,380	11,083	24.42%	60,756	03/05/2019
Apr	58,419	57,493	1.61%	52,814	5,605	10.61%	58,419	04/05/2022
May	71,645	65,858	8.79%	62,832	8,813	14.03%	71,645	05/31/2022
Jun	76,718	72,356	6.03%	70,257	6,460	9.20%	76,718	06/23/2022
Jul	80,148	74,984	6.89%	73,145	7,003	9.57%	80,148	07/20/2022
Aug	78,505	77,579	1.19%	73,687	4,818	6.54%	78,505	08/02/2022
Sep	71,075	71,902	-1.15%	72,370	-1,295	-1.79%	72,370	09/01/2021
Oct	66,153	64,650	2.32%	62,476	3,677	5.89%	66,153	10/12/2022
Nov	53,336	55,240	-3.45%	48,983	4,352	8.89%	56,446	11/12/2019
Dec	74,525	58,667	27.03%	49,192	25,333	51.50%	74,525	12/23/2022
Annual	80,148	77,579	3.31%	73,687				

Source: ERCOT 2022 Demand and Energy Report.

Want to know more about the energy industry in Texas?
Be sure to read this year's feature article
TEXAS: THE ENERGY STATE
starting on page 602.

Texas Oil Production History

The table shows the year of oil or gas discovery in each county, oil production in 2021 and 2022, and total oil production from date of discovery to Jan. 1, 2023. The 15 counties omitted have not produced oil.

The table has been compiled by the Texas Almanac from information provided in past years by the Texas Mid-Continent Oil & Gas Assoc., which used data from the U.S. Bureau of Mines and the Texas state comptroller. Since 1970, production figures have been compiled from records of the Railroad Commission of Texas. The figures in the final column are cumulative of all previously published figures. The change in sources, due to different techniques, may create some discrepancies in year-to-year comparisons among counties. ☆

County	Year of Discovery	Production in Barrels*		Total Production to Jan. 1, 2023
		2021	2022	
Anderson	1928	501,938	501,706	311,616,408
Andrews	1929	46,424,029	49,095,120	3,389,031,303
Angelina	1936	2,941	2,977	1,015,392
Aransas	1936	121,845	79,865	89,831,323
Archer	1911	746,966	752,554	512,280,758
Atascosa	1917	19,024,073	19,709,099	372,919,111
Austin	1915	299,922	308,924	122,848,606
Bandera	1995	893	1,212	48,514
Bastrop	1913	61,146	61,050	19,074,236
Baylor	1924	55,515	57,458	59,756,767
Bee	1929	262,701	267,433	115,973,834
Bell	1980	0	0	446
Bexar	1889	56,119	45,145	37,613,805
Borden	1949	5,081,862	6,304,419	481,241,763
Bosque	2006	0	0	309
Bowie	1944	25,667	26,044	7,303,153
Brazoria	1902	2,919,417	2,905,703	1,323,665,293
Brazos	1942	5,956,262	5,204,293	213,238,027
Brewster	1969	0	0	56
Briscoe	1982	0	0	4,065
Brooks	1935	321,091	313,243	184,470,147
Brown	1917	68,482	70,103	55,193,812
Burleson	1938	11,999,755	9,920,597	298,718,306
Caldwell	1922	909,475	935,832	301,290,299
Calhoun	1935	105,055	137,180	109,020,192
Callahan	1923	92,481	79,711	88,815,365
Cameron	1944	690	137	482,809
Camp	1940	73,816	79,247	31,600,087
Carson	1921	123,319	130,353	184,502,731
Cass	1936	558,345	1,034,546	121,054,362
Chambers	1916	2,049,224	1,871,564	947,309,543
Cherokee	1926	270,919	301,994	77,881,081
Childress	1961	2,349	2,557	1,819,198
Clay	1917	380,440	404,955	213,501,585
Cochran	1936	2,387,907	2,531,848	561,105,262
Coke	1942	237,702	222,194	232,317,474
Coleman	1902	133,557	140,201	99,152,382
Collin	1963	0	0	53,000
Collngswrth	1936	5,256	3,640	1,312,944
Colorado	1932	447,951	447,026	50,050,371
Comanche	1918	27,656	32,782	6,696,960
Concho	1940	183,260	159,157	31,553,475
Cooke	1924	1,038,263	1,005,238	422,900,138
Coryell	1964	0	0	1,100
Cottle	1955	113,680	148,100	6,998,254
Crane	1926	7,836,124	10,554,023	1,902,570,001
Crockett	1925	4,880,910	4,485,282	481,352,163
Crosby	1955	605,604	594,724	39,813,461
Culberson	1953	36,288,776	37,564,851	246,876,108
Dallam	2015	0	0	116
Dallas	1986	0	0	232
Dawson	1934	3,433,865	3,830,153	448,368,082
Delta	1984	0	0	65,089
Denton	1937	139,865	163,750	12,596,588
DeWitt	1930	47,889,585	39,376,344	717,708,065
Dickens	1953	321,223	357,821	31,116,762
Dimmit	1943	34,415,227	35,728,548	642,459,057
Donley	1967	0	204	3,633
Duval	1905	719,210	691,284	605,327,455
Eastland	1917	130,288	137,047	160,828,277
Ector	1926	15,524,218	18,332,178	3,472,532,151
Edwards	1946	2,599	4,545	624,768
Ellis	1953	3	6	844,869
Erath	1917	1,538	1,635	2,306,954
Falls	1937	981	357	897,693
Fannin	1980	0	0	13,354
Fayette	1943	3,267,744	2,759,383	190,681,950
Fisher	1928	2,142,662	4,283,894	269,338,515
Floyd	1952	0	0	268,610
Foard	1929	66,110	94,252	25,686,187
Fort Bend	1919	753,902	641,509	717,016,344
Franklin	1936	336,383	330,762	184,721,251
Freestone	1916	50,777	45,513	47,486,530
Frio	1934	6,648,186	6,429,262	219,702,020
Gaines	1935	20,234,893	19,747,670	2,606,923,909
Galveston	1922	163,795	167,686	465,537,244
Garza	1926	1,807,976	1,769,739	385,696,713
Glasscock	1925	42,378,168	49,537,084	666,748,854
Goliad	1930	178,847	152,668	90,062,372
Gonzales	1902	36,781,020	33,810,879	453,829,257
Gray	1925	843,749	884,156	690,579,015
Grayson	1930	935,552	1,074,648	278,212,553
Gregg	1931	1,161,839	1,255,909	3,324,170,585
Grimes	1952	293,381	250,451	27,653,817
Guadalupe	1922	610,960	705,374	220,252,237
Hale	1946	920,168	898,106	208,403,748
Hamilton	1938	15	12	164,747
Hansford	1937	169,637	147,582	43,143,616
Hardeman	1944	578,015	624,846	98,435,847
Hardin	1893	930,530	896,451	466,670,212
Harris	1905	1,021,891	1,111,910	1,399,098,947
Harrison	1928	701,431	921,503	107,335,968
Hartley	1937	202,910	203,594	11,917,895
Haskell	1929	677,825	621,002	125,747,471
Hays	1956	0	0	296

**Total includes condensate production.*

County	Year of Discovery	Production in Barrels*		Total Production to Jan. 1, 2023
		2021	2022	
Hemphill	1955	1,565,459	1,276,235	81,972,165
Henderson	1934	267,729	261,606	184,999,024
Hidalgo	1934	493,504	431,308	138,301,993
Hill	1929	8	16	80,700
Hockley	1937	10,512,280	10,107,402	1,897,466,701
Hood	1958	50,031	49,147	3,079,771
Hopkins	1936	122,036	122,955	93,413,789
Houston	1934	411,409	398,357	80,443,242
Howard	1925	111,359,178	123,009,702	1,443,717,886
Hudspeth	2008	0	0	59
Hunt	1942	940	1,058	2,029,942
Hutchnson	1923	447,595	412,866	542,524,386
Irion	1928	7,634,644	8,689,873	231,179,483
Jack	1923	823,686	766,059	222,055,521
Jackson	1934	1,075,161	958,486	702,860,337
Jasper	1928	660,531	696,318	48,799,796
Jeff Davis	1980	0	0	20,866
Jefferson	1901	564,524	527,421	580,221,400
Jim Hogg	1921	68,185	71,381	114,680,546
Jim Wells	1931	63,528	75,160	464,837,008
Johnson	1962	7,634	8,823	590,401
Jones	1926	707,894	624,139	231,988,598
Karnes	1930	108,185,102	112,220,940	1,245,745,362
Kaufman	1948	41,686	43,707	25,849,838
Kenedy	1947	427,327	408,148	44,642,347
Kent	1946	2,445,759	1,903,842	635,597,239
Kerr	1982	0	0	79,044
Kimble	1939	373	248	103,242
King	1943	1,349,915	1,398,743	207,106,341
Kinney	1960	0	0	402
Kleberg	1919	119,865	171,601	343,207,547
Knox	1946	185,890	150,047	65,456,310
Lamb	1945	45,125,230	38,663,615	628,330,338
Lampasas	1985	195,749	182,524	44,705,144
La Salle	1940	0	0	111
Lavaca	1941	7,177,509	8,775,665	105,978,413
Lee	1939	2,346,396	2,360,780	162,225,360
Leon	1936	440,298	423,298	80,795,184
Liberty	1904	744,740	811,690	564,847,669
Limestone	1920	82,383	82,287	121,628,025
Lipscomb	1956	1,564,480	1,438,605	105,163,807
Live Oak	1930	13,514,259	15,885,601	258,096,960
Llano	1978	0	0	647
Loving	1921	136,439,729	139,697,393	897,006,188
Lubbock	1941	846,292	824,460	90,696,716
Lynn	1950	187,074	154,038	24,935,556
Madison	1946	1,739,662	1,528,723	73,586,729
Marion	1910	429,909	420,967	60,875,626
Martin	1945	165,733,677	180,683,704	1,314,097,068
Matagorda	1901	431,060	389,896	293,327,989
Maverick	1929	1,397,701	1,394,281	72,749,426
McCulloch	1938	37,936	33,069	2,766,339
McLennan	1902	267	108	351,552
McMullen	1922	23,857,129	20,275,905	460,330,192
Medina	1901	79,879	75,163	12,668,378
Menard	1946	76,354	67,763	9,619,464

County	Year of Discovery	Production in Barrels*		Total Production to Jan. 1, 2023
		2021	2022	
Midland	1945	197,642,745	218,194,435	1,954,632,785
Milam	1921	1,970,410	1,776,599	35,782,289
Mills	1982	0	0	28,122
Mitchell	1920	1,921,008	1,850,676	281,597,964
Montague	1919	1,041,547	994,808	359,477,175
Montgmry	1931	777,612	742,906	792,450,567
Moore	1926	235,913	220,066	34,909,084
Morris	2004	60,876	140,835	331,335
Motley	1957	31,668	23,397	11,542,571
Nacgdches	1866	50,671	49,240	7,564,699
Navarro	1894	122,218	126,488	223,092,769
Newton	1937	807,366	801,363	76,652,315
Nolan	1939	1,071,512	1,051,722	222,239,556
Nueces	1930	263,584	309,845	575,968,465
Ochiltree	1951	2,932,610	3,168,498	231,166,048
Oldham	1957	238,249	204,402	21,200,298
Orange	1913	466,174	451,876	173,680,043
Palo Pinto	1902	91,581	80,744	28,980,613
Panola	1917	1,586,765	1,510,485	128,127,706
Parker	1942	51,290	34,996	5,837,617
Parmer	1963	0	0	144,000
Pecos	1926	34,048,911	31,456,027	2,064,722,416
Polk	1930	788,259	761,333	147,851,966
Potter	1925	369,143	314,796	16,154,542
Presidio	1980	0	0	4,641
Rains	1955	0	0	148,911
Reagan	1923	46,290,978	45,146,544	939,029,721
Real	2003	423	338	31,992
Red River	1951	54,879	58,538	9,578,022
Reeves	1939	170,155,244	162,545,770	1,169,803,296
Refugio	1920	1,676,632	1,962,537	1,374,965,817
Roberts	1945	1,038,238	1,149,553	80,612,208
Robertson	1944	1,700,952	1,928,117	51,961,017
Runnels	1927	261,635	239,152	155,174,144
Rusk	1930	1,745,929	1,712,640	1,872,628,603
Sabine	1981	117	74	497,828,509
S.Augustine	1947	26,243	21,477	30,136,715
S. Jacinto	1940	117,074	93,283	5,455,669
S. Patricio	1930	268,151	282,392	4,976,008
San Saba	1982	0	0	499,480
Schleicher	1934	253,710	226,600	95,336,026
Scurry	1923	15,039,607	14,487,857	2,306,737,658
Shackelford	1910	290,628	279,400	191,901,406
Shelby	1917	33,857	32,262	6,237,130
Sherman	1938	67,992	77,672	10,599,047
Smith	1931	1,106,839	1,348,857	289,447,722
Somervell	1978	2,546	2,456	107,664
Starr	1929	485,056	504,235	319,740,053
Stephens	1916	1,551,126	1,562,976	376,330,889
Sterling	1947	519,899	467,725	105,538,859
Stonewall	1938	1,045,211	954,639	288,991,869
Sutton	1948	50,617	46,860	9,426,388
Swisher	1981	0	0	6
Tarrant	1969	6,517	5,739	394,601
Taylor	1929	332,065	304,141	151,635,578

**Total includes condensate production.*

County	Year of Discovery	Production in Barrels* 2021	Production in Barrels* 2022	Total Production to Jan. 1, 2023
Terrell	1952	78,266	66,801	11,114,844
Terry	1940	2,339,793	2,434,445	505,565,899
Thrckmrton	1925	570,471	543,509	234,333,302
Titus	1936	328,643	317,942	219,405,204
Tm Green	1940	337,444	284,535	100,717,930
Travis	1934	3,534	4,370	810,873
Trinity	1946	15,837	15,162	1,736,047
Tyler	1937	1,286,894	1,888,153	80,458,053
Upshur	1931	220,621	210,771	294,787,067
Upton	1925	77,850,212	92,424,837	1,536,457,067
Uvalde	1950	0	0	1,814
Val Verde	1935	1,205	922	163,524
Van Zandt	1929	460,687	474,101	561,175,068
Victoria	1931	943,668	1,306,391	269,238,509
Walker	1934	86,594	72,319	1,499,904
Waller	1934	123,669	132,769	35,992,494
Ward	1928	52,266,066	50,583,423	1,182,205,059
Washngtn	1915	5,406,005	4,857,809	54,192,502

County	Year of Discovery	Production in Barrels* 2021	Production in Barrels* 2022	Total Production to Jan. 1, 2023
Webb	1921	11,691,972	14,925,041	337,174,216
Wharton	1925	719,326	615,522	368,286,836
Wheeler	1910	2,213,363	1,928,081	187,322,733
Wichita	1910	1,206,443	1,169,422	861,226,524
Wilbarger	1915	648,541	721,972	276,755,952
Willacy	1936	210,658	218,451	122,627,068
Williamson	1915	8,145	8,665	9,709,453
Wilson	1941	2,076,094	2,737,590	77,500,397
Winkler	1926	22,086,943	20,312,273	1,234,934,270
Wise	1942	447,247	515,538	118,278,162
Wood	1940	3,371,400	3,411,032	1,263,297,466
Yoakum	1936	25,676,484	26,512,097	2,492,723,146
Young	1917	788,342	797,878	329,324,270
Zapata	1919	75,448	71,955	51,199,550
Zavala	1937	7,172,705	7,514,100	124,662,956

Source: Railroad Commission, 2021–22 production reports.

**Total includes condensate production.*

Rig Counts and Wells Drilled by Year

Year	Rotary rigs active*		Permits†	Texas wells completed		Wells drilled**
	Texas	U.S.	Texas	Oil	Gas	Texas
2022	347	772	11,027	14,384	3,533	17,917
2021	225	475	8,728	10,485	3,244	13,729
2020	206	436	5322	8867	2032	10899
2019	463	944	9514	6936	1694	8630
2018	513	1,032	13,307	8,588	1,813	10,986
2017	430	876	12,600	5,394	1,022	6,914
2016	236	510	8,113	7,813	2,129	10,468
2015	430	977	10,549	15,578	2,787	19,503
2014	882	1,862	25,792	24,999	3,585	29,554
2013	835	1,761	21,471	19,249	4,917	24,166
2012	899	1,919	22,479	10,936	3,580	14,535
2011	838	1,875	22,480	5,380	3,008	8,391
2010	659	1,541	18,029	5,392	4,071	9,477
2009	432	1,086	12,212	5,860	8,706	14,585
2008	898	1,880	24,073	6,208	10,361	16,615
2007	834	1,769	19,994	5,084	8,643	13,778
2006	746	1,649	18,952	4,761	8,534	12,764
2005	614	1,381	16,914	3,454	7,197	11,154
2004	506	1,192	14,700	3,446	7,118	11,587
2003	449	1,032	12,664	3,111	6,336	10,420
2002	338	830	9,716	3,268	5,474	9,877
2001	462	1,156	12,227	3,082	5,787	10,005
2000	343	918	12,021	3,111	4,580	8,854
1999	226	622	8,430	2,049	3,566	6,658
1998	303	827	9,385	4,509	4,907	11,057
1997	358	945	13,933	4,482	4,594	10,778
1996	283	779	12,669	4,061	4,060	9,747

*Texas Railroad Commission. *Source for rig count: Baker Hughes Inc. This is an annual average from monthly reports.*
†Totals after 1988 are number of drilling permits issued; data for previous years were total drilling applications received.
Wells drilled are oil and gas well **completions and dry holes drilled/plugged.

Top Oil-Producing Counties since Discovery

Source: Texas Railroad Commission.

There are 44 counties that have produced more than 500 million barrels of oil since discovery. The counties are ranked below. The column at right lists the number of regular producing oil wells in the county in February 2023. ☆

Rank	County	Barrels	Oil Wells
1	Ector	3,472,532,151	5,492
2	Andrews	3,389,031,303	9,187
3	Gregg	3,324,170,585	2,816
4	Gaines	2,606,923,909	3,477
5	Yoakum	2,492,723,146	3,612
6	Scurry	2,306,737,658	2,325
7	Pecos	2,064,722,416	3,285
8	Midland	1,954,632,785	6,286
9	Crane	1,902,570,001	3,821
10	Hockley	1,897,466,701	3,299
11	Rusk	1,872,628,603	1,780
12	Upton	1,536,457,067	4,744
13	Howard	1,443,717,886	5,031
14	Harris	1,399,098,947	239
15	Refugio	1,374,965,817	389
16	Brazoria	1,323,665,293	228
17	Martin	1,314,097,068	5,714
18	Wood	1,263,297,466	595
19	Karnes	1,245,745,362	3,661
20	Winkler	1,234,934,270	1,843
21	Ward	1,182,205,059	3,270
22	Reeves	1,169,803,296	2,581
23	Chambers	947,309,543	149
24	Reagan	939,029,721	4,338
25	Loving	897,006,188	1,663
26	Wichita	861,226,524	4,336
27	Montgomery	792,450,567	109
28	DeWitt	717,708,065	1,238
29	Fort Bend	717,016,344	219
30	Jackson	702,860,337	249
31	Gray	690,579,015	2,217
32	Glasscock	666,748,854	3,950
33	Dimmit	642,459,057	2,212
34	Kent	635,597,239	561
35	La Salle	628,330,338	3,041
36	Duval	605,327,455	511
37	Jefferson	580,221,400	169
38	Nueces	575,968,465	104
39	Liberty	564,847,669	501
40	Van Zandt	561,175,068	322
41	Cochran	561,105,262	1,396
42	Hutchinson	542,524,386	1,304
43	Archer	512,280,758	2,157
44	Terry	505,565,899	740

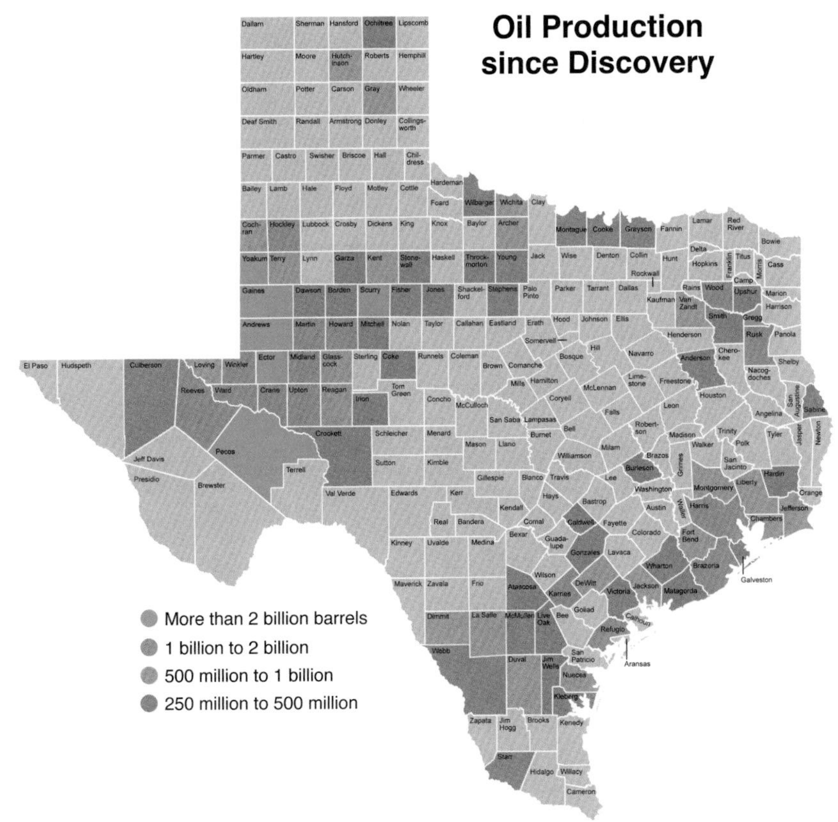

Oil and Gas Production by County, 2022

Source: Texas Railroad Commission.

In 2022 in Texas, the total natural gas production from gas wells was 7,182,028,696 thousand cubic feet (MCF) and total crude oil production from oil wells was 1,516,562,174 (BBL). Total condensate was 285,662,000 barrels. Total casinghead production was 4,330,746,114 MCF. Counties not listed in the chart below had no production in 2022. ☆

County	Oil (BBL)	Casinghead (MCF)	GW Gas (MCF)	Condensate (BBL)
Anderson	472,836	620,153	1,612,134	28,870
Andrews	48,187,178	82,501,298	7,224,240	907,942
Angelina	0	0	65,713,755	2,977
Aransas	24,199	182,776	1,842,035	55,666
Archer	752,431	219,494	12,567	123
Atascosa	19,685,714	20,751,756	1,385,758	23,385
Austin	292,046	153,854	7,593,546	16,878
Bandera	1,212	0	0	0
Bastrop	55,997	34,435	32,215	5,053
Baylor	57,458	0	0	0
Bee	197,257	117,082	8,383,380	70,176
Bexar	45,145	12	0	0
Borden	6,304,419	7,188,870	0	0
Bowie	20,727	0	12,210	5,317
Brazoria	2,540,598	599,333	8,815,157	365,105
Brazos	5,086,481	7,418,639	1,859,373	117,812
Brooks	127,818	155,169	10,615,367	185,425
Brown	69,444	160,998	452,275	659
Burleson	9,853,389	9,444,811	1,189,423	67,208
Caldwell	935,832	31,275	0	0
Calhoun	130,491	941,325	125,024	6,689
Callahan	78,680	211,820	239,378	1,031
Cameron	0	0	8,714	137
Camp	79,247	0	0	0
Carson	96,915	257,085	6,772,650	33,438
Cass	1,030,346	370,869	206,121	4,200
Chambers	1,864,016	325,269	1,066,905	7,548
Cherokee	137,422	371,209	20,397,515	164,572
Childress	2,557	0	0	0
Clay	400,489	846,469	191,460	4,466
Cochran	2,531,846	1,393,376	49,271	2
Coke	215,219	896,459	274,812	6,975
Coleman	139,288	259,520	141,956	913
Collingsworth	3,640	32,685	724,584	0
Colorado	123,198	253,942	11,604,723	323,828
Comanche	32,210	48,129	281,900	572
Concho	159,042	32,938	214,873	115
Cooke	921,487	1,297,026	9,047,548	83,751
Cottle	134,979	14,041	1,468,745	13,121
Crane	10,490,313	49,311,435	6,900,323	63,710
Crockett	4,376,635	46,657,787	34,186,417	108,647
Crosby	594,724	0	0	0
Culberson	284,462	1,724,906	455,357,193	37,280,389
Dallas	0	0	12,447,788	0
Dawson	3,830,153	1,875,548	0	0
Denton	10,177	154,732	131,615,165	153,573
DeWitt	23,238,150	68,186,091	163,117,322	16,138,194
Dickens	357,821	20,060	0	0
Dimmit	24,904,475	93,148,840	105,010,026	10,824,073
Donley	0	0	8,459	204
Duval	670,264	80,166	4,793,448	21,020
Eastland	120,582	307,140	1,392,895	16,465
Ector	18,327,350	37,080,999	1,960,249	4,828
Edwards	4,542	0	3,295,511	3
Ellis	6	12	2,032,725	0
Erath	277	542	1,764,474	1,358
Falls	357	0	0	0
Fayette	1,671,684	6,663,104	26,410,902	1,087,699
Fisher	4,283,773	6,864,545	8,801	121
Foard	94,252	8,410	49,974	0
Fort Bend	586,514	412,880	3,051,935	54,995
Franklin	309,119	75,647	685,511	21,643
Freestone	17,163	43,064	64,226,774	28,350
Frio	6,425,492	14,512,960	568,632	3,770
Gaines	19,744,209	17,835,945	1,771,597	3,461
Galveston	111,954	35,267	1,438,987	55,732
Garza	1,769,739	850,897	0	0
Glasscock	49,531,170	227,801,073	462,366	5,914
Goliad	115,386	79,110	3,980,895	37,282
Gonzales	31,622,126	43,890,486	8,982,153	2,188,753
Gray	865,786	1,560,666	4,927,540	18,370
Grayson	1,063,912	2,764,032	975,071	10,736
Gregg	1,156,410	1,343,873	18,305,544	99,499
Grimes	232,571	1,375,979	5,087,612	17,880
Guadalupe	705,374	0	0	0
Hale	898,106	1,279,103	0	0
Hamilton	12	0	43,440	0
Hansford	130,842	954,110	8,242,842	16,740
Hardeman	624,846	237,827	0	0
Hardin	687,713	648,753	2,999,359	208,738
Harris	1,036,774	699,454	5,028,011	75,136
Harrison	515,495	880,435	409,027,236	406,008
Hartley	203,594	51,535	838,179	0
Haskell	621,002	675,203	0	0
Hemphill	249,075	2,307,990	62,164,091	1,027,160
Henderson	247,880	1,909,838	4,179,785	13,726
Hidalgo	22,701	3,254	31,038,875	408,607
Hill	0	0	7,390,440	16
Hockley	10,106,027	6,032,699	15,213	1,375
Hood	0	0	25,817,757	49,147
Hopkins	120,751	59,794	16,505	2,204
Houston	328,076	322,246	2,382,052	70,281
Howard	123,008,179	288,652,826	149,453	1,523
Hunt	1,058	0	0	0
Hutchinson	341,982	1,628,796	3,830,502	70,884
Irion	8,675,656	131,707,005	1,137,022	14,217
Jack	702,952	6,496,099	5,667,882	63,107
Jackson	903,209	328,083	2,871,744	55,277
Jasper	292,312	284,367	7,041,684	404,006
Jefferson	352,402	216,216	3,006,930	175,019
Jim Hogg	15,742	1,692	4,872,339	55,639
Jim Wells	59,776	146,774	2,109,509	15,384

County	Oil (BBL)	Casinghead (MCF)	GW Gas (MCF)	Condensate (BBL)
Johnson	0	0	120,050,711	8,823
Jones	624,102	560,156	7,445	37
Karnes	97,791,585	202,480,156	111,562,231	14,429,355
Kaufman	43,707	27,860	0	0
Kenedy	93,713	152,507	35,513,763	314,435
Kent	1,903,842	4,868,574	0	0
Kimble	248	0	0	0
King	1,398,735	142,809	58,374	8
Kleberg	39,743	93,038	6,123,625	131,858
Knox	150,047	124,794	0	0
La Salle	33,727,696	74,806,333	241,863,057	4,935,919
Lamb	182,524	194,750	0	0
Lavaca	7,869,542	10,583,496	20,362,634	906,123
Lee	2,337,758	5,568,235	465,110	23,022
Leon	398,363	1,043,741	22,432,621	24,935
Liberty	639,288	342,459	4,988,257	172,402
Limestone	65,927	0	24,801,562	16,360
Lipscomb	621,503	7,278,483	25,389,344	817,102
Live Oak	7,749,716	24,551,354	70,110,598	8,135,885
Loving	81,535,977	186,739,559	353,410,415	58,161,416
Lubbock	824,460	66,379	0	0
Lynn	154,038	34,142	0	0
Madison	1,462,968	3,731,058	1,447,804	65,755
Marion	403,865	227,590	895,193	17,102
Martin	180,683,622	429,783,128	5,706	82
Matagrda	130,909	69,321	8,103,667	258,987
Maverick	1,370,842	2,912,944	989,824	23,439
McCulloch	33,069	0	0	0
McLennan	108	0	0	0
McMullen	17,067,153	30,504,947	56,085,977	3,208,752
Medina	75,163	0	9,297	0
Menard	67,681	2,733	1,919	82
Midland	218,132,800	709,262,066	3,165,812	61,635
Milam	1,776,392	2,851,188	9,503	207
Mitchell	1,850,676	491,015	0	0
Montague	754,445	6,396,352	33,534,366	240,363
Montgomry	707,020	899,728	1,562,395	35,886
Moore	215,154	1,015,374	22,614,597	4,912
Morris	140,835	18,595	0	0
Motley	23,397	2,125	0	0
Nacgdches	8,072	28,932	116,823,232	41,168
Navarro	119,302	115,906	255,095	7,186
Newton	706,692	1,198,525	1,974,111	94,671
Nolan	1,050,347	1,682,085	260,605	1,375
Nueces	117,932	233,981	8,027,345	191,913
Ochiltree	3,037,268	16,319,022	8,722,276	131,230
Oldham	204,402	461,413	30,323	0
Orange	289,365	523,644	1,726,129	162,511
Palo Pinto	62,660	917,042	4,037,524	18,084
Panola	213,755	1,078,191	763,367,329	1,296,730
Parker	210	85,139	43,805,874	34,786
Pecos	31,095,933	89,040,989	41,313,628	360,094
Polk	376,682	263,151	10,688,083	384,651
Potter	278,877	2,352,654	6,863,863	35,919
Rains	0	0	833,158	0
Reagan	45,134,347	341,526,743	1,303,724	12,197
Real	338	0	0	0

County	Oil (BBL)	Casinghead (MCF)	GW Gas (MCF)	Condensate (BBL)
Red River	58,538	0	0	0
Reeves	71,785,561	235,053,390	927,173,893	90,760,209
Refugio	1,915,301	11,716,301	6,803,820	47,236
Roberts	811,595	9,644,394	17,968,694	337,958
Robertson	1,925,140	1,223,542	49,699,983	2,977
Runnels	238,854	399,426	91,634	298
Rusk	1,207,860	1,544,852	80,828,857	504,780
Sabine	74	0	494,173	0
S.Augustine	7,586	134,604	228,478,277	13,891
SanJacinto	33,674	50,162	1,898,265	59,609
SanPatricio	208,947	298,415	2,089,482	73,445
Schleicher	199,526	1,823,681	3,479,972	27,074
Scurry	14,487,857	45,547,889	0	0
Shacklford	269,571	397,240	778,037	9,829
Shelby	11,451	221,419	84,867,312	20,811
Sherman	73,236	81,139	12,104,957	4,436
Smith	1,213,637	1,277,378	13,526,269	135,220
Somervell	0	0	3,435,875	2,456
Starr	254,853	463,623	23,183,075	249,382
Stephens	1,532,342	1,852,244	5,204,768	30,634
Sterling	443,198	3,901,117	2,107,020	24,527
Stonewall	954,639	1,233,863	0	0
Sutton	18,968	54,417	17,096,476	27,892
Tarrant	0	0	312,287,017	5,739
Taylor	304,141	101,022	10,653	0
Terrell	17,179	319,474	16,186,706	49,622
Terry	2,434,445	339,194	0	0
Throckmrtn	540,755	1,672,552	97,938	2,754
Titus	317,942	968	0	0
TomGreen	280,099	2,105,070	310,143	4,436
Travis	4,370	0	0	0
Trinity	13,911	0	47,020	1,251
Tyler	286,872	252,542	12,390,290	1,601,281
Upshur	69,426	11,631	17,530,251	141,345
Upton	92,302,429	352,706,991	7,069,116	122,408
Val Verde	836	0	3,426,475	86
Van Zandt	473,854	201,250	433,908	247
Victoria	1,212,026	931,614	5,082,197	94,365
Walker	39,614	1,602,563	477,174	32,705
Waller	122,596	7,549	1,176,892	10,173
Ward	44,020,716	100,051,764	65,455,171	6,562,707
Washngton	2,442,970	8,680,297	63,074,607	2,414,839
Webb	4,512,877	15,244,943	900,558,989	10,412,164
Wharton	550,858	645,187	5,373,951	64,664
Wheeler	767,485	5,867,150	55,616,944	1,160,596
Wichita	1,169,422	221,765	0	0
Wilbarger	721,972	71,265	0	0
Willacy	179,287	56,313	2,249,963	39,164
Willimson	8,665	0	0	0
Wilson	2,737,590	1,312,147	0	0
Winkler	18,896,032	37,717,297	18,649,892	1,416,241
Wise	121,633	2,185,239	153,864,009	393,905
Wood	3,319,820	50,666,674	2,976,934	91,212
Yoakum	26,512,097	51,240,920	56,762	0
Young	782,517	1,046,941	786,014	15,361
Zapata	32,098	74,663	55,490,848	39,857
Zavala	7,514,100	7,515,215	193,134	0

Top Gas-Producing Counties, 1993–2022

The top 37 natural gas-producing counties are listed in the chart below. The fourth column at the right lists the number of producing gas wells in the county in February 2022. Seventy-five counties have produced more than 500 billion cubic feet of natural gas since 1993 (see map). MCF is thousand cubic feet. ☆

Rank	County	Gas (MCF)	Gas Wells
1.	Webb	12,077,090,696	6,123
2.	Panola	8,225,902,264	4,781
3.	Tarrant	8,209,296,370	3,989
4.	Zapata	6,505,149,450	2,661
5.	Hidalgo	5,247,132,874	1,204
6.	Johnson	5,106,839,554	2,843
7.	Freestone	4,562,558,413	2,918
8.	Wise	4,486,680,589	4,085
9.	Pecos	4,194,566,316	1,200
10.	Denton	3,729,452,041	2,742
11.	Reeves	3,324,471,873	1,596
12.	Hemphill	3,142,196,211	2,227
13.	Starr	3,034,741,424	1,046
14.	Harrison	2,993,972,409	2,119
15.	Wheeler	2,941,751,975	1,663
16.	Rusk	2,756,155,235	2,152
17.	Robertson	2,670,875,707	873
18.	Crockett	2,654,199,501	5,492
19.	Loving	2,087,389,189	855
20.	Nacogdoches	1,992,090,444	1,238
21.	DeWitt	1,951,772,817	960
22.	Dimmit	1,646,503,074	1,802
23.	Culberson	1,626,443,526	656
24.	Limestone	1,621,203,990	1,091
25.	Sutton	1,601,547,344	5,257
26.	Lavaca	1,571,944,409	429
27.	La Salle	1,501,020,653	1,052
28.	Terrell	1,450,695,723	638
29.	San Augustine	1,449,883,612	309
30.	Karnes	1,443,865,314	988
31.	Parker	1,415,735,465	1,439
32.	Leon	1,341,748,235	547
33.	Shelby	1,328,615,245	603
34.	Brooks	1,327,773,404	357
35.	Gregg	1,317,820,663	782
36.	Duval	1,300,852,074	323
37.	Lipscomb	1,289,140,673	1,315

Source: Texas Railroad Commission.

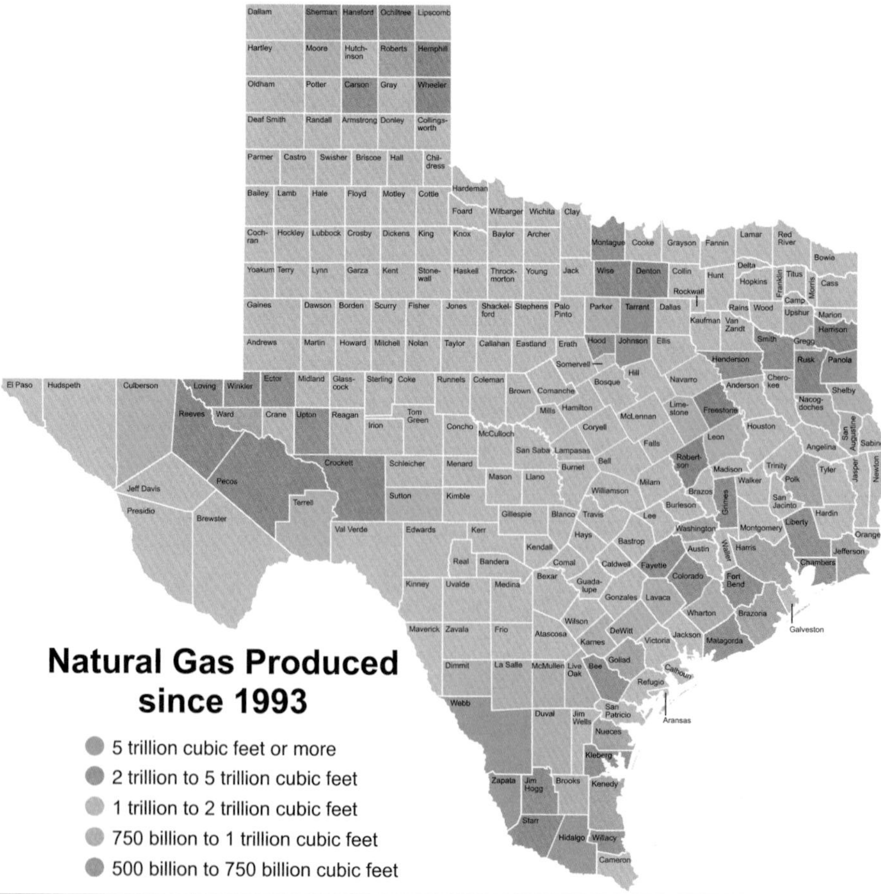

Natural Gas Produced since 1993

- 5 trillion cubic feet or more
- 2 trillion to 5 trillion cubic feet
- 1 trillion to 2 trillion cubic feet
- 750 billion to 1 trillion cubic feet
- 500 billion to 750 billion cubic feet

Petroleum Production and Income in Texas

Year	Crude Oil				Natural Gas		
	Production (Thousand Barrels)	Value (in Thousands)	Average Price per Barrel (Nominal)	*Average Price per Barrel (2005 $)	Production (Million Cubic Feet)	Value (in Thousands)	Wellhead Price (Cents per **MCF)
2022	1,846,806	$175,982,144	$95.29	—	10,482,080	—	—
2021	1,744,882	$118,355,346	$67.83	—	9,875,390	—	—
2020	1,495,495	$58,563,584	$39.16	—	6,593,494	$11,802,354	179.00
2019	1,586,337	$90,405,346	$56.99	—	6,775,942	$14,907,072	220.00
2018	1,274,569	$76,359,429	$59.91	—	5,742,978	$19,468,695	339.00
2017	1,026,765	$49,869,976	$48.57	—	6,300,292	$20,664,957	328.00
2016	974,612	$32,854,310	$42.40	—	6,996,000	$20,566,930	255.00
2015	1,004,774	$48,132,920	$48.79	—	7,871,200	$8,827,180	263.00
2014	927,417	$85,962,300	$87.02	—	8,171,230	$18,034,000	428.00
2013	749,876	$73,666,700	$95.80	—	7,725,119	$15,358,900	373.00
2012	724,422	$55,145,600	$92.50	—	7,128,775	$12,959,100	266.00
2011	448,903	$39,420,500	$91.99	$81.15	7,051,594	$13,646,300	395.00
2010	369,953	$26,054,900	$76.23	$68.88	7,246,042	$11,796,700	448.00
2009	349,391	$18,455,530	$57.40	$52.31	7,573,033	$12,167,800	367.00
2008	315,896	$30,409,170	$96.85	$89.28	7,271,815	$34,415,890	797.00
2007	311,830	$21,341,100	$68.30	$64.30	6,421,375	$22,968,420	625.00
2006	314,600	$19,353,500	$61.31	$59.38	6,077,786	$23,500,800	639.00
2005	327,600	$12,744,600	$52.61	$52.61	5,700,613	$16,399,400	733.00
2004	327,910	$12,762,650	$38.79	$40.08	5,817,227	$17,077,700	546.00
2003	333,300	$9,708,600	$29.13	$30.96	5,671,689	$14,797,800	488.00
2002	335,600	$8,150,400	$23.77	$25.80	5,611,958	$9,840,800	295.00
2001	325,500	$7,770,500	$23.41	$25.82	5,668,602	$13,708,700	400.00
2000	348,900	$10,037,300	$28.60	$32.26	5,645,972	$12,837,600	368.00
1999	337,100	$5,855,800	$17.29	$19.93	5,538,929	$6,789,700	219.00
1998	440,600	$5,472,400	$12.28	$14.36	5,772,080	$6,362,900	196.00
1997	464,900	$8,516,800	$18.66	$22.07	5,814,745	$8,134,200	232.00
1996	478,100	$9,560,800	$20.31	$24.44	5,770,255	$6,945,000	217.00
1995	503,200	$8,177,700	$16.38	$20.09	5,672,105	$5,305,200	155.00
1994	533,900	$7,977,500	$14.98	$18.76	5,675,748	$6,220,300	185.00
1993	572,600	$9,288,800	$16.19	$20.70	5,606,498	$7,365,800	204.00
1992	642,059	$11,820,306	$18.32	$23.94	5,436,408	$8,643,888	174.00
1991	672,810	$12,836,080	$19.04	$25.47	5,509,990	$7,713,986	143.00
1990	672,081	$15,047,902	$22.37	$30.98	5,533,771	$8,281,372	149.70
1989	679,575	$12,123,624	$17.81	$25.62	5,595,190	$8,113,026	145.00
1988	727,928	$10,729,660	$14.71	$21.96	5,702,643	$7,983,700	141.00
1987	754,213	$13,221,345	$17.55	$27.10	5,516,224	$7,612,389	138.00
1986	813,620	$11,976,488	$14.73	$23.40	5,663,491	$8,778,410	155.00
1985	860,300	$23,159,286	$26.80	$43.52	5,805,098	$12,665,114	218.00
1984	874,079	$25,138,520	$28.87	$48.31	5,864,224	$13,487,715	230.00
1983	876,205	$22,947,814	$29.35	$50.95	5,643,183	$14,672,275	225.00
1982	923,868	$29,074,126	$31.77	$57.33	6,497,678	$13,567,151	208.80
1975	1,221,929	$9,336,570	$7.64	—	7,485,764	$3,885,112	51.90
1970	1,249,697	$4,104,005	$3.28	—	8,357,716	$1,203,511	14.40
1965	1,000,749	$2,962,119	$2.96	—	6,636,555	$858,396	12.90
1955	1,053,297	$2,989,330	$2.84	—	4,730,798	$378,464	8.00
1945	754,710	$914,410	$1.21	—	1,711,401	$44,839	2.60
1935	392,666	$367,820	$0.94	—	642,366	$13,233	2.10

Revised September 2023. NA, not available.

*In chained (2005) dollars, from the U.S. Energy Information Administration (EIA).

**MCF (thousand cubic feet)

Sources: Previously from the Texas Railroad Commission, Texas Mid-Continent Oil & Gas Association and, beginning in 1979, data are from Department of Energy. Data since 1993 are from the state comptroller and EIA and the railroad commission. Federal figures do not include gas that is vented or flared or used for pressure maintenance and repressuring, but do include non-hydrocarbon gases.

Offshore Production History—Oil and Gas

The cumulative offshore natural gas production as of Jan. 1, 2019, was 4,207,288,591 thousand cubic feet (Mcf). The cumulative offshore oil production was 42,538,000 barrels. ☆

Production in Recent Years

Year	Crude Oil BBL	Casinghead MCF	Gas Well Gas MCF	Condensate BBL
2022	54,617	52,978	2,081,515	70,876
2021	73,946	244,494	1,398,188	95,175
2020	105,514	56,486	2,477,909	126,695
2019	132,838	78,601	3,282,580	174,754
2017	118,474	35,054	6,049,351	183,464
2016	154,005	48,816	8,337,712	231,975
2015	291,428	233,094	9,982,738	281,510
2014	424,191	574,464	12,280,841	354,585
2013	500,209	460,876	15,053,574	370,290
2012	605,389	902,900	17,011,234	435,049
2011	522,307	925,166	23,916,678	566,425
2010	477,303	1,160,607	28,143,515	866,959
2005	450,378	389,301	38,589,312	451,692
2000	548,046	335,415	44,086,237	220,309

2022 Production by Area

Offshore Area	Crude Oil BBL	Casinghead MCF	Gas Well Gas MCF	Condensate BBL
Brazos-LB	0	0	0	0
Brazos-SB	0	0	0	0
Galveston-LB	33,337	42,093	74,607	36,518
Galveston-SB	0	0	1,014,027	1,218
High Island-LB	0	0	0	0
High Island-SB	20,852	9,994	6	1
Matagrda Is.-LB	0	0	0	0
Matagrda Is.-SB	0	0	556,860	9,034
Mustang Is.-LB	428	891	436,015	24,105
Mustang Is.-SB	2,247	2,928	1,252,230	44,535
Total	**54,617**	**52,978**	**2,081,515**	**70,876**

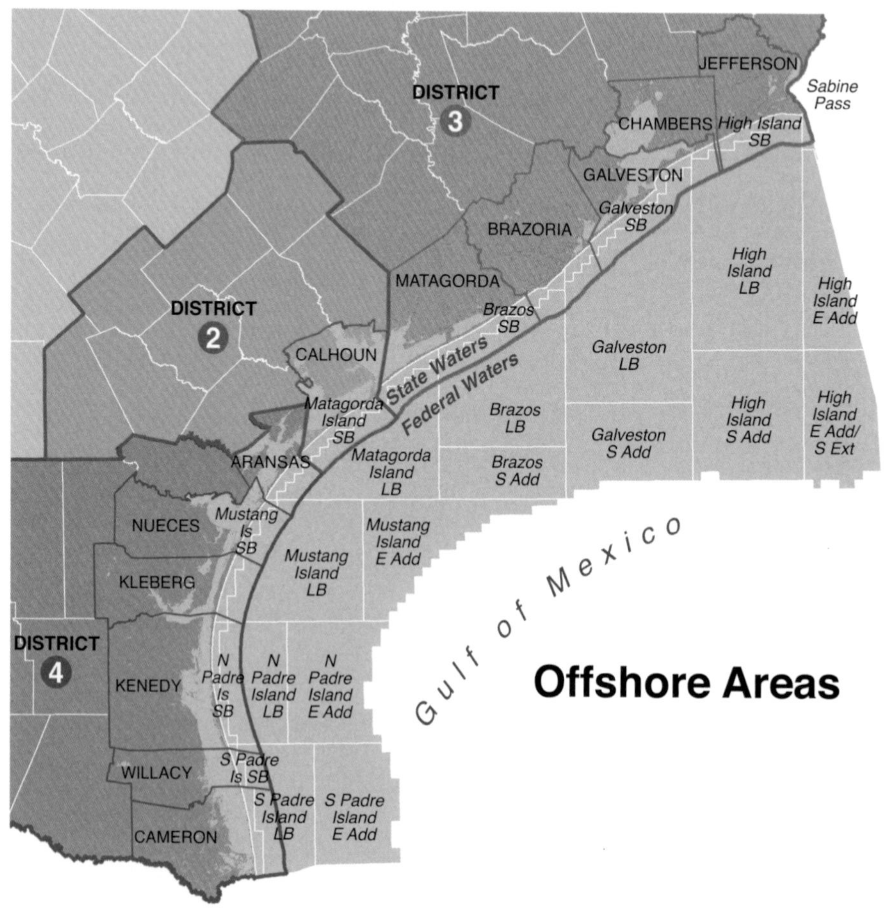

Receipts by Texas from Tidelands

The Republic of Texas had proclaimed its Gulf boundaries as three marine leagues, recognized by international law as traditional national boundaries. These boundaries were never seriously questioned when Texas joined the Union in 1845.

In 1930 a congressional resolution authorized the U.S. Attorney General to file suit to establish offshore lands as properties of the federal government. Congress returned the disputed lands to Texas in 1953, and the U.S. Supreme Court confirmed Texas' ownership in 1960.

In 1978, the federal government also granted states a "fair and equitable" share of the revenues from offshore leases within three miles of the states' outermost boundary. States did not receive any such revenue until 1986. ☆

The table shows annual receipts from tidelands in the Gulf of Mexico by the Texas General Land Office from 1963 to Aug. 31, 2018. It does not include revenue from bays and other submerged area owned by Texas. Totals include previous years not shown in this chart.

Source: General Land Office.

From	To	Total	Bonus	Rental	Royalty	Lease
9-01-1963	8-31-1964	$ 3,656,236.75	$ 2,435,244.36	$ 525,315.00	$ 695,677.39	...
9-01-1964	8-31-1965	54,654,576.96	53,114,943.63	755,050.12	784,583.21	...
9-01-1965	8-31-1966	22,148,825.44	18,223,357.84	3,163,475.00	761,992.60	...
9-01-1966	8-31-1967	8,469,680.86	3,641,414.96	3,711,092.65	1,117,173.25	...
9-01-1967	8-31-1968	6,305,851.00	1,251,852.50	2,683,732.50	2,370,266.00	...
9-01-1968	8-31-1969	6,372,268.28	1,838,118.33	1,491,592.50	3,042,557.45	...
9-01-1969	8-31-1970	10,311,030.48	5,994,666.32	618,362.50	3,698,001.66	...
9-01-1970	8-31-1971	9,969,629.17	4,326,120.11	726,294.15	4,917,214.91	...
9-01-1971	8-31-1972	7,558,327.21	1,360,212.64	963,367.60	5,234,746.97	...
9-01-1972	8-31-1973	9,267,975.68	3,701,737.30	920,121.60	4,646,116.78	...
9-01-1973	8-31-1974	41,717,670.04	32,981,619.28	1,065,516.60	7,670,534.16	...
9-01-1974	8-31-1975	27,321,536.62	5,319,762.85	2,935,295.60	19,066,478.17	...
9-01-1975	8-31-1976	38,747,074.09	6,197,853.00	3,222,535.84	29,326,685.25	...
9-01-1976	8-31-1977	84,196,228.27	41,343,114.81	2,404,988.80	40,448,124.66	...
9-01-1977	8-31-1978	118,266,812.05	49,807,750.45	4,775,509.92	63,683,551.68	...
9-01-1978	8-31-1979	100,410,268.68	34,578,340.94	7,318,748.40	58,513,179.34	...
9-01-1979	8-31-1980	200,263,803.03	34,733,270.02	10,293,153.80	155,237,379.21	...
9-01-1980	8-31-1981	219,126,876.54	37,467,196.97	13,100,484.25	168,559,195.32	...
9-01-1981	8-31-1982	250,824,581.69	27,529,516.33	14,214,478.97	209,080,586.39	...
9-01-1982	8-31-1983	165,197,734.83	10,180,696.40	12,007,476.70	143,009,561.73	...
9-01-1983	8-31-1984	152,755,934.29	32,864,122.19	8,573,996.87	111,317,815.23	...
9-01-1984	8-31-1985	140,561,690.79	32,650,127.75	6,837,603.70	101,073,959.34	...
9-01-1985	8-31-1986	516,503,771.08	6,365,426.23	4,241,892.75	78,289,592.27	$427,606,859.83
9-01-1986	8-31-1987	60,066,571.05	4,186,561.63	1,933,752.50	44,691,907.22	9,254,349.70
9-01-1987	8-31-1988	56,875,069.22	14,195,274.28	1,817,058.90	28,068,202.53	12,794,533.51
9-01-1988	8-31-1989	61,793,380.04	12,995,892.74	1,290,984.37	35,160,568.40	12,345,934.53
9-01-1989	8-31-1990	68,701,751.51	7,708,449.54	1,289,849.87	40,331,537.06	19,371,915.04
9-01-1990	8-31-1991	90,885,856.99	3,791,832.77	1,345,711.07	70,023,601.01	15,724,712.14
9-01-1991	8-31-1992	51,154,511.34	4,450,850.00	1,123,585.54	26,776,191.35	18,803,884.45
9-01-1992	8-31-1993	60,287,712.60	3,394,230.00	904,359.58	34,853,679.68	21,135,443.34
9-01-1993	8-31-1994	57,825,043.59	3,570,657.60	694,029.30	32,244,987.95	21,315,368.74
9-01-1994	8-31-1995	62,143,227.78	8,824,722.93	674,479.79	34,691,023.35	17,951,001.71
9-01-1995	8-31-1996	68,166,645.51	13,919,246.80	1,102,591.39	32,681,315.73	20,463,491.59
9-01-1996	8-31-1997	90,614,935.93	22,007,378.46	1,319,614.78	41,605,792.50	25,682,150.19
9-01-1997	8-31-1998	104,016,006.75	36,946,312.49	2,070,802.90	38,760,320.91	26,238,570.45
9-01-1998	8-31-1999	53,565,810.30	5,402,171.00	2,471,128.47	23,346,515.93	22,345,994.90
9-01-1999	8-31-2000	55,465,763.99	3,487,564.80	2,171,636.35	24,314,241.99	25,492,320.85
9-01-2000	8-31-2001	68,226,347.58	9,963,608.68	1,830,378.11	23,244,034.74	33,188,326.05
9-01-2001	8-31-2002	30,910,283.91	9,286,015.20	1,545,583.01	13,369,771.56	6,708,914.14
9-01-2002	8-31-2003	50,881,515.90	15,152,092.40	1,071,377.60	19,648,641.39	15,009,404.51
9-01-2003	8-31-2004	54,379,791.20	14,448,555.70	1,094,201.41	25,199,635.21	13,637,398.88
9-01-2004	8-31-2005	53,594,809.87	9,148,220.20	1,624,666.50	32,406,328.78	10,415,594.39
9-01-2005	8-31-2006	60,829,271.63	22,565,845.14	1,605,090.30	23,287,994.53	13,370,341.66
9-01-2006	8-31-2007	52,513,621.85	15,879,784.44	2,022,859.80	18,785,626.55	15,825,351.06
9-01-2007	8-31-2008	86,705,980.28	4,632,175.50	1,485,080.97	68,408,943.01	12,179,780.80
9-01-2008	8-31-2009	65,835,625.76	3,896,795.20	1,020,204.33	53,166,364.50	7,752,261.73
9-01-2009	8-31-2010	49,647,832.14	3,352,431.20	603,406.00	41,901,754.81	3,790,240.13
9-01-2010	8-31-2011	50,360,843.36	4,088,819.06	546,404.80	43,602,027.62	2,123,591.88
9-01-2011	8-31-2012	37,561,595.54	2,436,420.00	217,356.00	33,327,417.09	1,580,402.45
9-01-2012	8-31-2013	32,676,026.13	1,079,400.00	339,941.00	30,353,820.49	902,864.64
9-01-2013	8-31-2014	28,103,953.40	217,000.00	193,125.00	26,665,893.97	1,027.934.53
9-01-2014	8-31-2015	17,922,043.53	969,600.00	71,894.00	16,302,558.59	577,990.94
9-01-2015	8-31-2016	7,053,383.42	0.00	112,350.00	6,819,050.31	121,983.11
9-01-2016	8-31-2017	7,422,396.66	100,800.00	48,712.00	7,172,244.48	100,640.18
9-01-2017	8-31-2018	10,237,935.90	0.00	48,000.00	5,759,255.41	4,430,680.49
Totals		$ 3,974,612.907.55	$ 774,513,049,71	$ 147,166,154.10	$ 2,213,663,471.20	$ 839,270.232.54
Inside three-mile line		$ 533,256,002.78	$ 180,838,499.91	$ 39,193,553.27	$ 313,223,949.60	0.00
Between three-mile and three marine-league line		$ 2,599,261,306.65	$ 591,022,465.41	$ 107,734,519.64	$1,900,439,521.60	0.00
Outside three marine-league line		$ 842,095,598,12	$ 2,652,084.39	$ 173,281.19	0.00	$ 839,270,232,54

Nonpetroleum Minerals

Sources: U.S. Geological Survey's mineral industry surveys, www.usgs.gov/centers/nmic/mineral-industry-surveys; Bureau of Economic Geology, The University of Texas at Austin, www.beg.utexas.edu

There are many nonpetroleum, or nonfuel, minerals found in Texas. Although they are overshadowed by production of petroleum, natural gas, and natural gas liquids, many are important to the economy.

In 2022, Texas nonfuel mineral production was valued at $8.0 billion, a 39.4% increase from the $5.8 billion in total value for 2021, and accounted for 8.2% of the total U.S. nonfuel mineral production value of $98.2 billion. Among all 50 states, Texas ranked third in nonfuel mineral production for the eighth year in a row (since 2015), behind Nevada ($8.9 billion in 2022) and Arizona ($10.1 billion).

The nonfuel mineral commodities produced in Texas in 2018 include: ammonia, barite, cement, fluorspar, gold, gypsum, helium, iron and steel, lime, salt, sand and gravel (both construction and industrial) selenium, stone (both crushed and dimension), sulfur, talc, tellurium, and zeolites (clinoptilolite).

In 2022, Texas was the leader in crushed stone production as well as cement, and second to California in sand and gravel (construction). Texas is one of only two states that produced tellurium; the other is Utah. The amount and value has been withheld to avoid disclosing proprietary data for the companies involved.

ALUMINUM: No aluminum ores are mined in Texas, but three Texas plants process aluminum materials in one or more ways. Plants in San Patricio and Calhoun counties produce aluminum oxide (alumina) from imported raw ore (bauxite), and a plant in Milam County reduces the oxide to aluminum.

ASBESTOS: Small occurrences of amphibole-type asbestos have been found in the state. In West Texas, richterite, a white, long-fibered amphibole, is associated with some of the talc deposits northwest of Allamoore in Hudspeth County. Another type, tremolite, has been found in the Llano Uplift of Central Texas where it is associated with serpentinite in eastern Gillespie and western Blanco counties. No asbestos is mined in Texas.

ASPHALT (NATIVE): Asphalt-bearing Cretaceous limestones crop out in Burnet, Kinney, Pecos, Reeves, Uvalde, and other counties. The most significant deposit is in southwestern Uvalde County, where asphalt occurs naturally in pore spaces of the Anacacho Limestone. The material is quarried and used extensively as road-paving material. Asphalt-bearing sandstones occur in Anderson, Angelina, Cooke, Jasper, Maverick, Montague, Nacogdoches, Uvalde, Zavala, and other counties.

BARITE: Deposits of a heavy, nonmetallic mineral, barite (barium sulphate), have been found in many localities, including Baylor, Brown, Brewster, Culberson, Gillespie, Howard, Hudspeth, Jeff Davis, Kinney, Llano, Live Oak, Taylor, Val Verde, and Webb counties. During the 1960s, there was small, intermittent production in the Seven Heart Gap area of the Apache Mountains in Culberson County, where barite was mined from open pits. Most of the deposits are known to be relatively small, but the Webb County deposit has not been evaluated. Grinding plants, which prepare barite mined outside of Texas for use chiefly as a weighting agent in well-drilling muds and as a filler, are located in Brownsville, Corpus Christi, El Paso, Galena Park, Galveston, and Houston.

BASALT (TRAP ROCK): Masses of basalt: a hard, dark-colored, fine-grained igneous rock: crop out in Kinney, Travis, Uvalde, and several other counties along the Balcones Fault Zone, and also in the Trans-Pecos area of West Texas. Basalt is quarried near Knippa in Uvalde County for use as road-building material, railroad ballast, and other aggregate.

BENTONITE (see CLAYS).

BERYLLIUM: Occurrences of beryllium minerals at several Trans-Pecos localities have been recognized for several years.

BRINE (see also SALT, SODIUM SULPHATE): Many wells in Texas produce brine by solution mining of subsurface salt deposits, mostly in West Texas counties such as Andrews, Crane, Ector, Loving, Midland, Pecos, Reeves, Ward, and others. These wells in the Permian Basin dissolve salt from the Salado Formation, an enormous salt deposit that extends in the subsurface from north of the Big Bend northward to Kansas, has an east-west width of 150 to 200 miles, and may have several hundred feet of net salt thickness. The majority of the brine is used in the petroleum industry, but it also is used in water softening, the chemical industry, and other uses. Three Gulf Coast counties, Fort Bend, Duval, and Jefferson, have brine stations that produce from salt domes.

BUILDING STONE (DIMENSION STONE): Granite and limestone currently are quarried for use as dimension stone. The granite quarries are located in Burnet, Gillespie, Llano, and Mason counties; the limestone quarries are in Shackelford and Williamson counties. Past production of limestone for use as dimension stone has been reported in Burnet, Gillespie, Jones, Tarrant, Travis, and several other counties. There also has been production of sandstone in various counties for use as dimension stone.

CEMENT MATERIALS: Cement is currently manufactured in Bexar, Comal, Dallas, Ector, Ellis, Hays, McLennan, Nolan, and Potter counties. Many of these plants utilize Cretaceous limestones and shales or clays as raw materials for the cement. On the Texas High Plains, a cement plant near Amarillo uses impure caliche as the chief raw material. Iron oxide, also a constituent of cement, is available from the iron ore deposits of East Texas and from smelter slag. Gypsum, added to the cement as a retarder, is found chiefly in the North-Central, Central, and Trans-Pecos areas.

A new greenfields white cement production plant has been proposed near Brady, but it has been delayed due to local opposition. It would be the third of its kind in the U.S.

CHROMIUM: Chromite-bearing rock has been found in several small deposits around the margin of the Coal Creek

Cement Production in Texas
(metric tons)

Type	2022	2021	2020	2019	2018	2017
Portland and Blended	12,037,615	11,345,634	11,858,581	12,490,915	11,757,243	11,465,785
Masonry	298,625	295,687	297,338	301,000	291,718	304,320
Clinker	10,986,489	10,659,335	10,864,668	11,236,968	10,573,886	10,128,636

Source: Industry surveys at USGS

serpentinite mass in northeastern Gillespie County and northwestern Blanco County. Exploration has not revealed significant deposits.

CLAYS: Texas has an abundance and variety of ceramic and non-ceramic clays and is one of the country's leading producers of clay products.

Almost any kind of clay, ranging from common clay used to make brick and tile to clays suitable for manufacture of specialty whitewares, can be used for ceramic purposes. Fire clay suitable for use as refractories occurs chiefly in East and North-Central Texas; ball clay, a high-quality plastic ceramic clay, is found in East Texas.

Ceramic clay suitable for quality structural clay products, such as structural building brick, paving brick, and drain tile, is especially abundant in East and North-Central Texas. Common clay suitable for use in the manufacture of cement and ordinary brick is found in most counties of the state. Many of the Texas clays will expand or bloat upon rapid firing and are suitable for the manufacture of lightweight aggregate, which is used mainly in concrete blocks and highway surfacing.

Nonceramic clays are utilized without firing. They are used primarily as bleaching and absorbent clays, fillers, coaters, additives, bonding clays, drilling muds, catalysts, and potentially as sources of alumina. Most of the nonceramic clays in Texas are bentonites and fuller's earth. These occur extensively in the Coastal Plain and locally in the High Plains and Big Bend areas. Kaolin clays in parts of East Texas are potential sources of such nonceramic products as paper coaters and fillers, rubber fillers, and drilling agents. Relatively high in alumina, these clays also are a potential source of metallic aluminum.

COAL (see also LIGNITE): Bituminous coal, which occurs in North-Central, South, and West Texas, was a significant energy source in Texas prior to the large-scale development of oil and gas. During the period from 1895–1943, Texas mines produced more than 25 million tons of coal. The mines were inactive for many years, but the renewed interest in coal as a major energy source prompted a revaluation of Texas' coal deposits. In the late 1970s, bituminous coal production resumed in the state on a limited scale when mines were opened in Coleman, Erath, and Webb counties.

Much of the state's bituminous coal occurs in North-Central Texas. Deposits are found there in Pennsylvanian rocks within a large area that includes Coleman, Eastland, Erath, Jack, McCulloch, Montague, Palo Pinto, Parker, Throckmorton, Wise, Young, and other counties. Before the general availability of oil and gas, underground coal mines near Thurber, Bridgeport, Newcastle, Strawn, and other points annually produced significant coal tonnages. Preliminary evaluations indicate substantial amounts of coal may remain in the North-Central Texas area. The coal seams there are generally no more than 30 inches thick and are commonly covered by well-consolidated overburden. Ash and sulphur content are high. Beginning in 1979, two bituminous coal mine operations in North-Central Texas: one in southern Coleman County and one in northwestern Erath County: produced coal to be used as fuel by the cement industry. Neither mine is currently operating.

In South Texas, bituminous coal occurs in the **Eagle Pass district of Maverick County**, and bituminous cannel coal is present in the Santo Tomas district of Webb County. The Eagle Pass area was a leading coal-producing district in Texas during the late 1800s and early 1900s. The bituminous coal in that area, which occurs in the Upper Cretaceous Olmos Formation, has a high ash content and a moderate moisture and sulfur content. According to reports, Maverick County coal beds range from four to seven feet thick.

The cannel coals of western Webb County occur near the Rio Grande in middle Eocene strata. They were mined for more than 50 years and used primarily as a boiler fuel. Mining ceased from 1939 until 1978, when a surface mine was opened 30 miles northwest of Laredo to produce cannel coal for use as fuel in the cement industry and for export. An additional mine has since been opened in that county. Tests show that the coals of the Webb County Santo Tomas district have a high hydrogen content and yield significant amounts of gas and oil when distilled. They also have a high sulfur content. A potential use might be as a source of various petrochemical products.

Coal deposits in the Trans-Pecos country of West Texas include those in the Cretaceous rocks of the Terlingua area of Brewster County, the Eagle Spring area of Hudspeth County, and the San Carlos area of Presidio County. The coal deposits in these areas are believed to have relatively little potential for development as a fuel. They have been sold in the past as a soil amendment (see **LEONARDITE**).

COPPER: Copper minerals have been found in the Trans-Pecos area of West Texas, in the Llano Uplift area of Central Texas, and in redbed deposits of North Texas. No copper has been mined in Texas during recent years, and the total copper produced in the state has been relatively small. Past attempts to mine the North Texas and Llano Uplift copper deposits resulted in small shipments.

Practically all the copper production in the state has been from the Van Horn–Allamoore district of Culberson and Hudspeth counties in the Trans-Pecos area. Chief output was from the Hazel copper-silver mine of Culberson County that yielded over 1 million pounds of copper during 1891–1947. Copper ores and concentrates from outside of Texas are processed at smelters in El Paso and Amarillo.

CRUSHED STONE: Texas is among the leading states in the production of crushed stone. Most production consists of limestone; other kinds of crushed stone produced in the state include basalt (trap rock), dolomite, granite, marble, rhyolite, sandstone, and serpentinite. Large tonnages of crushed stone are used as aggregate in concrete, as road material, and in the manufacture of cement and lime. Some is used as riprap, terrazzo, roofing chips, filter material, fillers, as well as other purposes. In 2022, Texas lead the country in the production of crushed stone, followed by Missouri, Florida, and Pennsylvania.

Crushed Stone Production

Year	Quantity (thous. met. tons)	Value ($ millions)
2022	179,000*	—
2021	189,251	$2,693
2020	188,513	$2,617
2019	191,043	$2,643

*Estimation.

Source: Industry surveys at USGS

DIATOMITE (DIATOMACEOUS EARTH): Diatomite is a very lightweight siliceous material consisting of the remains of microscopic aquatic plants (diatoms). It is used chiefly as a filter and filler; other uses are for thermal insulation, as an abrasive, as an insecticide carrier, as a lightweight aggregate, and for other purposes. The diatomite was deposited in shallow, fresh-water lakes that were present in the High Plains during portions of the Pliocene and Pleistocene epochs. Deposits have been found in Armstrong, Crosby, Dickens, Ector, Hartley, and Lamb counties. No diatomite is mined in Texas.

DOLOMITE ROCK: Dolomite rock, which consists largely of the mineral dolomite (calcium-magnesium carbonate), commonly is associated with limestone in Texas. Areas in which dolomite rock occurs include Central Texas, the Callahan Divide, and parts of the Edwards Plateau, High Plains, and West Texas. Some of the principal deposits of dolomite rock are found in Bell, Brown, Burnet, Comanche,

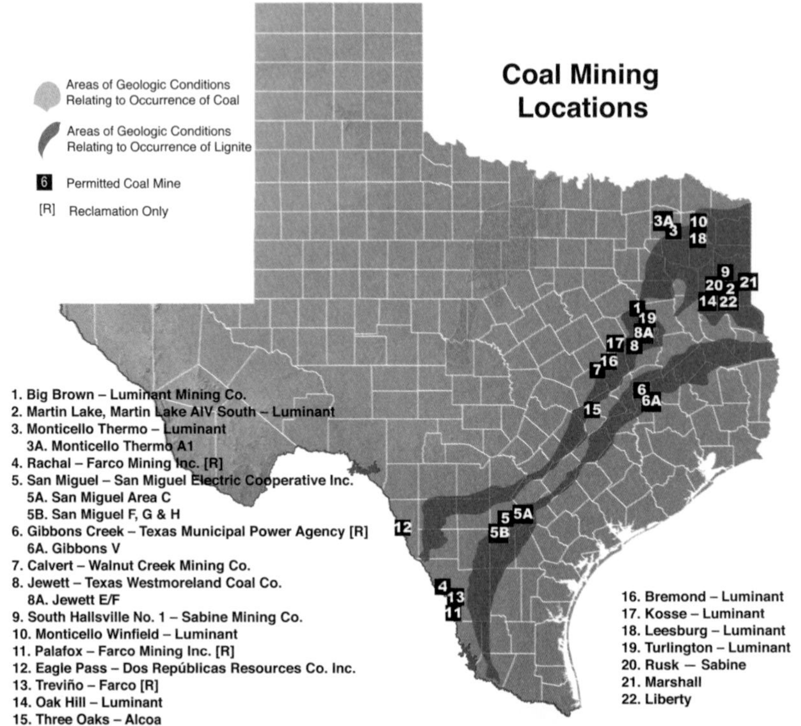

Coal and Lignite Mine Production
(in short tons)

Mine	Acres Bonded	2019	2020	2021	Cumulative Total
1. Big Brown	4,364.0	0	0	0	171,155,954
2. Martin Lake	17,098.0	924,947	0	0	315,950,912
Martin Lake AIV South	2,308.0	0	0	0	6,771,850
3. Monticello-Thermo	1,879.0	0	0	0	42,849,720
Monticello-Thermo A-1	279.0	0	0	0	792,213
4. Rachal	615.9	0	0	0	963,827
5. San Miguel	5,830.0	700,709	655,269	473,030	91,386,397
San Miguel Area C	3,357.3	0	0	0	22,747,139
San Miguel F, G, & H	1,968.0	2,303,071	1,992,447	2,196,647	7,279,809
6. Gibbons Creek	684.1	0	0	0	30,431,174
Gibbons Creek V	271.3	0	0	0	12,547,611
7. Calvert	5,867.0	2,156,794	1,972,073	2,063,647	59,632,933
8. Jewett	10,940.2	0	0	0	173,220,612
Jewett E/F	4,457.7	0	0	0	35,937,586
9. South Hallsville No. 1	19,783.0	1,065,829	693,180	850,117	115,153,367
10. Monticello-Winfield	13,269.0	0	0	0	277,049,944
12. Eagle Pass	2,578.4	1,638,483	250,766	0	8,916,057
13. Oak Hill	18,065.0	0	0	0	129,763,914
14. Three Oaks	11,429.0	0	0	0	75,274,333
15. Bremond	4,363.0	0	0	0	236
16. Kosse	12,751.0	9,594,365	10,104,902	8,754,648	108,134,458
17. Leesburg	4,293.0	0	0	0	0
18. Turlington	3,615.0	0	0	0	16,504,979
19. Rusk	9,070.0	2,073,093	933,156	1,015,508	15,761,541
20. Marshall	1,126.0	185,718	83,235	0	1,120,462
21. Liberty	3,425.0	2,663,711	2,954,048	2,102,030	18,270,206
Statewide Total	**163,686.9**	**23,306,720**	**19,639,076**	**17,455,627**	***1,904,093,860**

* Statewide cumulative total includes the cumulative amount mined from the following "no longer permitted" mines: Darco (6,798,881), Little Bull Creek (428,932), Powell Bend (1,569,875), Thurber (465,984), and Sandow (150,966,982). Also included are Palafox (5,355,519) and Treviño (890,453).

Source: Coal Production through 2018 report, Railroad Commission of Texas

Edwards, El Paso, Gillespie, Lampasas, Mills, Nolan, Taylor, and Williamson counties. Dolomite rock can be used as crushed stone (although much of Texas dolomite is soft and not a good aggregate material), in the manufacture of lime, and as a source of magnesium.

FELDSPAR: Large crystals and crystal fragments of feldspar minerals occur in the Precambrian pegmatite rocks that crop out in the Llano Uplift area of Central Texas: including Blanco, Burnet, Gillespie, Llano, and Mason counties: and in the Van Horn area of Culberson and Hudspeth counties in West Texas. Feldspar has been mined in Llano County for use as roofing granules and as a ceramic material. Feldspar is currently mined in Burnet County for use as an aggregate.

FLUORSPAR: The mineral fluorite (calcium fluoride), which is known commercially as fluorspar, occurs in both Central and West Texas. In Central Texas, the deposits that have been found in Burnet, Gillespie, and Mason counties are not considered adequate to sustain mining operations. In West Texas, deposits have been found in Brewster, El Paso, Hudspeth, Jeff Davis, and Presidio counties. Fluorspar has been mined in the Christmas Mountains of Brewster County and processed in Marathon. Former West Texas mining activity in the Eagle Mountains district of Hudspeth County resulted in the production of approximately 15,000 short tons of fluorspar during the peak years of 1942–1950. No production has been reported in Hudspeth County since that period. Imported fluorspar is processed in Brownsville, Eagle Pass, El Paso, and Houston. Fluorspar is used in the steel, chemical, aluminum, magnesium, ceramics, and glass industries, and for various other purposes.

FULLER'S EARTH (see CLAY).

GOLD: No major deposits of gold are known in Texas. Small amounts have been found in the Llano Uplift region of Central Texas and in West Texas; minor occurrences have been reported on the Edwards Plateau and the Gulf Coastal Plain of Texas. Nearly all of the gold produced in the state came as a by-product of silver and lead mining at Presidio mine, near Shafter in Presidio County. Additional small quantities were produced as a by-product of copper mining in Culberson County and from residual soils developed from gold-bearing quartz stringers in metamorphic rocks in Llano County. No gold mining has been reported in Texas since 1952. Total gold production in the state from 1889–1952 amounted to more than 8,419 troy ounces, according to U.S. Bureau of Mines figures. At least 73% of all production, and probably more, came from the Presidio mine.

GRANITE: Granites in shades of red and gray and related intrusive igneous rocks occur in the Llano Uplift of Central Texas and in the Trans-Pecos country of West Texas. Deposits are found in Blanco, Brewster, Burnet, El Paso, Gillespie, Hudspeth, Llano, McCulloch, Mason, Presidio, and other counties. Quarries in Burnet, Gillespie, Llano, and Mason counties produce Precambrian granite for a variety of uses as dimension stone and crushed stone.

GRAPHITE: Graphite, a soft, dark-gray mineral, is a form of very high-grade carbon. It occurs in Precambrian schist rocks of the Llano Uplift of Central Texas, notably in Burnet and Llano counties. Crystalline-flake graphite ore formerly was mined from open pits in the Clear Creek area of western Burnet County and processed at a plant near the mine. The mill now occasionally grinds imported material. Uses of natural crystalline graphite are refractories, steel production, pencil leads, lubricants, foundry facings, and crucibles, as well as other purposes.

GRINDING PEBBLES (ABRASIVE STONES): Flint pebbles, suitable for use in tube-mill grinding, are found in the Gulf Coastal Plain, where they occur in gravel deposits along rivers and in upland areas. Grinding pebbles are produced from Frio River terrace deposits near the McMullen–Live Oak county line, but the area is now part of the Choke Canyon Reservoir area.

GYPSUM: Gypsum is widely distributed in Texas. Chief deposits are bedded gypsum in the area east of the High Plains, in the Trans-Pecos country, and in Central Texas. It also occurs in salt-dome caprocks of the Gulf Coast. The massive, granular variety, which is known as rock gypsum, is the kind most commonly used by industry. Other varieties include alabaster, satin spar, and selenite.

Gypsum is one of the important industrial minerals in Texas. Bedded gypsum is produced from surface mines in Culberson, Fisher, Gillespie, Hardeman, Hudspeth, Kimble, Nolan, and Stonewall counties. Gypsum was formerly mined at Gyp Hill salt dome in Brooks County and at Hockley salt dome in Harris County. Most of the gypsum is calcined and used in the manufacture of gypsum wallboard, plaster, joint compounds, and other construction products. Crude gypsum is used chiefly as a retarder in portland cement and as a soil conditioner.

HELIUM: Helium is a very light, nonflammable, chemically inert gas. The U.S. Interior Department has ended its helium operation near Masterson in the Panhandle. The storage facility at Cliffside gas field near Amarillo and the 425-mile pipeline system will remain in operation until the government sells its remaining unrefined, crude helium. Helium is used in cryogenics, welding, pressurizing and purging, leak detection, synthetic breathing mixtures, and for other purposes. In 2022, there were three helium extraction plants in Texas.

IRON: Iron oxide (limonite, goethite, and hematite) and iron carbonate (siderite) deposits occur widely in East Texas, notably in Cass, Cherokee, Marion, and Morris counties, and also in Anderson, Camp, Harrison, Henderson, Nacogdoches, Smith, Upshur, and other counties. Magnetite (magnetic, black iron oxide) occurs in Central Texas, including a deposit at Iron Mountain in Llano County. Hematite occurs in the Trans-Pecos area and in the Llano Uplift of Central Texas. The extensive deposits of glauconite (a complex silicate containing iron) that occur in East Texas and the hematitic and goethitic Cambrian sandstone that crops out in the northwestern Llano Uplift region are potential sources of low-grade iron ore.

Limonite and other East Texas iron ores are mined from open pits in Cherokee and Henderson counties for use in the preparation of portland cement, as a weighting agent in well-drilling fluids, as an animal feed supplement, and for other purposes. East Texas iron ores also were mined in the past for use in the iron-steel industry.

KAOLIN (see CLAY).

LEAD AND ZINC: The lead mineral galena (lead sulfide) commonly is associated with zinc and silver. It formerly was produced as a by-product of West Texas silver mining, chiefly from the Presidio mine at Shafter in Presidio County, although lesser amounts were obtained at several other mines and prospects. Deposits of galena also are known to occur in Blanco, Brewster, Burnet, Gillespie, and Hudspeth counties.

Zinc, primarily from the mineral sphalerite (zinc sulphide), was produced chiefly from the Bonanza and Alice Ray mines in the Quitman Mountains of Hudspeth County. In addition, small production was reported from several other areas, including the Chinati and Montezuma mines of Presidio County and the Buck Prospect in the Apache Mountains of Culberson County. Zinc mineralization also occurs in association with the lead deposits in Cambrian rocks of Central Texas.

LEONARDITE: Deposits of weathered (oxidized) low-Btu value bituminous coals, generally referred to as "leonardite," occur in Brewster County. The name leonardite is used for a mixture of chemical compounds that is high in humic acids. In the past, material from these deposits was sold as soil conditioner. Other uses of leonardite include modification of viscosity of drill fluids and as sorbants in water-treatment.

LIGHTWEIGHT AGGREGATE (see CLAY, DIATOMITE, PERLITE, VERMICULITE).

LIGNITE: Almost all current coal production in Texas is located in the Tertiary-aged lignite belts that extend across the Texas Gulf Coastal Plain from the Rio Grande in South Texas to the Arkansas and Louisiana borders in East Texas. The Railroad Commission of Texas (RRC) reported that in 2018, Texas produced 24.8 million short tons of lignite from 12 mines. Cumulative production in 2018 was 1.8 billion short tons of lignite and coal. See the map and table opposite for more detail on coal and lignite mining.

Texas Coal and Lignite Production
(short tons)

Year	Total
2021	17,455,627
2020	19,639,076
2019	23,306,720
2018	24,842,955
2017	35,415,535
2016	39,139,879
2015	36,277,112
2014	43,633,881
2013	42,449,594
2012	43,536,176
2011	45,587,404
2010	41,419,857
2009	37,099,067
2008	40,152,112
2007	38,403,681
2006	46,128,231
2005	47,168,916
Pre-2005	1,282,438,037

Source: Railroad Commission of Texas

The near-surface lignite resources, occurring at depths of less than 200 feet in seams of three feet or thicker, are estimated at 23 billion short tons. Recoverable reserves of strippable lignite: those that can be economically mined under current conditions of price and technology: are estimated by the EIA to be 722 million short tons.

Additional lignite resources of the Texas Gulf Coastal Plain occur as deep-basin deposits. Deep-basin resources, those that occur at depths of 200 to 2,000 feet in seams of five feet or thicker, are comparable in magnitude to near-surface resources. The deep-basin lignites are a potential energy resource that conceivably could be utilized by in situ (in place) recovery methods such as underground gasification.

As with bituminous coal, lignite production was significant prior to the general availability of oil and gas. Remnants of old underground mines are common throughout the area of lignite occurrence. Large reserves of strippable lignite have again attracted the attention of energy suppliers, and Texas is now the nation's sixth leading producer of coal, 99 percent of it lignite. Twelve large strip mines are now producing lignite that is burned for mine-mouth electric-power generation, and additional mines are planned. Mines are located in Atascosa, Franklin, Freestone, Harrison, Hopkins, Leon, Limestone, McMullen, Milam, Panola, Robertson, Rusk, and Titus counties.

LIME MATERIAL: Limestones, which are abundant in some areas of Texas, are heated to produce lime (calcium oxide) at a number of plants in the state. High-magnesium limestone and dolomite are used to prepare lime at a plant in Burnet County. Other lime plants are located in Bexar, Bosque, Comal, Hill, Johnson, and Travis counties. Lime production captive to the kiln's operator occurs in several Texas counties. Lime is used in soil stabilization, water purification, paper and pulp manufacture, metallurgy, sugar refining, agriculture, construction, removal of sulfur from stack gases, and for many other purposes.

LIMESTONE (see also BUILDING STONE): Texas is one of the nation's leading producers of limestone, which is quarried in more than 60 counties. Limestone occurs in nearly all areas of the state with the exception of most of the Gulf Coastal Plain and High Plains. Although some of the limestone is quarried for use as dimension stone, most of the output is crushed for uses such as bulk building materials (crushed stone, road base, concrete aggregate), chemical raw materials, fillers or extenders, lime and portland cement raw materials, agricultural limestone, and removal of sulfur from stack gases.

MAGNESITE: Small deposits of magnesite (natural magnesium carbonate) have been found in Precambrian rocks in Llano and Mason counties of Central Texas. At one time, there was small-scale mining of magnesite in the area; some of the material was used as agricultural stone and as terrazzo chips. Magnesite also can be calcined to form magnesia, which is used in metallurgical furnace refractories and other products.

MAGNESIUM: On the Texas Gulf Coast in Brazoria County, magnesium chloride is extracted from sea water at a plant in Freeport and used to produce magnesium compounds and magnesium metal. During World War II, high-magnesium Ellenburger dolomite rock from Burnet County was used as magnesium ore at a plant near Austin.

MANGANESE: Deposits of manganese minerals, such as braunite, hollandite, and pyrolusite, have been found in several areas, including Jeff Davis, Llano, Mason, Presidio, and Val Verde counties. Known deposits are not large. Small shipments have been made from Jeff Davis, Mason, and Val Verde counties, but no manganese mining has been reported in Texas since 1954.

MARBLE: Metamorphic and sedimentary marbles suitable for monument and building stone are found in the Llano Uplift and nearby areas of Central Texas and the Trans-Pecos area of West Texas. Gray, white, black, greenish black, light green, brown, and cream-colored marbles occur in Central Texas in Burnet, Gillespie, Llano, and Mason counties. West Texas metamorphic marbles include the bluish-white and the black marbles found southwest of Alpine in Brewster County and the white marble from Marble Canyon north of Van Horn in Culberson County. Marble can be used as dimension stone, terrazzo, and roofing aggregate, and for other purposes.

MERCURY (QUICKSILVER): Mercury minerals, chiefly cinnabar, occur in the Terlingua district and nearby districts of southern Brewster and southeastern Presidio counties. Mining began there about 1894, and from 1905–1935, Texas was one of the nation's leading producers of quicksilver. Following World War II, a sharp drop in demand and price, along with depletion of developed ore reserves, caused abandonment of all the Texas mercury mines.

With a rise in the price, sporadic mining took place between 1951–1960. In 1965, when the price of mercury moved to a record high, renewed interest in the Texas mercury districts resulted in the reopening of several mines and the discovery of new ore reserves. By April 1972, however, the price had declined and the mines have reported no production since 1973.

MICA: Large crystals of flexible, transparent mica minerals in igneous pegmatite rocks and mica flakes in metamorphic schist rocks are found in the Llano Uplift area of Central Texas and the Van Horn area of West Texas. Most Central Texas deposits do not meet specifications for sheet mica, and although several attempts have been made to produce West Texas sheet mica in Culberson and Hudspeth counties, sustained production has not been achieved. A mica quarry operated for a short time in the early 1980s in the Van Horn Mountains of Culberson and Hudspeth counties to mine mica schist for use as an additive in rotary drilling fluids.

MOLYBDENUM: Small occurrences of molybdenite have been found in Burnet and Llano counties, and wulfenite, another molybdenum mineral, has been noted in rocks in the Quitman Mountains of Hudspeth County. Molybdenum minerals also occur at Cave Peak north of Van Horn in Culberson County, in the Altuda Mountain area of northwestern Brewster County, and in association with uranium ores of the Gulf Coastal Plain.

PEAT: This spongy organic substance forms in bogs from plant remains. It has been found in the Gulf Coastal Plain in several localities including Gonzales, Guadalupe, Lee, Milam, Polk, and San Jacinto counties. There has been intermittent, small-scale production of some of the peat for use as a soil conditioner.

PERLITE: Perlite, a glassy igneous rock, expands to a lightweight, porous mass when heated. It can be used as a lightweight aggregate, filter aid, horticultural aggregate, and for other purposes. Perlite occurs in Presidio County, where it has been mined in the Pinto Canyon area north of the Chinati Mountains. No perlite is currently mined in Texas, but perlite mined outside of Texas is expanded at plants in Bexar, Dallas, El Paso, Guadalupe, Harris, and Nolan counties.

PHOSPHATE: Rock phosphate is present in Paleozoic rocks in several areas of Brewster and Presidio counties in West Texas and in Central Texas, but the known deposits are not large. In Northeast Texas, sedimentary rock phosphate occurs in thin conglomeratic lenses in Upper Cretaceous and Tertiary rock units; possibly some of these low-grade phosphorites could be processed on a small scale for local use as a fertilizer. Imported phosphate rock is processed at a plant in Brownsville.

POTASH: The potassium mineral polyhalite is widely distributed in the subsurface Permian Basin of West Texas and has been found in many wells in that area. During 1927–1931, the federal government drilled a series of potash-test wells in Crane, Crockett, Ector, Glasscock, Loving, Reagan, Upton, and Winkler counties. In addition to polyhalite, which was found in all of the counties, these wells revealed the presence of the potassium minerals carnallite and sylvite in Loving County and carnallite in Winkler County. The known Texas potash deposits are not as rich as those in the New Mexico portion of the Permian Basin and have not been developed.

PUMICITE (VOLCANIC ASH): Deposits of volcanic ash occur in Brazos, Fayette, Gonzales, Karnes, Polk, Starr, and other counties of the Texas Coastal Plain. Deposits also have been found in the Trans-Pecos area, High Plains, and in several counties east of the High Plains. Volcanic ash is used to prepare pozzolan cement, cleansing and scouring compounds, and soaps and sweeping compounds; as a carrier for insecticides, and for other purposes. It has been mined in Dickens, Lynn, Scurry, Starr, and other counties.

QUICKSILVER (see MERCURY).

RARE-EARTH ELEMENTS AND METALS: The term, "rare-earth elements," is commonly applied to elements of the lanthanide group (atomic numbers 57 through 71) plus yttrium. Yttrium, atomic number 39 and not a member of the lanthanide group, is included as a rare-earth element because it has similar properties to members of that group and usually occurs in nature with them. The metals thorium and scandium are sometimes termed "rare metals" because their occurence is often associated with the rare-earth elements.

The majority of rare-earth elements are consumed as catalysts in petroleum cracking and other chemical industries. Rare earths are widely used in the glass industry for tableware, specialty glasses, optics, and fiber optics. Cerium oxide has growing use as a polishing compound for glass, gem stones, cathode-ray tube faceplates, and other polishing. Rare earths are alloyed with various metals to produce materials used in the aeronautic, space, and electronics industries. The addition of rare-earth elements may improve resistance to metal fatigue at high temperatures, reduce potential for corrosion, and selectively increase conductivity and magnetism of the metal.

Various members of this group, including thorium, have anomalous concentrations in the rhyolitic and related igneous rocks of the Quitman Mountains and the Sierra Blanca area of Trans-Pecos.

SALT (SODIUM CHLORIDE) (see also BRINES): Salt resources of Texas are virtually inexhaustible. Enormous deposits occur in the subsurface Permian Basin of West Texas and in the salt domes of the Gulf Coastal Plain. Salt also is found in the alkali playa lakes of the High Plains, the alkali flats or salt lakes in the Salt Basin of Culberson and Hudspeth counties, and along some of the bays and lagoons of the South Texas Gulf Coast.

Texas is one of the leading salt-producing states. Rock salt is obtained from underground mines in salt domes at Grand Saline in Van Zandt County and Hockley Dome in Harris County. Salt is produced from rock salt and by solution mining as brines from wells drilled into the underground salt deposits.

SAND, INDUSTRIAL: Sands used for special purposes, due to high silica content or to unique physical properties, command higher prices than common sand. Industrial sands in Texas occur mainly in the Central Gulf Coastal Plain and in North-Central Texas. They include abrasive, blast, chemical, engine, filtration, foundry, glass, hydraulic-fracturing (propant), molding, and pottery sands. Recent production of industrial sands has been from Atascosa, Colorado, Hardin, Harris, Liberty, Limestone, McCulloch, Newton, Smith, Somervell, and Upshur counties.

SAND AND GRAVEL (CONSTRUCTION): Sand and gravel are among the most extensively utilized resources in Texas. Principal occurrence is along the major streams and in stream terraces. Sand and gravel are important bulk construction materials, used as railroad ballast, base materials, and for other purposes. In 2018, Texas was second only to California in production of sand and gravel (construction). Arizona and Washington were the next two largest producers.

SANDSTONE: Sandstones of a variety of colors and textures are widely distributed in a number of geologic formations in Texas. Some of the sandstones have been quarried for use as dimension stone in El Paso, Parker, Terrell, Ward, and other counties. Crushed sandstone is produced in Freestone, Gaines, Jasper, McMullen, Motley, and other counties for use as road-building material, terrazzo stone, and aggregate.

SERPENTINITE: Several masses of serpentinite, which formed from the alteration of basic igneous rocks, are associated with other Precambrian metamorphic rocks of the Llano Uplift. The largest deposit is the Coal Creek serpentinite mass in northern Blanco and Gillespie counties from which terrazzo chips have been produced. Other deposits are present in Gillespie and Llano counties. (The features that are associated with surface and subsurface Cretaceous rocks in several counties in or near the Balcones Fault Zone and that are commonly known as "serpentine plugs" are not serpentine at all, but are altered igneous volcanic necks and pipes, and mounds of altered volcanic ash: palagonite: that accumulated around the former submarine volcanic pipes.)

SHELL: Oyster shells and other shells in shallow coastal waters and in deposits along the Texas Gulf Coast have been produced in the past chiefly by dredging. They were used to a limited extent as raw material in the manufacture of cement, as concrete aggregate and road base, and for other purposes. No shell has been produced in Texas since 1981.

SILVER: During the period 1885–1952, the production of silver in Texas, as reported by the U.S. Bureau of Mines, totaled about 33 million troy ounces. For about 70 years, silver was the most consistently produced metal in Texas, although always in moderate quantities. All of the production came from the Trans-Pecos country of West Texas, where the silver was mined in Brewster County (Altuda Mountain), Culberson and Hudspeth counties (Van Horn Mountains and Van Horn–Allamoore district), Hudspeth County (Quitman Mountains and Eagle Mountains), and Presidio County (Chinati Mountains area, Loma Plata mine, and Shafter district).

Chief producer was the Presidio mine in the Shafter district, which began operations in the late 1800s, and, through September 1942, produced more than 30 million ounces of silver: more than 92 percent of Texas' total silver production. Water in the lower mine levels, lean ores, and low price of silver resulted in the closing of the mine in 1942. Another important silver producer was the Hazel copper-silver mine in the Van Horn–Allamoore district in Culberson County, which accounted for more than 2 million ounces.

An increase in the price of silver in the late 1970s stimulated prospecting for new reserves, and exploration began near the old Presidio mine, near the old Plata Verde mine in the Van Horn Mountains district, at the Bonanza mine in the Quitman Mountains district, and at the old Hazel mine.

A decline in the price of silver in the early 1980s, however, resulted in reduction of exploration and mine development in the region. The recent rise in value of silver has sparked new interest in the Shafter mining district of West Texas.

SOAPSTONE (see TALC AND SOAPSTONE).

SODIUM SULFATE (SALT CAKE): Sodium sulfate minerals occur in salt beds and brines of the alkali playa lakes of the High Plains in West Texas. In some lakes, the sodium sulfate minerals are present in deposits a few feet beneath the lake-beds. Sodium sulfate also is found in underground brines in the Permian Basin. Current production is from brines and dry salt beds at alkali lakes in Gaines and Terry counties. Past production was reported in Lynn and Ward counties. Sodium sulfate is used chiefly by the detergent and paper and pulp industries. Other uses are in the preparation of glass and other products.

STONE (see BUILDING STONE and CRUSHED STONE).

STRONTIUM: Deposits of the mineral celestite (strontium sulfate) have been found in a number of places, including localities in Brown, Coke, Comanche, Fisher, Lampasas, Mills, Nolan, Real, Taylor, Travis, and Williamson counties. Most of the occurrences are very minor, and no strontium is currently produced in the state.

SULFUR: Texas is one of the world's principal sulfur-producing areas. The sulfur is mined from deposits of native sulfur, and it is extracted from sour (sulfur-bearing) natural gas and petroleum. Recovered sulfur is a growing industry and accounted for approximately 60 percent of all 1987 sulfur production in the United States, but only approximately 40 percent of Texas production. Native sulfur is found in large deposits in the caprock of some of the salt domes along the Texas Gulf Coast and in some of the surface and subsurface Permian strata of West Texas, notably in Culberson and Pecos counties.

Native sulfur obtained from the underground deposits is known as Frasch sulfur, so-called because of Herman Frasch, the chemist who devised the method of drilling wells into the deposits, melting the sulfur with superheated water, and forcing the molten sulfur to the surface. Most of the production now goes to the users in molten form.

Frasch sulfur is produced from only one Gulf Coast salt dome in Wharton County and from West Texas underground Permian strata in Culberson County. Operations at several Gulf Coast domes have been closed in recent years. During the 1940s, acidic sulfur earth was produced in the Rustler Springs district in Culberson County for use as a fertilizer and soil conditioner. Sulfur is recovered from sour natural gas and petroleum at plants in numerous Texas counties.

Sulfur is used in the preparation of fertilizers and organic and inorganic chemicals, in petroleum refining, and for many other purposes.

TALC AND SOAPSTONE: Deposits of talc are found in the Precambrian metamorphic rocks of the Allamoore area of eastern Hudspeth and western Culberson counties. Soapstone, containing talc, occurs in the Precambrian metamorphic rocks of the Llano Uplift area, notably in Blanco, Gillespie, and Llano counties. Current production is from surface mines in the Allamoore area. Talc is used in ceramic, roofing, paint, paper, plastic, synthetic rubber, and other products.

TIN: Tin minerals have been found in El Paso and Mason counties. Small quantities were produced during the early 1900s in the Franklin Mountains north of El Paso. Cassiterite (tin dioxide) occurrences in Mason County are believed to be very minor. The only tin smelter in the United States, built at Texas City by the federal government during World War II and later sold to a private company, processes tin concentrates from ores mined outside of Texas, tin residues, and secondary tin-bearing materials.

TITANIUM: The titanium mineral rutile has been found in small amounts at the Mueller prospect in Jeff Davis County. Another titanium mineral, ilmenite, occurs in sandstones in Burleson, Fayette, Lee, Starr, and several other counties. Deposits that would be considered commercial under present conditions have not been found.

TRAP ROCK (see BASALT).

TUNGSTEN: The tungsten mineral scheelite has been found in small deposits in Gillespie and Llano counties and in the Quitman Mountains in Hudspeth County. Small deposits of other tungsten minerals have been prospected in the Cave Peak area north of Van Horn in Culberson County.

URANIUM: Uranium deposits were discovered in the Texas Coastal Plain in 1954 when abnormal radioactivity was detected in the Karnes County area. A number of uranium deposits have since been discovered within a belt of strata extending more than 250 miles from the middle Coastal Plain southwestward to the Rio Grande.

Various uranium minerals also have been found in other areas of Texas, including the Trans-Pecos, the Llano Uplift, and the High Plains. With the exception of small shipments from the High Plains during the 1950s, all the uranium production in Texas has been from the Coastal Plain. Uranium has been obtained from surface mines extending from northern Live Oak County, southeastern Atascosa County, across northern Karnes County, and into southern Gonzales County. Uranium is produced by in-situ leaching, brought to the surface through wells, and stripped from the solution at recovery operations.

In 1999, uranium mining shut down because of decreased value and demand. Production resumed in Texas in late 2004, when inventories were depleted and market prices rose to economic levels that allowed resumption of production. A total of 1.38 million pounds (606.5 tons) of eU3O8 was produced in South Texas in 2007.

There are no active uranium recovery operations in Texas, though as of 2017 there are 10 permits for uranium exploration in seven counties: Bee, Brooks, Duval, Goliad, Jim Hogg, Kleburg, and Live Oak.

VERMICULITE: Vermiculite, a mica-like mineral that expands when heated, occurs in Burnet, Gillespie, Llano, Mason, and other counties in the Llano Uplift region. It has been produced at a surface mine in Llano County. Vermiculite, mined outside of Texas, is exfoliated (expanded) at plants in Dallas, Houston, and San Antonio. Exfoliated vermiculite is used for lightweight concrete aggregate, horticulture, insulation, and other purposes.

VOLCANIC ASH (see PUMICITE).

ZEOLITES: The zeolite minerals clinoptilolite and analcime occur in Tertiary lavas and tuffs in Brewster, Jeff Davis, and Presidio counties in West Texas. Clinoptilolite also is found associated with Tertiary tuffs in the southern Texas Coastal Plain, including deposits in Karnes, McMullen, and Webb counties, and currently is produced in McMullen County. Zeolites, sometimes called "molecular sieves," can be used in ion-exchange processes to reduce pollution, as a catalyst in oil cracking, in obtaining high-purity oxygen and nitrogen from air, in water purification, and for many other purposes.

ZINC (see LEAD AND ZINC). ☆

Construction Sand and Gravel Production

Year	Quantity (thous. met. tons)	Value ($ millions)
2019	121,500	$2,326
2018	99,100	$1,000
2017	84,300	$828
2016	81,700	$817

Source: Industry surveys at USGS;

Texas Newspapers, Radio, and Television Stations

Sources: 2023 Texas Newspaper Directory; FCC, fcc.gov/media/filing-systems-and-databases

Texas is rich with newspapers and broadcast media, many of which have long histories. In the following list, only printed, subscription newspapers appear, and their frequency of publication is indicated by the following codes: (D) daily or at least four days a week, (TW) triweekly, (S) semiweekly, (SM) semimonthly, (M) monthly; all others are weeklies.

Radio and TV stations are those with valid operating licenses as of May 2023. Not included are those with construction permits or pending applications. ☆

—A—

Abernathy: Newspaper: *Abernathy Advocate.*

Abilene: Newspaper: *Abilene Reporter-News* (D). **Radio-AM:** KSLI, 1280 kHz; KWKC, 1340; KYYW, 1470; KZQQ, 1560. **Radio-FM:** KGNZ, 88.1 MHz; KACU, 89.5; KAGT, 90.5; KAQD, 91.3; KMWX, 92.5; KULL, 100.7; KEAN, 105.1; KKHR, 106.3; KEYJ, 107.9. **TV Stations:** KXVA-Ch. 15; KRBC-Ch. 29; KTAB-Ch. 30.

Agua Dulce: Radio-FM: KOUL, 107.7 MHz.

Alamo: Radio-FM: KJAV, 104.9 MHz.

Alamo Heights: Radio-AM: KDRY, 1100 kHz.

Albany: Newspaper: *Albany News.* **Radio-FM:** KQOS, 91.7 MHz.

Aledo: Newspaper: *The Community News.*

Alice: Newspaper: *Alice Echo-News Journal* (S). **Radio-AM:** KOPY, 1070 kHz. **Radio-FM:** KAWV, 88.3 MHz; KOPY, 92.1; KNDA, 102.9.

Allen: Newspaper: *Allen American.* **Radio-FM:** KESN, 103.3 MHz.

Alpine: Newspaper: *Alpine Avalanche.* **Radio-AM:** KVLF, 1240 kHz. **Radio-FM:** KRTP, 91.7 MHz; KALP, 92.7.

Alvin: Newspaper: *Alvin Sun.* **Radio-AM:** KTEK, 1110 kHz. **Radio-FM:** KACC, 89.7 MHz. **TV Station:** KFTH-Ch. 36.

Amarillo: Newspaper: *Amarillo Globe-News* (D). **Radio-AM:** KGNC, 710 kHz; KIXZ, 940; KDJW, 1010; KZIP, 1310; KTNZ, 1360; KPUR, 1440. **Radio-FM:** KJRT, 88.3 MHz; KXLV, 89.1; KACV, 89.9; KAVW, 90.7; KXRI, 91.9; KQIZ, 93.1; KMXJ, 94.1; KXSS, 96.9; KGNC, 97.9; KPRF, 98.7; KBZD, 99.7; KXGL, 100.9; KATP, 101.9; KVWE, 102.9; KJJP, 105.7. **TV Stations:** KACV-Ch. 9; KFDA-Ch. 10; KCIT-Ch. 15; KAMR-Ch. 19; KVII-Ch. 20.

Anahuac: Newspaper: *The Progress.*

Andrews: Newspaper: *Andrews County News* (S). **Radio-AM:** KACT, 1360 kHz. **Radio-FM:** KACT, 105.5 MHz.

Anna: Newspaper: *Anna-Melissa Tribune.*

Anson: Newspaper: *Western Observer.* **Radio-FM:** KTLT, 98.1 MHz.

Aransas Pass: Newspaper: *Aransas Pass Progress.* **Radio-FM:** KKWV, 88.1 MHz.

Archer City: Newspaper: *Archer County News.* **Radio-FM:** KPMA, 91.9 MHz.

Arlington: Radio-FM: KLTY, 94.9 MHz. **TV Station:** KPXD-Ch. 25.

Arroyo: Radio-FM: KVJS, 88.1 MHz.

Athens: Newspaper: *Athens Daily Review* (TW). **Radio-AM:** KLVQ, 1410 kHz.

Atlanta: Newspaper: *Cass County Citizen's Journal-Sun.* **Radio-AM:** KPYN, 900 kHz. **Radio-FM:** KNRB, 100.1 MHz.

Austin: Newspapers: *Austin American-Statesman* (D); *Austin Business Journal; West Austin News* (SM). **Radio-AM:** KLBJ, 590 kHz; KVET, 1300; KJFK, 1490. **Radio-FM:** KAZI, 88.7 MHz; KMFA, 89.5; KUT, 90.5; KVRX, 91.7; KLBJ, 93.7; KKMJ, 95.5; KVET, 98.1; KASE, 100.7; KPEZ, 102.3; KBPA, 103.5. **TV Stations:** KTBC-Ch. 7; KXAN-Ch. 21; KLRU-Ch. 22; KNVA-Ch. 23; KVUE-Ch. 33; KEYE-Ch. 34.

Austwell: Radio-FM: KIBQ, 105.9 MHz.

Azle: Newspaper: *Azle News.* **Radio-FM:** KYDA,101.7 MHz.

—B—

Baird: Newspaper: *Baird Banner.* **Radio-FM:** KABW, 95.1 MHz.

Balch Springs: Radio-AM: KSKY, 660 kHz.

Balcones Heights: Radio-FM: KZAI, 103.7 MHz.

Ballinger: Newspaper: *Runnels County Register.* **Radio-AM:** KRUN, 1400 kHz. **Radio-FM:** KKCN, 103.1 MHz.

Bandera: Newspaper: *Bandera Bulletin.* **Radio-FM:** KEEP, 103.1 MHz.

Bangs: Radio-FM: KBNX, 97.9 MHz.

Bartlett: Newspaper: *Tribune-Progress.*

Bastrop: Newspaper: *Bastrop Advertiser* (S). **Radio-FM:** KHIB, 88.5 MHz; KLZT, 107.1.

Batesville: Radio-FM: KRZU, 90.7 MHz; KQSA, 97.9.

Bay City: Newspaper: *The Bay City Tribune* (S). **Radio-FM:** KQUE, 88.1 MHz; KVUD, 89.5; KNTE, 101.7; KBBB, 102.5.

Baytown: Newspaper: *Baytown Sun* (TW). **Radio-AM:** KWWJ, 1360. **TV Station:** KUBE-Ch. 31.

Beaumont: Newspaper: *The Beaumont Enterprise* (D). **Radio-AM:** KLVI, 560 kHz; KZZB, 990; KIKR, 1450. **Radio-FM:** KLBT, 88.1 MHz; KGHY, 88.5; KTXB, 89.7; KVLU, 91.3; KQXY, 94.1; KYKR, 95.1; KTCX, 102.5; KQQK, 107.9. **TV Stations:** KBMT-Ch. 12; KFDM-Ch. 15; KITU-Ch. 29.

Bee Cave: Radio-FM: KTXX, 104.9 MHz.

Beeville: Newspaper: *Beeville Bee-Picayune.* **Radio-AM:** KIBL, 1490 kHz. **Radio-FM:** KVFM, 91.3 MHz; KTKO, 105.7; KRXB, 107.1.

Bellaire: Radio-AM: KGOW, 1560 kHz.

Bellmead: Radio-FM: KBHT, 104.9 MHz.

Bells: Radio-FM: KMKT, 93.1 MHz.

Bellville: Newspaper: *The Bellville Times.*

Belton: Newspaper: *The Belton Journal.* **Radio-FM:** KOOC, 106.3 MHz. **TV Station:** KNCT-Ch. 17.

Benavides: Radio-FM: KXTM, 94.3 MHz.

Benbrook: Radio-AM: KFLC, 1270 kHz. **Radio-FM:** KESS, 107.1 MHz.

Big Lake: Newspaper: *Big Lake Wildcat.*

Big Sandy: Newspaper: *Big Sandy–Hawkins Journal.* **Radio-FM:** KTAA, 90.7 MHz.

Big Spring: Newspaper: *Big Spring Herald* (D). **Radio-AM:** KBYG, 1400 kHz; KBST, 1490. **Radio-FM:** KBCX, 91.5 MHz; KBTS, 94.3; KBST, 95.7; KBUG, 100.9. **TV Station:** KWAB-Ch. 33.

Big Wells: Radio-FM: KHBE, 102.1 MHz.

Bishop: Radio-FM: KMZZ, 106.9 MHz.

Blanco: Newspaper: *Blanco County News.* **TV Station:** KNIC-Ch. 18.

Blanket: Radio-FM: KQMJ, 104.7 MHz

Bloomington: Radio-FM: KHVT, 91.5 MHz; KLUB, 106.9.

Blossom: Radio-FM: KISY, 92.7 MHz

Blowout: Radio-FM: KTSN, 88.9 MHz.

Boerne: Newspaper: *The Boerne Star.* **Radio-AM:** KBRN,

1500 kHz.

Bonham: Newspaper: *The Fannin County Leader.* **Radio-AM:** KFYN, 1420 kHz.

Booker: Newspaper: *The Booker News.*

Borger: Newspaper: *Borger News-Herald* (D). **Radio-FM:** KWAS, 88.1 MHz; KQFX, 104.3; KQTY, 106.7. **TV Station:** KEYU-Ch. 31.

Bovina: Radio-FM: KKNM, 96.5 MHz.

Bowie: Newspaper: *The Bowie News* (S). **Radio-AM:** KNTX, 1410 kHz.

Brackettville: Newspaper: *Kinney County Post.* **Radio-FM:** KEDV, 90.3 MHz; KVDR, 94.7.

Brady: Newspaper: *Brady Standard-Herald.* **Radio-AM:** KNEL, 1490 kHz. **Radio-FM:** KNEL, 95.3 MHz.

Breckenridge: Newspaper: *Breckenridge American.* **Radio-AM:** KROO, 1430 kHz. **Radio-FM:** KQXB, 89.9 MHz; KLXK, 93.5.

Brenham: Newspaper: *The Banner-Press* (TW). **Radio-AM:** KWHI, 1280 kHz. **Radio-FM:** KUBJ, 89.7 MHz; KLTR, 94.1; KTTX, 106.1.

Bridgeport: Radio-FM: KBOC, 98.3 MHz.

Brookshire: Radio-AM: KCHN, 1050 kHz.

Brownfield: Newspaper: *Brownfield News* (S). **Radio-AM:** KKUB, 1300 kHz. **Radio-FM:** KLTB, 89.7 MHz; KHLK, 104.3.

Brownsville: Newspapers: *The Brownsville Herald* (D); *El Nuevo Heraldo* (D). **Radio-AM:** KVNS, 1700 kHz. **Radio-FM:** KBNR, 88.3 MHz; KKPS, 99.5. **TV Station:** KVEO-Ch. 24.

Brownwood: Newspaper: *Brownwood Bulletin* (TW). **Radio-AM:** KXYL, 1240 kHz; KBWD, 1380. **Radio-FM:** KBUB, 90.3 MHz; KHBW, 91.7; KQBZ, 96.9; KPSM, 99.3; KOXE, 101.3.

Bryan: Newspaper: *The Eagle* (D). **Radio-AM:** KTAM, 1240 kHz; KAGC, 1510. **Radio-FM:** KORA, 98.3 MHz; KNFX, 99.5; KKYS, 104.7. **TV Stations:** KBTX-Ch. 16; KYLE-Ch. 29.

Buda: Radio-FM: KROX, 101.5 MHz.

Buffalo: Newspaper: *Buffalo Express.* **Radio-FM:** WTAW, 103.5 MHz.

Buffalo Gap: Radio-FM: KBGT, 93.3 MHz.

Bullard: Radio-FM: KZXM, 94.3 MHz.

Burkburnett: Newspaper: *Burkburnett Informer Star.* **Radio-FM:** KYYI, 104.7 MHz.

Burke: Radio-FM: KAGZ, 97.7 MHz.

Burleson: Radio-AM: KCLE, 1460 kHz.

Burnet: Newspapers: *Burnet Bulletin; Citizens Gazette.* **Radio-FM:** KMPN 95.9 MHz; KBEY, 103.9.

Bushland: Radio-FM: KTXP, 91.5 MHz.

—C—

Caldwell: Newspaper: *Burleson County Tribune.* **Radio-FM:** KALD, 91.9 MHz; KAPN, 107.3.

Callisburg: Radio-FM: KPFC, 91.9 MHz.

Cameron: Newspaper: *The Cameron Herald.* **Radio-AM:** KTON, 1330 kHz. **Radio-FM:** KMIL, 105.1 MHz.

Campbell: Radio-FM: KRVA, 107.1 MHz.

Canadian: Newspaper: *The Canadian Record.* **Radio-FM:** KHHC, 91.9 MHz.

Canton: Newspapers: *Canton Herald; Van Zandt News.* **Radio-AM:** KWJB, 1510 kHz.

Canyon: Newspaper: *The Canyon News* (S). **Radio-FM:** KWTS, 91.1 MHz; KARX, 107.1; KZRK, 107.9.

Carbon: Radio-FM: KJDE, 100.1 MHz.

Carrizo Springs: Newspaper: *The Carrizo Springs Javelin.* **Radio-AM:** KBEN, 1450 kHz. **Radio-FM:** KCZO, 92.1 MHz.

Carrollton: Newspaper: *Carrollton Leader.* **Radio-AM:** KJON, 850 kHz.

Carthage: Newspaper: *The Panola Watchman* (S). **Radio-AM:** KGAS, 1590 kHz. **Radio-FM:** KRTG, 88.3 MHz; KTUX, 98.9; KGAS, 104.3.

Cedar Lake: Radio-FM: KQVI, 89.9 MHz.

Cedar Park: Newspaper: *Hill Country News.* **Radio-FM:** KGSR, 93.3 MHz.

Celina: Newspaper: *Celina Record.*

Center: Newspaper: *The Light and Champion.* **Radio-AM:** KDET, 930 kHz. **Radio-FM:** KQBB, 100.5 MHz.

Centerville: Newspaper: *Centerville News.* **Radio-FM:** KKEE, 101.3 MHz; KUZN, 105.9.

Channing: Radio-FM: KAMT, 105.1 MHz.

Charlotte: Radio-FM: KSAQ, 102.3 MHz.

Childress: Newspaper: *The Red River Sun.* **Radio-AM:** KCTX, 1510 kHz. **Radio-FM:** KCTX, 96.1 MHz; KCHT 99.7.

Chillicothe: Radio-FM: KVRG, 89.7 MHz.

Christine: Radio-FM: KWYU, 96.9 MHz.

Christoval: Radio-FM: KQTC, 99.5 MHz.

Clarendon: Newspaper: *The Clarendon Enterprise.* **Radio-FM:** KYCL, 88.9 MHz; KEFH, 99.3.

Clarksville: Radio-AM: KHDY, 1350 kHz. **Radio-FM:** KXQJ, 90.1 MHz; KHDY, 98.5.

Claude: Newspaper: *The Claude News.* **Radio-FM:** KPUR, 95.7 MHz.

Cleburne: Newspaper: *Cleburne Times-Review* (TW). **Radio-AM:** KHFX, 1140 kHz.

Cleveland: Radio-FM: KTHT, 97.1 MHz.

Clifton: Newspaper: *The Clifton Record.* **Radio-FM:** KWOW, 104.1 MHz.

Clute: Newspaper: *The Facts* (D).

Clyde: Newspaper: *Clyde Journal.*

Coahoma: Radio-FM: KXCS, 105.5 MHz.

Cockrell Hill: Radio-AM: KRVA, 1600 kHz.

Coleman: Newspaper: *Chronicle & Democrat-Voice.* **Radio-AM:** KSTA, 1000 kHz. **Radio-FM:** KXYL, 102.3 MHz.

College Station: Radio-AM: KZNE, 1150 kHz; KWBC, 1550; WTAW, 1620. **Radio-FM:** KEOS, 89.1 MHz; KLGS, 89.9; KAMU, 90.9; KNDE, 95.1. **TV Station:** KAMU-Ch. 12.

Colorado City: Newspaper: *Colorado City Record.* **Radio-AM:** KVMC, 1320 kHz. **Radio-FM:** KEHM, 99.3 MHz; KAUM, 107.1

Columbus: Newspapers: *The Banner-Press Newspaper; The Colorado County Citizen.* **Radio-FM:** KULM, 98.3 MHz.

Comanche: Newspaper: *The Comanche Chief.* **Radio-AM:** KCOM, 1550 kHz. **Radio-FM:** KYOX, 94.3 MHz; KCXX 103.9.

Comfort: Newspaper: *The Comfort News.* **Radio-FM:** KMYO, 95.1 MHz.

Commerce: Radio-FM: KETR, 88.9 MHz; KYJC, 91.3.

Comstock: Radio-FM: KDER, 99.3 MHz.

Concan: Radio-FM: KHCU, 93.1 MHz.

Conroe: Newspaper: *The Courier* (D). **Radio-AM:** KJOZ, 880 kHz; KYOK, 1140. **Radio-FM:** KHPT, 106.9 MHz. **TV Stations:** KPXB-Ch. 32; KTBU-Ch. 33.

Converse: Radio-AM: KTMR, 1130 kHz.

Cooper: Newspaper: *Cooper Review.* **Radio-FM:** KPCO, 89.9 MHz; KIKT, 93.5.

Coppell: Newspaper: *Coppell Gazette.*

Copperas Cove: Newspaper: *Copperas Cove Leader-Press* (S). **Radio-FM:** KSSM, 103.1 MHz.

Corpus Christi: Newspapers: *Corpus Christi Caller-Times* (D); *Coastal Bend Daily Legal & Business News* (D). **Radio-AM:** KCTA, 1030 kHz; KCCT, 1150; KSIX, 1230;

KKTX, 1360; KUNO, 1400; KEYS, 1440. **Radio-FM:** KPLV, 88.7 MHz; KEDT, 90.3; KBNJ, 91.7; KMXR, 93.9; KBSO, 94.7; KZFM, 95.5; KLTG, 96.5; KRYS, 99.1. **TV Stations:** KIII-Ch. 8; KZTV-Ch. 10; KSCC, Ch. 19; KEDT-Ch. 23; KRIS-Ch. 26; KORO-Ch. 27.

Corrigan: Radio-FM: KYTM, 99.3 MHz.

Corsicana: Newspaper: *Corsicana Daily Sun* (S). **Radio-AM:** KAND, 1340 kHz.

Cotulla: Radio-FM: KCOT, 96.3 MHz; KWMJ, 100.7.

Crane: Newspaper: *Crane News.* **Radio-AM:** KXOI, 810 kHz. **Radio-FM:** KMMZ, 101.3 MHz.

Creedmoor: Radio-AM: KZNX, 1530 kHz.

Crockett: Newspaper: *Houston County Messenger* (S). **Radio-AM:** KIVY, 1290 kHz. **Radio-FM:** KCKT, 88.5 MHz; KIVY, 92.7; KBPC, 93.5.

Crosbyton: Radio-FM: KEVQ, 100.7 MHz.

Cross Plains: Newspaper: *Cross Plains Review.*

Crowell: Newspaper: *Foard County News.* **Radio-FM:** KTUT, 98.9 MHz.

Crystal City: Newspaper: *Zavala County Sentinel.* **Radio-FM:** KHER, 94.3 MHz.

Cuero: Newspaper: *Cuero Record.* **Radio-FM:** KTLZ, 89.9 MHz.

Cuney: Radio-FM: KVUT, 99.7 MHz.

Cypress: Radio-AM: KYND, 1520 kHz.

—D—

Daingerfield: Newspaper: *The Steel Country Bee.*

Dalhart: Newspaper: *Dalhart Texan* (S). **Radio-AM:** KXIT, 1240 kHz. **Radio-FM:** KTDH, 89.3 MHz; KTDA, 91.7; KBEX 96.1.

Dallas: Newspapers: *The Dallas Morning News* (D); *Daily Commercial Record* (D); *Dallas Business Journal; The Dallas Examiner; Texas Jewish Post.* **Radio-AM:** KLIF, 570 kHz; KGGR, 1040; KRLD, 1080; KFXR, 1190; KTCK, 1310; KNGO, 1480. **Radio-FM:** KNON, 89.3 MHz; KERA, 90.1; KCBI, 90.9; KKXT, 91.7; KZPS, 92.5; KBFB, 97.9; KLUV, 98.7; KJKK, 100.3; WRR, 101.1; KDMX, 102.9; KKDA, 104.5; KRLD, 105.3. **TV Stations:** WFAA-Ch. 8; KERA-Ch. 14; KDTX-Ch. 21; KDFI-Ch. 27; KDAF-Ch. 32; KDFW-Ch. 35; KXTX-Ch. 36.

Decatur: Newspaper: *Wise County Messenger* (S). **Radio-FM:** KDKR, 91.3 MHz; KRNB, 105.7. **TV Station:** KMPX-Ch. 30.

Deer Park: Radio-FM: KAMA, 104.9 MHz.

De Leon: Newspaper: *De Leon Free Press.*

Dell City: Newspaper: *Hudspeth County Herald.*

Del Mar Hills: Radio-AM: KVOZ, 890 kHz.

Del Rio: Newspaper: *The 830 Times.* **Radio-AM:** KDRN, 1230 kHz; KWMC, 1490. **Radio-FM:** KVFE, 88.5 MHz; KTPD, 89.3; KDLI, 89.9; KDLK, 94.1; KTDR, 96.3. **TV Station:** KYVV-Ch. 28.

Del Valle: Radio-AM: KIXL, 970 kHz.

Denison: Radio-FM: KYFB, 91.5 MHz.

Denton: Newspaper: *Denton Record-Chronicle.* **Radio-FM:** KNTU, 88.1 MHz; KFZO, 99.1; KHKS, 106.1. **TV Station:** KDTN-Ch. 29.

Denver City: Newspaper: *Denver City Press.*

DeSoto: Newspaper: *Focus Daily News* (D).

Detroit: Radio-FM: KFYN, 104.3 MHz.

Devine: Newspaper: *The Devine News.* **Radio-FM:** KRPT, 92.5 MHz.

Diboll: Radio-AM: KSML, 1260 kHz. **Radio-FM:** KAFX, 95.5 MHz.

Dilley: Radio-FM: KKDL, 93.7 MHz; KVWG, 95.3; KLMO, 98.9.

Dimmitt: Newspaper: *The Castro County News.* **Radio-AM:** KDHN, 1470 kHz. **Radio-FM:** KNNK, 100.5 MHz.

Doss: Radio-FM: KGKV, 88.1 MHz.

Dripping Springs: Newspapers: *Dripping Springs Century News; News-Dispatch.* **Radio-FM:** KLLR, 91.9 MHz.

Driscoll: Radio-FM: KUKA, 105.9 MHz.

Dublin: Newspaper: *The Dublin Citizen.* **Radio-FM:** KSTV, 93.1 MHz.

Dumas: Newspaper: *Moore County News-Press* (S). **Radio-AM:** KDDD, 800 kHz. **Radio-FM:** KDDD, 95.3 MHz.

—E—

Eagle Lake: Radio-FM: KJJB, 95.3 MHz.

Eagle Pass: Radio-AM: KEPS, 1270 kHz. **Radio-FM:** KEPI, 88.7 MHz; KEPX, 89.5; KINL, 92.7. **TV Station:** KVAW-Ch. 18.

Early: Radio-FM: KJKB, 106.7 MHz.

East Bernard: Newspaper: *East Bernard Express.*

Eastland: Newspaper: *Eastland County Today.* **Radio-FM:** KQXE, 91.1 MHz; KATX, 97.7.

Eden: Newspaper: *Eden Echo.* **Radio-FM:** KPDE, 91.5 MHz.

Edinburg: Radio-AM: KURV, 710 kHz. **Radio-FM:** KOIR, 88.5 MHz; KBFM, 104.1; KVLY, 107.9.

Edna: Newspaper: *Jackson County Herald-Tribune.* **Radio-FM:** KIOX, 96.1 MHz.

El Campo: Newspaper: *El Campo Leader-News* (S). **Radio-AM:** KULP, 1390 kHz. **Radio-FM:** KXBJ, 96.9 MHz.

Eldorado: Newspaper: *Eldorado Success.* **Radio-FM:** KLDE, 104.9 MHz; KPEP, 106.5.

Electra: Newspaper: *Electra Star-News.* **Radio-FM:** KOLI, 94.9 MHz.

Elgin: Newspaper: *Elgin Courier.* **Radio-AM:** KTAE, 1260 kHz.

Elkhart: Radio-FM: KATG, 88.1 MHz.

Ellinger: Radio-FM: KTIM, 89.1 MHz.

El Paso: Newspaper: *El Paso Times* (D). **Radio-AM:** KROD, 600 kHz; KTSM, 690; KAMA, 750; KQBU, 920; KHRO, 1150; KVIV, 1340; KHEY, 1380; KELP, 1590; KSVE, 1650. **Radio-FM:** KTEP, 88.5 MHz; KKLY; 89.5; KVER, 91.1; KOFX, 92.3; KSII, 93.1; KINT, 93.9; KYSE, 94.7; KLAQ, 95.5; KHEY, 96.3; KBNA, 97.5; KTSM, 99.9; KPRR, 102.1. **TV Stations:** KCOS-Ch. 13; KFOX-Ch. 15; KTSM-Ch. 16; KVIA-Ch. 17; KDBC-Ch. 18; KTFN-Ch. 20; KSCE-Ch. 21; KINT-Ch. 25.

Emory: Newspaper: *Rains County Leader.*

Encinal: Radio-FM: KQBI, 91.7 MHz; KELT, 102.5; KZPL, 105.1.

Encino: Radio-FM: KZTX, 91.1 MHz.

Ennis: Newspaper: *The Ennis News.*

Escobares: Radio-FM: KERG, 104.7 MHz.

Estelline: Radio-FM: KZES, 91.3 MHz.

—F—

Fabens: Radio-FM: KPAS, 103.1 MHz.

Fairfield: Newspapers: *The Fairfield Recorder; Freestone County Times.* **Radio-FM:** KNES, 99.1 MHz.

Falfurrias: Newspaper: *Falfurrias Facts.* **Radio-AM:** KLDS, 1260 kHz. **Radio-FM:** KRVP, 91.5 MHz; KDFM, 103.3; KPSO, 106.3.

Fannett: Radio-FM: KZFT, 90.5 MHz.

Farmersville: Newspaper: *Farmersville Times.* **Radio-AM:** KFCD, 990 kHz. **Radio-FM:** KXEZ, 92.1 MHz.

Farwell: Newspaper: *The State Line Tribune.* **Radio-AM:** KIJN, 1060 kHz. **Radio-FM:** KIJN, 92.3 MHz; KICA, 98.3. **TV Station:** KPTF-Ch. 18.

Ferris: Newspaper: *The Ellis County Press.* **Radio-AM:** KDFT, 540 kHz.

Flatonia: Newspaper: *The Flatonia Argus.*

Floresville: Newspaper: *Wilson County News.* **Radio-FM:** KJMA, 89.7 MHz; KTFM, 94.1.

Flower Mound: Radio-FM: KTCK, 96.7 MHz.

Floydada: Newspaper: *The Floyd County Hesperian-Beacon.* **Radio-AM:** KFLP, 900 kHz. **Radio-FM:** KFLP, 106.1 MHz.

Forney: Newspaper: *Forney Messenger.*

Fort Davis: Newspaper: *Jeff Davis County Mountain Dispatch.*

Fort Stockton: Newspaper: *Fort Stockton Pioneer.* **Radio-AM:** KFST, 860 kHz. **Radio-FM:** KRAF, 88.3 MHz; KFST, 94.3.

Fort Worth: Newspapers: *Fort Worth Star-Telegram* (D); *Commercial Recorder* (D); *Tarrant County Commercial Record* (S); *Fort Worth Business Press* (SM). **Radio-AM:** WBAP, 820 kHz; KFJZ, 870; KHVN, 970; KKGM, 1630. **Radio-FM:** KTCU, 88.7 MHz; KLNO, 94.1; KSCS, 96.3; KEGL, 97.1; KPLX, 99.5; KDGE, 102.1; KMVK, 107.5. **TV Stations:** KFWD-Ch. 9; KTXA-Ch. 18; KTVT-Ch. 19; KXAS-Ch. 24.

Franklin: Newspapers: *Franklin Advocate; Franklin News Weekly.* **Radio-FM:** KVLX, 103.9 MHz.

Frankston: Radio-FM: KOYE, 96.7 MHz.

Fredericksburg: Newspaper: *Fredericksburg Standard-Radio Post.* **Radio-AM:** KNAF, 910 kHz. **Radio-FM:** KIVM, 91.1 MHz; KBLC, 91.5; KNAF, 105.7. **TV Station:** KCWX-Ch. 5.

Freer: Radio-FM: KBTD, 89.1 MHz; KQCI, 91.5; KBRA, 95.9.

Friona: Newspaper: *Friona Star.* **Radio-FM:** KGRW, 94.7 MHz.

Frisco: Newspaper: *Frisco Enterprise.* **Radio-AM:** KATH, 910 kHz.

Fritch: Newspaper: *The Eagle Press.*

—G—

Gail: Newspaper: *Borden Star.*

Gainesville: Newspaper: *Gainesville Daily Register* (S). **Radio-AM:** KGAF, 1580 kHz. **Radio-FM:** KZMJ, 94.5 MHz.

Galveston: Newspaper: *The Galveston County Daily News* (D). **Radio-AM:** KGBC, 1540 kHz. **Radio-FM:** KOVE, 106.5 MHz. **TV Stations:** KTMD-Ch. 22; KLTJ-Ch. 23.

Ganado: Radio-FM: KEON, 94.9 MHz.

Gardendale: Radio-FM: KFZX, 102.1 MHz.

Garland: Radio-AM: KAAM, 770 kHz. **TV Station:** KUVN-Ch. 33.

Garwood: Radio-FM: KPUY, 97.3 MHz.

Gatesville: Newspaper: *The Gatesville Messenger* (S). **Radio-FM:** KVLW, 88.1 MHz.

Georgetown: Newspaper: *Williamson County Sun* (S). **Radio-FM:** KHFI, 96.7 MHz; KLJA, 107.7.

George West: Radio-FM: KGWT, 93.5 MHz; KXAF 97.9.

Giddings: Newspaper: *Giddings Times & News.* **Radio-FM:** KANJ, 91.1 MHz; KGID 96.3.

Gilmer: Newspaper: *Gilmer Mirror.* **Radio-FM:** KFRO, 95.3 MHz.

Ginger: Radio-FM: KYFA, 91.5 MHz.

Gladewater: Newspaper: *Gladewater Mirror.* **Radio-AM:** KEES, 1430 kHz.

Glen Rose: Newspaper: *Glen Rose Reporter.* **Radio-FM:** KTFW, 92.1 MHz.

Goldsmith: Radio-FM: KTXO, 94.7 MHz.

Goldthwaite: Newspaper: *The Goldthwaite Eagle.* **Radio-FM:** KRNR, 92.7 MHz.

Goliad: Newspaper: *Goliad Advance-Guard.* **Radio-FM:** KHMC, 95.9 MHz; KPQG 104.3.

Gonzales: Newspaper: *The Gonzales Inquirer.* **Radio-AM:** KCTI, 1450 kHz. **Radio-FM:** KCTI, 88.1 MHz; KMLR, 106.3.

Graham: Newspaper: *The Graham Leader* (S). **Radio-AM:** KSWA, 1330 kHz. **Radio-FM:** KWKQ, 94.7 MHz.

Granbury: Newspaper: *Hood County News* (S). **Radio-AM:** KPIR, 1420 kHz.

Grand Prairie: Radio-AM: KKDA, 730 kHz.

Grand Saline: Newspaper: *Grand Saline Sun.*

Granite Shoals: Radio-FM: KAJZ, 106.5 MHz.

Grape Creek: Radio-FM: KPTJ 104.5 MHz.

Grapeland: Newspaper: *The Messenger* (S).

Greenville: Newspaper: *Herald-Banner* (TW). **Radio-AM:** KGVL, 1400 kHz. **Radio-FM:** KTXG, 90.5 MHz. **TV Station:** KTXD-Ch. 23.

Greenwood: Radio-FM: KAGP 89.1 MHz.

Gregory: Radio-FM: KPUS, 104.5 MHz.

Groesbeck: Newspaper: *Groesbeck Journal.*

Groom: Newspaper: *The Groom News.*

Groves: Radio-FM: KCOL, 92.5 MHz.

Groveton: Newspaper: *Trinity County News-Standard.* **Radio-FM:** KFON, 93.9 MHz.

Guthrie: Radio-FM: KJAG, 107.7 MHz

—H—

Hallettsville: Newspaper: *Hallettsville Tribune-Herald.* **Radio-FM:** KTXM, 99.9 MHz.

Hallsville: Radio-FM: KTLH, 107.9 MHz.

Haltom City: Radio-FM: KLIF, 93.3 MHz.

Hamilton: Newspaper: *Hamilton Herald-News.* **Radio-AM:** KCLW, 900 kHz.

Hamlin: Newspaper: *The Hamlin Herald.* **Radio-FM:** KCDD, 103.7 MHz.

Hardin: Radio-FM: KGBV, 90.7 MHz.

Harker Heights: Radio-FM: KUSJ, 105.5 MHz.

Harlingen: Newspaper: *The Valley Morning Star* (D). **Radio-AM:** KGBT, 1530 kHz. **Radio-FM:** KJJF, 88.9 MHz; KFRQ, 94.5; KBTQ, 96.1. **TV Stations:** KMBH-Ch. 16; KGBT-Ch. 18; KLUJ-Ch. 21.

Harper: Radio-FM: KZAH, 99.1 MHz.

Hartley: Radio-FM: KOGW, 90.5 MHz.

Haskell: Radio-FM: KVRP, 97.1 MHz.

Hawley: Radio-FM: KTJK, 101.7 MHz.

Hearne: Newspaper: *Robertson County News.* **Radio-FM:** KEDC, 88.5 MHz; KVJM, 103.1.

Hebbronville: Newspaper: *The Enterprise.* **Radio-FM:** KOTX 98.7 MHz; KEKO, 101.7; KUFA, 104.3.

Helotes: Radio-FM: KONO, 101.1 MHz.

Hemphill: Newspaper: *The Sabine County Reporter.* **Radio-FM:** KTHP, 103.9 MHz.

Hempstead: The Waller County Express. **Radio-FM:** KTWL, 105.3 MHz.

Henderson: Newspaper: *The Henderson News* (S). **Radio-AM:** KWRD, 1470 kHz.

Henrietta: Newspaper: *Clay County Leader.*

Hereford: Newspaper: *Hereford Brand* (S). **Radio-AM:** KPAN, 860 kHz. **Radio-FM:** KRLH, 90.9 MHz; KPAN, 106.3.

Hewitt: Radio-FM: KIXT, 106.7 MHz.

Hico: Newspaper: *The Hico News Review.* **Radio-FM:** KCBN, 107.7.

Highland Park: Radio-AM: KBDT, 1160 kHz. **Radio-FM:** KVIL, 103.7 MHz.

Highlands: Newspaper: *Highlands Star-Crosby Courier.*

Highland Village: Radio-FM: KWRD, 100.7 MHz.

Hillsboro: **Newspaper:** *Hillsboro Reporter* (S). **Radio-AM:** KHBR, 1560 kHz. **Radio-FM:** KBRQ, 102.5 MHz.

Holliday: **Radio-FM:** KGVB, 90.9 MHz; KWFB, 100.9.

Hondo: **Newspaper:** *Hondo Anvil Herald.* **Radio-AM:** KCWM, 1460 kHz. **Radio-FM:** KZIC, 89.9 MHz; KAHL, 105.9.

Hooks: **Radio-FM:** KTRG, 94.1 MHz; KPWW, 95.9.

Horizon City: **Newspaper:** *West Texas County Courier.*

Hornsby: **Radio-FM:** KOOP, 91.7 MHz.

Houston: **Newspapers:** *Houston Chronicle* (D); *Daily Court Review* (D); *Houston Business Journal; Jewish Herald-Voice.* **Radio-AM:** KILT, 610 kHz; KTRH, 740; KBME, 790; KEYH, 850; KPRC, 950; KLAT, 1010; KNTH, 1070; KCOH, 1230; KXYZ, 1320; KSHJ, 1430; KMIC, 1590. **Radio-FM:** KUHF, 88.7 MHz; KPFT, 90.1; KTSU, 90.9; KHVU, 91.7; KQBT, 93.7; KTBZ, 94.5; KKHH, 95.7; KHMX, 96.5; KBXX, 97.9; KODA, 99.1; KILT, 100.3; KLOL, 101.1; KMJQ, 102.1; KLTN, 102.9; KRBE, 104.1; KHCB, 105.7. **TV Stations:** KUHT-Ch. 8; KHOU-Ch. 11; KTRK-Ch. 13; KTXH-Ch. 19; KZJL-Ch. 21; KETH-Ch. 24; KRIV-Ch. 26; KIAH-Ch. 34; KPRC-Ch. 35.

Howe: **Radio-FM:** KHYI, 95.3 MHz.

Hudson: **Radio-FM:** KZXL, 96.3 MHz.

Humble: **Radio-AM:** KGOL, 1180 kHz. **Radio-FM:** KSBJ, 89.3 MHz.

Hunt: **Radio-FM:** KYRT, 97.9 MHz; KLKV, 99.9.

Huntington: **Radio-FM:** KSML, 101.9 MHz.

Huntsville: **Newspaper:** *The Huntsville Item* (TW). **Radio-AM:** KHCH, 1410 kHz; KHVL, 1490. **Radio-FM:** KSHU, 90.5 MHz; KVST, 99.7; KSAM, 101.7.

Hurst: **Radio-AM:** KMNY, 1360 kHz.

Hutto: **Radio-FM:** KYLR, 92.1 MHz.

—I—

Idalou: **Newspaper:** *Idalou Beacon.* **Radio-FM:** KRBL, 105.7 MHz; KLZK, 107.7.

Ingleside: **Newspaper:** *The Ingleside Index.* **Radio-FM:** KAJE, 107.3 MHz.

Ingram: **Newspaper:** *West Kerr Current.* **Radio-FM:** KTXI, 90.1 MHz; KFXE, 96.5.

Iowa Park: **Radio-FM:** KXXN, 97.5 MHz.

Irving: **Newspaper:** *The Irving Rambler.* **TV Station:** KSTR-Ch. 34.

—J—

Jacksboro: **Newspaper:** *Jacksboro Herald-Gazette.* **Radio-FM:** KFWR, 95.9 MHz.

Jacksonville: **Newspaper:** *Jacksonville Progress* (S). **Radio-AM:** KEBE, 1400 kHz. **Radio-FM:** KBJS, 90.3 MHz; KEBE, 95.1; KLFZ, 102.3; KOOI, 106.5. **TV Station:** KETK-Ch. 22.

Jasper: **Newspaper:** *The Jasper Newsboy.* **Radio-AM:** KCOX, 1350 kHz. **Radio-FM:** KTXJ, 102.7 MHz; KJAS, 107.3.

Jefferson: **Newspaper:** *Jefferson Jimplecute.* **Radio-FM:** KHCJ, 91.9 MHz; KJTX, 104.5.

Johnson City: **Newspaper:** *Johnson City Record Courier.* **Radio-FM:** KFAN, 107.9 MHz.

Jourdanton: **Radio-FM:** KLEY, 95.7 MHz.

Junction: **Newspaper:** *Junction Eagle.* **Radio-AM:** KMBL, 1450 kHz. **Radio-FM:** KYKK, 93.5 MHz.

—K—

Karnes City: **Newspaper:** *The Karnes Countywide.* **Radio-FM:** KZKV, 103.1 MHz.

Katy: **Newspaper:** *Katy Times.* **TV Station:** KYAZ-Ch. 25.

Kaufman: **Newspaper:** *The Kaufman Herald.*

Keene: **Radio-FM:** KJRN, 88.3 MHz.

Kempner: **Radio-FM:** KOOV, 106.9 MHz.

Kenedy: **Radio-AM:** KAML, 990 kHz. **Radio-FM:** KCAF, 92.1 MHz.

Kerens: **Radio-FM:** KRVF, 106.9 MHz.

Kermit: **Radio-FM:** KDCJ, 91.5 MHz; KWXW, 93.7.

Kerrville: **Newspapers:** *The Kerrville Daily Times* (TW); *Hill Country Community Journal.* **Radio-AM:** KERV, 1230 kHz. **Radio-FM:** KKER, 88.7 MHz; KHKV, 91.1; KRNH, 92.3; KRVL, 94.3; KKVR, 106.1. **TV Station:** KMYS-Ch. 32.

Kilgore: **Newspaper:** *Kilgore News Herald.* **Radio-AM:** KDOK, 1240 kHz. **Radio-FM:** KZLO, 88.7 MHz; KKTX, 96.1.

Killeen: **Newspaper:** *Killeen Daily Herald* (D). **Radio-FM:** KNCT, 91.3 MHz; KIIZ, 92.3. **TV Station:** KAKW-Ch. 13.

Kingsland: **Radio-FM:** KHSB, 104.7 MHz.

Kingsville: **Newspaper:** *The Kingsville Record.* **Radio-AM:** KINE, 1330 kHz. **Radio-FM:** KTAI, 91.1 MHz; KKBA, 92.7; KFTX, 97.5.

Kirbyville: **Newspaper:** *East Texas Banner.*

Krum: **Radio-FM:** KNOR, 93.7 MHz.

Kurten: **Radio-FM:** KPWJ, 107.7 MHz.

Kyle: **Newspaper:** *Hays Free Press.*

—L—

La Feria: **Newspaper:** *La Feria News.*

La Grange: **Newspaper:** *The Fayette County Record* (S). **Radio-AM:** KVLG, 1570 kHz. **Radio-FM:** KBUK, 104.9 MHz.

Lake Dallas: **TV Station:** KAZD-Ch. 31.

Lake Jackson: **Radio-FM:** KVUJ, 91.1 MHz; KGLK, 107.5.

Lakeway: **Newspaper:** *Lake Travis View.*

Lamesa: **Newspaper:** *Lamesa Press Reporter* (S). **Radio-AM:** KPET, 690 kHz. **Radio-FM:** KBKN, 91.3 MHz; KTXC, 104.7.

Lampasas: **Newspaper:** *Lampasas Dispatch Record* (S). **Radio-AM:** KCYL, 1450 kHz.

La Porte: **Newspaper:** *Bay Area Observer.* **Radio-FM:** KHJK, 103.7 MHz.

Laredo: **Newspaper:** *Laredo Morning Times* (D). **Radio-AM:** KLAR, 1300 kHz; KLNT, 1490. **Radio-FM:** KHOY, 88.1 MHz; KBNL, 89.9; KJBZ, 92.7; KQUR, 94.9; KRRG, 98.1; KNEX, 106.1. **TV Stations:** KGNS-Ch. 8; KLDO-Ch. 19.

Laughlin AFB: **Radio-FM:** KDRX, 106.9 MHz.

La Vernia: **Newspaper:** *La Vernia News.*

League City: **Radio-AM:** KHCB, 1400 kHz.

Leander: **Radio-FM:** KUTX, 98.9 MHz.

Lefors: **Radio-FM:** KHNZ, 101.3 MHz.

Leonard: **Newspaper:** *The Leonard Graphic.*

Levelland: **Newspaper:** *Levelland & Hockley County News-Press* (S). **Radio-AM:** KLVT, 1230 kHz. **Radio-FM:** KJDL, 105.3 MHz.

Lewisville: **Newspaper:** *Lewisville Leader.* **Radio-FM:** KDXX, 107.9 MHz.

Lexington: **Newspaper:** *Lexington Leader.*

Liberty: **Newspaper:** *The Vindicator.* **Radio-FM:** KHIH, 99.9 MHz.

Liberty Hill: **Newspaper:** *Liberty Hill Monthly (M).*

Lindale: **Newspaper:** *Lindale News & Times.*

Lindsay: **Newspaper:** *Lindsay Letter.*

Little Elm: **Newspaper:** *The Lakeside Journal.*

Littlefield: **Newspaper:** *The Lamb County Leader-News* (S). **Radio-AM:** KZZN, 1490 kHz.

Livingston: **Newspaper:** *Polk County Enterprise* (S). **Radio-AM:** KETX, 1440 kHz. **Radio-FM:** KEHH, 92.3 MHz.

Llano: **Newspaper:** *The Llano News.* **Radio-FM:** KVHL, 91.7 MHz; KTHE, 96.3; KITY, 102.9. **TV Station:** KBVO-Ch. 27.

Lockhart: **Newspaper:** *Lockhart Post-Register.* **Radio-AM:** KTSN, 1060 kHz.

Lometa: **Radio-FM:** KACQ, 101.9 MHz.

Longview: **Newspaper:** *Longview News-Journal* (TW). **Radio-AM:** KFRO, 1370 kHz. **Radio-FM:** KYKX, 105.7 MHz. **TV Stations:** KFXK-Ch. 20; KCEB-Ch. 28.

Lorena: **Radio-FM:** KYAR, 98.3 MHz.

Lorenzo: **Radio-FM:** KKCL, 98.1 MHz.

Louise: **Radio-FM:** KABA, 90.3 MHz.

Lovelady: **Radio-FM:** KHMR, 104.3 MHz.

Lubbock: **Newspaper:** *Lubbock Avalanche-Journal* (D). **Radio-AM:** KRFE, 580 kHz; KFYO, 790; KJTV, 950; KKAM, 1340; KWBF, 1420; KBZO, 1460; KDAV, 1590. **Radio-FM:** KTXT, 88.1 MHz; KTTZ, 89.1; KAMY, 90.1; KKLU, 90.9; KLBB, 93.7; KFMX, 94.5; KLLL, 96.3; KQBR, 99.5; KONE, 101.1; KZII, 102.5; KXTQ, 106.5. **TV Stations:** KCBD-Ch. 11; KPTB-Ch. 16; KTTZ-Ch. 25; KAMC-Ch. 27; KLBK-Ch. 31; KJTV-Ch. 35.

Lufkin: **Newspaper:** *The Lufkin Daily News* (TW). **Radio-AM:** KRBA, 1340 kHz. **Radio-FM:** KLDN, 88.9 MHz; KSWP, 90.9; KAVX, 91.9; KYBI, 100.1; KYKS, 105.1. **TV Station:** KTRE-Ch. 9.

Luling: **Newspaper:** *Luling Newsboy and Signal.* **Radio-FM:** KAMX, 94.7 MHz.

Lumberton: **Radio-AM:** KHTW, 1300 kHz. **Radio-FM:** KKHT, 100.7 MHz.

Lytle: **Radio-FM:** KZLV, 91.3 MHz.

—M—

Mabank: **Newspaper:** *The Monitor* (S). **Radio-AM:** KTXV, 890 kHz.

Madisonville: **Newspaper:** *Madisonville Meteor.* **Radio-AM:** KMVL, 1220 kHz. **Radio-FM:** KHML, 91.5 MHz; KAGG, 96.1; KMVL, 100.5.

Malakoff: **Radio-FM:** KCKL, 95.9 MHz.

Manor: **Radio-AM:** KTXW, 1120 kHz; KELG, 1440.

Marble Falls: **Newspaper:** *The Highlander* (S). **Radio-FM:** KBMD, 88.5 MHz.

Marathon: **Radio-FM:** KDKY, 91.5 MHz.

Marfa: **Newspaper:** *The Big Bend Sentinel.* **Radio-FM:** KRTS, 93.5 MHz.

Marion: **Radio-AM:** KBIB, 1000 kHz.

Markham: **Radio-FM:** KKHA, 92.5 MHz; KBYC, 104.5.

Marlin: **Newspaper:** *The Marlin Democrat.* **Radio-FM:** KRMX, 92.9 MHz.

Marshall: **Newspaper:** *Marshall News Messenger* (TW). **Radio-AM:** KMHT, 1450 kHz. **Radio-FM:** KBWC, 91.1 MHz; KDPM, 92.3; KMHT, 103.9.

Mart: **Radio-FM:** KWAA, 88.9 MHz.

Mason: **Newspaper:** *Mason County News.* **Radio-FM:** KZZM, 101.7 MHz; KHLB, 102.5; KMSN, 104.1.

Matagorda: **Radio-FM:** KPYM, 106.1 MHz.

McAllen: **Newspaper:** *The Monitor* (D). **Radio-AM:** KRIO, 910 kHz. **Radio-FM:** KHID, 88.1 MHz; KVMV, 96.9; KGBT, 98.5. **TV Station:** KNVO-Ch. 17.

McCook: **Radio-FM:** KCAS, 91.5 MHz.

McCoy: **Radio-FM:** KMPI, 90.5 MHz.

McKinney: **Newspapers:** *Collin County Commercial Record* (S); *McKinney Courier-Gazette.* **Radio-FM:** KNTU, 88.1 MHz.

McQueeney: **Radio-FM:** KZAR, 97.7 MHz.

Memphis: **Radio-FM:** KLSR, 105.3 MHz.

Menard: **Newspaper:** *Menard News and Messenger.* **Radio-FM:** KTCY, 105.3 MHz.

Mercedes: **Newspaper:** *The Mercedes Enterprise.* **Radio-FM:** KTEX, 100.3 MHz.

Meridian: **Newspaper:** *Meridian Tribune.* **Radio-FM:** KITT, 106.5 MHz.

Merkel: **Radio-AM:** KMXO, 1500 kHz. **Radio-FM:** KHXS, 102.7 MHz.

Mertzon: **Radio-FM:** KMEO, 91.9 MHz; KBTP, 101.1; KBJX, 103.5.

Mesquite: **Newspaper:** *Mesquite News.* **Radio-FM:** KEOM, 88.5 MHz.

Mexia: **Newspaper:** *The Mexia News* (S). **Radio-AM:** KEKR, 1590 kHz.

Meyersville: **Radio-FM:** KQBQ, 100.1 MHz.

Miami: **Newspaper:** *Miami Chief.*

Midland: **Newspaper:** *Midland Reporter-Telegram* (D). **Radio-AM:** KCRS, 550 kHz; KWEL, 1070; KLPF, 1180; KMND, 1510. **Radio-FM:** KVDG, 90.9 MHz; KNFM, 92.3; KZBT, 93.3; KQRX, 95.1; KCRS, 103.3; KCHX, 106.7. **TV Stations:** KUPB-Ch. 18; KMID-Ch. 26.

Midlothian: **Newspaper:** *Midlothian Mirror.*

Miles: **Newspaper:** *Miles Messenger.* **Radio-FM:** KMLS, 95.5 MHz.

Mineola: **Newspaper:** *Wood County Monitor.* **Radio-FM:** KMOO, 99.9 MHz.

Mineral Wells: **Newspaper:** *Palo Pinto Press.* **Radio-AM:** KVTT, 1110 kHz. **Radio-FM:** KYQX, 89.3 MHz.

Mirando City: **Radio-FM:** KBDR, 100.5 MHz.

Mission: **Newspaper:** *Progress Times.* **Radio-AM:** KIRT, 1580 kHz. **Radio-FM:** KQXX, 105.5 MHz.

Missouri City: **Radio-AM:** KBRZ, 1460 kHz.

Monahans: **Newspaper:** *The Monahans News.* **Radio-AM:** KCKM, 1330 kHz. **Radio-FM:** KMRA, 91.1 MHz; KBAT, 99.9.

Mont Belvieu: **Radio-FM:** KFNC, 97.5 MHz.

Moody: **Radio-FM:** KLTO, 99.1 MHz.

Moran: **Radio-FM:** KCKB, 104.1 MHz.

Morton: **Radio-FM:** KQOA, 91.1 MHz; KPGA, 91.9.

Moulton: **Newspaper:** *Moulton Eagle.*

Mountain Home: **Radio-FM:** KAXA, 103.7 MHz.

Mount Pleasant: **Newspaper:** *Mount Pleasant Tribune* (S). **Radio-AM:** KIMP, 960 kHz. **Radio-FM:** KYZQ, 88.3 MHz.

Mount Vernon: **Radio-FM:** KEUT, 100.5 MHz.

Muenster: **Newspaper:** *Muenster Enterprise.* **Radio-FM:** KTMU, 88.7 MHz; KZZA, 106.7.

Muleshoe: **Newspaper:** *Muleshoe Journal.* **Radio-FM:** KIXV, 91.5 MHz; KVRQ, 93.3.

Munday: **Newspaper:** *The Knox County News-Courier.*

Murphy: **Newspaper:** *Murphy Monitor.*

—N—

Nacogdoches: **Newspaper:** *The Daily Sentinel* (S). **Radio-AM:** KSFA, 860 kHz. **Radio-FM:** KSAU, 90.1 MHz; KJCS, 103.3; KTBQ, 107.7. **TV Station:** KYTX-Ch. 15.

Naples: **Newspaper:** *The Monitor.*

Natalia: **Radio-FM:** KYRQ, 90.3 MHz.

Navasota: **Newspaper:** *The Navasota Examiner.* **Radio-FM:** KWUP, 92.5 MHz.

Nederland: **Radio-AM:** KBED, 1510 kHz.

Needville: **Newspaper:** *Hometown Journal.*

New Boston: **Newspaper:** *Bowie County Citizens Tribune.* **Radio-FM:** KEWL, 95.1 MHz; KZRB, 103.5; KTTY, 105.1.

New Braunfels: **Newspaper:** *New Braunfels Herald-Zeitung* (D). **Radio-AM:** KGNB, 1420 kHz. **Radio-FM:** KNBT, 92.1 MHz.

Newcastle: **Radio-FM:** KBLY, 100.5 MHz.

New Deal: **Radio-FM:** KTTU, 97.3 MHz.

Newton: **Newspaper:** *Newton County News.*

New Ulm: Newspaper: *New Ulm Enterprise.* **Radio-FM:** KNRG, 92.3 MHz.

New Waverly: Radio-FM: KNLY, 91.1 MHz.

Nocona: Newspaper: *Nocona News.*

Nolanville: Radio-FM: KLFX, 107.3 MHz.

Normangee: Newspaper: *The Normangee Star.*

—O—

Oakwood: Radio-FM: KDNT, 94.5 MHz.

O'Brien: Radio-FM: KZOB, 105.5 MHz.

Odem: Radio-FM: KXAI, 103.7 MHz.

Odessa: Newspaper: *Odessa American* (S). **Radio-AM:** KFLB, 920 kHz. **Radio-FM:** KBMM, 89.5 MHz; KLVW, 90.5; KXWT, 91.3; KMRK, 96.1; KMCM, 96.9; KODM, 97.9; KHKX, 99.1; KQLM, 107.9. **TV Stations:** KOSA-Ch. 7; KWES-Ch. 9; KMLM-Ch. 15; KPEJ-Ch. 23; KPBT-Ch. 28; KWWT-Ch. 30.

O'Donnell: Newspaper: *O'Donnell Index-Press.*

Olney: Newspaper: *Olney Enterprise.* **Radio-FM:** KBVP, 104.3 MHz.

Orange: Newspaper: *The Orange Leader* (S). **Radio-FM:** KKMY, 104.5 MHz; KIOC, 106.1.

Ore City: Radio-FM: KAZE, 106.9 MHz.

Overton: Radio-FM: KTYK, 100.7 MHz.

Ozona: Newspaper: *Ozona Stockman.* **Radio-FM:** KYXX, 94.3 MHz; KCMZ, 105.5.

—P—

Paducah: Newspaper: *Paducah Post.* **Radio-FM:** KPZX, 94.7 MHz.

Paint Rock: Newspaper: *The Concho Herald.*

Palacios: Newspaper: *Palacios Beacon.* **Radio-FM:** KPAL, 91.3 MHz; KPLU, 100.7.

Palestine: Newspaper: *Palestine Herald-Press* (TW). **Radio-AM:** KNET, 1450 kHz. **Radio-FM:** KYFP, 89.1 MHz; KYYK, 98.3.

Pampa: Newspaper: *The Pampa News* (TW). **Radio-AM:** KGRO, 1230 kHz. **Radio-FM:** KAVO, 90.9 MHz; KOMX, 100.3; KDRL, 103.3.

Panhandle: Newspaper: *Panhandle Herald & White Deer News.* **Radio-FM:** KPQP, 106.1 MHz.

Paris: Newspaper: *The Paris News* (TW). **Radio-AM:** KZHN, 1250 kHz; KPLT, 1490. **Radio-FM:** KHCP, 89.3 MHz; KQPA, 91.9; KOYN, 93.9; KBUS, 101.9; KPLT, 107.7.

Pasadena: Radio-AM: KIKK, 650 kHz; KLVL, 1480. **Radio-FM:** KFTG, 88.1 MHz; KKBQ, 92.9.

Pearland: Newspaper: *Reporter News.*

Pearsall: Newspaper: *Frio-Nueces Current.* **Radio-AM:** KMFR, 1280 kHz. **Radio-FM:** KSAG, 103.3 MHz; KSAH, 104.1.

Pecan Grove: Radio-AM: KREH, 900 kHz.

Pecos: Newspaper: *Pecos Enterprise.* **Radio-AM:** KIUN, 1400 kHz. **Radio-FM:** KPKO, 91.3 MHz; KDNZ, 97.3; KPTX, 98.3.

Perryton: Newspaper: *Perryton Herald.* **Radio-AM:** KEYE, 1400 kHz. **Radio-FM:** KEYE, 93.7 MHz.

Pflugerville: Radio-AM: KOKE, 1600 kHz.

Pharr: Newspaper: *Advance News Journal.* **Radio-AM:** KVJY, 840 kHz.

Pilot Point: Newspaper: *Pilot Point Post-Signal.* **Radio-FM:** KZMP, 104.9 MHz.

Pineland: Radio-FM: KFAH, 99.1 MHz.

Pittsburg: Newspaper: *The Pittsburg Gazette.* **Radio-FM:** KGWP, 91.1 MHz; KPIT, 91.7; KSCN, 96.9; KHFZ, 103.1.

Plainview: Newspaper: *Plainview Herald* (TW). **Radio-AM:** KVOP, 1090 kHz; KREW, 1400. **Radio-FM:** KPMB, 88.5 MHz; KBAH, 90.5; KWLD, 91.5; KRIA, 103.9; KKYN, 106.9.

Plano: Newspaper: *Plano Star Courier.* **Radio-AM:** KTNO, 620 kHz.

Pleasanton: Newspaper: *Pleasanton Express.* **Radio-AM:** KWMF, 1380 kHz.

Pleasant Valley: Radio-FM: KZAM, 98.7 MHz.

Point Comfort: Radio-FM: KJAZ, 94.1 MHz.

Port Aransas: Newspaper: *Port Aransas South Jetty.*

Port Arthur: Newspaper: *The Port Arthur News* (TW). **Radio-AM:** KDEI, 1250 kHz; KOLE, 1340. **Radio-FM:** KQBU, 93.3 MHz; KTJM, 98.5. **TV Station:** KBTV-Ch. 27.

Port Isabel: Newspaper: *Port Isabel-South Padre Press.* **Radio-FM:** KNVO, 101.1 MHz; KRIX, 105.5.

Portland: Radio-FM: KSGR, 91.1 MHz; KLHB, 105.5.

Port Lavaca: Newspaper: *Port Lavaca Wave.* **Radio-FM:** KNAL, 93.3 MHz.

Port Neches: Radio-AM: KBPO, 1150 kHz.

Port O'Connor: Radio-FM: KHPO, 91.9 MHz.

Post: Newspaper: *The Post Dispatch.* **Radio-FM:** KSSL, 107.3 MHz.

Prairie View: Radio-FM: KPVU, 91.3 MHz.

Premont: Radio-FM: KLBD, 88.1 MHz.

Presidio: Newspaper: *The Presidio International.* FM-Radio: KRBP, 88.1 MHz; KOJP, 95.3.

Princeton: Newspaper: *Princeton Herald.*

—Q—

Quanah: Newspaper: *Quanah Tribune-Chief.* **Radio-AM:** KOLJ, 1150 kHz. **Radio-FM:** KQTX, 98.1 MHz.

Quemado: Radio-FM: KQMD, 88.1 MHz.

Quitaque: Newspaper: *Valley Tribune.*

—R—

Ralls: Newspaper: *Crosby County News.*

Ranchitos Las Lomas: Radio-FM: KLIT, 93.3 MHz.

Ranger: Radio-FM: KWBY, 98.5 MHz.

Rankin: Radio-FM: KXFS, 93.7 MHz.

Raymondville: Newspaper: *Raymondville Chronicle/Willacy County News.* **Radio-AM:** KSOX, 1240 kHz. **Radio-FM:** KVHI, 88.7 MHz; KBUC, 102.1; KBIC, 105.7.

Refugio: Newspaper: *Refugio County Press.* **Radio-FM:** KRIK, 100.5 MHz; KXHM, 106.1.

Reno: Radio-FM: KLOW, 98.9 MHz.

Richardson: Radio-AM: KKLF, 1700 kHz.

Riesel: Newspaper: *Riesel Rustler.*

Rio Grande City: Radio-FM: KXJT, 88.3 MHz; KRGX, 95.1; KQBO, 107.5. **TV Station:** KTLM-Ch. 14.

Robert Lee: Newspaper: *Observer/Enterprise.* **Radio-FM:** KJVI, 105.7 MHz.

Robinson: Radio-FM: KWPW, 107.9 MHz.

Robstown: Radio-AM: KROB, 1510 kHz. **Radio-FM:** KLUX, 89.5 MHz; KSAB, 99.9; KMIQ, 104.9.

Rockdale: Newspaper: *Rockdale Reporter.* **Radio-FM:** KRXT, 98.5 MHz.

Rockport: Newspaper: *The Rockport Pilot* (S). **Radio-FM:** KKPN, 102.3 MHz.

Rollingwood: Radio-AM: KJCE, 1370 kHz.

Roma: Radio-FM: KRIO, 97.7 MHz.

Rosebud: Newspaper: *The Rosebud News.*

Rosenberg: Newspaper: *Fort Bend Herald and Texas Coaster* (TW). **Radio-AM:** KQUE, 980 kHz. **TV Station:** KXLN-Ch. 30.

Rotan: Newspaper: *Double Mountain Chronicle.*

Round Rock: Newspaper: *Round Rock Leader* (S). **Radio-FM:** KNLE, 88.1 MHz; KFMK, 105.9.

Rowena: Newspaper: *The Rowena Press.*

Roxton: Newspaper: *Roxton Progress* (SM).

Royse City: Newspaper: *Royse City Herald Banner.*

Rusk: Newspaper: *Cherokeean Herald.* **Radio-AM:** KTLU, 1580 kHz.

—S—

Sabinal: Radio-FM: KHAV, 107.1 MHz.

Sachse: Newspaper: *Sachse News.*

Saint Jo: Newspaper: *Saint Jo Tribune.*

Salado: Newspaper: *Salado Village Voice.*

San Angelo: Newspaper: *San Angelo Standard-Times* (D). **Radio-AM:** KGKL, 960 kHz; KKSA, 1260; KCCE, 1340. **Radio-FM:** KLRW, 88.5 MHz; KNAR, 89.3; KNCH, 90.1; KLTP, 90.9; KDCD, 92.9; KSAO, 93.9; KIXY, 94.7; KGKL, 97.5; KELI, 98.7; KCLL, 100.1; KWFR, 101.9; KMDX, 106.1; KSJT, 107.5. **TV Stations:** KLST-Ch. 11; KSAN-Ch. 16; KIDY-Ch. 19.

San Antonio: Newspapers: *San Antonio Express-News* (D); *The Hart Beat* (TW); *San Antonio Business Journal.* **Radio-AM:** KTSA, 550 kHz; KSLR, 630; KKYX, 680; KTKR, 760; KONO, 860; KRDY, 1160; WOAI, 1200; KZDC, 1250; KAHL, 1310; KXTN, 1350; KCHL, 1480; KEDA, 1540. **Radio-FM:** KPAC, 88.3 MHz; KSTX, 89.1; KSYM, 90.1; KYFS, 90.9; KRTU, 91.7; KROM, 92.9; KXXM, 96.1; KAJA, 97.3; KISS, 99.5; KCYY, 100.3; KQXT, 101.9; KJXK, 102.7; KZEP, 104.5; KVBH, 107.5. **TV Stations:** KLRN-Ch. 9; KSAT-Ch. 12; KVDA-Ch. 15; KHCE-Ch. 16; KWEX-Ch. 24; WOAI-Ch. 28; KENS-Ch. 29; KABB-Ch. 30.

San Augustine: Newspaper: *San Augustine Tribune.* **Radio-FM:** KXXE, 92.5 MHz.

San Benito: Newspaper: *San Benito News.* **Radio-FM:** KHKZ, 106.3 MHz.

Sanderson: Radio-FM: KEVK, 105.1 MHz.

San Diego: Radio-FM: KXAM, 102.5 MHz.

Sanger: Radio-FM: KAWA, 89.7 MHz; KTCG, 104.1.

San Juan: Radio-AM: KUBR, 1210 kHz.

San Marcos: Newspaper: *San Marcos Daily Record* (D). **Radio-FM:** KTSW, 89.9 MHz.

San Saba: Newspaper: *San Saba News & Star.* **Radio-AM:** KROY, 1410 kHz. **Radio-FM:** KNUZ, 106.1 MHz.

Santa Anna: Radio-FM: KXXU, 104.3 MHz; KSZX, 105.5.

Santa Fe: Radio-FM: KJIC, 90.5 MHz.

Savoy: Radio-FM: KQDR, 107.3 MHz.

Schertz: Radio-FM: KBBT, 98.5 MHz.

Schulenburg: Newspaper: *Schulenburg Sticker.*

Scotland: Radio-FM: KTWF, 95.5 MHz.

Seabrook: Radio-FM: KROI, 92.1 MHz.

Seadrift: Radio-FM: KMAT, 105.1 MHz.

Sealy: Newspaper: *The Sealy News.* **Radio-FM:** KQLC, 90.7 MHz.

Seguin: Newspaper: *The Seguin Gazette* (S). **Radio-AM:** KWED, 1580 kHz. **Radio-FM:** KSMG, 105.3 MHz.

Seminole: Newspaper: *Seminole Sentinel* (S). **Radio-AM:** KIKZ, 1250 kHz. **Radio-FM:** KSEM, 106.3 MHz.

Seymour: Newspaper: *The Baylor County Banner.* **Radio-AM:** KSEY, 1230 kHz. **Radio-FM:** KSEY, 94.3 MHz.

Shamrock: Newspaper: *County Star-News.* **Radio-FM:** KSNZ, 92.9 MHz.

Shepherd: Newspaper: *San Jacinto News-Times.*

Shenandoah: Radio-AM: KRCM, 1380 kHz.

Sherman: Newspaper: *Herald Democrat* (D). **Radio-AM:** KJIM, 1500 kHz. **TV Station:** KXII-Ch. 12.

Shiner: Newspaper: *The Shiner Gazette.*

Silsbee: Newspaper: *The Silsbee Bee.* **Radio-FM:** KAYD, 101.7 MHz.

Silverton: Newspaper: *The Caprock Courier.*

Sinton: Newspaper: *The News of San Patricio.* **Radio-AM:** KDAE, 1590 kHz. **Radio-FM:** KNCN, 101.3 MHz.

Slaton: Newspaper: *The Slatonite.* **Radio-FM:** KVCE, 92.7 MHz.

Smiley: Radio-FM: KSXT, 90.3 MHz; KBQQ, 103.9.

Smithville: Newspaper: *Smithville Times.*

Snyder: Newspaper: *The Snyder News* (S). **Radio-AM:** KSNY, 1450 kHz. **Radio-FM:** KGWB, 91.1 MHz; KHMZ 94.9; KLYD, 98.9; KSNY, 101.5. **TV Station:** KPCB-Ch. 17.

Somerset: Radio-AM: KYTY, 810 kHz.

Somerville: Radio-FM: KXBT, 88.1 MHz.

Sonora: Newspaper: *The Devil's River News.* **Radio-FM:** KHOS, 92.1 MHz.

South Padre Island: Radio-FM: KESO, 92.7 MHz.

Spearman: Newspaper: *The Hansford County Reporter-Statesman.* **Radio-FM:** KTOT, 89.5 MHz; KXDJ, 98.3.

Springtown: Newspaper: *Springtown Epigraph.* **Radio-FM:** KSQX, 89.1 MHz.

Spur: Newspaper: *Texas Spur.*

Stamford: Newspapers: *The New Stamford American; The Stamford Star.* **Radio-AM:** KVRP, 1400 kHz. **Radio-FM:** KLGD, 106.9 MHz.

Stanton: Newspapers: *Greenwood Messenger; Martin County Messenger.* **Radio-FM:** KFLB, 88.1 MHz; KTPR, 89.9; KXQT, 105.9.

Stephenville: Newspaper: *Stephenville Empire Tribune* (S). **Radio-AM:** KSTV, 1510 kHz. **Radio-FM:** KQXS, 89.1 MHz; KEQX, 89.5; KTRL, 90.5.

Sterling City: Radio-FM: KNRX, 96.5 MHz.

Stinnett: Radio-FM: KPWD, 91.7 MHz.

Stockdale: Radio-AM: KQQB, 1520 kHz.

Stratford: Newspaper: *Sherman County Gazette.* **Radio-FM:** KUHC, 91.5 MHz.

Sulphur Bluff: Radio-FM: KETE, 99.7 MHz.

Sulphur Springs: Newspaper: *Sulphur Springs News-Telegram* (S). **Radio-AM:** KSST, 1230 kHz. **Radio-FM:** KGPF, 91.1 MHz; KZRF, 91.9; KSCH, 95.9.

Sunset Valley: Radio-FM: KVLR, 92.5 MHz.

Sweetwater: Newspaper: *Sweetwater Reporter* (TW). **Radio-AM:** KXOX, 1240 kHz. **Radio-FM:** KXOX, 96.7 MHz. **TV Station:** KTXS-Ch. 20.

—T—

Taft: Radio-FM: KYRK, 106.5 MHz.

Tahoka: Newspaper: *Lynn County News.* **Radio-FM:** KMMX, 100.3 MHz; KAMZ, 103.5.

Tatum: Radio-FM: KZQX, 100.3 MHz.

Taylor: Newspaper: *Taylor Press* (S). **Radio-FM:** KLQB, 104.3 MHz.

Teague: Newspaper: *Teague Chronicle.*

Temple: Newspaper: *Temple Daily Telegram* (D). **Radio-AM:** KTEM, 1400 kHz. **Radio-FM:** KVLT, 88.5 MHz; KBDE, 89.9; KLTD, 101.7. **TV Station:** KCEN-Ch. 9.

Terrell: Newspaper: *The Terrell Tribune.* **Radio-AM:** KPYK, 1570 kHz.

Terrell Hills: Radio-AM: KLUP, 930 kHz. **Radio-FM:** KTKX, 106.7 MHz.

Texarkana: Newspaper: *Texarkana Gazette* (D). **Radio-AM:** KCMC, 740 kHz; KTFS, 940; KKTK, 1400. **Radio-FM:** KTXK, 91.5 MHz; KTAL, 98.1; KKYR, 102.5. **TV Station:** KTAL-Ch. 26.

Texas City: Newspaper: *The Post Newspaper* (S). **Radio-AM:** KYST, 920 kHz.

Thorndale: Newspaper: *Thorndale Champion.* **Radio-FM:** KOKE, 99.3 MHz.

Three Rivers: Newspaper: *The Progress.* **Radio-FM:** KEMA, 94.5 MHz.

Throckmorton: Newspaper: *Throckmorton Tribune.*

Tolar: Radio-FM: KOME, 95.5 MHz.

Tomball: Radio-AM: KSEV, 700 kHz.

Tom Bean: Radio-FM: KLAK, 97.5 MHz.

Trinity: Radio-FM: KTYR, 89.7 MHz.

Troup: Radio-FM: KTBB, 97.5 MHz.

Tulia: Newspaper: *Swisher County News.* **Radio-FM:** KBTE, 104.9 MHz.

Tye: Radio-FM: KBCY, 99.7 MHz.

Tyler: Newspaper: *Tyler Morning Telegraph* (TW). **Radio-AM:** KTBB, 600 kHz; KGLD, 1330; KYZS, 1490. **Radio-FM:** KVNE, 89.5 MHz; KGLY, 91.3; KRWR, 92.1; KTYL, 93.1; KNUE, 101.5; KKUS, 104.1. **TV Station:** KLTV-Ch. 7.

—U—

Umbarger: Radio-FM: KRBG, 88.7 MHz.

Universal City: Radio-AM: KSAH, 720 kHz.

University Park: Radio-AM: KEXB, 1440 kHz; KZMP, 1540.

Uvalde: Newspaper: *Uvalde Leader-News* (S). **Radio-AM:** KGWU, 1400 kHz. **Radio-FM:** KHPS, 88.9 MHz; KBNU, 93.9; KUVA, 102.3; KVOU, 104.9. **TV Station:** KPXL-Ch. 26.

Uvalde Estates: Radio-FM: KEWP, 103.5 MHz.

—V—

Valley Mills: Newspaper: *Valley Mills Progress* (SM).

Valley View: Radio-FM: KQFZ, 89.1 MHz.

Van Alstyne: Newspaper: *Van Alstyne Leader.*

Van Horn: Newspaper: *The Van Horn Advocate.* **Radio-FM:** KVHR, 91.5 MHz.

Vega: Newspaper: *Vega Enterprise.*

Vernon: Newspaper: *Vernon Record.* **Radio-AM:** KVWC, 1490 kHz. **Radio-FM:** KVED, 88.5 MHz; KVWC, 103.1.

Victoria: Newspaper: *Victoria Advocate* (TW). **Radio-AM:** KVNN, 1340 kHz; KITE, 1410. **Radio-FM:** KAYK, 88.5 MHz; KBRZ, 89.3; KVRT, 90.7; KQVT, 92.3; KTXN, 98.7; KBAR, 100.9; KVIC, 104.7; KIXS, 107.9. **TV Stations:** KVCT-Ch. 11; KAVU-Ch. 20.

Vidor: Newspaper: *Vidor Vidorian.*

—W—

Waco: Newspaper: *Waco Tribune-Herald* (D). **Radio-AM:** KBBW, 1010 kHz; KWTX, 1230; KRZI, 1660. **Radio-FM:** KWBT, 94.5; KBGO, 95.7; KWTX, 97.5; WACO, 99.9; KWBU, 103.3. **TV Stations:** KWTX-Ch. 10; KXXV-Ch. 26; KWKT-Ch. 28.

Wake Village: Radio-FM: KHTA, 92.5 MHz.

Waskom: Radio-FM: KQHN, 97.3 MHz.

Waxahachie: Newspapers: *Waxahachie Daily Light* (S); *The Waxahachie Sun* (S). **Radio-AM:** KBEC, 1390 kHz.

Weatherford: Newspaper: *Weatherford Democrat* (S). **Radio-AM:** KZEE, 1220 kHz. **Radio-FM:** KMQX, 88.5 MHz.

Weimar: Newspaper: *Weimar Mercury.*

Wellington: Radio-FM: KSIF 91.7 MHz.

Wells: Radio-FM: KVLL, 94.7 MHz.

Weslaco: Radio-AM: KRGE, 1290 kHz. **TV Station:** KRGV-Ch. 13.

West: Newspaper: *The West News.*

West Lake Hills: Radio-AM: KTXZ, 1560 kHz.

West Odessa: Radio-FM: KFRI, 88.7 MHz.

Wharton: Newspaper: *Wharton Journal-Spectator* (S). **Radio-AM:** KANI, 1500 kHz.

Wheeler: Newspaper: *The Wheeler Times.* **Radio-FM:** KPDR, 90.3 MHz; KXNZ, 98.9.

Wheelock: Radio-FM: KVMK 100.9 MHz.

Whitehouse: Radio-FM: KISX, 107.3 MHz.

White Oak: Newspaper: *White Oak Independent.* **Radio-FM:** KAPW, 99.3 MHz.

Whitesboro: Newspaper: *Whitesboro News-Record.* **Radio-FM:** KMAD, 102.5 MHz.

Whitewright: Newspaper: *The Whitewright Sun.*

Wichita Falls: Newspaper: *Times Record News* (D). **Radio-AM:** KWFS, 1290. **Radio-FM:** KMCU, 88.7 MHz; KMOC, 89.5; KZKL, 90.5; KNIN, 92.9; KLUR, 99.9; KWFS, 102.3; KQXC, 103.9; KBZS, 106.3. **TV Stations:** KJTL-Ch. 15; KAUZ-Ch. 22; KFDX-Ch. 28.

Willis: Radio-FM: KAFR, 88.3 MHz.

Wills Point: Newspaper: *Wills Point Chronicle.*

Wimberley: Newspaper: *Wimberley View.*

Winfield: Radio-FM: KALK, 97.7 MHz.

Winnie: Newspapers: *The Hometown Press; The Seabreeze Beacon.* **Radio-FM:** KXXF 105.3 MHz.

Winnsboro: Newspaper: *Winnsboro News.* **Radio-FM:** KWNS, 104.7 MHz.

Winona: Radio-FM: KBLZ, 102.7 MHz.

Winters: Radio-FM: KORQ, 96.1 MHz.

Wixon Valley: Radio-FM: KBXT, 101.9 MHz.

Wolfforth: Radio-FM: KAIQ, 95.5 MHz. **TV Station:** KLCW-Ch. 23.

Woodville: Newspaper: *Tyler County Booster.*

Wylie: Newspaper: *The Wylie News.* **Radio-AM:** KHSE, 700 kHz.

—Y—

Yoakum: Newspaper: *Yoakum Herald-Times.* **Radio-FM:** KYKM, 94.3 MHz.

Yorktown: Newspaper: *Yorktown News-View.* **Radio-FM:** KGGB, 96.3 MHz.

—Z—

Zapata: Newspaper: *Zapata County News.* **Radio-FM:** KHEM, 89.3 MHz; KQHM 102.7; KJJS, 103.9. ∎

TRANSPORTATION

RAILROADS

HIGHWAYS & MOTOR VEHICLES

CONSULATES & FOREIGN TRADE ZONES

PORTS & FREIGHT GATEWAYS

PUBLIC ADMINISTRATION, DRONES, & AVIATION

Freight Railroads in Texas

Source: Association of American Railroads.

In Texas in 2021, there were three Class I railroad companies operating. Short line railroads made up about 14% of the state's total track mileage. In 2021, railroads in the state carried some 110.9 million tons of freight. The leading commodities handled are listed below.

A complete list of the 54 railroads in the state is in the Counties section on page 208. ☆

Railroads in State	Miles Operated
Class I (3, *see list at right*)	**12,742**
Regional (0)	0
Short Line Railroads (51)	2,075
Total	14,817
Total excluding trackage rights*	**10,370**

Railroads in State	Miles Operated
Class I	**12,742**
Union Pacific Railroad Co.	6,438
BNSF Railway Co.	5,365
Canadian Pacific Kansas City	939

*Trackage rights — track provided by another railroad. Numbers in parentheses represent the number of railroad companies in each category.

Freight Traffic in Texas by Kind – 2021

Carloads Originated		Tons (Mil.)
Chemicals	438,100	41.8
Nonmetallic minerals	206,800	21.5
Petroleum products	185,500	14.8
Intermodal	1,058,600	14.6
Primary metal products	51,500	4.7
All Other	220,800	13.5
Total	2,161,300	110.9

Carloads Terminated		Tons (Mil.)
Nonmetallic minerals	312,600	32.4
Coal	345,500	40.4
Chemicals	306,900	29.3
Farm products	194,600	20.1
Intermodal	1,092,700	15.1
All Other	623,600	44.6
Total	2,875,900	181.9

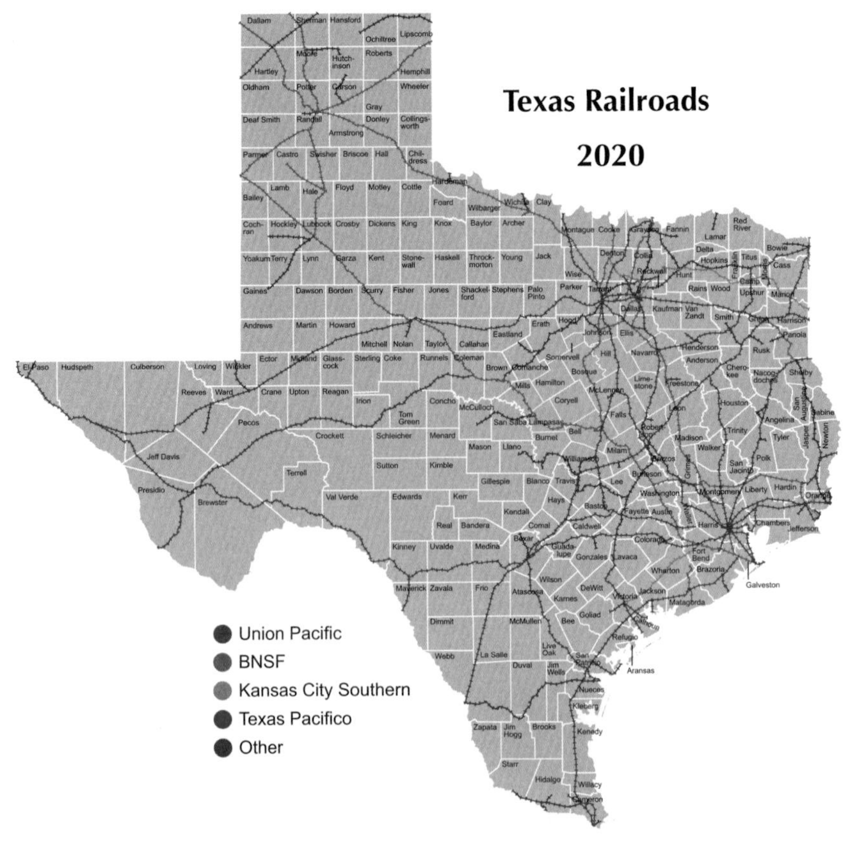

Highway Miles, Construction, Maintenance, Vehicles: 2021

Sources: Texas Department of Transportation and Department of Motor Vehicles.

Texans drove more than 22 million motor vehicles in 2021 over 322,153 miles of roadways, including city- and county-maintained roads. That driving is calculated to have included more than 574 million miles driven daily on the 200,060 miles of state-maintained highways alone.

The Texas Department of Transportation (TxDOT) is responsible for state highway construction and maintenance, planning for future road expansion, administering Texas tollways and toll tags, and operating the state's 12 official Texas Travel Information Centers and 76 safety rest areas.

Mileage, maintenance, and construction figures (listed by county) refer only to roads that are maintained by the state: Interstates, U.S. highways, state highways, farm-to-market roads, and some loops around urban areas. Not included are city- or county-maintained streets and roads. A lane mile is one lane for one mile; i.e., one mile of four-lane highway equals four lane miles. ☆

County	Vehicles Registered	Lane Miles of Highway	Vehicle Miles Driven Daily	State Construction Expenditures	Combined Construction Maintenance Expenditures	Total Vehicle Registration Fees	State Net Receipts	County Net Receipts
Anderson	49,200	1,013	1,242,694	$2,887,478	$16,700,255	$3,556,456	$2,586,736	$967,644
Andrews	22,618	556	958,208	$13,762,594	$28,835,162	$2,256,926	$1,760,221	$495,269
Angelina	82,226	952	2,204,610	$65,338,812	$82,102,527	$6,347,201	$4,979,475	$1,363,799
Aransas	27,846	203	542,943	$3,440,857	$7,630,106	$1,796,994	$1,214,540	$578,038
Archer	12,125	572	414,395	$7,511,603	$26,936,783	$838,113	$378,728	$458,359
Armstrong	2,749	379	450,558	$690,118	$1,458,141	$173,319	$9,495	$163,781
Atascosa	52,944	1,022	2,133,212	$3,489,518	$13,153,038	$3,803,566	$2,887,936	$913,285
Austin	43,094	660	1,669,439	$117,749,759	$130,558,158	$3,027,565	$2,207,904	$815,674
Bailey	6,351	491	249,928	$2,002,577	$9,842,945	$486,476	$101,093	$385,261
Bandera	30,152	414	489,564	$1,531,730	$6,733,995	$1,847,630	$1,200,741	$643,526
Bastrop	107,120	816	2,701,492	$25,237,944	$41,832,698	$7,915,658	$6,124,570	$1,780,744
Baylor	4,190	531	254,263	$2,261,984	$9,321,230	$274,885	$35,156	$239,433
Bee	22,462	679	609,260	$12,828,297	$18,544,216	$1,565,022	$965,596	$598,488
Bell	330,475	1,652	7,844,882	$54,882,467	$77,197,633	$22,826,699	$18,393,049	$4,409,564
Bexar	1,645,704	3,508	33,784,163	$484,979,719	$664,229,514	$150,336,338	$110,630,831	$39,601,804
Blanco	19,980	463	760,626	$1,734,776	$7,096,936	$1,351,985	$874,824	$475,031
Borden	1,024	344	71,391	$718,961	$2,783,342	$48,806	$3,306	$45,456
Bosque	24,900	697	577,320	$3,547,435	$16,727,899	$1,456,326	$852,573	$601,487
Bowie	85,695	1,212	3,204,858	$23,744,081	$55,769,110	$6,098,026	$4,752,333	$1,340,186
Brazoria	345,874	1,428	5,693,480	$126,743,850	$160,835,854	$25,202,271	$20,764,972	$4,409,875
Brazos	166,739	979	3,669,804	$24,990,029	$52,263,923	$12,988,299	$10,373,750	$2,584,127
Brewster	11,134	606	227,366	$548,157	$2,296,063	$692,172	$329,588	$358,937
Briscoe	1,880	325	56,867	$242,426	$2,348,442	$111,471	$6,584	$104,843
Brooks	6,193	354	657,929	$702,589	$4,467,630	$404,987	$128,586	$276,247
Brown	43,426	774	772,391	$3,611,873	$11,520,384	$3,151,887	$2,262,118	$887,480
Burleson	25,351	542	806,411	$15,112,697	$30,156,862	$1,771,307	$1,127,465	$642,029
Burnet	65,429	792	1,754,654	$7,604,101	$13,789,302	$4,716,241	$3,537,719	$1,170,792
Caldwell	47,291	711	1,434,598	$18,149,117	$21,321,603	$3,328,552	$2,410,092	$915,826
Calhoun	23,563	405	722,556	$16,911,282	$25,126,810	$1,831,840	$1,251,599	$578,829
Callahan	17,408	745	1,161,531	$7,396,351	$13,850,296	$1,362,728	$792,790	$568,767
Cameron	348,578	1,947	6,995,674	$42,424,498	$75,859,494	$29,693,918	$21,209,079	$8,470,831
Camp	18,277	263	285,970	$3,297,485	$5,281,598	$1,590,757	$1,103,085	$486,916
Carson	7,834	780	932,052	$4,257,462	$11,971,027	$543,680	$129,063	$414,224
Cass	33,595	980	890,784	$2,106,421	$14,765,279	$2,083,823	$1,384,992	$697,830
Castro	8,525	535	279,763	$521,381	$2,675,914	$1,045,782	$589,173	$456,438
Chambers	53,676	823	3,035,739	$20,984,963	$31,423,708	$3,784,448	$2,887,586	$893,161
Cherokee	51,461	1,145	1,254,440	$21,036,266	$38,417,752	$3,415,698	$2,493,543	$919,954
Childress	6,348	497	483,444	$2,600,361	$10,320,729	$384,148	$67,831	$316,042
Clay	13,695	756	906,987	$661,834	$4,808,491	$1,007,098	$482,120	$523,973
Cochran	2,894	469	92,602	$394,350	$2,234,743	$201,488	$9,952	$191,430
Coke	4,782	369	183,472	$963,419	$4,145,275	$264,513	$41,985	$222,333
Coleman	11,110	753	379,268	$508,104	$4,475,012	$672,105	$202,942	$468,675
Collin	892,924	1,578	9,753,992	$151,744,687	$197,793,653	$69,257,077	$56,594,866	$12,574,744

County	Vehicles Registered	Lane Miles of Highway	Vehicle Miles Driven Daily	State Construction Expenditures	Combined Construction Maintenance Expenditures	Total Vehicle Registration Fees	State Net Receipts	County Net Receipts
Collingsworth	3,353	454	92,261	$363,221	$3,315,808	$209,449	$11,699	$197,508
Colorado	30,125	765	2,160,962	$24,034,988	$41,657,778	$2,382,110	$1,661,619	$717,962
Comal	199,873	743	5,316,620	$33,980,198	$73,771,177	$16,404,283	$13,501,039	$2,876,380
Comanche	17,747	748	448,304	$11,879,800	$21,903,436	$1,310,518	$751,249	$558,794
Concho	3,589	478	296,627	$127,478	$1,822,364	$194,322	$11,665	$182,415
Cooke	57,807	848	2,100,214	$79,133,624	$87,609,827	$4,330,439	$3,287,783	$1,039,312
Coryell	64,146	782	1,162,173	$13,723,486	$17,500,352	$3,579,139	$2,610,010	$965,220
Cottle	1,578	390	62,378	$330,359	$3,325,080	$87,439	$5,448	$81,903
Crane	5,146	319	284,176	$15,732,376	$26,135,162	$362,361	$136,426	$225,870
Crockett	5,140	786	624,065	$870,180	$4,000,341	$590,710	$240,329	$350,316
Crosby	5,629	569	204,871	$543,096	$4,089,962	$342,035	$35,097	$306,507
Culberson	2,464	756	904,782	$34,994,958	$56,725,489	$150,771	$9,071	$141,390
Dallam	7,977	698	470,056	$2,451,737	$5,363,682	$709,120	$262,903	$445,947
Dallas	2,101,685	3,563	39,725,910	$901,760,003	$1,028,555,818	$171,631,654	$142,133,156	$29,370,793
Dawson	11,448	741	599,229	$11,467,545	$19,406,117	$1,044,984	$519,226	$524,004
Deaf Smith	21,068	603	510,936	$11,806,574	$21,321,059	$2,041,926	$1,421,288	$619,205
Delta	6,719	373	201,658	$3,387,799	$6,925,000	$398,315	$108,649	$289,492
Denton	763,677	1,822	11,973,908	$186,078,103	$216,733,811	$55,606,935	$45,638,670	$9,894,288
DeWitt	25,265	673	753,766	$10,142,545	$31,487,418	$1,723,393	$1,102,450	$619,698
Dickens	2,627	468	106,037	$96,661	$2,272,589	$144,092	$8,233	$135,837
Dimmit	10,727	506	478,590	$5,288,523	$8,159,670	$908,272	$535,979	$371,995
Donley	3,417	469	649,538	$2,897,205	$11,071,925	$227,033	$12,639	$214,196
Duval	11,061	642	385,008	$1,249,322	$3,616,377	$706,009	$270,635	$435,055
Eastland	24,645	1,026	1,363,606	$11,164,882	$34,163,113	$2,070,851	$1,421,216	$648,764
Ector	174,516	971	2,981,167	$45,199,056	$73,745,867	$17,565,118	$15,036,626	$2,523,239
Edwards	3,191	499	104,051	$2,516,588	$7,315,178	$188,592	$10,633	$177,849
Ellis	201,810	1,627	6,228,127	$74,009,258	$101,232,602	$13,573,544	$11,077,664	$2,483,170
El Paso	702,935	1,783	11,856,471	$172,252,518	$218,877,656	$58,940,229	$43,761,666	$15,157,525
Erath	44,886	850	1,264,065	$25,422,588	$35,688,855	$3,229,260	$2,381,011	$843,826
Falls	18,070	752	790,827	$2,616,273	$13,241,187	$1,249,950	$673,835	$575,825
Fannin	39,811	1,000	940,872	$16,213,037	$26,171,691	$2,629,647	$1,850,655	$776,474
Fayette	36,639	1,034	2,007,597	$18,725,610	$36,460,048	$2,458,627	$1,721,273	$733,837
Fisher	4,644	558	162,628	$2,179,121	$8,406,594	$257,188	$14,851	$242,209
Floyd	6,793	702	165,749	$276,690	$2,601,086	$479,793	$99,089	$380,121
Foard	1,654	298	58,540	$1,925,895	$10,819,505	$102,638	$5,338	$97,299
Fort Bend	687,281	1,397	8,748,466	$114,589,415	$126,271,403	$51,413,244	$42,132,336	$9,226,480
Franklin	12,971	344	525,476	$227,331	$4,339,033	$758,741	$348,963	$409,140
Freestone	23,478	823	1,638,880	$6,544,560	$18,833,263	$1,556,467	$956,127	$599,212
Frio	15,332	761	1,332,078	$19,878,975	$25,435,776	$1,025,708	$536,736	$488,736
Gaines	24,376	662	797,711	$16,985,543	$26,470,592	$2,095,618	$1,460,798	$634,007
Galveston	303,822	1,075	5,099,256	$164,855,364	$194,980,854	$21,090,912	$17,304,791	$3,756,360
Garza	4,904	457	530,002	$576,674	$2,260,271	$341,528	$80,977	$260,278
Gillespie	40,174	684	895,210	$1,426,562	$6,927,541	$2,611,660	$1,779,392	$826,304
Glasscock	2,912	357	247,095	$6,283,269	$24,733,104	$157,583	$9,454	$147,998
Goliad	9,622	535	356,802	$17,647,174	$21,007,959	$554,607	$157,739	$396,275
Gonzales	25,751	894	1,695,036	$9,244,535	$25,639,218	$1,829,106	$1,207,648	$620,396
Gray	22,067	762	707,311	$4,881,306	$20,621,661	$1,668,143	$1,046,821	$619,996
Grayson	144,617	1,273	3,995,003	$73,043,583	$97,794,468	$10,416,385	$8,355,698	$2,049,069
Gregg	130,817	824	3,021,195	$33,362,259	$45,249,762	$11,410,481	$9,584,652	$1,818,592
Grimes	36,453	627	1,263,692	$49,985,849	$60,624,422	$2,383,210	$1,649,820	$730,614
Guadalupe	173,318	1,016	4,069,668	$52,364,276	$67,114,689	$12,415,087	$9,897,604	$2,504,340
Hale	28,282	1,057	935,593	$806,711	$8,398,924	$2,108,970	$1,420,730	$686,744
Hall	2,910	459	278,732	$7,447,600	$10,074,444	$183,473	$10,318	$172,979
Hamilton	12,332	580	348,496	$5,325,116	$12,904,172	$758,538	$281,365	$476,391
Hansford	6,312	526	152,893	$1,163,921	$4,595,294	$471,049	$101,355	$369,533
Hardeman	4,012	465	430,932	$1,687,205	$5,819,977	$245,923	$13,468	$232,301

County	Vehicles Registered	Lane Miles of Highway	Vehicle Miles Driven Daily	State Construction Expenditures	Combined Construction Maintenance Expenditures	Total Vehicle Registration Fees	State Net Receipts	County Net Receipts
Hardin	61,058	586	1,345,486	$5,308,159	$12,879,889	$4,475,047	$3,383,667	$1,087,889
Harris	3,493,246	5,667	62,878,539	$394,669,119	$540,877,633	$295,386,758	$245,780,179	$49,370,476
Harrison	71,771	1,178	2,853,701	$13,807,628	$26,615,780	$5,165,956	$3,896,184	$1,265,227
Hartley	7,231	550	500,593	$16,112,367	$23,569,682	$887,997	$533,303	$354,230
Haskell	5,888	669	246,863	$4,200,712	$6,826,696	$425,689	$75,732	$349,715
Hays	218,342	749	5,755,441	$45,153,758	$116,631,446	$16,216,290	$13,360,120	$2,828,374
Hemphill	5,278	384	132,227	$3,145,433	$7,610,999	$363,643	$73,637	$289,633
Henderson	96,892	1,068	1,890,242	$7,664,182	$26,629,374	$6,295,851	$4,893,368	$1,397,636
Hidalgo	687,249	2,517	11,794,684	$193,083,034	$253,727,475	$60,700,101	$45,369,235	$15,308,471
Hill	46,707	1,163	2,687,340	$46,562,563	$57,106,815	$3,462,658	$2,615,818	$844,215
Hockley	25,348	752	665,279	$624,700	$3,717,452	$1,936,642	$1,305,362	$628,866
Hood	75,863	407	1,147,553	$10,371,359	$14,558,112	$5,957,288	$4,667,269	$1,281,197
Hopkins	44,737	1,006	1,815,197	$8,718,408	$23,838,362	$3,201,325	$2,304,629	$894,174
Houston	23,130	872	676,981	$11,592,327	$23,612,733	$1,353,200	$771,800	$579,389
Howard	29,367	912	1,384,103	$9,191,442	$23,428,502	$2,059,579	$1,378,112	$680,019
Hudspeth	4,016	828	1,625,886	$7,024,451	$16,978,658	$247,936	$13,409	$234,483
Hunt	107,436	1,371	3,284,010	$21,571,409	$37,434,521	$7,571,698	$5,899,493	$1,665,703
Hutchinson	23,794	489	376,890	$1,335,391	$7,995,356	$1,649,264	$1,082,923	$565,347
Irion	3,454	246	200,310	$109,300	$789,756	$294,688	$87,590	$206,876
Jack	11,007	583	317,450	$2,842,369	$5,781,866	$799,689	$358,573	$440,551
Jackson	18,229	638	1,200,268	$12,018,197	$23,753,796	$1,182,934	$636,471	$545,487
Jasper	40,514	778	1,204,026	$2,380,913	$8,633,548	$2,617,368	$1,824,354	$791,689
Jeff Davis	2,760	472	207,753	$3,090,350	$5,606,192	$164,796	$34,506	$129,582
Jefferson	208,338	1,120	5,507,072	$147,932,584	$192,030,436	$15,767,294	$12,937,054	$2,818,102
Jim Hogg	4,498	288	143,805	$871,397	$2,622,703	$318,684	$94,859	$223,781
Jim Wells	39,083	716	1,256,064	$25,397,916	$28,685,806	$2,938,098	$2,116,066	$820,319
Johnson	193,601	1,006	3,862,293	$25,354,387	$45,185,866	$15,476,564	$12,539,715	$2,923,070
Jones	18,557	1,006	516,782	$15,049,247	$20,817,705	$1,399,891	$828,677	$569,816
Karnes	19,918	709	703,701	$18,304,116	$28,953,105	$1,279,519	$743,321	$535,846
Kaufman	151,162	1,225	4,864,337	$59,611,136	$91,374,736	$10,246,184	$8,061,420	$2,176,487
Kendall	67,991	458	1,401,717	$16,130,526	$24,127,386	$6,601,376	$5,132,192	$1,455,738
Kenedy	904	191	505,211	$3,555,225	$6,386,655	$44,509	$3,035	$41,276
Kent	1,142	323	45,079	$780,543	$2,445,046	$50,156	$3,515	$46,597
Kerr	62,364	712	1,482,943	$1,283,413	$7,116,192	$4,450,921	$3,293,724	$1,142,316
Kimble	6,499	686	692,382	$1,417,915	$5,354,309	$400,246	$93,592	$305,977
King	531	229	86,461	$199,487	$1,560,936	$31,148	$1,681	$29,445
Kinney	3,717	407	239,435	$882,464	$2,816,816	$233,168	$63,821	$169,063
Kleberg	25,851	379	800,258	$22,150,335	$26,591,723	$1,839,915	$1,282,812	$555,173
Knox	4,256	470	150,256	$1,558,629	$6,173,678	$288,162	$32,218	$255,746
Lamar	53,212	1,013	1,374,863	$8,828,856	$19,306,816	$3,988,876	$3,003,598	$982,507
Lamb	12,928	802	486,240	$574,122	$4,870,890	$891,324	$390,589	$500,043
Lampasas	28,659	528	683,568	$4,204,448	$7,654,919	$1,981,406	$1,287,932	$691,434
La Salle	8,067	649	1,193,811	$19,224,796	$39,308,832	$658,406	$318,385	$339,887
Lavaca	30,088	670	660,184	$2,347,866	$9,740,313	$1,846,212	$1,200,487	$643,877
Lee	25,531	519	770,259	$10,839,020	$15,183,758	$1,918,303	$1,296,759	$620,186
Leon	23,610	840	1,723,126	$5,924,030	$22,187,529	$1,540,128	$961,125	$577,688
Liberty	94,125	871	2,247,037	$40,302,285	$53,986,280	$6,812,837	$5,408,587	$1,401,310
Limestone	25,663	770	642,565	$1,311,348	$6,838,931	$1,678,109	$1,047,282	$629,573
Lipscomb	4,044	414	93,373	$5,097,292	$10,140,072	$306,010	$37,095	$268,724
Live Oak	14,869	1,013	1,641,634	$3,223,757	$10,133,488	$1,027,457	$514,662	$511,788
Llano	30,493	514	566,661	$9,133,701	$14,203,560	$1,916,095	$1,204,507	$707,264
Loving	209	68	210,754	$1,551,103	$4,206,745	$9,483	$708	$8,776
Lubbock	258,030	1,722	4,343,111	$73,409,638	$99,771,826	$21,218,521	$17,601,948	$3,583,197
Lynn	6,735	709	472,821	$367,152	$2,930,097	$396,607	$60,657	$335,078
Madison	14,527	585	1,181,036	$10,331,367	$17,864,805	$1,375,123	$899,819	$474,055
Marion	10,551	330	285,857	$4,151,627	$6,896,469	$664,551	$243,269	$420,858

County	Vehicles Registered	Lane Miles of Highway	Vehicle Miles Driven Daily	State Construction Expenditures	Combined Construction Maintenance Expenditures	Total Vehicle Registration Fees	State Net Receipts	County Net Receipts
Martin	7,419	642	1,010,083	$8,891,534	$13,916,110	$606,006	$172,912	$432,736
Mason	6,796	421	206,844	$1,377,484	$7,147,073	$368,700	$83,451	$284,633
Matagorda	36,767	709	976,115	$2,845,189	$10,615,505	$2,408,871	$1,655,713	$750,363
Maverick	51,613	510	888,465	$2,888,848	$32,381,503	$4,068,548	$3,159,680	$907,103
McCulloch	9,772	616	336,224	$1,646,324	$10,388,243	$653,778	$211,470	$441,278
McLennan	231,153	1,766	6,583,447	$99,942,295	$133,573,387	$18,043,136	$14,587,940	$3,439,227
McMullen	1,819	324	181,898	$10,819,243	$17,009,675	$83,377	$5,740	$77,371
Medina	60,190	767	1,620,625	$4,475,728	$14,897,205	$4,512,901	$3,438,852	$1,070,414
Menard	2,984	348	158,789	$263,388	$1,572,948	$166,883	$19,886	$146,713
Midland	221,299	1,078	4,067,617	$67,422,428	$88,353,070	$21,387,230	$18,553,212	$2,820,320
Milam	31,170	712	893,403	$4,672,421	$10,901,041	$1,900,257	$1,232,728	$665,584
Mills	7,289	463	247,431	$836,737	$3,400,841	$463,620	$98,656	$364,447
Mitchell	7,192	662	729,812	$1,514,848	$16,360,545	$439,674	$87,240	$352,110
Montague	27,096	860	812,210	$22,466,564	$32,200,577	$1,808,051	$1,162,292	$643,685
Montgomery	596,714	1,580	11,187,451	$135,348,660	$153,489,038	$43,263,334	$36,107,464	$7,097,091
Moore	23,906	487	618,344	$5,442,610	$24,948,501	$1,858,224	$1,284,750	$573,013
Morris	13,678	359	484,194	$1,304,085	$5,875,761	$886,888	$468,698	$417,836
Motley	1,667	330	50,465	$1,036	$1,338,191	$88,171	$5,384	$82,761
Nacogdoches	59,219	981	1,787,416	$18,529,544	$31,554,191	$4,367,628	$3,267,687	$1,095,798
Navarro	54,161	1,276	2,326,883	$28,737,474	$47,097,331	$3,980,644	$2,990,291	$987,790
Newton	13,584	554	389,850	$3,154,512	$7,438,127	$844,218	$342,463	$501,357
Nolan	14,209	689	1,216,715	$9,548,734	$27,185,471	$947,572	$440,208	$506,033
Nueces	285,182	1,629	6,911,049	$177,833,282	$213,018,583	$22,388,585	$18,566,575	$3,803,072
Ochiltree	11,700	432	235,767	$2,143,891	$11,360,085	$1,069,033	$574,798	$493,581
Oldham	2,914	471	963,908	$3,124,543	$7,543,088	$215,178	$38,832	$176,236
Orange	80,778	657	2,936,950	$11,882,445	$23,275,795	$5,379,201	$4,144,860	$1,230,022
Palo Pinto	33,153	837	1,152,076	$13,590,814	$31,109,383	$2,299,931	$1,619,550	$677,882
Panola	26,740	774	1,002,260	$4,740,334	$17,206,563	$1,638,529	$1,184,964	$452,299
Parker	176,670	900	4,183,918	$34,919,347	$60,589,828	$13,393,987	$10,532,656	$2,841,006
Parmer	10,204	613	499,753	$4,284,470	$14,152,552	$781,117	$308,161	$472,476
Pecos	15,821	1,686	1,352,118	$17,270,189	$23,652,032	$1,222,001	$684,281	$536,719
Polk	58,417	868	1,845,931	$9,487,808	$20,001,799	$4,552,642	$3,483,824	$1,065,571
Potter	105,069	932	2,862,746	$57,351,112	$100,048,602	$8,838,179	$7,281,378	$1,546,282
Presidio	7,956	554	245,992	$4,890,655	$13,980,080	$554,187	$216,884	$337,079
Rains	16,438	269	350,061	$762,444	$5,056,313	$1,037,632	$573,591	$463,140
Randall	145,052	910	1,798,016	$36,032,198	$61,885,143	$11,554,939	$9,257,568	$2,281,689
Reagan	5,094	319	205,607	$6,956,276	$27,822,445	$414,236	$123,935	$290,247
Real	4,883	295	108,550	$239,369	$2,740,513	$313,693	$84,751	$228,394
Red River	14,556	759	449,268	$6,341,390	$23,317,210	$863,182	$363,269	$499,337
Reeves	15,108	1,179	1,699,460	$24,208,933	$54,847,544	$1,497,831	$945,846	$551,665
Refugio	8,080	464	815,561	$7,108,101	$12,235,688	$548,660	$217,633	$330,577
Roberts	1,282	244	76,854	$1,606,495	$8,407,510	$62,856	$4,266	$58,546
Robertson	21,053	661	873,547	$3,201,146	$8,065,023	$1,471,463	$872,222	$598,289
Rockwall	107,015	365	2,619,699	$34,015,706	$38,409,354	$8,436,070	$6,861,117	$1,562,799
Runnels	12,808	734	414,280	$2,133,957	$10,985,500	$829,013	$343,998	$484,006
Rusk	52,778	1,176	1,276,607	$550,572	$11,043,988	$3,639,213	$2,669,434	$967,253
Sabine	13,247	482	292,811	$580,431	$4,997,733	$838,961	$381,344	$456,720
San Augustine	9,684	536	299,324	$10,246,997	$15,690,664	$753,766	$324,112	$429,288
San Jacinto	31,005	534	922,066	$5,700,631	$10,148,253	$2,020,245	$1,308,120	$709,990
San Patricio	67,996	995	2,411,414	$36,340,167	$60,650,259	$4,760,506	$3,562,382	$1,193,464
San Saba	8,173	437	184,648	$1,097,540	$4,742,314	$486,337	$102,636	$383,234
Schleicher	4,251	361	146,081	$27,466	$1,207,391	$252,151	$45,196	$206,689
Scurry	18,868	687	641,937	$7,184,051	$12,981,345	$1,688,902	$1,101,091	$587,414
Shackelford	4,676	355	164,444	$3,751,348	$12,542,308	$439,273	$132,599	$306,540

County	Vehicles Registered	Lane Miles of Highway	Vehicle Miles Driven Daily	State Construction Expenditures	Combined Construction Maintenance Expenditures	Total Vehicle Registration Fees	State Net Receipts	County Net Receipts
Shelby	27,537	877	746,110	$2,287,483	$10,169,218	$2,065,717	$1,367,262	$697,535
Sherman	2,876	445	312,086	$488,154	$3,213,693	$262,229	$16,186	$245,978
Smith	233,611	1,618	5,895,008	$25,238,310	$53,079,435	$18,423,725	$14,786,618	$3,619,886
Somervell	11,897	199	253,653	$1,657,354	$5,377,282	$717,906	$347,339	$368,956
Starr	58,698	547	1,053,422	$13,800,340	$17,072,553	$4,068,435	$3,028,881	$1,038,427
Stephens	10,170	559	225,107	$2,775,908	$8,530,411	$694,379	$282,061	$411,788
Sterling	2,326	309	220,296	$372,444	$2,374,885	$127,516	$26,402	$101,071
Stonewall	1,885	327	71,518	$2,397,570	$6,035,249	$108,492	$5,854	$102,550
Sutton	5,453	591	648,726	$3,109,769	$14,857,694	$343,733	$94,353	$249,055
Swisher	6,891	804	450,864	$1,102,538	$6,846,938	$447,284	$83,408	$363,226
Tarrant	1,746,575	3,484	34,641,376	$308,750,319	$409,514,897	$145,249,334	$122,824,014	$22,232,913
Taylor	131,964	1,196	2,770,161	$15,343,986	$36,369,087	$10,637,631	$8,695,905	$1,931,607
Terrell	1,175	374	79,868	$14,277	$1,165,858	$56,631	$3,878	$52,707
Terry	11,506	628	559,690	$193,799	$2,077,916	$836,450	$339,602	$496,320
Throckmorton	2,168	343	92,795	$52,338	$1,589,171	$143,557	$6,616	$136,873
Titus	31,672	580	1,195,979	$13,851,857	$29,004,422	$2,411,183	$1,677,650	$732,439
Tom Green	118,749	1,047	1,888,285	$18,685,753	$39,624,958	$9,164,036	$7,184,524	$1,969,811
Travis	977,767	2,196	20,800,912	$253,844,247	$351,661,353	$75,138,054	$61,917,480	$13,088,595
Trinity	16,504	443	394,294	$818,780	$6,237,112	$1,032,196	$525,722	$505,606
Tyler	22,620	517	513,387	$17,693,976	$28,142,630	$1,447,950	$838,752	$608,556
Upshur	44,945	789	1,072,632	$5,494,796	$12,367,143	$2,725,911	$1,891,271	$832,988
Upton	5,193	392	311,817	$2,320,662	$3,715,742	$487,914	$224,992	$262,795
Uvalde	27,913	765	763,295	$581,421	$6,196,187	$2,021,560	$1,415,224	$605,053
Val Verde	48,930	748	601,305	$10,791,719	$18,199,319	$3,621,534	$2,721,529	$896,377
Van Zandt	66,114	1,173	2,645,106	$6,030,091	$17,758,926	$4,323,316	$3,188,518	$1,131,542
Victoria	89,662	935	2,696,419	$30,458,179	$43,595,581	$6,847,831	$5,276,421	$1,562,986
Walker	56,956	839	2,810,069	$60,453,492	$72,911,115	$4,209,867	$3,129,480	$1,075,176
Waller	58,654	607	2,155,552	$35,880,339	$41,396,297	$4,427,968	$3,406,866	$1,017,986
Ward	15,135	668	1,223,568	$3,522,334	-$2,109,441	$1,288,934	$987,615	$300,759
Washington	44,149	655	1,538,672	$5,826,882	$15,001,979	$3,298,477	$2,441,962	$852,992
Webb	225,598	1,224	3,611,950	$152,014,342	$179,056,264	$23,631,686	$18,392,662	$5,232,761
Wharton	48,282	926	2,051,665	$53,891,918	$65,392,164	$3,744,108	$2,835,838	$906,107
Wheeler	6,388	674	608,061	$509,764	$3,081,608	$433,411	$72,892	$360,204
Wichita	110,134	1,134	2,347,824	$7,018,507	$27,447,140	$7,896,399	$6,293,319	$1,595,430
Wilbarger	12,323	726	653,821	$4,107,342	$16,419,394	$847,807	$346,716	$500,272
Willacy	16,051	515	511,539	$13,778,496	$18,781,120	$1,066,094	$549,954	$515,429
Williamson	525,789	1,717	9,973,751	$61,604,236	$116,611,954	$41,523,598	$33,923,754	$7,530,929
Wilson	62,824	741	1,219,025	$5,486,478	$14,902,094	$4,080,584	$3,077,069	$999,110
Winkler	9,903	292	609,741	$45,049,114	$61,872,884	$959,158	$635,376	$323,345
Wise	96,086	914	2,542,384	$13,714,026	$24,599,560	$7,163,863	$5,727,801	$1,430,414
Wood	55,388	910	961,998	$2,260,859	$13,209,008	$3,764,394	$2,707,048	$1,052,603
Yoakum	10,412	431	278,526	$234,090	$2,226,761	$871,863	$403,305	$467,963
Young	23,420	703	377,179	$1,400,552	$8,155,678	$1,709,363	$1,098,358	$609,435
Zapata	12,128	289	318,623	$3,072,211	$4,787,625	$767,089	$384,779	$382,010
Zavala	9,315	541	434,692	$4,574,821	$9,437,525	$661,370	$306,414	$354,858
Total	**25,625,601**	**200,060**	**573,976,125**	**$7,151,191,904**	**$10,584,584,665**	**$2,033,992,884**	**$1,596,637,608**	**$435,377,918**

Texas Major Toll Roads						
Facilities	**Authority**	**2020**	**2019**	**2018**	**2017**	**2016**
Roads	(**Tolls Collected** in thousands of dollars)					
Central Texas Toll Facilities[1]	Central Texas Turnpike System and Regional Authority	$446,408	$306,830	$474,778	$466,552	$239,165
East Texas Toll Facilities	North East Texas Regional Authority	$11,307	$12,222	$9,111	$8,953	$8,731
Fort Bend Toll Roads	Fort Bend Toll Road Authority	$47,024	$40,167	$48,580	$27,283	$29,481
Harris County Toll Facilities[2]	Harris County Toll Road Authority	$960,117	$854,849	$1,397,750	$972,777	$759,276
North Texas Toll Facilities	North Texas Tollway Authority	$1,077,391	$911,046	$995,797	$1,366,845	$671,961
Total, roads		**$2,542,247**	**$2,125,114**	**$2,926,016**	**$2,842,410**	**$1,708,614**

[1]Including U.S. 183A and Manor Expressway. [2]Including Jesse Jones Memorial Toll Bridge.

Source: Highway Statistics annual, Federal Highway Administration; and local toll authorities.

Toll Bridges							
Facilities	**Authority**	**2019**	**2018**	**2016**	**2015**	**2014**	**2010**
Bridge	(**Tolls Collected** in thousands of dollars)						
Cameron County International Toll Bridge	Cameron County	$20,789	$20,664	$19,412	$21,273	$15,172	$22,102
Del Rio International	City of Del Rio	$8,313	$8,321	$10,268	$6,558	$5,216	$4,144
Eagle Pass International	City of Eagle Pass	$15,662	$13,857	$14,017	$10,737	$9,701	$8,106
Laredo International	City of Laredo	$71,036	$68,733	$68,887	$69,215	$54,402	$41,449
McAllen International	City of McAllen	$18,734	$19,013	$21,096	$19,799	$13,548	$11,036
Pharr International	City of Pharr	$14,539	$14,736	$18,156	$13,196	$12,362	$10,639
Roma International	Starr County	$2,420	$2,683	$2,561	$2,988	$1,871	$2,081
San Luis Pass–Vacek	Galveston County	$4,032	$579	$548	$3,128	$507	$1,265
Zaragosa	City of El Paso	$23,875	$25,275	$22,252	$21,499	$19,625	$16,094
TOTAL, bridges		**$179,400**	**$173,861**	**$177,197**	**$168,393**	**$132,404**	**$116,916**

Source: Highway Statistics annual, Federal Highway Administration.

Driver Licenses

The following list shows the number of licensed drivers by year for Texas and for all the states. Sources are the Texas Department of Public Safety (for state figures) and the Federal Highway Administration.

Year	Texas Licensed Drivers	Total U.S. Licensed Drivers
2021	18,297,900	232,781,797
2020	17,667,039	228,195,802
2019	17,822,760	228,679,719
2018	18,000,274	227,558,385
2017	17,675,389	225,346,257
2016	17,326,113	221,711,918
2015	16,970,365	218,084,465
2014	16,579,591	214,092,472
2013	16,230,209	212,159,728
2012	15,950,297	211,814,830
2011	16,880,877	211,874,649
2010	16,808,359	210,114,939
2009	16,602,416	209,618,386
2008	16,551,156	208,320,601

Year	Texas Licensed Drivers	Total U.S. Licensed Drivers
2007	16,330,825	205,741,845
2006	16,096,985	202,810,438
2005	15,831,852	200,548,972
2000	14,024,305	190,625,023
1995	12,369,243	176,628,482
1990	11,136,694	167,015,250
1985	10,809,078	156,868,277
1980	9,287,286	145,295,036
1975	7,509,497	129,790,666
1970	6,380,057	111,542,787
1965	5,413,887	98,502,152
1960	4,352,168	87,252,563
1955	3,874,834	74,685,949
1950	2,687,349	59,322,278

Motor Vehicles Crashes, Losses in Texas

Year	Number killed	†Number injured	Crashes by Kind				Vehicle Miles Traveled		Economic loss (in millions)
			Fatal	†Injury	†Non-injury	†Total	Number (in millions)	Deaths per 100 mill miles	
2022	4,481	244,092	4,037	165,792	362,808	532,637	289,965	1.55	$55,900
2021	4,497	239,709	4,068	163,438	360,941	528,447	285,224	1.58	56,100
2020	3,896	205,722	3,543	141,136	308,630	453,309	260,580	1.50	44,600
2019	3,623	256,338	3,288	172,768	363,111	539,167	288,227	1.26	40,400
2018	3,657	249,652	3,314	167,984	350,178	521,476	282,037	1.30	39,700
2017	3,726	253,852	3,432	160,926	343,680	537,970	272,981	1.36	38,401
2016	3,794	265,077	3,404	176,381	351,153	551,971	271,263	1.40	38,800
2015	3,582	247,652	3,186	165,199	332,891	521,389	258,122	1.39	36,600
2014	3,538	237,941	3,189	158,833	297,934	476,875	242,989	1.46	38,000
2013	3,407	232,599	3,065	154,458	272,601	445,829	244,536	1.39	27,800
2012	3,417	230,957	3,037	152,301	247,679	417,707	237,831	1.44	26,000
2011	3,015	211,006	2,751	138,624	226,949	381,463	235,602	1.28	21,900
2010	3,050	‡‡ 217,381	2,772	141,554	233,573	391,101	234,261	1.30	22,200
2009	3,108	234,704	2,807	154,685	251,850	428,273	232,055	1.34	20,300
2008	3,477	243,547	3,116	159,760	257,154	438,996	234,593	1.48	22,900
2007	3,463	267,305	3,098	173,052	264,098	459,689	241,746	1.43	20,600
2006	3,523	272,779	3,120	173,861	243,970	439,027	236,852	1.49	20,400
2005	3,559	293,583	3,157	184,093	257,532	464,541	234,232	1.52	19,200
2004	3,725	288,715	3,286	180,556	245,000	447,691	229,345	1.62	19,400
2003	3,823	308,543	3,372	190,926	§ 245,607	†† 460,025	218,209	1.75	20,700
2002	3,826	315,061	3,544	196,211	113,089	** 324,651	215,873	1.77	21,100
2001	3,739	340,554	3,319	207,043	113,596	323,958	216,276	1.73	9,348
2000	3,775	341,097	3,247	205,569	110,174	318,990	210,340	1.80	9,163
1999	3,519	339,448	3,106	203,220	105,375	311,701	213,847	1.60	8,729
1998	3,576	338,661	3,160	202,223	102,732	308,115	201,989	1.80	8,780
1997	3,508	347,881	3,079	205,595	97,315	305,989	194,665	1.80	7,662
1996	3,738	350,397	3,247	204,635	§ 90,261	298,143	187,064	2.00	7,766
1995	3,172	334,259	2,790	196,093	152,190	351,073	183,103	1.70	13,005
1994	3,142	326,837	2,710	192,014	219,890	414,614	172,976	1.80	12,505
1993	3,037	298,891	2,690	178,194	209,533	390,417	167,988	1.80	11,784
1992	3,057	282,025	2,690	170,513	209,152	382,355	162,769	1.90	6,725
1990	3,243	262,576	2,882	162,424	216,140	381,446	163,103	2.00	4,994
1985	3,682	231,009	3,270	151,657	300,531	452,188	143,500	2.60	3,755
1980	‡ 4,424	185,964	‡ 3,863	123,577	305,500	432,940	103,255	4.30	3,010
1975	3,429	138,962	2,945	92,510	373,141	468,596	84,575	4.10	1,440
1970	3,560	223,000	2,965	124,000	886,000	1,012,965	* 68,031	5.20	1,042
1965	3,028	186,062	2,460	103,368	365,160	470,988	* 52,163	5.80	498
1960	2,254	127,980	1,842	71,100	239,300	312,242	46,353	4.90	$350

(Note: The highest death rate was in 1966 at 6.2.)

*Method of calculating vehicle miles traveled revised. Last changed in 1982 by TxDOT.

†In August 1967, amended estimating formula received from National Safety Council (NCS). Starting 1972, actual reported injuries are listed rather than estimates.

‡Change in counting fatalities. In 1978, counted when injury results in death within 90 days of accident. In 1983, counted when injury results in death within 30 days.

§Change in counting Non-injury accidents. For 1996–2002, only crashes having at least **one vehicle towed** were tabulated.

¶Economic loss formula changed. Last changed in 2002, when figures are calculated using NCS Average Calculable Cost on a per death basis figure for the year identified. Figures are rounded to the nearest hundred million. For 1996–2001, only property damage in crashes having at least one vehicle towed was tabulated.

**Beginning with 2002 data, the "Total" crash figure includes "Unknown Severity Crashes" which are not included on this chart. Prior to 2002 these crashes were counted in the Non-injury or Injury category.

††Beginning with 2003 crashes, only those resulting in injury or death or damage to property to the apparent extent of $1,000 are tabulated.

‡‡Beginning in 2010, number injured includes incapacitating, non-incapacitating, and possible injuries.

Source: Texas Department of Transportation (TxDOT) since 2001. Earlier statistics are from the Texas Department of Public Safety (DPS).

Foreign Consulates in Texas

Source: Compiled from "Foreign Consular Offices in the United States," U.S. Dept. of State, September 2023; also Texas Secretary of State and individual consulates.

In the list below, these abbreviations appear after the name of the city: (CG) Consulate General; (C) Consulate; (VC) Vice Consulate. The letter "H" before the designation indicates honorary status. ☆

ALBANIA: **Houston (CG);** 23 Kingscote Way, The Woodlands, 77382. (281) 548-4740.

ANGOLA: **Houston; (CG);** 3040 Post Oak Blvd., Ste. 780, 77056. (713) 212-3840. angolaconsulate-tx.org

ARGENTINA: **Houston (CG);** 2200 West Loop South, Ste. 1025, 77027. (713) 871-8935. chous.cancilleria.gob.ar/en

AUSTRALIA: **Houston (CG);** 3009 Post Oak Blvd., Ste. 1310, 77056. (832) 962-8420. usa.embassy.gov.au/houston

AUSTRIA: **Houston (C);** 11000 Brittmoore Park Dr. Houston, 77041. (713) 723-9979. austrianconsulate-houston.org

BAHAMAS: **Houston (HC);** 7026 Old Katy Rd., Ste. 259, 77024. (713) 980-8791. bahamasembdc.org

BANGLADESH: **Houston (HCG);** 6060 Richmond Ave., Ste. 315 Houston, 77057. (713) 953-1056.

BARBADOS: **Houston (C);** 3027 Sleepy Hollow Dr., Sugar Land, 77479. (832) 725-5566. embassy-worldwide.com/embassy/consulate-of-barbados-in-houston-united-states

BELGIUM: **Austin (HC);** Allen-Fowler House, 1404 Wilson St., Bastrop, 78602. (512) 571-3125. unitedstates.diplomatie.belgium.be/en
Dallas (HC); 2525 East Southlake Blvd., Ste. B, Southlake, 76092. (817) 748-4367. unitedstates.diplomatie.belgium.be/en
Houston (HC); 2406 Cutter Ct., Seabrook, 77586. (770) 402-4988. unitedstates.diplomatie.belgium.be/en

BELIZE: **Houston (HC);** 1120 NASA Pkwy., Ste. 220R, 77058. (832) 390-4164.

BOLIVIA: **Houston (C);** 2401 Fountain View Dr., Ste. 110, 77057. (832) 916-4200. boliviatx.org

BOTSWANA: **Houston (HC);** 3330 Chevy Chase Dr., 77019. (713) 256-1517. botswanaembassy.org/page/honorary-consuls

BRAZIL: **Houston (CG);** 5444 Westheimer Rd., Ste. 1900, 77056. (713) 961-3063. houston.itamaraty.gov.br/en-us

CANADA: **Dallas (CG);** 500 N. Akard St., Ste. 2900, 75201. (214) 922-9806. international.gc.ca/country-pays/us-eu/dallas.aspx
Houston (C); 4201 Main St., Ste. 200, 77002. (713) 922-0822.
Austin (HC); 1701 Nueces St., 78701. (571) 217-4377.

CHILE: **Houston (CG);** 1300 Post Oak Blvd., Ste. 1130, 77056. (713) 621-5853. chile.gob.cl/houston/en
Dallas (HC); 3500 Oak Lawn Ave., Ste. 230, 75219. (214) 526-3267.

COLOMBIA: **Houston (CG);** 5599 San Felipe St., Ste. 600, 77056. (346) 204-4664. houston.consulado.gov.co

COSTA RICA: **Houston (CG);** 3100 Wilcrest Dr., Ste. 260, 77042. (713) 266-0484. costarica.org/facts/consulate

CÔTE D'IVOIRE: **Houston (HCG);** 1302 Waugh Dr., Ste. 482, 77019. (713) 410-0472.

CROATIA: **Houston (HC);** 2336 Albans Rd., 77005. (713) 444-1442.

CYPRUS: **Houston (HC);** 206 Voss Rd., 77024. (281) 704-6779.

CZECH REPUBLIC: **Temple (HC);** 520 N. Main St., 76501. (254) 931-4095.

DENMARK: **Houston (CG);** Williams Tower, 2800 Post Oak Blvd., Ste. 1910, 77056. (713) 622-9018.
Dallas (HC); 2701 Hibernia St., 75204. (214) 680-7778.

ECUADOR: **Dallas (CG);** 7510 Acorn Ln., Frisco, 75034. (972) 712-9107.
Houston (CG); 4200 Westheimer, Ste. 218, 77057. (713) 622-1787.

EGYPT: **Houston (C);** 5718 Westheimer, Ste. 1350, 77057. (713) 961-4915. egyptembassy.net/consular-services/egyptian-consulate-in-us

EL SALVADOR: **Dallas (CG);** 7610 Stemmons Fwy. Ste. 400, 75247. (214) 637-1500. rree.gob.sv/embajadas-consulados-y-misiones-permanentes-de-la-republica-de-el-salvador
El Paso (CG); 400 W. San Antonio St., Ste. B, 79901. (915) 600-5423.
Houston (CG); 8300 Bissonnet St., Ste. 400, 77074. (346) 571-5198.
Laredo (CG); 6010 McPherson Rd., Ste 140, 78041. (956) 701-3852.
McAllen (CG); 701 S. Broadway St., 78501. (956) 800-1363.

EQUATORIAL GUINEA: **Houston (CG);** 6401 Southwest Fwy., 77074. (713) 776-9900.

ESTONIA: **Dallas (HC);** 4444 Belfort Pl., 75205. (214) 417-2020. washington.mfa.ee/estonian-honorary-consuls-in-usa
Houston (HC); 3318 Spring Trail Dr., Sugar Land 77479. (281) 770-3009.

ETHIOPIA: **Houston (HC);** 9301 Southwest Fwy., Ste. 250, 77074. (713) 271-7567.

FINLAND: **Dallas (HC);** 2021 McKinney Ave., Ste. 1600, 75201. (214) 999-4672. finlandabroad.fi/web/usa/honorary-consulates
Houston (HC); 2001 Kirby Dr., Ste. 1300, 77019. (281) 216-5132.

FRANCE: **Houston (CG);** 777 Post Oak Blvd., Ste. 600, 77056. (346) 272-5363. houston.consulfrance.org
Dallas (HC); 1911 N. Lamar St., Ste. 300, 75202.
El Paso (HC); 12270 Rojas Dr., 79936. (915) 892-1660.
San Antonio (HC); 6106 Broadway, 78209.

(210) 859-1308.

GEORGIA: **Houston (HC);** 410 Pierce St., Ste. 220, 77002. (281) 766-7784.

GERMANY: **Houston (CG);** 1330 Post Oak Blvd., Ste. 1850, 77056. (713) 627-7770. germany.info/houston
Austin (HC); 912 S. Capital of. Hwy., Ste. 450, 78746. (512) 852-4162.
Dallas (HC); 17130 Dallas Parkway, Ste. 240, 75248. (972) 354-7000.

GHANA: **Houston (HC);** 3535 Westheimer Rd., Ste. 235, 77027. (713) 960-1950.

GREECE: **Houston (C);** 2401 Fountain View Dr., Ste. 850, 77057. (713) 840-7522. mfa.gr/usa/en/consulate-in-houston

GUATEMALA: **Houston (CG);** 6300 Richmond Ave., Ste. 103, 77057. (713) 953-9531. conshouston.minex.gob.gt/home/home.aspx
Del Rio (C); 106 Foster Dr., 78840. (830) 422-2230. consdelrio.minex.gob.gt
McAllen (C); 709 Broadway St., 78501. (956) 429-3413. consmcallen.minex.gob.gt

GUYANA: **Houston (C);** 1810 Woodland Park Dr., 77077. (281) 497-4466.

HONDURAS: **Dallas (CG);** 2520 W. Irving Blvd., Ste. 400, Irving, 75061. (214) 347-4441.
Houston (CG); 7400 Harwin St., 2nd Fl., 77036. (713) 785-5932.
McAllen (C); 1209 Galveston Ave., 78501. (956) 627-3172.

HUNGARY: **Houston (VC);** 5847 San Felipe St., Ste. 1700, 77057. (713) 914-1675. hungary.honoraryconsulate.network/houston

ICELAND: **Dallas (HC);** 6827 Northwood Rd., 75225. (214) 415-2331.
Houston (HC); 11110 South Country Sq., 77024. (713) 382-3546.

INDIA: **Houston (CG);** 4300 Scotland St., 77007. (713) 626-2148. cgihouston.gov.in

INDONESIA: **Houston (CG);** 10900 Richmond Ave., 77042. (713) 785-1691. kemlu.go.id

IRELAND: **Austin (CG);** 515 Congress Ave., Ste. 1720, 78701. (512) 792-5500. dfa.ie/irish-consulate/austin
Houston (HC); 2630 Sutton Ct.,, 77027. (713) 961-5263.

ISRAEL: **Houston (CG);** 24 Greenway Plaza, Ste. 1500, 77046. (832) 301-3500. embassies.gov.il/houston

ITALY: **Houston (CG);** 1330 Post Oak Blvd., Ste. 1950, 77056. (713) 850-7520. conshouston.esteri.it
Dallas (HC); 8303 Elmbrook Dr.,, 75247. (214) 754-1832.
San Antonio (HC); 2255 W. Mistletoe Ave., 78201. (210) 735-7232.

JAMAICA: **Houston (HC);** 6001 Savoy Dr., Ste. 509, 77036. (713) 541-3333.

JAPAN: **Houston (CG);** 2 Houston Center, 909 Fannin St., Ste. 3000, 77010. (713) 652-2977. houston.us.emb-japan.go.jp/itprtop_en
Dallas (HC); 4524 Bentley Dr. Plano, 75093. (972) 596-5012.

KOREA: **Houston (CG);** 1990 Post Oak Blvd., Ste. 1250, 77056. (713) 961-0186. overseas.mofa.go.kr/us-houston-en/index.do
Dallas (C); 14001 N. Dallas Pkwy., Ste. 450, 75240. (972) 701-0180. overseas.mofa.go.kr/us-houston-en/index.do

KYRGYZSTAN: **Houston (HC);** 15600 Barkers Landing Rd., #1, 77079. (281) 920-1841.

LATVIA: **Houston (HC);** 2120 Troon Rd., 77019. (713) 304-3831.

LITHUANIA: **Houston (HC);** 4030 Case St., 77005. (713) 665-4218.

LUXEMBOURG: **Austin (HC);** 2700 Via Fortuna Dr., Ste. 500, 78746. (512) 413-3603.

MALAWI: **Wimberley (HC);** 35 Champion Circle, 78676. (512) 569-7998.

MALI: **Austin (HC);** 2000 Lipanese Trail, 78733.

MALTA: **Dallas (HC);** 7739 Southwestern Blvd., 75227. (972) 883-4785.

MEXICO: **Austin (CG);** 5202 E. Ben White Blvd., Ste. 150, 78741. (512) 478-2866. consulmex.sre.gob.mx/austin/index.php

MEXICO: **Dallas (CG);** 1210 River Bend Dr., 75247. (214) 932-8670. consulmex.sre.gob.mx/dallas
Del Rio (CG); 2207 N. Bedell Ave., 78840. (830) 775-2352. consulmex.sre.gob.mx/delrio
Eagle Pass (CG); 2252 E. Garrison St., 78852. (830) 773-9255. consulmex.sre.gob.mx/eaglepass
El Paso (CG); 910 E. San Antonio Ave., 79901. (915) 747-3259. consulmex.sre.gob.mx/elpaso
Houston (CG); 10555 Richmond Ave., 77042. (713) 271-6800. consulmex.sre.gob.mx/houston
Laredo (CG); 1612 Farragut St., 78040. (956) 723-0990 consulmex.sre.gob.mx/laredo
Presidio (CG); 319 W. 21 de Marzo St., 79845. (432) 229-2788. consulmex.sre.gob.mx/presidio
San Antonio (CG); 127 Navarro St. San Antonio, 78205. (210) 227-9145. consulmex.sre.gob.mx/sanantonio
Brownsville (C); 301 Mexico Blvd., Ste. F2, 78520. (956) 542-4431 consulmex.sre.gob.mx/brownsville/index.php
McAllen (C); 600 S. Broadway St., 78501. (956) 686-0243. consulmex.sre.gob.mx/laredo

MONGOLIA: **Comfort (HC);** 622 High St., 78013. (830) 995-5014. mongolianembassy.us/honoraryconsuls

MOROCCO: **Dallas (HC);** 325 N. St. Paul St., Ste. 4200, 75201. (972) 839-2234.

NAMIBIA: **Houston (HC);** 617 Caroline St., #3, 77002. (832) 242-2426. namibiaembassyusa.org/about-embassy/honorary-consuls
San Antonio (HC); 106 S. St. Mary's St., Ste. 200, 78205. (210) 846-0630.

NETHERLANDS: **Houston (HC);** 10777 Westheimer Rd., Ste. 1055, 77042. (713) 783-7743.

NEW ZEALAND: **Houston (HC);** 3300 N. Sam Houston Pkwy. E., 77032. (713) 670-4384. mfat.govt.nz/en/countries-and-regions/americas/united-states-of-america/new-zealand-embassy-to-the-united-states-of-america

NICARAGUA: **Houston (CG);** 6009 Richmond Ave., Ste. 100, 77057. (713) 789-2762.

NORWAY: **Dallas (HC);** 100 Crescent Ct., 75201. (214) 880-4604.

PAKISTAN: **Houston (CG);** 11850 Jones Rd., 77070. (281) 890-1433. pakistanconsulatehouston.org

PANAMA: **Houston (CG);** 24 Greenway Plz., Ste. 710, 77046. (713) 622-4451. conpahouston.com
Austin (HC); 101 Knarr St., 78734. (512) 386-1461

PARAGUAY: **Houston (HC);** 4707 Welford Dr., Bellaire, 77401. (713) 444-9887.

PERU: **Dallas (CG);** 13601 Preston Rd., Ste. E-650, 75240. (972) 234-0005. consulado.pe/es/Dallas/Paginas/Inicio.aspx
Houston (CG); 5177 Richmond Ave., Ste. 695, 77056. (713) 355-9517. consulado.pe/es/Houston/Paginas/Inicio.aspx

PHILIPPINES: **Houston (CG);** 9990 Richmond Ave., Ste. 100N, 77042. (346) 293-8773.

POLAND: **Houston (CG);** 3040 Post Oak Blvd., Ste. 525, 77056. (713) 479-6770. gov.pl/web/usa-en/consulate-houston

PORTUGAL: **Houston (HC);** 721 Buckingham Dr., 77024. (713) 515-5272.

QATAR: **Houston (CG);** 1990 Post Oak Blvd., Ste. 900, 77056. (713) 355-8221. houston.consulate.qa/en/the-consulate/contact

ROMANIA: **Houston (HCG);** 19927 Parsons Green Ct., Katy, 77450. (713) 629-1551. washington.mae.ro/en/node/411
Dallas (HC); Hartford Bldg., 400 N. St. Paul St., Ste. 505, 75201. (214) 522-3799.

RUSSIA: **Houston (CG);** 1333 West Loop South, Ste. 1300, 77027. (713) 337-3300. washington.mid.ru/en/consular-services/consulate/contacts

RWANDA: **Houston (HCG);** 70 Terra Bella Dr., Manvel, 77578. (832) 687-0753.

SAUDI ARABIA: **Houston (CG);** 5718 Westheimer Rd, Ste. 1500, 77057. (713) 785-5577. saudiembassy.net/saudi-offices

SIERRA LEONE: **Dallas (HC);** 1919 S. Shiloh Rd., Ste. 540, Garland, 75042. (214) 552-5613.

SLOVAKIA: **Dallas (HC);** 10670 N. Central Expwy., Ste. 300, 75231. (214) 224-0075. mzv.sk/en/web/washington-en/contact-us

SLOVENIA: **Houston (HC);** 11300 Kingsworthy Ln., 77024. (713) 278-1366

SOUTH AFRICA: **Dallas (HC);** 400 S. Zang Blvd., Ste. 1018, 75208. (214) 943-4120

SPAIN: **Houston (C);** 1800 Bering Dr., Ste. 750, 77057. (713) 783-6200. exteriores.gob.es/Consulados/houston/en/Paginas/index.aspx
Austin (HC); 303 Colorado St., Ste. 2000, 78701. (512) 297-5884.
Corpus Christi (HC); 7314 Kolda Dr., 78414. (361) 994-7517.
Dallas (HC); 5454 La Sierra Dr., Ste. 200, 75231. (214) 373-1200.
El Paso (HC); 14 Cumberland Cir., 79903. (915) 274-9563.
San Antonio (HC); 9601 McAllister Fwy., Ste. 401, 78216. (210) 569-8484.

SRI LANKA: **Houston (HC);** 6200 Savoy Dr., Ste. 270,, 77036. (832) 287-1677.

SWEDEN: **Houston (CG);** River Oaks Tower, 3730 Kirby Dr., Ste. 805, 77098. (713) 953-1417. swedishconsulate.org
Dallas (C); 6301 Gaston Ave., Ste. 1322, 75205. (214) 308-2590.

SWITZERLAND: **Dallas (HC);** 2501 N. Harwood St., Ste. 1400, 75201. (214) 965-1025. eda.admin.ch/countries/usa/en/home/representations/embassy-washington/honorary-consulates.html
Houston (HC); 9114 N. Allegro St., 77080. (713) 854-3758.

THAILAND: **Houston (HCG);** 3 Greenway Plaza, Ste. 800, 77046. (713) 335-3907. thaiconsulatehouston.com

TRINIDAD AND TOBAGO: **Houston (HC);** 9 Parkside Rd., The Hills, 78738. (713) 816-6477. foreign.gov.tt/missions-consuls/tt-missions-abroad/honorary-consuls

TURKEY: **Houston (CG);** 5333 Westheimer Rd., Ste. 1050, 77056. (713) 622-5849. houston.cg.mfa.gov.tr

UGANDA: **Dallas (HC);** 12801 N. Central Expwy., Ste. 750, 75243. (214) 675-7330. washington.mofa.go.ug/consuls/texas

UKRAINE: **Houston (CG);** 3040 Post Oak Blvd., Suite 1250, 77056. (281) 822-0432. houston.mfa.gov.ua/en

UNITED ARAB EMIRATES: **Houston (CG);** 2200 Post Oak Blvd., Ste. 1500, 77056. (832) 956-6666. mofa.gov.ae/en/missions/houston

UNITED KINGDOM: **Houston (CG);** 1301 Fannin St., Ste. 2400, 77002. (713) 210-4000. gov.uk/world/organisations/british-consulate-general-houston

URUGUAY: **Dallas (HCG);** 700 N. Pearl St., Ste. 1100, 75225. (214) 586-0651.
Houston (HCG); 1220 S. Ripple Creek Dr., 77057. (713) 974-7855.

VIETNAM: **Houston (CG);** 5251 Westheimer Rd., 77056. (713) 850-1233.

Foreign-Trade Zones in Texas

Source: U.S. Department of Commerce.

Foreign-trade-zone status endows a domestic site with certain customs privileges, causing it to be considered outside customs territory and therefore available for activities that might otherwise be carried on overseas.

Operated as public utilities for qualified corporations, the zones are established under grants of authority from the Foreign-Trade Zones board, which is chaired by the U.S. Secretary of Commerce. Zone facilities are available for operations involving storage, repacking, inspection, exhibition, assembly, manufacturing, and other processing.

A foreign-trade zone is especially suitable for export processing or manufacturing operations when foreign components or materials with a high U.S. duty are needed to make the end product competitive in markets abroad.

In 2023, there were 34 Foreign-Trade Zones in Texas. ☆

Zone	Location	Port of Entry	Address	Phone
012	McAllen	Hidalgo	6401 S. 33rd Street, 78503	(956) 682-4306
036	Galveston	Galveston	P.O. Box 328, 77553	(409) 766-6203
039	Dallas/Fort Worth Airport	Dallas-Fort Worth	P.O. Box 619428, 2400 Aviation Drive, DFW Airport 75261	(972) 973-4649
062	Brownsville	Brownsville-Cameron	1000 Foust Road, 78521	(956) 592-3961
068	El Paso	El Paso	501 George Perry, Suite I, 79925	(915) 212-0480
080	San Antonio	San Antonio	100 W. Houston, Ste. 1800, 78205	(210) 207-3906
084	Houston	Houston	111 East Loop North, 77029-4327	(713) 670-2576
094	Laredo	Laredo	5210 Bob Bullock Loop, 78041	(956) 795-2000
095	Starr County	Rio Grande City	P.O. Box 502, Rio Grande City 78582	(956) 487-2709
096	Eagle Pass	Eagle Pass	100 S. Monroe, 78852	(830) 773-1111 x2003
113	Ellis County	Dallas-Fort Worth	P.O. Box 788, Midlothian 75065	(972) 723-5522
115	Beaumont	Port Arthur	P.O. Drawer 2297, 77704	(409) 835-5367
116	Port Arthur	Port Arthur	P.O. Drawer 2297, Beaumont 77704	(409) 835-5367
117	Orange	Port Arthur	P.O. Drawer 2297, Beaumont 77704	(409) 835-5367
122	Corpus Christi	Corpus Christi	400 Harbor Drive, 78401	(361) 885-6187
149	Freeport	Freeport	1100 Cherry Street, 77541	(979) 233-2667 x4320
150	El Paso	El Paso	1865 Northwestern Dr., 79912	(915) 877-4300
155	Calhoun/Victoria counties	Port Lavaca	P.O. Drawer 397, Point Comfort 77978	(361) 987-2813
156	Hidalgo County	Progreso	100 E. Cano, Suite 201, Edinburg 78539	(956) 318-2600
165	Midland	Midland International Airport	9506 Laforce Blvd., P.O. Box 60305, Midland 79711	(432) 560-2200
168	Dallas	Dallas-Fort Worth	P.O. Box 613307, 75261	(972) 357-1044
171	Liberty County	Houston	117 Cook Street, Dayton 77535	(281) 659-7213
183	Austin	Austin	Greater Austin Chamber of Commerce, 535 E. 5th Street, 78701	(512) 595-0741
196	Fort Worth	Fort Worth Alliance Airport	9800 Hillwood Parkway, Suite 300, 76177	(817) 224-6011
199	Texas City	Houston	1801 9th Avenue N., 77590	(409) 643-5927
234	Gregg County	Shreveport-Bossier Cty, LA	269 Terminal Circle, Longview 75603	(903) 643-3031
246	Waco	Dallas-Fort Worth	P.O. Box 1220, 76703	(254) 752-6551
252	Amarillo	Amarillo	600 S. Tyler St., Suite 1600, 79101	(806) 379-6411
258	Bowie County	Shreveport-Bossier Cty, LA	107 Chapel Lane, New Boston 75570	(903) 223-9841
260	Lubbock	Lubbock	500 Broadway, 6th Floor, 79401	(806) 723-8227
265	Conroe (Montgomery County)	Houston	P.O. Box 3066, 77305	(936) 522-3530
269	Athens	Dallas-Fort Worth	201 W. Corsicana St., Suite 3, 75751	(903) 675-4617
297	Lufkin	Port Arthur	P.O. Box 190, 300 E. Shepherd, 75902	(936) 633-0221
299	Smith County	LA, Shreveport-Bossier Cty	315 N. Broadway, Suite 300, Tyler 75702	(903) 595-1064

Annual Tonnage Handled by Major/Minor Texas Ports

Source: U.S. Corps of Engineers.

Table below gives consolidated tonnage (x1,000) handled by Texas ports. All figures are in short tons (2,000 lbs.). Note that "—" indicates no commerce was reported and "0" means tonnage reported was less than 500 tons. ☆

Port	2020	2019	2018	2017	2015	2010	2005	2000	1995	1990
Beaumont	70,567	101,090	100,244	89,437	87,170	76,959	78,887	76,894	20,937	26,729
Brownsville	6,782	6,633	8,348	7,763	7,779	4,616	5,105	3,268	2,656	1,372
Corpus Christi	150,755	111,224	93,236	87,323	85,647	73,663	77,637	81,164	70,218	60,165
Freeport	38,749	29,844	25,258	24,484	21,133	26,676	33,602	28,966	19,662	14,526
Galveston	11,945	10,958	9,112	7,836	10,381	13,949	8,008	10,402	10,465	9,620
Houston	275,940	284,944	227,834	224,374	240,933	227,133	211,666	186,567	135,231	126,178
Matagorda Channel (Port Lavaca)	4,760	5,221	5,380	4,279	11,821	8,879	11,607	10,552	9,237	6,097
Port Arthur	41,222	33,944	39,852	39,203	35,787	30,232	26,385	20,524	49,800	30,681
Sabine Pass	23,000	22,002	18,801	13,887	418	2,494	641	910	231	631
Texas City	33,347	40,889	42,682	39,662	42,924	56,591	57,839	58,109	50,403	48,052
Victoria Channel	2,033	2,673	3,861	4,337	6,733	2,792	3,224	5,104	4,624	3,740
Anahuac	—	—	—	—	—	—	—	—	—	0
Aransas Pass	38	45	640	280	917	173	128	6	181	169
Arroyo Colorado	1,658	666	330	271	260	411	791	837	994	765
Cedar Bayou	1,071	1,811	1,656	1,785	1,271	931	1,172	1,002	473	219
Chocolate Bayou	1,134	1,103	1,177	1,108	1,171	1,005	3,537	3,488	3,480	3,463
Clear Creek	—	—	—	—	—	—	—	—	—	0
Colorado River	781	760	875	541	848	671	501	445	576	476
Dickinson	365	450	512	545	491	93	688	904	657	556
Double Bayou	—	—	—	—	—	—	257	0	—	0
Greens Bayou	3,984	6,645	6,993	6,416	6,427	5,523	3,768	0	0	0
Harbor Island (Port Aransas)	77	121	232	27	28	1	10	151	209	—
Liberty Channel	808	3	—	—	16	5	—	—	—	0
Orange	4,095	1,574	1,236	659	838	684	627	681	693	710
Palacios	—	—	—	—	—	—	—	—	—	0
Port Isabel	31	—	0	8	0	0	—	5	130	269
Port Mansfield	—	—	—	—	—	—	—	—	20	102
Rockport	—	—	—	—	—	—	—	—	—	644
San Bernard River	41,203	194	171	117	317	371	773	633	653	534
TOTAL*	**638,340**	**574,061**	**524,583**	**524,583**	**514,012**	**486,658**	**487,100**	**452,991**	**371,021**	**335,312**

*Excludes duplication.

Foreign/Domestic Commerce: Breakdown for 2020

Data below represent inbound and outbound tonnage for major ports. Note that "—" means no tonnage was reported. All figures in short tons x1000.

Source: U.S. Corps of Engineers

Port	Foreign		Domestic		
	Imports	Exports	Receipts	Shipments	Local
Beaumont	16,171	29,610	6,992	15,634	2,159
Brownsville	3,696	309	2,395	376	6
Corpus Christi	17,606	108,093	3,995	16,986	4,075
Freeport	6,560	28,017	1,668	2,319	13
Galveston	1,525	5,177	—	—	—
Houston	42,310	113,001	2,742	8,189	70,998
Matagorda Chl. (Port Lavaca)	482	1,657	85	570	1,968
Port Arthur	7,317	16,609	7,600	9,154	543
Sabine Pass	224	20,641	1,812	340	—
Texas City	7,601	13,579	3,869	8,476	196
Victoria	—	—	637	1,396	—

Gulf Intracoastal Waterway by Commodity (Texas portion)

All figures in short tons x1000.

Source: U.S. Army Corps of Engineers

Commodity	2020	2019	2015	2010	2005	2000	1995
Coal	242	365	125	93	335	121	162
Petroleum products	50,103	53,738	57,224	49,219	39,538	34,816	40,496
Chemicals	16,791	16,060	17,475	17,553	20,668	21,382	26,818
Raw materials	5,540	4,056	3,910	3,123	4,898	5,822	6,544
Manufactured goods	1,705	2,130	1,631	1,646	2,449	2,301	2,056
Food, farm products	433	399	903	574	473	960	1,216
Total	**74,814**	**76,748**	**81,268**	**72,917**	**69,549**	**66,440**	**78,386**

U.S. ports ranked by tonnage, 2020 (short tons)

1. **Houston Port Authority....... 275,940,289**
2. Port of South Louisiana.............. 225,086,697
3. **Corpus Christi......................... 150,755,485**
4. New York, NY & NJ...................... 123,697,438
5. New Orleans, LA............................. 81,067,448
6. Port of Long Beach, CA................ 79,178,087
7. Port of Greater Baton Rouge, LA. 71,686,872
8. **Beaumont.......................................70,567,386**
9. Port of Los Angeles, CA................ 59,452,139
10. Port of Virginia, VA........................ 58,048,785

States ranked by tonnage, 2020 (x1,000 short tons)

1. **Texas...........................607,805**
2. Louisiana.......................485,439
3. California.......................214,920
4. New Jersey....................131,877
5. Washington...................109,703
6. Florida................................90,297
7. Kentucky............................76,730
8. Illinois................................75,112
9. Ohio....................................68,511
10. Alabama..............................63,979

U.S. Freight Gateways, 2020

Source: U.S. Bureau of Transportation Statistics, National Transportation Statistics, annual.

Top gateways ranked by value of shipments, with Texas gateways highlighted. In billions of dollars ($214.8 represents $214,800,000,000). ☆

Rank	Port	Mode	Exports	Imports	Total Trade	Exports as a percent of total
1	John F. Kennedy International Airport, NY	Air	$78.5	$137	$215.5	36.4%
2	Chicago, IL (Port)	Air	52.6	161.6	214.2	24.6
3	Laredo, Texas	Land	79.9	121.6	201.4	39.7
4	Los Angeles, CA	Water	27.9	169.1	196.9	14.2
5	New York, NY	Water	38.1	149	187.1	20.4
6	Long Beach, CA	Water	29.2	118.4	147.5	19.8
7	Houston, TX	Water	72.8	51.8	124.7	58.4
8	Detroit, Michigan	Land	65.1	53.2	118.3	55.0
9	Los Angeles International Airport, CA (Port)	Air	48.2	69.1	117.3	41.1
10	Savannah, GA	Water	26.7	76.2	102.9	25.9
11	New Orleans, LA (Port)	Air	37.8	41.9	79.7	47.4
12	Charleston, SC	Water	26.1	46	72	36.3
13	Port Huron, Michigan	Land	33.6	37.9	71.5	47.0
14	Norfolk, VA	Water	27.1	43.6	70.7	38.3
15	Cleveland, OH (Port)	Air	39.1	29.9	68.9	56.7
16	Buffalo-Niagara Falls, New York	Land	32	30	61.9	51.7
17	San Francisco International Airport, CA (Port)	Air	32.3	26.6	58.8	54.9
18	Anchorage, AK (Port)	Air	15.2	39.7	54.9	27.7
19	Atlanta, GA (Port)	Air	15.1	38.9	54	28.0
20	Miami International Airport, FL (Port)	Air	30.7	21.9	52.6	58.4
21	Oakland, CA	Water	20.4	30.3	50.7	40.2
22	Baltimore, MD	Water	12.7	36.8	49.5	25.7
23	Dallas-Fort Worth, TX (Port)	Air	21.7	27	48.8	44.5
24	Otay Mesa, California	Land	15.1	29.4	44.5	33.9
25	Ysleta Port of Entry	Land	13.8	27.3	41.1	33.6
26	Tacoma, WA	Water	7.2	32.5	39.6	18.2
27	Newark, NJ (Port)	Air	6.7	30.1	36.8	18.2
28	Corpus Christi, TX	Water	32.5	3.9	36.4	89.3
29	Hidalgo, Texas	Land	11.5	20.3	31.8	36.2
30	El Paso, Texas	Land	15.1	14.1	29.3	51.5
31	New Orleans, LA	Water	16.6	12.2	28.8	57.6
32	Eagle Pass, Texas	Land	7.6	20.5	28	27.1
33	Santa Teresa, New Mexico	Land	9.9	13.8	23.7	41.8
34	Seattle, WA	Water	7.5	16.1	23.7	31.6
35	Pembina, North Dakota	Land	12.1	10.8	22.9	52.8
36	Miami, FL	Water	7.8	14.4	22.2	35.1
37	New Orleans Customs District n.e.c.	Land	13.1	8.9	22	59.5
38	Nogales, Arizona	Land	8.5	13.4	21.9	38.8
49	Brownsville, Texas	Land	$8.1	$7.1	$15.2	53.3%

Border Crossings at U.S. Ports of Entry, 2022

Below are statistics for selected states as to incoming border traffic at ports of entry into the United States. Data are from the U.S. Bureau of Transportation Statistics. Total in thousands. "%" refers to Texas' percent of U.S. total.

Entering at border	U.S. total	%	Texas	California	New York	Arizona	Michigan
Buses	110,402	53.7%	59,303	17,721	10,471	7,998	2,307
Bus Passengers	2,313,785	58.5%	1,352,569	231,211	247,185	230,224	24,546
Personal Vehicles	87,509,943	37.2%	32,590,240	30,246,680	4,622,006	9,404,110	3,512,469
Personal Vehicle Passengers	155,366,112	38.8%	60,224,826	49,210,767	9,439,951	16,978,897	6,068,372
Pedestrians	36,071,311	38.9%	14,034,169	16,104,055	143,837	5,466,508	0
Trucks	9,226,551	54.8%	5,053,160	1,572,053	1,430,298	452,848	2,320,769
Truck Containers (Empty)	3,408,765	42.0%	1,433,034	501,684	253,619	121,766	490,292
Truck Containers (Loaded)	9,226,551	37.8%	3,489,418	1,128,985	1,086,429	335,340	1,810,992
Trains	31,690	29.8%	9,431	425	2,896	810	5,227
Train Passengers	49,224	1.9%	918	501	12,866	2,028	7,863
Rail Containers (Empty)	1,423,007	38.1%	541,963	12,709	45,178	30,815	263,330
Rail Containers (Loaded)	2,219,093	21.7%	480,630	641	162,225	49,632	340,086

Public Administration

Source: Texas Transportation Institute

In 1945, the Texas Aeronautics Commission (TAC) was created and directed by the legislature to encourage, foster, and assist in the development of aeronautics within the state, and to encourage the establishment of airports and air navigational facilities. The Commission's first annual report of Dec. 31, 1946, stated that Texas had 592 designated airports and 7,756 civilian aircraft.

The TAC's commitment to providing air transportation was strengthened in 1989 when the TAC became the Texas Department of Aviation (TDA). And on Sept. 1, 1991, when the Texas Department of Transportation (TxDOT) was created, the TDA became the Aviation Division within the department.

The primary responsibilities of the Aviation Division include providing engineering and technical services for planning, constructing, and maintaining aeronautical facilities in the state. It is also responsible for long-range aviation facility development planning (statewide system of airports) and applying for, receiving, and disbursing federal funds.

In the Texas Airport System Plan, TxDOT has identified 289 airports and three heliports. Of the airports, 26 are commercial airports, 24 are reliever airports, and 239 are general aviation airports.

Additionally, TxDOT's Aviation Division has requested Federal Aviation Administration Reliever status for five airports. These include the privately owned Austin Executive and Houston Executive airports, as well as the publicly owned New Braunfels Municipal, Mid-Way Regional (at Midlothian), and Cleburne municipal airports.

Commercial-service airports provide scheduled passenger service. Reliever airports are a special class of general aviation airports designated by the Federal Aviation Administration (FAA). They provide alternative landing facilities in the metropolitan areas separate from the commercial-service airports and, together with the business/corporate airports, provide access for business and executive turbine-powered aircraft.

The community-service and basic-service airports provide access for single- and multi-engine, piston-powered aircraft to smaller communities throughout the state. Some community-service airports are also capable of accommodating light jets.

TxDOT is charged by the legislature with planning, programming, and implementing improvement projects at the general aviation airports. In carrying out these responsibilities, TxDOT channels the Airport Improvement Program (AIP) funds provided by the FAA for all general aviation airports in Texas.

Since 1993, TxDOT has participated in the FAA's state block grant demonstration program. Under this program, TxDOT assumes most of the FAA's responsibility for the administration of the AIP funds for airports.

The Aviation Facilities Development Program (AFDP) oversees planning and research, assists with engineering and technical services, and provides financial assistance through state grants to public bodies operating airports for the purpose of establishing, constructing, reconstructing, enlarging, or repairing airports, airstrips, or navigational facilities.

The 85th Legislature appropriated funds to TxDOT, which subsequently allocated a portion of those funds to the Aviation Division. TxDOT allocated approximately $15 million annually for the 2018-2019 biennium to the Aviation Division to help implement and administer the AFDP. These funds are in addition to the block grant funds received through the FAA's AIP. ☆

Passenger Enplanement by Airport

Airport	2022	2021	2020	2019	2017	2015	2013
Abilene	70,419	75,402	44,202	81,813	86,386	88,959	78,847
Amarillo	358,360	303,904	173,469	353,124	334,102	347,304	373,946
Austin	10,382,573	6,666,215	3,141,505	8,507,410	6,580,031	5,643,251	4,809,854
Beaumont	24,882	21,914	15,792	29,068	24,880	35,557	26,070
Brownsville	127,239	167,957	93,145	129,407	119,912	147,831	88,292
College Station	54,542	67,033	41,790	83,832	74,552	91,243	84,379
Corpus Christi	319,687	285,195	162,161	328,109	318,810	339,105	309,480
D/FW	35,345,138	30,005,266	18,593,421	35,778,573	31,433,095	31,356,173	28,946,438
Dallas/Love	7,819,129	6,487,563	3,669,930	8,080,506	7,537,325	6,495,869	3,971,077
Del Rio*	26,641	19,879	8,296	22,439	—	—	6,846
El Paso	1,931,067	1,438,321	760,165	1,745,770	1,442,605	1,370,243	1,377,876
Harlingen	508,867	355,190	172,878	335,381	271,086	263,423	354,717
Houston/Bush	19,814,052	16,242,821	8,682,558	21,905,309	19,556,778	20,346,164	18,821,429
Houston/Hobby	6,462,948	5,560,780	3,127,178	7,069,614	6,392,225	5,765,544	5,213,512
Killeen-Ft. Hood	126,160	142,253	102,324	176,630	131,836	153,698	175,992
Laredo	139,396	108,992	52,612	91,043	94,970	113,176	106,524
Longview	25,982	23,942	14,632	27,160	20,682	19,871	20,207
Lubbock	489,710	405,157	253,126	520,181	453,680	446,081	454,661
McAllen	452,925	477,636	191,497	422,434	339,132	390,358	332,769
Midland	633,964	504,264	319,570	672,382	498,248	533,049	502,303
San Angelo	54,347	60,115	35,595	66,390	60,061	64,901	60,127
San Antonio	4,751,610	3,677,643	1,919,958	5,022,980	4,300,499	4,057,345	3,998,343
Texarkana	35,590	26,888	17,340	37,492	34,574	35,469	31,214
Tyler	40,548	39,943	29,133	59,807	49,075	77,543	81,277
Victoria	7,505	6,610	2,837	5,734	3,259	3,129	4,204
Waco	54,899	47,541	27,704	62,907	61,340	63,256	59,809
Wichita Falls	27,720	32,038	21,272	40,418	39,064	45,426	43,994
TOTAL	**90,085,900**	**73,250,462**	**41,674,090**	**91,655,913**	**78,293,968**	**70,334,187**	**68,529,262**

*Del Rio lost commercial service in 2013 and regained service in 2018. Calendar year data.

Sources: FAA Terminal Area Forecasts and Passenger Enplanement for US Airports 2019.

Texas Air History

Source: Federal Aviation Administration.

Passengers enplaned in Texas by scheduled carriers. A scheduled airline runs on specific routes at specific times. Texarkana is not included here; fiscal year data. ☆

2022........................90,089,634
2021........................73,274,996
2020........................41,687,899
2019........................91,618,421
2018........................86,428,773
2017........................80,223,633
2016........................80,187,617
2015........................78,261,315
2014........................73,714,180
2013........................70,305,633
2012........................69,059,805
2011........................68,505,347
2010........................66,850,320
2009........................66,155,323
2008........................69,906,579
2005........................65,718,669
2000........................65,090,784
1995........................57,166,515
1990........................49,317,029
1985........................40,659,223
1980........................26,216,873
1975........................13,182,957
1970........................10,256,691
1965........................5,757,689
1960........................3,113,582
1950........................1,169,051

Leading US Airlines by Passengers, 2020

Rank	Airline	Passengers
1	**Southwest Airlines**	**67,785,236**
2	**American Airlines**	**65,746,004**
3	Delta Air Lines	55,052,730
4	United Airlines	37,853,386
5	SkyWest Airlines	20,315,865
6	Spirit Airlines	18,310,615
7	JetBlue Airways	14,299,267
8	Alaska Airlines	12,181,494
9	Frontier Airlines	11,203,318
10	Republic Airline	8,773,761

Texas-based airlines in bold. *Source: U.S. Department of Transportation.*

AGRICULTURE

MARES AND FOALS IN A FIELD AT CANNON QUARTER HORSE RANCH IN ELLIS COUNTY
PHOTO BY CAROL M. HIGHSMITH, PUBLIC DOMAIN

Texas farmers are leading the nation in switching to more efficient irrigation systems like this center-pivot system, located on a winter wheat cover crop in Morton, Cochran County. Photo by USDA NRCS Texas, Public Domain

Agriculture in Texas

Information was collected from Texas A&M AgriLife Extension specialists, Texas Agricultural Statistics Service, U.S. Department of Agriculture, and U.S. Department of Commerce. Caroline Gleaton, Administrative Associate V; John Robinson, Professor and Extension Specialist-Cotton Marketing; and Mark Welch, Extension Economist-Grain Marketing, Texas A&M AgriLife Extension Service compiled the information. All references are to Texas unless otherwise specified. For information on the lumber industry, see page 71 in the Environment chapter.

Agribusiness, the combined phases of food and fiber production, processing, transporting, and marketing, is a leading Texas industry. Most of the following discussion is devoted to the initial phase of production on farms and ranches.

Texas agriculture is an important industry. Agricultural production is associated with considerable upstream and downstream economic activity. Many businesses, financial institutions, and individuals are involved in providing supplies, credit, and services to farmers and ranchers, and in processing and marketing agricultural commodities.

The potential for further growth is favorable. With the increasing demand for food and fiber throughout the world, and because of the importance of agricultural exports to the nation's trade balance, agriculture in Texas is destined to play an important role in the future.

Major efforts of research and educational programs by the Texas A&M University System are directed toward developing the state's agricultural industry to its fullest potential. The goal is to capitalize on natural advantages that agriculture has in Texas because of the relatively warm climate, productive soils, and availability of excellent export and transportation facilities.

Texas Farms

The number and nature of farms have changed over time. The number of farms in Texas has decreased from 420,000 in 1940 to 246,000 in 2022 with an average size of 512 acres. The number of small farms is increasing—but part-time farmers and ranchers operate them.

Mechanization of farming continues as new and larger machines replace workforce and smaller equipment. Even though machinery price tags are higher than in the past, machines are technologically advanced and efficient. Tractors, mechanical harvesters, and numerous cropping machines have virtually eliminated menial tasks that for many years were traditional to farming.

Revolutionary agricultural chemicals and genetically engineered traits have appeared along with improved plants and animals. Many of the natural hazards of farming and ranching have been reduced by better use of weather information, machinery, and other improvements. However, the adoption of such technologies implies rising capital, labor, and energy costs.

Changes in Texas agriculture in the last 50 years include:

1. More detailed record keeping that assists in management and marketing decisions;
2. More restrictions on choice or inputs/practices;

3. Adoption of precision agriculture through the use of satellites, computers, global positioning systems (GPS), and other high-tech tools to help producers manage inputs such as seed, fertilizers, pesticides, and water.

Farms have become fewer, larger, specialized, and much more expensive to own and operate. They are also far more productive. Meanwhile, the number of small farms operated by part-time farmers is increasing. Land ownership is becoming more of a lifestyle for recreational purposes. The number of off-farm landowners is increasing.

Irrigation continues to be an important factor in crop production. Crops and livestock have made major changes in production areas, as in the concentration of cotton on the High Plains and livestock industries in Central and Eastern Texas. Pest and disease control methods have greatly improved. Herbicides are relied upon for weed control.

Feedlot finishing, commercial broiler production, artificial insemination, improved pastures and brush control, reduced feed requirements, and other changes have greatly increased livestock and poultry efficiency. Biotechnology and genetic engineering promise new breakthroughs in reaching even higher levels of productivity. Horticultural plant and nursery businesses have expanded. Improved wildlife management has increased deer, turkey, and other wildlife populations. The use of land for recreation and ecotourism is growing.

Farmers and ranchers are better educated and informed and more science and business oriented. Today, agriculture operates in a global, high-tech, consumer-driven environment.

Cooperation among farmers in marketing, promotion, and other fields has increased. Also, agricultural producers have become increasingly dependent on off-the-farm services to supply production inputs such as feeds, chemicals, credit, and other essentials.

Agribusiness

Texas farmers and ranchers have developed considerable dependence upon agribusiness. With many producers specializing in the production of certain crops and livestock, they look beyond the farm and ranch for supplies and services. On the input side, they rely on suppliers of production needs and services, and on the output side they need assemblers, processors, and distributors.

Since 1940, the proportion of Texans whose livelihood is linked to agriculture has changed greatly. In 1940, about 23% of Texans were producers on farms and ranches, and about 17% were suppliers or were engaged in assembly, processing, and distribution of agricultural products. The agribusiness alignment in 2008 reflected less than 2% on farms and ranches with about 15% of the labor force providing production or marketing supplies and services and retailing food and fiber products.

Cash Receipts by Commodities, 2017–2021

COMMODITIES	2017	2018	2019	2020	2021	Percent of 2021
	(All values in thousands of dollars)					
All Commodities	**$ 22,242,427**	**21,402,164**	**20,624,434**	**20,390,842**	**24,785,523**	**100.0%**
Animals and products	**14,437,152**	**14,268,806**	**14,348,704**	**14,387,381**	**16,776,174**	**67.7%**
Meat animals	9,095,448	8,696,035	8,682,144	9,016,656	10,413,821	42.0%
Cattle and calves	8,899,836	8,473,061	8,439,243	8,794,871	10,053,767	40.6%
Hogs	195,612	222,974	242,901	221,785	360,054	1.5%
Dairy products, milk	2,213,152	2,168,608	2,640,193	2,757,636	2,833,922	11.4%
Poultry and eggs	2,702,579	2,984,390	2,602,999	2,188,428	3,101,407	12.5%
Broilers	2,231,814	2,374,520	2,165,130	1,659,867	2,518,594	10.2%
Misc. livestock †	425,973	419,773	423,368	424,661	427,024	1.7%
Crops	**7,805,274**	**7,133,358**	**6,275,729**	**6,003,461**	**8,009,348**	**32.3%**
Food grains	348,966	500,477	473,760	440,359	678,387	2.7%
Rice	147,896	155,112	172,332	162,092	193,831	0.8%
Wheat	198,545	342,506	298,252	275,012	480,666	1.9%
Feed crops	1,742,490	1,681,655	1,839,677	1,873,724	2,888,703	11.7%
Corn	1,010,355	1,029,645	1,102,881	901,148	1,486,278	6.0%
Sorghum	319,035	226,114	308,846	394,310	601,701	2.4%
Hay	410,626	410,581	419,469	568,474	795,547	3.2%
Cotton	3,443,599	2,991,571	2,465,937	2,038,567	2,660,097	10.7%
Oil crops	227,383	217,182	147,356	201,209	192,075	0.8%
Vegetables and melons	438,316	440,654	274,056	360,383	333,445	1.4%
Fruits and nuts	221,729	156,682	163,350	128,410	136,685	0.6%
All other crops ‡	1,382,791	1,145,137	911,594	960,809	1,119,956	4.5%

† Includes catfish, honey, mohair, wool, chicken eggs, farm chickens, turkeys, and other animals and products.
‡ Includes miscellaneous vegetables and other field crops.
Values are rounded to the nearest thousand. Sub-categories may not sum to total because not all sub-categories are reported.

Source: USDA/ERS Farm Income and Wealth Statistics.

Cash Receipts

Farm and ranch cash receipts in 2021 totaled $24.8 billion, with estimates of $1.8 billion for direct government payments. Realized gross farm income totaled $30.6 billion, with farm production expenses of $22.5 billion and net farm income totaling $8.1 billion.

Percent of Income from Products

Livestock and livestock products accounted for 67.7% of the $24.8 billion cash receipts from farm marketings in 2021, with the remaining 32.3% from crops. Receipts from livestock have trended up largely because of increased feeding operations and reduced crop acreage associated with farm programs and low prices. However, these relationships change continuously because of variations in commodity prices and volume of marketings.

Cattle and calves accounted for 40.6% of total cash receipts (excluding government payments) received by Texas farmers and ranchers in 2021. Milk made up 11.4% of receipts, poultry and eggs 12.5%, hogs 1.5%, and miscellaneous livestock 1.7%.

Cotton accounted for 10.7% of total receipts, while feed crops was 11.7%, food grains 2.7%, vegetables and melons 1.4%, oil crops 0.8%, fruits and nuts 0.6%, and other crops 4.5%.

Texas' Rank Among States

Measured by cash receipts from crops and livestock, Texas ranked fourth in 2021; California ranked first; Iowa ranked second; and Nebraska ranked third.

Texas normally leads all other states in numbers of farms and ranches and farm and ranch land, cattle slaughtered, cattle on feed, calf births, sheep and lambs, goats, cash receipts from livestock marketings, cattle and calves, beef cows, sheep and lambs, wool production, mohair production, and exports of fats, oils, and greases. Texas also usually leads in production of cotton.

Texas Agricultural Exports

The value of Texas' share of agricultural exports in fiscal year 2021 was $7.3 billion. Cotton accounted for $2.0 billion of the exports; corn was $366.4 million and processed grain products was $141.1 million; feed and other feed grains, $390.1 million; wheat, $291.2 million; vegetable oils, $14.1 million; rice, $115.0 million; hides and skins, $120.6 million; beef and veal and pork, $1,556.2 million; broiler meat, $300.2 million; other poultry products, $104.1 million; fresh and processed fruits, $47.8 million; tree nuts, $77.0 million; soybeans and soybean meal, $24.9 million; fresh and processed vegetables, $134.0 million; dairy products, $516.5 million; and miscellaneous and other products, $1.1 billion.

Export Shares of Commodities

Commodity	2018	2019	2020	2021	2021 % of U.S. Total*
	(All values in millions of dollars)				
Beef and veal	1,056.2	1,030.8	1,064.7	1,451.9	13.8%
Pork	68.4	77.2	89.3	104.3	1.3%
Hides and skins	144.3	103.2	89.5	120.6	10.3%
Other livestock products [1]	219.4	232.1	254.6	302.9	6.1%
Dairy products	337.1	385.1	440.5	516.5	6.8%
Broiler meat	235.8	246.8	238.9	300.2	8.0%
Other poultry products [2]	86.4	76.1	81.7	104.1	4.0%
Vegetables, fresh	41.1	30.2	36.0	44.4	1.6%
Vegetables, processed	79.3	57.8	69.7	89.6	1.6%
Fruits, fresh	59.8	37.0	37.4	25.5	0.6%
Fruits, processed	51.1	32.1	31.0	22.3	0.6%
Tree nuts	63.3	71.2	68.3	77.0	0.9%
Rice	104.3	116.1	106.5	115.0	5.9%
Wheat	193.9	214.8	195.3	291.2	4.0%
Corn	264.3	172.5	174.8	366.4	2.0%
Feeds and other feed grains [3]	257.3	263.0	308.3	390.1	3.4%
Grain products, processed	113.5	128.7	130.6	141.1	3.6%
Soybeans	19.1	12.1	19.8	20.7	0.1%
Soybean meal	5.7	2.8	3.7	4.2	0.1%
Vegetable oils	17.4	12.1	15.1	14.1	0.4%
Other oilseeds and products[4]	125.2	105.0	143.2	108.9	5.2%
Cotton	2,622.7	2,222.2	1,783.9	1,969.6	34.6%
Other plant products [5]	714.1	562.8	564.6	686.7	3.4%
Total agricultural exports*	**6,879.9**	**6,191.9**	**5,947.4**	**7,267.3**	**4.2%**
Total animal products*	**2,147.5**	**2,151.3**	**2,259.3**	**2,900.5**	**7.5%**
Total plant products*	**4,732.3**	**4,040.6**	**3,688.2**	**4,366.8**	**3.3%**

* Totals may not add due to rounding.
1 Includes other nonpoultry meats, animal fat, live farm animals, and other animal parts.
2 Includes turkey meat, eggs, and other fowl products.
3 Includes processed feeds, fodder, barley, oats, rye, and sorghum.
4 Includes peanuts (oilstock), other oil crops, corn meal, other oilcake and meal, protein substances, bran, and residues.
5 Includes sweeteners and products, other horticulture products, planting seeds, cocoa, coffee, and other processed foods.

Data sources: USDA, Economic Research Service; USDA, Foreign Agricultural Service, Global Agricultural Trade System.

In 2021, Texas' exports of $7.3 billion of farm and ranch products compares with $6.0 billion in 2020 and $6.2 billion in 2019.

Hunting

The management of wildlife as an economic enterprise through leasing for hunting makes a significant contribution to the economy of many counties. Leasing the right of ingress on a farm or ranch for the purpose of hunting is the service marketed. After the leasing, the consumer—the hunter—goes onto the land to seek the harvest of the wildlife commodity. Hunting lease income to farmers and ranchers in 2022 was estimated at $810 million.

The demand for hunting opportunities is growing while the land capable of producing huntable wildlife is decreasing. As a result, farmers and ranchers are placing more emphasis on wildlife management practices to help meet requests for hunting leases.

Irrigation

Agricultural irrigation in Texas peaked in 1974 at 8.6 million acres. Over the next 20 years, irrigation declined due to many factors including poor farm economics, falling water tables in certain regions, energy costs for irrigation pumping, and the movement of much of the vegetable production from South Texas to Mexico. For the past 15 years, total irrigated area has stabilized and fluctuates from year to year between 6 million and 6.4 million acres. This puts Texas third in the nation, behind California and Nebraska in agricultural irrigation.

Although some irrigation is practiced in nearly every county of the state, about 60% of the total irrigated acreage is on the High Plains of Texas. Other concentrated areas of irrigation are the Upper Gulf Coast rice-producing area, the Lower Rio Grande Valley, the Winter Garden area of South Texas, and the Trans-Pecos area of West Texas.

Sprinkler irrigation is used on about 75% of the total irrigated acreage, with surface irrigation methods, primarily furrow and surge methods, on much of the remaining irrigated area. Texas growers are continuing the switch to center pivot irrigation machines. Texas farmers lead the nation in the adoption of efficient irrigation technologies, particularly LEPA (low energy precision application)

Realized Gross Income* and Net Income from Farming 1984–2021

Year	**Realized Gross Farm Income	Farm Production Expenses	†Net Change In Farm Inventories	***Total Net Farm Income	***Total Net Income Per Farm
	(Values in millions of dollars)				(dollars)
1984	11,692.6	10,257.3	186.1	1,435.3	7,398.30
1985	11,375.3	9,842.8	– 9.0	1,532.5	7,981.90
1986	10,450.1	9,272.8	– 349.0	1,177.3	6,196.60
1987	12,296.6	10,038.7	563.2	2,257.9	12,010.10
1988	12,842.3	10,331.7	– 128.4	2,510.6	13,076.20
1989	12,843.1	10,328.4	– 798.6	2,514.7	12,962.10
1990	14,421.5	11,012.9	343.9	3,408.6	17,391.00
1991	14,376.4	11,270.3	150.0	3,106.1	15,767.00
1992	14,482.5	10,617.6	464.1	3,864.9	19,519.80
1993	15,817.0	11,294.6	197.0	4,522.5	20,745.40
1994	15,394.5	11,134.7	107.7	4,259.9	19,363.00
1995	15,678.9	12,537.3	243.7	3,141.6	14,151.30
1996	15,025.0	12,006.6	– 290.1	3,018.4	13,475.10
1997	16,430.7	12,718.5	709.2	3,712.3	16,498.90
1998	15,506.0	12,047.4	– 817.1	3,458.6	15,269.70
1999	17,469.5	12,441.9	196.0	5,027.6	22,099.30
2000	16,810.1	12,707.8	– 50.2	4,102.3	17,968.90
2001	18,089.0	13,106.6	113.4	4,982.5	21,795.70
2002	16,567.9	11,372.8	436.8	5,195.1	22,686.00
2003	20,105.7	13,687.6	– 137.7	6,418.1	28,026.60
2004	21,826.4	14,343.8	539.0	7,482.5	32,674.70
2005	21,928.5	15,371.6	306.7	6,556.8	28,507.90
2006	20,329.6	16,010.9	– 753.8	4,318.7	18,777.00
2007	24,738.0	19,800.2	948.6	4,937.7	19,950.30
2008	22,523.4	19,674.0	– 1,174.8	2,849.4	14,282.10
2009	20,648.8	18,562.9	– 980.9	2,085.9	9,133.80
2010	23,474.2	18,807.4	46.6	4,666.6	22,404.40
2011	26,004.5	21,429.7	– 2,494.0	4,574.7	21,811.90
2012	27,430.8	23,842.1	– 1,075.4	3,588.8	NA
2013	29,303.2	24,202.8	– 171.2	5,100.4	NA
2014	30,319.8	26,512.7	407.2	3,807.1	NA
2015	29,218.7	23,186.3	– 416.4	6,032.4	NA
2016	24,629.3	22,105.5	– 77.5	2,523.9	NA
2017	26,374.2	22,250.2	– 789.1	4,124.0	NA
2018	25,707.6	21,545.2	– 1,177.7	4,162.4	NA
2019	26,139.9	20,584.6	– 998.9	5,555.3	NA
2020	26,401.2	20,625.5	–932.5	5,775.6	NA
2021	30,608.2	22,484.6	–$294.8	8,123.6	NA

* Details for items may not add to totals because of rounding.
**Cash receipts from farm marketings, government payments, value of home consumption and gross rental value of farm dwellings.
***Farm income of farm operators.
† A positive value of inventory change represents current-year production not sold by December 31. A negative value is an offset to production from prior years included in current-year sales.

Source: "Economic Indicators of the Farm Sector, State Financial Summary, 1985", 1987", 1989", 1993", USDA/ERS; "Farm Business Economics Report", August 1996, "Texas Agricultural Statistics Service, October, 2010". "Farm Income and Wealth Statistics", USDA/ERS. NA = Not available

A dust storm blows over cotton fields ahead of a late-summer thunderstorm in Terry County in August 2022. Photo by Justin Rex for The Texas Tribune

and LESA (low elevation spray application) center pivot systems, both of which were developed by Texas A&M AgriLife Research and the Texas A&M AgriLife Extension Service.

The use of drip irrigation continues to increase and accounts for about 10% of the total irrigated acreage. Drip irrigation is routinely used for vegetables, vineyards, and tree crops such as citrus, pecans, and peaches. Some drip irrigation of cotton, forages, and peanuts is being practiced in West Texas. Farmers continue to experiment with drip irrigation, but the relatively high costs and management requirements are limiting more widespread use. One exception is the Texas fast-growing wine industry, where drip irrigation is almost exclusively used for vineyards.

Agricultural irrigation uses about 53% of all freshwater in the state, and landscape irrigation accounts for about 40% of total municipal water use during the summer months. Texas is one of only a handful of states that require a state irrigator's license for the design and installation of landscape and residential irrigation systems. Cities of 20,000 persons or larger are required to have irrigation inspectors to ensure that landscape irrigation systems meet state design and installation requirements. However, no license or certification is required for the design or installation of agricultural irrigation systems.

To meet **future water demand for our rapidly growing cities and industries**, several regions of the state are looking at water transfers from agriculture. The largest water transfer project is likely the San Antonio Water System Vista Ridge Pipeline, which is designed to transfer 16 billion gallons per year from the Carrizo and Simsboro aquifers in Burleson County to San Antonio. The long-term effects on water availability in Burleson County and surrounding areas are uncertain.

Texas water planning documents estimate that as much as 30% of future water demand could be met through agricultural irrigation conservation. However, state funding for such programs continues to decline. In about 20% of the irrigated area, water is delivered to farms through canals and pipelines by irrigation and other types of water districts and by river authorities. Many of these delivery networks are aging, in poor condition, and have high seepage losses. It is estimated that over 30% of all water diverted by irrigation districts is lost in the conveyance systems.

Approximately 80% of the state's irrigated acreage is supplied with water pumped from wells. Surface water sources supply the remaining area. Periods of droughts continue to plague Texas. The droughts over the last 20 years, in particular have greatly impacted water availability from surface sources (rivers, reservoirs, etc.). As a result, the number of groundwater wells increased rapidly throughout South and West Texas, which could impact future water availability. Declining groundwater levels in several major aquifers is a serious problem, particularly in the Ogallala Aquifer in the Texas High Plains, and the southern portion of the Carrizo-Wilcox formation.

Texas common law grants the landowner with broad rights to exploit the underlying groundwater. Laws and regulations governing groundwater use enacted in Texas over the last 50 years attempt to recognize the landowner's right to beneficially use the water, while giving water districts certain powers to manage and restrict water use. Legal battles are ongoing between these two interests. However, an increasing number of groundwater conservation districts are establishing water use limits for agricultural irrigation. The Edwards Aquifer Authority has a voluntary irrigation "opt-out" program, the first of its kind in Texas, where farmers receive payments in exchange for not irrigating during drought years.

Irrigation is an important factor in the productivity of Texas agriculture. The value of crop production from irrigated acreage is 50% to 60% of the total value of all crop production, although only about 30% of the state's total harvested cropland acreage is irrigated.

The Irrigation section was provided by Guy Fipps, Professor and Extension Agricultural Engineer, Texas A&M University.

Main Crops

In 2021, the value of crop production in Texas was 32.3% of the total value of the state's agricultural output. Cash receipts from farm sales of crops are reduced somewhat because some grain and roughage is fed to livestock on farms where produced. Drought has reduced receipts in recent years.

Receipts from all Texas crops totaled $8.0 billion in 2021, $6.0 billion in 2020, and $6.3 billion in 2019.

Cotton, corn, grain sorghum, and wheat account for a large part of the total crop receipts. In 2021, cotton contributed about 33.2% of the crop total; corn, 18.6%; and wheat, 6.0%. Hay, cottonseed, vegetables, peanuts, rice, soybeans, and grain sorghum are other important cash crops.

Cotton

Cotton has been a major crop in Texas for more than a century. Since 1880, Texas has led all states in cotton production in most years, and today the annual Texas all cotton harvest amounts to around 21.5% of total production in the United States. The annual Texas all cotton crop has averaged 5.71 million 480-lb. bales since 1996.

Value of upland cotton produced in Texas in 2022 was $1.3 billion. Cottonseed value in 2022 was $406.4 million—making the value of the Texas crop around $1.7 billion.

Upland cotton was harvested from 2.0 million acres in 2022 and American-Pima from 29,000 acres, for a total of 2.03 million acres. The relatively low level of harvested acreage in 2022 was due to historically land drought conditions. Yield for upland cotton in 2022 was 734 pounds per harvested acre, with American-Pima yielding 728 pounds per acre. Total cotton production for 2022 was 3.1 million 480-lb. bales. Upland cotton acreage harvested in 2021 totaled 5.6 million and American-Pima harvested 16,000 acres for total cotton acreage of 5.6 million acres. The yield for upland cotton was 666 pounds per acre and 780 pounds per acre for American-Pima. Total cotton production amounted to 7.7 million 480-lb. bales in 2021 and 4.7 million 480-lb. bales in 2020.

Cotton is the raw material for processing operations at gins, oil mills, compresses, and a small number of textile mills in Texas. Cotton in Texas is machine harvested. Field storage of harvested seed cotton has become common practice as gins decline in number.

Most of the Texas cotton crop is exported. China, Turkey, Mexico, and various Pacific Rim countries are major buyers. With the continuing development of fiber spinning technology and the improved quality of Texas cotton, the export demand for Texas cotton has grown.

Grain Sorghum

Texas grain sorghum, in 2022, ranked number two in value of production in the U.S., with Kansas being number one. Much of the grain is exported, as well as used in livestock and poultry feed throughout the state. Ethanol production is a more recent demand source for Texas sorghum.

Total production of grain sorghum in 2022 was 50.4 million bushels, with 53 bushels per acre yield from 950,000 acres harvested. With an average price of $10.80 per cwt., the total value reached $304.5 million. In 2021, 1.9 million acres of grain sorghum were harvested, yielding

Value of Cotton & Cottonseed 1983–2022

	Upland Cotton		Cottonseed	
Crop Year	Production (Bales)	Value	Production (Tons)	Value
	(All figures in thousands)			
1983	2,380	$ 680,870	1,002	$ 162,324
1984	3,680	962,688	1,563	157,863
1985	3,910	968,429	1,635	102,156
1986	2,535	560,945	1,053	82,118
1987	4,635	1,325,981	1,915	157,971
1988	5,215	1,291,651	2,131	238,672
1989	2,870	812,784	1,189	141,491
1990	4,965	1,506,182	1,943	225,388
1991	4,710	1,211,789	1,903	134,162
1992	3,265	769,495	1,346	145,368
1993	5,095	1,308,396	2,147	255,493
1994	4,915	1,642,003	2,111	215,322
1995	4,460	1,597,037	1,828	201,080
1996	4,345	1,368,154	1,784	230,136
1997	5,140	1,482,787	1,983	226,062
1998	3,600	969,408	1,558	204,098
1999	5,050	993,840	1,987	160,947
2000	3,940	868,061	1,589	162,078
2001	4,260	580,723	1,724	159,470
2002	5,040	967,680	1,855	191,065
2003	4,330	1,199,237	1,616	202,000
2004	7,740	1,493,510	2,895	301,080
2005	8,440	1,879,757	2,869	289,739
2006	5,800	1,288,992	2,066	243,776
2007	8,250	2,391,840	2,861	443,409
2008	4,450	935,568	1,547	351,192
2009	4,620	1,328,342	1,634	254,904
2010	7,840	3,006,797	2,685	413,490
2011	3,500	1,375,920	1,228	354,892
2012	5,000	1,675,200	1,669	442,285
2013	4,170	1,493,194	1,368	347,472
2014	6,175	1,739,868	1,946	354,579
2015	5,720	1,564,992	1,844	413,056
2016	8,100	2,593,296	2,528	490,432
2017	9,270	2,950,085	2,852	393,576
2018	6,850	2,232,552	2,088	331,992
2019	6,320	1,762,522	1,902	317,634
2020	4,700	1,373,904	1,443	269,841
2021	7,700	3,444,672	2,403	600,750
2022	3,060	1,328,448	940	406,448

Source: Texas Agricultural Facts@, USDA/NASS Crop Production Annual Summary, January; and Crop Values Annual Summary, February. USDA/NASS Quick Stats data syster

an average of 61 bushels per acre for a total production of 114.1 million bushels. It was valued at $10.20 per cwt., for a total value of $651.6 million. In 2020, 1.5 million acres were harvested with an average of 63 bushels per acre, or 94.5 million bushels. The season's average price was $7.57 per cwt. for a total value of $400.6 million.

Although grown to some extent in all counties where crops are important, the largest concentrations are in the High Plains, Coastal Bend, and the Lower Rio Grande Valley areas.

Research to develop high-yielding hybrids resistant to diseases and insect damage continues. A history of grain sorghum appeared in the 1972–1973 edition of the *Texas Almanac*.

Rice

Rice, which is grown in about 20 counties on the Coastal Prairie of Texas, ranked third in value among Texas crops for a number of years. However, in 2022, cotton, hay, corn, wheat, and grain sorghum outranked rice.

Rice farms are highly mechanized, producing rice through irrigation and using airplanes for much of the planting, fertilizing, and application of insecticides and herbicides.

Texas farmers grow long- and medium-grain rice only. The Texas rice industry, which has grown from 110 acres in 1850 to a high of 642,000 planted acres in 1954, has been marked by significant yield increases and improved varieties. Record production was in 1981, with 27.2 million cwt. harvested. Highest yield was 8,370 pounds per acre in 2012.

Several different types of rice milling procedures are in use today. The simplest and oldest method produces a product known as **regular milled white rice**, the most prevalent on the market today.

During this process, rice grains are subjected to additional cleaning to remove chaff, dust, foreign seed, etc., and then husks are removed from the grains. This results in a product that is the whole unpolished grain of rice with only the outer hull and a small amount of bran removed. This product is called brown rice and is sometimes sold without further treatment other than grading. It has a delightful nutlike flavor and a slightly chewy texture.

When additional layers of the bran are removed, the rice becomes white in color and begins to appear as it is normally recognized at retail level. The removal of the bran layer from the grain is performed in a number of steps using two or three types of machines. After the bran is removed, the product is ready for classification as to size. Rice is more valuable if the grains are not broken. In many cases, additional vitamins are added to the grains to produce what is called "enriched rice."

Another process may be used in rice milling to produce a product called **parboiled rice**. In this process, the rice is subjected to a combination of steam and pressure prior to the time it is milled in the manner described above. This process gelatinizes the starch in the grain, the treatment aiding in the retention of much of the natural vitamin and mineral content. After cooking, parboiled rice tends to be fluffy, more separate, and plump.

Still another type of rice is **precooked rice**, which is actually milled rice that, after milling, has been cooked. Then the moisture is removed through a dehydration process. Precooked rice requires a minimum of preparation time since it needs merely to have the moisture restored to it.

The United States produces only a small part of the world's total rice, but it is one of the leading exporters. American rice is popular abroad and is exported to more than 100 foreign countries.

Texas rice production in 2022 totaled 12.1 million cwt. from 186,000 harvested acres, with a yield of 6,510 pounds per acre. The crop value totaled $207.0 million. Rice production was 12.4 million cwt. in 2021 on 181,000 harvested acres, yielding 6,860 pounds per acre. Total value in 2021 was $176.4 million. Rice production was 14.6 million cwt. in 2020 on 179,000 harvested acres. Production in 2020 was valued at $194.1 million, with a yield of 8,150 pounds per acre.

Wheat

Wheat for grain is one of the state's most valuable cash crops. In 2022, wheat was exceeded in value by cotton, hay, and corn. Wheat pastures also provide considerable winter forage for cattle that is reflected in value of livestock produced.

Texas wheat production totaled 39.0 million bushels in 2022 as yield averaged 30.0 bushels per acre. Planted acreage totaled 5.3 million acres and 1.3 million acres were harvested. With an average price of $9.10 per bushel, the 2022 wheat value totaled $354.9 million. In 2021, Texas wheat growers planted 5.5 million acres and harvested 2.0 million acres. The yield was 37.0 bushels per acre for 2021 with total production of 74.0 million bushels at $6.51 per bushel valued at $481.7 million.

Texas wheat growers planted 4.9 million acres in 2020 and harvested grain from 2.1 million acres. The yield was 30.0 bushels per acre for a total production of 61.5 million bushels valued at $314.8 million or $5.12 per bushel.

Wheat was first grown commercially in Texas near Sherman about 1833. The acreage expanded greatly in North Central Texas after 1850 because of rapid settlement of the state and introduction of the well-adapted Mediterranean strain of wheat. A major family flour industry was developed in the Fort Worth/Dallas/Sherman area between 1875 and 1900. Now, around half of the state's acreage is planted on the High Plains and about a third of this is irrigated. Most of the Texas wheat acreage is of the hard red winter class. Because of the development of varieties with improved disease resistance and the use of wheat for winter pasture, there has been a sizable expansion of acreage in Central and South Texas.

Most wheat harvested for grain is used in some phase of the milling industry. The better-quality hard red winter wheat is used in the production of commercial bakery flour. Lower grades and varieties of soft red winter wheat are used in family flours. By-products of milled wheat are used for feed.

Corn

Interest in corn production throughout the state has increased since the 1970's as yields improved with new varieties. Once the principal grain crop, corn acreage declined as plantings of grain sorghum increased. Only 500,000 acres were harvested annually until the mid-1970s when development of new hybrids occurred.

Harvested acreage was 1.6 million in 2022; 1.9 million in 2021; and 1.8 million in 2020. Yields for the corresponding years (2022–2020) were 95, 128, and 128 bushels per acre, respectively.

Most of the acreage and yield increase has occurred in Central and South Texas. In 2022, corn ranked third in value of production among the state's crops. It was valued at $1.1 billion in 2022, $1.5 billion in 2021, and $1.1 billion in 2020. The grain is largely used for livestock feed, but other important uses are in ethanol and food products.

Oats

Oats are grown extensively in Texas for winter pasture, hay, silage, and greenchop feeding, and some acreage is harvested for grain.

Of the 450,000 acres planted to oats in 2022, 35,000 acres were harvested. The average yield was 55 bushels per acre. Production totaled 1.9 million bushels with a value of $11.9 million, or $6.20 per bushel. In 2021, 460,000 acres were planted. From the plantings, 35,000 acres were harvested, with an average yield of 45 bushels per acre for a total production of 1.6 million bushels. Average price per bushel was $4.87 and total production value was $7.7 million.

Texas farmers planted 470,000 acres of oats in 2020. They harvested 60,000 acres that averaged 45 bushels per acre for a total production of 2.7 million bushels at an average price of $4.17 per bushel with an estimated value of $11.3 million. Most of the acreage was used for grazing.

Almost all oat grain produced in Texas is utilized as feed for livestock within the state. A small acreage is grown exclusively for planting seed.

Sugarcane, Sugar, and Seed

Sugarcane is grown from seed cane planted in late summer or fall. It is harvested 12 months later and milled to produce raw sugar and molasses. Raw sugar requires additional refining into its final form and is offered to consumers.

The sugarcane grinding mill operated at Santa Rosa in Cameron County is considered one of the most modern mills in the United States. Texas sugarcane-producing counties include Cameron, Hidalgo, and Willacy.

At a yield of 22.6 tons per acre, sugarcane, sugar, and seed production in 2022 totaled 705,000 tons from 31,200 harvested acres. In 2021, 36,400 acres were harvested for total production of 1.1 million tons valued at $29.5 million. The yield was 30.9 tons per acre. In 2020, 35,900 acres were harvested, from which 1.1 million tons of sugarcane were milled. The yield averaged 31.7 tons per acre for a total value of $26.5 million.

Texas Crop Production, 2022

Crop	Harvested Acres	Yield Per Acre	Unit	Total Production (thousands)	Cash Value (thousands of dollars)
Corn, grain	1,610,000	95.0	Bu.	152,950.0	1,147,125.0
Corn, silage	260,000	15.0	Ton	3,900.0	—
Cotton, American-Pima	29,000	728.0	Lb:Bale	44.0	—
Cotton, Upland	2,000,000	734.0	Lb:Bale	3,060.0	1,328,448.0
Cottonseed	—	—	Ton	940.0	406,448.0
Grapefruit*	12,000	140.0	Box	31,338.0	33,945.0
Hay, Alfalfa	90,000	4.2	Ton	378.0	94,500.0
Hay, excluding Alfalfa	4,100,000	1.5	Ton	6,150.0	1,045,500.0
Hay, All	**4,190,000**	**1.6**	**Ton**	**6,528.0**	**1,140,000.0**
Oats	35,000	55.0	Bu.	1,925.0	11,935.0
Onions (fresh market)	9,000	260.0	Cwt.	2,340.0	121,680.0
Oranges*	6,500	31.0	Box	3,419.0	3,769.0
Peanuts	120,000	2,800.0	Lb.	336,000.0	131,040.0
Pecans*	100,000	250.0	Lb.	25,000.0	42,364.0
Potatoes	12,500	575.0	Cwt.	7,188.0	112,852.0
Rice	186,000	6,510.0	Lb:cwt.	12,105.0	206,996.0
Sorghum, Grain	950,000	53.0	Bu:cwt.	50,350.0	304,517.0
Sorghum, Silage	175,000	15.0	Ton	2,625.0	—
Soybeans	85,000	20.0	Bu.	1,700.0	21,760.0
Sugarcane for sugar & seed	31,200	22.6	Ton	705.0	—
Sunflowers	45,000	1,363.0	Lb.	61,350.0	16,553.0
Wheat, Winter	1,300,000	30.0	Bu.	39,000.0	354,900.0
Total of Listed Crops	**11,291,200**	—	—	—	**5,532,382.0**

* Grapefruit, Texas 80-lb./box; Oranges, Texas 85-lb./box; Pecan production and value are utilized in-shell basis.

USDA/NASS, annual crop production, January; annual crop values, February.

Paul Bauer (right), NRCS Conservation Technician, discusses conservation plans with a cotton and sugarcane farmer near San Benito. Photo by USDA NRCS Texas, Public Domain

Hay, Silage, and Other Forage Crops

A large proportion of Texas' agricultural land is devoted to forage crop production. This acreage produces much of the feed requirements for the state's large domestic livestock population as well as game animals.

Approximately 87.9 million acres of pasture and rangeland, which are primarily in the western half of Texas, provide grazing for beef cattle, sheep, goats, horses, and game animals. An additional 8.3 million acres are devoted to cropland used only for pasture or grazing. The average annual acreage of forage land used for hay, silage, and other forms of machine-harvested forage is around 5 million acres.

All hay accounts for a large amount of this production with some corn and sorghum silage being produced. The most important hay crops are annual and perennial grasses and alfalfa. Production in 2022 totaled 6.5 million tons of hay from 4.2 million harvested acres at a yield of 1.6 tons per acre. Value of hay was $1.1 billion, or $189.00 per ton. In 2021, 10.7 million tons of hay were produced from 5.6 million harvested acres at a yield of 1.9 tons per acre. The value in 2021 was $1.6 billion or $156.00 per ton. In 2020, the production of hay was 9.6 million tons from 5.0 million harvested acres with a value of $1.4 billion or $146.00 per ton, at a yield of 1.9 tons per acre.

Alfalfa hay production in 2022 totaled 378,000 tons with 90,000 acres harvested with a yield of 4.2 tons per acre. At a value of $250.00 per ton, total value was $94.5 million. In 2021, 540,000 tons of alfalfa hay were harvested from 100,000 acres at a yield of 5.4 tons per acre. Value was $113.4 million, or $210.00 per ton. Alfalfa hay was harvested from 110,000 acres in 2020, producing an average of 4.9 tons per acre for total production of 539,000 tons valued at $104.0 million, or $193.00 per ton.

An additional sizable acreage of annual forage crops is grazed as well as much of the small grain acreage. Alfalfa, sweet corn, vetch, arrowleaf clover, grasses, and other forage plants also provide income as seed crops.

Peanuts

Well over three-fourths of the annual peanut production is from irrigated acreage. In 2022, Texas ranked fifth nationally in production of peanuts. Among Texas crops, peanuts ranked eighth in value.

Until 1973, essentially all of the Texas acreage was planted to the Spanish type, which was favored because of its earlier maturity and better drought tolerance than other types. The Spanish variety is also preferred for some uses due to its distinctive flavor. The Florunner variety, a runner market type, is now planted on a sizable proportion of the acreage where soil moisture is favorable. The variety is later maturing but better yielding than Spanish varieties under good growing conditions. Florunner peanuts have acceptable quality to compete with the Spanish variety in most products.

In 2022, peanut production totaled 336.0 million pounds from 160,000 acres planted and 120,000 harvested, yielding

2,800 pounds per acre. At 39.0 cents per pound, value of the crop was estimated at $131.0 million. In 2021, peanut production amounted to 578.3 million pounds from 180,000 acres planted and 162,000 harvested. With an average yield of 3,570 pounds per acre and average price of 31.0 cents per pound, the 2021 value of production was $180.4 million. Production in 2020 amounted to 484.5 million pounds of peanuts from 190,000 acres planted and 170,000 acres harvested, or an average of 2,850 pounds per harvested acre valued at 26.0 cents per pound for a $125.5 million value.

Soybeans

Soybean production is located in the areas of the Upper Coast, irrigated High Plains, and Red River Valley of Northeast Texas. Soybeans are adapted to the same general soil climate conditions as corn, cotton, or grain sorghum, provided moisture, disease, and insects are not limiting factors.

In low-rainfall areas, yields have been too low or inconsistent for profitable production under dryland conditions. Soybeans' need for moisture in late summer minimizes economic crop possibilities in the Blacklands and Rolling Plains. In the Blacklands, cotton root rot seriously hinders soybean production. Limited moisture at critical growth stages may occasionally prevent economical yields, even in high-rainfall areas of Northeast Texas and the Coastal Prairie.

Because of day length sensitivity, soybeans should be planted in Texas during the long days of May and June to obtain sufficient vegetative growth for optimum yields. Varieties planted during this period usually cease vegetative development and initiate reproductive processes during the hot, dry months of July and August. When moisture is insufficient during the blooming and fruiting period, yields are drastically reduced. In most areas of the state, July and August rainfall is insufficient to permit economical dryland production. The risk of dryland soybean production in the Coastal Prairie and Northeast Texas is considerably less when compared to other dryland areas because moisture is available more often during the critical fruiting period.

The 2022 soybean crop totaled 1.7 million bushels and was valued at $21.8 million, or $12.80 per bushel. Of the 155,000 acres planted, 85,000 were harvested with an average yield of 20.0 bushels per acre. In 2021, the Texas soybean crop averaged 38.0 bushels per acre from 100,000 acres harvested. Total production of 3.8 million bushels was valued at $44.5 million, or $11.70 per bushel. In 2020, the Texas soybean crop averaged 34.0 bushels per acre from 110,000 acres harvested. Total production of 3.7 million bushels was valued at $34.0 million, or $9.10 per bushel.

Sunflowers

Sunflowers constitute one of the most important annual oilseed crops in the world. The cultivated types, which are thought to be descendants of the common wild sunflower native to Texas, have been successfully grown in several countries including Russia, Argentina, Romania, Bulgaria, Uruguay, Western Canada, and portions of the northern United States. Extensive trial plantings conducted in the Cotton Belt states since 1968 showed sunflowers have considerable potential as an oilseed crop in much of this area including Texas. This crop exhibits good cold and drought tolerance, is adapted to a wide range of soil and climate conditions, and tolerates higher levels of hail, wind, and sand abrasion than other crops normally grown in the state.

In 2022, sunflower production totaled 61.4 million pounds and was harvested from 45,000 acres at a yield of 1,363 pounds per acre. With an average price of $27.00 per cwt., the crop was valued at $16.6 million. In 2021, 38,500 of the 41,000 acres planted to sunflowers were harvested with an average yield of 1,220 pounds per acre. Total production of 47.0 million pounds was valued at $10.9 million, or $23.20 per cwt.

In 2020, of 63,000 acres planted to sunflowers, 57,000 acres were harvested, yielding 1,403 pounds per acre for a total production of 80.0 million pounds valued at $18.3 million, or $22.90 per cwt.

Reasons for growing sunflowers include the need for an additional cash crop with low water and plant nutrient requirements, the development of sunflower hybrids, and interest by food processors in Texas sunflower oil which has high oleic acid content. Commercial users have found many advantages in this high oleic oil, including excellent cooking stability particularly for use as a deep-frying medium for potato chips, corn chips, and similar products.

Sunflower meal is a high-quality protein source free of nutritional toxins that can be included in rations for swine, poultry, and ruminants. The hulls constitute a source of roughage, which can also be included in livestock rations.

Nursery Crops

The trend to increase production of nursery crops continues to rise as transportation costs on long-distance hauling increases. This has resulted in a marked increase in the production of container-grown plants within the state. This increase is noted especially in the production of bedding plants, foliage plants, sod, and the woody landscape plants.

Plant rental services have become a multimillion-dollar business. This relatively new service provides the plants and maintains them in office buildings, shopping malls, public buildings, and even in some homes for a fee. The response has been good as evidenced by the growth of companies providing these services.

The interest in plants for interior landscapes is confined to no specific age group as both retail nurseries and florist shops report that people of all ages are buying their plants—from the elderly in retirement homes to high school and college students in dormitory rooms and apartments.

Texas A&M AgriLife Extension specialists estimated cash receipts from nursery crops in Texas to be around $2.0 billion in 2022. Texans are creating colorful and green surroundings by improving their landscape plantings.

Vegetable Crops

Some market vegetables are produced in almost all Texas counties. In 2017, Hidalgo County was the leading Texas county in vegetable acres harvested, followed by Hartley and Frio counties. Other leading producing counties are Terry, Guadalupe, Medina, Uvalde, Yoakum, and Waller.

In 2020, fresh market vegetable utilized (fresh market and processing combined) production of 12.7 million cwt. in Texas was valued at $216.0 million. In 2019, Texas growers harvested total fresh market vegetable crops valued at $184.9 million from 47,800 acres with a utilized production of 12.6 million cwt. Texas growers harvested 15.8 million cwt. of fresh market vegetable crops from 62,000 acres, valued at $298.0 million in 2018. *Note: Tables containing principal vegetable totals by state were discontinued beginning with the "Vegetables 2021 Summary" published by NASS/USDA in February 2022.*

Dry Onions

Onion utilized production in 2022 totaled 2.3 million cwt. from 9,000 harvested acres and was valued at $121.7 million, at a yield of 260 cwt. per acre. In 2021, 3.1 million cwt. of onions were harvested from 11,000 acres and valued at $87.8 million, at a yield of 280 cwt. per acre. A total of 3.7 million cwt. of onions were produced from 11,000 harvested acres and valued at $73.5 million in 2020, yielding 338 cwt. per acre in 2020.

All Potatoes

In 2022, all potatoes were harvested from 12,500 acres with production of 7.2 million cwt. valued at $112.9 million at a yield of 575 cwt. per acre. In 2021, all potatoes were harvested from 12,000 acres with a production of 5.5 million cwt. valued at $87.2 million, yielding 460 cwt. per acre. This compares with 15,300 acres harvested valued at $109.6 million in 2020 with a production of 7.1 million cwt. and a yield of 465 cwt. per acre.

Watermelons

Watermelon production in 2022 was 3.5 million cwt. from 16,900 harvested acres with a value of $84.9 million, yielding 210 cwt. per acre. In 2021, at a yield of 250 cwt. per acre, 4.6 million cwt. watermelons were harvested from 18,300 acres and valued at $79.0 million. Watermelon production was 5.5 million cwt. from 19,000 harvested acres in 2020, with a value of $61.6 million at a yield of 290 cwt. per acre.

Cabbage

In 2022, 6,000 acres of cabbage were harvested and yielded a total production of 1.5 million cwt. that was valued at $34.8 million. Yield was 250 cwt. per acre. In 2021, 6,000 acres of cabbage were harvested and yielded a total production of 1.6 million cwt. Value in 2021 was $37.4 million at a yield of 260 cwt. per acre. The 6,400 acres of cabbage harvested in Texas in 2020 brought a value of $40.1 million. At a yield of 290 cwt. per acre, total production was 1.9 million cwt.

Spinach

Utilized production for spinach in fresh market and processing in 2022 was 187,000 cwt., harvested from 1,700 acres, at a yield of 110 cwt. per acre. At $66.30 per cwt., value of utilized production was $12.4 million. In 2021, spinach was harvested from 1,200 acres with a utilized production of 130,700 cwt. and a yield of 110 cwt. per acre. Value of utilized production in 2021 was $9.60 million or $73.10 per cwt. In 2020, spinach was harvested from 2,200 acres at a yield of 125 per cwt. Utilized production was 275,000 at a value of $15.2 million or $55.40 per cwt.

Pumpkins

Pumpkin numbers were not reported in 2022. Pumpkin production in 2021 was 1.1 million cwt., harvested from 4,500 acres. The yield was 240 cwt. per acre and a value of $26.5 million. In 2020, pumpkin production of 999,000 cwt. was harvested from 3,700 acres with a yield of 270 cwt. per acre. The production value was $25.9 million.

Cucumbers

In 2022, 4,700 acres of cucumbers were harvested. Production totaled 455,900 cwt. and was valued at $9.1 million. The yield was 97 cwt. per acre. Cucumber production in 2021 was 371,000 cwt. from 5,300 harvested acres. At a yield of 70 cwt. per acre, value of production was $6.9 million. At a yield of 83 cwt. per acre, the 473,100-cwt. cucumber crop in Texas during 2020 was harvested from 5,700 acres and valued at $9.3 million.

Texas Vegetable Production, 2022

Crop	Harvested Acres	Yield Per Acre Cwt.	Production Cwt. (thousands)	Value (thousands)
Cabbage	6,000	250	1,500	$ 34,800
Cucumbers	4,700	97	456	9,078
Onions	9,000	260	2,340	121,680
Potatoes	12,500	575	7,188	112,852
Spinach	1,700	110	187	12,399
Watermelons	16,900	210	3,549	84,860
Total	50,800	—	15,220	$ 375,669

Numbers may not add due to rounding.

Source: USDA/NASS, Annual Vegetable Summary, February 2023; "2022 State Agriculture Overview, Texas".

Fruits and Nuts

Texas is noted for producing a wide variety of fruits. The pecan is the only commercial nut crop in the state. The pecan is native to most of the state's river valleys and is the Texas state tree. Citrus is produced commercially in the three southernmost counties in the Lower Rio Grande Valley. Peaches represent the next most important Texas fruit crop, and there is considerable interest in growing apples.

Citrus

Texas ranks with California and Florida as leading states in the production of citrus. Most of the Texas production is in Cameron, Hidalgo, and Willacy counties of the Lower Rio Grande Valley. In 2021/2022, grapefruit utilized production was estimated at 1.7 million boxes at $19.97 per box or $33.9 million. Bearing acreage was 12,000 acres at a yield of 140 boxes per acre. Grapefruit production in 2020/2021 was 2.4 million boxes for a total value of $45.8 million or $19.08 per box. Bearing acreage was 15,000 acres in 2020/2021 with a yield of 160 boxes per acre. Production in 2019/2020 was 4.4 million boxes with a value of $48.5 million or $11.01 per box. Bearing acreage was 16,000 acres with a yield of 275 boxes per acre.

Utilized production of oranges in 2021/2022 was 200,000 boxes for a total value of $3.8 million or $18.85 per box. The yield was 31 boxes from 6,500 bearing acreage. In 2020/2021, production was 1.1 million boxes from a bearing acreage of 7,800 with a yield of 135 boxes per acre. At $20.65 per box, total value was $21.7 million. Production was 1.3 million boxes in 2019/2020 for a value of $16.4 million or $12.25 per box. A bearing acreage of 7,800 acres yielded 172 boxes per acre.

Peaches

Primary production areas are East Texas, the Hill Country, and the West Cross Timbers. Production varies substantially due to adverse weather conditions. Low-chilling varieties for early marketings are being grown in Atascosa, Frio, Webb, Karnes, and Duval counties.

The Texas peach crop's production totaled 2,420 tons in 2018. In 2017, utilized production was 2,500 tons. Value of production was $6.3 million. In 2016, utilized production was 4,200 tons that was valued at $9.2 million. Numbers were not reported after 2018.

Pecans

The pecan, the state tree, is one of the most widely distributed trees in Texas. It is native to over 150 counties and is grown commercially in some 30 additional counties. The pecan is also widely used as a dual-purpose yard tree. The commercial plantings of pecans have accelerated in Central and West Texas with many of the new orchards being irrigated. Many new pecan plantings are being established under trickle-irrigation systems.

In 2022, pecan orchards yielded 250 pounds per acre from 100,000 harvested acres. The utilized production was 25.0 million pounds with a value of $42.4 million or $1.69 per pound. In 2021, a yield of 325 pounds per acre was harvested from 110,000 acres. The utilized production was 35.8 million pounds with a value of $69.2 million or $1.93 per pound. The 2020 crop totaled 41.8 million pounds from 113,000 harvested acres at a yield of 370 pounds per acre. The value was $63.5 million or $1.52 per pound.

Nationally, Texas ranked fourth with Georgia first, New Mexico second, and Arizona third in utilized pecan production in 2022.

Rancher Deborah Clark watches over cattle on the Birdwell Clark Ranch in Washington County. Photo by USDA NRCS Texas, Public Domain

Livestock and Animal Products

Livestock and animal products accounted for about **67.7% of the agricultural cash receipts in Texas in 2021**. The state ranks first nationally in all cattle, beef cattle, cattle on feed, sheep and lambs, wool, goats, and mohair. Sales of livestock and animal products in 2021 totaled $16.8 billion, up from $14.4 billion in 2020.

Cattle and calves dominate livestock production in Texas, contributing around 59.9% of cash receipts from livestock and animal products. The Jan. 1, 2023 inventory of all cattle and calves in Texas totaled 12.5 million head, valued at $13.9 billion, compared to 12.7 million as of Jan. 1, 2022, valued at $13.5 billion, and 13.1 million as of Jan. 1, 2021, valued at $12.7 billion.

On Jan. 1, 2023, the sheep and lamb inventory stood at 675,000 head, valued at $145.8 million, compared with 700,000 head as of Jan. 1, 2022, valued at $137.9 million. Jan. 1, 2021 showed an inventory of 730,000 valued at $132.9 million. Sheep and lambs numbered 3.2 million on Jan. 1, 1973, down from a high of 10.8 million in 1943. Wool production decreased from 26.4 million pounds valued at $23.2 million in 1973 to 1.1 million pounds valued at $1.9 million in 2022. Production was 1.2 million pounds in 2021 valued at $2.7 million, compared to 1.4 million pounds in 2020 and valued at $2.4 million. The price of wool per pound was 88 cents in 1973, compared to $1.70 in 2022, $2.30 in 2021, and $1.80 in 2020.

Mohair production in Texas has dropped from a 1965 high of 31.6 million pounds to 315,000 pounds in 2022. Production was valued at $2.8 million or $9.00 per pound. In 2021, production was 335,000 pounds valued at $2.6 million or $7.70 per pound. Mohair production in 2020 was 370,000 pounds valued at $2.7 million or $7.20 per pound.

Beef Cattle

Raising beef cattle is the most extensive agricultural operation in Texas. In 2021, cattle and calves were 40.6% of total cash receipts — $10.1 million of $24.8 million, compared with $8.8 million of $20.4 million in 2020 (43.1%) and $8.4 million of $20.6 million in 2019 (40.9%). The next leading commodity is poultry and eggs.

Nearly all of the 254 counties in Texas derive more revenue from cattle than from any other agricultural commodity, and those that don't usually rank cattle second in importance. Within the boundaries of Texas are 14.0% of all the cattle and calves in the U.S., as are 15.0% of the beef cows that have calved, and 13.2% of the calf crop as of Jan. 1, 2023 inventory. The number of all cattle and calves in Texas on Jan. 1, 2023 totaled 12.5 million, compared with 12.7 million on Jan. 1, 2022 and 13.1 million on Jan. 1, 2021.

Calves born on Texas farms and ranches in Jan. 1, 2023 totaled 4.5 million, compared with 4.6 million in 2022 and 4.8 million in 2021.

Dairy Product Manufacturing

The major dairy products manufactured in Texas include condensed, evaporated and dry milk, creamer, butter, and cheese. However, specifics of production and value are not available because of the small number of manufacturing plants producing these products.

Dairying

All cows' milk sold by Texas dairy farmers is marketed under the terms of Federal Marketing Orders. Most Texas dairy farmers are members of one of four marketing cooperatives. Associate Milk Producers, Inc. is the largest, representing the majority of the state's producers.

Texas dairy farmers received an average price for milk of $25.60 per hundred pounds in 2022, $18.20 in 2021, and $18.60 in 2020. A total of 16.5 billion pounds of milk was sold to plants and dealers in 2022, bringing in cash receipts from milk to dairy farmers of $4.2 billion. This compared with 15.6 billion pounds sold in 2021 that brought in $2.8 billion in cash receipts. In 2020, Texas dairy farmers sold 14.9 billion pounds of milk, which brought in cash receipts of $2.8 billion.

The annual average number of milk cows in Texas was 650,000 head as of Jan. 1, 2023 inventory. This compared with 625,000 head as of Jan. 1, 2022 and 615,000 as of Jan. 1, 2021. Average milk production per cow in the state has increased steadily over the past several decades. The average milk production per cow in 2022 was 25,579 pounds. Milk per cow in 2021 was 25,079 pounds. In 2020, milk per cow was 24,966 pounds. Total milk production in Texas was 16.5 billion pounds in 2022, 15.6 billion pounds in 2021, and 14.9 billion pounds in 2020.

There were 467 farms reporting milk cows in Texas in 2017. In 2012, 985 farms reported milk cows, and in 2007, 1,293 farms reported milk cows in Texas.

Swine

Texas had 1.2 million head of swine on hand, Dec. 1, 2022 — only 1.7% of the U.S. swine herd. Although the number of farms producing hogs has steadily decreased, the size of production units has increased substantially. There is favorable potential for increased production.

In 2022, 2.8 million head of hogs were marketed in Texas, producing 444.5 million pounds of pork valued at $338.0 million. In 2021, 3.1 million head of hogs were marketed, producing 524.3 million pounds of pork valued at $385.3 million. Comparable figures for 2020 were 3.5 million head marketed, and 506.9 million pounds of pork produced with a value of $201.0 million.

Goats and Mohair

All goats in Texas numbered 806,000 on Jan. 1, 2023. This compares with 835,000 on Jan. 1, 2022 and 831,000 on Jan. 1, 2021. Though data for the all-goat inventory is limited, the goat herd consists of Angora goats for mohair production. Angora goats totaled 59,000 as of Jan. 1, 2023, 61,000 as of 2022, and 65,000 as of Jan. 1, 2021.

Mohair production during 2022 totaled 315,000 pounds. This compares with 335,000 in 2021 and 370,000 pounds in 2020. Average price per pound in 2022 was $9.00 from

55,000 goats clipped for a total value of $2.8 million. In 2021, producers received $7.70 per pound from 61,000 goats clipped for a total value of $2.6 million. In 2020, producers received $7.20 per pound from 65,000 goats clipped for a total value of $2.7 million.

Over half of the world's mohair and 56% of the U.S. clipped are produced in Texas.

Sheep and Wool

Sheep and lambs in Texas numbered 675,000 head on Jan. 1, 2023, compared to 700,000 as of 2022, and 730,000 as of Jan. 1, 2021. All sheep were valued at $145.8 million on Jan. 1, 2023, compared with $137.9 million as of Jan. 1, 2022, and $132.9 million as of Jan. 1, 2021.

Breeding ewes one year old and over numbered 425,000 as of Jan. 1, 2023, 430,000 as of Jan. 1, 2022, and 445,000 as of Jan. 1, 2021. Replacement lambs less than one year old totaled 83,000 head as of Jan. 1, 2023, 88,000 as of Jan. 1, 2022, and 90,000 as of Jan. 1, 2021. Sheep and lamb farms in Texas were estimated to be 14,672 as of Jan. 1, 2017, compared to 10,674 in 2012.

Texas wool production in 2022 was 1.1 million pounds from 170,000 sheep. Value totaled $1.9 million or $1.70 per pound. This compared with 1.2 million pounds of wool from 160,000 sheep valued at $2.7 million or $2.30 per pound in 2021, and 1.4 million pounds from 180,000 sheep valued at $2.4 million or $1.80 per pound in 2020.

Most sheep and lambs in Texas are concentrated in the Edwards Plateau area of West Central Texas and nearby counties. San Angelo has long been the largest sheep and wool market in the nation and the center for wool and mohair warehouses, scouring plants, and slaughterhouses.

Poultry and Eggs

Poultry and eggs contribute about 12.5% of the total cash receipts of Texas farmers in 2021. On Jan. 1, 2022, Texas ranked fifth among the states in broilers produced and fifth in eggs produced. In 2021, cash receipts to Texas producers from the production of poultry and eggs totaled $3.1 billion. This compares with $2.2 billion in 2020 and $2.6 in 2019.

Broiler production in 2022 totaled 723.3 million birds, compared with 706.6 million in 2021 and 702.5 million in 2020.

Horses

Nationally, Texas ranks as one of the leading states in horse numbers and is the headquarters for many national horse organizations. The largest single breed registry in America, the American Quarter Horse Association, has its headquarters in Amarillo. The National Cutting Horse Association and the American Paint Horse Association are both located in Fort Worth. In addition to these national associations, Texas also has active state associations that include Palominos, Arabians, Thoroughbreds, Appaloosas, and ponies.

Horses are still used to support the state's giant beef cattle and sheep industries. However, the largest horse numbers within the state are near urban and suburban areas where they are mostly used for recreation activities. Horses are most abundant in the heavily populated areas of the state. State participation activities consist of horse shows, trail rides, play days, rodeos, polo, and horse racing. Residential subdivisions have been developed within the state to provide facilities for urban and suburban horse owners.

Hog Production, 1985–2022

Year	Production (thousand lbs.)	Average Price Per Cwt.	Gross Income (thousands)
1985	168,950	$ 43.40	$ 72,512
1986	176,660	47.30	82,885
1987	216,834	50.60	103,983
1988	236,658	41.30	100,029
1989	230,004	39.90	95,482
1990	196,225	48.20	92,222
1991	207,023	45.10	97,398
1992	217,554	36.40	79,436
1993	221,071	39.90	90,571
1994	224,397	35.10	78,394
1995	221,323	35.50	81,509
1996	204,476	45.90	94,962
1997	224,131	47.40	103,050
1998	271,444	30.70	86,349
1999	274,572	27.50	71,604
2000	328,732	36.60	115,105
2001	260,875	39.10	105,217
2002	223,441	28.70	67,255
2003	197,876	33.60	67,998
2004	202,199	44.90	90,349
2005	223,375	45.40	105,989
2006	257,644	40.80	108,844
2007	273,213	39.70	95,581
2008	328,356	40.50	143,249
2009	286,069	37.60	135,077
2010	149,934	$ 50.20	96,676
2011	168,718	NA	153,517
2012	414,904	NA	288,652
2013	285,822	NA	240,322
2014	305,146	NA	248,928
2015	376,691	NA	224,328
2016	365,980	NA	191,892
2017	366,121	NA	197,572
2018	442,476	NA	225,125
2019	494,912	NA	244,954
2020	506,915	NA	223,545
2021	524,302	NA	362,891
2022	444,517	NA	$ 334,595

NA = not available

Source: "1985 Texas Livestock, Dairy and Poultry Statistics," USDA, Bulletin 235, June 1986, pp. 32, 46; 1991 "Texas Livestock Statistics," USDA,; "1993 Texas Livestock Statistics," Bulletin 252, Texas Agricultural Statistics Service, August 1994; "Texas Agricultural Facts, 2009," October, 2010; "Texas Ag Facts," various years. "Meat Animals - Prod., Disp., & Income," April 2021 and April 2022; (December 1 previous year); USDA/NASS Quick Stats. Numbers from previous years revised.

Goats and Mohair 1980–2023

Year	Goats		Angora Goats		Mohair	
	Number	Farm Value	Number	Value	Production (lbs)	Value
1980	1,400,000	$64,400,000	NA	NA	8,800,000	$30,800,000
1981	1,380,000	53,130,000	NA	NA	10,100,000	35,350,000
1982	1,410,000	$ 57,810,000	NA	NA	10,000,000	$ 25,500,000
1983	1,420,000	53,250,000	NA	NA	10,600,000	42,930,000
1984	1,450,000	82,215,000	NA	NA	10,600,000	48,160,000
1985	1,590,000	76,797,000	NA	NA	13,300,000	45,885,000
1986	1,770,000	70,977,000	NA	NA	16,000,000	40,160,000
1987	1,780,000	82,592,000	NA	NA	16,200,000	42,606,000
1988	1,800,000	108,180,000	NA	NA	15,400,000	29,876,000
1989	1,850,000	100,270,000	NA	NA	15,400,000	24,794,000
1990	1,900,000	93,100,000	NA	NA	14,500,000	13,775,000
1991	1,830,000	73,200,000	NA	NA	14,800,000	19,388,000
1992	2,000,000	84,000,000	1,620,000	NA	14,200,000	12,354,000
1993	1,960,000	84,280,000	1,560,000	NA	13,490,000	11,197,000
1994	1,960,000	74,480,000	1,490,000	NA	11,680,000	30,602,000
1995	1,850,000	81,400,000	1,250,000	NA	11,319,000	20,940,000
1996	1,900,000	89,300,000	1,250,000	NA	7,490,000	14,606,000
1997	1,650,000	70,950,000	1,000,000	NA	6,384,000	14,556,000
1998	1,400,000	71,400,000	750,000	NA	4,650,000	12,044,000
1999	1,350,000	71,550,000	550,000	NA	2,550,000	9,384,000
2000	1,300,000	74,100,000	370,000	NA	2,346,000	10,088,000
2001	1,400,000	105,000,000	300,000	NA	1,716,000	3,775,000
2002	1,250,000	106,250,000	250,000	NA	1,944,000	3,110,400
2003	1,200,000	110,400,000	240,000	NA	1,680,000	2,856,000
2004	1,200,000	115,200,000	210,000	$ 13,860,000	1,620,000	3,402,000
2005	1,270,000	138,430,000	190,000	14,070,000	1,250,000	3,750,000
2006	1,310,000	137,388,000	178,000	15,200,000	1,100,000	4,400,000
2007	1,300,000	147,552,000	159,000	14,220,000	960,000	3,840,000
2008	1,185,000	120,870,000	134,000	11,250,000	820,000	3,116,000
2009	1,090,000	129,920,000	120,000	10,080,000	700,000	2,170,000
2010	1,020,000	$ 108,290,000	100,000	7,500,000	730,000	3,066,000
2011	980,000	NA	110,000	11,000,000	530,000	2,703,000
2012	905,000	NA	85,000	7,565,000	470,000	2,256,000
2013	872,000	NA	74,000	9,028,000	490,000	2,695,000
2014	906,000	NA	76,000	9,196,000	535,000	3,371,000
2015	906,000	NA	83,000	12,035,000	480,000	3,408,000
2016	847,000	NA	78,000	10,140,000	510,000	3,060,000
2017	866,000	NA	80,000	12,000,000	470,000	3,102,000
2018	869,000	NA	75,000	9,750,000	465,000	3,348,000
2019	842,000	NA	75,000	10,500,000	470,000	3,760,000
2020	869,000	NA	75,000	10,500,000	370,000	2,664,000
2021	831,000	NA	65,000	7,800,000	335,000	2,580,000
2022	835,000	NA	61,000	8,540,000	315,000	$ 2,835,000
2023	806,000	NA	59,000	$ 8,260,000	NA	NA

NA = Not Available

Sources: "1985 Texas Livestock, Dairy and Poultry Statistics," USDA Bulletin 235, June 1986. "Texas Agricultural Facts," Crop and Livestock Reporting Service, various years; "1993 Texas Livestock Statistics," Texas Agricultural Statistics Service, Bulletin 252, August 1994; "Texas Agricultural Statistics, 2009," October 2010; "Texas Ag Facts," February and March 2011. USDA/TASS Texas Goat and Mohair, January 31, 2023; NASS Quick Stats.

Sheep and Wool Production 1978–2023

Year	Sheep		Wool	
	Number	Value	Production (lbs)	Value
1978	2,460,000	111,930,000	18,500,000	15,355,000
1979	2,415,000	152,145,000	19,075,000	18,503,000
1980	2,400,000	138,000,000	18,300,000	17,751,000
1981	2,360,000	116,820,000	20,500,000	24,600,000
1982	2,400,000	100,800,000	19,300,000	16,212,000
1983	2,225,000	86,775,000	18,600,000	15,438,000
1984	1,970,000	76,830,000	17,500,000	16,100,000
1985	1,930,000	110,975,000	16,200,000	13,284,000
1986	1,850,000	107,300,000	16,400,000	13,284,000
1987	2,050,000	133,250,000	16,400,000	19,844,000
1988	2,040,000	155,040,000	18,200,000	35,854,000
1989	1,870,000	133,445,000	18,000,000	27,180,000
1990	2,090,000	$ 133,760,000	17,400,000	$ 19,662,000
1991	2,000,000	108,000,000	16,700,000	13,861,000
1992	2,140,000	111,280,000	17,600,000	16,896,000
1993	2,040,000	118,320,000	17,000,000	11,050,000
1994	1,895,000	106,120,000	14,840,000	15,582,000
1995	1,700,000	100,300,000	13,468,000	15,488,000
1996	1,650,000	108,900,000	9,900,000	8,316,000
1997	1,400,000	100,800,000	10,950,000	11,607,000
1998	1,530,000	122,400,000	9,230,000	5,815,000
1999	1,350,000	95,850,000	7,956,000	3,898,000
2000	1,200,000	94,800,000	7,506,000	3,678,000
2001	1,150,000	92,000,000	6,003,000	3,122,000
2002	1,130,000	88,140,000	5,950,000	4,046,000
2003	1,040,000	82,160,000	5,600,000	5,040,000
2004	1,100,000	105,600,000	5,600,000	5,712,000
2005	1,070,000	112,350,000	5,550,000	5,328,000
2006	1,070,000	124,260,000	4,900,000	4,459,000
2007	1,050,000	111,300,000	4,500,000	5,445,000
2008	960,000	97,920,000	4,200,000	4,872,000
2009	870,000	87,870,000	3,500,000	3,640,000
2010	830,000	83,000,000	3,450,000	5,451,000
2011	850,000	109,650,000	2,600,000	5,746,000
2012	670,000	102,510,000	2,100,000	3,507,000
2013	680,000	96,560,000	2,300,000	4,048,000
2014	730,000	118,990,000	2,100,000	3,297,000
2015	720,000	126,000,000	1,950,000	3,198,000
2016	725,000	131,950,000	1,800,000	3,150,000
2017	710,000	129,220,000	1,800,000	2,934,000
2018	750,000	138,750,000	1,760,000	3,168,000
2019	750,000	135,750,000	1,700,000	3,230,000
2020	735,000	134,505,000	1,350,000	2,430,000
2021	730,000	132,860,000	1,190,000	2,737,000
2022	700,000	137,900,000	1,110,000	$ 1,887,000
2023	675,000	$ 145,800,000	NA	NA

NA = not available

Source: "Texas Agricultural Facts" Annual Summary, Crop and Livestock Reporting Service, various years, "1993 Texas Livestock Statistics", Texas Agricultural Statistics Service, Bulletin 252, August 1994; "Texas Agricultural Statistics, 2009", October 2010, "Texas Ag Fact", February and March 2011; Texas Sheep and Wool report, January 31, 2023, Agricultural Prices, February 28, 2023, NASS/TASS Quick Stats.

APPENDIX

TEXAS OBITUARIES

PRONUNCIATION GUIDE

INDEX OF ADVERTISERS

INDEX OF ENTRIES

Obituaries: August 2021 – July 2023

Airshow Mid-Air Collision; Two World War II-era aircraft (a B-17 and a Bell P-63) collided during the Wings Over Dallas airshow, killing all six men aboard: Terry Michael Barker (pilot and former Keller city council member), Kevin Dimitri "K5" Michels (historian and media representative), Daniel Alexander Ragan (Navy veteran), Leonard Lloyd "Len" Root (retired pilot), Curtis James Rowe (Ohio Wing Civil Air Patrol member), and Craig Stephen Hutain (pilot). November 12, 2022.

Benavides, Fortunato, 76; judge (1994–2012) and senior judge (2012–2023) on the U.S. Court of Appeals for the Fifth Circuit. Born in Mission and received law degree from the University of Houston before opening private practice in McAllen. Became court-at-law judge for Hidalgo Co. in 1977. Also served on Supreme Court of Texas in 1993 as visiting judge before being appointed to Fifth Circuit by President Clinton. In Austin, May 5, 2023.

Biard, James Robert, 91; inventor and engineer at Texas Instruments, invented the first infrared light-emitting diode (LED) and held 73 patents. Born and raised in Paris and attended Paris Junior College. Earned B.S. and M.S. degrees in electrical engineering from Texas A&M before joining TI in 1957. Retired in 2015. Known in Dallas area as a harmonica player, performing at various local venues. In McKinney, September 23, 2022.

Blanks, Sidney "Sid," 80; professional running back for the Houston Oilers (1964–1968) and Boston Patriots (1969–1970). Born in Del Rio, he became the first-ever Black football player in the Lone Star Conference and the first Black player to receive a football scholarship at an integrated school in Texas when he played for Texas A&I (1960–1963). Sidney Blanks Park in Del Rio is named for him. In Webster, December 12, 2021.

Campbell, Dr. Randolph B. "Mike," 81; history professor, served as the inaugural Chief Historian for the TSHA, 2008–2017. Earned his PhD from University of Virginia, then joined the faculty at North Texas State University (now U of North Texas) in Denton. Author of numerous books, chapters, and articles on Texas history, his essays were collected and published in 2013 as *This Corner of Canaan: Essays on Texas in Honor of Randolph B. Campbell.* In Denton, August 13, 2022.

Caskey, C. Thomas, 83; internist, biomedical researcher, and medical geneticist, created the simple PCR test used as standard practice by police around the world to analyze DNA evidence at crime scenes. Born in South Carolina, he came to Texas in 1971 and founded the Department of Molecular and Human Genetics at Baylor College of Medicine. Later in his career he worked with the UT Health Science Center at Houston and served as president of the Texas Academy of Medicine, Engineering, Science & Technology in Austin. In Houston, January 13, 2022.

Catacalos, Rosemary, 78; first Latina to serve as Texas Poet Laureate (2013–2014). Raised in San Antonio of Greek and Mexican heritage, blended history, mythology, and folklore into her poems. Worked at *San Antonio Light* newspaper in 1960s as reporter and arts columnist. Her collection *Again for the First Time* won the 1985 Texas Institute of Letters poetry prize. In San Antonio, June 17, 2022.

Corcoran, Diane, 76; R.N., Ph.D. Col. USA (Ret), was one of the first female officers to command a hospital unit when she served as chief nurse for three months at the 86th Combat Support Hospital in Fort Campbell, Ky., in 1976. Native New Yorker left the position to earn her Ph.D. at UT Austin. Her interest in near-death experiences developed while serving as combat nurse during the Vietnam War and led to her becoming an expert in the field and president of the International Association for Near-Death Studies. In North Carolina, March 5, 2023.

Cornelius, Carl, 81; truck stop operator, founder, and longtime mayor and municipal judge of Carl's Corner on I-35E in Hill County. Founded town to legalize alcohol sales in the mostly dry area. Kingsville native hosted a Willie Nelson Fourth of July concert in 1987 near the truck stop, which was the first to offer Nelson's biodiesel fuel, BioWillie. In Woodway, September 21, 2021.

Cunningham, Walter, 90; the third civilian astronaut at NASA spent 263 hours in space as the lunar module pilot for Apollo 7 in 1968. Born in Iowa, raised in Calif. Served as active duty fighter pilot for the U.S. Marine Corps and flew 54 night missions in Korea. Retired as colonel from U.S. Marine Corps Reserve in 1975. Wrote *The All-American Boys* (1977) about life as an astronaut and joined the organization Back to Space as an astronaut consultant in 2018 to inspire younger generations to travel to Mars. In Houston, January 3, 2023. Interred at the Texas State Cemetery in Austin.

Curl, Robert Floyd Jr., 88; chemist, professor, and researcher, awarded the Nobel Prize in Chemistry in 1996. Born in Alice, was inspired by science at an early age (received his first chemistry set at age nine). Earned his B.S. from Rice in 1954 and his Ph.D. from UC, Berkeley, in 1957. Joined the faculty at Rice in 1958; Curl, Richard Smalley, and Harold Kroto jointly won the Nobel for their discovery of a class of molecules called fullerenes. Continued at Rice until retirement in 2008. In Houston, July 3, 2022.

DeLaune, Gary, 88; sportscaster and news reporter for San Antonio's KENS-TV 5. Native Kansan was reporter for KLIF-AM 1190 in Dallas when he was among the first to announce President Kennedy had been shot. Filed continuing reports in the aftermath and was reporting on-the-scene when Oswald was killed by Ruby. Served as color commentator for the Dallas Cowboys and San Antonio Spurs on the radio before making the move to TV. In San Antonio, February 6, 2022.

Duncan, Charles William Jr., 96; served as Deputy Secretary of Defense (1977–1979) and Secretary of Energy (1979–1981) under President Carter. Born in Houston and served in the U.S. Army Air Corps near the end of World War II. Studied chemistry at Rice and business administration at UT Austin before joining the family business, Duncan Coffee Company. As president he expanded the business, then merged it with Coca-Cola in 1964,

(Left to right) ***Mike Campbell**, historian, photo by TSHA* ***Rosemary Catacalos**, poet, photo by Larry D. Moore, CC by 4.0* ***Carl Cornelius**, founder of Carl's Corner, family photo courtesy of Linda Cornelius* ***Robert Curl**, Nobel laureate, photo by Douglas Lockard, CC by SA 3.0*

Jim Hines racing for Texas Southern in 1966. Photo by UPI, Public Domain

where he supervised the expansion of Coca-Cola Europe into Eastern Europe, Asia, and North Africa. After serving in the Carter administration, he joined the State Board of Education under Governor Mark White. In Houston, October 18, 2022.

Gagnier, Jenae Linn, 33; model, became famous as an influencer under the name "Miss Mercedes Morr" on Instagram, where she had 2.6 million followers. Murdered in her apartment by stalker who then killed himself. In Richmond, August 29, 2021.

Gaines, Gary, 73; football head coach for Odessa Permian HS team in 1988, the basis for the book *Friday Night Lights: A Town, a Team, and a Dream* by Buzz Bissinger and the movie *Friday Night Lights* (2004) starring Billy Bob Thornton. Over his 35-year career, the Crane native coached for seven high schools and two colleges, won three championships, and was inducted into the Texas High School Coaches Association Hall of Honor in 2013. Diagnosed with early onset Alzheimer's in 2017. In Lubbock, August 22, 2022.

Goodenough, John B., 100; multiple award-winning chemist, solid-state physicist, and materials scientist credited with the development of the lithium-ion battery. Became the oldest Nobel laureate in history, winning the Chemistry prize at 97, alongside M. Stanley Whittingham and Akira Yoshino. Born in Germany to American parents, earned his first advanced degree from Yale in 1944, then served as meteorologist in the U.S. Army during World War II. Became an engineering professor at UT Austin in 1986, where his studies included improved materials for batteries, especially for electric vehicles, to help reduce dependency on fossil fuels. In Austin, June 25, 2023.

Graves, Curtis, 84; civil rights activist, businessman, and politician, in 1967 became one of the first Blacks to serve in the Texas Legislature after Reconstruction, alongside Barbara Jordan and Joe Lockridge. Born in New Orleans, Graves attended Texas Southern and Princeton, worked as director for civil affairs for NASA, and was an artistic photographer. In Atlanta, Ga., July 26, 2023.

Gray, Claude Jr., 91; country music singer-songwriter nicknamed "The Tall Texan" (he was 6'5"). Born in Henderson, he worked as a salesman, radio announcer, and disc jockey before beginning recording career in 1959. Two of his biggest hits were "Family Bible" and "I'll Just Have a Cup of Coffee (Then I'll Go)," which was covered by Bob Marley. In Illinois, April 28, 2023.

Harrison, Adlene, 98; Dallas native and City Council member from 1973 through 1977. Became first Jewish woman mayor of Dallas and of any major U.S. city when she became acting mayor in 1976 following the resignation of Wes Wise. After term on the council, she joined the EPA as a regional administrator and served as first chair of the board responsible for overseeing Dallas Area Rapid Transit (DART). In Dallas, February 19, 2022.

Hayden, Casey, 85; civil rights worker and student activist known for defending direct action in the struggle to end racial segregation. Born Sandra Cason in Austin, raised in Victoria, was part of a successful sit-in campaign at Austin-area theaters and restaurants while studying English and philosophy at UT Austin. Worked with the Student Non-Violent Coordinating Committee, Students for a Democratic Society, among others, and was organizer and strategist for Freedom Summer in 1964, a volunteer campaign in Miss. aimed at registering as many Black voters as possible. Briefly married to activist Tom Hayden, was also an advocate for women's rights. In Arizona, January 4, 2023.

Hines, James "Jim," 76; track and field athlete and wide receiver for the Miami Dolphins and KC Chiefs. As a member of Texas Southern Univ. Tigers track team, the native Arkansan became the first man to run the 100 meters in under ten seconds. Competed in the controversial 1968 Summer Olympics and set two world records, one in the 100-meter race and the second with his teammates in the 4x100-meter relay. In 1994 was inducted into the Texas Sports Hall of Fame. In California, June 3, 2023.

Johnson, Brad, 62; actor and model who became famous as a Marlboro Man, a cowboy featured in ad campaigns for Marlboro cigarettes. Born in Arizona and raised in Dallas, competed in professional rodeos before being discovered by movie scout casting cowboys for a beer commercial. Acting credits include an episode of *Dallas*, Steven Spielberg's film *Always* (1989), *Flight of the Intruder*, and the role of Dr. Dominick O'Malley on *Melrose Place*. Retired from acting and founded Johnson Land and Home, real estate firm in North Texas. In Fort Worth, February 18, 2022.

Kane, Sharon Smith, 89; children's book author and illustrator, and one-time youngest syndicated cartoonist in the country. Produced single-panel cartoon strip and humorous advice column for her Indiana school paper and signed her first syndication contract at 17 to produce the comic *Buttons an' Beaux*. Wrote and illustrated her first children's book, *Where Are You Going Today?* (1957). *Little Mommy* (1967), her most popular book, has been in print for more than 50 years. Donated *Buttons an' Beaux* archive to the Cartoon Art Museum in San Francisco as foundation of the exhibit *The Teen Age: Youth Culture in Comics* (2019). Two-decade resident of Texas. In Plano, November 3, 2021.

Kleberg Groves, Helen, 94; cattle rancher and horsewoman, given the title "First Lady of Cutting" by San Antonio Express-News. Great-granddaughter of Richard King, founder of the King Ranch, she also bred and raised Quarter Horses, Thoroughbreds, and Santa Gertrudis cattle. Inducted in the National Cowgirl Museum and Hall of Fame in 1998. Famously led racehorse Assault to the winner's circle after winning the Preakness and becoming the first (and only) Texas-bred winner of the Triple Crown. In San Antonio, her birthplace, May 6, 2022.

Krueger, Robert Charles "Bob," 86; U.S. Congressman (1975–1979), Texas Railroad Commissioner (1991–1993), U.S. Senator (1993), Ambassador to Burundi (1994–1995) and Botswana (1996–1999). Became last Democrat to represent Texas in the Senate (as of 2023) upon appointment by Gov. Richards to replace Cabinet-bound Lloyd Bentsen. Before his political career, earned degrees from SMU, Duke, and Oxford and was professor of English, then vice provost and dean, at Duke. After government service, wrote a memoir about time in Burundi, *From Bloodshed to Hope in Burundi: Our Embassy Years during Genocide* (2007). Later returned to academic life with lecture positions at various Texas universities. In New Braunfels, April 30, 2022. Interred at the Texas State Cemetery in Austin.

Leach, Mike, 61; college football coach, two-time national coach of the year, and three-time conference coach of the year. California native led the Red Raiders at Texas Tech for 10 consecutive winning seasons (2000–2009), earning the title "winningest coach in school history." Suspended, then fired, for alleged inappropriate treatment of a player. Returned to coaching in 2012 at Washington State and later Mississippi State. In Jackson, Miss., December 12, 2022.

Marcus, Richard Cantrell, 84; well-respected former chairman and CEO of Neiman Marcus, which was founded by his grandfather and great-aunt in 1907. Dallas native left Neiman Marcus in

1988 and spent next 30 years serving as a director on various boards for public companies and retail-oriented startups. Also served as board chair for The Contemporary Austin, where was later named trustee emeritus. In Austin, February 4, 2023.

McCarthy, Cormac, 89; writer of 12 novels, three short stories, two plays, and five screenplays regarded as one of the great American novelists. Born in Rhode Island, grew up in Tennessee. Quit college to join the Air Force. Published first novel, *The Orchard Keeper*, in 1965. Other works include *Blood Meridian* (1985), *All the Pretty Horses* (1992), *No Country for Old Men* (2005), and *The Road* (2006), which won the 2007 Pulitzer Prize for Fiction. Other awards include a MacArthur Fellowship (1981) and a National Book Award (1992); movies based on his works have earned broad acclaim. Notably, *No Country for Old Men* (2007) was nominated for eight Academy Awards and won four. Moved to El Paso in 1976 and lived there until move to New Mexico in late 1990s. In Santa Fe, June 13, 2023.

Moncrief, William Alvin Jr., 101; wildcatter, oil/gas businessman, and billionaire. Saw his first gusher at age 10, inspiring his career. Native Arkansan earned a degree in petroleum engineering from UT Austin in 1942; commissioned in Naval Reserve when U.S. entered WWII and served in the Pacific as communication officer. Became a 50-50 partner with his father in Moncrief Oil, which successfully discovered and developed oil and gas fields in multiple states. When company was raided by the IRS in 1994, was charged with criminal tax fraud for deducting $900,000 in business expenses on his personal return. He paid a $23 million settlement agreement in 1996. Served on the board of regents for UT System, which he supported with millions in donations. In Fort Worth, December 29, 2021.

Mueller, John, 52; pitmaster and founder of John Mueller's BBQ, JMueller BBQ (with sister LeAnn), and barbecue truck John Mueller Meat Co., from which he famously served smoked beef ribs to President Obama in 2014. Named "the dark prince of barbecue" by *Texas Monthly* because of his "cranky" persona, he and two siblings represent the third generation of a BBQ dynasty that was started in Taylor when grandfather founded Louie Mueller Barbecue in 1949. John's celebrated dishes included smoked beef ribs (complimented by Anthony Bourdain on his show *No Reservations*), brisket, and a signature side, cheesy squash. In Frisco, December 17, 2021.

Mueller, LeAnn Christine, 51; pitmaster and co-founder of JMueller BBQ (with brother John). A year after founding, the Taylor native fired her brother and renamed business La Barbecue (they later reconciled). What started as a food truck in South Austin in 2012 became the first woman- and lesbian-owned barbecue restaurant when it moved into brick-and-mortar location in 2021. Before taking her place in the Mueller family's barbecue legacy, attended Texas Tech and the Brooks Institute of Photography and worked around the world as professional photographer. In Austin, June 14, 2023.

Murdock, Steven H., 74; sociologist and former director of U.S. Census Bureau (2008–2009); led Texas State Data Center and was named first official Texas State Demographer in 2001. Minnesota native taught sociology at Rice, UT San Antonio, and Texas A&M, where he was a Regents professor and head of the Department of Rural Sociology for 25 years. Wrote dozens of books and nearly 50 articles, including "Texas Population: Still Growing and Increasingly Diverse" (with colleague Mike Cline), one of the features published in the *Texas Almanac 2020–2021*. In Lakeway, April 7, 2023.

Nelson, Bobbie Lee, 91; pianist, singer, and longtime collaborator with brother and fellow musician Willie Nelson. Born in Abbott, started learning to play piano and pump organ at the age of five from grandmother. Grew up performing at gospel conventions, church, and Abbott H.S. Married at 16 and performed in husband's band until divorce in 1955. Worked briefly at TV repair shop, then got job touring and performing on Hammond organ to demonstrate instrument to potential buyers. Joined brother in studio and played piano for several of his albums, officially joining band while recording *Shotgun Willie*. Released solo album *Audiobiography* in 2008; inducted into the Texas Country Music Hall of Fame in 2017 (alongside Kenny Rogers). In Austin, March 10, 2022.

Patrick, Robert, 85; Kilgore-born playwright, had more than 300 productions of his plays staged in New York, several on Broadway, including **Kennedy's Children** in 1975. Won many awards, including Best Play (1969) from magazine **Show Business**; Best World Playwrighting (1973) from Glasgow Citizens Theatre; Robert Chesley Award for Lifetime Achievement in Gay Playwriting (1996); and Charles Rodman Award for 50 Years of Service to Gay Theatre (2014). Also published collection of poems and several anthologies. In Los Angeles, April 23, 2023.

Pausé, Caitlin Clare "Cat", 42; activist and researcher specializing in fat studies; born in Midland, earned degrees at Texas State and Texas Tech, where wrote doctoral dissertation about weight identity in women categorized as "morbidly obese." Continued studies focused on fat stigma, barriers to health for fat people, and fat ethics. Hosted international conferences about fat studies in 2012 and 2016. Provided commentary to wide variety of international media as recognized public intellectual in the field. Also disseminated her work through social media accounts and podcast under name Friend of Marilyn. Suddenly in her sleep in New Zealand, March 25, 2022.

Powell, Julie Anne, 49; Austin-born writer and author who conducted Julie/Julia Project, in which she attempted to cook all the recipes in book *Mastering the Art of French Cooking* by Julia Child and wrote about experience in blog on Salon. Soon a hit, was republished as book and later became film *Julie & Julia* (2009), starring Amy Adams and Meryl Streep. Published second book, *Cleaving: A Story of Marriage, Meat, and Obsession* in 2009. In upstate New York, October 26, 2022.

Price, (William) Rayford, 86; lawyer and politician, served in Texas House of Representatives from 1961 to 1973, finishing as Speaker (1972–1973). Born in Jacksonville, first engaged in politics at Lon Morris College as student body president. Transferred to UT Austin to finish undergraduate degree and attend law school. Elected as conservative Democrat in East Texas, eventually lost seat to liberal incumbent who moved into district and won primary runoff. Switched parties in 1973 and founded Rayford Price & Associates law firm in 1982. In Austin, February 21, 2023.

Starr, Kenneth "Ken," 76; lawyer, federal appellate judge on Court of Appeals for the District of Columbia Circuit (1983–1989), and U.S. Solicitor General

(Left to Right) ***John Mueller*** *in the kitchen, photo by F.D. Richards, CC by SA 2.0;* **Bobbie Nelson** *at the keyboard, photo by ChunkyGlasses, CC by 2.0;* **Cat Pausé**, *activist and researcher, Photo by New Zealand Tertiary Education Union, CC by SA 2.0*

(1989–1993). Vernon native became known for investigation he led as independent counsel for Whitewater controversy (1994–1998), which expanded far beyond its original scope, with resulting *Starr Report* criticized for exaggerating legal definition of perjury and failing to provide evidence for some claims. Later was a member of President Trump's legal team during first impeachment trial. Also served as president of Baylor until removal by board (2010–2016) and published three nonfiction books. In Houston, September 13, 2022.

Stenholm, Charles Walter, 84; businessman, politician, and lobbyist; served as Congressman for large West Texas district (1979–2005). Born in Stamford and raised on family's 2,000-acre farm, which he took over after earning two degrees (B.S. and M.S.) in agriculture education from Texas Tech. Worked as vocational teacher while raising cotton and cattle, and entered politics as appointee to U.S. Agricultural Stabilization and Conservation Service. Elected to Congress as conservative Democrat, became part of Blue Dog Coalition and was long-time ranking member of Agriculture Committee. Eventually lost re-election to a Republican after redistricting split district four ways. Lobbied for agricultural interests (2005–2018) and later taught agriculture policy at Tarleton State. In Granbury, May 17, 2023.

Summers, Carroll Erwin, 91; engineer, entrepreneur, and philanthropist posthumously honored with title 2023 Mr. South Texas for contributions to Laredo community. Born in South Carolina, earned a degree in civil engineering, then joined Air Force and was stationed at base in Laredo in 1956. Discharged in 1958, became engineer for Texas Department of Highways before taking over management of family ranches after father-in-law's death. Well-known for good works in the community: served on multiple school boards and as president of the United Independent School District; worked with youth through the Texas Wildlife Association; established endowments for nursing students at Laredo College and Texas A&M International. In Laredo, December 17, 2022.

Tough, Coulson, 95; architect on the design team for The Woodlands community in Montgomery County. Michigan native served in Army Air Corps and graduated from Univ. of Michigan. Supervised construction of Univ. of California, Irvine as lead architect and designed a barn remodel for future president Reagan before becoming VP of facilities and operations at Univ. of Houston in 1968. Met George Mitchell and joined The Woodlands project in 1973. Also supervised renovations and construction in Galveston, including Tremont House, San Luis Hotel, and Galvez Hotel. In Spring, January 27, 2022.

Uvalde Elementary School Shooting; an 18-year-old former student of Robb Elementary entered that school with an assault rifle where he shot and killed 21 and left 17 injured. Also shot and injured his grandmother earlier in the day. The controversial police response to the shooting led to multiple investigations. Those killed were: fourth-graders Nevaeh Bravo, Jacklyn Cazares, Makenna Elrod, Jose Flores, Eliahna Garcia, Uziyah Garcia, Amerie Garza, Xavier Lopez, Jayce Luevanos, Tess Mata, Maranda Mathis, Alithia Ramirez, Annabell Rodriguez, Maite Rodriguez, Lexi Rubio, Layla Salazar, Jailah Silguero, Eliahna Torres, Rojelio Torres, and their teachers Irma Garcia and Eva Mireles. On May 24, 2022.

Sarah Weddington *at the 2004 March for Women's Lives in D.C., Photo by Pattymooney, CC by 4.0*

Waldrep, Kent, 67; disability rights activist and founder and president of Waldrep Medical and Disability Solutions, a disability accommodation consulting firm in Addison. Austin native played running back for TCU before being critically injured during game in Alabama, leaving him paralyzed from neck down. Served on National Council on Disability, lobbied for Americans with Disabilities Act, founded the National Paralysis Foundation, and served on College Football Assistance Fund. Advocated for spinal cord research and partnered with UT Southwestern Medical Center in Dallas to create Kent Waldrep Foundation Center for Basic Research on Nerve Growth and Regeneration. In Louisiana, February 27, 2022.

Weddington, Sarah, 76; law professor and women's rights activist best known for representing "Jane Roe" in Roe v. Wade. Earned her law degree at UT (one of only five women in her class) but had difficulty getting a job at law firm. With co-counsel Linda Coffee, filed suit against Henry Wade in 1970, which ultimately went to U.S. Supreme Court and prevailed. Served as member of Texas House of Representatives (1973–1977) and later as White House director of political affairs for President Carter (1979–1981). Joined Texas Woman's Univ. as lecturer (1981–1990) and UT Austin as adjunct professor. In Austin, December 26, 2021.

West, Joseph Sonny, 85; musician and songwriter in "rockabilly" tradition. Co-writer of two hit songs by Buddy Holly: "Oh, Boy!" and "Rave On." Born near Lubbock, formed his first band in 1956 in Levelland, and continued his music and songwriting career in Odessa and later Phoenix. Also had songs covered by Waylon Jennings. Continued performing live until late in life. Is featured on West Texas Walk of Fame in Lubbock and was named Honored Friend of the Buddy Holly Educational Foundation. In Oklahoma, September 8, 2022.

Whittington, Harry, 95; real estate investor and attorney. Henderson native became headline news when then-VP Dick Cheney accidentally shot him while hunting quail on ranch in Kenedy County. Earned law degree at UT Austin in 1950. Aided future president George H.W. Bush in failed 1964 U.S. Senate effort; later financially backed both of George W. Bush's presidential election campaigns. Served on Texas Corrections Board, Office of Patient Protection Executive Committee, and Texas Funeral Service Commission. As real estate investor, fought City of Austin in several disputes over properties he owned there. Although suffered a minor heart attack after the shooting, he recovered and lived out remainder of life with about 30 pieces of birdshot in body. In Austin, February 4, 2023.

Whitworth, Kathrynne Ann "Kathy," 83; pro golfer and member of World Golf Hall of Fame. Native of Monahans began playing golf at 14, attended Odessa College, and won New Mexico amateur championships twice before going pro in 1958. Won her first tournament four years later. With 88 tournament wins, including six major championships, has won more than any player in the history of professional golf (both LPGA and PGA). In 1981 became first LPGA player to win $1 million. Was LPGA Player of the Year seven times, member of multiple sports halls of fame. Retired in 2005; published *Kathy Whitworth's Little Book of Golf Wisdom* (with Jay Golden) in 2007. In Flower Mound, December 23, 2022.

Wise, Westley "Wes," 94; sportscaster, journalist, and politician. Born and raised in Louisiana; dropped out of high school at 15, worked at radio station, later passed high school equivalency test. Became a play-by-play radio announcer, broadcasting live recreations of MLB games. Moved to Dallas and worked as sports director for KRLD-TV before becoming announcer for Cowboys games on CBS in 1960. Was on scene reporting during the assassination of President Kennedy. Encountered and spoke to Jack Ruby following day and was present when Oswald was shot. Co-authored a memoir about those events in 2004: *When the News Went Live: Dallas 1963.* Elected to Dallas City Council in 1969 and became mayor in 1971. Elected to three terms but resigned in 1976 to run for the U.S. House, then lost in Democratic primary. After leaving politics, worked as VP of international affairs for Dallas World Trade Center and gave lectures on politics and sports. In Eustace, December 9, 2022.

TEXAS ALMANAC PRONUNCIATION GUIDE

Texas' rich cultural diversity is reflected nowhere better than in the names of places. Standard pronunciation is used in many cases, but purely colloquial pronunciation often is used, too.

In the late 1940s, George Mitchel Stokes, a graduate student at Baylor University, developed a list of pronunciations of 2,300 place names across the state. Stokes earned his doctorate and eventually was the director of the speech division in the communications studies department at Baylor University. He retired in 1983.

In the following list based on Stokes' longer list, pronunciation is by respelling and diacritical marking. Respelling is employed as follows: "ah" as in the exclamation, ah, or the "o" in tot; "ee" as in meet; "oo" as in moot; "yoo" as in use; "ow" as in cow; "oo" as in brood; "oi" as in oil; "uh" as in mud.

Note that ah, uh and the apostrophe(') are used for varying degrees of neutral vowel sounds, the apostrophe being used where the vowel is barely sounded. Diacritical markings are used as follows: bāle, băd, lĕt, rīse, rĭll, ōak, fŏŏt.

The stressed syllable is capitalized. Secondary stress is indicated by an underline as in Atascosa — ăt uhs KŌ suh.

A

Abbott — Ă buht
Abernathy — Ă ber nă thĭ
Abilene — ĂB uh leen
Acala — uh KĀ luh
Ackerly — ĂK er lĭ
Acme — ĂK mĭ
Acton — ĂK t'n
Acuff — Ā kuhf
Adamsville — Ă d'mz vĭl
Addicks — Ă dĭks
Addielou — ă dĭ LOO
Addison — A di s'n
Adkins — ĂT kĭnz
Adrian — Ā drĭ uhn
Afton — ĂF t'n
Agua Dulce — ah wuh DOOL sĭ
Agua Nueva — ah wuh noo Ā vuh
Aiken — Ā kĭn
Alamo — ĂL uh moh
Alamo Heights — ăl uh moh HĪTS
Alanreed — ĂL uhn reed
Alba — ĂL buh
Albany — AWL buh nĭ
Aledo — uh LEE doh
Alexander — ĕl ĭg ZĂN der
Alfred — ĂL frĕd
Algoa — ăl GŌ uh
Alice — Ă lĭs
Alief — Ā leef
Allen — Ă lĭn
Allenfarm — ălĭn FAHRM
Alleyton — Ă lĭ t'n
Allison — ĂL uh s'n
Alma — AHL muh
Alpine — ĂL pīn
Altair — awl TĂR
Alto — ĂL toh
Altoga — ăl TŌ guh
Alvarado — ăl vuh RĀ doh
Alvin — ĂL vĭn
Alvord — ĂL vord
Amarillo — ăm uh RĬL oh
Amherst — AM herst
Ammannsville — ĂM 'nz vĭl
Anahuac — ĂN uh wăk
Anderson — ĂN der s'n
Andice — ĂN dīs
Andrews — ĂN drooz
Angelina — ăn juh LEE nuh
Angleton — ĂNG g'l t'n
Annona — ă NŌ nuh
Anson — ĂN s'n
Anton — ĂNT n
Appleby — Ă p'l bĭ
Aquilla — uh KWĬL uh
Aransas — uh RĂN zuhs
Aransas Pass — uh răn zuhs PĂS
Arbala — ahr BĀ luh
Arcadia — ahr KĀ dĭ uh
Archer — AHR cher
Archer City — ahr cher SĬT ĭ
Arcola — ahr KŌ luh
Argo — AHR goh
Argyle — ahr GĪL
Arlington — AHR lĭng t'n
Arneckeville — AHR nĭ kĭ vĭl
Arnett — AHR nĭt
Arp — ahrp
Artesia Wells — ahr tee zh' WĔLZ
Arthur City — ahr ther SĬT ĭ
Asherton — ĂSH er t'n
Aspermont — ĂS per mahnt
Atascosa — ăt uhs KŌ suh
Athens — Ă thĕnz
Atlanta — ăt LĂN tuh
Atlas — ĂT l's
Attoyac — AT uh yăk
Aubrey — AW brĭ
Augusta — aw GUHS tuh
Austin — AWS t'n
Austonio — aws TŌ nĭ oh
Austwell — AWS wĕl
Avalon — ĂV uhl n
Avery — Ā vuh rĭ
Avinger — Ā vĭn jer
Avoca — uh VŌ kuh
Axtell — ĂKS t'l
Azle — Ā z'l

B

Bagwell — BĂG w'l
Bailey — BĀ lĭ
Baileyboro — BĀ lĭ ber ruh
Baileyville — BĀ lĭ vĭl
Baird — bărd
Bakersfield — BĀ kers feeld
Balch Springs — bawlch or bawlk SPRĬNGZ
Ballinger — BĂL ĭn jer
Balmorhea — băl muh RĀ
Bandera — băn DĔR uh
Banquete — băn KĔ tĭ
Barclay — BAHRK lĭ
Bardwell — BAHRD w'l
Barker — BAHR ker
Barksdale — BAHRKS dāl
Barnhart — BAHRN hahrt
Barnum — BAHR n'm
Barstow — BAHRS toh
Bartlett — BAHRT lĭt
Bassett — BĂ sĭt
Bastrop — BĂS trahp
Batesville — BĀTS v'l
Batson — BĂT s'n
Baxter — BĂKS ter
Bay City — ba SĬT ĭ
Baylor — BĀ ler
Bayside — BĀ sīd
Baytown — BĀ town
Beasley — BEEZ lĭ
Beaukiss — boh KĬS
Beaumont — BŌ mahnt
Beckville — BĔK v'l
Becton — BĔK t'n
Bedias — BEE dīs
Beehouse — BEE hows
Beeville — BEE vĭl
Belcherville — BĔL cher vĭl
Bellaire — bĕl ĂR
Bellevue — BĔL vyoo
Bellmead — bĕl MEED
Bellville — BĔL vĭl
Belmont — BĔL mahnt
Belton — BĔL t'n
Ben Arnold — bĕn AHR n'ld
Benavides — bĕn uh VEE d's
Ben Bolt — bĕn BŌLT
Benbrook — BĬN brook
Benchley — BĔNCH lĭ
Ben Franklin — bĕn FRĂNGk lĭn
Ben Hur — bĕn HER
Benjamin — BĔN juh m'n
Bennett — BĔN ĭt
Bentonville — BĔNT n vĭl
Ben Wheeler — bĭn HWEE ler
Berclair — ber KLĂR
Bertram — BERT r'm
Bessmay — bĕs MĀ
Bexar — BA ăr or băr

Beyersville — BĪRZ vĭl
Biardstown — BĂRDZ t'n
Bigfoot — BĬG foot
Big Lake — bĭg LĀK
Big Sandy — bĭg SĂN dĭ
Big Spring — bĭg SPRĬNG
Big Wells — bĭg WĔLZ
Birdville — BERD vĭl
Birome — bī RŌM
Birthright — BERTH rīt
Bishop — BĬ sh'p
Bivins — BĬ vĭnz
Blackfoot — BLĂK foot
Blackwell — BLĂK w'l
Blair — blăr
Blanchard — BLĂN cherd
Blanco — BLĂNG koh
Blanket — BLĂNG kĭt
Bleakwood — BLEEK wood
Bledsoe — BLĔD soh
Blessing — BLĔ sĭng
Blewett — BLOO ĭt
Blooming Grove — bloo mĭng GRŌV
Bloomington — BLOOM ĭng t'n
Blossom — BLAH s'm
Blue Grove — blyoo GRŌV
Blue Ridge — blyoo RĬJ
Bluff Dale — BLUHF dāl
Bluffton — BLUHF t'n
Blum — bluhm
Boerne — BER nĭ
Bogata — buh GŌ duh
Boling — BŌL ĭng
Bolivar — BAH lĭ ver
Bomarton — BŌ mer t'n
Bonham — BAH n'm
Bonita — boh NEE tuh
Bonney — BAH nĭ
Bonus — BŌ n's
Bon Wier — bahn WEER
Boonsville — BOONZ vĭl
Booth — booth
Borden — BAWRD n
Borger — BŌR ger
Bosque — BAHS kĭ
Boston — BAWS t'n
Bovina — boh VEE nuh
Bowie — BOO Ĭ
Boxelder — bahks ĔL der
Boyce — bawĭs
Boyd — boĭd
Brachfield — BRĂCH feeld
Bracken — BRĂ kĭn
Brackettville — BRĂ kĭt vĭl
Bradford — BRĂD ferd
Bradshaw — BRĂD shaw
Brady — BRĀ dĭ
Brandon — BRĂN d'n
Brashear — bruh SHĬR
Brazoria — bruh ZŌ rĭ uh
Brazos — BRĂZ uhs
Breckenridge — BRĔK uhn rĭj
Bremond — bree MAHND
Brenham — BRĔ n'm
Brewster — BROO ster
Brice — brīs
Bridgeport — BRĬJ pohrt
Briggs — brĭgz
Briscoe — BRĬS koh
Britton — BRĬT n
Broaddus — BRAW d's
Brock — brahk
Bronson — BRAHN s'n
Bronte — brahnt
Brookeland — BROOK l'nd
Brookesmith — BROOK smith
Brookshire — BROOK sher
Brookston — BROOKS t'n
Brown — brown
Browndel — brown DĔL
Brownfield — BROWN feeld
Brownsboro — BROWNZ buh ruh
Brownsville — BROWNZ vĭl
Brownwood — BROWN wood
Bruceville — BROOS v'l
Brundage — BRUHN dĭj
Bruni — BROO nĭ
Brushy Creek — bruh shĭ KREEK
Bryan — BRĪ uhn
Bryans Mill — brī 'nz MĬL
Bryarly — BRĪ er lĭ
Bryson — BRĪ s'n
Buchanan Dam — buhk hăn uhn DĂM
Buckholts — BUHK hohlts
Buckhorn — BUHK hawrn
Buda — BYOO duh
Buena Vista — bwā nuh VEES tuh
Buffalo — BUHF uh loh
Buffalo Gap — buhf uh loh GĂP
Buffalo Springs — buhf uh loh SPRĬNGZ
Bula — BYOO luh
Bullard — BOOL erd
Bulverde — bool VER dĭ
Buna — BYOO nuh
Burkburnett — berk ber NET
Burkett — BER kĭt
Burkeville — BERK vĭl
Burleson — BER luh s'n
Burlington — BER lĭng t'n
Burnet — BER nĕt
Burton — BERT n
Bushland — BOOSH l'nd
Bustamante — buhs tuh MAHN tĭ
Butler — BUHT ler
Byers — BĪ erz
Bynum — BĪ n'm
Byrd — berd

C

Caddo Mills — kă doh MĬLZ
Calallen — kăl ĂL ĭn
Calaveras — kăl uh VĔR's
Caldwell — KAHL wĕl
Calhoun — kăl HOON
Call — kawl
Calliham — KĂL uh hăm
Callisburg — KĂ lĭs berg
Call Junction — kawl JUHNGK sh'n
Calvert — KĂL vert
Camden — KĂM dĭn
Cameron — KĂM uh r'n
Camilla — kuh MEEL yuh
Camp — kămp
Campbell — KĂM uhl
Campbellton — KĂM uhl t'n
Camp Wood — kămp WOOD
Canadian — kuh NĀ dĭ uhn
Candelaria — kăn duh LĔ rĭ uh
Canton — KĂNT n
Canyon — KĂN y'n
Caplen — KĂP lĭn
Caps — kăps
Caradan — KĂR uh dăn
Carbon — KAHR b'n
Carey — KĀ rĭ
Carlisle — KAHR līl
Carlsbad — KAHR uhlz băd
Carlton — KAHR uhl t'n
Carmine — kahr MEEN
Carmona — kahr MŌ nuh
Caro — KAH roh
Carrizo Springs — kuh ree zuh SPRĬNGZ
Carrollton — KĂR 'l t'n
Carson — KAHR s'n
Carthage — KAHR thĭj
Cash — kăsh
Cason — KĀ s'n
Cass — kăs
Castell — kăs TĔL
Castro — KĂS troh
Castroville — KĂS tro vĭl
Catarina — kăt uh REE nuh
Cat Spring — kăt SPRĬNG
Caviness — KĀ vĭ nĕs
Cayuga — kā YOO guh
Cedar Bayou — see der BĪ oh
Cedar Creek — see der KREEK
Cedar Hill — see der HĬL
Cedar Lake — see der LĀK
Cedar Lane — see der LĀN
Cedar Park — see der PAHRK
Cedar Valley — see der VA lĭ
Cee Vee — see VEE
Celeste — suh LĔST
Celina — suh LĪ nuh
Center — SENT er
Center City — sĕn ter SĬT ĭ
Center Point — sĕn ter POINT
Centerville — sĕn ter vĭl
Centralia — sĕn TRĀL yuh
Chalk — chawlk
Chalk Mountain — chawlk MOWNT n
Chambers — CHĀM berz
Chandler — CHĂND ler
Channelview — chăn uhl VYOO
Channing — CHĂN ĭng
Chapman Ranch — chăp m'n RĂNCH
Chappell Hill — chă p'l HĬL
Charco — CHAHR koh
Charleston — CHAHR uhls t'n
Charlie — CHAHR lĭ
Charlotte — SHAHR l't
Chatfield — CHĂT feeld
Cheapside — CHEEP sīd
Cherokee — CHĔR uh kee
Chester — CHĔS ter
Chico — CHEE koh
Chicota — chĭ KŌ tuh
Childress — CHĬL drĕs
Chillicothe — chĭl ĭ KAH thĭ
Chilton — CHĬL t'n
China — CHĪ nuh
China Spring — chī nuh SPRĬNG
Chireno — sh' REE noh
Chisholm — CHĬZ uhm
Chita — CHEE tuh
Chocolate Bayou — chah kuh lĭt BĪ oh
Choice — chois
Chriesman — KRĬS m'n
Christine — krĭs TEEN

Diacritical markings are used as follows: bāle, băd, lĕt, rīse, rĭll, ōak, fŏŏt. The stressed syllable is capitalized. Secondary stress is indicated by an underline as in Atascosa — ăt uhs KŌ suh.

Christoval — krĭs TŌ v'l
Cibolo — SEE boh loh
Circle Back — SER k'l băk
Circleville — SER k'l vĭl
Cisco — SĬS koh
Cistern — SĬS tern
Clairemont — KLĂR mahnt
Clairette — klăr ĭ ĔT
Clarendon — KLĂR ĭn d'n
Clareville — KLĂR vĭl
Clarksville — KLAHRKS vĭl
Clarkwood — KLAHRK wood
Claude — klawd
Clawson — KLAW s'n
Clay — klā
Clayton — KLĀT n
Clear Lake — KLĬR lāk
Clear Spring — klĭr SPRĬNG
Cleburne — KLEE bern
Clemville — KLĔM vĭl
Cleveland — KLEEV l'nd
Clifton — KLĬF t'n
Cline — klīn
Clodine — klaw DEEN
Clute — klyoot
Clyde — klīd
Coahoma — kuh HŌ muh
Cockrell Hill — kahk ruhl HĬL
Coke — kohk
Coldspring — KŌLD sprĭng
Coleman — KŌL m'n
Colfax — KAHL făks
Collegeport — kah lĭj PŌRT
College Station — <u>kah</u> lĭj STĀ sh'n
Collin — KAH lĭn
Collingsworth — KAH lĭnz werth
Collinsville — KAH lĭnz vĭl
Colmesneil — KŌL m's neel
Colorado — <u>kahl</u> uh RAH doh
Colorado City — kah luh <u>rā</u> duh or kah luh <u>rah</u> duh SĬT ĭ
Columbus — kuh LUHM b's
Comal — KŌ măl
Comanche — kuh MĂN chĭ
Combes — kohmz
Comfort — KUHM fert
Commerce — KAH mers
Como — KŌ moh
Comstock — KAHM stahk
Concan — KAHN kăn
Concepcion — kuhn sep sĭ ŌN
Concho — KAHN choh
Concord — KAHN kawrd
Concrete — kahn KREET
Cone — kohn
Conlen — KAHN lĭn
Conroe — KAHN roh
Converse — KAHN vers
Conway — KAHN wā
Cooke — kook
Cookville — KOOK vĭl
Coolidge — KOO lĭj
Copeville — KŌP v'l
Coppell — kahp pĕl or kuhp PĔL
Copperas Cove — kahp ruhs KŌV
Corbett — KAWR bĭt
Cordele — kawr DĔL
Corinth — KAH rĭnth
Corley — KAWR lĭ
Corpus Christi — <u>kawr</u> p's KRĬS tĭ
Corrigan — KAWR uh g'n
Corsicana — <u>kawr</u> sĭ KĂN uh
Coryell — koh rĭ ĔL
Cottle — KAH t'l
Cotton Center — <u>kaht</u> n SĔNT er
Cotton Gin — KAHT n jĭn
Cottonwood — KAHT n wood
Cotulla — kuh TOO luh
Coupland — KŌP l'n
Courtney — KŌRT nĭ
Covington — KUHV ĭng t'n
Coy City — koi SĬT ĭ
Craft — krăft
Crafton — KRĂF t'n
Crandall — KRĂN d'l
Crane — krān
Cranfills Gap — krăn f'lz GĂP
Crawford — KRAW ferd
Creedmoor — KREED mohr
Cresson — KRĔ s'n
Crockett — KRAH kĭt
Crosbyton — KRAWZ bĭ t'n
Cross Cut — KRAWS kuht
Cross Plains — kraws PLĀNZ
Cross Roads — KRAWS rohdz
Crowell — KRŌ uhl
Crowley — KROW li
Crystal City — krĭs t'l SĬT ĭ
Crystal Falls — krĭs t'l FAWLZ
Cuero — KWĔR o
Culberson — KUHL ber s'n
Cumby — KUHM bĭ
Cuney — KYOO nĭ
Cunningham — KUHN ĭng hăm
Currie — KER rĭ
Cushing — KOO shĭng
Cuthand — KUHT hănd

D

Dabney — DĂB nĭ
Dacosta — duh KAHS tuh
Dacus — DĀ k's
Daingerfield — DĀN jer feeld
Daisetta — dā ZĔT uh
Dalby Springs — dĂl bĭ SPRĬNGZ
Dalhart — DĂL hahrt
Dallam — DĂL uhm
Dallas — DĂ luhs
Damon — DĀ m'n
Danbury — DĂN bĕrĭ
Danciger — DĂN sĭ ger
Danevang — DĂN uh văng
Darrouzett — dăr uh ZĔT
Davilla — duh VĬL uh
Dawson — DAW s'n
Dayton — DĀT n
Deaf Smith — dĕf SMĬTH
Deanville — DEEN vĭl
DeBerry — duh BĔ rĭ
Decatur — <u>dee</u> KĀT er
De Kalb — dĭ KĂB
De Leon — da lee AHN
Del Rio — dĕl REE oh
Del Valle — dĕl VĂ lĭ
Delwin — DĔl wĭn
Denhawken — DĬN haw kĭn
Denison — DĔN uh s'n
Denning — DĔN ĭng
Denton — DĔNT n
Denver City — <u>dĕn</u> ver SĬT ĭ
Deport — DEE pohrt or dĭ PŌRT
Derby — DER bĭ
Desdemona — <u>dĕz</u> dĭ MŌ nuh
DeSoto — dĭ SŌ tuh
Detroit — dee TROIT
Devers — DĔ vers
Devine — duh VĪN
Dew — dyoo
Deweyville — DYOO ĭ vĭl
DeWitt — dĭ WĬT
Dewville — DYOO vĭl
Dexter — DĔKS ter
D'Hanis — duh HĂ nĭs
Dialville — DĪ uhl vil
Diboll — DĪ bawl
Dickens — DĬK ĭnz
Dickinson — DĬK ĭn s'n
Dike — dīk
Dilley — DĬL i
Dilworth — DĬL <u>werth</u>
Dimebox — dīm BAHKS
Dimmit — DĬM ĭt
Dinero — dĭ NĔ roh
Direct — duh RĔKT
Dixon — DĬK s'n
Dobbin — DAH bĭn
Dobrowolski — <u>dah</u> bruh WAHL skĭ
Dodd City — dahd SĬT ĭ
Dodson — DAHD s'n
Donie — DŌ nĭ
Donley — DAHN lĭ
Doole — DOO lĭ
Dorchester — dawr CHĔS ter
Doucette — DOO sĕt
Dougherty — DAHR tĭ
Douglass — DUHG l's
Douglassville — DUHG lĭs vĭl
Downing — DOWN ĭng
Downsville — DOWNZ vĭl
Dozier — DŌ zher
Driftwood — DRĬFT wood
Dripping Springs — drĭp ĭng SPRĬNGZ
Driscoll — DRĬS k'l
Dryden — DRĪD n
Dublin — DUHB lĭn
Duffau — DUHF oh
Dumas — DOO m's
Dumont — DYOO mahnt
Dundee — DUHN dĭ
Dunlap — DUHN lăp
Dunlay — DUHN lĭ
Durango — duh RĂNG goh
Duval — DOO vawl

E

Eagle Lake — <u>ee</u> g'l LĀK
Eagle Pass — <u>ee</u> g'l PĂS
East Bernard — <u>eest</u> ber NAHRD
Easterly — EES ter lĭ
Eastland — EEST l'nd
Easton — EES t'n
Ector — ĔK ter
Edcouch — ĕd KOWCH
Eddy — E di
Eden — EED n
Edge — ĕj
Edgewood — ĔJ wood
Edinburg — ĔD n <u>berg</u>
Edmonson — ĔD m'n s'n

Diacritical markings are used as follows: bāle, băd, lĕt, rīse, rĭll, ōak, fŏŏt. The stressed syllable is capitalized. Secondary stress is indicated by an underline as in Atascosa — <u>ăt</u> uhs KŌ suh.

Edna — ED nuh
Edom — EE d'm
Edroy — ĔD roi
Egan — EE g'n
Egypt — EE juhpt
Elbert — ĔL bert
El Campo — ĕl KĂM poh
Eldorado — ĕl duh RĀ duh
Electra — ĭ LĔK truh
Elgin — ĔL gĭn
Eliasville — ee LĪ uhs vĭl
El Indio — ĕl ĬN dĭ oh
Elkhart — ĔLK hahrt
Ellinger — ĔL ĭn jer
Elliott — ĔL ĭ 't
Ellis — ĔL uhs
Elmendorf — ĔLM 'n dawrf
Elm Mott — ĕl MAHT
Elmo — ĔL moh
Eloise — ĔL o eez
Elsa — ĔL suh
Elysian Fields — uh lee zh'n FEELDZ
Emhouse — ĔM hows
Emory — ĔM uh rĭ
Encinal — ĕn suh NAHL
Encino — ĕn SEE noh
Energy — ĔN er jĭ
Engle — ĔN g'l
Enloe — ĔN loh
Ennis — ĔN ĭs
Enochs — EE nuhks
Eola — ee Ō luh
Era — EE ruh
Erath — EE răth
Esperanza — ĕs per RĂN zuh
Estelline — ĔS tuh leen
Etoile — ĭ TOIL
Etter — ĔT er
Eula — YOO luh
Euless — YOO lĭs
Eureka — yoo REE kuh
Eustace — YOOS t's
Evadale — EE vuh dāl
Evant — EE vănt
Everman — Ĕ ver m'n

F

Fabens — FĀ b'nz
Fairbanks — FĂR bangks
Fairfield — FĂR feeld
Fairlie — FĂR lee
Fair Play — făr PLĀ
Fairview — FĂR vyoo
Fairy — FĀ rĭ
Falfurrias — făl FYOO rĭ uhs
Falls City — fawlz SĬT ĭ
Fannett — fă NĔT
Fannin — FĂN ĭn
Fargo — FAHR goh
Farmers Branch — fahr merz BRĂNCH
Farmersville — FAHRM erz vĭl
Farnsworth — FAHRNZ werth
Farrar — FĂR uh
Farrsville — FAHRZ vĭl
Farwell — FAHR w'l
Fashing — FĂ shĭng
Fayette — fā ĔT
Fayetteville — FĀ uht vĭl
Fentress — FĔN trĭs
Ferris — FĔR ĭs
Field Creek — feeld KREEK
Fieldton — FEEL t'n
Fife — fīf
Fischer — FĬ sher
Fisher — FĬSH er
Flagg — flăg
Flatonia — flă TŌN yuh
Flomot — FLŌ maht
Florence — FLAH ruhns
Floresville — FLŌRZ vil
Florey — FLŌ ri
Floydada — floi DĀ duh
Fluvanna — flyoo VĂN uh
Flynn — flĭn
Foard — fohrd
Foard City — fohrd SĬT ĭ
Fodice — FŌ dĭs
Follett — fah LĔT
Fordtran — fohrd TRĂN
Forest — FAW rĕst
Forestburg — FAW rĕst berg
Forney — FAWR nĭ
Forreston — FAW rĕs t'n
Forsan — FŌR săn
Fort Bend — fohrt BĔND
Fort Chadbourne — fohrt CHĂD bern
Fort Davis — fohrt DĀ vĭs
Fort Griffin — fohrt GRĬF ĭn
Fort Hancock — fohrt HĂN kahk
Fort McKavett — fohrt muh KĂ vĕt
Fort Stockton — fohrt STAHK t'n
Fort Worth — fohrt WERTH
Fowlerton — FOW ler t'n
Francitas — frăn SEE t's
Franklin — FRĂNGK lĭn
Frankston — FRĂNGS t'n
Fred — frĕd
Fredericksburg — FRĔD er rĭks berg
Fredonia — free DŌN yuh
Freeport — FREE pohrt
Freer — FREE er
Freestone — FREE stohn
Frelsburg — FRĔLZ berg
Fresno — FRĔZ noh
Friday — FRĪ dĭ
Friendswood — FRĔNZ wood
Frio — FREE oh
Friona — free Ō nuh
Frisco — FRĬS koh
Fritch — frĭch
Fruitland — FROOT lănd
Fruitvale — FROOT vāl
Frydek — FRĪ dĕk
Fulbright — FOOL brīt
Fulshear — FUHL sher
Fulton — FOOL t'n

G

Gail — gāl
Gaines — gānz
Gainesville — GĀNZ vuhl
Galena Park — guh lee nuh PAHRK
Gallatin — GĂL uh t'n
Galveston — GĂL vĕs t'n
Ganado — guh NĀ doh
Garceno — gahr SĀ noh
Garciasville — gahr SEE uhs vĭl
Garden City — GAHRD n sĭt ĭ
Gardendale — GAHRD n dāl
Garden Valley — gahrd n VĂ lĭ
Garland — GAHR l'nd
Garner — GAHR ner
Garrett — GĂR ĭt
Garrison — GĂ rĭ s'n
Garwood — GAHR wood
Gary — GĔ rĭ
Garza — GAHR zuh
Gatesville — GĀTS vil
Gause — gawz
Gay Hill — gā HĬL
Geneva — juh NEE vuh
Georgetown — JAWRJ town
George West — jawrj WĔST
Geronimo — juh RAH nĭ moh
Giddings — GĬD ĭngz
Gillespie — guh LĔS pĭ
Gillett — juh LĔT
Gilliland — GĬL ĭ l'nd
Gilmer — GĬL mer
Ginger — JĬN jer
Girard — juh RAHRD
Girvin — GER vĭn
Gladewater — GLĀD wah ter
Glasscock — GLĂS kahk
Glazier — GLĀ zher
Glen Cove — glĕn KŌV
Glendale — GLĔN dāl
Glenfawn — glĕn FAWN
Glen Flora — glĕn FLŌ ruh
Glenn — glĕn
Glen Rose — GLĔN rohz
Glidden — GLĬD n
Gober — GŌ ber
Godley — GAHD lĭ
Golden — GŌL d'n
Goldfinch — GŌLD fĭnch
Goldsboro — GŌLZ buh ruh
Goldsmith — GŌL smith
Goldthwaite — GŌLTH wāt
Goliad — GŌ lĭ ăd
Golinda — goh LĬN duh
Gonzales — guhn ZAH l's
Goodland — GOOD l'n
Goodlett — GOOD lĕt
Goodnight — GOOD nīt
Goodrich — GOOD rĭch
Gordon — GAWRD n
Gordonville — GAWRD n vĭl
Goree — GŌ ree
Gorman — GAWR m'n
Gouldbusk — GOOLD buhsk
Graford — GRĀ ferd
Graham — GRĀ 'm
Granbury — GRĂN bĕ rĭ
Grandfalls — grănd FAWLZ
Grand Saline — grăn suh LEEN
Grandview — GRĂN vyoo
Granger — GRĀN jer
Grapeland — GRĀP l'nd
Grapevine — GRĀP vīn
Grassland — GRĂS l'nd
Grassyville — GRĂ sĭ vĭl
Gray — grā
Grayburg — GRĀ berg
Grayson — GRA s'n
Green — green
Greenville — GREEN v'l
Greenwood — GREEN wood
Gregg — grĕg
Gregory — GRĔG uh rĭ
Grimes — grīmz
Groesbeck — GRŌZ bĕk

Diacritical markings are used as follows: bāle, băd, lĕt, rīse, rĭll, ōak, fŏŏt. The stressed syllable is capitalized. Secondary stress is indicated by an underline as in Atascosa — ăt uhs KŌ suh.

Groom — gryoom
Groveton — GRŌV t'n
Gruene — green
Grulla — GROOL yuh
Gruver — GROO ver
Guadalupe — gwah duh LOO pĭ or gwah duh LOO pā
Guerra — GWĔ ruh
Gunter — GUHN ter
Gustine — GUHS teen
Guthrie — GUHTH rĭ
Guy — gī

H

Hackberry — HĂK bĕ rĭ
Hagansport — HĀ gĭnz pohrt
Hainesville — HĀNZ v'l
Hale — hāl
Hale Center — hāl SĔNT er
Hall — hawl
Hallettsville — HĂL ĕts vĭl
Hallsville — HAWLZ vĭl
Hamilton — HĂM uhl t'n
Hamlin — HĂM lĭn
Hammond — HĂM 'nd
Hamon — HĀ m'n
Hamshire — HĂM sher
Handley — HĂND lĭ
Hankamer — HĂN kăm er
Hansford — HĂNZ ferd
Happy — HĂ pĭ
Hardeman — HAHR duh m'n
Hardin — HAHRD n
Hare — hăr
Hargill — HAHR gĭl
Harleton — HAHR uhl t'n
Harlingen — HAHR lĭn juhn
Harper — HAHR per
Harrison — HĂ rĭ s'n
Harrold — HĂR 'ld
Hartburg — HAHRT berg
Hartley — HAHRT lĭ
Harwood — HAHR wood
Haskell — HĂS k'l
Haslam — HĂZ l'm
Haslet — HĂS lĕt
Hasse — HĂ sĭ
Hatchell — HĂ ch'l
Hawkins — HAW kĭnz
Hawley — HAW lĭ
Hearne — hern
Heath — heeth
Hebbronville — HĔB r'n vĭl
Hebron — HEE br'n
Hedley — HĔD lĭ
Heidenheimer — HĪD n hīmer
Helena — HĔL uh nuh
Helotes — hĕl Ō tĭs
Hemphill — HĔMP hĭl
Hempstead — HĔM stĕd
Henderson — HĔN der s'n
Henly — HĔN lĭ
Henrietta — hĕn rĭ Ĕ tuh
Hereford — HER ferd
Hermleigh — HER muh lee
Hewitt — HYOO ĭt
Hico — HĪ koh
Hidalgo — hĭ DĂL goh
Higgins — HĬ gĭnz
Highbank — HĪ băngk
High Island — hī Ī l'nd
Highlands — HĪ l'ndz
Hightower — HĪ tow er
Hillister — HĬL ĭs ter
Hillsboro — HĬLZ buh ruh
Hindes — hīndz
Hiram — HĪ r'm
Hitchcock — HĬCH kahk
Hitchland — HĬCH l'nd
Hobson — HAHB s'n
Hochheim — HŌ hīm
Hockley — HAHK lĭ
Holland — HAHL 'nd
Holliday — HAH luh dā
Hondo — HAHN doh
Honey Grove — HUHN ĭ grohv
Honey Island — huhn ĭ Ī l'nd
Honey Springs — huhn ĭ SPRĬNGZ
Hopkins — HAHP kĭnz
Houston — HYOOS t'n or YOOS t'n
Howard — HOW erd
Howe — how
Howland — HOW l'nd
Hubbard — HUH berd
Huckabay — HUHK uh bĭ
Hudspeth — HUHD sp'th
Huffman — HUHF m'n
Hufsmith — HUHF smĭth
Hughes Springs — hyooz SPRĬNGZ
Humble — UHM b'l
Hungerford — HUHNG ger ferd
Hunter — HUHNT er
Huntington — HUHNT ĭng t'n
Huntsville — HUHNTS v'l
Hurlwood — HERL wood
Hutchins — HUH chĭnz
Hutchinson — HUH chĭn s'n
Hutto — HUH toh
Hye — hī
Hylton — HĬL t'n

I

Iago — ī Ā goh
Idalou — Ī duh lyoo
Imperial — ĭm PĬR ĭ uhl
Inadale — Ī nuh dāl
Independence — ĭn duh PĔN d'ns
Indian Creek — ĭn dĭ uhn KREEK
Indian Gap — ĭn dĭ uhn GĂP
Industry — ĬN duhs trĭ
Inez — ī NĔZ
Ingleside — ĬNG g'l sīd
Ingram — ĬNG gr'm
Iola — ī Ō luh
Iowa Park — ī uh wuh PAHRK
Ira — Ī ruh
Iraan — ī ruh ĂN
Iredell — Ī ruh dĕl
Ireland — Ī rĭ l'nd
Irene — ī REEN
Irion — ĬR i uhn
Ironton — ĪRN t'n
Irving — ER vĭng
Italy — ĬT uh lĭ
Itasca — ī TĂS kuh
Ivan — Ī v'n
Ivanhoe — Ī v'n hoh

J

Jacksboro — JĂKS buh ruh
Jackson — JĂK s'n
Jacksonville — JĂK s'n vĭl
Jamestown — JĀMZ town
Jardin — JAHRD n
Jarrell — JĂR uhl
Jasper — JĂS per
Jayton — JĀT n
Jean — jeen
Jeddo — JĔ doh
Jeff Davis — jĕf DA vĭs
Jefferson — JĔF er s'n
Jericho — JĔ rĭ koh
Jermyn — JER m'n
Jewett — JOO ĭt
Jiba — HEE buh
Jim Hogg — jĭm HAWG
Jim Wells — jĭm WĔLZ
Joaquin — waw KEEN
Johnson — JAHN s'n
Johnson City — jahn s'n SĬT ĭ
Johntown — JAHN town
Johnsville — JAHNZ vĭl
Joinerville — JOI ner vĭl
Jolly — JAH lĭ
Jollyville — JAH lĭ vĭl
Jonah — JŌ nuh
Jones — johnz
Jonesboro — JŌNZ buh ruh
Jonesville — JŌNZ vĭl
Josephine — JŌ suh feen
Joshua — JAH sh' wa
Jourdanton — JERD n t'n
Joyce — jawĭs
Juliff — JOO lĭf
Junction — JUHNGK sh'n
Juno — JOO noh
Justiceburg — JUHS tĭs berg

K

Kalgary — KĂL gĕ rĭ
Kamay — KĀ ĭm ā
Kanawha — KAHN uh wah
Karnack — KAHR năk
Karnes — kahrnz
Karnes City — kahrnz SĬT ĭ
Katemcy — kuh TĔM sĭ
Katy — KĀ tĭ
Kaufman — KAWF m'n
Keechi — KEE chī
Keene — keen
Kellerville — KĔL er vĭl
Kemah — KEE muh
Kemp — kĕmp or kĭmp
Kemp City — kĕmp SĬT ĭ
Kempner — KĔMP ner
Kendalia — kĕn DĀL yuh
Kenedy — KĔN uh dĭ
Kennard — kuh NAHRD
Kennedale — KĔN uh dāl
Kerens — KER 'nz
Kermit — KER mĭt
Kerrville — KER vĭl
Kildare — KĬL dăr
Kilgore — KĬL gohr
Killeen — kuh LEEN
Kimble — KĬM b'l
Kingsbury — KĬNGZ bĕ rĭ
Kingsland — KĬNGZ l'nd
Kingsmill — kĭngz MĬL
Kingston — KĬNGZ t'n
Kingsville — KĬNGZ vĭl
Kinney — KĬN ĭ
Kirby — KER bĭ

Diacritical markings are used as follows: bāle, băd, lĕt, rīse, rĭll, ōak, fŏŏt. The stressed syllable is capitalized. Secondary stress is indicated by an underline as in Atascosa — ăt uhs KŌ suh.

Kirbyville — KER bĭ vĭl
Kirkland — KERK l'nd
Kirvin — KER vĭn
Kleberg — KLĀ berg
Klondike — KLAHN dīk
Knickerbocker — NĬK uh bah ker
Knippa — kuh NĬP uh
Knox — nahks
Knox City — nahks SĬT ĭ
Kosciusko — kuh SHOOS koh
Kosse — KAH sĭ
Kountze — kyoontz
Kurten — KER t'n

L

La Blanca — lah BLAHN kuh
La Coste — luh KAWST
Ladonia — luh DŌN yuh
LaFayette — lah fĭ ĔT
Laferia — luh FĔ rĭ uh
Lagarto — luh GAHR toh
La Gloria — lah GLŌ rĭ uh
La Grange — luh GRĀNJ
Laguna — luh GOO nuh
Laird Hill — lărd HĬL
La Joya — luh HŌ yuh
Lake Creek — lāk KREEK
Lake Dallas — lāk DĂL uhs
Lake Jackson — lāk JĂK s'n
Laketon — LĀK t'n
Lake Victor — lāk VĬK ter
Lakeview — LĀK vyoo
Lamar — luh MAHR
La Marque — luh MAHRK
Lamasco — luh MĂS koh
Lamb — lăm
Lamesa — luh MEE suh
Lamkin — LĂM kĭn
Lampasas — lăm PĂ s's
Lancaster — LĂNG k's ter
Laneville — LĀN vĭl
Langtry — LĂNG trĭ
Lanier — luh NĬR
La Paloma — lah puh LŌ muh
La Porte — luh PŌRT
La Pryor — luh PRĪ er
Laredo — luh RĀ doh
Lariat — LĂ ri uht
Larue — luh ROO
La Salle — luh SĂL
Lasara — luh SĔ ruh
Lassater — LĂ sĭ ter
Latch — lĂch
Latexo — luh TĔKS oh
Lavaca — luh VĂ kuh
La Vernia — luh VER nĭ uh
La Villa — lah VĬL uh
Lavon — luh VAHN
La Ward — luh WAWRD
Lawrence — LAH r'ns
Lazbuddie — LĂZ buh dĭ
League City — leeg SĬT ĭ
Leakey — LĀ kĭ
Leander — lee ĂN der
Leary — LĬ er ĭ
Ledbetter — LĔD bĕt er
Leesburg — LEEZ berg
Leesville — LEEZ vĭl
Lefors — lĭ FŌRZ
Leggett — LĔ gĭt
Leigh — lee
Lela — LEE luh
Lelia Lake — leel yuh LĀK
Leming — LĔ mĭng
Lenorah — lĕ NŌ ruh
Leon — lee AHN
Leona — lee Ō nuh
Leonard — LĔN erd
Leon Springs — lee ahn SPRĬNGZ
Leroy — LEE roi
Levelland — LĔ v'l lănd
Levita — luh VĪ tuh
Lewisville — LOO ĭs vĭl
Lexington — LĔKS ĭng t'n
Liberty — LĬB er tĭ
Liberty Hill — lĭ ber tĭ HĬL
Lillian — LĬL yuhn
Limestone — LĪM stohn
Lincoln — LĬNG k'n
Lindale — LĬN dāl
Linden — LĬN d'n
Lindenau — lĭn duh NOW
Lindsay — LĬN zĭ
Lingleville — LĬNG g'l vĭl
Linn — lĭn
Lipan — lī PĂN
Lipscomb — LĬPS k'm
Lissie — LĬ sĭ
Little Elm — lĭt l ĔLM
Littlefield — LĬT uhl feeld
Little River — lĭt uhl RĬV er
Live Oak — LĬV ohk
Liverpool — LĬ ver pyool
Livingston — LĬV ĭngz t'n
Llano — LĂ noh
Locker — LAH ker
Lockett — LAH kĭt
Lockhart — LAHK hahrt
Lockney — LAHK nĭ
Lodi — LŌ dī
Lohn — lahn
Lolita — loh LEE tuh
Loma Alto — loh muh ĂL toh
Lometa — loh MEE tuh
London — LUHN d'n
Lone Grove — lohn GRŌV
Lone Oak — LŌN ohk
Long Branch — lawng BRĂNCH
Long Mott — lawng MAHT
Longview — LAWNG vyoo
Longworth — LAWNG werth
Loop — loop
Lopeno — loh PEE noh
Loraine — loh RĀN
Lorena — loh REE nuh
Los Angeles — laws AN juh l's
Los Ebanos — lohs ĔB uh nohs
Los Fresnos — lohs FRĔZ nohs
Los Indios — lohs ĬN dĭ ohs
Losoya — luh SAW yuh
Lott — laht
Louise — LOO eez
Lovelady — LUHV lā dĭ
Loving — LUH vĭng
Lowake — loh WĀ kĭ
Lubbock — LUH buhk or LUH b'k
Lueders — LOO derz
Luella — lyoo ĔL uh
Lufkin — LUHF kĭn
Luling — LOO lĭng
Lutie — LOO tĭ
Lyford — LĪ ferd
Lyons — LĪ 'nz
Lytton Springs — lĭt n SPRĬNGZ

M

Mabank — MĀ băngk
Macune — muh KOON
Madison — MĂ dĭ s'n
Madisonville — MĂ duh s'n vĭl
Magnolia — măg NŌL yuh
Magnolia Springs — măg nol yuh SPRĬNGZ
Malakoff — MĂL uh kawf
Malone — muh LŌN
Malta — MAWL tuh
Manchaca — MĂN shăk
Manchester — MĂN chĕs ter
Manheim — MĂN hīm
Mankins — MĂN kĭnz
Manor — MĀ ner
Mansfield — MĂNZ feeld
Manvel — MĂN v'l
Marathon — MĂR uh th'n
Marble Falls — mahr b'l FAWLZ
Marfa — MAHR fuh
Margaret — MAHR guh rĭt
Marietta — mĕ rĭ Ĕ tuh
Marion — MĔ rĭ uhn
Markham — MAHR k'm
Marlin — MAHR lĭn
Marquez — mahr KĀ
Marshall — MAHR sh'l
Martin — MAHRT n
Martindale — MAHRT n dāl
Martinsville — MAHRT nz vĭl
Maryneal — mā rĭ NEEL
Marysville — MĀ rĭz vĭl
Mason — MĀ s'n
Matador — MĂT uh dohr
Matagorda — măt uh GAWR duh
Mathis — MĂ thĭs
Maud — mawd
Mauriceville — maw REES vĭl
Maverick — MĂV rĭk
Maxey — MĂKS ĭ
Maxwell — MĂKS w'l
Maydell — MĀ dĕl
Maypearl — mā PERL
Maysfield — MĀZ feeld
McAdoo — MĂK uh dyoo
McAllen — măk ĂL ĭn
McCamey — muh KĀ mĭ
McCaulley — muh KAW lĭ
McCoy — muh KOI
McCulloch — muh KUH luhk
McFaddin — măk FĂD n
McGregor — muh GRĔ ger
McKinney — muh KĬN ĭ
McLean — muh KLĀN
McLennan — muhk LĔN uhn
McLeod — măk LOWD
McMahan — măk MĂN
McMullen — măk MUHL ĭn
McNary — măk NĀ rĭ
McNeil — măk NEEL
McQueeney — muh KWEE nĭ
Medicine Mound — mĕd uhs n MOWND
Medill — mĕ DĬL
Medina — muh DEE nuh
Megargel — muh GAHR g'l
Melissa — muh LĬS uh

Diacritical markings are used as follows: bāle, băd, lĕt, rīse, rĭll, ōak, fŏŏt. The stressed syllable is capitalized. Secondary stress is indicated by an underline as in Atascosa — ăt uhs KŌ suh.

Melrose — MĔL rohz
Melvin — MĔL vĭn
Memphis — MĔM fĭs
Menard — muh NAHRD
Mendoza — mĕn DŌ zuh
Mentone — mĕn TŌN
Mercedes — mer SĀ deez
Mercury — MER kyuh ri
Mereta — muh RĔT uh
Meridian — muh RĬ dĭ uhn
Merit — MĔR ĭt
Merkel — MER k'l
Mertens — mer TĔNZ
Mertzon — MERTS n
Mesquite — muhs KEET
Mexia — muh HĀ uh
Meyersville — MĪRZ vĭl
Miami — mī ĂM uh or mī ĂM ĭ
Mico — MEE koh
Middleton — MĬD uhl t'n
Midfields — MĬD feeldz
Midland — MĬD l'nd
Midlothian — mĭd LŌ thĭ n
Milam — MĪ l'm
Milano — mĭ LĂ noh
Mildred — MĬL drĕd
Miles — mīlz
Milford — MĬL ferd
Miller Grove — mĭl er GRŌV
Millersview — MĬL erz vyoo
Millett — MĬL ĭt
Millheim — MĬL hīm
Millican — MĬL uh kuhn
Mills — mĭlz
Millsap — MĬL săp
Minden — MĬN d'n
Mineola — mĭn ĭ Ō luh
Mineral — MĬN er uhl
Mineral Wells — mĭn er uhl WĔLZ
Minerva — mĭ NER vuh
Mingus — MĬNG guhs
Minter — MĬNT er
Mirando City — mĭ răn duh SĬT ĭ
Mission — MĬSH uhn
Mission Valley — mĭsh uhn VĂ lĭ
Missouri City — muh zoor uh SĬT ĭ
Mitchell — MĬ ch'l
Mobeetie — moh BEE tĭ
Moline — moh LEEN
Monahans — MAH nuh hănz
Monaville — MŌ nuh vĭl
Monkstown — MUHNGKS town
Monroe — MAHN roh
Monroe City — mahn roh SĬT ĭ
Montague — mahn TĀG
Montalba — mahnt ĂL buh
Mont Belvieu — mahnt BĔL vyoo
Montell — mahn TĔL
Montgomery — mahnt GUHM er ĭ
Monthalia — mahn THĀL yuh
Moore — mohr
Morales — muh RAH lĕs
Moran — moh RĂN
Morgan — MAWR g'n
Morgan Mill — mawr g'n MĬL
Morse — mawrs
Morton — MAWRT n
Moscow — MAHS kow
Mosheim — MŌ shīm
Moss Bluff — maws BLUHF
Motley — MAHT lĭ
Moulton — MŌL t'n
Mound — mownd
Mountain Home — mownt n HŌM
Mount Calm — mownt KAHM
Mount Enterprise — mownt ĔN ter prīz
Mount Pleasant — mownt PLĔ z'nt
Mount Selman — mownt SĔL m'n
Mount Sylvan — mownt SĬL v'n
Mount Vernon — mownt VER n'n
Muenster — MYOONS ter
Muldoon — muhl DOON
Muleshoe — MYOOL shyoo
Mullin — MUHL ĭn
Mumford — MUHM ferd
Munday — MUHN dĭ
Murchison — MER kuh s'n
Murphy — MER fĭ
Mykawa—mĭ KAH wuh
Myra — MĪ ruh
Myrtle Springs — mert l SPRĬNGZ

N

Nacogdoches — năk uh DŌ chĭs
Nada — NĀ duh
Naples — NĀ p'lz
Nash — năsh
Natalia — nuh TĂL yuh
Navarro — nuh VĂ roh
Navasota — năv uh SŌ tuh
Nazareth — NĂZ uh r'th
Neches — NĀ chĭs
Nederland — NEE der l'nd
Needville — NEED vĭl
Nelsonville — NĔL s'n vĭl
Neuville — NYOO v'l
Nevada — nuh VĀ duh
Newark — NOO erk
New Baden — nyoo BĂD n
New Berlin — nyoo BER lin
New Boston — nyoo BAWS t'n
New Braunfels — nyoo BRAHN f'ls or BROWN fĕlz
Newby — NYOO bĭ
New Caney — nyoo KĀ nĭ
Newcastle — NYOO kăs uhl
New Gulf — nyoo GUHLF
New Home — NYOO hohm
New Hope — nyoo HŌP
Newlin — NYOO lĭn
New London — nyoo LUHN d'n
Newman — NYOO m'n
Newport — NYOO pohrt
New Salem — nyoo SĀ l'm
Newsome — NYOO s'm
New Summerfield — nyoo SUHM er feeld
Newton — NYOOT n
New Ulm — nyoo UHLM
New Waverly — nyoo WĀ ver lĭ
New Willard — nyoo WĬL erd
Nimrod — NĬM rahd
Nineveh — NĬN uh vuh
Nixon — NĬKS uhn
Nocona — noh KŌ nuh
Nolan — NŌ l'n
Nolanville — NŌ l'n vĭl
Nome — nohm
Noonday — NOON dā
Nopal — NŌ păl
Nordheim — NAWRD hīm
Normandy — NAWR m'n dĭ
Normangee — NAWR m'n jee
Normanna — nawr MĂN uh
Northrup — NAWR thr'p
North Zulch — nawrth ZOOLCH
Norton — NAWRT n
Novice — NAH vĭs
Nueces — nyoo Ā sĭs
Nugent — NYOO j'nt

O

Oakalla — oh KĂL uh
Oakhurst — ŌK herst
Oakland — ŌK l'nd
Oakville — ŌK vĭl
Oakwood — ŌK wood
O'Brien — oh BRĪ uhn
Ochiltree — AH k'l tree
Odell — Ō dĕl or oh DĔL
Odem — Ō d'm
Odessa — oh DĔS uh
O'Donnell — oh DAH n'l
Oenaville — oh EEN uh v'l
Oglesby — Ō g'lz bĭ
Oilton — OIL t'n
Oklaunion — ohk luh YOON y'n
Olden — ŌL d'n
Oldenburg — ŌL dĭn berg
Oldham — ŌL d'm
Old Glory — ohld GLŌ rĭ
Olivia — oh LĬV ĭ uh
Olmito — awl MEE tuh
Olmos Park — ahl m's PAHRK
Olney — AHL nĭ
Olton — ŌL t'n
Omaha — Ō muh haw
Onalaska — uhn uh LĂS kuh
Oplin — AHP lĭn
Orange — AHR ĭnj
Orangefield — AHR ĭnj feeld
Orange Grove — AHR ĭnj GRŌV
Orchard — AWR cherd
Ore City — ohr SĬT ĭ
Osceola — oh sĭ Ō luh
Otey — Ō tĭ
Otis Chalk — oh tĭs CHAWLK
Ottine — ah TEEN
Otto — AH toh
Ovalo — oh VĂL uh
Overton — Ō ver t'n
Owens — Ō ĭnz
Ozona — oh ZŌ nuh

P

Paducah — puh DYOO kuh
Paige — pāj
Paint Rock — pānt RAHK
Palacios — puh LĂ sh's
Palestine — PAL uhs teen
Palito Blanco — p' lee to BLAHNG koh
Palmer — PAH mer
Palo Pinto — pă loh PĬN toh
Paluxy — puh LUHK sĭ
Pampa — PĂM puh
Pandora — păn DŌR uh
Panhandle — PĂN hăn d'l
Panna Maria — păn uh muh REE uh
Papalote — pah puh LŌ tĭ
Paradise — PĂR uh dīs
Parker — PAHR ker

Diacritical markings are used as follows: bāle, băd, lĕt, rīse, rĭll, ōak, fŏŏt. The stressed syllable is capitalized. Secondary stress is indicated by an underline as in Atascosa — ăt uhs KŌ suh.

Parmer — PAH mer
Parnell — pahr NĔL
Parsley Hill — pahrs lĭ HĬL
Pasadena — păs uh DEE nuh
Patricia — puh TRĬ shuh
Patroon — puh TROON
Pattison — PĂT uh s'n
Pattonville — PĂT n vĭl
Pawnee — paw NEE
Paxton — PĂKS t'n
Pearland — PĂR lănd
Pearsall — PEER sawl
Peaster — PEES ter
Pecan Gap — pĭ kahn GĂP
Pecos — PĀ k's
Penelope — puh NĔL uh pĭ
Penitas — puh NEE t's
Pennington — PĔN ĭng t'n
Penwell — PĬN wĕl
Peoria — pee Ō rĭ uh
Percilla — per SĬL uh
Perrin — PĔR ĭn
Perry — PĔ rĭ
Perryton — PĔ rĭ t'n
Peters — PEET erz
Petersburg — PEET erz berg
Petrolia — puh TRŌL yuh
Petteway — PĔT uh wā
Pettit — PĔT ĭt
Pettus — PĔT uhs
Pflugerville — FLOO ger vĭl
Pharr — fahr
Phelps — fĕlps
Phillips — FĬL uhps
Pickton — PĬK t'n
Pidcoke — PĬD k6k
Piedmont — PEED mahnt
Pierce — PĬ ers
Pilot Point — pī l't POINT
Pine Forest — pīn FAW rĕst
Pinehurst — PĪN herst
Pineland — PĪN land
Pine Mills — pīn MĬLZ
Pine Springs — pīn SPRĬNGZ
Pioneer — pī uh NĬR
Pipecreek — pīp KREEK
Pittsburg — PĬTS berg
Placedo — PLĂS ĭ doh
Placid — PLĂ sĭd
Plainview — PLĀN vyoo
Plano — PLĀ noh
Plantersville — PLĂN terz vĭl
Plaska — PLĂS kuh
Plateau — plă TŌ
Pleasant Grove—plĕ z'nt GRŌV
Pleasanton — PLĔZ uhn t'n
Pledger — PLĔ jer
Pointblank — pint BLĂNGK
Pollock — PAHL uhk
Ponder — PAHN der
Ponta — pahn TĀ
Pontotoc — PAHNT uh tahk
Poolville — POOL vĭl
Port Aransas — pohrt uh RĂN zuhs
Port Arthur — pohrt AHR ther
Port Bolivar — pohrt BAH lĭ ver
Porter Springs — pohr ter SPRĬNGZ
Port Isabel — pohrt ĬZ uh bĕl
Portland — PŌRT l'nd
Port Lavaca — pohrt luh VĀ kuh
Port Neches — pohrt NĀ chĭs
Port O'Connor — pohrt oh KAH ner
Posey — PŌ zĭ
Post — pohst
Postoak — PŌST ohk
Poteet — poh TEET
Poth — pohth
Potosi — puh TŌ sĭ
Potter — PAHT er
Pottsboro — PAHTS buh ruh
Pottsville — PAHTS vĭl
Powderly — POW der lĭ
Powell — POW w'l
Poynor — POI ner
Prairie Dell — prĕr ĭ DĔL
Prairie Hill — prĕr ĭ HĬL
Prairie Lea — prĕr ĭ LEE
Prairie View — prĕr ĭ VYOO
Prairieville — PRĔR ĭ vĭl
Premont — PREE mahnt
Presidio — pruh SĬ dĭ oh
Priddy — PRĬ dĭ
Primera — pree MĔ ruh
Princeton — PRĬNS t'n
Pritchett — PRĬ chĭt
Proctor — PRAHK ter
Progreso — proh GRĔ soh
Prosper — PRAHS per
Purdon — PERD n
Purley — PER lĭ
Purmela — per MEE luh
Putnam — PUHT n'm
Pyote — PĪ oht

Q

Quanah — KWAH nuh
Queen City — kween SĬT ĭ
Quemado — kuh MAH doh
Quihi — KWEE hee
Quinlan — KWĬN l'n
Quintana — kwĭn TAH nuh
Quitaque — KĬT uh kwa
Quitman — KWĬT m'n

R

Ralls — rahlz
Randall — RĂN d'l
Randolph — RĂN dahlf
Ranger — RĀN jer
Rangerville — RĀN jer vĭl
Rankin — RĂNG kĭn
Ratcliff — RĂT klĭf
Ravenna — rĭ VĔN uh
Rayburn — RĀ bern
Raymondville — RĀ m'nd vĭl
Raywood — RĀ wood
Reagan — RĀ g'n
Real — REE awl
Realitos — ree uh LEE t's
Reeves — reevz
Refugio — rĕ FYOO rĭ oh
Reilly Springs — rī lĭ SPRĬNGZ
Reklaw — RĔK law
Reno — REE noh
Rhineland — RĪN l'nd
Rhome — rohm
Rhonesboro — RŌNZ buh ruh
Ricardo — rĭ KAHR doh
Richards — RĬCH erdz
Richardson — RĬCH erd s'n
Richland — RĬCH l'nd
Richland Springs — rĭch l'nd SPRĬNGZ
Richmond — RĬCH m'nd
Ridge — rĭj
Ridgeway — RĬJ wā
Riesel — REE s'l
Ringgold — RĬNG gohld
Rio Frio — ree oh FREE oh
Rio Grande City — ree oh grahn dĭ or ree oh grăn SĬT ĭ
Rio Hondo — ree oh HAHN doh
Riomedina — ree oh muh DEE nuh
Rios — REE ohs
Rio Vista — ree oh VĬS tuh
Rising Star — rī zĭng STAHR
River Oaks — rĭ ver ŌKS
Riverside — RĬ ver sīd
Riviera — ruh VĬR uh
Roane — rohn
Roanoke — RŌN ohk or RŌ uh nohk
Roans Prairie — rohnz PRĔR Ĭ
Roaring Springs — rohr ĭng SPRĬNGZ
Robert Lee — rah bert LEE
Roberts — RAH berts
Robertson — RAH bert s'n
Robinson — RAH bĭn s'n
Robstown — RAHBZ town
Rochelle — roh SHĔL
Rochester — RAH chĕs ter
Rockdale — RAHK dāl
Rock Island — rahk Ī l'nd
Rockland — RAHK l'nd
Rockport — rahk PŌRT
Rocksprings — rahk SPRĬNGZ
Rockwall — rahk WAWL
Rockwood — RAHK wood
Roganville — RŌ g'n vĭl
Rogers — RAH jerz
Romayor — roh MĀ er
Roosevelt — RŌ suh v'lt or ROO suh v'lt
Ropesville — RŌPS vĭl
Rosanky — roh ZĂNG kĭ
Roscoe — RAHS koh
Rosebud — RŌZ b'd
Rose Hill — rohz HĬL
Rosenberg — RŌZ n berg
Rosenthal — RŌZ uhn thawl
Rosewood — RŌZ wood
Rosharon — roh SHĔ r'n
Rosita — roh SEE tuh
Rosser — RAW ser
Rosston — RAWS t'n
Rossville — RAWS vĭl
Roswell — RAHZ w'l
Rotan — roh TĂN
Round Rock — ROWND rahk
Round Top — ROWN tahp
Rowena — roh EE nuh
Rowlett — ROW lĭt
Roxton — RAHKS t'n
Royalty — ROI uhl tĭ
Royse City — roi SĬT ĭ
Royston — ROIS t'n
Rugby — RUHG bĭ
Ruidosa — ree uh DŌ suh
Rule — ryool
Runge — RUHNG ĭ

Diacritical markings are used as follows: bāle, băd, lĕt, rīse, rĭll, ōak, fŏŏt. The stressed syllable is capitalized. Secondary stress is indicated by an underline as in Atascosa — ăt uhs KŌ suh.

Runnels — RUHN 'lz
Rural Shade — roor uhl SHĀD
Rutersville — ROO ter vĭl

S

Sabinal — SĂB uh năl
Sabine — suh BEEN
Sabine Pass — suh been PĂS
Sabinetown — suh been TOWN
Sachse — SĂK sĭ
Sacul — SĂ k'l
Sadler — SĂD ler
Sagerton — SĂ ger t'n
Saginaw — SĂ guh naw
Saint Jo — sānt JŌ
Saint Paul — sānt PAWL
Salado — suh LĂ doh
Salesville — SĀLZ vĭl
Salineno — suh LEEN yoh
Salmon — SĂL m'n
Saltillo — săl TĬL oh
Samfordyce — săm FOR dis
Samnorwood — săm NAWR wood
San Angelo — săn ĂN juh loh
San Antonio — săn ăn TŌ nĭ oh
San Augustine — săn AW g's teen
San Benito — săn buh NEE tuh
Sanderson — SĂN der s'n
Sandia — săn DEE uh
San Diego — săn dĭ Ā goh
Sandy Point — săn dĭ POINT
San Elizario — săn ĕl ĭ ZAH rĭ oh
San Felipe — săn fuh LEEP
Sanford — SĂN ferd
San Gabriel — săn GĀ brĭ uhl
Sanger — SĂNG er
San Jacinto — săn juh SĬN tuh or juh SĬN toh
San Juan — săn WAHN
San Marcos — săn MAHR k's
San Patricio — săn puh TRĬSH ĭ oh
San Perlita — săn per LEE tuh
San Saba — săn SĂ buh
Santa Anna — săn tuh ĂN uh
Santa Elena — săn tuh LEE nuh
Santa Maria — săn tuh muh REE uh
Santa Rosa — săn tuh RŌ suh
Santo — SĂN toh
San Ygnacio — săn ĭg NAH sĭ oh
Saragosa — sĕ ruh GŌ suh
Saratoga — sĕ ruh TŌ guh
Sargent — SAHR juhnt
Sarita — suh REE tuh
Saspamco — suh SPĂM koh
Savoy — suh VOI
Schattel — SHĂT uhl
Schertz — sherts
Schleicher — SHLĪ ker
Schroeder — SHRĀ der
Schulenburg — SHOO lĭn berg
Schwertner — SWERT ner
Scotland — SKAHT l'nd
Scottsville — SKAHTS vĭl
Scranton — SKRĂNT n
Scurry — SKUH rĭ
Scyene — sĭ EEN
Seabrook — SEE brook
Seadrift — SEE drĭft
Seagoville — SEE goh vĭl
Seagraves — SEE grāvz
Sebastopol — suh BĂS tuh pyool
Sebastian — suh BĂS tĭ 'n
Security — sĭ KYOOR ĭ tĭ
Segno — SĔG noh
Segovia — sĭ GŌ vĭ uh
Seguin — sĭ GEEN
Selma — SĔL muh
Seminole — SĔM uh nohl
Seymour — SEE mohr
Shackelford — SHĂK uhl ferd
Shady Grove — shā dĭ GRŌV
Shafter — SHĂF ter
Shallowater — SHĂL uh wah ter
Shamrock — SHĂM rahk
Shannon — SHĂN uhn
Sheffield — SHĔ feeld
Shelby — SHĔL bĭ
Shelbyville — SHĔL bĭ vĭl
Sheldon — SHĔL d'n
Shepherd — SHĔ perd
Sheridan — SHĔ rĭ dn
Sherman — SHER m'n
Sherwood — SHER wood
Shiner — SHĪ ner
Shiro — SHĪ roh
Shive — shīv
Sidney — SĬD nĭ
Sierra Blanca — sĭer ruh BLĂNG kuh
Siloam — suh LŌM
Silsbee — SĬLZ bĭ
Silver Lake — sĭl ver LĀK
Silverton — SĬL ver t'n
Silver Valley — sĭl ver VĂ lĭ
Simonton — SĪ m'n t'n
Singleton — SĬNG g'l t'n
Sinton — SĬNT n
Sipe Springs — SEEP sprĭngz
Sisterdale — SĬS ter dāl
Sivells Bend — sĭ v'lz BĔND
Skellytown — SKĔ lĭ town
Skidmore — SKĬD mohr
Slaton — SLĀT n
Slayden — SLĀD n
Slidell — slī DĔL
Slocum — SLŌ k'm
Smiley — SMĪ lĭ
Smith — smĭth
Smithfield — SMĬTH feeld
Smithland — SMĬTH l'nd
Smithson Valley — smĭth s'n VĂ lĭ
Smithville — SMĬTH vĭl
Smyer — SMĪ er
Snyder — SNĪ der
Somerset — SUH mer sĕt
Somervell — SUH mer vĕl
Somerville — SUH mer vĭl
Sonora — suh NŌ ruh
Sour Lake — sowr LĀK
South Bend — sowth BĔND
South Bosque — sowth BAHS kĭ
South Houston — sowth HYOOS t'n
Southland — SOWTH l'nd
Southmayd — sowth MĀD
South Plains — sowth PLĀNZ
Spanish Fort — spă nĭsh FŌRT
Sparenberg — SPĂR ĭn berg
Speaks — speeks
Spearman — SPĬR m'n
Spicewood — SPĪS wood
Splendora — splĕn DŌ ruh
Spofford — SPAH ferd
Springdale — SPRĬNG dāl
Springlake — sprĭng LĀK
Springtown — SPRĬNG town
Spurger — SPER ger
Stacy — STĀ sĭ
Stafford — STĂ ferd
Stamford — STĂM ferd
Stanton — STĂNT n
Staples — STĀ p'lz
Stephens — STEE vĕnz
Stephenville — STEEV n vĭl
Sterley — STER lĭ
Sterling — STER lĭng
Sterling City — ster lĭng SĬT ĭ
Stiles — stīlz
Stinnett — stĭ NĔT
Stockdale — STAHK dāl
Stoneburg — STŌN berg
Stoneham — STŌN uhm
Stone Point — stohn POINT
Stonewall — STŌN wawl
Stout — stowt
Stowell — STO w'l
Stranger — STRĀN jer
Stratford — STRĂT ferd
Strawn — strawn
Streeter — STREET er
Streetman — STREET m'n
Study Butte — styoo dĭ BYOOT
Sudan — SOO dăn
Sugar Land — SHOO ger lănd
Sullivan City — suh luh v'n SĬT ĭ
Sulphur Bluff — suhl fer BLUHF
Sulphur Springs — suhl fer SPRĬNGZ
Summerfield — SUHM er feeld
Sumner — SUHM ner
Sundown — SUHN down
Suniland — SUH nĭ lănd
Sunny Side — SUH nĭ sīd
Sunray — SUHN rā
Sunset — SUHN sĕt
Sutherland Springs — suh ther l'nd SPRĬNGZ
Sutton — SUHT n
Swan — swahn
Sweeny — SWEE nĭ
Sweet Home — sweet HŌM
Sweetwater — SWEET wah ter
Swenson — SWĔN s'n
Swift — swĭft
Swisher — SWĬ sher
Sylvester — sil VES ter

T

Tahoka — tuh HŌ kuh
Talco — TĂL koh
Talpa — TĂL puh
Tanglewood — TĂNG g'l wood
Tankersley — TĂNG kers lĭ
Tarrant — TAR uhnt
Tarzan — TAHR z'n
Tascosa — tăs KŌ suh
Tatum — TĀ t'm
Tavener — TĂV uh ner
Taylor — TĀ ler
Teague — teeg
Tehuacana — tuh WAW kuh nuh
Telferner — TĔLF ner
Tenaha — TĔN uh haw

Diacritical markings are used as follows: bāle, băd, lĕt, rīse, rĭll, ōak, fŏŏt. The stressed syllable is capitalized. Secondary stress is indicated by an underline as in Atascosa — ăt uhs KŌ suh.

Tennyson — TĔN uh s'n
Terlingua — TER lĭng guh
Terrell — TĔR uhl
Terrell Hills — ter uhl HILZ
Texarkana — tĕks ahr KĂN uh
Texas City — tĕks ĕz SĬT ĭ
Texhoma — tĕks Ō muh
Texline — TĔKS līn
Texon — tĕks AHN
Thalia — THĀL yuh
Thomaston — TAHM uhs t'n
Thompsons — TAHMP s'nz
Thorndale — THAWRN dāl
Thornton — THAWRN t'n
Thorp Spring — thawrp SPRĬNG
Three Rivers — three RĬ verz
Throckmorton — THRAHK mawrt n
Thurber — THER ber
Tilden — TĬL d'n
Timpson — TĬM s'n
Tioga — tī Ō guh
Tivoli — tī VŌ luh
Tokio — TŌ kī oh
Tolar — TŌ ler
Tolbert — TAHL bert
Tolosa — tuh LŌ suh
Tomball — TAHM bawl
Tom Bean — tahm BEEN
Tom Green — tahm GREEN
Topsey — TAHP sī
Tornillo — tawr NEE yoh
Toyah — TOI yuh
Toyahvale — TOI yuh vāl
Trawick — TRĀ wĭk
Travis — TRĂ vĭs
Trent — trĕnt
Trenton — TRĔNT n
Trickham — TRĬK uhm
Trinidad — TRĬN uh dăd
Trinity — TRĬN ĭ tī
Troup — tryoop
Truby — TROO bī
Trumbull — TRUHM b'l
Truscott — TRUHS k't
Tucker — TUHK er
Tuleta — tyoo LEE tuh
Tulia — TOOL yuh
Tulsita — tuhl SEE tuh
Tundra — TUHN druh
Tunis — TOO nĭs
Turkey — TER kī
Turlington — TER lĭng t'n
Turnersville — TER nerz vĭl
Turnertown — TER ner town
Turney — TER nī
Tuscola — tuhs KŌ luh
Twitty — TWĬ tī
Tyler — TĪ ler
Tynan — TĪ nuhn

U

Uhland — YOO l'nd
Umbarger — UHM bahr ger
Union — YOON y'n
Upshur — UHP sher
Upton — UHP t'n
Urbana — er BĂ nuh
Utley — YOOT lī
Uvalde — yoo VĂL dī

V

Valdasta — văl DĂS tuh
Valera — vuh LĬ ruh
Van Alstyne — văn AWLZ teen
Vancourt — VĂN kohrt
Vanderbilt — VĂN der bĭlt
Vanderpool — VĂN der pyool
Van Horn — văn hawrn
Van Vleck — văn VLĔK
Van Zandt — văn ZĂNT
Vashti — VĂSH tī
Vaughan — vawn
Vega — VĀ guh
Velasco — vuh LĂS koh
Vera — VĬ ruh
Veribest — VĔR ĭ bĕst
Verhalen — ver HĀ lĭn
Vickery — VĬK er ĭ
Vidor — VĪ der
Vienna — vee ĔN uh
Village Mills — vĭl ĭj MĬLZ
Vinegarone — vĭn er guh RŌN
Vineyard — VĬN yerd
Voca — VŌ kuh
Von Ormy — vahn AHR mī
Voss — vaws
Votaw — VŌ taw

W

Waco — WĀ koh
Wadsworth — WAHDZ werth
Waelder — WĔL der
Waka — WAH kuh
Walberg — WAWL berg
Waldeck — WAWL dĕk
Walker — WAWL ker
Waller — WAW ler
Wallis — WAH lĭs
Wallisville — WAH lĭs vĭl
Walnut Springs — wawl n't SPRĬNGZ
Walton — WAWL t'n
Warda — WAWR duh
Waring — WĂR ĭng
Warren — WAW rĭn
Warrenton — WAW rĭn t'n
Washburn — WAHSH bern
Washington — WAHSH ĭng t'n
Waskom — WAHS k'm
Wastella — wahs TĔL uh
Watauga — wuh TAW guh
Water Valley — wah ter VĂ lī
Waxahachie — wawks uh HĂ chī
Wayland — WĀ l'nd
Weatherford — WĔ ther ferd
Webberville — WĔ ber vĭl
Webster — WĔBS ter
Weches — WEE chĭz
Weesatche — WEE săch
Weimar — WĪ mer
Weinert — WĪ nert
Weir — weer
Weldon — WĔL d'n
Wellborn — WĔL bern
Wellington — WĔL ĭng t'n
Wellman — WĔL m'n
Weser — WEE zer
Weslaco — WĔS luh koh
Westbrook — WĔST brook
Westfield — WĔST feeld
Westhoff — WĔS tawf
Westminster — wĕst MĬN ster
Weston — WĔS t'n
Westover — WĔS toh ver
Westphalia — wĕst FĀL yuh
Wharton — HWAWRT n
Wheeler — HWEE ler
Wheelock — HWEE lahk
White Deer — HWĪT Deer
Whiteface — HWĪT fās
Whiteflat — hwīt FLĂT
Whitehouse — HWĪT hows
Whitesboro — HWĪTS buh ruh
Whitewright — HWĪT rīt
Whitharral — HWĬT hăr uhl
Whitsett — HWĬT sĭt
Whitson — HWĬT s'n
Whitt — hwĭt
Whon — hwahn
Wichita — WĬCH ĭ taw
Wichita Falls — wĭch ĭ taw FAWLZ
Wickett — WĬ kĭt
Wiergate — WEER gāt
Wilbarger — WĬL bahr ger
Wildorado — wĭl duh RĀ doh
Willacy — WĬL uh sī
Williamson — WĬL yuhm s'n
Wills Point — wĭlz POINT
Wilmer — WĬL mer
Wilson — WĬL s'n
Wimberley — WĬM ber lī
Winchester — WĬN ches ter
Windom — WĬN d'm
Windthorst — WĬN thr'st
Winfield — WĬN feeld
Wingate — WĬN gāt
Winkler — WĬNGK ler
Winnsboro — WĬNZ buh ruh
Winona — wī NŌ nuh
Winterhaven — WĬN ter hā v'n
Winters — WĬN terz
Woden — WŌD n
Wolfe City — woolf SĬT ĭ
Wolfforth — WOOL forth
Woodbine — WOOD bīn
Woodlake — wood LĀK
Woodland — WOOD l'nd
Woodlawn — wood LAWN
Woodrow — WOOD roh
Woodsboro — WOODZ buh ruh
Woodson — WOOD s'n
Woodville — WOOD v'l
Wortham — WERTH uhm
Wright City — rīt SĬT ĭ
Wrightsboro — RĪTS buh ruh
Wylie — WĪ lī

Y

Yancey — YĂN sī
Yantis — YĂN tĭs
Yoakum — YŌ k'm
Yorktown — YAWRK town
Youngsport — YUHNGZ pohrt
Ysleta — ĭs LĔT uh

Z

Zapata — zuh PAH tuh
Zavalla — zuh VĂL uh
Zephyr — ZĔF er
Zuehl — ZEE uhl

Diacritical markings are used as follows: bāle, băd, lĕt, rīse, rĭll, ōak, fŏŏt. The stressed syllable is capitalized. Secondary stress is indicated by an underline as in Atascosa — ăt uhs KŌ suh.

ADVERTISER INDEX

GENERAL INDEX

- For cities and towns not listed in the index, see lists of towns on pages 390-417. For full information about cities, see "Cities and towns" entry in this index.
- For full information about counties, also look under the cities and towns in the county, as well as the "Counties" index entry.
- Page numbers in *italics* refer to photographs and artwork and their captions.

A

For CITIES and TOWNS not listed in the Index, see complete list on pages 390-4'

For CITIES and TOWNS not listed in the Index, see complete list on pages 390–41'

C

For CITIES and TOWNS not listed in the Index, see complete list on pages 390–417

D

For CITIES and TOWNS not listed in the Index, see complete list on pages 390

E

F

For CITIES and TOWNS not listed in the Index, see complete list on pages 390–41

G

H

For CITIES and TOWNS not listed in the Index, see complete list on pages 390–417.

I

J

K

L

For CITIES and TOWNS not listed in the Index, see complete list on pages 390–417

M

P

For CITIES and TOWNS not listed in the Index, see complete list on pages 390–417.

For CITIES and TOWNS not listed in the Index, see complete list on pages 390–417.

S

For CITIES and TOWNS not listed in the Index, see complete list on pages 390–417.

For CITIES and TOWNS not listed in the Index, see complete list on pages 390–417.

U

V

W

For CITIES and TOWNS not listed in the Index, see complete list on pages 390–417.

Y

Z